LaVern Borchages

THE LAYMAN'S PARALLEL NEW TESTAMENT

THE LAYMAN'S PARALLEL NEW TESTAMENT

KING JAMES VERSION

THE AMPLIFIED NEW TESTAMENT

THE LIVING NEW TESTAMENT

REVISED STANDARD VERSION

ZONDERVAN PUBLISHING HOUSE
Grand Rapids, Michigan

THE LAYMAN'S PARALLEL NEW TESTAMENT

Library of Congress Catalog Card Number: 78-132518

FIRST PRINTING AUGUST 1970
SECOND PRINTING SEPTEMBER 1970
THIRD PRINTING DECEMBER 1970
FOURTH PRINTING MARCH 1971
FIFTH PRINTING JUNE 1971
SIXTH PRINTING AUGUST 1971
SEVENTH PRINTING OCTOBER 1971
EIGHTH PRINTING FEBRUARY 1972
NINTH PRINTING APRIL 1972

Printed in the United States of America

Contents

Publishers Preface

Out of the multiplicity of modern language translations of the Scriptures published in recent years has come one of the most thrilling and rewarding methods of Bible study. Bible students have discovered that by comparing translations they can gain new insights into Scriptural truth, and a new awareness of the relevancy of the Word of God to contemporary life. *The Layman's Parallel New Testament* offers the Bible student three of the most popular modern translations—*The Amplified New Testament, The Living New Testament* and the *Revised Standard Version, New Testament*—in parallel columns alongside the classic King James Version for comparison and amplification.

The King James Version has been, for centuries, the most loved and used translation of the Scriptures, and its ministry of blessing seems destined to continue for many years to come. Its majestic style and rich cadence give it an undying quality that will live on in our contemporary world. It remains a standard of excellence in Bible translation.

The Revised Standard Version is, basically, a revision commissioned for the purpose of maintaining the standard of the Tyndale-King James tradition based on present knowledge of the Hebrew and Greek texts, as well as the current English word meanings.

The Amplified New Testament is designed primarily as a Bible study *tool*. It employs a unique amplifying device built into the text which permits readers, even though unschooled in the original language in which the New Testament was written, to grasp the various shades of meaning in the original Greek—meanings which cannot be transcribed by individual English words.

The Living New Testament is a paraphrase rather than a translation. A paraphrase does not attempt to translate word by word, but rather, thought by thought. A good paraphrase is a careful restatement of the Biblical author's thoughts (examples of paraphrasing may be found in the Bible itself, where New Testament writers rephrase a quotation from the Old Testament). In this sense, a paraphrase can often communicate more vividly than a good translation, since it provides in contemporary conversational style, the gist of what the author would have said if he had spoken to us today.

The Layman's Parallel New Testament is an indispensable study tool, a work you will want to use both in the study and in the discussion group. It will also be an invaluable reference aid as you compare these translations in public reading and in the exposition of the New Testament Scriptures.

THE PUBLISHERS

King James Version

Epistle Dedicatory

TO THE MOST HIGH *and* MIGHTY PRINCE JAMES *by the Grace of God* KING OF GREAT BRITAIN, FRANCE, *and* IRELAND, DEFENDER OF THE FAITH, &C. *The Translators of this Bible wish Grace, Mercy, and Peace, through* JESUS CHRIST *our Lord*

Great and manifold were the blessings, most dread Sovereign, which Almighty God, the Father of all mercies, bestowed upon us the people of England, when first he sent Your Majesty's Royal Person to rule and reign over us. For whereas it was the expectation of many, who wished not well unto our Sion, that upon the setting of that bright Occidental Star, Queen Elizabeth of most happy memory, some thick and palpable clouds of darkness would so have overshadowed this Land, that men should have been in doubt which way they were to walk; and that it should hardly be known, who was to direct the unsettled State; the appearance of Your Majesty, as of the Sun in his strength, instantly dispelled those supposed and surmised mists, and gave unto all that were well affected exceeding cause of comfort; especially when we beheld the Government established in Your Highness, and Your hopeful Seed, by an undoubted Title, and this also accompanied with peace and tranquillity at home and abroad.

But among all our joys, there was no one that more filled our hearts, than the blessed continuance of the preaching of God's sacred Word among us; which is that inestimable treasure, which excelleth all the riches of the earth; because the fruit thereof extendeth itself, not only to the time spent in this transitory world, but directeth and disposeth men unto that eternal happiness which is above in heaven.

Then not to suffer this to fall to the ground, but rather to take it up, and to continue it in that state, wherein the famous Predecessor of Your Highness did leave it: nay, to go forward with the confidence and resolution of a Man in maintaining the truth of Christ, and propagating it far and near, is that which hath so bound and firmly knit the hearts of all Your Majesty's loyal and religious people unto You, that Your very name is precious among them: their eye doth behold You with comfort, and they bless You in their hearts, as that sanctified Person, who, under God, is the immediate Author of their true happiness. And this their contentment doth not diminish or decay, but every day increaseth and taketh strength, when they observe, that the zeal of Your Majesty toward the house of God doth not slack or go backward, but is more and more kindled, manifesting itself abroad in the farthest parts of Christendom, by writing in defence of the Truth, (which hath given such a blow unto that man of sin, as will not be healed), and every day at home, by religious and learned discourse, by frequenting the house of God, by hearing the Word preached, by cherishing the Teachers thereof, by caring for the Church, as a most tender and loving nursing Father.

There are infinite arguments of this right Christian and religious affection in Your Majesty; but none is more forcible to declare it to others than the vehement and perpetuated desire of accomplishing and publishing of this work, which now with all humility we present unto Your Majesty. For when Your Highness had once out of deep judgment apprehended how convenient it was, that out of the Original Sacred Tongues, together with comparing of the labours, both in our own, and other foreign Languages, of many worthy men who went before us, there should be one more exact Translation of the Holy Scriptures into the English Tongue; Your Majesty did never desist to urge and to excite those to whom it was commended, that the work might be hastened, and that the business might be expedited in so decent a manner, as a matter of such importance might justly require.

And now at last, by the mercy of God, and the continuance of our labours, it being brought unto such a conclusion, as that we have great hopes that the Church of England shall reap good fruit thereby; we hold it our duty to offer it to Your Majesty, not only as to our King and Sovereign, but as to the principal Mover and Author of the work: humbly craving of Your most Sacred Majesty, that since things of this quality have ever been subject to the censures of illmeaning and discontented persons, it may receive approbation and patronage from so learned and judicious a Prince as Your Highness is, whose allowance and acceptance of our labours shall more honour and encourage us, than all the calumniations and hard interpretations of other men shall dismay us. So that if, on the one side, we shall be traduced by Popish Persons at home or abroad, who therefore will malign us, because we are poor instruments to make God's holy Truth to be yet more and more known unto the people, whom they desire still to keep in ignorance and darkness; or if, on the other side, we shall be maligned by selfconceited Brethren, who run their own ways, and give liking unto nothing, but what is framed by themselves, and hammered on their anvil; we may rest secure, supported within by the truth and innocency of a good conscience, having walked the ways of simplicity and integrity, as before the Lord; and sustained without by the powerful protection of Your Majesty's grace and favour, which will ever give countenance to honest and Christian endeavors against bitter censures and uncharitable imputations.

The Lord of heaven and earth bless Your Majesty with many and happy days, that, as his heavenly hand hath enriched Your Highness with many singular and extraordinary graces, so You may be the wonder of the world in this latter age for happiness and true felicity, to the honour of that great GOD, and the good of his Church, through Jesus Christ our Lord and only Saviour.

Amplified New Testament

Preface

Those responsible for the publication of this work, after twelve thousand hours of diligent research and prayerful study, have peaceful confidence that the merits of the *Amplified New Testament* are sufficient justification for its existence. The richness and clarity in the translation from the Greek of multi-shaded meanings are destined to fascinate and intrigue the hearts and minds of readers. At the same time, it will prove infinitely more; it will become beneficially enlightening and helpfully instructive. It is nonetheless the glorious Bread of God, so indispensable to the abundant life and blissful hope of men, though it be served in a pleasantly different way. The Truth is here—authoritative, authentic and accurate, but in a new garb.

God's ways are past finding out, and never more so than in His inimitable manner of raising up the right servant at the right time for a particular purpose. Serving as Research Secretary, Frances E. Siewert, B. Lit., B. D., M. A., D. Lit., (with training far beyond the suggestion of these listed degrees), has spent the major portion of a long life in humble, thorough preparation for such hallowed endeavor as this represents, memorizing chapter after chapter of the Greek text—translating, collating and correlating in an amazing display of ability and accomplishment.

The Lockman Foundation, a California corporation, not for profit, established for the express and stated purpose of promoting Christian evangelism, education and benevolence, came into the picture in a remarkable and needful manner. The leaders of this Christian organization, both in the discovery of the preliminary work of this translation and in the subsequent developments, have recorded incidents again and again which bear the undeniable earmarks of supernatural direction. These have unfolded with the exactness and amazing wonder of the unfolding petals of a beautiful rose, and with similar order and timing. All of this contributed weighty impetus to the desire and determination to complete the undertaking, making possible the publication of the *Amplified New Testament* for the glory of God and the good of man.

An Editorial Committee gave dedicated and diligent attention to the manuscript. The edited and proofed translation was then submitted to three qualified Greek consultants.

Twenty-seven translations and versions of the New Testament in whole or in part were assiduously examined and the greatest lexicographers of all times continually consulted. The Greek text of Westcott and Hort was pursued with meticulous care. A fourfold aim for this translation has been kept in view:

1. That it should be true to the original Greek.
2. That it should be grammatically correct.
3. That it should be understandable to the masses.
4. That it should give the Lord Jesus Christ His proper place which the Word gives Him. No work will be personalized.

It is statedly God's will that all men shall "come unto the knowledge of the truth" (1 Tim 2:4.) It is equally emphasized that, "Knowledge is easy unto [esteemed by] him that understandeth" (Prov. 14:6).

To this end, the Author of divine Truth, amid changing languages and discovered dialects, permits His changeless Word to become accommodated to the comprehension and appreciation of finite minds in every era. Is it not prophesied that "knowledge [of the Lord] shall be increased" (Dan. 12:4)? Is not such an increase facilitated by clarification of the divine Precepts?

It is the hope and prayer of all who have had part in this translation's development and publication that it may be welcome everywhere. It is the Word of our blessed Lord, the Word of divine wisdom and infinite love, the Word of mercy and peace, the Word of everlasting life.

—Editorial Committee

Explanation of Arbitrary Punctuation Marks, etc.

PARENTHESES ( ) and DASHES — --: signify additional phases of meaning included in the original word, phrase or clause, or varying texts. However, names of Deity may be set off only with commas.

BRACKETS [ ]: contain justified clarifying words or comments, whether implied or not, which are not actually expressed in the immediate original text. However, when the identification of a person or thing represented by a pronoun is certain, the noun may be substituted for the pronoun without brackets.

ITALICS: point out certain familiar passages now recognized as not adequately supported by the original manuscripts, or italics may be substituted for brackets. Also "and," "or" and other connectives *in italics* indicate that the portions so connected are to be found in the same original word or expression.

CAPITALS: are used in names and personal pronouns referring to Deity, but sparingly elsewhere.

REFERENCES: are intended to cover any part of the preceding verse to which they apply.

SYNONYMS: are limited to what the text seems to warrant, both as to number and wording.

Living New Testament

Preface

The basic text used for this paraphrase is the American Standard Version of 1901, generally accepted by Bible scholars everywhere as a masterful work. New readings in the light of research since the publication of that volume have, of course, been incorporated into the *Living New Testament, Paraphrased.*

Copies of this book should be in every Christian household as a companion to the favored translation in use in that home. Each member of the family needs this paraphrase to use alongside such standard translations as the King James Version. Many testimonies indicate that the use of this paraphrase has transformed Bible reading from a duty to a joy, and that Christian lives have been radically changed as a result.

This book is also an important text for nonreaders of the Bible who have heretofore found Bible reading in the standard versions too difficult. Here the reading is not only easy, but stimulating, even exciting.

May many lives be changed by the Holy Spirit of God as He uses this form of His Word to cut into hard, troubled, or confused hearts, flooding them with light, and to fill all willing hearts with new, heavenly riches.

What is a Paraphrase?

A paraphrase does not attempt to translate word by word, but rather, thought by thought. A good paraphrase is a careful restatement of the author's thoughts. It can communicate more vividly than a good translation. (Examples of paraphrasing are found in the Bible itself, as when New Testament writers rephrase a quotation from the Old Testament.)

The purpose of this book, then, is to say as exactly as possible what the writers of Scripture would say to us in good conversational English today if they were here among us.

For study purposes, a paraphrase should be checked against a rigid translation; but for rapid reading and for accurately acquiring the sweeping movement of this "greatest story ever told," we believe that a paraphrase is invaluable.

Kenneth N. Taylor

Revised Standard Version

Preface

The Revised Standard Version of the Bible is an authorized revision of the American Standard Version, published in 1901, which was a revision of the King James Version, published in 1611.

The first English version of the Scriptures made by direct translation from the original Hebrew and Greek, and the first to be printed, was the work of William Tyndale. He met bitter opposition. He was accused of willfully perverting the meaning of the Scriptures, and his New Testaments were ordered to be burned as "untrue translations." He was finally betrayed into the hands of his enemies, and in October 1536, was publicly executed and burned at the stake.

Yet Tyndale's work became the foundation of subsequent English versions, notably those of Coverdale, 1535; Thomas Matthew (probably a pseudonym for John Rogers), 1537; the Great Bible, 1539; the Geneva Bible, 1560; and the Bishops' Bible, 1568. In 1582 a translation of the New Testament, made from the Latin Vulgate by Roman Catholic scholars, was published at Rheims.

The translators who made the King James Version took into account all of these preceding versions; and comparison shows that it owes something to each of them. It kept felicitous phrases and apt expressions, from whatever source, which had stood the test of public usage. It owed most, especially in the New Testament, to Tyndale.

The King James Version had to compete with the Geneva Bible in popular use; but in the end it prevailed, and for more than two and a half centuries no other authorized translation of the Bible into English was made. The King James Version became the "Authorized Version" of the English-speaking peoples.

The King James Version has with good reason been termed "the noblest monument of English prose." Its revisers in 1881 expressed admiration for "its simplicity, its dignity, its power, its happy turns of expression . . . the music of its cadences, and the felicities of its rhythm." It entered, as no other book has, into the making of the personal character and the public institutions of the English-speaking peoples. We owe to it an incalculable debt.

Yet the King James Version has grave defects. By the middle of the nineteenth century, the development of Biblical studies and the discovery of many manuscripts more ancient than those upon which the King James Version was based, made it manifest that these defects are so many and so serious as to call for revision of the English translation. The task was undertaken, by authority of the Church of England, in 1870. The English Revised Version of the Bible was published in 1881-1885; and the American Standard Version, its variant embodying the preferences of the American scholars associated in the work, was published in 1901.

Because of unhappy experience with unauthorized publications in the two decades between 1881 and 1901, which tampered with the text of the English Revised Version in the supposed interest of the American public, the American Standard Version was copyrighted to protect the text from unauthorized changes. In 1928 this copyright was acquired by the International Council of Religious Education, and thus passed into the ownership of the churches of the United States and Canada which were associated in this Council through their boards of education and publication.

The Council appointed a committee of scholars to have charge of the text of the American Standard Version and to undertake inquiry as to whether further revision was necessary. For more than two years the Committee worked upon the problem of whether or not revision should be undertaken; and if so, what should be its nature and extent. In the end the decision was reached that there is need for a thorough revision of the version of 1901, which will stay as close to the Tyndale-King James tradition as it can in the light of our present knowledge of the Hebrew and Greek texts and their meaning on the one hand, and our present understanding of English on the other.

In 1937 the revision was authorized by vote of the Council, which directed that the resulting version should "embody the best results of modern scholarship as to the meaning of the Scriptures, and express this meaning in English diction which is designed for use in public and private worship, and preserves those qualities which have given to the King James Version a supreme place in English literature."

Thirty-two scholars have served as members of the Committee charged with making the revision, and they have secured the review and counsel of an Advisory Board of fifty representatives of the cooperating denominations. The Committee has worked in two sections, one dealing with the Old Testament and one with the New Testament. Each section has submitted its work to the scrutiny of the members of the other section; and the charter of the Committee requires that all changes be agreed upon by a two-thirds vote of the total membership of the Committee. The Revised Standard Version of the New Testament was published in 1946. The publication of the Revised Standard Version of the Bible, containing the Old and New Testaments, was authorized by vote of the National Council of the Churches of Christ in the U.S.A. in 1951.

The problem of establishing the correct Hebrew and Aramaic text of the Old Testament is very different from the corresponding problem in the New Testament. For the New Testament we have a large number of Greek manuscripts, preserving many variant forms of the text. Some of them were made only two or three centuries later than the original composition of the books. For the Old Testament, only late manuscripts survive, all (with the exception of the Dead Sea texts of Isaiah and Habakkuk and some fragments of other books) based on a standardized form of the text established many centuries after the books were written.

The present revision is based on the consonantal Hebrew and Aramaic text as fixed early in the Christian era and revised by Jewish scholars (the "Masoretes") of the sixth to ninth centuries. The vowel signs, which were added by the Masoretes, are accepted also in the main, but where a more probable and convincing reading can be obtained by assuming different vowels, this has been done. No notes are given in such cases, because the vowel points are less ancient and reliable than the consonants.

Departures from the consonantal text of the best manuscripts have been made only where it seems clear that errors in copying had been made before the text was standardized. Most of the corrections adopted are based on the ancient versions (translations into Greek, Aramaic, Syriac, and Latin), which were made before the time of the Masoretic revision and therefore reflect earlier forms of the text. In every such instance a footnote specifies the version or versions from which the correction has been derived, and also gives a translation of the Masoretic Text.

Sometimes it is evident that the text has suffered in transmission, but none of the versions provides a satisfactory restoration. Here we can only follow the best judgment of competent scholars as to the most probable reconstruction of the original text. Such corrections are indicated in the footnotes by the abbreviation *Cn*, and a translation of the Masoretic Text is added.

The discovery of the meaning of the text, once the best readings have been established, is aided by many new resources for understanding the original languages. Much progress has been made in the historical and comparative study of these languages. A vast quantity of writings in related Semitic languages, some of them only recently discovered, has greatly enlarged our knowledge of the vocabulary and grammar of Biblical Hebrew and Aramaic. Sometimes the present translation will be found to render a Hebrew word in a sense quite different from that of the traditional interpretation. It has not been felt necessary in such cases to attach a footnote, because no change in the text is involved and it may be assumed that the new rendering was not adopted without convincing evidence. The analysis of religious texts from the ancient Near East has made clearer the significance of ideas and practices recorded in the Old Testament. Many difficulties and obscurities, of course, remain. Where the choice between two meanings is particularly difficult or doubtful, we have given an alternative rendering in a footnote. If in the judgment of the Committee the meaning of a passage is quite uncertain or obscure, either because of corruption in the text or because of the inadequacy of our present knowledge of the language, that fact is indicated by a note. It should not be assumed, however, that the Committee was entirely sure or unanimous concerning every rendering not so indicated. To record all minority views was obviously out of the question.

A major departure from the practice of the American Standard Version is the rendering of the Divine Name, the "Tetragrammaton." The American Standard Version used the term "Jehovah"; the King James Version had employed this in four places, but everywhere else, except in three cases where it was employed as part of a proper name, used the English word LORD (or in certain cases GOD) printed in capitals. The present revision returns to the procedure of the King James Version, which follows the precedent of the ancient Greek and Latin translators and the long established practice in the reading of the Hebrew scriptures in the synagogue. While it is almost, if not quite, certain that the Name was originally pronounced "Yahweh," this pronunciation was not indicated when the Masoretes added vowel signs to the consonantal Hebrew text. To the four consonents YHWH of the Name, which had come to be regarded as too sacred to be pronunced, they attached vowel signs indicating that in its place should be read the Hebrew word *Adonai* meaning "Lord" (or *Elohim* meaning "God"). The ancient Greek translators substituted the word *Kyrios* (Lord) for the Name. The Vulgate likewise used the Latin word *Dominus.* The form "Jehovah" is of late medieval origin; it is a combination of the consonants of the Divine Name and the vowels attached to it by the Masoretes but belonging to an entirely different word. The sound of Y is represented by J and the sound of W by V, as in Latin. For two reasons the Committee has returned to the more familiar usage of the King James Version: (1) the word "Jehovah" does not accurately represent any form of the Name ever used in Hebrew; and (2) the use of any proper name for the one and only God, as though there were other gods from whom He had to be distinguished, was discontinued in Judaism before the Christian era and is entirely inappropriate for the universal faith of the Christian Church.

The King James Version of the New Testament was based upon a Greek text that was marred by mistakes, containing the accumulated errors of fourteen centuries of manuscript copying. It was essentially the Greek text of the New Testament as edited by Beza, 1589, who closely followed that published by Erasmus, 1516-1535, which was based upon a few medieval manuscripts. The earliest and best of the eight manuscripts which Erasmus consulted was from the tenth century, and he made the least use of it because it differed most from the commonly received text; Beza had access to two manuscripts of great value dating from the fifth and sixth centuries, but he made very little use of them because they differed from the text published by Erasmus.

We now possess many more ancient manuscripts of the New Testament, and are far better equipped to seek to recover the original wording of the Greek text. The evidence for the text of the books of the New Testament is better than for any other ancient book, both in the number of extant manuscripts and in the nearness of the date of some of these manuscripts to the date when the book was originally written.

The revisers in the 1870's had most of the evidence that we now have for the Greek text, though the most ancient of all extant manuscripts of the Greek New Testament were not discovered until 1931. But they lacked the resources which discoveries within the past eighty years have afforded for understanding the vocabulary, grammar and idioms of the Greek New Testament. An amazing body of Greek papyri has been unearthed in Egypt since the 1870's—private letters, official reports, wills, business accounts, petitions, and other such trivial, everyday recordings of the activities of human beings. In 1895 appeared the first of Adolf Deissmann's studies of these ordinary materials. He proved that many words which had hitherto been assumed to belong to what was called "Biblical Greek" were current in the spoken vernacular of the first century A.D. The New Testament was written in the Koiné, the common Greek which was spoken and understood practically everywhere throughout the Roman Empire in the early centuries of the Christian era. This development in the study of New Testament Greek has come since the work on the English Revised Version and the American Standard Version was done, and at many points sheds new light upon the meaning of the Greek text.

A major reason for revision of the King James Version, which is valid for both the Old Testament and the New Testament, is the change since 1611 in English usage. Many forms of expression have become archaic, while still generally intelligible—the use of thou, thee, thy, thine and the verb endings -est and -edst, the verb endings -eth and -th, it came to pass that, whosoever, whatsoever, insomuch that, because that, for that, unto, howbeit, peradventure, holden, aforetime, must needs, would fain, behooved, to you-ward, etc. Other words are obsolete and no longer understood by the common reader. The greatest problem, however, is presented by the English words which are still in constant use but now convey a different meaning from that which they had in 1611 and in the King James Version. These words were once accurate translations of the Hebrew and Greek Scriptures; but now, having changed in meaning, they have become misleading. They no longer say what the King James translators meant them to say.

The King James Version uses the word "let" in the sense of "hinder," "prevent" to mean "preceed," "allow" in the sense of "approve," "communicate" for "share," "conversation" for "conduct," "comprehend" for "overcome," "ghost" for "spirit," "wealth" for "well-being," "allege" for "prove," "demand" for "ask," "take no thought" for "be not anxious," "purchase a good degree" for "gain a good standing," etc. The Greek word for "immediately" is translated in the King James Version not only by "immediately" and "straightway" but also by the terms "anon," "by and by," and "presently." There are more than three hundred English words which are used in the King James Version in a sense substantially different from that which they now convey. It not only does the King James translators no honor, but it is quite unfair to them and to the truth which they understood and expressed, to retain these words which now convey meanings they did not intend.

The Revised Standard Version of the Bible, containing the Old and New Testaments, was published on September 30, 1952, and has met with wide acceptance. This preface does not undertake to set forth in detail the lines along which the revision proceeded. That is done in pamphlets entitled *An Introduction to the Revised Standard Version of the Old Testament* and *An Introduction to the Revised Standard Version of the New Testament*, written by members of the Committee and designed to help the general public to understand the main principles which have guided this comprehensive revision of the King James and American Standard versions.

These principles were reaffirmed by the Committee in 1959, in connection with a study of criticisms and suggestions from various readers. As a result, a few changes have been authorized for the present and subsequent editions. Most of these are corrections of punctuation, capitalization, or footnotes. Some changes of words or phrases are made in the interest of consistency, clarity or accuracy of translation. Examples of such changes are "from," Job 19.26; "bread," Matthew 7.9, 1 Corinthians 10.17; "is he," Matthew 21.9 and parallels; "the Son," Matthew 27.54, Mark 15.39; "ask nothing of me," John 16.23; "for this life only," 1 Corinthians 15.19; "the husband of one wife," 1 Timothy 3.2,12; 5.9; Titus 1.6.

All the reasons which led to the demand for revision of the King James Version in the nineteenth century are still valid, and are even more cogent now than then. We have had a freer charter than our predecessors in the 1870's in that we have not been required, as they were, to limit the language of the English Bible to the vocabulary of the Elizabethan age. But we hope that we have not taken undue advantage of that freedom. The Revised Standard Version is not a new translation in the language of today. It is not a paraphrase which aims at striking idioms. It is a revision which seeks to preserve all that is best in the English Bible as it has been known and used through the years. It is intended for use in public and private worship, not merely for reading and instruction. We have resisted the temptation to use phrases that are merely current usage, and have sought to put the message of the Bible in simple, enduring words that are worthy to stand in the great Tyndale-King James tradition. We are glad to say, with the King James translators: "Truly (good Christian Reader) we never thought from the beginning, that we should need to make a new Translation, nor yet to make of a bad one a good one . . . but to make a good one better."

The Bible is more than a historical document to be preserved. And it is more than a classic of English literature to be cherished and admired. It is a record of God's dealing with men, of God's revelation of Himself and His will. It records the life and work of Him in whom the Word of God became flesh and dwelt among men. The Bible carries its full message, not to those who regard it simply as a heritage of the past or praise its literary style, but to those who read it that they may discern and understand God's Word to men. That Word must not be disguised in phrases that are no longer clear, or hidden under words that have changed or lost their meaning. It must stand forth in language that is direct and plain and meaningful to people today. It is our hope and our earnest prayer that this Revised Standard Version of the Bible may be used by God to speak to men in these momentous times, and to help them to understand and believe and obey His Word.

THE LAYMAN'S PARALLEL NEW TESTAMENT

King James

THE GOSPEL ACCORDING TO

St. Matthew

CHAPTER 1

THE book of the generation of Jesus Christ, the son of David, the son of Abraham.

2 Abraham begat Isaac; and Isaac begat Jacob; and Jacob begat Judas and his brethren;

3 And Judas begat Phares and Zara of Thamar; and Phares begat Esrom; and Esrom begat Aram;

4 And Aram begat Aminadab; and Aminadab begat Naasson; and Naasson begat Salmon;

5 And Salmon begat Booz of Rachab; and Booz begat Obed of Ruth; and Obed begat Jesse;

6 And Jesse begat David the king; and David the king begat Solomon of her *that had been the wife* of Urias;

7 And Solomon begat Roboam; and Roboam begat Abia; and Abia begat Asa;

8 And Asa begat Josaphat; and Josaphat begat Joram; and Joram begat Ozias;

9 And Ozias begat Joatham; and Joatham begat Achaz; and Achaz begat Ezekias;

10 And Ezekias begat Manasses; and Manasses begat Amon; and Amon begat Josias;

11 And Josias begat Jechonias and his brethren, about the time they were carried away to Babylon:

12 And after they were brought to Babylon, Jechonias begat Salathiel; and Salathiel begat Zorobabel;

13 And Zorobabel begat Abiud; and Abiud begat Eliakim; and Eliakim begat Azor;

14 And Azor begat Sadoc; and Sadoc begat Achim; and Achim begat Eliud;

15 And Eliud begat Eleazar; and Eleazar begat Matthan; and Matthan begat Jacob;

16 And Jacob begat Joseph the husband of Mary, of whom was born Jesus, who is called Christ.

17 So all the generations from Abraham to David *are* fourteen generations; and from David until the carrying away into Babylon *are* fourteen generations; and from the carrying away into Babylon unto Christ *are* fourteen generations.

18 ¶Now the birth of Jesus Christ was on this wise: When as his mother Mary was espoused to Joseph, before they came together, she was found with child of the Holy Ghost.

19 Then Joseph her husband, being a just *man,* and not willing to make her a public example, was minded to put her away privily.

Amplified

THE GOSPEL ACCORDING TO

Matthew

CHAPTER 1

The book of the ancestry (genealogy) of Jesus Christ, the Messiah, the Anointed, the son (descendant) of David, the son (descendant) of Abraham. [Ps. 132:11; Isa. 11:1.]

2 Abraham was the father of Isaac, Isaac the father of Jacob, Jacob the father of Judah and his brothers.

3 Judah the father of Perez and Zerah, whose mother was Tamar; Perez the father of Hezron, Hezron the father of Aram,

4 Aram the father of Aminadab, Aminadab the father of Nashon, Nashon the father of Salmon,

5 Salmon the father of Boaz, whose mother was Rahab; Boaz the father of Obed, whose mother was Ruth; Obed the father of Jesse,

6 Jesse the father of King David, King David the father of Solomon, whose mother had been the wife of Uriah; [Ruth 4:18-22; I Chron. 2:13-15.]

7 Solomon the father of Rehoboam, Rehoboam the father of Abijah, Abijah the father of Asa,

8 Asa the father of Jehoshaphat, Jehoshaphat the father of Joram, Joram the father of Uzziah,

9 Uzziah the father of Jotham, Jotham the father of Ahaz, Ahaz the father of Hezekiah,

10 Hezekiah the father of Manasseh, Manasseh the father of Amon, Amon the father of Josiah,

11 And Josiah became the father of Jechoniah and his brothers, about the time of the removal (deportation) to Babylon. [II Kings 24:14; I Chron. 3:15, 16.]

12 After the exile to Babylon, Jechoniah became the father of Shealtiel (Salathiel), Shealtiel the father of Zerubbabel,

13 Zerubbabel the father of Abiud, Abiud the father of Eliakim, Eliakim the father of Azor,

14 Azor the father of Sadoc, Sadoc the father of Achim, Achim the father of Elihud,

15 Elihud the father of Eliazar, Eliazar the father of Matthan, Matthan the father of Jacob,

16 Jacob the father of Joseph, the husband of Mary of whom was born Jesus Who is called the Christ.

17 So all the generations from Abraham to David are fourteen, from David to the Babylonian Exile (deportation) fourteen, from the Babylonian Exile to the Christ fourteen generations.

18 Now the birth of Jesus Christ took place under these circumstances: When His mother Mary had been promised in marriage to Joseph, before they came together she was found to be pregnant [through the power] of the Holy Spirit.

19 And her [promised] husband Joseph, being a just *and* upright man and not willing to expose her publicly *and* shame *and* disgrace her, decided to repudiate *and* dismiss (divorce) her quietly *and* secretly.

Living New Testament

Matthew

CHAPTER 1

These are the ancestors of Jesus Christ, a descendant of
King David and of Abraham:
2 Abraham was the father of Isaac; Isaac was the
father of Jacob; Jacob was the father of Judah
and his brothers.
3 Judah was the father of Perez and Zerah (Tamar
was their mother); Perez was the father of
Hezron; Hezron was the father of Aram;
4 Aram was the father of Amminadab; Amminadab was
the father of Nahshon; Nahshon was the
father of Salmon;
5 Salmon was the father of Boaz (Rahab was his
mother); Boaz was the father of Obed (Ruth
was his mother); Obed was the father of Jesse;
6 Jesse was the father of King David. David was the
father of Solomon (his mother was the ex-wife
of Uriah);
7 Solomon was the father of Rehoboam; Rehoboam
was the father of Abijah; Abijah was the
father of Asa;
8 Asa was the father of Jehoshaphat; Jehoshaphat was
the father of Joram; Joram was the father of
Uzziah;
9 Uzziah was the father of Jotham; Jotham was
the father of Ahaz; Ahaz was the father of
Hezekiah;
10 Hezekiah was the father of Manasseh; Manasseh
was the father of Amos; Amos was the
father of Josiah;
11 Josiah was the father of Jechoniah and his brothers
(born at the time of the exile to Babylon).
12 After the exile:
Jechoniah was the father of Shealtiel; Shealtiel
was the father of Zerubbabel;
13 Zerubbabel was the father of Abiud; Abiud was the
father of Eliakim; Eliakim was the father of
Azor;
14 Azor was the father of Zadok; Zadok was the father
of Achim; Achim was the father of Eliud.
15 Eliud was the father of Eleazar; Eleazar was the
father of Matthan; Matthan was the father of
Jacob;
16 Jacob was the father of Joseph (who was the husband of Mary, the mother of Jesus Christ
the Messiah).
17 These are[1] fourteen of the generations from Abraham to King David; and fourteen from King David's
time to the exile; and fourteen from the exile to Christ.

* * * * *

18 These are the facts concerning the birth of Jesus
Christ: His mother, Mary, was engaged to be married to
Joseph. But while she was still a virgin she became pregnant by the Holy Spirit.
19 Then Joseph, her fiancé,[2] being a man of stern
principle,[3] decided to break the engagement but to do it
quietly, as he didn't want to publicly disgrace her.

[1]Literally, "So all the generations from Abraham unto David are fourteen."
[2]Literally, "her husband."
[3]Literally, "a just man."

Revised Standard

THE GOSPEL ACCORDING TO

Matthew

1 The book of the genealogy of Jesus
Christ, the son of David, the son of
Abraham.

The genealogy of Jesus

2 Abraham was the father of Isaac, and
Isaac the father of Jacob, and Jacob the
father of Judah and his brothers, [3]and
Judah the father of Perez and Zerah by
Tamar, and Perez the father of Hezron, and
Hezron the father of Ram,[a] [4]and Ram[a]
the father of Amminadab, and Amminadab
the father of Nahshon, and Nahshon the
father of Salmon, [5]and Salmon the father of
Boaz by Rahab, and Boaz the father of
Obed by Ruth, and Obed the father of Jesse,
[6]and Jesse the father of David the
king.
And David was the father of Solomon
by the wife of Uriah, [7]and Solomon the
father of Rehoboam, and Rehoboam the
father of Abijah, and Abijah the father of
Asa,[b] [8]and Asa[b] the father of Jehoshaphat,
and Jehoshaphat the father of Joram, and
Joram the father of Uzziah, [9]and Uzziah
the father of Jotham, and Jotham the father
of Ahaz, and Ahaz the father of Hezekiah,
[10]and Hezekiah the father of Manasseh,
and Manasseh the father of Amos,[c] and
Amos[c] the father of Josiah, [11]and Josiah
the father of Jechoniah and his brothers,
at the time of the deportation to Babylon.
12 And after the deportation to Babylon:
Jechoniah was the father of Shealtiel,[d] and
Shealtiel[d] the father of Zerubbabel, [13]and
Zerubbabel the father of Abiud, and Abiud
the father of Eliakim, and Eliakim the father of Azor, [14]and Azor the father of
Zadok, and Zadok the father of Achim, and
Achim the father of Eliud, [15]and Eliud the
father of Eleazar, and Eleazar the father of
Matthan, and Matthan the father of Jacob,
[16]and Jacob the father of Joseph the husband of Mary, of whom Jesus was born,
who is called Christ.
17 So all the generations from Abraham
to David were fourteen generations, and
from David to the deportation to Babylon
fourteen generations, and from the deportation to Babylon to the Christ fourteen generations.

The birth of Jesus

18 Now the birth of Jesus Christ[f] took
place in this way. When his mother Mary
had been betrothed to Joseph, before they
came together she was found to be with
child of the Holy Spirit; [19]and her husband
Joseph, being a just man and unwilling to

[a] Greek *Aram*
[b] Greek *Asaph*
[c] Other authorities read *Amon*
[d] Greek *Sala thiel*
[f] Other ancient authorities read *of the Christ*

King James

20 But while he thought on these things, behold, the angel of the Lord appeared unto him in a dream, saying, Joseph, thou son of David, fear not to take unto thee Mary thy wife: for that which is conceived in her is of the Holy Ghost.

21 And she shall bring forth a son, and thou shalt call his name JESUS: for he shall save his people from their sins.

22 Now all this was done, that it might be fulfilled which was spoken of the Lord by the prophet, saying,

23 Behold, a virgin shall be with child, and shall bring forth a son, and they shall call his name Emmanuel, which being interpreted is, God with us.

24 Then Joseph being raised from sleep did as the angel of the Lord had bidden him, and took unto him his wife:

25 And knew her not till she had brought forth her firstborn son: and he called his name JESUS.

Amplified

20 But as he was thinking this over, behold, an angel of the Lord appeared to him in a dream, saying, Joseph, descendant of David, do not be afraid to take Mary [as] your wife, for that which is conceived in her is of (from, out of) the Holy Spirit.

21 She will bear a Son, and you shall call His name Jesus [in Hebrew means Savior], for He will save His people from their sins [that is, prevent their [a]failing and missing the true end and scope of life, which is God].

22 All this took place that it might be fulfilled which the Lord had spoken through the prophet.

23 Behold, the virgin shall become pregnant and give birth to a Son, and they shall call His name Emmanuel, which when translated means, God with us. [Isa. 7:14.]

24 Then Joseph being aroused from his sleep, did as the angel of the Lord had commanded him; he took [her to his side as] his wife,

25 But he had no union with her as her husband until she had borne *her first-born* Son, and he called His name Jesus.

CHAPTER 2

NOW when Jesus was born in Bethlehem of Judæa in the days of Herod the king, behold, there came wise men from the east to Jerusalem,

2 Saying, Where is he that is born King of the Jews? for we have seen his star in the east, and are come to worship him.

3 When Herod the king had heard *these things,* he was troubled, and all Jerusalem with him.

4 And when he had gathered all the chief priests and scribes of the people together, he demanded of them where Christ should be born.

5 And they said unto him, In Bethlehem of Judæa: for thus it is written by the prophet,

6 And thou Bethlehem, *in* the land of Juda, art not the least among the princes of Juda: for out of thee shall come a Governor, that shall rule my people Israel.

7 Then Herod, when he had privily called the wise men, inquired of them diligently what time the star appeared.

8 And he sent them to Bethlehem, and said, Go and search diligently for the young child; and when ye have found *him,* bring me word again, that I may come and worship him also.

9 When they had heard the king, they departed; and, lo, the star, which they saw in the east, went before them, till it came and stood over where the young child was.

10 When they saw the star, they rejoiced with exceeding great joy.

CHAPTER 2

NOW when Jesus was born in Bethlehem of Judea in the days of Herod the king, behold, wise men [astrologers] from the East came to Jerusalem, asking,

2 Where is He Who has been born King of the Jews? For we have seen His star in the East [b]at its rising, and have come to worship Him. [Jer. 23:5; Zech. 9:9; Num. 24:17.]

3 When Herod the king heard this, he was disturbed *and* troubled, and the whole of Jerusalem with him;

4 So he called together all the chief priests and learned men (scribes) of the people, and [c]anxiously asked them where the Christ was to be born.

5 They replied to him, In Bethlehem of Judea; for so it is written by the prophet:

6 And you Bethlehem, in the land of Judah, you are not in any way least *or* insignificant among the [d]chief cities of Judah; for from you shall come a Ruler ([e]Leader) Who will govern *and* [f]shepherd My people Israel. [Mic. 5:2.]

7 Then Herod sent for the wise men [astrologers] secretly, and [f]accurately to the last point ascertained from them the time of the appearing of the star—that is, [f]how long the star had made itself visible since its rising in the East.

8 Then he sent them to Bethlehem, saying, Go and search out the Child carefully *and* diligently, and when you have found [g]Him bring me word, that I too may come and worship Him.

9 When they had listened to the king they went their way, and lo, the star which had been seen in the East [h]in its rising went before them, until it came and stood over the place where the young Child was.

10 When they saw the star, they were thrilled with ecstatic joy.

---

a) Vincent's "Word Studies in the New Testament."
b) Alternate reading.
c) Williams' "The New Testament in the Language of the People."
d) Thayer's "Greek-English Lexicon of the New Testament—Grimm."
e) Moulton and Milligan's "The Vocabulary of the Greek Testament."
f) Vincent.
g) Capitalized because of what He is, the spotless Son of God, not what the speaker may have thought He was.
h) Alternate reading.

Living New Testament

20 As he lay awake[4] considering this, he fell into a dream, and saw an angel standing beside him. "Joseph, son of David," the angel said, "don't hesitate to take Mary as your wife! For the child within her has been conceived by the Holy Spirit!

21 And she will have a son, and you shall name Him Jesus (meaning 'Savior'), for He will save His people from their sins.

22 This will fulfill God's message through His prophets—

23 '*Listen! The virgin shall conceive a child!* She shall give birth to a Son, and He shall be called "Emmanuel" (meaning "God is with us").' "

24 When Joseph awoke, he did as the angel commanded, and brought Mary home to be his wife,

25 But she remained a virgin until her Son was born; and Joseph named Him "Jesus."

Revised Standard

put her to shame, resolved to divorce her
quietly. 20 But as he considered this, behold,
an angel of the Lord appeared to him in a
dream, saying, "Joseph, son of David, do
not fear to take Mary your wife, for that
which is conceived in her is of the Holy
Spirit; 21 she will bear a son, and you shall
call his name Jesus, for he will save his
people from their sins." 22 All this took
place to fulfil what the Lord had spoken
by the prophet:
23 "Behold, a virgin shall conceive and bear
a son,
and his name shall be called Emmanuel"
(which means, God with us). 24 When
Joseph woke from sleep, he did as the
angel of the Lord commanded him; he took
his wife, 25 but knew her not until she had
borne a son; and he called his name Jesus.

CHAPTER 2

Jesus was born in the town of Bethlehem, in Judea, during the reign of King Herod. At about that time some astrologers from eastern lands arrived in Jerusalem, asking,

2 "Where is the newborn King of the Jews? for we have seen His star in far-off eastern lands, and have come to worship Him."

3 King Herod was deeply disturbed by their question, and all Jerusalem was filled with rumors.[1]

4 He called a meeting of the Jewish religious leaders. "Did the prophets tell us where the Messiah would be born?" he asked.

5 "Yes, in Bethlehem," they said, "for this is what the prophet Micah[2] wrote:

6 'O little town of Bethlehem, you are not just an unimportant Judean village, for a Governor shall rise from you to rule My people Israel.' "

7 Then Herod sent a private message to the astrologers, asking them to meet him; at this meeting he found out from them the exact time when they first saw the star. Then he told them,

8 "Go to Bethlehem and search for the child. And when you find him, come back and tell me so that I can go and worship him too!"

9 After this interview the astrologers started out again. And look! The star appeared to them again, standing over Bethlehem.[3]

10 Their joy knew no bounds!

The coming of the wise men

2 Now when Jesus was born in Bethlehem of Judea in the days of Herod the
king, behold, wise men from the East came
to Jerusalem, saying, 2 "Where is he who has
been born king of the Jews? For we have
seen his star in the East, and have come to
worship him." 3 When Herod the king
heard this, he was troubled, and all Jerusalem with him; 4 and assembling all the chief
priests and scribes of the people, he inquired of them where the Christ was to be
born. 5 They told him, "In Bethlehem of
Judea; for so it is written by the prophet:
6 'And you, O Bethlehem, in the land of
Judah,
are by no means least among the rulers
of Judah;
for from you shall come a ruler who will
govern my people Israel.' "
7 Then Herod summoned the wise men
secretly and ascertained from them what
time the star appeared; 8 and he sent them
to Bethlehem, saying, "Go and search diligently for the child, and when you have
found him bring me word, that I too may
come and worship him." 9 When they had
heard the king they went their way; and
lo, the star which they had seen in the East
went before them, till it came to rest over
the place where the child was. 10 When they
saw the star, they rejoiced exceedingly with

---

[4] Implied in remainder of verse.
[1] Literally, "and all Jerusalem with him."
[2] Implied. Micah 5:2.
[3] Literally, "went before them until it came and stood over where the baby was."

King James

11 ¶ And when they were come into the house, they saw the young child with Mary his mother, and fell down, and worshipped him: and when they had opened their treasures, they presented unto him gifts; gold, and frankincense, and myrrh.

12 And being warned of God in a dream that they should not return to Herod, they departed into their own country another way.

13 And when they were departed, behold, the angel of the Lord appeareth to Joseph in a dream, saying, Arise, and take the young child and his mother, and flee into Egypt, and be thou there until I bring thee word: for Herod will seek the young child to destroy him.

14 When he arose, he took the young child and his mother by night, and departed into Egypt:

15 And was there until the death of Herod: that it might be fulfilled which was spoken of the Lord by the prophet, saying, Out of Egypt have I called my son.

16 ¶ Then Herod, when he saw that he was mocked of the wise men, was exceeding wroth, and sent forth, and slew all the children that were in Bethlehem, and in all the coasts thereof, from two years old and under, according to the time which he had diligently inquired of the wise men.

17 Then was fulfilled that which was spoken by Jeremy the prophet, saying,

18 In Rama was there a voice heard, lamentation, and weeping, and great mourning, Rachel weeping *for* her children, and would not be comforted, because they are not.

19 ¶ But when Herod was dead, behold, an angel of the Lord appeareth in a dream to Joseph in Egypt,

20 Saying, Arise, and take the young child and his mother, and go into the land of Israel: for they are dead which sought the young child's life.

21 And he arose, and took the young child and his mother, and came into the land of Israel.

22 But when he heard that Archelaus did reign in Judæa in the room of his father Herod, he was afraid to go thither: notwithstanding, being warned of God in a dream, he turned aside into the parts of Galilee:

23 And he came and dwelt in a city called Nazareth: that it might be fulfilled which was spoken by the prophets, He shall be called a Nazarene.

Amplified

11 And going into the house they saw the Child with Mary His mother, and they fell down and worshipped Him. Then opening their treasure bags, they presented to Him gifts, gold and frankincense and myrrh.

12 And [f]receiving an answer to their asking, they were divinely instructed *and* warned in a dream not to go back to Herod; so they departed to their own country by a different way.

13 Now after they had gone, behold, an angel of the Lord appeared to Joseph in a dream and said, Get up! [[i]Tenderly] take unto you the young Child and His mother and flee to Egypt, and remain there till I tell you [otherwise]; for Herod intends to search for the Child in order to destroy Him.

14 And having risen, he took the Child and His mother by night and withdrew to Egypt,

15 And remained there until Herod's death. This was to fulfill what the Lord had spoken by the prophet, Out of Egypt have I called My Son. [Hos. 11:1.]

16 Then Herod, when he realized that he had been misled by the wise men, was furiously enraged, and he sent and put to death all the male children in Bethlehem and in all that territory who were two years old or under, reckoning according to the date which he had investigated diligently *and* learned exactly from the wise men.

17 Then was fulfilled what was spoken by the prophet Jeremiah:

18 A voice was heard in Ramah, wailing and loud lamentation, Rachel weeping for her children; she refused to be comforted, because they were no more. [Jer. 31:15.]

19 But when Herod died, behold, an angel of the Lord appeared in a dream to Joseph in Egypt, and said,

20 Rise, [[j]tenderly] take unto you the Child and His mother, and go to the land of Israel, for those who sought the Child's life are dead.

21 Then he awoke and arose and [[j]tenderly] took the Child and His mother, and came into the land of Israel.

22 But because he heard that Archelaus was ruling over Judea in the place of his father Herod, he was afraid to go there; and being divinely warned in a dream he withdrew to the region of Galilee.

23 He went and dwelt in a town called Nazareth, so that what was spoken through the prophets might be fulfilled, He shall be called a Nazarene (meaning Branch, Separated One). [Isa. 11:1.]

CHAPTER 3

King James

IN those days came John the Baptist, preaching in the wilderness of Judæa,

Amplified

IN those days there appeared John the Baptist, preaching in the wilderness (desert) of Judea, and saying,

---

f) Williams.
i) Williams.
j) Williams.

Living New Testament

11 Entering the house where the baby and Mary His mother were, they threw themselves down before Him, worshiping. Then they opened their presents and gave Him gold, frankincense and myrrh.

12 And when they returned to their own land, they didn't go through Jerusalem to report to Herod, for God had warned them in a dream to go home another way.

13 After they were gone, an angel of the Lord appeared to Joseph in a dream. "Get up and flee to Egypt with the baby and His mother," the angel said, "and stay there until I tell you to return, for King Herod is going to try to kill the child."

14 That same night[4] he left for Egypt with Mary and the baby,

15 And stayed there until King Herod's death. This fulfilled the prophet's prediction, "I have called My Son from Egypt."[5]

16 Herod was furious when he learned that the astrologers had disobeyed him. Sending soldiers to Bethlehem, he ordered them to kill every baby boy two years old and under, both in town and on the nearby farms, for the astrologers had told him the star first appeared to them two years before.

17 This brutal action of Herod's fulfilled the prophecy of Jeremiah,[6]

18 "Screams of anguish come from Ramah,[7]
Weeping unrestrained;
Rachel weeping for her children,
Uncomforted—
For they are dead."

19 When Herod died, an angel of the Lord appeared in a dream to Joseph in Egypt, and told him,

20 "Get up and take the baby and His mother back to Israel, for those who were trying to kill the child are dead."

21 So he returned immediately to Israel with Jesus and His mother.

22 But on the way he was frightened to learn that the new king was Herod's son, Archelaus. Then, in another dream, he was warned not to go to Judea, so they went to Galilee instead,

23 And lived in Nazareth. This fulfilled the prediction of the prophets concerning the Messiah,
"He shall be called a Nazarene."

Revised Standard

great joy; 11 and going into the house they
saw the child with Mary his mother, and
they fell down and worshiped him. Then,
opening their treasures, they offered him
gifts, gold and frankincense and myrrh.
12 And being warned in a dream not to return to Herod, they departed to their own
country by another way.

The flight into Egypt

13 Now when they had departed, behold, an angel of the Lord appeared to
Joseph in a dream and said, "Rise, take
the child and his mother, and flee to Egypt,
and remain there till I tell you; for Herod
is about to search for the child, to destroy
him." 14 And he rose and took the child
and his mother by night, and departed to
Egypt, 15 and remained there until the
death of Herod. This was to fulfil what the
Lord had spoken by the prophet, "Out of
Egypt have I called my son."
16 Then Herod, when he saw that he
had been tricked by the wise men, was in a
furious rage, and he sent and killed all the
male children in Bethlehem and in all that
region who were two years old or under,
according to the time which he had ascertained from the wise men. 17 Then was fulfilled what was spoken by the prophet
Jeremiah:
18 "A voice was heard in Ramah,
wailing and loud lamentation,
Rachel weeping for her children;
she refused to be consoled,
because they were no more."

From Egypt to Nazareth

19 But when Herod died, behold, an
angel of the Lord appeared in a dream to
Joseph in Egypt, saying, 20 "Rise, take the
child and his mother, and go to the land
of Israel, for those who sought the child's
life are dead." 21 And he rose and took the
child and his mother, and went to the land
of Israel. 22 But when he heard that Archelaus reigned over Judea in place of his father
Herod, he was afraid to go there, and being warned in a dream he withdrew to the
district of Galilee. 23 And he went and dwelt
in a city called Nazareth, that what was
spoken by the prophets might be fulfilled,
"He shall be called a Nazarene."

CHAPTER 3

While they were still living in Nazareth,[1] John the Baptist began preaching out in the Judean wilderness. His constant theme was,

The preaching of John the Baptist

3 In those days came John the Baptist,
preaching in the wilderness of Judea,

---

[4]Implied.
[5]Hosea 11:1.
[6]Jeremiah 31:15.
[7]Or, "the region of Ramah."
[1]Literally, "in those days."

King James

2 And saying, Repent ye: for the kingdom of heaven is at hand.

3 For this is he that was spoken of by the prophet Esaias, saying, The voice of one crying in the wilderness, Prepare ye the way of the Lord, make his paths straight.

4 And the same John had his raiment of camel's hair, and a leathern girdle about his loins; and his meat was locusts and wild honey.

5 Then went out to him Jerusalem, and all Judæa, and all the region round about Jordan,

6 And were baptized of him in Jordan, confessing their sins.

7 ¶ But when he saw many of the Pharisees and Sadducees come to his baptism, he said unto them, O generation of vipers, who hath warned you to flee from the wrath to come?

8 Bring forth therefore fruits meet for repentance:

9 And think not to say within yourselves, We have Abraham to *our* father: for I say unto you, that God is able of these stones to raise up children unto Abraham.

10 And now also the axe is laid unto the root of the trees: therefore every tree which bringeth not forth good fruit is hewn down, and cast into the fire.

11 I indeed baptize you with water unto repentance: but he that cometh after me is mightier than I, whose shoes I am not worthy to bear: he shall baptize you with the Holy Ghost, and *with* fire:

12 Whose fan *is* in his hand, and he will throughly purge his floor, and gather his wheat into the garner; but he will burn up the chaff with unquenchable fire.

13 ¶ Then cometh Jesus from Galilee to Jordan unto John, to be baptized of him.

14 But John forbad him, saying, I have need to be baptized of thee, and comest thou to me?

15 And Jesus answering said unto him, Suffer *it to be so* now: for thus it becometh us to fulfil all righteousness. Then he suffered him.

16 And Jesus, when he was baptized, went up straightway out of the water: and, lo, the heavens were opened unto him, and he saw the Spirit of God descending like a dove, and lighting upon him:

17 And lo a voice from heaven, saying, This is my beloved Son, in whom I am well pleased.

Amplified

2 Repent—that is, [k]think differently; change your mind, regretting your sins and changing your conduct—for the kingdom of heaven is at hand.

3 This is he who was mentioned by the prophet Isaiah when he said, The voice of one crying in the wilderness—shouting in the desert: Prepare the road for the Lord; make His highways straight (level, [l]direct). [Isa. 40:4.]

4 This John's garments were made of camel's hair, and he wore a leather girdle about his waist, and his food was locusts and wild honey. [II Kings 1:8; Zech. 13:4; Lev. 11:22.]

5 Then Jerusalem and all Judea and all the country round about the Jordan went out to him,

6 And they were baptized in the Jordan by him, confessing their sins.

7 But when he saw many of the Pharisees and Sadducees coming for baptism, he said to them, You brood of vipers, who warned you to flee *and* escape from the wrath *and* indignation [of God against disobedience,] that is coming?

8 Bring forth fruit that is consistent with repentance—let your lives prove your change of heart;

9 And do not presume to say to yourselves, We have Abraham for our forefather; for I tell you God is able to raise up descendants for Abraham from these stones!

10 And already the ax is lying at the root of the trees; every tree therefore that does not bear good fruit is cut down and thrown into the fire.

11 I indeed baptize you [m]in (with) water [n]because of repentance—that is, because of your [o]changing your minds for the better, heartily amending your ways with abhorrence of your past sins; but He Who is coming after me is mightier than I, Whose sandals I am not worthy *or* fit to take off *or* carry; He will baptize you with the Holy Spirit and with fire.

12 His winnowing fan (shovel, fork) is in His hand, and He will thoroughly clear out *and* clean His threshing floor, and gather *and* store His wheat in His barn; but the chaff He will burn up with fire that cannot be put out.

13 Then Jesus came from Galilee to the Jordan to John to be baptized by him.

14 But John [p]protested strenuously, having in mind to prevent Him, saying, It is I who have need to be baptized by You, and do You come to me?

15 But Jesus replied to him, [q]Permit it just now, for this is the fitting way for [both of] us to fulfill all righteousness—that is, to [q]perform completely whatever is right.

16 And when Jesus was baptized, He went up at once out of the water, and behold, the heavens were opened, and he [John] saw the Spirit of God descending like a dove and alighting on Him;

17 And lo, a voice out from heaven said, This is My Son, My Beloved, in Whom I delight! [Ps. 2:7; Isa. 42:1.]

---

k) Vincent.
l) Abbott-Smith's "Manual Greek Lexicon of the New Testament."
m) "En," the preposition used here, is translated both "in" and "with" in the Greek lexicons and concordances generally. The *Authorized Version* gives preference to "with," putting "in" in the margin; the *American "Revised" Version* gives preference to "in," putting "with" in the margin; the many modern versions choose one or the other about equally.
n) Williams.
o) Thayer.
p) Vincent.
q) Thayer.

Living New Testament

2 "Turn from your sins . . . turn to God . . . for the Kingdom of Heaven is coming soon."[2]

3 Isaiah the prophet had told about John's ministry centuries before! He had written,

"I hear[3] a shout from the wilderness,
'Prepare a road for the Lord—straighten out the path where He will walk.' "

4 John's clothing was woven from camel's hair and he wore a leather belt; his food was locusts and wild honey.

5 People from Jerusalem and from all over the Jordan Valley, and, in fact, from every section of Judea went out to the wilderness to hear him preach,

6 And when they confessed their sins, he baptized them in the Jordan River.

7 But when he saw many Pharisees[4] and Saducees[5] coming to be baptized, he denounced them. "You sons of snakes!" he warned. "Who said that you could escape the coming wrath of God?

8 Before being baptized, prove that you have turned from sin by doing worthy deeds.

9 Don't try to get by as you are, thinking, 'We are safe for we are Jews—descendants of Abraham.' That proves nothing. God can change these stones here into Jews![6]

10 And even now the axe of God's judgment is poised to chop down every unproductive tree. They will be chopped and burned.

11 With[7] water I baptize those who repent of their sins; but Someone else is coming, far greater than I am, so great that I am not worthy to carry His shoes! He shall baptize you with[8] the Holy Spirit and with fire.

12 He will separate the chaff from the grain, burning the chaff with never-ending fire, and storing away the grain."

13 Then Jesus went from His home[9] in Galilee to the Jordan River to be baptized there by John.

14 John didn't want to do it. "This isn't proper," he said. "I am the one who needs to be baptized by You."

15 But Jesus said, "Please do it, for I must do all that is right."[10] So then John baptized Him.

16 After His baptism, as soon as Jesus came up out of the water, the heavens were opened to Him and He saw the Spirit of God coming down in the form of a dove.

17 And a voice from heaven said, "This is My beloved Son, and I am wonderfully pleased with Him."

---

[2]Or, "has arrived." Literally, "is at hand."
[3]Implied. Isaiah 40:3.
[4]Jewish religious leaders who strictly followed the letter of the law but often violated its intent.
[5]Jewish political leaders.
[6]Literally, "God is able of these stones to raise up children unto Abraham."
[7]Or, "in water."
[8]Or, "in the Holy Spirit and in fire."
[9]Implied.
[10]Literally, "to fulfill all righteousness."

Revised Standard

2"Repent, for the kingdom of heaven is at
hand." 3For this is he who was spoken of
by the prophet Isaiah when he said,
"The voice of one crying in the wilderness:
Prepare the way of the Lord,
make his paths straight."
4Now John wore a garment of camel's
hair, and a leather girdle around his waist;
and his food was locusts and wild honey.
5Then went out to him Jerusalem and all
Judea and all the region about the Jordan,
6and they were baptized by him in the river Jordan, confessing their sins.
7 But when he saw many of the Pharisees
and Sadducees coming for baptism, he said
to them, "You brood of vipers! Who warned
you to flee from the wrath to come? 8Bear
fruit that befits repentance, 9and do not
presume to say to yourselves, 'We have
Abraham as our father'; for I tell you, God
is able from these stones to raise up children to Abraham. 10Even now the axe is
laid to the root of the trees; every tree
therefore that does not bear good fruit is
cut down and thrown into the fire.
11 "I baptize you with water for repentance, but he who is coming after me is
mightier than I, whose sandals I am not
worthy to carry; he will baptize you with
the Holy Spirit and with fire. 12His winnowing fork is in his hand, and he will clear
his threshing floor and gather his wheat
into the granary, but the chaff he will burn
with unquenchable fire."

The baptism of Jesus

13 Then Jesus came from Galilee to the
Jordan to John, to be baptized by him.
14John would have prevented him, saying,
"I need to be baptized by you, and do you
come to me?" 15But Jesus answered him,
"Let it be so now; for thus it is fitting
for us to fulfil all righteousness." Then he
consented. 16And when Jesus was baptized,
he went up immediately from the water,
and behold, the heavens were opened[g] and
he saw the Spirit of God descending like a
dove, and alighting on him; 17and lo, a
voice from heaven, saying, "This is my beloved Son,[h] with whom I am well pleased."

---

[g] Other ancient authorities add *to him*
[h] Or *my Son, my* (or *the*) *Beloved*

King James

CHAPTER 4

THEN was Jesus led up of the Spirit into the wilderness to be tempted of the devil.

2 And when he had fasted forty days and forty nights, he was afterward an hungered.

3 And when the tempter came to him, he said, If thou be the Son of God, command that these stones be made bread.

4 But he answered and said, It is written, Man shall not live by bread alone, but by every word that proceedeth out of the mouth of God.

5 Then the devil taketh him up into the holy city, and setteth him on a pinnacle of the temple,

6 And saith unto him, If thou be the Son of God, cast thyself down: for it is written, He shall give his angels charge concerning thee: and in *their* hands they shall bear thee up, lest at any time thou dash thy foot against a stone.

7 Jesus said unto him, It is written again, Thou shalt not tempt the Lord thy God.

8 Again, the devil taketh him up into an exceeding high mountain, and sheweth him all the kingdoms of the world, and the glory of them;

9 And saith unto him, All these things will I give thee, if thou wilt fall down and worship me.

10 Then saith Jesus unto him, Get thee hence, Satan: for it is written, Thou shalt worship the Lord thy God, and him only shalt thou serve.

11 Then the devil leaveth him, and, behold, angels came and ministered unto him.

12 ¶ Now when Jesus had heard that John was cast into prison, he departed into Galilee;

13 And leaving Nazareth, he came and dwelt in Capernaum, which is upon the sea coast, in the borders of Zabulon and Nephthalim:

14 That it might be fulfilled which was spoken by Esaias the prophet, saying,

15 The land of Zabulon, and the land of Nephthalim, *by* the way of the sea, beyond Jordan, Galilee of the Gentiles;

16 The people which sat in darkness saw great light; and to them which sat in the region and shadow of death light is sprung up.

17 ¶ From that time Jesus began to preach, and to say, Repent: for the kingdom of heaven is at hand.

18 ¶ And Jesus, walking by the sea of Galilee saw two brethren, Simon called Peter, and Andrew his brother, casting a net into the sea: for they were fishers.

19 And he saith unto them, Follow me, and I will make you fishers of men.

Amplified

CHAPTER 4

THEN Jesus was led (guided) by the (Holy) Spirit into the wilderness (desert) to be tempted—that is, tested and tried—by the devil.

2 And He went without food for forty days and forty nights, and later He was hungry. [Exod. 34:28; I Kings 19:8.]

3 And the tempter came and said to Him, If You are God's Son, command these stones to be made [[r]loaves of] bread.

4 But He replied, It has been written, Man shall not live *and* be upheld *and* sustained by bread alone, but by every word that comes forth from the mouth of God. [Deut. 8:3.]

5 Then the devil took Him into the holy city, and placed Him on [s]a turret (pinnacle, [t]gable) of the temple [u]sanctuary, [Neh. 11:1; Dan. 9:24.]

6 And he said to Him, If You are the Son of God, throw Yourself down; for it is written, He will give His angels charge over you, and they will bear you up on their hands, lest you strike your foot against a stone. [Ps. 91:11, 12.]

7 Jesus said to him, [v]On the other hand it is written also, You shall not tempt, [w]test thoroughly *or* [x]try exceedingly the Lord your God. [Deut. 6:16.]

8 Again the devil took Him up on a very high mountain, and showed Him all the kingdoms of the world and the glory—the splendor, magnificence, preeminence and excellence—of them;

9 And he said to Him, These things all taken together I will give You, if You will prostrate Yourself before me and do homage *and* worship me.

10 Then Jesus said to him, Begone, Satan! for it has been written, You shall worship the Lord your God and Him alone shall you serve. [Deut. 6:13.]

11 Then the devil departed from Him, and behold, angels came and ministered to Him.

12 Now when Jesus heard that John had been arrested *and* put in prison, He withdrew into Galilee.

13 And leaving Nazareth He went *and* dwelt in Capernaum by the sea, in the country of Zebulun and Naphtali,

14 That what was spoken by the prophet Isaiah might be brought to pass:

15 The land of Zebulun and the land of Naphtali in the [y]way to the sea beyond the Jordan, Galilee of the Gentiles [that is, of the [y]peoples who are not of Israel]; [Isa. 9:1-2.]

16 The people who sat [z](dwelt enveloped) in darkness have seen a great Light, and for those who sat in the land and shadow of death Light has dawned.

17 From that time Jesus began to preach, [a]crying out, Repent—that is, [b]change your mind for the better, heartily amend your ways, with abhorrence of your past sins—for the kingdom of heaven is at hand.

18 As He was walking by the sea of Galilee, He noticed two brothers, Simon who is called Peter and Andrew his brother, throwing a dragnet into the sea, for they were fishermen.

19 And He said to them, Come [b]after Me [as disciples] —letting Me be your Guide, follow Me—and I will make you fishers of men!

---

r) Wycliffe's "Version of the New Testament."
s) Abbott-Smith.
t) Moulton and Milligan.
u) Trench.
v) Vincent.
w) Thayer
x) Young's "Analytical Concordance."
y) Cremer's "Biblico-Theological Lexicon of New Testament Greek."
z) Wycliffe.
a) Vincent.
b) Thayer.

Living New Testament

CHAPTER 4

Then Jesus was led out into the wilderness by the Holy Spirit, to be tempted there by Satan.

2 For forty days and forty nights He ate nothing and became very hungry.

3 Then Satan tempted Him to get food by changing stones into loaves of bread. "It will prove You are the Son of God," he said.

4 But Jesus told him, "No! For the Scriptures tell us that bread won't feed men's souls: obedience to every word of God is what we need."

5 Then Satan took Him to Jerusalem to the roof of the Temple.

6 "Jump off," he said, "and prove You are the Son of God; for the Scriptures declare, 'God will send His angels to keep you from harm,' . . . They will prevent You from smashing on the rocks below."

7 Jesus retorted, "It also says not to put the Lord God to a foolish test!"[1]

8 Next Satan took Him to the peak of a very high mountain and showed Him the nations of the world and all their glory.

9 "I'll give it all to You," he said, "if You will only kneel and worship me."

10 "Get out of here, Satan," Jesus told him. "The Scriptures say, 'Worship only the Lord God. Obey only Him.' "

11 Then Satan went away, and angels came and cared for Jesus.

* * * * * *

12, 13 When Jesus heard that John had been arrested, He left Judea and returned [home[2]] to Nazareth in Galilee; but soon He moved to Capernaum, beside the Lake of Galilee, close to Zebulun and Naphtali.

14 This fulfilled Isaiah's prophecy:

15 "The land of Zebulun and the land of Naphtali, beside the Lake, and the countryside beyond the Jordan River, and Upper Galilee where so many foreigners live—

16 There the people who sat in darkness have seen a great Light; they sat in the land of death, and the Light broke through upon them."[3]

17 From then on, Jesus began to preach, "Turn from sin, and turn to God, for the Kingdom of Heaven is near."[4]

18 One day as He was walking along the beach beside the Lake of Galilee, He saw two brothers—Simon, also called Peter, and Andrew—[out in a boat[5]] fishing with a net, for they were commercial fishermen.

19 Jesus called out, "Come along with Me and I will show you how to fish for the souls of men!"

Revised Standard

The temptation in the wilderness

4 Then Jesus was led up by the Spirit
into the wilderness to be tempted by
the devil. 2And he fasted forty days and
forty nights, and afterward he was hungry.
3And the tempter came and said to him,
"If you are the Son of God, command
these stones to become loaves of bread."
4But he answered, "It is written,
'Man shall not live by bread alone,
but by every word that proceeds from
the mouth of God.' "
5Then the devil took him to the holy city,
and set him on the pinnacle of the temple,
6and said to him, "If you are the Son of
God, throw yourself down; for it is written,
'He will give his angels charge of you,'
and
'On their hands they will bear you up,
lest you strike your foot against a stone.' "
7Jesus said to him, "Again it is written,
'You shall not tempt the Lord your God.' "
8Again, the devil took him to a very high
mountain, and showed him all the kingdoms
of the world and the glory of them; 9and
he said to him, "All these I will give you,
if you will fall down and worship me."
10Then Jesus said to him, "Begone, Satan!
for it is written,
'You shall worship the Lord your God
and him only shall you serve.' "
11Then the devil left him, and behold,
angels came and ministered to him.

The beginning of Jesus' ministry

12 Now when he heard that John had
been arrested, he withdrew into Galilee;
13and leaving Nazareth he went and dwelt
in Capernaum by the sea, in the territory
of Zebulun and Naphtali, 14that what was
spoken by the prophet Isaiah might be fulfilled: 15"The land of Zebulun and the land
of Naphtali,
toward the sea, across the Jordan,
Galilee of the Gentiles—
16the people who sat in darkness
have seen a great light,
and for those who sat in the region
and shadow of death
light has dawned."
17From that time Jesus began to preach,
saying, "Repent, for the kingdom of heaven
is at hand."

Jesus calls four disciples

18 As he walked by the Sea of Galilee,
he saw two brothers, Simon who is called
Peter and Andrew his brother, casting a net
into the sea; for they were fishermen. 19And
he said to them, "Follow me, and I will
make you fishers of men." 20Immediately

1Literally, "you must not make trial of the Lord your God."
2Implied.
3Isaiah 9:1,2.
4Or, "is at hand," or, "has arrived."
5Implied.

King James

20 And they straightway left *their* nets, and followed him.

21 And going on from thence, he saw other two brethren, James *the son* of Zebedee, and John his brother, in a ship with Zebedee their father, mending their nets; and he called them.

22 And they immediately left the ship and their father, and followed him.

23 ¶ And Jesus went about all Galilee, teaching in their synagogues, and preaching the gospel of the kingdom, and healing all manner of sickness and all manner of disease among the people.

24 And his fame went throughout all Syria: and they brought unto him all sick people that were taken with divers diseases and torments, and those which were possessed with devils, and those which were lunatic, and those that had the palsy; and he healed them.

25 And there followed him great multitudes of people from Galilee, and *from* Decapolis, and *from* Jerusalem, and *from* Judæa, and *from* beyond Jordan.

Amplified

20 At once they left their nets and [b]became His disciples—sided with His party and followed Him.

21 And going on further from there He noticed two other brothers, James the son of Zebedee and John his brother, in the boat with their father Zebedee, mending their nets *and* putting them to rights, and He called them.

22 At once they left the boat and their father and [c]joined Jesus as disciples—sided with His party and followed Him.

23 And He went about all Galilee, teaching in their synagogues and preaching the good news (Gospel) of the kingdom and healing every disease and every weakness *and* infirmity among the people.

24 So the report of Him spread throughout all Syria, and they brought Him all that were sick, those afflicted with various diseases and torments, those under the power of demons, and epileptics, and paralyzed people; and He healed them.

25 And great crowds joined *and* accompanied Him about, coming from Galilee and Decapolis [the district of the ten cities east of the Sea of Galilee] and Jerusalem and Judea and from the other [the east] side of the Jordan.

CHAPTER 5 (King James)

AND seeing the multitudes, he went up into a mountain: and when he was set, his disciples came unto him:

2 And he opened his mouth, and taught them, saying,

3 Blessed *are* the poor in spirit: for theirs is the kingdom of heaven.

4 Blessed *are* they that mourn: for they shall be comforted.

5 Blessed *are* the meek: for they shall inherit the earth.

6 Blessed *are* they which do hunger and thirst after righteousness: for they shall be filled.

7 Blessed *are* the merciful: for they shall obtain mercy.

8 Blessed *are* the pure in heart: for they shall see God.

CHAPTER 5 (Amplified)

SEEING the crowds, He went up on the mountain, and when He was seated His disciples came to Him.

2 Then He opened His mouth and taught them saying:

3 Blessed—happy, [d]to be envied, and [e]spiritually prosperous [that is, [f]with life-joy and satisfaction in God's favor and salvation, regardless of their outward conditions] —are the poor in spirit (the humble, rating themselves insignificant), for theirs is the kingdom of heaven!

4 Blessed *and* enviably happy, [with a [f]happiness produced by experience of God's favor and especially conditioned by the revelation of His matchless grace] are those who mourn, for they shall be comforted! [Isa. 61:2.]

5 Blessed—happy, blithesome, joyous, [g]spiritually prosperous [that is, [h]with life-joy and satisfaction in God's favor and salvation, regardless of their outward conditions] —are the meek (the mild, patient, long-suffering), for they shall inherit the earth! [Ps. 37:11.]

6 Blessed *and* fortunate *and* happy *and* [g]spiritually prosperous [that is, in that state in which the born-again child of God [h]enjoys His favor and salvation] are those who hunger and thirst for righteousness (uprightness and right standing with God), for they shall be [g]completely satisfied! [Isa. 55:1, 2.]

7 Blessed—happy, [i]to be envied, and [g]spiritually prosperous [that is, [h]with life-joy and satisfaction in God's favor and salvation, regardless of their outward conditions] —are the merciful, for they shall obtain mercy!

8 Blessed—happy, [i]enviably fortunate, and [g]spiritually prosperous [that is, possessing the [h]happiness produced by experience of God's favor and especially conditioned by the revelation of His grace, regardless of their outward condi-

---

b) Thayer.
c) Thayer.
d) Souter's "A Pocket Lexicon to the Greek New Testament."
e) Wuest's "Mark in the Greek New Testament."
f) Cremer.
g) Vincent.
h) Cremer.
i) Souter's "Pocket Lexicon to the Greek New Testament."

Living New Testament

20 And they left their nets at once and went with Him!

21 A little farther up the beach He saw two other brothers, James and John, sitting in a boat with their father Zebedee, mending their nets; and He called to them to come too.

22 At once they stopped their work and, leaving their father behind, went with Him.

23 Jesus traveled all through Galilee teaching in the Jewish synagogues, everywhere preaching the Good News about the Kingdom of Heaven. And He healed every kind of sickness and disease.

24 The report of His miracles spread far beyond the borders of Galilee so that sick folk were soon coming to be healed from as far away as Syria. And whatever their illness and pain, or if they were possessed by demons, or were insane, or paralyzed—He healed them all.

25 Enormous crowds followed Him wherever He went—people from Galilee, and the Ten Cities, and Jerusalem, and from all over Judea, and even from across the Jordan River.

Revised Standard

they left their nets and followed him. [21]And
going on from there he saw two other
brothers, James the son of Zebedee and
John his brother, in the boat with Zebedee
their father, mending their nets, and he
called them. [22]Immediately they left the
boat and their father, and followed him.

23 And he went about all Galilee,
teaching in their synagogues and preaching
the gospel of the kingdom and healing every
disease and every infirmity among the people. [24]So his fame spread throughout all
Syria, and they brought him all the sick,
those afflicted with various diseases and
pains, demoniacs, epileptics, and paralytics,
and he healed them. [25]And great crowds
followed him from Galilee and the Decapolis and Jerusalem and Judea and from beyond the Jordan.

CHAPTER 5

One day as the crowds were gathering, He went up the hillside with His disciples and sat down and taught them there.

3 "Humble men are very fortunate!" He told them, "for the Kingdom of Heaven is given to them.

4 Those who mourn are fortunate! for they shall be comforted.

5 The meek and lowly are fortunate! for the whole wide world belongs to them.

6 Happy are those who long for justice, for they shall surely have it.

7 Happy are the kind and merciful, for they shall be shown mercy.

8 Happy are those whose hearts are pure, for they shall see God.

Sermon on the Mount: Beatitudes

5 Seeing the crowds, he went up on the
mountain, and when he sat down his
disciples came to him. [2]And he opened
his mouth and taught them, saying:

3 "Blessed are the poor in spirit, for theirs is the kingdom of heaven.

4 "Blessed are those who mourn, for they shall be comforted.

5 "Blessed are the meek, for they shall inherit the earth.

6 "Blessed are those who hunger and thirst for righteousness, for they shall be satisfied.

7 "Blessed are the merciful, for they shall obtain mercy.

8 "Blessed are the pure in heart, for they shall see God.

King James

9 Blessed *are* the peacemakers: for they shall be called the children of God.

10 Blessed *are* they which are persecuted for righteousness' sake: for theirs is the kingdom of heaven.

11 Blessed are ye, when *men* shall revile you, and persecute *you*, and shall say all manner of evil against you falsely, for my sake.

12 Rejoice, and be exceeding glad: for great *is* your reward in heaven: for so persecuted they the prophets which were before you.

13 ¶ Ye are the salt of the earth: but if the salt have lost his savour, wherewith shall it be salted? it is thenceforth good for nothing, but to be cast out, and to be trodden under foot of men.

14 Ye are the light of the world. A city that is set on an hill cannot be hid.

15 Neither do men light a candle, and put it under a bushel, but on a candlestick; and it giveth light unto all that are in the house.

16 Let your light so shine before men, that they may see your good works, and glorify your Father which is in heaven.

17 ¶ Think not that I am come to destroy the law, or the prophets: I am not come to destroy, but to fulfil.

18 For verily I say unto you, Till heaven and earth pass, one jot or one tittle shall in no wise pass from the law, till all be fulfilled.

19 Whosoever therefore shall break one of these least commandments, and shall teach men so, he shall be called the least in the kingdom of heaven: but whosoever shall do and teach *them*, the same shall be called great in the kingdom of heaven.

20 For I say unto you, That except your righteousness shall exceed *the righteousness* of the scribes and Pharisees, ye shall in no case enter into the kingdom of heaven.

21 ¶ Ye have heard that it was said by them of old time, Thou shalt not kill; and whosoever shall kill shall be in danger of the judgment:

22 But I say unto you, That whosoever is angry with his brother without a cause shall be in danger of the judgment: and whosoever shall say to his brother, Raca, shall be in danger of the council: but whosoever shall say, Thou fool, shall be in danger of hell fire.

Amplified

tions]—are the pure in heart, for they shall see God! [Ps. 24:3, 4.]

9 Blessed—enjoying [i]enviable happiness, [g]spiritually prosperous [that is, [h]with life-joy and satisfaction in God's favor and salvation, regardless of their outward conditions]—are the makers *and* [j]maintainers of peace, for they shall be called the sons of God!

10 Blessed *and* happy *and* [k]enviably fortunate and [l]spiritually prosperous [that is, [m]in the state in which one enjoys and finds satisfaction in God's favor and salvation, regardless of his outward conditions], are those who are persecuted for righteousness' sake (for being and doing right), for theirs is the kingdom of heaven!

11 Blessed—happy, [k]to be envied, and [l]spiritually prosperous [that is, [m]with life-joy and satisfaction in God's favor and salvation, regardless of your outward conditions]—are you when people revile you and persecute you and say all kinds of evil things against you falsely on My account.

12 Be glad *and* supremely joyful, for your reward in heaven is great (strong and intense), for in this same way people persecuted the prophets who were before you. [II Chron. 36:16.]

13 You are the salt of the earth, but if salt has lost its taste—its strength, its quality—how can its saltness be restored? It is not good for anything any longer but to be thrown out and trodden under foot by men.

14 You are the light of the world. A city set on a hill cannot be hid.

15 Nor do men light a lamp and put it under a peck-measure but on a lamp stand, and it gives light to all in the house.

16 Let your light so shine before men that they may see your [m]moral excellence *and* your praiseworthy, noble *and* good deeds, and [m]recognize *and* honor *and* praise *and* glorify your Father Who is in heaven.

17 Do not think that I have come to do away with *or* [n]undo the Law and the prophets; I have come not to do away with *or* undo, but to complete *and* fulfill them.

18 For truly, I tell you, until the sky and earth pass away *and* perish not one smallest letter nor one little hook [identifying certain Hebrew letters] will pass from the Law until all things [it foreshadows] have been accomplished.

19 Whoever then breaks *or* does away with *or* relaxes one of the least important of these commandments and teaches men so, shall be called least important in the kingdom of heaven; but he who practices them and teaches others to do so shall be called great in the kingdom of heaven.

20 For I tell you, unless your righteousness (your uprightness and your right standing with God) is more than that of the scribes and Pharisees, you will never enter the kingdom of heaven.

21 You have heard that it was said to the men of old, You shall not kill; and whoever kills shall be [o]liable *so* that he cannot escape the punishment imposed by the court. [Exod. 20:13; Deut. 5:17; 16:18.]

22 But I say to you that every one who continues to be [p]angry with his brother *or* harbors malice [enmity of heart] against him shall be [o]liable to *and* unable to escape the punishment imposed by the court; and whoever speaks contemptuously *and* insultingly to his brother shall be [o]liable to *and* unable to escape the punishment imposed by the Sanhedrin, and whoever says, You [q]cursed fool!—You

g) Vincent.
h) Cremer.
i) Souter's "Pocket Lexicon to the Greek New Testament."
j) Tyndale's "Version of the New Testament."
k) Souter's "Pocket Lexicon to the Greek New Testament."
l) Wuest.
m) Cremer.
n) Wycliffe.
o) Thayer.
p) Many ancient authorities insert "without cause."
q) Williams.

Living New Testament

9 Happy are those who strive for peace—they shall be called the sons of God.

10 Happy are those who are persecuted because they are good, for the Kingdom of Heaven is theirs.

11 When you are reviled and persecuted and lied about because you are My followers—wonderful!

12 Be *happy* about it! Be *very glad!* for a *tremendous reward* awaits you up in heaven. And remember, the ancient prophets were persecuted too.

13 You are the world's seasoning, to make it tolerable. If you lose your flavor, what will happen to the world? And you yourselves will be thrown out and trampled underfoot as worthless.

14 You are the world's light—a city on a hill, glowing in the night for all to see.

15, 16 Don't hide your light! Let it shine for all; let your good deeds glow for all to see, so that they will praise your heavenly Father.

17 Don't misunderstand why I have come—it isn't to cancel the Old Testament laws and the warnings of the prophets. No, I came to fulfill them, and to make them all come true.

18 With all the earnestness I have I say: Every law in the Book will continue until its purpose is achieved.[1]

19 And so if anyone breaks the least commandment, and teaches others to, he shall be the least in the Kingdom of Heaven. But those who teach God's laws *and obey them* shall be great in the Kingdom of Heaven.

20 But I warn you—unless your goodness[2] is greater than that of the Pharisees and other Jewish leaders, you can't get into the Kingdom of Heaven at all!

21 Under the laws of Moses the rule was, 'If you kill, you must die.'

22 But I have added to that rule,[3] and tell you that if you are only *angry*, even in your own home,[4] you are in danger of judgment![5] If you call your friend an idiot, you are in danger of being brought before the court. And if you curse him, you are in danger of the fires of hell.[6]

---

[1]Literally, "until all things be accomplished."
[2]Literally, "righteousness."
[3]Literally, "But I say."
[4]Literally, "with your brother."
[5]Literally, "the hell of fire."

Revised Standard

9 "Blessed are the peacemakers, for they shall be called sons of God.

10 "Blessed are those who are persecuted for righteousness' sake, for theirs is the kingdom of heaven.

11 "Blessed are you when men revile you
and persecute you and utter all kinds of evil
against you falsely on my account. 12Re-
joice and be glad, for your reward is great
in heaven, for so men persecuted the prophets who were before you.

Teaching about salt and light

13 "You are the salt of the earth; but if salt has lost its taste, how shall its saltness be restored? It is no longer good for anything except to be thrown out and trodden under foot by men.

14 "You are the light of the world. A
city set on a hill cannot be hid. 15Nor do
men light a lamp and put it under a bushel,
but on a stand, and it gives light to all in the
house. 16Let your light so shine before men,
that they may see your good works and give
glory to your Father who is in heaven.

The higher righteousness

17 "Think not that I have come to abolish the law and the prophets; I have come
not to abolish them but to fulfil them. 18For
truly, I say to you, till heaven and earth pass
away, not an iota, not a dot, will pass from
the law until all is accomplished. 19Whoever
then relaxes one of the least of these commandments and teaches men so, shall be
called least in the kingdom of heaven; but
he who does them and teaches them shall
be called great in the kingdom of heaven.
20For I tell you, unless your righteousness
exceeds that of the scribes and Pharisees,
you will never enter the kingdom of
heaven.

Anger and reconciliation

21 "You have heard that it was said to
the men of old, 'You shall not kill; and
whoever kills shall be liable to judgment.'
22But I say to you that every one who is
angry with his brother[i] shall be liable to
judgment; whoever insults[j] his brother shall
be liable to the council, and whoever says,
'You fool!' shall be liable to the hell[k] of fire.

---

[i] Other ancient authorities insert *without cause*
[j] Greek *says Raca to* (an obscure term of abuse)
[k] Greek *Gehenna*

King James

23 Therefore if thou bring thy gift to the altar, and there rememberest that thy brother hath aught against thee;

24 Leave there thy gift before the altar, and go thy way; first be reconciled to thy brother, and then come and offer thy gift.

25 Agree with thine adversary quickly, whiles thou art in the way with him; lest at any time the adversary deliver thee to the judge, and the judge deliver thee to the officer, and thou be cast into prison.

26 Verily I say unto thee, Thou shalt by no means come out thence, till thou hast paid the uttermost farthing.

27 ¶ Ye have heard that it was said by them of old time, Thou shalt not commit adultery:

28 But I say unto you, That whosoever looketh on a woman to lust after her hath committed adultery with her already in his heart.

29 And if thy right eye offend thee, pluck it out, and cast *it* from thee: for it is profitable for thee that one of thy members should perish, and not *that* thy whole body should be cast into hell.

30 And if thy right hand offend thee, cut it off, and cast *it* from thee: for it is profitable for thee that one of thy members should perish, and not *that* thy whole body should be cast into hell.

31 It hath been said, Whosoever shall put away his wife, let him give her a writing of divorcement:

32 But I say unto you, That whosoever shall put away his wife, saving for the cause of fornication, causeth her to commit adultery: and whosoever shall marry her that is divorced committeth adultery.

33 ¶ Again, ye have heard that it hath been said by them of old time, Thou shalt not forswear thyself, but shalt perform unto the Lord thine oaths:

34 But I say unto you, Swear not at all; neither by heaven; for it is God's throne:

35 Nor by the earth; for it is his footstool: neither by Jerusalem; for it is the city of the great King.

36 Neither shalt thou swear by thy head, because thou canst not make one hair white or black.

37 But let your communication be, Yea, yea; Nay, nay: for whatsoever is more than these cometh of evil.

38 ¶ Ye have heard that it hath been said, An eye for an eye, and a tooth for a tooth:

39 But I say unto you, That ye resist not evil: but whosoever shall smite thee on thy right cheek, turn to him the other also.

40 And if any man will sue thee at the law, and take away thy coat, let him have *thy* cloak also.

41 And whosoever shall compel thee to go a mile, go with him twain.

42 Give to him that asketh thee, and from him that would borrow of thee turn not thou away.

43 ¶ Ye have heard that it hath been said, Thou shalt love thy neighbour, and hate thine enemy.

Amplified

empty-headed idiot! shall be [r]liable to *and* unable to escape the hell (Gehenna) of fire.

23 So if, when you are offering your gift at the altar you there remember that your brother has any [grievance] against you,

24 Leave your gift at the altar and go; first make peace with your brother, and then come back *and* present your gift.

25 Come to terms quickly with your accuser while you are on the way travelling with him, lest your accuser hand you over to the judge, and the judge to the guard, and you be put in prison;

26 Truly, I say to you, you will never be released until you have paid the last fraction of a penny.

27 You have heard that it was said, You shall not commit adultery, [Exod. 20:14; Deut. 5:18.]

28 But I say to you that every one who so much as looks at a woman with evil desire for her has already committed adultery with her in his heart.

29 If your right eye serves as a trap to ensnare you *or* is an occasion for you to stumble *and* sin, pluck it out and throw it away. It is better that you lose one of your members than that your whole body be cast into hell (Gehenna).

30 And if your right hand serves as a trap to ensnare you *or* is an occasion for you to stumble *and* sin, cut it off and cast it from you. It is better that you lose one of your members than that your entire body should be cast into hell (Gehenna).

31 It was also said, Whoever divorces his wife must give her a certificate of divorcement.

32 But I tell you, Whoever dismisses *and* repudiates *and* divorces his wife, except on the grounds of unfaithfulness (sexual immorality), causes her to commit adultery; and whoever marries a woman who has been divorced commits adultery. [Deut. 24:1-4].

33 Again, you have heard that it was said to the men of old, You shall not swear falsely, but you shall perform your oaths to the Lord—as a religious duty.

34 But I tell you, Do not bind yourselves by an oath at all, either by heaven, for it is the throne of God,

35 Or by the earth, for it is the footstool of His feet, or by Jerusalem, for it is the city of the great King. [Isa. 66:1; Ps. 48:2.]

36 And do not swear by your head, for you are not able to make a single hair white or black.

37 Let your Yes be simply Yes, and your No be simply No; anything more than that comes from the evil one. [Lev. 19:12; Num. 30:2; Deut. 23:21.]

38 You have heard that it was said, An eye for an eye and a tooth for a tooth, [Exod. 21:24; Lev. 24:20; Deut. 19:21.]

39 But I say to you, Do not resist the evil man [who injures you]; but if any one strikes you on the right jaw *or* cheek, turn to him the other one too;

40 And if any one wants to sue you and take your undershirt (tunic), let him have your coat also;

41 And if any one forces you to go one mile, go with him two [miles].

42 Give to him who keeps on begging from you, and do not turn away from him who would borrow ([s]at interest) from you, [Deut. 15:8; Prov. 24:29.]

43 You have heard that it was said, You shall love your neighbor and hate your enemy;

---

r) Thayer.
s) Vincent.

Living New Testament

23 So if you are standing before the altar in the Temple, offering a sacrifice to God, and suddenly remember that a friend has something against you,

24 Leave your sacrifice there beside the altar and go and apologize and be reconciled to him, and then come and offer your sacrifice to God.

25 Come to terms quickly with your enemy before it is too late and he drags you into court and you are thrown into a debtor's cell,

26 For you will stay there until you have paid the last penny.

27 The laws of Moses said, 'You shall not commit adultery.'

28 But I say, Anyone who even looks at a woman with lust in his eye has already committed adultery with her in his heart.

29 So if your eye—even if it is your best[6] eye!—causes you to lust, gouge it out and throw it away. Better for part of you to be destroyed than for all of you to be cast into hell.

30 And if your hand—even your right hand—causes you to sin, cut it off and throw it away. Better that than find yourself in hell.

31 The law of Moses says, 'If anyone wants to be rid of his wife, he can divorce her merely by giving her a letter of dismissal.'

32 But I say that a man who divorces his wife, except for unfaithfulness, causes her to commit adultery. And he who marries her commits adultery.

33 Again, the law of Moses says, 'You shall not break your vows to God, but must fulfill them all.'

34 But I say, Don't make any vows! And even to say, 'By heavens!' is a sacred vow to God, for the heavens are God's throne.

35 And if you say 'By the earth!' it is a sacred vow, for the earth is His footstool. And don't swear 'By Jerusalem!' for Jerusalem is the capital of the great King.

36 Don't even swear 'By my head!' for you can't turn one hair white or black.

37 Say just a simple 'Yes, I will' or 'No, I won't.' Your word is enough. To strengthen your promise with a vow shows that something is wrong.

38 The law of Moses says, 'If a man gouges out another's eye, he must pay with his own eye. If a tooth gets knocked out, knock out the tooth of the one who did it.'[7]

39 But I say: Don't resist violence! If you are slapped on one cheek, turn the other too.

40 If you are ordered to court, and your shirt is taken from you, give your coat too.

41 If the military demand that you carry their gear for a mile, carry it two.

42 Give to those who ask, and don't turn away from those who want to borrow.

43 There is a saying, 'Love your *friends* and hate your enemies.'

---

[6]Literally, "your right eye."
[7]Literally, "an eye for an eye and a tooth for a tooth."

Revised Standard

23 So if you are offering your gift at the
altar, and there remember that your brother
has something against you, 24 leave your gift
there before the altar and go; first be reconciled to your brother, and then come and
offer your gift. 25 Make friends quickly with
your accuser, while you are going with him
to court, lest your accuser hand you over to
the judge, and the judge to the guard, and
you be put in prison; 26 truly, I say to you,
you will never get out till you have paid the
last penny.

Adultery and divorce

27 "You have heard that it was said,
'You shall not commit adultery.' 28 But I say
to you that every one who looks at a woman
lustfully has already committed adultery
with her in his heart. 29 If your right eye
causes you to sin, pluck it out and throw it
away; it is better that you lose one of your
members than that your whole body be
thrown into hell.[k] 30 And if your right hand
causes you to sin, cut it off and throw it
away; it is better that you lose one of your
members than that your whole body go into
hell.[k]

31 "It was also said, 'Whoever divorces
his wife, let him give her a certificate of
divorce.' 32 But I say to you that every one
who divorces his wife, except on the ground
of unchastity, makes her an adulteress; and
whoever marries a divorced woman commits
adultery.

Oaths and retaliation

33 "Again you have heard that it was
said to the men of old, 'You shall not swear
falsely, but shall perform to the Lord what
you have sworn.' 34 But I say to you, Do not
swear at all, either by heaven, for it is the
throne of God, 35 or by the earth, for it is
his footstool, or by Jerusalem, for it is the
city of the great King. 36 And do not swear
by your head, for you cannot make one hair
white or black. 37 Let what you say be simply 'Yes' or 'No'; anything more than this
comes from evil.[l]

38 "You have heard that it was said, 'An
eye for an eye and a tooth for a tooth.'
39 But I say to you, Do not resist one who is
evil. But if any one strikes you on the right
cheek, turn to him the other also; 40 and if
any one would sue you and take your coat,
let him have your cloak as well; 41 and if
any one forces you to go one mile, go with
him two miles. 42 Give to him who begs
from you, and do not refuse him who would
borrow from you.

Neighbors and enemies

43 "You have heard that it was said,
'You shall love your neighbor and hate your

---

[k] Greek *Gehenna*
[l] Or *the evil one*

King James

44 But I say unto you, Love your enemies, bless them that curse you, do good to them that hate you, and pray for them which despitefully use you, and persecute you;

45 That ye may be the children of your Father which is in heaven: for he maketh his sun to rise on the evil and on the good, and sendeth rain on the just and on the unjust.

46 For if ye love them which love you, what reward have ye? do not even the publicans the same?

47 And if ye salute your brethren only, what do ye more *than others?* do not even the publicans so?

48 Be ye therefore perfect, even as your Father which is in heaven is perfect.

Amplified

44 But I tell you, Love your enemies and pray for those who persecute you, [Prov. 25:21, 22.]

45 [u]To show that you are the children of your Father Who is in heaven; for He makes His sun rise on the wicked and on the good, and makes the rain fall upon the upright and the wrongdoers [alike].

46 For if you love those who love you, what reward can you have? Do not even the tax collectors do that?

47 And if you greet only your brethren, what more than others are you doing? Do not even the Gentiles (the heathen) do that?

48 You, therefore, must be perfect, as your heavenly Father is perfect [that is, grow into complete [t]maturity of godliness in mind and character, [u]having reached the proper height of virtue and integrity]. [Lev. 19:2, 18.]

CHAPTER 6

TAKE heed that ye do not your alms before men, to be seen of them: otherwise ye have no reward of your Father which is in heaven.

2 Therefore when thou doest *thine* alms, do not sound a trumpet before thee, as the hypocrites do in the synagogues and in the streets, that they may have glory of men. Verily I say unto you, They have their reward.

3 But when thou doest alms, let not thy left hand know what thy right hand doeth:

4 That thine alms may be in secret: and thy Father which seeth in secret himself shall reward thee openly.

5 ¶ And when thou prayest, thou shalt not be as the hypocrites *are:* for they love to pray standing in the synagogues and in the corners of the streets, that they may be seen of men. Verily I say unto you, They have their reward.

6 But thou, when thou prayest, enter into thy closet, and when thou hast shut thy door, pray to thy Father which is in secret; and thy Father which seeth in secret shall reward thee openly.

7 But when ye pray, use not vain repetitions, as the heathen *do:* for they think that they shall be heard for their much speaking.

8 Be not ye therefore like unto them: for your Father knoweth what things ye have need of, before ye ask him.

9 After this manner therefore pray ye: Our Father which art in heaven, Hallowed be thy name.

10 Thy kingdom come. Thy will be done in earth, as *it is* in heaven.

11 Give us this day our daily bread.

12 And forgive us our debts, as we forgive our debtors.

13 And lead us not into temptation, but deliver us from evil: For thine is the kingdom, and the power, and the glory, for ever. Amen.

CHAPTER 6

TAKE care not to do your good deeds publicly *or* before men in order to be seen by them; otherwise you will have no reward [[s]reserved for and awaiting you] with *and* from your Father Who is in heaven.

2 Thus, whenever you give to the poor, do not blow a trumpet before you, as the hypocrites in the synagogues and in the streets like to do, that they may be [v]recognized *and* honored *and* praised by men. Truly, I tell you, they have their reward—[w]in full already.

3 But when you give to charity, do not let your left hand know what your right hand is doing,

4 So that your deeds of charity may be in secret; and your Father Who sees in secret will reward you *openly.*

5 Also when you pray you must not be like the hypocrites, for they love to pray standing in the synagogues and on the corners of the streets, that they may be seen by people. Truly, I tell you, they have their reward—[w]in full already.

6 But when you pray, go into your most private room, and closing the door, pray to your Father Who is in secret; and your Father Who sees in secret will reward you *in the open.*

7 And when you pray do not (multiply words, repeating the same ones over and over, and) heap up phrases as the Gentiles do, for they think they will be heard for their much speaking. [I Kings 18:25-29.]

8 Do not be like them, for your Father knows what you need before you ask Him.

9 Pray therefore like this: Our Father Who is in heaven, hallowed (kept holy) be Your name.

10 Your kingdom come, Your will be done, on earth as it is in heaven.

11 Give us this day our daily bread,

12 And forgive us our debts, as we also have forgiven ([x]left, remitted and let go the debts, and [y]given up resentment against) our debtors.

13 And lead (bring) us not into temptation, but deliver us from the evil one. *For Yours is the kingdom and the power and the glory forever. Amen.*

---

s) Vincent.
t) Wuest.
u) Thayer.
v) Cremer.
w) Vincent.
x) Moulton and Milligan.
y) Webster for "forgive."

Living New Testament

44 But I say, Love your *enemies!* Pray for those who *persecute* you!

45 In that way you will be acting as true sons of your Father in heaven. For He gives His sunlight to both the evil and the good, and sends rain on the just and on the unjust too.

46 If you love only those who love you, what good is that? Even scoundrels do that much.

47 If you are friendly only to your friends, how are you different from anyone else? Even the heathen do that.

48 But you are to be perfect, even as your Father in heaven is perfect.

Revised Standard

enemy.' 44But I say to you, Love your enemies and pray for those who persecute you,
45so that you may be sons of your Father
who is in heaven; for he makes his sun rise
on the evil and on the good, and sends rain
on the just and on the unjust. 46For if you
love those who love you, what reward have
you? Do not even the tax collectors do the
same? 47And if you salute only your brethren, what more are you doing than others?
Do not even the Gentiles do the same?
48You, therefore, must be perfect, as your
heavenly Father is perfect.

CHAPTER 6

Take care! Don't do your good deeds publicly, to be admired, for then you will lose the reward from your Father in heaven.

2 When you give a gift to a beggar, don't shout about it as the hypocrites do—blowing trumpets in the synagogues and streets to call attention to their acts of charity! I tell you in all earnestness, they have received all the reward they will ever get.

3 But when you do a kindness to someone, do it secretly—don't tell your left hand what your right hand is doing.

4 And your Father who knows all secrets will reward you.

5 And now about prayer. When you pray, don't be like the hypocrites who pretend piety by praying publicly on street corners and in the synagogues where everyone can see them. Truly, that is all the reward they will ever get.

6 But when you pray, go away by yourself, all alone, and shut the door behind you and pray to your Father secretly, and your Father, who knows your secrets, will reward you.

7, 8 Don't recite the same prayer over and over as the heathen do, who think prayers are answered only by repeating them again and again. Remember, your Father knows exactly what you need even before you ask Him!

9 Pray along these lines: 'Our Father in heaven, we honor Your holy name.

10 We ask that Your kingdom will come soon. May Your will be done here on earth, just as it is in heaven.

11 Give us our food again today, as usual,

12 And forgive us our sins, just as we have forgiven those who have sinned against us.

13 Don't bring us into temptation, but deliver us from the Evil One.[1] Amen.'

[1]Or "from evil." Some manuscripts add here, "For yours is the kingdom and the power and the glory forever. Amen."

Piety and almsgiving

6 "Beware of practicing your piety before men in order to be seen by them;
for then you will have no reward from
your Father who is in heaven.
2 "Thus, when you give alms, sound no
trumpet before you, as the hypocrites do in
the synagogues and in the streets, that they
may be praised by men. Truly, I say to you,
they have their reward. 3But when you give
alms, do not let your left hand know what
your right hand is doing, 4so that your alms
may be in secret; and your Father who sees
in secret will reward you.

Prayer and fasting

5 "And when you pray, you must not be
like the hypocrites; for they love to stand
and pray in the synagogues and at the
corners, that they may be seen by men.
Truly, I say to you, they have their reward.
6But when you pray, go into your room and
shut the door and pray to your Father who
is in secret; and your Father who sees in
secret will reward you.
7 "And in praying do not heap up empty
phrases as the Gentiles do; for they think
that they will be heard for their many
words. 8Do not be like them, for your
Father knows what you need before you
ask him. 9Pray then like this:
Our Father who art in heaven,
Hallowed be thy name.
10Thy kingdom come,
Thy will be done,
On earth as it is in heaven.
11Give us this day our daily bread;[m]
12And forgive us our debts,
As we also have forgiven our
debtors;
13And lead us not into temptation,
But deliver us from evil.[n]

[m] Or *our bread for the morrow*

[n] Or *the evil one*. Other authorities, some ancient, add in some form, *For thine is the kingdom and the power and the glory, for ever. Amen.*

King James

14 For if ye forgive men their trespasses, your heavenly Father will also forgive you:

15 But if ye forgive not men their trespasses, neither will your Father forgive your trespasses.

16 ¶ Moreover when ye fast, be not, as the hypocrites, of a sad countenance: for they disfigure their faces, that they may appear unto men to fast. Verily I say unto you, They have their reward.

17 But thou, when thou fastest, anoint thine head, and wash thy face;

18 That thou appear not unto men to fast, but unto thy Father which is in secret: and thy Father, which seeth in secret, shall reward thee openly.

19 ¶ Lay not up for yourselves treasures upon earth, where moth and rust doth corrupt, and where thieves break through and steal:

20 But lay up for yourselves treasures in heaven, where neither moth nor rust doth corrupt, and where thieves do not break through nor steal:

21 For where your treasure is, there will your heart be also.

22 The light of the body is the eye: if therefore thine eye be single, thy whole body shall be full of light.

23 But if thine eye be evil, thy whole body shall be full of darkness. If therefore the light that is in thee be darkness, how great *is* that darkness!

24 ¶ No man can serve two masters: for either he will hate the one, and love the other; or else he will hold to the one, and despise the other. Ye cannot serve God and mammon.

25 Therefore I say unto you, Take no thought for your life, what ye shall eat, or what ye shall drink; nor yet for your body, what ye shall put on. Is not the life more than meat, and the body than raiment?

26 Behold the fowls of the air: for they sow not, neither do they reap, nor gather into barns; yet your heavenly Father feedeth them. Are ye not much better than they?

27 Which of you by taking thought can add one cubit unto his stature?

28 And why take ye thought for raiment? Consider the lilies of the field, how they grow; they toil not, neither do they spin:

29 And yet I say unto you, That even Solomon in all his glory was not arrayed like one of these.

30 Wherefore, if God so clothe the grass of the field, which to-day is, and to-morrow is cast into the oven, *shall he* not much more *clothe* you, O ye of little faith?

31 Therefore take no thought, saying, What shall we eat? or, What shall we drink? or, Wherewithal shall we be clothed?

Amplified

14 For if you forgive people their trespasses—that is, their reckless and wilful sins, [z]leaving them, letting them go and [a]giving up resentment—your heavenly Father will also forgive you.

15 But if you do not forgive others their trespasses—their [b]reckless and wilful sins, [z]leaving them, letting them go and [a]giving up resentment—neither will your Father forgive you your trespasses.

16 And whenever you are fasting, do not look gloomy *and* [c]sour *and* [d]dreary like the hypocrites, for they put on a dismal countenance that their fasting may be apparent *and* seen by men. Truly, I say to you, they have their reward—[b]in full already. [Isa. 58:5.]

17 But when you fast, perfume your head and wash your face,

18 So that your fasting may not be noticed by men but by your Father Who sees in secret; and your Father Who sees in secret will reward you *in the open.*

19 Do not [e]gather *and* heap up *and* store for yourselves treasures on earth, where moth and rust *and* [f]worm consume *and* destroy, and where thieves break through and steal;

20 But [e]gather *and* heap up *and* store for yourselves treasures in heaven, where neither moth nor rust *nor* [f]worm consume *and* destroy, and where thieves do not break through and steal;

21 For where your treasure is, there will your heart be also.

22 The eye is the lamp of the body. So, if your eye is sound, your entire body will be full of light;

23 But if your eye is unsound, your whole body will be full of darkness. If then the very light in you [your [g]conscience] is darkened, how dense is that darkness!

24 No one can serve two masters; for either he will hate the one and love the other, or he will stand by *and* be devoted to the one and despise and be [h]against the other. You cannot serve God and mammon [that is, [g]deceitful riches, money, possessions or [i]what is trusted in].

25 Therefore I tell you, stop being [j]perpetually uneasy (anxious and worried) about your life, what you shall eat *or what you shall drink,* and about your body, what you shall put on. Is not life greater [in quality] than food, and the body [far above and more excellent] than clothing?

26 Look at the birds of the air; they neither sow nor reap nor gather into barns, and yet your heavenly Father keeps feeding them. Are you not worth more than they?

27 And which of you by worrying *and* being anxious can add one unit of measure [cubit] to his stature *or* to the [k]span of his life? [Ps. 39:5-7].

28 And why should you be anxious about clothes? Consider the lilies of the field *and* [i]learn thoroughly how they grow; they neither toil nor spin;

29 Yet I tell you, even Solomon in all his [i]magnificence (excellence, dignity and grace) was not arrayed like one of these. [I Kings 10:4-7.]

30 But if God so clothes the grass of the field, which today is alive *and* green and tomorrow is tossed into the furnace, will He not much more surely clothe you, O you men with little faith?

31 Therefore do not worry *and* be anxious, saying, What are we going to have to eat? or, What are we going to have to drink? or, What are we going to have to wear?

---

z) Moulton and Milligan.
a) Webster for "forgive."
b) Vincent.
c) Luther.
d) Trench.
e) Thayer.
f) Alternate reading.
g) Cremer.
h) Vincent.
i) Thayer.
j) Wuest.
k) Souter: [cubit] used as a measurement of time.

Living New Testament

14, 15 Your heavenly Father will forgive you if you forgive those who sin against you; but if *you* refuse to forgive *them, He* will not forgive *you.*

16 And now about fasting. When you fast, declining your food for a spiritual purpose, don't do it publicly, as the hypocrites do, who try to look wan and disheveled so people will feel sorry for them! Truly, that is the only reward they will ever get.

17 But when you fast, put on festive clothing,

18 So that no one will suspect you are hungry, except your Father who knows every secret. And He will reward you.

19 Don't store your profits here on earth where they can erode away or may be stolen.

20 Store them in heaven where they will never lose their value, and are safe from thieves!

21 If your profits are in heaven your heart will be there too.

22 If your eye is pure, there will be sunshine in your soul.

23 But if your eye is clouded with evil thoughts and desires, you are in deep spiritual darkness. And oh, how deep that darkness can be.

24 You cannot serve two masters: God and money. For you will hate one and love the other, or else the other way around.

25 So my counsel is, Don't worry about *things*—food, drink, money[2], and clothes. For you already have life and a body—and they are far more important than what to eat and wear.

26 Look at the birds! They don't worry about what to eat—they don't need to sow or reap or store up food—for your heavenly Father feeds them. And you are far more valuable to Him than they are.

27 Will all your worries add a single moment to your life?

28 And why worry about your clothes? Look at the field lilies! They don't worry about theirs.

29 Yet King Solomon in all his glory was not clothed as beautifully as they.

30 And if God cares so wonderfully for flowers that are here today and gone tomorrow, won't He more surely care for you, O men of little faith?

31, 32 So don't worry at all about having enough food and clothing. Why be like the heathen? For they take

[2]Implied.

Revised Standard

14For if you forgive men their trespasses,
your heavenly Father also will forgive you;
15but if you do not forgive men their trespasses, neither will your Father forgive
your trespasses.
16 "And when you fast, do not look dismal, like the hypocrites, for they disfigure
their faces that their fasting may be seen by
men. Truly, I say to you, they have their
reward. 17But when you fast, anoint your
head and wash your face, 18that your fasting may not be seen by men but by your
Father who is in secret; and your Father
who sees in secret will reward you.

Possessions and masters

19 "Do not lay up for yourselves treasures on earth, where moth and rust[o] consume and where thieves break in and steal,
20but lay up for yourselves treasures in
heaven, where neither moth nor rust[o] consumes and where thieves do not break in
and steal. 21For where your treasure is,
there will your heart be also.
22 "The eye is the lamp of the body. So,
if your eye is sound, your whole body will
be full of light; 23but if your eye is not
sound, your whole body will be full of
darkness. If then the light in you is
darkness, how great is the darkness!
24 "No one can serve two masters; for
either he will hate the one and love the
other, or he will be devoted to the one and
despise the other. You cannot serve God
and mammon.

Anxiety and God's kingdom

25 "Therefore I tell you, do not be anxious about your life, what you shall eat or
what you shall drink, nor about your body,
what you shall put on. Is not life more than
food, and the body more than clothing?
26Look at the birds of the air: they neither
sow nor reap nor gather into barns, and yet
your heavenly Father feeds them. Are you
not of more value than they? 27And which
of you by being anxious can add one cubit
to his span of life?[p] 28And why are you
anxious about clothing? Consider the lilies of
the field, how they grow; they neither toil
nor spin; 29yet I tell you, even Solomon in
all his glory was not arrayed like one of
these. 30But if God so clothes the grass of
the field, which today is alive and tomorrow
is thrown into the oven, will he not much
more clothe you, O men of little faith?
31Therefore do not be anxious, saying,
'What shall we eat?' or 'What shall we

[o] Or *worm*
[p] Or *to his stature*

King James

32 (For after all these things do the Gentiles seek:) for your heavenly Father knoweth that ye have need of all these things.
33 But seek ye first the kingdom of God, and his righteousness; and all these things shall be added unto you.
34 Take therefore no thought for the morrow: for the morrow shall take thought for the things of itself. Sufficient unto the day *is* the evil thereof.

Amplified

32 For the Gentiles (heathen) wish for *and* crave *and* diligently seek after all these things; and your heavenly Father well knows that you need them all.
33 But seek for ([l]aim at and strive after) first of all His kingdom, and His righteousness [[m]His way of doing and being right], and then all these things [l]taken together will be given you besides.
34 So do not worry *or* be anxious about tomorrow, for tomorrow will have worries *and* anxieties of its own. Sufficient for each day is its own trouble.

King James

CHAPTER 7

JUDGE not, that ye be not judged.
2 For with what judgment ye judge, ye shall be judged: and with what measure ye mete, it shall be measured to you again.
3 And why beholdest thou the mote that is in thy brother's eye, but considerest not the beam that is in thine own eye?
4 Or how wilt thou say to thy brother, Let me pull out the mote out of thine eye; and, behold, a beam *is* in thine own eye?
5 Thou hypocrite, first cast out the beam out of thine own eye; and then shalt thou see clearly to cast out the mote out of thy brother's eye.
6 ¶ Give not that which is holy unto the dogs, neither cast ye your pearls before swine, lest they trample them under their feet, and turn again and rend you.
7 ¶ Ask, and it shall be given you; seek, and ye shall find; knock, and it shall be opened unto you:
8 For every one that asketh receiveth; and he that seeketh findeth; and to him that knocketh it shall be opened.
9 Or what man is there of you, whom if his son ask bread, will he give him a stone?
10 Or if he ask a fish, will he give him a serpent?
11 If ye then, being evil, know how to give good gifts unto your children, how much more shall your Father which is in heaven give good things to them that ask him?
12 Therefore all things whatsoever ye would that men should do to you, do ye even so to them: for this is the law and the prophets.
13 ¶ Enter ye in at the strait gate: for wide *is* the gate, and broad *is* the way, that leadeth to destruction, and many there be which go in thereat:
14 Because strait *is* the gate, and narrow *is* the way, which leadeth unto life, and few there be that find it.

Amplified

CHAPTER 7

DO not judge *and* criticize *and* condemn others, so that you may not be judged *and* criticized *and* condemned yourselves.
2 For just as you judge *and* criticize *and* condemn others you will be judged *and* criticized *and* condemned, and in accordance with the measure you deal out to others it will be dealt out again to you.
3 Why do you [n]stare from without at the [o]very small particle that is in your brother's eye, but do not become aware of *and* consider the beam [p]of timber that is in your own eye?
4 Or how can you say to your brother, Let me get the tiny particle out of your eye, when there is the beam [p]of timber in your own eye?
5 You hypocrite, first get the beam of timber out of your own eye, and then you will see clearly to take the tiny particle out of your brother's eye.
6 Do not give that which is holy—the sacred thing—to the dogs; and do not throw your pearls before hogs, lest they trample upon them with their feet and turn *and* tear you in pieces.
7 [q]Keep on asking and it will be given you; [q]keep on seeking and you will find; [q]keep on knocking [reverently] and the door will be opened to you.
8 For every one who keeps on asking receives, and he who keeps on seeking finds, and to him who keeps on knocking it will be opened.
9 Or what man is there of you, if his son asks him for a loaf of bread, will hand him a stone?
10 Or if he asks for a fish, will hand him a serpent?
11 If you then, evil as you are, know how to give good *and* [r]advantageous gifts to your children, how much more will your Father Who is in heaven [perfect as He is] give good *and* [r]advantageous things to those who [q]keep on asking Him!
12 So then whatever you desire that others would do to *and* for you, even so do you also to *and* for them, for this is [sums up,] the Law and the prophets.
13 Enter through the narrow gate, for wide is the gate and spacious *and* broad is the way that leads away to destruction, and many are those who are entering it.
14 But the gate is narrow—contracted [s]by pressure—and the way is straitened *and* compressed that leads away to life, and few are they who find it. [Jer. 21:8; Deut. 30:19.]

---

l) Thayer.
m) Williams.
n) Vincent.
o) Moulton and Milligan.
p) Abbott-Smith.
q) Wuest's "Golden Nuggets from the Greek New Testament."
r) Cremer.
s) Souter.

Living New Testament

pride in all these things and are deeply concerned about them. But your heavenly Father already knows perfectly well that you need them,

33 And He will gladly give them to you if you give Him first place in your life.

34 So don't be anxious about tomorrow. God will take care of your tomorrow too. Live one day at a time.[3]

Revised Standard

drink?' or 'What shall we wear?' [32]For the Gentiles seek all these things; and your heavenly Father knows that you need them all. [33]But seek first his kingdom and his righteousness, and all these things shall be yours as well.

34 "Therefore do not be anxious about tomorrow, for tomorrow will be anxious for itself. Let the day's own trouble be sufficient for the day.

CHAPTER 7

Don't criticize, and then you won't be criticized!

2 For others will treat you as you treat them.

3 And why worry about a speck in the eye of a brother when you have a board in your own?

4 Should you say, 'Friend, let me help you get that speck out of your eye,' when you can't even see because of the board in your own?

5 Hypocrite! First get rid of the board. Then you can see to help your brother.

6 Don't give pearls to swine! They will trample the pearls and turn and attack you.

7 Ask, and you will be given what you ask for. Seek, and you will find. Knock, and the door will be opened.

8 For everyone who asks, receives. Anyone who seeks, finds. If only you will knock, the door will open.

9 If a child asks his father for a loaf of bread, will he be given a stone instead?

10 If he asks for fish, will he be given a poisonous snake? Of course not!

11 And if you hardhearted, sinful men know how to give good gifts to your children, won't your Father in heaven even more certainly give good gifts to those who ask Him for them?

12 Do for others what you want them to do for you. This is the teaching of the Old Testament in a nutshell.[1]

13 Heaven can be entered only through the narrow gate! The highway to hell[2] is broad, and its gate is wide enough for all the multitudes who choose its easy way.

14 But the Gateway to Life is small, and the road is narrow, and only a few ever find it.

Judging and hypocrisy

7 "Judge not, that you be not judged. [2]For with the judgment you pronounce you will be judged, and the measure you give will be the measure you get. [3]Why do you see the speck that is in your brother's eye, but do not notice the log that is in your own eye? [4]Or how can you say to your brother, 'Let me take the speck out of your eye,' when there is the log in your own eye? [5]You hypocrite, first take the log out of your own eye, and then you will see clearly to take the speck out of your brother's eye.

6 "Do not give dogs what is holy; and do not throw your pearls before swine, lest they trample them under foot and turn to attack you.

Prayer and the Golden Rule

7 "Ask, and it will be given you; seek, and you will find; knock, and it will be opened to you. [8]For every one who asks receives, and he who seeks finds, and to him who knocks it will be opened. [9]Or what man of you, if his son asks him for bread, will give him a stone? [10]Or if he asks for a fish, will give him a serpent? [11]If you then, who are evil, know how to give good gifts to your children, how much more will your Father who is in heaven give good things to those who ask him! [12]So whatever you wish that men would do to you, do so to them; for this is the law and the prophets.

The narrow and wide gates

13 "Enter by the narrow gate; for the gate is wide and the way is easy,[q] that leads to destruction, and those who enter by it are many. [14]For the gate is narrow and the way is hard, that leads to life, and those who find it are few.

---

[3]Literally, "sufficient unto the day is the evil thereof."
[1]Literally, "this is the law and the prophets."
[2]Literally, "the way that leads to destruction."

[q] Other ancient authorities read *for the way is wide and easy*

King James

15 ¶ Beware of false prophets, which come to you in sheep's clothing, but inwardly they are ravening wolves.

16 Ye shall know them by their fruits. Do men gather grapes of thorns, or figs of thistles?

17 Even so every good tree bringeth forth good fruit; but a corrupt tree bringeth forth evil fruit.

18 A good tree cannot bring forth evil fruit, neither *can* a corrupt tree bring forth good fruit.

19 Every tree that bringeth not forth good fruit is hewn down, and cast into the fire.

20 Wherefore by their fruits ye shall know them.

21 ¶ Not every one that saith unto me, Lord, Lord, shall enter into the kingdom of heaven; but he that doeth the will of my Father which is in heaven.

22 Many will say to me in that day, Lord, Lord, have we not prophesied in thy name? and in thy name have cast out devils? and in thy name done many wonderful works?

23 And then will I profess unto them, I never knew you: depart from me, ye that work iniquity.

24 ¶ Therefore whosoever heareth these sayings of mine, and doeth them, I will liken him unto a wise man, which built his house upon a rock:

25 And the rain descended, and the floods came, and the winds blew, and beat upon that house; and it fell not: for it was founded upon a rock.

26 And every one that heareth these sayings of mine, and doeth them not, shall be likened unto a foolish man, which built his house upon the sand:

27 And the rain descended, and the floods came, and the winds blew, and beat upon that house; and it fell: and great was the fall of it.

28 And it came to pass, when Jesus had ended these sayings, the people were astonished at his doctrine:

29 For he taught them as *one* having authority, and not as the scribes.

Amplified

15 Beware of false prophets, who come to you dressed as sheep, but inside they are devouring wolves. [Ezek. 22: 27.]

16 You will [t]fully recognize them by their fruits. Do people pick grapes from thorns, or figs from thistles?

17 Even so every healthy (sound) tree bears good fruit—[u]worthy of admiration; but the sickly (decaying, worthless) tree bears bad *and* worthless fruit.

18 A good (healthy) tree cannot bear bad (worthless) fruit; nor can a bad (diseased) tree bear [u]excellent fruit—worthy of admiration.

19 Every tree that does not bear good fruit is cut down and cast into the fire.

20 Therefore you will [t]fully know them by their fruits.

21 Not every one who says to Me, Lord, Lord, will enter the kingdom of heaven, but he who does the will of My Father Who is in heaven.

22 Many will say to Me on that day, Lord, Lord, have we not prophesied in Your name, and driven out demons in Your name, and done many mighty works in Your name?

23 And then I will say to them openly (publicly), I never knew you; depart from Me, you who act wickedly—disregarding My commands. [Ps. 6:8.]

24 So every one who hears these words of Mine and acts upon them—obeying them—will be like a [v]sensible (prudent, practical, wise) man who built his house upon the rock;

25 And the rain fell and the floods came, and the winds blew and beat against that house, but it did not fall, because it had been founded on the rock.

26 And every one who hears these words of Mine and does not do them will be like a stupid (foolish) man who built his house upon the sand;

27 And the rain fell and the floods came, and the winds blew and beat against that house, and it fell; and great *and* complete was the fall of it.

28 When Jesus had finished these sayings [the Sermon on the Mount], the crowds were astonished *and* overwhelmed with bewildered wonder at His teaching,

29 For He was teaching as [One] Who had [and was] authority, and not as did the scribes.

King James

CHAPTER 8

WHEN he was come down from the mountain, great multitudes followed him.

2 And, behold, there came a leper and worshipped him, saying, Lord, if thou wilt, thou canst make me clean.

3 And Jesus put forth *his* hand, and touched him, saying, I will; be thou clean. And immediately his leprosy was cleansed.

Amplified

CHAPTER 8

WHEN Jesus came down from the mountain, great throngs followed Him.

2 And behold, a leper came up to Him and prostrating himself, worshipped Him, saying, Lord, if You will, You are able to [w]cleanse me by curing me.

3 And He reached out His hand and touched him, saying, I will; be cleansed [w]by being cured. And instantly his leprosy was cured *and* cleansed.

---

t) Vincent.
u) Cremer.
v) Abbott-Smith.
w) Thayer.

Living New Testament

15 Beware of false teachers who come disguised as harmless sheep, but are wolves and will tear you apart.

16 You can detect them by the way they act, just as you can identify a tree by its fruit. You need never confuse grapevines with thorn bushes! Or figs with thistles!

17 Different kinds of fruit trees can quickly be identified by examining their fruit.

18 A variety that produces delicious fruit never produces an inedible kind! And a tree producing an inedible kind can't produce what is good!

19 So the trees having the inedible fruit are chopped down and thrown on the fire.

20 Yes, the way to identify a tree or a person[3] is by the kind of fruit produced.

21 Not all who talk like godly people are. They may refer to Me as 'Lord,' but still won't get to heaven. For the decisive question is whether they obey My Father in heaven.

22 At the Judgment[4] many will tell me, 'Lord, Lord, we told others about You and used Your name to cast out demons and to do many other great miracles.'

23 But I will reply, 'You have never been Mine.[5] Go away, for your deeds are evil.'

24 All who listen to My instructions and follow them are wise, like a man who builds his house on solid rock.

25 Though the rain comes in torrents, and the floods rise and the storm winds beat against his house, it won't collapse, for it is built on rock.

26 But those who hear My instructions and ignore them are foolish, like a man who builds his house on sand.

27 For when the rains and floods come, and storm winds beat against his house, it will fall with a mighty crash."

28 The crowds were amazed at Jesus' sermons,

29 For He taught as one who had great authority, and not as their Jewish leaders.[6]

Revised Standard

The test of false prophets

15 "Beware of false prophets, who come
to you in sheep's clothing but inwardly are
ravenous wolves. 16You will know them by
their fruits. Are grapes gathered from
thorns, or figs from thistles? 17So, every
sound tree bears good fruit, but the bad tree
bears evil fruit. 18A sound tree cannot bear
evil fruit, nor can a bad tree bear good
fruit. 19Every tree that does not bear good
fruit is cut down and thrown into the fire.
20Thus you will know them by their fruits.
21 "Not every one who says to me,
'Lord, Lord,' shall enter the kingdom of
heaven, but he who does the will of my
Father who is in heaven. 22On that day
many will say to me, 'Lord, Lord, did we
not prophesy in your name, and cast out
demons in your name, and do mighty works
in your name?' 23And then will I declare
to them, 'I never knew you; depart from
me, you evildoers.'

The wise and foolish builders

24 "Every one then who hears these
words of mine and does them will be like a
wise man who built his house upon the rock;
25and the rain fell, and the floods came, and
the winds blew and beat upon that house,
but it did not fall, because it had been
founded on the rock. 26And every one who
hears these words of mine and does not do
them will be like a foolish man who built his
house upon the sand; 27and the rain fell, and
the floods came, and the winds blew and
beat against that house, and it fell; and
great was the fall of it."
28 And when Jesus finished these sayings,
the crowds were astonished at his teaching,
29for he taught them as one who had authority, and not as their scribes.

CHAPTER 8

Large crowds followed Jesus as He came down the hillside.

2 *Look! A leper is approaching. He kneels before Him, worshiping. "Sir," the leper pleads, "if You want to, You can heal me."*

3 *Jesus touches the man, "I want to," He says; "be healed." And instantly the leprosy disappears!*

[3]Implied.
[4]Literally, "in that day."
[5]Literally, "I never knew you."
[6]Literally, "not as the scribes." These leaders only quoted others, and did not presume to present any fresh revelation.

The leper cleansed

8 When he came down from the mountain, great crowds followed him; 2and
behold, a leper came to him and knelt
before him, saying, "Lord, if you will, you

King James

4 And Jesus saith unto him, See thou tell no man; but go thy way, shew thyself to the priest, and offer the gift that Moses commanded, for a testimony unto them.

5 ¶ And when Jesus was entered into Capernaum, there came unto him a centurion, beseeching him,

6 And saying, Lord, my servant lieth at home sick of the palsy, grievously tormented.

7 And Jesus saith unto him, I will come and heal him.

8 The centurion answered and said, Lord, I am not worthy that thou shouldest come under my roof: but speak the word only, and my servant shall be healed.

9 For I am a man under authority, having soldiers under me: and I say to this *man,* Go, and he goeth; and to another, Come, and he cometh; and to my servant, Do this, and he doeth *it.*

10 When Jesus heard *it,* he marvelled, and said to them that followed, Verily I say unto you, I have not found so great faith, no, not in Israel.

11 And I say unto you, That many shall come from the east and west, and shall sit down with Abraham, and Isaac, and Jacob, in the kingdom of heaven.

12 But the children of the kingdom shall be cast out into outer darkness: there shall be weeping and gnashing of teeth.

13 And Jesus said unto the centurion, Go thy way; and as thou hast believed, *so* be it done unto thee. And his servant was healed in the selfsame hour.

14 ¶ And when Jesus was come into Peter's house, he saw his wife's mother laid, and sick of a fever.

15 And he touched her hand, and the fever left her: and she arose, and ministered unto them.

16 ¶ When the even was come, they brought unto him many that were possessed with devils: and he cast out the spirits with *his* word, and healed all that were sick:

17 That it might be fulfilled which was spoken by Esaias the prophet, saying, Himself took our infirmities, and bare *our* sicknesses.

18 ¶ Now when Jesus saw great multitudes about him, he gave commandment to depart unto the other side.

19 And a certain scribe came, and said unto him, Master, I will follow thee whithersoever thou goest.

20 And Jesus saith unto him, The foxes have holes, and the birds of the air *have* nests; but the Son of man hath not where to lay *his* head.

21 And another of his disciples said unto him, Lord, suffer me first to go and bury my father.

22 But Jesus said unto him, Follow me; and let the dead bury their dead.

23 ¶ And when he was entered into a ship, his disciples followed him.

24 And, behold, there arose a great tempest in the sea, insomuch that the ship was covered with the waves: but he was asleep.

25 And his disciples came to *him,* and awoke him, saying, Lord, save us: we perish.

Amplified

4 And Jesus said to him, See that you tell nothing about this to any one; but go, show yourself to the priest, and present the offering that Moses commanded, for a testimony [to your healing] *and* as an evidence to the people. [Lev. 14:2.]

5 As Jesus went into Capernaum, a centurion came up to Him, begging Him

6 And saying, Lord, my servant boy is lying at the house paralyzed *and* [w]distressed with intense pains.

7 And Jesus said to him, I will come and restore him.

8 But the centurion replied to Him, Lord, I am not worthy *or* fit to have You come under my roof; but only speak the word, and my servant boy will be cured.

9 For I also am a man subject to authority, with soldiers subject to me; and I say to one, Go, and he goes; and to another, Come, and he comes; and to my slave, Do this, and he does it.

10 When Jesus heard him, He marveled, and said to those who followed Him [that is, [w]who adhered steadfastly to Him, conforming to His example in living and if need be in dying also], I tell you, truly I have not found so much faith as this [x]with any one, even in Israel.

11 I tell you, many will come from east and west and sit at table with Abraham, Isaac, and Jacob in the kingdom of heaven,

12 While the sons *and* heirs of the kingdom will be driven out into the darkness outside, where there will be weeping and grinding of teeth. [Isa. 49:12; 59:19; Mal. 1:11; Ps. 107:2, 3.]

13 Then to the centurion Jesus said, Go; it shall be done for you as you have believed. And the servant boy was restored to health at that very [y]moment.

14 And when Jesus went into Peter's house, He saw his mother-in-law lying ill with a fever;

15 He touched her hand and the fever left her, and she got up and began waiting on Him.

16 When evening came they brought to Him many who were [z]under the power of demons, and He drove out the spirits with a word, and restored to health all who were sick;

17 And thus He fulfilled what was spoken by the prophet Isaiah, He Himself took ([z]in order to carry away) our weaknesses *and* infirmities and bore [a]away our diseases. [Isa. 53:4.]

18 Now Jesus, when He saw great throngs around Him, gave orders to cross to the other side [of the lake].

19 And a scribe came up and said to Him, Master, I will accompany you wherever you go.

20 And Jesus replied to him, Foxes have holes, and the birds of the air have lodging places; but the Son of man has nowhere to lay His head.

21 Another of the disciples said to Him, Lord, let me first go and bury [[b]care for till death] my father.

22 But Jesus said to him, Follow Me, and leave the dead [[c]in sin] to bury their own dead.

23 And after He got into the boat, His disciples followed Him.

24 And [d]suddenly, behold, there arose a violent storm on the sea, so that the boat was being covered up by the waves; but He was sleeping.

25 And they went and awakened Him, saying, Lord, rescue *and* preserve us! We are perishing!

---

w) Thayer.
x) Alternate reading.
y) Moulton and Milligan.
z) Thayer.
a) Abbott-Smith. Berry. Souter. Thayer. Hickie. (Greek-English lexicons to the New Testament.)
b) Most commentators.
c) Barnes.
d) Vincent.

Living New Testament

4 *Then Jesus says to him, "Don't stop to talk*[1] *to anyone; go right over to the priest to be examined; and take with you the offering required by Moses' law for lepers who are healed—a public testimony of your cure."*

5, 6 When Jesus arrived in Capernaum, a Roman army captain came and pled with Him to come to his home and heal his servant boy who was in bed paralyzed and racked with pain.

7 "Yes," Jesus said, "I will come and heal him."

8, 9 Then the officer said, "Sir, I am not worthy to have You in my home; [and it isn't necessary for You to come[2]]. If You will only stand here and say, 'Be healed,' my servant will get well! I know, because I am under the authority of my superior officers and I have authority over my soldiers, and I say to one, 'Go,' and he goes, and to another 'Come,' and he comes, and to my slave boy, 'Do this or that,' and he does it. And I know You have authority to tell his sickness to go—and it will go!"

10 Jesus stood there amazed! Turning to the crowd He said, "I haven't seen faith like this in all the land of Israel!

11 And I tell you this, that many Gentiles [like this Roman officer[2]], shall come from all over the world and sit down in the Kingdom of Heaven with Abraham, Isaac, and Jacob.

12 And many an Israelite—those for whom the Kingdom was prepared—shall be cast into outer darkness, into the place of weeping and torment."

13 Then Jesus said to the Roman officer, "Go on home. What you have believed has happened!" And the boy was healed that same hour!

14 When Jesus arrived at Peter's house, Peter's mother-in-law was in bed with a high fever.

15 But when Jesus touched her hand, the fever left her; and she got up and prepared a meal[3] for them!

16 That evening several demon-possessed people were brought to Jesus; and when He spoke a single word, all the demons fled; and all the sick were healed.

17 This fulfilled the prophecy of Isaiah, "He took our sicknesses and bore our diseases."[4]

18 When Jesus noticed how large the crowd was growing, He instructed His disciples to get ready to cross to the other side of the lake.

19 Just then[5] one of the Jewish religious teachers[6] said to Him, "Teacher, I will follow You no matter where You go!"

20 But Jesus said, "Foxes have dens and birds have nests, but I, the Son of Mankind, have no home of My own—no place to lay My head."

21 Another of His followers said, "Sir, let me first go and bury my father."[7]

22 But Jesus told him, "Follow Me *now!*[8] Let those who are spiritually[8] dead care for their own dead."

23 Then He got into a boat and started across the lake with His disciples.

24 Suddenly a terrible storm came up, with waves higher than the boat. But Jesus was asleep.

25 The disciples went to Him and wakened Him, shouting, "Lord, save us! We're sinking!"

---

[1]Literally, "See you tell no man."
[2]Implied.
[3]Literally, "ministered unto them."
[4]Isaiah 53:4.
[5]Implied.
[6]Literally, "a scribe."
[7]This probably does not mean his father was awaiting burial. A possible paraphrase would be, "Let me wait until my father dies."
[8]Implied.

Revised Standard

can make me clean." [3]And he stretched out
his hand and touched him, saying, "I will; be
clean." And immediately his leprosy was
cleansed. [4]And Jesus said to him, "See that
you say nothing to any one; but go, show
yourself to the priest, and offer the gift that
Moses commanded, for a proof to the people."[r]

The centurion's servant healed

5 As he entered Capernaum, a centurion
came forward to him, beseeching him [6]and
saying, "Lord, my servant is lying paralyzed
at home, in terrible distress." [7]And he said
to him, "I will come and heal him." [8]But
the centurion answered him, "Lord, I am
not worthy to have you come under my
roof; but only say the word, and my servant
will be healed. [9]For I am a man under
authority, with soldiers under me; and I say
to one, 'Go,' and he goes, and to another,
'Come,' and he comes, and to my slave, 'Do
this,' and he does it." [10]When Jesus heard
him, he marveled, and said to those who
followed him, "Truly, I say to you, not
even[s] in Israel have I found such faith. [11]I
tell you, many will come from east and west
and sit at table with Abraham, Isaac, and
Jacob in the kingdom of heaven, [12]while the
sons of the kingdom will be thrown into the
outer darkness; there men will weep and
gnash their teeth." [13]And to the centurion
Jesus said, "Go; be it done for you as you
have believed." And the servant was healed
at that very moment.

Peter's mother-in-law healed

14 And when Jesus entered Peter's house,
he saw his mother-in-law lying sick with a
fever; [15]he touched her hand, and the fever
left her, and she rose and served him.
[16]That evening they brought to him many
who were possessed with demons; and he
cast out the spirits with a word, and healed
all who were sick. [17]This was to fulfil what
was spoken by the prophet Isaiah, "He took
our infirmities and bore our diseases."

Teaching about discipleship

18 Now when Jesus saw great crowds
around him, he gave orders to go over to
the other side. [19]And a scribe came up and
said to him, "Teacher, I will follow you
wherever you go." [20]And Jesus said to him,
"Foxes have holes, and birds of the air have
nests; but the Son of man has nowhere to
lay his head." [21]Another of the disciples
said to him, "Lord, let me first go and bury
my father." [22]But Jesus said to him, "Follow me, and leave the dead to bury their
own dead."

The storm stilled

23 And when he got into the boat, his
disciples followed him. [24]And behold, there
arose a great storm on the sea, so that the
boat was being swamped by the waves; but

---

[r] Greek *to them*
[s] Other ancient authorities read *with no one*

King James

26 And he saith unto them, Why are ye fearful, O ye of little faith? Then he arose, and rebuked the winds and the sea; and there was a great calm.

27 But the men marvelled, saying, What manner of man is this, that even the winds and the sea obey him!

28 ¶ And when he was come to the other side into the country of the Gergesenes, there met him two possessed with devils, coming out of the tombs, exceeding fierce, so that no man might pass by that way.

29 And, behold, they cried out, saying, What have we to do with thee, Jesus, thou Son of God? art thou come hither to torment us before the time?

30 And there was a good way off from them an herd of many swine feeding.

31 So the devils besought him, saying, If thou cast us out, suffer us to go away into the herd of swine.

32 And he said unto them, Go. And when they were come out, they went into the herd of swine: and, behold, the whole herd of swine ran violently down a steep place into the sea, and perished in the waters.

33 And they that kept them fled, and went their ways into the city, and told every thing, and what was befallen to the possessed of the devils.

34 And, behold, the whole city came out to meet Jesus: and when they saw him, they besought *him* that he would depart out of their coasts.

Amplified

26 And He said to them, Why are you timid *and* afraid, O you of little faith? Then He got up and rebuked the winds and the sea, and there was a great *and* wonderful calm ([e]a perfect peaceableness).

27 And the men were stunned with bewildered wonder *and* marveled, saying, What kind of Man is this, that even the winds and the sea obey Him!

28 And when He arrived at the other side, at the country of the Gadarenes, two men under the control of demons went to meet Him, coming out of the tombs, so fierce *and* savage that no one was able to pass that way.

29 And behold, they shrieked *and* screamed, What have You to do with us, *Jesus,* Son of God? Have You come to torment us before the appointed time? [Judg. 11:12; II Sam. 16:10.]

30 Now at some distance from there a drove of many hogs was grazing.

31 And the demons begged Him, If You drive us out, send us into the drove of hogs.

32 And He said to them, Begone! So they came out and went into the hogs; and behold, the whole drove rushed down the steep bank into the sea, and died in the water.

33 The herdsmen fled, and went into the town and reported everything, including what had happened to the men under the power of demons.

34 And behold, the whole town went out to meet Jesus, and as soon as they saw Him, they begged Him to depart from their locality.

CHAPTER 9

AND he entered into a ship, and passed over, and came into his own city.

2 And, behold, they brought to him a man sick of the palsy, lying on a bed: and Jesus seeing their faith said unto the sick of the palsy; Son, be of good cheer; thy sins be forgiven thee.

3 And, behold, certain of the scribes said within themselves, This *man* blasphemeth.

4 And Jesus knowing their thoughts said, Wherefore think ye evil in your hearts?

5 For whether is easier, to say, *Thy* sins be forgiven thee; or to say, Arise, and walk?

6 But that ye may know that the Son of man hath power on earth to forgive sins, (then saith he to the sick of the palsy,) Arise, take up thy bed, and go unto thine house.

7 And he arose, and departed to his house.

8 But when the multitudes saw *it*, they marvelled, and glorified God, which had given such power unto men.

CHAPTER 9

AND Jesus getting into a boat crossed to the other side and came to His own town [Capernaum].

2 And behold, they brought to Him a man paralyzed *and* prostrated by illness, lying on a sleeping pad, and when Jesus saw their faith He said to the paralyzed man, Take courage, son; your sins are forgiven *and* the [f]penalty remitted.

3 And behold, some of the scribes said to themselves, This man blasphemes—He claims the rights and prerogatives of God!

4 But Jesus, knowing ([g]seeing) their thoughts, said, Why do you think evil *and* harbor [f]malice in your hearts?

5 For which is easier, to say, Your sins are forgiven *and* the [f]penalty remitted, or say, Get up and walk?

6 And in order that you may know that the Son of man has authority on earth to forgive sins *and* [f]remit the penalty, He then said to the paralyzed man, Get up! Pick up your sleeping pad and go to your own house.

7 And he got up and went away to his own house.

8 When the crowds saw it, they were struck with fear *and* awe, and they [h]recognized God *and* praised *and* thanked Him, Who had given such power *and* authority to men.

---

e) Wycliffe.
f) Thayer.
g) Many ancient authorities so read.
h) Cremer.

Living New Testament

26 But Jesus answered, "O you men of little faith! Why are you so frightened?" Then He stood up and rebuked the wind and waves, and the storm subsided and all was calm!

27 The disciples just sat there, awed! "Who is this," they asked themselves, "that even the winds and the sea obey Him?"

28 When they arrived on the other side of the lake, in the country of the Gadarenes, two men with demons in them met Him. They lived in a cemetery and were so dangerous that no one could go through that area.

29 They began screaming at Him, "What do You want with us, O Son of God? You have no right to torment us yet."[9]

30 A herd of pigs was feeding in the distance,

31 So the demons begged, "If You cast us out, send us into that herd of pigs."

32 "All right," Jesus told them. "Begone." And they came out of the men and entered the pigs, and the whole herd rushed over a cliff and drowned in the water below.

33 The herdsmen fled to the nearest city with the story of what had happened,

34 And the entire population came rushing out to see Jesus, and begged Him to go away and leave them alone.

Revised Standard

he was asleep. 25And they went and woke
him, saying, "Save, Lord; we are perishing."
26And he said to them, "Why are you
afraid, O men of little faith?" Then he rose
and rebuked the winds and the sea; and
there was a great calm. 27And the men
marveled, saying, "What sort of man is this,
that even winds and sea obey him?"

Demons cast out

28 And when he came to the other side,
to the country of the Gadarenes,[t] two
demoniacs met him, coming out of the
tombs, so fierce that no one could pass that
way. 29And behold, they cried out, "What
have you to do with us, O Son of God?
Have you come here to torment us before
the time?" 30Now a herd of many swine
was feeding at some distance from them.
31And the demons begged him, "If you cast
us out, send us away into the herd of
swine." 32And he said to them, "Go." So
they came out and went into the swine; and
behold, the whole herd rushed down the
steep bank into the sea, and perished in the
waters. 33The herdsmen fled, and going into
the city they told everything, and what had
happened to the demoniacs. 34And behold,
all the city came out to meet Jesus; and
when they saw him, they begged him to
leave their neighborhood.

CHAPTER 9

So Jesus climbed into a boat and went across the lake to Capernaum, His home[1] town.

2 Soon some men brought Him a paralyzed boy on a mat. When Jesus saw their faith, He said to the sick boy, "Cheer up, son! For I have forgiven your sins!"

3 "Blasphemy! This man is saying he is God!" exclaimed some of the religious leaders to themselves.

4 Jesus knew what they were thinking and asked them, "Why are you thinking such evil thoughts?

5 Is it any harder to forgive his sins than to heal him?

6 Consequently, to prove that I[2] have authority here on earth to forgive sins"—turning to the paralyzed boy He said, "Get up, roll up your mat and walk home!"

7 And the boy jumped up and left!

8 A chill of fear swept through the crowd as they saw this happen right before their eyes. How they praised God for giving such authority to a man!

A paralytic healed and forgiven

9 And getting into a boat he crossed over
and came to his own city. 2And behold, they brought to him a paralytic, lying on his bed; and when Jesus saw their
faith he said to the paralytic, "Take heart,
my son; your sins are forgiven." 3And behold, some of the scribes said to themselves, "This man is blaspheming." 4But
Jesus, knowing[u] their thoughts, said, "Why
do you think evil in your hearts? 5For which
is easier, to say, 'Your sins are forgiven,' or
to say, 'Rise and walk'? 6But that you may
know that the Son of man has authority on
earth to forgive sins"—he then said to the
paralytic—"Rise, take up your bed and go
home." 7And he rose and went home.
8When the crowds saw it, they were afraid,
and they glorified God, who had given such
authority to men.

[9]Literally, "Have you come here to torment us before the time?"
[1]Literally, "his own city."
[2]Literally, "that the Son of man."

[t] Other ancient authorities read *Gergesenes;* some *Gerasene*
[u] Other ancient authorities read *seeing*

King James

9 ¶ And as Jesus passed forth from thence, he saw a man, named Matthew, sitting at the receipt of custom: and he saith unto him, Follow me. And he arose, and followed him.

10 ¶ And it came to pass, as Jesus sat at meat in the house, behold, many publicans and sinners came and sat down with him and his disciples.

11 And when the Pharisees saw *it*, they said unto his disciples, Why eateth your Master with publicans and sinners?

12 But when Jesus heard *that*, he said unto them, They that be whole need not a physician, but they that are sick.

13 But go ye and learn what *that* meaneth, I will have mercy, and not sacrifice: for I am not come to call the righteous, but sinners to repentance.

14 ¶ Then came to him the disciples of John, saying, Why do we and the Pharisees fast oft, but thy disciples fast not?

15 And Jesus said unto them, Can the children of the bridechamber mourn, as long as the bridegroom is with them? but the days will come, when the bridegroom shall be taken from them, and then shall they fast.

16 No man putteth a piece of new cloth unto an old garment, for that which is put in to fill it up taketh from the garment, and the rent is made worse.

17 Neither do men put new wine into old bottles: else the bottles break, and the wine runneth out, and the bottles perish: but they put new wine into new bottles, and both are preserved.

18 ¶ While he spake these things unto them, behold, there came a certain ruler, and worshipped him, saying, My daughter is even now dead: but come and lay thy hand upon her, and she shall live.

19 And Jesus arose, and followed him, and *so did* his disciples.

20 ¶ And, behold, a woman, which was diseased with an issue of blood twelve years, came behind *him*, and touched the hem of his garment:

21 For she said within herself, If I may but touch his garment, I shall be whole.

22 But Jesus turned him about, and when he saw her, he said, Daughter, be of good comfort; thy faith hath made thee whole. And the woman was made whole from that hour.

23 And when Jesus came into the ruler's house, and saw the minstrels and the people making a noise,

24 He said unto them, Give place: for the maid is not dead, but sleepeth. And they laughed him to scorn.

25 But when the people were put forth, he went in, and took her by the hand, and the maid arose.

26 And the fame hereof went abroad into all that land.

27 ¶ And when Jesus departed thence, two blind men followed him, crying, and saying, *Thou* Son of David, have mercy on us.

28 And when he was come into the house, the blind men came to him: and

Amplified

9 As Jesus passed on from there, He saw a man named Matthew sitting at the tax collector's office; and He said to him, [i]Be My disciple—side with My party and follow Me. And he rose and followed Him.

10 And as Jesus reclined at table in the house, behold, many tax collectors and especially wicked sinners came and sat (reclined) with Him and His disciples.

11 And when the Pharisees saw this, they said to His disciples, Why does your Master eat with tax collectors and those pre-eminently sinful?

12 But when Jesus heard it, He replied, Those who are strong *and* well have no need of a physician, but those who are weak *and* sick.

13 Go and learn what this means, I desire mercy [that is, [i]readiness to help those in trouble] and not sacrifice *and* sacrificial victims. For I came not to call *and* invite [to repentance] the righteous—those who are upright and in right standing with God; but sinners—the erring ones *and* all those not free from sin. [Hos. 6:6.]

14 Then the disciples of John came to Jesus, inquiring, Why is it that we and the Pharisees fast [j]*often,* [that is, abstain from food and drink, as a religious exercise], but Your disciples do not fast?

15 And Jesus replied to them, Can the wedding guests mourn while the bridegroom is still with them? The days will come when the bridegroom is taken away from them, and then they will fast.

16 And no one puts a piece of cloth that has not been shrunk on an old garment, for such a patch tears away from the garment and a worse rent is made.

17 Neither is new wine put in old wineskins, for if it is, the skins burst and are [k]torn in pieces, and the wine is spilled and the skins ruined; but new wine is put into fresh wineskins, and so both are preserved.

18 While He was talking this way to them, behold, a ruler entered and kneeling down, worshipped Him, saying, My daughter has just [l]now died; but come and lay Your hand on her and she will come to life.

19 And Jesus got up and accompanied him, with His disciples.

20 And behold, a woman who had suffered from a flow of blood for twelve years came up behind Him and touched the fringe of His garment; [Num. 15:38; Deut. 22:12.]

21 For she kept saying to herself, If I only touch His garment, I shall be restored to health.

22 Jesus turned around and seeing her He said, Take courage, daughter! Your faith has made you well. And at once the woman was restored to health.

23 And when Jesus came to the ruler's house and saw the flute players, and the crowd making an uproar *and* din,

24 He said, Go away; for the girl is not dead but sleeping. And they laughed *and* jeered at Him.

25 But when the crowd had been ordered to go outside, He went in and took her by the hand, and the girl arose.

26 And the news about this spread through all that district.

27 As Jesus was passing on from there, two blind men followed Him, shouting loudly, Have pity *and* mercy on us, Son of David!

28 When He reached the house and went in, the blind men came to Him. And Jesus said to them, Do you believe that I am able to do this? They said to Him, Yes, Lord.

---

i) Thayer.
j) Many ancient authorities so read.
k) Thayer.
l) Vincent.

Living New Testament

9 As Jesus was going on down the road, He saw a tax collector, Matthew,[3] sitting at a tax collection booth. "Come and be My disciple," Jesus said to him, and Matthew jumped up and went along with Him.

10 Later, as Jesus and His disciples were eating dinner [at Matthew's house[4]], there were many notorious swindlers there as guests!

11 The Pharisees were indignant. "Why does your teacher associate with men like that?"

12 "Because people who are well don't need a doctor! It's the sick people who do!" was Jesus' reply.

13 Then He added, "Go away and learn the meaning of this verse of Scripture, 'It isn't your sacrifices and your gifts I care about—it's that you have some pity.'[5] My job down here on earth is to get sinners back to God—not to worry about the good people."

14 One day the disciples of John the Baptist came to Jesus and asked Him, "Why don't your disciples fast as we do and as the Pharisees do?"

15 "Should the Bridegroom's friends mourn and go without food while He is with them?" Jesus asked. "But the time is coming when I[6] will be taken from them. Time enough then for them to refuse to eat.

16 And who would patch an old garment with unshrunk cloth? For the patch would tear away and make the hole worse.

17 And who would use old wineskins[7] to store new wine? For the old skins would burst with the pressure, and the wine would be spilled and the skins ruined. Only new wineskins are used to store new wine. That way both are preserved."

18 As He was saying this, the rabbi of the local synagogue came and worshiped Him. "My little daughter has just died," he said, "but You can bring her back to life again if You will only come and touch her."

19 As Jesus and the disciples were going to the rabbi's home,

20 A woman who had been sick for twelve years with internal bleeding came up behind Him and touched a tassel of His robe,

21 For she thought, "If I only touch Him, I will be healed."

22 Jesus turned around and spoke to her. "Daughter," He said, "all is well! Your faith has healed you." And the woman was well from that moment.

23 When Jesus arrived at the rabbi's home and saw the noisy crowds and heard the funeral music,

24 He said, "Get them out, for the little girl isn't dead; she is only sleeping!" Then how they all scoffed and sneered at Him!

25 When the crowd was finally outside, Jesus went in where the little girl was lying and took her by the hand, and she jumped up and was all right again!

26 The report of this wonderful miracle swept the entire countryside.

27 As Jesus was leaving her home, two blind men followed along behind, shouting, "O Son of King David, have mercy on us."

28 They went right into the house where He was staying, and Jesus asked them, "Do you believe I can make you see?"

"Yes, Lord," they told Him, "we do."

[3]The Matthew who wrote this book.
[4]Implied.
[5]Hosea 6:6.
[6]Literally, "the bridegroom."
[7]These were leather bags for storing wine.

Revised Standard

Matthew called

9 As Jesus passed on from there, he saw
a man called Matthew sitting at the tax
office; and he said to him, "Follow me."
And he rose and followed him.
10 And as he sat at table[v] in the house,
behold, many tax collectors and sinners
came and sat down with Jesus and his disciples. 11And when the Pharisees saw this,
they said to his disciples, "Why does your
teacher eat with tax collectors and sinners?"
12But when he heard it, he said, "Those
who are well have no need of a physician,
but those who are sick. 13Go and learn what
this means, 'I desire mercy, and not sacrifice.' For I came not to call the righteous,
but sinners."

The question about fasting

14 Then the disciples of John came to
him, saying, "Why do we and the Pharisees
fast,[w] but your disciples do not fast?"
15And Jesus said to them, "Can the wedding
guests mourn as long as the bridegroom is
with them? The days will come, when the
bridegroom is taken away from them, and
then they will fast. 16And no one puts a
piece of unshrunk cloth on an old garment,
for the patch tears away from the garment,
and a worse tear is made. 17Neither is new
wine put into old wineskins; if it is, the skins
burst, and the wine is spilled, and the skins
are destroyed; but new wine is put into fresh
wineskins, and so both are preserved."

A ruler's daughter raised; a suffering woman healed

18 While he was thus speaking to them,
behold, a ruler came in and knelt before
him, saying, "My daughter has just died; but
come and lay your hand on her, and she will
live." 19And Jesus rose and followed him,
with his disciples. 20And behold, a woman
who had suffered from a hemorrhage for
twelve years came up behind him and
touched the fringe of his garment; 21for she
said to herself, "If I only touch his garment,
I shall be made well." 22Jesus turned, and
seeing her he said, "Take heart, daughter;
your faith has made you well." And instantly the woman was made well. 23And when
Jesus came to the ruler's house, and saw the
flute players, and the crowd making a tumult, 24he said, "Depart; for the girl is not
dead but sleeping." And they laughed at
him. 25But when the crowd had been put
outside, he went in and took her by the
hand, and the girl arose. 26And the report
of this went through all that district.

The blind and dumb healed

27 And as Jesus passed on from there,
two blind men followed him, crying aloud,

[v] Greek *reclined*
[w] Other ancient authorities add *much* or *often*

King James

Jesus saith unto them, Believe ye that I am able to do this? They said unto him, Yea, Lord.

29 Then touched he their eyes, saying, According to your faith be it unto you.

30 And their eyes were opened; and Jesus straitly charged them, saying, See *that* no man know *it*.

31 But they, when they were departed, spread abroad his fame in all that country.

32 ¶ As they went out, behold, they brought to him a dumb man possessed with a devil.

33 And when the devil was cast out, the dumb spake: and the multitudes marvelled, saying, It was never so seen in Israel.

34 But the Pharisees said, He casteth out devils through the prince of the devils.

35 And Jesus went about all the cities and villages, teaching in their synagogues, and preaching the gospel of the kingdom, and healing every sickness and every disease among the people.

36 ¶ But when he saw the multitudes, he was moved with compassion on them, because they fainted, and were scattered abroad, as sheep having no shepherd.

37 Then saith he unto his disciples, The harvest truly *is* plenteous, but the labourers are few;

38 Pray ye therefore the Lord of the harvest, that he will send forth labourers into his harvest.

Amplified

29 Then he touched their eyes, saying, According to your faith *and* trust *and* reliance [on the power invested in Me] be it done to you.

30 And their eyes were opened. And Jesus earnestly *and* sternly charged them, See that you let no one know about this.

31 But they went off and blazed *and* spread His fame abroad throughout that whole district.

32 And while they were going away, behold, a dumb man under the power of a demon was brought to Jesus.

33 And when the demon had been driven out, the dumb man spoke; and the crowds were stunned with bewildered wonder, saying, Never before has anything like this been seen in Israel.

34 But the Pharisees said, He drives out demons through *and* with the help of the prince of demons.

35 And Jesus went about all the cities and villages, teaching in their synagogues and proclaiming the good news (the Gospel) of the kingdom, and curing all kinds of disease and every weakness *and* infirmity.

36 When He saw the throngs, He was moved with pity *and* sympathy for them, because they were bewildered—harassed and distressed and dejected and helpless—like sheep without a shepherd. [Zech. 10:2.]

37 Then He said to His disciples, The harvest is indeed plentiful, but the laborers are few.

38 So pray the Lord of the harvest to [m]force out *and* thrust laborers into His harvest.

CHAPTER 10

AND when he had called unto *him* his twelve disciples, he gave them power *against* unclean spirits, to cast them out, and to heal all manner of sickness and all manner of disease.

2 Now the names of the twelve apostles are these; The first, Simon, who is called Peter, and Andrew his brother; James *the son* of Zebedee, and John his brother;

3 Philip, and Bartholomew; Thomas, and Matthew the publican; James, *the son* of Alphæus, and Lebbæus, whose surname was Thaddæus;

4 Simon the Canaanite, and Judas Iscariot, who also betrayed him.

5 These twelve Jesus sent forth, and commanded them, saying, Go not into the way of the Gentiles, and into *any* city of the Samaritans enter ye not.

6 But go rather to the lost sheep of the house of Israel.

7 And as ye go, preach, saying, The kingdom of heaven is at hand.

8 Heal the sick, cleanse the lepers, raise the dead, cast out devils: freely ye have received, freely give.

9 Provide neither gold, nor silver, nor brass in your purses,

10 Nor scrip for *your* journey, neither two coats, neither shoes, nor yet staves: for the workman is worthy of his meat.

CHAPTER 10

AND Jesus summoned to Him His twelve disciples and gave them power *and* authority over unclean spirits, to drive them out, and to cure all kinds of disease and all kinds of weakness *and* infirmity.

2 Now these are the names of the twelve apostles; first Simon, who is called Peter, and Andrew his brother; James the son of Zebedee, and John his brother;

3 Philip and Bartholomew [Nathaniel]; Thomas and Matthew the tax collector; James the son of Alphaeus, and Thaddaeus [Judas, not Iscariot];

4 Simon the Cananaean, and Judas Iscariot, who also betrayed Him.

5 Jesus sent out these twelve, charging them, Go nowhere among the Gentiles, and do not go into any town of the Samaritans,

6 But go rather to the lost sheep of the house of Israel.

7 And as you go, preach saying, The kingdom of heaven is at hand!

8 Cure the sick; raise the dead; cleanse the lepers; drive out demons. Freely (without pay) you have received; freely (without charge) give.

9 Take no gold, nor silver, nor [even] copper money in your purses (belts),

10 And do not take a provision-bag *or* a [n]wallet for a collection-bag for your journey, nor two undergarments, nor sandals, nor a staff, for the workman deserves his support— his living, his food.

---

m) Vincent.
n) Moulton and Milligan.

Living New Testament

29 Then He touched their eyes and said, "Because of your faith it will happen!"

30 And suddenly they could see! Jesus sternly warned them not to tell anyone about it,

31 But instead they spread His fame all over the town.[8]

32 Leaving that place, Jesus met a man who couldn't speak because a demon was inside him.

33 So Jesus cast out the demon, and instantly the man could talk. How the crowds marveled! "Never in all our lives have we seen anything like this," they exclaimed.

34 But the Pharisees said, "The reason he can cast out demons is that he is demon-possessed himself—possessed by Satan, the demon king!"

35 Jesus traveled around through all the cities and villages of that area, teaching in the Jewish synagogues and announcing the good news about the Kingdom. And wherever He went He healed people of every sort of illness.

36 And what pity He felt for the crowds that came, because their problems were so great and they didn't know what to do or where to go for help. They were like sheep without a shepherd.

37 "The harvest is so great, and the workers are so few," He told His disciples.

38 "So pray to the one in charge of the harvesting, and ask Him to recruit more workers for His harvest fields."

Revised Standard

"Have mercy on us, Son of David." 28When
he entered the house, the blind men came to
him; and Jesus said to them, "Do you believe that I am able to do this?" They said
to him, "Yes, Lord." 29Then he touched
their eyes, saying, "According to your faith
be it done to you." 30And their eyes were
opened. And Jesus sternly charged them,
"See that no one knows it." 31But they went
away and spread his fame through all that
district.
32 As they were going away, behold, a
dumb demoniac was brought to him. 33And
when the demon had been cast out, the
dumb man spoke; and the crowds marveled,
saying, "Never was anything like this seen in
Israel." 34But the Pharisees said, "He casts
out demons by the prince of demons."

The need for workers

35 And Jesus went about all the cities
and villages, teaching in their synagogues
and preaching the gospel of the kingdom,
and healing every disease and every infirmity. 36When he saw the crowds, he had compassion for them, because they were
harassed and helpless, like sheep without a
shepherd. 37Then he said to his disciples,
"The harvest is plentiful, but the laborers
are few; 38pray therefore the Lord of the
harvest to send out laborers into his harvest."

CHAPTER 10

Jesus called His twelve disciples to Him, and gave them authority to cast out evil spirits and to heal every kind of sickness and disease.

2 Here are the names of His twelve disciples:
Simon (also called Peter),
Andrew (Peter's brother),
James (Zebedee's son),
John (James' brother),

3 Philip,
Bartholomew,
Thomas,
Matthew (the tax collector),
James (Alphaeus' son),
Thaddeus,

4 Simon (a member of "The Zealots," a subversive political party),
Judas Iscariot (the one who betrayed Him).

5 Jesus sent them out with these instructions:
"Don't go to the Gentiles or the Samaritans,

6 But only to the people of Israel—God's lost sheep.

7 Go and announce to them that the Kingdom of Heaven is near.[1]

8 Heal the sick, raise the dead, cure the lepers, and cast out demons. Give as freely as you have received!

9 Don't take any money with you;

10 Don't even carry a duffle bag with extra clothes and shoes, or even a walking stick; for those you help should feed and care for you.

Names and mission of the twelve

10 And he called to him his twelve
disciples and gave them authority
over unclean spirits, to cast them out, and to
heal every disease and every infirmity. 2The
names of the twelve apostles are these: first,
Simon, who is called Peter, and Andrew his
brother; James the son of Zebedee, and John
his brother; 3Philip and Bartholomew;
Thomas and Matthew the tax collector;
James the son of Alphaeus, and Thaddaeus;[x]
4Simon the Cananaean, and Judas Iscariot,
who betrayed him.
5 These twelve Jesus sent out, charging
them, "Go nowhere among the Gentiles, and
enter no town of the Samaritans, 6but go
rather to the lost sheep of the house of
Israel. 7And preach as you go, saying, 'The
kingdom of heaven is at hand.' 8Heal the
sick, raise the dead, cleanse lepers, cast out
demons. You received without pay, give
without pay. 9Take no gold, nor silver, nor
copper in your belts, 10no bag for your
journey, nor two tunics, nor sandals, nor a
staff; for the laborer deserves his food.

8Literally, "in all that land."
1Or, "at hand," or, "has arrived."

x Other ancient authorities read *Lebbaeus* or *Lebbaeus called Thaddaeus*.

King James

11 And into whatsoever city or town ye shall enter, inquire who in it is worthy; and there abide till ye go thence.

12 And when ye come into an house, salute it.

13 And if the house be worthy, let your peace come upon it: but if it be not worthy, let your peace return to you.

14 And whosoever shall not receive you, nor hear your words, when ye depart out of that house or city, shake off the dust of your feet.

15 Verily I say unto you, It shall be more tolerable for the land of Sodom and Gomorrha in the day of judgment, than for that city.

16 ¶ Behold, I send you forth as sheep in the midst of wolves: be ye therefore wise as serpents, and harmless as doves.

17 But beware of men: for they will deliver you up to the councils, and they will scourge you in their synagogues;

18 And ye shall be brought before governors and kings for my sake, for a testimony against them and the Gentiles.

19 But when they deliver you up, take no thought how or what ye shall speak: for it shall be given you in that same hour what ye shall speak.

20 For it is not ye that speak, but the Spirit of your Father which speaketh in you.

21 And the brother shall deliver up the brother to death, and the father the child: and the children shall rise up against *their* parents, and cause them to be put to death.

22 And ye shall be hated of all *men* for my name's sake: but he that endureth to the end shall be saved.

23 But when they persecute you in this city, flee ye into another: for verily I say unto you, Ye shall not have gone over the cities of Israel, till the Son of man be come.

24 The disciple is not above *his* master, nor the servant above his lord.

25 It is enough for the disciple that he be as his master, and the servant as his lord. If they have called the master of the house Beelzebub, how much more *shall they call* them of his household?

26 Fear them not therefore: for there is nothing covered, that shall not be revealed; and hid, that shall not be known.

27 What I tell you in darkness, *that* speak ye in light: and what ye hear in the ear, *that* preach ye upon the housetops.

28 And fear not them which kill the body, but are not able to kill the soul: but rather fear him which is able to destroy both soul and body in hell.

29 Are not two sparrows sold for a farthing? and one of them shall not fall on the ground without your Father.

30 But the very hairs of your head are all numbered.

Amplified

11 And into whatever town or village you go, inquire who in it is deserving, and stay there [at his house] until you leave [that vicinity].

12 As you go into the house, give your greetings *and* wish it well.

13 Then if indeed that house is deserving, let come upon it your peace [that is, [o]freedom from all the distresses that are experienced as the result of sin]. But if it is not deserving, let your peace return to you.

14 And whoever will not receive *and* accept *and* welcome you nor listen to your message, as you leave that house or town shake the dust of it from your feet.

15 Truly, I tell you, it shall be more tolerable on the day of judgment for the land of Sodom and Gomorrah than for that town.

16 Lo, I am sending you out as sheep in the midst of wolves; be [p]wary *and* wise as serpents, and be innocent—harmless, guileless and [q]without falsity—as doves. [Gen. 3:1.]

17 Be on guard against the men [whose [r]way or nature is to act in opposition to God]; for they will deliver you up to councils and flog you in their synagogues,

18 And you will be brought before governors and kings for My sake, for a witness to bear testimony before them and to the Gentiles (the nations).

19 But when they deliver you up, do not be anxious about how *or* what you are to speak; for what you are to say will be given you in that very hour *and* [s]moment.

20 For it is not you who are speaking, but the Spirit of your Father speaking through you.

21 Brother will deliver up brother to death, and the father his child, and children will take a stand against their parents, and will have them put to death;

22 And you will be hated by all for My name's sake. But he who perseveres *and* endures to the end will be saved [[t]from spiritual disease and death in the world to come].

23 When they persecute you in one town [that is, pursue you in a manner to injure you and cause you to suffer because of your belief], flee to another town; for truly, I tell you, you will not have gone through all the towns of Israel before [u]the Son of man comes.

24 A disciple is not above his teacher, nor is a servant *or* slave above his master.

25 It is sufficient for the disciple to be like his teacher, and the servant *or* slave like his master. If they have called the Master of the house Beelzebub [[v]meaning master of the dwelling], how much more will they speak evil of those of His household. [II Kings 1:2.]

26 So have no fear of them; for nothing is concealed that will not be revealed, *or* kept secret that will not become known.

27 What I say to you in the dark, tell in the light; and what you hear whispered in the ear, proclaim upon the housetops.

28 And do not be afraid of those who kill the body but cannot kill the soul, but rather be afraid of him who can destroy both soul and body in hell (Gehenna).

29 Are not two [w]little sparrows sold for a penny? And yet not one of them will fall to the ground without your Father's leave *and* notice.

30 But even the very hairs of your head are all numbered.

---

o) Cremer.
p) Wycliffe.
q) Luther (-Vincent).
r) Cremer.
s) Moulton and Milligan.
t) Abbott-Smith.
u) Believed by many to mean the coming of the Holy Spirit at Pentecost.
v) Davis' "Dictionary of the Bible."
w) Vincent.

Living New Testament

11 Whenever you enter a city or village, search for a godly man and stay in his home until you leave for the next town.

12 When you ask permission to stay, be friendly,

13 And if it turns out to be a godly home, give it your blessing; if not, keep the blessing.

14 Any city or home that doesn't welcome you—shake off the dust of that place from your feet as you leave.

15 Truly, the wicked cities of Sodom and Gomorrah will be better off at Judgment Day than they.

16 I am sending you out as sheep among wolves. Be as wary as serpents and harmless as doves.

17 But beware! For you will be arrested and tried, and whipped in the synagogues.

18 Yes, and you must stand trial before governors and kings for My sake. This will give you the opportunity to tell them about Me, yes, to witness to the world.

19 When you are arrested, don't worry about what to say at your trial, for you will be given the right words at the right time.

20 For it won't be you doing the talking—it will be the Spirit of your heavenly Father speaking through you!

21 Brother shall betray brother to death, and fathers shall betray their own children. And children shall rise against their parents, and cause their deaths.

22 Everyone shall hate you because you belong to Me. But all of you who endure to the end shall be saved.

23 When you are persecuted in one city, flee to the next! I[2] will return before you have reached them all!

24 A student is not greater than his teacher. A servant is not above his master.

25 The student shares his teacher's fate. The servant shares his master's! And since I, the master of the household, have been called 'Satan,'[3] how much more will you!

26 But don't be afraid of those who threaten you. For the time is coming when the truth will be revealed: their secret plots will become public information.

27 What I tell you now in the gloom, shout abroad when daybreak comes. What I whisper in your ears, proclaim from the housetops!

28 Don't be afraid of those who can kill only your bodies—but can't touch your souls! Fear only God who can destroy both soul and body in hell.

29 Not one sparrow (What do they cost? Two for a penny?) can fall to the ground without your Father knowing it.

30 And the very hairs of your head are all numbered.

[2]Literally, "the Son of man."
[3]See Matthew 9:34, where they called Him this.

Revised Standard

11And whatever town or village you enter,
find out who is worthy in it, and stay with
him until you depart. 12As you enter the
house, salute it. 13And if the house is
worthy, let your peace come upon it; but if
it is not worthy, let your peace return to
you. 14And if any one will not receive you
or listen to your words, shake off the dust
from your feet as you leave that house or
town. 15Truly, I say to you, it shall be more
tolerable on the day of judgment for the
land of Sodom and Gomorrah than for that
town.

Facing persecution

16 "Behold, I send you out as sheep in
the midst of wolves; so be wise as serpents
and innocent as doves. 17Beware of men;
for they will deliver you up to councils, and
flog you in their synagogues, 18and you will
be dragged before governors and kings for
my sake, to bear testimony before them and
the Gentiles. 19When they deliver you up,
do not be anxious how you are to speak or
what you are to say; for what you are to say
will be given to you in that hour; 20for it is
not you who speak, but the Spirit of your
Father speaking through you. 21Brother will
deliver up brother to death, and the father
his child, and children will rise against parents and have them put to death; 22and you
will be hated by all for my name's sake. But
he who endures to the end will be saved.
23When they persecute you in one town,
flee to the next; for truly, I say to you, you
will not have gone through all the towns of
Israel, before the Son of man comes.
24 "A disciple is not above his teacher,
nor a servant[y] above his master; 25it is
enough for the disciple to be like his teacher, and the servant[y] like his master. If they
have called the master of the house Beelzebul, how much more will they malign those
of his household.

The value of life

26 "So have no fear of them; for nothing
is covered that will not be revealed, or hidden that will not be known. 27What I tell
you in the dark, utter in the light; and what
you hear whispered, proclaim upon the
housetops. 28And do not fear those who kill
the body but cannot kill the soul; rather fear
him who can destroy both soul and body in
hell.[z] 29Are not two sparrows sold for a
penny? And not one of them will fall to the
ground without your Father's will. 30But
even the hairs of your head are all num-

[y] Or *slave*
[z] Greek *Gehenna*

King James

31 Fear ye not therefore, ye are of more value than many sparrows.
32 Whosoever therefore shall confess me before men, him will I confess also before my Father which is in heaven.
33 But whosoever shall deny me before men, him will I also deny before my Father which is in heaven.
34 Think not that I am come to send peace on earth: I came not to send peace, but a sword.
35 For I am come to set a man at variance against his father, and the daughter against her mother, and the daughter in law against her mother in law.
36 And a man's foes *shall be* they of his own household.
37 He that loveth father or mother more than me is not worthy of me: and he that loveth son or daughter more than me is not worthy of me.
38 And he that taketh not his cross, and followeth after me is not worthy of me.
39 He that findeth his life shall lose it: and he that loseth his life for my sake shall find it.
40 ¶ He that receiveth you receiveth me, and he that receiveth me receiveth him that sent me.
41 He that receiveth a prophet in the name of a prophet shall receive a prophet's reward; and he that receiveth a righteous man in the name of a righteous man shall receive a righteous man's reward.
42 And whosoever shall give to drink unto one of these little ones a cup of cold *water* only in the name of a disciple, verily I say unto you, he shall in no wise lose his reward.

Amplified

31 Fear not, then; you are of more value than many sparrows.
32 Therefore, every one who acknowledges Me before men *and* confesses Me [[w]out of a state of oneness with Me], I will also acknowledge before My Father Who is in heaven, *and* [w]confess [abiding] in him.
33 But whoever denies *and* disowns Me before men, I also will deny *and* disown before My Father Who is in heaven.
34 Do not think that I have come to bring peace upon the earth; I have not come to bring peace but a sword.
35 For I have come to part asunder a man from his father, and a daughter from her mother, and a [x]newly married wife from her mother-in-law;
36 And a man's foes will be they of his own household. [Mic. 7:6.]
37 He who loves *and* [y]takes more pleasure in father or mother than in Me is not worthy of Me; and he who loves *and* takes more pleasure in son or daughter than in Me is not worthy of Me;
38 And he who does not take up his cross and follow Me [that is, [z]cleave steadfastly to Me, conforming wholly to My example in living and if need be in dying also] is not worthy of Me.
39 Whoever finds his [[y]lower] life will lose [the higher life], and whoever loses his [lower] life on My account will find [the higher life].
40 He who receives *and* welcomes *and* accepts you, receives *and* welcomes *and* accepts Me; and he who receives *and* welcomes *and* accepts Me, receives *and* welcomes *and* accepts Him Who sent Me.
41 He who receives *and* welcomes *and* accepts a prophet because he is a prophet shall receive a prophet's reward, and he who receives *and* welcomes *and* accepts a righteous man because he is a righteous man shall receive a righteous man's reward.
42 And whoever gives to one of these little ones [in rank or influence] even a cup of cold water because he is My disciple, surely, I declare to you, he shall not lose his reward.

CHAPTER 11

AND it came to pass, when Jesus had made an end of commanding his twelve disciples, he departed thence to teach and to preach in their cities.
2 Now when John had heard in the prison the works of Christ, he sent two of his disciples,
3 And said unto him, Art thou he that should come, or do we look for another?
4 Jesus answered and said unto them, Go and shew John again those things which ye do hear and see:
5 The blind receive their sight, and the lame walk, the lepers are cleansed, and the deaf hear, the dead are raised up, and the poor have the gospel preached to them.
6 And blessed is *he*, whosoever shall not be offended in me.

CHAPTER 11

WHEN Jesus had finished His charge to His twelve disciples, He left there to teach and to preach in their [Galilean] cities.
2 Now when John in prison heard about the activities of Christ, he sent a message by his disciples,
3 And asked Him, Are You He Who was to come, or should we keep on expecting a different one? [Gen. 49:10; Num. 24:17.]
4 And Jesus replied to them, Go and report to John what you hear and see:
5 The blind receive their sight, and the lame walk, lepers are cleansed (by healing), and the deaf hear, and the dead are raised up, and the poor have good news (the Gospel) preached to them. [Isa. 35:5, 6; 61:1].
6 And blessed—happy, fortunate and [a]to be envied—is he who takes no offense at Me, *and* finds no cause for stumbling in *or* through Me, *and* is not hindered from seeing the Truth.

w) Vincent.
x) Vincent.
y) Wuest.
z) Thayer.
a) Souter.

Living New Testament

31 So don't worry! You are more valuable to Him than many sparrows.

32 If anyone publicly acknowledges Me as his friend, I will openly acknowledge him as My friend before My Father in heaven.

33 But if anyone publicly denies Me, I will openly deny him before My Father in heaven.

34 Don't imagine that I came to bring peace to the earth! No, rather, a sword.

35 I have come to set a man against his father, and a daughter against her mother, and a daughter-in-law against her mother-in-law—

36 A man's worst enemies will be right in his own home!

37 If you love your father and mother more than you love Me, you are not worthy of being Mine; or if you love your son or daughter more than Me, you are not worthy of being Mine.

38 If you refuse to take up your cross and follow Me, you are not worthy of being Mine.

39 If you cling to your life, you will lose it; but if you give it up for Me, you will save it.

40 Those who welcome you are welcoming Me. And when they welcome Me they are welcoming God who sent Me.

41 If you welcome a prophet because he is a man of God, you will be given the same reward a prophet gets. And if you welcome good and godly men because of their godliness, you will be given a reward like theirs.

42 And if, as My representatives, you give even a cup of cold water to a little child, you will surely be rewarded."

Revised Standard

bered. [31]Fear not, therefore; you are of
more value than many sparrows. [32]So every
one who acknowledges me before men, I
also will acknowledge before my Father
who is in heaven; [33]but whoever denies me
before men, I also will deny before my
Father who is in heaven.

The reward of the righteous

34 "Do not think that I have come to
bring peace on earth; I have not come to
bring peace, but a sword. [35]For I have
come to set a man against his father, and a
daughter against her mother, and a daughter-in-law against her mother-in-law; [36]and
a man's foes will be those of his own household. [37]He who loves father or mother
more than me is not worthy of me; and he
who loves son or daughter more than me is
not worthy of me; [38]and he who does not
take his cross and follow me is not worthy
of me. [39]He who finds his life will lose it,
and he who loses his life for my sake will
find it.

40 "He who receives you receives me,
and he who receives me receives him who
sent me. [41]He who receives a prophet because he is a prophet shall receive a prophet's reward, and he who receives a righteous
man because he is a righteous man shall receive a righteous man's reward. [42]And
whoever gives to one of these little ones
even a cup of cold water because he is a
disciple, truly, I say to you, he shall not lose
his reward."

CHAPTER 11

When Jesus had finished giving these instructions to His twelve disciples, He went off preaching in the cities where they were scheduled to go.[1]

2 John the Baptist, who was now in prison, heard about all the miracles the Messiah was doing, so he sent his disciples to ask Jesus,

3 "Are you really the one we are waiting for, or shall we keep on looking?"

4 Jesus told them, "Go back to John and tell him about the miracles you've seen Me do—

5 The blind people I've healed, and the lame people now walking without help, and the cured lepers, and the deaf who hear, and the dead raised to life; and tell him about My preaching the Good News to the poor.

6 Then give him this message, 'Blessed are those who don't doubt Me.' "

11 And when Jesus had finished instructing his twelve disciples, he went on
from there to teach and preach in their
cities.

Tribute to John the Baptist

2 Now when John heard in prison about
the deeds of the Christ, he sent word by his
disciples [3]and said to him, "Are you he who
is to come, or shall we look for another?"
[4]And Jesus answered them, "Go and tell
John what you hear and see: [5]the blind
receive their sight and the lame walk, lepers
are cleansed and the deaf hear, and the dead
are raised up, and the poor have good news
preached to them. [6]And blessed is he who
takes no offense at me."

---

[1]Literally, "to teach and preach in their cities." Luke 10:1 remarks, "the Lord appointed 70 others and sent them two and two before his face, into every city and place where He Himself was about to come."

King James

7 ¶ And as they departed, Jesus began to say unto the multitudes concerning John, What went ye out into the wilderness to see? A reed shaken with the wind?

8 But what went ye out for to see? A man clothed in soft raiment? behold, they that wear soft *clothing* are in kings' houses.

9 But what went ye out for to see? A prophet? yea, I say unto you, and more than a prophet.

10 For this is *he*, of whom it is written, Behold, I send my messenger before thy face, which shall prepare thy way before thee.

11 Verily I say unto you, Among them that are born of women there hath not risen a greater than John the Baptist: notwithstanding he that is least in the kingdom of heaven is greater than he.

12 And from the days of John the Baptist until now the kingdom of heaven suffereth violence, and the violent take it by force.

13 For all the prophets and the law prophesied until John.

14 And if ye will receive *it*, this is Elias, which was for to come.

15 He that hath ears to hear, let him hear.

16 ¶ But whereunto shall I liken this generation? It is like unto children sitting in the markets, and calling unto their fellows,

17 And saying, We have piped unto you, and ye have not danced; we have mourned unto you, and ye have not lamented.

18 For John came neither eating nor drinking, and they say, He hath a devil.

19 The Son of man came eating and drinking, and they say, Behold a man gluttonous, and a winebibber, a friend of publicans and sinners. But wisdom is justified of her children.

20 ¶ Then began he to upbraid the cities wherein most of his mighty works were done, because they repented not:

21 Woe unto thee, Chorazin! woe unto thee, Bethsaida! for if the mighty works, which were done in you, had been done in Tyre and Sidon, they would have repented long ago in sackcloth and ashes.

22 But I say unto you, It shall be more tolerable for Tyre and Sidon at the day of judgment, than for you.

23 And thou, Capernaum, which art exalted unto heaven, shalt be brought down to hell: for if the mighty works, which have been done in thee, had been done in Sodom, it would have remained until this day.

24 But I say unto you, That it shall be more tolerable for the land of Sodom in the day of judgment, than for thee.

25 ¶ At that time Jesus answered and said, I thank thee, O Father, Lord of heaven and earth, because thou hast hid these things from the wise and prudent, and hast revealed them unto babes.

26 Even so, Father: for so it seemed good in thy sight.

Amplified

7 Then as these men went their way, Jesus began to speak to the crowds about John: What did you go out in the wilderness (desert) to see? A reed swayed by the wind?

8 What did you go out to see then? A man clothed in soft garments? Behold, those who wear soft clothing are in the houses of kings.

9 But what did you go out to see? A prophet? Yes, I tell you, and one ([b]out of the common, more eminent, more remarkable and) [b]superior to a prophet.

10 This is the one of whom it is written, Behold I send My messenger on ahead of You, who shall make ready Your way before You. [Mal. 3:1.]

11 Truly, I tell you, among those born of women there has not risen one greater than John the Baptist; yet he who is least in the kingdom of heaven is greater than he.

12 And from the days of John the Baptist until the present time the kingdom of heaven has endured violent assault, and violent men seize it by force [as a precious prize]—a [c]share in the heavenly kingdom is sought for with most ardent zeal and intense exertion.

13 For all the Law and the prophets prophesied up until John,

14 And if you are willing to receive *and* accept it, John himself is Elijah who was to come [before the kingdom]. [Mal. 4:5.]

15 He who has ears to hear, let him be listening, *and* consider *and* [d]perceive *and* comprehend by hearing.

16 But to what shall I liken this generation? It is like little children sitting in the market places who call to their playmates,

17 We piped to you [playing wedding], and you did not dance; we wailed dirges [playing funeral], and you did not mourn *and* beat your breasts *and* weep aloud.

18 For John came neither eating nor drinking with others, and they say, He has a demon!

19 The Son of man came eating and drinking with others and they say, Behold, a glutton and a wine drinker, a friend of tax collectors *and* [d]especially wicked sinners! Yet wisdom is justified *and* vindicated by what she does (her deeds) *and* by [e]*her children.*

20 Then He began to censure *and* reproach the cities in which most of His mighty works had been performed, because they did not repent—their hearts were not changed.

21 Woe to you, Chorazin! Woe to you, Bethsaida! for if the mighty works done in you had been done in Tyre and Sidon, they would long ago have repented in sackcloth and ashes—and their hearts have been changed.

22 I tell you [further], it shall be more endurable for Tyre and Sidon on the day of judgment than for you.

23 And you, Capernaum, are you to be lifted up to heaven? You shall be brought down to Hades [the region of the dead]! For if the mighty works done in you had been done in Sodom, it would have continued until today.

24 But I tell you, it shall be more endurable for the land of Sodom on the day of judgment than for you.

25 At that time Jesus began to say, I thank You, Father, Lord of heaven and earth, *and* [f]acknowledge openly *and* joyfully to Your honor that you have hidden these things from the wise *and* clever and learned, and revealed them to babies— to the [f]childish, untaught and unskilled.

26 Yes, Father, [I praise You that] such was Your gracious will *and* good pleasure.

---

b) Abbott-Smith.
c) Thayer.
d) Abbott-Smith.
e) Many ancient authorities read *children,* as in Luke 7:35.
f) Thayer.

Living New Testament

7 When John's disciples had gone, Jesus began talking about him to the crowds. "When you went out into the barren wilderness to see John, what did you expect him to be like? Grass blowing in the wind?

8 Or were you expecting to see a man dressed as a prince in a palace?

9 Or a prophet of God? Yes, and he is more than just a prophet.

10 For John is the man mentioned in the Scriptures—a messenger to precede Me, to announce My coming, and prepare people to receive Me.[2]

11 Truly, of all men ever born, none shines more brightly than John the Baptist. And yet, even the lesser lights in the Kingdom of Heaven will be greater than he is!

12 And from the time John the Baptist began preaching and baptizing until now, ardent multitudes have been crowding toward the Kingdom of Heaven.[3]

13 For all the laws and prophets looked forward [to the Messiah[4]]. Then John appeared,

14 And if you are willing to understand what I mean, he is Elijah, the one the prophets said would come [at the time the Kingdom begins[4]].

15 If ever you were willing to listen, listen now!

16 What shall I say about this nation? These people are like children playing, who say to their little friends,

17 'We played wedding and you weren't happy, so we played funeral but you weren't sad.'

18 For John the Baptist doesn't even drink wine and often goes without food, and you say, 'He's crazy.'[5]

19 And I, the Son of Mankind, feast and drink, and you complain that I am 'a glutton and a drinking man, and hang around with the worst sort of sinners!' But brilliant men like you can justify your every inconsistency!"[6]

20 Then He began to pour out His denunciations against the cities where He had done most of His miracles, because they hadn't turned to God.

21 "Woe to you, Chorazin, and woe to you, Bethsaida! For if the miracles I did in your streets had been done in wicked Tyre and Sidon[7] their people would have repented long ago in shame and humility.

22 Truly, Tyre and Sidon will be better off on the Judgment Day than you!

23 And Capernaum, though highly honored,[8] shall go down to hell! For if the marvelous miracles I did in you had been done in Sodom,[9] it would still be here today.

24 Truly, Sodom will be better off at the Judgment Day than you."

25 And Jesus prayed this prayer: "O Father, Lord of heaven and earth, thank You for hiding the truth from those who think themselves so wise, and for revealing it to little children!

26 Yes, Father, for it pleased You to do it this way!"

* * * * *

[2]Implied.
[3]Literally, "the kingdom of heaven suffers violence and men of violence take it by force."
[4]Implied.
[5]Literally, "he has a demon."
[6]Literally, "wisdom is justified by her children."
[7]Cities destroyed by God for their wickedness.
[8]Highly honored by Christ's being there.
[9]Cities destroyed by God for their wickedness.

Revised Standard

7 As they went away, Jesus began to
speak to the crowds concerning John:
"What did you go out into the wilderness to
behold? A reed shaken by the wind? [8]Why
then did you go out? To see a man[a] clothed
in soft raiment? Behold, those who wear
soft raiment are in kings' houses. [9]Why then
did you go out? To see a prophet?[b] Yes, I
tell you, and more than a prophet. [10]This is
he of whom it is written,
'Behold, I send my messenger before
thy face,
who shall prepare thy way before
thee.'
[11]Truly, I say to you, among those born of
women there has risen no one greater than
John the Baptist; yet he who is least in the
kingdom of heaven is greater than he.
[12]From the days of John the Baptist until
now the kingdom of heaven has suffered
violence,[c] and men of violence take it by
force. [13]For all the prophets and the law
prophesied until John; [14]and if you are
willing to accept it, he is Elijah who is to
come. [15]He who has ears to hear,[d] let him
hear.
16 "But to what shall I compare this generation? It is like children sitting in the market places and calling to their playmates,
[17]'We piped to you, and you did not dance;
we wailed, and you did not mourn.'
[18]For John came neither eating nor drinking, and they say, 'He has a demon'; [19]the
Son of man came eating and drinking, and
they say, 'Behold, a glutton and a drunkard,
a friend of tax collectors and sinners!' Yet
wisdom is justified by her deeds."[e]

The judgment of the unrepentant

20 Then he began to upbraid the cities
where most of his mighty works had been
done, because they did not repent. [21]"Woe
to you, Chorazin! woe to you, Bethsaida! for
if the mighty works done in you had been
done in Tyre and Sidon, they would have
repented long ago in sackcloth and ashes.
[22]But I tell you, it shall be more tolerable
on the day of judgment for Tyre and Sidon
than for you. [23]And you, Capernaum, will
you be exalted to heaven? You shall be
brought down to Hades. For if the mighty
works done in you had been done in Sodom,
it would have remained until this day. [24]But
I tell you that it shall be more tolerable on
the day of judgment for the land of Sodom
than for you."

Jesus reveals the Father

25 At that time Jesus declared, "I thank
thee, Father, Lord of heaven and earth, that
thou hast hidden these things from the wise
and understanding and revealed them to
babes; [26]yea, Father, for such was thy gra-

[a] Or *What then did you go out to see? A man . . .*
[b] Other ancient authorities read *What then did you go out to see? A prophet?*
[c] Or *has been coming violently*
[d] Other ancient authorities omit *to hear*
[e] Other ancient authorities read *children* (Luke 7.35)

King James

27 All things are delivered unto me of my Father: and no man knoweth the Son, but the Father; neither knoweth any man the Father, save the Son, and *he* to whomsoever the Son will reveal *him*.

28 ¶ Come unto me, all *ye* that labour and are heavy laden, and I will give you rest.

29 Take my yoke upon you, and learn of me; for I am meek and lowly in heart: and ye shall find rest unto your souls.

30 For my yoke *is* easy, and my burden is light.

Amplified

27 All things were entrusted *and* delivered to Me by My Father; and no one [h]fully knows *and* [g]accurately understands the Son except the Father; and no one [h]fully knows *and* [g]accurately understands the Father except the Son and any one to whom the Son [g]deliberately wills to make Him known.

28 Come to Me, all you who labor and are heavy-laden *and* over burdened, and I will cause you to rest—I will [i]ease *and* relieve *and* [j]refresh [g]your souls.

29 Take My yoke upon you, and learn of Me; for I am gentle (meek) *and* humble (lowly) in heart, and you will find rest—[k]relief, ease and refreshment and [g]recreation and blessed quiet—for your souls. [Jer. 6:16.]

30 For My yoke is wholesome (useful, [l]good)—not harsh, hard, sharp or pressing, but comfortable, gracious and pleasant; and My burden is light *and* easy to be borne.

CHAPTER 12

AT that time Jesus went on the sabbath day through the corn; and his disciples were an hungered, and began to pluck the ears of corn, and to eat.

2 But when the Pharisees saw *it*, they said unto him, Behold, thy disciples do that which is not lawful to do upon the sabbath day.

3 But he said unto them, Have ye not read what David did, when he was an hungered, and they that were with him;

4 How he entered into the house of God, and did eat the shewbread, which was not lawful for him to eat, neither for them which were with him, but only for the priests?

5 Or have ye not read in the law, how that on the sabbath days the priests in the temple profane the sabbath, and are blameless?

6 But I say unto you, That in this place is *one* greater than the temple.

7 But if ye had known what *this* meaneth, I will have mercy, and not sacrifice, ye would not have condemned the guiltless.

8 For the Son of man is Lord even of the sabbath day.

9 And when he was departed thence, he went into their synagogue:

10 ¶ And, behold, there was a man which had *his* hand withered. And they asked him, saying, Is it lawful to heal on the sabbath days? that they might accuse him.

11 And he said unto them, What man shall there be among you, that shall have one sheep, and if it fall into a pit on the sabbath day, will he not lay hold on it, and lift *it* out?

12 How much then is a man better than a sheep? Wherefore it is lawful to do well on the sabbath days.

13 Then saith he to the man, Stretch forth thine hand. And he stretched *it* forth; and it was restored whole, like as the other.

CHAPTER 12

AT that [h]particular time Jesus went through the fields of standing grain on the Sabbath, and His disciples were hungry, and they began to pick off the spikes of grain and to eat. [Deut. 23:25.]

2 And when the Pharisees saw it, they said to Him, See there! Your disciples are doing what is unlawful *and* not permitted on the Sabbath.

3 He said to them, Have you not even read what David did when he was hungry, and those who accompanied him? [I Sam. 21:1-6; Lev. 24:9.]

4 How he went into the house of God and ate the loaves of the showbread, which it was not lawful for him to eat, nor for the men who accompanied him, but for the priests only?

5 Or have you never read in the Law how on the Sabbath the priests in the temple violate the sanctity of the Sabbath, breaking it, and yet are guiltless? [Num. 28:9, 10.]

6 But I tell you, Something greater *and* [m]more exalted *and* more majestic than the temple is here!

7 And if you had only known what this saying means, I want mercy [readiness to help, to spare, to forgive] rather than sacrifice *and* sacrificial victims, you would not have condemned the guiltless. [Hos. 6:6.]

8 For the Son of man is Lord [even] of the Sabbath.

9 And going on from there, He went into their synagogue.

10 And behold, a man was there with one withered hand. And they said to Him, Is it lawful *or* allowable to cure people on the Sabbath days?

11 But He said to them, What man is there among you, if he has only one sheep, and it falls into a pit *or* ditch on the Sabbath, will not take hold of it and lift it out?

12 How much better *and* of more value is a man than a sheep! So it is lawful *and* allowable to do good on the Sabbath days.

13 Then He said to the man, Reach out your hand. And the man reached it out, and it was restored, sound as the other one.

---

g) Thayer.
h) Vincent.
i) Tyndale.
j) Wycliffe.
k) Souter.
l) Moulton and Milligan.
m) Thayer.

Living New Testament

27 "All truth[10] has been entrusted to Me by My Father. Only the Father knows the Son, and the Father is known only by the Son and by those to whom the Son reveals Him.

28 Come to Me and I will give you rest—all of you who work so hard beneath a heavy yoke.

29, 30 Wear My yoke—for it fits perfectly—and let Me teach you; for I am gentle and humble, and you shall find rest for your souls; for I give you only light burdens."

CHAPTER 12

About that time Jesus was walking one day through some grainfields with His disciples. It was on the Sabbath, the Jewish day of worship, and His disciples were hungry; so they began breaking off heads of wheat and eating the grain.

2 But some Pharisees saw them do it and protested, "Your disciples are breaking the law." "They are harvesting on the Sabbath!"[1]

3 But Jesus said to them, "Haven't you ever read what King David did when he and his friends were hungry?

4 He went into the Temple and all ate the special bread[2] permitted to the priests alone. That was breaking the law too!

5 And haven't you ever read in the law of Moses how the priests on duty in the Temple may work on the Sabbath?

6 And truly, one is here who is greater than the Temple!

7 But if you had known the meaning of this Scripture verse, 'I want you to be merciful more than I want your offerings,' you would not have condemned those who aren't guilty!

8 For I, the Son of Mankind, am master even of the Sabbath."

9 Then He went over to the synagogue,

10 And noticed there a man with a deformed hand. The Pharisees[3] asked Jesus, "Is it legal to work by healing on the Sabbath day?" (They were, of course, hoping He would say "yes," so they could arrest[4] Him!)

11 This was His answer: "If you had just one sheep, and it fell into a well on the Sabbath, would you work to rescue it that day? Of course you would![5]

12 And how much more valuable is a person than a sheep! Yes, it is right to do good on the Sabbath!"

13 Then He said to the man, "Stretch out your arm." And as he did, his hand became normal, just like the other one!

[10]Literally, "all things."
[1]Implied.
[2]Literally, "the shewbread."
[3]Implied.
[4]Literally, "accuse."
[5]Implied.

Revised Standard

cious will.[f] 27All things have been delivered
to me by my Father; and no one knows the
Son except the Father, and no one knows
the Father except the Son and any one to
whom the Son chooses to reveal him.
28Come to me, all who labor and are heavy
laden, and I will give you rest. 29Take my
yoke upon you, and learn from me; for I am
gentle and lowly in heart, and you will find
rest for your souls. 30For my yoke is easy,
and my burden is light."

Jesus the Lord of the Sabbath

12 At that time Jesus went through the
grainfields on the sabbath; his disciples
were hungry, and they began to pluck ears
of grain and to eat. 2But when the Pharisees
saw it, they said to him, "Look, your disciples
are doing what is not lawful to do
on the sabbath." 3He said to them, "Have
you not read what David did, when he was
hungry, and those who were with him:
4how he entered the house of God and
ate the bread of the Presence, which it
was not lawful for him to eat nor for
those who were with him, but only for the
priests? 5Or have you not read in the law
how on the sabbath the priests in the temple
profane the sabbath, and are guiltless? 6I
tell you, something greater than the temple
is here. 7And if you had known what this
means, 'I desire mercy, and not sacrifice,'
you would not have condemned the guiltless.
8For the Son of man is lord of the sabbath."

The healing on the Sabbath

9 And he went on from there, and entered
their synagogue. 10And behold, there
was a man with a withered hand. And they
asked him, "Is it lawful to heal on the sabbath?"
so that they might accuse him. 11He
said to them, "What man of you, if he has
one sheep and it falls into a pit on the
sabbath, will not lay hold of it and lift it
out? 12Of how much more value is a man
than a sheep! So it is lawful to do good on
the sabbath." 13Then he said to the man,
"Stretch out your hand." And the man
stretched it out, and it was restored, whole

[f] Or *so it was well-pleasing before thee*

King James

14 ¶ Then the Pharisees went out, and held a council against him, how they might destroy him.

15 But when Jesus knew it, he withdrew himself from thence: and great multitudes followed him, and he healed them all;

16 And charged them that they should not make him known:

17 That it might be fulfilled which was spoken by Esaias the prophet, saying,

18 Behold my servant, whom I have chosen; my beloved, in whom my soul is well pleased: I will put my spirit upon him, and he shall shew judgment to the Gentiles.

19 He shall not strive, nor cry; neither shall any man hear his voice in the streets.

20 A bruised reed shall he not break, and smoking flax shall he not quench, till he send forth judgment unto victory.

21 And in his name shall the Gentiles trust.

22 ¶ Then was brought unto him one possessed with a devil, blind, and dumb: and he healed him, insomuch that the blind and dumb both spake and saw.

23 And all the people were amazed, and said, Is not this the son of David?

24 But when the Pharisees heard *it*, they said, This *fellow* doth not cast out devils, but by Beelzebub the prince of the devils.

25 And Jesus knew their thoughts, and said unto them, Every kingdom divided against itself is brought to desolation; and every city or house divided against itself shall not stand:

26 And if Satan cast out Satan, he is divided against himself; how shall then his kingdom stand?

27 And if I by Beelzebub cast out devils, by whom do your children cast *them* out? therefore they shall be your judges.

28 But if I cast out devils by the Spirit of God, then the kingdom of God is come unto you.

29 Or else how can one enter into a strong man's house, and spoil his goods, except he first bind the strong man? and then he will spoil his house.

30 He that is not with me is against me; and he that gathereth not with me scattereth abroad.

31 ¶ Wherefore I say unto you, All manner of sin and blasphemy shall be forgiven unto men: but the blasphemy *against* the *Holy* Ghost shall not be forgiven unto men.

32 And whosoever speaketh a word against the Son of man, it shall be forgiven him: but whosoever speaketh against the Holy Ghost, it shall not be forgiven him, neither in this world, neither in the *world* to come.

33 Either make the tree good, and his fruit good; or else make the tree corrupt, and his fruit corrupt: for the tree is known by *his* fruit.

Amplified

14 But the Pharisees went out and held a consultation against Him, how they might do away with Him.

15 But being aware of this, Jesus went away from there. And many people [n]joined *and* accompanied Him, and He cured all of them,

16 And strictly charged them *and* sharply warned [them] not to make Him [o]publicly known.

17 This was in fulfillment of what was spoken by the prophet Isaiah,

18 Behold, My Servant Whom I have chosen, My Beloved in *and* with Whom My soul is well pleased *and* [o]has found its delight. I will put My Spirit upon Him, and He shall proclaim *and* [o]show forth judgment to the nations.

19 He will not strive *or* wrangle or cry out loudly, nor will any one hear His voice in the streets;

20 A bruised reed He will not break, and a smoldering (dimly burning) wick He will not quench till He brings [n]justice *and* a just cause to victory.

21 And in *and* on His name will the Gentiles—the [p]peoples outside of Israel—set their hopes. [Isa. 42:1-4.]

22 Then a blind and dumb man, under the power of a demon, was brought to Jesus, and He cured him, so that the blind and dumb man both spoke and saw.

23 And all the [crowds of] people were stunned with bewildered wonder, and said, This cannot be the Son of David, can it?

24 But the Pharisees hearing it said, This [q]Man drives out demons only by *and* with the help of Beelzebub, the prince of demons.

25 And knowing their thoughts, He said to them, Any kingdom that is divided against itself is being brought to desolation *and* laid waste, and no city *or* house divided against itself will last *or* continue to stand.

26 And if Satan drives out Satan, he has become divided against himself *and* disunited; how then will his kingdom last *or* continue to stand?

27 And if I drive out the demons by [help of] Beelzebub, by whose [help] do your sons drive them out? [r]For this reason they shall be your judges.

28 But if it is by the Spirit of God that I drive out the demons, then the kingdom of God has come upon you [[s]before you expected it].

29 Or how can a person go into a strong man's house and carry off his goods—the entire equipment of his house—without first binding the strong man? Then indeed he may plunder his house.

30 He who is not with Me (definitely [t]on My side), is against Me, and he who does not (definitely) gather with Me *and* for [t]My side, scatters.

31 Therefore I tell you, every sin and blasphemy—that is, every evil, abusive, [u]injurious speaking or indignity against sacred things—can be forgiven men, but blasphemy against the (Holy) Spirit shall not *and* [u]cannot be forgiven.

32 And whoever speaks a word against the Son of man will be forgiven, but whoever speaks against the Spirit, the Holy One, will not be forgiven, either in this world *and* age or in the world *and* age to come.

33 Either make the tree sound (healthy and good), and its fruit sound (healthy and good), or make the tree rotten (diseased and bad) and its fruit rotten (diseased and bad); for the tree is known *and* recognized *and* judged by its fruit.

---

n) Thayer.
o) Darby's "The New Testament, a New Translation."
p) Cremer.
q) Capitalized because of what He is, the spotless Son of God, not what the speakers may have thought He was.
r) Darby's "The New Testament, a New Translation."
s) Vincent.
t) Thayer.
u) Williams.

Living New Testament

14 Then the Pharisees called a meeting to plot Jesus' arrest and death.

15 But He knew what they were planning, and left the synagogue, with many following Him. He healed all the sick among them,

16 But He cautioned them against spreading the news about His miracle.

17 This fulfilled the prophecy of Isaiah concerning Him:

18 "Look at My Servant.
See My Chosen One.
He is My Beloved, in whom My soul delights.
I will put My Spirit upon Him,
And He will judge the nations.
19 He does not fight nor shout;
He does not raise His voice!
20 He does not crush the weak,
Or quench the smallest hope;
He will end all conflict with His final victory,
21 And His name shall be the hope
Of all the world."[6]

22 Then a demon-possessed man—he was both blind and unable to talk—was brought to Jesus, and Jesus healed him so that he could both speak and see.

23 The crowd was amazed. "Maybe Jesus is the Messiah!"[7] they exclaimed.

24 But when the Pharisees heard about the miracle they said, "He can cast out demons because He is Satan,[8] king of devils."

25 Jesus knew their thoughts and replied, "A divided kingdom ends in ruin. A city or home divided against itself cannot stand.

26 And if Satan is casting out Satan, he is fighting himself, and destroying his own kingdom.

27 And if, as you claim, I am casting out demons by invoking the powers of Satan, then what power do your own people use when they cast them out? Let them answer your accusation!

28 But if I am casting out demons by the Spirit of God, then the Kingdom of God has arrived among you.

29 One cannot rob Satan's kingdom without first binding Satan.[9] Only then can his demons be cast out![10]

30 Anyone who isn't helping Me is harming Me.

31, 32 Even blasphemy against Me,[11] or any other sin, can be forgiven—all except one: speaking against the Holy Spirit shall never be forgiven, either in this world or in the world to come.

33 A tree is identified by its fruit. A tree from a select variety produces good fruit; poor varieties don't.

Revised Standard

like the other. 14 But the Pharisees went out
and took counsel against him, how to destroy him.

Jesus heals many

15 Jesus, aware of this, withdrew from
there. And many followed him, and he
healed them all, 16 and ordered them not to
make him known. 17 This was to fulfil what
was spoken by the prophet Isaiah:
18 "Behold, my servant whom I have
chosen,
my beloved with whom my soul
is well pleased.
I will put my Spirit upon him,
and he shall proclaim justice to
the Gentiles.
19 He will not wrangle or cry aloud,
nor will any one hear his voice in
the streets;
20 he will not break a bruised reed
or quench a smoldering wick,
till he brings justice to victory;
21 and in his name will the Gentiles
hope."

Jesus answers the Pharisees' slander

22 Then a blind and dumb demoniac was
brought to him, and he healed him, so that
the dumb man spoke and saw. 23 And all the
people were amazed, and said, "Can this be
the Son of David?" 24 But when the Pharisees heard it they said, "It is only by Beelzebul, the prince of demons, that this
man casts out demons." 25 Knowing their
thoughts, he said to them, "Every kingdom
divided against itself is laid waste, and no
city or house divided against itself will
stand; 26 and if Satan casts out Satan, he is
divided against himself; how then will his
kingdom stand? 27 And if I cast out demons
by Beelzebul, by whom do your sons cast
them out? Therefore they shall be your
judges. 28 But if it is by the Spirit of God
that I cast out demons, then the kingdom of
God has come upon you. 29 Or how can one
enter a strong man's house and plunder his
goods, unless he first binds the strong man?
Then indeed he may plunder his house.
30 He who is not with me is against me, and
he who does not gather with me scatters.
31 Therefore I tell you, every sin and blasphemy will be forgiven men, but the blasphemy against the Spirit will not be forgiven.
32 And whoever says a word against
the Son of man will be forgiven; but whoever speaks against the Holy Spirit will not
be forgiven, either in this age or in the age
to come.
33 "Either make the tree good, and its
fruit good; or make the tree bad, and its
fruit bad; for the tree is known by its fruit.

---

6 Isaiah 42:1-4.
7 Literally, "the Son of David."
8 Literally, "Beelzebub."
9 Literally, "the strong."
10 Literally, "then will he spoil his house."
11 Literally, "the Son of man."

King James

34 O generation of vipers, how can ye, being evil, speak good things? for out of the abundance of the heart the mouth speaketh.

35 A good man out of the good treasure of the heart bringeth forth good things: and an evil man out of the evil treasure bringeth forth evil things.

36 But I say unto you, That every idle word that men shall speak, they shall give account thereof in the day of judgment.

37 For by thy words thou shalt be justified, and by thy words thou shalt be condemned.

38 ¶ Then certain of the scribes and of the Pharisees answered, saying, Master, we would see a sign from thee.

39 But he answered and said unto them, An evil and adulterous generation seeketh after a sign; and there shall no sign be given to it, but the sign of the prophet Jonas:

40 For as Jonas was three days and three nights in the whale's belly; so shall the Son of man be three days and three nights in the heart of the earth.

41 The men of Nineveh shall rise in judgment with this generation, and shall condemn it: because they repented at the preaching of Jonas; and, behold, a greater than Jonas is here.

42 The queen of the south shall rise up in the judgment with this generation, and shall condemn it: for she came from the uttermost parts of the earth to hear the wisdom of Solomon; and, behold, a greater than Solomon *is* here.

43 When the unclean spirit is gone out of a man, he walketh through dry places, seeking rest, and findeth none.

44 Then he saith, I will return into my house from whence I came out; and when he is come, he findeth *it* empty, swept, and garnished.

45 Then goeth he, and taketh with himself seven other spirits more wicked than himself, and they enter in and dwell there: and the last *state* of that man is worse than the first. Even so shall it be also unto this wicked generation.

46 ¶ While he yet talked to the people, behold, *his* mother and his brethren stood without, desiring to speak with him.

47 Then one said unto him, Behold, thy mother and thy brethren stand without, desiring to speak with thee.

48 But he answered and said unto him that told him, Who is my mother? and who are my brethren?

49 And he stretched forth his hand toward his disciples, and said, Behold my mother and my brethren!

50 For whosoever shall do the will of my Father which is in heaven, the same is my brother, and sister, and mother.

Amplified

34 You offspring of vipers! How can you speak good things when you are evil—wicked? For out of the fullness—the overflow, the [v]superabundance—of the heart the mouth speaks.

35 The good man from his inner good treasure [w]flings forth good things, and the evil man out of his inner evil storehouse [w]flings forth evil things.

36 But I tell you, on the day of judgment men will have to give account for every [w]idle (inoperative, non-working) word they speak.

37 For by your words you will be justified *and* acquitted, and by your words you will be condemned *and* sentenced.

38 Then some of the scribes and Pharisees said to Him, Teacher, we desire to see a sign *or* miracle from You [proving that You are what You claim to be].

39 But He replied to them, An evil and adulterous generation [that is, a generation [w]morally unfaithful to God] seeks *and* demands a sign; but no sign shall be given to it except the sign of the prophet Jonah.

40 For even as Jonah was three days and three nights in the belly of the sea monster, so will the Son of man be three days and three nights in the heart of the earth. [Jonah 1:17.]

41 The men of Nineveh will stand up at the judgment with this generation and condemn it; for they repented at the preaching of Jonah, and behold, Something more *and* greater than Jonah is here! [Jonah 3:5.]

42 The queen of the South will stand up at the judgment with this generation and condemn it; for she came from the ends of the earth to listen to the wisdom of Solomon, and behold, Something more *and* greater than Solomon is here. [I Kings 10:1; II Chron. 9:1.]

43 But when the unclean spirit has gone out of a man, he roams through dry places in search of rest, but he does not find any.

44 Then he says, I will go back to my house from which I came out. And when he arrives he finds the place unoccupied, swept, put in order *and* decorated.

45 Then he goes and brings with him seven other spirits more wicked than himself, and they go in and make their home there. And the last condition of that man becomes worse than the first. So also shall it be with this wicked generation.

46 Jesus was still speaking to the people when behold, His mother and brothers stood outside, seeking to speak to Him.

47 *Some one said to Him, Listen! Your mother and Your brothers are standing outside, seeking to speak to You.*

48 But He replied to the man who told Him, Who is My mother, and who are My brothers?

49 And stretching out His hand toward [not only the twelve disciples but all] [x]His adherents, He said, Here are My mother and My brothers.

50 For whoever does the will of My Father in heaven is My brother and sister and mother!

---

v) Souter.
w) Vincent.
x) Cremer.

Living New Testament

34 You brood of snakes! How could evil men like you speak what is good and right? For a man's heart determines his speech.

35 A good man's speech reveals the rich treasures within him. An evil-hearted man is filled with venom, and his speech reveals it.

36 And I tell you this, that you must give account on Judgment Day for every idle word you speak.

37 Your words now reflect your fate then; either you will be justified by them or you will be condemned."

* * * * *

38 One day some of the Jewish leaders, including some Pharisees, came to Jesus asking to see a miracle[12] to prove that He was really the Messiah.[13]

39, 40 But Jesus replied, "Only an evil, faithless nation would ask for further proof; and none will be given except what happened to Jonah the prophet! For as Jonah was in the sea monster for three days and three nights, so I, the Son of Mankind, shall be in the heart of the earth three days and three nights.

41 The men of Nineveh shall arise against this nation at the judgment and condemn you. For when Jonah preached to them, they repented and turned to God from all their evil ways. And now a greater than Jonah is here—and you refuse to believe Him.[13]

42 The Queen of Sheba shall rise against this nation in the judgment, and condemn it; for she came from a distant land to hear the wisdom of Solomon; and now a greater than Solomon is here—and you refuse to believe Him.[13]

43, 44, 45 This evil nation is like a man possessed by a demon. For if the demon leaves, it goes into the deserts[14] for a while, seeking rest but finding none. Then it says, 'I will return to the man I came from.' So it returns and finds the man's heart clean but empty! Then the demon finds seven other spirits more evil than itself, and all enter the man and live in him. And so he is worse off than before."

46, 47 As Jesus was speaking in a crowded house[15] His mother and brothers were outside, wanting to talk with Him. When someone told Him they were there,

48 He remarked, "Who is My mother? Who are My brothers?"

49 He pointed to His disciples. "Look!" He said, "these are My mother and brothers."

50 Then He added, "Anyone who obeys My Father in heaven is My brother, sister and mother!"

[12]Literally, "to see a sign."
[13]Implied.
[14]Literally, "passes through waterless places."
[15]Implied.

Revised Standard

[34]You brood of vipers! how can you speak good, when you are evil? For out of the abundance of the heart the mouth speaks. [35]The good man out of his good treasure brings forth good, and the evil man out of his evil treasure brings forth evil. [36]I tell you, on the day of judgment men will render account for every careless word they utter; [37]for by your words you will be justified, and by your words you will be condemned."

Warning against seeking signs

38 Then some of the scribes and Pharisees said to him, "Teacher, we wish to see a sign from you." [39]But he answered them, "An evil and adulterous generation seeks for a sign; but no sign shall be given to it except the sign of the prophet Jonah. [40]For as Jonah was three days and three nights in the belly of the whale, so will the Son of man be three days and three nights in the heart of the earth. [41]The men of Nineveh will arise at the judgment with this generation and condemn it; for they repented at the preaching of Jonah, and behold, something greater than Jonah is here. [42]The queen of the South will arise at the judgment with this generation and condemn it; for she came from the ends of the earth to hear the wisdom of Solomon, and behold, something greater than Solomon is here.

Return of the unclean spirits

43 "When the unclean spirit has gone out of a man, he passes through waterless places seeking rest, but he finds none. [44]Then he says, 'I will return to my house from which I came.' And when he comes he finds it empty, swept, and put in order. [45]Then he goes and brings with him seven other spirits more evil than himself, and they enter and dwell there; and the last state of that man becomes worse than the first. So shall it be also with this evil generation."

Jesus' true family

46 While he was still speaking to the people, behold, his mother and his brothers stood outside, asking to speak to him.[g] [48]But he replied to the man who told him, "Who is my mother, and who are my brothers?" [49]And stretching out his hand toward his disciples, he said, "Here are my mother and my brothers! [50]For whoever does the will of my Father in heaven is my brother, and sister, and mother."

[g] **Other ancient authorities insert verse 47, *Some one told him, "Your mother and your brothers are standing outside, asking to speak to you"***

King James

CHAPTER 13

THE same day went Jesus out of the house, and sat by the sea side.

2 And great multitudes were gathered together unto him, so that he went into a ship, and sat; and the whole multitude stood on the shore.

3 And he spake many things unto them in parables, saying, Behold, a sower went forth to sow;

4 And when he sowed, some *seeds* fell by the way side, and the fowls came and devoured them up:

5 Some fell upon stony places, where they had not much earth: and forthwith they sprung up, because they had no deepness of earth:

6 And when the sun was up, they were scorched; and because they had no root, they withered away.

7 And some fell among thorns; and the thorns sprung up, and choked them:

8 But other fell into good ground, and brought forth fruit, some an hundredfold, some sixtyfold, some thirtyfold.

9 Who hath ears to hear, let him hear.

10 And the disciples came, and said unto him, Why speakest thou unto them in parables?

11 He answered and said unto them, Because it is given unto you to know the mysteries of the kingdom of heaven, but to them it is not given.

12 For whosoever hath, to him shall be given, and he shall have more abundance; but whosoever hath not, from him shall be taken away even that he hath.

13 Therefore speak I to them in parables: because they seeing see not; and hearing they hear not, neither do they understand.

14 And in them is fulfilled the prophecy of Esaias, which saith, By hearing ye shall hear, and shall not understand; and seeing ye shall see, and shall not perceive:

15 For this people's heart is waxed gross, and *their* ears are dull of hearing, and their eyes they have closed; lest at any time they should see with *their* eyes, and hear with *their* ears, and should understand with *their* heart, and should be converted, and I should heal them.

16 But blessed *are* your eyes, for they see: and your ears, for they hear.

17 For verily I say unto you, That many prophets and righteous *men* have desired to see *those things* which ye see, and have not seen *them;* and to hear *those things* which ye hear and have not heard *them.*

18 ¶ Hear ye therefore the parable of the sower.

19 When any one heareth the word of the kingdom, and understandeth *it* not, then cometh the wicked *one,* and catcheth away that which was sown in his heart. This is he which received seed by the way side.

20 But he that received the seed into stony places, the same is he that heareth the word, and anon with joy receiveth it;

Amplified

CHAPTER 13

THAT same day Jesus went out of the house and was sitting beside the sea.

2 But such great crowds gathered about Him that He got into a boat and remained sitting there, while all the throng stood on the shore.

3 And He told them many things in parables—that is, stories by way of illustration; saying, A sower went out to sow,

4 And as he sowed, some seeds fell by the roadside, and the birds came and ate them up.

5 Other seeds fell on rocky ground, where they had not much soil, and at once they sprang up, because they had no depth of soil;

6 But when the sun rose they were scorched, and because they had no root they dried up *and* withered away.

7 Other seeds fell among thorns, and the thorns grew up and choked them out.

8 Other seeds fell on good soil and yielded grain, some a hundred times as much as was sown, some sixty times as much, and some thirty.

9 He who has ears [to hear], let him be listening *and* [y]consider and [z]perceive *and* comprehend by hearing.

10 Then the disciples came to Him and said, Why do You speak to them in parables?

11 And He replied to them, To you it has been given to know the secrets *and* mysteries of the kingdom of heaven, but to them it has not been given.

12 For whoever has [spiritual knowledge], to him will more be given *and* he will [a]be furnished richly, *so that* he will have abundance; but from him who has not, even what he has will be taken away.

13 This is the reason that I speak to them in parables, because [a]having the power of seeing they do not see, and [a]having the power of hearing they do not hear, nor do they grasp *and* understand.

14 In them indeed is [b]the process of fulfillment of the prophecy of Isaiah which says: You shall indeed hear *and* hear, but never grasp *and* understand; and you shall indeed look *and* look, but never see *and* perceive.

15 For this nation's heart has grown gross—fat and dull; and their ears heavy *and* difficult of hearing, and their eyes they have tightly closed, lest they see *and* perceive with their eyes, and hear *and* comprehend the sense with their ears, and grasp *and* understand with their heart, and turn *and* I should heal them. [Isa. 6:9, 10.]

16 But blessed—happy, fortunate and [c]to be envied—are your eyes, because they do see, and your ears, because they do hear.

17 Truly, I tell you, many prophets and righteous men—men who were upright and in right standing with God—yearned to see what you see, and did not see it, and to hear what you hear, and did not hear it.

18 Listen then to the parable of the sower.

19 [d]While any one is hearing the Word of the kingdom and does not grasp *and* comprehend it, the evil one comes and snatches away what is sown in his heart. This is what was sown along the roadside.

20 As for what was sown on thin (rocky) soil, this is he who hears the Word and at once welcomes *and* accepts it with joy;

---

y) Thayer.
z) Abbott-Smith.
a) Thayer.
b) Vincent.
c) Souter.
d) Vincent.

Living New Testament

CHAPTER 13

Later that same day, Jesus left the house and went down to the shore,

2, 3 Where an immense crowd soon gathered. He got into a boat and taught from it while the people listened on the beach. He used many illustrations such as this one in His sermon: "A farmer was sowing grain in his fields.

4 As he scattered the seed across the ground, some fell beside a path, and the birds came and ate it.

5 And some fell on rocky soil where there was little depth of earth; the plants sprang up quickly enough in the shallow soil,

6 But the hot sun soon scorched them and they withered and died, for they had so little root.

7 Other seeds fell among thorns, and the thorns choked out the tender blades.

8 But some fell on good soil, and produced a crop that was 30, 60 and even 100 times as much as he had planted.

9 If you have ears, listen!"

10 His disciples came and asked Him, "Why do You always use these hard-to-understand[1] illustrations?"

11 Then He explained to them that only they were permitted to understand about the Kingdom of Heaven, and others were not.

12, 13 "For to him who has will more be given," He told them, "and he will have great plenty; but from him who has not, even the little he has will be taken away. That is why I use these illustrations, so people will hear and see but not understand.[2]

14 This fulfills the prophecy of Isaiah, 'They hear, but don't understand; they look, but don't see!

15 For their hearts are fat and heavy, and their ears are dull, and they have closed their eyes in sleep,

16 So they won't see and hear and understand and turn to God again, and let Me heal them.' But blessed are your eyes, for they see; and your ears, for they hear.

17 Many a prophet and godly man has longed to see what you have seen, and hear what you have heard, but couldn't.

18 Now here is the explanation of the story I told about the farmer planting grain:

19 The hard path where some of the seed fell represents the heart of a person who hears the good news about the Kingdom and doesn't understand it; then Satan[3] comes and snatches away the seeds from his heart.

20 The shallow, rocky soil represents the heart of a man who hears the message and receives it with real joy,

[1]Implied.
[2]Those who were receptive to spiritual truth understood the illustrations. To others it was only a story without meaning.
[3]Literally, "the evil."

Revised Standard

The parable of the sower

13 That same day Jesus went out of the
house and sat beside the sea. [2]And
great crowds gathered about him, so that
he got into a boat and sat there; and the
whole crowd stood on the beach. [3]And
he told them many things in parables, saying: "A sower went out to sow. [4]And as he
sowed, some seeds fell along the path, and
the birds came and devoured them. [5]Other
seeds fell on rocky ground, where they had
not much soil, and immediately they sprang
up, since they had no depth of soil, [6]but
when the sun rose they were scorched; and
since they had no root they withered away.
[7]Other seeds fell upon thorns, and the
thorns grew up and choked them. [8]Other
seeds fell on good soil and brought forth
grain, some a hundredfold, some sixty, some
thirty. [9]He who has ears,[h] let him hear."

The reason for parables

10 Then the disciples came and said to
him, "Why do you speak to them in parables?" [11]And he answered them, "To you it
has been given to know the secrets of the
kingdom of heaven, but to them it has not
been given. [12]For to him who has will more
be given, and he will have abundance; but
from him who has not, even what he has
will be taken away. [13]This is why I speak to
them in parables, because seeing they do not
see, and hearing they do not hear, nor do
they understand. [14]With them indeed is
fulfilled the prophecy of Isaiah which says:
'You shall indeed hear but never understand,
and you shall indeed see but never perceive.
[15]For this people's heart has grown dull,
and their ears are heavy of hearing,
and their eyes they have closed,
lest they should perceive with their eyes,
and hear with their ears,
and understand with their heart,
and turn for me to heal them.'
[16]But blessed are your eyes, for they see,
and your ears, for they hear. [17]Truly, I say
to you, many prophets and righteous men
longed to see what you see, and did not see
it, and to hear what you hear, and did not
hear it.

Parable of the sower explained

18 "Hear then the parable of the sower.
[19]When any one hears the word of the
kingdom and does not understand it, the evil
one comes and snatches away what is sown
in his heart; this is what was sown along the
path. [20]As for what was sown on rocky
ground, this is he who hears the word and
immediately receives it with joy; [21]yet he

[h] Other ancient authorities add here and in verse 43 *to hear*

King James

21 Yet hath he not root in himself, but dureth for a while: for when tribulation or persecution ariseth because of the word, by and by he is offended.

22 He also that received seed among the thorns is he that heareth the word; and the care of this world, and the deceitfulness of riches, choke the word, and he becometh unfruitful.

23 But he that received seed into the good ground is he that heareth the word, and understandeth *it;* which also beareth fruit, and bringeth forth, some an hundredfold, some sixty, some thirty.

24 ¶ Another parable put he forth unto them, saying, The kingdom of heaven is likened unto a man which sowed good seed in his field:

25 But while men slept, his enemy came and sowed tares among the wheat, and went his way.

26 But when the blade was sprung up, and brought forth fruit, then appeared the tares also.

27 So the servants of the householder came and said unto him, Sir, didst not thou sow good seed in thy field? from whence then hath it tares?

28 He said unto them, An enemy hath done this. The servants said unto him, Wilt thou then that we go and gather them up?

29 But he said, Nay; lest while ye gather up the tares, ye root up also the wheat with them.

30 Let both grow together until the harvest: and in the time of harvest I will say to the reapers, Gather ye together first the tares, and bind them in bundles to burn them: but gather the wheat into my barn.

31 ¶ Another parable put he forth unto them, saying, The kingdom of heaven is like to a grain of mustard seed, which a man took, and sowed in his field:

32 Which indeed is the least of all seeds: but when it is grown, it is the greatest among herbs, and becometh a tree, so that the birds of the air come and lodge in the branches thereof.

33 ¶ Another parable spake he unto them; The kingdom of heaven is like unto leaven, which a woman took, and hid in three measures of meal, till the whole was leavened.

34 All these things spake Jesus unto the multitude in parables; and without a parable spake he not unto them:

35 That it might be fulfilled which was spoken by the prophet, saying, I will open my mouth in parables; I will utter things which have been kept secret from the foundation of the world.

36 Then Jesus sent the multitude away, and went into the house: and his disciples came unto him, saying, Declare unto us the parable of the tares of the field.

37 He answered and said unto them, He that soweth the good seed is the Son of man;

38 The field is the world; the good seed are the children of the kingdom; but the tares are the children of the wicked *one;*

Amplified

21 Yet it has no real root in himself, but is temporary—inconstant, [e]lasts but a little while and when affliction *or* trouble *or* persecution comes on account of the Word, at once he is caused to stumble—he is repelled and [f]begins to distrust and desert Him Whom he ought to trust and obey, and he falls away.

22 As for what was sown among thorns, this is he who hears the Word, but the cares of the world and the pleasure *and* delight *and* glamour *and* deceitfulness of riches choke *and* suffocate the Word, and it yields no fruit.

23 As for what was sown on good soil, this is he who hears the Word and grasps *and* comprehends it; he indeed bears fruit, and yields in one case a hundred times as much as was sown, in another sixty times as much, and in another thirty.

24 Another parable He set forth before them, saying, The kingdom of heaven is like a man who sowed good seed in his field;

25 But while he was sleeping, his enemy came and sowed also darnel [black, wild wheat] among the wheat, and went his way.

26 So when the plants sprouted and formed grain, the darnel [weeds resembling wheat] appeared also.

27 And the servants of the owner came to him and said, Sir, did you not sow good seed in your field? Then how does it have darnel shoots in it?

28 He replied to them, An enemy has done this. The servants said to him, Then do you want us to go and weed them out?

29 But he said, No, lest in gathering the wild wheat you root up the [true] wheat along with it.

30 Let them grow together until the harvest; and at harvest time I will say to the reapers, Gather the darnel first and bind it in bundles to be burned, but gather the wheat into my granary.

31 Another story by way of comparison He set forth before them, saying, The kingdom of heaven is like a grain of mustard seed which a man took and sowed in his field.

32 Of all the seeds it is the smallest, but when it has grown it is the largest of the garden herbs and becomes a tree, so that the birds of the air come and find shelter in its branches.

33 He told them another parable: The kingdom of heaven is like leaven ([g]sour dough) which a woman took and covered over in three measures of meal *or* flour, till all of it was leavened. [Gen. 18:6.]

34 These things [h]all taken together Jesus said to the crowds in parables; indeed without a parable He said nothing to them.

35 This was in fulfillment of what was spoken by the prophet: I will open My mouth in parables; I will utter things that have been hidden since the foundation of the world. [Ps. 78:2.]

36 Then He left the throngs and went into the house. And His disciples came to Him saying, Explain to us the parable of the darnel in the field.

37 He answered, He Who sows the good seed is the Son of man;

38 The field is the world, and the good seed means the children of the kingdom; the darnel is the children of the evil one,

---

e) Wycliffe.
f) Thayer.
g) Wycliffe.
h) Thayer.

Living New Testament

21 But he doesn't have much depth in his life, and the seeds don't root very deeply, and after a while when trouble comes, or persecution begins because of his beliefs, his enthusiasm fades, and he drops out.

22 The ground covered with thistles represents a man who hears the message, but the cares of this life and his longing for money choke out God's Word, and he does less and less for God.

23 The good ground represents the heart of a man who listens to the message and understands it and goes out and brings 30, 60 or even 100 others into the Kingdom."[4]

24 Here is another illustration Jesus used: "The Kingdom of Heaven is like a farmer sowing good seed in his field;

25 But one night as he slept, his enemy came and sowed thistles among the wheat.

26 When the crop began to grow, the thistles grew too.

27 The farmer's men came and told him, 'Sir, the field where you planted that choice seed is full of thistles!'

28 'An enemy has done it,' he exclaimed. 'Shall we pull out the thistles?' they asked.

29 'No,' he replied. 'You'll hurt the wheat if you do.

30 Let both grow together until the harvest, and I will tell the reapers to sort out the thistles first and burn them, and put the wheat in the barn.' "

31, 32 Here is another of His illustrations: "The Kingdom of Heaven is like a tiny mustard seed planted in a field. It is the smallest of all seeds, but becomes the largest of plants, and grows into a tree where birds can come and find shelter."

33 He also used this example: "The Kingdom of Heaven can be compared to a woman making bread. She takes a measure of flour and mixes in the yeast until it permeates every part of the dough."

34, 35 Jesus constantly used these illustrations when speaking to the crowds. In fact, because the prophets said that He would use so many, He never spoke to them without at least one illustration. For it had been prophesied, "I will talk in parables; I will explain mysteries hidden since the beginning of time."[5]

36 Then, leaving the crowds outside, He went into the house. His disciples asked Him to explain to them the illustration of the thistles and the wheat.

37 "All right," He said, "I[6] am the farmer who sows the choice seed.

38 The field is the world, and the seed represents the people of the Kingdom; the thistles are the people belonging to Satan.

[4]Literally, "produces a crop many times greater than the amount planted—30, 60, or even 100 times as much."
[5]Psalm 78:2.
[6]Literally, "the Son of man."

Revised Standard

has no root in himself, but endures for a
while, and when tribulation or persecution
arises on account of the word, immediately
he falls away.[i] [22]As for what was sown
among thorns, this is he who hears the
word, but the cares of the world and the
delight in riches choke the word, and it
proves unfruitful. [23]As for what was sown
on good soil, this is he who hears the word
and understands it; he indeed bears fruit,
and yields, in one case a hundredfold, in
another sixty, and in another thirty."

Parables about the kingdom

24 Another parable he put before them,
saying, "The kingdom of heaven may be
compared to a man who sowed good seed in
his field; [25]but while men were sleeping, his
enemy came and sowed weeds among the
wheat, and went away. [26]So when the
plants came up and bore grain, then the
weeds appeared also. [27]And the servants[j] of
the householder came and said to him, 'Sir,
did you not sow good seed in your field?
How then has it weeds?' [28]He said to them,
'An enemy has done this.' The servants[j] said
to him, 'Then do you want us to go and
gather them?' [29]But he said, 'No; lest in
gathering the weeds you root up the wheat
along with them. [30]Let both grow together
until the harvest; and at harvest time I will
tell the reapers, Gather the weeds first and
bind them in bundles to be burned, but
gather the wheat into my barn.' "

31 Another parable he put before them,
saying, "The kingdom of heaven is like a
grain of mustard seed which a man took and
sowed in his field; [32]it is the smallest of all
seeds, but when it has grown it is the
greatest of shrubs and becomes a tree, so
that the birds of the air come and make
nests in its branches."

33 He told them another parable. "The
kingdom of heaven is like leaven which a
woman took and hid in three measures of
meal, till it was all leavened."

34 All this Jesus said to the crowds in
parables; indeed he said nothing to them
without a parable. [35]This was to fulfil what
was spoken by the prophet:[k]

"I will open my mouth in parables,
I will utter what has been hidden since the
foundation of the world."

Parable of the weeds explained

36 Then he left the crowds and went into
the house. And his disciples came to him,
saying, "Explain to us the parable of the
weeds of the field." [37]He answered, "He who
sows the good seed is the Son of man;
[38]the field is the world, and the good seed
means the sons of the kingdom; the weeds

[i] Or *stumbles*
[j] Or *slaves*
[k] Other ancient authorities read *the prophet Isaiah*

King James

39 The enemy that sowed them is the devil; the harvest is the end of the world; and the reapers are the angels.
40 As therefore the tares are gathered and burned in the fire; so shall it be in the end of this world.
41 The Son of man shall send forth his angels, and they shall gather out of his kingdom all things that offend, and them which do iniquity;
42 And shall cast them into a furnace of fire: there shall be wailing and gnashing of teeth.
43 Then shall the righteous shine forth as the sun in the kingdom of their Father. Who hath ears to hear, let him hear.
44 ¶ Again, the kingdom of heaven is like unto treasure hid in a field; the which when a man hath found, he hideth, and for joy thereof goeth and selleth all that he hath, and buyeth that field.
45 ¶ Again, the kingdom of heaven is like unto a merchant man, seeking goodly pearls:
46 Who, when he had found one pearl of great price, went and sold all that he had, and bought it.
47 ¶ Again, the kingdom of heaven is like unto a net, that was cast into the sea, and gathered of every kind:
48 Which, when it was full, they drew to shore, and sat down, and gathered the good into vessels, but cast the bad away.
49 So shall it be at the end of the world: the angels shall come forth, and sever the wicked from among the just,
50 And shall cast them into the furnace of fire: there shall be wailing and gnashing of teeth.
51 Jesus saith unto them, Have ye understood all these things? They say unto him, Yea, Lord.
52 Then said he unto them, Therefore every scribe *which is* instructed unto the kingdom of heaven is like unto a man *that is* an householder, which bringeth forth out of his treasure *things* new and old.
53 ¶ And it came to pass, *that* when Jesus had finished these parables, he departed thence.
54 And when he was come into his own country, he taught them in their synagogue, insomuch that they were astonished, and said, Whence hath this *man* this wisdom, and *these* mighty works?
55 Is not this the carpenter's son? is not his mother called Mary? and his brethren, James, and Joses, and Simon, and Judas?
56 And his sisters, are they not all with us? Whence then hath this *man* all these things?
57 And they were offended in him. But Jesus said unto them, A prophet is not without honour, save in his own country, and in his own house.
58 And he did not many mighty works there because of their unbelief.

Amplified

39 And the enemy who sowed it is the devil; the harvest is the close *and* consummation of the age, and the reapers are angels.
40 Just as the darnel (wild wheat) is gathered and burned with fire, so it will be at the close of the age.
41 The Son of man will send forth His angels, and they will gather out of His kingdom all causes of offense—[i]persons by whom others are drawn into error *or* sin—and all who do iniquity *and* act wickedly,
42 And cast them into the furnace of fire; there will be weeping *and* wailing and grinding of teeth.
43 Then will the righteous—those who are upright and in right standing with God—shine forth as the sun in the kingdom of their Father. Let him who has ears be listening, *and* [i]consider *and* perceive *and* understand by listening.
44 The kingdom of heaven is like [i]something precious buried in a field, which a man found and hid again; then in his joy he goes and sells all he has and buys that field.
45 Again the kingdom of heaven is like a man who is a dealer in search of fine *and* [j]precious pearls,
46 Who, on finding a single pearl of great price, went and sold all he had and bought it.
47 Again, the kingdom of heaven is like a [k]dragnet which was cast into the sea and gathered in fish of every sort;
48 When it was full, men dragged it up on the beach and sat down and sorted out the good fish into vessels, but the worthless ones they threw away.
49 So it will be at the close *and* consummation of the age. The angels will go forth and separate the wicked from the righteous—those who are upright and in right standing with God—
50 And cast [the wicked] into the furnace of fire; there will be weeping *and* wailing and grinding of teeth.
51 Have you understood [j]all these [parables] taken together? They said to Him, Yes, *Lord.*
52 He said to them, Therefore every [j]teacher *and* interpreter of the Sacred Writings who has been instructed *and* trained for the kingdom of heaven and [k]become a disciple, is like a householder who brings forth out of his storehouse treasure that is new and [treasure that is] old—the fresh [as well as] the familiar.
53 When Jesus had finished these parables—these comparisons—He left there.
54 And coming to His own country [Capernaum] He taught in their synagogue so that they were amazed with bewildered wonder, and said, Where did this Man get this wisdom and these miraculous powers?
55 Is not this the carpenter's Son? Is not His mother called Mary? And are not His brothers James and Joseph and Simon and Judas?
56 And do not all His sisters live here among us? Where then did this Man get all this?
57 And they took offense at Him—[that is], they were repelled and hindered from acknowledging His authority and caused to stumble. But Jesus said to them, A prophet is not without honor except in his own country and in his own house.
58 And He did not do many works of power there, because of their unbelief—their lack of faith [[l]in the divine mission of Jesus].

---

i) Thayer.
j) Thayer.
k) Vincent.
l) Vincent.

Living New Testament

39 The enemy who sowed the thistles among the wheat is the devil; the harvest is the end of the world,[7] and the reapers are the angels.

40 Just as in this story the thistles are separated and burned, so shall it be at the end of the world:[7]

41 I[6] will send My angels and they will separate out of the Kingdom every temptation and all who are evil,

42 And throw them into the furnace and burn them. There shall be weeping and gnashing of teeth.

43 Then the godly shall shine as the sun in their Father's Kingdom. Let those with ears, listen!

44 The Kingdom of Heaven is like a treasure a man discovered in a field. In his excitement, he sells everything he owns to get enough money to buy the field—and get the treasure, too!

45 Again the Kingdom of Heaven is like a pearl merchant on the lookout for choice pearls.

46 He discovered a real bargain—a pearl of great value—and sold everything he owned to purchase it!

47, 48 Again, the Kingdom of Heaven can be illustrated by a fisherman—he casts a net into the water and gathers in fish of every kind, valuable and worthless. When the net is full, he drags it up onto the beach and sits down and sorts out the edible ones into crates and throws the others away.

49 That is the way it will be at the end of the world[7]—the angels will come and separate the wicked people from the godly,

50 Casting the wicked into the fire; there shall be weeping and gnashing of teeth.

51 Do you understand?"

"Yes," they said, "we do."

52 Then He added, "Those experts in Jewish law who are now My disciples have double treasures—from the Old Testament as well as from the New!"[8]

53, 54 When Jesus had finished giving these illustrations, He returned to His home town—Nazareth in Galilee[9], and taught there in the synagogue and astonished everyone with His wisdom and His miracles.

55 "How is this possible?" the people exclaimed. "He's just a carpenter's son, and we know Mary his mother and his brothers—James, Joseph, Simon, and Judas.

56 And his sisters—they all live here. How can he be so great?"

57 And they became angry with Him! Then Jesus told them, "A prophet is honored everywhere except in his own country, and among his own people!"

58 And so He did only a few great miracles there, because of their unbelief.

[6]Literally, "the Son of man."
[7]Or, "age."
[8]Literally, "brings back out of his treasure things both new and old." The paraphrase is of course highly anachronistic!
[9]Implied.

Revised Standard

are the sons of the evil one, 39and the
enemy who sowed them is the devil; the
harvest is the close of the age, and the
reapers are angels. 40Just as the weeds are
gathered and burned with fire, so will it be
at the close of the age. 41The Son of man
will send his angels, and they will gather out
of his kingdom all causes of sin and all
evildoers, 42and throw them into the furnace of fire; there men will weep and gnash
their teeth. 43Then the righteous will shine
like the sun in the kingdom of their Father.
He who has ears, let him hear.

Further parables of the kingdom

44 "The kingdom of heaven is like treasure hidden in a field, which a man found
and covered up; then in his joy he goes and
sells all that he has and buys that field.
45 "Again, the kingdom of heaven is like
a merchant in search of fine pearls, 46who,
on finding one pearl of great value, went
and sold all that he had and bought it.
47 "Again, the kingdom of heaven is like
a net which was thrown into the sea and
gathered fish of every kind; 48when it was
full, men drew it ashore and sat down and
sorted the good into vessels but threw away
the bad. 49So it will be at the close of the
age. The angels will come out and separate
the evil from the righteous, 50and throw
them into the furnace of fire; there men will
weep and gnash their teeth.
51 "Have you understood all this?" They
said to him, "Yes." 52And he said to them,
"Therefore every scribe who has been
trained for the kingdom of heaven is like a
householder who brings out of his treasure
what is new and what is old."

Jesus rejected at Nazareth

53 And when Jesus had finished these
parables, he went away from there, 54and
coming to his own country he taught them
in their synagogue, so that they were astonished, and said, "Where did this man get this
wisdom and these mighty works? 55Is not
this the carpenter's son? Is not his mother
called Mary? And are not his brothers
James and Joseph and Simon and Judas?
56And are not all his sisters with us? Where
then did this man get all this?" 57And they
took offense at him. But Jesus said to them,
"A prophet is not without honor except in
his own country and in his own house."
58And he did not do many mighty works
there, because of their unbelief.

King James

CHAPTER 14

AT that time Herod the tetrarch heard of the fame of Jesus,

2 And said unto his servants, This is John the Baptist; he is risen from the dead; and therefore mighty works do shew forth themselves in him.

3 ¶ For Herod had laid hold on John, and bound him, and put *him* in prison for Herodias' sake, his brother Philip's wife.

4 For John said unto him, It is not lawful for thee to have her.

5 And when he would have put him to death, he feared the multitude, because they counted him as a prophet.

6 But when Herod's birthday was kept, the daughter of Herodias danced before them, and pleased Herod.

7 Whereupon he promised with an oath to give her whatsoever she would ask.

8 And she, being before instructed of her mother, said, Give me here John Baptist's head in a charger.

9 And the king was sorry: nevertheless for the oath's sake, and them which sat with him at meat, he commanded *it* to be given *her*.

10 And he sent, and beheaded John in the prison.

11 And his head was brought in a charger, and given to the damsel: and she brought *it* to her mother.

12 And his disciples came, and took up the body, and buried it, and went and told Jesus.

13 ¶ When Jesus heard *of it*, he departed thence by ship into a desert place apart: and when the people had heard *thereof*, they followed him on foot out of the cities.

14 And Jesus went forth, and saw a great multitude, and was moved with compassion toward them, and he healed their sick.

15 ¶ And when it was evening, his disciples came to him, saying, This is a desert place, and the time is now past; send the multitude away, that they may go into the villages, and buy themselves victuals.

16 But Jesus said unto them, They need not depart; give ye them to eat.

17 And they say unto him, We have here but five loaves, and two fishes.

18 He said, Bring them hither to me.

19 And he commanded the multitude to sit down on the grass, and took the five loaves, and the two fishes, and looking up to heaven, he blessed, and brake, and gave the loaves to *his* disciples, and the disciples to the multitude.

20 And they did all eat, and were filled: and they took up of the fragments that remained twelve baskets full.

21 And they that had eaten were about five thousand men, beside women and children.

22 ¶ And straightway Jesus constrained his disciples to get into a ship, and to go before him unto the other side, while he sent the multitudes away.

23 And when he had sent the multitudes away, he went up into a mountain apart to pray: and when the evening was come, he was there alone.

Amplified

CHAPTER 14

AT that time Herod the governor heard the reports about Jesus.

2 And he said to his attendants, This is John the Baptist; He has been raised from the dead, and that is why the powers [l]of performing miracles are at work in Him.

3 For Herod had arrested John and bound him and (to [m]stow him out of the way) put him in prison, on account *and* for the sake of Herodias, his brother Philip's wife; for John had said to him,

4 It is not lawful *or* right for you to have her. [Lev. 18:16; 20:21.]

5 Although he wished to have him put to death, he was afraid of the people, for they regarded John as a prophet.

6 But when Herod's birthday came, the daughter of Herodias danced in the midst [before the company], and pleased *and* fascinated Herod,

7 And so he promised with an oath to give her whatever she might ask.

8 And she, being put forward *and* prompted by her mother, said, Give me the head of John the Baptist right here on a [n]platter.

9 And the king was distressed *and* sorry; but because of his oaths and his guests he ordered it to be given her;

10 He sent and had John beheaded in the prison.

11 And his head was brought in on a [n]platter and given [o]to the little maid, and she brought it to her mother.

12 And John's disciples came and took up the body and buried it. Then they went and told Jesus.

13 When Jesus heard it, He withdrew from there privately in a boat to a solitary place. But when the crowds heard of it, they followed Him by land on foot from the towns.

14 When He went ashore and saw a great throng of people, He had compassion (pity and deep sympathy) for them and cured their sick.

15 When evening came, the disciples came to Him and said, This is a remote *and* barren place, and the day is now over; send the throngs away into the villages to buy food for themselves.

16 Jesus said, They do not need to go away; you give them something to eat.

17 They said to Him, We have nothing here but five loaves and two fish.

18 He said, Bring them here to Me.

19 Then He ordered the crowds to recline on the grass; and He took the five loaves and two fish, and looking up to heaven He gave thanks, and blessed and broke the loaves and handed the pieces to the disciples, and the disciples gave them to the people.

20 And they all ate and were satisfied. And they picked up twelve [[p]small hand] baskets full of the broken pieces left over.

21 And those who ate were about five thousand men, not including women and children.

22 Then He directed the disciples to get into the boat and go before Him to the other side, while He sent away the crowds.

23 And after He had dismissed the multitude, He went up into the hills by Himself to pray. When it was evening He was still there alone.

---

l) Vincent.
m) Abbott-Smith.
n) Tyndale.
o) Luther (-Vincent).
p) Vincent. But Moulton and Milligan: Term *"refers to material, not size."*

Living New Testament

CHAPTER 14

When King[1] Herod heard about Jesus,

2 He said to his men, "This must be John the Baptist, come back to life again. That is why he can do these miracles."

3 For Herod had arrested John and chained him in prison at the demand of[2] his wife Herodias, his brother Philip's ex-wife,

4 Because John had told him it was wrong for him to marry her.

5 He would have killed John but was afraid of a riot, for all the people believed John was a prophet.

6 But at a birthday party for Herod, Herodias' daughter performed a dance that greatly pleased him,

7 So he vowed to give her anything she wanted!

8 Consequently, at her mother's urging, the girl asked for John the Baptist's head on a tray!

9 The king was grieved, but because of his oath, and because he didn't want to back down in front of his guests, he issued the necessary orders.

10 So John was beheaded in the prison,

11 And his head was brought on a tray and given to the girl, who took it to her mother.

12 Then John's disciples came for his body and buried it, and came to tell Jesus what had happened.

13 As soon as Jesus heard the news, He went off by Himself in a boat to a remote area to be alone. But the crowds saw where He was headed, and followed by land from many villages.

14 So when Jesus came out of the wilderness, a vast crowd was waiting for Him and He pitied them and healed their sick.

15 That evening the disciples came to Him and said, "It is already past time for supper, and there is nothing to eat here in the desert; send the crowds away so they can go to the villages and buy some food."

16 But Jesus replied, "That isn't necessary—you feed them!"

17 "What!" they exclaimed. "We have exactly five small loaves of bread and two fish!"

18 "Bring them here," He said.

19 Then He told the people to sit down on the grass; and He took the five loaves and two fish, looked up into the sky and asked God's blessing on the meal, then broke the loaves apart and gave them to the disciples to place before the people.

20 And everyone ate until full! And when the scraps were picked up afterwards, there were twelve basketfuls left over!

21 (About 5,000 men were in the crowd that day, besides all the women and children.)

22 Immediately after this, Jesus told His disciples to get into their boat and cross to the other side of the lake while He stayed to get the people started home.

23, 24 Then afterwards He went up into the hills to pray. Night fell, and out on the lake the disciples were in trouble. For the wind had risen and they were fighting heavy seas.

[1]Literally, "the Tetrarch"—he was one of four "kings" over the area, his sovereignty being Galilee and Peraea.
[2]Literally, "on account of."

Revised Standard

Death of John the Baptist

14 At that time Herod the tetrarch heard about the fame of Jesus; [2]and he said to his servants, "This is John the Baptist, he has been raised from the dead; that is why these powers are at work in him." [3]For Herod had seized John and bound him and put him in prison, for the sake of Herodias, his brother Philip's wife;[l] [4]because John said to him, "It is not lawful for you to have her." [5]And though he wanted to put him to death, he feared the people, because they held him to be a prophet. [6]But when Herod's birthday came, the daughter of Herodias danced before the company, and pleased Herod, [7]so that he promised with an oath to give her whatever she might ask. [8]Prompted by her mother, she said, "Give me the head of John the Baptist here on a platter." [9]And the king was sorry; but because of his oaths and his guests he commanded it to be given; [10]he sent and had John beheaded in the prison, [11]and his head was brought on a platter and given to the girl, and she brought it to her mother. [12]And his disciples came and took the body and buried it; and they went and told Jesus.

The five thousand fed

13 Now when Jesus heard this, he withdrew from there in a boat to a lonely place apart. But when the crowds heard it, they followed him on foot from the towns. [14]As he went ashore he saw a great throng; and he had compassion on them, and healed their sick. [15]When it was evening, the disciples came to him and said, "This is a lonely place, and the day is now over; send the crowds away to go into the villages and buy food for themselves." [16]Jesus said, "They need not go away; you give them something to eat." [17]They said to him, "We have only five loaves here and two fish." [18]And he said, "Bring them here to me." [19]Then he ordered the crowds to sit down on the grass; and taking the five loaves and the two fish he looked up to heaven, and blessed, and broke and gave the loaves to the disciples. and the disciples gave them to the crowds. [20]And they all ate and were satisfied. And they took up twelve baskets full of the broken pieces left over. [21]And those who ate were about five thousand men, besides women and children.

Jesus walks on the sea

22 Then he made the disciples get into the boat and go before him to the other side, while he dismissed the crowds. [23]And after he had dismissed the crowds, he went up into the hills by himself to pray. When

[l] Other ancient authorities read *his brother's wife*

King James

24 But the ship was now in the midst of the sea, tossed with waves: for the wind was contrary.
25 And in the fourth watch of the night Jesus went unto them, walking on the sea.
26 And when the disciples saw him walking on the sea, they were troubled, saying, It is a spirit; and they cried out for fear.
27 But straightway Jesus spake unto them, saying, Be of good cheer; it is I; be not afraid.
28 And Peter answered him and said, Lord, if it be thou, bid me come unto thee on the water.
29 And he said, Come. And when Peter was come down out of the ship, he walked on the water, to go to Jesus.
30 But when he saw the wind boisterous, he was afraid; and beginning to sink, he cried, saying, Lord, save me.
31 And immediately Jesus stretched forth *his* hand, and caught him, and said unto him, O thou of little faith, wherefore didst thou doubt?
32 And when they were come into the ship, the wind ceased.
33 Then they that were in the ship came and worshipped him, saying, Of a truth thou art the Son of God.
34 ¶ And when they were gone over, they came into the land of Gennesaret.
35 And when the men of that place had knowledge of him, they sent out into all that country round about, and brought unto him all that were diseased;
36 And besought him that they might only touch the hem of his garment: and as many as touched were made perfectly whole.

Amplified

24 But the boat was by this time out on the sea, *many furlongs* [one-eighth miles] *distant from the land,* beaten and tossed by the waves, for the wind was against them.
25 And in the fourth watch [between three and six o'clock] of the night, Jesus came to them, walking on the sea.
26 And when the disciples saw Him walking on the sea, they were terrified, and said, It is a ghost! And they screamed out with fright.
27 But instantly He spoke to them, saying, Take courage! I AM; stop being afraid! [Exod. 3:14.]
28 And Peter answered Him, Lord, if it is You, command me to come to You on the water.
29 He said, Come! So Peter got out of the boat and walked on the water, and he came to Jesus;
30 But when he perceived *and* felt the strong wind, he was frightened, and as he began to sink, he cried out, Lord, save me [from death]!
31 Instantly Jesus reached out His hand and caught *and* held him, saying to him, O you of little faith, why did you doubt?
32 And when they got into the boat, the wind ceased.
33 And those in the boat knelt and worshipped Him, saying, Truly, You are the Son of God!
34 And when they had crossed over to the other side, they went ashore at Gennesaret.
35 And when the men of that place recognized Him, they sent around into all the surrounding country and brought to Him all that were sick,
36 And begged Him to let them merely touch the fringe of His garment; and as many as touched it were perfectly restored. [Num. 15:38.]

CHAPTER 15

THEN came to Jesus scribes and Pharisees, which were of Jerusalem, saying,
2 Why do thy disciples transgress the tradition of the elders? for they wash not their hands when they eat bread.
3 But he answered and said unto them, Why do ye also transgress the commandment of God by your tradition?
4 For God commanded, saying, Honour thy father and mother: and, He that curseth father or mother, let him die the death.
5 But ye say, Whosoever shall say to *his* father or *his* mother, *It is* a gift, by whatsoever thou mightest be profited by me;
6 And honour not his father or his mother, *he shall be free.* Thus have ye made the commandment of God of none effect by your tradition.
7 *Ye* hypocrites, well did Esaias prophesy of you, saying,

CHAPTER 15

THEN from Jerusalem there came scribes and Pharisees and said,
2 Why do Your disciples transgress *and* violate the rules handed down by the elders of the past? For they do not practice [ceremonially] washing their hands before they eat.
3 He replied to them, And why also do you transgress *and* violate the commandment of God for the sake of the rules handed down to you by your forefathers—the elders?
4 For God commanded, Honor your father and your mother, and, He who curses *or* reviles *or* speaks evil of *or* abuses *or* treats improperly his father or mother, let him surely come to his end by death. [Exod. 20:12; Deut. 5:16; Exod. 21:17; Lev. 20:9.]
5 But you say, If any one tells his father or mother, What you would have gained from me [that is, the money and whatever I have that might be used for helping you] is already dedicated as a gift to God, then he is exempt *and* no longer under obligation to honor *and* help his father *and his mother.*
6 So for the sake of your tradition (the rules handed down by your forefathers), you have set aside the Word of God—depriving it of force and authority and making it of no effect.
7 You pretenders—hypocrites! Admirably *and* truly did Isaiah prophesy of you when he said:

Living New Testament

25 About four o'clock in the morning Jesus came to them, walking on the water!

26 They screamed in terror, for they thought He was a ghost.

27 But Jesus immediately spoke to them, reassuring them. "Don't be afraid!" He said.

28 Then Peter called to Him: "Sir, if it is really You, tell me to come over to You, walking on the water."

29 "All right," the Lord said, "come along!" So Peter went over the side of the boat and walked on the water toward Jesus.

30 But when he looked around at the high waves, he was terrified and began to sink. "Save me, Lord!" he shouted.

31 Instantly Jesus reached out His hand and rescued him. "O man of little faith," Jesus said. "Why did you doubt?"

32 And when they had climbed back into the boat, the wind stopped.

33 The others sat there, awestruck. "You really are the Son of God," they exclaimed.

34 They landed at Gennesaret.

35 The news of their arrival spread quickly throughout the city, and soon people were rushing around, telling everyone to bring in their sick to be healed.

36 The sick begged Him to let them touch even the tassel of His robe, and all who did were healed.

Revised Standard

evening came, he was there alone, 24but the
boat by this time was many furlongs distant
from the land,[m] beaten by the waves; for
the wind was against them. 25And in the
fourth watch of the night he came to them,
walking on the sea. 26But when the disciples
saw him walking on the sea, they were terrified, saying, "It is a ghost!" And they cried
out for fear. 27But immediately he spoke to
them, saying, "Take heart, it is I; have no
fear."

28 And Peter answered him, "Lord, if it
is you, bid me come to you on the water."
29He said, "Come." So Peter got out of the
boat and walked on the water and came to
Jesus; 30but when he saw the wind,[n] he was
afraid, and beginning to sink he cried out,
"Lord, save me." 31Jesus immediately
reached out his hand and caught him, saying
to him, "O man of little faith, why did you
doubt?" 32And when they got into the boat,
the wind ceased. 33And those in the boat
worshiped him, saying, "Truly you are the
Son of God."

34 And when they had crossed over, they
came to land at Gennesaret. 35And when
the men of that place recognized him, they
sent round to all that region and brought to
him all that were sick, 36and besought him
that they might only touch the fringe of his
garment; and as many as touched it were
made well.

Living New Testament

CHAPTER 15

Some Pharisees and other Jewish leaders now arrived from Jerusalem to interview Jesus.

2 "Why do Your disciples disobey the ancient Jewish traditions?" they demanded. "For they ignore our ritual of ceremonial handwashing before they eat."

3 He replied, "And why do your traditions violate the direct commandments of God?

4 For instance, God's law is 'Honor your father and mother; anyone who reviles his parents must die.'

5, 6 But you say, 'Even if your parents are in need, you may give their support money to the church[1] instead.' And so, by your man-made rule, you nullify the direct command of God to honor and care for your parents.

7 You hypocrites! Well did Isaiah prophesy of you,

[1]Literally, "to God."

Revised Standard

The tradition of the elders

15 Then Pharisees and scribes came to
Jesus from Jerusalem and said, 2"Why
do your disciples transgress the tradition
of the elders? For they do not wash their
hands when they eat." 3He answered them,
"And why do you transgress the commandment of God for the sake of your tradition?
4For God commanded, 'Honor your father
and your mother,' and, 'He who speaks
evil of father or mother, let him surely
die.' 5But you say, 'If any one tells his
father or his mother, What you would
have gained from me is given to God,[o] he
need not honor his father.' 6So, for the
sake of your tradition, you have made
void the word[p] of God. 7You hypocrites!
Well did Isaiah prophesy of you, when
he said:

[m] Other ancient authorities read *was out on the sea*
[n] Other ancient authorities read *strong wind*
[o] Or *an offering*
[p] Other ancient authorities read *law*

King James

8 This people draweth nigh unto me with their mouth, and honoureth me with *their* lips; but their heart is far from me.

9 But in vain they do worship me, teaching *for* doctrines the commandments of men.

10 ¶ And he called the multitude, and said unto them, Hear, and understand:

11 Not that which goeth into the mouth defileth a man; but that which cometh out of the mouth, this defileth a man.

12 Then came his disciples, and said unto him, Knowest thou that the Pharisees were offended, after they heard this saying?

13 But he answered and said, Every plant, which my heavenly Father hath not planted, shall be rooted up.

14 Let them alone: they be blind leaders of the blind. And if the blind lead the blind, both shall fall into the ditch.

15 Then answered Peter and said unto him, Declare unto us this parable.

16 And Jesus said, Are ye also yet without understanding?

17 Do not ye yet understand, that whatsoever entereth in at the mouth goeth into the belly, and is cast out into the draught?

18 But those things which proceed out of the mouth come forth from the heart; and they defile the man.

19 For out of the heart proceed evil thoughts, murders, adulteries, fornications, thefts, false witness, blasphemies:

20 These are *the things* which defile a man: but to eat with unwashen hands defileth not a man.

21 ¶ Then Jesus went thence, and departed into the coasts of Tyre and Sidon.

22 And, behold, a woman of Canaan came out of the same coasts, and cried unto him, saying, Have mercy on me, O Lord, *thou* son of David; my daughter is grievously vexed with a devil.

23 But he answered her not a word. And his disciples came and besought him, saying, Send her away; for she crieth after us.

24 But he answered and said, I am not sent but unto the lost sheep of the house of Israel.

25 Then came she and worshipped him, saying, Lord, help me.

26 But he answered and said, It is not meet to take the children's bread, and to cast *it* to dogs.

27 And she said, Truth, Lord: yet the dogs eat of the crumbs which fall from their masters' table.

28 Then Jesus answered and said unto her, O woman, great *is* thy faith: be it unto thee even as thou wilt. And her daughter was made whole from that very hour.

29 And Jesus departed from thence, and came nigh unto the sea of Galilee; and went up into a mountain, and sat down there.

30 And great multitudes came unto him, having with them *those that were* lame, blind, dumb, maimed, and many others, and cast them down at Jesus' feet; and he healed them:

31 Insomuch that the multitude wondered, when they saw the dumb to speak, the maimed to be whole, the lame to walk,

Amplified

8 This people *draw near Me with their mouth and* honor Me with their lips, but their heart holds off *and* is far away from Me;

9 Uselessly do they worship Me, for they teach as doctrines the commands of men. [Isa. 29:13.]

10 And Jesus called the people to Him and said to them, Listen, and grasp *and* comprehend this:

11 It is not what goes into the mouth of a man that makes him unclean *and* defiled, but what comes out of the mouth; this makes a man unclean *and* defiles [him].

12 Then the disciples came and said to Him, Do You know that the Pharisees were displeased *and* offended *and* indignant when they heard this saying?

13 He answered, Every plant which My heavenly Father has not planted will be torn up by the roots. [Isa. 60:21.]

14 Let them alone *and* disregard them; they are blind guides *and* teachers. And if a blind man leads a blind man, both will fall into a ditch.

15 But Peter said to Him, Explain this [q]proverb—this [r]maxim—to us.

16 And He said, Are you also even yet dull *and* ignorant—without understanding and [s]unable to put things together?

17 Do you not see *and* understand that whatever goes into the mouth passes into the [t]abdomen, and so passes on into the place where discharges are deposited?

18 But what comes out of the mouth comes from the heart, and this is what makes a man unclean *and* defiles [him].

19 For out of the heart come evil thoughts (reasonings and disputings and designs) such as murder, adultery, sexual vice, theft, false witnessing, slander *and* irreverent speech.

20 These are what make a man unclean *and* defile [him]; but eating with hands unwashed does not make him unclean *or* defile [him].

21 And going away from there, Jesus withdrew to the district of Tyre and Sidon.

22 And behold, a woman who was a Canaanite of that district came out and with a (loud, troublesomely urgent) cry begged, Have mercy on me, O Lord, Son of David! My daughter is miserably *and* distressingly *and* cruelly possessed by a demon!

23 But He did not answer her a word. And His disciples came and implored Him, saying, Send her away, for she is crying after us.

24 He answered, I was sent only to the lost sheep of the house of Israel.

25 But she came and kneeling, worshipped Him, and kept praying, Lord, help me!

26 And he answered, It is not right—proper, becoming or fair—to take the children's bread and throw it to the [u]little dogs.

27 She said, Yes, Lord, yet even the [v]little pups eat the crumbs that fall from their (young) masters' table.

28 Then Jesus answered her, O woman, great is your faith! Be it done for you as you wish. And her daughter was cured from that [w]moment.

29 And Jesus went on from there and passed along the shore of the sea of Galilee. Then He went up into the hills and kept sitting there.

30 And a great multitude came to Him, bringing with them the lame, the maimed, the blind, the dumb, and many others, and they put them down at His feet and He cured them.

---

q) Abbott-Smith.
r) Thayer.
s) Cremer.
t) Moulton and Milligan.
u) Vincent.
v) Wycliffe: "little whelps."
w) Moulton and Milligan.

Living New Testament

8 'These people say they honor Me, but their hearts are far away.

9 Their worship is worthless, for they teach their man-made laws instead of those from God.' "[2]

10 Then Jesus called to the crowds and said, "Listen to what I say and try to understand:

11 You aren't made unholy by eating non-kosher food! It is what you *say* and *think*[3] that makes you unclean."

12 Then the disciples came and told Him, "You offended the Pharisees by that remark."

13, 14 Jesus replied, "Every plant not planted by My Father shall be rooted up, so ignore them. They are blind guides leading the blind, and both will fall into a ditch."

15 Then Peter asked Jesus to explain what He meant when He said that people are not defiled by non-kosher food.

16 "Don't you understand?" Jesus asked him.

17 "Don't you see that anything you eat passes through the digestive tract and out again?

18 But evil words came from an evil heart, and defile the man who says them.

19 For from the heart come evil thoughts, murder, adultery, fornication, theft, lying and slander.

20 These are what defile; but there is no spiritual defilement from eating without first going through the ritual of ceremonial handwashing!"

21 Jesus then left that part of the country and walked the fifty miles[4] to Tyre and Sidon.

22 A woman from Canaan who was living there came to Him, pleading, "Have mercy on me, O Lord, King David's Son! For my daughter has a demon within her, and it torments her constantly."

23 But Jesus gave her no reply—not even a word! Then His disciples urged Him to send her away. "Tell her to get going," they said, "for she is bothering us with all her begging."

24 Then He said to the woman, "I was sent to help the Jews, not the Gentiles."

25 But she came and worshiped Him and pled again, "Sir, help me!"

26 "It doesn't seem right to take bread from the children and throw it to the dogs," He said.

27 "Yes, it is!" she replied, "for even the puppies beneath the table are permitted to eat the crumbs that fall."

28 "Woman," Jesus told her, "your faith is large, and your request is granted." And her daughter was healed right then.

29 Jesus now returned to the Sea of Galilee, and climbed a hill and sat there.

30 And a vast crowd brought Him their lame, blind, maimed, and those who couldn't speak, and many others, and laid them before Jesus, and He healed them all.

[2]Isaiah 29:13.
[3]Implied.
[4]Implied. Literally, "withdrew into the parts of Tyre and Sidon."

Revised Standard

8'This people honors me with their lips,
but their heart is far from me;
9in vain do they worship me,
teaching as doctrines the precepts of men.' "

What defiles a man

10 And he called the people to him and
said to them, "Hear and understand: 11not
what goes into the mouth defiles a man, but
what comes out of the mouth, this defiles a
man." 12Then the disciples came and said to
him, "Do you know that the Pharisees were
offended when they heard this saying?"
13He answered, "Every plant which my
heavenly Father has not planted will be
rooted up. 14Let them alone; they are blind
guides. And if a blind man leads a blind
man, both will fall into a pit." 15But Peter
said to him, "Explain the parable to us."
16And he said, "Are you also still without
understanding? 17Do you not see that whatever goes into the mouth passes into the
stomach, and so passes on?[q] 18But what
comes out of the mouth proceeds from the
heart, and this defiles a man. 19For out of
the heart come evil thoughts, murder, adultery, fornication, theft, false witness, slander. 20These are what defile a man; but to
eat with unwashed hands does not defile a man.

The faith of a Canaanite woman

21 And Jesus went away from there and
withdrew to the district of Tyre and Sidon.
22And behold, a Canaanite woman from
that region came out and cried, "Have mercy on me, O Lord, Son of David; my daughter is severely possessed by a demon." 23But
he did not answer her a word. And his
disciples came and begged him, saying,
"Send her away, for she is crying after us."
24He answered, "I was sent only to the lost
sheep of the house of Israel." 25But she
came and knelt before him, saying, "Lord,
help me." 26And he answered, "It is not fair
to take the children's bread and throw it
to the dogs." 27She said, "Yes, Lord, yet
even the dogs eat the crumbs that fall from
their master's table." 28Then Jesus answered
her, "O woman, great is your faith! Be it
done for you as you desire." And her daughter was healed instantly.

Multitudes healed

29 And Jesus went on from there and
passed along the Sea of Galilee. And he
went up into the hills, and sat down there.
30And great crowds came to him, bringing
with them the lame, the maimed, the blind,
the dumb, and many others, and they put
them at his feet, and he healed them, 31so

[q] Or *is evacuated*

King James

and the blind to see: and they glorified the
God of Israel.
32 ¶ Then Jesus called his disciples *unto*
him, and said, I have compassion on the
multitude, because they continue with me
now three days, and have nothing to eat:
and I will not send them away fasting, lest
they faint in the way.
33 And his disciples say unto him,
Whence should we have so much bread in
the wilderness, as to fill so great a multitude?
34 And Jesus saith unto them, How many
loaves have ye? And they said, Seven, and a
few little fishes.
35 And he commanded the multitude to
sit down on the ground.
36 And he took the seven loaves and the
fishes, and gave thanks, and brake *them*, and
gave to his disciples, and the disciples to the
multitude.
37 And they did all eat, and were filled:
and they took up of the broken *meat* that
was left seven baskets full.
38 And they that did eat were four thousand men, beside women and children.
39 And he sent away the multitude, and
took ship, and came into the coasts of Magdala.

Amplified

31 So that the crowd was amazed when they saw the
dumb speaking, the maimed whole, the lame walking, and
the blind seeing, *and* they [x]recognized *and* praised *and*
thanked *and* glorified the God of Israel.
32 Then Jesus called His disciples to Him and said, I
have pity *and* sympathy *and* am deeply moved for the
crowd, because they have been with Me now three days,
and they have nothing [at all left] to eat, and I am not willing to send them away hungry lest they faint *or* become
exhausted on the way.
33 And the disciples said to Him, Where are we to get
bread sufficient to feed so great a crowd in this isolated *and*
desert place?
34 And Jesus asked them, How many loaves of bread do
you have? They replied, Seven and a few small fish.
35 And ordering the crowd to recline on the ground,
36 He took the seven loaves and the fish, and when He
had given thanks He broke them and gave them to the disciples, and the disciples gave them to the people.
37 And they all ate and were satisfied: and they gathered
up seven [[y]large provision] baskets full of the broken pieces
that were left.
38 Those who ate were four thousand men, not including
the women and the children.
39 Then He dismissed the crowds, got into the boat, and
went to the district of Magadan.

CHAPTER 16

THE Pharisees also with the Sadducees
came, and tempting desired him that he
would shew them a sign from heaven.
2 He answered and said unto them, When
it is evening, ye say, *It will be* fair weather:
for the sky is red.
3 And in the morning, *It will be* foul
weather to-day: for the sky is red and lowering. O *ye* hypocrites, ye can discern the
face of the sky; but can ye not *discern* the
signs of the times?
4 A wicked and adulterous generation
seeketh after a sign; and there shall no sign
be given unto it, but the sign of the prophet
Jonas. And he left them, and departed.
5 And when his disciples were come to
the other side, they had forgotten to take
bread.
6 ¶ Then Jesus said unto them, Take
heed and beware of the leaven of the Pharisees and of the Sadducees.
7 And they reasoned among themselves,
saying, *It is* because we have taken no bread.
8 *Which* when Jesus perceived, he said
unto them, O ye of little faith, why reason
ye among yourselves, because ye have
brought no bread?
9 Do ye not yet understand, neither
remember the five loaves of the five thousand, and how many baskets ye took up?
10 Neither the seven loaves of the four
thousand, and how many baskets ye took
up?
11 How is it that ye do not understand
that I spake *it* not to you concerning bread,
that ye should beware of the leaven of the
Pharisees and of the Sadducees?

CHAPTER 16

NOW the Pharisees and Sadducees came up to Jesus
and they asked Him to show them a sign (spectacular miracle) from heaven—attesting His divine authority.
2 He replied to them, *When it is evening you say, It will*
be fair weather, for the sky is red.
3 *And in the morning, It will be stormy today, for the*
sky is red and has a gloomy and *threatening look. You know*
how to interpret the appearance of the sky, but you cannot
interpret the signs of the times.
4 A wicked and morally unfaithful generation craves for
a sign, but no sign shall be given to it except the sign of *the*
prophet Jonah. Then He left them and went away. [Jonah
3:4, 5.]
5 When the disciples reached the other side of the sea,
they found they had forgotten to bring any bread.
6 Jesus said to them, Be careful *and* on your guard
against the leaven (ferment) of the Pharisees and Sadducees.
7 And they reasoned among themselves about it, saying,
[It is] because we did not bring any bread.
8 But Jesus, aware of this asked, Why are you discussing
among yourselves the fact that you have no bread? O [men,
how] little trust [you have in Me, how]—little faith!
9 Do you not yet discern—perceive *and* understand? Do
you not remember the five loaves of the five thousand, and
how many [[z]small hand] baskets you gathered?
10 Nor the seven loaves for the four thousand, and how
many [[a]large] provision baskets you took up?
11 How is it that you fail to understand that I was not
talking to you about bread? But beware of the leaven (ferment) of the Pharisees and Sadducees.

---

x) Cremer.
y) Vincent. But Moulton and Milligan think size not indicated.
z) Vincent. (Moulton and Milligan think size not indicated, but material.)
a) Vincent. But Moulton and Milligan do not agree.

Living New Testament

31 What a spectacle it was! Those who hadn't been able to say a word before were talking excitedly, and those with missing arms and legs had new ones; the crippled were walking and jumping around, and those who had been blind were gazing about them! The crowds just marveled, and praised the God of Israel.

32 Then Jesus called His disciples to Him and said, "I pity these people—they've been here with Me for three days now, and have nothing left to eat; I don't want to send them away hungry or they will faint along the road."

33 The disciples replied, "And where would we get enough here in the desert for all this mob to eat?"

34 Jesus asked them, "How much food do you have?" And they replied, "Seven loaves of bread and a few small fish!"

35 Then Jesus told all of the people to sit down on the ground,

36 And He took the seven loaves and the fish, and gave thanks to God for them, and divided them into pieces, and gave them to the disciples who presented them to the crowd.

37, 38 And everyone ate until full—4,000 men besides the women and children! And afterwards, when the scraps were picked up, there were seven basketfuls left over!

39 Then Jesus sent the people home and got into the boat and crossed to Magadan.

Revised Standard

that the throng wondered, when they saw
the dumb speaking, the maimed whole, the
lame walking, and the blind seeing; and they
glorified the God of Israel.

The four thousand fed

32 Then Jesus called his disciples to him
and said, "I have compassion on the crowd,
because they have been with me now three
days, and have nothing to eat; and I am
unwilling to send them away hungry, lest
they faint on the way." 33And the disciples
said to him, "Where are we to get bread
enough in the desert to feed so great a
crowd?" 34And Jesus said to them, "How
many loaves have you?" They said, "Seven,
and a few small fish." 35And commanding
the crowd to sit down on the ground, 36he
took the seven loaves and the fish, and having given thanks he broke them and gave
them to the disciples, and the disciples gave
them to the crowds. 37And they all ate and
were satisfied; and they took up seven baskets full of the broken pieces left over.
38Those who ate were four thousand men,
besides women and children. 39And sending
away the crowds, he got into the boat and
went to the region of Magadan.

CHAPTER 16

One day the Pharisees and Sadducees[1] came to test Jesus' claim of being the Messiah by asking Him to show them some great demonstration in the skies.

2, 3 He replied, "You are good at reading the weather signs of the skies—red sky tonight means fair weather tomorrow; red sky in the morning means foul weather all day—but you can't read the obvious signs of the times!

4 This evil, unbelieving nation is asking for some strange sign in the heavens, but no further proof will be given except the kind given to Jonah." Then Jesus walked out on them.

5 Arriving across the lake, the disciples discovered they had forgotten to bring any food.

6 "Watch out!" Jesus warned them; "beware of the yeast of the Pharisees and Sadducees."

7 They thought He was saying this because they had forgotten to bring bread.

8 Jesus knew what they were thinking and told them, "O men of little faith! Why are you so worried about having no food?

9 Won't you ever understand? Don't you remember at all the 5,000 I fed with five loaves, and the basketfuls left over?

10 Don't you remember the 4,000 I fed, and all that was left?

11 How could you even think I was talking about food? But again I say, 'Beware of the yeast of the Pharisees and Sadducees.' "

[1]Jewish politico-religious leaders of two different parties.

Pharisees ask for a sign

16 And the Pharisees and the Sadducees
came, and to test him they asked
him to show them a sign from heaven. 2He
answered them,[r] "When it is evening, you
say, 'It will be fair weather; for the sky is
red.' 3And in the morning, 'It will be stormy
today, for the sky is red and threatening.'
You know how to interpret the appearance
of the sky, but you cannot interpret the
signs of the times. 4An evil and adulterous
generation seeks for a sign, but no sign shall
be given to it except the sign of Jonah." So
he left them and departed.
5 When the disciples reached the other
side, they had forgotten to bring any bread.
6Jesus said to them, "Take heed and beware
of the leaven of the Pharisees and Sadducees." 7And they discussed it among
themselves, saying, "We brought no bread."
8But Jesus, aware of this, said, "O men of
little faith, why do you discuss among yourselves the fact that you have no bread? 9Do
you not yet perceive? Do you not remember
the five loaves of the five thousand, and how
many baskets you gathered? 10Or the seven
loaves of the four thousand, and how many
baskets you gathered? 11How is it that you
fail to perceive that I did not speak about
bread? Beware of the leaven of the Phar-

[r] Other ancient authorities omit the following words to the end of verse 3

King James

12 Then understood they how that he bade *them* not beware of the leaven of bread, but of the doctrine of the Pharisees and of the Sadducees.

13 ¶ When Jesus came into the coasts of Cæsarea Philippi, he asked his disciples, saying, Whom do men say that I the Son of man am?

14 And they said, Some *say that thou art* John the Baptist: some, Elias; and others, Jeremias, or one of the prophets.

15 He saith unto them, But whom say ye that I am?

16 And Simon Peter answered and said, Thou art the Christ, the Son of the living God.

17 And Jesus answered and said unto him, Blessed art thou, Simon Barjona: for flesh and blood hath not revealed *it* unto thee, but my Father which is in heaven.

18 And I say also unto thee, That thou art Peter, and upon this rock I will build my church; and the gates of hell shall not prevail against it.

19 And I will give unto thee the keys of the kingdom of heaven: and whatsoever thou shalt bind on earth shall be bound in heaven: and whatsoever thou shalt loose on earth shall be loosed in heaven.

20 Then charged he his disciples that they should tell no man that he was Jesus the Christ.

21 ¶ From that time forth began Jesus to shew unto his disciples, how that he must go unto Jerusalem, and suffer many things of the elders and chief priests and scribes, and be killed, and be raised again the third day.

22 Then Peter took him, and began to rebuke him, saying, Be it far from thee, Lord: this shall not be unto thee.

23 But he turned, and said unto Peter, Get thee behind me, Satan: thou art an offence unto me: for thou savourest not the things that be of God, but those that be of men.

24 ¶ Then said Jesus unto his disciples, If any *man* will come after me, let him deny himself, and take up his cross, and follow me.

25 For whosoever will save his life shall lose it: and whosoever will lose his life for my sake shall find it.

26 For what is a man profited, if he shall gain the whole world, and lose his own soul? or what shall a man give in exchange for his soul?

27 For the Son of man shall come in the glory of his Father with his angels; and then he shall reward every man according to his works.

28 Verily I say unto you, There be some standing here, which shall not taste of death, till they see the Son of man coming in his kingdom.

Amplified

12 Then they discerned that He did not tell them to beware of the leaven of bread, but of the teaching of the Pharisees and Sadducees.

13 Now when Jesus went into the region of Caesarea Philippi, He asked His disciples, Who do people say that the Son of man is?

14 And they answered, Some say John the Baptist, others say Elijah, and others Jeremiah or one of the prophets.

15 He said to them, But who do you [yourselves] say that I am?

16 Simon Peter replied, You are the Christ, the Son of the living God.

17 Then Jesus answered him, Blessed—happy, fortunate and [b]to be envied—are you, Simon Bar-Jonah. For flesh and blood [men] have not revealed this to you, but My Father Who is in heaven.

18 And I tell you, you are Peter [Petr*os,* masculine, a large piece of rock], and on this rock [petr*a,* feminine, a [c]huge rock like Gibraltar] I will build My church, and the gates of Hades (the powers of the [c]infernal region) shall [d]not overpower it—or be strong to its detriment, or hold out against it.

19 I will give you the keys of the kingdom of heaven, and whatever you bind—that is, declare to be improper and unlawful—on earth [e]must be already bound in heaven; and whatever you loose on earth—declare lawful—[e]must be what is already loosed in heaven. [Isa. 22:22.]

20 Then He sternly *and* strictly charged *and* warned the disciples to tell no one that He was *Jesus* the Christ.

21 From that time forth Jesus began [clearly] to show His disciples that He must go to Jerusalem and suffer many things at the hands of the elders and the high priests and scribes, and be killed, and on the third day be raised [f]from death.

22 Then Peter took Him aside [g]to speak to Him privately, and began to reprove and [h]charge Him sharply, saying, God forbid, Lord! This must never happen to You!

23 But Jesus turned [g]away from Peter and said to him, Get behind Me, Satan! You are in My way—an offense and a hindrance and a snare to Me; for you are [g]minding what partakes not of the nature *and* quality of God, but of men.

24 Then Jesus said to His disciples, If any one desires to be My disciple, let him deny himself—that is, disregard, lose sight of and forget himself and his own interests—and take up his cross and follow me [[h]cleave steadily to Me, conform wholly to My example in living and if need be in dying, also].

25 For whoever is bent on saving his [temporal] life [his comfort and security here], shall lose [eternal life]; and whoever loses his life [his comfort and security here] for My sake, shall find [life everlasting].

26 For what will it profit a man if he gains the whole world and forfeits his life—his [blessed] [i]life in the kingdom of God? Or what would a man give as an exchange for his [blessed] [i]life—in the kingdom of God?

27 For the Son of man is going to come in the glory (majesty, splendor) of His Father, with His angels, and then He will render account *and* reward every man in accordance with what he has done.

28 Truly, I tell you, there are some standing here who will not taste of death before they see the Son of man coming in (into) His kingdom.

---

b) Souter.
c) Wuest.
d) Thayer.
e) Williams: "Perfect passive participle, so things in a state of having been already forbidden [or permitted]."
f) Cremer.
g) Vincent.
h) Thayer.
i) Thayer.

Living New Testament

12 Then at last they understood that by "yeast" He meant the *wrong teaching* of the Pharisees and Sadducees.

13 When Jesus came to Caesarea Philippi, He asked His disciples, "Who are the people saying I[2] am?"

14 "Well," they replied, "some say John the Baptist; some, Elijah; some, Jeremiah or one of the other prophets."

15 Then He asked them, "Who do *you* think I am?"

16 Simon Peter answered, "The Christ, the Messiah, the Son of the living God."

17 "God has blessed you, Simon, son of Jonah," Jesus said, "for My Father in heaven has personally revealed this to you—this is not from any human source.

18 You are Peter, a stone; and upon this rock I will build My church; and all the powers of hell shall not prevail against it.

19 And I will give you the keys of the Kingdom of Heaven; whatever doors you lock on earth shall be locked in heaven; and whatever doors you open on earth shall be open in heaven!"

20 Then He warned the disciples against telling others that He was the Messiah.

21 From then on Jesus began to speak plainly to His disciples about going to Jerusalem, and what would happen to Him there—that He would suffer at the hands of the Jewish leaders,[3] that He would be killed, and that three days later He would be raised to life again.

22 But Peter took Him aside to remonstrate with Him. "Heaven forbid, sir," he said. "This is not going to happen to You!"

23 Jesus turned on Peter and said, "Get away from Me, you Satan! You are a dangerous trap to Me. You are thinking merely from a human point of view, and not from God's."

24 Then Jesus said to the disciples, "If anyone wants to be a follower of Mine, let him deny himself and take up his cross and follow Me.

25 For anyone who keeps his life for himself shall lose it; and anyone who loses his life for Me shall find it again.

26 What profit is there if you gain the whole world—and lose eternal life? What can be compared with the value of eternal life?

27 For I, the Son of Mankind, shall come with My angels in the glory of My Father and judge each person according to his deeds.

28 And some of you standing right here now will certainly live to see Me coming in My Kingdom."

[2]Literally, "the Son of man."
[3]Literally, "of the elders, and chief priests, and scribes."

Revised Standard

isees and Sadducees." 12 Then they understood that he did not tell them to beware of
the leaven of bread, but of the teaching of
the Pharisees and Sadducees.

Peter's confession of faith

13 Now when Jesus came into the district
of Caesarea Philippi, he asked his disciples,
"Who do men say that the Son of man is?"
14 And they said, "Some say John the Baptist, others say Elijah, and others Jeremiah
or one of the prophets." 15 He said to them,
"But who do you say that I am?" 16 Simon
Peter replied, "You are the Christ, the Son
of the living God." 17 And Jesus answered
him, "Blessed are you, Simon Bar-jona! For
flesh and blood has not revealed this to you,
but my Father who is in heaven. 18 And I
tell you, you are Peter,[s] and on this rock[t] I
will build my church, and the powers of
death[u] shall not prevail against it. 19 I will
give you the keys of the kingdom of heaven,
and whatever you bind on earth shall be
bound in heaven, and whatever you loose on
earth shall be loosed in heaven." 20 Then he
strictly charged the disciples to tell no one
that he was the Christ.

Future events foretold

21 From that time Jesus began to show
his disciples that he must go to Jerusalem
and suffer many things from the elders and
chief priests and scribes, and be killed, and
on the third day be raised. 22 And Peter
took him and began to rebuke him, saying,
"God forbid, Lord! This shall never happen
to you." 23 But he turned and said to Peter,
"Get behind me, Satan! You are a hindrance[v] to me; for you are not on the side
of God, but of men."
24 Then Jesus told his disciples, "If
any man would come after me, let him
deny himself and take up his cross and
follow me. 25 For whoever would save his
life will lose it, and whoever loses his life
for my sake will find it. 26 For what will it
profit a man, if he gains the whole world and
forfeits his life? Or what shall a man give in
return for his life? 27 For the Son of man is
to come with his angels in the glory of his
Father, and then he will repay every man
for what he has done. 28 Truly, I say to
you, there are some standing here who
will not taste death before they see the
Son of man coming in his kingdom."

[s] Greek *Petros*
[t] Greek *petra*
[u] Greek *the gates of Hades*
[v] Greek *stumbling block*

King James

CHAPTER 17

AND after six days Jesus taketh Peter, James, and John his brother, and bringeth them up into an high mountain apart,

2 And was transfigured before them: and his face did shine as the sun, and his raiment was white as the light.

3 And, behold, there appeared unto them Moses and Elias talking with him.

4 Then answered Peter, and said unto Jesus, Lord, it is good for us to be here: if thou wilt, let us make here three tabernacles; one for thee, and one for Moses, and one for Elias.

5 While he yet spake, behold, a bright cloud overshadowed them: and behold a voice out of the cloud, which said, This is my beloved Son, in whom I am well pleased; hear ye him.

6 And when the disciples heard *it,* they fell on their face, and were sore afraid.

7 And Jesus came and touched them, and said, Arise, and be not afraid.

8 And when they had lifted up their eyes, they saw no man, save Jesus only.

9 And as they came down from the mountain, Jesus charged them, saying, Tell the vision to no man, until the Son of man be risen again from the dead.

10 And his disciples asked him, saying, Why then say the scribes that Elias must first come?

11 And Jesus answered and said unto them, Elias truly shall first come, and restore all things.

12 But I say unto you, That Elias is come already, and they knew him not, but have done unto him whatsoever they listed. Likewise shall also the Son of man suffer of them.

13 Then the disciples understood that he spake unto them of John the Baptist.

14 ¶ And when they were come to the multitude, there came to him a *certain* man, kneeling down to him, and saying,

15 Lord, have mercy on my son: for he is lunatic, and sore vexed: for ofttimes he falleth into the fire, and oft into the water.

16 And I brought him to thy disciples, and they could not cure him.

17 Then Jesus answered and said, O faithless and perverse generation, how long shall I be with you? how long shall I suffer you? bring him hither to me.

18 And Jesus rebuked the devil; and he departed out of him: and the child was cured from that very hour.

19 Then came the disciples to Jesus apart, and said, Why could not we cast him out?

20 And Jesus said unto them, Because of your unbelief: for verily I say unto you, If ye have faith as a grain of mustard seed, ye shall say unto this mountain, Remove hence to yonder place; and it shall remove; and nothing shall be impossible unto you.

21 Howbeit this kind goeth not out but by prayer and fasting.

Amplified

CHAPTER 17

AND six days after this Jesus took with Him Peter and James and John his brother, and led them up on a high mountain by themselves.

2 And His appearance underwent a change in their presence, and His face shone [j]clear and bright like the sun, and His clothing became white as light.

3 And behold, there appeared to them Moses and Elijah, who kept talking with Him.

4 Then Peter began to speak and said to Jesus, Lord, it is good *and* delightful that we are here; if You approve, I will put up three booths here, one for You and one for Moses and one for Elijah.

5 While he was still speaking, lo, a shining cloud ([k]composed of light) overshadowed them, and a voice from the cloud said, This is My Son, My Beloved, with Whom I am [and [l]have always been] delighted. Listen to Him! [Isa. 42:1; Ps. 2:7.]

6 When the disciples heard it, they fell on their faces and were [k]seized with alarm *and* struck with fear.

7 But Jesus came and touched them, and said, Get up, and do not be afraid.

8 And when they raised their eyes they saw no one but Jesus only.

9 And as they were going down the mountain, Jesus cautioned *and* commanded them, Do not mention to any one what you have seen, until the Son of man is raised from the dead.

10 The disciples asked Him, Then why do the scribes say that first Elijah must come?

11 He replied, Elijah does come and will get everything restored *and* ready;

12 But I tell you that Elijah has come already, and they did not know *or* recognize him, but did to him as they liked. So also the Son of man is going to be treated *and* suffer at their hands.

13 Then the disciples understood that He spoke to them about John the Baptist. [Mal. 4:5.]

14 And when they approached the multitude, a man came up to Him, kneeling before Him and saying,

15 Lord, do pity *and* have mercy on my son, for he has epilepsy (is [m]moonstruck) and he suffers terribly, for frequently he falls into the fire, and many times into the water.

16 And I brought him to Your disciples, and they were not able to cure him.

17 And Jesus answered, O you unbelieving ([n]warped, wayward, rebellious) and [o]thoroughly perverse generation! How long am I to remain with you? How long am I to bear with you? Bring him here to Me.

18 And Jesus rebuked the demon, and it came out of him; and the boy was cured instantly.

19 Then the disciples came to Jesus and asked privately, Why could we not drive it out?

20 He said to them, Because of the littleness of your faith—that is, your lack of [p]firmly relying trust. For truly, I say to you, if you have faith [[q]that is living] like a grain of mustard seed, you can say to this mountain, Move from here to yonder place, and it will move, and nothing will be impossible to you.

21 *But this kind does not go out except by prayer and fasting.*

---

j) Cremer.
k) Thayer.
l) Williams: "suggested by the aorist."
m) Thayer: "Epilepsy being supposed to return and increase with the increase of the moon."
n) Vincent.
o) Literally, "throughout" (*dia*).
p) Cremer.
q) Williams.

Living New Testament

CHAPTER 17

Six days later Jesus took Peter, James and his brother John to the top of a high and lonely hill,

2 And as they watched, His appearance changed so that His face shone like the sun and His clothing became dazzling white.

3 Suddenly Moses and Elijah appeared and were talking with Him.

4 Peter blurted out, "Sir, it's wonderful that we can be here! If You want me to, I'll make three shelters,[1] one for You and one for Moses and one for Elijah."

5 But even as he said it, a bright cloud came over them, and a voice from the cloud said, *"This* is My beloved Son, and I am wonderfully pleased with Him. Obey[2] *Him."*

6 At this the disciples fell face downward to the ground, terribly frightened.

7 Jesus came over and touched them. "Get up," He said, "don't be afraid."

8 And when they looked, only Jesus was with them.

9 As they were going down the mountain, Jesus commanded them not to tell anyone what they had seen until after He had risen from the dead.

10 His disciples asked, "Why do the Jewish leaders insist Elijah must return before the Messiah comes?"[3]

11 Jesus replied, "They are right. Elijah must come and set everything in order.

12 And, in fact, he has already come, but he wasn't recognized, and was badly mistreated by many. And I, the Son of Mankind, shall also suffer at their hands."

13 Then the disciples realized He was speaking of John the Baptist.

14 When they arrived at the bottom of the hill, a huge crowd was waiting for them. A man came and knelt before Jesus and said,

15 "Sir, have mercy on my son, for he is mentally deranged, and in great trouble, for he often falls into the fire or into the water;

16 So I brought him to Your disciples, but they couldn't cure him."

17 Jesus replied, "Oh, you stubborn, faithless people! How long shall I bear with you? Bring him here to Me."

18 Then Jesus rebuked the demon in the boy and it left him, and from that moment the boy was well.

19 Afterwards the disciples asked Jesus privately, "Why couldn't we cast that demon out?"

20 "Because of your little faith," Jesus told them. "For if you had faith even as small as a tiny mustard seed you could say to this mountain, 'Move!' and it would go far away. Nothing would be impossible.

21 But this kind of demon won't leave unless you have prayed and gone without food."[4]

[1]Literally, "three tabernacles" or "tents." What was in Peter's mind is not explained.
[2]Literally, "hear Him."
[3]Implied.
[4]This verse is omitted in many of the ancient manuscripts.

Revised Standard

The transfiguration

17 And after six days Jesus took with
him Peter and James and John his
brother, and led them up a high mountain
apart. 2And he was transfigured before
them, and his face shone like the sun,
and his garments became white as light.
3And behold, there appeared to them Moses
and Elijah, talking with him. 4And Peter
said to Jesus, "Lord, it is well that we are
here; if you wish, I will make three booths
here, one for you and one for Moses and
one for Elijah." 5He was still speaking,
when lo, a bright cloud overshadowed
them, and a voice from the cloud said,
"This is my beloved Son,[w] with whom I am
well pleased; listen to him." 6When the
disciples heard this, they fell on their faces,
and were filled with awe. 7But Jesus came
and touched them, saying, "Rise, and have
no fear." 8And when they lifted up their
eyes, they saw no one but Jesus only.
9 And as they were coming down the
mountain, Jesus commanded them, "Tell
no one the vision, until the Son of man
is raised from the dead." 10And the disciples
asked him, "Then why do the scribes say
that first Elijah must come?" 11He replied,
"Elijah does come, and he is to restore
all things; 12but I tell you that Elijah has
already come, and they did not know him,
but did to him whatever they pleased. So
also the Son of man will suffer at their
hands." 13Then the disciples understood that
he was speaking to them of John the Baptist.

An epileptic boy healed

14 And when they came to the crowd,
a man came up to him and kneeling before him said, 15"Lord, have mercy on my
son, for he is an epileptic and he suffers
terribly; for often he falls into the fire, and
often into the water. 16And I brought him
to your disciples, and they could not heal
him." 17And Jesus answered, "O faithless
and perverse generation, how long am I to
be with you? How long am I to bear with
you? Bring him here to me." 18And Jesus
rebuked him, and the demon came out of
him, and the boy was cured instantly.
19Then the disciples came to Jesus privately
and said, "Why could we not cast it out?"
20He said to them, "Because of your little
faith. For truly, I say to you, if you have
faith as a grain of mustard seed, you will
say to this mountain, 'Move hence to yonder place,' and it will move; and nothing will
be impossible to you."[x]

[w] Or *my Son, my* (or *the*) *Beloved*
[x] Other ancient authorities insert verse 21, *"But this kind never comes out except by prayer and fasting"*

King James

22 ¶ And while they abode in Galilee, Jesus said unto them, The Son of man shall be betrayed into the hands of men:

23 And they shall kill him, and the third day he shall be raised again. And they were exceeding sorry.

24 ¶ And when they were come to Capernaum, they that received tribute *money* came to Peter, and said, Doth not your master pay tribute?

25 He saith, Yes. And when he was come into the house, Jesus prevented him, saying, What thinkest thou, Simon? of whom do the kings of the earth take custom or tribute? of their own children, or of strangers?

26 Peter saith unto him, Of strangers. Jesus saith unto him, Then are the children free.

27 Notwithstanding, lest we should offend them, go thou to the sea, and cast an hook, and take up the fish that first cometh up; and when thou hast opened his mouth, thou shalt find a piece of money: that take, and give unto them for me and thee.

Amplified

22 When they were going about here and there in Galilee, Jesus said to them, The Son of man is going to be turned over to the hands of men.

23 And they will kill Him, and He will rise [to life] again on the third day. And they were deeply *and* exceedingly grieved *and* distressed.

24 When they arrived in Capernaum, the collectors of the half-shekel [the temple tax] went up to Peter and said, Does not your Teacher pay the half-shekel? [Exod. 30:13; 38:26.]

25 He answered, Yes. And when he came home, Jesus spoke to him [about it] first, saying, What do you think, Simon? From whom do earthly rulers collect duties *or* tribute? from their own sons or from others [r]not of their own family?

26 And when Peter said, From other people—[r]not of their own family—Jesus said to him, Then the sons are exempt.

27 However, in order not to give offense *and* cause them to stumble—that is, [r]to judge unfavorably and unjustly—go down to the sea and throw in a hook; take the first fish that comes up, and when you open its mouth you will find there a shekel. Take it and give it to them to pay the temple tax for Me and for yourself.

CHAPTER 18

AT the same time came the disciples unto Jesus, saying, Who is the greatest in the kingdom of heaven?

2 And Jesus called a little child unto him, and set him in the midst of them,

3 And said, Verily I say unto you, Except ye be converted, and become as little children, ye shall not enter into the kingdom of heaven.

4 Whosoever therefore shall humble himself as this little child, the same is greatest in the kingdom of heaven.

5 And whoso shall receive one such little child in my name receiveth me.

6 But whoso shall offend one of these little ones which believe in me, it were better for him that a millstone were hanged about his neck, and *that* he were drowned in the depth of the sea.

7 ¶ Woe unto the world because of offences! for it must needs be that offences come; but woe to that man by whom the offence cometh!

8 Wherefore if thy hand or thy foot offend thee, cut them off, and cast *them* from thee: it is better for thee to enter into life halt or maimed, rather than having two hands or two feet to be cast into everlasting fire.

9 And if thine eye offend thee, pluck it out, and cast *it* from thee: it is better for thee to enter into life with one eye, rather than having two eyes to be cast into hell fire.

CHAPTER 18

AT that time the disciples came up and asked Jesus, Who then is [really] the greatest in the kingdom of heaven?

2 And He called a little child to Him and put him in the midst of them,

3 And said, Truly, I say to you, unless you repent (change, turn about) and become like little children [trusting, lowly, loving, forgiving] you can never enter the kingdom of heaven at all.

4 Whoever will humble himself therefore, and becomes [trusting, lowly, loving, forgiving] as this little child, is greatest in the kingdom of heaven;

5 And whoever receives *and* accepts *and* welcomes one little child like this for My sake and in My name receives *and* accepts *and* welcomes Me.

6 But whoever causes one of these little ones who believe in *and* [s]acknowledge *and* cleave to Me to stumble and sin—that is, who entices him, or hinders him in right conduct or thought—it would be better ([t]more expedient and profitable or advantageous) for him to have a great millstone fastened around his neck and to be sunk in the depth of the sea.

7 Woe to the world for such temptations to sin *and* influences to do wrong! It is necessary that temptations come, but woe to the person on whose account *or* by whom the temptation comes!

8 And if your hand or your foot cause you to stumble *and* sin, cut it off and throw it away from you; it is better (more profitable and wholesome) for you to enter life maimed or lame than with two hands or two feet to be thrown into everlasting fire.

9 And if your eye causes you to stumble *and* sin, pluck it out and throw it away from you; it is better, (more profitable and wholesome) for you to enter life with only one eye than with two eyes to be thrown into the hell (Gehenna) of fire.

r) Thayer.
s) Cremer.
t) Abbott-Smith.

Living New Testament

22, 23 One day while they were still in Galilee, Jesus told them, "I am going to be betrayed into the power of those who will kill Me, and on the third day afterwards I will be brought back to life again." And the disciples' hearts were filled with sorrow and dread.

24 On their arrival in Capernaum, the Temple tax collectors came to Peter and asked him, "Doesn't your master pay taxes?"

25 "Of course He does," Peter replied. Then he went into the house to talk to Jesus about it, but before he had a chance to speak, Jesus asked him, "What do you think, Peter? Do kings levy assessments against their own people, or against conquered foreigners?"

26, 27 "Against the foreigners," Peter replied.

"Well, then," Jesus said, "the citizens are free! However, we don't want to offend them, so go down to the shore and throw in a line, and open the mouth of the first fish you catch. You will find a coin to cover the taxes for both of us; take it and pay them."

Revised Standard

Death and resurrection foretold again

22 As they were gathering[y] in Galilee,
Jesus said to them, "The Son of man is to
be delivered into the hands of men, 23and
they will kill him, and he will be raised on
the third day." And they were greatly distressed.

The coin in the fish's mouth

24 When they came to Capernaum, the
collectors of the half-shekel tax went up to
Peter and said, "Does not your teacher pay
the tax?" 25He said, "Yes." And when he
came home, Jesus spoke to him first, saying,
"What do you think, Simon? From whom
do kings of the earth take toll or tribute?
From their sons or from others?" 26And
when he said, "From others," Jesus said
to him, "Then the sons are free. 27However,
not to give offense to them, go to the sea
and cast a hook, and take the first fish that
comes up, and when you open its mouth
you will find a shekel; take that and give it
to them for me and for yourself."

CHAPTER 18

About that time the disciples came to Jesus to ask which of them would be greatest in the Kingdom of Heaven!

2 Jesus called a small child over to Him and set the little fellow down among them,

3 And said, "Unless you turn to God from your sins and become as little children, you will never get into the Kingdom of Heaven.

4 Therefore anyone who humbles himself as this little child, is the greatest in the Kingdom of Heaven.

5 And any of you who welcomes a little child like this because you are Mine, is welcoming Me and caring for Me.

6 But if any of you causes one of these little ones who trusts in Me to lose his faith,[1] it would be better for you to have a rock tied to your neck and be thrown into the sea.

7 Woe upon the world for all its evils.[2] Temptation to do wrong is inevitable, but woe to the man who does the tempting.

8 So if your hand or foot causes you to sin, cut it off and throw it away. Better to enter heaven crippled than to be in hell with both of your hands and feet.

9 And if your eye causes you to sin, gouge it out and throw it away. Better to enter heaven with one eye than to be in hell with two.

[1]Literally, "cause to stumble."
[2]Literally, "because of occasions of stumbling."

The greatest in the kingdom

18 At that time the disciples came to
Jesus, saying, "Who is the greatest
in the kingdom of heaven?" 2And calling
to him a child, he put him in the midst of
them, 3and said, "Truly, I say to you, unless
you turn and become like children, you
will never enter the kingdom of heaven.
4Whoever humbles himself like this child,
he is the greatest in the kingdom of heaven.
5 "Whoever receives one such child in
my name receives me; 6but whoever causes
one of these little ones who believe in me
to sin,[z] it would be better for him to have
a great millstone fastened round his neck
and to be drowned in the depth of the sea.
7 "Woe to the world for temptations to
sin![a] For it is necessary that temptations
come, but woe to the man by whom the
temptation comes! 8And if your hand or
your foot causes you to sin,[z] cut it off and
throw it from you; it is better for you to
enter life maimed or lame than with two
hands or two feet to be thrown into the
eternal fire. 9And if your eye causes you to
sin,[z] pluck it out and throw it from you;
it is better for you to enter life with one
eye than with two eyes to be thrown into
the hell[b] of fire.

[y] Other ancient authorities read *abode*
[z] Greek *causes . . . to stumble*
[a] Greek *stumbling blocks*
[b] Greek *Gehenna*

King James

10 Take heed that ye despise not one of these little ones; for I say unto you, That in heaven their angels do always behold the face of my Father which is in heaven.

11 For the Son of man is come to save that which was lost.

12 How think ye? if a man have an hundred sheep, and one of them be gone astray, doth he not leave the ninety and nine, and goeth into the mountains, and seeketh that which is gone astray?

13 And if so be that he find it, verily I say unto you, he rejoiceth more of that *sheep*, than of the ninety and nine which went not astray.

14 Even so it is not the will of your Father which is in heaven, that one of these little ones should perish.

15 ¶ Moreover if thy brother shall trespass against thee, go and tell him his fault between thee and him alone: if he shall hear thee, thou hast gained thy brother.

16 But if he will not hear *thee*, *then* take with thee one or two more, that in the mouth of two or three witnesses every word may be established.

17 And if he shall neglect to hear them, tell *it* unto the church: but if he neglect to hear the church, let him be unto thee as an heathen man and a publican.

18 Verily I say unto you, Whatsoever ye shall bind on earth shall be bound in heaven: and whatsoever ye shall loose on earth shall be loosed in heaven.

19 Again I say unto you, That if two of you shall agree on earth as touching any thing that they shall ask, it shall be done for them of my Father which is in heaven.

20 For where two or three are gathered together in my name, there am I in the midst of them.

21 ¶ Then came Peter to him, and said, Lord, how oft shall my brother sin against me, and I forgive him? till seven times?

22 Jesus saith unto him, I say not unto thee, Until seven times: but, Until seventy times seven.

23 ¶ Therefore is the kingdom of heaven likened unto a certain king, which would take account of his servants.

24 And when he had begun to reckon, one was brought unto him, which owed him ten thousand talents.

25 But forasmuch as he had not to pay, his lord commanded him to be sold, and his wife, and children, and all that he had, and payment to be made.

26 The servant therefore fell down, and worshipped him, saying, Lord, have patience with me, and I will pay thee all.

27 Then the lord of that servant was moved with compassion, and loosed him, and forgave him the debt.

28 But the same servant went out, and found one of his fellow-servants, which owed him an hundred pence: and he laid hands on him, and took *him* by the throat, saying, Pay me that thou owest.

29 And his fellow-servant fell down at his feet, and besought him, saying, Have patience with me, and I will pay thee all.

Amplified

10 Beware that you do not despise *or* feel scornful toward *or* think little of one of these little ones, for I tell you that in heaven their angels always are in the presence of *and* look upon the face of My Father Who is in heaven.

11 *For the Son of man came to save* ([u]*from the penalty of eternal death) that which was lost.*

12 What do you think? If a man has a hundred sheep, and one of them has gone astray *and* gets lost, will he not leave the ninety-nine on the mountain and go in search of the one that is lost?

13 And if it should be that he finds it, truly I say to you, he rejoices more over it than over the ninety-nine that did not get lost.

14 Just so it is not the will of My Father Who is in heaven that one of these little ones should be lost *and* perish.

15 If your brother wrongs you, go and show him his fault, between you and him privately. If he listens to you, you have won back your brother.

16 But if he does not listen, take along with you one or two others, so that every word may be confirmed *and* upheld by the testimony of two or three witnesses.

17 If he pays no attention to them—refusing to listen and obey—tell it to the church; and if he refuses to listen even to the church, let him be to you as a pagan and a tax collector. [Lev. 19:17; Deut. 19:15.]

18 Truly, I tell you, whatever you forbid *and* declare to be improper *and* unlawful on earth must be [v]what is already forbidden in heaven, and whatever you permit and declare proper and lawful on earth must be [v]already permitted in heaven.

19 Again I tell you, if two of you on earth agree (harmonize together, together make a symphony) about—anything and [w]everything—whatever they shall ask, it will come to pass *and* be done for them by My Father in heaven.

20 For wherever two or three are gathered (drawn together as My followers) in (into) My name, there I AM in the midst of them. [Exod. 3:14.]

21 Then Peter came up to Him and said, Lord, how many times may my brother sin against me, and I forgive him *and* [x]let it go? As many as up to seven times?

22 Jesus answered him, I tell you, not up to seven times, but seventy times seven! [Gen. 4:24.]

23 Therefore the kingdom of heaven is like a human king who wished to settle accounts with his attendants.

24 When he began the accounting, one was brought to him who owed him ten thousand talents [probably about $10,000,000],

25 And because he could not pay, his master ordered him to be sold, with his wife and his children and everything that he possessed, and payment to be made.

26 So the attendant fell on his knees, begging him, Have patience with me and I will pay you everything.

27 And his master's heart was moved with compassion, and he released him and forgave him (cancelling) the debt.

28 But that same attendant, as he went out, found one of his fellow attendants who owed him a hundred denarii [about twenty dollars]; and he caught him by the throat and said, Pay what you owe!

29 So his fellow attendant fell down and begged him earnestly, Give me time, and I will pay you *all*!

---

u) Cremer.
v) Williams: See footnote on Mt. 16:19.
w) Wycliffe.
x) Thayer.

Living New Testament

10 Beware that you don't look down upon a single one of these little children. For I tell you that in heaven their angels have constant access[3] to My Father.

11 And I, the Son of Mankind, came to save the lost.[4]

12 If a man has a hundred sheep, and one wanders away and is lost, what will he do? Won't he leave the ninety-nine others and go out into the hills to search for the lost one?

13 And if he finds it, he will rejoice over it more than over the ninety-nine others safe at home!

14 Just so, it is not My Father's will that even one of these little ones should perish.

15 If a brother sins against you, go to him privately and confront him with his fault. If he listens and confesses it, you have won back a brother.

16 But if not, then take one or two others with you and go back to him again, proving everything you say by these witnesses.

17 If he still refuses to listen, then take your case to the church, and if the church's verdict favors you, but he won't accept it, then the church should excommunicate him.[5]

18 And I tell you this—whatever you bind on earth is bound in heaven, and whatever you free on earth will be freed in heaven.

19 I also tell you this—if two of you agree down here on earth concerning anything you ask for, My Father in heaven will do it for you.

20 For where two or three gather together because they are Mine, I will be right there among them.

21 Then Peter came to Him and asked, "Sir, how often should I forgive a brother who sins against me? Seven times?"

22 "No!" Jesus replied, "seventy times seven!

23 The Kingdom of Heaven can be compared to a king who decided to bring his accounts up to date.

24 In the process, one of his debtors was brought in who owed him $10,000,000![6]

25 He couldn't pay, so the king ordered him sold for the debt, also his wife and children and everything he had.

26 But the man fell down before the king, his face in the dust, and said, 'Oh, sir, be patient with me and I will pay it all.'

27 Then the king was filled with pity for him and released him and forgave his debt.

28 But when the man left the king, he went to a man who owed him $2,000[7] and grabbed him by the throat and demanded instant payment.

29 The man fell down before him and begged him to give him a little time. 'Be patient and I will pay it,' he pled.

[3]"Do always behold . . ."
[4]This verse is omitted in many manuscripts, some ancient.
[5]Literally, "let him be to you as the Gentile and the publican."
[6]Literally, "10,000 talents." Approximately £3,000,000.
[7]Approximately £700.

Revised Standard

The parable of the lost sheep

10 "See that you do not despise one of
these little ones; for I tell you that in heav-
en their angels always behold the face of
my Father who is in heaven.[c] [12]What do
you think? If a man has a hundred sheep,
and one of them has gone astray, does he
not leave the ninety-nine on the hills and
go in search of the one that went astray?
[13]And if he finds it, truly, I say to you, he
rejoices over it more than over the ninety-
nine that never went astray. [14]So it is not
the will of my[d] Father who is in heaven
that one of these little ones should perish.

Sin and forgiveness

15 "If your brother sins against you, go
and tell him his fault, between you and him
alone. If he listens to you, you have gained
your brother. [16]But if he does not listen,
take one or two others along with you, that
every word may be confirmed by the evidence of two or three witnesses. [17]If he
refuses to listen to them, tell it to the
church; and if he refuses to listen even to
the church, let him be to you as a Gentile
and a tax collector. [18]Truly, I say to you,
whatever you bind on earth shall be bound
in heaven, and whatever you loose on
earth shall be loosed in heaven. [19]Again
I say to you, if two of you agree on earth
about anything they ask, it will be done
for them by my Father in heaven. [20]For
where two or three are gathered in my
name, there am I in the midst of them."

21 Then Peter came up and said to him,
"Lord, how often shall my brother sin
against me, and I forgive him? As many
as seven times?" [22]Jesus said to him, "I do
not say to you seven times, but seventy
times seven.[e]

Parable of the unforgiving servant

23 "Therefore the kingdom of heaven
may be compared to a king who wished to
settle accounts with his servants. [24]When
he began the reckoning, one was brought
to him who owed him ten thousand talents;[f]
[25]and as he could not pay, his lord ordered
him to be sold, with his wife and children
and all that he had, and payment to be
made. [26]So the servant fell on his knees,
imploring him, 'Lord, have patience with
me, and I will pay you everything.' [27]And
out of pity for him the lord of that servant
released him and forgave him the debt.
[28]But that same servant, as he went out,
came upon one of his fellow servants who
owed him a hundred denarii;[g] and seizing
him by the throat he said, 'Pay what you
owe.' [29]So his fellow servant fell down
and besought him, 'Have patience with me,

[c] Other ancient authorities add verse 11, *For the Son of man came to save the lost*
[d] Other ancient authorities read *your*
[e] Or *seventy-seven times*
[f] This talent was probably worth about a thousand dollars.
[g] The denarius was worth about twenty cents

King James

30 And he would not: but went and cast him into prison, till he should pay the debt.

31 So when his fellow-servants saw what was done, they were very sorry, and came and told unto their lord all that was done.

32 Then his lord, after that he had called him, said unto him, O thou wicked servant, I forgave thee all that debt, because thou desiredst me:

33 Shouldest not thou also have had compassion on thy fellow-servant, even as I had pity on thee?

34 And his lord was wroth, and delivered him to the tormentors, till he should pay all that was due unto him.

35 So likewise shall my heavenly Father do also unto you, if ye from your hearts forgive not every one his brother their trespasses.

Amplified

30 But he was unwilling and went out and had him put in prison till he should pay the debt.

31 When his fellow attendants saw what had happened, they were greatly distressed, and they went and told everything that had taken place to their master.

32 Then his master called him and said to him, You contemptible *and* wicked attendant! I forgave *and* cancelled all that [great] debt of yours because you begged me;

33 And should you not have had pity *and* mercy on your fellow attendant, as I had pity *and* mercy on you?

34 And in wrath his master turned him over to the torturers (the jailers), till he should pay all that he owed.

35 So also My heavenly Father will deal with every one of you, if you do not freely forgive your brother from your heart *his offenses*.

CHAPTER 19

AND it came to pass, *that* when Jesus had finished these sayings, he departed from Galilee, and came into the coasts of Judæa beyond Jordan;

2 And great multitudes followed him; and he healed them there.

3 ¶ The Pharisees also came unto him, tempting him, and saying unto him, Is it lawful for a man to put away his wife for every cause?

4 And he answered and said unto them, Have ye not read, that he which made *them* at the beginning made them male and female,

5 And said, For this cause shall a man leave father and mother, and shall cleave to his wife: and they twain shall be one flesh?

6 Wherefore they are no more twain, but one flesh. What therefore God hath joined together, let not man put asunder.

7 They say unto him, Why did Moses then command to give a writing of divorcement, and to put her away?

8 He saith unto them, Moses because of the hardness of your hearts suffered you to put away your wives: but from the beginning it was not so.

9 And I say unto you, Whosoever shall put away his wife, except *it be* for fornication, and shall marry another, committeth adultery: and whoso marrieth her which is put away doth commit adultery.

10 ¶ His disciples say unto him, If the case of the man be so with *his* wife, it is not good to marry.

11 But he said unto them, All *men* cannot receive this saying, save *they* to whom it is given.

12 For there are some eunuchs, which were so born from *their* mother's womb: and there are some eunuchs, which were made eunuchs of men: and there be eunuchs, which have made themselves eunuchs for the kingdom of heaven's sake. He that is able to receive *it*, let him receive *it*.

CHAPTER 19

NOW when Jesus had finished saying these things, He left Galilee and went into the part of Judea that is beyond the Jordan;

2 And great throngs accompanied Him, and He cured them there.

3 And Pharisees came to Him and put Him to the test by asking, Is it lawful *and* right to dismiss *and* repudiate *and* divorce one's wife for any *and* [y]every cause?

4 He replied, Have you never read that He Who made them from the beginning made them male and female,

5 And said, For this reason a man shall leave his father and mother and shall be united firmly (joined inseparably) to his wife, and the two shall become one flesh? [Gen. 1:27; 2:24.]

6 So they are no longer two but one flesh. What therefore God has joined together, let not man put asunder (separate).

7 They said to Him, Why then did Moses command [us] to give a certificate of divorce, and thus to dismiss *and* repudiate a wife? [Deut. 24:1-4.]

8 He said to them, Because of the hardness (stubbornness and perversity) of your hearts Moses permitted you to dismiss *and* repudiate *and* divorce your wives; but from the beginning it has not been [z]so [ordained].

9 I say to you: whoever dismisses (repudiates, divorces) his wife, except for unchastity, and marries another, commits adultery, *and he who marries a divorced woman commits adultery*.

10 The disciples said to Him, If the case of a man with his wife is like that, it is neither profitable *nor* advisable to marry.

11 But He said to them, Not all men can accept this saying, but it is for those to whom [the capacity to receive] it has been given.

12 For there are eunuchs who have been born incapable of marriage, and there are eunuchs who have been made so by men, and there are eunuchs who have made themselves incapable of marriage for the sake of the kingdom of heaven. Let him who is able to accept this, accept it.

---

y) Vincent.
z) Thayer.

Living New Testament

30 But his creditor wouldn't wait. He had the man arrested and jailed until the debt would be paid in full.

31 Then the man's friends went to the king and told him what had happened.

32 And the king called before him the man he had forgiven and said, 'You evil-hearted wretch! Here I forgave you all that tremendous debt, just because you asked me to—

33 Shouldn't you have mercy on others, just as I had mercy on you?'

34 Then the angry king sent the man to the torture chamber until he had paid every last penny due.

35 So shall My heavenly Father do to you if you refuse to truly forgive your brothers."

Revised Standard

and I will pay you.' 30 He refused and went
and put him in prison till he should pay
the debt. 31 When his fellow servants saw
what had taken place, they were greatly
distressed, and they went and reported to
their lord all that had taken place. 32 Then
his lord summoned him and said to him,
'You wicked servant! I forgave you all that
debt because you besought me; 33 and should
not you have had mercy on your fellow
servant, as I had mercy on you?' 34 And in
anger his lord delivered him to the jailers,[h]
till he should pay all his debt. 35 So also my
heavenly Father will do to every one of
you, if you do not forgive your brother
from your heart."

CHAPTER 19

After Jesus had finished this address, He left Galilee and circled back to Judea from across the Jordan River.

2 Vast crowds followed Him, and He healed their sick.

3 Some Pharisees came to interview Him, and tried to trap Him into saying something that would ruin Him. "Do you permit divorce?" they asked.

4 "Don't you read the Scriptures?" He replied, "In them it is written that at the beginning God created man and woman,

5, 6 And that a man should leave his father and mother, and be forever united to his wife. The two shall become one—no longer two, but one! And no man may divorce what God has joined together."

7 "Then, why," they asked, "did Moses say a man may divorce his wife by merely writing her a letter of dismissal?"

8 Jesus replied, "Moses did that in recognition of your hard and evil hearts, but it was not what God had originally intended.

9 And I tell you this, that anyone who divorces his wife, except for fornication, and marries another, commits adultery."[1]

10 Jesus' disciples then said to Him, "If that is how it is, it is better not to marry!"

11 "Not everyone can accept this statement," Jesus said. "Only those whom God helps.

12 Some are born without the ability to marry,[2] and some are disabled by men, and some refuse to marry for the sake of the Kingdom of Heaven. Let anyone who can, accept My statement."

* * * * *

Teaching on marriage and divorce

19 Now when Jesus had finished these
sayings, he went away from Galilee
and entered the region of Judea beyond
the Jordan; 2 and large crowds followed
him, and he healed them there.
3 And Pharisees came up to him and
tested him by asking, "Is it lawful to divorce one's wife for any cause?" 4 He
answered, "Have you not read that he who
made them from the beginning made them
male and female, 5 and said, 'For this reason
a man shall leave his father and mother and
be joined to his wife, and the two shall become one'?[i] 6 So they are no longer two but
one.[i] What therefore God has joined together, let no man put asunder." 7 They
said to him, "Why then did Moses command one to give a certificate of divorce,
and to put her away?" 8 He said to them,
"For your hardness of heart Moses allowed
you to divorce your wives, but from the
beginning it was not so. 9 And I say to you:
whoever divorces his wife, except for unchastity,[j] and marries another, commits
adultery."[k]
10 The disciples said to him, "If such
is the case of a man with his wife, it is not
expedient to marry." 11 But he said to them,
"Not all men can receive this precept, but
only those to whom it is given. 12 For there
are eunuchs who have been so from birth,
and there are eunuchs who have been made
eunuchs by men, and there are eunuchs
who have made themselves eunuchs for
the sake of the kingdom of heaven. He who
is able to receive this, let him receive it."

[1] "And the man who marries a divorced woman commits adultery." This sentence is added in some ancient manuscripts.
[2] Literally, "born eunuchs," or, "born emasculated."

[h] Greek *torturers*
[i] Greek *one flesh*
[j] Other ancient authorities, after *unchastity*, read *makes her commit adultery*
[k] Other ancient authorities insert *and he who marries a divorced woman commits adultery*

King James

13 ¶ Then were there brought unto him little children, that he should put *his* hands on them, and pray: and the disciples rebuked them.
14 But Jesus said, Suffer little children, and forbid them not, to come unto me: for of such is the kingdom of heaven.
15 And he laid *his* hands on them, and departed thence.
16 ¶ And, behold, one came and said unto him, Good Master, what good thing shall I do, that I may have eternal life?
17 And he said unto him, Why callest thou me good? *there is* none good but one, *that is,* God: but if thou wilt enter into life, keep the commandments.
18 He saith unto him, Which? Jesus said, Thou shalt do no murder, Thou shalt not commit adultery, Thou shalt not steal, Thou shalt not bear false witness,
19 Honour thy father and *thy* mother: and, Thou shalt love thy neighbour as thyself.
20 The young man saith unto him, All these things have I kept from my youth up: what lack I yet?
21 Jesus said unto him, If thou wilt be perfect, go *and* sell that thou hast, and give to the poor, and thou shalt have treasure in heaven: and come *and* follow me.
22 But when the young man heard that saying, he went away sorrowful: for he had great possessions.
23 ¶ Then said Jesus unto his disciples, Verily I say unto you, That a rich man shall hardly enter into the kingdom of heaven.
24 And again I say unto you, It is easier for a camel to go through the eye of a needle, than for a rich man to enter into the kingdom of God.
25 When his disciples heard *it,* they were exceedingly amazed, saying, Who then can be saved?
26 But Jesus beheld *them,* and said unto them, With men this is impossible; but with God all things are possible.
27 ¶ Then answered Peter and said unto him, Behold, we have forsaken all, and followed thee; what shall we have therefore?
28 And Jesus said unto them, Verily I say unto you, that ye which have followed me, in the regeneration when the Son of man shall sit in the throne of his glory, ye also shall sit upon twelve thrones, judging the twelve tribes of Israel.
29 And every one that hath forsaken houses, or brethren, or sisters, or father, or mother, or wife, or children, or lands, for my name's sake, shall receive an hundredfold, and shall inherit everlasting life.
30 But many *that are* first shall be last; and the last *shall be* first.

Amplified

13 Then little children were brought to Jesus that He might put His hands on them and pray, but the disciples rebuked those who brought them.
14 But He said, Leave the children alone! Allow the little ones to come to Me, and do not forbid *or* restrain *or* hinder them, for of such [as these] the kingdom of heaven is composed.
15 And He put His hands upon them, and then went His way.
16 And behold, there came a man up to Him, saying, Teacher, what excellent, *and* perfectly *and* essentially good deed must I do to possess eternal life? [Lev. 18:5.]
17 And He said to him, Why do you ask Me about the perfectly *and* essentially good? One only there is who is good—perfectly and essentially; God. If you would enter into the Life, you must continually keep the commandments.
18 He said to Him, What [a]sort of commandments?—*Or,* which ones? And Jesus answered, You shall not kill, You shall not commit adultery, You shall not steal, You shall not bear false witness, [Exod. 20:12-16; Deut. 5:16-20.]
19 Honor your father and your mother, and, You shall love your neighbor as yourself. [Lev. 19:18.]
20 The young man said, I have observed all these *from my youth;* what still do I lack?
21 Jesus answered him, If you would be perfect [that is, [b]have that spiritual maturity which accompanies self-sacrificing character], go and sell what you have and give to the poor, and you will have riches in heaven; and come, [c]be My disciple—side with My party and follow Me.
22 But when the young man heard this, he went away sad (grieved and in much distress), for he had great possessions.
23 And Jesus said to His disciples, Truly, I say to you, it will be difficult for a rich man to get into the kingdom of heaven.
24 Again I tell you, it is easier for a camel to go through the eye of a needle than for a rich man to go into the kingdom of heaven.
25 When the disciples heard this, they were utterly puzzled (astonished, bewildered), saying, Who then can be saved [[d]from eternal death]?
26 But Jesus looked at them and said, With men this is impossible, but all things are possible with God. [Gen. 18:14; Job 42:2.]
27 Then Peter answered Him saying, Lo, we have left [our] all and have become [c]Your disciples—sided with Your party and followed You. What then shall we receive?
28 Jesus said to them, Truly, I say to you, in the new age—the [e]Messianic rebirth of the world—when the Son of man shall sit down on the throne of His glory, you [who have become My disciples, sided with My party and followed Me] will also sit on twelve thrones and judge the twelve tribes of Israel.
29 And any one *and* every one who has left houses or brothers or sisters or father or mother or children or lands for My name's sake, will receive [f]many—even a hundred—times more, and inherit eternal life.
30 But many that [now] are first will be last [then], and many who [now] are last will be first [then].

---

a) Williams: "Interrogative of quality."
b) Wuest.
c) Thayer.
d) Cremer.
e) Moulton and Milligan.
f) Some ancient authorities read "manifold."

Living New Testament

13 Little children were brought for Jesus to lay His hands on them and pray. But the disciples scolded those who brought them. "Don't bother Him," they said.

14 But Jesus said, "Let the little children come to Me, and don't prevent them. For of such is the Kingdom of Heaven."

15 And He put His hands on their heads and blessed them before He left.

* * * * *

16 Someone came to Jesus with this question: "Good sir, what good thing shall I do to get eternal life?"

17 "Good?" He asked. "There is only one who is truly good—and that is God.[3] But to answer your question, you can get to heaven if you keep the commandments."

18 "Which ones?" the man asked.

And Jesus replied, "Don't kill, don't commit adultery, don't steal, don't lie,

19 Honor your father and mother, and love your neighbor as yourself!"

20 "I've always obeyed every one of them," the youth replied. "What else must I do?"

21 Jesus told him, "If you want to be perfect, go and sell everything you have and give the money to the poor, and you will have treasure in heaven; and come, follow Me."

22 But when the young man heard this, he went away sadly, for he was very rich.

23 Then Jesus said to His disciples, "It is almost impossible for a rich man to get into the Kingdom of Heaven.

24 I say it again—it is easier for a camel to go through the eye of a needle than for a rich man to enter the Kingdom of God!"

25 This remark confounded the disciples. "Then who in the world can be saved?" they asked.

26 Jesus looked at them intently and said, "Humanly speaking, no one. But with God, everything is possible."

27 Then Peter said to Him, "We left everything to follow You. What will we get out of it?"

28 And Jesus replied, "When I, the Son of Mankind, shall sit upon My glorious throne in the Kingdom,[4] you My disciples shall certainly sit on twelve thrones judging the twelve tribes of Israel.

29 And anyone who gives up his home, brothers, sisters, father, mother, wife,[5] children, or property, to follow Me, shall receive a hundred times as much in return, and shall have eternal life.

30 But many who are first now will be last then; and some who are last now will be first then."

[3]Implied from Luke 18:19.
[4]Literally, "in the regeneration."
[5]Omitted in many manuscripts, but included in Luke 18:29.

Revised Standard

Jesus blesses the little children

13 Then children were brought to him
that he might lay his hands on them and
pray. The disciples rebuked the people; 14 but
Jesus said, "Let the children come to me,
and do not hinder them; for to such belongs
the kingdom of heaven." 15 And he laid his
hands on them and went away.

The rich young ruler

16 And behold, one came up to him,
saying, "Teacher, what good deed must I
do, to have eternal life?" 17 And he said to
him, "Why do you ask me about what is
good? One there is who is good. If you
would enter life, keep the commandments."
18 He said to him, "Which?" And Jesus said,
"You shall not kill, You shall not commit
adultery, You shall not steal, You shall not
bear false witness, 19 Honor your father
and mother, and, You shall love your
neighbor as yourself." 20 The young man
said to him, "All these I have observed;
what do I still lack?" 21 Jesus said to him,
"If you would be perfect, go, sell what you
possess and give to the poor, and you will
have treasure in heaven; and come, follow
me." 22 When the young man heard this he
went away sorrowful; for he had great
possessions.

Teaching on the kingdom of heaven

23 And Jesus said to his disciples, "Truly,
I say to you, it will be hard for a rich man
to enter the kingdom of heaven. 24 Again I
tell you, it is easier for a camel to go through
the eye of a needle than for a rich man to
enter the kingdom of God." 25 When the
disciples heard this they were greatly astonished, saying, "Who then can be saved?"
26 But Jesus looked at them and said to them,
"With men this is impossible, but with God
all things are possible." 27 Then Peter said in
reply, "Lo, we have left everything and followed you. What then shall we have?"
28 Jesus said to them, "Truly, I say to you,
in the new world, when the Son of man
shall sit on his glorious throne, you who
have followed me will also sit on twelve
thrones, judging the twelve tribes of Israel.
29 And every one who has left houses or
brothers or sisters or father or mother or
children or lands, for my name's sake, will
receive a hundredfold,[1] and inherit eternal
life. 30 But many that are first will be last,
and the last first.

[1] Other ancient authorities read *manifold*

King James

CHAPTER 20

FOR the kingdom of heaven is like unto a man *that is* an householder, which went out early in the morning to hire labourers into his vineyard.

2 And when he had agreed with the labourers for a penny a day, he sent them into his vineyard.

3 And he went out about the third hour, and saw others standing idle in the marketplace,

4 And said unto them; Go ye also into the vineyard, and whatsoever is right I will give you. And they went their way.

5 Again he went out about the sixth and ninth hour, and did likewise.

6 And about the eleventh hour he went out, and found others standing idle, and saith unto them, Why stand ye here all the day idle?

7 They say unto him, Because no man hath hired us. He saith unto them, Go ye also into the vineyard; and whatsoever is right, *that* shall ye receive.

8 So when even was come, the lord of the vineyard saith unto his steward, Call the labourers, and give them *their* hire, beginning from the last unto the first.

9 And when they came that *were hired* about the eleventh hour, they received every man a penny.

10 But when the first came, they supposed that they should have received more; and they likewise received every man a penny.

11 And when they had received *it*, they murmured against the goodman of the house,

12 Saying, These last have wrought *but* one hour, and thou hast made them equal unto us, which have borne the burden and heat of the day.

13 But he answered one of them, and said, Friend, I do thee no wrong: didst not thou agree with me for a penny?

14 Take *that* thine *is*, and go thy way: I will give unto this last, even as unto thee.

15 Is it not lawful for me to do what I will with mine own? Is thine eye evil, because I am good?

16 So the last shall be first, and the first last: for many be called, but few chosen.

17 ¶ And Jesus going up to Jerusalem took the twelve disciples apart in the way, and said unto them,

18 Behold, we go up to Jerusalem; and the Son of man shall be betrayed unto the chief priests and unto the scribes, and they shall condemn him to death,

19 And shall deliver him to the Gentiles to mock, and to scourge, and to crucify *him:* and the third day he shall rise again.

20 ¶ Then came to him the mother of Zebedee's children with her sons, worshipping *him*, and desiring a certain thing of him.

21 And he said unto her, What wilt thou? She saith unto him, Grant that these my two sons may sit, the one on thy right hand, and the other on the left, in thy kingdom.

22 But Jesus answered and said, Ye know not what ye ask. Are ye able to drink of the

Amplified

CHAPTER 20

FOR the kingdom of heaven is like the owner of an estate who went out in the morning [g]along with the dawn to hire workmen for his vineyard.

2 After agreeing with the laborers for a denarius a day, he sent them into his vineyard.

3 And going out about the third hour (nine o'clock) he saw others standing idle in the market place;

4 And he said to them, You go also into the vineyard, and whatever is right I will pay you. And they went.

5 He went out again about the sixth hour (noon), and the ninth hour (three o'clock) he did the same.

6 And about the eleventh hour (five o'clock) he went out and found still others standing around, and said to them, Why do you stand here idle all day?

7 They answered him, Because nobody has hired us. He told them, You go out into the vineyard also *and you will get whatever is just and fair.*

8 When evening came, the owner of the vineyard said to his manager, Call the workmen and pay them their wages, beginning with the last and ending with the first. [Lev. 19:13; Deut. 24:15.]

9 And they who had been hired at the eleventh hour (five o'clock) came, and received a denarius each.

10 Now when the first came, they supposed they would get more, but each of them also received a denarius.

11 And when they received it they grumbled at the owner of the estate,

12 Saying, These who came last worked no more than an hour, and yet you have made them rank with us who have borne the burden and the [h]scorching heat of the day.

13 But he answered one of them, Friend, I am doing you no injustice. Did you not agree with me for a denarius?

14 Take what belongs to you and go. I choose to give to this man hired last the same as I give to you.

15 Am I not permitted to do what I choose with what is mine? Or do you begrudge my being generous? Is your eye evil because I am good?

16 So those who [now] are last will be first [then], and those who [now] are first will be last [then]. *For many are called, but few chosen.*

17 And as Jesus was going up to Jerusalem, He took the twelve disciples aside along the way, and said to them,

18 Behold, we are going up to Jerusalem; and the Son of man will be handed over to the chief priests and scribes and they will sentence Him to death,

19 And deliver Him over to the Gentiles to be mocked and whipped and crucified, and He will be raised [to life] on the third day.

20 Then the mother of Zebedee's children came up to Him with her sons, and kneeling, worshipped Him and asked a favor of Him.

21 And He asked her, What do you wish? She answered Him, Give orders that these two sons of mine may sit, one at Your right hand and one at Your left in Your kingdom.

22 But Jesus replied, You do not realize what you are asking. Are you able to drink the cup that I am about to drink *and to be baptized with the baptism with which I am baptized?* They answered, We are able.

---

g) Vincent.
h) Vincent.

Living New Testament

CHAPTER 20

Here is another illustration of the Kingdom of Heaven.

"The owner of an estate went out early one morning to hire workers for his harvest field.[1]

2 He agreed to pay them $20 a day[2] and sent them off to work.

3 A couple of hours later he was passing a hiring hall and saw some men standing around waiting for jobs,

4 So he sent them also into his fields, telling them he would pay them whatever was right at the end of the day.

5 At noon and again around three o'clock in the afternoon he did the same thing.

6 At five o'clock that evening he was in town again and saw some more men standing around and asked them, 'Why have you been idle all day?'

7 'Because no one has hired us,' they replied. 'Then go on out and join the others in my fields,' he told them.

8 That evening he told the paymaster to call the men in and pay them, beginning with the last men first.

9 When the men hired at five o'clock were paid, each received $20.

10 So when the men hired earlier came to get theirs, they assumed they would receive much more. But they, too, were paid $20.

11, 12 They protested, 'Those fellows worked only one hour, and yet you've paid them just as much as those of us who worked all day in the scorching heat.'

13 'Friend,' he answered to one of them, 'I did you no wrong! Didn't you agree to work all day for $20?

14 Take it and go. It is my desire to pay all the same;

15 Is it against the law to give away my money if I want to? Should you be angry because I am kind?'

16 And so it is that the last shall be first, and the first, last."

* * * * *

17 As Jesus was on the way to Jerusalem, He took the twelve disciples aside,

18 And talked to them about what would happen to Him when they arrived. "I[3] will be betrayed to the chief priests and other Jewish leaders, and they will condemn Me to die.

19 And they will hand Me over to the Roman government, and I will be mocked and crucified, and the third day I will rise to life again."

20 Then the mother of James and John, the sons of Zebedee, brought them to Jesus, bowed, and asked a favor.

21 "What is your request?" He asked. She replied, "In Your Kingdom, will You let my two sons sit on two thrones[4] next to Yours?"

22 But Jesus told her, "You don't know what you are asking!" Then He turned to James and John and asked them, "Are you able to drink from the terrible cup I am about to drink from?"

"Yes," they replied, "we are able!"

[1]Literally, "vineyard."
[2]Literally, "a denarii," the payment for a day's labor; equivalent to $20 in modern times, or £7.
[3]Literally, "the Son of man."
[4]Implied.

Revised Standard

Parable of the worker in the vineyard

20 "For the kingdom of heaven is like a
householder who went out early in
the morning to hire laborers for his vineyard.
2After agreeing with the laborers for a
denarius[m] a day, he sent them into his vineyard. 3And going out about the third hour
he saw others standing idle in the market
place; 4and to them he said, 'You go into
the vineyard too, and whatever is right I will
give you.' So they went. 5Going out again
about the sixth hour and the ninth hour, he
did the same. 6And about the eleventh hour
he went out and found others standing; and
he said to them, 'Why do you stand here
idle all day?' 7They said to him, 'Because
no one has hired us.' He said to them, 'You
go into the vineyard too.' 8And when evening
came, the owner of the vineyard said to his
steward, 'Call the laborers and pay them
their wages, beginning with the last, up to
the first.' 9And when those hired about the
eleventh hour came, each of them received
a denarius. 10Now when the first came, they
thought they would receive more; but each
of them also received a denarius. 11And on
receiving it they grumbled at the householder, 12saying, 'These last worked only one
hour, and you have made them equal to us
who have borne the burden of the day and
the scorching heat.' 13But he replied to one
of them, 'Friend, I am doing you no wrong;
did you not agree with me for a denarius?
14Take what belongs to you, and go; I
choose to give to this last as I give to you.
15Am I not allowed to do what I choose
with what belongs to me? Or do you begrudge my generosity?'[n] 16So the last will
be first, and the first last."

Crucifixion and resurrection foretold

17 And as Jesus was going up to Jerusalem, he took the twelve disciples aside, and
on the way he said to them, 18"Behold,
we are going up to Jerusalem; and the Son
of man will be delivered to the chief priests
and scribes, and they will condemn him to
death, 19and deliver him to the Gentiles to
be mocked and scourged and crucified,
and he will be raised on the third day."

The ambition of James and John

20 Then the mother of the sons of Zebedee came up to him, with her sons, and
kneeling before him she asked him for
something. 21And he said to her, "What
do you want?" She said to him, "Command
that these two sons of mine may sit, one at
your right hand and one at your left, in
your kingdom." 22But Jesus answered, "You
do not know what you are asking. Are you
able to drink the cup that I am to drink?"
They said to him, "We are able." 23He said

[m] The denarius was worth about twenty cents
[n] Or *is your eye evil because I am good?*

King James

cup that I shall drink of, and to be baptized with the baptism that I am baptized with? They say unto him, We are able.
23 And he saith unto them, Ye shall drink indeed of my cup, and be baptized with the baptism that I am baptized with: but to sit on my right hand, and on my left, is not mine to give, but *it shall be given to them* for whom it is prepared of my Father.
24 And when the ten heard *it*, they were moved with indignation against the two brethren.
25 But Jesus called them *unto him*, and said, Ye know that the princes of the Gentiles exercise dominion over them, and they that are great exercise authority upon them.
26 But it shall not be so among you: but whosoever will be great among you, let him be your minister;
27 And whosoever will be chief among you, let him be your servant:
28 Even as the Son of man came not to be ministered unto, but to minister, and to give his life a ransom for many.
29 And as they departed from Jericho, a great multitude followed him.
30 ¶ And, behold, two blind men sitting by the way side, when they heard that Jesus passed by, cried out, saying. Have mercy on us, O Lord, *thou* son of David.
31 And the multitude rebuked them, because they should hold their peace: but they cried the more, saying, Have mercy on us, O Lord, *thou* son of David.
32 And Jesus stood still, and called them, and said, What will ye that I shall do unto you?
33 They say unto him, Lord, that our eyes may be opened.
34 So Jesus had compassion *on them*, and touched their eyes: and immediately their eyes received sight, and they followed him.

Amplified

23 He said to them, You will drink My cup, but seats at My right hand and at My left are not Mine to give, but they are for those for whom they have been [i]ordained *and* prepared by My Father.
24 But when the ten [other disciples] heard this, they were indignant at the two brothers.
25 And Jesus called them to Him and said, You know that the rulers of the Gentiles lord it over them, and their great men hold them in subjection, tyrannizing over them.
26 Not so shall it be among you; but whoever wishes to be great among you must be your servant,
27 And whoever desires to be first among you must be your slave;
28 Just as the Son of man came not to be waited on but to serve, and to give His life as a ransom for many—the price paid to set them free.
29 And as they were going out of Jericho, a great throng accompanied Him.
30 And behold, two blind men were sitting by the roadside, and when they heard that Jesus was passing by, they cried out, Lord, have pity *and* mercy on us, [You] Son of David!
31 The crowds reproved them and told them to keep still; but they cried out the more, Lord, have pity *and* mercy on us, [You] Son of David!
32 And Jesus stopped and called them, and asked, What do you want Me to do for you?
33 They answered Him, Lord, we want our eyes to be opened!
34 And Jesus in pity touched their eyes, and instantly they received their sight and followed Him.

CHAPTER 21

AND when they drew nigh unto Jerusalem, and were come to Bethphage, unto the mount of Olives, then sent Jesus two disciples,
2 Saying unto them, Go into the village over against you, and straightway ye shall find an ass tied, and a colt with her: loose *them*, and bring *them* unto me.
3 And if any *man* say aught unto you, ye shall say, The Lord hath need of them, and straightway he will send them.
4 All this was done, that it might be fulfilled which was spoken by the prophet, saying,
5 Tell ye the daughter of Sion, Behold, thy King cometh unto thee, meek, and sitting upon an ass, and a colt the foal of an ass.
6 And the disciples went, and did as Jesus commanded them,

CHAPTER 21

AND when they came near Jerusalem and had reached Bethphage, at the Mount of Olives, Jesus sent two disciples on ahead,
2 Saying to them, Go into the village that is opposite you, and at once you will find a donkey tied, and a colt with her; untie her and bring them to Me.
3 If any one says anything to you, you shall reply, The Lord needs them, and he will let them go without delay.
4 This happened that what was spoken by the prophet might be fulfilled, saying,
5 Say to the daughter of Zion [inhabitants of Jerusalem], Behold your King is coming to you, lowly and riding on a donkey, and on a colt, the foal of a donkey [a beast of burden]. [Isa. 62:11; Zech. 9:9.]
6 Then the disciples went and did as Jesus had directed them.

i) Thayer.

Living New Testament

23 "You shall indeed drink from it," He told them. "But I have no right to say who will sit on the thrones[4] next to Mine. Those places are reserved for the persons My Father selects."

24 The other ten disciples were indignant when they heard what James and John had asked for.

25 But Jesus called them together and said, "Among the heathen, kings are tyrants and each minor official lords it over those beneath him.

26 But among you it is quite different. Anyone wanting to be a leader among you must be your servant.

27 And if you want to be right at the top, you must serve like a slave.

28 Your attitude[4] must be like My own, for I, the Son of Mankind, did not come to be served, but to serve, and to give My life as a ransom for many."

29 As Jesus and the disciples left the city of Jericho, a vast crowd surged along behind.

30 Two blind men were sitting beside the road and when they heard that Jesus was coming that way, they began shouting, "Sir, King David's Son, have mercy on us!"

31 The crowd told them to be quiet, but they only yelled the louder.

32, 33 When Jesus came to the place where they were He stopped in the road and called, "What do you want Me to do for you?"

"Sir," they said, "we want to see!"

34 Jesus was moved with pity for them and touched their eyes. And instantly they could see, and followed Him.

Revised Standard

to them, "You will drink my cup, but to
sit at my right hand and at my left is not
mine to grant, but it is for those for whom
it has been prepared by my Father." 24 And
when the ten heard it, they were indignant
at the two brothers. 25 But Jesus called them
to him and said, "You know that the rulers
of the Gentiles lord it over them, and their
great men exercise authority over them.
26 It shall not be so among you; but whoever would be great among you must be
your servant, 27 and whoever would be first
among you must be your slave; 28 even as
the Son of man came not to be served but
to serve, and to give his life as a ransom
for many."

Healing of two blind men

29 And as they went out of Jericho, a
great crowd followed him. 30 And behold,
two blind men sitting by the roadside, when
they heard that Jesus was passing by, cried
out,[o] "Have mercy on us, Son of David!"
31 The crowd rebuked them, telling them to
be silent; but they cried out the more,
"Lord, have mercy on us, Son of David!"
32 And Jesus stopped and called them, saying, "What do you want me to do for you?"
33 They said to him, "Lord, let our eyes be
opened." 34 And Jesus in pity touched their
eyes, and immediately they received their
sight and followed him.

CHAPTER 21

As Jesus and the disciples approached Jerusalem, and were near the town of Bethphage on the Mount of Olives, Jesus sent two of them into the village ahead.

2 "Just as you enter," He said, "you will see a donkey tied there, with its colt beside it. Untie them and bring them here.

3 If anyone asks you what you are doing, just say, 'The Master needs them,' and there will be no trouble."

4 This was done to fulfill the ancient prophecy,

5 "Tell Jerusalem her King is coming to her, riding humbly on a donkey's colt!"

6 The two disciples did as Jesus said,

The triumphal entry

21 And when they drew near to Jerusalem and came to Bethphage, to
the Mount of Olives, then Jesus sent two
disciples, 2 saying to them, "Go into the village opposite you, and immediately you
will find an ass tied, and a colt with her;
untie them and bring them to me. 3 If any
one says anything to you, you shall say,
'The Lord has need of them,' and he will
send them immediately." 4 This took place
to fulfil what was spoken by the prophet,
saying,
5 "Tell the daughter of Zion,
Behold, your king is coming to you,
humble, and mounted on an ass,
and on a colt, the foal of an ass."
6 The disciples went and did as Jesus had

[4]Implied.

[o] Other ancient authorities insert *Lord*

King James

7 And brought the ass, and the colt, and put on them their clothes, and they set *him* thereon.

8 And a very great multitude spread their garments in the way; others cut down branches from the trees, and strawed *them* in the way.

9 And the multitudes that went before, and that followed, cried, saying, Hosanna to the son of David: Blessed is he that cometh in the name of the Lord; Hosanna in the highest.

10 And when he was come into Jerusalem, all the city was moved, saying, Who is this?

11 And the multitude said, This is Jesus the prophet of Nazareth of Galilee.

12 ¶ And Jesus went into the temple of God, and cast out all them that sold and bought in the temple, and overthrew the tables of the moneychangers, and the seats of them that sold doves,

13 And said unto them, It is written, My house shall be called the house of prayer; but ye have made it a den of thieves.

14 And the blind and the lame came to him in the temple; and he healed them.

15 And when the chief priests and scribes saw the wonderful things that he did, and the children crying in the temple, and saying, Hosanna to the son of David; they were sore displeased,

16 And said unto him, Hearest thou what these say? And Jesus saith unto them, Yea; have ye never read, Out of the mouth of babes and sucklings thou hast perfected praise?

17 ¶ And he left them, and went out of the city into Bethany; and he lodged there.

18 Now in the morning as he returned into the city, he hungered.

19 And when he saw a fig tree in the way, he came to it, and found nothing thereon, but leaves only, and said unto it, Let no fruit grow on thee henceforward for ever. And presently the fig tree withered away.

20 And when the disciples saw *it*, they marvelled, saying, How soon is the fig tree withered away!

21 Jesus answered and said unto them, Verily I say unto you, If ye have faith, and doubt not, ye shall not only do this *which is done* to the fig tree, but also if ye shall say unto this mountain, Be thou removed, and be thou cast into the sea; it shall be done.

22 And all things, whatsoever ye shall ask in prayer, believing, ye shall receive.

23 ¶ And when he was come into the temple, the chief priests and the elders of the people came unto him as he was teaching, and said, By what authority doest thou these things? and who gave thee this authority?

Amplified

7 They brought the donkey and the colt and laid their coats upon them, and He seated Himself on [the clothing].

8 And most of the crowd kept spreading their garments on the road, and others kept cutting branches from the trees and scattering them on the road.

9 And the crowds that went ahead of Him and those that followed Him kept shouting, Hosanna ([j]O be propitious, graciously inclined) to the Son of David, [j]the Messiah! Blessed (praised, glorified) be He Who comes in the name of the Lord! Hosanna (O be favorably disposed) in the highest (heaven)! [Ps. 118:26.]

10 And when He entered Jerusalem, all the city became agitated, and [k]trembling with excitement said, Who is [l]This?

11 And the crowds replied, This is the prophet Jesus from Nazareth of Galilee.

12 And Jesus went into the temple ([m]whole temple enclosure) and drove out all who bought and sold in the [j]sacred place, and He turned over the [n]fourfooted tables of the money-changers and the chairs of those who sold pigeons.

13 He said to them, The Scripture says, My house shall be called a house of prayer, but you have made it a den of robbers. [Isa. 56:7; Jer. 7:11.]

14 And the blind and the lame came to Him in the [o]porches *and* courts of the temple, and He cured them.

15 But when the chief priests and the scribes saw the wonderful things that He did, and the boys *and* the girls *and* the [p]youths *and* the maidens crying out in the [o]porches *and* courts of the temple, Hosanna (O be propitious, graciously inclined) to the Son of David! they were indignant.

16 And they said to Him, Do You hear what these are saying? And Jesus replied to them, Yes; have you never read, Out of the mouths of children and infants You have made (provided) perfect praise? [Ps. 8:2.]

17 And leaving them, He departed from the city and went out to Bethany and lodged there.

18 In the early dawn next morning, as He was coming back to the city He was hungry.

19 And as He saw [q]one single leafy fig tree [r]above the roadside He went to it [[s]seeing that in the fig tree the fruit appears at the same time as the leaves], but He found nothing but leaves on it. And he said to it, Never again shall fruit grow on you! And the fig tree withered up at once.

20 When the disciples saw it they marveled greatly and asked, How is it that the fig tree has withered away all at once?

21 And Jesus answered them, Truly, I say to you, if you have faith—a [t]firm relying trust—and do not doubt, you will not only do what has been done to the fig tree, but even if you say to this mountain, Be taken up and cast into the sea, it will be done.

22 And whatever you ask for in prayer, having faith *and* [really] believing, you will receive.

23 And when He entered the sacred [u]enclosure of the temple, the chief priests and elders of the people came up to Him as He was teaching and said, By what [v]power of authority are You doing these things, and who gave You this power of authority?

---

j) Thayer.
k) Literal meaning.
l) Capitalized because of what He is, the spotless Son of God, not what the speakers may have thought Him to be.
m) Trench's "Synonyms of the New Testament."
n) Moulton and Milligan.
o) Trench's "Synonyms of the New Testament."
p) Abbott-Smith.
q) Literal meaning.
r) Thayer.
s) International Standard Bible Encyclopedia.
t) Cremer.
u) Trench.
v) Thayer.

Living New Testament

7 And brought the animals to Him and threw their garments over the colt[1] for Him to ride on.

8 And some in the crowd threw down their coats along the road ahead of Him, and others cut branches from the trees and spread them out before Him.

9 Then the crowds surged on ahead and pressed along behind, shouting, "God bless King David's son!" ... "Praise Him!" ... "God's man is here"[2] ... "Bless Him, Lord!"

10 The entire city of Jerusalem was stirred as He entered. "Who is this?" they asked.

11 And the crowds replied, "It's Jesus, the prophet from Nazareth up in Galilee."

* * * * *

12 Jesus went into the Temple, drove out the merchants, and knocked over the money-changers' tables and the stalls of those selling doves.

13 "The Scriptures say My Temple is a place of prayer," He declared, "but you have turned it into a den of thieves."

14 And now the blind and crippled came to Him and He healed them there in the Temple.

15 But when the chief priests and other Jewish leaders saw these wonderful miracles, and heard even the little children in the Temple shouting, "God bless the Son of David," they were disturbed and indignant and asked Him, "Do you hear what these children are saying?"

16 "Yes," Jesus replied. "Didn't you ever read the Scriptures? For they say, 'Even little babies shall praise Him!' "

17 Then He returned to Bethany, where He stayed overnight.

18 In the morning, as He was returning to Jerusalem, He was hungry,

19 And noticed a fig tree beside the road. He went over to see if there were any figs, but there were only leaves. Then He said to it, "Never bear fruit again!" And soon[3] the fig tree withered up.

20 The disciples were utterly amazed and asked, "How did the fig tree wither so quickly?"

21 Then Jesus told them, "Truly, if you have faith, and don't doubt, you can do things like this and much more. You can even say to this Mount of Olives, 'Move over into the ocean,' and it will.

22 You can get anything—*anything* you ask for in prayer—if you believe."

23 When He had returned to the Temple and was teaching, the chief priests and other Jewish leaders came up to Him and demanded to know by whose authority He had thrown the merchants out the day before.[4]

---

[1]Implied.
[2]Literally, "Blessed is He who comes in the name of the Lord."
[3]Or, "immediately."
[4]Literally, "By what authority do you do these things?"

Revised Standard

directed them; 7they brought the ass and the colt, and put their garments on them, and he sat thereon. 8Most of the crowd spread their garments on the road, and others cut branches from the trees and spread them on the road. 9And the crowds that went before him and that followed him shouted, "Hosanna to the Son of David! Blessed is he who comes in the name of the Lord! Hosanna in the highest!" 10And when he entered Jerusalem, all the city was stirred, saying, "Who is this?" 11And the crowds said, "This is the prophet Jesus from Nazareth of Galilee."

Cleansing of the temple

12 And Jesus entered the temple of God[p] and drove out all who sold and bought in the temple, and he overturned the tables of the money-changers and the seats of those who sold pigeons. 13He said to them, "It is written, 'My house shall be called a house of prayer'; but you make it a den of robbers."

14 And the blind and the lame came to him in the temple, and he healed them. 15But when the chief priests and the scribes saw the wonderful things that he did, and the children crying out in the temple, "Hosanna to the Son of David!" they were indignant; 16and they said to him, "Do you hear what these are saying?" And Jesus said to them, "Yes; have you never read,

'Out of the mouth of babes and sucklings
thou hast brought perfect praise'?"

17And leaving them, he went out of the city to Bethany and lodged there.

The barren fig tree

18 In the morning, as he was returning ing to the city, he was hungry. 19And seeing a fig tree by the wayside he went to it, and found nothing on it but leaves only. And he said to it, "May no fruit ever come from you again!" And the fig tree withered at once. 20When the disciples saw it they marveled, saying, "How did the fig tree wither at once?" 21And Jesus answered them, "Truly, I say to you, if you have faith and never doubt, you will not only do what has been done to the fig tree, but even if you say to this mountain, 'Be taken up and cast into the sea,' it will be done. 22And whatever you ask in prayer, you will receive, if you have faith."

Jesus' authority challenged

23 And when he entered the temple, the chief priests and the elders of the people came up to him as he was teaching, and said, "By what authority are you doing these things, and who gave you this author-

---

[p] Other ancient authorities omit *of God*

King James

24 And Jesus answered and said unto them, I also will ask you one thing, which if ye tell me, I in like wise will tell you by what authority I do these things.

25 The baptism of John, whence was it? from heaven, or of men? And they reasoned with themselves, saying, If we shall say, From heaven; he will say unto us, Why did ye not then believe him?

26 But if we shall say, Of men; we fear the people; for all hold John as a prophet.

27 And they answered Jesus, and said, We cannot tell. And he said unto them, Neither tell I you by what authority I do these things.

28 ¶ But what think ye? A *certain* man had two sons; and he came to the first, and said, Son, go work to-day in my vineyard.

29 He answered and said, I will not: but afterward he repented, and went.

30 And he came to the second, and said likewise. And he answered and said, I *go*, sir: and went not.

31 Whether of them twain did the will of *his* father? They say unto him, The first. Jesus saith unto them, Verily I say unto you, That the publicans and the harlots go into the kingdom of God before you.

32 For John came unto you in the way of righteousness, and ye believed him not: but the publicans and the harlots believed him: and ye, when ye had seen *it*, repented not afterward, that ye might believe him.

33 ¶ Hear another parable: There was a certain householder, which planted a vineyard, and hedged it round about, and digged a winepress in it, and built a tower, and let it out to husbandmen, and went into a far country:

34 And when the time of the fruit drew near, he sent his servants to the husbandmen, that they might receive the fruits of it.

35 And the husbandmen took his servants, and beat one, and killed another, and stoned another.

36 Again, he sent other servants more than the first: and they did unto them likewise.

37 But last of all he sent unto them his son, saying, They will reverence my son.

38 But when the husbandmen saw the son, they said among themselves, This is the heir; come, let us kill him, and let us seize on his inheritance.

39 And they caught him, and cast *him* out of the vineyard, and slew *him*.

40 When the lord therefore of the vineyard cometh, what will he do unto those husbandmen?

41 They say unto him, He will miserably destroy those wicked men, and will let out *his* vineyard unto other husbandmen, which shall render him the fruits in their seasons.

42 Jesus saith unto them, Did ye never read in the scriptures, The stone which the builders rejected, the same is become the head of the corner: this is the Lord's doing, and it is marvellous in our eyes?

43 Therefore say I unto you, The kingdom of God shall be taken from you, and given to a nation bringing forth the fruits thereof.

Amplified

24 Jesus answered them, I also will ask you a question, and if you give Me the answer, then I also will tell you by what [v]power of authority I do these things.

25 The baptism of John, from whence was it? From heaven or from men? And they reasoned *and* argued with one another, If we say, From heaven, [w]He will ask us, Why then did you not believe him?

26 But if we say, From men, we are afraid of *and* must reckon with the multitude for they all regard John as a prophet.

27 So they answered Jesus, We do not know. And He said to them, Nor will I tell you by what [v]power of authority I do these things.

28 What do you think? There was a man who had two sons. He came to the first and said, Son, go and work today in the vineyard.

29 And he answered, I will not; but afterward he changed his mind and went.

30 Then the man came to the second and said the same [thing], and he replied, I will [go], sir; but he did not go.

31 Which of the two did the will of the father? They replied, The first one. Jesus said to them, Truly, I tell you, the tax collectors and the harlots will get into the kingdom of heaven before you.

32 For John came to you walking in the way of an upright man in right standing with God, and you did not believe him, but the tax collectors and the harlots did believe him; and you, even when you saw that, did not afterward change your minds and believe him—adhere to, trust in and rely on what he told you.

33 Listen to another parable. There was a master of a house who planted a vineyard, and put a hedge around it, and dug a wine vat in it, and built a watchtower. Then he let it out to tenants, and went into another country.

34 When the fruit season drew near, he sent his servants to the tenants, to get his [share of the] fruit;

35 But the tenants took his servants and beat one, killed another, and stoned another.

36 Again he sent other servants, more than the first time, and they treated them the same way.

37 Finally he sent his own son to them, saying, They will respect *and* give heed to my son.

38 But when the tenants saw the son, they said to themselves, This is the heir; come on, let us kill him, and have his inheritance.

39 And they took him, and threw him out of the vineyard, and killed him.

40 Now when the owner of the vineyard comes back, what will he do to those tenants?

41 They said to Him, He will put those wretches to a miserable death, and rent the vineyard to other tenants [x]of such a character that they will give him the fruits promptly in their season. [Isa. 5:1-7.]

42 Jesus asked them, Have you never read in the Scriptures, The very Stone which the builders rejected *and* threw away has become the Cornerstone; this was the Lord's doings, and it is marvelous in our eyes? [Ps. 118: 22, 23.]

43 I tell you, for this reason the kingdom of God will be taken away from you and given to a people who will produce the fruits of it.

---

w) Capitalized because of what He is, the spotless Son of God, not what the speakers may have thought He was.

Living New Testament

24 "I'll tell you if you answer one question first," Jesus replied.

25 "Was John the Baptist sent from God, or not?" They talked it over among themselves. "If we say, 'From God,' " they said, "then He will ask why we didn't believe what John said.

26 And if we deny that God sent him, we'll be mobbed, for the crowd all think he was a phophet!"

27 So they finally replied, "We don't know!"

And Jesus said, "Then I won't answer your question either.

28 But what do you think about this? A man with two sons told the older boy, 'Son, go out and work on the farm today.'

29 'I won't,' he answered, but later he changed his mind and went.

30 Then the father told the youngest, 'You go!' and he said 'Yes, sir, I will.' But he didn't.

31 Which of the two was obeying his father?"

They replied, "The first, of course."

Then Jesus explained His meaning: "Surely evil men and prostitutes will get into the Kingdom before you do.

32 For John the Baptist told you to repent and turn to God, and you wouldn't, while very evil men and prostitutes did. And even when you saw this happening, you refused to repent so you couldn't believe.

33 Now listen to this story: A certain landowner planted a vineyard with a hedge around it, and built a platform for the watchman, then leased the vineyard to some farmers on a sharecrop basis, and went away to live in another country.

34 At the time of the grape harvest he sent his agents to the farmers to collect his share.

35 But the farmers attacked his men, beat one, killed one and stoned another.

36 Then he sent a larger group of his men to collect for him, but the results were the same.

37 Finally the owner sent his son, thinking they would surely respect him.

38 But when these farmers saw the son coming they said among themselves, 'Here comes the heir to this estate; come on, let's kill him and get it for ourselves!'

39 So they dragged him out of the vineyard and killed him.

40 When the owner returns, what do you think he will do to those farmers?"

41 The Jewish leaders replied, "He will put the wicked men to a horrible death, and lease the vineyard to others who will pay him promptly."

42 Then Jesus asked them, "Didn't you ever read in the Scriptures, 'The stone rejected by the builders has been made the honored cornerstone;[5] How remarkable! What an amazing thing the Lord has done'?

43 What I mean is that the Kingdom of God shall be taken away from you, and given to a nation that will give God His share of the crop.[6]

[5]Literally, "the head of the corner."
[6]Literally, "bringing forth the fruits."

Revised Standard

ity?" [24]Jesus answered them, "I also will
ask you a question; and if you tell me the
answer, then I also will tell you by what
authority I do these things. [25]The baptism
of John, whence was it? From heaven or
from men?" And they argued with one
another, "If we say, 'From heaven,' he will
say to us, 'Why then did you not believe
him?' [26]But if we say, 'From men,' we are
afraid of the multitude; for all hold that
John was a prophet." [27]So they answered
Jesus, "We do not know." And he said to
them, "Neither will I tell you by what
authority I do these things.

The parable of the two sons

28 "What do you think? A man had two
sons; and he went to the first and said,
'Son, go and work in the vineyard today.'
[29]And he answered, 'I will not'; but afterward he repented and went. [30]And he went
to the second and said the same; and he
answered, 'I go, sir,' but did not go. [31]Which
of the two did the will of his father?" They
said, "The first." Jesus said to them, "Truly,
I say to you, the tax collectors and the harlots go into the kingdom of God before
you. [32]For John came to you in the way of
righteousness, and you did not believe him,
but the tax collectors and the harlots believed him; and even when you saw it, you
did not afterward repent and believe him.

The parable of the wicked tenants

33 "Hear another parable. There was a
householder who planted a vineyard, and
set a hedge around it, and dug a wine press
in it, and built a tower, and let it out to
tenants, and went into another country.
[34]When the season of fruit drew near, he
sent his servants to the tenants, to get his
fruit; [35]and the tenants took his servants
and beat one, killed another, and stoned
another. [36]Again he sent other servants, more
than the first; and they did the same to them.
[37]Afterward he sent his son to them, saying,
'They will respect my son.' [38]But when the
tenants saw the son, they said to themselves,
'This is the heir; come, let us kill him and
have his inheritance.' [39]And they took him
and cast him out of the vineyard, and killed
him. [40]When therefore the owner of the
vineyard comes, what will he do to those
tenants?" [41]They said to him, "He will put
those wretches to a miserable death, and
let out the vineyard to other tenants who
will give him the fruits in their seasons."

42 Jesus said to them, "Have you never
read in the scriptures:

'The very stone which the builders rejected
has become the head of the corner;
this was the Lord's doing,
and it is marvelous in our eyes'?

[43]Therefore I tell you, the kingdom of God
will be taken away from you and given to a
nation producing the fruits of it."[q]

[q] Other ancient authorities add verse 44, *"And he who falls on this stone will be broken to pieces; but when it falls on any one, it will crush him"*

King James

44 And whosoever shall fall on this stone shall be broken: but on whomsoever it shall fall, it will grind him to powder.

45 And when the chief priests and Pharisees had heard his parables, they perceived that he spake of them.

46 But when they sought to lay hands on him, they feared the multitude, because they took him for a prophet.

Amplified

44 *And whoever falls on this Stone will be broken to pieces, but he on whom it falls will be crushed to powder, and it will* [y]*winnow him,* [x]*scattering him as dust.* [Isa. 8:14; Dan. 2:34, 35.]

45 And when the chief priests and the Pharisees heard His parables (comparisons, stories used to illustrate and explain), they perceived that He was talking about them;

46 And although they were trying to arrest Him, they feared the throngs, because they regarded Him as a prophet.

CHAPTER 22

AND Jesus answered and spake unto them again by parables, and said,

2 The kingdom of heaven is like unto a certain king, which made a marriage for his son,

3 And sent forth his servants to call them that were bidden to the wedding: and they would not come.

4 Again, he sent forth other servants, saying, Tell them which are bidden, Behold, I have prepared my dinner: my oxen and *my* fatlings *are* killed, and all things *are* ready: come unto the marriage.

5 But they made light of *it,* and went their ways, one to his farm, another to his merchandise:

6 And the remnant took his servants, and entreated *them* spitefully, and slew *them.*

7 But when the king heard *thereof,* he was wroth: and he sent forth his armies, and destroyed those murderers, and burned up their city.

8 Then saith he to his servants, The wedding is ready, but they which were bidden were not worthy.

9 Go ye therefore into the highways, and as many as ye shall find, bid to the marriage.

10 So those servants went out into the highways, and gathered together all as many as they found, both bad and good: and the wedding was furnished with guests.

11 ¶ And when the king came in to see the guests, he saw there a man which had not on a wedding garment:

12 And he saith unto him, Friend, how camest thou in hither not having a wedding garment? And he was speechless.

13 Then said the king to the servants, Bind him hand and foot, and take him away, and cast *him* into outer darkness; there shall be weeping and gnashing of teeth.

14 For many are called, but few *are* chosen.

15 ¶ Then went the Pharisees, and took counsel how they might entangle him in *his* talk.

16 And they sent out unto him their disciples with the Herodians, saying, Master, we know that thou art true, and teachest the way of God in truth, neither carest thou for any *man:* for thou regardest not the person of men.

CHAPTER 22

AND again Jesus spoke to them in parables (comparisons, stories used to illustrate and explain), saying,

2 The kingdom of heaven is like a king who gave a wedding banquet for his son,

3 And sent his servants to summon those who had been invited to the wedding banquet, but they refused to come.

4 Again he sent other servants, saying, Tell those who are invited, Behold, I have prepared my banquet; my bullocks and my fat calves are killed, and everything is prepared; come to the wedding feast.

5 But they were not concerned *and* paid no attention—they ignored and made light of the summons, treating it with contempt—and they went away, one to his farm, another to his business,

6 While the others seized his servants, treated them shamefully and put them to death.

7 [Hearing this] the king was infuriated, and he sent his soldiers and put those murderers to death and burned their city.

8 Then he said to his servants, the wedding [feast] is prepared, but those invited were not worthy.

9 So go to the thoroughfares where they leave the city—where the main roads and those from the country end—and invite to the wedding feast as many as you find.

10 And those servants went out on the crossroads and got together as many as they found, both bad and good, so [the room in which] the wedding feast [was held] was filled with guests.

11 But when the king came in to view the guests, he looked intently at a man there who had on no wedding garment;

12 And he said, Friend, how did you come in here without putting on the [appropriate] wedding garment? And he was speechless ([z]muzzled, gagged).

13 Then the king said to the attendants, Tie him hand and foot, and throw him into the darkness outside; there will be weeping and the grinding of teeth.

14 For many are called (invited and summoned), but few chosen.

15 Then the Pharisees went and consulted *and* plotted together how they might entangle Jesus in His talk.

16 And they sent their disciples to Him, along with the Herodians, saying, Teacher, we know that You are [a]sincere *and* what You profess to be, and that You teach the way of God truthfully, regardless of consequences *and* being afraid of no man; for You are impartial *and* do not regard either the person *or* the position of any one.

---

x) Vincent.
y) Thayer.
z) Literal translation.
a) Cremer.

Living New Testament

44 All who stumble on this rock of truth[7] shall be broken, but those it falls on will be scattered as dust."

45 When the chief priests and other Jewish leaders realized that Jesus was talking about them—that they were the farmers in His story—

46 They wanted to get rid of Him, but were afraid to try because of the crowds, for they accepted Jesus as a prophet.

Revised Standard

45 When the chief priests and the Pharisees heard his parables, they perceived
that he was speaking about them. 46 But
when they tried to arrest him, they feared
the multitudes, because they held him to be
a prophet.

CHAPTER 22

Jesus told several other stories to show what the Kingdom of Heaven is like. "For instance," He said, "it can be illustrated by the story of a king who prepared a great wedding dinner for his son.

3 Many guests were invited, and when the banquet was ready he sent messengers to notify everyone that it was time to come. But all refused!

4 So he sent other servants to tell them, 'Everything is ready and the roast is in the oven. Hurry!'[1]

5 But the guests he had invited merely laughed and went on about their business, one to his farm, another to his store;

6 Others beat up his messengers and treated them shamefully, even killing some of them.

7 Then the angry king sent out his army and destroyed the murderers and burned their city.

8 And he said to his servants, 'The wedding feast is ready, and the guests I invited aren't worthy of the honor.

9 Now go out to the street corners and invite everyone you see.'

10 So the servants did, and brought in all they could find, good and bad alike; and the banquet hall was filled with guests.

11 But when the king came in to meet the guests he noticed a man who wasn't wearing the wedding robe [provided for him[2]].

12 'Friend,' he asked, 'how does it happen that you are here without a wedding robe?' And the man had no reply.

13 Then the king said to his aides, 'Bind him hand and foot and throw him out into the outer darkness where there is weeping and gnashing of teeth.'

14 For many are called, but few are chosen."

15 Then the Pharisees met together to try to think of some way to trap Jesus into saying something for which they could arrest Him.

16 They decided to send some of their men along with the Herodians[3] to ask Him this question: "Sir, we know you are very honest and teach the truth regardless of the consequences, without fear or favor.

The parable of the marriage feast

22 And again Jesus spoke to them in
parables, saying, 2 "The kingdom of
heaven may be compared to a king who
gave a marriage feast for his son, 3 and
sent his servants to call those who were
invited to the marriage feast; but they
would not come. 4 Again he sent other
servants, saying, 'Tell those who are invited, Behold, I have made ready my dinner, my oxen and my fat calves are killed,
and everything is ready; come to the marriage feast.' 5 But they made light of it and
went off, one to his farm, another to his
business, 6 while the rest seized his servants,
treated them shamefully, and killed them.
7 The king was angry, and he sent his troops
and destroyed those murderers and burned
their city. 8 Then he said to his servants,
'The wedding is ready, but those invited
were not worthy. 9 Go therefore to the
thoroughfares, and invite to the marriage
feast as many as you find.' 10 And those
servants went out into the streets and
gathered all whom they found, both bad
and good; so the wedding hall was filled
with guests.
11 "But when the king came in to look
at the guests, he saw there a man who had
no wedding garment; 12 and he said to him,
'Friend, how did you get in here without
a wedding garment?' And he was speechless.
13 Then the king said to the attendants, 'Bind
him hand and foot, and cast him into the
outer darkness; there men will weep and
gnash their teeth.' 14 For many are called,
but few are chosen."

Taxes to Caesar

15 Then the Pharisees went and took
counsel how to entangle him in his talk.
16 And they sent their disciples to him, along
with the Herodians, saying, "Teacher, we
know that you are true, and teach the way
of God truthfully, and care for no man; for

---

[7] Literally, "on this stone."
[1] Literally, "come to the wedding feast."
[2] Implied.
[3] The Herodians were a Jewish political party.

King James

17 Tell us therefore, What thinkest thou? Is it lawful to give tribute unto Cæsar, or not?

18 But Jesus perceived their wickedness, and said, Why tempt ye me, *ye* hypocrites?

19 Shew me the tribute money. And they brought unto him a penny.

20 And he saith unto them, Whose *is* this image and superscription?

21 They say unto him, Cæsar's. Then saith he unto them, Render therefore unto Cæsar the things which are Cæsar's; and unto God the things that are God's.

22 When they had heard *these words*, they marvelled, and left him, and went their way.

23 ¶ The same day came to him the Sadducees, which say that there is no resurrection, and asked him,

24 Saying, Master, Moses said, If a man die, having no children, his brother shall marry his wife, and raise up seed unto his brother.

25 Now there were with us seven brethren: and the first, when he had married a wife, deceased, and, having no issue, left his wife unto his brother:

26 Likewise the second also, and the third, unto the seventh.

27 And last of all the woman died also.

28 Therefore in the resurrection whose wife shall she be of the seven? for they all had her.

29 Jesus answered and said unto them, Ye do err, not knowing the scriptures, nor the power of God.

30 For in the resurrection they neither marry, nor are given in marriage, but are as the angels of God in heaven.

31 But as touching the resurrection of the dead, have ye not read that which was spoken unto you by God, saying,

32 I am the God of Abraham, and the God of Isaac, and the God of Jacob? God is not the God of the dead, but of the living.

33 And when the multitude heard *this*, they were astonished at his doctrine.

34 ¶ But when the Pharisees had heard that he had put the Sadducees to silence, they were gathered together.

35 Then one of them, *which was* a lawyer, asked *him a question*, tempting him, and saying,

36 Master, which *is* the great commandment in the law?

37 Jesus said unto him, Thou shalt love the Lord thy God with all thy heart, and with all thy soul, and with all thy mind.

38 This is the first and great commandment.

39 And the second *is* like unto it, Thou shalt love thy neighbour as thyself.

40 On these two commandments hang all the law and the prophets.

41 ¶ While the Pharisees were gathered together, Jesus asked them,

42 Saying, What think ye of Christ? whose son is he? They say unto him, *The son* of David.

43 He saith unto them, How then doth David in spirit call him Lord, saying,

Amplified

17 Tell us, then, what You think about this: Is it lawful to pay tribute [levied on the individuals and to be paid yearly] to Caesar, or not?

18 But Jesus, aware of their malicious plot, asked, Why do you put Me to the test *and* try to entrap Me, you pretenders—hypocrites?

19 Show me the money for the tribute. And they brought Him a denarius.

20 And Jesus said to them, Whose likeness and title are these?

21 They said, Caesar's. Then He said to them, Pay therefore to Caesar the things that are due to Caesar, and pay to God the things that are due to God.

22 When they heard it they were amazed *and* marveled, and they left Him and departed.

23 The same day some Sadducees came to Him, who say that there is no resurrection [of the dead], and they asked Him a question,

24 Saying, Teacher, Moses said, If a man dies, leaving no children, his brother shall marry the widow and raise up a family for his brother. [Deut. 25:5.]

25 Now there were seven brothers among us; the first married and died, and having no children left his wife to his brother.

26 The second also died childless, and the third, down to the seventh.

27 Last of all, the woman died also.

28 Now in the resurrection to which of the seven will she be wife? For they all had her.

29 But Jesus replied to them, You are wrong, because you know neither the Scriptures nor God's power.

30 For in the resurrected state neither do [men] marry nor are [women] given in marriage, but they are as the angels in heaven.

31 But as to the resurrection of the dead, have you never read what was said to you by God,

32 I am the God of Abraham, and the God of Isaac, and the God of Jacob? He is not the God of the dead, but of the living! [Exod. 3:6.]

33 And when the throng heard it, they were astonished *and* filled with [[b]glad] amazement at His teaching.

34 Now when the Pharisees heard that He had silenced ([c]muzzled) the Sadducees, they gathered together;

35 And one of their number, a lawyer, asked Him a question to test Him.

36 Teacher, which [d]kind of commandment is great and important—the principal kind—in the Law? [Some are light; which are heavy?]

37 And He replied to him, You shall love the Lord your God with all your heart, and with all your soul, and with all your mind (intellect). [Deut. 6:5.]

38 This is the great (most important, principal) and first commandment.

39 And a second is like it, You shall love your neighbor as [you do] yourself. [Lev. 19:18.]

40 These two commandments [e]sum up *and* upon them depends all the Law and the prophets.

41 Now while the Pharisees were still assembled there, Jesus asked them a question,

42 Saying, What do you think of the Christ? Whose Son is He? They said to Him, The Son of David.

43 He said to them, How is it then that David, under the influence of the (Holy) Spirit, calls Him Lord, saying,

---

b) Thayer.
c) Literal translation.
d) Vincent.
e) Thayer.

Living New Testament

17 Now tell us, is it right to pay taxes to the Roman government or not?"

18 But Jesus saw what they were after. "You hypocrites!" He exclaimed, "who are you trying to fool with your trick questions?

19 Here, show Me a coin." And they handed Him a penny.

20 "Whose picture is stamped on it?" He asked them. "And whose name is this beneath the picture?"

21 "Caesar's," they replied.

"Well then," He said, "give it to Caesar if it is his, and give God everything that belongs to God."

22 His reply surprised and baffled them and they went away.

23 But that same day some of the Sadducees, who say there is no resurrection after death, came to Him and asked,

24 "Sir, Moses said that if a man died without children, his brother should marry the widow and their children would get all the dead man's property.

25 Well, we had among us a family of seven brothers. The first of these men married and then died, without children, so his widow became the second brother's wife.

26 This brother also died without children, and the wife was passed to the next brother, and so on until she had been the wife of each of them.

27 And then she also died.

28 So whose wife will she be in the resurrection? For she was the wife of all seven of them!"

29 But Jesus said, "Your error is caused by your ignorance of the Scriptures and of God's power!

30 For in the resurrection there is no marriage; everyone is as the angels in heaven.

31 But now, as to whether there is a resurrection of the dead—don't you ever read the Scriptures? Don't you realize that God was speaking directly to you when He said,

32 'I *am* the God of Abraham, Isaac and Jacob'? So God is not the God of the dead, but of the *living*."[4]

33 The crowds were profoundly impressed by His answers—

34, 35 But not the Pharisees! When they heard that He had routed the Sadducees with His reply, they thought up a fresh question of their own to ask Him. One of them, a lawyer, spoke up:

36 "Sir, which is the most important command in the laws of Moses?"

37 Jesus replied, " 'Love the Lord your God with all your heart, soul, and mind.'

38, 39 This is the first and greatest commandment.

The second most important is similar, 'Love your neighbor as much as you love yourself.'

40 All the other commandments and all the demands of the prophets stem from these two laws and are fulfilled if you obey them. Keep only these and you will find that you are obeying all the others."

41 Then, surrounded by the Pharisees, He asked them a question:

42 "What about the Messiah? Whose son is He?"

"The son of David," they replied.

43 "Then why does David, speaking under the inspiration of the Holy Spirit, call Him 'Lord'?" Jesus asked. "For David said,

---

[4]i.e., if Abraham, Isaac, and Jacob, long dead, were not alive in the presence of God, then God would have said, "I *was* the God of Abraham, etc."

Revised Standard

you do not regard the position of men. 17 Tell
us, then, what you think. Is it lawful to pay
taxes to Caesar, or not?" 18 But Jesus, aware
of their malice, said, "Why put me to the
test, you hypocrites? 19 Show me the money
for the tax." And they brought him a coin.[r]
20 And Jesus said to them, "Whose likeness
and inscription is this?" 21 They said, "Caesar's."
Then he said to them, "Render therefore
to Caesar the things that are Caesar's,
and to God the things that are God's."
22 When they heard it, they marveled; and
they left him and went away.

Sadducees and the resurrection

23 The same day Sadducees came to
him, who say that there is no resurrection;
and they asked him a question, 24 saying,
"Teacher, Moses said, 'If a man dies, having
no children, his brother must marry the
widow, and raise up children for his brother.'
25 Now there were seven brothers among
us; the first married, and died, and having
no children left his wife to his brother.
26 So too the second and third, down to the
seventh. 27 After them all, the woman died.
28 In the resurrection, therefore, to which
of the seven will she be wife? For they all
had her."
29 But Jesus answered them, "You are
wrong, because you know neither the scriptures
nor the power of God. 30 For in the
resurrection they neither marry nor are
given in marriage, but are like angels[s] in
heaven. 31 And as for the resurrection of the
dead, have you not read what was said to
you by God, 32 'I am the God of Abraham,
and the God of Isaac, and the God of
Jacob'? He is not God of the dead, but of
the living." 33 And when the crowd heard
it, they were astonished at his teaching.

The great commandment

34 But when the Pharisees heard that he
had silenced the Sadducees, they came together.
35 And one of them, a lawyer, asked
him a question, to test him. 36 "Teacher,
which is the great commandment in the
law?" 37 And he said to him, "You shall
love the Lord your God with all your heart,
and with all your soul, and with all your
mind. 38 This is the great and first commandment.
39 And a second is like it, You shall
love your neighbor as yourself. 40 On these
two commandments depend all the law and
the prophets."

The question about David's son

41 Now while the Pharisees were gathered
together, Jesus asked them a question,
42 saying, "What do you think of the Christ?
Whose son is he?" They said to him, "The
son of David." 43 He said to them, "How is
it then that David, inspired by the Spirit,[t]
calls him Lord, saying,

---

[r] Greek *a denarius*
[s] Other ancient authorities add *of God*
[t] Or *David in the Spirit*

King James

44 The LORD said unto my Lord, Sit thou on my right hand, till I make thine enemies thy footstool?

45 If David then call him Lord, how is he his son?

46 And no man was able to answer him a word, neither durst any *man* from that day forth ask him any more *questions*.

CHAPTER 23

THEN spake Jesus to the multitude, and to his disciples,

2 Saying, The scribes and the Pharisees sit in Moses' seat:

3 All therefore whatsoever they bid you observe, *that* observe and do; but do not ye after their works: for they say, and do not.

4 For they bind heavy burdens and grievous to be borne, and lay *them* on men's shoulders; but they *themselves* will not move them with one of their fingers.

5 But all their works they do for to be seen of men: they make broad their phylacteries, and enlarge the borders of their garments,

6 And love the uppermost rooms at feasts, and the chief seats in the synagogues,

7 And greetings in the markets, and to be called of men, Rabbi, Rabbi.

8 But be not ye called Rabbi: for one is your Master, *even* Christ; and all ye are brethren.

9 And call no *man* your father upon the earth: for one is your Father, which is in heaven.

10 Neither be ye called masters: for one is your Master, *even* Christ.

11 But he that is greatest among you shall be your servant.

12 And whosoever shall exalt himself shall be abased; and he that shall humble himself shall be exalted.

13 ¶ But woe unto you, scribes and Pharisees, hypocrites! for ye shut up the kingdom of heaven against men: for ye neither go in *yourselves*, neither suffer ye them that are entering to go in.

14 Woe unto you, scribes and Pharisees, hypocrites! for ye devour widows' houses, and for a pretence make long prayer: therefore ye shall receive the greater damnation.

15 Woe unto you, scribes and Pharisees, hypocrites! for ye compass sea and land to make one proselyte, and when he is made, ye make him twofold more the child of hell than yourselves.

16 Woe unto you, *ye* blind guides, which say, Whosoever shall swear by the temple, it is nothing; but whosoever shall swear by the gold of the temple, he is a debtor!

17 *Ye* fools and blind: for whether is greater, the gold, or the temple that sanctifieth the gold?

Amplified

44 The Lord said to My Lord, Sit at My right hand until I put Your enemies under Your feet? [Ps. 110:1.]

45 If then David thus calls Him Lord, how is He His Son?

46 And no one was able to answer Him a word, nor from that day did any one venture *or* dare to question Him.

CHAPTER 23

THEN Jesus said to the multitudes and to His disciples,

2 The scribes and Pharisees sit on Moses' seat [of authority],

3 So observe and practice all they tell you; but do not do what they do, for they preach, but do not practice.

4 They tie up heavy loads, *hard to bear*, and place them on men's shoulders, but they themselves will not lift a finger to help bear them.

5 They do all their works to be seen of men; for they make wide their phylacteries [[f]small cases enclosing certain Scripture passages, worn during prayer on left arm and forehead], and make long their fringes [worn by all male Israelites, according to the command]. [Num. 15:38; Exod. 13:9; Deut. 6:8.]

6 And they [g]take pleasure in *and* [thus] love the place of honor at feasts and the best seats in the synagogues,

7 And to be greeted with honor in the market places, and to have people call them rabbi.

8 But you are not to be called rabbi (teacher), for One is your Teacher, and you are all brothers.

9 And do not call any one [in the church] on earth father, for you have one Father, Who is in heaven.

10 And you must not be called masters (leaders), for you have one Master (Leader), the Christ.

11 He who is greatest among you shall be your servant.

12 Whoever exalts himself [[h]with haughtiness and empty pride] shall be humbled (brought low); and whoever humbles himself—who has a modest opinion of himself and behaves accordingly—shall be [h]raised to honor.

13 But woe to you, scribes and Pharisees, pretenders—hypocrites! because you shut the kingdom of heaven in men's faces; for you neither enter yourselves, nor do you allow those who are about to go in to do so.

14 *Woe to you, scribes and Pharisees, pretenders—hypocrites! for you swallow up widows' houses, and for a pretense to cover it up make long prayers; therefore you will receive the greater condemnation and the heavier sentence.*

15 Woe to you scribes and Pharisees, pretenders—hypocrites! for you travel over sea and land to make a single proselyte, and when he becomes [a proselyte], you make him doubly as much a child of hell (Gehenna) as you are.

16 Woe to you, blind guides, who say, If any one swears by the [i]sanctuary of the temple, it is nothing; but if any one swears by the gold of the [i]sanctuary, he is a debtor—bound by his oath.

17 You blind fools! For which is greater, the gold or the [i]sanctuary of the temple that has made the gold sacred? [Exod. 30:29.]

---

f) Condensed from "Davis Dictionary of the Bible."
g) Wuest.
h) Thayer.
i) Trench.

Living New Testament

44 God said to my Lord, Sit at My right hand until I put Your enemies beneath Your feet.'
45 Since David called Him 'Lord,' how can He be merely his son?"
46 They had no answer. And after that no one dared ask Him any more questions.

Revised Standard

44'The Lord said to my Lord,
Sit at my right hand,
till I put thy enemies under thy feet'?
45If David thus calls him Lord, how is he
his son?" 46And no one was able to answer
him a word, nor from that day did any one
dare to ask him any more questions.

CHAPTER 23

Then Jesus said to the crowds, and to His disciples,
"You would think these Jewish leaders and these Pharisees were Moses,[1] the way they keep making up so many laws!
3 And of course you should obey their every whim! It may be all right to do what they say, but above anything else, *don't follow their example.* For they don't do what they tell you to do.
4 They load you with impossible demands that they themselves don't even try to keep.
5 Everything they do is done for show. They act holy[2] by wearing on their arms large prayer boxes with Scripture verses inside,[3] and by lengthening the memorial fringes of their robes.
6 And how they love to sit at the head table at banquets, and in the reserved pews in the synagogue.
7 How they enjoy the deference paid them on the streets, and to be called 'Rabbi' and 'Master'!
8 Don't ever let anyone call you that. For only God is your Rabbi and all of you are on the same level, as brothers.
9 And don't address anyone here on earth as 'Father,' for only God in heaven should be addressed like that.
10 And don't be called 'Master,' for only one is your master, even the Messiah.
11 The more lowly your service to others, the greater you are. To be the greatest, be a servant.
12 But those who think themselves great shall be disappointed and humbled; and those who humble themselves shall be exalted.
13, 14 Woe to you, Pharisees, and you other religious leaders. Hypocrites! For you won't let others enter the Kingdom of Heaven, and won't go in yourselves. And you pretend to be holy, with all your long, public prayers in the streets, while you are evicting widows from their homes. Hypocrites!
15 Yes, woe upon you hypocrites. For you go to all lengths to make one convert, and then turn him into twice the son of hell you are yourselves.
16 Blind guides! Woe upon you! For your rule is that to swear 'By God's Temple' means nothing—you can break that oath; but to swear 'By the gold in the Temple' is binding!
17 Blind fools! Which is greater, the gold, or the Temple that sanctifies the gold?

[1]Literally, "sit on Moses' seat."
[2]Implied.
[3]Literally, "enlarge their phylacteries."

The warning against Pharisaism

23 Then said Jesus to the crowds and
to his disciples, 2"The scribes and
the Pharisees sit on Moses' seat; 3so practice
and observe whatever they tell you, but not
what they do; for they preach, but do not
practice. 4They bind heavy burdens hard
to bear,[u] and lay them on men's shoulders;
but they themselves will not move them
with their finger. 5They do all their deeds
to be seen by men; for they make their
phylacteries broad and their fringes long,
6and they love the place of honor at feasts
and the best seats in the synagogues, 7and
salutations in the market places, and being
called rabbi by men. 8But you are not to
be called rabbi, for you have one teacher,
and you are all brethren. 9And call no man
your father on earth, for you have one
Father, who is in heaven. 10Neither be
called masters, for you have one master,
the Christ. 11He who is greatest among you
shall be your servant; 12whoever exalts
himself will be humbled, and whoever
humbles himself will be exalted.

The woes upon the Pharisees

13 "But woe to you, scribes and Pharisees, hypocrites! because you shut the kingdom of heaven against men; for you neither enter yourselves, nor allow those who would enter to go in.[v] 15Woe to you,
scribes and Pharisees, hypocrites! for you
traverse sea and land to make a single proselyte, and when he becomes a proselyte, you
make him twice as much a child of hell[w]
as yourselves.
16 "Woe to you, blind guides, who say,
'If any one swears by the temple, it is nothing; but if any one swears by the gold of
the temple, he is bound by his oath.' 17You
blind fools! For which is greater, the gold
or the temple that has made the gold sacred?

[u] Other ancient authorities omit *hard to bear*
[v] Other authorities add here (or after verse 12) verse 14, *Woe to you, scribes and Pharisees, hypocrites! for you devour widows' houses and for a pretense you make long prayers; therefore you will receive the greater condemnation*
[w] Greek *Gehenna*

King James

18 And, Whosoever shall swear by the altar, it is nothing; but whosoever sweareth by the gift that is upon it, he is guilty.

19 *Ye* fools and blind: for whether *is* greater, the gift, or the altar that sanctifieth the gift?

20 Whoso therefore shall swear by the altar, sweareth by it, and by all things thereon.

21 And whoso shall swear by the temple, sweareth by it, and by him that dwelleth therein.

22 And he that shall swear by heaven, sweareth by the throne of God, and by him that sitteth thereon.

23 Woe unto you, scribes and Pharisees, hypocrites! for ye pay tithe of mint and anise and cummin, and have omitted the weightier *matters* of the law, judgment, mercy, and faith: these ought ye to have done, and not to leave the other undone.

24 *Ye* blind guides, which strain at a gnat, and swallow a camel.

25 Woe unto you, scribes and Pharisees, hypocrites! for ye make clean the outside of the cup and of the platter, but within they are full of extortion and excess.

26 *Thou* blind Pharisee, cleanse first that *which is* within the cup and platter, that the outside of them may be clean also.

27 Woe unto you, scribes and Pharisees, hypocrites! for ye are like unto whited sepulchres, which indeed appear beautiful outward, but are within full of dead *men's* bones, and of all uncleanness.

28 Even so ye also outwardly appear righteous unto men, but within ye are full of hypocrisy and iniquity.

29 Woe unto you, scribes and Pharisees, hypocrites! because ye build the tombs of the prophets, and garnish the sepulchres of the righteous,

30 And say, If we had been in the days of our fathers, we would not have been partakers with them in the blood of the prophets.

31 Wherefore ye be witnesses unto yourselves, that ye are the children of them which killed the prophets.

32 Fill ye up then the measure of your fathers.

33 *Ye* serpents, *ye* generation of vipers, how can ye escape the damnation of hell?

34 ¶ Wherefore, behold, I send unto you prophets, and wise men, and scribes: and *some* of them ye shall kill and crucify; and *some* of them shall ye scourge in your synagogues, and persecute *them* from city to city:

35 That upon you may come all the righteous blood shed upon the earth, from the blood of righteous Abel unto the blood of Zacharias son of Barachias, whom ye slew between the temple and the altar.

36 Verily I say unto you, All these things shall come upon this generation.

37 O Jerusalem, Jerusalem, *thou* that killest the prophets, and stonest them which are sent unto thee, how often would I have gathered thy children together, even as a hen gathereth her chickens under *her* wings, and ye would not!

Amplified

18 You say too, Whoever swears by the altar is not duty bound, but whoever swears by the offering on the altar, his oath is binding.

19 You blind men! Which is greater, the gift or the altar which makes the gift sacred?

20 So whoever swears by the altar, swears by it and by everything on it;

21 And he who swears by the [j]sanctuary of the temple, swears by it and by Him Who dwells in it; [I Kings 8:13; Ps. 26:8.]

22 And whoever swears by heaven, swears by the throne of God and by Him Who sits upon it.

23 Woe to you, scribes and Pharisees, pretenders—hypocrites! for you give a tenth of your mint and dill and cummin, and have neglected *and* omitted the weightier (more important) matters of the Law, right *and* justice and mercy and fidelity. These you ought [particularly] to have done, without neglecting the others.

24 You blind guides, filtering out a gnat and gulping down a [k]camel! [Lev. 27:30; Mic. 6:8.]

25 Woe to you, scribes and Pharisees, pretenders—hypocrites! for you clean the outside of the cup and of the platter, but within they are full of extortion—prey, spoil, plunder—and grasping self-indulgence.

26 You blind Pharisee! First clean the inside of the cup and of the plate, so that the outside may be clean also.

27 Woe to you, scribes and Pharisees, pretenders—hypocrites! for you are like tombs that have been whitewashed, which look beautiful on the outside, but inside are full of dead men's bones and everything impure.

28 Just so, you also outwardly seem to people to be just *and* upright, but inside you are full of pretense and lawlessness *and* iniquity. [Ps. 5:9.]

29 Woe to you, scribes and Pharisees, pretenders—hypocrites! for you build tombs for the prophets and decorate the monuments of the righteous,

30 Saying, If we had lived in the days of our forefathers, we would not have aided them in shedding the blood of the prophets.

31 Thus you are testifying [against] yourselves that you are the descendants of those who murdered the prophets.

32 Fill up then the measure of your fathers' sins to the brim [so [l]that nothing may be wanting to a full measure].

33 You serpents! You spawn of vipers! How can you escape the [l]penalty to be suffered in hell (Gehenna)?

34 Because of this, take notice, I am sending you prophets and wise men (interpreters and teachers) and scribes (men learned in the Mosaic Law and the prophets); some of them you will kill, even crucify, and some you will flog in your synagogues, and pursue *and* persecute from town to town,

35 So that upon your heads may come all the blood of the righteous [[m]those who correspond to the divine standard of right] shed on earth from the blood of the righteous Abel to the blood of Zechariah son of Barachiah, whom you murdered between the sanctuary and the altar [of burnt offering]. [Gen. 4:8; II Chron. 24:21.]

36 Truly, I declare to you, all these [[n]evil, calamitous times] will come upon this generation. [II Chron. 36:15, 16.]

37 O Jerusalem, Jerusalem, murdering the prophets and stoning those who are sent to you! How often would I have gathered your children together as a mother fowl gathers her brood under her wings, and you refused!

---

j) Trench.
k) The camel was also unclean (Lev. 11:4).
l) Thayer.
m) Abbott-Smith.
n) Thayer.

Living New Testament

18 And you say that to take an oath 'By the altar' can be broken, but to swear 'By the gifts on the altar' is binding!

19 Blind! For which is greater, the gift on the altar, or the altar itself that sanctifies the gift?

20 When you swear 'By the altar' you are swearing by it and everything on it,

21 And when you swear 'By the Temple' you are swearing by it, and by God who lives in it.

22 And when you swear 'By heavens' you are swearing by the Throne of God and by God Himself.

23 Yes, woe upon you, Pharisees, and you other religious leaders—hypocrites! For you tithe down to the last mint leaf in your garden, but ignore the important things—justice and mercy and faith. Yes, you should tithe, but you shouldn't leave the more important things undone.

24 Blind guides! You strain out a gnat and swallow a camel.

25 Woe to you, Pharisees, and you religious leaders—hypocrites! You are so careful to polish the outside of the cup, but the inside is foul with extortion and greed.

26 Blind Pharisees! First cleanse the inside of the cup, and then the whole cup will be clean.

27 Woe to you, Pharisees, and you religious leaders! You are like beautiful mausoleums—full of dead men's bones, and of foulness and corruption.

28 You try to look like saintly men, but underneath those pious robes of yours are hearts besmirched with every sort of hypocrisy and sin.

29, 30 Yes, woe to you, Pharisees, and you religious leaders—hypocrites! For you build monuments to the prophets killed by your fathers and lay flowers on the graves of the godly men they destroyed, and say, 'We certainly would never have acted as our fathers did.'

31 In saying that, you are accusing yourselves of being the sons of wicked men.

32 And you are following in their steps, filling up the full measure of their evil.

33 Snakes! Sons of vipers! How shall you escape the judgment of hell?

34 I will send you prophets, and spirit-filled men, and inspired writers, and you will kill some by crucifixion, and rip open the backs of others with whips in your synagogues, and hound them from city to city,

35 So that you will become guilty of all the blood of murdered godly men from righteous Abel to Zechariah (son of Barachiah), slain by you in the Temple between the altar and the sanctuary.

36 Yes, all the accumulated judgment of the centuries shall break upon the heads of this very generation.

37 O Jerusalem, Jerusalem, the city that kills the prophets, and stones all those God sends to her! How often I have wanted to gather your children together as a hen gathers her chicks beneath her wings, but you wouldn't let Me.

Revised Standard

18 And you say, 'If any one swears by the
altar, it is nothing; but if any one swears
by the gift that is on the altar, he is bound
by his oath.' 19 You blind men! For which
is greater, the gift or the altar that makes
the gift sacred? 20 So he who swears by the
altar, swears by it and by everything on it;
21 and he who swears by the temple, swears
by it and by him who dwells in it; 22 and
he who swears by heaven, swears by the
throne of God and by him who sits upon
it.

23 "Woe to you, scribes and Pharisees,
hypocrites! for you tithe mint and dill and
cummin, and have neglected the weightier
matters of the law, justice and mercy and
faith; these you ought to have done, without neglecting the others. 24 You blind guides,
straining out a gnat and swallowing a camel!

25 "Woe to you, scribes and Pharisees,
hypocrites! for you cleanse the outside of
the cup and of the plate, but inside they
are full of extortion and rapacity. 26 You
blind Pharisee! first cleanse the inside of the
cup and of the plate, that the outside also
may be clean.

27 "Woe to you, scribes and Pharisees,
hypocrites! for you are like whitewashed
tombs, which outwardly appear beautiful,
but within they are full of dead men's bones
and all uncleanness. 28 So you also outwardly appear righteous to men, but within you
are full of hypocrisy and iniquity.

29 "Woe to you, scribes and Pharisees,
hypocrites! for you build the tombs of the
prophets and adorn the monuments of the
righteous, 30 saying, 'If we had lived in the
days of our fathers, we would not have taken part with them in shedding the blood of
the prophets.' 31 Thus you witness against
yourselves, that you are sons of those who
murdered the prophets. 32 Fill up, then, the
measure of your fathers. 33 You serpents,
you brood of vipers, how are you to escape
being sentenced to hell?[w] 34 Therefore I send
you prophets and wise men and scribes,
some of whom you will kill and crucify,
and some you will scourge in your synagogues and persecute from town to town,
35 that upon you may come all the righteous
blood shed on earth, from the blood of
innocent Abel to the blood of Zechariah
the son of Barachiah, whom you murdered
between the sanctuary and the altar. 36 Truly,
I say to you, all this will come upon this
generation.

The lament over Jerusalem

37 "O Jerusalem, Jerusalem, killing the
prophets and stoning those who are sent to
you! How often would I have gathered
your children together as a hen gathers her
brood under her wings, and you would not!

[w] Greek *Gehenna*

King James

38 Behold, your house is left unto you desolate.

39 For I say unto you, Ye shall not see me henceforth, till ye shall say, Blessed *is* he that cometh in the name of the Lord.

Amplified

38 Behold, your house is forsaken and desolate—abandoned and left destitute [of God's help]. [I Kings 9:7; Jer. 22:5.]

39 For I declare to you, you will not see Me again until you say, Blessed—magnified in worship, adored and exalted—be He Who comes in the name of the Lord! [Ps. 118:26.]

CHAPTER 24

AND Jesus went out, and departed from the temple: and his disciples came to *him* for to shew him the buildings of the temple.

2 And Jesus said unto them, See ye not all these things? verily I say unto you, There shall not be left here one stone upon another, that shall not be thrown down.

3 ¶ And as he sat upon the mount of Olives, the disciples came unto him privately, saying, Tell us, when shall these things be? and what *shall be* the sign of thy coming, and of the end of the world?

4 And Jesus answered and said unto them, Take heed that no man deceive you.

5 For many shall come in my name, saying, I am Christ; and shall deceive many.

6 And ye shall hear of wars and rumours of wars: see that ye be not troubled: for all *these things* must come to pass, but the end is not yet.

7 For nation shall rise against nation, and kingdom against kingdom: and there shall be famines, and pestilences, and earthquakes, in divers places.

8 All these *are* the beginning of sorrows.

9 Then shall they deliver you up to be afflicted, and shall kill you: and ye shall be hated of all nations for my name's sake.

10 And then shall many be offended, and shall betray one another, and shall hate one another.

11 And many false prophets shall rise, and shall deceive many.

12 And because iniquity shall abound, the love of many shall wax cold.

13 But he that shall endure unto the end, the same shall be saved.

14 And this gospel of the kingdom shall be preached in all the world for a witness unto all nations; and then shall the end come.

15 When ye therefore shall see the abomination of desolation, spoken of by Daniel the prophet, stand in the holy place, (whoso readeth, let him understand:)

16 Then let them which be in Judæa flee into the mountains:

17 Let him which is on the housetop not come down to take any thing out of his house:

18 Neither let him which is in the field return back to take his clothes.

CHAPTER 24

JESUS departed from the temple [o]area and was going on His way, when His disciples came up to Him to call His attention to the buildings of the temple *and* point them out to Him.

2 But He answered them, Do you see all these? Truly, I tell you, there will not be left here one stone upon another that will not be thrown down.

3 While He was seated on the Mount of Olives, the disciples came to Him privately and said, Tell us, when will this take place, and what will be the sign of Your coming and of the end—that is, the completion, the consummation—of the age?

4 Jesus answered them, Be careful that no one misleads you—deceiving you and leading you into error.

5 For many will come in (on the strength of) My name—[p]appropriating the name which belongs to Me—saying, I am the Messiah, the Christ; and they will lead many astray.

6 And you will hear of wars and rumors of wars; see that you are not frightened *or* troubled, for this must take place, but the end is not yet.

7 For nation will rise against nation, and kingdom against kingdom, and there will be famines and earthquakes in place after place;

8 All this is but the beginning—the early pains of the [q]birth pangs—of the [p]intolerable anguish.

9 Then they will hand you over to suffer affliction *and* tribulation, and put you to death; and you will be hated by all nations for My name's sake.

10 And then many will be offended *and* repelled *and* [p]begin to distrust and desert [Him Whom they ought to trust and obey] *and* will stumble and fall away, and betray one another *and* pursue one another with hatred.

11 And many false prophets will rise up and deceive *and* lead many into error.

12 And the love of [r]the great body of people will grow cold, because of the multiplied lawlessness *and* iniquity.

13 But he who endures to the end will be saved.

14 And this good news of the kingdom (the Gospel) will be preached throughout the whole world as a testimony to all the nations, and then will come the end.

15 So when you see the appalling sacrilege spoken of by the prophet Daniel, standing in the Holy Place, [and] let the reader take notice *and* [s]ponder *and* consider *and* heed [this], [Dan. 9:27; 11:31; 12:11.]

16 Then let those who are in Judea flee to the mountains;

17 Let him who is on the housetop not come down *and* go into the house to take anything;

18 And let him who is in the field not turn back to get his overcoat.

---

o) Trench's "Synonyms of the New Testament."
p) Thayer.
q) Literal translation.
r) Vincent.
s) Thayer.

Living New Testament

38 And now your house is left to you, desolate.

39 For I tell you this, you will never see Me again until you are ready to welcome the One sent to you from God."[4]

CHAPTER 24

As Jesus was leaving the Temple grounds, His disciples came along and wanted to take Him on a tour of the various Temple buildings.

2 But He told them, "All these buildings will be knocked down, with not one stone left on top of another!"

3 "When will this happen?" the disciples asked Him later, as He sat on the slopes of the Mount of Olives. "What events will signal your return, and the end of the world?"[1]

4 Jesus told them, "Don't let anyone fool you.

5 For many will come claiming to be the Messiah, and will lead many astray.

6 When you hear of wars beginning, this does not signal My return; these must come, but the end is not yet.

7 The nations and kingdoms of the earth will rise against each other and there will be famines and earthquakes in many places.

8 But all this will be only the beginning of the horrors to come.

9 Then you will be tortured and killed and hated all over the world because you are Mine,

10 And many of you shall fall back into sin and betray and hate each other.

11 And many false prophets will appear and lead many astray.

12 Sin will be rampant everywhere and will cool the love of many.

13 But those enduring to the end shall be saved.

14 And the Good News about the Kingdom will be preached throughout the whole world, so that all nations will hear it, and then, finally, the end will come.

15 So, when you see the horrible thing[2] (told about by Daniel[3] the prophet) standing in a holy place (Note to the reader: You know what is meant!),[4]

16 Then those in Judea must flee into the Judean hills.

17 Those on their porches[5] must not even go inside to pack before they flee.

18 Those in the fields should not return to their homes for their clothes.

[4]Literally, "in the name of the Lord."
[1]Literally, "age."
[2]Literally, "the abomination of desolation."
[3]Daniel 9:27, 11:31, 12:11.
[4]Literally, "Let the reader take note."
[5]Literally, "roof tops" which, being flat, were used as porches at that time. See Acts 10:9.

Revised Standard

38Behold, your house is forsaken and desolate.[x] 39For I tell you, you will not see me
again, until you say, 'Blessed is he who
comes in the name of the Lord.' "

The course of this age

24 Jesus left the temple and was going
away, when his disciples came to
point out to him the buildings of the temple.
2But he answered them, "You see all these,
do you not? Truly, I say to you, there will
not be left here one stone upon another,
that will not be thrown down."
3 As he sat on the Mount of Olives, the
disciples came to him privately, saying,
"Tell us, when will this be, and what will
be the sign of your coming and of the close
of the age?" 4And Jesus answered them,
"Take heed that no one leads you astray.
5For many will come in my name, saying,
'I am the Christ,' and they will lead many
astray. 6And you will hear of wars and
rumors of wars; see that you are not
alarmed; for this must take place, but the
end is not yet. 7For nation will rise against
nation, and kingdom against kingdom, and
there will be famines and earthquakes in
various places: 8all this is but the beginning
of the sufferings.
9 "Then they will deliver you up to tribulation, and put you to death; and you
will be hated by all nations for my name's
sake. 10And then many will fall away,[y] and
betray one another, and hate one another.
11And many false prophets will arise and
lead many astray. 12And because wickedness is multiplied, most men's love will
grow cold. 13But he who endures to the
end will be saved. 14And this gospel of the
kingdom will be preached throughout the
whole world, as a testimony to all nations;
and then the end will come.

The time of tribulation

15 "So when you see the desolating
sacrilege spoken of by the prophet Daniel,
standing in the holy place (let the reader
understand), 16then let those who are in
Judea flee to the mountains; 17let him who
is on the housetop not go down to take
what is in his house; 18and let him who is
in the field not turn back to take his mantle.

[x] Other ancient authorities omit *and desolate*
[y] Or *stumble*

King James

19 And woe unto them that are with child, and to them that give suck in those days!

20 But pray ye that your flight be not in the winter, neither on the sabbath day:

21 For then shall be great tribulation, such as was not since the beginning of the world to this time, no, nor ever shall be.

22 And except those days should be shortened, there should no flesh be saved: but for the elect's sake those days shall be shortened.

23 Then if any man shall say unto you, Lo, here *is* Christ, or there; believe *it* not.

24 For there shall arise false Christs, and false prophets, and shall shew great signs and wonders; insomuch that, if *it were* possible, they shall deceive the very elect.

25 Behold, I have told you before.

26 Wherefore if they shall say unto you, Behold, he is in the desert; go not forth: behold, *he is* in the secret chamber; believe *it* not.

27 For as the lightning cometh out of the east, and shineth even unto the west; so shall also the coming of the Son of man be.

28 For wheresoever the carcase is, there will the eagles be gathered together.

29 ¶ Immediately after the tribulation of those days shall the sun be darkened, and the moon shall not give her light, and the stars shall fall from heaven, and the powers of the heavens shall be shaken:

30 And then shall appear the sign of the Son of man in heaven: and then shall all the tribes of the earth mourn, and they shall see the Son of man coming in the clouds of heaven with power and great glory.

31 And he shall send his angels with a great sound of a trumpet, and they shall gather together his elect from the four winds, from one end of heaven to the other.

32 Now learn a parable of the fig tree; When his branch is yet tender, and putteth forth leaves, ye know that summer *is* nigh:

33 So likewise ye, when ye shall see all these things, know that it is near, *even* at the doors.

34 Verily I say unto you, This generation shall not pass, till all these things be fulfilled.

35 Heaven and earth shall pass away, but my words shall not pass away.

36 ¶ But of that day and hour knoweth no *man*, no, not the angels of heaven, but my Father only.

37 But as the days of Noe *were*, so shall also the coming of the Son of man be.

38 For as in the days that were before the flood they were eating and drinking, marrying and giving in marriage, until the day that Noe entered into the ark,

39 And knew not until the flood came, and took them all away; so shall also the coming of the Son of man be.

40 Then shall two be in the field; the one shall be taken, and the other left.

Amplified

19 And alas for the women who are pregnant and for those who have nursing babies in those days!

20 Pray that your flight may not be in winter or on a Sabbath,

21 For then there will be great tribulation—affliction, distress and oppression—such as has not been from the beginning of the world until now; no, and never will be [again]. [Dan. 12:1; Joel 2:2.]

22 And if those days had not been shortened, no human being would endure *and* survive; but for the sake of the elect (God's chosen ones) those days will be shortened.

23 If any one says to you then, Lo, here is Christ, the Messiah! or, There He is! do not believe it.

24 For false Christs and false prophets will arise, and they will show great signs and wonders, so as to deceive *and* lead astray, if possible, even the elect (God's chosen ones).

25 See, I have warned you beforehand.

26 So if they say to you, Lo, He is in the wilderness (desert), do not go out there; if they tell you, Lo, He is in the secret places *or* inner rooms, do not believe it.

27 For just as the lightning flashes from the east and shines *and* [t]is seen as far as the west, so will the coming of the Son of man be.

28 Wherever there is a fallen body (a corpse), there the vultures (or eagles) will flock together. [Job 39:30.]

29 Immediately after the tribulation of those days the sun will be darkened, and the moon will not shed her light, and the stars will fall from the sky, and the powers of the heavens will be shaken. [Isa. 13:10; 34:4; Joel 2:10, 11; Zeph. 1:15.]

30 Then the sign of the Son of man will appear in the sky, and then all the tribes of the earth will mourn *and* [t]beat their breasts *and* lament in anguish, and they will see the Son of man coming on the clouds of heaven with power and great glory—in brilliancy and splendor. [Dan. 7:13.]

31 And He will send out His angels with a loud trumpet call, and they will gather His elect [His chosen ones] from the four winds, [even] from one end of the [u]universe to the other. [Isa. 27:13; Zech. 9:14.]

32 From the fig tree learn its lesson: as soon as its [t]young shoots become soft and tender and it puts out its leaves, you know [v]of a surety that summer is near.

33 So also when you see these signs [v]all taken together coming to pass, you may know [v]of a surety that He is near, at the very doors.

34 Truly, I tell you, this generation—that is, [v]the whole multitude of people living at the same time, [w]in a definite, [x]given period—will not pass away till all these things [y]taken together take place.

35 [z]Sky and earth will pass away, but My words will not pass away.

36 But of that [exact] day and hour no one knows, not even the angels of heaven, nor the Son, but only the Father.

37 As were the days of Noah, so will be the coming of the Son of man.

38 For just as in those days before the flood they were eating and drinking, [men] marrying and [women] being given in marriage, until the [very] day when Noah went into the ark,

39 And they did not know *or* understand until the flood came and swept them all away, so will be the coming of the Son of man. [Gen. 6:5-8; 7:6-24.]

40 At that time two men will be in the field; one will be taken and one will be left.

---

t) Vincent.
u) Abbott-Smith.
v) Thayer.
w) Cremer.
x) Abbott-Smith.
y) Thayer.
z) Moulton and Milligan.

Living New Testament

19 And woe to pregnant women and to those with babies in those days.

20 And pray that your flight will not be in winter, or on the Sabbath.[6]

21 For there will be persecution such as the world has never before seen in all its history, and will never see again.

22 In fact, unless those days are shortened, all mankind will perish. But they will be shortened for the sake of God's chosen[7] people.

23 Then if anyone tells you, 'The Messiah has arrived at such and such a place, or has appeared here or there, or in the village yonder,' don't believe it.

24 For false Christs shall arise, and false prophets, and will do wonderful miracles, so that if it were possible, even God's chosen[7] ones would be deceived.

25 See, I have warned you.

26 So if someone tells you the Messiah has returned and is out in the desert, don't bother to go and look. Or, that He is hiding at a certain place, don't believe it!

27 For as the lightning flashes across the sky from east to west, so shall My coming be, when I, the Son of all Mankind, return.

28 And wherever the carcass is, there the vultures will gather.

29 Immediately after the persecution of those days the sun will be darkened, and the moon will turn black, and the stars will seem[8] to fall from the heavens, and the powers overshadowing the earth will be convulsed.[9]

30 And then at last[10] the signal of My coming will appear in the heavens and there will be deep mourning all around the earth. And the nations of the world will see Me arrive in the clouds of heaven, with power and great glory.

31 And I shall send forth My angels with the sound of a mighty trumpet blast, and they shall gather My chosen ones from the farthest ends of the earth and heaven.[11]

32 Now learn a lesson from the fig tree. When her branch is tender and the leaves begin to sprout, you know that summer is almost here.

33 Just so, when you see all these things beginning to happen, you can know that My[12] return is near, even at the doors.

34 Then at last this age will come to its close.

35 Heaven and earth will disappear, but My words remain forever.

36 But no one knows the date and hour when the end will be—not even the angels. No, nor even God's Son.[13] Only the Father knows.

37, 38 The world will be at ease[14]—banquets and parties and weddings—just as it was in Noah's time before the sudden coming of the flood;

39 People wouldn't believe[15] what was going to happen until the flood actually arrived and took them all away. So shall My coming be.

40 Two men will be working together in the fields, and one will be taken, the other left.

[6]The city gates were to be closed on the Sabbath.
[7]Literally, "the elect."
[8]Literally, "the stars shall fall from heaven."
[9]Literally, "the powers of the heavens shall be shaken." See Eph. 6:12.
[10]Literally, "of the coming of the Son of man."
[11]"From the four winds, from one end of heaven to the other."
[12]Literally, "He is nigh."
[13]Literally, "neither the Son." Many ancient manuscripts omit this phrase.
[14]Implied.
[15]Literally, "knew not."

Revised Standard

19 And alas for those who are with child and
for those who give suck in those days!
20 Pray that your flight may not be in winter
or on a sabbath. 21 For then there will be
great tribulation, such as has not been from
the beginning of the world until now, no,
and never will be. 22 And if those days had
not been shortened, no human being would
be saved; but for the sake of the elect those
days will be shortened. 23 Then if any one
says to you, 'Lo, here is the Christ!' or
'There he is!' do not believe it. 24 For false
Christs and false prophets will arise and
show great signs and wonders, so as to
lead astray, if possible, even the elect. 25 Lo,
I have told you beforehand. 26 So, if they
say to you, 'Lo, he is in the wilderness,'
do not go out; if they say, 'Lo, he is in
the inner rooms,' do not believe it. 27 For
as the lightning comes from the east and
shines as far as the west, so will be the
coming of the Son of man. 28 Wherever the
body is, there the eagles[z] will be gathered
together.

The coming of the Son of man

29 "Immediately after the tribulation of
those days the sun will be darkened, and
the moon will not give its light, and the
stars will fall from heaven, and the powers
of the heavens will be shaken; 30 then will
appear the sign of the Son of man in heav-
en, and then all the tribes of the earth will
mourn, and they will see the Son of man
coming on the clouds of heaven with power
and great glory; 31 and he will send out his
angels with a loud trumpet call, and they
will gather his elect from the four winds,
from one end of heaven to the other.

Signs of the end

32 "From the fig tree learn its lesson:
as soon as its branch becomes tender and
puts forth its leaves, you know that summer
is near. 33 So also, when you see all these
things, you know that he is near, at the
very gates. 34 Truly, I say to you, this generation will not pass away till all things
take place. 35 Heaven and earth will pass
away, but my words will not pass away.
36 "But of that day and hour no one
knows, not even the angels of heaven, nor
the Son,[a] but the Father only. 37 As were
the days of Noah, so will be the coming of
the Son of man. 38 For as in those days
before the flood they were eating and
drinking, marrying and giving in marriage,
until the day when Noah entered the ark,
39 and they did not know until the flood
came and swept them all away, so will be
the coming of the Son of man. 40 Then two

[z] Or *vultures*
[a] Other ancient authorities omit *nor the Son*

King James

41 Two *women shall be* grinding at the mill; the one shall be taken, and the other left.

42 ¶ Watch therefore: for ye know not what hour your Lord doth come.

43 But know this, that if the goodman of the house had known in what watch the thief would come, he would have watched, and would not have suffered his house to be broken up.

44 Therefore be ye also ready: for in such an hour as ye think not the Son of man cometh.

45 Who then is a faithful and wise servant, whom his lord hath made ruler over his household, to give them meat in due season?

46 Blessed *is* that servant, whom his lord when he cometh shall find so doing.

47 Verily I say unto you, That he shall make him ruler over all his goods.

48 But and if that evil servant shall say in his heart, My lord delayeth his coming;

49 And shall begin to smite *his* fellowservants, and to eat and drink with the drunken;

50 The lord of that servant shall come in a day when he looketh not for *him*, and in an hour that he is not aware of,

51 And shall cut him asunder, and appoint *him* his portion with the hypocrites: there shall be weeping and gnashing of teeth.

Amplified

41 Two women will be grinding at the hand mill; one will be taken and one will be left.

42 Watch, therefore—[y]give strict attention, be cautious and active—for you do not know in what kind of a day [[a]whether a near or remote one] your Lord is coming.

43 But understand this: that had the householder known in what [part of the night, whether in [a]night or a morning] watch the thief was coming, he would have watched and would not have allowed his house to be [b]undermined *and* broken through.

44 You also must be ready therefore; for the Son of man is coming at an hour when you do not expect Him.

45 Who then is the faithful, thoughtful *and* wise servant, whom his master has put in charge of his household, to give to the others the food *and* supplies at the proper time?

46 Blessed—happy, fortunate and [c]to be envied—is that servant whom when his master comes he will find so doing.

47 I solemnly declare to you, he will set him over all his possessions.

48 But if that servant is wicked and says to himself, My master is delayed *and* is going to be gone a long time,

49 And begins to beat his fellow servants, and to eat and drink with the drunken,

50 The master of that servant will come on a day when he does not expect him and at an hour of which he is not aware,

51 And will punish him—[d]cut him up [by scourging]—and put him with the pretenders (hypocrites); there will be weeping and grinding of teeth.

CHAPTER 25

THEN shall the kingdom of heaven be likened unto ten virgins, which took their lamps, and went forth to meet the bridegroom.

2 And five of them were wise, and five *were* foolish.

3 They that *were* foolish took their lamps, and took no oil with them:

4 But the wise took oil in their vessels with their lamps.

5 While the bridegroom tarried, they all slumbered and slept.

6 And at midnight there was a cry made, Behold, the bridegroom cometh; go ye out to meet him.

7 Then all those virgins arose, and trimmed their lamps.

8 And the foolish said unto the wise, Give us of your oil; for our lamps are gone out.

9 But the wise answered, saying, *Not so;* lest there be not enough for us and you: but go ye rather to them that sell, and buy for yourselves.

10 And while they went to buy, the bridegroom came; and they that were ready went in with him to the marriage: and the door was shut.

11 Afterward came also the other virgins, saying, Lord, Lord, open to us.

CHAPTER 25

THEN the kingdom of heaven shall be likened to ten virgins who took their lamps and went to meet the bridegroom.

2 Five of them were foolish—thoughtless, without forethought; and five were wise—sensible, intelligent and prudent.

3 For when the foolish took their lamps, they did not take any [extra] oil with them;

4 But the wise took flasks of oil along with them [also] with their lamps.

5 While the bridegroom lingered *and* was slow in coming, they all began nodding their heads and fell asleep.

6 But at midnight there was a shout, Behold, the bridegroom! Go out to meet him!

7 Then all those virgins got up and put their own lamps in order.

8 And the foolish said to the wise, Give us some of your oil, for our lamps are going out.

9 But the wise replied, There will not be enough for us and for you; go instead to the dealers and buy for yourselves.

10 But while they were gone away to buy, the bridegroom came, and those who were prepared went in with him to the marriage feast; and the door was shut.

11 Later the other virgins also came, and said, Lord, Lord, open [the door] to us!

---

y) Thayer.
a) Vincent.
b) Wycliffe.
c) Souter.
d) Thayer.

Living New Testament

41 Two women will be going about their household tasks; one will be taken, the other left.

42 So be prepared, for you don't know what day your Lord is coming.

43 Just as a man can prevent trouble from thieves by keeping watch for them,

44 So you can avoid trouble by always being ready for My unannounced return.

45 Are you a wise and faithful servant of the Lord? Have I given you the task of managing My household, to feed My children day by day?

46 Blessings on you if I return and find you faithfully doing your work.

47 I will put such faithful ones in charge of everything I own!

48 But if you are evil and say to yourself, 'My Lord won't be coming for awhile,'

49 And begin oppressing your fellow servants, partying and getting drunk,

50 Your Lord will arrive unannounced and unexpected,

51 And severely whip you and send you off to the judgment of the hypocrites; there will be weeping and gnashing of teeth.

Revised Standard

men will be in the field; one is taken and one is left. 41 Two women will be grinding at the mill; one is taken and one is left. 42 Watch therefore, for you do not know on what day your Lord is coming. 43 But know this, that if the householder had known in what part of the night the thief was coming, he would have watched and would not have let his house be broken into. 44 Therefore you also must be ready; for the Son of man is coming at an hour you do not expect.

Faithful and unfaithful servants

45 "Who then is the faithful and wise servant, whom his master has set over his household, to give them their food at the proper time? 46 Blessed is that servant whom his master when he comes will find so doing. 47 Truly, I say to you, he will set him over all his possessions. 48 But if that wicked servant says to himself, 'My master is delayed,' 49 and begins to beat his fellow servants, and eats and drinks with the drunken, 50 the master of that servant will come on a day when he does not expect him and at an hour he does not know, 51 and will punish[b] him, and put him with the hypocrites; there men will weep and gnash their teeth.

CHAPTER 25

The Kingdom of Heaven can be illustrated by the story of ten bridesmaids[1] who took their lamps and went to meet the bridegroom.

2, 3, 4 But only five of them were wise enough to fill their lamps with oil, while the other five were foolish and forgot.

5, 6 So, when the bridegroom was delayed, they lay down to rest until midnight, when they were roused by the shout, 'The bridegroom is coming! Come out and welcome him!'

7, 8 All the girls jumped up and trimmed their lamps.

Then the five who hadn't any oil begged the others to share with them, for their lamps were going out.

9 But the others replied, 'We haven't enough. Go instead to the shops and buy some for yourselves.'

10 But while they were gone, the bridegroom came, and those who were ready went in with him to the marriage feast, and the door was locked.

11 Later, when the other five returned, they stood outside, calling, 'Sir, open the door for us!'

The parable of the ten maidens

25 "Then the kingdom of heaven shall be compared to ten maidens who took their lamps and went to meet the bridegroom.[c] 2 Five of them were foolish, and five were wise. 3 For when the foolish took their lamps, they took no oil with them; 4 but the wise took flasks of oil with their lamps. 5 As the bridegroom was delayed, they all slumbered and slept. 6 But at midnight there was a cry, 'Behold, the bridegroom! Come out to meet him.' 7 Then all those maidens rose and trimmed their lamps. 8 And the foolish said to the wise, 'Give us some of your oil, for our lamps are going out.' 9 But the wise replied, 'Perhaps there will not be enough for us and for you; go rather to the dealers and buy for yourselves.' 10 And while they went to buy, the bridegroom came, and those who were ready went in with him to the marriage feast; and the door was shut. 11 Afterward the other maidens came also, saying, 'Lord, lord, open to us.' 12 But he

[1]Literally, "virgins."

[b] Or *cut him in pieces*
[c] Other ancient authorities add *and the bride*

King James

12 But he answered and said, Verily I say unto you, I know you not.

13 Watch therefore, for ye know neither the day nor the hour wherein the Son of man cometh.

14 ¶ For *the kingdom of heaven is* as a man travelling into a far country, *who* called his own servants, and delivered unto them his goods.

15 And unto one he gave five talents, to another two, and to another one; to every man according to his several ability; and straightway took his journey.

16 Then he that had received the five talents went and traded with the same, and made *them* other five talents.

17 And likewise he that *had received* two, he also gained other two.

18 But he that had received one went and digged in the earth, and hid his lord's money.

19 After a long time the lord of those servants cometh, and reckoneth with them.

20 And so he that had received five talents came and brought other five talents, saying, Lord, thou deliveredst unto me five talents: behold, I have gained beside them five talents more.

21 His lord said unto him, Well done, *thou* good and faithful servant: thou hast been faithful over a few things, I will make thee ruler over many things: enter thou into the joy of thy lord.

22 He also that had received two talents came and said, Lord, thou deliveredst unto me two talents: behold, I have gained two other talents beside them.

23 His lord said unto him, Well done, good and faithful servant; thou hast been faithful over a few things, I will make thee ruler over many things: enter thou into the joy of thy lord.

24 Then he which had received the one talent came and said, Lord, I knew thee that thou art an hard man, reaping where thou hast not sown, and gathering where thou hast not strawed:

25 And I was afraid, and went and hid thy talent in the earth: lo, *there* thou hast *that is* thine.

26 His lord answered and said unto him, *Thou* wicked and slothful servant, thou knewest that I reap where I sowed not, and gather where I have not strawed:

27 Thou oughtest therefore to have put my money to the exchangers, and *then* at my coming I should have received mine own with usury.

28 Take therefore the talent from him, and give *it* unto him which hath ten talents.

29 For unto every one that hath shall be given, and he shall have abundance: but from him that hath not shall be taken away even that which he hath.

30 And cast ye the unprofitable servant into outer darkness: there shall be weeping and gnashing of teeth.

31 ¶ When the Son of man shall come in his glory, and all the holy angels with him, then shall he sit upon the throne of his glory:

Amplified

12 But He replied, I solemnly declare to you, I do not know you—I am not acquainted with you.

13 Watch therefore—give strict attention and be cautious and active—for you know neither the day nor the hour *when the Son of man will come.*

14 For it is as a man who was about to take a long journey, and he called his servants together and entrusted them with his property.

15 To one he gave five talents [probably about $5,000], to another two, to another one; to each in proportion to his own [e]personal ability. Then he departed *and* left the country.

16 He who had received the five talents went at once and traded with them, and he gained five talents more.

17 And likewise he who had received the two talents; he also gained two talents more.

18 But he who had received the one talent went and dug a hole in the ground and hid his master's money.

19 Now after a long time the master of those servants returned and settled accounts with them.

20 And he who had received the five talents came and brought him five more, saying, Master, you entrusted to me five talents; see, here I have gained five talents more.

21 His master said to him, Well done, you upright (honorable, [f]admirable) and faithful servant! You have been faithful *and* trustworthy over a little; I will put you in charge of much. Enter into *and* share the joy—the delight, the [d]blessedness—which your master [enjoys].

22 And he also who had the two talents came forward, saying, Master, you entrusted two talents to me; here I have gained two talents more.

23 His master said to him, Well done, you upright (honorable, [f]admirable) and faithful servant! You have been faithful *and* trustworthy over a little; I will put you in charge of much. Enter into *and* share the joy—the delight, the [g]blessedness—which your master [enjoys].

24 He who had received one talent also came forward, saying, Master, I knew you to be a harsh *and* hard man, reaping where you did not sow, and gathering where you had not winnowed [the grain];

25 So I was afraid, and I went and hid your talent in the ground. Here you have what is your own.

26 But his master answered him, You wicked *and* lazy *and* idle servant! Did you indeed know that I reap where I have not sowed, and gather grain where I have not winnowed?

27 Then you should have invested my money with the bankers, and at my coming I could have received what was my own with interest.

28 So take the talent away from him, and give it to the one who has the ten talents.

29 For to every one who has will more be given, and he will be [h]furnished richly so that he will have abundance.

30 And throw the good-for-nothing servant into the outer darkness; there will be weeping and grinding of teeth.

31 When the Son of man comes in His glory (His majesty and splendor) and all the *holy* angels with Him, then He will sit on the throne of His glory.

---

d) Thayer.
e) Vincent.
f) Cremer.
g) Thayer.
h) Thayer.

Living New Testament

12 But he called back, 'Go away! It is too late!'[2]

13 So stay awake and be prepared, for you do not know the date or moment of My return.[3]

14 Again, the Kingdom of Heaven can be illustrated by the story of a man going into another country, who called together his servants and loaned them money to invest for him while he was gone.

15 He gave $5,000 to one, $2,000 to another, and $1,000 to the last—dividing it in proportion to their abilities—and then left on his trip.

16 The man who received the $5,000 began immediately to buy and sell with it and soon earned another $5,000.

17 The man with $2,000 went right to work, too, and earned another $2,000.

18 But the man who received the $1,000 dug a hole in the ground and hid the money for safekeeping.

19 After a long time their master returned from his trip and called them to him to account for his money.

20 The man to whom he had entrusted the $5,000 brought him $10,000.

21 His master praised him for good work. 'You have been faithful in handling this small amount,' he told him, 'so now I will give you many more responsibilities. Begin the joyous tasks I have assigned to you.'

22 Next came the man who had received the $2,000, with the report, 'Sir, you gave me $2,000 to use, and I have doubled it.'

23 'Good work,' his Master said, 'You are a good and faithful servant. You have been faithful over this small amount, so now I will give you much more.'

24, 25 Then the man with the $1,000 came and said, 'Sir, I knew you were a hard man, and I was afraid you would rob me of what I earned,[4] so I hid your money in the earth and here it is!'

26 But his master replied, 'Wicked man! Lazy slave! Since you knew I would demand your profit,

27 You should at least have put my money into the bank so I could have some interest.

28 Take the money from this man and give it to the man with the $10,000.

29 For the man who uses well what he is given shall be given more, and he shall have abundance. But from the man who is unfaithful, even what little responsibility he has shall be taken from him.

30 And throw the useless[5] servant out into outer darkness: there shall be weeping and gnashing of teeth.'

31 But when I, the Son of Mankind, shall come in My glory, and all the angels with Me, then I shall sit upon My throne of glory.

[2]Literally, "I know you not!"
[3]Implied.
[4]Literally, "reaping where you didn't sow, and gathering where you didn't scatter, and I was afraid . . ."
[5]Literally, "unprofitable servant."

Revised Standard

replied, 'Truly, I say to you, I do not know
you.' 13 Watch therefore, for you know
neither the day nor the hour.

The parable of the talents

14 "For it will be as when a man going
on a journey called his servants and entrusted to them his property; 15 to one he gave
five talents,[d] to another two, to another one,
to each according to his ability. Then he
went away. 16 He who had received the five
talents went at once and traded with them;
and he made five talents more. 17 So also,
he who had the two talents made two
talents more. 18 But he who had received
the one talent went and dug in the ground
and hid his master's money. 19 Now after
a long time the master of those servants
came and settled accounts with them. 20 And
he who had received the five talents came
forward, bringing five talents more, saying, 'Master, you delivered to me five talents; here I have made five talents more.'
21 His master said to him, 'Well done, good
and faithful servant; you have been faithful
over a little, I will set you over much; enter
into the joy of your master.' 22 And he also
who had the two talents came forward, saying, 'Master, you delivered to me two
talents; here I have made two talents more.'
23 His master said to him, 'Well done, good
and faithful servant; you have been faithful
over a little, I will set you over much;
enter into the joy of your master.' 24 He
also who had received the one talent came
forward, saying, 'Master, I knew you to be
a hard man, reaping where you did not
sow, and gathering where you did not winnow; 25 so I was afraid, and I went and
hid your talent in the ground. Here you
have what is yours.' 26 But his master answered him, 'You wicked and slothful servant! You knew that I reap where I have
not sowed, and gather where I have not
winnowed? 27 Then you ought to have invested my money with the bankers, and at
my coming I should have received what
was my own with interest. 28 So take the
talent from him, and give it to him who
has the ten talents. 29 For to every one who
has will more be given, and he will have
abundance; but from him who has not,
even what he has will be taken away.
30 And cast the worthless servant into the
outer darkness; there men will weep and
gnash their teeth.'

The judgment

31 "When the Son of man comes in his
glory, and all the angels with him, then he
will sit on his glorious throne. 32 Before

[d] This talent was probably worth about a thousand dollars.

King James

32 And before him shall be gathered all nations: and he shall separate them one from another, as a shepherd divideth *his* sheep from the goats:

33 And he shall set the sheep on his right hand, but the goats on the left.

34 Then shall the King say unto them on his right hand, Come, ye blessed of my Father, inherit the kingdom prepared for you from the foundation of the world:

35 For I was an hungered, and ye gave me meat: I was thirsty, and ye gave me drink: I was a stranger, and ye took me in:

36 Naked, and ye clothed me: I was sick, and ye visited me: I was in prison, and ye came unto me.

37 Then shall the righteous answer him, saying, Lord, when saw we thee an hungered, and fed *thee?* or thirsty, and gave *thee* drink?

38 When saw we thee a stranger, and took *thee* in? or naked, and clothed *thee?*

39 Or when saw we thee sick, or in prison, and came unto thee?

40 And the King shall answer and say unto them, Verily I say unto you, Inasmuch as ye have done *it* unto one of the least of these my brethren, ye have done *it* unto me.

41 Then shall he say also unto them on the left hand, Depart from me, ye cursed, into everlasting fire, prepared for the devil and his angels:

42 For I was an hungered, and ye gave me no meat: I was thirsty, and ye gave me no drink:

43 I was a stranger, and ye took me not in: naked, and ye clothed me not: sick, and in prison, and ye visited me not.

44 Then shall they also answer him, saying, Lord, when saw we thee an hungered, or athirst, or a stranger, or naked, or sick, or in prison, and did not minister unto thee?

45 Then shall he answer them, saying, Verily I say unto you, Inasmuch as ye did *it* not to one of the least of these, ye did *it* not to me.

46 And these shall go away into everlasting punishment: but the righteous into life eternal.

Amplified

32 All nations shall be gathered before Him, and He will separate [the people] them from one another as a shepherd separates his sheep from the goats, [Ezek. 34:17.]

33 And He will cause the sheep to stand at His right hand, but the goats at His left.

34 Then the King will say to those at His right hand, Come, you blessed of My Father [that is, you [i]favored of God and appointed to eternal salvation], inherit—receive as your own—the kingdom prepared for you from the foundation of the world.

35 For I was hungry and you gave Me food; I was thirsty and you gave Me something to drink; I was a stranger and you [j]brought Me together with yourselves *and* welcomed *and* entertained *and* [k]lodged Me;

36 I was naked and you clothed Me; I was sick and you visited Me [l]with help *and* ministering care; I was in prison and you came to see Me. [Isa. 58:7.]

37 Then the just *and* upright will answer Him, Lord, when did we see You hungry and gave You food, or thirsty and gave You something to drink?

38 And when did we see You a stranger and welcomed *and* entertained You, or naked and clothed You?

39 And when did we see You sick or in prison and came to visit You?

40 And the King will reply to them, Truly, I tell you, in as far as you did it to one of the least [[l]in the estimation of men] of these My brethren, you did it to Me. [Prov. 19:17.]

41 Then He will say to those at His left hand, Be gone from Me, you cursed, into the eternal fire prepared for the devil and his angels!

42 For I was hungry and you gave Me no food; I was thirsty and you gave Me nothing to drink;

43 I was a stranger and you did not welcome Me *and* entertain Me; I was naked and you did not clothe Me; I was sick and in prison and you did not visit Me [l]with help *and* ministering care.

44 Then they also [in their turn] will answer, Lord, when did we see You hungry or thirsty or a stranger or naked or sick or in prison, and did not minister to You?

45 And He will reply to them, Solemnly I declare to you, in so far as you failed to do it for the least of these [[m]in the estimation of men] you failed to do it for Me.

46 Then they will go away into eternal punishment, but those who are just *and* upright *and* in right standing with God into eternal life. [Dan. 12:2.]

King James

CHAPTER 26

AND it came to pass, when Jesus had finished all these sayings, he said unto his disciples,

2 Ye know that after two days is *the feast of* the passover, and the Son of man is betrayed to be crucified.

3 Then assembled together the chief priests, and the scribes, and the elders of the people, unto the palace of the high priest, who was called Caiaphas,

4 And consulted that they might take Jesus by subtilty, and kill *him*.

Amplified

CHAPTER 26

WHEN Jesus had ended this discourse, He said to His disciples,

2 You know that the Passover is in two days, and the Son of man will be delivered up [m]treacherously to be crucified.

3 Then the chief priests and the elders of the people gathered in the [[n]open] court of the palace of the high priest, whose name was Caiaphas,

i) Thayer.
j) Literal meaning.
k) Tyndale.
l) Wuest's "Treasures from the Greek New Testament."
m) Thayer.
n) Vincent.

Living New Testament

32 And all the nations shall be gathered before Me. And I will separate the people[6] as a shepherd separates the sheep from the goats,

33 And place the sheep at My right hand, and the goats at My left.

34 Then I, the King, shall say to those at My right, 'Come, blessed of My Father, into the Kingdom prepared for you from the founding of the world.

35 For I was hungry and you fed Me; I was thirsty and you gave Me water; I was a stranger and you invited Me into your homes;

36 Naked and you clothed Me; sick and in prison, and you visited Me.'

37 Then these righteous ones will reply, 'Sir, when did we ever see you hungry and feed You? Or thirsty and give You anything to drink?

38 Or a stranger, and help You? Or naked, and clothe You?

39 When did we ever see You sick or in prison, and visit You?'

40 And I, the King, will tell them, 'When you did it to these My brothers you were doing it to Me!'

41 Then I will turn to those on My left and say, 'Away with you, you cursed ones, into the eternal fire prepared for the devil and his demons.

42 For I was hungry and you wouldn't feed Me; thirsty, and you wouldn't give Me anything to drink;

43 A stranger, and you refused Me hospitality; naked, and you wouldn't clothe Me; sick, and in prison, and you didn't visit Me.'

44 Then they will reply, 'Lord, when did we ever see You hungry or thirsty or a stranger or naked or sick or in prison, and not help You?'

45 And I will answer, 'When you refused to help the least of these My brothers, you were refusing help to Me.'

46 And they shall go away into eternal punishment; but the righteous into everlasting life."

Revised Standard

him will be gathered all the nations, and
he will separate them one from another as
a shepherd separates the sheep from the
goats, 33and he will place the sheep at his
right hand, but the goats at the left. 34Then
the King will say to those at his right hand,
'Come, O blessed of my Father, inherit the
kingdom prepared for you from the foundation of the world; 35for I was hungry and
you gave me food, I was thirsty and you
gave me drink, I was a stranger and you
welcomed me, 36I was naked and you
clothed me, I was sick and you visited me,
I was in prison and you came to me.' 37Then
the righteous will answer him, 'Lord, when
did we see thee hungry and feed thee, or
thirsty and give thee drink? 38And when
did we see thee a stranger and welcome
thee, or naked and clothe thee? 39And
when did we see thee sick or in prison and
visit thee?' 40And the King will answer
them, 'Truly, I say to you, as you did it to
one of the least of these my brethren, you
did it to me.' 41Then he will say to those
at his left hand, 'Depart from me, you
cursed, into the eternal fire prepared for
the devil and his angels; 42for I was hungry
and you gave me no food, I was thirsty and
you gave me no drink, 43I was a stranger
and you did not welcome me, naked and
you did not clothe me, sick and in prison
and you did not visit me.' 44Then they also
will answer, 'Lord, when did we see thee
hungry or thirsty or a stranger or naked or
sick or in prison, and did not minister to
thee?' 45Then he will answer them, 'Truly,
I say to you, as you did it not to one of
the least of these, you did it not to me.'
46And they will go away into eternal punishment, but the righteous into eternal life."

CHAPTER 26

When Jesus had finished this talk with His disciples, He told them,

2 "As you know, the Passover celebration begins in two days, and I[1] shall be betrayed and crucified."

3 At that very moment the chief priests and other Jewish officials were meeting at the residence of Caiaphas the High Priest,

The plot to kill Jesus

26 When Jesus had finished all these
sayings, he said to his disciples,
2"You know that after two days the Passover is coming, and the Son of man will
be delivered up to be crucified."

3 Then the chief priests and the elders
of the people gathered in the palace of the
high priest, who was called Caiaphas, 4and

[6]Or, "separate the nations."
[1]Literally, "The Son of man."

King James

5 But they said, Not on the feast *day*, lest there be an uproar among the people.

6 ¶ Now when Jesus was in Bethany, in the house of Simon the leper,

7 There came unto him a woman having an alabaster box of very precious ointment, and poured in on his head, as he sat *at meat*.

8 But when his disciples saw *it*, they had indignation, saying, To what purpose *is* this waste?

9 For this ointment might have been sold for much, and given to the poor.

10 When Jesus understood it, he said unto them, Why trouble ye the woman? for she hath wrought a good work upon me.

11 For ye have the poor always with you; but me ye have not always.

12 For in that she hath poured this ointment on my body, she did *it* for my burial.

13 Verily I say unto you, Wheresoever this gospel shall be preached in the whole world, *there* shall also this, that this woman hath done, be told for a memorial of her.

14 ¶ Then one of the twelve, called Judas Iscariot, went unto the chief priests,

15 And said *unto them*, What will ye give me, and I will deliver him unto you? And they covenanted with him for thirty pieces of silver.

16 And from that time he sought opportunity to betray him.

17 ¶ Now the first *day* of the *feast of* unleavened bread the disciples came to Jesus, saying unto him, Where wilt thou that we prepare for thee to eat the passover?

18 And he said, Go into the city to such a man, and say unto him, The Master saith, My time is at hand; I will keep the passover at thy house with my disciples.

19 And the disciples did as Jesus had appointed them; and they made ready the passover.

20 Now when the even was come, he sat down with the twelve.

21 And as they did eat, he said, Verily I say unto you, that one of you shall betray me.

22 And they were exceeding sorrowful, and began every one of them to say unto him, Lord, is it I?

23 And he answered and said, He that dippeth *his* hand with me in the dish, the same shall betray me.

24 The Son of man goeth as it is written of him: but woe unto that man by whom the Son of man is betrayed! it had been good for that man if he had not been born.

25 Then Judas, which betrayed him, answered and said, Master, is it I? He said unto him, Thou hast said.

26 ¶ And as they were eating, Jesus took bread, and blessed it, and brake it, and gave *it* to the disciples, and said, Take, eat; this is my body.

27 And he took the cup, and gave thanks, and gave *it* to them, saying, Drink ye all of it;

28 For this is my blood of the new testament, which is shed for many for the remission of sins.

Amplified

4 And consulted together in order to arrest Jesus by stratagem secretly, and put Him to death.

5 But they said, It must not be during the feast, for fear there will be a riot among the people.

6 Now when Jesus came back to Bethany and was in the house of Simon the leper,

7 A woman came up to Him with an alabaster flask of very precious perfume, and she poured it on His head as He reclined at table.

8 And when the disciples saw it, they were indignant, saying, For what purpose is all this waste?

9 For this perfume might have been sold for a large sum, and the money given to the poor.

10 But Jesus, fully aware of this, said to them, Why do you bother the woman? She has done a noble (praiseworthy and beautiful) thing to Me.

11 For you always have the poor among you, but you will not always have Me. [Deut. 15:11.]

12 In pouring this perfume on My body she has done something to prepare Me for My burial.

13 Truly, I tell you, wherever this good news (the Gospel) is preached in the whole world, what this woman has done will be told also in memory of her.

14 Then one of the twelve [apostles], who was called Judas Iscariot, went to the chief priests

15 And said, What are you willing to give me if I hand Him over to you? And they weighed out *and* paid him thirty pieces of silver [about twenty-one dollars and sixty cents]. [Exod. 21:32; Zech. 11:12.]

16 And from that moment he sought for a fitting opportunity to betray Him.

17 Now on the first day of Unleavened Bread [Passover week], the disciples came to Jesus and said *to Him*, Where do You wish us to prepare for You to eat the passover supper?

18 He said, Go into the city to a certain man, and say to him, The Master says, My time is near; I will keep the passover at your house with My disciples.

19 And accordingly the disciples did as Jesus had directed them, and they made ready the passover supper. [Deut. 16:5-8.]

20 When it was evening, He was reclining at table with the twelve disciples;

21 And as they were eating He said, Solemnly I say to you, one of you will betray Me!

22 They were exceedingly pained *and* distressed *and* deeply hurt *and* sorrowful, and began to say to Him one after another, [o]Surely, it cannot be I, Lord, can it?

23 He replied, He who has [just] dipped his hand in the same dish with Me will betray Me!

24 The Son of man is going as it is written of Him, but woe to that man by whom the Son of man is betrayed! It would have been better (more profitable and wholesome) for that man if he had never been born! [Ps. 41:9.]

25 Judas, the betrayer, said, [o]Surely, it is not I, is it, Master? He said to him, You have stated [the fact].

26 Now as they were eating, Jesus took a loaf of bread, and [p]praising God gave thanks *and* asked Him to bless it to their use, and when He had broken it He gave it to the disciples and said, Take, eat; this is My body.

27 And He took a cup, and when He had given thanks He gave it to them, saying, Drink of it, all of you;

28 For this is My blood of the *new* covenant, which [[p]ratifies the agreement and] is [o]being poured out for many for the forgiveness of sins. [Exod. 24:6-8.]

---

o) Vincent.
p) Thayer.

Living New Testament

4 To discuss ways of capturing Jesus quietly, and killing Him.

5 "But not during the Passover celebration," they agreed, "for there would be a riot."

6 Jesus now proceeded to Bethany, to the home of Simon the leper.

7 While He was eating, a woman came in with a bottle of very expensive perfume, and poured it over His head.

8, 9 The disciples were indignant. "What a waste of good money," they said. "Why, she could have sold it for a fortune and given it to the poor."

10 Jesus knew what they were thinking, and said, "Why are you criticizing her? For she has done a good thing to Me.

11 You will always have the poor among you, but you won't always have Me.

12 She has poured this perfume on Me to prepare My body for burial.

13 And she will always be remembered for this deed. The story of what she has done will be told throughout the whole world, wherever the Good News is preached."

14 Then, Judas Iscariot, one of the twelve apostles, went to the chief priests,

15 And asked, "How much will you pay me to get Jesus into your hands?" And they gave him thirty silver coins.

16 From that time on, Judas watched for an opportunity to betray Jesus to them.

17 On the first day of the Passover ceremonies, when bread made with yeast was purged from every Jewish home, the disciples came to Jesus and asked, "Where shall we plan to eat the Passover?"

18 He replied, "Go into the city and see Mr. So-and-So, and tell him, 'Our Master says, My time has come, and I will eat the Passover meal with My disciples at your house.' "

19 So the disciples did as He told them, and prepared the supper there.

20, 21 That evening as He sat eating with the Twelve He said, "One of you will betray Me."

22 Sorrow chilled their hearts, and each one asked, "Am I the one?"

23 He replied, "It is the one I served first.[2]

24 For I must die[3] just as was prophesied, but woe to the man by whom I am betrayed. Far better for that one if he had never been born."

25 Judas, too, had asked him, "Rabbi, am I the one?" And Jesus had told him, "Yes."

26 As they were eating, Jesus took a small loaf of bread and blessed it and broke it apart and gave it to the disciples and said, "Take it and eat it, for this is My body."

27 And He took a cup of wine and gave thanks for it and gave it to them and said, "Each one drink from it,

28 For this is My blood, sealing the new covenant. It is poured out to forgive the sins of multitudes.

[2]Literally, "he that dipped his hand with me in the dish."
[3]Literally, "the Son of man goes."

Revised Standard

took counsel together in order to arrest
Jesus by stealth and kill him. 5But they
said, "Not during the feast, lest there be a
tumult among the people."

Anointing of Jesus at Bethany

6 Now when Jesus was at Bethany in
the house of Simon the leper, 7a woman
came up to him with an alabaster jar of
very expensive ointment, and she poured it
on his head, as he sat at table. 8But when
the disciples saw it, they were indignant,
saying, "Why this waste? 9For this ointment
might have been sold for a large sum, and
given to the poor." 10But Jesus, aware of
this, said to them, "Why do you trouble the
woman? For she has done a beautiful thing
to me. 11For you always have the poor
with you, but you will not always have me.
12In pouring this ointment on my body she
has done it to prepare me for burial.
13Truly, I say to you, wherever this gospel
is preached in the whole world, what she
has done will be told in memory of her."

The bargain of Judas Iscariot

14 Then one of the twelve, who was
called Judas Iscariot, went to the chief
priests 15and said, "What will you give
me if I deliver him to you?" And they paid
him thirty pieces of silver. 16And from that
moment he sought an opportunity to betray
him.

The Last Supper

17 Now on the first day of Unleavened
Bread the disciples came to Jesus, saying,
"Where will you have us prepare for you
to eat the passover?" 18He said, "Go into
the city to such a one, and say to him, 'The
Teacher says, My time is at hand; I will
keep the passover at your house with my
disciples.' " 19And the disciples did as Jesus
had directed them, and they prepared the
passover.
20 When it was evening, he sat at table
with the twelve disciples;[e] 21and as they
were eating, he said, "Truly, I say to you,
one of you will betray me." 22And they
were very sorrowful, and began to say to
him one after another, "Is it I, Lord?" 23He
answered, "He who has dipped his hand in
the dish with me, will betray me. 24The
Son of man goes as it is written of him, but
woe to that man by whom the Son of man
is betrayed! It would have been better for
that man if he had not been born." 25Judas,
who betrayed him, said, "Is it I, Master?"[f]
He said to him, "You have said so."
26 Now as they were eating, Jesus took
bread, and blessed, and broke it, and gave
it to the disciples and said, "Take, eat; this
is my body." 27And he took a cup, and
when he had given thanks he gave it to
them, saying, "Drink of it, all of you; 28for

[e] Other authorities omit *disciples*
[f] Or *Rabbi*

King James

29 But I say unto you, I will not drink henceforth of this fruit of the vine, until that day when I drink it new with you in my Father's kingdom.

30 And when they had sung an hymn, they went out into the mount of Olives.

31 Then saith Jesus unto them, All ye shall be offended because of me this night: for it is written, I will smite the shepherd, and the sheep of the flock shall be scattered abroad.

32 But after I am risen again, I will go before you into Galilee.

33 Peter answered and said unto him, Though all *men* shall be offended because of thee, *yet* will I never be offended.

34 Jesus said unto him, Verily I say unto thee, That this night, before the cock crow, thou shalt deny me thrice.

35 Peter said unto him. Though I should die with thee, yet will I not deny thee. Likewise also said all the disciples.

36 ¶ Then cometh Jesus with them unto a place called Gethsemane, and saith unto the disciples, Sit ye here, while I go and pray yonder.

37 And he took with him Peter and the two sons of Zebedee, and began to be sorrowful and very heavy.

38 Then saith he unto them, My soul is exceeding sorrowful, even unto death: tarry ye here, and watch with me.

39 And he went a little farther, and fell on his face, and prayed, saying, O my Father, if it be possible, let this cup pass from me: nevertheless not as I will, but as thou *wilt*.

40 And he cometh unto the disciples, and findeth them asleep, and saith unto Peter, What, could ye not watch with me one hour?

41 Watch and pray, that ye enter not into temptation: the spirit indeed *is* willing, but the flesh *is* weak.

42 He went away again the second time, and prayed, saying, O my Father, if this cup may not pass away from me, except I drink it, thy will be done.

43 And he came and found them asleep again: for their eyes were heavy.

44 And he left them, and went away again, and prayed the third time, saying the same words.

45 Then cometh he to his disciples, and saith unto them, Sleep on now, and take *your* rest: behold, the hour is at hand, and the Son of man is betrayed into the hands of sinners.

46 Rise, let us be going: behold, he is at hand that doth betray me.

47 ¶ And while he yet spake, lo, Judas, one of the twelve, came, and with him a great multitude with swords and staves, from the chief priests and elders of the people.

48 Now he that betrayed him gave them a sign, saying, Whomsoever I shall kiss, that same is he: hold him fast.

49 And forthwith he came to Jesus, and said, Hail, master; and kissed him.

50 And Jesus said unto him, Friend, wherefore art thou come? Then came they, and laid hands on Jesus, and took him.

Amplified

29 I say to you, I shall not drink again of this fruit of the vine until that day when I drink it with you new *and* [q]of superior quality in My Father's kingdom.

30 And when they had sung a hymn, they went out to the Mount of Olives.

31 Then Jesus said to them, You will all be offended *and* stumble *and* fall away because of Me this night—distrusting and deserting Me; for it is written, I will strike the Shepherd, and the sheep of the flock will be scattered. [Zech. 13:7.]

32 But after I am raised up [to life again], I will go ahead of you to Galilee.

33 Peter declared to Him, Though they all are offended *and* stumble *and* fall away because of You *and* distrust *and* desert You, I will never do so.

34 Jesus said to him, Solemnly I declare to you, this very night before a [r]single rooster crows you will deny *and* disown Me three times.

35 Peter said to Him, Even if I must die with You, I will not deny *or* disown You! And all the disciples said the same thing.

36 Then Jesus went with them to a place called Gethsemane, and He told His disciples, Sit down here, while I go over yonder and pray.

37 And taking with Him Peter and the two sons of Zebedee, He began to [r]show grief *and* distress of mind and was [s]deeply depressed.

38 Then He said to them, My soul is very sad *and* deeply grieved, so that [q]I am almost dying of sorrow. Stay here and keep awake *and* watch with Me.

39 And going a little farther, He threw Himself upon the ground on His face and prayed saying, My Father, if it is possible, let this cup pass away from Me; nevertheless, not what I will—not what I desire—but as You will *and* desire.

40 And He came to the disciples and found them sleeping, and He said to Peter, What! Are you so utterly unable to stay awake *and* watch with Me for one hour?

41 All of you must keep awake (give strict attention, be cautious) *and* watch and pray that you may not come into temptation. The spirit indeed is willing, but the flesh is weak.

42 Again, a second time, He went away and prayed, My Father, if this cannot pass by unless I drink it, Your will be done.

43 And again He came and found them sleeping, for their eyes were weighed down with sleep.

44 So, leaving them again, He went away and prayed for the third time, using the same words.

45 Then He returned to the disciples and said to them, Are you still sleeping and taking your rest? Behold, the hour is at hand, and the Son of man is betrayed into the hands of [t]especially wicked sinners—[u]whose way or nature it is to act in opposition to God.

46 Get up, let us be going! See, My betrayer is at hand!

47 As He was still speaking, Judas, one of the twelve [apostles], came up and with him a great crowd with swords and clubs, from the chief priests and elders of the people.

48 Now the betrayer had given them a sign, saying, The One I shall kiss is the Man. Seize Him.

49 And he came up to Jesus at once and said, Hail (greeting, good health to You, long life to You), Master! And he [v]embraced Him and kissed Him [w]with [pretended] warmth and devotion.

50 Jesus said to him, Friend, for what are you here? Then they came up and laid hands on Jesus and arrested Him.

---

q) Thayer.
r) Vincent.
s) Berry's "Greek-English New Testament Lexicon."
t) Abbott-Smith.
u) Cremer.
v) Meyer's "Commentary on Matthew."
w) Wuest.

Living New Testament

29 Mark my words—I will not drink this wine again until the day I drink it new with you in my Father's kingdom."

30 And when they had sung a hymn, they went out to the Mount of Olives.

31 Then Jesus said to them, "Tonight you will all desert me. For it is written in the Scriptures[4] that God will smite the Shepherd, and the sheep of the flock will be scattered.

32 But after I have been brought back to life again I will go to Galilee, and meet you there."

33 Peter declared, "If everyone else deserts you, I won't!"

34 Jesus told him, "The truth is that this very night, before the cock crows at dawn, you will deny Me three times!"

35 "I would die first!" Peter insisted. And all the other disciples said the same thing.

36 Then Jesus brought them to a garden grove, Gethsemane, and told them to sit down and wait while He went on ahead to pray.

37 He took Peter with him and Zebedee's two sons James and John, and began to be filled with anguish and despair.

38 Then He told them, "My soul is crushed with horror and sadness to the point of death . . . stay here . . . stay awake with Me."

39 He went forward a little, and fell face downward on the ground, and prayed, "My Father! If it is possible, let this cup be taken away from Me. But I want Your will, not Mine."

40 Then He returned to the three disciples and found them asleep. "Peter," He called, "couldn't you even stay awake with Me one hour?

41 Keep alert and pray. Otherwise temptation will overpower you. For the spirit indeed is willing, but how weak the body is."

42 Again He left them and prayed, "My Father! If this cup cannot go away until I drink it all, Your will be done."

43 He returned to them again and found them sleeping, for their eyes were heavy,

44 So He went back to prayer the third time, saying the same things again.

45 Then He came to the disciples and said, "Sleep on now and take your rest . . . but no! The time has come! I[5] am betrayed into the hands of evil men!

46 Up! Let's be going! Look! Here comes the man who is betraying Me!"

47 At that very moment while He was still speaking, Judas, one of the Twelve, arrived with a great crowd armed with swords and clubs, sent by the Jewish leaders.

48 Judas had told them to arrest the man he greeted, for that would be the one they were after.

49 So now Judas came straight to Jesus and said, "Hello, Master!" and embraced[6] Him in friendly fashion.

50 Jesus said, "My friend, go ahead and do what you have come for." Then the others grabbed Him.

[4]Zechariah 13:7.
[5]Literally, "the Son of man."
[6]Literally, "kissed," the greeting still used among men in Eastern lands.

Revised Standard

this is my blood of the[g] covenant, which is
poured out for many for the forgiveness of
sins. 29 I tell you I shall not drink again of
this fruit of the vine until that day when
I drink it new with you in my Father's
kingdom."

30 And when they had sung a hymn,
they went out to the Mount of Olives.
31 Then Jesus said to them, "You will all fall
away because of me this night; for it is
written, 'I will strike the shepherd, and the
sheep of the flock will be scattered.' 32 But
after I am raised up, I will go before you
to Galilee." 33 Peter declared to him,
"Though they all fall away because of you,
I will never fall away." 34 Jesus said to him,
"Truly, I say to you, this very night, before the cock crows, you will deny me three
times." 35 Peter said to him, "Even if I
must die with you, I will not deny you."
And so said all the disciples.

Jesus' agony in Gethsemane

36 Then Jesus went with them to a place
called Gethsemane, and he said to his disciples, "Sit here, while I go yonder and
pray." 37 And taking with him Peter and
the two sons of Zebedee, he began to be
sorrowful and troubled. 38 Then he said to
them, "My soul is very sorrowful, even to
death; remain here, and watch[h] with me."
39 And going a little farther he fell on his
face and prayed, "My Father, if it be possible, let this cup pass from me; nevertheless, not as I will, but as thou wilt." 40 And
he came to the disciples and found them
sleeping; and he said to Peter, "So, could
you not watch[h] with me one hour? 41 Watch[h]
and pray that you may not enter into temptation; the spirit indeed is willing, but the
flesh is weak." 42 Again, for the second
time, he went away and prayed, "My Father, if this cannot pass unless I drink it,
thy will be done." 43 And again he came
and found them sleeping, for their eyes
were heavy. 44 So, leaving them again, he
went away and prayed for the third time,
saying the same words. 45 Then he came
to the disciples and said to them, "Are you
still sleeping and taking your rest? Behold,
the hour is at hand, and the Son of man
is betrayed into the hands of sinners. 46 Rise,
let us be going; see, my betrayer is at hand."

Jesus' betrayal and arrest

47 While he was still speaking, Judas
came, one of the twelve, and with him a
great crowd with swords and clubs, from
the chief priests and the elders of the people.
48 Now the betrayer had given them a sign,
saying, "The one I shall kiss is the man;
seize him." 49 And he came up to Jesus at
once and said, "Hail, Master!"[i] And he
kissed him. 50 Jesus said to him, "Friend,
why are you here?"[j] Then they came up
and laid hands on Jesus and seized him.

[g] Other ancient authorities insert *new*
[h] Or *keep awake*
[i] Or *Rabbi*
[j] Or *do that for which you have come*

King James

51 And, behold, one of them which were with Jesus stretched out *his* hand, and drew his sword, and struck a servant of the high priest's, and smote off his ear.

52 Then said Jesus unto him, Put up again thy sword into his place: for all they that take the sword shall perish with the sword.

53 Thinkest thou that I cannot now pray to my Father, and he shall presently give me more than twelve legions of angels?

54 But how then shall the scriptures be fulfilled, that thus it must be?

55 In that same hour said Jesus to the multitudes, Are ye come out as against a thief with swords and staves for to take me? I sat daily with you teaching in the temple, and ye laid no hold on me.

56 But all this was done, that the scriptures of the prophets might be fulfilled. Then all the disciples forsook him, and fled.

57 ¶ And they that had laid hold on Jesus led *him* away to Caiaphas the high priest, where the scribes and the elders were assembled.

58 But Peter followed him afar off unto the high priest's palace, and went in, and sat with the servants, to see the end.

59 Now the chief priests, and elders, and all the council, sought false witness against Jesus, to put him to death;

60 But found none: yea, though many false witnesses came, *yet* found they none. At the last came two false witnesses,

61 And said, This *fellow* said, I am able to destroy the temple of God, and to build it in three days.

62 And the high priest arose, and said unto him, Answerest thou nothing? what *is it which* these witness against thee?

63 But Jesus held his peace. And the high priest answered and said unto him, I adjure thee by the living God, that thou tell us whether thou be the Christ, the Son of God.

64 Jesus saith unto him, Thou hast said: nevertheless I say unto you, Hereafter shall ye see the Son of man sitting on the right hand of power, and coming in the clouds of heaven.

65 Then the high priest rent his clothes, saying, He hath spoken blasphemy; what further need have we of witnesses? behold, now ye have heard his blasphemy.

66 What think ye? They answered and said, He is guilty of death.

67 Then did they spit in his face, and buffeted him; and others smote *him* with the palms of their hands,

68 Saying, Prophesy unto us, thou Christ, Who is he that smote thee?

69 ¶ Now Peter sat without in the palace: and a damsel came unto him, saying, Thou also wast with Jesus of Galilee.

70 But he denied before *them* all, saying, I know not what thou sayest.

71 And when he was gone out into the porch, another *maid* saw him, and said unto them that were there, This *fellow* was also with Jesus of Nazareth.

72 And again he denied with an oath, I do not know the man.

Amplified

51 And behold, one of those who were with Jesus reached out his hand and drew his sword, and striking the body servant of the high priest, cut off his ear.

52 Then Jesus said to him, Put your sword back into its place, for all who draw the sword will die by the sword. [Gen. 9:6.]

53 Do you suppose that I cannot appeal to My Father, and He will immediately provide Me with more than twelve legions [[x]more than 80,000] of angels?

54 But how then should the Scripture be fulfilled that it must come about this way?

55 At that moment Jesus said to the crowds, Have you come out as against a robber with swords and clubs to capture Me? Day after day I was [y]accustomed to sit in the [z]porches *and* courts of the temple teaching, and you did not arrest Me.

56 But all this has taken place in order that the Scriptures of the prophets might be fulfilled. Then all the disciples deserted Him and fleeing escaped.

57 But those who had seized Jesus took Him away to Caiaphas the high priest, where the scribes and the elders had assembled.

58 But Peter followed Him at a distance as far as the courtyard of the high priest's home; he even went inside and sat with the guards to see the end.

59 Now the chief priests and the whole council [the Sanhedrin] sought to get false witnesses to testify against Jesus, so that they might put Him to death;

60 But they found none, though many witnesses came forward [to testify]. At last two men came forward

61 And testified, This [a]Fellow said, I am able to tear down the [b]sanctuary of the temple of God and to build it up again in three days.

62 And the high priest stood up and said, Have You no answer to make? What about this that these men testify against You?

63 But Jesus kept silent. And the high priest said to Him, [c]I call upon you to swear by the living God, and tell us whether you are the Christ, the Son of God.

64 Jesus said to him, [c]You have stated [the fact]. More than that, I tell you, You will in the future see the Son of man seated at the right hand of [d]the Almighty, and coming on the clouds of the sky. [Dan. 7:13; Ps. 110:1.]

65 Then the high priest tore his clothes and exclaimed, He has uttered blasphemy! What need have we of further evidence? You have now heard His blasphemy. [Num. 14:6; Lev. 24:16.]

66 What do you think now? They answered, He deserves to be put to death.

67 Then they spat in His face, and struck Him with their fists; and some [e]slapped Him in the face, [Isa. 50:6.]

68 Saying, Prophesy to us, You Christ, the Messiah! Who was it that struck You?

69 Now Peter was sitting outside in the courtyard and [f]one maid came up to him and said, You were also with Jesus the Galilean!

70 But he denied it [g]falsely before them all, saying, I do not know what you mean.

71 And when he had gone out to the porch, another maid saw him, and she said to the bystanders, This [fellow] was with Jesus the Nazarene!

72 And again he denied it and [g]disowned Him with an oath, saying, I do not know the Man!

---

x) Thayer.
y) Vincent.
z) Trench.
a) Capitalized because of what He is, the spotless Son of God, not what the speakers may have thought He was.
b) Trench.
c) Vincent.
d) Thayer.
e) Thayer.
f) Vincent.
g) Cremer.

Living New Testament

51 One of the men with Jesus pulled a sword and slashed off the ear of the High Priest's servant.

52 "Put away your sword," Jesus told him. "Those using swords will get killed.

53 Don't you realize that I could ask My Father for thousands of angels to protect us, and He would send them instantly?

54 But if I did, how would the Scriptures be fulfilled that describe what is happening now?"

55 Then Jesus spoke to the crowd. "Am I some dangerous criminal," He asked, "that you had to arm yourselves with swords and clubs before you could arrest Me? I was with you teaching daily in the Temple and you didn't stop Me then.

56 But this is all happening to fulfill the words of the prophets as recorded in the Scriptures."

At that point, all the disciples deserted Him and fled.

57 Then the mob led Him to the home of Caiaphas the High Priest, where all the Jewish leaders were gathering.

58 Meanwhile, Peter was following far to the rear, and came to the courtyard of the High Priest's house and went in and sat with the soldiers, and waited to see what was going to be done to Jesus.

59 The chief priests and, in fact, the entire Jewish Supreme Court assembled there and looked for witnesses who would lie about Jesus, in order to build a case against Him that would result in a death sentence.

60, 61 But even though they found many who agreed to be false witnesses, these always contradicted each other. Finally two men were found who declared, "This man said, 'I am able to destroy the Temple of God and rebuild it in three days.' "

62 Then the High Priest stood up and said to Jesus, "Well, what about it? Did you say that, or didn't you?"

63 But Jesus remained silent. Then the High Priest said to Him, "I demand in the name of the living God that you tell us whether you claim to be the Messiah, the Son of God."

64 "Yes," Jesus said, "I am. And in the future you will see Me, the Son of Mankind, sitting at the right hand of God and returning on the clouds of heaven."

65, 66 Then the High Priest tore at his own clothing, shouting, "Blasphemy! What need have we for other witnesses? You have all heard Him say it! What is your verdict?"

They shouted, "Death!—Death!—Death!"

67 Then they spat in His face and struck Him and some slapped Him.

68 Saying, "Prophesy to us, you Messiah! Who struck you that time?"

69 Meanwhile, as Peter was sitting in the courtyard a girl came over and said to him, "You were with Jesus, for both of you are from Galilee."[7]

70 But Peter denied it loudly. "I don't even know what you are talking about," he angrily declared.

71 Later, out by the gate, another girl noticed him and said to those standing around, "This man was with Jesus—from Nazareth."

72 Again Peter denied it, this time with an oath. "I don't even know the man," he said.

[7]Literally, "with Jesus the Galilean."

Revised Standard

51And behold, one of those who were with Jesus stretched out his hand and drew his sword, and struck the slave of the high priest, and cut off his ear. 52Then Jesus said to him, "Put your sword back into its place; for all who take the sword will perish by the sword. 53Do you think that I cannot appeal to my Father, and he will at once send me more than twelve legions of angels? 54But how then should the scriptures be fulfilled, that it must be so?" 55At that hour Jesus said to the crowds, "Have you come out as against a robber, with swords and clubs to capture me? Day after day I sat in the temple teaching, and you did not seize me. 56But all this has taken place, that the scriptures of the prophets might be fulfilled." Then all the disciples forsook him and fled.

Jesus before Caiaphas

57 Then those who had seized Jesus led him to Caiaphas the high priest, where the scribes and the elders had gathered. 58But Peter followed him at a distance, as far as the courtyard of the high priest, and going inside he sat with the guards to see the end. 59Now the chief priests and the whole council sought false testimony against Jesus that they might put him to death, 60but they found none, though many false witnesses came forward. At last two came forward 61and said, "This fellow said, 'I am able to destroy the temple of God, and to build it in three days.' " 62And the high priest stood up and said, "Have you no answer to make? What is it that these men testify against you?" 63But Jesus was silent. And the high priest said to him, "I adjure you by the living God, tell us if you are the Christ, the Son of God." 64Jesus said to him, "You have said so. But I tell you, hereafter you will see the Son of man seated at the right hand of Power, and coming on the clouds of heaven." 65Then the high priest tore his robes, and said, "He has uttered blasphemy. Why do we still need witnesses? You have now heard his blasphemy. 66What is your judgment?" They answered, "He deserves death." 67Then they spat in his face, and struck him; and some slapped him, 68saying, "Prophesy to us, you Christ! Who is it that struck you?"

Peter's denial of Jesus

69 Now Peter was sitting outside in the courtyard. And a maid came up to him, and said, "You also were with Jesus the Galilean." 70But he denied it before them all, saying, "I do not know what you mean." 71And when he went out to the porch, another maid saw him, and she said to the bystanders, "This man was with Jesus of

King James

73 And after a while came unto *him* they that stood by, and said to Peter, Surely thou also art *one* of them; for thy speech bewrayeth thee.

74 Then began he to curse and to swear, *saying*, I know not the man. And immediately the cock crew.

75 And Peter remembered the word of Jesus, which said unto him, Before the cock crow, thou shalt deny me thrice. And he went out, and wept bitterly.

Amplified

73 After a little while the bystanders came up and said to Peter, You certainly are one of them too, for even your accent betrays you.

74 Then Peter began to invoke a curse on himself and to swear, I do not even know the Man! And at that moment a rooster crowed.

75 And Peter remembered Jesus' words when He said, Before a [f]single rooster crows, you will deny *and* disown Me three times. And he went outside and wept bitterly.

CHAPTER 27

WHEN the morning was come, all the chief priests and elders of the people took counsel against Jesus to put him to death:

2 And when they had bound him, they led *him* away, and delivered him to Pontius Pilate the governor.

3 ¶ Then Judas, which had betrayed him, when he saw that he was condemned, repented himself, and brought again the thirty pieces of silver to the chief priests and elders,

4 Saying, I have sinned in that I have betrayed the innocent blood. And they said, What *is that* to us? see thou *to that*.

5 And he cast down the pieces of silver in the temple, and departed, and went and hanged himself.

6 And the chief priests took the silver pieces, and said, It is not lawful for to put them into the treasury, because it is the price of blood.

7 And they took counsel, and bought with them the potter's field, to bury strangers in.

8 Wherefore that field was called, The field of blood, unto this day.

9 Then was fulfilled that which was spoken by Jeremy the prophet, saying, And they took the thirty pieces of silver, the price of him that was valued, whom they of the children of Israel did value;

10 And gave them for the potter's field, as the Lord appointed me.

11 And Jesus stood before the governor: and the governor asked him, saying, Art thou the King of the Jews? And Jesus said unto him, Thou sayest.

12 And when he was accused of the chief priests and elders, he answered nothing.

13 Then said Pilate unto him, Hearest thou not how many things they witness against thee?

14 And he answered him to never a word; insomuch that the governor marvelled greatly.

15 Now at *that* feast the governor was wont to release unto the people a prisoner, whom they would.

16 And they had then a notable prisoner, called Barabbas.

CHAPTER 27

WHEN it was morning, all the chief priests and the elders of the people held a consultation against Jesus to put Him to death;

2 And they bound Him, and led Him away and handed Him over to Pilate the governor.

3 When Judas, His betrayer, saw that [Jesus] was condemned, (he was [h]afflicted in mind and troubled for his former folly; and) with remorse [that is, [i]an after care and little more than a selfish dread of the consequences] he brought back the thirty pieces of silver to the chief priests and the elders, [Exod. 21:32.]

4 Saying, I have sinned in betraying innocent blood. They replied, What is that to us? See to that yourself.

5 And casting the pieces of silver [forward] into the Holy Place *of* the [j]sanctuary of the temple, he departed, and he went off and hanged himself.

6 But the chief priests, picking up the pieces of silver, said, It is not legal to put these in the [consecrated] treasury, for it is the price of blood. [Deut. 23:18.]

7 So after consultation they bought with them the potter's field in which to bury strangers.

8 Therefore that piece of ground has been called the Field of Blood to the present day.

9 Then were fulfilled the words spoken by Jeremiah the prophet when he said, And they took the thirty pieces of silver, the price of Him on Whom a price had been set by some of the sons of Israel, [Zech. 11:12, 13.]

10 And they gave them for the potter's field, as the Lord directed me.

11 Now Jesus stood before the governor [Pilate]; and the governor asked Him, Are you the King of the Jews? Jesus said to him, You have stated [the fact].

12 But when the charges were made against Him by the chief priests and elders, He made no answer. [Isa. 53:7.]

13 Then Pilate said to Him, Do You not hear how many *and* how serious are the things they are testifying against You?

14 But He made no reply to him, not even to a single accusation, so that the governor marveled greatly.

15 Now at the feast (of the Passover) the governor was in the habit of setting free for the people any one prisoner whom they chose.

16 And at that time they had a notorious prisoner whose name was Barabbas.

---

f) Vincent.
h) Jeremy Taylor, and, i) Aristotle; both quoted in Trench's "Synonyms of the New Testament."
j) Trench.

Living New Testament

73 But after a while the men who had been standing there came over to him and said, "We know you are one of His disciples, for we can tell by your Galilean[8] accent."
74 Peter began to curse and swear. "I don't even know the man," he said. And immediately the cock crowed.
75 Then Peter remembered what Jesus had said, "Before the cock crows, you will deny Me three times." And he went away, crying bitterly.

Revised Standard

Nazareth." 72 And again he denied it with
an oath, "I do not know the man." 73 After
a little while the bystanders came up and
said to Peter, "Certainly you are one of
them, for your accent betrays you." 74 Then
he began to invoke a curse on himself
and to swear, "I do not know the man."
And immediately the cock crowed. 75 And
Peter remembered the saying of Jesus,
"Before the cock crows, you will deny me
three times." And he went out and wept
bitterly.

CHAPTER 27

When it was morning, the chief priests and Jewish leaders met again to discuss how to induce the Roman government to sentence Jesus to death.[1]
2 Then they sent Him in chains to Pilate, the Roman governor.
3 About that time Judas, who betrayed Him, when he saw that Jesus had been condemned to die, changed his mind and deeply regretted what he had done,[2] and brought back the money to the chief priests and other Jewish leaders.
4 "I have sinned," he declared, "for I have betrayed an innocent man."
"That's your problem," they retorted.
5 Then he threw the money onto the floor of the Temple and went out and hanged himself.
6 The chief priests picked the money up. "We can't put it in the collection," they said, "since it's against our laws to accept money paid for murder."
7 They talked it over and finally decided to buy a certain field where the clay was used by potters, and to make it into a cemetery for foreigners who died in Jerusalem.
8 That is why the cemetery is still called "The Field of Blood."
9 This fulfilled the prophecy of Jeremiah which says, "They took the thirty pieces of silver—the price at which He was valued by the people of Israel—
10 And purchased a field from the potters as the Lord directed me."
11 Now Jesus was standing before Pilate, the Roman governor. "Are you the Jews' Messiah?"[3] the governor asked Him.
"Yes," Jesus replied.
12 But when the chief priests and other Jewish leaders made their many accusations against Him, Jesus remained silent.
13 "Don't you hear what they are saying?" Pilate demanded.
14 But Jesus said nothing, much to the governor's surprise.
15 Now the governor's custom was to release one Jewish prisoner each year during the Passover celebration—anyone they wanted.
16 This year there was a particularly notorious criminal in jail named Barabbas,

[8]Implied.
[1]Literally, "took counsel against Jesus to put Him to death." They did not have the authority themselves.
[2]Literally, "repented himself."
[3]Literally, "King of the Jews."

Jesus delivered to Pilate

27 When morning came, all the chief
priests and the elders of the people
took counsel against Jesus to put him to
death; 2 and they bound him and led him
away and delivered him to Pilate the governor.

The death of Judas Iscariot

3 When Judas, his betrayer, saw that he
was condemned, he repented and brought
back the thirty pieces of silver to the chief
priests and the elders, 4 saying, "I have
sinned in betraying innocent blood." They
said, "What is that to us? See to it yourself."
5 And throwing down the pieces of
silver in the temple, he departed; and he
went and hanged himself. 6 But the chief
priests, taking the pieces of silver, said,
"It is not lawful to put them into the
treasury, since they are blood money." 7 So
they took counsel, and bought with them
the potter's field, to bury strangers in.
8 Therefore that field has been called the
Field of Blood to this day. 9 Then was fulfilled what had been spoken by the prophet
Jeremiah, saying, "And they took the thirty
pieces of silver, the price of him on whom
a price had been set by some of the sons
of Israel, 10 and they gave them for the
potter's field, as the Lord directed me."

Jesus before Pontius Pilate

11 Now Jesus stood before the governor;
and the governor asked him, "Are you the
King of the Jews?" Jesus said to him, "You
have said so." 12 But when he was accused
by the chief priests and elders, he made no
answer. 13 Then Pilate said to him, "Do
you not hear how many things they testify
against you?" 14 But he gave him no answer, not even to a single charge; so that
the governor wondered greatly.
15 Now at the feast the governor was
accustomed to release for the crowd any
one prisoner whom they wanted. 16 And they
had then a notorious prisoner, called Barab-

King James

17 Therefore when they were gathered together, Pilate said unto them, Whom will ye that I release unto you? Barabbas, or Jesus which is called Christ?

18 For he knew that for envy they had delivered him.

19 ¶ When he was set down on the judgment seat, his wife sent unto him, saying, Have thou nothing to do with that just man: for I have suffered many things this day in a dream because of him.

20 But the chief priests and elders persuaded the multitude that they should ask Barabbas, and destroy Jesus.

21 The governor answered and said unto them, Whether of the twain will ye that I release unto you? They said, Barabbas.

22 Pilate saith unto them, What shall I do then with Jesus which is called Christ? *They* all say unto him, Let him be crucified.

23 And the governor said, Why, what evil hath he done? But they cried out the more, saying, Let him be crucified.

24 ¶ When Pilate saw that he could prevail nothing, but *that* rather a tumult was made, he took water, and washed *his* hands before the multitude, saying, I am innocent of the blood of this just person: see ye *to it*.

25 Then answered all the people, and said, His blood *be* on us, and on our children.

26 ¶ Then released he Barabbas unto them: and when he had scourged Jesus, he delivered *him* to be crucified.

27 Then the soldiers of the governor took Jesus into the common hall, and gathered unto him the whole band *of soldiers*.

28 And they stripped him, and put on him a scarlet robe.

29 ¶ And when they had platted a crown of thorns, they put it upon his head, and a reed in his right hand: and they bowed the knee before him, and mocked him, saying, Hail, King of the Jews!

30 And they spit upon him, and took the reed, and smote him on the head.

31 And after that they had mocked him, they took the robe off from him, and put his own raiment on him, and led him away to crucify *him*.

32 And as they came out, they found a man of Cyrene, Simon by name: him they compelled to bear his cross.

33 And when they were come unto a place called Golgotha, that is to say, a place of a skull,

34 ¶ They gave him vinegar to drink mingled with gall: and when he had tasted *thereof*, he would not drink.

35 And they crucified him, and parted his garments, casting lots: that it might be fulfilled which was spoken by the prophet, They parted my garments among them, and upon my vesture did they cast lots.

36 And sitting down they watched him there;

37 And set up over his head his accusation written, THIS IS JESUS THE KING OF THE JEWS.

38 Then were there two thieves crucified with him, one on the right hand, and another on the left.

Amplified

17 So when they had assembled for this purpose, Pilate said to them, Whom do you want me to set free for you, Barabbas, or Jesus Who is called Christ?

18 For he knew that it was because of envy that they had handed Him over to him.

19 Also, while he was seated on the judgment bench, his wife sent him a message, saying, Have nothing to do with that just *and* upright Man, for I have had a painful experience because of Him today in a dream.

20 But the chief priests and the elders prevailed on the people to ask for Barabbas and put Jesus to death.

21 Again the governor said to them, Which of the two do you wish me to release for you? And they said, Barabbas!

22 Pilate said to them, Then what shall I do with Jesus Who is called Christ?

23 They all replied, Let Him be crucified! And he said, Why, what has He done that is evil? But they shouted all the louder, Let Him be crucified!

24 So when Pilate saw that he was getting nowhere, but rather that a riot was about to break out, he took water and washed his hands in the presence of the crowd, saying, I am not guilty of *nor* responsible for this [k]*righteous* Man's blood; see to it yourselves. [Deut. 21:6-9; Ps. 26:6.]

25 And all the people answered, His blood be on us and on our children! [Josh. 2:19.]

26 So he set free for them Barabbas, and [had] Jesus whipped, and delivered Him up to be crucified.

27 Then the governor's soldiers took Jesus into the palace, and they gathered the whole battalion about Him.

28 And they stripped off His clothes and put a scarlet robe [[l]garment of dignity and office, worn by Roman officers of rank] upon Him,

29 And weaving a crown of thorns they put it on His head, and put a reed-staff in His right hand. And kneeling before Him they made sport of Him, saying, Hail (greeting, good health to you, long life to you), King of the Jews!

30 And they spat on Him, and took the reed-staff and struck Him on the head.

31 And when they finished making sport of Him, they stripped Him of the robe and put His own garments on Him, and led Him away to be crucified.

32 As they were marching forth, they came upon a man of Cyrene named Simon; this man they forced to carry the cross of Jesus.

33 And when they came to a place called Golgotha [Calvary, in Latin], which means the place of a skull,

34 They offered Him wine mingled with gall to drink, but when He tasted it, He refused to drink it.

35 And when they had crucified Him, they divided *and* distributed His garments [among them] by casting lots *so that the prophet's saying was fulfilled, They parted My garments among them and over My apparel they cast lots.* [Ps. 22:18.]

36 Then they sat down there and kept watch over Him.

37 And over His head they put the accusation against Him ([m]the cause of His death), which read, This is Jesus the King of the Jews.

38 At the same time two robbers were crucified with Him, one on the right hand and one on the left.

---

k) Some authorities so read.
l) Trench.
m) Tyndale.

Living New Testament

17 And as the crowds gathered before Pilate's house that morning he asked them, "Which shall I release to you—Barabbas, or Jesus, your Messiah?"[4]

18 For he knew very well that the Jewish leaders had arrested Jesus out of envy because of His popularity with the people.

19 Just then, as he was presiding over the court, Pilate's wife sent him this message: "Leave that good man alone; for I had a terrible nightmare concerning Him last night."

20 Meanwhile the chief priests and Jewish officials persuaded the crowds to ask for Barabbas' release, and for Jesus' death.

21 So when the governor asked again,[5] "Which of these two shall I release to you?" the crowd shouted back their reply: "Barabbas!"

22 "Then what shall I do with Jesus, your Messiah?" Pilate asked.

And they shouted, "Crucify him!"

23 "Why?" Pilate demanded. "What has He done wrong?"

But they kept shouting, "Crucify! Crucify!"

24 When Pilate saw that he wasn't getting anywhere, and that a riot was developing, he sent for a bowl of water and washed his hands before the crowd, saying, "I am innocent of the blood of this good man. The responsibility is yours!"

25 And the mob yelled back, "His blood be on us and on our children!"

26 Then Pilate released Barabbas to them. And after he had whipped Jesus, he gave Him to the Roman soldiers to take away and crucify.

27 But first they took Him into the armory and called out the entire contingent.

28 They stripped Him and put a scarlet robe on Him,

29 And made a crown from long thorns and put it on His head, and placed a stick in His right hand as a scepter and knelt before Him in mockery. "Hail, King of the Jews," they yelled.

30 And they spat on Him and grabbed the stick and beat Him on the head with it.

31 After the mockery, they took off the robe and put His own garment on Him again, and took Him out to crucify Him.

32 As they were on the way to the execution grounds they came across a man from Cyrene, in Africa—Simon was his name—and forced him to carry Jesus' cross.

33 Then they went out to an area known as Golgotha, that is, "Skull Hill,"[6]

34 Where the soldiers gave Him drugged wine to drink, but when He had tasted it, He refused.

* * * * * * *

35 After the crucifixion, the soldiers threw dice to divide up His clothes among themselves.

36 Then they sat around and watched Him as He hung there.

37 And they put a sign above His head, "This is Jesus, the King of the Jews."

38 Two robbers were also crucified there that morning, one on either side of Him.

[4]Literally, "Jesus who is called Christ."
[5]Implied.
[6]Literally, "The place of a skull."

Revised Standard

bas[k]. 17 So when they had gathered, Pilate
said to them, "Whom do you want me to
release for you, Barabbas[k] or Jesus who
is called Christ?" 18 For he knew that it was
out of envy that they had delivered him up.
19 Besides, while he was sitting on the judgment seat, his wife sent word to him,
"Have nothing to do with that righteous
man, for I have suffered much over him,
today in a dream." 20 Now the chief priests
and the elders persuaded the people to ask
for Barabbas and destroy Jesus. 21 The governor again said to them, "Which of the
two do you want me to release for you?"
And they said, "Barabbas." 22 Pilate said
to them, "Then what shall I do with Jesus
who is called Christ?" They all said, "Let
him be crucified." 23 And he said, "Why,
what evil has he done?" But they shouted
all the more, "Let him be crucified."

24 So when Pilate saw that he was gaining nothing, but rather that a riot was beginning, he took water and washed his
hands before the crowd, saying, "I am innocent of this man's blood;[l] see to it yourselves." 25 And all the people answered,
"His blood be on us and on our children!"
26 Then he released for them Barabbas, and
having scourged Jesus, delivered him to be
crucified.

Jesus crowned with thorns

27 Then the soldiers of the governor
took Jesus into the praetorium, and they
gathered the whole battalion before him.
28 And they stripped him and put a scarlet
robe upon him, 29 and plaiting a crown of
thorns they put it on his head, and put a
reed in his right hand. And kneeling before
him they mocked him, saying, "Hail, King
of the Jews!" 30 And they spat upon him,
and took the reed and struck him on the
head. 31 And when they had mocked him,
they stripped him of the robe, and put his
own clothes on him, and led him away to
crucify him.

Jesus crucified

32 As they were marching out, they
came upon a man of Cyrene, Simon by
name; this man they compelled to carry his
cross. 33 And when they came to a place
called Golgotha (which means the place of
a skull), 34 they offered him wine to drink,
mingled with gall; but when he tasted it,
he would not drink it. 35 And when they
had crucified him, they divided his garments
among them by casting lots; 36 then they
sat down and kept watch over him there.
37 And over his head they put the charge
against him, which read, "This is Jesus the
King of the Jews." 38 Then two robbers
were crucified with him, one on the right

[k] Other ancient authorities read *Jesus Barabbas*
[l] Other authorities read *this righteous blood* or *this righteous man's blood*

King James

39 ¶ And they that passed by reviled him, wagging their heads,

40 And saying, Thou that destroyest the temple, and buildest it in three days, save thyself. If thou be the Son of God, come down from the cross.

41 Likewise also the chief priests mocking *him,* with the scribes and elders, said,

42 He saved others; himself he cannot save. If he be the King of Israel, let him now come down from the cross, and we will believe him.

43 He trusted in God; let him deliver him now, if he will have him: for he said, I am the Son of God.

44 The thieves also, which were crucified with him, cast the same in his teeth.

45 Now from the sixth hour there was darkness over all the land unto the ninth hour.

46 And about the ninth hour Jesus cried with a loud voice, saying, Eli, Eli, lama sabachthani? that is to say, My God, my God, why hast thou forsaken me?

47 Some of them that stood there, when they heard *that,* said, This *man* calleth for Elias.

48 And straightway one of them ran, and took a sponge, and filled *it* with vinegar, and put *it* on a reed, and gave him to drink.

49 The rest said, Let be, let us see whether Elias will come to save him.

50 ¶ Jesus, when he had cried again with a loud voice, yielded up the ghost.

51 And, behold, the veil of the temple was rent in twain from the top to the bottom; and the earth did quake, and the rocks rent;

52 And the graves were opened; and many bodies of the saints which slept arose,

53 And came out of the graves after his resurrection, and went into the holy city, and appeared unto many.

54 Now when the centurion, and they that were with him, watching Jesus, saw the earthquake, and those things that were done, they feared greatly, saying, Truly this was the Son of God.

55 And many women were there beholding afar off, which followed Jesus from Galilee, ministering unto him:

56 Among which was Mary Magdalene, and Mary the mother of James and Joses, and the mother of Zebedee's children.

57 When the even was come, there came a rich man of Arimathæa, named Joseph, who also himself was Jesus' disciple:

58 He went to Pilate, and begged the body of Jesus. Then Pilate commanded the body to be delivered.

59 And when Joseph had taken the body, he wrapped it in a clean linen cloth,

60 And laid it in his own new tomb, which he had hewn out in the rock: and he rolled a great stone to the door of the sepulchre, and departed.

Amplified

39 And those who passed by spoke reproachfully *and* abusively *and* jeered at Him, wagging their heads, [Ps. 22:7, 8; 109:25.]

40 And they said, You Who would tear down the [n]sanctuary of the temple and rebuild it in three days, rescue Yourself [o]from death. If You are the Son of God, come down from the cross.

41 In the same way the chief priests with the scribes and elders made sport of Him, saying,

42 He rescued others [o]from death; Himself He cannot rescue [o]from death. He is the King of Israel? Let Him come down from the cross now, and we will believe *and* [o]acknowledge *and* cleave to Him.

43 He trusts in God; let God deliver Him now, if He cares for Him *and* will [have] Him, for He said, I am the Son of God.

44 And the robbers who were crucified with Him also abused *and* reproached *and* made sport of Him in the same way.

45 Now from the sixth hour [noon] there was darkness over all the land until the ninth hour [three o'clock].

46 And about the ninth hour [three o'clock] Jesus cried with a loud voice, Eli, Eli, lama sabachthani? that is, My God, My God, why have You abandoned Me—leaving Me [p]helpless, forsaking and failing Me in My need? [Ps. 22:1.]

47 And some of the bystanders when they heard it said, This Man is calling for Elijah!

48 And one of them immediately ran and took a sponge, soaked it with vinegar [a sour wine], and put it on a reed-staff and was [q]about to give it to Him to drink. [Ps. 69:21.]

49 But the others said, Wait! Let us see whether Elijah will come to save Him [q]from death.

50 And Jesus cried again with a loud voice, and gave up His spirit.

51 And at once the curtain of the [r]sanctuary of the temple was torn in two from top to bottom; the earth shook, and the rocks were split; [Exod. 26:31-35.]

52 The tombs were opened, and many bodies of the saints who had fallen asleep [s]in death were raised.

53 And coming out of the tombs after His resurrection, they went into the holy city and appeared to many people.

54 When the centurion and those that were with him keeping watch over Jesus, observed the earthquake and all that was happening, they were terribly frightened *and* filled with awe, and said, Truly this was God's Son!

55 There were also numerous women there looking on from a distance, who were of those who had accompanied Jesus from Galilee, ministering to Him;

56 Among them were Mary of Magdala, and Mary the mother of James and Joseph, and the mother of Zebedee's sons.

57 When it was evening, there came a rich man from Arimathea, named Joseph, who also was a disciple of Jesus.

58 He went to Pilate and asked for the body of Jesus, and Pilate ordered that it be given him.

59 And Joseph took the body and [t]rolled it up in a clean linen cloth [u]used for swathing dead bodies,

60 And laid it in his own fresh [[v]undefiled] tomb, which he had hewn in the rock; and he rolled a big boulder over the door of the tomb and went away.

---

n) Trench.
o) Cremer
p) Wuest.
q) Vincent.
r) Trench.
s) Cremer.
t) Young's Concordance.
u) Moulton and Milligan.
v) Vincent.

Living New Testament

39 And the people passing by hurled abuse, shaking their heads at Him and saying,

40 "So! You can destroy the Temple and build it again in three days, can You? Well, then, come on down from the cross if you are the Son of God!"

41, 42, 43 And the chief priests and Jewish leaders also mocked Him. "He saved others," they scoffed, "but he can't save himself! So you are the King of Israel, are you? Come down from the cross and we'll believe you! He trusted God—let God show His approval by delivering him! Didn't he say, 'I am God's Son?' "

* * * * *

44 And the robbers also threw the same in His teeth.

* * * * *

45 That afternoon, the whole earth[7] was covered with darkness for three hours, from noon until three o'clock.

* * * * *

46 About three o'clock, Jesus shouted, "Eli, Eli, lama sabachthani," which means, "My God, My God, why have You forsaken Me?"

47 Some of the bystanders misunderstood and thought He was calling for Elijah.

48 One of them ran and filled a sponge with sour wine and put it on a stick and held it up to Him to drink.

49 But the rest said, "Leave him alone. Let's see whether Elijah will come and save him."

* * * * *

50 Then Jesus shouted out again, dismissed His spirit, and died.

51 And look! The curtain secluding the Holiest Place[8] in the Temple was split apart from top to bottom; and the earth shook, and rocks broke,

52 And tombs opened, and many godly men and women who had died came back to life again.

53 After Jesus' resurrection, they left the cemetery and went into Jerusalem, and appeared to many people there.

* * * * *

54 The soldiers at the crucifixion and their sergeant were terribly frightened by the earthquake and all that happened. They exclaimed, "Surely this was God's son."[9]

* * * * *

55 And many women who had come down from Galilee with Jesus to care for Him were watching from a distance.

56 Among them were Mary Magdalene and Mary the mother of James and Joseph, and the mother of James and John (the sons of Zebedee).

* * * * *

57 When evening came, a rich man from Arimathaea named Joseph, one of Jesus' followers,

58 Went to Pilate and asked for Jesus' body. And Pilate issued an order to release it to him.

59 Joseph took the body and wrapped it in a clean linen cloth,

60 And placed it in his own new rock-hewn tomb, and rolled a great stone across the entrance as he left.

[7]Or, "land."
[8]Implied.
[9]Or, "a godly man."

Revised Standard

and one on the left. 39 And those who
passed by derided him, wagging their heads
40 and saying, "You who would destroy the
temple and build it in three days, save
yourself! If you are the Son of God, come
down from the cross." 41 So also the chief
priests, with the scribes and elders, mocked
him, saying, 42 "He saved others; he cannot save himself. He is the King of Israel;
let him come down now from the cross,
and we will believe in him. 43 He trusts in
God; let God deliver him now, if he desires
him; for he said, 'I am the Son of God.' "
44 And the robbers who were crucified with
him also reviled him in the same way.

The death of Jesus

45 Now from the sixth hour there was
darkness over all the land[m] until the ninth
hour. 46 And about the ninth hour Jesus
cried with a loud voice, "Eli, Eli, lama
sabach-thani?" that is, "My God, my God,
why hast thou forsaken me?" 47 And some
of the bystanders hearing it said, "This man
is calling Elijah." 48 And one of them at
once ran and took a sponge, filled it with
vinegar, and put it on a reed, and gave it
to him to drink. 49 But the others said, "Wait,
let us see whether Elijah will come to save
him."[n] 50 And Jesus cried again with a loud
voice and yielded up his spirit.
51 And behold, the curtain of the temple
was torn in two, from top to bottom; and
the earth shook, and the rocks were split;
52 the tombs also were opened, and many
bodies of the saints who had fallen asleep
were raised, 53 and coming out of the tombs
after his resurrection they went into the
holy city and appeared to many. 54 When
the centurion and those who were with
him, keeping watch over Jesus, saw the
earthquake and what took place, they were
filled with awe, and said, "Truly this was
the Son of God!"
55 There were also many women there,
looking on from afar, who had followed
Jesus from Galilee, ministering to him;
56 among whom were Mary Magdalene,
and Mary the mother of James and Joseph,
and the mother of the sons of Zebedee.

Jesus laid in the tomb

57 When it was evening, there came a
rich man from Arimathea, named Joseph,
who also was a disciple of Jesus. 58 He went
to Pilate and asked for the body of Jesus.
Then Pilate ordered it to be given to him.
59 And Joseph took the body, and wrapped
it in a clean linen shroud, 60 and laid it in
his own new tomb, which he had hewn
in the rock; and he rolled a great stone to
the door of the tomb, and departed. 61 Mary

[m] Or *earth*
[n] Other ancient authorities insert *And another took a spear and pierced his side, and out came water and blood*

King James

61 And there was Mary Magdalene, and
the other Mary, sitting over against the sepulchre.
62 ¶ Now the next day, that followed the
day of the preparation, the chief priests and
Pharisees came together unto Pilate,
63 Saying, Sir, we remember that that
deceiver said, while he was yet alive, After
three days I will rise again.
64 Command therefore that the sepulchre
be made sure until the third day, lest his
disciples come by night, and steal him away,
and say unto the people, He is risen from
the dead: so the last error shall be worse
than the first.
65 Pilate said unto them, Ye have a
watch: go your way, make *it* as sure as ye
can.
66 So they went, and made the sepulchre
sure, sealing the stone, and setting a watch.

Amplified

61 And Mary of Magdala and the other Mary kept sitting
there opposite the tomb.
62 The next day, that is, the day after the day of
preparation [for the Sabbath], the chief priests and the
Pharisees assembled before Pilate
63 And said, Sir, we have just remembered how that
[v]vagabond [w]Imposter said, while He was still alive, After
three days I will arise again.
64 Therefore give an order to have the tomb made secure
and safeguarded until the third day, for fear His disciples go
and steal Him away, and tell the people that He has risen
from the dead, and the last deception *and* fraud will be worse
than the first.
65 Pilate said to them, You have a guard of soldiers; [take
them and] go, make it as secure as you can.
66 So they went off and made the tomb secure by sealing
the boulder, a guard of soldiers being with them *and*
remaining to watch.

CHAPTER 28

IN the end of the sabbath, as it began to
dawn toward the first *day* of the week,
came Mary Magdalene and the other Mary
to see the sepulchre.
2 And, behold, there was a great earthquake: for the angel of the Lord descended
from heaven, and came and rolled back the
stone from the door, and sat upon it.
3 His countenance was like lightning, and
his raiment white as snow:
4 And for fear of him the keepers did
shake, and became as dead *men*.
5 And the angel answered and said unto
the women, Fear not ye: for I know that ye
seek Jesus, which was crucified.
6 He is not here: for he is risen, as he
said. Come, see the place where the Lord
lay.
7 And go quickly, and tell his disciples
that he is risen from the dead; and, behold,
he goeth before you into Galilee; there shall
ye see him: lo, I have told you.
8 And they departed quickly from the
sepulchre with fear and great joy; and did
run to bring his disciples word.
9 ¶ And as they went to tell his disciples,
behold, Jesus met them, saying, All hail.
And they came and held him by the feet,
and worshipped him.
10 Then said Jesus unto them, Be not
afraid: go tell my brethren that they go into
Galilee, and there shall they see me.
11 ¶ Now when they were going, behold,
some of the watch came into the city, and
shewed unto the chief priests all the things
that were done.

CHAPTER 28

NOW after the Sabbath, near dawn of the first day of the
week, Mary of Magdala and the other Mary went to take
a look at the tomb.
2 And behold, there was a great earthquake, for an angel
of the Lord descended from heaven and came and rolled the
boulder back and sat upon it.
3 His appearance was like lightning, and his garments as
white as snow.
4 And those keeping guard were so frightened at sight of
him that they were agitated *and* trembled, and became like
dead men.
5 But the angel said to the women, Do not be alarmed
and frightened, for I know that you are looking for Jesus
Who was crucified.
6 He is not here; He has risen, as He said [He would do].
Come, see the place where He lay.
7 Then go quickly and tell His disciples, He has risen from
the dead, and behold, He is going before you to Galilee;
there you will see Him. Lo, I have told you.
8 So they left the tomb hastily with fear and great joy,
and ran to tell the disciples.
9 And *as they went,* behold, Jesus met them and said, Hail
(greeting)! And they went up to Him and clasped His feet
and worshipped Him.
10 Then Jesus said to them, Do not be alarmed *and*
afraid; go and tell My brethren to go into Galilee, and there
they will see Me.
11 While they were on their way, behold, some of the
guard went into the city and reported to the chief priests
everything that had occurred.

---

v) Vincent.
w) Capitalized because of what He is, the spotless Son of God, not what the speakers may have thought He was.

Living New Testament

61 Both Mary Magdalene and the other Mary were sitting nearby watching.

* * * * *

62 The next day—at the close of the first day of the Passover ceremonies[10]—the chief priests and Pharisees went to Pilate,

63 And told him, "Sir, that liar once said, 'After three days I will come back to life again.'

64 So we request an order from you sealing the tomb until the third day, to prevent his disciples from coming and stealing his body and then telling everyone he came back to life! If that happens we'll be worse off than we were at first."

65 "Use your own Temple police," Pilate told them. "They can guard it safely enough."

66 So they sealed[11] the stone and posted guards to protect it from intrusion.

Revised Standard

Magdalene and the other Mary were there, sitting opposite the sepulchre.

The tomb sealed and guarded

62 Next day, that is, after the day of Preparation, the chief priests and the Pharisees gathered before Pilate 63 and said, "Sir, we remember how that imposter said, while he was still alive, 'After three days I will rise again.' 64 Therefore order the sepulchre to be made secure until the third day, lest his disciples go and steal him away, and tell the people, 'He has risen from the dead,' and the last fraud will be worse than the first." 65 Pilate said to them, "You have a guard[o] of soldiers; go, make it as secure as you can."[p] 66 So they went and made the sepulchre secure by sealing the stone and setting a guard.

CHAPTER 28

Early the next morning,[1] as the new day was dawning, Mary Magdalene and the other Mary went out to the tomb.

2 Suddenly there was a great earthquake; for an angel of the Lord came down from heaven and rolled aside the stone and sat on it.

3 His face shone like lightning and his clothing was a brilliant white.[2]

4 The guards shook with fear when they saw him, and fell into a dead faint.

5 Then the angel spoke to the women. "Don't be frightened!" he said, "I know you are looking for Jesus, who was crucified,

6 But He isn't here! For He has come back to life again, just as He said He would. Come in and see where His body was lying . . .

7 And now, go quickly and tell His disciples that He has risen from the dead, and that He is going to Galilee to meet them there. That is my message to them."

8 The women ran from the tomb, badly frightened, but also filled with joy, and rushed to find the disciples to give them the angel's message.

9 And as they were running, suddenly Jesus was there in front of them! "Good morning!"[3] He said. And they fell to the ground before Him, holding His feet and worshiping Him.

10 Then Jesus said to them, "Don't be frightened! Go tell My brothers to leave at once for Galilee, to meet Me there."

* * * * *

11 As the women were on the way into the city, some of the Temple police who had been guarding the tomb went to the chief priests and told them what had happened.

The resurrection of Jesus

28 Now after the sabbath, toward the dawn of the first day of the week, Mary Magdalene and the other Mary went to see the sepulchre. 2 And behold, there was a great earthquake; for an angel of the Lord descended from heaven and came and rolled back the stone, and sat upon it. 3 His appearance was like lightning, and his raiment white as snow. 4 And for fear of him the guards trembled and became like dead men. 5 But the angel said to the women, "Do not be afraid; for I know that you seek Jesus who was crucified. 6 He is not here; for he has risen, as he said. Come, see the place where he[q] lay. 7 Then go quickly and tell his disciples that he has risen from the dead, and behold, he is going before you to Galilee; there you will see him. Lo, I have told you." 8 So they departed quickly from the tomb with fear and great joy, and ran to tell his disciples. 9 And behold, Jesus met them and said, "Hail!" And they came up and took hold of his feet and worshiped him. 10 Then Jesus said to them, "Do not be afraid; go and tell my brethren to go to Galilee, and there they will see me."

The bribing of the soldiers

11 While they were going, behold, some of the guard went into the city and told the chief priests all that had taken place.

---

[10] Implied; literally, "on the morrow, which is after the Preparation."
[11] This was done by stringing a cord across the rock, the cord being sealed at each end with clay.
[1] Literally, "late on the Sabbath day as it began to dawn . . ."
[2] Literally, "white as snow."
[3] Literally, "All hail!"

---

[o] Or *Take a guard*
[p] Greek *know*
[q] Other ancient authorities read *the Lord*

King James

12 And when they were assembled with the elders, and had taken counsel, they gave large money unto the soldiers,

13 Saying, Say ye, His disciples came by night, and stole him *away* while we slept.

14 And if this come to the governor's ears, we will persuade him, and secure you.

15 So they took the money, and did as they were taught: and this saying is commonly reported among the Jews until this day.

16 ¶ Then the eleven disciples went away into Galilee, into a mountain where Jesus had appointed them.

17 And when they saw him, they worshipped him: but some doubted.

18 And Jesus came and spake unto them, saying, All power is given unto me in heaven and in earth.

19 ¶ Go ye therefore, and teach all nations, baptizing them in the name of the Father, and of the Son, and of the Holy Ghost:

20 Teaching them to observe all things whatsoever I have commanded you: and, lo, I am with you alway, *even* unto the end of the world. Amen.

Amplified

12 And when they had gathered with the elders and had consulted together, they gave a sufficient sum of money to the soldiers,

13 And said, Tell people, His disciples came at night and stole Him away while we were sleeping.

14 And if the governor hears of it, we will appease him and make you safe *and* free from trouble *and* care.

15 So they took the money and did as they were instructed, and this story has been current among the Jews to the present day.

16 Now the eleven disciples went to Galilee, to the mountain to which Jesus had directed *and* made appointment with them.

17 And when they saw Him they fell down and worshipped Him, but some doubted.

18 Jesus approached and [x]breaking the silence said to them, All authority—all power of rule—in heaven and on earth has been given to Me.

19 Go then and make disciples of all the nations, baptizing them [y]into the name of the Father and of the Son and of the Holy Spirit;

20 Teaching them to observe everything that I have commanded you, and lo, I am with you [z]all the days,—[a]perpetually, uniformly and on every occasion—to the [very] close *and* consummation of the age. *Amen—so let it be.*

---

x) Vincent.
y) Vincent.
z) Wycliffe.
a) Webster's definition of "alway."

Living New Testament

12, 13 A meeting of all the Jewish leaders was called, and it was decided to bribe the police to say they had all been asleep when Jesus' disciples came during the night and stole His body.

14 "If the governor hears about it," the Council promised, "we'll stand up for you and everything will be all right."

15 So the police accepted the bribe and said what they were told to. Their story spread widely among the Jews, and is still believed by them to this very day.

16 Then the eleven disciples left for Galilee, going to the mountain where Jesus had said they would find Him.

17 There they met Him and worshiped Him—but some of them weren't sure it really was Jesus!

18 He told His disciples, "I have been given all authority in heaven and earth.

19 Therefore go and make disciples in[4] all the nations, baptizing them into the name of the Father and of the Son and of the Holy Spirit.

20 And then teach these new disciples to obey all the commands I have given you; and be sure of this—that I am with you always, even to the end of the world."[5]

[4]Literally, "of."
[5]Or, "age."

Revised Standard

12And when they had assembled with the
elders and taken counsel, they gave a sum
of money to the soldiers 13and said, "Tell
people, 'His disciples came by night and
stole him away while we were asleep.' 14And
if this comes to the governor's ears, we will
satisfy him and keep you out of trouble."
15So they took the money and did as they
were directed; and this story has spread
among the Jews to this day.

The great commission

16 Now the eleven disciples went to Galilee, to the mountain to which Jesus had directed them. 17And when they saw him they
worshiped him; but some doubted. 18And
Jesus came and said to them, "All authority
in heaven and on earth has been given to
me. 19Go therefore and make disciples of
all nations, baptizing them in the name of
the Father and of the Son and of the Holy
Spirit, 20teaching them to observe all that
I have commanded you; and lo, I am with
you always, to the close of the age."

King James

THE GOSPEL ACCORDING TO

St. Mark

CHAPTER 1

THE beginning of the gospel of Jesus Christ, the Son of God;

2 As it is written in the prophets, Behold, I send my messenger before thy face, which shall prepare thy way before thee.

3 The voice of one crying in the wilderness, Prepare ye the way of the Lord, make his paths straight.

4 John did baptize in the wilderness, and preach the baptism of repentance for the remission of sins.

5 And there went out unto him all the land of Judæa, and they of Jerusalem, and were all baptized of him in the river of Jordan, confessing their sins.

6 And John was clothed with camel's hair, and with a girdle of a skin about his loins; and he did eat locusts and wild honey;

7 And preached, saying, There cometh one mightier than I after me, the latchet of whose shoes I am not worthy to stoop down and unloose.

8 I indeed have baptized you with water: but he shall baptize you with the Holy Ghost.

9 And it came to pass in those days, that Jesus came from Nazareth of Galilee, and was baptized of John in Jordan.

10 And straightway coming up out of the water, he saw the heavens opened, and the Spirit like a dove descending upon him:

11 And there came a voice from heaven, *saying*, Thou art my beloved Son, in whom I am well pleased.

12 And immediately the Spirit driveth him into the wilderness.

13 And he was there in the wilderness forty days, tempted of Satan; and was with the wild beasts; and the angels ministered unto him.

14 Now after that John was put in prison, Jesus came into Galilee, preaching the gospel of the kingdom of God,

15 And saying, The time is fulfilled, and the kingdom of God is at hand: repent ye, and believe the gospel.

16 Now as he walked by the sea of Galilee, he saw Simon and Andrew his brother casting a net into the sea: for they were fishers.

Amplified

THE GOSPEL ACCORDING TO

Mark

CHAPTER 1

THE beginning [of the facts] of the good news (the Gospel) of Jesus Christ, *the Son of God.*

2 [a]Just as it is written in the prophet Isaiah: Behold, I send My messenger before Your face, who will make ready Your way; [Mal. 3:1.]

3 A voice of one crying in the wilderness—shouting in the desert—Prepare the way of the Lord, make His [b]beaten-tracks straight (level and passable)! [Isa. 40:3.]

4 John the Baptist appeared in the wilderness (desert), preaching a baptism [[a]obligating] repentance— [that is] [c]a change of one's mind for the better and heartily to amend one's ways with abhorrence of his past sins—in order [d]to obtain forgiveness of *and* release from sins.

5 And there kept going out to him (continuously) all the country of Judea, and all the inhabitants of Jerusalem; and they were baptized by him in the river Jordan, [f]as they were confessing their sins.

6 And John wore clothing woven of camel's hair, and had a leather girdle around his loins, and ate locusts and wild honey.

7 And he preached, saying, After me comes He Who is stronger—more powerful and more valiant—than I, the strap of Whose sandals I am not worthy *or* fit to stoop down and unloose.

8 I have baptized you with water, but He will baptize you with the Holy Spirit.

9 In those days Jesus came from Nazareth of Galilee and was baptized by John in the Jordan.

10 And when He came up out of the water, at once [e]he saw the heavens torn open and the [Holy] Spirit like a dove, coming down [[f]to enter] [g]into Him;

11 And there came a voice [f]out from within heaven, You are My Beloved Son; in You I am well pleased. [Ps. 2:7; Isa. 42:1.]

12 Immediately the [Holy] Spirit [from within] drove Him out into the wilderness (desert).

13 And He stayed in the wilderness (desert) forty days, being tempted [the while] by Satan; and He was with the wild beasts, and the angels ministered to Him (continually).

14 Now after John was arrested *and* put in prison, Jesus came into Galilee, preaching the good news (the Gospel) *of the kingdom* of God,

15 And saying, The [appointed period of] time is (completed) fulfilled, and the kingdom of God is at hand; repent ([h]have a change of mind which issues in regret for past sins and in change of conduct for the better) and believe—trust in, rely on and adhere to the good news—the Gospel.

16 And passing along the shore of the sea of Galilee, He saw Simon [Peter] and Andrew the brother of Simon casting a net (to and fro) in the sea, for they were fishermen.

---

a) Wuest's "Mark in the Greek Testament."
b) Moulton and Milligan's "The Vocabulary of the Greek Testament."
c) Thayer's "Greek-English Lexicon of the New Testament—Grimm."
d) Williams' "The New Testament in the Language of the People."
e) John 1:32.
f) Wuest's "Mark in the Greek Testament."
g) Literal translation of "eis."
h) Vincent.

Living New Testament

Mark

CHAPTER 1

Here begins the wonderful story of Jesus the Messiah, the Son of God.

2 In the book written by the prophet Isaiah, God announced the He would send His Son[1] to earth, and that a special messenger would arrive first to prepare the world for His coming.

2 "This messenger will live out in the barren wilderness," Isaiah[2] said, "and will proclaim that everyone must straighten out his life to be ready for the Lord's arrival."[3]

4 This messenger was John the Baptist. He lived in the wilderness and taught that all should be baptized as a public announcement of their decision to turn their backs on sin, so that God could forgive them.[4]

5 People from Jerusalem and from all over Judea traveled out into the Judean wastelands to see and hear John, and when they confessed their sins he baptized them in the Jordan River.

6 His clothes were woven from camel's hair and he wore a leather belt; locusts and wild honey were his food.

7 Here is a sample of his preaching: "Someone is coming soon who is far greater than I am, so much greater that I am not even worthy to be His slave.[5]

8 I baptize you with[6] water but He will baptize you with[6] God's Holy Spirit!"

9 Then one day Jesus came from Nazareth in Galilee, and was baptized by John there in the Jordan River.

10 The moment Jesus came up out of the water, He saw the heavens open and the Holy Spirit in the form of a dove descending on Him,

11 And a voice from heaven said, "You are My beloved Son; You are My Delight."

12, 13 Immediately the Holy Spirit urged Jesus into the desert. There, for 40 days, alone except for desert animals, He was subjected to Satan's temptations to sin. And afterwards the angels came and cared for Him.

14 Later on, after John was arrested by King Herod,[7] Jesus went to Galilee to preach God's Good News.

15 "At last the time has come!" He announced. "God's Kingdom is near! Turn from your sins and act on this glorious news!"

16 One day as Jesus was walking along the shores of the Sea of Galilee, He saw Simon and his brother Andrew fishing with nets, for they were commercial fishermen.

---

[1]Implied.

[2]Some ancient manuscripts read, "the prophets said." This quotation, unrecorded in the book of Isaiah, also appears in Malachi 3:1.

[3]Literally, "make ready the way of the Lord; make His paths straight."

[4]Literally, "preaching a baptism of repentance for the forgiveness of sins."

[5]Literally, "Whose shoes I am not worthy to unloose."

[6]Or, "in." The Greek word is not clear on this controversial point.

[7]Implied.

Revised Standard

THE GOSPEL ACCORDING TO

Mark

1 The beginning of the gospel of Jesus Christ, the Son of God.[a]

2 As it is written in Isaiah the prophet,[b]
"Behold, I send my messenger before
thy face,
who shall prepare thy way;
3 the voice of one crying in the wilderness:
Prepare the way of the Lord,
make his paths straight—"

The preaching of John the Baptist

4 John the baptizer appeared[c] in the wilderness, preaching a baptism of repentance for the forgiveness of sins.
5 And there went out to him all the country of Judea, and all the people of Jerusalem; and they were baptized by him in the river Jordan, confessing their sins.
6 Now John was clothed with camel's hair, and had a leather girdle around his waist, and ate locusts and wild honey.
7 And he preached, saying, "After me comes he who is mightier than I, the thong of whose sandals I am not worthy to stoop down and untie.
8 I have baptized you with water; but he will baptize you with the Holy Spirit."

Baptism and temptation of Jesus

9 In those days Jesus came from Nazareth of Galilee and was baptized by John in the Jordan.
10 And when he came up out of the water, immediately he saw the heavens opened and the Spirit descending upon him like a dove;
11 and a voice from heaven, "Thou art my beloved Son;[d] with thee I am well pleased."

12 The Spirit immediately drove him out into the wilderness.
13 And he was in the wilderness forty days, tempted by Satan; and he was with the wild beasts; and the angels ministered to him.

The beginning of Jesus' ministry

14 Now after John was arrested, Jesus came into Galilee, preaching the gospel of God,
15 and saying, "The time is fulfilled, and the kingdom of God is at hand; repent, and believe in the gospel."

Jesus calls four disciples

16 And passing along by the Sea of Galilee, he saw Simon and Andrew the brother of Simon casting a net in the sea;

---

[a] Other ancient authorities omit *the Son of God*

[b] Other ancient authorities read *in the prophets*

[c] Other ancient authorities read *John was baptizing*

[d] Or *my Son, my* (or *the*) *Beloved*

King James

17 And Jesus said unto them, Come ye after me, and I will make you to become fishers of men.

18 And straightway they forsook their nets, and followed him.

19 And when he had gone a little farther thence, he saw James the *son* of Zebedee, and John his brother, who also were in the ship mending their nets.

20 And straightway he called them: and they left their father Zebedee in the ship with the hired servants, and went after him.

21 And they went into Capernaum; and straightway on the sabbath day he entered into the synagogue, and taught.

22 And they were astonished at his doctrine: for he taught them as one that had authority, and not as the scribes.

23 And there was in their synagogue a man with an unclean spirit; and he cried out,

24 Saying, Let *us* alone; what have we to do with thee, thou Jesus of Nazareth? art thou come to destroy us? I know thee who thou art, the Holy One of God.

25 And Jesus rebuked him, saying, Hold thy peace, and come out of him.

26 And when the unclean spirit had torn him, and cried with a loud voice, he came out of him.

27 And they were all amazed, insomuch that they questioned among themselves, saying, What thing is this? what new doctrine *is* this? for with authority commandeth he even the unclean spirits, and they do obey him.

28 And immediately his fame spread abroad throughout all the region round about Galilee.

29 And forthwith, when they were come out of the synagogue, they entered into the house of Simon and Andrew, with James and John.

30 But Simon's wife's mother lay sick of a fever, and anon they tell him of her.

31 And he came and took her by the hand, and lifted her up; and immediately the fever left her, and she ministered unto them.

32 And at even, when the sun did set, they brought unto him all that were diseased, and them that were possessed with devils.

33 And all the city was gathered together at the door.

34 And he healed many that were sick of divers diseases, and cast out many devils; and suffered not the devils to speak, because they knew him.

35 And in the morning, rising up a great while before day, he went out, and departed into a solitary place, and there prayed.

36 And Simon and they that were with him followed after him.

37 And when they had found him, they said unto him, All *men* seek for thee.

38 And he said unto them, Let us go into the next towns, that I may preach there also: for therefore came I forth.

Amplified

17 And Jesus said to them, Come after Me *and* [i]be My disciples, and I will make you to become fishers of men.

18 And at once they left their nets *and* [i]yielding up all claim to them followed [with] Him—[i]joining Him as disciples and siding with His party.

19 He went on a little farther and saw James the [son] of Zebedee and John his brother, who were in [their] boat putting their nets in order.

20 And immediately He called out to them, and [[i]abandoning all mutual claims] they left their father Zebedee in the boat with the hired men, and went off after Him—[i]to be His disciples, side with His party and follow Him.

21 And they entered into Capernaum, and immediately on the Sabbath He went into the synagogue and began to teach.

22 And they were completely astonished at His teaching, for He was teaching as one who possessed authority, and not as the scribes.

23 Just at that time there was in their synagogue a man [who was in the power] of an unclean spirit; and now immediately he raised a deep *and* terrible cry from the depths of his throat, saying,

24 What have You to do with us, Jesus of Nazareth? Have You come to destroy us? I know who You are, the Holy [One] of God!

25 And Jesus rebuked him, saying, Hush up (be muzzled, gagged), and come out of him!

26 And the unclean spirit, throwing the man into convulsions and [j]screeching with a loud voice, came out of him.

27 And they were all so amazed *and* [k]almost terrified that they kept questioning *and* demanding one of another, saying, What is this? What new (fresh) teaching! With authority He gives orders even to the unclean spirits and they obey Him!

28 And immediately rumors concerning Him spread [everywhere] throughout all the region surrounding Galilee.

29 And at once He left the synagogue and went into the house of Simon [Peter] and Andrew, accompanied by James and John.

30 Now Simon's mother-in-law [l]had for some time been lying sick with a fever, and at once they told Him about her.

31 And He went up to her, and took her by the hand, and raised her up; and the fever left her, and she began to wait on them.

32 Now when it was evening, after the sun had set, they brought to Him all who were sick and those under the power of demons,

33 Until the whole town was gathered together about the door.

34 And He cured many who were afflicted with various diseases, and He drove out many demons; and would not allow the demons to talk, because they knew Him [[m]intuitively].

35 And in the morning, long before daylight, He got up and went out to a [n]deserted place, and there He prayed.

36 And Simon [Peter] and those who were with him followed Him—[o]pursuing Him eagerly and hunting Him out;

37 And they found Him, and said to Him, Everybody is looking for You.

38 And He said to them, Let us be going on into the neighboring country towns, that I may preach there also, for that is why I came out.

---

i) Thayer.
j) Robertson's "Word Pictures in the New Testament."
k) Souter's "Pocket Lexicon to the Greek New Testament."
l) Wuest.
m) Williams.
n) Moulton and Milligan.
o) Vincent.

Living New Testament

17 Jesus called out to them, "Come, follow Me! And I will make you fishermen for the souls of men!"

18 At once they left their nets and went along with Him.

19 A little farther up the beach, He saw Zebedee's sons, James and John, in a boat mending their nets.

20 He called them, too, and immediately they left their father Zebedee in the boat with the hired men and went with Him.

21 Jesus and His companions now arrived at the town of Capernaum and on Saturday[8] morning went into the Jewish place of worship—the synagogue—where He preached.

22 The congregation was surprised at His sermon because He spoke as an authority, and didn't try to prove His points by quoting others—quite unlike what they were used to hearing![9]

23 A man possessed by a demon was present and began shouting,

24 "Why are You bothering us, Jesus of Nazareth—have You come to destroy us demons? I know who You are—the holy Son of God!"

25 Jesus curtly commanded the demon to say no more and to come out of the man.

26 At that the evil spirit screamed and convulsed the man violently and left him.

27 Amazement gripped the audience and they began discussing what had happened. "What sort of new religion is this?" they asked excitedly. "Why, even evil spirits obey His orders!"

28 The news of what He had done spread quickly through that entire area of Galilee.

29, 30 Then leaving the synagogue, He and His disciples went over to Simon and Andrew's home, where they found Simon's mother-in-law sick in bed with a high fever. They told Jesus about her right away.

31 He went to her bedside, and as He took her by the hand and helped her to sit up, the fever suddenly left, and she got up and prepared dinner for them!

32, 33 By sunset the courtyard was filled with the sick and demon-possessed, brought to Him for healing; and a huge crowd of people from all over the city of Capernaum gathered outside the door to watch.

34 So Jesus healed great numbers of sick folk that evening and ordered many demons to come out of their victims. (But He refused to allow the demons to speak, because they knew who He was.)

35 The next morning He was up long before daybreak and went out alone into the wilderness to pray.

36, 37 Later, Simon and the others went out to find Him, and told Him, "Everyone is asking for You."

38 But He replied, "We must go on to other towns as well, and give My message to them too, for that is why I came."

[8]Sabbath.
[9]Literally, "not as the scribes."

Revised Standard

for they were fishermen. 17 And Jesus said
to them, "Follow me and I will make you
become fishers of men." 18 And immediately they left their nets and followed him.
19 And going on a little farther, he saw
James the son of Zebedee and John his
brother, who were in their boat mending
the nets. 20 And immediately he called
them; and they left their father Zebedee
in the boat with the hired servants, and
followed him.

The unclean spirit cast out

21 And they went into Capernaum; and
immediately on the sabbath he entered the
synagogue and taught. 22 And they were
astonished at his teaching, for he taught
them as one who had authority, and not
as the scribes. 23 And immediately there was
in their synagogue a man with an unclean
spirit; 24 and he cried out, "What have you
to do with us, Jesus of Nazareth? Have you
come to destroy us? I know who you are,
the Holy One of God." 25 But Jesus rebuked him, saying, "Be silent, and come
out of him!" 26 And the unclean spirit, convulsing him and crying with a loud voice,
came out of him. 27 And they were all
amazed, so that they questioned among
themselves, saying, "What is this? A new
teaching! With authority he commands even
the unclean spirits, and they obey him."
28 And at once his fame spread everywhere
throughout all the surrounding region of
Galilee.

Peter's mother-in-law healed

29 And immediately, he[e] left the synagogue, and entered the house of Simon and
Andrew, with James and John. 30 Now
Simon's mother-in-law lay sick with a fever,
and immediately they told him of her. 31 And
he came and took her by the hand and
lifted her up, and the fever left her; and
she served them.

The sick healed; demons cast out

32 That evening, at sundown, they
brought to him all who were sick or possessed with demons. 33 And the whole city
was gathered together about the door. 34 And
he healed many who were sick with various
diseases, and cast out many demons; and
he would not permit the demons to speak,
because they knew him.

Jesus preaches in Galilee

35 And in the morning, a great while
before day, he rose and went out to a lonely
place, and there he prayed. 36 And Simon
and those who were with him followed
him, 37 and they found him and said to him,
"Every one is searching for you." 38 And
he said to them, "Let us go on to the next
towns, that I may preach there also; for

[e] Other ancient authorities read *they*

King James

39 And he preached in their synagogues throughout all Galilee, and cast out devils.

40 And there came a leper to him, beseeching him, and kneeling down to him, and saying unto him, If thou wilt, thou canst make me clean.

41 And Jesus, moved with compassion, put forth *his* hand, and touched him, and saith unto him, I will; be thou clean.

42 And as soon as he had spoken, immediately the leprosy departed from him, and he was cleansed.

43 And he straitly charged him, and forthwith sent him away;

44 And saith unto him, See thou say nothing to any man: but go thy way, shew thyself to the priest, and offer for thy cleansing those things which Moses commanded, for a testimony unto them.

45 But he went out, and began to publish *it* much, and to blaze abroad the matter, insomuch that Jesus could no more openly enter into the city, but was without in desert places: and they came to him from every quarter.

Amplified

39 [So] He went throughout the whole of Galilee, preaching in their synagogues and driving out demons.

40 And a leper came to Him, begging Him on his knees and saying to Him, If You will, You are able to make me clean.

41 And being moved with pity *and* sympathy, Jesus reached out His hand and touched him, and said to him, I will; be made clean!

42 And at once the leprosy [completely] left him, and he was made clean (by being healed).

43 And Jesus charged him sternly (sharply and threateningly, and with earnest admonition), and (acting with deep feeling thrust him forth and) sent him away at once;

44 And said to him, See that you tell nothing [of this] to any one; but begone, show yourself to the priest, and offer for your purification what Moses commanded, as a proof (an evidence and witness) to the people [that you are really healed]. [Lev. 13:49; 14:2-32.]

45 But he went out and began to talk so freely about it and blaze abroad the news (spreading it everywhere), that [Jesus] could no longer openly go into a town, but was outside in (lonely) desert places. But the people kept on coming to Him from [p]all sides *and* every quarter.

CHAPTER 2

AND again he entered into Capernaum after *some* days; and it was noised that he was in the house.

2 And straightway many were gathered together, insomuch that there was no room to receive *them*, no, not so much as about the door: and he preached the word unto them.

3 And they come unto him, bringing one sick of the palsy, which was borne of four.

4 And when they could not come nigh unto him for the press, they uncovered the roof where he was: and when they had broken *it* up, they let down the bed wherein the sick of the palsy lay.

5 When Jesus saw their faith, he said unto the sick of the palsy, Son, thy sins be forgiven thee.

6 But there were certain of the scribes sitting there, and reasoning in their hearts,

7 Why doth this *man* thus speak blasphemies? who can forgive sins but God only?

8 And immediately when Jesus perceived in his spirit that they so reasoned within themselves, he said unto them, Why reason ye these things in your hearts?

9 Whether is it easier to say to the sick of the palsy, *Thy* sins be forgiven thee; or to say, Arise, and take up thy bed, and walk?

CHAPTER 2

AND Jesus having returned to Capernaum, after some days it was rumored about that He was in the house [Peter's, probably].

2 And so many people gathered together there that there was no longer room [for them], not even around the door; and He was discussing the Word.

3 Then they came bringing a paralytic to Him, who had been picked up *and* was being carried by four men.

4 And when they could not get him to a place in front of Jesus because of the throng, they dug through the roof above Him; and when they had [q]scooped out an opening, they let down the ([q]thickly padded) quilt *or* mat upon which the paralyzed man lay.

5 And when Jesus saw their faith [that is, their confidence in God through Him], He said to the paralyzed man, Son, your sins are forgiven [you] *and* put away—[that is,] the [r]penalty is remitted, the sense of guilt removed, and you are made upright and in right standing with God.

6 Now some of the scribes were sitting there, holding a dialogue with themselves as they questioned in their hearts,

7 Why does this [s]Man talk like this? He is blaspheming! Who can forgive sins—[that is] [t]remove guilt, remit the penalty and bestow righteousness instead—except God alone?

8 And at once Jesus, becoming fully aware in His spirit that they thus debated within themselves, said to them, Why do you argue (debate, reason) about all this in your hearts?

---

p) Moulton and Milligan.
q) Vincent.
r) Wuest.
s) Capitalized because of what He is, the spotless Son of God, not for what the speakers may have thought He was.
t) Wuest.

Living New Testament

39 So He traveled throughout the province of Galilee, preaching in the synagogues and releasing many from the power of demons.

40 Once a leper came and knelt in front of Him and begged to be healed. "If You want to, You can make me well again," he pled.

41 And Jesus, moved with pity, touched him and said, "I want to! Be healed!"

42 Immediately the leprosy was gone—the man was healed!

43, 44 Jesus then told him sternly, "Go and be examined immediately by the Jewish priest. Don't stop to speak to anyone along the way. Take along the offering prescribed by Moses for a leper who is healed, so that everyone will have proof that you are well again."

45 But as the man went on his way he began to shout the good news that he was healed; as a result, such throngs soon surrounded Jesus that He couldn't publicly enter a city anywhere, but had to stay out in the barren wastelands. And people from everywhere came to Him there.

CHAPTER 2

Several days later He returned to Capernaum, and the news of His arrival spread quickly through the city.

2 Soon the house where He was staying was so packed with visitors that there wasn't room for a single person more, not even outside the door. And He preached the Word to them.

3 Four men arrived carrying a paralyzed man on a stretcher.

4 They couldn't get to Jesus through the crowd, so they dug through the clay roof above His head and lowered the sick man on his stretcher, right down in front of Jesus.[1]

5 When Jesus saw how strongly they believed that He would help their friend, Jesus said to the sick man, "Son, your sins are forgiven!"

6 But some of the Jewish religious leaders[2] said to themselves as they sat there,

7 "What? This is blasphemy! Does he think he is God? For only God can forgive sins."

8 Jesus could read their minds and said to them at once, "Why does this bother you?

[1]Implied.
[2]Literally, "teachers of the law."

Revised Standard

that is why I came out." 39And he went
throughout all Galilee, preaching in their
synagogues and casting out demons.

The leper cleansed

40 And a leper came to him beseeching him, and kneeling said to him, "If you
will, you can make me clean." 41Moved with
pity, he stretched out his hand and touched
him, and said to him, "I will; be clean."
42And immediately the leprosy left him, and
he was made clean. 43And he sternly
charged him, and sent him away at once,
44and said to him, "See that you say nothing
to any one; but go, show yourself to the
priest, and offer for your cleansing what
Moses commanded, for a proof to the
people."[f] 45But he went out and began to
talk freely about it, and to spread the news,
so that Jesus[g] could no longer openly enter
a town, but was out in the country; and
people came to him from every quarter.

A paralytic healed and forgiven

2 And when he returned to Capernaum
after some days, it was reported that
he was at home. 2And many were gathered
together, so that there was no longer room
for them, not even about the door; and he
was preaching the word to them. 3And they
came, bringing to him a paralytic carried
by four men. 4And when they could not
get near him because of the crowd, they
removed the roof above him; and when
they had made an opening, they let down
the pallet on which the paralytic lay. 5And
when Jesus saw their faith, he said to the
paralytic, "My son, your sins are forgiven."
6Now some of the scribes were sitting there,
questioning in their hearts, 7"Why does this
man speak thus? It is blasphemy! Who can
forgive sins but God alone?" 8And immediately Jesus, perceiving in his spirit that
they thus questioned within themselves, said
to them, "Why do you question thus in your

[f] Greek *to them*
[g] Greek *he*

King James

10 But that ye may know that the Son of man hath power on earth to forgive sins, (he saith to the sick of the palsy,)

11 I say unto thee, Arise, and take up thy bed, and go thy way into thine house.

12 And immediately he arose, took up the bed, and went forth before them all; insomuch that they were all amazed, and glorified God, saying, We never saw it on this fashion.

13 And he went forth again by the sea side; and all the multitude resorted unto him, and he taught them.

14 And as he passed by, he saw Levi the *son* of Alphæus sitting at the receipt of custom, and said unto him, Follow me. And he arose and followed him.

15 And it came to pass, that, as Jesus sat at meat in his house, many publicans and sinners sat also together with Jesus and his disciples: for there were many, and they followed him.

16 And when the scribes and Pharisees saw him eat with publicans and sinners, they said unto his disciples, How is it that he eateth and drinketh with publicans and sinners?

17 When Jesus heard *it*, he saith unto them, They that are whole have no need of the physician, but they that are sick: I came not to call the righteous, but sinners to repentance.

18 And the disciples of John and of the Pharisees used to fast: and they come and say unto him, Why do the disciples of John and of the Pharisees fast, but thy disciples fast not?

19 And Jesus said unto them, Can the children of the bridechamber fast, while the bridegroom is with them? as long as they have the bridegroom with them, they cannot fast.

20 But the days will come, when the bridegroom shall be taken away from them, and then shall they fast in those days.

21 No man also seweth a piece of new cloth on an old garment: else the new piece that filled it up taketh away from the old, and the rent is made worse.

22 And no man putteth new wine into old bottles: else the new wine doth burst the bottles, and the wine is spilled, and the bottles will be marred: but new wine must be put into new bottles.

23 And it came to pass, that he went through the corn fields on the sabbath day; and his disciples began, as they went, to pluck the ears of corn.

24 And the Pharisees said unto him, Behold, why do they on the sabbath day that which is not lawful?

25 And he said unto them, Have ye never read what David did, when he had need, and was an hungered, he, and they that were with him?

Amplified

9 Which is easier, to say to the paralyzed man, Your sins are forgiven *and* [t]put away, or to say, Rise, take up your sleeping pad and start walking about—and [t]keep on walking?

10 But that you may know positively *and* beyond a doubt that the Son of man has right *and* authority *and* power on earth to forgive sins, He said to the paralyzed man,

11 I say to you, arise, pick up *and* carry your sleeping pad and be going on home.

12 And he arose at once and picked up the pallet and went out before them all; so that they were all amazed and [u]recognized *and* praised *and* thanked God, saying, We have never seen anything like this before!

13 [Jesus] went out again along the seashore, and all the multitude kept gathering about Him, and He kept teaching them.

14 And as He was passing by, He saw Levi [Matthew] the son of Alphaeus sitting at the tax office, and He said to him, (Be [v]joined to Me as a disciple, side with My party and) follow Me! And he arose and joined Him as His disciple *and* sided with His party *and* accompanied Him.

15 And as Jesus together with His disciples sat at table in his [Levi's] house, many tax collectors and persons ([w]definitely stained) with sin were dining with Him, for there were many who walked the same road (followed) with Him.

16 And the scribes (belonging to the party) of the Pharisees, when they saw that He was eating with (those [w]definitely known to be especially wicked) sinners and tax collectors, said to His disciples, Why does He eat *and drink* with tax collectors and (notorious) sinners?

17 And when Jesus heard it, He said to them, Those who are strong *and* well have no need of a physician, but those who are weak *and* sick; I came not to call the righteous ones *to repentance*, but sinners—the [x]erring ones and [w]all those not free from sin.

18 Now John's disciples and the Pharisees were observing a fast, and [some people] came and asked Jesus, Why are John's disciples and the disciples of the Pharisees fasting, but Your disciples are not doing so?

19 Jesus answered them, Can the wedding guests fast (abstain from food and drink) while the bridegroom is with them? As long as they have the bridegroom with them they cannot fast.

20 But the days will come when the bridegroom is taken away from them, and they will fast in that day.

21 No one sews a patch of (new) unshrunken goods on an old garment; if he does, the patch tears away from it, the new from the old, and the rent becomes bigger *and* worse [than it was before].

22 And no one puts new wine into old wineskins; if he does, the wine will burst the skins, and the wine is lost and the bottles destroyed; *but new wine is to be put in new (fresh) wineskins.*

23 One Sabbath He was going along beside the fields of standing grain; and as they made their way, His disciples began to [y]pick off the grains. [Deut. 23:25.]

24 And the Pharisees said to Him, Look! Why are they doing what is not permitted *or* lawful on the Sabbath?

25 And He said to them, Have you never [even] read what David did, when he was in need and was hungry, he and those who were accompanying him?

---

t) Wuest.
u) Cremer's "Biblico—Theological Lexicon of New Testament Greek."
v) Thayer.
w) Thayer.
x) Young's Concordance.
y) Wuest.

Living New Testament

9 Is it any harder to forgive his sins than to heal him?

10, 11 So, to prove that I, the Man from Heaven,[3] have forgiven his sins,"—turning to the paralyzed man He said, "You are healed.[4] Pick up your stretcher and go home!"

12 The man jumped up, took the stretcher, and pushed his way through the stunned onlookers! Then how they praised God. "We've never seen anything like this before!" they all exclaimed.

13 Then Jesus went out to the seashore again, and preached to the crowds that gathered around Him.

14 As He was walking up the beach He saw Levi, the son of Alphaeus, sitting at his tax collection booth. "Come with Me," Jesus told him. "Come be My disciple." And Levi jumped to his feet and went along.

15 That night Levi invited his fellow tax collectors and many other notorious sinners to be his dinner guests so that they could meet Jesus and His disciples. (There were many men of this type among the crowds that followed Him.)

16 But when some of the Jewish religious leaders[5] saw Him eating with these men of ill repute, they said to His disciples, "How can He stand it, to eat with such scum?"

17 When Jesus heard what they were saying, He told them, "Sick people need the doctor, not healthy ones! I haven't come to tell good people to repent, but the bad ones."

* * * * *

18 John's disciples and the Jewish leaders sometimes fasted, that is, went without food as part of their religion. One day they came to Jesus and asked why His disciples didn't do this too.

19 Jesus replied, "Do friends of the bridegroom refuse to eat at the wedding feast? Should they be sad while he is with them?

20 But some day he will be taken away from them, and then they will mourn.

21 [Besides, going without food is part of the old way of doing things.[6]] It is like patching an old garment with unshrunk cloth! What happens? The patch pulls away and leaves the hole worse than before.

22 You know better than to put new wine into old wineskins. They would burst. The wine would be spilled out and the wineskins ruined. New wine needs fresh wineskins."

23 Another time, on a Sabbath day as Jesus and His disciples were walking through the fields, the disciples were breaking off heads of wheat and eating the grain.[6]

24 Some of the Jewish religious leaders said to Jesus, "They shouldn't be doing that! It's against our laws to harvest grain on the Sabbath."

25, 26 But Jesus replied, "Didn't you ever hear about the time King David and his companions were hungry, and he went into the house of God—Abiathar was high priest then—and they ate the special bread[7] only priests were allowed to eat? That was against the law too.

[3]Literally, "Son of man"—a term full of meaning to Jesus and His contemporaries, but very difficult for us today. "Man from Heaven" is one part of its connotation.
[4]Literally, "stand up, pick up your mat and walk."
[5]Literally, "the scribes and Pharisees."
[6]Implied.
[7]Literally, "shewbread."

Revised Standard

hearts? 9 Which is easier, to say to the paralytic, 'Your sins are forgiven,' or to say,
'Rise, take up your pallet and walk'? 10 But
that you may know that the Son of man
has authority on earth to forgive sins"—he
said to the paralytic—11 "I say to you, rise,
take up your pallet and go home." 12 And
he rose, and immediately took up the pallet
and went out before them all; so that they
were all amazed and glorified God, saying,
"We never saw anything like this!"

Matthew called

13 He went out again beside the sea;
and all the crowd gathered about him, and
he taught them. 14 And as he passed on, he
saw Levi the son of Alphaeus sitting at the
tax office, and he said to him, "Follow me."
And he rose and followed him.
15 And as he sat at table in his house,
many tax collectors and sinners were sitting
with Jesus and his disciples; for there were
many who followed him. 16 And the scribes
of[h] the Pharisees, when they saw that he
was eating with sinners and tax collectors,
said to his disciples, "Why does he eat[i] with
tax collectors and sinners?" 17 And when
Jesus heard it, he said to them, "Those who
are well have no need of a physician, but
those who are sick; I came not to call the
righteous, but sinners."

The question about fasting

18 Now John's disciples and the Pharisees
were fasting; and people came and said to
him, "Why do John's disciples and the disciples of the Pharisees fast, but your disciples do not fast? 19 And Jesus said to them,
"Can the wedding guests fast while the
bridegroom is with them? As long as they
have the bridegroom with them, they cannot fast. 20 The days will come, when the
bridegroom is taken away from them, and
then they will fast in that day. 21 No one
sews a piece of unshrunk cloth on an old
garment; if he does, the patch tears away
from it, the new from the old, and a worse
tear is made. 22 And no one puts new wine
into old wineskins; if he does, the wine will
burst the skins, and the wine is lost, and
so are the skins; but new wine is for fresh
skins."[j]

Jesus the Lord of the Sabbath

23 One sabbath he was going through
the grainfields; and as they made their way
his disciples began to pluck ears of grain.
24 And the Pharisees said to him, "Look,
why are they doing what is not lawful on
the sabbath?" 25 And he said to them, "Have
you never read what David did, when he
was in need and was hungry, he and those

[h] Other ancient authorities read *and*
[i] Other ancient authorities add *and drink*
[j] Other ancient authorities omit *but new wine is for fresh skins*

King James

26 How he went into the house of God in the days of Abiathar the high priest, and did eat the shewbread, which is not lawful to eat but for the priests, and gave also to them which were with him?

27 And he said unto them, The sabbath was made for man, and not man for the sabbath:

28 Therefore the Son of man is Lord also of the sabbath.

CHAPTER 3

AND he entered again into the synagogue; and there was a man there which had a withered hand.

2 And they watched him, whether he would heal him on the sabbath day; that they might accuse him.

3 And he saith unto the man which had the withered hand, Stand forth.

4 And he saith unto them, Is it lawful to do good on the sabbath days, or to do evil? to save life, or to kill? But they held their peace.

5 And when he had looked round about on them with anger, being grieved for the hardness of their hearts, he saith unto the man, Stretch forth thine hand. And he stretched *it* out: and his hand was restored whole as the other.

6 And the Pharisees went forth, and straightway took counsel with the Herodians against him, how they might destroy him.

7 But Jesus withdrew himself with his disciples to the sea: and a great multitude from Galilee followed him, and from Judæa,

8 And from Jerusalem, and from Idumæa, and *from* beyond Jordan; and they about Tyre and Sidon, a great multitude, when they had heard what great things he did, came unto him.

9 And he spake to his disciples, that a small ship should wait on him because of the multitude, lest they should throng him.

10 For he had healed many; insomuch that they pressed upon him for to touch him, as many as had plagues.

11 And unclean spirits, when they saw him, fell down before him, and cried, saying, Thou art the Son of God.

12 And he straitly charged them that they should not make him known.

13 And he goeth up into a mountain, and calleth *unto him* whom he would: and they came unto him.

14 And he ordained twelve, that they should be with him, and that he might send them forth to preach,

15 And to have power to heal sicknesses, and to cast out devils:

16 And Simon he surnamed Peter;

17 And James the *son* of Zebedee, and John the brother of James; and he surnamed them Boanerges, which is, The sons of thunder:

Amplified

26 How he went into the house of God, when Abiathar was the high priest, and ate the sacred loaves set forth [before God], which it is not permitted *or* lawful for any but the priests to eat, and [how he] also gave [them] to those who were with him? [I Sam. 21:1-6; II Sam. 8:17.]

27 And Jesus said to them, The Sabbath was made on account *and* for the sake of man, not man for the Sabbath; [Exod. 23:12; Deut. 5:14.]

28 So the Son of man is Lord even of the Sabbath.

CHAPTER 3

AGAIN Jesus went into a synagogue, and a man was there who had one withered hand ([z]as the result of accident or disease).

2 And [the Pharisees] kept watching Jesus (closely), to see whether He would cure on the Sabbath, so that they might get a charge to bring against Him ([a]formally).

3 And He said to the man that had the withered hand, Get up [and stand here] in the midst.

4 And He said to them, Is it lawful *and* right on the Sabbath to do good or to do evil, to save life or to take it? But they kept silence.

5 And He glanced around at them with vexation *and* anger, grieved at the hardening of their hearts, and said to the man, Hold out your hand. He held it out, and his hand was (completely) restored.

6 Then the Pharisees went out and immediately held a consultation with the Herodians against Him, how they might (devise some means to) put Him to death.

7 And Jesus retired with His disciples to the lake, and a great throng from Galilee followed Him. Also from Judea

8 And from Jerusalem and Idumea and from beyond the Jordan and from about Tyre and Sidon a vast multitude, hearing all the many things that He was doing, came to Him.

9 And He told His disciples to have a little boat in [constant] readiness for Him because of the crowd, lest they press hard upon Him *and* crush Him;

10 For He had healed so many that all who had distressing bodily diseases kept falling upon Him *and* pressing upon Him in order that they might touch Him.

11 And the spirits, the unclean ones, [b]as often as they might see Him, fell down before Him and kept screaming out, You are the Son of God!

12 And He charged them strictly *and* severely under penalty again *and* again that they should not make Him known.

13 And He went up on the hillside, and called to Him ([c]for Himself those) whom He wanted *and* chose, and they came to Him.

14 And He appointed twelve to [c]continue to be with Him, and that He might send them out to preach (as apostles),

15 And to have authority *and* power to *heal the sick and to* drive out demons.

16 [They were] Simon, and He surnamed [him] Peter;

17 James the son of Zebedee and John the brother of James, and He surnamed them Boanerges, that is, Sons of Thunder; and

z) Vincent.
a) Wuest.
b) Vincent.
c) Wuest.

Living New Testament

27 But the Sabbath was made to benefit man, and not man to benefit the Sabbath.

28 And I, the Man from Heaven,[8] have authority even to decide what men can do on Sabbath days!"

Revised Standard

who were with him: [26]how he entered the
house of God, when Abiathar was high
priest, and ate the bread of the Presence,
which it is not lawful for any but the priests
to eat, and also gave it to those who were
with him?" [27]And he said to them, "The
sabbath was made for man, not man for
the sabbath; [28]so the Son of man is lord
even of the sabbath."

CHAPTER 3

While in Capernaum Jesus went over to the synagogue again, and noticed a man there with a deformed hand.

2 Since it was the Sabbath, Jesus' enemies watched Him closely. Would He heal the man's hand? If He did, they planned to arrest Him!

3 Jesus asked the man to come and stand in front of the congregation.

4 Then turning to His enemies He asked, "Is it all right to do kind deeds on Sabbath days? Or is this a day for doing harm? Is it a day to save lives or to destroy them?" But they wouldn't answer Him.

5 Looking around at them angrily, for He was deeply disturbed by their indifference to human need, He said to the man, "Reach out your hand." He did, and instantly his hand was healed!

6 At once the Pharisees[1] went away and met with the Herodians[2] to discuss plans for killing Jesus.

7, 8 Meanwhile Jesus and His disciples withdrew to the beach, followed by a huge crowd from all over Galilee, Judea, Jerusalem, Idumea, from beyond the Jordan River, and even from as far away as Tyre and Sidon. For the news about His miracles had spread far and wide and vast numbers came to see Him for themselves.

9 He instructed His disciples to bring around a boat and to have it standing ready to rescue Him in case He was crowded off the beach.

10 For there had been many healings that day and as a result great numbers of sick people were crowding around Him, trying to touch Him.

11 And whenever those possessed by demons caught sight of Him they would fall down before Him shrieking, "You are the Son of God!"

12 But He strictly warned them not to make Him known.

13 Afterwards He went up into the hills and summoned certain ones He chose, inviting them to come and join Him there; and they did.

14, 15 Then He selected twelve of them to be His regular companions and to go out to preach, and to cast out demons.

16-19 These are the names of the twelve He chose:
Simon, (He renamed him "Peter"),
James and John (the sons of Zebedee, but Jesus called them, "Sons of Thunder"),

Jesus heals on the Sabbath

3 Again he entered the synagogue, and a
man was there who had a withered
hand. [2]And they watched him, to see
whether he would heal him on the sabbath,
so that they might accuse him. [3]And he
said to the man who had the withered
hand, "Come here." [4]And he said to them,
"Is it lawful on the sabbath to do good
or to do harm, to save life or to kill?" But
they were silent. [5]And he looked around
at them with anger, grieved at their hardness of heart, and said to the man, "Stretch
out your hand." He stretched it out, and his
hand was restored. [6]The Pharisees went out,
and immediately held counsel with the
Herodians against him, how to destroy him.

Jesus heals many by the sea

7 Jesus withdrew with his disciples to
the sea, and a great multitude from Galilee
followed; also from Judea [8]and Jerusalem
and Idumea and from beyond the Jordan
and from about Tyre and Sidon a great
multitude, hearing all that he did, came to
him. [9]And he told his disciples to have a
boat ready for him because of the crowd,
lest they should crush him; [10]for he had
healed many, so that all who had diseases
pressed upon him to touch him. [11]And
whenever the unclean spirits beheld him,
they fell down before him and cried out,
"You are the Son of God." [12]And he strictly ordered them not to make him known.

The appointing of the twelve

13 And he went up into the hills, and
called to him those whom he desired; and
they came to him. [14]And he appointed
twelve,[k] to be with him, and to be sent
out to preach [15]and have authority to cast
out demons: [16]Simon whom he surnamed
Peter; [17]James the son of Zebedee and John
the brother of James, whom he surnamed
Boanerges, that is, sons of thunder; [18]An-

[8]Literally, "the son of man," a term of highest honor and acclaim.
[1]The Pharisees were a religious sect of the Jews.
[2]A pro-Roman political party.

[k] Other ancient authorities add *whom also he named apostles*

King James

18 And Andrew, and Philip, and Bartholomew, and Matthew, and Thomas, and James the *son* of Alphæus, and Thaddæus, and Simon the Canaanite,
19 And Judas Iscariot, which also betrayed him: and they went into an house.
20 And the multitude cometh together again, so that they could not so much as eat bread.
21 And when his friends heard *of it*, they went out to lay hold on him: for they said, He is beside himself.
22 ¶ And the scribes which came down from Jerusalem said, He hath Beelzebub, and by the prince of devils casteth he out devils.
23 And he called them *unto him*, and said unto them in parables, How can Satan cast out Satan?
24 And if a kingdom be divided against itself, that kingdom cannot stand.
25 And if a house be divided against itself, that house cannot stand.
26 And if Satan rise up against himself, and be divided, he cannot stand, but hath an end.
27 No man can enter into a strong man's house, and spoil his goods, except he will first bind the strong man; and then he will spoil his house.
28 Verily I say unto you, All sins shall be forgiven unto the sons of men, and blasphemies wherewith soever they shall blaspheme:
29 But he that shall blaspheme against the Holy Ghost hath never forgiveness, but is in danger of eternal damnation:
30 Because they said, He hath an unclean spirit.
31 ¶ There came then his brethren and his mother, and, standing without, sent unto him, calling him.
32 And the multitude sat about him, and they said unto him, Behold, thy mother and thy brethren without seek for thee.
33 And he answered them, saying, Who is my mother, or my brethren?
34 And he looked round about on them which sat about him, and said, Behold my mother and my brethren!
35 For whosoever shall do the will of God, the same is my brother, and my sister, and mother.

Amplified

18 Andrew, and Philip, and Bartholomew [Nathaniel], and Matthew, and Thomas, and James the son of Alphaeus, and Thaddaeus [Judas, not Iscariot], and Simon the Cananaean [also called Zelotes],
19 And Judas Iscariot, he who betrayed Him. Then He went to a house [probably Peter's].
20 But a throng came together again, so that Jesus and His disciples could not even take food.
21 And when those [d]who belonged to Him ([e]His kinsmen) heard it, they went out to take Him by force, for they kept saying, He is out of [f]His mind—beside Himself, deranged!
22 And the scribes who came down from Jerusalem said, He is possessed by Beelzebub, and by [the help of] the prince of demons He is casting out demons.
23 And He summoned them to Him, and said to them in parables, How can Satan drive out Satan?
24 And if a kingdom is divided *and* rebelling against itself, that kingdom cannot stand.
25 And if a house is divided—split into factions and rebelling—against itself that house will not be able to last.
26 And if Satan has raised an insurrection against himself and is divided, he cannot stand, but is [surely] coming to an end.
27 But no one can go into a strong man's house and ransack his household goods right and left *and* seize them as plunder, unless he first binds the strong man; then indeed he may [thoroughly] plunder his house. [Isa. 49:24,25.]
28 Truly *and* solemnly I say to you, all sins will be forgiven the sons of men, and whatever abusive *and* blasphemous things they utter;
29 But whoever speaks abusively against *or* maliciously misrepresents the Holy Spirit can never get forgiveness, but is guilty of *and* is in the grasp of [g]an everlasting trespass.
30 For they [h]persisted in saying, [i]He has an unclean spirit.
31 Then His mother and His brothers came, and standing outside they sent word to Him, calling [for] Him.
32 And a crowd was sitting around Him, and they said to Him, Your mother and Your brothers *and Your sisters* are outside, asking for You.
33 And He replied, Who are My mother and My brothers?
34 And looking around on those who sat in a circle about Him, He said, See! Here are My mother and My brothers,
35 For whoever does the things God wills is My brother, and sister, and mother!

King James

CHAPTER 4

AND he began again to teach by the sea side: and there was gathered unto him a great multitude, so that he entered into a ship, and sat in the sea; and the whole multitude was by the sea on the land.

Amplified

CHAPTER 4

AGAIN Jesus began to teach beside the lake. And a very great crowd gathered about Him, so that He got into a ship in order to sit in it on the sea; and the whole crowd was at the lakeside on the shore.

---

d) Tyndale.
e) Wycliffe.
f) Capitalized for what He is, the spotless Son of God, not what the speakers may have thought He was.
g) Wycliffe.
h) Vincent.
i) Capitalized for what He is, the spotless Son of God, not what the speakers may have thought He was.

Living New Testament

Andrew,
Philip,
Bartholomew,
Matthew,
Thomas,
James (the son of Alphaeus),
Thaddaeus,
Simon (a member of a political party advocating violent overthrow of the Roman government),
Judas Iscariot (who later betrayed Him).

20 When He returned to the house where He was staying, the crowds began to gather again, and soon it was so full of visitors that He couldn't even find time to eat.

21 When His friends heard what was happening they came to try to take Him home with them. "He's out of His mind," they said.

22 But the Jewish teachers of religion who had arrived from Jerusalem said, "His trouble is that he's possessed by Satan, king of demons. That's why demons obey him."

23 Jesus summoned these men and asked them (using proverbs they all understood), "How can Satan cast out Satan?

24 A kingdom divided against itself will collapse.

25 A home filled with strife and division destroys itself.

26 And if Satan is fighting against himself, how can he accomplish anything? He would never survive.

27 [Satan must be bound before his demons are cast out[3]], just as a strong man must be tied up before his house can be ransacked and his property robbed.

28 I solemnly declare that any sin of man can be forgiven, even blasphemy against My Father,

29 But blasphemy against the Holy Spirit can never be forgiven. It is an eternal sin."

30 He told them this because they were saying He did His miracles by Satan's power [instead of acknowledging it was by the Holy Spirit's power[4]].

31, 32 Now His mother and brothers arrived at the crowded house where He was teaching, and they sent word for Him to come out and talk with them. "Your mother and brothers are outside and want to see You," He was told.

33 He replied, "Who is My mother? Who are My brothers?"

34 Looking at those around Him He said, "These are My mother and brothers!

35 Anyone who does God's will is My brother, and My sister, and My mother."

CHAPTER 4

Once again an immense crowd gathered around Him on the beach as He was teaching, so He got into a boat and sat down and talked from there.

[3]Implied.
[4]Implied.

Revised Standard

drew, and Philip, and Bartholomew, and
Matthew, and Thomas, and James the son
of Alphaeus, and Thaddaeus, and Simon
the Cananaean, 19 and Judas Iscariot, who
betrayed him.

Jesus answers the Pharisees' slander

Then he went home; 20 and the crowd
came together again, so that they could
not even eat. 21 And when his friends heard
it, they went out to seize him, for they said,
"He is beside himself." 22 And the scribes
who came down from Jerusalem said, "He
is possessed by Beelzebul, and by the prince
of demons he casts out the demons." 23 And
he called them to him, and said to them in
parables, "How can Satan cast out Satan?
24 If a kingdom is divided against itself, that
kingdom cannot stand. 25 And if a house is
divided against itself, that house will not be
able to stand. 26 And if Satan has risen up
against himself and is divided, he cannot
stand, but is coming to an end. 27 But no
one can enter a strong man's house and
plunder his goods, unless he first binds the
strong man; then indeed he may plunder
his house.
28 "Truly, I say to you, all sins will be
forgiven the sons of men, and whatever
blasphemies they utter; 29 but whoever blasphemes against the Holy Spirit never has
forgiveness, but is guilty of an eternal
sin"—30 for they had said, "He has an unclean spirit."

Jesus' true family

31 And his mother and his brothers
came; and standing outside they sent to him
and called him. 32 And a crowd was sitting
about him; and they said to him, "Your
mother and your brothers[1] are outside, asking for you." 33 And he replied, "Who are
my mother and my brothers?" 34 And looking around at those who sat about him, he
said, "Here are my mother and my brothers!
35 Whoever does the will of God is my
brother, and sister, and mother."

The parable of the sower

4 Again he began to teach beside the sea.
And a very large crowd gathered about
him, so that he got into a boat and sat in
it on the sea; and the whole crowd was
beside the sea on the land. 2 And he taught

[1] Other early authorities add *and your sisters*

King James

2 And he taught them many things by parables, and said unto them in his doctrine,

3 Hearken; Behold, there went out a sower to sow:

4 And it came to pass, as he sowed, some fell by the way side, and the fowls of the air came and devoured it up.

5 And some fell on stony ground, where it had not much earth; and immediately it sprang up, because it had no depth of earth:

6 But when the sun was up, it was scorched; and because it had no root, it withered away.

7 And some fell among thorns, and the thorns grew up, and choked it, and it yielded no fruit.

8 And other fell on good ground, and did yield fruit that sprang up and increased; and brought forth, some thirty, and some sixty, and some an hundred.

9 And he said unto them, He that hath ears to hear, let him hear.

10 And when he was alone, they that were about him with the twelve asked of him the parable.

11 And he said unto them, Unto you it is given to know the mystery of the kingdom of God: but unto them that are without, all *these* things are done in parables:

12 That seeing they may see, and not perceive; and hearing they may hear, and not understand; lest at any time they should be converted, and *their* sins should be forgiven them.

13 And he said unto them, Know ye not this parable? and how then will ye know all parables?

14 ¶ The sower soweth the word.

15 And these are they by the way side, where the word is sown; but when they have heard, Satan cometh immediately, and taketh away the word that was sown in their hearts.

16 And these are they likewise which are sown on stony ground; who, when they have heard the word, immediately receive it with gladness;

17 And have no root in themselves, and so endure but for a time: afterward, when affliction or persecution ariseth for the word's sake, immediately they are offended.

18 And these are they which are sown among thorns; such as hear the word,

19 And the cares of this world, and the deceitfulness of riches, and the lusts of other things entering in, choke the word, and it becometh unfruitful.

20 And these are they which are sown on good ground; such as hear the word, and receive *it*, and bring forth fruit, some thirtyfold, some sixty, and some an hundred.

21 ¶ And he said unto them, Is a candle brought to be put under a bushel, or under a bed? and not to be set on a candlestick?

Amplified

2 And He taught them many things in parables [concrete illustrations put beside truths to explain them], and in His teaching He said to them:

3 Give attention to this. Behold, a sower went out to sow.

4 And as he was sowing, some seed fell along the path, and the birds came and ate it up.

5 Other seed [of the same kind] fell on ground full of rocks, where it had not much soil, and at once it sprang up, because it had no depth of soil;

6 And when the sun came up, it was scorched, and because it had not taken root withered away.

7 Other seed [of the same kind] fell among thorn-plants, and the thistles grew *and* pressed together *and* utterly choked *and* suffocated it, and it yielded no grain.

8 And other seed [of the same kind] fell into good (well adapted) soil, and brought forth grain, growing up and increasing, and yielded up to thirty times as much, and sixty times as much, and even a hundred times as much as had been sown.

9 And he said, He who has ears to hear, let him be hearing—and [j]consider, and comprehend.

10 And as soon as He was alone, those who were around Him with the twelve [apostles] began to ask Him about the parables.

11 And He said to them, To you has been entrusted the mystery of the kingdom of God, [that is, [k]the secret counsels of God which are hidden from the ungodly;] but for those outside [[l]of our circle] everything becomes a parable,

12 In order that they may [indeed] look *and* look but not perceive, and may hear *and* hear but not grasp *and* comprehend; [m]lest haply they should turn again, and it [[k]their wilful rejection of the truth] should be forgiven them. [Isa. 6:9,10.]

13 And He said to them, Do you not discern *and* understand this parable? How then [is it possible for] you to discern *and* understand all the parables?

14 The sower sows the Word.

15 The ones along the path are those who have the Word sown [in their hearts], but when they hear, Satan comes at once and (by force) takes away the message which is sown in them.

16 And in the same way the ones sown upon stony ground are those who, when they hear the Word, at once receive *and* accept *and* welcome it with joy;

17 And they have no real root in themselves, and so they endure for a little while, then when trouble or persecution arises on account of the Word, they immediately are offended—become displeased, indignant, resentful; *and* they stumble *and* fall away.

18 And the ones sown among the thorns are others who hear the Word,

19 Then the cares *and* anxieties of the world, *and* distractions of the age, and the pleasure *and* delight *and* false glamour *and* deceitfulness of riches, and the craving *and* passionate desire for other things creep in and choke *and* suffocate the Word, and it becomes fruitless.

20 And those that were sown on the good (well-adapted) soil are the ones who hear the Word, and receive *and* accept *and* welcome it and bear fruit, some thirty times as much as was sown, some sixty times as much, and some [even] a hundred times as much.

21 And He said to them, Is the lamp brought in to be put under a [n]peck-measure, or under a bed, and not on the [lamp] stand?

---

j) Thayer.
k) Wuest.
l) Vincent.
m) Robertson.
n) Moulton and Milligan.

Living New Testament

2 His usual method of teaching was to tell the people stories. One of them went like this:

3 "Listen! A farmer decided to sow some grain. As he scattered it across his field

4 Some of it fell on a path, and the birds came and picked it off the hard ground and ate it.

5, 6 Some fell on thin soil with underlying rock. It grew up quickly enough, but soon wilted beneath the hot sun and died because the roots had no nourishment in the shallow soil.

7 Other seeds fell among thorns that shot up and crowded the young plants so that they produced no grain.

8 But some of the seeds fell into good soil and yielded 30 times as much as he had planted—some of it even 60 or 100 times as much!

9 If you have ears, listen!"

10 Afterwards, when He was alone with the Twelve and with His other disciples, they asked Him, "What does Your story mean?"

11, 12 He replied, "You are permitted to know some truths about the Kingdom of God that are hidden to those outside the Kingdom. As Isaiah[1] the prophet says: 'Though they see and hear, they will not understand or turn to God, or be forgiven for their sins.'

13 But if you can't understand *this* simple illustration, what will you do about all the others I am going to tell?

14 The farmer I talked about is anyone who brings God's message to others, trying to plant good seed within their lives.

15 The hard pathway, where some of the seed fell, represents the hard hearts of some of those who hear God's message; Satan comes at once to try to make them forget it.

16 The rocky soil represents the hearts of those who hear the message with joy,

17 But, like young plants in such soil, their roots don't go very deep, and though at first they get along fine, as soon as persecution begins, they wilt.

18 The thorny ground represents the hearts of people who listen to the Good News and receive it,

19 But all too quickly the attractions of this world and the delights of wealth, and the search for success and lure of nice things come in and crowd out God's message from their hearts, so that no crop is produced.

20 But the good soil represents the hearts of those who truly accept God's message and produce a plentiful harvest for God—30, 60, or even 100 times as much as was planted in their hearts."

21 Then He asked them, "When someone lights a lamp, does he put a box over it to shut out the light? Of course not! The light couldn't be seen or used. A lamp is placed on a stand to shine and be useful.

[1]Implied.

Revised Standard

them many things in parables, and in his
teaching he said to them: 3"Listen! A
sower went out to sow. 4And as he sowed,
some seed fell along the path, and the birds
came and devoured it. 5Other seed fell on
rocky ground, where it had not much soil,
and immediately it sprang up, since it had
no depth of soil; 6and when the sun rose
it was scorched, and since it had no root it
withered away. 7Other seed fell among
thorns and the thorns grew up and choked
it, and it yielded no grain. 8And other seeds
fell into good soil and brought forth grain,
growing up and increasing and yielding
thirtyfold and sixtyfold and a hundredfold."
9And he said, "He who has ears to hear,
let him hear."

Parable of the sower explained

10 And when he was alone, those who
were about him with the twelve asked him
concerning the parables. 11And he said to
them, "To you has been given the secret
of the kingdom of God, but for those outside everything is in parables; 12so that
they may indeed see but not perceive, and
may indeed hear but not understand; lest
they should turn again, and be forgiven."
13And he said to them, "Do you not understand this parable? How then will you
understand all the parables? 14The sower
sows the word. 15And these are the ones
along the path, where the word is sown;
when they hear, Satan immediately comes
and takes away the word which is sown in
them. 16And these in like manner are the
ones sown upon rocky ground, who, when
they hear the word, immediately receive it
with joy; 17and they have no root in themselves, but endure for a while; then, when
tribulation or persecution arises on account
of the word, immediately they fall away.[m]
18And others are the ones sown among
thorns; they are those who hear the word,
19but the cares of the world, and the delight in riches, and the desire for other things,
enter in and choke the word, and it proves
unfruitful. 20But those that were sown upon
the good soil are the ones who hear the
word and accept it and bear fruit, thirtyfold
and sixtyfold and a hundredfold."

Parables about the kingdom

21 And he said to them, "Is a lamp
brought in to be put under a bushel, or
under a bed, and not on a stand? 22For

[m] Or *stumble*

King James

22 For there is nothing hid, which shall not be manifested; neither was any thing kept secret, but that it should come abroad.
23 If any man have ears to hear, let him hear.
24 And he said unto them, Take heed what ye hear: with what measure ye mete, it shall be measured to you: and unto you that hear shall more be given.
25 For he that hath, to him shall be given: and he that hath not, from him shall be taken even that which he hath.
26 ¶ And he said, So is the kingdom of God, as if a man should cast seed into the ground;
27 And should sleep, and rise night and day, and the seed should spring and grow up, he knoweth not how.
28 For the earth bringeth forth fruit of herself; first the blade, then the ear, after that the full corn in the ear.
29 But when the fruit is brought forth, immediately he putteth in the sickle, because the harvest is come.
30 ¶ And he said, Whereunto shall we liken the kingdom of God? or with what comparison shall we compare it?
31 *It is* like a grain of mustard seed, which, when it is sown in the earth, is less than all the seeds that be in the earth:
32 But when it is sown, it groweth up, and becometh greater than all herbs, and shooteth out great branches; so that the fowls of the air may lodge under the shadow of it.
33 And with many such parables spake he the word unto them, as they were able to hear *it*.
34 But without a parable spake he not unto them: and when they were alone, he expounded all things to his disciples.
35 And the same day, when the even was come, he saith unto them, Let us pass over unto the other side.
36 And when they had sent away the multitude, they took him even as he was in the ship. And there were also with him other little ships.
37 And there arose a great storm of wind, and the waves beat into the ship, so that it was now full.
38 And he was in the hinder part of the ship, asleep on a pillow: and they awake him, and say unto him, Master, carest thou not that we perish?
39 And he arose, and rebuked the wind, and said unto the sea, Peace, be still. And the wind ceased, and there was a great calm.
40 And he said unto them, Why are ye so fearful? how is it that ye have no faith?
41 And they feared exceedingly, and said one to another, What manner of man is this, that even the wind and the sea obey him?

Amplified

22—[o]Things are hidden [temporarily] only as a means to revelation. For there is nothing hidden except to be revealed, nor is anything [temporarily] kept secret except in order that it may be made known.
23 If any man has ears to hear, let him be listening, *and* perceive *and* comprehend.
24 And He said to them, Be careful what you are hearing. The measure [p][of thought and study] you give [to [q]the truth you hear] will be the measure [r][of virtue and knowledge] that comes back to you, and more [besides] will be given to you *who hear.*
25 For to him who has will more be given, and from him who has nothing, even what he has will be taken away ([s]by force),
26 And He said, The kingdom of God is like a man who scatters seed upon the ground,
27 Then continues sleeping and rising night and day while the seed sprouts and grows *and* [s]increases, he knows not how.
28 The earth produces [acting] by itself, first the blade, then the ear, then the full grain in the ear.
29 But when the grain is ripe *and* permits, immediately he [t]sends forth [the reapers] *and* puts in the sickle, because the harvest stands ready.
30 And He said, With what can we compare the kingdom of God, or what parable shall we use to illustrate *and* explain it?
31 It is like a grain of mustard seed, which when sown upon the ground is the smallest of all seeds upon the earth;
32 Yet after it is sown it grows up and becomes the greatest of all garden herbs, and puts out large branches, so that the birds of the air are able to make nests *and* dwell in its shade.
33 With many such parables [Jesus] spoke the Word to them, as they were able to hear *and* [u]to comprehend *and* understand.
34 He did not tell them anything without a parable, but privately to His disciples [[v]those who were peculiarly His own] He explained everything [fully].
35 On that same day [when] evening had come, He said to them, Let us go over to the other side [of the lake].
36 And leaving the throng, they took Him with them, [just] as He was, in the boat [in which He was sitting]. And other boats were with Him.
37 And a furious storm of wind ([v]of hurricane proportions) arose, and the waves kept beating into the boat, so that it was already becoming filled.
38 But He [Himself] was in the stern [of the boat] asleep on the [leather] cushion; and they awoke Him and said to Him, Master, do You not care that we are perishing?
39 And He arose and rebuked the wind, and said to the sea, Hush now! Be still (muzzled)! And the wind ceased, [that is, [w]sank to rest as if exhausted by its beating] and there was (immediately) a great calm—[x]a perfect peacefulness.
40 He said to them, Why are you so timid *and* fearful? How is it that you have no faith—no [y]firmly relying trust?
41 And they were filled with great awe *and* [w]feared exceedingly, and said one to another, Who then is this, that even wind and sea obey Him?

---

o) After Swete, Robertson, Vincent, etc.
p) After "Expositor's Greek Testament."
q) After Gray and Adams' "Bible Commentary," Euthy, Wuest, Barnes, etc.
r) After "Expositor's Greek Testament," etc.
s) Thayer.
t) Vincent.
u) Thayer.
v) Wuest.
w) Vincent.
x) After Wycliffe.
y) Cremer.

Living New Testament

22 All that is now hidden will someday come to light.
23 If you have ears, listen!
24 And be sure to put into practice what you hear. The more you do this, the more you will understand what I tell you.
25 To him who has shall be given; from him who has not shall be taken away even what he has.
26 Here is another story illustrating what the Kingdom of God is like: a farmer sowed his field,
27 And went away, and as the days went by, the seeds grew and grew without his help.
28 For the soil made the seeds grow. First a leaf-blade pushed through, and later the wheat-heads formed and finally the grain ripened,
29 And then the farmer came at once with his sickle and harvested it."
30 Jesus asked. "How can I describe the Kingdom of God? What story shall I use to illustrate it?
31, 32 It is like a tiny mustard seed! Though this is one of the smallest of seeds, yet it grows to become one of the largest of plants, with long branches where birds can build their nests and be sheltered."
33 He used many such illustrations to teach the people as much as they were ready to understand.[2]
34 In fact, He taught only by illustrations in His public teaching, but afterwards, when He was alone with His disciples, He would explain His meaning to them.

* * * * *

35 As evening fell, Jesus said to His disciples, "Let's cross to the other side of the lake."
36 So they took Him just as He was and started out, leaving the crowds behind (though other boats followed).
37 But soon a terrible storm arose. High waves began to break into the boat until it was nearly full of water and about to sink.
38 Jesus was asleep at the back of the boat with His head on a cushion. Frantically they wakened Him, shouting, "Teacher, don't You even care that we are all about to drown?"
39 Then He rebuked the wind and said to the sea, "Quiet down!" And the wind fell, and there was a great calm!
40 And He asked them, "Why were you so fearful? Don't you even yet have confidence in Me?"
41 And they were filled with awe and said among themselves, "Who is this man, that even the winds and seas obey Him?"

Revised Standard

there is nothing hid, except to be made
manifest; nor is anything secret, except to
come to light. [23]If any man has ears to
hear, let him hear." [24]And he said to them,
"Take heed what you hear; the measure
you give will be the measure you get, and
still more will be given you. [25]For to him
who has will more be given; and from him
who has not, even what he has will be
taken away."
26 And he said, "The kingdom of God
is as if a man should scatter seed upon the
ground, [27]and should sleep and rise night
and day, and the seed should sprout and
grow, he knows not how. [28]The earth produces of itself, first the blade, then the
ear, then the full grain in the ear. [29]But
when the grain is ripe, at once he puts in
the sickle, because the harvest has come."
30 And he said, "With what can we
compare the kingdom of God, or what
parable shall we use for it? [31]It is like a
grain of mustard seed, which, when sown
upon the ground, is the smallest of all the
seeds on earth; [32]yet when it is sown it
grows up and becomes the greatest of all
shrubs, and puts forth large branches, so
that the birds of the air can make nests
in its shade."
33 With many such parables he spoke
the word to them, as they were able to hear
it; [34]he did not speak to them without a
parable, but privately to his own disciples
he explained everything.

The storm stilled

35 On that day, when evening had come,
he said to them, "Let us go across to the
other side." [36]And leaving the crowd, they
took him with them, just as he was, in the
boat. And other boats were with him. [37]And
a great storm of wind arose, and the waves
beat into the boat, so that the boat was already filling. [38]But he was in the stern,
asleep on the cushion; and they woke him
and said to him, "Teacher, do you not care
if we perish?" [39]And he awoke and rebuked
the wind, and said to the sea, "Peace! Be
still!" And the wind ceased, and there was
a great calm. [40]He said to them, "Why are
you afraid? Have you no faith?" [41]And
they were filled with awe, and said to one
another, "Who then is this, that even wind
and sea obey him?"

---

[2]Literally, "as they were able to hear."

King James

CHAPTER 5

AND they came over unto the other side of the sea, into the country of the Gadarenes.

2 And when he was come out of the ship, immediately there met him out of the tombs a man with an unclean spirit,

3 Who had *his* dwelling among the tombs; and no man could bind him, no, not with chains:

4 Because that he had been often bound with fetters and chains, and the chains had been plucked asunder by him, and the fetters broken in pieces: neither could any *man* tame him.

5 And always, night and day, he was in the mountains, and in the tombs, crying, and cutting himself with stones.

6 But when he saw Jesus afar off, he ran and worshipped him,

7 And cried with a loud voice, and said, What have I to do with thee, Jesus, *thou* Son of the most high God? I adjure thee by God, that thou torment me not.

8 For he said unto him, Come out of the man, *thou* unclean spirit.

9 And he asked him, What *is* thy name? And he answered, saying, My name *is* Legion: for we are many.

10 And he besought him much that he would not send them away out of the country.

11 Now there was there nigh unto the mountains a great herd of swine feeding.

12 And all the devils besought him, saying, Send us into the swine, that we may enter into them.

13 And forthwith Jesus gave them leave. And the unclean spirits went out, and entered into the swine: and the herd ran violently down a steep place into the sea, (they were about two thousand;) and were choked in the sea.

14 And they that fed the swine fled, and told *it* in the city, and in the country. And they went out to see what it was that was done.

15 And they come to Jesus, and see him that was possessed with the devil, and had the legion, sitting, and clothed, and in his right mind: and they were afraid.

16 And they that saw *it* told them how it befell to him that was possessed with the devil, and *also* concerning the swine.

17 And they began to pray him to depart out of their coasts.

18 And when he was come into the ship, he that had been possessed with the devil prayed him that he might be with him.

19 Howbeit Jesus suffered him not, but saith unto him, Go home to thy friends, and tell them how great things the Lord hath done for thee, and hath had compassion on thee.

20 And he departed, and began to publish in Decapolis how great things Jesus had done for him: and all *men* did marvel.

21 And when Jesus was passed over again by ship unto the other side, much people gathered unto him: and he was nigh unto the sea.

Amplified

CHAPTER 5

THEY came to the other side of the sea, to the region of the Gerasenes.

2 And as soon as He got out of the boat, there met Him a man out of the tombs [under the power of] an unclean spirit.

3 This man [z]continually lived among the tombs, and no one could subdue him any more, even with a chain;

4 For he had been bound often with shackles for the feet, and [a]handcuffs, but the handcuffs [of light] chains he wrenched apart, and the shackles he rubbed *and* ground together *and* broke in pieces; and no one had strength enough to restrain *or* tame him.

5 Night and day among the tombs and on the mountains he was always [a]shrieking *and* screaming, and [b]beating *and* bruising *and* [c]cutting himself with stones.

6 And when from a distance he saw Jesus, he ran and fell on his knees before Him in homage,

7 And crying out with a loud voice, he said, What have You to do with me, Jesus, Son of the Most High God? What is there in common between us? I [z]solemnly implore you by God, do not begin to torment me!

8 For Jesus was commanding, Come out of the man, you unclean spirit!

9 And He asked him, What is your name? He replied, My name is Legion, for we are many.

10 And he kept begging Him urgently not to send them [himself and the other demons] away out of that region.

11 Now a great herd of hogs was grazing there on the hillside;

12 And *the demons* begged Him, saying, Send us to the hogs that we may go into them!

13 So He gave them permission. And the unclean spirits came out [of the man] and entered into the hogs, and the herd, numbering about two thousand, rushed headlong down the steep slope into the lake, and were drowned in the sea.

14 The hog-feeders ran away, and told [it] in the town and in the country. And [the people] came to see what it was that had taken place.

15 And they came to Jesus, and looked intently *and* searchingly at the man who had been a demoniac, sitting there clothed and in his right mind, [the same man] who had had the legion [of demons]; and they were [d]seized with alarm *and* struck with fear.

16 And those who had seen it related in full what had happened to the man possessed by demons and to the hogs.

17 And they began to beg [Jesus] to leave their neighborhood.

18 And when He had stepped into the boat, the man who had been controlled by the unclean spirits kept begging Him that he might be with Him.

19 But Jesus refused to permit him, but said to him, Go home to your own [family and relatives and friends], and bring back word to them of how much the Lord has done for you, and [how He has] had sympathy for you *and* mercy on you.

20 And he departed and began to publicly proclaim in Decapolis [the region of the ten cities] how much Jesus had done for him, and all the people were astonished *and* marveled.

21 And when Jesus had recrossed in the boat to the other side, a great throng gathered about Him, and He was at the lakeshore.

---

z) Wuest.
a) Thayer.
b) Moulton and Milligan.
c) Abbott-Smith.
d) Thayer.

Living New Testament

CHAPTER 5

When they arrived at the other side of the lake a demon-possessed man ran out from a graveyard, just as Jesus was climbing from the boat.

3, 4 This man lived among the gravestones, and had such strength that whenever he was put into handcuffs and shackles—as he often was—he snapped the handcuffs from his wrists and smashed the shackles and walked away. No one was strong enough to control him.

5 All day long and through the night he would wander among the tombs and in the wild hills, screaming and cutting himself with sharp pieces of stone.

6 When Jesus was still far out on the water, the man had seen Him and had run to meet Him, and fell down before Him.

7, 8 Then Jesus spoke to the demon within the man and said, "Come out, you evil spirit." It gave a terrible scream, shrieking, "What are You going to do to me, Jesus, Son of the Most High God? For God's sake, don't torture me!"

9 "What is your name?" Jesus asked, and the demon replied, "Legion, for there are many of us here within this man."

10 Then the demons begged Him again and again not to send them to some distant land.

11 Now as it happened there was a huge herd of hogs rooting around on the hill above the lake.

12 "Send us into those hogs," the demons begged.

13 And Jesus gave them permission. Then the evil spirits came out of the man and entered the hogs, and the entire herd plunged down the steep hillside into the lake and drowned.

14 The herdsmen fled to the nearby towns and countryside, spreading the news as they ran. Everyone rushed out to see for themselves,

15 And a large crowd soon gathered where Jesus was; but as they saw the man sitting there, fully clothed and perfectly sane, they were frightened.

16 Those who saw what happened were telling everyone about it,

17 And the crowd began pleading with Jesus to go away and leave them alone!

18 So He got back into the boat. The man who had been possessed by the demons begged Jesus to let him go along.

19 But Jesus said no. "Go home to your friends," He told him, "and tell them what wonderful things God has done for you; and how merciful He has been."

20 So the man started off to visit the Ten Towns[1] of that region and began to tell everyone about the great things Jesus had done for him; and they were awestruck by his story.

* * * * *

21 When Jesus had gone across by boat to the other side of the lake, a vast crowd gathered around Him on the shore.

[1]Or, "to visit Decapolis."

Revised Standard

Demons cast out

5 They came to the other side of the sea,
to the country of the Gerasenes.[n] [2]And
when he had come out of the boat, there
met him out of the tombs a man with an
unclean spirit, [3]who lived among the tombs;
and no one could bind him any more, even
with a chain; [4]for he had often been bound
with fetters and chains, but the chains he
wrenched apart, and the fetters he broke
in pieces; and no one had the strength to
subdue him. [5]Night and day among the
tombs and on the mountains he was always
crying out, and bruising himself with stones.
[6]And when he saw Jesus from afar, he ran
and worshiped him; [7]and crying out with
a loud voice, he said, "What have you to
do with me, Jesus, Son of the Most High
God? I adjure you by God, do not torment
me." [8]For he had said to him, "Come out
of the man, you unclean spirit!" [9]And
Jesus[o] asked him, "What is your name?"
He replied, "My name is Legion; for we
are many." [10]And he begged him eagerly
not to send them out of the country. [11]Now
a great herd of swine was feeding there
on the hillside; [12]and they begged him,
"Send us to the swine, let us enter them."
[13]So he gave them leave. And the unclean
spirits came out, and entered the swine;
and the herd, numbering about two thousand, rushed down the steep bank into the
sea, and were drowned in the sea.
14 The herdsmen fled, and told it in the
city and in the country. And people came
to see what it was that had happened. [15]And
they came to Jesus, and saw the demoniac
sitting there, clothed and in his right mind,
the man who had had the legion; and they
were afraid. [16]And those who had seen it
told what had happened to the demoniac
and to the swine. [17]And they began to beg
Jesus[p] to depart from their neighborhood.
[18]And as he was getting into the boat, the
man who had been possessed with demons
begged him that he might be with him.
[19]But he refused, and said to him, "Go
home to your friends, and tell them how
much the Lord has done for you, and how
he has had mercy on you." [20]And he went
away and began to proclaim in the Decapolis how much Jesus had done for him; and
all men marveled.

Jairus' daughter raised; a suffering woman healed

21 And when Jesus had crossed again in
the boat to the other side, a great crowd
gathered about him; and he was beside the

[n] Other ancient authorities read *Gergesenes,* some *Gadarenes*
[o] Greek *he*
[p] Greek *him*

King James

22 And, behold, there cometh one of the rulers of the synagogue, Jairus by name; and when he saw him, he fell at his feet,

23 And besought him greatly, saying, My little daughter lieth at the point of death: *I pray thee*, come and lay thy hands on her, that she may be healed; and she shall live.

24 And *Jesus* went with him; and much people followed him, and thronged him.

25 And a certain woman, which had an issue of blood twelve years,

26 And had suffered many things of many physicians, and had spent all that she had, and was nothing bettered, but rather grew worse,

27 When she had heard of Jesus, came in the press behind, and touched his garment.

28 For she said, If I may touch but his clothes, I shall be whole.

29 And straightway the fountain of her blood was dried up; and she felt in *her* body that she was healed of that plague.

30 And Jesus, immediately knowing in himself that virtue had gone out of him, turned him about in the press, and said, Who touched my clothes?

31 And his disciples said unto him, Thou seest the multitude thronging thee, and sayest thou, Who touched me?

32 And he looked round about to see her that had done this thing.

33 But the woman fearing and trembling, knowing what was done in her, came and fell down before him, and told him all the truth.

34 And he said unto her, Daughter, thy faith hath made thee whole; go in peace, and be whole of thy plague.

35 While he yet spake, there came from the ruler of the synagogue's *house certain* which said, Thy daughter is dead: why troublest thou the Master any further?

36 As soon as Jesus heard the word that was spoken, he saith unto the ruler of the synagogue, Be not afraid, only believe.

37 And he suffered no man to follow him, save Peter, and James, and John the brother of James.

38 And he cometh to the house of the ruler of the synagogue, and seeth the tumult, and them that wept and wailed greatly.

39 And when he was come in, he saith unto them, Why make ye this ado, and weep? the damsel is not dead, but sleepeth.

40 And they laughed him to scorn. But when he had put them all out, he taketh the father and the mother of the damsel, and them that were with him, and entereth in where the damsel was lying.

41 And he took the damsel by the hand, and said unto her, Talitha cumi; which is, being interpreted, Damsel, I say unto thee, arise.

42 And straightway the damsel arose, and walked; for she was *of the age* of twelve years. And they were astonished with a great astonishment.

Amplified

22 Then one of the rulers of the synagogue came up, Jairus by name; and seeing Him, he prostrated himself at His feet,

23 And begged Him earnestly, saying, My little daughter is at the point of death. Come and lay Your hands on her, so that she may be healed *and* live.

24 And Jesus went with him, and a great crowd kept following Him, and pressed Him [e]from all sides—so as almost to suffocate Him.

25 And there was a woman who had had a flow of blood for twelve years,

26 And who had endured much [f]suffering under [the hands of] many physicians, and had spent all that she had; and was no better but instead grew worse.

27 She had heard the reports concerning Jesus, and she came up behind Him in the throng and touched His garment,

28 For she kept saying, If I only touch His garments, I shall be restored to health.

29 And immediately her (flow of) blood was dried up at the source, and ([g]suddenly) she felt in her body that she was healed of her ([e]distressing) ailment.

30 And Jesus, recognizing in Himself that the power proceeding from Him had gone forth, turned around immediately in the crowd, and said, Who touched My clothes?

31 And the disciples kept saying to Him, You see the crowd pressing hard around You (from all sides), and You ask, Who touched Me?

32 Still He kept looking around to see her who had done it.

33 But the woman, knowing what had been done for her, though alarmed *and* frightened and trembling, fell down before Him, and told Him the whole truth.

34 And He said to her, Daughter, your faith [that is, your [h]trust and confidence in Me, springing from faith in God] has restored you to health. Go [i]in (to) peace, and be continually healed *and* free from your ([h]distressing bodily) disease.

35 While He was still speaking, there came some from the ruler's house who said [to Jairus], Your daughter has died. Why bother *and* distress the Teacher any further?

36 ([j]Overhearing) but ignoring what they said, Jesus said to the ruler of the synagogue, Do not be seized with alarm *and* have no fear, only keep on believing.

37 And He permitted no one to accompany Him except Peter and James and John the brother of James.

38 When they arrived at the house of the ruler of the synagogue, He [i]looked (carefully and with understanding) at [the] tumult and [the people] weeping and wailing loudly.

39 And when He had gone in, He said to them, Why do you make an uproar and weep? The little girl is not dead, but is sleeping.

40 And they laughed *and* [k]jeered at Him. But He put them all out, and taking the child's father and mother and those who were with Him, He went in where the little girl was *lying*.

41 Gripping her (firmly) by the hand, He said to her, Talitha cumi, which translated is, Little girl, I say to you, arise ([l]from the sleep of death)!

42 And instantly the girl got up and started walking around, for she was twelve years [old]. And they were utterly astonished *and* overcome with amazement.

---

e) Thayer.
f) Vincent.
g) Wuest.
h) Thayer.
i) Wuest.
j) Alternate reading.
k) Abbott-Smith.
l) Thayer.

Living New Testament

22 The leader of the local synagogue, whose name was Jairus, came and fell down before Him,

23 Pleading with Him to heal his little daughter. "She is at the point of death," he said in desperation. "Please come and place Your hands on her and make her live."

24 Jesus went with him, and the crowd thronged behind.

25 In the crowd was a woman who had been sick for twelve years with a hemorrhage.

26 She had suffered much from many doctors through the years and had become poor from paying them, and was no better but, in fact, was worse.

27 She had heard all about the wonderful miracles Jesus did, and that is why she came up behind Him through the crowd and touched His clothes.

28 For she thought to herself, "If I can just touch His clothing, I will be healed."

29 And sure enough, as soon as she had touched Him, the bleeding stopped and she knew she was well!

30 Jesus realized at once that healing power had gone out from Him, so He turned around in the crowd and asked, "Who touched My clothes?"

31 His disciples said to Him, "All this crowd pressing around You, and You ask who touched You?"

32 But He kept on looking around to see who it was who had done it.

33 Then the frightened woman, trembling at the realization of what had happened to her, came and fell at His feet and told Him what she had done.

34 And He said to her, "Daughter, your faith has made you well; go in peace, healed of your disease."

35 While He was still talking to her, messengers arrived from Jairus' home with the news that it was too late—his daughter was dead and there was no point in Jesus' coming now.

36 But Jesus ignored their comments and said to Jairus, "Don't be afraid. Just trust Me."

37 Then Jesus halted the crowd and wouldn't let anyone go on with Him to Jairus' home except Peter and James and John.

38 When they arrived, Jesus saw that all was in great confusion, with unrestrained weeping and wailing.

39 He went inside and spoke to the people. "Why all this weeping and commotion?" He asked. "The child isn't dead; she is only asleep!"

40 They laughed at Him in bitter derision, but He told them all to leave, and taking the little girl's father and mother and His three disciples, He went into the room where she was lying.

41, 42 Taking her by the hand He said to her, "Get up, little girl!" (She was twelve years old.) And she jumped up and walked around! Her parents just couldn't get over it.

Revised Standard

sea. 22 Then came one of the rulers of the
synagogue, Jairus by name; and seeing him,
he fell at his feet, 23 and besought him, saying, "My little daughter is at the point of
death. Come and lay your hands on her, so
that she may be made well, and live." 24 And
he went with him.
And a great crowd followed him and
thronged about him. 25 And there was a
woman who had had a flow of blood for
twelve years, 26 and who had suffered much
under many physicians, and had spent all
that she had, and was no better but rather
grew worse. 27 She had heard the reports
about Jesus, and came up behind him in the
crowd and touched his garment. 28 For she
said, "If I touch even his garments, I shall
be made well." 29 And immediately the hemorrhage ceased; and she felt in her body
that she was healed of her disease. 30 And
Jesus, perceiving in himself that power had
gone forth from him, immediately turned
about in the crowd, and said, "Who touched
my garments?" 31 And his disciples said to
him, "You see the crowd pressing around
you, and yet you say, 'Who touched me?' "
32 And he looked around to see who had
done it. 33 But the woman, knowing what
had been done to her, came in fear and
trembling and fell down before him, and
told him the whole truth. 34 And he said to
her, "Daughter, your faith has made you
well; go in peace, and be healed of your
disease."
35 While he was still speaking, there
came from the ruler's house some who said,
"Your daughter is dead. Why trouble the
Teacher any further?" 36 But ignoring[q] what
they said, Jesus said to the ruler of the synagogue, "Do not fear, only believe." 37 And
he allowed no one to follow him except
Peter and James and John the brother of
James. 38 When they came to the house of
the ruler of the synagogue, he saw a tumult,
and people weeping and wailing loudly.
39 And when he had entered, he said to
them, "Why do you make a tumult and
weep? The child is not dead but sleeping."
40 And they laughed at him. But he put them
all outside, and took the child's father and
mother and those who were with him, and
went in where the child was. 41 Taking her
by the hand he said to her, "Talitha cumi";
which means, "Little girl, I say to you,
arise." 42 And immediately the girl got up
and walked; for she was twelve years old.
And immediately they were overcome with

[q] Or *overhearing.* Other ancient authorities read *hearing*

King James

43 And he charged them straitly that no man should know it; and commanded that something should be given her to eat.

CHAPTER 6

AND he went out from thence, and came into his own country; and his disciples follow him.

2 And when the sabbath day was come, he began to teach in the synagogue: and many hearing *him* were astonished, saying, From whence hath this *man* these things? and what wisdom *is* this which is given unto him, that even such mighty works are wrought by his hands?

3 Is not this the carpenter, the son of Mary, the brother of James, and Joses, and of Juda, and Simon? and are not his sisters here with us? And they were offended at him.

4 But Jesus said unto them, A prophet is not without honour, but in his own country, and among his own kin, and in his own house.

5 And he could there do no mighty work, save that he laid his hands upon a few sick folk, and healed *them*.

6 And he marvelled because of their unbelief. And he went round about the villages, teaching.

7 ¶ And he called *unto him* the twelve, and began to send them forth by two and two; and gave them power over unclean spirits;

8 And commanded them that they should take nothing for *their* journey, save a staff only; no scrip, no bread, no money in *their* purse:

9 But *be* shod with sandals; and not put on two coats.

10 And he said unto them, In what place soever ye enter into an house, there abide till ye depart from that place.

11 And whosoever shall not receive you, nor hear you, when ye depart thence, shake off the dust under your feet for a testimony against them. Verily I say unto you, It shall be more tolerable for Sodom and Gomorrha in the day of judgment, than for that city.

12 And they went out, and preached that men should repent.

13 And they cast out many devils, and anointed with oil many that were sick, and healed *them*.

14 And king Herod heard *of him;* (for his name was spread abroad:) and he said, That John the Baptist was risen from the dead, and therefore mighty works do shew forth themselves in him.

Amplified

43 And He strictly commanded *and* warned them that no one should know this, and He ([l]expressly) told them to give her [something] to eat.

CHAPTER 6

JESUS went away from there and came to His [own] country *and* home town [Nazareth], and His disciples followed (with) Him.

2 And on the Sabbath He began to teach in the synagogue; and many who listened to Him were utterly astonished, saying, Where did this [Man] acquire all this? What is the wisdom—the broad and full intelligence—[which has been] given to [m]Him? What mighty works *and* exhibitions of power are wrought by His hands!

3 Is not this the Carpenter, the son of Mary and the brother of James and Joses and Judas and Simon, and are not His sisters here among us? And they took offense at Him *and* [n]were hurt [that is, they [o]disapproved of Him and it hindered them from acknowledging His authority]; *and* they were caused to stumble *and* fall.

4 But Jesus said to them, A prophet is not without honor (deference, reverence), except in his [own] country and among [his] relatives and in his [own] house.

5 And He was not able to do [p]even one work of power there, except that He laid His hands on a few sickly people [and] cured them.

6 And He marveled because of their unbelief—their lack of faith in Him. And He went about among the surrounding villages [and] continued teaching.

7 And He called to Him the twelve [apostles], and began to send them out [as His ambassadors] two by two, and gave them authority *and* power over the unclean spirits.

8 He charged them to take nothing for their journey except a walking stick; no bread, [q]no wallet for a collection bag, no money in their belts (girdles, purses);

9 But to go with sandals on their feet and not put on two tunics (undergarments).

10 And He told them, Where you go into a house, stay there until you leave that place.

11 And if any [community] will not receive *and* accept *and* welcome you, and they refuse to listen to you, when you depart shake off the dust that is on your feet for a testimony against them. *Truly, I tell you, it will be more tolerable for Sodom and Gomorrah in the judgment day than for that town.*

12 So they went out and preached that men should repent [that is [r]that they should change their minds for the better, and heartily amend their ways with abhorrence for their past sins].

13 And they drove out many unclean spirits, and anointed with oil many who were sick, and cured them.

14 King Herod heard of it, for [Jesus'] name had become well known. [s]He *and* they [of his court] said, John the Baptist has been raised from the dead; that is why these mighty powers ([t]of performing miracles)are at work in Him.

l) Thayer.
m) Capitalized because of what He is, the spotless Son of God, not what the speakers may have thought He was.
n) Tyndale.
o) Wuest.
p) Wuest.
q) Moulton and Milligan.
r) Thayer.
s) Some ancient authorities read "he."
t) Abbott-Smith.

Living New Testament

43 Jesus instructed them very earnestly not to tell what had happened, and told them to give her something to eat.

CHAPTER 6

Soon afterwards He left that section of the country and returned with His disciples to Nazareth, His home town.

2, 3 The next Sabbath He went to the synagogue to teach, and the people were astonished at His wisdom and His miracles because He was just a local man like themselves. "He's no better than we are," they said. "He's just a carpenter, Mary's boy, and a brother of James and Joseph, Judas and Simon. And His sisters live right here among us." And they were offended!

4 Then Jesus told them, "A prophet is honored everywhere except in his home town and among his relatives and by his own family."

5 And because of their unbelief He couldn't do any mighty miracles among them except to place His hands on a few sick people and heal them.

6 And He could hardly accept the fact that they wouldn't believe in Him. Then He went out among the villages, teaching.

7 And He called His twelve disciples together and sent them out two by two, with power to cast out demons.

8, 9 He told them to take nothing with them except their walking sticks—no food, no knapsack, no money, not even an extra pair of shoes or a change of clothes.

10 "Stay at one home in each village—don't shift around from house to house while you are there," He said.

11 "And whenever a village won't accept you or listen to you, shake off the dust from your feet as you leave; it is a sign that you have abandoned it to its fate."

12 So the disciples went out, telling everyone they met to turn from sin.

13 And they cast out many demons, and healed many sick people, anointing them with olive oil.

14 King Herod soon heard about Jesus, for His miracles were talked about everywhere. The king thought Jesus was John the Baptist come back to life again. So the people were saying, "No wonder he can do such miracles."

Revised Standard

amazement. 43 And he strictly charged them
that no one should know this, and told them
to give her something to eat.

Jesus rejected at Nazareth

6 He went away from there and came to
his own country; and his disciples followed him. 2 And on the sabbath he began
to teach in the synagogue; and many who
heard him were astonished, saying, "Where
did this man get all this? What is the wisdom given to him? What mighty works are
wrought by his hands! 3 Is not this the carpenter, the son of Mary and brother of
James and Joses and Judas and Simon, and
are not his sisters here with us?" And they
took offense[r] at him. 4 And Jesus said to
them, "A prophet is not without honor, except in his own country, and among his
own kin, and in his own house." 5 And he
could do no mighty work there, except that
he laid his hands upon a few sick people
and healed them. 6 And he marveled because
of their unbelief.

And he went about among the villages
teaching.

The mission of the twelve

7 And he called to him the twelve, and
began to send them out two by two, and
gave them authority over the unclean spirits.
8 He charged them to take nothing for their
journey except a staff; no bread, no bag, no
money in their belts; 9 but to wear sandals
and not put on two tunics. 10 And he said to
them, "Where you enter a house, stay there
until you leave the place. 11 And if any place
will not receive you and they refuse to hear
you, when you leave, shake off the dust
that is on your feet for a testimony against
them." 12 So they went out and preached
that men should repent. 13 And they cast out
many demons, and anointed with oil many
that were sick and healed them.

Death of John the Baptist

14 King Herod heard of it; for Jesus's[s]
name had become known. Some[t] said, "John
the baptizer has been raised from the dead;
that is why these powers are at work in

[r] Or *stumbled*
[s] Greek *his*
[t] Other ancient authorities read *he*

King James

15 Others said, That it is Elias. And others said, That it is a prophet, or as one of the prophets.

16 But when Herod heard *thereof*, he said, It is John, whom I beheaded: he is risen from the dead.

17 For Herod himself had sent forth and laid hold upon John, and bound him in prison for Herodias' sake, his brother Philip's wife: for he had married her.

18 For John had said unto Herod, It is not lawful for thee to have thy brother's wife.

19 Therefore Herodias had a quarrel against him, and would have killed him; but she could not:

20 For Herod feared John, knowing that he was a just man and an holy, and observed him; and when he heard him, he did many things, and heard him gladly.

21 And when a covenient day was come, that Herod on his birthday made a supper to his lords, high captains, and chief *estates* of Galilee;

22 And when the daughter of the said Herodias came in, and danced, and pleased Herod and them that sat with him, the king said unto the damsel, Ask of me whatsoever thou wilt, and I will give it thee.

23 And he sware unto her, Whatsoever thou shalt ask of me, I will give *it* thee, unto the half of my kingdom.

24 And she went forth, and said unto her mother, What shall I ask? And she said, The head of John the Baptist.

25 And she came in straightway with haste unto the king, and asked, saying, I will that thou give me by and by in a charger the head of John the Baptist.

26 And the king was exceeding sorry; *yet* for his oath's sake, and for their sakes which sat with him, he would not reject her.

27 And immediately the king sent an executioner, and commanded his head to be brought: and he went and beheaded him in the prison,

28 And brought his head in a charger, and gave it to the damsel: and the damsel gave it to her mother.

29 And when his disciples heard *of it*, they came and took up his corpse, and laid it in a tomb.

30 And the apostles gathered themselves together unto Jesus, and told him all things, both what they had done, and what they had taught.

31 And he said unto them, Come ye yourselves apart into a desert place, and rest a while: for there were many coming and going, and they had no leisure so much as to eat.

32 And they departed into a desert place by ship privately.

33 And the people saw them departing, and many knew him, and ran afoot thither out of all cities, and outwent them, and came together unto him.

34 And Jesus, when he came out, saw much people, and was moved with compassion toward them, because they were as sheep not having a shepherd: and he began to teach them many things.

Amplified

15 [But] others kept saying, It is Elijah! And others said, It is a prophet, like one of the prophets [of old].

16 But when Herod heard [of it], he said, ([u]This very) John, whom I beheaded, has been raised [from the dead].

17 For this Herod himself had sent and seized John, and bound him in prison for the sake of Herodias, his brother Philip's wife, because he [Herod] had married her.

18 For John had told Herod, It is not lawful *and* you have no right to have your brother's wife.

19 And Herodias was angry (enraged) with him, *and* held a grudge against him, and wanted to kill him, but she could not.

20 For Herod had ([t]a reverential) fear of John, knowing that he was a righteous and holy man, and (continually) kept him safe [[u]under guard]. When he heard [John speak] he was much perplexed. And [yet] he heard him gladly.

21 But an opportune time came [for Herodias] when Herod on his birthday gave a banquet for his nobles and the high military and chief men of Galilee.

22 For when the daughter [v]of Herodias herself came in and danced, she pleased *and* [v]fascinated Herod and his guests; and the king said to the girl, Ask me for whatever you desire, and I will give it to you.

23 And he put himself under oath to her, Whatever you ask me, I will give it to you, even to the half of my kingdom. [Esth. 5:3, 6.]

24 Then she left the room and said to her mother, What shall I ask [for myself]? And she replied, The head of John the Baptist!

25 And she rushed back instantly to the king, and requested, saying, I wish you to give me right now the head of John the Baptist on a platter.

26 And the king was deeply pained *and* grieved *and* exceedingly sorry; but because of his oaths and his guests he did not want to slight her [by breaking faith with her].

27 And immediately the king sent off one [of the soldiers] of his bodyguard, and gave him orders to bring [John's] head. He went and beheaded him in the prison,

28 And brought his head on a platter, and handed it to the girl, and the girl gave it to her mother.

29 When his disciples learned of it, they came and took [John's] body and laid it in a tomb.

30 The apostles [sent out as missionaries] came back *and* gathered together to Jesus, and told Him all that they had done and taught.

31 And He said to them, [[v]As for you] come away by yourselves to a deserted place, and rest a while. For many were (continually) coming and going, and they had not even leisure enough to eat.

32 And they went away in a boat to a solitary place by themselves.

33 Now many [people] saw them going and recognized them, and they ran there on foot from all the surrounding towns, and they got there ahead [of those in the boat].

34 As Jesus landed He saw a great crowd waiting, and He was moved with compassion for them, because they were like sheep without a shepherd; and He began to teach them many things.

---

t) Abbott-Smith.
u) Vincent.
v) Wuest.

Living New Testament

15 Others thought Jesus was Elijah the ancient prophet, now returned to life again; still others claimed He was a new prophet like the great ones of the past.

16 "No," Herod said, "it is John, the man I beheaded. He has come back from the dead."

17, 18 For Herod had sent soldiers to arrest and imprison John because he kept saying it was wrong for the king to marry Herodias, his brother Philip's wife.

19 Herodias wanted John killed in revenge, but without Herod's approval she was powerless.

20 And Herod respected John, knowing that he was a good and holy man, and so he kept him under his protection. Herod was disturbed whenever he talked with John, but even so he liked to listen to him.

21 Herodias' chance finally came. It was Herod's birthday and he gave a stag party for his palace aides, army officers, and the leading citizens of Galilee.

22, 23 Then Herodias' daughter came in and danced before them and greatly pleased them all. "Ask me for anything you like," the king vowed, "even half of my kingdom, and I will give it to you!"

24 She went out and consulted her mother, who told her, "Ask for John the Baptist's head!"

25 So she hurried back to the king and told him, "I want the head of John the Baptist—right now—on a tray!"

26 Then the king was sorry, but he was embarrassed to break his oath in front of his guests.

27 So he sent one of his bodyguards to the prison to cut off John's head and bring it to him. The soldier killed John in the prison,

28 And brought back his head on a tray, and gave it to the girl and she took it to her mother.

29 When John's disciples heard what had happened, they came for his body and buried it in a tomb.

* * * * *

30 The apostles now returned to Jesus from their tour and told Him all they had done and what they had said to the people they visited.

31 Then Jesus suggested, "Let's get away from the crowds for a while and rest." For so many people were coming and going that they scarcely had time to eat.

32 So they left by boat for a quieter spot.

33 But many people saw them leaving and ran on ahead along the shore and met them as they landed.

34 So the usual vast crowd was there as He stepped from the boat; and He had pity on them because they were like sheep without a shepherd, and He taught them many things they needed to know.

Revised Standard

him." [15]But others said, "It is Elijah." And
others said, "It is a prophet, like one of the
prophets of old." [16]But when Herod heard
of it he said, "John, whom I beheaded, has
been raised." [17]For Herod had sent and
seized John, and bound him in prison for
the sake of Herodias, his brother Philip's
wife; because he had married her. [18]For
John said to Herod, "It is not lawful for you
to have your brother's wife." [19]And Herodias had a grudge against him, and wanted
to kill him. But she could not, [20]for Herod
feared John, knowing that he was a righteous and holy man, and kept him safe.
When he heard him, he was much perplexed; and yet he heard him gladly. [21]But
an opportunity came when Herod on his
birthday gave a banquet for his courtiers
and officers and the leading men of Galilee.
[22]For when Herodias' daughter came in and
danced, she pleased Herod and his guests;
and the king said to the girl, "Ask me for
whatever you wish, and I will grant it."
[23]And he vowed to her, "Whatever you ask
me, I will give you, even half of my kingdom." [24]And she went out, and said to her
mother, "What shall I ask?" And she said,
"The head of John the baptizer." [25]And she
came in immediately with haste to the king,
and asked, saying, "I want you to give me
at once the head of John the Baptist on a
platter." [26]And the king was exceedingly
sorry; but because of his oaths and his
guests he did not want to break his word
to her. [27]And immediately the king sent a
soldier of the guard and gave orders to
bring his head. He went and beheaded him
in the prison, [28]and brought his head on a
platter, and gave it to the girl; and the girl
gave it to her mother. [29]When his disciples
heard of it, they came and took his body,
and laid it in a tomb.

The five thousand fed

30 The apostles returned to Jesus, and
told him all that they had done and taught.
[31]And he said to them, "Come away by
yourselves to a lonely place, and rest a
while." For many were coming and going,
and they had no leisure even to eat. [32]And
they went away in the boat to a lonely
place by themselves. [33]Now many saw them
going, and knew them, and they ran there
on foot from all the towns, and got there
ahead of them. [34]As he landed he saw a
great throng, and he had compassion on
them, because they were like sheep without
a shepherd; and he began to teach them

King James

35 And when the day was now far spent,
his disciples came unto him, and said, This is
a desert place, and now the time *is* far
passed:
36 Send them away, that they may go
into the country round about, and into the
villages, and buy themselves bread: for they
have nothing to eat.
37 He answered and said unto them,
Give ye them to eat. And they say unto
him, Shall we go and buy two hundred pennyworth of bread, and give them to eat?
38 He saith unto them, How many loaves
have ye? go and see. And when they knew,
they say, Five, and two fishes.
39 And he commanded them to make all
sit down by companies upon the green grass.
40 And they sat down in ranks, by hundreds, and by fifties.
41 And when he had taken the five loaves
and the two fishes, he looked up to heaven,
and blessed, and brake the loaves, and gave
them to his disciples to set before them; and
the two fishes divided he among them all.
42 And they did all eat, and were filled.
43 And they took up twelve baskets full
of the fragments, and of the fishes.
44 And they that did eat of the loaves
were about five thousand men.
45 And straightway he constrained his
disciples to get into the ship, and to go to
the other side before unto Bethsaida, while
he sent away the people.
46 And when he had sent them away, he
departed into a mountain to pray.
47 And when even was come, the ship
was in the midst of the sea, and he alone on
the land.
48 And he saw them toiling in rowing;
for the wind was contrary unto them: and
about the fourth watch of the night he cometh unto them, walking upon the sea, and
would have passed by them.
49 But when they saw him walking upon
the sea, they supposed it had been a spirit,
and cried out:
50 For they all saw him, and were troubled. And immediately he talked with them,
and saith unto them, Be of good cheer: it is
I; be not afraid.
51 And he went up unto them into the
ship; and the wind ceased: and they were
sore amazed in themselves beyond measure,
and wondered.
52 For they considered not *the miracle* of
the loaves: for their heart was hardened.
53 And when they had passed over, they
came into the land of Gennesaret, and drew
to the shore.
54 And when they were come out of the
ship, straightway they knew him,
55 And ran through that whole region
round about, and began to carry about in
beds those that were sick, where they heard
he was.

Amplified

35 And when [w]the day was already far gone, His
disciples came to Him and said, This is a desolate *and*
isolated place, and the hour is now late;
36 Send the crowds away to go into the country and
villages round about and buy themselves something to
eat.
37 But He replied to them, Give them something to eat
yourselves. And they said to Him, Shall we go and buy
two hundred denarii [about forty dollars] worth of bread,
and give it to them to eat? [II Kings 4:42-44.]
38 And He said to them, How many loaves do you
have? Go and see. And when they [had looked and] knew,
they said, Five [loaves] and two fish.
39 Then He commanded the people all to recline on
the green grass by companies.
40 So they threw themselves down in ranks in hundreds
and fifties—with the [x]regularity of arrangement of beds of
herbs, looking [y]like so many garden plots.
41 And taking the five loaves and two fish, He looked
up to heaven, and praising God gave thanks, and broke
the loaves, and kept on giving them to the disciples to set
before the people; and He [also] divided the two fish
among [them] all.
42 And they all ate and were satisfied.
43 And they took up twelve [[z]small hand] baskets full of
broken pieces [from the loaves] and of the fish.
44 And those who ate the loaves were five thousand
men.
45 And at once He insisted that the disciples get into
the boat and go ahead of Him to the other side, to
Bethsaida, while He was sending the throng away.
46 And after He had taken leave of them, He went off
into the hills to pray.
47 Now when evening had come, the boat was out in
the middle of the lake, and He was by Himself on the
land.
48 And having seen that they were troubled *and* tormented in rowing, for the wind was against them, about
the fourth watch of the night [3:00 o'clock] He came to
them, walking (directly) on the sea. And He acted as if
He meant to pass by them,
49 But when they saw Him walking on the sea they
thought [it] was a ghost, and [a]raised a (deep, throaty)
shriek of terror.
50 For they all saw Him, and were agitated—troubled
and filled with fear and dread. But immediately He talked
with them and said, Take heart! I AM! Stop being
alarmed *and* afraid. [Exod. 3:14.]
51 And He went up into the boat with them and the
wind ceased, [[b]sank to rest as if exhausted by its own
beating]. And they were astonished exceedingly—beyond
measure.
52 For they failed to consider *or* understand [the
teaching and meaning of the miracle of] the loaves; [in
fact] their hearts had [c]grown callous—had become dull
and had [c]lost the power of understanding.
53 And when they had crossed over they reached the
land of Gennesaret, and [c]came to (anchor at) the
shore.
54 As soon as they got out of the boat [the people]
recognized Him,
55 And they ran about the whole countryside, and
began to carry around sick people on their pallets (sleeping pads) to any place where they heard that He was.

w) Wuest.
x) Moulton and Milligan.
y) Trench's "Notes on the Miracles of our Lord."
z) Vincent. But Moulton and Milligan do not think size is meant.
a) Thayer.
b) Vincent.
c) Thayer.

Living New Testament

35, 36 Late in the afternoon His disciples came to Him and said, "Tell the people to go away to the nearby villages and farms and buy themselves some food, for there is nothing to eat here in this desolate spot, and it is getting late."
37 But Jesus said, "*You* feed them."
"With what?" they asked. "It would take a fortune[1] to buy food for all this crowd!"
38 "How much food do we have?" He asked. "Go and find out." They came back to report that there were five loaves of bread and two fish.
39, 40 Then Jesus told the crowd to sit down, and soon colorful groups of 50 or 100 each were sitting on the green grass.
41 He took the five loaves and two fish and looking up to heaven, gave thanks for the food. Breaking the loaves into pieces, He gave some of the bread and fish to each disciple to place before the people.
42 And the crowd ate until they could hold no more!
43, 44 There were about 5,000 men there for that meal, and afterwards twelve basketfuls of scraps were picked up off the grass!
45 Immediately after this Jesus instructed His disciples to get back into the boat and strike out across the lake to Bethsaida, where He would join them later. He Himself would stay and tell the crowds good-bye and get them started home.
46 Afterwards He went up into the hills to pray.
47 During the night, as the disciples in their boat were out in the middle of the lake, and He was alone on land,
48 He saw that they were in serious trouble, rowing hard and struggling against the wind and waves. About three o'clock in the morning He walked out to them on the water. He started past them,
49 But when they saw something walking along beside them they screamed in terror, thinking it was a ghost,
50 For they all saw Him. But He spoke to them at once. "It's all right," He said. "It is I! Don't be afraid."
51 Then He climbed into the boat and the wind stopped! They just sat there, unable to take it in!
52 For they still didn't realize who He was, even after the miracle the evening before! For they didn't want to believe![2]
53 When they arrived at Gennesaret on the other side of the lake they moored the boat,
54 And climbed out. The people standing around there recognized Him at once,
55 And ran throughout the whole area to spread the news of His arrival, and began carrying sick folks to Him on mats and stretchers.

[1]Literally, "200 denarii," a year's wage.
[2]Literally, "for their hearts were hardened," perhaps implying jealousy, as in Mark 6:2-6.

Revised Standard

many things. 35 And when it grew late, his
disciples came to him and said, "This is a
lonely place, and the hour is now late;
36send them away, to go into the country
and villages round about and buy themselves something to eat." 37But he answered
them, "You give them something to eat."
And they said to him, "Shall we go and
buy two hundred denarii[u] worth of bread,
and give it to them to eat? 38And he said
to them, "How many loaves have you? Go
and see." And when they had found out,
they said, "Five, and two fish." 39Then he
commanded them all to sit down by companies upon the green grass. 40So they sat
down in groups, by hundreds and by fifties.
41And taking the five loaves and the two
fish he looked up to heaven, and blessed,
and broke the loaves, and gave them to the
disciples to set before the people; and he
divided the two fish among them all. 42And
they all ate and were satisfied. 43And they
took up twelve baskets full of broken pieces
and of the fish. 44And those who ate the
loaves were five thousand men.

Jesus walks on the sea

45 Immediately he made his disciples
get into the boat and go before him to the
other side, to Bethsaida, while he dismissed
the crowd. 46And after he had taken leave
of them, he went into the hills to pray.
47And when evening came, the boat was
out on the sea, and he was alone on the
land. 48And he saw that they were distressed in rowing, for the wind was against
them. And about the fourth watch of the
night he came to them, walking on the sea.
He meant to pass by them, 49but when they
saw him walking on the sea they thought
it was a ghost, and cried out; 50for they all
saw him, and were terrified. But immediately he spoke to them and said, "Take
heart, it is I; have no fear." 51And he got
into the boat with them and the wind
ceased. And they were utterly astounded.
52for they did not understand about the
loaves, but their hearts were hardened.

Jesus' healings at Gennesaret

53 And when they had crossed over,
they came to land at Gennesaret, and
moored to the shore. 54And when they
got out of the boat, immediately the people
recognized him, 55and ran about the whole
neighborhood and began to bring sick people on their pallets to any place where they

[u] The denarius was worth about twenty cents

King James

56 And whithersoever he entered, into villages, or cities, or country, they laid the sick in the streets, and besought him that they might touch if it were but the border of his garment: and as many as touched him were made whole.

Amplified

56 And wherever He came into villages or cities or the country, they would lay the sick in the market places, and beg Him that they might touch even the fringe of His outer garment; and as many as touched Him were restored to health.

CHAPTER 7

THEN came together unto him the Pharisees, and certain of the scribes, which came from Jerusalem.

2 And when they saw some of his disciples eat bread with defiled, that is to say, with unwashen, hands, they found fault.

3 For the Pharisees, and all the Jews, except they wash *their* hands oft, eat not, holding the tradition of the elders.

4 And *when they come* from the market, except they wash, they eat not. And many other things there be, which they have received to hold, *as* the washing of cups, and pots, brasen vessels, and of tables.

5 Then the Pharisees and scribes asked him, Why walk not thy disciples according to the tradition of the elders, but eat bread with unwashen hands?

6 He answered and said unto them, Well hath Esaias prophesied of you hypocrites, as it is written, This people honoureth me with *their* lips, but their heart is far from me.

7 Howbeit in vain do they worship me, teaching *for* doctrines the commandments of men.

8 For laying aside the commandment of God, ye hold the tradition of men, *as* the washing of pots and cups: and many other such like things ye do.

9 And he said unto them, Full well ye reject the commandment of God, that ye may keep your own tradition.

10 For Moses said, Honour thy father and thy mother; and, Whoso curseth father or mother, let him die the death:

11 But ye say, If a man shall say to his father or mother, *It is* Corban, that is to say, a gift, by whatsoever thou mightest be profited by me; *he shall be free.*

CHAPTER 7

NOW there gathered together to [Jesus] the Pharisees and some of the scribes who had come from Jerusalem,

2 For they had seen that some of His disciples ate with [d]common hands, that is, [with hands defiled and unhallowed, because] they had not [given them a [e]ceremonial] washing.

3 For the Pharisees and all of the Jews do not eat unless [merely for ceremonial reasons] they wash their hands (diligently [f]up to the elbow) with clenched fist, adhering (carefully and faithfully) to the tradition of (practices and customs handed down to them by) their forefathers—to be observed.

4 And [when they come] from the market place, they do not eat unless they purify themselves; and there are many other traditions—[that is] oral, man-made laws handed down to them, which they observe faithfully and diligently—washing of cups and wooden pitchers and wide-mouthed jugs and utensils of copper and [g]beds.

5 And the Pharisees and scribes kept asking [Jesus], Why do Your disciples not order their way of living according to the tradition handed down by the forefathers to be observed, but eat with hands unwashed *and* ceremonially not purified?

6 But He said to them, Excellently *and* truly—[h]so that there will be no room for blame—did Isaiah prophesy of you, the pretenders *and* hypocrites, as it stands written: This people (constantly) honor Me with their lips, but their heart holds itself off *and* is far distant from Me.

7 In vain—fruitlessly and without profit—do they worship Me, ordering *and* teaching to be obeyed as doctrines the commandments *and* precepts of men. [Isa. 29:13.]

8 You disregard *and* give up *and* bid depart from you the commandment of God, and cling to the tradition of men—keeping it carefully and faithfully.

9 And He said to them, You have a fine way of rejecting (thus thwarting and nullifying and doing away with) the commandment of God, in order to keep your tradition—your own human regulations!

10 For Moses said, Honor (revere with tenderness of feeling and deference) your father and your mother; and, He who speaks ill of, *or* reviles *or* abuses *or* treats improperly father or mother, let him (surely) die. [Exod. 20:12; Deut. 5:16; Exod. 21:17; Lev. 20:9.]

11 But [as for you] you say, A man is exempt if he tells [his] father or [his] mother, What you would otherwise have gained from me (everything I have that would have been of use to you) is Corban, that is, is a gift—already given as an offering to God.

---

d) Tyndale.
e) Williams.
f) Abbott-Smith.
g) Rendered "beds" in most lexicons, and by Moulton and Milligan, and Young; mistranslated "tables" by the Authorized Version; omitted by Nestle.
h) Thayer.

Living New Testament

56 Wherever He went—in villages and cities, and out on the farms—they laid the sick in the market plazas and streets, and begged Him to let them at least touch the fringes of His clothes; and as many as touched Him were healed.

Revised Standard

heard he was. 56 And wherever he came, in villages, cities, or country, they laid the sick in the market places, and besought him that they might touch even the fringe of his garment; and as many as touched it were made well.

CHAPTER 7

One day some Jewish religious leaders arrived from Jerusalem to investigate Him,

2 And noticed that some of His disciples failed to follow the usual Jewish rituals before eating.

3 (For the Jews, especially the Pharisees, will never eat until they have sprinkled their arms to the elbows,[1] as required by their ancient traditions.

4 So when they come home from the market they must always sprinkle themselves in this way before touching any food. This is but one of many examples of laws and regulations they have clung to for centuries, and still follow, such as their ceremony of cleansing for pots, pans and dishes.)

5 So the religious leaders asked Him, "Why don't your disciples follow our age-old customs? For they eat without first performing the washing ceremony."

6, 7 Jesus replied, "You bunch of hypocrites! Isaiah the prophet described you very well when he said, 'These people speak very prettily about the Lord but they have no love for Him at all. Their worship is a farce, for they claim that God commands the people to obey their petty rules.' How right Isaiah was!

8 For you ignore God's specific orders and substitute your own traditions.

9 You are simply rejecting God's laws and trampling them under your feet for the sake of tradition.

10 For instance, Moses gave you this law from God: 'Honor your father and mother.' And he said that anyone who speaks against his father or mother must die.

11 But you say it is perfectly all right for a man to disregard his needy parents, telling them, 'Sorry, I can't help you! for I have given to God what I could have given to you.

[1]Literally, "to wash with the fist."

The tradition of the elders

7 Now when the Pharisees gathered together to him, with some of the scribes, who had come from Jerusalem, 2 they saw that some of his disciples ate with hands defiled, that is, unwashed. 3 (For the Pharisees, and all the Jews, do not eat unless they wash their hands,[v] observing the tradition of the elders; 4 and when they come from the market place, they do not eat unless they purify[w] themselves; and there are many other traditions which they observe, the washing of cups and pots and vessels of bronze.[x]) 5 And the Pharisees and the scribes asked him, "Why do your disciples not live[y] according to the tradition of the elders, but eat with hands defiled?" 6 And he said to them, "Well did Isaiah prophesy of you hypocrites, as it is written,

'This people honors me with their lips,
but their heart is far from me;
7 in vain do they worship me,
teaching as doctrines the precepts of men.'

8 You leave the commandment of God, and hold fast the tradition of men."

9 And he said to them, "You have a fine way of rejecting the commandment of God, in order to keep your tradition! 10 For Moses said, 'Honor your father and your mother'; and, 'He who speaks evil of father or mother, let him surely die'; 11 but you say, 'If a man tells his father or his mother, What you would have gained

[v] One Greek word is of uncertain meaning and is not translated
[w] Other ancient authorities read *baptize*
[x] Other ancient authorities add *and beds*
[y] Greek *walk*

King James

12 And ye suffer him no more to do aught for his father or his mother;

13 Making the word of God of none effect through your tradition, which ye have delivered: and many such like things do ye.

14 ¶ And when he had called all the people *unto him,* he said unto them, Hearken unto me every one *of you,* and understand:

15 There is nothing from without a man, that entering into him can defile him: but the things which come out of him, those are they that defile the man.

16 If any man have ears to hear, let him hear.

17 And when he was entered into the house from the people, his disciples asked him concerning the parable.

18 And he saith unto them, Are ye so without understanding also? Do ye not perceive, that whatsoever thing from without entereth into the man, *it* cannot defile him;

19 Because it entereth not into his heart, but into the belly, and goeth out into the draught, purging all meats?

20 And he said, That which cometh out of the man, that defileth the man.

21 For from within, out of the heart of men, proceed evil thoughts, adulteries, fornications, murders,

22 Thefts, covetousness, wickedness, deceit, lasciviousness, an evil eye, blasphemy, pride, foolishness:

23 All these evil things come from within, and defile the man.

24 ¶ And from thence he arose, and went into the borders of Tyre and Sidon, and entered into an house, and would have no man know *it:* but he could not be hid.

25 For a *certain* woman, whose young daughter had an unclean spirit, heard of him, and came and fell at his feet:

26 The woman was a Greek, a Syrophenician by nation; and she besought him that he would cast forth the devil out of her daughter.

27 But Jesus said unto her, Let the children first be filled: for it is not meet to take the children's bread, and to cast *it* unto the dogs.

28 And she answered and said unto him, Yes, Lord: yet the dogs under the table eat of the children's crumbs.

29 And he said unto her, For this saying go thy way; the devil is gone out of thy daughter.

30 And when she was come to her house, she found the devil gone out, and her daughter laid upon the bed.

31 ¶ And again, departing from the coasts of Tyre and Sidon, he came unto the sea of Galilee, through the midst of the coasts of Decapolis.

Amplified

12 Then you no longer are permitting him to do anything for [his] father or mother—but are letting him off from doing for them.

13 Thus you are nullifying *and* making void *and* of no effect [the authority of] the Word of God through your tradition, which you [in turn] hand on. And many [things] of this kind you are doing.

14 And He called the people to [Him] again, and said to them, Listen to Me, all of you, and understand [what I say].

15 There is not [even] one thing outside a man which by going into him can pollute *and* defile him, but the things which come out of a man are what defile him *and* make him unhallowed *and* unclean.

16 *If any man has ears to hear, let him be listening—and* [i]*perceive, comprehend by hearing.*

17 And when He had left the crowd and had gone into the house, His disciples began asking Him about the parable.

18 And He said to them, Then are you also unintelligent *and* dull *and* without understanding? Do you not discern *and* see that whatever goes into a man from the outside cannot make him unhallowed *or* unclean,

19 Since it does not reach *and* enter his heart but [only his] digestive tract, and so passes on (into the place designed to receive waste)? Thus He was making *and* declaring all foods (ceremonially) clean [that is, [j]abolishing the ceremonial distinctions of the Levitical Law].

20 And He said, What comes out of a man is what makes a man unclean *and* renders [him] unhallowed.

21 For from within, [that is] out of the heart of men, come base *and* wicked thoughts: sexual immorality, stealing, murder, adultery,

22 Coveting (a greedy desire to have more wealth), dangerous *and* destructive wickedness, deceit; [k]unrestrained (indecent) conduct; an evil eye (envy), slander (evil speaking, malicious misrepresentation, abusiveness); pride —[that is] [l]the sin of an uplifted heart against God and man; foolishness (folly, lack of sense, recklessness, thoughtlessness).

23 All these evil [purposes and desires] come from within, and they make the man unclean *and* render him unhallowed.

24 And Jesus arose and went away from there to the region of Tyre *and Sidon.* And He went into a house and did not want any one to know [that He was there], but it was not possible for Him to be hidden [from public notice].

25 Instead, at once a woman whose little daughter (was under the control of) an unclean spirit, heard about Him, and came and flung herself down at His feet.

26 Now the woman was a Greek [Gentile in religion], a Syrophoenician by race. And she kept begging Him to drive the demon out of her little daughter.

27 And He said to her, First let the children be fed, for it is not becoming *or* proper *or* right to take the children's bread and throw it to the (little house) dogs.

28 But she answered Him, Yes, Lord; yet even the small pups under the table eat the little children's scraps of food.

29 And He said to her, Because of this saying you may go your way; the demon has gone out of your daughter [permanently].

30 And she went home, and found the child thrown on the couch, and the demon departed.

31 Soon after this Jesus coming back from the region of Tyre, passed through Sidon on to the Sea of Galilee through the region of Decapolis [the ten cities].

---

i) Abbott-Smith.
j) "Expositor's Greek Testament."
k) Souter.
l) Vincent.

Living New Testament

12, 13 And so you break the law of God in order to protect your man-made tradition. And this is only one example. There are many, many others."

14 Then Jesus called to the crowd to come and hear. "All of you listen," He said, "and try to understand.

15, 16[2] Your souls aren't harmed by what you eat, but by what you think and say!"[3]

17 Then He went into a house to get away from the crowds, and His disciples asked Him what He meant by the statement He had just made.

18 "Don't you understand either?" He asked. "Can't you see that what you eat won't harm your soul?

19 For food doesn't come in contact with your heart, but only passes through the digestive system." (By saying this He showed that every kind of food is kosher.)

20 And then He added, "It is the thought-life that pollutes.

21 For from within, out of men's hearts, come evil thoughts of lust, theft, murder, adultery,

22 Wanting what belongs to others, wickedness, deceit, lewdness, envy, slander, pride, and all other folly.

23 All these vile things come from within; they are what pollute you and make you unfit for God."

* * * * *

24 Then He left Galilee and went to the region of Tyre and Sidon,[4] and tried to keep it a secret that He was there, but couldn't. For as usual the news of His arrival spread fast.

25 Right away a woman came to Him whose little girl was possessed by a demon. She had heard about Jesus and now she came and fell at His feet,

26 And pled with Him to release her child from the demon's control. (But she was Syrophoenician—a "despised Gentile!")

27 Jesus told her, "First I should help My own family—the Jews.[5] It isn't right to take the children's food and throw it to the dogs."

28 She replied, "That's true, sir, but even the puppies under the table are given some scraps from the children's plates."

29 "Good!" He said, "You have answered well—so well that I have healed your little girl. Go on home, for the demon has left her!"

30 And when she arrived home, her little girl was lying quietly in bed, and the demon was gone.

31 From Tyre He went to Sidon, then back to the Sea of Galilee by way of the Ten Towns.

[2]Verse 16 is omitted in many of the ancient manuscripts. "If any man has ears to hear, let him hear."
[3]Literally, "what proceeds out of the man defiles the man."
[4]About 50 miles away.
[5]Literally, "Let the children eat first."

Revised Standard

from me is Corban, (that is, given to God)
[z]—12then you no longer permit him to do
anything for his father or mother, 13thus
making void the word of God through your
tradition which you hand on. And many
such things you do."

What defiles a man

14 And he called the people to him
again, and said to them, "Hear me, all of
you, and understand: 15there is nothing
outside a man which by going into him
can defile him; but the things which come
out of a man are what defile him."[a] 17And
when he had entered the house, and left
the people, his disciples asked him about
the parable. 18And he said to them, "Then
are you also without understanding? Do
you not see that whatever goes into a man
from outside cannot defile him, 19since it
enters, not his heart but his stomach, and
so passes on?"[b] (Thus he declared all foods
clean.) 20And he said, "What comes out of
a man is what defiles a man. 21For from
within, out of the heart of man, come evil
thoughts, fornication, theft, murder, adultery, 22coveting, wickedness, deceit, licentiousness, envy, slander, pride, foolishness.
23All these evil things come from within,
and they defile a man."

A Greek woman's faith

24 And from there he arose and went
away to the region of Tyre and Sidon.[c]
And he entered a house, and would not
have any one know it; yet he could not be
hid. 25But immediately a woman, whose
little daughter was possessed by an unclean
spirit, heard of him, and came and fell
down at his feet. 26Now the woman was a
Greek, a Syrophoenician by birth. And she
begged him to cast the demon out of her
daughter. 27And he said to her, "Let the
children first be fed, for it is not right to
take the children's bread and throw it to
the dogs." 28But she answered him, "Yes,
Lord; yet even the dogs under the table
eat the children's crumbs." 29And he said
to her, "For this saying you may go your
way; the demon has left your daughter."
30And she went home, and found the child
lying in bed, and the demon gone.

A deaf-mute healed

31 Then he returned from the region
of Tyre, and went through Sidon to the
Sea of Galilee, through the region of the

[z] Or *an offering*
[a] Other ancient authorities add verse 16, *"If any man has ears to hear, let him hear"*
[b] Or *is evacuated*
[c] Other ancient authorities omit *and Sidon*

King James

32 And they bring unto him one that was deaf, and had an impediment in his speech; and they beseech him to put his hands upon him.

33 And he took him aside from the multitude, and put his fingers into his ears, and he spit, and touched his tongue;

34 And looking up to heaven, he sighed, and saith unto him, Ephphatha, that is, Be opened.

35 And straightway his ears were opened, and the string of his tongue was loosed, and he spake plain.

36 And he charged them that they should tell no man: but the more he charged them, so much the more a great deal they published *it;*

37 And were beyond measure astonished, saying, He hath done all things well: he maketh both the deaf to hear, and the dumb to speak.

Amplified

32 And they brought to Him a man who was deaf and had difficulty in speaking, and they begged Jesus to place His hand upon him.

33 And taking him aside from the crowd privately, He thrust His fingers into the man's ears, and spat and touched his tongue;

34 And looking up to heaven, He sighed as He said, Ephphatha, which means, Be opened.

35 And his ears were opened, his tongue was loosed, and he began to speak distinctly *and* as he should.

36 And Jesus [[m]in his own interest] admonished *and* ordered them sternly *and* expressly to tell no one, but the more He commanded them, the more zealously they proclaimed it.

37 And they were overwhelmingly astonished, saying, He has done everything excellently—commendably and nobly! He even makes the deaf to hear and the dumb to speak!

CHAPTER 8

IN those days the multitude being very great, and having nothing to eat, Jesus called his disciples *unto him,* and saith unto them,

2 I have compassion on the multitude, because they have now been with me three days, and have nothing to eat:

3 And if I send them away fasting to their own houses, they will faint by the way: for divers of them came from far.

4 And his disciples answered him, From whence can a man satisfy these *men* with bread here in the wilderness?

5 And he asked them, How many loaves have ye? And they said, Seven.

6 And he commanded the people to sit down on the ground: and he took the seven loaves, and gave thanks, and brake, and gave to his disciples to set before *them;* and they did set *them* before the people.

7 And they had a few small fishes: and he blessed, and commanded to set them also before *them.*

8 So they did eat, and were filled: and they took up of the broken *meat* that was left seven baskets.

9 And they that had eaten were about four thousand: and he sent them away.

10 ¶ And straightway he entered into a ship with his disciples, and came into the parts of Dalmanutha.

11 And the Pharisees came forth, and began to question with him, seeking of him a sign from heaven, tempting him.

12 And he sighed deeply in his spirit, and saith, Why doth this generation seek after a sign? verily I say unto you, There shall no sign be given unto this generation.

CHAPTER 8

IN those days when [again] an immense crowd had gathered, and they had nothing to eat, Jesus called His disciples to Him, and told them,

2 I have pity *and* sympathy for the people *and* My heart goes out to them, for they have been with Me now three days, and have nothing [left] to eat;

3 And if I send them away to their homes hungry, they will be feeble through exhaustion *and* faint along the road; and some of them have come a long way.

4 And His disciples replied to Him, How can any one fill *and* satisfy [these people] with loaves of bread here in [this] desolate *and* uninhabited region?

5 And He asked them, How many loaves have you? They said, Seven.

6 And He commanded the multitude to recline upon the ground, and He [then] took the seven loaves [of bread], and having given thanks, He broke them and kept on giving them to His disciples to put before [the people]; and they placed them before the crowd.

7 And they had a few small fish; and when He had [n]praised God *and* given thanks *and* asked Him to bless them [to their use], He ordered that these also should be set before [them].

8 And they ate and were satisfied, and they took up seven [[o]large provision] baskets full of the broken pieces left over.

9 And there were about four thousand people. And He dismissed them,

10 And at once He got into the boat with His disciples, and went to the district of Dalmanutha (or Magdala).

11 The Pharisees came and began to argue with *and* question Him, demanding from Him a sign—an attesting miracle from heaven—[maliciously] to test Him.

12 And He groaned *and* sighed deeply in His spirit, and said, Why does this generation seek for a sign? Positively I say to you, no sign shall be given this generation.

---

m) Wuest: In the middle voice showing charge given with speaker's personal interest in view.
n) Thayer.
o) Vincent. But Moulton and Milligan: *Size not meant.*

Living New Testament

32 A deaf man with a speech impediment was brought to Him, and everyone begged Jesus to lay His hands on the man and heal him.

33 Jesus led him away from the crowd and put His fingers into the man's ears, then spat and touched the man's tongue with the spittle.

34 Then, looking up to heaven, He sighed and commanded, "Open!"

35 Instantly the man could hear perfectly and speak plainly!

36 Jesus told the crowd not to spread the news, but the more He forbade them, the more they made it known,

37 For they were overcome with utter amazement. Again and again they said, "Everything He does is wonderful; He even corrects deafness and stammering!"

Revised Standard

Decapolis. 32And they brought to him a
man who was deaf and had an impediment
in his speech; and they besought him to lay
his hand upon him. 33And taking him aside
from the multitude privately, he put his
fingers into his ears, and he spat and
touched his tongue; 34and looking up to
heaven, he sighed, and said to him, "Ephphatha," that is, "Be opened." 35And his
ears were opened, his tongue was released,
and he spoke plainly. 36And he charged
them to tell no one; but the more he
charged them, the more zealously they proclaimed it. 37And they were astonished beyond measure, saying, "He has done all
things well; he even makes the deaf hear
and the dumb speak."

CHAPTER 8

One day about this time as another great crowd gathered, the people ran out of food again. Jesus called His disciples to discuss the situation. "I pity these people," He said, "for they have been here three days, and have nothing left to eat.

3 And if I send them home without feeding them, they will faint along the road! For some of them have come a long distance."

4 "Are we supposed to find food for them here in the desert?" His disciples scoffed.

5 "How many loaves of bread do you have?" He asked. "Seven," they replied.

6 So He told the crowd to sit down on the ground. Then He took the seven loaves, thanked God for them, broke them into pieces and passed them to His disciples; and the disciples placed them before the people.

7 A few small fish were found, too, so Jesus also blessed these and told the disciples to serve them.

8, 9 And the whole crowd ate until they were full, and afterwards He sent them home. There were about 4,000 people in the crowd that day and when the scraps were picked up after the meal, there were seven very large basketfuls left over!

10 Immediately after this He got into a boat with His disciples and came to the region of Dalmanutha.

11 When the local Jewish leaders learned of His arrival they came to argue with Him. "Do a miracle for us," they said. "Make something happen in the sky. Then we will believe in you."[1]

12 His heart fell[2] when He heard this and He said, "Certainly not. How many more miracles do you people need?"[3]

The four thousand fed

8 In those days, when again a great crowd
had gathered, and they had nothing to
eat, he called his disciples to him, and said
to them, 2"I have compassion on the
crowd, because they have been with me
now three days, and have nothing to eat;
3and if I send them away hungry to their
homes, they will faint on the way; and
some of them have come a long way."
4And his disciples answered him, "How
can one feed these men with bread here
in the desert?" 5And he asked them, "How
many loaves have you?" They said, "Sev-
en." 6And he commanded the crowd to
sit down on the ground; and he took the
seven loaves, and having given thanks he
broke them and gave them to his disciples
to set before the people; and they set
them before the crowd. 7And they had
a few small fish; and having blessed them,
he commanded that these also should be
set before them. 8And they ate, and were
satisfied; and they took up the broken
pieces left over, seven baskets full. 9And
there were about four thousand people.
10And he sent them away; and immediately
he got into the boat with his disciples, and
went to the district of Dalmanutha.[d]

Pharisees ask for a sign

11 The Pharisees came and began to
argue with him, seeking from him a sign
from heaven, to test him. 12And he sighed
deeply in his spirit, and said, "Why does
this generation seek a sign? Truly, I say
to you, no sign shall be given to this gen-

1Literally, "to test Him."
2Literally, "He sighed deeply."
3Literally, "Why does this generation seek a sign?"

d Other ancient authorities read *Magadan* or *Magdala*

King James

13 And he left them, and entering into the ship again departed to the other side.

14 ¶ Now *the disciples* had forgotten to take bread, neither had they in the ship with them more than one loaf.

15 And he charged them, saying, Take heed, beware of the leaven of the Pharisees, and *of* the leaven of Herod.

16 And they reasoned among themselves, saying, *It is* because we have no bread.

17 And when Jesus knew *it,* he saith unto them, Why reason ye, because ye have no bread? perceive ye not yet, neither understand? have ye your heart yet hardened?

18 Having eyes, see ye not? and having ears, hear ye not? and do ye not remember?

19 When I brake the five loaves among five thousand, how many baskets full of fragments took ye up? They say unto him, Twelve.

20 And when the seven among four thousand, how many baskets full of fragments took ye up? And they said, Seven.

21 And he said unto them, How is it that ye do not understand?

22 ¶ And he cometh to Bethsaida; and they bring a blind man unto him, and besought him to touch him.

23 And he took the blind man by the hand, and led him out of the town; and when he had spit on his eyes, and put his hands upon him, he asked him if he saw aught.

24 And he looked up, and said, I see men as trees, walking.

25 After that he put *his* hands again upon his eyes, and made him look up: and he was restored, and saw every man clearly.

26 And he sent him away to his house, saying, Neither go into the town, nor tell *it* to any in the town.

27 ¶ And Jesus went out, and his disciples, into the towns of Cæsarea Philippi: and by the way he asked his disciples, saying unto them, Whom do men say that I am?

28 And they answered, John the Baptist: but some *say,* Elias; and others, One of the prophets.

29 And he saith unto them, But whom say ye that I am? And Peter answereth and saith unto him, Thou art the Christ.

30 And he charged them that they should tell no man of him.

31 And he began to teach them, that the Son of man must suffer many things, and be rejected of the elders, and *of* the chief priests, and scribes, and be killed, and after three days rise again.

32 And he spake that saying openly. And Peter took him, and began to rebuke him.

33 But when he had turned about and looked on his disciples, he rebuked Peter, saying, Get thee behind me, Satan: for thou savourest not the things that be of God, but the things that be of men.

Amplified

13 And He went away *and* left them, and getting into the boat again He departed to the other side.

14 Now they had [[p]completely] forgotten to bring bread, and they had only one loaf with them in the boat.

15 And Jesus (repeatedly expressly) charged *and* admonished them saying, Look out; keep on your guard *and* beware of the leaven of the Pharisees and the leaven of Herod [[q]and the Herodians].

16 And they discussed it *and* reasoned with one another, [It is] because we have no bread.

17 And being aware [of it], Jesus said to them, Why are you reasoning *and* saying [it is] because you have no bread? Do you not yet discern or understand? Are your hearts in (a settled state of) hardness? [Jer. 5:21; Isa. 6:9, 10.]

18 Having eyes do you not see [with them], and having ears do you not hear *and* perceive *and* understand the sense of what is said? And do you not remember?

19 When I broke the five loaves for the five thousand, how many [[r]small hand] baskets full of broken pieces did you take up? They said to Him, Twelve.

20 And the seven loaves for the four thousand, how many [[r]large provision] baskets full of broken pieces did you take up? And they said to Him, Seven.

21 And He ([s]kept repeating), Do you not yet understand?

22 And they came to Bethsaida. And [people] brought to Him a blind man, and begged Him to touch him.

23 And He [t]caught the blind man by the hand, and led him out of the village; and when He had spit on his eyes and put His hands upon him, He asked him, Do you ([s]possibly) see anything?

24 And he looked up and said, I see people, but [they look] like trees, walking.

25 Then He put His hands on his eyes again, and the man looked intently [that is, fixed his eyes on definite objects], and he was restored, and saw everything distinctly—even what was [u]at a distance.

26 And He sent him away to his house, telling [him], Do not [even] enter the village *or tell any one there.*

27 And Jesus went on with His disciples to the villages of Caesarea Philippi, and on the way He asked His disciples, Who do people say that I am?

28 And they answered [Him], John the Baptist; and others, Elijah, but others, One of the prophets.

29 And He asked them, But who do you yourselves say that I am? Peter replied to Him, You are the Christ, the Messiah, the Anointed One.

30 And He charged them sharply to tell no one about Him.

31 And He began to teach them that the Son of man must of necessity suffer many things, and be tested *and* disapproved *and* rejected by the elders and the chief priests and the scribes, and be put to death, and after three days rise [again [v]from death].

32 And He said this freely—frankly, plainly and explicitly, making it unmistakable. And Peter took Him [u]by the hand *and* led Him aside, then [facing Him] began to rebuke Him.

33 But turning around [His back to Peter], and seeing His disciples, He rebuked Peter, saying, Get behind Me, Satan! For you do not have a mind [w]intent on promoting what God wills, but what pleases men—you are not on God's side, but that of men.

---

p) Wuest.
q) Some ancient authorities so read.
r) Vincent.
s) "Expositor's Greek Testament."
t) Tyndale.
u) Thayer.
v) Cremer.
w) Thayer.

Living New Testament

13 So He got back into the boat and left them, and crossed to the other side of the lake.

14 But the disciples had forgotten to stock up on food before they left, and had only one loaf of bread in the boat.

15 As they were crossing, Jesus said to them very solemnly, "Beware of the yeast of King Herod and of the Pharisees."

16 "What does He mean?" the disciples asked each other. They finally decided that He must be talking about their forgetting to bring bread.

17 Jesus realized what they were discussing and said, "No, that isn't it at all! Can't you understand? Are your hearts too hard to take it in?

18 As Isaiah[4] declared, 'Your eyes are to see with—why don't you look? Why don't you open your ears and listen?' Don't you remember anything at all?

19 What about the 5,000 men I fed with five loaves of bread? How many basketfuls of scraps did you pick up afterwards?"

"Twelve," they said.

20 "And when I fed the 4,000 with seven loaves, how much was left?"

"Seven basketfuls," they said.

21 "And yet you think I'm worried that we have no bread?"[5]

22 When they arrived at Bethsaida, some people brought a blind man to Him and begged Him to touch and heal him.

23 Jesus took the blind man by the hand and led him out of the village, and spat upon his eyes, and laid His hands over them. "Can you see anything now?" Jesus asked him.

24 The man looked around. "Yes!" He said, "I see men! But I can't see them very clearly; they look like tree trunks walking around!"

25 Then Jesus placed His hands over the man's eyes again and as the man stared intently, his sight was completely restored, and he saw everything clearly, drinking in the sights around him.

26 Jesus sent him home to his family. "Don't even go back to the village first," He said.

* * * * *

27 Jesus and His disciples now left Galilee and went out to the villages of Caesarea Philippi. As they were walking along He asked them, "Who do the people think I am? What are they saying about Me?"

28 "Some of them think You are John the Baptist," the disciples replied, "and others say You are Elijah or some other ancient prophet come back to life again."

29 Then He asked, "Who do you think I am?" Peter replied, "You are the Messiah."

30 But Jesus warned them not to tell anyone!

31 Then He began to tell them about the terrible things He[6] would suffer, and that He would be rejected by the elders and the Chief Priests and the other Jewish leaders—and be killed, and that He would rise again three days afterwards.

32 He talked about it quite frankly with them, so Peter took Him aside and chided Him.[7] "You shouldn't say things like that," he told Jesus.

33 Jesus turned and looked at His disciples and then said to Peter very sternly, "Satan, get behind Me! You are looking at this only from a human point of view and not from God's."

[4]Implied.
[5]Literally, "Do you not yet understand?"
[6]Literally, "the Son of man."
[7]Literally, "Peter began to rebuke Him."

Revised Standard

eration." 13And he left them, and getting into the boat again he departed to the other side.

14 Now they had forgotten to bring bread; and they had only one loaf with them in the boat. 15And he cautioned them, saying, "Take heed, beware of the leaven of the Pharisees and the leaven of Herod."[e] 16And they discussed it with one another, saying, "We have no bread." 17And being aware of it, Jesus said to them, "Why do you discuss the fact that you have no bread? Do you not yet perceive or understand? Are your hearts hardened? 18Having eyes do you not see, and having ears do you not hear? And do you not remember? 19When I broke the five loaves for the five thousand, how many baskets full of broken pieces did you take up?" They said to him, "Twelve." 20"And the seven for the four thousand, how many baskets full of broken pieces did you take up?" And they said to him, "Seven." 21And he said to them, "Do you not yet understand?"

The blind man of Beth-saida healed

22 And they came to Beth-saida. And some people brought to him a blind man, and begged him to touch him. 23And he took the blind man by the hand, and led him out of the village; and when he had spit on his eyes and laid his hands upon him, he asked him, "Do you see anything?" 24And he looked up and said, "I see men; but they look like trees, walking." 25Then again he laid his hands upon his eyes; and he looked intently and was restored, and saw everything clearly. 26And he sent him away to his home, saying, "Do not even enter the village."

Peter's confession of faith

27 And Jesus went on with his disciples, to the villages of Caesarea Philippi; and on the way he asked his disciples, "Who do men say that I am?" 28And they told him, "John the Baptist; and others say, Elijah; and others one of the prophets." 29And he asked them, "But who do you say that I am?" Peter answered him, "You are the Christ." 30And he charged them to tell no one about him.

Future events foretold

31 And he began to teach them that the Son of man must suffer many things, and be rejected by the elders and the chief priests and the scribes, and be killed, and after three days rise again. 32And he said this plainly. And Peter took him, and began to rebuke him. 33But turning and seeing his disciples, he rebuked Peter, and said, "Get behind me, Satan! For you are not on the side of God, but of men."

[e] Other ancient authorities read *the Herodians*

King James

34 ¶ And when he had called the people *unto him* with his disciples also, he said unto them, Whosoever will come after me, let him deny himself, and take up his cross, and follow me.
35 For whosoever will save his life shall lose it; but whosoever shall lose his life for my sake and the gospel's, the same shall save it.
36 For what shall it profit a man, if he shall gain the whole world, and lose his own soul?
37 Or what shall a man give in exchange for his soul?
38 Whosoever therefore shall be ashamed of me and of my words in this adulterous and sinful generation; of him also shall the Son of man be ashamed, when he cometh in the glory of his Father with the holy angels.

CHAPTER 9

AND he said unto them, Verily I say unto you, That there be some of them that stand here, which shall not taste of death, till they have seen the kingdom of God come with power.
2 ¶ And after six days Jesus taketh *with him* Peter, and James, and John, and leadeth them up into an high mountain apart by themselves: and he was transfigured before them.
3 And his raiment became shining, exceeding white as snow; so as no fuller on earth can white them.
4 And there appeared unto them Elias with Moses: and they were talking with Jesus.
5 And Peter answered and said to Jesus, Master, it is good for us to be here: and let us make three tabernacles; one for thee, and one for Moses, and one for Elias.
6 For he wist not what to say; for they were sore afraid.
7 And there was a cloud that overshadowed them: and a voice came out of the cloud, saying, This is my beloved Son: hear him.
8 And suddenly, when they had looked round about, they saw no man any more, save Jesus only with themselves.
9 And as they came down from the mountain, he charged them that they should tell no man what things they had seen, till the Son of man were risen from the dead.

Amplified

34 And Jesus called to [Him] the throng with His disciples, and said to them, If any one intends to come after Me, let him deny himself—forget, ignore, disown, [w]lose sight of himself and his own interests—and take up his cross, and ([w]joining Me as a disciple and siding with My party) follow [x]with Me—continually, [that is,] cleave steadfastly to Me.
35 For whoever wants to save his [[y]higher, spiritual, eternal] life, will lose [the [y]lower, natural, temporal life [w]which is lived (only) on earth]; and whoever gives up his life [which is lived (only) on earth], for My sake and the Gospel's, will save [his [y]higher, spiritual life [w]in the eternal kingdom of God].
36 For what does it profit a man to gain the whole world, and forfeit his life [[w]in the eternal kingdom of God]?
37 For what can a man give as an exchange—[z]a compensation, a ransom, in return—for his [blessed] life [[w]in the eternal kingdom of God]?
38 For whoever [a]is ashamed [here and now] of Me and My words in this adulterous (unfaithful) and (preeminently) sinful generation, of him will the Son of man also be ashamed, when He comes in the glory (splendor and majesty) of His Father with the holy angels.

CHAPTER 9

AND Jesus said to them, Truly *and* solemnly, I say to you, there are some standing here who will in no way taste death before they see the Kingdom of God come in [its] power.
2 Six days after this Jesus took with Him Peter and James and John, and led them up on a high mountain, apart by themselves. And He was transfigured before them *and* became resplendent with divine brightness.
3 And His garments became glistening, intensely white, as no fuller (cloth dresser) on earth could bleach them.
4 And Elijah appeared [there] to them, accompanied by Moses, and they were [b]holding (a protracted) conversation with Jesus.
5 And [c]Peter took up the conversation saying, Master, it is good *and* suitable *and* beautiful for us to be here. Let us make three booths (tents), one for You and one for Moses and one for Elijah.
6 For he did not [really] know what to say, for they were in a violent fright—[d]aghast [with] dread.
7 And a cloud threw a shadow upon them, and a voice came out of the cloud, saying, This is My Son, the ([d]most dear-worthy) Beloved One; be [b]constantly listening to *and* obeying Him.
8 And looking around they suddenly no longer saw any one with them except Jesus only.
9 And as they were coming back down the mountain, He admonished *and* [e]expressly ordered them to tell no one what they had seen, until the Son of man should rise from among the dead.

---

w) Thayer.
x) Wuest.
y) Jamieson, Fausett and Brown.
z) Cremer.
a) Robertson.
b) Wuest.
c) Kennedy's "Sources of New Testament Greek."
d) Wycliffe.
e) Abbott-Smith.

Living New Testament

34 Then He called His disciples and the crowds to come over and listen. "If any of you wants to be My follower," He told them, "you must put aside your own pleasures and shoulder your cross, and follow Me closely.

35 If you insist on saving your life, you will lose it. Only those who throw away their lives for My sake and for the sake of the Good News will ever know what it means to really live.

36 And how does a man benefit if he gains the whole world and loses his soul in the process?

37 For is anything worth more than his soul?

38 And anyone who is ashamed of Me and My message in these days of unbelief and sin, I, the Man of Glory,[8] will be ashamed of him when I return in the glory of My Father, with the holy angels."

Revised Standard

34 And he called to him the multitude
with his disciples, and said to them, "If
any man would come after me, let him
deny himself and take up his cross and
follow me. [35]For whoever would save
his life will lose it; and whoever loses his
life for my sake and the gospel's will save
it. [36]For what does it profit a man, to gain
the whole world and forfeit his life? [37]For
what can a man give in return for his life?
[38]For whoever is ashamed of me and of
my words in this adulterous and sinful
generation, of him will the Son of man
also be ashamed, when he comes in the
glory of his Father with the holy angels."

CHAPTER 9

Jesus went on to say to His disciples, "Some of you who are standing here right now will live to see the Kingdom of God arrive in great power!"

2 Six days later Jesus took Peter, James and John to the top of a mountain. No one else was there. Suddenly His face began to shine with glory,

3 And His clothing became dazzling white, far more glorious than any earthly process could ever make it!

4 Then Elijah and Moses appeared and began talking with Jesus!

5 "Teacher, this is wonderful!" Peter exclaimed. "We will make three shelters here, one for each of you. . . ."

6 He said this just to be talking, for he didn't know what else to say and they were all terribly frightened.

7 But while he was still speaking these words, a cloud covered them, blotting out the sun, and a voice from the cloud said, "*This* is My beloved Son. Listen to *Him*."

8 Then suddenly they looked around and Moses and Elijah were gone, and only Jesus was with them.

9 As they descended the mountainside He told them never to mention what they had seen until after He[1] had risen from the dead.

9 And he said to them, "Truly, I say to
you, there are some standing here who
will not taste death before they see the
kingdom of God come with power."

The transfiguration

2 And after six days Jesus took with
him Peter and James and John, and led
them up a high mountain apart by themselves; and he was transfigured before them,
[3]and his garments became glistening, intensely white, as no fuller on earth could
bleach them. [4]And there appeared to them
Elijah with Moses; and they were talking
to Jesus. [5]And Peter said to Jesus, "Master,[f] it is well that we are here; let us make
three booths, one for you and one for
Moses and one for Elijah." [6]For he did
not know what to say, for they were exceedingly afraid. [7]And a cloud overshadowed them, and a voice came out of the
cloud, "This is my beloved Son;[g] listen
to him." [8]And suddenly looking around
they no longer saw any one with them but
Jesus only.
9 And as they were coming down the
mountain, he charged them to tell no one
what they had seen, until the Son of man
should have risen from the dead. [10]So they

[8]Literally, "Son of man." The above paraphrase reveals another facet of this interesting term.
[1]Literally, "the Son of man."

[f] Or *Rabbi*
[g] Or *my Son, my* (or *the*) *Beloved*

King James

10 And they kept that saying with themselves, questioning one with another what the rising from the dead should mean.

11 ¶ And they asked him, saying, Why say the scribes that Elias must first come?

12 And he answered and told them, Elias verily cometh first, and restoreth all things; and how it is written of the Son of man, that he must suffer many things, and be set at nought.

13 But I say unto you, That Elias is indeed come, and they have done unto him whatsoever they listed, as it is written of him.

14 ¶ And when he came to *his* disciples, he saw a great multitude about them, and the scribes questioning with them.

15 And straightway all the people, when they beheld him, were greatly amazed, and running to *him* saluted him.

16 And he asked the scribes, What question ye with them?

17 And one of the multitude answered and said, Master, I have brought unto thee my son, which hath a dumb spirit;

18 And wheresoever he taketh him, he teareth him: and he foameth, and gnasheth with his teeth, and pineth away: and I spake to thy disciples that they should cast him out; and they could not.

19 He answereth him, and saith, O faithless generation, how long shall I be with you? how long shall I suffer you? bring him unto me.

20 And they brought him unto him: and when he saw him, straightway the spirit tare him; and he fell on the ground, and wallowed foaming.

21 And he asked his father, How long is it ago since this came unto him? And he said, Of a child.

22 And ofttimes it hath cast him into the fire, and into the waters, to destroy him: but if thou canst do any thing, have compassion on us, and help us.

23 Jesus said unto him, If thou canst believe, all things *are* possible to him that believeth.

24 And straightway the father of the child cried out, and said with tears, Lord, I believe; help thou mine unbelief.

25 When Jesus saw that the people came running together, he rebuked the foul spirit, saying unto him, *Thou* dumb and deaf spirit, I charge thee, come out of him, and enter no more into him.

26 And *the spirit* cried, and rent him sore, and came out of him: and he was as one dead; insomuch that many said, He is dead.

27 But Jesus took him by the hand, and lifted him up; and he arose.

28 And when he was come into the house, his disciples asked him privately, Why could not we cast him out?

Amplified

10 So they carefully *and* faithfully kept the matter to themselves, questioning *and* disputing with one another about what rising from among the dead [meant].

11 And they asked Him, Why do the scribes say that it is necessary for Elijah first to come? [Mal. 4:5, 6.]

12 And He said to them, Elijah, it is true, does come first to restore all things *and* [f]set them to right; and how is it written of the Son of man that He will suffer many things *and* be utterly despised *and* be treated with contempt *and* rejected? [Isa. 53:3.]

13 But I tell you that Elijah has already come, and [people] did to him whatever they desired, as it is written of him.

14 And when they came to the [nine] disciples, they saw a great crowd around them, and scribes questioning *and* disputing with them.

15 And immediately all the crowd, when they saw Jesus [[g]returning from the holy mount, His face and person yet glistening] were greatly amazed, and ran up to Him [and] greeted Him.

16 And He asked them, About what are you questioning *and* discussing with them?

17 And one of the throng replied to Him, Teacher, I brought my son to You, for he has a dumb spirit.

18 And wherever it lays hold of him (so as to make him its own), it dashes him down *and* convulses him, and he foams (at the mouth) and grinds his teeth, *and* he [[h]falls into a motionless stupor] and is wasting away; and I asked Your disciples to drive it out, and they were not able [to do it].

19 And He answered them, O unbelieving generation—without any faith! How long [h]shall I (have to do) with you? How long am I to bear with you? Bring him to Me.

20 So they brought [the boy] to Him, and when the spirit saw Him, at once it completely convulsed the boy, and he fell to the ground and kept rolling about, foaming [at the mouth].

21 And [Jesus] asked his father, How long has he had this? And he answered, From the time he was a little boy.

22 And it has often thrown him both into fire and into water, intending to kill him; but if You can do anything, do have pity on us and help us.

23 And Jesus said, [You say to Me], If You can do anything? [Why,] all things can be—are possible—to him who believes!

24 At once the father of the boy gave (an [i]eager, [j]piercing, inarticulate) cry *with tears*, and he said, Lord, I believe! Constantly help my [k]weakness of faith!

25 But when Jesus noticed that a crowd [of people] came running together, He rebuked the unclean spirit, saying to it, You dumb and deaf spirit, I charge you to come out of him and never go into him again.

26 And after giving a (hoarse, clamoring, fear-stricken) shriek of anguish and convulsing him terribly, it came out; and the boy lay (pale and motionless) like a corpse, so that many of them said, He is dead.

27 But Jesus took ([l]a strong grip of) his hand and began lifting him up, and he stood.

28 And when He had gone indoors His disciples asked Him privately, Why could not we drive it out?

---

f) Henry's "Commentary."
g) Trench's "Notes on the Miracles of Our Lord."
h) Wuest.
i) "Expositor's Greek Testament."
j) Swete in "Mark."
k) Thayer.
l) Wuest.

Living New Testament

10 So they kept it to themselves, but often talked about it, and wondered what He meant by "rising from the dead."

11 Now they began asking Him about something the Jewish religious leaders often spoke of, that Elijah must return [before the Messiah could come[2]].

12, 13 Jesus agreed that Elijah must come first and prepare the way—and that he had, in fact, already come! And that he had been terribly mistreated, just as the prophets had predicted. Then Jesus asked them what the prophets could have been talking about when they predicted that the Messiah[1] would suffer and be treated with utter contempt.

14 At the bottom of the mountain they found a great crowd surrounding the other nine disciples, as some Jewish leaders argued with them.

15 The crowd watched Jesus in awe as He came toward them, and then ran to greet Him.

16 "What's all the argument about?" He asked.

17 One of the men in the crowd spoke up and said, "Teacher, I brought my son for You to heal—he can't talk because he is possessed by a demon.

18 And whenever the demon is in control of him it dashes him to the ground and makes him foam at the mouth and grind his teeth and become rigid.[3] So I begged your disciples to cast out the demon, but they couldn't do it."

19 Jesus said [to His disciples[4]], "Oh, what tiny faith you have;[5] how much longer must I be with you until you believe? How much longer must I be patient with you? Bring the boy to Me."

20 So they brought the boy, but when he saw Jesus the demon convulsed the child horribly, and he fell to the ground writhing and foaming at the mouth.

21 "How long has he been this way?" Jesus asked the father.

And he replied, "Since he was very small,

22 And the demon often makes him fall into the fire or into water to kill him. Oh, have mercy on us and do something if You can."

23 "If I can?" Jesus asked. "*Anything* is possible if you have faith."

24 The father instantly replied, "I *do* have faith; oh, help me to have *more*!"

25 When Jesus saw that the crowd was growing He rebuked the demon. "O demon of deafness and dumbness," He said, "I command you to come out of this child and enter him no more!"

26 Then the demon screamed terribly and convulsed the boy again and left him; and the boy lay there limp and motionless, to all appearance dead. A murmur ran through the crowd—"He is dead."

27 But Jesus took him by the hand and helped him to his feet and he stood up and was all right!

28 Afterwards, when Jesus was alone in the house with His disciples, they asked Him, "Why couldn't we cast that demon out?"

---

[2]Implied.
[3]Or, "is growing weaker day by day."
[4]Implied.
[5]Literally, "O unbelieving generation."

Revised Standard

kept the matter to themselves, questioning
what the rising from the dead meant. [11]And
they asked him, "Why do the scribes say
that first Elijah must come?" [12]And he
said to them, "Elijah does come first to restore all things; and how is it written of
the Son of man, that he should suffer many
things and be treated with contempt? [13]But
I tell you that Elijah has come, and they
did to him whatever they pleased, as it is
written of him."

The demoniac boy cured

14 And when they came to the disciples,
they saw a great crowd about them, and
scribes arguing with them. [15]And immediately all the crowd, when they saw him,
were greatly amazed, and ran up to him
and greeted him. [16]And he asked them,
"What are you discussing with them?"
[17]And one of the crowd answered him,
"Teacher, I brought my son to you, for
he has a dumb spirit; [18]and wherever it
seizes him, it dashes him down; and he
foams and grinds his teeth and becomes
rigid; and I asked your disciples to cast it
out, and they were not able." [19]And he
answered them, "O faithless generation,
how long am I to be with you? How long
am I to bear with you? Bring him to me."
[20]And they brought the boy to him; and
when the spirit saw him, immediately it
convulsed the boy, and he fell on the
ground and rolled about, foaming at the
mouth. [21]And Jesus[h] asked his father, "How
long has he had this?" And he said, "From
childhood. [22]And it has often cast him into
the fire and into the water, to destroy him;
but if you can do anything, have pity on us
and help us." [23]And Jesus said to him, "If
you can! All things are possible to him
who believes." [24]Immediately the father of
the child cried out[i] and said, "I believe;
help my unbelief!" [25]And when Jesus saw
that a crowd came running together, he
rebuked the unclean spirit, saying to it,
"You dumb and deaf spirit, I command
you, come out of him, and never enter him
again." [26]And after crying out and convulsing him terribly, it came out, and the
boy was like a corpse; so that most of them
said, "He is dead." [27]But Jesus took him
by the hand and lifted him up, and he
arose. [28]And when he had entered the
house, his disciples asked him privately,
"Why could we not cast it out?" [29]And he

---

[h] Greek *he*
[i] Other ancient authorities add *with tears*

King James

29 And he said unto them, This kind can come forth by nothing, but by prayer and fasting.

30 ¶ And they departed thence, and passed through Galilee; and he would not that any man should know *it*.

31 For he taught his disciples, and said unto them, The Son of man is delivered into the hands of men, and they shall kill him; and after that he is killed, he shall rise the third day.

32 But they understood not that saying, and were afraid to ask him.

33 ¶ And he came to Capernaum: and being in the house he asked them, What was it that ye disputed among yourselves by the way?

34 But they held their peace: for by the way they had disputed among themselves, who *should be* the greatest.

35 And he sat down, and called the twelve, and saith unto them, If any man desire to be first, *the same* shall be last of all, and servant of all.

36 And he took a child, and set him in the midst of them: and when he had taken him in his arms, he said unto them,

37 Whosoever shall receive one of such children in my name, receiveth me: and whosoever shall receive me, receiveth not me, but him that sent me.

38 ¶ And John answered him, saying, Master, we saw one casting out devils in thy name, and he followeth not us: and we forbad him, because he followeth not us.

39 But Jesus said, Forbid him not: for there is no man which shall do a miracle in my name, that can lightly speak evil of me.

40 For he that is not against us is on our part.

41 For whosoever shall give you a cup of water to drink in my name, because ye belong to Christ, verily I say unto you, he shall not lose his reward.

42 And whosoever shall offend one of *these* little ones that believe in me, it is better for him that a millstone were hanged about his neck, and he were cast into the sea.

43 And if thy hand offend thee, cut it off: it is better for thee to enter into life maimed, than having two hands to go into hell, into the fire that never shall be quenched.

44 Where their worm dieth not, and the fire is not quenched.

45 And if thy foot offend thee, cut it off: it is better for thee to enter halt into life, than having two feet to be cast into hell, into the fire that never shall be quenched:

46 Where their worm dieth not, and the fire is not quenched.

47 And if thine eye offend thee, pluck it out: it is better for thee to enter into the kingdom of God with one eye, than having two eyes to be cast into hell fire:

48 Where their worm dieth not, and the fire is not quenched.

49 For every one shall be salted with fire, and every sacrifice shall be salted with salt.

Amplified

29 And He replied to them, This kind cannot be driven out by anything but prayer *and fasting*.

30 They went on from there, and passed along through Galilee. And He did not wish to have any one know it,

31 For He was [engaged for the time in] teaching His disciples. He said to them, The Son of man is being delivered into the hands of men, and they will put Him to death; and when He is killed, after three days He will rise [[m]from death].

32 But they did not comprehend what He was saying, and they were afraid to ask Him [what this statement meant].

33 And they arrived at Capernaum; and when [they were] in the house He asked them, What were you discussing *and* arguing about on the road?

34 But they kept still, for on the road they had discussed *and* disputed with one another as to who [was the] greatest.

35 And He sat down and called the twelve [apostles], and He said to them, If any one desires to be first, he must be last of all and servant of all.

36 And He took a little child, and put him in the center of their group; and taking him in [His] arms, He said to them,

37 Whoever in My name *and* for My sake accepts *and* receives *and* welcomes one such child, also accepts *and* receives *and* welcomes Me; and whoever so receives Me, receives not only Me, but Him Who sent Me.

38 John said to Him, Teacher, we saw a man driving out demons in Your name who does not follow along with us, and we forbade him to do it, because he [n]is not of our band [of Your disciples].

39 But Jesus said, Do not restrain *or* hinder *or* forbid him; for no one who does a mighty work in My name will soon afterward be able to speak evil of Me.

40 For he who is not against us is for us. [Num. 11:27-29.]

41 For I tell you truly, whoever gives you a cup of water to drink because you belong to *and* bear the name of Christ, will by no means fail to get his reward.

42 And whoever causes one of (these believers,) these little ones who [o]acknowledge *and* cleave to Me, to stumble *and* sin, it would be better—more profitable and wholesome—for him if a (huge) millstone were hung about his neck, and he were thrown into the sea.

43 And if your hand puts a stumbling block before you *and* causes you to sin, cut it off; it is more profitable *and* wholesome for you to go into the life [[p]that is really worthwhile] maimed, than with two hands to go to hell (Gehenna), into the fire that cannot be put out. [q]

45 And if your foot is a cause of stumbling *and* sin to you, cut it off! It is more profitable *and* wholesome for you to enter into the life [that is really worthwhile] crippled, than having two feet to be cast into hell (Gehenna)[r].

47 And if your eye causes you to stumble *and* sin, pluck it out! It is more profitable *and* wholesome for you to enter the kingdom of God with one eye, than with two eyes to be thrown into hell (Gehenna),

48 Where their worm [[s]which preys on the inhabitants, (and is a symbol of) the wounds inflicted on the man himself by his sins] does not die, and the fire is not put out. [Isa. 66:24.]

49 For everyone shall be salted with fire.

m) Cremer.
n) Thayer.
o) Cremer.
p) Wuest.
q) See footnote, verse 45.
r) Verses 44 and 46 (identical with verse 48) are omitted by the best ancient authorities.
s) Gould, quoted by Robertson, and by Swete.

Living New Testament

29 Jesus replied, "Cases like this require prayer."[6]

30, 31 Leaving that region they traveled through Galilee where He tried to avoid all publicity in order to spend more time with His disciples, teaching them. He would say to them, "I, the Son of Mankind, am going to be betrayed and killed and three days later I will return to life again."

32 But they didn't understand and were afraid to ask Him what He meant.

33 And so they arrived at Capernaum. When they were settled in the house where they were to stay He asked them, "What were you discussing out on the road?"

34 But they were ashamed to answer, for they had been arguing about which of them was the greatest!

35 He sat down and called them around Him and said, "Anyone wanting to be the greatest must be the least—the servant of all!"

36 Then He placed a little child among them; and taking the child in His arms He said to them,

37 "Anyone who welcomes a little child like this in My name is welcoming Me, and anyone who welcomes Me is welcoming My Father who sent Me!"

* * * * *

38 One of His disciples, John, told Him one day, "Teacher, we saw a man using Your name to cast out demons; but we told him not to, for he isn't one of our group."

39 "Don't forbid him!" Jesus said, "For no one doing miracles in My name will quickly turn against Me.[7]

40 Anyone who isn't against us is for us.

40 If anyone so much as gives you a cup of water because you are Christ's—I say this solemnly—he won't lose his reward.

42 But if someone causes one of these little ones who believe in Me to lose his faith—it would be better for that man if a huge millstone were tied around his neck and he were thrown into the sea.

* * * * *

43, 44[8] If your hand does wrong, cut it off. Better live forever with one hand than be thrown into the unquenchable fires of hell with two!

45, 46[8] If your foot carries you toward evil, cut it off! Better be lame and live forever than have two feet that carry you to hell.

47 And if your eye is sinful, gouge it out. Better enter the Kingdom of God half blind than have two eyes and see the fires of hell,

48 Where the worm never dies, and the fire never goes out—

49 Where all are salted with fire.[9]

[6]"And fasting" is added in some manuscripts, but not the most ancient.
[7]Literally, "will be able to speak evil of Me."
[8]Verses 44 and 46 (which are identical with verse 48) are omitted in some of the ancient manuscripts.
[9]Literally, "For everyone shall be salted with fire."

Revised Standard

said to them, "This kind cannot be driven
out by anything but prayer."[j]

Death and resurrection foretold again

30 They went on from there and passed
through Galilee. And he would not have
any one know it; 31for he was teaching his
disciples, saying to them, "The Son of man
will be delivered into the hands of men,
and they will kill him; and when he is
killed, after three days he will rise." 32But
they did not understand the saying, and
they were afraid to ask him.

True discipleship

33 And they came to Capernaum; and
when he was in the house he asked them,
"What were you discussing on the way?"
34But they were silent; for on they way
they had discussed with one another who
was the greatest. 35And he sat down and
called the twelve; and he said to them, "If
any one would be first, he must be last of
all and servant of all." 36And he took a
child, and put him in the midst of them;
and taking him in his arms, he said to
them, 37"Whoever receives one such child
in my name receives me; and whoever receives me, receives not me but him who
sent me."
38 John said to him, "Teacher, we saw
a man casting out demons in your name,[k]
and we forbade him, because he was not
following us." 39But Jesus said, "Do not
forbid him; for no one who does a mighty
work in my name will be able soon after
to speak evil of me. 40For he that is not
against us is for us. 41For truly, I say to
you, whoever gives you a cup of water to
drink because you bear the name of Christ,
will by no means lose his reward.
42 "Whoever causes one of these little
ones who believe in me to sin,[l] it would
be better for him if a great millstone were
hung round his neck and he were thrown
into the sea. 43And if your hand causes
you to sin,[l] cut it off; it is better for you
to enter life maimed than with two hands
to go to hell,[m] to the unquenchable fire.[n]
45And if your foot causes you to sin,[l] cut
it off; it is better for you to enter life lame
than with two feet to be thrown into hell.[m,n]
47And if your eye causes you to sin,[l] pluck
it out; it is better for you to enter the kingdom of God with one eye than with two
eyes to be thrown into hell,[m] 48where their
worm does not die, and the fire is not
quenched. 49For every one will be salted

[j] Other ancient authorities add *and fasting*
[k] Other ancient authorities add *who does not follow us*
[l] Greek *stumble*
[m] Greek *Gehenna*
[n] Verses 44 and 46 (which are identical with verse 48) are omitted by the best ancient authorities

King James

50 Salt *is* good: but if the salt have lost his saltness, wherewith will ye season it? Have salt in yourselves, and have peace one with another.

CHAPTER 10

AND he arose from thence, and cometh into the coasts of Judæa by the farther side of Jordan: and the people resort unto him again; and, as he was wont, he taught them again.

2 ¶ And the Pharisees came to him, and asked him, Is it lawful for a man to put away *his* wife? tempting him.

3 And he answered and said unto them, What did Moses command you?

4 And they said, Moses suffered to write a bill of divorcement, and to put *her* away.

5 And Jesus answered and said unto them, For the hardness of your heart he wrote you this precept.

6 But from the beginning of the creation God made them male and female.

7 For this cause shall a man leave his father and mother, and cleave to his wife;

8 And they twain shall be one flesh: so then they are no more twain, but one flesh.

9 What therefore God hath joined together, let not man put asunder.

10 And in the house his disciples asked him again of the same *matter*.

11 And he saith unto them, Whosoever shall put away his wife, and marry another, committeth adultery against her.

12 And if a woman shall put away her husband, and be married to another, she committeth adultery.

13 ¶ And they brought young children to him, that he should touch them: and *his* disciples rebuked those that brought *them*.

14 But when Jesus saw *it*, he was much displeased, and said unto them, Suffer the little children to come unto me, and forbid them not: for of such is the kingdom of God.

15 Verily I say unto you, Whosoever shall not receive the kingdom of God as a little child, he shall not enter therein.

16 And he took them up in his arms, put *his* hands upon them, and blessed them.

17 ¶ And when he was gone forth into the way, there came one running, and kneeled to him, and asked him, Good Master, what shall I do that I may inherit eternal life?

18 And Jesus said unto him, Why callest thou me good? *there is* none good but one, *that is,* God.

Amplified

50 Salt is good (beneficial); but if salt has lost its saltness, how will you restore [the saltness to] it? Have salt within yourselves, and be at peace *and* live in harmony with one another.

CHAPTER 10

AND [Jesus] left there [Capernaum] and went to the region of Judea and beyond [east of] the Jordan, and crowds (constantly) gathered around Him again; and again, as was His custom, He began to teach them.

2 And some Pharisees came up, and in order to test Him *and* try to find a weakness in Him asked, Is it lawful for a man to [t]dismiss *and* repudiate *and* divorce his wife?

3 He answered them, What did Moses command you?

4 They replied, Moses allowed a man to write a bill of divorce, and to put her away. [Deut. 24:1-4.]

5 But Jesus said to them, Because of your hardness of heart [that is, of [u]your condition of insensibility to the call of God] he wrote you this [v]precept in your Law.

6 But from the beginning of creation God made them male and female. [Gen. 1:27; 5:2.]

7 For this reason a man shall leave (behind) his father and his mother *and be* [w]*joined to his wife, and cleave closely to her (permanently).*

8 And the two shall become one flesh, so that they are no longer two, but one flesh. [Gen. 2:24.]

9 What therefore God has united—joined together—let not man separate *or* divide.

10 And indoors the disciples questioned Him again about this subject.

11 And He said to them, Whoever [u]dismisses (repudiates and divorces) his wife and marries another, commits adultery against her;

12 And if a woman dismisses (repudiates and divorces) her husband and marries another, she commits adultery.

13 And they kept bringing young children to Him that He might touch them; and the disciples were reproving them [for it].

14 But when Jesus saw [it], He was indignant *and* [x]pained, and said to them, Allow the children to come to Me—do not forbid or prevent or hinder them—for to such belongs the kingdom of God.

15 Truly I tell you, whoever does not receive *and* accept *and* welcome the kingdom of God as a little child [does], positively shall not enter it at all.

16 And He took [the children up [y]one by one] in His arms and ([z]fervently invoked a) blessing, placing His hands upon them.

17 And as He was setting out on His journey, a man ran up and knelt before Him, and asked Him, Teacher, (You are [a]essentially and perfectly [b]morally) good, what must I do to inherit eternal life (that is, [a]to partake of eternal salvation in the Messiah's kingdom)?

18 And Jesus said to him, Why do you call Me ([a]essentially and perfectly [b]morally) good? There is no one ([a]essentially and perfectly [b]morally) good except God alone.

---

t) Thayer.
u) Swete in "Mark."
v) Thayer.
w) Moulton and Milligan.
x) Robertson.
y) "Expositor's Greek Testament."
z) Alford's Greek Testament.
a) Thayer.
b) Cremer.

Living New Testament

50 Good salt is worthless if it loses its saltiness; it can't season anything. So don't lose your flavor! Live in peace with each other."

CHAPTER 10

Then He left Capernaum[1] and went southward to the Judean borders and into the area east of the Jordan River. And as always there were the crowds; and as usual He taught them.

2 Some Pharisees came and asked Him, "Do you permit divorce?" Of course they were trying to trap Him.

3 "What did Moses say about divorce?" Jesus asked them.

4 "He said it was all right," they replied. "He said that all a man has to do is write his wife a letter of dismissal."

5 "And why did he say that?" Jesus asked. "I'll tell you why—it was a concession to your hard-hearted wickedness.

6, 7 But it certainly isn't God's way. For from the very first He made man and woman to be joined together permanently in marriage; therefore a man is to leave his father and mother,

8 And he and his wife are united so that they are no longer two, but one.

9 And no man may separate what God has joined together."

10 Later, when He was alone with His disciples in the house, they brought up the subject again.

11 He told them, "When a man divorces his wife to marry someone else, he commits adultery against her.

12 And if a wife divorces her husband and remarries, she too commits adultery."

* * * * *

13 Once when some mothers[2] were bringing their children to Jesus to bless them, the disciples shooed them away, telling them not to bother Him.

14 But when Jesus saw what was happening He was very much displeased with His disciples and said to them, "Let the children come to Me, for the Kingdom of God belongs to such as they. Don't send them away!

15 I tell you as seriously as I know how that anyone who refuses to come to God as a little child will never be allowed into His Kingdom."

16 Then He took the children into His arms and placed His hands on their heads and He blessed them.

* * * * *

17 As He was starting out on a trip, a man came running to Him and knelt down and asked, "Good Teacher, what must I do to get to heaven?"

18 "Why do you call Me good?" Jesus asked. "Only God is truly good!

[1]Literally, "and rising up, He went from there." Mentioned here so quietly, this was His final farewell to Galilee. He never returned until after His death and resurrection.
[2]Implied.

Revised Standard

with fire.[o] [50]Salt is good; but if the salt has lost its saltness, how will you season it? Have salt in yourselves, and be at peace with one another."

Teaching on marriage and divorce

10 And he left there and went to the region of Judea and beyond the Jordan, and crowds gathered to him again; and again, as his custom was, he taught them.

2 And Pharisees came up and in order to test him asked, "Is it lawful for a man to divorce his wife?" [3]He answered them, "What did Moses command you?" [4]They said, "Moses allowed a man to write a certificate of divorce, and to put her away." [5]But Jesus said to them, "For your hardness of heart he wrote you this commandment. [6]But from the beginning of creation, 'God made them male and female.' [7]'For this reason a man shall leave his father and mother and be joined to his wife,[p] [8]and the two shall become one.'[q] [9]What therefore God has joined together, let not man put asunder."

10 And in the house the disciples asked him again about this matter. [11]And he said to them, "Whoever divorces his wife and marries another, commits adultery against her; [12]and if she divorces her husband and marries another, she commits adultery."

Jesus blesses the little children

13 And they were bringing children to him, that he might touch them; and the disciples rebuked them. [14]But when Jesus saw it he was indignant, and said to them, "Let the children come to me, do not hinder them; for to such belongs the kingdom of God. [15]Truly, I say to you, whoever does not receive the kingdom of God like a child shall not enter it." [16]And he took them in his arms and blessed them, laying his hands upon them.

The rich young ruler

17 And as he was setting out on his journey, a man ran up and knelt before him, and asked him, "Good Teacher, what must I do to inherit eternal life?" [18]And Jesus said to him, "Why do you call me good? No one is good but God alone.

[o] Other ancient authorities add *and every sacrifice will be salted with salt*
[p] Other ancient authorities omit *and be joined to his wife*
[q] Greek *one flesh*

King James

19 Thou knowest the commandments, Do not commit adultery, Do not kill, Do not steal, Do not bear false witness, Defraud not, Honour thy father and mother.

20 And he answered and said unto him, Master, all these have I observed from my youth.

21 Then Jesus beholding him loved him, and said unto him, One thing thou lackest: go thy way, sell whatsoever thou hast, and give to the poor, and thou shalt have treasure in heaven: and come, take up the cross, and follow me.

22 And he was sad at that saying, and went away grieved: for he had great possessions.

23 ¶ And Jesus looked round about, and saith unto his disciples, How hardly shall they that have riches enter into the kingdom of God!

24 And the disciples were astonished at his words. But Jesus answereth again, and saith unto them, Children, how hard is it for them that trust in riches to enter into the kingdom of God!

25 It is easier for a camel to go through the eye of a needle, than for a rich man to enter into the kingdom of God.

26 And they were astonished out of measure, saying among themselves, Who then can be saved?

27 And Jesus looking upon them saith, With men *it is* impossible, but not with God: for with God all things are possible.

28 ¶ Then Peter began to say unto him, Lo, we have left all, and have followed thee.

29 And Jesus answered and said, Verily I say unto you, There is no man that hath left house, or brethren, or sisters, or father, or mother, or wife, or children, or lands, for my sake, and the gospel's,

30 But he shall receive an hundredfold now in this time, houses, and brethren, and sisters, and mothers, and children, and lands, with persecutions; and in the world to come eternal life.

31 But many *that are* first shall be last; and the last first.

32 ¶ And they were in the way going up to Jerusalem; and Jesus went before them: and they were amazed; and as they followed, they were afraid. And he took again the twelve, and began to tell them what things should happen unto him,

33 *Saying,* Behold, we go up to Jerusalem; and the Son of man shall be delivered unto the chief priests, and unto the scribes; and they shall condemn him to death, and shall deliver him to the Gentiles:

34 And they shall mock him, and shall scourge him, and shall spit upon him, and shall kill him: and the third day he shall rise again.

35 ¶ And James and John, the sons of Zebedee, come unto him, saying, Master, we would that thou shouldest do for us whatsoever we shall desire.

36 And he said unto them, What would ye that I should do for you?

Amplified

19 You know the commandments: Do not kill; do not commit adultery; do not steal; do not bear false witness; do not defraud; honor your father and mother [Exod. 20:12-16; Deut. 5:16-20.]

20 And he replied to Him, Teacher, I have carefully guarded *and* observed all these *and* taken care not to violate them from my boyhood.

21 And Jesus looking upon him loved him, and He said to Him, You lack one thing; go and sell all you have, and give [the money] to the poor, and you will have treasure in heaven; and come [and] accompany Me—[c]walking the same road that I walk.

22 At that saying the man's countenance fell *and* was gloomy, and he went away grieved *and* sorrowing, for he was holding great possessions.

23 And Jesus looked around and said to His disciples, With what difficulty will those who possess wealth *and* [d]keep on holding it enter the kingdom of God!

24 And the disciples were amazed *and* bewildered *and* perplexed at His words. But Jesus said to them again, Children, how hard it is *for those who trust* (*place their confidence, their sense of safety*) *in riches* to enter the kingdom of God!

25 It is easier for a camel to go through the eye of a needle than [for] a rich man to enter the kingdom of God.

26 And they were shocked *and* exceedingly astonished, and said to Him *and* [e]to one another, Then who can be saved?

27 Jesus glanced around at them and said, With men [it is] impossible, but not with God; for all things are possible with God.

28 Peter started to say to Him, Lo, we have [d]yielded up *and* abandoned everything (once and for all and [f]joined You as Your disciples, sided with Your party) and accompanied You—[g]walking the same road that You walk.

29 Jesus said, Truly, I tell you, there is no one who has given up *and* left house or brothers or sisters or mother or father or children or lands, for My sake and for the Gospel,

30 Who will not receive a hundred times as much now in this time, houses and brothers and sisters and mothers and children and lands, with persecutions, and in the age to come eternal life.

31 But many [that are now] first will be last [then], and many [who are now] last will be first [then].

32 They were on the way going up to Jerusalem, and Jesus was walking on in front of them; and they were bewildered *and* perplexed *and* greatly astonished, and [those who were still] following were seized with alarm *and* were afraid. And He took the twelve [apostles] again, and began to tell them what was about to happen to Him.

33 [Saying], Behold, we are going up to Jerusalem; and the Son of man will be turned over to the chief priests and the scribes, and they will condemn *and* sentence Him to death and turn Him over to the Gentiles.

34 And they will mock Him, and spit on Him, and whip Him, and put Him to death; but after three days He will rise again [[h]from death].

35 And James and John, the sons of Zebedee, approached Him, and said to Him, Teacher, we desire You to do for us whatever we ask of You.

36 And He replied to them, What do you desire Me to do for you?

---

c) Literal translation.
d) Wuest.
e) Many ancient authorities read "to one another."
f) Thayer.
g) Literal translation.
h) Cremer.

Living New Testament

19 But as for your question—you know the commandments: don't kill, don't commit adultery, don't steal, don't lie, don't cheat, respect your father and mother."

20 "Teacher," the man replied, "I've never once[3] broken a single one of those laws."

21 Jesus felt genuine love for this man as He looked at him. "You lack only one thing," He told him; "go and sell all you have and give the money to the poor—and you shall have treasure in heaven—and come, follow Me."

22 Then the man's face fell, and he went sadly away, for he was very rich.

23 Jesus watched him go, then turned around and said to His disciples, "It's almost impossible for the rich to get into the Kingdom of God!"

24 This amazed them. So Jesus said it again: "Dear children, how hard it is for those who trust in riches[4] to enter the Kingdom of God.

25 It is easier for a camel to go through the eye of a needle than for a rich man to enter the Kingdom of God."

26 The disciples were incredulous! "Then who in the world can be saved, if not a rich man?" they asked.

27 Jesus looked at them intently, then said, "Without God, it is utterly impossible. But with God everything is possible."

28 Then Peter began to mention all that he and the other disciples had left behind. "We've given up everything to follow You," he said.

29 And Jesus replied, "Let Me assure you that no one has ever given up anything—home, brothers, sisters, mother, father, children, or property—for love of Me and to tell others the Good News,

30 Who won't be given back, a hundred times over, homes, brothers, sisters, mothers, children, and land—with persecutions! All these will be his here on earth, and in the world to come he shall have eternal life.

31 But many people who seem to be important now will be the least important then; and many who are considered least here shall be greatest there."

* * * * *

32 Now they were on the way to Jerusalem, and Jesus was walking along ahead; and as the disciples were following they were filled with terror and dread. Taking them aside, Jesus once more began describing all that was going to happen to Him when they arrived at Jerusalem.

33 "When we get there," He told them, "I, the Son of Mankind, will be arrested and taken before the chief priests and the Jewish leaders, who will sentence Me to die and hand Me over to the Romans to be killed.

34 They will mock Me and spit on Me and flog Me with their whips and kill Me; but after three days I will come back to life again."

35 Then James and John, the sons of Zebedee, came over and spoke to Him in a low voice.[5] "Master," they said, "we want You to do us a favor."

36 "What is it?" He asked.

[3]Literally, "from my youth."
[4]Some of the ancient manuscripts do not contain the words, "for those who trust in riches."
[5]Literally, "came up to Him."

Revised Standard

[19]You know the commandments: 'Do not kill, Do not commit adultery. Do not steal, Do not bear false witness, Do not defraud, Honor your father and mother.' " [20]And he said to him, "Teacher, all these I have observed from my youth." [21]And Jesus looking upon him loved him, and said to him, "You lack one thing; go, sell what you have, and give to the poor, and you will have treasure in heaven; and come, follow me." [22]At that saying his countenance fell, and he went away sorrowful; for he had great possessions.

Teaching on the kingdom of God

23 And Jesus looked around and said to his disciples, "How hard it will be for those who have riches to enter the kingdom of God!" [24]And the disciples were amazed at his words. But Jesus said to them again, "Children, how hard it is[r] to enter the kingdom of God! [25]It is easier for a camel to go through the eye of a needle than for a rich man to enter the kingdom of God." [26]And they were exceedingly astonished, and said to him,[s] "Then who can be saved?" [27]Jesus looked at them and said, "With men it is impossible, but not with God; for all things are possible with God." [28]Peter began to say to him, "Lo, we have left everything and followed you." [29]Jesus said, "Truly, I say to you, there is no one who has left house or brothers or sisters or mother or father or children or lands, for my sake and for the gospel, [30]who will not receive a hundred-fold now in this time, houses and brothers and sisters and mothers and children and lands, with persecutions, and in the age to come eternal life. [31]But many that are first will be last, and the last first."

Crucifixion and resurrection foretold

32 And they were on the road, going up to Jerusalem, and Jesus was walking ahead of them; and they were amazed, and those who followed were afraid. And taking the twelve again, he began to tell them what was to happen to him, [33]saying, "Behold, we are going up to Jerusalem; and the Son of man will be delivered to the chief priests and the scribes, and they will condemn him to death, and deliver him to the Gentiles; [34]and they will mock him, and spit upon him, and scourge him, and kill him; and after three days he will rise."

The ambition of James and John

35 And James and John, the sons of Zebedee, came forward to him, and said to him, "Teacher, we want you to do for us whatever we ask of you." [36]And he said to them, "What do you want me to do

[r] Other ancient authorities add *for those who trust in riches*
[s] Other ancient authorities read *to one another*

King James

37 They said unto him, Grant unto us
that we may sit, one on thy right hand, and
the other on thy left hand, in thy glory.
38 But Jesus said unto them, Ye know
not what ye ask: can ye drink of the cup
that I drink of? and be baptized with the
baptism that I am baptized with?
39 And they said unto him, We can. And
Jesus said unto them, Ye shall indeed drink
of the cup that I drink of; and with the
baptism that I am baptized withal shall ye
be baptized:
40 But to sit on my right hand and on
my left hand is not mine to give; but *it shall
be given to them* for whom it is prepared.
41 And when the ten heard *it*, they began
to be much displeased with James and John.
42 But Jesus called them *to him*, and
saith unto them, Ye know that they which
are accounted to rule over the Gentiles exercise lordship over them; and their great
ones exercise authority upon them.
43 But so shall it not be among you: but
whosoever will be great among you, shall be
your minister:
44 And whosoever of you will be the
chiefest, shall be servant of all.
45 For even the Son of man came not to
be ministered unto, but to minister, and to
give his life a ransom for many.
46 ¶ And they came to Jericho: and as
he went out of Jericho with his disciples and
a great number of people, blind Bartimæus,
the son of Timæus, sat by the highway side
begging.
47 And when he heard that it was Jesus
of Nazareth, he began to cry out, and say,
Jesus, *thou* son of David, have mercy on
me.
48 And many charged him that he should
hold his peace: but he cried the more a
great deal, *Thou* son of David, have mercy
on me.
49 And Jesus stood still, and commanded
him to be called. And they call the blind
man, saying unto him, Be of good comfort,
rise; he calleth thee.
50 And he, casting away his garment,
rose, and came to Jesus.
51 And Jesus answered and said unto
him, What wilt thou that I should do unto
thee? The blind man said unto him, Lord,
that I might receive my sight.
52 And Jesus said unto him, Go thy way;
thy faith hath made thee whole. And immediately he received his sight, and followed
Jesus in the way.

CHAPTER 11

AND when they came nigh to Jerusalem,
unto Bethphage and Bethany, at the
mount of Olives, he sendeth forth two of his
disciples,

Amplified

37 And they said to Him, Grant that we may sit one at
Your right hand and one at [Your] left hand, in Your
glory—Your majesty and splendor.
38 But Jesus said to them, You do not know what you
are asking. Are you able to drink the cup that I drink, or
be baptized with the baptism [of affliction] with which I
am baptized?
39 And they replied to Him, We are able. And Jesus
told them, The cup that I drink you will drink, and you
will be baptized with the baptism with which I am baptized;
40 But to sit at My right hand or at My left hand is
not Mine to give; but [will be given those] for whom it is
ordained *and* prepared.
41 And when the other ten [apostles] heard it, they
began to be indignant with James and John.
42 But Jesus called them to [Him], and said to them,
You know that those who are recognized as governing *and*
are supposed to rule the Gentiles (the nations) lord it
over them—ruling with absolute power, holding them in
subjection—and their great men exercise authority *and*
dominion over them.
43 But this is not to be so among you; instead, whoever
desires to be great among you must be your servant,
44 And whoever wishes to be most important *and* first
in rank among you must be the slave of all.
45 For even the Son of man came not to have service
rendered to Him, but to serve, and to give His life as a
ransom for ([i]instead of) many.
46 Then they came to Jericho; and as He was leaving
Jericho with His disciples and a great crowd, Bartimaeus,
a blind beggar, a son of Timaeus, was sitting by the
roadside.
47 And when he heard that it was Jesus of Nazareth,
he began to shout saying, Jesus, Son of David, have pity
and mercy on me ([j]now)!
48 And many [k]severely censured *and* reproved him,
telling him to keep still; but he kept on shouting out all
the more, You Son of David, have pity *and* mercy on me
(now)!
49 And Jesus stopped and said, Call him. And they
called the blind man, telling him, Take courage; get up,
He is calling you.
50 And throwing off his outer garment, he leaped up
and came to Jesus.
51 And Jesus said to him, What do you want Me to do
for you? And the blind man said to Him, Master, let me
receive my sight.
52 And Jesus said to him, Go your way; your faith has
healed you. And at once he received his sight and accompanied Jesus on the road. [Isa. 42:6, 7.]

CHAPTER 11

WHEN they were getting near to Jerusalem, to Bethphage and Bethany at the Mount of Olives, He sent
ahead two of His disciples,

---

i) Vincent.
j) In the aorist imperative. (Wuest.)
k) Thayer.

Living New Testament

37 "We want to sit on the thrones next to Yours in Your kingdom," they said, "one at Your right and the other at Your left!"

38 But Jesus answered, "You don't know what you are asking! Are you able to drink from the bitter cup of sorrow I must drink from? Or to be baptized with the baptism of suffering I must be baptized with?"

39 "Oh, yes," they said, "we are!" And Jesus said, "You shall indeed drink from My cup and be baptized with My baptism,

40 But I do not have the right to place you on thrones next to Mine. Those appointments have already been made."

41 When the other disciples discovered what James and John had asked, they were very indignant.

42 So Jesus called them to Him and said, "As you know, the kings and great men of the earth lord it over the people;

43 But among you it is different. Whoever wants to be great among you must be your servant.

44 And whoever wants to be greatest of all must be the slave of all.

45 For even I, the Man from Heaven,[6] am not here to be served, but to help others; and to give My life as a ransom for many."

46 And so they reached Jericho. Later, as they left town, a great crowd was following. Now it happened that a blind beggar named Bartimaeus (the son of Timaeus) was sitting beside the road as Jesus was going by.

47 When Bartimaeus heard that Jesus from Nazareth was near, he began to shout out, "Jesus, Son of David, have mercy on me!"

48 "Shut up!" some of the people yelled at him.

But he only shouted the louder, again and again, "O Son of David, have mercy on me!"

49 When Jesus heard him He stopped there in the road and said, "Tell him to come here."

So they called the blind man. "You lucky fellow,"[7] they said, "come on, He's calling you!"

50 Bartimaeus yanked off his old coat and flung it aside, jumped up and came to Jesus.

51 "What do you want Me to do for you?" Jesus asked.

"O Teacher," the blind man said, "I want to see!"

52 And Jesus said to him, "All right, it's done.[8] Your faith has healed you." And instantly the blind man could see, and followed Jesus down the road!

Revised Standard

for you?" [37]And they said to him, "Grant
us to sit, one at your right hand and one
at your left, in your glory." [38]But Jesus
said to them, "You do not know what you
are asking. Are you able to drink the cup
that I drink, or to be baptized with the
baptism with which I am baptized?" [39]And
they said to him, "We are able." And Jesus said to them, "The cup that I drink you
will drink; and with the baptism with which
I am baptized, you will be baptized; [40]but
to sit at my right hand or at my left is
not mine to grant, but it is for those for
whom it has been prepared." [41]And when
the ten heard it, they began to be indignant
at James and John. [42]And Jesus called
them to him and said to them, "You know
that those who are supposed to rule over
the Gentiles lord it over them, and their
great men exercise authority over them.
[43]But it shall not be so among you; but
whoever would be great among you must
be your servant, [44]and whoever would be
first among you must be slave of all. [45]For
the Son of man also came not to be served
but to serve, and to give his life as a ransom for many."

Bartimaeus receives his sight

46 And they came to Jericho; and as
he was leaving Jericho with his disciples
and a great multitude, Bartimaeus, a blind
beggar, the son of Timaeus, was sitting by
the roadside. [47]And when he heard that
it was Jesus of Nazareth, he began to cry
out and say, "Jesus, Son of David, have
mercy on me!" [48]And many rebuked him,
telling him to be silent; but he cried out
all the more, "Son of David, have mercy
on me!" [49]And Jesus stopped and said,
"Call him." And they called the blind
man, saying to him, "Take heart; rise, he
is calling you." [50]And throwing off his
mantle he sprang up and came to Jesus.
[51]And Jesus said to him, "What do you
want me to do for you?" And the blind
man said to him, "Master,[t] let me receive
my sight." [52]And Jesus said to him, "Go
your way; your faith has made you well."
And immediately he received his sight and
followed him on the way.

CHAPTER 11

As they neared Bethphage and Bethany on the outskirts of Jerusalem and came to the Mount of Olives, Jesus sent two of His disciples on ahead.

The triumphal entry

11 And when they drew near to Jerusalem, to Bethphage and Bethany, at the
Mount of Olives, he sent two of his dis-

[6]Literally, "the Son of man."
[7]Literally, "Be of good cheer."
[8]Literally, "Go your way."

[t] Or *Rabbi*

King James

2 And saith unto them, Go your way into the village over against you: and as soon as ye be entered into it, ye shall find a colt tied, whereon never man sat; loose him, and bring *him*.

3 And if any man say unto you, Why do ye this? say ye that the Lord hath need of him; and straightway he will send him hither.

4 And they went their way, and found the colt tied by the door without in a place where two ways met; and they loose him.

5 And certain of them that stood there said unto them, What do ye, loosing the colt?

6 And they said unto them even as Jesus had commanded: and they let them go.

7 And they brought the colt to Jesus, and cast their garments on him; and he sat upon him.

8 And many spread their garments in the way: and others cut down branches off the trees, and strawed *them* in the way.

9 And they that went before, and they that followed, cried, saying, Hosanna; Blessed *is* he that cometh in the name of the Lord:

10 Blessed *be* the kingdom of our father David, that cometh in the name of the Lord: Hosanna in the highest.

11 And Jesus entered into Jerusalem, and into the temple: and when he had looked round about upon all things, and now the eventide was come, he went out unto Bethany with the twelve.

12 ¶ And on the morrow, when they were come from Bethany, he was hungry:

13 And seeing a fig tree afar off having leaves, he came, if haply he might find any thing thereon: and when he came to it, he found nothing but leaves; for the time of figs was not *yet*.

14 And Jesus answered and said unto it, No man eat fruit of thee hereafter for ever. And his disciples heard *it*.

15 ¶ And they come to Jerusalem: and Jesus went into the temple, and began to cast out them that sold and bought in the temple, and overthrew the tables of the moneychangers, and the seats of them that sold doves;

16 And would not suffer that any man should carry *any* vessel through the temple.

17 And he taught, saying unto them, Is it not written, My house shall be called of all nations the house of prayer? but ye have made it a den of thieves.

18 And the scribes and chief priests heard *it*, and sought how they might destroy him: for they feared him, because all the people were astonished at his doctrine.

19 And when even was come, he went out of the city.

20 ¶ And in the morning, as they passed by, they saw the fig tree dried up from the roots.

21 And Peter calling to remembrance saith unto him, Master, behold, the fig tree which thou cursedst is withered away.

22 And Jesus answering saith unto them, Have faith in God.

Amplified

2 And instructed them, Go into the village in front of you, and as soon as you enter it you will find a colt tied which has never been ridden by any one; unfasten it and bring it [here].

3 If any one asks you, Why are you doing this? answer The Lord needs it, and He will send it back here presently.

4 So they went away and found a colt tied at the door out in the (winding) open street, and they loosed it.

5 And some who were standing there said to them, What are you doing, untying the colt?

6 And they replied as Jesus had directed them, and they allowed them to go.

7 And they brought the colt to Jesus, and threw their outer garments upon it, and He sat on it.

8 And many [of the people] spread their garments on the road, and others *scattered* (a layer of) leafy branches which they had cut from the fields.

9 And those who went before and those who followed cried out, [l]Hosanna! (Be graciously inclined and propitious [to Him]!) Praised *and* blessed be He Who comes in the name of the Lord! [Ps. 118:26.]

10 Praised *and* blessed *in the name of the Lord* be the coming kingdom of our father David! Hosanna (O save us) in the highest (heaven)!

11 And Jesus went into Jerusalem, and entered the temple ([m]enclosure); and when He had looked around, surveying *and* observing everything, as it was already late He went out to Bethany together with the twelve [apostles].

12 On the day following, when they had come away from Bethany, He was hungry.

13 And seeing in the distance a fig tree [covered] with leaves, He went to see if He could find any [fruit] on it [[n]for in the fig tree the fruit appears at the same time as the leaves]. But when He came up to it, He found nothing but leaves, for the fig season had not yet come.

14 And He said to it, No one ever again shall eat fruit from you. And His disciples were listening [to what He said].

15 And they came to Jerusalem. And He went into the temple (area, [m]porches and courts) and began to drive out those who sold and bought in the temple area, and He overturned the ([o]four-footed) tables of the money-changers and the seats of those who dealt in doves;

16 And He would not permit any one to carry any household equipment through the temple enclosure [thus making the temple area a short-cut traffic lane].

17 And He taught, and said to them, Is it not written, My house shall be called a house of prayer for all the nations? But you have turned it into a den of robbers. [Isa. 56:7; Jer. 7:11.]

18 And the chief priests and the scribes heard [of this] and kept seeking some way to destroy Him, for they feared Him, because the entire multitude was struck with astonishment at His teaching.

19 And when evening came on, He *and* [[p]His disciples] as accustomed went out of the city.

20 In the morning when they were passing along, they noticed that the fig tree was withered (completely) away to its roots.

21 And Peter remembered and said to Him, Master, look! The fig tree which You doomed has withered away!

22 And Jesus replying said to them, Have faith in God (constantly).

---

l) A cry of happiness (—Souter).
m) Trench's "Synonyms of the New Testament."
n) International Standard Bible Encyclopedia.
o) Moulton and Milligan.
p) Some authorities read "they."

Living New Testament

2 "Go into that village over there," He told them, "and just as you enter you will see a colt tied up that has never been ridden. Untie him and bring him here.

3 And if anyone asks you what you are doing, just say, 'Our Master needs him and will return him soon.' "

4, 5 Off went the two men and found the colt standing in the street, tied outside a house. As they were untying it, some who were standing there demanded, "What are you doing, untying that colt?"

6 So they said what Jesus had told them to, and then the men agreed.

7 So the colt was brought to Jesus and the disciples threw their cloaks across its back for him to ride on.

8 Then many in the crowd spread out their coats along the road before Him, while others threw down leafy branches from the fields.

9 He was in the center of the procession with crowds ahead and behind, and all of them shouting, "Long live the King!"[1] "Blessed is He who comes in the name of the Lord!" . . .

10 "Blessed is the Kingdom He is bringing, the Kingdom of our father David!" . . . "God save the King!"[2]

11 And so He entered Jerusalem and went into the Temple. He looked around carefully at everything and then left—for now it was late in the afternoon—and went out to Bethany with the twelve disciples.

12 The next morning as they left Bethany, He felt hungry.

13 A little way off He noticed a fig tree in full leaf, so He went over to see if He could find any figs on it. But no, there were only leaves, for it was too early in the season for fruit.

14 Then Jesus said to the tree, "You shall never bear fruit again!" And the disciples heard Him say it.

15 When they arrived back in Jerusalem He went to the Temple and began to drive out the merchants and their customers, and knocked over the tables of the moneychangers, and the stalls of those selling doves,

16 And stopped everyone from bringing in loads of merchandise.

17 He told them, "It is written in the Scriptures, 'My Temple is to be a place of prayer for all nations,' but you have turned it into a den of robbers."

18 When the chief priests and other Jewish leaders heard what He had done they began planning how best to get rid of Him. Their problem was their fear of riots because the people were so enthusiastic about Jesus' teaching.

19 That evening as usual they left the city.

20 Next morning, as the disciples passed the fig tree He had cursed, they saw that it was withered from the roots!

21 Then Peter remembered what Jesus had said to the tree on the previous day, and exclaimed, "Look, Teacher! The fig tree You cursed has withered!"

22, 23 In reply Jesus said to the disciples, "If you only have faith in God—this is the absolute truth—you can say

[1]Literally, "Hosanna."
[2]Literally, "Hosanna in the highest."

Revised Standard

ciples, 2and said to them, "Go into the
village opposite you, and immediately as
you enter it you will find a colt tied, on
which no one has ever sat; untie it and
bring it. 3If any one says to you, 'Why
are you doing this?' say, 'The Lord has
need of it and will send it back here immediately.' " 4And they went away, and
found a colt tied at the door out in the
open street; and they untied it. 5And those
who stood there said to them, "What are
you doing, untying the colt?" 6And they
told them what Jesus had said; and they
let them go. 7And they brought the colt
to Jesus, and threw their garments on it;
and he sat upon it. 8And many spread their
garments on the road, and others spread
leafy branches which they had cut from
the fields. 9And those who went before,
and those who followed cried out, "Hosanna! Blessed is he who comes in the
name of the Lord! 10Blessed is the kingdom of our father David that is coming!
Hosanna in the highest!"
11 And he entered Jerusalem, and went
into the temple; and when he had looked
round at everything, as it was already late,
he went out to Bethany with the twelve.

The barren fig tree

12 On the following day, when they
came from Bethany, he was hungry. 13And
seeing in the distance a fig tree in leaf, he
went to see if he could find anything on
it. When he came to it, he found nothing
but leaves, for it was not the season for
figs. 14And he said to it, "May no one ever
eat fruit from you again." And his disciples
heard it.

The cleansing of the temple

15 And they came to Jerusalem. And
he entered the temple and began to drive
out those who sold and those who bought
in the temple, and he overturned the tables
of the moneychangers and the seats of those
who sold pigeons; 16and he would not allow any one to carry anything through the
temple. 17And he taught, and said to them,
"Is it not written, 'My house shall be called
a house of prayer for all the nations'? But
you have made it a den of robbers." 18And
the chief priests and the scribes heard it
and sought a way to destroy him; for they
feared him, because all the multitude was
astonished at his teaching. 19And when
evening came they[u] went out of the city.

The power of faith

20 As they passed by in the morning,
they saw the fig tree withered away to its
roots. 21And Peter remembered and said
to him, "Master,[v] look! The fig tree which
you cursed has withered." 22And Jesus answered them, "Have faith in God. 23Truly,

[u] Other ancient authorities read *he*
[v] Or *Rabbi*

King James

23 For verily I say unto you, That whosoever shall say unto this mountain, Be thou removed, and be thou cast into the sea; and shall not doubt in his heart, but shall believe that those things which he saith shall come to pass; he shall have whatsoever he saith.

24 Therefore I say unto you, What things soever ye desire, when ye pray, believe that ye receive *them*, and ye shall have *them*.

25 And when ye stand praying, forgive, if ye have aught against any: that your Father also which is in heaven may forgive you your trespasses.

26 But if ye do not forgive, neither will your Father which is in heaven forgive your trespasses.

27 ¶ And they come again to Jerusalem: and as he was walking in the temple, there come to him the chief priests, and the scribes, and the elders,

28 And say unto him, By what authority doest thou these things? and who gave thee this authority to do these things?

29 And Jesus answered and said unto them, I will also ask of you one question, and answer me, and I will tell you by what authority I do these things.

30 The baptism of John, was *it* from heaven, or of men? answer me.

31 And they reasoned with themselves, saying, If we shall say, From heaven; he will say, Why then did ye not believe him?

32 But if we shall say, Of men; they feared the people: for all *men* counted John, that he was a prophet indeed.

33 And they answered and said unto Jesus, We cannot tell. And Jesus answering saith unto them, Neither do I tell you by what authority I do these things.

Amplified

23 Truly, I tell you, whoever says to this mountain, Be lifted up and thrown into the sea! and does not doubt at all in his heart, but believes that what he says will take place, it will be done for him.

24 For this reason I am telling you, whatever you ask for in prayer, believe—trust and be confident—that it is granted to you, and you will [get it].

25 And whenever you stand praying, if you have anything against any one, forgive him *and* [q]let it drop—leave it, let it go—in order that your Father Who is in heaven may also forgive you your [own] failings *and* shortcomings *and* let them drop.

26 *But if you do not forgive, neither will your Father in heaven forgive your failings and shortcomings.*

27 And they came again to Jerusalem. And when Jesus was walking about in the ([r]courts and porches of the) temple, the chief priests and the scribes and the elders came to Him,

28 And they kept saying to Him, By what (sort of) authority are You doing these things, or who gave You this authority to do them?

29 Jesus told them, I will ask you a question. Answer Me, and then I will tell you by what (sort of) authority I do these things.

30 Was the baptism of John from heaven or from men? Answer Me.

31 And they reasoned *and* argued with one another, If we say, From heaven, He will say, Why then did you not believe him?

32 But [on the other hand] can we say, from men? For they were afraid of the people, because everybody considered *and* held John actually to be a prophet.

33 So they replied to Jesus, We do not know. And Jesus said to them, Neither am I going to tell you what (sort of) authority I have for doing these things.

CHAPTER 12

AND he began to speak unto them by parables. A *certain* man planted a vineyard, and set an hedge about *it*, and digged *a place for* the winevat, and built a tower, and let it out to husbandmen, and went into a far country.

2 And at the season he sent to the husbandmen a servant, that he might receive from the husbandmen of the fruit of the vineyard.

3 And they caught *him*, and beat him, and sent *him* away empty.

4 And again he sent unto them another servant; and at him they cast stones, and wounded *him* in the head, and sent *him* away shamefully handled.

5 And again he sent another; and him they killed, and many others; beating some, and killing some.

6 Having yet therefore one son, his wellbeloved, he sent him also last unto them, saying, They will reverence my son.

CHAPTER 12

AND [Jesus] started to speak to them in parables—[that is,] with comparisons and illustrations. A man planted a vineyard, and put a hedge about it, and dug a pit for the wine press, and built a tower, and let it out [for rent] to vinedressers, and went into another country.

2 When the season came, he sent a bond servant to the tenants, to collect from them some of the fruit of the vineyard.

3 But they took him and beat him, and sent him away without anything.

4 Again he sent to them another bond servant, and they *stoned him and* wounded him in the head and treated him shamefully—sending him away with insults.

5 And he sent another, and that one they killed; then many others, some they beat and some they put to death.

6 He had still one left, a beloved son; last of all he sent him to them, saying, They will respect my son.

---

q) Moulton and Milligan.
r) Trench.

Living New Testament

to this Mount of Olives, 'Rise up and fall into the Mediterranean,' and your command will be obeyed. All that's required is that you really believe and have no doubt!

24 Listen to me! You can pray for *anything,* and *if you believe, you have it*; it's yours!

25 But when you are praying, first forgive anyone you are holding a grudge against, so that your Father in heaven will forgive you your sins too."

26,[3], 27, 28 By this time they had arrived in Jerusalem again, and as He was walking through the Temple area, the chief priests and other Jewish leaders[4] came up to Him demanding, "What's going on here? Who gave you the authority to drive out the merchants?"

29 Jesus replied, "I'll tell you if you answer one question!

30 What about John the Baptist? Was he sent by God, or not? Answer Me!"

31 They talked it over among themselves. "If we reply that God sent him, then he will say, 'All right, why didn't you accept him?'

32 But if we say God didn't send him, then the people will start a riot." (For the people all believed strongly that John was a prophet.)

33 So they said, "We can't answer. We don't know." To which Jesus replied, "Then I won't answer your question either!"

Revised Standard

I say to you, whoever says to this mountain, 'Be taken up and cast into the sea,'
and does not doubt in his heart, but believes that what he says will come to pass,
it will be done for him. 24Therefore I tell
you, whatever you ask in prayer, believe
that you receive it, and you will. 25And
whenever you stand praying, forgive, if
you have anything against any one; so that
your Father also who is in heaven may
forgive you your trespasses."[w]

Jesus' authority challenged

27 And they came again to Jerusalem.
And as he was walking in the temple, the
chief priests and the scribes and the elders
came to him, 28and they said to him, "By
what authority are you doing these things,
or who gave you this authority to do them?"
29Jesus said to them, "I will ask you a
question; answer me, and I will tell you
by what authority I do these things. 30Was
the baptism of John from heaven or from
men? Answer me." 31And they argued with
one another, "If we say, 'From heaven,'
he will say, 'Why then did you not believe
him?' 32But shall we say, 'From men'?"
—they were afraid of the people, for all
held that John was a real prophet. 33So
they answered Jesus, "We do not know."
And Jesus said to them, "Neither will I
tell you by what authority I do these
things."

CHAPTER 12

Here are some of the story-illustrations Jesus gave to the people at that time:

"A man planted a vineyard and built a wall around it and dug a pit for pressing out the grape juice, and built a watchman's tower. Then he leased the farm to tenant farmers and went on a trip to a distant[1] land.

2 At grape-picking time he sent one of his men to collect his share of the crop.

3 But the farmers beat up the man and sent him back empty-handed.

4 The owner then sent another of his men, who received the same treatment, only worse, for his head was seriously injured.

5 The next man he sent was killed; and later, others were either beaten or killed, until

6 There was only one left—his only son. He finally sent him, thinking they would surely give him their full respect.

The parable of the wicked tenants

12 And he began to speak to them in
parables. "A man planted a vineyard,
and set a hedge around it, and dug a pit
for the wine press, and built a tower, and
let it out to tenants, and went into another
country. 2When the time came, he sent a
servant to the tenants, to get from them
some of the fruit of the vineyard. 3And
they took him and beat him, and sent him
away empty-handed. 4Again he sent to
them another servant, and they wounded
him in the head, and treated him shamefully. 5And he sent another, and him they
killed; and so with many others, some they
beat and some they killed. 6He had still
one other, a beloved son; finally he sent
him to them, saying, 'They will respect my

[3]Many ancient authorities add verse 26, "but if you do not forgive, neither will your Father who is in heaven forgive your trespasses." All include this in Matthew 6:15.
[4]Literally, "scribes and elders."
[1]Implied.

[w] *Other ancient authorities add verse 26, "But if you do not forgive, neither will your Father who is in heaven forgive your trespasses"*

King James

7 But those husbandmen said among themselves, This is the heir; come, let us kill him, and the inheritance shall be ours.

8 And they took him, and killed *him*, and cast *him* out of the vineyard.

9 What shall therefore the lord of the vineyard do? he will come and destroy the husbandmen, and will give the vineyard unto others.

10 And have ye not read this scripture; The stone which the builders rejected is become the head of the corner:

11 This was the Lord's doing, and it is marvellous in our eyes?

12 And they sought to lay hold on him, but feared the people: for they knew that he had spoken the parable against them: and they left him, and went their way.

13 ¶ And they send unto him certain of the Pharisees and of the Herodians, to catch him in *his* words.

14 And when they were come, they say unto him, Master, we know that thou art true, and carest for no man: for thou regardest not the person of men, but teachest the way of God in truth: Is it lawful to give tribute to Cæsar, or not?

15 Shall we give, or shall we not give? But he, knowing their hypocrisy, said unto them, Why tempt ye me? bring me a penny, that I may see *it*.

16 And they brought *it*. And he saith unto them, Whose *is* this image and superscription? And they said unto him, Cæsar's.

17 And Jesus answering said unto them, Render to Cæsar the things that are Cæsar's, and to God the things that are God's. And they marvelled at him.

18 ¶ Then come unto him the Sadducees, which say there is no resurrection; and they asked him, saying,

19 Master, Moses wrote unto us, If a man's brother die, and leave *his* wife *behind him*, and leave no children, that his brother should take his wife, and raise up seed unto his brother.

20 Now there were seven brethren: and the first took a wife, and dying left no seed.

21 And the second took her, and died, neither left he any seed: and the third likewise.

22 And the seven had her, and left no seed: last of all the woman died also.

23 In the resurrection therefore, when they shall rise, whose wife shall she be of them? for the seven had her to wife.

24 And Jesus answering said unto them, Do ye not therefore err, because ye know not the scriptures, neither the power of God?

25 For when they shall rise from the dead, they neither marry, nor are given in marriage; but are as the angels which are in heaven.

26 And as touching the dead, that they rise: have ye not read in the book of Moses, how in the bush God spake unto him, saying, I *am* the God of Abraham, and the God of Isaac, and the God of Jacob?

27 He is not the God of the dead, but the God of the living: ye therefore do greatly err.

Amplified

7 But those tenants said to one another, Here is the heir; come on, let us put him to death, and [then] the inheritance will be ours.

8 And they took him and killed him, and threw [his body] outside the vineyard.

9 Now what will the owner of the vineyard do? He will come and destroy the tenants, and give the vineyard to others.

10 Have you not even read this [passage of] Scripture: The very Stone which [[s]after putting It to the test] the builders rejected, has become the Head of the corner;

11 This is from the Lord *and* is His doing, and it is marvelous in our eyes? [Ps. 118:22, 23.]

12 And they were trying to get hold of Him, but they were afraid of the people, for they knew that He spoke this parable with reference to *and* against them. So they left Him and departed. [Isa. 5:1-7.]

13 But they sent some of the Pharisees and of the Herodians to Him, for the purpose of entrapping Him in His speech.

14 And they came up and said to Him, Teacher, we know that You are [t]sincere *and* what You profess to be; that You cannot lie *and* that You have no personal bias for any one; for You are not influenced by partiality *and* have no [u]regard for any one's external condition *or* position, but [on the basis of] truth You teach the way of God. Is it lawful (permissible and right) to give tribute ([u]poll taxes) to Caesar, or not?

15 Should we pay [them], or should we not pay [them]? But knowing their hypocrisy, He asked them, Why do you put Me to the test? Bring Me a coin (a denarius), so I may see it.

16 And they brought [Him one]. Then He asked them, Whose image (picture) is this, and whose superscription ([v]title)? They said to Him, Caesar's.

17 Jesus said to them, Pay to Caesar the things that are Caesar's, and to [w]God the things that are God's. And they [v]stood marveling *and* greatly amazed at Him.

18 And [some] Sadducees came to Him, [of that party] that say there is no resurrection; and they asked Him a question, saying,

19 Teacher, Moses gave us [a law] that if a man's brother died leaving a wife but no child, the man must marry the widow, and raise up offspring for his brother. [Deut. 25:5.]

20 Now there were seven brothers; the first one took a wife and died leaving no children;

21 And the second [brother] married her, and died, leaving no children; and the third did the same,

22 And all seven, leaving no children. Last of all the woman died also.

23 Now in the resurrection, whose wife will she be? For the seven were married to her.

24 Jesus said to them, Is not this where you wander out of the way *and* go wrong, because you know neither the Scriptures nor the power of God?

25 For when they arise from among the dead, [men] do not marry nor are [women] given in marriage, but are like the angels in heaven.

26 But concerning the dead being raised, have you not read in the book of Moses, [in the passage] about the [burning] bush, how God said to him, I am the God of Abraham, and the God of Isaac, and the God of Jacob? [Exod. 3:2-6.]

27 He is not the God of [the] dead, but of [the] living! You are very wrong.

---

s) Wuest.
t) Cremer.
u) Thayer.
v) Wuest.
w) A rebuke of Emperor worship.

Living New Testament

7 But when the farmers saw him coming they said, 'He will own the farm when his father dies. Come on, let's kill him—and then the farm will be ours!'

8 So they caught him and murdered him and threw his body out of the vineyard.

9 What do you suppose the owner will do when he hears what happened? He will come and kill them all, and lease the vineyard to others.

10 Don't you remember reading this verse in the Scriptures? 'The Cornerstone—the most honored stone in the building—is a Rock the builders threw away!

11 This is the Lord's doing and it is an amazing thing to see.' "

12 The Jewish leaders wanted to arrest Him then and there for using this illustration, for they knew He was pointing at them—they were the wicked farmers in His story. But they were afraid to touch Him for fear of a mob. So they left Him and went away.

13 But they sent other religious and political leaders[2] to talk with Him and try to trap Him into saying something He could be arrested for.

14 "Teacher," these spies said, "we know You tell the truth no matter what! You aren't influenced by the opinions and desires of men, but sincerely teach the ways of God. Now tell us, is it right to pay taxes to Rome, or not?"

15 Jesus saw their trick and said, "Show Me a coin and I'll tell you."

16 When they handed it to Him He asked, "Whose picture and title is this on the coin?"

They replied, "The emperor's."

17 "All right," He said, "if it is his, give it to him. But everything that belongs to God must be given to God!" And they scratched their heads in bafflement at His reply.

18 Then the Sadducees stepped forward—a group of men who say there is no resurrection. Here was their question:

19 "Teacher, Moses gave us a law that when a man dies without children, the man's brother should marry his widow and have children in his brother's name.

20, 21, 22 Well, there were seven brothers and the oldest married and died, and left no children. So the second brother married the widow, but soon he died too, and left no children. Then the next brother married her, and died without children, and so on until all were dead, and still there were no children; and last of all, the woman died too.

23 What we want to know is this:[3] In the resurrection, whose wife will she be, for she had been the wife of each of them?"

24 Jesus replied, "Your trouble is that you don't know the Scriptures, and don't know the power of God.

25 For when these seven brothers and the woman rise from the dead, they won't be married—they will be like the angels.

26 But now as to whether there will be a resurrection—have you never read in the book of Exodus about Moses and the burning bush? God said to Moses, 'I *am* the God of Isaac, and I *am* the God of Jacob.'

27 God was telling Moses that these men, though dead for hundreds of years,[3] were still very much alive, for He would not have said, 'I *am* the God' of those who don't exist! You have made a serious error."

---

[2]Literally, "Pharisees and Herodians."
[3]Implied.

Revised Standard

son.' [7]But those tenants said to one another, 'This is the heir; come, let us kill him, and the inheritance will be ours.' [8]And they took him and killed him, and cast him out of the vineyard. [9]What will the owner of the vineyard do? He will come and destroy the tenants, and give the vineyard to others. [10]Have you not read this scripture:

'The very stone which the builders rejected
has become the head of the corner;
[11]this was the Lord's doing,
and it is marvelous in our eyes'?"

12 And they tried to arrest him, but feared the multitude, for they perceived that he had told the parable against them; so they left him and went away.

Taxes to Caesar

13 And they sent to him some of the Pharisees and some of the Herodians, to entrap him in his talk. [14]And they came and said to him, "Teacher, we know that you are true, and care for no man; for you do not regard the position of men, but truly teach the way of God. Is it lawful to pay taxes to Caesar, or not? [15]Should we pay them, or should we not? But knowing their hypocrisy, he said to them, "Why put me to the test? Bring me a coin,[x] and let me look at it." [16]And they brought one. And he said to them, "Whose likeness and inscription is this?" They said to him, "Caesar's." [17]Jesus said to them, "Render to Caesar the things that are Caesar's, and to God the things that are God's." And they were amazed at him.

Sadducees and the resurrection

18 And Sadducees came to him, who say that there is no resurrection; and they asked him a question, saying, [19]"Teacher, Moses wrote for us that if a man's brother dies and leaves a wife, but leaves no child, the man[y] must take the wife, and raise up children for his brother. [20]There were seven brothers; the first took a wife, and when he died left no children; [21]and the second took her, and died, leaving no children; and the third likewise; [22]and the seven left no children. Last of all the woman also died. [23]In the resurrection whose wife will she be? For the seven had her as wife."

24 Jesus said to them, "Is not this why you are wrong, that you know neither the scriptures, nor the power of God? [25]For when they rise from the dead, they neither marry nor are given in marriage, but are like angels in heaven. [26]And as for the dead being raised, have you not read in the book of Moses, in the passage about the bush, how God said to him, 'I am the God of Abraham, and the God of Isaac, and the God of Jacob'? [27]He is not God of the dead, but of the living; you are quite wrong."

---

[x] Greek *a denarius*
[y] Greek *his brother*

King James

28 ¶ And one of the scribes came, and having heard them reasoning together, and perceiving that he had answered them well, asked him, Which is the first commandment of all?

29 And Jesus answered him, The first of all the commandments *is*, Hear, O Israel; The Lord our God is one Lord:

30 And thou shalt love the Lord thy God with all thy heart, and with all thy soul, and with all thy mind, and with all thy strength: this *is* the first commandment.

31 And the second *is* like, *namely* this, Thou shalt love thy neighbour as thyself. There is none other commandment greater than these.

32 And the scribe said unto him, Well, Master, thou hast said the truth: for there is one God; and there is none other but he:

33 And to love him with all the heart, and with all the understanding, and with all the soul, and with all the strength, and to love *his* neighbour as himself, is more than all whole burnt offerings and sacrifices.

34 And when Jesus saw that he answered discreetly, he said unto him, Thou art not far from the kingdom of God. And no man after that durst ask him *any question*.

35 ¶ And Jesus answered and said, while he taught in the temple, How say the scribes that Christ is the son of David?

36 For David himself said by the Holy Ghost, The LORD said to my Lord, Sit thou on my right hand, till I make thine enemies thy footstool.

37 David therefore himself calleth him Lord; and whence is he *then* his son? And the common people heard him gladly.

38 ¶ And he said unto them in his doctrine, Beware of the scribes, which love to go in long clothing, and *love* salutations in the marketplaces,

39 And the chief seats in the synagogues, and the uppermost rooms at feasts:

40 Which devour widows' houses, and for a pretence make long prayers: these shall receive greater damnation.

41 ¶ And Jesus sat over against the treasury, and beheld how the people cast money into the treasury: and many that were rich cast in much.

42 And there came a certain poor widow, and she threw in two mites, which make a farthing.

43 And he called *unto him* his disciples, and saith unto them, Verily I say unto you, That this poor widow hath cast more in, than all they which have cast into the treasury:

44 For all *they* did cast in of their abundance; but she of her want did cast in all that she had, *even* all her living.

Amplified

28 Then one of the scribes came up and listened to them disputing with one another, and noticing that Jesus answered them fitly *and* admirably, he asked Him, Which commandment is first *and* most important of all ([x]in its nature)?

29 Jesus answered, The first *and* principal *one of all commands* is, Hear, O Israel: The Lord our God is one Lord;

30 And you shall love the Lord your God [x]out of *and* with your whole heart, and out of *and* with all your soul (your [y]life) and out of *and* with all your mind—[that is] with [x]your faculty of thought and your moral understanding—and out of *and* with all your strength. *This is the first and principal commandment*. [Deut. 6:4, 5.]

31 The second *is like it and* is this, You shall love your neighbor as yourself. There is no other commandment greater than these. [Lev. 19:18.]

32 And the scribe said to Him, Excellently *and* fitly *and* admirably answered, Teacher! You have said truly that He is One, and there is no other but He;

33 And to love Him out of all the heart, and with all the understanding—[that is,] with the [x]faculty of quick apprehension and intelligence and keenness of discernment—and with all the strength, and to love one's neighbor as oneself, is much more than all the whole burnt offerings and sacrifices. [I Sam. 15:22; Hos. 6:6; Mic. 6:6-8.]

34 And when Jesus saw that he answered intelligently—discreetly and [x]having his wits about him—He said to him, You are not far from the kingdom of God. And after that no one ventured *or* dared to ask Him any further question.

35 And as Jesus taught in (a [z]porch or court of) the temple, He said, How can the scribes say that the Christ is David's Son?

36 David, himself (inspired), in the Holy Spirit declared, The Lord said to my Lord, Sit at My right hand until I make Your enemies (a footstool) under Your feet. [Ps. 110:1.]

37 David himself calls Him Lord, so how can it be that He is his Son? Now the great mass of the people heard [Jesus] gladly—listening to Him with delight.

38 And in [the course of] His teaching He said, Beware of the scribes, who like to go around in long robes, and [to get] greetings in the market places [public forums],

39 And the front seats in the synagogues and the [z]chief couches (places of honor) at feasts,

40 Who devour widows' houses and to cover it up make long prayers. They will receive the heavier (sentence of) condemnation.

41 And He sat down opposite the treasury and saw how the crowd was casting money into the treasury. Many rich [people] were throwing in large sums.

42 And a widow who was poverty-stricken came and put in two copper mites [the smallest of coins], which together make [a]half of a cent.

43 And He called His disciples to [Him] and said to them, Truly *and* surely I tell you, this widow, (and she) poverty-stricken, has put in more than all those contributing to the treasury.

44 For they all threw in out of their abundance, but she out of her deep poverty has put in everything that she had, [even] all she had on which to live.

---

x) Vincent.
y) Cremer.
z) Trench.
a) Davis' "Dictionary of the Bible."

Living New Testament

28 One of the teachers of religion who was standing there listening to the discussion realized that Jesus had answered well. So he asked, "Of all the commandments, which is the most important?"

29 Jesus replied, "The one that says, 'Hear, O Israel! The Lord our God is the one and only God.

30 And you must love Him with all your heart and soul and mind and strength.'

31 The second is: 'You must love others as much as yourself.' No other commandments are greater than these."

32 The teacher of religion replied, "Sir, You have spoken a true word in saying that there is only one God and no other.

33 And I know it is far more important to love Him with all my heart and understanding and strength, and to love others as myself, than to offer all kinds of sacrifices on the altar of the Temple."

34 Realizing this man's understanding, Jesus said to him, "You are not far from the Kingdom of God." And after that, no one dared ask Him any more questions.

35 Later, as Jesus was teaching the people in the Temple area, He asked them this question: "Why do your religious teachers claim that the Messiah must be a descendant of King David?

36 For David himself said—and the Holy Spirit was speaking through him when he said it—'God said to my Lord, sit at My right hand until I make Your enemies Your footstool.'

37 Since David called Him his *Lord*, how can He be his *son*?" (This sort of reasoning delighted the crowd and they listened to Him with great interest.)

38 Here are some of the other things He taught them at this time: "Beware of the teachers of religion! For they love to wear the robes of the rich and scholarly, and to have everyone bow to them as they walk through the markets.

39 They love to sit in the best seats in the synagogues, and at the places of honor at banquets—

40 But they shamelessly cheat widows out of their homes and then, to cover up the kind of men they really are, they pretend to be pious by praying long prayers in public. Because of this, their punishment will be the greater."

41 Then He went over to the collection boxes in the Temple and sat and watched as the crowds dropped in their money. Some who were rich put in large amounts.

42 Then a poor widow came and dropped in two pennies.

43, 44 He called His disciples to Him and remarked, 'That poor widow has given more than all those rich men put together! For they gave a little of their extra fat,[4] while she gave up her last penny."

[4]Literally, "out of their surplus."

Revised Standard

The great commandment

28 And one of the scribes came up and
heard them disputing with one another,
and seeing that he answered them well,
asked him, "Which commandment is the
first of all?" 29Jesus answered, "The first
is, 'Hear, O Israel: The Lord our God, the
Lord is one; 30and you shall love the Lord
your God with all your heart, and with all
your soul, and with all your mind, and with
all your strength.' 31The second is this,
'You shall love your neighbor as yourself.'
There is no other commandment greater
than these." 32And the scribe said to him,
"You are right, Teacher; you have truly
said that he is one, and there is no other
but he; 33and to love him with all the heart,
and with all the understanding, and with all
the strength, and to love one's neighbor
as oneself, is much more than all whole
burnt offerings and sacrifices." 34And when
Jesus saw that he answered wisely, he said
to him, "You are not far from the kingdom
of God." And after that no one dared to
ask him any question.

The question about David's son

35 And as Jesus taught in the temple,
he said, "How can the scribes say that the
Christ is the son of David? 36David himself, inspired by[z] the Holy Spirit, declared,
'The Lord said to my Lord,
Sit at my right hand,
till I put thy enemies under thy feet.'
37David himself calls him Lord; so how
is he his son?" And the great throng heard
him gladly.

Jesus' warning against the scribes

38 And in his teaching he said, "Beware of the scribes, who like to go about in
long robes, and to have salutations in the
market places 39and the best seats in the
synagogues and the places of honor at
feasts, 40who devour widows' houses and
for a pretense make long prayers. They
will receive the greater condemnation."

The widow's penny

41 And he sat down opposite the treasury, and watched the multitude putting
money into the treasury. Many rich people
put in large sums. 42And a poor widow
came, and put in two copper coins, which
make a penny. 43And he called his disciples
to him, and said to them, "Truly, I say to
you, this poor widow has put in more than
all those who are contributing to the treasury. 44For they all contributed out of their
abundance; but she out of her poverty
has put in everything she had, her whole
living."

[z] Or *himself, in*

King James

CHAPTER 13

AND as he went out of the temple, one of his disciples saith unto him, Master, see what manner of stones and what buildings *are here!*

2 And Jesus answering said unto him, Seest thou these great buildings? there shall not be left one stone upon another, that shall not be thrown down.

3 And as he sat upon the mount of Olives over against the temple, Peter and James and John and Andrew asked him privately,

4 Tell us, when shall these things be? and what *shall be* the sign when all these things shall be fulfilled?

5 And Jesus answering them began to say, Take heed lest any *man* deceive you:

6 For many shall come in my name, saying, I am *Christ;* and shall deceive many.

7 And when ye shall hear of wars and rumours of wars, be ye not troubled: for *such things* must needs be; but the end *shall* not *be* yet.

8 For nation shall rise against nation, and kingdom against kingdom: and there shall be earthquakes in divers places, and there shall be famines and troubles: these *are* the beginnings of sorrows.

9 ¶ But take heed to yourselves: for they shall deliver you up to councils; and in the synagogues ye shall be beaten: and ye shall be brought before rulers and kings for my sake, for a testimony against them.

10 And the gospel must first be published among all nations.

11 But when they shall lead *you,* and deliver you up, take no thought beforehand what ye shall speak, neither do ye premeditate: but whatsoever shall be given you in that hour, that speak ye: for it is not ye that speak, but the Holy Ghost.

12 Now the brother shall betray the brother to death, and the father the son; and children shall rise up against *their* parents, and shall cause them to be put to death.

13 And ye shall be hated of all *men* for my name's sake: but he that shall endure unto the end, the same shall be saved.

14 ¶ But when ye shall see the abomination of desolation, spoken of by Daniel the prophet, standing where it ought not, (let him that readeth understand,) then let them that be in Judæa flee to the mountains:

15 And let him that is on the housetop not go down into the house, neither enter *therein,* to take any thing out of his house:

16 And let him that is in the field not turn back again for to take up his garment.

17 But woe to them that are with child, and to them that give suck in those days!

18 And pray ye that your flight be not in the winter.

Amplified

CHAPTER 13

AND as [Jesus] was coming out of the temple ([b]area) one of His disciples said to Him, Look, Teacher! Notice the sort *and* quality of these stones and buildings!

2 And Jesus replied to him, You see these great buildings? There will not be left here one stone upon another that will not be loosened *and* torn down.

3 And as He sat on the Mount of Olives opposite the temple ([b]enclosure), Peter and James and John and Andrew asked Him privately,

4 Tell us when is this to take place and what will be the sign when these things, all [of them], are about to be accomplished?

5 And Jesus began to tell them, Be careful *and* watchful that no one misleads you [about it].

6 Many will come ([c]appropriating to themselves) the name (of Messiah) which belongs to Me—[d]basing their claims on the use of My name—saying I am [He]! and they will mislead many.

7 And when you hear of wars and rumors of wars, do not get alarmed—troubled and frightened; it is necessary [that these things] take place, but the end is not yet.

8 For nation will rise against nation, and kingdom against kingdom; there will be earthquakes in various places; there will be famines *and calamities;* this is but a beginning of the [e]intolerable anguish *and* sufferings—only the first of the [f]birth pangs.

9 But look to yourselves, for they will turn you over to councils, and you will be beaten in the synagogues, and you will stand before governors and kings for My sake for a testimony to them.

10 And the good news (the Gospel) must first be preached to all nations.

11 Now when they take you [to court] and put you under arrest, do not be anxious beforehand about what you are to say *nor* [*even*] *meditate about it;* but say whatever is given you in that hour *and* at [g]the moment for it is not you who will be speaking but the Holy Spirit.

12 And brother will hand over brother to death, and the father his child, and children will take a stand against their parents and [have] them put to death,

13 And you will be hated *and* detested by everybody for My name's sake. But he who patiently perseveres *and* endures to the end will be saved [that is, [e]made a partaker of the salvation by Christ, and delivered [e]from spiritual death].

14 But when you see the abomination of desolation *mentioned by Daniel the prophet* standing where it ought not to be, [and] let the one who reads take notice *and* consider *and* understand *and* heed [this], then let those who are in Judea flee to the mountains. [Dan. 11:31; 12:11.]

15 Let him who is on the housetop not go down *into the house,* nor go inside to take anything out of his house;

16 And let him who is in the field not turn back again to get his mantle (cloak).

17 And alas for those who are pregnant and for those who have nursing babies in those days!

18 Pray that it may not occur in winter,

---

b) Trench.
c) Thayer.
d) Vincent.
e) Thayer.
f) Literal meaning.
g) Moulton and Milligan.

Living New Testament

CHAPTER 13

As He was leaving the Temple that day, one of His
disciples said, "Teacher, what beautiful buildings
ese are! Look at the decorated stonework on the walls."
2 Jesus replied, "Yes, look! For not one stone will be
ft upon another, except as ruins."
3, 4 And as He sat on the slopes of the Mount of
lives across the valley from Jerusalem, Peter, James,
ohn, and Andrew got alone with Him and asked Him,
Just when is all this going to happen to the Temple? Will
ere be some warning ahead of time?"
5 So Jesus launched into an extended reply. "Don't let
nyone mislead you," He said,
6 "For many will come declaring themselves to be your
lessiah, and will lead many astray.
7 And wars will break out near and far, but this is not
ie signal of the end-time.
8 For nations and kingdoms will proclaim war against
ach other, and there will be earthquakes in many lands,
nd famines. These herald only the early stages of the
nguish ahead.
9 But when these things begin to happen, watch out!
or you will be in great danger. You will be dragged
efore the courts, and beaten in the synagogues, and
ccused before governors and kings of being My follow-
rs. This is your opportunity to tell them the Good News.
10 And the Good News must first be made known in
very nation before the end-time finally comes.[1]
11 But when you are arrested and stand trial, don't
orry about what to say in your defense. Just say what
od tells you to. Then you will not be speaking, but the
Ioly Spirit will.
12 Brothers will betray each other to death, fathers
vill betray their own children, and children will betray
heir parents to be killed.
13 And everyone will hate you because you are Mine.
ut all who endure to the end without renouncing Me
hall be saved.
14 When you see the horrible thing standing in the
emple[2]—reader, pay attention!—flee, if you can to the
udean hills.
15, 16 Hurry! If you are on your rooftop porch, don't
ven go back into the house. If you are out in the fields,
on't even return for your money or clothes.
17 Woe to pregnant women in those days, and to
nothers nursing their children.
18 And pray that your flight will not be in winter.

Revised Standard

The course of this age

13 And as he came out of the temple,
one of his disciples said to him, "Look,
Teacher, what wonderful stones and what
wonderful buildings!" [2]And Jesus said to
him, "Do you see these great buildings?
There will not be left here one stone upon
another, that will not be thrown down."
3 And as he sat on the Mount of Olives
opposite the temple, Peter and James and
John and Andrew asked him privately,
[4]"Tell us, when will this be, and what will
be the sign when these things are all to be
accomplished?" [5]And Jesus began to say
to them, "Take heed that no one leads you
astray. [6]Many will come in my name, saying, 'I am he!' and they will lead many
astray. [7]And when you hear of wars and
rumors of wars, do not be alarmed; this
must take place, but the end is not yet.
[8]For nation will rise against nation, and
kingdom against kingdom; there will be
earthquakes in various places, there will
be famines; this is but the beginning of
the sufferings.
9 "But take heed to yourselves; for they
will deliver you up to councils; and you
will be beaten in synagogues; and you
will stand before governors and kings for
my sake, to bear testimony before them.
[10]And the gospel must first be preached
to all nations. [11]And when they bring you
to trial and deliver you up, do not be anxious beforehand what you are to say; but
say whatever is given you in that hour,
for it is not you who speak, but the Holy
Spirit. [12]And brother will deliver up brother to death, and the father his child, and
children will rise against parents and have
them put to death; [13]and you will be hated
by all for my name's sake. But he who
endures to the end will be saved.

The time of tribulation

14 "But when you see the desolating
sacrilege set up where it ought not to be
(let the reader understand), then let those
who are in Judea flee to the mountains; [15]let
him who is on the housetop not go down,
nor enter his house, to take anything away;
[16]and let him who is in the field not turn
back to take his mantle. [17]And alas for
those who are with child and for those
who give suck in those days! [18]Pray that
it may not happen in winter. [19]For in

Implied.
Literally, "standing where it ought not."

King James

19 For *in* those days shall be affliction, such as was not from the beginning of the creation which God created unto this time, neither shall be.

20 And except that the Lord had shortened those days, no flesh should be saved: but for the elect's sake, whom he hath chosen, he hath shortened the days.

21 And then if any man shall say to you, Lo, here *is* Christ; or, lo, *he is* there; believe *him* not:

22 For false Christs and false prophets shall rise, and shall shew signs and wonders, to seduce, if *it were* possible, even the elect.

23 But take ye heed: behold, I have foretold you all things.

24 ¶ But in those days, after that tribulation, the sun shall be darkened, and the moon shall not give her light,

25 And the stars of heaven shall fall, and the powers that are in heaven shall be shaken.

26 And then shall they see the Son of man coming in the clouds with great power and glory.

27 And then shall he send his angels, and shall gather together his elect from the four winds, from the uttermost part of the earth to the uttermost part of heaven.

28 Now learn a parable of the fig tree; When her branch is yet tender, and putteth forth leaves, ye know that summer is near:

29 So ye in like manner, when ye shall see these things come to pass, know that it is nigh, *even* at the doors.

30 Verily I say unto you, that this generation shall not pass, till all these things be done.

31 Heaven and earth shall pass away: but my words shall not pass away.

32 ¶ But of that day and *that* hour knoweth no man, no, not the angels which are in heaven, neither the Son, but the Father.

33 Take ye heed, watch and pray: for ye know not when the time is.

34 *For the Son of man is* as a man taking a far journey, who left his house, and gave authority to his servants, and to every man his work, and commanded the porter to watch.

35 Watch ye therefore: for ye know not when the master of the house cometh, at even, or at midnight, or at the cockcrowing, or in the morning:

36 Lest coming suddenly he find you sleeping.

37 And what I say unto you I say unto all, Watch.

Amplified

19 For at that time there will be such affliction—oppression and tribulation—as has not been from the beginning of the creation which God created until this particular time, and [h]positively never will be [again].

20 And unless the Lord had shortened the days, no human being would be saved (rescued); but for the sake of the elect, His chosen ones—those whom He [i]picked out for Himself—He has shortened the days. [Dan. 12:1.]

21 And then if any one says to you, See, here is the Christ! or, Look, there He is! do not believe it.

22 False Christs (Messiahs) and false prophets will arise and show signs and (work) miracles to deceive *and* lead astray, if possible, even the elect—those God has chosen out for Himself.

23 But look to yourselves *and* be on your guard; I have told you everything beforehand.

24 But in those days, after (the affliction and oppression and distress of) that tribulation, the sun will be darkened, and the moon will not give its light. [Isa. 13:10.]

25 And the stars will be falling from the sky, and the powers in the heavens will be shaken. [Isa. 34:4.]

26 And then they will see the Son of man coming in clouds with great (kingly) power and glory (majesty and splendor). [Dan. 7:13, 14.]

27 And then He will send out the angels and will gather together His elect—those He has [j]picked out for Himself—from the four winds, from the farthest bounds of the earth to the farthest bounds of heaven.

28 Now learn a lesson from the fig tree; as soon as its branch becomes tender, and it puts forth its leaves, you recognize *and* know that summer is near.

29 So also, when you see these things happening, you will recognize *and* know that He is near, at [the very] door.

30 Surely, I say to you, this generation [[k]the whole multitude of people living at that one time] positively will not perish *or* pass away before all these things take place.

31 Heaven and earth will perish *and* pass away, but My words will not perish *or* pass away.

32 But of that day or that hour not a [single] person knows, not even the angels in heaven, nor the Son, but only the Father.

33 Be on your guard (constantly alert) and watch *and pray,* for you do not know when the time will come.

34 It is like a man ([l]already) going on a journey; when he leaves home he puts his servants in charge, each with his particular task, and he gives orders to the doorkeeper to be constantly alert *and* on the watch.

35 Therefore watch—give strict attention, be cautious and alert—for you do not know when the Master of the house is coming, in the evening, or at midnight, or at cockcrowing, or in the morning.

36 [Watch, I say] lest He come suddenly *and* unexpectedly and find you asleep.

37 And what I say to you I say to everybody: (Give strict attention, be cautious, active, alert, and) watch!

---

h) Wuest.
i) Abbott-Smith.
j) Abbott-Smith.
k) Cremer; Thayer, and Abbott-Smith.
l) Wycliffe; Tyndale.

Living New Testament

19 For those will be days of such horror as have never been since the beginning of God's creation, nor will ever be again.

20 And unless the Lord shortens that time of calamity, not a soul in all the earth will survive. But for the sake of His chosen ones He will limit those days.

21 And then if anyone tells you, 'This is the Messiah,' or, 'That one is,' don't pay any attention.

22 For there will be many false Messiahs and false prophets who will do wonderful miracles that would deceive, if possible, even God's own children.[3]

23 Take care! I have warned you!

24 After the tribulation ends, then the sun will grow dim and the moon will not shine,

25 And the stars will fall—the heavens will convulse.

26 Then all mankind will see Me, the Son of Mankind, coming in the clouds with great power and glory.

27 And I will send out the angels to gather together My chosen ones from all over the world—from the farthest bounds of earth and heaven.

28 Now, here is a lesson from a fig tree. When its buds become tender and its leaves begin to sprout, you know that spring has come.

29 And when you see these things happening that I've described, you can be sure that My return is very near, that I am right at the door.

30 Yes, these are the events that will signal the end of the age.[4]

31 Heaven and earth shall disappear, but My words stand sure forever.

32 However, no one, not even the angels in heaven, nor I Myself,[5] knows the day or hour when these things will happen; only the Father knows.

33 And since you don't know when it will happen, stay alert. Be on the watch [for My return].[6]

34 My coming[7] can be compared with that of a man who went on a trip to another country. He laid out his employees' work for them to do while he was gone, and told the gatekeeper to watch for his return.

35, 36, 37 Keep a sharp lookout! For you do not know when I[6] will come, at evening, at midnight, early dawn or late daybreak. Don't let Me find you sleeping. *Watch for My return*! This is My message to you and to everyone else."

[3]Literally, "elect of God."
[4]Literally, "this generation."
[5]Literally, "The Son."
[6]Implied.
[7]Literally, "the Lord of the house."

Revised Standard

those days there will be such tribulation
as has not been from the beginning of the
creation which God created until now,
and never will be. 20And if the Lord had
not shortened the days, no human being
would be saved; but for the sake of the
elect, whom he chose, he shortened the
days. 21And then if any one says to you,
'Look, here is the Christ!' or 'Look, there
he is!' do not believe it. 22False Christs
and false prophets will arise and show
signs and wonders, to lead astray, if possible, the elect. 23But take heed; I have told
you all things beforehand.

The coming of the Son of man

24 "But in those days, after that tribulation, the sun will be darkened, and the
moon will not give its light, 25and the stars
will be falling from heaven, and the powers
in the heavens will be shaken. 26And then
they will see the Son of man coming in
clouds with great power and glory. 27And
then he will send out the angels, and gather
his elect from the four winds, from the
ends of the earth to the ends of heaven.

Signs of the end

28 "From the fig tree learn its lesson:
as soon as its branch becomes tender and
puts forth its leaves, you know that summer is near. 29So also, when you see these
things taking place, you know that he is
near, at the very gates. 30Truly, I say to
you, this generation will not pass away before all these things take place. 31Heaven
and earth will pass away, but my words
will not pass away.

32 "But of that day or that hour no one
knows, not even the angels in heaven, nor
the Son, but only the Father. 33Take heed,
watch;[a] for you do not know when the
time will come. 34It is like a man going
on a journey, when he leaves home and
puts his servants in charge, each with his
work, and commands the doorkeeper to be
on the watch. 35Watch therefore—for you
do not know when the master of the house
will come, in the evening, or at midnight,
or at cockcrow, or in the morning—36lest
he come suddenly and find you asleep.
37And what I say to you I say to all:
Watch."

[a] Other ancient authorities add *and pray*

King James

CHAPTER 14

AFTER two days was *the feast of* the passover, and of unleavened bread: and the chief priests and the scribes sought how they might take him by craft, and put *him* to death.

2 But they said, Not on the feast *day*, lest there be an uproar of the people.

3 ¶ And being in Bethany in the house of Simon the leper, as he sat at meat, there came a woman having an alabaster box of ointment of spikenard very precious; and she brake the box, and poured *it* on his head.

4 And there were some that had indignation within themselves, and said, Why was this waste of the ointment made?

5 For it might have been sold for more than three hundred pence, and have been given to the poor. And they murmured against her.

6 And Jesus said, Let her alone; why trouble ye her? she hath wrought a good work on me.

7 For ye have the poor with you always, and whensoever ye will ye may do them good: but me ye have not always.

8 She hath done what she could: she is come aforehand to anoint my body to the burying.

9 Verily I say unto you, Wheresoever this gospel shall be preached throughout the whole world, *this* also that she hath done shall be spoken of for a memorial of her.

10 ¶ And Judas Iscariot, one of the twelve, went unto the chief priests, to betray him unto them.

11 And when they heard it, they were glad, and promised to give him money. And he sought how he might conveniently betray him.

12 ¶ And the first day of unleavened bread, when they killed the passover, his disciples said unto him, Where wilt thou that we go and prepare that thou mayest eat the passover?

13 And he sendeth forth two of his disciples, and saith unto them, Go ye into the city, and there shall meet you a man bearing a pitcher of water: follow him.

14 And wheresoever he shall go in, say ye to the goodman of the house, The Master saith, Where is the guestchamber, where I shall eat the passover with my disciples?

15 And he will shew you a large upper room furnished *and* prepared: there make ready for us.

16 And his disciples went forth, and came into the city, and found as he had said unto them: and they made ready the passover.

17 And in the evening he cometh with the twelve.

18 And as they sat and did eat, Jesus said, Verily I say unto you, One of you which eateth with me shall betray me.

19 And they began to be sorrowful, and to say unto him one by one, *Is* it I? and another *said, Is* it I?

20 And he answered and said unto them, *It is* one of the twelve, that dippeth with me in the dish.

Amplified

CHAPTER 14

IT was now two days before the Passover and the feast of Unleavened Bread. And the chief priests and the scribes were all the while seeking to arrest [Jesus] by secrecy *and* deceit, and put [Him] to death,

2 For they kept saying, It must not be during the feast, for fear there might be a riot of the people.

3 And while He was in Bethany, [a guest] in the house of Simon the leper, as He was reclining [at table,] a woman came with an alabaster jar of ointment ([m]perfume) of pure nard, very costly *and* precious, and she broke the jar and poured [the perfume] over His head.

4 But there were some who were moved with indignation and said to themselves, To what purpose was the ointment ([m]perfume) thus wasted?

5 For it was possible to have sold this [perfume] for more than three hundred denarii [a laboring man's wages for a year], and to have given [them] to the poor. And they censured *and* reproved her.

6 But Jesus said, Let her alone; why are you troubling her? She has done a good *and* beautiful thing to Me—praiseworthy and noble.

7 For you always have the poor with you, and whenever you wish you can do good to them; but you will not always have Me. [Deut. 15:11.]

8 She has done what she could; she came beforehand to anoint My body for the burial.

9 And surely, I tell you, wherever the good news (the Gospel) is proclaimed in the entire world, what she has done will be told for a memorial of her.

10 Then Judas Iscariot, who was one of the twelve [apostles], went off to the chief priests in order to betray *and* hand Him over to them.

11 And when they heard it they rejoiced *and* were delighted, and they promised to give him money. And he (busying himself continually) sought an opportunity to betray Him.

12 On the first day [of the feast] of Unleavened Bread, when [as was customary] they killed the passover lamb, [Jesus'] disciples said to Him, Where do You wish us to go [and] prepare the passover [supper] for You to eat?

13 And He sent two of His disciples, and said to them, Go into the city, and a man carrying an (earthenware) jar *or* pitcher of water will meet you; follow him.

14 And whatever [house] he enters, say to the master of the house, The Teacher says, Where is My guest room, where I may eat the passover [supper] with My disciples?

15 And he will [himself] show you a large upper room furnished [that is, with carpets and with dining couches properly spread] and ready; there prepare for us.

16 Then the disciples set out and came to the city, and found [everything] as He had told them; and they prepared the passover.

17 And when it was evening He came with the twelve [apostles].

18 And while they were at the table eating, Jesus said, Surely, I say to you, one of you will betray Me, [one] who is eating [here] with Me. [Ps. 41:9.]

19 And they began to show that they were sad *and* hurt, and to say to Him one after another, Is it I? *or*, It is not I, is it?

20 He replied to them, It is one of the twelve [apostles], one who is dipping [bread] into the (same deep) dish with Me.

---

m) Moulton and Milligan.

Living New Testament

CHAPTER 14

The Passover observance began two days later—an annual Jewish holiday when no bread made with yeast was eaten. The chief priests and other Jewish leaders were still looking for an opportunity to arrest Jesus secretly and put Him to death.

2 "But we can't do it during the Passover," they said, "or there will be a riot."

3 Meanwhile Jesus was in Bethany, at the home of Simon the leper; during supper a woman came in with a beautiful flask of expensive perfume. Then, breaking the seal, she poured it over His head.

4, 5 Some of those at the table were indignant among themselves about this "waste," as they called it. "Why, she could have sold that perfume for a fortune and given the money to the poor!" they snarled.

6 But Jesus said, "Let her alone; why berate her for doing a good thing?

7 You always have the poor among you, and they badly need your help, and you can aid them whenever you want to; but I won't be here much longer.

8 She has done what she could, and has anointed My body ahead of time for burial.

9 And I tell you this in solemn truth, that wherever the Good News is preached throughout the world, this woman's deed will be remembered and praised."

10 Then Judas Iscariot, one of His disciples, went to the chief priests to arrange to betray Jesus to them.

11 When the chief priests heard why he had come, they were excited and happy and promised him a reward. So he began looking for the right time and place to betray Jesus.

12 On the first day of the Passover, the day the lambs were sacrificed, His disciples asked Him where He wanted to go to eat the traditional Passover supper.

13 He sent two of them into Jerusalem to make the arrangements. "As you are walking along," He told them, "you will see a man coming towards you carrying a pot of water. Follow him.

14 At the house he enters, tell the man in charge, 'Our Master sent us to see the room you have ready for us, where we will eat the Passover supper this evening!'

15 He will take you upstairs to a large room all set up. Prepare our supper there."

16 So the two disciples went on ahead into the city and found everything as Jesus had said, and prepared the Passover.

17 In the evening Jesus arrived with the other disciples,

18 And as they were sitting around the table eating, Jesus said, "I solemnly declare that one of you will betray Me, one of you who is here eating with Me."

19 A great sadness swept over them, and one by one they asked Him, "Am I the one?"

20 He replied, "It is one of you twelve eating with Me now.

Revised Standard

The plot to kill Jesus

14 It was now two days before the Passover and the feast of Unleavened
Bread. And the chief priests and the scribes
were seeking how to arrest him by stealth,
and kill him; 2for they said, "Not during
the feast, lest there be a tumult of the
people."

Anointing of Jesus at Bethany

3 And while he was at Bethany in the
house of Simon the leper, as he sat at table,
a woman came with an alabaster jar of
ointment of pure nard, very costly, and
she broke the jar and poured it over his
head. 4But there were some who said to
themselves indignantly, "Why was the ointment thus wasted? 5For this ointment
might have been sold for more than three
hundred denarii,[b] and given to the poor."
And they reproached her. 6But Jesus said,
"Let her alone; why do you trouble her?
She has done a beautiful thing to me. 7For
you always have the poor with you, and
whenever you will, you can do good to
them; but you will not always have me.
8She has done what she could; she has
anointed my body beforehand for burying.
9And truly, I say to you, wherever the gospel is preached in the whole world, what
she has done will be told in memory of
her."

The bargain of Judas Iscariot

10 Then Judas Iscariot, who was one of
the twelve, went to the chief priests in order
to betray him to them. 11And when they
heard it they were glad, and promised to
give him money. And he sought an opportunity to betray him.

The Last Supper

12 And on the first day of Unleavened
Bread, when they sacrificed the passover
lamb, his disciples said to him, "Where will
you have us go and prepare for you to eat
the passover?" 13And he sent two of his
disciples, and said to them, "Go into the
city, and a man carying a jar of water will
meet you; follow him, 14and wherever he
enters, say to the householder, 'The Teacher
says, Where is my guest room, where I am
to eat the passover with my disciples?'
15And he will show you a large upper room
furnished and ready; there prepare for us."
16And the disciples set out and went to the
city, and found it as he had told them; and
they prepared the passover.

17 And when it was evening he came
with the twelve. 18And as they were at table
eating, Jesus said, "Truly, I say to you, one
of you will betray me, one who is eating
with me." 19They began to be sorrowful,
and to say to him one after another, "Is it
I?" 20He said to them, "It is one of the
twelve, one who is dipping bread in the

---

[b] The denarius was worth about twenty cents

King James

21 The Son of man indeed goeth, as it is written of him: but woe to that man by whom the Son of man is betrayed! good were it for that man if he had never been born.

22 ¶ And as they did eat, Jesus took bread, and blessed, and brake *it*, and gave to them, and said, Take, eat: this is my body.

23 And he took the cup, and when he had given thanks, he gave *it* to them: and they all drank of it.

24 And he said unto them, This is my blood of the new testament, which is shed for many.

25 Verily I say unto you, I will drink no more of the fruit of the vine, until that day that I drink it new in the kingdom of God.

26 ¶ And when they had sung an hymn, they went out into the mount of Olives.

27 And Jesus saith unto them, All ye shall be offended because of me this night: for it is written, I will smite the shepherd, and the sheep shall be scattered.

28 But after that I am risen, I will go before you into Galilee.

29 But Peter said unto him, Although all shall be offended, yet *will* not I.

30 And Jesus saith unto him, Verily I say unto thee, That this day, *even* in this night, before the cock crow twice, thou shalt deny me thrice.

31 But he spake the more vehemently, If I should die with thee, I will not deny thee in any wise. Likewise also said they all.

32 And they came to a place which was named Gethsemane: and he saith to his disciples, Sit ye here, while I shall pray.

33 And he taketh with him Peter and James and John, and began to be sore amazed, and to be very heavy;

34 And saith unto them, My soul is exceeding sorrowful unto death: tarry ye here, and watch.

35 And he went forward a little, and fell on the ground, and prayed that, if it were possible, the hour might pass from him.

36 And he said, Abba, Father, all things *are* possible unto thee; take away this cup from me: nevertheless not what I will, but what thou wilt.

37 And he cometh, and findeth them sleeping, and saith unto Peter, Simon, sleepest thou? couldest not thou watch one hour?

38 Watch ye and pray, lest ye enter into temptation. The spirit truly *is* ready, but the flesh *is* weak.

39 And again he went away, and prayed, and spake the same words.

40 And when he returned, he found them asleep again, (for their eyes were heavy,) neither wist they what to answer him.

41 And he cometh the third time, and saith unto them, Sleep on now, and take *your* rest: it is enough, the hour is come; behold, the Son of man is betrayed into the hands of sinners.

Amplified

21 For the Son of man goes as it stands written concerning Him, but woe to that man by whom the Son of man is betrayed! It would have been good (profitable and wholesome) for that man if he had never been born. [Ps. 41:9.]

22 And while they were eating, He took a loaf [of bread], praised God *and* gave thanks *and* asked Him to bless it to their use. [Then] He broke [it], and gave to them, and said, Take. *Eat.* This is My body.

23 He also took a cup [of juice of grapes], and when He had given thanks He gave [it] to them, and they all drank of it.

24 And He said to them, This is My blood [which ratifies] the *new* covenant, [the blood] which is being poured out for (on account of,) many. [Exod. 24:8.]

25 Solemnly *and* surely, I tell you, I shall not again drink of the fruit of the vine till that day when I drink it [n]of a new *and* a higher quality in God's kingdom.

26 And when they had sung a hymn, they went out to the Mount of Olives.

27 And Jesus said to them, You will all fall away *this night*—[that is,] you will be caused to stumble and will begin to distrust and desert Me; for it stands written, I will strike the shepherd, and the sheep will be scattered. [Zech. 13:7.]

28 But after I am raised [to life], I will go before you into Galilee.

29 But Peter said to Him, Even if they all fall away *and* are caused to stumble *and* distrust *and* desert You, yet I will not [do so]!

30 And Jesus said to him, Truly, I tell you, this very night, before a cock crows twice, you will utterly deny Me—disclaiming all connection with Me—three times.

31 But [Peter] said more vehemently *and* repeatedly, [Even] if it should be necessary for me to die with You, I will not deny *or* disown You! And they all kept saying the same thing.

32 Then they went to a place called Gethsemane, and He said to His disciples, Sit down here while I pray.

33 And He took with Him Peter and James and John, and began to be [o]struck with terror *and* amazement and deeply troubled *and* depressed.

34 And He said to them, My soul is exceedingly sad—overwhelmed with grief—so that it almost kills Me! Remain here, and [p]keep awake *and* be watching.

35 And going a little farther, He fell on the ground and kept praying that, if it were possible, the [[o]fatal] hour might pass from Him.

36 And He was saying, Abba, [which means] Father, everything is possible for You; take away this cup from Me; yet not what I will, but what You [will].

37 And He came back and found them sleeping, and He said to Peter, Simon, are you asleep? Have you not the strength to [q]keep awake *and* watch [with Me] one hour?

38 [q]Keep awake *and* watch and pray (constantly) that you may not enter into temptation; the spirit indeed is willing, but the flesh is weak.

39 He went away again and prayed, saying the same words.

40 And again He came back and found them sleeping, for their eyes were very heavy; and they did not know what answer to give Him.

41 And He came back a third time, and said to them, Are you still sleeping and resting? It is enough [of that]. The hour has come. The Son of man is betrayed into the

---

n) Vincent.
o) Thayer.
p) Alternate reading.
q) Alternate reading.

Living New Testament

21 I[1] must die, as the prophets declared long ago; but, oh, the misery ahead for the man by whom I[1] am betrayed. Oh, that he had never been born!"

22 As they were eating, Jesus took a small loaf of bread and asked God's blessing on it and broke it in pieces and gave it to them and said, "Eat it—this is My body."

23 Then He took a cup of wine and gave thanks to God for it and gave it to them; and they all drank from it.

24 And He said to them, "This is My blood, poured out for many, sealing[2] the new agreement between God and man.

25 I solemnly declare that I shall never again taste wine until the day I drink a far better kind[3] in the Kingdom of God."

26 Then they sang a hymn and went out to the Mount of Olives.

27 "All of you will desert Me," Jesus told them, "for God has declared through the prophets, 'I will kill the Shepherd, and the sheep will scatter.'

28 But after I am raised to life again, I will go to Galilee and meet you there."

29 Peter said to Him, "I will never desert You no matter what the others do!"

30 "Peter," Jesus said, "before the cock crows a second time tomorrow morning you will deny Me three times."

31 "No!" Peter exploded. "Not even if I have to die with You! I'll *never* deny You!" And all the others vowed the same.

32 And now they came to an olive grove called the Garden of Gethsemane, and He instructed His disciples, "Sit here, while I go and pray."

33 He took Peter, James and John with Him and began to be filled with horror and deepest distress.

34 And He said to them, "My soul is crushed by sorrow to the point of death; stay here and watch with Me."

35 He went on a little farther and fell to the ground and prayed that if it were possible the awful hour awaiting Him might never come.[4]

36 "Father, Father," He said, "everything is possible for You. Take away this cup from Me. Yet I want Your will, not Mine."

37 Then He returned to the three disciples and found them asleep. "Simon!" He said. "Asleep? Couldn't you watch with Me for even one hour?

38 Watch with Me and pray lest the Tempter overpower you. For though the spirit is willing enough, the body is weak."

39 And He went away again and prayed, repeating His pleadings.

40 Again He returned to them and found them sleeping, for they were very tired. And they didn't know what to say.

41 The third time when He returned to them He said, "Sleep on; get your rest! But no! The time for sleep has ended! Look! I[5] am betrayed into the hands of wicked men.

[1]Literally, "the Son of man."
[2]Literally, "This is My blood of the covenant." Some ancient manuscripts read, "new covenant."
[3]Literally, "drink it new."
[4]Literally, "that the hour might pass away from Him."
[5]Literally, "the Son of man."

Revised Standard

same dish with me. 21For the Son of man
goes as it is written of him, but woe to that
man by whom the Son of man is betrayed!
It would have been better for that man if he
had not been born."

22 And as they were eating, he took
bread, and blessed, and broke it, and gave it
to them, and said, "Take; this is my body."
23And he took a cup, and when he had given
thanks he gave it to them, and they all
drank of it. 24And he said to them, "This
is my blood of the[c] covenant, which is
poured out for many. 25Truly, I say to you,
I shall not drink again of the fruit of the
vine until that day when I drink it new in
the kingdom of God."

Peter's denial foretold

26 And when they had sung a hymn, they
went out to the Mount of Olives. 27And
Jesus said to them, "You will all fall away;
for it is written, 'I will strike the shepherd,
and the sheep will be scattered.' 28But after
I am raised up, I will go before you to Galilee." 29Peter said to him, "Even though
they all fall away, I will not." 30And Jesus
said to him, "Truly, I say to you, this very
night, before the cock crows twice, you will
deny me three times." 31But he said vehemently, "If I must die with you, I will not
deny you." And they all said the same.

Jesus' agony in Gethsemane

32 And they went to a place which was
called Gethsemane; and he said to his disciples, "Sit here, while I pray." 33And he
took with him Peter and James and John,
and began to be greatly distressed and
troubled. 34And he said to them, "My soul
is very sorrowful, even to death; remain
here, and watch."[d] 35And going a little farther, he fell on the ground and prayed that,
if it were possible, the hour might pass from
him. 36And he said, "Abba, Father, all things
are possible to thee; remove this cup from
me; yet not what I will, but what thou wilt."
37And he came and found them sleeping, and
he said to Peter, "Simon, are you asleep?
Could you not watch[d] one hour? 38Watch[d]
and pray that you may not enter into temptation; the spirit indeed is willing, but the
flesh is weak." 39And again he went away
and prayed, saying the same words. 40And
again he came and found them sleeping, for
their eyes were very heavy; and they did
not know what to answer him. 41And he
came the third time, and said to them, "Are
you still sleeping and taking your rest? It
is enough; the hour has come; the Son of
man is betrayed into the hands of sinners.

[c] Other ancient authorities insert *new*
[d] Or *keep awake*

King James

42 Rise up, let us go; lo, he that betrayeth me is at hand.

43 ¶ And immediately, while he yet spake, cometh Judas, one of the twelve, and with him a great multitude with swords and staves, from the chief priests and the scribes and the elders.

44 And he that betrayed him had given them a token, saying, Whomsoever I shall kiss, that same is he; take him, and lead *him* away safely.

45 And as soon as he was come, he goeth straightway to him, and saith, Master, master; and kissed him.

46 ¶ And they laid their hands on him, and took him.

47 And one of them that stood by drew a sword, and smote a servant of the high priest, and cut off his ear.

48 And Jesus answered and said unto them, Are ye come out, as against a thief, with swords and *with* staves to take me?

49 I was daily with you in the temple teaching, and ye took me not: but the scriptures must be fulfilled.

50 And they all forsook him, and fled.

51 And there followed him a certain young man, having a linen cloth cast about *his* naked *body;* and the young men laid hold on him:

52 And he left the linen cloth, and fled from them naked.

53 ¶ And they led Jesus away to the high priest: and with him were assembled all the chief priests and the elders and the scribes.

54 And Peter followed him afar off, even into the palace of the high priest: and he sat with the servants, and warmed himself at the fire.

55 And the chief priests and all the council sought for witness against Jesus to put him to death; and found none.

56 For many bare false witness against him, but their witness agreed not together.

57 And there arose certain, and bare false witness against him, saying,

58 We heard him say, I will destroy this temple that is made with hands, and within three days I will build another made without hands.

59 But neither so did their witness agree together.

60 And the high priest stood up in the midst, and asked Jesus, saying, Answerest thou nothing? what *is it which* these witness against thee?

61 But he held his peace, and answered nothing. Again the high priest asked him, and said unto him, Art thou the Christ, the Son of the Blessed?

62 And Jesus said, I am: and ye shall see the Son of man sitting on the right hand of power, and coming in the clouds of heaven.

63 Then the high priest rent his clothes, and saith, What need we any further witnesses?

64 Ye have heard the blasphemy: what think ye? And they all condemned him to be guilty of death.

Amplified

hands of sinful men—[that is,] of men [r]whose way or nature is to act in opposition to God.

42 Get up; let us be going. See, My betrayer is at hand.

43 And at once, while He was still speaking, Judas came, one of the twelve [apostles], and with him a crowd of men with swords and clubs, [who came] from the chief priests and the scribes and the elders [of the Sanhedrin].

44 Now the betrayer had given them a signal, saying, The one I shall kiss is [the Man]; seize Him and lead [Him] away safely—so as to prevent His escape.

45 And when he came he went up to Jesus immediately, and said, Master! *Master!* and he [s]embraced Him *and* kissed Him fervently.

46 And they threw their hands on Him and arrested Him.

47 But one of the bystanders drew his sword, and struck the bond servant of the high priest and cut off his ear.

48 And Jesus said to them, Have you come out as against a robber, to capture Me with swords and clubs?

49 I was with you daily in the temple ([t]porches and courts) teaching, and you did not seize Me; but that the Scriptures be fulfilled.

50 Then [His disciples], forsaking Him, fled, all [of them].

51 And a young man was following Him, with nothing but a linen cloth ([u]sheet) thrown about [his] naked [body]; and they laid hold of him,

52 But leaving behind the linen cloth ([u]sheet), he fled from them naked.

53 And they led Jesus away to the high priest, and all the chief priests and the elders and the scribes were gathered together.

54 And Peter followed Him at a distance, even right into the courtyard of the high priest. And he was sitting ([v]in the firelight) with the guards, and warming himself at the fire.

55 Now the chief priests and the entire council (the Sanhedrin) were constantly seeking [to get] testimony against Jesus with a view to condemning Him *and* putting Him to death, but they did not find any.

56 For many were repeatedly bearing false witness against Him, but their testimonies did not agree.

57 And some stood up and were bearing false witness against Him, saying,

58 We heard Him say, I will destroy this temple (sanctuary) which is made with hands, and in three days I will build another, made without hands.

50 Still not even [in this] did their testimony agree.

60 And the high priest stood up in the midst, and asked Jesus, Have You not even one answer to make? What [about this which] these [men] are testifying against You?

61 But He kept still and did not answer at all. Again the high priest asked Him, Are You the Christ—the Messiah, the Anointed One—the Son of the Blessed?

62 And Jesus said, I AM; and you will (all) see the Son of man seated at the right hand of Power ([w]the Almighty), and coming with the clouds of heaven. [Ps. 110:1; Dan. 7:13.]

63 Then the high priest tore his garments, and said, What need have we for more witnesses? [Num. 14:6.]

64 You have heard His blasphemy. What is your decision? And they all condemned Him as being guilty *and* deserving death. [Lev. 24:16.]

---

r) Cremer.
s) Meyer's "Commentary on Mark."
t) Trench.
u) Souter.
v) Vincent.
w) Thayer.

Living New Testament

42 Come! Get up! We must go! Look! My betrayer is here!"

43 And immediately, while He was still speaking, Judas (one of His disciples) arrived with a mob equipped with swords and clubs, sent out by the chief priests and other Jewish leaders.

44 Judas had told them, "You will know which one to arrest when I go over and greet[6] Him. Then you can take Him easily."

45 So as soon as they arrived he walked up to Jesus. "Master!" he exclaimed, and embraced Him with a great show of friendliness.

46 Then the mob arrested Jesus and held Him fast.

47 But someone[7] pulled a sword and slashed at the high priest's servant, cutting off his ear.

48 Jesus asked them, "Am I some dangerous robber, that you come like this armed to the teeth to capture Me?

49 Why didn't you arrest Me in the Temple? I was there teaching every day. But these things are happening to fulfill the prophecies about Me."

50 Meanwhile all His disciples had fled.

51, 52 There was, however, a young man following along behind, clothed only in a linen nightshirt.[8] When the mob tried to grab him, he escaped, though his clothes were torn off in the process, so that he ran away completely naked.

53 Jesus was led to the High Priest's home where all of the chief priests and other Jewish leaders soon gathered.

54 Peter followed far behind and then slipped inside the gates of the High Priest's residence and crouched beside a fire among the servants.

55 Inside, the chief priests and the whole Jewish Supreme Court were trying to find something against Jesus that would be sufficient to condemn Him to death. But their efforts were in vain.

56 Many false witnesses volunteered, but they contradicted each other.

57 Finally some men stood up to lie about Him and said,

58 "We heard him say, 'I will destroy this Temple made with human hands and in three days I will build another, made without human hands!' "

59 But even then they didn't get their stories straight!

60 Then the High Priest stood up before the Court and asked Jesus, 'Do you refuse to answer this charge? What do you have to say for yourself?"

61 To this Jesus made no reply. Then the High Priest asked Him, "Are you the Messiah, the Son of God?"

62 Jesus said, "I am, and you will see Me[9] sitting at the right hand of God, and returning to earth in the clouds of heaven."

63, 64 Then the High Priest tore at his clothes and said, "What more do we need? Why wait for witnesses? You have heard his blasphemy. What is your verdict?" And the vote for the death sentence was unanimous.

[6]Literally, "kiss"—the usual oriental greeting, even to this day.
[7]It was Peter. John 18:10.
[8]Implied. Literally, "wearing only a linen cloth."
[9]Literally, "the Son of man."

Revised Standard

42 Rise, let us be going; see, my betrayer is at hand."

Jesus' betrayal and arrest

43 And immediately, while he was still speaking, Judas came, one of the twelve, and with him a crowd with swords and clubs, from the chief priests and the scribes and the elders. 44 Now the betrayer had given them a sign, saying, "The one I shall kiss is the man; seize him and lead him away safely." 45 And when he came, he went up to him at once, and said, "Master!"[e] And he kissed him. 46 And they laid hands on him and seized him. 47 But one of those who stood by drew his sword, and struck the slave of the high priest and cut off his ear. 48 And Jesus said to them, "Have you come out as against a robber, with swords and clubs to capture me? 49 Day after day I was with you in the temple teaching, and you did not seize me. But let the scriptures be fulfilled." 50 And they all forsook him, and fled.

51 And a young man followed him, with nothing but a linen cloth about his body; and they seized him, 52 but he left the linen cloth and ran away naked.

Jesus before Caiaphas

53 And they led Jesus to the high priest; and all the chief priests and the elders and the scribes were assembled. 54 And Peter had followed him at a distance, right into the courtyard of the high priest; and he was sitting with the guards, and warming himself at the fire. 55 Now the chief priests and the whole council sought testimony against Jesus to put him to death; but they found none. 56 For many bore false witness against him, and their witness did not agree. 57 And some stood up and bore false witness against him, saying, 58 "We heard him say, 'I will destroy this temple that is made with hands, and in three days I will build another, not made with hands.' " 59 Yet not even so did their testimony agree. 60 And the high priest stood up in the midst, and asked Jesus, "Have you no answer to make? What is it that these men testify against you?" 61 But he was silent and made no answer. Again the high priest asked him, "Are you the Christ, the Son of the Blessed?" 62 And Jesus said, "I am; and you will see the Son of man sitting at the right hand of Power, and coming with the clouds of heaven." 63 And the high priest tore his mantle, and said, "Why do we still need witnesses? 64 You have heard his blasphemy. What is your decision?" And they all condemned him as deserving death. 65 And some began to spit

[e] Or *Rabbi*

King James

65 And some began to spit on him, and to cover his face, and to buffet him, and to say unto him, Prophesy: and the servants did strike him with the palms of their hands.

66 ¶ And as Peter was beneath in the palace, there cometh one of the maids of the high priest:

67 And when she saw Peter warming himself, she looked upon him, and said, And thou also wast with Jesus of Nazareth.

68 But he denied, saying, I know not, neither understand I what thou sayest. And he went out into the porch; and the cock crew.

69 And a maid saw him again, and began to say to them that stood by, This is *one* of them.

70 And he denied it again. And a little after, they that stood by said again to Peter, Surely thou art *one* of them: for thou art a Gallilæan, and thy speech agreeth *thereto*.

71 But he began to curse and to swear, *saying*, I know not this man of whom ye speak.

72 And the second time the cock crew. And Peter called to mind the word that Jesus said unto him, Before the cock crow twice, thou shalt deny me thrice. And when he thought thereon, he wept.

Amplified

65 And some of them began to spit on Him, and to blindfold Him, and to strike Him with their fists, saying to Him, Prophesy! And the guards received Him with blows *and* by slapping Him.

66 While Peter was down below in the courtyard, one of the (serving) maids of the high priest came;

67 And when she saw Peter warming himself, she gazed intently at him, and said, You were with Jesus of Nazareth too.

68 But he denied it [x]falsely *and* disowned Him, saying, I neither know nor understand what you say. Then he went outside [the courtyard and was] in the [y]vestibule to it. *And a cock crowed.*

69 And the maid servant saw him, and began again to say to the bystanders, This [man] is [one] of them.

70 But again he denied it [x]falsely *and* disowned Him. And after a short while again the bystanders said to Peter, [x]Really you are one of them, for you are a Galilean, *and your dialect shows it.*

71 Then he commenced invoking a curse on himself [if he were not telling the truth] and to swear, I do not know the Man about Whom you are talking!

72 And at once for the second time a cock crowed. And Peter remembered how Jesus said to him, Before a cock crows twice, you will ([y]utterly) deny Me—disclaiming all connection with Me—three times. And [z]having put his thought upon it, he broke down *and* wept aloud *and* [a]lamented.

CHAPTER 15

AND straightway in the morning the chief priests held a consultation with the elders and scribes and the whole council, and bound Jesus, and carried *him* away, and delivered *him* to Pilate.

2 And Pilate asked him, Art thou the King of the Jews? And he answering said unto him, Thou sayest *it*.

3 And the chief priests accused him of many things: but he answered nothing.

4 And Pilate asked him again, saying, Answerest thou nothing? behold how many things they witness against thee.

5 But Jesus yet answered nothing; so that Pilate marvelled.

6 Now at *that* feast he released unto them one prisoner, whomsoever they desired.

7 And there was *one* named Barabbas, *which lay* bound with them that had made insurrection with him, who had committed murder in the insurrection.

8 And the multitude crying aloud began to desire *him to do* as he had ever done unto them.

9 But Pilate answered them, saying, Will ye that I release unto you the King of the Jews?

10 For he knew that the chief priests had delivered him for envy.

CHAPTER 15

AND immediately when it was morning the chief priests, with the elders and scribes and the whole council, held a consultation; and when they had bound Jesus they took Him away [[a]violently] and handed Him over to Pilate. [Isa. 53:8.]

2 And Pilate inquired of Him, Are You the King of the Jews? And He replied, It is as you say.

3 And the chief priests kept accusing Him of many things.

4 And Pilate again asked Him, Have [b]You no answer to make? See how many charges they are bringing against You!

5 But Jesus made no further answer at all, so that Pilate wondered *and* marveled. [Isa. 53:7.]

6 Now at the feast he [was accustomed] to set free for them any one prisoner whom they requested.

7 And among the rioters in the prison who had committed murder in the insurrection there was a man named Barabbas.

8 And the throng came up and began asking Pilate to do as he usually did for them.

9 And he replied to them, Do you wish me to set free for you the King of the Jews?

10 For he was aware that it was ([c]because they were prompted) by envy that the chief priests had delivered Him up.

---

x) Cremer.
y) Vincent.
z) Wuest.
a) Thayer.
b) Capitalized because of what He is, the spotless Son of God, not what the speaker may have thought He was.
c) Thayer.

Living New Testament

65 Then some of them began to spit at Him, and they blindfolded Him and began to hammer His face with their fists. "Who hit you that time, you prophet?" they jeered. And even the bailiffs were using their fists on Him as they led Him away.

66, 67 Meanwhile Peter was below in the courtyard. One of the maids who worked for the High Priest noticed Peter warming himself at the fire. She looked at him closely and then announced, "*You* were with Jesus, the Nazarene."

68 Peter denied it. "I don't know what you're talking about!" he said, and walked over to the edge of the courtyard. Just then, a rooster crowed.[10]

69 The maid saw him standing there and began telling the others, "There he is! There's that disciple of Jesus!"

70 Peter denied it again. A little later others standing around the fire began saying to Peter, "You are, too, one of them, for you are from Galilee!"

71 He began to curse and swear. "I don't even know this fellow you are talking about," he said.

72 And immediately the rooster crowed the second time. Suddenly Jesus' words flashed through Peter's mind, "Before the cock crows twice, you will deny Me three times." And he began to cry.

Revised Standard

on him, and to cover his face, and to strike him, saying to him, "Prophesy!" And the guards received him with blows.

Peter's denial of Jesus

66 And as Peter was below in the courtyard, one of the maids of the high priest
came; 67and seeing Peter warming himself,
she looked at him, and said, "You also were
with the Nazarene, Jesus." 68But he denied
it, saying, "I neither know nor understand
what you mean." And he went out into the
gateway.[f] 69And the maid saw him, and began again to say to the bystanders, "This
man is one of them." 70But again he denied
it. And after a little while again the bystanders said to Peter, "Certainly you are one of
them; for you are a Galilean." 71But he began to invoke a curse on himself and to
swear, "I do not know this man of whom
you speak." 72And immediately the cock
crowed a second time. And Peter remembered how Jesus had said to him, "Before
the cock crows twice, you will deny me
three times." And he broke down and wept.

CHAPTER 15

Early in the morning the chief priests, elders and teachers of religion—the entire Supreme Court—met to discuss their next steps. Their decision was to send Jesus under armed guard to Pilate, the Roman governor.[1]

2 Pilate asked Him, "Are you the King of the Jews?"

"Yes," Jesus replied, "it is as you say."

3, 4 Then the chief priests accused Him of many crimes, and Pilate asked Him, "Why don't you say something? What about all these charges against you?"

5 But Jesus said no more, much to Pilate's amazement.

6 Now, it was Pilate's custom to release one Jewish prisoner each year at Passover time—any prisoner the people requested.

7 One of the prisoners at that time was Barabbas, convicted along with others for murder during an insurrection.

8 Now a mob began to crowd in toward Pilate, asking him to release a prisoner as usual.

9 "How about giving you the 'King of Jews'?" Pilate asked. "Is he the one you want released?"

10 (For he realized by now that this was a frame-up, backed by the chief priests because they envied Jesus' popularity.)

Jesus before Pontius Pilate

15 And as soon as it was morning the
chief priests, with the elders and
scribes, and the whole council held a consultation; and they bound Jesus and led
him away and delivered him to Pilate. 2And
Pilate asked him, "Are you the King of the
Jews?" And he answered him, "You have
said so." 3And the chief priests accused him
of many things. 4And Pilate again asked
him, "Have you no answer to make? See
how many charges they bring against you."
5But Jesus made no further answer, so that
Pilate wondered.
6 Now at the feast he used to release for
them one prisoner whom they asked. 7And
among the rebels in prison, who had committed murder in the insurrection, there was
a man called Barabbas. 8And the crowd
came up and began to ask Pilate to do as he
was wont to do for them. 9And he answered
them, "Do you want me to release for you
the King of the Jews?" 10For he perceived
that it was out of envy that the chief priests
had delivered him up. 11But the chief priests

[10]This statement is found in only some of the manuscripts.
[1] Implied.

[f] Or *fore-court*. Other ancient authorities add ***and the cock crowed***

King James

11 But the chief priests moved the people, that he should rather release Barabbas unto them.

12 And Pilate answered and said again unto them, What will ye then that I shall do *unto him* whom ye call the King of the Jews?

13 And they cried out again, Crucify him.

14 Then Pilate said unto them, Why, what evil hath he done? And they cried out the more exceedingly, Crucify him.

15 ¶ And *so* Pilate, willing to content the people, released Barabbas unto them, and delivered Jesus, when he had scourged *him*, to be crucified.

16 And the soldiers led him away into the hall, called Prætorium; and they call together the whole band.

17 And they clothed him with purple, and platted a crown of thorns, and put it about his *head*,

18 And began to salute him, Hail, King of the Jews!

19 And they smote him on the head with a reed, and did spit upon him, and bowing *their* knees worshipped him.

20 And when they had mocked him, they took off the purple from him, and put his own clothes on him, and led him out to crucify him.

21 And they compel one Simon a Cyrenian, who passed by, coming out of the country, the father of Alexander and Rufus, to bear his cross.

22 And they bring him unto the place Golgotha, which is, being interpreted, The place of a skull.

23 And they gave him to drink wine mingled with myrrh: but he received *it* not.

24 And when they had crucified him, they parted his garments, casting lots upon them, what every man should take.

25 And it was the third hour, and they crucified him.

26 And the superscription of his accusation was written over, THE KING OF THE JEWS.

27 And with him they crucify two thieves; the one on his right hand, and the other on his left.

28 And the scripture was fulfilled, which saith, And he was numbered with the transgressors.

29 And they that passed by railed on him, wagging their heads, and saying, Ah, thou that destroyest the temple, and buildest *it* in three days,

30 Save thyself, and come down from the cross.

31 Likewise also the chief priests mocking said among themselves with the scribes, He saved others; himself he cannot save.

32 Let Christ the King of Israel descend now from the cross, that we may see and believe. And they that were crucified with him reviled him.

33 And when the sixth hour was come, there was darkness over the whole land until the ninth hour.

Amplified

11 But the chief priests stirred up the crowd [to get him to release for them Barabbas instead.

12 And again Pilate said to them, Then what shall I do [with the Man] Whom you call the King of the Jews?

13 And they shouted back again, Crucify Him!

14 But Pilate said to them, (Why?) What has He done that is evil? But they shouted with all their might the more, Crucify Him [[d]at once]!

15 So Pilate, wishing to satisfy the crowd, set Barabbas free for them; and after having whipped Jesus, he handed [Him] over to be crucified. [Isa. 53:5.]

16 Then the soldiers led Him away to the courtyard inside the palace which is the praetorium, and they called the entire detachment of soldiers together.

17 And they dressed Him in a purple [robe], and weaving together a crown of thorns they placed it on Him.

18 And they began to salute Him, Hail (greeting, good health to You, long life to You), King of the Jews!

19 And they struck His head with a staff made of a [bamboo-like] reed, and spat on Him, and kept bowing their knees in homage to Him. [Isa. 50:6.]

20 And when they had [finished] making sport of Him, they took the purple [robe] off of Him, and put His own clothes on Him. And they led Him out [of the city] to crucify Him.

21 And they forced a passerby, Simon of Cyrene, the father of Alexander and Rufus, who was coming in from the field (country), to carry His cross.

22 And they led Him to Golgotha [in Latin, Calvary], meaning the place of a skull.

23 And they (attempted to) give Him wine mingled with myrrh, but He would not take it.

24 And they crucified Him, and divided His garments *and* distributed them among them, throwing lots for them, to decide who should take each. [Ps. 22:18.]

25 And it was the third hour (about nine o'clock in the morning) when they crucified Him. [Ps. 22:14-16.]

26 And the inscription of the accusation against Him was written above, The King of the Jews.

27 And with Him they crucified two robbers, one on [His] right hand and one on His left.

28 *And the Scripture was fulfilled which says, He was counted among the transgressors.* [Isa. 53:12.]

29 And those who passed by kept reviling Him *and* reproaching Him abusively in harsh *and* insolent language, wagging their heads and saying, Aha! You Who would destroy the temple and build it in three days.

30 Now rescue [e]Yourself ([f]from death), coming down from the cross!

31 So also the chief priests with the scribes made sport of Him to one another, saying, He rescued others ([f]from death); Himself He is unable to rescue. [Ps. 22:7, 8.]

32 Let the Christ, the Messiah, the King of Israel, come down now from the cross, that we may see [it] and trust in *and* rely on Him *and* adhere to Him! Those who were crucified with Him also reviled *and* reproached Him—speaking abusively, harshly and insolently.

33 And when the sixth hour had come (about midday), there was darkness over the whole land until the ninth hour (about three o'clock).

---

d) Wuest.
e) Capitalized because of what He is, the spotless Son of God, not what the speakers may have thought He was.
f) Cremer.

Living New Testament

11 But at this point the chief priests whipped up the mob to demand the release of Barabbas instead of Jesus.

12 "But if I release Barabbas," Pilate asked them, "what shall I do with this man you call your king?"

13 They shouted back, "Crucify him!"

14 "But why?" Pilate demanded. "What has he done wrong?" They only roared the louder, "Crucify him!"

15 Then Pilate, afraid of a riot and anxious to please the people, released Barabbas to them. And he ordered Jesus flogged with a leaded whip, and handed him over to be crucified.

16, 17 Then the Roman soldiers took Him into the barracks of the palace, called out the entire palace guard, dressed Him in a purple robe, and made a crown of long, sharp thorns and put it on His head.

18 Then they saluted, yelling, "Yea! King of the Jews!"

19 And they beat Him on the head with a cane, and spit on Him and went down on their knees to "worship" Him.

20 When they finally tired of their sport, they took off the purple robe and put His own clothes on Him again, and led Him away to be crucified.

21 Simon of Cyrene, who was coming in from the country just then, was pressed into service to carry Jesus' cross. (Simon is the father of Alexander and Rufus.)

22 And they brought Jesus to a place called Golgotha. (Golgotha means skull.)

23 Wine drugged with bitter herbs was offered to Him there, but He refused it.

24 And then they crucified Him—and threw dice for His clothes.

* * * * *

25 It was about nine o'clock in the morning when the crucifixion took place.

* * * *

26 A signboard was fastened to the cross above His head, announcing His crime. It read, "The King of the Jews."

* * * * *

27 Two robbers were also crucified that morning, their crosses on either side of His.

28[2] And so the Scripture was fulfilled that said, "He was counted among evil men."

* * * * *

29, 30 The people jeered at Him as they walked by, and wagged their heads in mockery. "Ha! Look at you now!" they yelled at Him. "Sure, you can destroy the Temple and rebuild it in three days! If you're so wonderful, save yourself and come down from the cross."

* * * * *

31 The chief priests and religious leaders were also standing around joking about Jesus. "He's quite clever at 'saving' others," they said, "but he can't save himself!"

32 "Hey there, Messiah!" they yelled at Him. "You 'King of Israel'! Come on down from the cross and we'll believe you!" And even the two robbers dying with Him, cursed Him.

* * * * *

33 About noon, darkness fell across the entire land,[3] lasting until three o'clock that afternoon.

---

[2]Verse 28 is omitted in some of the ancient manuscripts. The quotation is from Isaiah 53:12.

[3]Or, "over the entire world."

Revised Standard

stirred up the crowd to have him release
for them Barabbas instead. 12 And Pilate
again said to them, "Then what shall I do
with the man whom you call the King of
the Jews?" 13 And they cried out again,
"Crucify him." 14 And Pilate said to them,
"Why, what evil has he done?" But they
shouted all the more, "Crucify him." 15 So
Pilate, wishing to satisfy the crowd, released
for them Barabbas; and having scourged
Jesus, he delivered him to be crucified.

Jesus crowned with thorns

16 And the soldiers led him away inside
the palace (that is, the praetorium); and
they called together the whole battalion.
17 And they clothed him in a purple cloak,
and plaiting a crown of thorns they put it
on him. 18 And they began to salute him,
"Hail, King of the Jews!" 19 And they struck
his head with a reed, and spat upon him,
and they knelt down in homage to him.
20 And when they had mocked him, they
stripped him of the purple cloak, and put
his own clothes on him. And they led him
out to crucify him.

Jesus crucified

21 And they compelled a passer-by,
Simon of Cyrene, who was coming in from
the country, the father of Alexander and
Rufus, to carry his cross. 22 And they brought
him to the place called Golgotha (which
means the place of a skull). 23 And they offered him wine mingled with myrrh; but he
did not take it. 24 And they crucified him,
and divided his garments among them,
casting lots for them, to decide what each
should take. 25 And it was the third hour,
when they crucified him. 26 And the inscription of the charge against him read, "The
King of the Jews." 27 And with him they
crucified two robbers, one on his right and
one on his left.[g] 29 And those who passed by
derided him, wagging their heads, and saying, "Aha! You who would destroy the
temple and build it in three days, 30 save
yourself, and come down from the cross!"
31 So also the chief priests mocked him to
one another with the scribes, saying, "He
saved others; he cannot save himself. 32 Let
the Christ, the King of Israel, come down
now from the cross, that we may see and
believe." Those who were crucified with
him also reviled him.

The death of Jesus

33 And when the sixth hour had come,
there was darkness over the whole land[h] until the ninth hour. 34 And at the ninth hour

---

[g] Other ancient authorities insert verse 28, *And the scripture was fulfilled which says, "He was reckoned with the transgressors"*

[h] Or *earth*

King James

34 And at the ninth hour Jesus cried with a loud voice, saying, Eloi, Eloi, lama sabachthani? which is, being interpreted, My God, my God, why hast thou forsaken me?

35 And some of them that stood by, when they heard *it*, said, Behold, he calleth Elias.

36 And one ran and filled a sponge full of vinegar, and put *it* on a reed, and gave him to drink, saying, Let alone; let us see whether Elias will come to take him down.

37 And Jesus cried with a loud voice, and gave up the ghost.

38 And the veil of the temple was rent in twain from the top to the bottom.

39 ¶ And when the centurion, which stood over against him, saw that he so cried out, and gave up the ghost, he said, Truly this man was the Son of God.

40 There were also women looking on afar off: among whom was Mary Magdalene, and Mary the mother of James the less and of Joses, and Salome;

41 (Who also, when he was in Galilee, followed him, and ministered unto him;) and many other women which came up with him unto Jerusalem.

42 ¶ And now when the even was come, because it was the preparation, that is, the day before the sabbath,

43 Joseph of Arimathæa, an honourable counsellor, which also waited for the kingdom of God, came, and went in boldly unto Pilate, and craved the body of Jesus.

44 And Pilate marvelled if he were already dead: and calling *unto him* the centurion, he asked him whether he had been any while dead.

45 And when he knew *it* of the centurion, he gave the body to Joseph.

46 And he bought fine linen, and took him down, and wrapped him in the linen, and laid him in a sepulchre which was hewn out of a rock, and rolled a stone unto the door of the sepulchre.

47 And Mary Magdalene and Mary *the mother* of Joses beheld where he was laid.

Amplified

34 And at the ninth hour Jesus cried with a loud voice, Eloi, Eloi, lama sabachthani? which means, My God, My God, why have You forsaken Me—[g]deserting Me and leaving Me helpless and abandoned? [Ps. 22:1.]

35 And some of those standing by [and] hearing it said, See! He is calling Elijah!

36 And one man ran, and, filling a sponge with vinegar [a [h]mixture of sour wine and water], put it on a staff made of a [bamboo-like] reed, and gave it to Him to drink, saying, Hold off! Let us see whether Elijah [does] come to take Him down. [Ps. 69:21.]

37 And Jesus uttered a loud cry, and breathed out His life.

38 And the curtain [of the Holy of Holies] of the temple was torn in two from top to bottom.

39 And when the centurion who stood facing Him saw Him expire this way, he said, [i]Really this Man was God's Son!

40 Now some women were there also, looking on from a distance, among whom were Mary Magdalene, and Mary the mother of James the younger and of Joses, and Salome,

41 Who, when [Jesus] was in Galilee, were in the habit of accompanying and ministering to Him; and also many other [women] who came up with Him to Jerusalem.

42 As evening had already come, since it was the day of Preparation, that is, [the day] before the Sabbath, [Deut. 21:22, 23.]

43 Joseph, he of Arimathea, noble *and* honorable in rank *and* a respected member of the council (Sanhedrin), who was himself waiting for the kingdom of God, daring the consequences, took courage *and* ventured to go to Pilate, and asked for the body of Jesus.

44 But Pilate wondered whether He was dead so soon, and having called the centurion, he asked him whether [Jesus] was already dead.

45 And when he learned from the centurion [that He was indeed dead], he gave the body to Joseph.

46 And Joseph bought a (fine) linen cloth [[j]for swathing dead bodies], and taking Him down from the cross, he [k]rolled Him up in the (fine) linen cloth; and placed Him in a tomb which had been hewn out of a rock. Then he rolled a [[l]very large] stone against the door of the tomb. [Isa. 53:9.]

47 And Mary Magdalene and Mary [the mother] of Joses were [[m]attentively] observing where He was laid.

CHAPTER 16

AND when the sabbath was past, Mary Magdalene, and Mary the *mother* of James, and Salome, had bought sweet spices, that they might come and anoint him.

CHAPTER 16

AND when the Sabbath was past [that is, after the sun had set], Mary Magdalene, and Mary [the mother] of James, and Salome purchased sweet-smelling spices, so that they might go and anoint [Jesus' body].

---

g) Thayer.
h) Thayer.
i) Cremer.
j) Moulton and Milligan.
k) Young.
l) Chap. 16:4.
m) Vincent.

Living New Testament

* * * * *

34 Then Jesus called out with a loud voice, "Eli, Eli, lama sabachthani?"[4] ("My God, My God, why have You deserted Me?")

35 Some of the people standing there thought He was calling for the prophet Elijah.

36 So one man ran and got a sponge and filled it with sour wine and held it up to Him on a stick. "Let's see if Elijah will come and take him down!" he said.

* * * * *

37 Then Jesus uttered another loud cry, and dismissed His spirit.

* * * * *

38 And the curtain[5] in the Temple was split apart from top to bottom.

* * * * *

39 When the Roman officer standing beside His cross saw how He dismissed His spirit, he exclaimed, "Truly, this was the Son of God!"

* * * * *

40 Some women were there watching from a distance—Mary Magdalene, Mary (mother of James the Younger and of Joses), Salome, and others.

41 They and many other Galilean women who were His followers had ministered to Him when He was up in Galilee, and had come with Him to Jerusalem.

* * * * *

42, 43 This all happened the day before the Sabbath. Late that afternoon Joseph from Arimathaea, an honored member of the Jewish Supreme Court (who personally was eagerly expecting the arrival of God's Kingdom), gathered his courage and went to Pilate and asked for Jesus' body.

44 Pilate couldn't believe that Jesus was already dead so he called for the Roman officer in charge and asked him.

45 The officer confirmed the fact, and Pilate told Joseph he could have the body.

46 Joseph bought a long sheet of linen cloth and taking Jesus' body down from the cross wound it in the cloth and laid it in a rock-hewn tomb, and rolled a stone in front of the entrance.

47 (Mary Magdalene and Mary the mother of Joses were watching as Jesus was laid away.)

Revised Standard

Jesus cried with a loud voice, "Eloi, Eloi,
lama sabachthani?" which means, "My God,
my God, why hast thou forsaken me?"
35 And some of the bystanders hearing it
said, "Behold, he is calling Elijah." 36 And
one ran and, filling a sponge full of vinegar,
put it on a reed and gave it to him to
drink, saying, "Wait, let us see whether Elijah will come to take him down." 37 And
Jesus uttered a loud cry, and breathed his
last. 38 And the curtain of the temple was
torn in two, from top to bottom. 39 And
when the centurion, who stood facing him,
saw that he thus[i] breathed his last, he said,
"Truly this man was the Son[x] of God!"
40 There were also women looking on
from afar, among whom were Mary Magdalene, and Mary the mother of James the
younger and of Joses, and Salome, 41 who,
when he was in Galilee, followed him, and
ministered to him; and also many other
women who came up with him to Jerusalem.

Jesus laid in the tomb

42 And when evening had come, since
it was the day of Preparation, that is, the
day before the sabbath, 43 Joseph of Arimathea, a respected member of the council,
who was also himself looking for the kingdom of God, took courage and went to
Pilate, and asked for the body of Jesus.
44 And Pilate wondered if he were already
dead; and summoning the centurion, he
asked him whether he was already dead.[j]
45 And when he learned from the centurion
that he was dead, he granted the body to
Joseph. 46 And he brought a linen shroud,
and taking him down, wrapped him in the
linen shroud, and laid him in a tomb which
had been hewn out of the rock; and he
rolled a stone against the door of the tomb.
47 Mary Magdalene and Mary the mother
of Joses saw where he was laid.

CHAPTER 16

That next evening, when the Sabbath ended, Mary Magdalene and Salome and Mary the mother of James went out and purchased embalming spices. Early the following morning, just at sunrise, they carried them out to the tomb.

The resurrection of Jesus

16 And when the sabbath was past, Mary
Magdalene, and Mary the mother of
James, and Salome, bought spices, so that
they might go and anoint him. 2 And very

[4] He spoke here in Aramaic. The onlookers, who spoke Greek and Latin, misunderstood His first two words ("Eloi, Eloi") and thought He was calling for the prophet Elijah.

[5] A heavy veil hung in front of the room in the Temple, called "The Holy of Holies," a place reserved by God for Himself; the veil separated Him from sinful mankind. Now this veil was split from above, showing that Christ's death, for man's sin, had opened up access to the holy God.

[i] Other ancient authorities insert *cried out and*

[x] Or *a son*

[j] Other ancient authorities read *whether he had been some time dead*

King James

2 And very early in the morning the first *day* of the week, they came unto the sepulchre at the rising of the sun.

3 And they said among themselves, Who shall roll us away the stone from the door of the sepulchre?

4 And when they looked, they saw that the stone was rolled away: for it was very great.

5 And entering into the sepulchre, they saw a young man sitting on the right side, clothed in a long white garment; and they were affrighted.

6 And he saith unto them, Be not affrighted: Ye seek Jesus of Nazareth, which was crucified: he is risen; he is not here: behold the place where they laid him.

7 But go your way, tell his disciples and Peter that he goeth before you into Galilee: there shall ye see him, as he said unto you.

8 And they went out quickly, and fled from the sepulchre; for they trembled and were amazed: neither said they any thing to any *man;* for they were afraid.

9 ¶ Now when *Jesus* was risen early the first *day* of the week, he appeared first to Mary Magdalene, out of whom he had cast seven devils.

10 *And* she went and told them that had been with him, as they mourned and wept.

11 And they, when they had heard that he was alive, and had been seen of her, believed not.

12 ¶ After that he appeared in another form unto two of them, as they walked, and went into the country.

13 And they went and told *it* unto the residue: neither believed they them.

14 ¶ Afterward he appeared unto the eleven as they sat at meat, and upbraided them with their unbelief and hardness of heart, because they believed not them which had seen him after he was risen.

15 And he said unto them, Go ye into all the world, and preach the gospel to every creature.

16 He that believeth and is baptized shall be saved; but he that believeth not shall be damned.

17 And these signs shall follow them that believe; In my name shall they cast out devils; they shall speak with new tongues;

18 They shall take up serpents; and if they drink any deadly thing, it shall not hurt them; they shall lay hands on the sick, and they shall recover.

19 ¶ So then after the Lord had spoken unto them, he was received up into heaven, and sat on the right hand of God.

20 And they went forth, and preached every where, the Lord working with *them,* and confirming the word with signs following. Amen.

Amplified

2 And very early on the first day of the week they came to the tomb; [by then] the sun had risen.

3 And they said to one another, Who will roll back the stone for us out of [the groove across the floor at] the door of the tomb?

4 And when they looked up, they [distinctly] saw that the stone was already rolled back, for it was very large.

5 And going into the tomb, they saw a young man sitting [there] on the right [side], clothed in a ([n]long, stately, sweeping) robe of white, and they were utterly amazed *and* struck with terror.

6 And he said to them, Do not be amazed *and* terrified; you are looking for Jesus of Nazareth Who was crucified. He is risen; He is not here. See the place where they laid Him. [Ps. 16:10.]

7 But be going; tell the disciples and Peter, He goes before you into Galilee; you will see Him there, [just] as He told you.

8 Then they went out [and] fled from the tomb, for trembling and bewilderment *and* consternation had seized them. And they said nothing about it to any one, for they were held by alarm *and* fear.

9 [o]Now Jesus, having risen ([p]from death) early on the first day of the week, appeared first to Mary Magdalene, from whom He had driven out seven demons.

10 She went and reported it to those who had been with Him, as they grieved and wept.

11 And when they heard that He was alive and that she had seen Him, they did not believe it.

12 After this He appeared in a different form to two of them, as they were walking [along the way] into the country.

13 And they returned [to Jerusalem] and told the others, but they did not believe them either.

14 Afterward He appeared to the eleven [apostles, themselves] as they reclined at table; and He reproved *and* reproached them for their unbelief (their lack of faith) and their hardness of heart, because they had refused to believe those who had seen Him *and* looked at Him attentively after He was risen ([p]from death).

15 And He said to them, Go into all the world and preach *and* publish openly the good news (the Gospel) to every creature (of the whole [q]human race).

16 He who believes—[that is,] who adheres to and trusts in and relies on the Gospel and Him Whom it sets forth—and is baptized will be saved [[r]from the penalty of eternal death]; but he who does not believe—who does not adhere to and trust in and rely on the Gospel and Him Whom it sets forth—will be condemned.

17 And these attesting signs will accompany those who believe: in My name they will drive out demons; they will speak in new languages;

18 They will pick up serpents, and [even] if they drink anything deadly, it will not hurt them; they will lay their hands on the sick, and they will get well.

19 So then the Lord Jesus, after He had spoken to them, was taken up into heaven and He sat down at the right hand of God. [Ps. 110:1.]

20 And they went out and preached everywhere, while the Lord kept working with them and confirming the message by the attesting signs *and* miracles that closely accompanied [it]. Amen—so be it.

---

n) Trench.
o) Verses 9 to 20 not in the two earliest manuscripts.
p) Cremer.
q) Thayer.
r) Cremer.

Living New Testament

3 On the way they were discussing how they could ever roll aside the huge stone from the entrance.

4 But when they arrived they looked up and saw that the stone—a *very* heavy one—was already moved away and the entrance was open!

5 So they entered the tomb—and there on the right sat a young man clothed in white. The women were startled,

6 But the angel said, "Don't be so surprised. Aren't you looking for Jesus, the Nazarene who was crucified? He isn't here! He has come back to life! Look, that's where His body was lying.

7 Now go and give this message to His disciples including Peter: 'Jesus is going ahead of you to Galilee. You will see Him there, just as He told you before He died.' "

8 The women fled from the tomb, trembling and bewildered, too frightened to talk.

* * * * *

9[1] It was early on Sunday morning when Jesus came back to life, and the first person who saw Him was Mary Magdalene—the woman from whom He had cast out seven demons.

10, 11 She found the disciples wet-eyed with grief and exclaimed that she had seen Jesus, and He was alive! But they didn't believe her!

* * * * *

12 Later that day[2] He appeared to two men walking from Jerusalem into the country, but they didn't recognize Him at first because He had changed His appearance.

13 When they finally realized who He was, they rushed back to Jerusalem to tell the others, but no one believed them.

* * * * *

14 Still later He appeared to the eleven disciples as they were eating together. He rebuked them for their unbelief—their stubborn refusal to believe those who had seen Him alive from the dead.

15 And then He told them, "You are to go into all the world and preach the Good News to everyone, everywhere.

16 Those who believe and are baptized will be saved. But those who refuse to believe will be condemned.

17 And those who believe shall use My authority to cast out demons, and they shall speak new languages.[3]

18 They will be able even to handle snakes with safety, and if they drink anything poisonous, it won't hurt them; and they will be able to place their hands on the sick and heal them."

19 When the Lord Jesus had finished talking with them, He was taken up into heaven and sat down at God's right hand.

20 And the disciples went everywhere preaching, and the Lord was with them and confirmed what they said by the miracles that followed their messages.

---

[1]Verses 9 through 20 are not found in the most ancient manuscripts, but may be considered an appendix giving additional facts.
[2]Literally, "after these things."
[3]Literally, "tongues." Some ancient manuscripts omit "new."

Revised Standard

early on the first day of the week they went
to the tomb when the sun had risen. 3And
they were saying to one another, "Who will
roll away the stone for us from the door of
the tomb?" 4And looking up, they saw that
the stone was rolled back; for it was very
large. 5And entering the tomb, they saw a
young man sitting on the right side, dressed
in a white robe; and they were amazed.
6And he said to them, "Do not be amazed;
you seek Jesus of Nazareth, who was crucified. He has risen, he is not here; see the
place where they laid him. 7But go, tell his
disciples and Peter that he is going before
you to Galilee; there you will see him, as
he told you." 8And they went out and fled
from the tomb; for trembling and astonishment had come upon them; and they said
nothing to any one, for they were afraid.[k]

---

[k] Other texts and versions add as 16.9-20 the following passage:

*9 Now when he rose early on the first day of the
week, he appeared first to Mary Magdalene, from whom
he had cast out seven demons. 10She went and told those
who had been with him, as they mourned and wept. 11But
when they heard that he was alive and had been seen by
her, they would not believe it.*

*12 After this he appeared in another form to two of
them, as they were walking into the country. 13And they
went back and told the rest, but they did not believe
them.*

*14 Afterward he appeared to the eleven themselves as
they sat at table; and he upbraided them for their unbelief and hardness of heart, because they had not believed those who saw him after he had risen. 15And he
said to them, "Go into all the world and preach the
gospel to the whole creation. 16He who believes and is
baptized will be saved; but he who does not believe will
be condemned. 17And these signs will accompany those
who believe: in my name they will cast out demons; they
will speak in new tongues; 18they will pick up serpents,
and if they drink any deadly thing, it will not hurt them;
they will lay their hands on the sick, and they will recover."*

*19 So then the Lord Jesus, after he had spoken to
them, was taken up into heaven, and sat down at the
right hand of God. 20And they went forth and preached
everywhere, while the Lord worked with them and confirmed the message by the signs that attended it. Amen.*

Other ancient authorities add after verse 8 the following: *But they reported briefly to Peter and those with him all that they had been told. And after this, Jesus himself sent out by means of them, from east to west, the sacred and imperishable proclamation of eternal salvation.*

King James

THE GOSPEL ACCORDING TO

St. Luke

CHAPTER 1

FORASMUCH as many have taken in hand to set forth in order a declaration of those things which are most surely believed among us,

2 Even as they delivered them unto us, which from the beginning were eyewitnesses, and ministers of the word;

3 It seemed good to me also, having had perfect understanding of all things from the very first, to write unto thee in order, most excellent Theophilus,

4 That thou mightest know the certainty of those things, wherein thou hast been instructed.

5 ¶ THERE was in the days of Herod, the king of Judæa, a certain priest named Zacharias, of the course of Abia: and his wife *was* of the daughters of Aaron, and her name *was* Elisabeth.

6 And they were both righteous before God, walking in all the commandments and ordinances of the Lord blameless.

7 And they had no child, because that Elisabeth was barren, and they both were *now* well stricken in years.

8 And it came to pass, that while he executed the priest's office before God in the order of his course,

9 According to the custom of the priest's office, his lot was to burn incense when he went into the temple of the Lord.

10 And the whole multitude of the people were praying without at the time of incense.

11 And there appeared unto him an angel of the Lord standing on the right side of the altar of incense.

12 And when Zacharias saw *him*, he was troubled, and fear fell upon him.

13 But the angel said unto him, Fear not, Zacharias: for thy prayer is heard; and thy wife Elisabeth shall bear thee a son, and thou shalt call his name John.

14 And thou shalt have joy and gladness; and many shall rejoice at his birth.

15 For he shall be great in the sight of the Lord, and shall drink neither wine nor strong drink; and he shall be filled with the Holy Ghost, even from his mother's womb.

16 And many of the children of Israel shall he turn to the Lord their God.

17 And he shall go before him in the spirit and power of Elias, to turn the hearts of the fathers to the children, and the disobedient to the wisdom of the just; to make ready a people prepared for the Lord.

Amplified

THE GOSPEL ACCORDING TO

Luke

CHAPTER 1

SINCE ([a]as is well known) many have undertaken to put in order *and* draw up a ([a]thorough) narrative of the surely established deeds which have been accomplished *and* fulfilled [b]in *and* among us,

2 Exactly as they were handed down to us by those who from the ([a]official) beginning [of Jesus' ministry] were eye-witnesses and ministers of the Word [that is, of [c]the doctrine concerning the attainment through Christ of salvation in the kingdom of God],

3 It seeming good *and* desirable to me, [I have determined] also after [d]having searched out diligently *and* followed all things closely *and* traced accurately the course from the highest to the minutest detail from the very first, to write an orderly account for you, most excellent Theophilus.

4 [My purpose is] that you may know the full truth, *and* understand with certainty *and* security against error the accounts (histories) *and* doctrines of the faith of which you have been informed *and* in which you have been [a]orally instructed.

5 In the days when Herod was king of Judea, there was a certain priest whose name was Zachariah, [a]of the daily service (the division) of Abia; and his wife was also a descendant of Aaron, and her name was Elizabeth.

6 And they both were righteous in the sight of God, walking blamelessly in all the commandments and requirements of the Lord.

7 But they had no child, for Elizabeth was barren, and both were [e]far advanced in years.

8 Now while on duty, serving as priest before God in the order of his division,

9 As was the custom of the priesthood, it fell to him by lot to enter (the [f]sanctuary of) the temple of the Lord and burn incense. [Exod. 30:7.]

10 And all the throng of people were praying outside [in the court] at the hour of incense [burning].

11 And there appeared to him an angel of the Lord, standing at [the] right side of the altar of incense.

12 And when Zachariah saw him he was troubled, and fear took possession of him.

13 But the angel said to him, Do not be afraid, Zachariah, because your petition [g]was heard, and your wife Elizabeth will bear you a son, and you must call his name John [meaning God is favorable].

14 And you shall have joy and exultant delight, and many will rejoice over his birth,

15 For he will be great *and* distinguished in the sight of the Lord. And he must drink no wine nor strong drink, and he will be filled with *and* controlled by the Holy Spirit, even [g]in *and* from his mother's womb. [Num. 6:3.]

16 And he will turn *and* cause to return many of the sons of Israel to the Lord their God,

17 And he will [himself] go before Him in the spirit and power of Elijah, to turn back the hearts of the fathers to the children, and the disobedient *and* incredulous *and*

---

a) Vincent's "Word Studies in the New Testament."
b) Wycliffe's Version of the New Testament.
c) Thayer's "Greek-English Lexicon of the New Testament—Grimm."
d) Tyndale's Version of the New Testament.
e) Wycliffe.
f) Trench's "Synonyms of the New Testament."
g) Tyndale.

Living New Testament

Luke

CHAPTER 1

Dear Friend who loves God:[1]

1, 2 Several biographies of Christ have already been written using as their source material the reports circulating among us from the early disciples and other eyewitnesses.

3 However, it occurred to me that it would be well to recheck all these accounts from first to last and after thorough investigation to pass this summary on to you,[2]

4 To reassure you of the truth of all you were taught.

* * * * *

5 My story begins with a Jewish priest, Zacharias, who lived when Herod was king of Judea. Zacharias was a member of the Abijah division of the Temple service corps. (His wife Elizabeth was, like himself, a member of the priest tribe of the Jews, a descendant of Aaron.)

6 Zacharias and Elizabeth were godly folk, careful to obey all of God's laws in spirit as well as in letter.

7 But they had no children, for Elizabeth was barren; and now they were both very old.

8, 9 One day as Zacharias was going about his work in the Temple—for his division was on duty that week—the honor fell to him by lot[3] to enter the inner sanctuary and burn incense before the Lord.

10 Meanwhile, a great crowd stood outside in the Temple court, praying as they always did during that part of the service when the incense was being burned.

11, 12 Zacharias was in the sanctuary when suddenly an angel appeared, standing to the right of the altar of incense! Zacharias was startled and terrified.

13 But the angel said, "Don't be afraid, Zacharias! For I have come to tell you that God has heard your prayer, and your wife Elizabeth will bear you a son! And you are to name him John.

14 You will both have great joy and gladness at his birth, and many will rejoice with you.

15 For he will be one of the Lord's great men. He must never touch wine or hard liquor—and he will be filled with the Holy Spirit, even from before his birth!

16 And he will persuade many a Jew to turn to the Lord his God.

17 He will be a man of rugged[4] spirit and power like Elijah, the prophet of old; and he will precede the coming of the Messiah, preparing the people for His arrival. He will teach them to love the Lord just as their ancestors did, and to live as godly men."

[1] From verse 3. Literally, "most excellent Theophilus." The name means "one who loves God."
[2] Literally, "an account of the things accomplished among us."
[3] Probably by throwing dice or something similar—"drawing straws" would be a modern equivalent.
[4] Implied.

Revised Standard

THE GOSPEL ACCORDING TO

Luke

Preface

1 Inasmuch as many have undertaken to compile a narrative of the things which have been accomplished among us, [2]just as they were delivered to us by those who from the beginning were eyewitnesses and ministers of the word, [3]it seemed good to me also, having followed all things closely[a] for some time past, to write an orderly account for you, most excellent Theophilus, [4]that you may know the truth concerning the things of which you have been informed.

Birth of John the Baptist foretold

5 In the days of Herod, king of Judea, there was a priest named Zechariah,[b] of the division of Abijah; and he had a wife of the daughters of Aaron, and her name was Elizabeth. [6]And they were both righteous before God, walking in all the commandments and ordinances of the Lord blameless. [7]But they had no child, because Elizabeth was barren, and both were advanced in years.

8 Now while he was serving as priest before God when his division was on duty, [9]according to the custom of the priesthood, it fell to him by lot to enter the temple of the Lord and burn incense. [10]And the whole multitude of the people were praying outside at the hour of incense. [11]And there appeared to him an angel of the Lord standing on the right side of the altar of incense. [12]And Zechariah was troubled when he saw him, and fear fell upon him. [13]But the angel said to him, "Do not be afraid, Zechariah, for your prayer is heard, and your wife Elizabeth will bear you a son, and you shall call his name John.

The song to Zechariah

[14]And you will have joy and gladness,
and many will rejoice at his birth;
[15]for he will be great before the Lord, and
he shall drink no wine nor strong drink,
and he will be filled with the Holy Spirit,
even from his mother's womb.
[16]And he will turn many of the sons of Israel to the Lord their God,
[17]and he will go before him in the spirit
and power of Elijah,
to turn the hearts of the fathers to the children,
and the disobedient to the wisdom of the just,
to make ready for the Lord a people prepared."

[a] Or *accurately*
[b] Greek *Zacharias*

King James

18 And Zacharias said unto the angel, Whereby shall I know this? for I am an old man, and my wife well stricken in years.

19 And the angel answering said unto him, I am Gabriel, that stand in the presence of God; and am sent to speak unto thee, and to shew thee these glad tidings.

20 And, behold, thou shalt be dumb, and not able to speak, until the day that these things shall be performed, because thou believest not my words, which shall be fulfilled in their season.

21 And the people waited for Zacharias, and marvelled that he tarried so long in the temple.

22 And when he came out, he could not speak unto them: and they perceived that he had seen a vision in the temple: for he beckoned unto them, and remained speechless.

23 And it came to pass, that, as soon as the days of his ministration were accomplished, he departed to his own house.

24 And after those days his wife Elisabeth conceived, and hid herself five months, saying,

25 Thus hath the Lord dealt with me in the days wherein he looked on *me*, to take away my reproach among men.

26 And in the sixth month the angel Gabriel was sent from God unto a city of Galilee, named Nazareth,

27 To a virgin espoused to a man whose name was Joseph, of the house of David; and the virgin's name *was* Mary.

28 And the angel came in unto her, and said, Hail, *thou that art* highly favoured, the Lord *is* with thee: blessed *art* thou among women.

29 And when she saw *him*, she was troubled at his saying, and cast in her mind what manner of salutation this should be.

30 And the angel said unto her, Fear not, Mary: for thou hast found favour with God.

31 And, behold, thou shalt conceive in thy womb, and bring forth a son, and shalt call his name JESUS.

32 He shall be great, and shall be called the Son of the Highest: and the Lord God shall give unto him the throne of his father David:

33 And he shall reign over the house of Jacob for ever; and of his kingdom there shall be no end.

34 Then said Mary unto the angel, How shall this be, seeing I know not a man?

35 And the angel answered and said unto her, The Holy Ghost shall come upon thee, and the power of the Highest shall overshadow thee: therefore also that holy thing which shall be born of thee shall be called the Son of God.

Amplified

unpersuadable to the wisdom of the upright [which is [h]the knowledge and holy love of the will of God], in order to make ready for the Lord a people [perfectly] prepared—in spirit, [i]adjusted and disposed and placed in the right moral state. [Mal. 4:5, 6; Isa. 40:3.]

18 And Zachariah said to the angel, By what shall I know *and* be sure of this? For I am an old man, and my wife is well advanced in years.

19 And the angel replied to him, I am Gabriel; I stand in the [very] presence of God, and I was sent to talk to you, and to bring you this good news. [Dan. 8:16; 9:21.]

20 And lo, you will be *and* [i]will continue to be silent, and not able to speak till the day when these things take place, because you have not believed what I told you; but my words are [i]of a kind which will be fulfilled in the appointed *and* proper time.

21 Now the people kept waiting for Zachariah, and they wondered at his delaying [so long] in the [j]sanctuary.

22 But when he did come out, he was unable to speak to them, and they ([i]clearly) perceived that he had seen a vision in the [j]sanctuary; and he kept making signs to them, still he remained dumb.

23 And when his time of performing priestly functions was ended, he returned to his [own] house.

24 Now after this his wife Elizabeth became pregnant, and for five months she secluded herself [j]entirely, saying, [I have hid myself]

25 [i]Because thus the Lord has dealt with me in the days when He deigned to look on me, to take away my reproach among men. [Gen. 30:23; Isa. 4:1.]

26 Now in the sixth month [after that], the angel Gabriel was sent from God to a town of Galilee named Nazareth,

27 To a girl never having been married *and* a [k]virgin, engaged to be married to a man whose name was Joseph, a descendant of the house of David; and the virgin's name was Mary.

28 And he came to her and said, Hail, O favored one ([l]endued with grace), the Lord is with you! *Blessed—favored of God—are you before all other women!*

29 But *when she saw him,* she was greatly troubled *and* disturbed *and* confused at what he said, and kept revolving in her mind what such a greeting might mean.

30 And the angel said to her, Do not be afraid, Mary, for you have found grace—[m]free, spontaneous, absolute favor and loving kindness—with God.

31 And listen! You will become pregnant and will give birth to a Son, and you shall call His name Jesus.

32 He will be great (eminent) and will be called the Son of the Most High; and the Lord God will give to Him the throne of His forefather David,

33 And He will reign over the house of Jacob throughout the ages, and of His reign there will be no end. [Isa. 9:6, 7; Dan. 2:44.]

34 And Mary said to the angel, How can this be, since I have no [intimacy with any man as a] husband?

35 Then the angel said to her, The Holy Spirit will come upon you, and the power of the Most High will overshadow you (as a shining cloud); and so the holy (pure, sinless) Thing which shall be born *of you,* will be called the Son of God. [Exod. 40:34; Isa. 7:14.]

---

h) Thayer.
i) Vincent.
j) Trench.
k) This Greek word, *parthenos* (virgin) is used in Isa. 7:14 in the Septuagint, the Greek O. T. translation Jesus read and quoted.
l) Literal translation.
m) Vincent.

Living New Testament

18 Zacharias said to the angel, "But this is impossible! I'm an old man now, and my wife is also well along in years."

19 Then the angel said, "I am Gabriel! I stand in the very presence of God. It was He who sent me to you with this good news!

20 And now, because you haven't believed me, you are to be stricken silent, unable to speak until the child is born. For my words will certainly come true at the proper time."

21 Meanwhile the crowds outside were waiting for Zacharias to appear and wondered why he was taking so long.

22 When he finally came out, he couldn't speak to them, and they realized from his gestures that he must have seen a vision in the Temple.

23 He stayed on at the Temple for the remaining days of his Temple duties and then returned home.

24 Soon afterwards Elizabeth his wife became pregnant and went into seclusion for five months.

25 "How kind the Lord is," she exclaimed, "to take away my disgrace of having no children!"

26 The following month God sent the angel Gabriel to Nazareth, a village in Galilee,

27 To a virgin, Mary, engaged to be married to a man named Joseph, a descendant of King David.

28 Gabriel appeared to her and said, "Congratulations, favored lady! The Lord is with you!"[5]

29 Confused and disturbed, Mary tried to think what the angel could mean.

30 "Don't be frightened, Mary," the angel told her, "for God has decided to wonderfully bless you!

31 Very soon now, you will become pregnant and have a baby boy, and you are to name Him 'Jesus.'

32 He shall be very great and shall be called the Son of God. And the Lord God shall give Him the throne of His ancestor David.

33 And He shall reign over Israel forever; His Kingdom shall never end!"

34 Mary asked the angel, "But how can I have a baby? I am a virgin."

35 The angel replied, "The Holy Spirit shall come upon you, and the power of God shall overshadow you; so the baby born to you will be utterly holy—the Son of God.

[5] Some ancient versions add, "Blessed are you among women," as in verse 42 which appears in all the manuscripts.

Revised Standard

[18]And Zechariah said to the angel, "How
shall I know this? For I am an old man,
and my wife is advanced in years." [19]And
the angel answered him, "I am Gabriel, who
stand in the presence of God; and I was
sent to speak to you, and to bring you this
good news. [20]And behold, you will be silent
and unable to speak until the day that these
things come to pass, because you did not
believe my words, which will be fulfilled in
their time." [21]And the people were waiting
for Zechariah, and they wondered at his
delay in the temple. [22]And when he came
out, he could not speak to them, and they
perceived that he had seen a vision in the
temple; and he made signs to them and
remained dumb. [23]And when his time of
service was ended, he went to his home.
24 After these days his wife Elizabeth
conceived, and for five months she hid herself, saying, [25]"Thus the Lord has done to
me in the days when he looked on me, to
take away my reproach among men."

The birth of Jesus foretold

26 In the sixth month the angel Gabriel
was sent from God to a city of Galilee
named Nazareth, [27]to a virgin betrothed to
a man whose name was Joseph, of the house
of David; and the virgin's name was Mary.
[28]And he came to her and said, "Hail, O
favored one, the Lord is with you!"[c] [29]But
she was greatly troubled at the saying and
considered in her mind what sort of greeting this might be. [30]And the angel said to
her, "Do not be afraid, Mary, for you have
found favor with God. [31]And behold, you
will conceive in your womb and bear a son,
and you shall call his name Jesus.
[32]He will be great, and will be called the
Son of the Most High;
and the Lord God will give to him the
throne of his father David,
[33]and he will reign over the house of Jacob
for ever;
and of his kingdom there will be no
end."
[34]And Mary said to the angel, "How can
this be, since I have no husband?"
[35]And the angel said to her,
"The Holy Spirit will come upon you,
and the power of the Most High will
overshadow you;
therefore the child to be born[d] will be
called holy,
the Son of God.

[c] Other ancient authorities add *"Blessed are you among women!"*

[d] Other ancient authorities add *of you*

King James

36 And, behold, thy cousin Elisabeth, she hath also conceived a son in her old age: and this is the sixth month with her, who was called barren.

37 For with God nothing shall be impossible.

38 And Mary said, Behold the handmaid of the Lord; be it unto me according to thy word. And the angel departed from her.

39 And Mary arose in those days, and went into the hill country with haste, into a city of Juda;

40 And entered into the house of Zacharias, and saluted Elisabeth.

41 And it came to pass, that, when Elisabeth heard the salutation of Mary, the babe leaped in her womb; and Elisabeth was filled with the Holy Ghost:

42 And she spake out with a loud voice, and said, Blessed *art* thou among women, and blessed *is* the fruit of thy womb.

43 And whence *is* this to me, that the mother of my Lord should come to me?

44 For, lo, as soon as the voice of thy salutation sounded in mine ears, the babe leaped in my womb for joy.

45 And blessed *is* she that believed: for there shall be a performance of those things which were told her from the Lord.

46 And Mary said, My soul doth magnify the Lord,

47 And my spirit hath rejoiced in God my Saviour.

48 For he hath regarded the low estate of his handmaiden: for, behold, from henceforth all generations shall call me blessed.

49 For he that is mighty hath done to me great things; and holy *is* his name.

50 And his mercy *is* on them that fear him from generation to generation.

51 He hath shewed strength with his arm; he hath scattered the proud in the imagination of their hearts.

52 He hath put down the mighty from *their* seats, and exalted them of low degree.

53 He hath filled the hungry with good things; and the rich he hath sent empty away.

54 He hath holpen his servant Israel, in remembrance of *his* mercy;

55 As he spake to our fathers, to Abraham, and to his seed for ever.

56 And Mary abode with her about three months, and returned to her own house.

57 Now Elisabeth's full time came that she should be delivered; and she brought forth a son.

58 And her neighbours and her cousins heard how the Lord had shewed great mercy upon her; and they rejoiced with her.

59 And it came to pass, that on the eighth day they came to circumcise the child; and they called him Zacharias, after the name of his father.

60 And his mother answered and said, Not *so;* but he shall be called John.

Amplified

36 And listen! Your relative Elizabeth in her old age has also conceived a son, and this is now the sixth month with her who was called barren;

37 For with God nothing is ever impossible, *and* no word from God shall be without power *or* impossible of fulfillment.

38 Then Mary said, Behold I am the handmaiden of the Lord; let it be done to me according to what you have said. And the angel left her.

39 And at that time Mary arose and went with haste into the hill country, to a town of Judah,

40 And she went to the house of Zachariah and entering it saluted Elizabeth.

41 And it occurred that when Elizabeth heard Mary's greeting, the baby leaped in her womb; and Elizabeth was filled with *and* controlled by the Holy Spirit,

42 And she cried out with a loud cry, then exclaimed, Blessed—favored of God—above all other women are you! And blessed—favored of God—is the Fruit of your womb!

43 And how [have I deserved that this honor should] be granted to me, that the mother of my Lord should come to me?

44 For lo, the instant the sound of your salutation reached my ears, the baby in my womb leaped for joy.

45 And blessed—happy, [n]to be envied—is she who believed that there would be a fulfillment of the things that were spoken to her from the Lord.

46 And Mary said, My soul magnifies *and* extols the Lord,

47 And my spirit rejoices in God my Savior;

48 For He has looked upon the low station *and* humiliation of His handmaiden. For behold, from now on all generations (of all ages) will call me blessed *and* declare me happy *and* [o]to be envied!

49 For He Who is almighty has done great things for me, and holy is His name—to be venerated in His purity, majesty and glory!

50 And His mercy—His compassion and kindness toward the miserable and afflicted—is on those who fear Him with godly reverence, from generation to generation *and* age to age.

51 He has shown strength *and* [p]made might with His arm; He has scattered the proud *and* haughty in *and* by the imagination *and* purpose *and* designs of their hearts;

52 He has put down the mighty from their thrones, and exalted those of low degree.

53 He has filled *and* satisfied the hungry with good things, and the rich He has sent away empty-handed—without a gift.

54 He has laid hold on His servant Israel (to help him, to espouse his cause), in remembrance of His mercy,

55 Even as He promised to our forefathers, to Abraham and to his descendants forever. [I Sam. 2:1-10; Mic. 7:20; Gen. 17:7; 18:18; 22:17.]

56 And Mary remained with [Elizabeth] for about three months, and [then] returned to her [own] home.

57 Now the time that Elizabeth should be delivered came, and she gave birth to a son.

58 And her neighbors and relatives heard that the Lord had shown great mercy on her, and they rejoiced with her.

59 And it occurred that on the eighth day when they came to circumcise the child, they were intending to call him Zachariah after his father; [Lev. 12:3; Gen. 17:12.]

60 But his mother answered, Not so, but he shall be called John.

---

n) Souter's "Pocket Lexicon to the Greek New Testament."
o) Souter.
p) Wycliffe.

Living New Testament

36 Furthermore, six months ago your cousin[6] Elizabeth—'the barren one,' they called her—became pregnant in her old age!

37 For every promise from God shall surely come true."

38 Mary said, "I am the Lord's servant, and I am willing to do whatever He wants. May everything you said come true." And then the angel disappeared.

39, 40 A few days later Mary hurried to the highlands of Judea to the town where Zacharias lived, to visit Elizabeth.

41 At the sound of Mary's greeting, Elizabeth's child leaped within her and she was filled with the Holy Spirit.

42 She gave a glad cry and exclaimed to Mary, "You are favored by God above all other women, and your child is destined for God's mightiest praise.

43 What an honor this is, that the mother of my Lord should visit me!

44 When you came in and greeted me, the instant I heard your voice, my baby moved in me for joy!

45 You believed that God would do what He said; that is why He has given you this wonderful blessing."

46 Mary responded, "Oh, how I praise the Lord.

47 How I rejoice in God my Savior!

48 For He took notice of His lowly servant girl, and now generation after generation forever shall call me blest of God.

49 For He, the mighty Holy One, has done great things to me.

50 His mercy goes on from generation to generation, to all who reverence Him.

51 How powerful is His mighty arm! How He scatters the proud and haughty ones!

52 He has torn princes from their thrones and exalted the lowly.

53 He has satisfied the hungry hearts and sent the rich away with empty hands.

54 And how He has helped His servant Israel! He has not forgotten His promise to be merciful.

55 For He promised our fathers—Abraham and his children—to be merciful to them forever."

56 Mary stayed with Elizabeth about three months and then went back to her own home.

57 By now Elizabeth's waiting was over, for the time had come for the baby to be born—and it was a boy.

58 The word spread quickly to her neighbors and relatives of how kind the Lord had been to her, and everyone rejoiced.

59 When the baby was eight days old, all the relatives and friends came for the circumcision ceremony. They all assumed the baby's name would be Zacharias, after his father.

60 But Elizabeth said, "No! He must be named John!"

[6] Literally, "relative."

Revised Standard

36 And behold, your kinswoman Elizabeth
in her old age has also conceived a son; and
this is the sixth month with her who was
called barren. 37 For with God nothing will
be impossible." 38 And Mary said, "Behold,
I am the handmaid of the Lord; let it be to
me according to your word." And the angel
departed from her.

Mary visits Elizabeth

39 In those days Mary arose and went
with haste into the hill country, to a city of
Judah, 40 and she entered the house of Zechariah and greeted Elizabeth. 41 And when
Elizabeth heard the greeting of Mary, the
babe leaped in her womb; and Elizabeth was
filled with the Holy Spirit 42 and she exclaimed with a loud cry, "Blessed are you
among women, and blessed is the fruit of
your womb! 43 And why is this granted me,
that the mother of my Lord should come to
me? 44 For behold, when the voice of your
greeting came to my ears, the babe in my
womb leaped for joy. 45 And blessed is she
who believed that there would be[e] a fulfilment of what was spoken to her from the
Lord." 46 And Mary said,

The song of Mary

"My soul magnifies the Lord,
47 and my spirit rejoices in God my Savior,
48 for he has regarded the low estate of his handmaiden.
For behold, henceforth all generations will call me blessed;
49 for he who is mighty has done great things for me,
and holy is his name.
50 And his mercy is on those who fear him from generation to generation.
51 He has shown strength with his arm,
he has scattered the proud in the imagination of their hearts,
52 he has put down the mighty from their thrones,
and exalted those of low degree;
53 he has filled the hungry with good things,
and the rich he has sent empty away.
54 He has helped his servant Israel,
in remembrance of his mercy,
55 as he spoke to our fathers,
to Abraham and to his posterity for ever."
56 And Mary remained with her about three
months, and returned to her home.

The birth of John the Baptist

57 Now the time came for Elizabeth to
be delivered, and she gave birth to a son.
58 And her neighbors and kinsfolk heard that
the Lord had shown great mercy to her, and
they rejoiced with her. 59 And on the eighth
day they came to circumcise the child; and
they would have named him Zechariah after

[e] Or *believed, for there will be*

King James

61 And they said unto her, There is none of thy kindred that is called by this name.

62 And they made signs to his father, how he would have him called.

63 And he asked for a writing table, and wrote, saying, His name is John. And they marvelled all.

64 And his mouth was opened immediately, and his tongue *loosed*, and he spake, and praised God.

65 And fear came on all that dwelt round about them: and all these sayings were noised abroad throughout all the hill country of Judæa.

66 And all they that heard *them* laid *them* up in their hearts, saying, What manner of child shall this be! And the hand of the Lord was with him.

67 And his father Zacharias was filled with the Holy Ghost, and prophesied, saying,

68 Blessed *be* the Lord God of Israel; for he hath visited and redeemed his people,

69 And hath raised up an horn of salvation for us in the house of his servant David;

70 As he spake by the mouth of his holy prophets, which have been since the world began:

71 That we should be saved from our enemies, and from the hand of all that hate us;

72 To perform the mercy *promised* to our fathers, and to remember his holy covenant;

73 The oath which he sware to our father Abraham,

74 That he would grant unto us, that we being delivered out of the hand of our enemies might serve him without fear,

75 In holiness and righteousness before him, all the days of our life.

76 And thou, child, shalt be called the prophet of the Highest: for thou shalt go before the face of the Lord to prepare his ways;

77 To give knowledge of salvation unto his people by the remission of their sins,

78 Through the tender mercy of our God; whereby the dayspring from on high hath visited us,

79 To give light to them that sit in darkness and *in* the shadow of death, to guide our feet into the way of peace.

80 And the child grew, and waxed strong in spirit, and was in the deserts till the day of his shewing unto Israel.

Amplified

61 And they said to her, None of your relatives is called by that name.

62 And they inquired with signs of his father what he wanted to have him called.

63 Then Zachariah asked for a writing tablet and wrote, His name is John. And they were all astonished.

64 And at once his mouth was opened and his tongue [loosed], and he began to speak, blessing *and* praising *and* thanking God.

65 And awe *and* reverential fear came on all their neighbors. And all these things were discussed throughout the hill country of Judea;

66 And all who heard them laid them up in their hearts, saying, Whatever will this little boy be then? For the hand of the Lord was [[q]so evidently] with him—protecting and aiding him.

67 Now Zachariah his father was filled with *and* controlled by the Holy Spirit, and prophesied saying,

68 Blessed—praised and extolled and thanked—be the Lord God of Israel, because He has come and brought deliverance *and* redemption to His people!

69 And He has raised up a Horn of salvation [that is, a mighty and valiant Helper, the Author of salvation] for us in the house of David His servant.

70 This is as He promised by the mouth of His holy prophets from the most ancient times (in the memory of man),

71 That we should have deliverance *and* be saved from our enemies, and from the hand of all who detest *and* pursue us with hatred;

72 To make true *and* show the mercy *and* compassion *and* kindness [promised] to our forefathers, and to remember *and* carry out His Holy covenant [to bless, which is [r]the more sacred because made by God Himself].

73 That covenant He sealed by oath to our forefather Abraham,

74 To grant us that we, being delivered from the hand of our foes, might serve Him fearlessly,

75 In holiness (divine consecration) and righteousness (that is, in accordance with the everlasting principles of right) within His presence all the days of our life.

76 And you, little one, shall be called prophet of the Most High; for you shall go before the face of the Lord to make ready His ways, [Isa. 40:3; Mal. 4:5.]

77 To bring *and* give the knowledge of salvation to His people in the forgiveness *and* remission of their sins.

78 Because of *and* through the heart of tender mercy *and* loving kindness of our God, a Light from on high will dawn upon us *and* visit [us], [Mal. 4:2.]

79 To shine upon *and* give light to those who sit in darkness and in the shadow of death, to direct *and* guide our feet in a straight line into [the] way of peace. [Isa. 9:2.]

80 And the little boy grew and became strong in spirit, and he was in the deserts (wildernesses) until the day of his appearing to Israel [the commencement of his public ministry].

CHAPTER 2

AND it came to pass in those days, that there went out a decree from Cæsar Augustus, that all the world should be taxed.

CHAPTER 2

IN those days it occurred that a decree went out from Caesar Augustus that the whole [s]Roman Empire should be registered.

---

q) Some translators, quoted in Barnes' "Notes on Luke and John."
r) Thayer.
s) Berry's "Greek-English New Testament Lexicon."

Living New Testament

61 "What?" they exclaimed. "There is no one in all your family by that name."

62 So they asked the baby's father, talking to him by gestures.[7]

63 He motioned for a piece of paper and to everyone's surprise wrote, "His name is JOHN!"

64 Instantly Zacharias could speak again, and he began praising God.

65 Wonder fell upon the whole neighborhood, and the news of what had happened spread through the Judean hills.

66 And everyone who heard about it thought long thoughts and asked, "I wonder what this child will turn out to be? For the hand of the Lord is surely upon him in some special way."

67 Then his father Zacharias was filled with the Holy Spirit and gave this prophecy:

68 "Praise the Lord, the God of Israel, for He has come to visit His people and has redeemed them.

69 He is sending us a Mighty Savior from the royal line of His servant David,

70 Just as He promised through His holy prophets long ago—

71 Someone to save us from our enemies, from all who hate us;

72, 73 He has been merciful to our ancestors, yes, to Abraham himself, by remembering His sacred promise to him,

74 And by granting us the privilege of serving God fearlessly, freed from our enemies,

75 And by making us holy and acceptable, ready to stand in His presence forever.

76 And you, my little son, shall be called the prophet of the glorious God, for you will prepare the way for the Messiah.

77 You will tell His people how to find salvation through forgiveness of their sins.

78 All this will be because the mercy of our God is very tender, and heaven's dawn is about to break upon us,

79 To give light to those who sit in darkness and death's shadow, and to guide us to the path of peace."

80 The little boy greatly loved God and when he grew up he lived out in the lonely wilderness until he began his public ministry to Israel.

Revised Standard

his father, 60 but his mother said, "Not so;
he shall be called John." 61 And they said to
her, "None of your kindred is called by this
name." 62 And they made signs to his father,
inquiring what he would have him called.
63 And he asked for a writing tablet, and
wrote, "His name is John." And they all
marveled. 64 And immediately his mouth was
opened and his tongue loosed, and he spoke,
blessing God. 65 And fear came on all their
neighbors. And all these things were talked
about through all the hill country of Judea;
66 and all who heard them laid them up in
their hearts, saying, "What then will this
child be?" For the hand of the Lord was
with him.

The song of Zechariah

67 And his father Zechariah was filled
with the Holy Spirit, and prophesied, saying,
68 "Blessed be the Lord God of Israel,
for he has visited and redeemed his
people,
69 and has raised up a horn of salvation
for us
in the house of his servant David,
70 as he spoke by the mouth of his holy
prophets from of old,
71 that we should be saved from our enemies,
and from the hand of all who hate us;
72 to perform the mercy promised to our
fathers,
and to remember his holy covenant,
73 the oath which he swore to our father
Abraham, 74 to grant us that we, being
delivered from the hand of our enemies,
might serve him without fear,
75 in holiness and righteousness before him
all the days of our life.
76 And you, child, will be called the prophet
of the Most High;
for you will go before the Lord to prepare his ways,
77 to give knowledge of salvation to his
people
in the forgiveness of their sins,
78 through the tender mercy of our God,
when the day shall dawn upon[f] us from
on high
79 to give light to those who sit in darkness
and in the shadow of death,
to guide our feet into the way of peace."
80 And the child grew and became strong in
spirit, and he was in the wilderness till the
day of his manifestation to Israel.

CHAPTER 2

About this time Caesar Augustus, the Roman Emperor, decreed that a census should be taken throughout the nation.[1]

The birth of Jesus

2 In those days a decree went out from
Caesar Augustus that all the world
should be enrolled. 2 This was the first en-

[7] Zacharias was apparently stone deaf as well as speechless, and had not heard what his wife had said.

[1] Literally, "all the land."

[f] Or *whereby the dayspring will visit.* Other ancient authorities read *since the dayspring has visited*

King James

2 (*And* this taxing was first made when Cyrenius was governor of Syria.)
3 And all went to be taxed, every one into his own city.
4 And Joseph also went up from Galilee, out of the city of Nazareth, into Judæa, unto the city of David, which is called Bethlehem; (because he was of the house and lineage of David:)
5 To be taxed with Mary his espoused wife, being great with child.
6 And so it was, that, while they were there, the days were accomplished that she should be delivered.
7 And she brought forth her firstborn son, and wrapped him in swaddling clothes, and laid him in a manger; because there was no room for them in the inn.
8 And there were in the same country shepherds abiding in the field, keeping watch over their flock by night.
9 And, lo, the angel of the Lord came upon them, and the glory of the Lord shone round about them: and they were sore afraid.
10 And the angel said unto them, Fear not: for, behold, I bring you good tidings of great joy, which shall be to all people.
11 For unto you is born this day in the city of David a Saviour, which is Christ the Lord.
12 And this *shall be* a sign unto you; Ye shall find the babe wrapped in swaddling clothes, lying in a manger.
13 And suddenly there was with the angel a multitude of the heavenly host praising God, and saying,
14 Glory to God in the highest, and on earth peace, good will toward men.
15 And it came to pass, as the angels were gone away from them into heaven, the shepherds said one to another, Let us now go even unto Bethlehem, and see this thing which is come to pass, which the Lord hath made known unto us.
16 And they came with haste, and found Mary, and Joseph, and the babe lying in a manger.
17 And when they had seen *it*, they made known abroad the saying which was told them concerning this child.
18 And all they that heard *it* wondered at those things which were told them by the shepherds.
19 But Mary kept all these things, and pondered *them* in her heart.
20 And the shepherds returned, glorifying and praising God for all the things that they had heard and seen, as it was told unto them.
21 And when eight days were accomplished for the circumcising of the child, his name was called JESUS, which was so named of the angel before he was conceived in the womb.
22 And when the days of her purification according to the law of Moses were accomplished, they brought him to Jerusalem, to present *him* to the Lord;
23 (As it is written in the law of the Lord, Every male that openeth the womb shall be called holy to the Lord;)

Amplified

2 This was the first enrollment and it was made when Quirinius was governor of Syria.
3 And all the people were going to be registered, each to his own city *or* town.
4 And Joseph also went up from Galilee from the town of Nazareth to Judea, to the town of David which is called Bethlehem, because he was of the house and family of David,
5 To be enrolled with Mary, his espoused ([t]married) wife, who was about to become a mother.
6 And while they were there, the time came for her delivery.
7 And she gave birth to her Son, her first-born, and she wrapped Him in swaddling clothes, and laid Him in a manger, because there was no room *or* place for them in the inn.
8 And in that vicinity there were shepherds living (out under the open sky) in the field, watching (in shifts) over their flock by night.
9 And *behold*, an angel of the Lord stood by them, and the glory of the Lord flashed *and* shone all about them, and they were terribly frightened.
10 But the angel said to them, Do not be afraid, for behold, I bring you good news of a great joy which will come to all the people.
11 For to you is born this day in the town of David a Savior, Who is Christ, the Messiah, the Lord! [Mic. 5:2.]
12 And this will be a sign for you [by which you will recognize Him]: you will find [u]after searching, a Baby wrapped in swaddling clothes and lying in a manger. [I Sam. 2:34; II Kings 19:29; Isa. 7:14.]
13 Then suddenly there appeared with the angel an army of the troops of heaven—[v]a heavenly knighthood—praising God and saying,
14 Glory to God in the highest [heaven], and on earth peace among men with whom He is well-pleased—[v]men of good will, of His favor.
15 When the angels went away from them into heaven, the shepherds said one to another, Let us go over to Bethlehem and see this thing ([w]saying) that has come to pass, which the Lord has made known to us.
16 So they went with haste, and ([x]by searching) found Mary and Joseph, and the Baby lying in a manger.
17 And when they saw it, they made known what had been told them concerning this Child;
18 And all who heard it were astounded *and* marvelled at what the shepherds told them.
19 But Mary was keeping [w]within herself all these things ([w]sayings), weighing *and* pondering them in her heart.
20 And the shepherds returned, glorifying and praising God for all things they had heard and seen, just as it had been told them.
21 And at the end of eight days, when [the Baby] was to be circumcised, He was called Jesus, the name given by the angel before He was conceived in the womb.
22 And when the time for their purification [the mother's purification and the Baby's dedication] came according to the Law of Moses, they brought Him up to Jerusalem to present Him to the Lord, [Lev. 12:1-4.]
23 As it is written in the Law of the Lord, Every [first-born] male that opens the womb shall be set apart *and* dedicated *and* called holy to the Lord. [Exod. 13:1, 2, 12; Num. 8:17.]

---

t) Vincent. Compare Matthew 1:20, 24, 25. Also Matthew 1:18, 19.
u) Thayer.
v) Wycliffe.
w) Vincent.
x) Thayer.

Living New Testament

2 (This census was taken when Quirinius was governor of Syria.)

3 Everyone was required to return to his ancestral home for this registration.

4 And because Joseph was a member of the royal line, he had to go to Bethlehem in Judea, King David's ancient home—journeying there from the Galilean province of Nazareth.

5 He took with him Mary, his fiancée, who was obviously pregnant by this time.

6 And while they were there, the time came for her baby to be born;

7 And she gave birth to her first child, a son. She wrapped Him in a blanket[2] and laid Him in a manger, because there was no room for them in the village inn.

8 That night some shepherds were in the fields outside the village, guarding their flocks of sheep.

9 Suddenly an angel appeared among them, and the landscape shone bright with the glory of the Lord. They were badly frightened,

10 But the angel reassured them. "Don't be afraid!" he said. "I bring you the most joyful news ever announced, and it is for everyone!

11 The Savior—yes, the Messiah, the Lord—has been born tonight in Bethlehem![3]

12 How will you recognize Him? You will find a baby wrapped in a blanket,[4] lying in a manger!"

13 Suddenly, the angel was joined by a vast host of others—the armies of heaven—praising God:

14 "Glory to God in the highest heaven," they sang,[5] "and peace on earth for all those pleasing Him."

15 When this great army of angels had returned again to heaven, the shepherds said to each other, "Come on! Let's go to Bethlehem! Let's see this wonderful thing that has happened, which the Lord has told us about."

16 They ran to the village and found their way to Mary and Joseph. And there was the baby, lying in the manger.

17 The shepherds told everyone what had happened and what the angel had said to them about this child.

18 All who heard the shepherds' story expressed astonishment,

19 But Mary quietly treasured these things in her heart and often thought about them.

20 Then the shepherds went back again to their fields and flocks, praising God for the visit of the angels, and because they had seen the child, just as the angel had told them.

21 Eight days later, at the baby's circumcision ceremony, He was named Jesus, the name given Him by the angel before He was even conceived.

22 When the time came for Mary's purification offering at the Temple, as required by the laws of Moses after the birth of a child, His parents took Him to Jerusalem to present Him to the Lord;

23 For in these laws God had said, "If a woman's first child is a boy, he shall be dedicated to the Lord."

[2] Literally, "swaddling clothes."
[3] Literally, "in the City of David."
[4] Literally, "swaddling clothes."
[5] Literally, "said."

Revised Standard

rollment, when Quirinius was governor of
Syria. 3 And all went to be enrolled, each to
his own city. 4 And Joseph also went up from
Galilee, from the city of Nazareth, to Judea,
to the city of David, which is called Bethlehem, because he was of the house and
lineage of David, 5 to be enrolled with Mary,
his betrothed, who was with child. 6 And
while they were there, the time came for her
to be delivered. 7 And she gave birth to her
first-born son and wrapped him in swaddling
clothes, and laid him in a manger, because
there was no place for them in the inn.

The angels and the shepherds

8 And in that region there were shepherds out in the field, keeping watch over
their flock by night. 9 And an angel of the
Lord appeared to them, and the glory of
the Lord shone around them, and they were
filled with fear. 10 And the angel said to
them, "Be not afraid; for behold, I bring
you good news of a great joy which will
come to all the people; 11 for to you is born
this day in the city of David a Savior, who
is Christ the Lord. 12 And this will be a sign
for you: you will find a babe wrapped in
swaddling clothes and lying in a manger."
13 And suddenly there was with the angel a
multitude of the heavenly host praising God
and saying,
14 "Glory to God in the highest,
and on earth peace among men with
whom he is pleased!"[g]
15 When the angels went away from
them into heaven, the shepherds said to one
another, "Let us go over to Bethlehem and
see this thing that has happened, which the
Lord has made known to us." 16 And they
went with haste, and found Mary and
Joseph, and the babe lying in a manger.
17 And when they saw it they made known
the saying which had been told them concerning this child; 18 and all who heard it
wondered at what the shepherds told them.
19 But Mary kept all these things, pondering them in her heart. 20 And the shepherds
returned, glorifying and praising God for all
they had heard and seen, as it had been told
them.

The circumcision and presentation

21 And at the end of eight days, when he
was circumcised, he was called Jesus, the
name given by the angel before he was conceived in the womb.
22 And when the time came for their
purification according to the law of Moses,
they brought him up to Jerusalem to present
him to the Lord 23 (as it is written in the law
of the Lord, "Every male that opens the
womb shall be called holy to the Lord")

[g] Other ancient authorities read *peace, good will among men*

King James

24 And to offer a sacrifice according to that which is said in the law of the Lord, A pair of turtledoves, or two young pigeons.

25 And, behold, there was a man in Jerusalem, whose name *was* Simeon; and the same man *was* just and devout, waiting for the consolation of Israel: and the Holy Ghost was upon him.

26 And it was revealed unto him by the Holy Ghost, that he should not see death, before he had seen the Lord's Christ.

27 And he came by the Spirit into the temple: and when the parents brought in the child Jesus, to do for him after the custom of the law,

28 Then took he him up in his arms, and blessed God, and said,

29 Lord, now lettest thou thy servant depart in peace, according to thy word:

30 For mine eyes have seen thy salvation,

31 Which thou hast prepared before the face of all people;

32 A light to lighten the Gentiles, and the glory of thy people Israel.

33 And Joseph and his mother marvelled at those things which were spoken of him.

34 And Simeon blessed them, and said unto Mary his mother, Behold, this *child* is set for the fall and rising again of many in Israel; and for a sign which shall be spoken against;

35 (Yea, a sword shall pierce through thy own soul also,) that the thoughts of many hearts may be revealed.

36 And there was one Anna, a prophetess, the daughter of Phanuel, of the tribe of Aser: she was of a great age, and had lived with an husband seven years from her virginity;

37 And she *was* a widow of about fourscore and four years, which departed not from the temple, but served *God* with fastings and prayers night and day.

38 And she coming in that instant gave thanks likewise unto the Lord, and spake of him to all them that looked for redemption in Jerusalem.

39 And when they had performed all things according to the law of the Lord, they returned into Galilee, to their own city Nazareth.

40 And the child grew, and waxed strong in spirit, filled with wisdom: and the grace of God was upon him.

41 Now his parents went to Jerusalem every year at the feast of the passover.

42 And when he was twelve years old, they went up to Jerusalem after the custom of the feast.

43 And when they had fulfilled the days, as they returned, the child Jesus tarried behind in Jerusalem; and Joseph and his mother knew not *of it*.

44 But they, supposing him to have been in the company, went a day's journey; and they sought him among *their* kinsfolk and acquaintance.

Amplified

24 And [they came also] to offer a sacrifice according to what is said in the Law of the Lord, a pair of turtledoves or two young pigeons. [Lev. 12:6-8.]

25 Now there was a man in Jerusalem whose name was Simeon, and this man was righteous and devout—cautiously and carefully observing the divine Law—and looking for the Consolation of Israel.

26 And the Holy Spirit was upon him and it had been divinely revealed (communicated) to him by the Holy Spirit that he should not see death before he had seen the Lord's Christ, the Messiah, the Anointed One.

27 And prompted by the (Holy) Spirit he came into the temple [y]enclosure; and when the parents brought in the little child Jesus, to do for Him what was customary according to the Law,

28 [Simeon] took Him up in his arms and praised *and* thanked God and said,

29 And now, Lord, You are releasing Your servant to depart (leave this world) in peace, according to Your word.

30 For with my [own] eyes I have seen Your Salvation [Isa. 52:10.]

31 Which You have ordained *and* prepared before (in the presence of) all peoples,

32 A Light for [z]revelation to the Gentiles—to disclose what was before unknown—and [to bring] praise *and* honor *and* glory to Your people Israel. [Isa. 42:6; 49:6.]

33 And His [legal] father and [His] mother were marvelling at what was said about Him;

34 And Simeon blessed them and said to Mary His mother, Behold, this Child is appointed *and* destined for the fall and rising of many in Israel, and for a sign that is spoken against, [Isa. 8:14, 15.]

35 And a sword will pierce through your own soul also, that the secret thoughts *and* purposes of many hearts may be brought out *and* disclosed.

36 And there was also a prophetess, Anna, the daughter of Phanuel of the tribe of Asher. She was very old, having lived with her husband seven years from her maidenhood, [Josh. 19:24.]

37 And as a widow even for eighty-four years. She did not go out from the temple [a]enclosure, but was worshiping night and day with fasting and prayer.

38 And she too came up that same hour and she returned thanks to God, and talked of [Jesus] to all who were looking for the redemption (deliverance) of Jerusalem.

39 And when they had done everything according to the Law of the Lord, they went back into Galilee to their own town, Nazareth.

40 And the Child grew and became strong *in spirit*, filled with wisdom, and the grace (favor and spiritual blessing) of God was upon Him. [Judg. 13:24; I Sam. 2:26.]

41 Now His parents went to Jerusalem every year to the Passover feast. [Deut. 16:1-8; Exod. 23:15.]

42 And when He was twelve years [old], they went up as was their custom.

43 And when the feast was ended, as they were returning, the boy Jesus remained behind in Jerusalem. Now His parents did not know this,

44 But supposing Him to be in the caravan they travelled on a day's journey, and [then] they sought Him (diligently, looking up and down for Him) among their kinsfolk and acquaintances.

---

y) Trench.
z) Vincent.
a) Trench.

Living New Testament

24 At that time Jesus' parents also offered their sacrifice for purification—"either a pair of turtledoves or two young pigeons" was the legal requirement.

25 That day a man named Simeon, a Jerusalem resident, was in the Temple. He was a good man, very devout, filled with the Holy Spirit and constantly expecting the Messiah[6] to come soon.

26 For the Holy Spirit had revealed to him that he would not die until he had seen Him—God's anointed King.

27 The Holy Spirit had impelled him to go to the Temple that day; and so, when Mary and Joseph arrived to present the baby Jesus to the Lord in obedience to the law,

28 Simeon was there and took the child in his arms, praising God.

29, 30, 31 "Lord," he said, "now I can die content! For I have seen Him as You promised me I would. I have seen the Savior You have given to the world.

32 He is the Light that will shine upon the nations, and He will be the glory of Your people Israel!"

33 Joseph and Mary just stood there, marveling at what was being said about Jesus.

34, 35 Simeon blessed them but then said to Mary, "A sword shall pierce your soul, for this child shall be rejected by many in Israel, and this to their undoing. But He will be the greatest joy of many others.

And the deepest thoughts of many hearts shall be revealed."

* * * * *

36, 37 Anna, a prophetess, was also there in the Temple that day. She was the daughter of Phanuel, of the Jewish tribe of Asher, and was very old, for she had been a widow for 84 years following seven years of marriage. She never left the Temple but stayed there night and day, worshiping God by praying and often going without food.

38 She came along just as Simeon was talking with Mary and Joseph, and she also began thanking God and publicly proclaiming the Messiah's arrival to everyone in Jerusalem who had been awaiting the coming of the Savior.[7]

38 When Jesus' parents had fulfilled all the requirements of the Law of God they returned home to Nazareth in Galilee.

40 There the child became a strong, robust lad, and was known for wisdom beyond His years; and God poured out His blessings on Him.

* * * * *

41, 42 When Jesus was 12 years old He accompanied His parents to Jerusalem for the annual Passover Festival, which they attended each year.

43 After the celebration was over they started home to Nazareth, but Jesus stayed behind in Jerusalem. His parents didn't miss Him the first day,

44 For they assumed He was with friends among the other travelers. But when He didn't show up that evening, they started to look for Him among their relatives and friends;

[6] Literally, "the Consolation of Israel."
[7] Literally, "looking for the redemption of Jerusalem."

Revised Standard

24 and to offer a sacrifice according to what
is said in the law of the Lord, "a pair of
turtledoves, or two young pigeons." 25 Now
there was a man in Jerusalem, whose name
was Simeon, and this man was righteous
and devout, looking for the consolation of
Israel, and the Holy Spirit was upon him.
26 And it had been revealed to him by the
Holy Spirit that he should not see death
before he had seen the Lord's Christ. 27 And
inspired by the Spirit[h] he came into the
temple; and when the parents brought in
the child Jesus, to do for him according to
the custom of the law, 28 he took him up in
his arms and blessed God and said,

The song of Simeon

29 "Lord, now lettest thou thy servant depart
in peace,
according to thy word;
30 for mine eyes have seen thy salvation
31 which thou hast prepared in the presence
of all peoples,
32 a light for revelation to the Gentiles,
and for glory to thy people Israel."

33 And his father and his mother marveled at what was said about him; 34 and
Simeon blessed them and said to Mary his
mother,
"Behold, this child is set for the fall and
rising of many in Israel,
and for a sign that is spoken against
35 (and a sword will pierce through your
own soul also),
that thoughts out of many hearts may
be revealed."

Anna gives thanks to God

36 And there was a prophetess, Anna,
the daughter of Phanuel, of the tribe of
Asher; she was of a great age, having lived
with her husband seven years from her virginity, 37 and as a widow till she was eighty-four. She did not depart from the temple,
worshiping with fasting and prayer night
and day. 38 And coming up at that very hour
she gave thanks to God, and spoke of him
to all who were looking for the redemption
of Jerusalem.

39 And when they had performed everything according to the law of the Lord, they
returned into Galilee, to their own city,
Nazareth. 40 And the child grew and became
strong, filled with wisdom; and the favor of
God was upon him.

The boy Jesus in the temple

41 Now his parents went to Jerusalem
every year at the feast of the Passover.
42 And when he was twelve years old, they
went up according to custom; 43 and when
the feast was ended, as they were returning,
the boy Jesus stayed behind in Jerusalem.
His parents did not know it, 44 but supposing
him to be in the company they went a day's
journey, and they sought him among their
kinsfolk and acquaintances; 45 and when they

[h] Or *in the Spirit*

King James

45 And when they found him not, they turned back again to Jerusalem, seeking him.

46 And it came to pass, that after three days they found him in the temple, sitting in the midst of the doctors, both hearing them, and asking them questions.

47 And all that heard him were astonished at his understanding and answers.

48 And when they saw him, they were amazed: and his mother said unto him, Son, why hast thou thus dealt with us? behold, thy father and I have sought thee sorrowing.

49 And he said unto them, How is it that ye sought me? wist ye not that I must be about my Father's business?

50 And they understood not the saying which he spake unto them.

51 And he went down with them, and came to Nazareth, and was subject unto them: but his mother kept all these sayings in her heart.

52 And Jesus increased in wisdom and stature, and in favour with God and man.

CHAPTER 3

NOW in the fifteenth year of the reign of Tiberius Cæsar, Pontius Pilate being governor of Judæa, and Herod being tetrarch of Galilee, and his brother Philip tetrarch of Ituræa and of the region of Trachonitis, and Lysanias the tetrarch of Abilene,

2 Annas and Caiaphas being the high priests, the word of God came unto John the son of Zacharias in the wilderness.

3 And he came into all the country about Jordan, preaching the baptism of repentance for the remission of sins;

4 As it is written in the book of the words of Esaias the prophet, saying, The voice of one crying in the wilderness, Prepare ye the way of the Lord, make his paths straight.

5 Every valley shall be filled, and every mountain and hill shall be brought low; and the crooked shall be made straight, and the rough ways *shall be* made smooth;

6 And all flesh shall see the salvation of God.

7 Then said he to the multitude that came forth to be baptized of him, O generation of vipers, who hath warned you to flee from the wrath to come?

Amplified

45 And when they failed to find Him, they went back to Jerusalem, looking for Him (up and down) all the way.

46 After three days they found Him; [came upon Him] in the [b](court of the) temple, sitting among the teachers, listening to them and asking them questions.

47 And all who heard Him were astonished *and* overwhelmed with bewildered wonder at His intelligence *and* understanding and His replies.

48 And when they [Joseph and Mary] saw Him they were amazed, and His mother said to Him, Child, why have You treated us like this? Here Your father and I have been anxiously looking for You—distressed *and* tormented.

49 And He said to them, How is it that you had to look for Me? Did you not see *and* know that it is necessary (as a duty) for Me [c]to be in My Father's house, *and* [occupied] about My Father's business?

50 But they did not comprehend what He was saying to them.

51 And He went down with them and came to Nazareth, and was (habitually) obedient to them; and his mother kept *and* closely *and* persistently guarded all these things in her heart.

52 And Jesus increased in wisdom (in broad and full understanding), and in stature *and* [d]years, and in favor with God and man.

CHAPTER 3

IN the fifteenth year of Tiberius Caesar's reign, when Pontius Pilate was governor of Judea, and Herod was tetrarch of Galilee, and his brother Philip tetrarch of the region of Ituraea and Trachonitis, and Lysanias tetrarch of Abilene,

2 In the high priesthood of Annas and Caiaphas, the Word of God [[e]concerning the attainment through Christ of salvation in the kingdom of God], came to John the son of Zachariah in the wilderness (desert).

3 And he went into all the country round about the Jordan, preaching a baptism of repentance (that is, [e]of hearty amending of their ways with abhorrence for past wrongdoing) unto the forgiveness of sin.

4 As it is written in the book of the words of Isaiah the prophet, The voice of one crying in the wilderness (shouting in the desert): Prepare the way of the Lord; make His beaten paths straight.

5 Every valley *and* ravine shall be filled up, and every mountain and hill shall be leveled down, and the crooked places shall be made straight, and the rough roads shall be made smooth;

6 And all mankind shall see (behold and [f]understand [and at last acknowledge]) the salvation of God—the deliverance from eternal death [e]decreed by God. [Isa. 40:3-5.]

7 So he said to the crowds that came out to be baptized by him, You offspring of vipers! Who [g]secretly warned you to flee from the coming wrath?

---

b) Trench.
c) Literally, "in the things of My Father."
d) Alternate reading.
e) Thayer.
f) Gray and Adams Bible Commentary.
g) Literal meaning.

Living New Testament

45 And when they couldn't find Him, they went back to Jerusalem to search for Him there.

46, 47 Three days later they finally discovered Him. He was in the Temple, sitting among the teachers of Law, discussing deep questions with them and amazing everyone with His understanding and answers.

48 His parents didn't know what to think when they saw Him sitting there so calmly.[8] "Son!" His mother said to Him, "Why have You done this to us? Your father and I have been frantic, searching for You everywhere."

49 "But why did you need to search?" He asked. "Didn't you realize that I would be here at the Temple, in My Father's House?"

50 But they didn't understand what He meant.

51 Then He returned to Nazareth with them and was obedient to them; and His mother stored away all these things in her heart.

52 So Jesus grew both tall and wise, and was loved by God and man.

Revised Standard

did not find him, they returned to Jerusalem, seeking him. [46]After three days they
found him in the temple, sitting among the
teachers, listening to them and asking them
questions; [47]and all who heard him were
amazed at his understanding and his answers. [48]And when they saw him they were
astonished; and his mother said to him,
"Son, why have you treated us so? Behold,
your father and I have been looking for you
anxiously." [49]And he said to them, "How is
it that you sought me? Did you not know
that I must be in my Father's house?" [50]And
they did not understand the saying which
he spoke to them. [51]And he went down
with them and came to Nazareth, and was
obedient to them; and his mother kept all
these things in her heart.

52 And Jesus increased in wisdom and
in stature,[i] and in favor with God and man.

CHAPTER 3

In the fifteenth year of the reign of Emperor Tiberius Caesar, a message came from God to John (the son of Zacharias), as he was living out in the deserts. (Pilate was governor over Judea at that time; Herod, over Galilee; his brother Philip, over Iturea and Trachonitis; Lysanias, over Abilene; and Annas and Caiaphas were the Jewish High Priests.)

3 Then John went from place to place on both sides of the Jordan River, preaching that people should be baptized to show that they had turned to God and away from their sins, in order to be forgiven.[1]

4 In the words of Isaiah the prophet, John was "a voice shouting from the barren wilderness, 'Prepare a road for the Lord to travel on! Widen the pathway before Him!

5 Level the mountains! Fill up the valleys! Straighten the curves! Smooth out the ruts!

6 And then all mankind shall see the Savior sent from God.' "

7 Here is a sample of John's preaching to the crowds that came for baptism: "You brood of snakes! You are trying to escape hell without truly turning to God! That is why you want to be baptized!

The preaching of John the Baptist

3 In the fifteenth year of the reign of
Tiberius Caesar, Pontius Pilate being
governor of Judea, and Herod being tetrarch
of Galilee, and his brother Philip tetrarch
of the region of Ituraea and Trachonitis,
and Lysanias tetrarch of Abilene, [2]in the
high-priesthood of Annas and Caiaphas, the
word of God came to John the son of
Zechariah in the wilderness; [3]and he went
into all the region about the Jordan, preaching a baptism of repentance for the forgiveness of sins. [4]As it is written in the
book of the words of Isaiah the prophet,

"The voice of one crying in the wilderness:
Prepare the way of the Lord,
make his paths straight.
5 Every valley shall be filled,
and every mountain and hill shall be
brought low,
and the crooked shall be made straight,
and the rough ways shall be made
smooth;
6 and all flesh shall see the salvation of
God."

7 He said therefore to the multitudes
that came out to be baptized by him, "You
brood of vipers! Who warned you to flee
from the wrath to come? [8]Bear fruits that

[8] Implied.
[1] Or, "preaching the baptism of repentance for remission of sins."

[i] Or *years*

King James

8 Bring forth therefore fruits worthy of repentance, and begin not to say within yourselves, We have Abraham to *our* father: for I say unto you, That God is able of these stones to raise up children unto Abraham.

9 And now also the axe is laid unto the root of the trees: every tree therefore which bringeth not forth good fruit is hewn down, and cast into the fire.

10 And the people asked him, saying, What shall we do then?

11 He answereth and saith unto them, He that hath two coats, let him impart to him that hath none; and he that hath meat, let him do likewise.

12 Then came also publicans to be baptized, and said unto him, Master, what shall we do?

13 And he said unto them, Exact no more than that which is appointed you.

14 And the soldiers likewise demanded of him, saying, And what shall we do? And he said unto them, Do violence to no man, neither accuse *any* falsely; and be content with your wages.

15 And as the people were in expectation, and all men mused in their hearts of John, whether he were the Christ, or not;

16 John answered, saying unto *them* all, I indeed baptize you with water; but one mightier than I cometh, the latchet of whose shoes I am not worthy to unloose: he shall baptize you with the Holy Ghost and with fire:

17 Whose fan *is* in his hand, and he will throughly purge his floor, and will gather the wheat into his garner; but the chaff he will burn with fire unquenchable.

18 And many other things in his exhortation preached he unto the people.

19 But Herod the tetrarch, being reproved by him for Herodias his brother Philip's wife, and for all the evils which Herod had done,

20 Added yet this above all, that he shut up John in prison.

21 Now when all the people were baptized, it came to pass, that Jesus also being baptized, and praying, the heaven was opened,

22 And the Holy Ghost descended in a bodily shape like a dove upon him, and a voice came from heaven, which said, Thou art my beloved Son; in thee I am well pleased.

23 And Jesus himself began to be about thirty years of age, being (as was supposed) the son of Joseph, which was *the son* of Heli,

24 Which was *the son* of Matthat, which was *the son* of Levi, which was *the son* of Melchi, which was *the son* of Janna, which was *the son* of Joseph,

25 Which was *the son* of Mattathias, which was *the son* of Amos, which was *the son* of Naum, which was *the son* of Esli, which was *the son* of Nagge,

26 Which was *the son* of Maath, which was *the son* of Mattathias, which was *the son* of Semei, which was *the son* of Joseph, which was *the son* of Juda,

Amplified

8 Bear fruits that are deserving *and* consistent with [h]your repentance—[that is,] [i]conduct worthy of a heart changed and abhorring sin. And do not begin to say to yourselves, We have Abraham as our father; for I tell you God is able from these stones to raise up descendants for Abraham.

9 Even now the ax is laid to the root of the trees, so that every tree that does not bear good fruit is cut down and cast into the fire.

10 And the multitudes asked him, Then what shall we do?

11 And he replied to them, He who has two tunics (undergarments), let him share with him who has none; and he who has food, let him do the same way.

12 Even tax collectors came to be baptized, and they said to him, Teacher, what shall we do?

13 And he said to them, Exact *and* collect no more than the fixed amount appointed you.

14 Those serving as soldiers also asked him, And we, what shall we do? And he replied to them, Never demand *or* enforce [j]by terrifying people or by accusing wrongfully, and always be satisfied with your rations (supplies) *and* with your allowance (wages).

15 As the people were in suspense *and* waiting expectantly, and everybody reasoned *and* questioned in their hearts concerning John whether he perhaps might be the Christ, the Messiah, the Anointed One,

16 John answered them all by saying, I baptize you with water, but He Who is mightier than I is coming, the strap of Whose sandals I am not fit to unfasten; He will baptize you with the Holy Spirit and with fire.

17 His winnowing shovel (fork) is in His hand, to thoroughly clear *and* cleanse His [threshing] floor, and to gather the wheat *and* store it in His granary, but the chaff He will burn with fire that cannot be extinguished.

18 So, with many other (various) appeals and admonitions, he preached the good news (the Gospel) to the people.

19 But Herod the tetrarch, who had been (repeatedly) told his fault *and* reproved *with* rebuke [k]producing conviction, by *John* for [having] Herodias, his brother's wife, and for all the wicked things that Herod had done,

20 Added this to them all, that he shut up John in prison.

21 Now when all the people were baptized, and when Jesus also had been baptized, and [while He was still] praying, the (visible) heaven was opened,

22 And the Holy Spirit descended upon Him in bodily form, like a dove, and a voice came from heaven, *saying,* You are My Son, the Beloved! In You I am well pleased *and* find delight! [Ps. 2:7; Isa. 42:l.]

23 Jesus Himself, when He began [His ministry], was about thirty years of age, being the Son, as was supposed, of Joseph, the son of Heli,

24 The son of Matthat, the son of Levi, the son of Melchi, the son of Jannai, the son of Joseph,

25 The son of Mattathias, the son of Amos, the son of Nahum, the son of Esli, the son of Naggai,

26 The son of Maath, the son of Mattathias, the son of Semein, the son of Josech, the son of Joda,

---

h) Alternate reading (ASV).
i) Thayer.
j) Vincent.
k) Vincent.

Living New Testament

8 First go and prove by the way you live that you really have repented. And don't think you are safe because you are descendants of Abraham. That isn't enough, God can produce children of Abraham from these desert stones!

9 The axe of His judgment is poised over you, ready to sever your roots and cut you down. Yes, every tree that does not produce good fruit will be chopped down and thrown into the fire."

10 The crowd replied, "What do you want us to do?"

11 "If you have two coats," he replied, "give one to the poor. If you have extra food, give it away to those who are hungry."

12 Even tax collectors—notorious for their corruption—came to be baptized and asked, "How shall we prove to you that we have abandoned our sins?"

13 "By your honesty," he replied. "Make sure you collect no more taxes than the Roman[2] government requires you to."

14 "And us," asked some soldiers, "what about us?" John replied, "Don't extort money by threats and violence; don't accuse anyone of what you know he didn't do; and be content with your pay!"

15 Everyone was expecting the Messiah to come soon, and eager to know whether or not John was He. This was the question of the hour, and was being discussed everywhere.

16 John answered the question by saying, "I baptize only with water; but someone is coming soon who has far higher authority than mine; in fact, I am not even worthy of being His slave.[3] He will baptize you with fire—with the Holy Spirit.

17 He will separate chaff from grain, and burn up the chaff with eternal fire and store away the grain."

18 He used many such warnings as he announced the Good News to the people.

19, 20 (But after John had publicly criticized Herod, governor of Galilee, for marrying Herodias, his brother's wife, and for many other wrongs he had done, Herod put John in prison, thus adding this sin to all his many others.)

21 Then one day Jesus Himself joined the crowds being baptized by John. And after He was baptized, and was praying, the heavens opened,

22 And the Holy Spirit in the form of a dove settled upon Him, and a voice from heaven said, "You are My much loved Son, yes, My delight."

23 Jesus was about 30 years old when He began His public ministry.

Jesus was known as the son of Joseph.
Joseph's father was Heli;
24 Heli's father was Matthat;
Matthat's father was Levi;
Levi's father was Melchi;
Melchi's father was Jannai;
Jannai's father was Joseph;
25 Joseph's father was Mattathias;
Mattathias' father was Amos;
Amos' father was Nahum;
Nahum's father was Esli;
Esli's father was Naggai;
26 Naggai's father was Maath;
Maath's father was Mattathais;
Mattathias' father was Semein;
Semein's father was Josech;
Josech's father was Joda;

---

[2] Implied.
[3] Literally, "of loosing (the sandal strap of) His shoe."

Revised Standard

befit repentance, and do not begin to say to
yourselves, 'We have Abraham as our father'; for I tell you, God is able from these
stones to raise up children to Abraham.
9 Even now the axe is laid to the root of the
trees; every tree therefore that does not bear
good fruit is cut down and thrown into the
fire."
10 And the multitudes asked him, "What
then shall we do?" 11 And he answered them,
"He who has two coats, let him share with
him who has none; and he who has food,
let him do likewise." 12 Tax collectors also
came to be baptized, and said to him "Teacher, what shall we do?" 13 And he said to
them, "Collect no more than is appointed
you." 14 Soldiers also asked him, "And we,
what shall we do?" And he said to them,
"Rob no one by violence or by false accusation, and be content with your wages."
15 As the people were in expectation,
and all men questioned in their hearts concerning John, whether perhaps he were the
Christ, 16 John answered them all, "I baptize you with water; but he who is mightier
than I is coming, the thong of whose sandals
I am not worthy to untie; he will baptize
you with the Holy Spirit and with fire. 17 His
winnowing fork is in his hand, to clear his
threshing floor, and to gather the wheat into
his granary, but the chaff he will burn with
unquenchable fire."
18 So, with many other exhortations, he
preached good news to the people. 19 But
Herod the tetrarch, who had been reproved
by him for Herodias, his brother's wife, and
for all the evil things that Herod had done,
20 added this to them all, that he shut up
John in prison.

The baptism of Jesus

21 Now when all the people were baptized, and when Jesus also had been baptized
and was praying, the heaven was opened,
22 and the Holy Spirit descended upon him in
bodily form, as a dove, and a voice came
from heaven, "Thou art my beloved Son;[j]
with thee I am well pleased."[k]

The genealogy of Jesus

23 Jesus, when he began his ministry, was
about thirty years of age, being the son (as
was supposed) of Joseph, the son of Heli,
24 the son of Matthat, the son of Levi, the
son of Melchi, the son of Jannai, the son of
Joseph, 25 the son of Mattathias, the son of
Amos, the son of Nahum, the son of Esli,
the son of Naggai, 26 the son of Maath, the
son of Mattathias, the son of Semein, the
son of Josech, the son of Joda, 27 the son of

---

[j] Or *my Son, my* (or *the*) *Beloved*
[k] Other ancient authorities read *today I have begotten thee*

King James

27 Which was *the son* of Joanna, which was *the son* of Rhesa, which was *the son* of Zorobabel, which was *the son* of Salathiel, which was *the son* of Neri,

28 Which was *the son* of Melchi, which was *the son* of Addi, which was *the son* of Cosam, which was *the son* of Elmodam, which was *the son* of Er,

29 Which was *the son* of Jose, which was *the son* of Eliezer, which was *the son* of Jorim which was *the son* of Matthat, which was *the son* of Levi,

30 Which was *the son* of Simeon, which was *the son* of Juda, which was *the son* of Joseph, which was *the son* of Jonan, which was *the son* of Eliakim,

31 Which was *the son* of Melea, which was *the son* of Menan, which was *the son* of Mattatha, which was *the son* of Nathan, which was *the son* of David,

32 Which was *the son* of Jesse, which was *the son* of Obed, which was *the son* of Booz, which was *the son* of Salmon, which was *the son* of Naasson,

33 Which was *the son* of Aminadab, which was *the son* of Esrom, which was *the son* of Phares, which was *the son* of Juda,

34 Which was *the son* of Jacob, which was *the son* of Isaac, which was *the son* of Abraham, which was *the son* of Thara, which was *the son* of Nachor,

35 Which was *the son* of Saruch, which was *the son* of Ragau, which was *the son* of Phalec, which was *the son* of Heber, which was *the son* of Sala,

36 Which was *the son* of Cainan, which was *the son* of Arphaxad, which was *the son* of Sem, which was *the son* of Noe, which was *the son* of Lamech,

37 Which was *the son* of Mathusala, which was *the son* of Enoch, which was *the son* of Jared, which was *the son* of Maleleel, which was *the son* of Cainan,

38 Which was *the son* of Enos, which was *the son* of Seth, which was *the son* of Adam, which was *the son* of God.

CHAPTER 4

AND Jesus being full of the Holy Ghost returned from Jordan, and was led by the Spirit into the wilderness,

Amplified

27 The son of Joanan, the son of Rhesa, the son of Zerubbabel, the son of Shealtiel, the son of Neri,

28 The son of Melchi, the son of Addi, the son of Cosam, the son of Elmadam, the son of Er,

29 The son of Jesus, the son of Eliezer, the son of Jorim, the son of Matthat, the son of Levi,

30 The son of Symeon, the son of Judas, the son of Joseph, the son of Jonam, the son of Eliakim,

31 The son of Melea, the son of Menna, the son of Mattatha, the son of Nathan, the son of David,

32 The son of Jesse, the son of Obed, the son of Boaz, the son of Salmon (Sala), the son of Nahshon,

33 The son of Adminadab, (the son of Admin), the son of Arni, the son of Hezron, the son of Perez, the son of Judah,

34 The son of Jacob, the son of Isaac, the son of Abraham, the son of Terah, the son of Nahor,

35 The son of Serug, the son of Reu, the son of Peleg, the son of Eber, the son of Shelah,

36 The son of Cainan, the son of Arphaxad, the son of Shem, the son of Noah, the son of Lamech,

37 The son of Methuselah, the son of Enoch, the son of Jared, the son of Mahalaleel, the son of Cainan,

38 The son of Enos, the son of Seth, the son of Adam, the son of God. [Gen. 5:3-32; 11:10-26; Ruth 4:18-22; I Chron. 1:1-4, 24-28; 2:1-15.]

CHAPTER 4

THEN Jesus, full of *and* controlled by the Holy Spirit, returned from the Jordan and was led in (by) the (Holy) Spirit

Living New Testament

27 Joda's father was Joanan;
Joanan's father was Rhesa;
Rhesa's father was Zerubbabel;
Zerubbabel's father was Shealtiel;
Shealtiel's father was Neri;
28 Neri's father was Melchi;
Melchi's father was Addi;
Addi's father was Cosam;
Cosam's father was Elmadam;
Elmadam's father was Er;
29 Er's father was Joshua;
Joshua's father was Eliezer;
Eliezer's father was Jorim;
Jorim's father was Matthat;
Matthat's father was Levi;
30 Levi's father was Simeon;
Simeon's father was Judas;
Judas' father was Joseph;
Joseph's father was Jonam;
Jonam's father was Eliakim;
31 Eliakim's father was Melea;
Melea's father was Menna;
Menna's father was Mattatha;
Mattatha's father was Nathan;
Nathan's father was David;
32 David's father was Jesse;
Jesse's father was Obed;
Obed's father was Boaz;
Boaz' father was Salmon;[4]
Salmon's father was Nahshon;
33 Nahshon's father was Amminadab;
Amminadab's father was Admin;
Admin's father was Arni;
Arni's father was Hezron;
Hezron's father was Perez;
Perez' father was Judah;
34 Judah's father was Jacob;
Jacob's father was Isaac;
Isaac's father was Abraham;
Abraham's father was Terah;
Terah's father was Nahor;
35 Nahor's father was Serug;
Serug's father was Reu;
Reu's father was Peleg;
Peleg's father was Eber;
Eber's father was Shelah;
36 Shelah's father was Cainan;
Cainan's father was Arphaxad;
Arphaxad's father was Shem;
Shem's father was Noah;
Noah's father was Lamech;
37 Lamech's father was Methuselah;
Methuselah's father was Enoch;
Enoch's father was Jared;
Jared's father was Mahalaleel;
Mahalalee's father was Cainan;
38 Cainan's father was Enos;
Enos' father was Seth;
Seth's father was Adam;
Adam's father was God.

CHAPTER 4

Then Jesus, full of the Holy Spirit, left the Jordan River being urged by the Spirit out into the barren wastelands of Judea, where Satan tempted Him for 40 days. He ate nothing all that time, and was very hungry.

[4] "Sala."

Revised Standard

Joanan, the son of Rhesa, the son of Zerubbabel, the son of Shealtiel,[1] the son of Neri,
28the son of Melchi, the son of Addi, the
son of Cosam, the son of Elmadam, the son
of Er, 29the son of Joshua, the son of Eliezer, the son of Jorim, the son of Matthat,
the son of Levi, 30the son of Simeon, the
son of Judah, the son of Joseph, the son of
Jonam, the son of Eliakim, 31the son of
Melea, the son of Menna, the son of Mattatha, the son of Nathan, the son of David,
32the son of Jesse, the son of Obed, the son
of Boaz, the son of Sala, the son of
Nahshon, 33the son of Amminadab, the son
of Admin, the son of Arni, the son of
Hezron, the son of Perez, the son of Judah,
34the son of Jacob, the son of Isaac, the son
of Abraham, the son of Terah, the son of
Nahor, 35the son of Serug, the son of Reu,
the son of Peleg, the son of Eber, the son
of Shelah, 36the son of Cainan, the son of
Arphaxad, the son of Shem, the son of
Noah, the son of Lamech, 37the son of
Methuselah, the son of Enoch, the son of
Jared, the son of Mahalaleel, the son of
Cainan, 38the son of Enos, the son of Seth,
the son of Adam, the son of God.

The temptation in the wilderness

4 And Jesus, full of the Holy Spirit, returned from the Jordan, and was led by
the Spirit 2for forty days in the wilderness,
tempted by the devil. And he ate nothing

[1] Greek *Salathiel*

King James

2 Being forty days tempted of the devil. And in those days he did eat nothing: and when they were ended, he afterward hungered.

3 And the devil said unto him, If thou be the Son of God, command this stone that it be made bread.

4 And Jesus answered him, saying, It is written, That man shall not live by bread alone, but by every word of God.

5 And the devil, taking him up into an high mountain, shewed unto him all the kingdoms of the world in a moment of time.

6 And the devil said unto him, All this power will I give thee, and the glory of them: for that is delivered unto me; and to whomsoever I will I give it.

7 If thou therefore wilt worship me, all shall be thine.

8 And Jesus answered and said unto him, Get thee behind me, Satan: for it is written, Thou shalt worship the Lord thy God, and him only shalt thou serve.

9 And he brought him to Jerusalem, and set him on a pinnacle of the temple, and said unto him, If thou be the Son of God, cast thyself down from hence:

10 For it is written, He shall give his angels charge over thee, to keep thee:

11 And in *their* hands they shall bear thee up, lest at any time thou dash thy foot against a stone.

12 And Jesus answering said unto him, It is said, Thou shalt not tempt the Lord thy God.

13 And when the devil had ended all the temptation, he departed from him for a season.

14 ¶ And Jesus returned in the power of the Spirit into Galilee: and there went out a fame of him through all the region round about.

15 And he taught in their synagogues, being glorified of all.

16 ¶ And he came to Nazareth, where he had been brought up: and, as his custom was, he went into the synagogue on the sabbath day, and stood up for to read.

17 And there was delivered unto him the book of the prophet Esaias. And when he had opened the book, he found the place where it was written,

18 The Spirit of the Lord *is* upon me, because he hath anointed me to preach the gospel to the poor; he hath sent me to heal the brokenhearted, to preach deliverance to the captives, and recovering of sight to the blind, to set at liberty them that are bruised,

19 To preach the acceptable year of the Lord.

Amplified

2 For (during) forty days in the wilderness (desert), where He was tempted ([l]tried, tested exceedingly) by the devil. And He ate nothing during those days, and when they were completed, He was hungry. [Deut. 9:9; I Kings 19:8.]

3 Then the devil said to Him, If You are the Son of God, order this stone to turn into a loaf [of bread].

4 And Jesus replied to him, It is written, Man shall not live *and* be sustained by (on) bread alone *but by every word* and *expression of God*. [Deut. 8:3.]

5 Then the devil took Him up *to a high mountain,* and showed Him all the kingdoms of the habitable world in a moment of time—[m]in the twinkling of an eye;

6 And he said to Him, To You I will give all this power *and* authority and their glory, (that is, all their magnificence, excellence, pre-eminence, dignity and grace,) for it has been turned over to me, and I give it to whom I will;

7 Therefore if You will do homage to *and* worship me ([n]just once), it shall all be Yours.

8 And Jesus replied to him, *Get behind Me, Satan!* It is written, You shall do homage to *and* worship the Lord your God; and Him only shall you serve. [Deut. 6:13; 10:20.]

9 Then he took Him to Jerusalem, and set Him on [o]a gable of the temple, and said to Him, If You are the Son of God, cast Yourself down from here;

10 For it is written, He will give His angels charge of you, to guard *and* watch over you closely *and* carefully;

11 And on their hands they will bear you up, lest you strike your foot against a stone. [Ps. 91:11, 12.]

12 And Jesus replied to him, [The Scripture] says, You shall not tempt (try, [p]test exceedingly) the Lord your God. [Deut. 6:16.]

13 And when the devil had ended every [the complete cycle of] temptation, he left Him—temporarily, that is, [q]stood off from Him until another more opportune *and* favorable time.

14 Then Jesus went back full of *and* under the power of the (Holy) Spirit into Galilee, and the fame of Him spread through the whole region round about.

15 And He Himself conducted ([r]a course of) teaching in their synagogues, being [s]recognized *and* honored *and* praised by all.

16 So He came to Nazareth, [[o]that Nazareth] where He had been brought up; and He entered the synagogue, as was His custom on the Sabbath day. And He stood up to read.

17 And there was handed to Him [the roll of] the book of the prophet Isaiah. He opened (unrolled) the book, and found the place where it was written, [Isa. 61:1, 2.]

18 The Spirit of the Lord [is] upon Me, because He has anointed Me [the Anointed One, the Messiah] to preach the good news (the Gospel) to the poor; He has sent Me to announce release to the captives, and recovery of sight to the blind; to send forth delivered those who are oppressed—who are downtrodden, bruised, crushed and broken down by calamity;

19 To proclaim the accepted *and* acceptable year of the Lord—the day [t]when salvation and the free favors of God profusely abound. [Isa. 61:1, 2.]

---

l) Young's Analytical Concordance.
m) Tyndale.
n) Williams' New Testament, "expressed by the aorist."
o) Moulton and Milligan's "Vocabulary of the Greek Testament."
p) Young's Analytical Concordance.
q) Wuest's "Golden Nuggets from the Greek New Testament."
r) Vincent: in imperfect tense.
s) Cremer's "Biblico-Theological Lexicon of New Testament Greek."
t) Thayer.

Living New Testament

3 Satan said, "If You are God's Son, tell this stone to become a loaf of bread."

4 But Jesus replied, "It is written in the Scriptures, 'Other things in life are much more important than bread!' "[1]

5 Then Satan took Him up and revealed to Him all the kingdoms of the world in a moment of time;

6, 7 And the Devil told Him, "I will give You all these splendid kingdoms and their glory—for they are mine to give to anyone I wish—if You will only get down on Your knees and worship me."

8 Jesus replied, "We must worship God, and Him alone. So it is written in the Scriptures."

9, 10, 11 Then Satan took Him to Jerusalem to a high roof of the Temple and said, "If You are the Son of God, jump off! For the Scriptures say that God will send His angels to guard You and to keep You from crashing to the pavement below!"

12 Jesus replied, "The Scriptures also say, 'Don't experiment with God's patience.' "[2]

13 When the Devil had ended all the temptations, he left Jesus for a while and went away.

14 Then Jesus returned to Galilee, full of the Holy Spirit's power. Soon He became well known throughout all that region

15 For His sermons in the synagogues; everyone praised Him.

16 When He came to the village of Nazareth, His boyhood home, He went as usual to the synagogue on Saturday,[3] and stood up to read the Scriptures.

17 The book of Isaiah the prophet was handed to Him, and He opened it to the place where it says:

18, 19 "The Spirit of the Lord is upon Me; He has appointed Me to preach Good News to the poor; He has sent Me to announce that captives shall be released and the blind shall see, that the downtrodden shall be freed from their oppressors, and that God is ready to give blessings to all who come to Him."[4]

Revised Standard

in those days; and when they were ended,
he was hungry. 3The devil said to him, "If
you are the Son of God, command this stone
to become bread." 4And Jesus answered him,
"It is written, 'Man shall not live by bread
alone.' " 5And the devil took him up, and
showed him all the kingdoms of the world
in a moment of time, 6and said to him,
"To you I will give all this authority and
their glory; for it has been delivered to me,
and I give it to whom I will. 7If you, then,
will worship me, it shall all be yours." 8And
Jesus answered him, "It is written,

'You shall worship the Lord your God,
and him only shall you serve.' "

9And he took him to Jerusalem, and set
him on the pinnacle of the temple, and said
to him, "If you are the Son of God, throw
yourself down from here; 10for it is written,

'He will give his angels charge of you,
to guard you,'

11 and

'On their hands they will bear you up,
lest you strike your foot against a stone.' "

12 And Jesus answered him, "It is said, 'You
shall not tempt the Lord your God.' " 13And
when the devil had ended every temptation,
he departed from him until an opportune
time.

The beginning of Jesus' ministry

14 And Jesus returned in the power of
the Spirit into Galilee, and a report concerning him went out through all the surrounding country. 15And he taught in their
synagogues, being glorified by all.

Jesus rejected at Nazareth

16 And he came to Nazareth, where he
had been brought up; and he went to the
synagogue, as his custom was, on the sabbath day. And he stood up to read; 17and
there was given to him the book of the
prophet Isaiah. He opened the book and
found the place where it was written,

18"The Spirit of the Lord is upon me,
because he has anointed me to preach
good news to the poor.
He has sent me to proclaim release to
the captives
and recovering of sight to the blind,
to set at liberty those who are oppressed,
19to proclaim the acceptable year of the
Lord."

[1] Literally, "Man shall not live by bread alone." Deuteronomy 8:3.
[2] Literally, "Do not make trial of the Lord your God."
[3] Literally, "the Sabbath day."
[4] Literally, "to proclaim the acceptable year of the Lord."

King James

20 And he closed the book, and he gave *it* again to the minister, and sat down. And the eyes of all them that were in the synagogue were fastened on him.

21 And he began to say unto them, This day is this scripture fulfilled in your ears.

22 And all bare him witness, and wondered at the gracious words which proceeded out of his mouth. And they said, Is not this Joseph's son?

23 And he said unto them, Ye will surely say unto me this proverb, Physician, heal thyself: whatsoever we have heard done in Capernaum, do also here in thy country.

24 And he said, Verily I say unto you, No prophet is accepted in his own country.

25 But I tell you of a truth, many widows were in Israel in the days of Elias, when the heaven was shut up three years and six months, when great famine was throughout all the land;

26 But unto none of them was Elias sent, save unto Sarepta, *a city* of Sidon, unto a woman *that was* a widow.

27 And many lepers were in Israel in the time of Eliseus the prophet; and none of them was cleansed, saving Naaman the Syrian.

28 And all they in the synagogue, when they heard these things, were filled with wrath,

29 And rose up, and thrust him out of the city, and led him unto the brow of the hill whereon their city was built, that they might cast him down headlong.

30 But he passing through the midst of them went his way,

31 And came down to Capernaum, a city of Galilee, and taught them on the sabbath days.

32 And they were astonished at his doctrine: for his word was with power.

33 ¶ And in the synagogue there was a man, which had a spirit of an unclean devil, and cried out with a loud voice,

34 Saying, Let *us* alone; what have we to do with thee, *thou* Jesus of Nazareth? art thou come to destroy us? I know thee who thou art; the Holy One of God.

35 And Jesus rebuked him, saying, Hold thy peace, and come out of him. And when the devil had thrown him in the midst, he came out of him, and hurt him not.

36 And they were all amazed, and spake among themselves, saying, What a word *is* this! for with authority and power he commandeth the unclean spirits, and they come out.

37 And the fame of him went out into every place of the country round about.

38 ¶ And he arose out of the synagogue, and entered into Simon's house. And Simon's wife's mother was taken with a great fever; and they besought him for her.

39 And he stood over her, and rebuked the fever; and it left her: and immediately she arose and ministered unto them.

Amplified

20 Then He rolled up the book, and gave it back to the attendant and sat down; and the eyes of all in the synagogue were gazing (attentively) at Him.

21 And He began to speak to them: Today this Scripture has been fulfilled [t]while you are present *and* hearing.

22 And all spoke well of Him, and marveled at the words of grace that came forth from His mouth; and they said, Is not this Joseph's [u]Son?

23 So He said to them, You will doubtless quote to Me this proverb, Physician, heal Yourself! What we have learned by hearsay that You did in Capernaum, do here also in Your [own] town.

24 Then He said, Solemnly I say to you, no prophet is acceptable *and* welcome in his [own] town (country).

25 But in truth I tell you, there were many widows in Israel in the days of Elijah, when the heavens were closed up for three years and six months, so that there came a great famine over all the land;

26 And yet Elijah was not sent to a single one of them, but only to Zarephath in the country of Sidon, to a woman who was a widow. [I Kings 17:1, 8-16; 18:1.]

27 And there were many lepers in Israel in the time of Elisha the prophet, and yet not one of them was cleansed (by being healed), but only Naaman the Syrian. [II Kings 5:1-14.]

28 When they heard these things, all the people in the synagogue were filled with rage.

29 And rising up they pushed *and* drove Him out of the town, and (laying hold of Him) they led Him to the (projecting) upper part of the hill on which their town was built, that they might hurl Him headlong down [over the cliff].

30 But passing through their midst, He went on His way.

31 And He descended to Capernaum, a town of Galilee, and there He continued to teach the people on the Sabbath days.

32 And they were amazed at His teaching, for His word was with authority *and* ability *and* weight *and* power.

33 Now in the synagogue there was a man who was possessed by the foul spirit of a demon; and he cried out with a loud (deep, terrible) cry,

34 Ah, [v]let us alone! What have You to do with us?—What have [w]we in common—Jesus of Nazareth? Have You come to destroy us? I know Who You are, the Holy One of God!

35 But Jesus rebuked him, saying, Be silent (muzzled, gagged), and come out of him! And when the demon had thrown the man down in their midst, he came out of him, without injuring him in any [x]possible way.

36 And they were all amazed and said to one another, What kind of talk is this? For with authority and power He commands the foul spirits, and they come out!

37 And a rumor about Him spread into every place in the surrounding country.

38 Then He arose and left the synagogue, and went into Simon's (Peter's) house. Now Simon's mother-in-law was suffering in the grip of a burning fever, and they pleaded with Him for her.

39 And standing over her, He rebuked the fever, and it left her; and immediately she got up and began waiting on them.

---

t) Thayer.
u) Capitalized because of what He is, the spotless Son of God, not what the speakers may have thought He was.
v) Alternate reading.
w) After Wycliffe's translation.
x) Literal meaning.

Living New Testament

20 He closed the book and handed it back to the attendant and sat down, while everyone in the synagogue gazed at Him intently.

21 Then He added, "These Scriptures came true today!"

22 All who were there spoke well of Him and were amazed by the beautiful words that fell from His lips. "How can this be?" they asked. "Isn't this Joseph's son?"

23 Then He said, "Probably you will quote Me that proverb, 'Physician, heal yourself'—meaning, 'Why don't you do miracles here in your home town like those you did in Capernaum?'

24 But I solemnly declare to you that no prophet is accepted in his own home town!

25, 26 For example, remember how Elijah the prophet used a miracle to help the widow of Zarephath—a foreigner from the land of Sidon. There were many Jewish widows needing help in those days of famine, for there had been no rain for three and one-half years, and hunger stalked the land; yet Elijah was not sent to them.

27 Or think of the prophet Elisha, who healed Naaman, a Syrian, rather than the many Jewish lepers needing help."

28 These remarks stung them to fury;

29 And jumping up, they mobbed Him and took Him to the edge of the hill on which the city was built, to push Him over the cliff.

30 But He walked away through the crowd and left them.

31 Then He returned to Capernaum, a city in Galilee, and preached there in the synagogue every Saturday.

32 Here, too, the people were amazed at the things He said. For He spoke as one who knew the truth, instead of merely quoting the opinions of others as His authority.

33 Once as He was teaching in the synagogue, a man possessed by a demon began shouting at Jesus,

34 "Go away! We want nothing to do with You, Jesus from Nazareth. You have come to destroy us. I know who You are—the Holy Son of God."

35 Jesus cut him short. "Be silent!" He told the demon. "Come out!" The demon threw the man to the floor as the crowd watched, and then left him without hurting him further.

36 Amazed, the people asked, "What is in this man's words that even demons obey Him?"

37 The story of what He had done spread like wildfire throughout the whole region.

38 After leaving the synagogue that day, He went to Simon's home where He found Simon's mother-in-law very sick with a high fever. "Please heal her," everyone begged.

39 Standing at her bedside He spoke to the fever, rebuking it, and immediately her temperature returned to normal and she got up and prepared a meal[5] for them!

[5] Literally, "ministered unto them."

Revised Standard

[20]And he closed the book, and gave it back
to the attendant, and sat down; and the eyes
of all in the synagogue were fixed on him.
[21]And he began to say to them, "Today
this scripture has been fulfilled in your hearing." [22]And all spoke well of him, and
wondered at the gracious words which proceeded out of his mouth; and they said, "Is
not this Joseph's son?" [23]And he said to
them, "Doubtless you will quote to me this
proverb, 'Physician, heal yourself; what we
have heard you did at Capernaum, do here
also in your own country.'" [24]And he said,
"Truly, I say to you, no prophet is acceptable in his own country. [25]But in truth, I
tell you, there were many widows in Israel
in the days of Elijah, when the heaven was
shut up three years and six months, when
there came a great famine over all the
land; [26]and Elijah was sent to none of them
but only to Zarephath, in the land of Sidon,
to a woman who was a widow. [27]And there
were many lepers in Israel in the time of
the prophet Elisha; and none of them was
cleansed, but only Naaman the Syrian."
[28]When they heard this, all in the synagogue
were filled with wrath. [29]And they rose up
and put him out of the city, and led him
to the brow of the hill on which their city
was built, that they might throw him down
headlong. [30]But passing through the midst
of them he went away.

The unclean spirit cast out

31 And he went down to Capernaum, a
city of Galilee. And he was teaching them
on the sabbath; [32]and they were astonished
at his teaching, for his word was with authority. [33]And in the synagogue there was a
man who had the spirit of an unclean demon; and he cried out with a loud voice,
[34]"Ah![m] What have you to do with us,
Jesus of Nazareth? Have you come to destroy us? I know who you are, the Holy
One of God." [35]But Jesus rebuked him,
saying, "Be silent, and come out of him!"
And when the demon had thrown him
down in the midst, he came out of him,
having done him no harm. [36]And they were
all amazed and said to one another, "What
is this word? For with authority and power
he commands the unclean spirits, and they
come out." [37]And reports of him went
out into every place in the surrounding
region.

Peter's mother-in-law healed

38 And he arose and left the synagogue,
and entered Simon's house. Now Simon's
mother-in-law was ill with a high fever,
and they besought him for her. [39]And he
stood over her and rebuked the fever, and
it left her; and immediately she rose and
served them.

[m] Or *Let us alone*

King James

40 ¶ Now when the sun was setting, all they that had any sick with divers diseases brought them unto him; and he laid his hands on every one of them, and healed them.

41 And devils also came out of many, crying out, and saying, Thou art Christ the Son of God. And he rebuking *them* suffered them not to speak: for they knew that he was Christ.

42 And when it was day, he departed and went into a desert place: and the people sought him, and came unto him, and stayed him, that he should not depart from them.

43 And he said unto them, I must preach the kingdom of God to other cities also: for therefore am I sent.

44 And he preached in the synagogues of Galilee.

Amplified

40 Now at the setting of the sun [indicating the end of the Sabbath], all those who had [any that were] sick with various diseases brought them to Him, and He laid His hands upon every one of them and cured them.

41 And demons even came out of many people, screaming *and* crying out, You are the Son of God! But He rebuked them, and would not permit them to speak, because they knew that He was the Christ, the Messiah.

42 And when daybreak came He left [Peter's house] and went into an isolated (desert) place. And the people looked for Him until they came up to Him, and tried to prevent Him from leaving them.

43 But He said to them, I must preach the good news (the Gospel) of the kingdom of God to the other cities and towns also; for I was sent for this [purpose].

44 And He continued to preach in the synagogues of Galilee.

CHAPTER 5

AND it came to pass, that, as the people pressed upon him to hear the word of God, he stood by the lake of Gennesaret,

2 And saw two ships standing by the lake: but the fishermen were gone out of them, and were washing *their* nets.

3 And he entered into one of the ships, which was Simon's, and prayed him that he would thrust out a little from the land. And he sat down, and taught the people out of the ship.

4 Now when he had left speaking, he said unto Simon, Launch out into the deep, and let down your nets for a draught.

5 And Simon answering said unto him, Master, we have toiled all the night, and have taken nothing: nevertheless at thy word I will let down the net.

6 And when they had this done, they enclosed a great multitude of fishes: and their net brake.

7 And they beckoned unto *their* partners, which were in the other ship, that they should come and help them. And they came, and filled both the ships, so that they began to sink.

8 When Simon Peter saw *it*, he fell down at Jesus' knees, saying, Depart from me; for I am a sinful man, O Lord.

9 For he was astonished, and all that were with him, at the draught of the fishes which they had taken:

10 And so *was* also James, and John, the sons of Zebedee, which were partners with Simon. And Jesus said unto Simon, Fear not; from henceforth thou shalt catch men.

11 And when they had brought their ships to land, they forsook all, and followed him.

12 ¶ And it came to pass, when he was in a certain city, behold a man full of leprosy: who seeing Jesus fell on *his* face, and besought him, saying, Lord, if thou wilt, thou canst make me clean.

CHAPTER 5

NOW it occurred that while the people pressed upon Jesus to hear the message of God, He was standing by the lake of Gennesaret [Sea of Galilee].

2 And He saw two boats drawn up by the lake, but the fishermen had gone down from them and were washing their nets.

3 And getting into one of the boats, [the one] that belonged to Simon (Peter), He requested him to draw away a little from the shore. Then He sat down and continued to teach the crowd (of people) from the boat.

4 When He had stopped speaking, He said to Simon (Peter), Put out into the deep [water], and lower your nets for a haul.

5 And Simon (Peter) answered, Master, we toiled all night ([y]exhaustingly) and caught nothing [in our nets]. But [y]on the ground of Your word, I will lower the nets [again].

6 And when they had done this, they caught a great number of fish; and as their nets were ([z]at the point of) breaking,

7 They signaled to their partners in the other boat to come and take hold with them. And they came and filled both the boats, so that they began to sink.

8 But when Simon Peter saw this, he fell down at Jesus' knees, saying, Depart from me, for I am a sinful man, O Lord.

9 For he was gripped with bewildering amazement—allied to terror—and all that were with him, at the haul of fish which they had made;

10 And so also were James and John, sons of Zebedee, who were partners with Simon (Peter). And Jesus said to Simon, Have no fear; from now on you will be catching men!

11 And after they had run their boats on shore, they left everything and joined Him as His disciples *and* sided with His party *and* accompanied Him.

12 While He was in one of the towns, there came a man full of (covered with) leprosy; and when he saw Jesus, he fell on his face and implored Him, saying, Lord, if You will, You are able to cure me *and* make me clean.

---

y) Vincent.
z) Trench.

Living New Testament

40 As the sun went down that evening, all the villagers who had any sick people in their homes, no matter what their diseases were, brought them to Jesus; and the touch of His hands healed every one!

41 Some were possessed by demons; and the demons came out at His command, shouting, "You are the Son of God." But because they knew He was the Christ, He stopped them and told them to be silent.

42 Early the next morning He went out into the desert. The crowds searched everywhere for Him and when they finally found Him they begged Him not to leave them, but to stay at Capernaum.

43 But He replied, "I must preach the Good News of the Kingdom of God in other places too, for that is why I was sent."

44 So He continued to travel around preaching in synagogues throughout Judea.

Revised Standard

The sick healed; demons cast out

40 Now when the sun was setting, all
those who had any that were sick with
various diseases brought them to him; and
he laid his hands on every one of them
and healed them. 41And demons also came
out of many, crying, "You are the Son of
God!" But he rebuked them, and would not
allow them to speak, because they knew
that he was the Christ.
42 And when it was day he departed
and went into a lonely place. And the
people sought him and came to him, and
would have kept him from leaving them;
43but he said to them, "I must preach the
good news of the kingdom of God to the
other cities also; for I was sent for this
purpose." 44And he was preaching in the
synagogues of Judea.[n]

CHAPTER 5

One day as he was preaching on the shore of Lake Gennesaret, great crowds pressed in on Him to listen to the Word of God.

2 He noticed two empty boats standing at the water's edge while the fishermen washed their nets.

3 Stepping into one of the boats, Jesus asked Simon, its owner, to push out a little into the water, so that He could sit in the boat and speak to the crowds from there.

4 When He had finished speaking, He said to Simon, "Now go out where it is deeper and let down your nets and you will catch a lot of fish!"

5 "Sir," Simon replied, "we worked hard all last night and didn't catch a thing. But if You say so, we'll try again."

6 And this time their nets were so full that they began to tear!

7 A shout for help brought their partners in the other boat and soon both boats were filled with fish and on the verge of sinking.

8 When Simon Peter realized what had happened, he fell to his knees before Jesus and said, "Oh, sir, please leave us—I'm too much of a sinner for You to have around."

9 For he was awestruck by the size of their catch, as were the others with him,

10 And his partners too—James and John, the sons of Zebedee.

Jesus replied, "Don't worry! From now on you'll be fishing for the souls of men!"

11 And as soon as they landed, they left everything and went with Him.

12 One day in a certain village He was visiting, there was a man with an advanced case of leprosy. When he saw Jesus he fell to the ground before Him, face downward in the dust, begging to be healed. "Sir," he said, "if You only will, You can clear me of every trace of my disease."

The call of the first disciples

5 While the people pressed upon him to
hear the word of God, he was standing
by the lake of Gennesaret. 2And he saw
two boats by the lake; but the fishermen
had gone out of them and were washing
their nets. 3Getting into one of the boats,
which was Simon's, he asked him to put
out a little from the land. And he sat
down and taught the people from the boat.
4And when he had ceased speaking, he
said to Simon, "Put out into the deep and
let down your nets for a catch." 5And Simon answered, "Master, we toiled all night
and took nothing! But at your word I will
let down the nets." 6And when they had
done this, they enclosed a great shoal of
fish; and as their nets were breaking, 7they
beckoned to their partners in the other
boat to come to help them. And they
came and filled both the boats, so that
they began to sink. 8But when Simon
Peter saw it, he fell down at Jesus' knees,
saying, "Depart from me, for I am a sinful
man, O Lord." 9For he was astonished, and
all that were with him, at the catch of fish
which they had taken; 10and so also were
James and John, sons of Zebedee, who
were partners with Simon. And Jesus said
to Simon, "Do not be afraid; henceforth
you will be catching men." 11And when
they had brought their boats to land, they
left everything and followed him.

The leper cleansed

12 While he was in one of the cities,
there came a man full of leprosy; and
when he saw Jesus, he fell on his face
and besought him, "Lord, if you will, you

[n] Other ancient authorities read *Galilee*

King James

13 And he put forth *his* hand, and touched him, saying, I will: be thou clean. And immediately the leprosy departed from him.

14 And he charged him to tell no man: but go, and shew thyself to the priest, and offer for thy cleansing, according as Moses commanded, for a testimony unto them.

15 But so much the more went there a fame abroad of him: and great multitudes came together to hear, and to be healed by him of their infirmities.

16 ¶ And he withdrew himself into the wilderness, and prayed.

17 And it came to pass on a certain day, as he was teaching, that there were Pharisees and doctors of the law sitting by, which were come out of every town of Galilee, and Judæa, and Jerusalem: and the power of the Lord was *present* to heal them.

18 ¶ And, behold, men brought in a bed a man which was taken with a palsy: and they sought *means* to bring him in, and to lay *him* before him.

19 And when they could not find by what *way* they might bring him in because of the multitude, they went upon the housetop, and let him down through the tiling with *his* couch into the midst before Jesus.

20 And when he saw their faith, he said unto him, Man, thy sins are forgiven thee.

21 And the scribes and the Pharisees began to reason, saying, Who is this which speaketh blasphemies? Who can forgive sins, but God alone?

22 But when Jesus perceived their thoughts, he answering said unto them, What reason ye in your hearts?

23 Whether is easier, to say, Thy sins be forgiven thee; or to say, Rise up and walk?

24 But that ye may know that the Son of man hath power upon earth to forgive sins, (he said unto the sick of the palsy,) I say unto thee, Arise, and take up thy couch, and go into thine house.

25 And immediately he rose up before them, and took up that whereon he lay, and departed to his own house, glorifying God.

26 And they were all amazed, and they glorified God, and were filled with fear, saying, We have seen strange things to-day.

27 ¶ And after these things he went forth, and saw a publican, named Levi, sitting at the receipt of custom: and he said unto him, Follow me.

28 And he left all, rose up, and followed him.

29 And Levi made him a great feast in his own house: and there was a great company of publicans and of others that sat down with them.

30 But their scribes and Pharisees murmured against his disciples, saying, Why do ye eat and drink with publicans and sinners?

31 And Jesus answering said unto them, They that are whole need not a physician; but they that are sick.

Amplified

13 And [Jesus] reached out His hand and touched him, saying, I will; be cleansed! And immediately the leprosy left him.

14 And [Jesus] charged him to tell no one ([a]that he might chance to meet), [b]Until, *He said,* you go and show yourself to the priest, and make an offering for your purification, as Moses commanded, for a testimony *and* proof to the people, that they may have evidence [of your healing]. [Lev. 13:49; 14:2-32.]

15 But so much the more the news spread abroad concerning Him and great crowds kept coming together to hear and to be healed by Him of their infirmities.

16 But He Himself withdrew [in retirement] to the wilderness (desert) and prayed.

17 One of those days, as He was teaching, there were Pharisees and teachers of the Law sitting by, who had come from every village *and* town of Galilee and Judea and from Jerusalem. And the power of the Lord was with Him ([c]present) to heal (them).

18 And behold, some men were bringing on a stretcher a man who was paralyzed, and they tried to carry him in and lay him before [Jesus].

19 But finding no way to bring him in, because of the crowd, they went up on the roof, and lowered him with his stretcher down through the tiles into the midst in front of Jesus.

20 And when He saw [their confidence in Him, springing from] their faith, He said, Man, your sins are forgiven you!

21 And the scribes and the Pharisees began to reason *and* question *and* argue, saying, Who is this [Man] Who speaks blasphemies? Who can forgive sins but God alone?

22 But Jesus, knowing their thoughts *and* questionings, answered them, Why do you question in your hearts?

23 Which is easier, to say, Your sins are forgiven you, or to say, Arise and walk (about)?

24 But that you may know that the Son of man has the ([d]power of) authority *and* right on earth to forgive sins, He said to the paralyzed man, I say to you, arise, pick up your litter (little bed), and go to your own house!

25 And instantly *the man* stood up before them, and picked up what he had been lying on, and went away to his house, [e]recognizing *and* praising *and* thanking God.

26 And overwhelming astonishment *and* ecstasy seized them all, and they [e]recognized *and* praised *and* thanked God, and they were filled with *and* controlled by reverential fear, and kept saying, We have seen wonderful *and* strange *and* incredible *and* unthinkable things today!

27 And after this Jesus went out and looked attentively at a tax collector named Levi, sitting at the tax office; and He said to him, Join Me as a disciple *and* side with My party *and* accompany Me.

28 And he forsook everything, and got up [and] followed Him—becoming His disciple and siding with His party.

29 And Levi [Matthew] made a great banquet for Him in his own house, and there was a large company of tax collectors and others who were reclining [at the table] with them.

30 Now the Pharisees and their scribes were grumbling against Jesus' disciples, saying. Why are you eating and drinking with tax collectors and pre-eminently sinful people?

31 And Jesus replied to them, It is not those who are healthy who need a physician, but those who are sick.

---

a) Vincent.
b) Trench.
c) Some ancient authorities so read.
d) Thayer.
e) Cremer.

Living New Testament

13 Jesus reached out and touched the man and said, "Of course I will. Be healed." And the leprosy left him instantly!

14 Then Jesus instructed him to go at once without telling anyone what had happened and be examined by the Jewish priest. "Offer the sacrifice Moses' law requires for lepers who are healed," He said. "This will prove to everyone that you are well."

15 Now the report of His power spread even faster and vast crowds came to hear Him preach and to be healed of their diseases.

16 But He often withdrew to the wilderness for prayer.

17 One day while He was teaching, some Jewish religious leaders[1] and teachers of the Law were sitting nearby. (It seemed that these men showed up from every village in all Galilee and Judea, as well as from Jerusalem.) And the Lord's healing power was upon Him.

18, 19 Then—look! Some men came carrying a paralyzed man on a sleeping mat. They tried to push through the crowd to Jesus but couldn't reach Him. So they went up on the roof above Him, took off some tiles and lowered the sick man down into the crowd, still on his sleeping mat, right in front of Jesus.

20 Seeing their faith, Jesus said to the man, "My friend, your sins are forgiven!"

21 "Who does this fellow think he is?" the Pharisees and teachers of the Law exclaimed among themselves. "This is blasphemy! Who but God can forgive sins?"

22 Jesus knew what they were thinking, and He replied, "Why is it blasphemy?

23 Is it any harder to forgive his sins than to heal him?

24 Now I will prove My[2] authority to forgive sin by demonstrating My power to heal disease." Then He said to the paralyzed man, "Get up, roll up your sleeping mat and go on home."

25 And immediately, as everyone watched, the man jumped to his feet, picked up his mat and went home praising God!

26 Everyone present was gripped with awe and fear. And they praised God, remarking over and over again, "We have seen strange things today."

27 Later on as Jesus left the town He saw a tax collector—with the usual reputation for cheating—sitting at a tax collection booth. The man's name was Levi. Jesus said to him, "Come and be one of My disciples!"

28 So Levi left everything, sprang up and went with Him!

29 Soon Levi held a reception in his home with Jesus as the guest of honor. Many of Levi's fellow tax collectors and other guests were there.

30 But the Pharisees and teachers of the Law complained bitterly to Jesus' disciples about His eating with such notorious sinners.

31 Jesus answered them, "It is the sick who need a doctor, not those in good health.

[1] Literally, "Pharisees."
[2] Literally, "the Son of Man's."

Revised Standard

can make me clean." [13]And he stretched out his hand, and touched him, saying, "I will; be clean." And immediately the leprosy left him. [14]And he charged him to tell no one; but "go and show yourself to the priest, and make an offering for your cleansing, as Moses commanded, for a proof to the people."[o] [15]But so much the more the report went abroad concerning him; and great multitudes gathered to hear and to be healed of their infirmities. [16]But he withdrew to the wilderness and prayed.

A paralytic healed and forgiven

17 On one of those days, as he was teaching, there were Pharisees and teachers of the law sitting by, who had come from every village of Galilee and Judea and from Jerusalem; and the power of the Lord was with him to heal.[p] [18]And behold, men were bringing on a bed a man who was paralyzed, and they sought to bring him in and lay him before Jesus;[q] [19]but finding no way to bring him in, because of the crowd, they went up on the roof and let him down with his bed through the tiles into the midst before Jesus. [20]And when he saw their faith he said, "Man, your sins are forgiven you." [21]And the scribes and the Pharisees began to question, saying, "Who is this that speaks blasphemies? Who can forgive sins but God only?" [22]When Jesus perceived their questionings, he answered them, "Why do you question in your hearts? [23]Which is easier, to say, 'Your sins are forgiven you,' or to say, 'Rise and walk'? [24]But that you may know that the Son of man has authority on earth to forgive sins"—he said to the man who was paralyzed—"I say to you, rise, take up your bed and go home." [25]And immediately he rose before them, and took up that on which he lay, and went home, glorifying God. [26]And amazement seized them all, and they glorified God and were filled with awe, saying, "We have seen strange things today."

The call of Levi

27 After this he went out, and saw a tax collector, named Levi, sitting at the tax office; and he said to him, "Follow me." [28]And he left everything, and rose and followed him.

29 And Levi made him a great feast in his house; and there was a large company of tax collectors and others sitting at table[r] with them. [30]And the Pharisees and their scribes murmured against his disciples, saying, "Why do you eat and drink with tax collectors and sinners?" [31]And Jesus answered them, "Those who are well have no need of a physician, but those who are

[o] Greek *to them*
[p] Other ancient authorities read *was present to heal them*
[q] Greek *him*
[r] Greek *reclining*

King James

32 I came not to call the righteous, but sinners to repentance.
33 ¶ And they said unto him, Why do the disciples of John fast often, and make prayers, and likewise *the disciples* of the Pharisees; but thine eat and drink?
34 And he said unto them, Can ye make the children of the bridechamber fast, while the bridegroom is with them?
35 But the days will come, when the bridegroom shall be taken away from them, and then shall they fast in those days.
36 ¶ And he spake also a parable unto them; No man putteth a piece of a new garment upon an old; if otherwise, then both the new maketh a rent, and the piece that was *taken* out of the new agreeth not with the old.
37 And no man putteth new wine into old bottles; else the new wine will burst the bottles, and be spilled, and the bottles shall perish.
38 But new wine must be put into new bottles; and both are preserved.
39 No man also having drunk old *wine* straightway desireth new: for he saith, The old is better.

Amplified

32 I have not come to arouse *and* invite *and* call the righteous, but [f]the erring ones ([g]those not free from sin) to repentance—[that is], [g]to change their minds for the better and heartily to amend their ways, with abhorrence of their past sins.
33 Then they said to Him, The disciples of John practice fasting often and offer up prayers of [special] petition, and so do [the disciples] of the Pharisees also, but Yours eat and drink.
34 And Jesus said to them, Can you make the wedding guests fast as long as the bridegroom is with them?
35 But the days will come when the bridegroom is taken from them, and then they will fast in those days.
36 He told them a [h]proverb also: No one puts a patch from a new garment on an old garment; if he does, he will both tear the new one, and the patch from the new [one] will not match the old [garment].
37 And no one pours new wine into old wineskins; if he does, the fresh wine will burst the skins and it will be spilled, and the skins will be ruined (destroyed).
38 But new wine must be put in fresh wineskins;
39 And no one after drinking old wine immediately desires new wine, for he says, The old is good *or* [i]better.

CHAPTER 6

AND it came to pass on the second sabbath after the first, that he went through the corn fields; and his disciples plucked the ears of corn, and did eat, rubbing *them* in *their* hands.
2 And certain of the Pharisees said unto them, Why do ye that which is not lawful to do on the sabbath days?
3 And Jesus answering them said, Have ye not read so much as this, what David did, when himself was an hungered, and they which were with him;
4 How he went into the house of God, and did take and eat the shewbread, and gave also to them that were with him; which it is not lawful to eat but for the priests alone?
5 And he said unto them, That the Son of man is Lord also of the sabbath.
6 And it came to pass also on another sabbath, that he entered into the synagogue and taught: and there was a man whose right hand was withered.
7 And the scribes and Pharisees watched him, whether he would heal on the sabbath day; that they might find an accusation against him.
8 But he knew their thoughts, and said to the man which had the withered hand, Rise up, and stand forth in the midst. And he arose and stood forth.
9 Then said Jesus unto them, I will ask you one thing; Is it lawful on the sabbath days to do good, or to do evil? to save life, or to destroy *it?*

CHAPTER 6

ONE Sabbath while Jesus was passing through the fields of standing grain, it occurred that His disciples picked some of the spikes and ate [of the grain], rubbing it out in their hands. [Deut. 23:25.]
2 But some of the Pharisees asked them, Why are you doing what is not permitted to be done on the Sabbath days? [Exod. 20:10; 23:12; Deut. 5:14.]
3 And Jesus replied to them saying, Have you never so much as read what David did when he was hungry, he and those who were with him? [I Sam. 21:1-6.]
4 How he went into the house of God, and took and ate the [sacred] loaves of the showbread, which it is not permitted for any except only the priests to eat, and also gave to those [who were] with him? [Lev. 24:9.]
5 And He said to them, The Son of man is Lord even over the Sabbath.
6 And it occurred on another Sabbath that when He went into the synagogue and taught, a man was present whose right hand was withered.
7 And the scribes and the Pharisees kept watching Jesus to see whether He would [actually] heal on the Sabbath, in order that they might get [some ground for] accusation against Him.
8 But He was aware all along of their thoughts, and He said to the man with the withered hand, Come and stand here in the midst. And he arose and stood there.
9 Then Jesus said to them, I ask you, is it lawful *and* right on the Sabbath to do good ([j]so that someone derives advantage from it), or to do evil? to save a life (and [k]make a soul safe) or to destroy it?

---

f) Young.
g) Thayer.
h) Abbott-Smith's "Manual Greek Lexicon of the New Testament."
i) Many ancient authorities read "better."
j) Cremer.
k) Wycliffe.

Living New Testament

32 My purpose is to invite sinners to turn from their sins, not to spend My time with those who think themselves already good enough."

33 Their next complaint was that Jesus' disciples were feasting instead of fasting. "John the Baptist's disciples are constantly going without food and praying," they declared, "and so do the disciples of the Pharisees. Why are yours wining and dining?"

34 Jesus asked, "Do happy men fast? Do wedding guests go hungry while celebrating with the groom?

35 But the time will come when the bridegroom will be killed;[3] then they won't want to eat."

36 Then Jesus used this illustration: "No one tears up unshrunk cloth to make patches for old clothes, for the new garment is ruined and the old one isn't helped when the patch tears out again.

37 And no one puts new wine into old wineskins, for the new wine bursts the old skins, ruining the skins and spilling the wine.

38 New wine must be put into new wineskins.

39 But no one after drinking the old wine seems to want the fresh and the new. 'The old ways are best,' they say."

Revised Standard

sick; 32 I have not come to call the righteous, but sinners to repentance."

The question about fasting

33 And they said to him, "The disciples
of John fast often and offer prayers, and
so do the disciples of the Pharisees, but
yours eat and drink." 34 And Jesus said to
them, "Can you make wedding guests fast
while the bridegroom is with them? 35 The
days will come, when the bridegroom is
taken away from them, and then they will
fast in those days." 36 He told them a
parable also: "No one tears a piece from
a new garment and puts it upon an old
garment; if he does, he will tear the new,
and the piece from the new will not match
the old. 37 And no one puts new wine into
old wine-skins; if he does, the new wine
will burst the skins and it will be spilled,
and the skins will be destroyed. 38 But new
wine must be put into fresh wineskins.
39 And no one after drinking old wine desires new; for he says, 'The old is good.' "[s]

CHAPTER 6

One Sabbath as Jesus and His disciples were walking through some grainfields, they were breaking off the heads of wheat, rubbing off the husks in their hands and eating the grains.

2 But some Pharisees said, "That's illegal! Your disciples are harvesting grain, and it's against the Jewish law to work on the Sabbath."

3 Jesus replied, "Don't you read the Scriptures? Haven't you ever read what King David did when he and his men were hungry?

4 He went into the Temple and took the shewbread, the special bread that was placed before the Lord, and ate it—illegal as this was—and shared it with others."

5 And Jesus added, "I[1] am master even of the Sabbath."

6 On another Sabbath He was in the synagogue teaching, and a man was present whose right hand was deformed.

7 The teachers of the Law and the Pharisees watched closely to see whether He would heal the man that day, since it was the Sabbath. For they were eager to find some charge to bring against Him.

8 How well He knew their thoughts! But He said to the man with the deformed hand, "Come and stand here where everyone can see." So he did.

9 Then Jesus said to the Pharisees and teachers of the Law. "I have a question for you. Is it right to do good on the Sabbath day, or to do harm? To save life, or to destroy it?"

Jesus the Lord of the Sabbath

6 On a sabbath,[t] while he was going
through the grainfields, his disciples
plucked and ate some ears of grain, rubbing them in their hands. 2 But some of
the Pharisees said, "Why are you doing
what is not lawful to do on the sabbath?"
3 And Jesus answered, "Have you not read
what David did when he was hungry, he
and those who were with him: 4 how he
entered the house of God, and took and
ate the bread of the Presence, which it is
not lawful for any but the priests to eat,
and also gave it to those with him?" 5 And
he said to them, "The Son of man is lord
of the sabbath."

Jesus heals on the Sabbath

6 On another sabbath, when he entered
the synagogue and taught, a man was there
whose right hand was withered. 7 And the
scribes and the Pharisees watched him, to
see whether he would heal on the sabbath,
so that they might find an accusation
against him. 8 But he knew their thoughts,
and he said to the man who had the withered hand, "Come and stand here." And
he rose and stood there. 9 And Jesus said
to them, "I ask you, is it lawful on the
sabbath to do good or to do harm, to save

---

[3] Literally, "taken away from them."
[1] Literally, "the Son of man."

[s] Other ancient authorities read *better*
[t] Other ancient authorities read *On the second first sabbath* (on the second sabbath after the first)

King James

10 And looking round about upon them all, he said unto the man, Stretch forth thy hand. And he did so: and his hand was restored whole as the other.

11 And they were filled with madness; and communed one with another what they might do to Jesus.

12 And it came to pass in those days, that he went out into a mountain to pray, and continued all night in prayer to God.

13 ¶ And when it was day, he called *unto him* his disciples: and of them he chose twelve, whom also he named apostles;

14 Simon, (whom he also named Peter,) and Andrew his brother, James and John, Philip and Bartholomew,

15 Matthew and Thomas, James the *son* of Alphæus, and Simon called Zelotes,

16 And Judas *the brother* of James, and Judas Iscariot, which also was the traitor.

17 ¶ And he came down with them, and stood in the plain, and the company of his disciples, and a great multitude of people out of all Judæa and Jerusalem, and from the sea coast of Tyre and Sidon, which came to hear him, and to be healed of their diseases;

18 And they that were vexed with unclean spirits: and they were healed.

19 And the whole multitude sought to touch him: for there went virtue out of him, and healed *them* all.

20 ¶ And he lifted up his eyes on his disciples, and said, Blessed *be ye* poor: for yours is the kingdom of God.

21 Blessed *are ye* that hunger now: for ye shall be filled. Blessed *are ye* that weep now: for ye shall laugh.

22 Blessed are ye, when men shall hate you, and when they shall separate you *from their company,* and shall reproach *you,* and cast out your name as evil, for the Son of man's sake.

23 Rejoice ye in that day, and leap for joy: for, behold, your reward *is* great in heaven: for in the like manner did their fathers unto the prophets.

24 But woe unto you that are rich! for ye have received your consolation.

25 Woe unto you that are full! for ye shall hunger. Woe unto you that laugh now! for ye shall mourn and weep.

Amplified

10 Then He glanced around at them all, and said to tl man, Stretch out your hand! And he did so, and his har was fully restored *like the other one.*

11 But they were filled with lack of understanding *an* senseless rage, and discussed (consulted) with one anoth what they might do to Jesus.

12 Now in those days it occurred that He went up in a mountain to pray, and spent the whole night in pray to God.

13 And when it was day, He summoned His disciple and selected from them twelve, whom He named apostl (special messengers).

14 They were Simon, whom He named Peter, and h brother Andrew, and James and John, and Philip an Bartholomew,

15 And Matthew and Thomas, and James the son Alphaeus, and Simon who was called the Zealot,

16 And Judas the son of James, and Judas Iscario who became a traitor—a treacherous, basely faithless pe son.

17 And Jesus came down with them and took His stan on a level spot, with a great crowd of His disciples and vast throng of people from all over Judea and Jerusale and the seacoast of Tyre and Sidon, who came to listen Him and to be cured of their diseases;

18 Even those who were disturbed *and* troubled wi unclean spirits, and they were being healed [also].

19 And all the multitude were seeking to touch Hin for healing power was all the while going forth from Hi and cured them all [that is, [l]saving them from sever illnesses or calamities].

20 And solemnly lifting up His eyes on His disciples H said: Blessed—happy [[m]with life-joy and satisfaction God's favor and salvation, apart from your outward co dition] and [n]to be envied—are you poor *and* [o]lowly *an* afflicted (destitute of wealth, influence, position and hor ors), for the kingdom of God is yours!

21 Blessed—happy [[m]with life-joy and satisfaction God's favor and salvation, apart from your outward co dition] and [n]to be envied—are you that hunger *and* see with eager desire now, for you shall be filled *and* con pletely satisfied! Blessed—happy [[p]with life-joy and sati faction in God's favor and salvation, apart from you outward condition] and [q]to be envied—are you who wee *and* sob now, for you shall laugh!

22 Blessed—happy [[p]with life-joy and satisfaction God's favor and salvation, apart from your outward cor dition] and [q]to be envied—are you when people despis (hate) you, and when they exclude *and* excommunica you (as disreputable), and revile *and* denounce you, an defame *and* cast out *and* spurn your name as evil (wick ed) on account of the Son of man.

23 Rejoice *and* be glad at such a time, and exult *an* leap for joy, for behold, your reward is rich *and* great *an* strong *and* intense *and* abundant in heaven; for even s their forefathers treated the prophets.

24 But woe to (alas for) you rich—[r]abounding in mate rial resources—for you already are receiving your cons lation [the solace and sense of strengthening and chee that come from prosperity]; and have taken *and* enjoye your comfort in full [having nothing left to be awarde you].

25 Woe to (alas for) you who are full now— completely filled, luxuriously gorged and satiated; for yo shall hunger *and* suffer want! Woe to (alas for) you th laugh now, for you shall mourn and weep *and* wail!

l) Vincent.
m) Cremer.
n) Souter.
o) Thayer.
p) Cremer.
q) Souter.
r) Thayer.

Living New Testament

10 He looked around at them one by one and then said to the man, "Reach out your hand." And as he did, it became completely normal again!

11 At this, the enemies of Jesus were wild with rage, and began to plot His murder.

* * * * *

12 One day soon afterwards He went out into the mountains to pray, and prayed all night.

13 At daybreak He called together His followers and chose twelve of them to be the inner circle of His disciples. (They were appointed as His "apostles," or "missionaries.")

14, 15, 16 Here are their names:
Simon (He also called him Peter),
Andrew (Simon's brother),
James,
John,
Philip,
Bartholomew,
Matthew,
Thomas,
James (the son of Alphaeus),
Simon (also called "Zealotes"),
Judas (son of James),
Judas Iscariot (who later betrayed Him).

17, 18 When they came down from the slopes of the mountain, they stood with Jesus on a large, level area, surrounded by many of His followers who, in turn, were surrounded by the crowds. For people from all over Judea and from Jerusalem and from as far north as the seacoasts of Tyre and Sidon had come to hear Him or to be healed. And He cast out many demons.

19 Everyone was trying to touch Him, for when they did, healing power went out from Him and they were cured.

20 Then He turned to His disciples and said, "What happiness there is for you who are poor, for the Kingdom of God is yours!

21 What happiness there is for you who are now hungry, for you are going to be satisfied! What happiness there is for you who weep, for the time will come when you shall laugh with joy!

22 What happiness it is when others hate you and exclude you and insult you and smear your name because you are Mine![2]

23 When that happens, rejoice! Yes, leap for joy! For you will have a great reward awaiting you in heaven. And you will be in good company—the ancient prophets were treated that way too!

24 But, oh, the sorrows that await the rich. For they have their only happiness down here.

25 They are fat and prosperous now, but a time of awful hunger is before them. Their careless laughter now means sorrow then.

Revised Standard

life or to destroy it?" [10]And he looked
around on them all, and said to him,
"Stretch out your hand." And he did so,
and his hand was restored. [11]But they were
filled with fury and discussed with one another what they might do to Jesus.

The choosing of the twelve

12 In these days he went out into the
hills to pray; and all night he continued
in prayer to God. [13]And when it was day,
he called his disciples, and chose from them
twelve, whom he named apostles; [14]Simon,
whom he named Peter, and Andrew his
brother, and James and John, and Philip,
and Bartholomew, [15]and Matthew, and
Thomas, and James the son of Alphaeus,
and Simon who was called the Zealot, [16]and
Judas the son of James, and Judas Iscariot,
who became a traitor.

The sermon on the plain

17 And he came down with them and
stood on a level place, with a great crowd
of his disciples and a great multitude of
people from all Judea and Jerusalem and
the seacoast of Tyre and Sidon, who came
to hear him and to be healed of their diseases;
[18]and those who were troubled with
unclean spirits were cured. [19]And all the
crowd sought to touch him, for power came
forth from him and healed them all.

Beatitudes and woes

20 And he lifted up his eyes on his disciples, and said:
"Blessed are you poor, for yours is the kingdom of God.

21 "Blessed are you that hunger now, for you shall be satisfied.
"Blessed are you that weep now, for you shall laugh.

22 "Blessed are you when men hate
you, and when they exclude you and revile
you, and cast out your name as evil, on
account of the Son of man! [23]Rejoice in
that day, and leap for joy, for behold, your
reward is great in heaven; for so their
fathers did to the prophets.

24 "But woe to you that are rich, for you have received your consolation.

25 "Woe to you that are full now, for you shall hunger.
"Woe to you that laugh now, for you shall mourn and weep.

[2] Literally, "the Son of man."

King James

26 Woe unto you, when all men shall speak well of you! for so did their fathers to the false prophets.

27 ¶ But I say unto you which hear, Love your enemies, do good to them which hate you,

28 Bless them that curse you, and pray for them which despitefully use you.

29 And unto him that smiteth thee on the *one* cheek offer also the other; and him that taketh away thy cloak forbid not *to take thy* coat also.

30 Give to every man that asketh of thee; and of him that taketh away thy goods ask *them* not again.

31 And as ye would that men should do to you, do ye also to them likewise.

32 For if ye love them which love you, what thank have ye? for sinners also love those that love them.

33 And if ye do good to them which do good to you, what thank have ye? for sinners also do even the same.

34 And if ye lend *to them* of whom ye hope to receive, what thank have ye? for sinners also lend to sinners, to receive as much again.

35 But love ye your enemies, and do good, and lend, hoping for nothing again; and your reward shall be great, and ye shall be the children of the Highest: for he is kind unto the unthankful and *to* the evil.

36 Be ye therefore merciful, as your Father also is merciful.

37 Judge not, and ye shall not be judged: condemn not, and ye shall not be condemned: forgive, and ye shall be forgiven:

38 Give, and it shall be given unto you; good measure, pressed down, and shaken together, and running over, shall men give into your bosom. For with the same measure that ye mete withal it shall be measured to you again.

39 And he spake a parable unto them, Can the blind lead the blind? shall they not both fall into the ditch?

40 The disciple is not above his master: but every one that is perfect shall be as his master.

41 And why beholdest thou the mote that is in thy brother's eye, but perceivest not the beam that is in thine own eye?

Amplified

26 Woe to (alas for) you when everyone speaks fairly *and* handsomely of you *and* praises you, for even so their forefathers did to the false prophets.

27 But I say to you who are listening now to Me ([s]in order to heed, make it a practice to) love your enemies; treat well (do good to, act nobly toward) those who detest you *and* pursue you with hatred.

28 Invoke blessings upon *and* pray for the happiness of those who curse you; implore God's blessing (favor) upon those who abuse you—who revile, reproach, disparage and high-handedly misuse you.

29 To the one who strikes you on the [t]jaw *or* cheek, offer the other [t]jaw *or* cheek also; and from him who takes away your outer garment, do not withhold your undergarment as well.

30 Give away to every one who begs of you [who is [t]in want of necessities]; and of him who takes away from you your goods, do not demand *or* require them back again.

31 And as you would like *and* desire that men would do to you, do exactly so to them.

32 If you [merely] love those who love you, what [u]quality of credit *and* thanks is that to you? For even [v]the [very] sinners love their lovers—those who love them.

33 And if you are kind *and* good *and* do favors to *and* benefit those who are kind *and* good *and* do favors to *and* benefit you, what [u]quality of credit *and* thanks is that to you? For even [t]the pre-eminently sinful do the same.

34 And if you lend money [u]at interest to those from whom you hope to receive, what [u]quality of credit *and* thanks is that to you? Even notorious sinners lend money [u]at interest to sinners, so as to recover as much again.

35 But love your enemies, and be kind *and* do good—doing favors [w]so that someone derives benefit from them; and lend expecting *and* hoping for nothing in return, *but* [x]considering nothing as lost *and* [y]despairing of no one; and then your recompense (your reward) will be great—rich, strong, intense and abundant—and you will be sons of the Most High; for He is kind *and* charitable *and* good to the ungrateful *and* the selfish and wicked.

36 So be merciful—sympathetic, tender, responsive and compassionate—even as your Father is [all these].

37 Judge not—neither pronouncing judgment nor subjecting to censure—and you will not be judged; do not condemn *and* pronounce guilty, and you will not be condemned *and* pronounced guilty; acquit *and* forgive *and* [z]release (give up resentment, let it drop), and you will be acquitted *and* forgiven *and* [z]released.

38 Give, and [gifts] will be given you, good measure, pressed down, shaken together and running over will they pour [x]into [the pouch formed by] the bosom [of your robe and used as a bag]. For with the measure you deal out—that is, with the measure you use when you confer benefits on others—it will be measured back to you.

39 He further told them [a]a proverb: Can a blind [man] guide *and* direct a blind [man]? Will they not both stumble into a ditch or a [b]hole in the ground?

40 A pupil is not superior to his teacher, but every one [when he is] completely trained—readjusted, restored, set to rights and perfected—will be like his teacher.

41 Why do you see the speck that is in your brother's eye, but do not notice *or* consider the beam [of timber] that is in your own eye?

---

s) Vincent.
t) Thayer.
u) Vincent.
v) Tyndale.
w) Cremer.
x) Vincent.
y) Some ancient authorities so read.
z) Literal meaning.
a) Abbott-Smith.
b) Souter.

Living New Testament

26 And what sadness is ahead for those praised by the crowds—for *false* prophets have *always* been praised.

27 Listen, all of you. Love your *enemies*. Do *good* to those who *hate* you.

28 Pray for the happiness of those who *curse* you; implore God's blessing on those who *hurt* you.

29 If someone slaps you on one cheek, let him slap the other too! If someone demands your coat, give him your shirt besides.

30 Give what you have to anyone who asks you for it; and when things are taken away from you, don't worry about getting them back.

31 Treat others as you want them to treat you.

32 Do you think you deserve credit for merely loving those who love you? Even the godless do that!

33 And if you do good only to those who do you good—is that so wonderful? Even sinners do that much!

34 And if you lend money only to those who repay you, what good is that? Even the most wicked will lend to their own kind for full return!

35 Love your *enemies!* Do good to *them!* Lend to *them!* And don't be concerned about the fact that they won't repay. Then your reward from heaven will be very great, and you will truly be acting as sons of God: for He is kind to the *unthankful* and to those who are *very wicked.*

36 Try to show as much compassion as your Father does.

37 Never criticize or condemn—or it will all come back on you. Go easy on others; then they will do the same for you.[3]

38 For if you give, you will get! Your gift will return to you in full and overflowing measure, pressed down, shaken together to make room for more, and running over. Whatever measure you use to give—large or small—will be used to measure what is given back to you."

39 Here are some of the story-illustrations Jesus used in His sermons: "What good is it for one blind man to lead another? He will fall into a ditch and pull the other down with him.

40 How can a student know more than his teacher? But if he works hard, he may learn as much.

41 And why quibble about the speck in someone else's eye—his little fault[4]—when a board is in your own?

[3] Literally, "release, and you shall be released."
[4] Implied.

Revised Standard

26 "Woe to you, when all men speak well of you, for so their fathers did to the false prophets.

The law of love

27 "But I say to you that hear, Love
your enemies, do good to those who hate
you, [28]bless those who curse you, pray for
those who abuse you. [29]To him who strikes
you on the cheek, offer the other also; and
from him who takes away your cloak do
not withhold your coat as well. [30]Give to
every one who begs from you; and of him
who takes away your goods do not ask
them again. [31]And as you wish that men
would do to you, do so to them.

32 "If you love those who love you,
what credit is that to you? For even sinners love those who love them. [33]And if
you do good to those who do good to you,
what credit is that to you? For even sinners
do the same. [34]And if you lend to those
from whom you hope to receive, what
credit is that to you? Even sinners lend
to sinners, to receive as much again. [35]But
love your enemies, and do good, and lend,
expecting nothing in return;[v] and your reward will be great, and you will be sons
of the Most High; for he is kind to the
ungrateful and the selfish. [36]Be merciful,
even as your Father is merciful.

The teaching about judging others

37 "Judge not, and you will not be
judged; condemn not, and you will not
be condemned; forgive, and you will be
forgiven; [38]give, and it will be given to
you; good measure, pressed down, shaken
together, running over, will be put into
your lap. For the measure you give will be
the measure you get back."

39 He also told them a parable: "Can
a blind man lead a blind man? Will they
not both fall into a pit? [40]A disciple is not
above his teacher, but every one when he
is fully taught will be like his teacher.
[41]Why do you see the speck that is in
your brother's eye, but do not notice the
log that is in your own eye? [42]Or how can

[v] Other ancient authorities read *despairing of no man*

King James

42 Either how canst thou say to thy brother, Brother, let me pull out the mote that is in thine eye, when thou thyself beholdest not the beam that is in thine own eye? Thou hypocrite, cast out first the beam out of thine own eye, and then shalt thou see clearly to pull out the mote that is in thy brother's eye.

43 For a good tree bringeth not forth corrupt fruit; neither doth a corrupt tree bring forth good fruit.

44 For every tree is known by his own fruit. For of thorns men do not gather figs, nor of a bramble bush gather they grapes.

45 A good man out of the good treasure of his heart bringeth forth that which is good; and an evil man out of the evil treasure of his heart bringeth forth that which is evil: for of the abundance of the heart his mouth speaketh.

46 ¶ And why call ye me, Lord, Lord, and do not the things which I say?

47 Whosoever cometh to me, and heareth my sayings, and doeth them, I will shew you to whom he is like:

48 He is like a man which built an house, and digged deep, and laid the foundation on a rock: and when the flood arose, the stream beat vehemently upon that house, and could not shake it: for it was founded upon a rock.

49 But he that heareth, and doeth not, is like a man that without a foundation built an house upon the earth; against which the stream did beat vehemently, and immediately it fell; and the ruin of that house was great.

Amplified

42 Or how can you say to your brother, Brother, allow me to take out the speck that is in your eye, when you yourself do not see the beam that is in your own eye? You actor—pretender, hypocrite! First take the beam out of your own eye, and then you will see clearly to take out the speck that is in your brother's eye.

43 For there is no good (healthy) tree that bears decayed (worthless, stale) fruit; nor on the other hand does a decayed (worthless, sickly) tree bear good fruit.

44 For each tree is known *and* identified by its own fruit; for figs are not gathered from thornbushes, nor is a cluster of grapes picked from a bramblebush.

45 The upright (honorable, intrinsically good) man out of the good treasure [stored] in his heart produces what is upright (honorable and intrinsically good); and the evil man out of the evil storehouse brings forth that which is depraved (wicked and intrinsically evil), for out of the abundance (overflow) of the heart his mouth speaks.

46 Why do you call Me, Lord, Lord, and do not [practice] what I tell you?

47 For every one who comes to Me and listens to My words (in order to heed their teaching) and does them, I will show you what he is like:

48 He is like a man building a house, who dug and went down deep, and laid a foundation upon the rock; and when a flood arose, the torrent broke against that house and could not shake *or* move it, because it had been securely built—[c]founded on a rock.

49 But he who merely hears, and does not practice doing My words, is like a man who built a house on the ground, without a foundation; against which the torrent burst and immediately it collapsed *and* fell, and the breaking *and* ruin of that house was great.

CHAPTER 7 (King James)

NOW when he had ended all his sayings in the audience of the people, he entered into Capernaum.

2 And a certain centurion's servant, who was dear unto him, was sick, and ready to die.

3 And when he heard of Jesus, he sent unto him the elders of the Jews, beseeching him that he would come and heal his servant.

4 And when they came to Jesus, they besought him instantly, saying, That he was worthy for whom he should do this:

5 For he loveth our nation, and he hath built us a synagogue.

6 Then Jesus went with them. And when he was now not far from the house, the centurion sent friends to him, saying unto him, Lord, trouble not thyself: for I am not worthy that thou shouldest enter under my roof:

7 Wherefore neither thought I myself worthy to come unto thee: but say in a word, and my servant shall be healed.

CHAPTER 7 (Amplified)

AFTER Jesus had finished all that He had to say in the hearing of the people [on the mountain], He entered Capernaum.

2 Now a centurion had a bond servant who was held in honor *and* highly valued by him, who was sick and at the point of death.

3 And when the centurion heard of Jesus, he sent some Jewish elders to Him, requesting Him to come and make his bond servant well.

4 And when they reached Jesus, they begged Him earnestly, saying, He is worthy that You should do this for him,

5 For he loves our nation, and he built us our synagogue [at his own expense].

6 And Jesus went with them. But when He was not far from the house, the centurion sent [some] friends to Him, saying, Lord, do not trouble [Yourself], for I am not [d]sufficiently worthy to have You come under my roof;

7 Neither did I consider myself worthy to come to You. But [just] speak a word, and my servant boy will be healed.

---

c) Alternate reading.
d) Literal reading, "sufficient."

Living New Testament

42 How can you think of saying to him, 'Brother, let me help you get rid of that speck in your eye,' when you can't see past the board in yours? Hypocrite! First get rid of the board, and then perhaps you can see well enough to deal with his speck!

43 A tree from good stock doesn't produce scrub fruit nor do trees from poor stock produce choice fruit.

44 A tree is identified by the kind of fruit it produces. Figs never grow on thorns, or grapes on bramble bushes!

45 A good man produces good deeds from a good heart. And an evil man produces evil deeds from his hidden wickedness. Whatever is in the heart overflows into speech.

46 So why do you call Me 'Lord' when you won't obey Me?

47, 48 But all those who come and listen and obey Me are like a man who builds a house on a strong foundation laid upon the underlying rock. When the floodwaters rise and break against the house, it stands firm, for it is strongly built.

49 But those who listen and don't obey are like a man who builds a house without a foundation. When the floods sweep down against that house, it crumbles into a heap of ruins."

Revised Standard

you say to your brother, 'Brother, let me
take out the speck that is in your eye,'
when you yourself do not see the log
that is in your own eye? You hypocrite,
first take the log out of your own eye, and
then you will see clearly to take out the
speck that is in your brother's eye.
43 "For no good tree bears bad fruit,
nor again does a bad tree bear good fruit;
44for each tree is known by its own fruit.
For figs are not gathered from thorns, nor
are grapes picked from a bramble bush.
45The good man out of the good treasure
of his heart produces good, and the evil
man out of his evil treasure produces evil;
for out of the abundance of the heart his
mouth speaks.

The wise and foolish builders

46 "Why do you call me 'Lord, Lord,'
and not do what I tell you? 47Every one
who comes to me and hears my words and
does them, I will show you what he is like:
48he is like a man building a house, who
dug deep, and laid the foundation upon
rock; and when a flood arose, the stream
broke against that house, and could not
shake it, because it had been well built.[w]
49But he who hears and does not do them
is like a man who built a house on the
ground without a foundation; against which
the stream broke, and immediately it fell,
and the ruin of that house was great."

CHAPTER 7

When Jesus had finished His sermon He went back into the city of Capernaum.

2 Just at that time the highly prized slave of a Roman[1] army captain was sick and near death.

3 When the captain heard about Jesus, he sent some respected Jewish elders to ask Him to come and heal his slave.

4 So they began pleading earnestly with Jesus to come with them and help the man. They told Him what a wonderful person the captain was. "If anyone deserves your help, it is he," they said,

5 "For he loves the Jews and even paid personally to build us a synagogue!"

6, 7 Jesus went with them; but just before arriving at the house, the captain sent some friends to say, "Sir, don't inconvenience Yourself by coming to my home, for I am not worthy of any such honor or even to come and meet You. Just speak a word from where You are, and my servant boy will be healed!

[1] Implied.

The centurion's servant healed

7 After he had ended all his sayings in
the hearing of the people he entered
Capernaum. 2Now a centurion had a
slave who was dear[x] to him, who was sick
and at the point of death. 3When he heard
of Jesus, he sent to him elders of the Jews,
asking him to come and heal his slave.
4And when they came to Jesus, they besought him earnestly, saying, "He is worthy
to have you do this for him, 5for he loves
our nation, and he built us our synagogue."
6And Jesus went with them. When he was
not far from the house, the centurion sent
friends to him, saying to him, "Lord, do
not trouble yourself, for I am not worthy
to have you come under my roof; 7there-
fore I did not presume to come to you.
But say the word, and let my servant be

[w] Other ancient authorities read *founded upon the rock*
[x] Or *valuable*

King James

8 For I also am a man set under authority, having under me soldiers, and I say unto one, Go, and he goeth; and to another, Come, and he cometh; and to my servant, Do this, and he doeth *it*.

9 When Jesus heard these things, he marvelled at him, and turned him about, and said unto the people that followed him, I say unto you, I have not found so great faith, no, not in Israel.

10 And they that were sent, returning to the house, found the servant whole that had been sick.

11 ¶ And it came to pass the day after, that he went into a city called Nain; and many of his disciples went with him, and much people.

12 Now when he came nigh to the gate of the city, behold, there was a dead man carried out, the only son of his mother, and she was a widow: and much people of the city was with her.

13 And when the Lord saw her, he had compassion on her, and said unto her, Weep not.

14 And he came and touched the bier: and they that bare *him* stood still. And he said, Young man, I say unto thee, Arise.

15 And he that was dead sat up, and began to speak. And he delivered him to his mother.

16 And there came a fear on all: and they glorified God, saying, That a great prophet is risen up among us; and, That God hath visited his people.

17 And this rumour of him went forth throughout all Judæa, and throughout all the region round about.

18 And the disciples of John shewed him of all these things.

19 ¶ And John calling *unto him* two of his disciples sent *them* to Jesus, saying, Art thou he that should come? or look we for another?

20 When the men were come unto him, they said, John Baptist hath sent us unto thee, saying, Art thou he that should come? or look we for another?

21 And in that same hour he cured many of *their* infirmities and plagues, and of evil spirits; and unto many *that were* blind he gave sight.

22 Then Jesus answering said unto them, Go your way, and tell John what things ye have seen and heard; how that the blind see, the lame walk, the lepers are cleansed, the deaf hear, the dead are raised, to the poor the gospel is preached.

23 And blessed is *he*, whosoever shall not be offended in me.

24 ¶ And when the messengers of John were departed, he began to speak unto the people concerning John, What went ye out into the wilderness for to see? A reed shaken with the wind?

25 But what went ye out for to see? A man clothed in soft raiment? Behold, they which are gorgeously apparelled, and live delicately, are in kings' courts.

26 But what went ye out for to see? A prophet? Yea, I say unto you, and much more than a prophet.

Amplified

8 For I also am a man daily subject to authority, with soldiers under me; and I say to one, Go, and he goes; and to another, Come, and he comes; and to my bond servant, Do this, and he does it.

9 Now when Jesus heard this He marveled at him, and He turned and said to the crowd that followed Him, I tell you, not even in [all] Israel have I found such great faith [as this].

10 And when the messengers who had been sent returned to the house, they found the bond servant *who had been ill* quite well again.

11 [e]Soon afterward Jesus went to a town called Nain, and His disciples and a great throng accompanied Him.

12 [Just] as He drew near the gate of the town, behold, a man who had died was being carried out, the only son of his mother, and she was a widow; and a large gathering from the town was accompanying her.

13 And when the Lord saw her, He had compassion on her and said to her, Do not weep.

14 And He went forward and touched the funeral couch, and the pallbearers stood still. And He said, Young man, I say to you, arise [[f]from death]!

15 And the man [who was] dead sat up, and began to speak. And [Jesus] gave him [back] to his mother.

16 Profound *and* reverent fear seized them all; and they began [g]to recognize God *and* praise *and* give thanks, saying, A great prophet has appeared among us! And God has visited His people (in order to help and care for and provide for them)!

17 And this report concerning [Jesus] spread through the whole of Judea and all the country round about. [I Kings 17:17-24; II Kings 4:32-37.]

18 And John's disciples brought him [now in prison] word of all these things.

19 And John summoned to him a certain two of his disciples and sent them to the Lord saying, Are You He Who is to come, or shall we (continue to) look for another?

20 So the men came to Jesus and said, John the Baptist sent us to You to ask, Are You the One Who is to come, or shall we (continue to) look for another?

21 In that very hour Jesus was healing many of sicknesses and distressing bodily plagues and evil spirits, and to many who were blind He gave ([h]a free, gracious, joy-giving gift of) sight.

22 So He replied to them, Go and tell John what you have seen and heard: the blind are receiving their sight; the lame are walking; the lepers are cleansed; the deaf are hearing; the dead are raised up, and the poor have the good news (the Gospel) preached to them. [Isa. 29:18, 19; 35:5, 6; 61:1.]

23 And blessed—happy [[i]with life-joy and satisfaction in God's favor and salvation apart from outward conditions] and [j]to be envied—is he who takes no offense in Me *and* who is not hurt *or* resentful *or* annoyed *or* repelled *or* made to stumble, [[h]whatever may occur].

24 And the messengers of John having departed, Jesus began to speak to the crowds about John: What did you go out into the desert to gaze on? A reed shaken *and* swayed by the wind?

25 Then what did you go out to see? A man dressed up in soft garments? Behold, those who wear fine apparel and live in luxury are in the courts *or* palaces of kings.

26 What then did you go out to see? A prophet—a forth-teller? Yes, I tell you, and far more than a prophet.

---

e) Many ancient authorities read "the next day."
f) Cremer.
g) Thayer.
h) Vincent.
i) Cremer.
j) Souter.

Living New Testament

8 I know, because I am under the authority of my superior officers, and I have authority over my men. I only need to say 'Go!' and they go; or 'Come!' and they come; and to my slave, 'Do this or that,' and he does it. [So just say, 'Be healed!' and my servant will be well again!"[2]]

9 Jesus was amazed. Turning to the crowd He said, "Never among all the Jews in Israel have I met a man with faith like this."

10 And when the captain's friends returned to his house, they found the slave completely healed!

11 Not long afterwards Jesus went with His disciples to the village of Nain, with the usual great crowd at His heels.

12 A funeral procession was coming out as He approached the village gate. The boy who had died was the only son of his widowed mother, and many mourners from the village were with her.

13 When the Lord saw her, His heart overflowed with sympathy. "Don't cry!" He said.

14 Then He walked over to the coffin and touched it, and the bearers stopped. "Laddie," He said, "come back to life again."

15 Then the boy sat up and began to talk to those around him! And Jesus gave him back to his mother.

16 A great fear swept the crowd, and they exclaimed with praises to God, "A mighty prophet has risen among us," and, "We have seen the hand of God at work today."

17 The report of what He did that day raced from end to end of Judea and even out across the borders.

18 The disciples of John the Baptist soon heard of all that Jesus was doing. When they told John about it,

19 He sent two of his disciples to Jesus to ask Him, "Are You really the Messiah?[3] Or shall we keep on looking for Him?"

20, 21, 22 The two disciples found Jesus while He was curing many sick people of their various diseases—healing the lame and the blind and casting out evil spirits. When they asked Him John's question, this was His reply: "Go back to John and tell him all you have seen and heard here today: how those who were blind can see! The lame are walking without a limp! The lepers are completely healed! The deaf can hear again! The dead come back to life! And the poor are hearing the Good News!

23 And tell him, 'Blessed is the one who does not lose his faith in Me.' "[4]

24 After they left, Jesus talked to the crowd about John. "Who is this man you went out into the Judean wilderness to see?" He asked. "Did you find him weak as grass, moved by every breath of wind?

25 Did you find him dressed in expensive clothes? No! Men who live in luxury are found in palaces, not out in the wilderness.

26 But did you find a prophet? Yes! And more than a prophet.

[2] This sentence implied from the previous verse.
[3] Literally, "the one who is coming."
[4] Literally, "Blessed is he who keeps from stumbling over Me."

Revised Standard

healed. 8For I am a man set under authority, with soldiers under me: and I say to
one, 'Go,' and he goes; and to another,
'Come,' and he comes; and to my slave,
'Do this,' and he does it." 9When Jesus
heard this he marveled at him, and turned
and said to the multitude that followed
him, "I tell you, not even in Israel have I
found such faith." 10And when those who
had been sent returned to the house, they
found the slave well.

The raising of the widow's son

11 Soon afterward[y] he went to a city
called Nain, and his disciples and a great
crowd went with him. 12As he drew near
to the gate of the city, behold, a man who had
died was being carried out, the only son
of his mother, and she was a widow; and
a large crowd from the city was with her.
13And when the Lord saw her, he had compassion on her and said to her, "Do not
weep." 14And he came and touched the
bier, and the bearers stood still. And he
said, "Young man, I say to you, arise."
15And the dead man sat up, and began to
speak. And he gave him to his mother.
16Fear seized them all; and they glorified
God, saying, "A great prophet has arisen
among us!" and "God has visited his people!" 17And this report concerning him
spread through the whole of Judea and
all the surrounding country.

Tribute to John the Baptist

18 The disciples of John told him of all
these things. 19And John, calling to him
two of his disciples, sent them to the Lord,
saying, "Are you he who is to come, or
shall we look for another?" 20And when
the men had come to him, they said, "John
the Baptist has sent us to you, saying, 'Are
you he who is to come, or shall we look
for another?' " 21In that hour he cured
many of diseases and plagues and evil spirits, and on many that were blind he bestowed sight. 22And he answered them,
"Go and tell John what you have seen and
heard: the blind receive their sight, the
lame walk, lepers are cleansed, and the deaf
hear, the dead are raised up, the poor have
good news preached to them. 23And blessed
is he who takes no offense at me."
24 When the messengers of John had
gone, he began to speak to the crowds concerning John: "What did you go out into
the wilderness to behold? A reed shaken
by the wind? 25What then did you go out
to see? A man clothed in soft raiment?
Behold, those who are gorgeously appareled
and live in luxury are in kings' courts.

[y] Other ancient authorities read *Next day*

King James

27 This is *he*, of whom it is written, Behold, I send my messenger before thy face, which shall prepare thy way before thee.

28 For I say unto you, Among those that are born of women there is not a greater prophet than John the Baptist: but he that is least in the kingdom of God is greater than he.

29 And all the people that heard *him*, and the publicans, justified God, being baptized with the baptism of John.

30 But the Pharisees and lawyers rejected the counsel of God against themselves, being not baptized of him.

31 ¶ And the Lord said, Whereunto then shall I liken the men of this generation? and to what are they like?

32 They are like unto children sitting in the marketplace, and calling one to another, and saying, We have piped unto you, and ye have not danced; we have mourned to you, and ye have not wept.

33 For John the Baptist came neither eating bread nor drinking wine; and ye say, He hath a devil.

34 The Son of man is come eating and drinking; and ye say, Behold a gluttonous man, and a winebibber, a friend of publicans and sinners!

35 But wisdom is justified of all her children.

36 ¶ And one of the Pharisees desired him that he would eat with him. And he went into the Pharisee's house, and sat down to meat.

37 And, behold, a woman in the city, which was a sinner, when she knew that *Jesus* sat at meat in the Pharisee's house, brought an alabaster box of ointment,

38 And stood at his feet behind *him* weeping, and began to wash his feet with tears, and did wipe *them* with the hairs of her head, and kissed his feet, and anointed *them* with the ointment.

39 Now when the Pharisee which had bidden him saw *it*, he spake within himself, saying, This man, if he were a prophet, would have known who and what manner of woman *this is* that toucheth him: for she is a sinner.

40 And Jesus answering said unto him, Simon, I have somewhat to say unto thee. And he saith, Master, say on.

41 There was a certain creditor which had two debtors: the one owed five hundred pence, and the other fifty.

42 And when they had nothing to pay, he frankly forgave them both. Tell me therefore, which of them will love him most?

43 Simon answered and said, I suppose that *he*, to whom he forgave most. And he said unto him, Thou hast rightly judged.

44 And he turned to the woman, and said unto Simon, Seest thou this woman? I entered into thine house, thou gavest me no water for my feet: but she hath washed my feet with tears, and wiped *them* with the hairs of her head.

45 Thou gavest me no kiss: but this woman since the time I came in hath not ceased to kiss my feet.

Amplified

27 This is he concerning whom it is written, Behold, I send My messenger before Your face, who shall make ready Your way before You. [Mal. 3:1.]

28 I tell you, among those born of women there is not a greater than John; but [k]he that is inferior [to the other citizens] in the kingdom of God is greater [in incomparable privilege] than he.

29 And all the people who heard Him, even the tax collectors, acknowledged the justice of God [in [k]calling them to repentance, and in pronouncing future wrath on the impenitent], being baptized with the baptism of John;

30 But the Pharisees and the lawyers [of the Mosaic Law] annulled *and* rejected *and* brought to nothing God's purpose concerning themselves, by [refusing and] not being baptized by [John].

31 So to what shall I compare the men of this generation, and what are they like?

32 They are like little children sitting in the market place, calling to one another and saying, We piped [playing wedding] to you, and you did not dance; we sang dirges *and* wailed [playing funeral], and you did not weep.

33 For John the Baptist has come neither eating bread nor drinking wine, and you say, He has a demon.

34 The Son of man has come eating and drinking, and you say, Behold, a Man Who is a glutton and a wine-drinker, a friend of tax collectors and notorious sinners.

35 Yet wisdom is vindicated [[l]shown to be true and divine] by all her children [that is, [l]by their life, character and deeds].

36 One of the Pharisees asked Jesus to dine with him, and He went into the Pharisee's house and reclined at table.

37 And behold, a woman of the town, who was [m]an especially wicked sinner, when she learned that He was reclining at table in the Pharisee's house, brought an alabaster flask of ointment (perfume).

38 And standing behind Him at His feet weeping, she began to wet His feet with [her] tears, and she wiped them with the hair of her head; and kissed His feet affectionately, and anointed them with the ointment (perfume).

39 Now when the Pharisee who had invited Him saw it, he said to himself, If this Man were a prophet, He would surely know who and what sort of woman this is who is touching Him, for she is a notorious sinner—a social outcast, devoted to sin.

40 And Jesus replying said to him, Simon, I have something to say to you. And he answered, Teacher, say it.

41 A certain lender of money at interest had two debtors; one owed him five hundred denarii, and the other fifty.

42 When they had no means of paying, he freely forgave them both. Now which of them will love him more?

43 Simon answered, The one, I take it, for whom he forgave *and* canceled more. And Jesus said to him, You have decided correctly.

44 Then turning toward the woman, He said to Simon, Do you see this woman? When I came into your house, you gave Me no water for My feet, but she has wet My feet with her tears and wiped them with her hair.

45 You gave Me no kiss, but she from the moment I came in has not ceased ([n]intermittently) to kiss My feet tenderly *and* caressingly.

---

k) Thayer.
l) Barnes' "Notes on the New Testament."
m) Thayer.
n) Vincent.

Living New Testament

27 He is the one to whom the Scriptures refer when they say, 'Look! I am sending My messenger ahead of You, to prepare the way before You.'

28 In all humanity there is no one greater than John. And yet the least citizen of the Kingdom of God is greater than he."

29 And all who heard John preach—even the most wicked of them[5]—agreed that God's requirements were right and they were baptized by him.

30 All, that is, except the Pharisees and teachers of Moses' Law. They rejected God's plan for them and refused John's baptism.

31 "What can I say about such men?" Jesus asked, "With what shall I compare them?

32 They are like a group of children who complain to their friends, 'You don't like it if we play "wedding" and you don't like it if we play "funeral" '![6]

33 For John the Baptist used to go without food and never took a drop of liquor in his life, and you said, 'He must be crazy!'[7]

34 But I eat My food and drink My wine, and you say, 'What a glutton Jesus is! And He drinks! And has the lowest sort of friends!'[8]

35 But I am sure you can always justify your inconsistencies."[9]

36 One of the Pharisees asked Jesus to come to his home for lunch and Jesus accepted the invitation. As they sat down to eat,

37 A woman of the streets—a prostitute—heard He was there and brought an exquisite flask filled with expensive perfume.

38 Going in, she knelt behind Him at His feet, weeping, until His feet were wet with her tears; and she wiped them off with her hair and kissed them and poured the perfume on them.

39 When Jesus' host, a Pharisee, saw what was happening and who the woman was, he said to himself, "This proves that Jesus is no prophet, for if God had really sent him, he would know what kind of woman this one is!"

40 Then Jesus spoke up and answered his thoughts. "Simon," He said to the Pharisee, "I have something to say to you."

"All right, Teacher," Simon replied, "go ahead."

41 Then Jesus told him this story: "A man loaned money to two people—$5,000 to one and $500 to the other.

42 But neither of them could pay him back, so he kindly forgave them both, letting them keep the money! Which do you suppose loved him most after that?"

43 "I suppose the one who had owed him the most," Simon answered. "Correct," Jesus agreed.

44 Then He turned to the woman and said to Simon, "Look! See this woman kneeling here! When I entered your home, you didn't bother to offer Me water to wash the dust from My feet, but she has washed them with her tears and wiped them with her hair!

45 You refused Me the customary kiss of greeting, but she has kissed My feet again and again from the time I first came in.

[5] Literally, "even the tax collectors"; i.e., the publicans.
[6] Literally, "we played the flute for you and you didn't dance; we sang a dirge and you didn't weep."
[7] Literally, "He has a demon."
[8] Literally, "is a friend of tax gatherers and sinners."
[9] Literally, "but wisdom is justified of all her children."

Revised Standard

26 What then did you go out to see? A
prophet? Yes, I tell you, and more than a
prophet. 27 This is he of whom it is written,
'Behold, I send my messenger before
thy face,
who shall prepare thy way before thee.'
28 I tell you, among those born of women
none is greater than John; yet he who is
least in the kingdom of God is greater than
he." 29 (When they heard this all the people and the tax collectors justified God,
having been baptized with the baptism of
John; 30 but the Pharisees and the lawyers
rejected the purpose of God for themselves, not having been baptized by him.)
31 "To what then shall I compare the
men of this generation, and what are they
like? 32 They are like children sitting in
the market place and calling to one another,
'We piped to you, and you did not dance;
we wailed, and you did not weep.'
33 For John the Baptist has come eating
no bread and drinking no wine; and
you say, 'He has a demon.' 34 The Son of
man has come eating and drinking; and
you say, 'Behold, a glutton and a drunkard,
a friend of tax collectors and sinners!'
35 Yet wisdom is justified by all her children."

Jesus anointed by the sinful woman

36 One of the Pharisees asked him to
eat with him, and he went into the Pharisee's house, and sat at table. 37 And behold,
a woman of the city, who was a sinner,
when she learned that he was sitting at
table in the Pharisee's house, brought an
alabaster flask of ointment, 38 and standing
behind him at his feet, weeping, she began
to wet his feet with her tears, and wiped
them with the hair of her head, and kissed
his feet, and anointed them with the ointment. 39 Now when the Pharisee who had
invited him saw it, he said to himself,
"If this man were a prophet, he would
have known who and what sort of woman
this is who is touching him, for she is a
sinner." 40 And Jesus answering said to
him, "Simon, I have something to say to
you." And he answered, "What is it, Teacher?" 41 "A certain creditor had two debtors;
one owed five hundred denarii, and the
other fifty. 42 When they could not pay, he
forgave them both. Now which of them
will love him more?" 43 Simon answered,
"The one, I suppose, to whom he forgave
more." And he said to him, "You have
judged rightly." 44 Then turning toward
the woman he said to Simon, "Do you see
this woman? I entered your house, you
gave me no water for my feet, but she
has wet my feet with her tears and wiped
them with her hair. 45 You gave me no kiss,
but from the time I came in she has not

King James

46 My head with oil thou didst not anoint: but this woman hath anointed my feet with ointment.

47 Wherefore I say unto thee, Her sins, which are many, are forgiven; for she loved much: but to whom little is forgiven, *the same* loveth little.

48 And he said unto her, Thy sins are forgiven.

49 And they that sat at meat with him began to say within themselves, Who is this that forgiveth sins also?

50 And he said to the woman, Thy faith hath saved thee; go in peace.

Amplified

46 You did not anoint My head with [o][cheap, ordi nary] oil, but she has anointed My feet with [o][costly, rare perfume.

47 Therefore I tell you, her sins, many [as they are] are forgiven her, because she has loved much; but he who is forgiven little, loves little.

48 And He said to her, Your sins are forgiven!

49 Then those who were at table with Him began to say among themselves, Who is this, Who even forgive sins?

50 But Jesus said to the woman, Your faith has saved you; go (enter) [n]into peace—[o]in freedom from all the distresses that are experienced as the result of sin.

CHAPTER 8

AND it came to pass afterward, that he went throughout every city and village, preaching and shewing the glad tidings of the kingdom of God: and the twelve *were* with him,

2 And certain women, which had been healed of evil spirits and infirmities, Mary called Magdalene, out of whom went seven devils,

3 And Joanna the wife of Chuza Herod's steward, and Susanna, and many others, which ministered unto him of their substance.

4 ¶ And when much people were gathered together, and were come to him out of every city, he spake by a parable:

5 A sower went out to sow his seed: and as he sowed, some fell by the way side; and it was trodden down, and the fowls of the air devoured it.

6 And some fell upon a rock; and as soon as it was sprung up, it withered away, because it lacked moisture.

7 And some fell among thorns; and the thorns sprang up with it, and choked it.

8 And other fell on good ground, and sprang up, and bare fruit an hundredfold. And when he had said these things, he cried, He that hath ears to hear, let him hear.

9 And his disciples asked him, saying, What might this parable be?

10 And he said, Unto you it is given to know the mysteries of the kingdom of God: but to others in parables; that seeing they might not see, and hearing they might not understand.

11 Now the parable is this: The seed is the word of God.

12 Those by the way side are they that hear; then cometh the devil, and taketh away the word out of their hearts, lest they should believe and be saved.

CHAPTER 8

SOON afterward [Jesus] went on through towns and villages, preaching and bringing the good news (the Gospel) of the kingdom of God. And the twelve [apostles] were with Him,

2 And also some women who had been cured of evil spirits and diseases: Mary, called Magdalene, from whom seven demons had been expelled;

3 And Joanna, the wife of Chuza, Herod's household manager, and Susanna, and many others, who ministered to *and* provided for [p]Him *and* them out of their property *and* personal belongings.

4 And when a very great throng was gathering together, and people from town after town kept coming to Jesus, He said in a parable:

5 A sower went out to sow seed, and as he sowed some fell along the traveled path, and was trodden underfoot; and the birds of the air ate it up.

6 And some [seed] fell on the rock, and as soon as it sprouted, it withered away, because it had no moisture.

7 And other [seed] fell in the midst of the thorns, and the thorns grew up with it and choked it (off).

8 And some seed fell into good soil, and grew up and yielded a crop a hundred times [as great]. As He said these things, He called out, He who has ears to hear, let him be listening *and* [q]consider *and* understand by hearing!

9 And when His disciples asked Him the meaning of this parable,

10 He said to them, To you it has been given to (come progressively to) know—that is, to recognize and understand more strongly and clearly—the mysteries *and* secrets of the kingdom of God; but for others they are in parables, so that looking they may not see, and hearing they may not comprehend. [Isa. 6:9, 10; Jer. 5:21; Ezek 12:2.]

11 Now the meaning of the parable is this: The seed is the Word of God.

12 Those along the traveled road are the people who have heard; then the devil comes and carries away the message out of their hearts, that they may not believe [[r]acknowledge Me as their Savior and devote themselves to Me], and be saved [here and hereafter].

---

n) Vincent.
o) Cremer.
p) Some ancient authorities read "Him" instead of "them."
q) Thayer.
r) Thayer.

Living New Testament

46 You neglected the usual courtesy of olive oil to anoint My head, but she has covered My feet with rare perfume.
47 Therefore her sins—and they are many—are forgiven, for she loved Me much; but one who is forgiven little, shows little love."
48 And He said to her, "Your sins are forgiven."
49 Then the men at the table said to themselves, "Who does this man think He is, going around forgiving sins?"
50 And Jesus said to the woman, "Your faith has saved you; go in peace."

Revised Standard

ceased to kiss my feet. 46You did not anoint
my head with oil, but she has anointed my
feet with ointment. 47Therefore I tell you,
her sins, which are many, are forgiven, for
she loved much; but he who is forgiven
little, loves little." 48And he said to her,
"Your sins are forgiven." 49Then those
who were at table with him began to say
among themselves, "Who is this, who even
forgives sins?" 50And he said to the woman,
"Your faith has saved you; go in peace."

CHAPTER 8

Not long afterwards He began a tour of the cities and villages of Galilee[1] to announce the coming of the Kingdom of God, and took His twelve disciples with Him.
2 Some women went along, from whom He had cast out demons or whom He had healed; among them were Mary Magdalene (Jesus had cast out seven demons from her),
3 Joanna, Chuza's wife (Chuza was King Herod's business manager and was in charge of his palace and domestic affairs), Susanna, and many others who were contributing from their private means to the support of Jesus and His disciples.
4 One day He gave this illustration to a large crowd that was gathering to hear Him—while many others were still on the way, coming from other towns.
5 "A farmer went out to his field to sow grain. As he scattered the seed on the ground, some of it fell on a footpath and was trampled on; and the birds came and ate it as it lay exposed.
6 Other seed fell on shallow soil with rock beneath. This seed began to grow, but soon withered and died for lack of moisture.
7 Other seed landed in thistle patches, and the young grain stalks were soon choked out.
8 Still other fell on fertile soil; this seed grew and produced a crop 100 times as large as he had planted." (As He was giving this illustration He said, "If anyone has listening ears, use them now!")
9 His apostles asked Him what the story meant.
10 He replied, "God has granted you to know the meaning of these parables, for they tell a great deal about the Kingdom of God. But these crowds hear the words and do not understand, just as the ancient prophets predicted.
11 This is its meaning: The seed is God's message to men.
12 The hard path where some seed fell represents the hard hearts of those who hear the words of God, but then the devil comes and steals the words away and prevents people from believing and being saved.

[1] Implied.

Jesus and his followers

8 Soon afterward he went on through
cities and villages, preaching and bringing the good news of the kingdom of God.
And the twelve were with him, 2and also
some women who had been healed of evil
spirits and infirmities: Mary, called Magdalene, from whom seven demons had gone
out, 3and Joanna, the wife of Chuza,
Herod's steward, and Susanna, and many
others, who provided for them[z] out of their
means.

The parable of the sower

4 And when a great crowd came together and people from town after town
came to him, he said in a parable: 5"A
sower went out to sow his seed; and as he
sowed, some fell along the path, and was
trodden under foot, and the birds of the
air devoured it. 6And some fell on the rock;
and as it grew up, it withered away, because it had no moisture. 7And some fell
among thorns; and the thorns grew with
it and choked it. 8And some fell into good
soil and grew, and yielded a hundredfold."
As he said this, he called out, "He who
has ears to hear, let him hear."

Parable of the sower explained

9 And when his disciples asked him
what this parable meant, 10he said, "To
you it has been given to know the secrets
of the kingdom of God; but for others they
are in parables, so that seeing they may
not see, and hearing they may not understand. 11Now the parable is this: The seed
is the word of God. 12The ones along the
path are those who have heard; then the
devil comes and takes away the word from
their hearts, that they may not believe and

[z] Other ancient authorities read *him*

King James

13 They on the rock *are they*, which, when they hear, receive the word with joy; and these have no root, which for a while believe, and in time of temptation fall away.

14 And that which fell among thorns are they, which, when they have heard, go forth, and are choked with cares and riches and pleasures of *this* life, and bring no fruit to perfection.

15 But that on the good ground are they, which in an honest and good heart, having heard the word, keep *it*, and bring forth fruit with patience.

16 ¶ No man, when he hath lighted a candle, covereth it with a vessel, or putteth *it* under a bed; but setteth *it* on a candlestick, that they which enter in may see the light.

17 For nothing is secret, that shall not be made manifest; neither *any thing* hid, that shall not be known and come abroad.

18 Take heed therefore how ye hear: for whosoever hath, to him shall be given; and whosoever hath not, from him shall be taken even that which he seemeth to have.

19 ¶ Then came to him *his* mother and his brethren, and could not come at him for the press.

20 And it was told *by certain* which said, Thy mother and thy brethren stand without, desiring to see thee.

21 And he answered and said unto them, My mother and my brethren are these which hear the word of God, and do it.

22 ¶ Now it came to pass on a certain day, that he went into a ship with his disciples: and he said unto them, Let us go over unto the other side of the lake. And they launched forth.

23 But as they sailed he fell asleep: and there came down a storm of wind on the lake; and they were filled *with water*, and were in jeopardy.

24 And they came to him, and awoke him, saying, Master, master, we perish. Then he arose, and rebuked the wind and the raging of the water: and they ceased, and there was a calm.

25 And he said unto them, Where is your faith? And they being afraid wondered, saying one to another, What manner of man is this! for he commandeth even the winds and water, and they obey him.

26 ¶ And they arrived at the country of the Gadarenes, which is over against Galilee.

27 And when he went forth to land, there met him out of the city a certain man, which had devils long time, and ware no clothes, neither abode in *any* house, but in the tombs.

28 When he saw Jesus, he cried out, and fell down before him, and with a loud voice said, What have I to do with thee, Jesus, *thou* Son of God most high? I beseech thee, torment me not.

29 (For he had commanded the unclean spirit to come out of the man. For oftentimes it had caught him; and he was kept bound with chains and in fetters; and he brake the bands, and was driven of the devil into the wilderness.)

Amplified

13 And those upon the rock [are the people] who, when they hear [the Word], receive *and* welcome it with joy; but these have no root; they believe for a while, and in time of trial *and* temptation fall away—withdraw and stand aloof.

14 And as for what fell among the thorns, these are [the people] who hear, but as they go on their way they are choked *and* suffocated with the anxieties *and* cares and riches and pleasures of life, and their fruit does not ripen —come to maturity and perfection.

15 But as for that in the good soil, these are [the people] who hearing the Word, hold it fast in a just—[s]noble, virtuous—and worthy heart, and steadily bring forth fruit with patience.

16 No one after he has lighted a lamp covers it with a vessel, or puts it under a [dining table-]couch; but he puts it on a [lamp]stand, that those who come in may see the light.

17 For there is nothing hid that shall not be disclosed, nor anything secret that shall not be known and come out into the open.

18 Be careful therefore how you listen, for to him who has [spiritual knowledge] will more be given, and from him who does not have [spiritual knowledge] even what he thinks *and* [t]guesses *and* [u]supposes that he has will be taken away.

19 Then Jesus' mother and His brothers came along toward Him, but they could not get to Him for the crowd.

20 And it was told Him, Your mother and Your brothers are standing outside, desiring to have an interview with You.

21 But He answered them, My mother and My brothers are those who listen to the Word of God and do it!

22 One of those days He and His disciples got into a boat, and He said to them, Let us go across to the other side of the lake. So they put off to sea.

23 But as they were sailing, He fell off to sleep. And a [v]whirlwind revolving from below upwards swept down on the lake, and the boat was filling with water, and they were in great danger.

24 And the disciples came and woke Him, saying, Master, Master, we are perishing! And He, being thoroughly awakened, [w]censured *and* [t]blamed *and* rebuked the wind and the raging waves; and they ceased, and there came a calm.

25 And He said to them, (Why are you so fearful?) Where is your faith—your trust, your confidence in Me, [in My veracity and My integrity]? And they were seized with alarm *and* profound *and* reverent dread, and they marveled, saying to one another, Who then is this, that He commands even wind and sea, and they obey Him?

26 Then they came to the country of the Gerasenes, which is opposite Galilee.

27 Now when Jesus stepped out on land, there met Him a certain man out of the town who had [was possessed by] demons. For a long time he had worn no clothes, and he lived not in a house but in the tombs.

28 And when he saw Jesus, he raised a deep (terrible) cry (from the depths of his throat), and fell down before Him [in terror], and shouted loudly, What have You [to do] with me, Jesus, Son of the Most High God?—What have we in common? I beg You, do not torment me!

29 For Jesus was already commanding the unclean spirit to come out of the man. For many times it snatched *and* held him; he was kept under guard and bound with chains and fetters, but he would break the bonds and be driven by the demon into the wilderness (desert).

s) Vincent.
t) Wycliffe.
u) Tyndale.
v) Schmidt's "Synonymik der Griechischen Sprache." (-Thayer).
w) Moulton and Milligan.

Living New Testament

13 The stony ground represents those who enjoy listening to sermons, but somehow the message never really gets through to them and doesn't take root and grow. They know the message is true, and sort of believe for awhile; but when the hot winds of persecution blow, they lose interest.

14 The seed among the thorns represents those who listen and believe God's words but whose faith afterwards is choked out by worry and riches and the responsibilities and pleasures of life. And so they are never able to help anyone else to believe the Good News.

15 But the good soil represents honest, good-hearted people. They listen to God's words and cling to them and steadily spread them to others who also soon believe."

* * * * *

16 [Another time He asked,[2]] "Who ever heard of someone lighting a lamp and then covering it up to keep it from shining? No, lamps are mounted in the open where they can be seen.

17 This illustrates the fact that someday everything [in men's hearts[2]] shall be brought to light and made plain to all.

18 So be careful how you listen; for whoever has, to him shall be given more; and whoever does not have, even what he thinks he has shall be taken away from him.

* * * * *

19 Once when His mother and brothers came to see Him, they couldn't get into the house where He was teaching, because of the crowds.

20 When Jesus heard they were standing outside and wanted to see Him,

21 He remarked, "My mother and My brothers are all those who hear the message of God and obey it."

* * * * *

22 One day about that time, as He and His disciples were out in a boat, He suggested that they cross to the other side of the lake.

23 On the way across He lay down for a nap, and while He was sleeping the wind began to rise. A fierce storm developed that threatened to swamp them, and they were in real danger.

24 They rushed over and woke Him up. "Master, Master, we are sinking!" they screamed. So He spoke to the storm: "Quiet down," He said, and the wind and waves subsided and all was calm!

25 Then He asked them, "Where is your faith?" And they were filled with awe and fear of Him and said to one another, "Who is this man, that even the winds and waves obey Him?"

26 So they arrived at the other side, in the Gerasene country across the lake from Galilee.

27 As He was climbing out of the boat a man from the city of Gadara came to meet Him, a man who had been demon-possessed for a long time. Homeless and naked, he lived in a cemetery among the tombs.

28 As soon as he saw Jesus he shrieked and fell to the ground before Him, screaming, "What do You want with me, Jesus, Son of God Most High? Please, I beg You, oh, don't torment me!"

29 For Jesus was already commanding the demon to leave him. This demon had often taken control of the man so that even when he was shackled with chains he simply broke them apart and rushed out into the desert, completely under the demon's power.

[2] Implied. See Matthew 5:16.

Revised Standard

be saved. [13]And the ones on the rock are
those who, when they hear the word, receive it with joy; but these have no root,
they believe for a while and in time of
temptation fall away. [14]And as for what
fell among the thorns, they are those who
hear, but as they go on their way they are
choked by the cares and riches and pleasures of life, and their fruit does not mature.
[15]And as for that in the good soil, they
are those who, hearing the word, hold it
fast in an honest and good heart, and bring
forth fruit with patience.

16 "No one after lighting a lamp covers
it with a vessel, or puts it under a bed, but
puts it on a stand, that those who enter
may see the light. [17]For nothing is hid that
shall not be made manifest, nor anything
secret that shall not be known and come to
light. [18]Take heed then how you hear; for
to him who has will more be given, and
from him who has not, even what he thinks
that he has will be taken away."

Jesus' true family

19 Then his mother and his brothers
came to him, but they could not reach him
for the crowd. [20]And he was told, "Your
mother and your brothers are standing outside, desiring to see you." [21]But he said
to them, "My mother and my brothers are
those who hear the word of God and do it."

The storm stilled

22 One day he got into a boat with his
disciples, and he said to them, "Let us go
across to the other side of the lake." So
they set out, [23]and as they sailed he fell
asleep. And a storm of wind came down
on the lake, and they were filling with
water, and were in danger. [24]And they
went and woke him, saying, "Master, Master, we are perishing!" And he awoke and
rebuked the wind and the raging waves;
and they ceased, and there was a calm.
[25]He said to them, "Where is your faith?"
And they were afraid, and they marveled,
saying to one another, "Who then is this,
that he commands even wind and water,
and they obey him?"

Demons cast out

26 Then they arrived at the country of
the Gerasenes,[a] which is opposite Galilee.
[27]And as he stepped out on land, there met
him a man from the city who had demons;
for a long time he had worn no clothes,
and he lived not in a house but among the
tombs. [28]When he saw Jesus, he cried out
and fell down before him, and said with
a loud voice, "What have you to do with
me, Jesus, Son of the Most High God?
I beseech you, do not torment me." [29]For
he had commanded the unclean spirit to
come out of the man. (For many a time
it had seized him; he was kept under guard,
and bound with chains and fetters, but he
broke the bonds and was driven by the

[a] Other ancient authorities read *Gadarenes*, others *Gergesenes*

King James

30 And Jesus asked him, saying, What is thy name? And he said, Legion: because many devils were entered into him.

31 And they besought him that he would not command them to go out into the deep.

32 And there was there an herd of many swine feeding on the mountain: and they besought him that he would suffer them to enter into them. And he suffered them.

33 Then went the devils out of the man, and entered into the swine: and the herd ran violently down a steep place into the lake, and were choked.

34 When they that fed *them* saw what was done, they fled, and went and told *it* in the city and in the country.

35 Then they went out to see what was done; and came to Jesus, and found the man, out of whom the devils were departed, sitting at the feet of Jesus, clothed, and in his right mind: and they were afraid.

36 They also which saw *it* told them by what means he that was possessed of the devils was healed.

37 ¶ Then the whole multitude of the country of the Gadarenes round about besought him to depart from them; for they were taken with great fear: and he went up into the ship, and returned back again.

38 Now the man out of whom the devils were departed besought him that he might be with him: but Jesus sent him away, saying,

39 Return to thine own house, and shew how great things God hath done unto thee. And he went his way, and published throughout the whole city how great things Jesus had done unto him.

40 And it came to pass, that, when Jesus was returned, the people *gladly* received him: for they were all waiting for him.

41 ¶ And, behold, there came a man named Jairus, and he was a ruler of the synagogue: and he fell down at Jesus' feet, and besought him that he would come into his house:

42 For he had one only daughter, about twelve years of age, and she lay a-dying. But as he went the people thronged him.

43 ¶ And a woman having an issue of blood twelve years, which had spent all her living upon physicians, neither could be healed of any,

44 Came behind *him,* and touched the border of his garment: and immediately her issue of blood stanched.

45 And Jesus said, Who touched me? When all denied, Peter and they that were with him said, Master, the multitude throng thee and press *thee,* and sayest thou, Who touched me?

46 And Jesus said, Somebody hath touched me: for I perceive that virtue is gone out of me.

47 And when the woman saw that she was not hid, she came trembling, and falling down before him, she declared unto him before all the people for what cause she had touched him, and how she was healed immediately.

48 And he said unto her, Daughter, be of good comfort: thy faith hath made thee whole; go in peace.

Amplified

30 Jesus then asked him, What is your name? And he answered, Legion; for many demons had entered him.

31 And they begged [Jesus] not to command them to depart into the bottomless pit (abyss).

32 Now a great herd of swine was there feeding on the hillside, and [the demons] begged Him to give them leave to enter these. And He allowed them [to do so].

33 Then the demons came out of the man and entered into the swine, and the herd rushed down the steep cliff into the lake and were drowned.

34 When the herdsmen saw what had happened, they ran away, and told it in the town and in the country.

35 And [people] went out to see what had occurred, and they came to Jesus and found the man from whom the demons had gone, sitting at the feet of Jesus, clothed and in his right (sound) mind, and they were seized with alarm *and* fear.

36 And those *also* who had seen it, told them how he who had been possessed with demons was restored (to health).

37 Then all the people of the country surrounding the Gerasenes district asked [Jesus] to depart from them, for they were possessed *and* suffering with dread *and* terror; so He entered a boat and returned [to the west side of the sea of Galilee].

38 But the man from whom the demons had gone kept begging *and* [x]praying that he might accompany Him *and* be with Him, but [Jesus] sent him away, saying,

39 Return to your home, and recount [the story] throughout of how many *and* great things God has done for you. And [the man] departed, proclaiming throughout the whole city how much Jesus had done for him.

40 Now when Jesus came back [to Galilee], the crowd received *and* welcomed Him gladly, for they were all waiting *and* looking for Him.

41 And there came a man named Jairus, who had (for a [y]long time) been a director of the synagogue; and falling at the feet of Jesus he begged Him to come to his house,

42 For he had an only daughter, about twelve years of age, and she was dying. As [Jesus] went, the people pressed together around Him—almost suffocating Him;

43 And a woman who had suffered from a flow of blood for twelve years *and had spent all her living upon physicians* and could not be healed by any one,

44 Came up behind Him and touched the tassel of His garment; and immediately her flow of blood ceased.

45 And Jesus said, Who is it that touched Me? When all were denying it, Peter *and those who were with him* said, Master, the multitudes surround You *and* press You on every side!

46 But Jesus said, Some one did touch Me; for I perceived that [healing] power has gone forth from Me.

47 And when the woman saw that she had not escaped notice, she came up trembling, and falling down before Him she declared in the presence of all the people for what reason she had touched Him, and how she had been instantly cured.

48 And He said to her, Daughter, your faith—that is, your confidence and trust in Me—has made you well! Go (enter) [z]into peace—[a]untroubled, undisturbed well-being.

---

x) Vincent.
y) Williams: "Imperfect expresses this idea of duration."
z) Trench.
a) Cremer.

Living New Testament

30 "What is your name?" Jesus asked the demon. "Legion," they replied—for the man was filled with thousands[3] of them!

31 They kept begging Him not to order them into the Bottomless Pit.

32 A herd of pigs was feeding on the mountainside nearby, and the demons pled with Him to let them enter into the pigs. And Jesus said they could.

33 So they left the man and went into the pigs, and immediately the whole herd rushed down the mountainside and fell over a cliff into the lake below, where they drowned.

34 The herdsmen rushed away to the nearby city, spreading the news as they ran.

35 Soon a crowd came out to see for themselves what had happened and saw the man who had been demon-possessed sitting quietly at Jesus' feet, clothed and sane! And the whole crowd was badly frightened.

36 Then those who had seen it happen told how the demon-possessed man had been healed.

37 And everyone begged Jesus to go away and leave them alone (for a deep wave of fear had swept over them). So He returned to the boat and left, crossing back to the other side of the lake.

38 The man who had been demon-possessed begged to go too, but Jesus said no.

39 "Go back to your family," He told him, "and tell them what a wonderful thing God has done for you." So he went all through the city telling everyone about Jesus' mighty miracle.

40 On the other side of the lake the crowds received Him with open arms, for they had been waiting for Him.

41 And now a man named Jairus, a leader of a Jewish synagogue, came and fell down at Jesus' feet and begged Him to come home with him,

42 For his only child was dying, a little girl twelve years old. Jesus went with him, pushing through the crowds.

43, 44 As they went a woman who wanted to be healed came up behind and touched Him, for she had been slowly bleeding for twelve years, and could find no cure (though she had spent everything she had on doctors[4]). But the instant she touched the edge of His robe, the bleeding stopped.

45 "Who touched Me?" Jesus asked. Everyone denied it, and Peter said, "Master, so many are crowding against You. . . ."

46 But Jesus told him, "No, it was someone who deliberately touched Me, for I felt healing power go out from Me."

47 When the woman realized that Jesus knew, she began to tremble and fell to her knees before Him and told why she had touched Him and that now she was well

48 "Daughter," He said to her, "your faith has healed you. Go in peace."

[3] Implied; a legion consisted of 6,000 troops. Whether the demons were speaking literally is, of course, unknown.
[4] This clause is not included in some of the ancient manuscripts.

Revised Standard

demon into the desert.) 30 Jesus then asked
him, "What is your name?" And he said,
"Legion"; for many demons had entered
him. 31 And they begged him not to command them to depart into the abyss. 32 Now
a large herd of swine was feeding there on
the hillside; and they begged him to let
them enter these. So he gave them leave.
33 Then the demons came out of the man
and entered the swine, and the herd rushed
down the steep bank into the lake and
were drowned.

34 When the herdsmen saw what had
happened, they fled, and told it in the city
and in the country. 35 Then people went
out to see what had happened, and they
came to Jesus, and found the man from
whom the demons had gone, sitting at the
feet of Jesus, clothed and in his right mind;
and they were afraid. 36 And those who had
seen it told them how he who had been
possessed with demons was healed. 37 Then
all the people of the surrounding country
of the Gerasenes[a] asked him to depart
from them; for they were seized with great
fear; so he got into the boat and returned.
38 The man from whom the demons had
gone begged that he might be with him;
but he sent him away, saying, 39 "Return
to your home, and declare how much God
has done for you." And he went away, proclaiming throughout the whole city how
much Jesus had done for him.

A ruler's daughter raised; a suffering woman healed

40 Now when Jesus returned, the crowd
welcomed him, for they were all waiting
for him. 41 And there came a man named
Jairus, who was a ruler of the synagogue;
and falling at Jesus' feet he besought him
to come to his house, 42 for he had an only
daughter, about twelve years of age, and
she was dying.

As he went, the people pressed round
him. 43 And a woman who had had a flow
of blood for twelve years[b] and could not be
healed by any one, 44 came up behind him,
and touched the fringe of his garment; and
immediately her flow of blood ceased.
45 And Jesus said, "Who was it that touched
me?" When all denied it, Peter[c] said, "Master, the multitudes surround you and press
upon you!" 46 But Jesus said, "Some one
touched me; for I perceive that power has
gone forth from me." 47 And when the
woman saw that she was not hidden, she
came trembling, and falling down before
him declared in the presence of all the
people why she had touched him, and how
she had been immediately healed. 48 And
he said to her, "Daughter, your faith has
made you well; go in peace."

[a] Other ancient authorities read *Gadarenes*, others *Gergesenes*
[b] Other ancient authorities add *and had spent all her living upon physicians*
[c] Other ancient authorities add *and those who were with him*

King James

49 ¶ While he yet spake, there cometh one from the ruler of the synagogue's *house*, saying to him, Thy daughter is dead; trouble not the Master.

50 But when Jesus heard *it*, he answered him, saying, Fear not: believe only, and she shall be made whole.

51 And when he came into the house, he suffered no man to go in, save Peter, and James, and John, and the father and the mother of the maiden.

52 And all wept, and bewailed her: but he said, Weep not; she is not dead, but sleepeth.

53 And they laughed him to scorn, knowing that she was dead.

54 And he put them all out, and took her by the hand, and called, saying, Maid, arise.

55 And her spirit came again, and she arose straightway: and he commanded to give her meat.

56 And her parents were astonished: but he charged them that they should tell no man what was done.

Amplified

49 While He was still speaking, a man from the h of the director of the synagogue came and said [to Jai Your daughter is dead; do not [z]weary *and* trouble Teacher any further.

50 But Jesus on hearing this answered him, Do no seized with alarm *or* struck with fear; simply believe Me as able to do this], and she shall be well.

51 And when He came to the house, He permitte one to enter with Him, except Peter and John and Ja and the girl's father and mother.

52 And all were weeping and bewailing her; but said, Do not weep, for she is not dead but sleeping.

53 And they laughed Him to scorn, knowing well she was dead.

54 And grasping her hand He called, saying, C arise [[c]from the sleep of death]!

55 And her spirit returned [[d]from death], and she a immediately; and He directed that she should be g something to eat.

56 And her parents were amazed, but He charged t to tell no one what had occurred.

CHAPTER 9

THEN he called his twelve disciples together, and gave them power and authority over all devils, and to cure diseases.

2 And he sent them to preach the kingdom of God, and to heal the sick.

3 And he said unto them, Take nothing for *your* journey, neither staves, nor scrip, neither bread, neither money; neither have two coats apiece.

4 And whatsoever house ye enter into, there abide, and thence depart.

5 And whosoever will not receive you, when ye go out of that city, shake off the very dust from your feet for a testimony against them.

6 And they departed, and went through the towns, preaching the gospel, and healing every where.

7 ¶ Now Herod the tetrarch heard of all that was done by him: and he was perplexed, because that it was said of some, that John was risen from the dead;

8 And of some, that Elias had appeared; and of others, that one of the old prophets was risen again.

9 And Herod said, John have I beheaded: but who is this, of whom I hear such things? And he desired to see him.

10 ¶ And the apostles, when they were returned, told him all that they had done. And he took them, and went aside privately into a desert place belonging to the city called Bethsaida.

11 And the people, when they knew *it*, followed him: and he received them, and spake unto them of the kingdom of God, and healed them that had need of healing.

CHAPTER 9

THEN Jesus called together the twelve *apostles*, and them power and authority over all demons an cure diseases,

2 And He sent them out to announce *and* preach kingdom of God and to bring healing.

3 And He said to them, Do not take anything for journey, neither walking stick, nor [e]wallet [for a co tion-bag], nor food of any kind, nor money, and do have two undergarments (tunics).

4 And whatever house you enter, stay there until go away [from that place].

5 And wherever they do not receive *and* accept welcome you, when you leave that town shake off the dust from your feet as a testimony against them.

6 And departing they went about from village to lage, preaching the Gospel and restoring the afflicte health everywhere.

7 Now Herod the tetrarch heard of all that was b done by [Jesus], and he was (thoroughly) perplexed troubled, because it was said by some that John Baptist] had been raised from the dead;

8 And by others that Elijah had appeared; and others, that one of the prophets of old had come bac life.

9 But Herod said, John I beheaded; but Who is about Whom I [learn] such things by hearsay? And sought to see Him.

10 On their return the apostles reported to Jesus that they had done. And He took them [along with F and withdrew into privacy near a town called B saida.

11 But when the crowds learned of it, [they] follo Him; and He welcomed them [and] talked to them a the kingdom of God, and healed those who needed re ation to health.

---

z) Trench
b) Thayer.
c) Thayer.
d) Cremer.
e) Moulton and Milligan.

Living New Testament

49 While He was still speaking to her, a messenger arrived from the Jairus' home with the news that the little girl was dead. "She's gone," he told her father; "there's no use troubling the Teacher now."

50 But when Jesus heard what had happened, He said to the father, "Don't be afraid! Just trust Me, and she'll be all right."

51 When they arrived at the house Jesus wouldn't let anyone into the room except Peter, James and John, and the little girl's father and mother.

52 The home was filled with mourning people, but He said, "Stop the weeping! She isn't dead; she is only asleep!"

53 This brought scoffing and laughter, for they all knew she was dead.

54 Then He took her by the hand and called, "Get up, little girl!"

55 And at that moment her life returned and she jumped up! "Give her something to eat," He said.

56 Her parents were overcome with happiness, but Jesus insisted that they not tell anyone the details of what had happened.

Revised Standard

49 While he was still speaking, a man
from the ruler's house came and said,
"Your daughter is dead; do not trouble
the Teacher any more." 50But Jesus on
hearing this answered him, "Do not fear;
only believe, and she shall be well." 51And
when he came to the house, he permitted
no one to enter with him, except Peter and
John and James, and the father and mother
of the child. 52And all were weeping and
bewailing her; but he said, "Do not weep;
for she is not dead but sleeping." 53And
they laughed at him, knowing that she was
dead. 54But taking her by the hand he
called, saying, "Child, arise." 55And her
spirit returned, and she got up at once; and
he directed that something should be given
her to eat. 56And her parents were amazed;
but he charged them to tell no one what
had happened.

CHAPTER 9

One day Jesus called together His twelve apostles and gave them authority over all demons—power to cast them out—and to heal all diseases.

2 Then He sent them away to tell everyone about the coming of the Kingdom of God and to heal the sick.

3 "Don't even take along a walking stick," He instructed them, "nor a beggar's bag, nor food, nor money. Not even an extra coat!

4 Be a guest in only one home at each village.

5 If the people of a town won't listen to you when you enter it, turn around and leave, demonstrating God's anger against it by shaking its dust from your feet as you go.[1]

6 So they began their circuit of the villages, preaching the Good News and healing the sick.

7 When reports of Jesus' miracles reached Herod,[2] the governor, he was worried and puzzled, for some were saying, "This is John the Baptist come back to life again";

8 And others, "It is Elijah or some other ancient prophet risen from the dead." These rumors were circulating all over the land.

9 "I beheaded John," Herod said, "so who is this man about whom I hear such strange stories?" And he tried to see Him.

10 After the apostles returned to Jesus and reported what they had done, He slipped quietly away with them to the city of Bethsaida.

11 But the crowds found out where He was going, and followed. And He welcomed them, teaching them again about the Kingdom of God and curing those who were ill.

The mission of the twelve

9 And he called the twelve together and
gave them power and authority over
all demons and to cure diseases, 2and he
sent them out to preach the kingdom of
God and to heal. 3And he said to them,
"Take nothing for your journey, no staff,
nor bag, nor bread, nor money; and do not
have two tunics. 4And whatever house you
enter, stay there, and from there depart.
5And wherever they do not receive you,
when you leave that town shake off the
dust from your feet as a testimony against
them." 6And they departed and went
through the villages, preaching the gospel
and healing everywhere.

Death of John the Baptist

7 Now Herod the tetrarch heard of all
that was done, and he was perplexed, because it was said by some that John had
been raised from the dead, 8by some that
Elijah had appeared, and by others that
one of the old prophets had risen. 9Herod
said, "John I beheaded; but who is this
about whom I hear such things?" And he
sought to see him.

The five thousand fed

10 On their return the apostles told him
what they had done. And he took them
and withdrew apart to a city called Bethsaida. 11When the crowds learned it, they
followed him; and he welcomed them and
spoke to them of the kingdom of God,
and cured those who had need of healing.

[1] Literally, "as a testimony against them."
[2] Literally, "Herod the Tetrarch."

King James

12 And when the day began to wear away, then came the twelve, and said unto him, Send the multitude away, that they may go into the towns and country round about, and lodge, and get victuals: for we are here in a desert place.

13 But he said unto them, Give ye them to eat. And they said, We have no more but five loaves and two fishes; except we should go and buy meat for all this people.

14 For they were about five thousand men. And he said to his disciples, Make them sit down by fifties in a company.

15 And they did so, and made them all sit down.

16 Then he took the five loaves and the two fishes, and looking up to heaven, he blessed them, and brake, and gave to the disciples to set before the multitude.

17 And they did eat, and were all filled: and there was taken up of fragments that remained to them twelve baskets.

18 ¶ And it came to pass, as he was alone praying, his disciples were with him: and he asked them, saying, Whom say the people that I am?

19 They answering said, John the Baptist; but some *say*, Elias; and others *say*, that one of the old prophets is risen again.

20 He said unto them, But whom say ye that I am? Peter answering said, The Christ of God.

21 And he straitly charged them, and commanded *them* to tell no man that thing;

22 Saying, The Son of man must suffer many things, and be rejected of the elders and chief priests and scribes, and be slain, and be raised the third day.

23 ¶ And he said to *them* all, If any *man* will come after me, let him deny himself, and take up his cross daily, and follow me.

24 For whosoever will save his life shall lose it: but whosoever will lose his life for my sake, the same shall save it.

25 For what is a man advantaged, if he gain the whole world, and lose himself, or be cast away?

26 For whosoever shall be ashamed of me and of my words, of him shall the Son of man be ashamed, when he shall come in his own glory, and *in his* Father's, and of the holy angels.

27 But I tell you of a truth, there be some standing here, which shall not taste of death, till they see the kingdom of God.

28 ¶ And it came to pass about an eight days after these sayings, he took Peter and John and James, and went up into a mountain to pray.

Amplified

12 Now the day began to decline, and the twelve came and said to Him, Dismiss the crowds *and* send them away, so that they may go to the neighboring hamlets *and* villages and the surrounding country and find lodging, and get a [f]supply of provisions; for we are here in an uninhabited (barren, solitary) place.

13 But He said to them, You [yourselves] give them [food] to eat. They said, We have not more than five loaves and two fishes, unless we are to go and buy food for all this crowd, [II Kings 4:42-44.]

14 For there were about five thousand men. And [Jesus] said to His disciples, Have them [sit down] reclining in table-groups (companies), of about fifty each.

15 And they did so, and made them all recline.

16 And taking the five loaves and the two fishes, He looked up to heaven, and (praising God) gave thanks *and* asked Him to bless them [to their use]. Then He broke them and gave them to the disciples to place before the multitude.

17 And all the people ate and were satisfied. And they gathered up what remained over, twelve [[g]small hand] baskets of broken pieces.

18 Now it occurred that as Jesus was praying privately the disciples were with Him, and He asked them, Who do men say that I am?

19 And they answered, John the Baptist; but some say, Elijah, and others, that one of the ancient prophets has come back to life.

20 And He said to them, But who do you [yourselves] say that I am? And Peter replied, The Christ of God!

21 But He strictly charged and sharply commanded them ([h]under penalty) to tell this to no one—no one, [h]whoever he might be,

22 Saying, The Son of man must suffer many things, and be ([h]deliberately) disapproved *and* repudiated *and* rejected on the part of the elders and chief priests and scribes, and be put to death, and on the third day be raised [again].

23 And He said to all, If any person wills to come after Me, let him deny himself—that is, [i]disown himself, [j]forget, lose sight of himself and his own interests, [k]refuse and give up himself—and take up his cross daily, and follow Me [that is, [j]cleave steadfastly to Me, conform wholly to My example, in living and if need be in dying also].

24 For whoever would preserve his life *and* save it, will lose *and* destroy it; but whoever loses his life for My sake, he will preserve *and* save it [[k]from the penalty of eternal death].

25 For what does it profit a man, if he gains the whole world and ruins or forfeits (loses) himself?

26 Because whoever is ashamed of Me and of My teachings, of him will the Son of man be ashamed when He comes in the [[l]threefold] glory (that is, the splendor and majesty) of Himself and of the Father and of the holy angels.

27 However I tell you truly, there are some of those standing here who will not taste of death before they see the kingdom of God.

28 Now about eight days after these teachings, Jesus took with Him Peter and John and James, and went up on the mountain to pray.

---

f) Vincent.
g) Vincent. But Moulton and Milligan think size not meant.
h) Vincent.
i) Moulton and Milligan.
j) Thayer.
k) Cremer.
l) Vincent.

Living New Testament

12 Late in the afternoon all twelve of the disciples came and urged Him to send the people away to the nearby villages and farms to find food and lodging for the night. "For there is nothing to eat here in this deserted spot," they said.

13 But Jesus replied, "*You* feed them!"

"Why, we have only five loaves of bread and two fish among the lot of us," they protested; "or are You expecting us to go and buy enough for this whole mob?"

14 For there were about 5,000 men there! "Just tell them to sit down on the ground in groups of about fifty each," Jesus replied.

15 So they did.

16 Jesus took the five loaves and two fish and looked up into the sky and gave thanks, then broke off pieces for His disciples to set before the crowd.

17 And everyone ate and ate; still twelve basketfuls of scraps were picked up afterwards!

* * * * *

18 One day as He was alone praying, with His disciples nearby, He came over and asked them, "Who are the people saying I am?"

19 "John the Baptist," they told Him, "or perhaps Elijah or one of the other ancient prophets risen from the dead."

20 Then He asked them, "Who do you think I am?" Peter replied, "The Messiah—the Christ of God!"

21 He gave them strict orders not to speak of this to anyone.

22 "For I[3] must suffer much," He said, "and be rejected by the Jewish leaders—the elders, chief priests, and teachers of the Law—and be killed; and three days later I will come back to life again!"

23 Then He said to all, "Anyone who wants to follow Me must put aside his own desires and conveniences and carry his cross with him every day and *keep close to Me!*

24 Whoever loses his life for My sake will save it, but whoever insists on saving his life will lose it:

25 And what profit is there in gaining the whole world when it means forfeiting one's self?

26 When I, the Man of Glory,[4] come in My glory and in the glory of the Father and the holy angels, I will be ashamed then of all who are ashamed of Me and My words now.

27 But this is the simple truth—some of you who are standing here right now will not die until you have seen the Kingdom of God!"

28 Eight days later He took Peter, James, and John with Him into the hills to pray.

[3] Literally, "the Son of man," a term filled with exalted meanings as well as describing His perfect humanity.

[4] Literally, "the Son of man."

Revised Standard

12Now the day began to wear away; and
the twelve came and said to him, "Send
the crowd away, to go into the villages
and country round about, to lodge and get
provisions; for we are here in a lonely
place." 13But he said to them, "You give
them something to eat." They said, "We
have no more than five loaves and two
fish—unless we are to go and buy food for
all these people." 14For there were about
five thousand men. And he said to his disciples,
"Make them sit down in companies,
about fifty each." 15And they did so, and
made them all sit down. 16And taking the
five loaves and the two fish he looked up
to heaven, and blessed and broke them,
and gave them to the disciples to set before
the crowd. 17And all ate and were satisfied.
And they took up what was left over,
twelve baskets of broken pieces.

Peter's confession of faith

18 Now it happened that as he was
praying alone the disciples were with him;
and he asked them, "Who do the people
say that I am?" 19And they answered,
"John the Baptist; but others say, Elijah;
and others, that one of the old prophets
has risen." 20And he said to them, "But
who do you say that I am?" And Peter
answered, "The Christ of God." 21But he
charged and commanded them to tell this
to no one,

Future events foretold

22saying, "The Son of man must suffer
many things, and be rejected by the elders
and chief priests and scribes, and be killed,
and on the third day be raised."

23 And he said to all, "If any man
would come after me, let him deny himself
and take up his cross daily and follow
me. 24For whoever would save his life will
lose it; and whoever loses his life for my
sake, he will save it. 25For what does it
profit a man if he gains the whole world
and loses or forfeits himself? 26For whoever
is ashamed of me and of my words,
of him will the Son of man be ashamed
when he comes in his glory and the glory
of the Father and of the holy angels. 27But
I tell you truly, there are some standing
here who will not taste death before they
see the kingdom of God."

The transfiguration

28 Now about eight days after these
sayings he took with him Peter and John
and James, and went up on the mountain

King James

29 And as he prayed, the fashion of his countenance was altered, and his raiment *was* white *and* glistering.

30 And, behold, there talked with him two men, which were Moses and Elias:

31 Who appeared in glory, and spake of his decease which he should accomplish at Jerusalem.

32 But Peter and they that were with him were heavy with sleep: and when they were awake, they saw his glory, and the two men that stood with him.

33 And it came to pass, as they departed from him, Peter said unto Jesus, Master, it is good for us to be here: and let us make three tabernacles; one for thee, and one for Moses, and one for Elias: not knowing what he said.

34 While he thus spake, there came a cloud, and overshadowed them: and they feared as they entered into the cloud.

35 And there came a voice out of the cloud, saying, This is my beloved Son: hear him.

36 And when the voice was past, Jesus was found alone. And they kept *it* close, and told no man in those days any of those things which they had seen.

37 ¶ And it came to pass, that on the next day, when they were come down from the hill, much people met him.

38 And, behold, a man of the company cried out, saying, Master, I beseech thee, look upon my son: for he is mine only child.

39 And, lo, a spirit taketh him, and he suddenly crieth out; and it teareth him that he foameth again, and bruising him hardly departeth from him.

40 And I besought thy disciples to cast him out; and they could not.

41 And Jesus answering said, O faithless and perverse generation, how long shall I be with you, and suffer you? Bring thy son hither.

42 And as he was yet a-coming, the devil threw him down, and tare *him*. And Jesus rebuked the unclean spirit, and healed the child, and delivered him again to his father.

43 ¶ And they were all amazed at the mighty power of God. But while they wondered every one at all things which Jesus did, he said unto his disciples,

44 Let these sayings sink down into your ears: for the Son of man shall be delivered into the hands of men.

45 But they understood not this saying, and it was hid from them, that they perceived it not: and they feared to ask him of that saying.

46 ¶ Then there arose a reasoning among them, which of them should be greatest.

47 And Jesus, perceiving the thought of their heart, took a child, and set him by him,

Amplified

29 And as He was praying, the appearance of His countenance became altered (different), and His raiment became dazzling white—[l]flashing with the brilliance of lightning.

30 And behold, two men were conversing with Him, Moses and Elijah,

31 Who appeared in splendor *and* majesty *and* brightness and were speaking of His exit [from life], which He was about to bring to realization at Jerusalem.

32 Now Peter and those with him were weighed down with sleep. But when they fully awoke they saw His glory (splendor and majesty and brightness) and the two men who stood with Him.

33 And it occurred as the men were parting from Him, that Peter said to Jesus, Master, it is delightful *and* good that we are here; and let us construct three booths *or* huts, one for You and one for Moses and one for Elijah! not noticing *or* knowing what he was saying.

34 But even as he was saying this, a cloud came and began to overshadow them; and they were seized with alarm *and* struck with fear as they entered into the cloud.

35 Then there came a voice out of the cloud, saying, This is My Son, My Chosen One—[m]My Beloved; listen to *and* yield to *and* obey Him!

36 And when the voice had died away, Jesus was found there alone. And they kept still and told no one at that time any of these things that they had seen.

37 Now it occurred the next day, when they had come down from the mountain, that a great multitude met Him.

38 And behold, a man from the crowd shouted out, Master, I implore You to look at my son, for he is my only child;

39 And behold, a spirit seizes him and suddenly he cries out; it convulses him so that he foams at the mouth, and he is sorely shattered, and it will scarcely leave him.

40 And I implored Your disciples to drive it out, but they could not.

41 Jesus answered, O (faithless ones,) unbelieving *and* without trust in God, a perverse ([n]wayward, [o]crooked and [p]warped) generation! Until when am I to be with you and bear with you? Bring your son here [to Me].

42 And even while he was coming the demon threw him down, and (completely) convulsed him. But Jesus censured *and* severely rebuked the unclean spirit and healed the child, and restored him to his father.

43 And all were astounded at the evidence of God's mighty power *and* His majesty *and* magnificence. But [while] they were all marveling at everything Jesus was doing, He said to His disciples,

44 Let these words sink into your ears: the Son of man is about to be delivered into the hands of men [[q]whose conduct is opposed to God].

45 However, they did not comprehend this saying, and it was kept hidden from them so that they should not grasp it *and* understand, and they were afraid to ask Him about the statement.

46 But a controversy arose among them as to which of them might be the greatest—that is, be surpassing the others in excellence, worth and authority.

47 But Jesus, as He perceived the thought of their heart, took a little child and put him at His side,

---

l) Vincent.
m) Many ancient authorities so read.
n) Wycliffe.
o) Tyndale.
p) Vincent.
q) Cremer.

Living New Testament

29 And as He was praying, His face began to shine,[5] and His clothes became dazzling white and blazed with light.

30 Then two men appeared and began talking with Him—Moses and Elijah!

31 They were splendid in appearance, glorious to see; and they were speaking of His death at Jerusalem, to be carried out in accordance with God's plan.

32 Peter and the others had been very drowsy and had fallen asleep. Now they woke up and saw Jesus covered with brightness and glory, and the two men standing with Him.

33 As Moses and Elijah were starting to leave, Peter, all confused and not even knowing what he was saying, blurted out, "Master, this is wonderful! We'll put up three shelters—one for You and one for Moses and one for Elijah!"

34 But even as he was saying this, a bright[6] cloud formed above them; and terror gripped them as it covered them.

35 And a voice from the cloud said, *"This* is My Son, My Chosen One; listen to *Him."*

36 Then, as the voice died away, Jesus was there alone with His disciples. They didn't tell anyone what they had seen until long afterwards.

37 The next day as they descended from the hill, a huge crowd met Him,

38 And a man in the crowd called out to Him, "Teacher, this boy here is my only son,

39 And a demon keeps seizing him, making him scream; and it throws him into convulsions so that he foams at the mouth; it is always hitting him and hardly ever leaves him alone.

40 I begged Your disciples to cast the demon out, but they couldn't."

41 "O you stubborn, faithless people," Jesus said [to His disciples[6]], "How long should I put up with you? Bring him here."

42 As the boy was coming the demon knocked him to the ground and threw him into a violent convulsion. But Jesus ordered the demon to come out, and healed the boy and handed him over to his father.

43 Awe gripped the people as they saw this display of the power of God. Meanwhile, as they were exclaiming over all the wonderful things He was doing, Jesus said to His disciples,

44 "Listen to Me and remember what I say. I, the Son of Mankind, am going to be betrayed."

45 But the disciples didn't know what He meant, for their minds had been sealed and they were afraid to ask Him.

46 Now came an argument among them as to which of them would be greatest [in the coming Kingdom[7]]!

47 But Jesus knew their thoughts, so He stood a little child beside Him

[5] Literally, "the appearance of His face changed."
[6] Implied.
[7] Implied.

Revised Standard

to pray. 29 And as he was praying the appearance of his countenance was altered,
and his raiment became dazzling white.
30 And behold, two men talked with him,
Moses and Elijah, 31 who appeared in glory
and spoke of his departure, which he was
to accomplish at Jerusalem. 32 Now Peter
and those who were with him were heavy
with sleep but kept awake, and they saw
his glory and the two men who stood with
him. 33 And as the men were parting from
him, Peter said to Jesus, "Master, it is
well that we are here; let us make three
booths, one for you and one for Moses
and one for Elijah"—not knowing what
he said. 34 As he said this, a cloud came
and overshadowed them; and they were
afraid as they entered the cloud. 35 And
a voice came out of the cloud, saying,
"This is my Son, my Chosen;[d] listen to
him!" 36 And when the voice had spoken,
Jesus was found alone. And they kept silence and told no one in those days anything of what they had seen.

An unclean spirit cast out

37 On the next day, when they had
come down from the mountain, a great
crowd met him. 38 And behold, a man from
the crowd cried, "Teacher, I beg you to
look upon my son, for he is my only
child; 39 and behold, a spirit seizes him,
and he suddenly cries out; it convulses him
till he foams, and shatters him, and will
hardly leave him. 40 And I begged your
disciples to cast it out, but they could not."
41 Jesus answered, "O faithless and perverse generation, how long am I to be with
you and bear with you? Bring your son
here." 42 While he was coming, the demon
tore him and convulsed him. But Jesus rebuked the unclean spirit, and healed the
boy, and gave him back to his father.
43 And all were astonished at the majesty of
God.

Death and resurrection foretold again

But while they were all marveling at
everything he did, he said to his disciples,
44 "Let these words sink into your ears; for
the Son of man is to be delivered into the
hands of men." 45 But they did not understand this saying, and it was concealed
from them, that they should not perceive
it; and they were afraid to ask him about
this saying.

True discipleship

46 And an argument arose among them
as to which of them was the greatest. 47 But
when Jesus perceived the thought of their
hearts, he took a child and put him by his

[d] Other ancient authorities read *my Beloved*

King James

48 And said unto them, Whosoever shall receive this child in my name receiveth me: and whosoever shall receive me receiveth him that sent me: for he that is least among you all, the same shall be great.

49 ¶ And John answered and said, Master, we saw one casting out devils in thy name; and we forbad him, because he followeth not with us.

50 And Jesus said unto him, Forbid *him* not: for he that is not against us is for us.

51 ¶ And it came to pass, when the time was come that he should be received up, he stedfastly set his face to go to Jerusalem,

52 And sent messengers before his face: and they went, and entered into a village of the Samaritans, to make ready for him.

53 And they did not receive him, because his face was as though he would go to Jerusalem.

54 And when his disciples James and John saw *this*, they said, Lord, wilt thou that we command fire to come down from heaven, and consume them, even as Elias did?

55 ¶ But he turned, and rebuked them, and said, Ye know not what manner of spirit ye are of.

56 For the Son of man is not come to destroy men's lives, but to save *them*. And they went to another village.

57 ¶ And it came to pass, that, as they went in the way, a certain *man* said unto him, Lord, I will follow thee whithersoever thou goest.

58 And Jesus said unto him, Foxes have holes, and birds of the air *have* nests; but the Son of man hath not where to lay *his* head.

59 And he said unto another, Follow me. But he said, Lord, suffer me first to go and bury my father.

60 Jesus said unto him, Let the dead bury their dead: but go thou and preach the kingdom of God.

61 And another also said, Lord, I will follow thee; but let me first go bid them farewell, which are at home at my house.

62 And Jesus said unto him, No man, having put his hand to the plough, and looking back, is fit for the kingdom of God.

CHAPTER 10

AFTER these things the Lord appointed other seventy also, and sent them two and two before his face into every city and place, whither he himself would come.

Amplified

48 And told them, Whoever receives *and* accepts *a* welcomes this child in My name *and* for My sake receiv *and* accepts *and* welcomes Me; and whoever so receiv Me so also receives Him Who sent Me; for he who is le *and* lowliest among you all, he is [the one who is tru great.

49 John said, Master, we saw a man driving c demons in Your name, and we commanded him to stop for he does not follow along with us.

50 But Jesus told him, Do not forbid [people]; f whoever is not against you is for you.

51 Now when the time was almost come for Jesus be received up, He steadfastly *and* determinedly set H face to go to Jerusalem. And He sent messengers befc Him.

52 And they reached and entered a Samaritan villa to make ready for Him;

53 But [the people] would not welcome *or* receive accept Him, because His face was [set as if He we going to Jerusalem.

54 And when His disciples James and John observ this, they said, Lord, do You wish us to command fire come down from heaven and consume them, *even Elijah did?* [II Kings 1:9-16.]

55 But He turned and rebuked *and* severely censur them. *He said, You do not know of what sort of spirit y* are,

56 *For the Son of man did not come to destroy me lives, but to save (them* [r]*from the penalty of etern death).* And they journeyed on to another village.

57 And it occurred that, as they were going along t road, a man said to Him, *Lord,* I will follow You wh ever You go.

58 And Jesus told him, Foxes have lurking-holes, a the birds of the air have roosts *and* nests; but the Son man has no place to lay His head.

59 And He said to another, [s]Become My disciple, si with My party, and accompany Me! But he replied, *Lo* permit me first to go and bury [[t]await the death of] n father.

60 But Jesus said to him, Allow the dead to bury th own dead; but as for you, go *and* publish abro [u]throughout all regions the kingdom of God.

61 Another also said, I will follow You, Lord, *a* become Your disciple, *and* side with Your party; but l me first say goodbye to those at my home.

62 Jesus said to him, No one who puts his hand to t plow and looks back [to the things behind] is fit for t kingdom of God.

CHAPTER 10

NOW after this the Lord chose *and* appointed seven others, and sent them out ahead of Him, two by tw into every town and place where He Himself was about come (visit).

---

r) Cremer.
s) Thayer.
t) Many commentators.
u) Vincent.

Living New Testament

48 And said to them, "Anyone who takes care of a little child like this is caring for Me! And whoever cares for Me is caring for God who sent Me. Your care for others is the measure of your greatness."

49 His disciple John came to Him and said, "Master, we saw someone using Your name to cast out demons. And we told him not to. After all, he isn't in our group."

50 But Jesus said, "You shouldn't have done that! For anyone who is not against you is for you."

51 As the time drew near for His return to heaven, He moved steadily onward towards Jerusalem with an iron will.

52 One day He sent messengers ahead to reserve rooms for them in a Samaritan village.

53 But they were turned away! The people of the village refused to have anything to do with them because they were headed for Jerusalem.[8]

54 When word came back of what had happened, James and John said to Jesus, "Master, shall we order fire down from heaven to burn them up?"

55 But Jesus turned and rebuked them,[9]

56 And they went on to another village.

57 As they were walking along someone said to Jesus, "I will always follow You no matter where You go."

58 But Jesus replied, "Remember, I don't even own a place to lay My head. Foxes have dens to live in, and birds have nests, but I, the Man from Heaven,[10] have no earthly home at all."

59 Another time, when He invited a man to come with Him and to be His disciple, the man agreed—but wanted to wait until his father's death.[11]

60 Jesus replied, "Let those without eternal life concern themselves with things like that.[12] Your duty is to come and preach the coming of the Kingdom of God to all the world."

61 Another said, "Yes, Lord, I will come, but first let me ask permission of those at home."[13]

62 But Jesus told him, "Anyone who lets himself be distracted from the work I plan for him is not fit for the Kingdom of God."

Revised Standard

side, 48 and said to them, "Whoever receives this child in my name receives me,
and whoever receives me receives him who
sent me; for he who is least among you all
is the one who is great."
49 John answered, "Master, we saw a
man casting out demons in your name, and
we forbade him, because he does not follow with us." 50 But Jesus said to him, "Do
not forbid him; for he that is not against
you is for you."

James and John rebuked

51 When the days drew near for him to
be received up, he set his face to go to
Jerusalem. And he sent messengers ahead
of him, 52 who went and entered a village
of the Samaritans, to make ready for him;
53 but the people would not receive him,
because his face was set toward Jerusalem.
54 And when his disciples James and John
saw it, they said, "Lord, do you want us
to bid fire come down from heaven and
consume them?"[e] 55 But he turned and rebuked them.[f] 56 And they went on to another village.

The teaching about discipleship

57 As they were going along the road,
a man said to him, "I will follow you wherever you go." 58 And Jesus said to him,
"Foxes have holes, and birds of the air
have nests; but the Son of man has nowhere to lay his head." 59 To another he
said, "Follow me." But he said, "Lord, let
me first go and bury my father." 60 But he
said to him, "Leave the dead to bury their
own dead; but as for you, go and proclaim
the kingdom of God." 61 Another said, "I
will follow you, Lord; but let me first say
farewell to those at my home." 62 Jesus said
to him, "No one who puts his hand to the
plow and looks back is fit for the kingdom
of God."

CHAPTER 10

The Lord now chose 70 other disciples and sent them on ahead in pairs to all the towns and villages He planned to visit later.

The mission of the seventy

10 After this the Lord appointed seventy[g]
others, and sent them on ahead of him,
two by two, into every town and place
where he himself was about to come. 2 And

[8] A typical case of discrimination. (cf. John 4:9). The Jews called the Samaritans "half-breeds," so the Samaritans naturally hated the Jews.

[9] Later manuscripts add to verses 55 and 56. "And Jesus said, You don't realize what your hearts are like. For the Son of man has not come to destroy men's lives, but to save them."

[10] Literally, "the Son of man."

[11] Literally, "But he said, 'Lord, suffer me first to go and bury my father' "—perhaps meaning that the man could, when his father died, collect the inheritance and have some security.

[12] Literally, "let the dead bury their dead."

[13] Literally, "bid them farewell at home."

[e] Other ancient authorities add *as Elijah did*

[f] Other ancient authorities add *and he said, "You do not know what manner of spirit you are of; for the Son of man came not to destroy men's lives but to save them"*

[g] Other ancient authorities read *seventy-two*

King James

2 Therefore said he unto them, The harvest truly *is* great, but the labourers *are* few: pray ye therefore the Lord of the harvest, that he would send forth labourers into his harvest.

3 Go your ways: behold, I send you forth as lambs among wolves.

4 Carry neither purse, nor scrip, nor shoes: and salute no man by the way.

5 And into whatsoever house ye enter, first say, Peace *be* to this house.

6 And if the son of peace be there, your peace shall rest upon it: if not, it shall turn to you again.

7 And in the same house remain, eating and drinking such things as they give: for the labourer is worthy of his hire. Go not from house to house.

8 And into whatsoever city ye enter, and they receive you, eat such things as are set before you:

9 And heal the sick that are therein, and say unto them, The kingdom of God is come nigh unto you.

10 But into whatsoever city ye enter, and they receive you not, go your ways out into the streets of the same, and say,

11 Even the very dust of your city, which cleaveth on us, we do wipe off against you: notwithstanding be ye sure of this, that the kingdom of God is come nigh unto you.

12 But I say unto you, that it shall be more tolerable in that day for Sodom, than for that city.

13 Woe unto thee, Chorazin! woe unto thee, Bethsaida! for if the mighty works had been done in Tyre and Sidon, which have been done in you, they had a great while ago repented, sitting in sackcloth and ashes.

14 But it shall be more tolerable for Tyre and Sidon at the judgment, than for you.

15 And thou, Capernaum, which art exalted to heaven, shalt be thrust down to hell.

16 He that heareth you heareth me; and he that despiseth you despiseth me; and he that despiseth me despiseth him that sent me.

17 ¶ And the seventy returned again with joy, saying, Lord, even the devils are subject unto us through thy name.

18 And he said unto them, I beheld Satan as lightning fall from heaven.

19 Behold, I give unto you power to tread on serpents and scorpions, and over all the power of the enemy: and nothing shall by any means hurt you.

20 Notwithstanding in this rejoice not, that the spirits are subject unto you; but rather rejoice, because your names are written in heaven.

21 ¶ In that hour Jesus rejoiced in spirit, and said, I thank thee, O Father, Lord of heaven and earth, that thou hast hid these things from the wise and prudent, and hast revealed them unto babes: even so, Father; for so it seemed good in thy sight.

22 All things are delivered to me of my Father: and no man knoweth who the Son is, but the Father; and who the Father is, but the Son, and *he* to whom the Son will reveal *him*.

Amplified

2 And He said to them, [v](There is much ripe *grain,*) the harvest indeed is abundant, but the farm hands are few. Pray therefore the Lord of the harvest to send out laborers into His harvest.

3 Go your way; behold, I send you out as lambs into the midst of wolves.

4 Carry no purse, no provisions bag, no [change of] sandals; refrain from [retarding your journey by] saluting *and* wishing well any one along the way.

5 Whatever house you enter, first say, Peace be to this household!—[that is,] [w]freedom from all the distresses that result from sin be with this family.

6 And if any one [worthy] of peace *and* blessedness is there, the peace *and* blessedness you wish shall come upon him; but if not, it shall come back to you.

7 And stay on in the same house, eating and drinking what they provide, for the laborer is worthy of his wages; do not keep moving from house to house. [Deut. 24:15.]

8 Whenever you go into a town and they receive *and* accept *and* welcome you, eat what is set before you;

9 And heal the sick in it and say to them, The kingdom of God has come close to you.

10 But whenever you go into a town and they do not receive *and* accept *and* welcome you, go out into its streets and say,

11 Even the dust of your town that clings to our feet we are wiping off against you; yet know *and* understand this, that the kingdom of God has come near you.

12 I tell you, it shall be more tolerable in that day for Sodom than for that town. [Gen. 19:24-28.]

13 Woe to you, Chorazin! Woe to you, Bethsaida! For if the mighty miracles performed in you had been performed in Tyre and Sidon, they would have repented long ago, sitting in sackcloth and ashes.

14 However it shall be more tolerable in the judgment for Tyre and Sidon than for you.

15 And you, Capernaum, will you be exalted unto heaven? You shall be brought down to Hades (the regions of the dead).

16 He who hears *and* heeds you [disciples] hears *and* heeds Me; and he who slights *and* rejects you, slights *and* rejects Me; *and* he who slights *and* rejects Me, slights *and* rejects Him who sent Me.

17 The seventy returned with joy, saying, Lord, even the demons are subject to us in Your name!

18 And He said to them, I saw Satan falling like a lightning [flash] from heaven.

19 Behold! I have given you authority *and* power to trample upon serpents and scorpions, and (physical and mental strength and ability) over all the power that the enemy [possesses], and nothing shall in any way harm you.

20 Nevertheless do not rejoice at this, that the spirits are subject to you, but rejoice that your names are enrolled in heaven. [Exod. 32:32; Ps. 69:28; Dan. 12:1.]

21 In that same hour He rejoiced *and* gloried in the Holy Spirit and said, I thank You, Father, Lord of heaven and earth, that You have concealed these things [relating to salvation] from the wise and understanding *and* learned, and revealed them to babes—the childish, unskilled and untaught. Yes, Father, for such was Your gracious [x]will *and* choice *and* good pleasure.

22 All things have been given over into My power by My Father, and no one knows Who the Son is except the Father, or Who the Father is except the Son and any one to whom the Son may choose to reveal *and* make Him known.

---

v) Wycliffe.
w) Cremer.
x) Thayer.

Living New Testament

2 These were His instructions to them: "Plead with the Lord of the harvest to send out more laborers to help you, for the harvest is so plentiful and the workers so few.

3 Go now, and remember that I am sending you out as lambs among wolves.

4 Don't take any money with you, or a beggar's bag, or even an extra pair of shoes. And don't waste time along the way.[1]

5 Whenever you enter a home, give it your blessing.

6 If it is worthy of the blessing, the blessing will stand; if not, the blessing will return to you.

7 When you enter a village, don't shift around from home to home, but stay in one place, eating and drinking without question whatever is set before you. And don't hesitate to accept hospitality, for the workman is worthy of his wages!

8, 9 If a town welcomes you, follow these two rules:

(1) Eat whatever is set before you.

(2) Heal the sick; and as you help them, say, 'The Kingdom of God is very near you now.'

10 But if a town refuses you, go out into its streets and say,

11 'We wipe the dust of your town from our feet as a public announcement of your doom. Never forget how close you were to the Kingdom of God!'

12 Even wicked Sodom will be better off than such a city on the Judgment Day.

13 What horrors await you, you cities of Chorazin and Bethsaida! For if the miracles I did for you had been done in the cities of Tyre and Sidon,[2] their people would have sat in deep repentance long ago, clothed in sackcloth and throwing ashes on their heads to show their remorse.

14 Yes, Tyre and Sidon will receive less punishment on the Judgment Day than you.

15 And you people of Capernaum, what shall I say about you? Will you be exalted to heaven? No, you shall be brought down to hell."

16 Then He said to the disciples, "Those who welcome you are welcoming Me. And those who reject you are rejecting Me. And those who reject Me are rejecting God who sent Me."

17 When the 70 disciples returned, they joyfully reported to Him, "Even the demons obey us when we use Your name."

18 "Yes," He told them, "I saw Satan falling from heaven as a flash of lightning!

19 And I have given you authority over all the power of the Enemy, and to walk among serpents and scorpions and to crush them! Nothing shall injure you!

20 However, the important thing is not that demons obey you, but that your names are registered as citizens of heaven."

21 Then He was filled with the joy of the Holy Spirit and said, "I praise You, O Father, Lord of heaven and earth, for hiding these things from the intellectuals and worldly wise and for revealing them to those who are as trusting as little children.[3] Yes, thank You, Father, for that is the way You wanted it.

22 I am the Agent of My Father in everything; and no one really knows the Son except the Father, and no one really knows the Father except the Son and those to whom the Son chooses to reveal Him."

[1] Literally, "Salute no one in the way."
[2] Cities destroyed by God in judgment for their wickedness. For a description of this event, see Ezekiel, chapters 26-28.
[3] Literally, "babies."

Revised Standard

he said to them, "The harvest is plentiful,
but the laborers are few; pray therefore the
Lord of the harvest to send out laborers
into his harvest. [3]Go your way; behold, I
send you out as lambs in the midst of
wolves. [4]Carry no purse, no bag, no sandals; and salute no one on the road. [5]What-
ever house you enter, first say, 'Peace be
to this house!' [6]And if a son of peace is
there, your peace shall rest upon him; but
if not, it shall return to you. [7]And remain
in the same house, eating and drinking
what they provide, for the laborer deserves
his wages; do not go from house to house.
[8]Whenever you enter a town and they receive you, eat what is set before you; [9]heal
the sick in it and say to them, 'The kingdom of God has come near to you.' [10]But
whenever you enter a town and they do not
receive you, go into its streets and say,
[11]'Even the dust of your town that clings
to our feet, we wipe off against you; nevertheless know this, that the kingdom of
God has come near.' [12]I tell you, it shall
be more tolerable on that day for Sodom
than for that town.

13 "Woe to you, Chorazin! woe to you,
Bethsaida! for if the mighty works done in
you had been done in Tyre and Sidon,
they would have repented long ago, sitting
in sackcloth and ashes. [14]But it shall be
more tolerable in the judgment for Tyre
and Sidon than for you. [15]And you, Capernaum, will you be exalted to heaven?
You shall be brought down to Hades.

16 "He who hears you hears me, and
he who rejects you rejects me, and he who
rejects me rejects him who sent me."

The return of the seventy

17 The seventy[g] returned with joy, saying, "Lord, even the demons are subject
to us in your name!" [18]And he said to
them, "I saw Satan fall like lightning from
heaven. [19]Behold, I have given you authority to tread upon serpents and scorpions,
and over all the power of the enemy; and
nothing shall hurt you. [20]Nevertheless do
not rejoice in this, that the spirits are subject to you; but rejoice that your names
are written in heaven."

21 In that same hour he rejoiced in the
Holy Spirit and said, "I thank thee, Father,
Lord of heaven and earth, that thou hast
hidden these things from the wise and understanding and revealed them to babes;
yea, Father, for such was thy gracious will.[h]
[22]All things have been delivered to me by
my Father; and no one knows who the Son
is except the Father, or who the Father is
except the Son and any one to whom the
Son chooses to reveal him."

[g] Other ancient authorities read *seventy-two*
[h] Or *so it was well-pleasing before thee*

King James

23 ¶ And he turned him unto *his* disciples, and said privately, Blessed *are* the eyes which see the things that ye see:

24 For I tell you, that many prophets and kings have desired to see those things which ye see, and have not seen *them;* and to hear those things which ye hear, and have not heard *them.*

25 ¶ And, behold, a certain lawyer stood up, and tempted him, saying, Master, what shall I do to inherit eternal life?

26 He said unto him, What is written in the law? how readest thou?

27 And he answering said, Thou shalt love the Lord thy God with all thy heart, and with all thy soul, and with all thy strength, and with all thy mind; and thy neighbour as thyself.

28 And he said unto him, Thou hast answered right: this do, and thou shalt live.

29 But he, willing to justify himself, said unto Jesus, And who is my neighbour?

30 And Jesus answering said, A certain *man* went down from Jerusalem to Jericho, and fell among thieves, which stripped him of his raiment, and wounded *him,* and departed, leaving *him* half dead.

31 And by chance there came down a certain priest that way: and when he saw him, he passed by on the other side.

32 And likewise a Levite, when he was at the place, came and looked *on him,* and passed by on the other side.

33 But a certain Samaritan, as he journeyed, came where he was: and when he saw him, he had compassion *on him,*

34 And went to *him,* and bound up his wounds, pouring in oil and wine, and set him on his own beast, and brought him to an inn, and took care of him.

35 And on the morrow when he departed, he took out two pence, and gave *them* to the host, and said unto him, Take care of him; and whatsoever thou spendest more, when I come again, I will repay thee.

36 Which now of these three, thinkest thou, was neighbour unto him that fell among the thieves?

37 And he said, He that shewed mercy on him. Then said Jesus unto him, Go, and do thou likewise.

38 ¶ Now it came to pass, as they went, that he entered into a certain village: and a certain woman named Martha received him into her house.

39 And she had a sister called Mary, which also sat at Jesus' feet, and heard his word.

40 But Martha was cumbered about much serving, and came to him, and said, Lord, dost thou not care that my sister hath left me to serve alone? bid her therefore that she help me.

41 And Jesus answered and said unto her, Martha, Martha, thou art careful and troubled about many things:

42 But one thing is needful: and Mary hath chosen that good part, which shall not be taken away from her.

Amplified

23 Then turning to His disciples He said private Blessed—happy, [y]to be envied—are those whose eyes s what you see!

24 For I tell you that many prophets and kings long to see what you see, and they did not see it, and to he what you hear, and they did not hear it.

25 And then a certain lawyer arose to try (test, tem Him, saying, Teacher, what am I to do to inherit everla ing life—[that is,] to partake of eternal salvation in t Messiah's kingdom?

26 Jesus said to him, What is written in the Law? Ho do you read it?

27 And he replied, You must love the Lord your G with all your heart, and with all your soul, and with your strength, and with all your mind; and your neighb as yourself. [Deut. 6:5; Lev. 19:18.]

28 And Jesus said to him, You have answered corre ly; do this, and you will live—enjoy active, blessed, endle life in the kingdom of God.

29 And he, [z]determined to acquit himself of reproac said to Jesus, And who is my neighbor?

30 Jesus [z]taking him up replied, A certain man w going from Jerusalem down to Jericho and he fell amo robbers, who stripped him of his clothes and belonging and beat him, and went their way [[z]unconcernedly] lea ing him half dead, as it happened.

31 Now by [z]coincidence a certain priest was goi down along that road; and when he saw him he passed on the other side.

32 A Levite likewise came down to the place and sa him, and passed by on the other side [of the road].

33 But a certain Samaritan, as he traveled along can down to where he was, and when he saw him was mov with pity *and* sympathy [for him],

34 And went to him and dressed his wounds, pouri on [them] oil and wine. Then he set him on his own bea and brought him to an inn, and took care of him.

35 And the next day he took out two denarii [two day wages], and gave [them] to the innkeeper, saying, Ta care of him; and whatever more you spend, I [myself] w repay you when I return.

36 Which of these three, do you think, proved himse neighbor to him who fell among the robbers?

37 He answered, The one who showed pity *and* merc to him. And Jesus said to him, Go and do likewise.

38 Now while they were on their way, it occurred th Jesus entered a certain village, and a woman named Ma tha received *and* welcomed Him into her house.

39 And she had a sister named Mary, who seate herself at the Lord's feet and was listening to H teaching.

40 But Martha (overoccupied and too busy) was di tracted about much serving; and she came up to Him ar said, Lord, is it nothing to You that my sister has left n to serve alone? Tell her then to help me—to lend a har and do her part along with me.

41 But the Lord replied to her by saying, Marth Martha, you are anxious and troubled about mar things;

42 There is need of (but [a]a few things, or) [a]only on Mary has chosen the good portion—[b]that which is advantage—which shall not be taken away from her.

---

y) Souter.
z) Vincent.
a) Many ancient authorities read "few things" or "only one."
b) Cremer.

Living New Testament

23 Then, turning to the twelve disciples, He said quietly, "How privileged you are to see what you have seen.

24 Many a prophet and king of old has longed for these days, to see and hear what you have seen and heard!"

25 One day an expert on Moses' laws came to test Jesus' orthodoxy by asking Him this question: "Teacher, what does a man need to do to live forever in heaven?"

26 Jesus replied, "What does Moses' law say about it?"

27 "It says," he replied, "that you must love the Lord your God with all your heart, and with all your soul, and with all your strength, and with all your mind. And you must love your neighbor just as much as you love yourself."

28 "Right!" Jesus told him. *"Do* this and *you* shall live!"

29 The man wanted to justify (his lack of love for some kinds of people),[4] so he asked, "Which neighbors?"

30 Jesus replied with an illustration: "A Jew going on a trip from Jerusalem to Jericho was attacked by bandits. They stripped him of his clothes and money and beat him up and left him lying half dead beside the road.

31 By chance a Jewish priest came along; and when he saw the man lying there, he crossed to the other side of the road and passed him by.

32 A Jewish Temple-assistant[5] did the same thing; he, too, left him lying there.

33 But a despised Samaritan[6] came along, and when he saw him, he felt deep pity.

34 Kneeling beside him the Samaritan soothed his wounds with medicine and bandaged them. Then he put the man on his donkey and walked along beside him till they came to an inn, where he nursed him through the night.

35 And the next day he handed the innkeeper two twenty-dollar bills[7] and told him to take care of the man. 'If his bill runs higher than that,' he said, 'I'll pay the difference the next time I am here.'

36 Now which of these three would you say was a neighbor to the bandits' victim?"

37 The man replied, "The one who showed him some pity."

Then Jesus said, "Yes, now go and do the same."

38 As Jesus and the disciples continued on their way to Jerusalem[8] they came to a village where a woman named Martha welcomed them into her home.

39 Her sister Mary sat on the floor, listening to Jesus as He talked.

40 But Martha was the jittery type, and was worrying over the big dinner she was preparing. She came to Jesus and said "Sir, doesn't it seem unfair to You that my sister just sits here while I do all the work? Tell her to come and help me."

41 But the Lord said to her, "Martha, dear friend,[9] you are so upset over all these details!

42 There is really only one thing worth being concerned about. Mary has discovered it—and I won't take it away from her!"

---

[4] Literally, "wanting to justify himself."
[5] Literally, "Levite."
[6] Literally, "a Samaritan." All Samaritans were despised by Jews, and the feeling was mutual, due to historical reasons.
[7] Literally, "two denarii," each the equivalent of a day's wage.
[8] Implied.
[9] Literally, "Martha, Martha."

Revised Standard

23 Then turning to the disciples he said
privately, "Blessed are the eyes which see
what you see! 24 For I tell you that many
prophets and kings desired to see what you
see, and did not see it, and to hear what
you hear, and did not hear it."

The good Samaritan

25 And behold, a lawyer stood up to
put him to the test, saying, "Teacher, what
shall I do to inherit eternal life?" 26 He
said to him, "What is written in the law?
How do you read?" 27 And he answered,
"You shall love the Lord your God with
all your heart, and with all your soul, and
with all your strength, and with all your
mind; and your neighbor as yourself."
28 And he said to him, "You have answered
right; do this, and you will live."
29 But he, desiring to justify himself,
said to Jesus, "And who is my neighbor?"
30 Jesus replied, "A man was going down
from Jerusalem to Jericho, and he fell
among robbers, who stripped him and beat
him, and departed, leaving him half dead.
31 Now by chance a priest was going down
that road; and when he saw him he passed
by on the other side. 32 So likewise a Levite,
when he came to the place and saw him,
passed by on the other side. 33 But a Samaritan, as he journeyed, came to where
he was; and when he saw him, he had compassion, 34 and went to him and bound up
his wounds, pouring on oil and wine; then
he set him on his own beast and brought
him to an inn, and took care of him.
35 And the next day he took out two denarii[i] and gave them to the innkeeper,
saying, 'Take care of him; and whatever
more you spend, I will repay you when I
come back.' 36 Which of these three, do you
think, proved neighbor to the man who
fell among the robbers?" 37 He said, "The
one who showed mercy on him." And Jesus said to him, "Go and do likewise."

Jesus visits Mary and Martha

38 Now as they went on their way, he
entered a village; and a woman named
Martha received him into her house. 39 And
she had a sister called Mary, who sat
at the Lord's feet and listened to his teaching. 40 But Martha was distracted with
much serving; and she went to him and
said, "Lord, do you not care that my sister
has left me to serve alone? Tell her then
to help me." 41 But the Lord answered her,
"Martha, Martha, you are anxious and
troubled about many things; 42 one thing
is needful.[j] Mary has chosen the good
portion, which shall not be taken away
from her."

---

[i] The denarius was worth about twenty cents
[j] Other ancient authorities read *few things are needful, or only one*

King James

CHAPTER 11

AND it came to pass, that, as he was praying in a certain place, when he ceased, one of his disciples said unto him, Lord, teach us to pray, as John also taught his disciples.

2 And he said unto them, When ye pray, say, Our Father which art in heaven, Hallowed be thy name. Thy kingdom come. Thy will be done, as in heaven, so in earth.

3 Give us day by day our daily bread.

4 And forgive us our sins; for we also forgive every one that is indebted to us. And lead us not into temptation; but deliver us from evil.

5 And he said unto them, Which of you shall have a friend, and shall go unto him at midnight, and say unto him, Friend, lend me three loaves;

6 For a friend of mine in his journey is come to me, and I have nothing to set before him?

7 And he from within shall answer and say, Trouble me not: the door is now shut, and my children are with me in bed; I cannot rise and give thee.

8 I say unto you, Though he will not rise and give him, because he is his friend, yet because of his importunity he will rise and give him as many as he needeth.

9 And I say unto you, Ask, and it shall be given you; seek, and ye shall find; knock, and it shall be opened unto you.

10 For every one that asketh receiveth; and he that seeketh findeth; and to him that knocketh it shall be opened.

11 If a son shall ask bread of any of you that is a father, will he give him a stone? or if *he ask* a fish, will he for a fish give him a serpent?

12 Or if he shall ask an egg, will he offer him a scorpion?

13 If ye then, being evil, know how to give good gifts unto your children: how much more shall *your* heavenly Father give the Holy Spirit to them that ask him?

14 ¶ And he was casting out a devil, and it was dumb. And it came to pass, when the devil was gone out, the dumb spake; and the people wondered.

15 But some of them said, He casteth out devils through Beelzebub the chief of the devils.

16 And others, tempting *him,* sought of him a sign from heaven.

17 But he, knowing their thoughts, said unto them, Every kingdom divided against itself is brought to desolation; and a house *divided* against a house falleth.

18 If Satan also be divided against himself, how shall his kingdom stand? because ye say that I cast out devils through Beelzebub.

19 And if I by Beelzebub cast out devils, by whom do your sons cast *them* out? therefore shall they be your judges.

20 But if I with the finger of God cast out devils, no doubt the kingdom of God is come upon you.

21 When a strong man armed keepeth his palace, his goods are in peace:

Amplified

CHAPTER 11

THEN He was praying in a certain place, and when He stopped, one of His disciples said to Him, Lord, teach us to pray, as John taught his disciples.

2 And He said to them, When you pray, say, [Our] Father, [Who is in heaven,] hallowed be Your name. Your kingdom come. *Your will be done—held holy and revered —on earth as it is in heaven.*

3 Give us daily our bread ([c]food for the morrow),

4 And forgive us our sins, for we ourselves also forgive every one who is indebted to us—who has offended us or done us wrong; and bring us not into temptation, *but rescue us from evil.*

5 And He said to them, Which of you who has a friend will go to him at midnight and will say to him, Friend, lend me three loaves [of bread],

6 For a friend of mine who is on a journey has just come, and I have nothing to put before him;

7 And he from within will answer, Do not disturb me; the door is now closed, and my children are with me in bed; I cannot get up and supply you [with anything]?

8 I tell you, although he will not get up and supply him anything because he is his friend, yet because of his shameless persistence *and* insistence, he will get up and give him as much as he needs.

9 So I say to you, Ask *and* [d]keep on asking, and it shall be given you; seek *and* [d]keep on seeking, and you shall find; knock *and* [d]keep on knocking, and the door shall be opened to you.

10 For every one who asks *and* [d]keeps on asking receives, and he who seeks and [d]keeps on seeking finds, and to him who knocks and [d]keeps on knocking the door shall be opened.

11 What father among you, if his son asks for *a loaf of bread, will give him a stone; or if he asks for* a fish, will instead of a fish give him a serpent;

12 Or if he asks for an egg, will give him a scorpion?

13 If you then, evil-minded as you are, know how to give good gifts—gifts [e]that are to advantage—to your children, how much more will your heavenly Father give the Holy Spirit to those who ask *and* [d]continue to ask Him!

14 Now Jesus was driving out a demon that was dumb, and it occurred that when the demon had gone out, the dumb man spoke. And the crowds marveled.

15 But some of them said, He drives out demons [because He is in league with, and] by Beelzebub, the prince of demons;

16 While others, to try *and* test *and* tempt Him, demanded a sign of Him from heaven.

17 But He, [well] aware of their intent *and* purpose, said to them, Every kingdom split up against itself is doomed *and* brought to desolation, and so house falls upon house.—The disunited household will collapse.

18 And if Satan also is divided against himself, how will his kingdom last? For you say that I expel demons with the help of *and* by Beelzebub.

19 Now if I expel demons with the help of *and* by Beelzebub, with whose help *and* by whom do your sons drive them out? Therefore they shall be your judges.

20 But if I drive out the demons by the finger of God, then the kingdom of God has (already) come upon you.

21 When the strong man, fully armed, ([f]from his courtyard) guards his own dwelling, his belongings are undisturbed—his property is at peace (secure).

---

c) Moulton and Milligan.
d) Williams: "This continuance is in the present imperative and present participles often repeated."
e) Cremer.
f) Vincent.

Living New Testament

CHAPTER 11

Once when Jesus had been out praying, one of His disciples came to Him as He finished and said, "Lord teach us a prayer to recite[1] just as John taught one to his disciples."

2 And this is the prayer He taught them: "Father, may Your name be honored for its holiness; send Your Kingdom soon.

3 Give us our food day by day.

4 And forgive our sins—for we have forgiven those who sinned against us. And don't allow us to be tempted."

5, 6 Then, teaching them more about prayer,[2] He used this illustration: "Suppose you went to a friend's house at midnight, wanting to borrow three loaves of bread. You would shout up to him, 'A friend of mine has just arrived for a visit and I've nothing to give him to eat.'

7 He would call down from his bedroom, 'Please don't ask me to get up. The door is locked for the night and we are all in bed. I just can't help you this time.'

8 But I'll tell you this—though he won't do it as a friend, if you keep knocking long enough he will get up and give you everything you want—just because of your persistence.

9 And so it is with prayer—keep on asking and you will keep on getting; keep on looking and you will keep on finding; knock and the door will be opened.

10 Everyone who asks, receives; all who seek, find; and the door is opened to everyone who knocks.

11 You men who are fathers—if your boy asks for bread, do you give him a stone? If he asks for fish, do you give him a snake?

12 If he asks for an egg, do you give him a scorpion? [Of course not![3]]

13 And if even sinful persons like yourselves give children what they need, don't you realize that your heavenly Father will do at least as much, and give the Holy Spirit to those who ask for Him?"

14 Once, when Jesus cast out a demon from a man who couldn't speak, his voice returned to him. The crowd was excited and enthusiastic,

15 But some said, "No wonder He can cast them out. He gets His power from Satan,[4] the king of demons!"

16 Others asked for something to happen in the sky to prove His claim of being the Messiah.[5]

17 He knew the thoughts of each of them, so He said, "Any kingdom filled with civil war is doomed; so is a home filled with argument and strife.

18 Therefore, if what you say is true, that Satan is fighting against himself by empowering Me to cast out his demons, how can his kingdom survive?

19 And if I am empowered by Satan, what about your own followers? For they cast out demons! Do you think this proves they are possessed by Satan? Ask *them* if you are right!

20 But if I am casting out demons because of power from God, it proves that the Kingdom of God has arrived.

21 For when Satan,[6] strong and fully armed, guards his palace, it is safe—

[1] Implied.
[2] Some ancient manuscripts add at this point additional portions of the Lord's Prayer as recorded in Matthew 6:9-13.
[3] Implied.
[4] Literally, "from Beelzebub."
[5] Implied; literally, "Others, tempting, sought of Him a sign from heaven."
[6] Literally, "the Strong."

Revised Standard

Jesus' teaching on prayer

11 He was praying in a certain place,
and when he ceased, one of his disciples said to him, "Lord, teach us to pray,
as John taught his disciples." 2And he said
to them, "When you pray, say:
"Father, hallowed be thy name. Thy
kingdom come. 3Give us each day our
daily bread;[k] 4and forgive us our sins,
for we ourselves forgive every one who is
indebted to us; and lead us not into temptation."
5 And he said to them, "Which of you
who has a friend will go to him at midnight and say to him, 'Friend, lend me
three loaves; 6for a friend of mine has
arrived on a journey, and I have nothing
to set before him'; 7and he will answer
from within, 'Do not bother me; the door
is now shut, and my children are with me
in bed; I cannot get up and give you anything'? 8I tell you, though he will not get
up and give him anything because he is
his friend, yet because of his importunity
he will rise and give him whatever he
needs. 9And I tell you, Ask, and it will
be given you; seek, and you will find;
knock, and it will be opened to you. 10For
every one who asks receives, and he who
seeks finds, and to him who knocks it will
be opened. 11What father among you, if
his son asks for[l] a fish, will instead of a
fish give him a serpent; 12or if he asks for
an egg, will give him a scorpion? 13If you
then, who are evil, know how to give good
gifts to your children, how much more will
the heavenly Father give the Holy Spirit to
those who ask him!"

Jesus answers the Pharisees' slander

14 Now he was casting out a demon that
was dumb; when the demon had gone out,
the dumb man spoke, and the people marveled. 15But some of them said, "He casts
out demons by Beelzebul, the prince of demons"; 16while others, to test him, sought
from him a sign from heaven. 17But he,
knowing their thoughts, said to them, "Every kingdom divided against itself is laid
waste, and house falls upon house. 18And
if Satan also is divided against himself,
how will his kingdom stand? For you say
that I cast out demons by Beelzebul. 19And
if I cast out demons by Beelzebul, by
whom do your sons cast them out? Therefore they shall be your judges. 20But if it
is by the finger of God that I cast out demons, then the kingdom of God has come
upon you. 21When a strong man, fully
armed, guards his own palace, his goods

[k] Or *our bread for the morrow*
[l] Other ancient authorities insert *bread, will give him a stone; or if he asks for*

King James

22 But when a stronger than he shall come upon him, and overcome him, he taketh from him all his armour wherein he trusted, and divideth his spoils.

23 He that is not with me is against me: and he that gathereth not with me scattereth.

24 When the unclean spirit is gone out of a man, he walketh through dry places, seeking rest; and finding none, he saith, I will return unto my house whence I came out.

25 And when he cometh, he findeth *it* swept and garnished.

26 Then goeth he, and taketh *to him* seven other spirits more wicked than himself; and they enter in, and dwell there: and the last *state* of that man is worse than the first.

27 ¶ And it came to pass, as he spake these things, a certain woman of the company lifted up her voice, and said unto him, Blessed *is* the womb that bare thee, and the paps which thou hast sucked.

28 But he said, Yea rather, blessed *are* they that hear the word of God, and keep it.

29 ¶ And when the people were gathered thick together, he began to say, This is an evil generation: they seek a sign; and there shall no sign be given it but the sign of Jonas the prophet.

30 For as Jonas was a sign unto the Ninevites, so shall also the Son of man be to this generation.

31 The queen of the south shall rise up in the judgment with the men of this generation, and condemn them: for she came from the utmost parts of the earth to hear the wisdom of Solomon; and, behold, a greater than Solomon is here.

32 The men of Nineve shall rise up in the judgment with this generation, and shall condemn it: for they repented at the preaching of Jonas; and, behold, a greater than Jonas *is* here.

33 No man, when he hath lighted a candle, putteth *it* in a secret place, neither under a bushel, but on a candlestick, that they which come in may see the light.

34 The light of the body is the eye: therefore when thine eye is single, thy whole body also is full of light; but when *thine eye* is evil, thy body also *is* full of darkness.

35 Take heed therefore that the light which is in thee be not darkness.

36 If thy whole body therefore *be* full of light, having no part dark, the whole shall be full of light, as when the bright shining of a candle doth give thee light.

37 ¶ And as he spake, a certain Pharisee besought him to dine with him: and he went in, and sat down to meat.

38 And when the Pharisee saw *it*, he marvelled that he had not first washed before dinner.

39 And the Lord said unto him, Now do ye Pharisees make clean the outside of the cup and the platter; but your inward part is full of ravening and wickedness.

40 *Ye* fools, did not he that made that which is without make that which is within also?

Amplified

22 But when one stronger than he attacks him and conquers him, he robs him of his whole armor on which he had relied, and divides up *and* distributes all his goods as plunder (spoil).

23 He who is not with Me—siding and believing with Me—is against Me, and he who does not gather with Me (engage in My interest), scatters.

24 When the unclean spirit has gone out of a person, he roams through waterless places in search [of a place] of rest (release, refreshing, ease); and finding none he says, I will go back to my house from which I came.

25 And when he arrives, he finds [the place] swept *and* put in order and furnished *and* decorated.

26 And he goes and brings other spirits, seven [of them], more evil than himself, and they enter in, settle down *and* dwell there; and the last state of that person is worse than the first.

27 Now it occurred that as He was saying these things, a certain woman in the crowd raised her voice and said to Him, Blessed—happy and [g]to be envied—is the womb that bore You, and the breasts that You sucked!

28 But He said, Blessed—happy and [g]to be envied—rather are they who hear the Word of God and obey *and* practice it!

29 Now as the crowds were (increasingly) thronging Him, He began to say, This present generation is a wicked one; it seeks *and* demands a sign (miracle), but no sign shall be given to it except the sign of Jonah [the prophet]. [Jonah 1:17 with Matt. 12:40.]

30 For [just] as Jonah became a sign to the people of Nineveh, so will also the Son of man be [a sign] to this age *and* generation. [Jonah 3:4-10.]

31 The queen of the South will arise in the judgment with the people of this age *and* generation and condemn them; for she came from the ends of the (inhabited) earth to listen to the wisdom of Solomon, and notice, [h]here is more than Solomon. [I Kings. 10: 1-13; II Chron. 9:1-12.]

32 The men of Nineveh will appear as witnesses at the judgment with this generation and will condemn it; for they repented at the preaching of Jonah, and behold, [h]here is more than Jonah. [Jonah 3:4-10.]

33 No one after lighting a lamp puts it in a cellar *or* crypt or under a bushel measure, but on a [lamp]stand, that those who are coming in may see the light.

34 Your eye is the lamp of your body; when your eye [[i]your conscience] is sound *and* fulfilling its office, your whole body is full of light; but when it is not sound *and* is not fulfilling its office, your body is full of darkness.

35 Be careful therefore that the light that is in you be not darkness.

36 If then your entire body is illuminated, having no part dark, it will be wholly bright [with light], as when a lamp with its bright rays gives you light.

37 Now while Jesus was speaking, a Pharisee invited Him to take dinner with him, so He entered and reclined at table.

38 The Pharisee noticed and was astonished [to see] that Jesus did not first wash before dinner.

39 But the Lord said to him, Now you Pharisees cleanse the outside of the cup and of the plate, but inside you yourselves are full of greed *and* robbery *and* extortion and malice *and* wickedness.

40 You senseless (foolish, stupid) ones—acting without reflection *or* intelligence! Did not He Who made the outside make the inside also?

---

g) Souter.
h) Wycliffe.
i) Cremer.

Living New Testament

22 Until someone stronger and better-armed attacks and overcomes him and strips him of his weapons and carries off his belongings.

23 Anyone who is not for Me is against Me; if he isn't helping Me, he is hurting My cause.

24 When a demon is cast out of a man, it goes to the deserts, searching there for rest; but finding none, it returns to the person it left,

25 And finds that its former home is all swept and clean.[7]

26 Then it goes and gets seven other demons more evil than itself, and they all enter the man. And so the poor fellow is seven times worse off than he was before."

27 As He was speaking, a woman in the crowd called out, "God bless Your mother—the womb from which You came, and the breasts that gave You suck!"

28 He replied, "Yes, but even more blessed are all who hear the Word of God and put it into practice."

29, 30 As the crowd pressed in upon Him, He preached them this sermon: "These are evil times, with evil people. They keep asking for some strange happening in the skies [to prove I am the Messiah[8]], but the only proof I will give them is a miracle like that of Jonah, whose experiences proved to the people of Nineveh that God had sent him. My similar experience will prove that God has sent Me to these people.

31 And at the Judgment Day the Queen of Sheba[9] shall arise and point her finger at this generation, condemning it, for she went on a long, hard journey to listen to the wisdom of Solomon; but one far greater than Solomon is here [and few pay any attention[10]].

32 The men of Nineveh, too, shall arise and condemn this nation, for they repented at the preaching of Jonah; and someone far greater than Jonah is here [but this nation won't listen[10]].

* * * * *

33 No one lights a lamp and hides it! Instead he puts it on a lampstand to give light to all who enter the room.

34 Your eye lights up your inward being.

A pure eye lets sunshine into your soul. A lustful eye shuts out the light and plunges you into darkness.

35 So watch out that the sunshine isn't blotted out.

36 If you are filled with light within, with no dark corners, then the outside will be radiant too, as though a floodlight is beamed upon you."

37, 38 As He was speaking, one of the Pharisees asked Him home for a meal. When Jesus arrived, He sat down to eat without first performing the ceremonial washing required by Jewish custom. This greatly surprised His host.

39 Then Jesus said to him, "You Pharisees wash the outside, but inside you are still dirty—full of greed and wickedness!

40 Fools! Didn't God make the inside as well as the outside?

Revised Standard

are in peace; 22but when one stronger than
he assails him and overcomes him, he takes
away his armor in which he trusted, and
divides his spoil. 23He who is not with me
is against me, and he who does not gather
with me scatters.
24 "When the unclean spirit has gone
out of a man, he passes through waterless
places seeking rest; and finding none he
says, 'I will return to my house from which
I came.' 25And when he comes he finds it
swept and put in order. 26Then he goes
and brings seven other spirits more evil
than himself, and they enter and dwell
there; and the last state of that man becomes worse than the first."
27 As he said this, a woman in the
crowd raised her voice and said to him,
"Blessed is the womb that bore you, and
the breasts that you sucked!" 28But he said,
"Blessed rather are those who hear the
word of God and keep it!"

Warning against seeking signs

29 When the crowds were increasing,
he began to say, "This generation is an
evil generation; it seeks a sign, but no sign
shall be given to it except the sign of
Jonah. 30For as Jonah became a sign to
the men of Nineveh, so will the Son of
man be to this generation. 31The queen of
the South will arise at the judgment with
the men of this generation and condemn
them; for she came from the ends of the
earth to hear the wisdom of Solomon, and
behold, something greater than Solomon
is here. 32The men of Nineveh will arise
at the judgment with this generation and
condemn it; for they repented at the
preaching of Jonah, and behold, something
greater than Jonah is here.

The parable of the lighted lamp

33 "No one after lighting a lamp puts
it in a cellar or under a bushel, but on a
stand, that those who enter may see the
light. 34Your eye is the lamp of your
body; when your eye is sound, your whole
body is full of light; but when it is not
sound, your body is full of darkness. 35Therefore be careful lest the light in you be darkness. 36If then your whole body is full of
light, having no part dark, it will be wholly
bright, as when a lamp with its rays gives you
light."

The warning against Pharisaism

37 While he was speaking, a Pharisee
asked him to dine with him; so he went
in and sat at table. 38The Pharisee was
astonished to see that he did not first wash
before dinner. 39And the Lord said to him,
"Now you Pharisees cleanse the outside
of the cup and of the dish, but inside you
are full of extortion and wickedness. 40You
fools! Did not he who made the outside

---

[7] But empty, since the person is neutral about Christ.
[8] Implied.
[9] Literally, "Queen of the South." See 1 Kings, Chapter 10.
[10] Implied.

King James

41 But rather give alms of such things as ye have; and, behold, all things are clean unto you.

42 But woe unto you, Pharisees! for ye tithe mint and rue and all manner of herbs, and pass over judgment and the love of God: these ought ye to have done, and not to leave the other undone.

43 Woe unto you, Pharisees! for ye love the uppermost seats in the synagogues, and greetings in the markets.

44 Woe unto you, scribes and Pharisees, hypocrites! for ye are as graves which appear not, and the men that walk over *them* are not aware *of them.*

45 ¶ Then answered one of the lawyers, and said unto him, Master, thus saying thou reproachest us also.

46 And he said, Woe unto you also, *ye* lawyers! for ye lade men with burdens grievous to be borne, and ye yourselves touch not the burdens with one of your fingers.

47 Woe unto you! for ye build the sepulchres of the prophets, and your fathers killed them.

48 Truly ye bear witness that ye allow the deeds of your fathers: for they indeed killed them, and ye build their sepulchres.

49 Therefore also said the wisdom of God, I will send them prophets and apostles, and *some* of them they shall slay and persecute:

50 That the blood of all the prophets, which was shed from the foundation of the world, may be required of this generation;

51 From the blood of Abel unto the blood of Zacharias, which perished between the altar and the temple: verily I say unto you, It shall be required of this generation.

52 Woe unto you, lawyers! for ye have taken away the key of knowledge: ye entered not in yourselves, and them that were entering in ye hindered.

53 And as he said these things unto them, the scribes and the Pharisees began to urge *him* vehemently, and to provoke him to speak of many things:

54 Laying wait for him, and seeking to catch something out of his mouth, that they might accuse him.

Amplified

41 But [dedicate your inner self and] give for donations to the poor of those things which are within [of inward righteousness] and behold, everything is purified *and* clean for you.

42 But woe to you, Pharisees! Because you tithe mint and rue and every (little) herb, and disregard *and* neglect justice and the love of God. These you ought to have done without leaving the others undone. [Lev. 27:30; Mic. 6:8.]

43 Woe to you, Pharisees! For you love the best seats in the synagogues and to be greeted *and* bowed down to in the market (public) places.

44 Woe to you! For you are like graves which are not marked *or* seen, and men walk over them without being aware of it [and are ceremonially defiled].

45 One of the experts of the [Mosaic] Law answered Him, Teacher, in saying this You reproach *and* outrage *and* affront even us!

46 But He said, Woe to you, the lawyers, also! For you load men with oppressive burdens hard to bear, and you do not personally [even [j]gently] touch the burdens with one of your fingers.

47 Woe to you! For you are [k]rebuilding *and* repairing the tombs of the prophets whom your fathers killed (destroyed).

48 So you bear witness, and give your full approval *and* consent to the deeds of your fathers; for they actually killed them, and you rebuild *and* repair monuments to them.

49 For this reason also the Wisdom of God said, I will send them prophets and apostles, [some] of whom they will put to death and persecute,

50 So that the blood of all the prophets shed from the foundation of the world may be charged against *and* required of this age *and* generation,

51 From the blood of Abel to the blood of Zechariah, who was slain between the altar and the sanctuary. Yes, I tell you, it shall be charged against *and* required of this age *and* generation. [Gen. 4:8; II Chron. 24:20, 21; Zech. 1:1.]

52 Woe to you, lawyers—experts in the [Mosaic] Law! For you have taken away the key to knowledge; you did not go in yourselves, and you hindered *and* prevented those who were entering.

53 As He left there, the scribes and the Pharisees [followed Him closely, and they] began [l]to be enraged with *and* set themselves violently against Him, and to draw Him out *and* provoke Him to speak of many things,

54 Secretly watching *and* plotting *and* lying in wait for Him, to seize upon something He might say [that they might accuse Him].

CHAPTER 12

IN the mean time, when there were gathered together an innumerable multitude of people, insomuch that they trode one upon another, he began to say unto his disciples first of all, Beware ye of the leaven of the Pharisees, which is hypocrisy.

CHAPTER 12

IN the meanwhile, when so many thousands of the people had gathered that they were trampling on one another, Jesus commenced by saying, primarily to His disciples, Be on your guard against the leaven (ferment) of the Pharisees which is hypocrisy [producing unrest and violent agitation].

---

j) Vincent.
k) Thayer.
l) Thayer.

Living New Testament

41 Purity is best demonstrated by generosity!

42 But woe to you Pharisees! For though you are careful to tithe even the smallest part of your income, you completely forget about justice and the love of God. You should tithe, yes, but you should not leave these other things undone.

43 Woe to you Pharisees! For how you love the seats of honor in the synagogues and the respectful greetings from everyone as you walk through the markets!

44 Yes, awesome judgment is awaiting you. For you are like hidden graves in a field. Men go by you with no knowledge of the corruption they are passing."

45 "Sir," said an expert in religious law who was standing there, "You have insulted my profession, too, in what you just said."

46 "Yes," said Jesus, "the same horrors await you! For you crush men beneath impossible religious demands—demands that you yourselves would never think of trying to keep.

47 Woe to you! For you are exactly like your ancestors who killed the prophets long ago.

48 Murderers! You agree with your fathers that what they did was right—you would have done the same yourselves.

49 This is what God says about you: 'I will send prophets and apostles to you, and you will kill some of them and chase away the others.'

50 And you of this generation will be held responsible for the murder of God's servants from the founding of the world—

51 From the murder of Abel to the murder of Zechariah who perished between the altar and the sanctuary. Yes, it will surely be charged against you.

52 Woe to you experts in religion! For you hide the truth from the people. You won't accept it for yourselves, and you prevent others from having a chance to believe it."

53, 54 The Pharisees and legal experts were furious; and from that time on they plied Him fiercely with a host of questions, trying to trap Him into saying something for which they could have Him arrested.

Revised Standard

make the inside also? [41]But give for alms
those things which are within; and behold,
everything is clean for you.
42 "But woe to you Pharisees! for you
tithe mint and rue and every herb, and
neglect justice and the love of God; these
you ought to have done, without neglecting
the others. [43]Woe to you Pharisees! for you
love the best seat in the synagogues and
salutations in the market places. [44]Woe
to you! for you are like graves which are
not seen, and men walk over them without
knowing it."
45 One of the lawyers answered him,
"Teacher, in saying this you reproach us
also." [46]And he said, "Woe to you lawyers
also! for you load men with burdens hard
to bear, and you yourselves do not touch
the burdens with one of your fingers.
[47]Woe to you! for you build the tombs of
the prophets whom your fathers killed. [48]So
you are witnesses and consent to the deeds
of your fathers; for they killed them, and
you build their tombs. [49]Therefore also the
Wisdom of God said, 'I will send them
prophets and apostles, some of whom they
will kill and persecute,' [50]that the blood of
all the prophets, shed from the foundation
of the world, may be required of this
generation, [51]from the blood of Abel to
the blood of Zechariah, who perished between the altar and the sanctuary. Yes, I
tell you, it shall be required of this generation. [52]Woe to you lawyers! for you have
taken away the key of knowledge; you did
not enter yourselves, and you hindered
those who were entering."
53 As he went away from there, the
scribes and the Pharisees began to press
him hard, and to provoke him to speak of
many things, [54]lying in wait for him, to
catch at something he might say.

CHAPTER 12

Meanwhile the crowds grew until thousands upon thousands were milling about and crushing each other. He turned now to His disciples and warned them, "More than anything else, beware of these Pharisees and the way they pretend to be good when they aren't. But such hypocrisy cannot be hidden forever.

The value of life

12 In the meantime, when so many thousands of the multitude had gathered
together that they trod upon one another,
he began to say to his disciples first, "Beware of the leaven of the Pharisees, which

King James

2 For there is nothing covered, that shall not be revealed; neither hid, that shall not be known.

3 Therefore whatsoever ye have spoken in darkness shall be heard in the light; and that which ye have spoken in the ear in closets shall be proclaimed upon the housetops.

4 And I say unto you my friends, Be not afraid of them that kill the body, and after that have no more that they can do.

5 But I will forewarn you whom ye shall fear: Fear him, which after he hath killed hath power to cast into hell; yea, I say unto you, Fear him.

6 Are not five sparrows sold for two farthings, and not one of them is forgotten before God?

7 But even the very hairs of your head are all numbered. Fear not therefore: ye are of more value than many sparrows.

8 Also I say unto you, Whosoever shall confess me before men, him shall the Son of man also confess before the angels of God:

9 But he that denieth me before men shall be denied before the angels of God.

10 And whosoever shall speak a word against the Son of man, it shall be forgiven him: but unto him that blasphemeth against the Holy Ghost it shall not be forgiven.

11 And when they bring you unto the synagogues, and *unto* magistrates, and powers, take ye no thought how or what thing ye shall answer, or what ye shall say:

12 For the Holy Ghost shall teach you in the same hour what ye ought to say.

13 ¶ And one of the company said unto him, Master, speak to my brother, that he divide the inheritance with me.

14 And he said unto him, Man, who made me a judge or a divider over you?

15 And he said unto them, Take heed, and beware of covetousness: for a man's life consisteth not in the abundance of the things which he possesseth.

16 And he spake a parable unto them, saying, The ground of a certain rich man brought forth plentifully:

17 And he thought within himself, saying, What shall I do, because I have no room where to bestow my fruits?

18 And he said, This will I do: I will pull down my barns, and build greater; and there will I bestow all my fruits and my goods.

19 And I will say to my soul, Soul, thou hast much goods laid up for many years; take thine ease, eat, drink, *and* be merry.

20 But God said unto him, *Thou* fool, this night thy soul shall be required of thee: then whose shall those things be, which thou hast provided?

Amplified

2 Nothing is [so closely] covered up that it will not be revealed, or hidden that will not be known.

3 Whatever you have spoken in the darkness shall be heard *and* listened to in the light, and what you have whispered in [people's] ears and behind closed doors, will be proclaimed upon the housetops.

4 I tell you, My friends, do not dread *and* be afraid of those who kill the body, and after that have nothing more that they can do.

5 But I will warn you whom you should fear: fear Him Who, after killing, has power to hurl into hell (Gehenna); yes, I say to you, fear Him!

6 Are not five sparrows sold for two pennies? And [yet] not one of them is forgotten *or* uncared for in the presence of God.

7 But [even] the very hairs of your head are all numbered. Do not be struck with fear *or* seized with alarm; you are of greater worth than many [flocks] of sparrows.

8 And I tell you: Whoever declares openly—speaking out freely—*and* confesses that he is My worshipper *and* acknowledges Me before men, the Son of man also will declare *and* confess *and* acknowledge him before the angels of God.

9 But he who disowns *and* denies *and* rejects *and* refuses to acknowledge Me before men will be disowned *and* denied *and* rejected *and* refused acknowledgment in the presence of the angels of God.

10 And everyone who makes a statement *or* speaks a word against the Son of man, it will be forgiven him; but he who blasphemes against the Holy Spirit [that is, whoever [m]intentionally comes short of the reverence due the Holy Spirit], it will not be forgiven him—for him there is no forgiveness.

11 And when they bring you before the synagogues and the magistrates and the authorities, do not be anxious [beforehand] how you shall reply in defense or what you are to say.

12 For the Holy Spirit will teach you in that very hour *and* [n]moment what [you] ought to say.

13 Someone from the crowd said to Him, Master, order my brother to divide the inheritance *and* share it with me.

14 But He told him, Man, who has appointed Me a judge or umpire *and* divider over you?

15 And He said to them, Guard yourselves and keep free from all covetousness—the immoderate desire for wealth, the greedy longing to have more; for a man's life does not consist *and* is not derived from possessing [o]overflowing abundance, *or* that which is [p]over and above his needs.

16 Then He told them a parable, saying, The land of a rich man was fertile *and* yielded plentifully;

17 And he considered *and* debated within himself, What shall I do? I have no place to gather together my harvest.

18 And he said, I will do this: I will pull down my storehouses and build larger ones; and there I will store all [q]my grain (produce) and my goods.

19 And I will say to my soul, Soul, you have many good things laid up, [enough] for many years; take your ease, eat, drink *and* enjoy yourself merrily.

20 But God said to him, You fool! This very night [r]they [that is, the messengers of God] demand your soul of you; and all the things that you have prepared, whose will they be? [Jer. 17:11; Job 28:8.]

---

m) Thayer.
n) Moulton and Milligan.
o) Souter.
p) Abbott-Smith.
q) Some ancient texts read "grain."
r) Vincent: "The indefiniteness is impressive."

Living New Testament

2 It will become as evident as yeast in dough.

3 Whatever they[1] have said in the dark shall be heard in the light, and what you have whispered in the inner rooms shall be broadcast from the housetops for all to hear!

4 Dear friends, don't be afraid of these who want to murder you. They can only kill the body; they have no power over your souls.

5 But I'll tell you whom to fear—fear God who has the power to kill and then cast into hell.

6 What is the price of five sparrows? A couple of pennies? Not much more than that. Yet God does not forget a single one of them.

7 And He knows the number of hairs on your head! Never fear, you are far more valuable to Him than a whole flock of sparrows.

8 And I assure you of this: I, the Man from Heaven,[2] will publicly honor you in the presence of God's angels if you publicly acknowledge Me here on earth as your Friend.

9 But I will deny before the angels those who deny Me here among men.

10 (Yet those who speak against Me[3] may be forgiven—while those who speak against the Holy Spirit shall never be forgiven.)

11 And when you are brought to trial before these Jewish rulers and authorities in the synagogues, don't be concerned about what to say in your defense,

12 For the Holy Spirit will give you the right words even as you are standing there."

13 Then someone called from the crowd, "Sir, please tell my brother to divide my father's estate with me."

14 But Jesus replied, "Man, who made Me a judge over you to decide such things as that?

15 Beware! Don't always be wishing for what you don't have."

16 Then He gave an illustration: "A rich man had a fertile farm that produced fine crops.

17 In fact, his barns were full to overflowing—he couldn't get everything in. He thought about his problem,

18 And finally exclaimed, 'I know—I'll tear down my barns and build bigger ones! Then I'll have room enough.

19 And I'll sit back and say to myself, "Friend, you have enough stored away for years to come. Now take it easy! Wine, women, and song for you" '[4]

20 But God said to him, 'Fool! Tonight you die. Then who will get it all?'

---

[1] Literally, "you."
[2] Literally, "the Son of man."
[3] Literally, "the Son of man."
[4] Literally, "eat, drink and be merry."

Revised Standard

is hypocrisy. 2Nothing is covered up that
will not be revealed, or hidden that will not
be known. 3Whatever you have said in the
dark shall be heard in the light, and what
you have whispered in private rooms shall
be proclaimed upon the housetops.
4 "I tell you, my friends, do not fear
those who kill the body, and after that
have no more that they can do. 5But I will
warn you whom to fear: fear him who, after he has killed, has power to cast into
hell;[m] yes, I tell you, fear him! 6Are not
five sparrows sold for two pennies? And
not one of them is forgotten before God.
7Why, even the hairs of your head are all
numbered. Fear not; you are of more
value than many sparrows.
8 "And I tell you, every one who acknowledges me before men, the Son of man
also will acknowledge before the angels of
God; 9but he who denies me before men
will be denied before the angels of God.
10And every one who speaks a word against
the Son of man will be forgiven; but he
who blasphemes against the Holy Spirit
will not be forgiven. 11And when they
bring you before the synagogues and the
rulers and the authorities, do not be anxious how or what you are to answer or
what you are to say; 12for the Holy Spirit
will teach you in that very hour what you
ought to say."

The parable of the rich fool

13 One of the multitude said to him,
"Teacher, bid my brother divide the inheritance with me." 14But he said to him,
"Man, who made me a judge or divider
over you?" 15And he said to them, "Take
heed, and beware of all covetousness; for
a man's life does not consist in the abundance of his possessions." 16And he told
them a parable, saying, "The land of a
rich man brought forth plentifully; 17and
he thought to himself, 'What shall I do,
for I have nowhere to store my crops?'
18And he said, 'I will do this: I will pull
down my barns, and build larger ones;
and there I will store all my grain and my
goods. 19And I will say to my soul, Soul,
you have ample goods laid up for many
years; take your ease, eat, drink, be merry.'
20But God said to him, 'Fool! This night
your soul is required of you; and the
things you have prepared, whose will they

---

[m] Greek *Gehenna*

King James

21 So *is* he that layeth up treasure for himself, and is not rich toward God.

22 ¶ And he said unto his disciples, Therefore I say unto you, Take no thought for your life, what ye shall eat; neither for the body, what ye shall put on.

23 The life is more than meat, and the body *is more* than raiment.

24 Consider the ravens: for they neither sow nor reap; which neither have storehouse nor barn; and God feedeth them: how much more are ye better than the fowls?

25 And which of you with taking thought can add to his stature one cubit?

26 If ye then be not able to do that thing which is least, why take ye thought for the rest?

27 Consider the lilies how they grow: they toil not, they spin not; and yet I say unto you, that Solomon in all his glory was not arrayed like one of these.

28 If then God so clothe the grass, which is today in the field, and tomorrow is cast into the oven; how much more *will he clothe* you, O ye of little faith?

29 And seek not ye what ye shall eat, or what ye shall drink, neither be ye of doubtful mind.

30 For all these things do the nations of the world seek after: and your Father knoweth that ye have need of these things.

31 ¶ But rather seek ye the kingdom of God; and all these things shall be added unto you.

32 Fear not, little flock; for it is your Father's good pleasure to give you the kingdom.

33 Sell that ye have, and give alms; provide yourselves bags which wax not old, a treasure in the heavens that faileth not, where no thief approacheth, neither moth corrupteth.

34 For where your treasure is, there will your heart be also.

35 Let your loins be girded about, and *your* lights burning;

36 And ye yourselves like unto men that wait for their lord, when he will return from the wedding; that when he cometh and knocketh, they may open unto him immediately.

37 Blessed *are* those servants, whom the lord when he cometh shall find watching: verily I say unto you, that he shall gird himself, and make them to sit down to meat, and will come forth and serve them.

38 And if he shall come in the second watch, or come in the third watch, and find *them* so, blessed are those servants.

39 And this know, that if the goodman of the house had known what hour the thief would come, he would have watched, and not have suffered his house to be broken through.

Amplified

21 So it is with him who continues to lay up *and* hoard possessions for himself, and is not rich [in his relation] to God—this is how he fares.

22 And [Jesus] said to His disciples, Therefore I tell you, do not be anxious *and* troubled [with cares] about your life, as to what you will [have to] eat, or about your body, as to what you will [have to] wear;

23 For life is more than food, and the body [more] than clothes.

24 Observe *and* consider the ravens, for they neither sow nor reap, they have neither storehouse nor barns, and [yet] God feeds them. Of how much more worth are you than the birds!

25 And which of you by being over-anxious *and* troubled with cares can add a [s]cubit to his stature, *or* a moment [unit] of time to his [s]age—the length of his life?

26 If then you are not able to do such a little thing as that, why are you anxious *and* troubled with cares about the rest?

27 Consider the lilies, how they grow; they neither [wearily] toil nor spin *nor* [t]*weave;* yet I tell you, even Solomon in all his glory—his splendor and magnificence—was not arrayed like one of these. [I Kings 10:4-7.]

28 But if God so clothes the grass in the field, which is alive today and tomorrow is thrown into the furnace, how much more will He clothe you, O you [people] of little faith?

29 And you, do not seek [by meditating and reasoning to inquire into] what you are to eat and what you are to drink, nor be of anxious (troubled) mind—[u]unsettled, excited, worried and [v]in suspense;

30 For all the pagan world is [greedily] seeking after these things, and your Father knows that you need them.

31 Only aim at *and* strive for *and* seek after His kingdom, and all these things shall be supplied to you also.

32 Do not be seized with alarm *and* struck with fear, little flock, for it is your Father's good pleasure to give you the kingdom!

33 Sell what you possess and give donations to the poor; provide yourselves with purses *and* handbags that do not grow old, an unfailing *and* inexhaustible treasure in the heavens, where no thief comes near and no moth destroys.

34 For where your treasure is, there will your heart be also.

35 Keep your loins girded and your lamps burning,

36 And be yourselves like men who are waiting for their master to return home from the marriage feast, so that when he shall return from the wedding and comes and knocks, they may open to him immediately.

37 Blessed—happy, fortunate and [w]to be envied—are those servants whom the master finds awake *and* alert *and* watching when he comes. Truly, I say to you, he will gird himself and have them recline at table and will come and serve them!

38 If he comes in the second watch (before midnight), or the third watch (after midnight), and finds them so, blessed—happy, fortunate and [w]to be envied—are those servants!

39 But of this be assured, that if the householder had known at what time the burglar was coming, he would have been awake *and* alert *and* watching, and would not have permitted his house to be dug through *and* broken open.

---

s) Abbott-Smith: "A stage of growth whether measured by age or stature."
t) Some ancient authorities read "weave."
u) Vincent.
v) Abbott-Smith.
w) Souter.

Living New Testament

21 Yes, every man is a fool who gets rich on earth but not in heaven."

22 Then turning to His disciples He said, "Don't worry about whether you have enough food to eat or clothes to wear.

23 For life consists of far more than food and clothes.

24 Look at the ravens—they don't plant or harvest or have barns to store away their food, and yet they get along all right—for God feeds them. And you are far more valuable to Him than any birds!

25 And besides, what's the use of worrying? What good does it do? Will it add a single day to your life? Of course not!

26 And if worry can't even do such little things as that, what's the use of worrying over bigger things?

27 Look at the lilies! They don't toil and spin, and yet Solomon in all his glory was not robed as well as they are.

28 And if God provides clothing for the flowers that are here today and gone tomorrow, don't you suppose that He will provide clothing for you, you doubters?

29 And don't worry about food—what to eat and drink; don't worry at all that God will provide it for you.

30 All mankind scratches for its daily bread, but your heavenly Father knows your needs.

31 He will always give you all you need from day to day if you will make the Kingdom of God your primary concern.

32 So don't be afraid, little flock. For it gives your Father great happiness to give you the Kingdom.

33 Sell what you have and give to those in need. This will fatten your purses in heaven! And the purses of heaven have no rips or holes in them. Your treasures there will never disappear; no thief can steal them; no moth can destroy them.

34 Wherever your treasure is, there your heart and thoughts will also be.

35 Be prepared—all dressed and ready—

36 For your Lord's return from the wedding feast. Then you will be ready to open the door and let Him in the moment He arrives and knocks.

37 There will be great joy for those who are ready and waiting for His return. He Himself will seat them and put on a waiter's uniform and serve them as they sit and eat!

38 He may come at nine o'clock at night—or even at midnight. But whenever He comes there will be joy for His servants who are ready!

39 Everyone would be ready for Him if they knew the exact hour of His return—just as they would be ready for a thief if they knew when he was coming.

Revised Standard

be?' 21So is he who lays up treasure for
himself, and is not rich toward God."

The teaching about anxiety

22 And he said to his disciples, "Therefore I tell you, do not be anxious about
your life, what you shall eat, nor about
your body, what you shall put on. 23For
life is more than food, and the body more
than clothing. 24Consider the ravens: they
neither sow nor reap, they have neither
storehouse nor barn, and yet God feeds
them. Of how much more value are you
than the birds! 25And which of you by
being anxious can add a cubit to his span
of life?[n] 26If then you are not able to do
as small a thing as that, why are you anxious about the rest? 27Consider the lilies,
how they grow; they neither toil nor spin;[o]
yet I tell you, even Solomon in all his glory
was not arrayed like one of these. 28But
if God so clothes the grass which is alive
in the field today and tomorrow is thrown
into the oven, how much more will he
clothe you, O men of little faith! 29And
do not seek what you are to eat and what
you are to drink, nor be of anxious mind.
30For all the nations of the world seek
these things; and your Father knows that
you need them. 31Instead, seek his[p] kingdom, and these things shall be yours as
well.

32 "Fear not, little flock, for it is your
Father's good pleasure to give you the
kingdom. 33Sell your possessions, and give
alms; provide yourselves with purses that
do not grow old, with a treasure in the
heavens that does not fail, where no thief
approaches and no moth destroys. 34For
where your treasure is, there will your
heart be also.

Parable of the watching servants

35 "Let your loins be girded and your
lamps burning, 36and be like men who are
waiting for their master to come home
from the marriage feast, so that they may
open to him at once when he comes and
knocks. 37Blessed are those servants whom
the master finds awake when he comes;
truly, I say to you, he will gird himself
and have them sit at table, and he will
come and serve them. 38If he comes in the
second watch, or in the third, and finds
them so, blessed are those servants! 39But
know this, that if the householder had
known at what hour the thief was coming,
he would have been awake and[q] would not
have left his house to be broken into. 40You

[n] Or *to his stature*

[o] Other ancient authorities read *Consider the lilies; they neither spin nor weave*

[p] Other ancient authorities read *God's*

[q] Other ancient authorities omit *would have been awake and*

King James

40 Be ye therefore ready also: for the
Son of man cometh at an hour when ye
think not.
41 ¶ Then Peter said unto him, Lord,
speakest thou this parable unto us, or even
to all?
42 And the Lord said, Who then is that
faithful and wise steward, whom *his* lord
shall make ruler over his household, to give
them their portion of meat in due season?
43 Blessed *is* that servant, whom his lord
when he cometh shall find so doing.
44 Of a truth I say unto you, that he will
make him ruler over all that he hath.
45 But and if that servant say in his
heart, My lord delayeth his coming; and
shall begin to beat the menservants and
maidens, and to eat and drink, and to be
drunken;
46 The lord of that servant will come in
a day when he looketh not for *him*, and at
an hour when he is not aware, and will cut
him in sunder, and will appoint him his
portion with the unbelievers.
47 And that servant, which knew his lord's
will, and prepared not *himself*, neither did
according to his will, shall be beaten with
many *stripes*.
48 But he that knew not, and did commit
things worthy of stripes, shall be beaten with
few *stripes*. For unto whomsoever much is
given, of him shall be much required: and
to whom men have committed much, of him
they will ask the more.
49 ¶ I am come to send fire on the earth;
and what will I, if it be already kindled?
50 But I have a baptism to be baptized
with; and how am I straitened till it be
accomplished!
51 Suppose ye that I am come to give
peace on earth? I tell you, Nay; but rather
division:
52 For from henceforth there shall be
five in one house divided, three against two,
and two against three.
53 The father shall be divided against the
son, and the son against the father; the
mother against the daughter, and the daughter against the mother; the mother in law
against her daughter in law, and the daughter in law against her mother in law.
54 ¶ And he said also to the people,
When ye see a cloud rise out of the west,
straightway ye say, There cometh a shower;
and so it is.
55 And when *ye see* the south wind blow,
ye say, There will be heat; and it cometh to
pass.
56 *Ye* hypocrites, ye can discern the face
of the sky and of the earth; but how is it
that ye do not discern this time?
57 Yea, and why even of yourselves judge
ye not what is right?
58 ¶ When thou goest with thine adversary to the magistrate, *as thou art* in the
way, give diligence that thou mayest be delivered from him; lest he hale thee to the
judge, and the judge deliver thee to the
officer, and the officer cast thee into prison.
59 I tell thee, thou shalt not depart
thence, till thou hast paid the very last mite.

Amplified

40 You also must be ready, for the Son of man i
coming at an hour *and* a [x]moment when you do nc
anticipate it.
41 Peter said, Lord, are You telling this parable for u
or for all alike?
42 And the Lord said, Who then is that faithful stew
ard, the wise men whom his master will set over those i
his household service, to supply them their allowance c
food at the appointed time?
43 Blessed—happy, and [y]to be envied—is that servar
whom his master finds so doing when he arrives.
44 Truly, I tell you, he will set him in charge over a
his possessions.
45 But if that servant says in his heart, My master i
late in coming, and begins to strike the menservants an
the maids, and to eat and drink and get drunk,
46 The master of that servant will come on a day whe
he does not expect him and at an hour of which he doe
not know, and will punish him *and* [z]cut him off and assig
his lot with [a]the unfaithful.
47 And that servant who knew his master's will, but di
not get ready or act as he would wish him to act, shall b
beaten with many [lashes].
48 But he who did not know and did things worthy o
a beating shall be beaten with few [lashes]. For every on
to whom much is given, of him shall much be required
and of him to whom men entrust much they will requir
and demand the more. [Deut. 25:2, 3; Num. 15:29
30.]
49 I have come to cast fire upon the earth, and how
wish that it were already kindled!
50 I have a baptism with which to be baptized, an
how greatly *and* sorely I am urged—impelled, [a]con
strained—until it is accomplished!
51 Do you suppose that I have come to give peac
upon earth? No, I say to you, but rather division;
52 For from now on in one house there will be fiv
divided [among themselves], three against two and tw
against three.
53 They will be divided, father against son and so
against father, mother against daughter and daughter agains
mother, mother-in-law against her daughter-in-law an
daughter-in-law against her mother-in-law. [Mic. 7:6.]
54 He also said to the crowds of people, When you se
a cloud rising in the west, at once you say, It is going t
rain! And so it does.
55 And when [you see that] a south wind is blowing
you say, There will be severe heat! And it occurs.
56 You play actors—hypocrites! You know how [inte
ligently] to discern *and* interpret *and* [a]prove the looks o
the earth and sky, but how is it you do not know how t
discern *and* interpret *and* apply the proof to the presen
time?
57 And why do you not judge what is just, *and* person
ally decide what is right?
58 Then, as you go with your accuser before a magis
trate, on the way make diligent effort to settle *and* be qui
of him, lest he drag you to the judge, and the judge tur
you over to the officer, and the officer put you i
prison.
59 I tell you, you will never get out until you have pai
the very last (fraction of a) cent.

---

x) Moulton and Milligan.
y) Souter.
z) Alternate reading.
a) Wycliffe.

Living New Testament

40 So be ready all the time. For I, the Man of Glory,[5] will come when least expected."

41 Peter asked, "Lord, are You talking just to us or to everyone?"

42, 43, 44 And the Lord replied, "I'm talking to any faithful, sensible man whose master gives him the responsibility of feeding the other servants. If his master returns and finds that he has done a good job, there will be a reward—his master will put him in charge of all he owns.

45 But if the man begins to think, 'My Lord won't be back for a long time,' and begins to whip the men and women he is supposed to protect, and to spend his time at drinking parties and in drunkenness—

46 Well, his Master will return without notice and remove him from his position of trust and assign him to the place of the unfaithful.

47 He will be severely punished, for though he knew his duty he refused to do it.

48 But anyone who is not aware that he is doing wrong will be punished only lightly. Much is required from those to whom much is given, for their responsibility is greater.

49 I have come to bring fire to the earth, and, oh, that My task were completed!

50 There is a terrible baptism ahead of Me, and how I am pent up until it is accomplished.

51 Do you think I have come to give peace to the earth? *No!* Rather, strife and division!

52 From now on families will be split apart, three in favor of Me, and two against—or perhaps the other way around.

53 A father will decide one way about Me; his son, the other; mother and daughter will disagree; and the decision of an honored[6] mother-in-law will be spurned by her daughter-in-law."

54 Then He turned to the crowd and said, "When you see clouds beginning to form in the west, you say, 'Here comes a shower.' And you are right.

55 When the south wind blows you say, 'Today will be a scorcher.' And it is.

56 Hypocrites! You interpret the sky well enough, but you refuse to notice the warnings all around you about the crisis ahead.

57 Why do you refuse to see for yourselves what is right?

58 If you meet your accuser on the way to court, try to settle the matter before it reaches the judge, lest he sentence you to jail;

59 For if that happens you won't be free again until the last penny is paid in full."

[5] Literally, "the Son of man."
[6] Implied from ancient custom.

Revised Standard

also must be ready; for the Son of man is
coming at an hour you do not expect."

Faithful and unfaithful servants

41 Peter said, "Lord, are you telling
this parable for us or for all?" 42And the
Lord said, "Who then is the faithful and
wise steward, whom his master will set
over his household, to give them their portion of food at the proper time? 43Blessed
is that servant whom his master when he
comes will find so doing. 44Truly I tell you,
he will set him over all his possessions.
45But if that servant says to himself, 'My
master is delayed in coming,' and begins
to beat the menservants and the maidservants, and to eat and drink and get drunk,
46the master of that servant will come on
a day when he does not expect him and at
an hour he does not know, and will punish[r]
him, and put him with the unfaithful.
47And that servant who knew his master's
will, but did not make ready or act according to his will, shall receive a severe beating. 48But he who did not know, and did
what deserved a beating, shall receive a
light beating. Every one to whom much is
given, of him will much be required; and
of him to whom men commit much they
will demand the more.

Jesus the divider

49 "I came to cast fire upon the earth;
and would that it were already kindled!
50I have a baptism to be baptized with;
and how I am constrained until it is accomplished! 51Do you think that I have
come to give peace on earth? No, I tell
you, but rather division; 52for henceforth
in one house there will be five divided,
three against two and two against three;
53they will be divided, father against son
and son against father, mother against
daughter and daughter against her mother,
mother-in-law against her daughter-in-law
and daughter-in-law against her mother-in-
law."

Interpreting the present time

54 He also said to the multitudes, "When
you see a cloud rising in the west, you say
at once, 'A shower is coming'; and so it
happens. 55And when you see the south
wind blowing, you say, 'There will be
scorching heat'; and it happens. 56You hypocrites! You know how to interpret the appearance of earth and sky; but why do you
not know how to interpret the present
time?

Settlement with an accuser

57 "And why do you not judge for
yourselves what is right? 58As you go with
your accuser before the magistrate, make
an effort to settle with him on the way, lest
he drag you to the judge, and the judge
hand you over to the officer, and the officer put you in prison. 59I tell you, you
will never get out till you have paid the
very last copper."

[r] Or *cut him in pieces*

King James

CHAPTER 13

THERE were present at that season some that told him of the Galilæans, whose blood Pilate had mingled with their sacrifices.

2 And Jesus answering said unto them, Suppose ye that these Galilæans were sinners above all the Galilæans, because they suffered such things?

3 I tell you, Nay: but, except ye repent, ye shall all likewise perish.

4 Or those eighteen, upon whom the tower in Siloam fell, and slew them, think ye that they were sinners above all men that dwelt in Jerusalem?

5 I tell you, Nay: but, except ye repent, ye shall all likewise perish.

6 ¶ He spake also this parable; A certain *man* had a fig tree planted in his vineyard; and he came and sought fruit thereon, and found none.

7 Then said he unto the dresser of his vineyard, Behold, these three years I come seeking fruit on this fig tree, and find none: cut it down; why cumbereth it the ground?

8 And he answering said unto him, Lord, let it alone this year also, till I shall dig about it, and dung *it:*

9 And if it bear fruit, *well:* and if not, *then* after that thou shalt cut it down.

10 And he was teaching in one of the synagogues on the sabbath.

11 ¶ And, behold, there was a woman which had a spirit of infirmity eighteen years, and was bowed together, and could in no wise lift up *herself.*

12 And when Jesus saw her, he called *her to him,* and said unto her, Woman, thou art loosed from thine infirmity.

13 And he laid *his* hands on her: and immediately she was made straight, and glorified God.

14 And the ruler of the synagogue answered with indignation, because that Jesus had healed on the sabbath day, and said unto the people, There are six days in which men ought to work: in them therefore come and be healed, and not on the sabbath day.

15 The Lord then answered him, and said, *Thou* hypocrite, doth not each one of you on the sabbath loose his ox or *his* ass from the stall, and lead *him* away to watering?

16 And ought not this woman, being a daughter of Abraham, whom Satan hath bound, lo, these eighteen years, be loosed from this bond on the sabbath day?

17 And when he had said these things, all his adversaries were ashamed: and all the people rejoiced for all the glorious things that were done by him.

18 ¶ Then said he, Unto what is the kingdom of God like? and whereunto shall I resemble it?

19 It is like a grain of mustard seed, which a man took, and cast into his garden; and it grew, and waxed a great tree; and the fowls of the air lodged in the branches of it.

Amplified

CHAPTER 13

JUST at that time there [arrived] some people who informed Jesus about the Galileans whose blood Pilate mixed with their sacrifices.

2 And He replied by saying to them, Do you think that those Galileans were greater sinners than all the other Galileans, because they have suffered in this way?

3 I tell you, No; but unless you repent—[that is,] [b]change your mind for the better and heartily amend your ways with abhorrence of your past sins—you will all likewise perish *and* be lost [[c]eternally].

4 Or those eighteen on whom the tower in Siloam fell and killed them, do you think that they were more guilty offenders (debtors) than all the others who dwelt in Jerusalem?

5 I tell you, No; but unless you repent—[that is,] [b]change your mind for the better and heartily amend your ways with abhorrence of your past sins—you will all likewise perish *and* be lost [[c]eternally].

6 And He told them this parable: A certain man had a fig tree planted in his vineyard, and he came looking for fruit on it, but did not find [any].

7 So he said to the vinedresser, See here! For these three years I have come looking for fruit on this fig tree and I find none. Cut it down; why should it continue also to use up the ground—that is, to [d]deplete the soil, intercept the sun and take up room?

8 But he replied to him, Leave it alone, sir, [just] this one more year, till I dig around it and put manure [on the soil];

9 Then perhaps it will bear fruit after this, but if not, you can cut it down *and* out.

10 Now Jesus was teaching in one of the synagogues on the Sabbath.

11 And there was a woman there who for eighteen years had had an [e]infirmity caused by a spirit [[f]a demon of sickness]. She was [g]bent completely forward and utterly unable to straighten herself *or* to [h]look upward.

12 And when Jesus saw her, He called [her to Him] and said to her, Woman, you are released from your infirmity!

13 Then He laid [His] hands on her and instantly she was made straight, and she [d]recognized *and* thanked *and* praised God.

14 But the [h]leader of the synagogue, indignant because Jesus had healed on the Sabbath, said to the crowd, There are six days on which work ought to be done, so come on those days and be cured, and not on the Sabbath day. [Exod. 20:9, 10.]

15 But the Lord replied to him, saying, You play actors—hypocrites! Does not each one of you on the Sabbath loose his ox or his donkey from the stall, and lead it out to water it?

16 And ought not this woman, a daughter of Abraham whom Satan has kept bound for eighteen years, be loosed from this bond on the Sabbath day?

17 Even as He said this, all His opponents were put to shame, and all the people were rejoicing over all the glorious things that were being done by Him.

18 This led Him to say, What is the kingdom of God like? And to what shall I compare it?

19 It is like a grain of mustard seed which a man took and planted in his own garden; and it grew and became a tree, and the wild birds [i]found shelter *and* roosted *and* nested in its branches.

---

b) Thayer.
c) Jamieson, Fausett and Brown; George W. Clark; Matthew Henry, etc.
d) Bengel's "Gnomon Novi Testamenti." (-Vincent)
e) Vincent.
f) Cremer.
g) Thayer.
h) Souter.
i) Moulton and Milligan.

Living New Testament

CHAPTER 13

About this time He was informed that Pilate had butchered some Jews from Galilee as they were sacrificing at the Temple in Jerusalem.

2 "Do you think they were worse sinners than other men from Galilee?" He asked. "Is that why they suffered?

3 Not at all! And don't you realize that you also will perish unless you leave your evil ways and turn to God?

4 And what about the 18 men who died when the Tower of Siloam fell on them? Were they the worst sinners in Jerusalem?

5 Not at all! And you, too will perish, unless you repent."

6 Then He used this illustration: "A man planted a fig tree in his garden and came again and again to see if he could find any fruit on it, but he was always disappointed.

7 Finally he told his gardener to cut it down. 'I've waited three years and there hasn't been a single fig!' he said. 'Why bother with it any longer? It's taking up space we can use for something else.'

8 'Give it one more chance,' the gardener answered. 'Leave it another year, and I'll give it special attention and plenty of fertilizer.

9 If we get figs next year, fine; if not, I'll cut it down.' "

* * * * *

10 One Sabbath as He was teaching in a synagogue,

11 He saw a seriously handicapped woman who had been bent double for 18 years and was unable to straighten herself.

12 Calling her over to Him Jesus said, "Woman, you are healed of your sickness!"

13 He touched her, and instantly she could stand straight. How she praised and thanked God!

14 But the local Jewish leader in charge of the synagogue was very angry about it because Jesus had healed her on the Sabbath day. "There are six days of the week to work," he shouted to the crowd. "Those are the days to come for healing, not on the Sabbath!"

15 But the Lord replied, "You hypocrite! You work on the Sabbath! Don't you untie your cattle from their stalls on the Sabbath and lead them out for water?

16 And is it wrong for Me, just because it is the Sabbath day, to free this Jewish woman from Satan's 18 years of bondage?"

17 This shamed His enemies. And all the people rejoiced at the wonderful things He did.

18 Now He began teaching them again about the Kingdom of God: "What is the Kingdom like?" He asked. "How can I illustrate it?

19 It is like a tiny mustard seed planted in a garden; soon it grows into a tall bush, and the birds live among its branches.

Revised Standard

Jesus' call to repentance

13 There were some present at that very time who told him of the Galileans whose blood Pilate had mingled with their sacrifices. 2And he answered them, "Do you think that these Galileans were worse sinners than all the other Galileans, because they suffered thus? 3I tell you, No; but unless you repent you will all likewise perish. 4Or those eighteen upon whom the tower in Siloam fell and killed them, do you think that they were worse offenders than all the others who dwelt in Jerusalem? 5I tell you, No; but unless you repent you will all likewise perish."

The parable of the fig tree

6 And he told this parable: "A man had a fig tree planted in his vineyard; and he came seeking fruit on it and found none. 7And he said to the vinedresser, 'Lo, these three years I have come seeking fruit on this fig tree, and I find none. Cut it down; why should it use up the ground?' 8And he answered him, 'Let it alone, sir, this year also, till I dig about it and put on manure. 9And if it bears fruit next year, well and good; but if not, you can cut it down.' "

A woman healed on the Sabbath

10 Now he was teaching in one of the synagogues on the sabbath. 11And there was a woman who had had a spirit of infirmity for eighteen years; she was bent over and could not fully straighten herself. 12And when Jesus saw her, he called her and said to her, "Woman, you are freed from your infirmity." 13And he laid his hands upon her, and immediately she was made straight, and she praised God. 14But the ruler of the synagogue, indignant because Jesus had healed on the sabbath, said to the people, "There are six days on which work ought to be done; come on those days and be healed, and not on the sabbath day." 15Then the Lord answered him, "You hypocrites! Does not each of you on the sabbath untie his ox or his ass from the manger, and lead it away to water it? 16And ought not this woman, a daughter of Abraham whom Satan bound for eighteen years, be loosed from this bond on the sabbath day?" 17As he said this, all his adversaries were put to shame; and all the people rejoiced at all the glorious things that were done by him.

Parables about the kingdom

18 He said therefore, "What is the kingdom of God like? And to what shall I compare it? 19It is like a grain of mustard seed which a man took and sowed in his garden; and it grew and became a tree, and the birds of the air made nests in its branches."

King James

20 And again he said, Whereunto shall I liken the kingdom of God?

21 It is like leaven, which a woman took and hid in three measures of meal, till the whole was leavened.

22 And he went through the cities and villages, teaching, and journeying toward Jerusalem.

23 Then said one unto him, Lord, are there few that be saved? And he said unto them,

24 ¶ Strive to enter in at the strait gate: for many, I say unto you, will seek to enter in, and shall not be able.

25 When once the master of the house is risen up, and hath shut to the door, and ye begin to stand without, and to knock at the door, saying, Lord, Lord, open unto us; and he shall answer and say unto you, I know you not whence ye are:

26 Then shall ye begin to say, We have eaten and drunk in thy presence, and thou hast taught in our streets.

27 But he shall say, I tell you, I know you not whence ye are; depart from me, all *ye* workers of iniquity.

28 There shall be weeping and gnashing of teeth, when ye shall see Abraham, and Isaac, and Jacob, and all the prophets, in the kingdom of God, and you *yourselves* thrust out.

29 And they shall come from the east, and *from* the west, and from the north, and *from* the south, and shall sit down in the kingdom of God.

30 And, behold, there are last which shall be first, and there are first which shall be last.

31 ¶ The same day there came certain of the Pharisees, saying unto him, Get thee out, and depart hence: for Herod will kill thee.

32 And he said unto them, Go ye, and tell that fox, Behold, I cast out devils, and I do cures today and tomorrow, and the third *day* I shall be perfected.

33 Nevertheless I must walk today, and tomorrow, and the *day* following: for it cannot be that a prophet perish out of Jerusalem.

34 O Jerusalem, Jerusalem, which killest the prophets, and stonest them that are sent unto thee; how often would I have gathered thy children together, as a hen *doth gather* her brood under *her* wings, and ye would not!

35 Behold, your house is left unto you desolate: and verily I say unto you, Ye shall not see me, until *the time* come when ye shall say, Blessed *is* he that cometh in the name of the Lord.

Amplified

20 And again He said, To what shall I liken the kingdom of God?

21 It is like leaven which a woman took and hid in three measures of wheat flour *or* meal, until it was all leavened (fermented).

22 [Jesus] journeyed on through towns and villages, teaching, and making His way toward Jerusalem.

23 And one asked Him, Lord, will only a few be saved [that is, rescued, delivered from the penalties of the last judgment, and made partakers of the salvation by Christ]? And He said to them,

24 Strive to enter by the narrow door—force yourselves through it—for many, I tell you, will try to enter and will not be able.

25 When once the Master of the house gets up and closes the door, and you begin to stand outside and to knock at the door (again and again) saying, Lord, open to us! He will answer you, I do not know where [[j]what household, certainly not Mine] you come from.

26 Then you will begin to say, We ate and drank in Your presence, and You taught in our streets.

27 But He will say, I tell you, I do not know where [[j]what household—certainly not Mine] you come from; depart from Me, all you wrongdoers!

28 There will be weeping and grinding of teeth, when you see Abraham and Isaac and Jacob and all the prophets in the kingdom of God, but you yourselves being cast forth—banished, driven away.

29 And [people] will come from east and west, and from north and south, and sit down [feast at table] in the kingdom of God.

30 And behold, there are some [now] last who will be first [then], and there are some [now] first who will be last [then].

31 At that very hour some Pharisees came up and said to Him, Go away from here, for Herod is determined to kill You.

32 And He said to them, Go and tell that fox [sly and crafty, skulking and cowardly], Behold, I drive out demons and perform healings today and tomorrow, and on the third day I finish (complete) My course.

33 Nevertheless I must continue on My way today and tomorrow and the day after that, for it will never do for a prophet to be destroyed away from Jerusalem!

34 O Jerusalem, Jerusalem, you who continue to kill the prophets and to stone those who are sent to you! How often I have desired *and* yearned to gather your children together [around Me], as a hen [gathers] her young under her wings, but you would not!

35 Behold, your house is forsaken—abandoned, left to you destitute [of God's help]! And I tell you, you will not see Me again until the time comes when you shall say, Blessed (to be celebrated with praises) is He Who comes in the name of the Lord! [Jer. 22:5; Ps. 118:26.]

---

j) Vincent.

Living New Testament

20, 21 It is like yeast kneaded into dough, which works unseen until it has risen high and light."

22 He went from city to city and village to village, teaching as He went, always pressing onward toward Jerusalem.

23 Someone asked Him, "Will only a few be saved?" And He replied,

24, 25 "The door to heaven is narrow. Work hard to get in, for the truth is that many will try to enter but when the head of the house has locked the door, it will be too late. Then if you stand outside knocking, and pleading, 'Lord, open the door for us,' He will reply, 'I do not know you.'

26 'But we ate with You, and You taught in our streets,' you will say.

27 And He will reply, 'I tell you, I don't know you. You can't come in here, guilty as you are. Go away.'

28 And there will be great weeping and gnashing of teeth as you stand outside and see Abraham, Isaac, Jacob, and all the prophets within the Kingdom of God—

29 For people will come from all over the world to take their places there.

30 And note this: some who are despised now will be greatly honored then; and some who are highly thought of now will be least important then."

31 A few minutes later some Pharisees said to Him, "Get out of here if you want to live, for King Herod is after you!"

32 Jesus replied, "Go tell that fox that I will keep on casting out demons and doing miracles of healing today and tomorrow; and the third day I will reach my destination.

33 Yes, today, tomorrow, and the next day! For it wouldn't do for a prophet of God to be killed except in Jerusalem!

34 O Jerusalem, Jerusalem! The city that murders the prophets. The city that stones those sent to help her. How often I have wanted to gather your children together even as a hen protects her brood under her wings, but you wouldn't let Me.

35 And now—now your house is left desolate. And you will never again see Me until you say, 'Welcome to Him who comes in the name of the Lord.' "

Revised Standard

20 And again he said, "To what shall I compare the kingdom of God? [21]It is like leaven which a woman took and hid in three measures of meal, till it was all leavened."

The narrow door

22 He went on his way through towns and villages, teaching, and journeying toward Jerusalem. [23]And some one said to him, "Lord, will those who are saved be few?" And he said to them, [24]"Strive to enter by the narrow door; for many, I tell you, will seek to enter and will not be able. [25]When once the householder has risen up and shut the door, you will begin to stand outside and to knock at the door, saying, 'Lord, open to us.' He will answer you, 'I do not know where you come from.' [26]Then you will begin to say, 'We ate and drank in your presence, and you taught in our streets.' [27]But he will say, 'I tell you, I do not know where you come from; depart from me, all you workers of iniquity!' [28]There you will weep and gnash your teeth, when you see Abraham and Isaac and Jacob and all the prophets in the kingdom of God and you yourselves thrust out. [29]And men will come from east and west, and from north and south, and sit at table in the kingdom of God. [30]And behold, some are last who will be first, and some are first who will be last."

The lament over Jerusalem

31 At that very hour some Pharisees came, and said to him, "Get away from here, for Herod wants to kill you." [32]And he said to them, "Go and tell that fox, 'Behold, I cast out demons and perform cures today and tomorrow, and the third day I finish my course. [33]Nevertheless I must go on my way today and tomorrow and the day following; for it cannot be that a prophet should perish away from Jerusalem.' [34]O Jerusalem, Jerusalem, killing the prophets and stoning those who are sent to you! How often would I have gathered your children together as a hen gathers her brood under her wings, and you would not! [35]Behold, your house is forsaken. And I tell you, you will not see me until you say, 'Blessed is he who comes in the name of the Lord!' "

King James

CHAPTER 14

AND it came to pass, as he went into the house of one of the chief Pharisees to eat bread on the sabbath day, that they watched him.

2 And, behold, there was a certain man before him which had the dropsy.

3 And Jesus answering spake unto the lawyers and Pharisees, saying, Is it lawful to heal on the sabbath day?

4 And they held their peace. And he took *him*, and healed him, and let him go;

5 And answered them, saying, Which of you shall have an ass or an ox fallen into a pit, and will not straightway pull him out on the sabbath day?

6 And they could not answer him again to these things.

7 ¶ And he put forth a parable to those which were bidden, when he marked how they chose out the chief rooms; saying unto them,

8 When thou art bidden of any *man* to a wedding, sit not down in the highest room; lest a more honourable man than thou be bidden of him;

9 And he that bade thee and him come and say to thee, Give this man place; and thou begin with shame to take the lowest room.

10 But when thou art bidden, go and sit down in the lowest room; that when he that bade thee cometh, he may say unto thee, Friend, go up higher: then shalt thou have worship in the presence of them that sit at meat with thee.

11 For whosoever exalteth himself shall be abased; and he that humbleth himself shall be exalted.

12 ¶ Then said he also to him that bade him, When thou makest a dinner or a supper, call not thy friends, nor thy brethren, neither thy kinsmen, nor *thy* rich neighbours; lest they also bid thee again, and a recompence be made thee.

13 But when thou makest a feast, call the poor, the maimed, the lame, the blind:

14 And thou shalt be blessed; for they cannot recompense thee: for thou shalt be recompensed at the resurrection of the just.

15 ¶ And when one of them that sat at meat with him heard these things, he said unto him, Blessed *is* he that shall eat bread in the kingdom of God.

16 Then said he unto him, A certain man made a great supper, and bade many:

17 And sent his servant at supper time to say to them that were bidden, Come; for all things are now ready.

18 And they all with one *consent* began to make excuse. The first said unto him, I have bought a piece of ground, and I must needs go and see it: I pray thee have me excused.

19 And another said, I have bought five yoke of oxen, and I go to prove them: I pray thee have me excused.

20 And another said, I have married a wife, and therefore I cannot come.

Amplified

CHAPTER 14

IT occurred one Sabbath, when [Jesus] went for a meal at the house of one of the ruling Pharisees, that they were (engaged in) watching Him (closely).

2 And behold, [just] in front of Him there was a man who had dropsy.

3 And Jesus asked the lawyers and the Pharisees, Is it lawful *and* right to cure on the Sabbath, or not?

4 But they kept silent. Then He took hold [of the man and] cured him and [k]sent him away.

5 And He said to them, Which of you, having [l]a son *or* a donkey or an ox that has fallen into a well, will not at once pull him out on the Sabbath day?

6 And they were unable to reply to this.

7 Now He told a parable to those who were invited, [when] He noticed how they were selecting the places of honor, saying to them,

8 When you are invited by any one to a marriage feast, do not recline on the chief seat—in the place of honor—lest a more distinguished person than you has been invited by him; [Prov. 25: 6, 7.]

9 And he who invited both of you will come to you and say, Let this man have the place [you have taken]. Then with humiliation *and* a guilty sense of impropriety you will begin to take the lowest place.

10 But when you are invited, go and recline in the lowest place, so that when your host comes in he may say to you, Friend, go up higher! Then you will be honored in the presence of all who sit [at table] with you.

11 For every one who exalts himself will be humbled [that is, ranked below others who are honored or rewarded], and he who humbles himself [that is, keeps a modest opinion of himself and behaves accordingly] will be exalted—elevated in rank.

12 Jesus also said to the man who had invited Him, When you give a dinner or a supper, do not invite your friends or your brothers or your relatives or your wealthy neighbors, lest perhaps they also invite you in return and you be paid back.

13 But when you give a banquet *or* a reception, invite the poor, the disabled, the lame, and the blind.

14 Then you will be blessed—happy, fortunate and [m]to be envied—because they have no way of repaying you, and you will be recompensed at the resurrection of the just (upright).

15 When one of those who reclined [at the table] with [Him] heard this, he said to Him, Blessed—happy, fortunate and [m]to be envied—is he who shall eat bread in the kingdom of God!

16 But Jesus said to him, A man was once giving a great supper and invited many;

17 And at the hour for the supper he sent his servant to say to those who had been invited, Come, for all is now ready.

18 But they all alike began to make excuses *and* to beg off. The first said to him, I have bought a piece of land, and I have to go out and see it; I beg you, have me excused.

19 And another said, I have bought five yoke of oxen, and I am going to examine *and* [n]put my approval on them; I beg you, have me excused.

20 And another said, I have married a wife, and because of this I am unable to come. [Deut. 24:5.]

---

k) Thayer.
l) Many ancient authorities so read.
m) Souter.
n) Wuest's "Treasures from the Greek New Testament."

Living New Testament

CHAPTER 14

One Sabbath as He was in the home of a member of the Jewish Council, the Pharisees were watching Him like hawks to see if He would heal a man who was present who was suffering from dropsy.

3 Jesus said to the Pharisees and legal experts standing around, "Well, is it within the Law to heal a man on the Sabbath day, or not?"

4 And when they refused to answer, Jesus took the sick man by the hand and healed him and sent him away.

5 Then He turned to them: "Which of you doesn't work on the Sabbath?" He asked. "If your cow falls into a pit, don't you proceed at once to get it out?"

6 Again they had no answer.

* * * * *

7 When He noticed that all who came to the dinner were trying to sit near the head of the table, He gave them this advice:

8 "If you are invited to a wedding feast, don't always head for the best seat. For if someone more respected than you shows up,

9 The host will bring him over to where you are sitting and say, 'Let this man sit here instead.' And you, embarrassed, will have to take whatever seat is left at the foot of the table!

10 Do this instead—start at the foot; and when your host sees you he will come and say, 'Friend, we have a better place than this for you!' Thus you will be honored in front of all the other guests!

11 For everyone who tries to honor himself shall be humbled; and he who humbles himself shall be honored."

12 Then He turned to His host. "When you put on a dinner," He said, "don't invite friends, brothers, relatives and rich neighbors! For they will return the invitation.

13 Instead, invite the poor, the crippled, the lame, and the blind.

14 Then at the resurrection of the godly, God will reward you for inviting those who can't repay you."

15 Hearing this, a man sitting at the table with Jesus exclaimed, "What a privilege it would be to get into the Kingdom of God!"

16 Jesus replied with this illustration: "A man prepared a great feast and sent out many invitations.

17 When all was ready, he sent his servant around to notify the guests that it was time for them to arrive.

18 But they all began making excuses. One said he had just bought a field and wanted to inspect it, and asked to be excused.

19 Another said he had just bought five pair of oxen and wanted to try them out.

20 Another had just been married and for that reason couldn't come.

Revised Standard

Jesus heals on the Sabbath

14 One sabbath when he went to dine at
the house of a ruler who belonged
to the Pharisees, they were watching him.
2And behold, there was a man before him
who had dropsy. 3And Jesus spoke to the
lawyers and Pharisees, saying, "Is it lawful to heal on the sabbath, or not?" 4But
they were silent. Then he took him and
healed him, and let him go. 5And he said
to them, "Which of you, having an ass[s] or
an ox that has fallen into a well, will not
immediately pull him out on a sabbath day?"
6And they could not reply to this.

The parable of the marriage feast

7 Now he told a parable to those who
were invited, when he marked how they
chose the places of honor, saying to them,
8"When you are invited by any one to a
marriage feast, do not sit down in a place
of honor, lest a more eminent man than you
be invited by him; 9and he who invited you
both will come and say to you, 'Give place
to this man,' and then you will begin with
shame to take the lowest place. 10But when
you are invited, go and sit in the lowest
place, so that when your host comes he may
say to you, 'Friend, go up higher'; then you
will be honored in the presence of all who
sit at table with you. 11For every one who
exalts himself will be humbled, and he who
humbles himself will be exalted."
12 He said also to the man who had invited him, "When you give a dinner or a
banquet, do not invite your friends or your
brothers or your kinsmen or rich neighbors,
lest they also invite you in return, and you
be repaid. 13But when you give a feast, invite the poor, the maimed, the lame, the
blind, 14and you will be blessed, because
they cannot repay you. You will be repaid
at the resurrection of the just."

The parable of the great banquet

15 When one of those who sat at table
with him heard this, he said to him, "Blessed
is he who shall eat bread in the kingdom
of God!" 16But he said to him, "A man once
gave a great banquet, and invited many;
17and at the time for the banquet he sent
his servant to say to those who had been
invited, 'Come; for all is now ready.' 18But
they all alike began to make excuses. The
first said to him, 'I have bought a field, and
I must go out and see it; I pray you, have
me excused.' 19And another said, 'I have
bought five yoke of oxen, and I go to examine them; I pray you, have me excused.'
20And another said, 'I have married a wife,
and therefore I cannot come.' 21So the

[s] Other ancient authorities read *a son*

King James

21 So that servant came, and shewed his lord these things. Then the master of the house being angry said to his servant, Go out quickly into the streets and lanes of the city, and bring in hither the poor, and the maimed, and the halt, and the blind.
22 And the servant said, Lord, it is done as thou hast commanded, and yet there is room.
23 And the lord said unto the servant, Go out into the highways and hedges, and compel *them* to come in, that my house may be filled.
24 For I say unto you, That none of those men which were bidden shall taste of my supper.
25 ¶ And there went great multitudes with him: and he turned, and said unto them,
26 If any *man* come to me, and hate not his father, and mother, and wife, and children, and brethren, and sisters, yea, and his own life also, he cannot be my disciple.
27 And whosoever doth not bear his cross, and come after me, cannot be my disciple.
28 For which of you, intending to build a tower, sitteth not down first, and counteth the cost, whether he have *sufficient* to finish *it?*
29 Lest haply, after he hath laid the foundation, and is not able to finish *it*, all that behold *it* begin to mock him,
30 Saying, This man began to build, and was not able to finish.
31 Or what king, going to make war against another king, sitteth not down first, and consulteth whether he be able with ten thousand to meet him that cometh against him with twenty thousand?
32 Or else, while the other is yet a great way off, he sendeth an ambassage, and desireth conditions of peace.
33 So likewise, whosoever he be of you that forsaketh not all that he hath, he cannot be my disciple.
34 ¶ Salt *is* good: but if the salt have lost his savour, wherewith shall it be seasoned?
35 It is neither fit for the land, nor yet for the dunghill; *but* men cast it out. He that hath ears to hear, let him hear.

CHAPTER 15

THEN drew near unto him all the publicans and sinners for to hear him.
2 And the Pharisees and scribes murmured, saying, This man receiveth sinners, and eateth with them.

Amplified

21 So the servant came and reported these [answers] to his master. Then the master of the house said in wrath to his servant, Go quickly to the [o]great streets and the small streets of the city, and bring in here the poor and the disabled and the blind and the lame.
22 And the servant [returning] said, Sir, what you have commanded me to do has been done, and yet there is room.
23 Then the master said to the servant, Go out into the highways and hedges and urge *and* constrain [them] to yield *and* come in, so that my house may be filled;
24 For I tell you, that no one of those who were invited shall taste my supper.
25 Now huge crowds were going along with [Jesus]; and He turned and said to them,
26 If any one comes to Me and does not hate his [own] father and mother [that is, [p]in the sense of indifference to or relative disregard for them in comparison with his attitude toward God] and [likewise] his wife and children and brothers and sisters, [yes] and even his own life also, he cannot be My disciple.
27 Whoever does not persevere *and* carry his own cross and come after (follow) Me, cannot be My disciple.
28 For which of you, wishing to build a [q]farm-building, does not first sit down and calculate the cost, whether he has sufficient means to finish it?
29 Otherwise, when he has laid the foundation and is unable to complete [the building], all who see it begin to mock *and* jeer at him,
30 Saying, This man began to build, and was not able ([r]worth enough) to finish.
31 Or what king going to engage in conflict with another king, will not first sit down and consider *and* take counsel whether he is able with ten thousand to meet him who comes against him with twenty thousand?
32 And if he cannot [do so], when the other king is still a great way off, he sends an envoy and asks the [terms] of peace.
33 So then, whoever of you does not forsake—renounce, surrender claim to, give up, [r]say goodbye to—all that he has cannot be My disciple.
34 Salt is good—an excellent thing; but if salt has lost its strength *and* has become saltless (insipid, flat), how shall its saltness be restored?
35 It is fit neither for the land nor for the manure heap; men throw it away. He who has ears to hear, let him listen *and* consider *and* comprehend by hearing!

CHAPTER 15

NOW the tax collectors and (notorious and [s]especially wicked) sinners were all coming near to [Jesus] to listen to Him.
2 And the Pharisees and the scribes kept muttering *and* indignantly complaining, saying, This man accepts *and* receives *and* welcomes ([s]pre-eminently wicked) sinners and eats with them.

---

o) Wycliffe.
p) Abbott-Smith.
q) Moulton and Milligan.
r) Vincent.
s) Thayer.

Living New Testament

21 The servant returned and reported to his master what they had said. His master was angry and told him to go quickly into the streets and alleys of the city and to invite the beggars, crippled, lame, and blind.

22 But even then, there was still room!

23 'Well, then,' said his master, 'go out into the country lanes and out behind the hedges and urge anyone you find to come, so that the house will be full.

24 For none of those I invited first will get even the smallest taste of what I had prepared for them.' "

* * * * *

25 Great crowds were following Him. He turned around and addressed them as follows:

26 "Anyone who wants to be My follower must love Me far more than[1] he does his own father, mother, wife, children, brothers or sisters—yes, more than his own life—otherwise he cannot be My disciple.

27 And no one can be My disciple who does not carry his own cross and follow Me.

28 But don't begin until you count the cost.[2] For who would begin construction of a building without first getting estimates and then checking to see if he has enough money to pay the bills?

29 Otherwise he might only complete the foundation before running out of funds. And then how everyone would laugh!

30 'See that fellow there?' they would mock. 'He started that building and ran out of money before it was finished!'

31 Or what king would ever dream of going to war without first sitting down with his counselors and discussing whether his army of 10,000 is strong enough to defeat the 20,000 men who are marching against him?

32 If the decision is negative, then while the enemy troops are still far away, he will send a truce team to discuss terms of peace.

33 So no one can become My disciple unless he first sits down and counts his blessings—and then renounces them all for Me!

34 What good is salt that has lost its saltiness?[3]

35 Flavorless salt is fit for nothing—not even for fertilizer. It is worthless and must be thrown out. Listen well, if you would understand My meaning."

Revised Standard

servant came and reported this to his master.
Then the householder in anger said to his
servant, 'Go out quickly to the streets and
lanes of the city, and bring in the poor and
maimed and blind and lame.' 22And the
servant said, 'Sir, what you commanded
has been done, and still there is room.'
23And the master said to the servant, 'Go
out to the highways and hedges, and compel
people to come in, that my house may be
filled. 24For I tell you, none of those men
who were invited shall taste my banquet.' "

Parables of the tower and the king

25 Now great multitudes accompanied
him; and he turned and said to them, 26"If
any one comes to me and does not hate his
own father and mother and wife and children
and brothers and sisters, yes, and even
his own life, he cannot be my disciple.
27Whoever does not bear his own cross and
come after me, cannot be my disciple. 28For
which of you, desiring to build a tower,
does not first sit down and count the cost,
whether he has enough to complete it?
29Otherwise, when he has laid a foundation,
and is not able to finish, all who see it begin
to mock him, 30saying, 'This man began to
build, and was not able to finish.' 31Or what
king, going to encounter another king in
war, will not sit down first and take counsel
whether he is able with ten thousand to
meet him who comes against him with
twenty thousand? 32And if not, while the
other is yet a great way off, he sends an
embassy and asks terms of peace. 33So
therefore, whoever of you does not renounce
all that he has cannot be my disciple.

The parable of the salt

34 "Salt is good; but if salt has lost its
taste, how shall its saltness be restored? 35It
is fit neither for the land nor for the dunghill;
men throw it away. He who has ears
to hear, let him hear."

CHAPTER 15

Dishonest tax collectors and other notorious sinners often came to listen to Jesus' sermons;

2 But this caused complaints from the Jewish religious leaders and the experts on Jewish law because He was associating with such despicable people—even eating with them!

15 Now the tax collectors and sinners
were all drawing near to hear him.
2And the Pharisees and the scribes murmured,
saying, "This man receives sinners
and eats with them."

---

[1] Literally, "if anyone comes to me and does not hate his father and mother . . . ."

[2] Implied from verse 33.

[3] Perhaps the reference is to impure salt; when wet, the salt dissolves and drains out, leaving a tasteless residue. Matthew 5:13.

King James

3 ¶ And he spake this parable unto them, saying,

4 What man of you, having an hundred sheep, if he lose one of them, doth not leave the ninety and nine in the wilderness, and go after that which is lost, until he find it?

5 And when he hath found it, he layeth *it* on his shoulders, rejoicing.

6 And when he cometh home, he calleth together *his* friends and neighbours, saying unto them, Rejoice with me; for I have found my sheep which was lost.

7 I say unto you, that likewise joy shall be in heaven over one sinner that repenteth, more than over ninety and nine just persons, which need no repentance.

8 ¶ Either what woman having ten pieces of silver, if she lose one piece, doth not light a candle, and sweep the house, and seek diligently till she find *it?*

9 And when she hath found *it,* she calleth *her* friends and *her* neighbours together, saying, Rejoice with me; for I have found the piece which I had lost.

10 Likewise, I say unto you, there is joy in the presence of the angels of God over one sinner that repenteth.

11 ¶ And he said, A certain man had two sons:

12 And the younger of them said to *his* father, Father, give me the portion of goods that falleth *to me.* And he divided unto them *his* living.

13 And not many days after the younger son gathered all together, and took his journey into a far country, and there wasted his substance with riotous living.

14 And when he had spent all, there arose a mighty famine in that land; and he began to be in want.

15 And he went and joined himself to a citizen of that country; and he sent him into his fields to feed swine.

16 And he would fain have filled his belly with the husks that the swine did eat: and no man gave unto him.

17 And when he came to himself, he said, How many hired servants of my father's have bread enough and to spare, and I perish with hunger!

18 I will arise and go to my father, and will say unto him, Father, I have sinned against heaven, and before thee,

19 And am no more worthy to be called thy son: make me as one of thy hired servants.

20 And he arose, and came to his father. But when he was yet a great way off, his father saw him, and had compassion, and ran, and fell on his neck, and kissed him.

21 And the son said unto him, Father, I have sinned against heaven, and in thy sight, and am no more worthy to be called thy son.

22 But the father said to his servants, Bring forth the best robe, and put *it* on him; and put a ring on his hand, and shoes on *his* feet:

Amplified

3 So He told them this parable:

4 What man of you, if he has a hundred sheep and should lose one of them, does not leave the ninety-nine in the wilderness (desert), and go after the one that is lost, until he finds it?

5 And when he has found it, he lays it on his [own] shoulders rejoicing.

6 And when he gets home, he summons together [his] friends and [his] neighbors, saying to them, Rejoice with me, because I have found my sheep which was lost.

7 Thus, I tell you, there will be more joy in heaven over one ([s]especially) wicked person who repents—[that is,] [s]changes his mind, abhorring his errors and misdeeds, and determines to enter upon a better course of life—than over ninety-nine righteous persons who have no need of repentance.

8 Or what woman, having ten (silver) drachmas [each one equal to a day's wages], if she loses one coin, does not light a lamp and sweep the house and look carefully *and* diligently until she finds it?

9 And when she has found it, she summons her (women) friends and neighbors, saying, Rejoice with me, for I have found the silver coin which I had lost.

10 Even so, I tell you, there is joy among *and* in the presence of the angels of God over one ([t]especially) wicked person who repents—[t]changes his mind for the better, heartily amending his ways with abhorrence for his past sins.

11 And He said, There was a certain man who had two sons;

12 And the younger of them said to his father, Father, give me the part of the property that falls [to me]. And he divided the livelihood [between] them. [Deut. 21:15-17.]

13 And not many days after that the younger son gathered up all that he had and journeyed into a distant country, and there he wasted his fortune in reckless *and* loose-from-restraint living.

14 And when he had spent all he had, a [u]mighty famine came upon that country, and he began to fall behind *and* be in want.

15 So he went and forced (glued) himself upon one of the citizens of that country, who sent him into his fields to feed hogs.

16 And he would gladly have fed on (and [v]filled his belly with) the [u]carob pods that the hogs were eating, but [they could not satisfy his hunger and] nobody gave him anything [better]. [Jer. 30:14.]

17 Then when he came to himself, he said, How many hired servants of my father have enough food and to spare, but I am perishing (dying) here of hunger!

18 I will get up and go to my father, and I will say to him, Father, I have sinned against heaven and in your sight;

19 I am no longer worthy to be called your son; [just] make me as one of your hired servants.

20 So he got up and came to his [own] father. But while he was still a long way off, his father saw him and was moved with pity *and* tenderness [for him], and he ran and embraced him and kissed him—[w]fervently.

21 And the son said to him, Father, I have sinned against heaven and in your sight; I am no longer worthy to be called your son—I no longer deserve to be recognized as a son of yours!

22 But the father said to his bond servants, Bring quickly the best robe—the festive, honor robe—and put it on him, and give him a ring for his hand and sandals for his feet; [Gen. 41:42; Zech. 3:4.]

---

s) Thayer.
t) Thayer.
u) Abbott-Smith.
v) Many ancient authorities so read.
w) Abbott-Smith.

Living New Testament

3, 4 So Jesus used this illustration: "If you had 100 sheep and one of them strayed away and was lost in the wilderness, wouldn't you leave the 99 others to go and search for the lost one, until you found it?

5 And then you would joyfully carry it home on your shoulders.

6 When you arrived you would call together your friends and neighbors to rejoice with you because your lost sheep was found.

7 Well, in the same way heaven will be happier over one lost sinner who returns to God than over 99 others who haven't strayed away!

8 Or take another illustration: A woman has ten valuable silver coins and loses one. Won't she light a lamp and look in every corner of the house and sweep every nook and cranny until she finds it?

9 And then won't she call her friends and neighbors to rejoice with her?

10 In the same way there is joy in the presence of the angels of God when one sinner repents."

To further illustrate the point, He told them this story:

11 "A man had two sons.

12 When the younger told his father, 'I want my share of your estate now, instead of waiting until you die!' his father agreed to divide his wealth between his sons.

13 A few days later this younger son packed all his belongings and took a trip to a distant land, and there wasted all his money on parties and prostitutes.

14 About the time his money was gone a great famine swept over the land, and he began to starve.

15 He persuaded a local farmer to hire him to feed his pigs.

16 The boy became so hungry that even the pods he was feeding the swine looked good to him. And no one gave him anything.

17 When he finally came to his senses, he said to himself, 'At home even the hired men have food enough and to spare and here I am, dying of hunger!

18 I will go home to my father and say, "Father, I have sinned against both heaven and you,

19 And am no longer worthy of being called your son. Please take me on as a hired man."

20 So he returned home to his father. And while he was still a long distance away, his father saw him coming, and was filled with loving pity and ran and embraced him and kissed him.

21 His son said to him, 'Father, I have sinned against heaven and you, and am not worthy of being called your son—'

22 But his father said to the slaves, 'Quick! Bring the finest robe in the house and put it on him. And a jeweled ring for his finger; and shoes!

Revised Standard

The parable of the lost sheep

3 So he told them this parable: 4"What man of you, having a hundred sheep, if he has lost one of them, does not leave the ninety-nine in the wilderness, and go after the one which is lost, until he finds it? 5And when he has found it, he lays it on his shoulders, rejoicing. 6And when he comes home, he calls together his friends and his neighbors, saying to them, 'Rejoice with me, for I have found my sheep which was lost.' 7Just so, I tell you, there will be more joy in heaven over one sinner who repents than over ninety-nine righteous persons who need no repentance.

The parable of the lost coin

8 "Or what woman, having ten silver coins,[t] if she loses one coin, does not light a lamp and sweep the house and seek diligently until she finds it? 9And when she has found it, she calls together her friends and neighbors, saying, 'Rejoice with me, for I have found the coin which I had lost.' 10Just so, I tell you, there is joy before the angels of God over one sinner who repents."

The parable of the lost son

11 And he said, "There was a man who had two sons; 12and the younger of them said to his father, 'Father, give me the share of property that falls to me.' And he divided his living between them. 13Not many days later, the younger son gathered all he had and took his journey into a far country, and there he squandered his property in loose living. 14And when he had spent everything, a great famine arose in that country, and he began to be in want. 15So he went and joined himself to one of the citizens of that country, who sent him into his fields to feed swine. 16And he would gladly have fed on[u] the pods that the swine ate; and no one gave him anything. 17But when he came to himself he said, 'How many of my father's hired servants have bread enough and to spare, but I perish here with hunger! 18I will arise and go to my father, and I will say to him, "Father, I have sinned against heaven and before you; 19I am no longer worthy to be called your son; treat me as one of your hired servants." ' 20And he arose and came to his father. But while he was yet at a distance, his father saw him and had compassion, and ran and embraced him and kissed him. 21And the son said to him, 'Father, I have sinned against heaven and before you; I am no longer worthy to be called your son.'[v] 22But the father said to his servants, 'Bring quickly the best robe, and put it on him; and put a ring on his

[t] The drachma, rendered here by *silver coin*, was about sixteen cents

[u] Other ancient authorities read *filled his belly with*

King James

23 And bring hither the fatted calf, and kill *it;* and let us eat, and be merry:

24 For this my son was dead, and is alive again; he was lost, and is found. And they began to be merry.

25 Now his elder son was in the field: and as he came and drew nigh to the house, he heard music and dancing.

26 And he called one of the servants, and asked what these things meant.

27 And he said unto him, Thy brother is come; and thy father hath killed the fatted calf, because he hath received him safe and sound.

28 And he was angry, and would not go in: therefore came his father out, and entreated him.

29 And he answering said to *his* father, Lo, these many years do I serve thee, neither transgressed I at any time thy commandment: and yet thou never gavest me a kid, that I might make merry with my friends:

30 But as soon as this thy son was come, which hath devoured thy living with harlots, thou hast killed for him the fatted calf.

31 And he said unto him, Son, thou art ever with me, and all that I have is thine.

32 It was meet that we should make merry, and be glad: for this thy brother was dead, and is alive again; and was lost, and is found.

Amplified

23 And bring out [x]that [wheat-]fattened calf and kill i
and let us [y]revel *and* feast *and* be happy *and* merry;

24 Because this my son was dead, and is alive again; h
was lost, and is found! And they began to [y]revel *and* fea
and make merry.

25 But his older son was in the field, and as he returne
and came near to the house, he heard music and dancing

26 And having called one of the servant (boys) to hin
he began to ask what this meant.

27 And he said to him, Your brother has come, an
your father has killed [z]that [wheat-]fattened calf, becaus
he has received him safe and well.

28 But [the elder brother] was angry—with deep-seate
wrath—and resolved not to go in. Then his father cam
out [and] began to plead with him,

29 But he answered his father, Lo, these many years
have served you, and I have never disobeyed your con
mand; yet you never gave me [so much as] a (little) ki
that I might [a]revel *and* feast *and* be happy *and* mak
merry with my friends;

30 But when this son of yours arrived, who has d
voured your living with immoral women, you have kille
for him [z]that [wheat-]fattened calf!

31 And the father said to him, Son, you are alway
with me, and all that is mine is yours.

32 But it was fitting to make merry, to [a]revel *and* fea
and rejoice, for this brother of yours was dead, and i
alive again! He was lost and is found!

CHAPTER 16

AND he said also unto his disciples, There was a certain rich man, which had a steward; and the same was accused unto him that he had wasted his goods.

2 And he called him, and said unto him, How is it that I hear this of thee? give an account of thy stewardship; for thou mayest be no longer steward.

3 Then the steward said within himself, What shall I do? for my lord taketh away from me the stewardship: I cannot dig; to beg I am ashamed.

4 I am resolved what to do, that, when I am put out of the stewardship, they may receive me into their houses.

5 So he called every one of his lord's debtors *unto him,* and said unto the first, How much owest thou unto my lord?

6 And he said, An hundred measures of oil. And he said unto him, Take thy bill, and sit down quickly, and write fifty.

CHAPTER 16

ALSO [Jesus] said to the disciples, There was a certai
rich man who had a [b]manager of his estate, an
accusations [against this man were brought] to him, th
he was squandering his [master's] possessions.

2 And he called him and said to him, What is this th
I hear about you? Turn in the account of your manag
ment [of my affairs], for you can be [my] manager n
longer.

3 And the manager of the estate said to himself, Wh
shall I do, seeing that my master is taking the manag
ment away from me? I am not able to dig, and I a
ashamed to beg.

4 I have come to know what I will do, so that they [m
master's debtors] may accept *and* welcome me into the
houses when I am put out of the management.

5 So he summoned his master's debtors one by on
and he said to the first, How much do you owe m
master?

6 He said, A hundred measures [about nine hundre
gallons] of oil. And he said to him, Take back you
written acknowledgment of [c]obligation, and sit dow
quickly and write fifty [about four hundred fifty ga
lons].

x) Tyndale.
y) Souter.
z) Tyndale.
a) Souter.
b) Moulton and Milligan.
c) Wycliffe.

Living New Testament

23 And kill the calf we have in the fattening pen. We must celebrate with a feast,

24 For this son of mine was dead and has returned to life. He was lost and is found.' So the party began.

25 Meanwhile the older son was in the fields working; when he returned home, he heard dance music coming from the house,

26 And he asked one of the servants what was going on.

27 'Your brother is back,' he was told, 'and your father has killed the calf we were fattening and has prepared a great feast to celebrate his coming home again unharmed.'

28 The older brother was angry and wouldn't go in. His father came out and begged him,

29 But he replied, 'All these years I've worked hard for you and never once refused to do a single thing you told me to; and in all that time you never gave me even one young goat for a feast with my friends.

30 Yet when this son of yours comes back after spending your money on prostitutes, you celebrate by killing the finest calf we have on the place.'

31 'Look, dear son,' his father said to him, 'you and I are very close, and everything I have is yours.

32 But it is right to celebrate. For he is your brother; and he was dead and has come back to life!

He was lost and is found!' "

Revised Standard

hand, and shoes on his feet; [23]and bring the
fatted calf and kill it, and let us eat and
make merry; [24]for this my son was dead,
and is alive again; he was lost, and is found.'
And they began to make merry.
25 "Now his elder son was in the field;
and as he came and drew near to the house,
he heard music and dancing. [26]And he
called one of the servants and asked what
this meant. [27]And he said to him, 'Your
brother has come, and your father has killed
the fatted calf, because he has received him
safe and sound.' [28]But he was angry and refused to go in. His father came out and entreated him, [29]but he answered his father,
'Lo, these many years I have served you,
and I never disobeyed your command; yet
you never gave me a kid, that I might make
merry with my friends. [30]But when this son
of yours came, who has devoured your living with harlots, you killed for him the fatted
calf!' [31]And he said to him, 'Son, you are always with me, and all that is mine is yours.
[32]It was fitting to make merry and be glad,
for this your brother was dead, and is alive;
he was lost, and is found.' "

CHAPTER 16

Jesus now told this story to His disciples: "A rich man hired an accountant to handle his affairs, but soon a rumor went around that the accountant was thoroughly dishonest.

2 So his employer called him in and said, 'What's this I hear about your stealing from me? Get your report in order, for you are to be dismissed.'

3 The accountant thought to himself, 'Now what? I'm through here, and I haven't the strength to go out and dig ditches, and I'm too proud to beg.

4 I know just the thing! And then I'll have plenty of friends to take care of me when I leave!'

5, 6 So he invited each one who owed money to his employer to come and discuss the situation. He asked the first one, 'How much do you owe him?' 'My debt is 850 gallons of olive oil,' the man replied. 'Yes, here is the contract you signed,' the accountant told him. 'Tear it up and write another one for half that much!'

Parable of the unrighteous steward

16 He also said to the disciples, "There
was a rich man who had a steward,
and charges were brought to him that this
man was wasting his goods. [2]And he called
him and said to him, 'What is this that I hear
about you? Turn in the account of your
stewardship, for you can no longer be
steward.' [3]And the steward said to himself,
'What shall I do, since my master is taking
the stewardship away from me? I am not
strong enough to dig, and I am ashamed to
beg. [4]I have decided what to do, so that
people may receive me into their houses
when I am put out of the stewardship.' [5]So,
summoning his master's debtors one by one,
he said to the first, 'How much do you owe
my master?' [6]He said, 'A hundred measures
of oil.' And he said to him, 'Take your bill,
and sit down quickly and write fifty.' [7]Then

[v] Other ancient authorities add *treat me as one of your hired servants*

King James

7 Then said he to another, And how much owest thou? And he said, An hundred measures of wheat. And he said unto him, Take thy bill, and write fourscore.

8 And the lord commended the unjust steward, because he had done wisely: for the children of this world are in their generation wiser than the children of light.

9 And I say unto you, Make to yourselves friends of the mammon of unrighteousness; that, when ye fail, they may receive you into everlasting habitations.

10 He that is faithful in that which is least is faithful also in much; and he that is unjust in the least is unjust also in much.

11 If therefore ye have not been faithful in the unrighteous mammon, who will commit to your trust the true *riches?*

12 And if ye have not been faithful in that which is another man's, who shall give you that which is your own?

13 ¶ No servant can serve two masters: for either he will hate the one, and love the other; or else he will hold to the one, and despise the other. Ye cannot serve God and mammon.

14 And the Pharisees also, who were covetous, heard all these things: and they derided him.

15 And he said unto them, Ye are they which justify yourselves before men; but God knoweth your hearts: for that which is highly esteemed among men is abomination in the sight of God.

16 ¶ The law and the prophets *were* until John: since that time the kingdom of God is preached, and every man presseth into it.

17 And it is easier for heaven and earth to pass, than one tittle of the law to fail.

18 Whosoever putteth away his wife, and marrieth another, committeth adultery: and whosoever marrieth her that is put away from *her* husband committeth adultery.

19 ¶ There was a certain rich man, which was clothed in purple and fine linen, and fared sumptuously every day:

20 And there was a certain beggar named Lazarus, which was laid at his gate, full of sores,

21 And desiring to be fed with the crumbs which fell from the rich man's table: moreover the dogs came and licked his sores.

22 And it came to pass, that the beggar died, and was carried by the angels into Abraham's bosom: the rich man also died, and was buried;

Amplified

7 After that he said to another, And how much do yo owe? He said, A hundred measures [about nine hundre bushels] of wheat. He said to him, Take back your writte acknowledgment of [c]obligation, and write eighty [abou seven hundred bushels].

8 And [his] master praised the dishonest (unjust) mai ager for acting [d]shrewdly *and* [e]prudently; for the sons o this age are shrewder *and* more prudent *and* wiser i [[d]relation to] their own generation—that is, to their ow age and [e]kind—than are the sons of light.

9 And I tell you, make friends for yourselves by mear of unrighteous mammon [that is, [f]deceitful riches, mone possessions], so that when it fails, they [those you hav favored] may receive *and* welcome you into the everlastir habitations (dwellings).

10 He who is faithful in a very little [thing], is faithfu also in much; and he who is dishonest *and* unjust in a ver little [thing], is dishonest *and* unjust also in much.

11 Therefore, if you have not been faithful in the [cas of] the unrighteous mammon—the [g]deceitful riches, mo ey, possessions—who will entrust to you the true riches?

12 And if you have not proved faithful in that whic belongs to another [whether God or man], who will giv you that which is your own [that is, [h]the true riches]?

13 No servant is able to serve two masters; for eithe he will hate the one and love the other, or he will stand b *and* be devoted to the one and despise the other. Yo cannot serve God and mammon—riches, that is, or [i]any thing in which you trust and on which you rely.

14 Now the Pharisees, who were covetous *and* lovers c money, heard all these things (taken together), and the began to sneer *and* ridicule *and* scoff at Him.

15 But He said to them, You are they who declar yourselves just *and* upright before men, but God know your hearts. For what is exalted *and* highly thought c among men is detestable *and* abhorrent (an abominatior in the sight of God. [I Sam. 16:7; Prov. 21:2.]

16 Until John came, there were the Law and th prophets; since then the good news (the Gospel) of th kingdom of God is being preached, and every one strive violently to go in—would force his [[j]own way, rather tha God's] way into it.

17 Yet it is easier for heaven and earth to pass away than for one dot of the Law to become void *and* fail.

18 Whoever (dismisses, repudiates and) divorces hi wife and marries another commits adultery, and he wh marries a woman who is divorced from her husban commits adultery.

19 There was a certain rich man, who (habituall clothed himself in purple and fine linen, and [k]reveled *an* feasted *and* made merry in splendor every day.

20 And at his gate there [l]was (carelessly) droppe down *and* left a certain [l]utterly destitute man, name Lazarus, (reduced to begging alms) and covered with ([l]u cerated) sores.

21 He [eagerly] desired to be satisfied with what fe from the rich man's table; moreover the dogs even cam and licked his sores.

22 And it occurred that the man (reduced to) beggin died, and was carried by the angels to Abraham's boson The rich man also died and was buried.

---

c) Wycliffe.
d) Vincent.
e) Tyndale.
f) Souter.
g) Souter.
h) Vincent.
i) Thayer.
j) Berkeley Version.
k) Souter.
l) Vincent.

Living New Testament

7 'And how much do you owe him?' he asked the next man. 'A thousand bushels of wheat,' was the reply. 'Here,' the accountant said, 'take your note and replace it with one for only 800 bushels!'

8 The rich man had to admire the rascal for being so shrewd.[1] And it is true that the citizens of this world are more clever [in dishonesty![2]] than the godly[3] are.

9 But shall I tell *you* to act that way, to buy friendship through cheating? Will this ensure your entry into an everlasting home in heaven?[4]

10 NO![5] For unless you are honest in small matters, you won't be in large ones. If you cheat even a little, you won't be honest with greater responsibilities.

11 And if you are untrustworthy about worldly wealth, who will trust you with the true riches of heaven?

12 And if you are not faithful with other people's money, why should you be entrusted with money of your own?

13 For neither you nor anyone else can serve two masters. You will hate one and show loyalty to the other, or else the other way around—you will be enthusiastic about one and despise the other. You cannot serve both God and money."

14 The Pharisees, who dearly loved their money, naturally scoffed at all this.

15 Then He said to them, "You wear a noble, pious expression in public, but God knows your evil hearts. Your pretense brings you honor from the people, but it is an abomination in the sight of God.

16 Until John the Baptist began to preach, the laws of Moses and the messages of the prophets were your guides. But John introduced the Good News that the Kingdom of God would come soon. And now eager multitudes are pressing in.

17 But that doesn't mean that the Law has lost its force in even the smallest point. It is as strong and unshakable as heaven and earth.

18 So anyone who divorces his wife and marries someone else commits adultery, and anyone who marries a divorced woman commits adultery."

* * * * *

19 "There was a certain rich man," Jesus said, "who was splendidly clothed and lived each day in mirth and luxury.

20 One day Lazarus, a diseased beggar, was laid at his door.

21 As he lay there longing for scraps from the rich man's table, the dogs would come and lick his open sores.

22 Finally the beggar died and was carried by the angels to be with Abraham in the place of the righteous dead.[6] The rich man also died and was buried.

[1] Or, "Do you think the rich man commended the scoundrel for being so shrewd?"
[2] Implied.
[3] Literally, "sons of the light."
[4] Literally, and probably ironically, "make to yourselves friends by means of the mammon of unrighteousness; that when it shall fail you, they may receive you into the eternal tabernacles!" Some commentators would interpret this to mean: "Use your money for good, so that it will be waiting to befriend you when you get to heaven." But this would imply that the end justifies the means, an idea never found in the Bible.
[5] Implied.
[6] Literally, "into Abraham's bosom."

Revised Standard

he said to another, 'And how much do you
owe?' He said, 'A hundred measures of
wheat.' He said to him, 'Take your bill, and
write eighty.' 8The master commended the
dishonest steward for his prudence; for the
sons of this world[w] are wiser in their own
generation than the sons of light. 9And I
tell you, make friends for yourselves by
means of unrighteous mammon, so that
when it fails they may receive you into the
eternal habitations.

10 "He who is faithful in a very little is
faithful also in much; and he who is dishonest in a very little is dishonest also in
much. 11If then you have not been faithful
in the unrighteous mammon, who will entrust to you the true riches? 12And if you
have not been faithful in that which is
another's, who will give you that which is
your own? 13No servant can serve two
masters; for either he will hate the one and
love the other, or he wil be devoted to the
one and despise the other. You cannot serve
God and mammon."

Jesus answers the Pharisees

14 The Pharisees, who were lovers of
money, heard all this, and they scoffed at
him. 15But he said to them, "You are those
who justify yourselves before men, but God
knows your hearts; for what is exalted
among men is an abomination in the sight
of God.

16 "The law and the prophets were until John; since then the good news of the
kingdom of God is preached, and every
one enters it violently. 17But it is easier for
heaven and earth to pass away, than for one
dot of the law to become void.

18 "Every one who divorces his wife
and marries another commits adultery, and
he who marries a woman divorced from her
husband commits adultery.

The rich man and Lazarus

19 "There was a rich man, who was
clothed in purple and fine linen and who
feasted sumptuously every day. 20And at his
gate lay a poor man named Lazarus, full of
sores, 21who desired to be fed with what
fell from the rich man's table; moreover the
dogs came and licked his sores. 22The poor
man died and was carried by the angels to
Abraham's bosom. The rich man also died

[w] Greek *age*

King James

23 And in hell he lift up his eyes, being in torments, and seeth Abraham afar off, and Lazarus in his bosom.

24 And he cried and said, Father Abraham, have mercy on me, and send Lazarus, that he may dip the tip of his finger in water, and cool my tongue; for I am tormented in this flame.

25 But Abraham said, Son, remember that thou in thy lifetime receivedst thy good things, and likewise Lazarus evil things: but now he is comforted, and thou art tormented.

26 And beside all this, between us and you there is a great gulf fixed: so that they which would pass from hence to you cannot; neither can they pass to us, that *would come* from thence.

27 Then he said, I pray thee therefore, father, that thou wouldest send him to my father's house:

28 For I have five brethren; that he may testify unto them, lest they also come into this place of torment.

29 Abraham saith unto him, They have Moses and the prophets; let them hear them.

30 And he said, Nay, father Abraham: but if one went unto them from the dead, they will repent.

31 And he said unto him, If they hear not Moses and the prophets, neither will they be persuaded, though one rose from the dead.

Amplified

23 And in Hades [the realm of the dead], being in torment, he lifted up his eyes and saw Abraham far away and Lazarus in his bosom.

24 And he cried out and said, Father Abraham, have pity *and* mercy upon me, and send Lazarus to dip the tip of his finger in water and cool my tongue; for I am in anguish in this flame.

25 But Abraham said, Child, remember that you in your lifetime fully received (what is due you) in comforts *and* delights, and Lazarus in like manner the discomforts *and* distresses; but now he is comforted here, and you are in anguish.

26 And besides all this, between us and you there is a great chasm fixed, in order that those who want to pass from this [place] to you may not be able, and no one may pass from there to us.

27 And [the man] said, Then, father, I beseech you to send him to my father's house,

28 For I have five brothers, so that he may give (solemn) testimony *and* warn them, lest they too come into this place of torment.

29 But Abraham said, They have Moses and the prophets; let them hear *and* listen to them.

30 But he answered, No, father Abraham; but if some one from the dead goes to them, they will repent ([m]change their minds for the better and heartily amend their ways with abhorrence of their past sins).

31 He said to him, If they do not hear *and* listen to Moses and the prophets, neither will they be persuaded *and* convinced *and* believe if some one should rise from the dead.

CHAPTER 17

King James

THEN said he unto the disciples, It is impossible but that offences will come: but woe *unto him,* through whom they come!

2 It were better for him that a millstone were hanged about his neck, and he cast into the sea, than that he should offend one of these little ones.

3 ¶ Take heed to yourselves: If thy brother trespass against thee, rebuke him; and if he repent, forgive him.

4 And if he trespass against thee seven times a day, and seven times a day turn again to thee, saying, I repent; thou shalt forgive him.

5 And the apostles said unto the Lord, Increase our faith.

6 And the Lord said, If ye had faith as a grain of mustard seed, ye might say unto this sycamine tree, Be thou plucked up by the root, and be thou planted in the sea; and it should obey you.

7 But which of you, having a servant plowing or feeding cattle, will say unto him by and by, when he is come from the field, Go and sit down to meat?

Amplified

AND [Jesus] said to His disciples, Temptations [that is, snares, traps set to entice to sin] are sure to come; but woe to him by *or* through whom they come!

2 It would be more profitable for him if a millstone were hung around his neck and he were hurled into the sea, than that he should cause to sin *or* be a snare to one of these little ones [[n]lowly in rank or influence].

3 [o]Pay attention *and* always be on your guard—looking out for one another; if your brother sins (misses the mark), solemnly tell him so *and* reprove him, and if he repents (feels sorry for having sinned), forgive him.

4 And even if he sins against you seven times in a day, and turns to you seven times and says, I repent (I am sorry), you must forgive him—[that is,] give up resentment and consider the offense as recalled and annulled.

5 The apostles said to the Lord, Increase our faith—that trust and confidence that springs from our belief in God.

6 And the Lord answered, If you had faith (trust and confidence in God) even as a grain of mustard seed, you could say to this mulberry tree, Be pulled up by the roots, and be planted in the sea, and it would obey you.

7 Will any man of you, who has a servant plowing or tending sheep, say to him when he has come in from the field, Come at once and take your place at the table?

---

m) Thayer.
n) Abbott-Smith.
o) Moulton and Milligan.

Living New Testament

23 And his soul went into hell.[7] There, in torment, he saw Lazarus in the far distance with Abraham.

24 'Father Abraham,' he shouted, 'have some pity. Send Lazarus over here if only to dip the tip of his finger in water and cool my tongue, for I am in anguish in these flames.'

25 But Abraham said to him, 'Son, remember that during your lifetime you had everything you wanted, and Lazarus had nothing. So now he is here being comforted and you are in anguish.

26 And besides, there is a great chasm separating us, and anyone wanting to come to you from here is stopped at its edge; and no one over there can cross to us.'

27 Then the rich man said, 'O Father Abraham, then please send him to my father's home—

28 For I have five brothers—to warn them about this place of torment lest they come here when they die.'

29 But Abraham said, 'The Scriptures have warned them again and again. Your brothers can read them any time they want to.'

30 The rich man replied, 'No, Father Abraham, they won't bother to read them. But if someone is sent to them from the dead, then they will turn from their sins.'

31 But Abraham said, 'If they won't listen to Moses and the prophets, they won't listen even though someone rises from the dead.' "[8]

Revised Standard

and was buried; 23 and in Hades, being in
torment, he lifted up his eyes, and saw
Abraham far off and Lazarus in his bosom.
24 And he called out, 'Father Abraham, have
mercy upon me, and send Lazarus to dip
the end of his finger in water and cool my
tongue; for I am in anguish in this flame.'
25 But Abraham said, 'Son, remember that
you in your lifetime received your good
things, and Lazarus in like manner evil
things; but now he is comforted here, and
you are in anguish. 26 And besides all this,
between us and you a great chasm has been
fixed, in order that those who would pass
from here to you may not be able, and
none may cross from there to us.' 27 And
he said, 'Then I beg you, father, to send
him to my father's house, 28 for I have five
brothers, so that he may warn them, lest
they also come into this place of torment.'
29 But Abraham said, 'They have Moses and
the prophets; let them hear them.' 30 And
he said, 'No, father Abraham; but if some
one goes to them from the dead, they will
repent.' 31 He said to him, 'If they do not
hear Moses and the prophets, neither will
they be convinced if some one should rise
from the dead.' "

CHAPTER 17

There will always be temptations to sin," Jesus said one day to His disciples, "but woe to the man who does the tempting.

2, 3 If he were thrown into the sea with a huge rock tied to his neck, he would be far better off than facing the punishment in store for those who harm these little children's souls. I am warning you!

Rebuke your brother if he sins, and forgive him if he is sorry.

4 Even if he wrongs you seven times a day and each time turns again and asks forgiveness, forgive him."

* * * * *

5 One day the apostles said to the Lord, "We need more faith; tell us how to get it."

6 "If your faith were only the size of a mustard seed," Jesus answered, "it would be large enough to uproot that mulberry tree over there and send it hurtling into the sea! Your command would bring immediate results!

7, 8, 9 When a servant comes in from plowing or taking care of sheep, he doesn't just sit down and eat, but first

Teaching on faith and forgiveness

17 And he said to his disciples, "Temptations to sin[x] are sure to come; but
woe to him by whom they come! 2 It would
be better for him if a millstone were hung
round his neck and he were cast into the
sea, than that he should cause one of these
little ones to sin.[y] 3 Take heed to yourselves;
if your brother sins, rebuke him, and if he
repents, forgive him; 4 and if he sins against
you seven times in the day, and turns to
you seven times, and says, 'I repent,' you
must forgive him."
5 The apostles said to the Lord, "Increase
our faith!" 6 And the Lord said, "If you had
faith as a grain of mustard seed, you could
say to this sycamine tree, 'Be rooted up,
and be planted in the sea,' and it would
obey you.
7 "Will any one of you, who has a servant plowing or keeping sheep, say to him
when he has come in from the field, 'Come
at once and sit down at table'? 8 Will he not

---

7 Literally, "in Hades."
8 Even Christ's Resurrection failed to convince the Pharisees, to whom He gave this illustration.

x Greek *stumbling blocks*
y Greek *stumble*

King James

8 And will not rather say unto him, Make ready wherewith I may sup, and gird thyself, and serve me, till I have eaten and drunken; and afterward thou shalt eat and drink?

9 Doth he thank that servant because he did the things that were commanded him? I trow not.

10 So likewise ye, when ye shall have done all those things which are commanded you, say, We are unprofitable servants: we have done that which was our duty to do.

11 ¶ And it came to pass, as he went to Jerusalem, that he passed through the midst of Samaria and Galilee.

12 And as he entered into a certain village, there met him ten men that were lepers, which stood afar off:

13 And they lifted up *their* voices, and said, Jesus, Master, have mercy on us.

14 And when he saw *them*, he said unto them, Go shew yourselves unto the priests. And it came to pass, that, as they went, they were cleansed.

15 And one of them, when he saw that he was healed, turned back, and with a loud voice glorified God,

16 And fell down on *his* face at his feet, giving him thanks: and he was a Samaritan.

17 And Jesus answering said, Were there not ten cleansed? but where *are* the nine?

18 There are not found that returned to give glory to God, save this stranger.

19 And he said unto him, Arise, go thy way: thy faith hath made thee whole.

20 ¶ And when he was demanded of the Pharisees, when the kingdom of God should come, he answered them and said, The kingdom of God cometh not with observation:

21 Neither shall they say, Lo here! or, lo there! for, behold, the kingdom of God is within you.

22 And he said unto the disciples, The days will come, when ye shall desire to see one of the days of the Son of man, and ye shall not see *it*.

23 And they shall say to you, See here; or, see there: go not after *them*, nor follow them.

24 For as the lightning, that lighteneth out of the one *part* under heaven, shineth unto the other *part* under heaven; so shall also the Son of man be in his day.

25 But first must he suffer many things, and be rejected of this generation.

26 And as it was in the days of Noe, so shall it be also in the days of the Son of man.

27 They did eat, they drank, they married wives, they were given in marriage, until the day that Noe entered into the ark, and the flood came, and destroyed them all.

28 Likewise also as it was in the days of Lot; they did eat, they drank, they bought, they sold, they planted, they builded;

29 But the same day that Lot went out of Sodom it rained fire and brimstone from heaven, and destroyed *them* all.

30 Even thus shall it be in the day when the Son of man is revealed.

Amplified

8 Will he not instead tell him, Get my supper ready, and gird yourself and serve me till I eat and drink; then afterward you yourself shall eat and drink?

9 Is he grateful *and* does he praise the servant because he did what he was ordered to do?

10 Even so on your part, when you have done everything that was assigned *and* commanded you, say, We are unworthy servants—possessing no merit, for we have not gone beyond our obligation; we have [merely] done what was our duty to do.

11 As He went His way to Jerusalem, it occurred that [Jesus] was passing [along the border] between Samaria and Galilee.

12 And as He was going into one village, He was met by ten lepers, who stood at a distance.

13 And they raised up their voices and called, Jesus, Master, take pity *and* have mercy on us!

14 And when He saw them He said to them, Go (at once) and show yourselves to the priests. And as they went they were cured *and* made clean. [Lev. 14:2-32.]

15 Then one of them, upon seeing that he was cured, turned back, [p]recognizing *and* thanking *and* praising God with a loud voice;

16 And he fell prostrate at Jesus' feet, thanking Him (over and over). And he was a Samaritan.

17 Then Jesus asked, Were not ten cleansed? Where are the nine?

18 Was there no one found to return and to [p]recognize *and* give thanks *and* praise to God except this alien?

19 And He said to him, Get up and go on your way. Your faith [that is, your trust and confidence that spring from your belief in God] has restored you to health.

20 Asked by the Pharisees when the kingdom of God would come, He replied to them by saying, The kingdom of God does not come with signs to be observed *or* with visible display.

21 Nor will people say, Look! Here [it is]! or, See, [it is] there! For behold, the kingdom of God is within you (in your hearts) *and* among you (surrounding you).

22 And He said to the disciples, The time is coming when you will long to see [even] one of the days of the Son of man, and you will not see [it].

23 And they will say to you, Lo, [He is] there! or, Lo [He is] here! But do not go out or follow [them].

24 For as the lightning that flashes and lights up the sky from [one end] to the [other], so will the Son of man be in His [own] day.

25 But first He must suffer many things and be disapproved *and* repudiated *and* rejected by this age *and* generation.

26 And [just] as it was in the days of Noah, so will it be in the time of the Son of man.

27 [People] ate, they drank, they married, they were given in marriage, right up to the day when Noah went into the ark, and the flood came and destroyed them all. [Gen. 6:5-8; 7:6-24.]

28 So also as it was in the days of Lot: [people] ate, they drank, they bought, they sold, they planted, they built;

29 But on the [very] day that Lot went out of Sodom it rained fire and brimstone from heaven and destroyed [them] all.

30 That is the way it will be on the day that the Son of man is revealed. [Gen. 18:20-33; 19:24, 25.]

p) Cremer.

Living New Testament

prepares his master's meal and serves him his supper before he eats his own. And he is not even thanked, for he is merely doing what he is supposed to do.

10 Just so, if you merely obey Me, you should not consider yourselves worthy of praise. For you have simply done your duty!"

* * * * *

11 As they continued onward toward Jerusalem, they reached the border between Galilee and Samaria,

12 And as they entered a village there, ten lepers stood at a distance,

13 Crying out, "Jesus, sir, have mercy on us!"

14 He looked at them and said, "Go to the Jewish priest and show him that you are healed!" And as they were going, their leprosy disappeared!

15 One of them came back to Jesus, shouting, "Glory to God, I'm healed!"

16 He fell flat on the ground in front of Jesus, face downward in the dust, thanking Him for what He had done. This man was a despised[1] Samaritan.

17 Jesus asked, "Didn't I heal ten men? Where are the nine?

18 Does only this foreigner return to give glory to God?"

19 And Jesus said to the man, "Stand up and go; your faith has made you well."

* * * * *

20 One day the Pharisees asked Jesus, "When will the Kingdom of God begin?" Jesus replied, "The Kingdom of God isn't ushered in with visible signs.

21 You won't be able to say, 'It has begun here in this place or there in that part of the country.' For the Kingdom of God is within you."[2]

22 Later He talked again about this with His disciples. "The time is coming when you will long for Me[3] to be with you even for a single day, but I won't be here," He said.

23 "Reports will reach you that I have returned and that I am in this place or that; don't believe it or go out to look for Me.

24 For when I return, you will know it beyond all doubt. It will be as evident as the lightning that flashes across the skies.

25 But first I must suffer terribly and be rejected by this whole nation.

26 [When I return[4]] the world will be [as indifferent to the things of God[4]] as the people were in Noah's day.

27 They ate and drank and married—everything just as usual right up to the day when Noah went into the ark and the flood came and destroyed them all.

28 And the world will be as it was in the days of Lot: people went about their daily business—eating and drinking, buying and selling, farming and building—

29 Until the morning Lot left Sodom. Then fire and brimstone rained down from heaven and destroyed them all.

30 Yes, it will be 'business as usual' right up to the hour of My return.[5]

[1] Implied. Samaritans were despised by Jews as being only "half-breed" Hebrews.
[2] Or, "among you."
[3] Literally, "the Son of man."
[4] Implied.
[5] Or, "the hour I am revealed."

Revised Standard

rather say to him, 'Prepare supper for me,
and gird yourself and serve me, till I eat
and drink; and afterward you shall eat and
drink'? 9 Does he thank the servant because
he did what was commanded? 10 So you also,
when you have done all that is commanded
you, say, 'We are unworthy servants; we have
only done what was our duty.'"

The healing of the ten lepers

11 On the way to Jerusalem he was passing along between Samaria and Galilee.
12 And as he entered a village, he was met
by ten lepers, who stood at a distance 13 and
lifted up their voices and said, "Jesus, Master, have mercy on us." 14 When he saw
them he said to them, "Go and show yourselves to the priests." And as they went
they were cleansed. 15 Then one of them,
when he saw that he was healed, turned
back, praising God with a loud voice; 16 and
he fell on his face at Jesus' feet, giving him
thanks. Now he was a Samaritan. 17 Then
said Jesus, "Were not ten cleansed? Where
are the nine? 18 Was no one found to return
and give praise to God except this foreigner?" 19 And he said to him, "Rise and go
your way; your faith has made you well."

The coming of the kingdom

20 Being asked by the Pharisees when
the kingdom of God was coming, he
answered them, "The kingdom of God is
not coming with signs to be observed; 21 nor
will they say, 'Lo, here it is!' or 'There!' for
behold, the kingdom of God is in the midst
of you."[z]
22 And he said to the disciples, "The
days are coming when you will desire to see
one of the days of the Son of man, and
you will not see it. 23 And they will say to
you, 'Lo, there!' or 'Lo, here!' Do not go,
do not follow them. 24 For as the lightning
flashes and lights up the sky from one side
to the other, so will the Son of man be in
his day.[a] 25 But first he must suffer many
things and be rejected by this generation.
26 As it was in the days of Noah, so will it
be in the days of the Son of man. 27 They
ate, they drank, they married, they were
given in marriage, until the day when Noah
entered the ark, and the flood came and
destroyed them all. 28 Likewise as it was in
the days of Lot—they ate, they drank, they
bought, they sold, they planted, they built,
29 but on the day when Lot went out from
Sodom fire and brimstone rained from heav-
en and destroyed them all—30 so will it be
on the day when the Son of man is revealed.

[z] Or *within you*
[a] Other ancient authorities omit ***in his day***

King James

31 In that day, he which shall be upon
the housetop, and his stuff in the house, let
him not come down to take it away: and he
that is in the field, let him likewise not
return back.
32 Remember Lot's wife.
33 Whosoever shall seek to save his life
shall lose it; and whosoever shall lose his life
shall preserve it.
34 I tell you, in that night there shall be
two *men* in one bed; the one shall be taken,
and the other shall be left.
35 Two *women* shall be grinding together; the one shall be taken, and the other
left.
36 Two *men* shall be in the field; the one
shall be taken, and the other left.
37 And they answered and said unto him,
Where, Lord? And he said unto them,
Wheresoever the body *is,* thither will the
eagles be gathered together.

Amplified

31 On that day, let him that is on the housetop and his
belongings in the house, not come down [and go inside] to
carry them away; and likewise let him who is in the field
not turn back.
32 Remember Lot's wife! [Gen. 19:26.]
33 Whoever tries to preserve his life will lose it, but
whoever loses his life will preserve and [q]quicken it.
34 I tell you, in that night there will be two men in one
bed; one will be taken and the other will be left.
35 There will be two women grinding together; one
will be taken and the other will be left.
36 *Two men will be in the field; one will be taken and
the other will be left.*
37 Then they asked Him, Where, Lord? He said to
them, Wherever the dead body is, there will the vultures
([r]or eagles) be gathered together.

CHAPTER 18

AND he spake a parable unto them *to
this end,* that men ought always to
pray, and not to faint;
2 Saying, There was in a city a judge,
which feared not God, neither regarded man:
3 And there was a widow in that city;
and she came unto him, saying, Avenge me
of mine adversary.
4 And he would not for a while: but
afterward he said within himself, Though I
fear not God, nor regard man;
5 Yet because this widow troubleth me, I
will avenge her, lest by her continual coming
she weary me.
6 And the Lord said, Hear what the
unjust judge saith.
7 And shall not God avenge his own
elect, which cry day and night unto him,
though he bear long with them?
8 I tell you that he will avenge them
speedily. Nevertheless when the Son of man
cometh, shall he find faith on the earth?
9 And he spake this parable unto certain
which trusted in themselves that they were
righteous, and despised others:
10 Two men went up into the temple to
pray; the one a Pharisee, and the other a
publican.

CHAPTER 18

ALSO [Jesus] told them a parable, to the effect that they
ought always to pray and not to [s]turn coward—faint,
lose heart and give up.
2 He said, In a certain city there was a judge who
neither reverenced *and* feared God nor respected *or* considered man.
3 And there was a widow in that city who kept coming
to him and saying, Protect *and* defend *and* give me justice
against my adversary.
4 And for a time he would not; but later he said to
himself, Though I have neither reverence *or* fear for God
nor respect *or* consideration for man,
5 Yet because this widow continues to bother me, I
will defend *and* protect *and* avenge her; lest she give me
[t]intolerable annoyance *and* wear me out by her continual
coming, or [u]at the last she come and rail on me, *or* [s]assault
me, *or* [v]strangle me.
6 Then the Lord said, Listen to what the unjust judge
says!
7 And will not [our just] God defend *and* protect *and*
avenge His elect (His chosen ones) who cry to Him day
and night? Will He [w]defer them *and* [x]delay help on their
behalf?
8 I tell you, He will defend *and* protect *and* avenge
them speedily. However, when the Son of man comes will
He find ([x]persistence in) the faith on the earth?
9 He also told this parable to some people who trusted
in themselves *and* were confident that they were righteous
[that is, that they were upright and in right standing with
God], and scorned *and* made nothing of all the rest of
men:
10 Two men went up into the temple ([y]enclosure) to
pray, the one a Pharisee and the other a tax collector.

---

q) Wycliffe.
r) Alternate reading.
s) Vincent.
t) Thayer.
u) Tyndale.
v) Wycliffe.
w) Tyndale.
x) Vincent.
y) Trench.

Living New Testament

31 Those away from home that day must not return to pack; those in the fields must not return to town—

32 Remember what happened to Lot's wife!

33 Whoever clings to his life shall lose it, and whoever loses his life shall save it.

34 That night two men will be asleep in the same room, and one will be taken away, the other left.

35, 36 Two women will be working together at household tasks; one will be taken, the other left; and so it will be with men working side by side in the fields."

37 "Lord, where will they be taken?" the disciples asked.

Jesus replied, "Where the body is, the vultures gather!"[6]

Revised Standard

31 On that day, let him who is on the housetop, with his goods in the house, not come
down to take them away; and likewise let
him who is in the field not turn back. 32 Remember Lot's wife. 33 Whoever seeks to gain
his life will lose it, but whoever loses his
life will preserve it. 34 I tell you, in that night
there will be two men in one bed; one will
be taken and the other left. 35 There will be
two women grinding together; one will be
taken and the other left."[b] 37 And they said
to him, "Where, Lord?" He said to them,
"Where the body is, there the eagles[c] will
be gathered together."

CHAPTER 18

One day Jesus told His disciples a story to illustrate their need for constant prayer and to show them that they must keep praying until the answer comes.

2 "There was a city judge," He said, "a very godless man who had great contempt for everyone.

3 A widow of that city came to him frequently to appeal for justice against a man who had harmed her.

4, 5 The judge ignored her for a while, but eventually she got on his nerves. 'I fear neither God nor man,' he said to himself, 'but this woman bothers me. I'm going to see that she gets justice, for she is wearing me out with her constant coming!' "

6 Then the Lord said, "If even an evil judge can be worn down like that,

7 Don't you think that God will surely give justice to His people who plead with Him day and night?

8 Yes! He will answer them quickly! But the question is: When I, the Son of Mankind, return, how many will I find who have faith [and are praying[1]]?"

9 Then He told this story to some who boasted of their virtue and scorned everyone else:

10 "Two men went to the Temple to pray. One was a proud, self-righteous Pharisee, and the other a cheating tax collector.

Parable of the widow and the judge

18 And he told them a parable, to the
effect that they ought always to pray
and not lose heart. 2 He said, "In a certain
city there was a judge who neither feared
God nor regarded man; 3 and there was a
widow in that city who kept coming to
him and saying, 'Vindicate me against my
adversary.' 4 For a while he refused; but
afterward he said to himself, 'Though I
neither fear God nor regard man, 5 yet because this widow bothers me, I will vindicate her, or she will wear me out by her
continual coming.' " 6 And the Lord said,
"Hear what the unrighteous judge says. 7 And
will not God vindicate his elect, who cry to
him day and night? Will he delay long over
them? 8 I tell you, he will vindicate them
speedily. Nevertheless, when the Son of man
comes, will he find faith on earth?"

The Pharisee and the publican

9 He also told this parable to some who
trusted in themselves that they were righteous and despised others: 10 "Two men went
up into the temple to pray, one a Pharisee
and the other a tax collector. 11 The Pharisee

[6] This may mean that God's people will be taken out to the execution grounds and their bodies left to the vultures.
[1] Implied.

[b] Other ancient authorities add verse 36, *"Two men will be in the field; one will be taken and the other left"*
[c] Or *vultures*

King James

11 The Pharisee stood and prayed thus with himself, God, I thank thee, that I am not as other men *are*, extortioners, unjust, adulterers, or even as this publican.

12 I fast twice a week, I give tithes of all that I possess.

13 And the publican, standing afar off, would not lift up so much as *his* eyes unto heaven, but smote upon his breast, saying, God be merciful to me a sinner.

14 I tell you, this man went down to his house justified *rather* than the other: for every one that exalteth himself shall be abased; and he that humbleth himself shall be exalted.

15 And they brought unto him also infants, that he would touch them: but when *his* disciples saw *it*, they rebuked them.

16 But Jesus called them *unto him*, and said, Suffer little children to come unto me, and forbid them not: for of such is the kingdom of God.

17 Verily I say unto you, Whosoever shall not receive the kingdom of God as a little child shall in no wise enter therein.

18 And a certain ruler asked him, saying Good Master, what shall I do to inherit eternal life?

19 And Jesus said unto him, Why callest thou me good? none *is* good, save one, *that is*, God.

20 Thou knowest the commandments, Do not commit adultery, Do not kill, Do not steal, Do not bear false witness, Honour thy father and thy mother.

21 And he said, All these have I kept from my youth up.

22 Now when Jesus heard these things, he said unto him, Yet lackest thou one thing: sell all that thou hast, and distribute unto the poor, and thou shalt have treasure in heaven: and come, follow me.

23 And when he heard this, he was very sorrowful: for he was very rich.

24 And when Jesus saw that he was very sorrowful, he said, How hardly shall they that have riches enter into the kingdom of God!

25 For it is easier for a camel to go through a needle's eye, than for a rich man to enter into the kingdom of God.

26 And they that heard *it* said, Who then can be saved?

27 And he said, The things which are impossible with men are possible with God.

28 Then Peter said, Lo, we have left all, and followed thee.

29 And he said unto them, Verily I say unto you, There is no man that hath left house, or parents, or brethren, or wife, or children, for the kingdom of God's sake,

30 Who shall not receive manifold more in this present time, and in the world to come life everlasting.

31 ¶ Then he took *unto him* the twelve, and said unto them, Behold, we go up to Jerusalem, and all things that are written by the prophets concerning the Son of man shall be accomplished.

Amplified

11 The Pharisee [x]took his stand ostentatiously, and began to pray thus before *and* with himself: God, I thank You that I am not as the rest of men, extortioners (robbers), swindlers—unrighteous in heart and life—adulterers, or even like this tax collector here.

12 I fast twice a week; I give tithes of all that I gain.

13 But the tax collector, [merely] standing at a distance, would not even lift up his eyes to heaven; but kept striking his breast, saying, O God, be favorable (be gracious, be merciful) to me, the [z]especially wicked sinner that I am!

14 I tell you, this man went down to his home justified—forgiven and made upright and in right standing with God—rather than the other man; for every one who exalts himself will be humbled, but he who humbles himself will be exalted.

15 Now they were also bringing even babies to Him that He might touch them, and when the disciples noticed it, they reproved them.

16 But Jesus called them [[a]the parents] to Him, saying, Allow the little children to come to Me, and do not hinder them, for to such [as these] belongs the kingdom of God.

17 Truly, I say to you, whoever does not accept *and* receive *and* welcome the kingdom of God as a little child [does], shall not in any way enter it (at all).

18 And a certain ruler asked Him, Good Teacher, (You who are [b]essentially and perfectly [c]morally good) what shall I do to inherit eternal life [that is, to partake of eternal salvation in the Messiah's kingdom]?

19 Jesus said to him, Why do you call Me ([b]essentially and perfectly [c]morally) good? No one (is [b]essentially and perfectly [c]morally) good except God only.

20 You know the commandments: Do not commit adultery; do not kill; do not steal; do not witness falsely; honor your father and your mother. [Exod. 20:12-16; Deut. 5:16-20.]

21 And he replied, All these I have kept from my youth.

22 And when Jesus heard it, He said to him, One thing you still lack. Sell everything that you have and [b]divide [the money] among the poor, and you will have rich treasure in heaven; and come back [and] follow Me—become My disciple, join My party and accompany Me.

23 But when he heard this, he became distressed *and* very sorrowful, for he was rich, exceedingly so.

24 Jesus observing him said, How difficult it is for those who have wealth to enter into the kingdom of God!

25 For it is easier for a camel to enter in through a needle's eye than [for] a rich man to enter into the kingdom of God.

26 And those who heard it said, Then who can be saved?

27 But He said, What is impossible with men is possible with God. [Gen. 18:14; Jer. 32:17.]

28 And Peter said, See, we have left our own [things]—home, family and business—and have followed You.

29 And He said to them, I say to you, truly there is no one who has left house or wife or brothers or parents or children for the sake of the kingdom of God,

30 Who will not receive in return many times more in this world, and in the coming age eternal life.

31 Then taking the twelve (apostles) aside, He said to them, Listen! We are going up to Jerusalem, and all things that are written about the Son of man through *and* by the prophets will be fulfilled. [Isa. 53:1-12.]

---

x) Vincent.
z) Thayer.
a) Henry.
b) Thayer.
c) Cremer.

Living New Testament

11 The proud Pharisee 'prayed' this prayer: 'Thank God, I am not a sinner like everyone else, especially like that tax collector over there! For I never cheat, I don't commit adultery,

12 I go without food twice a week, and I give to God a tenth of everything I earn.'

13 But the corrupt tax collector stood at a distance and dared not even lift his eyes to heaven as he prayed, but beat upon his chest in sorrow, exclaiming, 'God, be merciful to me, a sinner.'

14 I tell you, this sinner, not the Pharisee, returned home forgiven! For the proud shall be humbled, but the humble shall be honored."

* * * * *

15 One day some mothers brought their babies to Him to touch and bless. But the disciples told them to go away.

16, 17 Then Jesus called the children over to Him and said to the disciples, "Let the little children come to Me! Never send them away! For the Kingdom of God belongs to men who have hearts as trusting as these little children's. And anyone who doesn't have their kind of faith will never get within the Kingdom's gates."

* * * * *

18 Once a Jewish religious leader asked Him this question: "Good sir, what shall I do to get to heaven?"

19 "Do you realize what you are saying when you call me 'good'?" Jesus asked him. "Only God is truly good, and no one else.

20 But as to your question, you know what the ten commandments say—don't commit adultery, don't murder, don't steal, don't lie, honor your parents, and so on."

21 The man replied, "I've obeyed every one of these laws since I was a small child."

22 "There is still one thing you lack," Jesus said. "Sell all you have and give the money to the poor—it will become treasure for you in heaven—and come, follow Me."

23 But when the man heard this he went sadly away, for he was very rich.

24 Jesus watched him go and then said to His disciples, "How hard it is for the rich to enter the Kingdom of God!

25 It is easier for a camel to go through the eye of a needle than for a rich man to enter the Kingdom of God!"

26 Those who heard Him say this exclaimed, "If it is that hard, how can *anyone* be saved?"

27 He replied, "God can do what men can't!"

28 And Peter said, "We have left our homes and followed You."

29 "Yes," Jesus replied, "and everyone who has done as you have, leaving home, wife, brothers, parents, or children for the sake of the Kingdom of God,

30 Will be repaid many times over now, as well as receiving eternal life in the world to come."

* * * * *

31 Gathering the Twelve around Him He told them, "As you know, we are going to Jerusalem. And when we get there, all the predictions of the ancient prophets concerning Me will come true.

Revised Standard

stood and prayed thus with himself, 'God,
I thank thee that I am not like other men,
extortioners, unjust, adulterers, or even like
this tax collector. [12]I fast twice a week, I
give tithes of all that I get.' [13]But the tax
collector, standing far off, would not even
lift up his eyes to heaven, but beat his
breast, saying, 'God, be merciful to me a
sinner!' [14]I tell you, this man went down to
his house justified rather than the other; for
every one who exalts himself will be humbled, but he who humbles himself will be
exalted."

Jesus and the little children

15 Now they were bringing even infants
to him that he might touch them; and when
the disciples saw it, they rebuked them.
[16]But Jesus called them to him, saying, "Let
the children come to me, and do not hinder
them; for to such belongs the kingdom of
God. [17]Truly, I say to you, whoever does
not receive the kingdom of God like a
child shall not enter it."

The rich young ruler

18 And a ruler asked him, "Good Teacher, what shall I do to inherit eternal life?"
[19]And Jesus said to him, "Why do you call
me good? No one is good but God alone.
[20]You know the commandments: 'Do not
commit adultery, Do not kill, Do not steal,
Do not bear false witness, Honor your father and mother.'" [21]And he said, "All these
I have observed from my youth." [22]And
when Jesus heard it, he said to them, "One
thing you still lack. Sell all that you have
and distribute to the poor, and you will have
treasure in heaven; and come, follow me."
[23]But when he heard this he became sad,
for he was very rich. [24]Jesus looking at him
said, "How hard it is for those who have
riches to enter the kingdom of God! [25]For
it is easier for a camel to go through the
eye of a needle than for a rich man to enter
the kingdom of God." [26]Those who heard
it said, "Then who can be saved?" [27]But he
said, "What is impossible with men is possible with God." [28]And Peter said, "Lo, we
have left our homes and followed you."
[29]And he said to them, "Truly, I say to
you, there is no man who has left house or
wife or brothers or parents or children, for
the sake of the kingdom of God, [30]who will
not receive manifold more in this time, and
in the age to come eternal life."

Crucifixion and resurrection foretold

31 And taking the twelve, he said to
them, "Behold, we are going up to Jerusalem,
and everything that is written of the Son of
man by the prophets will be accomplished.

King James

32 For he shall be delivered unto the Gentiles, and shall be mocked, and spitefully entreated, and spitted on:
33 And they shall scourge *him*, and put him to death: and the third day he shall rise again.
34 And they understood none of these things: and this saying was hid from them, neither knew they the things which were spoken.
35 ¶ And it came to pass, that as he was come nigh unto Jericho, a certain blind man sat by the way side begging:
36 And hearing the multitude pass by, he asked what it meant.
37 And they told him, that Jesus of Nazareth passeth by.
38 And he cried, saying, Jesus, *thou* son of David, have mercy on me.
39 And they which went before rebuked him, that he should hold his peace: but he cried so much the more, *Thou* son of David, have mercy on me.
40 And Jesus stood, and commanded him to be brought unto him: and when he was come near, he asked him,
41 Saying, What wilt thou that I shall do unto thee? And he said, Lord, that I may receive my sight.
42 And Jesus said unto him, Receive thy sight: thy faith hath saved thee.
43 And immediately he received his sight, and followed him, glorifying God: and all the people, when they saw *it*, gave praise unto God.

Amplified

32 For He will be handed over to the Gentiles, and will be made sport of *and* scoffed *and* jeered at and insulted and spit upon; [Isa. 50:6.]
33 They will flog Him and kill Him, and on the third day He will rise again. [Ps. 16:10.]
34 But they understood nothing of these things; His words were a mystery *and* hidden from them, and they did not comprehend what He was telling them.
35 As He came near to Jericho, it occurred that a blind man was sitting by the roadside begging;
36 And hearing a crowd going by, he asked what it meant.
37 They told him, Jesus of Nazareth is passing by.
38 And he shouted, saying, Jesus, Son of David, take pity *and* have mercy on me!
39 But those who were in front reproved him, [telling him] to keep quiet; yet he [d]screamed *and* shrieked so much the more, Son of David, take pity *and* have mercy on me!
40 Then Jesus stood still, and ordered that he be led to Him; and when he came near, Jesus asked him,
41 What do you want Me to do for you? He said, Lord, let me receive my sight!
42 And Jesus said to him, Receive your sight! Your faith [that is, [e]your trust and confidence springing from your faith in God] has healed you.
43 And instantly he received his sight and began to follow Jesus—[f]recognizing, praising and honoring God; and all the people, when they saw it, praised God.

CHAPTER 19

AND *Jesus* entered and passed through Jericho.
2 And, behold, *there was* a man named Zacchæus, which was the chief among the publicans, and he was rich.
3 And he sought to see Jesus who he was; and could not for the press, because he was little of stature.
4 And he ran before, and climbed up into a sycomore tree to see him: for he was to pass that *way*.
5 And when Jesus came to the place, he looked up, and saw him, and said unto him, Zacchæus, make haste, and come down; for to-day I must abide at thy house.
6 And he made haste, and came down, and received him joyfully.
7 And when they saw *it*, they all murmured, saying, That he was gone to be guest with a man that is a sinner.

CHAPTER 19

AND [Jesus] entered Jericho and was passing on through it,
2 And there was a man called Zacchaeus, a chief tax collector and rich.
3 And he was trying to see Jesus, which [one] He was; but he could not on account of the crowd, because he was small in stature.
4 So he ran on ahead, and climbed up in a sycamore tree in order to see Him, for He was about to pass that way.
5 And when Jesus reached the place, He looked up and said to him, Zacchaeus, hurry and come down; for I must stay at your house today.
6 So he hurried and came down, and he received *and* welcomed Him joyfully.
7 And when the people saw it, they all [g]muttered among themselves *and* indignantly complained, He has gone in to be the guest of *and* lodge with a man who is devoted to sin *and* preeminently a sinner.
8 So then Zacchaeus stood up and solemnly declared to the Lord, See, Lord, the half of my goods I [now] give [by way of restoration] to the poor; and if I have cheated any one out of anything, I [now] restore four times as much. [Exod. 22:1; Lev. 6:5; Num. 5:6, 7.]

---

d) Vincent.
e) Thayer.
f) Cremer.
g) Abbott-Smith.

Living New Testament

32 I will be handed over to the Gentiles to be mocked and treated shamefully and spat upon,

33 And lashed and killed. And the third day I will rise again."

34 But they didn't understand a thing He said. He seemed to be talking in riddles.

35 As they approached Jericho, a blind man was sitting beside the road, begging from travelers.

36 When he heard the noise of a crowd going past, he asked what was happening.

37 He was told that Jesus from Nazareth was going by,

38 So he began shouting, "Jesus, Son of David, have mercy on me!"

39 The crowds ahead of Jesus tried to hush the man, but he only yelled the louder, "Son of David, have mercy on me!"

40 When Jesus arrived at the spot, He stopped. "Bring the blind man over here," He said.

41 Then Jesus asked the man, "What do you want?" "Lord," he pleaded, "I want to see!"

42 And Jesus said, "All right, begin seeing! Your faith has healed you!"

43 And instantly the man could see, and followed Jesus, praising God. And all who saw it happen praised God too.

Revised Standard

32 For he will be delivered to the Gentiles,
and will be mocked and shamefully treated
and spit upon; 33 they will scourge him and
kill him, and on the third day he will rise."
34 But they understood none of these things;
this saying was hid from them, and they did
not grasp what was said.

Healing the blind man near Jericho

35 As he drew near to Jericho, a blind
man was sitting by the roadside begging;
36 and hearing a multitude going by, he inquired what this meant. 37 They told him,
"Jesus of Nazareth is passing by." 38 And he
cried, "Jesus, Son of David, have mercy on
me!" 39 And those who were in front rebuked
him, telling him to be silent; but he cried
out all the more, "Son of David, have mercy
on me!" 40 And Jesus stopped, and commanded him to be brought to him; and when he
came near, he asked him, 41 "What do you
want me to do for you?" He said, "Lord, let
me receive my sight." 42 And Jesus said to
him, "Receive your sight; your faith has
made you well." 43 And immediately he received his sight and followed him, glorifying
God; and all the people, when they saw it,
gave praise to God.

CHAPTER 19

As Jesus was passing through Jericho, a man named Zacchaeus, one of the most influential Jews in the Roman tax-collecting business (and, of course, a very rich man),

3 Tried to get a look at Jesus, but he was too short to see over the crowds.

4 So he ran ahead and climbed into a sycamore tree beside the road, to watch from there.

5 When Jesus came by He looked up at Zacchaeus and called him by name! "Zacchaeus!" He said. "Quick! Come down! For I am going to be a guest in your home today!"

6 Zacchaeus hurriedly climbed down and took Jesus to his house in great excitement and joy.

7 But the crowds were displeased. "He has gone to be the guest of a notorious sinner," they grumbled.

8 Meanwhile, Zacchaeus stood before the Lord and said, "Sir, from now on I will give half my wealth to the poor, and if I find I have overcharged anyone on his taxes, I will penalize myself by giving him back four times as much!"

The conversion of Zacchaeus

19 He entered Jericho and was passing
through. 2 And there was a man named
Zacchaeus; he was a chief tax collector, and
rich. 3 And he sought to see who Jesus was,
but could not, on account of the crowd, because he was small of stature. 4 So he ran
on ahead and climbed up into a sycamore
tree to see him, for he was to pass that
way. 5 And when Jesus came to the place,
he looked up and said to him, "Zacchaeus,
make haste and come down; for I must stay
at your house today." 6 So he made haste and
came down, and received him joyfully. 7 And
when they saw it they all murmured, "He
has gone in to be the guest of a man who
is a sinner." 8 And Zacchaeus stood and said
to the Lord, "Behold, Lord, the half of my
goods I give to the poor; and if I have defrauded any one of anything, I restore it

King James

8 And Zacchæus stood, and said unto the Lord; Behold, Lord, the half of my goods I give to the poor; and if I have taken any thing from any man by false accusation, I restore *him* fourfold.

9 And Jesus said unto him, This day is salvation come to this house, forsomuch as he also is a son of Abraham.

10 For the Son of man is come to seek and to save that which was lost.

11 And as they heard these things, he added and spake a parable, because he was nigh to Jerusalem, and because they thought that the kingdom of God should immediately appear.

12 He said therefore, A certain nobleman went into a far country to receive for himself a kingdom, and to return.

13 And he called his ten servants, and delivered them ten pounds, and said unto them, Occupy till I come.

14 But his citizens hated him, and sent a message after him, saying, We will not have this *man* to reign over us.

15 And it came to pass, that when he was returned, having received the kingdom, then he commanded these servants to be called unto him, to whom he had given the money, that he might know how much every man had gained by trading.

16 Then came the first, saying, Lord, thy pound hath gained ten pounds.

17 And he said unto him, Well, thou good servant: because thou hast been faithful in a very little, have thou authority over ten cities.

18 And the second came, saying, Lord, thy pound hath gained five pounds.

19 And he said likewise to him, Be thou also over five cities.

20 And another came, saying, Lord, behold, *here* is thy pound, which I have kept laid up in a napkin:

21 For I feared thee, because thou art an austere man: thou takest up that thou layedst not down, and reapest that thou didst not sow.

22 And he saith unto him, Out of thine own mouth will I judge thee, *thou* wicked servant. Thou knewest that I was an austere man, taking up that I laid not down, and reaping that I did not sow:

23 Wherefore then gavest not thou my money into the bank, that at my coming I might have required mine own with usury?

24 And he said unto them that stood by, Take from him the pound, and give *it* to him that hath ten pounds.

25 (And they said unto him, Lord, he hath ten pounds.)

26 For I say unto you, That unto every one which hath shall be given; and from him that hath not, even that he hath shall be taken away from him.

27 But those mine enemies, which would not that I should reign over them, bring hither, and slay *them* before me.

28 ¶ And when he had thus spoken, he went before, ascending up to Jerusalem.

29 And it came to pass, when he was come nigh to Bethphage and Bethany, at the mount called *the mount* of Olives, he sent two of his disciples,

Amplified

9 And Jesus said to him, Today is ([h]Messianic and spiritual) salvation come to [all the members of] this household, since Zacchaeus too is a [real spiritual] son of Abraham;

10 For the Son of man came to seek and to save that which was lost.

11 Now as they were listening to these things, He proceeded to tell a parable, because He was approaching Jerusalem, and because they thought that the kingdom of God was going to be brought to light *and* shown forth immediately.

12 He therefore said, A certain nobleman went into a distant country to obtain for himself a kingdom and then return.

13 Calling ten of his [own] bond servants, he gave them ten minas [each equal to about one hundred days' wages or nearly twenty dollars], and said to them, [i]Buy *and* sell with these [j]while I go *and* return.

14 But his citizens detested him, and sent an embassy after him to say, We do not want this man to become ruler over us.

15 When he returned, having received the kingdom, he ordered these bond servants to whom he had given the money to be called to him, that he might know how much each one had made by [i]buying *and* selling.

16 The first one came before him, and he said, Lord, your mina has made ten [additional] minas.

17 And he said to him, Well done, excellent bond servant! Because you have been faithful *and* trustworthy in a very little, you shall have authority over ten cities.

18 The second one also came, and said, Lord, your mina has made five more minas.

19 And he said also to him, And you will have charge over five cities.

20 Then another came and said, Lord, here is your mina, which I have kept laid up in a [k]handkerchief.

21 For I was constantly afraid of you, because you are a stern (hard, severe) man; you pick up what you did not lay down, and you reap what you did not sow.

22 He said to the servant, I will judge *and* condemn you out of your own mouth, you wicked slave! You knew [did you], that I was a stern (hard, severe) man, picking up what I did not lay down, and reaping what I did not sow?

23 Then why did you not put my money in a bank, so that on my return I might have collected it with interest?

24 And he said to the bystanders, Take the mina away from him, and give it to him who has the ten minas.

25 And they said to him, Lord, he has ten minas [already]!

26 And [said Jesus,] I tell you, that to every one who gets *and* has, will more be given; but from the man who does not get, *and* does not have, will be taken away even what he has.

27 [The indignant king ended by saying,] But as for these enemies of mine, who did not want me to reign over them, bring them here and [l]slaughter them in my presence!

28 And after saying these things, Jesus went on ahead of them, going up to Jerusalem.

29 When He came near Bethphage and Bethany, at the mount called Olives, He sent two of His disciples,

---

h) Moulton and Milligan.
i) Tyndale.
j) Vincent.
k) Moulton and Milligan.
l) Vincent.

Living New Testament

9, 10 Jesus told him, "This shows[1] that salvation has come to this home today. This man was one of the lost sons of Abraham, and I, the Son of Mankind, have come to search for and save such souls as his."

11 And because Jesus was nearing Jerusalem, He told a story to correct the impression that the Kingdom of God would begin right away.

12 "A nobleman living in a certain province was called away to the distant capital of the empire to be crowned king of his province.

13 Before he left he called together ten assistants and gave them each $2,000 to invest while he was gone.

14 But some of his people hated him and sent him their declaration of independence, stating that they had rebelled and would not acknowledge him as their king.

15 Upon his return he called in the men to whom he had given the money, to find out what they had done with it, and what their profits were.

16 The first man reported a tremendous gain—ten times as much as the original amount!

17 'Fine!' the king exclaimed. 'You are a good man. You have been faithful with the little I entrusted to you, and as your reward, you shall be governor of ten cities.'

18 The next man also reported a splendid gain—five times the original amount.

19 'All right!' his master said. 'You can be governor over five cities.'

20 But the third man brought back only the money he had started with. 'I've kept it safe,' he said,

21 'Because I was afraid [you would demand my profits[2]], for you are a hard man to deal with, taking what isn't yours and even confiscating the crops that others plant!'

22 'You vile and wicked slave,' the king roared. 'Hard, am I? That's exactly how I'll be toward you! If you knew so much about me and how tough I am,

23 Then why didn't you deposit the money in the bank so that I could at least get some interest on it?'

24 Then turning to the others standing by he ordered, 'Take the money away from him and give it to the man who earned the most.'

25 'But, sir,' they said, 'he has enough already!'

26 'Yes,' the king replied, 'but it is always true that those who have, get more, and those who have little, soon lose even that.

27 And now about these enemies of mine who revolted—bring them in and execute them before me.' "

28 After telling this story, Jesus went on towards Jerusalem, walking along ahead of His disciples.

29 As they came to the towns of Bethphage and Bethany, on the Mount of Olives, He sent two disciples ahead.

[1] Implied.
[2] Implied.

Revised Standard

fourfold." 9And Jesus said to him, "Today
salvation has come to this house, since he
also is a son of Abraham. 10For the Son
of man came to seek and to save the lost."

The parable of the pounds

11 As they heard these things, he proceeded to tell a parable, because he was
near to Jerusalem, and because they supposed that the kingdom of God was to appear immediately. 12He said therefore, "A
nobleman went into a far country to receive kingly power[d] and then return. 13Call-
ing ten of his servants, he gave them ten
pounds,[e] and said to them, 'Trade with these
till I come.' 14But his citizens hated him
and sent an embassy after him, saying, 'We
do not want this man to reign over us.'
15When he returned, having received the
kingly power,[d] he commanded these servants, to whom he had given the money,
to be called to him, that he might know
what they had gained by trading. 16The first
came before him, saying, 'Lord, your pound
has made ten pounds more.' 17And he said
to him, 'Well done, good servant! Because
you have been faithful in a very little, you
shall have authority over ten cities.' 18And
the second came, saying, 'Lord, your pound
has made five pounds.' 19And he said to
him, 'And you are to be over five cities.'
20Then another came, saying, 'Lord, here is
your pound, which I kept laid away in a
napkin; 21for I was afraid of you, because
you are a severe man; you take up what
you did not lay down, and reap what you
did not sow.' 22He said to him, 'I will condemn you out of your own mouth, you
wicked servant! You knew that I was a
severe man, taking up what I did not lay
down and reaping what I did not sow?
23Why then did you not put my money into the bank, and at my coming I should
have collected it with interest?' 24And he
said to those who stood by, 'Take the pound
from him, and give it to him who has ten
pounds.' 25(And they said to him, 'Lord,
he has ten pounds!') 26'I tell you, that to
every one who has will more be given; but
from him who has not, even what he has
will be taken away. 27But as for these enemies of mine, who did not want me to reign
over them, bring them here and slay them
before me.' "

The triumphal entry

28 And when he had said this, he went
on ahead, going up to Jerusalem. 29When
he drew near to Bethphage and Bethany,
at the mount that is called Olivet, he sent

[d] Greek *a kingdom*
[e] The mina, rendered here by *pound*, was equal to about twenty dollars

King James

30 Saying, Go ye into the village over against *you;* in the which at your entering ye shall find a colt tied, whereon yet never man sat: loose him, and bring *him hither.*

31 And if any man ask you, Why do ye loose *him?* thus shall ye say unto him, Because the Lord hath need of him.

32 And they that were sent went their way, and found even as he had said unto them.

33 And as they were loosing the colt, the owners thereof said unto them, Why loose ye the colt?

34 And they said, The Lord hath need of him.

35 And they brought him to Jesus: and they cast their garments upon the colt, and they set Jesus thereon.

36 And as he went, they spread their clothes in the way.

37 And when he was come nigh, even now at the descent of the mount of Olives, the whole multitude of the disciples began to rejoice and praise God with a loud voice for all the mighty works that they had seen;

38 Saying, Blessed *be* the King that cometh in the name of the Lord: peace in heaven, and glory in the highest.

39 And some of the Pharisees from among the multitude said unto him, Master, rebuke thy disciples.

40 And he answered and said unto them, I tell you that, if these should hold their peace, the stones would immediately cry out.

41 ¶ And when he was come near, he beheld the city, and wept over it,

42 Saying, If thou hadst known, even thou, at least in this thy day, the things *which belong* unto thy peace! but now they are hid from thine eyes.

43 For the days shall come upon thee, that thine enemies shall cast a trench about thee, and compass thee round, and keep thee in on every side,

44 And shall lay thee even with the ground, and thy children within thee; and they shall not leave in thee one stone upon another; because thou knewest not the time of thy visitation.

45 And he went into the temple, and began to cast out them that sold therein, and them that bought;

46 Saying unto them, It is written, My house is the house of prayer: but ye have made it a den of thieves.

47 And he taught daily in the temple. But the chief priests and the scribes and the chief of the people sought to destroy him,

48 And could not find what they might do: for all the people were very attentive to hear him.

Amplified

30 Telling [them], Go into the village yonder; there as you go in you will find a donkey's colt tied, on which no man has ever yet sat; loose it and bring [it here].

31 If anybody asks you, Why are you untying [it]? you shall say this, Because the Lord has need of it.

32 So those who were sent went away, and found it as He had told them.

33 And as they were loosening the colt, its owners said to them, Why are you untying the colt?

34 And they said, The Lord has need of it.

35 And they brought it to Jesus; then they threw their garments over the colt, and set Jesus upon it, [Zech. 9:9.]

36 And as He rode along, the people kept spreading their garments on the road. [II Kings 9:13.]

37 As He was approaching [the city], at the descent of the Mount of Olives, the whole crowd of the disciples began to rejoice and to praise God, (extolling Him exultantly and) loudly for all the mighty miracles *and* works of power that they had witnessed,

38 Crying, Blessed—celebrated with praises—be the King Who comes in the name of the Lord! Peace in heaven— [that is,] [m]freedom [there] from all the distresses that are experienced as the result of sin; and glory (majesty and splendor) in the highest [heaven]! [Ps. 118:26.]

39 And some of the Pharisees from the throng said to Jesus, Teacher, reprove Your disciples!

40 He replied, I tell you that if these kept silent, the very stones would cry out. [Hab. 2:11.]

41 And when as He approached He saw the city, He wept ([n]audibly) over it,

42 Exclaiming, Would that you had known personally, even at least in this your day, the things that make for peace (for [m]freedom from all the distresses that are experienced as the result of sin and upon which your peace, that is, your [o]security, safety, prosperity and happiness depends)! But now they are hidden from your eyes.

43 For a time is coming upon you when your enemies will throw up a [p]bank (with pointed stakes) about you, and surround you, and shut you in on every side: [Isa. 29:3; Jer. 6:6; Ezek. 4:2.]

44 And they will dash you down to the ground, you [Jerusalem] and your children within you, and they will not leave in you one stone upon another; [all] because you did not come progressively to recognize *and* know *and* understand [from observation and experience] the time of your visitation [that is, when God was visiting you, the time [q]in which God showed Himself gracious toward you and offered you salvation through Christ].

45 Then He went into the temple ([r]enclosure) and began to drive out those who were selling,

46 Telling them, It is written, My house shall be a house of prayer, but you have made it a [s]cave of robbers. [Isa. 56:7; Jer. 7:11.]

47 And He continued to teach day after day in the temple ([r]porches and courts). The chief priests and scribes and the leading men of the people were seeking to put Him to death,

48 But they did not discover anything they could do, for all the people hung upon His words *and* [t]stuck by Him.

---

m) Cremer.
n) Vincent.
o) Thayer.
p) Vincent.
q) Thayer.
r) Trench's "Synonyms of the New Testament."
s) Moulton and Milligan.
t) Tyndale.

Living New Testament

30 With instructions to go to the next village, and as they entered they were to look for a donkey tied beside the road. It would be a colt, not yet broken for riding. "Untie him," Jesus said, "and bring him here.

31 And if anyone asks you what you are doing, just say, 'The Lord needs him.' "

32 They found the colt as Jesus said,

33 And sure enough, as they were untying it, the owners demanded an explanation. "What are you doing?" they asked. "Why are you untying our colt?"

34 And the disciples simply replied, "The Lord needs him!"

35 So they brought the colt to Jesus and threw some of their clothing across its back for Jesus to sit on.

36, 37 Then the crowds spread out their robes along the road ahead of Him, and as they reached the place where the road started down from the Mount of Olives, the whole procession began to shout and sing as they walked along, praising God for all the wonderful miracles Jesus had done.

38 "God has given us a King!" they exulted. "Long live the King! Let all heaven rejoice! Glory to God in the highest heavens!"

39 But some of the Pharisees among the crowd said, "Sir, rebuke your followers for saying things like that!"

40 He replied, "If they keep quiet, the stones along the road will burst into cheers!"

41 But as they came closer to Jerusalem and He saw the city ahead, He began to cry.

42 "Eternal peace was within your reach and you turned it down," He wept, "and now it is too late.

43 Your enemies will pile up earth against your walls and encircle you and close in on you,

44 And crush you to the ground, and your children within you; your enemies will not leave one stone upon another—for you have rejected the opportunity God offered you."

45 Then He entered the Temple and began to drive out the merchants from their stalls,

46 Saying to them, "The Scriptures declare, 'My Temple is a place of prayer; but you have turned it into a den of thieves.' "

47 After that He taught daily in the Temple, but the chief priests and other religious leaders and the business community[3] were trying to find some way to get rid of Him.

48 But they could think of nothing, for He was a hero to the people—they hung on every word He said.

Revised Standard

two of the disciples, 30 saying, "Go into the
village opposite, where on entering you will
find a colt tied, on which no one has ever yet
sat; untie it and bring it here. 31 If any one
asks you, 'Why are you untying it?' you
shall say this, 'The Lord has need of it.' "
32 So those who were sent went away and
found it as he had told them. 33 And as they
were untying the colt, its owners said to
them, "Why are you untying the colt?"
34 And they said, "The Lord has need of it."
35 And they brought it to Jesus, and throwing their garments on the colt they set Jesus
upon it. 36 And as he rode along, they
spread their garments on the road. 37 As he
was now drawing near, at the descent of
the Mount of Olives, the whole multitude
of the disciples began to rejoice and praise
God with a loud voice for all the mighty
works that they had seen, 38 saying, "Blessed
is the King who comes in the name of the
Lord! Peace in heaven and glory in the
highest!" 39 And some of the Pharisees in
the multitude said to him, "Teacher, rebuke
your disciples." 40 He answered, "I tell you,
if these were silent, the very stones would
cry out."

Jesus weeps over Jerusalem

41 And when he drew near and saw
the city he wept over it, 42 saying, "Would
that even today you knew the things that
make for peace! But now they are hid from
your eyes. 43 For the days shall come upon
you, when your enemies will cast up a bank
about you and surround you, and hem you
in on every side, 44 and dash you to the
ground, you and your children within you,
and they will not leave one stone upon
another in you; because you did not know
the time of your visitation."

The cleansing of the temple

45 And he entered the temple and began
to drive out those who sold, 46 saying to
them, "It is written, 'My house shall be a
house of prayer'; but you have made it a
den of robbers."

47 And he was teaching daily in the
temple. The chief priests and the scribes
and the principal men of the people sought
to destroy him; 48 but they did not find
anything they could do, for all the people
hung upon his words.

---

[3] Literally, "the leading men among the people."

King James

CHAPTER 20

AND it came to pass, *that* on one of those days, as he taught the people in the temple, and preached the gospel, the chief priests and the scribes came upon *him* with the elders,

2 And spake unto him, saying, Tell us, by what authority doest thou these things? or who is he that gave thee this authority?

3 And he answered and said unto them, I will also ask you one thing; and answer me:

4 The baptism of John, was it from heaven, or of men?

5 And they reasoned with themselves, saying, If we shall say, From heaven; he will say, Why then believed ye him not?

6 But and if we say, Of men; all the people will stone us: for they be persuaded that John was a prophet.

7 And they answered, that they could not tell whence *it was*.

8 And Jesus said unto them, Neither tell I you by what authority I do these things.

9 Then began he to speak to the people this parable; A certain man planted a vineyard, and let it forth to husbandmen, and went into a far country for a long time.

10 And at the season he sent a servant to the husbandmen, that they should give him of the fruit of the vineyard: but the husbandmen beat him, and sent *him* away empty.

11 And again he sent another servant: and they beat him also, and entreated *him* shamefully, and sent *him* away empty.

12 And again he sent a third: and they wounded him also, and cast *him* out.

13 Then said the lord of the vineyard, What shall I do? I will send my beloved son: it may be they will reverence *him* when they see him.

14 But when the husbandmen saw him, they reasoned among themselves, saying, This is the heir: come, let us kill him, that the inheritance may be ours.

15 So they cast him out of the vineyard, and killed *him*. What therefore shall the lord of the vineyard do unto them?

16 He shall come and destroy these husbandmen, and shall give the vineyard to others. And when they heard it, they said, God forbid.

17 And he beheld them, and said, What is this then that is written, The stone which the builders rejected, the same is become the head of the corner?

18 Whosoever shall fall upon that stone shall be broken; but on whomsoever it shall fall it will grind him to powder.

19 ¶ And the chief priests and the scribes the same hour sought to lay hands on him; and they feared the people; for they perceived that he had spoken this parable against them.

Amplified

CHAPTER 20

ONE day as Jesus was instructing the people in the temple [[r]porches] and preaching the good news (the Gospel), the chief priests and the scribes came up with the elders [members of the Sanhedrin]

2 And said to Him, Tell us by what (sort of) authority You are doing these things? Or who is it who gave You this authority?

3 He replied to them, I will also ask you a question. Now answer Me:

4 Was the baptism of John from heaven or from men?

5 And they argued *and* discussed [it] *and* reasoned together [u]with themselves, saying, If we reply, From heaven, He will say, Why then did you not believe him?

6 But if we answer, From men, all the people will stone us [u]to death; for they are [u]long since firmly convinced that John was a prophet.

7 So they replied that they did not know from where it came.

8 Then Jesus said to them, Neither do I tell you by what authority I do these things.

9 Then He began to relate to the people this parable—[v]this story to figuratively portray what He had to say: A man planted a vineyard, and leased it to some vinedressers and went into another country for a long stay. [Isa. 5:1-7.]

10 When the [right] season came, he sent a bond servant to the tenants, that they might give him [his part] of the fruit of the vineyard; but the tenants beat ([v]thrashed) him and sent him away empty-handed.

11 And he sent still another servant; him they also beat ([v]thrashed) and dishonored, *and* insulted him [w]disgracefully, and sent him away empty-handed.

12 And he sent yet a third; this one they wounded and threw out [of the vineyard].

13 Then the owner of the vineyard said, What shall I do? I will send my beloved son; it is [x]probable that they will respect him.

14 But when the tenants saw him, they argued with themselves, saying, This is the heir; let us kill him, so that the inheritance may be ours.

15 So they drove him out of the vineyard [and] killed him. What then will the owner of the vineyard do to them?

16 He will come and ([y]utterly) put an end to those tenants, and will give the vineyard to others. When they [the chief priests and the scribes and the elders] heard this, they said, May it never be!

17 But [Jesus] looked at them and said, What then is [the meaning of] this that is written: The [very] Stone which the builders rejected has become the chief Stone of the corner? [Ps. 118:22, 23.]

18 Every one who falls on that Stone will be broken [in pieces]; but upon whomever It falls, It will crush him—winnow him and [z]scatter him as dust. [Isa. 8:14, 15; Dan. 2:34, 35.]

19 The scribes and the chief priests desired *and* tried to find a way to arrest Him at that very hour, but they were afraid of the people; for they discerned that He had related this parable against themselves.

---

r) Trench's "Synonyms of the New Testament."
u) Vincent.
v) Thayer.
w) Souter.
x) Vincent.
y) Thayer.
z) Moulton and Milligan.

Living New Testament

CHAPTER 20

On one of those days when He was teaching and preaching the Good News in the Temple, He was confronted by the chief priests and other religious leaders and councilmen.

2 They demanded to know by what authority He had driven out the merchants from the Temple.

3 "I'll ask you a question before I answer," He replied.

4 "Was John sent by God, or was he merely acting under his own authority?"

5 They talked it over among themselves. "If we say his message was from heaven, then we are trapped because he will ask, 'Then why didn't you believe him?'

6 But if we say John was not sent from God, the people will mob us, for they are convinced that he was a prophet."

7 Finally they replied, "We don't know!"

8 And Jesus responded, "Then I won't answer your question either."

9 Now He turned to the people again and told them this story: "A man planted a vineyard and rented it out to some farmers, and went away to a distant land to live for several years.

10 When harvest time came, he sent one of his men to the farm to collect his share of the crops. But the tenants beat him up and sent him back empty-handed.

11 Then he sent another, but the same thing happened; he was beaten up and insulted and sent away without collecting.

12 A third man was sent and the same thing happened. He, too, was wounded and chased away.

13 'What shall I do?' the owner asked himself. 'I know! I'll send my cherished son. Surely they will show respect for him.'

14 But when the tenants saw his son, they said, 'This is our chance! This fellow will inherit all the land when his father dies. Come on. Let's kill him, and then it will be ours.'

15 So they dragged him out of the vineyard and killed him. What do you think the owner will do?

16 I'll tell you—he will come and kill them and rent the vineyard to others."

"But they would never do a thing like that," His listeners protested.

17 Jesus looked at them and said, "Then what does the Scripture mean where it says, 'The Stone rejected by the builders was made the cornerstone'?"

18 And He added, "Whoever stumbles over that Stone shall be broken; and those on whom it falls will be crushed to dust."

19 When the chief priests and religious leaders heard about this story He had told, they wanted Him arrested immediately, for they realized that He was talking about them. They were the wicked tenants in His illustration. But they were afraid that if they themselves arrested Him there would be a riot. So they tried to get Him to say something that could be reported to the Roman governor as a reason for Pilate to arrest him.

Revised Standard

Jesus' authority challenged

20 One day, as he was teaching the people in the temple and preaching the
gospel, the chief priests and the scribes with
the elders came up 2and said to him, "Tell
us by what authority you do these things,
or who it is that gave you this authority."
3He answered them, "I also will ask you a
question; now tell me, 4Was the baptism of
John from heaven or from men?" 5And they
discussed it with one another, saying, "If
we say, 'From heaven,' he will say, 'Why
did you not believe him?' 6But if we say,
'From men,' all the people will stone us;
for they are convinced that John was a
prophet." 7So they answered that they did
not know whence it was. 8And Jesus said
to them, "Neither will I tell you by what
authority I do these things."

The parable of the wicked tenants

9 And he began to tell the people this
parable: "A man planted a vineyard, and
let it out to tenants, and went into another
country for a long while. 10When the time
came, he sent a servant to the tenants, that
they should give him some of the fruit of
the vineyard; but the tenants beat him,
and sent him away empty-handed. 11And
he sent another servant; him also they beat
and treated shamefully, and sent him away
empty-handed. 12And he sent yet a third;
this one they wounded and cast out. 13Then
the owner of the vineyard said, 'What shall
I do? I will send my beloved son; it may
be they will respect him.' 14But when the
tenants saw him, they said to themselves,
'This is the heir; let us kill him, that the
inheritance may be ours.' 15And they cast
him out of the vineyard and killed him.
What then will the owner of the vineyard
do to them? 16He will come and destroy
those tenants, and give the vineyard to
others." When they heard this, they said,
"God forbid!" 17But he looked at them and
said, "What then is this that is written:

'The very stone which the builders rejected
has become the head of the corner'?

18 Every one who falls on that stone will be
broken to pieces; but when it falls on any
one it will crush him."

Taxes to Caesar

19 The scribes and the chief priests tried
to lay hands on him at that very hour, but
they feared the people; for they perceived
that he had told this parable against them.

King James

20 And they watched *him*, and sent forth spies, which should feign themselves just men, that they might take hold of his words, that so they might deliver him unto the power and authority of the governor.
21 And they asked him, saying, Master, we know that thou sayest and teachest rightly, neither acceptest thou the person *of any* but teachest the way of God truly:
22 Is it lawful for us to give tribute unto Cæsar, or no?
23 But he perceived their craftiness, and said unto them, Why tempt ye me?
24 Shew me a penny. Whose image and superscription hath it? They answered and said, Cæsar's.
25 And he said unto them, Render therefore unto Cæsar the things which he Cæsar's, and unto God the things which be God's.
26 And they could not take hold of his words before the people: and they marvelled at his answer, and held their peace.
27 ¶ Then came to *him* certain of the Sadducees, which deny that there is any resurrection; and they asked him,
28 Saying, Master, Moses wrote unto us, If any man's brother die, having a wife, and he die without children, that his brother should take his wife, and raise up seed unto his brother.
29 There were therefore seven brethren: and the first took a wife, and died without children.
30 And the second took her to wife, and he died childless.
31 And the third took her; and in like manner the seven also: and they left no children, and died.
32 Last of all the woman died also.
33 Therefore in the resurrection whose wife of them is she? for seven had her to wife.
34 And Jesus answering said unto them, The children of this world marry, and are given in marriage:
35 But they which shall be accounted worthy to obtain that world, and the resurrection from the dead, neither marry, nor are given in marriage:
36 Neither can they die any more: for they are equal unto the angels; and are the children of God, being the children of the resurrection.
37 Now that the dead are raised, even Moses shewed at the bush, when he calleth the Lord the God of Abraham, and the God of Isaac, and the God of Jacob.
38 For he is not a God of the dead, but of the living: for all live unto him.
39 ¶ Then certain of the scribes answering said, Master, thou hast well said.
40 And after that they durst not ask him any *question at all.*
41 And he said unto them, How say they that Christ is David's son?
42 And David himself saith in the book of Psalms. The LORD said unto my Lord, Sit thou on my right hand,
43 Till I make thine enemies thy footstool.
44 David therefore calleth him Lord, how is he then his son?

Amplified

20 So they watched (for an opportunity to ensnare) Him, and sent spies who pretended to be upright (honest and sincere), that they might lay hold of something He might say, so as to turn Him over to the control and authority of the governor.
21 They asked Him, Teacher, we know that You speak and teach what is right, and show no partiality to any one, but teach the way of God honestly *and* in truth.
22 Is it lawful for us to give tribute to Caesar, or not?
23 But He recognized *and* understood their cunning *and* [a]unscrupulousness, and said to them,
24 Show Me (a coin,) a denarius! Whose image and inscription has it? They answered, Caesar's.
25 He said to them, Then render to Caesar the things that are Caesar's, [b]and to God the things that are God's.
26 So they could not in the presence of the people take hold of anything He said to turn it against Him, but marveling at His reply they were silent.
27 Also there came to Him some Sadducees, those who say that there is no resurrection.
28 And they asked Him a question, saying, Teacher, Moses wrote for us a law that if a man's brother dies, leaving a wife and no children, the man shall take the woman and raise up offspring for his brother. [Deut. 25:5, 6.]
29 Now there were seven brothers, and the first took a wife and died without [having any] children,
30 And the second,
31 Then the third took her, and in like manner all seven, and they died leaving no children.
32 Last of all the woman died also.
33 Now in the resurrection, whose wife will the woman be? For the seven married her.
34 And Jesus said to them, The people of this world *and* present age marry and are given in marriage;
35 But those who are considered worthy to gain that other world *and* that future age and to attain to the resurrection from the dead neither marry nor are given in marriage.
36 For they cannot die again, but they are [c]angel-like *and* [d]equal to angels; and being sons of [that is, [c]sharers in] the resurrection, they are sons of God.
37 But that the dead are raised [[e]from death], even Moses made known *and* showed in the passage concerning the [burning] bush, where he calls the Lord, The God of Abraham, the God of Isaac, and the God of Jacob. [Exod. 3:6.]
38 Now He is not the God of the dead, but of the living; for, to Him, all men are alive [whether in the body or out of it]; *and* they are alive [not dead] unto Him [in definite relationship to Him].
39 And some of the scribes replied, Teacher, you have spoken well *and* expertly—[e]so that there is no room for blame.
40 For they did not dare to question Him more.
41 But He asked them, How can people say that the Christ, the Messiah, the Anointed One, is David's Son?
42 For David himself says in [the] Book of Psalms, The Lord said to my Lord, Sit at My right hand
43 Till I make Your enemies a footstool for Your feet. [Ps. 110:1.]
44 So David calls Him Lord; how then is He his Son?

---

a) Vincent.
b) A protest against Emperor-worship.
c) Cremer.
d) Abbott-Smith.
e) Thayer.

Living New Testament

20 Watching their opportunity, they sent secret agents pretending to be honest men.

21 They said to Jesus, "Sir, we know what an honest teacher you are. You always tell the truth and don't budge an inch in the face of what others think, but teach the ways of God.

22 Now tell us—is it right to pay taxes to the Roman government or not?"

23 He saw through their trickery and said,

24 "Show Me a coin. Whose portrait is this on it? And whose name?" They replied, "Caesar's—the Roman emperor's."

25 He said, "Then give the emperor all that is his—and give to God all that is His!"

26 Thus their attempt to outwit Him before the people failed; and marveling at His answer, they were silent.

27 Then some Sadducees—men who believe that death is the end of existence, that there is no resurrection—

28 Came to Jesus with this: "The laws of Moses state that if a man dies without children, the man's brother shall marry the widow and their children will legally belong to the dead man, to carry on his name.

29 We know of a family of seven brothers. The oldest married and then died without any children.

30 His brother married the widow and he, too, died. Still no children.

31 And so it went, one after the other, until each of the seven had married her and died, leaving no children.

32 Finally the woman died also.

33 Now here is our question: Whose wife will she be in the resurrection? For all of them were married to her!"

34, 35 Jesus replied, "Marriage is for people here on earth, but when those who are counted worthy of being raised from the dead get to heaven they do not marry.

36 And they never die again; in these respects they are like angels, and are sons of God, for they are raised up in new life from the dead.

37, 38 But as to your real question—whether or not there is a resurrection—why, even the writings of Moses himself prove this. For when he describes how God appeared to him in the burning bush, he speaks of God as 'the God of Abraham, the God of Isaac, and the God of Jacob.' To say that the Lord *is*[1] some person's God means that person is *alive,* not dead! So from God's point of view, all men are living."

39 "Well said, sir!" remarked some of the experts in the Jewish law who were standing there.

40 And that ended their questions, for they dared ask no more!

41 Then He presented *them* with a question. "Why is it," He asked, "that Christ, the Messiah, is said to be a descendant of King David?

42, 43 For David himself wrote in the book of Psalms: 'God said to my Lord, the Messiah, "Sit at My right hand until I place Your enemies beneath Your feet." '

44 How can the Messiah be both David's son and David's God at the same time?"

[1] Otherwise the statement would be, "He *had been* that person's God."

Revised Standard

20 So they watched him, and sent spies, who
pretended to be sincere, that they might
take hold of what he said, so as to deliver
him up to the authority and jurisdiction of
the governor. 21 They asked him, "Teacher,
we know that you speak and teach rightly,
and show no partiality, but truly teach the
way of God. 22 Is it lawful for us to give
tribute to Caesar, or not?" 23 But he perceived their craftiness, and said to them,
24 "Show me a coin.[f] Whose likeness and
inscription has it?" They said, "Caesar's."
25 He said to them, "Then render to Caesar
the things that are Caesar's, and to God the
things that are God's." 26 And they were not
able in the presence of the people to catch
him by what he said; but marveling at his
answer they were silent.

Sadducees and the resurrection

27 There came to him some Sadducees,
those who say that there is no resurrection,
28 and they asked him a question, saying,
"Teacher, Moses wrote for us that if a man's
brother dies, having a wife but no children,
the man[g] must take the wife and raise up
children for his brother. 29 Now there were
seven brothers; the first took a wife, and
died without children; 30 and the second
31 and the third took her, and likewise all
seven left no children and died. 32 Afterward the woman also died. 33 In the resurrection, therefore, whose wife will the
woman be? For the seven had her as wife."
34 And Jesus said to them, "The sons of
this age marry and are given in marriage;
35 but those who are accounted worthy to
attain to that age and to the resurrection
from the dead neither marry nor are given
in marriage, 36 for they cannot die any
more, because they are equal to angels and
are sons of God, being sons of the resurrection. 37 But that the dead are raised, even
Moses showed, in the passage about the
bush, where he calls the Lord the God of
Abraham and the God of Isaac and the God
of Jacob. 38 Now he is not God of the dead,
but of the living; for all live to him." 39 And
some of the scribes answered, "Teacher,
you have spoken well." 40 For they no longer dared to ask him any question.

The question about David's son

41 But he said to them, "How can they
say that the Christ is David's son? 42 For
David himself says in the Book of Psalms,
'The Lord said to my Lord,
Sit at my right hand,
43 till I make thy enemies a stool for thy
feet.'
44 David thus calls him Lord; so how is
he his son?"

[f] Greek *denarius*
[g] Greek *his brother*

King James

45 ¶ Then in the audience of all the people he said unto his disciples,
46 Beware of the scribes, which desire to walk in long robes, and love greetings in the markets, and the highest seats in the synagogues, and the chief rooms at feasts;
47 Which devour widows' houses, and for a shew make long prayers: the same shall receive greater damnation.

CHAPTER 21

AND he looked up, and saw the rich men casting their gifts into the treasury.
2 And he saw also a certain poor widow casting in thither two mites.
3 And he said, Of a truth I say unto you, that this poor widow hath cast in more than they all:
4 For all these have of their abundance cast in unto the offerings of God: but she of her penury hath cast in all the living that she had.
5 ¶ And as some spake of the temple, how it was adorned with goodly stones and gifts, he said,
6 *As for* these things which ye behold, the days will come, in the which there shall not be left one stone upon another, that shall not be thrown down.
7 And they asked him, saying, Master, but when shall these things be? and what sign *will there be* when these things shall come to pass?
8 And he said, Take heed that ye be not deceived: for many shall come in my name, saying, I am *Christ;* and the time draweth near: go ye not therefore after them.
9 But when ye shall hear of wars and commotions, be not terrified: for these things must first come to pass; but the end *is* not by and by.
10 Then said he unto them, Nation shall rise against nation, and kingdom against kingdom:
11 And great earthquakes shall be in divers places, and famines, and pestilences; and fearful sights and great signs shall there be from heaven.
12 But before all these, they shall lay their hands on you, and persecute *you*, delivering *you* up to the synagogues, and into prisons, being brought before kings and rulers for my name's sake.
13 And it shall turn to you for a testimony.
14 Settle *it* therefore in your hearts, not to meditate before what ye shall answer:
15 For I will give you a mouth and wisdom, which all your adversaries shall not be able to gainsay nor resist.

Amplified

45 And with all the people listening, He said to His disciples,
46 Beware of the scribes, who like to walk about in long robes, and love to be saluted (with honor) in places where people congregate, and love the front *and* best seats in the synagogues, and places of distinction at feasts,
47 Who make away with *and* devour widows' houses, and (to cover it up) with pretense make long prayers. They will receive the greater condemnation—the heavier sentence, the severer punishment.

CHAPTER 21

LOOKING up [Jesus] saw the rich people putting their gifts into the treasury,
2 And He saw also a poor widow putting in two mites [copper coins].
3 And He said, Truly I say to you, this poor widow has put in more than all of them;
4 For they all gave out of their abundance—their surplus—but she has contributed out of her lack *and* her want, putting in all that she had on which to live.
5 And as some were saying of the temple that it was decorated with handsome (shapely and magnificent) stones and consecrated offerings ([f]laid up to be kept), He said,
6 As for all this that you (thoughtfully) behold, the time will come when there shall not be left here one stone upon another that will not be thrown down.
7 And they asked Him, Teacher, when will this happen, and what sign will there be when this is about to occur?
8 And He said, Be on your guard *and* be careful that you are not led astray; for many will come in My name ([g]appropriating to themselves the name [Messiah] which belongs to Me), saying, I am He! and, The time is at hand! Do not go out after them.
9 And when you hear of wars and insurrections—disturbances, disorder and confusion—do not become alarmed *and* panic-stricken *and* terrified; for all this must take place first, but the end will not [come] immediately.
10 Then He told them, Nation will rise against nation, and kingdom against kingdom. [II Chron. 15:6; Isa. 19:2.]
11 There will be mighty *and* violent earthquakes, and in various places famines and pestilences (plagues, [h]malignant and contagious or infectious epidemic diseases, deadly and devastating). And there will be sights of terror and great signs from heaven.
12 But previous to all this they will lay their hands on you and persecute you, turning you over to the synagogues and prisons, and you will be led away before kings and governors for My name's sake.
13 This will be a time (an opportunity) for you to bear testimony.
14 Resolve *and* settle it in your minds, not to meditate *and* prepare beforehand how you are to make your defense *and* how you will answer;
15 For I [Myself] will give you a mouth *and* such utterance and wisdom as all of your foes combined will be unable to stand against or refute.

---

f) Thayer.
g) Thayer.
h) Webster's definition of "plague" and "pestilence."

Living New Testament

45 Then, with the crowds listening, He turned to His disciples and said,

46 "Beware of these experts in religion, for they love to parade in dignified robes and to be bowed to by the people as they walk along the street. And how they love the seats of honor in the synagogues and at religious festivals!

47 But even while they are praying long prayers with great outward piety, they are planning schemes to cheat widows out of their property. Therefore God's heaviest sentence awaits these men."

CHAPTER 21

As He stood in the Temple, He was watching the rich men tossing their gifts into the collection box.

2 Then a poor widow came by and dropped in two small copper coins.

3 "Really," He remarked, "this poor widow has given more than all the rest of them combined.

4 For they have given a little of what they didn't need, but she, poor as she is, has given everything she has."

5 Some of His disciples began talking about the beautiful stonework of the Temple and the memorial decorations on the walls.

6 But Jesus said, "The time is coming when all these things you are admiring will be knocked down, and not one stone will be left on top of another; all will become one vast heap of rubble."

7 "Master!" they exclaimed. "When? And will there be any warning ahead of time?"

8 He replied, "Don't let anyone mislead you. For many will come announcing themselves as the Messiah,[1] and saying, 'The time has come.' But don't believe them!

9 And when you hear of wars and insurrections beginning, don't panic. True, wars must come, but the end won't follow immediately—

10 For nation shall rise against nation and kingdom against kingdom,

11 And there will be great earthquakes, and famines in many lands, and epidemics, and terrifying things happening in the heavens.

12 But before all this occurs, there will be a time of special persecution, and you will be dragged into synagogues and prisons and before kings and governors for My name's sake.

13 But as a result, the Messiah will be widely known and honored.[2]

14 Therefore, don't be concerned about how to answer the charges against you,

15 For I will give you the right words and such logic that none of your opponents will be able to reply!

[1] Literally, "will come in My Name."
[2] Literally, "It shall turn out unto you for a testimony."

Revised Standard

The warning against scribes

45 And in the hearing of all the people
he said to his disciples, 46"Beware of the
scribes, who like to go about in long robes,
and love salutations in the market places
and the best seats in the synagogues and the
places of honor at feasts, 47who devour
widows' houses and for a pretense make
long prayers. They will receive the greater
condemnation."

The widow's offering

21 He looked up and saw the rich putting their gifts into the treasury;
2and he saw a poor widow put in two copper coins. 3And he said, "Truly I tell you,
this poor widow has put in more than all of
them; 4for they all contributed out of their
abundance, but she out of her poverty put
in all the living that she had."

The course of this age

5 And as some spoke of the temple, how
it was adorned with noble stones and offerings, he said, 6"As for these things which
you see, the days will come when there shall
not be left here one stone upon another
that will not be thrown down." 7And they
asked him, "Teacher, when will this be,
and what will be the sign when this is about
to take place?" 8And he said, "Take heed
that you are not led astray; for many will
come in my name, saying, 'I am he!' and,
'The time is at hand!' Do not go after them.
9And when you hear of wars and tumults,
do not be terrified; for this must first take
place, but the end will not be at once."
10 Then he said to them, "Nation will
rise against nation, and kingdom against
kingdom; 11there will be great earthquakes,
and in various places famines and pestilences;
and there will be terrors and great signs
from heaven. 12But before all this they will
lay their hands on you and persecute you,
delivering you up to the synagogues and
prisons, and you will be brought before
kings and governors for my name's sake.
13This will be a time for you to bear testimony. 14Settle it therefore in your minds,
not to meditate beforehand how to answer;
15for I will give you a mouth and wisdom,
which none of your adversaries will be able
to withstand or contradict. 16You will be

King James

16 And ye shall be betrayed both by parents, and brethren, and kinsfolks, and friends; and *some* of you shall they cause to be put to death.

17 And ye shall be hated of all *men* for my name's sake.

18 But there shall not an hair of your head perish.

19 In your patience possess ye your souls.

20 And when ye shall see Jerusalem compassed with armies, then know that the desolation thereof is nigh.

21 Then let them which are in Judæa flee to the mountains; and let them which are in the midst of it depart out; and let not them that are in the countries enter thereinto.

22 For these be the days of vengeance, that all things which are written may be fulfilled.

23 But woe unto them that are with child, and to them that give suck, in those days! for there shall be great distress in the land, and wrath upon this people.

24 And they shall fall by the edge of the sword, and shall be led away captive into all nations: and Jerusalem shall be trodden down of the Gentiles, until the times of the Gentiles be fulfilled.

25 ¶ And there shall be signs in the sun, and in the moon, and in the stars; and upon the earth distress of nations, with perplexity; the sea and the waves roaring;

26 Men's hearts failing them for fear, and for looking after these things which are coming on the earth: for the powers of heaven shall be shaken.

27 And then shall they see the Son of man coming in a cloud with power and great glory.

28 And when these things begin to come to pass, then look up, and lift up your heads; for your redemption draweth nigh.

29 And he spake to them a parable; Behold the fig tree, and all the trees;

30 When they now shoot forth, ye see and know of your own selves that summer is now nigh at hand.

31 So likewise ye, when ye see these things come to pass, know ye that the kingdom of God is nigh at hand.

32 Verily I say unto you, This generation shall not pass away, till all be fulfilled.

33 Heaven and earth shall pass away: but my words shall not pass away.

Amplified

16 You will be delivered up *and* betrayed even by parents and brothers and relatives and friends, and [some] of you they will put to death.

17 And you will be hated (despised) by everyone because [you bear] My name *and* for its sake.

18 But not a hair of your head shall perish. [I Sam. 14:45.]

19 By your steadfastness *and* patient endurance you [i]shall win the [j]true life of your souls.

20 But when you see Jerusalem surrounded by armies, then know *and* understand that its desolation has come near.

21 Then let those who are in Judea flee to the mountains, and let those who are inside [the city] get out of it, and let not those who are out in the country come into it;

22 For those are days of vengeance (that is, of rendering full justice or satisfaction), that all things that are written may be fulfilled.

23 Alas for those who are pregnant and for those who have babies which they are nursing in those days! For great misery *and* anguish *and* distress shall be upon the land, and indignation *and* punishment *and* retribution upon this people.

24 They will fall by [k]the mouth *and* the edge of the sword, and be led away as captives to *and* among all nations, and Jerusalem will be trodden down by the Gentiles until the times of the Gentiles are fulfilled—completed. [Isa. 63:18; Dan. 8:13.]

25 And there will be signs in the sun and moon and stars, and upon the earth distress (trouble and anguish) of nations in bewilderment *and* perplexity (that is, [l]without resources, left wanting, embarrassed, in doubt, not knowing which way to turn) at ([m]the echo) the roaring of the tossing of the sea; [Isa. 13:10; Joel 2:10; Zeph. 1:15.]

26 Men swooning away *or* expiring with fear *and* dread *and* apprehension and expectation of the things that are coming on the world; for the [very] powers of the heavens will be shaken *and* [l]caused to totter.

27 And then they will see the Son of man coming in a cloud with great (transcendent and overwhelming) power and [all His kingly] glory (majesty and splendor). [Dan. 7:13, 14.]

28 Now when these things begin to occur, look up and lift up your heads, because your redemption (deliverance) is drawing near.

29 And He told them a parable: Look at the fig tree, and all the trees;

30 When they put forth their buds *and* come out in leaf, you see for yourselves and perceive *and* know that the summer is already near.

31 Even so, when you see these things taking place, understand *and* know that the kingdom of God is at hand.

32 Truly, I tell you, this generation (that is, [n]those living at that definite period of time), will not perish *and* pass away until all has taken place.

33 The [o]sky and the earth (that is, [p]the universe, the world) will pass away; but My words will not pass away.

---

i) Vincent.
j) Thayer.
k) Wycliffe.
l) Thayer.
m) Vincent.
n) Cremer.
o) Moulton and Milligan.
p) Thayer.

Living New Testament

16 Even those closest to you—your parents, brothers, relatives, and friends will betray you and have you arrested; and some of you will be killed.

17 And everyone will hate you because you are Mine and are called by My Name.

18 But not a hair of your head will perish!

19 For if you stand firm, you will win your souls.

20 But when you see Jerusalem surrounded by armies, then you will know that the time of its destruction has arrived.

21 Then let the people of Judea flee to the hills. Let those in Jerusalem try to escape, and those outside the city must not attempt to return.

22 For those will be days of God's judgment,[3] and the words of the ancient Scriptures written by the prophets will be abundantly fulfilled.

23 Woe to expectant mothers in those days, and those with tiny babies. For there will be great distress upon the nation[4] and wrath upon this people.

24 They will be brutally killed by enemy weapons, or sent away as exiles and captives to all the nations of the world; and Jerusalem shall be conquered and trampled down by the Gentiles until the period of Gentile triumph ends in God's good time.

25 Then there will be strange events in the skies—warnings, evil omens and portents in the sun, moon and stars; and down here on earth the nations will be in turmoil, perplexed by the roaring seas and strange tides.

26 The courage of many people will falter because of the fearful fate they see coming upon the earth, for the stability of the very heavens will be broken up.

27 Then the peoples of the earth shall see Me,[5] the Man from Heaven, coming in a cloud with power and great glory.

28 So when all these things begin to happen, stand straight and look up! For your salvation is near."

29 Then He gave them this illustration: "Notice the fig tree, or any other tree.

30 When the leaves come out, you know without being told that summer is near.

31 In the same way, when you see the events taking place that I've described you can be just as sure that the Kingdom of God is near.

32 I solemnly declare to you that when these things happen, the end of this age[6] has come.

33 And though all heaven and earth shall pass away, yet My words remain forever true.

Revised Standard

delivered up even by parents and brothers
and kinsmen and friends, and some of you
they will put to death; 17 you will be hated
by all for my name's sake. 18 But not a hair
of your head will perish. 19 By your endurance you will gain your lives.

The destruction of Jerusalem

20 "But when you see Jerusalem surrounded by armies, then know that its desolation has come near. 21 Then let those who
are in Judea flee to the mountains, and let
those who are inside the city depart, and
let not those who are out in the country
enter it; 22 for these are days of vengeance,
to fulfil all that is written. 23 Alas for those
who are with child and for those who give
suck in those days! For great distress shall
be upon the earth and wrath upon this
people; 24 they will fall by the edge of the
sword, and be led captive among all nations;
and Jerusalem will be trodden down by the
Gentiles, until the times of the Gentiles are
fulfilled.

Signs of the end

25 "And there will be signs in sun and
moon and stars, and upon the earth distress
of nations in perplexity at the roaring of
the sea and the waves, 26 men fainting with
fear and with foreboding of what is coming
on the world; for the powers of the heavens
will be shaken. 27 And then they will see the
Son of man coming in a cloud with power
and great glory. 28 Now when these things
begin to take place, look up and raise your
heads, because your redemption is drawing
near."

29 And he told them a parable: "Look
at the fig tree, and all the trees; 30 as soon
as they come out in leaf, you see for yourselves and know that the summer is already
near. 31 So also, when you see these things
taking place, you know that the kingdom
of God is near. 32 Truly, I say to you, this
generation will not pass away till all has
taken place. 33 Heaven and earth will pass
away, but my words will not pass away.

---

[3] Literally, "days of vengeance."
[4] Literally, "upon the land," or, "upon the earth."
[5] Literally, "the Son of man."
[6] Or, "this generation."

King James

34 ¶ And take heed to yourselves, lest at any time your hearts be overcharged with surfeiting, and drunkenness, and cares of this life, and *so* that day come upon you unawares.

35 For as a snare shall it come on all them that dwell on the face of the whole earth.

36 Watch ye therefore, and pray always, that ye may be accounted worthy to escape all these things that shall come to pass, and to stand before the Son of man.

37 And in the day time he was teaching in the temple; and at night he went out, and abode in the mount that is called *the mount* of Olives.

38 And all the people came early in the morning to him in the temple, for to hear him.

Amplified

34 But take heed to yourselves *and* be on your guard lest your hearts be overburdened *and* depressed—weighed down—with the [p]giddiness *and* headache *and* [q]nausea of self-indulgence, drunkenness, and worldly worries *and* cares pertaining to (the [r]business of) this life, and that day come upon you suddenly like a trap *or* a noose;

35 For it will come upon all who live upon the face of the entire earth.

36 Keep awake then *and* watch at all times (that is, be discreet, attentive and ready); praying that you may have the full strength *and* ability *and* be accounted worthy to escape all these things [taken together] that will take place, and to stand in the presence of the Son of man.

37 Now in the daytime Jesus was teaching in ([s]the porches and courts of) the temple, but at night He would go out and stay on the mount called Olivet.

38 And early in the morning all the people came to Him in the temple ([s]porches *or* courts) to listen to Him.

CHAPTER 22

NOW the feast of unleavened bread drew nigh, which is called the Passover.

2 And the chief priests and scribes sought how they might kill him; for they feared the people.

3 ¶ Then entered Satan into Judas surnamed Iscariot, being of the number of the twelve.

4 And he went his way, and communed with the chief priests and captains, how he might betray him unto them.

5 And they were glad, and covenanted to give him money.

6 And he promised, and sought opportunity to betray him unto them in the absence of the multitude.

7 ¶ Then came the day of unleavened bread, when the passover must be killed.

8 And he sent Peter and John, saying, Go and prepare us the passover, that we may eat.

9 ¶ And they said unto him, Where wilt thou that we prepare?

10 And he said unto them, Behold, when ye are entered into the city, there shall a man meet you, bearing a pitcher of water; follow him into the house where he entereth in.

11 And ye shall say unto the goodman of the house, The Master saith unto thee, Where is the guestchamber, where I shall eat the passover with my disciples?

12 And he shall shew you a large upper room furnished: there make ready.

13 And they went, and found as he had said unto them: and they made ready the passover.

14 And when the hour was come, he sat down, and the twelve apostles with him.

15 And he said unto them, With desire I have desired to eat this passover with you before I suffer:

CHAPTER 22

NOW the festival of Unleavened Bread was drawing near, which is called the Passover.

2 And the chief priests and the scribes were seeking how to make away with [Jesus], for they feared the people.

3 But [then] Satan entered into Judas called Iscariot, who was one of the twelve [apostles];

4 And he went away and discussed with the chief priests and captains how he might betray Him *and* deliver Him up to them.

5 And they were delighted, and pledged [themselves] to give him money.

6 So he agreed [to this] and sought for an opportunity to betray Him to them [without an uprising] in the absence of the throng.

7 Then the day of Unleavened Bread came, on which the passover [lamb] had to be slain. [Exod. 12:18-20; Deut. 16:5-8.]

8 So Jesus sent Peter and John, saying, Go and prepare for us the passover meal, that we may eat it.

9 They said to Him, Where do You want us to prepare [it]?

10 He said to them, Behold, when you have gone into the city, a man carrying an earthen jug *or* pitcher of water will meet you; follow him into the house which he enters,

11 And say to the master of the house, The Teacher asks you, Where is the guest room, where I may eat the passover [meal] with My disciples?

12 And he will show you a large room upstairs, furnished [that is, with carpets and with couches properly spread]; there make [your] preparations.

13 And they went and found it as He had said to them, and they made ready the passover [supper].

14 And when the hour came [Jesus] reclined at table, and the apostles with Him.

15 And He said to them, I have earnestly *and* intensely desired to eat this passover with you before I suffer;

---

p) Thayer.
q) Abbott-Smith.
r) Wycliffe.
s) Trench.

Living New Testament

34, 35 Watch out! Don't let My sudden coming catch you unawares; don't let Me find you living in careless ease, carousing and drinking, and occupied with the problems of this life, like all the rest of the world.

36 Keep a constant watch. And pray that if possible you may arrive in My presence without having to experience these horrors.[7]

37, 38 Every day Jesus went to the Temple to teach, and the crowds began gathering early in the morning to hear Him. And each evening He returned to spend the night on the Mount of Olives.

Revised Standard

34 "But take heed to yourselves lest your hearts be weighed down with dissipation and drunkenness and cares of this life, and that day come upon you suddenly like a snare; [35]for it will come upon all who dwell upon the face of the whole earth. [36]But watch at all times, praying that you may have strength to escape all these things that will take place, and to stand before the Son of man."

37 And every day he was teaching in the temple, but at night he went out and lodged on the mount called Olivet. [38]And early in the morning all the people came to him in the temple to hear him.

CHAPTER 22

And now the Passover celebration was drawing near—the Jewish festival when only bread made without yeast was used.

2 The chief priests and other religious leaders were actively plotting Jesus' murder, trying to find a way to kill Him without starting a riot—a possibility they greatly feared.

3 Then Satan entered into Judas Iscariot, who was one of the twelve disciples,

4 And he went over to the chief priests and captains of the Temple guards to discuss the best ways to betray Jesus to them.

5 They were, of course, delighted to know that he was ready to help them and promised him a reward.

6 So he began to look for an opportunity for them to arrest Jesus quietly when the crowds weren't around.

7 Now the day of the Passover celebration arrived, when the Passover lamb was killed and eaten with the unleavened bread.

8 Jesus sent Peter and John ahead to find a place to prepare their Passover meal.

9 "Where do You want us to go?" they asked.

10 And He replied, "As soon as you enter Jerusalem,[1] you will see a man walking along carrying a pitcher of water. Follow him into the house he enters,

11 And say to the man who lives there, 'Our Teacher says for you to show us the guest room where He can eat the Passover meal with His disciples.'

12 He will take you upstairs to a large room all ready for us. That is the place. Go ahead and prepare the meal there."

13 They went off to the city and found everything just as Jesus had said, and prepared the Passover supper.

14 Then Jesus and the others arrived, and at the proper time all sat down together at the table;

15 And He said, "I have looked forward to this hour with deep longing, anxious to eat this Passover meal with you before My suffering begins.

The plot to kill Jesus

22 Now the feast of Unleavened Bread drew near, which is called the Passover. [2]And the chief priests and the scribes were seeking how to put him to death; for they feared the people.

3 Then Satan entered into Judas called Iscariot, who was of the number of the twelve; [4]he went away and conferred with the chief priests and captains how he might betray him to them. [5]And they were glad, and engaged to give him money. [6]So he agreed, and sought an opportunity to betray him to them in the absence of the multitude.

The Last Supper

7 Then came the day of Unleavened Bread, on which the passover lamb had to be sacrificed. [8]So Jesus[h] sent Peter and John, saying, "Go and prepare the passover for us, that we may eat it." [9]They said to him, "Where will you have us prepare it?" [10]He said to them, "Behold, when you have entered the city, a man carrying a jar of water will meet you; follow him into the house which he enters, [11]and tell the householder, 'The Teacher says to you, Where is the guest room, where I am to eat the passover with my disciples?' [12]And he will show you a large upper room furnished; there make ready." [13]And they went, and found it as he had told them; and they prepared the passover.

14 And when the hour came, he sat at table, and the apostles with him. [15]And he said to them, "I have earnestly desired to eat this passover with you before I suffer;

---

[7] Or, "pray for strength to pass safely through these coming horrors."

[1] Literally, "the city."

[h] Greek *he*

King James

16 For I say unto you, I will not any more eat thereof, until it be fulfilled in the kingdom of God.

17 And he took the cup, and gave thanks, and said, Take this, and divide *it* among yourselves:

18 For I say unto you, I will not drink of the fruit of the vine, until the kingdom of God shall come.

19 ¶ And he took bread, and gave thanks, and brake *it,* and gave unto them, saying, This is my body which is given for you: this do in remembrance of me.

20 Likewise also the cup after supper, saying, This cup *is* the new testament in my blood, which is shed for you.

21 ¶ But, behold, the hand of him that betrayeth me *is* with me on the table.

22 And truly the Son of man goeth, as it was determined: but woe unto that man by whom he is betrayed!

23 And they began to inquire among themselves, which of them it was that should do this thing.

24 ¶ And there was also a strife among them, which of them should be accounted the greatest.

25 And he said unto them, The kings of the Gentiles exercise lordship over them; and they that exercise authority upon them are called benefactors,

26 But ye *shall* not *be* so: but he that is greatest among you, let him be as the younger; and he that is chief, as he that doth serve.

27 For whether *is* greater, he that sitteth at meat, or he that serveth? *is* not he that sitteth at meat? but I am among you as he that serveth.

28 Ye are they which have continued with me in my temptations.

29 And I appoint unto you a kingdom, as my Father hath appointed unto me;

30 That ye may eat and drink at my table in my kingdom, and sit on thrones judging the twelve tribes of Israel.

31 ¶ And the Lord said, Simon, Simon, behold, Satan hath desired *to have* you, that he may sift *you* as wheat:

32 But I have prayed for thee, that thy faith fail not: and when thou art converted, strengthen thy brethren.

33 And he said unto him, Lord, I am ready to go with thee, both into prison, and to death.

34 And he said, I tell thee, Peter, the cock shall not crow this day, before that thou shalt thrice deny that thou knowest me.

35 And he said unto them, When I sent you without purse, and scrip, and shoes, lacked ye any thing? And they said, Nothing.

36 Then said he unto them, But now, he that hath a purse, let him take *it*, and likewise *his* scrip; and he that hath no sword, let him sell his garment, and buy one.

37 For I say unto you, that this that is written must yet be accomplished in me, And he was reckoned among the transgressors: for the things concerning me have an end.

38 And they said, Lord, behold, here *are* two swords. And he said unto them, It is enough.

Amplified

16 For I say to you, I shall eat it no more until it is fulfilled in the kingdom of God.

17 And He took a cup, and when He had given thanks He said, Take this, and divide *and* distribute it among yourselves;

18 For I say to you that from now on I shall not drink of the fruit of the vine at all until the kingdom of God comes.

19 Then He took a loaf [of bread], and when He had given thanks He broke [it] and gave it to them saying, This is My body which is given for you. Do this in remembrance of Me.

20 And in like manner He took the cup after supper, saying, This cup is the new testament *or* covenant [ratified] in My blood, which is shed (poured out) for you.

21 But, lo, the hand of him who [t]is now engaged in betraying Me is with Me on the table. [Ps. 41:9.]

22 For the Son of man goes as it has been determined *and* appointed, but woe to that man by whom He is betrayed *and* delivered up!

23 And they began to inquire among themselves, which of them it was who was about to do this. [Ps. 41:9.]

24 Now [t]an eager contention arose among them, which of them it was who was about to do this. [Ps. 41:9.]

25 But Jesus said to them, The kings of the Gentiles [u]are deified by them *and* exercise lordship [[u]ruling as emperor-gods] over them; and those in authority over them are called benefactors *and* well-doers.

26 But this is not to be so with you; on the contrary let him who is the greatest among you become as the youngest, and him who is the chief *and* leader as one who serves.

27 For which is the greater, he who reclines at table (the master), or he who serves? Is it not he who reclines at table? But I am in your midst as one who serves.

28 And you are those who have remained (throughout) *and* persevered with Me in My trials;

29 And as My Father has appointed a kingdom *and* conferred it on Me, so do I confer on you [the privilege and decree]

30 That you may eat and drink at My table in My kingdom, and sit on thrones, judging the twelve tribes of Israel.

31 Simon, Simon (Peter), listen! Satan [v]has asked excessively that (all of) you be given up to him—out of the power and keeping of God—that he might sift (all of) you like grain, [Job 1:6-12; Amos 9:9.]

32 But I have prayed especially for you [Peter] that your [own] faith may not fail; and when you yourself have turned again, strengthen *and* establish your brethren.

33 And [Simon Peter] said to Him, Lord, I am ready to go with You both to prison and to death.

34 But Jesus said, I tell you, Peter, before a [single] cock shall crow this day, you will three times [utterly] deny that you know Me.

35 And He said to them, When I sent you out with no purse or (provision) bag or sandals, did you lack anything? They answered, Nothing!

36 Then He said to them, But now let him who has a purse take it, and also (his provision) bag; and let him who has no sword sell his mantle and buy a sword.

37 For I tell you that this Scripture must yet be fulfilled in Me, And He was counted *and* classed among the wicked (the outlaws, the criminals); for what is written about Me has its fulfillment—has reached its end, and is finally settled. [Isa. 53:12.]

38 And they said, Look, Lord! Here are two swords. And He said to them, It is enough.

---

t) Vincent.
u) Wuest's "Bypaths in the Greek New Testament."
v) Thayer.

Living New Testament

16 For I tell you now that I won't eat it again until what it represents has occurred in the Kingdom of God."

17 Then He took a glass of wine, and when He had given thanks for it, He said, "Take this and share it among yourselves.

18 For I will not drink wine again until the Kingdom of God has come."

19 Then He took a loaf of bread; and when He had thanked God for it, He broke it apart and gave it to them, saying, "This is My body, given for you. Eat it in remembrance of Me."

20 After supper He gave them another glass of wine, saying, "This wine is the token of God's new agreement to save you—an agreement sealed with the blood I shall pour out to purchase back your souls.[2]

21 But here at this table, sitting among us as a friend, is the man who will betray Me.

22 I[3] must die. It is part of God's plan. But, oh, the horror awaiting that man who betrays Me."

23 Then the disciples wondered among themselves which of them would ever do such a thing.

24 And they began to argue among themselves as to who would have the highest rank [in the coming Kingdom].[4]

25 Jesus told them, "In this world the kings and great men order their slaves around, and the slaves have no choice but to like it![5]

26 But among you, the one who serves you best will be your leader.

27 Out in the world the master sits at the table and is served by his servants. But not here! For I am your servant.

28 Nevertheless, because you have stood true to Me in these terrible days,[6]

29 And because My Father has granted Me a Kingdom, I, here and now, grant you the right

30 To eat and drink at My table in that Kingdom; and you will sit on thrones judging the twelve tribes of Israel.

31 Simon, Simon, Satan has asked to have you, to sift you like wheat,

32 But I have pleaded in prayer for you that your faith should not completely fail.[7] So when you have repented and turned to Me again, strengthen and build up the faith of your brothers."

33 Simon said, "Lord, I am ready to go to jail with You, and even to die with You."

34 But Jesus said, "Peter, let Me tell you something. Between now and tomorrow morning when the rooster crows, you will deny Me three times, declaring that you don't even know Me."

35 Then Jesus asked them, "When I sent you out to preach the Good News and you were without money, duffle bag, or extra clothing, how did you get along?"

"Fine," they replied.

36 "But now," He said, "take a duffle bag if you have one, and your money. And if you don't have a sword, better sell your clothes and buy one!

37 For the time has come for this prophecy about Me to come true: 'He will be condemned as a criminal!' Yes, everything written about Me by the prophets will come true."

38 "Master," they replied, "we have two swords among us."

"Enough!" He said.

---

[2] Literally, "This cup is the new covenant in My blood, poured out for you."
[3] Literally, "the Son of man."
[4] Implied.
[5] Literally, "they (the kings and great men) are called 'benefactors.'"
[6] Literally, "you have continued with Me in My temptation."
[7] Literally, "fail not."

Revised Standard

16for I tell you I shall not eat[i] until it is
fulfilled in the kingdom of God." 17And he
took a cup, and when he had given thanks
he said, "Take this, and divide it among
yourselves; 18for I tell you that from now
on I shall not drink of the fruit of the vine
until the kingdom of God comes." 19And
he took bread, and when he had given
thanks he broke it and gave it to them, saying, "This is my body.[j] 21But behold the
hand of him who betrays me is with me on
the table. 22For the Son of man goes as it
has been determined; but woe to that man
by whom he is betrayed!" 23And they began to question one another, which of them
it was that would do this.

24 A dispute also arose among them,
which of them was to be regarded as the
greatest. 25And he said to them, "The kings
of the Gentiles exercise lordship over them;
and those in authority over them are called
benefactors. 26But not so with you; rather
let the greatest among you become as the
youngest, and the leader as one who serves.
27For which is the greater, one who sits at
table, or one who serves? Is it not the one
who sits at table? But I am among you as
one who serves.

28 "You are those who have continued
with me in my trials; 29as my Father appointed a kingdom for me, so do I appoint
for you 30that you may eat and drink at
my table in my kingdom, and sit on thrones
judging the twelve tribes of Israel.

Peter's denial foretold

31 "Simon, Simon, behold, Satan demanded to have you,[k] that he might sift
you[k] like wheat, 32but I have prayed for
you that your faith may not fail; and when
you have turned again, strengthen your
brethren." 33And he said to him, "Lord, I
am ready to go with you to prison and to
death." 34He said, "I tell you, Peter, the
cock will not crow this day, until you three
times deny that you know me."

35 And he said to them, "When I sent
you out with no purse or bag or sandals,
did you lack anything?" They said, "Nothing." 36He said to them, "But now, let him
who has a purse take it, and likewise a bag.
And let him who has no sword sell his
mantle and buy one. 37For I tell you that
this scripture must be fulfilled in me, 'And
he was reckoned with transgressors'; for
what is written about me has its fulfilment."
38And they said, "Look, Lord, here are two
swords." And he said to them, "It is
enough."

---

[i] Other ancient authorities read *never eat it again*
[j] Other ancient authorities add *which is given for you. Do this in remembrance of me." 20 And likewise the cup after supper, saying, "This cup which is poured out for you is the new covenant in my blood*
[k] The Greek word for *you* here is plural; in verse 32 it is singular

King James

39 ¶ And he came out, and went, as he was wont, to the mount of Olives; and his disciples also followed him.

40 And when he was at the place, he said unto them, Pray that ye enter not into temptation.

41 And he was withdrawn from them about a stone's cast, and kneeled down, and prayed,

42 Saying, Father, if thou be willing, remove this cup from me: nevertheless not my will, but thine, be done.

43 And there appeared an angel unto him from heaven, strengthening him.

44 And being in an agony he prayed more earnestly: and his sweat was as it were great drops of blood falling down to the ground.

45 And when he rose up from prayer, and was come to his disciples, he found them sleeping for sorrow,

46 And said unto them, Why sleep ye? rise and pray, lest ye enter into temptation.

47 ¶ And while he yet spake, behold a multitude, and he that was called Judas, one of the twelve, went before them, and drew near unto Jesus to kiss Him.

48 But Jesus said unto him, Judas, betrayest thou the Son of man with a kiss?

49 When they which were about him saw what would follow, they said unto him, Lord, shall we smite with the sword?

50 ¶ And one of them smote the servant of the high priest, and cut off his right ear.

51 And Jesus answered and said, Suffer ye thus far. And he touched his ear, and healed him.

52 Then Jesus said unto the chief priests, and captains of the temple, and the elders, which were come to him, Be ye come out, as against a thief, with swords and staves?

53 When I was daily with you in the temple, ye stretched forth no hands against me: but this is your hour, and the power of darkness.

54 ¶ Then took they him, and led *him*, and brought him into the high priest's house. And Peter followed afar off.

55 And when they had kindled a fire in the midst of the hall, and were set down together, Peter sat down among them.

56 But a certain maid beheld him as he sat by the fire, and earnestly looked upon him, and said, This man was also with him.

57 And he denied him, saying, Woman, I know him not.

58 And after a little while another saw him, and said, Thou art also of them. And Peter said, Man, I am not.

59 And about the space of one hour after another confidently affirmed, saying, Of a truth this *fellow* also was with him: for he is a Galilæan.

60 And Peter said, Man, I know not what thou sayest. And immediately, while he yet spake, the cock crew.

61 And the Lord turned, and looked upon Peter. And Peter remembered the word of the Lord, how he had said unto him, Before the cock crow, thou shalt deny me thrice.

Amplified

39 And He came out, and went, as was His habit, to the Mount of Olives; and the disciples also followed Him.

40 And when [He] came to the place He said to them, Pray that you may not [at all] enter into temptation.

41 And He withdrew from them about a stone's throw, and knelt down and prayed,

42 Saying, Father, if You are willing, remove this cup from Me; yet not My will, but ([w]always) Yours, be done.

43 And there appeared to Him an angel from heaven, strengthening Him in spirit.

44 And being in an agony [of mind] He prayed [the] more earnestly *and* intently; and His sweat became like great [x]clots of blood dropping down upon the ground.

45 And when He got up from prayer, He came to the disciples and found them sleeping for grief,

46 And He said to them, Why do you sleep? Get up and pray that you may not enter [at all] into temptation.

47 And while He was still speaking, behold, there came a crowd, and the man called Judas, one of the twelve [apostles], was going before [leading] them. He drew near to Jesus to kiss Him;

48 But Jesus said to Him, Judas! Would you betray *and* deliver up the Son of man with a kiss?

49 And when those who were around Him saw what was about to happen, they said, Lord, shall we strike with the sword?

50 And one of them struck the bond servant of the high priest and cut off his ear, the right one.

51 But Jesus said, Permit [y]them to go so far [as to seize Me]. And He touched the [z]little [insignificant] ear and healed him.

52 Then Jesus said to those who had come out against Him, the chief priests and captains of the temple and elders [of the Sanhedrin], Have you come out with swords and clubs as against a robber?

53 When I was with you day after day in the temple ([a]enclosure), you did not stretch forth [your] hands against Me. But this is your hour, and the power [which] darkness [gives you has its way].

54 Then they seized Him and led Him away, bringing Him into the house of the high priest. Peter was following at a distance.

55 And when they had kindled a fire in the middle of the courtyard and were seated together, Peter sat among them.

56 Then a servant girl, seeing him as he sat in the firelight and gazing (intently) at him said, This man too was with [b]Him.

57 But he denied it and said, Woman, I do not know Him!

58 And a little later someone else saw him and said, You are one of them also. But Peter said, Man, I am not!

59 And when about an hour more had elapsed still another emphatically insisted, It is the truth that this man also was with Him, for he too is a Galilean!

60 But Peter said, Man, I do not know what you are talking about. And instantly, while he was still speaking, the cock crowed.

61 And the Lord turned and looked at Peter. And Peter recalled the Lord's words, how He had told him, Before the cock crows today, you will deny Me thrice.

---

w) Williams: "in the present imperative."
x) Vincent.
y) Vincent.
z) Wycliffe.
a) Trench.
b) Capitalized because of what He is, the spotless Son of God, not what the speaker may have thought He was.

Living New Testament

39 Then, accompanied by the disciples, He left the upstairs room and went as usual to the Mount of Olives.

40 There He told them, "Pray God that you will not be overcome[8] by temptation."

41, 42 He walked away, perhaps a stone's throw, and knelt down and prayed this prayer: "Father, if You are willing, please take away this cup of horror from Me. But I want Your will, not Mine."

43 Then an angel from heaven appeared and strengthened Him,

44 For He was in such agony of spirit that He broke into a sweat of blood, with great drops falling to the ground as He prayed more and more earnestly.

45 At last He stood up again and returned to the disciples—only to find them asleep, exhausted from grief.

46 "Asleep!" He said. "Get up! Pray God that you will not fall when you are tempted."

47 But even as He said this, a mob approached, led by Judas, one of His twelve disciples. Judas walked over to Jesus and kissed Him on the cheek in friendly greeting.[9]

48 But Jesus said, "Judas, how can you do this—betray the Messiah with a kiss?"

49 When the other disciples saw what was about to happen, they exclaimed, "Master, shall we fight? We brought along the swords!"

50 And one of them slashed at the High Priest's servant, and cut off his right ear.

51 But Jesus said, "Don't resist any more." And He touched the place where the man's ear had been and restored it.

52 Then Jesus addressed the chief priests and captains of the Temple guards and the religious leaders who headed the mob. "Am I a robber," He asked, "that you have come armed with swords and clubs to get Me?

53 Why didn't you arrest Me in the Temple? I was there every day! But this is your moment—the time when Satan's power reigns supreme."

54 So they seized Him and led Him to the High Priest's residence, and Peter followed at a distance.

55 The soldiers lit a fire in the courtyard and sat around it for warmth, and Peter joined them there.

56 A servant girl noticed him in the firelight and began staring at him. Finally she spoke: "This man was with Jesus!"

57 Peter denied it! "Woman," he said, "I don't even know the man!"

58 After a while someone else looked at him and said, "You must be one of them!"

"No sir, I am not!" Peter replied.

59 About an hour later someone else flatly stated, "I know this fellow is one of Jesus' disciples, for both are from Galilee."

60 But Peter said, "Man, I don't know what you are talking about." And as he said the words, a rooster crowed.

61 At that moment Jesus turned and looked at Peter. Then Peter remembered what He had said—"Before the rooster crows tomorrow morning, you will deny Me three times."

[8] Literally, "that you enter not into temptation."
[9] Literally, "approached Jesus to kiss Him." This is still the traditional greeting among men in eastern lands.

Revised Standard

Jesus' agony in Gethsemane

39 And he came out, and went, as was
his custom, to the Mount of Olives; and the
disciples followed him. 40 And when he
came to the place he said to them, "Pray
that you may not enter into temptation."
41 And he withdrew from them about a
stone's throw, and knelt down and prayed,
42 "Father, if thou art willing, remove this
cup from me; nevertheless not my will, but
thine, be done." 43 And there appeared to
him an angel from heaven, strengthening
him. 44 And being in an agony he prayed
more earnestly; and his sweat became like
great drops of blood falling down upon the
ground.[1] 45 And when he rose from prayer,
he came to the disciples and found them
sleeping for sorrow, 46 and he said to them,
"Why do you sleep? Rise and pray that you
may not enter into temptation."

Jesus' betrayal and arrest

47 While he was still speaking, there
came a crowd, and the man called Judas,
one of the twelve, was leading them. He
drew near to Jesus to kiss him; 48 but Jesus
said to him, "Judas, would you betray the
Son of man with a kiss?" 49 And when those
who were about him saw what would follow,
they said, "Lord, shall we strike with the
sword?" 50 And one of them struck the slave
of the high priest and cut off his right ear.
51 But Jesus said, "No more of this!" And he
touched his ear and healed him. 52 Then
Jesus said to the chief priests and captains
of the temple and elders, who had come
out against him, "Have you come out as
against a robber, with swords and clubs?
53 When I was with you day after day in
the temple, you did not lay hands on me.
But this is your hour, and the power of
darkness."

Peter's denial of Jesus

54 Then they seized him and led him
away, bringing him into the high priest's
house. Peter followed at a distance; 55 and
when they had kindled a fire in the middle
of the courtyard and sat down together,
Peter sat among them. 56 Then a maid, seeing him as he sat in the light and gazing at
him, said, "This man also was with him."
57 But he denied it, saying, "Woman, I do
not know him." 58 And a little later some
one else saw him and said, "You also are
one of them." But Peter said, "Man, I am
not." 59 And after an interval of about an
hour still another insisted, saying, "Certainly this man also was with him; for he is a
Galilean." 60 But Peter said, "Man, I do not
know what you are saying." And immediately, while he was still speaking, the cock
crowed. 61 And the Lord turned and looked
at Peter. And Peter remembered the word
of the Lord, how he had said to him, "Before the cock crows today, you will deny

[1] Other ancient authorities omit verses 43 and 44

King James

62 And Peter went out, and wept bitterly.

63 ¶ And the men that held Jesus mocked him, and smote *him*.

64 And when they had blindfolded him, they struck him on the face, and asked him, saying, Prophesy, who is it that smote thee?

65 And many other things blasphemously spake they against him.

66 ¶ And as soon as it was day, the elders of the people and the chief priests and the scribes came together, and led him into their council, saying,

67 Art thou the Christ? tell us. And he said unto them, If I tell you, ye will not believe:

68 And if I also ask *you*, ye will not answer me, nor let *me* go.

69 Hereafter shall the Son of man sit on the right hand of the power of God.

70 Then said they all, Art thou then the Son of God? And he said unto them, Ye say that I am,

71 And they said, What need we any further witness? for we ourselves have heard of his own mouth.

Amplified

62 And he went out, and wept bitterly [that is, with painfully moving grief].

63 Now the men who had Jesus in custody treated Him with contempt *and* scoffed at *and* ridiculed Him and beat Him;

64 They blindfolded Him also, and asked Him, Prophesy! Who is it that struck [b]You?

65 And they said many other evil *and* slanderous *and* insulting words against Him, reviling Him.

66 As soon as it was day, the assembly of the elders of the people gathered together, both chief priests and scribes; and they led Him into their council [the Sanhedrin], and they said,

67 If You are the Christ, the Messiah, tell us. But He said to them, If I tell you, you will not believe—trust in, cleave to and rely on what I say;

68 And if I question you, you will not answer.

69 But hereafter (from this time on) the Son of man shall be seated at the right hand of the power of God. [Ps. 110:1.]

70 And they all said, You are the Son of God, then? And He said to them, [c]It is just as you say; I am.

71 And they said, What further evidence do we need? For we have heard [it] ourselves from His own mouth!

King James

CHAPTER 23

AND the whole multitude of them arose, and led him unto Pilate.

2 And they began to accuse him, saying, We found this *fellow* perverting the nation, and forbidding to give tribute to Cæsar, saying that he himself is Christ a King.

3 And Pilate asked him, saying, Art thou the King of the Jews? And he answered him and said, Thou sayest *it*.

4 Then said Pilate to the chief priests and *to* the people, I find no fault in this man.

5 And they were the more fierce, saying, He stirreth up the people, teaching throughout all Jewry, beginning from Galilee to this place.

6 When Pilate heard of Galilee, he asked whether the man were a Galilæan.

7 And as soon as he knew that he belonged unto Herod's jurisdiction, he sent him to Herod, who himself also was at Jerusalem at that time.

8 ¶ And when Herod saw Jesus, he was exceeding glad: for he was desirous to see him of a long *season*, because he had heard many things of him; and he hoped to have seen some miracle done by him.

9 Then he questioned with him in many words; but he answered him nothing.

10 And the chief priests and scribes stood and vehemently accused him.

11 And Herod with his men of war set him at nought, and mocked *him*, and arrayed him in a gorgeous robe, and sent him again to Pilate.

Amplified

CHAPTER 23

THEN the whole assembly of them got up, and conducted [Jesus] before Pilate.

2 And they began to accuse Him, asserting, We found this [d]Man perverting (misleading, corrupting and turning away) our nation, and forbidding to pay tribute to Caesar, saying that He Himself is Christ, the Messiah, the Anointed One, a King!

3 So Pilate asked Him, Are You the King of the Jews? And He answered him, [[c]It is just as] you say; [I am.]

4 And Pilate said to the chief priests and the throngs, I find no guilt *or* crime in this Man.

5 But they were urgent *and* emphatic, saying, He stirs up and excites the people, teaching throughout all Judea, from Galilee where He began, even to this place.

6 Upon hearing this, Pilate asked whether the Man was a Galilean.

7 And when he found out certainly that He belonged to Herod's jurisdiction, he sent Him up to Herod, [a higher authority,] who was also in Jerusalem in those days.

8 Now when Herod saw Jesus, he was exceedingly glad, for he had eagerly desired to see Him for a long time, because of what he had heard concerning Him, and he was hoping to witness some sign—some striking evidence or spectacular performance—done by Him.

9 So he asked Him many questions, but He made no reply. [Isa. 53:7.]

10 Meanwhile the chief priests and the scribes stood by, continuing vehemently *and* violently to accuse Him.

11 And Herod with his soldiers treated Him with contempt, and scoffed at *and* ridiculed Him; then, dressing Him up in bright *and* gorgeous apparel, he sent Him back to Pilate. [Isa. 53:8.]

b) Capitalized because of what He is, the spotless Son of God, not what the speaker may have thought He was.
c) Thayer.
d) Capitalized because of what He is, the spotless Son of God, not what the speaker may have thought He was.

Living New Testament

62 And Peter walked out of the courtyard, crying bitterly.

63, 64 Now the guards in charge of Jesus began mocking Him. They blindfolded Him and hit Him with their fists and asked, "Who hit you that time, prophet?"

65 And they threw all sorts of other insults at Him.

66 Early the next morning at daybreak the Jewish Supreme Court assembled, including the chief priests and all the top religious authorities of the nation. Jesus was led before this council,

67, 68 And instructed to state whether or not He claimed to be the Messiah. But He replied, "If I tell you, you won't believe Me or let Me present My case.

69 But the time is soon coming when I, the Man of Glory,[10] shall be enthroned beside Almighty God."

70 They all shouted, "Then you claim you are the Son of God?"

And He replied, "Yes, I am."

71 "What need do we have for other witnesses?" they shouted, "for we ourselves have heard him say it."

Revised Standard

me three times." 62And he went out and
wept bitterly.
63 Now the men who were holding Jesus
mocked him and beat him; 64they also
blindfolded him and asked him, "Prophesy!
Who is it that struck you?" 65And they
spoke many other words against him, reviling him.
66 When day came, the assembly of the
elders of the people gathered together, both
chief priests and scribes; and they led him
away to their council, and they said, 67"If
you are the Christ, tell us." But he said to
them, "If I tell you, you will not believe;
68and if I ask you, you will not answer.
69But from now on the Son of man shall
be seated at the right hand of the power of
God." 70And they all said, "Are you the
Son of God, then?" And he said to them,
"You say that I am." 71And they said,
"What further testimony do we need? We
have heard it ourselves from his own lips."

CHAPTER 23

Then the entire Council took Jesus over to Pilate, the governor.[1]

2 They began at once accusing Him: "This fellow has been leading our people to ruin by telling them not to pay their taxes to the Roman government and by claiming he is our Messiah—a King."

3 So Pilate asked Him, "Are you their Messiah—their King?"[2]

"Yes," Jesus replied, "It is as you say."

4 Then Pilate turned to the chief priests and to the mob and said, "So? That isn't a crime!"

5 Then they became desperate. "But he is causing riots against the government everywhere he goes, all over Judea, from Galilee to Jerusalem!"

6 "Is he then a Galilean?" Pilate asked.

7 When they told him yes, Pilate said to take Him to King Herod, for Galilee was under Herod's jurisdiction; and Herod happened to be in Jerusalem at the time.

8 Herod was delighted at the opportunity to see Jesus, for he had heard a lot about Him and had been hoping to see Him perform a miracle.

9 He asked Jesus question after question, but there was no reply.

10 Meanwhile the chief priests and the other religious leaders stood there shouting their accusations.

11 Now Herod and his soldiers began mocking and ridiculing Jesus; and putting a kingly robe on Him, they sent Him back to Pilate.

Jesus before Pontius Pilate

23 Then the whole company of them
arose, and brought him before Pilate.
2And they began to accuse him, saying, "We
found this man perverting our nation, and
forbidding us to give tribute to Caesar, and
saying that he himself is Christ a king."
3And Pilate asked him, "Are you the King
of the Jews?" And he answered him, "You
have said so." 4And Pilate said to the chief
priests and the multitudes, "I find no crime
in this man." 5But they were urgent, saying, "He stirs up the people, teaching
throughout all Judea, from Galilee even to
this place."
6 When Pilate heard this, he asked
whether the man was a Galilean. 7And
when he learned that he belonged to Herod's
jurisdiction, he sent him over to Herod,
who was himself in Jerusalem at that time.
8When Herod saw Jesus, he was very glad,
for he had long desired to see him, because
he had heard about him, and he was hoping to see some sign done by him. 9So he
questioned him at some length; but he made
no answer. 10The chief priests and the
scribes stood by, vehemently accusing him.
11And Herod with his soldiers treated him
with contempt and mocked him; then, arraying him in gorgeous apparel, he sent

---

10 Literally, "the Son of man."
1 Implied.
2 Literally, "Are you the King of the Jews?"

King James

12 ¶ And the same day Pilate and Herod were made friends together: for before they were at enmity between themselves.
13 ¶ And Pilate, when he had called together the chief priests and the rulers and the people,
14 Said unto them, Ye have brought this man unto me, as one that perverteth the people: and, behold, I, having examined *him* before you, have found no fault in this man touching those things whereof ye accuse him:
15 No, nor yet Herod: for I sent you to him; and, lo, nothing worthy of death is done unto him.
16 I will therefore chastise him, and release *him*.
17 (For of necessity he must release one unto them at the feast.)
18 And they cried out all at once, saying, Away with this *man*, and release unto us Barabbas:
19 (Who for a certain sedition made in the city, and for murder, was cast into prison.)
20 Pilate therefore, willing to release Jesus, spake again to them.
21 But they cried, saying, Crucify *him*, crucify him.
22 And he said unto them the third time, Why, what evil hath he done? I have found no cause of death in him: I will therefore chastise him, and let *him* go.
23 And they were instant with loud voices, requiring that he might be crucified. And the voices of them and of the chief priests prevailed.
24 And Pilate gave sentence that it should be as they required.
25 And he released unto them him that for sedition and murder was cast into prison, whom they had desired; but he delivered Jesus to their will.
26 And as they led him away, they laid hold upon one Simon, a Cyrenian, coming out of the country, and on him they laid the cross, that he might bear *it* after Jesus.
27 ¶ And there followed him a great company of people, and of women, which also bewailed and lamented him.
28 But Jesus turning unto them said, Daughters of Jerusalem, weep not for me, but weep for yourselves, and for your children.
29 For, behold, the days are coming, in the which they shall say, Blessed *are* the barren, and the wombs that never bare, and the paps which never gave suck.
30 Then shall they begin to say to the mountains, Fall on us; and to the hills, Cover us.
31 For if they do these things in a green tree, what shall be done in the dry?
32 And there were also two other malefactors, led with him to be put to death.
33 And when they were come to the place, which is called Calvary, there they crucified him, and the malefactors, one on the right hand, and the other on the left.
34 ¶ Then said Jesus, Father, forgive them; for they know not what they do. And they parted his raiment, and cast lots.

Amplified

12 And that very day Herod and Pilate became friends with each other, [though] they had been at enmity before this.
13 Pilate then called together the chief priests and the rulers and the people,
14 And said to them, You brought this Man before me as one Who was perverting *and* misleading *and* [e]turning away *and* corrupting the people; and behold, after examining Him before you, I have not found any offense, (crime or guilt) in this Man in regard to your accusations against Him;
15 No, nor indeed did Herod, for he sent him back to us. Behold, He has done nothing deserving of death.
16 I will therefore chastise Him *and* [f]deliver Him amended (reformed, taught His lesson) and release Him.
17 *For it was necessary for him to release to them one prisoner at the feast.*
18 But they all together raised a deep cry (from the depths of their throats), saying, Away with this Man! Release to us Barabbas!
19 He was a man who had been thrown into prison for raising a riot in the city and for murder.
20 Once more Pilate called to them, wishing to release Jesus;
21 But they kept shouting out, Crucify, crucify Him!
22 A third time he said to them, Why, what wrong has He done? I have found (no offense *or* crime *or* guilt) in Him, nothing deserving of death; I will therefore chastise Him ([g]in order to teach Him better) and release Him.
23 But they were insistent *and* urgent, demanding with loud cries that He should be crucified. And their voices prevailed—accomplished their purpose.
24 And Pilate gave sentence that what they asked should be done.
25 So he released the man who had been thrown into prison for riot and murder, for whom they continued to ask, but Jesus he delivered up to be done with as they willed.
26 And as they led Him away, they seized one Simon of Cyrene, who was coming in from the country, and laid on him the cross and made him carry it behind Jesus.
27 And there accompanied [Jesus] a great multitude of the people, [including] women who bewailed and lamented Him.
28 But Jesus turning toward them said, Daughters of Jerusalem, do not weep for Me, but weep for yourselves and for your children.
29 For behold, the days are coming during which they will say, Blessed—happy, fortunate and [h]to be envied—[are] the barren, and the wombs that have not borne, and the breasts that have never nursed [babies]!
30 Then they will begin to say to the mountains, Fall on us; and to the hills, cover (conceal, hide) us!
31 For if they do these things when the timber is green, what will happen when it is dry?
32 Two others also, who were criminals, were led away to be executed with Him. [Isa. 53:12.]
33 And when they came to the place which is called The Skull [Calvary, from the Latin; Golgotha, the Hebrew equivalent], there they crucified Him [along with] the criminals, one on the right and one on the left.
34 And Jesus prayed, Father, forgive them, for they know not what they do. And they divided His garments *and* distributed them by casting lots for them. [Ps. 22:18.]

---

e) Wycliffe.
f) Wycliffe.
g) Vincent.
h) Souter.

Living New Testament

12 That day Herod and Pilate—enemies before—became fast friends.

13 Then Pilate called together the chief priests and other Jewish leaders, along with the people,

14 And announced his verdict: "You brought this man to me, accusing him of leading a revolt against the Roman government.[3] I have examined him thoroughly on this point and find him innocent.

15 Herod came to the same conclusion and sent him back to us—nothing this man has done calls for the death penalty.

16 I will therefore have him scourged with leaded thongs, and release him."

17,[4] 18 But now a mighty roar rose from the crowd as with one voice they shouted, "Kill him, and release Barabbas to us!"

19 (Barabbas was in prison for starting an insurrection in Jerusalem against the government, and for murder.)

20 Pilate argued with them, for he wanted to release Jesus.

21 But they shouted, "Crucify him! Crucify him!"

22 Once more, for the third time, he demanded, "Why? What crime has he committed? I have found no reason to sentence him to death. I will therefore scourage him and let him go."

23 But they shouted louder and louder for Jesus' death, and their voices prevailed.

24 So Pilate sentenced Jesus to die as they demanded.

25 And he released Barabbas, the man in prison for insurrection and murder, at their request. But he delivered Jesus over to them to do with as they would.

26 As the crowd led Jesus away to His death, Simon of Cyrene, who was just coming into Jerusalem from the country, was forced to follow, carrying Jesus' cross.

27 Great crowds trailed along behind, and many grief-stricken women.

28 But Jesus turned and said to them, "Daughters of Jerusalem, don't weep for Me, but for yourselves and for your children.

29 For the days are coming when the women who have no children will be counted fortunate indeed.

30 Mankind will beg the mountains to fall on them and crush them, and the hills to bury them.

31 For if such things as this are done to Me, the Living Tree, what will they do to you?"[5]

* * * * *

32, 33 Two others, criminals, were led out to be executed with Him at a place called "The Skull." There all three were crucified—Jesus on the center cross, and the two criminals on either side.

34 "Father, forgive these people," Jesus said, "for they don't know what they are doing."

And the soldiers gambled for His clothing, throwing dice for each piece.

[3] Literally, "as one who perverts the people."
[4] Some ancient authorities add verse 17, "For it was necessary for him to release unto them at the feast one (prisoner)."
[5] Literally, "For if they do this when the tree is green, what will happen when it is dry?"

Revised Standard

him back to Pilate. [12]And Herod and Pilate
became friends with each other that very
day, for before this they had been at enmity
with each other.
13 Pilate then called together the chief
priests and the rulers and the people, [14]and
said to them, "You brought me this man
as one who was perverting the people; and
after examining him before you, behold, I
did not find this man guilty of any of your
charges against him; [15]neither did Herod,
for he sent him back to us. Behold, nothing
deserving death has been done by him; [16]I
will therefore chastise him and release
him."[m]
18 But they all cried out together, "Away
with this man, and release to us Barabbas"—[19]a man who had been thrown into
prison for an insurrection started in the
city, and for murder. [20]Pilate addressed
them once more, desiring to release Jesus;
[21]but they shouted out, "Crucify, crucify
him!" [22]A third time he said to them, "Why,
what evil has he done? I have found in him
no crime deserving death; I will therefore
chastise him and release him." [23]But they
were urgent, demanding with loud cries
that he should be crucified. And their voices
prevailed. [24]So Pilate gave sentence that
their demand should be granted. [25]He released the man who had been thrown into
prison for insurrection and murder, whom
they asked for; but Jesus he delivered up to
their will.

Jesus on the way to Calvary

26 And as they led him away, they
seized one Simon of Cyrene, who was coming in from the country, and laid on him the
cross, to carry it behind Jesus. [27]And there
followed him a great multitude of the
people, and of women who bewailed and
lamented him. [28]But Jesus turning to them
said, "Daughters of Jerusalem, do not weep
for me, but weep for yourselves and for
your children. [29]For behold, the days are
coming when they will say, 'Blessed are the
barren, and the wombs that never bore,
and the breasts that never gave suck!' [30]Then
they will begin to say to the mountains,
'Fall on us'; and to the hills, 'Cover us.'
[31]For if they do this when the wood is
green, what will happen when it is dry?"

Jesus crucified

32 Two others also, who were criminals,
were led away to be put to death with
him. [33]And when they came to the place
which is called The Skull, there they crucified him, and the criminals, one on the

[m] Here, or after verse 19, other ancient authorities add verse 17, *Now he was obliged to release one man to them at the festival*

King James

35 And the people stood beholding. And the rulers also with them derided *him,* saying, He saved others; let him save himself, if he be Christ, the chosen of God.

36 And the soldiers also mocked him, coming to him, and offering him vinegar,

37 And saying, If thou be the king of the Jews, save thyself.

38 And a superscription also was written over him in letters of Greek, and Latin, and Hebrew, THIS IS THE KING OF THE JEWS.

39 ¶And one of the malefactors which were hanged railed on him, saying, If thou be Christ, save thyself and us.

40 But the other answering rebuked him, saying, Dost not thou fear God, seeing thou art in the same condemnation?

41 And we indeed justly; for we receive the due reward of our deeds: but this man hath done nothing amiss.

42 And he said unto Jesus, Lord, remember me when thou comest into thy kingdom.

43 And Jesus said unto him, Verily I say unto thee, To-day shalt thou be with me in paradise.

44 And it was about the sixth hour, and there was a darkness over all the earth until the ninth hour.

45 And the sun was darkened, and the veil of the temple was rent in the midst.

46 ¶ And when Jesus had cried with a loud voice, he said, Father, into thy hands I commend my spirit: and having said thus, he gave up the ghost.

47 Now when the centurion saw what was done, he glorified God, saying, Certainly this was a righteous man.

48 And all the people that came together to that sight, beholding the things which were done, smote their breasts, and returned.

49 And all his acquaintance, and the women that followed him from Galilee, stood afar off, beholding these things.

50 ¶ And, behold, *there was* a man named Joseph, a counsellor; *and he was a* good man, and a just:

51 (The same had not consented to the counsel and deed of them;) *he was* of Arimathæa, a city of the Jews: who also himself waited for the kingdom of God.

52 This *man* went unto Pilate, and begged the body of Jesus.

53 And he took it down, and wrapped it in linen, and laid it in a sepulchre that was hewn in stone, wherein never man before was laid.

54 And that day was the preparation, and the sabbath drew on.

55 And the women also, which came with him from Galilee, followed after, and beheld the sepulchre, and how his body was laid.

Amplified

35 Now the people stood by, ([i]calmly and leisurely) watching; but the rulers scoffed *and* sneered ([j]turned up their noses) at Him, saying, He rescued others ([k]from death), let Him now rescue Himself, if He is the Christ, the Messiah of God, His Chosen One!

36 The soldiers also ridiculed *and* made sport of Him, coming up and offering Him vinegar [a sour wine mixed with water], [Ps. 69:21.]

37 And saying, If you are the King of the Jews, save (rescue) Yourself ([k]from death).

38 For there was also an inscription above Him *in letters of Greek and Latin and Hebrew,* This is the King of the Jews.

39 One of the criminals who were suspended kept up a railing at Him, saying, Are You not the Christ, the Messiah? Rescue Yourself and us ([k]from death)!

40 But the other one reproved him, saying, Do you not even fear God, seeing you yourself are under the same sentence of condemnation *and* suffering the same penalty?

41 And we indeed suffer it justly, receiving the due reward of our actions; but this Man has done nothing out of the way—nothing [i]strange or eccentric or perverse or unreasonable.

42 Then he said *to* Jesus, *Lord,* remember me when You come [l]in Your kingly glory!

43 And He answered him, Truly, I tell you, today you shall be with Me in Paradise.

44 It was now about the sixth hour [midday], and darkness enveloped the whole land *and* earth until the ninth hour [about three o'clock in the afternoon],

45 While the sun's light faded—[l]was darkened; and the curtain [of the Holy of Holies] of the temple was torn in two. [Exod. 26:31-35.]

46 And Jesus, crying out with a loud voice, said, Father, into Your hands I commit My spirit! And with these words He expired. [Ps. 31:5.]

47 Now the centurion, having seen what had taken place, [m]recognized God *and* thanked *and* praised Him, and said, Indeed, without question, this Man was upright—just and innocent!

48 And all the throngs that had gathered to see this spectacle, when they saw what had taken place, returned to their homes beating their breasts.

49 And all the acquaintances of [Jesus] and the women who had followed Him from Galilee stood at a distance and watched these things.

50 Now notice, there was a man named Joseph from the Jewish town of Arimathea. He was a member of the council [the Sanhedrin], and a good (upright, [m]advantageous) man and righteous—in right standing with God and man,

51 Who had not agreed with *or* assented to the purpose and action of the others, and he was expecting *and* waiting for the kingdom of God.

52 This man went to Pilate and asked for the body of Jesus.

53 Then he took it down and [n]rolled it up in a linen cloth [o]for swathing dead bodies, and laid Him in a rock-hewn tomb, where no one had ever yet been laid.

54 It was the day of preparation [for the Sabbath], and the Sabbath was dawning (approaching).

55 The women who had come with [Jesus] from Galilee followed closely, and saw the tomb, and how His body was laid;

---

i) Vincent.
j) Literal meaning.
k) Cremer.
l) Many ancient manuscripts so read.
m) Cremer.
m) Cremer.
n) Young's Concordance.
o) Moulton and Milligan.

Living New Testament

35 The crowd watched.

And the Jewish leaders laughed and scoffed. "He was so good at helping others," they said, "let's see him save himself if he is really God's Chosen One, the Messiah."

36 The soldiers mocked Him, too, by offering Him a drink—of sour wine.

37 And they called to Him, "If you are the King of the Jews, save yourself!"

38 A signboard was nailed to the cross above Him with these words: "THIS IS THE KING OF THE JEWS."

39 One of the criminals hanging beside Him scoffed, "So you're the Messiah, are you? Prove it by saving yourself—and us, too, while you're at it!"

40, 41 But the other criminal protested. "Don't you even fear God when you are dying? We deserve to die for our evil deeds, but this man hasn't done one thing wrong."

42 Then he said, "Jesus, remember me when You come into Your Kingdom."

43 And Jesus replied, "Today you will be with Me in Paradise. This is a solemn promise."

44 By now it was noon, and darkness fell across the whole land[6] for three hours, until 3 o'clock.

45 The light from the sun was gone—and suddenly[7] the thick veil hanging in the Temple split apart.

46 Then Jesus shouted, "Father, I commit My spirit to You," and with those words He died.[8]

47 When the captain of the Roman military unit handling the executions saw what had happened, he was stricken with awe before God and said, "Surely this man was innocent."[9]

48 And when the crowd that came to see the crucifixion saw that Jesus was dead, they went home in deep sorrow.

49 Meanwhile, Jesus' friends, including the women who had followed Him down from Galilee, stood in the distance watching.

50, 51, 52 Then a man named Joseph, a member of the Jewish Supreme Court, from the city of Arimathea in Judea, went to Pilate and asked for the body of Jesus. He was a godly man who had been expecting the Messiah's coming and had not agreed with the decision and actions of the other Jewish leaders.

53 So he took down Jesus' body and wrapped it in a long linen cloth and laid it in a new, unused tomb hewn into the rock [at the side of a hill].[10]

54 This was done late on Friday afternoon, the day of preparation for the Sabbath.

55 As the body was taken away, the women from Galilee followed and saw it carried into the tomb.

---

[6] Or, "the whole world."
[7] Implied.
[8] Literally, "yielded up the spirit."
[9] Literally, "righteous."
[10] Implied.

Revised Standard

right and one on the left. 34And Jesus said,
"Father, forgive them; for they know not
what they do"[n] And they cast lots to divide his garments. 35And the people stood
by, watching; but the rulers scoffed at him,
saying, "He saved others; let him save himself, if he is the Christ of God, his Chosen
One!" 36The soldiers also mocked him, coming up and offering him vinegar, 37and
saying, "If you are the King of the Jews,
save yourself!" 38There was also an inscription over him,[o] "This is the King of the
Jews."

The penitent thief

39 One of the criminals who were hanged
railed at him, saying, "Are you not the
Christ? Save yourself and us!" 40But the
other rebuked him, saying, "Do you not
fear God, since you are under the same
sentence of condemnation? 41And we indeed justly; for we are receiving the due
reward of our deeds; but this man has done
nothing wrong." 42And he said, "Jesus, remember me when you come in your kingly
power."[p] 43And he said to him, "Truly, I
say to you, today you will be with me in
Paradise."

The death of Jesus

44 It was now about the sixth hour, and
there was darkness over the whole land[q]
until the ninth hour, 45while the sun's light
failed;[r] and the curtain of the temple was
torn in two. 46Then Jesus, crying with a
loud voice, said, "Father, into thy hands
I commit my spirit!" And having said this
he breathed his last. 47Now when the centurion saw what had taken place, he praised
God, and said, "Certainly this man was innocent!" 48And all the multitudes who assembled to see the sight, when they saw
what had taken place, returned home beating their breasts. 49And all his acquaintances
and the women who had followed him from
Galilee stood at a distance and saw these
things.

Jesus laid in the tomb

50 Now there was a man named Joseph
from the Jewish town of Arimathea. He was
a member of the council, a good and righteous man, 51who had not consented to their
purpose and deed, and he was looking for
the kingdom of God. 52This man went to
Pilate and asked for the body of Jesus.
53Then he took it down and wrapped it in
a linen shroud, and laid him in a rock-
hewn tomb, where no one had ever yet been
laid. 54It was the day of Preparation, and
the sabbath was beginning.[s] 55The women
who had come with him from Galilee followed, and saw the tomb, and how his body

---

[n] Other ancient authorities omit the sentence *And Jesus . . . what they do*
[o] Other ancient authorities add *in letters of Greek and Latin and Hebrew*
[p] Greek *kingdom*
[q] Or *earth*
[r] Or *the sun was eclipsed.* Other ancient authorities read *the sun was darkened*
[s] Greek *was dawning*

King James

56 And they returned, and prepared spices and ointments; and rested the sabbath day according to the commandment.

CHAPTER 24

NOW upon the first *day* of the week, very early in the morning, they came unto the sepulchre, bringing the spices which they had prepared, and certain *others* with them.

2 And they found the stone rolled away from the sepulchre.

3 And they entered in, and found not the body of the Lord Jesus.

4 And it came to pass, as they were much perplexed thereabout, behold, two men stood by them in shining garments:

5 And as they were afraid, and bowed down *their* faces to the earth, they said unto them, Why seek ye the living among the dead?

6 He is not here, but is risen: remember how he spake unto you when he was yet in Galilee,

7 Saying, The Son of man must be delivered into the hands of sinful men, and be crucified, and the third day rise again.

8 And they remembered his words,

9 And returned from the sepulchre, and told all these things unto the eleven, and to all the rest.

10 It was Mary Magdalene, and Joanna, and Mary *the mother* of James, and other *women that were* with them, which told these things unto the apostles.

11 And their words seemed to them as idle tales, and they believed them not.

12 Then arose Peter, and ran unto the sepulchre; and stooping down, he beheld the linen clothes laid by themselves, and departed, wondering in himself at that which was come to pass.

13 ¶ And, behold, two of them went that same day to a village called Emmaus, which was from Jerusalem *about* threescore furlongs.

14 And they talked together of all these things which had happened.

15 And it came to pass, that, while they communed *together* and reasoned, Jesus himself drew near, and went with them.

16 But their eyes were holden that they should not know him.

17 And he said unto them, What manner of communications *are* these that ye have one to another, as ye walk, and are sad?

18 And the one of them, whose name was Cleopas, answering said unto him, Art thou only a stranger in Jerusalem, and hast not known the things which are come to pass there in these days?

Amplified

56 Then they went back, and made ready spices and ointments (perfumes). On the Sabbath day they rested in accordance with the commandment. [Exod. 12:16; 20:10.]

CHAPTER 24

BUT on the first day of the week at early dawn [the women] went to the tomb, taking the spices which they had made ready.

2 And they found the stone rolled back from the tomb,

3 But when they went inside they did not find the body of the Lord Jesus.

4 And while they were perplexed *and* wondering what to do about this, behold, two men in dazzling raiment suddenly stood beside them.

5 And as [the women] were frightened and were bowing their faces to the ground, the men said to them, Why do you look for the living among [those who are] dead?

6 He is not here, but has risen! Remember how He told you while He was still in Galilee,

7 That the Son of man must be given over into the hands of sinful men [that is, men [p]whose way or nature is to act in opposition to God], and be crucified, and on the third day rise ([p]from death). [Ps. 16:10.]

8 And they remembered His words,

9 And having returned from the tomb they reported all these things (taken together) to the eleven apostles and to all the rest.

10 Now it was Mary Magdalene and Joanna and Mary the mother of James, and the other women with them who reported these things to the apostles;

11 But these reports seemed to the men an idle tale—[q]madness, [r]feigned things, [s]nonsense—and they did not believe the women.

12 But Peter got up and ran to the tomb, and stooping down and looking in, he saw the linen cloths alone by themselves, and he went away wondering about *and* marveling at what had happened.

13 And behold, that very day two of [the disciples] were going to a village called Emmaus, [which is] about seven miles from Jerusalem,

14 And they were talking with each other about all these things that had occurred.

15 And while they were conversing and discussing together, Jesus Himself caught up with them and was already accompanying them.

16 But their eyes were held, so that they did not recognize Him.

17 And He said to them, What is this discussion that you are exchanging ([t]throwing back and forth) between you as you walk along? And they stood still, looking sad *and* downcast.

18 Then one of them named Cleopas answered Him, Do you alone dwell as a stranger in Jerusalem and not know the things that have occurred there in these days?

---

p) Cremer.
q) Wycliffe.
r) Tyndale.
s) Moulton and Milligan.
t) Literal meaning.

Living New Testament

56 Then they went home and prepared spices and ointments to embalm Him; but by the time they were finished it was the Sabbath, so they rested all that day as required by the Jewish law.

Revised Standard

was laid; 56 then they returned, and prepared
spices and ointments.
On the sabbath they rested according to
the commandment.

CHAPTER 24

But very early on Sunday morning they took the ointments to the tomb—

2 And found that the huge stone covering the entrance had been rolled aside.

3 So they went in—but the Lord Jesus' body was gone.

4 They stood there puzzled, trying to think what could have happened to it. Suddenly two men appeared before them, clothed in shining robes so bright their eyes were dazzled.

5 The women were terrified and bowed low before them. Then the men asked, "Why are you looking in a tomb for someone who is alive?

6, 7 He isn't here! He has come back to life again! Don't you remember what He told you back in Galilee—that the Messiah[1] must be betrayed into the power of evil men and be crucified and that He would rise again the third day?"

8 Then they remembered,

9 And rushed back to Jerusalem[2] to tell His eleven disciples—and everyone else—what had happened.

10 (The women who went to the tomb were Mary Magdalene and Joanna and Mary the mother of James, and several others.)

11 But the story sounded like a fairy tale to the men—they didn't believe it.

12 However, Peter ran to the tomb to look. Stooping, he peered in and saw the empty linen wrappings; and then he went back home again, wondering what had happened.

13 That same day, Sunday, two of Jesus' followers were walking to the village of Emmaus, seven miles out of Jerusalem.

14 As they walked along they were talking of Jesus' death,

15 When suddenly Jesus Himself came along and joined them and began walking beside them!

16 But they didn't recognize Him, for God kept them from it.

17 "You seem to be in a deep discussion about something," He said. "What are you so concerned about?" They stopped short, sadness written across their faces.

18 And one of them, Cleopas, replied, "You must be the only person in Jerusalem who hasn't heard about the terrible things that happened there last week."[3]

[1] Literally, "the Son of man."
[2] Literally, "returned from the tomb."
[3] Literally, "in these days."

The resurrection of Jesus

24 But on the first day of the week, at
early dawn, they went to the tomb,
taking the spices which they had prepared.
2 And they found the stone rolled away
from the tomb, 3 but when they went in
they did not find the body.[t] 4 While they
were perplexed about this, behold, two men
stood by them in dazzling apparel; 5 and as
they were frightened and bowed their faces
to the ground, the men said to them, "Why
do you seek the living among the dead?[u]
6 Remember how he told you, while he was
still in Galilee, 7 that the Son of man must
be delivered into the hands of sinful men,
and be crucified, and on the third day rise."
8 And they remembered his words, 9 and returning from the tomb they told all this to
the eleven and to all the rest. 10 Now it was
Mary Magdalene and Joanna and Mary
the mother of James and the other women
with them who told this to the apostles;
11 but these words seemed to them an idle
tale, and they did not believe them.[v]

The walk to Emmaus

13 That very day two of them were going
to a village named Emmaus, about seven
miles[w] from Jerusalem, 14 and talking with
each other about all these things that had
happened. 15 While they were talking and
discussing together, Jesus himself drew near
and went with them. 16 But their eyes were
kept from recognizing him. 17 And he said
to them, "What is this conversation which
you are holding with each other as you
walk?" And they stood still, looking sad.
18 Then one of them, named Cleopas, answered him, "Are you the only visitor to
Jerusalem who does not know the things
that have happened in these days?"

[t] Other ancient authorities add *of the Lord Jesus*
[u] Other ancient authorities add *He is not here, but has risen*
[v] Other ancient authorities add verse 12, *But Peter rose and ran to the tomb; stooping and looking in, he saw the line cloths by themselves; and he went home wondering at what had happened*
[w] Greek *sixty stadia;* some ancient authorities read *a hundred and sixty stadia*

King James

19 And he said unto them, What things? And they said unto him, Concerning Jesus of Nazareth, which was a prophet mighty in deed and word before God and all the people:

20 And how the chief priests and our rulers delivered him to be condemned to death, and have crucified him.

21 But we trusted that it had been he which should have redeemed Israel: and beside all this, to-day is the third day since these things were done.

22 Yea, and certain women also of our company made us astonished, which were early at the sepulchre;

23 And when they found not his body, they came, saying, that they had also seen a vision of angels, which said that he was alive.

24 And certain of them which were with us went to the sepulchre, and found *it* even so as the women had said: but him they saw not.

25 Then he said unto them, O fools, and slow of heart to believe all that the prophets have spoken:

26 Ought not Christ to have suffered these things, and to enter into his glory?

27 And beginning at Moses and all the prophets, he expounded unto them in all the scriptures the things concerning himself.

28 And they drew nigh unto the village, whither they went: and he made as though he would have gone further.

29 But they constrained him, saying, Abide with us: for it is toward evening, and the day is far spent. And he went in to tarry with them.

30 And it came to pass, as he sat at meat with them, he took bread, and blessed *it*, and brake, and gave them.

31 And their eyes were opened, and they knew him; and he vanished out of their sight.

32 And they said one to another, Did not our heart burn within us, while he talked with us by the way, and while he opened to us the scriptures?

33 And they rose up the same hour, and returned to Jerusalem, and found the eleven gathered together, and them that were with them,

34 Saying, The Lord is risen indeed, and hath appeared to Simon.

35 And they told what things *were done* in the way, and how he was known of them in breaking of bread.

36¶ And as they thus spake, Jesus himself stood in the midst of them, and saith unto them, Peace *be* unto you.

37 But they were terrified and affrighted, and supposed that they had seen a spirit.

38 And he said unto them, Why are ye troubled? and why do thoughts arise in your hearts?

39 Behold my hands and my feet, that it is I myself: handle me, and see; for a spirit hath not flesh and bones, as ye see me have.

40 And when he had thus spoken, he shewed them *his* hands and *his* feet.

Amplified

19 And He said to them, What (kind of) things? And they said to Him, About Jesus of Nazareth, Who was a Prophet mighty in work and word before God and all the people.

20 And how our chief priests and rulers gave Him up to be sentenced to death and crucified Him.

21 But we were hoping that it was He Who would redeem *and* set Israel free. [Yes] and besides all this, it is now the third day since these things occurred.

22 And moreover, some women of our company astounded us *and* [u]drove us out of our senses. They were at the tomb early [in the morning],

23 But did not find His body; and they returned saying that they had [even] seen a vision of angels who said that He was alive!

24 So some of those [who were] with us went to the tomb, and they found it just as the women had said; but Him they did not see.

25 And [Jesus] said to them, O foolish ones (sluggish in mind, dull of perception) and slow of heart to believe—to adhere to and trust in and rely on—everything that the prophets have spoken!

26 Was it not necessary *and* [v]essentially fitting that the Christ, the Messiah, should suffer all these things before entering into His glory (His majesty and splendor)?

27 Then beginning with Moses and (throughout) all the prophets, He went on explaining *and* interpreting to them in all the Scriptures the things concerning *and* referring to Himself.

28 Then they drew near to the village to which they were going; and He acted as if He would go further,

29 But they urged *and* insisted, saying to Him, Remain with us, for it is toward evening and the day is now far spent. So He went in to stay with them.

30 And it occurred that as He reclined at table with them, He took [a loaf of] bread and praised [God] *and* gave thanks *and* asked a blessing, then broke it and was giving it to them,

31 When their eyes were [instantly] opened and they (clearly) recognized Him; and He vanished ([w]departed invisibly).

32 And they said to one another, Was not our heart greatly moved *and* burning within us while He was talking with us on the road [and] as He opened *and* explained to us [the sense of] the Scriptures?

33 And rising up that very hour they went back to Jerusalem, where they found the eleven [apostles] gathered together and those who were with them,

34 Who said, The Lord really is risen, and has appeared to Simon [Peter]!

35 Then they [themselves] [w]related in full what had happened on the road, and how He was known *and* recognized by them in the breaking of bread.

36 Now while they were talking about this, Jesus Himself took His stand among them and said to them, Peace [that is, [x]freedom from all the distresses that are experienced as the result of sin] be to you!

37 But they were so startled and terrified that they thought they saw a spirit.

38 And He said to them, Why are you disturbed *and* troubled, and why do such doubts *and* questionings arise in your hearts?

39 See My hands and My feet, that it is I Myself; feel of *and* handle Me and see, for a spirit does not have flesh and bones as you see that I have.

40 And when He had said this, He showed them His hands and His feet.

---

u) Literal meaning.
v) Vincent.
w) Vincent.
x) Cremer.

Living New Testament

19 "What things?" Jesus asked.

"The things that happened to Jesus, the Man from Nazareth," they said. "He was a Prophet who did incredible miracles and was a mighty Teacher, highly regarded by both God and man.

20 But the chief priests and our religious leaders arrested Him and handed Him over to the Roman government to be condemned to death, and they crucified Him.

21 We had thought He was the glorious Messiah and that He had come to rescue Israel. And now, besides all this—which happened three days ago—

22, 23 Some women from our group of His followers were at His tomb early this morning and came back with an amazing report that His body was missing, and that they had seen some angels there who told them Jesus is alive!

24 Some of our men ran out to see, and sure enough, Jesus' body was gone just as the women had said."

25 Then Jesus said to them, "You are such foolish, foolish people! You find it so hard to believe all that the prophets wrote in the Scriptures!

26 Wasn't it clearly predicted by the prophets that the Messiah would have to suffer all these things before entering His time of glory?"

27 Then Jesus quoted them passage after passage from the writings of the prophets, beginning with the book of Genesis and going right on through the Old Testament, explaining what the passages meant and what they said about Himself.

28 By this time they were nearing Emmaus and the end of their journey. Jesus would have gone on,

29 But they begged Him to stay the night with them, as it was getting late. So He went home with them.

30 As they sat down to eat, He asked God's blessing on the food and then took a small loaf of bread and broke it and was passing it over to them,

31 When suddenly—it was as though their eyes were opened—they recognized Him! And at that moment He disappeared!

32 They began telling each other how their hearts had felt strangely warm as He talked with them and explained the Scriptures during the walk down the road.

33, 34 Within the hour they were on their way back to Jerusalem, where the eleven disciples and the other followers of Jesus greeted them with these words, "The Lord has really risen! He appeared to Peter!"

35 Then the two from Emmaus told their story of how Jesus had appeared to them as they were walking along the road and how they had recognized Him as He was breaking the bread.

36 And just as they were telling about it, Jesus Himself was suddenly standing there among them, and greeted them!

37 But the whole group was terribly frightened, thinking they were seeing a ghost!

38 "Why are you frightened?" He asked. "Why do you doubt that it is really I?

39 Look at My hands! Look at My feet! You can see that it is I, Myself! Touch Me and make sure that I am not a ghost! For ghosts don't have bodies, as you see that I do!"

40 As He spoke, He held out His hands for them to see [the marks of the nails[4]], and showed them [the wounds in[4]] His feet.

[4] Implied.

Revised Standard

[19]And he said to them, "What things?" And
they said to him, "Concerning Jesus of
Nazareth, who was a prophet mighty in
deed and word before God and all the people, [20]and how our chief priests and rulers
delivered him up to be condemned to death,
and crucified him. [21]But we had hoped that
he was the one to redeem Israel. Yes, and
besides all this, it is now the third day since
this happened. [22]Moreover, some women of
our company amazed us. They were at the
tomb early in the morning [23]and did not
find his body; and they came back saying
that they had even seen a vision of angels,
who said that he was alive. [24]Some of those
who were with us went to the tomb, and
found it just as the women had said; but
him they did not see." [25]And he said to
them, "O foolish men, and slow of heart to
believe all that the prophets have spoken!
[26]Was it not necessary that the Christ should
suffer these things and enter into his glory?"
[27]And beginning with Moses and all the
prophets, he interpreted to them in all the
scriptures the things concerning himself.
28 So they drew near to the village to
which they were going. He appeared to be
going further, [29]but they constrained him,
saying, "Stay with us, for it is toward evening and the day is now far spent." So he
went in to stay with them. [30]When he was
at table with them, he took the bread and
blessed, and broke it, and gave it to them.
[31]And their eyes were opened and they
recognized him; and he vanished out of
their sight. [32]They said to each other, "Did
not our hearts burn within us while he
talked to us on the road, while he opened
to us the scriptures?" [33]And they rose that
same hour and returned to Jerusalem; and
they found the eleven gathered together and
those who were with them, [34]who said, "The
Lord has risen indeed, and has appeared to
Simon!" [35]Then they told what had happened
on the road, and how he was known to them
in the breaking of the bread.

Jesus appears to the ten

36 As they were saying this, Jesus himself
stood among them.[x] [37]But they were startled
and frightened, and supposed that they saw
a spirit. [38]And he said to them, "Why are
you troubled, and why do questionings rise
in your hearts? [39]See my hands and my feet,
that it is I myself; handle me, and see; for a
spirit has not flesh and bones as you see that

[x] Other ancient authorities add *and said to them, "Peace to you!"*

King James

41 And while they yet believed not for joy, and wondered, he said unto them, Have ye here any meat?

42 And they gave him a piece of a broiled fish, and of an honeycomb.

43 And he took *it*, and did eat before them.

44 And he said unto them, These *are* the words which I spake unto you, while I was yet with you, that all things must be fulfilled, which were written in the law of Moses, and *in* the prophets, and *in* the psalms, concerning me.

45 Then opened he their understanding, that they might understand the scriptures,

46 And said unto them, Thus it is written, and thus it behoved Christ to suffer, and to rise from the dead the third day:

47 And that repentance and remission of sins should be preached in his name among all nations, beginning at Jerusalem.

48 And ye are witnesses of these things.

49 ¶ And, behold, I send the promise of my Father upon you: but tarry ye in the city of Jerusalem, until ye be endued with power from on high.

50 ¶ And he led them out as far as to Bethany, and he lifted up his hands, and blessed them.

51 And it came to pass, while he blessed them, he was parted from them, and carried up into heaven.

52 And they worshipped him, and returned to Jerusalem with great joy:

53 And were continually in the temple, praising and blessing God. Amen.

Amplified

41 And while [since] they still could not believe it for sheer joy, and marveled, He said to them, Have you anything here to eat?

42 They gave Him a piece of broiled fish,

43 And He took [it] and ate [it] before them.

44 Then He said to them, This is what I told you while I was still with you, that everything which is written concerning Me in the Law of Moses and the prophets and the Psalms must be fulfilled.

45 Then He (thoroughly) opened up their minds to understand the Scriptures,

46 And said to them, Thus it is written, that the Christ, the Messiah, should suffer and on the third day rise from ([y]among) the dead. [Hos. 6:2.]

47 And that repentance [with a view to and as the condition of] forgiveness of sins should be preached in His name to all nations, beginning from Jerusalem.

48 You are witnesses of these things.

49 And behold, I will send forth upon you what My Father has promised; but remain in the city [Jerusalem] until you are clothed with power from on high.

50 Then He conducted them out as far as Bethany, and lifting up His hands He invoked a blessing on them.

51 And it occurred that while He was blessing them, He parted from them and was taken up into heaven.

52 And they worshipping Him went back to Jerusalem with great joy,

53 And they were continually in the temple *celebrating with praises and* blessing *and* extolling God. *Amen.—So be it.*

---

y) Berry's "New Testament."

Living New Testament

41 Still they stood there undecided, filled with joy and doubt. Then He asked them, "Do you have anything here to eat?"

42 They gave Him a piece of broiled fish,

43 And He ate it as they watched!

44 Then He said, "When I was with you before, don't you remember My telling you that everything written about Me by Moses and the prophets and in the Psalms must all come true?"

45 Then He opened their minds to understand at last these many Scriptures!

46 And He said, "Yes, it was written long ago that the Messiah must suffer and die and rise again from the dead on the third day;

47 And that this message of salvation should be taken from Jerusalem to all the nations: *There is forgiveness of sins for all who turn to Me.*

48 You have seen these prophecies come true

49 And now I will send the Holy Spirit[5] upon you, just as My Father promised. Don't begin telling others[6] yet—stay here in the city until the Holy Spirit comes and fills you with power from heaven."

50 Then Jesus led them out along the road[7] to Bethany, and lifting His hands to heaven, He blessed them,

51 And then began rising into the sky, and went on to heaven.

52 And they worshiped Him, and returned to Jerusalem filled with mighty joy,

53 And were continually in the Temple, praising God.

[5] Implied. Literally, "the promise of My Father."
[6] Literally, "but wait here in the city until. . . ." The paraphrase relates this to verse 47.
[7] Implied. Bethany was a mile or so away, across the valley on the Mount of Olives.

Revised Standard

I have."[y] 41 And while they still disbelieved
for joy, and wondered, he said to them,
"Have you anything here to eat?" 42 They
gave him a piece of broiled fish, 43 and he
took it and ate before them.

The great commission

44 Then he said to them, "These are my
words which I spoke to you, while I was
still with you, that everything written about
me in the law of Moses and the prophets
and the psalms must be fulfilled." 45 Then he
opened their minds to understand the scriptures, 46 and said to them, "Thus it is written, that the Christ should suffer and on the
third day rise from the dead, 47 and that
repentance and forgiveness of sins should
be preached in his name to all nations,[z] beginning from Jerusalem. 48 You are witnesses of these things. 49 And behold, I send the
promise of my Father upon you; but stay
in the city, until you are clothed with power
from on high."

Jesus' ascension

50 Then he led them out as far as Bethany, and lifting up his hands he blessed
them. 51 While he blessed them, he parted
from them.[a] 52 And they[b] returned to Jerusalem with great joy, 53 and were continually
in the temple blessing God.

[y] Other ancient authorities add verse 40, *And when he had said this, he showed them his hands and his feet*
[z] Or *nations. Beginning from Jerusalem you are witnesses*
[a] Other ancient authorities add *and was carried up into heaven*
[b] Other ancient authorities add *worshipped him, and*

King James

THE GOSPEL ACCORDING TO

St. John

CHAPTER 1

IN the beginning was the Word, and the Word was with God, and the Word was God.

2 The same was in the beginning with God.

3 All things were made by him; and without him was not any thing made that was made.

4 In him was life; and the life was the light of men.

5 And the light shineth in darkness; and the darkness comprehended it not.

6 ¶ There was a man sent from God, whose name *was* John.

7 The same came for a witness, to bear witness of the Light, that all *men* through him might believe.

8 He was not that Light, but *was sent* to bear witness of that Light.

9 *That* was the true Light, which lighteth every man that cometh into the world.

10 He was in the world, and the world was made by him, and the world knew him not.

11 He came unto his own, and his own received him not.

12 But as many as received him, to them gave he power to become the sons of God, *even* to them that believe on his name:

13 Which were born, not of blood, nor of the will of the flesh, nor of the will of man, but of God.

14 And the Word was made flesh, and dwelt among us, (and we beheld his glory, the glory as of the only begotten of the Father,) full of grace and truth.

15 ¶ John bare witness of him, and cried, saying, This was he of whom I spake, He that cometh after me is preferred before me: for he was before me.

16 And of his fulness have all we received, and grace for grace.

17 For the law was given by Moses, *but* grace and truth came by Jesus Christ.

Amplified

THE GOSPEL ACCORDING TO

John

CHAPTER 1

IN the beginning [before all time] was the Word [[a]Christ], and the Word was with God, and the Word was God [b]Himself. [Isa. 9:6.]

2 He was present originally with God.

3 All things were made *and* came into existence through Him; and without Him was not even one thing made that has come into being.

4 In Him was Life and the Life was the Light of men.

5 And the Light shines on in the darkness, for the darkness has never overpowered it—put it out, or has not absorbed it, has not appropriated it, and is unreceptive to it.

6 There came a man, sent from God, whose name was John. [Mal. 3:1.]

7 This man came to witness, that he might testify of the Light, that all men might believe in it—adhere to it, trust it and rely upon it—through him.

8 He was not the Light himself, but came that he might bear witness regarding the Light.

9 There it was; the true Light [was then] coming into the world—the genuine, perfect, steadfast Light—that illumines every person. [Isa. 49:6.]

10 He came into the world, and though the world was made through Him, the world did not recognize Him—did not know Him.

11 He came to that which belonged to Him—to His own [domain, creation, things, world]—and they who were His own did not receive Him *and* did not welcome Him.

12 But to as many as did receive *and* welcome Him, He gave the authority [power, privilege, right] to become the children of God, that is, to those who believe in—adhere to, trust in and rely on—His name; [Isa. 56:5.]

13 Who owe their birth neither to [c]bloods, nor to the will of the flesh [that of physical impulse], nor to the will of man [that of a natural father], but to God.—They are born of God!

14 And the Word [Christ] became flesh (human, incarnate) and tabernacled—fixed His tent of flesh, lived awhile—among us; and we [actually] saw His glory—His honor, His majesty; such glory as an only begotten son receives from his father, full of grace (favor, loving kindness) and truth. [Isa. 40:5.]

15 John testified about Him and cried out, This is He of Whom I said, He that comes after me has priority over me, for He was before me—He takes rank above me, for He existed before I did. [He has advanced before me, because He is my Chief.]

16 For out of His fullness (abundance) we all received—all had a share and we were all supplied with—one grace after another *and* spiritual blessing upon spiritual blessing, *and* even favor upon favor *and* gift [heaped] upon gift.

17 For while the Law was given through Moses, grace—[d]unearned, undeserved favor and spiritual blessing—and truth came through Jesus Christ. [Exod. 20:1.]

---

a) Rev. 19:13, 16, "His name is called The Word of God . . . and Lord of Lords."
b) "God," emphatic, so "God Himself." (Williams' N. T.)
c) Literal translation.
d) Trench's "Synonyms of the New Testament."

Living New Testament

John

CHAPTER 1

Before anything else existed,[1] there was Christ,[2] with God. He has always[1] been alive and is Himself God.

3 He created everything there is—nothing exists that He didn't make.

4 Eternal life is in Him, and this life gives light to all mankind.

5 His life is the light that shines through the darkness—and the darkness can never extinguish it.

6, 7 God sent John the Baptist as a witness to the fact that Jesus Christ is the true Light.

8 John himself was not the Light; he was only a witness to identify it.

9 Later on, the One who is the true Light arrived to shine on everyone coming into the world.

10 But although He made the world, the world didn't recognize Him when He came.

11, 12 Even in His own land and among His own people, the Jews, He was not accepted. Only a few would welcome and receive Him. But to all who received Him, He gave the right to become children of God. All they needed to do was to trust Him to save them.[3]

13 All those who believe this are reborn!—not a physical rebirth[4] resulting from human passion or plan—but from the will of God.

14 And Christ[5] became a human being and lived here on earth among us and was full of loving forgiveness[6] and truth. And some of us have seen His glory[7]—the glory of the only Son of the heavenly Father![8]

15 John pointed Him out to the people, telling the crowds, "This is the one I was talking about when I said, 'Someone is coming who is greater by far than I am—for He existed long before I did!' "

16 We have all benefited from the rich blessings He brought to us—blessing upon blessing heaped upon us!

17 For Moses gave us only the Law with its rigid demands and merciless justice, while Jesus Christ brought us loving forgiveness as well.

[1] Literally, "In the beginning."
[2] Literally, "the Word," meaning Christ, the wisdom and power of God and the first cause of all things; God's personal expression of Himself to men.
[3] Literally, "to believe on His name."
[4] Literally, "not of blood."
[5] Literally, "the Word," meaning Christ, the wisdom and power of God and the first cause of all things; God's personal expression of Himself to men.
[6] Literally, "grace."
[7] See Matthew 17:2.
[8] Or, "His unique Son."

Revised Standard

THE GOSPEL ACCORDING TO

John

The Word became flesh

1 In the beginning was the Word, and the
word was with God, and the Word was
God. 2He was in the beginning with God;
3all things were made through him, and
without him was not anything made that
was made. 4In him was life,[a] and the life
was the light of men. 5The light shines in
the darkness, and the darkness has not overcome it.
6 There was a man sent from God, whose
name was John. 7He came for testimony,
to bear witness to the light, that all might
believe through him. 8He was not the light,
but came to bear witness to the light.
9 The true light that enlightens every
man was coming into the world. 10He was
in the world, and the world was made
through him, yet the world knew him not.
11He came to his own home, and his own
people received him not. 12But to all who
received him, who believed in his name, he
gave power to become children of God;
13who were born, not of blood nor of the
will of the flesh nor of the will of man, but
of God.
14 And the Word became flesh and dwelt
among us, full of grace and truth; we have
beheld his glory, glory as of the only Son
from the Father. 15(John bore witness to
him, and cried, "This was he of whom I
said, 'He who comes after me ranks before
me, for he was before me.' ") 16And from
his fulness have we all received, grace upon
grace. 17For the law was given through
Moses; grace and truth came through Jesus

[a] Or *was not anything made. That which has been made was life in him*

King James

18 No man hath seen God at any time; the only begotten Son, which is in the bosom of the Father, he hath declared *him*.

19 ¶ And this is the record of John, when the Jews sent priests and Levites from Jerusalem to ask him, Who art thou?

20 And he confessed, and denied not; but confessed, I am not the Christ.

21 And they asked him, What then? Art thou Elias? And he saith, I am not. Art thou that prophet? And he answered, No.

22 Then said they unto him, Who art thou? that we may give an answer to them that sent us. What sayest thou of thyself?

23 He said, I *am* the voice of one crying in the wilderness, Make straight the way of the Lord, as said the prophet Esaias.

24 And they which were sent were of the Pharisees.

25 And they asked him, and said unto him, Why baptizest thou then, if thou be not that Christ, nor Elias, neither that prophet?

26 John answered them, saying, I baptize with water: but there standeth one among you, whom ye know not;

27 He it is, who coming after me is preferred before me, whose shoe's latchet I am not worthy to unloose.

28 These things were done in Bethabara beyond Jordan, where John was baptizing.

29 ¶ The next day John seeth Jesus coming unto him, and saith, Behold the Lamb of God, which taketh away the sin of the world.

30 This is he of whom I said, After me cometh a man which is preferred before me: for he was before me.

31 And I knew him not: but that he should be made manifest to Israel, therefore am I come baptizing with water.

32 And John bare record, saying, I saw the Spirit descending from heaven like a dove, and it abode upon him.

33 And I knew him not: but he that sent me to baptize with water, the same said unto me, Upon whom thou shalt see the Spirit descending, and remaining on him, the same is he which baptizeth with the Holy Ghost.

34 And I saw, and bare record that this is the Son of God.

35 ¶ Again the next day after John stood, and two of his disciples;

36 And looking upon Jesus as he walked, he saith, Behold the Lamb of God!

37 And the two disciples heard him speak, and they followed Jesus.

38 Then Jesus turned, and saw them following, and saith unto them, What seek ye? They said unto him, Rabbi, (which is to say, being interpreted, Master,) where dwellest thou?

Amplified

18 No man has ever seen God at any time; the only [e]unique Son, [f]the only-begotten God, Who is in the bosom [that is, in the intimate presence] of the Father, He has declared Him—He has revealed Him, brought Him out where He can be seen; He has interpreted Him, *and* He has made Him known. [Prov. 8:30.]

19 And this is the testimony of John, when the Jews sent priests and Levites to him from Jerusalem to ask him, Who are you?

20 He confessed—admitted the truth—and did not try to conceal it, but acknowledged, I am not the Christ!

21 They asked him, What then? Are you Elijah? And he said, I am not! Are you the prophet? And he answered, No! [Mal. 4:5.]

22 Then they said to him, Who are you? Tell us, so that we may give an answer to them that sent us. What do you say about yourself?

23 He said, I am the voice of one crying aloud in the wilderness—the voice of one shouting in the desert—Prepare the way of the Lord (level, straighten out, the path of the Lord), as the prophet Isaiah said. [Isa. 40:3.]

24 The messengers had been sent from the Pharisees.

25 And they asked him, Why then are you baptizing, if you are not the Christ, nor Elijah, nor the prophet?

26 John answered them, I [only] baptize [g]in (with) water. Among you there stands One Whom you do not recognize *and* with Whom you are not acquainted *and* of Whom you know nothing. [Mal. 3:1.]

27 It is He Who coming after me is preferred before me, the string of Whose sandal I am not worthy to unloose.

28 These things occurred in Bethany (Bethabara) across the Jordan [[h]at the Jordan crossing] where John was then baptizing.

29 The next day John saw Jesus coming to him and said, Look! There is the Lamb of God, Who takes away the sin of the world! [Exod. 12:3; Isa. 53:7.]

30 This is He of Whom I said, After me comes a Man Who has priority over me—Who takes rank above me—because He was before me *and* existed before I did.

31 And I did not know Him *and* did not recognize Him [myself]; but it is in order that He should be made manifest *and* be revealed to Israel—be brought out where we can see Him—that I came baptizing [g]in (with) water.

32 John gave further evidence, saying, I have seen the Spirit descending as a dove out of heaven; and it dwelt on Him—not to depart.

33 And I did not know Him *nor* recognize Him; but He Who sent me to baptize [g]in (with) water said to me, Upon Whom you shall see the Spirit descend and remain, that One is He Who baptizes with the Holy Spirit.

34 And I have seen [that happen]—I actually did see it—and my testimony is that this is the Son of God!

35 Again the next day John was standing with two of his disciples,

36 And he looked at Jesus as He walked along and said, Look! There is the Lamb of God!

37 The two disciples heard him say this, and followed Him.

38 But Jesus turned and as He saw them following Him He said to them, What are you looking for? *And* what is it you wish? And they answered Him, Rabbi, which translated is teacher, when do you stay?

---

e) Moulton and Milligan's "Vocabulary of the Greek Testament."
f) Supported by "a great mass of ancient evidence" (Vincent).
g) King James version gives preference to "with," the American "Revised" Version to "in." Other versions are about equally divided in use of the two words.
h) Lamsa's "Modern New Testament."

Living New Testament

18 No one has ever actually seen God, but, of course, His only Son has, for He is the companion of the Father and has told us all about Him.

19 The Jewish leaders[9] sent priests and assistant priests from Jerusalem to ask John whether he claimed to be the Messiah.

20 He denied it flatly. "I am not the Christ," he said.

21 "Well then, who are you?" they asked. "Are you Elijah?"

"No," he replied.

"Are you the Prophet?"[10]

"No."

22 "Then who are you? Tell us, so we can give an answer to those who sent us. What do you have to say for yourself?"

23 He replied, "I am a voice from the barren wilderness, shouting as Isaiah prophesied, 'Get ready for the coming of the Lord!' "

24, 25 Then those who were sent by the Pharisees asked him, "If you aren't the Messiah or Elijah or the Prophet, what right do you have to baptize?"

26 John told them, "I merely baptize with[11] water, but right here in the crowd is Someone you have never met,

27 Who will soon begin His ministry among you, and I am not even fit to be His slave."

28 This incident took place at Bethany, a village on the other side of the Jordan River where John was baptizing.

29 The next day John saw Jesus coming toward Him and said, "Look! There is the Lamb of God who takes away the world's sin!

30 He is the one I was talking about when I said, 'Soon a man far greater than I am is coming, who existed long before me!'

31 I didn't know He was the one, but I am here baptizing with[11] water in order to point Him out to the nation of Israel."

32 Then John told about seeing the Holy Spirit in the form of a dove descending from heaven and resting upon Jesus.

33 "I didn't know He was the one," John said again, "but at the time God sent me to baptize He told me, 'When you see the Holy Spirit descending and resting upon someone—He is the one you are looking for. He is the one who baptizes with[11] the Holy Spirit.'

34 I saw it happen to this man, and I therefore testify that He is the Son of God."

35 The following day as John was standing with two of his disciples,

36 Jesus walked by. John looked at Him intently and then declared, "See! There is the Lamb of God!"

37 Then John's two disciples turned and followed Jesus!

38 Jesus looked around and saw them following. "What do you want?" He asked them.

"Sir," they replied, "where do You live?"

[9] Literally, "the Jews."
[10] See Deuteronomy 18:15.
[11] Or, "in."

Revised Standard

Christ. 18No one has ever seen God; the
only Son,[b] who is in the bosom of the Father, he has made him known.

John's witness to himself

19 And this is the testimony of John,
when the Jews sent priests and Levites from
Jerusalem to ask him, "Who are you?" 20He
confessed, he did not deny, but confessed,
"I am not the Christ." 21And they asked
him, "What then? Are you Elijah?" He said,
"I am not." "Are you the prophet?" And he
answered, "No." 22They said to him then,
"Who are you? Let us have an answer for
those who sent us. What do you say about
yourself?" 23He said, "I am the voice of one
crying in the wilderness, 'Make straight
the way of the Lord,' as the prophet Isaiah
said."

24 Now they had been sent from the
Pharisees. 25They asked him, "Then why
are you baptizing, if you are neither the
Christ, nor Elijah, nor the prophet?" 26John
answered them, "I baptize with water; but
among you stands one whom you do not
know, 27even he who comes after me, the
thong of whose sandal I am not worthy to
untie." 28This took place in Bethany beyond the Jordan, where John was baptizing.

John's witness to Jesus

29 The next day he saw Jesus coming
toward him, and said, "Behold, the Lamb
of God, who takes away the sin of the
world! 30This is he of whom I said, 'After
me comes a man who ranks before me, for
he was before me.' 31I myself did not know
him; but for this I came baptizing with
water, that he might be revealed to Israel."
32And John bore witness, "I saw the Spirit
descend as a dove from heaven, and it
remained on him. 33I myself did not know
him; but he who sent me to baptize with
water said to me, 'He on whom you see the
Spirit descend and remain, this is he who
baptizes with the Holy Spirit.' 34And I have
seen and have borne witness that this is
the Son of God."

Andrew and Peter follow Jesus

35 The next day again John was standing
with two of his disciples; 36and he looked at
Jesus as he walked, and said, "Behold, the
Lamb of God!" 37The two disciples heard
him say this, and they followed Jesus. 38Jesus
turned, and saw them following, and said to
them, "What do you seek?" And they said
to him, "Rabbi" (which means Teacher),

[b] Other ancient authorities read *God*

King James

39 He saith unto them, Come and see. They came and saw where he dwelt, and abode with him that day: for it was about the tenth hour.

40 One of the two which heard John *speak*, and followed him, was Andrew, Simon Peter's brother.

41 He first findeth his own brother Simon, and saith unto him, We have found the Messias, which is, being interpreted, the Christ.

42 And he brought him to Jesus. And when Jesus beheld him, he said, Thou art Simon the son of Jona: thou shalt be called Cephas, which is by interpretation, A stone.

43 ¶ The day following Jesus would go forth into Galilee, and findeth Philip, and saith unto him, Follow me.

44 Now Philip was of Bethsaida, the city of Andrew and Peter.

45 Philip findeth Nathanael, and saith unto him, We have found him, of whom Moses in the law, and the prophets, did write, Jesus of Nazareth, the son of Joseph.

46 And Nathanael said unto him, Can there any good thing come out of Nazareth? Philip saith unto him, Come and see.

47 Jesus saw Nathanael coming to him, and saith of him, Behold an Israelite indeed, in whom is no guile!

48 Nathanael saith unto him, Whence knowest thou me? Jesus answered and said unto him, Before that Philip called thee, when thou wast under the fig tree, I saw thee.

49 Nathanael answered and saith unto him, Rabbi, thou art the Son of God; thou art the King of Israel.

50 Jesus answered and said unto him, Because I said unto thee, I saw thee under the fig tree, believest thou? thou shalt see greater things than these.

51 And he saith unto him, Verily, verily, I say unto you, Hereafter ye shall see heaven open, and the angels of God ascending and descending upon the Son of man.

Amplified

39 He said to them, Come and see. So they went and saw where He was staying, and they remained with Him [i]that day. It was then about the tenth hour—about four o'clock in the afternoon.

40 One of the two who heard what John said and followed Jesus was Andrew, Simon Peter's brother.

41 He first sought out *and* found his own brother Simon and said to him, We have found (discovered) the Messiah! which translated is the Christ, the Anointed One.

42 Andrew then led (brought) Simon to Jesus. Jesus looked at him and said, You are Simon the son of John. You shall be called Cephas, which translated is Peter—meaning Stone.

43 The next day Jesus desired *and* decided to go into Galilee; and He found Philip and said to him, Join Me as My attendant *and* follow Me.

44 Now Philip was from Bethsaida, of the same city as Andrew and Peter.

45 Philip sought for *and* found Nathanael and told him, We have found (discovered) the One Moses in the Law and also the prophets wrote about, Jesus from Nazareth, the [legal] son of Joseph!

46 Nathanael answered him, [Nazareth!] Can any thing good come out of Nazareth? Philip replied, Come and see!

47 Jesus saw Nathanael coming toward Him and said concerning him, See! Here is an Israelite indeed—a true descendant of Jacob—in whom there is no guile *nor* deceit *nor* falsehood *nor* duplicity!

48 Nathanael said to Jesus, How do You know me?—How is it that You know these things about me?—Jesus answered him, Before ever Philip called you, when you were still under the fig tree, I saw you.

49 Nathanael answered, Teacher, You are the Son of God! You are the King of Israel!

50 Jesus replied, Because I said to you, I saw you beneath the fig tree, do you believe in *and* rely on *and* trust in Me? You shall see greater things than this!

51 Then He said to him, I assure you, most solemnly I tell you all, you shall see Heaven opened up, and the angels of God ascending and descending upon the Son of man! [Gen. 28:12; Dan. 7:13.]

CHAPTER 2

AND the third day there was a marriage in Cana of Galilee; and the mother of Jesus was there:

2 And both Jesus was called, and his disciples, to the marriage.

3 And when they wanted wine, the mother of Jesus saith unto him, They have no wine.

4 Jesus saith unto her, Woman, what have I to do with thee? mine hour is not yet come.

5 His mother saith unto the servants, Whatsoever he saith unto you, do *it*.

6 And there were set there six waterpots of stone, after the manner of the purifying of the Jews, containing two or three firkins apiece.

CHAPTER 2

ON the third day there was a wedding at Cana of Galilee, and the mother of Jesus was there.

2 Jesus also was invited with His disciples to the wedding.

3 And when the wine was all gone, the mother of Jesus said to Him, They have no more wine!

4 Jesus said to her, ([j]Dear) woman, what is that to you and to Me? [What have we in common? Leave it to Me.] My time (hour to act) is not come yet. [Eccl. 3:1.]

5 His mother said to the servants, Whatever He says to you, do it.

6 Now there were six waterpots of stone standing there, as the Jewish custom of purification (ceremonial washing) demanded, holding twenty to thirty gallons apiece.

---

i) In accordance with Oriental hospitality, the guests would be invited to remain that night also. (Lamsa's "Gospel Light.")
j) Abbott-Smith: "a term of respect and endearment."

Living New Testament

39 "Come and see," He said. So they went with Him to the place where He was staying and were with Him from about four o'clock that afternoon until the evening.

40 (One of these men was Andrew, Simon Peter's brother.)

41 Andrew then went to find his brother Peter and told him, "We have found the Messiah!"

42 And he brought Peter to meet Jesus. Jesus looked intently at Peter for a moment and then said, "You are Simon, John's son—but you shall be called Peter, the Rock!"

43 The next day Jesus decided to go to Galilee. He found Philip and told him, "Come with Me."

44 (Philip was from Bethsaida, Andrew and Peter's home town.)

45 Then Philip went off to look for Nathanael and told him, "We have found the Messiah!—the very person Moses and the prophets told about! His name is Jesus, the son of Joseph from Nazareth!"

46 "Nazareth!" exclaimed Nathanael. "Can anything good come from there?"

"Just come and see for yourself," Philip declared.

47 As they approached, Jesus said, "Here comes an honest man—a true son of Israel."

48 "How do you know what I am like?" Nathanael demanded.

And Jesus replied, "I could see you under that fig tree before Philip found you."

49 Nathanael replied, "Sir, You are the Son of God—the King of Israel!"

50 Jesus asked him, "Do you believe all this just because I told you I had seen you under the fig tree? You will see greater proofs than this.

51 You will even see heaven open and the angels of God coming back and forth to Me, the Man of Glory."[12]

Revised Standard

"where are you staying?" 39 He said to them,
"Come and see." They came and saw where
he was staying; and they stayed with him
that day, for it was about the tenth hour.
40 One of the two who heard John speak,
and followed him, was Andrew, Simon
Peter's brother. 41 He first found his brother
Simon, and said to him, "We have found
the Messiah" (which means Christ). 42 He
brought him to Jesus. Jesus looked at him,
and said, "So you are Simon the son of
John? You shall be called Çephas" (which
means Peter[c]).

Philip and Nathanael follow Jesus

43 The next day Jesus decided to go to
Galilee. And he found Philip and said to
him, "Follow me." 44 Now Philip was from
Bethsaida, the city of Andrew and Peter.
45 Philip found Nathanael, and said to him,
"We have found him of whom Moses in
the law and also the prophets wrote, Jesus
of Nazareth, the son of Joseph." 46 Nathanael
said to him, "Can anything good come out
of Nazareth?" Philip said to him, "Come
and see." 47 Jesus saw Nathanael coming to
him, and said to him, "Behold, an Israelite
indeed, in whom is no guile!" 48 Nathanael
said to him, "How do you know me?" Jesus
answered him, "Before Philip called you,
when you were under the fig tree, I saw
you." 49 Nathanael answered him, "Rabbi,
you are the Son of God! You are the King
of Israel!" 50 Jesus answered him, "Because
I said to you, I saw you under the fig tree,
do you believe? You shall see greater things
than these." 51 And he said to him, "Truly,
truly, I say to you, you will see heaven
opened, and the angels of God ascending
and descending upon the Son of man."

CHAPTER 2

Two days later Jesus' mother was a guest at a wedding in the village of Cana in Galilee,

2 And Jesus and His disciples were invited too.

3 The wine supply ran out during the festivities, and Jesus' mother came to Him with the problem.

4 "I can't help you now," He said.[1] "It isn't yet My time for miracles."

5 But His mother told the servants, "Do whatever He tells you to."

6 Six stone waterpots were standing there; they were used for Jewish ceremonial purposes and held perhaps 20 to 30 gallons each.

The miracle of water made into wine

2 On the third day there was a marriage
at Cana in Galilee, and the mother of
Jesus was there; 2 Jesus also was invited to
the marriage, with his disciples. 3 When the
wine failed, the mother of Jesus said to him,
"They have no wine." 4 And Jesus said to
her, "O woman, what have you to do with
me? My hour has not yet come." 5 His mother said to the servants, "Do whatever he
tells you." 6 Now six stone jars were standing there, for the Jewish rites of purification,
each holding twenty or thirty gallons. 7 Je-

---

[12] Literally, "the Son of man." This was a name of great exaltation and glory.

[1] Literally, "Woman, what have I to do with you?"

[c] From the word for *rock* in Aramaic and Greek, respectively

King James

7 Jesus saith unto them, Fill the waterpots with water. And they filled them up to the brim.
8 And he saith unto them, Draw out now, and bear unto the governor of the feast. And they bare *it*.
9 When the ruler of the feast had tasted the water that was made wine, and knew not whence it was: (but the servants which drew the water knew;) the governor of the feast called the bridegroom,
10 And saith unto him, Every man at the beginning doth set forth good wine; and when men have well drunk, then that which is worse: *but* thou hast kept the good wine until now.
11 This beginning of miracles did Jesus in Cana of Galilee, and manifested forth his glory; and his disciples believed on him.
12 ¶ After this he went down to Capernaum, he, and his mother, and his brethren, and his disciples: and they continued there not many days.
13 ¶ And the Jews' passover was at hand, and Jesus went up to Jerusalem,
14 And found in the temple those that sold oxen and sheep and doves, and the changers of money sitting:
15 And when he had made a scourge of small cords, he drove them all out of the temple, and the sheep, and the oxen; and poured out the changers' money, and overthrew the tables;
16 And said unto them that sold doves, Take these things hence; make not my Father's house an house of merchandise.
17 And his disciples remembered that it was written, The zeal of thine house hath eaten me up.
18 ¶ Then answered the Jews and said unto him, What sign shewest thou unto us, seeing that thou doest these things?
19 Jesus answered and said unto them, Destroy this temple, and in three days I will raise it up.
20 Then said the Jews, Forty and six years was this temple in building, and wilt thou rear it up in three days?
21 But he spake of the temple of his body.
22 When therefore he was risen from the dead, his disciples remembered that he had said this unto them; and they believed the scripture, and the word which Jesus had said.
23 ¶ Now when he was in Jerusalem at the passover, in the feast *day*, many believed in his name, when they saw the miracles which he did.
24 But Jesus did not commit himself unto them, because he knew all *men*,
25 And needed not that any should testify of man: for he knew what was in man.

Amplified

7 Jesus said to them, Fill the waterpots with water. So they filled them up to the brim.
8 Then He said to them, Draw some out now and take it to the manager of the feast—to the one presiding, the superintendent of the banquet. So they took him some.
9 And when the manager tasted the water just now turned into wine, not knowing where it came from, though the servants that had drawn the water knew, he called the bridegroom,
10 And said to him, Everyone else serves his best wine first, and when people have drunk freely, then he serves that which is not so good; but you have kept back the good wine until now!
11 This first of His signs (miracles, wonderworks) Jesus performed in Cana of Galilee and manifested His glory—by it He displayed His greatness *and* His power openly; and His disciples believed in Him—adhered to, trusted in and relied on Him. [Deut. 5:24; Ps. 72:18.]
12 After that He went down to Capernaum with His mother and brothers and disciples and they stayed there only a few days.
13 Now the Passover of the Jews was approaching, so Jesus went up to Jerusalem.
14 There He found in the temple [k]enclosure those who were selling oxen and sheep and doves, and the money changers sitting there [too at their stands].
15 And having made a lash (a whip) of cords, He drove them all out of the temple [k]enclosure, both the sheep and the oxen; spilling *and* scattering the brokers' money and upsetting *and* tossing around their trays—their stands.
16 Then to them that sold the doves He said, Take these things away—out of here! Make not My Father's house a house of merchandise—a market place, a sales shop! [Ps. 93:5.]
17 And His disciples remembered that it is written [in the Holy Scriptures], The zeal—the fervor of love—for Your house will eat Me up.—I will be consumed with jealousy for the honor of Your house. [Ps. 69:9.]
18 Then the Jews retorted, What sign can [l]You show us, seeing You do these things?—What sign, miracle, token, indication can You give us as evidence that You have authority *and* are commissioned to act in this way?
19 Jesus answered them, Destroy (undo) this temple and in three days I will raise it up again.
20 Then the Jews replied, It took forty-six years to build this temple (sanctuary), and will You raise it up in three days?
21 But He spoke of the temple which was His body.
22 When therefore He had risen from the dead, His disciples remembered that He said this: and so they believed *and* trusted in *and* relied on the Scripture and the word (message) Jesus had spoken. [Ps. 16:10.]
23 But when He was in Jerusalem during the Passover Feast, many believed on His name [identified themselves with His party] after seeing His signs (wonders, miracles) which He was doing.
24 But Jesus [for His part] did not trust Himself to them, because He knew all [men];
25 And He did not need that any one should witness concerning man—needed no evidence from any one about men; for He Himself knew what was in human nature. [He could read men's hearts.] [I Sam. 16:7.]

---

k) Trench's "Synonyms of the New Testament."
l) Capitalized because of what He is, the spotless Son of God, not what the speaker may have thought He was.

Living New Testament

7, 8 Then Jesus told the servants to fill them to the brim with water. When this was done He said, "Dip some out and take it to the master of ceremonies."

9 When the master of ceremonies tasted the water that was now wine, not knowing where it had come from (though, of course, the servants did), he called the bridegroom over.

10 "This is wonderful stuff!" he said. "You're different from most! Usually a host uses the best wine first, and afterwards, when everyone is full and doesn't care, then he brings out the less expensive brands. But you have kept the best for the last!"

11 This miracle at Cana in Galilee was Jesus' first public demonstration of His heaven-sent power. And His disciples believed that He really was the Messiah.[2]

12 After the wedding He left for Capernaum for a few days with His mother, brothers, and disciples.

13 Then it was time for the annual Jewish Passover celebration, and Jesus went to Jerusalem.

14 In the Temple area He saw merchants selling cattle, sheep, and doves for sacrifices, and money changers behind the counters.

15 Jesus made a whip from some ropes and chased them all out, and drove out the sheep and oxen, scattering the money changers' coins over the floor and turning over their tables!

16 Then, going over to the men selling doves, He told them, "Get these things out of here! Don't turn My Father's House into a market!"

17 Then His disciples remembered this prophecy from the Scriptures: "Concern for God's House will be My undoing."

18 "What right have you to order them out?" the Jewish leaders[3] demanded. "If you have this authority from God, show us a miracle to prove it."

19 "All right," Jesus replied, "this is the miracle I will do for you: Destroy this sanctuary and in three days I will raise it up!"

20 "What!" they exclaimed. "It took 46 years to build this Temple, and you can do it in three days?"

21 But by "this sanctuary" He meant His body.

22 After He came back to life again, the disciples remembered His saying this and realized that what He had quoted from the Scriptures really did refer to Him, and had all come true!

23 Because of the miracles He did in Jerusalem at the Passover celebration, many people were convinced that He was indeed the Messiah.

24, 25 But Jesus didn't trust them, for He knew mankind to the core. No one needed to tell Him how changeable human nature is!

[2] Literally, "His disciples believed on Him."
[3] Literally, "the Jews."

Revised Standard

sus said to them, "Fill the jars with water."
And they filled them up to the brim. [8]He
said to them, "Now draw some out, and
take it to the steward of the feast." So they
took it. [9]When the steward of the feast
tasted the water now become wine, and did
not know where it came from (though the
servants who had drawn the water knew),
the steward of the feast called the bridegroom [10]and said to him, "Every man serves
the good wine first; and when men have
drunk freely, then the poor wine; but you
have kept the good wine until now." [11]This,
the first of his signs, Jesus did at Cana in
Galilee, and manifested his glory; and his
disciples believed in him.

12 After this he went down to Capernaum, with his mother and his brothers and
his disciples; and there they stayed for a few
days.

The cleansing of the temple

13 The Passover of the Jews was at hand,
and Jesus went up to Jerusalem. [14]In the
temple he found those who were selling
oxen and sheep and pigeons, and the money-
changers at their business. [15]And making
a whip of cords, he drove them all, with the
sheep and oxen, out of the temple; and he
poured out the coins of the money-changers
and overturned their tables. [16]And he told
those who sold the pigeons, "Take these
things away; you shall not make my Father's house a house of trade." [17]His disciples
remembered that it was written, "Zeal for
thy house will consume me." [18]The Jews
then said to him, "What sign have you to
show us for doing this?" [19]Jesus answered
them, "Destroy this temple, and in three
days I will raise it up." [20]The Jews then
said, "It has taken forty-six years to build
this temple, and will you raise it up in three
days?" [21]But he spoke of the temple of his
body. [22]When therefore he was raised from
the dead, his disciples remembered that he
had said this; and they believed the scripture
and the word which Jesus had spoken.

23 Now when he was in Jerusalem at the
Passover feast, many believed in his name
when they saw the signs which he did;
[24]but Jesus did not trust himself to them,
[25]because he knew all men and needed no
one to bear witness of man; for he himself
knew what was in man.

King James

CHAPTER 3

THERE was a man of the Pharisees, named Nicodemus, a ruler of the Jews:

2 The same came to Jesus by night, and said unto him, Rabbi, we know that thou art a teacher come from God: for no man can do these miracles that thou doest, except God be with him.

3 Jesus answered and said unto him, Verily, verily, I say unto thee, Except a man be born again, he cannot see the kingdom of God.

4 Nicodemus saith unto him, How can a man be born when he is old? can he enter the second time into his mother's womb, and be born?

5 Jesus answered, Verily, verily, I say unto thee, Except a man be born of water and *of* the Spirit, he cannot enter into the kingdom of God.

6 That which is born of the flesh is flesh; and that which is born of the Spirit is spirit.

7 Marvel not that I said unto thee, Ye must be born again.

8 The wind bloweth where it listeth, and thou hearest the sound thereof, but canst not tell whence it cometh, and whither it goeth: so is every one that is born of the Spirit.

9 Nicodemus answered and said unto him, How can these things be?

10 Jesus answered and said unto him, Art thou a master of Israel, and knowest not these things?

11 Verily, verily, I say unto thee, We speak that we do know, and testify that we have seen; and ye receive not our witness.

12 If I have told you earthly things, and ye believe not, how shall ye believe, if I tell you *of* heavenly things?

13 And no man hath ascended up to heaven, but he that came down from heaven, *even* the Son of man which is in heaven.

14 ¶ And as Moses lifted up the serpent in the wilderness, even so must the Son of man be lifted up:

15 That whosoever believeth in him should not perish, but have eternal life.

16 ¶ For God so loved the world, that he gave his only begotten Son, that whosoever believeth in him should not perish, but have everlasting life.

17 For God sent not his Son into the world to condemn the world; but that the world through him might be saved.

18 ¶ He that believeth on him is not condemned: but he that believeth not is condemned already, because he hath not believed in the name of the only begotten Son of God.

Amplified

CHAPTER 3

NOW there was a certain man among the Pharisees named Nicodemus, a ruler—a leader, an authority—among the Jews;

2 Who came to Jesus at night and said to Him, Rabbi, we know *and* are certain that You are come from God [as] a Teacher; for no one can do these signs—these wonderworks, these miracles, and produce the proofs—that You do, unless God is with him.

3 Jesus answered him, I assure you, most solemnly I tell you, that unless a person is born again (anew, from above), he cannot ever see—know, be acquainted with [and experience]—the kingdom of God.

4 Nicodemus said to Him, How can a man be born when he is old? Can he enter his mother's womb again, and be born?

5 Jesus answered, I assure you, most solemnly I tell you, except a man be born of water and ([m]even) the Spirit, he cannot [ever] enter the kingdom of God. [Ezek. 36:25-27.]

6 What is born of [from] the flesh is flesh—of the physical is physical; and what is born of the Spirit is spirit.

7 Marvel not—do not be surprised, astonished—at My telling you, You must all be born anew (from above).

8 The wind blows (breathes) where it will; and though you hear its sound, yet you neither know where it comes from nor where it goes. So it is with every one who is born of the Spirit.

9 Nicodemus answered by asking, How can all this be possible?

10 Jesus replied, Are you the teacher of Israel and yet do not know *nor* understand these things? [Are they strange to you?]

11 I assure you, most solemnly I tell you, We speak only of what we know—we know absolutely what we are talking about; we have actually seen what we are testifying to—were eyewitnesses of it. And still you do not receive our testimony—you reject, refuse our evidence [that of Myself and of all those who are born of the Spirit].

12 If I have told you of things that happen right here on the earth, and yet none of you believes Me, how can you believe—trust Me, adhere to Me, rely on Me—if I tell you of heavenly things?

13 And yet no one has ever gone up to heaven; but there is One Who has come down from heaven, the Son of man [Himself], *Who is—dwells, Whose home is—in heaven.*

14 And just as Moses lifted up the serpent in the desert [on a pole], so must—so it is necessary that—the Son of man be lifted up [on the cross]; [Num. 21:9.]

15 In order that every one who believes in Him—who cleaves to Him, trusts Him and relies on Him—may *not perish, but* have eternal life *and* [actually] live forever!

16 For God so greatly loved *and* dearly prized the world that He [even] gave up His only-begotten ([n]unique) Son, so that whoever believes in (trusts, clings to, relies on) Him shall not perish—come to destruction, be lost—but have eternal (everlasting) life.

17 For God did not send the Son into the world in order to judge—to reject, to condemn, to pass sentence on—the world; but that the world might find salvation *and* be made safe *and* sound through Him.

18 He who believes on Him—who clings to, trusts in, relies on Him—is not judged (he who trusts in Him never comes up for judgment; for him there is no rejection, no condemnation; he incurs no damnation). But he who does

m) "Kai" may be rendered "even."
n) Moulton and Milligan.

Living New Testament

CHAPTER 3

After dark one night a Jewish religious leader named Nicodemus, a member of the sect of the Pharisees, came for an interview with Jesus. "Sir," he said, "we all know that God has sent You to teach us. Your miracles are proof enough of this."

3 Jesus replied, "With all the earnestness I possess I tell you this: Unless you are born again, you can never get into the Kingdom of God."

4 "Born again!" exclaimed Nicodemus. "What do You mean? How can an old man go back into his mother's womb and be born again?"

5 Jesus replied, "What I am telling you so earnestly is this: Unless one is born of water[1] and the Spirit, he cannot enter the Kingdom of God.

6 Men can only reproduce human life, but the Holy Spirit gives new life from heaven;

7 So don't be surprised at My statement that you must be born again!

8 Just as you can hear the wind but can't tell where it comes from or where it will go next, so it is with the Spirit. We do not know on whom He will next bestow this life from heaven."

9 "What do You mean?" Nicodemus asked.

10, 11 Jesus replied, "You, a respected Jewish teacher, and yet you don't understand these things? I am telling you what I know and have seen—and yet you won't believe Me.

12 But if you don't even believe Me when I tell you about such things as these that happen here among men, how can you possibly believe if I tell you what is going on in heaven?

13 For only I, the Man of Heaven,[2] have come to earth and will return to heaven again.

14 And as Moses in the wilderness lifted up the bronze image of a serpent on a pole, even so must I be lifted up upon a pole,

15 So that anyone who believes in Me will have eternal life.

16 For God loved the world so much that He gave His only[3] Son so that anyone who believes in Him shall not perish but have eternal life.

17 God did not send His Son into the world to condemn it, but to save it.

18 There is no eternal doom awaiting those who trust Him to save them. But those who don't trust Him have already been tried and condemned for not believing in the only[3] Son of God.

[1] Or, "Physical birth is not enough. You must also be born spiritually. . . ." This alternate paraphrase interprets "born of water" as meaning the normal process observed during every human birth.
[2] Literally, "the Son of man."
[3] Or, "the unique Son of God."

Revised Standard

Nicodemus visits Jesus

3 Now there was a man of the Pharisees,
named Nicodemus, a ruler of the Jews.
2This man came to Jesus[d] by night and said
to him, "Rabbi, we know that you are a
teacher come from God; for no one can do
these signs that you do, unless God is with
him." 3Jesus answered him, "Truly, truly,
I say to you, unless one is born anew,[e] he
cannot see the kingdom of God." 4Nicode-
mus said to him, "How can a man be born
when he is old? Can he enter a second time
into his mother's womb and be born?"
5Jesus answered, "Truly, truly, I say to you,
unless one is born of water and the Spirit,
he cannot enter the kingdom of God. 6That
which is born of the flesh is flesh, and that
which is born of the Spirit is spirit.[f] 7Do
not marvel that I said to you, 'You must be
born anew.'[e] 8The wind[f] blows where it
wills, and you hear the sound of it, but you
do not know whence it comes or whither
it goes; so it is with every one who is born
of the Spirit." 9Nicodemus said to him,
"How can this be?" 10Jesus answered him,
"Are you a teacher of Israel, and yet you
do not understand this? 11Truly, truly, I say
to you, we speak of what we know, and
bear witness to what we have seen; but you
do not receive our testimony. 12If I have
told you earthly things and you do not believe, how can you believe if I tell you
heavenly things? 13No one has ascended
into heaven but he who descended from
heaven, the Son of man.[g] 14And as Moses
lifted up the serpent in the wilderness, so
must the Son of man be lifted up, 15that
whoever believes in him may have eternal
life."[h]

16 For God so loved the world that he
gave his only Son, that whoever believes in
him should not perish but have eternal life.
17For God sent the Son into the world, not
to condemn the world, but that the world
might be saved through him. 18He who believes in him is not condemned; he who
does not believe is condemned already, because he has not believed in the name of

[d] Greek *him*
[e] Or *from above*
[f] The same Greek word means both *wind* and *spirit*
[g] Other ancient authorities add *who is in heaven*
[h] Some interpreters hold that the quotation continues through verse 21

King James

19 And this is the condemnation, that light is come into the world, and men loved darkness rather than light, because their deeds were evil.

20 For every one that doeth evil hateth the light, neither cometh to the light, lest his deeds should be reproved.

21 But he that doeth truth cometh to the light, that his deeds may be made manifest, that they are wrought in God.

22 ¶ After these things came Jesus and his disciples into the land of Judæa; there he tarried with them, and baptized.

23 ¶ And John also was baptizing in Ænon near to Salim, because there was much water there: and they came, and were baptized.

24 For John was not yet cast into prison.

25 ¶ Then there arose a question between *some* of John's disciples and the Jews about purifying.

26 And they came unto John, and said unto him, Rabbi, he that was with thee beyond Jordan, to whom thou barest witness, behold, the same baptizeth, and all *men* come to him.

27 John answered and said, A man can receive nothing, except it be given him from heaven.

28 Ye yourselves bear me witness, that I said, I am not the Christ, but that I am sent before him.

29 He that hath the bride is the bridegroom: but the friend of the bridegroom, which standeth and heareth him, rejoiceth greatly because of the bridegroom's voice: this my joy therefore is fulfilled.

30 He must increase, but I *must* decrease.

31 He that cometh from above is above all: he that is of the earth is earthly, and speaketh of the earth: he that cometh from heaven is above all.

32 And what he hath seen and heard, that he testifieth; and no man receiveth his testimony.

33 He that hath received his testimony hath set to his seal that God is true.

34 For he whom God hath sent speaketh the words of God: for God giveth not the Spirit by measure *unto him.*

Amplified

not believe (not cleave to, rely on, trust in Him) is judged already; (he has already been convicted; has already received his sentence) because he has not believed on *and* trusted in the name of the only begotten Son of God.—He is condemned for refusing to let his trust rest in Christ's name.

19 The [basis of the] judgment (indictment, the test by which men are judged, the ground for the sentence) lies in this: that the Light is come into the world, and people have loved the darkness rather than *and* more than the Light, for their works (deeds) were evil. [Isa. 5:20.]

20 For every wrongdoer hates (loathes, detests) the light and will not come out into the light, *but* shrinks from it, lest his works—his deeds, his activities, his conduct—be exposed *and* reproved.

21 But he who practices truth—who does what is right—comes out into the light; so that his works may be plainly shown to be what they are, wrought with God—divinely prompted, done with God's help, in dependence upon Him.

22 After this, Jesus and His disciples went into the land (the countryside) of Judea, where He remained with them and baptized.

23 But John also was baptizing at Aenon near Salim, for there was an abundance of water there; and the people kept coming and being baptized.

24 For John had not yet been thrown into prison.

25 Therefore there arose a controversy between some of John's disciples and a Jew in regard to purification.

26 So they came to John and reported to him, Rabbi, the Man Who was with you on the other side of the Jordan [[o]at the Jordan crossing], and to Whom you yourself have borne testimony, notice, here He is baptizing too, and everybody is flocking to Him!

27 John answered, A man can receive nothing—he can claim nothing, he can [p]take unto himself nothing—except as it has been granted to him from heaven. [A man must be content to receive the gift which is given him from heaven; there is no other source.]

28 You yourselves are my witnesses—you personally bear me out—that I stated, I am not the Christ, the Anointed One, the Messiah; but I have [only] been sent before Him—in advance of Him, as His appointed forerunner, His messenger, His announcer. [Mal. 3:1.]

29 He who has the bride is the bridegroom; but the groomsman, who stands by and listens to him, rejoices greatly *and* heartily on account of the bridegroom's voice. This then is my pleasure *and* joy, and it is now complete. [S. of Sol. 5:1.]

30 He must increase, but I must decrease—He must grow more prominent, I must grow less so. [Isa. 9:7.]

31 He Who comes from above (heaven) is [far] above all [others]. He who comes from the earth belongs to the earth, and talks the language of earth—his words are from an earthly standpoint. He Who comes from heaven is [far] above all others—far superior to all others in prominence and in excellence.

32 It is to what He has [actually] seen and heard that He bears testimony; and yet no one accepts His testimony—no one receives His evidence as true.

33 Whoever receives His testimony has set his seal of approval to this: that God is true—has definitely certified, acknowledged, declared once for all, is himself assured that it is divine truth, that God cannot lie.

34 For since He Whom God has sent speaks the words of God—proclaims God's own message—God does not give Him His Spirit sparingly *or* by measure, *but* boundless is the gift God makes of His Spirit! [Deut. 18:18.]

---

o) Lamsa's New Testament.
p) Thayer.

Living New Testament

19 Their sentence is based on this fact: that the Light from heaven came into the world, but they loved the darkness more than the Light, for their deeds were evil.

20 They hated the heavenly Light because they wanted to sin in the darkness. They stayed away from that Light for fear their sins would be exposed and they would be punished.

21 But those doing right come gladly to the Light to let everyone see that they are doing what God wants them to."

* * * * *

22 Afterwards Jesus and His disciples left Jerusalem and stayed for awhile in Judea and baptized there.

* * * * *

23, 24 At this time John the Baptist was not yet in prison. He was baptizing at Aenon, near Salim, because there was plenty of water there.

25 One day someone began an argument with John's disciples, telling them that Jesus' baptism was best.[4]

26 So they came to John and said, "Master, the man you met on the other side of the Jordan River—the one you said was the Messiah—He is baptizing too, and everybody is going over there instead of coming here to us."

27 John replied, "God in heaven appoints each man's work.

28 My work is to prepare the way for that man so that everyone will go to Him. You yourselves know how plainly I told you that I am not the Messiah. I am here to prepare the way for Him—that is all.

29 The crowds will naturally go to the main attraction[5]—the bride will go where the bridegroom is! A bridegroom's friends rejoice with him. I am the Bridegroom's friend, and I am filled with joy at His success.

30 He must become greater and greater, and I must become less and less.

31 He has come from heaven and is greater than anyone else. I am of the earth, and my understanding is limited to the things of earth.

32 He tells what He has seen and heard, but how few believe what He tells them!

33, 34 Those who believe Him discover that God is a fountain of truth. For this one—sent by God—speaks God's words, for God's Spirit is upon Him without measure or limit.

[4] Literally, "about purification."
[5] Implied.

Revised Standard

the only Son of God. [19]And this is the
judgment, that the light has come into the
world, and men loved darkness rather than
light, because their deeds were evil. [20]For
every one who does evil hates the light, and
does not come to the light, lest his deeds
should be exposed. [21]But he who does what
is true comes to the light, that it may be
clearly seen that his deeds have been
wrought in God.
22 After this Jesus and his disciples went
into the land of Judea; there he remained
with them and baptized. [23]John also was
baptizing at Aenon near Salim, because
there was much water there; and people
came and were baptized. [24]For John had
not yet been put in prison.

John's testimony to Jesus

25 Now a discussion arose between
John's disciples and a Jew over purifying.
[26]And they came to John, and said to him,
"Rabbi, he who was with you beyond the
Jordan, to whom you bore witness, here he
is, baptizing, and all are going to him."
[27]John answered, "No one can receive anything except what is given him from heaven.
[28]You yourselves bear me witness, that I said,
I am not the Christ, but I have been sent
before him. [29]He who has the bride is the
bridegroom; the friend of the bridegroom,
who stands and hears him, rejoices greatly
at the bridegroom's voice; therefore this joy
of mine is now full. [30]He must increase,
but I must decrease."[i]
31 He who comes from above is above
all; he who is of the earth belongs to the
earth, and of the earth he speaks; he who
comes from heaven is above all. [32]He bears
witness to what he has seen and heard, yet
no one receives his testimony; [33]he who
receives his testimony sets his seal to this,
that God is true. [34]For he whom God has
sent utters the words of God, for it is not
by measure that he gives the Spirit; [35]the

[i] Some interpreters hold that the quotation continues through verse 36

King James

35 The Father loveth the Son, and hath given all things into his hand.

36 He that believeth on the Son hath everlasting life: and he that believeth not the Son shall not see life; but the wrath of God abideth on him.

CHAPTER 4

WHEN therefore the Lord knew how the Pharisees had heard that Jesus made and baptized more disciples than John,

2 (Though Jesus himself baptized not, but his disciples,)

3 He left Judæa, and departed again into Galilee.

4 And he must needs go through Samaria.

5 Then cometh he to a city of Samaria, which is called Sychar, near to the parcel of ground that Jacob gave to his son Joseph.

6 Now Jacob's well was there. Jesus therefore, being wearied with *his* journey, sat thus on the well: *and* it was about the sixth hour.

7 There cometh a woman of Samaria to draw water: Jesus saith unto her, Give me to drink.

8 (For his disciples were gone away unto the city to buy meat.)

9 Then saith the woman of Samaria unto him, How is it that thou, being a Jew, askest drink of me, which am a woman of Samaria? for the Jews have no dealings with the Samaritans.

10 Jesus answered and said unto her, If thou knewest the gift of God, and who it is that saith to thee, Give me to drink; thou wouldest have asked of him, and he would have given thee living water.

11 The woman saith unto him, Sir, thou hast nothing to draw with, and the well is deep: from whence then hast thou that living water?

12 Art thou greater than our father Jacob, which gave us the well, and drank thereof himself, and his children, and his cattle?

13 Jesus answered and said unto her, Whosoever drinketh of this water shall thirst again:

14 But whosoever drinketh of the water that I shall give him shall never thirst; but the water that I shall give him shall be in him a well of water springing up into everlasting life.

15 The woman saith unto him, Sir, give me this water, that I thirst not, neither come hither to draw.

16 Jesus saith unto her, Go, call thy husband, and come hither.

Amplified

35 The Father loves the Son, and has given—entrusted, committed—everything into His hand. [Dan. 7:14.]

36 And he who believes on—has faith in, clings to, relies on—the Son has (now possesses) eternal life. But whoever disobeys—is unbelieving toward, refuses to trust in, disregards, is not subject to—the Son will never see (experience) life. But instead the wrath of God abides on him—God's displeasure remains on him; His indignation hangs over him continually. [Hab. 2:4.]

CHAPTER 4

NOW when the Lord knew (learned, was aware) that the Pharisees had been told that Jesus was winning and baptizing more disciples than John,

2 Though Jesus Himself did not baptize, but His disciples,

3 He left Judea and returned to Galilee.

4 It was necessary for Him to go through Samaria.

5 And in doing so He arrived at a Samaritan town called Sychar, near the tract of land that Jacob gave to his son Joseph.

6 And Jacob's well was there. So Jesus, tired as He was from His journey, sat down [to rest] by the well. It was then about the sixth hour (about noon).

7 Presently when a woman of Samaria came along to draw water, Jesus said to her, Give Me a drink.

8 For His disciples had gone off into the town to buy food.

9 The Samaritan woman said to Him, How is it that [q]You being a Jew ask me, a Samaritan [and a] woman, for a drink? For the Jews have nothing to do with the Samaritans.

10 Jesus answered her, if you had only known *and* had recognized God's gift, and Who this is that is saying to you, Give Me a drink, you would have asked Him instead and He would have given you living water.

11 She said to Him, Sir. [q]You have nothing to draw with (no draw-bucket) and the well is deep; how then can You provide living water?—Where do You get Your living water?

12 Are You greater than *and* superior to our ancestor Jacob, who gave us this well, and who used to drink from it himself, and his sons and his cattle also?

13 Jesus answered her, All who drink of this water will be thirsty again.

14 But whoever takes a drink of the water that I will give him shall never, no never, be thirsty any more. But the water that I will give him shall become a spring of water welling up (flowing, bubbling) continually within him unto (into, for) eternal life.

15 The woman said to Him, Sir, give me this water, so that I may never get thirsty, nor have to come [continually all the way] here to draw.

16 At this Jesus said to her, Go, call your husband and come back here.

q) Capitalized because of what He is, the spotless Son of God, not what the speaker may have thought He was.

Living New Testament

35 The Father loves this man because He is His Son, and God has given Him everything there is.

36 And all who trust Him—God's Son—to save them have eternal life; those who don't believe and obey Him shall never see heaven, but the wrath of God remains upon them."

Revised Standard

Father loves the Son, and has given all
things into his hand. 36 He who believes in
the Son has eternal life; he who does not
obey the Son shall not see life, but the
wrath of God rests upon him.

CHAPTER 4

When the Lord knew that the Pharisees had heard about the greater crowds coming to Him than to John to be baptized and to become His disciples—(though Jesus Himself didn't baptize them, but His disciples did)—

3 He left Judea and returned to the province of Galilee.

4 He had to go through Samaria on the way,

5, 6 And around noon as He approached the village of Sychar, He came to Jacob's Well, located on the parcel of ground Jacob gave to his son Joseph. Jesus was tired from the long walk in the hot sun and sat wearily beside the well.

7 Soon a Samaritan woman came to draw water, and Jesus asked her for a drink.

8 He was alone at the time as His disciples had gone into the village to buy some food.

9 The woman was surprised that a Jew would ask a "despised Samaritan" for anything—usually they won't even speak to them!—and she remarked about this to Jesus.

10 He replied, "If you only knew what a wonderful gift God has for you, and who I am, you would ask Me for some *living* water!"

11 "But you don't have a rope or a bucket," she said, "and this is a very deep well! From where would you get this living water?

12 And besides, are you greater than our ancestor Jacob? How can you offer better water than this which he and his sons and cattle enjoyed?"

13 Jesus replied that people soon became thirsty again after drinking this water.

14 "But the water I give them," He said, "becomes a perpetual spring within them, watering them forever with eternal life."

15 "Please, sir," the woman said, "give me some of that water! Then I'll never be thirsty again and won't have to make this long trip out here every day."

16 "Go and get your husband," Jesus told her.

Jesus and the woman of Samaria

4 Now when the Lord knew that the
Pharisees had heard that Jesus was making and baptizing more disciples than John
2 (although Jesus himself did not baptize,
but only his disciples), 3 he left Judea and
departed again to Galilee. 4 He had to pass
through Samaria. 5 So he came to a city of
Samaria, called Sychar, near the field that
Jacob gave to his son Joseph. 6 Jacob's well
was there, and so Jesus, wearied as he was
with his journey, sat down beside the well.
It was about the sixth hour.
7 There came a woman of Samaria to
draw water. Jesus said to her, "Give me a
drink." 8 For his disciples had gone away
into the city to buy food. 9 The Samaritan
woman said to him, "How is it that you, a
Jew, ask a drink of me, a woman of Samaria?" For Jews have no dealings with
Samaritans. 10 Jesus answered her, "If you
knew the gift of God, and who it is that is
saying to you, 'Give me a drink,' you would
have asked him, and he would have given
you living water." 11 The woman said to him,
"Sir, you have nothing to draw with, and the
well is deep; where do you get that living
water? 12 Are you greater than our father
Jacob, who gave us the well, and drank from
it himself, and his sons, and his cattle?"
13 Jesus said to her, "Every one who drinks
of this water will thirst again, 14 but whoever
drinks of the water that I shall give him will
never thirst; the water that I shall give him
will become in him a spring of water welling
up to eternal life." 15 The woman said to
him, "Sir, give me this water, that I may
not thirst, nor come here to draw."
16 Jesus said to her, "Go, call your hus-

King James

17 The woman answered and said, I have no husband. Jesus said unto her, Thou hast well said, I have no husband:

18 For thou hast had five husbands; and he whom thou now hast is not thy husband: in that saidst thou truly.

19 The woman saith unto him, Sir, I perceive that thou art a prophet.

20 Our fathers worshipped in this mountain; and ye say, that in Jerusalem is the place where men ought to worship.

21 Jesus saith unto her, Woman, believe me, the hour cometh, when ye shall neither in this mountain, nor yet at Jerusalem, worship the Father.

22 Ye worship ye know not what: we know what we worship: for salvation is of the Jews.

23 But the hour cometh, and now is, when the true worshippers shall worship the Father in spirit and in truth: for the Father seeketh such to worship him.

24 God *is* a Spirit: and they that worship him must worship *him* in spirit and in truth.

25 The woman saith unto him, I know that Messias cometh, which is called Christ: when he is come, he will tell us all things.

26 Jesus saith unto her, I that speak unto thee am *he*.

27 ¶ And upon this came his disciples, and marvelled that he talked with the woman: yet no man said, What seekest thou? or, Why talkest thou with her?

28 The woman then left her waterpot, and went her way into the city, and saith to the men,

29 Come, see a man, which told me all things that ever I did: is not this the Christ?

30 Then they went out of the city, and came unto him.

31 ¶ In the mean while his disciples prayed him, saying, Master, eat.

32 But he said unto them, I have meat to eat that ye know not of.

33 Therefore said the disciples one to another, Hath any man brought him *aught* to eat?

34 Jesus saith unto them, My meat is to do the will of him that sent me, and to finish his work.

35 Say not ye, There are yet four months, and *then* cometh harvest? behold, I say unto you, Lift up your eyes, and look on the fields; for they are white already to harvest.

36 And he that reapeth receiveth wages, and gathereth fruit unto life eternal: that both he that soweth and he that reapeth may rejoice together.

37 And herein is that saying true, One soweth, and another reapeth.

38 I sent you to reap that whereon ye bestowed no labour: other men laboured, and ye are entered into their labours.

39 ¶ And many of the Samaritans of that city believed on him for the saying of the woman, which testified, He told me all that ever I did.

Amplified

17 The woman answered, I have no husband. Jesus said to her, You have spoken truly in saying, I have no husband.

18 For you have had five husbands; but the man you are now living with is not your husband. In this you have spoken truly.

19 The woman said to Him, Sir, I see *and* understand that You are a prophet.

20 Our forefathers worshipped on this mountain, but you [Jews] say that Jerusalem is the place where it is necessary *and* proper to worship.

21 Jesus said to her, Woman, believe Me, a time is coming when you will worship the Father neither [merely] in this mountain nor [merely] in Jerusalem.

22 You [Samaritans] do not know what you are worshipping—you worship what you do not comprehend. We do know what we are worshipping—we worship what we have knowledge of and understand; for [after all] salvation comes from [among] the Jews.

23 A time will come, however, indeed it is already here, when the true (genuine) worshippers will worship the Father in spirit and in truth (reality); for the Father is seeking just such people as these as His worshippers.

24 God is a Spirit (a spiritual Being) and those who worship Him must worship *Him* in spirit and in truth (reality).

25 The woman said to Him, I know that Messiah is coming, He Who is called the Christ, the Anointed One, and when He arrives He will tell us everything we need to know *and* make it clear to us.

26 Jesus said to her, I Who am now speaking with you am He.

27 Just then His disciples came and they wondered (were surprised, astonished) to find Him talking with a woman [a married woman]. However, not one of them asked Him, What are You inquiring? *or* What do You want? or, Why do You speak with her?

28 Then the woman left her water jar and went away to the town. And she began telling the people,

29 Come, see a Man Who has told me everything that I ever did! Can this be (is not this) the Christ?—Must not this be the Messiah, the Anointed One?

30 So the people left the town and set out to go to Him.

31 Meanwhile the disciples urged Him saying, Rabbi, eat something.

32 But He assured them, I have food (nourishment) to eat of which you know nothing *and* have no idea.

33 So the disciples said one to another, Has someone brought Him something to eat?

34 Jesus said to them, My food (nourishment) is to do the will (pleasure) of Him Who sent Me and to accomplish *and* completely finish His work.

35 Do you not say, It is still four months until harvest time comes? Look! I tell you, raise your eyes and observe the fields *and* see how they are already white for harvesting.

36 Already the reaper is getting his wages—he who does the cutting now has his reward—for he is gathering fruit (crop) unto life eternal. So that he who does the planting and he who does the reaping may rejoice together.

37 For in this the saying holds true, One sows and another reaps.

38 I sent you to reap a crop on which you have not toiled. Other men labored and you step in to reap the results of their work.

39 Now numerous Samaritans from that town believed on *and* trusted in Him because of what the woman said when she declared *and* testified, He told me everything that I ever did.

Living New Testament

17, 18 "But I'm not married," the woman replied.

"All too true!" Jesus said. "For you have had five husbands, and you aren't even married to the man you're living with now. [You couldn't have spoken a truer word![1]]

19 "Sir," the woman said, "You must be a prophet.

20 But say, tell me, why is it that you Jews insist that Jerusalem is the only place of worship, while we Samaritans claim it is here [at Mount Gerazim[1]], where our ancestors worshiped?"

21, 22, 23, 24 Jesus replied, "The time is coming, Ma'am, when we will no longer be concerned about whether to worship the Father here or in Jerusalem. For it's not *where* we worship that counts, but *how* we worship—is our worship spiritual and real? Do we have the Holy Spirit's help? For God is Spirit, and we must have His help to worship as we should. The Father wants this kind of worship from us. But you Samaritans know so little about Him, worshiping blindly, while we Jews know all about Him, for salvation comes to the world through the Jews."

25 The woman said, "Well, at least I know that the Messiah will come—the one they call Christ—and when He does, He will explain everything to us."

26 Then Jesus told her, "I am the Messiah!"

27 Just then His disciples arrived. They were surprised to find Him talking to a woman, but none of them asked Him why, or what they had been discussing.

28, 29 Then the woman left her waterpot beside the well and went back to the village and told everyone, "Come and meet a man who told me everything I ever did! Can this be the Messiah?"

30 So the people came streaming from the village to see Him.

31 Meanwhile, the disciples were urging Jesus to eat.

32 "No," He said, "I have some food you don't know about."

33 "Who brought it to Him?" the disciples asked each other.

34 Then Jesus explained: "My nourishment comes from doing the will of God who sent Me, and from finishing His work.

35 Do you think the work of harvesting will not begin until the summer ends four months from now? Look around you! Vast fields of human souls are ripening all around us and are ready now for reaping.

36 The reapers will be paid good wages and will be gathering eternal souls into the granaries of heaven! What joys await the sower and the reaper, both together!

37 For it is true that one sows and someone else reaps.

38 I sent you to reap where you didn't sow; others did the work, and you received the harvest."

39 Many from that Samaritan village believed He was the Messiah because of the woman's report, "He told me everything I ever did!"

[1] Implied.

Revised Standard

band, and come here." [17]The woman answered him, "I have no husband." Jesus said to her, "You are right in saying, 'I have no husband'; [18]for you have had five husbands, and he whom you now have is not your husband; this you said truly." [19]The woman said to him, "Sir, I perceive that you are a prophet. [20]Our fathers worshiped on this mountain; and you say that in Jerusalem is the place where men ought to worship." [21]Jesus said to her, "Woman, believe me, the hour is coming when neither on this mountain nor in Jerusalem will you worship the Father. [22]You worship what you do not know; we worship what we know, for salvation is from the Jews. [23]But the hour is coming, and now is, when the true worshipers will worship the Father in spirit and truth, for such the Father seeks to worship him. [24]God is spirit, and those who worship him must worship in spirit and truth." [25]The woman said to him, 'I know that Messiah is coming (he who is called Christ); when he comes, he will show us all things." [26]Jesus said to her, "I who speak to you am he."

27 Just then his disciples came. They marveled that he was talking with a woman, but none said, "What do you wish?" or, "Why are you talking with her?" [28]So the woman left her water jar, and went away into the city, and said to the people, [29]"Come, see a man who told me all that I ever did. Can this be the Christ?" [30]They went out of the city and were coming to him.

31 Meanwhile the disciples besought him, saying, "Rabbi, eat." [32]But he said to them, "I have food to eat of which you do not know." [33]So the disciples said to one another, "Has any one brought him food?" [34]Jesus said to them, "My food is to do the will of him who sent me, and to accomplish his work. [35]Do you not say, 'There are yet four months, then comes the harvest'? I tell you, lift up your eyes, and see how the fields are already white for harvest. [36]He who reaps receives wages, and gathers fruit for eternal life, so that sower and reaper may rejoice together. [37]For here the saying holds true, 'One sows and another reaps.' [38]I sent you to reap that for which you did not labor; others have labored, and you have entered into their labor."

The conversion of Samaritans

39 Many Samaritans from that city believed in him because of the woman's testimony, "He told me all that I ever did." [40]So

King James

40 So when the Samaritans were come unto him, they besought him that he would tarry with them: and he abode there two days.

41 And many more believed because of his own word;

42 And said unto the woman, Now we believe, not because of thy saying: for we have heard *him* ourselves, and know that this is indeed the Christ, the Saviour of the world.

43 ¶ Now after two days he departed thence, and went into Galilee.

44 For Jesus himself testified, that a prophet hath no honour in his own country.

45 Then when he was come into Galilee, the Galilæans received him, having seen all the things that he did at Jerusalem at the feast: for they also went unto the feast.

46 So Jesus came again into Cana of Galilee, where he made the water wine. And there was a certain nobleman, whose son was sick at Capernaum.

47 When he heard that Jesus was come out of Judæa into Galilee, he went unto him, and besought him that he would come down, and heal his son: for he was at the point of death.

48 Then said Jesus unto him, Except ye see signs and wonders, ye will not believe.

49 The nobleman saith unto him, Sir, come down ere my child die.

50 Jesus saith unto him, Go thy way; thy son liveth. And the man believed the word that Jesus had spoken unto him, and he went his way.

51 And as he was now going down, his servants met him, and told *him*, saying, Thy son liveth.

52 Then inquired he of them the hour when he began to amend. And they said unto him, Yesterday at the seventh hour the fever left him.

53 So the father knew that *it was* at the same hour, in the which Jesus said unto him, Thy son liveth: and himself believed, and his whole house.

54 This *is* again the second miracle *that* Jesus did, when he was come out of Judæa into Galilee.

Amplified

40 So when the Samaritans arrived, they asked Him to remain with them, and He did stay there two days.

41 Then many more believed *and* adhered to *and* relied on Him because of His personal message—what He Himself said.

42 And they told the woman, Now we no longer believe (trust, have faith) just because of what you said; for we have heard Him ourselves—personally; and we know that He truly is the Savior of the world, *the Christ.*

43 But after these two days Jesus went on from there into Galilee,

44 Although He Himself declared that a prophet has no honor in his own country.

45 However, when He came into Galilee, the Galileans also welcomed Him *and* took Him to their hearts eagerly; for they had seen everything that He did in Jerusalem during the feast, for they too had attended the feast.

46 So Jesus came again to Cana of Galilee where He had turned the water into wine. And there was a certain royal official, whose son was lying ill in Capernaum.

47 Having heard that Jesus had come back from Judea into Galilee, he went away to meet Him and began to beg Him to come down and cure his son, for he was lying at the point of death.

48 Then Jesus said to him, Unless you see signs and miracles happen, you [people] never will believe (trust, have faith) at all.

49 The king's officer pleaded with Him, Sir, do come down at once before my little child is dead!

50 Jesus answered him, Go in peace; your son will live! And the man put his trust in what Jesus said and started home.

51 But even as he was on the road going down, his servants met him and reported, saying, Your son lives!

52 So he asked them at what time he had begun to get better. They said, Yesterday during the seventh hour [about one o'clock in the afternoon] the fever left him.

53 Then the father knew that it was at that very hour when Jesus had said to him, Your son lives. And he and his entire household believed—they adhered to, trusted in and relied on Jesus.

54 This is the second sign (wonderwork, miracle) that Jesus performed after He had come out of Judea into Galilee.

King James

CHAPTER 5

AFTER this there was a feast of the Jews; and Jesus went up to Jerusalem.

2 Now there is at Jerusalem by the sheep *market* a pool, which is called in the Hebrew tongue Bethesda, having five porches.

3 In these lay a great multitude of impotent folk, of blind, halt, withered, waiting for the moving of the water.

4 For an angel went down at a certain season into the pool, and troubled the water: whosoever then first after the troubling of the water stepped in was made whole of whatsoever disease he had.

5 And a certain man was there, which had an infirmity thirty and eight years.

Amplified

CHAPTER 5

LATER on there was a Jewish festival (feast), for which Jesus went up to Jerusalem.

2 Now there is in Jerusalem a pool near the Sheep Gate. This pool in the Hebrew is called Bethesda, having five porches (alcoves, colonnades, doorways).

3 In these lay a great number of sick folk, some blind, some crippled and some paralyzed (shriveled up), *waiting for the bubbling up of the water.*[r]

5 There was a certain man there who had suffered with a deep-seated *and* lingering disorder for thirty-eight years.

---

r) The best manuscripts omit verse 4, as does the American "Revised" Version (ASV).

Living New Testament

40, 41 When they came out to see Him at the well, they begged Him to stay at their village; and He did, for two days, long enough for many of them to believe in Him after hearing Him.

42 Then they said to the woman, "Now we believe because we have heard Him ourselves, not just because of what you told us. He is indeed the Savior of the world."

43, 44 At the end of the two days' stay He went on into Galilee,[2] for as Jesus used to say, "A prophet is honored everywhere except in his own country!"

45 But the Galileans welcomed Him with open arms, for they had been in Jerusalem at the Passover celebration and had seen some of His miracles.[3]

46, 47 In the course of His journey through Galilee He arrived at the town of Cana, where He had turned the water into wine. While He was there, a man in the city of Capernaum, a government official, whose son was very sick, heard that Jesus had come from Judea and was traveling in Galilee. This man went over to Cana, found Jesus, and begged Him to come to Capernaum with him and heal his son, who was now at death's door.

48 Jesus asked, "Won't any of you believe in Me unless I do more and more miracles?"

49 The official pled, "Sir, please come now before my child dies."

50 Then Jesus told him, "Go back home. Your son is healed!" And the man believed Jesus and started home.

51 While he was on his way, some of his servants met him with the news that all was well—his son had recovered!

52 He asked them when the lad had begun to feel better, and they replied, "Yesterday afternoon at about one o'clock his fever suddenly disappeared!"

53 Then the father realized it was the same moment that Jesus had told him, "Your son is healed." And the officer and his entire household believed that Jesus was the Messiah.

54 This was Jesus' second miracle in Galilee after coming from Judea.

Revised Standard

when the Samaritans came to him, they asked
him to stay with them; and he stayed there
two days. 41And many more believed because
of his word. 42They said to the woman, "It
is no longer because of your words that we
believe, for we have heard for ourselves,
and we know that this is indeed the Savior
of the world."

43 After the two days he departed to
Galilee. 44For Jesus himself testified that
a prophet has no honor in his own country.
45So when he came to Galilee, the Galileans welcomed him, having seen all that he
had done in Jerusalem at the feast, for they
too had gone to the feast.

The healing of the official's son

46 So he came again to Cana in Galilee,
where he had made the water wine. And at
Capernaum there was an official whose son
was ill. 47When he heard that Jesus had
come from Judea to Galilee, he went and
begged him to come down and heal his son,
for he was at the point of death. 48Jesus
therefore said to him, "Unless you see signs
and wonders you will not believe." 49The
official said to him, "Sir, come down before
my child dies." 50Jesus said to him, "Go;
your son will live." The man believed the
word that Jesus spoke to him and went his
way. 51As he was going down, his servants
met him and told him that his son was
living. 52So he asked them the hour when
he began to mend, and they said to him,
"Yesterday at the seventh hour the fever
left him." 53The father knew that was the
hour when Jesus had said to him, "Your
son will live"; and he himself believed, and
all his household. 54This was now the
second sign that Jesus did when he had come
from Judea to Galilee.

CHAPTER 5

Afterwards Jesus returned to Jerusalem for one of the Jewish religious holidays.

2 Inside the city, near the Sheep Gate, was Bethesda Pool, with five covered platforms or porches surrounding it.

3 Crowds of sick folks—lame, blind, or with paralyzed limbs—lay on the platforms (waiting for a certain movement of the water,

4 For an angel of the Lord came from time to time and disturbed the water, and the first person to step down into it afterwards was healed).[1]

5 One of the men lying there had been sick for 38 years.

[2] Apparently to avoid the crowds.
[3] See John 2:23.
[1] Many of the ancient manuscripts omit the material within the parentheses.

Jesus heals on the Sabbath

5 After this there was a feast of the Jews,
and Jesus went up to Jerusalem.

2 Now there is in Jerusalem by the Sheep
Gate a pool, in Hebrew called Bethzatha,[j]
which has five porticoes. 3In these lay a
multitude of invalids, blind, lame, paralyzed.[k] 5One man was there, who had been
ill for thirty-eight years. 6When Jesus saw

[j] Other ancient authorities read *Bethesda*, others *Bethsaida*
[k] Other ancient authorities insert, wholly or in part, *waiting for the moving of the water; 4 for an angel of the Lord went down at certain seasons into the pool, and troubled the water; whoever stepped in first after the troubling of the water was healed of whatever disease he had*

King James

6 When Jesus saw him lie, and knew that he had been now a long time *in that case*, he saith unto him, Wilt thou be made whole?

7 The impotent man answered him, Sir, I have no man, when the water is troubled, to put me into the pool: but while I am coming, another steppeth down before me.

8 Jesus saith unto him, Rise, take up thy bed, and walk.

9 And immediately the man was made whole, and took up his bed, and walked: and on the same day was the sabbath.

10 ¶ The Jews therefore said unto him that was cured, It is the sabbath day: it is not lawful for thee to carry *thy* bed.

11 He answered them, He that made me whole, the same said unto me, Take up thy bed, and walk.

12 Then asked they him, What man is that which said unto thee, Take up thy bed, and walk?

13 And he that was healed wist not who it was: for Jesus had conveyed himself away, a multitude being in *that* place.

14 Afterward Jesus findeth him in the temple, and said unto him, Behold, thou art made whole: sin no more, lest a worse thing come unto thee.

15 The man departed, and told the Jews that it was Jesus, which had made him whole.

16 And therefore did the Jews persecute Jesus, and sought to slay him, because he had done these things on the sabbath day.

17 ¶ But Jesus answered them, My Father worketh hitherto, and I work.

18 Therefore the Jews sought the more to kill him, because he not only had broken the sabbath, but said also that God was his Father, making himself equal with God.

19 Then answered Jesus and said unto them, Verily, verily, I say unto you, The Son can do nothing of himself, but what he seeth the Father do: for what things soever he doeth, these also doeth the Son likewise.

20 For the Father loveth the Son, and sheweth him all things that himself doeth: and he will shew him greater works than these, that ye may marvel.

21 For as the Father raiseth up the dead, and quickeneth *them;* even so the Son quickeneth whom he will.

22 For the Father judgeth no man, but hath committed all judgment unto the Son:

23 That all *men* should honour the Son, even as they honour the Father. He that honoureth not the Son honoureth not the Father which hath sent him.

24 Verily, verily, I say unto you, He that heareth my word, and believeth on him that sent me, hath everlasting life, and shall not come into condemnation; but is passed from death unto life.

Amplified

6 When Jesus noticed him lying there helpless, knowing that he had already been a long time in that condition, He said to him, Do you want to become well? [Are you really in earnest about getting well?]

7 The invalid answered, Sir, I have nobody when the water is moving to put me into the pool; but while I am trying to come myself, somebody else steps down ahead of me.

8 Jesus said to him, Get up; pick up your bed (sleeping pad) and walk!

9 Instantly the man became well *and* recovered his strength and picked up his bed and walked. But that happened on the Sabbath.

10 So the Jews kept saying to the man that had been healed, It is the Sabbath and you have no right to pick up your bed—it is not lawful.

11 He answered them, The [s]Man Who healed me *and* gave me back my strength, He Himself said to me, Pick up your bed and walk!

12 They asked him, Who is the Man Who told you, Pick up your bed and walk?

13 Now the invalid who had been healed did not know Who it was, for Jesus had quietly gone away (had passed on unnoticed), since there was a crowd in the place.

14 Afterward when Jesus found him in the temple, He said to him, See, you are well! Stop sinning, or something worse may happen to you.

15 The man went away and told the Jews that it was Jesus Who had made him well.

16 For this reason the Jews began to persecute (annoy, torment) Jesus, *and sought to kill Him,* because He was doing these things on the Sabbath.

17 But Jesus answered them, My Father has worked [even] until now.—He has never ceased working, He is still working—and I too must be at [divine] work.

18 This made the Jews more determined than ever to kill Him—to make away with Him; because He not only broke (weakened, violated) the Sabbath, but He actually spoke of God as being [in a special sense] His own Father, making Himself equal (putting Himself on a level) with God.

19 So Jesus answered them by saying, I assure you, most solemnly I tell you, the Son is able to do nothing from Himself—of His own accord; but He is able to do only what He sees the Father doing. For whatever the Father does is what the Son does in the same way [in His turn].

20 The Father dearly loves the Son and discloses (shows) to Him everything that He Himself does. And He will disclose to Him—let Him see—greater things yet than these, so that you may marvel *and* be full of wonder *and* astonishment.

21 Just as the Father raises up the dead and gives them life—makes them live on—so the Son also gives life to whomever He wills *and* is pleased to give it.

22 Even the Father judges no one; for He has given all judgment—the last judgment and the whole business of judging—entirely into the hands of the Son;

23 So that all men may give honor (reverence, homage) to the Son, just as they give honor to the Father. [In fact] whoever does not honor the Son, does not honor the Father Who has sent Him.

24 I assure you, most solemnly I tell you, the person whose ears are open to My words—who listens to My message—and believes *and* trusts in *and* clings to *and* relies on Him Who sent Me has (possesses now) eternal life. And he does not come into judgment—does not incur sentence of judgment, will not come under condemnation—but he has already passed over out of death into life.

---

s) Capitalized because of what He is, the spotless Son of God, not what the speaker may have thought He was.

Living New Testament

6 When Jesus saw him and knew how long he had been ill, He asked him, "Would you like to get well?"

7 "I can't," the sick man said, "for I have no one to help me into the pool at the movement of the water. While I am trying to get there, someone else always gets in ahead of me."

8 Jesus told him, "Stand up, roll up your sleeping mat and go on home!"

9 Instantly, the man was healed! He rolled up the mat and began walking! But it was on the Sabbath when this miracle was done.

10 So the Jewish leaders objected. They said to the man who was cured, "You can't work on the Sabbath! It's illegal to carry that sleeping mat!"

11 "The man who healed me told me to," was his reply.

12 "Who said such a thing as that?" they demanded.

13 The man didn't know, Jesus had disappeared into the crowd.

14 But afterwards Jesus found him in the Temple and told him, "Now you are well; don't sin as you did before,[2] or something even worse may happen to you."

15 Then the man went to find the Jewish leaders and told them it was Jesus who had healed him.

16 So they began harassing Jesus as a Sabbath breaker.

17 But Jesus replied, "My Father constantly does good,[3] and I'm following His example."

18 Then the Jewish leaders were all the more eager to kill Him because in addition to disobeying their Sabbath laws, He had spoken of God as His Father, thereby making Himself equal with God.

19 Jesus replied, "The Son can do nothing by Himself. He does only what He sees the Father doing, and in the same way.

20 For the Father loves the Son, and tells Him everything He is doing; and the Son will do far more awesome miracles than this man's healing!

21 He will even raise from the dead anyone He wants to, just as the Father does.

22 And the Father leaves all judgment of sin to His Son,

23 So that everyone will honor the Son, just as they honor the Father. But if you refuse to honor God's Son, whom He sent to you, then you are certainly not honoring the Father.

24 I say emphatically that anyone who listens to My message and believes in God who sent Me has eternal life, and will never be damned for his sins, but has already passed out of death into life.

Revised Standard

him and knew that he had been lying there
a long time, he said to him, "Do you want
to be healed?" 7The sick man answered
him, "Sir, I have no man to put me into the
pool when the water is troubled, and while
I am going another steps down before me."
8Jesus said to him, "Rise, take up your
pallet, and walk." 9And at once the man
was healed, and he took up his pallet and
walked.
Now the day was the sabbath. 10So the
Jews said to the man who was cured, "It is
the sabbath, it is not lawful for you to carry
your pallet." 11But he answered them, "The
man who healed me said to me, 'Take up
your pallet, and walk.'" 12They asked him,
"Who is the man who said to you, 'Take
up your pallet, and walk'?" 13Now the man
who had been healed did not know who it
was, for Jesus had withdrawn, as there was
a crowd in the place. 14Afterward, Jesus
found him in the temple, and said to him,
"See, you are well! Sin no more, that nothing worse befall you." 15The man went
away and told the Jews that it was Jesus
who had healed him. 16And this was why
the Jews persecuted Jesus, because he did
this on the sabbath. 17But Jesus answered
them, "My Father is working still, and I
am working." 18This was why the Jews
sought all the more to kill him, because he
not only broke the sabbath but also called
God his Father, making himself equal with
God.

The Son's witness to the Father

19 Jesus said to them, "Truly, truly, I
say to you, the Son can do nothing of his
own accord, but only what he sees the
Father doing; for whatever he does, that
the Son does likewise. 20For the Father loves
the Son, and shows him all that he himself
is doing; and greater works than these
will he show him, that you may marvel.
21For as the Father raises the dead and
gives them life, so also the Son gives life
to whom he will. 22The Father judges no
one, but has given all judgment to the Son,
23that all may honor the Son, even as they
honor the Father. He who does not honor
the Son does not honor the Father who
sent him. 24Truly, truly, I say to you, he
who hears my word and believes him who
sent me, has eternal life; he does not come
into judgment, but has passed from death
to life.

---

[2] Implied. Literally, "sin no more."
[3] Implied. Literally, "My Father works even until now, and I work."

King James

25 Verily, verily, I say unto you, The hour is coming, and now is, when the dead shall hear the voice of the Son of God: and they that hear shall live.

26 For as the Father hath life in himself; so hath he given to the Son to have life in himself;

27 And hath given him authority to execute judgment also, because he is the Son of man.

28 Marvel not at this: for the hour is coming, in the which all that are in the graves shall hear his voice,

29 And shall come forth; they that have done good, unto the resurrection of life; and they that have done evil, unto the resurrection of damnation.

30 I can of mine own self do nothing: as I hear, I judge: and my judgment is just; because I seek not mine own will, but the will of the Father which hath sent me.

31 If I bear witness of myself, my witness is not true.

32 ¶ There is another that beareth witness of me; and I know that the witness which he witnesseth of me is true.

33 Ye sent unto John, and he bare witness unto the truth.

34 But I receive not testimony from man: but these things I say, that ye might be saved.

35 He was a burning and a shining light: and ye were willing for a season to rejoice in his light.

36 ¶ But I have greater witness than *that* of John: for the works which the Father hath given me to finish, the same works that I do, bear witness of me, that the Father hath sent me.

37 And the Father himself, which hath sent me, hath borne witness of me. Ye have neither heard his voice at any time, nor seen his shape.

38 And ye have not his word abiding in you: for whom he hath sent, him ye believe not.

39 ¶ Search the scriptures; for in them ye think ye have eternal life: and they are they which testify of me.

40 And ye will not come to me, that ye might have life.

41 I receive not honour from men.

42 But I know you, that ye have not the love of God in you.

43 I am come in my Father's name, and ye receive me not: if another shall come in his own name, him ye will receive.

Amplified

25 Believe Me when I assure you, most solemnly I tell you, The time is coming and is here now when the dead shall hear the voice of the Son of God, and those who hear it shall live.

26 For even as the Father has life in Himself *and* is self-existent, so He has given to the Son to have life in Himself *and* be self-existent.

27 And He has given Him authority *and* granted Him power to execute (exercise, practice) judgment, because He is [t]a Son of man [very man].

28 Do not be surprised *and* wonder at this; for the time is coming when all those who are in the tombs shall hear His voice,

29 And they shall come out; those who have practiced doing good [will come out] to the resurrection of [new] life; and those who have done evil will be raised for judgment—raised to meet their sentence. [Dan. 12:2.]

30 I am able to do nothing from Myself—independently, of My own accord; but as I am taught by God *and* as I get His orders. [I decide as I am bidden to decide. As the voice comes to Me, so I give a decision.] Even as I hear, I judge and My judgment is right (just, righteous), because I do not seek *or* consult My own will—I have no desire to do what is pleasing to Myself, My own aim, My own purpose—but only the will *and* pleasure of the Father Who sent Me.

31 If I alone testify in My behalf, My testimony is not valid *and* can not be worth anything.

32 There is Another Who testifies concerning Me and I know *and* am certain that His evidence on My behalf is true and valid.

33 You yourselves have sent an inquiry to John and he has been a witness to the truth.

34 But I do not receive [a mere] human witness— the evidence which I accept on My behalf is not from man. But I simply mention all these things in order that you may be saved (made *and* kept safe *and* sound).

35 John was the lamp that kept on burning and shining [to show you the way], and you were willing for a while to delight (sun) yourselves in his light.

36 But I have as My witness something greater (weightier, higher, better) than that of John; for the works that the Father has appointed Me to accomplish *and* finish, the very same works that I am now doing, are a witness *and* proof that the Father has sent Me.

37 And the Father Who sent Me has Himself testified concerning Me. Not one of you has ever given ears to His voice, or seen His form (His face, what He is like).—You have always been deaf to His voice and blind to the vision of Him.

38 And you have not His word (His thought) living in your hearts, because you do not believe *and* adhere to, *and* trust in, *and* rely on Him Whom He has sent.—That is why you do not keep His message living in you, because you do not believe in the Messenger Whom He has sent.

39 You search *and* investigate *and* pore over the Scriptures diligently, because you suppose *and* trust that you have eternal life through them. And these [very Scriptures] testify about Me!

40 And still you are not willing (but refuse) to come to Me, so that you might have life.

41 I receive not glory from men—I crave no human honor, I look for no mortal fame.

42 But I know you *and* recognize *and* understand that you have not the love of God in you.

43 I have come in My Father's name *and* with His power and you do not receive Me—your hearts are not open to Me, you give Me no welcome. But if another comes in his own name *and* his own power *and* with no other authority but himself, you will receive him *and* give him your approval.

t) Vincent's "Word Studies in The New Testament."

Living New Testament

25 And I solemnly declare that the time is coming, in fact, it is here, when the dead shall hear My voice—the voice of the Son of God—and those who listen shall live.
26 The Father has life in Himself, and has granted His Son to have life in Himself,
27 And to judge the sins of all mankind because He is the Son of Man.
28 Don't be so surprised! Indeed the time is coming when all the dead in their graves shall hear the voice of God's Son,
29 And shall rise again—those who have done good, to eternal life; and those who have continued in evil, to judgment.
30 But I pass no judgment without consulting the Father. I judge as I am told. And My judgment is absolutely fair and just, for it is according to the will of God who sent Me and is not merely My own.
31 When I make claims about Myself they aren't believed,
32, 33 But someone else, yes, John the Baptist,[4] is making these claims for Me too. You have gone out to listen to his preaching, and I can assure you that all he says about Me is true!
34 But the truest witness I have is not from a man, though I have reminded you about John's witness so that you will believe in Me and be saved.
35 John shone brightly for awhile, and you benefitted and rejoiced,
36 But I have a greater witness than John. I refer to the miracles I do; these have been assigned Me by the Father, and they prove that the Father has sent Me.
37 And the Father Himself has also testified about Me, though not appearing to you personally, or speaking to you directly.
38 But you are not listening to Him, for you refuse to believe Me—the one sent to you with God's message.
39 You search the Scriptures, for you believe they give you eternal life. And the Scriptures point to Me!
40 Yet you won't come to Me so that I can give you this life eternal!
41, 42 Your approval or disapproval means nothing to Me, for as I know so well, you don't have God's love within you.
43 I know, because I have come to you representing My Father and you refuse to welcome Me, though you readily enough receive those who aren't sent from Him, but represent only themselves!

[4] Implied. However, most commentators believe the reference is to the witness of His Father. See verse 37.

Revised Standard

25 "Truly, truly, I say to you, the hour
is coming, and now is, when the dead will
hear the voice of the Son of God, and
those who hear will live. 26For as the Father has life in himself, so he has granted
the Son also to have life in himself, 27and
has given him authority to execute judgment, because he is the Son of man. 28Do
not marvel at this; for the hour is coming
when all who are in the tombs will hear
his voice 29and come forth, those who have
done good, to the resurrection of life, and
those who have done evil, to the resurrection of judgment.

The Father's witness to the Son

30 "I can do nothing on my own authority; as I hear, I judge; and my judgment
is just, because I seek not my own will
but the will of him who sent me. 31If I
bear witness to myself, my testimony is
not true; 32there is another who bears witness to me, and I know that the testimony
which he bears to me is true. 33You sent
to John, and he has borne witness to the
truth. 34Not that the testimony which I receive is from man; but I say this that you
may be saved. 35He was a burning and
shining lamp, and you were willing to rejoice for a while in his light. 36But the
testimony which I have is greater than that
of John; for the works which the Father
has granted me to accomplish, these very
works which I am doing, bear me witness
that the Father has sent me. 37And the
Father who sent me has himself borne witness to me. His voice you have never heard,
his form you have never seen; 38and you
do not have his word abiding in you, for
you do not believe him whom he has sent.
39You search the scriptures, because you
think that in them you have eternal life;
and it is they that bear witness to me; 40yet
you refuse to come to me that you may
have life. 41I do not receive glory from
men. 42But I know that you have not the
love of God within you. 43I have come
in my Father's name, and you do not receive me; if another comes in his own
name, him you will receive. 44How can

King James

44 How can ye believe, which receive honour one of another, and seek not the honour that *cometh* from God only?
45 Do not think that I will accuse you to the Father: there is *one* that accuseth you *even* Moses, in whom ye trust.
46 For had ye believed Moses, ye would have believed me: for he wrote of me.
47 But if ye believe not his writings, how shall ye believe my words?

Amplified

44 How is it possible for you to believe—how can you learn to believe—who [are content to seek for and] receive praise *and* honor *and* glory from one another, and do not seek the praise *and* honor *and* glory which come from Him Who alone is God?
45 Put out of your minds the thought *and* do not suppose [as some of you are supposing] that I will accuse you to the Father. There is one who accuses you; it is Moses, the very one on whom you have built your hopes—in whom you trust.
46 For if you believed in *and* relied on Moses, you would believe in *and* rely on Me, for he wrote about Me [personally].
47 But if you do not believe *and* trust his writings, how then will you believe *and* trust My teachings—how shall you cleave to *and* rely on My words?

King James

CHAPTER 6

AFTER these things Jesus went over the sea of Galilee, which is *the sea* of Tiberias.
2 And a great multitude followed him, because they saw his miracles which he did on them that were diseased.
3 And Jesus went up into a mountain, and there he sat with his disciples.
4 And the passover, a feast of the Jews, was nigh.
5 ¶ When Jesus then lifted up *his* eyes, and saw a great company come unto him, he saith unto Philip, Whence shall we buy bread, that these may eat?
6 And this he said to prove him: for he himself knew what he would do.
7 Philip answered him, Two hundred pennyworth of bread is not sufficient for them, that every one of them may take a little.
8 One of his disciples, Andrew, Simon Peter's brother, saith unto him,
9 There is a lad here, which hath five barley loaves, and two small fishes: but what are they among so many?
10 And Jesus said, Make the men sit down. Now there was much grass in the place. So the men sat down, in number about five thousand.
11 And Jesus took the loaves; and when he had given thanks, he distributed to the disciples, and the disciples to them that were set down; and likewise of the fishes as much as they would.
12 When they were filled, he said unto his disciples, Gather up the fragments that remain, that nothing be lost.
13 Therefore they gathered *them* together, and filled twelve baskets with the fragments of the five barley loaves, which remained over and above unto them that had eaten.
14 Then those men, when they had seen the miracle that Jesus did, said, This is of a truth that prophet that should come into the world.

Amplified

CHAPTER 6

AFTER this Jesus went to the farther side of the Sea of Galilee, that is, the Sea of Tiberias.
2 And a great crowd was following Him because they had seen the signs (miracles) which He [continually] performed upon those who were sick.
3 And Jesus walked up the mountain side and sat down there with His disciples.
4 Now the Passover, the feast of the Jews, was approaching.
5 Jesus looked up, then, and seeing that a vast multitude was coming toward Him, He said to Philip, Where are we to buy bread, so that all these people may eat?
6 But He said this to prove (test) him, for He well knew what He was about to do.
7 Philip answered Him, Two hundred pennies' [forty dollars'] worth of bread is not enough that every one may receive even a little.
8 Another of His disciples, Andrew, Simon Peter's brother, said to Him,
9 There is a little boy here, who has [with him] five barley loaves and two small fish; but what are they among so many people?
10 Jesus said, Make all the people recline (sit down). Now the ground [a pasture] was covered with thick grass at the spot, so the men threw themselves down, about five thousand in number.
11 Jesus took the loaves and when He had given thanks He distributed *to the disciples and the disciples* to the reclining people; so also with the small fish, as much as they wanted.
12 When they all had enough, He said to His disciples, Gather up now the fragments—the broken pieces that are left over—so that nothing may be lost *and* wasted.
13 So accordingly they gathered them up, and they filled twelve [u]hand baskets with fragments left over by those who had eaten from the five barley loaves.
14 When the people saw the sign (miracle) that Jesus had performed, they began saying, Surely *and* beyond a doubt this is the prophet who is to come into the world! [Deut. 18:18.]

u) Abbott-Smith.

Living New Testament

44 No wonder you can't believe! For you gladly honor each other, but you don't care about the honor that comes from the only God!

45 Yet it is not I who will accuse you of this to the Father—Moses will! Moses, on whose laws you set your hopes of heaven.

46 For you have refused to believe Moses. He wrote about Me, but you refuse to believe him, so you refuse to believe in Me.

47 And since you don't believe what he wrote, no wonder you don't believe Me either."

Revised Standard

you believe, who receive glory from one another and do not seek the glory that comes from the only God? 45 Do not think that I shall accuse you to the Father; it is Moses who accuses you, on whom you set your hope. 46 If you believed Moses, you would believe me, for he wrote of me. 47 But if you do not believe his writings, how will you believe my words?"

CHAPTER 6

After this, Jesus crossed over the Sea of Galilee (also known as the Sea of Tiberias).

2, 3, 4, 5 And a huge crowd, many of them pilgrims on their way to Jerusalem for the annual Passover celebration[1], were following Him wherever He went, to watch Him heal the sick. So when Jesus went up into the hills and sat down with His disciples around Him, He soon saw a great multitude of people climbing the hill, looking for Him. Turning to Philip He asked, "Philip, where can we buy bread to feed all these people?"

6 (He was testing Philip, for He already knew what He was going to do.)

7 Philip replied, "It would take a fortune[2] to begin to do it!"

8, 9 Then Andrew, Simon Peter's brother, spoke up. "There's a youngster here with five barley loaves and a couple of fish! But what good is that with all this mob?"

10 "Tell everyone to sit down," Jesus ordered. And all of them—the approximate count of the men only was 5,000—sat down on the grassy slopes.

11 Then Jesus took the loaves and gave thanks to God and passed them out to the people. Afterwards He did the same with the fish. And everyone ate until full!

12 "Now gather the scraps," Jesus told His disciples, "so that nothing is wasted."

13 And 12 baskets were filled with the leftovers!

14 When the people realized what a great miracle had happened, they exclaimed, "Surely, He is the Prophet we have been expecting!"

[1] Literally, "Now the Passover, the feast of the Jews, was at hand."
[2] Literally, 200 denarii, a denarii being a full day's wage.

The five thousand fed

6 After this Jesus went to the other side of the Sea of Galilee, which is the Sea of Tiberias. 2 And a multitude followed him, because they saw the signs which he did on those who were diseased. 3 Jesus went up into the hills, and there sat down with his disciples. 4 Now the Passover, the feast of the Jews, was at hand. 5 Lifting up his eyes, then; and seeing that a multitude was coming to him, Jesus said to Philip, "How are we to buy bread, so that these people may eat?" 6 This he said to test him, for he himself knew what he would do. 7 Philip answered him, "Two hundred denarii[l] would not buy enough bread for each of them to get a little." 8 One of his disciples, Andrew, Simon Peter's brother, said to him, 9 "There is a lad here who has five barley loaves and two fish; but what are they among so many?" 10 Jesus said, "Make the people sit down." Now there was much grass in the place; so the men sat down, in number about five thousand. 11 Jesus then took the loaves, and when he had given thanks, he distributed them to those who were seated; so also the fish, as much as they wanted. 12 And when they had eaten their fill, he told his disciples, "Gather up the fragments left over, that nothing may be lost." 13 So they gathered them up and filled twelve baskets with fragments from the five barley loaves, left by those who had eaten. 14 When the people saw the sign which he had done, they said, "This is indeed the prophet who is to come into the world!"

[l] The denarius was worth about twenty cents

King James

15 ¶ When Jesus therefore perceived that they would come and take him by force, to make him a king, he departed again into a mountain himself alone.

16 And when even was *now* come, his disciples went down unto the sea,

17 And entered into a ship, and went over the sea toward Capernaum. And it was now dark, and Jesus was not come to them.

18 And the sea arose by reason of a great wind that blew.

19 So when they had rowed about five and twenty or thirty furlongs, they see Jesus walking on the sea, and drawing nigh unto the ship: and they were afraid.

20 But he saith unto them, It is I; be not afraid.

21 Then they willingly received him into the ship: and immediately the ship was at the land whither they went.

22 ¶ The day following, when the people which stood on the other side of the sea saw that there was none other boat there, save that one whereinto his disciples were entered, and that Jesus went not with his disciples into the boat, but *that* his disciples were gone away alone;

23 (Howbeit there came other boats from Tiberias nigh unto the place where they did eat bread, after that the Lord had given thanks:)

24 When the people therefore saw that Jesus was not there, neither his disciples, they also took shipping, and came to Capernaum, seeking for Jesus.

25 And when they had found him on the other side of the sea, they said unto him, Rabbi, when camest thou hither?

26 Jesus answered them and said, Verily, verily, I say unto you, Ye seek me, not because ye saw the miracles, but because ye did eat of the loaves, and were filled.

27 Labour not for the meat which perisheth, but for that meat which endureth unto everlasting life, which the Son of man shall give unto you: for him hath God the Father sealed.

28 Then said they unto him, What shall we do, that we might work the works of God?

29 Jesus answered and said unto them, This is the work of God, that ye believe on him whom he hath sent.

30 They said therefore unto him, What sign shewest thou then, that we may see, and believe thee? what dost thou work?

31 Our fathers did eat manna in the desert; as it is written, He gave them bread from heaven to eat.

32 Then Jesus said unto them, Verily, verily, I say unto you, Moses gave you not that bread from heaven; but my Father giveth you the true bread from heaven.

33 For the bread of God is he which cometh down from heaven, and giveth life unto the world.

34 Then said they unto him, Lord, evermore give us this bread.

Amplified

15 Then Jesus, knowing that they meant to come and seize Him that they might make Him king, withdrew again to the hillside, Himself alone.

16 When evening came, His disciples went down to the sea.

17 And they took a boat and were going across the sea to Capernaum. It was now dark, and still Jesus had not [yet] come back to them.

18 Meanwhile the sea was getting rough *and* rising high because of a great *and* violent wind that was blowing.

19 [However,] when they had rowed three or four miles they saw Jesus walking on the sea and approaching the boat. And they were afraid—terrified.

20 But Jesus said to them, It is I; be not afraid!—I AM; stop being frightened! [Exod. 3:14.]

21 Then they were quite willing *and* glad for Him to come into the boat. And now the boat went at once to the land they steered for—and immediately they reached the shore toward which they had been [slowly] making.

22 The next day the crowd [that still remained] standing on the other side of the sea, realized that there had been only one small boat there, and that Jesus had not gone into it with His disciples, but that His disciples had gone away by themselves.

23 But now some other boats from Tiberias had come in near the place where they ate the bread after the Lord had given thanks.

24 So the people, finding that neither Jesus nor His disciples were there, themselves got into the small boats and came to Capernaum looking for Jesus.

25 And when they found Him on the other side of the lake, they said to Him, Rabbi! When did You come here?

26 Jesus answered them, I assure you, most solemnly I tell you, you have been searching for Me not because you saw the miracles *and* signs, but because you were fed with the loaves and were filled *and* satisfied.

27 Stop toiling *and* doing *and* producing for the food that perishes *and* decomposes in the using; but strive *and* work *and* produce rather for the lasting food which endures continually unto life eternal. The Son of man will give (furnish) you that, for God the Father has authorized *and* certified Him *and* put His seal of endorsement upon Him.

28 They then said, What are we to do that we may [habitually] be working the works of God?—What are we to do to carry out what God requires?

29 Jesus replied, This is the work (service) that God asks of you, that you believe in the One Whom He has sent—that you cleave to, trust, rely on and have faith in His Messenger.

30 Therefore they said to Him, What sign (miracle, wonderwork) will [v]You perform then, so that we may see it and believe *and* rely on *and* adhere to You?—What [supernatural] work have You to show what You can do?

31 Our forefathers ate the manna in the wilderness. As the Scripture says, He gave them bread out of heaven to eat. [Exod. 16:15; Ps 78:24.]

32 Jesus then said to them, I assure you, I most solemnly tell you, Moses did not give you the bread from heaven—what Moses gave you was not the Bread from heaven—but it is My Father Who gives you the true, heavenly Bread.

33 For the Bread of God is He Who comes down out of heaven and gives life to the world.

34 Then they said to Him, Lord, give us this bread always—all the time!

---

v) Capitalized because of what He is, the spotless Son of God, not what the speaker may have thought He was.

Living New Testament

15 Jesus saw that they were ready to take Him by force and make Him their king, so He went higher into the mountains alone.

16 That evening His disciples went down to the shore to wait for Him.

17 But as darkness fell and Jesus still hadn't come back, they got into the boat and headed out across the lake toward Capernaum.

18, 19 But soon a gale swept down upon them as they rowed, and the sea grew very rough. They were three or four miles out when suddenly they saw Jesus walking toward the boat! They were terrified,

20 But He called out to them and told them not to be afraid.

21 Then they were willing to let Him in, and immediately the boat was where they were going![3]

22, 23 The next morning, back across the lake, crowds began gathering on the shore, [waiting to see Jesus[4]]. For they knew that He and His disciples had come over together and that the disciples had gone off in their boat, leaving Him behind. Several small boats from Tiberias were nearby,

24 So when the people saw that Jesus wasn't there, nor His disciples, they got into the boats and went across to Capernaum to look for Him.

25 When they arrived and found Him, they said, "Sir, how did You get here?"

26 Jesus replied, "The truth of the matter is that you want to be with Me because I fed you, not because you believe in Me.

27 But you shouldn't be so concerned about perishable things like food. No, spend your energy seeking the eternal life that I the man from Heaven[5] can give you. For God the Father has sent Me for this very purpose."

28 They replied, "What should we do to satisfy God?"

29 Jesus told them, "This is the will of God, that you believe in the one He has sent."

30, 31 They replied, "You must show us more miracles if You want us to believe You are the Messiah. Give us free bread every day, like our fathers had while they journeyed through the wilderness! As the Scriptures say, 'Moses gave them bread from heaven.' "

32 Jesus said, "Moses didn't give it to them. My Father did.[6] And now He offers you true Bread from heaven.

33 The true Bread is a Person—the one sent by God from heaven, and He gives life to the world."

34 "Sir," they said, "give us that bread every day of our lives!"

[3] Literally, "and straightway the boat was at the land. . . ."
[4] Implied.
[5] Literally, "the Son of man."
[6] Implied.

Revised Standard

Jesus walks on the sea

15 Perceiving then that they were about
to come and take him by force to make him
king, Jesus withdrew again to the hills by
himself.
16 When evening came, his disciples
went down to the sea, 17 got into a boat,
and started across the sea to Capernaum.
It was now dark, and Jesus had not yet
come to them. 18 The sea rose because a
strong wind was blowing. 19 When they had
rowed about three or four miles,[m] they
saw Jesus walking on the sea and drawing
near to the boat. They were frightened,
20 but he said to them, "It is I; do not be
afraid." 21 Then they were glad to take
him into the boat, and immediately the
boat was at the land to which they were
going.

Jesus the bread of life

22 On the next day the people who
remained on the other side of the sea
saw that there had been only one boat
there, and that Jesus had not entered the
boat with his disciples, but that his disciples had gone away alone. 23 However,
boats from Tiberias came near the place
where they ate the bread after the Lord
had given thanks. 24 So when the people saw
that Jesus was not there, nor his disciples,
they themselves got into the boats and went
to Capernaum, seeking Jesus.
25 When they found him on the other
side of the sea, they said to him, "Rabbi,
when did you come here?" 26 Jesus answered them, "Truly, truly, I say to you,
you seek me, not because you saw signs,
but because you ate your fill of the loaves.
27 Do not labor for the food which perishes,
but for the food which endures to eternal
life, which the Son of man will give to
you; for on him has God the Father set
his seal." 28 Then they said to him, "What
must we do, to be doing the works of
God?" 29 Jesus answered them, "This is the
work of God, that you believe in him
whom he has sent." 30 So they said to him,
"Then what sign do you do, that we may
see, and believe you? What work do you
perform? 31 Our fathers ate the manna in
the wilderness; as it is written, 'He gave
them bread from heaven to eat.' " 32 Jesus
then said to them, "Truly, truly, I say to
you, it was not Moses who gave you the
bread from heaven; my Father gives you
the true bread from heaven. 33 For the
bread of God is that which comes down
from heaven, and gives life to the world."
34 They said to him, "Lord, give us this
bread always."

[m] Greek *twenty-five or thirty stadia*

King James

35 And Jesus said unto them, I am the bread of life: he that cometh to me shall never hunger; and he that believeth on me shall never thirst.

36 But I said unto you, That ye also have seen me, and believe not.

37 All that the Father giveth me shall come to me; and him that cometh to me I will in no wise cast out.

38 For I came down from heaven, not to do mine own will, but the will of him that sent me.

39 And this is the Father's will which hath sent me, that of all which he hath given me I should lose nothing, but should raise it up again at the last day.

40 And this is the will of him that sent me, that every one which seeth the Son, and believeth on him, may have everlasting life: and I will raise him up at the last day.

41 The Jews then murmured at him, because he said, I am the bread which came down from heaven.

42 And they said, Is not this Jesus, the son of Joseph, whose father and mother we know? how is it then that he saith, I came down from heaven?

43 Jesus therefore answered and said unto them, Murmur not among yourselves.

44 No man can come to me, except the Father which hath sent me draw him: and I will raise him up at the last day.

45 It is written in the prophets, And they shall be all taught of God. Every man therefore that hath heard, and hath learned of the Father, cometh unto me.

46 Not that any man hath seen the Father, save he which is of God, he hath seen the Father.

47 Verily, verily, I say unto you, He that believeth on me hath everlasting life.

48 I am that bread of life.

49 Your fathers did eat manna in the wilderness, and are dead.

50 This is the bread which cometh down from heaven, that a man may eat thereof, and not die.

51 I am the living bread which came down from heaven: if any man eat of this bread, he shall live for ever: and the bread that I will give is my flesh, which I will give for the life of the world.

52 The Jews therefore strove among themselves, saying, How can this man give us *his* flesh to eat?

53 Then Jesus said unto them, Verily, verily, I say unto you, Except ye eat the flesh of the Son of man, and drink his blood, ye have no life in you.

54 Whoso eateth my flesh, and drinketh my blood, hath eternal life; and I will raise him up at the last day.

55 For my flesh is meat indeed, and my blood is drink indeed.

56 He that eateth my flesh, and drinketh my blood, dwelleth in me, and I in him.

Amplified

35 Jesus replied, I am the Bread of Life. He who comes to Me will never be hungry and he who believes on *and* cleaves to *and* trusts in *and* relies on Me will never thirst any more—at any time.

36 But [as] I told you, Although you have seen *Me*, still you do not believe *and* trust *and* have faith.

37 All whom My Father has given (entrusted) to Me will come to Me; and him who comes to Me I will most certainly not cast out—I will never, no never reject one of them who comes to Me.

38 For I have come down from heaven, not to do My own will *and* purpose; but to do the will *and* purpose of Him Who sent Me.

39 And this is the will of Him Who sent Me, that I should not lose any of all that He has given Me; but that I should give new life *and* raise [them all] up at the last day.

40 For this is My Father's will *and* His purpose, that every one who sees the Son and believes *and* cleaves to *and* trusts *and* relies on Him should have eternal life, and I will raise him up [from the dead] at the last day.

41 Now the Jews murmured *and* found fault *and* grumbled about Jesus because He said, I am [Myself] the Bread which came down from heaven.

42 They kept asking, Is not this Jesus, the [w]Son of Joseph, Whose father and mother we know? How then can He say, I have come down from heaven?

43 So Jesus answered them, Stop grumbling *and* saying things against Me to one another.

44 No one is able to come to Me unless the Father Who sent Me attracts *and* draws him *and* gives him the desire to come to Me; and [then] I will raise him [from the dead] at the last day.

45 It is written in the book of the prophets, And they shall all be taught of God—have Him in person for their teacher. Every one, who has listened and learned from the Father, comes to Me. [Isa. 54:13.]

46 Which does not imply that any one has seen the Father—not that any one has ever seen Him—except He [Who was with the Father] Who comes from God. He [alone] has seen the Father.

47 I assure you, I most solemnly tell you, he who believes *in Me*—who adheres to, trusts in, relies on and has faith in Me—has (now possesses) eternal life.

48 I am the Bread of life—that gives life, the Living Bread.

49 Your forefathers ate the manna in the wilderness, and [yet] they died.

50 [But] this is the Bread that comes down from heaven, so that (any) one may eat of it and never die.

51 I [Myself] am this Living Bread which came down from heaven. If any one eats of this Bread, he will live forever; and also the Bread that I shall give for the life of the world is My flesh (body).

52 Then the Jews angrily contended with one another saying, How is He able to give us His flesh to eat?

53 And Jesus said to them, I assure you, most solemnly I tell you, you cannot have any life in yourselves unless you eat the flesh of the Son of man and drink His blood—unless you appropriate His life and [the saving merit of] His blood.

54 He who feeds on My flesh and drinks My blood has (possesses now) eternal life; and I will raise him up [from the dead] on the last day.

55 For My flesh is true *and* genuine food; and My blood is true *and* genuine drink.

56 He who feeds on My flesh and drinks My blood dwells continually in Me, and I [in like manner dwell continually] in him.

w) Capitalized because of what He is, the spotless Son of God, not what the speaker may have thought He was.

Living New Testament

35 Jesus replied, "I am the Bread of life. No one coming to Me will ever be hungry again. Those believing in Me will never thirst.

36 But the trouble is, as I have told you before, you haven't believed even though you have seen Me.

37 But some will come to Me—those the Father has given Me—and I will never, never reject them.

38 For I have come here from heaven to do the will of God who sent Me, not to have My own way.

39 And this is the will of God, that I should not lose even one of all those He has given Me, but that I should raise them to eternal life at the Last Day.

40 For it is My Father's will that everyone who sees His Son and believes on Him should have eternal life—that I should raise him at the Last Day."

41 Then the Jews began to murmur against Him because He claimed to be the Bread from heaven.

42 "What?" they exclaimed. "Why, He is merely Jesus the son of Joseph, whose father and mother we know. What is this He is saying, that He came down from heaven?"

43 But Jesus replied, "Don't murmur among yourselves about My saying that.

44 For no one can come to Me unless the Father who sent Me draws him to Me, and at the Last Day I will bring all such back to life.

45 As it is written in the Scriptures, 'They shall all be taught of God.' Those the Father speaks to, who learn the truth from Him, will be attracted to Me.

46 (Not that anyone actually sees the Father, for only I have seen Him.)

47 How earnestly I tell you this—anyone who believes in Me, already has eternal life!

48 Yes, I am the Bread of Life!

49 There was no real life[7] in that bread from the skies, which was given to your fathers in the wilderness, for they all died.

50, 51 But there is such a thing as Bread from heaven giving eternal life to everyone who eats it. And I am that Living Bread that came down out of heaven. Anyone eating this Bread shall live forever; My flesh is this Bread, given to redeem humanity."

52 Then the Jews began arguing with each other about what He meant. "How can this man give us His flesh to eat?" they asked.

53 So Jesus said it again, "With all the earnestness I possess I tell you this: Unless you eat the flesh of the Man of Glory[8] and drink His blood, you cannot have eternal life within you.

54 But anyone who does eat My flesh and drink My blood has eternal life, and I will raise him at the Last Day.

55 For My flesh is the true food, and My blood is the true drink.

56 Everyone who eats My flesh and drinks My blood is in Me, and I in him.

Revised Standard

35 Jesus said to them, "I am the bread
of life; he who comes to me shall not
hunger, and he who believes in me shall
never thirst. [36]But I said to you that you
have seen me and yet do not believe. [37]All
that the Father gives me will come to me;
and him who comes to me I will not cast
out. [38]For I have come down from heaven,
not to do my own will, but the will of him
who sent me; [39]and this is the will of him
who sent me, that I should lose nothing
of all that he has given me, but raise it up
at the last day. [40]For this is the will of my
Father, that every one who sees the Son
and believes in him should have eternal
life; and I will raise him up at the last day."

The Jews dispute Jesus' claim

41 The Jews then murmured at him,
because he said, "I am the bread which
came down from heaven." [42]They said, "Is
not this Jesus, the son of Joseph, whose
father and mother we know? How does he
now say, 'I have come down from heav-
en'?" [43]Jesus answered them, "Do not murmur among yourselves. [44] No one can come
to me unless the Father who sent me draws
him; and I will raise him up at the last
day. [45]It is written in the prophets, 'And
they shall all be taught by God.' Every one
who has heard and learned from the Father comes to me. [46]Not that any one
has seen the Father except him who is
from God; he has seen the Father. [47]Truly,
truly, I say to you, he who believes has
eternal life. [48]I am the bread of life. [49]Your
fathers ate the manna in the wilderness,
and they died. [50]This is the bread which
comes down from heaven, that a man may
eat of it and not die. [51]I am the living
bread which came down from heaven;
if any one eats of this bread, he will live
for ever; and the bread which I shall give
for the life of the world is my flesh."

52 The Jews then disputed among themselves, saying, "How can this man give us
his flesh to eat?" [53]So Jesus said to them,
"Truly, truly, I say to you, unless you eat
the flesh of the Son of man and drink his
blood, you have no life in you; [54]he who
eats my flesh and drinks my blood has
eternal life, and I will raise him up at the
last day. [55]For my flesh is food indeed,
and my blood is drink indeed. [56]He who
eats my flesh and drinks my blood abides
in me, and I in him. [57]As the living Father

[7] Implied.
[8] Implied. Literally, "Son of man."

King James

57 As the living Father hath sent me,
and I live by the Father: so he that eateth
me, even he shall live by me.
58 This is that bread which came down
from heaven: not as your fathers did eat
manna, and are dead: he that eateth of this
bread shall live for ever.
59 These things said he in the synagogue,
as he taught in Capernaum.
60 Many therefore of his disciples, when
they had heard *this*, said, This is an hard
saying; who can hear it?
61 When Jesus knew in himself that his
disciples murmured at it, he said unto them,
Doth this offend you?
62 *What* and if ye shall see the Son of
man ascend up where he was before?
63 It is the spirit that quickeneth; the
flesh profiteth nothing: the words that I
speak unto you, *they* are spirit, and *they* are
life.
64 But there are some of you that believe
not. For Jesus knew from the beginning who
they were that believed not, and who should
betray him.
65 And he said, Therefore said I unto
you, that no man can come unto me, except
it were given unto him of my Father.
66 ¶ From that *time* many of his disciples went back, and walked no more with
him.
67 Then said Jesus unto the twelve, Will
ye also go away?
68 Then Simon Peter answered him,
Lord, to whom shall we go? thou hast the
words of eternal life.
69 And we believe and are sure that
thou art that Christ, the Son of the living
God.
70 Jesus answered them, Have not I chosen you twelve, and one of you is a devil?
71 He spake of Judas Iscariot *the son* of
Simon: for he it was that should betray
him, being one of the twelve.

Amplified

57 Just as the living Father sent Me, and I live by
(through, because of) the Father, even so whoever continues to feed on Me—who takes Me for his food *and* is
nourished by Me—shall [in his turn] live through *and*
because of Me.
58 This is the Bread which came down from heaven. It
is not like the manna which our forefathers ate and yet
died. He who takes this Bread for his food shall live
forever.
59 He said these things in a synagogue while He was
teaching at Capernaum.
60 When His disciples heard this, many of them said,
This is a hard *and* difficult *and* strange saying—an offensive and unbearable message. Who can stand to hear
it?—Who can be expected to listen to such teaching?
61 But Jesus, knowing in Himself that His disciples
were complaining *and* protesting *and* grumbling about it,
said to them: Is this a stumbling block *and* an offense to
you?—Does this upset and displease and shock and scan-
dalize you?
62 What then [will be your reaction] if you should see
the Son of man ascending to the place where He was
before?
63 It is the Spirit that gives life—He is the Life-giver;
the flesh conveys no benefit whatever—there is no profit in
it. The words (truths) that I have been speaking to you
are spirit and life.
64 But [still] some of you fail to believe *and* trust *and*
have faith. For Jesus knew from the first who did not
believe *and* had no faith, and who would betray Him *and*
be false to Him.
65 And He said, This is why I told you that no one can
come to Me unless it is granted him—unless he is enabled
to do so—by the Father.
66 After this many of His disciples drew back—
returned to their old associations—and no longer accompanied Him.
67 Jesus said to the twelve, Will you also go away?
And do you too desire to leave Me?
68 Simon Peter answered, Lord, to whom shall we go?
You have the words (the message) of eternal life.
69 And we have learned to believe *and* trust; and
[more,] we have come to know [surely] that You are the
Christ, the Anointed One, the Son of the living God.
70 Jesus answered them, Did I not choose you, the
twelve? And [even] of you one is a devil—of the evil one
and a false accuser.
71 He was speaking of Judas, the son of Simon Iscariot, for he was about to betray Him, [although] he was one
of the twelve.

CHAPTER 7

AFTER these things Jesus walked in
Galilee: for he would not walk in
Jewry, because the Jews sought to kill him.
2 Now the Jews' feast of tabernacles was
at hand.
3 His brethren therefore said unto him,
Depart hence, and go into Judæa, that thy
disciples also may see the works that thou
doest.

CHAPTER 7

AFTER this Jesus went from place to place in Galilee;
for He would not travel in Judea, because the Jews
sought to kill Him.
2 Now the Jewish Feast of Tabernacles was drawing
near.
3 So His brothers said to Him, Leave here and go into
Judea, so that [x]Your disciples [there] may also see the
works that You do. [This is no place for You.]

---

x) Capitalized because of what He is, the spotless Son of God, not what the speaker may have thought He was.

Living New Testament

57 I live by the power of the living Father who sent Me, and in the same way those who partake of Me shall live because of Me!

58 I am the true Bread from heaven; and anyone who eats this Bread shall live forever, and not die as your fathers did—though they ate bread from heaven."

59 (He preached this sermon in the synagogue in Capernaum.

60 Even His disciples said, "This is very hard to understand. Who can tell what He means?"

61 Jesus knew within Himself that His disciples were complaining and said to them, "Does *this* offend you?

62 Then what will you think if you see Me, the Son of Mankind, return to heaven again?

63 Only the Holy Spirit gives eternal life.[9] Those born only once with physical birth[10] will never receive this gift. But now I have told you how to get this true spiritual life.

64 But some of you don't believe Me." (For Jesus knew from the beginning who didn't believe, and knew the one who would betray Him.)

65 And He remarked, "That is what I meant when I said that no one can come to Me unless the Father attracts him to Me."

66 At this point many of His disciples turned away and deserted Him.

67 Then Jesus turned to the Twelve and asked, "Are you going too?"

68 Simon Peter replied, "Master, to whom shall we go? You alone have the words that give eternal life,

69 And we believe them and know You are the holy Son of God."

70 Then Jesus said, "I chose the twelve of you, and one is a devil."

71 He was speaking of Judas, son of Simon Iscariot, one of the Twelve, who would betray Him.

Revised Standard

sent me, and I live because of the Father,
so he who eats me will live because of
me. 58 This is the bread which came down
from heaven, not such as the fathers ate
and died; he who eats this bread will live
for ever." 59 This he said in the synagogue,
as he taught at Capernaum.

The questioning disciples

60 Many of his disciples, when they
heard it, said, "This is a hard saying; who
can listen to it?" 61 But Jesus, knowing in
himself that his disciples murmured at it,
said to them, "Do you take offense at this?
62 Then what if you were to see the Son
of man ascending where he was before?
63 It is the spirit that gives life, the flesh is
of no avail; the words that I have spoken
to you are spirit and life. 64 But there are
some of you that do not believe." For
Jesus knew from the first who those were
that did not believe, and who it was that
should betray him. 65 And he said, "This
is why I told you that no one can come
to me unless it is granted him by the Father."

Peter's great affirmation

66 After this many of his disciples drew
back and no longer went about with him.
67 Jesus said to the twelve, "Will you also
go away?" 68 Simon Peter answered him,
"Lord, to whom shall we go? You have
the words of eternal life; 69 and we have
believed, and have come to know, that
you are the Holy One of God." 70 Jesus
answered them, "Did I not choose you,
the twelve, and one of you is a devil?"
71 He spoke of Judas the son of Simon
Iscariot, for he, one of the twelve, was to
betray him.

CHAPTER 7

After this Jesus went to Galilee, going from village to village, for he wanted to stay out of Judea where the Jewish leaders were plotting His death.

2 But soon it was time for the Tabernacle Ceremonies, one of the annual Jewish holidays,

3 And Jesus' brothers urged Him to go to Judea for the celebration. "Go where more people can see your miracles!" they scoffed.

[9] Literally, "It is the Spirit who quickens."
[10] See John 1:13. Literally, "the flesh profits nothing."

Jesus at the feast of Tabernacles

7 After this Jesus went about in Galilee;
he would not go about in Judea, because
the Jews[n] sought to kill him. 2 Now the
Jews' feast of Tabernacles was at hand.
3 So his brothers said to him, "Leave here
and go to Judea, that your disciples may
see the works you are doing. 4 For no man

[n] Or *Judeans*

King James

4 For *there is* no man *that* doeth any thing in secret, and he himself seeketh to be known openly. If thou do these things, shew thyself to the world.

5 For neither did his brethren believe in him.

6 Then Jesus said unto them, My time is not yet come: but your time is alway ready.

7 The world cannot hate you; but me it hateth, because I testify of it, that the works thereof are evil.

8. Go ye up unto this feast: I go not up yet unto this feast; for my time is not yet full come.

9 When he had said these words unto them, he abode *still* in Galilee.

10 ¶ But when his brethren were gone up, then went he also up unto the feast, not openly, but as it were in secret.

11 Then the Jews sought him at the feast, and said, Where is he?

12 And there was much murmuring among the people concerning him: for some said, He is a good man: others said, Nay; but he deceiveth the people.

13 Howbeit no man spake openly of him for fear of the Jews.

14 ¶ Now about the midst of the feast Jesus went up into the temple, and taught.

15 And the Jews marvelled, saying, How knoweth this man letters, having never learned?

16 Jesus answered them, and said, My doctrine is not mine, but his that sent me.

17 If any man will do his will, he shall know of the doctrine, whether it be of God, or *whether* I speak of myself.

18 He that speaketh of himself seeketh his own glory: but he that seeketh his glory that sent him, the same is true, and no unrighteousness is in him.

19 Did not Moses give you the law, and *yet* none of you keepeth the law? Why go ye about to kill me?

20 The people answered and said, Thou hast a devil: who goeth about to kill thee?

21 Jesus answered and said unto them, I have done one work, and ye all marvel.

22 Moses therefore gave unto you circumcision; (not because it is of Moses, but of the fathers;) and ye on the sabbath day circumcise a man.

23 If a man on the sabbath day receive circumcision, that the law of Moses should not be broken; are ye angry at me, because I have made a man every whit whole on the sabbath day?

24 Judge not according to the appearance, but judge righteous judgment.

Amplified

4 For no one does anything in secret, when he wishes to be conspicuous *and* secure publicity. If you [must] do these things—if [x]You must act like this—show Yourself openly *and* make Yourself known to the world!

5 For His brothers did not believe in *or* adhere to *or* trust in *or* rely on Him either.

6 Whereupon Jesus said to them, My time (opportunity) has not come yet; but any time is suitable for you *and* your opportunity is ready any time—is always here.

7 The world cannot [be expected to] hate you, but it does hate Me, because I denounce it for its wicked works *and* reveal that its doings are evil.

8 Go to the feast yourselves. I am not [yet] going up to the festival, because My time is not ripe—My term is not yet completed, it is not time for Me to go.

9 Having said these things to them, He stayed behind in Galilee.

10 But afterward, when His brothers had gone up to the feast, He went up also; not publicly, [not with a caravan] but by Himself quietly *and* as if He did not wish to be observed.

11 Therefore the Jews kept looking for Him at the feast and asking, Where can He be?—Where is that Fellow?

12 And there was among the mass of the people much whispered discussion *and* hot disputing about Him. Some were saying, He is good!—He is a good man! Others said, No, He misleads *and* deceives the people—gives them false ideas!

13 But no one dared speak out boldly about Him for fear of [the leaders of] the Jews.

14 When the feast was already half over, Jesus went up into the temple [y]court and began to teach.

15 The Jews were astonished. They said, How is it that this Man has learning—is so versed in the sacred Scriptures and in theology—when He has never studied?

16 Jesus answered them by saying, My teaching is not My own, but His Who sent Me.

17 If any man desires to do His will (God's pleasure) he will know—have the needed illumination to recognize, can tell for himself—whether the teaching is from God, or whether I am speaking from Myself *and* of My own accord *and* on My own authority.

18 He who speaks on his own authority seeks to win honor for himself—he whose teaching originates with himself seeks his own glory. But he who seeks the glory *and* is eager for the honor of him who sent him, he is true; and there is no unrighteousness *or* falsehood *or* deception in him.

19 Did not Moses give you the Law? And yet not one of you keeps the Law. [If that is the truth,] why do you seek to kill Me [for not keeping it]?

20 The crowd answered Him, You are possessed of a demon!—You are raving! Who seeks to kill You?

21 Jesus answered them, I did one work and you all were astounded. [John 5:1-9.]

22 Now, Moses established circumcision among you, though it did not originate with Moses but with previous patriarchs, and you circumcise a person [even] on the Sabbath day.

23 If to avoid breaking the Law of Moses a person undergoes circumcision on the Sabbath day, have you any cause to be angry with (indignant with, bitter against) Me for making a man's whole body well on the Sabbath?

24 Be honest in your judgment *and* do not decide at a glance—superficially *and* by appearances; but judge fairly *and* righteously.

---

x) Capitalized because of what He is, the spotless Son of God, not what the speaker may have thought He was.
y) Trench.

Living New Testament

4 "You can't be famous when you hide like this! If you're so great, prove it to the world!"

5 For even His brothers didn't believe in Him.

6 Jesus replied, "It is not the right time for Me to go now. But you can go anytime and it will make no difference,

7 For the world can't hate you; but it does hate Me, because I accuse it of sin and evil.

8 You go on, and I'll come later[1] when it is the right time."

9 So He remained in Galilee.

10 But after His brothers had left for the celebration, then He went too, though secretly, staying out of the public eye.

11 The Jewish leaders tried to find Him at the celebration and kept asking if anyone had seen Him.

12 There was a lot of discussion about Him among the crowds. Some said, "He's a wonderful man," while others said, "No, he's duping the public."

13 But no one had the courage to speak out for Him in public for fear of reprisals from the Jewish leaders.

14 Then, midway through the festival, Jesus went up to the Temple and preached openly.

15 The Jewish leaders were surprised when they heard Him. "How can he know so much when he's never been to our schools?" they asked.

16 So Jesus told them, "I'm not teaching you My own thoughts, but those of God who sent Me.

17 If any of you really determines to do God's will, then you will certainly know whether My teaching is from God or is merely My own.

18 Anyone presenting his own ideas is looking for praise for himself, but anyone seeking to honor the one who sent him is a good and true person.

19 None of *you* obeys the laws of Moses! So why pick on *Me* for breaking them? Why kill *Me* for this?"

20 The crowd replied, "You're out of your mind! Who's trying to kill you?"

21, 22, 23 Jesus replied, "I worked on the Sabbath by healing a man, and you were surprised. But you work on the Sabbath, too, whenever you obey Moses' law of circumcision (actually, however, this tradition of circumcision is older than the Mosaic law); for if the correct time for circumcising your children falls on the Sabbath, you go ahead and do it, as you should. So why should I be condemned for making a man completely well on the Sabbath?

24 Think this through and you will see that I am right."

[1] Literally, "I go not up (yet) unto this feast." The word "yet" is included in the text of many ancient manuscripts.

Revised Standard

works in secret if he seeks to be known
openly. If you do these things, show yourself to the world." [5]For even his brothers
did not believe in him. [6]Jesus said to them,
"My time has not yet come, but your time
is always here. [7]The world cannot hate
you, but it hates me because I testify of
it that its works are evil. [8]Go to the feast
yourselves; I am not[o] going up to this
feast, for my time has not yet fully come."
[9]So saying, he remained in Galilee.

10 But after his brothers had gone up to
the feast, then he also went up, not publicly but in private. [11]The Jews were looking for him at the feast, and saying, "Where
is he?" [12]And there was much muttering
about him among the people. While some
said, "He is a good man," others said, "No,
he is leading the people astray." [13]Yet for
fear of the Jews no one spoke openly of
him.

Jesus teaches in the temple

14 About the middle of the feast Jesus
went up into the temple and taught. [15]The
Jews marveled at it, saying, "How is it
that this man has learning,[p] when he has
never studied?" [16]So Jesus answered them,
"My teaching is not mine, but his who
sent me; [17]if any man's will is to do his
will, he shall know whether the teaching
is from God or whether I am speaking on
my own authority. [18]He who speaks on
his own authority seeks his own glory; but
he who seeks the glory of him who sent
him is true, and in him there is no falsehood. [19]Did not Moses give you the law?
Yet none of you keeps the law. Why do
you seek to kill me?" [20]The people answered, "You have a demon! Who is seeking to kill you?" [21]Jesus answered them,
"I did one deed, and you all marvel at
it. [22]Moses gave you circumcision (not that
it is from Moses, but from the fathers),
and you circumcise a man upon the sabbath. [23]If on the sabbath a man receives
circumcision, so that the law of Moses may
not be broken, are you angry with me because on the sabbath I made a man's whole
body well? [24]Do not judge by appearances,
but judge with right judgment."

[o] Other ancient authorities add *yet*
[p] Or *this man knows his letters*

King James

25 Then said some of them of Jerusalem, Is not this he, whom they seek to kill?

26 But, lo, he speaketh boldly, and they say nothing unto him. Do the rulers know indeed that this is the very Christ?

27 Howbeit we know this man whence he is: but when Christ cometh, no man knoweth whence he is.

28 Then cried Jesus in the temple as he taught, saying, Ye both know me, and ye know whence I am: and I am not come of myself, but he that sent me is true, whom ye know not.

29 But I know him: for I am from him, and he hath sent me.

30 Then they sought to take him: but no man laid hands on him, because his hour was not yet come.

31 And many of the people believed on him, and said, When Christ cometh, will he do more miracles than these which this *man* hath done?

32 ¶ The Pharisees heard that the people murmured such things concerning him; and the Pharisees and the chief priests sent officers to take him.

33 Then said Jesus unto them, Yet a little while am I with you, and *then* I go unto him that sent me.

34 Ye shall seek me, and shall not find *me:* and where I am, *thither* ye cannot come.

35 Then said the Jews among themselves, Whither will he go, that we shall not find him? will he go unto the dispersed among the Gentiles, and teach the Gentiles?

36 What *manner of* saying is this that he said, Ye shall seek me, and shall not find *me:* and where I am, *thither* ye cannot come?

37 In the last day, that great *day* of the feast, Jesus stood and cried, saying, If any man thirst, let him come unto me, and drink.

38 He that believeth on me, as the scripture hath said, out of his belly shall flow rivers of living water.

39 (But this spake he of the Spirit, which they that believe on him should receive: for the Holy Ghost was not yet *given;* because that Jesus was not yet glorified.)

40 ¶ Many of the people therefore, when they heard this saying, said, Of a truth this is the Prophet.

41 Others said, This is the Christ. But some said, Shall Christ come out of Galilee?

42 Hath not the scripture said, That Christ cometh of the seed of David, and out of the town of Bethlehem, where David was?

43 So there was a division among the people because of him.

44 And some of them would have taken him; but no man laid hands on him.

45 ¶ Then came the officers to the chief priests and Pharisees; and they said unto them, Why have ye not brought him?

46 The officers answered, Never man spake like this man.

Amplified

25 Then some of the Jerusalem people said, Is not this the Man they seek to kill?

26 And here He is speaking openly, and they say nothing to Him! Can it be possible that the rulers have discovered *and* know that this is *truly* the Christ?

27 No, we know where this Man comes from; when the Christ arrives, no one is to know from what place He comes.

28 Whereupon Jesus called out as He taught in the temple [z]porches, Do you know Me, and do you know where I am from? I have not come on My own authority *and* of My own accord *and* self-appointed, but the One Who sent Me is true (real, genuine, steadfast) and Him you do not know!

29 I know Him [Myself], because I come from His [very] presence, and it was He [personally] Who sent Me.

30 Therefore they were eager to arrest Him; but no one laid a hand on Him, for His hour (time) had not yet come.

31 And besides, many of the multitude believed in Him—adhered to Him, trusted Him, relied on Him. And they kept saying, When the Christ comes, will He do—can He be expected to do—more miracles *and* produce more proofs *and* signs than what this Man has done?

32 The Pharisees learned how the people said these things about Him under their breath, and the chief priests and Pharisees sent (attendants, guards) to arrest Him.

33 Therefore Jesus said, For a little while I am [still] with you, and then I go back to Him Who sent Me.

34 You will look for Me, but you will not be able to find Me; where I am you cannot come.

35 Then the Jews said among themselves, Where can this Man intend to go, that we shall not find Him? Will He go to the Jews that are scattered in the Dispersion among the Greeks and teach the Greeks?

36 What does this statement of His mean, You will look for Me and not be able to find Me, and, Where I am you cannot come?

37 Now on the final and most important day of the feast, Jesus stood forth and He cried in a loud voice, If any man is thirsty, let him come to Me and drink!

38 He who believes in Me—who cleaves to *and* trusts in *and* relies on Me—as the Scripture has said, Out from his innermost being springs *and* rivers of living water shall flow (continuously).

39 But He was speaking here of the Spirit, Whom those who believed—trusted, had faith—in Him were afterward to receive. For the (Holy) Spirit had not yet been given; because Jesus was not yet glorified (raised to honor).

40 Listening to those words, some of the multitude said, This is certainly *and* beyond doubt the prophet! [Deut. 18:18.]

41 Others said, This is the Christ, the Anointed One! But some said, What? Does the Christ come out of Galilee?

42 Does not the Scripture tell us that the Christ is to come from the offspring of David, and from Bethlehem, the village were David lived? [Ps. 89:3, 4; Mic. 5:2.]

43 So there arose a division *and* dissension among the people concerning Him.

44 Some of them wanted to arrest Him, but no one [ventured and] laid hands on Him.

45 Meanwhile the attendants (guards) had gone back to the chief priests and Pharisees, who asked them, Why have you not brought Him here with you?

46 The attendants replied, Never has a man talked as this Man talks!—No mere man has ever spoken as He speaks!

---

z) Trench.

Living New Testament

25 Some of the people who lived there in Jerusalem said among themselves, "Isn't this the man they are trying to kill?

26 But here he is preaching in public, and they say nothing to him. Can it be that our leaders have learned, after all, that he really is the Messiah?

27 But how could he be? For we know where this man was born; when Christ comes, He will just appear and no one will know where He comes from."

28 So Jesus, in a sermon in the Temple, called out "Yes, you know Me and where I was born and raised, but I am the representative of one you don't know, and He is Truth.

29 I know Him because I was with Him, and He sent Me to you."

30 Then the Jewish leaders sought to arrest Him; but no hand was laid on Him, for God's time had not yet come.

31 Many among the crowds at the Temple believed on Him. "After all," they said, "what miracles do you expect the Messiah to do that this man hasn't done?"

32 When the Pharisees heard that the crowds were in this mood, they and the chief priests sent officers to arrest Jesus.

33 But Jesus told them, ["Not yet![2]] I am to be here a little longer. Then I shall return to the one who sent Me.

34 You will search for Me but not find Me. And you won't be able to come where I am!"

35 The Jewish leaders were puzzled by this statement. "Where is he planning to go?" they asked. "Maybe he is thinking of leaving the country and going as a missionary among the Jews in other lands, or maybe even to the Gentiles!

36 What does he mean about our looking for him and not being able to find him, and, 'You won't be able to come where I am'?"

37 On the last day, the climax of the holidays, Jesus shouted to the crowds, "If anyone is thirsty, let him come to Me and drink.

38 For the Scriptures declare that rivers of living water shall flow from the inmost being of anyone who believes in Me."

39 (He was speaking of the Holy Spirit, who would be given to everyone believing in Him; but the Spirit had not yet been given, because Jesus had not yet returned to His glory in heaven.)

40 When the crowds heard Him say this, some of them declared, "This man surely is the prophet who will come just before the Messiah."

41, 42 Others said, "He *is* the Messiah." Still others, "But he *can't* be! Will the Messiah come from *Galilee?* For the Scriptures clearly state that the Messiah will be born of the royal line of David, in *Bethlehem*, the village where David was born."

43 So the crowd was divided about Him.

44 And some wanted Him arrested, but no one touched Him.

45 The Temple police who had been sent to arrest Him returned to the chief priests and Pharisees. "Why didn't you bring him in?" they demanded.

46 "He says such wonderful things!" they mumbled. "We've never heard anything like it."

[2] Implied.

Revised Standard

25 Some of the people of Jerusalem
therefore said, "Is not this the man whom
they seek to kill? [26]And here he is, speaking openly, and they say nothing to him!
Can it be that the authorities really know
that this is the Christ? [27]Yet we know
where this man comes from; and when
the Christ appears, no one will know where
he comes from." [28]So Jesus proclaimed,
as he taught in the temple, "You know me,
and you know where I come from? But
I have not come of my own accord; he who
sent me is true, and him you do not know.
[29]I know him, for I come from him, and
he sent me." [30]So they sought to arrest
him; but no one laid hands on him, because his hour had not yet come. [31]Yet
many of the people believed in him; they
said, "When the Christ appears, will he do
more signs than this man has done?"
32 The Pharisees heard the crowd thus
muttering about him, and the chief priests
and Pharisees sent officers to arrest him.
[33]Jesus then said, "I shall be with you a
little longer, and then I go to him who
sent me; [34]you will seek me and you will
not find me; where I am you cannot come."
[35]The Jews said to one another, "Where
does this man intend to go that we shall
not find him? Does he intend to go to the
Dispersion among the Greeks and teach
the Greeks? [36]What does he mean by saying, 'You will seek me and you will not
find me,' and, 'Where I am you cannot
come'? "

The last day of the feast

37 On the last day of the feast, the
great day, Jesus stood up and proclaimed,
"If any one thirst, let him come to me and
drink. [38]He who believes in me, as[q] the
scripture has said, 'Out of his heart shall
flow rivers of living water.' " [39]Now this he
said about the Spirit, which those who believed in him were to receive; for as yet
the Spirit had not been given, because
Jesus was not yet glorified.
40 When they heard these words, some
of the people said, "This is really the
prophet." [41]Others said, "This is the Christ."
But some said, "Is the Christ to come from
Galilee? [42]Has not the scripture said that the
Christ is descended from David, and comes
from Bethlehem, the village where David
was?" [43]So there was a division among the
people over him. [44]Some of them wanted to
arrest him, but no one laid hands on him.
45 The officers then went back to the
chief priests and Pharisees, who said to
them, "Why did you not bring him?"
[46]The officers answered, "No man ever
spoke like this man!" [47]The Pharisees an-

[q] Or *let him come to me, and let him who believes in me drink. As*

King James

47 Then answered them the Pharisees, Are ye also deceived?

48 Have any of the rulers or of the Pharisees believed on him?

49 But this people who knoweth not the law are cursed.

50 Nicodemus saith unto them, (he that came to Jesus by night, being one of them,)

51 Doth our law judge *any* man, before it hear him, and know what he doeth?

52 They answered and said unto him, Art thou also of Galilee? Search, and look: for out of Galilee ariseth no prophet.

53 And every man went unto his own house.

Amplified

47 The Pharisees said to them, Are you also deluded *and* led astray?—Are you also swept off your feet?

48 Have any of the authorities or of the Pharisees believed in Him?

49 As for this multitude (rabble) that does not know the Law, they are contemptible *and* doomed *and* accursed!

50 Then Nicodemus, who came to Jesus before at night and was one of them, asked,

51 Does our Law convict a man without giving him a hearing and finding out what he has done?

52 They answered him, Are you too from Galilee? Search [the Scriptures yourself] and you will see that no prophet comes—will rise to prominence—from Galilee.

53 [a]And they went [back], each to his own house.

CHAPTER 8 (King James)

JESUS went unto the mount of Olives.

2 And early in the morning he came again into the temple, and all the people came unto him; and he sat down, and taught them.

3 And the scribes and Pharisees brought unto him a woman taken in adultery; and when they had set her in the midst,

4 They say unto him, Master, this woman was taken in adultery, in the very act.

5 Now Moses in the law commanded us, that such should be stoned: but what sayest thou?

6 This they said, tempting him, that they might have to accuse him. But Jesus stooped down, and with *his* finger wrote on the ground, *as though he heard them not.*

7 So when they continued asking him, he lifted up himself, and said unto them, He that is without sin among you, let him first cast a stone at her.

8 And again he stooped down, and wrote on the ground.

9 And they which heard *it*, being convicted by *their own* conscience, went out one by one, beginning at the eldest, *even* unto the last: and Jesus was left alone, and the woman standing in the midst.

10 When Jesus had lifted up himself, and saw none but the woman, he said unto her, Woman, where are those thine accusers? hath no man condemned thee?

11 She said, No man, Lord. And Jesus said unto her, Neither do I condemn thee: go, and sin no more.

12 ¶ Then spake Jesus again unto them, saying, I am the light of the world: he that followeth me shall not walk in darkness, but shall have the light of life.

13 The Pharisees therefore said unto him, Thou bearest record of thyself; thy record is not true.

14 Jesus answered and said unto them, Though I bear record of myself, *yet* my record is true; for I know whence I came, and whither I go; but ye cannot tell whence I come, and whither I go.

CHAPTER 8 (Amplified)

BUT Jesus went to the mount of Olives.

2 Early in the morning (at dawn), He came back into the temple [b]court and the people came to Him in crowds. He sat down and was teaching them,

3 When the scribes and Pharisees brought a woman who had been caught in adultery. They made her stand in the middle of the court and put the case before Him.

4 Teacher, they said, this woman has been caught in the very act of adultery.

5 Now Moses in the Law commanded us that such [women, offenders] shall be stoned to death. But what do You say [to do with her]?—What is Your sentence? [Deut. 22:22-24.]

6 This they said to try (test) Him, hoping they might find a charge for which to accuse Him. But Jesus stooped down and wrote on the ground with His finger.

7 However, when they persisted with their question, He raised Himself up and said, Let him who is without sin among you be the first to throw a stone at her.

8 Then He bent down and went on writing on the ground with His finger.

9 They listened to Him and then they began going out conscience-stricken one by one, from the oldest down to the last one of them, till Jesus was left alone with the woman standing there before Him in the center of the court.

10 When Jesus raised up He said to her, Woman, where are your accusers? Has no man condemned you?

11 She answered, No one, Lord! And Jesus said, I do not condemn you either. Go on your way, and from now on sin no more.

12 Once more Jesus addressed the crowd. He said, I am the Light of the world. He who follows Me will not be walking in the dark, but will have the Light which is Life.

13 Whereupon the Pharisees told Him, You are testifying on Your own behalf; Your testimony is not valid *and* is worthless.

14 Jesus answered, Even if I do testify on My own behalf, My testimony is true *and* reliable *and* valid; for I know where I came from and where I am going; but you do not know where I came from or where I am going.

---

a) John 7:53 to 8:11 is not found in the older manuscripts, but it sounds so like Christ that we accept it as authentic, and feel that to omit it would be most unfortunate.
b) Trench.

Living New Testament

47 "So you also have been led astray?" the Pharisees mocked.

48 "Is there a single one of us Jewish rulers or Pharisees who believes he is the Messiah?

49 These stupid crowds do, yes; but what do they know about it? A curse upon them anyway!"[3]

50 Then Nicodemus spoke up. (Remember him? He was the Jewish leader who came secretly to interview Jesus.)

51 "Is it legal to convict a man before he is even tried?" he asked.

52 They replied, "Are you a wretched Galilean too? Search the Scriptures and see for youself—no prophets will come from Galilee!"

53[4] Then the meeting broke up and everybody went home.

Revised Standard

swered them, "Are you led astray, you also? 48 Have any of the authorities or of the Pharisees believed in him? 49 But this crowd, who do not know the law, are accursed." 50 Nicodemus, who had gone to him before, and who was one of them, said to them, 51 "Does our law judge a man without first giving him a hearing and learning what he does?" 52 They replied, "Are you from Galilee too? Search and you will see that no prophet is to rise from Galilee."[r] 53 *They went each to his own house.*

CHAPTER 8

Jesus returned to the Mount of Olives.

2 But early the next morning He was back again at the Temple. A crowd soon gathered, and He sat down and talked to them.

3 As He was speaking, the Jewish leaders and Pharisees brought a woman caught in adultery and placed her out in front of the staring crowd.

4 "Teacher," they said to Jesus, "this woman was caught in the very act of adultery.

5 Moses' law says to kill her. What about it?"

6 They were trying to trap Him into saying something they could use against Him, but Jesus stooped down and wrote in the dust with His finger.

7 They kept demanding an answer, so He stood up again and said, "All right, hurl the stones at her until she dies. But only he who never sinned may throw the first!"

8 Then He stooped down again and wrote some more in the dust.

9 And the Jewish leaders slipped away one by one, beginning with the eldest, until only Jesus was left in front of the crowd with the woman.

10 Then Jesus stood up again and said to her, "Where are your accusers? Didn't even one of them condemn you?"

11 "No, sir," she said.

And Jesus said, "Neither do I. Go and sin no more."

12 Later, in one of His talks, Jesus said to the people, "I am the Light of the world. So if you follow Me, you won't be stumbling through the darkness, for living light will flood your path."

13 The Pharisees replied, "You are boasting—and lying!"

14 Jesus told them, "These claims are true even though I make them concerning Myself. For I know where I came from and where I am going, but you don't know this about Me.

Jesus the light of the world

8 *But Jesus went to the Mount of Olives.* 2 *Early in the morning he came again to the temple; all the people came to him, and he sat down and taught them.* 3 *The scribes and the Pharisees brought a woman who had been caught in adultery, and placing her in the midst* 4 *they said to him, "Teacher, this woman has been caught in the act of adultery.* 5 *Now in the law Moses commanded us to stone such. What do you say about her?"* 6 *This they said to test him, that they might have some charge to bring against him. Jesus bent down and wrote with his finger on the ground.* 7 *And as they continued to ask him, he stood up and said to them, "Let him who is without sin among you be the first to throw a stone at her."* 8 *And once more he bent down and wrote with his finger on the ground.* 9 *But when they heard it, they went away, one by one, beginning with the eldest, and Jesus was left alone with the woman standing before him.* 10 *Jesus looked up and said to her, "Woman, where are they? Has no one condemned you?"* 11 *She said, "No one, Lord." And Jesus said, "Neither do I condemn you; go, and do not sin again."*

12 Again Jesus spoke to them, saying, "I am the light of the world; he who follows me will not walk in darkness, but will have the light of life." 13 The Pharisees then said to him, "You are bearing witness to yourself; your testimony is not true." 14 Jesus answered, "Even if I do bear witness to myself, my testimony is true, for I know whence I have come and whither I am going, but you do not know whence I come or whither I am going. 15 You

---

[3] Literally, "This multitude is accursed."
[4] Most ancient manuscripts omit John 7:53 - 8:11.

[r] Other ancient authorities add 7.53 – 8.11 either here or at the end of this gospel or after Luke 21.38, with variations of the text.

King James

15 Ye judge after the flesh; I judge no man.

16 And yet if I judge, my judgment is true: for I am not alone, but I and the Father that sent me.

17 It is also written in your law, that the testimony of two men is true.

18 I am one that bear witness of myself, and the Father that sent me beareth witness of me.

19 Then said they unto him, Where is thy Father? Jesus answered, Ye neither know me, nor my Father: if ye had known me, ye should have known my Father also.

20 These words spake Jesus in the treasury, as he taught in the temple: and no man laid hands on him; for his hour was not yet come.

21 Then said Jesus again unto them, I go my way, and ye shall seek me, and shall die in your sins: whither I go, ye cannot come.

22 Then said the Jews, Will he kill himself? because he saith, Whither I go, ye cannot come.

23 And he said unto them, Ye are from beneath; I am from above: ye are of this world; I am not of this world.

24 I said therefore unto you, that ye shall die in your sins: for if ye believe not that I am *he,* ye shall die in your sins.

25 Then said they unto him, Who art thou? And Jesus saith unto them, Even *the same* that I said unto you from the beginning.

26 I have many things to say and to judge of you: but he that sent me is true; and I speak to the world those things which I have heard of him.

27 They understood not that he spake to them of the Father.

28 Then said Jesus unto them, When ye have lifted up the Son of Man, then shall ye know that I am *he,* and *that* I do nothing of myself; but as my Father hath taught me, I speak these things.

29 And he that sent me is with me: the Father hath not left me alone; for I do always those things that please him.

30 As he spake these words, many believed on him.

31 Then said Jesus to those Jews which believed on him, If ye continue in my word, *then* are ye my disciples indeed;

32 And ye shall know the truth, and the truth shall make you free.

33 ¶ They answered him, We be Abraham's seed, and were never in bondage to any man: how sayest thou, Ye shall be made free?

34 Jesus answered them, Verily, verily, I say unto you, Whosoever committeth sin is the servant of sin.

35 And the servant abideth not in the house for ever: *but* the Son abideth ever.

Amplified

15 You [set yourselves up to] judge according to the flesh—by what you see; you condemn by external, human standards. I do not [set Myself up to] judge *or* condemn *or* sentence anyone.

16 Yet even if I do judge, My judgment is true—My decision is right; for I am not alone [in making it], but [there are two of Us], I and the Father Who sent Me.

17 In your [own] Law it is written that the testimony (evidence) of two persons is reliable *and* valid. [Deut. 19:15.]

18 I am one [of the Two] bearing testimony concerning Myself, and My Father Who sent Me, He also testifies about Me.

19 Then they said to Him, Where is this [c]Father of Yours? Jesus answered, You know My Father as little as you know Me. If you knew Me, you would know My Father also.

20 Jesus said these things in the treasury, while He was teaching in the temple [d]court; but no one ventured to arrest Him, because His hour had not yet come.

21 Therefore He said again to them, I am going away, and you will be looking for Me, but you will die in [under the curse of] your sin. Where I am going, it is not possible for you to come.

22 At this the Jews began to ask among themselves, Will He kill Himself? Is that why He says, Where I am going it is not possible for you to come?

23 He said to them, You are from below; I am from above. You are of this world—of this earthly order. I am not of this world.

24 That is why I told you that you will die in [under the curse of] your sins. For if you do not believe that I am He [Who I claim to be]—if you do not adhere to, trust in and rely on Me—you will die in your sins.

25 Then they said to Him, Who are You anyway? Jesus replied, Why do I even speak to you! I am exactly what I have been telling you from the first.

26 I have much to say about you and to judge *and* condemn. But He Who sent Me is true, and I tell the world [only] the things that I have heard from Him.

27 They did not perceive (know, understand) that He was speaking to them of the Father.

28 So Jesus added, When you have lifted up the Son of man [on the cross], you will realize (know, understand) that I am He [for Whom you look]; and that I do nothing from Myself—of My own accord, or on My own authority—but I say [exactly] what My Father has taught Me.

29 And He Who sent Me is ever with Me; My Father has not left Me alone, for I always do what pleases Him.

30 As He said these things, many believed on Him—trusted, relied on and adhered to Him.

31 So Jesus said to those Jews who had believed in Him, If you abide in My Word—hold fast to My teachings *and* live in accordance with them—you are truly My disciples.

32 And you will know the truth, and the truth will set you free.

33 They answered Him, We are Abraham's offspring (descendants) and have never been in bondage to anybody. What do You mean by saying, You will be set free?

34 Jesus answered them, I assure you, most solemnly I tell you, Whoever commits *and* practices sin is the slave of sin.

35 Now a slave does not remain in a household permanently (forever); the son [of the house] does remain forever.

---

c) Capitalized because of what He is, the spotless Son of God, not what the speaker may have thought He was.
d) Trench.

Living New Testament

15 You pass judgment on Me without knowing the facts. I am not judging you now;

16 But if I were, it would be an absolutely correct judgment in every respect, for I have with Me the Father who sent Me.

17 Your laws say that if two men agree on something that has happened, their witness is accepted as fact.

18 Well, I am one witness, and My Father who sent Me is the other."

19 "Where is your father?" they asked.

Jesus answered, "You don't know who I am, so you don't know who My Father is. If you knew Me, then you would know Him too."

20 Jesus made these statements while in the section of the Temple known as the Treasury. But He was not arrested, for His time had not yet run out.

21 Later He said to them again, "I am going away; and you will search for Me, and die in your sins. And you cannot come where I am going."

22 The Jews asked, "Is he planning suicide? What does he mean, 'You cannot come where I am going'?"

23 Then He said to them, "You are from below; I am from above. You are of this world; I am not.

24 That is why I said that you will die in your sins; for unless you believe that I am the Messiah, the Son of God, you will die in your sins."

25 "Tell us who you are," they demanded.

He replied, "I am the one I have always claimed to be.

26 I could condemn you for much and teach you much, but I won't, for I say only what I am told to by the one who sent Me; and He is Truth."

27 But they still didn't understand that He was talking to them about God.[1]

28 So Jesus said, "When you have killed the Man of Glory,[2] then you will realize that I am He and that I have not been telling you My own ideas, but have spoken what the Father taught Me.

29 And He who sent Me is with Me—He has not deserted Me—for I always do those things that are pleasing to Him."

30, 31 Then many of the Jewish leaders who heard Him say these things began believing Him to be the Messiah. Jesus said to them, "You are truly My disciples if you live as I tell you to,

32 And you will know the truth, and the truth will set you free."

33 "But we are descendants of Abraham," they said, "and have never been slaves to any man on earth! What do you mean, 'set free'?"

34 Jesus replied, "You are slaves to sin, every one of you.

35 And slaves don't have rights, but the Son has every right there is!

[1] Literally, "the Father."
[2] Literally, "when you have lifted up the Son of Man."

Revised Standard

judge according to the flesh, I judge no
one. 16Yet even if I do judge, my judgment is true, for it is not I alone that
judge, but I and he[s] who sent me. 17In
your law it is written that the testimony
of two men is true; 18I bear witness to myself, and the Father who sent me bears
witness to me." 19They said to him therefore, "Where is your Father?" Jesus answered, "You know neither me nor my
Father; if you knew me, you would know
my Father also." 20These words he spoke
in the treasury, as he taught in the temple;
but no one arrested him, because his hour
had not yet come.

Jesus warns against unbelief

21 Again he said to them, "I go away,
and you will seek me and die in your sin;
where I am going, you cannot come."
22Then said the Jews, "Will he kill himself, since he says, 'Where I am going, you
cannot come'?" 23He said to them, "You
are from below, I am from above; you are
of this world, I am not of this world. 24I
told you that you would die in your sins,
for you will die in your sins unless you
believe that I am he." 25They said to him,
"Who are you?" Jesus said to them, "Even
what I have told you from the beginning.[t]
26I have much to say about you and much
to judge; but he who sent me is true, and
I declare to the world what I have heard
from him." 27They did not understand
that he spoke to them of the Father. 28So
Jesus said, "When you have lifted up the
Son of man, then you will know that I
am he, and that I do nothing on my own
authority but speak thus as the Father
taught me. 29And he who sent me is with
me; he has not left me alone, for I always
do what is pleasing to him." 30As he spoke
thus, many believed in him.

The true children of Abraham

31 Jesus then said to the Jews who had
believed in him, "If you continue in my
word, you are truly my disciples, 32and
you will know the truth, and the truth will
make you free." 33They answered him, "We
are descendants of Abraham, and have
never been in bondage to any one. How
is it that you say, 'You will be made free'?"
34 Jesus answered them, "Truly, truly,
I say to you, every one who commits sin
is a slave to sin. 35The slave does not con-

[s] Other ancient authorities read *the Father*
[t] Or *Why do I talk to you at all?*

King James

36 If the Son therefore shall make you free, ye shall be free indeed.

37 I know that ye are Abraham's seed; but ye seek to kill me, because my word hath no place in you.

38 I speak that which I have seen with my Father: and ye do that which ye have seen with your father.

39 They answered and said unto him, Abraham is our father. Jesus saith unto them, If ye were Abraham's children, ye would do the works of Abraham.

40 But now ye seek to kill me, a man that hath told you the truth, which I have heard of God: this did not Abraham.

41 Ye do the deeds of your father. Then said they to him, We be not born of fornication; we have one Father, *even* God.

42 Jesus said unto them, If God were your Father, ye would love me: for I proceeded forth and came from God; neither came I of myself, but he sent me.

43 Why do ye not understand my speech? *even* because ye cannot hear my word.

44 Ye are of *your* father the devil, and the lusts of your father ye will do. He was a murderer from the beginning, and abode not in the truth, because there is no truth in him. When he speaketh a lie, he speaketh of his own: for he is a liar, and the father of it.

45 And because I tell *you* the truth, ye believe me not.

46 Which of you convinceth me of sin? And if I say the truth, why do ye not believe me?

47 He that is of God heareth God's words: ye therefore hear *them* not, because ye are not of God.

48 Then answered the Jews, and said unto him, Say we not well that thou art a Samaritan, and hast a devil?

49 Jesus answered, I have not a devil; but I honour my Father, and ye do dishonour me.

50 And I seek not mine own glory: there is one that seeketh and judgeth.

51 Verily, verily, I say unto you, If a man keep my saying, he shall never see death.

52 Then said the Jews unto him, Now we know that thou hast a devil. Abraham is dead, and the prophets; and thou sayest, If a man keep my saying, he shall never taste of death.

53 Art thou greater than our father Abraham, which is dead? and the prophets are dead: whom makest thou thyself?

Amplified

36 So if the Son liberates you—makes you free men—then you are really *and* unquestionably free.

37 [Yes] I know that you are Abraham's offspring; yet you plan to kill Me, because My word has no entrance—makes no progress, does not find any place—in you.

38 I tell the things which I have seen *and* learned at My Father's side, and your actions also reflect what you have heard *and* learned from your father.

39 They retorted, Abraham is our father. Jesus said, If you were truly Abraham's children, then you would do the works of Abraham—you would follow his example, do as Abraham did.

40 But now [instead] you are wanting *and* seeking to kill Me, a Man Who has told you the truth which I have heard from God. This is not the way Abraham did.

41 You do the works of your father. They said to Him, We are not illegitimate children *and* born of fornication; we have one Father, even God.

42 Jesus said to them, If God were your Father, you would love Me *and* respect Me *and* welcome Me gladly; for I proceeded (came forth) from God—out of His very presence. I did not even come on My own authority *or* of My own accord (self-appointed), but He sent Me.

43 Why do you misunderstand what I say? It is because you are unable to hear what I am saying—you cannot bear to listen to My message, your ears are shut to My teaching.

44 You are of your father the devil; and it is your will to practice the lusts *and* gratify the desires [which are characteristic] of your father. He was a murderer from the beginning, and does not stand in the truth, because there is no truth in him. When he speaks a falsehood, he speaks what is natural to him; for he is a liar [himself] and the father of lies *and* of all that is false.

45 But because I speak the truth, you do not believe Me—do not trust Me, do not rely on Me or adhere to Me.

46 Who of you convicts Me of wrongdoing *or* finds Me guilty of sin? Then if I speak truth, why do you not believe Me—trust Me, rely on and adhere to Me?

47 Whoever is of God listens to God.—Those who belong to God hear the words of God. This is the reason that you do not listen [to them, to Me], because you do not belong to *and* are not of God *or* in harmony with God.

48 The Jews answered Him, Are we not right when we say You are a Samaritan, and that You have a demon—that You are under the power of an evil spirit?

49 Jesus answered, I am not possessed by a demon. On the other hand, I honor *and* reverence My Father, and you dishonor—despise, vilify and scorn—Me.

50 However, I am not in search of honor for Myself—I do not seek and am not aiming for My own glory. There is One Who [looks after that; He] seeks [My glory] and He is the Judge.

51 I assure you, most solemnly I tell you, if any one observes My teaching—lives in accordance with My message, keeps My word—he will by no means ever see *and* experience death.

52 The Jews said to Him, Now we know that [e]You are under the power of a demon ([f]insane). Abraham died and also the prophets; yet You say, If a man keeps My word he will never taste of death to all eternity.

53 Are You greater than our father Abraham? He died and all the prophets died! Who do You make Yourself out to be?

---

e) Capitalized because of what He is, the spotless Son of God, not what the speaker may have thought He was.
f) Thayer.

Living New Testament

36 So if the Son sets you free, you will indeed be free—

37 (Yes, I realize that you are descendants of Abraham!) And yet some of you are trying to kill Me because My message does not find a home within your hearts.

38 I am telling you what I saw when I was with My Father. But you are following the advice of *your* father."

39 "Our father is Abraham," they declared.

"No!" Jesus replied, "for if he were, you would follow his good example.

40 But instead you are trying to kill Me—and all because I told you the truth I heard from God. Abraham wouldn't do a thing like that!

41 No, you are obeying your *real* father when you act that way."

They replied, "We were not born out of wedlock—our true Father is God Himself."

42 Jesus told them, "If that were so, then you would love Me, for I have come to you from God. I am not here on My own, but He sent Me.

43 Why can't you understand what I am saying? It is because you are prevented from doing so!

44 For you are children of your father the Devil and you love to do the evil things he does. He was a murderer from the beginning and a hater of truth—there is not an iota of truth in him. When he lies, it is perfectly normal; for he is the father of liars.

45 And so when I tell the truth, you just naturally don't believe it!

46 Which of you can truthfully accuse Me of one single sin? [No one![3]] And since I am telling you the truth, why don't you believe Me?

47 Anyone whose Father is God listens gladly to the words of God. Since you don't, it proves you aren't His children."

48 "You Samaritan! Foreigner! Devil!" the Jewish leaders snarled. "Didn't we say all along you were possessed by a demon?"

49 "No," Jesus said, "I have no demon in Me. For I honor My Father—and you dishonor Me.

50 And though I have no wish to make Myself great, God wants this for Me and judges [those who reject Me[4]].

51 With all the earnestness I have I tell you this—no one who obeys Me shall ever die!"

52 The leaders of the Jews said, "Now we know you are possessed by a demon. Even Abraham and the mightiest prophets died, and yet you say that obeying you will keep a man from dying!

53 So you are greater than our father Abraham who died? And greater than the prophets, who died? Who do you think you are?"

Revised Standard

tinue in the house for ever; the son continues for ever. 36So if the Son makes you
free, you will be free indeed. 37I know that
you are descendants of Abraham; yet you
seek to kill me, because my word finds no
place in you. 38I speak of what I have seen
with my Father, and you do what you have
heard from your father."
39 They answered him, "Abraham is
our father." Jesus said to them, "If you
were Abraham's children, you would do
what Abraham did, 40but now you seek to
kill me, a man who has told you the truth
which I heard from God; this is not what
Abraham did. 41You do what your father
did." They said to him, "We were not born
of fornication; we have one Father, even
God." 42Jesus said to them, "If God were
your Father, you would love me, for I
proceeded and came forth from God; I
came not of my own accord, but he sent
me. 43Why do you not understand what
I say? It is because you cannot bear to
hear my word. 44You are of your father
the devil, and your will is to do your
father's desires. He was a murderer from
the beginning, and has nothing to do with
the truth, because there is no truth in him.
When he lies, he speaks according to his
own nature, for he is a liar and the father
of lies. 45But, because I tell the truth, you
do not believe me. 46Which of you convicts me of sin? If I tell the truth, why do
you not believe me? 47He who is of God
hears the words of God; the reason why
you do not hear them is that you are not
of God."

Controversy with the Jews

48 The Jews answered him, "Are we not
right in saying that you are a Samaritan
and have a demon?" 49Jesus answered, "I
have not a demon; but I honor my Father,
and you dishonor me. 50Yet I do not seek
my own glory; there is One who seeks it
and he will be the judge. 51Truly, truly, I
say to you, if any one keeps my word, he
will never see death." 52The Jews said to
him, "Now we know that you have a demon. Abraham died, as did the prophets;
and you say, 'If any one keeps my word,
he will never taste death.' 53Are you greater
than our father Abraham, who died? And
the prophets died! Who do you claim to

---

[3] Implied.
[4] Implied. Literally, "There is one that seeketh and judgeth."

King James

54 Jesus answered, If I honour myself, my honour is nothing: it is my Father that honoureth me; of whom ye say, that he is your God:
55 Yet ye have not known him; but I know him: and if I should say, I know him not, I shall be a liar like unto you: but I know him, and keep his saying.
56 Your father Abraham rejoiced to see my day: and he saw *it,* and was glad.
57 Then said the Jews unto him, Thou art not yet fifty years old, and hast thou seen Abraham?
58 Jesus said unto them, Verily, verily, I say unto you, Before Abraham was, I am.
59 Then took they up stones to cast at him: but Jesus hid himself, and went out of the temple, going through the midst of them, and so passed by.

Amplified

54 Jesus answered, If I were to glorify Myself (magnify, praise and honor Myself) I should have no real glory, for My glory would be nothing *and* worthless.—My honor must come to Me from My Father. It is My Father Who glorifies Me—Who extols Me, magnifies and praises Me—of Whom you say that He is your God.
55 Yet you do not know Him *nor* recognize Him *and* are not acquainted with Him, but I know Him. If I should say that I do not know Him, I would be a liar like you. But I know Him and keep His word—obey His teachings, am faithful to His message.
56 Your forefather Abraham was extremely happy at the hope *and* prospect of seeing My day [My incarnation]. And he did see it and was delighted. [Heb. 11:13.]
57 Then the Jews said to Him, You are not yet fifty years old, and have You seen Abraham?
58 Jesus replied, I assure you, I most solemnly tell you, before Abraham was born, I AM. [Exod. 3:14.]
59 So they took up stones to throw at Him, but Jesus by mixing with the crowd concealed Himself and went out of the temple [g]enclosure.

CHAPTER 9

AND as *Jesus* passed by, he saw a man which was blind from *his* birth.
2 And his disciples asked him, saying, Master, who did sin, this man, or his parents, that he was born blind?
3 Jesus answered, Neither hath this man sinned, nor his parents: but that the works of God should be made manifest in him.
4 I must work the works of him that sent me, while it is day: the night cometh, when no man can work.
5 As long as I am in the world, I am the light of the world.
6 When he had thus spoken, he spat on the ground, and made clay of the spittle, and he anointed the eyes of the blind man with the clay,
7 And said unto him, Go, wash in the pool of Siloam, (which is by interpretation, Sent.) He went his way therefore, and washed, and came seeing.
8 ¶ The neighbours therefore, and they which before had seen him that he was blind, said, Is not this he that sat and begged?
9 Some said, This is he: others *said,* He is like him: *but* he said, I am *he.*
10 Therefore said they unto him, How were thine eyes opened?
11 He answered and said, A man that is called Jesus made clay, and anointed mine eyes, and said unto me, Go to the pool of Siloam, and wash: and I went and washed, and I received sight.
12 Then said they unto him, Where is he? He said, I know not.
13 ¶ They brought to the Pharisees him that aforetime was blind.
14 And it was the sabbath day when Jesus made the clay, and opened his eyes.
15 Then again the Pharisees also asked him how he had received his sight. He said unto them, He put clay upon mine eyes, and I washed, and do see.

CHAPTER 9

AS He passed along, He noticed a man blind from his birth.
2 His disciples asked Him, Rabbi, who sinned, this man or his parents, that he should be born blind?
3 Jesus answered, It was not that this man or his parents sinned; but he was born blind in order that the workings of God should be manifested—displayed and illustrated—in him.
4 We must work the works of Him Who sent Me, *and* be busy with His business while it is daylight; night is coming on when no man can work.
5 As long as I am in the world, I am the world's Light.
6 When He had said this, He spat on the ground and made clay (mud) with His saliva, and He spread it [as ointment] on the man's eyes.
7 And He said to him, Go, wash in the pool of Siloam, which means Sent. So he went and washed and came back seeing.
8 When the neighbors and those who used to know him by sight as a beggar saw him, they said, Is not this the man who used to sit and beg?
9 Some said, It is he. Others said, No, but he looks very much like him. But he said, Yes, I am the man.
10 So they said to him, How were your eyes opened?
11 He replied, The Man called Jesus made mud and smeared it on my eyes and said to me, Go to Siloam and wash. So I went and washed, and I obtained my sight!
12 They asked him, Where is He? He said, I do not know.
13 Then they conducted the man who had formerly been blind to the Pharisees.
14 Now it was on the Sabbath day that Jesus mixed the mud and opened the man's eyes.
15 So now again the Pharisees asked him how he received his sight. And he said to them, He smeared mud on my eyes and I washed and now I see.

g) Trench.

Living New Testament

54 Then Jesus told them this: "If I am merely boasting about Myself, it doesn't count. But it is My Father—and you claim Him as your God—who is saying these glorious things to Me.

55 But you do not even know Him. I do. If I said otherwise, I would be as great a liar as you! But it is true—I know Him and fully obey Him.

56 Your father Abraham rejoiced to see My day. He knew I was coming and was glad."

57 *The Jewish leaders:* "You aren't even 50 years old—sure, you've seen Abraham!"

58 *Jesus:* "The absolute truth is that I was in existence before Abraham was ever born!"

59 At that point the Jewish leaders picked up stones to kill Him. But Jesus was hidden from them, and walked past them and left the Temple.

Revised Standard

be?" [54]Jesus answered, "If I glorify myself,
my glory is nothing; it is my Father who
glorifies me, of whom you say that he is
your God. [55]But you have not known him;
I know him. If I said, I do not know him,
I should be a liar like you; but I do know
him and I keep his word. [56]Your father
Abraham rejoiced that he was to see my
day; he saw it and was glad." [57]The Jews
then said to him, "You are not yet fifty
years old, and have you seen Abraham?"[u]
[58]Jesus said to them, "Truly, truly, I say
to you, before Abraham was, I am." [59]So
they took up stones to throw at him; but
Jesus hid himself, and went out of the
temple.

CHAPTER 9

As He was walking along, He saw a man blind from birth.

2 "Master," His disciples asked Him, "why was this man born blind? Was it a result of his own sins or those of his parents?"

3 "Neither," Jesus answered. "But to demonstrate the power of God.

4 All of us must quickly carry out the tasks assigned us by the one who sent Me, for there is little time left before the night falls and all work comes to an end.

5 But while I am still here in the world, I give it My light."

6 Then He spat on the ground and made mud from the spittle and smoothed the mud over the blind man's eyes,

7 And told him, "Go and wash in the Pool of Siloam" (the word "Siloam" means "Sent"). So the man went where he was sent and washed and came back seeing!

8 His neighbors and others who knew him as a blind beggar asked each other, "Is this the same fellow—that beggar?"

9 Some said yes, and some said no. "It can't be the same man," they thought, "but he surely looks like him!"

And the beggar said, "I *am* the same man!"

10 Then they asked him how in the world he could see. What had happened?

11 And he told them, "A man they call Jesus made mud and smoothed it over my eyes and told me to go to the Pool of Siloam and wash off the mud. I did, and I can see!"

12 "Where is he now?" they asked.

"I don't know," he replied.

13 Then they took the man to the Pharisees.

14 Now as it happened, this all occurred on a Sabbath.[1]

15 Then the Pharisees asked him all about it. So he told them how Jesus had smoothed the mud over his eyes, and when it was washed away, he could see!

[1] i.e., on Saturday, the weekly Jewish holy day when all work was forbidden.

Jesus heals the man born blind

9 As he passed by, he saw a man blind
from his birth. [2]And his disciples asked
him, "Rabbi, who sinned, this man or his
parents, that he was born blind?" [3]Jesus
answered, "It was not that this man sinned,
or his parents, but that the works of God
might be made manifest in him. [4]We must
work the works of him who sent me, while
it is day; night comes, when no one can
work. [5]As long as I am in the world, I am
the light of the world." [6]As he said this,
he spat on the ground and made clay of
the spittle and anointed the man's eyes
with the clay, [7]saying to him, "Go, wash
in the pool of Siloam" (which means Sent).
So he went and washed and came back
seeing. [8]The neighbors and those who had
seen him before as a beggar, said, "Is not
this the man who used to sit and beg?"
[9]Some said, "It is he"; others said, "No,
but he is like him." He said, "I am the
man." [10]They said to him, "Then how were
your eyes opened?" [11]He answered, "The
man called Jesus made clay and anointed
my eyes and said to me, 'Go to Siloam
and wash'; so I went and washed and received my sight." [12]They said to him,
"Where is he?" He said, "I do not know."

Pharisees question the healed man

13 They brought to the Pharisees the
man who had formerly been blind. [14]Now
it was a sabbath day when Jesus made the
clay and opened his eyes. [15]The Pharisees
again asked him how he had received his
sight. And he said to them, "He put clay
on my eyes, and I washed, and I see."

[u] Other ancient authorities read *has Abraham seen you?*

King James

16 Therefore said some of the Pharisees, This man is not of God, because he keepeth not the sabbath day. Others said, How can a man that is a sinner do such miracles? And there was a division among them.

17 They say unto the blind man again, What sayest thou of him, that he hath opened thine eyes? He said, He is a prophet.

18 But the Jews did not believe concerning him, that he had been blind, and received his sight, until they called the parents of him that had received his sight.

19 And they asked them, saying, Is this your son, who ye say was born blind? how then doth he now see?

20 His parents answered them and said, We know that this is our son, and that he was born blind:

21 But by what means he now seeth, we know not; or who hath opened his eyes, we know not: he is of age; ask him: he shall speak for himself.

22 These *words* spake his parents, because they feared the Jews: for the Jews had agreed already, that if any man did confess that he was Christ, he should be put out of the synagogue.

23 Therefore said his parents, He is of age; ask him.

24 Then again called they the man that was blind, and said unto him, Give God the praise: we know that this man is a sinner.

25 He answered and said, Whether he be a sinner *or no*, I know not: one thing I know, that, whereas I was blind, now I see.

26 Then said they to him again, What did he to thee? how opened he thine eyes?

27 He answered them, I have told you already, and ye did not hear: wherefore would ye hear *it* again? will ye also be his disciples?

28 Then they reviled him, and said, Thou art his disciple; but we are Moses' disciples.

29 We know that God spake unto Moses: *as for* this *fellow*, we know not from whence he is.

30 The man answered and said unto them, Why herein is a marvellous thing, that ye know not from whence he is, and *yet* he hath opened mine eyes.

31 Now we know that God heareth not sinners: but if any man be a worshipper of God, and doeth his will, him he heareth.

32 Since the world began was it not heard that any man opened the eyes of one that was born blind.

33 If this man were not of God, he could do nothing.

34 They answered and said unto him, Thou wast altogether born in sins, and dost thou teach us? And they cast him out.

35 Jesus heard that they had cast him out; and when he had found him, he said unto him, Dost thou believe on the Son of God?

36 He answered and said, Who is he, Lord, that I might believe on him?

37 And Jesus said unto him, Thou hast both seen him, and it is he that talketh with thee.

38 And he said, Lord, I believe. And he worshipped him.

Amplified

16 Then some of the Pharisees said, This Man [Jesus] is not from God, because He does not observe the Sabbath. But others said, How can a man who is a sinner—a bad man—do such signs *and* miracles? So there was a difference of opinion among them.

17 Accordingly they said to the blind man again, What do you say about Him, seeing that He opened your eyes? And he said, He is—He must be—a prophet!

18 However the Jews did not believe that he had really been blind and that he had received his sight until they called (summoned) the parents of the man.

19 They asked them, Is this your son, whom you reported as having been born blind? How then does he see now?

20 His parents answered, We know that this is our son, and that he was born blind.

21 But as to how he can now see, we do not know; or who has opened his eyes we do not know. He is of age, ask him; let him speak for himself *and* give his own account of it.

22 His parents said this because they feared [the leaders of] the Jews. For the Jews had already agreed that if any one should acknowledge Jesus to be the Christ, he should be expelled *and* excluded from the synagogue.

23 On that account his parents said, He is of age, ask him.

24 So the second time they summoned the man who had been born blind, and said to him, Now give God the glory (praise). This [h]Fellow we know is only a sinner—a wicked person.

25 Then he answered, I do not know whether He is a sinner *and* wicked or not. But one thing I know, that whereas I was blind before, now I see.

26 So they said to him, What did He [actually] do to you? How did He open your eyes?

27 He answered, I already told you, and you would not listen. Why do you want to hear it again? Can it be that you wish to become His disciples also?

28 And they stormed at him—they jeered, they sneered, they reviled him—and retorted, You are His disciple yourself, but we are the disciples of Moses.

29 We know for certain that God spoke with Moses, but as for this Fellow, we know nothing about where He hails from.

30 The man replied, Well, this is astonishing! Here a Man has opened my eyes, and yet you do not know where He comes from—this is amazing!

31 We know that God does not listen to sinners; but if any one is God-fearing *and* a worshipper of Him and does His will, He listens to him.

32 Since the beginning of time it was never heard of that any one opened the eyes of a man born blind.

33 If that Man were not from God, He would not be able to do anything like this.

34 They retorted, You were wholly born in sin—from head to foot—and do you [presume to] teach us? So they cast him out—threw him clear outside the synagogue.

35 Jesus heard that they had put him out, and meeting him He said, Do you believe in *and* adhere to the Son of man—[i]the Son of God?

36 He answered, Who is He, Sir? Tell me, that I may believe in *and* adhere to Him.

37 Jesus said to him, You have seen Him; [in fact] He is talking to you right now.

38 He called out, Lord, I believe—I rely on, I trust, I cleave to You! And he worshipped Him.

---

h) Capitalized because of what He is, the spotless Son of God, not what the speaker may have thought He was.
i) Many ancient authorities read "the Son of God."

Living New Testament

16 Some of them said, "Then this fellow Jesus is not from God, because he is working on the Sabbath."

Others said, "But how could an ordinary sinner do such miracles?" So there was a deep division of opinion among them.

17 Then the Pharisees turned on the man who had been blind and demanded, "This man who opened your eyes—who do you say he is?"

"I think He must be a prophet sent from God," the man replied.

18 The Jewish leaders wouldn't believe he had been blind, until they called in his parents

19 And asked them, "Is this your son? Was he born blind? If so, how can he see?"

20 His parents replied, "We know this is our son and that he was born blind.

21 But we don't know what happened to make him see, or who did it. He is old enough to speak for himself. Ask him."

22, 23 They said this in fear of the Jewish leaders who had announced that anyone saying Jesus was the Messiah would be excommunicated.

24 So for the second time they called in the man who had been blind and told him, "Give the glory to God, not to Jesus, for we know Jesus is an evil person."

25 "I don't know whether He is good or bad," the man replied, "but I know this: *I was blind, and now I see!*"

26 "But what did he do?" they asked. "How did he heal you?"

27 "Look!" the man exclaimed. "I told you once; didn't you listen? Why do you want to hear it again? Do you want to become His disciples too?"

28 Then they cursed him and said, "You are his disciple, but we are disciples of Moses.

29 We know God has spoken to Moses, but as for this fellow, we don't know anything about him."

30 "Why, that's very strange!" the man replied. "He can heal blind men, and yet you don't know anything about Him!

31 Well, God doesn't listen to evil men, but He has open ears to those who worship Him and do His will.

32 Since the world began there has never been anyone who could open the eyes of someone born blind.

33 If this man were not from God, He couldn't do it."

34 "You illegitimate bastard,[2] you!" they shouted. "Are you trying to teach *us?*" And they threw him out.

35 When Jesus heard what had happened, He found the man and said, "Do you believe in the Messiah?"[3]

36 The man answered, "Who is He, sir, for I want to."

37 "You have seen Him," Jesus said, "and He is speaking to you!"

38 "Yes, Lord," the man said, "I believe!" And he worshiped Jesus.

[2] Literally, "You were altogether born in sin."
[3] Literally, "the Son of man."

Revised Standard

16 Some of the Pharisees said, "This man is
not from God, for he does not keep the
sabbath." But others said, "How can a man
who is a sinner do such signs?" There was
a division among them. 17 So they again
said to the blind man, "What do you say
about him, since he has opened your
eyes?" He said, "He is a prophet."

18 The Jews did not believe that he had
been blind and had received his sight, until they called the parents of the man who
had received his sight, 19 and asked them,
"Is this your son, who you say was born
blind? How then does he now see?" 20 His
parents answered, "We know that this is
our son, and that he was born blind; 21 but
how he now sees we do not know, nor do
we know who opened his eyes. Ask him;
he is of age, he will speak for himself."
22 His parents said this because they feared
the Jews, for the Jews had already agreed
that if any one should confess him to be
Christ, he was to be put out of the synagogue. 23 Therefore his parents said, "He
is of age, ask him."

24 So for the second time they called
the man who had been blind, and said to
him, "Give God the praise; we know that
this man is a sinner." 25 He answered,
"Whether he is a sinner, I do not know;
one thing I know, that though I was blind,
now I see." 26 They said to him, "What did
he do to you? How did he open your eyes?"
27 He answered them, "I have told you already, and you would not listen. Why do
you want to hear it again? Do you too
want to become his disciples?" 28 And they
reviled him, saying, "You are his disciple,
but we are disciples of Moses. 29 We know
that God has spoken to Moses, but as for
this man, we do not know where he comes
from." 30 The man answered, "Why, this
is a marvel! You do not know where he
comes from, and yet he opened my eyes.
31 We know that God does not listen to
sinners, but if any one is a worshiper of
God and does his will, God listens to him.
32 Never since the world began has it been
heard that any one opened the eyes of a
man born blind. 33 If this man were not
from God, he could do nothing." 34 They
answered him, "You were born in utter
sin, and would you teach us?" And they
cast him out.

Jesus talks to the healed man

35 Jesus heard that they had cast him
out, and having found him he said, "Do
you believe in the Son of man?"[v] 36 He
answered, "And who is he, sir, that I may
believe in him?" 37 Jesus said to him, "You
have seen him, and it is he who speaks to
you." 38 He said, "Lord, I believe"; and he

[v] Other ancient authorities read *the Son of God*

King James

39 ¶ And Jesus said, For judgment I am come into this world, that they which see not might see; and that they which see might be made blind.

40 And *some* of the Pharisees which were with him heard these words, and said unto him, Are we blind also?

41 Jesus said unto them, If ye were blind, ye should have no sin: but now ye say, We see; therefore your sin remaineth.

Amplified

39 Then Jesus said, I came into this world for judgment—as a Separator, in order that there may be [j]separation [between those who believe on Me and those who reject Me]—to make the sightless see, and that those who see may become blind.

40 Some Pharisees who were near, hearing this remark said to Him, Are we also blind?

41 Jesus said to them, If you were blind, you would have no sin; but because you now claim to have sight, your sin remains.—If you were blind, you would not be guilty of sin; but because you insist, We do see [clearly], you are unable to escape your guilt.

King James

CHAPTER 10

VERILY, verily, I say unto you, He that entereth not by the door into the sheepfold, but climbeth up some other way, the same is a thief and a robber.

2 But he that entereth in by the door is the shepherd of the sheep.

3 To him the porter openeth; and the sheep hear his voice; and he calleth his own sheep by name, and leadeth them out.

4 And when he putteth forth his own sheep, he goeth before them, and the sheep follow him: for they know his voice.

5 And a stranger will they not follow, but will flee from him: for they know not the voice of strangers.

6 This parable spake Jesus unto them: but they understood not what things they were which he spake unto them.

7 Then said Jesus unto them again, Verily, verily, I say unto you, I am the door of the sheep.

8 All that ever came before me are thieves and robbers: but the sheep did not hear them.

9 I am the door: by me if any man enter in, he shall be saved, and shall go in and out, and find pasture.

10 The thief cometh not, but for to steal, and to kill, and to destroy: I am come that they might have life, and that they might have *it* more abundantly.

11 I am the good shepherd: the good shepherd giveth his life for the sheep.

12 But he that is an hireling, and not the shepherd, whose own the sheep are not, seeth the wolf coming, and leaveth the sheep, and fleeth: and the wolf catcheth them, and scattereth the sheep.

13 The hireling fleeth, because he is an hireling, and careth not for the sheep.

14 I am the good shepherd, and know my *sheep,* and am known of mine.

15 As the Father knoweth me, even so know I the Father: and I lay down my life for the sheep.

Amplified

CHAPTER 10

I ASSURE you, most solemly I tell you, he who does not enter in by the door into the sheepfold, but climbs up some other way (elsewhere, from some other quarter) is a thief and a robber.

2 But he who enters by the door is the shepherd of the sheep.

3 The watchman opens the door for this man, and the sheep listen to his voice *and* heed it, and he calls his own sheep by name and brings (leads) them out.

4 When he has brought his own sheep outside, he walks on before them, and the sheep follow him, because they know his voice.

5 They will never [on any account] follow a stranger, but will run away from him, because they do not know the voice of strangers *or* recognize their call.

6 Jesus used this parable (illustration) with them, but they did not understand what He was talking about.

7 So Jesus said again, I assure you, most solemnly I tell you, that I Myself am the Door [k]for the sheep,

8 All others who came [as such] before Me are thieves and robbers; but the [true] sheep did not listen *and* obey them.

9 I am the Door. Any one who enters in through Me will be saved—will live; he will come in and he will go out [freely], and will find pasture.

10 The thief comes only in order that he may steal and may kill and may destroy. I came that they may have *and* enjoy life, and have it in abundance—to the full, till it [l]overflows.

11 I am the Good Shepherd. The good shepherd risks *and* lays down his [own] life for the sheep. [Ps. 23.]

12 But the hired servant—he who merely serves for wages—who is neither the shepherd nor the owner of the sheep, when he sees the wolf coming deserts the flock and runs away. And the wolf chases *and* snatches them and scatters [the flock].

13 Now *the hireling flees* because he merely serves for wages and is not himself concerned about the sheep—cares nothing for them.

14 I am the Good Shepherd and I know *and* recognize My own, and My own know *and* recognize Me,

15 Even as [truly as] the Father knows Me I also know the Father; and I am giving My [very own] life *and* laying it down in behalf of the sheep.

---

j) Vincent.
k) Vincent.
l) Souter's "Pocket Lexicon to the Greek New Testament."

Living New Testament

39 Then Jesus told him, "I have come into the world to give sight to those who are spiritually blind and to show those who think they see that they are blind."

40 The Pharisees who were standing there asked, "Are you saying we are blind?"

41 "If you were blind, you wouldn't be guilty," Jesus replied. "But your guilt remains because you claim to know what you are doing."

Revised Standard

worshiped him. 39Jesus said, "For judgment I came into this world, that those who
do not see may see, and that those who
see may become blind." 40Some of the
Pharisees near him heard this, and they
said to him, "Are we also blind?" 41Jesus
said to them, "If you were blind, you
would have no guilt; but now that you say,
'We see,' your guilt remains.

CHAPTER 10

Anyone refusing to walk through the gate into a sheepfold, who sneaks over the wall, must surely be a thief!

2 For a shepherd comes through the gate.

3 The gatekeeper opens the gate for him, and the sheep hear his voice and come to him; and he calls his own sheep by name and leads them out.

4 He walks ahead of them; and they follow him, for they recognize his voice.

5 They won't follow a stranger but will run from him, for they don't recognize his voice."

6 Those who heard Jesus use this illustration didn't understand what He meant,

7 So He explained it to them. "I am the Gate for the sheep," He said.

8 "All others who came before Me were thieves and robbers. But the true sheep did not listen to them.

9 Yes, I am the Gate. Those who came in by way of the gate will be saved and will go in and out and find green pastures.

10 The thief's purpose is to steal, kill and destroy. My purpose is to give eternal life—abundantly.

11 I am the Good Shepherd. The Good Shepherd lays down His life for the sheep.

12 A hired man will run when he sees a wolf coming and will leave the sheep, for they aren't his and he isn't their shepherd. And so the wolf leaps on them and scatters the flock.

13 The hired man runs because he is hired and has no real concern for the sheep.

14 I am the Good Shepherd and know My own sheep, and they know Me,

15 Just as My Father knows Me and I know the Father; and I lay down My life for the sheep.

Jesus the good shepherd

10 "Truly, truly, I say to you, he who
does not enter the sheepfold by the
door but climbs in by another way, that
man is a thief and a robber; 2but he who
enters by the door is the shepherd of the
sheep. 3To him the gatekeeper opens; the
sheep hear his voice, and he calls his own
sheep by name and leads them out. 4When
he has brought out all his own, he goes
before them, and the sheep follow him,
for they know his voice. 5A stranger they
will not follow, but they will flee from him,
for they do not know the voice of strangers." 6This figure Jesus used with them, but
they did not understand what he was saying
to them.

7 So Jesus again said to them, "Truly,
truly, I say to you, I am the door of the
sheep. 8All who came before me are thieves
and robbers; but the sheep did not heed
them. 9I am the door; if any one enters by
me, he will be saved, and will go in and
out and find pasture. 10The thief comes
only to steal and kill and destroy; I came
that they may have life, and have it abundantly. 11I am the good shepherd. The
good shepherd lays down his life for the
sheep. 12He who is a hireling and not a
shepherd, whose own the sheep are not,
sees the wolf coming and leaves the sheep
and flees; and the wolf snatches them and
scatters them. 13He flees because he is a
hireling and cares nothing for the sheep.
14I am the good shepherd; I know my
own and my own know me, 15as the Father knows me and I know the Father; and

King James

16 And other sheep I have, which are not of this fold: them also I must bring, and they shall hear my voice; and there shall be one fold, *and* one shepherd.

17 Therefore doth my Father love me, because I lay down my life, that I might take it again.

18 No man taketh it from me, but I lay it down of myself. I have power to lay it down, and I have power to take it again. This commandment have I received of my Father.

19 ¶ There was a division therefore again among the Jews for these sayings.

20 And many of them said, He hath a devil, and is mad; why hear ye him?

21 Others said, These are not the words of him that hath a devil. Can a devil open the eyes of the blind?

22 ¶ And it was at Jerusalem the feast of the dedication, and it was winter.

23 And Jesus walked in the temple in Solomon's porch.

24 Then came the Jews round about him, and said unto him, How long dost thou make us to doubt? If thou be the Christ, tell us plainly.

25 Jesus answered them, I told you, and ye believed not: the works that I do in my Father's name, they bear witness of me.

26 But ye believe not, because ye are not of my sheep, as I said unto you.

27 My sheep hear my voice, and I know them, and they follow me:

28 And I give unto them eternal life; and they shall never perish, neither shall any *man* pluck them out of my hand.

29 My Father, which gave *them* me, is greater than all; and no *man* is able to pluck *them* out of my Father's hand.

30 I and *my* Father are one.

31 Then the Jews took up stones again to stone him.

32 Jesus answered them, Many good works have I shewed you from my Father; for which of those works do ye stone me?

33 The Jews answered him, saying, For a good work we stone thee not; but for blasphemy; and because that thou, being a man, makest thyself God.

34 Jesus answered them, Is it not written in your law, I said, Ye are gods?

35 If he called them gods, unto whom the word of God came, and the scripture cannot be broken;

36 Say ye of him, whom the Father hath sanctified, and sent into the world, Thou blasphemest; because I said, I am the Son of God?

37 If I do not the works of my Father, believe me not.

Amplified

16 And I have other sheep [beside these], that are not of this fold. I must bring *and* [m]impel those also, and they will listen to My voice *and* heed My call, and so there will be (they will become) one flock under one Shepherd. [Ezek. 34:23.]

17 For this the Father loves Me, because I lay down My [own] life to take it back again.

18 No one takes it away from Me. On the contrary, I lay it down voluntarily—I put it from Myself. I am authorized *and* have power to lay it down—to resign it; and I am authorized *and* have power to take it back again. These are the instructions (orders) which I have received [as My charge] from My Father.

19 Then a fresh division of opinion arose among the Jews because of His saying these things.

20 And many of them said, He has a demon and He is mad—insane, He raves, He rambles. Why do you listen to Him?

21 Others argued, These are not the thoughts *and* the language of one possessed. Can a demon-possessed person open blind eyes?

22 After this the Feast of Dedication [of the reconsecration of the temple] was taking place at Jerusalem.

23 It was winter, and Jesus was walking in Solomon's porch in the temple area.

24 So the Jews surrounded Him and began asking Him, How long are You going to keep us in doubt *and* suspense? If You are really Christ, tell us so plainly *and* openly.

25 Jesus answered them, I have told you so, yet you do not believe Me—you do not trust Me *and* rely on Me. The very works that I do by the power of My Father *and* in My Father's name bear witness concerning Me—they are My credentials and evidence in support of Me.

26 But you do not believe *and* trust *and* rely on Me, because you do not belong to My fold—you are no sheep of Mine.

27 The sheep that are My own hear *and* are listening to My voice, and I know them and they follow Me,

28 And I give them eternal life, and they shall never lose it *or* perish throughout the ages—to all eternity they shall never by any means be destroyed. And no one is able to snatch them out of My hand.

29 My Father, Who has given them to Me, is greater *and* mightier than all else; and no one is able to snatch [them] out of the Father's hand.

30 I and the Father are One.

31 Again the Jews [n]brought up stones to stone Him.

32 Jesus said to them, My Father has enabled Me to do many good deeds—I have shown many acts of mercy in your presence. For which of these do you mean to stone Me?

33 The Jews replied, We are not going to stone You for a good act, but for blasphemy; because You, a mere man, make Yourself [out to be] God.

34 Jesus answered, Is it not written in your Law, I said, Ye are gods? [Ps. 82:6.]

35 So men are called gods—by the Law—men to whom God's message came, and the Scripture cannot be set aside *or* cancelled *or* broken *or* annulled. [If that is true] do you say [to Me],

36 The One Whom the Father consecrated *and* dedicated *and* set apart for Himself and sent into the world, You are blaspheming, because I said, I am the Son of God?

37 If I am not doing the works (performing the deeds) of My Father, then do not believe Me—do not adhere to Me and trust in and rely on Me.

---

m) Abbott-Smith.
n) Vincent.

Living New Testament

16 I have other sheep, too, in another fold. I must bring them also, and they will heed My voice; and there will be one flock with one Shepherd.

17 The Father loves Me because I lay down My life that I may have it back again.

18 No one can kill Me without My consent—I lay down My life voluntarily. For I have the right and power to lay it down when I want to and also the right and power to take it again. For the Father has given Me this right."

19 When He said these things, the Jewish leaders were again divided in their opinions about Him.

20 Some of them said, "He has a demon or else is crazy. Why listen to a man like that?"

21 Others said, "This doesn't sound to us like a man possessed by a demon! Can a demon open the eyes of blind men?"

* * * * *

22, 23 It was winter,[1] and Jesus was in Jerusalem at the time of the Dedication Celebration. He was at the Temple, walking through the section known as Solomon's Hall.

24 The Jewish leaders surrounded Him and asked, "How long are you going to keep us in suspense? If you are the Messiah, tell us plainly."

25 "I have already told you,[2] and you didn't believe Me," Jesus replied. "The proof is in the miracles I do in the name of My Father.

26 But you don't believe Me because you are not part of My flock.

27 My sheep recognize My voice, and I know them, and they follow Me.

28 I give them eternal life and they shall never perish. No one shall snatch them away from Me,

29 For My Father has given them to Me, and He is more powerful than anyone else, so no one can kidnap them from Me.

30 I and the Father are one."

31 Then again the Jewish leaders picked up stones to kill Him.

32 Jesus said, "At God's direction I have done many a miracle to help the people. For which one are you killing Me?"

33 They replied, "Not for any good work, but for blasphemy; you, a mere man, have declared yourself to be God."

34, 35, 36 "In your own Law it says that men are gods!" He replied. "So if the Scripture, which cannot be untrue, speaks of those as gods to whom the message of God came, do you call it blasphemy when the one sanctified and sent into the world by the Father says, 'I am the Son of God'?

37 Don't believe Me unless I do miracles of God.

[1] December 25 was the usual date for this celebration of the cleansing of the Temple.

[2] Chapter 5:19, 8:36, 56, 58, etc., etc.

Revised Standard

I lay down my life for the sheep. 16And I
have other sheep, that are not of this fold;
I must bring them also, and they will heed
my voice. So there shall be one flock, one
shepherd. 17For this reason the Father
loves me, because I lay down my life, that
I may take it again. 18No one takes it from
me, but I lay it down of my own accord.
I have power to lay it down, and I have
power to take it again; this charge I have
received from my Father."

19 There was again a division among
the Jews because of these words. 20Many
of them said, "He has a demon, and he
is mad; why listen to him?" 21Others said,
"These are not the sayings of one who has
a demon. Can a demon open the eyes of
the blind?"

Jesus at the feast of Dedication

22 It was the feast of the Dedication at
Jerusalem; 23it was winter, and Jesus was
walking in the temple, in the portico of
Solomon. 24So the Jews gathered round
him and said to him, "How long will you
keep us in suspense? If you are the Christ,
tell us plainly." 25Jesus answered them, "I
told you, and you do not believe. The
works that I do in my Father's name, they
bear witness to me; 26but you do not believe, because you do not belong to my
sheep. 27My sheep hear my voice, and I
know them, and they follow me; 28and I
give them eternal life, and they shall never
perish, and no one shall snatch them out
of my hand. 29My Father, who has given
them to me,[w] is greater than all, and no
one is able to snatch them out of the Father's hand. 30I and the Father are one."

The Jews try to arrest Jesus

31 The Jews took up stones again to
stone him. 32Jesus answered them, "I have
shown you many good works from the
Father; for which of these do you stone
me?" 33The Jews answered him, "We stone
you for no good work but for blasphemy;
because you, being a man, make yourself
God." 34Jesus answered them, "Is it not
written in your law, 'I said, you are gods'?
35If he called them gods to whom the word
of God came (and scripture cannot be
broken), 36do you say of him whom the
Father consecrated and sent into the world,
'You are blaspheming,' because I said, 'I
am the Son of God'? 37If I am not doing
the works of my Father, then do not be-

[w] Other ancient authorities read *What my Father has given to me*

King James

38 But if I do, though ye believe not me, believe the works: that ye may know, and believe that the Father *is* in me, and I in him.

39 Therefore they sought again to take him; but he escaped out of their hand,

40 And went away again beyond Jordan into the place where John at first baptized; and there he abode.

41 And many resorted unto him, and said, John did no miracle: but all things that John spake of this man were true.

42 And many believed on him there.

Amplified

38 But if I do them, even though you do not believe Me *nor* have faith in Me, [at least] believe the works *and* have faith in what I do, in order that you may know and understand [clearly] that the Father is in Me and I am in the Father—One with Him.

39 They sought again to arrest Him, but He escaped from their hands.

40 He went back again across the Jordan to the locality where John was when he first baptized, and there He remained.

41 And many came to Him, and they kept saying, John did not perform a [single] sign *or* miracle, but everything John said of this Man was true.

42 And many [people] there became believers on Him—they adhered to *and* trusted in *and* relied on Him.

CHAPTER 11

NOW a certain *man* was sick, *named* Lazarus, of Bethany, the town of Mary and her sister Martha.

2 (It was *that* Mary which anointed the Lord with ointment, and wiped his feet with her hair, whose brother Lazarus was sick.)

3 Therefore his sisters sent unto him, saying, Lord, behold, he whom thou lovest is sick.

4 When Jesus heard *that*, he said, This sickness is not unto death, but for the glory of God, that the Son of God might be glorified thereby.

5 Now Jesus loved Martha, and her sister, and Lazarus.

6 When he had heard therefore that he was sick, he abode two days still in the same place where he was.

7 Then after that saith he to *his* disciples, Let us go into Judæa again.

8 *His* disciples say unto him, Master, the Jews of late sought to stone thee; and goest thou thither again?

9 Jesus answered, Are there not twelve hours in the day? If any man walk in the day, he stumbleth not, because he seeth the light of this world.

10 But if a man walk in the night, he stumbleth, because there is no light in him.

11 These things said he: and after that he saith unto them, Our friend Lazarus sleepeth; but I go, that I may awake him out of sleep.

12 Then said his disciples, Lord, if he sleep, he shall do well.

13 Howbeit Jesus spake of his death: but they thought that he had spoken of taking of rest in sleep.

14 Then said Jesus unto them plainly, Lazarus is dead.

15 And I am glad for your sakes that I was not there, to the intent ye may believe; nevertheless let us go unto him.

16 Then said Thomas, which is called Didymus, unto his fellow disciples, Let us also go, that we may die with him.

17 Then when Jesus came, he found that he had *lain* in the grave four days already.

CHAPTER 11

NOW a certain man named Lazarus was ill. He was of Bethany, the village where Mary and her sister Martha lived.

2 This Mary was the one who anointed the Lord with perfume and wiped His feet with her hair. It was her brother Lazarus who was [now] sick.

3 So the sisters sent to Him saying, Lord, he whom You love [so well] is sick.

4 When Jesus received the message He said, This sickness is not to end in death; but [on the contrary] it is to honor God *and* to promote His glory, that the Son of God may be glorified through (by) it.

5 Now Jesus loved Martha and her sister and Lazarus; [they were His dear friends and He held them in loving esteem].

6 Therefore, [even] when He heard that Lazarus was sick, He still stayed two days longer in the same place where He was.

7 Then, after that interval He said to His disciples, Let us go back again to Judea.

8 The disciples said to Him, Rabbi, the Jews only recently were intending *and* trying to stone You, and are You [thinking of] going back there again?

9 Jesus answered, Are there not twelve hours in the day? Any one who walks about in the daytime does not stumble, because he sees the light of this world.

10 But if any one walks about in the night, he does stumble, because there is no light in him—the light is lacking to him.

11 He said these things and then added, Our friend Lazarus is at rest *and* sleeping, but I am going there that I may awaken him out of his sleep.

12 The disciples answered, Lord, if he is sleeping, he will recover.

13 However, Jesus had spoken of his death, but they thought that He referred to falling into a refreshing *and* natural sleep.

14 So then Jesus told them plainly, Lazarus is dead;

15 And for your sake I am glad that I was not there; it will help you to believe—to trust and rely on Me. However, let us go to him.

16 Then Thomas, who was called the Twin, said to his fellow disciples, Let us go too, that we may die [be killed] along with Him.

17 So when Jesus arrived, He found that he [Lazarus] had already been in the tomb four days.

Living New Testament

38 But if I do, believe them even if you don't believe Me. Then you will become convinced that the Father is in Me, and I in the Father."

39 Once again they started to arrest Him. But He walked away and left them,

40 And went beyond the Jordan River to stay near the place where John was first baptizing.

41 And many followed Him. "John didn't do miracles," they remarked to one another, "but all his predictions concerning this man have come true."

42 And many came to the decision that He was the Messiah.[3]

Revised Standard

lieve me; 38but if I do them, even though
you do not believe me, believe the works,
that you may know and understand that
the Father is in me and I am in the Father." 39Again they tried to arrest him, but
he escaped from their hands.
40 He went away again across the Jordan to the place where John at first baptized, and there he remained. 41And many
came to him; and they said, "John did no
sign, but everything that John said about
this man was true." 42And many believed
in him there.

CHAPTER 11

Do you remember Mary, who poured the costly perfume on Jesus' feet and wiped them with her hair?[1] Well, her brother Lazarus, who lived in Bethany with his sisters Mary and Martha, was sick.

3 So the two sisters sent a message to Jesus telling Him, "Sir, your good friend is very, very sick."

4 But when Jesus heard about it He said, "The purpose of his illness is not death, but for the glory of God. I, the Son of God, will receive glory from this situation."

5 Although Jesus was very fond of Martha, Mary, and Lazarus,

6 He stayed where He was for the next two days and made no move to go to them.

7 Finally, after the two days, He said to His disciples, "Let's go to Judea."

8 But His disciples objected. "Master," they said, "only a few days ago the Jewish leaders in Judea were trying to kill You. Are You going there again?"

9 Jesus replied, "There are 12 hours of daylight every day, and during every hour of it a man can walk safely and not stumble.

10 Only at night is there danger of a wrong step, because of the dark."

11 Then He said, "Our friend Lazarus has gone to sleep, but now I will go and awaken him!"

12, 13 The disciples, thinking Jesus meant Lazarus was having a good night's rest, said, "That means he is getting better!" But Jesus meant Lazarus had died.

14 And He told them plainly, "Lazarus is dead.

15 And for your sake, I am glad I wasn't there, for this will give you another opportunity to believe in Me. Come, let's go to him."

16 Thomas, nicknamed "The Twin", said to his fellow disciples, "Let's go too—and die with Him."

17 When they arrived in Bethany, they were told that Lazarus had already been in his tomb for four days.

[3] Literally, "Many believed on Him there."
[1] See John 12:3.

Jesus hears of Lazarus' death

11 Now a certain man was ill, Lazarus
of Bethany, the village of Mary and
her sister Martha. 2It was Mary who anointed the Lord with ointment and wiped his
feet with her hair, whose brother Lazarus
was ill. 3So the sisters sent to him, saying,
"Lord, he whom you love is ill." 4But when
Jesus heard it he said, "This illness is not
unto death; it is for the glory of God, so
that the Son of God may be glorified by
means of it."
5 Now Jesus loved Martha and her sister and Lazarus. 6So when he heard that
he was ill, he stayed two days longer in
the place where he was. 7Then after this
he said to the disciples, "Let us go into
Judea again." 8The disciples said to him,
"Rabbi, the Jews were but now seeking
to stone you, and are you going there
again?" 9Jesus answered, "Are there not
twelve hours in the day? If any one walks
in the day, he does not stumble, because he
sees the light of this world. 10But if any
one walks in the night, he stumbles, because
the light is not in him." 11Thus he spoke,
and then he said to them, "Our friend
Lazarus has fallen asleep, but I go to awake
him out of sleep. 12The disciples said to
him, "Lord if he has fallen asleep, he will
recover." 13Now Jesus had spoken of his
death, but they thought that he meant
taking rest in sleep. 14Then Jesus told
them plainly, "Lazarus is dead; 15and for
your sake I am glad that I was not there,
so that you may believe. But let us go to
him." 16Thomas, called the Twin, said to
his fellow disciples, "Let us also go, that
we may die with him."

Jesus the resurrection and the life

17 Now when Jesus came, he found that
Lazarus[x] had already been in the tomb

[x] Greek *he*

King James

18 Now Bethany was nigh unto Jerusalem, about fifteen furlongs off:

19 And many of the Jews came to Martha and Mary, to comfort them concerning their brother.

20 Then Martha, as soon as she heard that Jesus was coming, went and met him: but Mary sat *still* in the house.

21 Then said Martha unto Jesus, Lord, if thou hadst been here, my brother had not died.

22 But I know, that even now, whatsoever thou wilt ask of God, God will give *it* thee.

23 Jesus saith unto her, Thy brother shall rise again.

24 Martha saith unto him, I know that he shall rise again in the resurrection at the last day.

25 Jesus said unto her, I am the resurrection, and the life: he that believeth in me, though he were dead, yet shall he live:

26 And whosoever liveth and believeth in me shall never die. Believest thou this?

27 She saith unto him, Yea, Lord: I believe that thou art the Christ, the Son of God, which should come into the world.

28 And when she had so said, she went her way, and called Mary her sister secretly, saying, The Master is come, and calleth for thee.

29 As soon as she heard *that*, she arose quickly, and came unto him.

30 Now Jesus was not yet come into the town, but was in that place where Martha met him.

31 The Jews then which were with her in the house, and comforted her, when they saw Mary, that she rose up hastily and went out, followed her, saying, She goeth unto the grave to weep there.

32 Then when Mary was come where Jesus was, and saw him, she fell down at his feet, saying unto him, Lord, if thou hadst been here, my brother had not died.

33 When Jesus therefore saw her weeping, and the Jews also weeping which came with her, he groaned in the spirit, and was troubled,

34 And said, Where have ye laid him? They said unto him, Lord, come and see.

35 Jesus wept.

36 Then said the Jews, Behold how he loved him!

37 And some of them said, Could not this man, which opened the eyes of the blind, have caused that even this man should not have died?

38 Jesus therefore again groaning in himself cometh to the grave. It was a cave, and a stone lay upon it.

39 Jesus said, Take ye away the stone. Martha, the sister of him that was dead, saith unto him, Lord, by this time he stinketh: for he hath been *dead* four days.

40 Jesus saith unto her, Said I not unto thee, that, if thou wouldest believe, thou shouldest see the glory of God?

41 Then they took away the stone *from the place* where the dead was laid. And Jesus lifted up *his* eyes, and said, Father, I thank thee that thou hast heard me.

Amplified

18 Bethany was near Jerusalem, only about two miles away.

19 And a considerable number of the Jews had gone out to see Martha and Mary to console them concerning their brother.

20 When Martha heard that Jesus was coming, she went to meet Him, while Mary remained sitting in the house.

21 Martha then said to Jesus, Master, if You had been here, my brother would not have died.

22 And even now I know that whatever You ask from God He will grant it to You.

23 Jesus said to her, Your brother shall rise again.

24 Martha replied, I know that he will rise again at the resurrection in the last day.

25 Jesus said to her, I am [Myself] the Resurrection and the Life. Whoever believes in—adheres to, trusts in and relies on—Me, although he may die, yet he shall live.

26 And whoever continues to live and believes—has faith in, cleaves to and relies—on Me shall never [actually] die at all. Do you believe this?

27 She said to Him, Yes, Lord, I have believed—I do believe—that You are the Messiah, the Anointed One, the Son of God, [even He] Who was to come into the world. [It is for Your coming that the world has waited.]

28 After she had said this, she went back and called her sister Mary, privately whispering to her, The Teacher is close at hand and is asking for you.

29 When she heard this she sprang up quickly and went to Him.

30 Now Jesus had not yet entered the village, but was still at the same spot where Martha had met Him.

31 When the Jews who were sitting with her in the house and consoling her saw how hastily Mary had arisen and gone out, they followed her, supposing that she was going to the tomb to pour out her grief there.

32 When Mary came to the place where Jesus was and saw Him, she dropped down at His feet, saying to Him, Lord, if You had been here my brother would not have died.

33 When Jesus saw her sobbing, and the Jews who came with her [also] sobbing, He was deeply moved in spirit and troubled—He chafed in spirit, and sighed and was disturbed.

34 And He said, Where have you laid him? They said to Him, Lord, come and see.

35 Jesus wept.

36 The Jews said, See how tenderly He loved him!

37 But some of them said, Could not He, Who opened a blind man's eyes, have prevented this man from dying?

38 Now Jesus again sighing repeatedly *and* deeply disquieted, approached the tomb. It was a cave—a hole in the rock—and a boulder lay against [the entrance to close] it.

39 Jesus said, Take away the stone. Martha, the sister of the dead man, exclaimed, But Lord, by this time he [is decaying and] throws off an offensive odor, for he has been dead four days!

40 Jesus said to her, Did I not tell you *and* [o]promise you that if you would believe *and* rely on Me, you should see the glory of God?

41 So they took away the stone. And Jesus lifted up His eyes and said, Father, I thank You that You have heard Me.

---

o) Williams.

Living New Testament

18 Bethany was only a couple of miles down the road from Jerusalem,

19 And many of the Jewish leaders had come to pay their respects and to console Martha and Mary on their loss.

20 When Martha got word that Jesus was coming, she went to meet Him. But Mary stayed at home.

21 Martha said to Jesus, "Sir, if You had been here, my brother wouldn't have died.

22 And even now it's not too late, for I know that God will bring my brother back to life again, if You will only ask Him to."

23 Jesus told her, "Your brother will come back to life again."

24 "Yes," Martha said, "when everyone else does, on Resurrection Day."

25 Jesus told her, "I am the one who raises the dead and gives them life again. Anyone who believes in Me, even though he dies like anyone else, shall live again.

26 He is given eternal life for believing in Me and shall never perish.[2] Do you believe this, Martha?"

27 "Yes, Master," she told Him. "I believe You are the Messiah, the Son of God, the one we have so long awaited."

28 Then she left Him and returned to Mary and calling her aside from the mourners told her, "He is here and wants to see you."

29 So Mary went to Him at once.

30 Now Jesus had stayed outside the village, at the place where Martha met Him.

31 When the Jewish leaders who were at the house trying to console Mary saw her leave so hastily, they assumed she was going to Lazarus' tomb to weep; so they followed her.

32 When Mary arrived where Jesus was, she fell down at His feet, saying, "Sir, if You had been here, my brother would still be alive."

33 When Jesus saw her weeping and the Jewish leaders wailing with her, He was moved with indignation and deeply troubled.

34 "Where is he buried?" He asked them.

They told Him, "Come and see."

35 Tears came to Jesus' eyes.

36 "They were close friends," the Jewish leaders said. "See how much he loved him."

37, 38 But some said, "This fellow healed a blind man—why couldn't he keep Lazarus from dying?" And again Jesus was moved with deep anger. Then they came to the tomb. It was a cave with a heavy stone rolled across its door.

39 "Roll the stone aside," Jesus told them.

But Martha, the dead man's sister, said, "By now the smell will be terrible, for he has been dead four days."

40 "But didn't I tell you that you will see a wonderful miracle from God if you believe?" Jesus asked her.

41 So they rolled the stone aside. Then Jesus looked up to heaven and said, "Father, thank You for hearing Me."

Literally, "Whoever lives and believes on Me shall never die."

Revised Standard

four days. 18 Bethany was near Jerusalem,
about two miles[y] off, 19 and many of the
Jews had come to Martha and Mary to
console them concerning their brother.
20 When Martha heard that Jesus was coming, she went and met him, while Mary sat
in the house. 21 Martha said to Jesus, "Lord,
if you had been here, my brother would
not have died. 22 And even now I know
that whatever you ask from God, God
will give you." 23 Jesus said to her, "Your
brother will rise again." 24 Martha said to
him, "I know that he will rise again in
the resurrection at the last day." 25 Jesus
said to her, "I am the resurrection and
the life;[z] he who believes in me, though
he die, yet shall he live, 26 and whoever lives
and believes in me shall never die. Do you
believe this?" 27 She said to him, "Yes,
Lord; I believe that you are the Christ, the
Son of God, he who is coming into the
world."

Jesus talks with Mary

28 When she had said this, she went
and called her sister Mary, saying quietly,
"The Teacher is here and is calling for
you." 29 And when she heard it, she rose
quickly and went to him. 30 Now Jesus had
not yet come to the village, but was still in
the place where Martha had met him.
31 When the Jews who were with her in
the house, consoling her, saw Mary rise
quickly and go out, they followed her, supposing that she was going to the tomb to
weep there. 32 Then Mary, when she came
where Jesus was and saw him, fell at his
feet, saying to him, "Lord, if you had
been here, my brother would not have
died." 33 When Jesus saw her weeping, and
the Jews who came with her also weeping,
he was deeply moved in spirit and troubled;
34 and he said, "Where have you laid him?"
They said to him, "Lord, come and see."
35 Jesus wept. 36 So the Jews said, "See how
he loved him!" 37 But some of them said,
"Could not he who opened the eyes of the
blind man have kept this man from dying?"

Jesus raises Lazarus

38 Then Jesus, deeply moved again,
came to the tomb; it was a cave, and a
stone lay upon it. 39 Jesus said, "Take away
the stone." Martha, the sister of the dead
man, said to him, "Lord, by this time there
will be an odor, for he has been dead
four days." 40 Jesus said to her, "Did I
not tell you that if you would believe you
would see the glory of God?" 41 So they
took away the stone. And Jesus lifted up
his eyes and said, "Father, I thank thee

[y] Greek *fifteen stadia*

[z] Other ancient authorities omit *and the life*

King James

42 And I knew that thou hearest me always: but because of the people which stand by I said *it*, that they may believe that thou hast sent me.

43 And when he thus had spoken, he cried with a loud voice, Lazarus, come forth.

44 And he that was dead came forth, bound hand and foot with graveclothes: and his face was bound about with a napkin. Jesus saith unto them, Loose him, and let him go.

45 Then many of the Jews which came to Mary, and had seen the things which Jesus did, believed on him.

46 But some of them went their ways to the Pharisees, and told them what things Jesus had done.

47 ¶ Then gathered the chief priests and Pharisees a council, and said, What do we? for this man doeth many miracles.

48 If we let him thus alone, all *men* will believe on him: and the Romans shall come and take away both our place and nation.

49 And one of them, *named* Caiaphas, being the high priest that same year, said unto them, Ye know nothing at all,

50 Nor consider that it is expedient for us that one man should die for the people, and that the whole nation perish not.

51 And this spake he not of himself: but being high priest that year, he prophesied that Jesus should die for that nation;

52 And not for that nation only, but that also he should gather together in one the children of God that were scattered abroad.

53 Then from that day forth they took counsel together for to put him to death.

54 Jesus therefore walked no more openly among the Jews; but went thence unto a country near to the wilderness, into a city called Ephraim, and there continued with his disciples.

55 ¶ And the Jews' passover was nigh at hand: and many went out of the country up to Jerusalem before the passover, to purify themselves.

56 Then sought they for Jesus, and spake among themselves, as they stood in the temple, What think ye, that he will not come to the feast?

57 Now both the chief priests and the Pharisees had given a commandment, that, if any man knew where he were, he should shew *it*, that they might take him.

CHAPTER 12

THEN Jesus six days before the passover came to Bethany, where Lazarus was which had been dead, whom he raised from the dead.

2 There they made him a supper; and Martha served: but Lazarus was one of them that sat at the table with him.

Amplified

42 Yes, I know You always hear *and* listen to Me; but I have said this on account of *and* for the benefit of the people standing around, so that they may believe You did send Me—that You have made Me Your Messenger.

43 When He had said this, He shouted with a loud voice, Lazarus, come out!

44 And out walked the man who had been dead, his hands and feet wrapped in burial cloths (linen strips), and with a [burial] napkin bound around his face. Jesus said to them, Free him of the burial wrappings and let him go.

45 Upon seeing what Jesus had done, many of the Jews who had come with Mary believed on Him—they trusted in Him and adhered to Him and relied on Him.

46 But some of them went back to the Pharisees and told them what Jesus had done.

47 So the chief priests and Pharisees called a meeting of the council [the Sanhedrin] and said, What are we to do? For this Man performs many signs (evidences, miracles).

48 If we let Him alone to go on like this, everyone will believe in Him *and* adhere to Him, and the Romans will come and suppress *and* destroy *and* take away our [holy] place and our nation [[p]our temple and city, and our civil organization].

49 But one of them, Caiaphas, who was the high priest that year, declared, You know nothing at all.

50 Nor do you understand *or* reason out that it is expedient *and* better for your own welfare that one man should die on behalf of the people than that the whole nation should perish (be destroyed, ruined).

51 Now he did not say this simply of his own accord—he was not self-moved; but being the high priest that year, he prophesied that Jesus was to die for the nation; [Isa. 53:8.]

52 And not only for the nation, but also for the purpose of uniting into one body the children of God who have been scattered far and wide. [Isa. 49:6.]

53 So from that day on they took counsel *and* plotted together how they might put Him to death.

54 For that reason Jesus no longer appeared publicly among the Jews, but left there and retired to the district that borders on the wilderness (the desert), to a village called Ephraim, and there He stayed with the disciples.

55 Now the Jewish Passover was at hand, and many from the country went up to Jerusalem in order that they might purify *and* consecrate themselves before the Passover.

56 So they kept looking for Jesus and questioned among themselves as they were standing about in the temple [q]area, What do you think? Will He not come to the feast at all?

57 Now the chief priests and Pharisees had given orders that if any one knew where He was, he should report it to them, so that they might arrest Him.

CHAPTER 12

SO six days before the Passover Feast Jesus came to Bethany where Lazarus was, who had died and whom He had raised from the dead.

2 So they made Him a supper, and Martha served, but Lazarus was one of those at the table with Him.

---

p) Vincent: "Word Studies in the New Testament."
q) Trench.

Living New Testament

42 (You always hear Me, of course, but I said it because of all these people standing here, so that they will believe You sent Me.)"

43 Then He shouted, "Lazarus, come out!"

44 And Lazarus came—bound up in the gravecloth, his face muffled in a head swath. Jesus told them, "Unwrap him and let him go!"

45 And so at last many of the Jewish leaders who were with Mary and saw it happen, finally believed on Him!

46 But some went away to the Pharisees and reported it to them.

47 Then the chief priests and Pharisees convened a council to discuss the situation. "What are we going to do?" they asked each other, "for this man certainly does miracles.

48 If we let him alone the whole nation will follow him—and then the Roman army will come and kill us and take over the Jewish government."

49 And one of them, Caiaphas, who was High Priest that year, said, "You stupid idiots—

50 Let this one man die for the people—why should the whole nation perish?"

51 This prophecy that Jesus should die for the entire nation came from Caiaphas in his position as High Priest —he didn't think of it by himself, but was inspired to say it.

52 It was a prediction that Jesus' death would not be for Israel only, but for all the children of God scattered around the world.

53 So from that time on the Jewish leaders began plotting Jesus' death.

54 Jesus now stopped His public ministry and left Jerusalem; he went to the edge of the desert, to the village of Ephraim, and stayed there with His disciples.

55 The Passover, a Jewish holy day, was near, and many country people arrived in Jerusalem several days early so that they could go through the cleansing ceremony before the Passover began.

56 They wanted to see Jesus, and as they gossiped in the Temple, they asked each other, "What do you think? Will He come for the Passover?"

57 Meanwhile the chief priests and Pharisees had publicly announced that anyone seeing Jesus must report Him immediately so that they could arrest Him.

CHAPTER 12

Six days before Passover ceremonies began, Jesus arrived in Bethany where Lazarus was—the man He had brought back to life.

2 A banquet was prepared in Jesus' honor. Martha served, and Lazarus sat at the table with Him.

Revised Standard

that thou hast heard me. 42 I knew that
thou hearest me always, but I have said
this on account of the people standing by,
that they may believe that thou didst send
me." 43 When he had said this, he cried
with a loud voice, "Lazarus, come out."
44 The dead man came out, his hands and
feet bound with bandages, and his face
wrapped with a cloth. Jesus said to them,
"Unbind him, and let him go."

Pharisees plot to kill Jesus

45 Many of the Jews therefore, who had
come with Mary and had seen what he did,
believed in him; 46 but some of them went
to the Pharisees and told them what Jesus
had done. 47 So the chief priests and the
Phariseees gathered the council, and said,
"What are we to do? For this man performs many signs. 48 If we let him go on
thus, every one will believe in him, and
the Romans will come and destroy both
our holy place[a] and our nation." 49 But one
of them, Caiaphas, who was high priest that
year, said to them, "You know nothing at
all; 50 you do not understand that it is
expedient for you that one man should die
for the people, and that the whole nation
should not perish." 51 He did not say this
of his own accord, but being high priest
that year he prophesied that Jesus should
die for the nation, 52 and not for the nation only, but to gather into one the children of God who are scattered abroad. 53 So
from that day on they took counsel how
to put him to death.
54 Jesus therefore no longer went about
openly among the Jews, but went from there
to the country near the wilderness, to a town
called Ephraim; and there he stayed with
the disciples.
55 Now the Passover of the Jews was
at hand, and many went up from the country to Jerusalem before the Passover, to
purify themselves. 56 They were looking for
Jesus and saying to one another as they
stood in the temple, "What do you think?
That he will not come to the feast?" 57 Now
the chief priests and the Pharisees had
given orders that if any one knew where he
was, he should let them know, so that they
might arrest him.

Jesus anointed by Mary of Bethany

12 Six days before the Passover, Jesus
came to Bethany, where Lazarus was,
whom Jesus had raised from the dead.
2 There they made him a supper; Martha
served, and Lazarus was one of those at

[a] Greek *our place*

King James

3 Then took Mary a pound of ointment of spikenard, very costly, and anointed the feet of Jesus, and wiped his feet with her hair: and the house was filled with the odour of the ointment.

4 Then saith one of his disciples, Judas Iscariot, Simon's *son*, which should betray him,

5 Why was not this ointment sold for three hundred pence, and given to the poor?

6 This he said, not that he cared for the poor; but because he was a thief, and had the bag, and bare what was put therein.

7 Then said Jesus, Let her alone: against the day of my burying hath she kept this.

8 For the poor always ye have with you; but me ye have not always.

9 Much people of the Jews therefore knew that he was there: and they came not for Jesus' sake only, but that they might see Lazarus also, whom he had raised from the dead.

10 ¶ But the chief priests consulted that they might put Lazarus also to death;

11 Because that by reason of him many of the Jews went away, and believed on Jesus.

12 ¶ On the next day much people that were come to the feast, when they heard that Jesus was coming to Jerusalem,

13 Took branches of palm trees, and went forth to meet him, and cried, Hosanna: Blessed *is* the King of Israel that cometh in the name of the Lord.

14 And Jesus, when he had found a young ass, sat thereon; as it is written,

15 Fear not, daughter of Sion: behold, thy King cometh, sitting on an ass's colt.

16 These things understood not his disciples at the first: but when Jesus was glorified, then remembered they that these things were written of him, and *that* they had done these things unto him.

17 The people therefore that was with him when he called Lazarus out of his grave, and raised him from the dead, bare record.

18 For this cause the people also met him, for that they heard that he had done this miracle.

19 The Pharisees therefore said among themselves, Perceive ye how ye prevail nothing? behold, the world is gone after him.

20 ¶ And there were certain Greeks among them that came up to worship at the feast:

21 The same came therefore to Philip, which was of Bethsaida of Galilee, and desired him, saying, Sir, we would see Jesus.

22 Philip cometh and telleth Andrew: and again Andrew and Philip tell Jesus.

23 ¶ And Jesus answered them, saying, The hour is come, that the Son of man should be glorified.

24 Verily, verily, I say unto you, Except a corn of wheat fall into the ground and die, it abideth alone: but if it die, it bringeth forth much fruit.

Amplified

3 Mary took a pound of ointment of pure liquid nard [a rare perfume] that was very expensive, and she poured it on Jesus' feet and wiped them with her hair. And the whole house was filled with the fragrance of the perfume.

4 But Judas Iscariot, the one of His disciples who was about to betray Him, said,

5 Why was this perfume not sold for [r]three hundred denarii, and that given to the poor—the destitute?

6 Now he did not say this because he cared for the poor, but because he was a thief and having the bag [the money box, the purse of the twelve], he took for himself what was put into it—pilfering the collections.

7 But Jesus said, Let her alone. It was that she might keep it for the time of My preparation for burial—she has kept it that she might have it for the time of My [s]embalming.

8 You always have the poor with you, but you do not always have Me.

9 Now a great crowd of the Jews heard that He was at Bethany, and they came there, not only because of Jesus, but that they also might see Lazarus whom He had raised from the dead.

10 So the chief priests planned to put Lazarus to death also,

11 Because on account of him many of the Jews were going away—were withdrawing *and* leaving [the Judeans]—and believing in *and* adhering to Jesus.

12 The next day a vast crowd of those who had come to the Passover Feast heard that Jesus was coming to Jerusalem.

13 So they took branches of palm trees and went out to meet Him. And as they went they kept shouting, Hosanna! Blessed is He *and* praise to Him Who comes in the name of the Lord, even the King of Israel! [Ps. 118:26.]

14 And Jesus, having found a young donkey, rode upon it, [just] as it is written in the Scriptures,

15 Do not fear, O daughter of Zion! Look! Your King is coming, sitting on a donkey's colt! [Zech. 9:9.]

16 His disciples did not understand *and* could not comprehend the meaning of these things at first, but when Jesus was glorified *and* exalted, they remembered that these things had been written about Him and had been done to Him.

17 The group that had been with Jesus when He called Lazarus out of the tomb and raised him from among the dead, kept telling it to others—bearing witness.

18 It was for this reason that the crowd went out to meet Him, because they had heard that He had performed this sign (proof, miracle).

19 Then the Pharisees said among themselves, You see how futile your efforts are *and* how you accomplish nothing. See! The whole world is running after Him!

20 Now among those who went up to worship at the feast were some Greeks.

21 These came to Philip, who was from Bethsaida in Galilee, and they made this request, Sir, we desire to see Jesus.

22 Philip came and told Andrew. Then Andrew and Philip together [went] and told Jesus.

23 And Jesus answered them, The time has come for the Son of man to be glorified *and* exalted.

24 I assure you, most solemnly I tell you, Unless a grain of wheat falls into the earth and dies, it remains [just one grain; never becomes more but lives] by itself alone. But if it dies, it produces many others *and* yields a rich harvest.

---

r) The wages of an ordinary workman for a whole year.
s) Vincent.

Living New Testament

3 Then Mary took a jar of costly perfume made from essence of nard, and anointed Jesus' feet with it and wiped them with her hair. And the house was filled with fragrance.

4 But Judas Iscariot, one of His disciples—the one who would betray Him—said,

5 "That perfume was worth a fortune. It should have been sold and the money given to the poor."

6 Not that he cared for the poor, but he was in charge of the disciples' funds and often dipped into them for his own use!

7 Jesus replied, "Let her alone. She did it in preparation for My burial.

8 You can always help the poor, but I won't be with you very long."

9 When the ordinary people of Jerusalem heard of His arrival, they flocked to see Him and also to see Lazarus—the man who had come back to life again.

10 Then the chief priests decided to kill Lazarus too,

11 For it was because of him that many of the Jewish leaders had deserted and believed in Jesus as their Messiah.

12 The next day, the news that Jesus was on the way to Jerusalem swept through the city, and a huge crowd of Passover visitors

13 Took palm branches and went down the road to meet Him, shouting, "The Savior! God bless the King of Israel! Hail to God's Ambassador!"

14 Jesus rode along on a donkey, fulfilling the prophecy that said,

15 "Don't be afraid of your King, people of Israel, for He will come to you meekly, sitting on a donkey's colt!"

16 (His disciples didn't realize at the time that this was a fulfillment of prophecy; but after Jesus returned to His glory in heaven, then they noticed how many prophecies of Scripture had come true before their eyes.)

17 And those in the crowd who had seen Jesus call Lazarus back to life were telling about it.

18 That was the main reason why so many went out to meet Him—because they had heard about this mighty miracle.

19 Then the Pharisees said to each other, "We've lost. Look—the whole world has gone after him!"

20 Some Greeks who had come to Jerusalem to attend the Passover

21 Paid a visit to Philip,[1] who was from Bethsaida, and said, "Sir, we want to meet Jesus."

22 Philip told Andrew about it, and they went together to ask Jesus.

23, 24 Jesus replied that the time had come for Him to return to His glory in heaven, and that "I must fall and die like a kernel of wheat that falls between the furrows of the earth. Unless I die I will be alone—a single seed. But My death will produce many new wheat kernels—a plentiful harvest of new lives.

[1] Philip's name was Greek, though he was a Jew.

Revised Standard

table with him. [3]Mary took a pound of costly ointment of pure nard and anointed the feet of Jesus and wiped his feet with her hair; and the house was filled with the fragrance of the ointment. [4]But Judas Iscariot, one of his disciples (he who was to betray him), said, [5]"Why was this ointment not sold for three hundred denarii[b] and given to the poor?" [6]This he said, not that he cared for the poor but because he was a thief, and as he had the money box he used to take what was put into it. [7]Jesus said, "Let her alone, let her keep it for the day of my burial. [8]The poor you always have with you, but you do not always have me."

9 When the great crowd of the Jews learned that he was there, they came, not only on account of Jesus but also to see Lazarus, whom he had raised from the dead. [10]So the chief priests planned to put Lazarus also to death, [11]because on account of him many of the Jews were going away and believing in Jesus.

The triumphal entry

12 The next day a great crowd who had come to the feast heard that Jesus was coming to Jerusalem. [13]So they took branches of palm trees and went out to meet him, crying, "Hosanna! Blessed is he who comes in the name of the Lord, even the King of Israel!" [14]And Jesus found a young ass and sat upon it; as it is written,

[15]"Fear not, daughter of Zion;
behold, your king is coming,
sitting on an ass's colt!"

[16]His disciples did not understand this at first; but when Jesus was glorified, then they remembered that this had been written of him and had been done to him. [17]The crowd that had been with him when he called Lazarus out of the tomb and raised him from the dead bore witness. [18]The reason why the crowd went to meet him was that they heard he had done this sign. [19]The Pharisees then said to one another, "You see that you can do nothing; look, the world has gone after him."

Jesus sought by the Gentiles

20 Now among those who went up to worship at the feast were some Greeks. [21]So these came to Philip, who was from Bethsaida in Galilee, and said to him, "Sir, we wish to see Jesus." [22]Philip went and told Andrew; Andrew went with Philip and they told Jesus. [23]And Jesus answered them, "The hour has come for the Son of man to be glorified. [24]Truly, truly, I say to you, unless a grain of wheat falls into the earth and dies, it remains alone; but if it dies, it bears much fruit. [25]He

[b] The denarius was worth about twenty cents

King James

25 He that loveth his life shall lose it; and he that hateth his life in this world shall keep it unto life eternal.

26 If any man serve me, let him follow me; and where I am, there shall also my servant be: if any man serve me, him will *my* Father honour.

27 Now is my soul troubled; and what shall I say? Father, save me from this hour: but for this cause came I unto this hour.

28 Father, glorify thy name. Then came there a voice from heaven, *saying*, I have both glorified *it*, and will glorify *it* again.

29 The people therefore, that stood by, and heard *it*, said that it thundered: others said, An angel spake to him.

30 Jesus answered and said, This voice came not because of me, but for your sakes.

31 Now is the judgment of this world: now shall the prince of this world be cast out.

32 And I, if I be lifted up from the earth, will draw all *men* unto me.

33 This he said, signifying what death he should die.

34 The people answered him, We have heard out of the law that Christ abideth for ever: and how sayest thou, The Son of man must be lifted up? who is this Son of man?

35 Then Jesus said unto them, Yet a little while is the light with you. Walk while ye have the light, lest darkness come upon you: for he that walketh in darkness knoweth not whither he goeth.

36 While ye have light, believe in the light, that ye may be the children of light. These things spake Jesus, and departed, and did hide himself from them.

37 ¶ But though he had done so many miracles before them, yet they believed not on him:

38 That the saying of Esaias the prophet might be fulfilled, which he spake, Lord, who hath believed our report? and to whom hath the arm of the Lord been revealed?

39 Therefore they could not believe, because that Esaias said again,

40 He hath blinded their eyes, and hardened their heart; that they should not see with *their* eyes, nor understand with *their* heart, and be converted, and I should heal them.

41 These things said Esaias, when he saw his glory, and spake of him.

42 ¶ Nevertheless among the chief rulers also many believed on him; but because of the Pharisees they did not confess *him*, lest they should be put out of the synagogue:

Amplified

25 Any one who loves his life loses it. But any one who hates his life in this world will keep it to life eternal.—Whoever has no love for, no concern for, no regard for his life here on the earth, but despises it, preserves his life forever and ever.

26 If any one would serve Me, he must continue to follow Me—[t]to cleave steadfastly to Me, conform wholly to My example, in living and if need be in dying—and wherever I am, there will My servant be also. If any one serves Me, the Father will honor him.

27 Now My soul is troubled *and* distressed, and what shall I say? Father, save Me from this hour [of trial and agony]? But it was for this very purpose that I have come to this hour [that I might undergo it].

28 [Rather, I will say,] Father, glorify—honor and extol—Your own name! Then there came a voice out of heaven saying, I have already glorified it, and I will glorify it again.

29 The crowd of bystanders heard the sound and said that it had thundered. Others said, An angel has spoken to Him!

30 Jesus answered, This voice has not come for My sake, but for your sake.

31 Now the judgment (crisis) of this world is [coming on]—sentence is now being passed on this world. Now the ruler (evil genius, prince) of this world shall be cast out—expelled.

32 And I, if *and* when I am lifted up from the earth [on the cross], will draw *and* attract all men [Gentile as well as Jew] to Myself.

33 He said this to signify in what manner He would die.

34 At this the people answered Him, We have learned from the Law that the Christ is to remain forever. How then can You say, The Son of man must be lifted up [on the cross]? Who is this Son of man? [Ps. 110:4.]

35 So Jesus said to them, You will have the Light only a little while longer. Walk while you have the Light—keep on living by it—so that darkness may not overtake *and* overcome you. He who walks about in the dark does not know where he goes—he is drifting.

36 While you have the Light, believe in the Light—have faith in it, hold to it, rely on it—that you may become sons of the Light *and* be filled with light. Jesus said these things and then He went away and hid Himself from them—was lost to their view.

37 Even though He had done so many miracles before them—right before their eyes—yet they still did not trust in Him *and* failed to believe on Him.

38 So that what Isaiah the prophet said was fulfilled, Lord, who has believed our report *and* our message? And to whom has the arm (the power) of the Lord been shown—unveiled and revealed? [Isa. 53:1.]

39 Therefore, they could not believe—they were unable to believe. For Isaiah has also said,

40 He has blinded their eyes, and hardened *and* benumbed their [callous, degenerated] heart—He has made their minds dull—to keep them from seeing with their eyes and understanding with their heart *and* mind and repenting *and* turning to Me to heal them.

41 Isaiah said this because he saw His glory and spoke of Him. [Isa. 6:9, 10.]

42 And yet [in spite of all this] many even of the leading men—of the authorities and the nobles—believed *and* trusted in Him. But because of the Pharisees they did not confess it, for fear [that if they should acknowledge Him] they would be expelled from the synagogue.

---

t) Thayer.

Living New Testament

25 If you love your life down here—you will lose it. If you despise your life down here—you will exchange it for eternal glory.

26 If these Greeks[2] want to be My disciples, tell them to come and follow Me, for My servants must be where I am. And if they follow Me, the Father will honor them.

27 Now My soul is deeply troubled. Shall I pray, 'Father, save Me from what lies ahead'? But that is the very reason why I came!

28 Father, bring glory and honor to Your name."

Then a voice spoke from heaven saying, "I have already done this, and I will do it again."

29 When the crowd heard the voice, some of them thought it was thunder while others declared an angel had spoken to Him.

30 Then Jesus told them, "The voice was for your benefit, not Mine.

31 The time of judgment for the world has come—and the time when Satan,[3] the prince of this world, shall be cast out.

32 And when I am lifted up [on the cross[4]], I will draw everyone to Me."

33 He said this to indicate how He was going to die.

34 "Die?" asked the crowd. "We understood that the Messiah would live forever and never die. Why are you saying he will die? What Messiah are you talking about?"

35 Jesus replied, "My light will shine out for you just a little while longer. Walk in it while you can, and go where you want to go before the darkness falls, for then it will be too late for you to find your way.

36 Make use of the Light while there is still time; then you will become light bearers."[5] After saying these things, Jesus went away and was hidden from them.

37 But despite all the miracles He had done, most of the people would not believe He was the Messiah.

38 This is exactly what Isaiah the prophet had predicted: "Lord, who will believe us? Who will accept God's mighty miracles as proof?"[6]

39 But they couldn't believe, for as Isaiah also said:

40 "God[7] has blinded their eyes and hardened their hearts so that they can neither see nor understand nor turn to Me to heal them."

41 Isaiah was referring to Jesus when he made this prediction, for he had seen a vision of the Messiah's glory.

42 However, even many of the Jewish leaders believed Him to be the Messiah but wouldn't admit it to anyone because of their fear that the Pharisees would excommunicate them from the synagogue;

Revised Standard

who loves his life loses it, and he who
hates his life in this world will keep it for
eternal life. 26 If any one serves me, he
must follow me; and where I am, there
shall my servant be also; if any one serves
me, the Father will honor him.
27 "Now is my soul troubled. And what
shall I say? 'Father, save me from this
hour'? No, for this purpose I have come
to this hour. 28 Father, glorify thy name."
Then a voice came from heaven, "I have
glorified it, and I will glorify it again."
29 The crowd standing by heard it and
said that it had thundered. Others said,
"An angel has spoken to him." 30 Jesus
answered, "This voice has come for your
sake, not for mine. 31 Now is the judgment
of this world, now shall the ruler of this
world be cast out; 32 and I, when I am lifted
up from the earth, will draw all men to
myself." 33 He said this to show by what
death he was to die. 34 The crowd answered him, "We have heard from the law
that the Christ remains for ever. How
can you say that the Son of man must be
lifted up? Who is this Son of man?" 35 Jesus said to them, "The light is with you for
a little longer. Walk while you have the
light, lest the darkness overtake you; he
who walks in the darkness does not know
where he goes. 36 While you have the light,
believe in the light, that you may become
sons of light."

The cause of unbelief

When Jesus had said this, he departed
and hid himself from them. 37 Though he
had done so many signs before them, yet
they did not believe in him; 38 it was that
the word spoken by the prophet Isaiah
might be fulfilled:
"Lord, who has believed our report,
and to whom has the arm of the Lord
been revealed?"
39 Therefore they could not believe.
For Isaiah again said,
40 "He has blinded their eyes and hardened
their heart,
lest they should see with their eyes and
perceive with their heart,
and turn for me to heal them."
41 Isaiah said this because he saw his glory
and spoke of him. 42 Nevertheless many
even of the authorities believed in him,
but for fear of the Pharisees they did not
confess it, lest they should be put out

Literally, "if any man."
Implied. See 2 Corinthians 4:4, and Ephesians 2:2 and 6:12.
Implied.
Literally, "sons of light."
Literally, "To whom has the arm of the Lord been revealed?" Isaiah 53:1.
Literally, "He" Isaiah 6:10. The Greek here is a very free rendering, or paraphrase, of the original Hebrew.

King James

43 For they loved the praise of men more than the praise of God.

44 ¶ Jesus cried and said, He that believeth on me, believeth not on me, but on him that sent me.

45 And he that seeth me seeth him that sent me.

46 I am come a light into the world, that whosoever believeth on me should not abide in darkness.

47 And if any man hear my words, and believe not, I judge him not: for I came not to judge the world, but to save the world.

48 He that rejecteth me, and receiveth not my words, hath one that judgeth him: the word that I have spoken, the same shall judge him in the last day.

49 For I have not spoken of myself; but the Father which sent me, he gave me a commandment, what I should say, and what I should speak.

50 And I know that his commandment is life everlasting: whatsoever I speak therefore, even as the Father said unto me, so I speak.

Amplified

43 For they loved the approval *and* the praise *and* the glory that comes from men [instead of and] more than the glory that comes from God.—They valued their credit with men more than their credit with God.

44 But Jesus loudly declared, The one who believes on Me, does not [only] believe on *and* trust in *and* rely on Me, but [in believing on Me he believes] on Him Who sent Me.

45 And whoever sees Me sees Him Who sent Me.

46 I have come a light into the world, so that whoever believes on Me—who cleaves to *and* trusts in *and* relies on Me—may not continue to live in darkness.

47 If any one hears My teachings and fails to observe them—does not keep them, but disregards them—it is not I who judges him. For I have not come to judge *and* to condemn *and* to pass sentence *and* to inflict penalty on the world, but to save the world.

48 Any one who rejects Me *and* persistently sets Me at naught, refusing to accept My teachings, has his judge [however]; for the [very] message that I have spoken will itself judge *and* convict him on the last day.

49 This is because I have never spoken on My own authority *or* of My own accord *or* self-appointed, but the Father Who has sent Me has Himself given Me orders what to say and what to tell. [Deut. 18:18, 19.]

50 And I know that His commandment is (means,) eternal life. So whatever I speak, I am saying [exactly] what My Father has told Me to say *and* in accordance with His instructions.

CHAPTER 13

NOW before the feast of the passover, when Jesus knew that his hour was come that he should depart out of this world unto the Father, having loved his own which were in the world, he loved them unto the end.

2 And supper being ended, the devil having now put into the heart of Judas Iscariot, Simon's *son*, to betray him;

3 Jesus knowing that the Father had given all things into his hands, and that he was come from God, and went to God;

4 He riseth from supper, and laid aside his garments; and took a towel, and girded himself.

5 After that he poureth water into a basin, and began to wash the disciples' feet and to wipe *them* with the towel wherewith he was girded.

6 Then cometh he to Simon Peter: and Peter saith unto him, Lord, dost thou wash my feet?

7 Jesus answered and said unto him, What I do thou knowest not now; but thou shalt know hereafter.

8 Peter saith unto him, Thou shalt never wash my feet. Jesus answered him, If I wash thee not, thou hast no part with me.

9 Simon Peter saith unto him, Lord, not my feet only, but also *my* hands and *my* head.

CHAPTER 13

[NOW] before the Passover Feast began, Jesus knew (was fully aware) that the time had come for Him to leave this world *and* return to the Father. And as He had loved those who were His own in the world, He loved them to the last *and* [u]to the highest degree.

2 So during supper, Satan having already put the thought of betraying Jesus in the heart of Judas Iscariot, Simon's son,

3 Jesus, knowing (fully aware) that the Father had put everything into His hands, and that He had come from God and was [now] returning to God,

4 Got up from supper, took off His garments and taking a [servant's] towel, He fastened it around His waist.

5 Then He poured water into the washbasin and began to wash the disciples' feet and to wipe them with the [servant's] towel with which He was girded.

6 When He came to Simon Peter, [Peter] said to Him, Lord, are my feet to be washed by You?—Is it for You to wash my feet?

7 Jesus said to him, You do not understand now what I am doing, but you will understand later on.

8 Peter said to Him, You shall never wash my feet! Jesus answered him, Unless I wash you, you have no part with [[v]in] Me—no share in companionship with Me.

9 Simon Peter said to Him, Lord, [wash] not only my feet, but my hands and my head, too!

---

u) Chrysostom.

v) Origen; Adam Clarke, and others. cf. John 15:3-7, noticing "in Me . . . in Me . . . in Me . . . ," concerning the same subject the same evening.

Living New Testament

43 For they loved the praise of men more than the praise of God.

* * * * *

44 Jesus shouted to the crowds, "If you trust Me, you are really trusting God.

45 For when you see Me, you are seeing the one who sent Me.

46 I have come as a Light to shine in this dark world, so that all who put their trust in Me will no longer wander in the darkness.

47 If anyone hears Me and doesn't obey Me, I am not his judge—for I have come to save the world and not to judge it.

48 But all who reject Me and My message will be judged at the Day of Judgment by the truths I have spoken.

49 For these are not My own ideas, but I have told you what the Father said to tell you.

50 And I know His instructions lead to eternal life; so whatever He tells Me to say, I say!"

Revised Standard

of the synagogue: [43]for they loved the praise
of men more than the praise of God.

A summary of Jesus' claims

44 And Jesus cried out and said, "He
who believes in me, believes not in me but
in him who sent me. [45]And he who sees me
sees him who sent me. [46]I have come as
light into the world, that whoever believes
in me may not remain in darkness. [47]If
any one hears my sayings and does not
keep them, I do not judge him; for I did
not come to judge the world but to save
the world. [48]He who rejects me and does
not receive my sayings has a judge; the
word that I have spoken will be his judge
on the last day. [49]For I have not spoken
on my own authority; the Father who sent
me has himself given me commandment
what to say and what to speak. [50]And I
know that his commandment is eternal life.
What I say, therefore, I say as the Father
has bidden me."

CHAPTER 13

Jesus knew on the evening of Passover Day that it would be His last night on earth before returning to His Father. During supper the Devil had already suggested to Judas Iscariot, Simon's son, that this was the night to carry out his plan to betray Jesus. Jesus knew that the Father had given Him everything, and that He had come from God and would return to God. And how He loved His disciples!

4 So He got up from the supper table, took off His robe, wrapped a towel around His loins,[1]

5 Poured water into a basin, and began to wash the disciples' feet and to wipe them with the towel He had around Him.

6 When He came to Simon Peter, Peter said to Him, "Master, You shouldn't be washing our feet like this!"

7 Jesus replied, "You don't understand now why I am doing it; some day you will."

8 "No," Peter protested, "You shall never wash my feet!"

"But if I don't, you can't be My partner," Jesus replied.

9 Simon Peter exclaimed, "Then wash my hands and head as well—not just my feet!"

Washing the disciples' feet

13 Now before the feast of the Passover,
when Jesus knew that his hour had
come to depart out of this world to the
Father, having loved his own who were in
the world, he loved them to the end. [2]And
during supper, when the devil had already
put it into the heart of Judas Iscariot, Simon's son, to betray him, [3]Jesus, knowing
that the Father had given all things into
his hands, and that he had come from God
and was going to God, [4]rose from supper,
laid aside his garments, and girded himself
with a towel. [5]Then he poured water into
a basin, and began to wash the disciples'
feet, and to wipe them with the towel
with which he was girded. [6]He came to
Simon Peter; and Peter said to him, "Lord,
do you wash my feet?" [7]Jesus answered
him, "What I am doing you do not know
now, but afterward you will understand."
[8]Peter said to him, "You shall never wash
my feet." Jesus answered him, "If I do not
wash you, you have no part in me." [9]Si-
mon Peter said to him, "Lord, not my feet
only but also my hands and my head!"

---

[1] As the lowliest of slaves would dress.

King James

10 Jesus saith to him, He that is washed needeth not save to wash *his* feet, but is clean every whit: and ye are clean, but not all.

11 For he knew who should betray him; therefore said he, Ye are not all clean.

12 So after he had washed their feet, and had taken his garments, and was set down again, he said unto them, Know ye what I have done to you?

13 Ye call me Master and Lord: and ye say well; for *so* I am.

14 If I then, *your* Lord and Master, have washed your feet; ye also ought to wash one another's feet.

15 For I have given you an example that ye should do as I have done to you.

16 Verily, verily, I say unto you, The servant is not greater than his lord; neither he that is sent greater than he that sent him.

17 If ye know these things, happy are ye if ye do them.

18 ¶ I speak not of you all: I know whom I have chosen: but that the scripture may be fulfilled, He that eateth bread with me hath lifted up his heel against me.

19 Now I tell you before it come, that, when it is come to pass, ye may believe that I am *he*.

20 Verily, verily, I say unto you, He that receiveth whomsoever I send receiveth me; and he that receiveth me receiveth him that sent me.

21 When Jesus had thus said, he was troubled in spirit, and testified, and said, Verily, verily, I say unto you, that one of you shall betray me.

22 Then the disciples looked one on another, doubting of whom he spake.

23 Now there was leaning on Jesus' bosom one of his disciples, whom Jesus loved.

24 Simon Peter therefore beckoned to him, that he should ask who it should be of whom he spake.

25 He then lying on Jesus' breast saith unto him, Lord, who is it?

26 Jesus answered, He it is, to whom I shall give a sop, when I have dipped *it*. And when he had dipped the sop, he gave *it* to Judas Iscariot, *the son* of Simon.

27 And after the sop Satan entered into him. Then said Jesus unto him, That thou doest, do quickly.

28 Now no man at the table knew for what intent he spake this unto him.

29 For some *of them* thought, because Judas had the bag, that Jesus had said unto him, Buy *those things* that we have need of against the feast; or, that he should give something to the poor.

30 He then having received the sop went immediately out: and it was night.

Amplified

10 Jesus said to him, Any one who is bathed needs not to wash *except his feet* but is clean all over. And you [My disciples] are clean, but not all of you.

11 For He knew who was going to betray Him; that was the reason He said, You are not all of you clean.

12 So when He had finished washing their feet and had put on His garments and had sat down again, He said to them, Do you understand what I have done to you?

13 You call Me the Teacher (Master) and the Lord, and you are right in doing so, for that is what I am.

14 If I then, your Lord and Teacher (Master), have washed your feet, you ought—it is your duty, you are under obligation, you owe it—to wash one another's feet.

15 For I have given you this as an example, so that you should do [in your turn] what I have done to you.

16 I assure you, most solemnly I tell you, A servant is not greater than his master, and no one who is sent is superior to the one who sent him.

17 If you know these things, blessed *and* happy *and* [w]to be envied are you if you practice them—if you act accordingly and really do them.

18 I am not speaking of *and* I do not mean all of you. I know whom I have chosen; but it is that the Scripture may be fulfilled, He who eats [[x]his] bread with Me has raised up his heel against Me. [Ps. 41:9.]

19 I tell you this now before it occurs, so that when it does take place you may be persuaded *and* believe that I am He—what I say I am, the Christ, the Anointed One, the Messiah.

20 I assure you, most solemnly I tell you, he who receives *and* welcomes *and* takes into his heart any messenger of Mine, receives Me [in just that way]; and he who receives *and* welcomes *and* takes Me into his heart, receives Him Who sent Me [in that same way].

21 After Jesus had said these things, He was troubled (disturbed, agitated) in spirit, and said, I assure you, most solemnly I tell you that one of you will deliver Me up—be false to Me and betray Me!

22 The disciples kept looking at one another, puzzled as to whom He could mean.

23 One of His disciples whom Jesus loved—whom He esteemed and delighted in—was reclining [next to Him] on Jesus' bosom.

24 So Simon Peter motioned to him to ask of whom He was speaking.

25 Then leaning back against Jesus' breast, he asked Him, Lord, who is it?

26 Jesus answered, It is the one to whom I am going to give this morsel (bit) of food after I have dipped it. So when He had dipped the morsel of bread [into the dish], He gave it to Judas, Simon Iscariot's son.

27 Then, after [he had taken] the bit of food, Satan entered into *and* took possession of [Judas]. Jesus said to him, What you are going to do, do [[y]more swiftly than you seem to intend] *and* [z]make quick work of it.

28 But nobody reclining at the table knew why He spoke to him, *or* what He meant by telling him this.

29 Some thought that since Judas had the money box (the purse), Jesus was telling him, Buy what we need for the festival, or that he should give something to the poor.

30 So, after receiving the bit of bread, he went out immediately. And it was night.

---

w) Souter's "Pocket Lexicon of the Greek New Testament."
x) Many ancient authorities read "*his bread with Me.*"
y) Thayer: "Greek-English Lexicon of the New Testament—Grimm."
z) Williams: "New Testament in the Language of the People."

Living New Testament

10 Jesus replied, "One who has bathed all over needs only to have his feet washed to be entirely clean. Now you are clean—but that isn't true of everyone here."

11 For Jesus knew who would betray Him. That is what He meant when He said, "Not all of you are clean."

12 After washing their feet He put on His robe again and sat down and asked, "Do you understand what I was doing?

13 You call Me 'Master' and 'Lord,' and you do well to say it, for it is true.

14 And since I, the Lord and Teacher, have washed your feet, you ought to wash each other's feet.

15 I have given you an example to follow: do as I have done to you.

16 How true it is that a servant is not greater than his master. Nor is the messenger more important than the one who sends him.

17 You know these things—now do them! That is the path of blessing.

18 I am not saying these things to all of you; I know so well each one of you I chose. The Scripture declares, 'One who eats supper with Me will betray Me,' and this will soon come true.

19 I tell you this now so that when it happens, you will believe on Me.

* * * * *

20 Truly, anyone welcoming the Holy Spirit,[2] whom I will send, is welcoming Me. And to welcome Me is to welcome the Father who sent Me."

* * * * *

21 Now Jesus was in great anguish of spirit and exclaimed, "Yes, it is true—one of you will betray Me."

22 The disciples looked at each other wondering whom He could mean.

23 Since I[3] was sitting next[4] to Jesus at the table, being His closest friend,

24 Simon Peter motioned to me to ask Him who it was who would do this terrible deed.

25 So I turned[5] and asked Him, "Lord, who is it?"

26 He told me, "It is the one I honor by giving the bread dipped in the sauce."[6] And when He had dipped it, He gave it to Judas, son of Simon Iscariot.

27 As soon as he had eaten it, Satan entered into him. Then Jesus told him, "Hurry—do it now."

28 None of the others at the table knew what Jesus meant.

29 Some thought that since Judas was their treasurer, Jesus was telling him to go and pay for the food or to give some money to the poor.

30 Judas left at once, going out into the night.

[2] Implied. Literally, "whomsoever I send."
[3] Literally, "There was one at the table." All commentators believe him to be John, the writer of this book.
[4] Literally, "reclining on Jesus' bosom." The custom of the period was to recline around the table, leaning on the left elbow. John, next to Jesus, was at His side.
Literally, "leaning back against Jesus' chest," to whisper his inquiry.
Literally, "He it is for whom I shall dip the sop and give it him." The honored guest was thus singled out in the custom of that time.

Revised Standard

10Jesus said to him, "He who has bathed
does not need to wash, except for his feet,[c]
but he is clean all over; and you are clean,
but not all of you." 11For he knew who
was to betray him; that was why he said,
"You are not all clean."

12 When he had washed their feet, and
taken his garments, and resumed his place,
he said to them, "Do you know what I
have done to you? 13You call be Teacher
and Lord; and you are right, for so I am.
14If I then, your Lord and Teacher, have
washed your feet, you also ought to wash
one another's feet. 15For I have given you
an example, that you also should do as I
have done to you. 16Truly, truly, I say to
you, a servant[d] is not greater than his
master; nor is he who is sent greater than
he who sent him. 17If you know these
things, blessed are you if you do them.
18I am not speaking of you all; I know
whom I have chosen; it is that the scripture may be fulfilled, 'He who ate my
bread has lifted his heel against me.' 19I
tell you this now, before it takes place,
that when it does take place you may believe that I am he. 20Truly, truly, I say to
you, he who receives any one whom I send
receives me; and he who receives me receives him who sent me."

Jesus dismisses Judas, his betrayer

21 When Jesus had thus spoken, he
was troubled in spirit, and testified, "Truly,
truly, I say to you, one of you will betray
me." 22The disciples looked at one another, uncertain of whom he spoke. 23One
of his disciples, whom Jesus loved, was
lying close to the breast of Jesus; 24so
Simon Peter beckoned to him and said,
"Tell us who it is of whom he speaks."
25So lying thus, close to the breast of Jesus, he said to him, "Lord, who is it?"
26Jesus answered, "It is he to whom I
shall give this morsel when I have dipped
it." So when he had dipped the morsel, he
gave it to Judas, the son of Simon Iscariot. 27Then after the morsel, Satan entered into him. Jesus said to him, "What
you are going to do, do quickly." 28Now
no one at the table knew why he said this
to him. 29Some thought that, because Judas
had the money box, Jesus was telling him,
"Buy what we need for the feast"; or,
that he should give something to the poor.
30So, after receiving the morsel, he immediately went out; and it was night.

[c] Other ancient authorities omit *except for his feet*
[d] Or *slave*

King James

31 ¶ Therefore, when he was gone out, Jesus said, Now is the Son of man glorified, and God is glorified in him.

32 If God be glorified in him, God shall also glorify him in himself, and shall straightway glorify him.

33 Little children, yet a little while I am with you. Ye shall seek me: and as I said unto the Jews, Whither I go, ye cannot come; so now I say to you.

34 A new commandment I give unto you, That ye love one another; as I have loved you, that ye also love one another.

35 By this shall all *men* know that ye are my disciples, if ye have love one to another.

36 ¶ Simon Peter said unto him, Lord, whither goest thou? Jesus answered him, Whither I go, thou canst not follow me now; but thou shalt follow me afterwards.

37 Peter said unto him, Lord, why cannot I follow thee now? I will lay down my life for thy sake.

38 Jesus answered him, Wilt thou lay down thy life for my sake? Verily, verily, I say unto thee, The cock shall not crow, till thou hast denied me thrice.

Amplified

31 When he had left, Jesus said, Now is the Son of man glorified!—Now He has achieved His glory, His honor, His exaltation; and God has been glorified through *and* in Him.

32 And if God is glorified through *and* in Him, God will also glorify Him in Himself; and He will glorify Him at once *and* not delay.

33 [Dear] little children, I am to be with you only a little longer. You will look for Me and, as I told the Jews so I tell you now, you are not able to come where I am going.

34 I give you a new commandment, that you should love one another; just as I have loved you, so you too should love one another.

35 By this shall all [men] know that you are My disciples, if you love one another—if you keep on showing love among yourselves.

36 Simon Peter said to Him, Lord, where are You going? Jesus answered, You are not able to follow Me now where I am going; but you shall follow Me afterwards.

37 Peter said to Him, Lord, why cannot I follow You now? I will lay down my life for You.

38 Jesus answered, Will you lay down your life for Me? I assure you, most solemnly I tell you, Before a rooster crows you will deny Me—completely disown Me—three times.

CHAPTER 14

LET not your heart be troubled: ye believe in God, believe also in me.

2 In my Father's house are many mansions: if *it were* not *so*, I would have told you. I go to prepare a place for you.

3 And if I go and prepare a place for you, I will come again, and receive you unto myself; that where I am, *there* ye may be also.

4 And whither I go ye know, and the way ye know.

5 Thomas saith unto him, Lord, we know not whither thou goest; and how can we know the way?

6 Jesus saith unto him, I am the way, the truth, and the life: no man cometh unto the Father, but by me.

7 If ye had known me, ye should have known my Father also: and from henceforth ye know him, and have seen him.

8 Philip saith unto him, Lord, shew us the Father, and it sufficeth us.

9 Jesus saith unto him, Have I been so long time with you, and yet hast thou not known me, Philip? he that hath seen me hath seen the Father; and how sayest thou *then*, Shew us the Father?

10 Believest thou not that I am in the Father, and the Father in me? the words that I speak unto you I speak not of myself: but the Father that dwelleth in me, he doeth the works.

CHAPTER 14

DO not let your hearts be troubled (distressed, agitated). You believe in *and* adhere to *and* trust in *and* rely on God, believe in *and* adhere to *and* trust in *and* rely also on Me.

2 In My Father's house there are many dwelling places (homes). If it were not so, I would have told you, for I am going away to prepare a place for you.

3 And when (if) I go and make ready a place for you, I will come back again and will take you to Myself, that where I am you may be also.

4 And [to the place] where I am going you know the way.

5 Thomas said to Him, Lord, we do not know where You are going, so how can we know the way?

6 Jesus said to him, I am the Way and the Truth and the Life; no one comes to the Father except by (through) Me.

7 If you had known Me—had learned to recognize Me—you would also have known My Father. From now on you know Him and have seen Him.

8 Philip said to Him, Lord, show us the Father—cause us to see the Father, that is all we ask; then we shall be satisfied.

9 Jesus replied, Have I been with all of you for so long a time and do you not recognize *and* know Me yet, Philip? Any one who has seen Me has seen the Father. How can you say then, Show us the Father?

10 Do you not believe that I am in the Father and that the Father is in Me? What I am telling you I do not say on My own authority *and* of My own accord, but the Father Who lives continually in Me does the works— [a]His miracles, His own deeds of power.

---

a) Several ancient authorities read "His works."

Living New Testament

31 As soon as Judas left the room, Jesus said, "My time has come; the glory of God will soon surround Me—and God shall receive great praise because of all that happens to Me.

32 And God shall give Me His own glory, and this so very soon.

33 Dear, dear children, how brief are these moments before I must go away and leave you! Then, though you search for Me, you cannot come to Me—just as I told the Jewish leaders.

34 And so I am giving a new commandment to you now—love each other just as much as I love you.

35 Your strong love for each other will prove to the world that you are My disciples."

36 Simon Peter said, "Master, where are You going?" And Jesus replied, "You can't go with Me now; but you will follow Me later."

37 "But why can't I come now?" he asked, "for I am ready to die for You."

38 Jesus answered, "Die for Me? No—three times before the cock crows tomorrow morning, you will deny that you even know Me!

Revised Standard

The new commandment

31 When he had gone out, Jesus said,
"Now is the Son of man glorified, and in
him God is glorified; 32 if God is glorified
in him, God will also glorify him in himself, and glorify him at once. 33 Little children, yet a little while I am with you. You
will seek me; and as I said to the Jews
so now I say to you, 'Where I am going
you cannot come.' 34 A new commandment
I give to you, that you love one another;
even as I have loved you, that you also
love one another. 35 By this all men will
know that you are my disciples, if you
have love for one another."

Peter's denial foretold

36 Simon Peter said to him, "Lord,
where are you going?" Jesus answered,
"Where I am going you cannot follow me
now; but you shall follow afterward." 37 Peter said to him, "Lord, why cannot I follow you now? I will lay down my life for
you." 38 Jesus answered, "Will you lay
down your life for me? Truly, truly, I say
to you, the cock will not crow, till you
have denied me three times.

CHAPTER 14

Let not your heart be troubled. You are trusting God, now trust in Me.

2, 3 There are many homes up there where My Father lives, and I am going to prepare them for your coming. When everything is ready, then I will come and get you, so that you can always be with Me where I am. If this weren't so, I would tell you plainly.

4 And you know where I am going and how to get there."

5 "No, we don't," Thomas said. "We haven't any idea where You are going, so how can we know the way?"

6 Jesus told him, "I am the Way—yes, and the Truth and the Life. No one can get to the Father except by means of Me.

7 If you had known who I am, then you would have known who My Father is. From now on you know Him—and have seen Him!"

8 Philip said, "Sir, show us the Father and we will be satisfied."

9 Jesus replied, "Don't you even yet know who I am, Philip, even after all this time I have been with you? Anyone who has seen Me has seen the Father! So why are you asking to see Him?

10 Don't you believe that I am in the Father and the Father is in Me? The words I say are not My own but are from My Father who lives in Me. And He does His work through Me.

The way, the truth and the life

14 "Let not your hearts be troubled; believe[e] in God, believe also in me. 2 In
my Father's house are many rooms; if it
were not so, would I have told you that I
go to prepare a place for you? 3 And when
I go and prepare a place for you, I will
come again and will take you to myself,
that where I am you may be also. 4 And
you know the way where I am going."[f]
5 Thomas said to him, "Lord, we do not
know where you are going; how can we
know the way?" 6 Jesus said to him, "I am
the way, and the truth, and the life; no
one comes to the Father, but by me. 7 If
you had known me, you would have known
my Father also; henceforth you know him
and have seen him."
8 Philip said to him, "Lord, show us
the Father, and we shall be satisfied."
9 Jesus said to him, "Have I been with you
so long, and yet you do not know me,
Philip? He who has seen me has seen the
Father; how can you say, 'Show us the
Father'? 10 Do you not believe that I am
in the Father and the Father in me? The
words that I say to you I do not speak on
my own authority; but the Father who

[e] Or *you believe*

[f] Other ancient authorities read *where I am going you know, and the way you know*

King James

11 Believe me that I *am* in the Father, and the Father in me: or else believe me for the very work's sake.

12 Verily, verily, I say unto you, He that believeth on me, the works that I do shall he do also; and greater *works* than these shall he do; because I go unto my Father.

13 And whatsoever ye shall ask in my name, that will I do, that the Father may be glorified in the Son.

14 If ye shall ask any thing in my name, I will do *it*.

15 ¶ If ye love me, keep my commandments.

16 And I will pray the Father, and he shall give you another Comforter, that he may abide with you for ever;

17 *Even* the Spirit of truth; whom the world cannot receive, because it seeth him not, neither knoweth him: but ye know him; for he dwelleth with you, and shall be in you.

18 I will not leave you comfortless: I will come to you.

19 Yet a little while, and the world seeth me no more; but ye see me: because I live, ye shall live also.

20 At that day ye shall know that I *am* in my Father, and ye in me, and I in you.

21 He that hath my commandments, and keepeth them, he it is that loveth me: and he that loveth me shall be loved of my Father, and I will love him, and will manifest myself to him.

22 Judas saith unto him, not Iscariot, Lord, how is it that thou wilt manifest thyself unto us, and not unto the world?

23 Jesus answered and said unto him, If a man love me, he will keep my words: and my Father will love him, and we will come unto him, and make our abode with him.

24 He that loveth me not keepeth not my sayings: and the word which ye hear is not mine, but the Father's which sent me.

25 These things have I spoken unto you being *yet* present with you.

26 But the Comforter, *which is* the Holy Ghost, whom the Father will send in my name, he shall teach you all things, and bring all things to your remembrance, whatsoever I have said unto you.

27 Peace I leave with you, my peace I give unto you: not as the world giveth, give I unto you. Let not your heart be troubled, neither let it be afraid.

28 Ye have heard how I said unto you, I go away, and come *again* unto you. If ye loved me, ye would rejoice, because I said, I go unto the Father: for my Father is greater than I.

Amplified

11 Believe Me that I am in the Father and the Father in Me; or else believe Me for the sake of the [very] works themselves.—If you cannot trust Me, at least let these works that I do in My Father's name convince you.

12 I assure you, most solemnly I tell you, if any one steadfastly believes in Me, he will himself be able to do the things that I do; and he will do even greater things than these, because I go to the Father.

13 And I will do—I Myself will grant—whatever you may ask in My name [[b]presenting all I AM] so that the Father may be glorified *and* extolled in [through] the Son. [Exod. 3:14.]

14 [Yes] I will grant—will do for you—whatever you shall ask in My name [[b]presenting all I AM].

15 If you [really] love Me you will keep (obey) My commands.

16 And I will ask the Father, and He will give you another Comforter (Counselor, Helper, Intercessor, Advocate, Strengthener and Standby) that He may remain with you forever,

17 The Spirit of Truth, Whom the world cannot receive (welcome, take to its heart), because it does not see Him, nor know *and* recognize Him. But you know *and* recognize Him, for He lives with you [constantly] and will be in you.

18 I will not leave you orphans—comfortless, desolate, bereaved, forlorn, helpless—I will come [back] to you.

19 Just a little while now and the world will not see Me any more, but you will see Me; because I live, you will live also.

20 At that time—when that day comes—you will know [for yourselves] that I am in My Father, and you [are] in Me, and I [am] in you.

21 The person who has My commands and keeps them is the one who [really] loves Me, and whoever [really] loves Me will be loved by My Father. And I [too] will love him and will show (reveal, manifest) Myself to him—I will let Myself be clearly seen by him *and* make Myself real to him.

22 Judas, not Iscariot, asked Him, Lord, how is it that You will reveal Yourself—make Yourself real—to us and not to the world?

23 Jesus answered, If a person [really] loves Me, he will keep My word—obey My teaching; and My Father will love him, and We will come to him and make Our home (abode, special dwelling place) with him.

24 And one who does not [really] love Me does not observe *and* obey My teaching. And the teaching which you hear *and* heed is not Mine, but [comes] from the Father Who sent Me.

25 I have told you these things while I am still with you.

26 But the Comforter (Counselor, Helper, Intercessor Advocate, Strengthener, Standby), the Holy Spirit, Whom the Father will send in My name [in My place, to represent Me and act on My behalf], He will teach you all things. And He will cause you to recall—will remind you of, bring to your remembrance—everything I have told you.

27 Peace I leave with you; My [own] peace I now give *and* bequeath to you. Not as the world gives do I give to you. Do not let your heart be troubled, neither let it be afraid—stop allowing yourselves to be agitated and disturbed; and do not permit yourselves to be fearful *and* intimidated *and* cowardly *and* unsettled.

28 You heard Me tell you, I am going away, and I am coming [back] to you. If you [really] loved Me, you would have been glad because I am going to the Father; for the Father is greater *and* mightier than I am.

---

b) Cremer.

Living New Testament

11 Just believe it—that I am in the Father and the Father is in Me. Or else believe it because of the mighty miracles you have seen Me do.

12, 13 In solemn truth I tell you, anyone believing in Me shall do the same miracles I have done, and even greater ones, because I am going to be with the Father. You can ask Him for *anything*, using My name, and I will do it, for this will bring praise to the Father because of what I, the Son, will do for you.

14 Yes, ask *anything*, using My name, and I will do it!

15, 16 If you love Me, obey Me; and I will ask the Father and He will give you another Comforter, and He will never leave you.

17 He is the Holy Spirit, the Spirit who leads into all truth. The world at large cannot receive Him, for it isn't looking for Him and doesn't recognize Him. But you do, for He lives with you now and some day shall be in you.

18 No, I will not abandon you or leave you as orphans in the storm—I will come to you.

19 In just a little while I will be gone from the world, but I will still be present with you. For I will live again—and you will too.

20 When I come back to life again, you will know that I am in My Father, and you in Me, and I in you.

21 The one who obeys Me is the one who loves Me; and because he loves Me, My Father will love him; and I will too, and I will reveal Myself to him."

22 Judas (not Judas Iscariot, but His other disciple with that name) said to Him, "Sir, why are You going to reveal Yourself only to us disciples and not to the world at large?"

23 Jesus replied, "Because I will only reveal Myself to those who love Me and obey Me. The Father will love them too, and We will come to them and live with them.

24 Anyone who doesn't obey Me doesn't love Me. And remember, I am not making up this answer to your question! It is the answer given by the Father who sent Me.

25 I am telling you these things now while I am still with you.

26 But when the Father sends the Comforter[1] to represent Me[2]—and by the Comforter I mean the Holy Spirit—He will teach you much, as well as remind you of everything I Myself have told you.

27 I am leaving you with a gift—peace of mind and heart! And the peace I give isn't fragile like the peace the world gives. So don't be troubled or afraid.[3]

28 Remember what I told you—I am going away, but I will come back to you again. If you really love Me, you will be very happy for Me, for now I can go to the Father, who is greater than I am.

Or, "Advocate," or, "Lawyer."
Literally, "in My name."
Implied.

Revised Standard

dwells in me does his works. [11]Believe me
that I am in the Father and the Father in
me; or else believe me for the sake of the
works themselves.

The promise of greater works

12 "Truly, truly, I say to you, he who
believes in me will also do the works that
I do; and greater works than these will he
do, because I go to the Father. [13]Whatever
you ask in my name, I will do it, that the
Father may be glorified in the Son; [14]if
you ask[g] anything in my name, I will do
it.

The promise of the Spirit

15 "If you love me, you will keep my
commandments. [16]And I will pray the Father, and he will give you another Counselor, to be with you for ever, [17]even the
Spirit of truth, whom the world cannot
receive, because it neither sees him nor
knows him; you know him, for he dwells
with you, and will be in you.
18 "I will not leave you desolate; I will
come to you. [19]Yet a little while, and the
world will see me no more, but you will
see me; because I live, you will live also.
[20]In that day you will know that I am in
my Father, and you in me, and I in you.
[21]He who has my commandments and keeps
them, he it is who loves me; and he who
loves me will be loved by my Father, and
I will love him and manifest myself to
him." [22]Judas (not Iscariot) said to him,
"Lord, how is it that you will manifest
yourself to us, and not to the world?"
[23]Jesus answered him, "If a man loves me,
he will keep my word, and my Father will
love him, and we will come to him and
make our home with him. [24]He who does
not love me does not keep my words; and
the word which you hear is not mine but
the Father's who sent me.

The promise of peace

25 "These things I have spoken to you,
while I am still with you. [26]But the Counselor, the Holy Spirit, whom the Father
will send in my name, he will teach you
all things, and bring to your remembrance
all that I have said to you. [27]Peace I leave
with you; my peace I give to you; not as
the world gives do I give to you. Let not
your hearts be troubled, neither let them
be afraid. [28]You heard me say to you,
'I go away, and I will come to you.' If
you loved me, you would have rejoiced,
because I go to the Father; for the Father

[g] Other ancient authorities add *me*

King James

29 And now I have told you before it come to pass, that, when it is come to pass, ye might believe.

30 Hereafter I will not talk much with you: for the prince of this world cometh, and hath nothing in me.

31 But that the world may know that I love the Father; and as the Father gave me commandment, even so I do. Arise, let us go hence.

Amplified

29 And now I have told you [this] before it occurs, so that when it does take place you may believe *and* have faith in *and* rely on Me.

30 I will not talk with you much more, for the prince (evil genius, ruler) of the world is coming. And he has no claim on Me—he has nothing in common with Me, there is nothing in Me that belongs to him, he has no power over Me.

31 But [[c]Satan is coming and] I do as the Father has commanded Me, so that the world may know (be convinced) that I love the Father, and that I do only what the Father has instructed Me to do.—I act in full agreement with His orders. Rise, let us go away from here.

King James

CHAPTER 15

I AM the true vine, and my Father is the husbandman.

2 Every branch in me that beareth not fruit he taketh away: and every *branch* that beareth fruit, he purgeth it, that it may bring forth more fruit.

3 Now ye are clean through the word which I have spoken unto you.

4 Abide in me, and I in you. As the branch cannot bear fruit of itself, except it abide in the vine; no more can ye, except ye abide in me.

5 I am the vine, *ye are* the branches: He that abideth in me, and I in him, the same bringeth forth much fruit: for without me ye can do nothing.

6 If a man abide not in me, he is cast forth as a branch, and is withered; and men gather them, and cast *them* into the fire, and they are burned.

7 If ye abide in me, and my words abide in you, ye shall ask what ye will, and it shall be done unto you.

8 Herein is my Father glorified, that ye bear much fruit; so shall ye be my disciples.

9 As the Father hath loved me, so have I loved you: continue ye in my love.

10 If ye keep my commandments, ye shall abide in my love; even as I have kept my Father's commandments, and abide in his love.

11 These things have I spoken unto you, that my joy might remain in you, and *that* your joy might be full.

12 This is my commandment, That ye love one another, as I have loved you.

13 Greater love hath no man than this, that a man lay down his life for his friends.

14 Ye are my friends, if ye do whatsoever I command you.

Amplified

CHAPTER 15

I AM the True Vine and My Father is the Vinedresser.

2 Any branch in Me that does not bear fruit—that stops bearing—He cuts away (trims off, takes away). And He cleanses *and* repeatedly prunes every branch that continues to bear fruit, to make it bear more *and* richer *and* more excellent fruit.

3 You are cleansed *and* pruned already, because of the Word which I have given you—the teachings I have discussed with you.

4 Dwell in Me and I will dwell in you.—Live in Me and I will live in you. Just as no branch can bear fruit of itself without abiding in (vitally united to) the vine, neither can you bear fruit unless you abide in Me.

5 I am the Vine, you are the branches. Whoever lives in Me and I in him bears much (abundant) fruit. However, apart from Me—cut off from vital union with Me—you can do nothing.

6 If a person does not dwell in Me, he is thrown out as a [broken-off] branch and withers. Such branches are gathered up and thrown into the fire and they are burned.

7 If you live in Me—abide vitally united to Me—and My words remain in you *and* continue to live in your hearts, ask whatever you will and it shall be done for you.

8 When you bear (produce) much fruit. My Father is honored *and* glorified; and you show *and* prove yourselves to be true followers of Mine.

9 I have loved you [just] as the Father has loved Me; abide in My love—[d]continue in His love with Me.

10 If you keep My commandments—if you continue to obey My instructions—you will abide in My love *and* live on in it; just as I have obeyed My Father's commandments and live on in His love.

11 I have told you these things that My joy *and* delight may be in you, and that your joy *and* gladness may be full measure *and* complete *and* overflowing.

12 This is My commandment, that you love one another [just] as I have loved you.

13 No one has greater love—no one has shown stronger affection—than to lay down (give up) his own life for his friends.

14 You are My friends, if you keep on doing the things which I command you to do.

c) Vincent.
d) Cremer's "Biblico-Theological Lexicon."

Living New Testament

29 I have told you these things before they happen so that when they do, you will believe [in Me[4]].

30 I don't have much more time to talk to you, for the evil prince of this world approaches. He has no power over Me,

31 But I will freely do what the Father requires of Me so that the world will know that I love the Father. Come, let's be going."

Revised Standard

is greater than I. [29]And now I have told you before it takes place, so that when it does take place, you may believe. [30]I will no longer talk much with you, for the ruler of this world is coming. He has no power over me; [31]but I do as the Father has commanded me, so that the world may know that I love the Father. Rise, let us go hence.

CHAPTER 15

I am the true Vine, and My Father is the Gardener.

2 He lops off every branch that doesn't produce. And He prunes those branches that bear fruit for even larger crops.

3 He has already tended you by pruning you back for greater strength and usefulness by means of the commands I gave you.

4 Take care to live in Me, and let Me live in you. For a branch can't produce fruit when severed from the vine. Nor can you be fruitful apart from Me.

5 Yes, I am the Vine; you are the branches. Whoever lives in Me and I in him shall produce a large crop of fruit. For apart from Me you can't do a thing.

6 If anyone separates from Me, he is thrown away like a useless branch, withers, and is gathered into a pile with all the others and burned.

7 But if you stay in Me and obey My commands, you may ask any request you like, and it will be granted!

8 My true disciples produce bountiful harvests. This brings great glory to My Father.

9 I have loved you even as the Father has loved Me. Live within My love.

10 When you obey Me you are living in My love, just as I obey My Father and live in His love.

11 I have told you this so that you will be filled with My joy. Yes, your cup of joy will overflow!

12 I demand that you love each other as much as I love you.

13 And here is how to measure it—the greatest love is when a person lays down his life for his friends;

14 And you are My friends if you obey Me.

Jesus the true vine

15 "I am the true vine, and my Father is the vinedresser. [2]Every branch of mine that bears no fruit, he takes away, and every branch that does bear fruit he prunes, that it may bear more fruit. [3]You are already made clean by the word which I have spoken to you. [4]Abide in me, and I in you. As the branch cannot bear fruit by itself, unless it abides in the vine, neither can you, unless you abide in me. [5]I am the vine, you are the branches. He who abides in me, and I in him, he it is that bears much fruit, for apart from me you can do nothing. [6]If a man does not abide in me, he is cast forth as a branch and withers; and the branches are gathered, thrown into the fire and burned. [7]If you abide in me, and my words abide in you, ask whatever you will, and it shall be done for you. [8]By this my Father is glorified, that you bear much fruit, and so prove to be my disciples. [9]As the Father has loved me, so have I loved you; abide in my love. [10]If you keep my commandments, you will abide in my love, just as I have kept my Father's commandments and abide in his love. [11]These things I have spoken to you, that my joy may be in you, and that your joy may be full.

12 "This is my commandment, that you love one another as I have loved you. [13]Greater love has no man than this, that a man lay down his life for his friends. [14]You are my friends if you do what I command you. [15]No longer do I call you

[4]Implied.

King James

15 Henceforth I call you not servants; for the servant knoweth not what his lord doeth: but I have called you friends; for all things that I have heard of my Father I have made known unto you.

16 Ye have not chosen me, but I have chosen you, and ordained you, that ye should go and bring forth fruit, and *that* your fruit should remain: that whatsoever ye shall ask of the Father in my name, he may give it you.

17 These things I command you, that ye love one another.

18 If the world hate you, ye know that it hated me before *it hated* you.

19 If ye were of the world, the world would love his own: but because ye are not of the world, but I have chosen you out of the world, therefore the world hateth you.

20 Remember the word that I said unto you, The servant is not greater than his lord. If they have persecuted me, they will also persecute you; if they have kept my saying, they will keep yours also.

21 But all these things will they do unto you for my name's sake, because they know not him that sent me.

22 If I had not come and spoken unto them, they had not had sin: but now they have no cloak for their sin.

23 He that hateth me hateth my Father also.

24 If I had not done among them the works which none other man did, they had not had sin: but now have they both seen and hated both me and my Father.

25 But *this cometh to pass,* that the word might be fulfilled that is written in their law, They hated me without a cause.

26 But when the Comforter is come, whom I will send unto you from the Father, *even* the Spirit of truth, which proceedeth from the Father, he shall testify of me:

27 And ye also shall bear witness, because ye have been with me from the beginning.

Amplified

15 I do not call you servants (slaves) any longer, for the servant does not know what his master is doing (working out). But I have called you My friends, because I have made known to you everything that I have heard from My Father—I have revealed to you everything that I have learned from Him.

16 You have not chosen Me, but I have chosen you—I have appointed you, I have planted you—that you might go and bear fruit *and* keep on bearing; that your fruit may be lasting (that it may remain, abide); so that whatever you ask the Father in My name [as [e]presenting all that I AM] He may give it to you.

17 This is what I command you, that you love one another.

18 If the world hates you, know that it hated Me before it hated you.

19 If you belonged to the world, the world would treat you with affection *and* would love you as its own. But because you are not of the world—are no longer one with it—but I have chosen (selected) you out of the world, the world hates (detests) you.

20 Remember that I told you, A servant is not greater than his master—is not superior to him. If they persecuted Me, they will also persecute you; if they kept My word *and* obeyed My teachings, they will also keep *and* obey yours.

21 But they will do all this to you—inflict all this suffering on you—because of [your bearing] My name, *and* on My account, for they do not know *or* understand the One Who sent Me.

22 If I had not come and spoken to them, they would not be guilty of sin; but now they have no excuse for their sin.

23 Whoever hates Me also hates My Father.

24 If I had not done (accomplished) among them the works which no one else ever did, they would not be guilty of sin—would be blameless. But [the fact is] now they have both seen [these works] and have hated both Me and My Father.

25 But [this is so] that the word written in their Law might be fulfilled, They hated Me without a cause. [Ps. 35:19; 69:4.]

26 But when the Comforter (Counselor, Helper, Advocate, Intercessor, Strengthener) comes Whom I will send to you from the Father, the Spirit of Truth Who comes (proceeds) from the Father, He [Himself] will testify regarding Me.

27 But you also will testify *and* be My witnesses, because you have been with Me from the beginning.

CHAPTER 16

THESE things have I spoken unto you, that ye should not be offended.

2 They shall put you out of the synagogues: yea, the time cometh, that whosoever killeth you will think that he doeth God service.

3 And these things will they do unto you, because they have not known the Father, nor me.

4 But these things have I told you, that when the time shall come, ye may remember that I told you of them. And these things I said not unto you at the beginning, because I was with you.

CHAPTER 16

I HAVE told you all these things so that you should no[t] be offended—taken unawares and falter, or be cause[d] to stumble and fall away, *and* to keep you from bein[g] scandalized and repelled.

2 They will put you out of the synagogues—expel you[.] But an hour is coming when whoever kills you will thin[k] *and* claim that he has offered service to God.

3 And they will do this because they have not know[n] the Father nor Me.

4 But I have told you these things now so that whe[n] they occur you will remember that I told you of them. [I] did not say these things to you from the beginning, be[-]cause I was with you.

---

e) Cremer.

Living New Testament

15 I no longer call you slaves, for a master doesn't confide in his slaves; now you are My friends, proved by the fact that I have told you everything the Father told Me.

16 You didn't choose Me! I chose you! I appointed you to go and produce lovely fruit always, so that no matter what you ask for from the Father, using My name, He will give it to you.

17 I demand that you love each other,

18 For you get enough hate from the world! But then, it hated Me before it hated you.

19 The world would love you if you belonged to it; but you don't—for I chose you to come out of the world, and so it hates you.

20 Do you remember what I told you? 'A slave isn't greater than his master!' So since they persecuted Me, naturally they will persecute you. And if they had listened to Me, they would listen to you!

21 The people of the world will persecute you because you belong to Me, for they don't know God who sent Me.

22 They would not be guilty if I had not come and spoken to them. But now they have no excuse for their sin.

23 Anyone hating Me is also hating My Father.

24 If I hadn't done such mighty miracles among them they would not be counted guilty. But as it is, they saw these miracles and yet they hated both of us—Me and My Father.

25 This has fulfilled what the prophets said concerning the Messiah, 'They hated Me without reason.'

26 But I will send you the Comforter—the Holy Spirit, the source of all truth. He will come to you from the Father and will tell you all about Me.

27 And you also must tell everyone about Me, because you have been with Me from the beginning.

Revised Standard

servants,[h] for the servant[i] does not know
what his master is doing; but I have called
you friends, for all that I have heard
from my Father I have made known to
you. 16 You did not choose me, but I chose
you and appointed you that you should
go and bear fruit and that your fruit should
abide; so that whatever you ask the Father
in my name, he may give it to you. 17 This
I command you, to love one another.

The hatred of the world

18 "If the world hates you, know that
it has hated me before it hated you. 19 If
you were of the world, the world would
love its own; but because you are not of
the world, but I chose you out of the world,
therefore the world hates you. 20 Remember
the word that I said to you, 'A servant[i] is
not greater than his master.' If they persecuted me, they will persecute you; if they
kept my word, they will keep yours also.
21 But all this they will do to you on my account, because they do not know him who
sent me. 22 If I had not come and spoken to
them, they would not have sin; but now they
have no excuse for their sin. 23 He who hates
me hates my Father also. 24 If I had not done
among them the works which no one else did,
they would not have sin; but now they
have seen and hated both me and my Father. 25 It is to fulfil the word that is written in their law, 'They hated me without
a cause.' 26 But when the Counselor comes,
whom I shall send to you from the Father,
even the Spirit of truth, who proceeds from
the Father, he will bear witness to me;
27 and you also are witnesses, because you
have been with me from the beginning.

CHAPTER 16

I have told you these things so that you won't be staggered by all that lies ahead.[1]

2 For you will be excommunicated from the synagogues, and indeed the time is coming when those who kill you will think they are doing God a service.

3 This is because they have never known the Father or Me.

4 Yes, I'm telling you these things now so that when they happen you will remember I warned you. I didn't tell you earlier because I was going to be with you for a while longer.

16 "I have said all this to you to keep
you from falling away. 2 They will
put you out of the synagogues; indeed,
the hour is coming when whoever kills
you will think he is offering service to
God. 3 And they will do this because they
have not known the Father, nor me. 4 But
I have said these things to you, that when
their hour comes you may remember that
I told you of them.

[1] Implied.

[h] Or *slaves*
[i] Or *slave*

King James

5 But now I go my way to him that sent me; and none of you asketh me, Whither goest thou?

6 But because I have said these things unto you, sorrow hath filled your heart.

7 Nevertheless I tell you the truth; It is expedient for you that I go away: for if I go not away, the Comforter will not come unto you; but if I depart, I will send him unto you.

8 And when he is come, he will reprove the world of sin, and of righteousness, and of judgment:

9 Of sin, because they believe not on me;

10 Of righteousness, because I go to my Father, and ye see me no more;

11 Of judgment, because the prince of this world is judged.

12 I have yet many things to say unto you, but ye cannot bear them now.

13 Howbeit when he, the Spirit of truth, is come, he will guide you into all truth: for he shall not speak of himself; but whatsoever he shall hear, *that* shall he speak: and he will shew you things to come.

14 He shall glorify me: for he shall receive of mine, and shall shew *it* unto you.

15 All things that the Father hath are mine: therefore said I, that he shall take of mine, and shall shew *it* unto you.

16 A little while, and ye shall not see me: and again, a little while, and ye shall see me, because I go to the Father.

17 Then said *some* of his disciples among themselves, What is this that he saith unto us, A little while, and ye shall not see me: and again, a little while, and ye shall see me: and, Because I go to the Father?

18 They said therefore, What is this that he saith, A little while? we cannot tell what he saith.

19 Now Jesus knew that they were desirous to ask him, and said unto them, Do ye inquire among yourselves of that I said, A little while, and ye shall not see me: and again, a little while, and ye shall see me?

20 Verily, verily, I say unto you, That ye shall weep and lament, but the world shall rejoice: and ye shall be sorrowful, but your sorrow shall be turned into joy.

21 A woman when she is in travail hath sorrow, because her hour is come: but as soon as she is delivered of the child, she remembereth no more the anguish, for joy that a man is born into the world.

22 And ye now therefore have sorrow: but I will see you again, and your heart shall rejoice, and your joy no man taketh from you.

23 And in that day ye shall ask me nothing. Verily, verily, I say unto you, Whatsoever ye shall ask the Father in my name, he will give *it* you.

Amplified

5 But now I am going to Him Who sent Me; yet none of you asks Me, Where are You going?

6 But because I have said these things to you sorrow has filled your hearts—taken complete possession of them.

7 However, I am telling you nothing but the truth when I say, it is profitable—good, expedient, advantageous—for you that I go away. Because if I do not go away, the Comforter (Counselor, Helper, Advocate, Intercessor, Strengthener, Standby) will not come to you—into close fellowship with you. But if I go away, I will send Him to you—to be in close fellowship with you.

8 And when He comes, He will convict *and* convince the world *and* bring demonstration to it about sin and about righteousness—uprightness of heart and right standing with God—and about judgment.

9 About sin, because they do not believe on Me—trust in, rely on and adhere to Me.

10 About righteousness—uprightness of heart and right standing with God—because I go to My Father and you will see Me no longer.

11 About judgment, because the ruler (prince) of this world [Satan] is judged *and* condemned *and* sentence already is passed upon him.

12 I have still many things to say to you, but you are not able to bear them *nor* to take them upon you *nor* to grasp them now.

13 But when He, the Spirit of Truth (the truth-giving Spirit) comes, He will guide you into all the truth—the whole, full truth. For He will not speak His own message—on His own authority—but He will tell whatever He hears [from the Father, He will give the message that has been given to Him] and He will announce *and* declare to you the things that are to come—that will happen in the future.

14 He will honor *and* glorify Me, because He will take of (receive, draw upon) what is Mine and will reveal (declare, disclose, transmit) it to you.

15 Everything that the Father has is Mine. That is what I meant when I said that He will take the things that are Mine and will reveal (declare, disclose, transmit) them to you.

16 In a little while you will no longer see Me, and again after a short while you will see Me.

17 So some of His disciples questioned among themselves, What does He mean when He tells us, A little while and you will no longer see Me, and again after a short while you will see Me, and, Because I go to My Father?

18 What does He mean by a little while? We do not know *nor* understand what He is talking about.

19 Jesus knew that they wanted to ask Him, so He said to them, Are you wondering *and* inquiring among yourselves what I meant when I said, In a little while you will see Me no longer, and again after a short while you will see Me?

20 I assure you, most solemnly I tell you, that you shal weep and grieve, but the world will rejoice. You will be sorrowful, but your sorrow will be turned into joy.

21 A woman, when she gives birth to a child has grie (anguish, agony), because her time has come. But whe she is delivered of the child, she no longer remembers he pain (trouble, anguish), because she is so glad that a ma (a child, a human being) has been born into the world.

22 So for the present you are also in sorrow—in dis tress and depressed. But I will see you again and [then your hearts will rejoice, and no one can take from yo your joy (gladness, delight).

23 And when that time comes, you will ask nothing c Me—you will need to ask Me no questions. I assure you most solemnly I tell you, that My Father will grant yo

Living New Testament

5 But now I am going away to the one who sent Me; and none of you seems interested in the purpose of My going; none wonders why.[2]

6 Instead you are only filled with sorrow.

7 But the fact of the matter is that it is best for you that I go away, for if I don't, the Comforter won't come. If I do, He will—for I will send Him to you.

8 And when He has come He will convince the world of its sin, and of the availability of God's goodness, and of deliverance from judgment.[3]

9 The world's sin is unbelief in Me;

10 There is righteousness available because I go to the Father and you shall see Me no more;

11 There is deliverance from judgment because the prince of this world has already been judged.

12 Oh, there is so much more I want to tell you, but you can't understand it now.

13 When the Holy Spirit, who is truth, comes, He shall guide you into all truth, for He will not be presenting His own ideas, but will be passing on to you what He has heard. He will tell you about the future.

14 He shall praise Me and bring Me great honor by showing you My glory.

15 All the Father's glory is Mine; this is what I mean when I say that He will show you My glory.

16 In just a little while I will be gone, and you will see Me no more; but just a little while after that, and you will see Me again!"

17, 18 "Whatever is He saying?" some of His disciples asked. "What is this about 'going to the Father'? We don't know what He means."

19 Jesus realized they wanted to ask Him so He said, "Are you asking yourselves what I mean?

20 The world will greatly rejoice over what is going to happen to Me, and you will weep. But your weeping shall suddenly be turned to wonderful joy [when you see Me again[4]].

21 It will be the same joy as that of a woman in labor when her child is born—her anguish gives place to rapturous joy and the pain is forgotten.

22 You have sorrow now, but I will see you again and then you will rejoice; and no one can rob you of that joy.

23 At that time you won't need to ask Me for anything, for you can go directly to the Father and ask Him, and He will give you what you ask for because you use My name.

---

2 Literally, "none of you is asking Me whither I am going." The question had been asked before (John 13:36, 14:5), but apparently not in this deeper sense.
3 Literally, "He will convict the world of sin and righteousness and judgment."
4 Implied.

Revised Standard

The coming of the Spirit

"I did not say these things to you from
the beginning, because I was with you.
5But now I am going to him who sent me;
yet none of you asks me, 'Where are you
going?' 6But because I have said these
things to you, sorrow has filled your hearts.
7Nevertheless I tell you the truth: it is to
your advantage that I go away, for if I
do not go away, the Counselor will not
come to you; but if I go, I will send him
to you. 8And when he comes, he will convince the world of sin and of righteousness
and of judgment: 9of sin, because they do
not believe in me; 10of righteousness, because I go to the Father, and you will
see me no more; 11of judgment, because
the ruler of this world is judged.
12 "I have yet many things to say to you,
but you cannot bear them now. 13When
the Spirit of truth comes, he will guide you
into all the truth; for he will not speak on
his own authority, but whatever he hears
he will speak, and he will declare to you
the things that are to come. 14He will glorify me, for he will take what is mine and
declare it to you. 15All that the Father has
is mine; therefore I said that he will take
what is mine and declare it to you.

Jesus' farewell to his disciples

16 "A little while, and you will see me
no more; again a little while, and you will
see me." 17Some of his disciples said to one
another, "What is this that he says to us, 'A
little while, and you will not see me, and
again a little while, and you will see me';
and, 'because I go to the Father'?" 18They
said, "What does he mean by 'a little
while'? We do not know what he means."
19Jesus knew that they wanted to ask him;
so he said to them, "Is this what you are
asking yourselves, what I meant by saying,
'A little while, and you will not see me,
and again a little while, and you will see
me'? 20Truly, truly, I say to you, you will
weep and lament, but the world will rejoice;
you will be sorrowful, but your sorrow will
turn into joy. 21When a woman is in travail
she has sorrow, because her hour has come;
but when she is delivered of the child, she
no longer remembers the anguish, for joy
that a child[j] is born into the world. 22So you
have sorrow now, but I will see you again
and your hearts will rejoice, and no one will
take your joy from you. 23In that day you
will ask nothing of me. Truly, truly, I say
to you, if you ask anything of the Father,
he will give it to you in my name. 24Hither-

---

j Greek *a human being*

King James

24 Hitherto have ye asked nothing in my name: ask, and ye shall receive, that your joy may be full.

25 These things have I spoken unto you in proverbs: but the time cometh, when I shall no more speak unto you in proverbs, but I shall shew you plainly of the Father.

26 At that day ye shall ask in my name: and I say not unto you, that I will pray the Father for you:

27 For the Father himself loveth you, because ye have loved me, and have believed that I came out from God.

28 I came forth from the Father, and am come into the world: again, I leave the world, and go to the Father.

29 His disciples said unto him, Lo, now speakest thou plainly, and speakest no proverb.

30 Now are we sure that thou knowest all things, and needest not that any man should ask thee: by this we believe that thou comest forth from God.

31 Jesus answered them, Do ye now believe?

32 Behold, the hour cometh, yea, is now come, that ye shall be scattered, every man to his own, and shall leave me alone: and yet I am not alone, because the Father is with me.

33 These things I have spoken unto you, that in me ye might have peace. In the world ye shall have tribulation: but be of good cheer; I have overcome the world.

Amplified

whatever you ask in My name [[f]presenting all I AM]. [Exod. 3:14.]

24 Up to this time, you have not asked a [single] thing in My name [that is, [f]presenting all I AM] *but now* ask *and* keep on asking and you will receive, so that your joy (gladness, delight) may be full *and* complete.

25 I have told you these things in parables (veiled language, allegories, dark sayings). The hour is now coming when I shall no longer speak to you in figures of speech, but I shall tell you about the Father in plain words *and* openly—without reserve.

26 At that time you will ask (pray) in My name, and I am not saying that I will ask the Father on your behalf [for it will be unnecessary].

27 For the Father Himself tenderly loves you, because you have loved Me, and have believed that I came out from the Father.

28 I came out from the Father and have come into the world; again, I am leaving the world and going to the Father.

29 His disciples said, Ah, now You are speaking plainly to us, and not in parables—not in veiled language and figures of speech!

30 Now we know that You are acquainted with everything and have no need to be asked questions. Because of this, we believe that You [really] came from God.

31 Jesus answered them, Do you now believe—do you believe it at last?

32 But take notice, the hour is coming and it has arrived, when you will all be dispersed *and* scattered every man to his own home, leaving Me alone. Yet I am not alone, because the Father is with Me.

33 I have told you these things so that in Me you may have perfect peace *and* confidence. In the world you have tribulation *and* trials *and* distress *and* frustration; but be of good cheer—take courage, be confident, certain, undaunted—for I have overcome the world.—I have deprived it of power to harm, have conquered it [for you].

CHAPTER 17

THESE words spake Jesus, and lifted up his eyes to heaven, and said, Father, the hour is come; glorify thy Son, that thy Son also may glorify thee:

2 As thou hast given him power over all flesh, that he should give eternal life to as many as thou hast given him.

3 And this is life eternal, that they might know thee the only true God, and Jesus Christ, whom thou hast sent.

4 I have glorified thee on the earth: I have finished the work which thou gavest me to do.

5 And now, O Father, glorify thou me with thine own self with the glory which I had with thee before the world was.

6 I have manifested thy name unto the men which thou gavest me out of the world: thine they were, and thou gavest them me; and they have kept thy word.

CHAPTER 17

WHEN Jesus had spoken these things, He lifted up His eyes to heaven and said, Father, the hour is come. Glorify *and* exalt *and* honor *and* magnify Your Son, so that Your Son may glorify *and* extol *and* honor *and* magnify You.

2 Just as You have granted Him power *and* authority over all flesh (all human kind), *now glorify Him,* so that He may give eternal life to all whom You have given Him.

3 And this is eternal life: [it means] to know (to perceive, recognize, become acquainted with and understand) You, the only true *and* real God, and [likewise] to know Him, Jesus [as the] Christ, the Anointed One, the Messiah, Whom You have sent.

4 I have glorified You down here on the earth by completing the work that You gave Me to do.

5 And now, Father, glorify Me along with Yourself *and* restore Me to such majesty *and* honor in Your presence as I had with You before the world existed.

6 I have manifested Your name—I have revealed Your very Self, Your real Self—to the people whom You have given Me out of the world. They were Yours, and You gave them to Me, and they have obeyed *and* kept Your Word.

---

f) Cremer.

Living New Testament

24 You haven't tried this before, [but begin now[4]]. Ask, using My name, and you will receive, and your cup of joy will overflow.

25 I have spoken of these matters very guardedly, but the time will come when this will not be necessary and I will tell you plainly all about the Father.

26 Then you will present your petitions over My signature![5] And I won't need to ask the Father to grant you these requests,

27 For the Father Himself loves you dearly because you love Me and believe that I came from the Father.

28 Yes, I came from the Father into the world and will leave the world and return to the Father."

29 "At last You are speaking plainly," His disciples said, "and not in riddles.

30 Now we understand that You know everything and don't need anyone to tell You anything.[6] From this we believe that You came from God."

31 "Do you finally believe this?" Jesus asked.

32 "But the time is coming—in fact, it is here—when you will be scattered, each one returning to his own home, leaving Me alone. Yet I will not be alone, for the Father is with Me.

33 I have told you all this so that you will have peace of heart and mind. Here on earth you will have many trials and sorrows; but cheer up, for I have overcome the world."

Revised Standard

to you have asked nothing in my name;
ask, and you will receive, that your joy may
be full.
25 "I have said this to you in figures;
the hour is coming when I shall no longer
speak to you in figures but tell you plainly
of the Father. 26 In that day you will ask in
my name; and I do not say to you that I
shall pray the Father for you; 27 for the
Father himself loves you, because you have
loved me and have believed that I came
from the Father. 28 I came from the Father
and have come into the world; again, I am
leaving the world and going to the Father."
29 His disciples said, "Ah, now you
are speaking plainly, not in any figure!
30 Now we know that you know all things,
and need none to question you; by this we
believe that you came from God." 31 Jesus
answered them, "Do you now believe? 32 The
hour is coming, indeed it has come, when
you will be scattered, every man to his
home, and will leave me alone; yet I am
not alone, for the Father is with me. 33 I
have said this to you, that in me you may
have peace. In the world you have tribulation; but be of good cheer, I have overcome the world."

CHAPTER 17

When Jesus had finished saying all these things He looked up to heaven and said, "Father, the time has come. Reveal the glory of Your Son so that He can give the glory back to You.

2 For You have given Him authority over every man and woman in all the earth. He gives eternal life to each one You have given Him.

3 And this is the way to have eternal life—by knowing You, the only true God, and Jesus Christ, the one You sent to earth!

4 I brought glory to You here on earth by doing everything You told Me to.

5 And now, Father, reveal My glory as I stand in Your presence, the glory We shared before the world began.

6 I have told these men all about You. They were in the world, but then You gave them to Me. Actually, they were always Yours, and You gave them to Me; and they have obeyed You.

The prayer to be glorified

17 When Jesus had spoken these words,
he lifted up his eyes to heaven and
said, "Father, the hour has come; glorify
thy Son that the Son may glorify thee,
2 since thou hast given him power over all
flesh, to give eternal life to all whom thou
hast given him. 3 And this is eternal life,
that they know thee the only true God, and
Jesus Christ whom thou hast sent. 4 I glorified thee on earth, having accomplished the
work which thou gavest me to do; 5 and
now, Father, glorify thou me in thy own
presence with the glory which I had with
thee before the world was made.

The prayer for the disciples

6 "I have manifested thy name to the
men whom thou gavest me out of the
world; thine they were, and thou gavest
them to me, and they have kept thy word.

[4] Implied.
[5] Literally, "you shall ask *in My name*." The above paraphrase is the modern equivalent of this idea, otherwise obscure.
[6] Literally, "and need not that anyone should ask you," i.e., discuss what is true.

King James

7 Now they have known that all things whatsoever thou hast given me are of thee.

8 For I have given unto them the words which thou gavest me; and they have received *them,* and have known surely that I came out from thee, and they have believed that thou didst send me.

9 I pray for them: I pray not for the world, but for them which thou hast given me; for they are thine.

10 And all mine are thine, and thine are mine; and I am glorified in them.

11 And now I am no more in the world, but these are in the world, and I come to thee. Holy Father, keep through thine own name those whom thou hast given me, that they may be one, as we *are.*

12 While I was with them in the world, I kept them in thy name: those that thou gavest me I have kept, and none of them is lost, but the son of perdition; that the scripture might be fulfilled.

13 And now come I to thee; and these things I speak in the world, that they might have my joy fulfilled in themselves.

14 I have given them thy word; and the world hath hated them, because they are not of the world, even as I am not of the world.

15 I pray not that thou shouldest take them out of the world, but that thou shouldest keep them from the evil.

16 They are not of the world, even as I am not of the world.

17 Sanctify them through thy truth: thy word is truth.

18 As thou hast sent me into the world, even so have I also sent them into the world.

19 And for their sakes I sanctify myself, that they also might be sanctified through the truth.

20 Neither pray I for these alone, but for them also which shall believe on me through their word;

21 That they all may be one; as thou, Father, *art* in me, and I in thee, that they also may be one in us: that the world may believe that thou hast sent me.

22 And the glory which thou gavest me I have given them; that they may be one, even as we are one:

22 I in them, and thou in me, that they may be made perfect in one; and that the world may know that thou hast sent me, and hast loved them, as thou hast loved me.

Amplified

7 Now [at last] they know *and* understand that all You have given Me belongs to You—is really and truly Yours.

8 For the uttered words that You gave Me I have given them. And they have received *and* accepted [them], and have come to know positively *and* in reality—to believe with absolute assurance—that I came forth from Your presence. And they have believed *and* are convinced that You did send Me.

9 I am praying for them. I am not praying (requesting) for the world; but for those You have given Me, for they belong to You.

10 All Mine are Yours, and all that are Yours belong to Me; and I am glorified in (through) them—they have done Me honor, in them My glory is achieved.

11 And [now] I am no more in the world, but these are in the world and I am coming to You. Holy Father, keep in Your name [[g]in the knowledge of Yourself] them whom You have given Me, that they may be one, as We [are one].

12 While I was with them, I kept *and* preserved them in Your name [[g]in the knowledge and worship of You]. Those You have given Me I guarded *and* protected, and not one of them has perished *or* is lost except the son of perdition [Judas Iscariot]—the one who is now doomed to destruction, destined to be lost—that the Scripture might be fulfilled. [Ps. 41:9; John 6:70.]

13 And now I am coming to You. I say these things while I am still in the world, so that My joy may be made full *and* complete *and* perfect in them—that they may experience My delight fulfilled in them, that My enjoyment may be perfected in their own souls, that they may have My gladness within them filling their hearts.

14 I have given *and* delivered to them Your Word (message); and the world has hated them, because they are not of the world—do not belong to the world—[just] as I am not of the world.

15 I do not ask that You will take them out of the world, but that You will keep *and* protect them from the evil [one].

16 They are not of the world (worldly, belonging to the world), [just] as I am not of the world.

17 Sanctify them—purify, consecrate, separate them for Yourself, make them holy—by the Truth. Your Word is Truth.

18 Just as You sent Me into the world, I also have sent them into the world.

19 And so for their sake *and* on their behalf I sanctify (dedicate, consecrate) Myself, that they also may be sanctified (dedicated, consecrated, made holy) in the Truth.

20 Neither for these alone do I pray—it is not for their sake only that I make this request—but also for all those who will ever come to believe in (trust, cling to, rely on) Me through their word *and* teaching;

21 So that they all may be one [just] as You, Father, are in Me and I in You, that they also may be one in Us, so that the world may believe *and* be convinced that You have sent Me.

22 I have given to them the glory *and* honor which You have given Me, that they may be one, [even] as We are one:

23 I in them and You in Me, in order that they may become one *and* perfectly united, that the world may know *and* [definitely] recognize that You sent Me, and that You have loved them [even] as You have loved Me.

---

g) Barnes' "Notes on Luke and John."

Living New Testament

7 Now they know that everything I have is a gift from You,

8 For I have passed on to them the commands You gave Me; and they accepted them and know of a certainty that I came down to earth from You, and they believe You sent Me.

9 My plea is not for the world but for those You have given Me because they belong to You.

10 And all of them, since they are Mine, belong to You; and You have given them back to Me with everything else of Yours, and so *they are My glory!*

11 Now I am leaving the world, and leaving them behind, and coming to You. Holy Father, keep them in Your own care—all those You have given Me—so that they will be united just as We are, with none missing.

12 During My time here I have kept safe within Your family[1] all of these You gave to Me. I guarded them so that not one perished, except the son of hell, as the Scriptures foretold.

13 And now I am coming to You. I have told them many things while I was with them so that they would be filled with My joy.

14 I have given them Your commands. And the world hates them because they don't fit in with it, just as I don't.

15 I'm not asking You to take them out of the world, but to keep them safe from Satan's power.

16 They are not part of this world any more than I am.

17 Make them pure and holy through teaching them Your words of truth.

18 As You sent Me into the world, I am sending them into the world,

19 And I consecrate Myself to meet their need for growth in truth and holiness.

20 I am not praying for these alone but also for all future believers who will come to Me because of the testimony of these.

21 My prayer for all of them is that they will be of one heart and mind, just as You and I are, Father—that just as You are in Me and I am in You, so they will be in Us, and the world will believe you sent Me.

22 I have given them the glory You gave Me—the glorious unity of being one, as We are—

23 I in them and You in Me, all being perfected into one—so that the world will know You sent Me and will understand that You love them as much as You love Me.

[1]Literally, "kept in Your name those whom You have given Me."

Revised Standard

[7]Now they know that everything that thou
hast given me is from thee; [8]for I have
given them the words which thou gavest me,
and they have received them and know in
truth that I came from thee; and they have
believed that thou didst send me. [9]I am
praying for them; I am not praying for the
world but for those whom thou hast given
me, for they are thine; [10]all mine are thine,
and thine are mine, and I am glorified in
them. [11]And now I am no more in the
world, but they are in the world, and I am
coming to thee. Holy Father, keep them in
thy name, which thou hast given me, that
they may be one, even as we are one.
[12]While I was with them, I kept them in
thy name, which thou hast given me; I have
guarded them, and none of them is lost but
the son of perdition, that the scripture
might be fulfilled. [13]But now I am coming
to thee; and these things I speak in the
world, that they may have my joy fulfilled
in themselves. [14]I have given them thy
word; and the world has hated them because they are not of the world, even as
I am not of the world. [15]I do not pray that
thou shouldst take them out of the world,
but that thou shouldst keep them from the
evil one.[k] [16]They are not of the world, even
as I am not of the world. [17]Sanctify them
in the truth; thy word is truth. [18]As thou
didst send me into the world, so I have sent
them into the world. [19]And for their sake
I consecrate myself, that they also may be
consecrated in truth.

The prayer for the church

20 "I do not pray for these only, but
also for those who believe in me through
their word, [21]that they may all be one; even
as thou, Father, art in me, and I in thee,
that they also may be in us, so that the
world may believe that thou hast sent me.
[22]The glory which thou hast given me I
have given to them, that they may be one
even as we are one, [23]I in them and thou in
me, that they may become perfectly one,
so that the world may know that thou hast
sent me and hast loved them even as thou
hast loved me. [24]Father, I desire that

[k] Or *from evil*

King James

24 Father, I will that they also, whom thou hast given me, be with me where I am; that they may behold my glory, which thou hast given me: for thou lovedst me before the foundation of the world.

25 O righteous Father, the world hath not known thee: but I have known thee, and these have known that thou hast sent me.

26 And I have declared unto them thy name, and will declare *it:* that the love wherewith thou hast loved me may be in them, and I in them.

Amplified

24 Father, I desire that they also whom You have entrusted to Me [Your gift to Me,] may be with Me where I am, so that they may see My glory, which You have given Me—Your love gift to Me—for You loved Me before the foundation of the world.

25 O just *and* righteous Father, although the world has not known You *and* has failed to recognize You *and* has never acknowledged You, I have known You continually. And these men understand *and* know that You have sent Me.

26 I made Your name known to them *and* revealed Your character *and* Your very [h]Self, and I will continue to make [You] known, that the love which You have bestowed upon Me may be in them—felt in their hearts—and that I [Myself] may be in them.

King James — CHAPTER 18

WHEN Jesus had spoken these words, he went forth with his disciples over the brook Cedron, where was a garden, into the which he entered, and his disciples.

2 And Judas also, which betrayed him, knew the place: for Jesus ofttimes resorted thither with his disciples.

3 Judas then, having received a band *of men* and officers from the chief priests and Pharisees, cometh thither with lanterns and torches and weapons.

4 Jesus therefore, knowing all things that should come upon him, went forth, and said unto them, Whom seek ye?

5 They answered him, Jesus of Nazareth. Jesus saith unto them, I am *he.* And Judas also, which betrayed him, stood with them.

6 As soon then as he had said unto them, I am *he,* they went backward, and fell to the ground.

7 Then asked he them again, Whom seek ye? And they said, Jesus of Nazareth.

8 Jesus answered, I have told you that I am *he:* if therefore ye seek me, let these go their way:

9 That the saying might be fulfilled, which he spake, Of them which thou gavest me have I lost none.

10 Then Simon Peter having a sword drew it, and smote the high priest's servant, and cut off his right ear. The servant's name was Malchus.

11 Then said Jesus unto Peter, Put up thy sword into the sheath: the cup which my Father hath given me shall I not drink it?

12 Then the band and the captain and officers of the Jews took Jesus, and bound him,

13 And led him away to Annas first; for he was father in law to Caiaphas, which was the high priest that same year.

14 Now Caiaphas was he, which gave counsel to the Jews, that it was expedient that one man should die for the people.

15 ¶ And Simon Peter followed Jesus, and *so did* another disciple: that disciple was known unto the high priest, and went in with Jesus into the palace of the high priest.

Amplified — CHAPTER 18

HAVING said these things, Jesus went out with His disciples beyond (across) the winter torrent of the Kidron (in the Ravine of the Cedars). There was a garden there, which He and His disciples entered.

2 And Judas, who was betraying Him *and* delivering Him up, also knew the place, because Jesus had often retired there with His disciples.

3 So Judas, obtaining *and* taking charge of the band of soldiers and some guards (attendants) of the high priests and Pharisees, came there with lanterns and torches and weapons.

4 Then Jesus, knowing all that was about to befall Him, went out to them and said, Whom are you seeking—Whom do you want?

5 They answered Him, Jesus the Nazarene. Jesus said to them, I am He. Judas, who was betraying Him, was also standing with them.

6 When Jesus said to them, I am He, they went backwards—drew back, lurched backward—and fell to the ground.

7 Then again He asked them, Whom are you seeking? And they said, Jesus the Nazarene.

8 Jesus answered, I told you that I am He. So, if you want Me—if it is only I for Whom you are looking—let these men go their way.

9 Thus what He had said was fulfilled *and* verified, Of those whom You have given Me, I have not lost even one. [John 17:12.]

10 Then Simon Peter, who had a sword, drew it and struck the high priest's servant and cut off his right ear. The servant's name was Malchus.

11 Therefore, Jesus said to Peter, Put the sword [back] in the sheath! The cup which My Father has given Me, shall I not drink it?

12 So the troops and their captain and the guards (attendants) of the Jews seized Jesus and bound Him.

13 And they brought Him first to Annas, for he was the father-in-law of Caiaphas, who was the high priest that year.

14 It was Caiaphas who had counselled the Jews that it was expedient *and* for their welfare that one man should die for (instead of, in behalf of) the people.

15 Now Simon Peter and another disciple followed Jesus. And that disciple was known to the high priest, so he entered along with Jesus into the court of the palace of the high priest.

h) Thayer.

Living New Testament

24 Father, I want them with Me—these You've given Me—so that they can see My glory. You gave Me the glory because You loved Me before the world began!
25 O righteous Father, the world doesn't know You, but I do; and these disciples know You sent Me.
26 And I have revealed You to them, and will keep on revealing You so that the mighty love You have for Me may be in them, and I in them."

Revised Standard

they also, whom thou hast given me, may
be with me where I am, to behold my
glory which thou hast given me in thy love
for me before the foundation of the world.
[25]O righteous Father, the world has not
known thee, but I have known thee; and
these know that thou hast sent me. [26]I made
known to them thy name, and I will make
it known, that the love with which thou
hast loved me may be in them, and I in
them."

CHAPTER 18

After saying these things Jesus crossed the Kidron ravine with His disciples and entered a grove of olive trees.
2 Judas, the betrayer, knew this place, for Jesus had gone there many times with His disciples.
3 The chief priests and Pharisees had given Judas a squad of soldiers and police to accompany him. Now with blazing torches, lanterns, and weapons they arrived at the olive grove.
4, 5 Jesus fully realized all that was going to happen to Him. Stepping forward to meet them He asked, "Whom are you looking for?"
"Jesus of Nazareth," they replied.
"I am He," Jesus said.
6 And as He said it, they all fell backwards to the ground!
7 Once more He asked them, "Whom are you searching for?"
And again they replied, "Jesus of Nazareth."
8 "I told you I am He," Jesus said; "and since I am the one you are after, let these others go."
9 He did this to carry out the prophecy He had just made, "I have not lost a single one of those You gave Me . . . ."
10 Then Simon Peter drew a sword and slashed off the right ear of Malchus, the High Priest's servant.
11 But Jesus said to Peter, "Put your sword away. Shall I not drink from the cup the Father has given Me?"
12 So the Jewish police, with the soldiers and their lieutenant, arrested Jesus and tied Him.
13 First they took Him to Annas, the father-in-law of Caiaphas, the High Priest that year.
14 Caiaphas was the one who told the other Jewish leaders, "Better that one should die for all."
15 Simon Peter followed along behind, as did another of the disciples who was acquainted with the High Priest. So that other disciple was permitted into the courtyard along with Jesus,

Jesus' betrayal and arrest

18 When Jesus had spoken these words,
he went forth with his disciples across
the Kidron valley, where there was a garden,
which he and his disciples entered. [2]Now
Judas, who betrayed him, also knew the
place; for Jesus often met there with his
disciples. [3]So Judas, procuring a band of
soldiers and some officers from the chief
priests and the Pharisees, went there with
lanterns and torches and weapons. [4]Then
Jesus, knowing all that was to befall him,
came forward and said to them, "Whom
do you seek?" [5]They answered him, "Jesus
of Nazareth." Jesus said to them, "I am
he." Judas, who betrayed him, was standing
with them. [6]When he said to them, "I am
he," they drew back and fell to the ground.
[7]Again he asked them, "Whom do you
seek?" And they said, "Jesus of Nazareth."
[8]Jesus answered, "I told you that I am he;
so, if you seek me, let these men go." [9]This
was to fulfil the word which he had spoken,
"Of those whom thou gavest me I lost not
one." [10]Then Simon Peter, having a sword,
drew it and struck the high priest's slave
and cut off his right ear. The slave's name
was Malchus. [11]Jesus said to Peter, "Put
your sword into its sheath; shall I not drink
the cup which the Father has given me?"

Jesus before Jewish authorities

12 So the band of soldiers and their
captain and the officers of the Jews seized
Jesus and bound him. [13]First they led him
to Annas; for he was the father-in-law of
Caiaphas, who was high priest that year.
[14]It was Caiaphas who had given counsel
to the Jews that it was expedient that one
man should die for the people.
15 Simon Peter followed Jesus, and so
did another disciple. As this disciple was
known to the high priest, he entered the
court of the high priest along with Jesus,

King James

16 But Peter stood at the door without. Then went out that other disciple, which was known unto the high priest, and spake unto her that kept the door, and brought in Peter.

17 Then saith the damsel that kept the door unto Peter, Art not thou also *one* of this man's disciples? He saith, I am not.

18 And the servants and officers stood there, who had made a fire of coals; for it was cold: and they warmed themselves: and Peter stood with them, and warmed himself.

19 ¶ The high priest then asked Jesus of his disciples, and of his doctrine.

20 Jesus answered him, I spake openly to the world; I ever taught in the synagogue, and in the temple, whither the Jews always resort; and in secret have I said nothing.

21 Why askest thou me? ask them which heard me, what I have said unto them: behold, they know what I said.

22 And when he had thus spoken, one of the officers which stood by struck Jesus with the palm of his hand, saying, Answerest thou the high priest so?

23 Jesus answered him, If I have spoken evil, bear witness of the evil: but if well, why smitest thou me?

24 Now Annas had sent him bound unto Caiaphas the high priest.

25 And Simon Peter stood and warmed himself. They said therefore unto him, Art not thou also *one* of his disciples? He denied *it*, and said, I am not.

26 One of the servants of the high priest, being *his* kinsman whose ear Peter cut off, saith, Did not I see thee in the garden with him?

27 Peter then denied again: and immediately the cock crew.

28 ¶ Then led they Jesus from Caiaphas unto the hall of judgment: and it was early; and they themselves went not into the judgment hall, lest they should be defiled; but that they might eat the passover.

29 Pilate then went out unto them, and said, What accusation bring ye against this man?

30 They answered and said unto him, If he were not a malefactor, we would not have delivered him up unto thee.

31 Then said Pilate unto them, Take ye him, and judge him according to your law. The Jews therefore said unto him, It is not lawful for us to put any man to death:

32 That the saying of Jesus might be fulfilled, which he spake, signifying what death he should die.

33 Then Pilate entered into the judgment hall again, and called Jesus, and said unto him, Art thou the King of the Jews?

34 Jesus answered him, Sayest thou this thing of thyself, or did others tell it thee of me?

35 Pilate answered, Am I a Jew? Thine own nation and the chief priests have delivered thee unto me: what hast thou done?

36 Jesus answered, My kingdom is not of this world: if my kingdom were of this world, then would my servants fight, that I should not be delivered to the Jews: but now is my kingdom not from hence.

Amplified

16 But Peter was standing outside at the door. So the other disciple, who was known to the high priest, went out and spoke to the maid who kept the door and brought Peter inside.

17 Then the maid who was in charge at the door said to Peter, You are not also one of the disciples of this [i]Man, are you? He said, I am not!

18 Now the servants and the guards (the attendants) had made a fire of coals, for it was cold, and they were standing and warming themselves. And Peter was with them, standing and warming himself.

19 Then the high priest questioned Jesus about His disciples and about His teaching.

20 Jesus answered him, I have spoken openly to the world; I have always taught in a synagogue and in the temple area, where the Jews habitually congregate (assemble), and I have spoken nothing secretly.

21 Why do you ask Me? Ask those who have heard [Me] what I said to them. See! They know what I said.

22 But when He said this, one of the attendants who stood by struck Jesus, saying, Is that how [i]You answer the high priest?

23 Jesus replied, If I have said anything wrong—have spoken abusively, if there was evil in what I said—tell what was wrong with it. But if I spoke rightly *and* properly, why do you strike Me?

24 Then Annas sent Him bound to Caiaphas the high priest.

25 But Simon Peter [still] was standing and was warming himself. They said to him, You are not also one of His disciples, are you? He denied and said, I am not!

26 One of the high priest's servants, a relative of the man whose ear Peter cut off, said, Did I not see you in the garden with Him?

27 And again Peter denied it. And immediately a rooster crowed.

28 Then they brought Jesus from Caiaphas into the praetorium (judgment hall, governor's palace). And it was early. They themselves did not enter the praetorium, that they might not be defiled (become ceremonially unclean), but might be fit to eat the Passover [supper].

29 So Pilate went out to them and said, What accusations do you bring against this [j]Man?

30 They retorted, If He were not an evildoer (criminal) we would not have handed Him over to you.

31 Pilate said to them. Take Him yourselves and judge *and* sentence *and* punish Him according to your [own] law. The Jews answered, It is not lawful for us to put any one to death.

32 This was to fulfill the word which Jesus had spoken to show (indicate, predict) by what manner of death He was to die.

33 So Pilate went back again into the judgment hall and called Jesus and asked Him, Are You the King of the Jews?

34 Jesus replied, Are you saying this of yourself—on your own initiative—or have others told it to you about Me?

35 Pilate answered, Am I a Jew? Your [own] people *and* nation and their chief priests have delivered You to me. What have You done?

36 Jesus answered, My kingdom (kingship, royal power) belongs not to this world. If My kingdom were of this world, My followers would have been fighting to keep Me from being handed over to the Jews. But as it is, My kingdom is not from [this world]—has no such origin *or* source.

---

i and j) Capitalized because of what He is, the spotless Son of God, not what the speaker may have thought He was.

Living New Testament

16 While Peter stood outside the gate. Then the other disciple spoke to the girl watching at the gate, and she let Peter in.

17 The girl asked Peter, "Aren't you one of Jesus' disciples?"

"No," he said, "I am not!"

18 The police and the household servants were standing around a fire they had made, for it was cold. And Peter stood there with them, warming himself.

19 Inside, the High Priest began asking Jesus about His followers and what He had been teaching them.

20 Jesus replied, "What I teach is widely known, for I have preached regularly in the synagogue and Temple; I have been heard by all the Jewish leaders and teach nothing in private that I have not said in public.

21 Why are you asking Me this question? Ask those who heard Me. You have some of them here. They know what I said."

22 One of the soldiers standing there struck Jesus with his fist. "Is that the way to answer the High Priest?" he demanded.

23 "If I lied, prove it," Jesus replied. "Should you hit a man for telling the truth?"

24 Then Annas sent Jesus, bound, to Caiaphas the High Priest.

25 Meanwhile as Simon Peter was standing by the fire, he was asked again, "Aren't you one of His disciples?"

"Of course not," he replied.

26 But one of the household slaves of the High Priest—a relative of the man whose ear Peter had cut off—asked, "Didn't I see you out there in the olive grove with Jesus?"

27 Again Peter denied it. And immediately a rooster crowed.

28 Jesus' trial before Caiaphas ended in the early hours of the morning. Next he was taken to the palace of the Roman governor.[1] His accusers wouldn't go in themselves for that would "defile"[2] them, they said, and they wouldn't be allowed to eat the Passover lamb.

29 So Pilate, the governor, went out to them and asked, "What is your charge against this man? What are you accusing him of doing?"

30 "We wouldn't have arrested him if he weren't a criminal!" they retorted.

31 "Then take him away and judge him yourselves by your own laws," Pilate told them.

"But we want him crucified," they said, "and your approval is required."[3]

32 This fulfilled Jesus' prediction concerning the method of His execution.[4]

33 Then Pilate went back into the palace and called for Jesus to be brought to him, "Are you the King of the Jews?" he asked Him.

34 " 'King' as *you* use the word or as the *Jews* use it?" Jesus asked.[5]

35 "Am I a Jew?" Pilate retorted. "Your own people and their chief priests brought you here. Why? What have you done?"

36 Then Jesus answered, "I am not an earthly king. If I were, My followers would have fought when I was arrested by the Jewish leaders. But My Kingdom is not of the world.

---

[1] Literally, "the Praetorium."
[2] By Jewish law, entering the house of a Gentile was a serious offense.
[3] Literally, "It is not lawful for us to put any man to death."
[4] This prophecy is recorded in Matthew 20:19, which indicates His death by crucifixion, a practice under Roman law.
[5] A paraphrase of this verse—that goes beyond the limits of this book's paraphrasing—would be, "Do you mean their King, or their Messiah?" If Pilate was asking as the Roman governor, he would be inquiring whether Jesus was setting up a rebel government. But the Jews were using the word "King" to mean their religious ruler, the Messiah. Literally this verse reads, "Are you saying this of yourself, or did someone else say it about me?"

Revised Standard

16 while Peter stood outside at the door.
So the other disciple, who was known to
the high priest, went out and spoke to the
maid who kept the door, and brought Peter
in. 17 The maid who kept the door said to
Peter, "Are not you also one of this man's
disciples?" He said, "I am not." 18 Now
the servants[1] and officers had made a charcoal fire, because it was cold, and they
were standing and warming themselves;
Peter also was with them, standing and
warming himself.
19 The high priest then questioned Jesus
about his disciples and his teaching. 20 Jesus
answered him, "I have spoken openly to
the world; I have always taught in synagogues and in the temple, where all Jews
come together; I have said nothing secretly.
21 Why do you ask me? Ask those who have
heard me, what I said to them; they know
what I said." 22 When he had said this, one
of the officers standing by struck Jesus with
his hand, saying, "Is that how you answer
the high priest?" 23 Jesus answered him, "If
I have spoken wrongly, bear witness to the
wrong; but if I have spoken rightly, why
do you strike me?" 24 Annas then sent him
bound to Caiaphas the high priest.
25 Now Simon Peter was standing and
warming himself. They said to him, "Are
not you also one of his disciples?" He
denied it and said, "I am not." 26 One of
the servants[1] of the high priest, a kinsman
of the man whose ear Peter had cut off,
asked, "Did I not see you in the garden with
him?" 27 Peter again denied it; and at once
the cock crowed.

Jesus before Pontius Pilate

28 Then they led Jesus from the house
of Caiaphas to the praetorium. It was early.
They themselves did not enter the praetorium, so that they might not be defiled, but
might eat the passover. 29 So Pilate went out
to them and said, "What accusation do you
bring against this man?" 30 They answered
him, "If this man were not an evildoer,
we would not have handed him over."
31 Pilate said to them, "Take him yourselves
and judge him by your own law." The Jews
said to him, "It is not lawful for us to put
any man to death." 32 This was to fulfil the
word which Jesus had spoken to show by
what death he was to die.
33 Pilate entered the praetorium again
and called to Jesus, and said to him, "Are
you the King of the Jews?" 34 Jesus answered,
"Do you say this of your own accord, or
did others say it to you about me?" 35 Pilate
answered, "Am I a Jew? Your own nation
and the chief priests have handed you over
to me; what have you done?" 36 Jesus answered, "My kingship is not of this world;
if my kingship were of this world, my servants would fight, that I might not be handed over to the Jews; but my kingship is not

---

[1] Or *slaves*

King James

37 Pilate therefore said unto him, Art thou a king then? Jesus answered, Thou sayest that I am a king. To this end was I born, and for this cause came I into the world, that I should bear witness unto the truth. Every one that is of the truth heareth my voice.

38 Pilate saith unto him, What is truth? And when he had said this, he went out again unto the Jews, and saith unto them, I find in him no fault *at all*.

39 But ye have a custom, that I should release unto you one at the passover: will ye therefore that I release unto you the King of the Jews?

40 Then cried they all again, saying, Not this man, but Barabbas. Now Barabbas was a robber.

Amplified

37 Pilate said to Him, Then You are a King? Jesus answered, You say it! (You speak correctly,) for I am a King.—Certainly I am a King! This is why I was born, and for this I have come into the world, to bear witness to the Truth. Everyone who is of the Truth (who is a friend of the Truth, who belongs to the Truth) hears *and* listens to My voice.

38 Pilate said to Him, What is truth? On saying this he went out to the Jews again and told them, I find no fault in [k]Him.

39 But it is your custom that I release one [prisoner] for you at the Passover. So shall I release for you the King of the Jews?

40 Then they all shouted back again, Not Him—not this Man—but Barabbas! Now Barabbas was a robber.

CHAPTER 19

THEN Pilate therefore took Jesus, and scourged *him*.

2 And the soldiers platted a crown of thorns, and put *it* on his head, and they put on him a purple robe,

3 And said, Hail, King of the Jews! and they smote him with their hands.

4 Pilate therefore went forth again, and saith unto them, Behold, I bring him forth to you, that ye may know that I find no fault in him.

5 Then came Jesus forth, wearing the crown of thorns, and the purple robe. And *Pilate* saith unto them, Behold the man!

6 When the chief priests therefore and officers saw him, they cried out, saying, Crucify *him*, crucify *him*. Pilate saith unto them, Take ye him, and crucify *him*: for I find no fault in him.

7 The Jews answered him, We have a law, and by our law he ought to die, because he made himself the Son of God.

8 ¶ When Pilate therefore heard that saying, he was the more afraid;

9 And went again into the judgment hall, and saith unto Jesus, Whence art thou? But Jesus gave him no answer.

10 Then saith Pilate unto him, Speakest thou not unto me? knowest thou not that I have power to crucify thee, and have power to release thee?

11 Jesus answered, Thou couldest have no power *at all* against me, except it were given thee from above: therefore he that delivered me unto thee hath the greater sin.

12 And from thenceforth Pilate sought to release him: but the Jews cried out, saying, If thou let this man go, thou art not Caesar's friend: whosoever maketh himself a king speaketh against Caesar.

13 ¶ When Pilate therefore heard that saying, he brought Jesus forth, and sat down in the judgment seat in a place that is called the Pavement, but in the Hebrew, Gabbatha.

CHAPTER 19

SO then Pilate took Jesus and scourged (flogged, whipped) Him.

2 And the soldiers, having twisted a crown of thorns, put it on His head and threw a purple cloak around Him.

3 And they kept coming to Him and saying, Hail, King of the Jews! (Good health to you! Peace to you! Long life to you, King of the Jews!) And they struck Him with the palms of their hands. [Isa. 53:3, 5, 7.]

4 Then Pilate went out again and said to them, See, I bring Him out to you so that you may know I find no fault (crime, cause for accusation) in Him.

5 So Jesus came out, wearing the thorny crown and purple cloak, and Pilate said to them, See, [here is] the [l]Man!

6 When the chief priests and attendants (guards) saw Him, they cried out, Crucify Him! Crucify Him! Pilate said to them, Take Him yourselves and crucify Him, for I find no fault (crime) in Him.

7 The Jews answered him, We have a Law, and according to that Law He should die, because He has claimed *and* made Himself out to be the Son of God.

8 So, when Pilate heard this said, he was more alarmed *and* awe-stricken *and* afraid than before.

9 He went into the judgment hall again and said to Jesus, Where are You from?—To what world do You belong? But Jesus did not answer him.

10 So Pilate said to Him, Will You not speak [even] to me? Do You not know that I have power (authority) to release You and I have power to crucify You?

11 Jesus answered, You would not have any power *or* authority whatever against (over) Me, if it were not given you from above. For this reason the sin *and* guilt of the one who delivered Me over to you is greater.

12 Upon this Pilate wanted (sought, was anxious) to release Him, but the Jews kept shrieking, If you release this Man, you are no friend of Caesars! Anybody who makes himself a king sets himself up against Caesar—is a rebel against the emperor!

13 Hearing this, Pilate brought Jesus out and sat down on the judgment seat at a place called the Pavement—the Mosaic Pavement, the Stone Platform; but in Hebrew, Gabbatha.

---

k and l) Capitalized because of what He is, the spotless Son of God, not what the speaker may have thought He was.

Living New Testament

37 Pilate replied, "But you are a king then?"

"Yes," Jesus said. "I was born for that purpose. And I came to bring truth to the world. All who love the truth are My followers."

38 "What is truth?" Pilate exclaimed. Then he went out again to the people and told them, "He is not guilty of any crime.

39 But you have a custom of asking me to release someone from prison each year at Passover. So if you want me to, I'll release the 'King of the Jews.' "

40 But they screamed back, "No! Not this man, but Barabbas!" Barabbas was a robber.

Revised Standard

from the world." 37Pilate said to him, "So
you are a king?" Jesus answered, "You say
that I am a king. For this I was born, and
for this I have come into the world, to bear
witness to the truth. Every one who is of
the truth hears my voice." 38Pilate said to
him, "What is truth?"
After he had said this, he went out to
the Jews again, and told them, "I find no
crime in him. 39But you have a custom
that I should release one man for you at
the Passover; will you have me release for
you the King of the Jews?" 40They cried
out again, "Not this man, but Barabbas!"
Now Barabbas was a robber.

CHAPTER 19

Then Pilate laid open Jesus' back with a leaded whip,

2 And the soldiers made a crown of thorns and placed it on His head and robed Him in royal[1] purple.

3 "Hail, 'King of the Jews!' " they mocked, and struck Him with their fists.

4 Pilate went outside again and said to the Jews, "I am going to bring him out to you now, but understand clearly that I find him NOT GUILTY."

5 Then Jesus came out wearing the crown of thorns and the purple robe. And Pilate said, "Behold the man!"

6 At sight of Him the chief priests and Jewish officials began yelling, "Crucify! Crucify!"

"*You* crucify him," Pilate said. "I find him NOT GUILTY."

7 They replied, "By our laws he ought to die because he called himself the Son of God."

8 When Pilate heard this, he was more frightened than ever.

9 He took Jesus back into the palace again and asked Him, "Where are you from?" but Jesus gave no answer.

10 "You won't talk to me?" Pilate demanded. "Don't you realize that I have the power to release you or to crucify you?"

11 Then Jesus said, "You would have no power at all over Me unless it were given to you from above. So those[2] who brought Me to you have the greater sin."

12 Then Pilate tried to release Him, but the Jewish leaders told him, "If you release this man, you are no friend of Caesar's. Anyone who declares himself a king is a rebel against Caesar."

13 At these words Pilate brought Jesus out to them again and sat down at the judgment bench on the stone-paved platform.[3]

Jesus crowned with thorns

19 Then Pilate took Jesus and scourged
him. 2And the soldiers plaited a crown
of thorns, and put it on his head, and arrayed him in a purple robe; 3they came up
to him, saying, "Hail, King of the Jews!"
and struck him with their hands. 4Pilate
went out again, and said to them, "Behold,
I am bringing him out to you, that you may
know that I find no crime in him." 5So
Jesus came out, wearing the crown of
thorns and the purple robe. Pilate said to
them, "Here is the man!" 6When the chief
priests and the officers saw him, they cried
out, "Crucify him, crucify him!" Pilate said
to them, "Take him yourselves and crucify
him, for I find no crime in him." 7The Jews
answered him, "We have a law, and by that
law he ought to die, because he has made
himself the Son of God." 8When Pilate
heard these words, he was the more afraid;
9he entered the praetorium again and said
to Jesus, "Where are you from?" But Jesus
gave no answer. 10Pilate therefore said to
him, "You will not speak to me? Do you
not know that I have power to release you,
and power to crucify you?" 11Jesus answered
him, "You would have no power over me
unless it had been given you from above;
therefore he who delivered me to you has
the greater sin."
12 Upon this Pilate sought to release
him, but the Jews cried out, "If you release
this man, you are not Caesar's friend; every
one who makes himself a king sets himself
against Caesar." 13When Pilate heard these
words, he brought Jesus out and sat down
on the judgment seat at a place called The
Pavement, and in Hebrew, Gabbatha. 14Now

---

[1] Implied.
[2] Literally, "he."
[3] Literally, "the judgment seat in a place that is called The Pavement, but in Hebrew, Gabbatha."

King James

14 And it was the preparation of the passover, and about the sixth hour: and he saith unto the Jews, Behold your King!

15 But they cried out, Away with *him*, away with *him*, crucify him. Pilate saith unto them, Shall I crucify your King? The chief priests answered, We have no king but Caesar.

16 Then delivered he him therefore unto them to be crucified. And they took Jesus, and led *him* away.

17 And he bearing his cross went forth into a place called *the place* of a skull, which is called in the Hebrew Golgotha:

18 Where they crucified him, and two other with him, on either side one, and Jesus in the midst.

19 ¶ And Pilate wrote a title, and put *it* on the cross. And the writing was, JESUS OF NAZARETH THE KING OF THE JEWS.

20 This title then read many of the Jews: for the place where Jesus was crucified was nigh to the city: and it was written in Hebrew, *and* Greek, *and* Latin.

21 Then said the chief priests of the Jews to Pilate, Write not, The King of the Jews; but that he said, I am King of the Jews.

22 Pilate answered, What I have written I have written.

23 ¶ Then the soldiers, when they had crucified Jesus, took his garments, and made four parts, to every soldier a part; and also *his* coat: now the coat was without seam, woven from the top throughout.

24 They said therefore among themselves, Let us not rend it, but cast lots for it, whose it shall be: that the scripture might be fulfilled, which saith, They parted my raiment among them, and for my vesture they did cast lots. These things therefore the soldiers did.

25 ¶ Now there stood by the cross of Jesus his mother, and his mother's sister, Mary the *wife* of Cleophas, and Mary Magdalene.

26 When Jesus therefore saw his mother, and the disciple standing by, whom he loved, he saith unto his mother, Woman, behold thy son!

27 Then saith he to the disciple, Behold thy mother! And from that hour that disciple took her unto his own *home*.

28 ¶ After this, Jesus knowing that all things were now accomplished, that the scripture might be fulfilled, saith, I thirst.

29 Now there was set a vessel full of vinegar: and they filled a sponge with vinegar, and put it upon hyssop, and put *it* to his mouth.

30 When Jesus therefore had received the vinegar, he said, It is finished: and he bowed his head, and gave up the ghost.

31 The Jews therefore, because it was the preparation, that the bodies should not remain upon the cross on the sabbath day, (for that sabbath day was an high day,) besought Pilate that their legs might be broken, and *that* they might be taken away.

32 Then came the soldiers, and brake the legs of the first, and of the other which was crucified with him.

Amplified

14 Now it was the day of Preparation for the Passover, and it was about the sixth hour—about twelve o'clock noon. He said to the Jews, See, [here is] your King!

15 But they shouted, Away with Him! Away with Him! Crucify Him! Pilate said to them, Crucify your King? The chief priests answered, We have no king but Caesar!

16 Then he delivered Him over to them to be crucified.

17 And they took Jesus *and* led [Him] away; so He went out, bearing His own cross, to the spot called [Place of a] Skull; in Hebrew it is called Golgotha.

18 There they crucified Him, and with Him two others, one on either side and Jesus between them. [Isa. 53:12.]

19 And Pilate also wrote a title [an inscription on a placard] and put it on the cross. And the writing was, Jesus the Nazarene, the King of the Jews.

20 So many of the Jews read this title, for the place where Jesus was crucified was near the city, and it was written in Hebrew, in Latin [and] in Greek.

21 Then the chief priests of the Jews said to Pilate, Do not write, The King of the Jews, but, He said, I am King of the Jews.

22 Pilate replied, What I have written, I have written.

23 Then the soldiers when they had crucified Jesus took His garments and made four parts, one share for each soldier, and also the tunic [the long shirt-like undergarment]. But the tunic was seamless, woven from the top throughout.

24 So they said to one another, Let us not tear it, but let us cast lots to decide whose it shall be. This was to fulfill the Scripture, They parted My garments among them, and for My clothing they cast lots. So the soldiers did these things. [Ps. 22:18.]

25 But by the cross of Jesus stood His mother, and His mother's sister, Mary the [wife] of Clopas, and Mary Magdalene.

26 So Jesus, seeing His mother, and the disciple whom He loved standing near, said to His mother, [[m]Dear] lady, behold (see) your son!

27 Then He said to the disciple, Behold your mother! And from that hour the disciple took her to his own [keeping, own home].

28 After this, Jesus, knowing that all was now finished (ended), said in fulfillment of the Scripture, I thirst. [Ps. 69:21.]

29 A vessel (bowl) full of vinegar (a sour wine) was placed there. So they put a sponge soaked in the vinegar on [a stalk, reed of] hyssop and held it to [His] mouth.

30 When Jesus had received the vinegar, He said, It is finished! and He bowed His head and gave up His spirit.

31 Since it was the day of Preparation, in order to prevent the bodies from hanging on the cross on the Sabbath, for that Sabbath was a very solemn *and* important one, the Jews requested Pilate to have the legs broken and the bodies taken away.

32 So the soldiers came and broke the legs of the first one and of the other who had been crucified with Him.

---

m) Abbott-Smith: "A term of respect and endearment."

Living New Testament

14 It was now about noon of the day before Passover. And Pilate said to the Jews, "Here is your King!"

15 "Away with him," they yelled. "Away with him—crucify him!"

"What? Crucify your King?" Pilate asked.

"We have no king but Caesar," the chief priests shouted back.

16 Then Pilate gave Jesus to them to be crucified.

17 So they had Him at last, and He was taken out of the city, carrying His cross to the place known as "The Skull," in Hebrew, "Golgotha."

18 There they crucified Him and two others with Him, one on either side with Jesus between them.

19 And Pilate posted a sign over Him reading, "JESUS OF NAZARETH, THE KING OF THE JEWS."

20 The place where Jesus was crucified was near the city; and the signboard was written in Hebrew, Latin, and Greek, so that many people read it.

21 Then the chief priests said to Pilate, "Change it from 'The King of the Jews' to '*He said,* I am King of the Jews.' "

22 Pilate replied, "What I have written, I have written. It stays exactly as it is."

23, 24 When the soldiers had crucified Jesus, they put his garments into four piles, one for each of them. But they said, "Let's not tear up his robe," for it was seamless. "Let's throw dice to see who gets it." This fulfilled the Scripture that says, "They divided My clothes among them, and cast lots for My robe."[4]

25 So that is what they did.

Standing near the cross were Jesus' mother, Mary, His aunt, the wife of Cleopas, and Mary Magdalene.

26 When Jesus saw His mother standing there beside me, His close friend[5], He said to her, "He is your son."

27 And to me[6] He said, "She is your mother!" And from then on I took her into my home.

28 Jesus knew that everything was now finished, and to fulfill the Scriptures said, "I'm thirsty."

29 A jar of sour wine was sitting there, so a sponge was soaked in it and put on a hyssop branch and held up to His lips.

30 When Jesus had tasted[7] it, He said, "It is finished," and bowed His head and dismissed His spirit.

31 The Jewish leaders didn't want the victims hanging there the next day, which was the Sabbath (and a very special Sabbath at that, for it was the Passover), so they asked Pilate to order the legs of the men broken to hasten death; then their bodies could be taken down.

32 So the soldiers came and broke the legs of the two men crucified with Jesus;

Revised Standard

it was the day of Preparation of the Passover; it was about the sixth hour. He said
to the Jews, "Here is your King!" 15They
cried out, "Away with him, away with him,
crucify him!" Pilate said to them, "Shall I
crucify your King?" The chief priests answered, "We have no king but Caesar."
16Then he handed him over to them to be
crucified.

Jesus crucified

17 So they took Jesus, and he went out,
bearing his own cross, to the place called
the place of a skull, which is called in Hebrew Golgotha. 18There they crucified him,
and with him two others, one on either side,
and Jesus between them. 19Pilate also wrote
a title and put it on the cross; it read, "Jesus
of Nazareth, the King of the Jews." 20Many
of the Jews read this title, for the place
where Jesus was crucified was near the city;
and it was written in Hebrew, in Latin, and
in Greek. 21The chief priests of the Jews
then said to Pilate, "Do not write, 'The
King of the Jews,' but, 'This man said, I
am King of the Jews.' " 22Pilate answered,
"What I have written I have written."

23 When the soldiers had crucified Jesus
they took his garments and made four
parts, one for each soldier; also his tunic.
But the tunic was without seam, woven
from top to bottom; 24so they said to one
another, "Let us not tear it, but cast lots
for it to see whose it shall be." This was to
fulfil the scripture,

"They parted my garments among them,
and for my clothing they cast lots."

25 So the soldiers did this. But standing
by the cross of Jesus were his mother, and
his mother's sister, Mary the wife of Clopas,
and Mary Magdalene. 26When Jesus saw
his mother, and the disciple whom he loved
standing near, he said to his mother, "Woman, behold your son!" 27Then he said to
the disciple, "Behold, your mother!" And
from that hour the disciple took her to his
own home.

The death of Jesus

28 After this Jesus, knowing that all was
now finished, said (to fulfil the scripture),
"I thirst." 29A bowl full of vinegar stood
there; so they put a sponge full of the vinegar on hyssop and held it to his mouth.
30When Jesus had received the vinegar, he
said, "It is finished"; and he bowed his head
and gave up his spirit.

31 Since it was the day of Preparation,
in order to prevent the bodies from remaining on the cross on the sabbath (for that
sabbath was a high day), the Jews asked
Pilate that their legs might be broken, and
that they might be taken away. 32So the
soldiers came and broke the legs of the
first, and of the other who had been cruci-

---

[4] Psalm 22:18.
[5] Literally, "standing by the disciple whom He loved."
[6] Literally, "to the disciple."
[7] Literally, "had received."

King James

33 But when they came to Jesus, and saw that he was dead already, they brake not his legs:

34 But one of the soldiers with a spear pierced his side, and forthwith came there out blood and water.

35 And he that saw *it* bare record, and his record is true: and he knoweth that he saith true, that ye might believe.

36 For these things were done, that the scripture should be fulfilled, A bone of him shall not be broken.

37 And again another scripture saith, They shall look on him whom they pierced.

38 ¶ And after this Joseph of Arimathæa, being a disciple of Jesus, but secretly for fear of the Jews, besought Pilate that he might take away the body of Jesus: and Pilate gave *him* leave. He came therefore, and took the body of Jesus.

39 And there came also Nicodemus, which at the first came to Jesus by night, and brought a mixture of myrrh and aloes, about an hundred pound *weight.*

40 Then took they the body of Jesus, and wound it in linen clothes with the spices, as the manner of the Jews is to bury.

41 Now in the place where he was crucified there was a garden; and in the garden a new sepulchre, wherein was never man yet laid.

42 There laid they Jesus therefore because of the Jews' preparation *day;* for the sepulchre was nigh at hand.

Amplified

33 But when they came to Jesus, and they saw that He was already dead, they did not break His legs.

34 But one of the soldiers pierced His side with a spear, and immediately blood and water came (flowed) out.

35 And he who saw it—the eye-witness—gives this evidence and his testimony is true, and he knows that he tells the truth, that you may believe also.

36 For these things took place that the Scripture might be fulfilled (verified, carried out), Not one of His bones shall be broken. [Exod. 12:46; Num. 9:12; Ps. 34:20.]

37 And again another Scripture says, They shall look on Him Whom they have pierced. [Zech. 12:10.]

38 And after this Joseph of Arimathea, a disciple of Jesus, but secretly for fear of the Jews, asked Pilate to let him take away the body of Jesus. And Pilate granted him permission. So he came and took away His body.

39 And Nicodemus also, who at first had come to Jesus by night, came bringing a mixture of myrrh and aloes, [weighing] about a hundred pounds.

40 So they took Jesus' body, and bound it in linen cloths with the spices (aromatics), as is the Jews' customary way to prepare for burial.

41 Now there was a garden in the place where He was crucified and in the garden a new tomb, in which no one had ever [yet] been laid.

42 So there, because of the Jewish day of Preparation [and] as the tomb was near by, they laid Jesus.

CHAPTER 20

THE first *day* of the week cometh Mary Magadalene early, when it was yet dark, unto the sepulchre, and seeth the stone taken away from the sepulchre.

2 Then she runneth, and cometh to Simon Peter, and to the other disciple, whom Jesus loved, and saith unto them, They have taken away the Lord out of the sepulchre, and we know not where they have laid him.

3 Peter therefore went forth, and that other disciple, and came to the sepulchre.

4 So they ran both together: and the other disciple did outrun Peter, and came first to the sepulchre.

5 And he stooping down, *and looking in,* saw the linen clothes lying; yet went he not in.

6 Then cometh Simon Peter following him, and went into the sepulchre, and seeth the linen clothes lie,

7 And the napkin, that was about his head, not lying with the linen clothes, but wrapped together in a place by itself.

8 Then went in also that other disciple, which came first to the sepulchre, and he saw, and believed.

9 For as yet they knew not the scripture, that he must rise again from the dead.

CHAPTER 20

NOW on the first day of the week Mary Magdalene came to the tomb early, while it was still dark, and saw the stone had been removed from—lifted out of [the groove across the entrance of]—the tomb.

2 So she ran and went to Simon Peter and the other disciple whom Jesus tenderly loved, and said to them, They have taken away the Lord out of the tomb, and we do not know where they have laid Him!

3 Upon this Peter and the other disciple came out and they went toward the tomb.

4 And they came running together, but the other disciple outran Peter and arrived at the tomb first.

5 And stooping down he saw the linen cloths lying there, but he did not enter.

6 Then Simon Peter came up, following him, and went into the tomb, and saw the linen cloths lying there.

7 But the burial napkin (or kerchief) which had been around Jesus' head, was not lying with the other linen cloths, but was [still] [n]rolled up—wrapped round and round—in a place by itself.

8 Then the other disciple, who reached the tomb first, went in too, and he saw and was convinced *and* believed.

9 For as yet they did not know (understand) the statement of Scripture that He must rise again from the dead. [Ps. 16:10.]

---

n) ASV, Vincent, Thayer, etc.

Living New Testament

33 But when they came to Him, they saw that He was dead already, so they didn't break His.

34 However, one of the soldiers pierced His side with a spear, and blood and water flowed out.

35 I saw this all myself and have given an accurate report so that you also can believe.[8]

36, 37 The soldiers did this in fulfillment of the Scripture that says, "Not one of His bones shall be broken," and, "They shall look on Him whom they pierced."

38 Afterwards Joseph of Arimathea, who had been a secret disciple of Jesus for fear of the Jewish leaders, boldly asked Pilate for permission to take Jesus' body down; and Pilate told him to go ahead. So he came and took it away.

39 Nicodemus, the man who had come to Jesus at night,[9] came too, bringing a hundred pounds of embalming ointment made from myrrh and aloes.

40 Together they wrapped Jesus' body in a long linen cloth saturated with the spices, as is the Jewish custom of burial.

41 The place of crucifixion was near a grove of trees,[10] where there was a new tomb, never used before.

42 And so, because of the need for haste before the Sabbath, and because the tomb was close at hand, they laid Him there.

Revised Standard

fied with him; 33 but when they came to
Jesus and saw that he was already dead,
they did not break his legs. 34 But one of
the soldiers pierced his side with a spear,
and at once there came out blood and water.
35 He who saw it has borne witness—his testimony is true, and he knows that he tells the
truth—that you also may believe. 36 For these
things took place that the scripture might be
fulfilled, "Not a bone of him shall be broken." 37 And again another scripture says,
"They shall look on him whom they have
pierced."

Jesus laid in the tomb

38 After this Joseph of Arimathea, who
was a disciple of Jesus, but secretly, for fear
of the Jews, asked Pilate that he might take
away the body of Jesus, and Pilate gave
him leave. So he came and took away his
body. 39 Nicodemus also, who had at first
come to him by night, came bringing a
mixture of myrrh and aloes, about a hundred pounds' weight. 40 They took the body
of Jesus, and bound it in linen cloths with
the spices, as is the burial custom of the
Jews. 41 Now in the place where he was
crucified there was a garden, and in the
garden a new tomb where no one had ever
been laid. 42 So because of the Jewish day
of Preparation, as the tomb was close at
hand, they laid Jesus there.

CHAPTER 20

Early Sunday[1] morning, while it was still dark, Mary Magdalene came to the tomb and found that the stone was rolled aside from the entrance.

2 She ran and found Simon Peter and me[2] and said, "They have taken the Lord's body out of the tomb, and I don't know where they have put Him!"

3, 4 We[3] ran to the tomb to see; I[4] outran Peter and got there first,

5 And stooped and looked in and saw the linen cloth lying there, but I didn't go in.

6 Then Simon Peter arrived and went on inside. He also noticed the cloth lying there,

7 While the swath that had covered Jesus' head was rolled up in a bundle and was lying at the side.

8 Then I[5] went in too, and saw, and believed [that He had risen[5]]—

9 For until then we hadn't realized that the Scriptures said He would come to life again!

The resurrection of Jesus

20 Now on the first day of the week
Mary Magdalene came to the tomb
early, while it was still dark, and saw that
the stone had been taken away from the
tomb. 2 So she ran, and went to Simon
Peter and the other disciple, the one whom
Jesus loved, and said to them, "They have
taken the Lord out of the tomb, and we do
not know where they have laid him." 3 Peter
then came out with the other disciple, and
they went toward the tomb. 4 They both ran,
but the other disciple outran Peter and
reached the tomb first; 5 and stooping to
look in, he saw the linen cloths lying there,
but he did not go in. 6 Then Simon Peter
came, following him, and went into the
tomb; he saw the linen cloths lying, 7 and
the napkin, which had been on his head,
not lying with the linen cloths but rolled up
in a place by itself. 8 Then the other disciple,
who reached the tomb first, also went in,
and he saw and believed; 9 for as yet they
did not know the scripture, that he must

---

8 Literally, "And he who has seen has borne witness, and his witness is true; and he knows what he says is true, that you also may believe."
9 See chapter 3.
10 Literally, "a garden."
1 Literally, "on the first day of the week."
2 Literally, "the other disciple whom Jesus loved."
3 Literally, "Peter and the other disciple."
4 Literally, "the other disciple also, who came first."
5 Implied.

King James

10 Then the disciples went away again unto their own home.

11 ¶ But Mary stood without at the sepulchre weeping: and as she wept, she stooped down, *and looked* into the sepulchre.

12 And seeth two angels in white sitting, the one at the head, and the other at the feet, where the body of Jesus had lain.

13 And they say unto her, Woman, why weepest thou? She saith unto them, Because they have taken away my Lord, and I know not where they have laid him.

14 And when she had thus said, she turned herself back, and saw Jesus standing, and knew not that it was Jesus.

15 Jesus saith unto her, Woman, why weepest thou? whom seekest thou? She, supposing him to be the gardener, saith unto him, Sir, if thou have borne him hence, tell me where thou hast laid him, and I will take him away.

16 Jesus saith unto her, Mary. She turned herself, and saith unto him, Rabboni; which is to say, Master.

17 Jesus saith unto her, Touch me not; for I am not yet ascended to my Father: but go to my brethren, and say unto them, I ascend unto my Father, and your Father; and *to* my God, and your God.

18 Mary Magdalene came and told the disciples that she had seen the Lord, and *that* he had spoken these things unto her.

19 ¶ Then the same day at evening, being the first *day* of the week, when the doors were shut where the disciples were assembled for fear of the Jews, came Jesus and stood in the midst, and saith unto them, Peace *be* unto you.

20 And when he had so said, he shewed unto them *his* hands and his side. Then were the disciples glad, when they saw the Lord.

21 Then said Jesus to them again, Peace *be* unto you: as *my* Father hath sent me, even so send I you.

22 And when he had said this, he breathed on *them*, and saith unto them, Receive ye the Holy Ghost:

23 Whose soever sins ye remit, they are remitted unto them; *and* whose soever *sins* ye retain, they are retained.

24 ¶ But Thomas, one of the twelve, called Didymus, was not with them when Jesus came.

25 The other disciples therefore said unto him, We have seen the Lord. But he said unto them, Except I shall see in his hands the print of the nails, and put my finger into the print of the nails, and thrust my hand into his side, I will not believe.

26 ¶ And after eight days again his disciples were within, and Thomas with them: *then* came Jesus, the doors being shut, and stood in the midst, and said, Peace *be* unto you.

27 Then saith he to Thomas, Reach hither thy finger, and behold my hands; and reach hither thy hand, and thrust *it* into my side: and be not faithless, but believing.

28 And Thomas answered and said unto him, My Lord and my God.

Amplified

10 Then the disciples went back again to their [lodging places].

11 But Mary remained standing outside the tomb sobbing. As she wept, she stooped down [and looked] into the tomb.

12 And she saw two angels in white sitting there, one at the head and one at the feet, where the body of Jesus had lain.

13 And they said to her, Woman, why are you sobbing? She told them, Because they have taken away my Lord and I do not know where they have laid Him.

14 On saying this, she turned around and saw Jesus standing [there], but she did not know (recognize) that it was Jesus.

15 Jesus said to her, Woman, why are you crying [so]? For whom are you looking? Supposing that it was the gardener, she replied, Sir, if you carried Him from here, tell me where you put Him and I will take Him away.

16 Jesus said to her, Mary! Turning around she said to Him in Hebrew, Rabboni! which means Teacher *or* Master.

17 Jesus said to her, Do not cling to Me [do not hold Me] for I have not yet ascended to the Father. But go to My brethren and tell them, I am ascending to My Father and your Father, and to My God and your God.

18 Away came Mary Magdalene, bringing the disciples news [word] that she had seen the Lord and that He had said these things to her.

19 Then that same first day of the week, when it was evening, though the disciples were behind closed doors for fear of the Jews, Jesus came and stood among them, and said, Peace to you!

20 So saying, He showed them His hands and His side. And when the disciples saw the Lord they were filled with joy (delight, exultation, ecstasy, rapture).

21 Then Jesus said to them again, Peace to you! [Just] as the Father has sent Me forth, so I am sending you.

22 And having said this, He breathed on [them] and said to them, Receive (admit) the Holy Spirit!

23 [Now, having received the Holy Spirit and being [o]led and directed by Him] if you forgive the sins of any one they are forgiven; if you retain the sins of any one, they are retained.

24 But Thomas, one of the twelve, called the Twin, was not with them when Jesus came.

25 So the other disciples kept telling him, We have seen the Lord. But he said to them, Unless I see in His hands the mark made by the nails, and put my finger into the nail prints, and put my hand into His side, I will never believe [it].

26 Eight days later His disciples were again in the house, and Thomas was with them. Jesus came, though they were behind closed doors, and stood among them and said, Peace to you!

27 Then He said to Thomas, Reach out your finger here and see My hands; and put out your hand and place [it] in My side. Do not be faithless *and* incredulous, but [stop your unbelief and] believe!

28 Thomas answered Him, My Lord and my God!

---

o) Matthew Henry's Commentary.

Living New Testament

10 We[6] went on home,

11 And by that time Mary had returned[7] to the tomb and was standing outside crying. And as she wept, she stooped and looked in

12 And saw two white-robed angels sitting at the head and foot of the place where the body of Jesus had been lying.

13 "Why are you crying?" the angels asked her. "Because they have taken away my Lord," she replied, "and I don't know where they have put Him."

14 She glanced over her shoulder and saw someone standing behind her. It was Jesus, but she didn't recognize Him!

15 "Why are you crying?" He asked her. "Whom are you looking for?"

She thought He was the gardener. "Sir," she said, "if you have taken Him away, tell me where you have put Him, and I will go and get Him."

16 "Mary!" Jesus said. She turned toward Him.

"Master!" she exclaimed.

17 "Don't touch Me," He cautioned, "for I haven't yet ascended to the Father. But go find My brothers and tell them that I ascend to My Father and your Father, My God and your God."

18 Mary Magdalene found the disciples and told them, "I have seen the Lord!" Then she gave them His message.

19 That evening the disciples were meeting behind locked doors, in fear of the Jewish leaders, when suddenly Jesus was standing there among them! After greeting them,

20 He showed them His hands and side. And how wonderful was their joy as they saw their Lord!

21 He spoke to them again and said, "As the Father has sent Me, even so I am sending you."

22 Then He breathed on them and told them, "Receive the Holy Spirit.

23 If you forgive anyone's sins, they are forgiven. If you refuse to forgive them, they are unforgiven."

24 One of the disciples, Thomas, "The Twin," was not there at the time with the others.

25 When they kept telling him, "We have seen the Lord," he replied, "I won't believe it unless I see the nail wounds in His hands—and put my fingers into them—and place my hand into His side."

26 Eight days later the disciples were together again, and this time Thomas was with them. The doors were locked; but suddenly, as before, Jesus was standing among them and greeting them.

27 Then He said to Thomas, "Put your finger into My hands. Put your hand into My side. Don't be faithless any longer. Believe!"

28 "My Lord and my God!" Thomas said.

[6] Literally, "the disciples."
[7] Implied.

Revised Standard

rise from the dead. 10Then the disciples
went back to their homes.

Jesus appears to Mary Magdalene

11 But Mary stood weeping outside the
tomb, and as she wept she stooped to look
into the tomb; 12and she saw two angels in
white, sitting where the body of Jesus had
lain, one at the head and one at the feet.
13They said to her, "Woman, why are you
weeping?" She said to them, "Because they
have taken away my Lord, and I do not
know where they have laid him." 14Saying
this, she turned round and saw Jesus standing, but she did not know that it was Jesus.
15Jesus said to her, "Woman, why are you
weeping? Whom do you seek?" Supposing
him to be the gardener, she said to him,
"Sir, if you have carried him away, tell
me where you have laid him, and I will
take him away." 16Jesus said to her, "Mary."
She turned and said to him in Hebrew,
"Rabboni!" (which means Teacher). 17Jesus
said to her, "Do not hold me, for I have not
yet ascended to the Father; but go to my
brethren and say to them, I am ascending
to my Father and your Father, to my God
and your God." 18Mary Magdalene went
and said to the disciples, "I have seen the
Lord"; and she told them that he had said
these things to her.

Jesus appears to the disciples

19 On the evening of that day, the first
day of the week, the doors being shut where
the disciples were, for fear of the Jews, Jesus
came and stood among them and said to
them, "Peace be with you." 20When he had
said this, he showed them his hands and
his side. Then the disciples were glad when
they saw the Lord. 21Jesus said to them
again, "Peace be with you. As the Father
has sent me, even so I send you." 22And
when he had said this, he breathed on them,
and said to them, "Receive the Holy Spirit.
23If you forgive the sins of any, they are
forgiven; if you retain the sins of any, they
are retained."

Thomas' doubt and belief

24 Now Thomas, one of the twelve,
called the Twin, was not with them when
Jesus came. 25So the other disciples told
him, "We have seen the Lord." But he said
to them, "Unless I see in his hands the
print of the nails, and place my finger in
the mark of the nails, and place my hand
in his side, I will not believe."

26 Eight days later, his disciples were
again in the house, and Thomas was with
them. The doors were shut, but Jesus came
and stood among them, and said, "Peace
be with you." 27Then he said to Thomas,
"Put your finger here, and see my hands;
and put out your hand, and place it in my
side; do not be faithless, but believing."
28Thomas answered him, "My Lord and

King James

29 Jesus saith unto him, Thomas, because thou hast seen me, thou hast believed: blessed *are* they that have not seen, and *yet* have believed.

30 ¶ And many other signs truly did Jesus in the presence of his disciples, which are not written in this book:

31 But these are written, that ye might believe that Jesus is the Christ, the Son of God; and that believing ye might have life through his name.

Amplified

29 Jesus said to him, Because you have seen Me, *Thomas,* do you now believe (trust, have faith)? Blessed *and* happy *and* [p]to be envied are those who have never seen Me, and yet have believed *and* adhered to *and* trusted in *and* relied on Me.

30 There are also many other signs *and* miracles, which Jesus performed in the presence of the disciples, which are not written in this book.

31 But these are written (recorded) in order that you may believe that Jesus is the Christ, the Anointed One, the Son of God, and that through believing *and* cleaving to *and* trusting in *and* relying upon Him you may have life through (in) His name [that is, [q]through what He is]. [Ps. 2:7, 12.]

CHAPTER 21

AFTER these things Jesus shewed himself again to the disciples at the sea of Tiberias; and on this wise shewed he *himself.*

2 There were together Simon Peter, and Thomas called Didymus, and Nathanael of Cana in Galilee, and the *sons* of Zebedee, and two other of his disciples.

3 Simon Peter saith unto them, I go a-fishing. They say unto him, We also go with thee. They went forth, and entered into a ship immediately; and that night they caught nothing.

4 But when the morning was now come, Jesus stood on the shore: but the disciples knew not that it was Jesus.

5 Then Jesus saith unto them, Children, have ye any meat? They answered him, No.

6 And he said unto them, Cast the net on the right side of the ship, and ye shall find. They cast therefore, and now they were not able to draw it for the multitude of fishes.

7 Therefore that disciple whom Jesus loved saith unto Peter, It is the Lord. Now when Simon Peter heard that it was the Lord, he girt *his* fisher's coat *unto him,* (for he was naked,) and did cast himself into the sea.

8 And the other disciples came in a little ship; (for they were not far from land, but as it were two hundred cubits,) dragging the net with fishes.

9 As soon then as they were come to land, they saw a fire of coals there, and fish laid thereon, and bread.

10 Jesus saith unto them, Bring of the fish which ye have now caught.

11 Simon Peter went up, and drew the net to land full of great fishes, an hundred and fifty and three: and for all there were so many, yet was not the net broken.

12 Jesus saith unto them, Come *and* dine. And none of the disciples durst ask him, Who art thou? knowing that it was the Lord.

13 Jesus then cometh, and taketh bread, and giveth them, and fish likewise.

CHAPTER 21

AFTER this Jesus let Himself be seen *and* revealed [Himself] again to the disciples at the Sea of Tiberias. And He did it in this way:

2 There were together Simon Peter, and Thomas, called the Twin, and Nathanael from Cana of Galilee, also the sons of Zebedee and two others of His disciples.

3 Simon Peter said to them, I am going fishing! They said to him, And we are coming with you! So they went out and got into the boat, and throughout that night they caught nothing.

4 Morning was already breaking when Jesus came to the beach and stood there. However, the disciples did not know that it was Jesus.

5 So Jesus said to them, [r]Boys (children) [have you caught anything to eat with bread?] You do not have any meat (fish) do you? They answered Him, No!

6 But He said to them, Cast the net on the right side of the boat and you will find [some]. So they cast the net, and now they were not able to haul it in for such a big catch (mass, quantity) of fish [was in it].

7 Then the disciple whom Jesus loved said to Peter, It is the Lord! Simon Peter, hearing him say that it was the Lord, put (girded) on his upper garment—his fisherman's coat, his outer tunic—for he was stripped [for work], and sprang into the sea.

8 And the other disciples came in the small boat, for they were not far from shore, only some hundred yards away, dragging the net full of fish.

9 When they got out on land (the beach), they saw a fire of coals there and fish lying on it [cooking], and bread.

10 Jesus said to them, Bring some of the fish which you have just caught.

11 So Simon Peter went aboard and hauled the net to land, full of large fish, a hundred [and] fifty-three of them. And [though] there were so many of them, the net was not torn.

12 Jesus said to them, Come [and] have breakfast. But none of the disciples ventured *or* dared to ask Him, Who are You? Because they [well] knew that it was the Lord.

13 Jesus came and took the bread and gave it to them, and also the fish.

---

p) Souter.
q) Cremer: "Biblico-Theological Lexicon of New Testament Greek."
r) Souter.

Living New Testament

29 Then Jesus told him, "You believe because you have seen Me. But blessed are those who haven't seen Me and believe anyway."

30, 31 Jesus' disciples saw Him do many other miracles besides the ones told about in this book, but these are recorded so that you will believe that He is the Messiah, the Son of God, and that believing in Him you will have Life.

CHAPTER 21

Later Jesus appeared again to the disciples beside the Lake of Galilee. This is how it happened:

2 A group of us were there—Simon Peter, Thomas "The Twin," Nathanael from Cana, in Galilee, my brother James and I[1] and two other disciples.

3 Simon Peter said, "I'm going fishing."

"We'll come too," we all said. We did, but caught nothing all night.

4 At dawn we saw a man standing on the beach but couldn't see who he was.

5 He called, "Any fish, boys?"[2]

"No," we replied.

6 Then He said, "Throw out your net on the right-hand side of the boat, and you'll get plenty of them!" So we did, and couldn't draw in the net because of the weight of the fish, there were so many!

7 Then I[3] said to Peter, "It is the Lord!" At that, Simon Peter put on his tunic (for he was stripped to the waist) and jumped into the water [and swam ashore[4]].

8 The rest of us stayed in the boat and pulled the loaded net to the beach, about 300 feet away.

9 When we got there, we saw that a fire was kindled and fish were frying over it, and there was bread.

10 "Bring some of the fish you've just caught," Jesus said.

11 So Simon Peter went out and dragged the net ashore. By his count there were 153 large fish; and yet the net hadn't torn!

12 "Now come and have some breakfast!" Jesus said; and none of us dared ask Him if He really was the Lord, for we were quite sure of it.

13 Then Jesus went around serving us the bread and fish.

[1] Literally, "the sons of Zebedee."
[2] Literally, "children."
[3] Literally, "that disciple therefore whom Jesus loved."
[4] Implied.

Revised Standard

my God!" 29 Jesus said to him, "Have you believed because you have seen me? Blessed are those who have not seen and yet believe."

30 Now Jesus did many other signs in the presence of the disciples, which are not written in this book; 31 but these are written that you may believe that Jesus is the Christ, the Son of God, and that believing you may have life in his name.

The appearance beside the sea

21 After this Jesus revealed himself again to the disciples by the Sea of Tiberias; and he revealed himself in this way. 2 Simon Peter, Thomas called the Twin, Nathanael of Cana in Galilee, the sons of Zebedee, and two others of his disciples were together. 3 Simon Peter said to them, "I am going fishing." They said to him, "We will go with you." They went out and got into the boat; but that night they caught nothing.

4 Just as day was breaking, Jesus stood on the beach; yet the disciples did not know that it was Jesus. 5 Jesus said to them, "Children, have you any fish?" They answered him, "No." 6 He said to them, "Cast the net on the right side of the boat, and you will find some." So they cast it, and now they were not able to haul it in, for the quantity of fish. 7 That disciple whom Jesus loved said to Peter, "It is the Lord!" When Simon Peter heard that it was the Lord, he put on his clothes, for he was stripped for work, and sprang into the sea. 8 But the other disciples came in the boat, dragging the net full of fish, for they were not far from the land, but about a hundred yards[m] off.

9 When they got out on land, they saw a charcoal fire there, with fish lying on it, and bread. 10 Jesus said to them, "Bring some of the fish that you have just caught." 11 So Simon Peter went aboard and hauled the net ashore, full of large fish, a hundred and fifty-three of them; and although there were so many, the net was not torn. 12 Jesus said to them, "Come and have breakfast." Now none of the disciples dared ask him, "Who are you?" They knew it was the Lord. 13 Jesus came and took the bread and gave it to them, and so with the fish. 14 This was

[m] Greek *two hundred cubits*

King James

14 This is now the third time that Jesus shewed himself to his disciples, after that he was risen from the dead.

15 ¶ So when they had dined, Jesus saith to Simon Peter, Simon, *son* of Jonas, lovest thou me more than these? He saith unto him, Yea, Lord; thou knowest that I love thee. He saith unto him, Feed my lambs.

16 He saith to him again the second time, Simon, *son* of Jonas, lovest thou me? He saith unto him, Yea, Lord; thou knowest that I love thee. He saith unto him, Feed my sheep.

17 He saith unto him the third time, Simon, *son* of Jonas, lovest thou me? Peter was grieved because he said unto him the third time, Lovest thou me? And he said unto him, Lord, thou knowest all things; thou knowest that I love thee. Jesus saith unto him, Feed my sheep.

18 Verily, verily, I say unto thee, When thou wast young, thou girdedst thyself, and walkedst whither thou wouldest: but when thou shalt be old, thou shalt stretch forth thy hands, and another shall gird thee, and carry *thee* whither thou wouldest not.

19 This spake he, signifying by what death he should glorify God. And when he had spoken this, he saith unto him, Follow me.

20 Then Peter, turning about, seeth the disciple whom Jesus loved following; which also leaned on his breast at supper, and said, Lord, which is he that betrayeth thee?

21 Peter seeing him saith to Jesus, Lord, and what *shall* this man *do?*

22 Jesus saith unto him, If I will that he tarry till I come, what *is that* to thee? follow thou me.

23 Then went this saying abroad among the brethren, that that disciple should not die: yet Jesus said not unto him, He shall not die; but, If I will that he tarry till I come, what *is that* to thee?

24 This is the disciple which testifieth of these things, and wrote these things: and we know that his testimony is true.

25 And there are also many other things which Jesus did, the which, if they should be written every one, I suppose that even the world itself could not contain the books that should be written. Amen.

Amplified

14 This was now the third time that Jesus revealed Himself (appeared, was manifest) to the disciples after He had risen from the dead.

15 When they had eaten, Jesus said to Simon Peter, Simon, son of John, do you love Me more than these [others do]—with reasoning, intentional, spiritual devotion, as one loves the Father? He said to Him, Yes, Lord; You know that I love you—that I have deep, instinctive, personal affection for You, as for a close friend. He said to him, Feed My lambs.

16 Again He said to him the second time, Simon, son of John, do you love Me—with reasoning, intentional, spiritual devotion, as one loves the Father? He said to Him, Yes, Lord, You know that I love You—that I have a deep, instinctive, personal affection for You, as for a close friend. He said to him, Shepherd (tend) My sheep.

17 He said to him the third time, Simon, son of John, do you love Me—with a deep, instinctive, personal affection for Me, as for a close friend? Peter was grieved—took it ill—that He should ask him the third time, Do you love Me? And he said to Him, Lord, You know everything; You know that I love You—that I have a deep, instinctive, personal affection for You, as for a close friend. Jesus said to him, Feed My sheep.

18 I assure you, most solemnly I tell you, when you were young, you girded yourself—put on your own belt (girdle)—and you walked about wherever you pleased to go. But when you grow old you will stretch out your hands and someone else will put a girdle around you, and carry you where you do not wish to go.

19 He said this to indicate by what kind of death Peter would glorify God. And after this He said to him, Follow Me!

20 But Peter had turned and saw the disciple whom Jesus loved, following, who also had leaned back on His breast at the supper and had said, Lord, who is it that is going to betray You?

21 When Peter saw him, he said to Jesus, Lord, what about this man?

22 Jesus said to him, If I will have him to stay (survive, live) till I come, what is that to you?—What concern is it of yours? You follow Me!

23 So word went out among the brethren that this disciple was not to die; yet Jesus did not say to him that he was not to die, but, If I want him to stay (survive, live) till I come, what is that to you?

24 It is this same disciple who is bearing witness to these things, and who has recorded (written) them; and we [well] know that his testimony is true.

25 And there are also many other things which Jesus did. If they should be all recorded one by one [in detail], I suppose that even the world itself could not contain (have room for) the books that would be written.

Living New Testament

14 This was the third time Jesus had appeared to us since His return from the dead.

15 After breakfast Jesus said to Simon Peter, "Simon, son of John, do you love Me more than these others?"[5]

"Yes," Peter replied, "You know I am Your friend."

"Then feed My lambs," Jesus told him.

16 Jesus repeated the question: "Simon, son of John, do you *really* love Me?"

"Yes, Lord," Peter said, "You know I am Your friend."

"Then take care of My sheep," Jesus said.

17 Once more He asked him, "Simon, son of John, are you even My friend?"

Peter was grieved at the way Jesus asked the question this third time. "Lord, You know my heart;[6] You know I am," he said.

Jesus said, "Then feed My little sheep.

18 When you were young, you were able to do as you liked and go wherever you wanted to; but when you are old, you will stretch out your hands and others will direct you and take you where you don't want to go."

19 Jesus said this to let him know what kind of death he would die to glorify God. Then Jesus told him, "Follow Me."

20 Peter turned around and saw the disciple Jesus loved following, the one who had leaned around at supper that time to ask Jesus, "Master, which of us will betray You?"

21 Peter asked Jesus, "What about him, Lord? What sort of death will he die?"[7]

22 Jesus replied, "If I want him to live[8] until I return, what is that to you? *You* follow Me."

23 So the rumor spread among the brotherhood that this disciple wouldn't die! But that isn't what Jesus said at all! He only said, "If I want him to live[8] until I come, what is that to you?"

24 *I am that disciple!* I saw these events and have recorded them here. And we all know that my account of these things is accurate.

25 And I suppose that if all the other events in Jesus' life were written, the whole world could hardly contain the books!

Revised Standard

now the third time that Jesus was revealed to the disciples after he was raised from the dead.

Jesus questions Peter

15 When they had finished breakfast,
Jesus said to Simon Peter, "Simon, son of
John, do you love me more than these?"
He said to him, "Yes, Lord; you know that
I love you." He said to him, "Feed my
lambs." 16 A second time he said to him,
"Simon, son of John, do you love me?" He
said to him, "Yes, Lord; you know that I
love you." He said to him, "Tend my sheep."
17 He said to him the third time, "Simon,
son of John, do you love me?" Peter was
grieved because he said to him the third
time, "Do you love me?" And he said to
him, "Lord, you know everything; you
know that I love you." Jesus said to him,
"Feed my sheep. 18 Truly, truly, I say to
you, when you were young, you girded
yourself and walked where you would; but
when you are old, you will stretch out your
hands, and another will gird you and carry
you where you do not wish to go." 19 (This
he said to show by what death he was to
glorify God.) And after this he said to
him, "Follow me."
20 Peter turned and saw following them
the disciple whom Jesus loved, who had
lain close to his breast at the supper and had
said, "Lord, who is it that is going to betray
you?" 21 When Peter saw him, he said to
Jesus, "Lord, what about this man?" 22 Jesus
said to him, "If it is my will that he remain until I come, what is that to you? Follow me!" 23 The saying spread abroad among
the brethren that this disciple was not to die;
yet Jesus did not say to him that he was not
to die, but, "If it is my will that he remain
until I come, what is that to you?"

24 This is the disciple who is bearing witness to these things, and who has written these things; and we know that his testimony is true.

25 But there are also many other things which Jesus did; were every one of them to be written, I suppose that the world itself could not contain the books that would be written.

---

[5] Literally, "more than these." See Mark 14:29.
[6] Literally, "all things."
[7] Implied. Literally, "and this man, what?"
[8] Literally, "tarry."

King James

THE

Acts of the Apostles

CHAPTER 1

THE former treatise have I made, O Theophilus, of all that Jesus began both to do and teach,

2 Until the day in which he was taken up, after that he through the Holy Ghost had given commandments unto the apostles whom he had chosen:

3 To whom also he shewed himself alive after his passion by many infallible proofs, being seen of them forty days, and speaking of the things pertaining to the kingdom of God:

4 And, being assembled together with *them*, commanded them that they should not depart from Jerusalem, but wait for the promise of the Father, which, *saith he*, ye have heard of me.

5 For John truly baptized with water; but ye shall be baptized with the Holy Ghost not many days hence.

6 When they therefore were come together, they asked of him, saying, Lord, wilt thou at this time restore again the kingdom to Israel?

7 And he said unto them, It is not for you to know the times or the seasons, which the Father hath put in his own power.

8 But ye shall receive power, after that the Holy Ghost is come upon you: and ye shall be witnesses unto me both in Jerusalem, and in all Judæa, and in Samaria, and unto the uttermost part of the earth.

9 And when he had spoken these things, while they beheld, he was taken up; and a cloud received him out of their sight.

10 And while they looked stedfastly toward heaven as he went up, behold, two men stood by them in white apparel;

11 Which also said, Ye men of Galilee, why stand ye gazing up into heaven? this same Jesus, which is taken up from you into heaven, shall so come in like manner as ye have seen him go into heaven.

12 Then returned they unto Jerusalem from the mount called Olivet, which is from Jerusalem a sabbath day's journey.

13 And when they were come in, they went up into an upper room, where abode both Peter, and James, and John, and Andrew, Philip, and Thomas, Bartholomew, and Matthew, James *the son* of Alphæus, and Simon Zelotes, and Judas *the brother* of James.

14 These all continued with one accord in prayer and supplication, with the women, and Mary the mother of Jesus, and with his brethren.

15 ¶ And in those days Peter stood up in the midst of the disciples and said, (the number of names together were about an hundred and twenty,)

Amplified

THE ACTS OF THE

Apostles

CHAPTER 1

[IN] the former [account which I prepared] O Theophilus, I made a continuous report dealing with all the things which Jesus began to do and to teach,

2 Until the day when He ascended, after He through the Holy Spirit had instructed *and* commanded the apostles (special messengers) whom He had chosen.

3 To them also He showed Himself alive after His passion (His suffering in the garden and on the cross), by [a series of] many convincing demonstrations—unquestionable evidence and infallible proofs—appearing to them during forty days, and talking [to them] about the things of the kingdom of God.

4 And while being in their company *and* eating at the table with them, He commanded them not to leave Jerusalem, but to wait for what the Father had promised, Of which, He said, you have heard Me speak.

5 For John baptized with water, but not many days from now you shall be baptized with—[a]placed in, introduced into—the Holy Spirit.

6 So when they were assembled they asked Him, Lord, is this the time when You will re-establish the kingdom *and* restore it to Israel?

7 He said to them, It is not for you to become acquainted with *and* know [b]what time brings—the things and events of time and their definite periods—fixed [c]years and seasons (their critical nick of time), which the Father has appointed (fixed and reserved) by His own choice *and* authority *and* personal power.

8 But you shall receive power—ability, efficiency and might—when the Holy Spirit has come upon you; and you shall be My witnesses in Jerusalem and all Judea and Samaria and to the ends—the very bounds—of the earth.

9 And when He had said this, even as they were looking [at Him], He was caught up, and a cloud received *and* carried Him away out of their sight.

10 And while they were gazing intently into heaven as He went, behold, two men [dressed] in white robes suddenly stood beside them,

11 Who said, Men of Galilee, why do you stand gazing into heaven? This same Jesus, Who was caught away *and* lifted up from among you into heaven, will return in [just] the same way in which you saw Him go into heaven.

12 Then [the disciples] went back to Jerusalem from the hill called Olivet, which is near Jerusalem, [only] a Sabbath day's journey [three-quarters of a mile] away.

13 And when they had entered [the city], they mounted to the upper room where they were [d]indefinitely staying—Peter and John and James and Andrew, Philip and Thomas, Bartholomew and Matthew, James the son of Alphaeus and Simon the Zealot and Judas the [son] of James.

14 All of these with their minds in full agreement devoted themselves steadfastly to prayer, [waiting together] with the women and Mary the mother of Jesus, and with His brothers.

15 Now one of those days Peter arose among the brethren, the whole number of whom gathered together was about a hundred and twenty.

---

a) Wuest's "Untranslatable Riches from the Greek New Testament."
b) Thayer's "Greek-English Lexicon of the New Testament—Grimm."
c) Trench's "Synonyms of Greek New Testament."
d) Moulton and Milligan.

Living New Testament

Acts

CHAPTER 1

Dear Friend who loves God:

In my first letter[1] I told you about Jesus' life and teachings and how He returned to heaven after giving His chosen apostles further instructions from the Holy Spirit.

3 During the 40 days after His crucifixion He had appeared to the apostles from time to time in human form and proved to them in many ways that it was actually He Himself they were seeing. And on these occasions He talked to them about the Kingdom of God.

4 In one of these meetings He told them not to leave Jerusalem until the Holy Spirit came upon them in fulfillment of the Father's promise, a matter he had previously discussed with them.

5 "John baptized you with[2] water," He reminded them, "but you shall be baptized with[2] the Holy Spirit in just a few days."

6 And another time when He appeared to them, they asked Him, "Lord, are You going to free Israel (from Rome[3]) now and restore us as an independent nation?"

7 "The Father sets those dates," He replied, "and they are not for you to know.

8 But when the Holy Spirit has come upon you, you will receive power to preach with great effect to the people in Jerusalem, throughout Judea, in Samaria and to the ends of the earth, about My death and resurrection."

9 It was not long afterwards that He rose into the sky and disappeared into a cloud, leaving them staring after Him.

10 As they were straining their eyes for another glimpse, suddenly two white-robed men were standing there among them,

11 And said, "Men of Galilee, why are you standing here staring at the sky? Jesus has gone away to heaven, and some day, just as He went, He will return!"

12 They were at the Mount of Olives when this happened, so now they walked the half mile back to Jerusalem

13, 14 And held a prayer meeting in an upstairs room of the house where they were staying. Here is the list of those who were present at the meeting:

Peter,
John,
James,
Andrew,
Philip,
Thomas,
Bartholomew,
Matthew,
James (son of Alphaeus),
Simon (also called "The Zealot"),
Judas (son of James),
And the brothers of Jesus.
Several women, including Jesus' mother, were also there.

15 This prayer meeting went on for several days. During this time, on a day when about 120 people were present, Peter stood up and addressed them as follows:

[1] i.e., the book of Luke; see footnote Chapter 1, verse 1.
[2] Or, "in."
[3] Implied.

Revised Standard

THE

Acts of the Apostles

Preface

1 In the first book, O Theophilus, I have
dealt with all that Jesus began to do
and teach, [2]until the day when he was taken
up, after he had given commandment
through the Holy Spirit to the apostles
whom he had chosen. [3]To them he
presented himself alive after his passion by
many proofs, appearing to them during forty days, and speaking of the kingdom of
God. [4]And while staying[a] with them he
charged them not to depart from Jerusalem,
but to wait for the promise of the Father,
which, he said, "you heard from me, [5]for
John baptized with water, but before many
days you shall be baptized with the Holy
Spirit."

The ascension

6 So when they had come together, they
asked him, "Lord, will you at this time
restore the kingdom to Israel?" [7]He said to
them, "It is not for you to know times or
seasons which the Father has fixed by his
own authority. [8]But you shall receive power
when the Holy Spirit has come upon you;
and you shall be my witnesses in Jerusalem
and in all Judea and Samaria and to the
end of the earth." [9]And when he had said
this, as they were looking on, he was lifted
up, and a cloud took him out of their sight.
[10]And while they were gazing into heaven
as he went, behold, two men stood by them
in white robes, [11]and said, "Men of Galilee,
why do you stand looking into heaven? This
Jesus, who was taken up from you into
heaven, will come in the same way as you
saw him go into heaven."

Matthias chosen to replace Judas

12 Then they returned to Jerusalem from
the mount called Olivet, which is near
Jerusalem, a sabbath day's journey away;
[13]and when they had entered, they went up
to the upper room, where they were staying,
Peter and John and James and Andrew,
Philip and Thomas, Bartholomew and Matthew, James the son of Alphaeus and Simon
the Zealot and Judas the son of James.
[14]All these with one accord devoted themselves to prayer, together with the women
and Mary the mother of Jesus, and with his
brothers.

15 In those days Peter stood up among
the brethren (the company of persons was
in all about a hundred and twenty), and

[a] Or *eating*

King James

16 Men *and* brethren, this scripture must needs have been fulfilled, which the Holy Ghost by the mouth of David spake before concerning Judas, which was guide to them that took Jesus.

17 For he was numbered with us, and had obtained part of this ministry.

18 Now this man purchased a field with the reward of iniquity; and falling headlong, he burst asunder in the midst, and all his bowels gushed out.

19 And it was known unto all the dwellers at Jerusalem; insomuch as that field is called in their proper tongue, Aceldama, that is to say, The field of blood.

20 For it is written in the book of Psalms, Let his habitation be desolate, and let no man dwell therein: and his bishopric let another take.

21 Wherefore of these men which have companied with us all the time that the Lord Jesus went in and out among us,

22 Beginning from the baptism of John, unto that same day that he was taken up from us, must one be ordained to be a witness with us of his resurrection.

23 And they appointed two, Joseph called Barsabas, who was surnamed Justus, and Matthias.

24 And they prayed, and said, Thou, Lord, which knowest the hearts of all *men*, shew whether of these two thou hast chosen,

25 That he may take part of this ministry and apostleship, from which Judas by transgression fell, that he might go to his own place.

26 And they gave forth their lots; and the lot fell upon Matthias; and he was numbered with the eleven apostles.

Amplified

16 Brethren, he said, it was necessary that the Scripture be fulfilled, which the Holy Spirit foretold by the lips of David, about Judas who acted as guide to those who arrested Jesus.

17 For he was counted among us and received [by divine allotment] his portion of this ministry.

18 Now this [man] obtained a piece of land with the [money paid him as a] reward for his treachery *and* wickedness, and falling headlong he burst open in the middle [of his body] and all his intestines poured forth.

19 And all the residents of Jerusalem became acquainted with the facts, so that they called the piece of land in their own dialect, Akeldama, that is, Field of Blood.

20 For in the book of Psalms it is written, Let his place of residence become deserted *and* gloomy, and let there be no one to live in it; and [again], Let another take his position *or* overseership. [Ps. 69:25; 109:8.]

21 So one of the [other] men who have accompanied us [apostles] during all the time that the Lord Jesus went in and out among us,

22 From the baptism of John at the outset until the day when He was taken up from among us, one of these men must join with us and become a witness to testify to His resurrection.

23 And they accordingly proposed (nominated) two men, Joseph called Barsabbas, who was surnamed Justus, and Matthias.

24 And they prayed and said, You, Lord, Who know all hearts [e][their thoughts, passions, desires, appetites, purposes and endeavors], indicate to us which one of these two You have chosen

25 To take the place in this ministry and receive the position of an apostle from which Judas fell away *and* went astray to go (where he belonged,) to his own (proper) place.

26 And they drew lots [between the two], and the lot fell on Matthias; and he was added to *and* counted with the eleven apostles (special messengers).

King James

CHAPTER 2

AND when the day of Pentecost was fully come, they were all with one accord in one place.

2 And suddenly there came a sound from heaven as of a rushing mighty wind, and it filled all the house where they were sitting.

3 And there appeared unto them cloven tongues like as of fire, and it sat upon each of them.

4 And they were all filled with the Holy Ghost, and began to speak with other tongues, as the Spirit gave them utterance.

5 And there were dwelling at Jerusalem Jews, devout men, out of every nation under heaven.

6 Now when this was noised abroad, the multitude came together, and were confounded, because that every man heard them speak in his own language.

Amplified

CHAPTER 2

AND when the day of Pentecost had fully come, they were all assembled together in one place,

2 When suddenly there came a sound from heaven like the rushing of a violent tempest blast, and it filled the whole house in which they were sitting.

3 And there appeared to them tongues resembling fire, which were separated *and* distributed and that settled on each one of them.

4 And they were all filled—diffused throughout their souls—with the Holy Spirit and began to speak in other (different, foreign) languages, as the Spirit [f]kept giving them clear *and* loud expression (in each tongue in appropriate words).

5 Now there were then residing in Jerusalem Jews, devout *and* God-fearing men from every country under heaven.

6 And when this sound was heard, the multitude came together and they were astonished *and* bewildered, because each one heard them speaking in his own (particular) dialect.

---

e) Thayer.
f) Vincent's "Word Studies in the New Testament."

Living New Testament

16 "Brothers, it was necessary for the Scriptures to come true concerning Judas, who betrayed Jesus by guiding the mob to Him, for this was predicted long ago by the Holy Spirit, speaking through King David.

17 Judas was one of us, chosen to be an apostle just as we were.

18 He bought a field with the money he received for his treachery and falling headlong there, he burst open, spilling out his bowels.

19 The news of his death spread rapidly among all the people of Jerusalem, and they named the place 'The Field of Blood.'

20 King David's prediction of this appears in the Book of Psalms, where he says, 'Let his home become desolate with no one living in it.'[4] And again, 'Let his work be given to someone else to do.'[5]

21, 22 So now we must choose someone else to take Judas' place and to join us as witnesses of Jesus' resurrection. Let us select someone who has been with us constantly from our first association with the Lord—from the time He was baptized by John until the day He was taken from us into heaven."

23 The assembly nominated two men: Joseph Justus (also called Barsabbas) and Matthias.

24 Then they all prayed for the right man to be chosen. "O Lord," they said, "You know every heart; show us which of these men You have chosen as an apostle to replace Judas the traitor, who has gone on to his proper place."

25 Then they drew straws,[6] and in this manner Matthias was chosen and became an apostle with the other eleven.

Revised Standard

said, 16"Brethren, the scripture had to be
fulfilled, which the Holy Spirit spoke beforehand by the mouth of David, concerning
Judas who was guide to those who arrested
Jesus. 17For he was numbered among us,
and was allotted his share in this ministry.
18(Now this man bought a field with the
reward of his wickedness; and falling headlong[b] he burst open in the middle and all his
bowels gushed out. 19And it became known
to all the inhabitants of Jerusalem, so that
the field was called in their language Akeldama, that is, Field of Blood.) 20For it is
written in the book of Psalms,

'Let his habitation become desolate,
and let there be no one to live in it';

and

'His office let another take.'

21So one of the men who have accompanied us during all the time that the Lord
Jesus went in and out among us, 22begin-
ning from the baptism of John until the day
when he was taken up from us—one of
these men must become with us a witness to
his resurrection." 23And they put forward
two, Joseph called Barsabbas, who was surnamed Justus, and Matthias. 24And they
prayed and said, "Lord, who knowest the
hearts of all men, show which one of these
two thou hast chosen 25to take the place in
this ministry and apostleship from which
Judas turned aside, to go to his own place."
26And they cast lots for them, and the lot
fell on Matthias; and he was enrolled with
the eleven apostles.

CHAPTER 2

Seven weeks[1] had now gone by since Jesus' death and resurrection, and the Day of Pentecost[2] arrived. As the believers met together that day,

2 Suddenly there was a sound like the roaring of a mighty windstorm in the skies above them and it filled the house where they were meeting.

3 Then, what looked like flames or tongues of fire appeared and settled on their heads.

4 And everyone present was filled with the Holy Spirit and began speaking in languages they didn't know,[3] for the Holy Spirit gave them this ability.

5 Many godly Jews were in Jerusalem that day for the religious celebrations, having arrived from many nations.

6 And when they heard the roaring in the sky above the house, crowds came running to see what it was all about, and were stunned to hear their own languages being spoken by the disciples.

[4] Psalm 69:25.
[5] Psalm 109:8.
[6] Literally, "cast lots," or, "threw dice."
[1] Implied. See Leviticus 23:16.
[2] This annual celebration came 50 days after the Passover ceremonies, when Christ was crucified.
[3] Literally, "in other tongues."

The gift of the Holy Spirit

2 When the day of Pentecost had come,
they were all together in one place.
2And suddenly a sound came from heaven
like the rush of a mighty wind, and it filled
all the house where they were sitting. 3And
there appeared to them tongues as of fire,
distributed and resting on each one of them.
4And they were all filled with the Holy
Spirit and began to speak in other tongues,
as the Spirit gave them utterance.

5 Now there were dwelling in Jerusalem
Jews, devout men from every nation under
heaven. 6And at this sound the multitude
came together, and they were bewildered,
because each one heard them speaking in his

[b] Or *swelling up*

King James

7 And they were all amazed and marvelled, saying one to another, Behold, are not all these which speak Galilæans?

8 And how hear we every man in our own tongue, wherein we were born?

9 Parthians, and Medes, and Elamites, and the dwellers in Mesopotamia, and in Judæa, and Cappadocia, in Pontus, and Asia,

10 Phrygia, and Pamphylia, in Egypt, and in the parts of Libya about Cyrene, and strangers of Rome, Jews and proselytes,

11 Cretes and Arabians, we do hear them speak in our tongues the wonderful works of God.

12 And they were all amazed, and were in doubt, saying one to another, What meaneth this?

13 Others mocking said, These men are full of new wine.

14 ¶ But Peter, standing up with the eleven, lifted up his voice, and said unto them, Ye men of Judæa, and all *ye* that dwell at Jerusalem, be this known unto you, and hearken to my words:

15 For these are not drunken, as ye suppose, seeing it is *but* the third hour of the day.

16 But this is that which was spoken by the prophet Joel;

17 And it shall come to pass in the last days, saith God, I will pour out of my Spirit upon all flesh: and your sons and your daughters shall prophesy, and your young men shall see visions, and your old men shall dream dreams:

18 And on my servants and on my handmaidens I will pour out in those days of my Spirit; and they shall prophesy:

19 And I will shew wonders in heaven above, and signs in the earth beneath; blood, and fire, and vapour of smoke:

20 The sun shall be turned into darkness, and the moon into blood, before that great and notable day of the Lord come:

21 And it shall come to pass, *that* whosoever shall call on the name of the Lord shall be saved.

22 Ye men of Israel, hear these words; Jesus of Nazareth, a man approved of God among you by miracles and wonders and signs, which God did by him in the midst of you, as ye yourselves also know:

23 Him, being delivered by the determinate counsel and foreknowledge of God, ye have taken, and by wicked hands have crucified and slain:

24 Whom God hath raised up, having loosed the pains of death: because it was not possible that he should be holden of it.

25 For David speaketh concerning him, I foresaw the Lord always before my face, for he is on my right hand, that I should not be moved:

Amplified

7 And they were beside themselves with amazement, saying, Are not all these who are talking Galileans?

8 Then how is it that we hear, each of us in our own (particular) dialect to which we were born?

9 Parthians and Medes and Elamites and inhabitants of Mesopotamia, Judea and Cappadocia, Pontus and [the province of] Asia,

10 Phrygia and Pamphylia, Egypt and the parts of Libya about Cyrene, and the transient residents from Rome, both Jews and the proselytes [to Judaism from other religions];

11 Cretans and Arabians too—we all hear them speaking in our own native tongues [and telling of] the mighty works of God!

12 And all were beside themselves with amazement and were puzzled *and* bewildered, saying one to another, What can this mean?

13 But others made a joke of it *and* derisively said, They are simply drunk *and* full of sweet [intoxicating] wine.

14 But Peter, standing with the eleven, raised his voice and addressed them: You Jews and all you residents of Jerusalem, let this be [explained] to you so that you will know *and* understand; listen closely to what I have to say.

15 For these men are not drunk, as you imagine, for it is [only] the third hour [about nine o'clock] of the day;

16 But [instead], this is [the beginning of] what was spoken through the prophet Joel:

17 And it shall come to pass in the last days, God declares, that I will pour out of My Spirit upon all mankind, and your sons and your daughters shall prophesy—[g]telling forth the divine counsels—and your young men shall see visions (that is, [h]divinely granted appearances), and your old men shall dream [[h]divinely suggested] dreams.

18 Yes, and on My menservants also and on My maidservants in those days I will pour out of My Spirit, and they shall prophesy—[g]telling forth the divine counsels and [h]predicting future events pertaining especially to God's kingdom.

19 And I will show wonders in the sky above and signs on the earth beneath, blood and fire and smoking vapor;

20 The sun shall be turned into darkness and the moon into blood, before the obvious day of the Lord comes, that great and notable *and* conspicuous and renowned [day].

21 And it shall be that whosoever shall call upon the name of the Lord—that is, [h]invoking, adoring and worshipping the Lord (Christ)—shall be saved. [Joel 2:28-32.]

22 You men of Israel, listen to what I have to say: Jesus of Nazareth, a Man accredited *and* pointed out *and* shown forth *and* commended *and* attested to you by God, by the mighty works and [the power of performing] wonders and signs which God worked through Him [right] in your midst, as you yourselves know,

23 This Jesus, when delivered up according to the definite *and* fixed purpose *and* settled plan and foreknowledge of God, you crucified *and* put out of the way, [killing Him] by the hands of lawless *and* wicked men.

24 [But] God raised Him up, liberating Him from the pangs of death, seeing that it was not possible for Him to continue to be controlled *or* retained by it.

25 For David says in regard to Him, I saw the Lord constantly before me, for He is at my right hand that I may not be shaken *or* overthrown *or* cast down [from my secure and happy state].

---

g) Abbott-Smith's "Manual Greek Lexicon of the New Testament."
h) Thayer.

Living New Testament

7 "How can this be?" they exclaimed. "For these men are all from Galilee,

8 And yet we hear them speaking all the native languages of the lands where we were born!

9 Here we are—Parthians, Medes, Elamites, men from Mesopotamia, Judea, Cappadocia, Pontus, Ausia,[4]

10 Phrygia, Pamphylia, Egypt, the Cyrene language areas of Libya, visitors from Rome—both Jews and Jewish converts—

11 Cretans, and Arabians. And we all hear these men telling in our own languages about the mighty miracles of God!"

12 They stood there amazed and perplexed. "What can this mean?" they asked each other.

13 But others in the crowd were mocking. "They're drunk, that's all!" they said.

14 Then Peter stepped forward with the eleven apostles, and shouted to the crowd, "Listen, all of you, visitors and residents of Jerusalem alike!

15 Some of you are saying these men are drunk! It isn't true! It's much too early for that! People don't get drunk by 9 a.m.!

16 No! What you see this morning was predicted centuries ago by the prophet Joel—

17 'In the last days,' God said, 'I will pour out My Holy Spirit upon all mankind, and your sons and daughters shall prophesy, and your young men shall see visions, and your old men dream dreams.

18 Yes, the Holy Spirit shall come upon all My servants, men and women alike, and they shall prophesy.

19 And I will cause strange demonstrations in the heavens and on the earth—blood and fire and clouds of smoke;

20 The sun shall turn black and the moon blood-red before that awesome Day of the Lord arrives.

21 But anyone who asks for mercy from the Lord shall have it and shall be saved.'

22 O men of Israel, listen! God publicly endorsed Jesus of Nazareth by doing tremendous miracles through Him, as you well know.

23 But God, following His prearranged plan, let you use the Roman[5] government to nail Him to the cross and murder Him.

24 Then God released Him from the horrors of death and brought Him back to life again, for death could not keep this man within its grip.

25 King David quoted Jesus as saying, 'I know the Lord is always with Me. He is helping Me. God's mighty power supports Me.

[4] Literally, "Asia," a province of what is now Turkey.
[5] Literally, "men without the Law." See Romans 2:12.

Revised Standard

own language. [7]And they were amazed and
wondered, saying, "Are not all these who
are speaking Galileans? [8]And how is it that
we hear, each of us in his own native language? [9]Parthians and Medes and Elamites
and residents of Mesopotamia, Judea and
Cappadocia, Pontus and Asia, [10]Phrygia and
Pamphylia, Egypt and the parts of Libya
belonging to Cyrene, and visitors from
Rome, both Jews and proselytes, [11]Cretans
and Arabians, we hear them telling in our
own tongues the mighty works of God."
[12]And all were amazed and perplexed, saying to one another, "What does this mean?"
[13]But others mocking said, "They are filled
with new wine."

Peter's Pentecostal sermon

14 But Peter, standing with the eleven,
lifted up his voice and addressed them,
"Men of Judea and all who dwell in
Jerusalem, let this be known to you, and
give ear to my words. [15]For these men are
not drunk, as you suppose, since it is only
the third hour of the day; [16]but this is what
was spoken by the prophet Joel:
17 'And in the last days it shall be, God declares,
that I will pour out my Spirit upon all flesh,
and your sons and your daughters shall prophesy,
and your young men shall see visions,
and your old men shall dream dreams;
18 yea, and on my menservants and my maidservants in those days
I will pour out my Spirit; and they shall prophesy.
19 And I will show wonders in the heaven above
and signs on the earth beneath,
blood, and fire, and vapor of smoke;
20 the sun shall be turned into darkness and the moon into blood,
before the day of the Lord comes,
the great and manifest day.
21 And it shall be that whoever calls on the name of the Lord shall be saved.'

22 "Men of Israel, hear these words:
Jesus of Nazareth, a man attested to you by
God with mighty works and wonders and
signs which God did through him in your
midst, as you yourselves know—[23]this Jesus,
delivered up according to the definite plan
and foreknowledge of God, you crucified
and killed by the hands of lawless men.
[24]But God raised him up, having loosed the
pangs of death, because it was not possible
for him to be held by it. [25]For David says
concerning him,
'I saw the Lord always before me, for
he is at my right hand that I may not be shaken;

King James

26 Therefore did my heart rejoice, and my tongue was glad; moreover also my flesh shall rest in hope:

27 Because thou wilt not leave my soul in hell, neither wilt thou suffer thine Holy One to see corruption.

28 Thou hast made known to me the ways of life; thou shalt make me full of joy with thy countenance.

29 Men *and* brethren, let me freely speak unto you of the patriarch David, that he is both dead and buried, and his sepulchre is with us unto this day.

30 Therefore being a prophet, and knowing that God had sworn with an oath to him, that of the fruit of his loins, according to the flesh, he would raise up Christ to sit on his throne;

31 He seeing this before spake of the resurrection of Christ, that his soul was not left in hell, neither his flesh did see corruption.

32 This Jesus hath God raised up, whereof we all are witnesses.

33 Therefore being by the right hand of God exalted, and having received of the Father the promise of the Holy Ghost, he hath shed forth this, which ye now see and hear.

34 For David is not ascended into the heavens: but he saith himself, The LORD said unto my Lord, Sit thou on my right hand,

35 Until I make thy foes thy footstool.

36 Therefore let all the house of Israel know assuredly, that God hath made that same Jesus, whom ye have crucified, both Lord and Christ.

37 ¶ Now when they heard *this,* they were pricked in their heart, and said unto Peter and to the rest of the apostles, Men *and* brethren, what shall we do?

38 Then Peter said unto them, Repent, and be baptized every one of you in the name of Jesus Christ for the remission of sins, and ye shall receive the gift of the Holy Ghost.

39 For the promise is unto you, and to your children, and to all that are afar off, *even* as many as the Lord our God shall call.

40 And with many other words did he testify and exhort, saying, Save yourselves from this untoward generation.

41 ¶ Then they that gladly received his word were baptized: and the same day there were added *unto them* about three thousand souls.

42 And they continued stedfastly in the apostles' doctrine and fellowship, and in breaking of bread, and in prayers.

43 And fear came upon every soul: and many wonders and signs were done by the apostles.

Amplified

26 Therefore my heart rejoiced, and my tongue exulted exceedingly; moreover my flesh also will rest in hope—will encamp, pitch its tent and dwell on hope [in anticipation of the resurrection].

27 For You will not abandon My soul, leaving it helpless in Hades [the state of departed spirits], nor let Your Holy One know decay *or* see destruction [of the body after death].

28 You have made known to Me the ways of life; You will enrapture Me—diffusing My soul with joy—with *and* in Your presence. [Ps. 16:8-11.]

29 Brethren, it is permitted me to tell you confidently *and* with freedom concerning the patriarch David that he both died and was buried, and his tomb is with us to this day.

30 Being however a prophet, and knowing that God had sealed to him with an oath that He would set one of his descendants on his throne. [Ps. 132:11.]

31 He forseeing this, spoke (by foreknowledge) of the resurrection of the Christ, the Messiah, that He was not deserted [in death] *and* left in Hades [the state of departed spirits], nor did His body know decay *or* see destruction. [Ps. 16:10.]

32 This Jesus God raised up, and of that all we [His disciples] are witnesses.

33 Being therefore lifted high by the right hand of God, and having received from the Father [i]the promised [blessing which is the] Holy Spirit, He has made this outpouring which you yourselves both see and hear.

34 For David did not ascend into the heavens; yet he himself says, The Lord said to my Lord, Sit at My right hand, *and* share My throne

35 Till I make Your enemies a footstool for Your feet. [Ps. 110:1.]

36 Therefore let the whole house of Israel recognize beyond all doubt *and* acknowledge assuredly that God has made Him both Lord and Christ, the Messiah, this Jesus Whom you crucified.

37 Now when they heard this they were stung (cut) to the heart, and they said to Peter and the rest of the apostles (special messengers), Brethren, what shall we do?

38 And Peter answered them, Repent—change your views, and purpose to accept the will of God in your inner selves instead of rejecting it—and be baptized every one of you in the name of Jesus Christ for the forgiveness of *and* release from your sins; and you shall receive the gift of the Holy Spirit.

39 For the promise (of the Holy Spirit) is to *and* for you and your children, and to *and* for all that are far away, [even] to as many as the Lord our God invites *and* bids come to Himself. [Isa. 57:19; Joel 2:32.]

40 And [Peter] [j]solemnly *and* earnestly witnessed (testified) and admonished (exhorted) with much more continuous speaking *and* warned (reproved, advised, encouraged) them, saying, Be saved from this crooked (perverse, wicked, unjust) generation.

41 Therefore those who accepted *and* welcomed his message were baptized, and there were added that day about three thousand souls.

42 And they steadfastly persevered, devoting themselves constantly to the instruction and fellowship of the apostles, to the breaking of bread [including [k]the Lord's Supper] and prayers.

43 And a sense of awe (reverential fear) came upon every soul, and many wonders and signs were performed through the apostles—the special messengers.

---

i) Thayer.
j) Vincent: The preposition *dia* gives this force.
k) Many authorities.

Living New Testament

26 No wonder My heart is filled with joy and My tongue shouts His praises! For I know all will be well with Me in death—

27 You will not leave My soul in hell or let the body of Your Holy Son decay.

28 You will give Me back My life, and give Me wonderful joy in Your presence.'

29 Dear brothers, think! David wasn't referring to himself when he spoke these words I have quoted,[6] for he died and was buried, and his tomb is still here among us!

30 But he was a prophet, and knew God had promised with an unbreakable oath that one of David's own descendants would [be the Messiah and[6]] sit on David's throne.

31 David was looking far into the future and predicting the Messiah's resurrection, and saying that the Messiah's soul would not be left in hell and His body would not decay.

32 He was speaking of Jesus, and we all are witnesses that Jesus rose from the dead.

33 And now He sits on the throne of highest honor in heaven, next to God. And just as promised, the Father has sent the Holy Spirit—with the results you are seeing and hearing today.

34 [No, David was not speaking of himself in these words of his I have quoted[7]], for he never ascended into the skies. Moreover, he further stated, 'God spoke to my Lord, the Messiah, and said to Him, Sit here in honor beside Me

35 Until I bring Your enemies into complete subjection.'

36 Therefore I clearly state to everyone in Israel that God has made this Jesus you crucified to be the Lord, the Messiah!"

37 These words of Peter's moved them deeply, and they said to him and to the other apostles, "Brothers, what should we do?"

38 And Peter replied, "Each one of you must turn from sin, return to God, and be baptized in the name of Jesus Christ for the forgiveness of your sins; then you also shall receive this gift, the Holy Spirit.

39 For Christ promised Him to each one of you who has been called by the Lord our God, and to your children and even to those in distant lands!"

40 Then Peter preached a long sermon, telling about Jesus and strongly urging all his listeners to save themselves from the evils of their nation.

41 And those who believed Peter were baptized—about 3,000 in all!

42 They joined with the other believers in regular attendance at the apostles' teaching sessions and at the Communion services[8] and prayer meetings.

43 A deep sense of awe was on them all, and the apostles did many miracles.

Revised Standard

26 therefore my heart was glad, and my
tongue rejoiced;
moreover my flesh will dwell in hope.
27 For thou wilt not abandon my soul to
Hades,
nor let thy Holy One see corruption.
28 Thou hast made known to me the ways
of life;
thou wilt make me full of gladness with
thy presence.'

29 "Brethren, I may say to you confidently of the patriarch David that he both
died and was buried, and his tomb is with us
to this day. 30 Being therefore a prophet,
and knowing that God had sworn with an
oath to him that he would set one of his
descendants upon his throne, 31 he foresaw
and spoke of the resurrection of the Christ,
that he was not abandoned to Hades, nor
did his flesh see corruption. 32 This Jesus God
raised up, and of that we all are witnesses.
33 Being therefore exalted at the right hand
of God, and having received from the Father the promise of the Holy Spirit, he has
poured out this which you see and hear.
34 For David did not ascend into the heavens;
but he himself says,
'The Lord said to my Lord, Sit at my
right hand,
35 till I make thy enemies a stool for thy
feet.'
36 Let all the house of Israel therefore know
assuredly that God has made him both Lord
and Christ, this Jesus whom you crucified."

The community of the believers

37 Now when they heard this they were
cut to the heart, and said to Peter and the
rest of the apostles, "Brethren, what shall
we do?" 38 And Peter said to them, "Repent,
and be baptized every one of you in the
name of Jesus Christ for the forgiveness of
your sins; and you shall receive the gift of
the Holy Spirit. 39 For the promise is to you
and to your children and to all that are far
off, every one whom the Lord our God calls
to him." 40 And he testified with many other
words and exhorted them, saying, "Save
yourselves from this crooked generation."
41 So those who received his word were baptized, and there were added that day about
three thousand souls. 42 And they devoted
themselves to the apostles' teaching and
fellowship, to the breaking of bread and the
prayers.

43 And fear came upon every soul; and
many wonders and signs were done through

---

[6] Implied from verse 31.
[7] Implied.
[8] Literally, "the breaking of bread," i.e., "the Lord's Supper."

King James

44 And all that believed were together, and had all things common;

45 And sold their possessions and goods, and parted them to all *men*, as every man had need.

46 And they, continuing daily with one accord in the temple, and breaking bread from house to house, did eat their meat with gladness and singleness of heart,

47 Praising God, and having favour with all the people. And the Lord added to the church daily such as should be saved.

CHAPTER 3

NOW Peter and John went up together into the temple at the hour of prayer, *being* the ninth *hour*.

2 And a certain man lame from his mother's womb was carried, whom they laid daily at the gate of the temple which is called Beautiful, to ask alms of them that entered into the temple;

3 Who seeing Peter and John about to go into the temple asked an alms.

4 And Peter, fastening his eyes upon him with John, said, Look on us.

5 And he gave heed unto them, expecting to receive something of them.

6 Then Peter said, Silver and gold have I none; but such as I have give I thee: In the name of Jesus Christ of Nazareth rise up and walk.

7 And he took him by the right hand, and lifted *him* up: and immediately his feet and ankle bones received strength.

8 And he leaping up stood, and walked, and entered with them into the temple, walking, and leaping, and praising God.

9 And all the people saw him walking and praising God:

10 And they knew that it was he which sat for alms at the Beautiful gate of the temple: and they were filled with wonder and amazement at that which had happened unto him.

11 And as the lame man which was healed held Peter and John, all the people ran together unto them in the porch that is called Solomon's, greatly wondering.

12 ¶ And when Peter saw *it*, he answered unto the people, Ye men of Israel, why marvel ye at this? or why look ye so earnestly on us, as though by our own power or holiness we had made this man to walk?

13 The God of Abraham, and of Isaac, and of Jacob, the God of our fathers, hath glorified his Son Jesus; whom ye delivered up, and denied him in the presence of Pilate, when he was determined to let *him* go.

14 But ye denied the Holy One and the Just, and desired a murderer to be granted unto you;

Amplified

44 And all who believed—that is, who adhered to and trusted in and relied on Jesus Christ—were united, *and* together they had everything in common;

45 And they sold their possessions [both their landed property and their movable goods] and distributed the price among all, according as any had need.

46 And day after day they regularly assembled in the temple with united purpose, and in their homes they broke bread [including the Lord's Supper]. They partook of their food with gladness and simplicity *and* generous hearts,

47 Constantly praising God and being in favor *and* goodwill with all the people, and the Lord kept adding [to their number] daily those who were being saved (from spiritual death).

CHAPTER 3

NOW Peter and John were going up to the temple at the hour of prayer, the ninth hour (three o'clock in the afternoon),

2 [When] a certain man crippled from his birth was being carried along, who was laid each day at that gate of the temple [which is] called Beautiful, that he might beg for charitable gifts from those who entered the temple.

3 So when he saw Peter and John about to go into the temple, he asked them to give him a gift.

4 And Peter directed his gaze intently at him, and so did John, and said, Look at us!

5 And [the man] paid attention to them, expecting that he was going to get something from them.

6 But Peter said, Silver and gold [money], I have none; but what I do have, that I give to you: in (the [l]use of) the name of Jesus Christ of Nazareth, walk!

7 Then he took hold of the man's right hand with a firm grip and raised him up. And at once his feet and ankle bones became strong *and* steady,

8 And leaping forth he stood and [m]began to walk, and he went into the temple with them, walking and leaping and praising God.

9 And all the people saw him walking about and praising God,

10 And they recognized him as the man who usually sat [begging] of alms at the Beautiful Gate of the temple, and they were filled with wonder and amazement (bewilderment, consternation) over what had occurred to him.

11 Now while he [still] firmly clung to Peter and John, all the people in utmost amazement ran together *and* crowded around them in the covered porch (walk) called Solomon's.

12 And Peter seeing it, answered the people, You men, Israelites, why are you so surprised *and* wondering at this? Why do you keep staring at us, as though by our [own individual] power *or* [active] piety we had made [this man able] to walk?

13 The God of Abraham and of Isaac and of Jacob, the God of our forefathers, has glorified His Servant and [n]Son Jesus—doing Him this honor—Whom you indeed delivered up and denied *and* rejected *and* disowned in the presence of Pilate, when he had determined to let Him go. [Exod. 3:6; Isa. 52:13.]

l) Thayer.
m) Vincent.
n) Alternate reading.

Living New Testament

44 And all the believers met together constantly and shared everything with each other,

45 Selling their possessions and dividing with those in need.

46 They worshiped together regularly at the Temple each day, met in small groups in homes for Communion, and shared their meals with great joy and thankfulness,

47 Praising God. The whole city was favorable to them, and each day God added to them all who were being saved.

Revised Standard

the apostles. [44]And all who believed were together and had all things in common; [45]and they sold their possessions and goods and distributed them to all, as any had need. [46]And day by day, attending the temple together and breaking bread in their homes, they partook of food with glad and generous hearts, [47]praising God and having favor with all the people. And the Lord added to their number day by day those who were being saved.

CHAPTER 3

Peter and John went to the Temple one afternoon to take part in the three o'clock daily prayer meeting.

2 As they approached the Temple, they saw a man lame from birth carried along the street and laid beside the Temple gate—the one called The Beautiful Gate—as was his custom every day.

3 As Peter and John were passing by, he asked them for some money.

4 They looked at him intently, and then Peter said, "Look here!"

5 The lame man looked at them eagerly, expecting a gift.

6 But Peter said, "We don't have any money for you! But I'll give you something else! I command you in the name of Jesus Christ of Nazareth, *walk*!"

7, 8 Then Peter took the lame man by the hand and pulled him to his feet. And as he did, the man's feet and ankle-bones were healed and strengthened so that he came up with a leap, stood there a moment and began walking! Then, walking, leaping, and praising God, he went into the Temple with them.

9 When the people inside saw him walking and heard him praising God,

10 And realized he was the lame beggar they had seen so often at The Beautiful Gate, they were inexpressibly surprised!

11 They all rushed out to Solomon's Hall, where he was holding tightly to Peter and John! Everyone stood there awed by the wonderful thing that had happened.

12 Peter saw his opportunity and addressed the crowd! "Men of Israel," he said, "what is so surprising about this? And why look at us as though we by our own power and godliness had made this man walk?

13 For it is the God of Abraham, Isaac, Jacob and of all our ancestors who has brought glory to His servant Jesus by doing this. I refer to the Jesus whom you rejected before Pilate, despite Pilate's determination to release Him.

The healing of the lame man

3 Now Peter and John were going up to the temple at the hour of prayer, the ninth hour. [2]And a man lame from birth was being carried, whom they laid daily at that gate of the temple which is called Beautiful to ask alms of those who entered the temple. [3]Seeing Peter and John about to go into the temple, he asked for alms. [4]And Peter directed his gaze at him, with John, and said, "Look at us." [5]And he fixed his attention upon them, expecting to receive something from them. [6]But Peter said, "I have no silver and gold, but I give you what I have; in the name of Jesus Christ of Nazareth, walk." [7]And he took him by the right hand and raised him up; and immediately his feet and ankles were made strong. [8]And leaping up he stood and walked and entered the temple with them, walking and leaping and praising God. [9]And all the people saw him walking and praising God, [10]and recognized him as the one who sat for alms at the Beautiful Gate of the temple; and they were filled with wonder and amazement at what had happened to him.

Peter's sermon in the temple area

11 While he clung to Peter and John, all the people ran together to them in the portico called Solomon's, astounded. [12]And when Peter saw it he addressed the people, "Men of Israel, why do you wonder at this, or why do you stare at us, as though by our own power or piety we had made him walk? [13]The God of Abraham and of Isaac and of Jacob, the God of our fathers, glorified his servant[c] Jesus, whom you delivered up and denied in the presence of Pilate, when he had decided to release him. [14]But you denied

[c] Or *child*

King James

15 And killed the Prince of life, whom God hath raised from the dead; whereof we are witnesses.

16 And his name through faith in his name hath made this man strong, whom ye see and know: yea, the faith which is by him hath given him this perfect soundness in the presence of you all.

17 And now, brethren, I wot that through ignorance ye did *it*, as *did* also your rulers.

18 But those things, which God before had shewed by the mouth of all his prophets, that Christ should suffer, he hath so fulfilled.

19 ¶ Repent ye therefore, and be converted, that your sins may be blotted out, when the times of refreshing shall come from the presence of the Lord;

20 And he shall send Jesus Christ, which before was preached unto you:

21 Whom the heaven must receive until the times of restitution of all things, which God hath spoken by the mouth of all his holy prophets since the world began.

22 For Moses truly said unto the fathers, A prophet shall the Lord your God raise up unto you of your brethren, like unto me; him shall ye hear in all things whatsoever he shall say unto you.

23 And it shall come to pass, *that* every soul, which will not hear that prophet, shall be destroyed from among the people.

24 Yea, and all the prophets from Samuel and those that follow after, as many as have spoken, have likewise foretold of these days.

25 Ye are the children of the prophets, and of the covenant which God made with our fathers, saying unto Abraham, And in thy seed shall all the kindreds of the earth be blessed.

26 Unto you first God, having raised up his Son Jesus, sent him to bless you, in turning away every one of you from his iniquities.

CHAPTER 4

AND as they spake unto the people, the priests, and the captain of the temple, and the Sadducees, came upon them,

2 Being grieved that they taught the people, and preached through Jesus the resurrection from the dead.

3 And they laid hands on them, and put *them* in hold unto the next day: for it was now eventide.

Amplified

14 But you denied *and* rejected *and* disowned the Pure *and* Holy, the Just *and* Blameless One, and demanded [the pardon of] a murderer to be granted to you.

15 But you killed the very Source—the Author—of life, Whom God raised from the dead. To this we are witnesses.

16 And His name, through *and* by faith in His name, has made this man whom you see and recognize well *and* strong. [Yes,] the faith which is through *and* by Him [Jesus] has given the man this perfect soundness [of body] before all of you.

17 And now, brethren, I know that you acted in ignorance—not aware of what you were doing—as did your rulers also.

18 Thus has God fulfilled what He foretold by the mouth of all the prophets, that His Christ, the Messiah, should undergo ill treatment *and* be afflicted *and* suffer.

19 So repent—change your mind *and* purpose; turn around *and* return [to God], that your sins may be erased (blotted out, wiped clean), that times of refreshing—of recovering from the effects of heat, of [o]reviving with fresh air—may come from the presence of the Lord;

20 And that He may send [to you] the Christ, the Messiah, Who before was designated *and* appointed for you, Jesus,

21 Whom heaven must receive [and retain] until the time for the complete restoration of all that God spoke by the mouth of all His holy prophets for ages past—from the most ancient time in the memory of man.

22 Thus Moses said *to the forefathers,* The Lord God will raise up for you a Prophet from among your brethren as [He raised up] me; Him you shall listen to *and* understand by hearing, *and* heed in all things whatever He tells you.

23 And it shall be that every soul that does not listen to *and* understand by hearing *and* heed that Prophet shall be utterly [p]exterminated from among the people. [Deut. 18:15-19; Lev. 23:29.]

24 Indeed, all the prophets from Samuel and those who came afterwards, as many as have spoken also promised *and* foretold *and* proclaimed these days.

25 You are the descendants (sons) of the prophets and the heirs of the covenant which God made *and* gave to your forefathers, saying to Abraham, And in your Seed (Heir), shall all the families of the earth be blessed *and* benefited. [Gen. 22:18; cf. Gal. 3:16.]

26 It was to you first that God sent His Servant *and* [q]Son *Jesus,* when He raised Him up ([r]provided, gave Him) to bless you in turning every one of you from your wickedness *and* evil ways.

CHAPTER 4

AND while they [Peter and John] were talking to the people, the high priests and the military commander of the temple, and the Sadducees came upon them,

2 Being vexed *and* indignant through *and* through because they were teaching the people *and* proclaiming in [the case of] Jesus the resurrection from the dead.

3 So they laid hands on them (arrested them) and put them in prison until the following day, for it was already evening.

o) Vincent.
p) Souter.
q) Alternate reading.
r) Jamieson, Fausett and Brown.

Living New Testament

14 You didn't want Him freed—this holy, righteous one. Instead you demanded the release of a murderer.

15 And you killed the Author of Life; but God brought Him back to life again. And John and I are witnesses of this fact, for after you killed Him we saw Him alive!

16 Jesus' name has healed this man—and you know how lame he was before. Faith in Jesus' name—faith given us from God—has caused this perfect healing.

17 Dear brothers, I realize that what you did to Jesus was done in ignorance; and the same can be said of your leaders.

18 But God was fulfilling the prophecies that the Messiah must suffer all these things.

19 Now change your mind and attitude to God and turn to Him so He can cleanse away your sins and send you wonderful times of refreshment from the presence of the Lord

20 And send Jesus your Messiah back to you again.

21, 22 For He must remain in heaven until the final recovery of all things from sin, as prophesied from ancient times. Moses, for instance, said long ago, 'The Lord God will raise up a Prophet among you, who will resemble me![1] Listen carefully to everything He tells you.

23 Anyone who will not listen to Him shall be utterly destroyed.'[2]

24 Samuel and every prophet since have all spoken about what is going on today.

25 You are the children of those prophets; and you are included in God's promise to your ancestors to bless the entire world through the Jewish race—that is the promise God gave to Abraham.

26 And as soon as God had brought His servant to life again, He sent Him first of all to you men of Israel, to bless you by turning you back from your sins."

Revised Standard

the Holy and Righteous One, and asked for
a murderer to be granted to you, [15]and
killed the Author of life, whom God raised
from the dead. To this we are witnesses.
[16]And his name, by faith in his name, has
made this man strong whom you see and
know; and the faith which is through Jesus[d]
has given the man this perfect health in the
presence of you all.
17 "And now, brethren, I know that you
acted in ignorance, as did also your rulers.
[18]But what God foretold by the mouth of
all the prophets, that his Christ should
suffer, he thus fulfilled. [19]Repent therefore,
and turn again, that your sins may be
blotted out, that times of refreshing may
come from the presence of the Lord, [20]and
that he may send the Christ appointed for
you, Jesus, [21]whom heaven must receive
until the time for establishing all that God
spoke by the mouth of his holy prophets
from of old. [22]Moses said, 'The Lord God
will raise up for you a prophet from your
brethren as he raised me up. You shall listen
to him in whatever he tells you. [23]And it
shall be that every soul that does not listen
to that prophet shall be destroyed from the
people.' [24]And all the prophets who have
spoken, from Samuel and those who came
afterwards, also proclaimed these days.
[25]You are the sons of the prophets and of
the covenant which God gave to your fathers, saying to Abraham, 'And in your posterity shall all the families of the earth be
blessed.' [26]God, having raised up his servant,[c] sent him to you first, to bless you in
turning every one of you from your wickedness."

CHAPTER 4

While they were talking to the people, the chief priests, the captain of the Temple police, and some of the Sadducees[1] came over to them,

2 Very disturbed that Peter and John were claiming that Jesus had risen from the dead.

3 They arrested them and since it was already evening, jailed them overnight.

[1] Literally, "like unto me."

[2] Literally, "destroyed from among the people."

[1] The Sadducees were a Jewish religious sect that denied the resurrection of the dead.

Peter and John arrested

4 And as they were speaking to the people, the priests and the captain of the
temple and the Sadducees came upon them,
[2]annoyed because they were teaching the
people and proclaiming in Jesus the resurrection from the dead. [3]And they arrested
them and put them in custody until the
morrow, for it was already evening. [4]But

[c] Or *child*

[d] Greek *him*

King James

4 Howbeit many of them which heard the word believed; and the number of the men was about five thousand.

5 ¶ And it came to pass on the morrow, that their rulers, and elders, and scribes,

6 And Annas the high priest, and Caiaphas, and John, and Alexander, and as many as were of the kindred of the high priest, were gathered together at Jerusalem.

7 And when they had set them in the midst, they asked, By what power, or by what name, have ye done this?

8 Then Peter, filled with the Holy Ghost, said unto them, Ye rulers of the people, and elders of Israel,

9 If we this day be examined of the good deed done to the impotent man, by what means he is made whole;

10 Be it known unto you all, and to all the people of Israel, that by the name of Jesus Christ of Nazareth, whom ye crucified, whom God raised from the dead, *even* by him doth this man stand here before you whole.

11 This is the stone which was set at nought of you builders, which is become the head of the corner.

12 Neither is there salvation in any other: for there is none other name under heaven given among men, whereby we must be saved.

13 ¶ Now when they saw the boldness of Peter and John, and perceived that they were unlearned and ignorant men, they marvelled; and they took knowledge of them, that they had been with Jesus.

14 And beholding the man which was healed standing with them, they could say nothing against it.

15 But when they had commanded them to go aside out of the council, they conferred among themselves,

16 Saying, What shall we do to these men? for that indeed a notable miracle hath been done by them *is* manifest to all them that dwell in Jerusalem; and we cannot deny *it*.

17 But that it spread no further among the people, let us straitly threaten them, that they speak henceforth to no man in this name.

18 And they called them, and commanded them not to speak at all nor teach in the name of Jesus.

19 But Peter and John answered and said unto them, Whether it be right in the sight of God to hearken unto you more than unto God, judge ye.

20 For we cannot but speak the things which we have seen and heard.

21 So when they had further threatened them, they let them go, finding nothing how they might punish them, because of the people: for all *men* glorifed God for that which was done.

22 For the man was above forty years old, on whom this miracle of healing was shewed.

23 ¶ And being let go, they went to their own company, and reported all that the chief priests and elders had said unto them.

Amplified

4 But many of those who heard the message believed—adhered to and trusted in and relied on [Jesus as the Christ]. And their number grew *and* came to about five thousand.

5 Then on the following day their magistrates and elders and scribes were assembled in Jerusalem,

6 Including Annas the high priest and Caiaphas and John and Alexander, and all others who belonged to the high priestly relationship.

7 And they set the men in the midst and repeatedly demanded, By what sort of power or by what kind of authority did [such people as] you do this [healing]?

8 Then Peter, [because he was] filled with [and controlled by] the Holy Spirit, said to them, Rulers of the people and members of the council,

9 If we are being put on trial [here] today *and* examined concerning a good deed done to benefit a feeble (helpless) cripple, by what means this man has been restored to health,

10 Let it be known *and* understood by you all, and by the whole house of Israel, that in the name and through the power *and* authority of Jesus Christ of Nazareth, Whom you crucified, [but] Whom God raised from the dead, in Him *and* by means [of Him] this man is standing here before you well *and* sound in body.

11 This [Jesus] is the Stone which was despised *and* rejected by you, the builders, but which has become the Head [the external angle] of the corner—the Cornerstone. [Ps. 118:22.]

12 And there is salvation in *and* through no one else, for there is no other name under heaven given among men by *and* in which we must be saved.

13 Now when they saw the boldness *and* unfettered eloquence of Peter and John, and perceived that they were unlearned *and* untrained in the schools—common men with no advantages—they marvelled; and they recognized that they had been with Jesus.

14 And since they saw the man who had been cured standing there beside them, they could not contradict the fact *or* say anything in opposition.

15 But, having ordered [the prisoners] to go aside out of the council [chamber], they conferred (debated) among themselves,

16 Saying, What are we to do with these men? For that an extraordinary miracle has been performed by (through) them is plain to all the residents of Jerusalem, and we cannot deny it.

17 But in order that it may not spread further among the people *and* the nation, let us warn *and* forbid them with a stern threat to speak any more to any one in this name—or about this Person.

18 [So] they summoned them and imperatively instructed them not to converse in any way *or* teach at all in *or* about the name of Jesus.

19 But Peter and John replied to them, Whether it is right in the sight of God to listen to you *and* obey you rather than God, you must decide (judge).

20 But we [ourselves] cannot help telling what we have seen and heard.

21 Then when [the rulers and council members] had further threatened them, they let them go, not seeing how they could secure a conviction against them, because of the people; for everybody was praising *and* glorifying God for what had occurred,

22 For the man on whom this sign (miracle) of healing was performed was more than forty years old.

23 After they were permitted to go, [the apostles] returned to their own [company] and told all that the chief priests and elders had said to them.

Living New Testament

4 But many of the people who heard their message believed it, so that the number of believers now reached a new high of about 5,000 men!

5 The next day it happened that the Council of all the Jewish leaders was in session in Jerusalem—

6 Ananias the High Priest was there, and Caiaphas, John, Alexander, and others of the High Priest's relatives.

7 So the two disciples were brought in before them. "By what power, or by whose authority have you done this?" the Council demanded.

8 Then Peter, filled with the Holy Spirit, said to them, "Honorable leaders and elders of our nation,

9 If you mean the good deed done to the cripple, and how he was healed,

10 Let me clearly state to you and to all the people of Israel that it was done in the name and power of Jesus from Nazareth, the Messiah, the man you crucified —but God raised back to life again. It is by His authority that this man stands here healed!

11 For Jesus the Messiah is (the one referred to in the Scriptures when they speak of) a 'stone discarded by the builders which became the capstone of the arch.'[2]

12 There is salvation in no one else! Under all heaven there is no other name for men to call upon to save them."

13 When the Council saw the boldness of Peter and John, and could see that they were obviously uneducated non-professionals, they were amazed and realized what being with Jesus had done for them!

14 And the Council could hardly discredit the healing when the man they had healed was standing right there beside them!

15 So they sent them out of the Council chamber and conferred among themselves.

16 "What shall we do with these men?" they asked each other. "We can't deny that they have done a tremendous miracle, and everybody in Jerusalem knows about it.

17 But perhaps we can stop them from spreading their propaganda. We'll tell them that if they do it again we'll really throw the book at them."

18 So they called them back in, and told them never again to speak about Jesus.

19 But Peter and John replied, "You decide whether God wants us to obey you instead of Him!

20 We cannot stop telling about the wonderful things we saw Jesus do and heard Him say."

21 The Council then threatened them further, and finally let them go because they didn't know how to punish them without starting a riot. For everyone was praising God for this wonderful miracle—

22 The healing of a man who had been lame 40 years!

23 As soon as they were freed, Peter and John found the other disciples and told them what the council had said.

Revised Standard

many of those who heard the word believed; and the number of the men came to about five thousand.

Peter's defense

5 On the morrow their rulers and elders
and scribes were gathered together in
Jerusalem, 6 with Annas the high priest and
Caiaphas and John and Alexander, and all
who were of the high-priestly family. 7 And
when they had set them in the midst, they
inquired, "By what power or by what name
did you do this?" 8 Then Peter, filled with
the Holy Spirit, said to them, "Rulers of the
people and elders, 9 if we are being examined today concerning a good deed done to
a cripple, by what means this man has been
healed, 10 be it known to you all, and to all
the people of Israel, that by the name of
Jesus Christ of Nazareth, whom you
crucified, whom God raised from the dead,
by him this man is standing before you well.
11 This is the stone which was rejected by
you builders, but which has become the
head of the corner. 12 And there is salvation
in no one else, for there is no other name
under heaven given among men by which
we must be saved."

Peter and John set free

13 Now when they saw the boldness of
Peter and John, and perceived that they
were uneducated, common men, they wondered; and they recognized that they had
been with Jesus. 14 But seeing the man that
had been healed standing beside them, they
had nothing to say in opposition. 15 But
when they had commanded them to go aside
out of the council, they conferred with one
another, 16 saying, "What shall we do with
these men? For that a notable sign has been
performed through them is manifest to all
the inhabitants of Jerusalem, and we cannot
deny it. 17 But in order that it may spread
no further among the people, let us warn
them to speak no more to any one in this
name." 18 So they called them and charged
them not to speak or teach at all in the
name of Jesus. 19 But Peter and John answered them, "Whether it is right in the
sight of God to listen to you rather than to
God, you must judge; 20 for we cannot but
speak of what we have seen and heard."
21 And when they had further threatened
them, they let them go, finding no way to
punish them, because of the people; for all
men praised God for what had happened.
22 For the man on whom this sign of healing
was performed was more than forty years
old.

The report to the believers

23 When they were released they went to their friends and reported what the chief priests and the elders had said to them.

---

[2] Implied. Literally, "became the head of the corner."

King James

24 And when they heard that, they lifted up their voice to God with one accord, and said, Lord, thou *art* God, which hast made heaven, and earth, and the sea, and all that in them is:

25 Who by the mouth of thy servant David hast said, Why did the heathen rage, and the people imagine vain things?

26 The kings of the earth stood up, and the rulers were gathered together against the Lord, and against his Christ.

27 For of a truth against thy holy child Jesus, whom thou hast anointed, both Herod, and Pontius Pilate, with the Gentiles, and the people of Israel, were gathered together,

28 For to do whatsoever thy hand and thy counsel determined before to be done.

29 And now, Lord, behold their threatenings: and grant unto thy servants, that with all boldness they may speak thy word,

30 By stretching forth thine hand to heal; and that signs and wonders may be done by the name of thy holy child Jesus.

31 ¶ And when they had prayed, the place was shaken where they were assembled together; and they were all filled with the Holy Ghost, and they spake the word of God with boldness.

32 And the multitude of them that believed were of one heart and of one soul: neither said any *of them* that aught of the things which he possessed was his own; but they had all things common.

33 And with great power gave the apostles witness of the resurrection of the Lord Jesus: and great grace was upon them all.

34 Neither was there any among them that lacked: for as many as were possessors of lands or houses sold them, and brought the prices of the things that were sold,

35 And laid *them* down at the apostles' feet: and distribution was made unto every man according as he had need.

36 And Joses, who by the apostles was surnamed Barnabas, (which is, being interpreted, The son of consolation,) a Levite, *and* of the country of Cyprus,

37 Having land, sold *it*, and brought the money, and laid *it* at the apostles' feet.

Amplified

24 And they, when they heard it, lifted their voices together with one united mind to God and said, O Sovereign Lord, You are He Who made the heaven and the earth and the sea and everything that is in them, [Exod. 20:11; Ps. 146:6.]

25 Who by the mouth of our forefather David, Your servant *and* [s]child, said through the Holy Spirit, Why did the heathen [Gentiles] become wanton *and* insolent *and* rage, and the people imagine *and* study *and* plan vain (fruitless) things—that will not succeed?

26 The kings of the earth took their stand in array [for attack], and the rulers were assembled *and* combined together against the Lord and against His Anointed, Christ, the Messiah. [Ps. 2:1, 2.]

27 For in this city there actually met and plotted together against Your holy Child *and* [s]Servant Jesus, Whom You consecrated by anointing, both Herod and Pontius Pilate with the Gentiles and peoples of Israel, [Ps. 2:1, 2.]

28 To carry out all that Your hand and Your will *and* purpose had predestined (predetermined) should occur.

29 And now, Lord, observe their threats and grant to Your bond servants [full freedom] to declare Your message fearlessly,

30 While You stretch out Your hand to cure and to perform signs *and* wonders through the authority *and* by the power of the name of Your holy Child *and* [s]Servant Jesus.

31 And when they had prayed, the place in which they were assembled was shaken; and they were all filled with the Holy Spirit, and they continued to speak the Word of God with freedom *and* boldness *and* courage.

32 Now the company of believers was of one heart and soul, and not one of them claimed that anything which he possessed was [exclusively] his own, but everything they had was in common *and* for the use of all.

33 And with great strength *and* ability *and* power the apostles delivered their testimony to the resurrection of the Lord Jesus, and great grace—loving kindness and favor and goodwill—rested richly upon them all.

34 Nor was there a destitute *or* needy person among them, for as many as were owners of lands or houses proceeded to sell them, and one by one they brought (gave back) the amount received from the sales

35 And laid it at the feet of the apostles. Then distribution was made according as any one had need.

36 Now Joseph, a Levite and native of Cyprus who was surnamed Barnabas by the apostles (special messengers), which interpreted means, Son of Encouragement,

37 Sold a field which belonged to him, and brought the sum of money and laid it at the feet of the apostles.

CHAPTER 5

BUT a certain man named Ananias, with Sapphira his wife, sold a possession,

2 And kept back *part* of the price, his wife also being privy *to it*, and brought a certain part, and laid *it* at the apostles' feet.

3 But Peter said, Ananias, why hath Satan filled thine heart to lie to the Holy Ghost, and to keep back *part* of the price of the land?

CHAPTER 5

BUT a certain man named Ananias with his wife Sapphira sold a piece of property,

2 And with his wife's knowledge *and* connivance he kept back *and* wrongfully appropriated some of the proceeds, bringing a part only and putting it at the feet of the apostles.

3 But Peter said, Ananias, why has Satan filled your heart that you should lie to *and* attempt to deceive the Holy Spirit, and should [in violation of your promise] withdraw secretly *and* appropriate to your own use part of the price from the sale of the land?

---

s) Alternate reading.

Living New Testament

24 Then all the believers united in this prayer: "O Lord, Creator of heaven and earth and of the sea and everything in them—

25, 26 You spoke long ago by the Holy Spirit through our ancestor King David, your servant, saying, 'Why do the heathen rage against the Lord, and the foolish nations plan their little plots against Almighty God? The kings of the earth unite to fight against Him, against the anointed Son of God!'

27 That is what is happening here in this city today! For Herod the king, and Pontius Pilate the governor, and all the Romans—as well as the people of Israel—are united against Jesus, Your anointed Son, Your holy servant.

28 They won't stop at anything that You in Your wise power will let them do.

29 And now, O Lord, hear their threats, and grant to Your servants great boldness in their preaching,

30 And send Your healing power, and may miracles and wonders be done by the name of Your holy servant Jesus."

31 After this prayer, the building where they were meeting shook and they were all filled with the Holy Spirit and boldly preached God's message.

32 All the believers were of one heart and mind, and no one felt that what he owned was his own; everyone was sharing.

33 And the apostles preached powerful sermons about the resurrection of the Lord Jesus, and there was warm fellowship[3] among all the believers,

34, 35 And no poverty—for all who owned land or houses sold them and brought the money to the apostles to give to others in need.

36 For instance, there was Joseph (the one the apostles nicknamed "Barny the Preacher"! He was of the tribe of Levi, from the island of Cyprus).

37 He was one of those who sold a field he owned, and brought the money to the apostles for distribution to those in need.

Revised Standard

24 And when they heard it, they lifted their
voices together to God and said, "Sovereign
Lord, who didst make the heaven and the
earth and the sea and everything in them,
25 who by the mouth of our father David,
thy servant,[c] didst say by the Holy Spirit,

'Why did the Gentiles rage,
and the peoples imagine vain things?
26 The kings of the earth set themselves
in array,
and the rulers were gathered together,
against the Lord and against his Anointed'—[e]

27 for truly in this city there were gathered
together against thy holy servant[c] Jesus,
whom thou didst anoint, both Herod and
Pontius Pilate, with the Gentiles and the
peoples of Israel, 28 to do whatever thy hand
and thy plan had predestined to take place.
29 And now, Lord, look upon their threats,
and grant to thy servants[f] to speak thy word
with all boldness, 30 while thou stretchest
out thy hand to heal, and signs and wonders
are performed through the name of thy holy
servant[c] Jesus." 31 And when they had prayed,
the place in which they were gathered together was shaken; and they were filled with
the Holy Spirit and spoke the word of God
with boldness.

The community of possessions

32 Now the company of those who believed were of one heart and soul, and no
one said that any of the things which he
possessed was his own, but they had everything in common. 33 And with great power
the apostles gave their testimony to the resurrection of the Lord Jesus, and great
grace was upon them all. 34 There was not a
needy person among them, for as many as
were possessors of lands or houses sold
them, and brought the proceeds of what was
sold 35 and laid it at the apostles' feet; and
distribution was made to each as any had
need. 36 Thus Joseph who was surnamed by
the apostles Barnabas (which means, Son of
encouragement), a Levite, a native of Cyprus, 37 sold a field which belonged to him,
and brought the money and laid it at the
apostles' feet.

CHAPTER 5

But there was a man named Ananias (with his wife Sapphira) who sold some property,

2 And brought only part of the money, claiming it was the full price. (His wife had agreed to this deception.)

3 But Peter said, "Ananias, Satan has filled your heart. When you claimed this was the full price, you were lying to the Holy Spirit.

Ananias and Sapphira punished

5 But a man named Ananias with his
wife Sapphira sold a piece of property,
2 and with his wife's knowledge he kept back
some of the proceeds, and brought only a
part and laid it at the apostles' feet. 3 But
Peter said, "Ananias, why has Satan filled
your heart to lie to the Holy Spirit and to
keep back part of the proceeds of the land?

[3] Literally, "great grace was upon them all."

[c] Or *child*
[e] Or *Christ*
[f] Or *slaves*

King James

4 Whiles it remained, was it not thine own? and after it was sold, was it not in thine own power? why hast thou conceived this thing in thine heart? thou hast not lied unto men, but unto God.

5 And Ananias hearing these words fell down, and gave up the ghost: and great fear came on all them that heard these things.

6 And the young men arose, wound him up, and carried *him* out, and buried *him*.

7 And it was about the space of three hours after, when his wife, not knowing what was done, came in.

8 And Peter answered unto her, Tell me whether ye sold the land for so much? And she said, Yea, for so much.

9 Then Peter said unto her, How is it that ye have agreed together to tempt the Spirit of the Lord? behold, the feet of them which have buried thy husband *are* at the door, and shall carry thee out.

10 Then fell she down straightway at his feet, and yielded up the ghost: and the young men came in, and found her dead, and, carrying *her* forth, buried *her* by her husband.

11 And great fear came upon all the church, and upon as many as heard these things.

12 ¶ And by the hands of the apostles were many signs and wonders wrought among the people; (and they were all with one accord in Solomon's porch.

13 And of the rest durst no man join himself to them: but the people magnified them.

14 And believers were the more added to the Lord, multitudes both of men and women.)

15 Insomuch that they brought forth the sick into the streets, and laid *them* on beds and couches, that at the least the shadow of Peter passing by might overshadow some of them.

16 There came also a multitude *out* of the cities round about unto Jerusalem, bringing sick folks, and them which were vexed with unclean spirits: and they were healed every one.

17 ¶ Then the high priest rose up, and all they that were with him, (which is the sect of the Sadducees,) and were filled with indignation,

18 And laid their hands on the apostles, and put them in the common prison.

19 But the angel of the Lord by night opened the prison doors, and brought them forth, and said,

20 Go, stand and speak in the temple to the people all the words of this life.

21 And when they heard *that*, they entered into the temple early in the morning, and taught. But the high priest came, and they that were with him, and called the council together, and all the senate of the children of Israel, and sent to the prison to have them brought.

22 But when the officers came, and found them not in the prison, they returned, and told,

Amplified

4 As long as it remained unsold, was it not still your own? And [even] after it was sold, was not [the money] at your disposal *and* under your control? Why then, is it that you have proposed *and* purposed in your heart to do this thing?—How could you have the heart to do such a deed? You have not (simply) lied to men—playing false and showing yourself utterly deceitful—but to God.

5 Upon hearing these words, Ananias fell down and died. And great dread *and* terror took possession of all who heard of it.

6 And the young men arose and wrapped up [the body] and carried it out [and] buried it.

7 Now after an interval of about three hours his wife came in, not having learned of what had happened.

8 And Peter said to her, Tell me, did you sell the land for so much? Yes, she said, for so much.

9 Then Peter said to her, How could you two have agreed *and* conspired together to try to deceive the Spirit of the Lord? Listen! The feet of those who have buried your husband are at the door, and they will carry you out [also].

10 And instantly she fell down at his feet and died, and the young men entering found her dead, and they carried her out and buried her beside her husband.

11 And the whole church was appalled—great awe and strange terror and dread seized them—and all others who heard of these things.

12 Now by the hands of the apostles (special messengers) numerous *and* startling signs *and* wonders were being performed among the people. And by common consent they all met together [at the temple] in the porch *or* covered walk called Solomon's.

13 And none of those who were not of their number dared to join *and* associate with them, but the people held them in high regard *and* praised *and* made much of them.

14 More *and* more there were being added to the Lord those who believed—[that is,] those who acknowledged Jesus as their Savior and devoted themselves to Him, joined and gathered with them—crowds both of men and of women.

15 So that they [even] kept carrying out the sick into the streets and placing them on couches and sleeping pads, [in the hope] that as Peter passed by at least his shadow might fall on some of them.

16 And the people gathered also from the towns *and* hamlets around Jerusalem, bringing the sick and those troubled with foul spirits, and they were all cured.

17 But the high priest rose up and all who were his supporters, that is, the party of the Sadducees, and being filled with [t]jealousy *and* indignation *and* rage

18 They seized and arrested the apostles (special messengers) and put them in the public jail.

19 But during the night an angel of the Lord opened the prison doors and leading them out said,

20 Go, take your stand in the temple courts and declare to the people the whole doctrine concerning this Life [the eternal life which Christ revealed].

21 And when they heard this, they accordingly went into the temple about daybreak and began to teach. Now the high priest and his supporters who were with him arrived and called together the council (Sanhedrin) and [even] all the senate of the Jews, and they sent to the prison to have [the apostles] brought.

22 But when the attendants arrived there they failed to find them in the jail; so they came back and reported,

---

t) Abbott-Smith.

Living New Testament

4 The property was yours to sell or not, as you wished. And after selling it, it was yours to decide how much to give. How could you do a thing like this? You weren't lying to us, but to God."

5 As soon as Ananias heard these words, he fell to the floor, dead! Everyone was terrified,

6 And the younger men covered him with a sheet and took him out and buried him.

7 About three hours later his wife came in, not knowing what had happened.

8 Peter asked her, "Did you people sell your land for such and such a price?"

"Yes," she replied, "we did."

9 And Peter said, "How could you and your husband even think of doing a thing like this—conspiring together to test the Spirit of God's ability to know what is going on?[1] Just outside that door are the young men who buried your husband, and they will carry you out too."

10 Instantly she fell to the floor dead, and the young men came in and, seeing that she was dead, carried her out and buried her beside her husband.

11 Terror gripped the entire church and all others who heard what had happened.

12 Meanwhile, the apostles were meeting regularly at the Temple in the area known as Solomon's Hall, and they did many remarkable miracles among the people.

13 The other believers didn't dare join them, though, but all had the highest regard for them.

14 And more and more believers were added to the Lord, crowds both of men and women.

15 Sick people were brought out into the streets on beds and mats so that at least Peter's shadow would fall across some of them as he went by!

16 And crowds came in from the Jerusalem suburbs, bringing their sick folk and those possessed by demons; and every one of them was healed.

17 The High Priest and his relatives and friends among the Sadducees reacted with violent jealousy

18 And arrested the apostles, and put them in the public jail.

19 But an angel of the Lord came at night, opened the gates of the jail and brought them out. Then he told them,

20 "Go over to the Temple and preach about this Life!"

21 They arrived at the Temple about daybreak, and immediately began preaching! Later that morning[2] the High Priest and his courtiers arrived at the Temple, and, convening the Jewish Council and the entire Senate, they sent for the apostles to be brought for trial.

22 But when the police arrived at the jail, the men weren't there, so they returned to the Council and reported,

Revised Standard

[4]While it remained unsold, did it not remain
your own? And after it was sold, was it not
at your disposal? How is it that you have
contrived this deed in your heart? You have
not lied to men but to God." [5]When Ananias heard these words, he fell down and died.
And great fear came upon all who heard of
it. [6]The young men rose and wrapped him
up and carried him out and buried him.

7 After an interval of about three hours
his wife came in, not knowing what had
happened. [8]And Peter said to her, "Tell me
whether you sold the land for so much."
And she said, "Yes, for so much." [9]But
Peter said to her, "How is it that you have
agreed together to tempt the Spirit of the
Lord? Hark, the feet of those that have
buried your husband are at the door, and
they will carry you out." [10]Immediately she
fell down at his feet and died. When the
young men came in they found her dead,
and they carried her out and buried her
beside her husband. [11]And great fear came
upon the whole church, and upon all who
heard of these things.

Converts multiplied

12 Now many signs and wonders were
done among the people by the hands of the
apostles. And they were all together in Solomon's Portico. [13]None of the rest dared join
them, but the people held them in high hon-
or. [14]And more than ever believers were
added to the Lord, multitudes both of men
and women, [15]so that they even carried
out the sick into the streets, and laid them
on beds and pallets, that as Peter came by
at least his shadow might fall on some of
them. [16]The people also gathered from the
towns around Jerusalem, bringing the sick
and those afflicted with unclean spirits, and
they were all healed.

The apostles imprisoned

17 But the high priest rose up and all
who were with him, that is, the party of the
Sadducees, and filled with jealousy [18]they
arrested the apostles and put them in the
common prison. [19]But at night an angel of
the Lord opened the prison doors and
brought them out and said, [20]"Go and stand
in the temple and speak to the people all the
words of this Life." [21]And when they heard
this, they entered the temple at daybreak
and taught.

Now the high priest came and those who
were with him and called together the council and all the senate of Israel, and sent to
the prison to have them brought. [22]But
when the officers came, they did not find
them in the prison, and they returned and

---

[1] Literally, "to try the Spirit of the Lord."
[2] Implied.

King James

23 Saying, The prison truly found we shut with all safety, and the keepers standing without before the doors: but when we had opened, we found no man within.

24 Now when the high priest and the captain of the temple and the chief priests heard these things, they doubted of them whereunto this would grow.

25 Then came one and told them, saying, Behold, the men whom ye put in prison are standing in the temple, and teaching the people.

26 Then went the captain with the officers, and brought them without violence: for they feared the people, lest they should have been stoned.

27 And when they had brought them, they set *them* before the council: and the high priest asked them,

28 Saying, Did not we straitly command you that ye should not teach in this name? and, behold, ye have filled Jerusalem with your doctrine, and intend to bring this man's blood upon us.

29 ¶ Then Peter and the *other* apostles answered and said, We ought to obey God rather than men.

30 The God of our fathers raised up Jesus, whom ye slew and hanged on a tree.

31 Him hath God exalted with his right hand *to be* a Prince and a Saviour, for to give repentance to Israel, and forgiveness of sins.

32 And we are his witnesses of these things; and *so is* also the Holy Ghost, whom God hath given to them that obey him.

33 ¶ When they heard *that,* they were cut *to the heart,* and took counsel to slay them.

34 Then stood there up one in the council, a Pharisee named Gamaliel, a doctor of the law, had in reputation among all the people, and commanded to put the apostles forth a little space;

35 And said unto them, Ye men of Israel, take heed to yourselves what ye intend to do as touching these men.

36 For before these days rose up Theudas, boasting himself to be somebody; to whom a number of men, about four hundred, joined themselves: who was slain; and all, as many as obeyed him, were scattered, and brought to nought.

37 After this man rose up Judas of Galilee in the days of the taxing, and drew away much people after him: he also perished; and all, *even* as many as obeyed him, were dispersed.

38 And now I say unto you, Refrain from these men, and let them alone: for if this counsel or this work be of men, it will come to nought:

39 But if it be of God, ye cannot overthrow it; lest haply ye be found even to fight against God.

40 And to him they agreed: and when they had called the apostles, and beaten *them,* they commanded that they should not speak in the name of Jesus, and let them go.

41 ¶ And they departed from the presence of the council, rejoicing that they were counted worthy to suffer shame for his name.

Amplified

23 We found the prison quite safely locked up and the guards were on duty outside the doors, but when we opened [it] we found no one on the inside.

24 Now when the military leader of the temple area and the chief priests heard these facts, they were much perplexed *and* thoroughly at a loss about them, wondering into what this might grow.

25 But some man came and reported to them, saying, Listen! The men whom you put in jail are standing [right here] in the temple and teaching the people!

26 Then the military leader went with the attendants and brought [the prisoners], but without violence for they dreaded the people lest they be stoned by them.

27 So they brought them [and] set them before the council (Sanhedrin). And the high priest examined them by questioning,

28 Saying, We definitely commanded *and* strictly charged you not to teach in *or* about this Name; yet here you have flooded Jerusalem with your doctrine and you intend to bring this [u]Man's blood upon us.

29 Then Peter and the apostles replied, We must obey God rather than men.

30 The God of our forefathers raised up Jesus Whom you killed by hanging Him on a tree (cross). [Deut. 21:22, 23.]

31 God exalted Him to His right hand to be Prince *and* Leader and Savior *and* Deliverer *and* Preserver, in order to grant repentance to Israel and to bestow forgiveness *and* release from sins.

32 And we are witnesses of these things, and the Holy Spirit is also, Whom God has bestowed on those who obey Him.

33 Now when they heard this they were cut to the heart *and* infuriated and wanted to kill the disciples.

34 But a certain Pharisee in the council (Sanhedrin) named Gamaliel, a teacher of the Law, highly esteemed by all the people, standing up, ordered that the apostles be taken outside for a little while.

35 Then he [addressed the council] saying, Men of Israel, take care in regard to what you propose to do concerning these men.

36 For before our time there arose Theudas, asserting himself to be a person of importance, with whom a number of men allied themselves, about four hundred; but he was killed and all who had listened to *and* adhered to him were scattered and brought to nothing.

37 And after this one, rose up Judas the Galilean, [who led an uprising] during the time of the census and drew away a popular following after him; he also perished and all his adherents were scattered.

38 Now in the present case let me say to you, stand off (withdraw) from these men and let them alone. For if this doctrine *or* purpose or undertaking *or* movement is of human origin, it will fail—be overthrown and come to nothing;

39 But if it is of God, you will not be able to stop *or* overthrow or destroy them; you might even be found fighting against God!

40 So, convinced by him they took his advice, and summoning the apostles they flogged them and sternly forbade them to speak in *or* about the name of Jesus, and allowed them to go.

41 So they went out from the presence of the council (Sanhedrin), rejoicing that they were being counted worthy—dignified by the indignity—to suffer shame *and* be exposed to disgrace for [the sake of] His name.

---

u) Capitalized because of what He is, the spotless Son of God, not what the speakers may have thought Him to be.

Living New Testament

23 "The jail doors were locked, and the guards were standing outside, but when we opened the gates, no one was there!"

24 When the police captain[3] and the chief priests heard this, they were frantic, wondering what would happen next and where all this would end!

25 Then someone arrived with the news that the men they had jailed were out in the Temple, preaching to the people!

26, 27 The police captain went with his officers and arrested them (without violence, for they were afraid the people would kill them if they roughed up the disciples) and brought them in before the council.

28 "Didn't we tell you never again to preach about this Jesus?" the High Priest demanded. "And instead you have filled all Jerusalem with your teaching and intend to bring the blame for this man's death on us!"

29 But Peter and the apostles replied, "We must obey God rather than men.

30 The God of our ancestors brought Jesus back to life again after you had killed Him by hanging Him on a cross.

31 Then, with mighty power, God exalted Him to be a Prince and Savior, so that the people of Israel would have an opportunity for repentance, and for their sins to be forgiven.

32 And we are witnesses of these things, and so is the Holy Spirit, who is given by God to all who obey Him."

33 At this, the Council was furious, and decided to kill them.

34 But one of their members, a Pharisee named Gamaliel, (an expert on religious law and very popular with the people), stood up and requested that the apostles be sent outside the Council Chamber while he talked.

35 Then he addressed his colleagues as follows: "Men of Israel, take care what you are planning to do to these men!

36 Some time ago there was that fellow Theudas, who pretended to be someone great. About 400 others joined him, but he was killed, and his followers were harmlessly dispersed.

37 After him, at the time of the taxation, there was Judas of Galilee. He drew away some people as disciples, but he also died, and his followers scattered.

38 And so my advice is, leave these men alone. If what they teach and do is merely on their own, it will soon be overthrown.

39 But if it is of God, you will not be able to stop them, lest you find yourselves fighting even against God."

40 The Council accepted his advice, called in the apostles, had them beaten, and then told them never again to speak in the name of Jesus, and finally let them go.

41 They left the Council Chamber rejoicing that God had counted them worthy to suffer dishonor for His name.

[3] Literally, "the captain of the Temple."

Revised Standard

reported, 23"We found the prison securely
locked and the sentries standing at the
doors, but when we opened it we found no
one inside." 24Now when the captain of the
temple and the chief priests heard these
words, they were much perplexed about
them, wondering what this would come to.
25And some one came and told them, "The
men whom you put in prison are standing in
the temple and teaching the people."
26Then the captain with the officers went
and brought them, but without violence, for
they were afraid of being stoned by the
people.
27 And when they had brought them,
they set them before the council. And the
high priest questioned them, 28saying, "We
strictly charged you not to teach in this
name, yet here you have filled Jerusalem
with your teaching and you intend to bring
this man's blood upon us." 29But Peter and
the apostles answered, "We must obey God
rather than men. 30The God of our fathers
raised Jesus whom you killed by hanging
him on a tree. 31God exalted him at his
right hand as Leader and Savior, to give
repentance to Israel and forgiveness of sins.
32And we are witnesses to these things, and
so is the Holy Spirit whom God has given to
those who obey him."

The counsel of Gamaliel

33 When they heard this they were enraged and wanted to kill them. 34But a
Pharisee in the council named Gamaliel, a
teacher of the law, held in honor by all the
people, stood up and ordered the men to be
put outside for a while. 35And he said to
them, "Men of Israel, take care what you do
with these men. 36For before these days
Theudas arose, giving himself out to be
somebody, and a number of men, about
four hundred, joined him; but he was slain
and all who followed him were dispersed
and came to nothing. 37After him Judas the
Galilean arose in the days of the census and
drew away some of the people after him; he
also perished, and all who followed him
were scattered. 38So in the present case I
tell you, keep away from these men and let
them alone; for if this plan or this undertaking is of men, it will fail; 39but if it is of God,
you will not be able to overthrow them. You
might even be found opposing God!"
40 So they took his advice, and when
they had called in the apostles, they beat
them and charged them not to speak in the
name of Jesus, and let them go. 41Then
they left the presence of the council, rejoicing that they were counted worthy to suffer

King James

42 And daily in the temple, and in every house, they ceased not to teach and preach Jesus Christ.

CHAPTER 6

AND in those days, when the number of the disciples was multiplied, there arose a murmuring of the Grecians against the Hebrews, because their widows were neglected in the daily ministration.

2 Then the twelve called the multitude of the disciples *unto them*, and said, It is not reason that we should leave the word of God, and serve tables.

3 Wherefore, brethren, look ye out among you seven men of honest report, full of the Holy Ghost and wisdom, whom we may appoint over this business.

4 But we will give ourselves continually to prayer, and to the minstry of the word.

5 ¶ And the saying pleased the whole multitude: and they chose Stephen, a man full of faith and of the Holy Ghost, and Philip, and Prochorus, and Nicanor, and Timon, and Parmenas, and Nicolas a proselyte of Antioch:

6 Whom they set before the apostles: and when they had prayed, they laid *their* hands on them.

7 And the word of God increased; and the number of the disciples multiplied in Jerusalem greatly; and a great company of the priests were obedient to the faith.

8 And Stephen, full of faith and power, did great wonders and miracles among the people.

9 ¶ Then there arose certain of the synagogue, which is called *the synagogue* of the Libertines, and Cyrenians, and Alexandrians, and of them of Cilicia and of Asia, disputing with Stephen.

10 And they were not able to resist the wisdom and the spirit by which he spake.

11 Then they suborned men, which said, We have heard him speak blasphemous words against Moses, and *against* God.

12 And they stirred up the people, and the elders, and the scribes, and came upon *him*, and caught him, and brought *him* to the council,

13 And set up false witnesses, which said, This man ceaseth not to speak blasphemous words against this holy place, and the law:

14 For we have heard him say, that this Jesus of Nazareth shall destroy this place, and shall change the customs which Moses delivered us.

15 And all that sat in the council, looking stedfastly on him, saw his face as it had been the face of an angel.

Amplified

42 Yet [in spite of the threats] they never ceased for a single day both in the temple area and at home to teach *and* to proclaim the good news (Gospel) of Jesus [as] the Christ, the Messiah.

CHAPTER 6

NOW about this time, when the number of the disciples was greatly increasing, complaint was made by the Hellenists (the Greek-speaking Jews), against the [native] Hebrews because their widows were being overlooked *and* neglected in the daily ministration—distribution [of relief].

2 So the twelve (apostles) convened the multitude of the disciples and said, It is not seemly *or* desirable *or* right that we should have to give up *or* neglect [preaching] the Word of God in order to attend to serving at tables *and* superintending the distribution of food.

3 Therefore select out from among yourselves, brethren, seven men of good *and* attested character *and* repute, full of the (Holy) Spirit and wisdom, whom we may assign to look after this business *and* duty.

4 But we will continue to devote ourselves steadfastly to prayer and the ministry of the Word.

5 And the suggestion pleased the whole assembly, and they selected Stephen, a man full of faith [that is, of a strong and welcome belief that Jesus is the Messiah], and full of *and* controlled by the Holy Spirit; and Philip, and Prochorus, and Nicanor, and Timon, and Parmenas, and Nicolaus, a proselyte [convert] from Antioch.

6 These they presented to the apostles, who after prayer laid their hands on them.

7 And the message of God kept on spreading, and the number of disciples multiplied greatly in Jerusalem; and [besides] a large number of the priests were obedient to the faith [in Jesus as the Messiah, through Whom is obtained eternal salvation in the kingdom of God].

8 Now Stephen, full of grace—divine blessing and favor—worked great wonders and signs (miracles) among the people.

9 However, some of those who belonged to the synagogue of the Freedmen [freed Jewish slaves], as it was called, and [of the synagogues] of the Cyrenians, and of the Alexandrians, and of those from Cilicia and [the province of] Asia, arose [and undertook] to debate *and* dispute with Stephen.

10 But they were not able to resist the intelligence *and* the wisdom and [the inspiration of] the Spirit with which he spoke.

11 So they [secretly] instigated *and* instructed men to say, We have heard this man speak, using slanderous *and* abusive *and* blasphemous language against Moses and God.

12 [Thus] they incited the people as well as the elders and the scribes, and they came upon Stephen and arrested him and took him before the council (Sanhedrin).

13 And they brought forward false witnesses who asserted, This man never stops making statements against this sacred place and the Law [of Moses];

14 For we have heard him say that this Jesus the Nazarene will tear down *and* destroy this place, and will alter the institutions *and* usages which Moses transmitted to us.

15 Then all who sat in the council (Sanhedrin), as they gazed intently at Stephen, saw that his face [had the appearance of] the face of an angel.

Living New Testament

42 And every day, in the Temple and in the city,[4] they continued to teach and preach that Jesus is the Messiah.

Revised Standard

dishonor for the name. 42 And every day in
the temple and at home they did not cease
teaching and preaching Jesus as the
Christ.

CHAPTER 6

But with the believers multiplying rapidly, there were rumblings of discontent. Those who spoke only Greek complained that their widows were being discriminated against, that they were not being given as much food, in the daily distribution, as the widows who spoke Hebrew.

2 So the Twelve called a meeting of all the believers. "We should spend our time preaching, not administering a feeding program,"[1] they said.

3 "Now look around among yourselves, dear brothers, and select seven men, wise and full of the Holy Spirit, who are well thought of by everyone; and we will put them in charge of this business.

4 Then we can spend our time in prayer, preaching, and teaching."

5 This sounded reasonable to the whole assembly, and they elected the following:

Stephen (a man unusually full of faith and the Holy Spirit),
Philip,
Prochorus,
Nicanor,
Timon,
Parmenas,
Nicolaus of Antioch (a Gentile convert to the Jewish faith, who had become a Christian).

6 These seven were presented to the apostles, who prayed for them and laid their hands on them in blessing.

* * * * *

7 God's message was preached in ever-widening circles, and the number of disciples increased vastly in Jerusalem; and many of the Jewish priests were converted too.

8 Stephen, the man so full of faith and the Holy Spirit's power,[2] did spectacular miracles among the people.

9 But one day some of the men from the Jewish cult of "The Freedmen" started an argument with him, and they were soon joined by Jews from Cyrene, Alexandria in Egypt, and the Turkish provinces of Cilicia, and Ausia.

10 But none of them were able to stand against Stephen's wisdom and spirit.

11 So they brought in some men to lie about him, claiming they had heard Stephen curse Moses, and even God.

12 This accusation roused the crowds to fury against Stephen, and the Jewish leaders[3] arrested him and brought him before the Council.

13 The lying witnesses testified again that Stephen was constantly speaking against the Temple and against the laws of Moses.

14 They declared, "We have heard him say that this fellow Jesus of Nazareth will destroy the Temple, and throw out all of Moses' laws."

15 At this point everyone in the Council Chamber saw Stephen's face become as radiant as an angel's!

[4] Literally, "at home." Possibly, "from house to house," or perhaps, in their meeting halls."

[1] Literally, "it is not fit that we should forsake the Word of God and serve tables."

[2] Literally, "full of grace and power." See verse 5.

[3] Literally, "the elders and the Scribes."

The appointment of the seven

6 Now in these days when the disciples
were increasing in number, the Helen-
ists murmured against the Hebrews because
their widows were neglected in the daily
distribution. 2 And the twelve summoned the
body of the disciples and said, "It is not
right that we should give up preaching the
word of God to serve tables. 3 Therefore,
brethren, pick out from among you seven
men of good repute, full of the Spirit and of
wisdom, whom we may appoint to this duty.
4 But we will devote ourselves to prayer and
to the ministry of the word." 5 And what
they said pleased the whole multitude, and
they chose Stephen, a man full of faith and
of the Holy Spirit, and Philip, and Prochorus, and Nicanor, and Timon, and Parmenas, and Nicolaus, a proselyte of Antioch.
6 These they set before the apostles, and
they prayed and laid their hands upon
them. 7 And the word of God increased; and
the number of the disciples multiplied greatly in Jerusalem, and a great many of the
priests were obedient to the faith.

The arrest of Stephen

8 And Stephen, full of grace and power,
did great wonders and signs among the people. 9 Then some of those who belonged to
the synagogue of the Freedmen (as it was
called), and of the Cyrenians, and of the
Alexandrians, and of those from Cilicia and
Asia, arose and disputed with Stephen.
10 But they could not withstand the wisdom
and the spirit with which he spoke. 11 Then
they secretly instigated men, who said, "We
have heard him speak blasphemous words
against Moses and God." 12 And they stirred
up the people and the elders and the scribes,
and they came upon him and seized him and
brought him before the council, 13 and set
up false witnesses who said, "This man never ceases to speak words against this holy
place and the law; 14 for we have heard him
say that this Jesus of Nazareth will destroy
this place, and will change the customs
which Moses delivered to us." 15 And gazing
at him, all who sat in the council saw that
his face was like the face of an angel.

King James

CHAPTER 7

THEN said the high priest, Are these things so?

2 And he said, Men, brethren, and fathers, hearken; The God of glory appeared unto our father Abraham, when he was in Mesopotamia, before he dwelt in Charran,

3 And said unto him, Get thee out of thy country, and from thy kindred, and come into the land which I shall shew thee.

4 Then came he out of the land of the Chaldæans, and dwelt in Charran: and from thence, when his father was dead, he removed him into this land, wherein ye now dwell.

5 And he gave him none inheritance in it, no, not *so much as* to set his foot on: yet he promised that he would give it to him for a possession, and to his seed after him, when *as yet* he had no child.

6 And God spake on this wise, That his seed should sojourn in a strange land; and that they should bring them into bondage, and entreat *them* evil four hundred years.

7 And the nation to whom they shall be in bondage will I judge, said God: and after that shall they come forth, and serve me in this place.

8 And he gave him the covenant of circumcision: and so *Abraham* begat Isaac, and circumcised him the eighth day; and Isaac *begat* Jacob; and Jacob *begat* the twelve patriarchs.

9 And the patriarchs, moved with envy, sold Joseph into Egypt: but God was with him,

10 And delivered him out of all his afflictions, and gave him favour and wisdom in the sight of Pharaoh king of Egypt; and he made him governor over Egypt and all his house.

11 Now there came a dearth over all the land of Egypt and Chanaan, and great affliction: and our fathers found no sustenance.

12 But when Jacob heard that there was corn in Egypt, he sent out our fathers first.

13 And at the second *time* Joseph was made known to his brethren; and Joseph's kindred was made known unto Pharaoh.

14 Then sent Joseph, and called his father Jacob to *him*, and all his kindred, threescore and fifteen souls.

15 So Jacob went down into Egypt, and died, he, and our fathers,

16 And were carried over into Sychem, and laid in the sepulchre that Abraham bought for a sum of money of the sons of Emmor *the father* of Sychem.

17 But when the time of the promise drew nigh, which God had sworn to Abraham, the people grew and multiplied in Egypt,

Amplified

CHAPTER 7

AND the high priest asked [Stephen], Are these charges true?

2 And he answered, Brethren and fathers, listen to me. The God of glory appeared to our forefather Abraham, when he was still in Mesopotamia, before he [went to] live in Haran, [Ps. 29:3; Gen. 11:31; 15:7].

3 And He said to him, Leave your own country and your relatives and come into the land (region) that I will point out to you. [Gen. 12:1.]

4 So then he went forth from the land of the Chaldeans and settled in Haran. And from there, after his father died [God] transferred him to this country in which you are now dwelling. [Gen. 11:31; 15:7; 12:5.]

5 Yet He gave him no inheritable property in it, [no] not even enough ground to set his foot on; but He promised that He would give it to him for a [v]permanent possession and to his descendants after him, [even though as yet] he had no child. [Deut. 2:5; Gen. 12:7; 17:8.]

6 And this is [in effect] what God told him: That his descendants would be aliens (sojourners) in a land belonging to other people, who would bring them into bondage and ill-treat them four hundred years.

7 But I will judge the nation to whom they shall be slaves, said God, and after that they shall escape *and* come forth and worship Me in this [very] place. [Gen. 15:13, 14; Exod. 3:12.]

8 And [God] made with Abraham a covenant—an agreement to be religiously observed—[v]of which circumcision was the seal. And under these circumstances [Abraham] became the father of Isaac, and circumcised him on the eighth day; and Isaac [did so] when he became the father of Jacob, and Jacob [when each of his sons was born], the twelve patriarchs. [Gen. 17:10-14; 21:2-4; 25:26; 29:31-35; 30:1-24; 35:16-26.]

9 And the patriarchs [Jacob's sons] boiling with envy *and* hatred *and* anger, sold Joseph into slavery in Egypt, but God was with him, [Gen. 37:11, 28; 45:4.]

10 And delivered him from all his distressing afflictions, and won him goodwill *and* favor and wisdom *and* understanding in the sight of Pharaoh, king of Egypt, who made him governor over Egypt and all his house. [Gen. 39:2, 3, 21; 41:40-46; Ps. 105:21.]

11 Then there came a famine over all of Egypt and Canaan, with great distress, and our forefathers could find no fodder [for the cattle] *or* vegetable sustenance [for their households]. [Gen. 41:54, 55; 42:5.]

12 But when Jacob heard that there was grain in Egypt, he sent forth our forefathers [to go there on their] first trip. [Gen. 42:2.]

13 And on their second visit Joseph revealed [himself] to his brothers, and the family of Joseph became known to Pharaoh, *and* his origin *and* race. [Gen. 45:1-4.]

14 And Joseph sent an invitation calling to himself Jacob his father and all his kindred, seventy-five persons in all. [Gen. 45:9, 10.]

15 And Jacob went down into Egypt, where he himself died, as did [also] our forefathers; [Deut. 10:22.]

16 And their bodies were taken back to Shechem and laid in the tomb which Abraham had purchased for a sum of silver money from the sons of Hamor in Shechem. [Josh. 24:32; Gen. 50:13.]

17 But [in proportion] as the time for the fulfillment of the promise drew near, which God had made to Abraham, the [Hebrew] people increased and multiplied in Egypt,

---

v) Vincent.

Living New Testament

CHAPTER 7

Then the High Priest asked him, "Are these accusations true?"

2 This was Stephen's lengthy reply:

"The glorious God appeared to our ancestor Abraham in Iraq[1] before he moved to Syria,[2]

3 And told him to leave his native land, to say good-bye to his relatives and to start out for a country that God would direct him to.

4 So he left the land of the Chaldeans and lived in Haran, in Syria, until his father died. Then God brought him here to the land of Israel,

5 But gave him no property of his own, not one little tract of land. However, God promised that eventually the whole country would belong to him and his descendants—though as yet he had no children!

6 But God also told him that these descendants of his would leave the land and live in a foreign country and there become slaves for 400 years.

7 'But I will punish the nation that enslaves them,' God told him, 'and afterwards My people will return to this land of Israel and worship Me here.'

8 God also gave Abraham the ceremony of circumcision at that time, as evidence of the covenant between God and the people of Abraham. And so Isaac, Abraham's son, was circumcised when he was eight days old. Isaac became the father of Jacob, and Jacob was the father of the twelve patriarchs of the Jewish nation.

9 These men were very jealous of Joseph and sold him to be a slave in Egypt. But God was with him,

10 And delivered him out of all of his anguish, and gave him favor before Pharaoh, king of Egypt. God also gave Joseph unusual wisdom, so that Pharaoh appointed him governor over all Egypt, as well as putting him in charge of all the affairs of the palace.

11 But a famine developed in Egypt and Canaan and there was great misery for our ancestors. When their food was gone,

12 Jacob heard that there was still grain in Egypt, so he sent his sons[3] to buy some.

13 The second time they went, Joseph revealed his identity to his brothers, and they were introduced to Pharaoh.

14 Then Joseph sent for his father Jacob and all his brothers' families to come to Egypt, 75 persons in all.

15 So Jacob came to Egypt, where he died, and all his sons.

16 All of them were taken to Shechem and buried in the tomb Abraham bought from the sons of Hamor, Shechem's father.

17, 18 As the time drew near when God would fulfill His promise to Abraham to free his descendants from slavery, the Jewish people greatly multiplied in Egypt; but then

---

[1] Literally, "Mesopotamia."
[2] Literally, "Haran," a city in the area we now know as Syria.
[3] Literally, "our fathers."

Revised Standard

The defense of Stephen

7 And the high priest said, "Is this so?"
[2]And Stephen said:
"Brethren and fathers, hear me. The God
of glory appeared to our father Abraham,
when he was in Mesopotamia, before he
lived in Haran, [3]and said to him, 'Depart
from your land and from your kindred and
go into the land which I will show you.'
[4]Then he departed from the land of the
Chaldeans, and lived in Haran. And after his
father died, God removed him from there
into this land in which you are now living;
[5]yet he gave him no inheritance in it, not
even a foot's length, but promised to give it
to him in possession and to his posterity
after him, though he had no child. [6]And
God spoke to this effect, that his posterity
would be aliens in a land belonging to others, who would enslave them and ill-treat
them four hundred years. [7]'But I will judge
the nation which they serve,' said God, 'and
after that they shall come out and worship
me in this place.' [8]And he gave him the
covenant of circumcision. And so Abraham
became the father of Isaac, and circumcised
him on the eighth day; and Isaac became
the father of Jacob, and Jacob of the twelve
patriarchs.

The age of the patriarchs

9 "And the patriarchs, jealous of Joseph,
sold him into Egypt; but God was with him,
[10]and rescued him out of all his afflictions,
and gave him favor and wisdom before
Pharaoh, king of Egypt, who made him
governor over Egypt and over all his household. [11]Now there came a famine throughout all Egypt and Canaan, and great affliction, and our fathers could find no food.
[12]But when Jacob heard that there was
grain in Egypt, he sent forth our fathers
the first time. [13]And at the second visit
Joseph made himself known to his brothers,
and Joseph's family became known to Pharaoh. [14]And Joseph sent and called to him
Jacob his father and all his kindred, seventy-five souls; [15]and Jacob went down into
Egypt. And he died, himself and our fathers, [16]and they were carried back to
Shechem and laid in the tomb that Abraham
had bought for a sum of silver from the sons
of Hamor in Shechem.

The leadership of Moses

17 "But as the time of the promise drew near, which God had granted to Abraham, the people grew and multiplied in Egypt

King James

18 Till another king arose, which knew not Joseph.

19 The same dealt subtilly with our kindred, and evil entreated our fathers, so that they cast out their young children, to the end they might not live.

20 In which time Moses was born, and was exceeding fair, and nourished up in his father's house three months:

21 And when he was cast out, Pharaoh's daughter took him up, and nourished him for her own son.

22 And Moses was learned in all the wisdom of the Egyptians, and was mighty in words and in deeds.

23 And when he was full forty years old, it came into his heart to visit his brethren the children of Israel.

24 And seeing one *of them* suffer wrong, he defended *him,* and avenged him that was oppressed, and smote the Egyptian:

25 For he supposed his brethren would have understood how that God by his hand would deliver them: but they understood not.

26 And the next day he shewed himself unto them as they strove, and would have set them at one again, saying, Sirs, ye are brethren; why do ye wrong one to another?

27 But he that did his neighbour wrong thrust him away, saying, Who made thee a ruler and a judge over us?

28 Wilt thou kill me, as thou diddest the Egyptian yesterday?

29 Then fled Moses at this saying, and was a stranger in the land of Madian, where he begat two sons.

30 And when forty years were expired, there appeared to him in the wilderness of mount Sina an angel of the Lord in a flame of fire in a bush.

31 When Moses saw *it,* he wondered at the sight: and as he drew near to behold *it,* a voice of the Lord came unto him,

32 *Saying,* I *am* the God of thy fathers, the God of Abraham, and the God of Isaac, and the God of Jacob. Then Moses trembled, and durst not behold.

33 Then said the Lord to him, Put off thy shoes from thy feet: for the place where thou standest is holy ground.

34 I have seen, I have seen the affliction of my people which is in Egypt, and I have heard their groaning, and am come down to deliver them. And now come, I will send thee into Egypt.

35 This Moses whom they refused, saying, Who made thee a ruler and a judge? the same did God send *to be* a ruler and a deliverer by the hand of the angel which appeared to him in the bush.

36 He brought them out, after that he had shewed wonders and signs in the land of Egypt, and in the Red sea, and in the wilderness forty years.

Amplified

18 Until [the time when] there arose over Egypt another *and* a different king who did not know Joseph—his history and services, and did not recognize his merits. [Exod. 1:7, 8.]

19 He dealt treacherously with *and* defrauded our race; he abused *and* oppressed our forefathers, forcing them to expose their babies so that they might not be kept alive. [Exod. 1:7-11, 15-22.]

20 At this juncture Moses was born, and was exceedingly beautiful in God's sight; for three months he was nurtured in his father's house; [Exod. 2:2.]

21 Then when he was exposed [to perish], the daughter of Pharaoh rescued him and took him *and* reared him as her own son. [Exod. 2:5, 6, 10.]

22 So Moses was educated in all the wisdom *and* culture of the Egyptians, and he was mighty (powerful) in his speech and deeds.

23 And when he was in his fortieth year, it came into his heart to visit his kinsmen the children of Israel [w]with help and to care for them.

24 And on seeing one of them being unjustly treated, he defended the oppressed man and avenged him by striking down the Egyptian *and* slaying [him].

25 He expected his brethren to understand that God was granting them deliverance by his hand—taking it for granted that they would accept him; but they did not understand.

26 Then on the next day he [x]suddenly appeared to some who were quarreling *and* fighting among themselves, and he urged them to make peace *and* become reconciled, saying, Men, you are brethren; why do you abuse *and* wrong one another?

27 Whereupon the man who was abusing his neighbor pushed [Moses] aside, saying, Who appointed you a ruler (umpire) and a judge over us?

28 Do you intend to slay me as you slew the Egyptian yesterday?

29 At that reply Moses sought safety by flight, and he was an exile *and* an alien in the country of Midian, where he became the father of two sons. [Exod. 2:11-15, 22; 18:3, 4.]

30 And when forty years had gone by, there appeared to him in the wilderness (desert) of Mount Sinai an angel, in the flame of a burning bramble-bush.

31 When Moses saw it he was astonished *and* marvelled at the sight; but when he went close to investigate, there came to him the voice of the Lord, saying,

32 I am the God of your forefathers, the God of Abraham and of Isaac and of Jacob. And Moses trembled *and* was so terrified that he did not venture to look.

33 Then the Lord said to him, Remove the sandals from your feet, for the place where you are standing is holy ground *and* worthy of veneration.

34 Because I have most assuredly seen the abuse *and* oppression of My people in Eygpt, and have heard their sighing *and* groaning, I have come down to rescue them. So, now come! I will send you back to Egypt [as My messenger]. [Exod. 3:1-10.]

35 It was this very Moses whom they had denied—disowned and rejected—saying, Who made you our ruler (referee) and judge? whom God sent to be a ruler and deliverer *and* redeemer, by *and* with the [protecting and helping] hand of the Angel that appeared to him in the bramble-bush. [Exod. 2:14.]

36 He it was who led them forth, having worked wonders and signs in Egypt and at the Red Sea, and during the forty years in the wilderness (desert). [Exod. 7:3; 14:21; Num. 14:33.]

---

w) Abbott-Smith.
x) Vincent.

Living New Testament

a king was crowned who had no respect for Joseph's memory.

19 This king plotted against our race, forcing parents to abandon their children in the fields.

20 About that time Moses was born—a child of divine beauty. His parents hid him at home for three months,

21 And when at last they could no longer keep him hidden, and had to abandon him, Pharaoh's daughter found him and adopted him as her own son,

22 And taught him all the wisdom of the Egyptians, and he became a mighty prince and orator.[4]

23 One day as he was nearing his 40th birthday, it came into his mind to visit his brothers, the people of Israel.

24 During this visit he saw an Egyptian mistreating a man of Israel. So Moses killed the Egyptian.

25 Moses supposed his brothers would realize that God had sent him to help them, but they didn't.

26 The next day he visited them again and saw two men of Israel fighting. He tried to be a peacemaker. 'Gentlemen,' he said, 'you are brothers and shouldn't be fighting like this! It is wrong!'

27 But the man in the wrong told Moses to mind his own business. 'Who made *you* a ruler and judge over us?' he asked.

28 'Are you going to kill me as you killed that Egyptian yesterday?'

29 At this, Moses fled the country, and lived in the land of Midian, where his two sons were born.

30 Forty years later, in the desert near Mount Sinai, an Angel appeared to him in a flame of fire in a bush.

31 Moses saw it and wondered what it was, and as he ran to see, the voice of the Lord called out to him,

32 'I am the God of your ancestors—of Abraham, Isaac and Jacob.' Moses shook with terror and dared not look.

33 And the Lord said to him, 'Take off your shoes, for you are standing on holy ground.

34 I have seen the anguish of My people in Egypt and have heard their cries. I have come down to deliver them. Come, I will send you to Egypt.'

35 And so God sent back the same man His people had previously rejected with the question, 'Who made *you* a ruler and judge over us?' Moses was sent to be their ruler and savior.

36 And by means of many remarkable miracles he led them out of Egypt and through the Red Sea, and back and forth through the wilderness for 40 years.

37 Moses himself told the people of Israel, 'God will raise up a Prophet much like me[5] from among your brothers.'

Revised Standard

18 till there arose over Egypt another king
who had not known Joseph. 19 He dealt
craftily with our race and forced our fathers
to expose their infants, that they might not
be kept alive. 20 At this time Moses was
born, and was beautiful before God. And he
was brought up for three months in his
father's house; 21 and when he was exposed,
Pharaoh's daughter adopted him and
brought him up as her own son. 22 And
Moses was instructed in all the wisdom of
the Egyptians, and he was mighty in his
words and deeds.

23 "When he was forty years old, it came
into his heart to visit his brethren, the sons
of Israel. 24 And seeing one of them being
wronged, he defended the oppressed man
and avenged him by striking the Egyptian.
25 He supposed that his brethren understood that God was giving them deliverance
by his hand, but they did not understand.
26 And on the following day he appeared to
them as they were quarreling and would
have reconciled them, saying, 'Men, you are
brethren, why do you wrong each other?'
27 But the man who was wronging his neighbor thrust him aside, saying, 'Who made you
a ruler and a judge over us? 28 Do you want
to kill me as you killed the Egyptian yesterday?' 29 At this retort Moses fled, and became an exile in the land of Midian, where
he became the father of two sons.

30 "Now when forty years had passed, an
angel appeared to him in the wilderness of
Mount Sinai, in a flame of fire in a bush.
31 When Moses saw it he wondered at the
sight; and as he drew near to look the voice
of the Lord came, 32 'I am the God of your
fathers, the God of Abraham and of Isaac
and of Jacob.' And Moses trembled and did
not dare to look. 33 And the Lord said to
him, 'Take off the shoes from your feet, for
the place where you are standing is holy
ground. 34 I have surely seen the ill-treatment
of my people that are in Egypt and heard
their groaning, and I have come down to
deliver them. And now come, I will send
you to Egypt.'

Israel in the wilderness

35 "This Moses whom they refused, saying, 'Who made you a ruler and a judge?'
God sent as both ruler and deliverer by the
hand of the angel that appeared to him in
the bush. 36 He led them out, having performed wonders and signs in Egypt and at
the Red Sea, and in the wilderness for forty
years. 37 This is the Moses who said to the
Israelites, 'God will raise up for you a
prophet from your brethren as he raised me

---

[4] Literally, "mighty in word and works."
[5] Literally, "like unto me."

King James

37 ¶ This is that Moses, which said unto the children of Israel, A prophet shall the Lord your God raise up unto you of your brethren, like unto me; him shall ye hear.

38 This is he, that was in the church in the wilderness with the angel which spake to him in the mount Sina, and *with* our fathers: who received the lively oracles to give unto us:

39 To whom our fathers would not obey, but thrust *him* from them, and in their hearts turned back again into Egypt,

40 Saying unto Aaron, Make us gods to go before us: for *as for* this Moses, which brought us out of the land of Egypt, we wot not what is become of him.

41 And they made a calf in those days, and offered sacrifice unto the idol, and rejoiced in the works of their own hands.

42 Then God turned, and gave them up to worship the host of heaven; as it is written in the book of the prophets, O ye house of Israel, have ye offered to me slain beasts and sacrifices *by the space of* forty years in the wilderness?

43 Yea, ye took up the tabernacle of Moloch, and the star of your god Remphan, figures which ye made to worship them: and I will carry you away beyond Babylon.

44 Our fathers had the tabernacle of witness in the wilderness, as he had appointed, speaking unto Moses, that he should make it according to the fashion that he had seen.

45 Which also our fathers that came after brought in with Jesus into the possession of the Gentiles, whom God drave out before the face of our fathers, unto the days of David;

46 Who found favour before God, and desired to find a tabernacle for the God of Jacob.

47 But Solomon built him an house.

48 Howbeit the most High dwelleth not in temples made with hands; as saith the prophet,

49 Heaven *is* my throne, and earth *is* my footstool: what house will ye build me? saith the Lord: or what *is* the place of my rest?

50 Hath not my hand made all these things?

51 ¶ Ye stiffnecked and uncircumcised in heart and ears, ye do always resist the Holy Ghost: as your fathers *did*, so *do* ye.

52 Which of the prophets have not your fathers persecuted? and they have slain them which shewed before of the coming of the Just One; of whom ye have been now the betrayers and murderers:

53 Who have received the law by the disposition of angels, and have not kept *it*.

54 ¶ When they heard these things, they were cut to the heart, and they gnashed on him with *their* teeth.

Amplified

37 It was this [very] Moses who said to the children of Israel, God will raise up for you a Prophet from among your brethren as He raised me up. [Deut. 18:15, 18.]

38 This is he who in the assembly in the wilderness (desert) was the go-between for the Angel who spoke to him on Mount Sinai, and our forefathers; and he received to be handed down to us living oracles—words that still live. [Exod. 19.]

39 [And yet] our forefathers determined not to be subject to him—refusing to listen to *or* obey him; but thrusting him aside they rejected him, and in their hearts yearned for and turned back to Egypt. [Num. 14:3, 4.]

40 And they said to Aaron, Make us gods who shall [be our leaders and] go before us; as for this Moses who led us forth from the land of Egypt, we have no knowledge of what has happened to him. [Exod. 32:1, 23.]

41 And they [even] made a calf in those days, and offered sacrifice to the idol and made merry *and* exulted in the work of their [own] hands. [Exod. 32:4, 6.]

42 But God turned [away from them] and delivered them up to worship *and* serve the host (stars) of heaven, as it is written in the book of the prophets: Did you [really] offer to Me slain beasts and sacrifices for forty years in the wilderness (desert), O house of Israel? [Jer. 19:13.]

43 [No!] You took up the tent—the portable temple—of Moloch *and* carried it [with you], and the star-idol of the god Rephan, the images which you [yourselves made that you might worship them; and I will remove you—carrying you away [into exile]—beyond Babylon. [Amos 5:25-27.]

44 Our forefathers had the tent (tabernacle) of witness in the wilderness, even as He Who directed Moses to make it had ordered, according to the pattern *and* model he had seen. [Exod. 25:9-40.]

45 Our forefathers in turn brought [this tent of witness into the land with them when] with Joshua they dispossessed the nations which God drove out before the face of our forefathers. [So it remained there] until the time of David, [Josh. 3:14-17; Deut. 32:49.]

46 Who found grace (favor and spiritual blessing) in the sight of God and prayed that he might be allowed to find a dwelling place for the God of Jacob. [II Sam. 7:8-16; Ps. 132:1-5.]

47 But it was Solomon who built a house for Him. [I Kings 6.]

48 However the Most High does not dwell in houses *and* temples made with hands; as the prophet says, [Isa. 66:1, 2.]

49 Heaven [is] My throne, and earth the footstool for my feet. What [kind of] house can you build for Me, says the Lord, or what is the place in which I can rest?

50 Was it not My hand that made all these things? [Isa. 66:1, 2.]

51 You stubborn *and* stiff-necked people, still heathenish *and* uncircumcised in heart and ears, you are always [y]actively resisting the Holy Spirit. As your forefathers [were], so you [are and so you do]! [Exod. 33:3, 5; Jer. 9:26; 6:10; Num. 27:14; Isa. 63:10.]

52 Which of the prophets did your forefathers not persecute? And they slew those who proclaimed beforehand the coming of the Righteous One, Whom you now have betrayed and murdered,

53 You who received the Law as it was ordained *and* set in order *and* delivered by angels, and [yet] you did not obey it!

54 Now upon hearing these things, they [the Jews] were cut to the heart *and* infuriated, and they ground their teeth against [Stephen].

---

y) Vincent.

Living New Testament

38 How true this proved to be, for in the wilderness, Moses was the go-between—the mediator between the people of Israel and the Angel who gave them the Law of God—the Living Word—on Mount Sinai.

39 But our fathers rejected Moses and wanted to return to Egypt.

40 They told Aaron, ‘Make idols for us, so that we will have gods to lead us back; for we don't know what has become of this Moses, who brought us out of Egypt.’

41 So they made a calf-idol and sacrificed to it, and rejoiced in this thing they had made.

42 Then God turned away from them and gave them up, and let them serve the sun, moon and stars as their gods! In the book of Amos’ prophecies the Lord God asks, ‘Was it to Me you were sacrificing during those 40 years in the desert, Israel?

43 No, your real interest was in your heathen gods—Sakkuth, and the star god Kaiway, and in all the images you made. So I will send you into captivity far away beyond Babylon.’

44 Our ancestors carried along with them a portable Temple, or Tabernacle, through the wilderness. In it they kept the stone tablets with the Ten Commandments written on them. This building was constructed in exact accordance with the plan shown to Moses by the Angel.

45 Years later, when Joshua led the battles against the Gentile nations, this Tabernacle was taken with them into their new territory, and used until the time of King David.

46 God blessed David greatly, and David asked for the privilege of building a permanent Temple for the God of Jacob.

47 But it was Solomon who actually built it.

48, 49 However, God doesn't live in temples made by human hands. ‘The heaven is My throne,’ says the Lord through His prophets, ‘and earth is My footstool. What kind of home could you build,’ asks the Lord! ‘Would I stay in it?

50 Didn't I make both heaven and earth?’

51 You stiff-necked heathen! Must you forever resist the Holy Spirit? But your fathers did, and so do you!

52 Name one prophet your ancestors didn't persecute! They even killed the ones who predicted the coming of the Righteous One—the Messiah whom you betrayed and murdered.

53 Yes, and you deliberately destroyed God's Laws, though you received them from the hands of angels.”[6]

54 The Jewish leaders were stung to fury by Stephen's accusation, and ground their teeth in rage.

Revised Standard

up.’ 38This is he who was in the congregation in the wilderness with the angel who
spoke to him at Mount Sinai, and with our
fathers; and he received living oracles to
give to us. 39Our fathers refused to obey
him, but thrust him aside, and in their hearts
they turned to Egypt, 40saying to Aaron,
‘Make for us gods to go before us; as for
this Moses who led us out from the land of
Egypt, we do not know what has become of
him.’ 41And they made a calf in those days,
and offered a sacrifice to the idol and rejoiced in the works of their hands. 42But
God turned and gave them over to worship
the host of heaven, as it is written in the
book of the prophets:

‘Did you offer to me slain beasts and
sacrifices,
forty years in the wilderness, O house of
Israel?
43 And you took up the tent of Moloch,
and the star of the god Rephan,
the figures which you made to worship;
and I will remove you beyond Babylon.’

A place to worship God

44 “Our fathers had the tent of witness in
the wilderness, even as he who spoke to
Moses directed him to make it, according to
the pattern that he had seen. 45Our fathers
in turn brought it in with Joshua when they
dispossessed the nations which God thrust
out before our fathers. So it was until the
days of David, 46who found favor in the
sight of God and asked leave to find a
habitation for the God of Jacob. 47But it
was Solomon who built a house for him.
48Yet the Most High does not dwell in
houses made with hands; as the prophet
says,

49‘Heaven is my throne,
and earth my footstool.
What house will you build for me, says
the Lord,
or what is the place of my rest?
50 Did not my hand make all these things?’

51 “You stiff-necked people, uncircumcised in heart and ears, you always resist the
Holy Spirit. As your fathers did, so do you.
52Which of the prophets did not your fathers
persecute? And they killed those who announced beforehand the coming of the
Righteous One, whom you have now betrayed and murdered, 53you who received
the law as delivered by angels and did not
keep it.”

The stoning and death of Stephen

54 Now when they heard these things
they were enraged, and they ground their

[6] Literally, “the Law as it was ordained by angels.”

King James

55 But he, being full of the Holy Ghost, looked up stedfastly into heaven, and saw the glory of God, and Jesus standing on the right hand of God,

56 And said, Behold, I see the heavens opened, and the Son of man standing on the right hand of God.

57 Then they cried out with a loud voice, and stopped their ears, and ran upon him with one accord,

58 And cast *him* out of the city, and stoned *him:* and the witnesses laid down their clothes at a young man's feet, whose name was Saul.

59 And they stoned Stephen, calling upon *God*, and saying, Lord Jesus, receive my spirit.

60 And he kneeled down, and cried with a loud voice, Lord, lay not this sin to their charge. And when he had said this, he fell asleep.

CHAPTER 8

AND Saul was consenting unto his death. And at that time there was a great persecution against the church which was at Jerusalem; and they were all scattered abroad throughout the regions of Judæa and Samaria, except the apostles.

2 And devout men carried Stephen *to his burial*, and made great lamentation over him.

3 As for Saul, he made havoc of the church, entering into every house, and haling men and women committed *them* to prison.

4 Therefore they that were scattered abroad went every where preaching the word.

5 Then Philip went down to the city of Samaria, and preached Christ unto them.

6 And the people with one accord gave heed unto those things which Philip spake, hearing and seeing the miracles which he did.

7 For unclean spirits, crying with loud voice, came out of many that were possessed *with them:* and many taken with palsies, and that were lame, were healed.

8 And there was great joy in that city.

9 But there was a certain man, called Simon, which beforetime in the same city used sorcery, and bewitched the people of Samaria, giving out that himself was some great one:

10 To whom they all gave heed, from the least to the greatest, saying, This man is the great power of God.

Amplified

55 But he, full of the Holy Spirit *and* controlled by [Him], gazed into heaven and saw the glory—the splendor and majesty—of God, and Jesus standing at God's right hand;

56 And he said, Look! I see the heavens opened, and the Son of man standing at God's right hand!

57 But they raised a great shout and put their hands over their ears and rushed together upon him.

58 Then they dragged him out of the city and began to stone him, and the witnesses placed their garments at the feet of a young man named Saul.

59 And while they were stoning Stephen, he prayed, Lord Jesus, receive *and* accept *and* welcome my spirit!

60 And falling on his knees, he cried out loudly, Lord, [z]fix not this sin upon them—lay it not to their charge! And when he had said this, he fell asleep [a][in death].

CHAPTER 8

AND Saul was [not only] consenting to [Stephen's] death—[he was] [b]pleased and [c]entirely approving. On that day a great *and* severe persecution broke out against the church which was in Jerusalem; and they were all scattered throughout the regions of Judea and Samaria, except the apostles—the special messengers.

2 [A party of] devout men [b]with others helped to carry out *and* bury Stephen, and made great lamentation over him.

3 But Saul shamefully treated *and* laid waste the church continuously,—with cruelty *and* violence; and entering house after house, he dragged out men and women and committed them to prison.

4 Now those who were scattered abroad went about through [the land from place to place] preaching the glad tidings, the Word [that is, [b]the doctrine concerning the attainment through Christ of salvation in the kingdom of God].

5 Philip [the deacon, not the apostle] went down to the city of Samaria, and proclaimed the Christ, the Messiah, to them [the people]; [Acts 6:5.]

6 And great crowds of people with one accord listened to *and* heeded what was said by Philip, as they heard him *and* watched the miracles *and* wonders which he kept performing [from time to time].

7 For foul spirits came out of many who were possessed by them, screaming *and* shouting with a loud voice, and many who were suffering from palsy or were crippled were restored to health.

8 And there was great rejoicing in that city.

9 But there was a man named Simon who had formerly practiced magic arts in the city to the utter amazement of the Samaritan nation, claiming that he himself was an extraordinary *and* distinguished person.

10 They all paid earnest attention to him, from the least to the greatest, saying, This man is that exhibition of the power of God which is called Great (intense).

z) Literal translation.
a) Cremer.
b) Thayer.
c) Souter.

Living New Testament

55 But Stephen, full of the Holy Spirit, gazed steadily upward into heaven and saw the glory of God and Jesus standing at God's right hand.

56 And he told them, "Look, I see the heavens opened and Jesus the Messiah[7] standing beside God, at His right hand!"

57 Then they mobbed him, putting their hands over their ears, and drowning out his voice with their shouts,

58 And dragged him out of the city to stone him. The official witnesses—the executioners—took off their coats and laid them at the feet of a young man named Paul.[8]

59 And as the murderous stones came hurtling at him, Stephen prayed, "Lord Jesus, receive my spirit."

60 And he fell to his knees, shouting, "Lord, don't charge them with this sin!" and with that, he died.

Revised Standard

teeth against him. 55But he, full of the Holy
Spirit, gazed into heaven and saw the glory
of God, and Jesus standing at the right hand
of God; 56and he said, "Behold, I see the
heavens opened, and the Son of man standing at the right hand of God." 57But they
cried out with a loud voice and stopped
their ears and rushed together upon him.
58Then they cast him out of the city and
stoned him; and the witnesses laid down
their garments at the feet of a young man
named Saul. 59And as they were stoning
Stephen, he prayed, "Lord Jesus, receive my
spirit. 60And he knelt down and cried with
a loud voice, "Lord, do not hold this sin
against them." And when he had said this,

CHAPTER 8

Paul was in complete agreement with the killing of Stephen. And a great wave of persecution of the believers began that day, sweeping over the church in Jerusalem, and everyone except the apostles fled into Judea and Samaria.

2 (But some godly Jews[1] came and with great sorrow buried Stephen.)

3 Paul was like a wild man, going everywhere to devastate the believers, even entering private homes and dragging out men and women alike and jailing them.

4 But the believers[2] who had fled Jerusalem went everywhere preaching the Good News about Jesus!

5 Philip, for instance, went to the city of Samaria and told the people there about Christ.

6 Crowds listened intently to what he had to say because of the miracles he did.

7 Many evil spirits were cast out, screaming as they left their victims, and many who were paralyzed or lame were healed,

8 So there was much joy in that city!

9, 10, 11 A man named Simon had formerly been a sorcerer there for many years; he was a very influential, proud man because of the amazing things he could do—in fact, the Samaritan people often spoke of him as the Messiah.[3]

8 he fell asleep. 1And Saul was consenting to his death.

The persecution of the church

And on that day a great persecution arose
against the church in Jerusalem; and they
were all scattered throughout the region of
Judea and Samaria, except the apostles.
2Devout men buried Stephen, and made
great lamentation over him. 3But Saul laid
waste the church, and entering house after
house, he dragged off men and women and
committed them to prison.

Philip at Samaria

4 Now those who were scattered went
about preaching the word. 5Philip went
down to a city of Samaria and proclaimed
to them the Christ. 6And the multitudes
with one accord gave heed to what was said
by Philip, when they heard him and saw the
signs which he did. 7For unclean spirits
came out of many who were possessed, crying with a loud voice; and many who were
paralyzed or lame were healed. 8So there
was much joy in that city.

Conversion of Simon the sorcerer

9 But there was a man named Simon
who had previously practiced magic in the
city and amazed the nation of Samaria, saying that he himself was somebody great.
10They all gave heed to him, from the least
to the greatest, saying, "This man is that
power of God which is called Great."

---

[7] Literally, "the Son of man."
[8] Paul is also known as Saul.
[1] Literally, "devout men." It is not clear whether these were Christians who braved the persecution, or whether they were godly and sympathetic Jews.
[2] Literally, "the church."
[3] Literally, "this man is that Power of God which is called great."

King James

11 And to him they had regard, because that of long time he had bewitched them with sorceries.

12 But when they believed Philip preaching the things concerning the kingdom of God, and the name of Jesus Christ, they were baptized, both men and women.

13 Then Simon himself believed also: and when he was baptized, he continued with Philip, and wondered, beholding the miracles and signs which were done.

14 Now when the apostles which were at Jerusalem heard that Samaria had received the word of God, they sent unto them Peter and John:

15 Who, when they were come down, prayed for them, that they might receive the Holy Ghost:

16 (For as yet he was fallen upon none of them: only they were baptized in the name of the Lord Jesus.)

17 Then laid they *their* hands on them, and they received the Holy Ghost.

18 And when Simon saw that through laying on of the apostles' hands the Holy Ghost was given, he offered them money,

19 Saying, Give me also this power, that on whomsoever I lay hands, he may receive the Holy Ghost.

20 But Peter said unto him, Thy money perish with thee, because thou hast thought that the gift of God may be purchased with money.

21 Thou hast neither part nor lot in this matter: for thy heart is not right in the sight of God.

22 Repent therefore of this thy wickedness, and pray God, if perhaps the thought of thine heart may be forgiven thee.

23 For I perceive that thou art in the gall of bitterness, and *in* the bond of iniquity.

24 Then answered Simon, and said, Pray ye to the Lord for me, that none of these things which ye have spoken come upon me.

25 And they, when they had testified and preached the word of the Lord, returned to Jerusalem, and preached the gospel in many villages of the Samaritans.

26 And the angel of the Lord spake unto Philip, saying, Arise, and go toward the south unto the way that goeth down from Jerusalem unto Gaza, which is desert.

27 And he arose and went: and, behold, a man of Ethiopia, an eunuch of great authority under Candace queen of the Ethiopians, who had the charge of all her treasure, and had come to Jerusalem for to worship,

28 Was returning, and sitting in his chariot read Esaias the prophet.

29 Then the Spirit said unto Philip, Go near, and join thyself to this chariot.

30 And Philip ran thither to *him*, and heard him read the prophet Esaias, and said, Understandest thou what thou readest?

31 And he said, How can I, except some man should guide me? And he desired Philip that he would come up and sit with him.

Amplified

11 And they were attentive *and* made much of him, because for a long time he had amazed *and* bewildered *and* dazzled them with his skill in magic arts.

12 But when they believed the good news (the Gospel) about the kingdom of God and the name of Jesus Christ, the Messiah, as Philip preached it, they were baptized, both men and women.

13 Even Simon himself believed—[that is,] he adhered to, trusted in and relied on the teaching of Philip—and after being baptized devoted himself constantly to him. And seeing signs *and* miracles of great power which were being performed, he was utterly amazed.

14 Now when the apostles (special messengers) at Jerusalem heard that [the country of] Samaria had accepted *and* welcomed the Word of God, they sent Peter and John to them,

15 And they came down and prayed for them that the Samaritans might receive the Holy Spirit;

16 For He had not yet fallen upon any of them, but they had only been baptized into the name of the Lord Jesus.

17 Then [the apostles] laid their hands on them one by one and they received the Holy Spirit.

18 However, when Simon saw that the (Holy) Spirit was imparted through the laying on of the apostles' hands, he brought money *and* offered it to them,

19 Saying, Grant me also this power *and* authority, in order that any one on whom I place my hands may receive the Holy Spirit.

20 But Peter said to him, Destruction overtake your money and you, because you imagined you could obtain the [free] gift of God with money!

21 You have neither part nor lot in this matter, for your heart is all wrong in God's sight—[it is] not straightforward *or* right *or* true before God. [Ps. 78:37.]

22 So repent of this depravity *and* wickedness of yours, and pray to the Lord that, if possible, this [d]contriving thought *and* purpose of your heart may be removed *and* disregarded *and* forgiven you.

23 For I see that you are in the gall of bitterness and [e]a bond forged by iniquity [to fetter souls]. [Isa. 58:6.]

24 And Simon answered, Pray for me!—Beseech the Lord, both of you—that nothing of what you have said may befall me!

25 Now when [the apostles] had borne their testimony and preached the message of the Lord, they went back to Jerusalem, proclaiming the glad tidings (Gospel) to many villages of the Samaritans [on the way].

26 But an angel of the Lord said to Philip, Rise and proceed southward [f]at midday on the road that runs from Jerusalem down to Gaza. This is the desert [[g]route].

27 So he got up and went. And, behold, an Ethiopian, a eunuch, of great authority under Candace the queen of the Ethiopians, who was in charge of all her treasure, had come to Jerusalem to worship.

28 And he was [now] returning, and sitting in his chariot he was reading the book of the prophet Isaiah.

29 Then the (Holy) Spirit said to Philip, Go forward and join yourself to this chariot.

30 Accordingly Philip, running up to him, heard [the man] reading the prophet Isaiah, and asked, Do you really understand what you are reading?

31 And he said, How is it possible for me to do so, unless some one explains it to me *and* guides me [in the right way]? And he earnestly requested Philip to come up and sit beside him.

---

d) Vincent.
e) Thayer.
f) Alternate reading.
g) Vincent.

Living New Testament

12 But now they believed Philip's message that Jesus was the Messiah, and his words concerning the Kingdom of God; and many men and women were baptized.

13 Then Simon himself believed and was baptized and began following Philip wherever he went, and was amazed by the miracles he did.

14 When the apostles back in Jerusalem heard that the people of Samaria had accepted God's message, they sent down Peter and John.

15 As soon as they arrived, they began praying for these new Christians to receive the Holy Spirit,

16 For as yet He had not come upon any of them. For they had only been baptized in the name of the Lord Jesus.

17 Then Peter and John laid their hands upon these believers, and they received the Holy Spirit.

18 When Simon saw this—that the Holy Spirit was given when the apostles placed their hands upon peoples' heads—he offered money to buy this power.

19 "Let me have this power too," he exclaimed, "so that when I lay my hands on people, they will receive the Holy Spirit!"

20 But Peter replied, "Your money perish with you for thinking God's gift can be bought!

21 You can have no part in this, for your heart is not right before God.

22 Turn from this great wickedness and pray. Perhaps God will yet forgive your evil thoughts—

23 For I can see that there is jealousy[4] and sin in your heart."

24 "Pray for me," Simon exclaimed, "that these terrible things won't happen to me."

25 After testifying and preaching in Samaria, Peter and John returned to Jerusalem, stopping at several Samaritan villages along the way to preach the Good News to them too.

26 But as for Philip, an angel of the Lord said to him, "Go over to the road that runs from Jerusalem through the Gaza Desert, arriving around noon."

27 So he did, and who should be coming down the road but the Treasurer of Ethiopia, a eunuch of great authority under Candace the queen. He had gone to Jerusalem to worship at the Temple,

28 And was now returning in his chariot, reading aloud from the book of the prophet Isaiah.

29 The Holy Spirit said to Philip, "Go over and walk along beside the chariot!"

30 Philip ran over and heard what he was reading and asked, "Do you understand it?"

31 "Of course not!" the man replied. "How can I when there is no one to instruct me?" And he begged Philip to come up into the chariot and sit with him!

[4] Literally, "the gall of bitterness."

Revised Standard

[11]And they gave heed to him, because for a
long time he had amazed them with his
magic. [12]But when they believed Philip as
he preached good news about the kingdom
of God and the name of Jesus Christ, they
were baptized, both men and women.
[13]Even Simon himself believed, and after
being baptized he continued with Philip.
And seeing signs and great miracles performed, he was amazed.

14 Now when the apostles at Jerusalem
heard that Samaria had received the word
of God, they sent to them Peter and John,
[15]who came down and prayed for them that
they might receive the Holy Spirit; [16]for it
had not yet fallen on any of them, but they
had only been baptized in the name of the
Lord Jesus. [17]Then they laid their hands on
them and they received the Holy Spirit.
[18]Now when Simon saw that the Spirit was
given through the laying on of the apostles'
hands, he offered them money, [19]saying,
"Give me also this power, that any one on
whom I lay my hands may receive the Holy
Spirit." [20]But Peter said to him, "Your silver perish with you, because you thought
you could obtain the gift of God with money! [21]You have neither part nor lot in this
matter, for your heart is not right before
God. [22]Repent therefore of this wickedness
of yours, and pray to the Lord that, if
possible, the intent of your heart may be
forgiven you. [23]For I see that you are in
the gall of bitterness and in the bond of
iniquity." [24]And Simon answered, "Pray for
me to the Lord, that nothing of what you
have said may come upon me."

25 Now when they had testified and spoken the word of the Lord, they returned to
Jerusalem, preaching the gospel to many villages of the Samaritans.

Conversion of the Ethiopian

26 But an angel of the Lord said to Philip, "Rise and go toward the south[g] to the
road that goes down from Jerusalem to
Gaza." This is a desert road. [27]And he rose
and went. And behold, an Ethiopian, a eunuch, a minister of Candace the queen of
the Ethiopians, in charge of all her treasure,
had come to Jerusalem to worship [28]and
was returning; seated in his chariot, he was
reading the prophet Isaiah. [29]And the Spirit
said to Philip, "Go up and join this chariot."
[30]So Philip ran to him, and heard him reading Isaiah the prophet, and asked, "Do you
understand what you are reading?" [31]And
he said, "How can I, unless some one guides
me?" And he invited Philip to come up and
sit with him. [32]Now the passage of the

[g] Or *at noon*

King James

32 The place of the scripture which he read was this, He was led as a sheep to the slaughter; and like a lamb dumb before his shearer, so opened he not his mouth:
33 In his humiliation his judgment was taken away: and who shall declare his generation? for his life is taken from the earth.
34 And the eunuch answered Philip, and said, I pray thee, of whom speaketh the prophet this? of himself, or of some other man?
35 Then Philip opened his mouth, and began at the same scripture, and preached unto him Jesus.
36 And as they went on *their* way, they came unto a certain water: and the eunuch said, See, *here is* water; what doth hinder me to be baptized?
37 And Philip said, If thou believest with all thine heart, thou mayest. And he answered and said, I believe that Jesus Christ is the Son of God.
38 And he commanded the chariot to stand still: and they went down both into the water, both Philip and the eunuch; and he baptized him.
39 And when they were come up out of the water, the Spirit of the Lord caught away Philip, that the eunuch saw him no more: and he went on his way rejoicing.
40 But Philip was found at Azotus: and passing through he preached in all the cities, till he came to Cæsarea.

Amplified

32 Now this was the passage of Scripture which he was reading: Like a sheep He was led to the slaughter, and as a lamb before its shearer is dumb, so He opens not His mouth.
33 In His humiliation [h]He was taken away by distressing *and* oppressive judgment, *and* justice was denied Him (caused to cease). Who can describe *or* relate in full [g]the wickedness of His contemporaries (generation)? For His life is taken from the earth *and* [i]a bloody death inflicted upon Him. [Isa. 53:7, 8.]
34 And the eunuch said to Philip, I beg of you, tell me about whom does the prophet say this, about himself or about someone else?
35 Then Philip opened his mouth, and beginning with this portion of Scripture he announced to him the glad tidings (Gospel) of Jesus *and* about [Him].
36 And as they continued along on the way, they came to some water, and the eunuch exclaimed, See, [here is] water! What is to hinder my being baptized?
37 *And Philip said, If you believe with all your heart [that is, if you have [j]a conviction, full of joyful trust, that Jesus is the Messiah, and accept Him as the Author of your salvation in the kingdom of God, giving Him your obedience, then] you may. And he replied, I do believe that Jesus Christ is the Son of God,*
38 And he ordered that the chariot be stopped, and both Philip and the eunuch went down into the water, and [Philip] baptized him.
39 And when they came up out of the water, the Spirit of the Lord [[k]suddenly] caught away Philip; and the eunuch saw him no more, and he went on his way rejoicing.
40 But Philip was found at Azotus, and passing on he preached the good news (Gospel) to all the towns until he reached Caesarea.

King James

CHAPTER 9

AND Saul, yet breathing out threatenings and slaughter against the disciples of the Lord, went unto the high priest,
2 And desired of him letters to Damascus to the synagogues, that if he found any of this way, whether they were men or women, he might bring them bound unto Jerusalem.
3 And as he journeyed, he came near Damascus: and suddenly there shined round about him a light from heaven:
4 And he fell to the earth, and heard a voice saying unto him, Saul, Saul, why persecutest thou me?
5 And he said, Who art thou, Lord? And the Lord said, I am Jesus whom thou persecutest: *it is* hard for thee to kick against the pricks.
6 And he trembling and astonished said, Lord, what wilt thou have me to do? And the Lord *said* unto him, Arise, and go into the city, and it shall be told thee what thou must do.
7 And the men which journeyed with him stood speechless, hearing a voice, but seeing no man.

Amplified

CHAPTER 9

MEANWHILE Saul, [k]still drawing his breath hard from threatening and murderous desire against the disciples of the Lord, went to the high priest
2 And requested of him letters to the synagogues at Damascus [authorizing him], so that if he found any men or women belonging to the Way [of life as determined by faith in Jesus Christ], he might bring them bound [with chains] to Jerusalem.
3 Now as he traveled on, he came near to Damascus, and suddenly a light from heaven flashed around him,
4 And he fell to the ground. Then he heard a voice saying to him, Saul, Saul, why are you persecuting Me—harassing, troubling and molesting Me?
5 And Saul said, Who are You, Lord? And He said, I am Jesus, Whom you are persecuting. *It is dangerous and it turns out badly for you to keep kicking against the goad—that is, to offer vain and perilous resistance.*
6 *Trembling and astonished he asked, Lord, what do You desire me to do? The Lord said to him,* But arise and go into the city and you will be told what you must do.
7 The men who were accompanying him were unable to speak [for terror], hearing the voice but seeing no one.

h) Clarke quoting others.
i) Thayer.
j) Thayer.
k) Vincent.

Living New Testament

32 The passage of Scripture he had been reading from was this:

"He was led as a sheep to the slaughter,
And as a lamb is silent before the shearers, so He opened not His mouth;
33 In His humiliation, justice was denied Him; and who can express the wickedness of the people of His generation?[5] For His life is taken from the earth."

34 The eunuch asked Philip, "Was Isaiah talking about himself or someone else?"

35 So Philip began with this same Scripture and then used many others to tell him about Jesus.

36 As they rode along, they came to a small body of water, and the eunuch said, "Look! Water! Why can't I be baptized?"

37[6] "You can," Philip answered, "if you believe with all your heart."

And the eunuch replied, "I believe that Jesus Christ is the Son of God."

38 He stopped the chariot, and they went down into the water and Philip baptized him.

39 And when they came up out of the water, the Spirit of the Lord caught away Philip, and the eunuch never saw him again, but went on his way rejoicing.

40 Meanwhile, Philip discovered himself at Azotus! He preached the Good News there and in every city along the way, as he traveled to Caesarea.

Revised Standard

scripture which he was reading was this:
"As a sheep led to the slaughter
or a lamb before its shearer is dumb,
so he opens not his mouth.
33 In his humiliation justice was denied
him.
Who can describe his generation?
For his life is taken up from the earth."
34 And the eunuch said to Philip, "About
whom, pray, does the prophet say this,
about himself or about some one
else?" 35 Then Philip opened his mouth, and
beginning with this scripture he told him the
good news of Jesus. 36 And as they went
along the road they came to some water,
and the eunuch said, "See, here is water!
What is to prevent my being baptized?"[h]
38 And he commanded the chariot to stop,
and they both went down into the water,
Philip and the eunuch, and he baptized him.
39 And when they came up out of the water,
the Spirit of the Lord caught up Philip; and
the eunuch saw him no more, and went on
his way rejoicing. 40 But Philip was found at
Azotus, and passing on he preached the gospel to all the towns till he came to Caesarea.

CHAPTER 9

But Paul, threatening with every breath and eager to destroy every Christian, went to the High Priest in Jerusalem.

2 He requested a letter addressed to synagogues in Damascus, requiring their cooperation in the persecution of any believers he found there, both men and women, so that he could bring them in chains to Jerusalem.

3 As he was nearing Damascus on this mission, suddenly a brillant light from heaven spotted down upon him!

4 He fell to the ground and heard a voice saying to him, "Saul! Saul! Why are you persecuting Me?"

5 "Who is speaking, sir?" Paul asked.

And the voice replied, "I am Jesus, the one you are persecuting!

6 Now get up and go into the city and await My further instructions."

7 The men with Paul stood speechless with surprise, for they heard the sound of someone's voice but saw no one!

Conversion of Saul

9 But Saul, still breathing threats and
murder against the disciples of the
Lord, went to the high priest 2 and asked
him for letters to the synagogues at Damascus, so that if he found any belonging to the
Way, men or women, he might bring them
bound to Jerusalem. 3 Now as he journeyed
he approached Damascus, and suddenly a
light from heaven flashed about him. 4 And
he fell to the ground and heard a voice
saying to him, "Saul, Saul, why do you persecute me?" 5 And he said, "Who are you,
Lord?" And he said, "I am Jesus, whom you
are persecuting; 6 but rise and enter the city,
and you will be told what you are to do."
7 The men who were traveling with him
stood speechless, hearing the voice but

[5] Implied. Literally, "Who can declare His generation." Alternatively, "Who will be able to speak of His posterity? For . . ."

[6] Many ancient manuscripts omit verse 37 wholly or in part.

[h] Other ancient authorities add all or most of verse 37, *And Philip said, "If you believe with all your heart, you may." And he replied, "I believe that Jesus Christ is the Son of God."*

King James

8 And Saul arose from the earth; and when his eyes were opened, he saw no man: but they led him by the hand, and brought *him* into Damascus.

9 And he was three days without sight, and neither did eat nor drink.

10 ¶ And there was a certain disciple at Damascus, named Ananias; and to him said the Lord in a vision, Ananias. And he said, Behold, I *am here*, Lord.

11 And the Lord *said* unto him, Arise, and go into the street which is called Straight, and inquire in the house of Judas for *one* called Saul, of Tarsus: for, behold, he prayeth,

12 And hath seen in a vision a man named Ananias coming in, and putting *his* hand on him, that he might receive his sight.

13 Then Ananias answered, Lord, I have heard by many of this man, how much evil he hath done to thy saints at Jerusalem:

14 And here he hath authority from the chief priests to bind all that call on thy name.

15 But the Lord said unto him, Go thy way: for he is a chosen vessel unto me, to bear my name before the Gentiles, and kings, and the children of Israel:

16 For I will shew him how great things he must suffer for my name's sake.

17 And Ananias went his way, and entered into the house; and putting his hands on him said, Brother Saul, the Lord, *even* Jesus, that appeared unto thee in the way as thou camest, hath sent me, that thou mightest receive thy sight, and be filled with the Holy Ghost.

18 And immediately there fell from his eyes as it had been scales: and he received sight forthwith, and arose, and was baptized.

19 And when he had received meat, he was strengthened. Then was Saul certain days with the disciples which were at Damascus.

20 And straightway he preached Christ in the synagogues, that he is the Son of God.

21 But all that heard *him* were amazed, and said; Is not this he that destroyed them which called on this name in Jerusalem, and came hither for that intent, that he might bring them bound unto the chief priests?

22 But Saul increased the more in strength, and confounded the Jews which dwelt at Damascus, proving that this is very Christ.

23 ¶ And after that many days were fulfilled, the Jews took counsel to kill him:

24 But their laying await was known of Saul. And they watched the gates day and night to kill him.

25 Then the disciples took him by night, and let *him* down by the wall in a basket.

26 And when Saul was come to Jerusalem, he assayed to join himself to the disciples: but they were all afraid of him, and believed not that he was a disciple.

27 But Barnabas took him, and brought *him* to the apostles, and declared unto them how he had seen the Lord in the way, and that he had spoken to him, and how he had preached boldly at Damascus in the name of Jesus.

Amplified

8 Then Saul got up from the ground, but though his eyes were opened, he could see nothing; so they led him by the hand and brought him into Damascus.

9 And he was unable to see for three days, and he neither ate nor drank [anything].

10 Now there was in Damascus a disciple named Ananias. The Lord said to him in a vision, Ananias. And he answered, [Here am] I, Lord.

11 And the Lord said to him, Get up and go to the street called Straight, and ask at the house of Judas for a man of Tarsus named Saul, for behold, he is praying [there].

12 And he has seen *in a vision* a man named Ananias enter and lay his hands on him so that he might regain his sight.

13 But Ananias answered, Lord, I have heard many people tell about this man, especially how much evil *and* what great suffering he has brought on Your saints at Jerusalem;

14 Now he is here and has authority from the high priests to put in chains all who call upon Your name.

15 But the Lord said to him, Go, for this man is a chosen instrument of Mine to bear My name before the Gentiles and kings and the descendants of Israel;

16 For I will make clear to him how much he will be afflicted *and* must endure *and* suffer for My name's sake.

17 So Ananias left and went into the house. And he laid his hands on Saul and said, Brother Saul, the Lord Jesus Who appeared to you along the way by which you came here, has sent me that you may recover your sight and be filled with the Holy Spirit.

18 And instantly something like scales fell from [Saul's] eyes, and he recovered his sight. Then he arose and was baptized,

19 And after he took some food he was strengthened. For several days [afterward] he remained with the disciples at Damascus.

20 And immediately in the synagogues he proclaimed Jesus, saying, He is the Son of God!

21 And all who heard him were amazed, and said, Is not this the very man who harassed *and* overthrew *and* destroyed in Jerusalem those who called upon this Name? And he has come here for the express purpose of arresting them *and* bringing them in chains before the chief priests.

22 But Saul increased all the more in strength, and continued to confound *and* put to confusion the Jews who lived in Damascus by comparing *and* examining evidence *and* proving that Jesus is the Christ, the Messiah.

23 After considerable time had elapsed, the Jews conspired to put Saul out of the way by slaying him,

24 But [the knowledge of] their plot was made known to Saul. They were guarding the [city's] gates day and night to kill him,

25 But his disciples took him at night and let him down through the [city's] wall, lowering him in a basket *or* hamper.

26 And when he had arrived in Jerusalem he tried to associate himself with the disciples, but they were all afraid of him, for they did not believe he really was a disciple.

27 However, Barnabas took him and brought him to the apostles, and he explained to them how along the way he had seen the Lord, Who spoke to him, and how at Damascus he had preached freely *and* confidently *and* courageously in the name of Jesus.

Living New Testament

8 As Paul picked himself up off the ground, he found that he was blind. He had to be led into Damascus and was there three days, blind, going without food and water all that time.

10 Now there was in Damascus a believer named Ananias. The Lord spoke to him in a vision, calling, "Ananias!"

"Yes, Lord!" he replied.

11 And the Lord said, "Go over to Straight Street and find the house of a man named Judas and ask there for Paul of Tarsus. He is praying to Me right now, for

12 I have shown him a vision of a man named Ananias coming in and laying his hands on him so that he can see again!"

13 "But Lord," exclaimed Ananias, "I have heard about the terrible things this man has done to the believers in Jerusalem!

14 And we hear that he has arrest warrants with him from the chief priests, authorizing him to arrest every believer in Damascus!"

15 But the Lord said, "Go and do what I say. For Paul is my chosen instrument to take My message to the nations and before kings, as well as to the people of Israel.

16 And I will show him how much he must suffer for Me."

17 So Ananias went over and found Paul and laid his hands on him and said, "Brother Paul, the Lord Jesus, who appeared to you on the road, has sent me so that you may be filled with the Holy Spirit and get your sight back."

18 Instantly (it was as though scales fell from his eyes) Paul could see, and was immediately baptized.

19 Then he ate and was strengthened. He stayed with the believers in Damascus for a few days

20 And went at once to the synagogue to tell everyone there the Good News about Jesus—that He is indeed the Son of God!

21 All who heard him were amazed. "Isn't this the same man who persecuted Jesus' followers so bitterly in Jerusalem?" they asked. "And we understand that he came here to arrest them all and take them in chains to the chief priests."

22 Paul became more and more fervent in his preaching, and the Damascus Jews couldn't withstand his proofs that Jesus was indeed the Christ.

23 After a while the Jewish leaders determined to kill him.

24 But Saul was told about their plans, that they were watching the gates of the city day and night prepared to murder him.

25 So during the night some of his converts let him down in a basket through an opening in the city wall!

26 Upon arrival in Jerusalem he tried to meet with the believers, but they were all afraid of him. They thought he was faking!

27 Then Barnabas brought him to the apostles and told them how Paul had seen the Lord on the way to Damascus, what the Lord had said to him, and all about his powerful preaching in the name of Jesus.

Revised Standard

seeing no one. [8]Saul arose from the ground; and when his eyes were opened, he could see nothing; so they led him by the hand and brought him into Damascus. [9]And for three days he was without sight, and neither ate nor drank.

Ananias restores Paul's sight

10 Now there was a disciple at Damascus named Ananias. The Lord said to him in a vision, "Ananias." And he said, "Here I am, Lord." [11]And the Lord said to him, "Rise and go to the street called Straight, and inquire in the house of Judas for a man of Tarsus named Saul; for behold, he is praying, [12]and he has seen a man named Ananias come in and lay his hands on him so that he might regain his sight." [13]But Ananias answered, "Lord, I have heard from many about this man, how much evil he has done to thy saints at Jerusalem; [14]and here he has authority from the chief priests to bind all who call upon thy name." [15]But the Lord said to him, "Go, for he is a chosen instrument of mine to carry my name before the Gentiles and kings and the sons of Israel; [16]for I will show him how much he must suffer for the sake of my name." [17]So Ananias departed and entered the house. And laying his hands on him he said, "Brother Saul, the Lord Jesus who appeared to you on the road by which you came, has sent me that you may regain your sight and be filled with the Holy Spirit." [18]And immediately something like scales fell from his eyes and he regained his sight. Then he rose and was baptized, [19]and took food and was strengthened.

Paul preaches at Damascus

For several days he was with the disciples at Damascus. [20]And in the synagogues immediately he proclaimed Jesus, saying, "He is the Son of God." [21]And all who heard him were amazed, and said, "Is not this the man who made havoc in Jerusalem of those who called on this name? And he has come here for this purpose, to bring them bound before the chief priests." [22]But Saul increased all the more in strength, and confounded the Jews who lived in Damascus by proving that Jesus was the Christ.

Paul escapes to Jerusalem

23 When many days had passed, the Jews plotted to kill him, [24]but their plot became known to Saul. They were watching the gates day and night, to kill him; [25]but his disciples took him by night and let him down over the wall, lowering him in a basket.

26 And when he had come to Jerusalem he attempted to join the disciples; and they were all afraid of him, for they did not believe that he was a disciple. [27]But Barnabas took him, and brought him to the apostles, and declared to them how on the road he had seen the Lord, who spoke to him, and how at Damascus he had preached

King James

28 And he was with them coming in and going out at Jerusalem.

29 And he spake boldly in the name of the Lord Jesus, and disputed against the Grecians: but they went about to slay him.

30 *Which* when the brethren knew, they brought him down to Cæsarea, and sent him forth to Tarsus.

31 Then had the churches rest throughout all Judæa and Galilee and Samaria, and were edified; and walking in the fear of the Lord, and in the comfort of the Holy Ghost, were multiplied.

32 ¶ And it came to pass, as Peter passed throughout all *quarters*, he came down also to the saints which dwelt at Lydda.

33 And there he found a certain man named Æneas, which had kept his bed eight years, and was sick of the palsy.

34 And Peter said unto him, Æneas, Jesus Christ maketh thee whole: arise, and make thy bed. And he arose immediately.

35 And all that dwelt at Lydda and Saron saw him, and turned to the Lord.

36 ¶ Now there was at Joppa a certain disciple named Tabitha, which by interpretation is called Dorcas: this woman was full of good works and almsdeeds which she did.

37 And it came to pass in those days, that she was sick, and died: whom when they had washed, they laid *her* in an upper chamber.

38 And forasmuch as Lydda was nigh to Joppa, and the disciples had heard that Peter was there, they sent unto him two men, desiring *him* that he would not delay to come to them.

39 Then Peter arose and went with them. When he was come, they brought him into the upper chamber: and all the widows stood by him weeping, and shewing the coats and garments which Dorcas made, while she was with them.

40 But Peter put them all forth, and kneeled down, and prayed; and turning *him* to the body said, Tabitha, arise. And she opened her eyes: and when she saw Peter, she sat up.

41 And he gave her *his* hand, and lifted her up, and when he had called the saints and widows, presented her alive.

42 And it was known throughout all Joppa; and many believed in the Lord.

43 And it came to pass, that he tarried many days in Joppa with one Simon a tanner.

CHAPTER 10

THERE was a certain man in Cæsarea called Cornelius, a centurion of the band called the Italian *band*,

Amplified

28 So he went in and out [as one] among them at Jerusalem,

29 Preaching freely *and* confidently *and* boldly in the name of the Lord. And he spoke and discussed with *and* disputed against the Hellenists [the Grecian Jews], but they were seeking to slay him.

30 And when the brethren found it out, they brought him down to Caesarea, and sent him off to Tarsus [his home town].

31 So the church throughout the whole of Judea and Galilee and Samaria had peace and was edified—growing in wisdom, virtue and piety—and walking in the respect *and* reverential fear of the Lord and in the consolation *and* exhortation of the Holy Spirit, continued to increase *and* was multiplied.

32 Now as Peter went here and there among them all, he went down also to the saints who lived at Lydda.

33 There he found a man named Aeneas, who had been bedfast for eight years and was paralyzed.

34 And Peter said to him, Aeneas, Jesus Christ, the Messiah, [now] makes you whole. Get up and make your bed! And immediately [Aeneas] stood up.

35 Then all the inhabitants of Lydda and the plain of Sharon saw [what had happened to] him and they turned to the Lord.

36 Now there was at Joppa [a woman], a disciple named [in Aramaic] Tabitha, which [in Greek] means Dorcas *or* [in English] Gazelle. She was abounding in good deeds and acts of charity.

37 About that time she fell sick and died, and when they had cleansed her, they laid [her] in an upper room.

38 Since Lydda was near Joppa [however], the disciples hearing that Peter was there, sent two men to him begging him, Do come on to us without delay.

39 So Peter [immediately] rose and accompanied them. And when he had arrived, they took him to the upper room. All the widows stood around him crying, and displaying under-shirts (tunics) and [other] garments such as Dorcas was accustomed to make while she was with them.

40 But Peter put them all out [of the room] and knelt down and prayed; then turning to the body he said, Tabitha, get up! And she opened her eyes, and when she saw Peter she raised herself *and* sat upright.

41 And he gave her his hand and lifted her up. Then calling in God's people and the widows he presented her to them alive.

42 And this became known throughout all Joppa, and many came to believe on the Lord—that is, to adhere to and trust in and rely on Him as the Christ and as their Savior.

43 And Peter remained in Joppa for considerable time with one Simon, a tanner.

CHAPTER 10

NOW [living] at Caesarea there was a man whose name was Cornelius, a centurion of what was known as the Italian Regiment,

Living New Testament

28 Then they accepted him, and after that he was constantly with the believers

29 And preached boldly in the name of the Lord. But then some Greek-speaking Jews with whom he had argued plotted to murder him.

30 However, when the other believers heard about his danger, they took him to Caesarea and then sent him to his home[1] in Tarsus.

31 Meanwhile, the church had peace throughout Judea, Galilee and Samaria, and grew in strength and numbers. The believers learned how to walk in the fear of the Lord and in the comfort of the Holy Spirit.

32 Peter traveled from place to place to visit them,[1] and in his travels came to the believers in the town of Lydda.

33 There he met a man named Aeneas, paralyzed and bedridden for eight years.

34 Peter said to him, "Aeneas! Jesus Christ has healed you! Get up and make your bed!" And he was healed instantly.

35 Then the whole population of Lydda and Sharon turned to the Lord when they saw Aeneas walking around.

36 In the city of Joppa there was a woman named Dorcas ("Gazelle"), a believer who was always doing kind things for others, especially for the poor.

37 About this time she became ill and died. Her friends prepared her for burial and laid her in an upstairs room.

38 But when they learned that Peter was nearby at Lydda, they sent two men to beg him to return with them to Joppa.

39 This he did; as soon as he arrived, they took him upstairs where Dorcas lay. The room was filled with weeping widows who were showing one another the coats and other garments Dorcas had made for them.

40 But Peter asked them all to leave the room; then he knelt and prayed. Turning to the body he said, "Get up, Dorcas,"[2] and she opened her eyes! And when she saw Peter, she sat up!

41 He gave her his hand and helped her up and called in the believers and widows, presenting her to them!

42 The news raced through the town, and many believed in the Lord.

43 And Peter stayed a long time in Joppa, living with Simon, the tanner.

CHAPTER 10

In Caesarea there lived a Roman army officer, Cornelius, a captain of an Italian regiment.

Revised Standard

boldly in the name of Jesus. 28So he went in
and out among them at Jerusalem,
29preaching boldly in the name of the Lord.
And he spoke and disputed against the Hellenists; but they were seeking to kill him.
30And when the brethren knew it, they
brought him down to Caesarea, and sent
him off to Tarsus.
31 So the church throughout all Judea
and Galilee and Samaria had peace and was
built up; and walking in the fear of the Lord
and in the comfort of the Holy Spirit it was
multiplied.

Peter heals Aeneas

32 Now as Peter went here and there
among them all, he came down also to the
saints that lived at Lydda. 33There he found
a man named Aeneas, who had been bedridden for eight years and was paralyzed.
34And Peter said to him, "Aeneas, Jesus
Christ heals you; rise and make your bed."
And immediately he rose. 35And all the
residents of Lydda and Sharon saw him, and
they turned to the Lord.

Tabitha raised from the dead

36 Now there was at Joppa a disciple
named Tabitha, which means Dorcas or
Gazelle. She was full of good works and acts
of charity. 37In those days she fell sick and
died; and when they had washed her, they
laid her in an upper room. 38Since Lydda
was near Joppa, the disciples, hearing that
Peter was there, sent two men to him en-
treating him, "Please come to us without
delay." 39So Peter rose and went with
them. And when he had come, they took
him to the upper room. All the widows
stood beside him weeping, and showing
coats and garments which Dorcas made
while she was with them. 40But Peter put
them all outside and knelt down and prayed;
then turning to the body he said, "Tabitha,
rise." And she opened her eyes, and when
she saw Peter she sat up. 41And he gave her
his hand and lifted her up. Then calling the
saints and widows he presented her alive.
42And it became known throughout all Joppa, and many believed in the Lord. 43And
he stayed in Joppa for many days with one
Simon, a tanner.

Cornelius' vision

10 At Caesarea there was a man named
Cornelius, a centurion of what was
known as the Italian Cohort, 2a devout man

---

1 Implied.
2 Literally, "Tabitha," her name in Hebrew.

King James

2 A devout *man*, and one that feared God with all his house, which gave much alms to the people, and prayed to God alway.

3 He saw in a vision evidently about the ninth hour of the day an angel of God coming in to him, and saying unto him, Cornelius.

4 And when he looked on him, he was afraid, and said, What is it, Lord? And he said unto him, Thy prayers and thine alms are come up for a memorial before God.

5 And now send men to Joppa, and call for *one* Simon, whose surname is Peter:

6 He lodgeth with one Simon a tanner, whose house is by the sea side: he shall tell thee what thou oughtest to do.

7 And when the angel which spake unto Cornelius was departed, he called two of his household servants, and a devout soldier of them that waited on him continually;

8 And when he had declared all *these* things unto them, he sent them to Joppa.

9 ¶ On the morrow, as they went on their journey, and drew nigh unto the city, Peter went up upon the housetop to pray about the sixth hour:

10 And he became very hungry, and would have eaten: but while they made ready, he fell into a trance,

11 And saw heaven opened, and a certain vessel descending unto him, as it had been a great sheet knit at the four corners, and let down to the earth:

12 Wherein were all manner of fourfooted beasts of the earth, and wild beasts, and creeping things, and fowls of the air.

13 And there came a voice to him, Rise, Peter; kill, and eat.

14 But Peter said, Not so, Lord; for I have never eaten any thing that is common or unclean.

15 And the voice *spake* unto him again the second time, What God hath cleansed, *that* call not thou common.

16 This was done thrice: and the vessel was received up again into heaven.

17 Now while Peter doubted in himself what this vision which he had seen should mean, behold, the men which were sent from Cornelius had made inquiry for Simon's house, and stood before the gate,

18 And called, and asked whether Simon, which was surnamed Peter, were lodged there.

19 ¶ While Peter thought on the vision, the Spirit said unto him, Behold, three men seek thee.

20 Arise therefore, and get thee down, and go with them, doubting nothing: for I have sent them.

21 Then Peter went down to the men which were sent unto him from Cornelius; and said, Behold, I am he whom ye seek: what *is* the cause wherefore ye are come?

22 And they said, Cornelius the centurion, a just man, and one that feareth God, and of good report among all the nation of the Jews, was warned from God by an holy angel to send for thee into his house, and to hear words of thee.

Amplified

2 A devout man who venerated God *and* treated Him with reverential obedience, as did all his household, and he gave much alms to the people, and prayed continually to God.

3 About the ninth hour (three o'clock) of the day he saw clearly in a vision an angel of God entering and saying to him, Cornelius!

4 And he gazing intently at him became frightened, and said, What is it, Lord? And the angel said to him, Your prayers and your [generous] gifts to the poor have come up [as a sacrifice] to God *and* have been remembered by Him.

5 And now send men to Joppa, and have them call for *and* invite here one Simon whose surname is Peter;

6 He is lodging with Simon a tanner, whose house is by the seaside.

7 When the angel who spoke to him had left, Cornelius called two of his servants and a God-fearing soldier from among his own personal attendants.

8 And having rehearsed everything to them, he sent them to Joppa.

9 The next day as they were still on their way and were approaching the town, Peter went up to the roof of the house to pray, about the sixth hour (noon).

10 But he became very hungry, and wanted something to eat; and while the meal was being prepared a trance came over him,

11 And he saw the sky opened and something like a great sheet lowered by the four corners, descending to the earth.

12 It contained all kinds of quadrupeds *and wild beasts* and creeping things of the earth and birds of the air.

13 And there came a voice to him saying, Rise up, Peter, kill and eat.

14 But Peter said, No, by no means, Lord; for I have never eaten anything that is common *and* unhallowed or [ceremonially] unclean.

15 And the voice came to him again a second time, What God has cleansed *and* pronounced clean, do not you defile *and* profane by regarding *and* calling common *and* unhallowed or unclean.

16 This occurred three times, then immediately the sheet was taken up to heaven.

17 Now Peter was still inwardly perplexed *and* doubted as to what the vision which he had seen could mean, when [just then] behold the messengers that were sent by Cornelius, who had made inquiry for Simon's house, stopped *and* stood before the gate.

18 And they called out to inquire whether Simon who was surnamed Peter was staying there.

19 And while Peter was [1]earnestly revolving the vision in his mind *and* meditating on it, the (Holy) Spirit said to him, Behold, three men are looking for you!

20 Get up and go below and accompany them without any doubt [about its legality] *or* any discrimination *or* hesitation, for I have sent them.

21 Then Peter went down to the men and said, I am the man you seek; what is the purpose of your coming?

22 And they said, Cornelius, a centurion (captain) who is just and upright *and* in right standing with God, being God-fearing *and* obedient, and well spoken of by the whole Jewish nation, has been instructed by a holy angel to send for you to come to his house; and he [1]has received in answer [to prayer] a warning to listen to *and* act upon what you have to say.

---

1) Vincent.

Living New Testament

2 He was a godly man, deeply reverent, as was his entire household. He gave generously to charity and was a man of prayer.

3 While wide awake one afternoon he had a vision—it was about three o'clock—and in this vision he saw an angel of God coming toward him. "Cornelius!" the angel said.

4 Cornelius stared at him in terror. "What do you want, sir?" he asked the angel.

And the angel replied, "Your prayers and charities have not gone unnoticed by God!

5, 6 Now send some men to Joppa to find a man named Simon Peter, who is staying with Simon, the tanner, down by the shore, and ask him to come and visit you."

7 As soon as the angel was gone, Cornelius called two of his household servants and a godly soldier, one of his personal bodyguard,

8 And told them what had happened and sent them off to Joppa.

9, 10 The next day, as they were nearing the city, Peter went up on the flat roof of his house to pray. It was noon and he was hungry, but while lunch was being prepared, he fell into a trance.

11 He saw the sky open, and a great canvas sheet,[1] suspended by its four corners, settle to the ground.

12 In the sheet were all sorts of animals, snakes and birds [forbidden to the Jews for food[2]].

13 Then a voice said to him, "Go kill and eat any of them you wish."

14 "Never, Lord," Peter declared, "I have never in all my life eaten such creatures, for they are forbidden by our Jewish laws."

15 The voice spoke again, "Don't contradict God! If He says something is kosher, then it is!"

16 The same vision was repeated three times! Then the sheet was pulled up again to heaven!

17 Peter was very perplexed. What could the vision mean? What was he supposed to do? Just then the men sent by Cornelius had found the house and were standing outside at the gate,

18 Inquiring whether this was the place where Simon Peter lived!

19 Meanwhile, as Peter was puzzling over the vision, the Holy Spirit said to him, "Three men have come to see you.

20 Go down and meet them and go with them. All is well, I have sent them."

21 So Peter went down. "I'm the man you're looking for," he said. "Now what is it you want?"

22 Then they told him about Cornelius the Roman officer, a good and godly man, well thought of by the Jews, and how an angel had instructed him to send for Peter to come and tell him what God wanted him to do.

Revised Standard

who feared God with all his household, gave
alms liberally to the people, and prayed constantly to God. 3About the ninth hour of the
day he saw clearly in a vision an angel of
God coming in and saying to him, "Cornelius." 4And he stared at him in terror, and
said, "What is it, Lord?" And he said to
him, "Your prayers and your alms have ascended as a memorial before God. 5And
now send men to Joppa, and bring one Simon who is called Peter; 6he is lodging with
Simon, a tanner, whose house is by the
seaside." 7When the angel who spoke to him
had departed, he called two of his servants
and a devout soldier from among those that
waited on him, 8and having related everything to them, he sent them to Joppa.

Peter's vision

9 The next day, as they were on their
journey and coming near the city, Peter
went up on the housetop to pray, about the
sixth hour. 10And he became hungry and
desired something to eat; but while they
were preparing it, he fell into a trance
11and saw the heaven opened, and something descending, like a great sheet, let down
by four corners upon the earth. 12In it were
all kinds of animals and reptiles and birds of
the air. 13And there came a voice to him,
"Rise, Peter; kill and eat." 14But Peter said,
"No, Lord; for I have never eaten anything
that is common or unclean." 15And the
voice came to him again a second time,
"What God has cleansed, you must not call
common." 16This happened three times, and
the thing was taken up at once to heaven.

Cornelius sends for Peter

17 Now while Peter was inwardly perplexed as to what the vision which he had
seen might mean, behold, the men that were
sent by Cornelius, having made inquiry for
Simon's house, stood before the gate 18and
called out to ask whether Simon who was
called Peter was lodging there. 19And while
Peter was pondering the vision, the Spirit
said to him, "Behold, three men are looking
for you. 20Rise and go down, and accompany them without hesitation; for I have sent
them." 21And Peter went down to the men
and said, "I am the one you are looking for;
what is the reason for your coming?" 22And
they said, "Cornelius, a centurion, an upright
and God-fearing man, who is well spoken of
by the whole Jewish nation, was directed by
a holy angel to send for you to come to his
house, and to hear what you have to say."

---

[1] Implied.
[2] Implied; see Leviticus 11 for the forbidden list.

King James

23 Then called he them in, and lodged *them.* And on the morrow Peter went away with them, and certain brethren from Joppa accompanied him.

24 And the morrow after they entered into Cæsarea. And Cornelius waited for them, and had called together his kinsmen and near friends.

24 And as Peter was coming in, Cornelius met him, and fell down at his feet, and worshipped *him.*

26 But Peter took him up, saying, Stand up; I myself also am a man.

27 And as he talked with him, he went in, and found many that were come together.

28 And he said unto them, Ye know how that it is an unlawful thing for a man that is a Jew to keep company, or come unto one of another nation; but God hath shewed me that I should not call any man common or unclean.

29 Therefore came I *unto you* without gainsaying, as soon as I was sent for: I ask therefore for what intent ye have sent for me?

30 And Cornelius said, Four days ago I was fasting until this hour; and at the ninth hour I prayed in my house, and, behold, a man stood before me in bright clothing,

31 And said, Cornelius, thy prayer is heard, and thine alms are had in remembrance in the sight of God.

32 Send therefore to Joppa, and call hither Simon, whose surname is Peter; he is lodged in the house of *one* Simon a tanner by the sea side: who, when he cometh, shall speak unto thee.

33 Immediately therefore I sent to thee; and thou hast well done that thou art come. Now therefore are we all here present before God, to hear all things that are commanded thee of God.

34 ¶ Then Peter opened *his* mouth, and said, Of a truth I perceive that God is no respecter of persons:

35 But in every nation he that feareth him, and worketh righteousness, is accepted with him.

36 The word which *God* sent unto the children of Israel, preaching peace by Jesus Christ: (he is Lord of all:)

37 That word, *I say*, ye know, which was published throughout all Judæa, and began from Galilee, after the baptism which John preached;

38 How God anointed Jesus of Nazareth with the Holy Ghost and with power: who went about doing good, and healing all that were oppressed of the devil; for God was with him.

39 And we are witnesses of all things which he did both in the land of the Jews, and in Jerusalem; whom they slew and hanged on a tree:

40 Him God raised up the third day, and shewed him openly;

Amplified

23 So Peter invited them in to be his guests [for the night]. The next day he arose and went away with them, and some of the brethren from Joppa accompanied him.

24 And on the following day they entered Caesarea. Cornelius was waiting for *and* expecting them, and he had invited together his relatives and his intimate friends.

25 As Peter arrived, Cornelius met him, and falling down at his feet he made obeisance *and* paid worshipful reverence to him.

26 But Peter raised him up, saying, Get up; I myself am also a man.

27 And as [Peter] spoke with him, he entered the house and found a large group of persons assembled;

28 And he said to them, You yourselves are aware how it is not lawful *or* permissible for a Jew to keep company with *or* to visit *or* [even] to come near *or* to speak first to any one of another nationality, but God has shown *and* taught me by words that I should not call any human being common *or* unhallowed or (ceremonially) unclean.

29 Therefore when I was sent for, I came without hesitation *or* objection *or* misgivings. So now I ask for what reason you sent for me.

30 And Cornelius said, This is now the fourth day since about this time I was observing the ninth hour [three o'clock in the afternoon] of prayer in my lodging place, when [suddenly] a man stood before me in dazzling apparel;

31 And he said, Cornelius, your prayer has been heard *and* harkened to, and your donations to the poor have been known *and* [m]preserved before God—so that He heeds and is about to help you.

32 Send therefore to Joppa and ask for Simon who is surnamed Peter; he is staying in the house of Simon the tanner, by the seaside.

33 So at once I sent for you, and you [being a Jew] have done a kind *and* [n]courteous *and* handsome thing in coming. Now then, we are all present in the sight of God to listen to all that you have been instructed by the Lord to say.

34 And Peter opened his mouth and said: Most certainly *and* thoroughly I now perceive *and* understand that God shows no partiality *and* is no respecter of persons,

35 But in every nation he who venerates *and* has a reverential fear for God, treating Him with worshipful obedience and living uprightly, is acceptable to Him *and* [o]sure of being received and welcomed [by Him].

36 You know the contents of the message which He sent to Israel, announcing the good news (Gospel) of peace by Jesus Christ, Who is Lord of all,

37 The [same] message which was proclaimed throughout all Judea, starting from Galilee after the baptism preached by John:

38 How God anointed *and* consecrated Jesus of Nazareth with the (Holy) Spirit and with strength *and* ability *and* power; how He went about doing good and [p]in particular curing all that were harassed *and* oppressed by [the power of] the devil, for God was with Him.

39 And we are [eye and ear] witnesses of everything that He did both in the land of the Jews and in Jerusalem. And [yet] they put Him out of the way—murdered Him—by hanging Him on a tree;

40 But God raised Him to life on the third day and caused Him to be manifest—to be plainly seen—

---

m) Thayer.
n) Vincent.
o) Webster's definition of "acceptable."
p) Vincent.

Living New Testament

23 So Peter invited them in and lodged them overnight. The next day he went with them, accompanied by some other believers from Joppa.

24 They arrived in Caesarea the following day, and Cornelius was waiting for him, and had called together his relatives and close friends to meet Peter.

25 As Peter entered his home, Cornelius fell to the floor before him in worship.

26 But Peter said, "Stand up! I'm not a god!"

27 So he got up and they talked together for a while and then went in where the others were assembled.

28 Peter told them, "You know it is against the Jewish laws for me to come into a Gentile home like this. But God has shown me in a vision that I should never think of anyone as inferior.[3]

29 So I came as soon as I was sent for. Now tell me what you want."

30 Cornelius replied, "Four days ago I was praying as usual at this time of the afternoon, when suddenly a man was standing before me clothed in a radiant robe!

31 He told me, 'Cornelius, your prayers are heard and your charities have been noticed by God!

32 Now send some men to Joppa and summon Simon Peter, who is staying in the home of Simon, a tanner, down by the shore.'

33 So I sent for you at once, and you have done well to come so soon. Now here we are, waiting before the Lord, anxious to hear what He has told you to tell us!"

34 Then Peter replied, "I see very clearly that the Jews are not God's only favorites!

35 In every nation He has those who worship Him and do good deeds and are acceptable to Him.

36, 37 I'm sure you have heard about the Good News for the people of Israel—that there is peace with God through Jesus, the Messiah, who is Lord of all creation. This message has spread all through Judea, beginning with John the Baptist in Galilee.

38 And you no doubt know that Jesus of Nazareth was anointed by God with the Holy Spirit and with power, and He went around doing good and healing all who were possessed by demons, for God was with Him.

39 And we apostles are witnesses of all He did throughout Israel and in Jerusalem, where He was murdered on a cross.

40, 41 But God brought Him back to life again three days later and showed Him to certain witnesses God had selected beforehand—not to the general public, but to us who ate and drank with Him after He rose from the dead.

[3] Literally, "that I should not call any man common or unclean."

Revised Standard

23 So he called them in to be his guests.

Peter's visit to Cornelius

The next day he rose and went off with
them, and some of the brethren from Joppa
accompanied him. 24 And on the following
day they entered Caesarea. Cornelius was
expecting them and had called together his
kinsmen and close friends. 25 When Peter
entered, Cornelius met him and fell down at
his feet and worshiped him. 26 But Peter
lifted him up, saying, "Stand up; I too am a
man." 27 And as he talked with him, he
went in and found many persons gathered;
28 and he said to them, "You yourselves
know how unlawful it is for a Jew to associate with or to visit any one of another
nation; but God has shown me that I should
not call any man common or unclean. 29 So
when I was sent for, I came without objection. I ask then why you sent for me."
30 And Cornelius said, "Four days ago,
about this hour, I was keeping the ninth
hour of prayer in my house; and behold, a
man stood before me in bright apparel,
31 saying, 'Cornelius, your prayer has been
heard and your alms have been remembered
before God. 32 Send therefore to Joppa and
ask for Simon who is called Peter; he is
lodging in the house of Simon, a tanner, by
the seaside.' 33 So I sent to you at once, and
you have been kind enough to come. Now
therefore we are all here present in the sight
of God, to hear all that you have been
commanded by the Lord."

Peter's sermon to Cornelius

34 And Peter opened his mouth and said:
"Truly I perceive that God shows no partiality, 35 but in every nation any one who
fears him and does what is right is acceptable to him. 36 You know the word which he
sent to Israel, preaching good news of peace
by Jesus Christ (he is Lord of all), 37 the
word which was proclaimed throughout all
Judea, beginning from Galilee after the baptism which John preached: 38 how God
anointed Jesus of Nazareth with the Holy
Spirit and with power; how he went about
doing good and healing all that were oppressed by the devil, for God was with him.
39 And we are witnesses to all that he did
both in the country of the Jews and in
Jerusalem. They put him to death by hanging him on a tree; 40 but God raised him on
the third day and made him manifest; 41 not

King James

41 Not to all the people, but unto witnesses chosen before of God, *even* to us, who did eat and drink with him after he rose from the dead.
42 And he commanded us to preach unto the people, and to testify that it is he which was ordained of God *to be* the Judge of quick and dead.
43 To him give all the prophets witness, that through his name whosoever believeth in him shall receive remission of sins.
44 ¶ While Peter yet spake these words, the Holy Ghost fell on all them which heard the word.
45 And they of the circumcision which believed were astonished, as many as came with Peter, because that on the Gentiles also was poured out the gift of the Holy Ghost.
46 For they heard them speak with tongues, and magnify God. Then answered Peter,
47 Can any man forbid water, that these should not be baptized, which have received the Holy Ghost as well as we?
48 And he commanded them to be baptized in the name of the Lord. Then prayed they him to tarry certain days.

CHAPTER 11

AND the apostles and brethren that were in Judæa heard that the Gentiles had also received the word of God.
2 And when Peter was come up to Jerusalem, they that were of the circumcision contended with him,
3 Saying, Thou wentest in to men uncircumcised, and didst eat with them.
4 But Peter rehearsed *the matter* from the beginning, and expounded *it* by order unto them, saying,
5 I was in the city of Joppa praying: and in a trance I saw a vision, A certain vessel descend, as it had been a great sheet, let down from heaven by four corners; and it came even to me:
6 Upon the which when I had fastened mine eyes, I considered, and saw fourfooted beasts of the earth, and wild beasts, and creeping things, and fowls of the air.
7 And I heard a voice saying unto me, Arise, Peter; slay and eat.
8 But I said, Not so, Lord: for nothing common or unclean hath at any time entered into my mouth.
9 But the voice answered me again from heaven, What God hath cleansed, *that* call not thou common.
10 And this was done three times: and all were drawn up again into heaven.
11 And, behold, immediately there were three men already come unto the house where I was, sent from Cæsarea unto me.

Amplified

41 Not by all the people but to us who were chosen (designated) beforehand by God as witnesses, who ate and drank with Him after He arose from the dead.
42 And He charged us to preach to the people, and to bear solemn testimony that He is the God-appointed *and* God-ordained Judge of the living and the dead.
43 To Him all the prophets testify (bear witness) that every one who believes in Him—who adheres to, trusts in and relies on Him, giving himself up to Him—receives forgiveness of sins through His name.
44 While Peter was still speaking these words, the Holy Spirit fell on all who were listening to the message.
45 And the believers from among the circumcised [the Jews] who came with Peter were surprised *and* amazed, because the free gift of the Holy Spirit had been bestowed *and* poured out largely even on the Gentiles.
46 For they heard them talking in [unknown] languages and extolling *and* magnifying God. Then Peter asked,
47 Can any one forbid *or* refuse water for baptizing these people, seeing that they have received the Holy Spirit just as we have?
48 And he ordered that they be baptized in the name of Jesus Christ, the Messiah. Then they begged him to stay on there for some days.

CHAPTER 11

NOW the apostles (special messengers) and the brethren who were throughout Judea heard [with astonishment] that the Gentiles (heathen) also had received *and* accepted *and* welcomed the Word of God—that is, the doctrine concerning the attainment through Christ of salvation in the kingdom of God.
2 So when Peter went up to Jerusalem, the circumcision party [the Jewish Christians] found fault with him—separating themselves from him in a hostile spirit, opposing and disputing and contending with him—
3 Saying, Why do you go to uncircumcised men and [even] eat with them?
4 But Peter began [at the beginning] and narrated *and* explained to them step by step [the whole list of events]. He said:
5 I was in the town of Joppa praying, and [falling] in a trance I saw a vision, of something coming down from heaven, like a huge sheet lowered by the four corners; and it descended until it came to me.
6 Gazing intently *and* closely at it I observed in it [a variety] of four-footed animals and wild beasts and reptiles of the earth and birds of the air,
7 And I heard a voice saying to me, Get up, Peter; kill and eat.
8 But I said, [No] by no means, Lord; for nothing common *or* unhallowed or (ceremonially) unclean has ever entered my mouth.
9 But the voice answered a second time from heaven, What God has cleansed *and* pronounced clean, do not you defile *and* profane by regarding *or* calling it common *or* unhallowed or unclean.
10 This occurred three times, and then all was drawn up again into heaven.
11 And right then the three men sent to me from Caesarea arrived at the house in which we were.

Living New Testament

42 And He sent us to preach the Good News everywhere and to testify that Jesus is ordained of God to be the Judge of all—living and dead.

43 And all the prophets have written about Him, saying that everyone who believes in Him will have their sins forgiven through His name."

44 Even as Peter was saying these things, the Holy Spirit fell upon all those listening!

45 The Jews who came with Peter were amazed that the gift of the Holy Spirit would be given to Gentiles too!

46, 47 But there could be no doubt about it,[4] for they heard them speaking in tongues and praising God. Peter asked, "Can anyone object to my baptizing them, now that they have received the Holy Spirit just as we did?"

48 So he did,[4] baptizing them in the name of Jesus, the Messiah. Afterwards Cornelius begged him to stay with them for several days.

Revised Standard

to all the people but to us who were chosen
by God as witnesses, who ate and drank
with him after he rose from the dead.
[42]And he commanded us to preach to the
people, and to testify that he is the one
ordained by God to be judge of the living
and the dead. [43]To him all the prophets
bear witness that every one who believes in
him receives forgiveness of sins through his
name."

Gentiles receive the Holy Spirit

44 While Peter was still saying this, the
Holy Spirit fell on all who heard the word.
[45]And the believers from among the circumcised who came with Peter were
amazed, because the gift of the Holy Spirit
had been poured out even on the Gentiles.
[46]For they heard them speaking in tongues
and extolling God. Then Peter declared,
[47]"Can any one forbid water for baptizing
these people who have received the Holy
Spirit just as we have?" [48]And he commanded them to be baptized in the name of
Jesus Christ. Then they asked him to remain
for some days.

CHAPTER 11

Soon the news reached the apostles and other brothers in Judea that Gentiles also were being converted!

2 But when Peter arrived back in Jerusalem, the Jewish believers argued with him.

3 "You fellowshiped with Gentiles and even ate with them," they accused.

4 Then Peter told them the whole story.

5 "One day in Joppa," he said, "while I was praying, I saw a vision—a huge sheet, let down by its four corners from the sky.

6 Inside the sheet were all sorts of animals, reptiles and birds [which we are not to eat[1]].

7 And I heard a voice say, 'Kill and eat whatever you wish.'

8 'Never, Lord,' I replied. 'For I have never yet eaten anything forbidden by our Jewish laws!'

9 But the voice came again, 'Don't say it isn't right when God declares it is!'

10 This happened *three times* before the sheet and all it contained disappeared into heaven.

11 Just then three men who had come to take me with them to Caesarea arrived at the house where I was staying!

11 Now the apostles and the brethren
who were in Judea heard that the
Gentiles also had received the word of God.
[2]So when Peter went up to Jerusalem, the
circumcision party criticized him, [3]saying,
"Why did you go to uncircumcised men and
eat with them?" [4]But Peter began and explained to them in order: [5]"I was in the city
of Joppa praying; and in a trance I saw a
vision, something descending, like a great
sheet, let down from heaven by four corners; and it came down to me. [6]Looking at
it closely I observed animals and beasts of
prey and reptiles and birds of the air. [7]And
I heard a voice saying to me, 'Rise, Peter;
kill and eat.' [8]But I said, 'No, Lord; for
nothing common or unclean has ever entered my mouth.' [9]But the voice answered a
second time from heaven, 'What God has
cleansed you must not call common.' [10]This
happened three times, and all was drawn up
again into heaven. [11]At that very moment
three men arrived at the house in which we
were, sent to me from Caesarea. [12]And the

Implied.
Implied.

King James

12 And the Spirit bade me go with them, nothing doubting. Moreover these six brethren accompanied me, and we entered into the man's house:

13 And he shewed us how he had seen an angel in his house, which stood and said unto him, Send men to Joppa, and call for Simon, whose surname is Peter;

14 Who shall tell thee words, whereby thou and all thy house shall be saved.

15 And as I began to speak, the Holy Ghost fell on them, as on us at the beginning.

16 Then remembered I the word of the Lord, how that he said, John indeed baptized with water; but ye shall be baptized with the Holy Ghost.

17 Forasmuch then as God gave them the like gift as *he did* unto us, who believed on the Lord Jesus Christ; what was I, that I could withstand God?

18 When they heard these things, they held their peace, and glorified God, saying, Then hath God also to the Gentiles granted repentance unto life.

19 ¶ Now they which were scattered abroad upon the persecution that arose about Stephen travelled as far as Phenice, and Cyprus, and Antioch, preaching the word to none but unto the Jews only.

20 And some of them were men of Cyprus and Cyrene, which, when they were come to Antioch, spake unto the Grecians, preaching the Lord Jesus.

21 And the hand of the Lord was with them: and a great number believed, and turned unto the Lord.

22 ¶ Then tidings of these things came unto the ears of the church which was in Jerusalem: and they sent forth Barnabas, that he should go as far as Antioch.

23 Who, when he came, and had seen the grace of God, was glad, and exhorted them all, that with purpose of heart they would cleave unto the Lord.

24 For he was a good man, and full of the Holy Ghost and of faith: and much people was added unto the Lord.

25 Then departed Barnabas to Tarsus, for to seek Saul:

26 And when he had found him, he brought him unto Antioch. And it came to pass, that a whole year they assembled themselves with the church, and taught much people. And the disciples were called Christians first in Antioch.

27 ¶ And in these days came prophets from Jerusalem unto Antioch.

28 And there stood up one of them named Agabus, and signified by the Spirit that there should be great dearth throughout all the world: which came to pass in the days of Claudius Cæsar.

Amplified

12 And the (Holy) Spirit instructed me to accompany them without [the least] hesitation *or* misgivings *or* discrimination. So these six brethren accompanied me also and we went into the man's house.

13 And he related to us how he had seen the angel in his house which stood and said to him, Send men to Joppa and bring Simon who is surnamed Peter;

14 He will give *and* explain to you a message by means of which you and all your household [as well] will be saved [[q]from eternal death].

15 When I began to speak, the Holy Spirit fell on them just as on us at the beginning.

16 Then I recalled the declaration of the Lord, how He said, John indeed baptized with water, but you shall be baptized with—[r]be placed in, introduced into—the Holy Spirit.

17 If then God gave to them the same Gift [equally] as He gave to us when we believed—adhering to, trusting in and relying on—the Lord Jesus Christ, who was I *and* what power *or* authority had I to interfere *or* hinder *or* forbid *or* withstand God?

18 When they heard this they were quieted *and* made no further objection. And they glorified God, saying, Then God has also granted to the Gentiles repentance [s]unto [real] life [after resurrection].

19 Meanwhile those who were scattered because of the persecution that arose in connection with Stephen had traveled as far away as Phoenicia and Cyprus and Antioch, without delivering the message [concerning [t]the attainment through Christ of salvation in the kingdom of God] to any one except Jews.

20 But there were some of them, men of Cyprus and Cyrene, who on returning to Antioch spoke to the Greeks also, proclaiming [to them] the good news, the Lord Jesus.

21 And the presence of the Lord was with them with power, so that a great number [learned] to believe—to adhere to and trust in and rely on the Lord—and turned *and* surrendered themselves to Him.

22 The rumors of this came to the ears of the church (assembly) in Jerusalem, and they sent Barnabas to Antioch.

23 When he arrived and saw what grace (favor) God was bestowing upon them, he was full of joy; and he continuously exhorted—warned, urged and encouraged—them all to cleave unto *and* remain faithful *and* devoted to the Lord with [resolute and steady] purpose of heart.

24 For he was a good man [[t]good in himself and also at once for the good and the advantage of other people], full of *and* controlled by the Holy Spirit and full of faith [that is, of his [s]belief that Jesus is the Messiah, through Whom we obtain eternal salvation]. And a large company was added to the Lord.

25 [Barnabas] went on to Tarsus to hunt for Saul.

26 And when he had found him, he brought him back to Antioch. For a whole year they assembled together with *and* [u]were guests of the church, and instructed a large number of people; and in Antioch the disciples were first called Christians.

27 And during these days prophets—inspired teachers and interpreters of the divine will and purpose—came down from Jerusalem to Antioch.

28 And one of them named Agabus stood up and prophesied through the (Holy) Spirit that there would be a great *and* severe famine come upon the whole world And this did occur during the reign of Claudius.

---

q) Cremer.
r) Wuest's "Untranslatable Riches from the Greek New Testament."
s) Thayer.
t) Cremer's "Biblico-Theological Lexicon in New Testament Greek."
u) Alternate reading.

Living New Testament

12 The Holy Spirit told me to go with them and not
o worry about their being Gentiles! These six brothers
iere accompanied me, and we soon arrived at the home of
he man who had sent the messengers.
13 He told us how an angel had appeared to him and
old him to send messengers to Joppa to find Simon Peter!
14 'He will tell you how you and all your household
an be saved!' the angel had told him.
15 Well, I began telling them the Good News, but just
s I was getting started with my sermon, the Holy Spirit
ell on them, just as He fell on us at the beginning!
16 Then I thought of the Lord's words when He said,
Yes, John baptized with[2] water, but you shall be baptized
vith[2] the Holy Spirit.'
17 And since it was *God* who gave these Gentiles the
ame gift He gave us when we believed on the Lord Jesus
Christ, who was I to argue?"
18 When the others heard this, all their objections were
nswered and they began praising God! "Yes," they said,
God has given to the Gentiles, too, the privilege of turn-
ng to Him and receiving eternal life!"
19 Meanwhile, the believers who fled from Jerusalem
uring the persecution after Stephen's death traveled as
ar as Phoenicia, Cyprus, and Antioch, scattering the
Good News, but only to Jews.
20 However, some of the believers who went to Antioch
rom Cyprus and Cyrene also gave their message about the
Lord Jesus to some Greeks.
21 And the Lord honored this effort so that large num-
ers of these Gentiles became believers.
22 When the church at Jerusalem heard what had
appened, they sent Barnabas to Antioch to help the new
onverts.
23 When he arrived and saw the wonderful things God
vas doing, he was filled with excitement and joy, and
ncouraged the believers to stay close to the Lord, what-
ver the cost.
24 Barnabas was a kindly person, full of the Holy
Spirit and strong in faith. As a result large numbers of
eople were added to the Lord.
25 Then Barnabas went on to Tarsus to hunt for Saul.
26 When he found him, he brought him back to
Antioch; and both of them stayed there for a full year
eaching the many new converts. (It was there at Antioch
hat the believers were first called "Christians.")
27 During this time some prophets came down from
erusalem to Antioch,
28 And one of them, named Agabus, stood up in one
f the meetings to predict by the Spirit that a great
amine was coming upon the land of Israel.[3] (This was
ulfilled during the reign of Claudius.)

Or, "in."
Literally, "upon the earth."

Revised Standard

Spirit told me to go with them, making no
distinction. These six brethren also accompanied me, and we entered the man's house.
13 And he told us how he had seen the angel
standing in his house and saying, 'Send to
Joppa and bring Simon called Peter; 14 he
will declare to you a message by which you
will be saved, you and all your household.'
15 As I began to speak, the Holy Spirit fell
on them just as on us at the beginning.
16 And I remembered the word of the Lord,
how he said, 'John baptized with water, but
you shall be baptized with the Holy Spirit.'
17 If then God gave the same gift to them as
he gave to us when we believed in the Lord
Jesus Christ, who was I that I could withstand God?" 18 When they heard this they
were silenced. And they glorified God, saying, "Then to the Gentiles also God has
granted repentance unto life."

Barnabas and the church at Antioch

19 Now those who were scattered because of the persecution that arose over
Stephen traveled as far as Phoenicia and
Cyprus and Antioch, speaking the word to
none except Jews. 20 But there were some of
them, men of Cyprus and Cyrene, who on
coming to Antioch spoke to the Greeks[i]
also, preaching the Lord Jesus. 21 And the
hand of the Lord was with them, and a
great number that believed turned to the
Lord. 22 News of this came to the ears of
the church in Jerusalem, and they sent Barnabas to Antioch. 23 When he came and saw
the grace of God, he was glad; and he
exhorted them all to remain faithful to the
Lord with steadfast purpose; 24 for he was
a good man, full of the Holy Spirit and of
faith. And a large company was added to
the Lord. 25 So Barnabas went to Tarsus to
look for Saul; 26 and when he had found
him, he brought him to Antioch. For a
whole year they met with[j] the church, and
taught a large company of people; and in
Antioch the disciples were for the first time
called Christians.
27 Now in these days prophets came
down from Jerusalem to Antioch. 28 And
one of them named Agabus stood up and
foretold by the Spirit that there would be a
great famine over all the world; and this
took place in the days of Claudius. 29 And

[i] Other ancient authorities read *Hellenists*
[j] Or *were guests of*

King James

29 Then the disciples, every man according to his ability, determined to send relief unto the brethren which dwelt in Judæa:

30 Which also they did, and sent it to the elders by the hands of Barnabas and Saul.

CHAPTER 12

NOW about that time Herod the king stretched forth *his* hands to vex certain of the church.

2 And he killed James the brother of John with the sword.

3 And because he saw it pleased the Jews, he proceeded further to take Peter also. (Then were the days of unleavened bread.)

4 And when he had apprehended him, he put *him* in prison, and delivered *him* to four quaternions of soldiers to keep him; intending after Easter to bring him forth to the people.

5 Peter therefore was kept in prison: but prayer was made without ceasing of the church unto God for him.

6 And when Herod would have brought him forth, the same night Peter was sleeping between two soldiers, bound with two chains: and the keepers before the door kept the prison.

7 And, behold, the angel of the Lord came upon *him*, and a light shined in the prison: and he smote Peter on the side, and raised him up, saying, Arise up quickly. And his chains fell off from *his* hands.

8 And the angel said unto him, Gird thyself, and bind on thy sandals. And so he did. And he saith unto him, Cast thy garment about thee, and follow me.

9 And he went out, and followed him; and wist not that it was true which was done by the angel; but thought he saw a vision.

10 When they were past the first and the second ward, they came unto the iron gate that leadeth unto the city; which opened to them of his own accord: and they went out, and passed on through one street; and forthwith the angel departed from him.

11 And when Peter was come to himself, he said, Now I know of a surety, that the Lord hath sent his angel, and hath delivered me out of the hand of Herod, and *from* all the expectation of the people of the Jews.

12 And when he had considered *the thing*, he came to the house of Mary the mother of John, whose surname was Mark; where many were gathered together praying.

13 And as Peter knocked at the door of the gate, a damsel came to hearken, named Rhoda.

14 And when she knew Peter's voice, she opened not the gate for gladness, but ran in, and told how Peter stood before the gate.

Amplified

29 So the disciples resolved to send relief, every one according to his individual ability—in proportion as he had prospered—to the brethren who lived in Judea.

30 And so they did, sending [their contributions] to the elders by the hand of Barnabas and Saul.

CHAPTER 12

ABOUT that time Herod the king stretched forth his hands to afflict *and* oppress *and* torment some who belonged to the church (assembly).

2 And he killed James the brother of John with a sword;

3 And when he saw that it was pleasing to the Jews, he proceeded further and arrested Peter also. This was during the days of Unleavened Bread (the Passover week).

4 And when he had seized [Peter], he put him in prison and delivered him to four squads of soldiers of four each to guard him, purposing after the Passover to bring him forth to the people.

5 So Peter was kept in prison; but fervent prayer for him was persistently made to God by the church (assembly).

6 The very night before Herod was about to bring him forth, Peter was sleeping between two soldiers, fastened with two chains, and sentries before the door were guarding the prison.

7 And suddenly an angel of the Lord appeared, standing beside him, and a light shone in the place where he was. And the angel gently smote Peter on the side and awakened him, saying, Get up quickly! And the chains fell off his hands.

8 And the angel said to him, Tighten your girdle and bind on your sandals. And he did so. And he said to him, Wrap your outer garment around you and follow me.

9 And [Peter] went out [along] following him, and he was not conscious that what was apparently being done by the angel was real, but thought he was seeing a vision.

10 When they had passed through the first guard and the second, they came to the iron gate which leads into the city. Of its own accord [the gate] swung open, and they went out and passed on through one street; and at once the angel left him.

11 Then Peter came to himself, and said, Now I really know *and* am sure that the Lord has sent His angel and delivered me out of the hand of Herod and from all that the Jewish people were expecting to do to me.

12 When he at a glance became aware of this—[v]comprehending [all the elements of the case]—he went to the house of Mary, the mother of John whose surname was Mark, where a large number were assembled together and were praying.

13 And when he knocked at the gate of the porch, a maid named Rhoda [Rose, in English] came to answer.

14 And recognizing Peter's voice, in her joy she failed to open the gate, but ran in and told the people that Peter was standing before the porch gate.

---

v) Vincent.

Living New Testament

29 So the believers decided to send relief to the Christians in Judea, each giving as much as he could.

30 This they did, consigning their gifts to Barnabas and Paul to take to the elders of the church in Jerusalem.

Revised Standard

the disciples determined, every one according to his ability, to send relief to the
brethren who lived in Judea; [30]and they
did so, sending it to the elders by the hand
of Barnabas and Saul.

CHAPTER 12

About that time King Herod moved against some of the believers,

2 And killed the apostle[1] James (John's brother).

3 When Herod saw how much this pleased the Jewish leaders, he arrested Peter during the Passover celebration

4 And imprisoned him, placing him under the guard of 16 soldiers. Herod's intention was to deliver Peter to the Jews for execution after the Passover.

5 But earnest prayer was going up to God from the Church for his safety all the time he was in prison.

6 The night before he was to be executed, he was asleep, double-chained between two soldiers with others standing guard before the prison gate,

7 When suddenly there was a light in the cell and an angel of the Lord stood beside Peter! The angel slapped him on the side to awaken him and said, "Quick! Get up!" And the chains fell off his wrists!

8 Then the angel told him, "Get dressed and put on your shoes." And he did. "Now put on your coat and follow me!" the angel ordered.

9 So Peter left the cell, following the angel. But all the time he thought it was a dream or vision, and didn't believe it was really happening.

10 They passed the first and second cell blocks and came to the iron gate to the street, and this opened to them of its own accord! So they passed through and walked along together for a block, and then the angel left him.

11 Peter finally realized what had happened! "It's really true!" he said to himself. "The Lord has sent His angel and saved me from Herod and from what the Jews were hoping to do to me!"

12 After a little thought he went to the home of Mary, mother of John Mark, where many were gathered for a prayer meeting.

13 He knocked at the door in the gate, and a girl named Rhoda came to open it.

14 When she recognized Peter's voice, she was so overjoyed that she ran back inside to tell everyone that Peter was standing outside in the street!

James killed; Peter imprisoned

12 About that time Herod the king laid
violent hands upon some who belonged to the church. [2]He killed James the
brother of John with the sword; [3]and when
he saw that it pleased the Jews, he proceeded to arrest Peter also. This was during the
days of Unleavened Bread. [4]And when he
had seized him, he put him in prison, and
delivered him to four squads of soldiers to
guard him, intending after the Passover to
bring him out to the people. [5]So Peter was
kept in prison; but earnest prayer for him
was made to God by the church.

Peter delivered from prison

6 The very night when Herod was about
to bring him out, Peter was sleeping between two soldiers, bound with two chains,
and sentries before the door were guarding
the prison; [7]and behold, an angel of the
Lord appeared, and a light shone in the cell;
and he struck Peter on the side and woke
him, saying, "Get up quickly." And the
chains fell off his hands. [8]And the angel said
to him, "Dress yourself and put on your
sandals." And he did so. And he said to him,
"Wrap your mantle around you and follow
me." [9]And he went out and followed him;
he did not know that what was done by the
angel was real, but thought he was seeing a
vision. [10]When they had passed the first and
the second guard, they came to the iron gate
leading into the city. It opened to them out
of its own accord, and they went out and
passed on through one street; and immediately the angel left him. [11]And Peter came
to himself, and said, "Now I am sure that
the Lord has sent his angel and rescued me
from the hand of Herod and from all that
the Jewish people were expecting."

12 When he realized this, he went to the
house of Mary, the mother of John whose
other name was Mark, where many were
gathered together and were praying. [13]And
when he knocked at the door of the gateway, a maid named Rhoda came to answer.
[14]Recognizing Peter's voice, in her joy she
did not open the gate but ran in and told
that Peter was standing at the gate. [15]They

[1] Implied.

King James

15 And they said unto her, Thou art mad. But she constantly affirmed that it was even so. Then said they, It is his angel.

16 But Peter continued knocking: and when they had opened *the door*, and saw him, they were astonished.

17 But he, beckoning unto them with the hand to hold their peace, declared unto them how the Lord had brought him out of the prison. And he said, Go shew these things unto James, and to the brethren. And he departed, and went into another place.

18 Now as soon as it was day, there was no small stir among the soldiers, what was become of Peter.

19 And when Herod had sought for him, and found him not, he examined the keepers, and commanded that *they* should be put to death. And he went down from Judæa to Cæsarea, and *there* abode.

20 ¶ And Herod was highly displeased with them of Tyre and Sidon: but they came with one accord to him, and, having made Blastus the king's chamberlain their friend, desired peace; because their country was nourished by the king's *country*.

21 And upon a set day Herod, arrayed in royal apparel, sat upon his throne, and made an oration unto them.

22 And the people gave a shout, *saying, It is* the voice of a god, and not of a man.

23 And immediately the angel of the Lord smote him, because he gave not God the glory: and he was eaten of worms, and gave up the ghost.

24 ¶ But the word of God grew and multiplied.

25 And Barnabas and Saul returned from Jerusalem, when they had fulfilled *their* ministry, and took with them John, whose surname was Mark.

Amplified

15 They said to her, You are crazy! But she persistently *and* strongly *and* confidently affirmed that it was the truth. They said, It is his angel!

16 But meanwhile Peter continued knocking, and when they opened the gate and saw him, they were amazed.

17 But motioning to them with his hand to keep quiet *and* listen, he related to them how the Lord had delivered him out of the prison. And he said, Report all this to James [the less] and to the brethren. Then he left and went to some other place.

18 Now as soon as it was day, there was no small disturbance among the soldiers over what had become of Peter.

19 And when Herod had looked for him and could not find him, he placed the guards on trial and commanded that they should be led away [to execution]. Then [Herod] went down from Judea to Caesarea, and stayed on there.

20 Now [Herod] cherished bitter animosity *and* hostility for the people of Tyre and Sidon; and [their deputies] came to him in a united body, and having made Blastus the king's chamberlain their friend, they asked for peace, because their country was nourished by *and* depended on the king's [country] for food.

21 On an appointed day Herod arrayed himself in his royal robes, took his seat upon [his] throne, and addressed an oration to them.

22 And the assembled people shouted, It is the voice of a god, and not of a man!

23 And at once an angel of the Lord smote him *and* cut him down, because he did not give God the glory—that is, the pre-eminence and kingly majesty that belong to Him as the supreme Ruler; and he was eaten by worms and died.

24 But the Word of the Lord [concerning the attainment through Christ of salvation in the kingdom of God] continued to grow and spread.

25 And Barnabas and Saul came back from Jerusalem when they had completed their mission, bringing with them John whose surname was Mark.

CHAPTER 13

NOW there were in the church that was at Antioch certain prophets and teachers; as Barnabas, and Simeon that was called Niger, and Lucius of Cyrene, and Manaen, which had been brought up with Herod the tetrarch, and Saul.

2 As they ministered to the Lord, and fasted, the Holy Ghost said, Separate me Barnabas and Saul for the work whereunto I have called them.

3 And when they had fasted and prayed, and laid *their* hands on them, they sent *them* away.

4 ¶ So they, being sent forth by the Holy Ghost, departed unto Seleucia; and from thence they sailed to Cyprus.

5 And when they were at Salamis, they preached the word of God in the synagogues of the Jews: and they had also John to *their* minister.

CHAPTER 13

NOW in the church (assembly) at Antioch there were prophets—inspired interpreters of the will and purposes of God—and teachers, Barnabas, Symeon who was called Niger [black], Lucius of Cyrene, Manaen a member of the court of Herod the tetrarch, and Saul.

2 While they were worshipping the Lord and fasting, the Holy Spirit said, Separate now for Me Barnabas and Saul for the work to which I have called them.

3 Then after fasting and praying they put their hands on them and sent them away.

4 So then, being sent out by the Holy Spirit, they went down to Seleucia, and from [that port] they sailed away to Cyprus.

5 When they arrived at Salamis they preached the Word of God [concerning the attainment through Christ of salvation in the kingdom of God] in the synagogues of the Jews. And they had John [Mark] as an attendant to assist them.

Living New Testament

15 They didn't believe her. "You're out of your mind," they said. When she insisted they decided, "It must be his angel. [They must have killed him.[2]]"

16 Meanwhile Peter continued knocking! When they finally went out and opened the door, their surprise knew no bounds.

17 He motioned for them to quiet down and told them what had happened and how the Lord had brought him out of jail.

"Tell James and the others what happened," he said—and left for safer quarters.

18 At dawn, the jail was in great commotion. What had happened to Peter?

19 When Herod sent for him and found that he wasn't there, he had the 16 guards arrested, court-martialed and sentenced to death.[3] Afterwards he left to live in Caesarea for a while.

20 While he was in Caesarea, a delegation from Tyre and Sidon arrived to see him. He was highly displeased with the people of those two cities, but the delegates made friends with Blastus, the royal secretary, and asked for peace, for their cities were economically dependent upon trade with Herod's country.

21 An appointment with Herod was granted, and when the day arrived he put on his royal robes, sat on his throne and made a speech to them.

22 At its conclusion the people gave him a great ovation, shouting, "It is the voice of a god and not of a man!"

23 Instantly, an angel of the Lord struck Herod with a sickness so that he was filled with maggots and died—because he accepted the people's worship instead of giving the glory to God.

* * * * *

24 God's Good News was spreading rapidly and there were many new believers.

25 Barnabas and Paul now visited Jerusalem and, as soon as they had finished their business, returned to Antioch[3], taking John Mark with them.

Revised Standard

said to her, "You are mad." But she insisted that it was so, They said, "It is his angel!" 16But Peter continued knocking; and when they opened, they saw him and were amazed. 17But motioning to them with his hand to be silent, he described to them how the Lord had brought him out of the prison. And he said, "Tell this to James and to the brethren." Then he departed and went to another place.

The death of Herod

18 Now when day came, there was no small stir among the soldiers over what had become of Peter. 19And when Herod had sought for him and could not find him, he examined the sentries and ordered that they should be put to death. Then he went down from Judea to Caesarea, and remained there.

20 Now Herod was angry with the people of Tyre and Sidon; and they came to him in a body, and having persuaded Blastus, the king's chamberlain, they asked for peace, because their country depended on the king's country for food. 21On an appointed day Herod put on his royal robes, took his seat upon the throne, and made an oration to them. 22And the people shouted, "The voice of a god, and not of man!" 23Immediately an angel of the Lord smote him, because he did not give God the glory; and he was eaten by worms and died.

24 But the word of God grew and multiplied.

25 And Barnabas and Saul returned from[k] Jerusalem when they had fulfilled their mission, bringing with them John whose other name was Mark.

CHAPTER 13

Among the prophets and teachers of the church at Antioch were Barnabas and Symeon (also called "The Black Man"), Lucius (from Cyrene), Manaen (the foster-brother of King Herod), and Paul.

2 One day as these men were worshiping and fasting the Holy Spirit said, "Dedicate Barnabas and Paul for a special job I have for them."

3 So after more fasting and prayer, the men laid their hands on them—and sent them on their way.

4 Directed by the Holy Spirit they went to Seleucia and then sailed for Cyprus.

5 There, in the town of Salamis, they went to the Jewish synagogue and preached. (John Mark went with them as their assistant.)

[2] Implied.
[3] Implied.

Paul and Barnabas on Cyprus

13 Now in the church at Antioch there were prophets and teachers, Barnabas, Symeon who was called Niger, Lucius of Cyrene, Manaen a member of the court of Herod the tetrarch and Saul. 2While they were worshiping the Lord and fasting, the Holy Spirit said, "Set apart for me Barnabas and Saul for the work to which I have called them." 3Then after fasting and praying they laid their hands on them and sent them off.

4 So, being sent out by the Holy Spirit, they went down to Seleucia; and from there they sailed to Cyprus. 5When they arrived at Salamis, they proclaimed the word of God in the synagogues of the Jews. And they had John to assist them. 6When they

[k] Other ancient authorities read *to*

King James

6 And when they had gone through the isle unto Paphos, they found a certain sorcerer, a false prophet, a Jew, whose name *was* Bar-Jesus:

7 Which was with the deputy of the country, Sergius Paulus, a prudent man; who called for Barnabas and Saul, and desired to hear the word of God.

8 But Elymas the sorcerer (for so is his name by interpretation) withstood them, seeking to turn away the deputy from the faith.

9 Then Saul, (who also *is called* Paul,) filled with the Holy Ghost, set his eyes on him,

10 And said, O full of all subtilty and all mischief, *thou* child of the devil, *thou* enemy of all righteousness, wilt thou not cease to pervert the right ways of the Lord?

11 And now, behold, the hand of the Lord *is* upon thee, and thou shalt be blind, not seeing the sun for a season. And immediately there fell on him a mist and a darkness; and he went about seeking some to lead him by the hand.

12 Then the deputy, when he saw what was done, believed, being astonished at the doctrine of the Lord.

13 Now when Paul and his company loosed from Paphos, they came to Perga in Pamphylia: and John departing from them returned to Jerusalem.

14 ¶ But when they departed from Perga, they came to Antioch in Pisidia, and went into the synagogue on the sabbath day, and sat down.

15 And after the reading of the law and the prophets the rulers of the synagogue sent unto them, saying, *Ye* men *and* brethren, if ye have any word of exhortation for the people, say on.

16 Then Paul stood up, and beckoning with *his* hand said, Men of Israel, and ye that fear God, give audience.

17 The God of this people of Israel chose our fathers, and exalted the people when they dwelt as strangers in the land of Egypt, and with an high arm brought he them out of it.

18 And about the time of forty years suffered he their manners in the wilderness.

19 And when he had destroyed seven nations in the land of Chanaan, he divided their land to them by lot.

20 And after that he gave *unto them* judges about the space of four hundred and fifty years, until Samuel the prophet.

21 And afterward they desired a king: and God gave unto them Saul the son of Cis, a man of the tribe of Benjamin, by the space of forty years.

22 And when he had removed him, he raised up unto them David to be their king; to whom also he gave testimony, and said, I have found David the *son* of Jesse, a man after mine own heart, which shall fulfil all my will.

23 Of this man's seed hath God according to *his* promise raised unto Israel a Saviour, Jesus:

Amplified

6 When they had passed through the entire island of Cyprus as far as Paphos, they came upon a certain Jewish wizard *or* sorcerer, a false prophet named Bar-Jesus.

7 He was closely associated with the proconsul, Sergius Paulus, who was an intelligent *and* sensible man of sound understanding; he summoned to him Barnabas and Saul and sought to hear the Word of God [concerning salvation in the kingdom of God attained through Christ].

8 But Elymas [w]the wise man, for that is the translation of his name [[x]which he had given himself], opposed them, seeking to keep the proconsul from accepting the faith.

9 But Saul, who is also called Paul, filled with *and* controlled by the Holy Spirit, looked steadily at [Elymas]

10 And said, You master in every form of deception *and* recklessness, unscrupulousness *and* wickedness, you son of the devil, you enemy of everything that is upright *and* good, will you never stop perverting *and* making crooked the straight paths of the Lord *and* plotting against His saving purposes? [Hos. 14:9.]

11 And now, lo, the hand of the Lord is upon you, and you shall be blind, [so blind that you will be] unable to see the sun for a time. Instantly there fell upon him a mist and a darkness, and he groped about seeking persons who would lead him by the hand.

12 Then the proconsul believed—became a Christian—when he saw what had occurred, for he was astonished *and* deeply touched at the teaching concerning the Lord *and* from [Him].

13 Now Paul and his companions sailed from Paphos, and came to Perga in Pamphylia. And John [Mark] separated himself from them and went back to Jerusalem;

14 But they [themselves] came on from Perga and arrived at Antioch in Pisidia. And on the Sabbath day they went into the synagogue there and sat down.

15 After the reading of the Law and the prophets, the leaders [of the worship] of the synagogue sent to them saying, Brethren, if you have any word of exhortation *or* consolation *or* encouragement for the people, say it.

16 So Paul arose, and motioning with his hand said, Men of Israel, and you who reverence *and* fear God, listen!

17 The God of this people Israel selected our forefathers and made this people great *and* important during their stay in the land of Egypt, and then with uplifted arm He led them out from there. [Exod. 6:1, 6.]

18 And for about forty years [[y]as a nursing-father] He cared for them in the wilderness, *and* endured their behavior. [Deut. 1:31.]

19 When He had destroyed seven nations in the land of Canaan, He gave them [the Hebrews] their land as an inheritance—distributing it to them by lot; [all of which took] about four hundred and fifty years. [Deut. 7:1; Josh. 14:1.]

20 After that He gave them judges until the prophet Samuel.

21 Then they asked for a king; and God gave them Saul the son of Kish, a man of the tribe of Benjamin, for forty years.

22 And when He had deposed him, He raised up David to be their king; of him He bore witness and said, I have found David the Son of Jesse a man after My own heart, who will do all My will *and* carry out My program fully. [Ps. 89:20; I Sam. 13:14; Isa. 44:28.]

23 Of this man's descendants God has brought to Israel a Savior [in the person of Jesus], according to His promise.

---

w) Abbott-Smith.
x) Alford's "The Greek Testament, with Notes."
y) Some ancient authorities so read.

Living New Testament

6, 7 Afterwards they preached from town to town across the entire island until finally they reached Paphos where they met a Jewish sorcerer, a fake prophet named Bar-Jesus. He had attached himself to the governor, Sergius Paulus, a man of considerable insight and understanding. The governor invited Barnabas and Saul to visit him, for he wanted to hear their message from God.

8 But the sorcerer, Elymas (his name in Greek), interfered and urged the governor to pay no attention to what Paul and Barnabas said, trying to keep him from trusting the Lord.

9 Then Paul, filled with the Holy Spirit, glared angrily at the sorcerer and said,

10 "You son of the Devil, full of every sort of trickery and villainy, enemy of all that is good, will you never end your opposition to the Lord?

11 And now God has laid His hand of punishment upon you, and you will be stricken awhile with blindness." Instantly mist and darkness fell upon him, and he began wandering around begging for someone to take his hand and lead him.

12 When the governor saw what happened he believed and was astonished at the power of God's message.

13 Now Paul and those with him left Paphos by ship for Turkey,[1] landing at the port town of Perga. There John deserted[2] them and returned to Jerusalem.

14 But Barnabas and Paul went on to Antioch, a city in the province of Pisidia. On the Sabbath they went into the synagogue for the services.

15 After the usual readings from the Books of Moses and from the Prophets, those in charge of the service sent them this message: "Brothers, if you have any word of instruction for us come and give it!"

16 So Paul stood, waved a greeting to them[3] and began. "Men of Israel," he said, "and all others here who reverence God, [let me begin my remarks with a bit of history.[4]]

17 The God of this nation Israel chose our ancestors and honored them in Egypt by gloriously leading them out of their slavery.

18 And He nursed them through 40 years of wandering around in the wilderness.

19, 20 Then He destroyed seven nations in Canaan, and gave Israel their land as an inheritance. Judges ruled for about 450 years, and were followed by Samuel the prophet.

21 Then the people begged for a king, and God gave them Saul (son of Kish), a man of the tribe of Benjamin, who reigned for 40 years.

22 But God removed him and replaced him with David as king, a man about whom God said, 'David (son of Jesse) is a man after My own heart, for he will obey Me.'

23 And it is one of King David's descendants, Jesus, who is God's promised Savior of Israel!

[1] Literally, "Pamphylia."
[2] Literally, "departed from them." See chapter 15, verse 38.
[3] Literally, "beckoning with the hand."
[4] Implied.

Revised Standard

had gone through the whole island as far as Paphos, they came upon a certain magician, a Jewish false prophet, named Bar-Jesus. 7He was with the proconsul, Sergius Paulus, a man of intelligence, who summoned Barnabas and Saul and sought to hear the word of God. 8But Elymas the magician (for that is the meaning of his name) withstood them, seeking to turn away the proconsul from the faith. 9But Saul, who is also called Paul, filled with the Holy Spirit, looked intently at him 10and said, "You son of the devil, you enemy of all righteousness, full of all deceit and villainy, will you not stop making crooked the straight paths of the Lord? 11And now, behold, the hand of the Lord is upon you, and you shall be blind and unable to see the sun for a time." Immediately mist and darkness fell upon him and he went about seeking people to lead him by the hand. 12Then the proconsul believed, when he saw what had occurred, for he was astonished at the teaching of the Lord.

Preaching in Perga and Antioch

13 Now Paul and his company set sail from Paphos, and came to Perga in Pamphylia. And John left them and returned to Jerusalem; 14but they passed on from Perga and came to Antioch of Pisidia. And on the sabbath day they went into the synagogue and sat down. 15After the reading of the law and the prophets, the rulers of the synagogue sent to them, saying, "Brethren, if you have any word of exhortation for the people, say it." 16So Paul stood up, and motioning with his hand said:

"Men of Israel, and you that fear God, listen. 17The God of this people Israel chose our fathers and made the people great during their stay in the land of Egypt, and with uplifted arm he led them out of it. 18And for about forty years he bore with[m] them in the wilderness. 19And when he had destroyed seven nations in the land of Canaan, he gave them their land as an inheritance, for about four hundred and fifty years. 20And after that he gave them judges until Samuel the prophet. 21Then they asked for a king; and God gave them Saul the son of Kish, a man of the tribe of Benjamin, for forty years. 22And when he had removed him, he raised up David to be their king; of whom he testified and said, 'I have found in David the son of Jesse a man after my heart, who will do all my will.' 23Of this man's posterity God has brought to Israel a Savior, Jesus, as he promised. 24Before his

[m] Other ancient authorities read *cared for* (Deut. 1.31)

King James

24 When John had first preached before his coming the baptism of repentance to all the people of Israel.

25 And as John fulfilled his course, he said, Whom think ye that I am? I am not *he*. But, behold, there cometh one after me, whose shoes of *his* feet I am not worthy to loose.

26 Men *and* brethren, children of the stock of Abraham, and whosoever among you feareth God, to you is the word of this salvation sent.

27 For they that dwell at Jerusalem, and their rulers, because they knew him not, nor yet the voices of the prophets which are read every sabbath day, they have fulfilled *them* in condemning *him*.

28 And though they found no cause of death *in him*, yet desired they Pilate that he should be slain.

29 And when they had fulfilled all that was written of him, they took *him* down from the tree, and laid *him* in a sepulchre.

30 But God raised him from the dead:

31 And he was seen many days of them which came up with him from Galilee to Jerusalem, who are his witnesses unto the people.

32 And we declare unto you glad tidings, how that the promise which was made unto the fathers,

33 God hath fulfilled the same unto us their children, in that he hath raised up Jesus again; as it is also written in the second psalm, Thou art my Son, this day have I begotten thee.

34 And as concerning that he raised him up from the dead, *now* no more to return to corruption, he said on this wise, I will give you the sure mercies of David.

35 Wherefore he saith also in another *psalm*, Thou shalt not suffer thine Holy One to see corruption.

36 For David, after he had served his own generation by the will of God, fell on sleep, and was laid unto his fathers, and saw corruption:

37 But he, whom God raised again, saw no corruption.

38 ¶ Be it known unto you therefore, men *and* brethren, that through this man is preached unto you the forgiveness of sins:

39 And by him all that believe are justified from all things, from which ye could not be justified by the law of Moses.

40 Beware therefore, lest that come upon you, which is spoken of in the prophets;

41 Behold, ye despisers, and wonder, and perish: for I work a work in your days, a work which ye shall in no wise believe, though a man declare it unto you.

Amplified

24 Before His coming John had (already) preached baptism of repentance to all the people of Israel.

25 And as John was ending his course, he asked, What do you secretly think that I am? I am not He [the Christ. No], but note that after me One is coming, the sandals of Whose feet I am not worthy to untie!

26 Brethren, sons of the race of Abraham, and all those others among you who reverence *and* fear God, to us has been sent the message of this salvation—the salvation obtained through Jesus Christ. [Ps. 107:20.]

27 For those who dwell in Jerusalem and their rulers, because they did not know *or* recognize Him or understand the utterances of the prophets which are read every Sabbath, by condemning *and* sentencing [Him] have actually fulfilled these very predictions.

28 And although they could find no cause deserving death with which to charge Him, yet they asked Pilate to have Him executed *and* put out of the way.

29 And when they had finished *and* fulfilled everything that was written about Him, they took Him down from the tree and laid Him in a tomb.

30 But God raised Him from the dead.

31 And for many days He appeared to those who came up with Him from Galilee to Jerusalem, and they are His witnesses to the people.

32 So now we are bringing you the good news that what God promised to our forefathers,

33 This He has [z]completely fulfilled to us their children by raising up Jesus, as it is written in the second Psalm, You are My Son; today I have begotten You—[a]caused You to arise, to be born, [[a]formally shown You to be the Messiah by the resurrection]. [Ps. 2:7.]

34 And as to His having raised Him from among the dead, now no more to return to [undergo] putrefaction *and* dissolution [of the grave], He spoke in this way, I will fulfill *and* give to you the holy and sure mercies *and* blessings [that were promised and assured] to David. [Isa. 55:3.]

35 For this reason He says also in another Psalm, You will not allow Your Holy One to see corruption—to undergo putrefaction and dissolution [of the grave]. [Ps. 16:10.]

36 For David, after he had served God's will *and* purpose *and* counsel in his own generation, fell asleep [[b]in death], and was buried among his forefathers, and he did see corruption *and* undergo putrefaction *and* dissolution [of the grave].

37 But He Whom God raised up [to life] saw no corruption—did not experience putrefaction and dissolution [of the grave].

38 So let it be clearly known *and* understood by you, brethren, that through this Man forgiveness *and* removal of sins is now proclaimed to you;

39 And that through Him every one who believes, [that is, who [a]acknowledges Jesus as his Savior and devotes himself to Him] is absolved (cleared and freed) from every charge from which you could not be justified *and* freed by the Law of Moses, *and* given right standing with God.

40 Take care, therefore, lest there come upon you what is spoken in the prophets:

41 Look, you scoffers *and* scorners, and marvel, and perish, *and* vanish away; for I am doing a deed in your days, a deed which you will never have confidence in *or* believe, [even] if some one—[c]clearly describing it in detail—declares it to you. [Hab. 1:5.]

---

z) Vincent.
a) Thayer.
b) Cremer.
c) Vincent.

Living New Testament

24 But before He came, John the Baptist preached the need for everyone in Israel to turn from sin to God.

25 As John was finishing his work he asked, "Do you think I am the Messiah? No! But He is coming soon—and in comparison with Him, I am utterly worthless.'

26 Brothers—you sons of Abraham, and also all of you Gentiles here who reverence God—this salvation is for all of us!

27 The Jews in Jerusalem and their leaders fulfilled prophecy by killing Jesus; for they didn't recognize Him, or realize that He is the one the prophets had written about, though they heard the prophets' words read every Sabbath.

28 They found no just cause to execute Him, but asked Pilate to have Him killed anyway.

29 When they had fulfilled all the prophecies concerning His death, He was taken from the cross and placed in a tomb.

30 But God brought Him back to life again!

31 And He was seen many times during the next few days by the men who had accompanied Him to Jerusalem from Galilee—these men have constantly testified to this in public witness.

32, 33 And now Barnabas and I are here to bring you this Good News—that God's promise to our ancestors has come true in our own time, in that God brought Jesus back to life again. This is what the second Psalm is talking about when it says concerning Jesus, 'Today I have honored You as My Son.'[5]

34 For God had promised to bring Him back to life again, no more to die. This is stated in the Scripture that says, 'I will do for You the wonderful thing I promised David.'

35 In another Psalm He explained more fully, saying, 'God will not let His Holy One decay.'

36 This was not a reference to David, for after David had served his generation according to the will of God, he died and was buried, and his body decayed.

37 [No, it was a reference to another[6]]—Someone God brought back to life, whose body was not touched at all by the ravages of death.[7]

38 Brothers! Listen! In this man Jesus, there is forgiveness for your sins!

39 Everyone who trusts in Him is freed from all guilt and declared righteous—something the Jewish law could never do.

40 Oh, be careful! Don't let the prophets' words apply to you! For they said,

41 'Look and perish, you despisers [of the truth[8]], for I am doing something in your day—something that you won't believe when you hear it announced.' "

[5] Literally, "this day have I begotten You."
[6] Implied.
[7] Literally, "saw no corruption."
[8] Implied.

Revised Standard

coming John had preached a baptism of
repentance to all the people of Israel.
25 And as John was finishing his course, he
said, 'What do you suppose that I am? I am
not he. No, but after me one is coming, the
sandals of whose feet I am not worthy to
untie.'
26 "Brethren, sons of the family of Abraham, and those among you that fear God, to
us has been sent the message of this salvation.
27 For those who live in Jerusalem and
their rulers, because they did not recognize
him nor understand the utterances of the
prophets which are read every sabbath,
fulfilled these by condemning him.
28 Though they could charge him with nothing deserving death, yet they asked Pilate to
have him killed.
29 And when they had
fulfilled all that was written of him, they
took him down from the tree, and laid him
in a tomb.
30 But God raised him from the
dead;
31 and for many days he appeared to
those who came up with him from Galilee
to Jerusalem, who are now his witnesses to
the people.
32 And we bring you the good
news that what God promised to the fathers,
33 this he has fulfilled to us their children by raising Jesus; as also it is written in
the second psalm,
'Thou art my Son,
today I have begotten thee.'
34 And as for the fact that he raised him
from the dead, no more to return to corruption, he spoke in this way,
'I will give you the holy and sure
blessings of David.'
35 Therefore he says also in another
psalm,
'Thou wilt not let thy Holy One see
corruption.'
36 For David, after he had served the counsel of God in his own generation, fell asleep,
and was laid with his fathers, and saw corruption;
37 but he whom God raised up saw
no corruption.
38 Let it be known to you
therefore, brethren, that through this man
forgiveness of sins is proclaimed to you,
39 and by him every one that believes is
freed from everything from which you could
not be freed by the law of Moses.
40 Beware, therefore, lest there come upon you
what is said in the prophets:
41 'Behold, you scoffers, and wonder, and
perish;
for I do a deed in your days,
a deed you will never believe, if one
declares it to you.' "

King James

42 And when the Jews were gone out of the synagogue, the Gentiles besought that these words might be preached to them the next sabbath.

43 Now when the congregation was broken up, many of the Jews and religious proselytes followed Paul and Barnabas: who, speaking to them, persuaded them to continue in the grace of God.

44 ¶ And the next sabbath day came almost the whole city together to hear the word of God.

45 But when the Jews saw the multitudes, they were filled with envy, and spake against those things which were spoken by Paul, contradicting and blaspheming.

46 Then Paul and Barnabas waxed bold, and said, It was necessary that the word of God should first have been spoken to you: but seeing ye put it from you, and judge yourselves unworthy of everlasting life, lo, we turn to the Gentiles.

47 For so hath the Lord commanded us, *saying,* I have set thee to be a light of the Gentiles, that thou shouldest be for salvation unto the ends of the earth.

48 And when the Gentiles heard this, they were glad, and glorified the word of the Lord: and as many as were ordained to eternal life believed.

49 And the word of the Lord was published throughout all the region.

50 But the Jews stirred up the devout and honourable women, and the chief men of the city, and raised persecution against Paul and Barnabas, and expelled them out of their coasts.

51 But they shook off the dust of their feet against them, and came unto Iconium.

52 And the disciples were filled with joy, and with the Holy Ghost.

Amplified

42 As they [Paul and Barnabas] went out [of the synagogue], the people earnestly begged that these things might be told to them [further] the next Sabbath.

43 And when the congregation of the synagogue dispersed, many of the Jews and the devout converts to Judaism followed Paul and Barnabas, who talked to them and urged them to continue [to trust themselves to and stand fast] in the grace—that is, the unmerited favor and blessing—of God.

44 The next Sabbath almost the entire city gathered together to hear the Word of God—concerning [d]the attainment through Christ of salvation in the kingdom of God.

45 But when the Jews saw the crowds, filled with envy *and* jealousy they contradicted what was said by Paul, and talked abusively—reviling and slandering him.

46 And Paul and Barnabas spoke out plainly *and* boldly, saying, It was necessary that God's message (concerning [d]salvation through Christ) should be spoken to you first. But since you thrust it from you, you pass this judgment on yourselves that you are unworthy of eternal life, *and* out of your own mouth you shall be judged. [Now] behold, we turn to the Gentiles—the heathen.

47 For so the Lord has charged us, saying, I have set you to be a light for the Gentiles—the heathen—that you may bring (eternal) salvation to the uttermost parts of the earth. [Isa. 49:6.]

48 And when the Gentiles heard this, they rejoiced and glorified (praised and gave thanks for) the Word of God; and as many as were destined (appointed and ordained) to eternal life believed—adhered to, trusted in and relied on Jesus as the Christ and their Savior.

49 And so the Word of the Lord (concerning eternal salvation through Christ) scattered *and* spread throughout the whole region.

50 But the Jews stirred up the devout women of high rank and the outstanding men of the town, and instigated persecution against Paul and Barnabas, and drove them out of their boundaries.

51 But [the apostles] shook off the dust from their feet against them, and went to Iconium.

52 And the disciples were continually diffused [throughout their souls] with joy and the Holy Spirit.

CHAPTER 14

AND it came to pass in Iconium, that they went both together into the synagogue of the Jews, and so spake, that a great multitude both of the Jews and also of the Greeks believed.

2 But the unbelieving Jews stirred up the Gentiles, and made their minds evil affected against the brethren.

3 Long time therefore abode they speaking boldly in the Lord, which gave testimony unto the word of his grace, and granted signs and wonders to be done by their hands.

4 But the multitude of the city was divided: and part held with the Jews, and part with the apostles.

5 And when there was an assault made both of the Gentiles, and also of the Jews with their rulers, to use *them* despitefully, and to stone them,

CHAPTER 14

NOW at Iconium [also Paul and Barnabas] went into the Jewish synagogue together and spoke with such power that a great number both of Jews and of Greeks believed—became Christians;

2 But the unbelieving Jews (who rejected their message) aroused the Gentiles and embittered their minds against the brethren.

3 So [Paul and Barnabas] stayed on there for a long time, speaking freely *and* fearlessly *and* boldly in the Lord, Who continued to bear testimony to the Word of His grace, granting signs and wonders to be performed by their hands.

4 But the residents of the town were divided, some siding with the Jews and some with the apostles.

5 When there was an attempt both on the part of the Gentiles and the Jews together with their rulers, to insult *and* abuse *and* molest [Paul and Barnabas] and to stone them,

---

d) Thayer.

Living New Testament

42 As the people left the synagogue that day, they asked Paul to return and speak to them again the next week.

43 And many Jews and godly Gentiles who worshiped at the synagogue followed Paul and Barnabas down the street as the two men urged them to accept the mercies God was offering.

44 The following week almost the entire city turned out to hear them preach the Word of God.

45 But when the Jewish leaders[9] saw the crowds, they were jealous, and cursed[10] and argued against whatever Paul said.

46 Then Paul and Barnabas spoke out boldly and declared, "It was necessary that this Good News from God should be given first to you Jews. But since you have rejected it, and shown yourselves unworthy of eternal life —well, we will offer it to Gentiles.

47 For this is as the Lord commanded when He said, 'I have made you a light to the Gentiles, to lead them from the farthest corners of the earth[11] to My salvation.' "

48 When the Gentiles heard this, they were very glad and rejoiced in Paul's message; and as many as wanted[12] eternal life, believed.

49 So God's message spread all through that region.

50 Then the Jewish leaders stirred up both the godly women and the civic leaders of the city and incited a mob against Paul and Barnabas, and ran them out of town.

51 But they shook off the dust of their feet against the town and went on to the city of Iconium.

52 And their converts[13] were filled with joy and with the Holy Spirit.

Revised Standard

42 As they went out, the people begged
that these things might be told them the
next sabbath. 43And when the meeting of
the synagogue broke up, many Jews and
devout converts to Judaism followed Paul
and Barnabas, who spoke to them and urged
them to continue in the grace of God.

Jews oppose; Gentiles believe

44 The next sabbath almost the whole
city gathered together to hear the word of
God. 45But when the Jews saw the multitudes, they were filled with jealousy, and
contradicted what was spoken by Paul, and
reviled him. 46And Paul and Barnabas
spoke out boldly, saying, "It was necessary
that the word of God should be spoken first
to you. Since you thrust it from you, and
judge yourselves unworthy of eternal life,
behold, we turn to the Gentiles. 47For so
the Lord has commanded us, saying,

'I have set you to be a light for the
Gentiles,
that you may bring salvation to the
uttermost parts of the earth.' "

48 And when the Gentiles heard this,
they were glad and glorified the word of
God; and as many as were ordained to eternal life believed. 49And the word of the
Lord spread throughout all the region.
50But the Jews incited the devout women of
high standing and the leading men of the
city, and stirred up persecution against Paul
and Barnabas, and drove them out of their
district. 51But they shook off the dust from
their feet against them, and went to Iconium. 52And the disciples were filled with joy
and with the Holy Spirit.

CHAPTER 14

At Iconium, Paul and Barnabas went together to the synagogue and preached with such power that many —both Jews and Gentiles—believed.

2 But the Jews who spurned God's message stirred up distrust among the Gentiles against Paul and Barnabas, saying all sorts of evil things about them.

3 Nevertheless, they stayed there a long time, preaching boldly, and the Lord proved their message was from Him by giving them power to do great miracles.

4 But the people of the city were divided in their opinion about them. Some agreed with the Jewish leaders, and some backed the apostles.

5, 6 When Paul and Barnabas learned of a plot to incite a mob of Gentiles, Jews, and Jewish leaders to

Preaching at Iconium

14 Now at Iconium they entered together into the Jewish synagogue, and so
spoke that a great company believed, both of
Jews and of Greeks. 2But the unbelieving
Jews stirred up the Gentiles and poisoned
their minds against the brethren. 3So they
remained for a long time, speaking boldly
for the Lord, who bore witness to the word
of his grace, granting signs and wonders to
be done by their hands. 4But the people of
the city were divided; some sided with the
Jews, and some with the apostles. 5When an
attempt was made by both Gentiles and
Jews, with their rulers, to molest them and

---

[9] Literally, "the Jews."
[10] Or, "blasphemed."
[11] Literally, "from the uttermost part of the earth."
[12] Or, "were disposed to," or, "ordained to."
[13] Literally, "the disciples."

King James

6 They were ware of *it,* and fled unto Lystra and Derbe, cities of Lycaonia, and unto the region that lieth round about:

7 And there they preached the gospel.

8 ¶ And there sat a certain man at Lystra, impotent in his feet, being a cripple from his mother's womb, who never had walked:

9 The same heard Paul speak: who stedfastly beholding him, and perceiving that he had faith to be healed,

10 Said with a loud voice, Stand upright on thy feet. And he leaped and walked.

11 And when the people saw what Paul had done, they lifted up their voices, saying in the speech of Lycaonia, The gods are come down to us in the likeness of men.

12 And they called Barnabas, Jupiter; and Paul, Mercurius, because he was the chief speaker.

13 Then the priest of Jupiter, which was before their city, brought oxen and garlands unto the gates, and would have done sacrifice with the people.

14 *Which* when the apostles, Barnabas and Paul, heard *of,* they rent their clothes, and ran in among the people, crying out,

15 And saying, Sirs, why do ye these things? We also are men of like passions with you, and preach unto you that ye should turn from these vanities unto the living God, which made heaven, and earth, and the sea, and all things that are therein:

16 Who in times past suffered all nations to walk in their own ways.

17 Nevertheless he left not himself without witness, in that he did good, and gave us rain from heaven, and fruitful seasons, filling our hearts with food and gladness.

18 And with these sayings scarce restrained they the people, that they had not done sacrifice unto them.

19 ¶ And there came thither *certain* Jews from Antioch and Iconium, who persuaded the people, and, having stoned Paul, drew *him* out of the city, supposing he had been dead.

20 Howbeit, as the disciples stood round about him, he rose up, and came into the city: and the next day he departed with Barnabas to Derbe.

21 And when they had preached the gospel to that city, and had taught many, they returned again to Lystra, and *to* Iconium, and Antioch,

22 Confirming the souls of the disciples, *and* exhorting them to continue in the faith, and that we must through much tribulation enter into the kingdom of God.

23 And when they had ordained them elders in every church, and had prayed with fasting, they commended them to the Lord, on whom they believed.

24 And after they had passed throughout Pisidia, they came to Pamphylia.

25 And when they had preached the word in Perga, they went down into Attalia:

26 And thence sailed to Antioch, from whence they had been recommended to the grace of God for the work which they fulfilled.

Amplified

6 They, aware of the situation, made their escape to Lystra and Derbe, cities of Lycaonia, and the neighboring districts;

7 And there they continued to preach the glad tidings (Gospel).

8 Now at Lystra a man sat whose feet it was impossible for him to use, for he was a cripple from birth and had never walked.

9 He was listening to Paul as he talked, and [Paul] gazing intently at him and observing that he had faith to be healed,

10 Shouted at him, saying, Stand erect on your feet! And he leaped up and walked.

11 And the crowds, when they saw what Paul had done, lifted up their voices, shouting in the Lycaonian language, The gods have come down to us in human form!

12 They called Barnabas Zeus, and they called Paul, because he led in the discourse, Hermes [god of speech].

13 And the priest of Zeus, whose [temple] was at the entrance of the town, brought bulls and garlands to the [city's] gates and wanted to join the people in offering sacrifice.

14 But when the apostles Barnabas and Paul heard of it, they tore their clothing and dashed out among the crowd, shouting,

15 Men, why are you doing this? We also are [only] human beings, of nature like your own, and we bring you the good news that you should turn away from these foolish *and* vain things to the living God, Who made the heaven and the earth and the sea and everything that they contain. [Exod. 20:11; Ps. 146:6.]

16 In generations past He permitted all the nations to walk in their own ways;

17 Yet He did not neglect to leave some witness of Himself, for He did you good *and* kindnesses, and gave you rains from heaven and fruitful seasons, satisfying your hearts with nourishment and happiness.

18 Even in [the light of] these words they with difficulty prevented the people from offering sacrifice to them.

19 But some Jews arrived there from Antioch and Iconium; and having persuaded the people *and* won them over, they stoned Paul and [[e]afterward] dragged him out of the town, thinking that he was dead.

20 But the disciples formed a circle about him, and he got up and went back into the town; and on the morrow he went on with Barnabas to Derbe.

21 When they had preached the Gospel to that town and made disciples of many of the people, they went back to Lystra and Iconium and Antioch,

22 Establishing *and* strengthening the souls *and* the hearts of the disciples, urging *and* warning *and* encouraging them to stand firm in the faith, and telling them that it is through many hardships *and* tribulations we must enter the kingdom of God.

23 And when they had appointed *and* ordained elders for them in each church, with prayer and fasting, they committed them to the Lord in Whom they had come to believe [being full of joyful trust that He is the Christ, the Messiah].

24 Then they went through Pisidia and arrived at Pamphylia.

25 And when they had spoken the Word in Perga, [that is, the doctrine concerning the attainment through Christ of salvation in the kingdom of God], they went down to Attalia;

26 And from there they sailed back to Antioch, where they had [first] been commended to the grace of God for the work which they had [now] completed.

---

e) Alford.

Living New Testament

attack and stone them, they fled for their lives, going to the cities of Lycaonia, Lystra, Derbe, and the surrounding area,

7 And preaching the Good News there.

8 While they were at Lystra, they came upon a man with crippled feet who had been that way from birth, so he had never walked.

9 He was listening as Paul preached, and Paul noticed him and realized he had faith to be healed!

10 So Paul yelled at him, "Stand up!" and the man leaped to his feet and started walking!

11 When the listening crowd saw what Paul had done, they shouted (in their local dialect, of course), "These men are gods in human bodies!"

12 They decided that Barnabas was the Greek god Jupiter, and that Paul, because he was the chief speaker, was Mercury!

13 The local priest of the Temple of Jupiter, located on the outskirts of the city, brought them cartloads of flowers and sacrificed oxen to them at the city gates before the crowds.

14 But when Barnabas and Paul saw what was happening they ripped at their clothing in dismay and ran out among the people, shouting,

15 "Men! What are you doing? We are merely human beings like yourselves! We have come to bring you the Good News that you are invited to turn from the worship of these foolish things and to pray instead to the living God who made heaven and earth and sea and everything in them.

16 In bygone days He permitted the nations to go their own ways,

17 But He never left Himself without a witness; there were always His reminders—the kind things He did such as sending you rain and good crops and giving you food and gladness."

18 But even so, Paul and Barnabas could scarcely restrain the people from sacrificing to them!

19 Yet only a few days later, some Jews arrived from Antioch and Iconium and turned the crowds into a murderous mob that stoned Paul and dragged him out of the city, apparently dead!

20 But as the believers stood around him, he got up and went back into the city! The next day he left with Barnabas for Derbe.

21 After preaching the Good News there and making many disciples, they returned again to Lystra, Iconium and Antioch,

22 Where they helped the believers to grow in love for God and each other. They encouraged them to continue in the faith in spite of all the persecution, reminding them that they must enter into the Kingdom of God through many tribulations.

23 Paul and Barnabas also appointed elders in every church and prayed for them with fasting, turning them over to the care of the Lord in whom they trusted.

24 Then they traveled back through Pisidia to Pamphylia,

25 Preached again in Perga, and went on to Attalia.

26 Finally they returned by ship to Antioch, where their journey had begun, and where they had been committed to God for the work now completed.

Revised Standard

to stone them, [6]they learned of it and fled
to Lystra and Derbe, cities of Lycaonia, and
to the surrounding country; [7]and there they
preached the gospel.

Preaching at Lystra

8 Now at Lystra there was a man sitting,
who could not use his feet; he was a cripple
from birth, who had never walked. [9]He
listened to Paul speaking; and Paul, looking
intently at him and seeing that he had faith
to be made well, [10]said in a loud voice,
"Stand upright on your feet." And he sprang
up and walked. [11]And when the crowds saw
what Paul had done, they lifted up their
voices, saying in Lycaonian, "The gods have
come down to us in the likeness of men!"
[12]Barnabas they called Zeus, and Paul,
because he was the chief speaker, they
called Hermes. [13]And the priest of Zeus,
whose temple was in front of the city,
brought oxen and garlands to the gates and
wanted to offer sacrifice with the people.
[14]But when the apostles Barnabas and Paul
heard of it, they tore their garments and
rushed out among the multitude, crying,
[15]"Men, why are you doing this? We also
are men, of like nature with you, and bring
you good news, that you should turn from
these vain things to a living God who made
the heaven and the earth and the sea and all
that is in them. [16]In past generations he
allowed all the nations to walk in their own
ways; [17]yet he did not leave himself without
witness for he did good and gave you from
heaven rains and fruitful seasons, satisfying
your hearts with food and gladness." [18]With
these words they scarcely restrained the people from offering sacrifice to them.

Paul and Barnabas return to Antioch

19 But Jews came there from Antioch
and Iconium; and having persuaded the people, they stoned Paul and dragged him out
of the city, supposing that he was dead.
[20]But when the disciples gathered about
him, he rose up and entered the city; and on
the next day he went on with Barnabas to
Derbe. [21]When they had preached the
gospel to that city and had made many
disciples, they returned to Lystra and to
Iconium and to Antioch, [22]strengthening
the souls of the disciples, exhorting them to
continue in the faith, and saying that
through many tribulations we must enter the
kingdom of God. [23]And when they had
appointed elders for them in every church,
with prayer and fasting, they committed
them to the Lord in whom they believed.
24 Then they passed through Pisidia, and
came to Pamphylia. [25]And when they had
spoken the word in Perga, they went down
to Attalia; [26]and from there they sailed to
Antioch, where they had been commended
to the grace of God for the work which they

King James

27 And when they were come, and had gathered the church together, they rehearsed all that God had done with them, and how he had opened the door of faith unto the Gentiles.

28 And there they abode long time with the disciples.

Amplified

27 Arriving there, they gathered the church together and declared all that God had accomplished with them, and how He had opened to the Gentiles a door of faith [in Jesus as the Messiah, through Whom we obtain salvation in the kingdom of God].

28 And there they stayed no little time with the disciples.

CHAPTER 15

AND certain men which came down from Judæa taught the brethren, *and said*, Except ye be circumcised after the manner of Moses, ye cannot be saved.

2 When therefore Paul and Barnabas had no small dissension and disputation with them, they determined that Paul and Barnabas, and certain other of them, should go up to Jerusalem unto the apostles and elders about this question.

3 And being brought on their way by the church, they passed through Phenice and Samaria, declaring the conversion of the Gentiles: and they caused great joy unto all the brethren.

4 And when they were come to Jerusalem, they were received of the church, and *of* the apostles and elders, and they declared all things that God had done with them.

5 But there rose up certain of the sect of the Pharisees which believed, saying, That it was needful to circumcise them, and to command *them* to keep the law of Moses.

6 ¶ And the apostles and elders came together for to consider of this matter.

7 And when there had been much disputing, Peter rose up, and said unto them, Men *and* brethren, ye know how that a good while ago God made choice among us, that the Gentiles by my mouth should hear the word of the gospel, and believe.

8 And God, which knoweth the hearts, bare them witness, giving them the Holy Ghost, even as *he did* unto us;

9 And put no difference between us and them, purifying their hearts by faith.

10 Now therefore why tempt ye God, to put a yoke upon the neck of the disciples, which neither our fathers nor we were able to bear?

11 But we believe that through the grace of the Lord Jesus Christ we shall be saved, even as they.

12 ¶ Then all the multitude kept silence, and gave audience to Barnabas and Paul, declaring what miracles and wonders God had wrought among the Gentiles by them.

13 ¶ And after they had held their peace, James answered, saying, Men *and* brethren, hearken unto me:

14 Simeon hath declared how God at the first did visit the Gentiles, to take out of them a people for his name.

CHAPTER 15

BUT some men came down from Judea and were instructing the brethren, Unless you are circumcised in accordance with the Mosaic custom, you cannot be saved.

2 And when Paul and Barnabas had no small disagreement and discussion with them, it was decided that Paul and Barnabas and some of the others of their number should go up to Jerusalem [and confer] with the apostles (special messengers) and the elders about this matter.

3 So, being [f]fitted out *and* sent on their way by the church, they went through both Phoenicia and Samaria telling of the conversion of the Gentiles, and they caused great rejoicing among all the brethren.

4 When they arrived in Jerusalem, they were heartily welcomed by the church and the apostles and the elders, and they told them all that God had accomplished through them.

5 But some who believed [that is, who [f]acknowledged Jesus as their Savior and devoted themselves to Him] belonged to the sect of the Pharisees, and they rose up and said, It is necessary to circumcise [the Gentile converts], and to charge them to obey the Law of Moses.

6 The apostles and the elders were assembled together to look into *and* consider this matter.

7 And after there had been a long debate, Peter got up and said to them, Brethren, you know that quite a while ago God made a selection from among you, that by my mouth the Gentiles should hear the message of the Gospel [concerning the [g]attainment through Christ of salvation in the kingdom of God] and believe—that is, credit *and* place their confidence in it.

8 And God, Who is acquainted with *and* understands the heart, bore witness to them, giving them the Holy Spirit as also He did to us;

9 And He made no difference between us and them, but cleansed their hearts by faith [that is, [g]by a strong and welcome conviction that Jesus is the Messiah, through Whom we obtain eternal salvation in the kingdom of God].

10 Now then, why do you try to test God by putting a yoke on the necks of the disciples, such as neither our forefathers nor we [ourselves] were able to endure?

11 But we believe that we are saved through the grace [the undeserved favor and mercy] of the Lord Jesus, just as they [are].

12 Then the whole assembly remained silent, and they listened [attentively] as Barnabas and Paul rehearsed what signs and wonders God had performed through them among the Gentiles.

13 When they had finished talking, James replied, Brethren, listen to me.

14 Symeon [Peter] has rehearsed how God first visited the Gentiles, to take out of them a people [to bear and honor] His name.

f) Thayer.
g) Thayer.

Living New Testament

27 Upon arrival they called together the believers and reported on their trip, telling how God had opened the door of faith to the Gentiles too.

28 And they stayed there with the believers at Antioch for a long while.

CHAPTER 15

While Paul and Barnabas were at Antioch, some men from Judea arrived and began to teach the believers that unless they adhered to the ancient Jewish[1] custom of circumcision, they could not be saved.

2 Paul and Barnabas argued and discussed this with them at length, and finally the believers sent them to Jerusalem, accompanied by some local men, to talk to the apostles and elders there about this question.

3 After the entire congregation had escorted them out of the city the delegates went on to Jerusalem, stopping along the way in the cities of Phoenicia and Samaria to visit the believers, telling them—much to everyone's joy—that the Gentiles, too, were being converted.

4 Arriving in Jerusalem, they met with the church leaders—all the apostles and elders were present—and Paul and Barnabas reported on what God had been doing through their ministry.

5 But then some of the men who had been Pharisees before their conversion stood to their feet and declared that all Gentile converts must be circumcised and required to follow all the Jewish customs and ceremonies.[2]

6 So the apostles and church elders set a further meeting to decide this question.

7 At that meeting, after long discussion, Peter stood and addressed them as follows:

"Brothers, you all know that God chose me from among you long ago to preach the Good News to the Gentiles, so that they also could believe.

8 God, who knows men's hearts, confirmed the fact that He accepts Gentiles by giving them the Holy Spirit, just as He gave Him to us.

9 He made no distinction between them and us, for He cleansed their lives through faith, just as He did ours.

10 And now are you going to correct God by burdening the Gentiles with a yoke that neither we nor our fathers were able to bear?

11 Don't you believe that all are saved the same way, by the free gift of the Lord Jesus?"

12 There was no further discussion, and everyone now listened as Barnabas and Paul told about the miracles God had done through them among the Gentiles.

13 When they had finished, James took the floor. "Brothers," he said, "listen to me.

14 Peter[3] has told you about the time God first visited the Gentiles to take from them a people to bring honor to His name.

---

[1] Literally, "the custom of Moses."
[2] Literally, "to charge them to keep the laws of Moses."
[3] Literally, "Symeon."

Revised Standard

had fulfilled. [27]And when they arrived, they
gathered the church together and declared
all that God had done with them, and how
he had opened a door of faith to the Gentiles. [28]And they remained no little time
with the disciples.

The council at Jerusalem

15 But some men came down from
Judea and were teaching the brethren,
"Unless you are circumcised according to
the custom of Moses, you cannot be saved."
[2]And when Paul and Barnabas had no small
dissension and debate with them, Paul and
Barnabas and some of the others were appointed to go up to Jerusalem to the apostles and the elders about this question. [3]So,
being sent on their way by the church, they
passed through both Phoenicia and Samaria,
reporting the conversion of the Gentiles, and
they gave great joy to all the brethren.
[4]When they came to Jerusalem, they were
welcomed by the church and the apostles
and the elders, and they declared all that
God had done with them. [5]But some believers who belonged to the party of the Pharisees rose up, and said, "It is necessary to
circumcise them, and to charge them to
keep the law of Moses."
6 The apostles and the elders were
gathered together to consider this matter.
[7]And after there had been much debate,
Peter rose and said to them, "Brethren, you
know that in the early days God made
choice among you, that by my mouth the
Gentiles should hear the word of the gospel
and believe. [8]And God who knows the heart
bore witness to them, giving them the Holy
Spirit just as he did to us; [9]and he made no
distinction between us and them, but
cleansed their hearts by faith. [10]Now therefore why do you make trial of God by
putting a yoke upon the neck of the disciples
which neither our fathers nor we have been
able to bear? [11]But we believe that we shall
be saved through the grace of the Lord
Jesus, just as they will."

The decision of the council

12 And all the assembly kept silence; and
they listened to Barnabas and Paul as they
related what signs and wonders God had
done through them among the Gentiles.
[13]After they finished speaking, James replied, "Brethren, listen to me. [14]Symeon has
related how God first visited the Gentiles, to
take out of them a people for his name.

King James

15 And to this agree the words of the prophets; as it is written,

16 After this I will return, and will build again the tabernacle of David, which is fallen down; and I will build again the ruins thereof, and I will set it up:

17 That the residue of men might seek after the Lord, and all the Gentiles, upon whom my name is called, saith the Lord, who doeth all these things.

18 Known unto God are all his works from the beginning of the world.

19 Wherefore my sentence is, that we trouble not them, which from among the Gentiles are turned to God:

20 But that we write unto them, that they abstain from pollutions of idols, and *from* fornication, and *from* things strangled, and *from* blood.

21 For Moses of old time hath in every city them that preach him, being read in the synagogues every sabbath day.

22 Then pleased it the apostles and elders, with the whole church, to send chosen men of their own company to Antioch with Paul and Barnabas; *namely*, Judas surnamed Barsabas, and Silas, chief men among the brethren:

23 And they wrote *letters* by them after this manner; The apostles and elders and brethren *send* greeting unto the brethren which are of the Gentiles in Antioch and Syria and Cilicia:

24 Forasmuch as we have heard, that certain which went out from us have troubled you with words, subverting your souls, saying, *Ye must* be circumcised, and keep the law: to whom we gave no *such* commandment:

25 It seemed good unto us, being assembled with one accord, to send chosen men unto you with our beloved Barnabas and Paul,

26 Men that have hazarded their lives for the name of our Lord Jesus Christ.

27 We have sent therefore Judas and Silas, who shall also tell *you* the same things by mouth.

28 For it seemed good to the Holy Ghost, and to us, to lay upon you no greater burden than these necessary things;

29 That ye abstain from meats offered to idols, and from blood, and from things strangled, and from fornication: from which if ye keep yourselves, ye shall do well. Fare ye well.

30 So when they were dismissed, they came to Antioch: and when they had gathered the multitude together, they delivered the epistle:

31 *Which* when they had read, they rejoiced for the consolation.

32 And Judas and Silas, being prophets also themselves, exhorted the brethren with many words, and confirmed *them*.

33 And after they had tarried *there* a space, they were let go in peace from the brethren unto the apostles.

34 Notwithstanding it pleased Silas to abide there still.

35 Paul also and Barnabas continued in Antioch, teaching and preaching the word of the Lord, with many others also.

Amplified

15 And with this the predictions of the prophets agree, as it is written,

16 After this I will come back, and will rebuild the house of David, which has fallen; I will rebuild its [very] ruins, and I will set it up again,

17 So that the rest of men may seek the Lord, and all the Gentiles upon whom My name has been invoked,

18 Says the Lord Who has been making [h]these things known from the beginning of the world. [Amos 9:11, 12; Jer. 12:15; Isa. 45:21.]

19 Therefore it is my opinion that we should not put obstacles in the way *and* annoy *and* disturb those of the Gentiles who turn to God,

20 But we should send word to them in writing to abstain from *and* avoid anything that has been polluted by being offered to idols, and all sexual impurity, and [meat of animals] that have been strangled, and [tasting] of blood.

21 For from ancient generations Moses has had in every town his preachers, for he is read [aloud] every Sabbath in the synagogues.

22 Then the apostles and the elders, together with the whole church, resolved to select men from among their number and send them to Antioch with Paul and Barnabas. They chose Judas called Barsabbas, and Silas, [both] leading men among the brethren, *and* sent them.

23 With [them they sent] the following letter: The brethren, both the apostles and the elders, to the brethren who are of the Gentiles in Antioch and Syria and Cilicia, greeting:

24 As we have heard that some persons from our number have disturbed you with their teaching, unsettling your minds *and* [h]throwing you into confusion, although we gave them no express orders *or* instructions [on the points in question],

25 It has been resolved by us in assembly to select men and send them [as messengers] to you with our beloved Barnabas and Paul,

26 Men who have hazarded their lives for the sake of our Lord Jesus Christ.

27 So we have sent Judas and Silas, who themselves will bring you the same message by word of mouth.

28 For it has seemed good to the Holy Spirit and to us not to lay upon you any greater burden than these indispensable requirements:

29 That you abstain from what has been sacrificed to idols and from [tasting] blood and from [eating the meat of animals] that have been strangled and from sexual impurity. If you keep yourselves from these things, you will do well. Farewell—be strong!

30 So when [the messengers] were sent off, they went down to Antioch; and having assembled the congregation, they delivered the letter.

31 And when they read it, the people rejoiced at the consolation *and* encouragement [it brought them].

32 And Judas and Silas, who were themselves prophets (inspired interpreters of the will and purposes of God), urged *and* warned *and* consoled *and* encouraged the brethren with many words and strengthened them.

33 And after spending some time there, they were sent back by the brethren with [the greeting] Peace, to those who had sent them.

34 *Though Silas decided to stay on there.*

35 But Paul and Barnabas remained in Antioch and with many others also continued teaching and proclaiming the Word of the Lord [concerning the [i]attainment through Christ of eternal salvation in God's kingdom].

h) Vincent.
i) Thayer.

Living New Testament

15 And this fact of Gentile conversion agrees with what the prophets predicted. For instance, listen to this passage from the prophet Amos[4]:

16 'Afterwards,' [says the Lord[4]], 'I will return and renew the broken contract with David,[5]

17 So that Gentiles, too, will find the Lord—all those marked with My name.'

18 That is what the Lord says, who reveals His plans made from the beginning.

19 And so my judgment is that we should not insist that the Gentiles who turn to God must obey our Jewish laws,

20 Except that we should write to them to refrain from eating meat sacrificed to idols, from all fornication, and also from eating unbled meat of strangled animals.

21 For these things have been preached against in Jewish synagogues in every city on every Sabbath for many generations."

22 Then the apostles and elders and the whole congregation voted to send delegates to Antioch with Paul and Barnabas, to report on this decision. The men chosen were two of the church leaders—Judas (also called Barsabbas) and Silas.

23 This is the letter they took along with them:

"*From*: The apostles, elders and brothers in Jerusalem.

To: The Gentile brothers in Antioch, Syria and Cilicia. Greetings!

24 We understand that some believers from here have upset you and questioned your salvation,[6] but they had no such instructions from us.

25 So it seemed wise to us, having unanimously agreed on our decision, to send to you these two official representatives, along with our beloved Barnabas and Paul.

26 These men—Judas and Silas, who have risked their lives for the sake of our Lord Jesus Christ—will confirm orally what we have decided concerning your question.

27, 28, 29 For it seemed good to the Holy Spirit and to us to lay no greater burden of Jewish laws on you than to abstain from eating food offered to idols and from unbled meat of strangled animals,[7] and, of course, from fornication. If you do this, it is enough. Farewell."

30 The four messengers went at once to Antioch, where they called a general meeting of the Christians and gave them the letter.

31 And there was great joy throughout the church that day as they read it.

32 Then Judas and Silas, both being gifted speakers,[8] preached long sermons to the believers, strengthening their faith.

mplied. See Amos 9:11,12.
.iterally, "rebuild the tabernacle of David which is fallen."
.iterally, "subverted your souls."
.iterally, "and from blood."
)r, "prophets."

Revised Standard

15 And with this the words of the prophets
agree, as it is written,
16 'After this I will return,
And I will rebuild the dwelling of David,
which has fallen;
I will rebuild its ruins,
and I will set it up,
17 that the rest of men may seek the Lord,
and all the Gentiles who are called by
my name,
18 says the Lord, who has made these things
known from of old.'
19 Therefore my judgment is that we should
not trouble those of the Gentiles who turn
to God, 20 but should write to them to abstain from the pollutions of idols and from
unchastity and from what is strangled[n] and
from blood. 21 For from early generations
Moses has had in every city those who
preach him, for he is read every sabbath in
the synagogues."

The decision sent to the Gentiles

22 Then it seemed good to the apostles
and the elders, with the whole church, to
choose men from among them and send
them to Antioch with Paul and Barnabas.
They sent Judas called Barsabbas, and Silas,
leading men among the brethren, 23 with the
following letter: "The brethren, both the
apostles and the elders, to the brethren who
are of the Gentiles in Antioch and Syria and
Cilicia, greeting. 24 Since we have heard that
some persons from us have troubled you
with words, unsettling your minds, although
we gave them no instructions, 25 it has
seemed good to us in assembly to choose
men and send them to you with our beloved
Barnabas and Paul, 26 men who have risked
their lives for the sake of our Lord Jesus
Christ. 27 We have therefore sent Judas and
Silas, who themselves will tell you the same
things by word of mouth. 28 For it has
seemed good to the Holy Spirit and to us to
lay upon you no greater burden than these
necessary things: 29 that you abstain from
what has been sacrificed to idols and from
blood and from what is strangled[n] and from
unchastity. If you keep yourselves from
these, you will do well. Farewell."
30 So when they were sent off, they went
down to Antioch; and having gathered the
congregation together, they delivered the
letter. 31 And when they read it, they rejoiced at the exhortation. 32 And Judas and
Silas, who were themselves prophets, exhorted the brethren with many words and

[n] Other early authorities omit *and from what is strangled*

King James

36 ¶ And some days after Paul said
unto Barnabas, Let us go again and visit our
brethren in every city where we have
preached the word of the Lord, *and see* how
they do.
37 And Barnabas determined to take
with them John, whose surname was Mark.
38 But Paul thought not good to take
him with them, who departed from them
from Pamphylia, and went not with them to
the work.
39 And the contention was so sharp between them, that they departed asunder one
from the other: and so Barnabas took
Mark, and sailed unto Cyprus;
40 And Paul chose Silas, and departed,
being recommended by the brethren unto
the grace of God.
41 And he went through Syria and Cilicia, confirming the churches.

Amplified

36 And after some time Paul said to Barnabas, Come,
let us go back and again visit *and* help *and* minister to the
brethren in every town where we made known the message of the Lord, and see how they are getting along.
37 Now Barnabas wanted to take with them John
called Mark [his near relative].
38 But Paul did not think it best to have along with
them the one who had quit *and* deserted them in Pamphylia, and had not gone on with them to the work.
39 And there followed a sharp disagreement between
them, so that they separated from each other, and Barnabas took Mark with him and sailed away to Cyprus.
40 But Paul selected Silas and set out, being commended by the brethren to the grace—the favor and mercy—of
the Lord.
41 And he passed through Syria and Cilicia, establishing *and* strengthening the churches.

CHAPTER 16

THEN came he to Derbe and Lystra:
and, behold, a certain disciple was
there, named Timotheus, the son of a certain woman, which was a Jewess, and believed; but his father *was* a Greek:
2 Which was well reported of by the
brethren that were at Lystra and Iconium.
3 Him would Paul have to go forth with
him; and took and circumcised him because
of the Jews which were in those quarters:
for they knew all that his father was a
Greek.
4 And as they went through the cities,
they delivered them the decrees for to keep,
that were ordained of the apostles and elders which were at Jerusalem.
5 And so were the churches established in
the faith, and increased in number daily.
6 Now when they had gone throughout
Phrygia and the region of Galatia, and were
forbidden of the Holy Ghost to preach the
word in Asia,
7 After they were come to Mysia, they
assayed to go into Bithynia: but the Spirit
suffered them not.
8 And they passing by Mysia came down
to Troas.
9 And a vision appeared to Paul in the
night; There stood a man of Macedonia, and
prayed him, saying, Come over into Macedonia, and help us.
10 And after he had seen the vision,
immediately we endeavoured to go into
Macedonia, assuredly gathering that the
Lord had called us for to preach the gospel
unto them.
11 Therefore loosing from Troas, we
came with a straight course to Samothracia,
and the next *day* to Neapolis;

CHAPTER 16

AND [Paul] went down to Derbe and also to Lystra. A
disciple named Timothy was there, the son of a
Jewish woman who was a believer—that is, she had become convinced that Jesus is the Messiah, and the Author
of eternal salvation, and yielded obedience to Him; but
[Timothy's] father was a Greek.
2 He [Timothy] had a good reputation among the brethren at Lystra and Iconium.
3 Paul desired Timothy to go with him [[j]as a mission-
ary]; and he took him and circumcised him, because of the
Jews that were in those places, all of whom knew that his
father was a Greek.
4 As they went on their way from town to town, they
delivered over to the assemblies for their observance the
regulations decided upon by the apostles and elders who
were at Jerusalem.
5 So the churches were strengthened *and* made firm in
the faith, and they increased in number day after day.
6 And Paul and Silas passed through the territory of
Phrygia and Galatia, having been forbidden by the Holy
Spirit to proclaim the Word in [the province of] Asia.
7 And when they had come opposite Mysia, they tried
to go into Bithynia, but the Spirit of Jesus did not permit
them.
8 So passing by Mysia, they went down to Troas.
9 [There] a vision appeared to Paul in the night: a man
from Macedonia stood pleading with him and saying,
Come over to Macedonia and help us!
10 And when he had seen the vision, we at once
endeavored to go on into Macedonia, confidently inferring
that God had called us to proclaim the glad tidings (Gospel) to them.
11 Therefore, setting sail from Troas, we came in
direct course to Samothrace, and the next day went on to
Neapolis.

j) Vincent.

Living New Testament

33 They stayed several days,[9] and then Judas and Silas returned to Jerusalem taking greetings and appreciation to those who had sent them.

34, 35 Paul and Barnabas stayed on at Antioch to assist several others who were preaching and teaching there.

36 Several days later Paul suggested to Barnabas that they return again to Turkey, and visit each city where they had preached before,[10] to see how the new converts were getting along.

37 Barnabas agreed, and wanted to take along John Mark.

38 But Paul didn't like that idea at all, since John had deserted them in Pamphylia.

39 Their disagreement over this was so sharp that they separated. Barnabas took Mark with him and sailed for Cyprus,

40, 41 While Paul chose Silas and, with the blessing of the believers, left for Syria and Cilicia, to encourage the churches there.

CHAPTER 16

Paul and Silas went first to Derbe and then on to Lystra where they met Timothy, a believer whose mother was a Christian Jewess but his father a Greek.

2 Timothy was well thought of by the brothers in Lystra and Iconium,

3 So Paul asked him to join them on their journey. In deference to the Jews of the area, he circumcised Timothy before they left, for everyone knew that his father was a Greek [and hadn't permitted this before[1]].

4 Then they went from city to city, making known the decision concerning the Gentiles, as decided by the apostles and elders in Jerusalem.

5 So the church grew daily in faith and numbers.

6 Next they traveled through Phrygia and Galatia, because the Holy Spirit had told them not to go into the Turkish province of Ausia at that time.

7 Then going along the borders of Mysia they headed north for the province of Bithynia, but again the Spirit of Jesus said no.

8 So instead they went on through Mysia province to the city of Troas.

9 That night[2] Paul had a vision. In his dream he saw a man over in Macedonia, Greece, pleading with him, "Come over here and help us."

10 Well, that settled it. We[3] would go to Macedonia, for we could only conclude that God was sending us to preach the Good News there.

11 We went aboard a boat at Troas, and sailed straight across to Samothrace, and the next day on to Neapolis,

---

Literally, "spent some time."
Implied. Literally, "return now and visit every city wherein we proclaimed the word of the Lord."
Implied.
Literally, "in the night."
Luke, the writer of this book, now joined Paul and accompanied him on his journey.

Revised Standard

strengthened them. [33]And after they had
spent some time, they were sent off in peace
by the brethren to those who had sent them.[o]
[35]But Paul and Barnabas remained in Antioch, teaching and preaching the word of
the Lord, with many others also.

Separation of Paul and Barnabas

36 And after some days Paul said to Barnabas, "Come, let us return and visit the
brethren in every city where we proclaimed
the word of the Lord, and see how they
are." [37]And Barnabas wanted to take with
them John called Mark. [38]But Paul thought
best not to take with them one who had
withdrawn from them in Pamphylia, and
had not gone with them to the work. [39]And
there arose a sharp contention, so that they
separated from each other; Barnabas took
Mark with him and sailed away to Cyprus,
[40]but Paul chose Silas and departed, being
commended by the brethren to the grace of
the Lord. [41]And he went through Syria and
Cilicia, strengthening the churches.

The selection of Timothy

16 And he came also to Derbe and to
Lystra. A disciple was there, named
Timothy, the son of a Jewish woman who
was a believer; but his father was a Greek.
[2]He was well spoken of by the brethren at
Lystra and Iconium. [3]Paul wanted Timothy
to accompany him; and he took him and
circumcised him because of the Jews that
were in those places, for they all knew that
his father was a Greek. [4]As they went on
their way through the cities, they delivered
to them for observance the decisions which
had been reached by the apostles and elders
who were at Jerusalem. [5]So the churches
were strengthened in the faith, and they increased in numbers daily.

The Macedonian call

6 And they went through the region of
Phrygia and Galatia, having been forbidden
by the Holy Spirit to speak the word in
Asia. [7]And when they had come opposite
Mysia, they attempted to go into Bithynia,
but the Spirit of Jesus did not allow them;
[8]so, passing by Mysia, they went down to
Troas. [9]And a vision appeared to Paul in
the night: a man of Macedonia was standing
beseeching him and saying, "Come over to
Macedonia and help us." [10]And when he
had seen the vision, immediately we sought
to go on into Macedonia, concluding that
God had called us to preach the gospel to
them.

The conversion of Lydia

11 Setting sail therefore from Troas, we
made a direct voyage to Samothrace, and

---

o Other ancient authorities insert verse 34, *But it seemed good to Silas to remain there*

King James

12 And from thence to Philippi, which is the chief city of that part of Macedonia, *and* a colony: and we were in that city abiding certain days.

13 And on the sabbath we went out of the city by a river side, where prayer was wont to be made; and we sat down, and spake unto the women which resorted thither.

14 ¶ And a certain woman named Lydia, a seller of purple, of the city of Thyatira, which worshipped God, heard *us:* whose heart the Lord opened, that she attended unto the things which were spoken of Paul.

15 And when she was baptized, and her household, she besought *us,* saying, If ye have judged me to be faithful to the Lord, come into my house, and abide *there.* And she constrained us.

16 ¶ And it came to pass, as we went to prayer, a certain damsel possessed with a spirit of divination met us, which brought her masters much gain by soothsaying:

17 The same followed Paul and us, and cried, saying, These men are the servants of the most high God, which shew unto us the way of salvation.

18 And this did she many days. But Paul, being grieved, turned and said to the spirit, I command thee in the name of Jesus Christ to come out of her. And he came out the same hour.

19 ¶ And when her masters saw that the hope of their gains was gone, they caught Paul and Silas, and drew *them* into the marketplace unto the rulers,

20 And brought them to the magistrates, saying, These men, being Jews, do exceedingly trouble our city,

21 And teach customs, which are not lawful for us to receive, neither to observe, being Romans.

22 And the multitude rose up together against them: and the magistrates rent off their clothes, and commanded to beat *them.*

23 And when they had laid many stripes upon them, they cast *them* into prison, charging the jailer to keep them safely:

24 Who, having received such a charge, thrust them into the inner prison, and made their feet fast in the stocks.

25 ¶ And at midnight Paul and Silas prayed, and sang praises unto God: and the prisoners heard them.

26 And suddenly there was a great earthquake, so that the foundations of the prison were shaken: and immediately all the doors were opened, and every one's bands were loosed.

27 And the keeper of the prison awaking out of his sleep, and seeing the prison doors open, he drew out his sword, and would have killed himself, supposing that the prisoners had been fled.

28 But Paul cried with a loud voice, saying, Do thyself no harm: for we are all here.

29 Then he called for a light, and sprang in, and came trembling, and fell down before Paul and Silas,

Amplified

12 And from there [we came] to Philippi, which is the chief city of the district of Macedonia, and a [Roman] colony. We stayed on in this place some days;

13 And on the Sabbath day we went outside the [city's] gate to the bank of the river, where we supposed there was [an accustomed] place of prayer, and we sat down and addressed the women who had assembled there.

14 One of those who listened to us was a woman named Lydia, from the city of Thyatira, a dealer in fabrics dyed in purple. She was [already] a worshipper of God, and the Lord opened her heart to pay attention to what was said by Paul.

15 And when she was baptized along with her household, she earnestly entreated us, saying, If in your opinion I am one really convinced [that Jesus is the Messiah and the Author of salvation], *and* that I will be faithful to the Lord, come to my house and stay. And she induced us [to do it].

16 As we were on our way to the place of prayer, we were met by a slave girl who was possessed by a spirit of divination—claiming to foretell future events and to discover hidden knowledge—and she brought her owners much gain by her fortune-telling.

17 She kept following Paul and [the rest of] us, shouting loudly, These men are the servants of the Most High God! They announce to you the way of salvation!

18 And she did this for many days. Then Paul, being sorely annoyed *and* worn out, turned and said to the spirit within her, I charge you in the name of Jesus Christ to come out of her! And it came out that very [k]moment.

19 But when her owners discovered that their hope of profit was gone, they caught hold of Paul and Silas and dragged them before the authorities in the forum—market place [where trials are held].

20 And when they had brought them before the magistrates, they declared, These fellows are Jews and they are throwing our city into great confusion.

21 They encourage the practice of customs which it is unlawful for us Romans to accept or observe!

22 The crowd [also] joined in the attack upon them, and the rulers tore the clothes off of them and commanded that they be beaten with rods.

23 And when they had struck them with many blows, they threw them into prison, charging the jailer to keep them safely.

24 He, having received [so strict a] charge, put them into the inner prison [the dungeon] and fastened their feet in the stocks.

25 But about midnight, as Paul and Silas were praying and singing hymns of praise to God, and the [other] prisoners were listening to them,

26 Suddenly there was a great earthquake, so that the very foundations of the prison were shaken; and at once all the doors were opened and every one's shackles were unfastened.

27 When the jailer, startled out of his sleep, saw that the prison doors were open, he drew his sword and was on the point of killing himself, because he supposed that the prisoners had escaped.

28 But Paul shouted, Do not harm yourself, for we are all here!

29 Then [the jailer] called for lights and rushed in, and trembling *and* terrified he fell down before Paul and Silas.

---

k) Moulton and Milligan's "The Vocabulary of the Greek Testament."

Living New Testament

12 And finally reached Philippi, a Roman[4] colony just inside the Macedonian border, and stayed there several days.

13 On the Sabbath, we went a little way outside the city to a river bank where we understood some people met for prayer; and we taught the Scriptures to some women who came.

14 One of them was Lydia, a saleswoman from Thyatira, a merchant of purple cloth. She was already a worshiper of God and, as she listened to us, the Lord opened her heart and she accepted all that Paul was saying.

15 She was baptized along with all her household and asked us to be her guests. "If you agree that I am faithful to the Lord," she said, "come and stay at my home." And she urged us until we did.

16 One day as we were going down to the place of prayer beside the river, we met a demon-possessed slave girl who was a fortune-teller, and earned much money for her masters.

17 She followed along behind us shouting, "These men are servants of God and they have come to tell you how to have your sins forgiven."

18 This went on day after day until Paul, in great distress, turned and spoke to the demon within her. "I command you in the name of Jesus Christ to come out of her," he said. And instantly it left her.

19 Her masters' hopes of wealth were now shattered; they grabbed Paul and Silas and dragged them before the judges at the marketplace.

20, 21 "These Jews are corrupting our city," they shouted. "They are teaching the people to do things that are against the Roman laws."

22 A mob was quickly formed against Paul and Silas, and the judges ordered them stripped and beaten with wooden whips.

23 Again and again the rods slashed down across their bared backs, causing the blood to flow; and afterwards they were thrown into prison. The jailer was threatened with death if they escaped,[5]

24 So he took no chances, but put them into the inner dungeon and clamped their feet into the stocks.

25 Around midnight, as Paul and Silas were praying and singing hymns to the Lord—and the other prisoners were listening—

26 Suddenly there was a great earthquake; the prison was shaken to its foundations, all the doors flew open—and the chains of every prisoner fell off!

27 The jailer wakened to see the prison doors wide open, and assuming the prisoners had escaped, he drew his sword to kill himself.

28 But Paul yelled to him, "Don't do it! We are all here!"

29 Trembling with fear, the jailer called for lights and ran to the dungeon and fell down before Paul and Silas.

[4] Implied.
[5] Implied.

Revised Standard

the following day to Neapolis, 12and from
there to Philippi, which is the leading city of
the district[x] of Macedonia, and a Roman
colony. We remained in this city some days;
13and on the sabbath day we went outside
the gate to the riverside, where we supposed
there was a place of prayer; and we sat
down and spoke to the women who had
come together. 14One who heard us was a
woman named Lydia, from the city of Thyatira,
a seller of purple goods, who was a
worshiper of God. The Lord opened her
heart to give heed to what was said by Paul.
15And when she was baptized, with her
household, she besought us, saying, "If you
have judged me to be faithful to the Lord,
come to my house and stay." And she prevailed upon us.

Paul and Silas imprisoned

16 As we were going to the place of
prayer, we were met by a slave girl who had
a spirit of divination and brought her owners
much gain by soothsaying. 17She followed
Paul and us, crying, "These men are
servants of the Most High God, who proclaim
to you the way of salvation." 18And
this she did for many days. But Paul was
annoyed, and turned and said to the spirit,
"I charge you in the name of Jesus Christ to
come out of her." And it came out that very
hour.

19 But when her owners saw that their
hope of gain was gone, they seized Paul and
Silas and dragged them into the market
place before the rulers; 20and when they
had brought them to the magistrates they
said, "These men are Jews and they are
disturbing our city. 21They advocate customs
which it is not lawful for us Romans to
accept or practice." 22The crowd joined in
attacking them; and the magistrates tore the
garments off them and gave orders to beat
them with rods. 23And when they had inflicted
many blows upon them, they threw
them into prison, charging the jailer to keep
them safely. 24Having received this charge,
he put them into the inner prison and fastened
their feet in the stocks.

Conversion of the Philippian jailer

25 But about midnight Paul and Silas
were praying and singing hymns to God, and
the prisoners were listening to them, 26and
suddenly there was a great earthquake, so
that the foundations of the prison were
shaken; and immediately all the doors were
opened and every one's fetters were unfastened.
27When the jailer woke and saw that
the prison doors were open, he drew his
sword and was about to kill himself, supposing
that the prisoners had escaped.
28But Paul cried with a loud voice, "Do
not harm yourself, for we are all here."
29And he called for lights and rushed in,
and trembling with fear he fell down be-

[x] The Greek text is uncertain

King James

30 And brought them out, and said, Sirs, what must I do to be saved?

31 And they said, Believe on the Lord Jesus Christ, and thou shalt be saved, and thy house.

32 And they spake unto him the word of the Lord, and to all that were in his house.

33 And he took them the same hour of the night, and washed *their* stripes; and was baptized, he and all his, straightway.

34 And when he had brought them into his house, he set meat before them, and rejoiced, believing in God with all his house.

35 And when it was day, the magistrates sent the sergeants, saying, Let those men go.

36 And the keeper of the prison told this saying to Paul, The magistrates have sent to let you go: now therefore depart, and go in peace.

37 But Paul said unto them, They have beaten us openly uncondemned, being Romans, and have cast *us* into prison; and now do they thrust us out privily? nay verily; but let them come themselves and fetch us out.

38 And the sergeants told these words unto the magistrates: and they feared, when they heard that they were Romans.

39 And they came and besought them, and brought *them* out, and desired *them* to depart out of the city.

40 And they went out of the prison, and entered into *the house of* Lydia: and when they had seen the brethren, they comforted them, and departed.

Amplified

30 And he brought them out [of the dungeon] and said, Men, what is it necessary for me to do that I may be saved?

31 And they answered, Believe in *and* on the Lord Jesus Christ—that is, [l]give yourself up to Him, [m]take yourself out of your own keeping and entrust yourself into His keeping, and you will be saved; [and this applies both to] you and your household as well.

32 And they declared the Word of the Lord [that is, the doctrine concerning the [l]attainment through Christ of eternal salvation in the kingdom of God] to him and to all who were in his house.

33 And he took them the same hour of the night and [n]bathed [them because of their bloody] wounds, and he was baptized immediately and all [the members] of his [household].

34 Then he took them up into his house and set food before them; and he [o]leaped much for joy *and* exulted with all his family that he believed in God [accepting and joyously welcoming what He had made known through Christ].

35 But when it was day, the magistrates sent policemen, saying, Release those fellows *and* let them go.

36 And the jailer repeated the words to Paul, saying, The magistrates have sent to release you *and* let you go; now therefore come out and go in peace.

37 But Paul answered them, They have beaten us openly *and* publicly, without a trial *and* uncondemned, men who are Roman citizens, and have thrown us into prison; and do they now thrust us out secretly? No, indeed! Let them come here themselves and conduct us out!

38 The police reported this message to the magistrates, and they were frightened when they heard that the prisoners were Roman citizens;

39 So they came themselves and—striving to appease them by entreaty—apologized to them. And they brought them out and asked them to leave the city.

40 So [Paul and Silas] left the prison, and went to Lydia's house; and when they had seen the brethren, they warned *and* urged *and* consoled *and* encouraged them and departed.

CHAPTER 17

NOW when they had passed through Amphipolis and Apollonia, they came to Thessalonica, where was a synagogue of the Jews:

2 And Paul, as his manner was, went in unto them, and three sabbath days reasoned with them out of the scriptures,

3 Opening and alleging, that Christ must needs have suffered, and risen again from the dead; and that this Jesus, whom I preach unto you, is Christ.

4 And some of them believed, and consorted with Paul and Silas; and of the devout Greeks a great multitude, and of the chief women not a few.

CHAPTER 17

NOW after [Paul and Silas] had passed through Amphipolis and Apollonia, they came to Thessalonica, where there was a synagogue of the Jews.

2 And Paul entered, as he usually did, and for three Sabbaths he reasoned *and* argued with them from the Scriptures,

3 Explaining [them] *and* [quoting passages] setting forth *and* proving that it was necessary for Christ to suffer and to rise from the dead, and saying, This Jesus, Whom I proclaim to you, is the Christ, the Messiah.

4 And some of them [accordingly] were induced to believe, and associated themselves with Paul and Silas, as did a great number of the devout Greeks and not a few of the leading women.

---

l) Thayer.
m) Wuest's "Golden Nuggets from the Greek New Testament."
n) Vincent's "Word Studies in the New Testament."
o) Young's Concordance.

Living New Testament

30 He brought them out and begged them, "Sirs, what must I do to be saved?"

31 They replied, "Believe on the Lord Jesus and you will be saved, and your entire household."

32 Then they told him and all his household the Good News from the Lord.

33 That same hour he washed their stripes and he and all his family were baptized.

34 Then he brought them up into his house and set a meal before them. How he and his household rejoiced because all were now believers!

35 The next morning the judges sent police officers over to tell the jailer, "Let those men go!"

36 So the jailer told Paul they were free to leave.

37 But Paul replied, "Oh, no they don't! They have publicly beaten us without trial and jailed us—and we are Roman citizens! So now they want us to leave secretly? Never! Let them come themselves and release us!"

38 The police officers reported to the judges, who feared for their lives when they heard Paul and Silas were Roman citizens.

39 So they came to the jail and begged them to go, and brought them out and pled with them to leave the city.

40 Paul and Silas then returned to the home of Lydia where they met with the believers and preached to them once more before leaving town.

Revised Standard

fore Paul and Silas, 30and brought them out
and said, "Men, what must I do to be
saved?" 31And they said, "Believe in the
Lord Jesus, and you will be saved, you
and your household." 32And they spoke
the word of the Lord to him and to all
that were in his house. 33And he took
them the same hour of the night, and
washed their wounds, and he was baptized
at once, with all his family. 34Then he
brought them up into his house, and set
food before them; and he rejoiced with
all his household that he had believed in
God.

35 But when it was day, the magistrates sent the police, saying, "Let those
men go." 36And the jailer reported the
words to Paul, saying, "The magistrates
have sent to let you go; now therefore
come out and go in peace." 37But Paul
said to them, "They have beaten us publicly, uncondemned, men who are Roman
citizens, and have thrown us into prison;
and do they now cast us out secretly? No!
let them come themselves and take us out."
38The police reported these words to the
magistrates, and they were afraid when
they heard that they were Roman citizens;
39so they came and apologized to them.
And they took them out and asked them
to leave the city. 40So they went out of
the prison, and visited Lydia; and when
they had seen the brethren, they exhorted
them and departed.

CHAPTER 17

Now they traveled through the cities of Amphipolis and Apollonia and came to Thessalonica, where there was a Jewish synagogue.

2 As was Paul's custom, he went there to preach, and for three Sabbaths in a row he opened the Scriptures to the people,

3 Explaining the prophecies about the sufferings of the Messiah and His coming back to life, and proving that Jesus is the Messiah.

4 Some who listened were persuaded and became converts—including a large number of godly Greek men, and also many important women of the city.[1]

Paul at Thessalonica

17 Now when they had passed through
Amphipolis and Apollonia, they came
to Thessalonica, where there was a synagogue of the Jews. 2And Paul went in, as
was his custom, and for three weeks[p] he
argued with them from the scriptures, 3ex-
plaining and proving that it was necessary
for the Christ to suffer and to rise from
the dead, and saying, "This Jesus, whom
I proclaim to you, is the Christ." 4And
some of them were persuaded, and joined
Paul and Silas; as did a great many of the
devout Greeks and not a few of the leading

Some manuscripts read, "many of the wives of leading men."

[p] Or *sabbaths*

King James

5 ¶ But the Jews which believed not, moved with envy, took unto them certain lewd fellows of the baser sort, and gathered a company, and set all the city on an uproar, and assaulted the house of Jason, and sought to bring them out to the people.

6 And when they found them not, they drew Jason and certain brethren unto the rulers of the city, crying, These that have turned the world upside down are come hither also;

7 Whom Jason hath received: and these all do contrary to the decrees of Cæsar, saying that there is another king, *one* Jesus.

8 And they troubled the people and the rulers of the city, when they heard these things.

9 And when they had taken security of Jason, and of the other, they let them go.

10 ¶ And the brethren immediately sent away Paul and Silas by night unto Berea: who coming *thither* went into the synagogue of the Jews.

11 These were more noble than those in Thessalonica, in that they received the word with all readiness of mind, and searched the scriptures daily, whether those things were so.

12 Therefore many of them believed; also of honourable women which were Greeks, and of men, not a few.

13 But when the Jews of Thessalonica had knowledge that the word of God was preached of Paul at Berea, they came thither also, and stirred up the people.

14 And then immediately the brethren sent away Paul to go as it were to the sea: but Silas and Timotheus abode there still.

15 And they that conducted Paul brought him unto Athens: and receiving a commandment unto Silas and Timotheus for to come to him with all speed, they departed.

16 ¶ Now while Paul waited for them at Athens, his spirit was stirred in him, when he saw the city wholly given to idolatry.

17 Therefore disputed he in the synagogue with the Jews, and with the devout persons, and in the market daily with them that met with him.

18 Then certain philosophers of the Epicureans, and of the Stoics, encountered him. And some said, What will this babbler say? other some, He seemeth to be a setter forth of strange gods: because he preached unto them Jesus and the resurrection.

19 And they took him, and brought him unto Areopagus, saying, May we know what this new doctrine, whereof thou speakest, *is?*

20 For thou bringest certain strange things to our ears: we would know therefore what these things mean.

21 (For all the Athenians and strangers which were there spent their time in nothing else, but either to tell, or to hear some new thing.)

22 ¶ Then Paul stood in the midst of Mars' hill, and said, *Ye* men of Athens, I perceive that in all things ye are too superstitious.

Amplified

5 But the unbelieving Jews were aroused to jealousy, and getting hold of some loungers in the market place—ruffians *and* rascals—they gathered together a mob, set the town in an uproar, and attacked the house of Jason, seeking to bring [Paul and Silas] out to the people.

6 But when they failed to find them, they dragged Jason and some of the brethren before the city authorities, crying, These men who have turned the world upside down have come here also,

7 And Jason has received them to his house *and* privately protected them! And they are all ignoring *and* acting contrary to the decrees of Caesar, [actually] asserting that there is another king, one Jesus!

8 And both the crowd and the city authorities on hearing this were irritated—stirred up and troubled.

9 And when they had taken security [bail] from Jason and the others, they let them go.

10 Now the brethren at once sent Paul and Silas away by night to Beroea, and when they arrived they entered the synagogue of the Jews.

11 Now these [Jews] were better disposed *and* more noble than those in Thessalonica, for they were entirely ready and accepted *and* welcomed the message [[p]concerning the attainment through Christ of eternal salvation in the kingdom of God], with inclination of mind *and* eagerness, searching *and* examining the Scriptures daily to see if these things were so.

12 Many of them therefore became believers, together with not a few prominent Greeks, women as well as men;

13 But when the Jews of Thessalonica learned that the Word of God [[p]concerning the attainment through Christ of eternal salvation in the kingdom of God] was preached at Beroea also by Paul, they came there too, disturbing *and* inciting the masses.

14 At once the brethren sent Paul off on his way to the sea, but Silas and Timothy remained behind.

15 Those who escorted Paul brought him as far as Athens; and receiving instructions for Silas and Timothy that they should come to him as soon as possible, they departed.

16 Now while Paul was awaiting them at Athens, his spirit was grieved *and* roused to anger as he saw that the city was full of idols.

17 So he reasoned *and* argued in the synagogue with the Jews and those who worshipped there, and in the market place [where assemblies are held], day after day with any who chanced to be there.

18 And some also of the Epicurean and Stoic philosophers encountered him *and* began to engage in discussion. And some said, What is this blabber with his scrap-picked learning trying to say? Others said, He seems to be an announcer of foreign deities, because he preached Jesus and the resurrection.

19 And they took hold of him and brought him to the Areopagus [Mars Hill auditorium] saying, May we know what this novel—unheard of and unprecedented—teaching is which you are openly declaring?

20 For you set forth some startling things, foreign *and* strange to our ears; we wish to know therefore just what these things mean.

21 For the Athenians, all of them, and the foreign residents *and* visitors among them spent all their leisure time in nothing except telling or hearing something newer than the last.

22 So Paul, standing in the center of the Areopagus [Mars Hill auditorium] said: Men of Athens, I perceive in every way—on every hand and with every turn I make—that you are most religious (very reverent to demons).

---

p) Thayer.

Living New Testament

5 But the Jewish leaders were jealous and incited some worthless fellows from the streets to form a mob and start a riot. They attacked the home of Jason, planning to take Paul and Silas to the City Council for punishment.

6 Not finding them there, they dragged out Jason and some of the other believers, and took them before the Council instead. "Paul and Silas have turned the rest of the world upside down, and now they are here disturbing our city," they shouted,

7 "And Jason has let them into his house. They are all guilty of treason, for they claim another king, Jesus instead of Caesar."

8, 9 The people of the city, as well as the judges, were concerned at these reports and only let them go after they had posted bail.

10 That night the Christians hurried Paul and Silas to Beroea, and, as usual,[2] they went to the synagogue to preach.

11 But the people of Beroea were more open minded than those in Thessalonica, and gladly listened to the message. They searched the Scriptures day by day to check up on Paul and Silas' statements to see if they were really so.

12 As a result, many of them believed, including several prominent Greek women and many men also.

13 But when the Jews in Thessalonica learned that Paul was preaching in Beroea, they went over and stirred up trouble.

14 The believers acted at once, sending Paul on to the coast, while Silas and Timothy remained behind.

15 Those accompanying Paul went on with him to Athens, and then returned to Beroea with a message for Silas and Timothy to hurry and join him.

16 While Paul was waiting for them in Athens, he was deeply troubled by all the idols he saw everywhere throughout the city.

17 He went to the synagogue for discussions with the Jews and the devout Gentiles, and spoke daily in the public square to all who happened to be there.

18 He also had an encounter with some of the Epicurean and Stoic philosophers. Their reaction, when he told them about Jesus and His resurrection, was, "He's a dreamer," or, "He's pushing some foreign religion."

19 But they invited him to the forum at Mars Hill. "Come and tell us more about this new religion," they said,

20 "For you are saying some rather startling things and we want to hear more."

21 (I should explain that all the Athenians as well as the foreigners in Athens seemed to spend all their time discussing the latest new ideas!)

22 So Paul, standing before them at the Mars Hill forum, addressed them as follows:

"Men of Athens, I notice that you are very religious,

[2] Implied.

Revised Standard

women. [5]But the Jews were jealous, and
taking some wicked fellows of the rabble,
they gathered a crowd, set the city in an
uproar, and attacked the house of Jason,
seeking to bring them out to the people.
[6]And when they could not find them, they
dragged Jason and some of the brethren
before the city authorities, crying, "These
men who have turned the world upside
down have come here also, [7]and Jason
has received them; and they are all acting
against the decrees of Caesar, saying that
there is another king, Jesus." [8]And the
people and the city authorities were disturbed when they heard this. [9]And when
they had taken security from Jason and
the rest they let them go.

Paul at Beroea

10 The brethren immediately sent Paul
and Silas away by night to Beroea; and
when they arrived they went into the Jewish synagogue. [11]Now these Jews were
more noble than those in Thessalonica, for
they received the word with all eagerness,
examining the scriptures daily to see if
these things were so. [12]Many of them
therefore believed, with not a few Greek
women of high standing as well as men.
[13]But when the Jews of Thessalonica learned
that the word of God was proclaimed by
Paul at Beroea also, they came there too,
stirring up and inciting the crowds. [14]Then
the brethren immediately sent Paul off on
his way to sea, but Silas and Timothy remained there. [15]Those who conducted Paul
brought him as far as Athens; and receiving
a command for Silas and Timothy to come
to him as soon as possible, they departed.

Paul at Athens

16 Now while Paul was waiting for them
at Athens, his spirit was provoked within
him as he saw that the city was full of
idols. [17]So he argued in the synagogue with
the Jews and the devout persons, and in the
market place every day with those who
chanced to be there. [18]Some also of the
Epicurean and Stoic philosophers met him.
And some said, "What would this babbler
say?" Others said, "He seems to be a
preacher of foreign divinities"—because he
preached Jesus and the resurrection. [19]And
they took hold of him and brought him to
the Areopagus, saying, "May we know what
this new teaching is which you present?
[20]For you bring some strange things to our
ears; we wish to know therefore what these
things mean." [21]Now all the Athenians and
the foreigners who lived there spent their
time in nothing except telling or hearing
something new.

22 So Paul, standing in the middle of the
Areopagus, said: "Men of Athens, I perceive that in every way you are very relig-

King James

23 For as I passed by, and beheld your devotions, I found an altar with this inscription, TO THE UNKNOWN GOD. Whom therefore ye ignorantly worship, him declare I unto you.
24 God that made the world and all things therein, seeing that he is Lord of heaven and earth, dwelleth not in temples made with hands;
25 Neither is worshipped with men's hands, as though he needed any thing, seeing he giveth to all life, and breath, and all things;
26 And hath made of one blood all nations of men for to dwell on all the face of the earth, and hath determined the times before appointed, and the bounds of their habitation;
27 That they should seek the Lord, if haply they might feel after him, and find him, though he be not far from every one of us:
28 For in him we live, and move, and have our being; as certain also of your own poets have said, For we are also his offspring.
29 Forasmuch then as we are the offspring of God, we ought not to think that the Godhead is like unto gold, or silver, or stone, graven by art and man's device.
30 And the times of this ignorance God winked at; but now commandeth all men everywhere to repent:
31 Because he hath appointed a day, in the which he will judge the world in righteousness by *that* man whom he hath ordained; *whereof* he hath given assurance unto all *men*, in that he hath raised him from the dead.
32 ¶ And when they heard of the resurrection of the dead, some mocked: and others said, We will hear thee again of this *matter*.
33 So Paul departed from among them.
34 Howbeit certain men clave unto him, and believed: among the which *was* Dionysius the Areopagite, and a woman named Damaris, and others with them.

Amplified

23 For as I passed along and carefully observed your objects of worship, I came also upon an altar with this inscription, To the unknown god. Now what you are already worshipping as unknown, this I set forth to you.
24 The God Who produced *and* formed the world and all things in it, being Lord of heaven and earth, does not dwell in handmade shrines.
25 Neither is He served by human hands, as though He lacked anything, for it is He Himself Who gives life and breath and all things to all [people]. [Isa. 42:5.]
26 And He made from one [common origin, one source, one blood] all nations of men to settle on the face of the earth, having definitely determined [their] allotted periods of time and the fixed boundaries of their habitation—their settlements, lands and abodes;
27 So that they should seek God, in the hope that they might feel after Him and find Him, although He is not far from each one of us.
28 For in Him we live and move and have our being; as even some of your [own] poets have said, For we are also His offspring.
29 Since then we are God's offspring, we ought not to suppose that Deity—[q]the Godhead—is like gold or silver or stone, [that is, of the nature of] a representation by human art and imagination, *or* anything constructed *or* invented.
30 Such [former] ages of ignorance God, it is true, ignored *and* allowed to pass unnoticed; but now He charges all people everywhere to repent—[that is,] [r]to change their minds for the better and heartily to amend their ways, with abhorrence for their past sins.
31 Because He has fixed a day when He will judge the world righteously (justly) by a Man Whom He has destined *and* appointed for that task, and He has made this credible *and* given conviction *and* assurance *and* evidence to everyone by raising Him from the dead. [Ps. 9:8; 96:13; 98:9.]
32 Now when they had heard [that there had been] a resurrection from the dead, some scoffed; but others said, We will hear you again about this matter.
33 So Paul went out from among them.
34 But some men were on his side *and* joined him and believed (became Christians); among them were Dionysius, a judge of the Areopagus, and a woman named Damaris and some others with them.

CHAPTER 18

AFTER these things Paul departed from Athens, and came to Corinth;
2 And found a certain Jew named Aquila, born in Pontus, lately come from Italy, with his wife Priscilla; (because that Claudius had commanded all Jews to depart from Rome:) and came unto them.
3 And because he was of the same craft, he abode with them, and wrought: for by their occupation they were tentmakers.
4 And he reasoned in the synagogue every sabbath, and persuaded the Jews and the Greeks.

CHAPTER 18

AFTER this [Paul] departed from Athens and went to Corinth.
2 There he met a Jew named Aquila, a native of Pontus, recently arrived from Italy with Priscilla his wife, due to the fact that Claudius had issued an edict that all the Jews were to leave Rome. And [Paul] went to see them;
3 And because he was of the same occupation he stayed with them, and they worked [together], for they were tentmakers by trade.
4 But he discoursed *and* argued in the synagogue every Sabbath, and won over [both] Jews and Greeks.

---

q) King James Version.
r) Thayer.

Living New Testament

23 For as I was out walking I saw your many altars, and one of them had this inscription on it—'To the Unknown God.' You have been worshiping Him without knowing who He is, and now I wish to tell you about Him.

24 He made the world and everything in it, and since He is Lord of heaven and earth, He doesn't live in man-made temples;

25 And human hands can't minister to His needs—for He has no needs! He Himself gives life and breath to everything, and satisfies every need there is.

26 He created all the people of the world from one man, Adam,[3] and scattered the nations across the face of the earth. He decided beforehand which should rise and fall, and when. He determined their boundaries.

27 His purpose in all of this is that they should seek after God, and perhaps feel their way toward Him and find Him—though He is not far from any one of us.

28 For in Him we live and move and are! As one of your own poets says it, 'We are the sons of God.'

29 If this is true, we shouldn't think of God as an idol made by men from gold or silver or chipped from stone.

30 God tolerated man's past ignorance about these things, but now He commands everyone to put away idols and worship only Him.

31 For He has set a day for justly judging the world by the man He has appointed, and has pointed Him out by bringing Him back to life again."

32 When they heard Paul speak of the resurrection of a person who had been dead, some laughed, but others said, "We want to hear more about this later."

33 That ended Paul's discussion with them,

34 But a few joined him and became believers. Among them was Dionysius, a member of the City Council, and a woman named Damaris, and others.

Revised Standard

ious. 23 For as I passed along, and observed
the objects of your worship, I found also
an altar with this inscription, 'To an unknown god.' What therefore you worship
as unknown, this I proclaim to you. 24 The
God who made the world and everything
in it, being Lord of heaven and earth, does
not live in shrines made by man, 25 nor is he
served by human hands, as though he needed anything, since he himself gives to all
men life and breath and everything. 26 And
he made from one every nation of men to
live on all the face of the earth, having
determined allotted periods and the boundaries of their habitation. 27 that they should
seek God, in the hope that they might feel
after him and find him. Yet he is not far
from each one of us, 28 for
'In him we live and move and have our
being';
as even some of your poets have said,
'For we are indeed his offspring.'
29 Being then God's offspring, we ought not
to think that the Deity is like gold, or silver,
or stone, a representation by the art and
imagination of man. 30 The times of ignorance God overlooked, but now he commands all men everywhere to repent, 31 because he has fixed a day on which he will
judge the world in righteousness by a man
whom he has appointed, and of this he has
given assurance to all men by raising him
from the dead."

32 Now when they heard of the resurrection of the dead, some mocked; but others said, "We will hear you again about
this." 33 So Paul went out from among them.
34 But some men joined him and believed,
among them Dionysius the Areopagite and
a woman named Damaris and others with
them.

CHAPTER 18

Then Paul left Athens and went to Corinth.

2, 3 There he became acquainted with a Jew named Aquila, born in Pontus, who had recently arrived from Italy with his wife, Priscilla. They had been expelled from Italy as a result of Claudius Caesar's order to deport all Jews from Rome. Paul lived and worked with them, for they were tentmakers just as he was.

4 Each Sabbath found Paul at the synagogue, trying to convince the Jews and Greeks alike.

Paul at Corinth

18 After this he left Athens and went to
Corinth. 2 And he found a Jew named
Aquila, a native of Pontus, lately come from
Italy with his wife Priscilla, because Claudius had commanded all the Jews to leave
Rome. And he went to see them; 3 and because he was of the same trade he stayed
with them, and they worked, for by trade
they were tentmakers. 4 And he argued in
the synagogue every sabbath, and persuaded Jews and Greeks.

[3] Implied.

King James

5 And when Silas and Timotheus were come from Macedonia, Paul was pressed in the spirit, and testified to the Jews *that* Jesus *was* Christ.

6 And when they opposed themselves, and blasphemed, he shook *his* raiment, and said unto them, Your blood *be* upon your own heads; I *am* clean: from henceforth I will go unto the Gentiles.

7 And he departed thence, and entered into a certain *man's* house, named Justus, *one* that worshipped God, whose house joined hard to the synagogue.

8 And Crispus, the chief ruler of the synagogue, believed on the Lord with all his house; and many of the Corinthians hearing believed, and were baptized.

9 Then spake the Lord to Paul in the night by a vision, Be not afraid, but speak, and hold not thy peace:

10 For I am with thee, and no man shall set on thee to hurt thee: for I have much people in this city.

11 And he continued *there* a year and six months, teaching the word of God among them.

12 ¶ And when Gallio was the deputy of Achaia, the Jews made insurrection with one accord against Paul, and brought him to the judgment seat,

13 Saying, This *fellow* persuadeth men to worship God contrary to the law.

14 And when Paul was now about to open *his* mouth, Gallio said unto the Jews, If it were a matter of wrong or wicked lewdness, O *ye* Jews, reason would that I should bear with you:

15 But if it be a question of words and names, and *of* your law, look ye *to it;* for I will be no judge of such *matters.*

16 And he drave them from the judgment seat.

17 Then all the Greeks took Sosthenes, the chief ruler of the synagogue, and beat *him* before the judgment seat. And Gallio cared for none of those things.

18 ¶ And Paul *after this* tarried *there* yet a good while, and then took his leave of the brethren, and sailed thence into Syria, and with him Priscilla and Aquila; having shorn *his* head in Cenchrea: for he had a vow.

19 And he came to Ephesus, and left them there: but he himself entered into the synagogue, and reasoned with the Jews.

20 When they desired *him* to tarry longer time with them, he consented not;

21 But bade them farewell, saying, I must by all means keep this feast that cometh in Jerusalem: but I will return again unto you, if God will. And he sailed from Ephesus.

22 And when he had landed at Cæsarea, and gone up, and saluted the church, he went down to Antioch.

23 And after he had spent some time *there,* he departed, and went over *all* the country of Galatia and Phrygia in order, strengthening all the disciples.

24 ¶ And a certain Jew named Apollos, born at Alexandria, an eloquent man, *and* mighty in the scriptures, came to Ephesus.

Amplified

5 By the time Silas and Timothy arrived from Macedonia, Paul was completely engrossed with preaching, earnestly arguing *and* testifying to the Jews that Jesus [is] the Christ.

6 But since they kept opposing *and* abusing *and* reviling him, he shook out his clothing [against them] and said to them, Your blood be upon your [own] heads! I am innocent [of it]. From now on I will go to the Gentiles.

7 He then left there and went to the house of a man named Titus Justus, who worshipped God, and whose house was next door to the synagogue.

8 But Crispus, the leader of the synagogue, believed [that Jesus is the Messiah and acknowledged Him with joyful trust as Savior and Lord], together with his entire household; and many of the Corinthians who listened [to Paul also] believed and were baptized.

9 And one night the Lord said to Paul in a vision, Have no fear, but speak and do not keep silent;

10 For I am with you, and no man shall assault you to harm you; for I have many people in this city. [Isa. 43:5; Jer. 1:8.]

11 So he settled down among them for a year and six months, teaching the Word of God [concerning the [s]attainment through Christ of eternal salvation in the kingdom of God].

12 But when Gallio was proconsul of Achaia [most of Greece], the Jews unitedly made an attack upon Paul and brought him before the judge's seat.

13 Declaring, This fellow is advising *and* inducing *and* inciting people to worship God in violation of the Law [of Moses].

14 But when Paul was about to open his mouth to reply, Gallio said to the Jews, If it were a matter of some misdemeanor or villainy, O Jews, I should have cause to bear with you *and* listen;

15 But since it is merely a question (of doctrine) about words and names and your own law, see to it yourselves; I decline to be a judge of such matters *and* I have no intention of trying such cases.

16 And he drove them away from the judgment seat.

17 Then they [the Greeks] all seized Sosthenes, the leader of the synagogue, and beat him right in front of the judgment seat. But Gallio paid no attention to any of this.

18 Afterward Paul remained many days longer, and then told the brethren farewell and sailed for Syria, and he was accompanied by Priscilla and Aquila. At Cenchreae he [[t]Paul] cut his hair, for he had made a vow.

19 Then they arrived in Ephesus, and [Paul] left the others there; but he himself entered the synagogue and discoursed *and* argued with the Jews.

20 When they asked him to remain for a longer time, he would not consent,

21 But when he was leaving them he said, I will return to you if God is willing, and he set sail from Ephesus.

22 When he landed at Caesarea, he went up and saluted the church [at Jerusalem], and then went down to Antioch.

23 After staying there some time, he left and went from place to place in an orderly journey through the territory of Galatia and Phrygia, establishing the disciples *and* imparting new strength to them.

24 Meanwhile there was a Jew named Apollos, a native of Alexandria, who came to Ephesus. He was a cultured *and* eloquent man, well versed *and* mighty in the Scriptures.

---

s) Thayer.
t) Vincent. Alford. Stanley. Others think Aquila is meant.

Living New Testament

5 And after the arrival of Silas and Timothy from Macedonia, Paul spent his full time preaching and testifying to the Jews that Jesus is the Messiah.

6 But when the Jews opposed him and blasphemed, hurling abuse at Jesus, Paul shook off the dust from his robe and said, "Your blood be upon your own heads—I am innocent—from now on I will preach to the Gentiles."

7 After that he stayed with Titus Justus, a Gentile[1] who worshiped God and lived next door to the synagogue.

8 Crispus, the leader of the synagogue, and all his household believed in the Lord and were baptized—as were many others in Corinth.

9 One night the Lord spoke to Paul in a vision and told him, "Don't be afraid! Speak out! Don't quit!

10 For I am with you and no one can harm you. Many people here in this city belong to Me."

11 So Paul stayed there the next year and a half, teaching the truths of God.

12 But when Gallio became governor of Achaia, the Jews rose in concerted action against Paul and brought him before the governor for judgment.

13 They accused Paul of "persuading men to worship God in ways that are contrary to Roman law."

14 But just as Paul started to make his defense, Gallio turned to his accusers and said, "Listen, you Jews, if this were a case involving some crime, I would be obliged to listen to you,

15 But since it is merely a bunch of questions of semantics and personalities and your silly Jewish laws, you take care of it. I'm not interested and I'm not touching it."

16 And he drove them out of the courtroom.

17 Then the mob[2] grabbed Sosthenes, the new leader of the synagogue, and beat him outside the courtroom! But Gallio couldn't have cared less.

18 Paul stayed in the city several days after that and then said good-bye to the Christians and sailed for the coast of Syria, taking Priscilla and Aquila with him. At Cenchreae, Paul had his head shaved according to Jewish custom, for he had taken a vow.[3]

19 Arriving at the port of Ephesus, he left us aboard ship while he went over to the synagogue for a discussion with the Jews.

20 They asked him to stay for a few days, but he felt that he had no time to lose.[4]

21 "I must by all means be at Jerusalem for the holiday,"[5] he said. But he promised to return to Ephesus later if God permitted; and so we set sail again.

22 The next stop was at the port of Caesarea from where he visited the church [at Jerusalem[6]] and then sailed on to Antioch.

23 After spending some time there, he left for Turkey again, going through Galatia and Phrygia visiting all the believers, encouraging them and helping them grow in the Lord.

24 As it happened, a Jew named Apollos, a wonderful Bible teacher and preacher, had just arrived in Ephesus from Alexandria in Egypt.

---

1 Implied.
2 Implied.
3 Probably a vow to offer a sacrifice in Jerusalem in thanksgiving for answered prayer. The head was shaved 30 days before such gifts and sacrifices were given to God at the Temple.
4 Possibly in order to arrive in Jerusalem within the prescribed 30 days.
5 Literally, "feast." This entire sentence is omitted in many of the ancient manuscripts.
6 Implied.

Revised Standard

5 When Silas and Timothy arrived from Macedonia, Paul was occupied with preaching, testifying to the Jews that the Christ was Jesus. [6]And when they opposed and reviled him, he shook out his garments and said to them, "Your blood be upon your heads! I am innocent. From now on I will go to the Gentiles." [7]And he left there and went to the house of a man named Titius[q] Justus, a worshiper of God; his house was next door to the synagogue. [8]Crispus, the ruler of the synagogue, believed in the Lord, together with all his household; and many of the Corinthians hearing Paul believed and were baptized. [9]And the Lord said to Paul one night in a vision, "Do not be afraid, but speak and do not be silent; [10]for I am with you, and no man shall attack you to harm you; for I have many people in this city." [11]And he stayed a year and six months, teaching the word of God among them.

12 But when Gallio was proconsul of Achaia, the Jews made a united attack upon Paul and brought him before the tribunal, [13]saying, "This man is persuading men to worship God contrary to the law." [14]But when Paul was about to open his mouth, Gallio said to the Jews, "If it were a matter of wrongdoing or vicious crime, I should have reason to bear with you, O Jews; [15]but since it is a matter of questions about words and names and your own law, see to it yourselves; I refuse to be a judge of these things." [16]And he drove them from the tribunal. [17]And they all seized Sosthenes, the ruler of the synagogue, and beat him in front of the tribunal. But Gallio paid no attention to this.

Paul returns to Antioch

18 After this Paul stayed many days longer, and then took leave of the brethren and sailed for Syria, and with him Priscilla and Aquila. At Cenchreae he cut his hair, for he had a vow. [19]And they came to Ephesus, and he left them there; but he himself went into the synagogue and argued with the Jews. [20]When they asked him to stay for a longer period, he declined; [21]but on taking leave of them he said, "I will return to you if God wills," and he set sail from Ephesus.

22 When he had landed at Caesarea, he went up and greeted the church, and then went down to Antioch. [23]After spending some time there he departed and went from place to place through the region of Galatia and Phrygia, strengthening all the disciples.

Apollos' preaching at Ephesus

24 Now a Jew named Apollos, a native of Alexandria, came to Ephesus. He was an eloquent man, well versed in the scriptures.

---

q Other early authorities read *Titus*

King James

25 This man was instructed in the way of the Lord; and being fervent in the spirit, he spake and taught diligently the things of the Lord, knowing only the baptism of John.

26 And he began to speak boldly in the synagogue: whom when Aquila and Priscilla had heard, they took him unto *them,* and expounded unto him the way of God more perfectly.

27 And when he was disposed to pass into Achaia, the brethren wrote, exhorting the disciples to receive him: who, when he was come, helped them much which had believed through grace:

28 For he mightily convinced the Jews, *and that* publicly, shewing by the scriptures that Jesus was Christ.

Amplified

25 He had been instructed in the way of the Lord, and burning with spiritual zeal, he spoke and taught diligently *and* accurately the things concerning Jesus, though he was acquainted only with the baptism of John.

26 He began to speak freely—fearlessly and boldly—in the synagogue; but when Priscilla and Aquila heard him, they took him with them and expounded to him the way of God more definitely *and* accurately.

27 And when [Apollos] wished to cross to Achaia [most of Greece], the brethren wrote to the disciples there, urging *and* encouraging them to accept *and* welcome him heartily. When he arrived, he proved a great help to those who through grace—God's unmerited favor and mercy—had believed (adhered to, trusted in and relied on [Christ as Lord and Savior]).

28 For with great power he refuted the Jews in public [discussions], showing *and* proving by the Scriptures that Jesus is the Christ, the Messiah.

CHAPTER 19

AND it came to pass, that, while Apollos was at Corinth, Paul having passed through the upper coasts came to Ephesus: and finding certain disciples,

2 He said unto them, Have ye received the Holy Ghost since ye believed? And they said unto him, We have not so much as heard whether there be any Holy Ghost.

3 And he said unto them, Unto what then were ye baptized? And they said, Unto John's baptism.

4 Then said Paul, John verily baptized with the baptism of repentance, saying unto the people, that they should believe on him which should come after him, that is, on Christ Jesus.

5 When they heard *this,* they were baptized in the name of the Lord Jesus.

6 And when Paul had laid *his* hands upon them, the Holy Ghost came on them; and they spake with tongues, and prophesied.

7 And all the men were about twelve.

8 And he went into the synagogue, and spake boldly for the space of three months, disputing and persuading the things concerning the kingdom of God.

9 But when divers were hardened, and believed not, but spake evil of that way before the multitude, he departed from them, and separated the disciples, disputing daily in the school of one Tyrannus.

10 And this continued by the space of two years; so that all they which dwelt in Asia heard the word of the Lord Jesus, both Jews and Greeks.

11 And God wrought special miracles by the hands of Paul:

12 So that from his body were brought unto the sick handkerchiefs or aprons, and the diseases departed from them, and the evil spirits went out of them.

CHAPTER 19

WHILE Apollos was in Corinth, Paul went through the upper inland districts and came down to Ephesus. There he found some disciples.

2 And he asked them, Did you receive the Holy Spirit when you believed [on Jesus as the Christ]? And they said, No, we have not even heard that there is a Holy Spirit.

3 And he asked, Into what then were you baptized? They said, Into John's baptism.

4 And Paul said, John baptized with the baptism of repentance, continually telling the people that they should believe in the One Who was to come after him, that is, in Jesus [having a conviction full of joyful trust that He is Christ, the Messiah, and being obedient to Him].

5 On hearing this they were baptized [again, this time] in the name of the Lord Jesus.

6 And as Paul laid his hands upon them, the Holy Spirit came on them; and they spoke in foreign languages and prophesied.

7 There were about twelve of them in all.

8 And he went into the synagogue and for three months spoke boldly, persuading *and* arguing and pleading about the kingdom of God.

9 But when some became more and more stubborn (hardened and unbelieving), discrediting *and* reviling *and* speaking evil of the Way [of the Lord] before the congregation, he separated himself from them, taking the disciples with him, and went on holding daily discussions in the lecture room of Tyrannus [[u]from about ten o'clock till three].

10 This continued for two years, so that all the inhabitants of [the province of] Asia, Jews as well as Greeks, heard the Word of the Lord [concerning the [v]attainment through Christ of eternal salvation in the kingdom of God].

11 And God did unusual *and* extraordinary miracles by the hands of Paul,

12 So that handkerchiefs *or* towels or aprons which had touched his skin were carried away *and* put upon the sick, and their diseases left them, and the evil spirits came out of them.

---

u) Added by some ancient authorities.
v) Thayer.

Living New Testament

25, 26 While he was in Egypt, someone had told him about John the Baptist and what John had said about Jesus, but that is all he knew. He had never heard the rest of the story! So he was preaching boldly and enthusiastically in the synagogue, "The Messiah is coming! Get ready to receive Him!" Priscilla and Aquila were there and heard him—and it was a powerful sermon. Afterwards they met with him and explained what had happened to Jesus since the time of John, and all that it meant![7]

27 Apollos had been thinking about going to Greece, and the believers encouraged him in this. They wrote to their fellow-believers there, telling them to welcome him. And upon his arrival in Greece, he was greatly used of God to strengthen the church,

28 For he powerfully refuted all the Jewish arguments in public debate, showing by the Scriptures that Jesus is indeed the Messiah.

Revised Standard

25 He had been instructed in the way of
the Lord; and being fervent in spirit, he
spoke and taught accurately the things concerning Jesus, though he knew only the
baptism of John. 26 He began to speak boldly in the synagogue; but when Priscilla and
Aquila heard him, they took him and expounded to him the way of God more accurately. 27 And when he wished to cross
to Achaia, the brethren encouraged him,
and wrote to the disciples to receive him.
When he arrived, he greatly helped those
who through grace had believed, 28 for he
powerfully confuted the Jews in public,
showing by the scriptures that the Christ
was Jesus.

CHAPTER 19

While Apollos was in Corinth, Paul traveled through Turkey and arrived in Ephesus, where he found several disciples.

2 "Did you receive the Holy Spirit when you believed?" he asked them.

"No," they replied, "we don't know what you mean. What is the Holy Spirit?"

3 "Then what beliefs did you acknowledge at your baptism?" he asked.

And they replied, "What John the Baptist taught."

4 Then Paul pointed out to them that John's baptism was to demonstrate a desire to turn from sin to God and that those receiving his baptism must then go on to believe in Jesus, the one John said would come later.

5 As soon as they heard this, they were baptized in[1] the name of the Lord Jesus.

6 Then, when Paul laid his hands upon their heads, the Holy Spirit came on them, and they spoke in other languages and prophesied.

7 The men involved were about 12 in number.

8 Then Paul went to the synagogue and preached boldly each Sabbath day[2] for three months, telling what[3] he believed and why, and persuading many to believe in Jesus.

9 But some rejected his message and publicly spoke against Christ, so he left, refusing to preach to them again. Pulling out the believers he began a separate meeting at the lecture hall of Tryannus and preached there daily.

10 This went on for the next two years, so that everyone in the Turkish province of Ausia—both Jews and Greeks—heard the Lord's message.

11 And God gave Paul the power to do unusual miracles,

12 So that even when his handkerchiefs or parts of his clothing were placed upon sick people, they were healed, and any demons within them came out.

Paul baptizes John's disciples

19 While Apollos was at Corinth, Paul
passed through the upper country and
came to Ephesus. There he found some disciples. 2 And he said to them, "Did you receive the Holy Spirit when you believed?"
And they said, "No, we have never even
heard that there is a Holy Spirit." 3 And he
said, "Into what then were you baptized?"
They said, "Into John's baptism." 4 And
Paul said, "John baptized with the baptism
of repentance, telling the people to believe
in the one who was to come after him, that
is, Jesus." 5 On hearing this, they were baptized in the name of the Lord Jesus. 6 And
when Paul had laid his hands upon them,
the Holy Spirit came on them; and they
spoke with tongues and prophesied. 7 There
were about twelve of them in all.

Paul's work in Ephesus

8 And he entered the synagogue and for
three months spoke boldly, arguing and
pleading about the kingdom of God; 9 but
when some were stubborn and disbelieved,
speaking evil of the Way before the congregation, he withdrew from them, taking the
disciples with him, and argued daily in the
hall of Tyrannus.[r] 10 This continued for two
years, so that all the residents of Asia heard
the word of the Lord, both Jews and Greeks.
11 And God did extraordinary miracles
by the hands of Paul, 12 so that handkerchiefs
or aprons were carried away from his body
to the sick, and diseases left them and the
evil spirits came out of them. 13 Then some

---

[7] Literally, "explained to him the way of God more accurately."
[1] Or, "into."
[2] Implied.
[3] Literally, "concerning the Kingdom of God."

[r] Other ancient authorities add *from the fifth hour to the tenth*

King James

13 ¶ Then certain of the vagabond Jews, exorcists, took upon them to call over them which had evil spirits the name of the Lord Jesus, saying, We adjure you by Jesus whom Paul preacheth.

14 And there were seven sons of *one* Sceva, a Jew, *and* chief of the priests, which did so.

15 And the evil spirit answered and said, Jesus I know, and Paul I know; but who are ye?

16 And the man in whom the evil spirit was leaped on them, and overcame them, and prevailed against them, so that they fled out of that house naked and wounded.

17 And this was known to all the Jews and Greeks also dwelling at Ephesus; and fear fell on them all, and the name of the Lord Jesus was magnified.

18 And many that believed came, and confessed, and shewed their deeds.

19 Many of them also which used curious arts brought their books together, and burned them before all *men:* and they counted the price of them, and found *it* fifty thousand *pieces* of silver.

20 So mightily grew the word of God and prevailed.

21 ¶ After these things were ended, Paul purposed in the spirit, when he had passed through Macedonia and Achaia, to go to Jerusalem, saying, After I have been there, I must also see Rome.

22 So he sent into Macedonia two of them that ministered unto him, Timotheus and Erastus; but he himself stayed in Asia for a season.

23 And the same time there arose no small stir about that way.

24 For a certain *man* named Demetrius, a silversmith, which made silver shrines for Diana, brought no small gain unto the craftsmen;

25 Whom he called together with the workmen of like occupation, and said, Sirs, ye know that by this craft we have our wealth.

26 Moreover ye see and hear, that not alone at Ephesus, but almost throughout all Asia, this Paul hath persuaded and turned away much people, saying that they be no gods, which are made with hands:

27 So that not only this our craft is in danger to be set at nought; but also that the temple of the great goddess Diana should be despised, and her magnificence should be destroyed, whom all Asia and the world worshippeth.

28 And when they heard *these sayings,* they were full of wrath, and cried out, saying, Great *is* Diana of the Ephesians.

29 And the whole city was filled with confusion: and having caught Gaius and Aristarchus, men of Macedonia, Paul's companions in travel, they rushed with one accord into the theatre.

30 And when Paul would have entered in unto the people, the disciples suffered him not.

Amplified

13 Then some of the traveling Jewish exorcists [men who adjure evil spirits] also undertook to call the name of the Lord Jesus over those who had evil spirits, saying, I solemnly implore *and* charge you by the Jesus Whom Paul preaches!

14 Seven sons of a certain Jewish chief priest named Sceva were doing this.

15 But [one] evil spirit retorted, Jesus I know, and Paul I know [w]about, but who are you?

16 Then the man in whom the evil spirit dwelt, leaped upon them, mastering [x]two of them, and was so violent against them that they dashed out of that house [in fear], stripped naked and wounded.

17 This became known to all who lived in Ephesus, both Jews and Greeks, and alarm *and* terror fell upon them all; and the name of the Lord Jesus was extolled *and* magnified.

18 Many also of those who were now believers came making [y]full confession *and* thoroughly exposing their [former deceptive and evil] practices.

19 And many of those who had practiced curious magical arts collected their books and (throwing them [y]book after book on the pile) burned them in the sight of everybody. When they counted the value of them, they found it amounted to fifty thousand pieces of silver ([y]about $9,300).

20 Thus the Word of the Lord [concerning the [z]attainment through Christ of eternal salvation in the kingdom of God] grew *and* spread *and* intensified, prevailing mightily.

21 Now after these events Paul determined in the (Holy) Spirit that he would travel through Macedonia and Achaia [most of Greece], and go to Jerusalem, saying, After I have been there, I must visit Rome also.

22 And having sent two of his assistants, Timothy and Erastus, into Macedonia, he himself stayed on in [the province of] Asia for a while.

23 But as time went on there arose no little disturbance concerning the Way [of the Lord].

24 For a man named Demetrius, a silversmith, who made silver shrines of (the goddess) Artemis [not Diana], brought no small income to his craftsmen.

25 These he called together, along with the workmen of similar trades, and said, Men, you are acquainted with the facts *and* understand that from this business we derive our wealth *and* livelihood.

26 Now you notice and hear that not only at Ephesus but almost all over [the province of] Asia this Paul has persuaded *and* induced people to believe his teaching and has alienated a considerable company of them, saying that gods that are made with human hands are not really gods at all.

27 Now there is danger not merely that this trade of ours may be discredited, but also that the temple of the great goddess Artemis may come into disrepute *and* count for nothing, and that her glorious magnificence may be degraded and fall into contempt, she whom all Asia and the wide world worship.

28 As they listened to this they were filled with rage, and they continued to shout, Great is Artemis of the Ephesians!

29 Then the city was filled with confusion; and they rushed together into the amphitheater, dragging along with them Gaius and Aristarchus, Macedonians who were fellow travelers with Paul.

30 Paul wished to go in among the crowd, but the disciples would not permit him to do it.

---

w) A weaker verb.
x) The best texts read "both of them."
y) Vincent.
z) Thayer.

Living New Testament

13 A team of itinerant Jews who were traveling from town to town casting out demons planned to experiment by using the name of the Lord Jesus. The incantation they decided on was this: "I adjure you by Jesus, whom Paul preaches, to come out!"

14 Seven sons of Sceva, a Jewish priest, were doing this.

15 But when they tried it on a man possessed by a demon, the demon replied, "I know Jesus and I know Paul, but who are you?"

16 And he leaped on two of them and beat them up, so that they fled out of his house naked and badly injured.

17 The story of what happened spread quickly all through Ephesus, to Jews and Greeks alike; and a solemn fear descended on the city, and the name of the Lord Jesus was greatly honored.

18, 19 Many of the believers who had been practicing black magic confessed their deeds and brought their incantation books and charms and burned them at a public bonfire. (Someone estimated the value of the books at $10,000[4]).

20 This indicates how deeply the whole area was stirred by God's message.

21 Afterwards, Paul felt impelled by the Holy Spirit[5] to go across to Greece before returning to Jerusalem. "And after that," he said, "I must go on to Rome!"

22 He sent his two assistants, Timothy and Erastus, on ahead to Greece while he stayed awhile longer in Turkey.

23 But about that time, a big blowup developed in Ephesus concerning the Christians.

24 It began with Demetrius, a silversmith who employed many craftsmen to manufacture silver shrines of the Greek goddess Diana.

25 He called a meeting of his men, together with others employed in related trades, and addressed them as follows:

"Gentlemen, this business is our income.

26 As you know so well from what you've seen and heard, this man Paul has persuaded many, many people that handmade gods aren't gods at all. As a result, our sales volume is going down! And this trend is evident not only here in Ephesus, but throughout the entire province!

27 Of course, I am not only talking about the business aspects of this situation and our loss of income, but also of the possibility that the temple of the great goddess Diana will lose its influence, and that Diana—this magnificent goddess worshiped not only throughout this part of Turkey but all around the world—will be forgotten!"

28 At this their anger boiled and they began shouting, "Great is Diana of the Ephesians."

29 A crowd began to gather and soon the city was filled with confusion. Everyone rushed to the amphitheater, dragging along Gaius and Aristarchus, Paul's traveling companions, for trial.

30 Paul wanted to go in, but the disciples wouldn't let him.

---

[4] Approximately £3,500.
[5] Literally, "purposed in the spirit."

Revised Standard

of the itinerant Jewish exorcists undertook
to pronounce the name of the Lord Jesus
over those who had evil spirits, saying, "I
adjure you by the Jesus whom Paul preaches." [14]Seven sons of a Jewish high priest
named Sceva were doing this. [15]But the
evil spirit answered them, "Jesus I know,
and Paul I know; but who are you?" [16]And
the man in whom the evil spirit was leaped
on them, mastered all of them, and overpowered them, so that they fled out of that
house naked and wounded. [17]And this became known to all residents of Ephesus,
both Jews and Greeks; and fear fell upon
them all; and the name of the Lord Jesus
was extolled. [18]Many also of those who were
now believers came, confessing and divulg-
ing their practices. [19]And a number of those
who practiced magic arts brought their books
together and burned them in the sight of
all; and they counted the value of them and
found it came to fifty thousand pieces of
silver. [20]So the word of the Lord grew and
prevailed mightily.

21 Now after these events Paul resolved
in the Spirit to pass through Macedonia and
Achaia and go to Jerusalem, saying, "After
I have been there, I must also see Rome."
[22]And having sent into Macedonia two of
his helpers, Timothy and Erastus, he himself stayed in Asia for a while.

Demetrius and the riot at Ephesus

23 About that time there arose no little
stir concerning the Way. [24]For a man named
Demetrius, a silversmith, who made silver
shrines of Artemis, brought no little business
to the craftsmen. [25]These he gathered together, with the workmen of like occupation,
and said, "Men, you know that from this
business we have our wealth. [26]And you see
and hear that not only at Ephesus but almost
throughout all Asia this Paul has persuaded
and turned away a considerable company of
people, saying that gods made with hands are
not gods. [27]And there is danger not only that
this trade of ours may come into disrepute
but also that the temple of the great goddess
Artemis may count for nothing, and that she
may even be deposed from her magnificence,
she whom all Asia and the world worship."

28 When they heard this they were enraged, and cried out, "Great is Artemis of
the Ephesians!" [29]So the city was filled with
the confusion; and they rushed together into
the theater, dragging with them Gaius and
Aristarchus, Macedonians who were Paul's
companions in travel. [30]Paul wished to go in
among the crowd, but the disciples would

King James

31 And certain of the chief of Asia, which were his friends, sent unto him, desiring *him* that he would not adventure himself into the theatre.

32 Some therefore cried one thing, and some another: for the assembly was confused; and the more part knew not wherefore they were come together.

33 And they drew Alexander out of the multitude, the Jews putting him forward. And Alexander beckoned with the hand, and would have made his defence unto the people.

34 But when they knew that he was a Jew, all with one voice about the space of two hours cried out, Great *is* Diana of the Ephesians.

35 And when the townclerk had appeased the people, he said, *Ye* men of Ephesus, what man is there that knoweth not how that the city of the Ephesians is a worshipper of the great goddess Diana, and of the *image* which fell down from Jupiter?

36 Seeing then that these things cannot be spoken against, ye ought to be quiet, and to do nothing rashly.

37 For ye have brought hither these men, which are neither robbers of churches, nor yet blasphemers of your goddess.

38 Wherefore if Demetrius, and the craftsmen which are with him, have a matter against any man, the law is open, and there are deputies: let them implead one another.

39 But if ye inquire any thing concerning other matters, it shall be determined in a lawful assembly.

40 For we are in danger to be called in question for this day's uproar, there being no cause whereby we may give an account of this concourse.

41 And when he had thus spoken, he dismissed the assembly.

Amplified

31 Even some of the Asiarchs [presidents of athletic games in Asia] who were his friends, also sent to him and warned him not to risk venturing into the theater.

32 Now some shouted one thing and some another, for the gathering was in a tumult, and most of them did not know why they had come together.

33 Some of the crowd called upon Alexander [to speak], since the Jews had pushed *and* urged him forward. And Alexander motioned with his hand, wishing to make a defense *and* [was about] to apologize to the people.

34 But as soon as they saw him *and* recognized that he was a Jew, a shout went up from them as the voice of one man, as for about two hours they cried, Great is Artemis of the Ephesians!

35 And when the town clerk had calmed the crowd down, he said, Men of Ephesus, what man is there who does not know that the city of the Ephesians is guardian of the temple of the great Artemis, and of the sacred stone [image of her] that fell from the sky?

36 Seeing then that these things cannot be denied, you ought to (keep yourselves in check) be quiet and do nothing rashly.

37 For you have brought these men here, [who are guilty] neither of temple robberies nor of blasphemous speech about our goddess.

38 Now then, if Demetrius and his fellow tradesmen who are with him have a grievance against any one, the courts are open, and proconsuls are [available]; let them bring charges against one another [legally].

39 But if you require anything about this further *or* [a]about other matters, it must be decided *and* cleared up in the regular assembly.

40 For we are in danger of being called to render an account *and* of being accused of rioting because of [this commotion] today, there being no reason that we can offer to justify this disorder.

41 And when he had said these things, he dismissed the assembly.

CHAPTER 20

AND after the uproar was ceased, Paul called unto *him* the disciples, and embraced *them,* and departed for to go into Macedonia.

2 And when he had gone over those parts, and had given them much exhortation, he came into Greece,

3 And *there* abode three months. And when the Jews laid wait for him, as he was about to sail into Syria, he purposed to return through Macedonia.

4 And there accompanied him into Asia Sopater of Berea; and of the Thessalonians, Aristarchus and Secundus; and Gaius of Derbe, and Timotheus; and of Asia, Tychicus and Trophimus.

5 These going before tarried for us at Troas.

CHAPTER 20

AFTER the uproar had ceased, Paul sent for the disciples and warned *and* consoled *and* urged *and* encouraged them; then he embraced them *and* told them farewell, and set forth on his journey to Macedonia.

2 Then after he had gone through those districts and had warned *and* consoled *and* urged *and* encouraged the brethren with much discourse, he came to Greece.

3 Having spent three months there, when a plot was formed against him by the Jews as he was about to set sail for Syria, he resolved to go back through Macedonia.

4 He was accompanied by Sopater, the son of Pyrrhus from Beroea; and by the Thessalonians, Aristarchus and Secundus; and Gaius of Derbe, and Timothy; and the Asians, Tychicus and Trophimus.

5 These went on ahead and were waiting for us [including Luke] at Troas,

---

a) Alternate reading.

Living New Testament

31 Some of the Roman officers of the province, friends of Paul, also sent a message to him, begging him not to risk his life by entering.

32 Inside, the people were all shouting, some one thing and some another—everything was in confusion. In fact, most of them didn't even know why they were there.

33 Alexander was spotted among the crowd by some of the Jews and dragged forward. He motioned for silence and tried to speak.

34 But when the crowd realized he was a Jew, they started shouting again and kept it up for two hours: "Great is Diana of the Ephesians! Great is Diana of the Ephesians!"

35 At last the mayor was able to quiet them down enough to speak. "Men of Ephesus," he said, "everyone knows that Ephesus is the center[6] of the religion of the great Diana, whose image fell down to us from heaven.

36 Since this is an indisputable fact, you shouldn't be disturbed no matter what is said, and should do nothing rash.

37 Yet you have brought these men here who have stolen nothing from her temple and have not defamed her.

38 If Demetrius and the craftsmen have a case against them, the courts are currently in session and the judges can take the case at once. Let them go through legal channels.

39 And if there are complaints about other matters, they can be settled at the regular City Council meetings;

40 For we are in danger of being called to account by the Roman government for today's riot, since there is no cause for it. And if Rome demands an explanation, I won't know what to say."

41 Then he dismissed them, and they dispersed.

CHAPTER 20

When it was all over, Paul sent for the disciples, preached a farewell message to them, said good-bye and left for Greece,

2 Preaching to the believers along the way, in all the cities he passed through.

3 He was in Greece three months and was preparing to sail for Syria when he discovered a plot by the Jews against his life, so he decided to go north to Macedonia first.

4 Several men were traveling with him, going as far as Turkey;[1] they were Sopater of Beroea, the son of Pyrrhus; Aristarchus and Secundus, from Thessalonica; Gaius, from Derbe; and Timothy; and Tychicus and Trophimus, who were returning to their homes in Turkey,

5 And had gone on ahead and were waiting for us at Troas.

Literally, "is the temple-keeper."
Literally, "Asia."

Revised Standard

not let him: 31 some of the Asiarchs also, who
were friends of his, sent to him and begged
him not to venture into the theater. 32 Now
some cried one thing, some another; for the
assembly was in confusion, and most of
them did not know why they had come
together. 33 Some of the crowd prompted
Alexander, whom the Jews had put forward.
And Alexander motioned with his hand,
wishing to make a defense to the people.
34 But when they recognized that he was a
Jew, for about two hours they all with one
voice cried out, "Great is Artemis of the
Ephesians!" 35 And when the town clerk had
quieted the crowd, he said, "Men of Ephesus,
what man is there who does not know that
the city of the Ephesians is temple keeper
of the great Artemis, and of the sacred
stone that fell from the sky?[s] 36 Seeing then
that these things cannot be contradicted,
you ought to be quiet and do nothing rash.
37 For you have brought these men here who
are neither sacrilegious nor blasphemers of
our goddess. 38 If therefore Demetrius and
the craftsmen with him have a complaint
against any one, the courts are open, and
there are proconsuls; let them bring charges
against one another. 39 But if you seek anything further,[t] it shall be settled in the regular assembly. 40 For we are in danger of
being charged with rioting today, there being no cause that we can give to justify this
commotion." 41 And when he had said this,
he dismissed the assembly.

Paul visits Macedonia and Achaia

20 After the uproar ceased, Paul sent
for the disciples and having exhorted them took leave of them and departed
for Macedonia. 2 When he had gone through
these parts and had given them much encouragement, he came to Greece. 3 There he
spent three months, and when a plot was
made against him by the Jews as he was
about to set sail for Syria, he determined
to return through Macedonia. 4 Sopater of
Beroea, the son of Pyrrhus, accompanied
him; and of the Thessalonians, Aristarchus
and Secundus; and Gaius of Derbe, and
Timothy; and the Asians, Tychicus and
Trophimus.

From Philippi to Miletus

5 These went on and were waiting for us at

---

[s] The meaning of the Greek is uncertain
[t] Other ancient authorities read ***about other matters***

King James

6 And we sailed away from Philippi after the days of unleavened bread, and came unto them to Troas in five days; where we abode seven days.

7 And upon the first *day* of the week, when the disciples came together to break bread, Paul preached unto them, ready to depart on the morrow; and continued his speech until midnight.

8 And there were many lights in the upper chamber, where they were gathered together.

9 And there sat in a window a certain man named Eutychus, being fallen into a deep sleep: and as Paul was long preaching, he sunk down with sleep, and fell down from the third loft, and was taken up dead.

10 And Paul went down, and fell on him, and embracing *him* said, Trouble not yourselves; for his life is in him.

11 When he therefore was come up again, and had broken bread, and eaten, and talked a long while, even till break of day, so he departed.

12 And they brought the young man alive, and were not a little comforted.

13 ¶ And we went before to ship, and sailed unto Assos, there intending to take in Paul: for so had he appointed, minding himself to go afoot.

14 And when he met with us at Assos, we took him in, and came to Mitylene.

15 And we sailed thence, and came the next *day* over against Chios; and the next *day* we arrived at Samos, and tarried at Trogyllium; and the next *day* we came to Miletus.

16 For Paul had determined to sail by Ephesus, because he would not spend the time in Asia: for he hasted, if it were possible for him, to be at Jerusalem the day of Pentecost.

17 ¶ And from Miletus he sent to Ephesus, and called the elders of the church.

18 And when they were come to him, he said unto them, Ye know, from the first day that I came into Asia, after what manner I have been with you at all seasons,

19 Serving the Lord with all humility of mind, and with many tears, and temptations, which befell me by the lying in wait of the Jews:

20 *And* how I kept back nothing that was profitable *unto you*, but have shewed you, and have taught you publicly, and from house to house,

21 Testifying both to the Jews, and also to the Greeks, repentance toward God, and faith toward our Lord Jesus Christ.

22 And now, behold, I go bound in the spirit unto Jerusalem, not knowing the things that shall befall me there:

23 Save that the Holy Ghost witnesseth in every city, saying that bonds and afflictions abide me.

24 But none of these things move me, neither count I my life dear unto myself, so that I might finish my course with joy, and the ministry, which I have received of the Lord Jesus, to testify the gospel of the grace of God.

Amplified

6 But we [ourselves] sailed from Philippi after the days of Unleavened Bread [the Passover week], and in five days we joined them at Troas, where we remained for seven days.

7 And on the first day of the week, when we were assembled together to break bread [[b]the Lord's Supper], Paul discoursed with them, intending to leave the next morning; and he kept on with his message until midnight.

8 Now there were numerous lights in the upper room where we were assembled,

9 And there was a young man named Eutychus sitting in the window. He was borne down with deep sleep as Paul kept on talking still longer, and [finally] completely overcome by sleep, he fell down from the third story, and was picked up dead.

10 But Paul went down and bent over him and embraced him, saying, Make no ado; his life is within him.

11 When Paul had gone back upstairs and had broken bread and eaten [with them], and after he had (talked confidentially,) communing with them for considerable time, until daybreak [in fact], he departed.

12 They took the youth home alive, and were not a little comforted *and* cheered *and* refreshed *and* encouraged.

13 But going on before to the ship, the rest of us set sail for Assos, intending to take Paul aboard there, for that was what he had directed, intending himself to go by land—on foot.

14 So when he met us at Assos, we took him aboard and sailed on to Mitylene.

15 And sailing from there, we arrived the day after at a point opposite Chios; the following day we struck across to Samos, and the next day we arrived at Miletus.

16 For Paul had determined to sail on past Ephesus, lest he might have to spend time [unnecessarily] in [the province of] Asia; for he was hastening on that he might reach Jerusalem, if at all possible, by the day of Pentecost.

17 However from Miletus he sent to Ephesus and summoned the elders of the church [to come to him there].

18 And when they arrived he said to them: You yourselves are well acquainted with my manner of living among you from the first day that I set foot in [the province of] Asia, and how I continued afterward,

19 Serving the Lord with all humility in tears and in the midst of adversity (affliction) *and* trials which befell me, due to the plots of the Jews [against me];

20 How I did not shrink from telling you anything that was for your benefit, and teaching you in public meetings and from house to house,

21 But constantly *and* earnestly I bore testimony both to Jews and Greeks, urging them to turn in repentance [[c]that is due] to God and have the faith in our Lord Jesus Christ [[c]that is due Him].

22 And now, you see, I am going to Jerusalem, bound by the (Holy) Spirit, *and* obligated *and* compelled by the [convictions of my own] spirit, not knowing what will befall me there;

23 Except that the Holy Spirit clearly *and* emphatically affirms to me in city after city that imprisonment and suffering await me.

24 But *none of these things move me;* neither do I esteem my life dear to myself, if only I may finish my course *with joy,* and the ministry which I have obtained of [entrusted to me by] the Lord Jesus, faithfully to attest the good news (Gospel) of God's grace—His unmerited favor, spiritual blessing and mercy.

---

b) Thayer.
c) Vincent.

Living New Testament

6 As soon as the Passover ceremonies ended, we boarded ship at Philippi in northern Greece and five days later arrived in Troas, Turkey, where we stayed a week.

7 On Sunday, we gathered for a communion service, with Paul preaching. And since he was leaving the next day, he talked until midnight!

8 The upstairs room where we met was lighted with many flickering lamps;

9 And as Paul spoke on and on, a young man named Eutychus, sitting on the window sill, went fast asleep and fell three stories to his death below.

10, 11, 12 Paul went down and gathered him into his arms. "Don't worry," he said, "he's all right!" And he was! What a wave of awesome joy swept through the crowd! They all went back upstairs and ate the Lord's Supper together; then Paul preached another long sermon—so it was dawn when he finally left them!

13 Paul was going by land to Assos, and we went on ahead by ship.

14 He joined us there and we sailed together to Mitylene;

15 The next day we passed Chios; the next, we touched at Samos; and a day later we arrived at Miletus.

16 Paul had decided against stopping at Ephesus this time, as he was hurrying to get to Jerusalem, if possible, for the celebration of Pentecost.

17 But when we landed at Miletus, he sent a message to the elders of the church at Ephesus asking them to come down to the boat to meet him.

18 When they arrived he told them, "You men know that from the day I set foot in Turkey until now

19 I have done the Lord's work humbly—yes, and with tears—and have faced grave danger from the plots of the Jews against my life.

20 Yet I never shrank from telling you the truth, either publicly or in your homes.

21 I have had one message for Jews and Gentiles alike—the necessity of turning from sin to God through faith in our Lord Jesus Christ.

22 And now I am going to Jerusalem, drawn there irresistibly by the Holy Spirit,[2] not knowing what awaits me,

23 Except that the Holy Spirit has told me in city after city that jail and suffering lie ahead.

24 But life is worth nothing unless I use it for doing the work assigned me by the Lord Jesus—the work of telling others the Good News about God's mighty kindness and love.

[2] Or, "by an inner compulsion."

Revised Standard

Troas, 6 but we sailed away from Philippi
after the days of Unleavened Bread, and in
five days we came to them at Troas, where
we stayed for seven days.
7 On the first day of the week, when we
were gathered together to break bread, Paul
talked with them, intending to depart on the
morrow; and he prolonged his speech until
midnight. 8 There were many lights in the
upper chamber where we were gathered.
9 And a young man named Eutychus was
sitting in the window. He sank into a deep
sleep as Paul talked still longer; and being
overcome by sleep, he fell down from the
third story and was taken up dead. 10 But
Paul went down and bent over him, and
embracing him said, "Do not be alarmed,
for his life is in him." 11 And when Paul
had gone up and had broken bread and
eaten, he conversed with them a long while,
until daybreak, and so departed. 12 And they
took the lad away alive, and were not a little
comforted.
13 But going ahead to the ship, we set
sail for Assos, intending to take Paul aboard
there; for so he had arranged, intending
himself to go by land. 14 And when he met
us at Assos, we took him on board and
came to Mitylene. 15 And sailing from there
we came the following day opposite Chios; the next day we touched at Samos; and[u]
the day after that we came to Miletus. 16 For
Paul had decided to sail past Ephesus, so
that he might not have to spend time in Asia;
for he was hastening to be at Jerusalem, if
possible, on the day of Pentecost.

Paul speaks to the Ephesian elders

17 And from Miletus he sent to Ephesus
and called to him the elders of the church.
18 And when they came to him, he said to
them:
"You yourselves know how I lived among
you all the time from the first day that I
set foot in Asia, 19 serving the Lord with all
humility and with tears and with trials
which befell me through the plots of the
Jews; 20 how I did not shrink from declaring
to you anything that was profitable, and
teaching you in public and from house to
house, 21 testifying both to Jews and to
Greeks of repentance to God and of faith
in our Lord Jesus Christ. 22 And now, behold,
I am going to Jerusalem, bound in the Spirit,
not knowing what shall befall me there; 23 except that the Holy Spirit testifies to me in
every city that imprisonment and afflictions
await me. 24 But I do not account my life
of any value nor as precious to myself, if
only I may accomplish my course and the
ministry which I received from the Lord
Jesus, to testify to the gospel of the grace

[u] Other ancient authorities add *after remaining at Trogyllium*

King James

25 And now, behold, I know that ye all, among whom I have gone preaching the kingdom of God, shall see my face no more.
26 Wherefore I take you to record this day, that I *am* pure from the blood of all *men.*
27 For I have not shunned to declare unto you all the counsel of God.
28 ¶ Take heed therefore unto yourselves, and to all the flock, over the which the Holy Ghost hath made you overseers, to feed the church of God, which he hath purchased with his own blood.
29 For I know this, that after my departing shall grievous wolves enter in among you, not sparing the flock.
30 Also of your own selves shall men arise, speaking perverse things, to draw away disciples after them.
31 Therefore watch, and remember, that by the space of three years I ceased not to warn every one night and day with tears.
32 And now, brethren, I commend you to God, and to the word of his grace, which is able to build you up, and to give you an inheritance among all them which are sanctified.
33 I have coveted no man's silver, or gold, or apparel.
34 Yea, ye yourselves know, that these hands have ministered unto my necessities, and to them that were with me.
35 I have shewed you all things, how that so labouring ye ought to support the weak, and to remember the words of the Lord Jesus, how he said, It is more blessed to give than to receive.
36 ¶ And when he had thus spoken, he kneeled down, and prayed with them all.
37 And they all wept sore, and fell on Paul's neck, and kissed him,
38 Sorrowing most of all for the words which he spake, that they should see his face no more. And they accompanied him unto the ship.

Amplified

25 And now, observe, I perceive that all of you, among whom I have gone in and out proclaiming the kingdom, will see my face no more.
26 Therefore I testify *and* protest to you on this [our parting] day that I am clean *and* innocent *and* not responsible for the blood of any of you.
27 For I never shrank *or* kept back *or* fell short from declaring to you the whole purpose *and* plan *and* counsel of God.
28 Take care *and* be on guard for yourselves and the whole flock over which the Holy Spirit has appointed you bishops and guardians, to shepherd the church (that is, tend and feed and guide the church) of the Lord [d](God) which He obtained for Himself—buying it and saving it [for Himself]—with His own blood.
29 I know that after I am gone ferocious wolves will get in among you, not sparing the flock;
30 Even from among your own selves men will come to the front, who by saying perverse (distorted and corrupt) things will endeavor to draw away the disciples after them [to their own party].
31 Therefore be always alert *and* on your guard, being mindful that for three years I never stopped night or day seriously to admonish *and* advise *and* exhort you one by one with tears.
32 And now, *brethren,* I commit you to God—that is, I deposit you in His charge, entrusting you to His protection and care. And I commend you to the Word of His grace—to the commands and counsels and promises of His unmerited favor. It is able to build you up and to give you [your rightful] inheritance among all God's set-apart ones—those consecrated, purified *and* transformed of soul.
33 I coveted no man's silver or gold or [costly] garments.
34 You yourselves know personally that these hands ministered to my own needs and those [of the persons] who were with me.
35 In everything I have pointed out to you [by example] that, by working diligently thus we ought to assist the weak, being mindful of the words of the Lord Jesus, how He Himself said, It is more blessed—makes one happier and more [e]to be envied—to give than to receive.
36 Having spoken thus, he knelt down with them all and prayed.
37 And they all wept freely and threw their arms around Paul's neck and kissed him fervently *and* repeatedly,
38 Being especially distressed *and* sorrowful because he had stated that they were about to see his face no more. And they accompanied him to the ship.

CHAPTER 21 (King James)

AND it came to pass, that after we were gotten from them, and had launched, we came with a straight course unto Coos, and the *day* following unto Rhodes, and from thence unto Patara:
2 And finding a ship sailing over unto Phenicia, we went aboard, and set forth.
3 Now when we had discovered Cyprus, we left it on the left hand, and sailed into Syria, and landed at Tyre: for there the ship was to unlade her burden.

CHAPTER 21 (Amplified)

AND when we had torn ourselves away from them *and* withdrawn, we set sail and made a straight run to Cos, and on the following [day came] to Rhodes, and from there to Patara.
2 There we found a ship crossing over to Phoenicia, so we went aboard, and sailed away.
3 After we had sighted Cyprus, leaving it on our left we sailed on to Syria and put in at Tyre, for there the ship was to unload her cargo.

d) Many ancient authorities read "of God."
e) Souter.

Living New Testament

25 And now I know that none of you among whom I went about teaching the Kingdom will ever see me again.
26 Let me say plainly that no man's blood can be laid at my door,
27 For I didn't shrink from declaring all God's message to you.
28 And now beware! Be sure that you feed and shepherd God's flock—His church, purchased with His blood—for the Holy Spirit is holding you responsible as overseers.
29 I know full well that after I leave you, false teachers, like vicious wolves, will appear among you, not sparing the flock.
30 Some of you yourselves will distort the truth in order to draw a following.
31 Watch out! Remember the three years I was with you—my constant watchcare over you night and day and my many tears for you.
32 And now I entrust you to God and to His care and to His wonderful words which are able to build your faith and give you all the inheritance of those who are set apart for Himself.
33 I have never been hungry for money or fine clothing—
34 You know that these hands of mine worked to pay my own way and even to supply the needs of those who were with me.
35 And I was a constant example to you in helping the poor; for I remembered the words of the Lord Jesus, 'It is more blessed to give than to receive.' "
36 When he had finished speaking, he knelt and prayed with them,
37 And they wept aloud as they embraced him[3] in farewell,
38 Sorrowing most of all because he said that he would never see them again. Then they accompanied him down to the ship.

Revised Standard

of God. 25 And now, behold, I know that
all you among whom I have gone about
preaching the kingdom will see my face no
more. 26 Therefore I testify to you this day
that I am innocent of the blood of all of you,
27 for I did not shrink from declaring to
you the whole counsel of God. 28 Take heed
to yourselves and to all the flock, in which
the Holy Spirit has made you guardians, to
feed the church of the Lord[v] which he obtained with his own blood.[w]
29 I know that
after my departure fierce wolves will come
in among you, not sparing the flock; 30 and
from among your own selves will arise men
speaking perverse things, to draw away the
disciples after them. 31 Therefore be alert,
remembering that for three years I did not
cease night or day to admonish every one
with tears. 32 And now I commend you to
God and to the word of his grace, which is
able to build you up and to give you the
inheritance among all those who are sanctified. 33 I coveted no one's silver or gold or
apparel. 34 You yourselves know that these
hands ministered to my necessities, and to
those who were with me. 35 In all things I
have shown you that by so toiling one must
help the weak, remembering the words of
the Lord Jesus, how he said, 'It is more
blessed to give than to receive.' "
36 And when he had spoken thus, he
knelt down and prayed with them all. 37 And
they all wept and embraced Paul and kissed
him, 38 sorrowing most of all because of
the word he had spoken, that they should
see his face no more. And they brought
him to the ship.

CHAPTER 21

After parting from the Ephesian elders, we sailed straight to Cos. The next day we reached Rhodes and then went to Patara.
2 There we boarded a ship sailing for the Syrian province of Phoenicia.
3 We sighted the island of Cyprus, passed it on our left and landed at the harbor of Tyre, in Syria, where the ship unloaded.

[3] Literally, "fell on Paul's neck and kissed him."

Paul travels to Caesarea

21 And when we had parted from them
and set sail, we came by a straight
course to Cos, and the next day to Rhodes,
and from there to Patara.[x] 2 And having
found a ship crossing to Phoenicia, we went
aboard, and set sail. 3 When we had come
in sight of Cyprus, leaving it on the left
we sailed to Syria, and landed at Tyre;
for there the ship was to unload its cargo.

[v] Other ancient authorities read *of God*
[w] Or *with the blood of his Own*
[x] Other ancient authorities add *and Myra*

King James

4 And finding disciples, we tarried there seven days: who said to Paul through the Spirit, that he should not go up to Jerusalem.

5 And when we had accomplished those days, we departed and went our way; and they all brought us on our way, with wives and children, till *we were* out of the city: and we kneeled down on the shore, and prayed.

6 And when we had taken our leave one of another, we took ship; and they returned home again.

7 And when we had finished *our* course from Tyre, we came to Ptolemais, and saluted the brethren, and abode with them one day.

8 And the next *day* we that were of Paul's company departed, and came unto Cæsarea: and we entered into the house of Philip the evangelist, which was *one* of the seven; and abode with him.

9 And the same man had four daughters, virgins, which did prophesy.

10 And as we tarried *there* many days, there came down from Judæa a certain prophet, named Agabus.

11 And when he was come unto us, he took Paul's girdle, and bound his own hands and feet, and said, Thus saith the Holy Ghost, So shall the Jews at Jerusalem bind the man that owneth this girdle, and shall deliver *him* into the hands of the Gentiles.

12 And when we heard these things, both we, and they of that place, besought him not to go up to Jerusalem.

13 Then Paul answered, What mean ye to weep and to break mine heart? for I am ready not to be bound only, but also to die at Jerusalem for the name of the Lord Jesus.

14 And when he would not be persuaded, we ceased, saying, The will of the Lord be done.

15 And after those days we took up our carriages, and went up to Jerusalem.

16 There went with us also *certain* of the disciples of Cæsarea, and brought with them one Mnason of Cyprus, an old disciple, with whom we should lodge.

17 And when we were come to Jerusalem, the brethren received us gladly.

18 And the *day* following Paul went in with us unto James; and all the elders were present.

19 And when he had saluted them, he declared particularly what things God had wrought among the Gentiles by his ministry.

20 And when they heard *it,* they glorified the Lord, and said unto him, Thou seest, brother, how many thousands of Jews there are which believe; and they are all zealous of the law:

21 And they are informed of thee, that thou teachest all the Jews which are among the Gentiles to forsake Moses, saying that they ought not to circumcise *their* children, neither to walk after the customs.

22 What is it therefore? the multitude must needs come together: for they will hear that thou art come.

Amplified

4 And having looked up the disciples there, we remained with them for seven days. Prompted by the (Holy) Spirit they kept telling Paul not to set foot in Jerusalem.

5 But when our time there was ended, we left and proceeded on our journey; and all of them with their wives and children accompanied us on our way till we were outside the city. There we knelt down on the beach and prayed.

6 Then when we had told one another farewell we went on board the ship, and they returned to their own homes.

7 When we had completed the voyage from Tyre, we landed at Ptolemais, where we paid our respects to the brethren and remained with them for one day.

8 On the morrow we left there and came to Caesarea; and we went into the house of Philip the evangelist, who was one of the seven [first deacons], and stayed with him. [Acts 6:5.]

9 And he had four maiden daughters who had the gift of prophecy.

10 While we were remaining there for some time, a prophet named Agabus came down from Judea.

11 And coming to [see] us, he took Paul's belt and with it bound his own feet and hands, and said, Thus says the Holy Spirit, The Jews at Jerusalem shall bind like this the man who owns this belt, and they shall deliver him into the hands of the Gentiles (heathen).

12 When we heard this, both we and the residents of that place pleaded with him not to go up to Jerusalem.

13 Then Paul replied, What do you mean by weeping and breaking my heart like this? For I hold myself in readiness not only to be arrested *and* bound *and* imprisoned at Jerusalem, but also [even] to die for the name of the Lord Jesus.

14 And when he would not yield to [our] persuading, we stopped [urging and imploring him], saying, The Lord's will be done!

15 After these days we packed our baggage and went up to Jerusalem.

16 And some of the disciples from Caesarea came with us, conducting us to the house of Mnason, a man from Cyprus, one of the disciples of long standing, with whom we were to lodge.

17 When we arrived in Jerusalem, the brethren received *and* welcomed us gladly.

18 On the next day Paul went in with us to [see] James, and all the elders of the church were present [also].

19 After saluting them, Paul gave a detailed account of the things God had done among the Gentiles through his ministry.

20 And upon hearing it, they adored *and* exalted *and* praised *and* thanked God. And they said to [Paul], You see, brother, how many thousands of believers there are among the Jews, and all of them are enthusiastic upholders of the [Mosaic] Law.

21 Now they have been informed about you that you continually teach all the Jews who live among the Gentiles to turn back from *and* forsake Moses, advising them not to circumcise their children or pay any attention to the observance of the [Mosaic] customs.

22 What then [is it best] should be done? A multitude will come together, for they will surely hear that you have arrived.

Living New Testament

4 We went ashore, found the local believers and stayed with them a week. These disciples warned Paul—the Holy Spirit prophesying through them—not to go on to Jerusalem.

5 At the end of the week when we returned to the ship, the entire congregation including wives and children walked down to the beach with us where we prayed and said our farewells.

6 Then we went aboard and they returned home.

7 The next stop after leaving Tyre was Ptolemais where we greeted the believers, but stayed only one day.

8 Then we went on to Caesarea and stayed at the home of Philip the Evangelist, one of the first seven deacons.[1]

9 He had four unmarried[2] daughters who had the gift of prophecy.

10 During our stay of several days, a man named Agabus, who also had the gift of prophecy, arrived from Judea

11 And visited us. He took Paul's belt, bound his own feet and hands with it and said, "The Holy Spirit declares, 'So shall the owner of this belt be bound by the Jews in Jerusalem and turned over to the Romans.' "

12 Hearing this, all of us—the local believers and his traveling companions—begged Paul not to go on to Jerusalem.

13 But he said, "Why all this weeping? You are breaking my heart! For I am ready not only to be jailed at Jerusalem, but also to die for the sake of the Lord Jesus."

14 When it was clear that he wouldn't be dissuaded, we gave up and said, "The will of the Lord be done."

15 So shortly afterwards, we packed our things and left for Jerusalem.

16 Some disciples from Caesarea accompanied us, and on arrival we were guests at the home of Mnason, originally from Cyprus, one of the early believers;

17 And all the believers at Jerusalem welcomed us cordially.

18 The second day Paul took us with him to meet with James and the elders of the Jerusalem church.

19 After greetings were exchanged, Paul recounted the many things God had accomplished among the Gentiles through his work.

20 They praised God but then said, "You know, dear brother, how many thousands of Jews have also believed, and they are all very insistent that Jewish believers must continue to follow the Jewish traditions and customs.[3]

21 Our Jewish Christians here at Jerusalem have been told that you are against the laws of Moses, against our Jewish customs, and that you forbid the circumcision of their children.

22 Now what can be done? For they will certainly hear that you have come.

Revised Standard

[4]And having sought out the disciples, we
stayed there for seven days. Through the
Spirit they told Paul not to go on to Jerusalem. [5]And when our days there were ended, we departed and went on our journey;
and they all, with wives and children,
brought us on our way till we were outside
the city; and kneeling down on the beach
we prayed and bade one another farewell.
[6]Then we went on board the ship, and
they returned home.

7 When we had finished the voyage from
Tyre, we arrived at Ptolemais; and we
greeted the brethren and stayed with them
for one day. [8]On the morrow we departed
and came to Caesarea; and we entered
the house of Philip the evangelist, who was
one of the seven, and stayed with him.
[9]And he had four unmarried daughters, who
prophesied. [10]While we were staying for
some days, a prophet named Agabus came
down from Judea. [11]And coming to us he
took Paul's girdle and bound his own feet
and hands, and said, "Thus says the Holy
Spirit, 'So shall the Jews at Jerusalem bind
the man who owns this girdle and deliver
him into the hands of the Gentiles.' " [12]When
we heard this, we and the people there
begged him not to go up to Jerusalem.
[13]Then Paul answered, "What are you doing, weeping and breaking my heart? For
I am ready not only to be imprisoned but
even to die at Jerusalem for the name of
the Lord Jesus." [14]And when he would
not be persuaded, we ceased and said, "The
will of the Lord be done."

Paul in Jerusalem

15 After these days we made ready and
went up to Jerusalem. [16]And some of the
disciples from Caesarea went with us, bringing us to the house of Mnason of Cyprus,
an early disciple with whom we should
lodge.

17 When we had come to Jerusalem, the
brethren received us gladly. [18]On the following day Paul went in with us to James;
and all the elders were present. [19]After
greeting them, he related one by one the
things that God had done among the Gentiles through his ministry. [20]And when they
heard it, they glorified God. And they said
to him, "You see, brother, how many
thousands there are among the Jews of those
who have believed; they are all zealous for
the law, [21]and they have been told about you
that you teach all the Jews who are among
the Gentiles to forsake Moses, telling them
not to circumcise their children or observe
the customs. [22]What then is to be done? They
will certainly hear that you have come. [23]Do

---

[1] See Acts 6:5, 8:1-13.
[2] Literally, "virgins."
[3] Literally, "they are all zealous for the law."

King James

23 Do therefore this that we say to thee: We have four men which have a vow on them;

24 Them take, and purify thyself with them, and be at charges with them, that they may shave *their* heads: and all may know that those things, whereof they were informed concerning thee, are nothing; but *that* thou thyself also walkest orderly, and keepest the law.

25 As touching the Gentiles which believe, we have written *and* concluded that they observe no such thing, save only that they keep themselves from *things* offered to idols, and from blood, and from strangled, and from fornication.

26 Then Paul took the men, and the next day purifying himself with them entered into the temple, to signify the accomplishment of the days of purification, until that an offering should be offered for every one of them.

27 And when the seven days were almost ended, the Jews which were of Asia, when they saw him in the temple, stirred up all the people, and laid hands on him,

28 Crying out, Men of Israel, help: This is the man, that teacheth all *men* every where against the people, and the law, and this place: and further brought Greeks also into the temple, and hath polluted this holy place.

29 (For they had seen before with him in the city Trophimus an Ephesian, whom they supposed that Paul had brought into the temple.)

30 And all the city was moved, and the people ran together: and they took Paul, and drew him out of the temple: and forthwith the doors were shut.

31 And as they went about to kill him, tidings came unto the chief captain of the band, that all Jerusalem was in an uproar.

32 Who immediately took soldiers and centurions, and ran down unto them: and when they saw the chief captain and the soldiers, they left beating of Paul.

33 Then the chief captain came near, and took him, and commanded *him* to be bound with two chains; and demanded who he was, and what he had done.

34 And some cried one thing, some another, among the multitude: and when he could not know the certainty for the tumult, he commanded him to be carried into the castle.

35 And when he came upon the stairs, so it was, that he was borne of the soldiers for the violence of the people.

36 For the multitude of the people followed after, crying, Away with him.

37 And as Paul was to be led into the castle, he said unto the chief captain, May I speak unto thee? Who said, Canst thou speak Greek?

38 Art not thou that Egyptian, which before these days madest an uproar, and leddest out into the wilderness four thousand men that were murderers?

39 But Paul said, I am a man *which am* a Jew of Tarsus, *a city* in Cilicia, a citizen of no mean city: and, I beseech thee, suffer me to speak unto the people.

Amplified

23 Therefore do just what we tell you. With us are four men who have taken a vow upon themselves.

24 Take these men and purify yourself along with them, and pay their expenses [for the temple offering], so that they may have their heads shaved. Thus everybody will know that there is no truth in what they have been told about you, but that you yourself walk in observance of the Law.

25 But with regard to the Gentiles who have believed—adhered to, trusted in and relied on Christ—we have sent them a letter with our decision that they should keep themselves free from anything that has been sacrificed to idols and from [tasting] blood and [the meat of animals] which have been strangled and from all impurity *and* sexual immorality.

26 Then Paul took the [four] men with him and the following day [he went through the rites of] purifying himself along with them. And they entered the temple to give notice when the days of purification (the ending of each vow) would be fulfilled and the usual offering could be presented on behalf of each of them.

27 When the seven days were drawing to a close, some of the Jews from [the province of] Asia, who had caught sight of Paul in the temple, incited all the rabble, and laid hands on him,

28 Shouting, Men of Israel, help! [help!] This is the man who is teaching everybody everywhere against the people and the Law and this place! Moreover he has also [actually] brought Greeks into the temple; he has desecrated *and* polluted this holy place!

29 For they had previously seen Trophimus the Ephesian in the city with Paul and they supposed that he had brought the man into the temple—[that is,] into the inner court [forbidden to Gentiles].

30 Then the whole city was aroused *and* thrown into confusion, and the people rushed together; they laid hands on Paul and dragged him outside the temple, and immediately the gates were closed.

31 Now while they were trying to kill him, word came to the commandant of the regular Roman garrison that the whole of Jerusalem was in a state of ferment.

32 So immediately he took soldiers and centurions and hurried down among them; and when the people saw the commandant and the troops, they stopped beating Paul.

33 Then the commandant approached and arrested Paul, and ordered that he be secured with two chains. He then inquired who he was and what he had done.

34 Some in the crowd kept shouting back one thing and others something else, and since he could not ascertain the facts because of the furore, he ordered that Paul be removed to the barracks.

35 And when [Paul] came to mount the steps, he was actually being carried by the soldiers because of the violence of the mob;

36 For the mass of the people kept following them, shouting, Away with him!—Kill him!

37 Just as Paul was about to be taken into the barracks, he asked the commandant, May I say something to you? And the man replied, Can you speak Greek?

38 Are you not then [as I supposed] the Egyptian who not long ago stirred up a rebellion and led those four thousand men of the cutthroats out into the wilderness?

39 Paul answered, I am a Jew, from Tarsus in Cilicia, a citizen of no insignificant *or* undistinguished city. I beg you, allow me to address the people.

Living New Testament

23 We suggest this: We have four men here who are preparing to shave their heads and take some vows.

24 Go with them to the Temple and have your head shaved too—and pay for theirs to be shaved. Then everyone will know that you approve of this custom for the Hebrew Christians and that you yourself obey the Jewish laws and are in line with our thinking in these matters.

25 As for the Gentile Christians, we aren't asking them to follow these Jewish customs at all—except for the ones we wrote to them about: not to eat food offered to idols, not to eat unbled meat from strangled animals, and not to commit fornication."

26, 27 So Paul agreed to their request and the next day went with the men to the Temple for the ceremony, thus publicizing his vow to offer a sacrifice seven[4] days later with the others. The seven days were almost ended when some Jews from Turkey saw him in the Temple and roused a mob against him. They grabbed him,

28 Yelling, "Men of Israel! Help! Help! This is the man who preaches against our people and tells everybody to disobey the Jewish laws. He even talks against the Temple and defiles it by bringing Gentiles in!"

29 (For down in the city earlier that day, they had seen him with Trophimus, a Gentile[5] from Ephesus in Turkey, and assumed that Paul had taken him into the Temple.)

30 The whole population of the city was electrified by these accusations and a great riot followed. Paul was dragged out of the Temple, and immediately the gates were closed behind him.

31 As they were killing him, word reached the commander of the Roman garrison that all Jerusalem was in an uproar.

32 He quickly ordered out his soldiers and officers and ran down among the crowd. When the mob saw the troops coming, they quit beating Paul.

33 The commander arrested him and ordered him bound with double chains. Then he asked the crowd who he was and what he had done.

34 Some shouted one thing and some another. When he couldn't find out anything in all the uproar and confusion, he ordered Paul to be taken to the armory.[6]

35 As they reached the stairs, the mob grew so violent that the soldiers lifted Paul to their shoulders to protect him,

36 And the crowd surged behind shouting, "Away with him, away with him!"

37, 38 As Paul was about to be taken inside, he said to the commander, "May I have a word with you?"

"Do you know Greek?" the commander asked, surprised. "Aren't you that Egyptian who led a rebellion a few years ago[7] and took 4,000 members of the Assassins with him into the desert?"

39 "No," Paul replied, "I am a Jew from Tarsus in Cilicia which is no small town. I request permission to talk to these people."

[4] Literally, "the days of purification."
[5] Implied.
[6] Literally, "castle," or "fort."
[7] Literally, "before these days."

Revised Standard

therefore what we tell you. We have four
men who are under a vow; 24 take these
men and purify yourself along with them
and pay their expenses, so that they may
shave their heads. Thus all will know that
there is nothing in what they have been
told about you but that you yourself live in
observance of the law. 25 But as for the
Gentiles who have believed, we have sent
a letter with our judgment that they should
abstain from what has been sacrificed to
idols and from blood and from what is
strangled[y] and from unchastity." 26 Then Paul
took the men, and the next day he purified
himself with them and went into the temple,
to give notice when the days of purification
would be fulfilled and the offering
presented for every one of them.

Paul's arrest

27 When the seven days were almost
completed, the Jews from Asia, who had
seen him in the temple, stirred up all the
crowd, and laid hands on him, 28 crying out,
"Men of Israel, help! This is the man who
is teaching men everywhere against the people
and the law and this place; moreover he
also brought Greeks into the temple, and
he has defiled this holy place." 29 For they
had previously seen Trophimus the Ephesian
with him in the city, and they supposed
that Paul had brought him into the temple.
30 Then all the city was aroused, and the
people ran together; they seized Paul and
dragged him out of the temple, and at once
the gates were shut. 31 And as they were
trying to kill him, word came to the tribune
of the cohort that all Jerusalem was in confusion.
32 He at once took soldiers and centurions,
and ran down to them; and when
they saw the tribune and the soldiers, they
stopped beating Paul. 33 Then the tribune
came up and arrested him, and ordered him
to be bound with two chains. He inquired
who he was and what he had done. 34 Some
in the crowd shouted one thing, some another;
and as he could not learn the facts
because of the uproar, he ordered him to
be brought into the barracks. 35 And when
he came to the steps, he was actually carried
by the soldiers because of the violence
of the crowd; 36 for the mob of the people
followed, crying, "Away with him!"

Paul's defense

37 As Paul was about to be brought into
the barracks, he said to the tribune,
"May I say something to you?" And he
said, "Do you know Greek? 38 Are you not
the Egyptian, then, who recently stirred up
a revolt and led the four thousand men of
the Assassins out into the wilderness?" 39 Paul
replied, "I am a Jew, from Tarsus in Cilicia,
a citizen of no mean city; I beg you, let me

[y] Other early authorities omit *and from what is strangled*

King James

40 And when he had given him licence, Paul stood on the stairs, and beckoned with the hand unto the people. And when there was made a great silence, he spake unto *them* in the Hebrew tongue, saying,

CHAPTER 22

MEN, brethren, and fathers, hear ye my defence *which I make* now unto you.

2 (And when they heard that he spake in the Hebrew tongue to them, they kept the more silence: and he saith,)

3 I am verily a man *which am* a Jew, born in Tarsus, *a city* in Cilicia, yet brought up in this city at the feet of Gamaliel, *and* taught according to the perfect manner of the law of the fathers, and was zealous toward God, as ye all are this day.

4 And I persecuted this way unto the death, binding and delivering into prisons both men and women.

5 As also the high priest doth bear me witness, and all the estate of the elders: from whom also I received letters unto the brethren, and went to Damascus, to bring them which were there bound unto Jerusalem, for to be punished.

6 And it came to pass, that, as I made my journey, and was come nigh unto Damascus about noon, suddenly there shone from heaven a great light round about me.

7 And I fell unto the ground, and heard a voice saying unto me, Saul, Saul, why persecutest thou me?

8 And I answered, Who art thou, Lord? And he said unto me, I am Jesus of Nazareth, whom thou persecutest.

9 And they that were with me saw indeed the light, and were afraid; but they heard not the voice of him that spake to me.

10 And I said, What shall I do, Lord? And the Lord said unto me, Arise, and go into Damascus; and there it shall be told thee of all things which are appointed for thee to do.

11 And when I could not see for the glory of that light, being led by the hand of them that were with me, I came into Damascus.

12 And one Ananias, a devout man according to the law, having a good report of all the Jews which dwelt *there,*

13 Came unto me, and stood, and said unto me, Brother Saul, receive thy sight. And the same hour I looked up upon him.

14 And he said, The God of our fathers hath chosen thee, that thou shouldest know his will, and see that Just One, and shouldest hear the voice of his mouth.

15 For thou shalt be his witness unto all men of what thou hast seen and heard.

Amplified

40 And when the man had granted him permission, Paul, standing on the steps, gestured with his hand to the people; and there was a great hush. Then he spoke to them in a Hebrew dialect, saying:

CHAPTER 22

BRETHREN and fathers, listen to the defense which I now make in your presence.

2 And when they heard that he addressed them in the Hebrew tongue, they were all the more quiet. And he continued,

3 I am a Jew, born in Tarsus of Cilicia, but reared in this city. At the feet of Gamaliel I was educated according to the strictest care in the Law of our fathers, being ardent—even a zealot—for God, as all you are today.

4 [Yes,] I harassed (troubled, molested and persecuted) this Way [of the Lord] to the death, putting in chains and committing to prison both men and women,

5 As the high priest and whole council of elders [Sanhedrin] can testify; for from them indeed I received letters with which I was on my way to the brethren in Damascus in order to take also those [believers] who were there, and bring them in chains to Jerusalem that they might be punished.

6 But as I was on my journey and approached Damascus, about noon a great blaze of light flashed suddenly from heaven and shone about me.

7 And I fell to the ground and heard a voice saying to me, Saul, Saul, why do you persecute Me—harass and trouble and molest Me?

8 And I replied, Who are You, Lord? And He said to me, I am Jesus the Nazarene, Whom you are persecuting.

9 Now the men who were with me saw the light, but they did not hear [[f]the sound of the uttered words of] the voice of the One Who was speaking to me—so that they could [g]understand it.

10 And I asked, What shall I do, Lord? And the Lord answered me, Get up and go into Damascus, and there it will be told you all that it is destined *and* appointed for you to do.

11 And since I could not see, because (of the dazzlingly glorious intensity) of the brightness of that light, I was led by the hand by those who were with me, and [thus] I arrived in Damascus.

12 And one Ananias, a devout man according to the Law, well spoken of by all the Jews who resided there,

13 Came to see me, and standing by my side said to me, Brother Saul, [h]look up—and receive back your sight. And in that very [i]instant, I [recovered my sight and] looking up saw him.

14 And he said, The God of our forefathers has destined *and* appointed you to come progressively to know His will—that is, to perceive, to recognize more strongly and clearly and to become better and more intimately acquainted with His will; and to see the Righteous One *Jesus Christ, the Messiah* and to hear a voice from His [own] mouth *and* a message from His [own] lips;

15 For you will be His witness unto all men of everything that you have seen and heard.

---

f) Thayer.
g) Vincent.
h) Thayer.
i) Moulton and Milligan.

Living New Testament

40 The commander agreed, so Paul stood on the stairs and motioned to the people to be quiet; soon a deep silence enveloped the crowd, and he addressed them in Hebrew as follows:

Revised Standard

speak to the people."
40 And when he had
given him leave, Paul, standing on the steps,
motioned with his hand to the people; and
when there was a great hush, he spoke to
them in the Hebrew language, saying:

CHAPTER 22

Brothers and fathers, listen to me as I offer my defense."

2 (When they heard him speaking in Hebrew, the silence was even greater.)

3 "I am a Jew," he said, "born in Tarsus, a city in Cilicia, but educated here in Jerusalem under Gamaliel, at whose feet I learned to follow our Jewish laws and customs very carefully. I became very anxious to honor God in everything I did, just as you have tried to do today.

4 And I persecuted the Christians, hounding them to death, binding and delivering both men and women to prison.

5 The High Priest or any member of the Council can testify that this is so. For I asked them for letters to the Jewish leaders in Damascus, with instructions to let me bring any Christian I found to Jerusalem in chains to be punished.

6 As I was on the road, nearing Damascus, suddenly about noon a very bright light from heaven shone around me.

7 And I fell to the ground and heard a voice saying to me, 'Saul, Saul, why are you persecuting Me?"

8 'Who is it speaking to me, sir?' I asked. And He replied, 'I am Jesus of Nazareth, the one you are persecuting.'

9 The men with me saw the light but didn't understand what was said.

10 And I said, 'What shall I do, Lord?' And the Lord told me, 'Get up and go into Damascus, and there you will be told what awaits you in the years ahead.'

11 I was blinded by the intense light, and had to be led into Damascus by my companions.

12 There a man named Ananias, as godly a man as you could find for obeying the law, and well thought of by all the Jews of Damascus,

13 Came to me, and standing beside me said, 'Brother Saul, receive your sight!' And that very hour I could see him!

14 Then he told me, 'The God of our fathers has chosen you to know His will and to see the Messiah[1] and hear Him speak.

15 You are to take His message everywhere, telling what you have seen and heard.

22 "Brethren and fathers, hear the defense which I now make before
you."

2 And when they heard that he addressed
them in the Hebrew language, they were
the more quiet. And he said:

3 "I am a Jew, born at Tarsus in Cilicia,
but brought up in this city at the feet of
Gamaliel, educated according to the strict
manner of the law of our fathers, being
zealous for God as you all are this day.
4 I
persecuted this Way to the death, binding
and delivering to prison both men and
women,
5 as the high priest and the whole
council of elders bear me witness. From them
I received letters to the brethren, and I
journeyed to Damascus to take those also
who were there and bring them in bonds to
Jerusalem to be punished.

6 "As I made my journey and drew near
to Damascus, about noon a great light from
heaven suddenly shone about me.
7 And I
fell to the ground and heard a voice saying
to me, 'Saul, Saul, why do you persecute
me?'
8 And I answered, 'Who are you, Lord?'
And he said to me, 'I am Jesus of Nazareth
whom you are persecuting.'
9 Now those
who were with me saw the light but did not
hear the voice of the one who was speaking
to me.
10 And I said, "What shall I do, Lord?'
And the Lord said to me, 'Rise, and go into
Damascus, and there you will be told all
that is appointed for you to do.'
11 And when
I could not see because of the brightness of
that light, I was led by the hand by those
who were with me, and came into Damascus.

12 "And one Ananias, a devout man according to the law, well spoken of by all
the Jews who lived there,
13 came to me,
and standing by me said to me, 'Brother
Saul, receive your sight.' And in that very
hour I received my sight and saw him.
14 And he said, 'The God of our fathers
appointed you to know his will, to see the
Just One and to hear a voice from his
mouth;
15 for you will be a witness for him
to all men of what you have seen and

[1] Literally, "Righteous One."

King James

16 And now why tarriest thou? arise, and be baptized, and wash away thy sins, calling on the name of the Lord.

17 And it came to pass, that, when I was come again to Jerusalem, even while I prayed in the temple, I was in a trance;

18 And saw him saying unto me, Make haste, and get thee quickly out of Jerusalem: for they will not receive thy testimony concerning me.

19 And I said, Lord, they know that I imprisoned and beat in every synagogue them that believed on thee:

20 And when the blood of thy martyr Stephen was shed, I also was standing by, and consenting unto his death, and kept the raiment of them that slew him.

21 And he said unto me, Depart: for I will send thee far hence unto the Gentiles.

22 And they gave him audience unto this word, and *then* lifted up their voices, and said, Away with such a *fellow* from the earth: for it is not fit that he should live.

23 And as they cried out, and cast off *their* clothes, and threw dust into the air,

24 The chief captain commanded him to be brought into the castle, and bade that he should be examined by scourging; that he might know wherefore they cried so against him.

25 And as they bound him with thongs, Paul said unto the centurion that stood by, Is it lawful for you to scourge a man that is a Roman, and uncondemned?

26 When the centurion heard *that*, he went and told the chief captain, saying, Take heed what thou doest: for this man is a Roman.

27 Then the chief captain came, and said unto him, Tell me, art thou a Roman? He said, Yea.

28 And the chief captain answered, With a great sum obtained I this freedom. And Paul said, But I was *free* born.

29 Then straightway they departed from him which should have examined him: and the chief captain also was afraid, after he knew that he was a Roman, and because he had bound him.

30 On the morrow, because he would have known the certainty wherefore he was accused of the Jews, he loosed him from *his* bands, and commanded the chief priests and all their council to appear, and brought Paul down, and set him before them.

Amplified

16 And now, why do you delay? Rise and be baptized, and [j]by calling upon His name wash away your sins.

17 Then when I had come back to Jerusalem and was praying in the temple [k]enclosure, I fell into a trance—an ecstasy;

18 And I saw Him as He said to me, Hurry, get quickly out of Jerusalem, because they will not receive your testimony about Me.

19 And I said, Lord, they themselves well know that throughout all the synagogues I cast into prison and flogged those who believed—who adhered to and trusted in and relied—on You.

20 And when the blood of Your (martyr) witness Stephen was shed, I also was personally standing by and consenting *and* approving, and guarding the garments of those who slew him.

21 And the Lord said to me, Go, for I will send you far away unto the Gentiles (nations).

22 Up to the moment that Paul made this last statement, the people listened to him; but now they raised their voices and shouted, Away with such a fellow from the earth! He is not fit to live!

23 And as they were shouting and tossing *and* waving their garments and throwing dust into the air,

24 The commandant ordered that Paul be brought into the barracks, and that he be examined by scourging, in order that [the commandant] might learn why the people cried out thus against him.

25 But when they had stretched him out with the thongs [leather straps], Paul asked the centurion who was standing by, Is it legal for you to flog a man who is a Roman citizen, and without a trial (uncondemned)?

26 When the centurion heard that, he went to the commandant and said to him, What are you about to do? This man is a Roman citizen!

27 So the commandant came and said to [Paul], Tell me, are you a Roman citizen? And he said, Yes [indeed]!

28 The commandant replied, I purchased this citizenship (as a capital investment) for a big price. Paul said, But I was [Roman] born!

29 Instantly those who were about to examine (and flog) him withdrew from him; and the commandant also was frightened, for he realized that [Paul] was a Roman citizen and he had put him in chains.

30 But the next day, desiring to know the real cause for which the Jews accused him, he unbound him and ordered the chief priests and all the council [Sanhedrin] to assemble, and he brought Paul down and placed him before them.

King James — CHAPTER 23

AND Paul, earnestly beholding the council, said, Men *and* brethren, I have lived in all good conscience before God until this day.

Amplified — CHAPTER 23

THEN Paul, gazing earnestly at the council [Sanhedrin], said, Brethren, I have lived before God, doing my duty with a perfectly good conscience until this very day—[l]as a citizen, a true and loyal Jew.

j) Williams: Adverbial participle of means.
k) Trench.
l) Vincent.

Living New Testament

16 And now, why delay? Go and be baptized, and be cleansed from your sins, calling on the name of the Lord.'

17, 18 One day after my return to Jerusalem, while I was praying in the Temple, I fell into a trance and saw a vision of God saying to me, 'Hurry! Leave Jerusalem, for the people here won't believe you when you give them My message.'

19 'But Lord,' I argued, 'they certainly know that I imprisoned and beat those in every synagogue who believed on You.

20 And when Your witness Stephen was killed, I was standing there agreeing—keeping the coats they laid aside as they stoned him.'

21 But God said to me, 'Leave Jerusalem, for I will send you far away to the *Gentiles*!' "

22 The crowd listened until Paul came to that word, then with one voice they shouted, "Away with such a fellow! Kill him! He isn't fit to live!"

23 They yelled and threw their coats in the air and tossed up handfuls of dust.

24 So the commander brought him inside and ordered him lashed with whips to make him confess his crime. He wanted to find out why the crowd had become so furious!

25 As they tied Paul down to lash him, Paul said to an officer standing there, "Is it legal for you to whip a Roman citizen who hasn't even been tried?"

26 The officer went to the commander and asked, "What are you doing? This man is a Roman citizen!"

27 So the commander went over and asked Paul, "Tell me, are you a Roman citizen?"

"Yes, I certainly am."

28 "I am too," the commander muttered, "and it cost me plenty!"

"But I am a citizen by birth!"

29 The soldiers standing ready to lash him, quickly disappeared when they heard Paul was a Roman citizen, and the commander was frightened because he had ordered him bound and whipped.

30 The next day the commander freed him from his chains and ordered the chief priests into session with the Jewish Council. He had Paul brought in before them to try to find out what the trouble was all about.

Revised Standard

heard. 16And now why do you wait? Rise
and be baptized, and wash away your sins,
calling on his name.'
17 "When I had returned to Jerusalem
and was praying in the temple, I fell into
a trance 18and saw him saying to me, 'Make
haste and get quickly out of Jerusalem, because they will not accept your testimony
about me.' 19And I said, 'Lord, they themselves know that in every synagogue I imprisoned and beat those who believed in thee.
20And when the blood of Stephen thy witness was shed, I also was standing by and
approving, and keeping the garments of those
who killed him.' 21And he said to me, 'Depart; for I will send you far away to the
Gentiles.' "
22 Up to this word they listened to him;
then they lifted up their voices and said,
"Away with such a fellow from the earth!
For he ought not to live." 23And as they
cried out and waved their garments and
threw dust into the air, 24the tribune commanded him to be brought into the barracks,
and ordered him to be examined by scourging, to find out why they shouted thus
against him. 25But when they had tied him
up with the thongs, Paul said to the centurion
who was standing by, "Is it lawful for you
to scourge a man who is a Roman citizen,
and uncondemned?" 26When the centurion
heard that, he went to the tribune and said
to him, "What are you about to do? For
this man is a Roman citizen." 27So the tribune came and said to him, "Tell me, are
you a Roman citizen?" And he said, "Yes."
28The tribune answered, "I bought this citizenship for a large sum." Paul said, "But I
was born a citizen." 29So those who were
about to examine him withdrew from him
instantly; and the tribune also was afraid,
for he realized that Paul was a Roman citizen and that he had bound him.

Paul's trial before the Sanhedrin

30 But on the morrow, desiring to know the real reason why the Jews accused him, he unbound him, and commanded the chief priests and all the council to meet, and he brought Paul down and set him before them.

CHAPTER 23

Gazing intently at the Council, Paul began: "Brothers, I have always lived before God in all good conscience!"

23 And Paul, looking intently at the council, said, "Brethren, I have lived before God in all good conscience up to this

King James

2 And the high priest Ananias commanded them that stood by him to smite him on the mouth.

3 Then said Paul unto him, God shall smite thee, *thou* whited wall: for sittest thou to judge me after the law, and commandest me to be smitten contrary to the law?

4 And they that stood by said, Revilest thou God's high priest?

5 Then said Paul, I wist not, brethren, that he was the high priest: for it is written, Thou shalt not speak evil of the ruler of thy people.

6 But when Paul perceived that the one part were Sadducees, and the other Pharisees, he cried out in the council, Men *and* brethren, I am a Pharisee, the son of a Pharisee: of the hope and resurrection of the dead I am called in question.

7 And when he had so said, there arose a dissension between the Pharisees and the Sadducees: and the multitude was divided.

8 For the Sadducees say that there is no resurrection, neither angel, nor spirit: but the Pharisees confess both.

9 And there arose a great cry: and the scribes *that were* of the Pharisees' part arose, and strove, saying, We find no evil in this man: but if a spirit or an angel hath spoken to him, let us not fight against God.

10 And when there arose a great dissension, the chief captain, fearing lest Paul should have been pulled in pieces of them, commanded the soldiers to go down, and to take him by force from among them, and to bring *him* into the castle.

11 And the night following the Lord stood by him, and said, Be of good cheer, Paul: for as thou hast testified of me in Jerusalem, so must thou bear witness also at Rome.

12 And when it was day, certain of the Jews banded together, and bound themselves under a curse, saying that they would neither eat nor drink till they had killed Paul.

13 And they were more than forty which had made this conspiracy.

14 And they came to the chief priests and elders, and said, We have bound ourselves under a great curse, that we will eat nothing until we have slain Paul.

15 Now therefore ye with the council signify to the chief captain that he bring him down unto you to-morrow, as though ye would inquire something more perfectly concerning him: and we, or ever he come near, are ready to kill him.

16 And when Paul's sister's son heard of their lying in wait, he went and entered into the castle, and told Paul.

17 Then Paul called one of the centurions unto *him,* and said, Bring this young man unto the chief captain: for he hath a certain thing to tell him.

18 So he took him, and brought *him* to the chief captain, and said, Paul the prisoner called me unto *him,* and prayed me to bring this young man unto thee, who hath something to say unto thee.

19 Then the chief captain took him by the hand, and went *with him* aside privately, and asked *him,* What is that thou hast to tell me?

Amplified

2 At this the high priest Ananias ordered those who stood near him to strike him on the mouth.

3 Then Paul said to him, God is about to strike you, you whitewashed wall! Do you sit as a judge to try me in accordance with the Law, and yet in defiance of the Law you order me to be struck?

4 Those who stood near exclaimed, Do you rail at *and* insult the high priest of God?

5 And Paul said, I was not conscious, brethren, that he is a high priest; for the Scripture says, You shall not speak ill of a ruler of your people. [Exod. 22: 28.]

6 But Paul, when he perceived that one part of them were Sadducees and the other part Pharisees, cried out to the council [Sanhedrin], Brethren, I am a Pharisee, a son of Pharisees; it is with regard to the hope and the resurrection of the dead that I am indicted *and* being judged.

7 So when he had said this, an angry dispute arose between the Pharisees and the Sadducees; and the whole [crowded] assemblage was divided [into two factions].

8 For the Sadducees hold that there is no resurrection, nor angel nor spirit; but the Pharisees declare openly *and* speak out freely, acknowledging [their faith in] them both.

9 Then a great uproar ensued, and some of the scribes of the Pharisees' party stood up and thoroughly fought the case, (contending fiercely) and declaring, We find nothing evil *or* wrong in this man. But if a spirit or an angel [really] spoke to him—? *Let us not fight against God!*

10 And when the strife became more and more tense *and* violent, the commandant, fearing that Paul would be torn in pieces by them, ordered the troops to go down and take him forcibly from among them and conduct him back into the barracks.

11 And [that same] following night the Lord stood beside Paul and said, Take courage, *Paul,* for as you have borne faithful witness concerning Me at Jerusalem, so you must also bear witness at Rome.

12 Now when daylight came, the Jews formed a plot and bound themselves by an oath *and* under a curse neither to eat nor drink till they had done away with Paul.

13 There were more than forty [men of them], who formed this conspiracy—swearing together this oath and curse.

14 And they went to the chief priests and elders saying, We have strictly bound ourselves by an oath *and* under a curse not to taste any food until we have slain Paul.

15 So now, you along with the council [Sanhedrin] give notice to the commandant to bring [Paul] down to you, as if you were going to investigate his case more accurately. But we [ourselves] are ready to slay him before he comes near.

16 But the son of Paul's sister heard of their intended attack, and he went and got into the barracks and told Paul.

17 Then Paul, calling in one of the centurions, said, Take this young man to the commandant, for he has something to report to him.

18 So he took him and conducted him to the commandant and said, Paul the prisoner called me to him and requested me to conduct this young man to you, for he has something to report to you.

19 The commandant took him by the hand, and going aside with him asked privately, What is it that you have to report to me?

Living New Testament

2 Instantly Ananias the High Priest commanded those close to Paul to slap him on the mouth.

3 Paul said to him, "God shall slap you, you whitewashed pigpen.[1] What kind of judge are you to break the law yourself by ordering me struck like that?"

4 Those standing near Paul said to him, "Is that the way to talk to God's High Priest?"

5 "I didn't realize he was the High Priest, brothers," Paul replied, "for the Scriptures say, 'Never speak evil of any of your rulers.' "

6 Then Paul thought of something! Part of the Council were Sadducees, and part were Pharisees! So he shouted, "Brothers, I am a Pharisee, as were all my ancestors! And I am being tried here today because I believe in the resurrection of the dead!"

7 This divided the Council right down the middle—the Pharisees against the Sadducees—

8 For the Sadducees say there is no resurrection or angels or even eternal spirit within us,[2] but the Pharisees believe in all of these.

9 So a great clamor arose. Some of the Jewish leaders[3] jumped up to argue that Paul was all right. "We see nothing wrong with him," they shouted. "Perhaps a spirit or angel spoke to him [there on the Damascus road[4]]."

10 The shouting grew louder and louder, and the men were tugging at Paul from both sides, pulling him this way and that. Finally the commander, fearing they would tear him apart, ordered his soldiers to take him away from them by force and bring him back to the armory.

11 That night the Lord stood beside Paul and said, "Don't worry, Paul; just as you have told the people about Me here in Jerusalem, so you must also in Rome."

12, 13 The next morning some 40 or more of the Jews got together and bound themselves by a curse neither to eat nor drink until they had killed Paul!

14 Then they went to the chief priests and elders and told them what they had done.

15 "Ask the commander to bring Paul back to the Council again," they requested. "Pretend you want to ask a few more questions. We will kill him on the way."

16 But Paul's nephew got wind of their plan and came to the armory and told Paul.

17 Paul called one of the officers and said, "Take this boy to the commander. He has something important to tell him."

18 So the officer did, explaining, "Paul, the prisoner, called me over and asked me to bring this young man to you to tell you something."

19 The commander took the boy by the hand, and leading him aside asked, "What is it you want to tell me, lad?"

[1] Literally, "you whitewashed wall."
[2] Literally, "nor spirit."
[3] Literally, "scribes."
[4] Implied.

Revised Standard

day." 2 And the high priest Ananias commanded those who stood by him to strike him
on the mouth. 3 Then Paul said to him, "God
shall strike you, you whitewashed wall! Are
you sitting to judge me according to the
law, and yet contrary to the law you order
me to be struck?" 4 Those who stood by said,
"Would you revile God's high priest?" 5 And
Paul said, "I did not know, brethren, that
he was the high priest; for it is written,
'You shall not speak evil to a ruler of your
people.' "

6 But when Paul perceived that one part
were Sadducees and the other Pharisees, he
cried out in the council, "Brethren, I am a
Pharisee, a son of Pharisees; with respect to
the hope and the resurrection of the dead
I am on trial." 7 And when he had said this,
a dissension arose between the Pharisees and
the Sadducees; and the assembly was divided.
8 For the Sadducees say that there is no
resurrection, nor angel, nor spirit; but the
Pharisees acknowledge them all. 9 Then a
great clamor arose; and some of the scribes
of the Pharisees' party stood up and contended, "We find nothing wrong in this man.
What if a spirit or an angel spoke to him?"
10 And when the dissension became violent,
the tribune, afraid that Paul would be torn
in pieces by them, commanded the soldiers
to go down and take him by force from
among them and bring him into the barracks.

11 The following night the Lord stood by
him and said, "Take courage, for as you
have testified about me at Jerusalem, so
you must bear witness also at Rome."

The plot to kill Paul

12 When it was day, the Jews made a
plot and bound themselves by an oath
neither to eat nor drink till they had killed
Paul. 13 There were more than forty who
made this conspiracy. 14 And they went to
the chief priests and elders, and said, "We
have strictly bound ourselves by an oath to
taste no food till we have killed Paul. 15 You
therefore, along with the council, give notice
now to the tribune to bring him down to
you, as though you were going to determine
his case more exactly. And we are ready to
kill him before he comes near."

16 Now the son of Paul's sister heard of
their ambush; so he went and entered the
barracks and told Paul. 17 And Paul called
one of the centurions and said, "Bring this
young man to the tribune; for he has something to tell him." 18 So he took him and
brought him to the tribune and said, "Paul
the prisoner called me and asked me to bring
this young man to you, as he has something
to say to you." 19 The tribune took him by
the hand, and going aside asked him privately, "What is it that you have to tell me?"

King James

20 And he said, The Jews have agreed to desire thee that thou wouldest bring down Paul tomorrow into the council, as though they would inquire somewhat of him more perfectly.

21 But do not thou yield unto them: for there lie in wait for him of them more than forty men, which have bound themselves with an oath, that they will neither eat nor drink till they have killed him: and now are they ready, looking for a promise from thee.

22 So the chief captain *then* let the young man depart, and charged *him, See thou* tell no man that thou hast shewed these things to me.

23 And he called unto *him* two centurions, saying, Make ready two hundred soldiers to go to Cæsarea, and horsemen threescore and ten, and spearmen two hundred, at the third hour of the night;

24 And provide *them* beasts, that they may set Paul on, and bring *him* safe unto Felix the governor.

25 And he wrote a letter after this manner:

26 Claudius Lysias unto the most excellent governor Felix *sendeth* greeting.

27 This man was taken of the Jews, and should have been killed of them: then came I with an army, and rescued him, having understood that he was a Roman.

28 And when I would have known the cause wherefore they accused him, I brought him forth into their council:

29 Whom I perceived to be accused of questions of their law, but to have nothing laid to his charge worthy of death or of bonds.

30 And when it was told me how that the Jews laid wait for the man, I sent straightway to thee, and gave commandment to his accusers also to say before thee what *they had* against him. Farewell.

31 Then the soldiers, as it was commanded them, took Paul, and brought *him* by night to Antipatris.

32 On the morrow they left the horsemen to go with him, and returned to the castle:

33 Who, when they came to Cæsarea, and delivered the epistle to the governor, presented Paul also before him.

34 And when the governor had read *the letter,* he asked of what province he was. And when he understood that *he was* of Cilicia;

35 I will hear thee, said he, when thine accusers are also come. And he commanded him to be kept in Herod's judgment hall.

CHAPTER 24

AND after five days Ananias the high priest descended with the elders, and *with* a certain orator *named* Tertullus, who informed the governor against Paul.

Amplified

20 And he replied, The Jews have agreed to ask you to bring Paul down to the council [Sanhedrin] tomorrow, as if [they were] intending to examine him more exactly.

21 But do not yield to their persuasion, for more than forty of their men are lying in ambush waiting for him, having bound themselves by an oath *and* under a curse neither to eat nor drink till they have killed him; and even now they are all ready, [just] waiting for your promise.

22 So the commandant sent the youth away, charging him, Do not disclose to any one that you have given me this information.

23 Then summoning two of the centurions, he said, Have two hundred footmen ready by the third hour of tonight (about nine o'clock) to go as far as Caesarea, with seventy horsemen and two hundred spearmen.

24 Also provide beasts for mounts for Paul to ride, and bring him in safety to Felix the governor.

25 And he wrote a letter having this message:

26 Claudius Lysias sends greetings to His Excellency Felix the governor.

27 This man was seized [as prisoner] by the Jews, and was about to be killed by them, when I came upon them with the troops and rescued him, because I learned that he is a Roman citizen.

28 And wishing to know the exact accusation which they were making against him, I brought him down before their council [Sanhedrin].

29 [Where] I found that he was charged in regard to questions of their own law, but he was accused of nothing that would call for death or [even] for imprisonment.

30 [However] when it was pointed out to me that there would be a conspiracy against the man, I sent him to you immediately, directing his accusers also to present before you their charge against him.

31 So the soldiers, in compliance with their instructions, took Paul and conducted him during the night to Antipatris.

32 And the next day they returned to the barracks, leaving the mounted men to proceed with him.

33 When these came to Caesarea and gave the letter to the governor, they also presented Paul before him.

34 Having read the letter, he asked to what kind of a province [Paul] belonged. When he discovered that he was from Cilicia [an imperial province],

35 He said, I will hear your case [m]fully when your accusers also have come. And he ordered that an eye be kept on him in Herod's palace—the praetorium.

CHAPTER 24

FIVE days later, the high priest Ananias came down [from Jerusalem to Caesarea] with some elders, and a certain forensic advocate Tertullus—acting as spokesman and counsel. They presented to the governor their evidence against Paul.

---

m) Vincent.

Living New Testament

20 "Tomorrow," he told him, "the Jews are going to ask you to bring Paul before the Council again, pretending they want to get some more information.

21 But don't do it! There are more than 40 men hiding along the road ready to jump him and kill him. They have bound themselves under a curse to neither eat nor drink till he is dead. They are out there now, expecting you to agree to their request."

22 "Don't let a soul know you told me this," the commander warned the boy as he left.

23, 24 Then the commander called two of his officers and ordered, "Get 200 soldiers ready to leave for Caesarea at nine o'clock tonight! Take 200 spearmen and 70 mounted cavalry. Give Paul a horse to ride on and get him safely to Governor Felix."

25 Then he wrote this letter to the governor:

26 "*From*: Claudius Lysias

To: His Excellency, Governor Felix.

Greetings!

27 This man was seized by the Jews and they were killing him when I sent the soldiers to rescue him, for I learned that he was a Roman citizen.

28 Then I took him to their Council to try to find out what he had done.

29 I soon discovered it was something about their Jewish beliefs, certainly nothing worthy of imprisonment or death.

30 But when I was informed of a plot to kill him, I decided to send him on to you and will tell his accusers to bring their charges before you."

31 So that night, as ordered, the soldiers took Paul to Antipatris.

32 They returned to the armory the next morning, leaving him with the cavalry to take him on to Caesarea.

33 When they arrived in Caesarea, they presented Paul and the letter to the governor.

34 He read it and then asked Paul where he was from. "Cilicia," Paul answered.

35 "I will hear your case fully when your accusers arrive," the governor told him, and ordered him kept in the prison at King Herod's palace.

Revised Standard

20And he said, "The Jews have agreed to ask
you to bring Paul down to the council tomorrow, as though they were going to inquire
somewhat more closely about him. 21But do
not yield to them; for more than forty of their
men lie in ambush for him, having bound
themselves by an oath neither to eat nor
drink till they have killed him; and now they
are ready, waiting for the promise from
you." 22So the tribune dismissed the young
man, charging him, "Tell no one that you
have informed me of this."

Paul taken to Caesarea

23 Then he called two of the centurions
and said, "At the third hour of the night
get ready two hundred soldiers with seventy
horsemen and two hundred spearmen to go
as far as Caesarea. 24Also provide mounts
for Paul to ride, and bring him safely to
Felix the governor." 25And he wrote a letter
to this effect:
26 "Claudius Lysias to his Excellency the
governor Felix, greeting. 27This man was
seized by the Jews, and was about to be
killed by them, when I came upon them
with the soldiers and rescued him, having
learned that he was a Roman citizen. 28And
desiring to know the charge on which they
accused him, I brought him down to their
council. 29I found that he was accused about
questions of their law, but charged with
nothing deserving death or imprisonment.
30And when it was disclosed to me that
there would be a plot against the man, I
sent him to you at once, ordering his accusers also to state before you what they have
against him."
31 So the soldiers, according to their instructions, took Paul and brought him by
night to Antipatris. 32And on the morrow
they returned to the barracks, leaving the
horsemen to go on with him. 33When they
came to Caesarea and delivered the letter
to the governor, they presented Paul also
before him. 34On reading the letter, he asked
to what province he belonged. When he
learned that he was from Cilicia 35he said,
"I will hear you when your accusers arrive."
And he commanded him to be guarded in
Herod's praetorium.

Living New Testament

CHAPTER 24

Five days later Ananias the High Priest arrived with some of the Jewish leaders[1] and the lawyer[2] Tertullus, to make their accusations against Paul.

[1] Literally, "elders."
[2] Literally, "orator."

Revised Standard

Paul tried before Felix

24 And after five days the high priest
Ananias came down with some elders
and a spokesman, one Tertullus. They laid
before the governor their case against Paul;

King James

2 And when he was called forth, Tertullus began to accuse *him*, saying, Seeing that by thee we enjoy great quietness, and that very worthy deeds are done unto this nation by thy providence,

3 We accept *it* always, and in all places, most noble Felix, with all thankfulness.

4 Notwithstanding, that I be not further tedious unto thee, I pray thee that thou wouldest hear us of thy clemency a few words.

5 For we have found this man *a* pestilent *fellow*, and a mover of sedition among all the Jews throughout the world, and a ringleader of the sect of the Nazarenes:

6 Who also hath gone about to profane the temple: whom we took, and would have judged according to our law.

7 But the chief captain Lysias came *upon us*, and with great violence took *him* away out of our hands,

8 Commanding his accusers to come unto thee: by examining of whom thyself mayest take knowledge of all these things, whereof we accuse him.

9 And the Jews also assented, saying that these things were so.

10 Then Paul, after that the governor had beckoned unto him to speak, answered, Forasmuch as I know that thou hast been of many years a judge unto this nation, I do the more cheerfully answer for myself:

11 Because that thou mayest understand, that there are yet but twelve days since I went up to Jerusalem for to worship.

12 And they neither found me in the temple disputing with any man, neither raising up the people, neither in the synagogues, nor in the city:

13 Neither can they prove the things whereof they now accuse me.

14 But this I confess unto thee, that after the way which they call heresy, so worship I the God of my fathers, believing all things which are written in the law and in the prophets:

15 And have hope toward God, which they themselves also allow, that there shall be a resurrection of the dead, both of the just and unjust.

16 And herein do I exercise myself, to have always a conscience void of offence toward God, and *toward* men.

17 Now after many years I came to bring alms to my nation, and offerings.

18 Whereupon certain Jews from Asia found me purified in the temple, neither with multitude, nor with tumult.

19 Who ought to have been here before thee, and object, if they had aught against me.

20 Or else let these same *here* say, if they have found any evil doing in me, while I stood before the council,

21 Except it be for this one voice, that I cried standing among them, Touching the resurrection of the dead I am called in question by you this day.

Amplified

2 And when he was called, Tertullus began the complaint [against him] by saying:

3 Most Excellent Felix, since through you we obtain *and* enjoy much peace, and since by your foresight *and* provision wonderful reforms (amendments and improvements) are introduced *and* effected on behalf of this nation, in every way and in every place we accept *and* acknowledge this with deep appreciation *and* with all gratitude.

4 But not to hinder *or* detain you too long, I beg you in your clemency *and* courtesy *and* kindness to grant us a brief *and* [m]concise hearing.

5 For we have found this man a perfect pest—a real plague—an agitator *and* source of disturbance to all the Jews throughout the world, and a ringleader of the (heretical, [m]division-producing) sect of the Nazarenes.

6 He also [even] tried to desecrate *and* defile the temple, but we laid hands on him

7 *And would have sentenced him by our Law, but the commandant Lysias came and took him from us with violence and force, and ordered his accusers to present themselves to you.*

8 By examining *and* cross-questioning him yourself you will be able to ascertain the truth from him about all these things with which we charge him.

9 The Jews also agreed *and* joined in the accusation, declaring that all these things were exactly so.

10 And when the governor had beckoned to Paul to speak, he answered: Because I know that for many years you have been a judge over this nation, I find it easier to make my defense, *and* do it cheerfully *and* with good courage.

11 As you can readily verify, it is not more than twelve days since I went up to Jerusalem to worship;

12 And neither in the temple nor in the synagogues nor in the city did they find me disputing with anybody or bringing together a seditious crowd.

13 Neither can they present argument *or* evidence to prove to you what they now bring against me.

14 But this I confess to you, however, that in accordance with the Way [of the Lord], which they call (an heretical, division-producing) sect, I worship (serve) the God of our fathers, still persuaded of the truth of *and* believing *and* placing full confidence in everything laid down in the Law [of Moses] *or* written in the prophets;

15 Having [the same] hope in God which these themselves hold *and* look for, that there is to be a resurrection both of the righteous and the unrighteous—the just and the unjust.

16 Therefore I always exercise *and* discipline myself—mortifying my body [deadening my carnal affections, bodily appetites and worldly desires], endeavoring in all respects—to have a clear (unshaken, blameless) conscience, void of offense toward God and toward men.

17 Now after several years I came up to bring my race contributions of charity and offerings.

18 While I was engaged in presenting these, they found me [occupied in the rites of purification] in the temple, without any crowd or uproar. But some Jews from [the province of] Asia [were there],

19 Who ought to be here before you and to present their charges, if they have anything against me.

20 Or else let these men themselves tell of what crime *or* wrongdoing they found me guilty when I appeared before the council [Sanhedrin],

21 Unless it be this one sentence which I cried out as I stood among them, In regard to the resurrection of the dead I am indicted *and* on trial before you this day!

---

m) Vincent.

Living New Testament

2 When Tertullus was called forward, he laid charges against Paul in the following address to the governor:

"Your Excellency, you have given quietness and peace to us Jews and have greatly reduced the discrimination against us.

3 And for this we are very, very grateful to you.

4 But lest I bore you, kindly give me your attention for only a moment as I briefly outline our case against this man.

5 For we have found him to be a troublemaker, a man who is constantly inciting the Jews throughout the entire world to riots and rebellions against the Roman government. He is a ringleader of the sect known as the Nazarenes.

6 Moreover, he was trying to defile the Temple when we arrested him. We would have given him what he justly deserves,

7 But Lysias, the commander of the garrison, came and took him violently away from us,

8 Demanding that he be tried by Roman law. You can find out the truth of our accusations by examining him yourself."

9 Then all the other Jews chimed in, declaring that everything Tertullus said was true.

10 Now it was Paul's turn. The governor motioned for him to rise and speak. Paul began: "I know, sir, that you have been a judge of Jewish affairs for many years, and this gives me confidence as I make my defense.

11 You can quickly discover that it was no more than twelve days ago that I arrived in Jerusalem to worship at the Temple,

12 And you will discover that I have never incited a riot in any synagogue or on the streets of any city;

13 And these men certainly cannot prove the things they accuse me of doing.

14 But one thing I do confess, that I believe in the way of salvation, which they refer to as a sect; I follow that system of serving the God of our ancestors; I firmly believe in the Jewish law and everything written in the books of prophecy;

15 And I believe, just as these men do, that there will be a resurrection of both the righteousness and ungodly.

16 Because of this I try with all my strength to always maintain a clear conscience before God and man.

17 After several years away, I returned to Jerusalem with money to aid the Jews, and to offer a sacrifice to God.

18 My accusers saw me in the Temple as I was presenting my thank offering.[3] I had shaved my head as their laws required, and there was no crowd around me, and no rioting! But some Jews from Turkey were there,

19 (Who ought to be here if they have anything against me)—

20 But look! Ask these men right here what wrongdoing their Council found in me,

21 Except that I said one thing I shouldn't[4] when I shouted out, 'I am here before the Council to defend myself for believing that the dead will rise again!' "

[3] Implied.
[4] Literally, "except it be for this one voice."

Revised Standard

2and when he was called, Tertullus began to
accuse him, saying:
"Since through you we enjoy much peace,
and since by your provision, most excellent
Felix, reforms are introduced on behalf of
this nation, 3in every way and everywhere
we accept this with all gratitude. 4But, to detain you no further, I beg you in your kindness to hear us briefly. 5For we have found
this man a pestilent fellow, an agitator among
all the Jews throughout the world, and a
ringleader of the sect of the Nazarenes. 6He
even tried to profane the temple, but we
seized him.[z] 8By examining him yourself
you will be able to learn from him about
everything of which we accuse him."
9 The Jews also joined in the charge, af-
firming that all this was so.
10 And when the governor had motioned
to him to speak, Paul replied:
"Realizing that for many years you have
been judge over this nation, I cheerfully
make my defense. 11As you may ascertain,
it is not more than twelve days since I went
up to worship at Jerusalem; 12and they did
not find me disputing with any one or stirring up a crowd, either in the temple or in
the synagogues, or in the city. 13Neither can
they prove to you what they now bring up
against me. 14But this I admit to you, that
according to the Way, which they call a
sect, I worship the God of our fathers, believing everything laid down by the law or
written in the prophets, 15having a hope in
God which these themselves accept, that there
will be a resurrection of both the just and
the unjust. 16So I always take pains to have
a clear conscience toward God and toward
men. 17Now after some years I came to
bring to my nation alms and offerings. 18As
I was doing this, they found me purified in
the temple, without any crowd or tumult.
But some Jews from Asia—19they ought to
be here before you and to make an accusation, if they have anything against me. 20Or
else let these men themselves say what
wrongdoing they found when I stood before
the council, 21except this one thing which
I cried out while standing among them,
'With respect to the resurrection of the
dead I am on trial before you this day.' "

[z] Other ancient authorities add *and we woulr have judged him according to our law.* [7] *But the chief captain Lysias came and with great violence took him out of our hands,* [8] *commanding his accusers to come before you.*

King James

22 And when Felix heard these things, having more perfect knowledge of *that* way, he deferred them, and said, When Lysias the chief captain shall come down, I will know the uttermost of your matter.

23 And he commanded a centurion to keep Paul, and to let *him* have liberty, and that he should forbid none of his acquaintance to minister or come unto him.

24 And after certain days, when Felix came with his wife Drusilla, which was a Jewess, he sent for Paul, and heard him concerning the faith of Christ.

25 And as he reasoned of righteousness, temperance, and judgment to come, Felix trembled, and answered, Go thy way for this time; when I have a convenient season, I will call for thee.

26 He hoped also that money should have been given him of Paul, that he might loose him: wherefore he sent for him the oftener, and communed with him.

27 But after two years Porcius Festus came into Felix' room: and Felix, willing to shew the Jews a pleasure, left Paul bound.

Amplified

22 But Felix, having a rather accurate understanding of the Way [of the Lord], put them off *and* adjourned the trial, saying, When Lysias the commandant comes down, I will determine your case more fully.

23 Then he ordered the centurion to keep [Paul] in custody, but to treat him with indulgence—giving him some liberty—and not to hinder his friends from ministering to his needs *and* serving him.

24 Some days later Felix came with his wife Drusilla, who was a Jewess; and he sent for Paul and listened to him [talk] about faith in Christ Jesus.

25 But as he continued to argue about uprightness, purity of life—the control of the passions—and the judgment to come, Felix became alarmed *and* terrified and said, Go away for the present; when I have a convenient opportunity I will send for you.

26 At the same time he hoped to get money from Paul, for which reason he continued to send for him, and was in his company *and* conversed with him often.

27 But when two years had gone by, Felix was succeeded in office by Porcius Festus, and wishing to gain favor with the Jews, Felix left Paul still a prisoner in chains.

King James

CHAPTER 25

NOW when Festus was come into the province, after three days he ascended from Cæsarea to Jerusalem.

2 Then the high priest and the chief of the Jews informed him against Paul, and besought him,

3 And desired favour against him, that he would send for him to Jerusalem, laying wait in the way to kill him.

4 But Festus answered, that Paul should be kept at Cæsarea, and that he himself would depart shortly *thither*.

5 Let them therefore, said he, which among you are able, go down with *me,* and accuse this man, if there be any wickedness in him.

6 And when he had tarried among them more than ten days, he went down unto Cæsarea; and the next day sitting on the judgment seat commanded Paul to be brought.

7 And when he was come, the Jews which came down from Jerusalem stood round about, and laid many and grievous complaints against Paul, which they could not prove.

8 While he answered for himself, Neither against the law of the Jews, neither against the temple, not yet against Cæsar, have I offended any thing at all.

9 But Festus, willing to do the Jews a pleasure, answered Paul, and said, Wilt thou go up to Jerusalem, and there be judged of these things before me?

10 Then said Paul, I stand at Cæsar's judgment seat, where I ought to be judged: to the Jews have I done no wrong, as thou very well knowest.

Amplified

CHAPTER 25

NOW when Festus had entered into his own province, after three days he went up from Caesarea to Jerusalem.

2 And [there] the chief priests and the principal men of the Jews laid charges before him against Paul, and they kept begging *and* urging him,

3 Asking as a favor that he would have him brought to Jerusalem; [meanwhile] they were planning an ambush to slay him on the way.

4 Festus answered that Paul was in custody in Caesarea and that he himself planned to leave for there soon.

5 So, said he, let those who are in a position of authority *and* are influential among you go down with me, and if there is anything amiss *or* criminal about the man, let them so charge him.

6 So when Festus had remained among them not more than eight or ten days, he went down to Caesarea, took his seat next day on the judgment bench and ordered Paul to be brought before him.

7 And when he arrived, the Jews who had come down from Jerusalem stood all around him, bringing many grave accusations against him which they were not able to prove.

8 Paul declared in [his own] defense, Neither against the Law of the Jews, nor against the temple, nor against Caesar have I offended in any way.

9 But Festus, wishing to ingratiate himself with the Jews, answered Paul, Are you willing to go up to Jerusalem, and there be put on trial [[n]before the Jewish Sanhedrin] in my presence concerning these charges?

10 But Paul replied, I am standing before Caesar's judgment seat, where I ought to be tried. To the Jews I have done no wrong, as you know [n]better [than your question implies].

n) Vincent.

Living New Testament

22 Felix, who knew Christians didn't go around starting riots,[5] told the Jews to wait for the arrival of Lysias, the garrison commander, and then he would decide the case.

23 He ordered Paul to prison but instructed the guards to treat him gently and not to forbid any of his friends from visiting him or bringing him gifts to make his stay more comfortable.

24 A few days later Felix came with Drusilla, his legal[6] wife, a Jewess. Sending for Paul, they listened as he told them about faith in Christ Jesus.

25 And as he reasoned with them about righteousness and self-control and the judgment to come, Felix was terrified. "Go away for now," he replied, "and when I have a more convenient time, I'll call for you again."

26 He also hoped that Paul would bribe him, so he sent for him from time to time and talked with him.

27 Two years went by in this way; then Felix was succeeded by Porcius Festus. And because Felix wanted to gain favor with the Jews, he left Paul in chains.

Revised Standard

Felix defers the sentence

22 But Felix, having a rather accurate
knowledge of the Way, put them off, saying,
"When Lysias the tribune comes down, I
will decide your case." 23Then he gave orders
to the centurion that he should be kept in
custody but should have some liberty, and
that none of his friends should be prevented
from attending to his needs.
24 After some days Felix came with his
wife Drusilla, who was a Jewess; and he
sent for Paul and heard him speak upon
faith in Christ Jesus. 25And as he argued
about justice and self-control and future
judgment, Felix was alarmed and said, "Go
away for the present; when I have an opportunity I will summon you." 26At the
same time he hoped that money would be
given him by Paul. So he sent for him often
and conversed with him. 27But when two
years had elapsed, Felix was succeeded by
Porcius Festus; and desiring to do the Jews
a favor, Felix left Paul in prison.

CHAPTER 25

Three days after Festus arrived in Caesarea to take over his new responsibilities, he left for Jerusalem,

2 Where the chief priests and other Jewish leaders got hold of him and gave him their story about Paul.

3 They begged him to bring Paul to Jerusalem at once. (Their plan was to waylay and kill him.)

4 But Festus replied that since Paul was at Caesarea and he himself was returning there soon,

5 Those with authority in this affair should return with him for the trial.

6 Eight or ten days later he returned to Caesarea and the following day opened Paul's trial.

7 On Paul's arrival in court the Jews from Jerusalem gathered around, hurling many serious accusations which they couldn't prove.

8 Paul denied the charges: "I am not guilty," he said. "I have not opposed the Jewish laws or desecrated the Temple or rebelled against the Roman government."

9 Then Festus, anxious to please the Jews, asked him, "Are you willing to go to Jerusalem and stand trial before me?"

10, 11 But Paul replied, "No! I demand my privilege of a hearing before the Emperor himself. You know very

Paul tried before Festus

25 Now when Festus had come into his
province, after three days he went
up to Jerusalem from Caesarea. 2And the
chief priests and the principal men of the
Jews informed him against Paul; and they
urged him, 3asking as a favor to have the
man sent to Jerusalem, planning an ambush
to kill him on the way. 4Festus replied that
Paul was being kept at Caesarea, and that
he himself intended to go there shortly.
5"So," said he, "let the men of authority
among you go down with me, and if there
is anything wrong about the man, let them
accuse him."
6 When he had stayed among them not
more than eight or ten days, he went down
to Caesarea; and the next day he took his
seat on the tribunal and ordered Paul to be
brought. 7And when he had come, the
Jews who had gone down from Jerusalem
stood about him, bringing against him many
serious charges which they could not prove.
8Paul said in his defense, "Neither against
the law of the Jews, nor against the temple,
nor against Caesar have I offended at all."
9But Festus, wishing to do the Jews a favor,
said to Paul, "Do you wish to go up to
Jerusalem, and there be tried on these
charges before me?" 10But Paul said, "I am
standing before Caesar's tribunal, where I
ought to be tried; to the Jews I have done
no wrong, as you know very well. 11If then

[5] Literally, "having more accurate knowledge."
[6] Literally, "his own wife."

King James

11 For if I be an offender, or have committed any thing worthy of death, I refuse not to die: but if there be none of these things whereof these accuse me, no man may deliver me unto them. I appeal unto Cæsar.

12 Then Festus, when he had conferred with the council, answered, Hast thou appealed unto Cæsar? unto Cæsar shalt thou go.

13 And after certain days king Agrippa and Bernice came unto Cæsarea to salute Festus.

14 And when they had been there many days, Festus declared Paul's cause unto the king, saying, There is a certain man left in bonds by Felix:

15 About whom, when I was at Jerusalem, the chief priests and the elders of the Jews informed *me,* desiring *to have* judgment against him.

16 To whom I answered, It is not the manner of the Romans to deliver any man to die, before that he which is accused have the accusers face to face, and have licence to answer for himself concerning the crime laid against him.

17 Therefore, when they were come hither, without any delay on the morrow I sat on the judgment seat, and commanded the man to be brought forth.

18 Against whom when the accusers stood up, they brought none accusation of such things as I supposed:

19 But had certain questions against him of their own superstition, and of one Jesus, which was dead, whom Paul affirmed to be alive.

20 And because I doubted of such manner of questions, I asked *him* whether he would go to Jerusalem, and there be judged of these matters.

21 But when Paul had appealed to be reserved unto the hearing of Augustus, I commanded him to be kept till I might send him to Cæsar.

22 Then Agrippa said unto Festus, I would also hear the man myself. To-morrow, said he, thou shalt hear him.

23 And on the morrow, when Agrippa was come, and Bernice, with great pomp, and was entered into the place of hearing, with the chief captains, and principal men of the city, at Festus' commandment Paul was brought forth.

24 And Festus said, King Agrippa, and all men which are here present with us, ye see this man, about whom all the multitude of the Jews have dealt with me, both at Jerusalem, and *also* here, crying that he ought not to live any longer.

25 But when I found that he had committed nothing worthy of death, and that he himself hath appealed to Augustus, I have determined to send him.

26 Of whom I have no certain thing to write unto my lord. Wherefore I have brought him forth before you, and specially before thee, O king Agrippa, that, after examination had, I might have somewhat to write.

Amplified

11 If then I am a wrongdoer *and* a criminal, and have committed anything for which I deserve to die, I do not beg off *and* seek to escape death; but if there is no ground for their accusations against me, no one can give me up *and* [o]make a present of me to them. I appeal to Caesar.

12 Then Festus, when he had consulted with the [[n]men who formed his] council, answered, You have appealed to Caesar; to Caesar you shall go.

13 Now after an interval of some days, Agrippa the king and Bernice arrived at Caesarea to pay their respects to Festus—to welcome him and wish him well.

14 And while they remained there for many days, Festus acquainted the king with Paul's case, telling him, There is a man left a prisoner in chains by Felix;

15 And when I was at Jerusalem, the chief priests and the elders of the Jews informed me about him, petitioning for a judicial hearing *and* condemnation of him.

16 But I replied to them that it was not the custom of the Romans to give up freely any man for punishment before the accused had met the accusers face to face, and had opportunity to defend himself concerning the charge brought against him.

17 So when they came here together, I did not delay, but on the morrow took my place on the judgment seat and ordered that the man be brought before me.

18 [But] when the accusers stood up, they brought forward no accusation [in his case] of any such misconduct as I was expecting.

19 Instead they had some points of controversy with him about their own religion *or* superstition and concerning one Jesus, Who had died, but Whom Paul kept asserting [over and over] to be alive.

20 And I, being puzzled to know how to make inquiries into such questions, asked whether he would be willing to go to Jerusalem and there be tried regarding them.

21 But when Paul had appealed to have his case retained for examination *and* decision by the emperor, I ordered that he be detained until I could send him to Caesar.

22 Then Agrippa said to Festus, I am also desiring to hear the man myself. Tomorrow, [Festus] replied, you shall hear him.

23 So the next day Agrippa and Bernice approached with great display, and they went into the audience hall accompanied by the military commandants and the prominent citizens of the city. At the order of Festus Paul was brought in.

24 Then Festus said, King Agrippa and all the men present with us, you see this man about whom the whole Jewish people came to me *and* complained, both at Jerusalem and here, insisting *and* shouting that he ought not to live any longer.

25 But I found nothing that he had done deserving of death. Still, as he himself appealed to the emperor, I determined to send him to Rome.

26 [However] I have nothing in particular *and* definite to write to my lord concerning him. So I have brought him before you all, and especially before you, King Agrippa, that, after [further] examination has been made, I may have something to put in writing.

---

n) Vincent.
o) Abbott-Smith: "bestow, give freely."

Living New Testament

well I am not guilty. If I have done something worthy of death, I don't refuse to die! But if I am innocent, neither you nor anyone else has a right to turn me over to these men to kill me. *I appeal to Caesar.*"

12 Festus conferred with his advisors and then replied, "Very well! You have appealed to Caesar, and to Caesar you shall go!"

13 A few days later King Agrippa arrived with Bernice[1] for a visit with Festus.

14 During their stay of several days Festus discussed Paul's case with the king. "There is a prisoner here," he told him, "whose case was left for me by Felix.

15 When I was in Jerusalem, the chief priests and other Jewish leaders gave me their side of the story and asked me to have him killed.

16 Of course I quickly pointed out to them that Roman law does not convict a man before he is tried. He is given an opportunity to defend himself face to face with his accusers.

17 When they came here for the trial, I called the case the very next day and ordered Paul brought in.

18 But the accusations made against him weren't at all what I supposed they would be.

19 It was something about their religion, and about someone called Jesus who died, but Paul insists is alive!

20 I was perplexed as to how to decide a case of this kind and asked him whether he would be willing to stand trial on these charges in Jerusalem.

21 But Paul appealed to Caesar! So I ordered him back to jail until I could arrange to get him to the Emperor."

22 "I'd like to hear the man myself," Agrippa said. And Festus replied, "You shall—tomorrow!"

23 So the next day, after the king and Bernice had arrived at the courtroom with great pomp, accompanied by military officers and prominent men of the city, Festus ordered Paul brought in.

24 Then Festus addressed the audience: "King Agrippa and all present," he said, "this is the man whose death is demanded both by the local Jews and those in Jerusalem!

25 But in my opinion he has done nothing worthy of death. However, he appealed his case to Caesar, and I have no alternative but to send him.

26 But what shall I write the Emperor? For there is no real charge against him! So I have brought him before you all, and especially you, King Agrippa, to examine him and then tell me what to write.

[1] She was his sister.

Revised Standard

I am a wrongdoer, and have committed anything for which I deserve to die, I do not
seek to escape death; but if there is nothing
in their charges against me, no one can give
me up to them. I appeal to Caesar." [12]Then
Festus, when he had conferred with his
council, answered, "You have appealed to
Caesar; to Caesar you shall go."

Paul's case discussed

13 Now when some days had passed,
Agrippa the king and Bernice arrived at
Caesarea to welcome Festus. [14]And as they
stayed there many days, Festus laid Paul's
case before the king, saying, "There is a
man left prisoner by Felix; [15]and when I
was at Jerusalem, the chief priests and the
elders of the Jews gave information about
him, asking for sentence against him. [16]I
answered them that it was not the custom
of the Romans to give up any one before the
accused met the accusers face to face, and
had opportunity to make his defense concerning the charge laid against him. [17]When
therefore they came together here, I made
no delay, but on the next day took my seat
on the tribunal and ordered the man to be
brought in. [18]When the accusers stood up,
they brought no charge in his case of such
evils as I supposed; [19]but they had certain
points of dispute with him about their own
superstition and about one Jesus, who was
dead, but whom Paul asserted to be alive.
[20]Being at a loss how to investigate these
questions, I asked whether he wished to go
to Jerusalem and be tried there regarding
them. [21]But when Paul had appealed to be
kept in custody for the decision of the emperor, I commanded him to be held until I
could send him to Caesar." [22]And Agrippa
said to Festus, "I should like to hear the
man myself." "Tomorrow," said he, "you
shall hear him."

23 So on the morrow Agrippa and Bernice came with great pomp, and they entered
the audience hall with the military tribunes
and the prominent men of the city. Then by
command of Festus Paul was brought in.
[24]And Festus said, "King Agrippa and all
who are present with us, you see this man
about whom the whole Jewish people pe-
titioned me, both at Jerusalem and here,
shouting that he ought not to live any longer. [25]But I found that he had done nothing
deserving death; and as he himself appealed
to the emperor, I decided to send him. [26]But
I have nothing definite to write to my lord
about him. Therefore I have brought him
before you, and, especially before you, King
Agrippa, that, after we have examined him,
I may have something to write. [27]For it

King James

27 For it seemeth to me unreasonable to send a prisoner, and not withal to signify the crimes *laid* against him.

CHAPTER 26

THEN Agrippa said unto Paul, Thou art permitted to speak for thyself. Then Paul stretched forth the hand, and answered for himself:

2 I think myself happy, king Agrippa, because I shall answer for myself this day before thee touching all things whereof I am accused of the Jews:

3 Especially *because I know* thee to be expert in all customs and questions which are among the Jews: wherefore I beseech thee to hear me patiently.

4 My manner of life from my youth, which was at the first among mine own nation at Jerusalem, know all the Jews;

5 Which knew me from the beginning, if they would testify, that after the most straitest sect of our religion I lived a Pharisee.

6 And now I stand and am judged for the hope of the promise made of God unto our fathers:

7 Unto which *promise* our twelve tribes, instantly serving *God* day and night hope to come. For which hope's sake, king Agrippa, I am accused of the Jews.

8 Why should it be thought a thing incredible with you, that God should raise the dead?

9 I verily thought with myself, that I ought to do many things contrary to the name of Jesus of Nazareth.

10 Which thing I also did in Jerusalem: and many of the saints did I shut up in prison, having received authority from the chief priests; and when they were put to death, I gave my voice against *them*.

11 And I punished them oft in every synagogue, and compelled *them* to blaspheme; and being exceedingly mad against them, I persecuted *them* even unto strange cities.

12 Whereupon as I went to Damascus with authority and commission from the chief priests,

13 At midday, O king, I saw in the way a light from heaven, above the brightness of the sun, shining round about me and them which journeyed with me.

14 And when we were all fallen to the earth, I heard a voice speaking unto me, and saying in the Hebrew tongue, Saul, Saul, why persecutest thou me? *it is* hard for thee to kick against the pricks.

15 And I said, Who art thou, Lord? And he said, I am Jesus whom thou persecutest.

16 But rise, and stand upon thy feet: for I have appeared unto thee for this purpose to make thee a minister and a witness both of these things which thou hast seen, and of those things in the which I will appear unto thee;

Amplified

27 For it seems to me senseless *and* absurd to send a prisoner and not state the accusations against him.

CHAPTER 26

THEN Agrippa said to Paul, You are permitted to speak on your own behalf. At that Paul stretched forth his hand and made his defense [as follows]:

2 I consider myself fortunate, King Agrippa, that it is before you that I am to make my defense today in regard to all the charges brought against me by [the] Jews,

3 [Especially] because you are so fully *and* unusually conversant with all [the] Jewish customs and controversies; therefore, I beg you to hear me patiently.

4 My behavior *and* manner of living from my youth up is known by all the Jews; [they are aware] that from [its] commencement my youth was spent among my own race in Jerusalem.

5 They have had knowledge of me for a long time, if they are willing to testify to it, that in accordance with the [very] strictest sect of our religion I have lived as a Pharisee.

6 And now I stand here on trial (to be judged on the ground) of the hope of that promise made to our forefathers by God, [See Acts 13:32, 33.]

7 Which hope [of the Messiah and the resurrection] our twelve tribes confidently expect to realize, as they fervently worship (without ceasing) night and day. And for that hope, O king, I am accused by Jews *and* as a criminal!

8 Why is it thought incredible by any of you that God raises the dead?

9 I myself indeed was [once] persuaded that it was my duty to do many things contrary to *and* in defiance of the name of Jesus of Nazareth.

10 And that is what I did in Jerusalem; I [not only] shut up many of the faithful holy ones in prison by virtue of authority received from the chief priests, but when they were being condemned to death I cast my vote against them.

11 And frequently I punished them in all the synagogues to make them blaspheme; and in my bitter fury against them, I harassed (troubled, molested, persecuted) *and* pursued them even to foreign cities.

12 Thus engaged I proceeded to Damascus with the authority and orders of the chief priests,

13 When on the road at midday, O king, I saw a light from heaven surpassing the brightness of the sun, flashing about me and those who were traveling with me.

14 And when we had all fallen to the ground, I heard a voice in the Hebrew tongue saying to me, Saul, Saul, why do you continue to persecute Me—to harass and trouble and molest Me? It is dangerous *and* turns out badly for you to keep kicking against the goads—[that is,] to offer vain and perilous resistance.

15 And I said, Who are You, Lord? And the Lord said, I am Jesus Whom you are persecuting.

16 But arise and stand upon your feet; for I have appeared to you for this purpose, that I might appoint you to serve as [My] minister and to bear witness both to what you have seen of Me and to that in which I will appear to you,

Living New Testament

27 For it doesn't seem reasonable to send a prisoner to the Emperor without any charges against him!"

CHAPTER 26

Then Agrippa said to Paul, "Go ahead. Tell us your story." So Paul, with many gestures,[1] presented his defense:

2 "I am fortunate, King Agrippa," he began, "to be able to present my answer before you,

3 For I know you are an expert on Jewish laws and customs. Now please listen patiently!

4 As the Jews are well aware, I was given a thorough Jewish training from my earliest childhood in Tarsus[2] and later at Jerusalem, and I lived accordingly.

5 If they would admit it, they know that I have always been the strictest of Pharisees when it comes to obedience to Jewish laws and customs.

6 But the real reason behind their accusations is something else—it is because I am looking forward to the fulfillment of God's promise made to our ancestors.

7 The 12 tribes of Israel strive night and day to attain this same hope I have! Yet, O King, for me it is a crime, they say!

8 But is it a crime to believe in the resurrection of the dead? Does it seem incredible to you that God can bring men back to life again?

9 I used to believe that I ought to do many horrible things to the followers[3] of Jesus of Nazareth.

10 I imprisoned many of the saints in Jerusalem, as authorized by the High Priests; and when they were condemned to death, I cast my vote against them.

11 I used torture to try to make Christians everywhere curse Christ. I was so violently opposed to them that I even hounded them in distant cities in foreign lands.

12 I was on such a mission to Damascus, armed with the authority and commission of the chief priests,

13 When one day about noon, sir, a light from heaven brighter than the sun shone down on me and my companions.

14 We all fell down, and I heard a voice speaking to me in Hebrew, 'Saul, Saul, why are you persecuting Me? You are only hurting yourself.'[4]

15 'Who are you, sir?' I asked. And the Lord replied, 'I am Jesus, the one you are persecuting.

16 Now stand up! For I have appeared to you to appoint you as My servant and My witness. You are to tell the world about this experience and about the many other occasions when I shall appear to you.

[1] Literally, "stretched forth his hand."
[2] Literally, "my own nation."
[3] Literally, "the name."
[4] Literally, "it is hard for you to kick against the oxgoad!"

Revised Standard

seems to me unreasonable, in sending a
prisoner, not to indicate the charges against
him."

Paul tried before Agrippa

26 Agrippa said to Paul, "You have
permission to speak for yourself."
Then Paul stretched out his hand and made
his defense:
2 "I think myself fortunate that it is before you, King Agrippa, I am to make my
defense today against all the accusations of
the Jews, 3because you are especially familiar with all customs and controversies of the
Jews; therefore I beg you to listen to me
patiently.
4 "My manner of life from my youth,
spent from the beginning among my own
nation and at Jerusalem, is known by all
the Jews. 5They have known for a long time,
if they are willing to testify, that according
to the strictest party of our religion I have
lived as a Pharisee. 6And now I stand here
on trial for hope in the promise made by
God to our fathers, 7to which our twelve
tribes hope to attain, as they earnestly worship night and day. And for this hope I am
accused by Jews, O king! 8Why is it thought
incredible by any of you that God raises
the dead?
9 "I myself was convinced that I ought
to do many things in opposing the name of
Jesus of Nazareth. 10And I did so in Jerusalem; I not only shut up many of the saints
in prison, by authority from the chief priests,
but when they were put to death I cast my
vote against them. 11And I punished them
often in all the synagogues and tried to make
them blaspheme; and in raging fury against
them, I persecuted them even to foreign
cities.

Paul describes his conversion

12 "Thus I journeyed to Damascus with
the authority and commission of the chief
priests. 13At midday, O king, I saw on the
way a light from heaven, brighter than the
sun, shining round me and those who journeyed with me. 14And when we had all fallen
to the ground, I heard a voice saying to me
in the Hebrew language, 'Saul, Saul, why do
you persecute me? It hurts you to kick
against the goads.' 15And I said, 'Who are
you, Lord?' And the Lord said, 'I am Jesus
whom you are persecuting. 16But rise and
stand upon your feet; for I have appeared
to you for this purpose, to appoint you to
serve and bear witness to the things in which
you have seen me and to those in which I
will appear to you, 17delivering you from

King James

17 Delivering thee from the people, and *from* the Gentiles, unto whom now I send thee,

18 To open their eyes, *and* to turn *them* from darkness to light, and *from* the power of Satan unto God, that they may receive forgiveness of sins, and inheritance among them which are sanctified by faith that is in me.

19 Whereupon, O king Agrippa, I was not disobedient unto the heavenly vision:

20 But shewed first unto them of Damascus, and at Jerusalem, and throughout all the coasts of Judæa, and *then* to the Gentiles, that they should repent and turn to God, and do works meet for repentance.

21 For these causes the Jews caught me in the temple, and went about to kill *me*.

22 Having therefore obtained help of God, I continue unto this day, witnessing both to small and great, saying none other things than those which the prophets and Moses did say should come:

23 That Christ should suffer, *and* that he should be the first that should rise from the dead, and should shew light unto the people, and to the Gentiles.

24 And as he thus spake for himself, Festus said with a loud voice, Paul, thou art beside thyself; much learning doth make thee mad.

25 But he said, I am not mad, most noble Festus; but speak forth the words of truth and soberness.

26 For the king knoweth of these things, before whom also I speak freely: for I am persuaded that none of these things are hidden from him; for this thing was not done in a corner.

27 King Agrippa, believest thou the prophets? I know that thou believest.

28 Then Agrippa said unto Paul, Almost thou persuadest me to be a Christian.

29 And Paul said, I would to God, that not only thou, but also all that hear me this day, were both almost, and altogether such as I am, except these bonds.

30 And when he had thus spoken, the king rose up, and the governor, and Bernice, and they that sat with them:

31 And when they were gone aside, they talked between themselves, saying, This man doeth nothing worthy of death or of bonds.

32 Then said Agrippa unto Festus, This man might have been set at liberty, if he had not appealed unto Cæsar.

CHAPTER 27

AND when it was determined that we should sail into Italy, they delivered Paul and certain other prisoners unto *one* named Julius, a centurion of Augustus' band.

Amplified

17 [p]Choosing you out (selecting you for Myself) *and* [q]delivering you from among this [Jewish] people and the Gentiles to whom I am sending you, [Ezek. 2:1, 3.]

18 To open their eyes, that they may turn from darkness to light, and from the power of Satan to God, so that they may thus receive forgiveness *and* release from their sins and a place *and* portion among those who are consecrated *and* purified by faith in me. [Isa. 42:7, 16.]

19 Wherefore, O King Agrippa, I was not disobedient unto the heavenly vision,

20 But made known openly first of all to those at Damascus, then at Jerusalem and throughout the whole land of Judea, and also among the Gentiles, that they should repent and turn to God and do works *and* live lives consistent with *and* worthy of their repentance.

21 Because of these things the Jews seized me in the temple [r]enclosure and tried to do away with me.

22 [But] to this day I have had the help which comes from God (as my [s]ally), and so I stand here testifying to small and great alike, asserting nothing beyond what the prophets and Moses declared would come to pass;

23 That the Christ, the Anointed One, must suffer; and that He, by being the first to rise from the dead, would declare *and* show light both to the [Jewish] people and to the Gentiles.

24 And as he thus proceeded with his defense, Festus called out loudly, Paul, you are mad! Your great learning is driving you insane!

25 But Paul replied, I am not mad, most noble Festus, but I am uttering the straight, sound truth.

26 For the king understands about these things well enough, and [therefore] to him I speak with bold frankness *and* confidence. I am convinced that not one of these things has escaped his notice, for all this did not take place in a corner—in secret.

27 King Agrippa, do you believe the prophets?—Do you give credence to God's messengers and their words? I perceive *and* know that you do believe.

28 Then Agrippa said to Paul, You think it a small task to make a Christian of me—just off hand to induce me with little ado and persuasion, at very short notice.

29 And Paul replied, Whether short or long, I would to God that not only you but also all who are listening to me today might become such as I am, except for these chains.

30 Then the king arose, and the governor and Bernice and all those who were seated with them;

31 And after they had gone out, they said to one another, This man is doing nothing deserving of death or [even] of imprisonment.

32 And Agrippa said to Festus, This man could have been set at liberty, if he had not appealed to Caesar.

CHAPTER 27

NOW when it was determined that we should sail for Italy, they turned Paul and some other prisoners over to a centurion of the imperial regiment, named Julius.

---

p) Thayer.
q) Abbott-Smith.
r) Trench.
s) Cf. Abbott-Smith.

Living New Testament

17 And I will protect you from both your own people and the Gentiles. Yes, I am going to send you to the Gentiles

18 To open their eyes to their true condition so that they may repent and live in the light of God instead of in Satan's darkness, so that they may receive forgiveness for their sins and God's inheritance along with all people everywhere whose sins are cleansed away, who are set apart by faith in Me.'

19 And so, O King Agrippa, I was not disobedient to that vision from heaven!

20 I preached first to those in Damascus, then in Jerusalem and through Judea, and also to the Gentiles that all must forsake their sins and turn to God—and prove their repentance by doing good deeds.

21 The Jews arrested me in the Temple for preaching this and tried to kill me,

22 But God protected me so that I am still alive today to tell these facts to everyone, both great and small. I teach nothing except what the prophets and Moses said—

23 That the Messiah would suffer, and be the First to rise from the dead, to bring light to Jews and Gentiles alike."

24 Suddenly Festus shouted, "Paul, you are insane. Your long studying has broken your mind!"

25 But Paul replied, "I am not insane, Most Excellent Festus. I speak words of sober truth.

26 And King Agrippa knows about these things. I speak frankly for I am sure these events are all familiar to him, for they were not done in a corner!

27 King Agrippa, do you believe the prophets? But I know you do—"

28 Agrippa interrupted him. "With trivial proofs like these,[5] you expect me to become a Christian?"

29 And Paul replied, "Would to God that whether my arguments are trivial or strong, both you and everyone here in this audience might become the same as I am, except for these chains."

30 Then the king, the governor, Bernice, and all the others stood and left.

31 As they talked it over afterwards they agreed, "This man hasn't done anything worthy of death or imprisonment."

32 And Agrippa said to Festus, "He could be set free if he hadn't appealed to Caesar!"

CHAPTER 27

Arrangements were finally made to start us on our way to Rome by ship; so Paul and several other prisoners were placed in the custody of an officer named Julius, a member of the imperial guard.

[5] Literally, "with little (persuasion)."

Revised Standard

the people and from the Gentiles—to whom
I send you [18]to open their eyes, that they
may turn from darkness to light and from
the power of Satan to God, that they may
receive forgiveness of sins and a place among
those who are sanctified by faith in me.'
19 "Wherefore, O King Agrippa, I was
not disobedient to the heavenly vision, [20]but
declared first to those at Damascus, then at
Jerusalem and throughout all the country of
Judea, and also to the Gentiles, that they
should repent and turn to God and perform
deeds worthy of their repentance. [21]For this
reason the Jews seized me in the temple and
tried to kill me. [22]To this day I have had
the help that comes from God, and so I
stand here testifying both to small and great,
saying nothing but what the prophets and
Moses said would come to pass: [23]that the
Christ must suffer, and that, by being the
first to rise from the dead, he would proclaim light both to the people and to the
Gentiles."

Paul's appeal to Agrippa

24 And as he thus made his defense,
Festus said with a loud voice, "Paul, you
are mad; your great learning is turning you
mad." [25]But Paul said, "I am not mad, most
excellent Festus, but I am speaking the
sober truth. [26]For the king knows about these
things, and to him I speak freely; for I am
persuaded that none of these things have
escaped his notice, for this was not done in
a corner. [27]King Agrippa, do you believe
the prophets? I know that you believe."
[28]And Agrippa said to Paul, "In a short
time you think to make me a Christian!"
[29]And Paul said, "Whether short or long,
I would to God that not only you but also
all who hear me this day might become
such as I am—except for these chains."
30 Then the king rose, and the governor
and Bernice and those who were sitting with
them; [31]and when they had withdrawn, they
said to one another, "This man is doing
nothing to deserve death or imprisonment."
[32]And Agrippa said to Festus, "This man
could have been set free if he had not appealed to Caesar."

Paul sent to Rome

27 And when it was decided that we
should sail for Italy, they delivered
Paul and some other prisoners to a centurion of the Augustan Cohort, named Julius.

King James

2 And entering into a ship of Adramyttium, we launched, meaning to sail by the coasts of Asia; *one* Aristarchus, a Macedonian of Thessalonica, being with us.

3 And the next *day* we touched at Sidon. And Julius courteously entreated Paul, and gave *him* liberty to go unto his friends to refresh himself.

4 And when we had launched from thence, we sailed under Cyprus, because the winds were contrary.

5 And when we had sailed over the sea of Cilicia and Pamphylia, we came to Myra, *a city* of Lycia.

6 And there the centurion found a ship of Alexandria sailing into Italy; and he put us therein.

7 And when we had sailed slowly many days, and scarce were come over against Cnidus, the wind not suffering us, we sailed under Crete, over against Salmone;

8 And, hardly passing it, came unto a place which is called The fair havens; nigh whereunto was the city *of* Lasea.

9 Now when much time was spent, and when sailing was now dangerous, because the fast was now already past, Paul admonished *them,*

10 And said unto them, Sirs, I perceive that this voyage will be with hurt and much damage, not only of the lading and ship, but also of our lives.

11 Nevertheless the centurion believed the master and the owner of the ship, more than those things which were spoken by Paul.

12 And because the haven was not commodious to winter in, the more part advised to depart thence also, if by any means they might attain to Phenice, *and there* to winter; *which is* an haven of Crete, and lieth toward the south-west and north-west.

13 And when the south wind blew softly, supposing that they had obtained *their* purpose, loosing *thence,* they sailed close by Crete.

14 But not long after there arose against it a tempestuous wind, called Euroclydon.

15 And when the ship was caught, and could not bear up into the wind, we let *her* drive.

16 And running under a certain island which is called Clauda, we had much work to come by the boat:

17 Which when they had taken up, they used helps, undergirding the ship; and, fearing lest they should fall into the quicksands, strake sail, and so were driven.

18 And we being exceedingly tossed with a tempest, the next *day* they lightened the ship;

19 And the third *day* we cast out with our own hands the tackling of the ship.

20 And when neither sun nor stars in many days appeared, and no small tempest lay on *us,* all hope that we should be saved was then taken away.

21 But after long abstinence Paul stood forth in the midst of them, and said, Sirs, ye should have hearkened unto me, and not have loosed from Crete, and to have gained this harm and loss.

Amplified

2 And going aboard a ship of Adramyttium, which was about to sail for the ports along the coast of [the province of] Asia, we put out to sea, and Aristarchus, a Macedonian from Thessalonica, accompanied us.

3 The following day we landed at Sidon, and Julius treated Paul in a man-loving way, with much consideration (kindness and care), permitting him to go to his friends [there] and be refreshed *and* be cared for.

4 After putting to sea from there we passed to the leeward [south side] of Cyprus [for protection], for the winds were contrary to us.

5 And when we had sailed over [the whole length] of sea which lies off Cilicia and Pamphylia, we reached Myra in Lycia.

6 There the centurion found an Alexandrian ship bound for Italy, and he transferred us to it.

7 For a number of days we made slow progress, and arrived with difficulty off Cnidus; then, as the wind did not permit us to proceed, we went under the lee (shelter) of Crete off Salmone,

8 And coasting along it with difficulty, we arrived at a place called Fair Havens, near which is located the town of Lasea.

9 But [as the season was well advanced], for much time had been lost and navigation was already dangerous, for the time for the Fast [the day of Atonement, about the middle of September] had already gone by, Paul warned *and* advised them,

10 Saying, Sirs, I perceive [after careful observation] that this voyage will be attended with disaster and much heavy loss, not only of the cargo and the ship but of our lives also.

11 However, the centurion paid greater attention to the pilot and to the owner of the ship than to what Paul said.

12 And as the harbor was not well situated *and* so unsuitable to winter in, the majority favored the plan of putting to sea again from there, hoping somehow to reach Phoenice, a harbor of Crete facing northeast and southeast, and winter there.

13 So when the south wind blew softly, supposing they were gaining their object, they weighed anchor and sailed along Crete, hugging the coast.

14 But soon afterward a violent wind [of the character of a typhoon] called a northeaster, came bursting down from the island.

15 And when the ship was caught and was unable to head against the wind, we gave up and letting her drift were borne along.

16 We ran under the shelter of a small island called Cauda, where we managed with [much] difficulty to draw the [ship's small] boat on deck *and* secure it.

17 After hoisting it on board, they used supports with ropes to undergird *and* brace the ship; then afraid that they would be driven into the Syrtis [quicksands off the north coast of Africa], they lowered the gear [sails and ropes], and so were driven along.

18 As we were being dangerously tossed about by the violence of the storm, the next day they began to throw the freight overboard;

19 And the third day they threw out with their own hands the ship's equipment—the tackle *and* the furniture.

20 And when neither sun nor stars were visible for many days, and no small tempest kept raging about us, all hope of our being saved was finally abandoned.

21 Then as they had eaten nothing for a long time, Paul came forward into their midst and said, Men, you should have listened to me, and should not have put to sea from Crete and brought on this disaster and harm *and* misery *and* loss.

Living New Testament

2 We left on a boat bound for Greece,[1] which was scheduled to make several stops along the Turkish coast.[2] I should add that Aristarchus,[3] a Greek from Thessalonica, was with us.

3 The next day when we docked at Sidon, Julius was very kind to Paul and let him go ashore to visit with friends and receive their hospitality.

4 Putting to sea from there, we encountered headwinds that made it difficult to keep the ship on course, so we sailed north of Cyprus between the island and the mainland,[4]

5 And passed along the coast of the provinces of Cilicia and Pamphylia, landing at Myra, in the province of Lycia.

6 There our officer found an Egyptian ship from Alexandria, bound for Italy, and put us aboard.

7, 8 We had several days of rough sailing, and finally neared Cnidus;[5] but the winds had become too strong, so we ran across to Crete, passing the port of Salmone. Beating into the wind with great difficulty and moving slowly along the southern coast, we arrived at Fair Havens, near the city of Lasea.

9 There we stayed for several days. The weather was becoming dangerous for long voyages by then, because it was late in the year,[6] and Paul spoke to the ship's officers about it.

10 "Sirs," he said, "I believe there is trouble ahead if we go on—perhaps shipwreck, loss of cargo, injuries, and death."

11 But the officers in charge of the prisoners listened more to the ship's captain and the owner than to Paul.

12 And since Fair Havens was an exposed[7] harbor—a poor place to spend the winter—most of the crew advised trying to go further up the coast to Phoenix, in order to winter there; Phoenix was a good harbor with only a northwest and southwest exposure.

13 Just then a light wind began blowing from the south, and it looked like a perfect day for the trip; so they pulled up anchor and sailed along close to shore.

14, 15 But shortly afterwards, the weather changed abruptly and a heavy wind of typhoon strength (a "northeaster," they called it) caught the ship and blew it out to sea. They tried at first to face back to shore but couldn't, so they gave up and let the ship run before the gale.

16 We finally sailed behind a small island named Clauda, where with great difficulty we hoisted aboard the lifeboat that was being towed behind us,

17 And then banded the ship with ropes to strengthen the hull. The sailors were afraid of being driven across to the quicksands of the African coast,[8] so they lowered the topsails and were thus driven before the wind.

18 The next day as the seas grew higher, the crew began throwing the cargo overboard.

19 The following day they threw out the tackle and anything else they could lay their hands on.

20 The terrible storm raged unabated many days,[9] until at last all hope was gone.

[1] Literally, "Adramyttium," a Greek port.
[2] Literally, "the coast of Asia."
[3] See Acts 19:29, 20:4, Philemon 24.
[4] Implied. Literally, "we sailed under the lee of Cyprus." Narratives from that period interpret this as meaning what is indicated in the paraphrase above.
[5] Cnidus was a port on the southeast coast of Turkey.
[6] Literally, "because the Fast was now already gone by." It came at about the time of the autumn equinox.
[7] Implied.
[8] Literally, "fearing lest they should be cast upon the Syrtis."
[9] Literally, "neither sun nor stars shone upon us."

Revised Standard

2 And embarking in a ship of Adramyttium,
which was about to sail to the ports along
the coast of Asia, we put to sea, accompanied by Aristarchus, a Macedonian from
Thessalonica. 3 The next day we put in at
Sidon; and Julius treated Paul kindly, and
gave him leave to go to his friends and be
cared for. 4 And putting to sea from there
we sailed under the lee of Cyprus, because
the winds were against us. 5 And when we
had sailed across the sea which is off Cilicia
and Pamphylia, we came to Myra in Lycia.
6 There the centurion found a ship of Alexandria sailing for Italy, and put us on board.
7 We sailed slowly for a number of days,
and arrived with difficulty off Cnidus, and
as the wind did not allow us to go on, we
sailed under the lee of Crete off Salmone.
8 Coasting along it with difficulty, we came
to a place called Fair Havens, near which
was the city of Lasea.
9 As much time had been lost, and the
voyage was already dangerous because the
fast had already gone by, Paul advised them,
10 saying, "Sirs, I perceive that the voyage
will be with injury and much loss, not only
of the cargo and the ship, but also of
our lives." 11 But the centurion paid more
attention to the captain and to the owner of
the ship than to what Paul said. 12 And because the harbor was not suitable to winter
in, the majority advised to put to sea from
there, on the chance that somehow they
could reach Phoenix, a harbor of Crete,
looking northeast and southeast,[a] and winter
there.

The storm at sea

13 And when the south wind blew gently,
supposing that they had obtained their purpose, they weighed anchor and sailed along
Crete, close inshore. 14 But soon a tempestuous wind, called the northeaster, struck down
from the land; 15 and when the ship was
caught and could not face the wind, we gave
way to it and were driven. 16 And running
under the lee of a small island called Cauda,[b]
we managed with difficulty to secure the
boat; 17 after hoisting it up, they took measures[c] to undergird the ship; then, fearing
that they should run on the Syrtis, they
lowered the gear, and so were driven. 18 As
we were violently storm-tossed, they began
next day to throw the cargo overboard;
19 and the third day they cast out with their
own hands the tackle of the ship. 20 And
when neither sun nor stars appeared for
many a day, and no small tempest lay on
us, all hope of our being saved was at last
abandoned.

[a] Or *southwest and northwest*
[b] Other ancient authorities read *Clauda*
[c] Greek *helps*

King James

22 And now I exhort you to be of good cheer: for there shall be no loss of *any man's* life among you but of the ship.

23 For there stood by me this night the angel of God, whose I am, and whom I serve,

24 Saying, Fear not, Paul; thou must be brought before Cæsar: and, lo, God hath given thee all them that sail with thee.

25 Wherefore, sirs, be of good cheer: for I believe God, that it shall be even as it was told me.

26 Howbeit we must be cast upon a certain island.

27 But when the fourteenth night was come, as we were driven up and down in Adria, about midnight the shipmen deemed that they drew near to some country;

28 And sounded, and found *it* twenty fathoms: and when they had gone a little further, they sounded again, and found *it* fifteen fathoms.

29 Then fearing lest we should have fallen upon rocks, they cast four anchors out of the stern, and wished for the day.

30 And as the shipmen were about to flee out of the ship, when they had let down the boat into the sea, under colour as though they would have cast anchors out of the foreship,

31 Paul said to the centurion and to the soldiers, Except these abide in the ship, ye cannot be saved.

32 Then the soldiers cut off the ropes of the boat, and let her fall off.

33 And while the day was coming on, Paul besought *them* all to take meat, saying, This day is the fourteenth day that ye have tarried and continued fasting, having taken nothing.

34 Wherefore I pray you to take *some* meat: for this is for your health: for there shall not an hair fall from the head of any of you.

35 And when he had thus spoken, he took bread, and gave thanks to God in presence of them all: and when he had broken *it*, he began to eat.

36 Then were they all of good cheer, and they also took *some* meat.

37 And we were in all in the ship two hundred threescore and sixteen souls.

38 And when they had eaten enough, they lightened the ship, and cast out the wheat into the sea.

39 And when it was day, they knew not the land: but they discovered a certain creek with a shore, into the which they were minded, if it were possible, to thrust in the ship.

40 And when they had taken up the anchors, they committed *themselves* unto the sea, and loosed the rudder bands, and hoisted up the mainsail to the wind, and made toward shore.

41 And falling into a place where two seas met, they ran the ship aground; and the forepart stuck fast, and remained unmoveable, but the hinder part was broken with the violence of the waves.

Amplified

22 But [even] now I beg you be in good spirits *and* take heart, for there will be no loss of life among you but only of the ship.

23 For this [very] night there stood by my side an angel of the God to Whom I belong and Whom I serve *and* worship,

24 And he said, Do not be frightened, Paul! It is necessary for you to stand before Caesar; and behold, God has given you all those who are sailing with you.

25 So keep up your courage, men, for I have faith—complete confidence—in God that it will be exactly as it was told me;

26 But we shall have to be stranded on some island.

27 The fourteenth night had come and we were drifting *and* being driven about in the Adriatic Sea, when about midnight the sailors began to suspect that they were drawing near to some land.

28 So they took soundings and found twenty fathoms, and a little farther on they sounded again and found fifteen fathoms.

29 Then fearing that we might fall off [our course] onto rocks, they dropped four anchors from the stern, and kept wishing for daybreak to come.

30 And, as the sailors were trying to escape [secretly] from the ship, and were lowering the small boat into the sea, pretending that they were going to lay out anchors from the bow,

31 Paul said to the centurion and the soldiers, Unless these men remain in the ship, you cannot be saved.

32 Then the soldiers cut away the ropes that held the small boat, and let it fall *and* drift away.

33 While they waited until it should become day, Paul entreated them all to take some food, saying, This is the fourteenth day that you have been continually in suspense *and* on the alert without food, having eaten nothing.

34 So I urge you to take some food for your safety—it will give you strength; for not a hair is to perish from the head of any one of you.

35 Having said these words, he took bread, and giving thanks to God before them all he broke it and began to eat.

36 Then they all became more cheerful *and* were encouraged and took food themselves.

37 All told, there were [t]two hundred and seventy-six souls of us in the ship.

38 And after they had eaten sufficiently, [they proceeded] to lighten the ship, throwing out the wheat into the sea.

39 Now when it was day [and they saw] the land, they did not recognize [it], but they noticed a bay with a beach on which they—taking counsel—purposed to run the ship ashore if they possibly could.

40 So they cut the cables *and* severed the anchors and left them in the sea; at the same time unlashing the ropes that held the rudders, and hoisting the foresail to the wind they headed for the beach.

41 But striking a crosscurrent—a place open to two seas—they ran the ship aground. The prow stuck fast and remained immovable, and the stern began to break up under the violent force of the waves.

---

t) Some ancient authorities read "seventy-six."

Living New Testament

21 No one had eaten for a long time, but finally Paul called the crew together and said, "Men, you should have listened to me in the first place and not left Fair Havens—you would have avoided all this injury and loss!

22 But cheer up! Not one of us will lose our lives, even though the ship will go down.

23 For last night an angel of the God to whom I belong and whom I serve stood beside me,

24 And said, 'Don't be afraid, Paul—for you will surely stand trial before Caesar! What's more, God has granted your request and will save the lives of all those sailing with you.'

25 So take courage! For I believe God! It will be just as He said!

26 But we will be shipwrecked on an island."

27 About midnight on the 14th night of the storm, as we were being driven to and fro on the Adriatic Sea, the sailors suspected land was near.

28 They sounded, and found 120 feet of water below them. A little later they sounded again, and found only 90 feet.

29 At this rate they knew they would soon be driven ashore; and fearing rocks along the coast, they threw out four anchors from the stern and prayed for daylight.

30 Some of the sailors planned to abandon the ship, and lowered the emergency boat as though they were going to put out anchors from the prow.

31 But Paul said to the soldiers and commanding officer, "You will all die unless everyone stays aboard."

32 So the soldiers cut the ropes and let the boat fall off.

33 As the darkness gave way to the early morning light, Paul begged everyone to eat. "You haven't touched food for two weeks," he said.

34 "Please eat something now for your own good! For not a hair of your heads shall perish!"

35 Then he took some hardtack and gave thanks to God before them all, and broke off a piece and ate it.

36 Suddenly everyone felt better and began eating,

37 All two hundred seventy-six of us—for that is the number we had aboard.

38 After eating, the crew lightened the ship further by throwing all the wheat overboard.

39 When it was day, they didn't recognize the coastline, but noticed a bay with a beach and wondered whether they could get between the rocks and be driven up onto the beach.

40 They finally decided to try. Cutting off the anchors and leaving them in the sea, they lowered the rudders, raised the foresail and headed ashore.

41 But the ship hit a sandbar[10] and ran aground. The bow of the ship stuck fast, while the stern was exposed to the violence of the waves and began to break apart.

[10] Literally, "a place where two seas met."

Revised Standard

21 As they had been long without food,
Paul then came forward among them and
said, "Men, you should have listened to me,
and should not have set sail from Crete and
incurred this injury and loss. 22I now bid
you take heart; for there will be no loss of
life among you, but only of the ship. 23For
this very night there stood by me an angel
of the God to whom I belong and whom I
worship, 24and he said, 'Do not be afraid,
Paul; you must stand before Caesar; and
lo, God has granted you all those who sail
with you.' 25So take heart, men, for I have
faith in God that it will be exactly as I have
been told. 26But we shall have to run on
some island."

The shipwreck

27 When the fourteenth night had come,
as we were drifting across the sea of Adria,
about midnight the sailors suspected that
they were nearing land. 28So they sounded
and found twenty fathoms; a little farther
on they sounded again and found fifteen
fathoms. 29And fearing that we might run
on the rocks, they let out four anchors from
the stern, and prayed for day to come. 30And
as the sailors were seeking to escape from
the ship, and had lowered the boat into the
sea, under pretense of laying out anchors
from the bow, 31Paul said to the centurion
and the soldiers, "Unless these men stay in
the ship, you cannot be saved." 32Then the
soldiers cut away the ropes of the boat, and
let it go.
33 As day was about to dawn, Paul urged
them all to take some food, saying, "Today
is the fourteenth day that you have continued in suspense and without food, having
taken nothing. 34Therefore I urge you to take
some food; it will give you strength, since
not a hair is to perish from the head of any
of you." 35And when he had said this, he
took bread, and giving thanks to God in the
presence of all he broke it and began to eat.
36Then they all were encouraged and ate
some food themselves. 37(We were in all two
hundred and seventy-six[d] persons in the ship.)
38And when they had eaten enough, they
lightened the ship, throwing out the wheat
into the sea.
39 Now when it was day, they did not
recognize the land, but they noticed a bay
with a beach, on which they planned if
possible to bring the ship ashore. 40So they
cast off the anchors and left them in the
sea, at the same time loosening the ropes
that tied the rudders; then hoisting the foresail to the wind they made for the beach.
41But striking a shoal[e] they ran the vessel
aground; the bow stuck and remained immovable, and the stern was broken up by

[d] Other ancient authorities read *seventy-six* or *about seventy-six*
[e] Greek *place of two seas*

King James

42 And the soldiers' counsel was to kill the prisoners, lest any of them should swim out, and escape.

43 But the centurion, willing to save Paul, kept them from *their* purpose; and commanded that they which could swim should cast *themselves* first *into the sea,* and get to land:

44 And the rest, some on boards, and some on *broken pieces* of the ship. And so it came to pass, that they escaped all safe to land.

Amplified

42 It was the counsel of the soldiers to kill the prisoners, lest any of them should swim to land and escape;

43 But the centurion, wishing to save Paul, prevented their carrying out their purpose. He commanded those who could swim to throw themselves overboard first and make for the shore,

44 And the rest on heavy boards or pieces of the vessel. And so it was that all escaped safely to land.

CHAPTER 28

AND when they were escaped, then they knew that the island was called Melita.

2 And the barbarous people shewed us no little kindness: for they kindled a fire, and received us every one, because of the present rain, and because of the cold.

3 And when Paul had gathered a bundle of sticks, and laid *them* on the fire, there came a viper out of the heat, and fastened on his hand.

4 And when the barbarians saw the *venomous* beast hang on his hand, they said among themselves, No doubt this man is a murderer, whom, though he hath escaped the sea, yet vengeance suffereth not to live.

5 And he shook off the beast into the fire, and felt no harm.

6 Howbeit they looked when he should have swollen, or fallen down dead suddenly: but after they had looked a great while, and saw no harm come to him, they changed their minds, and said that he was a god.

7 In the same quarters were possessions of the chief man of the island, whose name was Publius; who received us, and lodged us three days courteously.

8 And it came to pass, that the father of Publius lay sick of a fever and of a bloody flux: to whom Paul entered in, and prayed, and laid his hands on him, and healed him.

9 So when this was done, others also, which had diseases in the island, came, and were healed:

10 Who also honoured us with many honours; and when we departed, they laded *us* with such things as were necessary.

11 And after three months we departed in a ship of Alexandria, which had wintered in the isle, whose sign was Castor and Pollux.

12 And landing at Syracuse, we tarried *there* three days.

13 And from thence we fetched a compass, and came to Rhegium: and after one day the south wind blew, and we came the next day to Puteoli:

14 Where we found brethren, and were desired to tarry with them seven days: and so we went toward Rome.

CHAPTER 28

AFTER we were safe on the island, we knew *and* recognized that it was called Malta.

2 And the natives showed us unusual *and* remarkable kindness, for they kindled a fire and welcomed *and* received us all, since it had begun to rain and was cold.

3 Now Paul had gathered a bundle of sticks, and he was laying them on the fire, when a viper crawled out because of the heat and fastened itself on his hand.

4 When the natives saw the little animal hanging from his hand, they said to one another, Doubtless this man is a murderer, for though he has been saved from the sea, Justice [[u]the goddess], avenging, has not permitted that he should live.

5 Then [Paul simply] shook off the small creature into the fire and suffered no evil effects.

6 However, they were waiting, expecting him to swell up or suddenly drop dead; but when they had watched him a long time and saw nothing fatal *or* harmful come to him, they changed their minds and kept saying over and over that he was a god.

7 In the vicinity of that place there were estates belonging to the head man of the island, named Publius, who accepted *and* welcomed *and* entertained us with hearty hospitality for three days.

8 And it happened that the father of Publius was sick in bed with recurring attacks of fever and dysentery; and Paul went to see him, and after praying and laying his hands on him he healed him.

9 After this had occurred, the other people on the island who had diseases also kept coming and were cured.

10 They showed us every respect, *and* presented many gifts to us, honoring us with many honors; and when we sailed, they provided *and* put on [board our ship] everything we needed.

11 It was after three months' stay there that we set sail in a ship which had wintered in the island, an Alexandrian ship, with the Twin Brothers [Castor and Pollux] as its figurehead.

12 We landed at Syracuse and remained there three days,

13 And from there we made a circuit—following the coast—and reached Rhegium, and one day later a south wind sprang up and the next day we arrived at Puteoli.

14 There we found some [Christian] brethren, and were entreated to stay with them for seven days. And so we came to Rome.

u) Souter, Thayer.

Living New Testament

42 The soldiers advised their commanding officer to let them kill the prisoners lest any of them swim ashore and escape.

43 But Julius[11] wanted to spare Paul, so he told them no. Then he ordered all who could swim to jump overboard and make for land.

44 And the rest to try for it on planks and debris from the broken ship. So everyone escaped safely ashore!

Revised Standard

the surf. 42The soldiers' plan was to kill the
prisoners, lest any should swim away and
escape; 43but the centurion, wishing to save
Paul, kept them from carrying out their
purpose. He ordered those who could swim
to throw themselves overboard first and
make for the land, 44and the rest on planks
or on pieces of the ship. And so it was that
all escaped to land.

CHAPTER 28

We soon learned that we were on the island of Malta. The people of the island were very kind to us, building a bonfire on the beach to welcome and warm us in the rain and cold.

3 As Paul gathered an armful of sticks to lay on the fire, a poisonous snake, driven out by the heat, fastened itself onto his hand!

4 The people of the island saw it hanging there and said to each other, "A murderer no doubt! Though he escaped the sea, justice will not permit him to live!"

5 But Paul shook off the snake into the fire and was unharmed.

6 The people waited for him to begin swelling or suddenly fall dead; but when they had waited a long time and no harm came to him, they changed their minds and decided he was a god.

7 Near the shore where we landed was an estate belonging to Publius, the governor of the island. He welcomed us courteously and fed us for three days.

8 As it happened, Publius' father was ill with fever and dysentery. Paul went in and prayed for him, and laying his hands on him, healed him!

9 Then all the other sick people in the island came and were cured.

10 As a result we were showered with gifts,[1] and when the time came to sail, people put on board all sorts of things we would need for the trip.

11 It was three months after the shipwreck before we set sail again, and this time it was in "The Twin Brothers" of Alexandria, a ship that had wintered at the island.

12 Our first stop was Syracuse, where we stayed three days.

13 From there we circled around to Rhegium; a day later a south wind began blowing, so the following day we arrived at Puteoli,

14 Where we found some believers! They begged us to stay with them seven days. Then, we sailed on to Rome.

The stopover at Malta

28 After we had escaped, we then
learned that the island was called
Malta. 2And the natives showed us unusual
kindness, for they kindled a fire and welcomed us all, because it had begun to rain
and was cold. 3Paul had gathered a bundle
of sticks and put them on the fire, when a
viper came out because of the heat and
fastened on his hand. 4When the natives
saw the creature hanging from his hand,
they said to one another, "No doubt this
man is a murderer. Though he has escaped
from the sea, justice has not allowed him
to live." 5He, however, shook off the creature
into the fire and suffered no harm. 6They
waited, expecting him to swell up or suddenly fall down dead; but when they had waited
a long time and saw no misfortune come to
him, they changed their minds and said that
he was a god.

7 Now in the neighborhood of that place
were lands belonging to the chief man of the
island, named Publius, who received us and
entertained us hospitably for three days. 8It
happened that the father of Publius lay sick
with fever and dysentery; and Paul visited
him and prayed, and putting his hands on
him healed him. 9And when this had taken
place, the rest of the people on the island
who had diseases also came and were cured.
10They presented many gifts to us;[f] and
when we sailed, they put on board whatever
we needed.

11 After three months we set sail in a
ship which had wintered in the island, a
ship of Alexandria, with the Twin Brothers
as figurehead. 12Putting in at Syracuse, we
stayed there for three days. 13And from
there we made a circuit and arrived at Rhegium; and after one day a south wind
sprang up, and on the second day we came
to Puteoli. 14There we found brethren, and
were invited to stay with them for seven
days. And so we came to Rome. 15And the

---

[11] Implied.
[1] Literally, "honors."

[f] Or *honored us with many honors*

King James

15 And from thence, when the brethren heard of us, they came to meet us as far as Appii forum, and The three taverns: whom when Paul saw, he thanked God, and took courage.

16 And when we came to Rome, the centurion delivered the prisoners to the captain of the guard: but Paul was suffered to dwell by himself with a soldier that kept him.

17 And it came to pass, that after three days Paul called the chief of the Jews together: and when they were come together, he said unto them, Men *and* brethren, though I have committed nothing against the people, or customs of our fathers, yet was I delivered prisoner from Jerusalem into the hands of the Romans.

18 Who, when they had examined me, would have let *me* go, because there was no cause of death in me.

19 But when the Jews spake against *it,* I was constrained to appeal unto Cæsar; not that I had aught to accuse my nation of.

20 For this cause therefore have I called for you to see *you,* and to speak with *you:* because that for the hope of Israel I am bound with this chain.

21 And they said unto him, We neither received letters out of Judæa concerning thee, neither any of the brethren that came shewed or spake any harm of thee.

22 But we desire to hear of thee what thou thinkest: for as concerning this sect, we know that every where it is spoken against.

23 And when they had appointed him a day, there came many to him into *his* lodging; to whom he expounded and testified the kingdom of God, persuading them concerning Jesus, both out of the law of Moses, and *out of* the prophets, from morning till evening.

24 And some believed the things which were spoken, and some believed not.

25 And when they agreed not among themselves, they departed, after that Paul had spoken one word, Well spake the Holy Ghost by Esaias the prophet unto our fathers,

26 Saying, Go unto this people, and say, Hearing ye shall hear, and shall not understand; and seeing ye shall see, and not perceive:

27 For the heart of this people is waxed gross, and their ears are dull of hearing, and their eyes have they closed; lest they should see with *their* eyes, and hear with *their* ears, and understand with *their* heart, and should be converted, and I should heal them.

28 Be it known therefore unto you, that the salvation of God is sent unto the Gentiles, and *that* they will hear it.

29 And when he had said these words, the Jews departed, and had great reasoning among themselves.

30 And Paul dwelt two whole years in his own hired house, and received all that came in unto him,

31 Preaching the kingdom of God, and teaching those things which concern the Lord Jesus Christ, with all confidence, no man forbidding him.

Amplified

15 And the [Christian] brethren there, having had news of us, came as far as the Forum of Appius and the Three Taverns to meet us. When Paul saw them, he thanked God and received new courage.

16 When we arrived at Rome, *the centurion delivered the prisoners to the captain of the guard, but* Paul was permitted to live by himself with the soldier who guarded him.

17 Three days after [our arrival], he called together the leading local Jews; and when they had gathered, he said to them, Brethren, though I have done nothing against the people or against the customs of our forefathers, yet I was turned over as a prisoner from Jerusalem into the hands of the Romans.

18 After they had examined me, they were ready to release me, because I was innocent of any offense deserving the death penalty.

19 But when the Jews protested, I was forced to appeal to Caesar, though it was not because I had any charge to make against my nation.

20 This is the reason therefore why I have begged to see you and to talk with you, since it is because of the Hope of Israel [the Messiah] that I am bound with this chain.

21 And they answered him, We have not received any letters about you from Judea, and none of the [Jewish] brethren coming here has reported or spoken anything evil about you.

22 But we think it fitting *and* are eager to hear from you what it is that you have in mind, *and* believe, *and* what your opinion is, for with regard to this sect it is known to all of us that it is everywhere denounced.

23 So when they had set a day with him, they came in large numbers to his lodging. And he fully set forth *and* explained the matter to them, from morning until night, testifying to the kingdom of God and trying to persuade them concerning Jesus both from the Law of Moses and from the prophets.

24 And some were convinced *and* believed what he said, and others did not believe.

25 And as they disagreed among themselves, they began to leave, [but not before] Paul had added one statement [more]: The Holy Spirit was right in saying through Isaiah the prophet to your forefathers:

26 Go to this people, and say to them, You will indeed hear *and* hear with your ears, but will not understand; and you will indeed look *and* look with your eyes, but will not see—not perceive, have knowledge of or become acquainted with what you look at, at all.

27 For the heart—the understanding, the soul—of this people has grown dull (stupid, hardened and calloused), and their ears are heavy *and* hard of hearing, and they have shut tight their eyes, so that they may not perceive *and* have knowledge *and* become acquainted with their eyes, and hear with their ears, and understand with their souls, and turn (to Me, be converted) that I may heal them. [Isa. 6:9, 10.]

28 So let it be understood by you then that [this message of] the salvation of God has been sent to the Gentiles, and they will listen [to it]! [Ps. 67:2.]

29 *And when he had said these things, the Jews went away, arguing and disputing among themselves.*

30 After this Paul lived there for two entire years at his own expense, in his own rented lodging, and he welcomed all who came to him,

31 Preaching to them the kingdom of God and teaching them about the Lord Jesus Christ with boldness *and* quite openly, and without being molested *or* hindered. *Amen—so be it.*

Living New Testament

15 The brothers in Rome had heard we were coming and came to meet us at the Forum[2] on the Appian Way. Others joined us at The Three Taverns.[3] When Paul saw them, he thanked God and took courage.

16 When we arrived in Rome, Paul was permitted to live wherever he wanted to, though guarded by a soldier.

17 Three days after his arrival, he called together the local Jewish leaders and spoke to them as follows:

"Brothers, I was arrested by the Jews in Jerusalem and handed over to the Roman government for prosecution, even though I had harmed no one nor violated the customs of our ancestors.

18 The Romans gave me a trial and wanted to release me, for they found no cause for the death sentence demanded by the Jewish leaders.

19 But when the Jews protested the decision, I felt it necessary, with no malice against them, to appeal to Caesar.

20 I asked you to come here today so we could get acquainted and I could tell you that it is because I believe the Messiah[4] has come that I am bound with this chain."

21 They replied, "We have heard nothing against you! We have had no letters from Judea or reports from those arriving from Jerusalem.[5]

22 But we want to hear what you believe, for the only thing we know about these Christians is that they are denounced everywhere!"

23 So a time was set and on that day large numbers came to his house. He told them about the Kingdom of God and taught them about Jesus from the Scriptures—from the five books of Moses and the books of prophecy. He began lecturing in the morning and went on into the evening!

24 Some believed, and some didn't.

25 But after they had argued back and forth among themselves, they left with this final word from Paul ringing in their ears: "The Holy Spirit was right when He said through Isaiah the prophet,

26 'Say to the Jews, "You will hear and see but not understand,

27 For your hearts are too fat and your ears don't listen and you have closed your eyes against understanding, for you don't want to see and hear and understand and turn to Me to heal you.'[6]

28, 29[7] So I want you to realize that this salvation from God is available to the Gentiles too, and they will accept it."

30 Paul lived for the next two years in his rented house[8] and welcomed all who visited him,

31 Telling them with all boldness about the Kingdom of God and about the Lord Jesus Christ; and no one tried to stop him.

---

[2] About 43 miles from Rome.
[3] About 35 miles from Rome.
[4] Literally, "the hope of Israel." But perhaps he is referring here as in his other defenses to his belief in the resurrection of the dead.
[5] Implied.
[6] Isaiah 6:9,10.
[7] Some of the ancient manuscripts add, "And when he had said these words, the Jews departed, having much dissenting among themselves."
[8] Or, "at his own expense."

Revised Standard

brethren there, when they heard of us, came
as far as the Forum of Appius and Three
Taverns to meet us. On seeing them Paul
thanked God and took courage. 16 And when
we came into Rome, Paul was allowed to
stay by himself, with the soldier that guarded him.

The arrival at Rome

17 After three days he called together the
local leaders of the Jews; and when they
had gathered, he said to them, "Brethren,
though I had done nothing against the
people or the customs of our fathers, yet I
was delivered prisoner from Jerusalem into
the hands of the Romans. 18 When they had
examined me, they wished to set me at liberty, because there was no reason for the
death penalty in my case. 19 But when the
Jews objected, I was compelled to appeal to
Caesar—though I had no charge to bring
against my nation. 20 For this reason therefore I have asked to see you and speak with
you, since it is because of the hope of Israel
that I am bound with this chain." 21 And
they said to him, "We have received no
letters from Judea about you, and none of
the brethren coming here has reported or
spoken any evil about you. 22 But we desire
to hear from you what your views are; for
with regard to this sect we know that everywhere it is spoken against."

23 When they had appointed a day for
him, they came to him at his lodging in
great numbers. And he expounded the matter to them from morning till evening, testifying to the kingdom of God and trying to
convince them about Jesus both from the
law of Moses and from the prophets. 24 And
some were convinced by what he said, while
others disbelieved. 25 So, as they disagreed
among themselves, they departed, after Paul
had made one statement: "The Holy Spirit
was right in saying to your fathers through
Isaiah the prophet:

26 'Go to this people, and say,
You shall indeed hear but never understand,
and you shall indeed see but never perceive.
27 For this people's heart has grown dull,
and their ears are heavy of hearing,
and their eyes they have closed;
lest they should perceive with their eyes,
and hear with their ears,
and understand with their heart,
and turn for me to heal them.'
28 Let it be known to you then that this salvation of God has been sent to the Gentiles;
they will listen."[g]

30 And he lived there two whole years
at his own expense,[h] and welcomed all who
came to him, 31 preaching the kingdom of
God and teaching about the Lord Jesus quite
openly and unhindered.

---

[g] Other ancient authorities add verse 29, *And when he had said these words, the Jews departed, holding much dispute among themselves*
[h] Or *in his own hired dwelling*

King James

THE EPISTLE OF PAUL THE APOSTLE
TO THE

Romans

CHAPTER 1

PAUL, a servant of Jesus Christ, called *to be* an apostle separated unto the gospel of God,

2 (Which he had promised afore by his prophets in the holy scriptures,)

3 Concerning his Son Jesus Christ our Lord, which was made of the seed of David according to the flesh;

4 And declared *to be* the Son of God with power, according to the spirit of holiness, by the resurrection from the dead:

5 By whom we have received grace and apostleship, for obedience to the faith among all nations, for his name:

6 Among whom are ye also the called of Jesus Christ:

7 To all that be in Rome, beloved of God, called *to be* saints: Grace to you and peace from God our Father, and the Lord Jesus Christ.

8 First, I thank my God through Jesus Christ for you all, that your faith is spoken of throughout the whole world.

9 For God is my witness, whom I serve with my spirit in the gospel of his Son, that without ceasing I make mention of you always in my prayers;

10 Making request, if by any means now at length I might have a prosperous journey by the will of God to come unto you.

11 For I long to see you, that I may impart unto you some spiritual gift, to the end ye may be established;

12 That is, that I may be comforted together with you by the mutual faith both of you and me.

13 Now I would not have you ignorant, brethren, that oftentimes I purposed to come unto you, (but was let hitherto,) that I might have some fruit among you also, even as among other Gentiles.

14 I am debtor both to the Greeks, and to the Barbarians; both to the wise, and to the unwise.

15 So, as much as in me is, I am ready to preach the gospel to you that are at Rome also.

16 For I am not ashamed of the gospel of Christ: for it is the power of God unto salvation to every one that believeth; to the Jew first, and also to the Greek.

Amplified

THE LETTER OF PAUL
TO THE

Romans

CHAPTER 1

FROM Paul, a bond servant of Jesus Christ, the Messiah, called to be an apostle, a (special messenger) set apart to [preach] the Gospel (good news) of *and* from God,

2 Which He promised in advance [long ago] through His prophets in the sacred Scriptures,

3 [The Gospel] regarding His Son, Who as to the flesh (His human nature) was descended from David;

4 And [as to His divine nature] according to the Spirit of holiness, was openly [a]designated the Son of God in power—in a striking, triumphant and miraculous manner —by His resurrection from the dead, even Jesus Christ our Lord, the Messiah, the Anointed One.

5 It is through Him that we have received grace—God's unmerited favor—and [our] apostleship to promote obedience to the faith *and* make disciples for His name's sake among all the nations,

6 And this includes yourselves, called of Jesus Christ *and* invited [as you are] to belong to Him.

7 To [you then,] all God's beloved ones in Rome, called to be saints *and* designated for a consecrated life: Grace *and* spiritual blessing and peace be yours from God our Father and from the Lord Jesus Christ.

8 First, I thank my God through Jesus Christ for all of you, because [the report of] your faith is made known to all the world *and* is [a]commended everywhere.

9 For God is my witness, Whom I serve with [all] my spirit—rendering priestly and spiritual service—in [preaching] the Gospel *and* telling the good news of His Son, how incessantly I always mention you when at my prayers.

10 I keep pleading that somehow by God's will I may now at last be prospered *and* come to you.

11 For I am yearning to see you, that I may impart *and* share with you some spiritual gift to strengthen *and* establish you;

12 That is, that we may be mutually strengthened *and* encouraged *and* comforted by each other's faith, both yours and mine.

13 I want you to know, brethren, that many times I have planned *and* intended to come to you, though thus far I have been hindered *and* prevented, in order that I might have some fruit—some result of my labors—among you, as I have among the rest of the Gentiles.

14 Both to Greeks and to barbarians (to the cultured and to the uncultured), both to the wise and the foolish I have an obligation to discharge *and* a duty to perform *and* a debt to pay.

15 So, for my part, I am willing *and* eagerly ready to preach the Gospel to you also who are in Rome.

16 For I am not ashamed of the Gospel (good news) *of Christ*; for it is God's power working unto salvation (for deliverance from eternal death) to every one who believes *with* a personal trust *and* a confident surrender *and* firm reliance, to the Jew first and also to the Greek,

---

a) Vincent.

Living New Testament

Romans

CHAPTER 1

Dear Friends in Rome,

1 This letter is from Paul, Jesus Christ's slave, chosen to be a missionary, and sent out to preach God's Good News.

2 This Good News was promised long ago by God's prophets in the Old Testament.

3 It is the Good News about His Son, Jesus Christ our Lord, who came as a human baby, born into King David's royal family line;

4 And by being raised from the dead He was proved to be the mighty Son of God, with the holy nature of God Himself.

5 And now, through Christ, all the kindness of God has been poured out upon us undeserving sinners; and now He is sending us out around the world to tell all people everywhere the great things God has done for them, so that they, too, will believe and obey Him.

6, 7 And you, dear friends in Rome, are among those He dearly loves; you, too, are invited by Jesus Christ to be God's very own—yes, His holy people. May all God's mercies and peace be yours from God our Father and from Jesus Christ our Lord.

* * * * * * *

8 Let me say first of all that wherever I go I hear you being talked about! For your faith in God is becoming known around the world. How I thank God through Jesus Christ for this good report, and for each one of you.

9 God knows how often I pray for you. Day and night I bring you and your needs in prayer to the one I serve with all my might, telling others the Good News about His Son.

10 And one of the things I keep on praying for is the opportunity, God willing,[1] to come at last to see you and, if possible, that I will have a safe trip.[2]

11, 12 For I long to visit you so that I can impart to you the faith[3] that will help your church grow strong in the Lord. Then, too, I need your help, for I want not only to share my faith with you but to be encouraged by yours: Each of us will be a blessing to the other.

13 I want you to know, dear brothers, that I planned to come many times before (but was prevented) so that I could work among you and see good results, just as I have among the other Gentile churches.[4]

14 For I owe a great debt to you and to everyone else, both to civilized peoples and heathen nations; yes, to the educated and uneducated alike.

15 So, to the fullest extent of my ability, I am ready to come also to you in Rome to preach God's Good News.

16 For I am not ashamed of this Good News about Christ. It is God's powerful method of bringing all who believe it to heaven. This message was preached first to the Jews alone, but now everyone is invited to come to God in this same way.

---

1 Literally, "in the will of God."
2 Or, "that I will finally succeed in coming."
3 Literally, "some spiritual gift . . . that is, . . . faith."
4 Literally, "among the Gentiles."

Revised Standard

Romans

Salutation

1 Paul, a servant[a] of Jesus Christ, called
to be an apostle, set apart for the gospel
of God 2which he promised beforehand
through his prophets in the holy scriptures,
3the gospel concerning his Son, who was
descended from David according to the flesh
4and designated Son of God in power according to the Spirit of holiness by his resurrection from the dead, Jesus Christ our Lord,
5through whom we have received grace and
apostleship to bring about the obedience of
faith for the sake of his name among all
the nations, 6including yourselves who are
called to belong to Jesus Christ;
7 To all God's beloved in Rome, who
are called to be saints:
Grace to you and peace from God our
Father and the Lord Jesus Christ.

Thanksgiving

8 First, I thank my God through Jesus
Christ for all of you, because your faith is
proclaimed in all the world. 9For God is
my witness, whom I serve with my spirit in
the gospel of his Son, that without ceasing
I mention you always in my prayers, 10asking
that somehow by God's will I may now at
last succeed in coming to you. 11For I long
to see you, that I may impart to you some
spiritual gift to strengthen you, 12that is, that
we may be mutually encouraged by each
other's faith, both yours and mine. 13I want
you to know, brethren, that I have often
intended to come to you (but thus far have
been prevented), in order that I may reap
some harvest among you as well as among
the rest of the Gentiles. 14I am under obligation both to Greeks and to barbarians,
both to the wise and to the foolish: 15so I
am eager to preach the gospel to you also
who are in Rome.

Theme

16 For I am not ashamed of the gospel:
it is the power of God for salvation to
every one who has faith, to the Jew first

---

[a] Or *slave*

King James

17 For therein is the righteousness of God revealed from faith to faith: as it is written, The just shall live by faith.

18 For the wrath of God is revealed from heaven against all ungodliness and unrighteousness of men, who hold the truth in unrighteousness;

19 Because that which may be known of God is manifest in them; for God hath shewed *it* unto them.

20 For the invisible things of him from the creation of the world are clearly seen, being understood by the things that are made, *even* his eternal power and Godhead; so that they are without excuse:

21 Because that, when they knew God, they glorified *him* not as God, neither were thankful; but became vain in their imaginations, and their foolish heart was darkened.

22 Professing themselves to be wise, they became fools,

23 And changed the glory of the uncorruptible God into an image made like to corruptible man, and to birds, and fourfooted beasts, and creeping things.

24 Wherefore God also gave them up to uncleanness through the lusts of their own hearts, to dishonour their own bodies between themselves:

25 Who changed the truth of God into a lie, and worshipped and served the creature more than the Creator, who is blessed for ever. Amen.

26 For this cause God gave them up unto vile affections: for even their women did change the natural use into that which is against nature:

27 And likewise also the men, leaving the natural use of the woman, burned in their lust one toward another; men with men working that which is unseemly, and receiving in themselves that recompence of their error which was meet.

28 And even as they did not like to retain God in *their* knowledge, God gave them over to a reprobate mind, to do those things which are not convenient;

29 Being filled with all unrighteousness, fornication, wickedness, covetousness, maliciousness; full of envy, murder, debate, deceit, malignity; whisperers,

30 Backbiters, haters of God, despiteful, proud, boasters, inventors of evil things, disobedient to parents,

31 Without understanding, covenantbreakers, without natural affection, implacable, unmerciful:

32 Who knowing the judgment of God, that they which commit such things are worthy of death, not only do the same, but have pleasure in them that do them.

Amplified

17 For in the Gospel a righteousness which God ascribes is revealed, both springing from faith and leading to faith—disclosed through the way of faith that arouses to more faith. As it is written, The man who through faith is just *and* upright shall live *and* [b]shall live by faith. [Hab. 2:4.]

18 For God's [holy] wrath *and* indignation are revealed from heaven against all ungodliness and unrighteousness of men, who in their wickedness repress *and* hinder the truth *and* make it inoperative.

19 For that which is known about God is evident to them *and* made plain in their inner consciousness, because God [Himself] has shown it to them.

20 For ever since the creation of the world His invisible nature *and* attributes, that is, His eternal power and divinity have been made intelligible *and* clearly discernible in *and* through the things that have been made—His handiworks. So [men] are without excuse—altogether without any defense or justification; [Ps. 19:1-4.]

21 Because when they knew *and* recognized Him as the God, they did not honor *and* glorify Him as God, or give Him thanks. But instead they became futile *and* [c]godless in their thinking — with vain imaginings, foolish reasoning and stupid speculations — and their senseless minds were darkened.

22 Claiming to be wise, they became fools — professing to be smart, they made simpletons of themselves.

23 And by them the glory and majesty *and* excellence of the immortal God were exchanged for *and* represented by images, resembling mortal man and birds and beasts and reptiles.

24 Therefore God gave them up in the lusts of their [own] hearts to sexual impurity, to the dishonoring of their bodies among themselves, abandoning them to the degrading power of sin.

25 Because they exchanged the truth of God for a lie and worshipped and served the creature rather than the Creator, Who is blessed forever! Amen — so be it. [Jer. 2:11.]

26 For this reason God gave them over *and* abandoned them to vile affections *and* degrading passions. For their women exchanged their natural function for an unnatural *and* abnormal one;

27 And the men also turned from natural relations with women and were set ablaze (burned out, consumed) with lust for one another, men committing shameful acts with men and suffering in their own [d]bodies *and* personalities the inevitable consequences *and* penalty of their wrong doing *and* going astray, which was [their] fitting retribution.

28 And so, since they did not see fit to acknowledge God *or* approve of Him *or* consider Him worth the knowing, God gave them over to a base *and* condemned mind to do things not proper *or* decent *but* loathsome;

29 Until they were filled — permeated and saturated — with every kind of unrighteousness, iniquity, grasping *and* covetous greed, [and] malice. [They were] full of envy *and* jealousy, murder, strife, deceit *and* treachery, ill will *and* cruel ways. [They were] secret backbiters *and* gossipers,

30 Slanderers, hateful to *and* hating God, full of insolence, arrogance [and] boasting; inventors of new forms of evil, disobedient *and* undutiful to parents.

31 [They were] without understanding, conscienceless *and* faithless, heartless *and* loveless [and] merciless.

32 Though they are fully aware of God's righteous decree that those who do such things deserve to die, they not only do them themselves but approve *and* applaud others who practice them.

---

b) Alternate reading.
c) Souter.
d) Webster, defining "selves."

Living New Testament

17 This Good News tells us that God makes us ready for heaven—makes us right in God's sight—when we put our faith and trust in Christ to save us. This is accomplished from start to finish by faith.[5] As the Scripture says it, "The man who finds life will find it through trusting God."[6]

18 But God shows His anger from heaven against all sinful, evil men who push away the truth from them.

19 For the truth about God is known to them instinctively[7]; God has put this knowledge in their hearts.

20 Since earliest times men have seen the earth and sky and all God made, and have known of His existence and great eternal power. So they will have no excuse [when they stand before God at Judgment Day[8]].

21 Yes, they knew about Him all right, but they wouldn't admit it or worship Him or even thank Him for all His daily care. And after awhile they began to think up silly ideas of what God was like and what He wanted them to do. The result was that their foolish minds became dark and confused.

22 Claiming themselves to be wise without God, they became utter fools instead.

23 And then, instead of worshiping the glorious, ever-living God, they took wood and stone and made idols for themselves, carving them to look like mere birds and animals and snakes and puny[9] men.

24 So God let them go ahead into every sort of sex sin, and do whatever they wanted to—yes, vile and sinful things with each other's bodies.

25 Instead of believing what they knew was the truth about God, they deliberately chose to believe lies. So they prayed to the things God made, but wouldn't obey the blessed God who made these things.

26 That is why God let go of them and let them do all these evil things, so that even their women turned against God's natural plan for them and indulged in sex sin with each other.

27 And the men, instead of having a normal sex relationship with women, burned with lust for each other, men doing shameful things with other men and, as a result, getting paid within their own souls with the penalty they so richly deserved.

28 So it was that when they gave God up and would not even acknowledge Him, God gave them up to doing everything their evil minds could think of.

29 Their lives became full of every kind of wickedness and sin, of greed and hate, envy, murder, fighting, lying, bitterness, and gossip.

30 They were backbiters, haters of God, insolent, proud braggarts, always thinking of new ways of sinning and continually being disobedient to their parents.

31 They tried to misunderstand,[10] broke their promises, and were heartless—without pity.

32 They were fully aware of God's death penalty for these crimes, yet they went right ahead and did them anyway, and encouraged others to do them, too.

[5] Literally: "(this) righteousness of God is *revealed* from faith to faith."
[6] Habakkuk 2:4.
[7] Literally, "is manifest in them."
[8] Implied. Or, "They have no excuse for saying there is no God."
[9] Literally, "mortal."
[10] Or, "were confused fools."

Revised Standard

and also to the Greek. 17For in it the righteousness of God is revealed through faith for faith; as it is written, "He who through faith is righteous shall live."[b]

The Gentiles: guilty before God

18 For the wrath of God is revealed from heaven against all ungodliness and wickedness of men who by their wickedness suppress the truth. 19For what can be known about God is plain to them, because God has shown it to them. 20Ever since the creation of the world his invisible nature, namely, his eternal power and deity, has been clearly perceived in the things that have been made. So they are without excuse; 21for although they knew God they did not honor him as God or give thanks to him, but they became futile in their thinking and their senseless minds were darkened. 22Claiming to be wise, they became fools, 23and exchanged the glory of the immortal God for images resembling mortal man or birds or animals or reptiles.

24 Therefore God gave them up in the lusts of their hearts to impurity, to the dishonoring of their bodies among themselves, 25because they exchanged the truth about God for a lie and worshiped and served the creature rather than the Creator, who is blessed for ever! Amen.

26 For this reason God gave them up to dishonorable passions. Their women exchanged natural relations for unnatural, 27and the men likewise gave up natural relations with women and were consumed with passion for one another, men committing shameful acts with men and receiving in their own persons the due penalty for their error.

28 And since they did not see fit to acknowledge God, God gave them up to a base mind and to improper conduct. 29They were filled with all manner of wickedness, evil, covetousness, malice. Full of envy, murder, strife, deceit, malignity, they are gossips, 30slanderers, haters of God, insolent, haughty, boastful, inventors of evil, disobedient to parents, 31foolish, faithless, heartless, ruthless. 32Though they know God's decree that those who do such things deserve to die, they not only do them but approve those who practice them.

[b] Or *The righteous shall live by faith*

King James

CHAPTER 2

THEREFORE thou art inexcusable, O man, whosoever thou art that judgest: for wherein thou judgest another, thou condemnest thyself; for thou that judgest doest the same things.

2 But we are sure that the judgment of God is according to truth against them which commit such things.

3 And thinkest thou this, O man, that judgest them which do such things, and doest the same, that thou shalt escape the judgment of God?

4 Or despisest thou the riches of his goodness and forbearance and longsuffering; not knowing that the goodness of God leadeth thee to repentance?

5 But after thy hardness and impenitent heart treasurest up unto thyself wrath against the day of wrath and revelation of the righteous judgment of God;

6 Who will render to every man according to his deeds:

7 To them who by patient continuance in well-doing seek for glory and honour and immortality, eternal life:

8 But unto them that are contentious, and do not obey the truth, but obey unrighteousness, indignation and wrath,

9 Tribulation and anguish, upon every soul of man that doeth evil, of the Jew first, and also of the Gentile;

10 But glory, honour, and peace, to every man that worketh good, to the Jew first, and also to the Gentile;

11 For there is no respect of persons with God.

12 For as many as have sinned without law shall also perish without law: and as many as have sinned in the law shall be judged by the law;

13 (For not the hearers of the law *are* just before God, but the doers of the law shall be justified.

14 For when the Gentiles, which have not the law, do by nature the things contained in the law, these, having not the law, are a law unto themselves:

15 Which shew the work of the law written in their hearts, their conscience also bearing witness, and *their* thoughts the mean while accusing or else excusing one another;)

16 In the day when God shall judge the secrets of men by Jesus Christ according to my gospel.

17 Behold, thou art called a Jew, and restest in the law, and makest thy boast of God,

Amplified

CHAPTER 2

THEREFORE you have no excuse *or* defense *or* justification, O man, whoever you are who judges *and* condemns another. For in posing as judge *and* passing sentence on another you condemn yourself, because you who judge are habitually practicing the very same things [that you censure and denounce].

2 [But] we know that the judgment (adverse verdict, sentence) of God falls justly *and* in accordance with truth upon those who practice such things.

3 And do you think *or* imagine, O man, when you judge *and* condemn those who practice such things and yet do them yourself, that you will escape God's judgment *and* elude His sentence *and* adverse verdict?

4 Or are you [so blind as] to trifle with *and* presume upon *and* despise *and* underestimate the wealth of His kindness and forbearance and long-enduring patience? Are you unmindful or actually ignorant [of the fact] that God's kindness is intended to lead you to repent — [e]to change your mind and inner man to accept God's will?

5 But by your callous stubbornness and impenitence of heart you are storing up wrath and indignation for yourself on the day of wrath and indignation, when God's righteous judgement (just doom) will be revealed.

6 For He will render to every man according to his works — justly, as his deeds deserve: [Ps. 62:12.]

7 To those who by patient persistence in welldoing [[f]springing from piety] seek for [unseen but sure] glory and honor and [[f]the eternal blessedness of] immortality, He will give eternal life.

8 But for those who are self-seeking *and* self-willed *and* disobedient to the Truth but responsive to wickedness, there will be indignation and wrath.

9 [And] there will be tribulation *and* anguish and calamity *and* constraint for every soul of man who (habitually) does evil, the Jew first and also the Greek.

10 But glory and honor and heart-peace shall be awarded to every one who (habitually) does good, the Jew first and also [g]the Greek.

11 For God shows no partiality ([h]undue favor, or unfairness; with Him one man is not different from another). [Deut. 10:17; II Chron. 19:7.]

12 All who have sinned without the Law will also perish without [regard to] the Law, and all who have sinned under the Law will be judged *and* condemned by the Law.

13 For it is not merely hearing the Law [read] that makes one righteous before God, but it is the doers of the Law who will be held guiltless *and* acquitted *and* justified.

14 When Gentiles who have not [the divine] Law do instinctively what the Law requires, they are a law to themselves, since they do not have the Law.

15 They show that the essential requirements of the Law are written in their hearts *and* are operating there; with which their conscience (sense of right and wrong) also bears witness; and their [moral] [i]decisions — their arguments of reason, their condemning or approving [j]thoughts — will accuse or perhaps defend *and* excuse [them]

16 On that day when, as my Gospel proclaims, God by Jesus Christ will judge men in regard to [j]the things which they conceal — their hidden thoughts. [Eccl. 12:14.]

17 But if you bear the name of Jew and rely upon the Law and pride yourselves in God *and* your relationship to Him,

---

e) Souter.
f) Thayer.
g) A Pauline term for Gentile.
h) Moulton and Milligan.
i) Thayer.
j) Alford, Vincent, AV, ASV, etc.

Living New Testament

CHAPTER 2

Well," you may be saying, "what terrible people you have been talking about!" But wait a minute! You are just as bad. When you say they are wicked and should be punished, you are talking about yourselves, for you do these very same things.

2 And we know that God, in justice, will punish anyone who does such things as these.

3 Do you think that God will judge and condemn others for doing them and overlook you when you do them, too?

4 Don't you realize how patient He is being with you? Or don't you care? Can't you see that He has been waiting all this time without punishing you, to give you time to turn from your sin? His kindness is meant to lead you to repentance.

5 But no, you won't listen; and so you are saving up terrible punishment for yourselves because of your stubbornness in refusing to turn from your sin; for there is going to come a day of wrath when God will be the just Judge of all the world.

6 He will give each one whatever his deeds deserve:

7 He will give eternal life to those who patiently do the will of God,[1] seeking for the unseen[2] glory and honor and eternal life that He offers.[2]

8 But He will terribly punish those who fight against the truth of God and walk in evil ways—God's anger will be poured out upon them.

9 There will be sorrow and suffering for Jews and Gentiles alike who keep on sinning.

10 But there will be glory and honor and peace from God for all who obey Him,[3] whether they are Jews or Gentiles.

11 For God treats everyone the same.

12, 13, 14, 15 He will punish sin wherever it is found. He will punish the heathen when they sin, even though they never had God's written laws, for down in their hearts they know right from wrong. God's laws are written within them; their own conscience accuses them, or sometimes excuses them. And God will punish the Jews for sinning because they have His written laws but don't obey them. They know what is right but don't do it. After all, salvation is not given to those who know what to do, unless they do it.

16 The day will surely come when at God's command Jesus Christ will judge the secret lives of everyone, their inmost thoughts and motives; this is all part of God's great plan which I proclaim.

17 You Jews think all is well between yourselves and God because He gave His laws to you;[4] you brag that you are His special friends.

---

[1] Literally, "who patiently do good."
[2] Implied.
[3] Literally, "all who do good."
[4] Or, "you rely upon the law for your salvation."

Revised Standard

God's principles of judgment

2 Therefore you have no excuse, O man,
whoever you are, when you judge another; for in passing judgment upon him
you condemn yourself, because you, the
judge, are doing the very same things. [2]We
know that the judgment of God rightly falls
upon those who do such things. [3]Do you
suppose, O man, that when you judge those
who do such things and yet do them yourself, you will escape the judgment of God?
[4]Or do you presume upon the riches of his
kindness and forbearance and patience? Do
you not know that God's kindness is meant
to lead you to repentance? [5]But by your
hard and impenitent heart you are storing
up wrath for yourself on the day of wrath
when God's righteous judgment will be revealed. [6]For he will render to every man
according to his works: [7]to those who by
patience in well-doing seek for glory and
honor and immortality, he will give eternal
life; [8]but for those who are factious and do
not obey the truth, but obey wickedness,
there will be wrath and fury. [9]There will
be tribulation and distress for every human
being who does evil, the Jew first and also
the Greek, [10]but glory and honor and peace
for every one who does good, the Jew first
and also the Greek. [11]For God shows no
partiality.

12 All who have sinned without the law
will also perish without the law, and all who
have sinned under the law will be judged
by the law. [13]For it is not the hearers of
the law who are righteous before God, but
the doers of the law who will be justified.
[14]When Gentiles who have not the law do
by nature what the law requires, they are
a law to themselves, even though they do
not have the law. [15]They show that what the
law requires is written on their hearts, while
their conscience also bears witness and their
conflicting thoughts accuse or perhaps excuse them [16]on that day when, according
to my gospel, God judges the secrets of
men by Christ Jesus.

The Jews guilty before God

17 But if you call yourself a Jew and
rely upon the law and boast of your rela-

King James

18 And knowest *his* will, and approvest the things that are more excellent, being instructed out of the law;

19 And art confident that thou thyself art a guide of the blind, a light of them which are in darkness,

20 An instructor of the foolish, a teacher of babes, which hast the form of knowledge and of the truth in the law.

21 Thou therefore which teachest another, teachest thou not thyself? thou that preachest a man should not steal, dost thou steal?

22 Thou that sayest a man should not commit adultery, dost thou commit adultery? thou that abhorrest idols, dost thou commit sacrilege?

23 Thou that makest thy boast of the law, through breaking the law dishonourest thou God?

24 For the name of God is blasphemed among the Gentiles through you, as it is written.

25 For circumcision verily profiteth, if thou keep the law: but if thou be a breaker of the law, thy circumcision is made uncircumcision.

26 Therefore if the uncircumcision keep the righteousness of the law, shall not his uncircumcision be counted for circumcision?

27 And shall not uncircumcision which is by nature, if it fulfil the law, judge thee, who by the letter and circumcision dost transgress the law?

28 For he is not a Jew, which is one outwardly; neither *is that* circumcision, which is outward in the flesh:

29 But he *is* a Jew, which is one inwardly; and circumcision *is that* of the heart, in the spirit, *and* not in the letter; whose praise *is* not of men, but of God.

Amplified

18 And know *and* understand His will and discerningly approve the better things *and* have a sense of what is vital, because you are instructed by the Law;

19 And if you are confident that you [yourself] are a guide to the blind, a light to those who are in darkness, and [that

20 You are] a corrector of the foolish, a teacher of the childish, having in the Law the embodiment of knowledge and truth;

21 Well then, you who teach others, do you not teach yourself? While you teach against stealing, do you steal — take what does not really belong to you?

22 You who say not to commit adultery, do you commit adultery — are you unchaste in action or in thought? You who abhor *and* loathe idols, do you rob temples — appropriate to your own use what is consecrated to God, thus robbing the sanctuary and [k]doing sacrilege?

23 You who boast in the Law, do you dishonor God by breaking the Law — by stealthily infringing upon or carelessly neglecting or openly breaking it?

24 For, as it is written, The name of God is maligned *and* blasphemed among the Gentiles because of you! — The words to this effect are from [your own] Scriptures. [Isa. 52:5; Ezek. 36:20.]

25 Circumcision does indeed profit if you keep the Law; but if you habitually transgress the Law; your circumcision is made uncircumcision.

26 So, if a man who is uncircumcised keeps the requirements of the Law, will not his uncircumcision be credited to him [as equivalent to] circumcision?

27 Then those who are physically uncircumcised but keep the Law will condemn you who, although you have the code in writing and have circumcision, break the Law.

28 For he is not a [real] Jew who is only one outwardly *and* publicly, nor is [true] circumcision something external and physical.

29 But he is a Jew who is one inwardly, and [true] circumcision is of the heart, a spiritual and not a literal [matter]. His praise is not from men but from God.

CHAPTER 3

WHAT advantage then hath the Jew? or what profit *is there* of circumcision?

2 Much every way: chiefly, because that unto them were committed the oracles of God.

3 For what if some did not believe? shall their unbelief make the faith of God without effect?

4 God forbid: yea, let God be true, but every man a liar; as it is written, That thou mightest be justified in thy sayings, and mightest overcome when thou art judged.

5 But if our unrighteousness commend the righteousness of God, what shall we say? *Is* God unrighteous who taketh vengeance? (I speak as a man)

CHAPTER 3

THEN what advantage remains to the Jew? — How is he favored? Or what is the value *or* benefit of circumcision?

2 Much in every way. To begin with, to the Jews were entrusted the oracles (the brief communications, the intentions, the utterances) of God. [Ps. 147:19.]

3 What if some did not believe *and* were without faith? Does their lack of faith *and* their faithlessness nullify *and* make ineffective *and* void the faithfulness of God *and* His fidelity [to His Word]?

4 By no means! Let God be found true though every human being be false *and* a liar, as it is written, That You may be justified *and* shown to be upright in what You say, and prevail when You are judged [by sinful men]. [Ps 51:4.]

5 But if our unrighteousness thus establishes *and* exhibits the righteousness of God, what shall we say? That God is unjust *and* wrong to inflict His wrath upon us [Jews]? I speak in a [purely] human way.

---

k) Moulton and Milligan.

Living New Testament

18 Yes, you know what He wants; you know right from wrong and favor the right because you have been taught His laws from earliest youth.

19 You are so sure of the way to God that you could point it out to a blind man. You think of yourselves as beacon lights, directing men lost in darkness to God.

20 You think that you can guide the simple and teach even children the affairs of God, for you really know His laws, which are full of all knowledge and truth.

21 Yes, you teach others—then why don't you teach yourselves? You tell others not to steal—do *you* steal?

22 You say it is wrong to commit adultery—do *you* do it? You say, "Don't pray to idols," and then make money your god instead.[5]

23 You are so proud of knowing God's laws, *but you dishonor Him by breaking them.*

24 No wonder the Scriptures say that the world speaks evil of God because of you.

25 Being a Jew is worth something if you obey God's laws; but if you don't, then you are no better off than the heathen.

26 And if the heathen obey God's laws, won't God give them all the rights and honors He planned to give the Jews?

27 In fact, those heathen will be much better off[6] than you Jews who know so much about God and have His promises but don't obey His laws.

28 For you are not real Jews just because you were born of Jewish parents or because you have gone through the Jewish initiation ceremony of circumcision.

29 No, a real Jew is anyone whose heart is right with God. For God is not looking for those who cut their bodies in actual body circumcision, but He is looking for those with changed hearts and minds. Whoever has that kind of change in his life will get his praise from God, even if not from you.

Revised Standard

tion to God 18and know his will and approve what is excellent, because you are instructed in the law, 19and if you are sure
that you are a guide to the blind, a light to
those who are in darkness, 20a corrector of
the foolish, a teacher of children, having in
the law the embodiment of knowledge and
truth—21you then who teach others, will
you not teach yourself? While you preach
against stealing, do you steal? 22You who
say that one must not commit adultery, do
you commit adultery? You who abhor idols,
do you rob temples? 23You who boast in
the law, do you dishonor God by breaking
the law? 24For, as it is written, "The name
of God is blasphemed among the Gentiles
because of you."

25 Circumcision indeed is of value if you
obey the law; but if you break the law, your
circumcision becomes uncircumcision. 26So,
if a man who is uncircumcised keeps the
precepts of the law, will not his uncircumcision be regarded as circumcision? 27Then
those who are physically uncircumcised but
keep the law will condemn you who have
the written code and circumcision but break
the law. 28For he is not a real Jew who is
one outwardly, nor is true circumcision
something external and physical. 29He is a
Jew who is one inwardly, and real circumcision is a matter of the heart, spiritual and
not literal. His praise is not from men but
from God.

CHAPTER 3

Then what's the use of being a Jew? Are there any special benefits for them from God? Is there any value in the Jewish circumcision ceremony?

2 Yes, being a Jew has many advantages. First of all, God trusted them with His laws [so that they could know and do His will[1]].

3 True, some of them were unfaithful, but just because they broke their promises to God, does that mean God will break His promises to those who love Him?

4 Of course not! Though everyone else in the world is a liar, God is not. Do you remember what the book of Psalms says about this?[2] That God's words will always prove true and right, no matter who questions them.

5 "But," some say, "our breaking faith with God is good, our sins serve a good purpose, for people will notice how good God is when they see how bad we are. Is it fair, then, for Him to punish us when our sins are helping Him?" (That is the way some people talk.)

[5] Literally, "do you rob temples?"
[6] Literally, "will condemn" you.
[1] Implied.
[2] Psalm 51:4.

3 Then what advantage has the Jew? Or
what is the value of circumcision?
2Much in every way. To begin with, the Jews
are entrusted with the oracles of God. 3What
if some were unfaithful? Does their unfaithfulness nullify the faithfulness of God? 4By
no means! Let God be true though every man
be false, as it is written.

"That thou mayest be justified in thy
words,
and prevail when thou art judged."

5But if our wickedness serves to show the
justice of God, what shall we say? That God
is unjust to inflict wrath on us? (I speak in

King James

6 God forbid: for then how shall God
judge the world?
7 For if the truth of God hath more
abounded through my lie unto his glory;
why yet am I also judged as a sinner?
8 And not *rather,* (as we be slanderously
reported, and as some affirm that we say,)
Let us do evil, that good may come? whose
damnation is just.
9 What then? are we better *than they?*
No, in no wise: for we have before proved
both Jews and Gentiles, that they are all
under sin;
10 As it is written, There is none righteous, no, not one:
11 There is none that understandeth,
there is none that seeketh after God.
12 They are all gone out of the way, they
are together become unprofitable; there is
none that doeth good, no, not one.
13 Their throat *is* an open sepulchre;
with their tongues they have used deceit; the
poison of asps *is* under their lips:
14 Whose mouth *is* full of cursing and
bitterness:
15 Their feet *are* swift to shed blood:
16 Destruction and misery *are* in their
ways:
17 And the way of peace have they not
known:
18 There is no fear of God before their
eyes.
19 Now we know that what things soever
the law saith, it saith to them who are under
the law: that every mouth may be stopped,
and all the world may become guilty before
God.
20 Therefore by the deeds of the law
there shall no flesh be justified in his sight:
for by the law *is* the knowledge of sin.
21 But now the righteousness of God
without the law is manifested, being witnessed by the law and the prophets;
22 Even the righteousness of God *which*
is by faith of Jesus Christ unto all and upon
all them that believe: for there is no difference:
23 For all have sinned, and come short
of the glory of God;
24 Being justified freely by his grace
through the redemption that is in Christ
Jesus:
25 Whom God hath set forth *to be* a
propitiation through faith in his blood, to
declare his righteousness for the remission of
sins that are past, through the forbearance
of God;
26 To declare, *I say,* at this time his
righteousness: that he might be just, and
the justifier of him which believeth in
Jesus.

Amplified

6 By no means! Otherwise, how could God judge the
world?
7 But [you say,] if through my falsehood God's integrity
is magnified *and* advertised *and* abounds to His glory,
why am I still being judged as a sinner?
8 And why should we not do evil that good may come?
as some slanderously charge us with teaching. Such [false
teaching] is justly condemned by them.
9 Well then, are we [Jews] superior *and* better off than
they? No, not at all. We have already charged that all
men, both Jews and Greeks, are under sin — held down
by and subject to its power and control.
10 As it is written, None is righteous, just *and* truthful
and upright *and* conscientious, no, not one. [Ps. 14:3.]
11 No one understands — no one intelligently discerns
or comprehends; no one seeks out God. [Ps. 14:2.]
12 All have turned aside; together they have gone
wrong *and* have become unprofitable *and* worthless; no
one does right, not even one!
13 Their throat is a yawning grave; they use their
tongues to deceive — to mislead and to deal treacherously. The venom of asps is beneath their lips. [Ps. 5:9;
140:3.]
14 Their mouth is full of cursing and bitterness. [Ps.
10:7.]
15 Their feet are swift to shed blood.
16 Destruction (as it dashes them to pieces) and misery mark their ways.
17 And they have no experience of the way of peace
— they know nothing about peace, for a peaceful way
they do not even recognize. [Isa. 59:7, 8.]
18 There is no (reverential) fear of God before their
eyes. [Ps. 36:1.]
19 Now we know that whatever the Law says it speaks
to those who are under the Law, so that [the murmurs
and excuses of] every mouth may be hushed, and all the
world may be held accountable to God.
20 For no person will be justified — made righteous,
acquitted and judged acceptable — in His sight by observing the works prescribed by the Law. For [the real function of] the Law is to make men recognize *and* be conscious of sin [[l]not mere perception, but an acquaintance
with sin which works toward repentance, faith and holy
character].
21 But now the righteousness of God has been revealed
independently *and* altogether apart from law, although
actually it is attested by the Law and the prophets,
22 Namely, the righteousness of God which comes by
believing *with* personal trust *and* confident reliance on
Jesus Christ, the Messiah. [And it is meant] for all who
believe. For there is no distinction,
23 Since all have sinned and are falling short of the
honor *and* glory [l]which God bestows *and* receives.
24 [All] are justified *and* made upright *and* in right
standing with God, freely *and* gratuitously by His grace
(His unmerited favor and mercy), through the redemption
which is [provided] in Christ Jesus,
25 Whom God put forward [[m]before the eyes of all] as
a mercy seat *and* propitiation by His blood — the cleansing and life-giving sacrifice of atonement and reconciliation — [to be received] through faith. This was to show
God's righteousness, because in His divine forbearance He
had passed over *and* ignored former sins without punishment.
26 It was to demonstrate *and* prove at the present
time ([n]in the now season) that He Himself is righteous
and that He justifies *and* accepts as righteous him who has
[true] faith in Jesus.

---

l) Vincent.
m) Bengel.
n) Literal translation.

Living New Testament

6 God forbid! Then what kind of God would He be, to overlook sin? How could He ever condemn anyone?

7 For He could not judge and condemn me as a sinner if my dishonesty brought Him glory by pointing up His honesty in contrast to my lies.

8 If you follow through with that idea you come to this: the worse we are, the better God likes it! But the damnation of those who say such things is just. Yet some claim that this is what I preach!

9 Well, then, are we Jews *better* than others? No, not at all, for we have already shown that all men alike are sinners, whether Jews or Gentiles.

10 As the Scriptures say, "No one is good—no one in all the world is innocent."[3]

11 No one has ever really followed God's paths, or even truly wanted to.

12 Every one has turned away; all have gone wrong. No one anywhere has kept on doing what is right; not one.

13 Their talk is foul and filthy like the stench from an open grave.[4] Their tongues are loaded with lies. Everything they say has in it the sting and poison of deadly snakes.

14 Their mouths are full of cursing and bitterness.

15 They are quick to kill, hating anyone who disagrees with them.[5]

16 Wherever they go they leave misery and trouble behind them,

17 And they have never known what it is to feel secure or enjoy God's blessing.

18 They care nothing about God nor what He thinks of them.

19 So the judgment of God lies very heavily upon the Jews, for they are responsible to keep God's law instead of doing all these evil things; not one of them has any excuse; in fact, all the world stands hushed and guilty before Almighty God.

20 Now do you see it? No one can ever be made right in God's sight by doing what the law commands. For the more we know of God's laws, the clearer it becomes that we aren't obeying them; His laws serve only to make us see that we are sinners.

21, 22 But now God has shown us a different way to heaven[6]—not by "being good enough" and trying to keep His laws, but by a new way (though not new, really, for the Old Testament told about it long ago). Now God says He will accept and acquit us—declare us "not guilty"—if we trust Jesus Christ to take away our sins. And we all can be saved in this same way, by coming to Christ, no matter who we are or what we have been like.

23 Yes, all have sinned; all fall short of God's glorious ideal;

24 Yet now God declares us "not guilty" of offending Him, if we trust in Jesus Christ, who in His kindness freely takes away our sins.

25 For God sent Christ Jesus to take the punishment for our sins and to end all God's anger against us. He used Christ's blood and our faith as the means of saving us from His wrath.[7] In this way He was being entirely fair, even though He did not punish those who sinned in former times. For He was looking forward to the time when Christ would come and take away those sins.

26 And now in these days also He can receive sinners in this same way, because Jesus took away their sins. But isn't this unfair for God to let criminals go free, and say that they are innocent? No, for He does it on the basis of their trust in Jesus who took away their sins.

---

[3] Psalm 14:13.
[4] Literally, "their throat is an open grave." Perhaps the meaning is "their speech injures others."
[5] Implied.
[6] Implied. Literally, "A righteousness of God has been manifested."
[7] Literally, "to be a propitiation."

Revised Standard

a human way.) 6By no means! For then how
could God judge the world? 7But if through
my falsehood God's truthfulness abounds to
his glory, why am I still being condemned
as a sinner? 8And why not do evil that good
may come?—as some people slanderously
charge us with saying. Their condemnation
is just.

The world: guilty before God

9 What then? Are we Jews any better
off?[c] No, not at all; for I[d] have already
charged that all men, both Jews and Greeks
are under the power of sin, 10as it is written:
"None is righteous, no, not one;
11 no one understands, no one seeks for God.
12 All have turned aside, together they have
gone wrong;
no one does good, not even one."
13 "Their throat is an open grave,
they use their tongues to deceive."
"The venom of asps is under their lips."
14 "Their mouth is full of curses and bitterness."
15 "Their feet are swift to shed blood,
16 in their paths are ruin and misery,
17 and the way of peace they do not know."
18 "There is no fear of God before their
eyes."

19 Now we know that whatever the law
says it speaks to those who are under the
law, so that every mouth may be stopped,
and the whole world may be held accountable to God. 20For no human being will be
justified in his sight by works of the law,
since through the law comes knowledge of
sin.

Faith: the means of salvation

21 But now the righteousness of God has
been manifested apart from law, although
the law and the prophets bear witness to it,
22the righteousness of God through faith in
Jesus Christ for all who believe. For there
is no distinction; 23since all have sinned and
fall short of the glory of God, 24they are
justified by his grace as a gift, through the
redemption which is in Christ Jesus, 25whom
God put forward as an expiation by his
blood, to be received by faith. This was to
show God's righteousness, because in his
divine forbearance he had passed over former sins; 26it was to prove at the present
time that he himself is righteous and that he
justifies him who has faith in Jesus.

---

[c] Or *at any disadvantage?*
[d] Greek *we*

King James

27 Where *is* boasting then? It is excluded. By what law? of works? Nay: but by the law of faith.

28 Therefore we conclude that a man is justified by faith without the deeds of the law.

29 *Is he* the God of the Jews only? *is he* not also of the Gentiles? Yes, of the Gentiles also:

30 Seeing *it is* one God which shall justify the circumcision by faith, and uncircumcision through faith.

31 Do we then make void the law through faith? God forbid: yea, we establish the law.

Amplified

27 Then what becomes of [our] pride *and* [our] boasting? It is excluded — banished, ruled out entirely. On what principle? [On the principle] of doing good deeds? No, but on the principle of faith.

28 For we hold that a man is justified *and* made upright by faith independent of *and* distinctly apart from good deeds (works of law). — The observance of the Law has nothing to do with justification.

29 Or is God merely [the God] of Jews? Is He not the God of Gentiles also? Yes, of Gentiles also,

30 Since it is one and the same God Who will justify the circumcised by faith [[o]which germinated from Abraham] and the uncircumcised through their [newly acquired] faith. — [For] it is the same trusting faith in both cases, a firmly relying faith [in Jesus Christ].

31 Do we then by [this] faith make the Law of no effect, overthrow it *or* make it a dead letter? Certainly not! On the contrary, we confirm *and* establish *and* uphold the Law.

CHAPTER 4

WHAT shall we say then that Abraham our father, as pertaining to the flesh, hath found?

2 For if Abraham were justified by works, he hath *whereof* to glory; but not before God.

3 For what saith the scripture? Abraham believed God, and it was counted unto him for righteousness.

4 Now to him that worketh is the reward not reckoned of grace, but of debt.

5 But to him that worketh not, but believeth on him that justifieth the ungodly, his faith is counted for righteousness.

6 Even as David also describeth the blessedness of the man, unto whom God imputeth righteousness without works,

7 *Saying*, Blessed *are* they whose iniquities are forgiven, and whose sins are covered.

8 Blessed *is* the man to whom the Lord will not impute sin.

9 *Cometh* this blessedness then upon the circumcision *only*, or upon the uncircumcision also? for we say that faith was reckoned to Abraham for righteousness.

10 How was it then reckoned? when he was in circumcision, or in uncircumcision? Not in circumcision, but in uncircumcision.

11 And he received the sign of circumcision, a seal of the righteousness of the faith which *he had yet* being uncircumcised: that he might be the father of all them that believe, though they be not circumcised: that righteousness might be imputed unto them also:

CHAPTER 4

[BUT] if so, what shall we say about Abraham, our forefather humanly speaking? (How does this affect his position, and what [p]was gained by him?)

2 For if Abraham was justified (that is, [q]established as just by acquittal from guilt) by good works [that he did, then] he has grounds for boasting. But not before God!

3 For what does the Scripture say? Abraham believed (trusted in) God, and it was credited to his account as righteousness — right living and right standing with God. [Gen. 15:6.]

4 Now to a laborer, his wages are not counted as a favor *or* a gift, but as an obligation — something owed to him.

5 But to one who not working [by Law] trusts (believes fully) in Him Who justifies the ungodly, his faith is credited to him as righteousness — the standing acceptable to God.

6 Thus David [r]congratulates the man *and* pronounces a blessing on him to whom God credits righteousness apart from the works he does:

7 Blessed *and* happy *and* [r]to be envied are those whose iniquities are forgiven and whose sins are covered up *and* completely buried.

8 Blessed *and* happy *and* [r]to be envied is the person of whose sin the Lord will take no account *nor* reckon it against him. [Ps. 32:1, 2.]

9 Is this blessing (this happiness) then meant only for the circumcised, or also for the uncircumcised? We say that faith was credited to Abraham as righteousness.

10 How then was it credited [to him]? Was it before or after he had been circumcised? It was not after, but before he was circumcised.

11 He received the mark of circumcision as a token *or* an evidence or seal of the righteousness which he had by faith while he was still uncircumcised, [faith] that he was to be made the father of all who [truly] believe though without circumcision and who thus have righteousness (right standing with God) imputed to them *and* credited to their account,

---

o) Vincent.
p) Some ancient authorities so read.
q) Cremer.
r) Souter.

Living New Testament

27 Then what can we boast about doing, to earn our salvation? Nothing at all. Why? Because our acquittal is not based on our good deeds; it is based on what Christ has done and our faith in Him.

28 So it is that we are saved[8] by faith in Christ and not by the good things we do.

29 And does God save only the Jews in this way? No, the Gentiles too may come to Him in this same manner.

30 God treats us all the same; all, whether Jews or Gentiles, are acquitted if they have faith.

31 Well then, if we are saved by faith, does this mean that we no longer need obey God's laws? Just the opposite! In fact, only when we trust Jesus can we truly obey Him.

Revised Standard

27 Then what becomes of our boasting?
It is excluded. On what principle? On the
principle of works? No, but on the principle of faith. 28 For we hold that a man is
justified by faith apart from works of law.
29 Or is God the God of Jews only? Is
he not the God of Gentiles also? Yes, of
Gentiles also, 30 since God is one; and he
will justify the circumcised on the ground
of their faith and the uncircumcised through
their faith. 31 Do we then overthrow the
law by this faith? By no means! On the
contrary, we uphold the law.

CHAPTER 4

Abraham was, humanly speaking, the founder of our Jewish nation. What were his experiences concerning this question of being saved by faith? Was it because of his good deeds that God accepted him? If so, then he would have something to boast about. But from God's point of view Abraham had no basis at all for pride.

3 For the Scriptures tell us Abraham *believed God,* and that is why God canceled his sins and declared him "not guilty."

4, 5 But didn't he earn his right to heaven by all the good things he did? No, for being saved is a gift; if a person could earn it by being good, then it wouldn't be free—but it is! It is *given* to those who do *not* work for it. For God declares sinners to be good in His sight if they have faith in Christ to save them from God's wrath.[1]

6 King David spoke of this, describing the happiness of an undeserving sinner who is declared "not guilty"[2] by God.

7 "Blessed, and to be envied," he said, "are those whose sins are forgiven and put out of sight.

8 Yes, what joy there is for anyone whose sins are no longer counted against him by the Lord."[3]

9 Now then, the question: Is this blessing given only to those who have faith in Christ but also keep the Jewish laws, or is the blessing also given to those who do not keep the Jewish rules, but only trust in Christ? Well, what about Abraham? We say that he received these blessings through his faith. Was it by faith alone? Or because he also kept the Jewish rules?

10 For the answer to that question, answer this one: *When* did God give this blessing to Abraham? It was *before he became a Jew*—before he went through the Jewish initiation ceremony of circumcision.

11 It wasn't until later on, *after* God had promised to bless him *because of his faith,* that he was circumcised. The circumcision ceremony was a sign that Abraham already had faith and that God had already accepted him and declared him just and good in His sight—before the ceremony took place. So Abraham is the spiritual father of those who believe and are saved without obeying Jewish laws. We see, then, that those who do not keep these rules are justified by God through faith.

---

[8] Literally, "justified."
[1] Literally, "Faith is reckoned for righteousness."
[2] Literally, "righteous."
[3] Psalm 32:1-2.

Abraham saved by faith

4 What then shall we say about[e] Abraham, our forefather according to the
flesh? 2 For if Abraham was justified by
works, he has something to boast about, but
not before God. 3 For what does the scripture say? "Abraham believed God, and it
was reckoned to him as righteousness."
4 Now to one who works, his wages are not
reckoned as a gift but as his due. 5 And to
one who does not work but trusts him who
justifies the ungodly, his faith is reckoned as
righteousness. 6 So also David pronounces a
blessing upon the man to whom God reck-
ons righteousness apart from works:
7 "Blessed are those whose iniquities are
forgiven, and whose sins are covered;
8 blessed is the man against whom the
Lord will not reckon his sin."
9 Is this blessing pronounced only upon
the circumcised, or also upon the uncircumcised? We say that faith was reckoned to
Abraham as righteousness. 10 How then was
it reckoned to him? Was it before or after
he had been circumcised? It was not after,
but before he was circumcised. 11 He received circumcision as a sign or seal of the
righteousness which he had by faith while
he was still uncircumcised. The purpose was
to make him the father of all who believe
without being circumcised and who thus
have righteousness reckoned to them, 12 and

---

[e] Other ancient authorities read *was gained by*

King James

12 And the father of circumcision to them who are not of the circumcision only, but who also walk in the steps of that faith of our father Abraham, which *he had* being *yet* uncircumcised.

13 For the promise, that he should be the heir of the world, *was* not to Abraham, or to his seed, through the law, but through the righteousness of faith.

14 For if they which are of the law *be* heirs, faith is made void, and the promise made of none effect:

15 Because the law worketh wrath: for where no law is, *there is* no transgression.

16 Therefore *it is* of faith, that *it might be* by grace; to the end the promise might be sure to all the seed; not to that only which is of the law, but to that also which is of the faith of Abraham; who is the father of us all,

17 (As it is written, I have made thee a father of many nations,) before him whom he believed, *even* God, who quickeneth the dead, and calleth those things which be not as though they were.

18 Who against hope believed in hope, that he might become the father of many nations, according to that which was spoken, So shall thy seed be.

19 And being not weak in faith, he considered not his own body now dead, when he was about an hundred years old, neither yet the deadness of Sarah's womb:

20 He staggered not at the promise of God through unbelief; but was strong in faith, giving glory to God;

21 And being fully persuaded that, what he had promised, he was able also to perform.

22 And therefore it was imputed to him for righteousness.

23 Now it was not written for his sake alone, that it was imputed to him;

24 But for us also, to whom it shall be imputed, if we believe on him that raised up Jesus our Lord from the dead;

25 Who was delivered for our offences, and was raised again for our justification.

Amplified

12 As well as to make him the father of those circumcised persons, who are not merely circumcised, but also walk in the way of that faith which our father Abraham had before he was circumcised.

13 For the promise to Abraham or his posterity, that he should inherit the world, did not come through [observing the commands of] the Law but through the righteousness of faith. [Gen. 17:4-6; 22:16-18.]

14 If it is the adherents of the Law who are to be the heirs, then faith is made futile *and* empty of all meaning, and the promise [of God] is made void — is annulled and has no power.

15 For the Law results in [divine] wrath, but where there is no law there is no transgression [of it either].

16 Therefore [inheriting] the promise is the outcome of faith *and* depends [entirely] on faith, in order that it might be given as an act of grace (unmerited favor), to make it stable *and* valid *and* guaranteed to all his descendants; not only to the devotees *and* adherents of the Law but also to those who share the faith of Abraham, who is [thus] the father of us all,

17 As it is written, I have made you the father of many nations. — He was appointed our father — in the sight of God in Whom he believed, Who gives life to the dead and speaks of the nonexistent things that [He has foretold and promised] as if they [already] existed. [Gen. 17:5.]

18 [For Abraham, human reason for] hope being gone, hoped on in faith that he should become the father of many nations, as he had been promised, So [numberless] shall your descendants be. [Gen. 15:5.]

19 He did not weaken in faith when he considered the [utter] impotence of his own body, which was as good as dead because he was about a hundred years old, or [when he considered] the barrenness of Sarah's (deadened) womb. [Gen. 17:17; 18:11.]

20 No unbelief *or* distrust made him waver *or* doubtingly question concerning the promise of God, but he grew strong *and* was empowered by faith as he gave praise *and* glory to God,

21 Fully satisfied *and* assured that God was able *and* mighty to keep His word *and* to do what He had promised.

22 That is why his faith was accredited to him as righteousness — right standing with God.

23 But [the words], it was accredited to him, were written not for his sake alone,

24 But [they were written] for our sakes too. [Righteousness, standing acceptable to God] will be granted *and* accredited to us also who believe — trust in, adhere to and rely on — God Who raised Jesus our Lord from the dead,

25 Who was betrayed and put to death because of our misdeeds and was raised to secure our justification — our [s]acquittal, and to make our account balance, absolving us from all guilt before God.

CHAPTER 5

THEREFORE being justified by faith, we have peace with God through our Lord Jesus Christ:

CHAPTER 5

THEREFORE, since we are justified — [s]acquitted, declared righteous, and given a right standing with God — through faith, let us [grasp the fact that we] have [the peace of reconciliation] to hold *and* to [t]enjoy, peace with God through our Lord Jesus Christ, the Messiah, the Anointed One.

s) Abbott-Smith.
t) Literally, "have" or "hold," so "enjoy."

Living New Testament

12 And Abraham is also the spiritual father of those Jews who have been circumcised. They can see from his example that it is not this ceremony that saves them, for Abraham found favor with God by faith alone, *before he was circumcised.*

13 It is clear, then, that God's promise to give the whole earth to Abraham and his descendants was not because Abraham obeyed God's law but because he trusted God to keep His promise.

14 So if you still claim that God's blessings go to those who are "good enough," then you are saying that God's promises to those who have faith are meaningless, and faith is foolish.

15 But the fact of the matter is this: when we try to gain God's blessing and salvation by keeping His laws we always end up under His anger, for we always fail to keep them. The only way we can keep from breaking laws is not to have any to break!

16 So God's blessings are given to us by faith, as a free gift; we are certain to get them whether or not we follow Jewish customs if we have faith like Abraham's, for Abraham is the father of us all when it comes to these matters of faith.

17 That is what the Scriptures mean when they say that God made Abraham the father of many nations. God will accept all people in every nation who trust God as Abraham did. And this promise is from God Himself, who makes the dead live again and speaks of future events with as much certainty as though they were already past!

18 So, when God told Abraham that He would give him a son who would have many descendants and become a great nation, Abraham believed God even though such a promise just couldn't come to pass!

19 And because his faith was strong, he didn't worry about the fact that he was far too old to be a father, at the age of one hundred, and that Sarah his wife, at ninety,[4] was also much too old to have a baby.

20 But Abraham never doubted. He believed God, for his faith and trust grew ever stronger, and he praised God for this blessing even before it happened.

21 He was completely sure that God was well able to do anything He promised.

22 And because of Abraham's faith God forgave his sins and declared him "not guilty."

23 Now this wonderful statement—that he was accepted and approved through his faith—wasn't just for Abraham's benefit.

24 It was for us, too, assuring us that God will accept us in the same way He accepted Abraham—when we believe the promises of God Who brought back Jesus our Lord from the dead.

25 He died for our sins and rose again to make us right with God, filling us with God's goodness.[5]

Revised Standard

likewise the father of the circumcised who are not merely circumcised but also follow the example of the faith which our father Abraham had before he was circumcised.

13 The promise to Abraham and his descendants, that they should inherit the world,
did not come through the law but through
the righteousness of faith. 14 If it is the adherents of the law who are to be the heirs,
faith is null and the promise is void. 15 For
the law brings wrath, but where there is no
law there is no transgression.
16 That is why it depends on faith, in
order that the promise may rest on grace
and be guaranteed to all his descendants—
not only to the adherents of the law but also
to those who share the faith of Abraham,
for he is the father of us all, 17 as it is written, "I have made you the father of many
nations"—in the presence of the God in
whom he believed, who gives life to the
dead and calls into existence the things that
do not exist. 18 In hope he believed against
hope, that he should become the father of
many nations; as he had been told, "So
shall your descendants be." 19 He did not
weaken in faith when he considered his own
body, which was as good as dead because
he was about a hundred years old, or when
he considered the barrenness of Sarah's
womb. 20 No distrust made him waver concerning the promise of God, but he grew
strong in his faith as he gave glory to God,
21 fully convinced that God was able to do
what he had promised. 22 That is why his
faith was "reckoned to him as righteousness." 23 But the words, "it was reckoned to
him," were written not for his sake alone,
24 but for ours also. It will be reckoned to
us who believe in him that raised from the
dead Jesus our Lord, 25 who was put to
death for our trespasses and raised for our
justification.

CHAPTER 5

So now, since we have been made right in God's sight by faith in His promises, we can have real peace with Him because of what Jesus Christ our Lord has done for us.

Results of justification by faith

5 Therefore, since we are justified by faith,
we[f] have peace with God through our
Lord Jesus Christ. 2 Through him we have

[4] Genesis 17:17.
[5] Literally, "raised for our justification."

[f] Other ancient authorities read *let us*

King James

2 By whom also we have access by faith into this grace wherein we stand, and rejoice in hope of the glory of God.

3 And not only *so*, but we glory in tribulations also: knowing that tribulation worketh patience;

4 And patience, experience; and experience, hope:

5 And hope maketh not ashamed; because the love of God is shed abroad in our hearts by the Holy Ghost which is given unto us.

6 For when we were yet without strength, in due time Christ died for the ungodly.

7 For scarcely for a righteous man will one die: yet peradventure for a good man some would even dare to die.

8 But God commendeth his love toward us, in that, while we were yet sinners, Christ died for us.

9 Much more then, being now justified by his blood, we shall be saved from wrath through him.

10 For if, when we were enemies, we were reconciled to God by the death of his Son, much more, being reconciled, we shall be saved by his life.

11 And not only *so*, but we also joy in God through our Lord Jesus Christ, by whom we have now received the atonement.

12 Wherefore, as by one man sin entered into the world, and death by sin; and so death passed upon all men, for that all have sinned:

13 (For until the law sin was in the world: but sin is not imputed when there is no law.

14 Nevertheless death reigned from Adam to Moses, even over them that had not sinned after the similitude of Adam's transgression who is the figure of him that was to come.

15 But not as the offence, so also *is* the free gift. For if through the offence of one many be dead, much more the grace of God, and the gift by grace, *which is* by one man, Jesus Christ, hath abounded unto many.

16 And not as *it was* by one that sinned, *so is* the gift: for the judgment *was* by one to condemnation, but the free gift *is* of many offences unto justification.

Amplified

2 Through Him also we have [our] access (entrance, introduction) by faith into this grace — state of God's favor — in which we [firmly and safely] stand. And [u]let us rejoice *and* exult in our hope of experiencing *and* enjoying the glory of God.

3 Moreover — let us also be full of joy now! [u]Let us exult *and* triumph in our troubles *and* rejoice in our sufferings, knowing that pressure *and* affliction *and* hardship produce patient *and* unswerving endurance.

4 And endurance (fortitude) develops maturity of [v]character — that is, approved faith and [w]tried integrity. And character [of this sort] produces [the habit of] [x]joyful and confident hope of eternal salvation.

5 Such hope never disappoints *or* deludes *or* shames us, for God's love has been poured out in our hearts through the Holy Spirit Who has been given to us.

6 While we were yet in weakness — powerless to help ourselves — at the fitting time Christ died for (in behalf of) the ungodly.

7 Now it is an extraordinary thing for one to give his life even for an upright man, though perhaps for a noble *and* lovable *and* generous benefactor someone might even dare to die.

8 But God shows *and* clearly proves His [own] love for us by the fact that while we were still sinners Christ, the Messiah, the Anointed One, died for us.

9 Therefore, since we are now justified — [y]acquitted, made righteous and brought into right relationship with God — by Christ's blood, how much more [certain is it that] we shall be saved by Him from the indignation *and* wrath of God.

10 For if while we were enemies we were reconciled to God through the death of His Son, it is much more [certain], now that we are reconciled, that we shall be saved [daily delivered from sin's dominion] through His [[y]resurrection] life.

11 Not only so, but we also rejoice *and* exultingly glory in God [His love and perfection] through our Lord Jesus Christ, through Whom we have now received *and* enjoy [our] reconciliation. [Jer. 9:24.]

12 Therefore as sin came into the world through one man and death as the result of sin, so death spread to all men, [[z]no one being able to stop it *or* to escape its power] because all men sinned.

13 [To be sure,] sin was in the world before ever the Law was given, but sin is not charged to men's account where there is no law [to transgress].

14 Yet death held sway from Adam to Moses [the Lawgiver], even over those who did not themselves transgress [a positive command] as Adam did. Adam was a type (prefigure) of the One Who was to come [in reverse, [z]the former destructive, the Latter saving]. [Gen. 5:5; 7:22; Deut. 34:5.]

15 But God's free gift is not at all to be compared to the trespass — His grace is out of all proportion to the fall of man. For if many died through one man's falling away — his lapse, his offense — much more profusely did God's grace and the free gift [that comes] through the undeserved favor of the one Man Jesus Christ, abound *and* overflow to *and* for [the benefit of] many.

16 Nor is the free gift at all to be compared to the effect of that one [man's] sin. For the sentence [following the trespass] of one [man] brought condemnation, whereas the free gift [following] many transgressions brings justification — [a]an act of righteousness.

---

u) Alternate reading.
v) Souter.
w) Vincent.
x) Thayer.
y) Abbott-Smith.
z) Thayer.
a) Literal meaning.

Living New Testament

2 For because of our faith, He has brought us into this place of highest privilege where we now stand, and we confidently and joyfully look forward to actually becoming all that God has had in mind for us to be.

3 We can rejoice, too, when we run into problems and trials for we know that they are good for us—they help us learn to be patient.

4 And patience develops strength of character in us and helps us trust God more each time we use it until finally our hope and faith are strong and steady.

5 Then, when that happens, we are able to hold our heads high no matter what happens and know that all is well, for we know how dearly God loves us, and we feel this warm love everywhere within us because God has given us the Holy Spirit to fill our hearts with His love.

6 When we were utterly helpless with no way of escape, Christ came at just the right time and died for us sinners who had no use for Him.

7 Even if we were good, we really wouldn't expect anyone to die for us, though of course that might be barely possible.

8 But God showed His great love for us by sending Christ to die for us while we were still sinners.

9 And since by His blood He did all this for us as sinners, how much more will He do for us now that He has declared us not guilty? Now He will save us from all of God's wrath to come.

10 And since, when we were His enemies, we were brought back to God by the death of His Son, what blessings He must have for us now that we are His friends, and He is living within us!

11 Now we rejoice in our wonderful new relationship with God—all because of what our Lord Jesus Christ has done in dying for our sins—making us friends of God.

* * * * * * *

12 When Adam sinned, sin entered the entire human race. His sin spread death throughout all the world, so everything began to grow old and die,[1] for all sinned.

13 [We know that it was Adam's sin that caused this[2]] because although, of course, people were sinning from the time of Adam until Moses, God did not in those days judge them guilty of death for breaking His laws—because He had not yet given His laws to them, nor told them what He wanted them to do.

14 So when their bodies died it was not for their own sins[2] since they themselves had never disobeyed God's special law against eating the forbidden fruit, as Adam had.

What a contrast between Adam and Christ who was yet to come.

15 And what a difference between man's sin and God's forgiveness! For this one man, Adam, brought death to many through his *sin*. But this one man, Jesus Christ, brought forgiveness to many through God's *mercy*.

16 Adam's *one* sin brought the penalty of death to many, while Christ freely takes away *many* sins and gives glorious life instead.

[1] Literally, "sin entered into the world, and death through sin."
[2] Implied.

Revised Standard

obtained access[g] to this grace in which we
stand, and we[h] rejoice in our hope of sharing
the glory of God. 3More than that, we[h] rejoice in our sufferings, knowing that suffering
produces endurance, 4and endurance produces character, and character produces
hope, 5and hope does not disappoint us, because God's love has been poured into our
hearts through the Holy Spirit which has
been given to us.
6 While we were yet helpless, at the right
time Christ died for the ungodly. 7Why, one
will hardly die for a righteous man—though
perhaps for a good man one will dare even
to die. 8But God shows his love for us in
that while we were yet sinners Christ died
for us. 9Since, therefore, we are now justified by his blood, much more shall we be
saved by him from the wrath of God. 10For
if while we were enemies we were reconciled to God by the death of his Son, much
more, now that we are reconciled, shall we
be saved by his life. 11Not only so, but we
also rejoice in God through our Lord Jesus
Christ, through whom we have now received
our reconciliation.

Christ the basis of our salvation

12 Therefore as sin came into the world
through one man and death through sin,
and so death spread to all men because all
men sinned—13sin indeed was in the world
before the law was given, but sin is not
counted where there is no law. 14Yet death
reigned from Adam to Moses, even over
those whose sins were not like the transgression of Adam, who was a type of the
one who was to come.
15 But the free gift is not like the trespass. For if many died through one man's
trespass, much more have the grace of God
and the free gift in the grace of that one
man Jesus Christ abounded for many. 16And
the free gift is not like the effect of that one
man's sin. For the judgment following one
trespass brought condemnation, but the free
gift following many trespasses brings justifi-

[g] Other ancient authorities add *by faith*
[h] Or *let us*

King James

17 For if by one man's offence death
reigned by one; much more they which receive abundance of grace and of the gift of
righteousness shall reign in life by one, Jesus
Christ.)
18 Therefore as by the offence of one
judgment came upon all men to condemnation; even so by the righteousness of one *the*
free gift came upon all men unto justification of life.
19 For as by one man's disobedience
many were made sinners, so by the obedience of one shall many be made righteous.
20 Moreover the law entered, that the
offence might abound. But where sin
abounded, grace did much more abound:
21 That as sin hath reigned unto death,
even so might grace reign through righteousness unto eternal life by Jesus Christ our
Lord.

Amplified

17 For if, because of one man's trespass (lapse,
offense) death reigned through that one, much more surely will those who receive [God's] overflowing grace (unmerited favor) and the free gift of righteousness (putting
them into right standing with Himself) reign as kings in
life through the One, Jesus Christ, the Messiah, the
Anointed One.
18 Well then, as one man's trespass — one man's false
step and falling away — [led] to condemnation for all
men, so one Man's act of righteousness [leads] to acquittal
and right standing with God, and life for all men.
19 For just as by one man's disobedience (failing to
hear, [b]heedlessness and carelessness) the many were constituted sinners, so by one Man's obedience the many will
be constituted righteous — made acceptable to God,
brought into right standing with Him.
20 But then Law came in, [only] to expand *and* in-
increase the trespass [making it more apparent and exciting
opposition]. But where sin increased *and* abounded, grace
(God's unmerited favor) has surpassed it *and* increased
the more *and* superabounded.
21 So that, [just] as sin has reigned in death, so grace
— His unearned and undeserved favor — might reign also
through righteousness (right standing with God) which
issues in eternal life through Jesus Christ, the Messiah, the
Anointed One, our Lord.

CHAPTER 6

WHAT shall we say then? Shall we continue in sin, that grace may abound?
2 God forbid. How shall we, that are
dead to sin, live any longer therein?
3 Know ye not, that so many of us as
were baptized into Jesus Christ were baptized into his death?
4 Therefore we are buried with him by
baptism into death: that like as Christ was
raised up from the dead by the glory of the
Father, even so we also should walk in newness of life.
5 For if we have been planted together in
the likeness of his death, we shall be also *in*
the likeness of *his* resurrection:
6 Knowing this, that our old man is
crucified with *him,* that the body of sin
might be destroyed, that henceforth we
should not serve sin.
7 For he that is dead is freed from sin.
8 Now if we be dead with Christ, we
believe that we shall also live with him:
9 Knowing that Christ being raised from
the dead dieth no more; death hath no more
dominion over him.
10 For in that he died, he died unto sin
once: but in that he liveth, he liveth unto
God.
11 Likewise reckon ye also yourselves
to be dead indeed unto sin, but alive unto
God through Jesus Christ our Lord.

CHAPTER 6

WHAT shall we say [to all this]? Are we to remain in
sin in order that God's grace (favor and mercy)
may multiply *and* overflow?
2 Certainly not? How can we who died to sin live in it
any longer?
3 Are you ignorant of the fact that all of us who have
been baptized into Christ Jesus were baptized into His
death?
4 We were buried therefore with Him by the baptism
into death, so that just as Christ was raised from the dead
by the glorious [power] of the Father, so we too might
habitually live *and* behave in newness of life.
5 For if we have become one with Him by sharing a
death like His, we shall also be [one with Him in sharing]
His resurrection [by a new life lived for God].
6 We know that our old (unrenewed) self was nailed
to the cross with Him in order that [our] body, [which is
the instrument] of sin, might be made ineffective *and*
inactive for evil, that we might no longer be the slaves of
sin.
7 For when a man dies he is freed — loosed, delivered
— from [the power of] sin [among men].
8 Now if we have died with Christ, we believe that we
shall also live with Him.
9 Because we know that Christ, the Anointed One,
being once raised from the dead will never die again;
death no longer has power over Him.
10 For by the death He died, He died to sin [ending
His relation to it] once for all, and the life that He lives
He is living to God — in unbroken fellowship with Him.
11 Even so consider yourselves also dead to sin *and*
your relation to it broken, but [that you are] alive to God
— living in unbroken fellowship with Him — in Christ
Jesus.

---

b) Vincent, Bengel.

Living New Testament

17 The sin of this one man, Adam, caused *death to be king over all,* but all who will take God's gift of forgiveness and acquittal are *kings of life*[3] because of this one man, Jesus Christ.

18 Yes, Adam's *sin* brought *punishment* to all, but Christ's *righteousness* makes men *right with God,* so that they can live.

19 Adam caused many to be sinners because he *disobeyed* God, and Christ caused many to be made acceptable to God because He *obeyed.*

20 The Ten Commandments were given so that all could see the extent of their failure to obey God's laws. But the more we see our sinfulness, the more we see God's abounding grace forgiving us.

21 Before, sin ruled over all men and brought them to death, but now God's kindness rules instead, giving us right standing with God and resulting in eternal life through Jesus Christ our Lord.

Revised Standard

cation. 17If, because of one man's trespass,
death reigned through that one man, much
more will those who receive the abundance
of grace and the free gift of righteousness
reign in life through the one man Jesus
Christ.

18 Then as one man's trespass led to condemnation for all men, so one man's act of
righteousness leads to acquittal and life for
all men. 19For as by one man's disobedience
many were made sinners, so by one man's
obedience many will be made righteous.
20Law came in, to increase the trespass; but
where sin increased, grace abounded all the
more, 21so that, as sin reigned in death,
grace also might reign through righteousness
to eternal life through Jesus Christ our Lord.

CHAPTER 6

Well then, shall we keep on sinning so that God can keep on showing us more and more kindness and forgiveness?

2, 3 Of course not! Should we keep on sinning when we don't have to? For sin's power over us was broken when we became Christians and were baptized to become a part of Jesus Christ; through His death the power of your sinful nature was shattered.

4 Your old sin-loving nature was buried with Him by baptism when He died, and when God the Father, with glorious power, brought Him back to life again, you were given His wonderful new life to enjoy.

5 For you have become a part of Him, and so you died with Him, so to speak, when He died[1]; and now you share His new life, and shall rise as He did.

6 Your old evil desires were nailed to the cross with Him; that part of you that loves to sin was crushed and fatally wounded, so that your sin-loving body is no longer under sin's control, no longer needs to be a slave to sin;

7 For when you are deadened to sin you are freed from all its allure and its power over you.

8 And since your old sin-loving nature "died" with Christ, we know that you will share His new life.

9 Christ rose from the dead and will never die again. Death no longer has any power over Him.

10 He died once for all to end sin's power, but now He lives forever in unbroken fellowship with God.

11 So look upon your old sin nature as dead and unresponsive to sin, instead be alive to God, alert to Him, through Jesus Christ our Lord.

Believers dead to sin

6 What shall we say then? Are we to continue in sin that grace may abound?
2By no means! How can we who died to
sin still live in it? 3Do you not know that
all of us who have been baptized into Christ
Jesus were baptized into his death? 4We
were buried therefore with him by baptism
into death, so that as Christ was raised
from the dead by the glory of the Father,
we too might walk in newness of life.

5 For if we have been united with him
in a death like his, we shall certainly be
united with him in a resurrection like his.
6We know that our old self was crucified
with him so that the sinful body might be
destroyed, and we might no longer be enslaved to sin. 7For he who has died is freed
from sin. 8But if we have died with Christ,
we believe that we shall also live with him.
9For we know that Christ being raised from
the dead will never die again; death no
longer has dominion over him. 10The death
he died he died to sin, once for all, but the
life he lives he lives to God. 11So you also
must consider yourselves dead to sin and
alive to God in Christ Jesus.

---

[3] Literally, "reign in life."
[1] Literally, "united with Him in the likeness of His death."

King James

12 Let not sin therefore reign in your mortal body, that ye should obey it in the lusts thereof.

13 Neither yield ye your members *as* instruments of unrighteousness unto sin: but yield yourselves unto God, as those that are alive from the dead, and your members *as* instruments of righteousness unto God.

14 For sin shall not have dominion over you: for ye are not under the law, but under grace.

15 What then? shall we sin, because we are not under the law, but under grace? God forbid.

16 Know ye not, that to whom ye yield yourselves servants to obey, his servants ye are to whom ye obey; whether of sin unto death, or of obedience unto righteousness?

17 But God be thanked, that ye were the servants of sin, but ye have obeyed from the heart that form of doctrine which was delivered you.

18 Being then made free from sin, ye became the servants of righteousness.

19 I speak after the manner of men because of the infirmity of your flesh: for as ye have yielded your members servants to uncleanness and to iniquity unto iniquity; even so now yield your members servants to righteousness unto holiness.

20 For when ye were the servants of sin, ye were free from righteousness.

21 What fruit had ye then in those things whereof ye are now ashamed? for the end of those things *is* death.

22 But now being made free from sin, and become servants to God, ye have your fruit unto holiness, and the end everlasting life.

23 For the wages of sin *is* death; but the gift of God *is* eternal life through Jesus Christ our Lord.

Amplified

12 Let not sin therefore rule as king in your mortal (short-lived, perishable) bodies, to make you yield to their cravings *and* be subject to their lusts *and* evil passions.

13 Do not continue offering or yielding your bodily members [and [c]faculties] to sin as instruments (tools) of wickedness. But offer *and* yield yourselves to God as though you have been raised from the dead to [perpetual] life, and your bodily members [and [c]faculties] to God, presenting them as implements of righteousness.

14 For sin shall not [any longer] exert dominion over you, since now you are not under Law [as slaves], but under grace — as subjects of God's favor and mercy.

15 What then [are we to conclude]? Shall we sin because we live not under Law but under God's favor *and* mercy? Certainly not!

16 Do you not know that if you continually surrender yourselves to any one to do his will, you are the slaves of him whom you obey, whether that be to sin, which leads to death, or to obedience which leads to righteousness — right doing and right standing with God?

17 But thank God, though you were once slaves of sin you have become obedient with all your heart to the standard of teaching in which you were instructed *and* to which you were committed.

18 And, having been set free from sin, you have become the servants of righteousness — of conformity to the divine will in thought, purpose and action.

19 I am speaking in familiar human terms, because of your natural limitations. For as you yielded your bodily members [and [d]faculties] as servants to impurity and ever increasing lawlessness, so now yield your bodily members [and [d]faculties] once for all as servants to righteousness — right being and doing — [which leads] to sanctification.

20 For when you were slaves of sin, you were free in regard to righteousness.

21 But then what benefit (return) did you get from the things of which you are now ashamed? [None,] for the end of those things is death.

22 But now since you have been set free from sin and have become the slaves of God, you have your present reward in holiness and its end is eternal life.

23 For the wages which sin pays is death; but the [bountiful] free gift of God is eternal life through (in union with) Jesus Christ our Lord.

CHAPTER 7

KNOW ye not, brethren, (for I speak to them that know the law,) how that the law hath dominion over a man as long as he liveth?

2 For the woman which hath an husband is bound by the law to *her* husband so long as he liveth; but if the husband be dead, she is loosed from the law of *her* husband.

3 So then if, while *her* husband liveth, she be married to another man, she shall be called an adulteress: but if her husband be dead, she is free from that law; so that she is no adulteress, though she be married to another man.

4 Wherefore, my brethren, ye also are become dead to the law by the body of Christ; that ye should be married to another, *even* to him who is raised from the dead, that we should bring forth fruit unto God.

CHAPTER 7

DO you not know, brethren, for I am speaking to men who are acquainted with the Law, that legal claims have power over a person only for so long as he is alive?

2 For [instance] a married woman is bound by law to her husband as long as he lives; but if her husband dies she is loosed *and* discharged from the law concerning her husband.

3 Accordingly, she will be held an adulteress if she unites herself to another man while her husband lives. But if her husband dies, the marriage law no longer is binding on her — she is free from that law — and if she unites herself to another man she is not an adulteress.

4 Likewise, my brethren, you have undergone death as to the Law through the [crucified] body of Christ, so that now you may belong to Another, to Him Who was raised from the dead in order that we may bear fruit for God.

---

c and d) *Mele* — "Physical; though some include mental faculties." — Vincent's "Word Studies in The New Testament."

Living New Testament

12 Do not let sin control your puny body any longer; do not give in to its sinful desires.

13 Do not let any part of your bodies become tools of wickedness, to be used for sinning; but give yourselves completely to God—every part of you—for you are back from death and you want to be tools in the hands of God, to be used for His good purposes.

14 Sin need[2] never again be your master, for now you are no longer tied to the law where sin enslaves you, but you are free under God's favor and mercy.

15 Does this mean that now we can go ahead and sin and not worry about it? (For our salvation does not depend on keeping the law, but on receiving God's grace!) Of course not!

16 Don't you realize that you can choose your own master? You can choose sin (with death) or else obedience (with acquittal). The one to whom you offer yourself—he will take you and be your master and you will be his slave.

17 Thank God that though you once chose to be slaves of sin, now you have obeyed with all your heart the teaching to which God has committed you.

18 And now you are free from your old master, sin; and you have become slaves to your new master, righteousness.

19 I speak this way, using the illustration of slaves and masters because it is easy to understand: just as you used to be slaves to all kinds of sin, so now you must let yourselves be slaves to all that is right and holy.

20 In those days when you were slaves of sin you didn't bother much with goodness.

21 And what was the result? Evidently not good, since you are ashamed now even to think about those things you used to do, for all of them end in eternal doom.

22 But now you are free from the power of sin and are slaves of God, and His benefits to you include holiness and everlasting life.

23 For the wages of sin is death, but the free gift of God is eternal life through Jesus Christ our Lord.

CHAPTER 7

Don't you understand yet, dear Jewish[1] brothers in Christ, that when a person dies the law no longer holds him in its power?

2 Let me illustrate: when a woman marries, the law binds her to her husband as long as he is alive. But if he dies, she is no longer bound to him; the laws of marriage no longer apply to her.

3 Then she can marry someone else if she wants to. That would be wrong while he was alive, but it is perfectly all right after he dies.

4 Your "husband," your master, used to be the Jewish law; but you "died," as it were, with Christ on the cross; and since you are "dead," you are no longer "married to the law," and it has no more control over you. Then you came back to life again when Christ did, and are a new person. And now you are "married," so

[2] Literally, "sin will never again be your master."

[1] Implied. Literally, "men who know (the law)."

Revised Standard

12 Let not sin therefore reign in your
mortal bodies, to make you obey their passions.
13 Do not yield your members to sin
as instruments of wickedness, but yield
yourselves to God as men who have been
brought from death to life, and your members
to God as instruments of righteousness.
14 For sin will have no dominion over you,
since you are not under law but under grace.

Slaves to righteousness

15 What then? Are we to sin because we
are not under law but under grace? By no
means! 16 Do you not know that if you yield
yourselves to any one as obedient slaves, you
are slaves of the one whom you obey, either
of sin, which leads to death, or of obedience,
which leads to righteousness? 17 But thanks
be to God, that you who were once slaves of
sin have become obedient from the heart to
the standard of teaching to which you were
committed, 18 and, having been set free from
sin, have become slaves of righteousness. 19 I
am speaking in human terms, because of your
natural limitations. For just as you once
yielded your members to impurity and to
greater and greater iniquity, so now yield
your members to righteousness for sanctification.

20 When you were slaves of sin, you were
free in regard to righteousness. 21 But then
what return did you get from the things of
which you are now ashamed? The end of
those things is death. 22 But now that you
have been set free from sin and have become
slaves of God, the return you get is sanctification
and its end, eternal life. 23 For the
wages of sin is death, but the free gift of
God is eternal life in Christ Jesus our Lord.

Married to Christ

7 Do you not know, brethren—for I am
speaking to those who know the law—
that the law is binding on a person only
during his life? 2 Thus a married woman is
bound by law to her husband as long as he
lives; but if her husband dies she is discharged
from the law concerning the husband.
3 Accordingly, she will be called an
adulteress if she lives with another man
while her husband is alive. But if her husband
dies she is free from that law, and if
she marries another man she is not an adulteress.

4 Likewise, my brethren, you have died
to the law through the body of Christ, so
that you may belong to another, to him who
has been raised from the dead in order that

King James

5 For when we were in the flesh, the motions of sins, which were by the law, did work in our members to bring forth fruit unto death.

6 But now we are delivered from the law, that being dead wherein we were held; that we should serve in newness of spirit, and not *in* the oldness of the letter.

7 What shall we say then? *Is* the law sin? God forbid. Nay, I had not known sin, but by the law: for I had not known lust, except the law had said, Thou shalt not covet.

8 But sin, taking occasion by the commandment, wrought in me all manner of concupiscence. For without the law sin *was* dead.

9 For I was alive without the law once: but when the commandment came, sin revived, and I died.

10 And the commandment, which *was ordained* to life, I found *to be* unto death.

11 For sin, taking occasion by the commandment, deceived me, and by it slew *me*.

12 Wherefore the law *is* holy, and the commandment holy, and just, and good.

13 Was then that which is good made death unto me? God forbid. But sin, that it might appear sin, working death in me by that which is good; that sin by the commandment might become exceeding sinful.

14 For we know that the law is spiritual: but I am carnal, sold under sin.

15 For that which I do I allow not: for what I would, that do I not; but what I hate, that do I.

16 If then I do that which I would not, I consent unto the law that *it is* good.

17 Now then it is no more I that do it, but sin that dwelleth in me.

18 For I know that in me (that is, in my flesh,) dwelleth no good thing: for to will is present with me; but *how* to perform that which is good I find not.

19 For the good that I would I do not: but the evil which I would not, that I do.

20 Now if I do that I would not, it is no more I that do it, but sin that dwelleth in me.

Amplified

5 When we were living in the flesh (mere physical lives) the sinful passions that were awakened *and* aroused up by [what] the Law [makes sin] were constantly operating in our natural powers — in our bodily organs, [e]in the sensitive appetites and wills of the flesh — so that we bore fruit for death.

6 But now we are discharged from the Law *and* have terminated all intercourse with it, having died to what once restrained *and* held us captive. So now we serve not under [obedience to] the old code of written regulations, but [under obedience to the promptings] of the Spirit in newness [of life].

7 What then do we conclude? Is the Law identical with sin? Certainly not! Nevertheless, if it had not been for the Law, I should not have recognized sin *or* have known its meaning. [For instance] I would not have known about covetousness — would have had no consciousness of sin or sense of guilt — if the Law had not [repeatedly] said, You shall not covet *and* have an evil desire [for one thing and another]. [Exod. 20:17; Deut. 5:21.]

8 But sin, finding opportunity in the commandment [to express itself] got a hold on me *and* aroused *and* stimulated all kinds of forbidden desires (lust, covetousness). For without the Law sin is dead — the sense of it is inactive and a lifeless thing.

9 Once I was alive but quite apart from *and* unconscious of the Law. But when the commandment came, sin lived again, and I died — was sentenced by the Law to death. [Ps. 73:22.]

10 And the very legal ordinance which was designed *and* intended to bring life, actually proved [to mean to me] death. [Lev. 18:5.]

11 For sin, seizing the opportunity *and* getting a hold on me [by taking its incentive] from the commandment, beguiled *and* entrapped *and* cheated me, and using it [as a weapon] killed me.

12 The Law therefore is holy, and [each] commandment is holy and just and good.

13 Did that which is good then prove fatal (bringing death) to me? Certainly not! It was sin, working death in me by using this good thing [as a weapon], in order that through the commandment sin might be shown up clearly to be sin, that the extreme malignity and immeasurable sinfulness of sin might plainly appear.

14 We know that the Law is spiritual; but I am a creature of the flesh (carnal, unspiritual), having been sold into slavery under [the control of] sin.

15 For I do not understand my own actions — I am baffled, bewildered. I do not practice *or* accomplish what I wish, but I do the very thing that I loathe [[f]which my moral instinct condemns].

16 Now if I do [habitually] what is contrary to my desire, [that means that] I acknowledge *and* agree that the Law is good (morally excellent) *and* that I take sides with it.

17 However, it is no longer I who do the deed, but the sin [principle] which is at home in me *and* has possession of me.

18 For I know that nothing good dwells within me, that is, in my flesh. I can will what is right, but I cannot perform it. — I have the intention and urge to do what is right, but no power to carry it out;

19 For I fail to practice the good deeds I desire to do, but the evil deeds that I do not desire to do are what I am [ever] doing.

20 Now if I do what I desire not to do, it is no longer I doing it — it is not myself that acts — but the sin [principle] which dwells within me [[g]fixed and operating in my soul].

e) Matthew Henry's Commentary.
f) Godet (—Vincent).
g) Thayer.

Living New Testament

to speak, to the one who rose from the dead, so that you can produce good fruit, that is good deeds for God.

5 When your old nature was still active, sinful desires were at work within you, making you want to do whatever God said not to, and producing sinful deeds, the rotting fruit of death.

6 But now you need no longer worry about the Jewish laws and customs[2] because you "died" while in their captivity, and now you can really serve God; not in the old way, mechanically obeying a set of rules, but in the new way, [with all of your hearts and minds[3]].

7 Well then, am I suggesting that these laws of God are evil? Of course not! No, the law is not sinful but it was the law that showed me my sin. I would never have known the sin in my heart—the evil desires that are hidden there—if the law had not said, "You must not have evil desires in your heart."

8 But sin used this law against evil desires by reminding me that such desires are wrong and arousing all kinds of forbidden desires within me! Only if there were no laws to break would there be no sinning.

9 That is why I felt fine so long as I did not understand what the law really demanded. But when I learned the truth, I realized that I had broken the law and was a sinner, doomed to die.

10 So as far as I was concerned, the good law which was supposed to show me the way of life resulted instead in my being given the death penalty.

11 Sin fooled me by taking the good laws of God and using them to make me guilty of death.

12 But still, you see, the law itself was wholly right and good.

13 But how can that be? Didn't the law cause my doom? How then can it be good? No, it was sin, devilish stuff that it is, that used what was good to bring about my condemnation. So you can see how cunning and deadly and damnable it is. For it uses God's good laws for its own evil purposes.

14 The law is good, then, and the trouble is not there but with *me*, because I am sold into slavery with Sin as my owner.

15 I don't understand myself at all, for I really want to do what is right, but I can't. I do what I don't want to—what I hate.

16 I know perfectly well that what I am doing is wrong, and my bad conscience proves that I agree with these laws I am breaking.

17 But I can't help myself, because I'm no longer doing it. It is sin inside me that is stronger than I am that makes me do these evil things.

18 I know I am rotten through and through so far as my old sinful nature is concerned. No matter which way I turn I can't make myself do right. I want to but I can't.

19 When I want to do good, I don't; and when I try not to do wrong, I do it anyway.

20 Now if I am doing what I don't want to, it is plain where the trouble is: sin still has me in its evil grasp.

Revised Standard

we may bear fruit for God. [5]While we were
living in the flesh, our sinful passions,
aroused by the law, were at work in our
members to bear fruit for death. [6]But now
we are discharged from the law, dead to
that which held us captive, so that we serve
not under the old written code but in the
new life of the Spirit.

The Christian struggle

7 What then shall we say? That the law
is sin? By no means! Yet, if it had not been
for the law, I should not have known sin.
I should not have known what it is to covet
if the law had not said, "You shall not
covet." [8]But sin, finding opportunity in the
commandment, wrought in me all kinds of
covetousness. Apart from the law sin lies
dead. [9]I was once alive apart from the law,
but when the commandment came, sin revived and I died; [10]the very commandment
which promised life proved to be death to
me. [11]For sin, finding opportunity in the
commandment, deceived me and by it killed
me. [12]So the law is holy, and the commandment is holy and just and good.

13 Did that which is good, then, bring
death to me? By no means! It was sin, working death in me through what is good, in order that sin might be shown to be sin, and
through the commandment might become
sinful beyond measure. [14]We know that the
law is spiritual; but I am carnal, sold under
sin. [15]I do not understand my own actions.
For I do not do what I want, but I do the
very thing I hate. [16]Now if I do what I do
not want, I agree that the law is good. [17]So
then it is no longer I that do it, but sin
which dwells within me. [18]For I know that
nothing good dwells within me, that is, in
my flesh. I can will what is right, but I
cannot do it. [19]For I do not do the good I
want, but the evil I do not want is what I
do. [20]Now if I do what I do not want, it is
no longer I that do it, but sin which dwells
within me.

---

[2] Literally, "Now we are delivered from the law."
[3] Implied.

King James

21 I find then a law, that, when I would do good, evil is present with me.
22 For I delight in the law of God after the inward man:
23 But I see another law in my members, warring against the law of my mind, and bringing me into captivity to the law of sin which is in my members.
24 O wretched man that I am! who shall deliver me from the body of this death?
25 I thank God through Jesus Christ our Lord. So then with the mind I serve the law of God; but with the flesh the law of sin.

Amplified

21 So I find it to be a law [of my being] that when I want to do what is right *and* good, evil is ever present with me *and* I am subject to its insistent demands.
22 For I endorse *and* delight in the Law of God in my inmost self — with my new nature. [Ps. 1:2.]
23 But I discern in my bodily members — [h]in the sensitive appetites and wills of the flesh — a different law (rule of action) at war against the law of my mind (my reason) and making me a prisoner to the law of sin that dwells in my bodily organs — [h]in the sensitive appetites and wills of the flesh.
24 O unhappy *and* pitiable *and* wretched man that I am! Who will release *and* deliver me from [the shackles of] this body of death?
25 O thank God! — He will! through Jesus Christ, the Anointed One, our Lord! So then indeed I of myself with the mind *and* heart serve the Law of God, but with the flesh the law of sin.

CHAPTER 8

THERE *is* therefore now no condemnation to them which are in Christ Jesus, who walk not after the flesh, but after the Spirit.
2 For the law of the Spirit of life in Christ Jesus hath made me free from the law of sin and death.
3 For what the law could not do, in that it was weak through the flesh, God sending his own Son in the likeness of sinful flesh, and for sin, condemned sin in the flesh:
4 That the righteousness of the law might be fulfilled in us, who walk not after the flesh, but after the Spirit.
5 For they that are after the flesh do mind the things of the flesh; but they that are after the Spirit the things of the Spirit.
6 For to be carnally minded *is* death; but to be spiritually minded *is* life and peace.
7 Because the carnal mind *is* enmity against God: for it is not subject to the law of God, neither indeed can be.
8 So then they that are in the flesh cannot please God.

CHAPTER 8

THEREFORE (there is] now no condemnation — no adjudging guilty of wrong — for those who are in Christ Jesus, *who live not after the dictates of the flesh, but after the dictates of the Spirit.* [cf. John 3:18.]
2 For the law of the Spirit of life [which is] in Christ Jesus [the law of our new being], has freed me from the law of sin and of death.
3 For God has done what the Law could not do, [its power] being weakened by the flesh [that is, [i]the entire nature of man without the Holy Spirit]. Sending His own Son in the guise of sinful flesh and [j]as an offering for sin, [God] condemned sin in the flesh — [k]subdued, overcame, [l]deprived it of its power [over all who accept that sacrifice]. [Lev. 7:37.]
4 So that the righteous *and* just requirement of the Law might be fully met in us, who live *and* move not in the ways of the flesh but in the ways of the Spirit — our lives governed not by the standards *and* according to the dictates of the flesh, but controlled by the (Holy) Spirit.
5 For those who are according to the flesh *and* controlled by its unholy desires, set their minds on *and* [k]pursue those things which gratify the flesh. But those who are according to the Spirit *and* [controlled by the desires] of the Spirit, set their minds on *and* [k]seek those things which gratify the (Holy) Spirit.
6 Now the mind of the flesh [which is sense and reason without the Holy Spirit] is death — death that [k]comprises all the miseries arising from sin, both here and hereafter. But the mind of the (Holy) Spirit is life and soul-peace [both now and forever].
7 [That is] because the mind of the flesh — with its carnal thoughts and purposes — is hostile to God; for it does not submit itself to God's Law, indeed it cannot.
8 So then those who are living the life of the flesh — catering to the appetites and impulses of their carnal nature — cannot please *or* satisfy God, *or* be acceptable to Him.

---

h) Matthew Henry's Commentary.
i) Melanchthon (—Vincent).
j) Alternate reading.
k) Thayer.
l) Vincent.

Living New Testament

21 It seems to be a fact of life that when I want to do what is right, I inevitably do what is wrong.

22 I love to do God's will so far as my new nature is concerned;

23, 24, 25 But there is something else deep within me, in my lower nature, that is at war with my mind and wins the fight and makes me a slave to the sin that is still within me. In my mind I want to be God's willing servant but instead I find myself still enslaved to sin.

So you see how it is: my new life tells me to do right, but the old nature that is still inside me loves to sin. Oh, what a terrible predicament I'm in! Who will free me from my slavery to this deadly lower nature? Thank God! It has been done[4] by Jesus Christ our Lord. He has set me free.

Revised Standard

21 So I find it to be a law that when I
want to do right, evil lies close at hand.
22For I delight in the law of God, in my inmost self, 23but I see in my members another
law at war with the law of my mind and
making me captive to the law of sin which
dwells in my members. 24Wretched man that
I am! Who will deliver me from this body
of death? 25Thanks be to God through
Jesus Christ our Lord! So then, I of myself
serve the law of God with my mind, but
with my flesh I serve the law of sin.

CHAPTER 8

So there is now no condemnation awaiting those who belong to Christ Jesus.

2 For the power of the life-giving Spirit—and this power is mine through Christ Jesus—has freed me from the vicious circle of sin and death.

3 We aren't saved from sin's grasp by knowing the commandments of God, because we can't and don't keep them, but God put into effect a different plan to save us. He sent His own Son, in a human body like ours—except that ours are sinful—and destroyed sin's control over us by giving Himself as a sacrifice for our sins.

4 So now we can obey God's laws if we follow after the Holy Spirit and no longer obey the old evil nature within us.

5 Those who let themselves be controlled by their lower natures live only to please themselves, but those who follow after the Holy Spirit find themselves doing those things that please God.

6 Following after the Holy Spirit leads to life and peace, but following after the old nature leads to death,

7 Because the old sinful nature within us is against God. It never did obey God's laws and it never will.

8 That's why those who are still under the control of their old sinful selves, bent on following their old evil desires, can never please God.

Life in the Spirit

8 There is therefore now no condemnation
for those who are in Christ Jesus. 2For
the law of the Spirit of life in Christ Jesus
has set me free from the law of sin and
death. 3For God has done what the law,
weakened by the flesh, could not do: sending his own Son in the likeness of sinful
flesh and for sin,[i] he condemned sin in the
flesh, 4in order that the just requirement of
the law might be fulfilled in us, who walk
not according to the flesh but according to
the Spirit. 5For those who live according to
the flesh set their minds on the things of the
flesh, but those who live according to the
Spirit set their minds on the things of the
Spirit. 6To set the mind on the flesh is death,
but to set the mind on the Spirit is life and
peace. 7For the mind that is set on the flesh
is hostile to God; it does not submit to
God's law, indeed it cannot; 8and those who
are in the flesh cannot please God.

[4] Or, "it will be done." Literally, "I thank God through Jesus Christ our Lord."

[i] Or *and as a sin offering*

King James

9 But ye are not in the flesh, but in the Spirit, if so be that the Spirit of God dwell in you. Now if any man have not the Spirit of Christ, he is none of his.

10 And if Christ *be* in you, the body *is* dead because of sin; but the Spirit *is* life because of righteousness.

11 But if the Spirit of him that raised up Jesus from the dead dwell in you, he that raised up Christ from the dead shall also quicken your mortal bodies by his Spirit that dwelleth in you.

12 Therefore, brethren, we are debtors, not to the flesh, to live after the flesh.

13 For if ye live after the flesh, ye shall die: but if ye through the Spirit do mortify the deeds of the body, ye shall live.

14 For as many as are led by the Spirit of God, they are the sons of God.

15 For ye have not received the spirit of bondage again to fear; but ye have received the Spirit of adoption, whereby we cry, Abba, Father.

16 The Spirit itself beareth witness with our spirit, that we are the children of God:

17 And if children, then heirs; heirs of God, and joint-heirs with Christ; if so be that we suffer with *him,* that we may be also glorified together.

18 For I reckon that the sufferings of this present time *are* not worthy *to be compared* with the glory which shall be revealed in us.

19 For the earnest expectation of the creature waiteth for the manifestation of the sons of God.

20 For the creature was made subject to vanity, not willingly, but by reason of him who hath subjected *the same* in hope,

21 Because the creature itself also shall be delivered from the bondage of corruption into the glorious liberty of the children of God.

22 For we know that the whole creation groaneth and travaileth in pain together until now.

23 And not only *they,* but ourselves also, which have the firstfruits of the Spirit, even we ourselves groan within ourselves, waiting for the adoption, *to wit,* the redemption of our body.

24 For we are saved by hope: but hope that is seen is not hope: for what a man seeth, why doth he yet hope for?

25 But if we hope for that we see not, *then* do we with patience wait for *it.*

Amplified

9 But you are not living the life of the flesh, you are living the life of the Spirit, if the (Holy) Spirit of God [really] dwells within you—directs *and* controls you. But if any one does not possess the (Holy) Spirit of Christ, he is none of His — he does not belong to Christ [is not truly a child of God]. [v. 14.]

10 But if Christ lives in you, [then although your natural] body is dead by reason of sin *and* guilt, the spirit is alive because of [the] righteousness [that He imputes to you].

11 And if the Spirit of Him Who raised up Jesus from the dead dwells in you, [then] He Who raised up Christ *Jesus* from the dead will also restore to life your mortal (short-lived, perishable) bodies through His Spirit Who dwells in you.

12 So then, brethren, we are debtors, but not to the flesh — we are not obligated to our carnal nature — to live [a life ruled by the standards set up by the dictates] of the flesh.

13 For if you live according to [the dictates of] the flesh you will surely die. But if through the power of the (Holy) Spirit you are habitually putting to death — making extinct, deadening — the [evil] deeds prompted by the body, you shall (really and genuinely) live forever.

14 For all who are led by the Spirit of God are sons of God.

15 For [the Spirit which] you have now received [is] not a spirit of slavery to put you once more in bondage to fear, but you have received the Spirit of adoption — the Spirit producing sonship — in [the bliss of] which we cry, Abba! [That is,] Father!

16 The Spirit Himself [thus] testifies together with our own spirit, [assuring us] that we are children of God.

17 And if we are [His] children, then we are [His] heirs also: heirs of God and fellow heirs with Christ — sharing His inheritance with Him; only we must share His suffering if we are to share His glory.

18 [But what of that?] For I consider that the sufferings of this present time (this present life) are not worth being compared with the glory that is about to be revealed to us *and* in us *and* [m]for us, *and* [n]conferred on us!

19 For (even the whole) creation (all nature) waits expectantly *and* longs earnestly for God's sons to be made known — waits for the revealing, the disclosing of their sonship.

20 For the creation (nature) was subjected to [n]frailty — to futility, condemned to frustration — not because of some intentional fault on its part, but by the will of Him Who so subjected it. [Yet] with the hope [Eccl. 1:2.]

21 That nature (creation) itself will be set free from its bondage to decay *and* corruption [and gain an entrance] into the glorious freedom of God's children.

22 We know that the whole creation (of irrational creatures) has been moaning together in the pains of labor until now. [Jer. 12:4, 11.]

23 And not only the creation, but we ourselves too, who have *and* enjoy the first fruits of the (Holy) Spirit — a foretaste of the blissful things to come — groan inwardly as we wait for the redemption of our bodies [from sensuality and the grave, which will reveal] our adoption (our manifestation as God's sons).

24 For in [this] hope we were saved. But hope [the object of] which is seen is not hope. For how can one hope for what he already sees?

25 But if we hope for what is still unseen by us, we wait for it with patience *and* composure.

---

m) Williams' "The New Testament in the Language of the People."
n) Thayer.

Living New Testament

9 But you are not like that. You are controlled by your new nature if you have the Spirit of God living in you. (And remember that if anyone doesn't have the Spirit of Christ living in him, he is not a Christian at all.)

10 Yet, even though Christ lives within you, your body will die because of sin; but your spirit will live, for Christ has pardoned it.[1]

11 And if the Spirit of God, who raised up Jesus from the dead, lives in you, He will make your dying bodies live again after you die, by means of this same Holy Spirit living within you.

12 So, dear brothers, you have no obligations whatever to your old sinful nature to do what it begs you to do.

13 For if you keep on following it you are lost and will perish, but if through the power of the Holy Spirit you crush it and its evil deeds, you shall live.

14 For all who are led by the Spirit of God are sons of God.

15 And so we should not be like cringing, fearful slaves, but we should behave like God's very own children, adopted into the bosom of His family, and calling to Him, "Father, Father."

16 For His Holy Spirit speaks to us deep in our hearts, and tells us that we really are God's children.

17 And since we are His children, we will share His treasures—for all God gives to His Son Jesus is now ours too. But if we are to share His glory, we must also share His suffering.

18 Yet what we suffer now is nothing compared to the glory He will give us later.

19 For all creation is waiting patiently and hopefully for that future day when God will resurrect His children.[2]

20, 21 For on that day thorns and thistles, sin, death, and decay[3]—the things that overcame the world against its will at God's command—will all disappear, and the world around us will share in the glorious freedom from sin which God's children enjoy.

22 For we know that even the things of nature, like animals and plants, suffer in sickness and death as they await this great event.[4]

23 And even we Christians, although we have the Holy Spirit within us as a foretaste of future glory, also groan to be released from pain and suffering. We, too, wait anxiously for that day when God will give us our full rights as His children, including the new bodies He has promised us—bodies that will never be sick again and will never die.

24 We are saved by trusting. And trusting means looking forward to getting something we do not yet have—for a man who already has something doesn't need to hope and trust that he will get it.

25 But if we must keep trusting God for something that hasn't happened yet, it teaches us to wait patiently and confidently.

[1] Or possibly, "but the Holy Spirit who lives in you will give you life, for He has already given you righteousness." Literally, "but the spirit is life because of righteousness."
[2] Literally, "waiting for the revelation of the sons of God."
[3] Implied.
[4] Literally, "the whole creation has been groaning in travail together until now."

Revised Standard

9 But you are not in the flesh, you are in
the Spirit, if the Spirit of God really dwells
in you. Any one who does not have the
Spirit of Christ does not belong to him.
10 But if Christ is in you, although your
bodies are dead because of sin, your spirits
are alive because of righteousness. 11 If the
Spirit of him who raised Jesus from the
dead dwells in you, he who raised Christ
Jesus from the dead will give life to your
mortal bodies also through his Spirit which
dwells in you.

12 So then, brethren, we are debtors, not
to the flesh, to live according to the flesh—
13 for if you live according to the flesh you
will die, but if by the Spirit you put to death
the deeds of the body you will live. 14 For
all who are led by the Spirit of God are
sons of God. 15 For you did not receive the
spirit of slavery to fall back into fear, but
you have received the spirit of sonship.
When we cry, "Abba! Father!" 16 it is the
Spirit himself bearing witness with our spirit
that we are children of God, 17 and if children, then heirs, heirs of God and fellow
heirs with Christ, provided we suffer with
him in order that we may also be glorified
with him.

The future glory

18 I consider that the sufferings of this
present time are not worth comparing with
the glory that is to be revealed to us. 19 For
the creation waits with eager longing for the
revealing of the sons of God; 20 for the creation was subjected to futility, not of its own
will but by the will of him who subjected
it in hope; 21 because the creation itself will
be set free from its bondage to decay and
obtain the glorious liberty of the children
of God. 22 We know that the whole creation
has been groaning in travail together until
now; 23 and not only the creation, but we
ourselves, who have the first fruits of the
Spirit, groan inwardly as we wait for adoption as sons, the redemption of our bodies.
24 For in this hope we were saved. Now hope
that is seen is not hope. For who hopes for
what he sees? 25 But if we hope for what we
do not see, we wait for it with patience.

King James

26 Likewise the Spirit also helpeth our infirmities: for we know not what we should pray for as we ought: but the Spirit itself maketh intercession for us with groanings which cannot be uttered.

27 And he that searcheth the hearts knoweth what *is* the mind of the Spirit, because he maketh intercession for the saints according to *the will of* God.

28 And we know that all things work together for good to them that love God, to them who are the called according to *his* purpose.

29 For whom he did foreknow, he also did predestinate *to be* conformed to the image of his Son, that he might be the firstborn among many brethren.

30 Moreover whom he did predestinate, them he also called: and whom he called, them he also justified: and whom he justified, them he also glorified.

31 What shall we then say to these things? If God *be* for us, who *can be* against us?

32 He that spared not his own Son, but delivered him up for us all, how shall he not with him also freely give us all things?

33 Who shall lay any thing to the charge of God's elect? *It is* God that justifieth.

34 Who *is* he that condemneth? *It is* Christ that died, yea rather, that is risen again, who is even at the right hand of God, who also maketh intercession for us.

35 Who shall separate us from the love of Christ? *shall* tribulation, or distress, or persecution, or famine, or nakedness, or peril, or sword?

36 As it is written, For thy sake we are killed all the day long; we are accounted as sheep for the slaughter.

37 Nay, in all these things we are more than conquerors through him that loved us.

38 For I am persuaded, that neither death, nor life, nor angels, nor principalities, nor powers, nor things present, nor things to come,

39 Nor height, nor depth, nor any other creature, shall be able to separate us from the love of God, which is in Christ Jesus our Lord.

Amplified

26 So too the (Holy) Spirit comes to our aid *and* bears us up in our weakness; for we do not know what prayer to offer *nor* how to offer it worthily as we ought, but the Spirit Himself goes to meet our supplication *and* pleads in our behalf with unspeakable yearnings *and* groanings too deep for utterance.

27 And He Who searches the hearts of men knows what is in the mind of the (Holy) Spirit — what His intent is — because the Spirit intercedes *and* pleads [before God] in behalf of the saints according to *and* in harmony with God's will. [Ps. 139:1, 2.]

28 We are assured *and* know that [[o]God being a partner in their labor], all things work together *and* are [fitting into a plan] for good to those who love God and are called according to [His] design *and* purpose.

29 For those whom He foreknew — of whom He was [p]aware and [q]loved beforehand — He also destined from the beginning (foreordaining them) to be molded into the image of His Son [and share inwardly His likeness], that He might become the first-born among many brethren.

30 And those whom He thus foreordained He also called; and those whom He called He also justified — acquitted, made righteous, putting them into right standing with Himself. And those whom He justified He also glorified — raising them to a heavenly dignity and condition [state of being].

31 What then shall we say to [all] this? If God be for us, who [can be] against us? — Who can be our foe, if God is on our side? [Ps. 118:6.]

32 He who did not withhold *or* spare [even] His own Son but gave Him up for us all, will He not also with Him freely *and* graciously give us all [other] things?

33 Who shall bring any charge against God's elect [when it is] God Who justifies — Who puts us in right relation to Himself? (Who shall come forward and accuse or impeach those whom God has chosen? Will God, Who acquits us?)

34 Who is there to condemn [us]? Will Christ Jesus, the Messiah, Who died, or rather Who was raised from the dead, Who is at the right hand of God actually pleading *as* He intercedes for us?

35 Who shall ever separate us from Christ's love? Shall suffering *and* affliction *and* tribulation? Or calamity *and* distress? Or persecution, or hunger, or destitution, or peril, or sword?

36 Even as it is written, For Thy sake we are put to death all the day long, we are regarded *and* counted as sheep for the slaughter. [Ps. 44:22.]

37 Yet amid all these things we are more than conquerors [r]*and* gain a surpassing victory through Him Who loved us.

38 For I am persuaded beyond doubt —am sure — that neither death, nor life, nor angels, nor principalities, nor things [s]impending *and* threatening, nor things to come, nor powers,

39 Nor height, nor depth, nor anything else in all creation will be able to separate us from the love of God which is in Christ Jesus our Lord.

---

o) Some authorities read, "God worketh all things with them."
p) Meyer [—Vincent].
q) John Murray's "The Sovereignty of God."
r) Thayer.
s) Vincent. Literal meaning, "standing in sight."

Living New Testament

26 And in the same way—by our faith[5]—the Holy Spirit helps us with our daily problems and in our praying. For we don't even know what we should pray for, nor how to pray as we should; but the Holy Spirit prays for us with such feeling that it cannot be expressed in words.

27 And the Father who knows all hearts knows, of course, what the Spirit is saying as He pleads for us in harmony with God's own will.

28 And we know that all that happens to us is working for our good if we love God and are fitting into His plans.

29 For from the very beginning God decided that those who came to Him—and all along He knew who would—should become like His Son, so that His Son would be the First, with many brothers.

30 And having chosen us, He called us to come to Him; and when we came, He declared us "not guilty," filled us with Christ's goodness, gave us right standing with Himself, and promised us His glory.

31 What can we ever say to such wonderful things as these? If God is on our side, who can ever be against us?

32 Since He did not spare even His own Son for us but gave Him up for us all, won't He also surely give us everything else?

33 Who dares accuse us whom God has chosen for His own? Will God? No! He is the one who has forgiven us and given us right standing with Himself.

34 Who then will condemn us? Will Christ? NO! For He is the one who died for us and came back to life again for us and is sitting at the place of highest honor next to God, pleading for us there in heaven.

35 Who then can ever keep Christ's love from us? When we have trouble or calamity, when we are hunted down or destroyed, is it because He doesn't love us anymore? And if we are hungry, or penniless, or in danger, or threatened with death, has God deserted us?

36 No, for the Scriptures tell us that for His sake we must be ready to face death at every moment of the day—we are like sheep awaiting slaughter;

37 But despite all this, overwhelming victory is ours through Christ who loved us enough to die for us.

38 For I am convinced that nothing can ever separate us from His love. Death can't, and life can't. The angels won't, and all the powers of hell itself cannot keep God's love away. Our fears for today, our worries about tomorrow,

39 Or where we are—high above the sky, or in the deepest ocean—nothing will ever be able to separate us from the love of God demonstrated by our Lord Jesus Christ when He died for us.

---

5 Implied. Literally, "in like manner."

Revised Standard

26 Likewise the Spirit helps us in our
weakness; for we do not know how to pray
as we ought, but the Spirit himself intercedes for us with sighs too deep for words.
27 And he who searches the hearts of men
knows what is the mind of the Spirit, because[j] the Spirit intercedes for the saints according to the will of God.
28 We know that in everything God works
for good[k] with those who love him,[l] who
are called according to his purpose. 29 For
those whom he foreknew he also predestined
to be conformed to the image of his Son,
in order that he might be the first-born
among many brethren. 30 And those whom
he predestined he also called; and those
whom he called he also justified; and those
whom he justified he also glorified.
31 What then shall we say to this? If
God is for us, who is against us? 32 He who
did not spare his own Son but gave him up
for us all, will he not also give us all things
with him? 33 Who shall bring any charge
against God's elect? It is God who justifies;
34 who is to condemn? Is it Christ Jesus, who
died, yes, who was raised from the dead,
who is at the right hand of God, who indeed intercedes for us?[m] 35 Who shall separate us from the love of Christ? Shall tribulation, or distress, or persecution, or famine,
or nakedness, or peril, or sword? 36 As it is
written,

> "For thy sake we are being killed all the day long;
> we are regarded as sheep to be slaughtered."

37 No, in all these things we are more than
conquerors through him who loved us. 38 For
I am sure that neither death, nor life, nor
angels, nor principalities, nor things present,
nor things to come, nor powers, 39 nor height,
nor depth, nor anything else in all creation,
will be able to separate us from the love of
God in Christ Jesus our Lord.

---

j Or *that*
k Other ancient authorities read *in everything he works for good*, or *everything works for good*
l Greek *God*
m Or *It is Christ Jesus . . . for us*

King James

CHAPTER 9

I SAY the truth in Christ, I lie not, my conscience also bearing me witness in the Holy Ghost,

2 That I have great heaviness and continual sorrow in my heart.

3 For I would wish that myself were accursed from Christ for my brethren, my kinsmen according to the flesh:

4 Who are Israelites; to whom *pertaineth* the adoption, and the glory, and the covenants, and the giving of the law, and the service *of God,* and the promises;

5 Whose *are* the fathers, and of whom as concerning the flesh Christ *came,* who is over all, God blessed for ever. Amen.

6 Not as though the word of God hath taken none effect. For they *are* not all Israel, which are of Israel:

7 Neither, because they are the seed of Abraham, *are they* all children: but, In Isaac shall thy seed be called.

8 That is, They which are the children of the flesh, these *are* not the children of God: but the children of the promise are counted for the seed.

9 For this *is* the word of promise, At this time will I come, and Sarah shall have a son.

10 And not only *this;* but when Rebecca also had conceived by one, *even* by our father Isaac;

11 (For *the children* being not yet born, neither having done any good or evil, that the purpose of God according to election might stand, not of works, but of him that calleth;)

12 It was said unto her, The elder shall serve the younger.

13 As it is written, Jacob have I loved, but Esau have I hated.

14 What shall we say then? *Is there* unrighteousness with God? God forbid.

15 For he saith to Moses, I will have mercy on whom I will have mercy, and I will have compassion on whom I will have compassion.

16 So then *it is* not of him that willeth, nor of him that runneth, but of God that sheweth mercy.

17 For the scripture saith unto Pharaoh, Even for this same purpose have I raised thee up, that I might shew my power in thee, and that my name might be declared throughout all the earth.

18 Therefore hath he mercy on whom he will *have mercy,* and whom he will he hardeneth.

19 Thou wilt say then unto me, Why doth he yet find fault? For who hath resisted his will?

Amplified

CHAPTER 9

I AM speaking the truth in Christ. I am not lying; my conscience [enlightened and prompted] by the Holy Spirit, bearing witness with me

2 That I have bitter grief and incessant anguish in my heart.

3 For I could wish that I myself were accursed *and* cut off *and* banished from Christ, for the sake of my brethren *and* instead of them, my natural kinsmen *and* my fellow countrymen. [Exod. 32:32.]

4 For they are Israelites, and to them belong God's adoption [as a nation] and the glorious (Shekinah) Presence. With them were the special covenants made, to them was the Law given. To them [the temple] worship was revealed and [God's own] promises announced. [Exod. 4:22; Hos. 11:1.]

5 To them belong the patriarchs, and as far as His natural descent was concerned from them is the Christ, Who is exalted *and* supreme over all, God, blessed forever! Amen — so let it be.

6 However, it is not as though God's Word had failed — coming to nothing. For it is not everybody who is a descendant of Jacob (Israel) who belongs to [the true] Israel.

7 And they are not all the children of Abraham because they are by blood his descendants. [No, the promise was,] Your descendants will be called *and* counted through the line of Isaac [though Abraham had an older son]. [Gen. 21:9-12.]

8 That is to say, it is not the children of the body [of Abraham] who are made God's children, but it is the offspring to whom the promise applies that shall be counted [as Abraham's true] descendants.

9 For this is what the promise said, About this time [next year] will I return and Sarah shall have a son. [Gen. 18:10.]

10 And not only that, but this too: Rebecca conceived [two sons under exactly the same circumstances] by our forefather Isaac.

11 And the children were yet unborn and had so far done nothing either good or evil. Even so, in order further to carry out God's purpose of selection (election, choice), which depends not on works *or* what men can do, but on Him Who calls [them],

12 It was said to her that the elder [son] should serve the younger [son]. [Gen. 25:21-23.]

13 As it is written, Jacob have I loved, but Esau have I hated [held in [t]relative disregard in comparison with My feeling for Jacob]. [Mal. 1:2, 3.]

14 What shall we conclude then? Is there injustice upon God's part? Certainly not!

15 For He says to Moses, I will have mercy on whom I will have mercy and I will have compassion (pity) on whom I will have compassion. [Exod. 33:19.]

16 So then [God's gift] is not a question of human will and human effort, but of God's mercy. — It depends not on one's own willingness nor on his strenuous exertion as in running a race, but on God's having mercy on him.

17 For the Scripture says to Pharaoh, I have raised you up for this very purpose of displaying My power in [dealing with] you, so that My name may be proclaimed the whole world over.

18 So then He has mercy on whomever He wills (chooses) and He hardens — makes stubborn and unyielding the heart of — whomever He wills.

19 You will say to me, Why then does He still find fault *and* blame us [for sinning]? For who can resist *and* withstand His will?

---

t) Abbott-Smith's "Manual Greek Lexicon of The New Testament."

Living New Testament

CHAPTER 9

Oh, Israel, my people! Oh, my Jewish brothers! How I long for you to come to Christ. My heart is heavy within me and I grieve bitterly day and night because of you. Christ knows and the Holy Spirit knows that it is no mere pretense when I say that I would be willing to be forever damned if that would save you.

4 God has given you so much, but still you will not listen to Him. He took you as His own special, chosen people and led you along with a bright cloud of glory and told you how very much He wanted to bless you. He gave you His rules for daily life so you would know what He wanted you to do. He let you worship Him, and gave you mighty promises.

5 Great men of God were your fathers, and Christ Himself was one of you, a Jew so far as His human nature is concerned, He who now rules over all things. Praise God forever!

6. Well then, has God failed to fulfill His promises to the Jews? No! [For these promises are only to those who are truly Jews.[1]] And not everyone born into a Jewish family is truly a Jew!

7 Just the fact that they come from Abraham doesn't make them truly Abraham's children. For the Scriptures say that the promises apply only to Abraham's son Isaac and Isaac's descendants, though Abraham had other children too.

8 This means that not all of Abraham's children are children of God, but only those who believe the promise of salvation which He made to Abraham.

9 For God had promised, "Next year I will give you and Sarah a son."

10, 11, 12, 13 And years later, when this son, Isaac, was grown up and married, and Rebecca his wife was about to bear him twin children, God told her that Esau, the child born first, would be a servant to Jacob, his twin brother. In the words of the Scripture, "I chose to bless Jacob, but not Esau." And God said this before the children were even born, before they had done anything either good or bad. This proves that God was doing what He had decided from the beginning; it was not because of what the children did but because of what God wanted and chose.

14 Was God being unfair? Of course not.

15 For God had said to Moses, "If I want to be kind to someone, I will. And I will take pity on anyone I want to."

16 And so God's blessings are not given just because someone decides to have them or works hard to get them. They are given because God takes pity on those He wants to.

17 Pharaoh, king of Egypt, was an example of this fact. For God told him He had given him the kingdom of Egypt for the very purpose of displaying the awesome power of God against him: so that all the world would hear about God's glorious name.[2]

18 So you see, God is kind to some just because He wants to be, and He makes some refuse to listen.

19 Well then, why does God blame them for not listening? Haven't they done what He made them do?

---

[1] Implied.
[2] Literally, "that My name might be published abroad in all the earth."

Revised Standard

Paul's sorrow for Israel

9 I am speaking the truth in Christ, I am
not lying; my conscience bears me witness in the Holy Spirit, [2]that I have great
sorrow and unceasing anguish in my heart.
[3]For I could wish that I myself were accursed and cut off from Christ for the sake
of my brethren, my kinsmen by race. [4]They
are Israelites, and to them belong the sonship,
the glory, the covenants, the giving of the
law, the worship, and the promises; [5]to them
belong the patriarchs, and of their race, according to the flesh, is the Christ. God who
is over all be blessed for ever.[n] Amen.
6 But it is not as though the word of
God had failed. For not all who are descended from Israel belong to Israel, [7]and
not all are children of Abraham because
they are his descendants; but "Through
Isaac shall your descendants be named."
[8]This means that it is not the children of the
flesh who are the children of God, but the
children of the promise are reckoned as
descendants. [9]For this is what the promise
said, "About this time I will return and
Sarah shall have a son." [10]And not only so,
but also when Rebecca had conceived children by one man, our forefather Isaac,
[11]though they were not yet born and had
done nothing either good or bad, in order
that God's purpose of election might continue, not because of works but because of
his call, [12]she was told, "The elder will serve
the younger." [13]As it is written, "Jacob
I loved, but Esau I hated."

God's justice and mercy

14 What shall we say then? Is there injustice on God's part? By no means! [15]For
he says to Moses, "I will have mercy on
whom I have mercy, and I will have compassion on whom I have compassion." [16]So
it depends not upon man's will or exertion,
but upon God's mercy. [17]For the scripture
says to Pharaoh, "I have raised you up for
the very purpose of showing my power in
you, so that my name may be proclaimed
in all the earth." [18]So then he has mercy
upon whomever he wills, and he hardens
the heart of whomever he wills.
19 You will say to me then, "Why does
he still find fault? For who can resist his

---

[n] Or *Christ, who is God over all, blessed for ever*

King James

20 Nay but, O man, who art thou that repliest against God? Shall the thing formed say to him that formed *it,* Why hast thou made me thus?

21 Hath not the potter power over the clay, of the same lump to make one vessel unto honour, and another unto dishonour?

22 *What* if God, willing to shew *his* wrath, and to make his power known, endured with much long-suffering the vessels of wrath fitted to destruction:

23 And that he might make known the riches of his glory on the vessels of mercy, which he had afore prepared unto glory,

24 Even us, whom he hath called, not of the Jews only, but also of the Gentiles?

25 As he saith also in Osee, I will call them my people, which were not my people; and her beloved, which was not beloved.

26 And it shall come to pass, *that* in the place where it was said unto them, Ye *are* not my people; there shall they be called the children of the living God.

27 Esaias also crieth concerning Israel, Though the number of the children of Israel be as the sand of the sea, a remnant shall be saved:

28 For he will finish the work, and cut *it* short in righteousness: because a short work will the Lord make upon the earth.

29 And as Esaias said before, Except the Lord of Sabaoth had left us a seed, we had been as Sodoma, and been made like unto Gomorrha.

30 What shall we say then? That the Gentiles, which followed not after righteousness, have attained to righteousness, even the righteousness which is of faith.

31 But Israel, which followed after the law of righteousness, hath not attained to the law of righteousness.

32 Wherefore? Because *they sought it* not by faith, but as it were by the works of the law. For they stumbled at that stumblingstone;

33 As it is written, Behold, I lay in Sion a stumblingstone and rock of offence: and whosoever believeth on him shall not be ashamed.

Amplified

20 But who are you, a mere man, to criticize *and* contradict *and* answer back to God? Will what is formed say to him that formed it, Why have you made me thus? [Isa. 29:16; 45:9.]

21 Has the potter no right over the clay, to make out of the same mass (lump) one vessel for beauty *and* distinction *and* honorable use, and another for menial *or* ignoble *and* dishonorable use?

22 What if God, although fully intending to show (the awfulness of) His wrath and to make known His power *and* authority, has tolerated with much patience the vessels (objects) of [His] anger which are ripe for destruction? [Prov. 16:4.]

23 And [what if] He thus purposes to make known *and* show the wealth of His glory in [dealing with] the vessels (objects) of His mercy which He has prepared beforehand for glory,

24 Even including ourselves whom He has called, not only from among the Jews but also from among the Gentiles (heathen)?

25 Just as He says in Hosea, Those who were not My people I will call My people, and her who was not beloved [I will call] My beloved. [Hos. 2:23.]

26 And it shall be in the very place where it was said to them, You are not My people, they shall be called sons of the living God. [Hos. 1:10.]

27 And Isaiah calls out (solemnly cries aloud) over Israel: Though the number of the sons of Israel be as the sand of the sea, only the remnant — a small part of them — will be saved [[u]from perdition, condemnation, judgment]!

28 For the Lord will execute His sentence upon the earth — He will conclude, close, His account with men completely and without delay — rigorously cutting it short in His justice. [Isa. 10:22, 23.]

29 It is as Isaiah predicted, If the Lord of hosts had not left us a seed [from which to propagate descendants], we (Israel) would have fared like Sodom and have been made like Gomorrah. [Isa. 1:9.]

30 What shall we say then? That Gentiles who did not follow after righteousness — who did not seek salvation by right relationship to God — have attained it by faith (that is, righteousness imputed by God, based on and produced by faith).

31 Whereas Israel, though ever in pursuit of a law [for the securing] of righteousness (right standing with God), actually did not succeed in fulfilling the Law. [Isa. 51:1.]

32 For what reason? Because [they pursued it] not through faith — they did not depend on faith but on what they could do — relying on the merit of their works. They have stumbled over the Stumbling Stone. [Isa. 28:16; 8:14.]

33 As it is written, Behold I am laying in Zion a Stone that will make men stumble, a Rock that will make them fall; but he who believes in Him (who adheres to, trusts in and relies on Him) shall not be put to shame *nor* be disappointed in his expectations. [Isa. 28:16.]

---

u) Cremer's "Biblico-Theological Lexicon of New Testament Greek."

Living New Testament

20 No, don't say that. Who are you to criticize God? Should the thing made say to the one who made it, "Why have you made me like this?"

21 When a man makes a jar out of clay, doesn't he have a right to use the same lump of clay to make one jar beautiful, to be used for holding flowers, and another to throw garbage into?

22 Does not God have a perfect right to show His fury and power against those who are fit only for destruction, those He has been patient with for all this time?

23, 24 And He has a right to take others such as ourselves, who have been made for pouring the riches of His glory into, whether we are Jews or Gentiles, and to be kind to us so that everyone can see how very great His glory is.

25 Remember what the prophecy of Hosea says? There God says that He will find other children for Himself (who are not from His Jewish family) and will love them, though no one had ever loved them before.

26 And the heathen, of whom it once was said, "You are not My people" shall be called "sons of the Living God."[3]

27 Isaiah the prophet cried out concerning the Jews that though there would be millions[4] of them, only a small number would ever be saved.

28 "For the Lord will execute His sentence upon the earth, quickly ending His dealings, justly cutting them short."[5]

29 And Isaiah says in another place that except for God's mercy all the Jews would be destroyed—all of them—just as everyone in the cities of Sodom and Gomorrah perished.[6]

30 Well then, what shall we say about these things? Just this, that God has given the Gentiles the opportunity to be acquitted by faith, even though they had not been really seeking God.

31 But the Jews, who tried so hard to get right with God by keeping His laws, never succeeded.

32 Why not? Because they were trying to be saved by keeping the law and being good instead of by depending on faith. They have stumbled over the great stumbling-stone.

33 God warned them of this in the Scriptures when He said, "I have put a Rock in the path of the Jews, and many will stumble over Him (Jesus). But those who believe in Him will never be disappointed."[7]

Revised Standard

will?" 20But who are you, a man, to answer
back to God? Will what is molded say to its
molder, "Why have you made me thus?"
21Has the potter no right over the clay, to
make out of the same lump one vessel for
beauty and another for menial use? 22What
if God, desiring to show his wrath and to
make known his power, has endured with
much patience the vessels of wrath made
for destruction, 23in order to make known
the riches of his glory for the vessels of
mercy, which he has prepared beforehand
for glory, 24even us whom he has called,
not from the Jews only but also from the
Gentiles? 25As indeed he says in Hosea,

"Those who were not my people
I will call 'my people,'
and her who was not beloved
I will call 'my beloved.' "
26"And in the very place where it was said
to them, 'You are not my people,'
they will be called 'sons of the living
God.' "

27 And Isaiah cries out concerning Israel:
"Though the number of the sons of Israel
be as the sand of the sea, only a remnant
of them will be saved; 28for the Lord will
execute his sentence upon the earth with
rigor and dispatch." 29And as Isaiah predicted,

"If the Lord of hosts had not left us
children,
we would have fared like Sodom and been
made like Gomorrah."

The gospel offered to the Jews

30 What shall we say, then? That Gentiles who did not pursue righteousness have
attained it, that is, righteousness through
faith; 31but that Israel who pursued the
righteousness which is based on law did not
succeed in fulfilling that law. 32Why? Because they did not pursue it through faith,
but as if it were based on works. They
have stumbled over the stumbling stone,
33as it is written,

"Behold, I am laying in Zion a stone that
will make men stumble,
a rock that will make them fall;
and he who believes in him will not be
put to shame."

---

[3] Hosea 2:23.
[4] Literally: "as the sand of the sea," *i.e.*, numberless.
[5] Isaiah 10:22, 28:22.
[6] Isaiah 1:9.
[7] Isaiah 28:16.

King James

CHAPTER 10

BRETHREN, my heart's desire and prayer to God for Israel is, that they might be saved.

2 For I bear them record that they have a zeal of God, but not according to knowledge.

3 For they being ignorant of God's righteousness, and going about to establish their own righteousness, have not submitted themselves unto the righteousness of God.

4 For Christ *is* the end of the law for righteousness to every one that believeth.

5 For Moses describeth the righteousness which is of the law, That the man which doeth those things shall live by them.

6 But the righteousness which is of faith speaketh on this wise, Say not in thine heart, Who shall ascend into heaven? (that is, to bring Christ down *from above:*)

7 Or, Who shall descend into the deep? (that is, to bring up Christ again from the dead.)

8 But what saith it? The word is nigh thee, *even* in thy mouth, and in thy heart: that is, the word of faith, which we preach;

9 That if thou shalt confess with thy mouth the Lord Jesus, and shalt believe in thine heart that God hath raised him from the dead, thou shalt be saved.

10 For with the heart man believeth unto righteousness; and with the mouth confession is made unto salvation.

11 For the scripture saith, Whosoever believeth on him shall not be ashamed.

12 For there is no difference between the Jew and the Greek: for the same Lord over all is rich unto all that call upon him.

13 For whosoever shall call upon the name of the Lord shall be saved.

14 How then shall they call on him in whom they have not believed? and how shall they believe in him of whom they have not heard? and how shall they hear without a preacher?

15 And how shall they preach, except they be sent? as it is written, How beautiful are the feet of them that preach the gospel of peace, and bring glad tidings of good things!

16 But they have not all obeyed the gospel. For Esaias saith, Lord, who hath believed our report?

17 So then faith *cometh* by hearing, and hearing by the word of God.

Amplified

CHAPTER 10

BRETHREN, [with all] my heart's desire *and* goodwill for (Israel) I long and pray to God that they may be saved.

2 I bear them witness that they have a [certain] zeal *and* enthusiasm for God, but it is not enlightened *and* according to [correct and vital] knowledge.

3 For being ignorant of the righteousness that God ascribes (which makes one acceptable to Him in word, thought and deed), and seeking to establish a *righteousness* (*a means of salvation*) of their own, they did not obey *or* submit themselves to God's righteousness.

4 For Christ is the end of the Law — the limit at which it ceases to be, for the Law leads up to Him Who is the fulfillment of its types, and in Him the purpose which it was designed to accomplish is fulfilled. — That is, the purpose of the Law is fulfilled in Him — as the means of righteousness (right relationship to God) for everyone who trusts in *and* adheres to *and* relies on Him.

5 For Moses writes that the man who [can] practice the righteousness (perfect conformity to God's will) which is based on the Law [with all its intricate demands] shall live by it. [Lev. 18:5.]

6 But the righteousness based on faith — imputed by God and bringing right relationship with Him — says, Do not say in your heart, Who will ascend into Heaven? that is, to bring Christ down,

7 Or who will descend into the abyss? that is, to bring Christ up from the dead [as if we could be saved by our own efforts], [Deut. 30:12, 13.]

8 But what does it say? The Word (God's message in Christ) is near you, on your lips and in your heart; that is, the Word — the message, the basis and object — of faith, which we preach. [Deut. 30:14.]

9 Because if you acknowledge *and* confess with your lips that Jesus is Lord and in your heart believe (adhere to, trust in and rely on the truth) that God raised Him from the dead, you will be saved.

10 For with the heart a person believes (adheres to, trusts in and relies on Christ) and so is justified (declared righteous, acceptable to God), and with the mouth he confesses — declares openly and speaks out freely his faith — *and* confirms [his] salvation.

11 The Scripture says, No man who believes in Him — who adheres to, relies on and trusts in Him — will [ever] be put to shame *or* be disappointed. [Isa. 28:16; 49:23; Jer. 17:7; Ps. 34:22.]

12 [No one,] for there is no distinction between Jew and Greek. The same Lord is Lord over all [of us] and He generously bestows His riches upon all who call upon Him [in faith].

13 For every one who calls upon the name of the Lord [invoking Him as Lord] will be saved. [Joel 2:32.]

14 But how are people to call upon Him Whom they have not believed — in Whom they have no faith, on Whom they have no reliance? And how are they to believe in Him — adhere to, trust in and rely upon Him — of Whom they have never heard? And how are they to hear without a preacher?

15 And how can men [be expected to] preach unless they are sent? As it is written, How beautiful are the feet of those who bring glad tidings! — How welcome is the coming of those who preach the good news of His good things! [Isa. 52:7.]

16 But they have not all heeded the Gospel; for Isaiah says, Lord, who has believed (had faith in) what he has heard from us? [Isa. 53:1.]

17 So faith comes by hearing [what is told], and what is heard comes by the preaching [of the message that came from the lips] of Christ, the Messiah [Himself].

Living New Testament

CHAPTER 10

Dear brothers, the longing of my heart and my prayer is that the Jewish people might be saved.

2 I know what enthusiasm you have for the honor of God, but it is misdirected zeal.

3 For you don't understand that Christ has died to make you right with God. Instead you are trying to make yourselves good enough to gain God's favor by keeping the Jewish laws and customs, but that is not God's way of salvation.

4 You don't understand that Christ gives to those who trust in Him everything you are trying to get by keeping His laws. He ends all that.

5 For Moses wrote that if a person could be perfectly good and hold out against temptation all his life and never sin once, only then could he be pardoned and saved.

6 But the salvation that comes through faith says, "You don't need to search the heavens to find Christ and bring Him down to help you," and,

7 "You don't need to go among the dead to bring Christ back to life again,"

8 For salvation that comes from trusting Christ—which is what we preach—is already within easy reach of each of us; in fact, it is as near as our own hearts and mouths.

9 For if you tell others with your own mouth that Jesus Christ is your Lord, and believe in your own heart that God has raised Him from the dead, you will be saved.

10 For it is by believing in his heart that a man becomes right with God; and with his mouth he tells others of his faith, confirming his salvation.[1]

11 For the Scriptures tell us that no one who believes in Christ will ever be disappointed.

12 Jew and Gentile are the same in this respect: they all have the same Lord who generously gives His riches to all those who ask Him for them.

13 Anyone who calls upon the name of the Lord will be saved.

14 But how shall they ask Him to save them unless they believe in Him? And how can they believe in Him if they have never heard about Him? And how can they hear about Him unless someone tells them?

15 And how will anyone go and tell them unless someone sends him? That is what the Scriptures are talking about when they say, "How beautiful are the feet of those who preach the Gospel of peace with God and bring glad tidings of good things."[2] In other words, how welcome are those who come preaching God's Good News!

16 But not everyone who hears the Good News has welcomed it, for Isaiah the prophet said, "Lord, who has believed me when I told them?"[3]

17 Yet faith comes from listening to this Good News —the Good News about Christ.

Revised Standard

10 Brethren, my heart's desire and prayer
to God for them is that they may be
saved. [2]I bear them witness that they have
a zeal for God, but it is not enlightened.
[3]For, being ignorant of the righteousness
that comes from God, and seeking to establish their own, they did not submit to
God's righteousness. [4]For Christ is the end
of the law, that every one who has faith
may be justified.
5 Moses writes that the man who practices the righteousness which is based on
the law shall live by it. [6]But the righteousness based on faith says, Do not say in
your heart, "Who will ascend into heaven?"
(that is, to bring Christ down) [7]or "Who
will descend into the abyss?" (that is, to
bring Christ up from the dead). [8]But what
does it say? The word is near you, on your
lips and in your heart (that is, the word of
faith which we preach); [9]because, if you
confess with your lips that Jesus is Lord
and believe in your heart that God raised
him from the dead, you will be saved. [10]For
man believes with his heart and so is justified, and he confesses with his lips and so is
saved. [11]The scripture says, "No one who
believes in him will be put to shame." [12]For
there is no distinction between Jew and
Greek; the same Lord is Lord of all and bestows his riches upon all who call upon him.
[13]For, "every one who calls upon the name
of the Lord will be saved."

The necessity of a preacher

14 But how are men to call upon him in
whom they have not believed? And how are
they to believe in him of whom they have
never heard? And how are they to hear
without a preacher? [15]And how can men
preach unless they are sent? As it is written,
"How beautiful are the feet of those who
preach good news!" [16]But they have not all
heeded the gospel; for Isaiah says, "Lord,
who has believed what he has heard from
us?" [17]So faith comes from what is heard,
and what is heard comes by the preaching
of Christ.

---

[1] Literally, "confession is made unto salvation."
[2] Isaiah 52:7.
[3] Isaiah 53:1.

King James

18 But I say, Have they not heard? Yes verily, their sound went into all the earth, and their words unto the ends of the world.

19 But I say, Did not Israel know? First Moses saith, I will provoke you to jealousy by *them that are* no people, *and* by a foolish nation I will anger you.

20 But Esaias is very bold, and saith, I was found of them that sought me not; I was made manifest unto them that asked not after me.

21 But to Israel he saith, All day long I have stretched forth my hands unto a disobedient and gainsaying people.

Amplified

18 But I ask, Have they not heard? Indeed they have; [for the Scripture says,] Their voice [that of nature bearing God's message] has gone out to all the earth, and their words to the far bounds of the world. [Ps. 19:4.]

19 Again I ask, Did Israel not understand? — Did the Jews have no warning that the Gospel was to go forth to the Gentiles, to all the earth? First, there is Moses who says, I will make you jealous of those who are not a nation; with a foolish nation I will make you angry. [Deut. 32:21.]

20 Then Isaiah is so bold as to say, I have been found by those who did not seek Me; I have shown (revealed) Myself to those who did not [consciously] ask for Me. [Isa. 65:1.]

21 But of Israel he says, All day long I have stretched out My hands to a people unyielding *and* disobedient and self-willed — to a fault-finding, contrary and contradicting people. [Isa. 65:2.]

CHAPTER 11

I SAY then, Hath God cast away his people? God forbid. For I also am an Israelite, of the seed of Abraham, *of* the tribe of Benjamin.

2 God hath not cast away his people which he foreknew. Wot ye not what the scripture saith of Elias? how he maketh intercession to God against Israel, saying,

3 Lord, they have killed thy prophets, and digged down thine altars; and I am left alone, and they seek my life.

4 But what saith the answer of God unto him? I have reserved to myself seven thousand men, who have not bowed the knee to *the image of* Baal.

5 Even so then at this present time also there is a remnant according to the election of grace.

6 And if by grace, then *is it* no more of works: otherwise grace is no more grace. But if *it be* of works, then is it no more grace: otherwise work is no more work.

7 What then? Israel hath not obtained that which he seeketh for; but the election hath obtained it, and the rest were blinded.

8 (According as it is written, God hath given them the spirit of slumber, eyes that they should not see, and ears that they should not hear;) unto this day.

9 And David saith, Let their table be made a snare, and a trap, and a stumblingblock, and a recompence unto them:

10 Let their eyes be darkened that they may not see, and bow down their back alway.

CHAPTER 11

I ASK then, has God totally rejected and disowned His people? Of course not! Why, I myself am an Israelite, a descendant of Abraham, a member of the tribe of Benjamin! [I Sam. 12:22; Jer. 31:37; 33:24-26.]

2 No, God has not rejected *and* disowned His people [whose destiny] He had marked out *and* appointed *and* foreknown from the beginning. Do you not know what the Scripture says of Elijah, how he pleads with God against Israel? [Ps. 94:14; I Kings 19.]

3 Lord, they have killed Your prophets, they have demolished Your altars, and I alone am left, and they seek my life.

4 But what is God's reply to him? I have kept for Myself seven thousand men who have not bowed the knee to Baal! [I Kings 19:18.]

5 So too at the present time there is a remnant (a small believing minority), selected (chosen) by grace — by God's unmerited favor and graciousness.

6 But if it is by grace — His unmerited favor and graciousness — it is no longer conditioned on works or anything men have done. Otherwise, grace would no longer be grace — it would be meaningless.

7 What then [shall we conclude]? Israel failed to obtain what it sought [God's favor by obedience to law]. Only the elect (those chosen few) obtained it; while the rest of them became callously indifferent — blinded, hardened and made insensible to it.

8 As it is written, God gave them a spirit (an attitude) of stupor, eyes that should not see and ears that should not hear, [that has continued] down to this very day. [Isa. 29:10; Deut. 29:4.]

9 And David says, Let their table (their feasting, banqueting) become a snare and a trap, a pitfall and a [v]just retribution — [w]rebounding as a boomerang upon them; [Ps. 69:22.]

10 Let their eyes be darkened (dimmed) so that they cannot see, and make them bend their back [stooping beneath their burden] forever. [Ps. 69:23.]

v) Vincent.
w) Greek, literally, *a return, a recompense, etc.*

Living New Testament

18 But what about the Jews? Have they heard God's Word? Yes, for it has gone wherever they are; the Good News has been told to the ends of the earth.

19 And did they understand [that God would give His salvation to others if they refused to take it[4]]? Yes, for even back in the time of Moses, God had said that He would make His people jealous and try to wake them up by giving His salvation to the foolish heathen nations.

20 And later on Isaiah said boldly that God would be found by people who weren't even looking for Him.[5]

21 In the meantime, He keeps on reaching out His hands to the Jews but they keep arguing[6] and refusing to come.

Revised Standard

18 But I ask, have they not heard? Indeed they have; for
"Their voice has gone out to all the
earth,
and their words to the ends of the world."
19 Again I ask, did Israel not understand?
First Moses says,
"I will make you jealous of those who
are not a nation;
with a foolish nation I will make you
angry."
20 Then Isaiah is so bold as to say,
"I have been found by those who did not
seek me;
I have shown myself to those who did
not ask for me."
21 But of Israel he says, "All day long I have
held out my hands to a disobedient and
contrary people."

CHAPTER 11

I ask then, has God rejected and deserted His people the Jews? Oh no, not at all. Remember that I myself am a Jew, a descendant of Abraham and a member of Benjamin's family.

2, 3 No, God has not discarded His own people whom He chose from the very beginning. Do you remember what the Scriptures say about this? Elijah the prophet was complaining to God about the Jews, telling God how they had killed the prophets and torn down God's altars; Elijah claimed that he was the only one left in all the land who still loved God, and now they were trying to kill him too.

4 And do you remember how God replied? God said, "No, you are not the only one left. I have seven thousand others besides you who still love Me and have not bowed down to idols!"[1]

5 It is the same today. Not all the Jews have turned away from God; there are a few being saved as a result of God's kindness in choosing them.

6 And if it is by God's kindness, then it is not by their being good enough. For in that case the free gift would no longer be free—it isn't free when it is earned.

7 So this is the situation: most of the Jews have not found the favor of God they are looking for. A few have—the ones God has picked out—but the eyes of the others have been blinded.

8 This is what our Scriptures refer to when they say that God has put them to sleep, shutting their eyes and ears so that they do not understand what we are talking about when we tell them of Christ. And so it is to this very day.

9 King David spoke of this same thing when he said, "Let their good food and other blessings trap them into thinking all is well between themselves and God. Let these things boomerang on them and fall back upon their heads to justly crush them.

10 Let their eyes be dim," he said, "so that they cannot see, and let them walk bent-backed forever with a heavy load."

The remnant of Israel

11 I ask, then, has God rejected his people? By no means! I myself am an
Israelite, a descendant of Abraham, a member of the tribe of Benjamin. 2 God has not
rejected his people whom he foreknew. Do
you not know what the scripture says of
Elijah, how he pleads with God against
Israel? 3 "Lord, they have killed thy prophets,
they have demolished thy altars, and I alone
am left, and they seek my life." 4 But what is
God's reply to him? "I have kept for myself
seven thousand men who have not bowed
the knee to Baal." 5 So too at the present
time there is a remnant, chosen by grace.
6 But if it is by grace, it is no longer on the
basis of works; otherwise grace would no
longer be grace.
7 What then? Israel failed to obtain what
it sought. The elect obtained it, but the
rest were hardened, 8 as it is written,
"God gave them a spirit of stupor, eyes
that should not see and ears that should
not hear,
down to this very day."
9 And David says,
"Let their feast become a snare and a
trap,
a pitfall and a retribution for them;
10 let their eyes be darkened so that they
cannot see,
and bend their backs for ever."

[4] Implied.
[5] Isaiah 65:1.
[6] Literally, "disobedient, obstinate."
[1] I Kings 19:18.

King James

11 I say then, Have they stumbled that they should fall? God forbid: but *rather* through their fall salvation *is come* unto the Gentiles, for to provoke them to jealousy.

12 Now if the fall of them *be* the riches of the world, and the diminishing of them the riches of the Gentiles; how much more their fulness?

13 For I speak to you Gentiles, inasmuch as I am the apostle of the Gentiles, I magnify mine office:

14 If by any means I may provoke to emulation *them which are* my flesh, and might save some of them.

15 For if the casting away of them *be* the reconciling of the world, what *shall* the receiving *of them be,* but life from the dead?

16 For if the firstfruit *be* holy, the lump *is* also *holy:* and if the root *be* holy, so *are* the branches.

17 And if some of the branches be broken off, and thou, being a wild olive tree, wert grafted in among them, and with them partakest of the root and fatness of the olive tree;

18 Boast not against the branches. But if thou boast, thou bearest not the root, but the root thee.

19 Thou wilt say then, The branches were broken off, that I might be grafted in.

20 Well; because of unbelief they were broken off, and thou standest by faith. Be not highminded, but fear:

21 For if God spared not the natural branches, *take heed* lest he also spare not thee.

22 Behold therefore the goodness and severity of God: on them which fell, severity; but toward thee, goodness, if thou continue in *his* goodness: otherwise thou also shalt be cut off.

23 And they also, if they abide not still in unbelief, shall be grafted in: for God is able to graft them in again.

24 For if thou wert cut out of the olive tree which is wild by nature, and wert grafted contrary to nature into a good olive tree: how much more shall these, which be the natural *branches,* be grafted into their own olive tree?

25 For I would not, brethren, that ye should be ignorant of this mystery, lest ye should be wise in your own conceits; that blindness in part is happened to Israel, until the fulness of the Gentiles be come in.

26 And so all Israel shall be saved: as it is written, There shall come out of Sion the Deliverer, and shall turn away ungodliness from Jacob:

27 For this *is* my covenant unto them, when I shall take away their sins.

Amplified

11 So I ask, have they stumbled so as to fall — to their utter spiritual ruin, irretrievably? By no means! But through their false step *and* transgression salvation [has come] to the Gentiles, so as to arouse Israel [to see and feel what they forfeited] and so to make them jealous.

12 Now if their stumbling — their lapse, their transgression — has so enriched the world [at large], and if [Israel's] failure means such riches for the Gentiles, think what an enrichment *and* greater advantage will follow their full reinstatement!

13 But now I am speaking to you who are Gentiles. Inasmuch then as I am an apostle to the Gentiles, I lay great stress on my ministry *and* magnify my office,

14 In the hope of making my fellow Jews jealous — in order to stir them up to imitate, copy and appropriate — and thus managing to save some of them.

15 For if their rejection *and* exclusive from the benefits of salvation were [overruled] for the reconciliation of a world to God, what will their acceptance *and* admission mean? [It will be nothing short of] life from the dead!

16 Now if the first handful of dough offered as the first fruits [Abraham and the patriarchs] is consecrated (holy), so is the whole mass [the nation of Israel]; and if the root [Abraham] is consecrated (holy), so are the branches. [Num. 15:19-21.]

17 But if some of the branches were broken off, while you, a wild olive shoot, were grafted in among them to share the richness [of the root and sap] of the olive tree,

18 Do not boast over the branches *and* pride yourself at their expense. If you do boast *and* feel superior, remember it is not you that support the root, but the root [that supports] you.

19 You will say then, Branches were broken (pruned) off so that I might be grafted in!

20 That is true. But they were broken (pruned) off because of their unbelief — their lack of real faith, and you are established through faith — because you do believe. So do not become proud *and* conceited, but rather stand in awe *and* be reverently afraid.

21 For if God did not spare the natural branches [because of unbelief], neither will He spare you [if you are guilty of the same offense].

22 Then note *and* appreciate the gracious kindness and the severity of God; severity toward those who have fallen, but God's gracious kindness to you. [That is, to you] provided you continue in His grace *and* to abide in His kindness; otherwise you too will be cut off — pruned away.

23 And even those others (the fallen branches, Jews), if they do not persist in [clinging to] their unbelief, will be grafted in, for God has the power to graft them in again.

24 For if you have been cut from what is by nature a wild olive tree, and against nature grafted into a cultivated olive tree, how much easier will it be to graft these natural [branches] back on [the original parent stock of] their own olive tree.

25 Lest you be self-opinionated — wise in your own conceits — I do not want you to miss this hidden truth *and* mystery, brethren: a hardening (insensibility) has [temporarily] befallen a part of Israel [to last] until the [x]full number of the ingathering of the Gentiles has come in,

26 And so all Israel will be saved. As it is written, The Deliverer will come from Zion, He will banish ungodliness from Jacob. [Isa. 59:20, 21.]

27 And this will be My covenant — My agreement — with them when I shall take away their sins. [Jer. 31:33; Isa. 27:9.]

---

x) Thayer.

Living New Testament

11 Does this mean that God has rejected His Jewish people forever? Of course not! His purpose was to make His salvation available to the Gentiles, and then the Jews would be jealous and begin to want God's salvation for themselves.

12 Now if the whole world became rich as a result of God's offer of salvation, when the Jews stumbled over it and turned it down, think how much greater a blessing the world will share in later on when the Jews too, come to Christ.

13 As you know, God has appointed me as a special messenger to you Gentiles. I lay great stress on this and remind the Jews about it as often as I can,

14 So that if possible I can make them want what you Gentiles have and in that way save some of them.

15 And how wonderful it will be when they become Christians. When God turned away from them it meant that He turned to the rest of the world to offer His salvation; and now it is even more wonderful when the Jews come to Christ. It will be like dead people coming back to life.

16 And since Abraham and the prophets are God's people, their children will be too. For if the roots of the tree are holy, the branches will be too.

17 But some of these branches from Abraham's tree, some of the Jews, have been broken off. And you Gentiles who were branches from, we might say, a wild olive tree, were grafted in. So now you, too, receive the blessing God has promised Abraham and his children, sharing in God's rich nourishment of His own special olive tree.

18 But you must be careful not to brag about being put in to replace the branches that were broken off. Remember that you are important only because you are now a part of God's tree; you are just a branch, not a root.

19 "Well," you may be saying, "those branches were broken off to make room for me so I must be pretty good."

20 Watch out! Remember that those branches, the Jews, were broken off because they didn't believe God, and you are there only because you do. Do not be proud; be humble and grateful—and careful.

21 For if God did not spare the branches He put there in the first place, He won't spare you either.

22 Notice how God is both so kind and so severe. He is very hard on those who disobey, but very good to you if you continue to love and trust Him. But if you don't, you too will be cut off.

23 On the other hand, if the Jews leave their unbelief behind them and come back to God, God will graft them back into the tree again. He has the power to do it.

24 For if God was willing to take you who were so far away from Him—being a part of a wild olive tree—and graft you into His own good tree—a very unusual thing to do—don't you see that He will be far more ready to put the Jews back again, who were there in the first place?

25 I want you to know about this truth from God, dear brothers, so that you will not feel proud and start bragging. Yes, it is true that some of the Jews have set themselves against the Gospel now, but this will last only until all of you Gentiles have come to Christ—those of you who will.

26 And then all Israel will be saved. Do you remember what the prophets said about this? "There shall come out of Zion a Deliverer, and He shall turn the Jews from all ungodliness.

27 At that time I will take away their sins, just as I promised."

Revised Standard

Israel's future salvation

11 So I ask, have they stumbled so as to
fall? By no means! But through their trespass salvation has come to the Gentiles, so
as to make Israel jealous. [12]Now if their
trespass means riches for the world, and if
their failure means riches for the Gentiles,
how much more will their full inclusion
mean!
13 Now I am speaking to you Gentiles.
Inasmuch then as I am an apostle to the
Gentiles, I magnify my ministry [14]in order
to make my fellow Jews jealous, and thus
save some of them. [15]For if their rejection
means the reconciliation of the world, what
will their acceptance mean but life from
the dead? [16]If the dough offered as first
fruits is holy, so is the whole lump; and if
the root is holy, so are the branches.
17 But if some of the branches were
broken off, and you, a wild olive shoot, were
grafted in their place to share the richness[o]
of the olive tree, [18]do not boast over the
branches. If you do boast, remember it is
not you that support the root, but the root
that supports you. [19]You will say, "Branches
were broken off so that I might be grafted
in." [20]That is true. They were broken off because of their unbelief, but you stand fast
only through faith. So do not become proud,
but stand in awe. [21]For if God did not spare
the natural branches, neither will he spare
you. [22]Note then the kindness and the
severity of God: severity toward those who
have fallen, but God's kindness to you, provided you continue in his kindness; otherwise you too will be cut off. [23]And even the
others, if they do not persist in their unbelief, will be grafted in, for God has the
power to graft them in again. [24]For if you
have been cut from what is by nature a
wild olive tree, and grafted, contrary to
nature, into a cultivated olive tree, how
much more will these natural branches be
grafted back into their own olive tree.
25 Lest you be wise in your own conceits, I want you to understand this mystery,
brethren: a hardening has come upon part
of Israel, until the full number of the Gentiles come in, [26]and so all Israel will be
saved; as it is written,

"The Deliverer will come from Zion,
he will banish ungodliness from Jacob";
27 "and this will be my covenant with them
when I take away their sins."

[o] Other ancient authorities read *rich root*

King James

28 As concerning the gospel, *they are* enemies for your sakes: but as touching the election, *they are* beloved for the fathers' sakes.

29 For the gifts and calling of God *are* without repentance.

30 For as ye in times past have not believed God, yet have now obtained mercy through their unbelief:

31 Even so have these also now not believed, that through your mercy they also may obtain mercy.

32 For God hath concluded them all in unbelief, that he might have mercy upon all.

33 O the depth of the riches both of the wisdom and knowledge of God! how unsearchable *are* his judgments, and his ways past finding out!

34 For who hath known the mind of the Lord? or who hath been his counsellor?

35 Or who hath first given to him, and it shall be recompensed unto him again?

36 For of him, and through him, and to him, *are* all things: to whom *be* glory for ever. Amen.

Amplified

28 From the point of view of the Gospel (good news) they [the Jews, at present] are enemies [of God], which is for your advantage *and* benefit. But from the point of view of God's choice — of election, of divine selection — they are still the beloved [dear to Him] for the sake of their forefathers.

29 For God's gifts and His call are irrevocable — He never withdraws them when once they are given, and He does not change His mind about those to whom He gives His grace or to whom He sends His call.

30 Just as you were once disobedient *and* rebellious toward God but now have obtained [His] mercy, through their disobedience,

31 So they also now are being disobedient (when you are receiving mercy, that they in turn may one day share the mercy [through you as messengers of the Gospel to them] which has been shown to you). Thus through the mercy you are enjoying, they may *now* also receive mercy.

32 For God has consigned (penned up) all men to disobedience, only that He may have mercy on them all [alike].

33 O the depth of the riches and wisdom and knowledge of God! How unfathomable (inscrutable, unsearchable) are His judgments — His decisions! And how untraceable (mysterious, undiscoverable) are His ways — His methods, His paths!

34 For who has known the mind of the Lord *and* who has understood His thoughts, or who has [ever] been His counselor? [Isa. 40:13, 14.]

35 Or who has first given God anything that he might be paid back *or* that he could claim a recompense?

36 For from Him and through Him and to Him are all things. — For all things originate with Him and come from Him; all things live through Him, and all things center in and tend to consummate and to end in Him. To Him be glory forever! Amen — so be it.

King James

CHAPTER 12

I BESEECH you therefore, brethren, by the mercies of God, that ye present your bodies a living sacrifice, holy, acceptable unto God, *which is* your reasonable service.

2 And be not conformed to this world: but be ye transformed by the renewing of your mind, that ye may prove what *is* that good, and acceptable, and perfect, will of God.

3 For I say, through the grace given unto me, to every man that is among you, not to think *of himself* more highly than he ought to think; but to think soberly, according as God hath dealt to every man the measure of faith.

4 For as we have many members in one body, and all members have not the same office:

Amplified

CHAPTER 12

I APPEAL to you therefore, brethren, *and* beg of you in view of [all] the mercies of God, to make a decisive dedication of your bodies — presenting all your members and faculties — as a living sacrifice, holy (devoted, consecrated) and well pleasing to God, which is your reasonable (rational, intelligent) service *and* spiritual worship.

2 Do not be conformed to this world — this [y]age, fashioned after and adapted to its external, superficial customs. But be transformed (changed) by the [entire] renewal of your mind — by its new ideals and its new attitude — so that you may prove [for yourselves] what is the good and acceptable and perfect will of God, [y]*even* the thing which is good and acceptable and perfect [in His sight for you].

3 For by the grace (unmerited favor of God) given to me I warn every one among you not to estimate *and* think of himself more highly than he ought — not to have an exaggerated opinion of his own importance; but to rate his ability with sober judgment, each according to the degree of faith apportioned by God to him.

4 For as in one physical body we have many parts (organs, members) and all of these parts do not have the same function *or* use,

---

y) Alternate reading.

Living New Testament

28 Now many of the Jews are enemies of the Gospel. They hate it. But this has been a benefit to you, for it has resulted in God giving His gifts to you Gentiles. Yet the Jews are still beloved of God because of His promises to Abraham, Isaac, and Jacob.

29 For God's gifts and His call can never be withdrawn; He will never go back on His promises.

30 Once you were rebels against God, but when the Jews refused His gifts God was merciful to you instead.

31 And now the Jews are the rebels, but some day they, too, will share in God's mercy upon you.

32 For God has given them all up to sin[2] so that He could have mercy upon all alike.

33 Oh, what a wonderful God we have! How great are His wisdom and knowledge and riches! How impossible it is for us to understand His decisions and His methods!

34 For who among us can know the mind of the Lord? Who knows enough to be His counselor and guide?

35 And who could ever offer to the Lord enough to induce Him to act?

36 For everything comes from God alone. Everything lives by His power, and everything is for His glory. To Him be glory evermore.

Revised Standard

28 As regards the gospel they are enemies of
God, for your sake; but as regards election
they are beloved for the sake of their forefathers. 29 For the gifts and the call of
God are irrevocable. 30 Just as you were
once disobedient to God but now have received mercy because of their disobedience,
31 so they have now been disobedient in
order that by the mercy shown to you they
also may[p] receive mercy. 32 For God has
consigned all men to disobedience, that he
may have mercy upon all.

33 O the depth of the riches and wisdom
and knowledge of God! How unsearchable
are his judgments and how inscrutable his
ways!

34 "For who has known the mind of the
Lord,
or who has been his counselor?"

35 "Or who has given a gift to him that he
might be repaid?"

36 For from him and through him and to
him are all things. To him be glory for
ever. Amen.

CHAPTER 12

And, so, dear brothers, I plead with you to give your bodies to God. Let them be a living sacrifice, holy—the kind He can accept. When you think of what He has done for you, is this too much to ask?

2 Don't copy the behavior and customs of this world, but be a new and different person with a fresh newness in all you do and think. Then you will learn from your own experience how His ways will really satisfy you.

3 As God's messenger I give each of you God's warning: be honest in your estimate of yourselves, measuring your value by how much faith God has given you.

4, 5 Just as there are many parts to our bodies, so it is with Christ's body. We are all parts of it, and it takes

Conduct in relation to God

12 I appeal to you therefore, brethren,
by the mercies of God, to present
your bodies as a living sacrifice, holy and
acceptable to God, which is your spiritual
worship. 2 Do not be conformed to this
world[q] but be transformed by the renewal
of your mind, that you may prove what is
the will of God, what is good and acceptable
and perfect.[r]

Conduct in relation to the church

3 For by the grace given to me I bid
every one among you not to think of himself
more highly than he ought to think, but to
think with sober judgment, each according
to the measure of faith which God has assigned him. 4 For as in one body we have
many members, and all the members do

[2] **Literally, "shut up all unto disobedience."**

[p] Other ancient authorities add *now*
[q] Greek *age*
[r] Or *what is the good and acceptable and perfect will of God*

King James

5 So we, *being* many, are one body in Christ, and every one members one of another.

6 Having then gifts differing according to the grace that is given to us, whether prophecy, *let us prophesy* according to the proportion of faith;

7 Or ministry, *let us wait* on *our* ministering: or he that teacheth, on teaching;

8 Or he that exhorteth, on exhortation: he that giveth, *let him do it* with simplicity; he that ruleth, with diligence; he that sheweth mercy, with cheerfulness.

9 *Let* love be without dissimulation. Abhor that which is evil; cleave to that which is good.

10 *Be* kindly affectioned one to another with brotherly love; in honour preferring one another;

11 Not slothful in business; fervent in spirit; serving the Lord;

12 Rejoicing in hope; patient in tribulation; continuing instant in prayer;

13 Distributing to the necessity of saints; given to hospitality.

14 Bless them which persecute you: bless, and curse not.

15 Rejoice with them that do rejoice, and weep with them that weep.

16 *Be* of the same mind one toward another. Mind not high things, but condescend to men of low estate. Be not wise in your own conceits.

17 Recompense to no man evil for evil. Provide things honest in the sight of all men.

18 If it be possible, as much as lieth in you, live peaceably with all men.

19 Dearly beloved, avenge not yourselves, but *rather* give place unto wrath: for it is written, Vengeance *is* mine; I will repay, saith the Lord.

20 Therefore if thine enemy hunger, feed him; if he thirst, give him drink: for in so doing thou shalt heap coals of fire on his head.

21 Be not overcome of evil, but overcome evil with good.

Amplified

5 So we, numerous as we are, are one body in Christ, the Messiah, and individually we are parts one of another — mutually dependent on one another.

6 Having gifts (faculties, talents, qualities) that differ according to the grace given us, let us use them: [He whose gift is] prophecy, [let him prophesy] according to the proportion of his faith;

7 [He whose gift is] practical service, let him give himself to serving; he who teaches, to his teaching;

8 (He who exhorts, encourages), to his exhortation; he who contributes, let him do it in simplicity *and* liberality; he who gives aid *and* superintends, with zeal *and* singleness of mind; he who does acts of mercy, with genuine cheerfulness *and* joyful eagerness.

9 [Let your] love be sincere — a real thing; hate what is evil (loathe all ungodliness, turn in horror from wickedness), but hold fast to that which is good.

10 Love one another with brotherly affection — as members of one family — giving precedence *and* showing honor to one another.

11 Never lag in zeal *and* in earnest endeavor; be aglow *and* burning with the Spirit, serving the Lord.

12 Rejoice *and* exult in hope; be steadfast and patient in suffering *and* tribulation; be constant in prayer.

13 Contribute to the needs of God's people — sharing in the necessities of the saints — pursuing the practice of hospitality.

14 Bless those who persecute you — who are cruel in their attitude toward you; bless and do not curse them.

15 [Share others' joy], rejoicing with those who rejoice; and [share others' grief], weeping with those who weep.

16 Live in harmony with one another; do not be haughty (snobbish, high-minded, exclusive), but readily adjust yourself to [people, things] *and* give yourselves to humble tasks. Never over-estimate yourself *or* be wise in your own conceits. [Prov. 3:7.]

17 Repay no one evil for evil, but take thought for what is honest *and* proper *and* noble — aiming to be above reproach — in the sight of every one. [Prov. 20:22.]

18 If possible, as far as it depends on you, live at peace with every one.

19 Beloved, never avenge yourselves, but leave the way open for [God's] wrath; for it is written, Vengeance is Mine, I will repay (requite), says the Lord. [Deut. 32:35.]

20 But, if your enemy is hungry, feed him; if he is thirsty, give him drink; for by so doing you will heap burning coals upon his head. [Prov. 25:21, 22.]

21 Do not let yourself be overcome by evil, but overcome (master) evil with good.

CHAPTER 13

LET every soul be subject unto the higher powers. For there is no power but of God: the powers that be are ordained of God.

2 Whosoever therefore resisteth the power, resisteth the ordinance of God: and they that resist shall receive to themselves damnation.

3 For rulers are not a terror to good works, but to the evil. Wilt thou then not be afraid of the power? do that which is good, and thou shalt have praise of the same:

CHAPTER 13

LET every person be loyally subject to the governing (civil) authorities. For there is no authority except from God — by His permission, His sanction; and those that exist do so by God's appointment. [Prov. 8:15.]

2 Therefore he who resists *and* sets himself up against the authorities resists what God has appointed *and* arranged — in divine order. And those who resist will bring down judgment upon themselves — receiving the penalty due them.

3 For civil authorities are not a terror to [people of] good conduct, but to [those of] bad behavior. Would you have no dread of him who is in authority? Then do what is right and you will receive his approval *and* commendation.

Living New Testament

every one of us to make it complete, for we each have different work to do. So we belong to each other, and each needs all the others.

6 God has given each of us the ability to do certain things well. So if God has given you the ability to prophesy, then prophesy whenever you can—as often as your faith is strong enough to receive a message from God.

7 If your gift is that of serving others, serve them well. If you are a teacher, do a good job of teaching.

8 If you are a preacher, see to it that your sermons are strong and helpful. If God has given you money, be generous in helping others with it. If God has given you administrative ability and put you in charge of the work of others, take the responsibility seriously. Those who offer comfort to the sorrowing should do so with Christian cheer.

9 Don't just pretend that you love others: really love them. Hate what is wrong. Stand on the side of the good.

10 Love each other with brotherly affection and take delight in honoring each other.

11 Never be lazy in your work but serve the Lord enthusiastically.

12 Be glad for all God is planning for you. Be patient in trouble, and prayerful always.

13 When God's children are in need, you be the one to help them out. And get into the habit of inviting guests home for dinner or, if they need lodging, for the night.

14 If someone mistreats you because you are a Christian, don't curse him; pray that God will bless him.

15 When others are happy, be happy with them. If they are sad, share their sorrow.

16 Work happily together. Don't try to act big. Don't try to get into the good graces of important people, but enjoy the company of ordinary folks. And don't think you know it all!

17 Never pay back evil for evil. Do things in such a way that everyone can see you are honest clear through.

19 Don't quarrel with anyone. Be at peace with everyone, just as much as possible.

19 Dear friends, never avenge yourselves. Leave that to God, for He has said that He will repay those who deserve it. [Don't take the law into your own hands.[1]]

20 Instead, feed your enemy if he is hungry. If he is thirsty give him something to drink and you will be "heaping coals of fire on his head." In other words, he will feel ashamed of himself for what he has done to you.

21 Don't let evil get the upper hand but conquer evil by doing good.

CHAPTER 13

Obey the government, for God is the one who has put it there. There is no government anywhere that God has not placed in power.

2 So those who refuse to obey the laws of the land are refusing to obey God, and punishment will follow.

3 For the policeman does not frighten people who are doing right; but those doing evil will always fear him. So if you don't want to be afraid, keep the laws and you will get along well.

Implied.

Revised Standard

not have the same function, 5so we, though
many, are one body in Christ, and individually members one of another. 6Having gifts
that differ according to the grace given to
us, let us use them: if prophecy, in proportion to our faith; 7if service, in our serving;
he who teaches, in his teaching; 8he who
exhorts, in his exhortation; he who contributes, in liberality; he who gives aid, with
zeal; he who does acts of mercy, with cheerfulness.

Conduct in relation to men

9 Let love be genuine; hate what is evil,
hold fast to what is good; 10love one another with brotherly affection; outdo one another in showing honor. 11Never flag in zeal,
be aglow with the Spirit, serve the Lord.
12Rejoice in your hope, be patient in tribulation, be constant in prayer. 13Contribute
to the needs of the saints, practice hospitality.
14 Bless those who persecute you; bless
and do not curse them. 15Rejoice with those
who rejoice, weep with those who weep.
16Live in harmony with one another; do not
be haughty, but associate with the lowly;[s]
never be conceited. 17Repay no one evil for
evil, but take thought for what is noble
in the sight of all. 18If possible, so far as it
depends upon you, live peaceably with all.
19Beloved, never avenge yourselves, but leave
it[t] to the wrath of God; for it is written,
"Vengeance is mine, I will repay, says the
Lord." 20No, "if your enemy is hungry, feed
him; if he is thirsty, give him drink; for by
so doing you will heap burning coals upon
his head." 21Do not be overcome by evil,
but overcome evil with good.

Conduct in relation to the state

13 Let every person be subject to the governing authorities. For there is no
authority except from God, and those that
exist have been instituted by God. 2There-
fore he who resists the authorities resists
what God has appointed, and those who resist will incur judgment. 3For rulers are not
a terror to good conduct, but to bad. Would
you have no fear of him who is in authority? Then do what is good, and you will receive his approval, 4for he is God's servant

[s] Or *give yourselves to humble tasks*
[t] Greek *give place*

King James

4 For he is the minister of God to thee for good. But if thou do that which is evil, be afraid; for he beareth not the sword in vain: for he is the minister of God, a revenger to *execute* wrath upon him that doeth evil.

5 Wherefore *ye* must needs be subject, not only for wrath, but also for conscience sake.

6 For for this cause pay ye tribute also: for they are God's ministers, attending continually upon this very thing.

7 Render therefore to all their dues: tribute to whom tribute *is due;* custom to whom custom; fear to whom fear; honour to whom honour.

8 Owe no man any thing, but to love one another: for he that loveth another hath fulfilled the law.

9 For this, Thou shalt not commit adultery, Thou shalt not kill, Thou shalt not steal, Thou shalt not bear false witness, Thou shalt not covet; and if *there be* any other commandment, it is briefly comprehended in this saying, namely, Thou shalt love thy neighbour as thyself.

10 Love worketh no ill to his neighbour: therefore love *is* the fulfilling of the law.

11 And that, knowing the time, that now *it is* high time to awake out of sleep: for now *is* our salvation nearer than when we believed.

12 The night is far spent, the day is at hand: let us therefore cast off the works of darkness, and let us put on the armour of light.

13 Let us walk honestly, as in the day; not in rioting and drunkenness, not in chambering and wantonness, not in strife and envying.

14 But put ye on the Lord Jesus Christ, and make not provision for the flesh, to *fulfil* the lusts *thereof.*

Amplified

4 For he is God's servant for your good. But if you do wrong, [you should dread him and] be afraid, for he does not bear *and* wear the sword for nothing. He is God's servant to execute His wrath (His punishment, His vengeance) on the wrongdoer.

5 Therefore one must be subject, not only to avoid God's wrath *and* escape punishment, but also as a matter of principle *and* for the sake of conscience.

6 For this same reason you pay taxes, for [the civil authorities] are official servants under God, devoting themselves to attending to this very service.

7 Render to all men their dues. [Pay] taxes to whom taxes are due, revenue to whom revenue is due, respect to whom respect is due, and honor to whom honor is due.

8 Keep out of debt *and* owe no man anything, except to love one another; for he who loves his neighbor — who practices loving others — has fulfilled the Law [relating to one's fellowmen], meeting all its requirements.

9 The commandments, You shall not commit adultery, You shall not kill, You shall not steal, You shall not covet (have an evil desire), and any other commandment, are summed up in the single command, You shall love your neighbor as yourself. [Exod. 20:13-17; Lev. 19:18.]

10 Love does no wrong to one's neighbor — it never hurts anybody. Therefore love meets all the requirements *and* is the fulfilling of the Law.

11 Besides this you know what [a critical] hour this is, how it is high time now for you to wake up out of your sleep — rouse to reality. For salvation (final deliverance) is nearer to us now than when we first believed — adhered to, trusted in and relied on Christ, the Messiah.

12 The night is far gone [and] the day is almost here. Let us then drop (fling away) the works *and* deeds of darkness and put on the [full] armor of light.

13 Let us live *and* conduct ourselves honorably *and* becomingly as in the [open light of] day; not in reveling (carousing) and drunkenness, not in immorality and debauchery (sensuality and licentiousness), not in quarreling and jealousy.

14 But clothe yourself with the Lord Jesus Christ, the Messiah, and make no provision for [indulging] the flesh — put a stop to thinking about the evil cravings of your physical nature — to [gratify its] desires (lusts).

CHAPTER 14

HIM that is weak in the faith receive ye, *but* not to doubtful disputations.

2 For one believeth that he may eat all things: another, who is weak, eateth herbs.

3 Let not him that eateth despise him that eateth not; and let not him which eateth not judge him that eateth: for God hath received him.

CHAPTER 14

AS for the man who is a weak believer, welcome him [into your fellowship], but not to criticize his opinions *or* pass judgment on his scruples *or* perplex him with discussions.

2 One [man's faith permits him] to believe he may eat anything, while a weaker one [limits his] eating to vegetables.

3 Let not him who eats look down on *or* despise him who abstains, and let not him who abstains criticize *and* pass judgment on him who eats; for God has accepted *and* welcomed him.

Living New Testament

4 The policeman is sent by God to help you. But if you are doing something wrong, of course you should be afraid, for he will have you punished. He is sent by God for that very purpose.

5 Obey the laws, then, for two reasons: first, to keep from being punished, and second, just because you know you should.

6 Pay your taxes too, for these same two reasons. For government workers need to be paid so that they can keep on doing God's work, serving you.

7 Pay everyone whatever he ought to have: pay your taxes and import duties gladly, obey those over you, and give honor and respect to all those to whom it is due.

8 Pay all your debts except the debt of love for others —never finish paying that! For if you love them, you will be obeying all of God's laws, fulfilling all His requirements.

If you love your neighbor as much as you love yourself you will not want to harm or cheat him, or kill him or steal from him. And you won't sin with his wife or want what is his, or do anything else the Ten Commandments say are wrong. All ten are wrapped up in this one, to love your neighbor as you love yourself.

10 Love does no wrong to anyone. That's why it fully satisfies all of God's requirements. It is the only law you need.

11 Another reason for right living is this: you know how late it is; time is running out. Wake up, for the coming of the Lord[1] is nearer now than when we first believed.

12, 13 The night is far gone, the day of His return[1] will soon be here. So quit the evil deeds of darkness and put on the armor of right living, as we who live in the daylight should! Be decent and true in everything you do so that all can approve your behavior. Don't spend your time in wild parties and getting drunk or in adultery and lust, or fighting, or jealousy.

14 But ask the Lord Jesus Christ to help you live as you should, and don't make plans to enjoy evil.

Revised Standard

for your good. But if you do wrong, be
afraid, for he does not bear the sword in
vain; he is the servant of God to execute
his wrath on the wrongdoer. [5]Therefore
one must be subject, not only to avoid God's
wrath but also for the sake of conscience.
[6]For the same reason you also pay taxes,
for the authorities are ministers of God, attending to this very thing. [7]Pay all of them
their dues, taxes to whom taxes are due,
revenue to whom revenue is due, respect to
whom respect is due, honor to whom honor
is due.

Conduct in relation to neighbors

8 Owe no one anything, except to love
one another; for he who loves his neighbor
has fulfilled the law. [9]The commandments,
"You shall not commit adultery, You shall
not kill, You shall not steal, You shall not
covet," and any other commandment, are
summed up in this sentence, "You shall
love your neighbor as yourself." [10]Love does
no wrong to a neighbor; therefore love is
the fulfilling of the law.

Conduct in the day of salvation

11 Besides this you know what hour it is,
how it is full time now for you to wake
from sleep. For salvation is nearer to us
now than when we first believed; [12]the night
is far gone, the day is at hand. Let us then
cast off the works of darkness and put on
the armor of light; [13]let us conduct ourselves
becomingly as in the day, not in reveling
and drunkenness, not in debauchery and
licentiousness, not in quarreling and jealousy.
[14]But put on the Lord Jesus Christ, and
make no provision for the flesh, to gratify
its desires.

CHAPTER 14

Give a warm welcome to any brother who wants to join you, even though his faith is weak. Don't criticize him for having different ideas from yours about what is right and wrong.[1]

2 For instance, don't argue with him about whether or not to eat meat that has been offered to idols. You may believe there is no harm in this, but the faith of others is weaker; they think it is wrong, and will go without any meat at all and eat vegetables rather than eat that kind of meat.

3 Those who think it is all right to eat such meat must not look down on those who won't. And if you are one of those who won't, don't find fault with those who do. For God has accepted them to be His children.

Literally, "our salvation."

Literally, "receive him that is weak in faith, not for decisions of scruples." Perhaps the meaning is, "Receive those whose consciences hurt them when they do things others have no doubts about." Accepting them might cause discord in the church, but Paul says to welcome them anyway.

Do not judge

14 As for the man who is weak in faith,
welcome him, but not for disputes over
opinions. [2]One believes he may eat anything,
while the weak man eats only vegetables.
[3]Let not him who eats despise him who
abstains, and let not him who abstains pass
judgment on him who eats; for God has

King James

4 Who art thou that judgest another man's servant? to his own master he standeth or falleth. Yea, he shall be holden up: for God is able to make him stand.

5 One man esteemeth one day above another: another esteemth every day *alike*. Let every man be fully persuaded in his own mind.

6 He that regardeth the day, regardeth *it* unto the Lord; and he that regardeth not the day, to the Lord he doth not regard *it*. He that eateth, eateth to the Lord, for he giveth God thanks; and he that eateth not, to the Lord he eateth not, and giveth God thanks.

7 For none of us liveth to himself, and no man dieth to himself.

8 For whether we live, we live unto the Lord; and whether we die, we die unto the Lord: whether we live therefore, or die, we are the Lord's.

9 For to this end Christ both died, and rose, and revived, that he might be Lord both of the dead and living.

10 But why dost thou judge thy brother? or why dost thou set at nought thy brother? for we shall all stand before the judgment seat of Christ.

11 For it is written, *As* I live, saith the Lord, every knee shall bow to me, and every tongue shall confess to God.

12 So then every one of us shall give account of himself to God.

13 Let us not therefore judge one another any more: but judge this rather, that no man put a stumblingblock or an occasion to fall in *his* brother's way.

14 I know, and am persuaded by the Lord Jesus, that *there is* nothing unclean of itself: but to him that esteemeth any thing to be unclean, to him *it is* unclean.

15 But if thy brother be grieved with *thy* meat, now walkest thou not charitably. Destroy not him with thy meat, for whom Christ died.

16 Let not then your good be evil spoken of:

17 For the kingdom of God is not meat and drink; but righteousness, and peace, and joy in the Holy Ghost.

18 For he that in these things serveth Christ *is* acceptable to God, and approved of men.

19 Let us therefore follow after the things which make for peace, and things wherewith one may edify another.

20 For meat destroy not the work of God. All things indeed *are* pure; but *it is* evil for that man who eateth with offence.

21 *It is* good neither to eat flesh, nor to drink wine, nor *any thing* whereby thy brother stumbleth, or is offended, or is made weak.

Amplified

4 Who are you to pass judgment on *and* censure anotl er's household servant? It is before his own Master that h stands or falls. And he shall stand *and* be upheld, for th Master — the Lord — is mighty to support him *and* mak him stand.

5 One man esteems one day as better than anothe while another man esteems all days alike [sacred]. Le every one be fully convinced (satisfied) in his own mind.

6 He who observes the day, observes it in honor of th Lord. He also who eats, eats in honor of the Lord, sinc he gives thanks to God; while he who abstains, abstains i honor of the Lord and gives thanks to God.

7 None of us lives to himself (but to the Lord), an none of us dies to himself (but to the Lord, for)

8 If we live, we live to the Lord, and if we die, we di to the Lord. So then, whether we live or we die, w belong to the Lord.

9 For Christ died and lived again for this very purpos that He might be Lord both of the dead and of the living.

10 Why do you criticize *and* pass judgment on you brother? Or you, why do you look down upon *or* despis your brother? For we shall all stand before the judgmer seat of God.

11 For it is written, As I live, says the Lord, ever knee shall bow to Me, and every tongue shall confess t God — that is, acknowledge Him to His honor and to H praise. [Isa. 45:23.]

12 And so each of us shall give an account of himse — give an answer in reference to judgment — to God.

13 Then let us no more criticize *and* blame *and* pas judgment on one another, but rather decide *and* endeavc never to put a stumbling block *or* an obstacle or a hir drance in the way of a brother.

14 I know and am convinced (persuaded) as one in th Lord Jesus, that nothing is [forbidden as] essentially ur clean — that is, defiled and unholy in itself. But [none th less] it is unclean (defiled and unholy) to any one wh thinks it is unclean.

15 But if your brother is being pained *or* his feelin hurt *or* if he is being injured by what you eat, [then] yo are no longer walking in love. — That is, you have cease to be living and conducting yourself by the standard c love toward him. Do not let what you eat hurt *or* caus the ruin of one for whom Christ died!

16 Do not therefore let what seems good to you b considered an evil thing [by someone else]. — [In oth words], do not give occasion for others to criticize th which is justifiable for you.

17 [After all,] the kingdom of God is not a matter c [getting the] food and drink [one likes], but instead, it righteousness — that state which makes a person accept ble to God — and heartpeace and joy in the Holy Spiri

18 He who serves Christ in this way is acceptable *ar* pleasing to God and is approved by men.

19 So let us then definitely aim for *and* eagerly purs what makes for harmony and for mutual upbuilding (e ification and development) of one another.

20 You must not, for the sake of food, undo *and* bre down and destroy the work of God! Everything is inde (ceremonially) clean *and* pure, but it is wrong for any or to hurt the conscience of others *or* to make them fall b what he eats.

21 The right thing is to eat no meat or drink no wi [at all], or [do anything else] if it [hurts your brothe conscience or] makes him stumble, *or* offends or weake him.

Living New Testament

4 They are God's servants, not yours. They are responsible to Him, not to you. Let Him tell them whether they are right or wrong. And God is able to make them do as they should.

5 Some think that Christians should observe the Jewish holidays as special days to worship God, but others say it is wrong and foolish to go to all that trouble for every day alike belongs to God. On questions of this kind everyone must decide for himself.

6 If you have special days for worshiping the Lord, you are trying to honor Him; you are doing a good thing. So is the person who eats meat that has been offered to idols; he is thankful to the Lord for it; he is doing right. And the person who won't touch such meat, he, too, is anxious to please the Lord, and is thankful.

7 We are not our own bosses to live or die as we ourselves might choose.

8 Living or dying we follow the Lord. Either way we are His.

9 Christ died and rose again for this very purpose, so that He can be our Lord both while we live and when we die.

10 You have no right to criticize your brother or look down on him. Remember, each of us will stand personally before the Judgment Seat of God.

11 For it is written, "As I live," says the Lord, "every knee shall bow to me and every tongue confess to God."

12 Yes, each of us will give an account of himself to God.

13 So don't criticize each other any more. Try instead to live in such a way that you will never make your brother stumble by letting him see you doing something he thinks is wrong.

14 As for myself, I am perfectly sure on the authority of the Lord Jesus that there is nothing really wrong with eating meat that has been offered to idols. But if someone believes it is wrong, then he shouldn't do it because for him it is wrong.

15 And if your brother is bothered by what you eat, you are not acting in love if you go ahead and eat it. Don't let your eating ruin someone for whom Christ died.

16 Don't do anything that will cause criticism against yourself even though you know that what you do is right.

17 For after all, the important thing for us as Christians is not what we eat or drink but stirring up goodness and peace and joy from the Holy Spirit.

18 If you let Christ be Lord in these affairs, God will be glad; and so will your friends.

19 In this way aim for harmony in the church and try to build each other up.

20 Don't undo the work of God for a chunk of meat. Remember, there is nothing wrong with the meat but it is wrong to eat it if it makes another stumble.

21 The right thing to do is to quit eating meat or drinking wine or doing anything else that offends your brother or makes him sin.

Revised Standard

welcomed him. 4 Who are you to pass judgment on the servant of another? It is before
his own master that he stands or falls. And
he will be upheld, for the Master is able to
make him stand.
5 One man esteems one day as better
than another, while another man esteems
all days alike. Let every one be fully convinced in his own mind. 6 He who observes
the day, observes it in honor of the Lord.
He also who eats, eats in honor of the Lord,
since he gives thanks to God; while he who
abstains, abstains in honor of the Lord and
gives thanks to God. 7 None of us lives to
himself, and none of us dies to himself. 8 If
we live, we live to the Lord, and if we die,
we die to the Lord; so then, whether we
live or whether we die, we are the Lord's.
9 For to this end Christ died and lived again,
that he might be Lord both of the dead and
of the living.
10 Why do you pass judgment on your
brother? Or you, why do you despise your
brother? For we shall all stand before the
judgment seat of God; 11 for it is written,

"As I live, says the Lord, every knee
shall bow to me,
and every tongue shall give praise[u] to
God."

12 So each of us shall give account of himself to God.

Do not be a stumbling block

13 Then let us no more pass judgment on
one another, but rather decide never to put
a stumbling block or hindrance in the way
of a brother. 14 I know and am persuaded
in the Lord Jesus that nothing is unclean
in itself; but it is unclean for anyone who
thinks it unclean. 15 If your brother is being
injured by what you eat, you are no longer
walking in love. Do not let what you eat
cause the ruin of one for whom Christ died.
16 So do not let what is good to you be spok-
en of as evil. 17 For the kingdom of God
does not mean food and drink but righteousness and peace and joy in the Holy Spirit;
18 he who thus serves Christ is acceptable to
God and approved by men. 19 Let us then
pursue what makes for peace and for mutual upbuilding. 20 Do not, for the sake of
food, destroy the work of God. Everything
is indeed clean, but it is wrong for any one
to make others fall by what he eats; 21 it is
right not to eat meat or drink wine or do
anything that makes your brother stumble.[v]

[u] Or *confess*

[v] Other ancient authorities add *or be upset or be weakened*

King James

22 Hast thou faith? have *it* to thyself before God. Happy *is* he that condemneth not himself in that thing which he alloweth.

23 And he that doubteth is damned if he eat, because *he eateth* not of faith: for whatsoever *is* not of faith is sin.

Amplified

22 Your personal convictions [on such matters] exercise as in God's presence, keeping them to yourself — striving only to know the truth and obey His will. Blessed, happy, [z]to be envied is he who has no reason to judge himself for what he approves — who does not convict himself by what he chooses to do.

23 But the man who has doubts — misgivings, an uneasy conscience — about eating, and then eats [perhaps because of you], stands condemned [before God], because he is not true to his convictions *and* he does not act from faith. For whatever does not originate *and* proceed from faith is sin — that is, whatever is done without a conviction of its approval by God is sinful.

CHAPTER 15

WE then that are strong ought to bear the infirmities of the weak, and not to please ourselves.

2 Let every one of us please *his* neighbour for *his* good to edification.

3 For even Christ pleased not himself; but, as it is written, The reproaches of them that reproached thee fell on me.

4 For whatsoever things were written aforetime were written for our learning, that we through patience and comfort of the scriptures might have hope.

5 Now the God of patience and consolation grant you to be likeminded one toward another according to Christ Jesus:

6 That ye may with one mind *and* one mouth glorify God, even the Father of our Lord Jesus Christ.

7 Wherefore receive ye one another, as Christ also received us to the glory of God.

8 Now I say that Jesus Christ was a minister of the circumcision for the truth of God, to confirm the promises *made* unto the fathers:

9 And that the Gentiles might glorify God for *his* mercy; as it is written, For this cause I will confess to thee among the Gentiles, and sing unto thy name.

10 And again he saith, Rejoice, ye Gentiles, with his people.

11 And again, Praise the Lord, all ye Gentiles; and laud him, all ye people.

12 And again, Esaias saith, There shall be a root of Jesse, and he that shall rise to reign over the Gentiles; in him shall the Gentiles trust.

CHAPTER 15

WE who are strong [in our convictions and of robust faith] ought to bear with the failings *and* the frailties *and* the tender scruples of the weak. — We ought to help carry the doubts and qualms of others — and not to please ourselves.

2 Let each one of us make it a practice to please (make happy) his neighbor for his good *and* for his true welfare, to edify him — that is, to strengthen him and build him up spiritually.

3 For Christ (gave no thought to His own interests) to please Himself; but, as it is written, The reproaches *and* abuses of those who reproached *and* abused you fell on Me. [Ps. 69:9.]

4 For whatever was thus written in former days was written for our instruction, that by [our steadfast and patient] endurance and the encouragement [drawn] from the Scriptures we might hold fast *and* cherish hope.

5 Now may the God Who gives the power of patient endurance (steadfastness) and Who supplies encouragement, grant you to live in such mutual harmony *and* such full sympathy with one another, in accord with Christ Jesus,

6 That together you may (unanimously) with united hearts *and* one voice, praise and glorify the God and Father of our Lord Jesus Christ, the Messiah.

7 Welcome *and* receive (to your hearts) one another, then, even as Christ has welcomed *and* received you, for the glory of God.

8 For I tell you that Christ, the Messiah, became a servant *and* a minister to the circumcised [the Jews] in order to show God's truthfulness *and* honesty by confirming (verifying) the promises [given to our] fathers.

9 And [also in order] that the Gentiles might glorify God for [His unconvenanted] mercy to them. As it is written, Therefore I will praise You among the Gentiles, and sing praises to Your name. [Ps. 18:49.]

10 Again it is said, Rejoice (exult), O Gentiles, along with His [own] people; [Deut. 32:43.]

11 And again, Praise the Lord, all you Gentiles (nations), and let all the peoples praise Him! [Ps. 117:1.]

12 And further Isaiah says, There shall be a [a]Sprout from the [b]Root of Jesse, He Who rises to rule over the Gentiles; in Him shall the Gentiles hope. [Isa. 11:1, 10.]

---

z) Souter.
a) Abbott-Smith.
b) Rev. 5:5; 22:16.

Living New Testament

22 You may know that there is nothing wrong with what you do, even from God's point of view, but keep it to yourself; don't flaunt your faith in front of others who might be hurt by it. In this situation, happy is the man who does not sin by doing what he knows is right.

23 But anyone who believes that something he wants to do is wrong shouldn't do it. He sins if he does, for he thinks it is wrong, and so for him it *is* wrong. Anything that is done apart from what he feels is right is sin.

Revised Standard

[22]The faith that you have, keep between yourself and God; happy is he who has no reason to judge himself for what he approves. [23]But he who has doubts is condemned, if he eats, because he does not act from faith; for whatever does not proceed from faith is sin.[w]

CHAPTER 15

Even if we believe that it makes no difference to the Lord that we do these things, still we cannot just go ahead and do them to please ourselves; for we must bear the "burden" of being considerate of the doubts and fears of others—of those who feel these things are wrong. Let's please the other fellow, not ourselves, and do what is for his good and thus build him up in the Lord.

3 Christ didn't please Himself. As the Psalmist said, "He came for the very purpose of suffering under the insults of those who were against the Lord."

4 These things that were written in the Scriptures so long ago are to teach us patience and to encourage us, so that we will look forward expectantly to the time when God will conquer sin and death.

5 May God who gives patience, steadiness, and encouragement help you to live in complete harmony with each other—each with the attitude of Christ toward the other.

6 And then all of us can praise the Lord together with one voice, giving glory to God, the Father of our Lord Jesus Christ.

7 So, warmly welcome each other into the church, just as Christ has warmly welcomed you; then God will be glorified.

8 Remember that Jesus Christ came to show that God is true to His promises and to help the Jews.

9 And remember that He came also so that the Gentiles might be saved and give glory to God for His mercies to them. That is what the Psalmist meant when he wrote: I will praise You among the Gentiles, and sing to Your name."

10 And in another place, "Be glad, O you Gentiles, along with His people the Jews."

11 And yet again, "Praise the Lord, O you Gentiles, let everyone praise Him."

12 And the prophet Isaiah said, "There shall be an Heir in the house of Jesse, and He will be King over the Gentiles; they will pin their hopes on Him alone."

Follow Christ's example

15 We who are strong ought to bear with
the failings of the weak, and not to
please ourselves; [2]let each of us please his
neighbor for his good, to edify him. [3]For
Christ did not please himself; but, as it is
written, "The reproaches of those who reproached thee fell on me." [4]For whatever
was written in former days was written for
our instruction, that by steadfastness and by
the encouragement of the scriptures we
might have hope. [5]May the God of steadfastness and encouragement grant you to
live in such harmony with one another, in
accord with Christ Jesus, [6]that together you
may with one voice glorify the God and
Father of our Lord Jesus Christ.
7 Welcome one another, therefore, as
Christ has welcomed you, for the glory of
God. [8]For I tell you that Christ became a
servant to the circumcised to show God's
truthfulness, in order to confirm the promises given to the patriarchs, [9]and in order
that the Gentiles might glorify God for his
mercy. As it is written,
"Therefore I will praise thee among the
Gentiles,
and sing to thy name";
10 and again it is said,
"Rejoice, O Gentiles, with his people";
11 and again,
"Praise the Lord, all Gentiles,
and let all the peoples praise him";
12 and further Isaiah says,
"The root of Jesse shall come,
he who rises to rule the Gentiles;
in him shall the Gentiles hope."

[w] Other authorities, some ancient, insert here Ch. 16.25-27

King James

13 Now the God of hope fill you with all joy and peace in believing, that ye may abound in hope, through the power of the Holy Ghost.

14 And I myself also am persuaded of you, my brethren, that ye also are full of goodness, filled with all knowledge, able also to admonish one another.

15 Nevertheless, brethren, I have written the more boldly unto you in some sort, as putting you in mind, because of the grace that is given to me of God,

16 That I should be the minister of Jesus Christ to the Gentiles, ministering the gospel of God, that the offering up of the Gentiles might be acceptable, being sanctified by the Holy Ghost.

17 I have therefore whereof I may glory through Jesus Christ in those things which pertain to God.

18 For I will not dare to speak of any of those things which Christ hath not wrought by me, to make the Gentiles obedient, by word and deed,

19 Through mighty signs and wonders, by the power of the Spirit of God; so that from Jerusalem, and round about unto Illyricum, I have fully preached the gospel of Christ.

20 Yea, so have I strived to preach the gospel, not where Christ was named, lest I should build upon another man's foundation:

21 But as it is written, To whom he was not spoken of, they shall see: and they that have not heard shall understand.

22 For which cause also I have been much hindered from coming to you.

23 But now having no more place in these parts, and having a great desire these many years to come unto you;

24 Whensoever I take my journey into Spain, I will come to you: for I trust to see you in my journey, and to be brought on my way thitherward by you, if first I be somewhat filled with your *company*.

25 But now I go unto Jerusalem to minister unto the saints.

26 For it hath pleased them of Macedonia and Achaia to make a certain contribution for the poor saints which are at Jerusalem.

27 It hath pleased them verily; and their debtors they are. For if the Gentiles have been made partakers of their spiritual things, their duty is also to minister unto them in carnal things.

28 When therefore I have performed this, and have sealed to them this fruit, I will come by you into Spain.

29 And I am sure that, when I come unto you, I shall come in the fulness of the blessing of the gospel of Christ.

30 Now I beseech you, brethren, for the Lord Jesus Christ's sake, and for the love of the Spirit, that ye strive together with me in *your* prayers to God for me;

31 That I may be delivered from them that do not believe in Judæa; and that my service which *I have* for Jerusalem may be accepted of the saints;

Amplified

13 May the God of your hope so fill you with all joy and peace in believing — through the experience of your faith — that by the power of the Holy Spirit you may abound *and* be overflowing (bubbling over) with hope.

14 Personally I am satisfied about you, my brethren, that you yourselves are rich in goodness, amply filled with all [spiritual] knowledge and competent to admonish *and* counsel *and* instruct one another also.

15 Still on some points I have written to you the more boldly *and* unreservedly by way of reminder. [I have done so] because of the grace — the unmerited favor — bestowed on me by God

16 In making me a minister of Christ Jesus to the Gentiles. I act in the priestly service of the Gospel (the good news) of God, in order that the sacrificial offering of the Gentiles may be acceptable [to God], consecrated *and* made holy by the Holy Spirit.

17 In Christ Jesus, then, I have legitimate reason to glory (to exult) in my work for God — in what through Christ Jesus I have accomplished concerning the things of God.

18 For [of course] I will not venture (presume) to speak thus of any work except what Christ has actually done through me — as an instrument in His hands — to win obedience from the Gentiles, by word and deed,

19 [And as my preaching has been accompanied] with the power of signs and wonders, [and all of it] by the power of the Holy Spirit. So that starting from Jerusalem and as far round as Illyricum I have fully preached the Gospel — faithfully executing, accomplishing, carrying out to the full the good news — of Christ, the Messiah, in its entirety.

20 Thus my ambition has been to preach the Gospel, not where Christ's name has already been known, lest I build on another man's foundation;

21 But [instead I would act on the principle], as it is written, They shall see who have never been told of Him, and they shall understand who have never heard [of Him]. [Isa. 52:15.]

22 This [ambition] is the reason why I have so frequently been hindered from coming to visit you.

23 But now since I have no further opportunity for work in these regions, and since I have longed for [c]enough years to come to you,

24 I hope to see you in passing [through Rome] as I go [on my intended trip] to Spain, and to be aided on my journey there by you, after I have enjoyed your company for a little while.

25 For the present, however, I am going to Jerusalem to bring aid (relief) for the saints — God's people there.

26 For it has been the good pleasure of Macedonia and Achaia to make some contribution for the poor among the saints of Jerusalem.

27 They were pleased to do it, and surely they are in debt to them, for if these Gentiles have come to share in their [the Jerusalem Jews'] spiritual blessings, then they ought also to be of service to them in material blessings.

28 When therefore I have completed this mission, and have delivered to them [at Jerusalem] what has been raised, I shall go on by way of you to Spain.

29 And I know that when I do come to you I shall come in the abundant blessing *of the Gospel* of Christ.

30 I appeal to you — I entreat you — brethren, for the sake of our Lord Jesus Christ and by the love [given by] the Spirit, to unite with me in earnest wrestling in prayer to God in my behalf.

31 [Pray] that I may be delivered (rescued) from the unbelievers in Judea, and that my mission of relief to Jerusalem may be acceptable *and* graciously received by the saints — God's people there.

c) Vincent.

Living New Testament

13 So I pray for you Gentiles that God who gives you hope will keep you happy and full of peace as you believe in Him. I pray that God will help you overflow with hope in Him through the Holy Spirit's power within you.

14 I know that you are wise and good, my brothers, and that you know these things so well that you are able to teach others all about them.

15, 16 But even so I have been bold enough to emphasize some of these points, knowing that all you need is this reminder from me; for I am, by God's grace, a special messenger from Jesus Christ to you Gentiles, bringing you the Gospel and offering you up as a fragrant sacrifice to God; for you have been made pure and pleasing to Him by the Holy Spirit.

17 So it is right for me to be a little proud of all Christ Jesus has done through me.

18 I dare not judge how effectively He has used others, but I know this: He has used me to win the Gentiles to God.

19 I have won them by my message and by the good way I have lived before them, and by miracles done through me as signs from God—all by the Holy Spirit's power. In this way I have preached the full[1] Gospel of Christ all the way from Jerusalem clear over into Illyricum.

20 But all the while my ambition has been to go still further, preaching where the name of Christ has never yet been heard, rather than where a church has already been started by someone else.

21 I have been following the plan spoken of in the Scriptures where Isaiah says that those who have never heard the name of Christ before will see and understand.

22 In fact that is the very reason I have been so long in coming to visit you.

23 But now at last I am through with my work here, and I am ready to come after all these long years of waiting.

24 For I am planning to take a trip to Spain, and when I do, I will stop off there in Rome; and after we have had a good time together for a little while, you can send me on my way again.

25 But before I come, I must go down to Jerusalem to take a gift to the Jewish Christians there.

26 For you see, the Christians in Macedonia and Achaia have taken up an offering for those in Jerusalem who are going through such hard times.

27 They were very glad to do this, for they feel that they owe a real debt to the Jerusalem Christians. Why? Because the news about Christ came to them from the church in Jerusalem. And since they received this wonderful spiritual gift of the Gospel from them, they feel that the least they can do in return is to give them some material aid.[2]

28 As soon as I have delivered this money and completed this good deed of theirs, I will come to see you on my way to Spain.

29 And I am sure that when I come the Lord will give me a great blessing for you.

30 Will you be my prayer partners? For the Lord Jesus Christ's sake, and because of your love for me—given to you by the Holy Spirit—pray much with me for my work.

31 Pray that I will be protected from those who are not Christians in Jerusalem. Pray also that the Christians there will be willing to accept the money I am bringing them.

---

[1] Or, "I have fully accomplished my Gospel ministry."

[2] Literally, "For if the Gentiles have come to share in their spiritual blessings, they ought also to be of service to them in material blessings."

Revised Standard

13 May the God of hope fill you with all
joy and peace in believing, so that by the
power of the Holy Spirit you may abound
in hope.

Paul's reason for writing

14 I myself am satisfied about you, my
brethren, that you yourselves are full of
goodness, filled with all knowledge, and able
to instruct one another. 15 But on some
points I have written to you very boldly by
way of reminder, because of the grace given
me by God 16 to be a minister of Christ Jesus
to the Gentiles in the priestly service of the
gospel of God, so that the offering of the
Gentiles may be acceptable, sanctified by
the Holy Spirit. 17 In Christ Jesus, then, I
have reason to be proud of my work for
God. 18 For I will not venture to speak of
anything except what Christ has wrought
through me to win obedience from the
Gentiles, by word and deed, 19 by the power
of signs and wonders, by the power of the
Holy Spirit, so that from Jerusalem and as
far round as Illyricum I have fully preached
the gospel of Christ, 20 thus making it my
ambition to preach the gospel, not where
Christ has already been named, lest I build
on another man's foundation, 21 but as it is
written,

"They shall see who have never been
told of him,
and they shall understand who have never
heard of him."

Paul's future plans

22 This is the reason why I have so often
been hindered from coming to you. 23 But
now, since I no longer have any room for
work in these regions, and since I have
longed for many years to come to you, 24 I
hope to see you in passing as I go to Spain,
and to be sped on my journey there by you,
once I have enjoyed your company for a little.
25 At present, however, I am going to Jerusalem with aid for the saints. 26 For Macedonia and Achaia have been pleased to make
some contribution for the poor among the
saints at Jerusalem; 27 they were pleased to do
it, and indeed they are in debt to them, for
if the Gentiles have come to share in their
spiritual blessings, they ought also to be of
service to them in material blessings. 28 When
therefore I have completed this, and have
delivered to them what has been raised,[x] I
shall go on by way of you to Spain; 29 and I
know that when I come to you I shall come
in the fulness of the blessing[y] of Christ.

30 I appeal to you, brethren, by our Lord
Jesus Christ and by the love of the Spirit,
to strive together with me in your prayers
to God on my behalf, 31 that I may be delivered from the unbelievers in Judea, and
that my service for Jerusalem may be ac-

---

[x] Greek *sealed to them this fruit*

[y] Other ancient authorities insert *of the gospel*

King James

32 That I may come unto you with joy by the will of God, and may with you be refreshed.

33 Now the God of peace *be* with you all. Amen.

CHAPTER 16

I COMMEND unto you Phebe our sister, which is a servant of the church which is at Cenchrea:

2 That ye receive her in the Lord, as becometh saints, and that ye assist her in whatsoever business she hath need of you: for she hath been a succourer of many, and of myself also.

3 Greet Priscilla and Aquila my helpers in Christ Jesus:

4 Who have for my life laid down their own necks: unto whom not only I give thanks, but also all the churches of the Gentiles.

5 Likewise *greet* the church that is in their house. Salute my well-beloved Epænetus, who is the firstfruits of Achaia unto Christ.

6 Greet Mary, who bestowed much labour on us.

7 Salute Andronicus and Junia, my kinsmen, and my fellow-prisoners, who are of note among the apostles, who also were in Christ before me.

8 Greet Amplias my beloved in the Lord.

9 Salute Urbane, our helper in Christ, and Stachys my beloved.

10 Salute Apelles approved in Christ. Salute them which are of Aristobulus' household.

11 Salute Herodion my kinsman. Greet them that be of the *household* of Narcissus, which are in the Lord.

12 Salute Tryphena and Tryphosa, who labour in the Lord. Salute the beloved Persis, which laboured much in the Lord.

13 Salute Rufus chosen in the Lord, and his mother and mine.

14 Salute Asyncritus, Phlegon, Hermas, Patrobas, Hermes, and the brethren which are with them.

15 Salute Philologus, and Julia, Nereus, and his sister, and Olympas, and all the saints which are with them.

16 Salute one another with an holy kiss. The churches of Christ salute you.

17 Now I beseech you, brethren, mark them which cause divisions and offences contrary to the doctrine which ye have learned; and avoid them.

18 For they that are such serve not our Lord Jesus Christ, but their own belly; and by good words and fair speeches deceive the hearts of the simple.

19 For your obedience is come abroad unto all *men*. I am glad therefore on your behalf: but yet I would have you wise unto that which is good, and simple concerning evil.

Amplified

32 So that by God's will I may subsequently come to you with joy — with a happy heart — and be refreshed [by the interval of rest] in your company.

33 May [our] peace-giving God be with you all! Amen — so be it.

CHAPTER 16

NOW I introduce *and* commend to you our sister Phoebe, a deaconess of the church at Cenchreae,

2 That you may receive her in the Lord — with a Christian welcome — as saints (God's people) ought to receive one another. And help her in whatever matter she may require assistance from you, for she has been a helper of many including myself — shielding us from suffering.

3 Give my greetings to Prisca and Aquila, my fellow workers in Christ Jesus,

4 Who risked their lives — endangering their very necks — for my life. To them not only I but also all the churches among the Gentiles give thanks.

5 [Remember me] also to the church [that meets] in their house. Greet my beloved Epaenetus, who was a first fruit (convert) to Christ in Asia.

6 Greet Mary, who has worked so hard among you.

7 Remember me to Andronicus and Junias, my tribal kinsmen and once my fellow prisoners. They are men held in high esteem among the apostles, who also were in Christ before I was.

8 Remember me to Ampliatus, my beloved in the Lord.

9 Salute Urbanus, our fellow worker in Christ, and my dear Stachys.

10 Greet Apelles, that one tried *and* approved in Christ, the Messiah. Remember me to those who belong to the household of Aristobulus.

11 Greet my tribal kinsman Herodion, and those in the Lord who belong to the household of Narcissus.

12 Salute those workers in the Lord, Tryphaena and Tryphosa. Greet my dear Persis, who has worked so hard in the Lord.

13 Remember me to Rufus, eminent in the Lord, also to his mother [who has been] a mother to me also.

14 Greet Asyncritus, Phlegon, Hermes, Patrobas, Hermas, and the brethren who are with them.

15 Greet Philologus, Julia, Nereus and his sister, and Olympas, and all the saints who are with them.

16 Greet one another with a holy (consecrated) kiss. All the churches of Christ, the Messiah, wish to be remembered to you.

17 I appeal to you, brethren, to be on your guard concerning those who create dissensions and difficulties *and* cause divisions, in opposition to the doctrine — the teaching — which you have been taught. [I warn you to turn aside from them, to] avoid them.

18 For such persons do not serve our Lord Christ but their own appetites *and* base desires, and by ingratiating and flattering speech they beguile the hearts of the unsuspecting *and* simple-minded [people].

19 For while your loyalty *and* obedience is known to all, so that I rejoice over you, I would have you well versed *and* wise as to what is good, and innocent *and* guileless as to what is evil.

Living New Testament

32 Then I will be able to come to you with a happy heart by the will of God, and we can refresh each other.

33 And now may our God, who gives peace, be with you all. Amen.

Revised Standard

ceptable to the saints, [32]so that by God's will
I may come to you with joy and be refreshed
in your company. [33]The God of peace be
with you all. Amen.

CHAPTER 16

Phoebe, a dear Christian woman from the town of Cenchreae, will be coming to see you soon. She has worked hard in the church there. Receive her as your sister in the Lord, giving her a warm Christian welcome. Help her in every way you can, for she has helped many in their needs, including me.

3 Tell Priscilla and Aquila "hello." They have been my fellow workers in the affairs of Christ Jesus.

4 In fact, they risked their lives for me; and I am not the only one who is thankful to them: so are all the Gentile churches.

5 Please give my greetings to all those who meet to worship in their home. Greet my good friend Epaenetus. He was the very first person to become a Christian in Asia.

6 Remember me to Mary, too, who has worked so hard to help us.

7 Then there are Andronicus and Junias, my relatives who were in prison with me. They are respected by the apostles, and became Christians before I did. Please give them my greetings.

8 Say "hello" to Amplias, whom I love as one of God's own children,

9 And Urbanus, our fellow worker, and beloved Stachys.

10 Then there is Apelles, a good man whom the Lord approves; greet him for me. And give my best regards to those working at the house of Aristobulus.

11 Remember me to Herodion my relative. Remember me to the Christian slaves over at Narcissus House.

12 Say "hello" to Tryphena and Tryphosa, the Lord's workers; and to dear Persis, who has worked so hard for the Lord.

13 Greet Rufus for me, whom the Lord picked out to be His very own; and also his dear mother who has been such a mother to me.

14 And please give my greetings to Asyncritus, Phlegon, Hermes, Patrobas, Hermas, and the other brothers who are with them.

15 Give my love to Philologus, Julia, Nereus and his sister, and to Olympas, and all the Christians who are with them.

16 Shake hands warmly with each other. All the churches here send you their greetings.

17 And now there is one more thing to say before I end this letter. Stay away from those who cause divisions and are upsetting people's faith, teaching things about Christ that are contrary to what you have been taught.

18 Such teachers are not working for our Lord Jesus, but only want gain for themselves. They are good speakers, and simple-minded people are often fooled by them.

19 But everyone knows that you stand loyal and true. This makes me very happy. I want you always to remain very clear about what is right, and to stay innocent of any wrong.

Commendations and greetings

16 I commend to you our sister Phoebe,
a deaconess of the church at Cenchreae, [2]that you may receive her in the Lord
as befits the saints, and help her in whatever she may require from you, for she has
been a helper of many and of myself as
well.

3 Greet Prisca and Aquila, my fellow
workers in Christ Jesus, [4]who risked their
necks for my life, to whom not only I but
also all the churches of the Gentiles give
thanks; [5]greet also the church in their house.
Greet my beloved Epaenetus, who was the
first convert in Asia for Christ. [6]Greet Mary,
who has worked hard among you. [7]Greet
Andronicus and Junias, my kinsmen and my
fellow prisoners; they are men of note among
the apostles, and they were in Christ before
me. [8]Greet Ampliatus, my beloved in the
Lord. [9]Greet Urbanus, our fellow worker in
Christ, and my beloved Stachys. [10]Greet
Apelles, who is approved in Christ. Greet
those who belong to the family of Aristobulus. [11]Greet my kinsman Herodion. Greet
those in the Lord who belong to the family
of Narcissus. [12]Greet those workers in the
Lord, Tryphaena and Tryphosa. Greet the
beloved Persis, who has worked hard in the
Lord. [13]Greet Rufus, eminent in the Lord,
also his mother and mine. [14]Greet Asyncritus, Phlegon, Hermes, Patrobas, Hermas,
and the brethren who are with them. [15]Greet
Philologus, Julia, Nereus and his sister, and
Olympas, and all the saints who are with
them. [16]Greet one another with a holy kiss.
All the churches of Christ greet you.

17 I appeal to you, brethren, to take note
of those who create dissensions and difficulties, in opposition to the doctrine which you
have been taught; avoid them. [18]For such
persons do not serve our Lord Christ, but
their own appetites,[z] and by fair and flattering words they deceive the hearts of the
simple-minded. [19]For while your obedience
is known to all, so that I rejoice over you,
I would have you wise as to what is good

[z] Greek *their own belly* (Phil 3.19)

King James

20 And the God of peace shall bruise Satan under your feet shortly. The grace of our Lord Jesus Christ *be* with you. Amen.
21 Timotheus my workfellow, and Lucius, and Jason, and Sosipater, my kinsmen, salute you.
22 I Tertius, who wrote *this* epistle, salute you in the Lord.
23 Gaius mine host, and of the whole church, saluteth you. Erastus the chamberlain of the city saluteth you, and Quartus a brother.
24 The grace of our Lord Jesus Christ *be* with you all. Amen.
25 Now to him that is of power to stablish you according to my gospel, and the preaching of Jesus Christ, according to the revelation of the mystery, which was kept secret since the world began,
26 But now is made manifest, and by the scriptures of the prophets, according to the commandment of the everlasting God, made known to all nations for the obedience of faith:
27 To God only wise, *be* glory through Jesus Christ for ever. Amen.

¶ Written to the Romans from Corinthus, and sent by Phebe servant of the church at Cenchrea.

Amplified

20 And the God of peace will soon crush Satan under your feet. The grace of our Lord Jesus Christ, the Messiah, be with you.
21 Timothy, my fellow worker, wishes to be remembered to you, as do Lucius and Jason and Sosipater, my tribal kinsmen.
22 I Tertius, the writer of this letter, greet you in the Lord.
23 Gaius, who is host to me and to the whole church here, greets you. So do Erastus, the city treasurer, and our brother Quartus.
24 *The grace of our Lord Jesus Christ, the Messiah, be with you all. Amen — so be it.*
25 Now to Him Who is able to strengthen you in the faith which is in accordance with my Gospel and the preaching of (concerning) Jesus Christ, the Messiah, according to the revelation — the unveiling — of the mystery of the plan of redemption which was kept in silence *and* secret for long ages,
26 But is now disclosed and through the prophetic Scriptures is made known to all nations, according to the command of the eternal God, [to win them] to obedience to the faith,
27 To [the] only wise God be glory for evermore through Jesus Christ, the Anointed One! Amen — so be it.

Living New Testament

20 The God of peace will soon crush Satan under your feet. The blessings from our Lord Jesus Christ be upon you.

21 Timothy my fellow-worker, and Lucius and Jason and Sosipater, my relatives, send you their good wishes.

22 I, Tertius, the one who is writing this letter for Paul, send my greetings too, as a Christian brother.

23 Gaius says to say "hello" to you for him. I am his guest, and the church meets here in his home. Erastus, the city treasurer, sends you his greetings and so does Quartus, a Christian brother.

24 Good-bye. May the grace of our Lord Jesus Christ be with you all.

25, 26, 27 I commit you to God, who is able to make you strong and steady in the Lord, just as the Gospel says, and just as I have told you. This is God's plan of salvation for you Gentiles, kept secret from the beginning of time. But now as the prophets foretold and as God commands, this message is being preached everywhere, so that people all around the world will have faith in Christ and obey Him. To God, who alone is wise, be the glory forever through Jesus Christ our Lord. Amen.

Sincerely,
Paul

Revised Standard

and guileless as to what is evil; [20]then the God of peace will soon crush Satan under your feet. The grace of our Lord Jesus Christ be with you.[a]

21 Timothy, my fellow worker, greets you; so do Lucius and Jason and Sosipater, my kinsmen.

22 I Tertius, the writer of this letter, greet you in the Lord.

23 Gaius, who is host to me and to the whole church, greets you. Erastus, the city treasurer, and our brother Quartus, greet you.[b]

Doxology

25 Now to him who is able to strengthen you according to my gospel and the preaching of Jesus Christ, according to the revelation of the mystery which was kept secret for long ages [26]but is now disclosed and through the prophetic writings is made known to all nations, according to the command of the eternal God, to bring about the obedience of faith—[27]to the only wise God be glory for evermore through Jesus Christ! Amen.

[a] Other ancient authorities omit this sentence
[b] Other ancient authorities insert verse 24, *The grace of our Lord Jesus Christ be with you all. Amen.*

King James

THE FIRST EPISTLE OF PAUL THE APOSTLE

TO THE

Corinthians

CHAPTER 1

PAUL, called *to be* an apostle of Jesus Christ through the will of God, and Sosthenes *our* brother,

2 Unto the church of God which is at Corinth, to them that are sanctified in Christ Jesus, called *to be* saints, with all that in every place call upon the name of Jesus Christ our Lord, both theirs and ours:

3 Grace *be* unto you, and peace, from God our Father, and *from* the Lord Jesus Christ.

4 I thank my God always on your behalf, for the grace of God which is given you by Jesus Christ;

5 That in every thing ye are enriched by him, in all utterance, and *in* all knowledge;

6 Even as the testimony of Christ was confirmed in you:

7 So that ye come behind in no gift; waiting for the coming of our Lord Jesus Christ.

8 Who shall also confirm you unto the end, *that ye may be* blameless in the day of our Lord Jesus Christ.

9 God *is* faithful, by whom ye were called unto the fellowship of his Son Jesus Christ our Lord.

10 Now I beseech you, brethren, by the name of our Lord Jesus Christ, that ye all speak the same thing, and *that* there be no divisions among you; but *that* ye be perfectly joined together in the same mind and in the same judgment.

11 For it hath been declared unto me of you, my brethren, by them *which are of the house* of Chloe, that there are contentions among you.

12 Now this I say, that every one of you saith, I am of Paul; and I of Apollos; and I of Cephas; and I of Christ.

13 Is Christ divided? was Paul crucified for you? or were ye baptized in the name of Paul?

14 I thank God that I baptized none of you, but Crispus and Gaius;

15 Lest any should say that I had baptized in mine own name.

Amplified

THE FIRST LETTER OF PAUL

TO THE

Corinthians

CHAPTER 1

PAUL, summoned by the will *and* purpose of God to be an apostle (special messenger) of Christ Jesus, and our brother Sosthenes,

2 To the church (assembly) of God which is in Corinth, to those consecrated *and* purified *and* made holy in Christ Jesus, [who are] selected *and* called to be saints (God's people) together with all those who in any place call upon *and* give honor to the name of our Lord Jesus Christ, both their Lord and ours:

3 Grace (favor and spiritual blessing) be to you and (heart) peace from God our Father and the Lord Jesus Christ.

4 I thank my God at all times for you because of the grace (the favor and spiritual blessing) of God which was bestowed on you in Christ Jesus.

5 [So] that in Him in every respect you were enriched, in full power *and* readiness of speech (to speak of your faith), and complete knowledge *and* illumination (to give you full insight into its meaning).

6 In this way [our] witnessing concerning Christ, the Messiah, was so confirmed *and* established *and* made sure in you.

7 That you are not (consciously) falling behind *or* lacking in any special spiritual endowment *or* Christian grace ([a]the reception of which is due to the power of divine grace operating in your souls by the Holy Spirit), while you wait *and* watch (constantly living in hope) for the coming of our Lord Jesus Christ *and* [His] being made visible to all.

8 And He will establish you to the end—keep you steadfast, give you strength, and guarantee your vindication, that is, be your warrant against all accusation or indictment—[so that you will be] guiltless *and* irreproachable in the day of our Lord Jesus Christ, the Messiah.

9 God is faithful—reliable, trustworthy and [therefore] ever true to His promise, and He can be depended on; by Him you were called into companionship *and* participation with His Son, Jesus Christ our Lord.

10 But I urge *and* entreat you, brethren, by the name of our Lord Jesus Christ, that all of you be in perfect harmony, *and* full agreement in what you say, and that there be no dissensions *or* factions *or* divisions among you; but that you be perfectly united in your common understanding and in your opinions *and* judgments.

11 For it has been made clear to me, my brethren, by those of Chloe's household that there are contentions *and* wrangling *and* factions among you.

12 What I mean is this, that each one of you [either] says, I belong to Paul, or I belong to Apollos, or I belong to Cephas (Peter), or I belong to Christ.

13 Is Christ, the Messiah, divided into parts? Was Paul crucified on behalf of you? Or were you baptized into the name of Paul?

14 I thank God that I did not baptize any of you except Crispus and Gaius,

15 Lest any one should say that I baptized in my own name.

---

a) Thayer's "Greek-English Lexicon of the New Testament — Grimm."

Living New Testament

I Corinthians

CHAPTER 1

From: Paul, chosen by God to be Jesus Christ's missionary, and from brother Sosthenes.

2 *To:* The Christians in Corinth, invited by God to be His people and made acceptable[1] to Him by Christ Jesus. *And to:* All Christians everywhere—whoever calls upon the name of Jesus Christ, our Lord and theirs.

3 May God our Father and the Lord Jesus Christ give you all of His blessings, and great peace of heart and mind.

4 I can never stop thanking God for all the wonderful gifts He has given you, now that you are Christ's:

5 He has enriched your whole life. He has helped you speak out for Him and has given you a full understanding of the truth;

6 What I told you Christ could do for you has happened!

7 Now you have every grace and blessing; every spiritual gift and power for doing His will are yours during this time of waiting for the return of our Lord Jesus Christ.

8 And He guarantees right up to the end that you will be counted free from all sin and guilt on that day when He returns.

9 God will surely do this for you, for He always does just what He says, and He is the one who invited you into this wonderful friendship with His Son; even Christ our Lord.

10 But, dear brothers, I beg you in the name of the Lord Jesus Christ to stop arguing among yourselves. Let there be real harmony so that there won't be splits in the church. I plead with you to be of one mind, united in thought and purpose.

11 For some of those who live at Chloe's house have told me of your arguments and quarrels, dear brothers.

12 Some of you are saying, "I am a follower of Paul"; and others say that they are for Apollos or for Peter; and some that they alone are the true followers of Christ.

13 And so, in effect, you have broken Christ into many pieces. But did I, Paul, die for your sins? Were any of you baptized in my name?

14 I am so thankful now that I didn't baptize any of you except Crispus and Gaius.

15 For now no one can think that I have been trying to start something new, beginning a "Church of Paul."

[1] Or, "chosen by Christ Jesus." Literally, "Sanctified in Christ Jesus."

Revised Standard

THE FIRST LETTER OF PAUL TO THE

Corinthians

Introduction

1 Paul, called by the will of God to be an
apostle of Christ Jesus, and our brother
Sosthenes,
2 To the church of God which is at
Corinth, to those sanctified in Christ Jesus,
called to be saints together with all those
who in every place call on the name of our
Lord Jesus Christ, both their Lord and ours:
3 Grace to you and peace from God our
Father and the Lord Jesus Christ.

4 I give thanks to God[a] always for you
because of the grace of God which was
given you in Christ Jesus, 5that in every
way you were enriched in him with all
speech and all knowledge—6even as the
testimony to Christ was confirmed among
you—7so that you are not lacking in any
spiritual gift, as you wait for the revealing
of our Lord Jesus Christ; 8who will sustain
you to the end, guiltless in the day of our
Lord Jesus Christ. 9God is faithful, by whom
you were called into the fellowship of his
Son, Jesus Christ our Lord.

An appeal for unity

10 I appeal to you, brethren, by the name
of our Lord Jesus Christ, that all of you
agree and that there be no dissensions among
you, but that you be united in the same
mind and the same judgment. 11For it has
been reported to me by Chloe's people that
there is quarreling among you, my brethren.
12What I mean is that each one of you says,
"I belong to Paul," or "I belong to Apollos,"
or "I belong to Cephas," or "I belong to
Christ." 13Is Christ divided? Was Paul crucified for you? Or were you baptized in the
name of Paul? 14I am thankful[b] that I baptized none of you except Crispus and Gaius;
15lest any one should say that you were bap-

[a] Other ancient authorities read *my God*
[b] Other ancient authorities read *I thank God*

King James

16 And I baptized also the household of Stephanas: besides, I know not whether I baptized any other.

17 For Christ sent me not to baptize, but to preach the gospel: not with wisdom of words, lest the cross of Christ should be made of none effect.

18 For the preaching of the cross is to them that perish foolishness; but unto us which are saved it is the power of God.

19 For it is written, I will destroy the wisdom of the wise, and will bring to nothing the understanding of the prudent.

20 Where *is* the wise? where *is* the scribe? where *is* the disputer of this world? hath not God made foolish the wisdom of this world?

21 For after that in the wisdom of God the world by wisdom knew not God, it pleased God by the foolishness of preaching to save them that believe.

22 For the Jews require a sign, and the Greeks seek after wisdom:

23 But we preach Christ crucified, unto the Jews a stumblingblock, and unto the Greeks foolishness;

24 But unto them which are called, both Jews and Greeks, Christ the power of God, and the wisdom of God.

25 Because the foolishness of God is wiser than men; and the weakness of God is stronger than men.

26 For ye see your calling, brethren, how that not many wise men after the flesh, not many mighty, not many noble, *are called:*

27 But God hath chosen the foolish things of the world to confound the wise; and God hath chosen the weak things of the world to confound the things which are mighty;

28 And base things of the world, and things which are despised, hath God chosen, *yea,* and things which are not, to bring to nought things that are:

29 That no flesh should glory in his presence.

30 But of him are ye in Christ Jesus, who of God is made unto us wisdom, and righteousness, and sanctification, and redemption:

31 That, according as it is written, He that glorieth, let him glory in the Lord.

Amplified

16 [Yes] I did baptize the household of Stephanas, also. More than these, I do not remember that I baptized any one.

17 For Christ, the Messiah, sent me out not to baptize but (to evangelize by) preaching the glad tidings (the Gospel); and that not with verbal eloquence, lest the cross of Christ should be deprived of force *and* emptied of its power *and* rendered vain—fruitless, void of value and of no effect.

18 For the story *and* message of the cross is sheer absurdity *and* folly to those who are perishing *and* on their way to perdition, but to us who are being saved it is the [manifestation of] the power of God.

19 For it is written, I will baffle *and* render useless *and* destroy the learning of the learned *and* the philosophy of the philosophers and the cleverness of the clever *and* the discernment of the discerning, I will frustrate *and* nullify [them] *and* bring [them] to nothing. [Isa. 29:14.]

20 Where is the wise man—the philosopher? Where is the scribe—the scholar? Where is the investigator—the logician, the debater—of this present time *and* age? Has not God shown up the nonsense *and* the folly of this world's wisdom?

21 For when the world with all its earthly wisdom failed to perceive *and* recognize *and* know God by means of its own philosophy, God in His wisdom was pleased through the foolishness of preaching [of salvation, procured by Christ and to be had through Him], to save those who believed—who clung to and trusted in and relied on Him.

22 For while Jews (demandingly) ask for signs *and* miracles, and Greeks pursue philosophy *and wisdom,*

23 We preach Christ, the Messiah, crucified, which to the Jews is a scandal *and* an offensive stumbling block (that springs a snare-trap), and to the Gentiles it is absurd *and* utterly unphilosophical nonsense.

24 But to those who are called, whether Jew or Greek (Gentile), Christ [is] the power of God and the wisdom of God.

25 [This is] because the foolish thing [that has its source in] God is wiser than men, and the weak thing [that springs from] God is stronger than men.

26 For [simply] consider your own call, brethren; not many [of you were considered to be] wise, according to human estimates *and* standards; not many influential *and* powerful; not many of high *and* noble birth.

27 [No,] for God selected—deliberately chose—what in the world is foolish to put the wise to shame, and what the world calls weak to put the strong to shame.

28 And God also selected—deliberately chose—[what] in the world [is] lowborn *and* insignificant, and branded *and* treated with contempt, even the things that are nothing, that He might depose *and* bring to nothing the things that are;

29 So that no mortal man should (have pretense for glorying and) boast in the presence of God.

30 But it is from Him that you have your life in Christ Jesus, Whom God made our Wisdom from God, [that is, revealed to us a knowledge of the divine plan of salvation previously hidden, manifesting itself as] our Righteousness *and thus* making us upright and putting us in right standing with God; and our Consecration—making us pure and holy; and our Redemption—providing our ransom from eternal penalty for sin.

31 So then, as it is written, Let him who boasts *and* proudly rejoices *and* glories, boast *and* proudly rejoice *and* glory in the Lord. [Jer. 9:24.]

Living New Testament

16 Oh, yes, and I baptized the family of Stephanas. I don't remember ever baptizing anyone else.

17 For Christ didn't send me to baptize, but to preach the Gospel; and even my preaching sounds poor, for I do not fill my sermons with profound words and high sounding ideas, for fear of diluting the mighty power there is in the simple message of the cross of Christ.

18 I know very well how foolish it sounds to those who are[2] lost when they hear that Jesus died to save them. But we who are[2] saved recognize this message as the very power of God.

19 For God says, "I will destroy all human plans of salvation no matter how wise they seem to be, and ignore the best ideas of men, even the most brilliant of them."

20 So what about these wise men, these scholars, these brilliant debaters of this world's great affairs? God has made them all look foolish, and shown their wisdom to be useless nonsense.

21 For God in His wisdom saw to it that the world would never find God through human brilliance, and then He stepped in and saved all those who believed His message, which the world calls foolish and silly.

22 It seems foolish to the Jews because they want a sign from heaven as proof that what is preached is true; and it is foolish to the Gentiles because they believe only what agrees with their philosophy and seems wise to them.

23 So when we preach about Christ dying to save them, the Jews are offended and the Gentiles say it's all nonsense.

24 But God has opened the eyes of those called to salvation, both Jews and Gentiles, to see that Christ is the mighty power of God to save them; Christ Himself is the center of God's wise plan for their salvation.

25 This so-called "foolish" plan of God is far wiser than the wisest plan of the wisest man, and God in His weakness—Christ dying on the cross—is far stronger than any man.

26 Notice among yourselves, dear brothers, that few of you who follow Christ have big names or power or wealth.

27 Instead, God has deliberately chosen to use ideas the world considers foolish and of little worth in order to shame those people considered by the world as wise and great.

28 He has chosen a plan despised by the world, counted as nothing at all, and used it to bring down to nothing those the world considers great,

29 So that no one anywhere can ever brag in the presence of God.

30 For it is from God alone that you have your life through Christ Jesus. He showed us God's plan of salvation; He was the one who made us acceptable to God; He made us pure and holy[3] and gave Himself to purchase our salvation.[4]

31 As it says in the Scriptures, "If anyone is going to boast, let him boast only of what the Lord has done."

Revised Standard

tized in my name. 16(I did baptize also the
household of Stephanas. Beyond that, I do
not know whether I baptized any one else.)
17For Christ did not send me to baptize but
to preach the gospel, and not with eloquent
wisdom, lest the cross of Christ be emptied
of its power.

Christ the power and wisdom of God

18 For the word of the cross is folly to
those who are perishing, but to us who are
being saved it is the power of God. 19For
it is written,

"I will destroy the wisdom of the wise,
and the cleverness of the clever I will
thwart."

20Where is the wise man? Where is the
scribe? Where is the debater of this age?
Has not God made foolish the wisdom of
the world? 21For since, in the wisdom of
God, the world did not know God through
wisdom, it pleased God through the folly
of what we preach to save those who believe. 22For Jews demand signs and Greeks
seek wisdom, 23but we preach Christ crucified, a stumbling block to Jews and folly to
Gentiles, 24but to those who are called, both
Jews and Greeks, Christ the power of God
and the wisdom of God. 25For the foolishness of God is wiser than men, and the
weakness of God is stronger than men.

26 For consider your call, brethren; not
many of you were wise according to worldly
standards, not many were powerful, not
many were of noble birth; 27but God chose
what is foolish in the world to shame the
wise, God chose what is weak in the world
to shame the strong, 28God chose what is
low and despised in the world, even things
that are not, to bring to nothing things that
are, 29so that no human being might boast
in the presence of God. 30He is the source
of your life in Christ Jesus, whom God
made our wisdom, our righteousness and
sanctification and redemption; 31therefore,
as it is written, "Let him who boasts, boast
of the Lord."

---

[2] Or, "are being . . ."
[3] Or, "He brought us near to God."
[4] Or, "to free us from slavery to sin."

King James

CHAPTER 2

AND I, brethren, when I came to you, came not with excellency of speech or of wisdom, declaring unto you the testimony of God.

2 For I determined not to know any thing among you, save Jesus Christ, and him crucified.

3 And I was with you in weakness, and in fear, and in much trembling.

4 And my speech and my preaching *was* not with enticing words of man's wisdom, but in demonstration of the Spirit and of power:

5 That your faith should not stand in the wisdom of men, but in the power of God.

6 Howbeit we speak wisdom among them that are perfect: yet not the wisdom of this world, nor of the princes of this world, that come to nought:

7 But we speak the wisdom of God in a mystery, *even* the hidden *wisdom,* which God ordained before the world unto our glory:

8 Which none of the princes of this world knew: for had they known *it,* they would not have crucified the Lord of glory.

9 But as it is written, Eye hath not seen, nor ear heard, neither have entered into the heart of man, the things which God hath prepared for them that love him.

10 But God hath revealed *them* unto us by his Spirit: for the Spirit searcheth all things, yea, the deep things of God.

11 For what man knoweth the things of a man, save the spirit of man which is in him? even so the things of God knoweth no man, but the Spirit of God.

12 Now we have received, not the spirit of the world, but the spirit which is of God; that we might know the things that are freely given to us of God.

13 Which things also we speak, not in the words which man's wisdom teacheth, but which the Holy Ghost teacheth; comparing spiritual things with spiritual.

Amplified

CHAPTER 2

AS for myself, brethren, when I came to you [I] did not come proclaiming to you the testimony *and* evidence *or* [b]mystery *or* secret of God [concerning what He has done through Christ for the salvation of men] in lofty words of eloquence or human philosophy *and* wisdom;

2 For I resolved to know nothing—to be acquainted with [nothing], to make a display of the knowledge of [nothing], and to be conscious of [nothing]—among you except Jesus Christ, the Messiah, and Him crucified.

3 And I ([c]passed into a state of) weakness and was in fear (dread) and great trembling [[c]after I had come] among you.

4 And my language and my message were not set forth in persuasive (enticing and plausible) words of wisdom, but they were in demonstration of the (Holy) Spirit and power [that is, [d]a proof by the Spirit and power of God, operating on me and stirring in the minds of my hearers the most holy emotions and thus persuading them],

5 So that your faith might not rest in the wisdom of men (human philosophy), but in the power of God.

6 Yet when we are among the fullgrown—spiritually mature Christians who are ripe in understanding—we do impart a (higher) wisdom [that is, the knowledge of the divine plan previously hidden]; but it is indeed not a wisdom of this present age nor of this world *or* of the leaders *and* rulers of this age, who are being brought to nothing *and* are doomed to pass away.

7 But rather what we are setting forth is a wisdom of God once hidden [from the human understanding] and now revealed to us by God; [that wisdom] which God devised *and* decreed before the ages for our glorification [that is, to lift us into the glory of His presence].

8 None of the rulers of this age *or* world perceived *and* recognized *and* understood this; for if they had, they would never have crucified the Lord of glory.

9 But, on the contrary, as the Scripture says, What eye has not seen, and ear has not heard, and has not entered into the heart of man, [all that,] God has prepared—made and keeps ready—for those who love Him [that is, for those who hold Him [e]in affectionate reverence, promptly obeying Him and gratefully recognizing the benefits He has bestowed]. [Isa. 64:4; 65:17.]

10 Yet to us God has unveiled *and* revealed them by *and* through His Spirit, for the (Holy) Spirit searches diligently, exploring *and* examining everything, even sounding the profound and bottomless things of God—the [e]divine counsels and things hidden and beyond man's scrutiny.

11 For what person perceives (knows and understands) what passes through a man's thoughts except the man's own spirit within him? Just so no one discerns (comes to know and comprehend) the thoughts of God except the Spirit of God.

12 Now we have not received the spirit (that belongs to) the world, but the (Holy) Spirit Who is from God, [given to us] that we might realize *and* comprehend *and* appreciate the gifts (of divine favor and blessing so freely and lavishly) bestowed on us by God.

13 And we are setting these truths forth in words not taught by human wisdom but taught by the (Holy) Spirit, combining *and* interpreting spiritual truths with spiritual language [to those who possess the (Holy) Spirit].

---

b) Many ancient authorities so read.
c) Vincent.
d) Thayer's "Greek-English Lexicon of the New Testament — Grimm."
e) Thayer.

Living New Testament

CHAPTER 2

Dear brothers, even when I first came to you I didn't use lofty words and brilliant ideas to tell you God's message.

2 For I decided that I would speak only of Jesus Christ and His death on the cross.

3 I came to you in weakness—timid and trembling.

4 And my preaching was very plain, not with a lot of oratory and human wisdom, but the Holy Spirit's power was in my words, proving to those who heard them that the message was from God.

5 I did this because I wanted your faith to stand firmly upon God, not on man's great ideas.

6 Yet when I am among mature Christians I do speak with words of great wisdom, but not the kind that comes from here on earth, and not the kind that appeals to the great men of this world, who are doomed to fall.

7 Our words are wise because they are from God, telling of God's wise plan to bring us into the glories of heaven. This plan was hidden in former times, though it was made for our benefit before the world began.

8 But the great men of the world have not understood it; if they had, they never would have crucified the Lord of Glory.

9 That is what is meant by the Scriptures which say that no mere man has ever seen, heard or even imagined what wonderful things God has ready for those who love the Lord.

10 But we know about these things because God has sent His Spirit to tell us, and His Spirit searches out and shows us all of God's deepest secrets.

11 No one can really know what anyone else is thinking, or what he is really like, except that person himself. And no one can know God's thoughts except God's own Spirit.

12 And God has actually given us His Spirit (not the world's spirit) to tell us about the wonderful free gifts of grace and blessing that God has given us.

13 In telling you about these gifts we have even used the very words given us by the Holy Spirit, not words that we as men might choose. So we use the Holy Spirit's words to explain the Holy Spirit's facts.[1]

[1] Or, "interpeting spiritual truth in spiritual language."

Revised Standard

2 When I came to you, brethren, I did not
come proclaiming to you the testimony[c]
of God in lofty words or wisdom. 2 For I
decided to know nothing among you except
Jesus Christ and him crucified. 3 And I was
with you in weakness and in much fear and
trembling; 4 and my speech and my message
were not in plausible words of wisdom, but
in demonstration of the Spirit and power,
5 that your faith might not rest in the wisdom of men but in the power of God.

True wisdom the gift of God

6 Yet among the mature we do impart
wisdom, although it is not a wisdom of this
age or of the rulers of this age, who are
doomed to pass away. 7 But we impart a
secret and hidden wisdom of God, which
God decreed before the ages for our glorification. 8 None of the rulers of this age understood this; for if they had, they would
not have crucified the Lord of glory. 9 But
as it is written,

"What no eye has seen, nor ear heard,
nor the heart of man conceived,
what God has prepared for those who
love him,"

10 God has revealed to us through the Spirit.
For the Spirit searches everything, even the
depths of God. 11 For what person knows
a man's thoughts except the spirit of the
man which is in him? So also no one comprehends the thoughts of God except the
Spirit of God. 12 Now we have received not
the spirit of the world, but the Spirit which
is from God, that we might understand the
gifts bestowed on us by God. 13 And we impart this in words not taught by human
wisdom but taught by the Spirit, interpreting spiritual truths to those who possess the
Spirit.[d]

[c] Other ancient authorities read *mystery* (or *secret*)
[d] Or *interpreting spiritual truths in spiritual language;* or *comparing spiritual things with spiritual*

King James

14 But the natural man receiveth not the things of the Spirit of God: for they are foolishness unto him: neither can he know *them,* because they are spiritually discerned.

15 But he that is spiritual judgeth all things, yet he himself is judged of no man.

16 For who hath known the mind of the Lord, that he may instruct him? But we have the mind of Christ.

Amplified

14 But the natural, nonspiritual man does not accept *or* welcome *or* admit into his heart the gifts *and* teachings *and* revelations of the Spirit of God, for they are folly (meaningless nonsense) to him; and he is incapable of knowing them—of progressively recognizing, understanding and becoming better acquainted with them—because they are spiritually discerned *and* estimated *and* appreciated.

15 But the spiritual man tries all things—[that is,] he [f]examines, investigates, inquires into, questions, and discerns all things; yet is himself to be put on trial and judged by no one.—He can read the meaning of everything, but no one can properly discern *or* appraise *or* get an insight into him.

16 For who has known *or* understood the mind (the counsels and purposes) of the Lord so as to guide *and* instruct [Him] *and* give Him knowledge? But we have the mind of Christ, the Messiah, *and* do hold the thoughts (feelings and purposes) of His heart. [Isa. 40:13.]

CHAPTER 3

AND I, brethren, could not speak unto you as unto spiritual, but as unto carnal, *even* as unto babes in Christ.

2 I have fed you with milk, and not with meat: for hitherto ye were not able *to bear it,* neither yet now are ye able.

3 For ye are yet carnal: for whereas *there* is among you envying, and strife, and divisions, are ye not carnal, and walk as men?

4 For while one saith, I am of Paul; and another, I am of Apollos; are ye not carnal?

5 Who then is Paul, and who *is* Apollos, but ministers by whom ye believed, even as the Lord gave to every man?

6 I have planted, Apollos watered; but God gave the increase.

7 So then neither is he that planteth any thing, neither he that watereth; but God that giveth the increase.

8 Now he that planteth and he that watereth are one: and every man shall receive his own reward according to his own labour.

9 For we are labourers together with God: ye are God's husbandry, *ye are* God's building.

10 According to the grace of God which is given unto me, as a wise masterbuilder, I have laid the foundation, and another buildeth thereon. But let every man take heed how he buildeth thereupon.

CHAPTER 3

HOWEVER, brethren, I could not talk to you as to spiritual [men], but as to nonspiritual (men of the flesh, in whom the carnal nature predominates), as to mere infants [in the new life] in Christ—[g]unable to talk yet!

2 I fed you with milk, not solid food, for you were not yet strong enough [to be ready for it]; but even yet you are not strong enough [to be ready for it],

3 For you are still (unspiritual, having the nature) of the flesh—under the control of ordinary impulses. For as long as [there are] envying and jealousy *and* wrangling and factions among you, are you not unspiritual *and* of the flesh, behaving yourselves after a human standard *and* like mere (unchanged) men?

4 For when one says, I belong to Paul, and another, I belong to Apollos, are you not [proving yourselves] ordinary (unchanged) men?

5 What then is Apollos? What is Paul? Ministering servants [not heads of parties], through whom you believed, even as the Lord appointed to each his task:

6 I planted, Apollos watered, but God [all the while] was making it grow, *and* [He] gave the increase.

7 So neither he who plants is anything nor he who waters, but [only] God Who makes it grow *and* become greater.

8 He who plants and he who waters are equal—one in aim, of the same importance and esteem—yet each shall receive his own reward (wages), according to his own labor.

9 For we are fellow workmen—joint promoters, laborers together—with *and* for God; *you* are God's [h]garden *and* vineyard *and* field under cultivation; [you are] God's building. [Isa. 61:3.]

10 According to the grace—the special endowment for my task—of God bestowed on me, like a skilful architect *and* master builder I laid [the] foundation, and now another [man] is building upon it. But let each [man] be careful how he builds upon it.

---

f) Lightfoot.
g) Literally, "non-speakers."
h) Bengel.

Living New Testament

14 But the man who isn't a Christian can't understand and can't accept these thoughts from God, which the Holy Spirit teaches us. They sound foolish to him, because only those who have the Holy Spirit within them can understand what the Holy Spirit means. Others just can't take it in.

15 But the spiritual man has insight into everything, and that bothers and baffles the man of the world, who can't understand him at all.

16 How could he? For certainly he has never been one to know the Lord's thoughts, or to discuss them with Him, or to move the hands of God by prayer.[2] But, strange as it seems, we Christians actually do have within us a portion of the very thoughts and mind of Christ.

Revised Standard

14 The unspiritual[e] man does not receive
the gifts of the Spirit of God, for they are
folly to him, and he is not able to understand them because they are spiritually discerned. [15]The spiritual man judges all things,
but is himself to be judged by no one.
[16]"For who has known the mind of the
Lord so as to instruct him?" But we have
the mind of Christ.

CHAPTER 3

Dear brothers, I have been talking to you as though you were still just babies in the Christian life, who are not following the Lord, but your own desires; I cannot talk to you as I would to healthy Christians, who are filled with the Spirit.

2 I have had to feed you with milk and not with solid food, because you couldn't digest anything stronger. And even now you still have to be fed on milk.

3 For you are still only baby Christians, controlled by your own desires, not God's. When you are jealous of one another and divide up into quarreling groups, doesn't that prove you are still babies, wanting your own way? In fact, you are acting like people who don't belong to the Lord at all.

4 There you are, quarreling about whether I am greater than Apollos and dividing the church. Doesn't this show how little you have grown in the Lord?[1]

5 Who am I, and who is Apollos, that we should be the cause of a quarrel? Why, we're just God's servants, each of us with certain special abilities, and with our help you believed.

6 My work was to plant the seed in your hearts, and Apollos' work was to water it, but it was God, not we, who made the garden grow in your hearts.

7 The person who does the planting or watering isn't very important, but God is important because He is the one who makes things grow.

8 Apollos and I are working as a team, with the same aim, though each of us will be rewarded for his own hard work.

9 We are only God's co-workers. You are *God's* garden, not ours; you are *God's* building, not ours.

10 God, in His kindness, has taught me how to be an expert builder. I have laid the foundation and Apollos[2] has built on it. But he who builds on the foundation must be very careful.

Fellow workmen for God

3 But I, brethren, could not address you
as spiritual men, but as men of the
flesh, as babes in Christ. [2]I fed you with
milk, not solid food; for you were not ready
for it; and even yet you are not ready, [3]for
you are still of the flesh. For while there is
jealousy and strife among you, are you not
of the flesh, and behaving like ordinary
men? [4]For when one says, "I belong to
Paul," and another, "I belong to Apollos,"
are you not merely men?
5 What then is Apollos? What is Paul?
Servants through whom you believed, as the
Lord assigned to each. [6]I planted, Apollos
watered, but God gave the growth. [7]So
neither he who plants nor he who waters
is anything, but only God who gives the
growth. [8]He who plants and he who waters
are equal, and each shall receive his wages
according to his labor. [9]For we are fellow
workers for God;[f] you are God's field, God's
building.

Christ, the foundation

10 According to the commission of God
given to me, like a skilled master builder I
laid a foundation, and another man is building upon it. Let each man take care how he

---

Or, "who can advise Him?"
Literally, "are you not (mere) men?"
Implied.

[e] Or *natural*
[f] Greek *God's fellow workers*

King James

11 For other foundation can no man lay than that is laid, which is Jesus Christ.
12 Now if any man build upon this foundation gold, silver, precious stones, wood, hay, stubble;
13 Every man's work shall be made manifest: for the day shall declare it, because it shall be revealed by fire; and the fire shall try every man's work of what sort it is.
14 If any man's work abide which he hath built thereupon, he shall receive a reward.
15 If any man's work shall be burned, he shall suffer loss: but he himself shall be saved; yet so as by fire.
16 Know ye not that ye are the temple of God, and *that* the Spirit of God dwelleth in you?
17 If any man defile the temple of God, him shall God destroy; for the temple of God is holy, which *temple* ye are.
18 Let no man deceive himself. If any man among you seemeth to be wise in this world, let him become a fool, that he may be wise.
19 For the wisdom of this world is foolishness with God. For it is written, He taketh the wise in their own craftiness.
20 And again, The Lord knoweth the thoughts of the wise, that they are vain.
21 Therefore let no man glory in men. For all things are yours;
22 Whether Paul, or Apollos, or Cephas, or the world, or life, or death, or things present, or things to come; all are yours;
23 And ye are Christ's; and Christ *is* God's.

Amplified

11 For no other foundation can any one lay than that which is [already] laid, which is Jesus Christ, the Messiah, the Anointed One.
12 But if any one builds upon the Foundation, whether it be with gold, silver, precious stones, wood, hay, straw,
13 The work of each [one] will become (plainly, openly) known—shown for what it is; for the day (of Christ) will disclose *and* declare it, because it will be revealed with fire, and the fire will test *and* critically appraise the character *and* worth of the work each person has done.
14 If the work which any person has built on this Foundation—any product of his efforts whatever—survives (this test), he will get his reward.
15 But if any person's work is burned up [under the test], he will suffer the loss (of it all, losing his reward), though he himself will be saved, but only as [one who has passed] through fire. [Job 23:10.]
16 Do you not discern *and* understand that you [the whole church at Corinth] are God's temple (His sanctuary), and that God's Spirit has His permanent dwelling in you—to be at home in you [[i]collectively as a church and also individually]?
17 If any one [j]does hurt to God's temple *or* corrupts [[i]it with false doctrines] *or* destroys it, God will [j]do hurt to him *and* bring him to the corruption of death *and* destroy him. For the temple of God is holy—sacred to Him—and that [temple] you [[i]the believing church and its individual believers] are.
18 Let no person deceive himself. If any one among you supposes that he is wise in this age—let him discard his [worldly] discernment and recognize himself as dull, stupid and foolish, without [true] learning and scholarship; let him become a fool that he may become [really] wise. [Isa. 5:21.]
19 For this world's wisdom is foolishness—absurdity and stupidity—with God. For it is written, He lays hold of the wise in their [own] craftiness; [Job 5:13.]
20 And again, The Lord knows the thoughts *and* reasonings of the [humanly] wise *and* recognizes how futile they are. [Ps. 94:11.]
21 So let no one exult proudly concerning men [boasting of having this or that man as a leader], for all things are yours,
22 Whether Paul or Apollos or Cephas (Peter), or the universe or life or death, or the immediate *and* [k]threatening present or the [subsequent and uncertain] future; all are yours,
23 And you are Christ's, and Christ is God's.

King James

CHAPTER 4

LET a man so account of us, as of the ministers of Christ, and stewards of the mysteries of God.
2 Moreover it is required in stewards, that a man be found faithful.
3 But with me it is a very small thing that I should be judged of you, or of man's judgment: yea, I judge not mine own self.

Amplified

CHAPTER 4

SO then let us [apostles] be looked upon as ministering servants of Christ and stewards (trustees) of the mysteries—that is, the secret purposes—of God.
2 Moreover, it is [essentially] required of stewards that a man should be found faithful—proving himself worthy of trust.
3 But (as for me personally) it matters very little to me that I should be put on trial by you [on this point], *and* that you or any other human tribunal should investigate *and* question *and* cross-question me. I do not even put myself on trial *and* judge myself.

---

i) Matthew Henry and many others.
j) Cambridge Bible.
k) Vincent.

Living New Testament

11 For no one can ever lay any other real foundation than the one we already have—Jesus Christ.

12 But there are various kinds of materials that can be used to build on that foundation. Some use gold and silver and jewels; and some build with sticks, and hay, or even straw!

13 There is going to come a time of testing at Christ's Judgment Day to see what kind of material each builder has used. Everyone's work will be put through the fire so that all can see whether or not it keeps its value, and what was really accomplished.

14 Then every workman who has built on the foundation with the right materials, and whose work still stands, will get his pay.

15 But if the house he has built burns up, he will have a great loss. He himself will be saved, but like a man escaping through a wall of flames.

16 Don't you realize that all of you together are the house of God, and that the Spirit of God lives among you in His house?

17 If anyone defiles and spoils God's home, God will destroy him. For God's home is holy and clean, and you are that home.

18 Stop fooling yourselves. If you count yourself above average in intelligence, as judged by this world's standards, you had better put this all aside and be a fool rather than let it hold you back from the true wisdom from above.

19 For the wisdom of this world is foolishness to God. As it says in the book of Job, God uses man's own brilliance to trap him; he stumbles over his own "wisdom" and falls.

20 And again, in the book of Psalms, we are told that the Lord knows full well how the human mind reasons, and how foolish and futile it is.

21 So don't be proud of following the wise men of this world.[3] For God has already given you everything you need.

22 He has given you Paul and Apollos and Peter as your helpers. He has given you the whole world to use, and life and even death are your servants. He has given you all of the present and all of the future. All are yours,

23 And you belong to Christ, and Christ is God's.

Revised Standard

builds upon it. 11For no other foundation
can any one lay than that which is laid,
which is Jesus Christ. 12Now if any one
builds on the foundation with gold, silver,
precious stones, wood, hay, stubble—13each
man's work will become manifest; for the
Day will disclose it, because it will be revealed with fire, and the fire will test what
sort of work each one has done. 14If the
work which any man has built on the foundation survives, he will receive a reward.
15If any man's work is burned up, he will
suffer loss, though he himself will be saved,
but only as through fire.
16 Do you not know that you are God's
temple and that God's Spirit dwells in you?
17If any one destroys God's temple, God will
destroy him. For God's temple is holy, and
that temple you are.
18 Let no one deceive himself. If any one
among you thinks that he is wise in this
age, let him become a fool that he may become wise. 19For the wisdom of this world
is folly with God. For it is written, "He
catches the wise in their craftiness," 20and
again, "The Lord knows that the thoughts
of the wise are futile." 21So let no one boast
of men. For all things are yours, 22whether
Paul or Apollos or Cephas or the world of
life or death or the present or the future,
all are yours; 23and you are Christ's; and
Christ is God's.

CHAPTER 4

So Apollos and I should be looked upon as Christ's servants who distribute God's blessings by explaining God's secrets.

2 Now the most important thing about a servant is that he does just what his master tells him to.

3 What about me? Have I been a good servant? Well, I don't worry over what you think about this, or what anyone else thinks. I don't even trust my own judgment on this point.

The humility of the apostles

4 This is how one should regard us, as
servants of Christ and stewards of the
mysteries of God. 2Moreover it is required
of stewards that they be found trustworthy.
3But with me it is a very small thing that I
should be judged by you or by any human
court. I do not even judge myself. 4I am

[3] Literally, "Let no one glory in men."

King James

4 For I know nothing by myself; yet am I not hereby justified: but he that judgeth me is the Lord.

5 Therefore judge nothing before the time, until the Lord come, who both will bring to light the hidden things of darkness, and will make manifest the counsels of the hearts: and then shall every man have praise of God.

6 And these things, brethren, I have in a figure transferred to myself and *to* Apollos for your sakes; that ye might learn in us not to think *of men* above that which is written, that no one of you be puffed up for one against another.

7 For who maketh thee to differ *from another?* and what hast thou that thou didst not receive? now if thou didst receive *it,* why dost thou glory, as if thou hadst not received *it?*

8 Now ye are full, now ye are rich, ye have reigned as kings without us: and I would to God ye did reign, that we also might reign with you.

9 For I think that God hath set forth us the apostles last, as it were appointed to death: for we are made a spectacle unto the world, and to angels, and to men.

10 We *are* fools for Christ's sake, but ye *are* wise in Christ; we *are* weak, but ye *are* strong; ye *are* honourable, but we *are* despised.

11 Even unto this present hour we both hunger, and thirst, and are naked, and are buffeted, and have no certain dwellingplace;

12 And labour, working with our own hands: being reviled, we bless; being persecuted, we suffer it:

13 Being defamed, we entreat: we are made as the filth of the world, *and are* the offscouring of all things unto this day.

14 I write not these things to shame you, but as my beloved sons I warn *you.*

15 For though ye have ten thousand instructors in Christ, yet *have ye* not many fathers: for in Christ Jesus I have begotten you through the gospel.

16 Wherefore I beseech you, be ye followers of me.

17 For this cause have I sent unto you Timotheus, who is my beloved son, and faithful in the Lord, who shall bring you into rememberance of my ways which be in Christ, as I teach every where in every church.

Amplified

4 I am not conscious of anything against myself, *and* I feel blameless; but I am not vindicated *and* acquitted before God on that account. It is the Lord [Himself] Who examines *and* judges me.

5 So do not make any hasty *or* premature judgments before the time when the Lord comes [again], for He will both bring to light the secret things that are (now hidden) in darkness, and disclose *and* expose the (secret) aims (motives and purposes) of hearts. Then every man will receive his (due) commendation from God.

6 Now I have applied all this [about parties and factions] to myself and Apollos for your sakes, brethren, so that from what I have said of us [as illustrations] you may learn [to think of men in accordance with Scripture and] not to go beyond that which is written; that none of you may be puffed up *and* inflated with pride *and* boast in favor of one [minister and teacher] against another.

7 For who separates you from the others [as a faction leader]?—Who makes you superior and sets you apart from another, giving you the pre-eminence? What have you that was not given to you? If then you received it [from someone], why do you boast as if you had not received (but had gained it by your own efforts)?

8 [[l]You behave as if] you are already filled *and* think you have enough—you are full and content, feeling no need of anything more! Already you have become rich (in spiritual gifts and graces)! [Without any counsel or instruction from us, that is, in your conceit], you have ascended your thrones *and* come into your kingdom without including us! And would that it were true *and* that you did reign, so that we might be sharing the kingdom with you!

9 For it seems to me that God has made an exhibit of us apostles, exposing us to view last [of all, like men in a triumphal procession who are] sentenced to death [and displayed at the end of the line]. For we have become a spectacle to the world—a show in the world's amphitheatre—with both men and angels (as spectators).

10 We are [looked upon as] fools on account of Christ *and* for His sake, but you are [supposedly] so amazingly wise *and* prudent in Christ! We are weak, but you are [so very] strong! You are highly esteemed, but we are in disrepute *and* contempt!

11 To this hour we have gone both hungry and thirsty; we [m]habitually wear but one undergarment [and shiver in the cold]; we are roughly knocked about and wander around homeless.

12 And we still toil unto weariness [for our living], working hard with our own hands. When men revile us—that is, [n]wound us with an accursed sting—we bless them. When we are persecuted, we take it patiently *and* endure it.

13 When we are slandered *and* defamed, we [try to] answer softly *and* bring comfort. We have been made and are now the rubbish *and* filth of the world—the offscouring of all things, the scum of the earth.

14 I do not write this to shame you, but to warn *and* counsel you as my beloved children.

15 After all, though you should have ten thousand teachers (guides to direct you) in Christ, yet you do not have many fathers. For I became your father in Christ Jesus through the glad tidings (the Gospel).

16 So I urge *and* implore you, be imitators of me.

17 For this very cause I sent to you Timothy who is my beloved and trustworthy child in the Lord, who will recall to your minds my methods of proceeding *and* course of conduct *and* way of life in Christ, such as I teach everywhere in each of the churches.

---

l) Alford.
m) Souter.
n) Wuest's "Byways in the Greek New Testament."

Living New Testament

4 My conscience is clear, but even that isn't final proof. It is the Lord Himself who must examine me and decide.

5 So be careful not to jump to conclusions before the Lord returns as to whether someone is a good servant or not. When the Lord comes, He will turn on the light so that everyone can see exactly what each one of us is really like, deep down in our hearts. Then everyone will know why we have been doing the Lord's work. At that time God will give to each one whatever praise is coming to him.

6 I have used Apollos and myself as examples to illustrate what I have been saying: that you must not have favorites. You must not be proud of one of God's teachers more than another.

7 What are you so puffed up about? What do you have that God hasn't given you? And if all you have is from God, why act as though you are so great, and as though you have accomplished something on your own?

8 You seem to think you already have all the spiritual food you need. You are full and spiritually contented, rich kings on your thrones, leaving us far behind! I wish you really were already on your thrones, for when that time comes you can be sure that we will be there, too, reigning with you.

9 Sometimes I think God has put us apostles at the very end of the line, like prisoners soon to be killed, put on display at the end of a victor's parade, to be stared at by men and angels alike.

10 Religion has made us foolish, you say, but of course you are all such wise and sensible Christians! We are weak, but not you! You are well thought of, while we are laughed at.

11 To this very hour we have gone hungry and thirsty, without even enough clothes to keep us warm. We have been kicked around without homes of our own.

12 We have worked wearily with our hands to earn our living. We have blessed those who cursed us. We have been patient with those who injured us.

13 We have replied quietly when evil things have been said about us. Yet right up to the present moment we are like dirt under foot, like garbage.

14 I am not writing about these things to make you ashamed, but to warn and counsel you as beloved children.

15 For although you may have ten thousand others to teach you about Christ, remember that you have only me as your father. For I was the one who brought you to Christ when I preached the Gospel to you.

16 So I beg you to follow my example, and do as I do.

17 That is the very reason why I am sending Timothy—to help you do this. For he is one of those I won to Christ, a beloved and trustworthy child in the Lord. He will remind you of what I teach in all the churches wherever I go.

Revised Standard

not aware of anything against myself, but
I am not thereby acquitted. It is the Lord
who judges me. 5 Therefore do not pronounce judgment before the time, before the
Lord comes, who will bring to light the
things now hidden in darkness and will disclose the purposes of the heart. Then every
man will receive his commendation from
God.

6 I have applied all this to myself and
Apollos for your benefit, brethren, that you
may learn by us to live according to scripture, that none of you may be puffed up in
favor of one against another. 7 For who sees
anything different in you? What have you
that you did not receive? If then you received it, why do you boast as if it were not
a gift?

The trials of the apostles

8 Already you are filled! Already you
have become rich! Without us you have become kings! And would that you did reign,
so that he might share the rule with you!
9 For I think that God has exhibited us
apostles as last of all, like men sentenced
to death; because we have become a spectacle to the world, to angels and to men.
10 We are fools for Christ's sake, but you
are wise in Christ. We are weak, but you
are strong. You are held in honor, but we
in disrepute. 11 To the present hour we
hunger and thirst, we are ill-clad and buffeted and homeless, 12 and we labor, working
with our own hands. When reviled, we bless;
when persecuted, we endure; 13 when slandered, we try to conciliate; we have become,
and are now, as the refuse of the world, the
offscouring of all things.

14 I do not write this to make you
ashamed, but to admonish you as my beloved children. 15 For though you have
countless guides in Christ, you do not have
many fathers. For I became your father in
Christ Jesus through the gospel. 16 I urge
you, then, be imitators of me. 17 Therefore
I sent[g] to you Timothy, my beloved and
faithful child in the Lord, to remind you of
my ways in Christ, as I teach them every-

[g] Or *am sending*

King James

18 Now some are puffed up, as though I would not come to you.

19 But I will come to you shortly, if the Lord will, and will know, not the speech of them which are puffed up, but the power.

20 For the kingdom of God *is* not in word, but in power.

21 What will ye? shall I come unto you with a rod, or in love, and *in* the spirit of meekness?

Amplified

18 Some of you have become conceited *and* arrogant *and* pretentious, counting on my not coming to you.

19 But I will come to you [and] shortly, if the Lord is willing, and then I will perceive *and* understand not what the talk of these puffed up *and* arrogant spirits amount to, but their force—that is, [o]the moral power and excellence of soul they really possess.

20 For the kingdom of God consists of *and* is based on not talk but power—[o]moral power and excellence of soul.

21 Now which do you prefer? Shall I come to you with a rod of correction, or with love and in a spirit of gentleness?

CHAPTER 5

IT is reported commonly *that there is* fornication among you, and such fornication as is not so much as named among the Gentiles, that one should have his father's wife.

2 And ye are puffed up, and have not rather mourned, that he that hath done this deed might be taken away from among you.

3 For I verily, as absent in body, but present in spirit, have judged already, as though I were present, *concerning* him that hath so done this deed,

4 In the name of our Lord Jesus Christ, when ye are gathered together, and my spirit, with the power of our Lord Jesus Christ,

5 To deliver such an one unto Satan for the destruction of the flesh, that the spirit may be saved in the day of the Lord Jesus.

6 Your glorying *is* not good. Know ye not that a little leaven leaveneth the whole lump?

7 Purge out therefore the old leaven, that ye may be a new lump, as ye are unleavened. For even Christ our passover is sacrificed for us:

8 Therefore let us keep the feast, not with old leaven, neither with the leaven of malice and wickedness; but with the unleavened *bread* of sincerity and truth.

9 I wrote unto you in an epistle not to company with fornicators:

10 Yet not altogether with the fornicators of this world, or with the covetous, or extortioners, or with idolaters; for then must ye needs go out of the world.

11 But now I have written unto you not to keep company, if any man that is called a brother be a fornicator, or covetous, or an idolater, or a railer, or a drunkard, or an extortioner; with such an one no not to eat.

CHAPTER 5

IT is actually reported that there is sexual immorality among you, impurity of a sort that is condemned *and* does not occur even among the heathen; for a man has [his own] father's wife. [Deut. 22:30; 27:20.]

2 And you are proud *and* arrogant! And you ought rather to mourn—bow in sorrow and in shame—until the person who has done this (shameful) thing is removed from your fellowship *and* your midst!

3 As for my attitude, though I am absent [from you] in body, I am present in spirit, and I have already decided *and* passed judgment, as if actually present,

4 In the name of the Lord Jesus *Christ,* on the man who has committed such a deed. When you and my own spirit are met together with the power of our Lord Jesus,

5 You are to deliver this man over to Satan [p]for physical discipline—to destroy carnal lusts [which prompted him to incest]—that [his] spirit may [yet] be saved in the day of the Lord Jesus.

6 [About the condition of your church] your boasting is not good—indeed it is most unseemly and entirely out of place. Do you not know that [just] a little leaven will ferment the whole lump [of dough]?

7 Purge (clean out) the old leaven that you may be fresh (new) dough, still uncontaminated (as you are), for Christ, our Passover [Lamb], has been sacrificed.

8 Therefore, let us keep the feast, not with old leaven, nor with leaven of vice *and* malice and wickedness, but with the unleavened [bread] of purity (nobility, honor) *and* sincerity and (unadulterated) truth. [Exod. 12:19; 13:7; Deut. 16:3.]

9 I wrote you in my [previous] letter not to associate (closely and habitually) with unchaste (impure) people;

10 Not [meaning of course that you must] altogether shun the immoral people of this world, or the greedy graspers and cheats *and* thieves or idolaters, since otherwise you would need to get out of the world *and* human society altogether!

11 But now I write to you not to associate with any one who bears the name of [Christian] brother, if he is known to be guilty of immorality or greed, or is an idolater—that is, whose soul is devoted to any object that usurps the place of God—or [is] a person with a foul tongue (railing, abusing, reviling, slandering), or is a drunkard, or a swindler *or* a robber. [No] you must not so much as eat with such a person.

---

o) Thayer's "Greek-English Lexicon of the New Testament — Grimm."
p) Abbott-Smith's "Manual Greek Lexicon of the New Testament."

Living New Testament

18 I know that some of you have become proud, thinking that I am afraid to come to deal with you.

19 But I will come, and soon, if the Lord will let me, and then I'll find out whether these proud men are just big talkers or whether they really have God's power.

20 The kingdom of God is not just talking; it is living by God's power.

21 Which do you choose? Shall I come with punishment and scolding, or shall I come with quiet love and gentleness?

Revised Standard

where in every church. 18Some are arrogant,
as though I were not coming to you. 19But
I will come to you soon, if the Lord wills,
and I will find out not the talk of these
arrogant people but their power. 20For the
kingdom of God does not consist in talk
but in power. 21What do you wish? Shall I
come to you with a rod, or with love in a
spirit of gentleness?

CHAPTER 5

Everyone is talking about the terrible thing that has happened there among you, something so evil that even the heathen don't do it: you have a man in your church who is living in sin with his father's wife.[1]

2 And are you still so conceited, so "spiritual"? Why aren't you mourning in sorrow and shame, and seeing to it that this man is removed from your membership?

3, 4 Although I am not there with you, I have been thinking a lot about this, and in the name of the Lord Jesus Christ I have already decided what to do, just as though I were there. You are to call a meeting of the church—and the power of the Lord Jesus will be with you as you meet, and I will be there in spirit—

5 And cast out this man from the fellowship of the church and into Satan's hands, to punish him,[2] in the hope that his soul will be saved when our Lord Jesus Christ returns.

6 What a terrible thing it is that you are boasting about your purity, and yet you let this sort of thing go on. Don't you realize that if even one person is allowed to go on sinning, soon all will be affected?

7 Remove this evil cancer—this wicked person—from among you, so that you can stay pure. Christ, God's Lamb, has been slain for us.

8 So let us feast upon Him and grow strong in the Christian life, leaving entirely behind us the cancerous old life with all its hatreds and wickedness. Let us feast instead upon the pure bread of honor and sincerity and truth.

9 When I wrote to you before I said not to mix with evil people.

10 But when I said that I wasn't talking about unbelievers who live in sexual sin, or are greedy cheats and thieves and idol worshipers. For you can't live in this world without being with people like that.

11 What I meant was that you are not to keep company with anyone who claims to be a brother Christian but indulges in sexual sins, or is greedy, or is a swindler, or worships idols, or is a drunkard, or abusive. Don't even eat lunch with such a person.

A report of immorality

5 It is actually reported that there is immorality among you, and of a kind that
is not found even among pagans; for a man
is living with his father's wife. 2And you
are arrogant! Ought you not rather to
mourn? Let him who has done this be removed from among you.

3 For though absent in body I am present in spirit, and as if present, I have already pronounced judgment 4in the name
of the Lord Jesus on the man who has done
such a thing. When you are assembled, and
my spirit is present, with the power of our
Lord Jesus, 5you are to deliver this man to
Satan for the destruction of the flesh, that
his spirit may be saved in the day of the Lord
Jesus.[h]

6 Your boasting is not good. Do you not
know that a little leaven leavens the whole
lump? 7Cleanse out the old leaven that you
may be a new lump, as you really are unleavened. For Christ, our paschal lamb, has
been sacrificed. 8Let us, therefore, celebrate
the festival, not with the old leaven, the
leaven of malice and evil, but with the unleavened bread of sincerity and truth.

Judgment of the immoral

9 I wrote to you in my letter not to associate with immoral men; 10not at all meaning the immoral of this world, or the greedy
and robbers, or idolaters, since then you
would need to go out of the world. 11But
rather I wrote[i] to you not to associate with
any one who bears the name of brother if
he is guilty of immorality or greed, or is an
idolater, reviler, drunkard, or robber—not
even to eat with such a one. 12For what have

Possibly his step-mother.
Literally, "for the destruction of the flesh."

---

[h] Other ancient authorities omit *Jesus*
[i] Or *now I write*

King James

12 For what have I to do to judge them also that are without? do not ye judge them that are within?
13 But them that are without God judgeth. Therefore put away from among yourselves that wicked person.

Amplified

12 What [business] of mine is it *and* what right have I to judge outsiders? Is it not those inside [the church] upon whom you are to pass disciplinary judgment—passing censuring sentence on them [as the facts require]?
13 God alone sits in judgment on those who are outside. Drive out that wicked one from among you—expel him from your church.

CHAPTER 6

King James

DARE any of you, having a matter against another, go to law before the unjust, and not before the saints?
2 Do ye not know that the saints shall judge the world? and if the world shall be judged by you, are ye unworthy to judge the smallest matters?
3 Know ye not that we shall judge angels? how much more things that pertain to this life?
4 If then ye have judgments of things pertaining to this life, set them to judge who are least esteemed in the church.
5 I speak to your shame. Is it so, that there is not a wise man among you? no, not one that shall be able to judge between his brethren?
6 But brother goeth to law with brother, and that before the unbelievers.
7 Now therefore there is utterly a fault among you, because ye go to law one with another. Why do ye not rather take wrong? why do ye not rather *suffer yourselves to* be defrauded?
8 Nay, ye do wrong, and defraud, and that *your* brethren.
9 Know ye not that the unrighteous shall not inherit the kingdom of God? Be not deceived: neither fornicators, nor idolaters, nor adulterers, nor effeminate, nor abusers of themselves with mankind,
10 Nor thieves, nor covetous, nor drunkards, nor revilers, nor extortioners, shall inherit the kingdom of God.
11 And such were some of you: but ye are washed, but ye are sanctified, but ye are justified in the name of the Lord Jesus, and by the Spirit of our God.
12 All things are lawful unto me, but all things are not expedient: all things are lawful for me, but I will not be brought under the power of any.

CHAPTER 6

Amplified

DOES any of you dare, when he has a matter of complaint against another [brother], to go to law before unrighteous men—men neither upright nor right with God, laying it before them—instead of before the saints (the people of God)?
2 Do you not know that the saints [the Christians] will [one day] judge *and* govern the world? And if the world [itself] is to be judged *and* ruled by you, are you unworthy *and* incompetent to try [such petty matters] of the smallest courts of justice?
3 Do you not know also that we [Christians] are to judge the [very] angels *and* pronounce opinion between right and wrong [for them]? How much more then [as to] matters pertaining to this world *and* of this life only!
4 If then you do have such cases of everyday life to decide, why do you appoint [as judges to lay them before], those who [from the standpoint] of the church count for least *and* are without standing?
5 I say this to move you to shame. Can it be that there really is not one man among you who [in action is governed by piety and integrity and] is wise *and* competent enough to decide [the private grievances, disputes and quarrels] between members of the brotherhood,
6 But brother goes to law against brother, and that before [Gentile judges] who are unbelievers—without faith or trust in the Gospel of Christ?
7 Why, the very fact of your having lawsuits with one another at all is a defect—a defeat, an evidence of positive moral loss for you. Why not rather let yourselves suffer wrong *and* be deprived of what is your due? Why not rather be cheated—defrauded and robbed?
8 But [instead it is you] yourselves who wrong and defraud, and that even your own brethren [by so treating them]!
9 Do you not know that the unrighteous *and* the wrongdoers will not inherit *or* have any share in the kingdom of God? Do not be deceived (misled); neither the impure *and* immoral, nor idolaters, nor adulterers, nor those who participate in homosexuality,
10 Nor cheats—swindlers and thieves; nor greedy graspers, nor drunkards, nor foulmouthed revilers *and* slanderers, nor extortioners *and* robbers will inherit *or* have any share in the kingdom of God.
11 And such some of you were (once). But you were washed clean [purified by a complete atonement for sin and made free from the guilt of sin]; and you were consecrated (set apart, hallowed); and you were justified (pronounced righteous, by trust) in the name of the Lord Jesus Christ and in the (Holy) Spirit of our God.
12 Everything is permissible for me—allowable and lawful; but not all things are helpful—good for me to do, expedient and profitable when considered with other things. Everything is lawful for me, but I will not become the slave of anything *or* be brought under its power.

Living New Testament

12 It isn't our job to judge outsiders. But it certainly is our job to judge and deal strongly with those who are members of the church, and who are sinning in these ways.

13 God alone is the Judge of those on the outside. But you yourselves must deal with this man and put him out of your church.

Revised Standard

I to do with judging outsiders? Is it not those
inside the church whom you are to judge?
[13]God judges those outside. "Drive out the
wicked person from among you."

CHAPTER 6

How is it that when you have something against another Christian, you "go to law" and ask a heathen court to decide the matter instead of taking it to other Christians to decide which of you is right?

2 Don't you know that some day we Christians are going to judge and govern the world? So why can't you decide even these little things among yourselves?

3 Don't you realize that we Christians will judge and reward the very angels in heaven? So you should be able to decide your problems down here on earth easily enough.

4 Why then go to outside judges who are not even Christians?[1]

5 I am trying to make you ashamed. Isn't there anyone in all the church who is wise enough to decide these arguments?

6 But, instead, one Christian sues another and accuses his Christian brother in front of unbelievers.

7 To have such lawsuits at all is a real defeat for you as Christians. Why not just accept mistreatment and leave it at that? It would be far more honoring to the Lord to let yourselves be cheated.

8 But, instead, you yourselves are the ones who do wrong, cheating others, even your own brothers.

9,10 Don't you know that those doing such things have no share in the kingdom of God? Don't fool yourselves. Those who live immoral lives, who are idol worshipers, adulterers or homosexuals—will have no share in His kingdom. Neither will thieves or greedy people, drunkards, slandermongers, or robbers.

11 There was a time when some of you were just like that but now your sins are washed away, and you are set apart for God, and He has accepted you because of what the Lord Jesus Christ and the Spirit of our God have done for you.

12 I can do anything I want to if Christ has not said no,[2] but some of these things aren't good for me. Even if I am allowed to do them, I'll refuse to if I think that they might get such a grip on me that I can't easily stop when I want to.

[1] Or, "Even the least capable people in the church should be able to decide these things for you." Both interpretations are possible.
[2] Literally, "all things are lawful for me." Obviously, Paul is not here permitting sins such as have just been expressly prohibited in verses 8 and 9. He is apparently quoting some in the church of lustful Corinth who were excusing their sins.

Lawsuits among brothers

6 When one of you has a grievance
against a brother, does he dare go to
law before the unrighteous instead of the
saints? [2]Do you not know that the saints
will judge the world? And if the world is to
be judged by you, are you incompetent to
try trivial cases? [3]Do you not know that we
are to judge angels? How much more, matters pertaining to this life! [4]If then you
have such cases, why do you lay them before those who are least esteemed by the
church? [5]I say this to your shame. Can it
be that there is no man among you wise
enough to decide between members of the
brotherhood, [6]but brother goes to law against
brother, and that before unbelievers?
7 To have lawsuits at all with one another is defeat for you. Why not rather suffer
wrong? Why not rather be defrauded? [8]But
you yourselves wrong and defraud, and that
even your own brethren.

God to be glorified in the body

9 Do you not know that the unrighteous
will not inherit the kingdom of God? Do
not be deceived; neither the immoral, nor
idolaters, nor adulterers, nor homosexuals,[j]
[10]nor thieves, nor the greedy, nor drunkards,
nor revilers, nor robbers will inherit the
kingdom of God. [11]And such were some of
you. But you were washed, you were sanctified, you were justified in the name of the
Lord Jesus Christ and in the Spirit of our
God.
12 "All things are lawful for me," but
not all things are helpful. "All things are
lawful for me," but I will not be enslaved

[j] Two Greek words are rendered by this expression

King James

13 Meats for the belly, and the belly for meats: but God shall destroy both it and them. Now the body *is* not for fornication, but for the Lord; and the Lord for the body.

14 And God hath both raised up the Lord, and will also raise up us by his own power.

15 Know ye not that your bodies are the members of Christ? shall I then take the members of Christ, and make *them* the members of an harlot? God forbid.

16 What? know ye not that he which is joined to an harlot is one body? for two, saith he, shall be one flesh.

17 But he that is joined unto the Lord is one spirit.

18 Flee fornication. Every sin that a man doeth is without the body; but he that committeth fornication sinneth against his own body.

19 What? know ye not that your body is the temple of the Holy Ghost *which is* in you, which ye have of God, and ye are not your own?

20 For ye are bought with a price: therefore glorify God in your body, and in your spirit, which are God's.

Amplified

13 Food [is intended] for the stomach and the stomach for food, but God will finally end [the functions of] both *and* bring them to nothing. The body is not intended for sexual immorality, but [is intended] for the Lord, and the Lord [is intended] for the body [[q]to save, sanctify and raise it again].

14 And God both raised the Lord to life and will also raise us up by His power.

15 Do you not see *and* know that your bodies are members (bodily parts) of Christ, the Messiah? Am I therefore to take the parts of Christ and make [them] parts of a prostitute? Never! Never!

16 Or do you not know *and* realize that when a man joins himself to a prostitute he becomes one body with her? The two, it is written, shall become one flesh [Gen. 2:24.]

17 But the person who is united to the Lord becomes one spirit with Him.

18 Shun immorality *and* all sexual looseness—flee from impurity [in thought, word or deed]. Any other sin which a man commits is one outside the body, but he who commits sexual immorality sins against his own body.

19 Do you not know that your body is the temple—the very sanctuary—of the Holy Spirit Who lives within you, Whom you have received [as a Gift] from God? You are not your own,

20 You were bought for a price—purchased with a [r]preciousness and paid for, [r]made His own. So then, honor God *and* bring glory to Him in your body.

CHAPTER 7

NOW concerning the things whereof ye wrote unto me: *It is* good for a man not to touch a woman.

2 Nevertheless, *to avoid* fornication, let every man have his own wife, and let every woman have her own husband.

3 Let the husband render unto the wife due benevolence: and likewise also the wife unto the husband.

4 The wife hath not power of her own body, but the husband: and likewise also the husband hath not power of his own body, but the wife.

5 Defraud ye not one the other, except *it be* with consent for a time, that ye may give yourselves to fasting and prayer; and come together again, that Satan tempt you not for your incontinency.

6 But I speak this by permission, *and* not of commandment.

7 For I would that all men were even as I myself. But every man hath his proper gift of God, one after this manner, and another after that.

8 I say therefore to the unmarried and widows, It is good for them if they abide even as I.

CHAPTER 7

NOW as to the matters of which you wrote me. It is well—[and by that I mean] advantageous, expedient, profitable and wholesome—for a man not to touch a woman (to cohabit with her), *but* to remain unmarried.

2 But because of the temptation to impurity *and* to avoid immorality, let each [man] have his own wife and let each [woman] have her own husband.

3 The husband should give to his wife her conjugal rights—goodwill, kindness and what is due her as his wife; and likewise the wife to her husband.

4 For the wife does not have [exclusive] authority *and* control over her own body, but the husband [has his rights]; likewise also the husband does not have [exclusive] authority *and* control over his body, but the wife [has her rights].

5 Do not refuse *and* deprive *and* defraud each other (of your due marital rights), except perhaps by mutual consent for a time, that you may devote yourselves unhindered to prayer. But afterwards resume marital relations, lest Satan tempt you [to sin] through your lack of restraint of sexual desire. [Exod. 19:15.]

6 But I am saying this more as a matter of permission *and* concession, not as a command *or* regulation.

7 I wish that all men were like I myself am [in this matter of self-control]. But each has his own special gift from God, one of this kind and one of another.

8 But to the unmarried people and to the widows, I declare that it is well—good, advantageous, expedient and wholesome—for them to remain [single] even as I do.

---

q) Cambridge Bible. (See Rom. 8:11; I Cor. 15:35-54).
r) Thayer.

Living New Testament

13 For instance, take the matter of eating. God has given us an appetite for food and stomachs to digest it. But that doesn't mean we should eat more than we need. Don't think of eating as important, because some day God will do away with both stomachs and food. But sexual sin is never right: our bodies were not made for that, but for the Lord, and the Lord wants to fill our bodies with Himself.

14 And God is going to raise our bodies from the dead by His power just as He raised up the Lord Jesus Christ.

15 Don't you realize that your bodies are actually parts and members of Christ? So should I take part of Christ and join Him to a prostitute? Never!

16 And don't you know that if a man joins himself to a prostitute she becomes a part of him and he becomes a part of her? For God tells us in the Scripture that in His sight the two become one person.

17 But if you give yourself to the Lord, you and Christ are joined together as one person.

18 That is why I say to run from sex sin. No other sin affects the body as this one does. When you sin this sin it is against your own body.

19 Haven't you yet learned that your body is the home of the Holy Spirit God gave you, and that He lives within you? Your own body does not belong to you,

20 For God has bought you with a great price. So use every part of your body to give glory back to God, because He owns it.

Revised Standard

by anything. [13]"Food is meant for the
stomach and the stomach for food"—and
God will destroy both one and the other.
The body is not meant for immorality, but
for the Lord, and the Lord for the body.
[14]And God raised the Lord and will also
raise us up by his power. [15]Do you not know
that your bodies are members of Christ?
Shall I therefore take the members of Christ
and make them members of a prostitute?
Never! [16]Do you not know that he who
joins himself to a prostitute becomes one
body with her? For, as it is written, "The
two shall become one."[k] [17]But he who is
united to the Lord becomes one spirit with
him. [18]Shun immorality. Every other sin
which a man commits is outside the body;
but the immoral man sins against his own
body. [19]Do you not know that your body is
a temple of the Holy Spirit within you,
which you have from God? You are not
your own; [20]you were bought with a price.
So glorify God in your body.

CHAPTER 7

Now about those questions you asked in your last letter: my answer is that if you do not marry, it is good.

2 But usually it is best to be married, each man having his own wife, and each woman having her own husband, because otherwise you might fall back into sin.

3 The man should give his wife all that is her right as a married woman, and the wife should do the same for her husband:

4 For a girl who marries no longer has full right to her own body, for her husband then has his rights to it, too; and in the same way the husband no longer has full right to his own body, for it belongs also to his wife.

5 So do not refuse these rights to each other. The only exception to this rule would be the agreement of both husband and wife to refrain from the rights of marriage for a limited time, so that they can give themselves more completely to prayer. Afterwards, they should come together again so that Satan won't be able to tempt them because of their lack of self-control.

6 I'm not saying you *must* marry; but you certainly *may* if you wish.

7 I wish everyone could get along without marrying, just as I do. But we are not all the same. God gives some the gift of a husband or wife, and others He gives the gift of being able to stay happily unmarried.

8 So I say to those who aren't married, and to widows—better to stay unmarried if you can, just as I am.

Rights of marriage

7 Now concerning the matters about which
you wrote. It is well for a man not to
touch a woman. [2]But because of the temptation to immorality, each man should have
his own wife and each woman her own husband. [3]The husband should give to his wife
her conjugal rights, and likewise the wife to
her husband. [4]For the wife does not rule
over her own body, but the husband does;
likewise the husband does not rule over his
own body, but the wife does. [5]Do not refuse one another except perhaps by agreement for a season, that you may devote
yourselves to prayer; but then come together again, lest Satan tempt you through
lack of self-control. [6]I say this by way of
concession, not of command. [7]I wish that
all were as I myself am. But each has his
own special gift from God, one of one kind
and one of another.
8 To the unmarried and the widows I
say that it is well for them to remain single

[k] Greek *one flesh*

King James

9 But if they cannot contain, let them marry: for it is better to marry than to burn.

10 And unto the married I command, *yet* not I, but the Lord, Let not the wife depart from *her* husband:

11 But and if she depart, let her remain unmarried, or be reconciled to *her* husband: and let not the husband put away *his* wife.

12 But to the rest speak I, not the Lord: If any brother hath a wife that believeth not, and she be pleased to dwell with him, let him not put her away.

13 And the woman which hath an husband that believeth not, and if he be pleased to dwell with her, let her not leave him.

14 For the unbelieving husband is sanctified by the wife, and the unbelieving wife is sanctified by the husband: else were your children unclean; but now are they holy.

15 But if the unbelieving depart, let him depart. A brother or a sister is not under bondage in such *cases:* but God hath called us to peace.

16 For what knowest thou, O wife, whether thou shalt save *thy* husband? or how knowest thou, O man, whether thou shalt save *thy* wife?

17 But as God hath distributed to every man, as the Lord hath called every one, so let him walk. And so ordain I in all churches.

18 Is any man called being circumcised? let him not become uncircumcised. Is any called in uncircumcision? let him not be circumcised.

19 Circumcision is nothing, and uncircumcision is nothing, but the keeping of the commandments of God.

20 Let every man abide in the same calling wherein he was called.

21 Art thou called *being* a servant? care not for it: but if thou mayest be made free, use *it* rather.

22 For he that is called in the Lord, *being* a servant, is the Lord's freeman: likewise also he that is called, *being* free, is Christ's servant.

23 Ye are bought with a price; be not ye the servants of men.

24 Brethren, let every man, wherein he is called, therein abide with God.

25 Now concerning virgins I have no commandment of the Lord: yet I give my judgment, as one that hath obtained mercy of the Lord to be faithful.

26 I suppose therefore that this is good for the present distress, *I say,* that *it is* good for a man so to be.

Amplified

9 But if they have not self-control (restraint of their passions), they should marry. For it is better to marry than to be aflame (with passion and tortured continually with ungratified desire).

10 But to the married [people] I give charge, not I but the Lord, that the wife is not to separate from her husband.

11 But if she does [separate from and divorce him], let her remain single or else be reconciled to her husband. And [I charge] the husband [also] that he should not put away *or* divorce his wife.

12 To the rest I declare, I, not the Lord [for Jesus did not discuss this], that if any brother has a wife who does not believe [on Christ], and she consents to live with him, he should not leave *or* divorce her.

13 And if any woman has an unbelieving husband, and he consents to live with her, she should not leave *or* divorce him.

14 For the unbelieving husband is set apart (separated, withdrawn from heathen contamination and affiliated with the Christian people) by union with his consecrated (set-apart) wife; and the unbelieving wife is set apart *and* separated through union with her consecrated husband. Otherwise your children would be unclean [unblessed heathen, [s]outside the Christian covenant], but as it is they are [t]prepared for God—pure and clean.

15 But if the unbelieving partner [actually] leaves, let him do so; in such [cases the remaining] brother or sister is not morally bound. But God has called us to peace.

16 For, wife, how can you be sure of converting *and* saving your husband? Husband, how can you be sure of converting *and* saving your wife?

17 Only, let each one (seek to conduct himself and regulate his affairs so as to) lead the life which the Lord has allotted *and* imparted to him, *and* to which God has invited *and* summoned him. This is my order in all the churches.

18 Was any one at the time of his summons [from God] already circumcised? Let him not seek to remove the evidence of circumcision. Was any one at the time [God] called him, uncircumcised? Let him not be circumcised.

19 For circumcision is nothing *and* counts for nothing, neither does uncircumcision, but [what counts is] keeping the commandments of God.

20 Every one should remain after God calls him in the station *or* condition of life in which the summons found him.

21 Were you a slave when you were called? Do not let that trouble you. But if you are able to gain your freedom, avail yourself of the opportunity.

22 For he who as a slave was summoned in [to union with] the Lord is a freedman of the Lord; just so he who was free when he was called is a bond servant of Christ, the Messiah.

23 You were bought with a price—purchased with a preciousness and paid for [by Christ]; then do not yield yourselves up to become [in your own estimation] slaves to men, [but consider yourselves slaves to Christ].

24 So, brethren, in whatever station *or* state *or* condition of life each one was when he was called, let him continue there, with *and* close to God.

25 Now concerning the virgins—the marriageable [u]maidens—I have no command of the Lord, but I give my opinion *and* advice as one who by the Lord's mercy is rendered trustworthy *and* faithful.

26 I think then, because of the impending distress (that is even now setting in), it is well—expedient, profitable and wholesome—for a person to remain as he *or* she is.

---

s) Jamieson, Fausset and Brown.
t) Thayer.
u) Vincent.

Living New Testament

9 But if you can't control yourselves, go ahead and marry. It is better to marry than to burn with lust.

10 Now, for those who are married I have a command, not just a suggestion. And it is not a command from me, for this is what the Lord Himself has said: a wife must not leave her husband.

11 But if she is separated from him, let her remain single or else go back to him again. And the husband must not divorce his wife.

12 Here I want to add some suggestions of my own. These are not direct commands from the Lord, but they seem right to me: If a Christian has a wife who is not a Christian, but she wants to stay with him anyway, he must not leave her or divorce her.

13 And if a Christian woman has a husband who isn't a Christian, and he wants her to stay with him, she must not leave him.

14 For perhaps the husband who isn't a Christian may become a Christian with the help of his Christian wife. And the wife who isn't a Christian may become a Christian with the help of her Christian husband. Otherwise, if the family separates, the children might never come to know the Lord; whereas a united family may, in God's plan, result in the children's salvation.

15 But if the husband or wife who isn't a Christian is eager to leave, it is permitted. In such cases the Christian husband or wife should not insist that the other stay, for God wants His children to live in peace and harmony.

16 For after all, there is no assurance to you wives that your husbands will be converted if they stay; and the same may be said to you husbands concerning your wives.

17 But be sure in deciding these matters that you are living as God intended, marrying or not marrying in accordance with God's direction and help, and accepting whatever situation God has put you into. This is my rule for all the churches.

18 For instance, a man who already has gone through the Jewish ceremony of circumcision before he became a Christian shouldn't worry about it; and if he hasn't been circumcised, he shouldn't do it now.

19 For it doesn't make any difference at all whether a Christian has gone through this ceremony or not. But it makes a lot of difference whether he is pleasing God and keeping God's commandments. That is the important thing.

20 Usually a person should keep on with the work he was doing when God called him.

21 Are you a slave? Don't let that worry you—but of course, if you get a chance to be free, take it.

22 If the Lord calls you, and you are a slave, remember that Christ has set you free from the awful power of sin; and if He has called you and you are free, remember that you are now a slave of Christ.

23 You have been bought and paid for by Christ, so you belong to Him—be free now from all these earthly prides and fears.[1]

24 So, dear brothers, whatever situation a person is in when he becomes a Christian, let him stay there, for now the Lord is there to help him.

25 Now I will try to answer your other question. What about girls who are not yet married? Should they be permitted to do so? In answer to this question, I have no special command for them from the Lord. But the Lord in His kindness has given me wisdom that can be trusted, and I will be glad to tell you what I think.

26 Here is the problem: we Christians are facing great dangers to our lives at present. In times like these I think it is best for a person to remain unmarried.

[1] Literally, "Become not bondservants of men."

Revised Standard

as I do. 9But if they cannot exercise self-
control, they should marry. For it is better
to marry than to be aflame with passion.

Responsibilities of marriage

10 To the married I give charge, not I
but the Lord, that the wife should not separate from her husband 11(but if she does,
let her remain single or else be reconciled
to her husband)—and that the husband
should not divorce his wife.
12 To the rest I say, not the Lord, that
if any brother has a wife who is an unbeliever, and she consents to live with him,
he should not divorce her. 13If any woman
has a husband who is an unbeliever, and he
consents to live with her, she should not
divorce him. 14For the unbelieving husband
is consecrated through his wife, and the unbelieving wife is consecrated through her
husband. Otherwise, your children would be
unclean, but as it is they are holy. 15But if
the unbelieving partner desires to separate,
let it be so; in such a case the brother or
sister is not bound. For God has called us[l]
to peace. 16Wife, how do you know whether
you will save your husband? Husband, how
do you know whether you will save your
wife?

The life God has assigned

17 Only, let every one lead the life which
the Lord has assigned to him, and in which
God has called him. This is my rule in all the
churches. 18Was any one at the time of
his call already circumcised? Let him not
seek to remove the marks of circumcision.
Was any one at the time of his call uncircumcised? Let him not seek circumcision.
19For neither circumcision counts for anything nor uncircumcision, but keeping the
commandments of God. 20Every one should
remain in the state in which he was called.
21Were you a slave when called? Never mind.
But if you can gain your freedom, avail
yourself of the opportunity.[x] 22For he who
was called in the Lord as a slave is a freedman of the Lord. Likewise he who was free
when called is a slave of Christ. 23You were
bought with a price; do not become slaves
of men. 24So, brethren, in whatever state
each was called, there let him remain with
God.

Counsel to the unmarried

25 Now concerning the unmarried, I have
no command of the Lord, but I give my
opinion as one who by the Lord's mercy is
trustworthy. 26I think that in view of the

[l] Other ancient authorities read *you*
[x] Or *make use of your present condition instead*

King James

27 Art thou bound unto a wife? seek not to be loosed. Art thou loosed from a wife? seek not a wife.

28 But and if thou marry, thou hast not sinned; and if a virgin marry, she hath not sinned. Nevertheless such shall have trouble in the flesh: but I spare you.

29 But this I say, brethren, the time *is* short: it remaineth, that both they that have wives be as though they had none;

30 And they that weep, as though they wept not; and they that rejoice, as though they rejoiced not; and they that buy, as though they possessed not;

31 And they that use this world, as not abusing *it:* for the fashion of this world passeth away.

32 But I would have you without carefulness. He that is unmarried careth for the things that belong to the Lord, how he may please the Lord:

33 But he that is married careth for the things that are of the world, how he may please *his* wife.

34 There is difference *also* between a wife and a virgin. The unmarried woman careth for the things of the Lord, that she may be holy both in body and in spirit: but she that is married careth for the things of the world, how she may please *her* husband.

35 And this I speak for your own profit; not that I may cast a snare upon you, but for that which is comely, and that ye may attend upon the Lord without distraction.

36 But if any man think that he behaveth himself uncomely toward his virgin, if she pass the flower of *her* age, and need so require, let him do what he will, he sinneth not: let them marry.

37 Nevertheless he that standeth stedfast in his heart, having no necessity, but hath power over his own will, and hath so decreed in his heart that he will keep his virgin, doeth well.

38 So then he that giveth *her* in marriage doeth well; but he that giveth *her* not in marriage doeth better.

39 The wife is bound by the law as long as her husband liveth; but if her husband be dead, she is at liberty to be married to whom she will; only in the Lord.

40 But she is happier if she so abide, after my judgment: and I think also that I have the Spirit of God.

CHAPTER 8

NOW as touching things offered unto idols, we know that we all have knowledge. Knowledge puffeth up, but charity edifieth.

Amplified

27 Are you bound to a wife? Do not seek to be free. Are you free from a wife? Do not seek a wife.

28 But if you do marry, you do not sin [in doing so], and if a virgin marries, she does not sin [in doing so]. Yet those who marry will have physical *and* earthly troubles, and I would like to spare you that.

29 I mean, brethren, the appointed time has been [u]winding up *and* it has grown very short. From now on, let even those who have wives be as if they had none.

30 And those who weep *and* mourn as though they were not weeping *and* mourning, and those who rejoice as though they were not rejoicing, and those who buy as though they did not possess anything,

31 And those who deal with this world—[u]over-using the enjoyments of this life—let them live as though they were not absorbed by it, *and* as if they had no dealings with it. For the outward form of this world—the present world order—is passing away.

32 My desire is to have you free from all anxiety *and* distressing care. The unmarried [man] is anxious about the things of the Lord, how he may please the Lord;

33 But the married man is anxious about worldly matters, how he may please his wife.

34 And he is drawn in diverging directions—his interests are divided, *and* he is distracted [from his devotion to God]. And the unmarried woman or girl is concerned *and* anxious about the matters of the Lord, how to be wholly separated *and* set apart in body and spirit; but the married woman has her cares [centered] in earthly affairs, how she may please her husband.

35 Now I say this for your own welfare *and* profit, not to put (a halter of) restraint upon you, but to promote what is seemly *and* good order and to secure your undistracted *and* undivided devotion to the Lord.

36 But if any man thinks that he is not acting properly toward *and* in regard to his virgin, [that he is preparing disgrace for her or incurring reproach] in case she is passing the bloom of her youth, and if there is need for it, let him do what to him seems right; he does not sin; let them marry.

37 But whoever is firmly established in his heart—strong in mind and purpose—not being forced by necessity but having control over his own will *and* desire, and has resolved this in his heart, to keep his own virginity, he is doing well.

38 So also then, he [the father] who gives [his daughter, virgin] in marriage does well; and he [the father] who does not give [her] in marriage does better.

39 A wife is bound to her husband by the law as long as he lives. If the husband dies, she is free to be married to whom she will, only [provided that he too is] in the Lord.

40 But in my opinion [a widow] is happier (more blessed and [v]to be envied) if she does not remarry. And also I think I have the Spirit of God.

CHAPTER 8

NOW about food offered to idols: of course we know that all of us possess knowledge [concerning these matters. Yet mere] knowledge causes people to be puffed up—to bear themselves loftily and be proud; but love, [that is,] affection *and* goodwill *and* benevolence, edifies *and* builds up *and* encourages one to grow [to his full stature].

u) Vincent.
v) Souter's "Pocket Lexicon to the Greek New Testament."

Living New Testament

27 Of course, if you already are married, don't separate because of this. But if you aren't, don't rush into it at this time.

28 But if you men decide to go ahead anyway and get married now, it is all right; and if a girl gets married in times like these, it is no sin. However, marriage will bring extra problems that I wish you didn't have to face right now.

29 The important thing to remember is that our remaining time is very short, [and so are our opportunities for doing the Lord's work[2]]. For that reason those who have wives should stay as free as possible for the Lord;[3]

30 Happiness or sadness or wealth should not keep anyone from doing God's work.

31 Those in frequent contact with the exciting things the world offers should make good use of their opportunities without stopping to enjoy them; for the world in its present form will soon be gone.

32 In all you do, I want you to be free from worry. An unmarried man can spend his time doing the Lord's work and thinking how to please Him.

33 But a married man can't do that so well; he has to think about his earthly responsibilities and how to please his wife.

34 His interests are divided. It is the same with a girl who marries. She faces the same problem. A girl who is not married is anxious to please the Lord in all she is and does.[4] But a married woman must consider other things such as housekeeping and the likes and dislikes of her husband.

35 I am saying this to help you, not to try to keep you from marrying. I want you to do whatever will help you serve the Lord best, with as few other things as possible to distract your attention from Him.

36 But if anyone feels he ought to marry because he has trouble controlling his passions, it is all right, it is not a sin; let him marry.

37 But if a man has the will power not to marry and decides that he doesn't need to and won't, he has made a wise decision.

38 So the person who marries does well, and the person who doesn't marry does even better.

39 The wife is part of her husband as long as he lives; if her husband dies, then she may marry again, but only if she marries a Christian.

40 But in my opinion she will be happier if she doesn't marry again; and I think I am giving you counsel from God's Spirit when I say this.

Revised Standard

impending[m] distress it is well for a person
to remain as he is. 27 Are you bound to a
wife? Do not seek to be free. Are you free
from a wife? Do not seek marriage. 28 But
if you marry, you do not sin, and if a girl
marries she does not sin. Yet those who
marry will have worldly troubles, and I
would spare you that. 29 I mean, brethren,
the appointed time has grown very short;
from now on, let those who have wives live
as though they had none, 30 and those who
mourn as though they were not mourning,
and those who rejoice as though they were
not rejoicing, and those who buy as though
they had no goods, 31 and those who deal
with the world as though they had no dealings with it. For the form of this world is
passing away.
32 I want you to be free from anxieties.
The unmarried man is anxious about the
affairs of the Lord, how to please the Lord;
33 but the married man is anxious about
worldly affairs, how to please his wife, 34 and
his interests are divided. And the unmarried
woman or girl is anxious about the affairs
of the Lord, how to be holy in body and
spirit; but the married woman is anxious
about worldly affairs, how to please her husband. 35 I say this for your own benefit, not
to lay any restraint upon you, but to promote good order and to secure your undivided devotion to the Lord.
36 If any one thinks that he is not behaving properly toward his betrothed, if his
passions are strong, and it has to be, let him
do as he wishes: let them marry—it is no
sin. 37 But whoever is firmly established in
his heart, being under no necessity but having his desire under control, and has determined this in his heart, to keep her as his
betrothed, he will do well. 38 So that he who
marries his betrothed does well; and he who
refrains from marriage will do better.

Counsel to widows

39 A wife is bound to her husband as
long as he lives. If the husband dies, she is
free to be married to whom she wishes,
only in the Lord. 40 But in my judgment she
is happier if she remains as she is. And I
think that I have the Spirit of God.

CHAPTER 8

Next is your question about eating food that has been sacrificed to idols. On this question everyone feels that only his answer is the right one! But although being a "know-it-all" makes us feel important, what is really needed to build the church is love.

Food offered to idols

8 Now concerning food offered to idols:
we know that "all of us possess knowledge." "Knowledge" puffs up, but love builds

---

Implied.
Literally, "(that) those who have wives may be as though they didn't."
Literally, "pure in body and in spirit."

---

m Or *present*

King James

2 And if any man think that he knoweth any thing, he knoweth nothing yet as he ought to know.

3 But if any man love God, the same is known of him.

4 As concerning therefore the eating of those things that are offered in sacrifice unto idols, we know that an idol *is* nothing in the world, and that *there is* none other God but one.

5 For though there be that are called gods, whether in heaven or in earth, (as there be gods many, and lords many,)

6 But to us *there is but* one God, the Father, of whom *are* all things, and we in him; and one Lord Jesus Christ, by whom *are* all things, and we by him.

7 Howbeit *there is* not in every man that knowledge: for some with conscience of the idol unto this hour eat *it* as a thing offered unto an idol; and their conscience being weak is defiled.

8 But meat commendeth us not to God: for neither, if we eat, are we the better; neither, if we eat not, are we the worse.

9 But take heed lest by any means this liberty of yours become a stumblingblock to them that are weak.

10 For if any man see thee which hast knowledge sit at meat in the idol's temple, shall not the conscience of him which is weak be emboldened to eat those things which are offered to idols;

11 And through thy knowledge shall the weak brother perish, for whom Christ died?

12 But when ye sin so against the brethren, and wound their weak conscience, ye sin against Christ.

13 Wherefore, if meat make my brother to offend, I will eat no flesh while the world standeth, lest I make my brother to offend.

Amplified

2 If any one imagines that he has come to know *and* understand much [of divine things, without love], he does not yet perceive *and* recognize *and* understand as strongly *and* clearly, *nor* has he become as intimately acquainted with anything as he ought *or* as is necessary.

3 But if one loves God truly—[w]with affectionate reverence, prompt obedience and grateful recognition of His blessing—he is known by God [that is, [v]recognized as worthy of His intimacy and love, and he is owned by Him].

4 In this matter, then, of the eating of food offered to idols, we know that an idol is nothing—has no real existence—and that there is no God but One. [Deut.6:4].

5 For although there may be so-called gods, whether in heaven or on earth, as indeed there are many of them, both of gods and of lords *and* masters,

6 Yet for us there is [only] one God, the Father, Who is the Source of all things, and for Whom we [have life], and one Lord, Jesus Christ, through *and* by Whom are all things and through *and* by Whom we [ourselves exist]. [Mal. 2:10.]

7 Nevertheless, not all [believers] possess this knowledge. But some, through being all their lives until now accustomed to [thinking of] idols [as real and living], still consider the food [offered to an idol] as that sacrificed to an [actual] god; and their weak conscience becomes defiled *and* injured [if they] eat [it].

8 Now food [itself] will not cause our acceptance by God *nor* commend us to Him. Eating [food offered to idols] gives us no advantage, neither do we come short *or* become any the worse if we do not eat [it].

9 Only be careful that this power of choice—this permission and liberty to do as you please—which is yours, does not [somehow] become a hindrance (cause of stumbling) to the weak *or* overscrupulous [giving them an impulse to sin].

10 For suppose any one sees you, a man having knowledge [of God, with an intelligent view of this subject] reclining at table in an idol's temple; might he not be encouraged *and* emboldened [to violate his own conscientious scruples], if he is weak *and* uncertain, and eat what [to him] is for the purpose of idol worship?

11 And so by your enlightenment (your knowledge of spiritual things), this weak man is ruined—is lost and perishes—the brother for whom Christ, the Messiah, died!

12 And when you sin against your brethren in this way, wounding *and* damaging their weak conscience, you sin against Christ.

13 Therefore, if [my eating a] food is a cause of my brother's falling *or* of hindering [his spiritual advancement], I will not eat [such] flesh forever, lest I cause my brother to be tripped up *and* fall *and* to offend.

CHAPTER 9

AM I not an apostle? am I not free? have I not seen Jesus Christ our Lord? are not ye my work in the Lord?

2 If I be not an apostle unto others, yet doubtless I am to you: for the seal of mine apostleship are ye in the Lord.

CHAPTER 9

AM I not an apostle (a special messenger)? Am I not free—unrestrained and exempt from any obligation? Have I not seen Jesus our Lord? Are you [yourselves] not (the product and proof of) my workmanship in the Lord?

2 Even if I am not considered an apostle (a special messenger) by others, at least I am one to you; for you are the seal (the certificate, the living evidence) of my apostleship in the Lord—confirming and authenticating it.

v) Souter's "Pocket Lexicon to the Greek New Testament."
w) Thayer's "Greek-English Lexicon of the New Testament — Grimm."

Living New Testament

2 If anyone thinks he knows all the answers, he is just showing his ignorance.

3 But the person who truly loves God is the one who is open to God's knowledge.

4 So now, what about it? Should we eat meat that has been sacrificed to idols? Well, we all know that an idol is not really a god, and that there is only one God, and no other.

5 According to some people, there are a great many gods, both in heaven and on earth.

6 But we know that there is only one God, the Father, who created all things[1] and made us to be His own; and one Lord Jesus Christ, who made everything and gives us life.

7 However, some Christians don't realize this. All their lives they have been used to thinking of idols as alive, and have believed that food offered to the idols is really being offered to actual gods. So when they eat such food it bothers them and hurts their tender consciences.

8 Just remember that God doesn't care whether we eat it or not. We are no worse off if we don't eat it, and no better off if we do.

9 But be careful not to use your freedom to eat it, lest you cause some Christian brother to sin whose conscience[2] is weaker than yours.

10 You see, this is what may happen: Someone who thinks it is wrong to eat this food will see you eating at a temple restaurant, for you know there is no harm in it. Then he will become bold enough to do it too, although all the time he still feels it is wrong.

11 So because you "know it is all right to do it," you will be responsible for causing great spiritual damage to a brother with a tender conscience for whom Christ died.

12 And it is a sin against Christ to sin against your brother by encouraging him to do something he thinks is wrong.

13 So if eating meat offered to idols is going to make my brother sin, I'll not eat any of it as long as I live, because I don't want to do this to him.

Revised Standard

up. [2]If any one imagines that he knows
something, he does not yet know as he
ought to know. [3]But if one loves God, one
is known by him.
4 Hence, as to the eating of food offered
to idols, we know that "an idol has no real
existence," and that "there is no God but
one." [5]For although there may be so-called
gods in heaven or on earth—as indeed
there are many "gods" and many "lords"
—[6]yet for us there is one God, the Father,
from whom are all things and for whom we
exist, and one Lord, Jesus Christ, through
whom are all things and through whom we
exist.
7 However, not all possess this knowledge.
But some, through being hitherto accustomed
to idols, eat food as really offered to
an idol; and their conscience, being weak, is
defiled. [8]Food will not commend us to God.
We are no worse off if we do not eat, and
no better off if we do. [9]Only take care lest
this liberty of yours somehow become a
stumbling block to the weak. [10]For if any
one sees you, a man of knowledge, at table
in an idol's temple, might he not be encouraged,
if his conscience is weak, to eat food
offered to idols? [11]And so by your knowledge
this weak man is destroyed, the brother
for whom Christ died. [12]Thus, sinning
against your brethren and wounding their
conscience when it is weak, you sin against
Christ. [13]Therefore, if food is a cause of my
brother's falling, I will never eat meat, lest
I cause my brother to fall.

CHAPTER 9

I am an apostle, God's messenger, responsible to no mere man. I am one who has actually seen Jesus our Lord with my own eyes. And your changed lives are the result of my hard work for Him.

2 If in the opinion of others, I am not an apostle, I certainly am to you, for you have been won to Christ through me.

Christian rights acknowledged

9 Am I not free? Am I not an apostle?
Have I not seen Jesus our Lord? Are
not you my workmanship in the Lord? [2]If
to others I am not an apostle, at least I am
to you; for you are the seal of my apostleship
in the Lord.

[1]Literally, "of whom are all things."
[2]Implied. Literally, "faith."

King James

3 Mine answer to them that do examine me is this,

4 Have we not power to eat and to drink?

5 Have we not power to lead about a sister, a wife, as well as other apostles, and *as* the brethren of the Lord, and Cephas?

6 Or I only and Barnabas, have not we power to forbear working?

7 Who goeth a warfare any time at his own charges? who planteth a vineyard, and eateth not of the fruit thereof? or who feedeth a flock, and eateth not of the milk of the flock?

8 Say I these things as a man? or saith not the law the same also?

9 For it is written in the law of Moses, Thou shalt not muzzle the mouth of the ox that treadeth out the corn. Doth God take care for oxen?

10 Or saith he *it* altogether for our sakes? For our sakes, no doubt, *this* is written: that he that ploweth should plow in hope; and that he that thresheth in hope should be partaker of his hope.

11 If we have sown unto you spiritual things, *is it* a great thing if we shall reap your carnal things?

12 If others be partakers of *this* power over you, *are* not we rather? Nevertheless we have not used this power; but suffer all things, lest we should hinder the gospel of Christ.

13 Do ye not know that they which minister about holy things live *of the things* of the temple? and they which wait at the altar are partakers with the altar?

14 Even so hath the Lord ordained that they which preach the gospel should live of the gospel.

15 But I have used none of these things: neither have I written these things, that it should be so done unto me: for *it were* better for me to die, than that any man should make my glorying void.

16 For though I preach the gospel, I have nothing to glory of: for necessity is laid upon me; yea, woe is unto me, if I preach not the gospel!

17 For if I do this thing willingly, I have a reward: but if against my will, a dispensation *of the gospel* is committed unto me.

18 What is my reward then? *Verily* that, when I preach the gospel, I may make the gospel of Christ without charge, that I abuse not my power in the gospel.

19 For though I be free from all *men*, yet have I made myself servant unto all, that I might gain the more.

20 And unto the Jews I became as a Jew, that I might gain the Jews; to them that are under the law, as under the law, that I might gain them that are under the law;

21 To them that are without law, as without law, (being not without law to God, but under the law to Christ,) that I might gain them that are without law.

Amplified

3 This is my [real ground of] defense—my vindication of myself—to those who would put me on trial *and* cross-examine me.

4 Have we not the right to our food and drink [at the expense of the churches]?

5 Have we not the right also to take along with us a Christian sister as wife, as do the other apostles and the Lord's brothers and Cephas (Peter)?

6 Or is it only Barnabas and I who have no right to refrain from doing manual labor for a livelihood [in order to go about the work of the ministry]?

7 [Consider this:] What soldier at any time serves at his own expense? Who plants a vineyard and does not eat any of the fruit of it? Who tends a flock and does not partake of the milk of the flock?

8 Do I say this only on human authority *and* as a man reasons? Does not the Law endorse the same principle?

9 For in the Law of Moses it is written, You shall not muzzle an ox when it is treading out the corn. Is it [only] for oxen that God is having a care? [Deut. 25:4.]

10 Or does He speak certainly *and* entirely for our sakes? [Assuredly] it is written for our sakes, because the plowman ought to plow in hope, and the thresher ought to thresh in expectation of partaking of the harvest.

11 If we have sown [the seed of] spiritual good among you, [is it too] much if we reap from your material benefits?

12 If others share in this rightful claim upon you, do not we [have a still better and greater claim]? However, we have never exercised this right, but we endure everything rather than put a hindrance in the way [of the spread] of the good news (the Gospel) of Christ.

13 Do you not know that those men who are employed in the services of the temple get their food from the temple? And that those who tend the altar share with the altar [in the offerings brought]? [Deut. 18:1.]

14 (On the same principle) the Lord directed that those who publish the good news (the Gospel) should live (get their maintenance) by the Gospel.

15 But I have not made use of any of these privileges, nor am I writing this [to suggest] that any such provision be made for me [now]. For it would be better for me to die than to have any one make void *and* deprive me of my [ground for] glorifying [in this matter].

16 For if I [merely] preach the Gospel, that gives me no reason to boast, for I feel compelled of necessity to do it. Woe is me if I do not preach the glad tidings (the Gospel)!

17 For if I do this work of my own free will, then I have my pay—my reward; but if it is not of my own will, but is done reluctantly *and* under compulsion, I am [still] entrusted with a [sacred] trusteeship *and* commission.

18 What then is the [actual] reward that I get? Just this: that in my preaching the good news (the Gospel), I may offer it [absolutely] free of expense [to anybody], not taking advantage of my rights *and* privileges [as a preacher of] the Gospel.

19 For although I am free in every way from any one's control, I have made myself a bond servant to everyone, so that I might gain the more [for Christ].

20 To the Jews I became as a Jew, that I might win Jews; to men under the Law, [I became] as one under the Law, though not myself being under the Law, that I might win those under the Law.

21 To those without law I became as one without law, not that I am without the law of God *and* lawless toward Him, but that I am [especially keeping] within *and* committed to the law of Christ, that I might win those who are without (outside) law.

Living New Testament

3 This is my answer to those who question my rights.

4 Or don't I have any rights at all? Can't I claim the same privilege the other apostles have of being a guest in your homes?

5 If[1] I had a wife, and if[1] she were a believer, couldn't I bring her along on these trips just as the other disciples do, and as the Lord's brothers do, and as Peter does?

6 And must Barnabas and I alone keep working for our living, while you supply these others?

7 What soldier in the army has to pay his own expenses? And have you ever heard of a farmer who harvests his crop and doesn't have the right to eat some of it? What shepherd takes care of a flock of sheep and goats and isn't allowed to drink some of the milk?

8 And I'm not merely quoting the opinions of men as to what is right. I'm telling you what God's law says.

9 For in the law God gave to Moses He said that you must not put a muzzle on an ox to keep it from eating when it is treading out the wheat. Do you suppose God was thinking only about oxen when He said this?

10 Wasn't He also thinking about us? Of course He was. He said this to show us that Christian workers should be paid by those they help. Those who do the plowing and threshing should expect some share of the harvest.

11 We have planted good spiritual seed in your souls. Is it too much to ask, in return, for mere food and clothing?

12 You give them to others who preach to you, and you should. But shouldn't we have an even greater right to them? Yet we have *never* used this right but supply our own needs without your help. We have never demanded payment of any kind for fear that, if we did, you might be less interested in our message to you from Christ.

13 Don't you realize that God told those working in His temple to take for their own needs some of the food brought there as gifts to Him? And those who work at the altar of God get a share of the food that is brought by those offering it to the Lord.

14 In the same way the Lord has given orders that those who preach the Gospel should be supported by those who accept it.

15 Yet I have never asked you for one penny. And I am not writing this to hint that I would like to start now. In fact, I would rather die of hunger than lose the satisfaction I get from preaching to you without charge.

16 For just preaching the Gospel isn't any special credit to me—I couldn't keep from preaching it if I wanted to. I would be utterly miserable. Woe unto me if I don't.

17 If I were volunteering my services of my own free will, then the Lord would give me a special reward; but that is not the situation, for God has picked me out and given me this sacred trust and I have no choice.

18 Under this circumstance, what is my pay? It is the special joy I get from preaching the Good News without expense to anyone, never demanding my rights.

19 And this has a real advantage: I am not bound to obey anyone just because he pays my salary; yet I have freely and happily become a servant of any and all so that I can win them to Christ.

20 When I am with the Jews I seem as one of them so that they will listen to the Gospel and I can win them to Christ. When I am with Gentiles who follow Jewish customs and ceremonies I don't argue, even though I don't agree, because I want to help them.

21 When with the heathen I agree with them as much as I can, except of course that I must always do what is right as a Christian. And so, by agreeing, I can win their confidence[2] and help them too.

---

[1] Implied. Literally, "Have we no right to lead about a wife that is a believer?"
[2] Implied.

Revised Standard

3 This is my defense to those who would
examine me. [4]Do we not have the right to
our food and drink? [5]Do we not have the
right to be accompanied by a wife,[n] as the
other apostles and the brothers of the Lord
and Cephas? [6]Or is it only Barnabas and I
who have no right to refrain from working
for a living? [7]Who serves as a soldier at his
own expense? Who plants a vineyard without eating any of its fruit? Who tends a
flock without getting some of the milk?

8 Do I say this on human authority?
Does not the law say the same? [9]For it is
written in the law of Moses, "You shall not
muzzle an ox when it is treading out the
grain." Is it for oxen that God is concerned?
[10]Does he not speak entirely for our sake?
It was written for our sake, because the
plowman should plow in hope and the thresher thresh in hope of a share in the crop.
[11]If we have sown spiritual good among you,
is it too much if we reap your material benefits? [12]If others share this rightful claim
upon you, do not we still more?

Nevertheless, we have not made use of this
right, but we endure anything rather than
put an obstacle in the way of the gospel of
Christ. [13]Do you not know that those who
are employed in the temple service get their
food from the temple, and those who serve
at the altar share in the sacrificial offerings?
[14]In the same way, the Lord commanded
that those who proclaim the gospel should
get their living by the gospel.

Christian rights surrendered

15 But I have made no use of any of
these rights, nor am I writing this to secure
any such provision. For I would rather die
than have any one deprive me of my ground
for boasting. [16]For if I preach the gospel,
that gives me no ground for boasting. For
necessity is laid upon me. Woe to me if I
do not preach the gospel! [17]For if I do this
of my own will, I have a reward; but if not
of my own will, I am entrusted with a commission. [18]What then is my reward? Just this:
that in my preaching I may make the gospel
free of charge, not making full use of my
right in the gospel.

19 For though I am free from all men, I
have made myself a slave to all, that I might
win the more. [20]To the Jews I became as a
Jew, in order to win Jews; to those under the
law I became as one under the law—though
not being myself under the law—that I might
win those under the law. [21]To those outside
the law I became as one outside the law—
not being without law toward God but under
the law of Christ—that I might win those

---

[n] Greek *a sister as wife*

King James

22 To the weak became I as weak, that I might gain the weak: I am made all things to all *men,* that I might by all means save some.

23 And this I do for the gospel's sake, that I might be partaker thereof with *you.*

24 Know ye not that they which run in a race run all, but one receiveth the prize? So run, that ye may obtain.

25 And every man that striveth for the mastery is temperate in all things. Now they *do it* to obtain a corruptible crown; but we an incorruptible.

26 I therefore so run, not as uncertainly; so fight I, not as one that beateth the air:

27 But I keep under my body, and bring *it* into subjection: lest that by any means, when I have preached to others, I myself should be a castaway.

Amplified

22 To the weak (wanting in discernment) I have become weak (wanting in discernment) that I might win the weak *and* overscrupulous. I have [in short] become all things to all men, that I might by all means—at all costs and in any and every way—save some [by winning them to faith in Jesus Christ].

23 And I do this for the sake of the good news (the Gospel), in order that I may become a participator in it *and* share in its [blessings along with you].

24 Do you not know that in a race all the runners compete, but [only] one receives the prize? So run [your race] that you may lay hold [of the prize] *and* make it yours.

25 Now every athlete who goes into training conducts himself temperately *and* restricts himself in all things. They do it to win a wreath that will soon wither, but we [do it to receive a crown of eternal blessedness] that cannot wither.

26 Therefore I do not run uncertainly—without definite aim. I do not box as one beating the air *and* striking without an adversary.

27 But [like a boxer] I buffet my body—handle it roughly, discipline it by hardships—and subdue it, for fear that after proclaiming to others the Gospel *and* things pertaining to it, I myself should become unfit—not stand the test and be unapproved—*and* rejected [as a counterfeit].

CHAPTER 10

MOREOVER, brethren, I would not that ye should be ignorant, how that all our fathers were under the cloud, and all passed through the sea;

2 And were all baptized unto Moses in the cloud and in the sea;

3 And did all eat the same spiritual meat;

4 And did all drink the same spiritual drink: for they drank of that spiritual Rock that followed them: and that Rock was Christ.

5 But with many of them God was not well pleased: for they were overthrown in the wilderness.

6 Now these things were our examples, to the intent we should not lust after evil things, as they also lusted.

7 Neither be ye idolaters, as *were* some of them; as it is written, The people sat down to eat and drink, and rose up to play.

8 Neither let us commit fornication, as some of them committed, and fell in one day three and twenty thousand.

9 Neither let us tempt Christ, as some of them also tempted, and were destroyed of serpents.

CHAPTER 10

FOR I do not want you to be ignorant, brethren, that our forefathers were every one of them under *and* protected by the cloud [in which God's Presence went before them], and every one of them passed safely through the (Red) sea, [Exod. 13:21; 14:22, 29.]

2 And every one of them (allowed himself too) to be baptized into Moses in the cloud and in the sea, [that is, they were thus brought under obligation to the Law, to Moses and to the covenant, consecrated and set apart to the service of God];

3 And all [of them] ate the same spiritual (supernaturally given) food, [Exod. 16:4, 35.]

4 And they all drank the same supernaturally given drink. For they drank from a spiritual Rock which followed them—produced by the sole power of God Himself without natural instrumentality—and the Rock was Christ. [Exod. 17:6; Num. 20:11.]

5 Nevertheless God was not pleased with the great majority of them, for they were overthrown *and* strewn down along [the ground] in the wilderness. [Num. 14:29, 30.]

6 Now these things are examples (warnings and admonitions) for us not to desire *or* crave *or* covet *or* lust after evil *and* carnal things as they did. [Num. 11:4, 34.]

7 Do not be worshippers of false gods as some of them were, as it is written, The people sat down to eat and drink [the sacrifices offered to the golden calf at Horeb] and rose to sport—to dance and give way to jesting and hilarity. [Exod. 32:4, 6.]

8 We must not gratify evil desire *and* indulge in immorality as some of them did, and twenty-three thousand [suddenly] fell *dead* in a single day! [Num. 25: 1-18.]

9 We should not tempt the Lord—try His patience, become a trial to Him, critically appraise Him and exploit His goodness—as some of them did and were killed by poisonous serpents; [Num. 21:5, 6.]

Living New Testament

22 When I am with those whose consciences bother them easily, I don't act as though I know it all and don't say they are foolish; the result is that they are willing to let me help them. Yes, whatever a person is like, I try to find common ground with him so that he will let me tell him about Christ and let Christ save him.

23 I do this to get the Gospel to them and also for the blessing I myself receive when I see them come to Christ.

24 In a race, everyone runs but only one person gets first prize. So run your race to win.

25 To win the contest you must deny yourselves many things that would keep you from doing your best. An athlete goes to all this trouble just to win a blue ribbon or a silver cup,[3] but we do it for a heavenly reward that never disappears.

26 So I run straight to the goal with purpose in every step. I fight to win. I'm not just shadow-boxing or playing around.

27 Like an athlete I punish my body, treating it roughly, training it to do what it should, not what it wants to. Otherwise I fear that after enlisting others for the race, I myself might be declared unfit and ordered to stand aside.

Revised Standard

outside the law. [22]To the weak I became
weak, that I might win the weak. I have
become all things to all men, that I might
by all means save some. [23]I do it all for the
sake of the gospel, that I may share in its
blessings.

24 Do you not know that in a race all
the runners compete, but only one receives
the prize? So run that you may obtain it.
[25]Every athlete exercises self-control in all
things. They do it to receive a perishable
wreath, but we an imperishable. [26]Well, I
do not run aimlessly, I do not box as one
beating the air; [27]but I pommel my body
and subdue it, lest after preaching to others
I myself should be disqualified.

CHAPTER 10

For we must never forget, dear brothers, what happened to our people in the wilderness long ago. God guided them by sending a cloud that moved along ahead of them; and He brought them all safely through the waters of the Red Sea.

2 This might be called their "baptism"—baptized both in sea and cloud!—as followers of Moses—their commitment to him as their leader.

3,4 And by a miracle[1] God sent them food to eat and water to drink there in the desert; they drank the water that Christ gave them.[2] He was there with them as a mighty Rock of spiritual refreshment.

5 Yet after all this most of them did not obey God, and He destroyed them in the wilderness.

6 From this lesson we are warned that we must not desire evil things as they did,

7 Nor worship idols as they did. (The Scriptures tell us, "The people sat down to eat and drink and then got up to dance" in worship of the golden calf.)

8 Another lesson for us is what happened when some of them sinned with other men's wives, and 23,000 fell dead in one day.

9 And don't try the Lord's patience—they did, and died from snake bites.

The idolatry in the wilderness

10 I want you to know, brethren, that
our fathers were all under the cloud,
and all passed through the sea, [2]and all were
baptized into Moses in the cloud and in the
sea, [3]and all ate the same supernatural[o]
food [4]and all drank the same supernatural[o]
drink. For they drank from the supernatural[o]
Rock which followed them, and the
Rock was Christ. [5]Nevertheless with most
of them God was not pleased; for they were
overthrown in the wilderness.

6 Now these things are warnings for us,
not to desire evil as they did. [7]Do not be
idolaters as some of them were; as it is
written, "The people sat down to eat and
drink and rose up to dance." [8]We must not
indulge in immorality as some of them did,
and twenty-three thousand fell in a single
day. [9]We must not put the Lord[p] to the
test, as some of them did and were destroyed
by serpents; [10]nor grumble, as some

Literally: "a wreath that quickly fades," given to the winners of the original Olympic races of Paul's time.
Implied. Literally, "spiritual food and drink."
Literally, "for they drank of a spiritual Rock that followed them, and the Rock was Christ."

---

[o] Greek *spiritual*
[p] Other ancient authorities read *Christ*

King James

10 Neither murmur ye, as some of them also murmured, and were destroyed of the destroyer.

11 Now all these things happened unto them for ensamples: and they are written for our admonition, upon whom the ends of the world are come.

12 Wherefore let him that thinketh he standeth take heed lest he fall.

13 There hath no temptation taken you but such as is common to man: but God *is* faithful, who will not suffer you to be tempted above that ye are able; but will with the temptation also make a way to escape, that ye may be able to bear *it*.

14 Wherefore, my dearly beloved, flee from idolatry.

15 I speak as to wise men; judge ye what I say.

16 The cup of blessing which we bless, is it not the communion of the blood of Christ? The bread which we break, is it not the communion of the body of Christ?

17 For we *being* many are one bread, *and* one body: for we are all partakers of that one bread.

18 Behold Israel after the flesh: are not they which eat of the sacrifices partakers of the altar?

19 What say I then? that the idol is any thing, or that which is offered in sacrifice to idols is any thing?

20 But *I say,* that the things which the Gentiles sacrifice, they sacrifice to devils, and not to God: and I would not that ye should have fellowship with devils.

21 Ye cannot drink the cup of the Lord, and the cup of devils: ye cannot be partakers of the Lord's table, and of the table of devils.

22 Do we provoke the Lord to jealousy? are we stronger than he?

23 All things are lawful for me, but all things are not expedient: all things are lawful for me, but all things edify not.

24 Let no man seek his own, but every man another's *wealth*.

Amplified

10 Nor discontentedly complain as some of them did and were [x]put out of the way entirely by the destroyer [death]. [Num. 16:41, 49.]

11 Now these things befell them by way of a figure—as an example and warning [to us]; they were written to admonish *and* fit us for right action by good instruction, we in whose days the ages have reached their climax—their consummation and concluding period.

12 Therefore let any one who thinks he stands—who feels sure that he has a steadfast mind and is standing firm—take heed lest he fall [into sin].

13 For no temptation—no trial regarded as enticing to sin [no matter how it comes or where it leads]—has overtaken you *and* laid hold on you that is not common to man—that is, no temptation or trial has come to you that is beyond human resistance and that is not [x]adjusted and [y]adapted and belonging to human experience, and such as man can bear. But God is faithful [to His Word and to His compassionate nature], and He [can be trusted] not to let you be tempted *and* tried *and* assayed beyond your ability *and* strength of resistance *and* power to endure, but with the temptation He will [always] also provide the way out—the means of escape to [z]a landing place—that you may be capable *and* strong *and* powerful patiently to bear up under it.

14 Therefore, my dearly beloved, shun—keep clear away from, avoid by flight if need be—any sort of idolatry (of loving or venerating anything more than God).

15 I am speaking as to intelligent (sensible) men. Think over *and* make up your minds [for yourselves] about what I say.—I appeal to your reason and your discernment in these matters.

16 The cup of blessing [of wine at the Lord's Supper] upon which we ask [God's] blessing, does it not mean [that in drinking it] we participate in *and* share a fellowship (a communion) in the blood of Christ, the Messiah? The bread which we break, does it not mean [that in eating it] we participate in *and* share a fellowship (a communion) in the body of Christ?

17 For we [no matter how] numerous we are, are one body, because we all partake of the one Bread [the One Whom the communion bread represents].

18 Consider those physically people of Israel. Are not those who eat the sacrifices partners of the altar—united in their worship of the same God? [Lev. 7:6.]

19 What do I imply then? That food offered to idols is [intrinsically changed by the fact and amounts to] anything *or* that an idol itself is a [living] thing?

20 No, I am suggesting that what the pagans sacrifice they offer [in effect] to demons—to evil spiritual powers—and not to God [at all]. I do not want you to fellowship *and* be partners with diabolical spirits [by eating at their feasts]. [Deut. 32:17.]

21 You cannot drink the Lord's cup and the demons' cup. You cannot partake of the Lord's table and the demons' table.

22 Shall we thus provoke the Lord to jealousy *and* anger *and* indignation? Are we stronger than He [that we should defy Him]? [Deut. 32:21; Eccl. 6:10; Isa. 45:9.]

23 All things are legitimate—permissible, and we are free to do anything we please; but not all things are helpful (expedient, profitable and wholesome). All things are legitimate, but not all things are constructive [to character] *and* edifying [to spiritual life].

24 Let not one then seek his own good *and* advantage *and* profit, but [rather let him seek the welfare of his neighbor] each one of the other.

---

x) Thayer.
y) Alford.
z) Vincent.

Living New Testament

10 And don't murmur against God and His dealings with you as some of them did, for that is why God sent His Angel to destroy them.

11 All these things happened to them as examples—as object lessons to us—to warn us against doing the same things; they were written down so that we could read about them and learn from them in these last days as the world nears its end.

12 So be careful. If you are thinking, "Oh, I would never behave like that"—let this be a warning to you. For you too may fall into sin.

13 But remember this—the wrong desires that come into your life aren't anything new and different. Many others have faced exactly the same problems before you. And no temptation is irresistible. You can trust God to keep the temptation from becoming so strong that you can't stand up against it, for He has promised this and will do what He says. He will show you how to escape temptation's power so that you can bear up patiently against it.

14 So, dear friends, carefully avoid idol-worship of every kind.

15 You are intelligent people. Look now and see for yourselves whether what I am about to say is true.

16 When we ask the Lord's blessing upon our drinking from the cup of wine at the Lord's Table, this means, doesn't it, that all who drink it are sharing together the blessing of Christ's blood? And when we break off pieces of the bread from the loaf to eat there together, this shows that we are sharing together in the benefits of His body.

17 No matter how many of us there are, we all eat from the same loaf, showing that we are all parts of the one body of Christ.

18 And the Jewish people, all who eat the sacrifices, are united by that act.

19 What am I trying to say? Am I saying that the idols to whom the heathen bring sacrifices are really alive and are real gods, and that these sacrifices are of some value? No, not at all.

20 What I am saying is that those who offer food to these idols are united together in sacrificing to demons, certainly not to God. And I don't want any of you to be partners with demons when you eat the same food, along with the heathen, that has been offered to these idols.

21 You cannot drink from the cup at the Lord's Table and at Satan's table, too. You cannot eat bread both at the Lord's Table and at Satan's table.

22 What? Are you tempting the Lord to be angry with you? Are you stronger than He is?

23 You are certainly free to eat food offered to idols if you want to; it's not against God's laws to eat such meat, but that doesn't mean that you should go ahead and do it. It may be perfectly legal, but it may not be best and helpful.

24 Don't think only of yourself. Try to think of the other fellow, too, and what is best for him.

Revised Standard

of them did and were destroyed by the
Destroyer. 11Now these things happened to
them as a warning, but they were written
down for our instruction, upon whom the
end of the ages has come. 12Therefore let
any one who thinks that he stands take
heed lest he fall. 13No temptation has overtaken you that is not common to man. God
is faithful, and he will not let you be tempted
beyond your strength, but with the temptation will also provide the way of escape,
that you may be able to endure it.

Prohibition of idol feasts

14 Therefore, my beloved, shun the worship of idols. 15I speak as to sensible men;
judge for yourselves what I say. 16The cup
of blessing which we bless, is it not a participation[q] in the blood of Christ? The bread
which we break, is it not a participation[q]
in the body of Christ? 17Because there is
one bread, we who are many are one body,
for we all partake of the one bread. 18Con-
sider the practice of Israel; are not those
who eat the sacrifices partners in the altar?
19What do I imply then? That food offered
to idols is anything, or that an idol is anything? 20No, I imply that what pagans sacrifice they offer to demons and not to God.
I do not want you to be partners with demons. 21You cannot drink the cup of the
Lord and the cup of demons. You cannot
partake of the table of the Lord and the
table of demons. 22Shall we provoke the
Lord to jealousy? Are we stronger than he?

Do all to the glory of God

23 "All things are lawful," but not all
things are helpful. "All things are lawful,"
but not all things build up. 24Let no one seek
his own good, but the good of his neighbor.

---

[q] Or *communion*

King James

25 Whatsoever is sold in the shambles, *that* eat, asking no question for conscience sake:
26 For the earth *is* the Lord's, and the fullness thereof.
27 If any of them that believe not bid you *to a feast,* and ye be disposed to go; whatsoever is set before you, eat, asking no question for conscience sake.
28 But if any man say unto you, This is offered in sacrifice unto idols, eat not for his sake that shewed it, and for conscience sake: for the earth *is* the Lord's, and the fulness thereof:
29 Conscience, I say, not thine own, but of the other: for why is my liberty judged of another *man's* conscience?
30 For if I by grace be a partaker, why am I evil spoken of for that for which I give thanks?
31 Whether therefore ye eat, or drink, or whatsoever ye do, do all to the glory of God.
32 Give none offence, neither to the Jews, nor to the Gentiles, nor to the church of God:
33 Even as I please all *men* in all *things,* not seeking mine own profit, but the *profit* of many, that they may be saved.

Amplified

25 [As to meat offered to idols] eat anything that is sold in the meat market without raising any question *or* investigating on the grounds of conscientious scruples,
26 For the (whole) earth is the Lord's and everything that is in it. [Ps. 24:1; 50:12.]
27 In case one of the unbelievers invites you to a meal and you want to go, eat whatever is served to you without examining into its source because of conscientious scruples.
28 But if some one tells you, This has been offered in sacrifice to an idol, do not eat it, out of consideration for the person who informed you, and for conscience's sake; [that is,]
29 I mean for the sake of his conscience, not yours [do not eat it]. For why should another man's scruples apply to me, *and* my liberty of action be determined by his conscience?
30 If I partake [of my food] with thankfulness, why am I accused *and* evil spoken of because of that for which I give thanks?
31 So then, whether you eat or drink, or whatever you may do, do all for the honor *and* glory of God.
32 Do not let yourselves be [hindrances by giving] offense to the Jews or to the Greeks or to the church of God—[a]do not lead others into sin by your mode of life;
33 Just as I myself strive to please—to accommodate myself to the opinions, desires and interests of others—[adapting myself to] all men in everything I do; not aiming at *or* considering my own profit *and* advantage, but that of the many in order that they may be saved.

CHAPTER 11

BE ye followers of me, even as I also *am* of Christ.
2 Now I praise you, brethren, that ye remember me in all things, and keep the ordinances, as I delivered *them* to you.
3 But I would have you know, that the head of every man is Christ; and the head of the woman *is* the man; and the head of Christ *is* God.
4 Every man praying or prophesying, having *his* head covered, dishonoureth his head.
5 But every woman that prayeth or prophesieth with *her* head uncovered dishonoureth her head: for that is even all one as if she were shaven.
6 For if the woman be not covered, let her also be shorn: but if it be a shame for a woman to be shorn or shaven, let her be covered.
7 For a man indeed ought not to cover *his* head, forasmuch as he is the image and glory of God: but the woman is the glory of the man.
8 For the man is not of the woman; but the woman of the man.

CHAPTER 11

PATTERN after me, follow my example, as I imitate *and* follow Christ, the Messiah.
2 I appreciate *and* commend you because you always remember me in everything and keep firm possession of the traditions (the substance of my instructions), just as I have (verbally) passed them on to you.
3 But I want you to know *and* realize that Christ is the head of every man, the head of a woman is her husband, and the Head of Christ is God.
4 Any man who prays or prophesies—that is, teaches, refutes, reproves, admonishes and comforts—with his head covered dishonors his Head (Christ).
5 And any woman who [publicly] prays or prophesies (teaches, refutes, reproves, admonishes or comforts) when she is bareheaded dishonors her head (her husband); it is the same as [if her head were] shaved.
6 For if a woman will not wear [a head] covering, then she should cut off her hair too; but if it is disgraceful for a woman to have her head shorn or shaven, let her cover [her head].
7 For a man ought not to wear anything on his head [in church], for he is the image and [reflected] glory of God, [that is, [b]his function of government reflects the majesty of the divine Rule]; but woman is [the expression of] man's glory (majesty, pre-eminence). [Gen. 1:26.]
8 For man was not [created] from woman, but woman from man; [Gen. 2:21-23.]

a) Thayer.
b) Thayer.

Living New Testament

25 Here's what you should do. Take any meat you want that is sold at the market. Don't ask whether or not it was offered to idols, lest the answer hurt your conscience.

26 For the earth and every good thing in it belongs to the Lord and is yours to enjoy.

27 If someone who isn't a Christian asks you out to dinner, go ahead; accept the invitation if you want to. Eat whatever is on the table and don't ask any questions about it. Then you won't know whether or not it had been used as a sacrifice to idols, and you won't risk a bad conscience over eating it.

28 But if someone warns you that this meat has been offered to idols, then don't eat it for the sake of the man who told you, and of his conscience.

29 In this case *his* feeling about it is the important thing, not yours. But why, you may ask, must I be guided and limited by what someone else thinks?

30 If I can thank God for the food and enjoy it, why let someone spoil everything just because he thinks I am wrong?

31 Well, I'll tell you why. It is because you must do everything for the glory of God, even your eating and drinking.

32 So don't be a stumbling block to anyone, whether they are Jews or Gentiles or Christians.

33 That is the plan I follow, too. I try to please everyone in everything I do, not doing what I like or what is best for me, but what is best for them, so that they may be saved.

Revised Standard

[25]Eat whatever is sold in the meat market
without raising any question on the ground
of conscience. [26]For "the earth is the Lord's,
and everything in it." [27]If one of the unbelievers invites you to dinner and you are
disposed to go, eat whatever is set before
you without raising any question on the
ground of conscience. [28](But if some one
says to you, "This has been offered in sacrifice," then out of consideration for the man
who informed you, and for conscience'
sake—[29]I mean his conscience, not yours—
do not eat it.) For why should my liberty
be determined by another man's scruples?
[30]If I partake with thankfulness, why am I
denounced because of that for which I
give thanks?

31 So, whether you eat or drink, or
whatever you do, do all to the glory of God.
[32]Give no offense to Jews or to Greeks or to
the church of God, [33]just as I try to please
all men in everything I do, not seeking my
own advantage, but that of many, that they

CHAPTER 11

And you should follow my example, just as I follow Christ's.

2 I am so glad, dear brothers, that you have been remembering and doing everything I taught you.

3 But there is one matter I want to remind you about: that a wife is responsible to her husband, her husband is responsible to Christ, and Christ is responsible to God.

4 That is why, if a man refuses to remove his hat while praying or preaching, he dishonors Christ.

5 And that is why a woman who publicly prays or prophesies without a covering on her head dishonors her husband [for her covering is a sign of her subjection to him[1]].

6 Yes, if she refuses to wear a head covering, then she should cut off all her hair. And if it is shameful for a woman to have her head shaved, then she should wear a covering.

7 But a man should *not* wear anything on his head [when worshiping, for his hat is a sign of subjection to men[2]]. God's glory is man made in His image, and man's glory is the woman.

8 The first man didn't come from woman, but the first woman came out of man.[3]

11 may be saved. [1]Be imitators of me, as
I am of Christ.

The veiling of women

2 I commend you because you remember
me in everything and maintain the traditions
even as I have delivered them to you. [3]But
I want you to understand that the head of
every man is Christ, the head of a woman
is her husband, and the head of Christ is
God. [4]Any man who prays or prophesies
with his head covered dishonors his head,
[5]but any woman who prays or prophesies
with her head unveiled dishonors her head
—it is the same as if her head were shaven.
[6]For if a woman will not veil herself, then
she should cut off her hair; but if it is disgraceful for a woman to be shorn or shaven,
let her wear a veil. [7]For a man ought not
to cover his head, since he is the image and
glory of God; but woman is the glory of
man. [8](For man was not made from woman,
but woman from man. [9]Neither was man
created for woman, but woman for man.)

---

[1] Implied from verses 7, 10.
[2] Implied.
[3] Genesis 2:21-22.

King James

9 Neither was the man created for the woman; but the woman for the man.

10 For this cause ought the woman to have power on *her* head because of the angels.

11 Nevertheless neither is the man without the woman, neither the woman without the man, in the Lord.

12 For as the woman *is* of the man, even so *is* the man also by the woman; but all things of God.

13 Judge in yourselves: is it comely that a woman pray unto God uncovered?

14 Doth not even nature itself teach you, that, if a man have long hair, it is a shame unto him?

15 But if a woman have long hair, it is a glory to her: for *her* hair is given her for a covering.

16 But if any man seem to be contentious, we have no such custom, neither the churches of God.

17 Now in this that I declare *unto you* I praise *you* not, that ye come together not for the better, but for the worse.

18 For first of all, when ye come together in the church, I hear that there be divisions among you; and I partly believe it.

19 For there must be also heresies among you, that they which are approved may be made manifest among you.

20 When ye come together therefore into one place, *this* is not to eat the Lord's supper.

21 For in eating every one taketh before *other* his own supper: and one is hungry, and another is drunken.

22 What? have ye not houses to eat and to drink in? or despise ye the church of God, and shame them that have not? What shall I say to you? shall I praise you in this? I praise *you* not.

23 For I have received of the Lord that which also I delivered unto you, That the Lord Jesus the *same* night in which he was betrayed took bread:

24 And when he had given thanks, he brake *it,* and said, Take, eat: this is my body, which is broken for you: this do in remembrance of me.

25 After the same manner also *he took* the cup, when he had supped, saying, This cup is the new testament in my blood: this do ye, as oft as ye drink *it,* in remembrance of me.

26 For as often as ye eat this bread, and drink this cup, ye do shew the Lord's death till he come.

27 Wherefore whosoever shall eat this bread, and drink *this* cup of the Lord, unworthily, shall be guilty of the body and blood of the Lord.

28 But let a man examine himself, and so let him eat of *that* bread, and drink of *that* cup.

Amplified

9 Neither was man created on account of *or* for the benefit of woman, but woman on account of *and* for the benefit of man. [Gen. 2:18.]

10 [c]Therefore she should [be subject to his authority and should] have a covering on her head [as a token, a symbol, of her submission] to authority, [[b]that she may show reverence as do] the angels *and* not displease them.

11 Nevertheless, in [the plan of] the Lord *and* from His point of view woman is not apart from *and* independent of man, nor is man aloof from *and* independent of woman;

12 For as woman was made from man, even so man is also born of woman. And all [whether male or female go forth] from God (as their Author).

13 Consider for yourselves; is it proper *and* decent [according to your customs] for a woman to offer prayer to God [publicly] with her head uncovered?

14 Does not (experience, common sense, reason and) [b]the native sense of propriety itself teach you that for a man to wear long hair is a dishonor (humiliating and degrading) to him,

15 But if a woman has long hair, it is her ornament *and* glory? For her hair is given to her for a covering.

16 Now if any one is disposed to be argumentative *and* contentious about this, we hold to *and* recognize no other custom [in worship] than this, nor do the churches of God generally.

17 But in what I instruct [you] next I do not commend [you], because when you meet together it is not for the better but for the worse.

18 For, in the first place, when you assemble as a congregation, I hear that there are cliques (divisions and factions) among you; and I in part believe it,

19 For doubtless there have to be factions *or* parties among you in order that they who are genuine *and* of approved fitness may become evident *and* plainly recognized among you.

20 So when you gather for your meetings, it is not the Supper instituted by the Lord that you eat,

21 For in eating each one [hurries] to get his own supper first [not waiting for the poor], and one goes hungry while another gets drunk.

22 What! Do you have no houses in which to eat and drink? Or do you despise the church of God, *and* mean to show contempt for it, while you humiliate those who are poor—have no homes and have brought no food? What shall I say to you? Shall I commend you in this? No, [most certainly] I will not!

23 For I received from the Lord Himself that which I passed on to you—it was given to me personally; that the Lord Jesus on the night when He was treacherously delivered up *and* while His betrayal was in progress took bread,

24 And when He had given thanks, He broke [it], and said, *Take, eat.* This is My body which is broken for you. Do this to call Me [affectionately] to remembrance.

25 Similarly when supper was ended, He took the cup also, saying, This cup is the new covenant [ratified and established] in My blood. Do this, as often as you drink [it], to call Me [affectionately] to remembrance.

26 For every time you eat this bread and drink this cup, you are representing *and* signifying *and* proclaiming the fact of the Lord's death until He comes [again].

27 So then whoever eats the bread or drinks the cup of the Lord in a way that is unworthy [of Him] will be guilty of (profaning and sinning against) the body and blood of the Lord.

28 Let a man [thoroughly] examine himself, and [only] when he has done so should he eat of the bread and drink of the cup.

---

b) Thayer.
c) Kypke, quoted in Clarke's Commentary.

Living New Testament

9 And Adam, the first man, was not made for Eve's benefit, but Eve was made for Adam.

10 So a woman should wear a covering on her head as a sign that she is under man's authority,[4] a fact for all the angels to notice and rejoice in.[5]

11 But remember that in God's plan men and women need each other.

12 For although the first woman came out of man, all men have been born from women ever since, and both men and women come from God their Creator.

13 What do you yourselves really think about this? Is it right for a woman to pray in public without covering her head?

14, 15 Doesn't even nature itself teach us that women's heads should be covered? For women are proud of their long hair, while a man with long hair tends to be ashamed.

16 But if anyone wants to argue about this, all I can say is that we never teach anything else than this—that a woman should wear a covering when prophesying or praying publicly in the church, and all the churches feel the same way about it.

17 Next on my list of items to write you about is something else I cannot agree with. For it sounds as if more harm is done than good when you meet together for your communion services.

18 Everyone keeps telling me about the arguing that goes on in these meetings, and the divisions developing among you, and I can just about believe it.

19 But I suppose you feel this is necessary so that you who are always right will become known and recognized!

20 When you come together to eat, it isn't the Lord's Supper you are eating,

21 But your own. For I am told that everyone hastily gobbles all the food he can without waiting to share with the others, so that one doesn't get enough and goes hungry while another has too much to drink and gets drunk.

22 What? Is this really true? Can't you do your eating and drinking at home, to avoid disgracing the church and shaming those who are poor and can bring no food? What am I supposed to say about these things? Do you want me to praise you? Well, I certainly do not!

23 For this is what the Lord Himself has said about His Table, and I have passed it on to you before: That on the night when Judas betrayed Him, the Lord Jesus took bread,

24 And when He had given thanks to God for it, He broke it and gave it to His disciples and said "Take this and eat it. This is My body, which is given[6] for you. Do this to remember Me."

25 In the same way, He took the cup of wine after supper, saying, "This cup is the new agreement between God and you that has been established and set in motion by My blood. Think of this in remembrance of Me whenever you drink it."

26 For every time you eat this bread and drink this cup you are re-telling the message of the Lord's death, that He has died for you. Do this until He comes again.

27 So if anyone eats this bread and drinks from this cup of the Lord in an unworthy manner, he is guilty of sin against the body and the blood of the Lord.

28 That is why a man should examine himself carefully before eating the bread and drinking from the cup.

[4] Literally, "For this cause ought the woman to have power on (her) head."
[5] Literally, "because of the angels."
[6] Some ancient manuscripts read, "broken."

Revised Standard

10 That is why a woman ought to have a veil[r]
on her head, because of the angels. 11 (Nevertheless, in the Lord woman is not independent of man nor man of woman; 12 for
as woman was made from man, so man is
now born of woman. And all things are
from God.) 13 Judge for yourselves; is it
proper for a woman to pray to God with
her head uncovered? 14 Does not nature itself
teach you that for a man to wear long hair
is degrading to him, 15 but if a woman has
long hair, it is her pride? For her hair is
given to her for a covering. 16 If any one
is disposed to be contentious, we recognize
no other practice, nor do the churches of
God.

The Lord's Supper

17 But in the following instructions I do
not commend you, because when you come
together it is not for the better but for the
worse. 18 For, in the first place, when you
assemble as a church, I hear that there are
divisions among you; and I partly believe it,
19 for there must be factions among you
in order that those who are genuine among
you may be recognized. 20 When you meet
together, it is not the Lord's supper that
you eat. 21 For in eating, each one goes
ahead with his own meal, and one is hungry
and another is drunk. 22 What! Do you not
have houses to eat and drink in? Or do you
despise the church of God and humiliate
those who have nothing? What shall I say
to you? Shall I commend you in this? No,
I will not.
23 For I received from the Lord what I
also delivered to you, that the Lord Jesus
on the night when he was betrayed took
bread, 24 and when he had given thanks, he
broke it, and said, "This is my body which
is for[s] you. Do this in remembrance of me."
25 In the same way also the cup, after supper, saying, "This cup is the new covenant
in my blood. Do this, as often as you drink
it, in remembrance of me." 26 For as often
as you eat this bread and drink the cup,
you proclaim the Lord's death until he
comes.
27 Whoever, therefore, eats the bread or
drinks the cup of the Lord in an unworthy
manner will be guilty of profaning the body
and blood of the Lord. 28 Let a man examine
himself, and so eat the bread and drink of

[r] Greek *authority* (the veil being a symbol of this)
[s] Other ancient authorities read *broken for*

King James

29 For he that eateth and drinketh unworthily, eateth and drinketh damnation to himself, not discerning the Lord's body.

30 For this cause many *are* weak and sickly among you, and many sleep.

31 For if we would judge ourselves, we should not be judged.

32 But when we are judged, we are chastened of the Lord, that we should not be condemned with the world.

33 Wherefore, my brethren, when ye come together to eat, tarry one for another.

34 And if any man hunger, let him eat at home; that ye come not together unto condemnation. And the rest will I set in order when I come.

Amplified

29 For any one who eats and drinks without discriminating *and* recognizing with due appreciation that [it is Christ's] body, eats and drinks a sentence—a verdict of judgment—upon himself.

30 That [careless and unworthy participation] is the reason many of you are weak and sickly, and quite enough of you are fallen into the sleep of death.

31 For if we searchingly examined ourselves—detecting our shortcomings and recognizing our own condition—we should not be judged *and* penalty decreed [by the divine judgement].

32 But when we [fall short and] are judged by the Lord, we are disciplined *and* chastened so that we may not (finally) be condemned (to eternal punishment along) with the world.

33 So then, my brothers, when you gather together to eat [the Lord's Supper], wait for one another.

34 If any one is hungry, let him eat at home, lest you come together to bring judgment [on yourselves]. About the other matters, I will give you directions (personally) when I come.

King James

CHAPTER 12

NOW concerning spiritual *gifts,* brethren, I would not have you ignorant.

2 Ye know that ye were Gentiles, carried away unto these dumb idols, even as ye were led.

3 Wherefore I give you to understand, that no man speaking by the Spirit of God calleth Jesus accursed: and *that* no man can say that Jesus is the Lord, but by the Holy Ghost.

4 Now there are diversities of gifts, but the same Spirit.

5 And there are differences of administrations, but the same Lord.

6 And there are diversities of operations, but it is the same God which worketh all in all.

7 But the manifestation of the Spirit is given to every man to profit withal.

8 For to one is given by the Spirit the word of wisdom; to another the word of knowledge by the same Spirit;

9 To another faith by the same Spirit; to another the gifts of healing by the same Spirit;

10 To another the working of miracles; to another prophecy; to another discerning of spirits; to another *divers* kinds of tongues; to another the interpretation of tongues:

Amplified

CHAPTER 12

NOW about the spiritual gifts (the special endowments of supernatural energy), brethren, I do not want you to be misinformed.

2 You know that [when] you were heathen, you were led off after idols that could not speak—habitually—as impulse directed *and* whenever the occasion might arise.

3 Therefore I want you to understand that no one speaking under the power *and* influence of the (Holy) Spirit of God [ever] can say, Jesus be cursed! And no one can [really] say, Jesus is [my] Lord, except by *and* under the power *and* influence of the Holy Spirit.

4 Now there are distinctive varieties *and* distributions of endowments [[d]extra-ordinary powers distinguishing certain Christians, due to the power of divine grace operating in their souls by the Holy Spirit] and they vary, but the (Holy) Spirit remains the same.

5 And there are distinctive varieties of service *and* ministration, but it is the same Lord [Who is served].

6 And there are distinctive varieties of operation—of working to accomplish things—but it is the same God Who inspires *and* energizes them all in all.

7 But to each one is given the manifestation of the (Holy) Spirit—that is, the evidence, the spiritual illumination of the Spirit—for good *and* profit.

8 To one is given in *and* through the (Holy) Spirit [the power to speak] a message of wisdom, and to another [the power to express] a word of knowledge *and* understanding according to the same (Holy) Spirit;

9 To another ([e]wonder-working) faith by the same (Holy) Spirit, to another the extraordinary powers of healing by the one Spirit;

10 To another the working of miracles, to another prophetic insight—that is, [f]the gift of interpreting the divine will and purpose; to another the ability to discern *and* distinguish between [the utterances of true] spirits [and false ones], to another various kinds of [unknown] tongues, to another the ability to interpret [such] tongues.

---

d) Thayer.
e) Vincent.
f) Abbott-Smith.

Living New Testament

29 For if he eats the bread and drinks from the cup unworthily, not thinking about the body of Christ and what it means, he is eating and drinking God's judgment upon himself; for he is trifling with the death of Christ.

30 That is why many of you are weak and sick, and some have even died.

31 But if you carefully examine yourselves before eating you will not need to be judged and punished.

32 Yet, when we are judged and punished by the Lord, it is so that we will not be condemned with the rest of the world.

33 So, dear brothers, when you gather for the Lord's Supper—the communion service—wait for each other;

34 If anyone is really hungry he should eat at home so that he won't bring punishment upon himself when you meet together.

I'll talk to you about the other matters after I arrive.

Revised Standard

the cup. 29For any one who eats and drinks
without discerning the body eats and drinks
judgment upon himself. 30That is why many
of you are weak and ill, and some have
died.[t] 31But if we judged ourselves truly, we
should not be judged. 32But when we are
judged by the Lord, we are chastened[u] so
that we may not be condemned along with
the world.
33 So then, my brethren, when you come
together to eat, wait for one another—34if
any one is hungry, let him eat at home—
lest you come together to be condemned.
About the other things I will give directions
when I come.

CHAPTER 12

And now, brothers, I want to write about the special abilities the Holy Spirit gives to each of you, for I don't want any misunderstanding about them.

2 You will remember that before you became Christians you went around from one idol to another, not one of which could speak a single word.

3 But now you are meeting people who claim to speak messages from the Spirit of God. How can you know whether they are really inspired by God or whether they are fakes? Here is the test: no one speaking by the power of the Spirit of God can curse Jesus, and no one can say "Jesus is Lord," and really mean it, unless the Holy Spirit is helping him.

4 Now God gives us many kinds of special abilities, but it is the same Holy Spirit who is the source of them all.

5 There are different kinds of service to God, but it is the same Lord we are serving.

6 There are many ways in which God works in our lives, but it is the same God who does the work in and through all of us who are His.

7 The Holy Spirit displays God's power through each of us as a means of helping the entire church.

8 To one person the Spirit gives the ability to give wise advice; someone else may be especially good at studying and teaching, and this is his gift from the same Spirit.

9 He gives special faith to another, and to someone else the power to heal the sick.

10 He gives power for doing miracles to some, and to others power to prophesy and preach. He gives someone else the power to know whether evil spirits are speaking through those who claim to be giving God's messages—or whether it is really the Spirit of God who is speaking. Still another person is able to speak in languages he never learned; and others, who do not know the language either, are given power to understand what he is saying.

The varieties of gifts

12 Now concerning spiritual gifts, brethren, I do not want you to be uninformed. 2You know that when you were
heathen, you were led astray to dumb idols,
however you may have been moved. 3There-
fore I want you to understand that no one
speaking by the Spirit of God ever says
"Jesus be cursed!" and no one can say
"Jesus is Lord" except by the Holy Spirit.
4 Now there are varieties of gifts, but
the same Spirit; 5and there are varieties of
service, but the same Lord; 6and there are
varieties of working, but it is the same God
who inspires them all in every one. 7To
each is given the manifestation of the
Spirit for the common good. 8To one is given
through the Spirit the utterance of wisdom,
and to another the utterance of knowledge
according to the same Spirit, 9to another
faith by the same Spirit, to another gifts of
healing by the one Spirit, 10to another the
working of miracles, to another prophecy,
to another the ability to distinguish between
spirits, to another various kinds of tongues,
to another the interpretation of tongues.

---

[t] Greek *have fallen asleep* (as in 15.6, 20)
[u] Or *when we are judged we are being chastened by the Lord*

King James

11 But all these worketh that one and the selfsame Spirit, dividing to every man severally as he will.

12 For as the body is one, and hath many members, and all the members of that one body, being many, are one body: so also *is* Christ.

13 For by one Spirit are we all baptized into one body, whether *we be* Jews or Gentiles, whether *we be* bond or free; and have been all made to drink into one Spirit.

14 For the body is not one member, but many.

15 If the foot shall say, Because I am not the hand, I am not of the body; is it therefore not of the body?

16 And if the ear shall say, Because I am not the eye, I am not of the body; is it therefore not of the body?

17 If the whole body *were* an eye, where *were* the hearing? If the whole *were* hearing, where *were* the smelling?

18 But now hath God set the members every one of them in the body, as it hath pleased him.

19 And if they were all one member, where *were* the body?

20 But now *are they* many members, yet but one body.

21 And the eye cannot say unto the hand, I have no need of thee: nor again the head to the feet, I have no need of you.

22 Nay, much more those members of the body, which seem to be more feeble, are necessary:

23 And those *members* of the body, which we think to be less honourable, upon these we bestow more abundant honour; and our uncomely *parts* have more abundant comeliness.

24 For our comely *parts* have no need: but God hath tempered the body together, having given more abundant honour to that *part* which lacked:

25 That there should be no schism in the body; but *that* the members should have the same care one for another.

26 And whether one member suffer, all the members suffer with it; or one member be honoured, all the members rejoice with it.

27 Now ye are the body of Christ, and members in particular.

28 And God hath set some in the church, first apostles, secondarily prophets, thirdly teachers, after that miracles, then gifts of healings, helps, governments, diversities of tongues.

29 *Are* all apostles? *are* all prophets? *are* all teachers? *are* all workers of miracles?

30 Have all the gifts of healing? do all speak with tongues? do all interpret?

Amplified

11 All these [achievements and abilities] are inspired *and* brought to pass by one and the same (Holy) Spirit, Who apportions to each person individually [exactly] as He chooses.

12 For just as the body is a unity and yet has many parts, and all the parts, though many, form [only] one body, so it is with Christ, the Messiah, the Anointed One.

13 For by ([g]means of the personal agency of) one (Holy) Spirit we were all, whether Jews or Greeks, slaves or free, baptized [and [h]by baptism united together] into one body, and all made to drink of one (Holy) Spirit.

14 For the body does not consist of one limb *or* organ but of many.

15 If the foot should say, Because I am not the hand, I do not belong to the body, would it be therefore not [a part] of the body?

16 If the ear should say, Because I am not the eye, I do not belong to the body, would it be therefore not [a part] of the body?

17 If the whole body were an eye, where [would be the sense of] hearing? If the whole body were an ear, where [would be the sense of] smell?

18 But as it is, God has placed *and* arranged the limbs *and* organs in the body, each (particular one) of them, just as He wished *and* saw fit *and* with the best adaption.

19 But if [the whole] were all a single organ, where would the body be?

20 And now there are [certainly] many limbs *and* organs, but a single body.

21 And the eye is not able to say to the hand, I have no need of you, nor again the head to the feet, I have no need of you.

22 But instead, there is [absolute] necessity for the parts of the body that are considered the more weak.

23 And those [parts] of the body which we consider rather ignoble are [the very parts] which we invest with additional honor; and our unseemly parts *and* those unsuitable for exposure are treated with seemliness (modesty and decorum),

24 Which our more presentable parts do not require. But God has so adjusted (mingled, harmonized and subtly proportioned the parts of the whole) body, giving the greater honor *and* richer endowment to the inferior parts which lack [apparent importance],

25 So that there is no division *or* discord *or* lack of adaptation (of the parts of the body to each other), but the members all alike have a mutual interest in *and* care for one another.

26 And if one member suffers, all the parts [share] the suffering; if one member is honored, all the members [share in] the enjoyment of it.

27 Now you (collectively) are Christ's body and (individually) you are members of it, each part severally *and* distinct—each with his own place and function.

28 So God has appointed some in the church ([i]for His own use): first apostles (special messengers); second prophets (inspired preachers and expounders); third teachers, then wonder-workers, then those with ability to heal the sick, helpers, administrators, [speakers in] different [unknown] tongues.

29 Are all apostles, (special messengers)? Are all prophets—inspired interpreters of the will and purposes of God? Are all teachers? Do all have the power of performing miracles?

30 Do all possess extraordinary powers of healing? Do all speak with tongues? Do all interpret?

---

g) Wuest's "Untranslatable Riches from the Greek New Testament."
h) Thayer.
i) Vincent.

Living New Testament

11 It is the same and only Holy Spirit who gives all these gifts and powers, deciding which each one of us should have.

12 Our bodies have many parts, but the many parts make up only one body when they are all put together. So it is with the "body" of Christ.

13 Each of us is a part of the one body of Christ. Some of us are Jews, some are Gentiles, some are slaves and some are free. But the Holy Spirit has fitted us all together into one body. We have been baptized into Christ's body by the one Spirit, and have been given that same Holy Spirit.

14 Yes, the body has many parts, not just one part.

15 If the foot says, "I am not a part of the body because I am not a hand," that does not make it any less a part of the body.

16 And what would you think if you heard an ear say, "I am not part of the body because I am only an ear, and not an eye"? Would that make it any less a part of the body'?

17 Suppose the whole body were an eye—then how would you hear? Or if your whole body were just one big ear, how could you smell anything?

18 But that isn't the way God has made us. He has made many parts for our bodies and has put each part just where He wants it.

19 What a strange thing a body would be if it had only one part!

20 So He has made many parts, but still there is only one body.

21 The eye can never say to the hand, "I don't need you." The head can't say to the feet, "I don't need you."

22 And some of the parts that seem weakest and least important are really the most necessary.

23 Yes, we are especially glad to have some parts that seem rather odd! And we carefully protect from the eyes of others those parts that should not be seen,

24 While of course the parts that may be seen do not require this special care. So God has put the body together in such a way that extra honor and care are given to those parts that might otherwise seem less important.

25 This makes for happiness among the parts, so that the parts have the same care for each other that they do for themselves.

26 If one part suffers, all the parts suffer with it, and if one part is honored, all the parts are glad.

27 Now here is what I am trying to say: all of you together are the one body of Christ and each one of you is a separate and necessary part of it.

28 Here is a list of some of the parts He has placed in His church, which is His body:

Apostles,
Prophets—those who preach God's Word,
Teachers,
Those who do miracles,
Those who have the gift of healing,
Those who can help others,
Those who can get others to work together,
Those who speak in languages they have
never learned.

29 Is everyone an apostle? Of course not. Is everyone a preacher? No. Are all teachers? Does everyone have the power to do miracles?

30 Can everyone heal the sick? Of course not. Does God give all of us the ability to speak in languages we've never learned? Can just anyone understand and translate what those are saying who have that gift of foreign speech?

Revised Standard

[11]All these are inspired by one and the same
Spirit, who apportions to each one individually as he wills.

Unity in diversity

12 For just as the body is one and has
many members, and all the members of the
body, though many, are one body, so it is
with Christ. [13]For by one Spirit we were
all baptized into one body—Jews or Greeks,
slaves or free—and all were made to drink
of one Spirit.
14 For the body does not consist of one
member but of many. [15]If the foot should
say, "Because I am not a hand, I do not belong to the body," that would not make it
any less a part of the body. [16]And if the
ear should say, "Because I am not an eye,
I do not belong to the body," that would
not make it any less a part of the body.
[17]If the whole body were an eye, where
would be the hearing? If the whole body
were an ear, where would be the sense of
smell? [18]But as it is, God arranged the organs in the body, each one of them, as he
chose. [19]If all were a single organ, where
would the body be? [20]As it is, there are
many parts, yet one body. [21]The eye cannot
say to the hand, "I have no need of you,"
nor again the head to the feet, "I have no
need of you." [22]On the contrary, the parts
of the body which seem to be weaker are
indispensable, [23]and those parts of the body
which we think less honorable we invest
with the greater honor, and our unpresent-
able parts are treated with greater modesty,
[24]which our more presentable parts do not
require. But God has so adjusted the body,
giving the greater honor to the inferior part,
[25]that there may be no discord in the body,
but that the members may have the same
care for one another. [26]If one member suffers, all suffer together; if one member is
honored, all rejoice together.

Specific gifts

27 Now you are the body of Christ and
individually members of it. [28]And God has
appointed in the church first apostles, second
prophets, third teachers, then workers of
miracles, then healers, helpers, administrators, speakers in various kinds of tongues.
[29]Are all apostles? Are all prophets? Are all
teachers? Do all work miracles? [30]Do all
possess gifts of healing? Do all speak with

King James

31 But covet earnestly the best gifts: and yet shew I unto you a more excellent way.

CHAPTER 13

THOUGH I speak with the tongues of men and of angels, and have not charity, I am become *as* sounding brass, or a tinkling cymbal.

2 And though I have *the gift of* prophecy, and understand all mysteries, and all knowledge; and though I have all faith, so that I could remove mountains, and have not charity, I am nothing.

3 And though I bestow all my goods to feed *the poor,* and though I give my body to be burned, and have not charity, it profiteth me nothing.

4 Charity suffereth long, *and* is kind; charity envieth not; charity vaunteth not itself, is not puffed up,

5 Doth not behave itself unseemly, seeketh not her own, is not easily provoked, thinketh no evil;

6 Rejoiceth not in iniquity, but rejoiceth in the truth;

7 Beareth all things, believeth all things, hopeth all things, endureth all things.

8 Charity never faileth: but whether *there be* prophecies, they shall fail; whether *there be* tongues, they shall cease; whether *there be* knowledge, it shall vanish away.

9 For we know in part, and we prophesy in part.

10 But when that which is perfect is come, then that which is in part shall be done away.

11 When I was a child, I spake as a child, I understood as a child, I thought as a child: but when I became a man, I put away childish things.

12 For now we see through a glass, darkly; but then face to face: now I know in part; but then shall I know even as also I am known.

Amplified

31 But earnestly desire *and* zealously cultivate the greatest *and* best—the higher [gifts] and the choicest [graces]. And yet I will show you a still more excellent way—one that is better by far and the highest of them all, [love].

CHAPTER 13

IF I [can] speak in the tongues of men and [even] of angels, but have not love [that reasoning, intentional, spiritual devotion, such [j]as is inspired by God's love for and in us], I am only a noisy gong *or* a clanging cymbal.

2 And if I have prophetic powers—that is, [k]the gift of interpreting the divine will and purpose; and understand all the secret truths *and* mysteries and possess all knowledge, and if I have (sufficient) faith so that I can remove mountains, but have not love [God's love in me] I am nothing—a useless nobody.

3 Even if I dole out all that I have [to the poor in providing] food, and if I surrender my body to be burned [or [l]in order that I may glory], but have not love [God's love in me], I gain nothing.

4 Love endures long *and* is patient and kind; love never is envious *nor* boils over with jealousy; is not boastful *or* vainglorious, does not display itself haughtily.

5 It is not conceited—arrogant and inflated with pride; it is not rude (unmannerly), *and* does not act unbecomingly. Love [God's love in us] does not insist on its own rights *or* its own way, *for* it is not self-seeking; it is not touchy *or* fretful *or* resentful; it takes no account of the evil done to it—pays no attention to a suffered wrong.

6 It does not rejoice at injustice *and* unrighteousness, but rejoices when right *and* truth prevail.

7 Love bears up under anything *and* everything that comes, is ever ready to believe the best of every person, its hopes are fadeless under all circumstances and it endures everything [without weakening].

8 Love never fails—never fades out or becomes obsolete or comes to an end. As for prophecy [that is, [m]the gift of interpreting the divine will and purpose], it will be fulfilled *and* pass away; as for tongues, they will be destroyed *and* cease; as for knowledge, it will pass away [that is, it will lose its value and be superseded by truth].

9 For our knowledge is fragmentary (incomplete and imperfect), and our prophecy (our teaching) is fragmentary (incomplete and imperfect).

10 But when the complete *and* perfect [total] comes, the incomplete *and* imperfect will vanish away—become antiquated, void and superseded.

11 When I was a child, I talked like a child, I thought like a child, I reasoned like a child; now that I have become a man, I am done with childish ways *and* have put them aside.

12 For now we are looking in a mirror that gives only a dim (blurred) reflection [of reality as [n]in a riddle or enigma], but then [when perfection comes] we shall see in reality *and* face to face! Now I know in part (imperfectly); and then I shall know *and* understand [n]fully *and* clearly, even in the same manner as I have been [n]fully *and* clearly known *and* understood [[o]by God].

---

j) Souter.
k) Abbott-Smith.
l) Some ancient authorities so read.
m) Abbott-Smith's "Manual Greek Lexicon of the New Testament."
n) Vincent's "Word Studies in the New Testament."
o) Matthew Henry and others.

Living New Testament

31 No, but try your best to have the more important of these gifts. First, however, let me tell you about something else that is better than any of them!

CHAPTER 13

If I had the gift of being able to speak in other languages without learning them, and could speak in every language there is in all of heaven and earth, but didn't love others, I would only be making noise.

2 If I had the gift of prophecy and knew all about what is going to happen in the future, knew everything about *everything,* but didn't love others, what good would it do? Even if I had the gift of faith so that I could speak to a mountain and make it move, I would still be worth nothing at all without love.

3 If I gave everything I have to poor people, and if I were burned alive for preaching the Gospel but didn't love others, it would be of no value whatever.

4 Love is very patient and kind, never jealous or envious, never boastful or proud,

5 Never haughty or selfish or rude. Love does not demand its own way. It is not irritable or touchy. It does not hold grudges and will hardly even notice when others do it wrong.

6 It is never glad about injustice, but rejoices whenever truth wins out.

7 If you love someone you will be loyal to him no matter what the cost. You will always believe in him, always expect the best of him, and always stand your ground in defending him.

8 All the special gifts and powers from God will someday come to an end, but love goes on forever. Someday prophecy, and speaking in unknown languages, and special knowledge—the gifts will disappear.

9 Now we know so little, even with our special gifts, and the preaching of those most gifted is still so poor.

10 But when we have been made perfect and complete, then the need for these inadequate special gifts will come to an end, and they will disappear.

11 It's like this: when I was a child I spoke and thought and reasoned as a child does. But when I became a man my thoughts grew far beyond those of my childhood, and now I have put away the childish things.

12 In the same way, we can see and understand only a little about God now, as if we were peering at His reflection in a poor mirror; but someday we are going to see Him in His completeness, face to face. Now all that I know is hazy and blurred, but then I will see everything clearly, just as clearly as God sees into my heart right now.

Revised Standard

tongues? Do all interpret? 31But earnestly
desire the higher gifts.

The way of love

And I will show you a still more excellent
way.

13 If I speak in the tongues of men and
of angels, but have not love, I am a
noisy gong or a clanging cymbal. 2And if I
have prophetic powers, and understand all
mysteries and all knowledge, and if I have
all faith, so as to remove mountains, but
have not love, I am nothing. 3If I give away
all I have, and if I deliver my body to be
burned,[v] but have not love, I gain nothing.
4 Love is patient and kind; love is not
jealous or boastful; 5it is not arrogant or
rude. Love does not insist on its own way;
it is not irritable or resentful; 6it does not
rejoice at wrong, but rejoices in the right.
7Love bears all things, believes all things,
hopes all things, endures all things.
8 Love never ends; as for prophecies,
they will pass away; as for tongues, they will
cease; as for knowledge, it will pass away.
9For our knowledge is imperfect and our
prophecy is inperfect; 10but when the perfect
comes, the imperfect will pass away. 11When
I was a child, I spoke like a child, I thought
like a child, I reasoned like a child; when
I became a man, I gave up childish ways.
12For now we see in a mirror dimly, but
then face to face. Now I know in part; then
I shall understand fully, even as I have been

[v] Other ancient authorities read *body that I may glory*

King James

13 And now abideth faith, hope, charity, these three; but the greatest of these *is* charity.

Amplified

13 And so faith, hope, love abide; [faith, conviction and belief respecting man's relation to God and divine things; hope, joyful and confident expectation of eternal salvation; love, true affection for God and man, growing out of God's love for and in us], these three, but the greatest of these is love.

CHAPTER 14

FOLLOW after charity, and desire spiritual *gifts,* but rather that ye may prophesy.

2 For he that speaketh in an *unknown* tongue speaketh not unto men, but unto God: for no man understandeth *him;* howbeit in the spirit he speaketh mysteries.

3 But he that prophesieth speaketh unto men *to* edification, and exhortation, and comfort.

4 He that speaketh in an *unknown* tongue edifieth himself; but he that prophesieth edifieth the church.

5 I would that ye all spake with tongues, but rather that ye prophesied: for greater *is* he that prophesieth than he that speaketh with tongues, except he interpret, that the church may receive edifying.

6 Now, brethren, if I come unto you speaking with tongues, what shall I profit you, except I shall speak to you either by revelation, or by knowledge, or by prophesying, or by doctrine?

7 And even things without life giving sound, whether pipe or harp, except they give a distinction in the sounds, how shall it be known what is piped or harped?

8 For if the trumpet give an uncertain sound, who shall prepare himself to the battle?

9 So likewise ye, except ye utter by the tongue words easy to be understood, how shall it be known what is spoken? for ye shall speak into the air.

10 There are, it may be, so many kinds of voices in the world, and none of them *is* without signification.

11 Therefore if I know not the meaning of the voice, I shall be unto him that speaketh a barbarian, and he that speaketh *shall be* a barbarian unto me.

12 Even so ye, forasmuch as ye are zealous of spiritual *gifts*, seek that ye may excel to the edifying of the church.

CHAPTER 14

EAGERLY pursue *and* seek to acquire [this] love—make it your aim, your great quest; and earnestly desire *and* cultivate the spiritual endowments, especially that you may prophesy—that is, [p]interpret the divine will and purpose in inspired preaching and teaching.

2 For one who speaks in an [unknown] tongue speaks not to men but to God, for no one understands *or* catches his meaning, because in the (Holy) Spirit he utters secret truths *and* hidden things [not obvious to the understanding].

3 But [on the other hand], the one who prophesies—who [p]interprets the divine will and purpose in inspired preaching and teaching—speaks to men for their upbuilding *and* constructive spiritual progress and encouragement and consolation.

4 He who speaks in a [strange] tongue edifies *and* improves himself, but he who prophesies—[p]interpreting the divine will and purpose and teaching with inspiration—edifies *and* improves the church *and* promotes growth [in Christian wisdom, piety, holiness and happiness].

5 Now I wish that you might all speak in [unknown] tongues, but more especially [I want you] to prophesy—to be inspired to preach and interpret the divine will and purpose. He who prophesies—who is inspired to preach and teach—is greater (more useful and more important) than he who speaks in [unknown] tongues, unless he should interpret [what he says], so that the church may be edified *and* get good out of it.

6 Now, brethren, if I come to you speaking in [unknown] tongues, how shall I make it to your advantage unless I speak to you either in revelation—disclosure of God's will to man—in knowledge or in prophecy or in instruction?

7 If even inanimate musical instruments, such as the flute or the harp, do not give distinct tones, how will any one [listening] know *or* understand what is played?

8 And if the war bugle gives an uncertain (indistinct) call, who will prepare for battle?

9 Just so it is with you; if you in the [unknown] tongue speak words that are not intelligible, how will any one understand what you are saying? For you will be talking into empty space!

10 There are, I suppose, all these many [to us unknown] tongues in the world [somewhere], and none is destitute of [its own power of] expression *and* meaning.

11 But if I do not know the force *and* significance of the speech (language), I shall seem to be a foreigner to the one who speaks [to me], and the speaker who addresses [me] will seem a foreigner to me.

12 So it is with yourselves; since you are so eager *and* ambitious to possess spiritual endowments *and* manifestations of the (Holy) Spirit, [concentrate on] striving to excel *and* to abound [in them] in ways that will build up the church.

p) Abbott-Smith.

Living New Testament

13 There are three things that remain—faith, hope and love—and the greatest of these is love.

CHAPTER 14

Let love be your greatest aim; nevertheless, ask also for the special abilities the Holy Spirit gives, and especially the gift of prophecy, being able to preach the messages of God.

2 But if your gift is that of being able to "speak in tongues," that is, to speak in languages you haven't learned, you will be talking to God but not to others, since they won't be able to understand you. You will be speaking by the power of the Spirit but it will all be a secret.

3 But one who prophesies, preaching the messages of God, is helping others grow in the Lord, encouraging and comforting them.

4 So a person "speaking in tongues" helps himself grow spiritually, but one who prophesies, preaching messages from God, helps the entire church grow in holiness and happiness.

5 I wish you all had the gift of "speaking in tongues" but, even more, I wish you were all able to prophesy, preaching God's messages, for that is a greater and more useful power than to speak in unknown languages—unless, of course, you can tell everyone afterwards what you were saying, so that they can get some good out of it too.

6 Dear friends, even if I myself should come to you talking in some language you don't understand, how would that help you? But if I speak plainly what God has revealed to me, and tell you the things I know, and what is going to happen, and the great truths of God's word—that is what you need; that is what will help you.

7 Even musical instruments—the flute, for instance, or the harp—are examples of the need for speaking in plain, simple English[1] rather than in unknown languages. For no one will recognize the tune the flute is playing unless each note is sounded clearly.

8 And if the army bugler doesn't play the right notes, how will the soldiers know that they are being called to battle?

9 In the same way, if you talk to a person in some language he doesn't understand, how will he know what you mean? You might as well be talking to an empty room.

10 I suppose that there are hundreds of different languages in the world, and all are excellent for those who understand them,

11 But to me they mean nothing. A person talking to me in one of these languages will be a stranger to me and I will be a stranger to him.

12 Since you are so anxious to have special gifts from the Holy Spirit, ask Him for the very best, for those that will be of real help to the whole church.

The local language, whatever it is.

Revised Standard

fully understood. 13So faith, hope, love a-
bide, these three; but the greatest of these
is love.

Prophecy and tongues

14 Make love your aim, and earnestly desire the spiritual gifts, especially that
you may prophesy. 2For one who speaks in
a tongue speaks not to men but to God; for
no one understands him, but he utters mysteries in the Spirit. 3On the other hand, he
who prophesies speaks to men for their upbuilding and encouragement and consolation. 4He who speaks in a tongue edifies
himself, but he who prophesies edifies the
church. 5Now I want you all to speak in
tongues, but even more to prophesy. He who
prophesies is greater than he who speaks in
tongues, unless some one interprets, so that
the church may be edified.
6 Now, brethren, if I come to you speaking in tongues, how shall I benefit you unless I bring you some revelation or knowledge or prophecy or teaching? 7If even lifeless instruments, such as the flute or the
harp, do not give distinct notes, how will
any one know what is played? 8And if the
bugle gives an indistinct sound, who will
get ready for battle? 9So with yourselves;
if you in a tongue utter speech that is not
intelligible, how will any one know what is
said? For you will be speaking into the air.
10There are doubtless many different languages in the world, and none is without
meaning; 11but if I do not know the meaning of the language, I shall be a foreigner
to the speaker and the speaker a foreigner
to me. 12So with yourselves; since you are
eager for manifestations of the Spirit, strive
to excel in building up the church.

King James

13 Wherefore let him that speaketh in an *unknown* tongue pray that he may interpret.

14 For if I pray in an *unknown* tongue, my spirit prayeth, but my understanding is unfruitful.

15 What is it then? I will pray with the spirit, and I will pray with the understanding also: I will sing with the spirit, and I will sing with the understanding also.

16 Else when thou shalt bless with the spirit, how shall he that occupieth the room of the unlearned say Amen at thy giving of thanks, seeing he understandeth not what thou sayest?

17 For thou verily givest thanks well, but the other is not edified.

18 I thank my God, I speak with tongues more than ye all:

19 Yet in the church I had rather speak five words with my understanding, that *by my voice* I might teach others also, than ten thousand words in an *unknown* tongue.

20 Brethren, be not children in understanding: howbeit in malice be ye children, but in understanding be men.

21 In the law it is written, With *men of* other tongues and other lips will I speak unto this people; and yet for all that will they not hear me, saith the Lord.

22 Wherefore tongues are for a sign, not to them that believe, but to them that believe not: but prophesying *serveth* not for them that believe not, but for them which believe.

23 If therefore the whole church be come together into one place, and all speak with tongues, and there come in *those that are* unlearned, or unbelievers, will they not say that ye are mad?

24 But if all prophesy, and there come in one that believeth not, or *one* unlearned, he is convinced of all, he is judged of all:

25 And thus are the secrets of his heart made manifest; and so falling down on *his* face, he will worship God, and report that God is in you of a truth.

26 How is it then, brethren? when ye come together, every one of you hath a psalm, hath a doctrine, hath a tongue, hath a revelation, hath an interpretation. Let all things be done unto edifying.

27 If any man speak in an *unknown* tongue, *let it be* by two, or at the most *by* three, and *that* by course; and let one interpret.

28 But if there be no interpreter, let him keep silence in the church; and let him speak to himself, and to God.

29 Let the prophets speak two or three, and let the other judge.

Amplified

13 Therefore, the person who speaks in an [unknown] tongue should pray [for the power] to interpret *and* explain what he says.

14 For if I pray in an [unknown] tongue, my spirit [by the [q]Holy Spirit within me] prays, but my mind is unproductive—bears no fruit and helps nobody.

15 Then what am I to do? I will pray with my spirit—by the [q]Holy Spirit that is within me; but I will also pray intelligently—with my mind and understanding; I will sing with my spirit—by the Holy Spirit that is within me; but I will sing (intelligently) with my mind *and* understanding also.

16 Otherwise, if you bless *and* render thanks with [your] spirit [[r]thoroughly aroused by the Holy Spirit], how can any one in the position of an outsider, or [s]he who is not gifted with [interpreting of unknown] tongues, say the Amen to your thanksgiving, since he does not know what you are saying? [1 Chron. 16:36; Ps. 106:48.]

17 To be sure, you may give thanks well (nobly), but the bystander is not edified—it does him no good.

18 I thank God that I speak in [strange] languages more than any of you *or* all of you put together;

19 Nevertheless, in public worship, I would rather say five words with my understanding, *and* intelligently in order to instruct others, than ten thousand words in a [strange] language.

20 Brethren, do not be children (immature) in your thinking; continue to be babes in [matters of] evil, but in your minds be mature [men].

21 It is written in the Law, By men of strange languages *and* by the lips of foreigners will I speak to this people, and not even then will they listen to Me, says the Lord. [Isa. 28:11,12.]

22 Thus [unknown] tongues are meant for a (supernatural) sign, not for believers but for unbelievers [on the point of believing], while prophecy (inspired preaching and teaching, interpreting the divine will and purpose) is not for unbelievers [on the point of believing] but for believers.

23 Therefore, if the whole church assembles and all of you speak in [unknown] tongues, and the ungifted *and* uninitiated or unbelievers come in, will they not say that you are demented?

24 But if all prophesy—giving inspired testimony and interpreting the divine will and purpose—and an unbeliever or untaught outsider comes in, he is told of his sin *and* reproved *and* convicted *and* convinced by all, and his defects *and* needs are examined (estimated, determined), *and* he is called to account by all,

25 The secrets of his heart are laid bare; and so, falling on [his] face, he will worship God, declaring that God is among you in very truth.

26 What then, brethren, is [the right course]? When you meet together, each one has a hymn, a teaching, a disclosure of special knowledge *or* information, an utterance in a [strange] tongue or an interpretation of it. [But] let everything be constructive *and* edifying *and* for the good of all.

27 If some speak in a [strange] tongue, let the number be limited to two or at the most three, and each one [taking his] turn, and let one interpret *and* explain [what is said].

28 But if there is no one to do the interpreting, let each of them keep still in church and talk to himself and to God.

29 So, let two or three prophets speak—those inspired to preach or teach—while the rest pay attention *and* weigh *and* discern what is said.

---

q) Vincent.
r) Thayer.
s) Alternate reading.

Living New Testament

13 If someone is given the gift of speaking in unknown tongues, he should pray also for the gift of knowing what he has said, so that he can tell people afterwards, plainly.

14 For if I pray in a language I don't understand, my spirit is praying but I don't know what I am saying.

15 Well, then, what shall I do? I will do both. I will pray in unknown tongues and also in ordinary language that everyone understands. I will sing in unknown tongues and also in ordinary language, so that I can understand the praise I am giving;

16 For if you praise and thank God with the spirit alone, speaking in another language, how can those who don't understand you be praising God along with you? How can they join you in giving thanks when they don't know what you are saying?

17 You will be giving thanks very nicely, no doubt, but the other people present won't be helped.

18 I thank God that I "speak in tongues" privately[2] more than any of the rest of you.

19 But in public worship I would much rather speak five words that people can understand and be helped by, than ten thousand words while "speaking in tongues" in an unknown language.

20 Dear brothers, don't be childish in your understanding of these things. Be innocent babies when it comes to planning evil, but be men of intelligence in understanding matters of this kind.

21 We are told in the ancient Scriptures that God would send men from other lands to speak in foreign languages to His people, but even then they would not listen.

22 So you see that being able to "speak in tongues" is not a help to God's children, but is to interest the unsaved. However, prophecy (preaching the deep truths of God) is what the Christians need, and unbelievers aren't yet ready for it.

23 Even so, if an unsaved person, or someone who doesn't have these gifts, comes to church and hears you all talking in other languages, he is likely to think you are crazy.

24 But if you all prophesy, preaching God's Word, [even though such preaching is mostly for believers[3]] and an unsaved person or a new Christian comes in who does not understand about these things, all these sermons will convince him of the fact that he is a sinner, and his conscience will be pricked by everything he hears.

25 As he listens, his secret thoughts will be laid bare and he will fall down on his knees and worship God, declaring that God is really there among you.

26 Well, my brothers, let's add up what I am saying. When you meet together some will sing, another will teach, or tell some special information God has given him, or speak in an unknown tongue, or tell what someone else is saying who is speaking in the unknown language, but everything that is done must be useful to all, and build them up in the Lord.

27 No more than two or three should speak in an unknown language, and they must speak one at a time, and someone must be ready to interpret what they are saying.

28 But if no one is present who can interpret, they must not speak out loud. They may talk silently to themselves and to God in the unknown language but not publicly.

29, 30 Two or three may prophesy, one at a time, if they have the gift, while all the others listen. But if, while

[2] Implied. See verses 19 and 28.
[3] Implied.

Revised Standard

The need to interpret tongues

13 Therefore, he who speaks in a tongue
should pray for the power to interpret. 14 For
if I pray in a tongue, my spirit prays but
my mind is unfruitful. 15 What am I to do?
I will pray with the spirit and I will pray
with the mind also; I will sing with the
spirit and I will sing with the mind also.
16 Otherwise, if you bless[w] with the spirit,
how can any one in the position of an outsider[x] say the "Amen" to your thanksgiving
when he does not know what you are saying? 17 For you may give thanks well enough,
but the other man is not edified. 18 I thank
God that I speak in tongues more than you
all; 19 nevertheless, in church I would rather
speak five words with my mind, in order
to instruct others, than ten thousand words
in a tongue.
20 Brethren, do not be children in your
thinking; be babes in evil, but in thinking
be mature. 21 In the law it is written, "By
men of strange tongues and by the lips of
foreigners will I speak to this people, and
even then they will not listen to me, says the
Lord." 22 Thus, tongues are a sign not for
believers but for unbelievers, while prophecy
is not for unbelievers but for believers. 23 If,
therefore, the whole church assembles and
all speak in tongues, and outsiders or unbelievers enter, will they not say that you are
mad? 24 But if all prophesy, and an unbeliever or outsider enters, he is convicted by
all, he is called to account by all, 25 the
secrets of his heart are disclosed; and so,
falling on his face, he will worship God
and declare that God is really among you.

The use of spiritual gifts

26 What then, brethren? When you come
together, each one has a hymn, a lesson, a
revelation, a tongue, or an interpretation.
Let all things be done for edification. 27 If
any speak in a tongue, let there be only two
or at most three, and each in turn; and let
one interpret. 28 But if there is no one to
interpret, let each of them keep silence in
church and speak to himself and to God.
29 Let two or three prophets speak, and let
the others weigh what is said. 30 If a revela-

[w] That is, *give thanks to God*
[x] Or *him that is without gifts*

King James

30 If *any thing* be revealed to another that sitteth by, let the first hold his peace.

31 For ye may all prophesy one by one, that all may learn, and all may be comforted.

32 And the spirits of the prophets are subject to the prophets.

33 For God is not *the author* of confusion, but of peace, as in all churches of the saints.

34 Let your women keep silence in the churches: for it is not permitted unto them to speak; but *they are commanded* to be under obedience, as also saith the law.

35 And if they will learn any thing, let them ask their husbands at home: for it is a shame for women to speak in the church.

36 What? came the word of God out from you? or came it unto you only?

37 If any man think himself to be a prophet, or spiritual, let him acknowledge that the things that I write unto you are the commandments of the Lord.

38 But if any man be ignorant, let him be ignorant.

39 Wherefore, brethren, covet to prophesy, and forbid not to speak with tongues.

40 Let all things be done decently and in order.

Amplified

30 But if an inspired revelation comes to another who is sitting by, then let the first one be silent.

31 For in this way you can give testimony—prophesying and thus interpreting the divine will and purpose—one by one, so that all may be instructed and all may be stimulated *and* encouraged;

32 For the spirits of the prophets [the speakers in tongues] are under the speaker's control [and subject to being silenced as may be necessary],

33 For He [Who is the source of their prophesying] is not a God of confusion *and* disorder but of peace *and* order. As [is the practice] in all the churches of the saints (God's people),

34 The women should keep quiet in the churches, for they are not authorized to speak, but should take a secondary *and* subordinate place, just as the Law also says. [Gen. 3:16.]

35 But if there is anything they want to learn, they should ask their own husbands at home, for it is disgraceful for a woman to talk in church [that is, [t]for her to usurp and exercise authority over men in the church].

36 What! Did the Word of the Lord originate with you [Corinthians], or has it reached only you?

37 If any one thinks *and* claims that he is a prophet—filled with and governed by the Holy Spirit of God and inspired to interpret the divine will and purpose in preaching or teaching—or [to have any other] spiritual endowment, let him understand (recognize and acknowledge) that what I am writing to you is a command of the Lord.

38 But if any one disregards *or* does not recognize [[u]that it is a command of the Lord], he is disregarded *and* not recognized—he is [v]one whom God knows not.

39 So [to conclude], my brethren, earnestly desire *and* set your hearts on prophesying—on being inspired to preach and teach and to interpret God's will and purpose—and do not forbid *or* hinder speaking in [unknown] tongues.

40 But all things should be done with regard to decency *and* propriety *and* in an orderly fashion.

CHAPTER 15

MOREOVER, brethren, I declare unto you the gospel which I preached unto you, which also ye have received, and wherein ye stand;

2 By which also ye are saved, if ye keep in memory what I preached unto you, unless ye have believed in vain.

3 For I delivered unto you first of all that which I also received, how that Christ died for our sins according to the scriptures;

4 And that he was buried, and that he rose again the third day according to the scriptures:

5 And that he was seen of Cephas, then of the twelve:

CHAPTER 15

AND now let me remind you [since it seems to have escaped you], brethren, of the Gospel—the glad tidings of salvation—which I proclaimed to you, which you welcomed *and* accepted and upon which your faith rests;

2 And by which you are saved, if you hold fast *and* keep firmly what I preached to you, unless you believed at first without effect *and* all for nothing.

3 For I passed on to you first of all what I also had received, that Christ, the Messiah, the Anointed One, died for our sins in accordance with [what] the Scriptures [foretold], [Isa. 53:5-12.]

4 That He was buried, that He arose on the third day as the Scriptures foretold, [Ps. 16:9, 10.]

5 And [also] that He appeared to Cephas [Peter], then to the twelve.

---

t) "Expositor's Greek Testament."
u) Thayer.
v) Vincent. Some authorities read "he is not known."

Living New Testament

someone is prophesying, someone else receives a message or idea from the Lord he must not interrupt. The one who is speaking should be allowed to finish before another begins.

31 In this way all who have the gift of prophecy can speak, one after the other, and everyone will learn and be encouraged and helped.

32 Remember that a person who has a message from God has the power to stop himself or wait his turn.[4]

33 God is not one who likes things to be disorderly and upset. He likes harmony, and He finds it in all the other churches.

34 Women should be silent during the church meetings. They are not to take part in the discussion, for they are subordinate to men[5] as the Scriptures also declare.

35 If they have any questions to ask, let them ask their husbands at home, for it is improper for women to express their opinions in church meetings.

36 You disagree? And do you think that the knowledge of God's will begins and ends with you Corinthians? Well, you are mistaken!

37 You who claim to have the gift of prophecy or any other special ability from the Holy Spirit should be the first to realize that what I am saying is a commandment from the Lord Himself.

38 But if anyone still disagrees—well, we will leave him in his ignorance.[6]

39 So, my fellow believers, long to be prophets so that you can preach God's message plainly; and never say it is wrong to "speak in tongues;"

40 However, be sure that everything is done properly in a good and orderly way.

Revised Standard

tion is made to another sitting by, let the
first be silent. 31For you can all prophesy
one by one, so that all may learn and all be
encouraged; 32and the spirits of prophets
are subject to prophets. 33For God is not a
God of confusion but of peace.
As in all the churches of the saints, 34the
women should keep silence in the churches.
For they are not permitted to speak, but
should be subordinate, as even the law says.
35If there is anything they desire to know,
let them ask their husbands at home. For
it is shameful for a woman to speak in
church. 36What! Did the word of God originate with you, or are you the only ones it
has reached?

37 If any one thinks that he is a prophet,
or spiritual, he should acknowledge that
what I am writing to you is a command of
the Lord. 38If any one does not recognize
this, he is not recognized. 39So, my brethren,
earnestly desire to prophesy, and do not forbid speaking in tongues; 40but all things
should be done decently and in order.

CHAPTER 15

Now let me remind you, brothers, of what the Gospel really is, for it has not changed—it is the same Good News I preached to you before. You welcomed it then and still do now, for your faith is squarely built upon this wonderful message;

2 And it is this Good News that saves you if you still firmly believe it, unless of course you never really believed it in the first place.

3 I passed on to you right from the first what had been told to me, that Christ died for our sins just as the Scriptures said He would,

4 And that He was buried, and that three days afterwards He arose from the grave just as the prophets foretold.

5 He was seen by Peter and later by the rest of "the Twelve."[1]

The fact of the resurrection

15 Now I would remind you, brethren,
in what terms I preached to you the
gospel, which you received, in which you
stand, 2by which you are saved, if you hold
it fast—unless you believed in vain.
3 For I delivered to you as of first importance what I also received, that Christ
died for our sins in accordance with the
scriptures, 4that he was buried, that he was
raised on the third day in accordance with
the scriptures, 5and that he appeared to
Cephas, then to the twelve. 6Then he ap-

Literally, "The spirits of the prophets are subject to the prophets."
Literally, "They are not authorized to speak." They were permitted to pray and prophesy (I Cor. 11:5), apparently in public meetings, but not to teach men (I Tim. 2:12).
Or, "If he disagrees, ignore his opinion."
The name given to Jesus' twelve disciples, and still used after Judas was gone from among them.

King James

6 After that, he was seen of above five hundred brethren at once; of whom the greater part remain unto this present, but some are fallen asleep.

7 After that, he was seen of James; then of all the apostles.

8 And last of all he was seen of me also, as of one born out of due time.

9 For I am the least of the apostles, that am not meet to be called an apostle, because I persecuted the church of God.

10 But by the grace of God I am what I am: and his grace which *was bestowed* upon me was not in vain; but I laboured more abundantly than they all: yet not I, but the grace of God which was with me.

11 Therefore whether *it were* I or they, so we preach, and so ye believed.

12 Now if Christ be preached that he rose from the dead, how say some among you that there is no resurrection of the dead?

13 But if there be no resurrection of the dead, then is Christ not risen:

14 And if Christ be not risen, then *is* our preaching vain, and your faith *is* also vain.

15 Yea, and we are found false witnesses of God; because we have testified of God that he raised up Christ: whom he raised not up, if so be that the dead rise not.

16 For if the dead rise not, then is not Christ raised:

17 And if Christ be not raised, your faith *is* vain; ye are yet in your sins.

18 Then they also which are fallen asleep in Christ are perished.

19 If in this life only we have hope in Christ, we are of all men most miserable.

20 But now is Christ risen from the dead, *and* become the firstfruits of them that slept.

21 For since by man *came* death, by man *came* also the resurrection of the dead.

22 For as in Adam all die, even so in Christ shall all be made alive.

23 But every man in his own order: Christ the firstfruits; afterward they that are Christ's at his coming.

24 Then *cometh* the end, when he shall have delivered up the kingdom to God, even the Father; when he shall have put down all rule and all authority and power.

25 For he must reign, till he hath put all enemies under his feet.

26 The last enemy *that* shall be destroyed *is* death.

27 For he hath put all things under his feet. But when he saith all things are put under *him, it is* manifest that he is excepted, which did put all things under him.

Amplified

6 Then later He showed Himself to more than five hundred brethren at one time, the majority of whom are still alive, but some have fallen asleep [in death].

7 Afterward He was seen by James, then by all the apostles (the special messengers),

8 And last of all He appeared to me also, as to one prematurely *and* dead born [[w]no better than an unperfected fetus among living men].

9 For I am least [worthy] of the apostles, who am not fit *or* deserving to be called an apostle, because I once wronged *and* pursued *and* molested the church of God—oppressing it with cruelty and violence.

10 But by the grace (the unmerited favor and blessing) of God, I am what I am, and His grace toward me was not [found to be] for nothing—fruitless and without effect. In fact, I worked harder than all of them [the apostles], though it was not really I, but the grace (the unmerited favor and blessing) of God which was with me.

11 So, whether then it was I or they, this is what we preach and this is what you believed—what you adhered to, trusted in and relied on.

12 But now if Christ, the Messiah, is preached as raised from the dead, how is it that some of you say that there is no resurrection of the dead?

13 But if there is no resurrection of the dead, then Christ has not risen;

14 And if Christ has not risen, then our preaching is in vain (amounts to nothing) and your faith is devoid of truth *and* is fruitless—without effect, empty, imaginary and unfounded.

15 We are even discovered to be misrepresenting God, for we testified of Him that He raised Christ Whom He did not raise, in case it is true that the dead are not raised.

16 For if the dead are not raised, then Christ has not been raised;

17 And if Christ has not been raised, your faith is mere delusion (futile, fruitless), and you are still in your sins—that is, under the control and penalty of sin;

18 And further, those who have died in ([x]spiritual fellowship and union with) Christ have perished—are lost!

19 If we who are [abiding] in Christ have hope only in this life *and* that is all, then we are of all people most miserable *and* to be pitied.

20 But the fact is that Christ, the Messiah, has been raised from the dead, *and He became* the first fruits of those who have fallen asleep [in death].

21 For since [it was] through a man that death [came into the world, it is] also through a Man that the resurrection of the dead [has come].

22 For just as [because of [y]union of nature] in Adam all people die, so also [by virtue of their [y]union of nature] shall all in Christ be made alive.

23 But each in his own rank *and* turn: Christ, the Messiah, [is] the first fruits, then those who are Christ's [own will be resurrected] at His coming.

24 After that comes the end (the completion), when He delivers over the kingdom to God the Father after rendering inoperative *and* abolishing every [other] rule and every authority and power.

25 For [Christ] must be King *and* reign until He has put all [His] enemies under His feet. [Ps. 110:1.]

26 The last enemy to be subdued *and* abolished is death.

27 For He [the Father] has put all things in subjection under His [Christ's] feet. But when it says, All things are put in subjection [under Him], it is evident that He [Himself] is excepted Who does the subjecting of all things to Him. [Ps. 8:6.]

---

w) Vincent's "Word Studies in the New Testament."
x) Thayer.
y) Jamieson, Fausset and Brown.

Living New Testament

6 After that he was seen by more than five hundred Christian brothers at one time, most of whom are still alive, though some have died by now.

7 Then James saw Him and later all the apostles.

8 Last of all I saw Him too, long after the others, as though I had been born almost too late for this.

9 For I am the least worthy of all the apostles, and I shouldn't even be called an apostle at all after the way I treated the church of God.

10 But whatever I am now it is all because God poured out such kindness and grace upon me—and not without results: for I have worked harder than all the other apostles, yet actually I wasn't doing it, but God working in me, to bless me.

11 It makes no difference who worked the hardest, I or they; the important thing is that we preached the Gospel to you, and you believed it.

12 But tell me this! Since you believe what we preach, that *Christ* rose from the dead, why are some of you saying that dead people will never come back to life again?

13 For if there is no resurrection of the dead, then Christ must still be dead.

14 And if He is still dead, then all our preaching is useless and your trust in God is empty, worthless, hopeless;

15 And we apostles are all liars because we have said that God raised Christ from the grave, and of course that isn't true if the dead do not come back to life again.

16 If they don't, then Christ is still dead,

17 And you are very foolish to keep on trusting God to save you, and you are still under condemnation for your sins;

18 In that case all Christians who have died are lost!

19 And if being a Christian is of value to us only now in this life, we are the most miserable of creatures.

20 But the fact is that Christ did actually rise from the dead, and has become the first of millions[2] who will come back to life again some day.

21 Death came into the world because of what one man (Adam) did, and it is because of what this other man (Christ) has done that now there is the resurrection from the dead.

22 Everyone dies because all of us are related to Adam, being members of his sinful race, and wherever there is sin, death results. But all who are related to Christ will rise again.

23 Each, however, in his own turn: Christ rose first; then when Christ comes back, all His people will become alive again.

24 After that the end will come when He will turn the kingdom over to God the Father, having put down all enemies of every kind.

25 For Christ will be King until He has defeated all His enemies,

26 Including the last enemy—death. This too must be defeated and ended.

27 For the rule and authority over all things has been given to Christ by His Father; except of course, Christ does not rule over the Father Himself, who gave Him this power to rule.

[2] Literally, "the first-fruits of them that are asleep."

Revised Standard

peared to more than five hundred brethren
at one time, most of whom are still alive,
though some have fallen asleep. 7Then he
appeared to James, then to all the apostles.
8Last of all, as to one untimely born, he
appeared also to me. 9For I am the least of
the apostles, unfit to be called an apostle,
because I persecuted the church of God.
10But by the grace of God I am what I am,
and his grace toward me was not in vain.
On the contrary, I worked harder than any
of them, though it was not I, but the grace
of God which it with me. 11Whether then it
was I or they, so we preach and so you
believed.

The necessity of the resurrection

12 Now if Christ is preached as raised
from the dead, how can some of you say
that there is no resurrection of the dead?
13But if there is no resurrection of the dead,
then Christ has not been raised; 14if Christ
has not been raised, then our preaching is
in vain and your faith is in vain. 15We are
even found to be misrepresenting God, because we testified of God that he raised
Christ, whom he did not raise if it is true
that the dead are not raised. 16For if the
dead are not raised, then Christ has not been
raised. 17If Christ has not been raised, your
faith is futile and you are still in your sins.
18Then those also who have fallen asleep
in Christ have perished. 19If for this life
only we have hoped in Christ, we are of all
men most to be pitied.

The assurance of the resurrection

20 But in fact Christ has been raised from
the dead, the first fruits of those who have
fallen asleep. 21For as by a man came death,
by a man has come also the resurrection of
the dead. 22For as in Adam all die, so also
in Christ shall all be made alive. 23But each
in his own order: Christ the first fruits, then
at his coming those who belong to Christ.
24Then comes the end, when he delivers the
kingdom to God the Father after destroying
every rule and every authority and power.
25For he must reign until he has put all his
enemies under his feet. 26The last enemy
to be destroyed is death. 27"For God[z] has
put all things in subjection under his feet."
But when it says, "All things are put in
subjection under him," it is plain that he is
excepted who put all things under him.

[z] Greek *he*

King James

28 And when all things shall be subdued unto him, then shall the Son also himself be subject unto him that put all things under him, that God may be all in all.

29 Else what shall they do which are baptized for the dead, if the dead rise not at all? why are they then baptized for the dead?

30 And why stand we in jeopardy every hour?

31 I protest by your rejoicing which I have in Christ Jesus our Lord, I die daily.

32 If after the manner of men I have fought with beasts at Ephesus, what advantageth it me, if the dead rise not? let us eat and drink; for to-morrow we die.

33 Be not deceived: evil communications corrupt good manners.

34 Awake to righteousness, and sin not; for some have not the knowledge of God: I speak *this* to your shame.

35 But some *man* will say, How are the dead raised up? and with what body do they come?

36 *Thou* fool, that which thou sowest is not quickened, except it die:

37 And that which thou sowest, thou sowest not that body that shall be, but bare grain, it may chance of wheat, or of some other *grain:*

38 But God giveth it a body as it hath pleased him, and to every seed his own body.

39 All flesh *is* not the same flesh: but *there is* one *kind of* flesh of men, another flesh of beasts, another of fishes, *and* another of birds.

40 *There are* also celestial bodies, and bodies terrestrial: but the glory of the celestial *is* one, and the *glory* of the terrestrial *is* another.

41 *There is* one glory of the sun, and another glory of the moon, and another glory of the stars: for *one* star differeth from *another* star in glory.

42 So also *is* the resurrection of the dead. It is sown in corruption; it is raised in incorruption:

43 It is sown in dishonour; it is raised in glory: it is sown in weakness; it is raised in power:

44 It is sown a natural body; it is raised a spiritual body. There is a natural body, and there is a spiritual body.

45 And so it is written, The first man Adam was made a living soul; the last Adam *was made* a quickening spirit.

46 Howbeit that *was* not first which is spiritual, but that which is natural; and afterward that which is spiritual.

47 The first man *is* of the earth, earthy: the second man *is* the Lord from heaven.

Amplified

28 However, when everything is subjected to Him, then the Son Himself will also subject Himself to [the Father] Who put all things under Him, so that God may be all in all—that is, be everything to everyone, supreme, the indwelling and controlling factor of life.

29 Otherwise, what do people mean by being [themselves] baptized in behalf of the dead? If the dead are not raised at all, why are people baptized for them?

30 [For that matter], why do I live [dangerously as I do, running such risks that I am] in peril every hour?

31 [I assure you] by the pride which I have in you in (your [z]fellowship and union with) Christ Jesus our Lord, that I die daily—that is, that I face death every day and die to self.

32 What do I gain if, merely from the human point of view, I fought with [wild] beasts at Ephesus? If the dead are not raised [at all], let us eat and drink, for tomorrow we will be dead. [Isa. 22:13.]

33 Do not be so deceived *and* misled! Evil companionships, (communion, associations) corrupt *and* deprave good manners *and* morals *and* character.

34 Awake ([a]from your drunken stupor and return) to sober sense *and* your right minds, and sin no more. For some of you have not the knowledge of God—you are utterly and wilfully and disgracefully ignorant, and continue to be so, lacking the sense of God's presence and all true knowledge of Him. I say this to your shame.

35 But some one will say, How can the dead be raised? With what [kind of] body will they come forth?

36 You foolish man! Every time you plant seed you sow something that does not come to life (germinating, springing up and growing) unless it dies first.

37 Nor is the seed you sow, then in the body which it is going to have [later], but it is a naked kernel, perhaps of wheat or some of the rest of the grains.

38 But God gives to it the body that He plans *and* sees fit, and to each kind of seed a body of his own. [Gen. 1:11.]

39 For all flesh is not the same, but there is one kind for humans, another for beasts, another for birds, and another for fish.

40 There are heavenly bodies [sun, moon and stars] and there are earthly bodies [of men, animals and plants], but the beauty *and* glory of the heavenly bodies is of one kind, while the beauty *and* glory of earthly bodies is a different kind.

41 The sun is glorious in one way, and the moon is glorious in another way, and the stars are glorious in their own (distinctive) way; for one star differs from *and* surpasses another in its beauty *and* brilliance.

42 So it is with the resurrection of the dead. [The body] that is sown is perishable *and* decays, but [the body] that is resurrected is imperishable—immune to decay, immortal. [Dan. 12:3.]

43 It is sown in dishonor *and* humiliation; it is raised in honor *and* glory. It is sown in infirmity *and* weakness; it is resurrected in strength *and* endued with power.

44 It is sown a natural (physical) body; it is raised a supernatural (a spiritual) body. [As surely as] there is a physical body, there is also a spiritual body.

45 Thus it is written, The first man Adam became a living being—an individual personality; the last Adam (Christ) became a life-giving Spirit—restoring the dead to life.

46 But [it is] not the spiritual life which came first, but the physical and then the spiritual.

47 The first man [was] from out of earth, made of dust—earth-minded; the second Man [is] *the Lord* from out of heaven. [Gen. 2:7.]

---

z) Thayer.
a) Vincent.

Living New Testament

28 When Christ has finally won the battle against all His enemies, then He, the Son of God, will put Himself also under His Father's orders, so that God who has given Him the victory over everything else will be utterly supreme.

29 If the dead will not come back to life again, then what point is there in people being baptized for those who are gone? Why do it unless you believe that the dead will some day rise again?

30 And why should we ourselves be continually risking our lives, facing death hour by hour?

31 For it is a fact that I face death daily; that is as true as my pride in your growth in the Lord.

32 And what value was there in fighting wild beasts—those men of Ephesus—if it was only for what I gain in this life down here? If we will never live again after we die, then we might as well go and have ourselves a good time: let us eat, drink, and be merry. What's the difference? For tomorrow we die, and that ends everything!

33 Don't be fooled by those who say such things. If you listen to them you will start acting like them.

34 Get some sense and quit your sinning. For to your shame I say it, some of you are not even Christians at all and have never really known God.[3]

35 But someone may ask, "How will the dead be brought back to life again? What kind of bodies will they have?"

36 What a foolish question! You will find the answer in your own garden! When you put a seed into the ground it doesn't grow into a plant unless it "dies" first.

37 And when the green shoot comes up out of the seed, it is very different from the seed you first planted. For all you put into the ground is a dry little seed of wheat, or whatever it is you are planting.

38 Then God gives it a beautiful new body—just the kind He wants it to have; a different kind of plant grows from each kind of seed.

39 And just as there are different kinds of seeds and plants, so also there are different kinds of flesh. Humans, animals, fish, and birds are all different.

40 The angels[4] in heaven have bodies far different from ours, and the beauty and the glory of their bodies is different from the beauty and the glory of ours.

41 The sun has one kind of glory while the moon and stars have another kind. And the stars differ from each other in their beauty and brightness.

42 In the same way, our earthly bodies which die and decay are different from the bodies we shall have when we come back to life again, for they will never die.

43 The bodies we have now embarrass us for they become sick and die; but they will be full of glory when we come back to life again. Yes, they are weak, dying bodies now, but when we live again they will be full of strength.

44 They are just human bodies at death, but when they come back to life they will be superhuman bodies. For just as there are natural, human bodies, there are also supernatural, spiritual bodies.

45 The Scriptures tell us that the first man, Adam, was given a natural human body[5] but Christ[6] is more[7] than that, for He was life-giving Spirit.

46 First, then, we have these human bodies and later on God gives us spiritual, heavenly bodies.

47 Adam was made from the dust of the earth, but Christ came from heaven above.

---

[3] Or, "there are some who know nothing of God."
[4] Literally, "there are celestial bodies." This may refer to the sun, moon, planets, and stars.
[5] Literally, "was made a living soul."
[6] Literally, "the last Adam."
[7] Implied.

Revised Standard

[28]When all things are subjected to him, then
the Son himself will also be subjected to
him who put all things under him, that God
may be everything to every one.

The logic of the resurrection

29 Otherwise, what do people mean by
being baptized on behalf of the dead? If the
dead are not raised at all, why are people
baptized on their behalf? [30]Why am I in peril
every hour? [31]I protest, brethren, by my
pride in you which I have in Christ Jesus
our Lord, I die every day! [32]What do I gain
if, humanly speaking, I fought with beasts
at Ephesus? If the dead are not raised, "Let
us eat and drink, for tomorrow we die."
[33]Do not be deceived: "Bad company ruins
good morals." [34]Come to your right mind,
and sin no more. For some have no knowledge of God. I say this to your shame.

The nature of the resurrection

35 But some one will ask, "How are
the dead raised? With what kind of body do
they come?" [36]You foolish man! What you
sow does not come to life unless it dies.
[37]And what you sow is not the body which
is to be, but a bare kernel, perhaps of
wheat or of some other grain. [38]But God
gives it a body as he has chosen, and to
each kind of seed its own body. [39]For not all
flesh is alike, but there is one kind for men,
another for animals, another for birds, and
another for fish. [40]There are celestial bodies
and there are terrestrial bodies; but the glory
of the celestial is one, and the glory of the
terrestrial is another. [41]There is one glory
of the sun, and another glory of the moon,
and another glory of the stars; for star differs
from star in glory.

42 So is it with the resurrection of the
dead. What is sown is perishable, what is
raised is imperishable. [43]It is sown in dishonor, it is raised in glory. It is sown in
weakness, it is raised in power. [44]It is sown
a physical body, it is raised a spiritual body.
If there is a physical body, there is also a
spiritual body. [45]Thus it is written, "The first
man Adam became a living being"; the last
Adam became a life-giving spirit. [46]But it is
not the spiritual which is first but the physical, and then the spiritual. [47]The first man
was from the earth, a man of dust; the

King James

48 As *is* the earthy, such *are* they also that are earthy: and as *is* the heavenly, such *are* they also that are heavenly.
49 And as we have borne the image of the earthy, we shall also bear the image of the heavenly.
50 Now this I say, brethren, that flesh and blood cannot inherit the kingdom of God; neither doth corruption inherit incorruption.
51 Behold, I shew you a mystery; We shall not all sleep, but we shall all be changed,
52 In a moment, in the twinkling of an eye, at the last trump: for the trumpet shall sound, and the dead shall be raised incorruptible, and we shall be changed.
53 For this corruptible must put on incorruption, and this mortal *must* put on immortality.
54 So when this corruptible shall have put on incorruption, and this mortal shall have put on immortality, then shall be brought to pass the saying that is written, Death is swallowed up in victory.
55 O death, where *is* thy sting? O grave, where *is* thy victory?
56 The sting of death *is* sin; and the strength of sin *is* the law.
57 But thanks *be* to God, which giveth us the victory through our Lord Jesus Christ.
58 Therefore, my beloved brethren, be ye stedfast, unmoveable, always abounding in the work of the Lord, forasmuch as ye know that your labour is not in vain in the Lord.

Amplified

48 Now those who are made of the dust are like him who was first made of the dust—earth-minded; and as is [the Man] from heaven, so also [are those] who are of heaven—heaven-minded.
49 And just as we have borne the image of the [man] of dust, so shall we *and* so [b]let us also bear the image of the [Man] of heaven.
50 But I tell you this, brethren, flesh and blood cannot (become partakers of eternal salvation and) inherit *or* share in the kingdom of God; nor does the perishable—that which is decaying—inherit *or* share in the imperishable (the immortal).
51 Take notice! I tell you a mystery—a secret truth, an event decreed by the hidden purpose or counsel of God. We shall not all fall asleep [in death], but we shall all be changed (transformed)
52 In a moment, in the twinkling of an eye, at the (sound of the) last trumpet call. For a trumpet will sound, and the dead [in Christ] will be raised imperishable—free and immune from decay—and we shall be changed (transformed).
53 For this perishable [part of us] must put on the imperishable [nature], and this mortal [part of us]—this nature that is capable of dying—must put on immortality (freedom from death).
54 And when this perishable puts on the imperishable and this [that was] capable of dying puts on freedom from death, then shall be fulfilled the Scripture that says, Death is swallowed up (utterly vanquished, [c]forever) in *and* unto victory. [Isa. 25:8.]
55 O death, where is your victory? O death, where is your sting? [Hos. 13:14.]
56 Now sin is the sting of death, and sin exercises its power [d][upon the soul] through [d][the abuse of] the Law.
57 But thanks be to God, Who gives us the victory—making us conquerors—through our Lord Jesus Christ.
58 Therefore, my beloved brethren, be firm (steadfast), immovable, always abounding in the work of the Lord—that is, always being superior (excelling, doing more than enough) in the service of the Lord, knowing *and* being continually aware that your labor in the Lord is not futile—never wasted or to no purpose.

King James

CHAPTER 16

NOW concerning the collection for the saints, as I have given order to the churches of Galatia, even so do ye.
2 Upon the first *day* of the week let every one of you lay by him in store, as *God* hath prospered him, that there be no gatherings when I come.
3 And when I come, whomsoever ye shall approve by *your* letters, them will I send to bring your liberality unto Jerusalem.
4 And if it be meet that I go also, they shall go with me.
5 Now I will come unto you, when I shall pass through Macedonia: for I do pass through Macedonia.
6 And it may be that I will abide, yea, and winter with you, that ye may bring me on my journey whithersoever I go.

Amplified

CHAPTER 16

NOW concerning the money contributed for [the relief of] the saints (God's people): you are to do the same as I directed the churches of Galatia to do.
2 On the first [day] of each week, let everyone of you (personally) put aside something and save it up as he has prospered—in proportion to what he is given—so that no collections will need to be taken after I come.
3 And when I arrive, I will send on those whom you approve *and* authorize with credentials to carry your gift (of charity) to Jerusalem.
4 If it seems worthwhile that I should go too, they will accompany me.
5 After passing through Macedonia, I will visit you, for I intend [only] to pass through Macedonia;
6 But it may be that I will stay with you [for a while], perhaps even spend the winter, so that you may bring me forward [on my journey] to wherever I may go.

---

b) Many ancient authorities read "let us."
c) Vincent's "Word Studies in the New Testament."
d) Thayer.

Living New Testament

48 Every human being has a body just like Adam's, made of dust, but all who become Christ's will have the same kind of body as His—a body from heaven.

49 Just as each of us now has a body like Adam's, so we shall some day have a body like Christ's.

50 I tell you this, my brothers: an earthly body made of flesh and blood cannot get into God's kingdom. These perishable bodies of ours are not the right kind to live forever.

51 But I am telling you this strange and wonderful secret: we shall not all die, but we shall all be given new bodies!

52 It will all happen in a moment, in the twinkling of an eye, when the last trumpet is blown. For there will be a trumpet blast from the sky[7] and all the Christians who have died will suddenly become alive with new bodies that will never, never die; and then we who are still alive shall suddenly have new bodies too.

53 For our earthly bodies, the ones we have now that can die, must be transformed into heavenly bodies that cannot perish but will live forever.

54 When this happens, then at last this Scripture will come true—"Death is swallowed up in victory."

55, 56 O death, where then your victory? Where then your sting? For sin—the sting that causes death—will all be gone; and the law, which reveals our sins, will no longer be our judge.

57 How we thank God for all of this! It is He who makes us victorious through Jesus Christ our Lord!

58 So my dear brothers, since future victory is sure, be strong and steady, always abounding in the Lord's work, for you know that nothing you do for the Lord is ever wasted as it would be if there were no resurrection.

Revised Standard

second man is from heaven. 48As was the
man of dust, so are those who are of the
dust; and as is the man of heaven, so are
those who are of heaven. 49Just as we have
borne the image of the man of dust, we
shall[a] also bear the image of the man of
heaven. 50I tell you this, brethren: flesh and
blood cannot inherit the kingdom of God,
nor does the perishable inherit the imperishable.

The triumph of the resurrection

51 Lo! I tell you a mystery. We shall not
all sleep, but we shall all be changed, 52in
a moment, in the twinkling of an eye, at
the last trumpet. For the trumpet will sound,
and the dead will be raised imperishable, and
we shall be changed. 53For this perishable
nature must put on the imperishable, and this
mortal nature must put on immortality.
54When the perishable puts on the imperishable, and the mortal puts on immortality,
then shall come to pass the saying that is
written:

"Death is swallowed up in victory."
55 "O death, where is thy victory?
O death, where is thy sting?"
56 The sting of death is sin, and the power
of sin is the law. 57But thanks be to God,
who gives us the victory through our Lord
Jesus Christ.

58 Therefore, my beloved brethren, be
steadfast, immovable, always abounding in
the work of the Lord, knowing that in the
Lord your labor is not in vain.

CHAPTER 16

Now here are the directions about the money you are collecting to send to the Christians in Jerusalem,[1] (and, by the way, these are the same directions I gave to the churches in Galatia).

2 Every Sunday each of you should put aside something from what you have earned during the week, and use it for this offering. The amount depends on how much the Lord has helped you earn. Don't wait until I get there and then try to collect it all at once.

3 When I come I will send your loving gift with a letter to Jerusalem, to be taken there by trustworthy messengers you yourselves will choose.

4 And if it seems wise for me to go along too, then we can travel together.

5 I am coming to visit you after I have been to Macedonia first, but I will be staying there only for a little while.

6 It could be that I will stay longer with you, perhaps all winter, and then you can send me on to my next destination.

Implied.
Implied.

The contribution for the poor

16 Now concerning the contribution for
the saints: as I directed the churches
of Galatia, so you also are to do. 2On the
first day of every week, each of you is to
put something aside and store it up, as he
may prosper, so that contributions need not
be made when I come. 3And when I arrive,
I will send those whom you accredit by
letter to carry your gift to Jerusalem. 4If it
seems advisable that I should go also, they
will accompany me.

Paul's itinerary

5 I will visit you after passing through
Macedonia, for I intend to pass through
Macedonia, 6and perhaps I will stay with you
or even spend the winter, so that you may
speed me on my journey, wherever I go.

[a] Other ancient authorities read *let us*

King James

7 For I will not see you now by the way; but I trust to tarry a while with you, if the Lord permit.

8 But I will tarry at Ephesus until Pentecost.

9 For a great door and effectual is opened unto me, and *there are* many adversaries.

10 Now if Timotheus come, see that he may be with you without fear: for he worketh the work of the Lord, as I also *do*.

11 Let no man therefore despise him: but conduct him forth in peace, that he may come unto me: for I look for him with the brethren.

12 As touching *our* brother Apollos, I greatly desired him to come unto you with the brethren: but his will was not at all to come at this time; but he will come when he shall have convenient time.

13 Watch ye, stand fast in the faith, quit you like men, be strong.

14 Let all your things be done with charity.

15 I beseech you, brethren, (ye know the house of Stephanas, that it is the firstfruits of Achaia, and *that* they have addicted themselves to the ministry of the saints,)

16 That ye submit yourselves unto such, and to every one that helpeth with *us*, and laboureth.

17 I am glad of the coming of Stephanas and Fortunatus and Achaicus: for that which was lacking on your part they have supplied.

18 For they have refreshed my spirit and yours: therefore acknowledge ye them that are such.

19 The churches of Asia salute you. Aquila and Priscilla salute you much in the Lord, with the church that is in their house.

20 All the brethren greet you. Greet ye one another with an holy kiss.

21 The salutation of *me* Paul with mine own hand.

22 If any man love not the Lord Jesus Christ, let him be Anathema Maranatha.

23 The grace of our Lord Jesus Christ *be* with you.

24 My love *be* with you all in Christ Jesus. Amen.

¶ The first *epistle* to the Corinthians was written from Philippi by Stephanas, and Fortunatus, and Achaicus, and Timotheus.

Amplified

7 For I am unwilling to see you right now [just] in passing, but I hope later to remain for some time with you, if the Lord permits.

8 I will remain in Ephesus [however] until Pentecost,

9 For a wide door of opportunity for effectual [service] has opened to me [there]—one great and promising—and many adversaries.

10 When Timothy arrives, look to it that [you put him at ease, so that] he may be fearless among you, for he is [devotedly] doing the Lord's work, just as I am.

11 [So see to it that] no one despises him, *or* treats him as if he were of no account *or* slights him. But send him off (cordially, speed him on his way) in peace, for I am expecting him [to come along] with the other brethren.

12 As for our brother Apollos, I have urgently encouraged him to visit you with the other brethren, but it was not at all (his will, or) [e]God's will that he should go now. He will come when he has opportunity.

13 Be alert *and* on your guard; stand firm in your faith [that is, in [f]your conviction respecting man's relationship to God and divine things, keeping the trust and holy fervor born of faith and a part of it]. Act like men *and* be courageous; grow in strength! [Ps. 31:24.]

14 Let everything you do be done in love [true love to God and man as inspired by God's love for us].

15 Now, brethren, you know that the household of Stephanas were the first converts *and* our first fruits in Achaia [most of Greece], and how they have consecrated *and* devoted themselves to the service of the saints (God's people).

16 I urge you to pay all deference to such leaders *and* to enlist under them *and* be subject to them, as well as to every one who joins *and* co-operates [with you] *and* labors earnestly.

17 I am happy because Stephanas and Fortunatus and Achaicus have come [to me], for they have made up for your absence.

18 For they gave me [g]respite from labor *and* rested me *and* refreshed my spirit as well as yours. Deeply appreciate *and* thoroughly know *and* fully recognize such men.

19 The churches of Asia send greetings *and* best wishes. Aquila and Prisca, together with the church [that meets] in their house, send you their hearty greetings in the Lord.

20 All the brethren wish to be remembered to you *and* wish you well. Greet one another with a holy kiss.

21 I, Paul, [add this final] greeting with my own hand.

22 If any one does not love the Lord—does not have a friendly affection for Him and is not kindly disposed toward Him—he shall be accursed! Our Lord will come! (Maranatha!)

23 The grace (favor and spiritual blessing) of our Lord Jesus *Christ* be with you.

24 My love [that true love growing out of sincere devotion to God] be with you all in Christ Jesus. *Amen—so be it.*

---

e) "His" may refer to Apollos, but probably means "God's."
f) Thayer.
g) Abbott-Smith.

Living New Testament

7 This time I don't want to make just a passing visit and then go right on; I want to come and stay awhile, if the Lord will let me.

8 I will be staying here at Ephesus until the holiday of Pentecost,

9 For there is a wide open door for me to preach and teach here. So much is happening, but there are many enemies.

10 If Timothy comes make him feel at home, for he is doing the Lord's work just as I am.

11 Don't let anyone despise or ignore him [because he is young[2]], but send him back to me happy with his time among you; I am looking forward to seeing him soon, along with the others who are returning.

12 I begged Apollos to visit you along with the others, but he thought that it was not at all God's will for him to go now. He will be seeing you later on when he has the opportunity.

13 Keep your eyes open for spiritual danger; stand true to the Lord; act like men; be strong;

14 And whatever you do, do it with kindness and love.

15 Do you remember Stephanas and his family? They were the first to become Christians in Greece and they are spending their lives helping and serving Christians everywhere.

16 Please follow their instructions and do everything you can to help them as well as all others like them who work hard at your side with such real devotion.

17 I am so glad that Stephanas, Fortunatus, and Achaicus have arrived here for a visit. They have been making up for the help you aren't here to give me.

18 They have cheered me greatly and have been a wonderful encouragement to me, as I am sure they were to you, too. I hope you properly appreciate the work of such men as these.

19 The churches here in Asia send you their loving greetings. Aquila and Priscilla send you their love and so do all the others who meet in their home for their church service.

20 All the friends here have asked me to say "hello" to you for them. And give each other a loving handshake when you meet.

21 I will write these final words of this letter with my own hand:

22 If anyone does not love the Lord, that person is cursed.

Lord Jesus, come!

23 May the love and favor of the Lord Jesus Christ rest upon you.

24 My love to all of you, for we all belong to Christ Jesus.

Sincerely,
Paul

Implied from I Timothy 4:12.

Revised Standard

7 For I do not want to see you now just in
passing; I hope to spend some time with
you, if the Lord permits. 8 But I will stay
in Ephesus until Pentecost, 9 for a wide door
for effective work has opened to me, and
there are many adversaries.

10 When Timothy comes, see that you
put him at ease among you, for he is doing
the work of the Lord, as I am. 11 So let no
one despise him. Speed him on his way in
peace, that he may return to me; for I am
expecting him with the brethren.

12 As for our brother Apollos, I strongly
urged him to visit you with the other brethren, but it was not at all his will[b] to come
now. He will come when he has opportunity.

Concluding message

13 Be watchful, stand firm in your faith,
be courageous, be strong. 14 Let all that you
do be done in love.

15 Now, brethren, you know that the
household of Stephanas were the first converts in Achaia, and they have devoted
themselves to the service of the saints; 16 I
urge you to be subject to such men and to
every fellow worker and laborer. 17 I rejoice
at the coming of Stephanas and Fortunatus
and Achaicus, because they have made up
for your absence; 18 for they refreshed my
spirit as well as yours. Give recognition to
such men.

19 The churches of Asia send greetings.
Aquila and Prisca, together with the church
in their house, send you hearty greetings
in the Lord. 20 All the brethren send greetings. Greet one another with a holy kiss.

21 I, Paul, write this greeting with my
own hand. 22 If any man has no love for the
Lord, let him be accursed. Our Lord, come![c]
23 The grace of the Lord Jesus be with you.
24 My love be with you all in Christ Jesus.
Amen.

---

[b] Or *God's will for him*
[c] Greek *Maranatha*

King James

THE SECOND EPISTLE OF PAUL THE APOSTLE

TO THE

Corinthians

CHAPTER 1

PAUL, an apostle of Jesus Christ by the will of God, and Timothy *our* brother, unto the church of God which is at Corinth, with all the saints which are in all Achaia:

2 Grace *be* to you and peace from God our Father, and *from* the Lord Jesus Christ.

3 Blessed *be* God, even the Father of our Lord Jesus Christ, the Father of mercies, and the God of all comfort;

4 Who comforteth us in all our tribulation, that we may be able to comfort them which are in any trouble, by the comfort wherewith we ourselves are comforted of God.

5 For as the sufferings of Christ abound in us, so our consolation also aboundeth by Christ.

6 And whether we be afflicted, *it is* for your consolation and salvation, which is effectual in the enduring of the same sufferings which we also suffer: or whether we be comforted, *it is* for your consolation and salvation.

7 And our hope of you *is* stedfast, knowing, that as ye are partakers of the sufferings, so *shall ye be* also of the consolation.

8 For we would not, brethren, have you ignorant of our trouble which came to us in Asia, that we were pressed out of measure, above strength, insomuch that we despaired even of life:

9 But we had the sentence of death in ourselves, that we should not trust in ourselves, but in God which raiseth the dead:

10 Who delivered us from so great a death, and doth deliver: in whom we trust that he will yet deliver *us;*

11 Ye also helping together by prayer for us, that for the gift *bestowed* upon us by the means of many persons thanks may be given by many on our behalf.

Amplified

THE SECOND LETTER OF PAUL TO THE

Corinthians

CHAPTER 1

PAUL, an apostle (a special messenger) of Christ Jesus by the will of God, and Timothy [our] brother, to the church (assembly) of God which is at Corinth, and to all the saints (the people of God) throughout Achaia [most of Greece]:

2 Grace (favor and spiritual blessing) to you and (heart) peace from God our Father and the Lord Jesus Christ, the Messiah, the Anointed One.

3 Blessed [be] the God and Father of our Lord Jesus Christ, the Father of sympathy (pity and mercies) and the God [Who is the Source] of every consolation *and* comfort *and* encouragement;

4 Who consoles *and* comforts *and* encourages us in every trouble (calamity and affliction), so that we may also be able to console (comfort and encourage) those who are in any kind of trouble *or* distress, with the consolation (comfort and encouragement) with which we ourselves are consoled *and* comforted *and* encouraged by God.

5 For just as Christ's ([a]own) sufferings fall to our lot [a][as they overflow upon His disciples, and we share and experience them] abundantly, so through Christ comfort *and* consolation *and* encouragement are also [shared and experienced] abundantly by us.

6 But if we are troubled (afflicted and distressed), it is for your comfort (consolation and encouragement) and [for your] salvation; and if we are comforted (consoled and encouraged), it is for your comfort *and* consolation *and* encouragement, which work [in you when you] patiently endure the same evils (misfortunes and calamities) that we also suffer *and* undergo.

7 And our hope for you—that is, our joyful and confident expectation of good for you—is ever unwavering, (assured and unshaken); for we know that just as you share *and* are partners in [our] sufferings *and* calamities, you also share *and* are partners in [our] comfort (consolation and encouragement).

8 For we do not want you to be uninformed, brethren, about the affliction *and* oppressing distress which befell us in [the province of] Asia, how we were so utterly and unbearably weighed down *and* crushed that we despaired even of life [itself].

9 Indeed, we felt within ourselves that we had received the [very] sentence of death; but that was to keep us from trusting *and* depending on ourselves instead of on God Who raises the dead.

10 [For it is He] Who rescued *and* saved us from such a perilous death, and He will still rescue *and* save us; in *and* on Him we have set our hope (our joyful and confident expectation) that He will again deliver us from danger *and* destruction *and* [b]draw [us] to Himself,

11 While you also co-operate by your prayers for us—helping *and* laboring together with us. Thus the lips of many persons Godward turned will [eventually] give thanks on our behalf for the grace (the blessing of deliverance) granted us at the request of the many who have prayed.

---

a) Vincent's "Word Studies in the New Testament."
b) Primary meaning, "to draw to one's self." (Thayer.)

Living New Testament

II Corinthians

CHAPTER 1

Dear Friends,
This letter is from me, Paul, appointed by God to
be Jesus Christ's messenger; and from our dear brother
Timothy. We are writing to all of you Christians there in
Corinth and throughout Greece.[1]
2 May God our Father and the Lord Jesus Christ
mightily bless each one of you, and give you peace.
3, 4 What a wonderful God we have—He is the Father
of our Lord Jesus Christ, the source of every mercy, and
the one who so wonderfully comforts and strengthens us
in our hardships and trials. And why does He do this? So
that when others are troubled, needing our sympathy and
encouragement, we can pass on to them this same help and
comfort God has given us.
5 You can be sure that the more we undergo sufferings
for Christ, the more He will shower us with His comfort
and encouragement.
6, 7 We are in deep trouble for bringing you God's comfort and salvation. But in our trouble God had comforted
us—and this, too, to help you: to show you from our
personal experience how God will tenderly comfort you
when you undergo these same sufferings. He will give you
the strength to endure.
8 I think you ought to know, dear brothers, about the
hard time we went through in Asia. We were really
crushed, and overwhelmed, and feared we would never
live through it.
9 We felt we were doomed to die and saw how powerless we were to help ourselves; but that was good, for then
we put everything into the hands of God, who alone could
save us, for He can even raise the dead.
10 And He did help us, and saved us from a terrible
death; yes, and we expect Him to do it again and again.
11 But you must help us too, by praying for us. For
much thanks and praise will go to God from you who see
His wonderful answers to your prayers for our safety!

[1] Or, "throughout Achaia."

Revised Standard

THE SECOND LETTER OF PAUL TO THE

Corinthians

Introduction

1 Paul, an apostle of Christ Jesus by the
will of God, and Timothy our brother.
To the church of God which is at Corinth,
with all the saints who are in the whole of
Achaia:
2 Grace to you and peace from God our
Father and the Lord Jesus Christ.

3 Blessed be the God and Father of our
Lord Jesus Christ, the Father of mercies
and God of all comfort, 4 who comforts us
in all our affliction, so that we may be able
to comfort those who are in any affliction,
with the comfort with which we ourselves
are comforted by God. 5 For as we share
abundantly in Christ's sufferings, so through
Christ we share abundantly in comfort too.[a]
6 If we are afflicted, it is for your comfort
and salvation; and if we are comforted, it
is for your comfort, which you experience
when you patiently endure the same sufferings that we suffer. 7 Our hope for you is
unshaken; for we know that as you share
in our sufferings, you will also share in our
comfort.
8 For we do not want you to be ignorant,
brethren, of the affliction we experienced in
Asia; for we were so utterly, unbearably
crushed that we despaired of life itself.
9 Why, we felt that we had received the
sentence of death; but that was to make
us rely not on ourselves but on God who
raises the dead; 10 he delivered us from so
deadly a peril, and he will deliver us; on
him we have set our hope that he will deliver us again. 11 You also must help us by
prayer, so that many will give thanks on our
behalf for the blessing granted us in answer
to many prayers.

[a] Or *For as the sufferings of Christ abound for us, so also our comfort abounds through Christ*

King James

12 For our rejoicing is this, the testimony of our conscience, that in simplicity and godly sincerity, not with fleshly wisdom, but by the grace of God, we have had our conversation in the world, and more abundantly to you-ward.

13 For we write none other things unto you, than what ye read or acknowledge; and I trust ye shall acknowledge even to the end;

14 As also ye have acknowledged us in part, that we are your rejoicing, even as ye also *are* ours in the day of the Lord Jesus.

15 And in this confidence I was minded to come unto you before, that ye might have a second benefit;

16 And to pass by you into Macedonia, and to come again out of Macedonia unto you, and of you to be brought on my way toward Judæa.

17 When I therefore was thus minded, did I use lightness? or the things that I purpose, do I purpose according to the flesh, that with me there should be yea yea, and nay nay?

18 But *as* God *is* true, our word toward you was not yea and nay.

19 For the Son of God, Jesus Christ, who was preached among you by us, *even* by me and Silvanus and Timotheus, was not yea and nay, but in him was yea.

20 For all the promises of God in him *are* yea, and in him Amen, unto the glory of God by us.

21 Now he which stablisheth us with you in Christ, and hath anointed us, *is* God;

22 Who hath also sealed us, and given the earnest of the Spirit in our hearts.

23 Moreover I call God for a record upon my soul, that to spare you I came not as yet unto Corinth.

24 Not for that we have dominion over your faith, but are helpers of your joy: for by faith ye stand.

Amplified

12 It is a reason for pride *and* exultation to which our conscience testifies, that we have conducted ourselves in the world [generally] and more especially toward you, with devout *and* pure motives and godly sincerity, not in fleshly wisdom but by the grace of God—the unmerited favor and [c]merciful kindness [by which God exerting His holy influence upon souls, turns them to Christ, and keeps, strengthens and increases them in Christian virtues].

13 For we write you nothing else but simply what you can read and understand—that is, there is no double meaning to what we say—and I hope that you will become thoroughly acquainted [with [c]divine things] *and* know *and* understand [them] accurately *and* well to the end,

14 [Just] as you have (already) partially known *and* understood *and* acknowledged us *and* recognized that you can [honestly] be proud of us, even as we [can be proud] of you on the day of our Lord Jesus.

15 It was with assurance of this that I wanted *and* planned to visit you first [of all], so that you might have a double *favor and* token of grace (good will).

16 [I wanted] to visit you on my way to Macedonia, and [then] to come again to you [on my return trip] from Macedonia and have you send me forward on my way to Judea.

17 Now because I changed my original plan was I being unstable *and* capricious? Or what I plan do I plan according to the flesh—like a worldly man—ready to say Yes, yes, [when it may mean] No, no?

18 As surely as God is trustworthy *and* faithful *and* means what He says, our speech *and* message to you have not been Yes [that might mean] No.

19 For the Son of God, Christ Jesus, the Messiah, Who has been preached among you by us, by myself, Silvanus and Timothy, was not Yes and No; but in Him it is [always the divine] Yes.

20 For as many as are the promises of God, they all find their Yes (answer) in Him (Christ). For this reason we also utter the Amen (so be it) to God through Him—that is, in His Person and by His agency—to the glory of God.

21 But it is God Who confirms *and* makes us steadfast *and* establishes us (in joint fellowship) with you in Christ, and has consecrated *and* anointed us—[d]enduing us with the gifts of the Holy Spirit.

22 [He has also appropriated and acknowledged us as His], putting His seal upon us and giving us His (Holy) Spirit in our hearts as the security deposit *and* guarantee [of the fulfillment of His promise].

23 But I call upon God as my soul's witness, it was to avoid hurting you that I refrained from coming to Corinth;

24 Not that we have dominion [over you] *and* lord it over your faith, but (rather that we work with you as) fellow laborers [to promote] your joy, for in [your] faith [that is, [e]in your strong and welcome conviction or belief that Jesus is the Messiah, through Whom we obtain eternal salvation in the kingdom of God] you stand firm.

---

c) Thayer's "Greek-English Lexicon of the New Testament—Grimm."
d) Thayer.
e) Cf. Westcott on I John 2:20.

Living New Testament

12 We are so glad that we can say with utter honesty that in all our dealings we have been pure and sincere, quietly depending upon the Lord for His help, and not on our own skills. And that is even more true, if possible, about the way we have acted toward you.

13, 14 My letters have been straightforward and sincere; nothing is written between the lines! And even though you don't know me very well (I hope someday you will), I want you to try to accept me and be proud of me, as you already are to some extent; just as I shall be of you on that day when our Lord Jesus comes back again.

15, 16 It was because I was so sure of your understanding and trust that I planned to stop and see you on my way to Macedonia, as well as afterwards when I returned, so that I could be a double blessing to you and so that you could send me on my way to Judea.

17 Then why, you may be asking, did I change my plan? Hadn't I really made up my mind yet? Or am I like a man of the world who says "yes" when he really means "no"?

18 Never! As surely as God is true, I am not that sort of person. My "yes" means "yes."

19 Timothy and Silvanus and I have been telling you about Jesus Christ the Son of God. He isn't one to say "yes" when He means "no." He always does exactly what He says.

20 He carries out and fulfills all of God's promises, no matter how many of them there are; and we have told everyone how faithful He is, giving glory to His name.

21 It is this God who has made you and me into faithful Christians and commissioned us apostles to preach the Good News.

22 He has put His brand upon us—His mark of ownership—and given us His Holy Spirit in our hearts as guarantee that we belong to Him, and as the first installment of all that He is going to give us.

23 I call upon this God to witness against me if I am not telling the absolute truth: the reason I haven't come to visit you yet is that I don't want to sadden you with a severe rebuke.

24 When I come, although I can't do much to help your faith, for it is strong already, I want to be able to do something about your joy: I want to make you happy, not sad.

Revised Standard

Paul's change of plans

12 For our boast is this, the testimony
of our conscience that we have behaved in
the world, and still more toward you, with
holiness and godly sincerity, not by earthly
wisdom but by the grace of God. 13For we
write you nothing but what you can read
and understand; I hope you will understand
fully, 14as you have understood in part,
that you can be proud of us as we can be
of you, on the day of the Lord Jesus.
15 Because I was sure of this, I wanted
to come to you first, so that you might
have a double pleasure;[b] 16I wanted to visit
you on my way back to Macedonia, and to
come back to you from Macedonia and have
you send me on my way to Judea. 17Was I
vacillating when I wanted to do this? Do I
make my plans like a worldly man, ready
to say Yes and No at once? 18As surely as
God is faithful, our word to you has not
been Yes and No. 19For the Son of God,
Jesus Christ, whom we preached among you,
Silvanus and Timothy and I, was not Yes
and No; but in him it is always Yes. 20For
all the promises of God find their Yes in
him. That is why we utter the Amen through
him, to the glory of God. 21But it is God
who establishes us with you in Christ, and
has commissioned us; 22he has put his seal
upon us and given us his Spirit in our hearts
as a guarantee.
23 But I call God to witness against
me—it was to spare you that I refrained
from coming to Corinth. 24Not that we lord
it over your faith; we work with you for
your joy, for you stand firm in your faith.

[b] Other ancient authorities read *favor*

King James

CHAPTER 2

BUT I determined this with myself; that I would not come again to you in heaviness.

2 For if I make you sorry, who is he then that maketh me glad, but the same which is made sorry by me?

3 And I wrote this same unto you, lest, when I came; I should have sorrow from them of whom I ought to rejoice; having confidence in you all, that my joy is *the joy* of you all.

4 For out of much affliction and anguish of heart I wrote unto you with many tears; not that ye should be grieved, but that ye might know the love which I have more abundantly unto you.

5 But if any have caused grief, he hath not grieved me, but in part: that I may not overcharge you all.

6 Sufficient to such a man *is* this punishment, which *was inflicted* of many.

7 So that contrariwise ye *ought* rather to forgive *him*, and comfort *him*, lest perhaps such a one should be swallowed up with overmuch sorrow.

8 Wherefore I beseech you that ye would confirm *your* love toward him.

9 For to this end also did I write, that I might know the proof of you, whether ye be obedient in all things.

10 To whom ye forgive any thing, I *forgive* also: for if I forgave any thing, to whom I forgave *it*, for your sakes *forgave I it* in the person of Christ;

11 Lest Satan should get an advantage of us: for we are not ignorant of his devices.

12 Furthermore, when I came to Troas to *preach* Christ's gospel, and a door was opened unto me of the Lord,

13 I had no rest in my spirit, because I found not Titus my brother: but taking my leave of them, I went from thence into Macedonia.

14 Now thanks *be* unto God, which always causeth us to triumph in Christ, and maketh manifest the savour of his knowledge by us in every place.

15 For we are unto God a sweet savour of Christ, in them that are saved, and in them that perish:

16 To the one *we are* the savour of death unto death; and to the other the savour of life unto life. And who *is* sufficient for these things?

17 For we are not as many, which corrupt the word of God: but as of sincerity, but as of God, in the sight of God speak we in Christ.

Amplified

CHAPTER 2

BUT I definitely made up my mind not to grieve you with another painful *and* distressing visit.

2 For if I cause you pain [with merited rebuke], who is there to provide me enjoyment but the [very] one whom I have grieved *and* made sad?

3 And I wrote the same to you so that when I came I might not be myself pained by those who are the [very] ones who ought to make me glad, for I trusted in you all *and* felt confident that my joy would be shared by all of you.

4 For I wrote you out of great sorrow and deep distress (with mental torture and anxiety) of heart, [yes, and] with many tears, not to cause you pain but in order to make you realize the overflowing love that I continue increasingly to have for you.

5 But if some one [the one among you who committed incest] has caused [all this] grief *and* pain, he has caused it not to me, but in some measure, not to put it too severely, [he has distressed] all of you.

6 For such a one this censure by the majority [which he has received is] sufficient [punishment].

7 So [instead of further rebuke, now] you should rather turn *and* (graciously) forgive and comfort *and* encourage [him], to keep him from being overwhelmed by excessive sorrow *and* despair.

8 I therefore beg you to reinstate him in your affections *and* assure him by your love for him;

9 For this is my purpose in writing you, to test your attitude *and* see if you would stand the test, whether you are obedient *and* altogether agreeable [to following my orders] in everything.

10 If you forgive any one anything, I too forgive that one; and what I have forgiven, if I have forgiven anything, has been for your sakes in the presence [and with the approval] of Christ, the Messiah,

11 To keep Satan from getting the advantage over us; for we are not ignorant of his wiles *and* intentions.

12 Now when I arrived at Troas [to preach] the good news (the Gospel) of Christ, a door of opportunity was opened for me in the Lord,

13 Yet my spirit could not rest (relax, get relief) because I did not find my brother Titus there. So I took leave from them *and* departed for Macedonia.

14 But thanks be to God, Who in Christ always leads us in triumph—as trophies of Christ's victory—and through us spreads *and* makes evident the fragrance of the knowledge of God everywhere,

15 For we are the sweet fragrance of Christ [which exhales] unto God, [discernible alike] among those who are being saved *and* among those who are perishing;

16 To the latter it is an aroma [wafted] from death to death—a fatal odor, the smell of doom; to the former it is an aroma from life to life—a vital fragrance, living and fresh. And who is qualified (fit and sufficient) for these things?—Who is able for such a ministry? [We?]

17 For we are not, like so many (as hucksters, tavern keepers, making a trade of) peddling God's Word—short-measuring and adulterating the divine message; but as [men] of sincerity *and* the purest motive, commissioned *and* sent by God, we speak [His message] in Christ, the Messiah, in the [very] sight *and* presence of God.

Living New Testament

CHAPTER 2

No," I said to myself, "I won't do it. I'll not make them unhappy with another painful visit."

2 For if I make you sad, who is going to make me happy? You are the ones to do it, and how can you if I cause you pain?

3 That is why I wrote as I did in my last letter, so that you will get things straightened out before I come.[1] Then, when I do come, I will not be made sad by the very ones who ought to give me greatest joy. I felt sure that your happiness was so bound up in mine that you would not be happy either, unless I came with joy.

4 Oh, how I hated to write that letter! It almost broke my heart and I tell you honestly that I cried over it. I didn't want to hurt you but I had to show you how very much I loved you and cared about what was happening to you.

5, 6 Remember that the man I wrote about, who caused all the trouble, has not caused sorrow to me as much as to all the rest of you—though I certainly have my share in it too. I don't want to be harder on him than I should. He has been punished enough by your united disapproval.

7 Now it is time to forgive him and comfort him. Otherwise he may become so bitter and discouraged that he won't be able to recover.

8 Please show him now that you still do love him very much.

9 I wrote to you as I did so that I could find out how far you would go in obeying me.

10 When you forgive anyone, I do too. And whatever I have forgiven (to the extent that this affected me too) has been by Christ's authority, and for your good.

11 A further reason for forgiveness is to keep from being outsmarted by Satan; for we know what he is trying to do.

12 Well, when I got as far as the city of Troas, the Lord gave me tremendous opportunities to preach the Gospel.

13 But Titus, my dear brother, wasn't there to meet me and I couldn't rest, wondering where he was and what had happened to him. So I said good-bye and went right on to Macedonia to try to find him.

14 But thanks be to God! For through what Christ has done, He has triumphed over us so that now wherever we go He uses us to tell others about the Lord and to spread the Gospel like a sweet perfume.

15 As far as God is concerned there is a sweet, wholesome fragrance in our lives. It is the fragrance of Christ within us, an aroma to both the saved and the unsaved all around us.

16 To those who are not being saved, we seem a fearful smell of death and doom, while to those who know Christ we are a life-giving perfume. But who is adequate for such a task as this?

17 Only those who, like ourselves, are men of integrity, sent by God, speaking with Christ's power, with God's eye upon us. We are not like those hucksters—and there are many of them—whose idea in getting out the Gospel is to make a good living out of it.

[1] Implied.

Revised Standard

2 For I made up my mind not to make you
another painful visit. [2]For if I cause
you pain, who is there to make me glad
but the one whom I have pained? [3]And I
wrote as I did, so that when I came I might
not be pained by those who should have
made me rejoice, for I felt sure of all of
you, that my joy would be the joy of you
all. [4]For I wrote you out of much affliction
and anguish of heart and with many tears,
not to cause you pain but to let you know
the abundant love that I have for you.

Forgiveness of an offender

5 But if any one caused pain, he has
caused it not to me, but in some measure—
not to put it too severely—to you all. [6]For
such a one this punishment by the majority
is enough; [7]so you should rather turn to
forgive and comfort him, or he may be
overwhelmed by excessive sorrow. [8]So I beg
you to reaffirm your love for him. [9]For this
is why I wrote, that I might test you and
know whether you are obedient in everything. [10]Any one whom you forgive, I also
forgive. What I have forgiven, if I have
forgiven anything, has been for your sake
in the presence of Christ, [11]to keep Satan
from gaining the advantage over us; for we
are not ignorant of his designs.

A triumphant ministry

12 When I came to Troas to preach the
gospel of Christ, a door was opened for me
in the Lord; [13]but my mind could not rest
because I did not find my brother Titus
there. So I took leave of them and went
on to Macedonia.

14 But thanks be to God, who in Christ
always leads us in triumph, and through us
spreads the fragrance of the knowledge of
him everywhere. [15]For we are the aroma
of Christ to God among those who are being saved and among those who are perishing, [16]to one a fragrance from death to
death, to the other a fragrance from life to
life. Who is sufficient for these things? [17]For
we are not, like so many, peddlers of God's
word; but as men of sincerity, as commissioned by God, in the sight of God we speak
in Christ.

King James

CHAPTER 3

DO we begin again to commend ourselves? or need we, as some *others*, epistles of commendation to you, or *letters* of commendation from you?

2 Ye are our epistle written in our hearts, known and read of all men:

3 *Forasmuch as ye are* manifestly declared to be the epistle of Christ ministered by us, written not with ink, but with the Spirit of the living God; not in tables of stone, but in fleshy tables of the heart.

4 And such trust have we through Christ to God-ward:

5 Not that we are sufficient of ourselves to think any thing as of ourselves; but our sufficiency *is* of God;

6 Who also hath made us able ministers of the new testament; not of the letter, but of the spirit: for the letter killeth, but the spirit giveth life.

7 But if the ministration of death, written *and* engraven in stones, was glorious, so that the children of Israel could not stedfastly behold the face of Moses for the glory of his countenance; which *glory* was to be done away:

8 How shall not the ministration of the spirit be rather glorious?

9 For if the ministration of condemnation *be* glory, much more doth the ministration of righteousness exceed in glory.

10 For even that which was made glorious had no glory in this respect, by reason of the glory that excelleth.

11 For if that which is done away *was* glorious, much more that which remaineth *is* glorious.

12 Seeing then that we have such hope, we use great plainness of speech:

13 And not as Moses, *which* put a veil over his face, that the children of Israel could not stedfastly look to the end of that which is abolished:

14 But their minds were blinded: for until this day remaineth the same veil untaken away in the reading of the old testament; which *veil* is done away in Christ.

15 But even unto this day, when Moses is read, the veil is upon their heart.

16 Nevertheless when it shall turn to the Lord, the veil shall be taken away.

17 Now the Lord is that Spirit: and where the Spirit of the Lord *is*, there *is* liberty.

Amplified

CHAPTER 3

ARE we starting to commend ourselves again? Or we do not, as some [false teachers], need written credentials *or* letters of recommendation to you or from you, [do we]?

2 [No, you] yourselves are our letter of recommendation (our credentials), written in [f]your hearts, to be (perceived, recognized,) known and read by everybody.

3 You show *and* make obvious that you are a letter from Christ delivered by us, not written with ink but with [the] Spirit of [the] living God, not on tablets of stone but on tablets of human hearts. [Exod. 24:12; 31:18; 32:15, 16; Jer. 31:33.]

4 Such is the reliance *and* confidence that we have through Christ toward *and* with reference to God.

5 Not that we are fit (qualified and sufficient in ability) of ourselves to form personal judgments *or* to claim *or* count anything as coming from us; but our power *and* ability *and* sufficiency are from God.

6 [It is He] Who has qualified us (making us to be fit and worthy and sufficient) as ministers *and* dispensers of a new covenant [of salvation through Christ], not [ministers] of the letter—that is, of legally written code—but of the Spirit; for the code [of the Law] kills, but the (Holy) Spirit makes alive. [Jer. 31:31.]

7 Now if (the ministration of the Law,) the dispensation of death engraved in letters on stone, was inaugurated with such glory *and* splendor that the Israelites were not able to look steadily at the face of Moses because of its brilliance, (a glory) that was to fade *and* pass away, [Exod. 34:29-35.]

8 Why should not the dispensation of the Spirit [that is, this spiritual [g]ministry whose task it is to cause men to obtain and be governed by the Holy Spirit] be attended with much greater *and* more splendid glory?

9 For if the service that condemns, (the ministration of doom,) had glory, how infinitely more abounding in splendor *and* glory must be the service that makes righteous—the ministry that produces and fosters righteous living and right standing with God!

10 Indeed, in view of this fact, what once had splendor [[h]the glory of the Law in the face of Moses] has come to have no splendor at all, because of the overwhelming glory that exceeds *and* excels it, [[h]the glory of the Gospel in the face of Jesus Christ].

11 For if that which was but passing *and* fading away came with splendor, how much more must that abide in glory *and* splendor which remains *and* is permanent!

12 Since we have such [glorious] hope—such [joyful and confident] expectation—we speak very freely *and* openly *and* fearlessly.

13 Nor [do we act] like Moses, who put a veil over his face so that the Israelites might not gaze upon the finish of the vanishing [splendor which had been upon it].

14 In fact, their minds were grown hard *and* calloused—they had become dull and had lost the power of understanding; for until this present day, when the Old Testament [the old covenant] is being read, that same veil still lies [on their hearts], not being lifted [to reveal] that in Christ it is made void *and* done away.

15 Yes, down to this [very] day whenever Moses is read a veil lies upon their minds *and* hearts.

16 But whenever a person turns (in repentance) to the Lord the veil is stripped off *and* taken away.

17 Now the Lord is the Spirit, and where the Spirit of the Lord is, there is liberty—emancipation from bondage, freedom. [Isa. 61:1, 2.]

---

f) Many ancient authorities read "our."
g) Thayer.
h) Vincent's "Word Studies in the New Testament."

Living New Testament

CHAPTER 3

Are we beginning to be like those false teachers of yours who must tell you all about themselves and bring long letters of recommendation with them? I think you hardly need someone's letter to tell you about us, do you? And we don't need a recommendation from you, either!

2 The only letter I need is you yourselves! By looking at the good change in your hearts, everyone can see that we have done a good work among you.

3 They can see that you are a letter from Christ, written by us. It is not a letter written with pen and ink, but by the Spirit of the living God; not one carved on stone, but in human hearts.

4 We dare to say these good things about ourselves only because of our great trust in God through Christ, that He will help us to be true to what we say,

5 And not because we think we can do anything of lasting value by ourselves. Our only power and success comes from God.

6 He is the one who has helped us tell others about His new agreement to save them. We do not tell them that they must obey every law of God or die; but we tell them there is life for them from the Holy Spirit. The old way, trying to be saved by keeping the Ten Commandments, ends in death; in the new way, the Holy Spirit gives them life.

7 Yet that old system of law that led to death began with such glory that people could not bear to look at Moses' face. For as he gave them God's law to obey, his face shone out with the very glory of God—though the brightness was already fading away.

8 Shall we not expect far greater glory in these days when the Holy Spirit is giving life?

9 If the plan that leads to doom was glorious, much more glorious is the plan that makes men right with God.

10 In fact, that first glory as it shone from Moses' face is worth nothing at all in comparison with the overwhelming glory of the new agreement.

11 So if the old system that faded into nothing was full of heavenly glory, the glory of God's new plan for our salvation[1] is certainly far greater, for it is eternal.

12 Since we know that this new glory will never go away, we can preach with great boldness,

13 And not as Moses did, who put a veil over his face so that the Israeli could not see the glory fade away.

14 Not only Moses' face was veiled, but his people's minds and understanding were veiled and blinded too. Even now when the Scripture is read it seems as though Jewish hearts and minds are covered by a thick veil, because they cannot see and understand the real meaning of the Scriptures. For this veil of misunderstanding can be removed only by believing in Christ.

15 Yes, even today when they read Moses' writings their hearts are blind and they think that obeying the Ten Commandments is the way to be saved.

16 But whenever anyone turns to the Lord from his sins, then the veil is taken away.

17 The Lord is the Spirit who gives them life, and where He is there is freedom [from trying to be saved by keeping the laws of God[2]].

[1] Implied.
[2] Implied.

Revised Standard

A commended ministry

3 Are we beginning to commend ourselves
again? Or do we need, as some do, letters of recommendation to you, or from
you? 2You yourselves are our letter of recommendation, written on your[c] hearts, to be
known and read by all men; 3and you show
that you are a letter from Christ delivered
by us, written not with ink but with the
Spirit of the living God, not on tablets of
stone but on tablets of human hearts.
4 Such is the confidence that we have
through Christ toward God. 5Not that we
are sufficient of ourselves to claim anything
as coming from us; our sufficiency is from
God, 6who has qualified us to be ministers
of a new covenant, not in a written code but
in the Spirit; for the written code kills, but
the Spirit gives life.

A ministry of splendor

7 Now if the dispensation of death, carved
in letters on stone, came with such splendor
that the Israelites could not look at Moses'
face because of its brightness, fading as
this was, 8will not the dispensation of the
Spirit be attended with greater splendor?
9For if there was splendor in the dispensation of condemnation, the dispensation of
righteousness must far exceed it in splendor.
10Indeed, in this case, what once had splendor has come to have no splendor at all,
because of the splendor that surpasses it.
11For if what faded away came with splendor, what is permanent must have much
more splendor.
12 Since we have such a hope, we are
very bold, 13not like Moses, who put a
veil over his face so that the Israelites might
not see the end of the fading splendor. 14But
their minds were hardened; for to this day,
when they read the old covenant, that same
veil remains unlifted, because only through
Christ is it taken away. 15Yes, to this day
whenever Moses is read a veil lies over their
minds; 16but when a man turns to the Lord
the veil is removed. 17Now the Lord is the
Spirit, and where the Spirit of the Lord is,

[c] Other ancient authorities read *our*

King James

18 But we all, with open face beholding as in a glass the glory of the Lord, are changed into the same image from glory to glory, *even* as by the Spirit of the Lord.

Amplified

18 And all of us, as with unveiled face, [because we] continued to behold [in the Word of God] as in a mirror the glory of the Lord, are constantly being transfigured into His *very own* image in ever increasing splendor *and* from one degree of glory to another; [for this comes] from the Lord [Who is] the Spirit.

CHAPTER 4 (King James)

THEREFORE seeing we have this ministry, as we have received mercy, we faint not;
2 But have renounced the hidden things of dishonesty, not walking in craftiness, nor handling the word of God deceitfully; but by manifestation of the truth commending ourselves to every man's conscience in the sight of God.
3 But if our gospel be hid, it is hid to them that are lost:
4 In whom the god of this world hath blinded the minds of them which believe not, lest the light of the glorious gospel of Christ, who is the image of God, should shine unto them.
5 For we preach not ourselves, but Christ Jesus the Lord; and ourselves your servants for Jesus' sake.
6 For God, who commanded the light to shine out of darkness, hath shined in our hearts, to *give* the light of the knowledge of the glory of God in the face of Jesus Christ.
7 But we have this treasure in earthen vessels, that the excellency of the power may be of God, and not of us.
8 *We are* troubled on every side, yet not distressed; *we are* perplexed, but not in despair;
9 Persecuted, but not forsaken; cast down, but not destroyed;
10 Always bearing about in the body the dying of the Lord Jesus, that the life also of Jesus might be made manifest in our body.
11 For we which live are alway delivered unto death for Jesus' sake, that the life also of Jesus might be made manifest in our mortal flesh.
12 So then death worketh in us, but life in you.

CHAPTER 4 (Amplified)

THEREFORE, since we do hold *and* engage in this ministry by the mercy of God [granting us favor, benefits, opportunities and especially salvation], we do not get discouraged—spiritless and despondent with fear, or become faint with weariness and exhaustion.
2 We have renounced disgraceful ways—secret thoughts, feelings, desires and underhandedness, methods and arts that men hide through shame; we refuse to deal craftily (to practice trickery and cunning) or to adulterate or handle dishonestly the Word of God; but we state the truth openly—clearly and candidly. And so we commend ourselves in the sight *and* presence of God to every man's conscience.
3 But even if our Gospel (the glad tidings) also be hid—obscured and covered up with a veil [that hinders the knowledge of God]—it is hid [only] to those who are perishing, *and* obscured [only] to those who are spiritually dying, *and* veiled [only] to those who are lost.
4 For the god of this world has blinded the unbelievers' minds (that they should not discern the truth), preventing them from seeing the illuminating light of the Gospel of the glory of Christ, the Messiah, Who is the image *and* likeness of God.
5 For what we preach is not ourselves, but Jesus Christ as Lord, and ourselves [merely] as your servants (slaves) for Jesus' sake.
6 For God Who said, Let light shine out of darkness, has shone in our hearts so as [to beam forth] the Light for the illumination of the knowledge of the majesty *and* glory of God [as it is manifest in the Person and is revealed] in the face of *Jesus* Christ, the Messiah. [Gen. 1:3.]
7 However, we possess this precious treasure [the divine Light of the Gospel] in [frail, human] vessels of earth, that the grandeur *and* exceeding greatness of the power may be shown to be of God and not from ourselves.
8 We are hedged in (pressed) on every side—troubled and oppressed in every way; but not cramped *or* crushed; we suffer embarrassments *and* are perplexed *and* unable to find a way out, but not driven to despair;
9 We are (persecuted and hard driven,) pursued, but not deserted—to stand alone; we are struck down to the ground, but never struck out *and* destroyed;
10 Always carrying about in the body the liability *and* exposure to the same putting to death that *the Lord* Jesus suffered, so that the [[i]resurrection-] life of Jesus also may be shown forth by *and* in our bodies.
11 For we who live are constantly [experiencing] being handed over to death for Jesus' sake, that the [[i]resurrection-] life of Jesus also may be evidenced through our flesh which is liable to death.
12 Thus death is actively at work in us, but [it is in order that [j]our] life [may be actively at work] in you.

---

i) Vincent.
j) Thayer.

Living New Testament

18 But we Christians have no veil over our faces; we can be mirrors that brightly reflect the glory of the Lord. And as the Spirit of the Lord works within us, we become more and more like Him.

Revised Standard

there is freedom. 18 And we all, with unveiled face, beholding[d] the glory of the
Lord, are being changed into his likeness
from one degree of glory to another; for
this comes from the Lord who is the Spirit.

CHAPTER 4

It is God Himself, in His mercy, who has given us this wonderful work [of telling His Good News to others,][1] and so we never give up.

2 We do not try to trick people into believing—we are not interested in fooling anyone. We never try to get anyone to believe that the Bible teaches what it doesn't. All such shameful methods we forgo. We stand in the presence of God as we speak and so we tell the truth, as all who know us will agree.

3 If the Good News we preach is hidden to anyone, it is hidden from the one who is on the road to eternal death.

4 Satan, who is the god of this evil world, has made him blind, unable to see the glorious light of the Gospel that is shining upon him, or to understand the amazing message we preach about the glory of Christ, who is God.[2]

5 We don't go around preaching about ourselves, but about Christ Jesus as Lord. All we say of ourselves is that we are your slaves because of what Jesus has done for us.

6 For God, who said, "Let there be light in the darkness," has made us understand that it is the brightness of His glory that is seen in the face of Jesus Christ.

7 But this precious treasure—this light and power that now shine within us[3]—is held in a perishable container, that is, in our weak bodies. Everyone can see that the glorious power within must be from God and is not our own.

8 We are pressed on every side by troubles, but not crushed and broken. We are perplexed because we don't know why things happen as they do, but we don't give up and quit.

9 We are hunted down, but God never abandons us. We get knocked down, but we get up again and keep going.

10 These bodies of ours are constantly facing death just as Jesus did; so it is clear to all that it is only the living Christ within [who keeps us safe[3]].

11 Yes, we live under constant danger to our lives because we serve the Lord, but this gives us constant opportunities to show forth the power of Jesus Christ within our dying bodies.

12 Because of our preaching we face death, but it has resulted in eternal life for you.

An honest ministry

4 Therefore, having this ministry by the
mercy of God,[e] we do not lose heart.
2 We have renounced disgraceful, underhand-
ed ways; we refuse to practice cunning or
to tamper with God's word, but by the open
statement of the truth we would commend
ourselves to every man's conscience in the
sight of God. 3 And even if our gospel is
veiled, it is veiled only to those who are
perishing. 4 In their case the god of this
world has blinded the minds of the unbelievers, to keep them from seeing the light
of the gospel of the glory of Christ, who is
the likeness of God. 5 For what we preach
is not ourselves, but Jesus Christ as Lord,
with ourselves as your servants[f] for Jesus'
sake. 6 For it is the God who said, "Let light
shine out of darkness," who has shone in our
hearts to give the light of the knowledge of
the glory of God in the face of Christ.

A tried ministry

7 But we have this treasure in earthen
vessels, to show that the transcendent power
belongs to God and not to us. 8 We are
afflicted in every way, but not crushed;
perplexed, but not driven to despair; 9 persecuted, but not forsaken; struck down, but
not destroyed; 10 always carrying in the body
the death of Jesus, so that the life of Jesus
may also be manifested in our bodies. 11 For
while we live we are always being given
up to death for Jesus' sake, so that the
life of Jesus may be manifested in our mortal flesh. 12 So death is at work in us, but
life in you.

---

[1] Implied.
[2] Literally, "the image of God."
[3] Implied.

---

[d] Or *reflecting*
[e] Greek *as we have received mercy*
[f] Or *slaves*

King James

13 We having the same spirit of faith, according as it is written, I believed, and therefore have I spoken; we also believe, and therefore speak;

14 Knowing that he which raised up the Lord Jesus shall raise up us also by Jesus, and shall present *us* with you.

15 For all things *are* for your sakes, that the abundant grace might through the thanksgiving of many redound to the glory of God.

16 For which cause we faint not; but though our outward man perish, yet the inward *man* is renewed day by day.

17 For our light affliction, which is but for a moment, worketh for us a far more exceeding *and* eternal weight of glory;

18 While we look not at the things which are seen, but at the things which are not seen: for the things which are seen *are* temporal; but the things which are not seen *are* eternal.

Amplified

13 Yet we have the same spirit of faith as he had who wrote, I have believed, and therefore have I spoken. We too believe, and therefore we speak. [Ps. 116:10.]

14 Assured that He Who raised up the Lord Jesus will raise us up also with Jesus and bring us [along) with you into His presence.

15 For all [these] things are [taking place] for your sake, so that the more the grace (divine favor and spiritual blessing) extends to more and more people *and* multiplies through the many, the more the thanksgiving may increase [and redound] to the glory of God.

16 Therefore we do not become discouraged—utterly spiritless, exhausted, and wearied out through fear. Though our outer man is (progressively) decaying *and* wasting away, yet our inner self is being (progressively) renewed day after day.

17 For our light, momentary affliction (this slight distress of the passing hour) is ever more and more abundantly preparing *and* producing *and* achieving for us an everlasting weight of glory—beyond all measure, excessively surpassing all comparisons and all calculations, a vast and transcendent glory and blessedness never to cease!

18 Since we consider *and* look not to the things that are seen but to the things that are unseen; for the things that are visible are temporal (brief and fleeting), but the things that are invisible are deathless *and* everlasting.

King James

CHAPTER 5

FOR we know that if our earthly house of *this* tabernacle were dissolved, we have a building of God, an house not made with hands, eternal in the heavens.

2 For in this we groan, earnestly desiring to be clothed upon with our house which is from heaven:

3 If so be that being clothed we shall not be found naked.

4 For we that are in *this* tabernacle do groan, being burdened: not for that we would be unclothed, but clothed upon, that mortality might be swallowed up of life.

5 Now he that wrought us for the selfsame thing *is* God, who also hath given unto us the earnest of the Spirit.

6 Therefore *we are* always confident, knowing that, whilst we are at home in the body, we are absent from the Lord:

7 (For we walk by faith, not by sight:)

8 We are confident, *I say*, and willing rather to be absent from the body, and to be present with the Lord.

Amplified

CHAPTER 5

FOR we know that if the tent which is our earthly home is destroyed (dissolved), we have from God a building, a house not made with hands, eternal in the heavens.

2 Here indeed, in this (present abode, body), we sigh *and* groan inwardly, because we yearn to be clothed over—to put on our celestial body like a garment, to be fitted out—with our heavenly dwelling;

3 So that by putting it on we may not be found naked—without a body.

4 For while we are still in this tent, we groan under the burden *and* sigh deeply—weighed down, depressed, oppressed; not that we want to put off the body (the clothing of the spirit), but rather that we would be further clothed, so that what is mortal (our dying body) may be swallowed up by life [[k]after the resurrection].

5 Now He Who has fashioned us (preparing and making us fit) for this very thing is God, Who also has given us the (Holy) Spirit as a guarantee [of the fulfillment of His promise].

6 So then, we are always full of good *and* hopeful *and* confident courage; we know that while we are at home in the body we are abroad from the home with the Lord [that is promised us].

7 For we walk by faith [that is, we [k]regulate our lives and conduct ourselves by our conviction or belief respecting man's relationship to God and divine things, with trust and holy fervor; thus we walk] not by sight *or* appearance.

8 [Yes] we have confident *and* hopeful courage, and are well-pleased rather to be away from home out of the body and be at home with the Lord.

---

k) Thayer.

Living New Testament

13 We boldly say what we believe, [trusting God to care for us[3]], just as the Psalm writer did when he said, "I believe and therefore I speak."

14 We know that the same God who brought the Lord Jesus back from death will also bring us back to life again with Jesus, and present us to Him along with you.

15 These sufferings of ours are for your benefit. And the more of you who are won to Christ, the more there are to thank Him for His great kindness, and the more the Lord is glorified.

16 That is why we never give up. Though our bodies are dying, our inner strength in the Lord is growing every day.

17 These troubles and sufferings of ours are, after all, quite small and won't last very long. Yet this short time of distress will result in God's richest blessing upon us forever and ever!

18 So we do not look at what we can see right now, the troubles all around us, but we look forward to the joys in heaven which we have not yet seen. The troubles will soon be over, but the joys to come will last forever.

Revised Standard

13 Since we have the same spirit of faith
as he had who wrote, "I believed, and so I
spoke," we too believe, and so we speak,
[14]knowing that he who raised the Lord
Jesus will raise us also with Jesus and bring
us with you into his presence. [15]For it is
all for your sake, so that as grace extends
to more and more people it may increase
thanksgiving, to the glory of God.
16 So we do not lose heart. Though our
outer nature is wasting away, our inner nature is being renewed every day. [17]For this
slight momentary affliction is preparing for
us an eternal weight of glory beyond all
comparison, [18]because we look not to the
things that are seen but to the things that
are unseen; for the things that are seen are
transient, but the things that are unseen are
eternal.

CHAPTER 5

For we know that when this tent we live in now is taken down—when we die and leave these bodies—we will have wonderful new bodies in heaven, homes that will be ours forevermore, made for us by God Himself, and not by human hands.

2 How weary we grow of our present bodies. That is why we look forward eagerly to the day when we shall have heavenly bodies which we shall put on like new clothes.

3 For we shall not be merely spirits without bodies.

4 These earthly bodies make us groan and sigh, but we wouldn't like to think of dying and having no bodies at all. We want to slip into our new bodies so that these dying bodies will, as it were, be swallowed up by everlasting life.

5 This is what God prepared for us and, as a guarantee, He has given us His Holy Spirit.

6 Now we look forward with confidence to our heavenly bodies, realizing that every moment we spend in these earthly bodies is time spent away from our eternal home in heaven with Jesus.

7 We know these things are true by believing, not by seeing.

8 And we are not afraid, but are quite content to die, for then we will be at home with the Lord.

A courageous ministry

5 For we know that if the earthly tent
we live in is destroyed, we have a building from God, a house not made with hands,
eternal in the heavens. [2]Here indeed we
groan, and long to put on our heavenly
dwelling, [3]so that by putting it on we may
not be found naked. [4]For while we are still
in this tent, we sigh with anxiety; not that
we would be unclothed, but that we would
be further clothed, so that what is mortal
may be swallowed up by life. [5]He who has
prepared us for this very thing is God, who
has given us the Spirit as a guarantee.
6 So we are always of good courage; we
know that while we are at home in the body
we are away from the Lord, [7]for we walk
by faith, not by sight. [8]We are of good
courage, and we would rather be away
from the body and at home with the Lord.

[3] Implied.

King James

9 Wherefore we labour, that, whether
present or absent, we may be accepted of
him.
10 For we must all appear before the
judgment seat of Christ; that every one may
receive the things *done* in *his* body, according to that he hath done, whether *it be*
good or bad.
11 Knowing therefore the terror of the
Lord, we persuade men; but we are made
manifest unto God; and I trust also are
made manifest in your consciences.
12 For we commend not ourselves again
unto you, but give you occasion to glory on
our behalf, that ye may have somewhat to
answer them which glory in appearance, and
not in heart.
13 For whether we be beside ourselves, *it
is* to God: or whether we be sober, *it is* for
your cause.
14 For the love of Christ constraineth us;
because we thus judge, that if one died for
all, then were all dead:
15 And *that* he died for all, that they
which live should not henceforth live unto
themselves, but unto him which died for
them, and rose again.
16 Wherefore henceforth know we no
man after the flesh: yea, though we have
known Christ after the flesh, yet now henceforth know we *him* no more.
17 Therefore if any man *be* in Christ, *he
is* a new creature: old things are passed
away; behold, all things are become new.
18 And all things *are* of God, who hath
reconciled us to himself by Jesus Christ, and
hath given to us the ministry of reconciliation;
19 To wit, that God was in Christ, reconciling the world unto himself, not imputing
their trespasses unto them; and hath committed unto us the word of reconciliation.
20 Now then we are ambassadors for
Christ, as though God did beseech *you* by
us: we pray *you* in Christ's stead, be ye
reconciled to God.
21 For he hath made him *to be* sin for
us, who knew no sin; that we might be made
the righteousness of God in him.

Amplified

9 Therefore, whether we are at home [on earth away
from Him], or away from home [and with Him], we are
constantly ambitious *and* strive earnestly to be well-
pleasing to Him.
10 For we must all appear *and* be revealed as we are
before the judgment seat of Christ, so that each one may
receive [his pay] according to what he has done in the
body, whether good or evil, [considering [l]what his purpose
and motive have been, and what he has [k]achieved, been
busy with and given himself and his attention to accom-
plishing].
11 Therefore, being conscious of fearing the Lord with
respect *and* reverence, we seek to win people over—to
persuade them. But [m]what sort of persons we are is
plainly recognized *and* thoroughly understood by God,
and I hope that it is plainly recognized *and* thoroughly
understood also by your consciences—that is, by your
inborn discernment.
12 We are not commending ourselves to you again, but
we are providing you with an occasion *and* incentive to be
[rightfully] proud of us, so that you may have a reply for
those who pride themselves on surface appearances—[m]on
the virtues they only appear to have—although their heart
is devoid of them.
13 For if we are beside ourselves [mad, as some say], it
is for God *and* concerns Him; if we are in our right mind,
it is for your benefit,
14 For the love of Christ controls *and* urges *and* impels
us, because we are of the opinion *and* conviction that [if]
One died for all, then all died;
15 And He died for all, so that all those who live might
live no longer to *and* for themselves, but to *and* for Him
Who died and was raised again for their sake.
16 Consequently, from now on we estimate *and* regard
no one from a [purely] human point of view—in terms of
natural standards of value. [No] even though we once did
estimate Christ from a human viewpoint *and* as a man,
yet now [we have such knowledge of Him that] we know
Him no longer [in terms of the flesh].
17 Therefore if any person is (ingrafted) in Christ, the
Messiah, he is (a new creature altogether,) a new
creation; the old (previous moral and spiritual condition)
has passed away. Behold, the fresh *and* new has come!
18 But all things are from God, Who through *Jesus*
Christ reconciled us to Himself (received us into favor,
brought us into harmony with Himself) and gave to us
the ministry of reconciliation—that by word and deed we
might aim to bring others into harmony with Him.
19 It was God (personally present) in Christ, reconciling *and* restoring the world to favor with Himself, not
counting up *and* holding against [men] their trespasses [but
cancelling them]; and committing to us the message of
reconciliation—of the restoration to favor.
20 So we are Christ's ambassadors, God making His
appeal as it were through us. We [as Christ's personal
representatives] beg you for His sake to lay hold of the
divine favor [now offered you] *and* be reconciled to God.
21 For our sake He made Christ [virtually] to be sin
Who knew no sin, so that in *and* through Him we might
become [[n]endued with, viewed as in and examples of] the
righteousness of God—what we ought to be, approved
and acceptable and in right relationship with Him, by His
goodness.

---

k) Thayer.
l) Souter's "Pocket Lexicon to the Greek New Testament."
m) Thayer.
n) Alford.

Living New Testament

9 So our aim is to please Him always in everything we do, whether we are here in this body or away from this body and with Him in heaven.

10 For we must all stand before Christ to be judged and our lives laid bare—before Him. Each of us will receive whatever he deserves for the good or bad things he has done in his earthly body.

11 It is because of this solemn fear of the Lord, which is ever present is our minds, that we work so hard to win others. God knows our hearts, that they are pure in this matter, and I hope that, deep within, you really know it too.

12 Are we trying to pat ourselves on the back again? No, I am giving you some good ammunition! You can use this on those preachers of yours who brag about how well they look and preach, but don't have true and honest hearts. You can boast about us that we at least are well intentioned and honest.

13, 14 Are we insane [to say such things about ourselves[1]]? If so, it is to bring glory to God. And if we are in our right minds, it is for your benefit. Whatever we do, it is certainly not for our own profit, but because Christ's love controls us now. Since we believe that Christ died for all of us, we should also believe that we have died to the old life we used to live.

15 He died for all so that all who live—having received eternal life from Him—might live no longer for themselves, to please themselves, but to spend their lives pleasing Christ who died and rose again for them.

16 So stop evaluating Christians by what the world thinks about them or by what they seem to be like on the outside. Once I mistakenly thought of Christ that way, merely as a human being like myself. How differently I feel now!

17 When someone becomes a Christian he becomes a brand new person inside. He is not the same any more. A new life has begun!

18 All these new things are from God who brought us back to Himself through what Christ Jesus did. And God has given us the privilege of urging everyone to come into His favor and be reconciled to Him.

19 For God was in Christ, restoring the world to Himself, no longer counting men's sins against them but blotting them out. This is the wonderful message He has given us to tell others.

20 We are Christ's ambassadors. God is using us to speak to you: we beg you, as though Christ Himself were here pleading with you, receive the love He offers you—be reconciled to God.

21 For God took the sinless Christ and poured into Him our sins. Then, in exchange, He poured God's goodness into us![2]

Implied.
Literally, "Him who knew no sin, He made sin in our behalf, that we might become the righteousness of God in Him."

Revised Standard

9 So whether we are at home or away, we make it our aim to please him. 10 For we must all appear before the judgment seat of Christ, so that each one may receive good or evil, according to what he has done in the body.

A reconciling ministry

11 Therefore, knowing the fear of the Lord, we persuade men; but what we are is known to God, and I hope it is known also to your conscience. 12 We are not commending ourselves to you again but giving you cause to be proud of us, so that you may be able to answer those who pride themselves on a man's position and not on his heart. 13 For if we are beside ourselves, it is for God; if we are in our right mind, it is for you. 14 For the love of Christ controls us, because we are convinced that one has died for all; therefore all have died. 15 And he died for all, that those who live might live no longer for themselves but for him who for their sake died and was raised.

16 From now on, therefore, we regard no one from a human point of view; even though we once regarded Christ from a human point of view, we regard him thus no longer. 17 Therefore, if any one is in Christ, he is a new creation;[g] the old has passed away, behold, the new has come. 18 All this is from God, who through Christ reconciled us to himself and gave us the ministry of reconciliation; 19 that is, God was in Christ reconciling[h] the world to himself, not counting their trespasses against them, and entrusting to us the message of reconciliation. 20 So we are ambassadors for Christ, God making his appeal through us. We beseech you on behalf of Christ, be reconciled to God. 21 For our sake he made him to be sin who knew no sin, so that in him we might become the righteousness of God.

[g] Or *creature*
[h] Or *in Christ God was reconciling*

King James

CHAPTER 6

WE then, *as* workers together *with him*, beseech *you* also that ye receive not the grace of God in vain.

2 (For he saith, I have heard thee in a time accepted, and in the day of salvation have I succoured thee: behold, now *is* the accepted time; behold, now *is* the day of salvation.)

3 Giving no offence in any thing, that the ministry be not blamed:

4 But in all *things* approving ourselves as the ministers of God, in much patience, in afflictions, in necessities, in distresses,

5 In stripes, in imprisonments, in tumults, in labours, in watchings, in fastings;

6 By pureness, by knowledge, by longsuffering, by kindness, by the Holy Ghost, by love unfeigned,

7 By the word of truth, by the power of God, by the armour of righteousness on the right hand and on the left,

8 By honour and dishonour, by evil report and good report: as deceivers, and *yet* true;

9 As unknown, and *yet* well known; as dying, and, behold, we live; as chastened, and not killed;

10 As sorrowful, yet alway rejoicing; as poor, yet making many rich; as having nothing, and *yet* possessing all things.

11 O *ye* Corinthians, our mouth is open unto you, our heart is enlarged.

12 Ye are not straitened in us, but ye are straitened in your own bowels.

13 Now for a recompence in the same, (I speak as unto *my* children,) be ye also enlarged.

14 Be ye not unequally yoked together with unbelievers: for what fellowship hath righteousness with unrighteousness? and what communion hath light with darkness?

15 And what concord hath Christ with Belial? or what part hath he that believeth with an infidel?

16 And what agreement hath the temple of God with idols? for ye are the temple of the living God; as God hath said, I will dwell in them, and walk in *them;* and I will be their God, and they shall be my people.

17 Wherefore come out from among them, and be ye separate, saith the Lord, and touch not the unclean *thing;* and I will receive you,

18 And will be a Father unto you, and ye shall be my sons and daughters, saith the Lord Almighty.

Amplified

CHAPTER 6

(AS God's fellow workers) laboring together with Him then, we beg of you not to receive the grace of God in vain—that [o]merciful kindness by which God exerts His holy influence on souls and turns them to Christ, keeping and strengthening them, do not receive it to no purpose.

2 For He says, In the time of favor (of an assured welcome) I have listened to *and* heeded your call, and I have helped you on the day of deliverance—the day of salvation. Behold, now is truly the time for a gracious welcome *and* acceptance [of you from God]; behold, now is the day of salvation! [Isa. 49:8.]

3 We (give no offense in anything,) put no obstruction in anybody's way, so that no fault may be found *and* [our] ministry blamed *and* discredited.

4 But we commend ourselves in every way as [true] servants of God: through great endurance, in tribulation *and* suffering, in hardships *and* privations, in sore straits *and* calamities,

5 In beatings, imprisonments, riots, labors, sleepless watching, hunger;

6 By innocence *and* purity, knowledge *and* spiritual insight, longsuffering *and* patience, kindness, in the Holy Spirit, in unfeigned love;

7 By [speaking] the word of truth, in the power of God, with the weapons of righteousness for the right hand [to attack] and for the left hand [to defend];

8 Amid honor and dishonor; in defaming *and* evil report and in praise *and* good report. [We are branded] as deceivers (impostors), and [yet vindicated as] truthful *and* honest.

9 [We are treated] as unknown *and* ignored [by the world], and [yet we are] well-known *and* recognized [by God and His people]; as dying, and yet here we are alive; as chastened by suffering and [yet] not killed;

10 As grieved *and* mourning, yet [we are] always rejoicing; as poor [ourselves, yet] bestowing riches on many; as having nothing, and [yet in reality] possessing all things.

11 Our mouth is open to you, Corinthians—we are hiding nothing, keeping nothing back; and our heart is expanded wide [for you]! [Ezek. 33:22; Isa. 60:5.]

12 There is no lack of room for you in [our hearts], but you lack room in your own affections [for us].

13 By way of return then, do this for me—I speak as to children—open wide your hearts also [to us].

14 Do not be unequally yoked up with unbelievers—do not make mismated alliances with them, or come under a different yoke with them [inconsistent with your faith]. For what partnership have right living *and* right standing with God with iniquity *and* lawlessness? Or how can light fellowship with darkness?

15 What harmony can there be between Christ and Belial [the devil]? Or what has a believer in common with an unbeliever?

16 What agreement [can there be between] a temple of God and idols? For we are the temple of the living God; even as God said, I will dwell in *and* with *and* among them and will walk in *and* with *and* among them, and I will be their God, and they shall be My people. [Exod. 25:8; 29:45; Lev. 26:12; Ezek. 37:27; Jer. 31:1.]

17 So, come out from among (unbelievers), and separate (sever) yourselves from them, says the Lord, and touch not [any] unclean thing; then I will receive you kindly *and* treat you with favor, [Isa. 52:11.]

18 And I will be a Father to you, and you shall be My sons and daughters, says the Lord Almighty. [Hos. 1:10; Isa. 43:6.]

---

o) Thayer.

Living New Testament

CHAPTER 6

As God's partners we beg you not to toss aside this marvelous message of God's great kindness.

2 For God says, "Your cry came to me at a favorable time, when the doors of welcome were wide open. I helped you on a day when salvation was being offered." Right now God is ready to welcome you. Today He is ready to save you.

3 We try to live in such a way that no one will ever be offended or kept back from finding the Lord by the way we act, so that no one can find fault with us and blame it on the Lord.

4 In fact, in everything we do we try to show that we are true ministers of God. We patiently endure suffering and hardship and trouble of every kind.

5 We have been beaten, put in jail, faced angry mobs, worked to exhaustion, stayed awake through sleepless nights of watching, and gone without food.

6 We have proved ourselves to be what we claim by our wholesome lives and by our understanding of the Gospel and by our patience. We have been kind and truly loving and filled with the Holy Spirit.

7 We have been truthful, with God's power helping us in all we do. All of the godly man's arsenal—weapons of defense, and weapons of attack—have been ours.

8 We stand true to the Lord whether others honor us or despise us, whether they criticize us or commend us. We are honest, but they call us liars.

9 The world ignores us, but we are known to God; we live close to death, but here we are, still very much alive. We have been injured but kept from death.

10 Our hearts ache, but at the same time we have the joy of the Lord. We are poor, but we give rich spiritual gifts to others. We own nothing, and yet we enjoy everything.

11 Oh, my dear Corinthian friends! I have told you all my feelings; I love you with all my heart.

12 Any coldness still between us is not because of any lack of love on my part, but because your love is too small and does not reach out to me and draw me in.

13 I am talking to you now as if you truly were my very own children. Open your hearts to us! Return our love!

14 Don't be teamed with those who do not love the Lord, for what do the people of God have in common with the people of sin? How can light live with darkness?

15 And what harmony can there be between Christ and the devil? How can a Christian be a partner with one who doesn't believe?

16 And what union can there be between God's temple and idols? For you are God's temple, the home of the living God, and God has said of you, "I will live in them and walk among them, and I will be their God and they shall be My people."

17 That is why the Lord has said, "Leave them; separate yourselves from them; don't touch their filthy things, and I will welcome you,

18 "And be a Father to you, and you will be My sons and daughters."

Revised Standard

A suffering ministry

6 Working together with him, then, we
entreat you not to accept the grace of
God in vain. [2]For he says,
"At the acceptable time I have listened
to you,
and helped you on the day of salvation."
Behold, now is the acceptable time; behold,
now is the day of salvation. [3]We put no
obstacle in any one's way, so that no fault
may be found with our ministry, [4]but as
servants of God we commend ourselves in
every way: through great endurance, in
afflictions, hardships, calamities, [5]beatings,
imprisonments, tumults, labors, watching,
hunger; [6]by purity, knowledge, forbearance,
kindness, the Holy Spirit, genuine love,
[7]truthful speech, and the power of God;
with the weapons of righteousness for the
right hand and for the left; [8]in honor and
dishonor, in ill repute and good repute. We
are treated as imposters, and yet are true;
[9]as unknown, and yet well known; as dying,
and behold we live; as punished, and yet
not killed; [10]as sorrowful, yet always rejoicing; as poor, yet making many rich; as
having nothing, and yet possessing everything.
11 Our mouth is open to you, Corinthians;
our heart is wide. [12]You are not restricted
by us, but you are restricted in your own
affections. [13]In return—I speak as to children—widen your hearts also.

Believers are the temple of God

14 Do not be mismated with unbelievers.
For what partnership have righteousness
and iniquity? Or what fellowship has light
with darkness? [15]What accord has Christ
with Belial?[i] Or what has a believer in common with an unbeliever? [16]What agreement
has the temple of God with idols? For we
are the temple of the living God; as God
said,
"I will live in them and move among
them,
and I will be their God,
and they shall be my people.
17 Therefore come out from them,
and be separate from them, says the
Lord,
and touch nothing unclean;
then I will welcome you,
18 and I will be a father to you,
and you shall be my sons and daughters,
says the Lord Almighty."

---

[i] Greek *Beliar*

King James

CHAPTER 7

HAVING therefore these promises, dearly beloved, let us cleanse ourselves from all filthiness of the flesh and spirit, perfecting holiness in the fear of God.

2 Receive us; we have wronged no man, we have corrupted no man, we have defrauded no man.

3 I speak not *this* to condemn *you:* for I have said before, that ye are in our hearts to die and live with *you.*

4 Great *is* my boldness of speech toward you, great *is* my glorying of you: I am filled with comfort, I am exceeding joyful in all our tribulation.

5 For, when we were come into Macedonia, our flesh had no rest, but we were troubled on every side; without *were* fightings, within *were* fears.

6 Nevertheless God, that comforteth those that are cast down, comforted us by the coming of Titus;

7 And not by his coming only, but by the consolation wherewith he was comforted in you, when he told us your earnest desire, your mourning, your fervent mind toward me; so that I rejoiced the more.

8 For though I made you sorry with a letter, I do not repent, though I did repent: for I perceive that the same epistle hath made you sorry, though *it were* but for a season.

9 Now I rejoice, not that ye were made sorry, but that ye sorrowed to repentance: for ye were made sorry after a godly manner, that ye might receive damage by us in nothing.

10 For godly sorrow worketh repentance to salvation not to be repented of: but the sorrow of the world worketh death.

11 For behold this selfsame thing, that ye sorrowed after a godly sort, what carefulness it wrought in you, yea, *what* clearing of yourselves, yea, *what* indignation, yea, what fear, yea, *what* vehement desire, yea, *what* zeal, yea, *what* revenge! In all *things* ye have approved yourselves to be clear in this matter.

12 Wherefore, though I wrote unto you, *I did it* not for his cause that had done the wrong, nor for his cause that suffered wrong, but that our care for you in the sight of God might appear unto you.

13 Therefore we were comforted in your comfort: yea, and exceedingly the more joyed we for the joy of Titus, because his spirit was refreshed by you all.

Amplified

CHAPTER 7

THEREFORE, since these [great] promises are ours, beloved, let us cleanse ourselves from everything that contaminates *and* defiles body and spirit, and bring [our] consecration to completeness in the (reverential) fear of God.

2 Do open your hearts to us again—enlarge them to take us in. We have wronged no one; we have betrayed *or* corrupted no one; we have cheated *or* taken advantage of no one.

3 I do not say this to reproach *or* condemn [you], for I have said before that you are (nested) in our hearts, [and you will remain there] whether we die or live, it will be together.

4 I have great boldness *and* free *and* fearless confidence *and* cheerful courage toward you; my pride in you is great; I am filled brimful with the comfort [of it]. With all our tribulation *and* in spite of it, I am filled with comfort, I am overflowing with joy.

5 For even when we arrived in Macedonia, our bodies had no ease *or* rest, but we were oppressed in every way *and* afflicted at every turn—fighting *and* contentions without, dread *and* fears within [us];

6 But God, Who comforts *and* encourages *and* refreshes *and* cheers the depressed *and* the sinking, comforted *and* encouraged *and* refreshed *and* cheered us by the arrival of Titus.

7 [Yes] and not only by his coming but also by [his account of] the comfort with which he was encouraged *and* refreshed *and* cheered as to you, while he told us of your yearning affection, of how sorry you were [for me] and how eagerly you took my part, so that I rejoiced still more.

8 For even though I did grieve you with my letter, I do not regret [it now], though I did regret it, for I see that that letter did pain you, though only for a little while;

9 Yet I am glad now, not because you were pained, but because you were pained into repentance (that turned you to God); for you felt a grief such as God meant you to feel, so that in nothing you might suffer loss through us *or* harm for what we did.

10 For godly grief *and* the pain God is permitted to direct, produce a repentance that leads *and* contributes to salvation *and* deliverance from evil, and it never brings regret; but worldly grief [the hopeless sorrow that is characteristic of the pagan world] is deadly—breeding *and* ending in death.

11 For [you can look back now and] observe what this same godly sorrow has done for you *and* has produced in you: what eagerness *and* earnest care to explain *and* clear yourselves [of all [p]complicity in the condoning of incest], what indignation [at the sin], what alarm, what yearning, what zeal [to do justice to all concerned], what readiness to mete out punishment [[p]to the offender]! At every point you have proved yourselves cleared *and* guiltless in the matter. [I Cor. 5.]

12 So although I did write to you [as I did], it was not for the sake *and* because of the one who did [the] wrong, nor on account of the one who suffered [the] wrong, but in order that you might realize before God [that your readiness to accept our authority revealed] how zealously you do care for us.

13 Therefore we are relieved *and* comforted *and* encouraged [at the result]. And in addition to our own (personal) consolation, we were especially delighted at the joy of Titus, because you have all set his mind at rest, soothing *and* refreshing his spirit.

---

p) Vincent.

Living New Testament

CHAPTER 7

Having such great promises as these, dear friends, let us turn away from everything wrong, whether of body or spirit, and purify ourselves, living in the wholesome fear of God, giving ourselves to Him alone.

2 Please open your hearts to us again, for not one of you has suffered any wrong from us. Not one of you was led astray. We have cheated no one nor taken advantage of anyone.

3 I'm not saying this to scold or blame you, for, as I have said before, you are in my heart forever and I live and die with you.

4 I have the highest confidence in you, and my pride in you is great. You have greatly encouraged me; you have made me so happy in spite of all my suffering.

5 When we arrived in Macedonia there was no rest for us; outside, trouble was on every hand and all around us; within us, our hearts were full of dread and fear.

6 Then God who cheers those who are discouraged refreshed us by the arrival of Titus.

7 Not only was his presence a joy, but also the news that he brought of the wonderful time he had with you. When he told me how much you were looking forward to my visit, and how sorry you were about what had happened, and about your loyalty and warm love for me, well, I overflowed with joy!

8 I am no longer sorry that I sent that letter to you, though I was very sorry for a time, realizing how painful it would be to you. But it hurt you only for a little while.

9 Now I am glad I sent it, not because it hurt you, but because the pain turned you to God. It was a good kind of sorrow you felt, the kind of sorrow God wants His people to have, so that I need not come to you with harshness.

10 For God sometimes uses sorrow in our lives to help us turn away from sin and seek eternal life. We should never regret His sending it. But the sorrow of the man who is not a Christian is not the sorrow of true repentance and does not prevent eternal death.

11 Just see how much good this grief from the Lord did for you! You no longer shrugged your shoulders, but became earnest and sincere, and very anxious to get rid of the sin that I wrote you about. You became frightened about what had happened, and longed for me to come and help. You went right to work on the problem and cleared it up [punishing the man who sinned[1]]. You have done everything you could to make it right.

12 I wrote as I did so the Lord could show how much you really do care for us. That was my purpose even more than to help the man[1] who sinned, or his father[1] to whom he did the wrong.

13 In addition to the encouragement you gave us by your love, we were made happier still by Titus' joy when you gave him such a fine welcome and set his mind at ease.

[1] Implied.

Revised Standard

7 Since we have these promises, beloved,
let us cleanse ourselves from every defilement of body and spirit, and make holiness perfect in the fear of God.

2 Open your hearts to us; we have
wronged no one, we have corrupted no one,
we have taken advantage of no one. [3]I do
not say this to condemn you, for I said before that you are in our hearts, to die together and to live together. [4]I have great
confidence in you; I have great pride in you;
I am filled with comfort. With all our affliction, I am overjoyed.

The joy of good news

5 For even when we came into Macedonia, our bodies had no rest but we were
afflicted at every turn—fighting without and
fear within. [6]But God, who comforts the
downcast, comforted us by the coming of
Titus, [7]and not only by his coming but also
by the comfort with which he was comforted in you, as he told us of your longing,
your mourning, your zeal for me, so that I
rejoiced still more. [8]For even if I made you
sorry with my letter, I do not regret it
(though I did regret it), for I see that that
letter grieved you, though only for a while.
[9]As it is, I rejoice, not because you were
grieved, but because you were grieved into
repenting; for you felt a godly grief, so that
you suffered no loss through us. [10]For
godly grief produces a repentance that leads
to salvation and brings no regret, but worldly grief produces death. [11]For see what
earnestness this godly grief has produced
in you, what eagerness to clear yourselves,
what indignation, what alarm, what longing,
what zeal, what punishment! At every point
you have proved yourselves guiltless in the
matter. [12]So although I wrote to you, it was
not on account of the one who did the
wrong, nor on account of the one who
suffered the wrong, but in order that your
zeal for us might be revealed to you in the
sight of God. [13]Therefore we are comforted.

And besides our own comfort we rejoiced
still more at the joy of Titus, because his
mind has been set at rest by you all. [14]For

King James

14 For if I have boasted any thing to him of you, I am not ashamed; but as we spake all things to you in truth, even so our boasting, which *I made* before Titus, is found a truth.

15 And his inward affection is more abundant toward you, whilst he remembereth the obedience of you all, how with fear and trembling ye received him.

16 I rejoice therefore that I have confidence in you in all *things*.

CHAPTER 8

MOREOVER, brethren, we do you to wit of the grace of God bestowed on the churches of Macedonia;

2 How that in a great trial of affliction the abundance of their joy and their deep poverty abounded unto the riches of their liberality.

3 For to *their* power, I bear record, yea, and beyond *their* power *they were* willing of themselves;

4 Praying us with much entreaty that we would receive the gift, and *take upon us* the fellowship of the ministering to the saints.

5 And *this they did*, not as we hoped, but first gave their own selves to the Lord, and unto us by the will of God.

6 Insomuch that we desired Titus, that as he had begun, so he would also finish in you the same grace also.

7 Therefore, as ye abound in every *thing*, *in* faith, and utterance, and knowledge, and *in* all diligence, and *in* your love to us, *see* that ye abound in this grace also.

8 I speak not by commandment, but by occasion of the forwardness of others, and to prove the sincerity of your love.

9 For ye know the grace of our Lord Jesus Christ, that, though he was rich, yet for your sakes he became poor, that ye through his poverty might be rich.

10 And herein I give *my* advice: for this is expedient for you, who have begun before, not only to do, but also to be forward a year ago.

11 Now therefore perform the doing *of it;* that as *there was* a readiness to will, so *there may be* a performance also out of that which ye have.

12 For if there be first a willing mind, *it is* accepted according to that a man hath, *and* not according to that he hath not.

Amplified

14 For if I had boasted to him at all concerning you, I was not disappointed *or* put to shame, but just as everything we ever said to you was true, so our boasting [about you] to Titus has proved true also.

15 And his heart goes out to you more abundantly than ever as he recalls how submissive [to his guidance] you all were, and the reverence *and* anxiety [to meet all requirements] with which you accepted *and* welcomed him.

16 I am very happy because I now am of good courage *and* have perfect confidence in you in all things.

CHAPTER 8

WE want to tell you further, brethren, about the grace (the favor and spiritual blessing) of God which has been evident in the churches of Macedonia [arousing in them the desire to give alms];

2 For in the midst of an ordeal of severe tribulation, their abundance of joy and their depth of poverty [together] have overflowed in a wealth of lavish generosity on their part.

3 For, as I can bear witness, [they gave] according to their ability, yes, and beyond their ability; and [they did it] voluntarily,

4 Begging us most insistently for the favor *and* the fellowship of contributing in this ministration for [the relief and support of] the saints [in Jerusalem].

5 Nor [was this gift of theirs merely the contribution] that we expected, but first they gave themselves to the Lord and to us [as His agents] by the will of God—that is, [q]entirely disregarding their personal interests, they gave as much as they possibly could, having put themselves at our disposal to be directed by the will of God.

6 So much so that we have urged Titus that as he began it, he should also complete this beneficent *and* gracious contribution among you, [the church at Corinth].

7 Now as you abound *and* excel *and* are at the front in everything, in faith, in expressing yourselves, in knowledge, in all zeal, and in your love for us, [see to it that you come to the front now and] abound *and* excel in this gracious work [of almsgiving] also.

8 I give this not as an order—to dictate to you—but to prove by [pointing out] the zeal of others the sincerity of your [own] love also.

9 For you are coming progressively to be acquainted with *and* to recognize more strongly *and* clearly the grace of our Lord Jesus Christ—His kindness, His gracious generosity, His undeserved favor and spiritual blessing; [in] that though He was [so very] rich, yet for your sakes He became [so very] poor, in order that by His poverty you might become enriched—abundantly supplied.

10 [It is then] my counsel *and* my opinion in this matter that I give [you, when I say], it is profitable *and* fitting for you [now to complete the enterprise], which more than a year ago you not only began, but were the first to wish to do anything [about contributions for the relief of the saints at Jerusalem].

11 So now finish doing it, that your (enthusiastic) readiness in desiring it may be equalled by your completion of it according to your ability *and* means.

12 For if the (eager) readiness to give is there, then it is acceptable *and* welcomed in proportion to what a person has, not according to what he does not have.

---

q) Thayer.

Living New Testament

14 I told him how it would be—told him before he left me of my pride in you—and you didn't disappoint me. I have always told you the truth and now my boasting to Titus has also proved true!

15 He loves you more than ever when he remembers the way you listened to him so willingly and received him so anxiously and with such deep concern.

16 How happy this makes me, now that I am sure all is well between us again. Once again I can have perfect confidence in you.

Revised Standard

if I have expressed to him some pride in
you, I was not put to shame; but just as
everything we said to you was true, so our
boasting before Titus has proved true. 15And
his heart goes out all the more to you, as
he remembers the obedience of you all, and
the fear and trembling with which you received him. 16I rejoice, because I have perfect confidence in you.

CHAPTER 8

Now I want to tell you what God in His grace has done for the churches in Macedonia.

2 Though they have been going through much trouble and hard times, they have mixed their wonderful joy with their deep poverty, and the result has been an overflow of giving to others.

3 They gave not only what they could afford, but far more; and I can testify that they did it because they wanted to, and not because of nagging on my part.

4 They begged us to take the money so they could share in the joy of helping the Christians in Jerusalem.

5 Best of all, they went beyond our highest hopes, for their first action was to dedicate themselves to the Lord and to us, for whatever directions God might give to them through us.

6 They were so enthusiastic about it that we have urged Titus, who encouraged your giving in the first place, to visit you and encourage you to complete your share in this ministry of giving.

7 You people there are leaders in so many ways—you have so much faith, so many good preachers, so much learning, so much enthusiasm, so much love for us. Now I want you to be leaders also in the spirit of cheerful giving.

8 I am not giving you an order; I am not saying you must do it, but others are eager for it. This is one way to prove that your love is real, that it goes beyond mere words.

9 You know how full of love and kindness our Lord Jesus was: though He was so very rich, yet to help you He became so very poor, so that by being poor He could make you rich.

10 I want to suggest that you finish what you started to do a year ago, for you were not only the first to propose this idea, but the first to begin doing something about it.

11 Having started the ball rolling so enthusiastically, you should carry this project through to completion just as gladly, giving whatever you can out of whatever you have. Let your enthusiastic idea at the start be equalled by your realistic action now.

12 If you are really eager to give, then it isn't important how much you have to give. God wants you to give what you have, not what you haven't.

The giving of the Macedonians

8 We want you to know, brethren, about
the grace of God which has been shown
in the churches of Macedonia, 2for in a
severe test of affliction, their abundance of
joy and their extreme poverty have overflowed in a wealth of liberality on their part.
3For they gave according to their means,
as I can testify, and beyond their means, of
their own free will, 4begging us earnestly
for the favor of taking part in the relief of
the saints—5and this, not as we expected,
but first they gave themselves to the Lord
and to us by the will of God. 6Accordingly
we have urged Titus that as he had already
made a beginning, he should also complete
among you this gracious work. 7Now as
you excel in everything—in faith, in utterance, in knowledge, in all earnestness, and
in your love for us—see that you excel in
this gracious work also.

The example of Jesus

8 I say this not as a command, but to
prove by the earnestness of others that your
love also is genuine. 9For you know the
grace of our Lord Jesus Christ, that though
he was rich, yet for your sake he became
poor, so that by his poverty you might
become rich. 10And in this matter I give my
advice: it is best for you now to complete what a year ago you began not only
to do but to desire, 11so that your readiness
in desiring it may be matched by your completing it out of what you have. 12For if the
readiness is there, it is acceptable according
to what a man has, not according to what

King James

13 For *I mean* not that other men be eased, and ye burdened:

14 But by an equality, *that* now at this time your abundance *may be a supply* for their want, that their abundance also may be *a supply* for your want: that there may be equality:

15 As it is written, He that *had gathered* much had nothing over; and he that *had gathered* little had no lack.

16 But thanks *be* to God, which put the same earnest care into the heart of Titus for you.

17 For indeed he accepted the exhortation; but being more forward, of his own accord he went unto you.

18 And we have sent with him the brother, whose praise *is* in the gospel throughout all the churches;

19 And not *that* only, but who was also chosen of the churches to travel with us with this grace, which is administered by us to the glory of the same Lord, and *declaration* of your ready mind:

20 Avoiding this, that no man should blame us in this abundance which is administered by us:

21 Providing for honest things, not only in the sight of the Lord, but also in the sight of men.

22 And we have sent with them our brother, whom we have oftentimes proved diligent in many things, but now much more diligent, upon the great confidence which *I have* in you.

23 Whether *any do inquire* of Titus, *he is* my partner and fellow-helper concerning you: or our brethren *be inquired of, they are* the messengers of the churches, *and* the glory of Christ.

24 Wherefore shew ye to them, and before the churches, the proof of your love, and of our boasting on your behalf.

Amplified

13 For it is not [intended] that other people be eased *and* relieved (of their responsibility) and you be burdened *and* suffer (unfairly),

14 But to have equality—share and share alike; your surplus over necessity at the present time going to meet their want *and* to equalize the difference created by it, so that [at some other time] their surplus in turn may be given to supply your want. Thus there may be equality.

15 As it is written, He who gathered much had nothing over, and he who gathered little did not lack. [Exod. 16:18.]

16 But thanks be to God Who planted the same earnest zeal *and* care for you in the heart of Titus.

17 For he not only welcomed *and* responded to our appeal, but was himself so keen in his enthusiasm *and* interest in you that he is going to you of his own accord.

18 But we are sending along with him that brother [Luke?] whose praise in the Gospel ministry [is spread] throughout all the churches;

19 And more than that, he has been appointed by the churches to travel as our companion in regard to this bountiful contribution which we are administering for the glory of the Lord Himself, and [to show] our eager readiness [as Christians to help one another].

20 [For] we are on our guard, intending that no one should find anything for which to blame us in regard to our administration of this large contribution.

21 For we take thought beforehand *and* aim to be honest *and* absolutely above suspicion not only in the sight of the Lord but also in the sight of men.

22 Moreover along with them we are sending our brother, whom we have often put to the test and have found him zealous (devoted and earnest) in many matters, but who is now more (eagerly) earnest than ever because of [his] absolute confidence in you.

23 As for Titus, he is my colleague and shares my work in your service; and as for the [other two] brethren, they are the (special) messengers of the churches, a credit *and* glory to Christ, the Messiah.

24 Show to these men, therefore, in the sight of the churches, the reality *and* plain truth of your love—your affection, goodwill and benevolence—and what [good reasons] I had for boasting about *and* being proud of you.

CHAPTER 9

FOR as touching the ministering to the saints, it is superfluous for me to write to you:

2 For I know the forwardness of your mind, for which I boast of you to them of Macedonia, that Achaia was ready a year ago; and your zeal hath provoked very many.

3 Yet have I sent the brethren, lest our boasting of you should be in vain in this behalf; that, as I said, ye may be ready:

4 Lest haply if they of Macedonia come with me, and find you unprepared, we (that we say not, ye) should be ashamed in this same confident boasting.

5 Therefore I thought it necessary to exhort the brethren, that they would go before unto you, and make up beforehand your bounty, whereof ye had notice before, that the same might be ready, as *a matter of* bounty, and not as *of* covetousness.

CHAPTER 9

NOW about the offering that is [to be made] for the saints—God's people [in Jerusalem]—it is quite superfluous that I should write you;

2 For I am well acquainted with your willingness—your readiness and your eagerness to promote it—and I have proudly told about you to the people of Macedonia, saying that Achaia [most of Greece] has been prepared since last year for this contribution; and [consequently] your enthusiasm has stimulated the majority of them.

3 Still, I am sending the brethren [on to you], lest our pride in you should be made an empty boast in this particular case, and so that you may be all ready, as I told them you would be;

4 Lest, if [any] Macedonians should come with me and find you unprepared [for this generosity], we, to say nothing of yourselves, be humiliated for our being so confident.

5 That is why I thought it necessary to urge these brethren to go to you before I do, and make arrangements in advance for this bountiful, promised gift of yours; so that it may be ready, not as an extortion—wrung out of you—but as a generous *and* willing gift.

Living New Testament

13 Of course, I don't mean that those who receive your gifts should have an easy time of it at your expense,

14 But you should divide with them. Right now you have plenty and can help them; then at some other time they can share with you when you need it. In this way each will have as much as he needs.

15 Do you remember what the Scriptures say about this? "He that gathered much had nothing left over, and he that gathered little had enough." So you also should share with those in need.

16 I am thankful to God that He has given Titus the same real concern for you that I have.

17 He is glad to follow my suggestion that he visit you again—but I think he would have come anyway, for he is very eager to see you!

18 I am sending another well-known brother with him, who is highly praised as a preacher of the Good News in all the churches.

19 In fact, this man was elected by the churches to travel with me to take the gift to Jerusalem. This will glorify the Lord and show our eagerness to help each other.

20 By traveling together we will guard against any suspicion, for we are anxious that no one should find fault with the way we are handling this large gift.

21 God knows we are honest, but I want everyone else to know it too. That is why we have made this arrangement.

22 And I am sending you still another brother, whom we know from experience to be an earnest Christian. He is especially interested, as he looks forward to this trip, because I have told him all about your eagerness to help.

23 If anyone asks who Titus is, say that he is my partner, my helper in helping you, and you can also say that the other two brothers represent the assemblies here and are splendid examples of those who belong to the Lord.

24 Please show your love for me to these men and do for them all that I have publicly boasted you would.

Revised Standard

he has not. 13 I do not mean that others should
be eased and you burdened, 14 but that as a
matter of equality your abundance at the
present time should supply their want, so
that their abundance may supply your want,
that there may be equality. 15 As it is written,
"He who gathered much had nothing over,
and he who gathered little had no lack."

Coming of Titus and the messengers

16 But thanks be to God who puts the
same earnest care for you into the heart of
Titus. 17 For he not only accepted our appeal, but being himself very earnest he is
going to you of his own accord. 18 With him
we are sending the brother who is famous
among all the churches for his preaching of
the gospel; 19 and not only that, but he has
been appointed by the churches to travel
with us in this gracious work which we are
carrying on, for the glory of the Lord and
to show our good will. 20 We intend that no
one should blame us about this liberal gift
which we are administering, 21 for we aim at
what is honorable not only in the Lord's
sight but also in the sight of men. 22 And
with them we are sending our brother whom
we have often tested and found earnest in
many matters, but who is now more earnest
than ever because of his great confidence
in you. 23 As for Titus, he is my partner and
fellow worker in your service; and as for
our brethren, they are messengers[j] of the
churches, the glory of Christ. 24 So give
proof, before the churches, of your love
and of our boasting about you to these men.

CHAPTER 9

I realize that I really don't even need to mention this to you, about helping God's people.

2 For I know how eager you are to do it, and I have boasted to the friends in Macedonia that you were ready to send an offering a year ago. In fact, it was this enthusiasm of yours that stirred up many of them to begin helping.

3 But I am sending these men just to be sure that you really are ready, as I told them you would be, with your money all collected; I don't want it to turn out that this time I was wrong in my boasting about you.

4 I would be very much ashamed—and so would you—if some of these Macedonian people come with me, only to find that you still aren't ready after all I have told them!

5 So I have asked these other brethren to arrive ahead of me to see that the gift you promised is on hand and waiting. I want it to be a real gift and not look as if it were being given under pressure.

The offering for the saints

9 Now it is superfluous for me to write to
you about the offering for the saints,
2 for I know your readiness, of which I boast
about you to the people of Macedonia, saying that Achaia has been ready since last
year; and your zeal has stirred up most of
them. 3 But I am sending the brethren so
that our boasting about you may not prove
vain in this case, so that you may be ready,
as I said you would be; 4 lest if some Macedonians come with me and find that you
are not ready, we be humiliated—to say
nothing of you—for being so confident. 5 So
I thought it necessary to urge the brethren
to go on to you before me, and arrange in
advance for this gift you have promised, so
that it may be ready not as an exaction but
as a willing gift.

---

[j] Greek *apostles*

King James

6 But this *I say*, He which soweth sparingly shall reap also sparingly; and he which soweth bountifully shall reap also bountifully.

7 Every man according as he purposeth in his heart, *so let him give;* not grudgingly, or of necessity: for God loveth a cheerful giver.

8 And God *is* able to make all grace abound toward you; that ye, always having all sufficiency in all *things*, may abound to every good work:

9 (As it is written, He hath dispersed abroad; he hath given to the poor: his righteousness remaineth for ever.

10 Now he that ministereth seed to the sower both minister bread for *your* food, and multiply your seed sown, and increase the fruits of your righteousness;)

11 Being enriched in every thing to all bountifulness, which causeth through us thanksgiving to God.

12 For the administration of this service not only supplieth the want of the saints, but is abundant also by many thanksgivings unto God;

13 Whiles by the experiment of this ministration they glorify God for your professed subjection unto the gospel of Christ, and for *your* liberal distribution unto them, and unto all *men;*

14 And by their prayer for you, which long after you for the exceeding grace of God in you.

15 Thanks *be* unto God for his unspeakable gift.

Amplified

6 [Remember] this: he who sows sparingly *and* grudgingly will also reap sparingly *and* grudgingly, and he who sows generously *and* [r]that blessings may come to someone, will also reap generously *and* with blessings.

7 Let each one [give] as he has made up his own mind *and* purposed in his heart, not reluctantly *or* sorrowfully or under compulsion, for God loves (that is, He [r]takes pleasure in, prizes above other things, and is unwilling to abandon or to do without) a cheerful (joyous, prompt-to-do-it) giver—whose heart is in his giving. [Prov. 22:9.]

8 And God is able to make all grace (every favor and [r]earthly blessing) come to you in abundance, so that you may always *and* under all circumstances *and* whatever the need, [s]be self-sufficient—possessing enough to require no aid or support and furnished in abundance for every good work and charitable donation.

9 As it is written, He [the benevolent person] scatters abroad, he gives to the poor; his deeds of justice *and* goodness *and* kindness *and* benevolence will go on *and* endure forever! [Ps. 112:9.]

10 And [God] Who provides seed for the sower and bread for eating will also provide and multiply your [resources for] sowing, and increase the fruits of your righteousness [[t]which manifests itself in active goodness, kindness and charity]. [Isa. 55:10; Hos. 10:12.]

11 Thus you will be enriched in all things *and* in every way, so that you can be generous, [and your generosity as it is] administered by us will bring forth thanksgiving to God.

12 For the service the ministering of this fund renders does not only fully supply what is lacking to the saints (God's people), but it also overflows in many [cries of] thanksgiving to God.

13 Because at [your] standing of the test of this ministry, they will glorify God at your loyalty *and* obedience to the Gospel of Christ which you confess, as well as for your generous-hearted liberality to them and to all [the other needy ones].

14 And they yearn for you while they pray for you, because of the surpassing measure of God's grace (His favor and mercy and spiritual blessing which is shown forth) in you.

15 Now thanks be to God for His Gift, [precious] beyond telling—His indescribable, inexpressible, free Gift!

CHAPTER 10

NOW I Paul myself beseech you by the meekness and gentleness of Christ, who in presence *am* base among you, but being absent am bold toward you:

2 But I beseech *you*, that I may not be bold when I am present with that confidence, wherewith I think to be bold against some, which think of us as if we walked according to the flesh.

3 For though we walk in the flesh, we do not war after the flesh:

4 (For the weapons of our warfare *are* not carnal, but mighty through God to the pulling down of strong holds;)

CHAPTER 10

NOW I myself, Paul, beseech you, by the gentleness and consideration of Christ [Himself; I] who [am] lowly enough [so they say] when among you face to face, but bold (fearless and outspoken to you when I am) absent from you!

2 I entreat you when I do come [to you] that I may not [be driven to such] boldness as I intend to show toward those few who suspect us of acting according to the flesh—on the low level of worldly motives and as if invested with only human powers.

3 For though we walk [live] in the flesh, we are not carrying on our warfare according to the flesh *and* using mere human weapons.

4 For the weapons of our warfare are not physical (weapons of flesh and blood), but they are mighty before God for the overthrow *and* destruction of strongholds,

r) Thayer.
s) Vincent.
t) Thayer.

Living New Testament

6 But remember this—if you give little, you will get little. A farmer who plants just a few seeds will get only a small crop, but if he plants much, he will reap much.

7 Every one must make up his own mind as to how much he should give. Don't force anyone to give more than he really wants to, for cheerful givers are the ones God prizes.

8 God is able to make it up to you by giving you everything you need and more, so that there will not only be enough for your own needs, but plenty left over to give joyfully to others.

9 It is as the Scriptures say: "The godly man gives generously to the poor. His good deeds will be an honor to him forever."

10 For God, who gives seed to the farmer to plant, and later on, good crops to harvest and eat, will give you more and more seed to plant and will make it grow so that you can give away more and more fruit from your harvest.

11 Yes, God will give you much so that you can give away much, and when we take your gifts to those who need them they will break out into thanksgiving and praise to God for your help.

12 So, two good things happen as a result of your gifts—those in need are helped, and they overflow with thanks to God.

13 Those you help will be glad not only because of your generous gifts to themselves and to others, but they will praise God for this proof that your deeds are as good as your doctrine.

14 And they will pray for you with deep fervor and feeling because of the wonderful grace of God shown through you.

15 Thank God for His Son—His Gift too wonderful for words.

Revised Standard

God loves a cheerful giver

6 The point is this: he who sows sparingly will also reap sparingly, and he who sows
bountifully will also reap bountifully. 7 Each
one must do as he has made up his mind,
not reluctantly or under compulsion, for
God loves a cheerful giver. 8 And God is
able to provide you with every blessing in
abundance, so that you may always have
enough of everything and may provide in
abundance for every good work. 9 As it is
written,

"He scatters abroad, he gives to the poor;
his righteousness[k] endures for ever."

10 He who supplies seed to the sower and
bread for food will supply and multiply
your resources[l] and increase the harvest of
your righteousness.[k] 11 You will be enriched
in every way for great generosity, which
through us will produce thanksgiving to God;
12 for the rendering of this service not only
supplies the wants of the saints but also
overflows in many thanksgivings to God.
13 Under the test of this service, you[m] will
glorify God by your obedience in acknowledging the gospel of Christ, and by the generosity of your contribution for them and
for all others; 14 while they long for you and
pray for you, because of the surpassing grace
of God in you. 15 Thanks be to God for his
inexpressible gift!

CHAPTER 10

I plead with you—yes, I, Paul—and I plead gently, as Christ Himself would do. Yet some of you are saying, "Paul's letters are bold enough when he is far away, but when he gets here he will be afraid to raise his voice!"

2 I hope I won't need to show you when I come how harsh and rough I can be. I don't want to carry out my present plans against some of you who seem to think my deeds and words are merely those of an ordinary man.

3 It is true that I am no ordinary weak human being, but I don't use human plans and methods to win my battles.

4 I use God's mighty weapons, not those made by men, to knock down the devil's strongholds.

Paul's reply to charges against him

10 I, Paul, myself entreat you, by the
meekness and gentleness of Christ—I
who am humble when face to face with you,
but bold to you when I am away!—2 I beg
of you that when I am present I may not
have to show boldness with such confidence
as I count on showing against some who
suspect us of acting in worldly fashion. 3 For
though we live in the world we are not carrying on a worldly war, 4 for the weapons
of our warfare are not worldly but have
divine power to destroy strongholds. 5 We

[k] Or *benevolence*
[l] Greek *sowing*
[m] Or *they*

King James

5 Casting down imaginations, and every high thing that exalteth itself against the knowledge of God, and bringing into captivity every thought to the obedience of Christ;
6 And having in a readiness to revenge all disobedience, when your obedience is fulfilled.
7 Do ye look on things after the outward appearance? If any man trust to himself that he is Christ's, let him of himself think this again, that, as he *is* Christ's, even so *are* we Christ's.
8 For though I should boast somewhat more of our authority, which the Lord hath given us for edification, and not for your destruction, I should not be ashamed:
9 That I may not seem as if I would terrify you by letters.
10 For *his* letters, say they, *are* weighty and powerful; but *his* bodily presence *is* weak, and *his* speech contemptible.
11 Let such an one think this, that, such as we are in word by letters when we are absent, such *will we be* also in deed when we are present.
12 For we dare not make ourselves of the number, or compare ourselves with some that commend themselves: but they measuring themselves by themselves, and comparing themselves among themselves, are not wise.
13 But we will not boast of things without *our* measure, but according to the measure of the rule which God hath distributed to us, a measure to reach even unto you.
14 For we stretch not ourselves beyond *our measure*, as though we reached not unto you: for we are come as far as to you also in *preaching* the gospel of Christ:
15 Not boasting of things without *our* measure, *that is*, of other men's labours; but having hope, when your faith is increased, that we shall be enlarged by you according to our rule abundantly,
16 To preach the gospel in the *regions* beyond you, *and* not to boast in another man's line of things made ready to our hand.
17 But he that glorieth, let him glory in the Lord.
18 For not he that commendeth himself is approved, but whom the Lord commendeth.

Amplified

5 [Inasmuch as we] refute arguments *and* theories *and* reasonings and every proud *and* lofty thing that sets itself up against the (true) knowledge of God; and we lead every thought *and* purpose away captive into the obedience of Christ, the Messiah, the Anointed One,
6 Being in readiness to punish every [insubordinate for his] disobedience, when your own submission *and* obedience [as a church] are fully secured *and* complete.
7 Look at [this obvious fact] which is before your eyes. If any one is confident that he is Christ's, let him reflect *and* remind himself that even as he is Christ's, so too are we.
8 For even though I boast rather freely about our power *and* authority, which the Lord gave for your upbuilding and not for demolishing you, yet I shall not be put to shame [for exceeding the truth],
9 Neither would I seem to be overawing *or* frightening you with my letters;
10 For they say, His letters are weighty *and* impressive and forceful *and* telling, but his personality *and* bodily presence are weak, and his speech *and* delivery are utterly contemptible—of no account.
11 Let such people realize that what we say by letters when we are absent, [we put] also into deeds when we are present.
12 Not that we [have the audacity to] venture to class or [even to] compare ourselves with some who exalt *and* furnish testimonials for themselves! However, when they measure themselves with themselves and compare themselves with one another, they are without understanding *and* behave unwisely.
13 We, on the other hand, will not boast beyond our legitimate province *and* proper limit, but will keep within the limits [of our commission which] God has allotted us as our measuring line, and which reaches *and* includes even you.
14 For we are not overstepping the limits of our province *and* stretching beyond our ability to reach, as though we (had no legitimate mission to) you, for we were [the very first] to come even as far as to you with the good news (the Gospel) of Christ.
15 We do not boast therefore beyond our proper limit, over other men's labors, but we have the hope *and* confident expectation that as your faith continues to grow our field among you may be greatly enlarged, still within the limits of our commission,
16 So that [we may even] preach the Gospel in lands [lying] beyond you, without making a boast of work already done in another [man's] sphere of activity [before we came on the scene].
17 However, let him who boasts *and* glories, boast *and* glory in the Lord. [Jer. 9:24.]
18 For [it is] not [the man] who praises *and* commends himself who is approved *and* accepted, but [it is the person] whom the Lord accredits *and* commends.

CHAPTER 11

WOULD to God ye could bear with me a little in *my* folly: and indeed bear with me.
2 For I am jealous over you with godly jealousy: for I have espoused you to one husband, that I may present *you* as a chaste virgin to Christ.

CHAPTER 11

I WISH you would bear with me while I indulge in a little [so-called] foolishness. Do bear with me!
2 For I am [u]zealous for you with a godly eagerness *and* a divine jealousy, for I have betrothed you to one Husband, to present you a chaste virgin to Christ. [Hos. 2:19, 20.]

u) Abbott-Smith, Thayer, Berry, etc.

Living New Testament

5 These weapons can break down every proud argument against God and every wall that can be built to keep men from finding Him. With these weapons I can capture rebels and bring them back to God, and change them into men whose hearts' desire is obedience to Christ.

6 I will use these weapons against every rebel who remains after I have first used them on you yourselves, and you surrender to Christ.

7 The trouble with you is that you look at me and I seem weak and powerless, but you don't look beneath the surface. Yet if anyone can claim the power and authority of Christ, I certainly can.

8 I may seem to be boasting more than I should about my authority over you—authority to help you, not to hurt you—but I shall make good every claim.

9 I say this so that you will not think I am just blustering when I scold you in my letters.

10 "Don't bother about his letters," some say. "He sounds big, but it's all noise. When he gets here you will see that there is nothing great about him, and you have never heard a worse preacher!"

11 This time my personal presence is going to be just as rough on you as my letters are!

12 Oh, don't worry, I wouldn't dare say that I am as wonderful as these other men who tell you how good they are! Their trouble is that they are only comparing themselves with each other, and measuring themselves against their own little ideas. What stupidity!

13 But we will not boast of authority we do not have. Our goal is to measure up to God's plan for us, and this plan includes our working there with you.

14 We are not going too far when we claim authority over you, for we were the first to come to you with the Good News concerning Christ.

15 It is not as though we were trying to claim credit for the work someone else has done among you. Instead, we hope that your faith will grow and that, still within the limits set for us, our work among you will be greatly enlarged.

16 After that, we will be able to preach the Good News to other cities that are far beyond you, where no one else is working; then there will be no question about being in someone else's field.

17 As the Scriptures say, "If anyone is going to boast, let him boast about what the Lord has done and not about himself."

18 When someone boasts about himself and how well he has done, it doesn't count for much. But when the Lord commends him, that's different!

Revised Standard

destroy arguments and every proud obstacle
to the knowledge of God, and take every
thought captive to obey Christ, 6being ready
to punish every disobedience, when your
obedience is complete.

7 Look at what is before your eyes. If
any one is confident that he is Christ's, let
him remind himself that as he is Christ's, so
are we. 8For even if I boast a little too much
of our authority, which the Lord gave for
building you up and not for destroying you,
I shall not be put to shame. 9I would not
seem to be frightening you with letters.
10For they say, "His letters are weighty and
strong, but his bodily presence is weak, and
his speech of no account." 11Let such people
understand that what we say by letter when
absent, we do when present. 12Not that we
venture to class or compare ourselves with
some of those who commend themselves.
But when they measure themselves by one
another, and compare themselves with one
another, they are without understanding.

Paul stays within God's limits

13 But we will not boast beyond limit,
but will keep to the limits God has apportioned us, to reach even to you. 14For we
are not overextending ourselves, as though
we did not reach you; we were the first to
come all the way to you with the gospel of
Christ. 15We do not boast beyond limit, in
other men's labors; but our hope is that as
your faith increases, our field among you
may be greatly enlarged, 16so that we may
preach the gospel in lands beyond you,
without boasting of work already done in
another's field. 17"Let him who boasts, boast
of the Lord." 18For it is not the man who
commends himself that is accepted, but
the man whom the Lord commends.

CHAPTER 11

I hope you will be patient with me as I keep on talking like a fool. Do bear with me and let me say what is on my heart.

2 I am anxious for you with the deep concern of God Himself—anxious that your love should be for Christ alone, just as a pure maiden reserves her love for one man only, for the one who will be her husband.

Paul's fear of false teachers

11 I wish you would bear with me in a
little foolishness. Do bear with me!
2I feel a divine jealousy for you, for I betrothed you to Christ to present you as a
pure bride to her one husband. 3But I am

King James

3 But I fear, lest by any means, as the serpent beguiled Eve through his subtilty, so your minds should be corrupted from the simplicity that is in Christ.

4 For if he that cometh preacheth another Jesus, whom we have not preached, or *if* ye receive another spirit, which ye have not received, or another gospel, which ye have not accepted, ye might well bear with *him.*

5 For I suppose I was not a whit behind the very chiefest apostles.

6 But though *I be* rude in speech, yet not in knowledge; but we have been throughly made manifest among you in all things.

7 Have I committed an offence in abasing myself that ye might be exalted, because I have preached to you the gospel of God freely?

8 I robbed other churches, taking wages *of them,* to do you service.

9 And when I was present with you, and wanted, I was chargeable to no man: for that which was lacking to me the brethren which came from Macedonia supplied: and in all *things* I have kept myself from being burdensome unto you, and *so* will I keep *myself.*

10 As the truth of Christ is in me, no man shall stop me of this boasting in the regions of Achaia.

11 Wherefore? because I love you not? God knoweth.

12 But what I do, that I will do, that I may cut off occasion from them which desire occasion; that wherein they glory, they may be found even as we.

13 For such *are* false apostles, deceitful workers, transforming themselves into the apostles of Christ.

14 And no marvel; for Satan himself is transformed into an angel of light.

15 Therefore *it is* no great thing if his ministers also be transformed as the ministers of righteousness; whose end shall be according to their works.

16 I say again, Let no man think me a fool; if otherwise, yet as a fool receive me, that I may boast myself a little.

17 That which I speak, I speak *it* not after the Lord, but as it were foolishly, in this confidence of boasting.

18 Seeing that many glory after the flesh, I will glory also.

19 For ye suffer fools gladly, seeing ye *yourselves* are wise.

20 For ye suffer, if a man bring you into bondage, if a man devour *you,* if a man take *of you,* if a man exalt himself, if a man smite you on the face.

21 I speak as concerning reproach, as though we had been weak. Howbeit whereinsoever any is bold, (I speak foolishly,) I am bold also.

22 Are they Hebrews? so *am* I. Are they Israelites? so *am* I. Are they the seed of Abraham? so *am* I.

Amplified

3 But [now] I am fearful lest that even as the serpent beguiled Eve by his cunning, so your minds may be corrupted *and* seduced from wholehearted *and* sincere *and* pure devotion to Christ. [Gen. 3:4.]

4 For [you seem readily to endure it] if a man comes and preaches another Jesus than the One we preached, or if you receive a different spirit from the [Spirit] you [once] received, or a different gospel from the one you [then] received *and* welcomed. You tolerate [all that] well enough!

5 Yet I consider myself as in no way inferior to these (precious) [v]extra-super [false] apostles.

6 But even if [I am] unskilled in speaking, yet [I am] not [unskilled] in knowledge—I know what I am talking about; we have made this evident to you in all things.

7 But did I perhaps make a mistake *and* do you a wrong in debasing *and* cheapening myself so that you might be exalted *and* enriched in dignity *and* honor *and* happiness, by preaching God's Gospel without expense to you?

8 Other churches I have robbed by accepting [more than their share of] support for my ministry [from them in order] to serve you.

9 And when I was with you and ran short financially, I did not burden any [of you], for what I lacked was abundantly made up by the brethren who came from Macedonia. So I kept myself from being burdensome to you in any way, and will continue to keep [myself from being so].

10 As the truth of Christ is in me, this my boast [of independence] shall not be debarred (silenced or checked) in the regions of Achaia [most of Greece].

11 And why? Because I do not love you—do not have a preference for you, wish you well and regard your welfare? God perceives *and* knows that I do!

12 But what I do I will continue to do, [for I am determined to maintain this independence] in order to cut off the claim of those who would like [to find an occasion and incentive] to claim that in their boasted [mission] they work on the same terms that we do.

13 For such men are false apostles—spurious, counterfeits—deceitful workmen, masquerading as apostles (special messengers) of Christ, the Messiah.

14 And it is no wonder, for Satan himself masquerades as an angel of light,

15 So it is not surprising if his servants also masquerade as ministers of righteousness. [But] their end will correspond with their deeds.

16 I repeat then, let no one think I have lost my wits; but even if you do, then bear with a witless man, so that I too may boast a little.

17 What I say by way of this confident boasting, I say not with the Lord's authority (by inspiration) but as it were in pure witlessness.

18 [For], since many boast of worldly things *and* according to the flesh, I will glory (boast) also.

19 For you readily *and* gladly bear with the foolish, since you are so smart *and* wise yourselves!

20 For you endure it if a man assumes control of your souls *and* makes slaves of you, or devours (your substance, spends your money) *and* preys upon you, or deceives *and* takes advantage of you, or is arrogant *and* puts on airs, or strikes you in the face.

21 To my discredit, I must say, we have shown ourselves too weak [for you to show such tolerance of us; for us to do strong, courageous things like that to you]! But in whatever any person is bold *and* dares [to boast], mind I am speaking in this foolish (witless) way, I also am bold *and* dare [to boast].

22 They are Hebrews? So am I! They are Israelites? So am I! They are descendants of Abraham? So am I!

---

v) Farrar's "Life and Work of Saint Paul."

Living New Testament

3 But I am frightened, fearing that in some way you will be led away from your pure and simple devotion to our Lord, just as Eve was deceived by Satan in the Garden of Eden.

4 You seem so gullible: you believe whatever anyone tells you even if he is preaching about another Jesus than the one we preach, or a different spirit than the Holy Spirit you received, or shows you a different way to be saved. You swallow it all.

5 Yet I don't feel that these marvelous "messengers from God," as they call themselves, are any better than I am.

6 If I am a poor speaker, at least I know what I am talking about, as I think you realize by now, for we have proved it again and again.

7 Did I do wrong and cheapen myself and make you look down on me because I preached God's Good News to you without charging you anything?

8, 9 Instead I "robbed" other churches by taking what they sent me, and using it up while I was with you, so that I could serve you without cost. And when that was gone,[1] and I was getting hungry I still didn't ask you for anything, for the Christians from Macedonia brought me another gift. I have never yet asked you for one cent, and I never will.

10 I promise this with every ounce of truth I possess—that I will tell everyone in Greece about it!

11 Why? Because I don't love you? God knows I do.

12 But I will do it to cut out the ground from under the feet of those who boast that they are doing God's work in just the same way we are.

13 God never sent those men at all; they are "phonies" who have fooled you into thinking they are Christ's apostles.

14 Yet I am not surprised! Satan can change himself into an angel of light,

15 So is it no wonder his servants can do it too, and seem like godly ministers. In the end they will get every bit of punishment their wicked deeds deserve.

16 Again I plead, don't think that I have lost my wits to talk like this; but even if you do, listen to me anyway—a witless man, a fool—while I also boast a little as they do.

17 Such bragging isn't something the Lord commanded me to do, for I am acting like a brainless fool.

18 Yet those other men keep telling you how wonderful they are, so here I go:

19, 20 (You think you are so wise—yet you listen gladly to those fools; you don't mind at all when they make you their slaves and take everything you have, and take advantage of you, and put on airs, and slap you in the face.

21 I'm ashamed to say that I'm not strong and daring like that! But whatever they can boast about—I'm talking like a fool again—I can boast about it, too.)

22 They brag that they are Hebrews, do they? Well, so am I. And they say that they are Israelites, God's chosen people? So am I. And they are descendents of Abraham? Well, I am too.

1 Implied.

Revised Standard

afraid that as the serpent deceived Eve by
his cunning, your thoughts will be led astray
from a sincere and pure devotion to Christ.
[4]For if some one comes and preaches another Jesus than the one we preached, or if you
receive a different spirit from the one you
received, or if you accept a different gospel
from the one you accepted, you submit to
it readily enough. [5]I think that I am not
in the least inferior to these superlative apostles. [6]Even if I am unskilled in speaking, I
am not in knowledge; in every way we have
made this plain to you in all things.

7 Did I commit a sin in abasing myself
so that you might be exalted, because I
preached God's gospel without cost to you?
[8]I robbed other churches by accepting support from them in order to serve you. [9]And
when I was with you and was in want, I did
not burden any one, for my needs were supplied by the brethren who came from Macedonia. So I refrained and will refrain from
burdening you in any way. [10]As the truth
of Christ is in me, this boast of mine shall
not be silenced in the regions of Achaia.
[11]And why? Because I do not love you? God
knows I do!

12 And what I do I will continue to do,
in order to undermine the claim of those
who would like to claim that in their boasted
mission they work on the same terms as
we do. [13]For such men are false apostles,
deceitful workmen, disguising themselves as
apostles of Christ. [14]And no wonder, for even
Satan disguises himself as an angel of light.
[15]So it is not strange if his servants also
disguise themselves as servants of righteousness. Their end will correspond to their
deeds.

Paul's rightful boasting

16 I repeat, let no one think me foolish;
but even if you do, accept me as a fool, so
that I too may boast a little. [17](What I am
saying I say not with the Lord's authority
but as a fool, in this boastful confidence;
[18]since many boast of worldly things, I too
will boast.) [19]For you gladly bear with fools,
being wise yourselves! [20]For you bear it if
a man makes slaves of you, or preys upon
you, or takes advantage of you, or puts on
airs, or strikes you in the face. [21]To my
shame, I must say, we were too weak for
that!

But whatever any one dares to boast of—I
am speaking as a fool—I also dare to boast
of that. [22]Are they Hebrews? So am I. Are
they Israelites? So am I. Are they descendants of Abraham? So am I. [23]Are they ser-

King James

23 Are they ministers of Christ? (I speak as a fool) I *am* more; in labours more abundant, in stripes above measure, in prisons more frequent, in deaths oft.

24 Of the Jews five times received I forty *stripes* save one.

25 Thrice was I beaten with rods, once was I stoned, thrice I suffered shipwreck, a night and a day I have been in the deep;

26 *In* journeyings often, *in* perils of waters, *in* perils of robbers, *in* perils by *mine own* countrymen, *in* perils by the heathen, *in* perils in the city, *in* perils in the wilderness, *in* perils in the sea, *in* perils among false brethren;

27 In weariness and painfulness, in watchings often, in hunger and thirst, in fastings often, in cold and nakedness.

28 Beside those things that are without, that which cometh upon me daily, the care of all the churches.

29 Who is weak, and I am not weak? who is offended, and I burn not?

30 If I must needs glory, I will glory of the things which concern mine infirmities.

31 The God and Father of our Lord Jesus Christ, which is blessed for evermore, knoweth that I lie not.

32 In Damascus the governor under Aretas the king kept the city of the Damascenes with a garrison, desirous to apprehend me:

33 And through a window in a basket was I let down by the wall, and escaped his hands.

Amplified

23 Are they (ministering) servants of Christ, the Messiah? I am talking like one beside himself, [but] I am more, with far more extensive *and* abundant labors, with far more imprisonments, [beaten] with countless stripes, and frequently [at the point of] death.

24 Five times I received from [the hands of] the Jews forty [lashes all] but one; [Deut. 25:3.]

25 Three times I have been beaten with rods; once I was stoned. Three times I have been aboard a ship wrecked at sea; a [whole] night and a day I have spent (adrift) on the deep;

26 Many times on journeys, [exposed to] perils from rivers, perils from bandits, perils from [my own] nation, perils from the Gentiles, perils in the city, perils in the desert places, perils in the sea, perils from those posing as believers—but destitute of Christian knowledge and piety;

27 In toil and hardship, watching often (through sleepless nights), in hunger and thirst, frequently driven to fasting by want, in cold and exposure *and* lack of clothing.

28 And besides those things that are without, there is the daily [inescapable pressure] of my care *and* anxiety for all the churches!

29 Who is weak, and I do not feel [his] weakness? Who is made to stumble *and* fall *and* have his faith hurt, and I am not on fire [with sorrow or indignation]?

30 If I must boast, I will boast of the things that [show] my infirmity—of the things by which I am made weak and contemptible [in the eyes of my opponents].

31 The God and Father of the Lord Jesus *Christ* knows, He Who is blessed *and* to be praised forevermore, that I do not lie.

32 In Damascus, the city governor acting under King Aretas guarded the city of Damascus [on purpose] to arrest me,

33 And I was [actually] let down in a (rope) basket *or* hamper, through a window [a small door] in the wall, and I escaped through his fingers.

CHAPTER 12

IT is not expedient for me doubtless to glory. I will come to visions and revelations of the Lord.

2 I knew a man in Christ above fourteen years ago, (whether in the body, I cannot tell; or whether out of the body, I cannot tell: God knoweth;) such an one caught up to the third heaven.

3 And I knew such a man, (whether in the body, or out of the body, I cannot tell: God knoweth;)

4 How that he was caught up into paradise, and heard unspeakable words, which it is not lawful for a man to utter.

5 Of such an one will I glory: yet of myself I will not glory, but in mine infirmities.

6 For though I would desire to glory, I shall not be a fool; for I will say the truth: but *now* I forbear, lest any man should think of me above that which he seeth me *to be*, or *that* he heareth of me.

7 And lest I should be exalted above measure through the abundance of the revelations, there was given to me a thorn in the flesh, the messenger of Satan to buffet me, lest I should be exalted above measure.

CHAPTER 12

TRUE, there is nothing to be gained by it, but [as I am obliged] to boast I will go on to visions and revelations of the Lord.

2 I know a man in Christ who fourteen years ago, whether in the body or out of the body I do not know, God knows, was caught up to the third heaven.

3 And I know that this man was caught up into Paradise, whether in the body or away from the body I do not know, God knows.

4 And he heard utterances beyond the power of man to put into words, which man is not permitted to utter.

5 Of this same [man's experiences] I will boast, but of myself (personally) I will not boast, except as regards my infirmities—my weaknesses.

6 Should I desire to boast, I shall not be a witless braggart, for I shall be speaking the truth. But I abstain [from it] so that no one may form a higher estimate of me than [is justified by] what he sees in me or hears from me.

7 And to keep me from being puffed up *and* too much elated by the exceeding greatness (pre-eminence) of these revelations, there was given me a thorn ([w]a splinter) in the flesh, a messenger of Satan, to rack *and* buffet *and* harass me, to keep me from being excessively exalted. [Job 2:6.]

---

w) Moulton and Milligan's "The Vocabulary of the Greek Testament."

Living New Testament

23 They say they serve Christ? But I have served Him far more! (Have I gone mad to boast like this?) I have worked harder, been put in jail oftener, been whipped times without number, and faced death again and again and again.

24 Five different times the Jews gave me their terrible thirty-nine lashes.

25 Three times I was beaten with rods. Once I was stoned. Three times I was shipwrecked. Once I was in the open sea all night and the whole next day.

26 I have traveled many weary miles and have been often in great danger from flooded rivers, and from robbers, and from my own people, the Jews, as well as from the hands of the Gentiles. I have faced grave dangers from mobs in the cities and from death in the deserts and in the stormy seas and from men who claim to be brothers in Christ but are not.

27 I have lived with weariness and pain and sleepless nights. Often I have been hungry and thirsty and have gone without food; often I have shivered with cold, without enough clothing to keep me warm.

28 Then, besides all this, I have the constant worry of how the churches are getting along:

29 Who makes a mistake and I do not feel his sadness? Who falls without my longing to help him? Who is spiritually hurt without my fury rising against the one who hurt him?

30 But if I must brag, I would rather brag about the things that show how weak I am.

31 God, the Father of our Lord Jesus Christ, who is to be praised forever and ever, knows I tell the truth.

32 For instance, in Damascus the governor under King Aretas kept guards at the city gates to catch me;

33 But I was let down by rope and basket from a hole in the city wall, and so I got away! [What popularity![2]]

Revised Standard

vants of Christ? I am a better one—I am
talking like a madman—with far greater
labors, far more imprisonments, with countless beatings, and often near death. 24Five
times I have received at the hands of the
Jews the forty lashes less one. 25Three times
I have been beaten with rods; once I was
stoned. Three times I have been shipwrecked;
a night and a day I have been adrift at sea;
26on frequent journeys, in danger from rivers, danger from robbers, danger from my
own people, danger from Gentiles, danger
in the city, danger in the wilderness, danger
at sea, danger from false brethren; 27in toil
and hardship, through many a sleepless night,
in hunger and thirst, often without food, in
cold and exposure. 28And, apart from other
things, there is the daily pressure upon me of
my anxiety for all the churches. 29Who is
weak, and I am not weak? Who is made to
fall, and I am not indignant?
30 If I must boast, I will boast of the
things that show my weakness. 31The God
and Father of the Lord Jesus, he who is
blessed for ever, knows that I do not lie.
32At Damascus, the governor under King
Aretas guarded the city of Damascus in order to seize me, 33but I was let down in a
basket through a window in the wall, and
escaped his hands.

CHAPTER 12

This boasting is all so foolish, but let me go on. Let me tell about the visions I've had, and revelations from the Lord.

2, 3 Fourteen years ago I[1] was taken up to heaven[2] for a visit. Don't ask me whether my body was there or just my spirit, for I don't know; only God can answer that. But anyway, there I was in paradise,

4 And heard things so astounding that they are beyond a man's power to describe or put in words (and anyway I am not allowed to tell them to others).

5 That experience is something worth bragging about, but I am not going to do it. I am going to boast only about how weak I am and how great God is to use such weakness for His glory.

6 I have plenty to boast about and would be no fool in doing it, but I don't want anyone to think more highly of me than he should from what he can actually see in my life and my message.

7 I will say this: because these experiences I had were so tremendous, God was afraid I might be puffed up by them; so I was given a sickness which has been a thorn in my flesh, a messenger from Satan to hurt and bother me, and prick my pride.

Paul's visions of the Lord

12 I must boast; there is nothing to be
gained by it, but I will go on to visions
and revelations of the Lord. 2I know a man
in Christ who fourteen years ago was caught
up to the third heaven—whether in the body
or out of the body I do not know, God
knows. 3And I know that this man was
caught up into Paradise—whether in the
body or out of the body I do not know,
God knows—4and he heard things that cannot be told, which man may not utter. 5On
behalf of this man I will boast, but on my
own behalf I will not boast, except of my
weaknesses. 6Though if I wish to boast, I
shall not be a fool, for I shall be speaking
the truth. But I refrain from it, so that no
one may think more of me than he sees in
me or hears from me. 7And to keep me from
being too elated by the abundance of revelations, a thorn was given me in the flesh, a
messenger of Satan, to harass me, to keep
me from being too elated. 8Three times I

Implied.
Literally, "A man in Christ."
Literally, "the third heaven."

King James

8 For this thing I besought the Lord thrice, that it might depart from me.

9 And he said unto me, My grace is sufficient for thee: for my strength is made perfect in weakness. Most gladly therefore will I rather glory in my infirmities, that the power of Christ may rest upon me.

10 Therefore I take pleasure in infirmities, in reproaches, in necessities, in persecutions, in distresses for Christ's sake: for when I am weak, then am I strong.

11 I am become a fool in glorying; ye have compelled me: for I ought to have been commended of you: for in nothing am I behind the very chiefest apostles, though I be nothing.

12 Truly the signs of an apostle were wrought among you in all patience, in signs, and wonders, and mighty deeds.

13 For what is it wherein ye were inferior to other churches, except *it be* that I myself was not burdensome to you? forgive me this wrong.

14 Behold, the third time I am ready to come to you; and I will not be burdensome to you: for I seek not yours, but you: for the children ought not to lay up for the parents, but the parents for the children.

15 And I will very gladly spend and be spent for you; though the more abundantly I love you, the less I be loved.

16 But be it so, I did not burden you: nevertheless, being crafty, I caught you with guile.

17 Did I make a gain of you by any of them whom I sent unto you?

18 I desired Titus, and with *him* I sent a brother. Did Titus make a gain of you? walked we not in the same spirit? *walked we* not in the same steps?

19 Again, think ye that we excuse ourselves unto you? we speak before God in Christ: but *we do* all things, dearly beloved, for your edifying.

20 For I fear, lest, when I come, I shall not find you such as I would, and *that* I shall be found unto you such as ye would not: lest *there be* debates, envyings, wraths, strifes, backbitings, whisperings, swellings, tumults:

21 *And* lest, when I come again, my God will humble me among you, and *that* I shall bewail many which have sinned already, and have not repented of the uncleanness and fornication and lasciviousness which they have committed.

Amplified

8 Three times I called upon the Lord *and* besought [Him] about this *and* begged that it might depart from me;

9 But He said to me, My grace—My favor and loving-kindness and mercy—are enough for you, [that is, sufficient against any danger and to enable you to bear the trouble manfully]; for *My* strength *and* power are made perfect—fulfilled and completed *and* [x]*show themselves most effective* —in [your] weakness. Therefore, I will all the more gladly glory in my weaknesses *and* infirmities, that the strength *and* power of Christ, the Messiah, may rest—yes, may [y]pitch a tent [over] and dwell—upon me!

10 So for the sake of Christ, I am well pleased *and* take pleasure in infirmities, insults, hardships, persecutions, perplexities *and* distresses; for when I am weak ([z]in human strength), then am I [truly] strong—able, powerful [z]in divine strength.

11 Now I have been [speaking like] a fool! But you forced me to it, for I ought to have been [[y]saved the necessity and] commended by you. For I have not fallen short one bit *or* proved myself at all inferior to those superlative [false] apostles [of yours], even if I am nothing—a nobody.

12 Indeed, the signs that indicate [a genuine] apostle were performed among you fully *and* most patiently in miracles and wonders and mighty works.

13 For in what respect were you put to a disadvantage in comparison with the rest of the churches, unless [it was for the fact] that I myself did not burden you [with my financial support]? Pardon me [for doing you] this injustice!

14 Now for the third time I am ready to come to [visit] you. And I will not burden you [financially], for it is not yours that I want but you; for children are not duty bound to lay up store for their parents, but parents for their children.

15 But I will most gladly spend and be utterly spent [myself] for your souls. If I love you exceedingly, am I to be loved [by you] the less?

16 But though granting that I did not burden you [with my support, some say] I was crafty, *and* that I cheated *and* got the better of you with my trickery.

17 Did I [then] take advantage of you *or* make any money out of you through any of those [messengers] whom I sent to you?

18 [Actually] I urged Titus [to go], and I sent the brother with [him]. Did Titus overreach *or* take advantage of you [in anything]? Did he *and* I not act in the same spirit? Did we not [take the] same steps?

19 Have you been supposing [all this time] that we have been defending ourselves *and* apologizing to you? [It is] in the sight *and* the [very] presence of God [and as one] in Christ, the Messiah, that we have been speaking, dearly beloved, and all in order to build you up [spiritually].

20 For I am fearful lest somehow or other I may come and find you not what I desire to find you, and that you may find me too not what you want to find me; lest perhaps there may be factions (quarreling), jealousy, temper (wrath, intrigues, rivalry, divided loyalties), selfishness, whispering, gossip, arrogance (self-assertion) and disorder among you.

21 [I am fearful] that when I come again my God may humiliate *and* humble me in your regard, and that I may have to sorrow over many of those who sinned before and have not repented of the impurity, sexual vice and sensuality which they formerly practiced.

---

x) Two Greek texts so read.
y) Vincent.
z) Thayer.

Living New Testament

8 Three different times I begged God to make me well again.

9 Each time He said, "No. But I am with you; that is all you need. My power shows up best in weak people." Now I am glad to boast about how weak I am; I am glad to be a living demonstration of Christ's power, instead of showing off my own power and abilities.

10 Since I know it is all for Christ's good, I am quite happy about "the thorn," and about insults and hardships, persecutions and difficulties; for when I am weak, then I am strong—the less I have, the more I depend on Him.

11 You have made me act like a fool—boasting like this—for you people ought to be writing about me and not making me write about myself. There isn't a single thing these other marvelous fellows have that I don't have too, even though I am really worth nothing at all.

12 When I was there I certainly gave you every proof that I was truly an apostle, sent to you by God Himself: for I patiently did many wonders and signs and mighty works among you.

13 The only thing I didn't do for you, that I do everywhere else in all other churches, was to become a burden to you—I didn't ask you to give me food to eat and a place to stay. Please forgive me for this wrong!

14 Now I am coming to you again, the third time; and it is still not going to cost you anything, for I don't want your money. I want *you!* And anyway, you are my children, and little children don't pay for their father's and mother's food—it's the other way around; parents supply food for their children.

15 I am glad to give you myself and all I have for your spiritual good, even though it seems that the more I love you, the less you love me.

16 Some of you are saying, "It's true that his visits didn't seem to cost us anything, but he is a sneaky fellow, that Paul, and he fooled us. As sure as anything he must have made money from us some way."

17 But how? Did any of the men I sent to you take advantage of you?

18 When I urged Titus to visit you, and sent our other brother with him, did they make any profit? No, of course not. For we have the same Holy Spirit, and walk in each other's steps, doing things the same way.

19 I suppose you think I am saying all this to get back into your good graces. That isn't it at all. I tell you, with God listening as I say it, that I have said this to help *you*, dear friends—to build you up spiritually and not to help myself.[3]

20 For I am afraid that when I come to visit you I won't like what I find, and then you won't like the way I will have to act. I am afraid that I will find you quarreling, and envying each other, and being angry with each other, and acting big, and saying wicked things about each other and whispering behind each other's backs, filled with conceit and disunity.

21 Yes, I am afraid that when I come God will humble me before you and I will be sad and mourn because many of you have kept on sinning and don't even care about the wicked, impure things you have done: your lust and immorality, and the taking of other men's wives.

Revised Standard

besought the Lord about this, that it should leave me; 9but he said to me, "My grace is sufficient for you, for my power is made perfect in weakness." I will all the more gladly boast of my weaknesses, that the power of Christ may rest upon me. 10For the sake of Christ, then, I am content with weaknesses, insults, hardships, persecutions, and calamities; for when I am weak, then I am strong.

The marks of a true apostle

11 I have been a fool! You forced me to it, for I ought to have been commended by you. For I am not at all inferior to these superlative apostles, even though I am nothing. 12The signs of a true apostle were performed among you in all patience, with signs and wonders and mighty works. 13For in what were you less favored than the rest of the churches, except that I myself did not burden you? Forgive me this wrong!

14 Here for the third time I am ready to come to you. And I will not be a burden, for I seek not what is yours but you; for children ought not to lay up for their parents, but parents for their children. 15I will most gladly spend and be spent for your souls. If I love you the more, am I to be loved the less? 16But granting that I myself did not burden you, I was crafty, you say, and got the better of you by guile. 17Did I take advantage of you through any of those whom I sent to you? 18I urged Titus to go, and sent the brother with him. Did Titus take advantage of you? Did we not act in the same spirit? Did we not take the same steps?

The appeal for repentance

19 Have you been thinking all along that we have been defending ourselves before you? It is in the sight of God that we have been speaking in Christ, and all for your upbuilding, beloved. 20For I fear that perhaps I may come and find you not what I wish, and that you may find me not what you wish; that perhaps there may be quarreling, jealousy, anger, selfishness, slander, gossip, conceit, and disorder. 21I fear that when I come again my God may humble me before you, and I may have to mourn over many of those who sinned before and have not repented of the impurity, immorality, and licentiousness which they have practiced.

---

[3] Implied.

King James

CHAPTER 13

THIS *is* the third *time* I am coming to you. In the mouth of two or three witnesses shall every word be established.

2 I told you before, and foretell you, as if I were present, the second time; and being absent now I write to them which heretofore have sinned, and to all other, that, if I come again, I will not spare:

3 Since ye seek a proof of Christ speaking in me, which to youward is not weak, but is mighty in you.

4 For though he was crucified through weakness, yet he liveth by the power of God. For we also are weak in him, but we shall live with him by the power of God toward you.

5 Examine yourselves, whether ye be in the faith; prove your own selves. Know ye not your own selves, how that Jesus Christ is in you, except ye be reprobates?

6 But I trust that ye shall know that we are not reprobates.

7 Now I pray to God that ye do no evil; not that we should appear approved, but that ye should do that which is honest, though we be as reprobates.

8 For we can do nothing against the truth, but for the truth.

9 For we are glad, when we are weak, and ye are strong: and this also we wish, *even* your perfection.

10 Therefore I write these things being absent, lest being present I should use sharpness, according to the power which the Lord hath given me to edification, and not to destruction.

11 Finally, brethren, farewell. Be perfect, be of good comfort, be of one mind, live in peace; and the God of love and peace shall be with you.

12 Greet one another with an holy kiss.

13 All the saints salute you.

14 The grace of the Lord Jesus Christ, and the love of God, and the communion of the Holy Ghost, *be* with you all. Amen.

¶ The second *epistle* to the Corinthians was written from Philippi, *a city* of Macedonia, by Titus and Lucas.

Amplified

CHAPTER 13

THIS is the third time that I am coming to you. By the testimony of two or three witnesses must any charge *and* every accusing statement be sustained *and* confirmed. [Deut. 19:15.]

2 I have already warned those who sinned formerly and all the rest also, and I warn them now again while I am absent, as I did when present on my second visit, that if I come back I will not spare [them],

3 Since you desire *and* seek (perceptible) proof of the Christ Who speaks in *and* through me. [For He] is not weak *and* feeble in dealing with you, but is a mighty power within you;

4 For though He was crucified in weakness, yet He goes on living by the power of God. And though we too are weak in Him [as He was humanly weak], yet in dealing with you [we shall show ourselves] alive *and* strong in (fellowship with) Him by the power of God.

5 Examine *and* test *and* evaluate your own selves, to see whether you are holding to your faith *and* showing the proper fruits of it. Test *and* prove yourselves, [[a]not Christ]. Do you not yourselves realize *and* know (thoroughly by an ever-increasing experience) that Jesus Christ is in you? unless you are [counterfeits] disapproved on trial *and* rejected!

6 But I hope you will recognize *and* know that we are not disapproved on trial and rejected.

7 But I pray to God that you may do nothing wrong, not in order that we [[a]our teaching] may appear to be approved, but that you may continue doing right, [though] we may seem to have failed *and* be unapproved.

8 For we can do nothing against the Truth [[b]not serve any party or personal interest], but only for the Truth [[c]which is the Gospel].

9 For we are glad when we are weak ([a]unapproved) and you are really strong. And this we also pray for, your all round strengthening *and* perfecting of soul.

10 So I write these things while I am absent from you, that when I come to you I may not have to deal sharply in my use of the authority which the Lord has given me, [to be employed, however] for building [you] up and not for tearing [you] down.

11 Finally, brethren, farewell—rejoice! Be strengthened—perfected, completed, made what you ought to be; be encouraged *and* consoled *and* comforted; be of the same (agreeable) mind one with another; live in peace, and [then] the God of love [Who is the Source]—of affection, goodwill, love and benevolence toward men—and the Author *and* Promoter of peace will be with you.

12 Greet one another with a consecrated kiss.

13 All the saints (the people of God here) salute you.

14 The grace (favor and spiritual blessing) of the Lord Jesus Christ and the love of God and the presence *and* fellowship (the communion and sharing together, and participation) in the Holy Spirit be with you all. *Amen—so be it.*

---

a) Vincent.
b) Gray and Adams' Commentary.
c) Thayer.

Living New Testament

CHAPTER 13

This is the third time I am coming to visit you. The Scriptures tell us that if two or three have seen a wrong, it must be punished. [Well, this is my third warning, as I come now for this visit.[1]]

2 I have already warned those who had been sinning when I was there last; now I warn them again, and all others, just as I did then, that this time I come ready to punish severely and I will not spare them.

3 I will give you all the proof you want that Christ speaks through me. Christ is not weak in His dealings with you, but is a mighty power within you.

4 His weak, human body died on the cross, but now He lives by the mighty power of God. We, too, are weak in our bodies, as He was, but now we live and are strong, as He is, and have all of God's power to use in dealing with you.

5 Check up on yourselves. Are you really Christians? Do you pass the test? Do you feel Christ's presence and power more and more within you? Or are you just pretending to be Christians when actually you aren't at all?

6 I hope you can agree that I have stood that test and truly belong to the Lord.

7 I pray that you will live good lives, not because that will be a feather in our caps,[2] proving that what we teach is right; no, for we want you to do right even if we ourselves are despised.

8 Our responsibility is to encourage the right at all times, not to hope for evil.[3]

9 We are glad to be weak and despised if you are really strong. Our greatest wish and prayer is that you will become mature Christians.

10 I am writing this to you now in the hope that I won't need to scold and punish when I come; for I want to use the Lord's authority which He has given me, not to punish you but to make you strong.

11 I close my letter with these last words:

Be happy.
Grow in Christ.
Pay attention to what I have said.
Live in harmony and peace.

And may the God of love and peace be with you.

12 Greet each other warmly in the Lord.

13 All the Christians here send you their best regards.

14 May the grace of our Lord Jesus Christ be with you all. May God's love and the Holy Spirit's friendship be yours.

Paul

[1] Implied.
[2] Literally, "not that we may appear approved."
[3] Literally, "For we can do nothing against the truth, but for the truth."

Revised Standard

13 This is the third time I am coming to
you. Any charge must be sustained
by the evidence of two or three witnesses.
[2]I warned those who sinned before and all
the others, and I warn them now while absent, as I did when present on my second
visit, that if I come again I will not spare
them—[3]since you desire proof that Christ is
speaking in me. He is not weak in dealing
with you, but is powerful in you. [4]For he
was crucified in weakness, but lives by the
power of God. For we are weak in him,
but in dealing with you we shall live with
him by the power of God.
5 Examine yourselves, to see whether you
are holding to your faith. Test yourselves.
Do you not realize that Jesus Christ is in
you?—unless indeed you fail to meet the
test! [6]I hope you will find out that we have
not failed. [7]But we pray God that you may
not do wrong—not that we may appear to
have met the test, but that you may do
what is right, though we may seem to have
failed. [8]For we cannot do anything against
the truth, but only for the truth. [9]For we
are glad when we are weak and you are
strong. What we pray for is your improvement. [10]I write this while I am away from
you, in order that when I come I may not
have to be severe in my use of the authority which the Lord has given me for building up and not for tearing down.

Farewell and benediction

11 Finally, brethren, farewell. Mend your
ways, heed my appeal, agree with one another, live in peace, and the God of love and
peace will be with you. [12]Greet one another
with a holy kiss. [13]All the saints greet you.
14 The grace of the Lord Jesus Christ and
the love of God and the fellowship of[n] the
Holy Spirit be with you all.

[n] Or *and participation in*

King James

THE EPISTLE OF PAUL THE APOSTLE
TO THE

Galatians

CHAPTER 1

PAUL, an apostle, (not of men, neither
by man, but by Jesus Christ, and God
the Father, who raised him from the dead;)
2 And all the brethren which are with
me, unto the churches of Galatia:
3 Grace *be* to you and peace from God
the Father, and *from* our Lord Jesus Christ,
4 Who gave himself for our sins, that he
might deliver us from this present evil
world, according to the will of God and our
Father:
5 To whom *be* glory for ever and ever.
Amen.
6 I marvel that ye are so soon removed
from him that called you into the grace of
Christ unto another gospel:
7 Which is not another; but there be
some that trouble you, and would pervert
the gospel of Christ.
8 But though we, or an angel from heav-
en, preach any other gospel unto you than
that which we have preached unto you, let
him be accursed.
9 As we said before, so say I now again,
If any *man* preach any other gospel unto
you than that ye have received, let him be
accursed.
10 For do I now persuade men, or God?
or do I seek to please men? for if I yet
pleased men, I should not be the servant of
Christ.
11 But I certify you, brethren, that the
gospel which was preached of me is not
after man.
12 For I neither received it of man, neither was I taught *it*, but by the revelation of
Jesus Christ.
13 For ye have heard of my conversation
in time past in the Jews' religion, how that
beyond measure I persecuted the church of
God, and wasted it:
14 And profited in the Jews' religion
above many my equals in mine own nation,
being more exceedingly zealous of the traditions of my fathers.
15 But when it pleased God, who separated me from my mother's womb, and
called *me* by his grace,

Amplified

THE LETTER OF PAUL
TO THE

Galatians

CHAPTER 1

PAUL, an apostle—special messenger appointed and commissioned and sent out—not from [any body of] men
nor by *or* through [a]any man, but by *and* through Jesus
Christ, the Messiah, and God the Father Who raised Him
from among the dead;
2 And all the brethren who are with me, to the churches
of Galatia:
3 Grace *and* spiritual blessing be to you and soul peace
from God the Father and our Lord Jesus Christ, the
Messiah,
4 Who gave (yielded) Himself up [[a]to atone] for our
sins (and [a]to save and sanctify us), in order to rescue *and*
deliver us from this present wicked age *and* world order,
in accordance with the will *and* purpose *and* plan of our
God and Father.
5 To Him [be ascribed all] the glory through all the ages
of the ages *and* the eternities of the eternities! Amen—so
be it.
6 I am surprised *and* astonished that you are so quickly
[b]turning renegade *and* deserting Him Who invited *and* called
you [a]by the grace (unmerited favor) of Christ, the Messiah,
[and that you are transferring your allegiance] to a different,
even an opposition gospel.
7 Not that there is [or could be] any other [genuine Gos-
pel], but there are [obviously] some who are troubling *and*
disturbing *and* bewildering you ([a]with a different kind of
teaching which they offer as a gospel) and want to pervert
and distort the Gospel of Christ, the Messiah [into something
which it absolutely is not].
8 But even if we or an angel from heaven should preach
to you a gospel contrary to *and* different from that which we
preached to you, let him be accursed—anathema, devoted to
destruction, doomed to eternal punishment!
9 As we said before, so I now say again, If any one is
preaching to you a gospel different from *or* contrary to that
which you received [from us], let him be accursed—
anathema, devoted to destruction, doomed to eternal punishment!
10 Now, am I trying to win the favor of men, or of
God? Do I seek to be a man-pleaser? If I were still seeking
popularity with men, I should not be a bondservant of
Christ, the Messiah.
11 For I want you to know, brethren, that the Gospe
which was proclaimed *and* made known by me is not man's
gospel—a human invention, according to or patterned afte
any human standard.
12 For indeed I did not receive it from man, nor was
taught it; [it came to me] through a [direct] revelation [giv
en] by Jesus Christ, the Messiah.
13 You have heard of my earlier career *and* former man
ner of life in the Jewish religion (Judaism), how I perse
cuted *and* abused the church of God furiously *and* exten
sively, and [with fanatical zeal did my best] to make havo
of it *and* destroy it.
14 And [have heard how] I outstripped many of the me
of my own generation among the people of my race, in [m
advancement in study and observance of the laws o
Judaism, so extremely enthusiastic *and* zealous I was for th
traditions of my ancestors.
15 But when He Who had chosen *and* set me apart [eve
before I was born, and had called me by His grace (H
undeserved favor and blessing), [Isa. 49:1; Jer. 1:5.]

a) Vincent.
b) Lightfoot.

Living New Testament

Galatians

CHAPTER 1

From: Paul the missionary and all the other Christians here.
To: The churches of Galatia.[1]

I was not called to be a missionary by any group or agency—my call is from Jesus Christ Himself, and from God the Father who raised Him from the dead.

3 May peace and blessing be yours from God the Father and from the Lord Jesus Christ.

4 He died for our sins just as God our Father planned, and rescued us from this evil world in which we live.

5 All glory to God through all the ages of eternity. Amen.

6 I am amazed that you are turning away so soon from God who, in His love and mercy, invited you to share the eternal life He gives through Christ; you are already following a different "way to heaven," which really doesn't go to heaven at all.

7 For there is no other way than the one we showed you; you are being fooled by those who twist and change the truth concerning Christ.

8 Let God's curses fall on anyone, including myself, who preaches any other way to be saved than the one we told you about; yes, if an angel comes from heaven and preaches any other message, let him be forever cursed.

9 I will say it again: if anyone preaches any other Gospel than the one you welcomed, let God's curse fall upon him.

10 You can see that I am not trying to please you by sweet talk and flattery; no, I am trying to please God. If I were still trying to please men I could not be Christ's servant.

11 Dear friends, I solemnly swear that the way to heaven which I preach is not based on some mere human whim or dream.

12 For my message comes from no less a person than Jesus Christ Himself, who told me what to say. No one else has taught me.

13 You know what I was like when I followed the Jewish religion—how I went after the Christians mercilessly, hunting them down and doing my best to get rid of them all.

14 I was one of the most religious Jews of my own age in the whole country, and tried as hard as I possibly could to follow all the old, traditional rules of my religion.

15 But then something happened! For even before I was born God had chosen me to be His, and called me—what kindness and grace—

---

[1] alatia was a city in what is now called Turkey.

Revised Standard

THE LETTER OF PAUL TO THE

Galatians

Salutation and occasion of letter

1 Paul an apostle—not from men nor
through man, but through Jesus Christ
and God the Father, who raised him from
the dead—2and all the brethren who are
with me,
To the churches of Galatia:
3 Grace to you and peace from God the
Father and our Lord Jesus Christ, 4who
gave himself for our sins to deliver us from
the present evil age, according to the will of
our God and Father; 5to whom be the glory
for ever and ever. Amen.
6 I am astonished that you are so quickly
deserting him who called you in the grace of
Christ and turning to a different gospel—
not that there is another gospel, but there
are some who trouble you and want to pervert the gospel of Christ. 8But even if we,
or an angel from heaven, should preach to
you a gospel contrary to that which we
preached to you, let him be accursed. 9As
we have said before, so now I say again,
If any one is preaching to you a gospel
contrary to that which you received, let him
be accursed.
10 Am I now seeking the favor of men,
or of God? Or am I trying to please men?
If I were still pleasing men, I should not be
a servant[a] of Christ.

Paul's authority of divine origin

11 For I would have you know, brethren,
that the gospel which was preached by me
is not man's[b] gospel. 12For I did not receive
it from man, nor was I taught it, but it
came through a revelation of Jesus Christ.
13For you have heard of my former life in
Judaism, how I persecuted the church of
God violently and tried to destroy it; 14and
I advanced in Judaism beyond many of my
own age among my people, so extremely
zealous was I for the traditions of my fathers. 15But when he who had set me apart
before I was born, and had called me

---

[a] Or *slave*
[b] Greek *according to man*

King James

16 To reveal his Son in me, that I might preach him among the heathen; immediately I conferred not with flesh and blood:

17 Neither went I up to Jerusalem to them which were apostles before me; but I went into Arabia, and returned again unto Damascus.

18 Then after three years I went up to Jerusalem to see Peter, and abode with him fifteen days.

19 But other of the apostles saw I none, save James the Lord's brother.

20 Now the things which I write unto you, behold, before God, I lie not.

21 Afterwards I came into the regions of Syria and Cilicia;

22 And was unknown by face unto the churches of Judaea which were in Christ:

23 But they had heard only, That he which persecuted us in times past now preacheth the faith which once he destroyed.

24 And they glorified God in me.

Amplified

16 Saw fit *and* was pleased to reveal (unveil, disclose) His Son within me so that I might proclaim Him among the Gentiles [the non-Jewish world] as the glad tidings, immediately I did not confer with flesh and blood—did not consult or counsel with any frail human being or communicate with any one.

17 Nor did I [even] go up to Jerusalem to those who were apostles—special messengers of Christ—before I was; but I went away *and* retired into Arabia, and afterward I came back again to Damascus.

18 Then three years later, I did go up to Jerusalem to become (personally) acquainted with Cephas (Peter), and remained with him for fifteen days.

19 But I did not see any of the other apostles—the special messengers of Christ—except James the brother of our Lord.

20 Now—[note carefully] what I am telling you, [for] it is the truth; I write it as if I were standing before the bar of God; I do not lie.

21 Then I went into the districts (countries, regions) of Syria and Cilicia.

22 And so far I was still unknown by sight to the churches of Christ in Judea [the country surrounding Jerusalem].

23 They were only hearing it said, He who used to persecute us is now proclaiming the very faith he once reviled *and* which he set out to ruin *and* tried [with all his might] to destroy.

24 And they glorified God [as the Author and Source of what had taken place] in me.

CHAPTER 2

THEN fourteen years after I went up again to Jerusalem with Barnabas, and took Titus with *me* also.

2 And I went up by revelation, and communicated unto them that gospel which I preach among the Gentiles, but privately to them which were of reputation, lest by any means I should run, or had run, in vain.

3 But neither Titus, who was with me, being a Greek, was compelled to be circumcised:

4 And that because of false brethren unawares brought in, who came in privily to spy out our liberty which we have in Christ Jesus, that they might bring us into bondage:

5 To whom we gave place by subjection, no, not for an hour; that the truth of the gospel might continue with you.

6 But of these who seemed to be somewhat, (whatsoever they were, it maketh no matter to me: God accepteth no man's person:) for they who seemed *to be somewhat* in conference added nothing to me:

CHAPTER 2

THEN after (an interval) of fourteen years I again went up to Jerusalem. [This time I went] with Barnabas, taking Titus along with [me] also.

2 I went because it was specially *and* divinely revealed to me that I should go, and I put before them the Gospel [declaring to them that] which I preach among the Gentiles However, [I presented the matter] privately before those o repute, [for I wanted to make certain, by thus at first confining my communication to this private conference] that was not running or had not run in vain—guarding agains being discredited either in what I was planning to do or ha already done.

3 But [all went well]; even Titus, who was with me, wa not compelled [as some had anticipated] to be circumcise although he was a Greek.

4 [My precaution was] because of [some men who we Christians in name only], false brethren who had bee secretly smuggled in [to the Christian brotherhood]; th had slipped in to spy on our liberty *and* the freedom whic we have in Christ Jesus, that they might again bring us int bondage [under the Law of Moses].

5 To them we did not yield submission even for a m ment, that the truth of the Gospel might continue to [preserved] for you [in its purity].

6 Moreover, [no new requirements were made] by th who were reputed to be something, though what was th individual position *and* whether they really were of imp tance or not makes no difference to me; God is not i pressed with the positions that men hold *and* He is not p tial *and* recognizes no external distinctions. Those [I s who were of repute imposed no new requirements u me—had nothing to add to my Gospel and from ther received no new suggestions. [Deut. 10:17.]

Living New Testament

16 To reveal His Son within me so that I could go to the Gentiles and show them the Good News about Jesus. When all this happened to me I didn't go at once and talk it over with anyone else;

17 I didn't go up to Jerusalem to consult with those who were apostles before I was. No, I went away into the deserts of Arabia, and then came back to the city of Damascus.

18 It was not until three years later that I finally went to Jerusalem for a visit with Peter, and stayed there with him for fifteen days.

19 And the only other apostle I met at that time was James, our Lord's brother.

20 (Listen to what I am saying, for I am telling you this in the very presence of God. This is exactly what happened—I am not lying to you.)

21 Then after this visit I went to Syria and Cilicia.

22 And still the Christians in Judea didn't even know what I looked like.

23 All they knew was what people were saying, that "our former enemy is now preaching the very faith he tried to wreck."

24 And they gave glory to God because of me.

Revised Standard

through his grace, [16]was pleased to reveal
his Son to[c] me, in order that I might preach
him among the Gentiles, I did not confer
with flesh and blood, [17]nor did I go up to
Jerusalem to those who were apostles before
me, but I went away into Arabia; and again
I returned to Damascus.
18 Then after three years I went up to
Jerusalem to visit Cephas, and remained
with him fifteen days. [19]But I saw none of
the other apostles except James the Lord's
brother. [20](In what I am writing to you,
before God, I do not lie!) [21]Then I went
into the regions of Syria and Cilicia. [22]And
I was still not known by sight to the churches
of Christ in Judea; [23]they only heard it said,
"He who once persecuted us is now preaching the faith he once tried to destroy." [24]And
they glorified God because of me.

CHAPTER 2

Then fourteen years later I went back to Jerusalem again, this time with Barnabas; and Titus came along oo.

2 I went there with definite orders from God to confer ith the brothers there about the message I was preaching the Gentiles. I talked privately to the leaders of the hurch so that they would all understand just what I had een teaching and, I hoped, agree that it was right.

3 And they did agree; they did not even demand that itus, my companion, should be circumcised, though he as a Gentile.

4 Even that question wouldn't have come up except for me so-called "Christians" there—false ones, really—who me to spy on us and see what freedom we enjoyed in hrist Jesus, as to whether we obeyed the Jewish laws or ot. They tried to get us all tied up in their rules, like ves in chains.

5 But we did not listen to them for a single moment, we did not want to confuse you into thinking that vation can be earned by being circumcised and by eying Jewish laws.

6 And the great leaders of the church who were there d nothing to add to what I was preaching. (By the way, ir being great leaders made no difference to me, for all the same to God.)

Paul accepted by the church

2 Then after fourteen years I went up
again to Jerusalem with Barnabas, taking Titus along with me. [2]I went up by revelation; and I laid before them (but privately before those who were of repute) the
gospel which I preach among the Gentiles,
lest somehow I should be running or had
run in vain. [3]But even Titus, who was with
me, was not compelled to be circumcised,
though he was a Greek. [4]But because of
false brethren secretly brought in, who
slipped in to spy out our freedom which we
have in Christ Jesus, that they might bring
us into bondage—[5]to them we did not yield
submission even for a moment, that the truth
of the gospel might be preserved for you.
[6]And from those who were reputed to be
something (what they were makes no difference to me; God shows no partiality)—
those, I say, who were of repute added

[c] Greek *in*

King James

7 But contrariwise, when they saw that the gospel of the uncircumcision was committed unto me, as *the gospel* of the circumcision *was* unto Peter;

8 (For he that wrought effectually in Peter to the apostleship of the circumcision, the same was mighty in me toward the Gentiles:)

9 And when James, Cephas, and John, who seemed to be pillars, perceived the grace that was given unto me, they gave to me and Barnabas the right hands of fellowship; that we *should go* unto the heathen, and they unto the circumcision.

10 Only *they would* that we should remember the poor; the same which I also was forward to do.

11 But when Peter was come to Antioch, I withstood him to the face, because he was to be blamed.

12 For before that certain came from James, he did eat with the Gentiles: but when they were come, he withdrew and separated himself, fearing them which were of the circumcision.

13 And the other Jews dissembled likewise with him; insomuch that Barnabas also was carried away with their dissimulation.

14 But when I saw that they walked not uprightly according to the truth of the gospel, I said unto Peter before *them* all, If thou, being a Jew, livest after the manner of Gentiles, and not as do the Jews, why compellest thou the Gentiles to live as do the Jews?

15 We *who are* Jews by nature, and not sinners of the Gentiles,

16 Knowing that a man is not justified by the works of the law, but by the faith of Jesus Christ, even we have believed in Jesus Christ, that we might be justified by the faith of Christ, and not by the works of the law: for by the works of the law shall no flesh be justified.

17 But if, while we seek to be justified by Christ, we ourselves also are found sinners, *is* therefore Christ the minister of sin? God forbid.

18 For if I build again the things which I destroyed, I make myself a transgressor.

19 For I through the law am dead to the law, that I might live unto God.

20 I am crucified with Christ: nevertheless I live; yet not I, but Christ liveth in me: and the life which I now live in the flesh I live by the faith of the Son of God, who loved me, and gave himself for me.

Amplified

7 But on the contrary, when they [really] saw that I had been entrusted [to carry] the Gospel to the uncircumcised [Gentiles, just as definitely] as Peter had been entrusted [to proclaim] the Gospel to the circumcised [Jews, they were agreeable];

8 For He Who motivated *and* fitted Peter *and* worked effectively through him for the mission to the circumcised, motivated *and* fitted me *and* worked through me also for [the mission to] the Gentiles.

9 And when they knew (perceived, recognized, understood and acknowledged) the grace (God's unmerited favor and spiritual blessing) that had been bestowed upon me, James and Cephas (Peter) and John, who were reputed to be pillars of the Jerusalem church, gave to me and Barnabas the right hand of fellowship, with the understanding that we should go to the Gentiles and they to the circumcised (Jews).

10 They only [made one stipulation], that we were to remember the poor, which very thing I was also eager to do.

11 But when Cephas (Peter) came to Antioch I protested *and* opposed him to his face [concerning his conduct there], for he was blameable *and* stood condemned.

12 For up to the time that certain persons came from James, he ate his meals with the Gentile [converts]; but when the men [from Jerusalem] arrived he withdrew *and* held himself aloof from the Gentiles and [ate] separately for fear of those of the circumcision [party].

13 And the rest of the Jews along with him also concealed their true convictions *and* acted insincerely, with the result that even Barnabas was carried away by their hypocrisy—that is, by their example of insincerity and pretense.

14 But as soon as I saw that they were not straightforward *and* were not living up to the truth of the Gospel, I said to Cephas (Peter) before everybody present, If you though born a Jew, can live [as you have been living] like a Gentile and not as a Jew, how do you dare now to urge *an* practically force the Gentiles to [comply with the ritual o Judaism and] live like Jews?

15 [I went on to say], Although we ourselves—you an I—are Jews by birth and not Gentile (heathen) sinners,

16 Yet we know that a man is justified *or* reckone righteous *and* in right standing with God, not by works c law but [only] through faith *and* [absolute] reliance on *an* adherence to *and* trust in Jesus Christ, the Messiah, th Anointed One. [Therefore] even we [ourselves] have be lieved on Christ Jesus, in order to be justified by faith i Christ and not by works of the Law—for we cannot b justified by any observance of [the ritual of] the Law [give by Moses]; because by keeping legal rituals *and* by wor no human being can ever be justified—declared righteo and put in right standing with God. [Ps. 143:2.]

17 But if, in our desire *and* endeavor to be justified Christ—to be declared righteous and put in right standi with God wholly and solely through Christ—we ha shown ourselves sinners also *and* convicted of sin, does th make Christ a minister (a party and contributor) to c sin? Banish the thought!—Of course not!

18 For if I [or any other]—who have taught that observance of the Law of Moses is not essential to be justified by God, should now by word or practice teach intimate that it is essential—building up again what I t down, I prove myself a transgressor.

19 For I through the Law—under the operation [of curse] of the Law—have [in Christ's death for me] my died to the Law *and* all the Law's demands upon me, so I may [henceforth] live to *and* for God.

20 I have been crucified with Christ—[in Him] I h shared His crucifixion; it is no longer I who live, but Ch the Messiah, lives in me; and the life I now live in the b I live by faith—by adherence to *and* reliance on *and* [c plete] trust—in the Son of God, Who loved me and Himself up for me.

Living New Testament

7, 8, 9 In fact, when Peter, James and John, who were known as the pillars of the church, saw how greatly God had used me in winning the Gentiles, just as Peter had been blessed so greatly in his preaching to the Jews—for the same God gave us each our special gifts—they shook hands with Barnabas and me and encouraged us to keep right on with our preaching to the Gentiles while they continued their work with the Jews.

10 The only thing they did suggest was that we must always remember to help the poor, and I, too, was eager for that.

11 But when Peter came to Antioch I had to oppose him publicly, speaking strongly against what he was doing, for it was very wrong.

12 For when he first arrived he ate with the Gentile Christians [who don't bother with circumcision and the many other Jewish laws[1]]. But afterwards when some Jewish friends of James came, he wouldn't eat with the Gentiles anymore because he was afraid of what these Jewish legalists, who insisted that circumcision was necessary for salvation, would say;

13 And then all the other Jewish Christians and even Barnabas, became hypocrites too, following Peter's example, though they certainly knew better.

14 When I saw what was happening and that they weren't being honest about what they really believed, and weren't following the truth of the Gospel, I said to Peter in front of all the others, "Though you are a Jew by birth, you have long since discarded the Jewish laws; so why, all of a sudden, are you trying to make these Gentiles obey them?

15 You and I are Jews by birth, not mere Gentile sinners,

16 And yet we Jewish Christians know very well that we cannot become right with God by obeying our Jewish laws, but only by faith in Jesus Christ to take away our sins. And so we, too, have trusted Jesus Christ, that we might be accepted by God because of faith—and not because we have obeyed the Jewish laws. For no one will ever be saved by obeying them."

17 But what if we trust Christ to save us and then find that we are wrong, and that we cannot be saved without being circumcised and obeying all the other Jewish laws? Wouldn't we need to say that faith in Christ had ruined us? God forbid that anyone should dare to think such things about our Lord.

18 Rather, we are sinners if we start rebuilding the old system I have been destroying, of trying to be saved by keeping Jewish laws.

19 For it was through reading the Scripture that I came to realize that I could never find God's favor by trying—and failing—to obey the laws. I came to realize that acceptance with God comes by believing in Christ.[2]

20 I have been crucified with Christ: and I myself no longer live, but Christ lives in me. And the real life I now have within this body is a result of my trusting in the Son of God, who loved me and gave Himself for me.

---

[1] Implied.
[2] Literally, "For I through the law died unto the law, that I might live unto God."

Revised Standard

nothing to me; 7but on the contrary, when
they saw that I had been entrusted with the
gospel to the uncircumcised, just as Peter
had been entrusted with the gospel to the
circumcised 8(for he who worked through
Peter for the mission to the circumcised
worked through me also for the Gentiles),
9and when they perceived the grace that was
given to me, James and Cephas and John,
who were reputed to be pillars, gave to me
and Barnabas the right hand of fellowship,
that we should go to the Gentiles and they
to the circumcised; 10only they would have
us remember the poor, which very thing I
was eager to do.

Paul's opposition to Cephas

11 But when Cephas came to Antioch I
opposed him to his face, because he stood
condemned. 12For before certain men came
from James, he ate with the Gentiles; but
when they came he drew back and separated himself, fearing the circumcision
party. 13And with him the rest of the Jews
acted insincerely, so that even Barnabas
was carried away by their insincerity. 14But
when I saw that they were not straightforward about the truth of the gospel, I said
to Cephas before them all, "If you, though
a Jew, live like a Gentile and not like a
Jew, how can you compel the Gentiles to
live like Jews?" 15We ourselves, who are
Jews by birth and not Gentile sinners, 16yet
who know that a man is not justified[d] by
works of the law but through faith in Jesus
Christ, even we have believed in Christ
Jesus, in order to be justified by faith in
Christ, and not by works of the law, because
by works of the law shall no one be justified. 17But if, in our endeavor to be justified
in Christ, we ourselves were found to be sinners, is Christ then an agent of sin? Certainly not! 18But if I build up again those
things which I tore down, then I prove myself a transgressor. 19For I through the law
died to the law, that I might live to God.
20I have been crucified with Christ; it is no
longer I who live, but Christ who lives in
me; and the life I now live in the flesh I live
by faith in the Son of God, who loved me

---

[d] Or *reckoned righteous:* and so elsewhere

King James

21 I do not frustrate the grace of God: for if righteousness *come* by the law, then Christ is dead in vain.

Amplified

21 [Therefore, I do not treat God's gracious gift as something of minor importance and defeat its very purpose]; I do not set aside *and* invalidate *and* frustrate *and* nullify the grace (unmerited favor) of God. For if justification (righteousness, acquittal from guilt) comes through [observing the ritual of] the Law, then Christ, the Messiah, died groundlessly *and* to no purpose *and* in vain.—His death was then wholly superfluous.

CHAPTER 3

O FOOLISH Galatians, who hath bewitched you, that ye should not obey the truth, before whose eyes Jesus Christ hath been evidently set forth, crucified among you?

2 This only would I learn of you, Received ye the Spirit by the works of the law, or by the hearing of faith?

3 Are ye so foolish? having begun in the Spirit, are ye now made perfect by the flesh?

4 Have ye suffered so many things in vain? if *it be* yet in vain.

5 He therefore that ministereth to you the Spirit, and worketh miracles among you, *doeth he it* by the works of the law, or by the hearing of faith?

6 Even as Abraham believed God, and it was accounted to him for righteousness.

7 Know ye therefore that they which are of faith, the same are the children of Abraham.

8 And the scripture, foreseeing that God would justify the heathen through faith, preached before the gospel unto Abraham, *saying*, In thee shall all nations be blessed.

9 So then they which be of faith are blessed with faithful Abraham.

10 For as many as are of the works of the law are under the curse: for it is written, Cursed *is* every one that continueth not in all things which are written in the book of the law to do them.

11 But that no man is justified by the law in the sight of God, *it is* evident: for, The just shall live by faith.

12 And the law is not of faith: but, The man that doeth them shall live in them.

CHAPTER 3

O YOU poor *and* silly *and* thoughtless *and* unreflecting *and* senseless Galatians! Who has fascinated *or* bewitched *or* cast a spell over you, unto whom—right before your very eyes—Jesus Christ, the Messiah, was openly *and* graphically set forth *and* portrayed as crucified?

2 Let me ask you this one question: Did you receive the (Holy) Spirit as the result of obeying the Law *and* doing its works, or was it by hearing [the message of the Gospel] and believing [it]?—Was it from observing a law of rituals or from a message of faith?

3 Are you so foolish *and* so senseless *and* so silly? Having begun [your new life spiritually] with the (Holy) Spirit, are you now reaching perfection [by dependence] on the flesh?

4 Have you suffered so many things *and* experienced so much all for nothing—to no purpose? if it really is to no purpose *and* in vain,

5 Then does He Who supplies you with His marvelous (Holy) Spirit, and works powerfully *and* miraculously among you, [do so on the grounds of your doing] what the Law demands, or because of your believing *and* adhering to *and* trusting in *and* relying on the message that you heard?

6 Thus Abraham believed *and* adhered to *and* trusted in *and* relied on God, and it was reckoned *and* placed to his account *and* accredited as righteousness—as conformity to the divine will in purpose, thought and action. [Gen. 15:6.]

7 Know *and* understand that it is [really] the people [who live] by faith who are [the true] sons of Abraham.

8 And the Scripture, foreseeing that God would justify—declare righteous, put in right standing with Himself—the Gentiles in consequence of faith, proclaimed the Gospe[l] [foretelling the glad tidings of a Savior long beforehand] t[o] Abraham in the promise, saying, In you shall all the nation[s] [of the earth] be blessed. [Gen. 12:3.]

9 So then, those who are people of faith are blessed *an[d]* made happy *and* favored by God [as partners in fellowship] with the believing *and* trusting Abraham.

10 And all who depend on the Law—who are seeking t[o] be justified by obedience to the Law of rituals—are under curse *and* doomed to disappointment *and* destruction; for is written in the Scriptures, Cursed (accursed, devoted t[o] destruction, doomed to eternal punishment) be everyo[ne] who does not continue to abide (live and remain) by all th[e] precepts *and* commands written in the book of the Law, a[nd] practice them. [Deut. 27:26.]

11 Now it is evident that no person is justified—declar[ed] righteous and brought into right standing with God—through the Law; for the Scripture says, The man in rig[ht] standing with God (the just, the righteous) shall live by *a[nd]* out of faith, *and* he who through *and* by faith is declar[ed] righteous *and* in right standing with God shall live. [Ha[b.] 2:4.]

12 But the Law does not rest on faith—does not requ[ire] faith, has nothing to do with faith—for it itself says, He w[ho] does them (the things prescribed by the Law) shall live [in] them, [not by faith]. [Lev. 18:5.]

Living New Testament

21 I am not one of those who treats Christ's death as meaningless. For if we could be saved by keeping Jewish laws, then there was no need for Christ to die.

Revised Standard

and gave himself for me. 21 I do not nullify
the grace of God; for if justification[e] were
through the law, then Christ died to no purpose.

Living New Testament

CHAPTER 3

Oh, foolish Galatians! What magician has hypnotized you and cast an evil spell upon you? For you used to see the meaning of Jesus Christ's death as clearly as though I had waved a placard before you with a picture on it of Christ dying on the cross.

2 Let me ask you this one question: Did you receive the Holy Spirit by trying to keep the Jewish laws? Of course not, for the Holy Spirit came upon you only after you heard about Christ and trusted Him to save you.

3 Then have you gone completely crazy? For if trying to obey the Jewish laws never gave you spiritual life in the first place, why do you think that trying to obey them now will make you stronger Christians?

4 You have suffered so much for the Gospel. Now are you going to just throw it all overboard? I can hardly believe it!

5 I ask you again, does God give you the power of the Holy Spirit and work miracles among you as a result of your trying to obey the Jewish laws? No, of course not. It is when you believe in Christ and fully trust Him.

6 Abraham had the same experience—God declared him fit for heaven only because he believed God's promises.

7 You can see from this that the real children of Abraham are all the men of faith who truly trust in God.

8, 9 What's more, the Scriptures looked forward to this time when God would save the Gentiles also, through their faith. God told Abraham about this long ago when He said, "I will bless those in every nation who trust in Me as you do." And so it is: all who trust in Christ share the same blessing Abraham received.

10 Yes, and those who depend on the Jewish laws to save them are under God's curse, for the Scriptures point out very clearly, "Cursed is everyone who at any time breaks a single one of these laws that are written in God's Book of the Law."

11 Consequently, it is clear that no one can ever win God's favor by trying to keep the Jewish laws, because God has said that the only way we can be right in His sight is by faith. As the prophet Habakkuk says it, "The man who finds life will find it through trusting God."

12 How different from this way of faith is the way of law which says that a man is saved by obeying every law of God, without one slip.

Revised Standard

Receiving the Spirit by faith

3 O foolish Galatians! Who has bewitched you, before whose eyes Jesus
Christ was publicly portrayed as crucified?
2 Let me ask you only this: Did you receive
the Spirit by works of the law, or by hearing
with faith? 3 Are you so foolish? Having
begun with the Spirit are you now ending
with the flesh? 4 Did you experience so many
things in vain?—if it really is in vain. 5 Does
he who supplies the Spirit to you and works
miracles among you do so by works of the
law, or by hearing with faith?

The example of Abraham

6 Thus Abraham "believed God, and it
was reckoned to him as righteousness." 7 So
you see that it is men of faith who are the
sons of Abraham. 8 And the scripture, foreseeing that God would justify the Gentiles
by faith, preached the gospel beforehand to
Abraham, saying, "In you shall all the nations be blessed." 9 So then, those who are
men of faith are blessed with Abraham who
had faith.

10 For all who rely on works of the law
are under a curse; for it is written, "Cursed
be every one who does not abide by all
things written in the book of the law, and
do them." 11 Now it is evident that no man
is justified before God by the law; for "He
who through faith is righteous shall live";[f]
12 but the law does not rest on faith, for "He
who does them shall live by them." 13 Christ

---

[e] Or *righteousness*

[f] Or *the righteous shall live by faith*

King James

13 Christ hath redeemed us from the curse of the law, being made a curse for us: for it is written, Cursed *is* every one that hangeth on a tree:

14 That the blessing of Abraham might come on the Gentiles through Jesus Christ; that we might receive the promise of the Spirit through faith.

15 Brethren, I speak after the manner of men; Though *it be* but a man's covenant, yet *if it be* confirmed, no man disannulleth, or addeth thereto.

16 Now to Abraham and his seed were the promises made. He saith not, And to seeds, as of many; but as of one, And to thy seed, which is Christ.

17 And this I say, *that* the covenant, that was confirmed before of God in Christ, the law, which was four hundred and thirty years after, cannot disannul, that it should make the promise of none effect.

18 For if the inheritance *be* of the law, *it is* no more of promise: but God gave *it* to Abraham by promise.

19 Wherefore then *serveth* the law? It was added because of transgressions, till the seed should come to whom the promise was made; *and it was* ordained by angels in the hand of a mediator.

20 Now a mediator is not a *mediator* of one, but God is one.

21 *Is* the law then against the promises of God? God forbid: for if there had been a law given which could have given life, verily righteousness should have been by the law.

22 But the scripture hath concluded all under sin, that the promise by faith of Jesus Christ might be given to them that believe.

23 But before faith came, we were kept under the law, shut up unto the faith which should afterwards be revealed.

24 Wherefore the law was our schoolmaster *to bring us* unto Christ, that we might be justified by faith.

25 But after that faith is come, we are no longer under a schoolmaster.

26 For ye are all the children of God by faith in Christ Jesus.

Amplified

13 Christ purchased our freedom (redeeming us) from the curse (doom) of the Law's (condemnation), by [Himself] becoming a curse for us, for it is written [in the Scriptures], Cursed is everyone who hangs on a tree (is crucified); [Deut. 21:23.]

14 To the end that through [their receiving] Christ Jesus, the blessing [promised] to Abraham might come upon the Gentiles, so that we through faith might [all] receive [the realization of] the promise of the (Holy) Spirit.

15 To speak in terms of human relations, brethren, [if] even a man makes a last will and testament [a merely human covenant], no one sets it aside *or* makes it void *or* adds to it, when once it has been drawn up *and* signed (ratified, confirmed).

16 Now the promises (covenants, agreements) were decreed *and* made to Abraham and his Seed (his Offspring, his Heir). He (God) does not say, And to seeds (descendants, heirs), as if referring to many persons; but, And to your Seed (your Descendant, your Heir), obviously referring to one individual, Who is [none other than] Christ, the Messiah. [Gen. 13:15; 17:8.]

17 This is my argument: The Law, which began four hundred and thirty years after the covenant [concerning the coming Messiah], does not *and* can not annul the covenant previously established (ratified) by God, so as to abolish the promise *and* make it void. [Exod. 12:40.]

18 For if the inheritance [of the promise depends on observing] the Law [as these false teachers would like you to believe], it no longer [depends] on the promise; however, God gave it to Abraham [as a free gift solely] by virtue of His promise.

19 What then was the purpose of the Law? It was added—later on, after the promise, to disclose and expose to men their guilt—because of transgressions *and* [to make men more conscious of the sinfulness] of sin; and it was intended to be in effect until the Seed (the Descendant, the Heir) should come, to *and* concerning Whom the promise had been made. And it (the Law) was arranged *and* ordained *and* appointed through the instrumentality of angels [and was given] by the hand (in the person) of a go-between—an intermediary person (Moses) between God and man.

20 Now a go-between (intermediary) has to do with *and* implies more than one party—there can be no mediator with just one person. Yet God is [only] one person—and He was the sole party [in giving that promise to Abraham. But the Law was a contract between two, God and Israel; its validity was dependent on both].

21 Is the Law then contrary *and* opposed to the promises of God? Of course not! For if a Law had been given which could confer [spiritual] life, then righteousness *and* righ[t] standing with God would certainly have come by Law.

22 But the Scripture [pictures all mankind as sinners] shu[t] up *and* imprisoned by sin, so that [the inheritance, blessing which was promised through faith in Jesus Christ, the Messiah, might be given (released, delivered and committed) t[o] [all] those who believe—who adhere to and trust in and rel[y] on Him.

23 Now before the faith came we were perpetuall[y] guarded under the Law, kept in custody in preparation fo[r] the faith that was destined to be revealed (unveiled, disclosed).

24 So that the Law served [c][to us Jews] as our trainer—our guardian, our guide to Christ, to lead us—until Chri[st] [came], that we might be justified (declared righteous, put [in] right standing with God) by *and* through faith.

25 But now that the faith has come, we are no long[er] under a trainer—the guardian of our childhood.

26 For in Christ Jesus you are all sons of God throu[gh] faith.

---

c) Vincent.

Living New Testament

13 But Christ has bought us out from under the doom of that impossible system by taking the curse for our wrongdoing upon Himself. For it is written in the Scripture, "Anyone who is hanged on a tree is cursed" [as Jesus was on the wooden cross [1]].

* * * * *

14 Now God can bless the Gentiles, too, with this same blessing He promised to Abraham; and all of us as Christians can have the promised Holy Spirit through this faith.

15 Dear brothers, even in everyday life a promise made by one man to another, if it is written down and signed, cannot be changed. He cannot decide afterward to do something else instead.

16 Now, God gave some promises to Abraham and his Child. And notice that it doesn't say the promises were to his *children,* as it would if all his sons—all the Jews—were being spoken of, but to his *Child*—and that of course means Christ.

17 Here's what I am trying to say: God's promise to save through faith—and God wrote this promise down and signed it—could not be canceled or changed four hundred and thirty years later when God gave the Ten Commandments.

18 If *obeying those laws* could save us, then it is obvious that this would be a different way of gaining God's favor than Abraham's way, for he simply accepted God's promise.

19 Well then, why were the laws given? They were added, after the promise was given, to show men how guilty they are of breaking God's laws. But this system of law was to last only until the coming of Christ, the Child to whom God's promise was made. (And there is this further difference: God gave His laws to angels to give to Moses, who then gave them to the people;

20 But when God gave His promise to Abraham, He did it by Himself alone, without angels or Moses as go-betweens.)

21, 22 Well then, are God's laws and God's promises against each other? Of course not! If we could be saved by His laws, then God would not have had to give us a different way to get out of the grip of sin—for the Scriptures insist we are all its prisoners. The only way out is through faith in Jesus Christ; the way of escape is open to all who believe Him.

23 Until Christ came we were guarded by the law, kept in protective custody, so to speak, until we could believe n the coming Savior.

24 Let me put it another way. The Jewish laws were our teacher and guide until Christ came to give us right standing with God through our faith.

25 But now that Christ has come, we don't need those laws any longer to guard us and lead us to Him.

26 For now we are all children of God through faith in esus Christ,

nplied.

Revised Standard

redeemed us from the curse of the law, having become a curse for us—for it is written,
"Cursed be every one who hangs on a tree"
—14that in Christ Jesus the blessing of
Abraham might come upon the Gentiles,
that we might receive the promise of the
Spirit through faith.
15 To give a human example, brethren:
no one annuls even a man's will,[g] or adds
to it, once it has been ratified. 16Now the
promises were made to Abraham and to his
offspring. It does not say, "And to off-
springs," referring to many; but, referring
to one, "And to your offspring," which is
Christ. 17This is what I mean: the law,
which came four hundred and thirty years
afterward, does not annul a covenant previously ratified by God, so as to make the
promise void. 18For if the inheritance is by
the law, it is no longer by promise; but
God gave it to Abraham by a promise.

The function of the law

19 Why then the law? It was added because of transgressions, till the offspring
should come to whom the promise had been
made; and it was ordained by angels
through an intermediary. 20Now an intermediary implies more than one; but God
is one.
21 Is the law then against the promises
of God? Certainly not; for if a law had
been given which could make alive, then
righteousness would indeed be by the law.
22But the scripture consigned all things to
sin, that what was promised to faith in Jesus
Christ might be given to those who believe.
23 Now before faith came, we were con-
fined under the law, kept under restraint
until faith should be revealed. 24So that the
law was our custodian until Christ came,
that we might be justified by faith. 25But
now that faith has come, we are no longer
under a custodian; 26for in Christ Jesus you
are all sons of God, through faith. 27For as

[g] Or *covenant* (as in verse 17)

King James

27 For as many of you as have been baptized into Christ have put on Christ.

28 There is neither Jew nor Greek, there is neither bond nor free, there is neither male nor female: for ye are all one in Christ Jesus.

29 And if ye *be* Christ's, then are ye Abraham's seed, and heirs according to the promise.

Amplified

27 For as many [of you] as were baptized into Christ—into a spiritual union and communion with Christ, the Anointed One, the Messiah—have put on (clothed yourselves with) Christ.

28 There is [now no distinction], neither Jew nor Greek, there is neither slave nor free, there is not male [d]and female; for you are all one in Christ Jesus.

29 And if you belong to Christ (are in Him, Who is Abraham's Seed), then you are Abraham's offspring and (spiritual) heirs according to promise.

CHAPTER 4

NOW I say, *That* the heir, as long as he is a child, differeth nothing from a servant, though he be lord of all;

2 But is under tutors and governors until the time appointed of the father.

3 Even so we, when we were children, were in bondage under the elements of the world:

4 But when the fulness of the time was come, God sent forth his Son, made of a woman, made under the law,

5 To redeem them that were under the law, that we might receive the adoption of sons.

6 And because ye are sons, God hath sent forth the Spirit of his Son into your hearts, crying, Abba, Father.

7 Wherefore thou art no more a servant, but a son; and if a son, then an heir of God through Christ.

8 Howbeit then, when ye knew not God, ye did service unto them which by nature are no gods.

9 But now, after that ye have known God, or rather are known of God, how turn ye again to the weak and beggarly elements, whereunto ye desire again to be in bondage?

10 Ye observe days, and months, and times, and years.

11 I am afraid of you, lest I have bestowed upon you labour in vain.

12 Brethren, I beseech you, be as I *am;* for I *am* as ye *are:* ye have not injured me at all.

13 Ye know how through infirmity of the flesh I preached the gospel unto you at the first.

14 And my temptation which was in my flesh ye despised not, nor rejected; but received me as an angel of God, *even* as Christ Jesus.

CHAPTER 4

NOW what I mean is that as long as the inheritor (heir) is a child and under age, he does not differ from a slave, although he is the master of all the estate;

2 But he is under guardians and administrators *or* trustees until the date fixed by his father.

3 So we [Jewish Christians] also, when we were minors were kept like slaves under (the rules of the Hebrew ritual and subject to) the elementary teachings of a system of external observations *and* regulations.

4 But when the proper time had fully come, God sent His Son, born of a woman, born subject to [the regulations of] the Law,

5 To purchase the freedom of (to ransom, to redeem, to [e]atone for) those who were subject to the Law, that we might be adopted *and* have sonship conferred upon us—be recognized as [God's] sons.

6 And because you [really] are (His) sons, God has sent the ([f]Holy) Spirit of His Son into our hearts, crying, Abba (Father)! Father!

7 Therefore, you are no longer a slave (bond servant) but a son; and if a son, then [it follows that you are] an heir [g]by the aid of God, *through Christ.*

8 But at that previous time, when you had not come to be acquainted with *and* understand *and* know the true God, you [Gentiles] were in bondage to gods that by their very nature could not be gods at all—gods that really did not exist.

9 Now however that you have come to be acquainted with *and* understand *and* know [the true] God, or rather to be understood *and* known by God, how can you turn back again to the weak and beggarly *and* worthless elementary things [[h]of all religions before Christ came] whose slaves you once more want to become?

10 You observe [particular] days, and months, and seasons and years!

11 I am alarmed [about you] lest I have labored among *and* over you to no purpose *and* in vain.

12 Brethren, I beg of you, become as I am [free from the bondage of Jewish ritualism and ordinances]; for I also have become as you are [[i]a Gentile]. You did me no wrong [[i]in those days, do not do it now].

13 On the contrary, you know that it was on account of bodily ailment that [I remained and] preached the Gospel to you the first time.

14 And [yet], although my physical condition was [such] a trial to you, you did not regard it with contempt, or scorn *and* loathe *and* reject me; but you received me as an angel of God, [even] as Christ Jesus [Himself]!

---

d) Literal translation.
e) Webster, defining "redeem."
f) Vincent.
g) Thayer.
h) Thayer.
i) Vincent.

Living New Testament

27 And we who have been baptized into union with Christ are enveloped by Him.

28 We are no longer Jews or Greeks or slaves or free men or even merely men or women, but we are all the same—we are Christians; we are one in Christ Jesus.

29 And now that we are Christ's we are the true descendants of Abraham, and all of God's promises to him belong to us.

Revised Standard

many of you as were baptized into Christ
have put on Christ. [28]There is neither Jew
nor Greek, there is neither slave nor free,
there is neither male nor female; for you
are all one in Christ Jesus. [29]And if you are
Christ's, then you are Abraham's offspring,
heirs according to promise.

CHAPTER 4

But remember this, that if a father dies and leaves great wealth for his little son, that child is not much better off than a slave until he grows up, even though he actually owns everything his father had.

2 He has to do what his guardians and managers tell him to, until he reaches whatever age his father set.

3 And that is the way it was with us before Christ came. We were slaves to Jewish laws and rituals for we thought they could save us.

4 But when the right time came, the time God decided on, He sent His Son, born of a woman, born as a Jew,

5 To buy freedom for us who were slaves to the law so that He could adopt us as His very own sons.

6 And because we are His sons God has sent the Spirit of His Son into our hearts, so now we can rightly speak of God as our dear Father.

7 Now we are no longer slaves, but God's own sons. And since we are His sons, everything He has belongs to us, for that is the way God planned.

8 Before you Gentiles knew God you were slaves to so-called gods that did not even exist.

9 And now that you have found God (or I should say, now that God has found you) how can it be that you want to go back again and become slaves once more to another poor, weak, useless religion of trying to get to heaven by obeying God's laws?

10 You are trying to find favor with God by what you do or don't do on certain days or months or seasons or years.

11 I fear for you. I am afraid that all my hard work for you was worth nothing.

* * * * *

12 Dear brothers, please feel as I do about these things, for I am as free from these chains as you used to be. You did not despise me then when I first preached to you,

13 Even though I was sick when I first brought you the Good News of Christ.

14 But even though my sickness was revolting to you, you didn't reject me and turn me away. No, you took me in and cared for me as though I were an angel from God, or even Jesus Christ Himself.

Appeal against return to bondage

4 I mean that the heir, as long as he is a
child, is no better than a slave, though
he is the owner of all the estate; [2]but he
is under guardians and trustees until the
date set by the father. [3]So with us; when
we were children, we were slaves to the
elemental spirits of the universe. [4]But when
the time had fully come, God sent forth his
Son, born of woman, born under the law,
[5]to redeem those who were under the law,
so that we might receive adoption as sons.
[6]And because you are sons, God has sent
the Spirit of his Son into our hearts, crying,
"Abba! Father!" [7]So through God you are
no longer a slave but a son, and if a son
then an heir.
8 Formerly, when you did not know
God, you were in bondage to beings that
by nature are no gods; [9]but now that you
have come to know God, or rather to be
known by God, how can you turn back
again to the weak and beggarly elemental
spirits, whose slaves you want to be once
more? [10]You observe days, and months, and
seasons, and years! [11]I am afraid I have
labored over you in vain.

Paul's concern for the Galatians

12 Brethren, I beseech you, become as
I am, for I also have become as you are.
You did me no wrong; [13]you know it was
because of a bodily ailment that I preached
the gospel to you at first; [14]and though my
condition was a trial to you, you did not
scorn or despise me, but received me as an

King James

15 Where is then the blessedness ye spake of? for I bear you record, that, if *it had been* possible, ye would have plucked out your own eyes, and have given them to me.

16 Am I therefore become your enemy, because I tell you the truth?

17 They zealously affect you, *but* not well; yea, they would exclude you, that ye might affect them.

18 But *it is* good to be zealously affected always in *a* good *thing,* and not only when I am present with you.

19 My little children, of whom I travail in birth again until Christ be formed in you,

20 I desire to be present with you now, and to change my voice; for I stand in doubt of you.

21 Tell me, ye that desire to be under the law, do ye not hear the law?

22 For it is written, that Abraham had two sons, the one by a bondmaid, the other by a freewoman.

23 But he *who was* of the bondwoman was born after the flesh; but he of the freewoman *was* by promise.

24 Which things are an allegory: for these are the two covenants; the one from the mount Sinai, which gendereth to bondage, which is Agar.

25 For this Agar is mount Sinai in Arabia, and answereth to Jerusalem which now is, and is in bondage with her children.

26 But Jerusalem which is above is free, which is the mother of us all.

27 For it is written, Rejoice, *thou* barren that bearest not; break forth and cry, thou that travailest not: for the desolate hath many more children than she which hath an husband.

28 Now we, brethren, as Isaac was, are the children of promise.

29 But as then he that was born after the flesh persecuted him *that was born* after the Spirit, even so *it is* now.

30 Nevertheless what saith the scripture? Cast out the bondwoman and her son: for the son of the bondwoman shall not be heir with the son of the freewoman.

31 So then, brethren, we are not children of the bondwoman, but of the free.

Amplified

15 What has become of that blessed enjoyment *and* satisfaction *and* self-congratulation that once was yours [in what I taught you and in your regard for me]? For I bear you witness that you would have torn out your own eyes and have given them to me [to replace mine], if that were possible.

16 Have I then become your enemy by telling the truth to you *and* dealing sincerely with you?

17 These men [the Judaizing teachers] are zealously trying to dazzle you—paying court to you, making much of you; but their purpose is not honorable *or* worthy *or* for any good. What they want to do is to isolate you [from us who oppose them], so that they may win you over to their side *and* get you to court their favor.

18 It is always a fine thing [of course] to be zealously sought after [as you are, provided that it is] for a good purpose *and* done [j]by reason of purity of heart and life, and not just when I am present with you!

19 My little children, for whom I am again suffering birth pangs until Christ is completely *and* permanently formed (molded) within you!

20 Would that I were with you now and could coax you vocally, for I am fearful *and* perplexed about you.

21 Tell me, you who are bent on being under law, will you listen to what the Law [really] says?

22 For it is written that Abraham had two sons, one by the bondmaid and one by the free [woman]. [Gen. 16:15; 21:2, 9.]

23 But whereas the child of the slave woman was born according to the flesh *and* had an ordinary birth, the son of the free [woman] was born in fulfillment of the promise.

24 Now all this is an allegory; these [two women] represent two covenants. One covenant originated from Mount Sinai [where the Law was given], and bears [children destined] for slavery; this is Hagar.

25 Now Hagar is (stands for) Mount Sinai in Arabia and she corresponds to *and* belongs in the same category with the present Jerusalem, for she is in bondage together with her children.

26 But the Jerusalem above, [[k]the Messianic kingdom of Christ], is free and she is our mother.

27 For it is written in the Scriptures, Rejoice, O barren woman who has not given birth to children; break forth into a joyful shout, you who are not feeling birth pangs, for the desolate woman has many more children than she who has a husband. [Isa. 54:1.]

28 But we, brethren, are children [[k]not by physical descent, as was Ishmael, but] like Isaac born [k]in virtue of promise.

29 Yet [just] as at that time the child (of ordinary birth,) born according to the flesh, despised *and* persecuted him [who was born remarkably,] according to [the promise and the working of] the (Holy) Spirit, so it is now also. [Gen. 21:9.]

30 But what does the Scripture say? Cast out *and* send away the slave woman and her son, for never shall the son of the slave woman be heir *and* share the inheritance with the son of the free [woman]. [Gen. 21:10.]

31 So, brethren, we [who are born again] are not children of a slave woman [[l]the natural], but of the free [[l]the supernatural].

---

j) Thayer.
k) Vincent.
l) The Biblical Illustrator.

Living New Testament

15 Where is that happy spirit that we felt together then? For in those days I know you would gladly have taken out your own eyes and given them to replace mine[1] if that would have helped me.

16 And now have I become your enemy because I tell you the truth?

17 Those false teachers who are so anxious to win your favor are not doing it for your good. What they are trying to do is to shut you off from me so that you will pay more attention to them.

18 It is a fine thing when people are nice to you with good motives and sincere hearts, especially if they aren't doing it just when I am with you!

19 Oh, my children, how you are hurting me. I am once again suffering for you the pains of a mother waiting for her child to be born—longing for the time when you will finally be filled with Christ.

20 How I wish I could be there with you right now and not have to reason with you like this, for at this distance I frankly don't know what to do.

21 Listen to me, you friends who think you have to obey the Jewish laws to be saved: Why don't you find out what those laws really mean?

22 For it is written that Abraham had two sons, one from his slave-wife and one from his freeborn wife.

23 There was nothing unusual about the birth of the slave-wife's baby. But the baby of the freeborn wife was born only after God had especially promised he would come.

24, 25 Now this true story is an illustration of God's two ways of helping people. One way was by giving them His laws to obey. He did this on Mount Sinai, when He gave the Ten Commandments to Moses. Mount Sinai, by the way, is called "Mount Hagar" by the Arabs—and in my illustration Abraham's slave-wife Hagar represents Jerusalem, the mother-city of the Jews, the center of that system of trying to please God by trying to obey the Commandments; and the Jews, who try to follow that system, are her slave children.

26 But our mother-city is the heavenly Jerusalem, and she is not a slave to Jewish laws.

27 That is what Isaiah meant when he prophesied, "Now you can rejoice, O childless woman; you can shout with joy though you never before had a child. For I am going to give you many children—more children than the slave-wife has."

28 You and I, dear brothers, are the children that God promised, just as Isaac was.

29 And so we who are born of the Holy Spirit are persecuted now by those who want us to keep the Jewish laws, just as Isaac the child of promise was persecuted by Ishmael the slave-wife's son.

30 But the Scriptures say that God told Abraham to send away the slave-wife and her son, for the slave-wife's son could not inherit Abraham's home and lands along with the free woman's son.

31 Dear brothers, we are not slave children, obligated to the Jewish laws, but children of the free woman, acceptable to God because of our faith.

It is traditional to suppose that Paul was handicapped by a disease of the eyes.

Revised Standard

angel of God, as Christ Jesus. 15What has
become of the satisfaction you felt? For I
bear you witness that, if possible, you would
have plucked out your eyes and given them
to me. 16Have I then become your enemy
by telling you the truth?[h] 17They make
much of you, but for no good purpose;
they want to shut you out, that you may
make much of them. 18For a good purpose
it is always good to be made much of, and
not only when I am present with you. 19My
little children, with whom I am again in
travail until Christ be formed in you! 20I
could wish to be present with you now and
to change my tone, for I am perplexed
about you.

The allegory of Abraham

21 Tell me, you who desire to be under
law, do you not hear the law? 22For it is
written that Abraham had two sons, one by
a slave and one by a free woman. 23But
the son of the slave was born according to
the flesh, the son of the free woman through
promise. 24Now this is an allegory: these
women are two covenants. One is from
Mount Sinai, bearing children for slavery;
she is Hagar. 25Now Hagar is Mount Sinai
in Arabia;[i] she corresponds to the present
Jerusalem, for she is in slavery with her
children. 26But the Jerusalem above is free,
and she is our mother. 27For it is written,

"Rejoice, O barren one that dost not
bear;
break forth and shout, thou who art not
in travail;
for the desolate hath more children than
she who hath a husband."

28Now we,[j] brethren, like Isaac, are children
of promise. 29But as at that time he who
was born according to the flesh persecuted
him who was born according to the Spirit,
so it is now. 30But what does the scripture
say? "Cast out the slave and her son; for
the son of the slave shall not inherit with
the son of the free woman." 31So, brethren,
we are not children of the slave but of the
free woman.

---

[h] Or *by dealing truly with you*

[i] Other ancient authorities read ***For Sinai is a mountain in Arabia***

[j] Other ancient authorities read ***you***

King James

CHAPTER 5

STAND fast therefore in the liberty
wherewith Christ hath made us free, and
be not entangled again with the yoke of
bondage.
2 Behold, I Paul say unto you, that if ye
be circumcised, Christ shall profit you nothing.
3 For I testify again to every man that is
circumcised, that he is a debtor to do the
whole law.
4 Christ is become of no effect unto you,
whosoever of you are justified by the law; ye
are fallen from grace.
5 For we through the Spirit wait for the
hope of righteousness by faith.
6 For in Jesus Christ neither circumcision
availeth any thing, nor uncircumcision; but
faith which worketh by love.
7 Ye did run well; who did hinder you
that ye should not obey the truth?
8 This persuasion *cometh* not of him that
calleth you.
9 A little leaven leaveneth the whole
lump.
10 I have confidence in you through the
Lord, that ye will be none otherwise minded: but he that troubleth you shall bear his
judgment, whosoever he be.
11 And I, brethren, if I yet preach circumcision, why do I yet suffer persecution?
then is the offence of the cross ceased.
12 I would they were even cut off which
trouble you.
13 For, brethren, ye have been called
unto liberty; only *use* not liberty for an
occasion to the flesh, but by love serve one
another.
14 For all the law is fulfilled in one
word, *even* in this; Thou shalt love thy
neighbour as thyself.
15 But if ye bite and devour one another,
take heed that ye be not consumed one of
another.
16 *This* I say then, Walk in the Spirit,
and ye shall not fulfil the lust of the flesh.
17 For the flesh lusteth against the Spirit,
and the Spirit against the flesh: and these
are contrary the one to the other: so that ye
cannot do the things that ye would.
18 But if ye be led of the Spirit, ye are
not under the law.
19 Now the works of the flesh are
manifest, which are *these;* Adultery, fornication, uncleanness, lasciviousness,

Amplified

CHAPTER 5

IN [this] freedom Christ has made us free—completely
liberated us; stand fast then, and do not be hampered
and held ensnared *and* submit again to a yoke of slavery—
which you have once put off.
2 Notice, it is I, Paul, who tells you that if you receive
circumcision, Christ will be of no profit (advantage, avail)
to you, [[m]for if you distrust Him, you can gain nothing from
Him].
3 I once more protest *and* testify to every man who receives circumcision that he is under obligation *and* bound to
practice the whole of the Law *and* its ordinances.
4 If you seek to be justified *and* declared righteous *and* to
be given a right standing with God through the Law, you
are brought to nothing *and* so separated (severed) from
Christ. You have fallen away from grace—from God's gracious favor and unmerited blessing.
5 For we [not relying on the Law], through the (Holy)
Spirit's [help] by faith anticipate *and* wait for the blessing
and good for which our righteousness *and* right standing
with God—our [n]conformity to His will in purpose, thought
and action—[causes us] to hope.
6 For [if we are] in Christ Jesus, neither circumcision nor
uncircumcision counts for anything, but only faith activated
and energized *and* expressed *and* working through love.
7 You were running the race nobly. Who has interfered
(hindered and stopped you) from heeding *and* following the
Truth?
8 This [evil] persuasion is not from Him Who called you
—Who invited you to freedom in Christ.
9 A little leaven [a slight inclination to error, or a few
false teachers] leavens the whole lump [perverts the whole
conception of faith, or misleads the whole church].
10 [For my part] I have confidence [toward you] in the
Lord that you will take no contrary view of the matter *but*
will come to think with me. But he who is unsettling you,
whoever he is, will have to bear the penalty.
11 But, brethren, if I still preach circumcision [as some
accuse me of doing, as necessary to salvation], why am I still
suffering persecution? In that case the cross has ceased to be
a stumbling block *and* is made meaningless—done away.
12 I wish those who unsettle *and* confuse you would [[o]go
all the way and] cut themselves off!
13 For you, brethren, were [indeed] called to freedom;
only [do not let your] freedom be an incentive to your flesh
and an opportunity *or* excuse [for [o]selfishness], but through
love you should serve one another.
14 For the whole Law [concerning human relationships] is
[o]complied with in the one precept, You shall love your
neighbor as yourself. [Lev. 19:18.]
15 But if you bite and devour one another [in partisan
strife], be careful that you [and your whole fellowship] are
not consumed by one another.
16 But I say, walk *and* live habitually in the (Holy) Spirit
—responsive to *and* controlled *and* guided by the Spirit;
then you will certainly not gratify the cravings *and* desires of
the flesh—of human nature without God.
17 For the desires of the flesh are opposed to the (Holy)
Spirit, and the [desires of the] Spirit are opposed to the flesh
(Godless human nature); for these are antagonistic to each
other—continually withstanding and in conflict with each
other—so that you are not free *but* are prevented from
doing what you desire to do.
18 But if you are guided (led) by the (Holy) Spirit you
are not subject to the Law.
19 Now the doings (practices) of the flesh are clear—
obvious: they are immorality, impurity, indecency;

---

m) Chrysostom.
n) Abbott-Smith.
o) Vincent.

Living New Testament

CHAPTER 5

So Christ has made us free. Now make sure that you stay free and don't get all tied up again in the chains of slavery to Jewish laws and ceremonies.

2 Listen to me, for this is serious: *if you are counting on circumcision and keeping the Jewish laws to make you right with God, then Christ cannot save you.*

3 I'll say it again. Anyone trying to find favor with God by being circumcised must always obey every other Jewish law or perish.

4 Christ is useless to you if you are counting on clearing your debt to God by keeping those laws; you are lost from God's grace.

5 But we by the help of the Holy Spirit are counting on Christ's death to clear away our sins and make us right with God.

6 And we to whom Christ has given eternal life don't need to worry about whether we have been circumcised or not, or whether we are obeying the Jewish ceremonies or not; for all we need is faith working through love.

7 You were getting along so well. Who has interfered with you to hold you back from following the truth?

8 It certainly isn't God who has done it, for He is the one who has called you to freedom in Christ.

9 But it takes only one wrong person among you to infect all the others.

10 I am trusting the Lord to bring you back to believing as I do about these things. God will deal with that person, whoever he is, who has been troubling and confusing you.

11 Some people even say that I myself am preaching that circumcision and Jewish laws are necessary to the plan of salvation. Well, if I preached that, I would be persecuted no more—for that message doesn't offend anyone. The fact that I am still being persecuted proves that I am still preaching salvation through faith in the cross of Christ alone.

12 I only wish these teachers who want you to cut yourselves by being circumcised would cut themselves off from you and leave you alone!

13 For, dear brothers, you have been given freedom: not freedom to do wrong, but freedom to love and serve each other.

14 For the whole Law can be summed up in this one command: "Love others as you love yourself."

15 But if instead of showing love among yourselves you are always critical and catty, watch out! Beware of ruining each other.

16 I advise you to obey only the Holy Spirit's instructions. He will tell you where to go and what to do, and then you won't always be doing the wrong things your evil nature wants you to.

17 For we naturally love to do evil things that are just the opposite from the things that the Holy Spirit tells us to do; and the good things we want to do when the Spirit has His way with us are just the opposite of our natural desires. These two forces within us are constantly fighting each other to win control over us and our wishes are never free from their pressures.

18 When you are guided by the Holy Spirit you need no longer force yourself to obey Jewish laws.

19 But when you follow your own wrong inclinations your lives will produce these evil results: impure thoughts, eagerness for lustful pleasure,

Revised Standard

Liberty threatened by legalism

5 For freedom Christ has set us free;
stand fast therefore, and do not submit
again to a yoke of slavery.
2 Now I, Paul, say to you that if you
receive circumcision, Christ will be of no
advantage to you. [3]I testify again to every
man who receives circumcision that he is
bound to keep the whole law. [4]You are
severed from Christ, you who would be
justified by the law; you have fallen away
from grace. [5]For through the Spirit, by
faith, we wait for the hope of righteousness.
[6]For in Christ Jesus neither circumcision
nor uncircumcision is of any avail, but faith
working through love. [7]You were running
well; who hindered you from obeying the
truth? [8]This persuasion is not from him who
called you. [9]A little leaven leavens the
whole lump. [10]I have confidence in the Lord
that you will take no other view than mine;
and he who is troubling you will bear his
judgment, whoever he is. [11]But if I, brethren,
still preach circumcision, why am I
still persecuted? In that case the stumbling
block of the cross has been removed. [12]I
wish those who unsettle you would mutilate
themselves!

Freedom defined

13 For you were called to freedom,
brethren; only do not use your freedom
as an opportunity for the flesh, but through
love be servants of one another. [14]For the
whole law is fulfilled in one word, "You
shall love your neighbor as yourself." [15]But
if you bite and devour one another take
heed that you are not consumed by one
another.
16 But I say, walk by the Spirit, and
do not gratify the desires of the flesh. [17]For
the desires of the flesh are against the Spirit,
and the desires of the Spirit are against the
flesh; for these are opposed to each other,
to prevent you from doing what you would.
[18]But if you are led by the Spirit you are
not under the law. [19]Now the works of the
flesh are plain: immorality, impurity, licen-

King James

20 Idolatry, witchcraft, hatred, variance, emulations, wrath, strife, seditions, heresies,

21 Envyings, murders, drunkenness, revellings, and such like: of the which I tell you before, as I have also told *you* in time past, that they which do such things shall not inherit the kingdom of God.

22 But the fruit of the Spirit is love, joy, peace, longsuffering, gentleness, goodness, faith,

23 Meekness, temperance: against such there is no law.

24 And they that are Christ's have crucified the flesh with the affections and lusts.

25 If we live in the Spirit, let us also walk in the Spirit.

26 Let us not be desirous of vain glory, provoking one another, envying one another.

Amplified

20 Idolatry, sorcery, enmity, strife, jealousy, anger (ill temper), selfishness, divisions (dissensions), party spirit (factions, sects, with peculiar opinions, heresies);

21 Envy, drunkenness, carousing, and the like. I warn you beforehand, just as I did previously, that those who do such things shall not inherit the kingdom of God.

22 But the fruit of the (Holy) Spirit, [the work which His presence within accomplishes]—is love, joy (gladness), peace, patience (an even temper, forbearance), kindness, goodness (benevolence), faithfulness;

23 (Meekness, humility) gentleness, self-control (self-restraint, continence). Against such things there is no law [[p]that can bring a charge].

24 And those who belong to Christ Jesus, the Messiah, have crucified the flesh—the Godless human nature—with its passions and appetites *and* desires.

25 If we live by the (Holy) Spirit, let us also walk by the Spirit.—If by the (Holy) Spirit [q]we have our life [in God], let us go forward [p]walking in line, our conduct controlled by the Spirit.

26 Let us not become vainglorious *and* self-conceited, competitive *and* challenging *and* provoking *and* irritating to one another, envying *and* being jealous of one another.

CHAPTER 6

BRETHREN, if a man be overtaken in a fault, ye which are spiritual, restore such an one in the spirit of meekness; considering thyself, lest thou also be tempted.

2 Bear ye one another's burdens, and so fulfil the law of Christ.

3 For if a man think himself to be something, when he is nothing, he deceiveth himself.

4 But let every man prove his own work, and then shall he have rejoicing in himself alone, and not in another.

5 For every man shall bear his own burden.

6 Let him that is taught in the word communicate unto him that teacheth in all good things.

7 Be not deceived; God is not mocked: for whatsoever a man soweth, that shall he also reap.

CHAPTER 6

BRETHREN, if any person is overtaken in misconduct *or* sin of any sort, you who are spiritual—who are responsive to and controlled by the Spirit—should set him right *and* restore *and* reinstate him, without any sense of superiority *and* with all gentleness, keeping an attentive eye on yourself, lest you should be tempted also.

2 Bear (endure, carry) one another's burdens *and* [r]troublesome moral faults, and in this way fulfill *and* observe perfectly the law of Christ, the Messiah, *and* complete [s]what is lacking [in your obedience to it].

3 For if any person thinks himself to be somebody [too important to condescend to shoulder another's load], when he is nobody [of superiority except in his own estimation], he deceives *and* deludes *and* cheats himself.

4 But let every person carefully scrutinize *and* examine *and* test his own conduct *and* his own work. He can then have the personal satisfaction *and* joy of doing something commendable [[s]in itself alone] without [resorting to] boastful comparison with his neighbor.

5 For every person will have to bear [r][be equal to understanding and calmly receive] his own ([t]little) load [r][of oppressive faults].

6 Let him who receives instruction in the Word [of God] share all good things with his teacher—contributing to his support.

7 Do not be deceived *and* deluded *and* misled; God will not allow Himself to be sneered at—scorned, disdained or mocked [[u]by mere pretensions or professions, or His precepts being set aside].—He inevitably deludes himself who attempts to delude God. For whatever a man sows, that *and* [v]that only is what he will reap.

---

p) Vincent.
q) Adam Clarke.
r) Thayer.
s) Vincent.
t) Diminutive form of the Greek word.
u) Matthew Henry.
v) Vincent.

Living New Testament

20 Idolatry, spiritism (that is, encouraging the activity of demons), hatred and fighting, jealousy and anger, constant effort to get the best for yourself, complaints and criticisms, the feeling that everyone else is wrong except those in your own little group—and there will be wrong doctrine,

21 Envy, murder, drunkenness, wild parties, and all that sort of thing. Let me tell you again as I have before, that anyone living that sort of life will not inherit the kingdom of God.

22 But when the Holy Spirit controls our lives He will produce this kind of fruit in us: love, joy, peace, patience, kindness, goodness, faithfulness,

23 Gentleness and self-control; and here there is no conflict with Jewish laws.

24 Those who belong to Christ have nailed their natural evil desires to His cross and crucified them there.

25 If we are living now by the Holy Spirit's power, let us follow the Holy Spirit's leading in every part of our lives.

26 Then we won't need to look for honors and popularity, which lead to jealousy and hard feelings.

Revised Standard

tiousness, [20]idolatry, sorcery, enmity, strife,
jealousy, anger, selfishness, dissension, party
spirit, [21]envy,[k] drunkenness, carousing, and
the like. I warn you, as I warned you before, that those who do such things shall
not inherit the kingdom of God. [22]But the
fruit of the Spirit is love, joy, peace,
patience, kindness, goodness, faithfulness,
[23]gentleness, self-control; against such there
is no law. [24]And those who belong to Christ
Jesus have crucified the flesh with its passions and desires.

Fulfilling the law of Christ

25 If we live by the Spirit, let us also
walk by the Spirit. [26]Let us have no self-conceit, no provoking of one another, no envy of one another.

CHAPTER 6

Dear brothers, if a Christian is overcome by some sin, you who are godly should gently and humbly help him back onto the right path, remembering that next time it might be one of you who is in the wrong.

2 Share each other's troubles and problems, and so obey our Lord's command.

3 If anyone thinks he is too great to stoop to this, he is fooling himself. He is really a nobody.

4 Let everyone be sure that he is doing his very best, for then he will have the personal satisfaction of work well done, and won't need to compare himself with someone else.

5 Each of us must bear some faults and burdens of his own. For none of us is perfect!

6 Those who are taught the Word of God should help their teachers by paying them.

7 Don't be misled; remember that you can't ignore God and get away with it: a man will always reap just the kind of crop he sows!

6 Brethren, if a man is overtaken in any trespass, you who are spiritual should restore him in a spirit of gentleness. Look to
yourself, lest you too be tempted. [2]Bear one
another's burdens, and so fulfil the law of
Christ. [3]For if any one thinks he is something, when he is nothing, he deceives himself. [4]But let each one test his own work,
and then his reason to boast will be in himself alone and not in his neighbor. [5]For
each man will have to bear his own load.
6 Let him who is taught the word share all good things with him who teaches.
7 Do not be deceived; God is not mocked, for whatever a man sows, that he

[k] Other ancient authorities add *murder*

King James

8 For he that soweth to his flesh shall of the flesh reap corruption; but he that soweth to the Spirit shall of the Spirit reap life everlasting.

9 And let us not be weary in well-doing: for in due season we shall reap, if we faint not.

10 As we have therefore opportunity, let us do good unto all *men*, especially unto them who are of the household of faith.

11 Ye see how large a letter I have written unto you with mine own hand.

12 As many as desire to make a fair shew in the flesh, they constrain you to be circumcised; only lest they should suffer persecution for the cross of Christ.

13 For neither they themselves who are circumcised keep the law; but desire to have you circumcised, that they may glory in your flesh.

14 But God forbid that I should glory, save in the cross of our Lord Jesus Christ, by whom the world is crucified unto me, and I unto the world.

15 For in Christ Jesus neither circumcision availeth any thing, nor uncircumcision, but a new creature.

16 And as many as walk according to this rule, peace *be* on them, and mercy, and upon the Israel of God.

17 From henceforth let no man trouble me: for I bear in my body the marks of the Lord Jesus.

18 Brethren, the grace of our Lord Jesus Christ *be* with your spirit. Amen.

¶Unto the Galatians written from Rome.

Amplified

8 For he who sows to his own flesh (lower nature, sensuality) will from the flesh reap decay *and* ruin *and* destruction; but he who sows to the Spirit will from the Spirit reap life eternal.

9 And let us not lose heart *and* grow weary *and* faint in acting nobly *and* doing right, for in due time *and* at the appointed season we shall reap, if we do not loosen *and* relax our courage *and* faint.

10 So then, as occasion *and* opportunity open to us, let us do good ([v]morally) to all people [not only [v]being useful or profitable to them, but also doing what is for their spiritual good and advantage]. Be mindful to be a blessing, especially to those of the household of faith—those who belong to God's family with you, the believers.

11 [[v]Mark carefully these closing words of mine.] See with what large letters I am writing them with my own hand.

12 Those who want to make a good impression *and* a fine show in the flesh, would try to compel you to receive circumcision simply so that they may escape being persecuted for allegiance to the cross of Christ, the Messiah, the Anointed One.

13 For even the circumcised [Jews] themselves do not [really] keep the Law, but they want to have you circumcised in order that they may glory in your flesh—your subjection to external rites.

14 But far be it from me to glory [in anything or any one] except in the cross of our Lord Jesus Christ, the Messiah, through Whom the world has been crucified to me, and I to the world!

15 For neither is circumcision [now] of any importance, nor uncircumcision, but [only] a new creation [the result of a new birth and a new nature in Christ Jesus, the Messiah].

16 Peace and mercy be upon all who walk by this rule—who discipline themselves and regulate their lives by this principle—even upon the [true] Israel of God! [Ps. 125:5.]

17 From now on let no person trouble me [by [w]making it necessary for me to vindicate my apostolic authority and the divine truth of my Gospel]; for I bear on my body the brand marks of the Lord Jesus, [the wounds, scars and other outward evidence of persecutions].—These testify to His ownership of me!

18 The grace (spiritual favor, blessing) of our Lord Jesus Christ, the Anointed One, the Messiah, be with your spirit, brethren. Amen — so be it.

---

v) Vincent.
w) Vincent.

Living New Testament

8 If he sows to please his own wrong desires, he will be planting seeds of evil and he will surely reap a harvest of spiritual decay and death; but if he plants the good things of the Spirit, he will reap the everlasting life which the Holy Spirit gives him.

9 And let us not get tired of doing what is right, for after a while we will reap a harvest of blessing if we don't get discouraged and give up.

10 That's why whenever we can we should always be kind to everyone, and especially to our Christian brothers.

11 I will write these closing words in my own handwriting. See how large I have to make the letters!

12 Those teachers of yours who are trying to convince you to be circumcised are doing it for just one reason: so that they can be popular and avoid the persecution they would get if they admitted that the cross of Christ alone can save.

13 And even those teachers who submit to circumcision don't try to keep the other Jewish laws; but they want you to be circumcised in order that they can boast that you are their disciples.

14 As for me, God forbid that I should boast about anything except the cross of our Lord Jesus Christ. Because of that cross my interest in all the attractive things of the world was killed long ago, and the world's interest in me is also long dead.

15 It doesn't make any difference now whether we have been circumcised or not; what counts is whether we really have been changed into new and different people.

16 May God's mercy and peace be upon all of you who live by this principle and upon those everywhere who are really God's own.

17 From now on please don't argue with me about these things, for I carry on my body the scars of the whippings and wounds from Jesus' enemies that mark me as His slave.

18 Dear brothers, may the grace of our Lord Jesus Christ be with you all.

Sincerely,
Paul

Revised Standard

will also reap. [8]For he who sows to his own
flesh will from the flesh reap corruption;
but he who sows to the Spirit will from the
Spirit reap eternal life. [9]And let us not grow
weary in well-doing, for in due season we
shall reap, if we do not lose heart. [10]So
then, as we have opportunity, let us do good
to all men, and especially to those who are
of the household of faith.

Paul's personal benediction

11 See with what large letters I am writing to you with my own hand. [12]It is those
who want to make a good showing in the
flesh that would compel you to be circumcised, and only in order that they may not
be persecuted for the cross of Christ. [13]For
even those who receive circumcision do not
themselves keep the law, but they desire to
have you circumcised that they may glory
in your flesh. [14]But far be it from me to
glory except in the cross of our Lord Jesus
Christ, by which[1] the world has been crucified to me, and I to the world. [15]For neither
circumcision counts for anything, nor uncircumcision, but a new creation. [16]Peace
and mercy be upon all who walk by this
rule, upon the Israel of God.

17 Henceforth let no man trouble me; for I bear on my body the marks of Jesus.

18 The grace of our Lord Jesus Christ be with your spirit, brethren. Amen.

[1] Or *through whom*

King James

THE EPISTLE OF PAUL THE APOSTLE TO THE

Ephesians

CHAPTER 1

PAUL, an apostle of Jesus Christ by the will of God, to the saints which are at Ephesus, and to the faithful in Christ Jesus:

2 Grace *be* to you, and peace, from God our Father, and *from* the Lord Jesus Christ.

3 Blessed *be* the God and Father of our Lord Jesus Christ, who hath blessed us with all spiritual blessings in heavenly *places* in Christ:

4 According as he hath chosen us in him before the foundation of the world, that we should be holy and without blame before him in love:

5 Having predestinated us unto the adoption of children by Jesus Christ to himself, according to the good pleasure of his will,

6 To the praise of the glory of his grace, wherein he hath made us accepted in the beloved.

7 In whom we have redemption through his blood, the forgiveness of sins, according to the riches of his grace;

8 Wherein he hath abounded toward us in all wisdom and prudence;

9 Having made known unto us the mystery of his will, according to his good pleasure which he hath purposed in himself:

10 That in the dispensation of the fulness of times he might gather together in one all things in Christ, both which are in heaven, and which are on earth; *even* in him:

11 In whom also we have obtained an inheritance, being predestinated according to the purpose of him who worketh all things after the counsel of his own will:

12 That we should be to the praise of his glory, who first trusted in Christ.

13 In whom ye also *trusted*, after that ye heard the word of truth, the gospel of your salvation: in whom also after that ye believed, ye were sealed with that holy Spirit of promise,

14 Which is the earnest of our inheritance until the redemption of the purchased possession, unto the praise of his glory.

Amplified

THE LETTER OF PAUL TO THE

Ephesians

CHAPTER 1

PAUL, an apostle (special messenger) of Christ Jesus, the Messiah, by the divine will—the purpose and the choice of God—to the saints (the consecrated, set-apart ones) [a]at Ephesus who are also faithful *and* loyal *and* steadfast in Christ Jesus:

2 May grace (which is God's unmerited favor) and spiritual peace (which means peace with God and harmony, unity and undisturbedness) be yours from God our Father and from the Lord Jesus Christ.

3 Blessing (praise, laudation and eulogy) be to the God and Father of our Lord Jesus Christ, the Messiah, Who has blessed us *in Christ* with every spiritual (Holy Spirit given) blessing in the heavenly realm!

4 Even as [[a]in His love] He chose us—actually picked us out for Himself as His own—in Christ before the foundation of the world; that we should be holy (consecrated and set apart for Him) and blameless in His sight, *even* above reproach before Him in love.

5 For He foreordained us (destined us, planned in love for us) to be adopted [revealed] as His own children through Jesus Christ, in accordance with the purpose of His will — [b]because it pleased Him and was His kind intent;

6 [So that we might be] to the praise *and* the commendation of His glorious grace—favor and mercy—which He so freely bestowed on us in the Beloved.

7 In Him we have redemption (deliverance and salvation) through His blood, the remission (forgiveness) of our offenses (shortcomings and trespasses), in accordance with the riches *and* the generosity of His gracious favor,

8 Which He lavished upon us in every kind of wisdom and understanding (practical insight and prudence),

9 Making known to us the mystery (secret) of His will—of His plan, of His purpose. [And it is this:] In accordance with His good pleasure (His merciful intention) which He had previously purposed *and* set forth in [c]Him,

10 [He planned] for the maturity of the times *and* the climax of the ages to unify all things *and* head them up *and* consummate them in Christ, [both] things in heaven and things on the earth.

11 In Him we also were made [God's] heritage (portion) *and* [d]we obtained an inheritance; for we had been foreordained (chosen and appointed beforehand) in accordance with His purpose, Who works out everything in agreement with the counsel *and* design of His [own] will.

12 So that we who first hoped in Christ—who first put our confidence in Him—[have been destined and appointed] to live for the praise of His glory!

13 In Him you also who have heard the Word of Truth, the glad tidings (Gospel) of your salvation, and have believed in *and* have adhered to *and* have relied on Him, were stamped with the seal of the long-promised Holy Spirit.

14 That [Spirit] is the guarantee of our inheritance—the first fruit, the pledge and foretaste, the down payment on our heritage—in anticipation of its full redemption *and* our acquiring [complete] possession of it, to the praise of His glory.

---

a) Many ancient authorities so read.
b) Vincent.
c) Some interpret "in Him" to mean "in Himself"; others, "in Christ."
d) Alternate reading.

Living New Testament

Ephesians

CHAPTER 1

Dear Christian friends at Ephesus, ever loyal to the Lord: This is Paul writing to you, chosen by God to be Jesus Christ's messenger.

2 May His blessings and peace be yours, sent to you from God our Father and Jesus Christ our Lord.

3 How we praise God, the Father of our Lord Jesus Christ, who has blessed us with every blessing in heaven because we belong to Christ.

4 Long ago, even before He made the world, God chose us to be His very own, through what Christ would do for us; He decided then to make us holy in His eyes, without a single fault—we who stand before Him covered with His love.

5 His unchanging plan has always been to adopt us into His own family by sending Jesus Christ to die for us. And He did this because He wanted to!

6 Now all praise to God for His wonderful kindness to us and His favor that He has poured out upon us, because we belong to His dearly loved Son.

7 So overflowing is His kindness towards us that He took away all our sins through the blood of His Son, by whom we are saved;

8 And He has showered down upon us the richness of His grace—for how well He understands us and knows what is best for us at all times.

9 God has told us His secret reason for sending Christ, a plan He decided on in mercy long ago;

10 And this was His purpose: that when the time is ripe He will gather us all together from wherever we are—in heaven or on earth—to be with Him, in Christ, forever.

11 Moreover, because of what Christ has done we have become gifts to God that He delights in, for as part of God's sovereign plan we were chosen from the beginning to be His, and all things happen just as He decided long ago.

12 God's purpose in this was that we should praise God and give glory to Him for doing these mighty things for us, who were the first to trust in Christ.

13 And because of what Christ did, all you others too, who heard the Good News about how to be saved, and trusted Christ, were marked as belonging to Christ by the Holy Spirit, who long ago had been promised to all of us Christians.

14 His presence within us is God's guarantee that He really will give us all that He promised; and the Spirit's seal upon us means that God has already purchased us and that He guarantees to bring us to Himself. This is just one more reason for us to praise our glorious God.

Revised Standard

THE LETTER OF PAUL
TO THE

Ephesians

Salutation

1 Paul, an apostle of Christ Jesus by the will of God,
To the saints who are also faithful[a] in Christ Jesus:
2 Grace to you and peace from God our Father and the Lord Jesus Christ.

Spiritual blessings through Christ

3 Blessed be the God and Father of our
Lord Jesus Christ, who has blessed us in
Christ with every spiritual blessing in the
heavenly places, 4even as he chose us in him
before the foundation of the world, that we
should be holy and blameless before him.
5He destined us in love[b] to be his sons
through Jesus Christ, according to the purpose of his will, 6to the praise of his glorious
grace which he freely bestowed on us in the
Beloved. 7In him we have redemption
through his blood, the forgiveness of our
trespasses, according to the riches of his
grace 8which he lavished upon us. 9For he
has made known to us in all wisdom and
insight the mystery of his will, according to
his purpose which he set forth in Christ 10as
a plan for the fulness of time, to unite all
things in him, things in heaven and things
on earth.
11 In him, according to the purpose of
him who accomplishes all things according
to the counsel of his will, 12we who first
hoped in Christ have been destined and appointed to live for the praise of his glory.
13In him you also, who have heard the word
of truth, the gospel of your salvation, and
have believed in him, were sealed with the
promised Holy Spirit, 14which is the guarantee of our inheritance until we acquire possession of it, to the praise of his glory.

[a] Other ancient authorities read *who are at Ephesus and faithful*
[b] Or *before him in love, having destined us*

King James

15 Wherefore I also, after I heard of your faith in the Lord Jesus, and love unto all the saints,
16 Cease not to give thanks for you, making mention of you in my prayers;
17 That the God of our Lord Jesus Christ, the Father of glory, may give unto you the spirit of wisdom and revelation in the knowledge of him:
18 The eyes of your understanding being enlightened; that ye may know what is the hope of his calling, and what the riches of the glory of his inheritance in the saints,
19 And what *is* the exceeding greatness of his power to us-ward who believe, according to the working of his mighty power,
20 Which he wrought in Christ, when he raised him from the dead, and set *him* at his own right hand in the heavenly *places*,
21 Far above all principality, and power, and might, and dominion, and every name that is named, not only in this world, but also in that which is to come:
22 And hath put all *things* under his feet, and gave him *to be* the head over all *things* to the church,
23 Which is his body, the fulness of him that filleth all in all.

Amplified

15 For this reason, because I have heard of your faith in the Lord Jesus and your love toward all the saints (the people of God),
16 I do not cease to give thanks for you, making mention of you in my prayers.
17 [For I always pray] the God of our Lord Jesus Christ, the Father of Glory, that He may grant you a spirit of wisdom and revelation—of insight into mysteries and secrets—in the [deep and intimate] knowledge of Him,
18 By having the eyes of your heart flooded with light, so that you can know *and* understand the hope to which He has called you and how rich is His glorious inheritance in the saints—His set-apart ones.
19 And [so that you can know and understand] what is the immeasurable *and* unlimited *and* surpassing greatness of His power in *and* for us who believe, as demonstrated in the working of His mighty strength,
20 Which He exerted in Christ when He raised Him from the dead and seated Him at His [own] right hand in the heavenly [places],
21 Far above all rule and authority and power and dominion, and every name that is named—above every title that can be conferred—not only in this age *and* in this world, but also in the age *and* the world which are to come.
22 And He has put all things under his feet and has appointed Him the universal and supreme Head of the church (a headship exercised throughout the church), [Ps. 8:6.]
23 Which is His body, the fullness of Him Who fills all in all—for in that body lives the full measure of Him Who makes everything complete, and Who fills everything everywhere [with Himself].

CHAPTER 2

AND you *hath he quickened*, who were dead in trespasses and sins;
2 Wherein in time past ye walked according to the course of this world, according to the prince of the power of the air, the spirit that now worketh in the children of disobedience:
3 Among whom also we all had our conversation in times past in the lusts of our flesh, fulfilling the desires of the flesh and of the mind; and were by nature the children of wrath, even as others.
4 But God, who is rich in mercy, for his great love wherewith he loved us,
5 Even when we were dead in sins, hath quickened us together with Christ, (by grace ye are saved;)

CHAPTER 2

AND you [He made alive], when you were dead [slain] by [your] trespasses and sins
2 In which at one time you walked habitually. You were following the course *and* fashion of this world—were under the sway of the tendency of this present age—following the prince of the power of the air. (You were obedient to him and were under his control,) the [demon] spirit that still constantly works in the sons of disobedience—the careless, the rebellious and the unbelieving, who go against the purposes of God.
3 Among these we as well as you once lived *and* conducted ourselves in the passions of our flesh—our behavior governed by our corrupt and sensual nature; obeying the impulses of the flesh and the thoughts of the mind—our cravings dictated by our senses and our dark imaginings. We were then by nature children of [God's] wrath *and* heirs of [His] indignation, like the rest of mankind.
4 But God! So rich is He in His mercy! Because of *and* in order to satisfy the great *and* wonderful *and* intense love with which He loved us,
5 Even when we were dead [slain] by [our own] shortcomings *and* trespasses, He made us alive together in fellowship *and* in union with Christ. —He gave us the very life of Christ Himself, the same new life with which He quickened Him. [For] it is by grace—by His favor and mercy which you did not deserve—that you are saved ([e]delivered from judgment *and* made partakers of Christ's salvation).

e) Thayer.

Living New Testament

15 That is why, ever since I heard of your strong faith in the Lord Jesus and of the love you have for Christians everywhere,

16, 17 I have never stopped thanking God for you. I pray for you constantly, asking God, the glorious Father of our Lord Jesus Christ, to give you wisdom to see clearly and really understand who Christ is and all that He has done for you.

18 I pray that your hearts will be flooded with light so that you can see something of the future He has called you to share. I want you to realize that God has been made rich because we who are Christ's have been given to Him!

19 I pray that you will begin to understand how incredibly great His power is to help those who believe Him. It is that same mighty power

20 That raised Christ from the dead and seated Him in the place of honor at God's right hand in heaven,

21 Far, far above any other king or ruler or dictator or leader. Yes, His honor is far more glorious than that of anyone else either in this world or in the world to come.

22 And God has put all things under His feet and made Him the supreme Head of the church—

23 Which is His body, filled with Himself, the Author and Giver of everything everywhere.

Revised Standard

Prayer for wisdom and knowledge

15 For this reason, because I have heard
of your faith in the Lord Jesus and your
love[c] toward all the saints, [16]I do not cease to
give thanks for you, remembering you in my
prayers, [17]that the God of our Lord Jesus
Christ, the Father of glory, may give you a
spirit of wisdom and of revelation in the
knowledge of him, [18]having the eyes of your
hearts enlightened, that you may know what
is the hope to which he has called you, what
are the riches of his glorious inheritance in
the saints, [19]and what is the immeasurable
greatness of his power in us who believe,
according to the working of his great might
[20]which he accomplished in Christ when he
raised him from the dead and made him sit
at his right hand in the heavenly places,
[21]far above all rule and authority and power
and dominion, and above every name that
is named, not only in this age but also in
that which is to come; [22]and he has put all
things under his feet and has made him the
head over all things for the church, [23]which
is his body, the fulness of him who fills all
in all.

CHAPTER 2

Once you were under God's curse, doomed forever for your sins.

2 You went along with the crowd and were just like all the others, full of sin, obeying Satan, the mighty prince of the power of the air, who is at work right now in the hearts of those who are against the Lord.

3 All of us used to be just as they are, our lives expressing the evil within us, doing every wicked thing that our passions or our evil thoughts might lead us into. We started out bad, being born with evil natures, and were under God's anger just like everyone else.

4 But God is so rich in mercy; He loved us so much

5 That even though we were spiritually dead and doomed by our sins, He gave us back our lives again[1] when He raised Christ from the dead—only by His undeserved favor have we ever been saved—

New life with Christ

2 And you he made alive, when you were
dead through the trespasses and sins [2]in
which you once walked, following the course
of this world, following the prince of the
power of the air, the spirit that is now at
work in the sons of disobedience. [3]Among
these we all once lived in the passions of our
flesh, following the desires of body and mind,
and so we were by nature children of wrath,
like the rest of mankind. [4]But God, who is
rich in mercy, out of the great love with
which he loved us, [5]even when we were dead
through our trespasses, made us alive together with Christ (by grace you have been

---

[1] Literally, "He made us alive."

[c] Other ancient authorities omit *your love*

King James

6 And hath raised *us* up together, and made *us* sit together in heavenly *places* in Christ Jesus:

7 That in the ages to come he might shew the exceeding riches of his grace in *his* kindness toward us through Christ Jesus.

8 For by grace are ye saved through faith; and that not of yourselves: *it is* the gift of God:

9 Not of works, lest any man should boast.

10 For we are his workmanship, created in Christ Jesus unto good works, which God hath before ordained that we should walk in them.

11 Wherefore remember, that ye *being* in time past Gentiles in the flesh, who are called Uncircumcision by that which is called the Circumcision in the flesh made by hands;

12 That at that time ye were without Christ, being aliens from the commonwealth of Israel, and strangers from the covenants of promise, having no hope, and without God in the world:

13 But now in Christ Jesus ye who sometimes were far off are made nigh by the blood of Christ.

14 For he is our peace, who hath made both one, and hath broken down the middle wall of partition *between us;*

15 Having abolished in his flesh the enmity, *even* the law of commandments *contained* in ordinances; for to make in himself of twain one new man, *so* making peace;

16 And that he might reconcile both unto God in one body by the cross, having slain the enmity thereby:

17 And came and preached peace to you which were afar off, and to them that were nigh.

18 For through him we both have access by one Spirit unto the Father.

19 Now therefore ye are no more strangers and foreigners, but fellow-citizens with the saints, and of the household of God;

20 And are built upon the foundation of the apostles and prophets, Jesus Christ himself being the chief corner *stone;*

Amplified

6 And He raised us up together with Him and made us sit down together—giving us [f]joint seating with Him—in the heavenly sphere [by virtue of our being] in Christ Jesus, the Messiah, the Anointed One.

7 He did this that He might clearly demonstrate through the ages to come the immeasurable (limitless, surpassing) riches of His free grace (His unmerited favor) in kindness *and* goodness of heart toward us in Christ Jesus.

8 For it is by free grace (God's unmerited favor) that you are saved ([e]delivered from judgment *and* made partakers of Christ's salvation) through [your] faith. And this [salvation] is not of yourselves—of your own doing, it came not through your own striving—but it is the gift of God;

9 Not because of works [not the fulfillment of the Law's demands], lest any man should boast. —It is not the result of what any one can possibly do, so no one can pride himself in it or take glory to himself.

10 For we are God's [own] handiwork (His workmanship), [g]recreated in Christ Jesus, [born anew] that we may do those good works which God predestined (planned beforehand) for us, (taking paths which He prepared ahead of time) that we should walk in them—living the good life which He prearranged and made ready for us to live.

11 Therefore remember that at one time you were Gentiles [heathen] in the flesh; called Uncircumcision by those who called themselves Circumcision, [itself a [g]mere mark] in the flesh made by human hands.

12 Remember that you were at that time separated (living apart) from Christ—excluded from all part in Him; utterly estranged *and* outlawed from the rights of Israel as a nation, and strangers with no share in the sacred compacts of the [Messianic] promise—with no knowledge of or right in God's agreements, His covenants. And you had no hope—no promise; you were in the world without God.

13 But now in Christ Jesus, you who once were [so] far away, through (by, in) the blood of Christ have been brought near.

14 For He is [Himself] our peace—our bond of unity and harmony. He has made us both [Jew and Gentile] one (body), and has broken down (destroyed, abolished) the hostile dividing wall between us.

15 By abolishing in His [own crucified] flesh the enmity [caused by] the Law with its decrees and ordinances—which He annulled; that He from the two might create in Himself one new man—one new quality of humanity out of the two—so making peace.

16 And [He designed] to reconcile to God both [Jew and Gentile, united] in a single body by means of His cross; thereby killing the mutual enmity *and* bringing the feud to an end.

17 And He came and preached the glad tidings of peace to you who were afar off and [peace] to those who were near. [Isa. 57:19.]

18 For it is through Him that we both [whether far off or near] now have an introduction (access) by one (Holy) Spirit to the Father—so that we are able to approach Him.

19 Therefore you are no longer outsiders—exiles, migrants and aliens, excluded from the rights of citizens; but you now share citizenship with the saints—God's own people, consecrated and set apart for Himself; and you belong to God's [own] household.

20 You are built upon the foundation of the apostles and prophets with Christ Jesus Himself the chief Cornerstone.

---

e) Thayer.
f) Meyer's Commentary.
g) Arthur S. Way: "The Letters of St. Paul and Hebrews."

Living New Testament

6 And lifted us up from the grave into glory along with Christ, where we sit with Him in the heavenly realms—all because of what Christ Jesus did.

7 And now God can always point to us as examples of how very, very rich His kindness is, as shown in all He has done for us through Jesus Christ.

8 Because of His kindness you have been saved through trusting Christ. And even trusting[2] is not of yourselves; it too is a gift from God.

9 Salvation is not a reward for the good we have done, so none of us can take any credit for it.

10 It is God Himself who has made us what we are and given us new lives from Christ Jesus; and long ages ago He planned that we should spend these lives in helping others.

11 Never forget that once you were heathen, and that you were called godless and "unclean" by the Jews. (But their hearts, too, were still unclean, even though they were going through the ceremonies and rituals of the godly, for they circumcised themselves as a sign of godliness.)

12 Remember that in those days you were living utterly apart from Christ; you were enemies of God's children and He had promised you no help. You were lost, without God, without hope.

13 But now you belong to Christ Jesus, and though you once were far away from God, now you have been brought very near to Him because of what Jesus Christ has done for you with His blood.

14 For Christ Himself is our way of peace. He has made peace between us Jews and you Gentiles by making us all one family,[3] breaking down the wall of contempt[4] that used to separate us.

15 By His death He ended the angry resentment between us, caused by the Jewish laws which favored the Jews and excluded the Gentiles, for He died to annul that whole system of Jewish laws. Then He took the two groups that had been opposed to each other and made them parts of Himself; thus He fused us together to become one new person, and at last there was peace.

16 As parts of the same body, our anger against each other has disappeared, for both of us have been reconciled to God. And so the feud ended at last at the cross.

17 And He has brought this Good News of peace to you Gentiles who were very far away from Him, and to us Jews who were near.

18 Now all of us, whether Jews or Gentiles, may come to God the Father with the Holy Spirit's help because of what Christ has done for us.

19 Now you are no longer strangers to God and foreigners to heaven, but you are members of God's very own family, citizens of God's country, and you belong in God's household with every other Christian.

20 What a foundation you stand on now: the apostles and the prophets; and the cornerstone of the building is Jesus Christ Himself!

Revised Standard

saved), 6 and raised us up with him, and
made us sit with him in the heavenly places
in Christ Jesus, 7 that in the coming ages he
might show the immeasurable riches of his
grace in kindness toward us in Christ Jesus.
8 For by grace you have been saved through
faith; and this is not your own doing, it is
the gift of God— 9 not because of works, lest
any man should boast. 10 For we are his
workmanship, created in Christ Jesus for
good works, which God prepared beforehand, that we should walk in them.

The household of God

11 Therefore remember that at one time
you Gentiles in the flesh, called the uncircumcision by what is called the circumcision, which is made in the flesh by hands
— 12 remember that you were at that time
separated from Christ, alienated from the
commonwealth of Israel, and strangers to
the covenants of promise, having no hope
and without God in the world. 13 But now in
Christ Jesus you who once were far off have
been brought near in the blood of Christ.
14 For he is our peace, who has made us both
one, and has broken down the dividing wall
of hostility, 15 by abolishing in his flesh the
law of commandments and ordinances, that
he might create in himself one new man in
place of the two, so making peace, 16 and
might reconcile us both to God in one body
through the cross, thereby bringing the hostility to an end. 17 And he came and preached
peace to you who were far off and peace to
those who were near; 18 for through him we
both have access in one Spirit to the Father.
19 So then you are no longer strangers and
sojourners, but you are fellow citizens with
the saints and members of the household of
God, 20 built upon the foundation of the
apostles and prophets, Christ Jesus himself

---

2 Or, "Salvation is not of yourselves."
3 Literally, "by making us one."
4 Implied.

King James

21 In whom all the building fitly framed
together groweth unto an holy temple in the
Lord:
22 In whom ye also are builded together
for an habitation of God through the Spirit.

Amplified

21 In Him the whole structure is joined (bound, weld-
ed) together harmoniously; and it continues to rise (grow,
increase) into a holy temple in the Lord—a sanctuary
dedicated, consecrated and sacred to the presence of the
Lord.
22 In Him—and in fellowship with one another—you
yourselves also are being built up [into this structure] with
the rest, to form a fixed abode (dwelling place) of God in
(by, through) the Spirit.

CHAPTER 3

FOR this cause I Paul, the prisoner of
Jesus Christ for you Gentiles,
2 If ye have heard of the dispensation of
the grace of God which is given me to
you-ward:
3 How that by revelation he made known
unto me the mystery; (as I wrote afore in
few words,
4 Whereby, when ye read, ye may understand my knowledge in the mystery of
Christ)
5 Which in other ages was not made
known unto the sons of men, as it is now
revealed unto his holy apostles and prophets
by the Spirit;
6 That the Gentiles should be fellow-
heirs, and of the same body and partakers
of his promise in Christ by the gospel:
7 Whereof I was made a minister, according to the gift of the grace of God given
unto me by the effectual working of his
power.
8 Unto me, who am less than the least of
all saints, is this grace given, that I should
preach among the Gentiles the unsearchable
riches of Christ;
9 And to make all *men* see what *is* the
fellowship of the mystery, which from the
beginning of the world hath been hid in
God, who created all things by Jesus Christ:
10 To the intent that now unto the principalities and powers in heavenly *places*
might be known by the church the manifold
wisdom of God,
11 According to the eternal purpose
which he purposed in Christ Jesus our Lord:
12 In whom we have boldness and access
with confidence by the faith of him.

CHAPTER 3

FOR this reason [[h]because I preached that you are thus
builded together], I, Paul, am the prisoner of Jesus the
Christ [h]for the sake *and* on behalf of you Gentiles.
2 Assuming that you have heard of the stewardship of
God's grace (His unmerited favor) that was entrusted to
me [to dispense to you] for your benefit;
3 And how the mystery (secret) was made known to
me *and* I was allowed to comprehend it by direct revelation, as I already briefly wrote you,
4 When you read this you can understand my insight
into the mystery of Christ.
5 [This mystery] was never disclosed to human beings
in past generations as it has now been revealed to His holy
apostles [consecrated messengers] and prophets by the
(Holy) Spirit.
6 [It is this:] that the Gentiles are now to be fellow
heirs [with the Jews], members of the same body, and joint
partakers (sharing) in the same divine promise in Christ
through [their acceptance of] the glad tidings (the Gospel).
7 Of this [Gospel] I was made a minister according to
the gift of God's free grace (undeserved favor), which
was bestowed on me by the exercise—the working in all
its effectiveness—of His power.
8 To me, though I am the very least of all the saints
(God's consecrated people), this grace (favor, privilege)
was granted *and* graciously entrusted: to proclaim to the
Gentiles the unending (boundless, fathomless, incalculable
and exhaustless) riches of Christ—wealth which no human
being could have searched out.
9 Also to enlighten all men *and* make plain to them
what is the plan [regarding the Gentiles and providing for
the salvation of all men,] of the mystery kept hidden
through the ages *and* concealed until now in [the mind of]
God Who created all things *by Christ Jesus.*
10 [The purpose is] that through the church the [i]com-
plicated, many-sided wisdom of God in all its infinite
variety *and* innumerable aspects might now be made
known to the angelic rulers and authorities (principalities
and powers) in the heavenly sphere.
11 This is in accordance with the terms of the eternal
and timeless purpose which He has realized *and* carried
into effect, in [the person of] Christ Jesus our Lord;
12 In Whom, because of our faith in Him, we dare to
have the boldness (courage and confidence) of free access
—an unreserved approach to God with freedom and without fear.

---

h) The Jews persecuted and imprisoned Paul because he was an apostle to the Gentiles and preached the gospel to them.—Matthew Henry.
i) Webster in defining "manifold" (the King James rendering of "polupoikilos").

Living New Testament

21 We who believe are carefully joined together with Christ as parts of a beautiful, constantly growing temple for God.

22 And you also are joined with Him and with each other by the Spirit, and are part of this dwelling place of God.

Revised Standard

being the cornerstone, [21]in whom the whole
structure is joined together and grows into
a holy temple in the Lord; [22]in whom you
also are built into it for a dwelling place of
God in the Spirit.

CHAPTER 3

I Paul, the servant of Christ, am here in jail because of you—for preaching that you Gentiles are a part of God's house.

2, 3 No doubt you already know that God has given me this special work of showing God's favor to you Gentiles, as I briefly mentioned before in one of my letters. God Himself showed me this secret plan of His, that the Gentiles, too, are included in His kindness.

4 I say this to explain to you how I know about these things.

5 In olden times God did not share this plan with His people, but now He has revealed it by the Holy Spirit to His apostles and prophets.

6 And this is the secret: that the Gentiles will have their full share with the Jews in all the riches inherited by God's sons; both are invited to belong to His church, and all of God's promises of mighty blessings through Christ apply to them both when they accept the Good News about Christ and what He has done for them.

7 God has given me the wonderful privilege of telling everyone about this plan of His; and He has given me His power and special ability to do it well.

8 Just think! Though I did nothing to deserve it, and though I am the most useless Christian there is, yet I was the one chosen for this special joy of telling the Gentiles the Glad News of the endless treasures available to them in Christ;

9 And to explain to everyone that God is the Savior of the Gentiles too, just as He who made all things had secretly planned from the very beginning.

10 And His reason? To show to all the powers of heaven how perfectly wise God is when they see all of His family—Jews and Gentiles—joined together in His church,

11 Just as He had always planned to do through Jesus Christ our Lord.

12 Now we can come fearlessly right into God's presence, assured of His glad welcome when we come with Christ and trust in Him.

Paul, apostle to the Gentiles

3 For this reason I, Paul, a prisoner for
Christ Jesus on behalf of you Gentiles—
[2]assuming that you have heard of the stewardship of God's grace that was given to me
for you, [3]how the mystery was made known
to me by revelation, as I have written briefly.
[4]When you read this you can perceive my
insight into the mystery of Christ, [5]which
was not made known to the sons of men in
other generations as it has now been revealed to his holy apostles and prophets by
the Spirit; [6]that is, how the Gentiles are fellow heirs, members of the same body, and
partakers of the promise in Christ Jesus
through the gospel.
7 Of this gospel I was made a minister
according to the gift of God's grace which
was given me by the working of his power.
[8]To me, though I am the very least of all
the saints, this grace was given, to preach to
the Gentiles the unsearchable riches of
Christ, [9]and to make all men see what is the
plan of the mystery hidden for ages in[d] God
who created all things; [10]that through the
church the manifold wisdom of God might
now be made known to the principalities and
powers in the heavenly places. [11]This was
according to the eternal purpose which he
has realized in Christ Jesus our Lord, [12]in
whom we have boldness and confidence of
access through our faith in him. [13]So I ask

[d] Or *by*

King James

13 Wherefore I desire that ye faint not at my tribulations for you, which is your glory.

14 For this cause I bow my knees unto the Father of our Lord Jesus Christ,

15 Of whom the whole family in heaven and earth is named,

16 That he would grant you, according to the riches of his glory, to be strengthened with might by his Spirit in the inner man;

17 That Christ may dwell in your hearts by faith; that ye, being rooted and grounded in love,

18 May be able to comprehend with all saints what *is* the breadth, and length, and depth, and height;

19 And to know the love of Christ, which passeth knowledge, that ye might be filled with all the fulness of God.

20 Now unto him that is able to do exceeding abundantly above all that we ask or think, according to the power that worketh in us,

21 Unto him *be* glory in the church by Christ Jesus throughout all ages, world without end. Amen.

Amplified

13 So I ask you not to lose heart—not to faint or become despondent through fear—at what I am suffering in your behalf. [Rather glory in it] for it is an honor to you.

14 For this reason [[j]seeing the greatness of this plan by which you are built together in Christ], I bow my knees before the Father *of our Lord Jesus Christ,*

15 For Whom every family in heaven and on earth is named—[that Father] from Whom all [k]fatherhood takes its title and derives its name.

16 May He grant you out of the rich treasury of His glory to be strengthened *and* reinforced with mighty power in the inner man by the (Holy) Spirit [Himself]—indwelling your innermost being and personality.

17 May Christ through your faith [actually] dwell—settle down, abide, make His permanent home—in your hearts! May you be rooted deep in love *and* founded securely on love,

18 That you may have the power *and* be strong to apprehend *and* grasp with all the saints (God's devoted people, the experience of that love) what is the breadth and length and height and depth [of it];

19 [That you may really come] to know—practically, [l]through experience for yourselves—the love of Christ, which far surpasses [l]mere knowledge (without experience); that you may be filled (through all your being) [l]unto all the fullness of God—[that is] may have the richest measure of the divine Presence, and [m]become a body wholly filled and flooded with God Himself!

20 Now to Him Who, by (in consequence of) the [action of His] power that is at work within us, is able to [carry out His purpose and] do superabundantly, far over *and* above all that we [dare] ask or think—infinitely beyond our highest prayers, desires, thoughts, hopes or dreams—

21 To Him be glory in the church and in Christ Jesus throughout all generations, for ever and ever. Amen—so be it.

CHAPTER 4

I THEREFORE, the prisoner of the Lord, beseech you that ye walk worthy of the vocation wherewith ye are called,

2 With all lowliness and meekness, with longsuffering, forbearing one another in love;

3 Endeavouring to keep the unity of the Spirit in the bond of peace.

4 *There is* one body, and one Spirit, even as ye are called in one hope of your calling;

5 One Lord, one faith, one baptism,

6 One God and Father of all, who *is* above all, and through all, and in you all.

7 But unto every one of us is given grace according to the measure of the gift of Christ.

CHAPTER 4

I THEREFORE, the prisoner for the Lord, appeal to *and* beg you to walk (lead a life) worthy of the [divine] calling to which you have been called—with behavior that is a credit to the summons to God's service,

2 Living as becomes you—with complete lowliness of mind (humility) and meekness (unselfishness, gentleness, mildness), with patience, bearing with one another *and* making allowances because you love one another.

3 Be eager *and* strive earnestly to guard *and* keep the harmony *and* oneness of [produced by] the Spirit in the binding power of peace.

4 [There is] one body and one Spirit, just as there is also one hope [that belongs] to the calling you received.

5 [There is] one Lord, one faith, one baptism,

6 One God and Father of [us] all, Who is above all (Sovereign over all), pervading all and [living] in [us] all.

7 Yet grace (God's unmerited favor) was given to each of us individually—not indiscriminately, but in different ways—in proportion to the measure of Christ's [rich and bounteous] gift.

j) Many authorities consider that Paul here resumes the thread of verse.
k) Alternate reading.
l) Vincent's Word Studies.
m) Thayer.

Living New Testament

13 So please don't lose heart at what they are doing to me here. It is for you I am suffering and you should feel honored and encouraged.

14, 15 When I think of the wisdom and scope of His plan I fall down on my knees and pray to the Father of all the great family of God—some of them already in heaven and some down here on earth—

16 That out of His glorious, unlimited resources He will give you the mighty inner strengthening of His Holy Spirit.

17 And I pray that Christ will be more and more at home in your hearts, living within you as you trust in Him. May your roots go down deep into the soil of God's marvelous love;

18, 19 And may you be able to feel and understand, as all God's children should, how long, how wide, how deep, and how high His love really is; and to experience this love for yourselves, though it is so great that you will never see the end of it or fully know or understand it. And so at last you will be filled up with God Himself.

20 Now glory be to God who by His mighty power at work within us is able to do far more than we would ever dare to ask or even dream of—infinitely beyond our highest prayers, desires, thoughts, or hopes.

21 May He be given glory forever and ever through endless ages because of His master plan of salvation for the church through Jesus Christ.

Revised Standard

you not to[e] lose heart over what I am suffering for you, which is your glory.

Strength through the Spirit

14 For this reason I bow my knees before the Father, [15]from whom every family
in heaven and on earth is named, [16]that according to the riches of his glory he may
grant you to be strengthened with might
through his Spirit in the inner man, [17]and
that Christ may dwell in your hearts through
faith; that you, being rooted and grounded
in love, [18]may have power to comprehend
with all the saints what is the breadth and
length and height and depth, [19]and to know
the love of Christ which surpasses knowledge,
that you may be filled with all the fulness of
God.

20 Now to him who by the power at work
within us is able to do far more abundantly
than all that we ask or think, [21]to him be
glory in the church and in Christ Jesus to all
generations, for ever and ever. Amen.

CHAPTER 4

I beg you—I, a prisoner here in jail for serving the Lord—to live and act in a way worthy of those who have been chosen for such wonderful blessings as these.

2 Be humble and gentle. Be patient with each other, making allowance for each other's faults because of your love.

3 Try always to be led along together by the Holy Spirit, and so be at peace with one another.

4 We are all parts of one body, we have the same Spirit, and we have all been called to the same glorious future.

5 For us there is only one Lord, one faith, one baptism,

6 And we all have the same God and Father who is over us all and in us all, and living through every part of us.

7 However, Christ has given each of us special abilities —whatever He wants us to have out of His rich storehouse of gifts.

The unity of the Spirit

4 I therefore, a prisoner for the Lord, beg
you to lead a life worthy of the calling
to which you have been called, [2]with all lowliness and meekness, with patience, forbearing one another in love, [3]eager to maintain
the unity of the Spirit in the bond of peace.
[4]There is one body and one Spirit, just as
you were called to the one hope that belongs
to your call, [5]one Lord, one faith, one baptism, [6]one God and Father of us all, who is
above all and through all and in all. [7]But

The gifts of the Spirit

grace was given to each of us according to

[e] Or *I ask that I may not*

King James

8 Wherefore he saith, When he ascended up on high, he led captivity captive, and gave gifts unto men.

9 (Now that he ascended, what is it but that he also descended first into the lower parts of the earth?

10 He that descended is the same also that ascended up far above all heavens, that he might fill all things.)

11 And he gave some, apostles; and some, prophets; and some, evangelists; and some, pastors and teachers;

12 For the perfecting of the saints, for the work of the ministry, for the edifying of the body of Christ:

13 Till we all come in the unity of the faith, and of the knowledge of the Son of God, unto a perfect man, unto the measure of the stature of the fulness of Christ:

14 That we *henceforth* be no more children, tossed to and fro, and carried about with every wind of doctrine, by the sleight of men, *and* cunning craftiness, whereby they lie in wait to deceive;

15 But speaking the truth in love, may grow up into him in all things, which is the head, *even* Christ:

16 From whom the whole body fitly joined together and compacted by that which every joint supplieth, according to the effectual working in the measure of every part, maketh increase of the body unto the edifying of itself in love.

17 This I say therefore, and testify in the Lord, that ye henceforth walk not as other Gentiles walk, in the vanity of their mind,

18 Having the understanding darkened, being alienated from the life of God through the ignorance that is in them, because of the blindness of their heart:

19 Who being past feeling have given themselves over unto lasciviousness, to work all uncleanness with greediness.

20 But ye have not so learned Christ;

21 If so be that ye have heard him, and have been taught by him, as the truth is in Jesus:

Amplified

8 Therefore it is said, When He ascended on high, He led captivity captive—He led a train of [n]vanquished foes—and He bestowed gifts on men. [Ps. 68:18.]

9 [But He ascended?] Now what can this, He ascended, mean but that He had previously descended from the height of heaven into [the depth], the lower parts of the earth?

10 He Who descended is the [very] same as He Who also has ascended high above all the heavens, that He [His presence] might fill all things—the whole universe, from the lowest to the highest.

11 And His gifts were [varied; He Himself appointed and gave men to us,] some to be apostles (special messengers), some prophets (inspired preachers and expounders), some evangelists (preachers of the Gospel, traveling missionaries), some pastors (shepherds of His flock) and teachers.

12 His intention was the perfecting *and* the full equipping of the saints (His consecrated people), [that they should do] the work of ministering toward building up Christ's body (the church),

13 [That it might develop] until we all attain oneness in the faith and in the comprehension of the [o]full and accurate knowledge of the Son of God; that [we might arrive] at really mature manhood—the completeness of personality which is nothing less than the standard height of Christ's own perfection—the measure of the stature of the fullness of the Christ, *and* the completeness found in Him.

14 So then, we may no longer be children, tossed [like ships] to and fro between chance gusts of teaching, *and* wavering with every changing wind of doctrine, [the prey of] the cunning *and* cleverness of [p]unscrupulous men, (gamblers engaged) in every shifting form of trickery in inventing errors to mislead.

15 Rather, let our lives lovingly [o]express truth in all things—speaking truly, dealing truly, living truly. Enfolded in love, let us grow up in every way *and* in all things into Him, Who is the Head, [even] Christ, the Messiah, the Anointed One.

16 For because of Him the whole body (the church, in all its various parts closely) joined and firmly knit together by the joints *and* ligaments with which it is supplied, when each part [with power adapted to its need] is working properly (in all its functions), grows to full maturity, building itself up in love.

17 So this I say and solemnly testify in [the name of] the Lord [as in His Presence], that you must no longer live as the heathen (the Gentiles) do in their perverseness—in the folly, vanity and emptiness of their souls and the futility—of their minds.

18 Their [q]moral understanding is darkened *and* their reasoning is beclouded. [They are] alienated (estranged, self-banished) from the life of God—with no share in it. [This is] because of the ignorance—the want of knowledge and perception, the willful blindness—that is [q]deep-seated in them, due to their hardness of heart (to the insensitiveness of their moral nature).

19 In their spiritual apathy they have become callous *and* past feeling *and* reckless, and have abandoned themselves [a prey] to unbridled sensuality, eager *and* greedy to indulge in every form of impurity [that their depraved desires may suggest and demand].

20 But you did not so learn Christ!

21 Assuming that you have really heard Him *and* been taught by Him, as [all] Truth is in Jesus—embodied and personified in Him:

---

n) "He conquered those who had conquered us; such as sin, the devil and death."—Matthew Henry.
o) Vincent.
p) Literally, *dice-playing*.
q) Vincent.

Living New Testament

8 The Psalmist tells about this, for he says that when Christ returned triumphantly to heaven after His resurrection and victory over Satan, He gave generous gifts to men.

9 Notice that it says He returned to heaven. This means that He had first come down from the heights of heaven, far down to the lowest parts of the earth.

10 The same one who came down is the one who went back up, that He might fill all things everywhere with Himself, from the very lowest to the very highest.[1]

11 Some of us have been given special ability as apostles; to others He has given the gift of being able to preach well; some have special ability in winning people to Christ, helping them to trust Him as their Savior; still others have a gift for caring for God's people as a shepherd does his sheep, leading and teaching them in the ways of God.

12 Why is it that He gives us these special abilities to do certain things best? It is that God's people will be equipped to do better work for Him, building up the church, the body of Christ, to a position of strength and maturity;

13 Until finally we all believe alike about our salvation and about our Savior, God's Son, and all become full-grown in the Lord—yes, to the point of being filled full with Christ.

14 Then we will no longer be like children, forever changing our minds about what we believe because someone has told us something different, or has cleverly lied to us and made the lie sound like the truth.

15, 16 Instead we will lovingly follow the truth at all times—speaking truly, dealing truly, living truly[2]—and so become more and more in every way like Christ who is the Head of His body, the church. Under His direction the whole body is fitted together perfectly, and each part in its own special way helps the other parts, so that the whole body is healthy and growing and full of love.

17, 18 Let me say this, then, speaking for the Lord: live no longer as the unsaved do, for they are blinded and confused. Their closed hearts are full of darkness; they are far away from the life of God because they have shut their minds against Him, and they cannot understand His ways.

19 They don't care anymore about right and wrong and have given themselves over to impure ways. They stop at nothing being driven by their evil minds and reckless lusts.

20 But that isn't the way Christ taught you!

21 If you have really heard His voice and learned from Him the truths concerning Himself,

Revised Standard

the measure of Christ's gift. 8 Therefore it is
said,
"When he ascended on high he led a host
of captives,
and he gave gifts to men."
9 (In saying, "He ascended," what does it
mean but that he had also descended into
the lower parts of the earth? 10 He who descended is he who also ascended far above
all the heavens, that he might fill all things.)
11 And his gifts were that some should be
apostles, some prophets, some evangelists,
some pastors and teachers, 12 for the equipment of the saints, for the work of the ministry, for building up the body of Christ,
13 until we all attain to the unity of the faith
and of the knowledge of the Son of God, to
mature manhood, to the measure of the
stature of the fulness of Christ; 14 so that we
may no longer be children, tossed to and fro
and carried about with every wind of doctrine, by the cunning of men, by their craftiness in deceitful wiles. 15 Rather, speaking
the truth in love, we are to grow up in every
way into him who is the head, into Christ,
16 from whom the whole body, joined and knit
together by every joint with which it is supplied, when each part is working properly,
makes bodily growth and upbuilds itself in
love.

The old life and the new

17 Now this I affirm and testify in the
Lord, that you must no longer live as the
Gentiles do, in the futility of their minds;
18 they are darkened in their understanding,
alienated from the life of God because of
the ignorance that is in them, due to their
hardness of heart; 19 they have become callous and have given themselves up to licentiousness, greedy to practice every kind of
uncleanness. 20 You did not so learn Christ!—
21 assuming that you have heard about him
and were taught in him, as the truth is in

---

[1] Literally, "that He might fill all things."
[2] Amplified New Testament.

King James

22 That ye put off concerning the former conversation the old man, which is corrupt according to the deceitful lusts;
23 And be renewed in the spirit of your mind;
24 And that ye put on the new man, which after God is created in righteousness and true holiness.
25 Wherefore putting away lying, speak every man truth with his neighbour: for we are members one of another.
26 Be ye angry, and sin not: let not the sun go down upon your wrath:
27 Neither give place to the devil.
28 Let him that stole steal no more: but rather let him labour, working with *his* hands the thing which is good, that he may have to give to him that needeth.
29 Let no corrupt communication proceed out of your mouth, but that which is good to the use of edifying, that it may minister grace unto the hearers.
30 And grieve not the holy Spirit of God, whereby ye are sealed unto the day of redemption.
31 Let all bitterness, and wrath, and anger, and clamour, and evil speaking, be put away from you, with all malice:
32 And be ye kind one to another, tenderhearted, forgiving one another, even as God for Christ's sake hath forgiven you.

Amplified

22 Strip yourselves of your former nature—put off and discard your old unrenewed self—which characterized your previous manner of life and becomes corrupt through lusts *and* desires that spring from delusion;
23 And be constantly renewed in the spirit of your mind—having a fresh mental and spiritual attitude;
24 And put on the new nature (the regenerate self) created in God's image, (Godlike) in true righteousness and holiness.
25 Therefore, rejecting all falsity *and* done now with it, let every one express the truth with his neighbor, for we are all parts of one body *and* members one of another. [Zech. 8:16.]
26 When angry, do not sin; do not ever let your wrath—your exasperation, your fury or indignation—last until the sun goes down.
27 Leave no [such] room *or* foothold for the devil—give no opportunity to him.
28 Let the thief steal no more, but rather let him be industrious, making an honest living with his own hands, so that he may be able to give to those in need.
29 Let no foul *or* polluting language, *nor* evil word, *nor* unwholesome *or* worthless talk [ever] come out of your mouth; but only such [speech] as is good *and* beneficial to the spiritual progress of others, as is fitting to the need *and* the occasion, that it may be a blessing *and* give grace (God's favor) to those who hear it.
30 And do not grieve the Holy Spirit of God, (do not offend, or vex, or sadden Him) by Whom you were sealed (marked, branded as God's own, secured) for the day of redemption—of final deliverance through Christ from evil and the consequences of sin.
31 Let all bitterness and indignation *and* wrath (passion, rage, bad temper) and resentment (anger, animosity) and quarreling (brawling, clamor, contention) and slander (evilspeaking, abusive or blasphemous language) be banished from you, with all malice (spite, ill will or baseness of any kind).
32 And become useful *and* helpful *and* kind to one another, tenderhearted (compassionate, understanding, loving-hearted), forgiving one another [readily and freely], as God in Christ forgave you.

CHAPTER 5

BE ye therefore followers of God, as dear children;
2 And walk in love, as Christ also hath loved us, and hath given himself for us an offering and a sacrifice to God for a sweet-smelling savour.
3 But fornication, and all uncleanness, or covetousness, let it not be once named among you, as becometh saints;
4 Neither filthiness, nor foolish talking, nor jesting, which are not convenient: but rather giving of thanks.

CHAPTER 5

THEREFORE be imitators of God—copy Him *and* follow His example—as well-beloved children [imitate their father].
2 And walk in love—esteeming and delighting in one another—as Christ loved us and gave Himself up for us, a [r]slain offering and sacrifice to God [for you, so that it became] a sweet fragrance. [Ezek. 20:41.]
3 But immorality (sexual vice) and all impurity [[s]of lustful, rich, wasteful living] or greediness must not even be named among you, as is fitting *and* proper among saints (God's consecrated people).
4 Let there be no filthiness (obscenity, indecency) nor foolish *and* sinful (silly and corrupt) talk, nor coarse jesting, which are not fitting *or* becoming; but instead voice your thankfulness [to God].

r) Vincent.
s) Thayer.

Living New Testament

22 Then throw off your old evil nature—the old you that was a partner in your evil ways—rotten through and through, full of lust and sham.

23 Now your attitudes and thoughts must all be constantly changing for the better.

24 Yes, you must be a new and different person, holy and good. Clothe yourself with this new nature.

25 Stop lying to each other; tell the truth, for we are parts of each other and when we lie to each other we are hurting ourselves.

26 If you are angry, don't sin by nursing your grudge. Don't let the sun go down with you still angry—get over it quickly;

27 For when you are angry you give a mighty foothold to the devil.

28 If anyone is stealing he must stop it and begin using those hands of his for honest work so he can give to others in need.

29 Don't use bad language. Say only what is good and helpful to those you are talking to, and what will give them a blessing.

30 Don't cause the Holy Spirit sorrow by the way you live. Remember, He is the one who marks you to be present[3] on that day when salvation from sin will be complete.

31 Stop being mean, bad-tempered and angry. Quarreling, harsh words, and dislike of others should have no place in your lives.

32 Instead, be kind to each other, tenderhearted, forgiving one another, just as God has forgiven you because you belong to Christ.

Revised Standard

Jesus. 22Put off your old nature which belongs to your former manner of life and is
corrupt through deceitful lusts, 23and be
renewed in the spirit of your minds, 24and
put on the new nature, created after the
likeness of God in true righteousness and
holiness.

25 Therefore, putting away falsehood, let
every one speak the truth with his neighbor,
for we are members one of another. 26Be
angry but do not sin; do not let the sun go
down on your anger, 27and give no opportunity to the devil. 28Let the thief no longer
steal, but rather let him labor, doing honest
work with his hands, so that he may be able
to give to those in need. 29Let no evil talk
come out of your mouths, but only such
as is good for edifying, as fits the occasion,
that it may impart grace to those who hear.
30And do not grieve the Holy Spirit of God,
in whom you were sealed for the day of redemption. 31Let all bitterness and wrath and
anger and clamor and slander be put away
from you, with all malice, 32and be kind to
one another, tenderhearted, forgiving one
another, as God in Christ forgave you.

CHAPTER 5

Follow God's example in everything you do just as a much loved child imitates his father.

2 Be full of love for others, following the example of Christ who loved you and gave Himself to God as a sacrifice to take away your sins. And God was pleased, for Christ's love for you was like sweet perfume to Him.

3 Let there be no sex sin, impurity or greed among you. Let no one be able to accuse you of any such things.

4 Dirty stories, foul talk and coarse jokes—these are not for you. Instead, remind each other of God's goodness and be thankful.

The works of light and darkness

5 Therefore be imitators of God, as beloved children. 2And walk in love, as
Christ loved us and gave himself up for us,
a fragrant offering and sacrifice to God.

3 But immorality and all impurity or
covetousness must not even be named among
you, as is fitting among saints. 4Let there be
no filthiness, nor silly talk, nor levity, which
are not fitting; but instead let there be
thanksgiving. 5Be sure of this, that no im-

Literally, "in whom you were sealed unto the day of redemption."

King James

5 For this ye know, that no whoremonger, nor unclean person, nor covetous man, who is an idolater, hath any inheritance in the kingdom of Christ and of God.

6 Let no man deceive you with vain words: for because of these things cometh the wrath of God upon the children of disobedience.

7 Be not ye therefore partakers with them.

8 For ye were sometimes darkness, but now *are ye* light in the Lord: walk as children of light:

9 (For the fruit of the Spirit *is* in all goodness and righteousness and truth;)

10 Proving what is acceptable unto the Lord.

11 And have no fellowship with the unfruitful works of darkness, but rather reprove *them*.

12 For it is a shame even to speak of those things which are done of them in secret.

13 But all things that are reproved are made manifest by the light: for whatsoever doth make manifest is light.

14 Wherefore he saith, Awake thou that sleepest, and arise from the dead, and Christ shall give thee light.

15 See then that ye walk circumspectly, not as fools, but as wise,

16 Redeeming the time, because the days are evil.

17 Wherefore be ye not unwise, but understanding what the will of the Lord *is*.

18 And be not drunk with wine, wherein is excess; but be filled with the Spirit;

19 Speaking to yourselves in psalms and hymns and spiritual songs, singing and making melody in your heart to the Lord;

20 Giving thanks always for all things unto God and the Father in the name of our Lord Jesus Christ;

21 Submitting yourselves one to another in the fear of God.

22 Wives, submit yourselves unto your own husbands, as unto the Lord.

23 For the husband is the head of the wife, even as Christ is the head of the church: and he is the saviour of the body.

24 Therefore as the church is subject unto Christ, so *let* the wives *be* to their own husbands in every thing.

25 Husbands, love your wives, even as Christ also loved the church, and gave himself for it;

26 That he might sanctify and cleanse it with the washing of water by the word,

27 That he might present it to himself a glorious church, not having spot, or wrinkle, or any such thing; but that it should be holy and without blemish.

28 So ought men to love their wives as their own bodies. He that loveth his wife loveth himself.

Amplified

5 For be sure of this, that no person practicing sexual vice or impurity in thought or in life, or one who is covetous—that is, who has lustful desire for the property of others and is greedy for gain—[for] that [in effect] is an idolater, has any inheritance in the kingdom of Christ and of God.

6 Let no one delude *and* deceive you with empty excuses *and* groundless arguments [for these sins], for through these things the wrath of God comes upon the sons of rebellion *and* disobedience.

7 So do not associate *or* be sharers with them.

8 For once you were darkness, but now you are light in the Lord; walk as children of light—lead the lives of those native-born to the Light.

9 For the fruit—the effect, the product—of the Light, [t]the Spirit, [consists] in every form of kindly goodness, uprightness of heart and trueness of life.

10 And try to learn [in your experience] what is pleasing to the Lord;—[let your lives be constant] proofs of what is most acceptable to Him.

11 Take no part in *and* have no fellowship with the fruitless deeds *and* enterprises of darkness, but instead [let your lives be so in contrast as to] [u]expose *and* reprove *and* convict them.

12 For it is a shame even to speak of *or* mention the things that [such people] practice in secret.

13 But when anything is exposed *and* reproved by the light, it is made visible *and* clear; and where everything is visible *and* clear there is light.

14 Therefore He says, Awake, O sleeper, and arise from the dead, and Christ shall shine [make day dawn] upon you *and* give you light. [Isa. 60:1, 2 with 26:19.]

15 Look carefully then how you walk! Live purposefully *and* worthily *and* accurately, not as the unwise *and* witless, but as wise—sensible, intelligent people;

16 Making the very most of the time—[v]buying up each opportunity—because the days are evil.

17 Therefore do not be vague *and* thoughtless *and* foolish, but understanding *and* firmly grasping what the will of the Lord is.

18 And do not get drunk with wine, for that is debauchery; but ever be filled *and* stimulated with the (Holy) Spirit. [Prov. 23:20.]

19 Speak out to one another in psalms and hymns and spiritual songs, offering praise with voices [[w]and instruments], and making melody with all your heart to the Lord,

20 At all times and for everything giving thanks in the name of our Lord Jesus Christ to God the Father.

21 Be subject to one another out of reverence for Christ, the Messiah, the Anointed One.

22 Wives, be subject—be submissive and adapt yourselves—to your own husbands as [a service] to the Lord.

23 For the husband is head of the wife as Christ is the Head of the church, Himself the Savior of [His] body.

24 As the church is subject to Christ, so let wives also be subject in everything to their husbands.

25 Husbands, love your wives, as Christ loved the church and gave Himself up for her,

26 So that He might sanctify her, having cleansed her by the washing of water with the Word,

27 That He might present the church to Himself in glorious splendor, without spot or wrinkle or any such things—that she might be holy and faultless.

28 Even so husbands should love their wives as [being in a sense] their own bodies. He who loves his own wife loves himself.

---

t) Some ancient authorities so read.
u) Thayer.
v) Alternate reading.
w) Berry's "Greek-English New Testament Lexicon."

Living New Testament

5 You can be sure of this: the kingdom of Christ and of God will never belong to anyone who is impure or greedy, for a greedy person is really an idol worshiper—[the loves and worships the good things of this life more than God[1]].

6 Don't be fooled by those who try to excuse these sins, for the terrible wrath of God is upon all those who do them.

7 Don't even associate with such people.

8 For though once your heart was full of darkness, now it is full of light from the Lord, and your behavior should show it!

9 Because of this light within you, you should do only what is good and right and true.

10 Learn as you go along what pleases the Lord.[2]

11 Take no part in the worthless pleasures of evil and darkness, but instead, rebuke and expose them.

12 It would be shameful even to mention here those pleasures of darkness which the ungodly do.

13 But when you expose them, the light shines in upon their sin and shows it up, and when they see how wrong they really are, some of them may even become children of light!

14 That is why God says, in the Scriptures, "Awake, O sleeper, and rise up from the dead; and Christ shall give you light."

15, 16 So be careful how you act; these are difficult days. Don't be fools; be wise: make the most of every opportunity you have for doing good.

17 Don't act thoughtlessly, but try to find out and do whatever the Lord wants you to.

18 Don't drink too much wine, for many evils lie along that path; be filled instead with the Holy Spirit, and controlled by Him.

19 Talk with each other much about the Lord, quoting psalms and hymns and singing sacred songs, making music in your hearts to the Lord.

20 Always give thanks for everything to our God and Father in the name of our Lord Jesus Christ.

21 Honor Christ by submitting to each other.

22 You wives must submit to your husband's leadership in the same way you submit to the Lord.

23 For a husband is in charge of his wife in the same way Christ is in charge of His body the church. (He gave His very life to take care of it and be its Savior!)

24 So you wives must willingly obey your husbands in everything, just as the church obeys Christ.

25 And you husbands, show the same kind of love to your wives as Christ showed to the church when He died for her,

26 To make her holy and clean, washed by baptism[3] and God's Word;

27 So that He could give her to Himself as a glorious church without a single spot or wrinkle or any other blemish, being holy and without a single fault.

28 That is how husbands should treat their wives, loving them as parts of themselves. For since a man and his wife are now one, a man is really doing himself a favor and loving himself when he loves his wife!

Implied.
Or, "your lives should be an example."
Literally, "having cleansed it by washing of water with the word."

Revised Standard

moral or impure man, or one who is covetous (that is, an idolater), has any inheritance in the kingdom of Christ and of God.
6 Let no one deceive you with empty words,
for it is because of these things that the
wrath of God comes upon the sons of disobedience. 7 Therefore do not associate with
them, 8 for once you were darkness, but now
you are light in the Lord; walk as children
of light 9 (for the fruit of light is found in
all that is good and right and true), 10 and
try to learn what is pleasing to the Lord.
11 Take no part in the unfruitful works of
darkness, but instead expose them. 12 For it
is a shame even to speak of the things that
they do in secret; 13 but when anything is exposed by the light it becomes visible, for
anything that becomes visible is light.
14 Therefore it is said,

"Awake, O sleeper, and arise from the dead,
and Christ shall give you light."

15 Look carefully then how you walk, not
as unwise men but as wise, 16 making the
most of the time, because the days are evil.
17 Therefore do not be foolish, but understand
what the will of the Lord is. 18 And do not
get drunk with wine, for that is debauchery;
but be filled with the Spirit, 19 addressing one
another in psalms and hymns and spiritual
songs, singing and making melody to the
Lord with all your heart, 20 always and for
everything giving thanks in the name of our
Lord Jesus Christ to God the Father.

Analogy of family and church

21 Be subject to one another out of
reverence for Christ. 22 Wives, be subject to
your husbands, as to the Lord. 23 For the
husband is the head of the wife as Christ is
the head of the church, his body, and is himself its Savior. 24 As the church is subject to
Christ, so let wives also be subject in everything to their husbands. 25 Husbands, love
your wives, as Christ loved the church and
gave himself up for her, 26 that he might
sanctify her, having cleansed her by the
washing of water with the word, 27 that he
might present the church to himself in splendor, without spot or wrinkle or any such
thing, that she might be holy and without
blemish. 28 Even so husbands should love
their wives as their own bodies. He who loves

King James

29 For no man ever yet hated his own flesh; but nourisheth and cherisheth it, even as the Lord the church:

30 For we are members of his body, of his flesh, and of his bones.

31 For this cause shall a man leave his father and mother, and shall be joined unto his wife, and they two shall be one flesh.

32 This is a great mystery: but I speak concerning Christ and the church.

33 Nevertheless let every one of you in particular so love his wife even as himself; and the wife *see* that she reverence *her* husband.

Amplified

29 For no man ever hated his own flesh, but nourishes *and* carefully protects and cherishes it, as Christ does the church,

30 Because we are members (parts) of His body.

31 For this reason a man shall leave his father and his mother and shall be joined to his wife, and the two shall become one flesh. [Gen. 2:24.]

32 This mystery is very great, but I speak concerning [the relation of] Christ and the church.

33 However, let each man of you (without exception) love his wife as [being in a sense] his very own self; and let the wife see that she respects *and* reverences her husband—[x]that she notices him, regards him, honors him, prefers him, venerates and esteems him; and [x]that she defers to him, praises him, and loves and admires him exceedingly.

King James

CHAPTER 6

CHILDREN, obey your parents in the Lord: for this is right.

2 Honour thy father and mother; which is the first commandment with promise;

3 That it may be well with thee, and thou mayest live long on the earth.

4 And, ye fathers, provoke not your children to wrath: but bring them up in the nurture and admonition of the Lord.

5 Servants, be obedient to them that are *your* masters according to the flesh, with fear and trembling, in singleness of your heart, as unto Christ;

6 Not with eye-service, as men-pleasers; but as the servants of Christ, doing the will of God from the heart;

7 With good will doing service, as to the Lord, and not to men:

8 Knowing that whatsoever good thing any man doeth, the same shall he receive of the Lord, whether *he be* bond or free.

9 And, ye masters, do the same things unto them, forbearing threatening: knowing that your Master also is in heaven; neither is there respect of persons with him.

10 Finally, my brethren, be strong in the Lord, and in the power of his might.

11 Put on the whole armour of God, that ye may be able to stand against the wiles of the devil.

12 For we wrestle not against flesh and blood, but against principalities, against powers, against the rulers of the darkness of this world, against spiritual wickedness in high *places*.

Amplified

CHAPTER 6

CHILDREN, obey your parents in the Lord [as His representatives], for this is just and right.

2 Honor (esteem and value as precious) your father and your mother; this is the first commandment with a promise: [Exod. 20:12.]

3 That all may be well with you and that you may live long on the earth.

4 Fathers, do not irritate *and* provoke your children to anger—do not exasperate them to resentment—but rear them [tenderly] in the training *and* discipline and the counsel *and* admonition of the Lord.

5 Servants (slaves), be obedient to those who are your physical masters, having respect for them and eager concern to please them, in singleness of motive *and* with all your heart, as [service] to Christ [Himself].

6 Not in the way of eyeservice—as if they were watching you—and only to please men; but as servants (slaves) of Christ, doing the will of God heartily *and* with your whole soul;

7 Rendering service readily with goodwill, as to the Lord and not to men,

8 Knowing that for whatever good any one does, he will receive his reward from the Lord, whether he is slave or free.

9 You masters, act on the same [principle] toward them, and give up threatening *and* using violent *and* abusive words, knowing that He Who is both their Master and yours is in heaven, and that there is no respect of persons—no partiality—with Him.

10 In conclusion, be strong in the Lord—be empowered through your union with Him; draw your strength from Him—that strength which His [boundless] might provides.

11 Put on God's whole armor—the armor of a heavy-armed soldier, which God supplies—that you may be able successfully to stand up against [all] the strategies *and* the deceits of the devil.

12 For we are not wrestling with flesh and blood—contending only with physical opponents—but against the despotisms, against the powers, against [the master spirits who are] the world rulers of this present darkness, against the spirit forces of wickedness in the heavenly (supernatural) sphere.

---

x) Webster's list of English words with the same or nearly the same essential meaning as "respect" and "reverence." The latter includes the word "adore" in the sense not applied to Deity.

Living New Testament

29, 30 No one hates his own body but lovingly cares for it, just as Christ cares for His body the church, of which we are parts.

31 (That the husband and wife are one body is proved by the Scripture which says, "A man must leave his father and mother when he marries, so that he can be perfectly joined to his wife, and the two shall be one.")

32 I know this is hard to understand, but it is an illustration of the way we are parts of the body of Christ.

33 So again I say, a man must love his wife as a part of himself; and the wife must see to it that she deeply respects her husband—obeying, praising and honoring him.

Revised Standard

his wife loves himself. [29]For no man ever
hates his own flesh, but nourishes and cherishes it, as Christ does the church, [30]because
we are members of his body. [31]"For this
reason a man shall leave his father and
mother and be joined to his wife, and the two
shall become one." [32]This is a great mystery,
and I take it to mean Christ and the church;
[33]however, let each one of you love his wife
as himself, and let the wife see that she
respects her husband.

CHAPTER 6

Children, obey your parents; this is the right thing to do because God has placed them in authority over you.

2 Honor your father and mother. This is the first of God's Ten Commandments that ends with a promise.

3 And this is the promise: that if you honor your father and mother, yours will be a long life, full of blessing.

4 And now a word to you parents. Don't keep on scolding and nagging your children, making them angry and resentful. Rather, bring them up with the loving discipline the Lord Himself approves, with suggestions and godly advice.

5 Slaves, obey your masters; be eager to give them your very best. Serve them as you would Christ.

6, 7 Don't work hard only when your master is watching and then shirk when he isn't looking; work hard and with gladness all the time, as though working for Christ, doing the will of God with all your hearts.

8 Remember, the Lord will pay you for each good thing you do, whether you are slave or free.

9 And you slave owners must treat your slaves right, just as I have told them to treat you. Don't keep threatening them; remember, you yourselves are slaves to Christ; you have the same Master they do, and He has no favorites.

10 Last of all I want to remind you that your strength must come from the Lord's mighty power within you.

11 Put on all of God's armor so that you will be able to stand safe against all strategies and tricks of Satan.

12 For we are not fighting against people made of flesh and blood, but against persons without bodies—the evil rulers of the unseen world, those mighty satanic beings and great evil princes of darkness who rule this world; and against huge numbers of wicked spirits in the spirit world.

6 Children, obey your parents in the Lord,
for this is right. [2]"Honor your father and
mother" (this is the first commandment with
a promise), [3]"that it may be well with you
and that you may live long on the earth."
[4]Fathers, do not provoke your children to
anger, but bring them up in the discipline
and instruction of the Lord.
5 Slaves, be obedient to those who are
your earthly masters, with fear and trembling, in singleness of heart, as to Christ;
[6]not in the way of eye-service, as men-
pleasers, but as servants[f] of Christ, doing the
will of God from the heart, [7]rendering service with a good will as to the Lord and not
to men, [8]knowing that whatever good any
one does, he will receive the same again
from the Lord, whether he is a slave or free.
[9]Masters, do the same to them, and forbear threatening, knowing that he who is
both their Master and yours is in heaven,
and that there is no partiality with him.

The whole armor of God

10 Finally, be strong in the Lord and in
the strength of his might. [11]Put on the whole
armor of God, that you may be able to
stand against the wiles of the devil. [12]For we
are not contending against flesh and blood,
but against the principalities, against the
powers, against the world rulers of this present darkness, against the spiritual hosts of
wickedness in the heavenly places. [13]There-

[f] Or *slaves*

King James

13 Wherefore take unto you the whole armour of God, that ye may be able to withstand in the evil day, and having done all, to stand.
14 Stand therefore, having your loins girt about with truth, and having on the breastplate of righteousness;
15 And your feet shod with the preparation of the gospel of peace;
16 Above all, taking the shield of faith, wherewith ye shall be able to quench all the fiery darts of the wicked.
17 And take the helmet of salvation, and the sword of the Spirit, which is the word of God:
18 Praying always with all prayer and supplication in the Spirit, and watching thereunto with all perseverance and supplication for all saints;
19 And for me, that utterance may be given unto me, that I may open my mouth boldly, to make known the mystery of the gospel,
20 For which I am an ambassador in bonds: that therein I may speak boldly, as I ought to speak.
21 But that ye also may know my affairs, *and* how I do, Tychicus, a beloved brother and faithful minister in the Lord, shall make known to you all things:
22 Whom I have sent unto you for the same purpose, that ye might know our affairs, and *that* he might comfort your hearts.
23 Peace be to the brethren, and love with faith, from God the Father and the Lord Jesus Christ.
24 Grace *be* with all them that love our Lord Jesus Christ in sincerity. Amen.
¶ Written from Rome unto the Ephesians by Tychicus.

Amplified

13 Therefore put on God's complete armor, that you may be able to resist *and* stand your ground on the evil day [of danger], and having done all [the crisis demands], to stand [firmly in your place].
14 Stand therefore—hold your ground—having tightened the belt of truth around your loins, and having put on the breastplate of integrity *and* of moral rectitude *and* right standing with God;
15 And having shod your feet in preparation [to face the enemy with the [y]firm-footed stability, the promptness and the readiness [z]produced by the good news] of the Gospel of peace. [Isa. 52:7.]
16 Lift up over all the (covering) shield of [y]saving faith, upon which you can quench all the flaming missiles of the wicked [one].
17 And take the helmet of salvation and the sword the Spirit [a]wields, which is the Word of God.
18 Pray at all times—on every occasion, in every season—in the Spirit, with all [manner of] prayer and entreaty. To that end keep alert and watch with strong purpose *and* perseverance, interceding in behalf of all the saints (God's consecrated people).
19 And also for me, that [freedom of] utterance may be given me, that I may open my mouth to proclaim boldly the mystery of the good news [of the Gospel],
20 For which I am an ambassador in a coupling chain [in prison. Pray] that I may declare it boldly *and* courageously as I ought to do.
21 Now that you may know how I am and what I am doing, Tychicus the beloved brother and faithful minister in the Lord [and His service] will tell you everything.
22 I have sent him to you for this very purpose, that you may know how we are and that he may [b]console *and* cheer *and* encourage *and* strengthen your hearts.
23 Peace be to the brethren, and love joined with faith, from God the Father and the Lord Jesus Christ, the Messiah, the Anointed One.
24 Grace (God's undeserved favor) be with all who love our Lord Jesus Christ with undying *and* incorruptible [love]. *Amen—so let it be.*

---

y) Vincent.
z) Thayer.
a) Williams: Subjective genitive.
b) Thayer.

Living New Testament

13 So use every piece of God's armor to resist the enemy whenever he attacks, and when it is all over, you will still be standing up.

14 But to do this, you will need the strong belt of truth and the breastplate of God's approval.

15 Wear shoes that are able to speed you on as you preach the Good News of peace with God.

16 In every battle you will need faith as your shield to stop the fiery arrows aimed at you by Satan,

17 And you will need the helmet of salvation and the sword of the Spirit—which is the Word of God.

18 Pray all the time. Ask God for anything in line with the Holy Spirit's wishes. Plead with Him, reminding Him of your needs, and keep praying earnestly for all Christians everywhere.

19 Pray for me, too, and ask God to give me the right words as I boldly tell others about the Lord, and as I explain to them that His salvation is for the Gentiles too.

20 I am in chains now for preaching this message from God. But pray that I will keep on speaking out boldly for Him even here in prison, as I should.

21 Tychicus, who is a much-loved brother and faithful helper in the Lord's work, will tell you all about how I am getting along.

22 I am sending him to you for just this purpose, to let you know how we are and be encouraged by his report.

23 May God give peace to you, my Christian brothers, and love, with faith from God the Father and the Lord Jesus Christ.

24 May God's grace and blessing be upon all who sincerely love our Lord Jesus Christ.

Sincerely,
Paul

Revised Standard

fore take the whole armor of God, that you
may be able to withstand in the evil day, and
having done all, to stand. 14 Stand therefore,
having girded your loins with truth, and
having put on the breastplate of righteousness, 15 and having shod your feet with the
equipment of the gospel of peace; 16 above
all taking the shield of faith, with which you
can quench all the flaming darts of the evil
one. 17 And take the helmet of salvation, and
the sword of the Spirit, which is the word of
God. 18 Pray at all times in the Spirit, with
all prayer and supplication. To that end keep
alert with all perseverance, making supplication for all the saints, 19 and also for me, that
utterance may be given me in opening my
mouth boldly to proclaim the mystery of the
gospel, 20 for which I am an ambassador in
chains; that I may declare it boldly, as I
ought to speak.

Concluding benediction

21 Now that you also may know how I am and what I am doing, Tychicus the beloved brother and faithful minister in the
Lord will tell you everything. 22 I have sent
him to you for this very purpose, that you may know how we are, and that he may encourage your hearts.

23 Peace be to the brethren, and love with faith, from God the Father and the
Lord Jesus Christ. 24 Grace be with all who
love our Lord Jesus Christ with love undying.

King James

THE EPISTLE OF PAUL THE APOSTLE TO THE

Philippians

CHAPTER 1

PAUL and Timotheus, the servants of Jesus Christ, to all the saints in Christ Jesus which are at Philippi, with the bishops and deacons:

2 Grace *be* unto you, and peace, from God our Father, and *from* the Lord Jesus Christ.

3 I thank my God upon every remembrance of you,

4 Always in every prayer of mine for you all making request with joy,

5 For your fellowship in the gospel from the first day until now;

6 Being confident of this very thing, that he which hath begun a good work in you will perform *it* until the day of Jesus Christ:

7 Even as it is meet for me to think this of you all, because I have you in my heart; inasmuch as both in my bonds, and in the defence and confirmation of the gospel, ye all are partakers of my grace.

8 For God is my record, how greatly I long after you all in the bowels of Jesus Christ.

9 And this I pray, that your love may abound yet more and more in knowledge and *in* all judgment;

10 That ye may approve things that are excellent; that ye may be sincere and without offence till the day of Christ;

11 Being filled with the fruits of righteousness, which are by Jesus Christ, unto the glory and praise of God.

12 But I would ye should understand, brethren, that the things *which happened* unto me have fallen out rather unto the furtherance of the gospel;

13 So that my bonds in Christ are manifest in all the palace, and in all other *places;*

Amplified

THE LETTER OF PAUL TO THE

Philippians

CHAPTER 1

PAUL and Timothy, bondservants of Christ Jesus, the Messiah, to all the saints (God's consecrated people) in Christ Jesus who are at Philippi, with the bishops [overseers] and deacons [assistants]:

2 Grace (favor and blessing) to you and heart peace from God our Father and the Lord Jesus Christ, the Messiah.

3 I thank my God in all my remembrance of you.

4 In every prayer of mine I always make my entreaty *and* petition for you all with joy (delight).

5 [I thank my God] for your fellowship—your [a]sympathetic co-operation and contributions and partnership—in advancing the good news (the Gospel) from the first day [you heard it] until now.

6 And I am convinced *and* sure of this very thing, that He Who began a good work in you will continue until the day of Jesus Christ—right up to the time of His return—developing [that good work] *and* perfecting *and* bringing it to full completion in you.

7 It is right *and* appropriate for me to have this confidence *and* feel this way about you all, because even as [b]you do me, I hold you in my heart as partakers *and* sharers, one *and* all with me, of grace (God's unmerited favor and spiritual blessing). [This is true] both when I am shut up in prison and when I am out in the defense and confirmation of the good news (the Gospel).

8 For God is my witness how I long for *and* [c]pursue you all with love, in the tender mercies of Christ Jesus [Himself]!

9 And this I pray, that your love may abound yet more and more *and* extend to its fullest development in knowledge and all keen insight—that is, that your love may [[d]display itself in] greater depth of acquaintance and more comprehensive discernment;

10 So that you may surely learn to sense what is vital, *and* approve *and* prize what is excellent *and* of real value—recognizing the highest and the best, and [e]distinguishing the moral differences; and that you may be untainted *and* pure and unerring *and* blameless, that—with hearts sincere and certain and unsullied—you may [approach] the day of Christ, not stumbling *nor* causing others to stumble.

11 May you abound in *and* be filled with the fruits of righteousness (of right standing with God and right doing) which come through Jesus Christ, the Anointed One, to the honor and praise of God—[d]that His glory may be both manifested and recognized.

12 Now I want you to know *and* continue to rest assured, brethren, that what [has happened] to me [this imprisonment,] has actually only served to advance *and* give a renewed impetus to the [spreading of the] good news—of the Gospel.

13 So much is this a fact that throughout the whole imperial guard and to all the rest [here], my imprisonment has become generally known to be in Christ—in that I am a prisoner in His service and for Him.

---

a) Vincent.
b) Alternate reading, "you have me in your heart."
c) Thayer.
d) Vincent.
e) Alternate reading, "distinguish the things that differ."

Living New Testament

Philippians

CHAPTER 1

From: Paul and Timothy, slaves of Jesus Christ.
To: The pastors and deacons and all the Christians in the city of Philippi.

2 May God bless you all. Yes, I pray that God our Father and the Lord Jesus Christ will give each of you His fullest blessings, and His peace in your hearts and your lives.

3 All my prayers for you are full of praise to God!

4 When I pray for you, my heart is full of joy,

5 Because of all your wonderful help in making known the Good News about Christ from the time you first heard it until now.

6 And I am sure that God who began the good work within you will keep right on helping you grow in His grace until His task within you is finally finished on that day when Jesus Christ returns.

7 How natural it is that I should feel as I do about you, for you have a very special place in my heart. We have shared together the blessings of God, both when I was in prison and when I was out, defending the truth and telling others about Christ.

8 Only God knows how deep is my love and longing for you—with the tenderness of Jesus Christ.

9 My prayer for you is that you will overflow more and more with love for others, and at the same time keep on growing in spiritual knowledge and insight,

10 For I want you always to see clearly the difference between right and wrong, and to be inwardly clean, no one being able to criticize you from now until our Lord returns.

11 May you always be doing those good, kind things which show that you are a child of God, for this will bring much praise and glory to the Lord.

* * * * *

12 And I want you to know this, dear brothers: Everything that has happened to me here has been a great boost in getting out the Good News concerning Christ.

13 For everyone around here, including all the soldiers over at the barracks, know that I am in chains simply because I am a Christian.

Revised Standard

THE LETTER OF PAUL TO THE

Philippians

Salutation

1 Paul and Timothy, servants[a] of Christ
Jesus,
To all the saints in Christ Jesus who are
at Philippi, with the bishops[b] and deacons:
2 Grace to you and peace from God our
Father and the Lord Jesus Christ.

Prayer of thankfulness

3 I thank my God in all my remembrance
of you, 4always in every prayer of mine for
you all making my prayer with joy, 5thankful
for your partnership in the gospel from the
first day until now. 6And I am sure that he
who began a good work in you will bring
it to completion at the day of Jesus Christ.
7It is right for me to feel thus about you all,
because I hold you in my heart, for you are
all partakers with me of grace, both in my
imprisonment and in the defense and confirmation of the gospel. 8For God is my witness, how I yearn for you all with the affection of Christ Jesus. 9And it is my prayer
that your love may abound more and more,
with knowledge and all discernment, 10so
that you may approve what is excellent, and
may be pure and blameless for the day of
Christ, 11filled with the fruits of righteousness which come through Jesus Christ, to
the glory and praise of God.

Paul's boldness in prison

12 I want you to know, brethren, that
what has happened to me has really served
to advance the gospel, 13so that it has become known throughout the whole praetor-
ian guard[c] and to all the rest that my im-

[a] Or *slaves*
[b] Or *overseers*
[c] Greek *in the whole praetorium*

King James

14 And many of the brethren in the Lord, waxing confident by my bonds, are much more bold to speak the word without fear.

15 Some indeed preach Christ even of envy and strife; and some also of good will:

16 The one preach Christ of contention, not sincerely, supposing to add affliction to my bonds:

17 But the other of love, knowing that I am set for the defence of the gospel.

18 What then? notwithstanding every way, whether in pretence, or in truth, Christ is preached; and I therein do rejoice, yea, and will rejoice.

19 For I know that this shall turn to my salvation through your prayer, and the supply of the Spirit of Jesus Christ,

20 According to my earnest expectation and *my* hope, that in nothing I shall be ashamed, but *that* with all boldness, as always, *so* now also Christ shall be magnified in my body, whether *it be* by life, or by death.

21 For to me to live *is* Christ, and to die *is* gain.

22 But if I live in the flesh, this *is* the fruit of my labour: yet what I shall choose I wot not.

23 For I am in a strait betwixt two, having a desire to depart, and to be with Christ; which is far better:

24 Nevertheless to abide in the flesh *is* more needful for you.

25 And having this confidence, I know that I shall abide and continue with you all for your furtherance and joy of faith;

26 That your rejoicing may be more abundant in Jesus Christ for me by my coming to you again.

27 Only let your conversation be as it becometh the gospel of Christ: that whether I come and see you, or else be absent, I may hear of your affairs, that ye stand fast in one spirit, with one mind striving together for the faith of the gospel;

28 And in nothing terrified by your adversaries: which is to them an evident token of perdition, but to you of salvation, and that of God.

29 For unto you it is given in the behalf of Christ, not only to believe on him, but also to suffer for his sake;

30 Having the same conflict which ye saw in me, and now hear *to be* in me.

Amplified

14 And [also] most of the brethren have derived fresh confidence in the Lord because of my chains, and are much more bold to speak *and* publish fearlessly the Word of God—acting with more freedom and indifference to the consequences.

15 Some, it is true, [actually] preach Christ, the Messiah, [for no better reason than] out of envy and rivalry (party spirit); but others are doing so out of a loyal spirit *and* goodwill.

16 [f]The latter [proclaim Christ] out of love, because they recognize *and* know that I am (providentially) put here for the defense of the good news (the Gospel).

17 [f]But the former preach Christ out of a party spirit insincerely—out of no pure motive, but thinking to annoy me—supposing they are making my bondage more bitter *and* my chains more galling.

18 But what does it matter, so long as either way, whether in pretense [for personal ends] or in all honesty [for the furtherance of the Truth], Christ is being proclaimed? And in that I [now] rejoice,

19 Yes, and I shall rejoice [hereafter] also. For I am well assured *and* indeed know that through your prayers and a [g]bountiful supply of the Spirit of Jesus Christ, the Messiah, this will turn out for my preservation [for the spiritual health and [g]welfare of my own soul and avail toward the saving work of the Gospel].

20 This is in keeping with my own eager desire *and* persistent expectation *and* hope, that I shall not disgrace myself *nor* be put to shame in anything; but that with the utmost freedom of speech *and* unfailing courage, now as always heretofore, Christ, the Messiah, will be magnified *and* get glory *and* praise in this body of mine *and* be boldly exalted in my person, whether through (by) life or through (by) death.

21 For me, to live is Christ—His life in me; and to die is gain—[the gain of the glory of eternity].

22 If, however, it is to be life in the flesh *and* I am to live on here, that means fruitful service for me; so I can say nothing as to my personal preference—I cannot choose.

23 But I am hard pressed between the two. My yearning desire is to depart—to be free of this world, to set forth—and be with Christ, for that is far, far better;

24 But to remain in my body is more needful *and* essential for your sake.

25 Since I am convinced of this, I know that I shall remain and stay by you all, to promote your progress and joy in believing.

26 So that in me you may have abundant cause for exultation *and* glorying in Christ Jesus, through my coming to you again.

27 Only be sure as citizens so to conduct yourselves *that* your manner of life will be worthy of the good news (the Gospel) of Christ, so that whether I [do] come and see you or am absent, I may hear this of you: that you are standing firm in united spirit *and* purpose, striving side by side *and* contending with a single mind for the faith of the glad tidings (the Gospel).

28 And do not [for a moment] be frightened *or* intimidated in anything by your opponents *and* adversaries, for such [constancy and fearlessness] will be a clear sign (proof and seal) to them of [their impending] destruction, but [a sure token and evidence] of your deliverance *and* salvation, and that from God.

29 For you have been granted [the privilege] for Christ's sake not only to believe—adhere to, rely on and trust—in Him but also to suffer in His behalf.

30 So you are engaged in the same conflict which you saw me [wage] and which you now hear to be mine [still].

---

f) The order of verses 16 and 17 has been reversed for the sake of clarity in almost all versions since the King James.
g) Vincent.

Living New Testament

14 And because of my imprisonment many of the Christians here seem to have lost their fear of chains! Somehow my patience has encouraged them and they have become more and more bold in telling others about Christ.

15 Some, of course, are preaching the Good News because they are jealous of the way God has used me. They want reputations as fearless preachers! But others have purer motives,

16, 17 Preaching because they love me, for they know that the Lord has brought me here to use me to defend the Truth. And some preach to make me jealous, thinking that their success will add to my sorrows here in jail!

18 But whatever their motive for doing it, the fact remains that the Good News about Christ is being preached and I am glad.

19 I am going to keep on being glad, for I know that as you pray for me, and as the Holy Spirit helps me, this is all going to turn out for my good.

20 For I live in eager expectation and hope that I will never do anything that will cause me to be ashamed of myself; but that I will always be ready to speak out boldly for Christ while I am going through all these trials here, just as I have in the past; and that I will always be an honor to Christ, whether I live or whether I must die.

* * * * *

21 For to me, living means opportunities for Christ, and dying—well, that's better yet!

22 But if living will give me more opportunities to win people to Christ, then I really don't know which is best, to live or die!

23 Sometimes I want to live and at other times I don't, for I long to go and be with Christ. How much happier for *me* than being here!

24 But the fact is that I can be of more help to *you* by staying!

25 Yes, I am still needed down here and so I feel certain I will be staying on earth a little longer, to help you grow and become happy in your faith;

26 My staying will make you glad and give you reason to glorify Christ Jesus for keeping me safe, when I return to visit you again.

* * * * *

27 But whatever happens to me, remember always to live as Christians should, so that, whether I ever see you again or not, I will keep on hearing good reports that you are standing side by side with one strong purpose—to tell the Good News

28 Fearlessly, no matter what your enemies may do. They will see this as a sign of their downfall, but for you it will be a clear sign from God that He is with you, and that He has given you eternal life with Him.

29 For to you has been given the privilege not only of trusting Him but also of suffering for Him.

30 We are in this fight together. You have seen me suffer for Him in the past; and I am still in the midst of a great and terrible struggle now, as you know so well.

Revised Standard

prisonment is for Christ; [14]and most of the
brethren have been made confident in the
Lord because of my imprisonment, and are
much more bold to speak the word of God
without fear.
15 Some indeed preach Christ from envy
and rivalry, but others from good will. [16]The
latter do it out of love, knowing that I am
put here for the defense of the gospel; [17]the
former proclaim Christ out of partisanship,
not sincerely but thinking to afflict me in my
imprisonment. [18]What then? Only that in
every way, whether in pretense or in truth,
Christ is proclaimed; and in that I rejoice.
19 Yes, and I shall rejoice. For I know
that through your prayers and the help of
the Spirit of Jesus Christ this will turn out
for my deliverance, [20]as it is my eager expectation and hope that I shall not be at all
ashamed, but that with full courage now as
always Christ will be honored in my body,
whether by life or by death. [21]For to me to
live is Christ, and to die is gain. [22]If it is to
be life in the flesh, that means fruitful labor
for me. Yet which I shall choose I cannot
tell. [23]I am hard pressed between the two.
My desire is to depart and be with Christ,
for this is far better. [24]But to remain in the
flesh is more necessary on your account.
[25]Convinced of this, I know that I shall remain and continue with you all, for your
progress and joy in the faith, [26]so that in me
you may have ample cause to glory in Christ
Jesus, because of my coming to you again.

The example of Christ

27 Only let your manner of life be worthy
of the gospel of Christ, so that whether I
come and see you or am absent, I may hear
of you that you stand firm in one spirit, with
one mind striving side by side for the faith
of the gospel, [28]and not frightened in anything by your opponents. This is a clear
omen to them of their destruction, but of
your salvation, and that from God. [29]For it
has been granted to you that for the sake
of Christ you should not only believe in him
but also suffer for his sake, [30]engaged in
the same conflict which you saw and now
hear to be mine.

King James

CHAPTER 2

IF *there be* therefore any consolation in Christ, if any comfort of love, if any fellowship of the Spirit, if any bowels and mercies,

2 Fulfil ye my joy, that ye be likeminded, having the same love, *being* of one accord, of one mind.

3 *Let* nothing *be done* through strife or vainglory; but in lowliness of mind let each esteem other better than themselves.

4 Look not every man on his own things, but every man also on the things of others.

5 Let this mind be in you, which was also in Christ Jesus:

6 Who, being in the form of God, thought it not robbery to be equal with God:

7 But made himself of no reputation, and took upon him the form of a servant, and was made in the likeness of men:

8 And being found in fashion as a man, he humbled himself, and became obedient unto death, even the death of the cross.

9 Wherefore God also hath highly exalted him, and given him a name which is above every name:

10 That at the name of Jesus every knee should bow, of *things* in heaven, and *things* in earth, and *things* under the earth;

11 And *that* every tongue should confess that Jesus Christ *is* Lord, to the glory of God the Father.

12 Wherefore, my beloved, as ye have always obeyed, not as in my presence only, but now much more in my absence, work out your own salvation with fear and trembling.

13 For it is God which worketh in you both to will and to do of *his* good pleasure.

14 Do all things without murmurings and disputings:

Amplified

CHAPTER 2

SO by whatever [appeal to you there is in our mutual dwelling in Christ, by whatever] strengthening *and* consoling *and* encouraging [our relationship] in Him [affords], by whatever persuasive [h]incentive there is in love, by whatever participation in the (Holy) Spirit [we share] and by whatever depth of affection and compassionate sympathy,

2 Fill up *and* complete my joy by living in harmony *and* being of the same mind *and* one in purpose, having the same love, being in full accord and of one harmonious mind *and* intention.

3 Do nothing from factional motives—through contentiousness, strife, selfishness or for unworthy ends—or prompted by conceit *and* empty arrogance. Instead, in the true spirit of humility (lowliness of mind) let each regard the others as better than *and* superior to himself—thinking more highly of one another than you do of yourselves.

4 Let each of you esteem *and* look upon *and* be concerned for not [merely] his own interests, but also each for the interests of others.

5 Let this same attitude *and* purpose *and* [humble] mind be in you which was in Christ Jesus.—Let Him be your example in humility—

6 Who, although being essentially one with God *and* in the form of God [[i]possessing the fullness of the attributes which make God God], did not [j]think this equality with God was a thing to be eagerly grasped [j]or retained;

7 But stripped Himself [of all privileges and [k]rightful dignity] so as to assume the guise of a servant (slave), in that He became like men *and* was born a human being.

8 And after He had appeared in human form He abased *and* humbled Himself [still further] and carried His obedience to the extreme of death, even the death of [the] cross!

9 Therefore [because He stooped so low], God has highly exalted Him and has [l]freely bestowed on Him the name that is above every name,

10 That in (at) the name of Jesus every knee [m]should (must) bow, in heaven and on earth and under the earth,

11 And every tongue [[l]frankly and openly] confess *and* acknowledge that Jesus Christ is Lord, to the glory of God the Father.

12 Therefore, my dear ones, as you have always obeyed [my suggestions], so now, not only [with the enthusiasm you would show] in my presence but much more because I am absent, work out—cultivate, carry out to the goal and fully complete—your own salvation with reverence *and* awe and trembling [self-distrust, that is, [n]with serious caution, tenderness of conscience, watchfulness against temptation; timidly shrinking from whatever might offend God and discredit the name of Christ].

13 [Not in your own strength] for it is God Who is all the while [n]effectually at work in you—energizing and creating in you the power and desire—both to will and to work for His good pleasure *and* satisfaction *and* [o]delight.

14 Do all things without grumbling *and* faultfinding *and* complaining [[n]against God] and [n]questioning *and* doubting [among yourselves],

---

h) Vincent.
i) Warfield's "Biblical Doctrines."
j) Thayer.
k) Berry.
l) Vincent.
m) "Should" is past tense of "shall," implying authority or compulsion.
n) Vincent.
o) Souter.

Living New Testament

CHAPTER 2

Is there any such thing as Christians cheering each other up? Do you love me enough to want to help me? Does it mean anything to you that we are brothers in the Lord, sharing the same Spirit? Are your hearts tender and sympathetic at all?

2 Then make me truly happy by loving each other and agreeing wholeheartedly with each other, working together with one heart and mind and purpose.

3 Don't be selfish; don't live to make a good impression on others. Be humble, thinking of others as better than yourself.

4 Don't just think about your own affairs, but be interested in others, too, and in what they are doing.

5 Your attitude should be the kind that was shown us by Jesus Christ,

6 Who, though He was God, did not demand and cling to His rights as God,

7 But laid aside His mighty power and glory, taking the disguise of a slave and becoming like men.[1]

8 And he humbled Himself even further, going so far as actually to die a criminal's death on a cross.[2]

9 Yet it was because of this that God raised Him up to the heights of heaven and gave Him a name which is above every other name,

10 That at the name of Jesus every knee shall bow in heaven and on earth and under the earth,

11 And every tongue shall confess that Jesus Christ is Lord, to the glory of God the Father.

* * * * *

12 Dearest friends, when I was there with you, you were always so careful to follow my instructions. And now that I am away you must be even more careful to do the good things that result from being saved, obeying God with deep reverence, shrinking back from all that might displease Him.

13 For God is at work within you, helping you want to obey Him, and then helping you do what He wants.

14 In everything you do, stay away from complaining and arguing,

[1] Literally, "was made in the likeness of men."
[2] Literally, "became obedient unto death, even the death of the cross."

Revised Standard

2 So if there is any encouragement in
Christ, any incentive of love, any participation in the Spirit, any affection and sympathy, 2complete my joy by being of the
same mind, having the same love, being in
full accord and of one mind. 3Do nothing
from selfishness or conceit, but in humility
count others better than yourselves. 4Let each
of you look not only to his own interests, but
also to the interests of others. 5Have this
mind among yourselves, which you have in
Christ Jesus, 6who, though he was in the
form of God, did not count equality with
God a thing to be grasped, 7but emptied himself, taking the form of a servant,[d] being
born in the likeness of men. 8And being
found in human form he humbled himself
and became obedient unto death, even death
on a cross. 9Therefore God has highly exalted him and bestowed on him the name
which is above every name, 10that at the
name of Jesus every knee should bow, in
heaven and on earth and under the earth,
11and every tongue confess that Jesus Christ
is Lord, to the glory of God the Father.

Obligations of Christians

12 Therefore, my beloved, as you have
always obeyed, so now, not only as in my
presence but much more in my absence, work
out your own salvation with fear and trembling; 13for God is at work in you, both to
will and to work for his good pleasure.
14 Do all things without grumbling or

[d] Or *slave*

King James

15 That ye may be blameless and harmless, the sons of God, without rebuke, in the midst of a crooked and perverse nation, among whom ye shine as lights in the world;

16 Holding forth the word of life; that I may rejoice in the day of Christ, that I have not run in vain, neither laboured in vain.

17 Yea, and if I be offered upon the sacrifice and service of your faith, I joy, and rejoice with you all.

18 For the same cause also do ye joy, and rejoice with me.

19 But I trust in the Lord Jesus to send Timotheus shortly unto you, that I also may be of good comfort, when I know your state.

20 For I have no man like-minded, who will naturally care for your state.

21 For all seek their own, not the things which are Jesus Christ's.

22 But ye know the proof of him, that, as a son with the father, he hath served with me in the gospel.

23 Him therefore I hope to send presently, as soon as I shall see how it will go with me.

24 But I trust in the Lord that I also myself shall come shortly.

25 Yet I supposed it necessary to send to you Epaphroditus, my brother, and companion in labour, and fellowsoldier, but your messenger, and he that ministered to my wants.

26 For he longed after you all, and was full of heaviness, because that ye had heard that he had been sick.

27 For indeed he was sick nigh unto death: but God had mercy on him; and not on him only, but on me also, lest I should have sorrow upon sorrow.

28 I sent him therefore the more carefully, that, when ye see him again, ye may rejoice, and that I may be the less sorrowful.

29 Receive him therefore in the Lord with all gladness; and hold such in reputation:

30 Because for the work of Christ he was nigh unto death, not regarding his life, to supply your lack of service toward me.

Amplified

15 That you may show yourselves to be blameless *and* guileless, innocent *and* uncontaminated, children of God without blemish (faultless, unrebukable) in the midst of a crooked *and* wicked generation—[spiritually] perverted and perverse. Among whom you are seen as bright lights—stars or beacons shining out clearly—in the [dark] world;

16 Holding out [to it] *and* offering [to all men] the Word of Life, so that in the day of Christ I may have something of which exultantly to rejoice *and* glory in that I did not run my race in vain or spend my labor to no purpose.

17 Even if [my lifeblood] must be poured out as a libation on the sacrificial offering of your faith [to God], still I am glad [to do it] and [p]congratulate you all on [your share in] it;

18 And you also in like manner be glad and [p]congratulate me on [my share in] it.

19 But I hope *and* trust in the Lord Jesus soon to send Timothy to you, so that I may also be encouraged *and* cheered by learning news of you.

20 For I have no one like him—no one of so kindred a spirit—who will be so genuinely interested in your welfare *and* devoted to your interests.

21 For the others all seek [to advance] their own interests, not those of Jesus Christ, the Messiah.

22 But Timothy's tested worth you know, how as a son with his father he has toiled with me zealously [serving and helping to advance] the good news (the Gospel).

23 I hope therefore to send him promptly, just as soon as I know how my case is going to turn out.

24 But [really] I am confident *and* fully trusting in the Lord that shortly I myself shall come to you also.

25 However, I thought it necessary to send Epaphroditus [back] to you. [He has been] my brother and companion in labor and my fellow soldier, as well as [having come as] your special messenger (apostle) and minister to my need.

26 For he has been (homesick,) longing for you all and has been distressed because you had heard that he was ill.

27 He certainly was ill [too], near to death. But God had compassion on him, and not only on him but also on me, lest I should have sorrow [over him] [q]coming upon sorrow.

28 So I have sent him the more willingly *and* eagerly, that you may be gladdened at seeing him again, and that I may be the less disquieted.

29 Welcome him [home] then in the Lord with all joy, and honor *and* highly appreciate men like him,

30 For it was through working for Christ that he came so near death, risking his [very] life to complete the deficiencies in your service to me [which distance prevented you yourselves from rendering].

CHAPTER 3

FINALLY, my brethren, rejoice in the Lord. To write the same things to you, to me indeed *is* not grievous, but for you *it is* safe.

2 Beware of dogs, beware of evil workers, beware of the concision.

CHAPTER 3

FOR the rest, my brethren, delight yourselves in the Lord *and* continue to rejoice that you are in Him. To keep writing to you [over and over] of the same things is not irksome to me, and it is [a precaution] for your safety.

2 Look out for those dogs [the Judaizers], look out for those mischief-workers, look out for those who mutilate the flesh.

p) Lightfoot: "St. Paul's Epistle to the Philippians"; Moulton and Milligan: "The Vocabulary of the Greek Testament."
q) Vincent.

Living New Testament

15 So that no one can speak a word of blame against you. You are to live clean, innocent lives as children of God in a dark world full of people who are crooked and stubborn. Shine out among them like beacon lights,
16 Holding out to them the Word of Life. Then when Christ returns how glad I will be that my work among you was so worthwhile.
17 And if my lifeblood is, so to speak, to be poured out over your faith which I am offering up to God as a sacrifice—that is, if I am to die for you—even then I will be glad, and will share my joy with each of you.
18 For you should be happy about this, too, and rejoice with me for having this privilege of dying for you.

* * * * *

19 If the Lord is willing, I will send Timothy to see you soon. Then when he comes back he can cheer me up by telling me all about you and how you are getting along.
20 There is no one like Timothy for having a real interest in you;
21 Everyone else seems to be worrying about his own plans and not those of Jesus Christ.
22 But you know Timothy. He has been just like a son to me in helping me preach the Good News.
23 I hope to send him to you just as soon as I find out what is going to happen to me here.
24 And I am trusting the Lord that soon I myself may come to see you.
25 Meanwhile, I thought I ought to send Epaphroditus back to you. You sent him to help me in my need; well, he and I have been real brothers, working and battling side by side.
26 Now I am sending him home again, for he has been homesick for all of you and upset because you heard that he was ill.
27 And he surely was; in fact, he almost died. But God had mercy on him, and on me too, not allowing me to have this sorrow on top of everything else.
28 So I am all the more anxious to get him back to you again, for I know how thankful you will be to see him, and that will make me happy and lighten all my cares.
29 Welcome him in the Lord with great joy, and show your appreciation,
30 For he risked his life for the work of Christ and was at the point of death while trying to do for me the things you couldn't do because you were far away.

Revised Standard

questioning, [15]that you may be blameless
and innocent, children of God without blemish in the midst of a crooked and preverse
generation, among whom you shine as lights
in the world, [16]holding fast the word of life,
so that in the day of Christ I may be proud
that I did not run in vain or labor in vain.
[17]Even if I am to be poured as a libation
upon the sacrificial offering of your faith, I
am glad and rejoice with you all. [18]Likewise
you also should be glad and rejoice with me.

Coming of Timothy and Epaphroditus

19 I hope in the Lord Jesus to send Timothy to you soon, so that I may be cheered
by news of you. [20]I have no one like him,
who will be genuinely anxious for your welfare. [21]They all look after their own interests,
not those of Jesus Christ. [22]But Timothy's
worth you know, how as a son with a father
he has served with me in the gospel. [23]I hope
therefore to send him just as soon as I see
how it will go with me; [24]and I trust in the
Lord that shortly I myself shall come also.
25 I have thought it necessary to send to
you Epaphroditus my brother and fellow
worker and fellow soldier, and your messenger and minister to my need, [26]for he has
been longing for you all, and has been distressed because you heard that he was ill.
[27]Indeed he was ill, near to death. But God
had mercy on him, and not only on him but
on me also, lest I should have sorrow upon
sorrow. [28]I am the more eager to send him,
therefore, that you may rejoice at seeing him
again, and that I may be less anxious. [29]So
receive him in the Lord with all joy; and
honor such men, [30]for he nearly died for the
work of Christ, risking his life to complete
your service to me.

CHAPTER 3

Whatever happens, dear friends, be glad in the Lord. I never get tired of telling you this and it is good for you to hear it again and again.

* * * * *

2 Watch out for those wicked men—dangerous dogs, I call them—who say you must be circumcised to be saved.

The example of Paul

3 Finally, my brethren, rejoice in the
Lord. To write the same things to you
is not irksome to me, and is safe for you.
2 Look out for the dogs, look out for the
evil-workers, look out for those who muti-

King James

3 For we are the circumcision, which worship God in the spirit, and rejoice in Christ Jesus, and have no confidence in the flesh.

4 Though I might also have confidence in the flesh. If any other man thinketh that he hath whereof he might trust in the flesh, I more:

5 Circumcised the eighth day, of the stock of Israel, *of* the tribe of Benjamin, an Hebrew of the Hebrews; as touching the law, a Pharisee;

6 Concerning zeal, persecuting the church; touching the righteousness which is in the law, blameless.

7 But what things were gain to me, those I counted loss for Christ.

8 Yea doubtless, and I count all things *but* loss for the excellency of the knowledge of Christ Jesus my Lord: for whom I have suffered the loss of all things, and do count them *but* dung, that I may win Christ,

9 And be found in him, not having mine own righteousness, which is of the law, but that which is through the faith of Christ, the righteousness which is of God by faith:

10 That I may know him, and the power of his resurrection, and the fellowship of his sufferings, being made conformable unto his death;

11 If by any means I might attain unto the resurrection of the dead.

12 Not as though I had already attained, either were already perfect: but I follow after, if that I may apprehend that for which also I am apprehended of Christ Jesus.

13 Brethren, I count not myself to have apprehended: but *this* one thing *I do*, forgetting those things which are behind, and reaching forth unto those things which are before,

14 I press toward the mark for the prize of the high calling of God in Christ Jesus.

15 Let us therefore, as many as be perfect, be thus minded: and if in any thing ye be otherwise minded, God shall reveal even this unto you.

Amplified

3 For we [Christians] are the true circumcision, who worship God [r]in spirit *and* by the Spirit of God, and exult *and* glory *and* pride ourselves in Jesus Christ, and put no confidence *or* dependence [on what we are] in the flesh *and* on outward privileges *and* physical advantages and external appearances.

4 Though for myself I have [at least grounds] to rely on the flesh. If any other man considers that he has *or* seems to have reason to rely on the flesh *and* his physical *and* outward advantages, still more have I!

5 Circumcised when I was eight days old, of the race of Israel, of the tribe of Benjamin, a Hebrew [and the son] of Hebrews; as to the observance of the Law I was of [the party of] the Pharisees,

6 As to my zeal I was a persecutor of the church, and by the Law's standard of righteousness—[supposed] justice, uprightness and right standing with God—I was proven to be blameless *and* no fault was found with me.

7 But whatever former things I had that might have been gains to me, I have come to consider as ([s]one combined) loss for Christ's sake.

8 Yes, furthermore I count everything as loss compared to the possession of the priceless privilege—the overwhelming preciousness, the surpassing worth and supreme advantage—of knowing Christ Jesus my Lord, *and* of progressively becoming more deeply *and* intimately acquainted with Him, of perceiving *and* recognizing *and* understanding Him more fully *and* clearly. For His sake I have lost everything, and consider it all to be mere rubbish (refuse, dregs), in order that I may win (gain) Christ, the Anointed One,

9 And that I may [actually] be found *and* known as in Him, not having any (self-achieved) righteousness that can be called my own, based on my obedience to the Law's demands—ritualistic uprightness and [supposed] right standing with God thus acquired—but possessing that [genuine righteousness] which comes through faith in Christ, the Anointed One, the [truly] right standing with God, which comes from God by (saving) faith.

10 [For my determined purpose is] that I may know Him—that I may progressively become more deeply and intimately acquainted with Him, perceiving and recognizing and understanding [the wonders of His Person] more strongly and more clearly. And that I may in that same way come to know the power outflowing from His resurrection [[t]which it exerts over believers]; and that I may so share His sufferings as to be continually transformed [in spirit into His likeness even] to His death, [in the hope]

11 That if possible I may attain to the [[u]spiritual and moral] resurrection [that lifts me] out from among the dead [even while in the body].

12 Not that I have now attained [this ideal] or am already made perfect, but I press on to lay hold of (grasp) *and* make my own, that for which Christ Jesus, the Messiah, has laid hold of me *and* made me His own.

13 I do not consider, brethren, that I have captured *and* made it my own [yet]; but one thing I do—it is my one aspiration: forgetting what lies behind and straining forward to what lies ahead,

14 I press on toward the goal to win the [supreme and heavenly] prize to which God in Christ Jesus is calling us upward.

15 So let those [of us] who are spiritually mature *and* full-grown have this mind *and* hold these convictions, and if in any respect you have a different attitude of mind, God will make that clear to you also.

---

r) Alternate reading.
s) His "gains" are plural, but they are all counted as one "loss,' singular. (-Vincent.)
t) Vincent.
u) Williams: Double compound "non," meaning a spiritual, moral resurrection, not the final, physical one, which will be the climax.

Living New Testament

3 For it isn't the *cutting of our bodies* that makes us children of God; it is *worshiping Him with our spirits*. That is the only true "circumcision." We Christians glory in what Christ Jesus has done for us and realize that we are helpless to save ourselves.

4 Yet if anyone ever had reason to hope that he could save himself, it would be I. If others could be saved by what they are, certainly I could!

5 For I went through the Jewish initiation ceremony when I was eight days old, having been born into a pure-blooded Jewish home that was a branch of the old original Benjamin family. So I was a real Jew if there ever was one! What's more, I was a member of the Pharisees who demand the strictest obedience to every Jewish law and custom.

6 And sincere? Yes, so much so that I greatly persecuted the church; and I tried to obey every Jewish rule and regulation right down to the very last point.

7 But all these things that I once thought very worthwhile—now I've thrown them all away so that I can put my trust and hope in Christ alone.

8 Yes, everything else is worthless when compared with the priceless gain of knowing Christ Jesus my Lord. I have put aside all else, counting it worth less than nothing, in order that I can have Christ,

9 And become one with Him, no longer counting on being saved by being good enough or by obeying God's laws, but by trusting Christ to save me; for God's way of making us right with Himself depends on faith—counting on Christ alone.

10 Now I have given up everything else—I have found it to be the only way to really know Christ and to experience the mighty power that brought Him back to life again, and to find out what it means to suffer and to die with Him,

11 So, whatever it takes, I will be one who lives in the fresh newness of life of those who are alive from the dead.

12 I don't mean to say I am perfect. I haven't learned all I should even yet, but I keep working toward that day when I will finally be all that Christ saved me for and wants me to be.

13 No, dear brothers, I am still not all I should be but I am bringing all my energies to bear on this one thing: Forgetting the past and looking forward to what lies ahead,

14 I strain to reach the end of the race and receive the prize for which God is calling us up to heaven because of what Christ Jesus did for us.

* * * * *

15 I hope all of you who are mature Christians will see eye-to-eye with me on these things, and if you disagree on some points I believe that God will make it plain to you—

Revised Standard

late the flesh. [3]For we are the true circumcision, who worship God in spirit,[e] and glory
in Christ Jesus, and put no confidence in the
flesh. [4]Though I myself have reason for confidence in the flesh also. If any other man
thinks he has reason for confidence in the
flesh, I have more: [5]circumcised on the
eighth day, of the people of Israel, of the
tribe of Benjamin, a Hebrew born of Hebrews; as to the law a Pharisee, [6]as to zeal
a persecutor of the church, as to righteousness under the law blameless. [7]But whatever
gain I had, I counted as loss for the sake of
Christ. [8]Indeed I count everything as loss
because of the surpassing worth of knowing
Christ Jesus my Lord. For his sake I have
suffered the loss of all things, and count them
as refuse, in order that I may gain Christ
[9]and be found in him, not having a righteousness of my own, based on law, but that which
is through faith in Christ, the righteousness
from God that depends on faith; [10] that I may
know him and the power of his resurrection,
and may share his sufferings, becoming like
him in his death, [11]that if possible I may
attain the resurrection from the dead.

The upward call of God

12 Not that I have already obtained this
or am already perfect; but I press on to
make it my own, because Christ Jesus has
made me his own. [13]Brethren, I do not consider that I have made it my own; but one
thing I do, forgetting what lies behind and
straining forward to what lies ahead, [14]I press
on toward the goal for the prize of the upward call of God in Christ Jesus. [15]Let those
of us who are mature be thus minded; and
if in anything you are otherwise minded,
God will reveal that also to you. [16]Only let

---

[e] Other ancient authorities read *worship by the Spirit of God*

King James

16 Nevertheless, whereto we have already attained, let us walk by the same rule, let us mind the same thing.

17 Brethren, be followers together of me, and mark them which walk so as ye have us for an ensample.

18 (For many walk, of whom I have told you often, and now tell you even weeping, *that they are* the enemies of the cross of Christ:

19 Whose end *is* destruction, whose God *is their* belly, and *whose* glory *is* in their shame, who mind earthly things.)

20 For our conversation is in heaven; from whence also we look for the Saviour, the Lord Jesus Christ:

21 Who shall change our vile body, that it may be fashioned like unto his glorious body, according to the working whereby he is able even to subdue all things unto himself.

Amplified

16 Only let us hold true to what we have alreac attained *and* walk *and* order our lives by that.

17 Brethren, together follow my example and obser those who live after the pattern we have set you.

18 For there are many, of whom I have often told yc and now tell you even with tears, who walk (live) enemies of the cross of Christ, the Anointed One.

19 They are doomed *and* their [v]fate [is] eternal mise (perdition); their god is their stomach (their appetite their sensuality) and they glory in their shame, [v]sidi with early things *and* being of their party.

20 But we are citizens of the state (commonwealt homeland) which is in heaven, and from it also we [w]ea nestly *and* patiently await [the coming of] the Lord Jes Christ, the Messiah, [as] Savior,

21 Who will [w]transform *and* fashion anew the body our humiliation to conform to *and* be like the body of H glory *and* majesty, be exerting that power which enabl Him even to subject everything to Himself.

CHAPTER 4

THEREFORE, my brethren dearly beloved and longed for, my joy and crown, so stand fast in the Lord, *my* dearly beloved.

2 I beseech Euodias, and beseech Syntyche, that they be of the same mind in the Lord.

3 And I entreat thee also, true yokefellow, help those women which laboured with me in the gospel, with Clement also, and *with* other my fellow-labourers, whose names *are* in the book of life.

4 Rejoice in the Lord alway: *and* again I say, Rejoice.

5 Let your moderation be known unto all men. The Lord *is* at hand.

6 Be careful for nothing; but in every thing by prayer and supplication with thanksgiving let your requests be made known unto God.

7 And the peace of God, which passeth all understanding, shall keep your hearts and minds through Christ Jesus.

8 Finally, brethren, whatsoever things are true, whatsoever things *are* honest, whatsoever things *are* just, whatsoever things *are* pure, whatsoever things *are* lovely, whatsoever things *are* of good report; if *there be* any virtue, and if *there be* any praise, think on these things.

9 Those things, which ye have both learned, and received, and heard, and seen in me, do: and the God of peace shall be with you.

CHAPTER 4

THEREFORE, my brethren, whom I love and yearn see, my delight and crown (wreath of victory), th stand firm in the Lord, my beloved.

2 I entreat *and* advise Euodia and I entreat *and* advi Syntyche to agree *and* to work in harmony in the Lord.

3 And I exhort you too, [my] genuine yokefellow, he these [two women to keep on co-operating], for they ha toiled along with me in [the spreading of] the good nev (the Gospel), as have Clement and the rest of my fello workers whose names are in the Book of Life.

4 Rejoice in the Lord always—delight, gladden you selves in Him; again I say, Rejoice! [Ps. 37:4.]

5 Let all men know *and* perceive *and* recognize yo unselfishness—your considerateness, your forbearing spir The Lord is near—He is [x]coming soon.

6 Do not fret *or* have any anxiety about anything, b in every circumstance *and* in everything by prayer ar petition [[x]definite requests] with thanksgiving continue make your wants known to God.

7 And God's peace [be yours, that [x]tranquil state of soul assured of its salvation through Christ, and so feari nothing from God and content with its earthly lot whatever sort that is, that peace] which transcends understanding, shall [y]garrison *and* mount guard over yo hearts and minds in Christ Jesus.

8 For the rest, brethren, whatever is true, whatever worthy of reverence *and* is honorable *and* seemly, whate er is just, whatever is pure, whatever is lovely *and* lovabl whatever is kind *and* winsome *and* gracious, if there is ar virtue *and* excellence, if there is anything worthy praise, think on *and* weigh *and* take account of the things—fix your minds on them.

9 Practice what you have learned and received ar heard and seen in me, *and* model your way of living on and the God of peace—of [z]untroubled, undisturbed we being—will be with you.

---

v) Thayer.
w) Vincent.
x) Thayer.
y) Gurnall (-Vincent.)
z) Cremer.

Living New Testament

16 If you fully obey the truth you have.

* * * * *

17 Dear brothers, pattern your lives after mine and notice who else lives up to my example.

18 For I have told you often before, and I say it again now with tears in my eyes, there are many who walk along the Christian road who are really enemies of the cross of Christ.

19 Their future is eternal loss for their god is their appetite: they are proud of what they should be ashamed of; and all they think about is this life here on earth.

20 But our homeland is in heaven, with our Savior the Lord Jesus Christ; and we are looking forward to His return from there.

* * * * *

21 When He comes back He will take these dying bodies of ours and change them into glorious bodies like His own, using the same mighty power that He will use to conquer all else everywhere.

Revised Standard

us hold true to what we have attained.
17 Brethren, join in imitating me, and
mark those who so live as you have an example in us. [18]For many, of whom I have
often told you and now tell you even with
tears, live as enemies of the cross of Christ.
[19]Their end is destruction, their god is the
belly, and they glory in their shame, with
minds set on earthly things. [20]But our commonwealth is in heaven, and from it we
await a Savior, the Lord Jesus Christ, [21]who
will change our lowly body to be like his
glorious body, by the power which enables
him even to subject all things to himself.

CHAPTER 4

Dear brother Christians, I love you and long to see you, for you are my joy and my reward for my work. My beloved friends, stay true to the Lord.

* * * * *

2 And now I want to plead with those two dear women, Euodias and Syntyche. Please, please, with the Lord's help, quarrel no more—be friends again.

3 And I ask you, my true teammate, to help these women, for they worked side by side with me in telling the Good News to others; and they worked with Clement too and the rest of my fellow workers whose names are written in the Book of Life.

* * * * *

4 Always be full of joy in the Lord; I say it again, rejoice!

5 Let everyone see that you are unselfish and considerate in all you do. Remember that the Lord is coming soon.

6 Don't worry about anything; instead, pray about everything; tell God your needs and don't forget to thank Him for His answers.

7 If you do this you will experience God's peace, which is far more wonderful than the human mind can understand. His peace will keep your thoughts and your hearts quiet and at rest as you trust in Christ Jesus.

* * * * *

8 And now, brothers, as I close this letter let me say this one more thing. Fix your thoughts on what is true and good and right. Think about things that are pure and lovely, and dwell on the fine, good things in others. Think about all you can praise God for and be glad about.

9 Keep putting into practice all you learned from me and saw me doing, and the God of peace will be with you.

Appeal to rejoice in the Lord

4 Therefore, my brethren, whom I love
and long for, my joy and crown, stand
firm thus in the Lord, my beloved.
2 I entreat Euodia and I entreat Syntyche
to agree in the Lord. [3]And I ask you also,
true yokefellow, help these women, for they
have labored side by side with me in the
gospel together with Clement and the rest of
my fellow workers, whose names are in the
book of life.
4 Rejoice in the Lord always; again I will
say, Rejoice. [5]Let all men know your forbearance. The Lord is at hand. [6]Have no
anxiety about anything, but in everything by
prayer and supplication with thanksgiving let
your requests be made known to God. [7]And
the peace of God, which passes all understanding, will keep your hearts and your
minds in Christ Jesus.
8 Finally, brethren, whatever is true, whatever is honorable, whatever is just, whatever
is pure, whatever is lovely, whatever is gracious, if there is any excellence, if there is
anything worthy of praise, think about these
things. [9]What you have learned and received
and heard and seen in me, do; and the God
of peace will be with you.

King James

10 But I rejoiced in the Lord greatly, that now at the last your care of me hath flourished again; wherein ye were also careful, but ye lacked opportunity.

11 Not that I speak in respect of want: for I have learned, in whatsoever state I am, *therewith* to be content.

12 I know both how to be abased, and I know how to abound: every where and in all things I am instructed both to be full and to be hungry, both to abound and to suffer need.

13 I can do all things through Christ which strengtheneth me.

14 Notwithstanding ye have well done, that ye did communicate with my affliction.

15 Now ye Philippians know also, that in the beginning of the gospel, when I departed from Macedonia, no church communicated with me as concerning giving and receiving, but ye only.

16 For even in Thessalonica ye sent once and again unto my necessity.

17 Not because I desire a gift: but I desire fruit that may abound to your account.

18 But I have all, and abound: I am full, having received of Epaphroditus the things *which were sent* from you, an odour of a sweet smell, a sacrifice acceptable, wellpleasing to God.

19 But my God shall supply all your need according to his riches in glory by Christ Jesus.

20 Now unto God and our Father *be* glory for ever and ever. Amen.

21 Salute every saint in Christ Jesus. The brethren which are with me greet you.

22 All the saints salute you, chiefly they that are of Caesar's household.

23 The grace of our Lord Jesus Christ *be* with you all. Amen.

¶ It was written to the Philippians from Rome by Epaphroditus.

Amplified

10 I was made very happy in the Lord that now you have revived your interest in my welfare after so long a time; you were indeed thinking of me, but you had no opportunity to show it.

11 Not that I am implying that I was in any personal want, for I have learned how to be content (satisfied to the point where I am not disturbed or disquieted) in whatever state I am.

12 I know how to be abased *and* live humbly in straitened circumstances, and I know also how to enjoy plenty *and* live in abundance. I have learned in any and all circumstances, the secret of facing every situation, whether well-fed or going hungry, having a sufficiency *and* to spare or going without *and* being in want.

13 I have strength for all things in Christ Who empowers me—I am ready for anything and equal to anything through Him Who [a]infuses inner strength into me, [that is, I am [b]self-sufficient in Christ's sufficiency].

14 But it was right *and* commendable *and* noble of you to contribute for my needs *and* to share my difficulties with me.

15 And you Philippians yourselves well know that in the early days of the Gospel ministry, when I left Macedonia, no church (assembly) entered into partnership with me *and* opened up [a debit and credit] account in giving and receiving except you only.

16 For even in Thessalonica you sent [me contributions] for my needs, not only once but a second time.

17 Not that I seek *or* am eager for [your] gift, but I do seek *and* am eager for the fruit which increases to your credit—the harvest of blessing that is accumulating to your account.

18 But I have [your full payment] and more; I have everything I need *and* am amply supplied, now that I have received from Epaphroditus the gifts you sent me. [They are the] fragrant odor [of] an offering *and* sacrifice which God welcomes *and* in which He delights.

19 And my God will liberally supply ([c]fill to the full) your every need according to His riches in glory in Christ Jesus.

20 To our God and Father by glory forever and ever—through the endless eternities of the eternities. *Amen, so be it.*

21 Remember me to every saint (every born-again believer) in Christ Jesus. The brethren (my [c]associates) who are with me greet you.

22 All the saints—God's consecrated ones here—wish to be remembered to you, especially those of Caesar's household.

23 The grace (spiritual favor and blessing) of the Lord Jesus Christ, the Anointed One, be with your spirit. *Amen—so be it.*

---

a) Vincent.
b) "Content" (v.11) literally means "self-sufficient."
c) Thayer.

Living New Testament

* * * * *

10 How grateful I am and how I praise the Lord that you are helping me again. I know you have always been anxious to send what you could, but for a while you didn't have the chance.

11 Not that I was ever in need, for I have learned how to get along happily whether I have much or little.

12 I know how to live on almost nothing or with everything. I have learned the secret of contentment in every situation, whether it be a full stomach or hunger, plenty or want;

13 For I can do everything God asks me to with the help of Christ who gives me the strength and power.

14 But even so, you have done right in helping me in my present difficulty.

15 As you well know, when I first brought the Gospel to you and then went on my way, leaving Macedonia, only you Philippians became my partners in giving and receiving. No other church did this.

16 Even when I was over in Thessalonica you sent help twice.

17 But though I appreciate your gifts, what makes me happiest is the well-earned reward you will have because of your kindness.

18 At the moment I have all I need—more than I need! I am generously supplied with the gifts you sent me when Epaphroditus came. They are a sweet smelling sacrifice that pleases God well.

19 And it is He who will supply all your needs from His riches in glory, because of what Christ Jesus has done for us.

20 Now unto God our Father be glory forever and ever. Amen.

Sincerely,
Paul

P.S.

21 Say "hello" for me to all the Christians there; the brothers with me send their greetings too.

22 And all the other Christians here want to be remembered to you, especially those who work in Caesar's palace.

23 The blessings of our Lord Jesus Christ be upon your spirits.

Revised Standard

Acknowledgment of Philippian gifts

10 I rejoice in the Lord greatly that now
at length you have revived your concern for
me; you were indeed concerned for me, but
you had no opportunity. [11]Not that I complain of want; for I have learned, in whatever
state I am, to be content. [12]I know how to be
abased, and I know how to abound; in any
and all circumstances I have learned the
secret of facing plenty and hunger, abundance and want. [13]I can do all things in him
who strengthens me.
14 Yet it was kind of you to share my
trouble. [15]And you Philippians yourselves
know that in the beginning of the gospel,
when I left Macedonia, no church entered
into partnership with me in giving and receiving except you only; [16]for even in Thessalonica you sent me help[f] once and again.
[17]Not that I seek the gift; but I seek the fruit
which increases to your credit. [18]I have received full payment, and more; I am filled,
having received from Epaphroditus the gifts
you sent, a fragrant offering, a sacrifice acceptable and pleasing to God. [19]And my God
will supply every need of yours according
to his riches in glory in Christ Jesus. [20]To
our God and Father be glory for ever and
ever. Amen.

Concluding benediction

21 Greet every saint in Christ Jesus. The
brethren who are with me greet you. [22]All
the saints greet you, especially those of
Caesar's household.
23 The grace of the Lord Jesus Christ be
with your spirit.

[f] Other ancient authorities read *money for my needs*

King James

THE EPISTLE OF PAUL THE APOSTLE
TO THE

Colossians

CHAPTER 1

PAUL, an apostle of Jesus Christ by the will of God, and Timotheus *our* brother,

2 To the saints and faithful brethren in Christ which are at Colosse: Grace *be* unto you, and peace, from God our Father and the Lord Jesus Christ.

3 We give thanks to God and the Father of our Lord Jesus Christ, praying always for you,

4 Since we heard of your faith in Christ Jesus, and of the love *which ye have* to all the saints,

5 For the hope which is laid up for you in heaven, whereof ye heard before in the word of the truth of the gospel;

6 Which is come unto you, as *it is* in all the world; and bringeth forth fruit, as *it doth* also in you, since the day ye heard *of it*, and knew the grace of God in truth:

7 As ye also learned of Epaphras our dear fellow-servant, who is for you a faithful minister of Christ;

8 Who also declared unto us your love in the Spirit.

9 For this cause we also, since the day we heard *it*, do not cease to pray for you, and to desire that ye might be filled with the knowledge of his will in all wisdom and spiritual understanding;

10 That ye might walk worthy of the Lord unto all pleasing, being fruitful in every good work, and increasing in the knowledge of God;

11 Strengthened with all might, according to his glorious power, unto all patience and longsuffering with joyfulness;

12 Giving thanks unto the Father, which hath made us meet to be partakers of the inheritance of the saints in light:

Amplified

THE LETTER OF PAUL
TO THE

Colossians

CHAPTER 1

PAUL, an apostle (special messenger) of Christ Jesus, the Messiah, by the will of God, and Timothy [our] brother,

2 To the saints (the consecrated people of God) and [a]believing *and* faithful brethren in Christ, who are at Colossae: Grace (spiritual favor and blessing) to you and heart peace from God our Father.

3 We [b]continually give thanks to God the Father of our Lord Jesus Christ, the Messiah, as we are praying for you,

4 For we have heard of your faith in Christ Jesus [[c]the leaning of your entire human personality on Him in absolute trust and confidence in His power, wisdom and goodness] and of the love which you [have and show] for all the saints (God's consecrated ones),

5 Because of the hope [of experiencing what is] laid up—[a]reserved and waiting—for you in heaven. Of this [hope] you heard in the past in the message of the truth of the Gospel,

6 Which has come to you. Indeed in the whole world [that Gospel] is bearing fruit *and* still is growing [c][by its own inherent power], even as it has done among yourselves ever since the day you first heard and came to know *and* understand the grace of God in truth.—[That is,] you came to know the grace (undeserved favor) of God in reality, deeply and clearly and thoroughly, becoming accurately and intimately acquainted with it.

7 You so learned it from Epaphras our beloved fellow servant. He is a faithful minister of Christ in our stead *and* as our representative, *and* [d]yours.

8 Also he has informed us of your love in the (Holy) Spirit.

9 For this reason we also, from the day we heard of it, have not ceased to pray *and* make [[e]special] request for you, [asking] that you may be filled with the [e]full (deep and clear) knowledge of His will in all spiritual wisdom [that is, [f]in comprehensive insight into the ways and purposes of God] and in understanding *and* discernment of spiritual things;

10 That you may walk (live and conduct yourselves) in a manner worthy of the Lord, fully pleasing to Him *and* [g]desiring to please Him in all things, bearing fruit in every good work and steadily growing *and* increasing in (and [h]by) the knowledge of God—with fuller, deeper and clearer insight, [i]acquaintance and recognition.

11 [We pray] that you may be invigorated *and* strengthened with all power, according to the might of His glory, [to exercise] every kind of endurance and patience (perseverance and forbearance) with joy,

12 Giving thanks to the Father, Who has qualified *and* made us fit to share the [e]portion which is the inheritance of the saints (God's holy people) in the Light.

---

a) Vincent.
b) *Always;* belongs with *give thanks,* not elsewhere (-Vincent.)
c) Souter's "Pocket Lexicon to the Greek New Testament."
d) Many ancient authorities read "your."
e) Vincent.
f) Souter.
g) Thayer.
h) The best texts read "by."
i) Abbott-Smith.

Living New Testament

Colossians

CHAPTER 1

From: Paul, chosen by God to be Jesus Christ's messenger, and from Brother Timothy.

2 *To:* The faithful Christian brothers—God's people—in the city of Colosse.

May God our Father shower you with blessings and fill you with His great peace.

3 Whenever we pray for you we always begin by giving thanks to God the Father of our Lord Jesus Christ,

4 For we have heard how much you trust the Lord, and how much you love His people.

5 And you are looking forward to the joys of heaven, and have been ever since the Gospel first was preached to you.

6 The same Good News that came to you is going out all over the world and changing lives everywhere, just as it changed yours that very first day you heard it and understood about God's great kindness to sinners.

7 Epaphras our much-loved fellow worker was the one who brought you this Good News. He is Jesus Christ's slave, here to help us in your stead.

8 And he is the one who has told us about the great love for others which the Holy Spirit has given you.

9 So ever since we first heard about you we have kept on praying and asking God to help you understand what He wants you to do, and to make you wise about spiritual things,

10 That the way you live will always please the Lord and honor Him, that you will always be doing good, kind things for others, all the time learning to know God better and better.

11 We are praying, too, that you will be filled up with His mighty, glorious strength so that you can keep going no matter what happens—always full of the joy of the Lord,

12 And always thankful to the Father who has made us fit to share all the wonderful things that belong to those who live in the kingdom of light.

Revised Standard

THE LETTER OF PAUL TO THE

Colossians

Salutation and thanksgiving

1 Paul, an apostle of Christ Jesus by the
will of God, and Timothy our brother,
2 To the saints and faithful brethren in
Christ at Colossae:
Grace to you and peace from God our
Father.
3 We always thank God, the Father of
our Lord Jesus Christ, when we pray for you,
[4]because we have heard of your faith in
Christ Jesus and of the love which you have
for all the saints, [5]because of the hope laid
up for you in heaven. Of this you have heard
before in the word of the truth, the gospel
[6]which has come to you, as indeed in the
whole world it is bearing fruit and growing
—so among yourselves, from the day you
heard and understood the grace of God in
truth, [7]as you learned it from Epaphras our
beloved fellow servant. He is a faithful minister of Christ on our[a] behalf [8]and has made
known to us your love in the Spirit.

Paul's prayer for the Colossians

9 And so, from the day we heard of it,
we have not ceased to pray for you, asking
that you may be filled with the knowledge
of his will in all spiritual wisdom and understanding, [10]to lead a life worthy of the Lord,
fully pleasing to him, bearing fruit in every
good work and increasing in the knowledge
of God. [11]May you be strengthened with all
power, according to his glorious might, for
all endurance and patience with joy, [12]giving
thanks to the Father, who has qualified us[b] to
share in the inheritance of the saints in light.

[a] Other ancient authorities read *your*
[b] Other ancient authorities read *you*

King James

13 Who hath delivered us from the power of darkness, and hath translated *us* into the kingdom of his dear Son:

14 In whom we have redemption through his blood, *even* the forgiveness of sins:

15 Who is the image of the invisible God, the firstborn of every creature:

16 For by him were all things created, that are in heaven, and that are in earth, visible and invisible, whether *they be* thrones, or dominions, or principalities, or powers: all things were created by him, and for him:

17 And he is before all things, and by him all things consist.

18 And he is the head of the body, the church: who is the beginning, the firstborn from the dead; that in all *things* he might have the preeminence.

19 For it pleased *the Father* that in him should all fulness dwell;

20 And, having made peace through the blood of his cross, by him to reconcile all things unto himself; by him, *I say,* whether *they be* things in earth, or things in heaven.

21 And you, that were sometime alienated and enemies in *your* mind by wicked works, yet now hath he reconciled

22 In the body of his flesh through death, to present you holy and unblameable and unreproveable in his sight:

23 If ye continue in the faith grounded and settled, and *be* not moved away from the hope of the gospel, which ye have heard, *and* which was preached to every creature which is under heaven; whereof I Paul am made a minister;

24 Who now rejoice in my sufferings for you, and fill up that which is behind of the afflictions of Christ in my flesh for his body's sake, which is the church:

25 Whereof I am made a minister, according to the dispensation of God which is given to me for you, to fulfil the word of God;

26 *Even* the mystery which hath been hid from ages and from generations, but now is made manifest to his saints:

27 To whom God would make known what *is* the riches of the glory of this mystery among the Gentiles; which is Christ in you, the hope of glory:

Amplified

13 [The Father] has delivered *and* [g]drawn us to Himself out of the control *and* the dominion of darkness and has transferred us into the kingdom of the Son [j]of His love,

14 In Whom we have our redemption *through His blood,* [which means] the forgiveness of our sins.

15 [Now] He is the [k]exact likeness of the unseen God—the visible representation of the invisible; He is the First-born—of all creation.

16 For it was in Him that all things were created, in heaven and on earth, things seen and things unseen, whether thrones, dominions, rulers or authorities; all things were created *and* exist through Him (by His service, intervention) *and* in and for Him.

17 And He Himself existed before all things and in Him all things consist—cohere, are held together. [Prov. 8:22-31.]

18 He also is the Head of [His] body, the church; seeing He is the Beginning, the First-born from among the dead, so that He alone in everything *and* in every respect might occupy the chief place—stand first and be pre-eminent.

19 For it has pleased [the Father] that all the divine fullness—the sum total of the divine perfection, powers and attributes—should dwell in Him [l]permanently.

20 And God purposed that through—[m]by the service, the intervention of—Him (the Son) all things should be completely reconciled [l]back to Himself, whether on earth or in heaven, as through Him [the Father] made peace by means of the blood of His cross.

21 And although you at one time were estranged *and* alienated from Him and of hostile attitude of mind in your wicked activities,

22 Yet now has [Christ, the Messiah,] reconciled [you to God] in the body of His flesh through death, in order to present you holy and faultless and irreproachable in His [the Father's] presence.

23 [And this He will do] provided that you continue to [n]stay with *and* in the faith [in Christ], well-grounded and settled *and* steadfast, not shifting *or* moving away from the hope [which rests on and is inspired by] the glad tidings (the Gospel), which you heard and which has been preached [o][as being designed for and offered without restrictions] to every person under heaven, and of which [Gospel] I, Paul, became a minister.

24 [Even] now I rejoice in [n]the midst of my sufferings on your behalf. And in my own person I am making up whatever is still lacking *and* remains to be completed [[n]on our part] of Christ's afflictions, for the sake of His body, which is the Church.

25 In it I became a minister in accordance with the divine [n]stewardship which was entrusted to me for you—as its object and for your benefit—to make the Word of God fully known [among you].

26 The mystery of which was hidden for ages and generations ([p]from angels and men), but is now revealed to His holy people (the saints),

27 To whom God was pleased to make known how great for the Gentiles are the riches of the glory of this mystery, which is, Christ within *and* among you the hope of [realizing] the glory.

---

g) Thayer.
j) Literal meaning.
k) Williams: "Strong terms; so *exact likeness.*"
l) Vincent.
m) Thayer.
n) Vincent.
o) Clarke's Commentary, and others.
p) Bengel. Alford (Jamieson, Fausset and Brown).

Living New Testament

13 For He has rescued us out of the darkness and gloom of Satan's kingdom and brought us into the kingdom of His dear Son,

14 Who bought our freedom with His blood and forgave us all our sins.

* * * * *

15 Christ is the exact likeness of the unseen God. He existed before God made anything at all,[1] and, in fact,

16 Christ Himself is the Creator who made everything in heaven and earth, the things we can see and the things we can't; the spirit world with its kings and kingdoms, its rulers and authorities: all were made by Christ for His own use and glory.

17 He was before all else began and it is His power that holds everything together.

18 He is the Head of the body made up of His people—that is, His church—which He began; and He is the Leader of all who arise from the dead,[2] so that He is first in everything;

19 For God wanted all of Himself to be in His Son.

20 It was through what His Son did that God cleared a path for everything to come to Him—all things in heaven and on earth—for Christ's death on the cross has made peace with God for all by His blood.

21 This includes you who were once so far away from God. You were His enemies and hated Him and were separated from Him by your evil thoughts and actions, yet now He has brought you back as His friends.

22 He has done this through the death on the cross of His own human body, and now as a result Christ has brought you into the very presence of God, and you are standing there before Him with nothing left against you—nothing left that He could even chide you for;

23 The only condition is that you fully believe the Truth, standing in it steadfast and firm, strong in the Lord, convinced of the Good News that Jesus died for you, and never shifting from trusting Him to save you. This is the wonderful news that came to each of you and is now spreading all over the world. And I, Paul, have the joy of telling it to others.

* * * * *

24 But part of my work is to suffer for you; and I am glad, for I am helping to finish up the remainder of Christ's sufferings for His body, the church.

* * * * *

25 God has sent me to help His church and to tell His secret plan to you Gentiles.

26, 27 He has kept this secret for centuries and generations past, but now at last it has pleased Him to tell it to those who love Him and live for Him, and the riches and glory of His plan are for you Gentiles too. And this is the secret: *that Christ in your hearts is your only hope of glory.*

[1] Literally, "the firstborn of all creation."
[2] Literally: "He is the Beginning, the firstborn from the dead."

Revised Standard

[13]He has delivered us from the dominion of
darkness and transferred us to the kingdom
of his beloved Son, [14]in whom we have redemption, the forgiveness of sins.

Christ the full expression of God

15 He is the image of the invisible God,
the first-born of all creation; [16]for in him all
things were created, in heaven and on earth,
visible and invisible, whether thrones or dominions or principalities or authorities—all
things were created through him and for
him. [17]He is before all things, and in him all
things hold together. [18]He is the head of the
body, the church; he is the beginning, the
firstborn from the dead, that in everything
he might be pre-eminent. [19]For in him all
the fulness of God was pleased to dwell,
[20]and through him to reconcile to himself all
things, whether on earth or in heaven, making peace by the blood of his cross.
21 And you, who once were estranged
and hostile in mind, doing evil deeds, [22]he
has now reconciled in his body of flesh by
his death, in order to present you holy and
blameless and irreproachable before him,
[23]provided that you continue in the faith,
stable and steadfast, not shifting from the
hope of the gospel which you heard, which
has been preached to every creature under
heaven, and of which I, Paul, became a minister.

The ministry of Paul

24 Now I rejoice in my sufferings for your
sake, and in my flesh I complete what is lacking in Christ's afflictions for the sake of his
body, that is, the church, [25]of which I became a minister according to the divine office which was given to me for you, to make
the word of God fully known, [26]the mystery
hidden for ages and generations[c] but now
made manifest to his saints. [27]To them God

[c] Or *from angels and men*

King James

28 Whom we preach, warning every man, and teaching every man in all wisdom; that we may present every man perfect in Christ Jesus:

29 Whereunto I also labour, striving according to his working, which worketh in me mightily.

CHAPTER 2

FOR I would that ye knew what great conflict I have for you, and *for* them at Laodicea, and *for* as many as have not seen my face in the flesh;

2 That their hearts might be comforted, being knit together in love, and unto all riches of the full assurance of understanding, to the acknowledgement of the mystery of God, and of the Father, and of Christ;

3 In whom are hid all the treasures of wisdom and knowledge.

4 And this I say, lest any man should beguile you with enticing words.

5 For though I be absent in the flesh, yet am I with you in the spirit, joying and beholding your order, and the stedfastness of your faith in Christ.

6 As ye have therefore received Christ Jesus the Lord, *so* walk ye in him:

7 Rooted and built up in him, and stablished in the faith, as ye have been taught, abounding therein with thanksgiving.

8 Beware lest any man spoil you through philosophy and vain deceit, after the tradition of men, after the rudiments of the world, and not after Christ.

9 For in him dwelleth all the fulness of the Godhead bodily.

Amplified

28 Him we preach *and* proclaim, warning *and* admonishing every one and instructing every one in all wisdom, [[q]in comprehensive insight into the ways and purposes of God], that we may present every person mature—full-grown, fully initiated, complete and perfect—in Christ, the Anointed One.

29 For this I labor [[r]unto weariness], striving with all the [r]superhuman energy which He so mightily enkindles *and* works within me.

CHAPTER 2

FOR I want you to know how great is my solicitude for you—in how severe an inward struggle I am engaged for you—and for those [believers] at Laodicea, and for all who ([r]like yourselves) have never seen my face *and* known me personally.

2 [For my concern is] that their hearts may be [r]braced (comforted, cheered and encouraged) as they are knit together in love, that they may come to have all the abounding wealth *and* blessings of assured conviction of understanding, and that they may become progressively [s]more intimately acquainted with, *and* may know more definitely *and* accurately *and* thoroughly, that mystic secret of God [which is] Christ, the Anointed One.

3 In Him all the treasures of [divine] wisdom, [of [q]comprehensive insight into the ways and purposes of God], and [all the riches of spiritual] knowledge *and* enlightenment are stored up *and* lie hidden.

4 I say this in order that no one may mislead *and* delude you by plausible *and* persuasive *and* attractive arguments *and* beguiling speech.

5 For though I am away from you in body, yet I am with you in spirit, delighted at the sight of your [standing shoulder to shoulder in such] orderly array and the firmness *and* the solid front *and* steadfastness of your faith in Christ, [that [t]leaning of the entire human personality on Him in absolute trust and confidence in His power, wisdom and goodness].

6 As you have therefore received the Christ, [even] Jesus the Lord, [so] walk—regulate your lives *and* conduct yourselves—in union with *and* conformity to Him.

7 Have the roots [of your being] firmly *and* deeply planted [in Him]—fixed and founded in Him—being continually built up in Him, becoming increasingly more confirmed *and* established in the faith, just as you were taught, and abounding *and* overflowing in it with thanksgiving.

8 See to it that no one carries you off as spoil *or* makes you yourselves captive by his so-called philosophy *and* intellectualism, and vain deceit (idle fancies and plain nonsense), following human tradition—men's ideas of the material [rather than the spiritual] world—just crude notions following the rudimentary *and* elemental teachings of the universe, and disregarding [the teachings of] Christ, the Messiah.

9 For in Him the whole fullness of Deity (the Godhead), continues to dwell in bodily form—giving complete expression of the divine nature.

---

q) Souter.
r) Vincent.
s) Trench.
t) Souter's "Pocket Lexicon to the New Testament."

Living New Testament

28 So everywhere we go we talk about Christ to all who will listen, warning them and teaching them as well as we know how. We want to be able to present each one to God, perfect because of what Christ has done for each of them.

29 This is my work, and I can do it only because Christ's mighty energy is at work within me.

Revised Standard

chose to make known how great among the
Gentiles are the riches of the glory of this
mystery, which is Christ in you, the hope of
glory. [28]Him we proclaim, warning every
man and teaching every man in all wisdom,
that we may present every man mature in
Christ. [29]For this I toil, striving with all the
energy which he mightily inspires within me.

CHAPTER 2

I wish you could know how much I have struggled in prayer for you and for the church at Laodicea, and for my many other friends who have never known me personally.

2 This is what I have asked of God for you: that you will be encouraged and knit together by strong ties of love, and that you will have the rich experience of knowing Christ with real certainty and clear understanding. *For God's secret plan, now at last made known, is Christ Himself.*

3 In Him lie hidden all the mighty, untapped treasures of wisdom and knowledge.

4 I am saying this because I am afraid that someone may fool you with smooth talk.

5 For though I am far away from you my heart is with you, happy because you are getting along so well, happy because of your strong faith in Christ.

6 And now just as you trusted Christ to save you, trust Him, too, for each day's problems; live in vital union with Him.

7 Let your roots grow down into Him and draw up nourishment from Him. See that you go on growing in the Lord, and become strong and vigorous in the truth. Let your lives overflow with joy and thanksgiving for all He has done.

8 Don't let others spoil your faith and joy with their philosophies, their wrong and shallow answers built on men's thoughts and ideas, instead of on what Christ has said.

9 For in Christ there is all of God in a human body;

2 For I want you to know how greatly I
strive for you, and for those at Laodicea,
and for all who have not seen my face, [2]that
their hearts may be encouraged as they are
knit together in love, to have all the riches
of assured understanding and the knowledge
of God's mystery, of Christ, [3]in whom are
hid all the treasures of wisdom and knowledge. [4]I say this in order that no one may
delude you with beguiling speech. [5]For
though I am absent in body, yet I am with
you in spirit, rejoicing to see your good order
and the firmness of your faith in Christ.
6 As therefore you received Christ Jesus
the Lord, so live in him, [7]rooted and built
up in him and established in the faith, just
as you were taught, abounding in thanksgiving.

The sufficiency of Christ

8 See to it that no one makes a prey of
you by philosophy and empty deceit, according to human tradition, according to the elemental spirits of the universe, and not according to Christ. [9]For in him the whole
fulness of deity dwells bodily, [10]and you

King James

10 And ye are complete in him, which is the head of all principality and power:

11 In whom also ye are circumcised with the circumcision made without hands, in putting off the body of the sins of the flesh by the circumcision of Christ:

12 Buried with him in baptism, wherein also ye are risen with *him* through the faith of the operation of God, who hath raised him from the dead.

13 And you, being dead in your sins and the uncircumcision of your flesh, hath he quickened together with him, having forgiven you all trespasses;

14 Blotting out the handwriting of ordinances that was against us, which was contrary to us, and took it out of the way, nailing it to his cross;

15 *And* having spoiled principalities and powers, he made a shew of them openly, triumphing over them in it.

16 Let no man therefore judge you in meat, or in drink, or in respect of an holyday, or of the new moon, or of the sabbath *days:*

17 Which are a shadow of things to come; but the body *is* of Christ.

18 Let no man beguile you of your reward in a voluntary humility and worshipping of angels, intruding into those things which he hath not seen, vainly puffed up by his fleshly mind,

19 And not holding the Head, from which all the body by joints and bands having nourishment ministered, and knit together, increaseth with the increase of God.

20 Wherefore if ye be dead with Christ from the rudiments of the world, why, as though living in the world, are ye subject to ordinances,

21 (Touch not; taste not; handle not;

22 Which all are to perish with the using;) after the commandments and doctrines of men?

23 Which things have indeed a shew of wisdom in will-worship, and humility, and neglecting of the body; not in any honour to the satisfying of the flesh.

Amplified

10 And you [u]are in Him, made full *and* have come to fullness of life—in Christ you too are filled with the Godhead: Father, Son and Holy Spirit, and reach full spiritual stature. And He is the Head of all rule and authority—of every angelic principality and power.

11 In Him also you were circumcised with a circumcision not made with hands, but in a [spiritual] circumcision [performed by] Christ by stripping off the body of the flesh [the whole corrupt, carnal nature with its passions and lusts].

12 [Thus [v]you were circumcised when] you were buried with Him in [your] baptism, in which you were also raised with Him [[u]to a new life] through [your] faith in the working of God [[u]as displayed] when He raised Him up from the dead.

13 And you, who were dead in trespasses and in the uncircumcision of your flesh—your sensuality, your sinful carnal nature—[God] brought to life together with [Christ], having (freely) forgiven us all our transgressions;

14 Having cancelled *and* blotted out *and* wiped away the handwriting of the note (or bond) with its legal decrees *and* demands, which was in force *and* stood against us—hostile to us. This [note with its regulations, decrees and demands] He set aside *and* cleared [u]completely out of our way by nailing it to [His] cross.

15 [God] disarmed the principalities and powers ranged against us and made a bold display *and* public example of them, in triumphing over them in Him *and* [w]in it [the cross].

16 Therefore let no one sit in judgment on you in matters of food and drink, or with regard to a feast day or a new moon or a Sabbath.

17 Such [things] are only the shadow of things that are to come, *and* they have only a symbolic value. But the reality—the substance, the solid fact of what is foreshadowed, the body of it— belongs to Christ.

18 Let no one defraud you by acting as an umpire *and* declaring you unworthy *and* disqualifying you for the prize, insisting on self-abasement and worship of angels, taking his stand on visions [he claims] he has seen, vainly puffed up by his sensuous notions *and* inflated by his unspiritual thoughts *and* fleshly conceit,

19 And not holding fast to the Head, from Whom the entire body, supplied and knit together by means of its joints and ligaments, grows with a growth that is from God.

20 If then you have died with Christ to material ways of looking at things *and* have escaped from the world's crude *and* elemental notions *and* teachings of externalism, why do you live as if you still belong to the world?—Why do you submit to rules *and* regulations? [such as],

21 Do not handle [this], Do not taste [that], Do not even touch [them],

22 Referring to things all of which perish with being used. To do this is to follow human precepts and doctrines. [Isa. 29:13.]

23 Such [practices] have indeed the outward appearance [that popularly passes] for wisdom, in promoting self-imposed rigor of devotion *and* delight in self-humiliation *and* severity of discipline of the body, but they are of no value in checking the indulgence of the flesh—the lower nature. [Instead, they do not honor God] but [x]serve only to indulge the flesh.

---

u) Vincent's "Word Studies in the New Testament."
v) "The aorist tense puts the burial as contemporaneous with the circumcision" (Vincent).
w) Alternate reading, "in it [the cross]."
x) Alternate reading.

Living New Testament

10 *So you have everything when you have Christ,* and you are filled with God through your union with Christ. He is the highest ruler, with authority over every other power.

* * * * *

11 When you came to Christ He set you free from your evil desires, not by a bodily operation of circumcision but by a spiritual operation, the baptism of your souls.

12 For in baptism you see how your old, evil nature died with Him and was buried with Him; and then you came up out of death with Him into a new life because you trusted the Word of the mighty God who raised Christ from the dead.

13 You were dead in sins, and your sinful desires were not yet cut away. Then He gave you a share in the very life of Christ, for He forgave all your sins,

14 And blotted out the charges proved against you, the list of His commandments which you had not obeyed. He took this list of sins and destroyed it by nailing it to Christ's cross.

15 In this way God took away Satan's power to accuse you of sin, and God openly displayed to the whole world Christ's triumph at the cross where your sins were all taken away.

16 So don't let anyone criticize you for what you eat or drink, or for not celebrating Jewish holidays and feasts or new moon ceremonies or Sabbaths.

17 For these were only temporary rules that ended when Christ came. They were only shadows of the real thing—of Christ Himself.

18 Don't let anyone declare you lost when you refuse to worship angels, as they say you must. They have seen a vision, they say, and know you should. These proud men have a very clever imagination.

19 But they are not connected to Christ, the Head to which all of us who are His body are joined; for we are joined together by His strong sinews and we grow only as we get our nourishment and strength from Him.

20 Since you died, as it were, with Christ and this has set you free from following the world's ideas of how to be saved—by doing good and obeying various rules[1]—why do you keep right on following it anyway, still bound by such rules as

21 Not eating, tasting, or even touching certain foods?

22 Such rules are mere human teachings, for food was made to be eaten and used up.

23 These rules may seem good, for rules of this kind require strong devotion and are humiliating and hard on the body, but they have no effect when it comes to conquering a person's evil thoughts and desires. They only make him proud.

[1] Literally: "If you died with Christ from the rudiments of the world."

Revised Standard

have come to fulness of life in him, who
is the head of all rule and authority. [11]In
him also you were circumcised with a circumcision made without hands, by putting
off the body of flesh in the circumcision of
Christ; [12]and you were buried with him in
baptism, in which you were also raised with
him through faith in the working of God,
who raised him from the dead. [13]And you,
who were dead in trespasses and the uncircumcision of your flesh, God made alive together with him, having forgiven us all our
trespasses, [14]having canceled the bond which
stood against us with its legal demands; this
he set aside, nailing it to the cross. [15]He disarmed the principalities and powers and made
a public example of them, triumphing over
them in him.[d]

Regulations and rituals condemned

16 Therefore let no one pass judgment on
you in questions of food and drink or with
regard to a festival or a new moon or a sabbath. [17]These are only a shadow of what is
to come; but the substance belongs to Christ.
[18]Let no one disqualify you, insisting on self-
abasement and worship of angels, taking his
stand on visions, puffed up without reason
by his sensuous mind, [19]and not holding fast
to the Head, from whom the whole body,
nourished and knit together through its joints
and ligaments, grows with a growth that is
from God.

20 If with Christ you died to the elemental spirits of the universe, why do you
live as if you still belonged to the world?
Why do you submit to regulations, [21]"Do
not handle, Do not taste, Do not touch"
[22](referring to things which all perish as they
are used), according to human precepts and
doctrines? [23]These have indeed an appearance of wisdom in promoting rigor of devotion and self-abasement and severity to the
body, but they are of no value in checking
the indulgence of the flesh.[e]

[d] Or *in it* (that is, the cross)
[e] Or *are of no value, serving only to indulge the flesh*

King James

CHAPTER 3

IF ye then be risen with Christ, seek those things which are above, where Christ sitteth on the right hand of God.

2 Set your affection on things above, not on things on the earth.

3 For ye are dead, and your life is hid with Christ in God.

4 When Christ, *who is* our life, shall appear, then shall ye also appear with him in glory.

5 Mortify therefore your members which are upon the earth; fornication, uncleanness, inordinate affection, evil concupisence, and covetousness, which is idolatry:

6 For which things' sake the wrath of God cometh on the children of disobedience:

7 In the which ye also walked some time, when ye lived in them.

8 But now ye also put off all these; anger, wrath, malice, blasphemy, filthy communication out of your mouth.

9 Lie not one to another, seeing that ye have put off the old man with his deeds;

10 And have put on the new *man,* which is renewed in knowledge after the image of him that created him:

11 Where there is neither Greek nor Jew, circumcision nor uncircumcision, Barbarian, Scythian, bond *nor* free: but Christ *is* all, and in all.

12 Put on therefore, as the elect of God, holy and beloved, bowels of mercies, kindness, humbleness of mind, meekness, longsuffering;

13 Forbearing one another, and forgiving one another, if any man have a quarrel against any: even as Christ forgave you, so also *do* ye.

14 And above all these things *put on* charity, which is the bond of perfectness.

15 And let the peace of God rule in your hearts, to the which also ye are called in one body; and be ye thankful.

16 Let the word of Christ dwell in you richly in all wisdom; teaching and admonishing one another in psalms and hymns and spiritual songs, singing with grace in your hearts to the Lord.

Amplified

CHAPTER 3

IF then you have been raised with Christ [to a new life, thus sharing His resurrection from the dead], aim at *and* seek the [rich, eternal treasures] that are above, where Christ is, seated at the right hand of God. [Ps. 110:1.]

2 And set your minds *and* keep them set on what is above—the higher things—not on the things that are on the earth.

3 For [as far as this world is concerned] you have died, and your [new, real] life is hid with Christ in God.

4 When Christ Who is our life appears, then you also will appear with Him in (the splendor of His) glory.

5 So kill (deaden, [y]deprive of power) the evil desire lurking in your members—those animal impulses and all that is earthly in you that is employed in sin: sexual vice, impurity, sensual appetites, unholy desires, and all greed *and* covetousness, for that is idolatry [the deifying of self and other created things instead of God].

6 It is on account of these [very sins] that the [holy] anger of God is ever coming upon (those who are obstinately opposed to the divine will) the sons of disobedience,

7 Among whom you also once walked, when you were living in *and* addicted to [such practices].

8 But now put away *and* rid yourselves [completely] of all these things: anger, rage, bad feeling toward others, curses *and* slander and foulmouthed abuse *and* shameful utterances from your lips!

9 Do not lie to one another, for you have stripped off the old (unregenerate) self with its evil practices,

10 And have clothed yourselves with the new [spiritual self], which is (ever in the process of being) renewed *and* remoulded into (fuller and more perfect [z]knowledge upon) knowledge, after the image (the likeness) of Him Who created it. [Gen. 1:26.]

11 [In this new creation all distinctions vanish]; there [a]is no room for *and* there can be neither Greek nor Jew, circumcised nor uncircumcised, [nor difference between nations whether alien] barbarians or Scythians [[a]who are the most savage of all], nor slave or free man; but Christ is all and in all—[b]everything and everywhere, to all men, without distinction of person.

12 Clothe yourselves therefore, as (God's own picked representatives,) His own chosen ones, [who are] purified *and* holy and well-beloved [by God Himself, by putting on behavior marked by] tenderhearted pity *and* mercy, kind feeling, a lowly opinion of yourselves, gentle ways, [and] patience—which is tireless, long-suffering and has the power to endure whatever comes, with good temper.

13 Be gentle *and* forbearing with one another and, if one has a difference (a grievance or complaint) against another, readily pardoning each other; even as the Lord has freely forgiven you, so must you also [forgive].

14 And above all these [put on] love *and* enfold yourselves with the bond of perfectness—which binds everything together completely in ideal harmony.

15 And let the peace (soul harmony which comes) from the Christ rule (act as umpire continually) in your hearts—deciding and settling with finality all questions that arise in your minds—[in that peaceful state] to which [as members of Christ's] one body you were also called [to live]. And be thankful—appreciative, giving praise to Go always.

16 Let the word [spoken by] the Christ, the Messiah have its home (in your hearts and minds) *and* dwell i you in [all its] richness, as you teach and admonish *an* train one another in all insight *and* intelligence *and* wis

---

y) Thayer.
z) Literal translation.
a) Vincent.
b) Gray and Adams' Commentary.

Living New Testament

CHAPTER 3

Since you became alive again, so to speak, when Christ arose from the dead, now set your sights on the rich treasures and joys of heaven where He sits beside God in the place of honor and power.

2 Let heaven fill your thoughts; don't spend your time worrying about things down here.

3 You should have as little desire for this world as a dead person does. Your real life is in heaven with Christ and God.

4 And when Christ who is our real life comes back again, you will shine with Him and share in all His glories.

5 Away then with sinful, earthly things; deaden the evil desires lurking within you; have nothing to do with sexual sin, impurity, lust and shameful desires; don't worship the good things of this life, for that is idolatry.

6 God's terrible anger is upon those who do such things.

7 You used to do them when your life was still part of this world;

8 But now is the time to cast off and throw away all these rotten garments of anger, hatred, cursing and dirty language.

9 Don't tell lies to each other; it was your old life with all its wickedness that did that sort of thing; now it is dead and gone.

10 You are living a brand new kind of life that is continually learning more and more of what is right, and trying constantly to be more and more like Christ who created this new life within you.

11 In this new life one's nationality or race or education or social position is unimportant; such things mean nothing. Whether a person has Christ is what matters, and He is equally available to all.

12 Since you have been chosen by God who has given you this new kind of life, and because of His deep love and concern for you, you should practice tenderhearted mercy and kindness to others. Don't worry about making a good impression on them but be ready to suffer quietly and patiently.

13 Be gentle and ready to forgive; never hold grudges. Remember, the Lord forgave you, so you must forgive others.

14 Most of all, let love guide your life for then the whole church will stay together in perfect harmony.

15 Let the peace of heart which comes from Christ be always present in your hearts and lives, for this is your responsibility and privilege as members of His body. And always be thankful.

16 Remember what Christ taught and let His words enrich your lives and make you wise; teach them to each other and sing them out in psalms and hymns and spiritual songs, singing to the Lord with thankful hearts.

Revised Standard

The true center of Christian life

3 If then you have been raised with Christ,
seek the things that are above, where
Christ is, seated at the right hand of God.
[2]Set your minds on things that are above,
not on things that are on earth. [3]For you
have died, and your life is hid with Christ
in God. [4]When Christ who is our life appears, then you also will appear with him in
glory.
5 Put to death therefore what is earthly
in you: immorality, impurity, passion, evil
desire, and covetousness, which is idolatry.
[6]On account of these the wrath of God is
coming.[f] [7]In these you once walked, when
you lived in them. [8]But now put them all
away: anger, wrath, malice, slander, and
foul talk from your mouth. [9]Do not lie to
one another, seeing that you have put off
the old nature with its practices [10]and have
put on the new nature, which is being renewed in knowledge after the image of its
creator. [11]Here there cannot be Greek and
Jew, circumcised and uncircumcised, barbarian, Scythian, slave, free man, but Christ
is all, and in all.
12 Put on then, as God's chosen ones,
holy and beloved, compassion, kindness, lowliness, meekness, and patience, [13]forbearing
one another and, if one has a complaint
against another, forgiving each other; as the
Lord has forgiven you, so you also must forgive. [14]And above all these put on love,
which binds everything together in perfect
harmony. [15]And let the peace of Christ rule
in your hearts, to which indeed you were
called in the one body. And be thankful.
[16]Let the word of Christ dwell in you richly,
as you teach and admonish one another in
all wisdom, and as you sing psalms and
hymns and spiritual songs with thankfulness

[f] Other ancient authorities add *upon the sons of disobedience*

King James

17 And whatsoever ye do in word or deed, *do* all in the name of the Lord Jesus, giving thanks to God and the Father by him.
18 Wives, submit yourselves unto your own husbands, as it is fit in the Lord.
19 Husbands, love *your* wives, and be not bitter against them.
20 Children, obey *your* parents in all things: for this is well pleasing unto the Lord.
21 Fathers, provoke not your children *to anger,* lest they be discouraged.
22 Servants, obey in all things *your* masters according to the flesh; not with eye-service, as men-pleasers; but in singleness of heart, fearing God:
23 And whatsoever ye do, do *it* heartily, as to the Lord, and not unto men;
24 Knowing that of the Lord ye shall receive the reward of the inheritance: for ye serve the Lord Christ.
25 But he that doeth wrong shall receive for the wrong which he hath done: and there is no respect of persons.

Amplified

dom [in spiritual things, and sing] psalms and hymns and spiritual songs, making melody to God with [His] grace in your hearts.
17 And whatever you do—no matter what it is—in word or deed, do everything in the name of the Lord Jesus *and* in [dependence upon] His Person, giving praise to God the Father through Him.
18 Wives, be subject to your husbands—subordinate and adapt yourselves to them—as is right *and* fitting *and* your proper duty in the Lord.
19 Husbands, love your wives—be affectionate and sympathetic with them—and do not be harsh *or* bitter *or* resentful toward them.
20 Children, obey your parents in everything, for this is well-pleasing to the Lord.
21 Fathers, do not provoke *or* irritate *or* fret your children—do not be hard on them or harass them; lest they become discouraged *and* sullen *and* morose *and* feel inferior *and* frustrated; do not break their spirit.
22 Servants, obey in everything those who are your earthly masters, not only when their eyes are on you, as pleasers of men, but in simplicity of purpose (with all your heart) because of your reverence for the Lord *and* as a sincere expression of your devotion to Him.
23 Whatever may be your task, work at it heartily (from the soul), as [something done] for the Lord and not for men,
24 Knowing (with all certainty) that it is from the Lord [and not from men] that you will receive the inheritance which is your (real) reward. [The One Whom] you are actually serving [is] the Lord Christ, the Messiah.
25 For he who deals wrongfully will [reap the fruit of his folly and] be punished for his wrongdoing. And [with God] there is no partiality [no matter what a person's position may be, whether he is the slave or the master].

King James — CHAPTER 4

MASTERS, give unto *your* servants that which is just and equal; knowing that ye also have a Master in heaven.
2 Continue in prayer, and watch in the same with thanksgiving;
3 Withal praying also for us, that God would open unto us a door of utterance, to speak the mystery of Christ, for which I am also in bonds:
4 That I may make it manifest, as I ought to speak.
5 Walk in wisdom toward them that are without, redeeming the time.
6 Let your speech *be* alway with grace, seasoned with salt, that ye may know how ye ought to answer every man.
7 All my state shall Tychicus declare unto you, *who is* a beloved brother, and a faithful minister and fellow-servant in the Lord:
8 Whom I have sent unto you for the same purpose, that he might know your estate, and comfort your hearts;

Amplified — CHAPTER 4

MASTERS, [on your part] deal with your slaves justly and fairly, knowing that also you have a Master in heaven. [Lev. 25:43, 53.]
2 Be earnest *and* unwearied *and* steadfast in your prayer [life], being [both] alert *and* intent in [your praying] with thanksgiving.
3 And at the same time pray for us also, that God may open a door to us for the Word (the Gospel), to proclaim the mystery concerning Christ, the Messiah, on account of which I am in prison;
4 That I may (speak boldly and unfold that mystery,) proclaim it fully *and* make it clear, as is my duty.
5 Behave yourselves wisely—living prudently and with discretion—in your relations with those of the outside world (the non-Christians), making the very most of the time *and* seizing (buying up) the opportunity.
6 Let your speech at all times be gracious (pleasant and winsome), seasoned [as it were] with salt, [so that you may never be at a loss] to know how you ought to answer any one [who puts a question to you].
7 Tychicus will give you full information about my affairs; [he is] a much-loved brother and faithful ministering assistant and fellow servant [with us] in the Lord.
8 I have sent him to you for this very purpose, that you may know how we are faring and that he may comfort *and* cheer *and* encourage your hearts.

Living New Testament

17 And whatever you do or say, let it be as a representative of the Lord Jesus, and come with Him into the presence of God the Father to give Him your thanks.

18 You wives, submit yourselves to your husbands, for that is what the Lord has planned for you.

19 And you husbands must be loving and kind to your wives and not bitter against them, nor harsh.

20 You children must always obey your fathers and mothers, for that pleases the Lord.

21 Fathers, don't scold your children so much that they become discouraged and quit trying.

22 You slaves must always obey your earthly masters, not only trying to please them when they are watching you but all the time; obey them willingly because of your love for the Lord and because you want to please Him.

23 Work hard and cheerfully at all you do, just as though you were working for the Lord and not merely for your masters,

24 Remembering that it is the Lord Christ who is going to pay you, giving you your full portion of all He owns. He is the one you are really working for.

25 And if you don't do your best for Him, He will pay you in a way that you won't like—for He has no special favorites who can get away with shirking.

Revised Standard

in your hearts to God. 17And whatever you
do, in word or deed, do everything in the
name of the Lord Jesus, giving thanks to
God the Father through him.

The Christian family

18 Wives, be subject to your husbands, as
is fitting in the Lord. 19Husbands, love your
wives, and do not be harsh with them.
20Children, obey your parents in everything,
for this pleases the Lord. 21Fathers, do not
provoke your children, lest they become discouraged. 22Slaves, obey in everything those
who are your earthly masters, not with eye-
service, as men-pleasers, but in singleness of
heart, fearing the Lord. 23Whatever your
task, work heartily, as serving the Lord and
not men, 24knowing that from the Lord you
will receive the inheritance as your reward;
you are serving the Lord Christ. 25For the
wrongdoer will be paid back for the wrong
he has done, and there is no partiality.

CHAPTER 4

You slave owners must be just and fair to all your slaves. Always remember that you too have a Master in heaven who is closely watching you.

* * * * *

2 Don't be weary in prayer; keep at it; watch for God's answers and remember to be thankful when they come.

3 Don't forget to pray for us too, that God will give us many chances to preach the Good News of Christ for which I am here in jail.

4 Pray that I will be bold enough to tell it freely and fully, and make it plain, as, of course, I should.

5 Make the most of your chances to tell others the Good News. Be wise in all your contacts with them.

6 Let your conversation be gracious as well as sensible, for then you will have the right answer for everyone.

* * * * *

7 Tychicus, our much loved brother, will tell you how I am getting along. He is a hard worker and serves the Lord with me.

8 I have sent him on this special trip just to see how you are, and to comfort and encourage you.

4 Masters, treat your slaves justly and
fairly, knowing that you also have a
Master in heaven.

2 Continue steadfastly in prayer, being
watchful in it with thanksgiving; 3and pray
for us also, that God may open to us a door
for the word, to declare the mystery of
Christ, on account of which I am in prison,
4that I may make it clear, as I ought to
speak.

5 Conduct yourselves wisely toward outsiders, making the most of the time. 6Let
your speech always be gracious, seasoned
with salt, so that you may know how you
ought to answer every one.

Introduction of Tychicus and Onesimus

7 Tychicus will tell you all about my affairs; he is a beloved brother and faithful
minister and fellow servant in the Lord. 8I
have sent him to you for this very purpose,
that you may know how we are and that he

King James

9 With Onesimus, a faithful and beloved brother, who is *one* of you. They shall make known unto you all things which *are done* here.

10 Aristarchus my fellow-prisoner saluteth you, and Marcus, sister's son to Barnabas, (touching whom ye received commandments: if he come unto you, receive him;)

11 And Jesus, which is called Justus, who are of the circumcision. These only *are my* fellow-workers unto the kingdom of God, which have been a comfort unto me.

12 Epaphras, who is *one* of you, a servant of Christ, saluteth you, always labouring fervently for you in prayers, that ye may stand perfect and complete in all the will of God.

13 For I bear him record, that he hath a great zeal for you, and them *that are* in Laodicea, and them in Hierapolis.

14 Luke, the beloved physician, and Demas, greet you.

15 Salute the brethren which are in Laodicea, and Nymphas, and the church which is in his house.

16 And when this epistle is read among you, cause that it be read also in the church of the Laodiceans; and that ye likewise read the *epistle* from Laodicea.

17 And say to Archippus, Take heed to the ministry which thou hast received in the Lord, that thou fulfil it.

18 The salutation by the hand of me Paul. Remember my bonds. Grace *be* with you. Amen.

¶ Written from Rome to the Colossians by Tychicus and Onesimus.

Amplified

9 And with [him is] Onesimus, [our] faithful and beloved brother, who is [one] of yourselves. They will let you know everything that has taken place here [in Rome].

10 Aristarchus my fellow prisoner wishes to be remembered to you, as does Mark the relative of Barnabas. You received instructions concerning him; if he comes to you give him a ([c]hearty) welcome.

11 And [greetings also from] Jesus who is called Justus. These [Hebrew Christians] alone of the circumcision are among my fellow workers for [the extension of] God's kingdom, and they have proved a relief *and* a comfort to me.

12 Epaphras, who is one of yourselves, a servant of Christ Jesus, sends you greetings. [He is] always striving for you earnestly in his prayers, [pleading] that you may—as persons of ripe character and clear conviction—stand firm *and* mature (in spiritual growth), convinced *and* fully assured in [d]everything willed by God.

13 For I bear him testimony that he has labored hard in your behalf and for [the believers] in Laodicea and those in Hierapolis.

14 Luke the beloved physician and Demas salute you.

15 Give my greetings to the brethren at Laodicea, and to Nympha and the assembly [the church] which meets in her house.

16 And when this epistle has been read before you, [see] that it is read also in the assembly [the church] of the Laodiceans; and also [see] that you yourselves in turn read the [letter that comes to you] from Laodicea.

17 And say to Archippus, See that you discharge carefully [the duties of] the ministry *and* fulfill the stewardship which you have received in the Lord.

18 I, Paul, [add this final] greeting, writing with my own hand. Remember I am still in prison *and* in chains. May grace (God's unmerited favor and blessing) be with you! *Amen, so be it.*

---

c) Williams: "A very strong verb, so *give him a hearty welcome.*"
d) Vincent.

Living New Testament

9 I am also sending Onesimus, a faithful and much loved brother, one of your own people. He and Tychicus will give you all the latest news.

10 Aristarchus, who is with me here as a prisoner, sends you his love, and so does Mark, a relative of Barnabas. And as I said before, give Barnabas a hearty welcome if he comes your way.

11 Jesus Justus also sends his love. These are the only Jewish Christians working with me here, and what a comfort they have been!

12 Epaphras, from your city, a servant of Christ Jesus, sends you his love. He is always earnestly praying for you, asking God to make you strong and perfect and to help you know His will in everything you do.

13 I can assure you that he has worked hard for you with his prayers, and also for the Christians in Laodicea and Hierapolis.

14 Dear doctor Luke sends his love, and so does Demas.

15 Please give my greeting to the Christian friends at Laodicea, and to Nymphas, and to those who meet in his home.

16 By the way, after you have read this letter will you pass it on to the church at Laodicea? And read the letter I wrote to them.

17 And say to Archippus, "Be sure that you do all the Lord has told you to."

18 Here is my own greeting in my own handwriting: Remember me here in jail. May God's blessings surround you.

Sincerely,
Paul

Revised Standard

may encourage your hearts, [9]and with him
Onesimus, the faithful and beloved brother,
who is one of yourselves. They will tell you
of everything that has taken place here.

Greetings and final instructions

10 Aristarchus my fellow prisoner greets
you, and Mark the cousin of Barnabas (concerning whom you have received instructions
—if he comes to you, receive him), [11]and
Jesus who is called Justus. These are the only
men of the circumcision among my fellow
workers for the kingdom of God, and they
have been a comfort to me. [12]Epaphras,
who is one of yourselves, a servant[g] of Christ
Jesus, greets you, always remembering you
earnestly in his prayers, that you may stand
mature and fully assured in all the will of
God. [13]For I bear him witness that he has
worked hard for you and for those in Laodicea and in Hierapolis. [14]Luke the beloved
physician and Demas greet you. [15]Give my
greetings to the brethren at Laodicea, and
to Nympha and the church in her house.
[16]And when this letter has been read among
you, have it read also in the church of the
Laodiceans; and see that you read also the
letter from Laodicea. [17]And say to Archippus, "See that you fulfil the ministry which
you have received in the Lord."

18 I, Paul, write this greeting with my own hand. Remember my fetters. Grace be with you.

[g] Or *slave*

King James

THE FIRST EPISTLE OF PAUL THE APOSTLE
TO THE

Thessalonians

CHAPTER 1

PAUL, and Silvanus, and Timotheus,
unto the church of the Thessalonians
which is in God the Father and *in* the Lord
Jesus Christ: Grace *be* unto you, and peace,
from God our Father, and the Lord Jesus
Christ.
2 We give thanks to God always for you
all, making mention of you in our prayers;
3 Remembering without ceasing your
work of faith, and labour of love, and patience of hope in our Lord Jesus Christ, in
the sight of God and our Father;
4 Knowing, brethren beloved, your election of God.
5 For our gospel came not unto you in
word only, but also in power, and in the
Holy Ghost, and in much assurance; as ye
know what manner of men we were among
you for your sake.
6 And ye became followers of us, and of
the Lord, having received the word in much
affliction, with joy of the Holy Ghost:
7 So that ye were ensamples to all that
believe in Macedonia and Achaia.
8 For from you sounded out the word of
the Lord not only in Macedonia and
Achaia, but also in every place your faith to
God-ward is spread abroad; so that we need
not to speak any thing.
9 For they themselves shew of us what
manner of entering in we had unto you, and
how ye turned to God from idols to serve
the living and true God;
10 And to wait for his Son from heaven,
whom he raised from the dead, *even* Jesus,
which delivered us from the wrath to come.

CHAPTER 2

FOR yourselves, brethren, know our entrance in unto you, that it was not in
vain:
2 But even after that we had suffered
before, and were shamefully entreated, as ye
know, at Philippi, we were bold in our God
to speak unto you the gospel of God with
much contention.

Amplified

THE FIRST LETTER OF PAUL
TO THE

Thessalonians

CHAPTER 1

PAUL, Silvanus (Silas) and Timothy to the assembly
(church) of the Thessalonians in God the Father and
the Lord Jesus Christ, the Messiah: Grace (spiritual blessing and divine favor) to you and heart peace.
2 We are ever giving thanks to God for all of you,
continually mentioning [you when engaged] in our prayers,
3 Recalling unceasingly before our God and Father
your work energized by faith and service motivated by
love, and unwavering hope in (the return of) our Lord
Jesus Christ, the Messiah. [1:10.]
4 [O] brethren beloved by God, we recognize *and* know
that He has selected (chosen) you;
5 For our [preaching of the] glad tidings (the Gospel)
came to you not only in word, but also in (its own
inherent) power and in the Holy Spirit, and with great
conviction *and* absolute certainty (on our part). You
know what kind of men we proved [ourselves] to be among
you for your good.
6 And you [set yourselves to] become imitators of us
and [through us] of the Lord Himself, for you welcomed
our message in [spite of the] much persecution, with joy
[inspired] of the Holy Spirit;
7 So that you [thus] became a pattern to all the believers—those who adhere to, trust in and rely on Christ
Jesus—in Macedonia and Achaia [most of Greece].
8 For not only has the Word concerning *and* from the
Lord resounded forth from you unmistakably in Macedonia and Achaia, but everywhere the report has gone forth
of your faith in God—of your [a]leaning of your whole
personality on Him in complete trust and confidence in
His power, wisdom and goodness. So we [find that we]
never need to tell people anything [further about it].
9 For they themselves volunteer testimony concerning us, telling what an entrance we had among you, and
how you turned to God from [your] idols to serve a God
Who is alive and true *and* genuine;
10 And [how you] look forward to *and* await the
coming of His Son from heaven, Whom He raised from
the dead, Jesus Who personally rescues *and* delivers us out
of *and* from the wrath (bringing punishment) which is
coming [upon the impenitent] *and* [b]draws us to Himself
[that is, [c]invests us with all the privileges and rewards of
the new life in Christ, the Messiah].

CHAPTER 2

FOR you yourselves know, brethren, that our coming
among you was not useless *and* fruitless.
2 But though we had already suffered and been
outrageously treated at Philippi, as you know, yet in [the
strength of] our God we summoned courage to proclaim
to you unfalteringly the good news (the Gospel) with
earnest contention, much conflict *and* great opposition.

---

a) Souter.
b) Literal meaning of the verb "to deliver."
c) Vincent.

Living New Testament

I Thessalonians

CHAPTER 1

From: Paul, Silas and Timothy.
To: The church of Thessalonica—to you who belong to God the Father and the Lord Jesus Christ: May blessing and peace of heart be your rich gifts from God our Father, and from Jesus Christ our Lord.

2 We always thank God for you and pray for you constantly.

3 We never forget your loving deeds as we talk to our God and Father about you, and your strong faith and steady looking forward to the return of our Lord Jesus Christ.

4 We know that God has chosen you, dear brothers, much beloved of God.

5 For when we brought you the Good News, it was not just meaningless chatter to you; no, you listened with great interest. What we told you produced a powerful effect upon you, for the Holy Spirit gave you great and full assurance that what we said was true. And you know how our very lives were further proof to you of the truth of our message.

6 So you became our followers and the Lord's; for you received our messages with joy from the Holy Spirit in spite of the trials and sorrows it brought you.

7 Then you yourselves became an example to all the other Christians in Macedonia and Achaia.

8 And now the Word of the Lord has spread out from you to others everywhere, far beyond the boundaries of Macedonia and Achaia, for wherever we go we find people telling us about your remarkable faith in God. We don't need to tell *them* about it,

9 For *they* keep telling *us* about the wonderful welcome you gave us, and how you turned away from your idols to God so that now the living and true God only is your master.

10 And they speak of how you are looking forward to the return of God's Son from heaven—Jesus, whom God brought back to life—and He is our only Savior from God's terrible anger against sin.

Revised Standard

THE FIRST LETTER OF PAUL TO THE

Thessalonians

Salutation and thanksgiving

1 Paul, Silvanus, and Timothy,
To the church of the Thessalonians in God the Father and the Lord Jesus Christ:
Grace to you and peace.

2 We give thanks to God always for
you all, constantly mentioning you in our
prayers, 3remembering before our God and
Father your work of faith and labor of love
and steadfastness of hope in our Lord Jesus
Christ. 4For we know, brethren beloved by
God, that he has chosen you; 5for our gospel
came to you not only in word, but also in
power and in the Holy Spirit and with full
conviction. You know what kind of men we
proved to be among you for your sake. 6And
you became imitators of us and of the Lord,
for you received the word in much affliction, with joy inspired by the Holy Spirit;
7so that you became an example to all the
believers in Macedonia and in Achaia. 8For
not only has the word of the Lord sounded
forth from you in Macedonia and Achaia,
but your faith in God has gone forth everywhere, so that we need not say anything.
9For they themselves report concerning us
what a welcome we had among you, and
how you turned to God from idols, to serve
a living and true God, 10and to wait for his
Son from heaven, whom he raised from the
dead, Jesus who delivers us from the wrath
to come.

CHAPTER 2

You yourselves know, dear brothers, how worthwhile that visit was.

2 You know how badly we had been treated at Philippi just before we came to you, and how much we suffered there. Yet God gave us the courage to boldly repeat the same message to you, even though we were surrounded by enemies.

Paul's work in Thessalonica

2 For you yourselves know, brethren, that
our visit to you was not in vain; 2but
though we had already suffered and been
shamefully treated at Philippi, as you know,
we had courage in our God to declare to you
the gospel of God in the face of great oppo-

King James

3 For our exhortation *was* not of deceit, nor of uncleanness, nor in guile:

4 But as we were allowed of God to be put in trust with the gospel, even so we speak; not as pleasing men, but God, which trieth our hearts.

5 For neither at any time used we flattering words, as ye know, nor a cloak of covetousness; God *is* witness:

6 Nor of men sought we glory, neither of you, nor *yet* of others, when we might have been burdensome, as the apostles of Christ.

7 But we were gentle among you, even as a nurse cherisheth her children:

8 So being affectionately desirous of you, we were willing to have imparted unto you, not the gospel of God only, but also our own souls, because ye were dear unto us.

9 For ye remember, brethren, our labour and travail: for labouring night and day, because we would not be chargeable unto any of you, we preached unto you the gospel of God.

10 Ye *are* witnesses, and God *also,* how holily and justly and unblameably we behaved ourselves among you that believe:

11 As ye know how we exhorted and comforted and charged every one of you, as a father *doth* his children,

12 That ye would walk worthy of God, who hath called you unto his kingdom and glory.

13 For this cause also thank we God without ceasing, because, when ye received the word of God which ye heard of us, ye received *it* not *as* the word of men, but as it is in truth, the word of God, which effectually worketh also in you that believe.

14 For ye, brethren, became followers of the churches of God which in Judaea are in Christ Jesus: for ye also have suffered like things of your own countrymen, even as they *have* of the Jews:

15 Who both killed the Lord Jesus, and their own prophets, and have persecuted us; and they please not God, and are contrary to all men:

16 Forbidding us to speak to the Gentiles that they might be saved, to fill up their sins alway: for the wrath is come upon them to the uttermost.

17 But we, brethren, being taken from you for a short time in presence, not in heart, endeavoured the more abundantly to see your face with great desire.

18 Wherefore we would have come unto you, even I Paul, once and again; but Satan hindered us.

19 For what *is* our hope, or joy, or crown of rejoicing? *Are* not even ye in the presence of our Lord Jesus Christ at his coming?

20 For ye are our glory and joy.

Amplified

3 For our appeal [in preaching] does not [originate] from delusion *or* error or impure purpose *or* motive, nor in fraud *or* deceit.

4 But just as we have been approved by God to be entrusted with the glad tidings (the Gospel), so we speak not to please men, but to please God, Who tests our hearts ([d]expecting them to be approved).

5 For, as you well know, we never resorted either to words of flattery or to any cloak to conceal greedy motives *or* pretexts for gain, [as] God is our witness.

6 Nor did we seek to extract praise *and* honor *and* glory from men, either from you or from any one else, though we might have asserted our authority (stood on our dignity and claimed honor) as apostles (special missionaries) of Christ, the Messiah.

7 But we behaved gently when we were among you, like a devoted mother nursing *and* cherishing her own children.

8 So, being thus tenderly *and* affectionately desirous of you, we continued to share with you not only God's good news (the Gospel) but also our own lives as well, for you had become so very dear to us.

9 For you recall our hard toil and struggles, brethren. We worked night and day [and plied our trade] in order not to be a burden to any of you [for our support] while we proclaimed the glad tidings (the Gospel) of God to you.

10 You are witnesses, [yes] and God [also], how unworldly and upright and blameless was our behavior toward you believers—who adhered to and trusted in and relied on our Lord Jesus Christ.

11 For you know how, like a father [dealing with] his children, we used to exhort each of you personally, stimulating *and* encouraging and charging you

12 To live lives worthy of God, Who calls you into His own kingdom and the glorious blessedness [[e]into which true believers will enter after Christ's return].

13 And we also [especially] thank God continually for this, that when you received the message of God [which you heard] from us, you welcomed it not as the word of [mere] men but as what it truly is, the Word of God, which is effectually at work in you who believe— [f]exercising its [superhuman] power in those who adhere to and trust in and rely on it.

14 For you, brethren, became imitators of the assemblies (churches) of God in Christ Jesus which are in Judea, for you too have suffered the same kind of treatment from your own fellow countrymen as they did [who were persecuted at the hands] of the Jews,

15 Who killed both the Lord Jesus and the prophets, and harassed *and* drove us out; and continue to make themselves hateful *and* offensive to God and to show themselves foes of all men,

16 Forbidding *and* hindering us from speaking to the Gentiles [the nations] that they may be saved. So as always they fill up (to the brim the measure of) their sins. But God's wrath has come upon them at last—completely and forever! [Gen. 15:16.]

17 But since we were bereft of you, brethren, for a little while in person, [of course] not in heart, we endeavored the more eagerly and with great longing to see you face to face,

18 Because it was our will to come to you. [I mean that] I, Paul, again and again [wanted to come], but Satan hindered *and* impeded us.

19 For what is our hope or happiness or our victor's wreath of exultant triumph when we stand in the presence of our Lord Jesus at His coming? Are not you?

20 For you are [indeed] our glory and our joy!

---

d) Abbott-Smith.
e) Thayer.
f) Vincent.

Living New Testament

3 So you can see that we were not preaching with any false motives or evil purposes in mind; we were perfectly straightforward and sincere.

4 For we speak as messengers from God, trusted by Him to tell the truth; we change His message not one bit to suit the taste of those who hear it; for we serve God alone, who examines our hearts' deepest thoughts.

5 Never once did we try to win you with flattery, as you very well know, and God knows we were not just pretending to be your friends so that you would give us money!

6 As for praise, we have never asked for it from you or anyone else, although as apostles of Christ we certainly had a right to some honor from you.

7 But we were as gentle among you as a mother feeding and caring for her own children.

8 We loved you dearly—so dearly that we gave you not only God's message, but our own lives too.

9 Don't you remember, dear brothers, how hard we worked among you? Night and day we toiled and sweated to earn enough to live on so that our expenses would not be a burden to anyone there, as we preached God's Good News among you.

10 You yourselves are our witnesses—as is God—that we have been pure and honest and faultless toward every one of you.

11 We talked to you as a father to his own children—don't you remember?—pleading with you, encouraging you and even demanding

12 That your daily lives should not embarrass God, but bring joy to Him who invited you into His kingdom to share His glory.

13 And we will never stop thanking God for this: that when we preached to you, you didn't think of the words we spoke as being just our own, but you accepted what we said as the very Word of God—which, of course, it was—and it changed your lives when you believed it.

14 And then, dear brothers, you suffered what the churches in Judea did, persecution from your own countrymen, just as they suffered from their own people the Jews.

15 After they had killed their own prophets, they even executed the Lord Jesus; and now they have brutally persecuted us and driven us out. They are against both God and man,

16 Trying to keep us from preaching to the Gentiles for fear some might be saved; and so their sins continue to grow. But the anger of God has caught up with them at last.

17 Dear brothers, after we left you and had been away from you but a very little while (though our hearts never left you), we tried hard to come back again to see you once more.

18 We wanted very much to come and I, Paul, tried again and again, but Satan stopped us.

19 For what is it we live for, that gives us hope and joy and is our proud reward and crown? It is you! Yes, you will bring us much joy as we stand together before our Lord Jesus Christ when He comes back again.

20 For you are our trophy and joy.

Revised Standard

sition. [3]For our appeal does not spring from
error or uncleanness, nor is it made with
guile; [4]but just as we have been approved by
God to be entrusted with the gospel, so we
speak, not to please men, but to please God
who tests our hearts. [5]For we never used
either words of flattery, as you know, or a
cloak for greed, as God is witness; [6]nor did
we seek glory from men, whether from you
or from others, though we might have made
demands as apostles of Christ. [7]But we were
gentle[a] among you, like a nurse taking care
of her children. [8]So, being affectionately desirous of you, we were ready to share with
you not only the gospel of God but also
our own selves, because you had become
very dear to us.

9 For you remember our labor and toil,
brethren; we worked night and day, that we
might not burden any of you, while we
preached to you the gospel of God. [10]You
are witnesses, and God also, how holy and
righteous and blameless was our behavior
to you believers; [11]for you know how, like
a father with his children, we exhorted each
one of you and encouraged you and charged
you [12]to lead a life worthy of God, who calls
you into his own kingdom and glory.

Paul's reception in Thessalonica

13 And we also thank God constantly for
this, that when you received the word of
God which you heard from us, you accepted
it not as the word of men but as what it
really is, the word of God, which is at work
in you believers. [14]For you, brethren, became
imitators of the churches of God in Christ
Jesus which are in Judea; for you suffered
the same things from your own countrymen
as they did from the Jews, [15]who killed both
the Lord Jesus and the prophets, and drove
us out, and displease God and oppose all
men [16]by hindering us from speaking to the
Gentiles that they may be saved—so as always to fill up the measure of their sins. But
God's wrath has come upon them at last![b]

17 But since we were bereft of you, brethren, for a short time, in person not in heart,
we endeavored the more eagerly and with
great desire to see you face to face; [18]because
we wanted to come to you—I, Paul, again
and again—but Satan hindered us. [19]For
what is our hope or joy or crown of boasting before our Lord Jesus at his coming? Is
it not you? [20]For you are our glory and joy.

---

[a] Other ancient authorities read *babes*
[b] Or *completely*, or *for ever*

King James

CHAPTER 3

WHEREFORE when we could no longer forbear, we thought it good to be left at Athens alone;

2 And sent Timotheus, our brother, and minister of God, and our fellow-labourer in the gospel of Christ, to establish you, and to comfort you concerning your faith:

3 That no man should be moved by these afflictions: for yourselves know that we are appointed thereunto.

4 For verily, when we were with you, we told you before that we should suffer tribulation; even as it came to pass, and ye know.

5 For this cause, when I could no longer forbear, I sent to know your faith, lest by some means the tempter have tempted you, and our labour be in vain.

6 But now when Timotheus came from you unto us, and brought us good tidings of your faith and charity, and that ye have good remembrance of us always, desiring greatly to see us, as we also *to see* you:

7 Therefore, brethren, we were comforted over you in all our affliction and distress by your faith:

8 For now we live, if ye stand fast in the Lord.

9 For what thanks can we render to God again for you, for all the joy wherewith we joy for your sakes before our God;

10 Night and day praying exceedingly that we might see your face, and might perfect that which is lacking in your faith?

11 Now God himself and our Father, and our Lord Jesus Christ, direct our way unto you.

12 And the Lord make you to increase and abound in love one toward another, and toward all *men*, even as we *do* toward you:

13 To the end he may stablish your hearts unblameable in holiness before God, even our Father, at the coming of our Lord Jesus Christ with all his saints.

Amplified

CHAPTER 3

THEREFORE when [the suspense of separation and our yearning for some personal communication from you] became intolerable, we consented to being left behind alone at Athens.

2 And we sent Timothy, our brother and God's servant in [spreading] the good news (the Gospel) of Christ, to strengthen *and* establish, exhort *and* comfort *and* encourage you in your faith,

3 That no one [of you] should be disturbed *and* beguiled *and* led astray by these afflictions *and* difficulties [to which I have referred]. For you yourselves know that this is [unavoidable in our position, and must be recognized as] our appointed lot.

4 For even when we were with you [you know] we warned you plainly beforehand that we were to be pressed with difficulties *and* made to suffer affliction, just as to your own knowledge has [since] happened.

5 That is the reason that, when I could bear [the suspense] no longer, I sent that I might learn [how you were standing the strain, and the endurance of] your faith, [for I was fearful] lest somehow the tempter had tempted you and our toil [among you should prove to] be fruitless *and* to no purpose.

6 But now that Timothy has just come back to us from [his visit to] you, and has brought us the good news of [the steadfastness of] your faith and [the warmth of your] love, and [reported] how kindly you cherish a constant *and* affectionate remembrance of us, [and that you are] longing to see us as we [are to see] you,

7 Brethren, for this reason, in [spite of all] our stress and crushing difficulties we have been filled with comfort *and* cheer about you [because of] your faith—[g]the leaning of your whole personality on God in complete trust and confidence.

8 Because now we [really] live, if you stand [firm] in the Lord.

9 For what [adequate] thanksgiving can we render to God for you, for all the gladness *and* delight which we enjoy for your sakes before our God?

10 [And we] continue to pray especially *and* with most intense earnestness night and day that we may see you face to face and mend *and* make good whatever may be imperfect *and* lacking in your faith.

11 Now may our God and Father Himself, and our Lord Jesus *Christ, the Messiah,* guide our steps to you.

12 And may the Lord make you to increase and excel *and* overflow in love for one another and for all people, just as we also do for you.

13 So that He may strengthen *and* confirm *and* establish your hearts faultlessly pure *and* unblamable in holiness in the sight of our God and Father, at the coming of our Lord Jesus *Christ, the Messiah,* with all His saints—the [h]holy and glorified people of God! *Amen, so be it!*

King James

CHAPTER 4

FURTHERMORE then we beseech you, brethren, and exhort *you* by the Lord Jesus, that as ye have received of us how ye ought to walk and to please God, *so* ye would abound more and more.

Amplified

CHAPTER 4

[h]FURTHERMORE, brethren, we beg and admonish you in [virtue of our union with] the Lord Jesus, that [you follow the instructions which] you learned from us about how you ought to walk so as to please *and* gratify God, as indeed you are doing; that you do so even more and more abundantly—attaining yet greater perfection in living this life.

---

g) Souter.
h) Vincent.

Living New Testament

CHAPTER 3

Finally, when I could stand it no longer, I decided to stay alone in Athens,

2, 3 And send Timothy, our brother and fellow worker, God's minister, to visit you to strengthen your faith and encourage you, and to keep you from becoming faint-hearted in all the troubles you were going through. (But of course you know that such troubles are a part of God's plan for us Christians.

4 Even while we were still with you we warned you ahead of time that suffering would soon come—and it did.)

5 As I was saying, when I could bear the suspense no longer I sent Timothy to find out whether your faith was still strong. I was afraid that perhaps Satan had gotten the best of you and that all our work had been useless.

6 And now Timothy has just returned and brings the welcome news that your faith and love are as strong as ever, and that you remember our visit with joy and want to see us just as much as we want to see you.

7 So we are greatly comforted, dear brothers, in all of our own crushing troubles and suffering here, now that we know you are standing true to the Lord.

8 We can bear anything as long as we know that you remain strong in Him.

9 How can we thank God enough for you and for the joy and delight you have given us in our praying for you?

10 For night and day we pray on and on for you, asking God to let us see you again, to fill up any little cracks there may yet be in your faith.

11 May God our Father Himself and our Lord Jesus send us back to you again.

12 And may the Lord make your love to grow and overflow to each other and to everyone else, just as our love does towards you.

13 This will result in your hearts' being made strong, sinless and holy by God our Father, so that you may stand before Him guiltless on that day when our Lord Jesus Christ returns with all those who belong to Him.[1]

Revised Standard

Timothy's visit and report

3 Therefore when we could bear it no longer, we were willing to be left behind
at Athens alone, 2and we sent Timothy, our
brother and God's servant in the gospel of
Christ, to establish you in your faith and to
exhort you, 3that no one be moved by these
afflictions. You yourselves know that this is
to be our lot. 4For when we were with you,
we told you beforehand that we were to
suffer affliction; just as it has come to pass,
and as you know. 5For this reason, when I
could bear it no longer, I sent that I might
know your faith, for fear that somehow the
tempter had tempted you and that our labor
would be in vain.
6 But now that Timothy has come to us
from you, and has brought us the good news
of your faith and love and reported that you
always remember us kindly and long to see
us, as we long to see you—7for this reason,
brethren, in all our distress and affliction we
have been comforted about you through your
faith; 8for now we live, if you stand fast in
the Lord. 9For what thanksgiving can we render to God for you, for all the joy which we
feel for your sake before our God, 10praying
earnestly night and day that we may see you
face to face and supply what is lacking in
your faith?

A prayer for holiness

11 Now may our God and Father himself, and our Lord Jesus, direct our way to
you; 12and may the Lord make you increase
and abound in love to one another and to all
men, as we do to you, 13so that he may establish your hearts unblamable in holiness
before our God and Father, at the coming of
our Lord Jesus with all his saints.

Living New Testament

CHAPTER 4

Let me add this, dear brothers: you already know how to please God in your daily living, for you know the commands we gave you from the Lord Jesus Himself. Now we beg you—yes, we demand of you in the name of the Lord Jesus—that you live more and more closely to that ideal.

Revised Standard

An appeal for purity

4 Finally, brethren, we beseech and exhort you in the Lord Jesus, that as you learned
from us how you ought to live and to please
God, just as you are doing, you do so more

---

[1] Literally, "with all His saints. Amen."

King James

2 For ye know what commandments we gave you by the Lord Jesus.

3 For this is the will of God, *even* your sanctification, that ye should abstain from fornication:

4 That every one of you should know how to possess his vessel in sanctification and honour;

5 Not in the lust of concupiscence, even as the Gentiles which know not God:

6 That no *man* go beyond and defraud his brother in *any* matter: because that the Lord *is* the avenger of all such, as we also have forewarned you and testified.

7 For God hath not called us unto uncleanness, but unto holiness.

8 He therefore that despiseth, despiseth not man, but God, who hath also given unto us his holy Spirit.

9 But as touching brotherly love ye need not that I write unto you: for ye yourselves are taught of God to love one another.

10 And indeed ye do it toward all the brethren which are in all Macedonia: but we beseech you, brethren, that ye increase more and more;

11 And that ye study to be quiet, and to do your own business, and to work with your own hands, as we commanded you;

12 That ye may walk honestly toward them that are without, and *that* ye may have lack of nothing.

13 But I would not have you to be ignorant, brethren, concerning them which are asleep, that ye sorrow not, even as others which have no hope.

14 For if we believe that Jesus died and rose again, even so them also which sleep in Jesus will God bring with him.

15 For this we say unto you by the word of the Lord, that we which are alive *and* remain unto the coming of the Lord shall not prevent them which are asleep.

16 For the Lord himself shall descend from heaven with a shout, with the voice of the archangel, and with the trump of God: and the dead in Christ shall rise first:

17 Then we which are alive *and* remain shall be caught up together with them in the clouds, to meet the Lord in the air: and so shall we ever be with the Lord.

18 Wherefore comfort one another with these words.

Amplified

2 For you know what charges *and* precepts we gave you [[i]on the authority and by the inspiration of] the Lord Jesus.

3 For this is the will of God, that you should be consecrated—separated and set apart for pure and holy living: that you should abstain *and* shrink from all sexual vice;

4 That each one of you should know how to [j]possess [control, manage] his own [k]body (in purity, separated from things profane, and) in consecration and honor,

5 Not [to be used] in the passion of lust, like the heathen who are ignorant of the true God *and* have no knowledge of His will,

6 That no man transgress, and overreach his brother *and* defraud him in this matter *or* defraud his brother in business. For the Lord is an avenger in all these things, as we have already warned you solemnly *and* [l]told you plainly.

7 For God has not called us to impurity, but to consecration [to dedicate ourselves to the most thorough purity].

8 Therefore whoever disregards—sets aside and rejects this—disregards not man but God, Whose [very] Spirit [Whom] He gives to you [is] holy—chaste, pure.

9 But concerning brotherly love [for all other Christians], you have no need to have any one write you, for you yourselves have been (personally) taught of God to love one another.

10 And indeed you already are [extending and displaying your love] to all the brethren throughout Macedonia. But we beseech *and* earnestly exhort you, brethren, that you [l]excel [in this matter] more and more;

11 To make it your ambition *and* definitely endeavor to live quietly *and* peacefully, to mind your own affairs, and to work with your hands, as we charged you;

12 So that you may bear yourselves becomingly, be correct *and* honorable *and* command the respect of the outside world, being (self-supporting,) dependent on nobody *and* having need of nothing.

13 Now also we would not have you ignorant, brethren, about those who fall asleep [in death], that you may not grieve [for them], as the rest do who have no hope [beyond the grave].

14 For since we believe that Jesus died and rose again, even so God will also bring with Him through Jesus those who have fallen asleep [[m]in death].

15 For this we declare to you by the Lord's [own] word, that we who are alive and remain until the coming of the Lord, shall in no way precede [into His presence] *or* have any advantage at all over those who have previously fallen asleep [in Him [m]in death].

16 For the Lord Himself will descend from heaven with a loud cry of summons, with the shout of an archangel, and with the blast of the trumpet of God. And those who have departed this life in Christ will rise first.

17 Then we, the still living who remain [on the earth], shall simultaneously be caught up along with (the resurrected dead) in the clouds to meet the Lord in the air; and so always—through the eternity of the eternities—we shall be with the Lord!

18 Therefore comfort *and* encourage one another with these words.

---

i) Abbott-Smith.
j) ASV and others.
k) Moulton and Milligan: " 'body' rather than 'wife'." Allowed by lexicons generally. Supported by Knox, Phillips, Way, etc. Early versions say "vessel."
l) Abbott-Smith.
m) Cremer.

Living New Testament

3, 4 For God wants you to be holy and pure, and to keep clear of all sexual sin so that each of you will marry in holiness and honor—

5 Not in lustful passion as the heathen do, in their ignorance of God and His ways.

6 And this also is God's will: that you never cheat in this matter by taking another man's wife, because the Lord will punish you terribly for this, as we have solemnly told you before.

7 For God has not called us to be dirty-minded and full of lust, but to be holy and clean.

8 If anyone refuses to live by these rules he is not disobeying the rules of men but of God who gives His *Holy* Spirit to you.

9 But concerning the pure brotherly love that there should be among God's people, I don't need to say very much, I'm sure! For God Himself is teaching you to love one another.

10 Indeed, your love is already strong toward all the Christian brothers throughout your whole nation. Even so, dear friends, we beg you to love them more and more.

11 This should be your ambition: to live a quiet life, minding your own business and doing your own work, just as we told you before.

12 As a result, people who are not Christians will trust and respect you, and you will not need to depend on others for enough money to pay your bills.

* * * * *

13 And now, dear brothers, I want you to know what happens to a Christian when he dies so that when it happens, you will not be full of sorrow, as those are who have no hope.

14 For since we believe that Jesus died and then came back to life again, we can also believe that when Jesus returns, God will bring back with Him all the Christians who have died.

15 I can tell you this directly from the Lord: that we who are still living when the Lord returns will not rise to meet Him ahead of those who are in their graves.

16 For the Lord Himself will come down from heaven with a mighty shout and with the soul-stirring cry of the archangel and the great trumpet-call of God. And the Christians who are dead will be the first to rise to meet the Lord.

17 Then we who are still alive and remain on the earth will be caught up with them in the clouds to meet the Lord in the air and remain with Him forever.

18 So comfort and encourage each other with this news.

Revised Standard

and more. 2For you know what instructions
we gave you through the Lord Jesus. 3For
this is the will of God, your sanctification:
that you abstain from immorality; 4that each
one of you know how to take a wife for
himself in holiness and honor, 5not in the
passion of lust like heathen who do not know
God; 6that no man transgress, and wrong
his brother in this matter,[c] because the Lord
is an avenger in all these things, as we solemnly forewarned you. 7For God has not
called us for uncleanness, but in holiness.
8Therefore whoever disregards this, disregards not man but God, who gives his Holy
Spirit to you.

An appeal for love and labor

9 But concerning love of the brethren you
have no need to have any one write to you,
for you yourselves have been taught by God
to love one another; 10and indeed you do
love all the brethren throughout Macedonia.
But we exhort you, brethren, to do so more
and more, 11to aspire to live quietly, to
mind your own affairs, and to work with
your hands, as we charged you; 12so that you
may command the respect of outsiders, and
be dependent on nobody.

Comfort in the resurrection hope

13 But we would not have you ignorant,
brethren, concerning those who are asleep,
that you may not grieve as others do who
have no hope. 14For since we believe that
Jesus died and rose again, even so, through
Jesus, God will bring with him those who
have fallen asleep. 15For this we declare to
you by the word of the Lord, that we who
are alive, who are left until the coming of
the Lord, shall not precede those who have
fallen asleep. 16For the Lord himself will
descend from heaven with a cry of command,
with the archangel's call, and with the sound
of the trumpet of God. And the dead in
Christ will rise first; 17then we who are alive,
who are left, shall be caught up together
with them in the clouds to meet the Lord in
the air; and so we shall always be with the
Lord. 18Therefore comfort one another with
these words.

[c] Or *defraud his brother in business*

King James

CHAPTER 5

BUT of the times and the seasons, brethren, ye have no need that I write unto you.

2 For yourselves know perfectly that the day of the Lord so cometh as a thief in the night.

3 For when they shall say, Peace and safety; then sudden destruction cometh upon them, as travail upon a woman with child; and they shall not escape.

4 But ye, brethren, are not in darkness, that that day should overtake you as a thief.

5 Ye are all the children of light, and the children of day: we are not of the night, nor of darkness.

6 Therefore let us not sleep, as *do* others; but let us watch and be sober.

7 For they that sleep sleep in the night; and they that be drunken are drunken in the night.

8 But let us, who are of the day, be sober, putting on the breastplate of faith and love; and for an helmet, the hope of salvation.

9 For God hath not appointed us to wrath, but to obtain salvation by our Lord Jesus Christ,

10 Who died for us, that, whether we wake or sleep, we should live together with him.

11 Wherefore comfort yourselves together, and edify one another, even as also ye do.

12 And we beseech you, brethren, to know them which labour among you, and are over you in the Lord, and admonish you;

13 And to esteem them very highly in love for their work's sake. *And* be at peace among yourselves.

14 Now we exhort you, brethren, warn them that are unruly, comfort the feebleminded, support the weak, be patient toward all *men.*

15 See that none render evil for evil unto any *man;* but ever follow that which is good, both among yourselves, and to all *men.*

16 Rejoice evermore.

17 Pray without ceasing.

18 In every thing give thanks: for this is the will of God in Christ Jesus concerning you.

19 Quench not the Spirit.

20 Despise not prophesyings.

21 Prove all things; hold fast that which is good.

22 Abstain from all appearance of evil.

Amplified

CHAPTER 5

BUT as to the suitable times and the precise seasons *and* dates, brethren, you have no necessity for anything being written to you.

2 For you yourselves know perfectly well that the day of the Lord['s return] will come [as unexpectedly and suddenly] as a thief in the night.

3 When people are saying, All is well and secure, *and,* There is peace and safety, then in a moment unforeseen destruction (ruin and death) will come upon them as suddenly as labor pains come upon a woman with child; and they shall by no means escape, *for* there will be no escape.

4 But you are not in [given up to the power of] darkness, brethren, for that day to overtake you by surprise like a thief.

5 For you are all sons of light and sons of the day; we do not belong either to the night or to darkness.

6 Accordingly then, let us not sleep, as the rest do, but let us keep wide awake (alert, watchful, cautious and on our guard) and let us be sober (calm, collected and circumspect).

7 For those who sleep sleep at night, and those who are drunk get drunk at night.

8 But we belong to the day, therefore let us be sober, and put on the breastplate (corslet) of faith and love and for a helmet the hope of salvation.

9 For God has not appointed us to [incur His] wrath—He did not select us to condemn us—but [that we might] obtain [His] salvation through our Lord Jesus Christ, the Messiah,

10 Who died for us so that whether we are still alive or are dead [at Christ's appearing] we might live together with Him *and* share His life.

11 Therefore encourage (admonish, exhort) one another and edify—strengthen and build up—one another, just as you are doing.

12 Now also we beseech you, brethren, get to know those who labor among you—recognize them for what they are, acknowledge and appreciate and respect them all—your leaders who are over you in the Lord, and those who warn *and* kindly reprove *and* exhort you.

13 And hold them in very high and most affectionate esteem in [intelligent and sympathetic] appreciation of their work. Be at peace among yourselves.

14 And we earnestly beseech you, brethren, admonish (warn and seriously advise) those who are out of line—the loafers, the disorderly and the unruly; encourage the timid *and* fainthearted, help *and* give your support to the weak souls [and] be very patient with everybody—always keeping your temper. [Isa. 35:4.]

15 See that none of you repays another with evil for evil, but always aim to show kindness *and* seek to do goo to one another and to everybody.

16 Be happy [in your faith] *and* rejoice *and* be glad hearted continually—always.

17 Be unceasing in prayer—praying perseveringly;

18 Thank [God] in everything—no matter what the cir cumstances may be, be thankful and give thanks; for thi is the will of God for you [who are] in Christ Jesus [th Revealer and Mediator of that will].

19 Do not quench (suppress or subdue) the (Holy Spirit.

20 Do not spurn the gifts *and* utterances of the prop ets—do not depreciate prophetic revelations nor despi inspired instruction or exhortation or warning.

21 But test *and* prove all things [until you can reco nize] what is good; [to that] hold fast.

22 Abstain from evil—shrink from it and keep alo from it—in whatever form *or* whatever kind it may be.

Living New Testament

CHAPTER 5

When is all this going to happen? I really don't need to say anything about that, dear brothers,

2 For you know perfectly well that no one knows. That day of the Lord will come unexpectedly like a thief in the night.

3 When people are saying, "All is well, everything is quiet and peaceful"—then, all of a sudden, disaster will fall upon them as suddenly as a woman's birth pains begin when her child is born. And these people will not be able to get away anywhere—there will be no place to hide.

4 But dear brothers, you are not in the dark about these things, and you won't be surprised as by a thief when that day of the Lord comes.

5 For you are all children of the light and of the day, and do not belong to darkness and night.

6 So be on your guard, not asleep like the others. Watch for His return and stay sober.

7 Night is the time for sleep and the time when people get drunk.

8 But let us who live in the light keep sober, protected by the armor of faith and love, and wearing as our helmet the happy hope of salvation.

9 For God has not chosen to pour out His anger upon us, but to save us through our Lord Jesus Christ;

10 He died for us so that we can live with Him forever, whether we are dead or alive at the time of His return.

11 So encourage each other and build each other up, just as you are already doing.

12 Dear brothers, honor the officers of your church who work hard among you and warn you against all that is wrong.

13 Think highly of them and give them your wholehearted love because they are straining to help you. And remember, no quarreling among yourselves.

14 Dear brothers, warn those who are lazy or wild; comfort those who are frightened; take tender care of those who are weak; and be patient with everyone.

15 See that no one pays back evil for evil, but always try to do good to each other and to everyone else.

16 Always be joyful.

17 Always keep on praying.

18 Always be thankful no matter what happens, for that is God's will for you who belong to Christ Jesus.

19 Do not smother the Holy Spirit.

20 Do not scoff at those who prophesy,

21 But test everything that is said to be sure it is true, and if it is, then accept it.

22 Keep away from every kind of evil.

Revised Standard

The sudden coming of the Lord

5 But as to the times and the seasons,
brethren, you have no need to have anything written to you. 2For you yourselves
know well that the day of the Lord will
come like a thief in the night. 3When people
say, "There is peace and security," then sudden destruction will come upon them as travail comes upon a woman with child, and
there will be no escape. 4But you are not in
darkness, brethren, for that day to surprise
you like a thief. 5For you are all sons of
light and sons of the day; we are not of the
night or of darkness. 6So then let us not
sleep, as others do, but let us keep awake
and be sober. 7For those who sleep sleep at
night, and those who get drunk are drunk
at night. 8But, since we belong to the day,
let us be sober, and put on the breastplate
of faith and love, and for a helmet the hope
of salvation. 9For God has not destined us
for wrath, but to obtain salvation through
our Lord Jesus Christ, 10who died for us
so that whether we wake or sleep we might
live with him. 11Therefore encourage one
another and build one another up, just as
you are doing.

Practical appeals

12 But we beseech you, brethren, to respect those who labor among you and are
over you in the Lord and admonish you,
13and to esteem them very highly in love
because of their work. Be at peace among
yourselves. 14And we exhort you, brethren,
admonish the idle, encourage the fainthearted, help the weak, be patient with them
all. 15See that none of you repays evil for
evil, but always seek to do good to one
another and to all. 16Rejoice always, 17pray
constantly, 18give thanks in all circumstances;
for this is the will of God in Christ Jesus for
you. 19Do not quench the Spirit, 20do not
despise prophesying, 21but test everything;
hold fast what is good, 22abstain from every
form of evil.

King James

23 And the very God of peace sanctify you wholly; and *I pray God* your whole spirit and soul and body be preserved blameless unto the coming of our Lord Jesus Christ.
24 Faithful *is* he that calleth you, who also will do *it*.
25 Brethren, pray for us.
26 Greet all the brethren with an holy kiss.
27 I charge you by the Lord that this epistle be read unto all the holy brethren.
28 The grace of our Lord Jesus Christ *be* with you. Amen.

¶ The first *epistle* unto the Thessalonians was written from Athens.

Amplified

23 And may the God of peace Himself sanctify you through and through—that is, separate you from profane things, make you pure and wholly consecrated to God—and may your spirit and soul and body be preserved sound *and* complete [and found] blameless at the coming of our Lord Jesus Christ, the Messiah.
24 Faithful is He Who is calling you [to Himself] ***and*** utterly trustworthy, and He will also do it [that is, fulfill His call by hallowing and keeping you].
25 Brethren, pray for us.
26 Greet all the brethren with a sacred kiss.
27 I solemnly charge you [in the name of] the Lord to have this letter read before all the brethren.
28 The grace (the unmerited favor and blessings) of our Lord Jesus Christ, the Messiah, be with you all. *Amen, so be it.*

Living New Testament

23 May the God of peace Himself make you entirely clean; and may your spirit and soul and body be kept strong and blameless until that day when our Lord Jesus Christ comes back again.

24 God who called you to become His child, will do all this for you, just as He promised.

25 Dear brothers, pray for us.

26 Shake hands for me with all the brothers there.

27 I command you in the name of the Lord to read this letter to all the Christians.

28 And may rich blessings from our Lord Jesus Christ be with you, every one.

Sincerely,
Paul

Revised Standard

Conclusion

23 May the God of peace himself sanctify
you wholly; and may your spirit and soul
and body be kept sound and blameless at
the coming of our Lord Jesus Christ. [24]He
who calls you is faithful, and he will do it.

25 Brethren, pray for us.

26 Greet all the brethren with a holy kiss.

27 I adjure you by the Lord that this letter be read to all the brethren.

28 The grace of our Lord Jesus Christ be with you.

King James

THE SECOND EPISTLE OF PAUL THE APOSTLE TO THE

Thessalonians

CHAPTER 1

PAUL, and Silvanus, and Timotheus, unto the church of the Thessalonians in God our Father and the Lord Jesus Christ:

2 Grace unto you, and peace, from God our Father and the Lord Jesus Christ.

3 We are bound to thank God always for you, brethren, as it is meet, because that your faith groweth exceedingly, and the charity of every one of you all toward each other aboundeth;

4 So that we ourselves glory in you in the churches of God for your patience and faith in all your persecutions and tribulations that ye endure:

5 *Which is* a manifest token of the righteous judgment of God, that ye may be counted worthy of the kingdom of God, for which ye also suffer:

6 Seeing *it is* a righteous thing with God to recompense tribulation to them that trouble you;

7 And to you who are troubled rest with us, when the Lord Jesus shall be revealed from heaven with his mighty angels,

8 In flaming fire taking vengeance on them that know not God, and that obey not the gospel of our Lord Jesus Christ:

9 Who shall be punished with everlasting destruction from the presence of the Lord, and from the glory of his power;

10 When he shall come to be glorified in his saints, and to be admired in all them that believe (because our testimony among you was believed) in that day.

11 Wherefore also we pray always for you, that our God would count you worthy of *this* calling, and fulfil all the good pleasure of *his* goodness, and the work of faith with power:

12 That the name of our Lord Jesus Christ may be glorified in you, and ye in him, according to the grace of our God and the Lord Jesus Christ.

Amplified

THE SECOND LETTER OF PAUL TO THE

Thessalonians

CHAPTER 1

PAUL, Silvanus (Silas) and Timothy to the church (assembly) of the Thessalonians in God our Father and the Lord Jesus Christ, the Messiah, the Anointed One:

2 Grace (unmerited favor) be to you and heart peace from God the Father and the Lord Jesus Christ, the Messiah, the Anointed One.

3 We ought *and* indeed are obligated [as those in debt] to give thanks always to God for you, brethren, as is fitting, because your faith is growing exceedingly, and the love of every one of you each toward the others is increasing *and* abounds.

4 And this is a cause of our mentioning you with pride among the churches (assemblies) of God for your steadfastness—your unflinching endurance and patience—and your firm faith in the midst of all the persecutions and crushing distresses *and* afflictions under which you are holding up.

5 This is positive proof of the just *and* right judgment of God to the end that you may be deemed deserving of His kingdom—a plain token of His fair verdict [which designs] that you should be made *and* counted worthy of the kingdom of God—for the sake of which you are also suffering.

6 [It is a fair decision] since it is a righteous thing with God to repay with distress *and* affliction those who distress *and* afflict you,

7 And to [[a]recompense] you who are so distressed *and* afflicted [by granting you] relief *and* rest along with us—your fellow sufferers—when the Lord Jesus is revealed from heaven with His mighty angels in a flame of fire;

8 To deal out retribution—chastisement and vengeance—upon those who do not know *or* perceive *or* become acquainted with God, and [upon those] who ignore *and* refuse to obey the Gospel of our Lord Jesus *Christ.*

9 Such people will pay the penalty *and* suffer the punishment of everlasting ruin (destruction and perdition) and [eternal exclusion and banishment] from the presence of the Lord and from the glory of His power,

10 When He comes to be glorified in His saints. (That is, on that day He will be made more glorious in His consecrated people) and [He will] be marveled at *and* admired [in His glory reflected] in all who have believed—who have adhered to, trusted in and relied on Him—because our witnessing among you was confidently accepted *and* believed [and confirmed in your lives].

11 With this in view we constantly pray for you, that our God may deem *and* count you worthy of [your] calling and [His] every gracious purpose of goodness, and with power complete in every particular [your] work of faith [faith which is that [b]leaning of the whole human personality on God in absolute trust and confidence in His power, wisdom and goodness].

12 Thus may the name of our Lord Jesus *Christ* be glorified *and* become more glorious through *and* in you and may you [also be glorified] in Him according to the grace (favor and blessing) of our God and the Lord Jesus Christ, the Messiah, the Anointed One.

---

a) Jamieson, Fausset and Brown.
b) Souter's "Pocket Lexicon to the Greek New Testament."

Living New Testament

II Thessalonians

CHAPTER 1

From: Paul, Silas and Timothy.
To: The church of Thessalonica—kept safe in God our Father and in the Lord Jesus Christ.

2 May God the Father and the Lord Jesus Christ give you rich blessings, and peace-filled hearts and minds.

3 Dear brothers, giving thanks to God for you is not only the right thing to do, but it is our duty to God, because of the really wonderful way your faith has grown, and because of your growing love for each other.

4 We are happy to tell other churches about your patience and complete faith in God, in spite of all the crushing troubles and hardships you are going through.

5 This is only one example of the fair, just way God does things, for He is using your sufferings to make you ready for His kingdom,

6 While at the same time He is preparing judgment and punishment for those who are hurting you.

7 And so I would say to you who are suffering, God will give you rest along with us when the Lord Jesus appears suddenly from heaven in flaming fire with His mighty angels,

8 Bringing judgment on those who do not wish to know God, and who refuse to accept His plan to save them through our Lord Jesus Christ.

9 They will be punished in everlasting hell, forever separated from the face of the Lord, never to see the glory of His power

10 When He comes to receive praise and admiration because of all He has done for His people, His saints. And you will be with Him, because you have believed God's word which we gave you.

11 And so we keep on praying for you that our God will make you the kind of children He wants to have—will make you as good as you wish you could be!—rewarding your faith with His power.

12 Then everyone will be praising the name of the Lord Jesus Christ because of the results they see in you; and your greatest glory will be that you belong to Him. The tender mercy of our God and of the Lord Jesus Christ has made all this possible for you.

Revised Standard

THE SECOND LETTER OF PAUL
TO THE

Thessalonians

Salutation and thanksgiving

1 Paul, Silvanus, and Timothy,
To the church of the Thessalonians in God our Father and the Lord Jesus Christ:
2 Grace to you and peace from God the Father and the Lord Jesus Christ.

Encouragement to endure suffering

3 We are bound to give thanks to God
always for you, brethren, as is fitting, because your faith is growing abundantly, and
the love of every one of you for one another
is increasing. 4 Therefore we ourselves boast
of you in the churches of God for your steadfastness and faith in all your persecutions
and in the afflictions which you are enduring.

The righteous judgment of God

5 This is evidence of the righteous judgment of God, that you may be made worthy
of the kingdom of God, for which you are
suffering— 6 since indeed God deems it just
to repay with affliction those who afflict you,
7 and to grant rest with us to you who are
afflicted, when the Lord Jesus is revealed
from heaven with his mighty angels in flaming fire, 8 inflicting vengeance upon those who
do not know God and upon those who do
not obey the gospel of our Lord Jesus. 9 They
shall suffer the punishment of eternal destruction and exclusion from the presence of the
Lord and from the glory of his might,
10 when he comes on that day to be glorified
in his saints, and to be marveled at in all who
have believed, because our testimony to you
was believed. 11 To this end we always pray
for you, that our God may make you worthy
of his call, and may fulfil every good resolve
and work of faith by his power, 12 so that the
name of our Lord Jesus may be glorified in
you, and you in him, according to the grace
of our God and the Lord Jesus Christ.

King James

CHAPTER 2

NOW we beseech you, brethren, by the coming of our Lord Jesus Christ, and *by* our gathering together unto him,

2 That ye be not soon shaken in mind, or be troubled, neither by spirit, nor by word, nor by letter as from us, as that the day of Christ is at hand.

3 Let no man deceive you by any means: for *that day shall not come,* except there come a falling away first, and that man of sin be revealed, the son of perdition;

4 Who opposeth and exalteth himself above all that is called God, or that is worshipped; so that he as God sitteth in the temple of God, shewing himself that he is God.

5 Remember ye not, that, when I was yet with you, I told you these things?

6 And now ye know what withholdeth that he might be revealed in his time.

7 For the mystery of iniquity doth already work: only he who now letteth *will let,* until he be taken out of the way.

8 And then shall that Wicked be revealed, whom the Lord shall consume with the spirit of his mouth, and shall destroy with the brightness of his coming:

9 *Even him,* whose coming is after the working of Satan with all power and signs and lying wonders,

10 And with all deceivableness of unrighteousness in them that perish; because they received not the love of the truth, that they might be saved.

11 And for this cause God shall send them strong delusion, that they should believe a lie:

12 That they all might be damned who believed not the truth, but had pleasure in unrighteousness.

13 But we are bound to give thanks alway to God for you, brethren beloved of the Lord, because God hath from the beginning chosen you to salvation through sanctification of the Spirit and belief of the truth:

14 Whereunto he called you by our gospel, to the obtaining of the glory of our Lord Jesus Christ.

15 Therefore, brethren, stand fast, and hold the traditions which ye have been taught, whether by word, or our epistle.

16 Now our Lord Jesus Christ himself, and God, even our Father, which hath loved us, and hath given *us* everlasting consolation and good hope through grace,

Amplified

CHAPTER 2

BUT relative to the coming of our Lord Jesus Christ, the Messiah, and our gathering together to [meet] Him, we beg you, brethren,

2 Not to allow your minds to be quickly unsettled *or* disturbed or kept excited *or* alarmed, whether it be by some [pretended] revelation of [the] Spirit or by word or by letter [alleged to be] from us, to the effect that the day of the Lord has [already] arrived *and* is here.

3 Let no one deceive *or* beguile you in any way, for that day will not come except the [c]apostasy comes first —that is, unless the [predicted] great [c]falling away of those who have professed to be Christians has come—and the man of lawlessness (sin) is revealed, who is the son of doom (of perdition), [I Tim. 4:1; Dan. 7:25; 8:25.]

4 Who opposes and exalts himself so proudly *and* insolently against *and* over all that is called God or that is worshiped, [even to his actually] taking his seat in the temple of God, proclaiming that he himself is God. [Dan. 11:36, 37; Ezek. 28:2.]

5 Do you not recollect that when I was still with you I told you these things?

6 And now you know what is restraining him [from being revealed at this time]; it is so that he may be manifested (revealed) in his own [appointed] time.

7 For the mystery of lawlessness—that hidden principle of rebellion against constituted authority—is already at work in the world, [but it is] restrained only until [d]he who restrains is taken out of the way.

8 And then the lawless one (the Antichrist) will be revealed and the Lord Jesus will slay him with the breath of His mouth and bring him to an end by His appearing *at* His coming. [Isa. 11:4.]

9 The coming [of the lawless one, the Antichrist] is through the activity *and* working of Satan, and will be attended by great power and with all sorts of [pretended] miracles and signs *and* delusive marvels—[all of them] lying wonders—

10 And by unlimited seduction to evil *and* with all wicked deception for those who are (going to perdition,) perishing because they did not welcome the Truth *but* refused to love it that they might be saved.

11 Therefore God sends upon them a misleading influence, a working of error *and* a strong delusion to make them believe what is false,

12 In order that all may be judged *and* condemned who did not believe—who refused to adhere to, trust in and rely on—the Truth, but [instead] took pleasure in unrighteousness.

13 But we, brethren beloved by the Lord, ought *and* are obligated [as those who are in debt] to give thanks always to God for you, because God chose you from the beginning [[e]to be the first converts] for salvation through the sanctifying work of the (Holy) Spirit and [your] belief in—adherence to, trust in and reliance on—the Truth.

14 [It was] to this end that He called you through our Gospel, so that you may obtain *and* share in the glory of our Lord Jesus Christ, the Messiah.

15 So then, brethren, stand firm and hold fast to the traditions *and* instructions which you were taught by us, whether by our word of mouth or by letter.

16 Now may our Lord Jesus Christ Himself, and God our Father, Who loved us and gave us everlasting consolation *and* encouragement and well-founded hope through [His] grace (unmerited favor),

---

c) A possible rendering of apostasia is "departure [of the church]."
d) Many believe this one who restrains the Antichrist to be the Holy Spirit, Who lives in all believers and will be removed with them at Christ's coming. A majority think it refers to the Roman Empire.
e) Many ancient authorities so read.

Living New Testament

CHAPTER 2

And now, what about the coming again of our Lord Jesus Christ, and our being gathered together to meet Him? Please don't be upset and excited, dear brothers, by the rumor that this day of the Lord has already begun.[1] If you hear of people having visions and special messages from God about this, or letters that are supposed to have come from me, don't believe them.

3 Don't be carried away and deceived regardless of what they say. For that day will not come until two things happen: first, there will be a time of great rebellion against God, and then the man of rebellion will come—the son of hell.

4 He will defy every god there is, and tear down every other object of adoration and worship. He will go in and sit as God in the temple of God, claiming that he himself is God.

5 Don't you remember that I told you this when I was with you?

6 And you know who is keeping him from being here already; for he can come only when his time is ready.

7 As for the work this man of rebellion and hell will do when he comes, it is already going on,[2] but he himself will not come until the one who is holding him back steps out of the way.

8 Then this wicked one will appear, whom the Lord Jesus will burn up with the breath of His mouth and destroy by His presence when He returns.

9 This man of sin will come as Satan's tool, full of Satanic power, and will trick everyone with strange demonstrations, and will pretend to do great miracles.

10 He will completely fool those who are on their way to hell because they have said "no" to the Truth; they have refused to believe it and love it, and let it save them,

11 So God will allow them to believe lies with all their hearts,

12 And all of them will be justly judged for believing falsehood, refusing the Truth, and enjoying their sins.

13 But we must forever give thanks to God for you, our brothers loved by the Lord, because God chose from the very first to give you salvation, cleansing you by the work of the Holy Spirit and by your trusting in the Truth.

14 Through us He told you the Good News. Through us He called you to share in the glory of our Lord Jesus Christ.

15 With all these things in mind, dear brothers, stand firm and keep a strong grip on the truth that we taught you in our letters and during the time we were with you.

16 May our Lord Jesus Christ Himself and God our Father, who has loved us and given us everlasting comfort and hope which we don't deserve,

Literally, "is just at hand."
Literally, "the mystery of lawlessness is already at work."

Revised Standard

The man of lawlessness

2 Now concerning the coming of our Lord
Jesus Christ and our assembling to meet
him, we beg you, brethren, [2]not to be quickly
shaken in mind or excited, either by spirit or
by word, or by letter purporting to be from
us, to the effect that the day of the Lord has
come. [3]Let no one deceive you in any way;
for that day will not come, unless the rebellion comes first, and the man of lawlessness[a]
is revealed, the son of perdition, [4]who opposes and exalts himself against every so-called god or object of worship, so that he
takes his seat in the temple of God, proclaiming himself to be God. [5]Do you not remember that when I was still with you I told
you this? [6]And you know what is restraining
him now so that he may be revealed in his
time. [7]For the mystery of lawlessness is already at work; only he who now restrains it
will do so until he is out of the way. [8]And
then the lawless one will be revealed, and the
Lord Jesus will slay him with the breath of
his mouth and destroy him by his appearing
and his coming. [9]The coming of the lawless
one by the activity of Satan will be with all
power and with pretended signs and wonders,
[10]and with all wicked deception for those
who are to perish, because they refused to
love the truth and so be saved. [11]Therefore
Gods sends upon them a strong delusion, to
make them believe what is false, [12]so that all
may be condemned who did not believe the
truth but had pleasure in unrighteousness.

Thanksgiving and appeal

13 But we are bound to give thanks to
God always for you, brethren beloved by the
Lord, because God chose you from the beginning[b] to be saved, through sanctification
by the Spirit[c] and belief in the truth. [14]To
this he called you through our gospel, so
that you may obtain the glory of our Lord
Jesus Christ. [15]So then, brethren, stand firm
and hold to the traditions which you were
taught by us, either by word of mouth or by
letter.

16 Now may our Lord Jesus Christ himself, and God our Father, who loved us and gave us eternal comfort and good hope

[a] Other ancient authorities read *sin*
[b] Other ancient authorities read *as the first converts*
[c] Or *of spirit*

King James

17 Comfort your hearts, and stablish you in every good word and work.

CHAPTER 3

FINALLY, brethren, pray for us, that the word of the Lord may have *free* course, and be glorified, even as *it is* with you:

2 And that we may be delivered from unreasonable and wicked men: for all *men* have not faith.

3 But the Lord is faithful, who shall stablish you, and keep *you* from evil.

4 And we have confidence in the Lord touching you, that ye both do and will do the things which we command you.

5 And the Lord direct your hearts into the love of God, and into the patient waiting for Christ.

6 Now we command you, brethren, in the name of our Lord Jesus Christ, that ye withdraw yourselves from every brother that walketh disorderly, and not after the tradition which he received of us.

7 For yourselves know how ye ought to follow us: for we behaved not ourselves disorderly among you;

8 Neither did we eat any man's bread for nought; but wrought with labour and travail night and day, that we might not be chargeable to any of you:

9 Not because we have not power, but to make ourselves an ensample unto you to follow us.

10 For even when we were with you, this we commanded you, that if any would not work, neither should he eat.

11 For we hear that there are some which walk among you disorderly, working not at all, but are busybodies.

12 Now them that are such we command and exhort by our Lord Jesus Christ, that with quietness they work, and eat their own bread.

13 But ye, brethren, be not weary in well-doing.

14 And if any man obey not our word by this epistle, note that man, and have no company with him, that he may be ashamed.

15 Yet count *him* not as an enemy, but admonish *him* as a brother.

16 Now the Lord of peace himself give you peace always by all means. The Lord *be* with you all.

Amplified

17 Comfort and encourage your hearts and strengthen them—make them steadfast and keep them unswerving—in every good work and word.

CHAPTER 3

FURTHERMORE, brethren, do pray for us, that the Word of the Lord may speed on (spread rapidly and run its course) and be glorified (extolled) *and* triumph, even as [it has done] with you.

2 And that we may be delivered from perverse (improper, unrighteous) and wicked (actively malicious) men, for not everybody has faith *and* is held by it.

3 Yet the Lord is faithful and He will strengthen [you] *and* set you on a firm foundation and guard you from the evil [one].

4 And we have confidence in the Lord concerning you, that you are doing and will continue to do the things which we suggest *and* with which we charge you.

5 May the Lord direct your hearts into [realizing and showing] the love of God, and into the steadfastness *and* patience of Christ *in* [f]waiting for His return.

6 Now we charge you, brethren, in the name *and* on the authority of our Lord Jesus Christ, the Messiah, that you withdraw *and* keep away from every brother (fellow believer) who is slack in the performance of duty *and* is disorderly, living as a shirker *and* not walking in accord with the traditions *and* instructions that you have received from us.

7 For you yourselves know how it is necessary to imitate our example, for we were not disorderly *or* shirking of duty when we were with you—we were not idle.

8 Nor did we eat any one's bread without paying for it, but with toil and struggle we worked night and day, that we might not be a burden *or* impose on any of you [for our support].

9 [It was] not because we do not have a right [to such support], but [we wished] to make ourselves an example for you to follow.

10 For while we were yet with you we gave you this rule *and* charge: If any one will not work, neither let him eat.

11 Indeed, we hear that some among you are disorderly—that they are passing their lives in idleness, neglectful of duty—being busy with other people's affairs instead of their own and doing no work.

12 Now we charge and exhort such persons [as [g]ministers in Him exhorting those] in the Lord Jesus Christ, the Messiah, that they work in quietness and earn their own food *and* other necessities.

13 And as for you, brethren, do not be weary *or* lose heart in doing right [but continue in well-doing without weakening].

14 But if any one [in the church] refuses to obey what we say in this letter, take note of that person, and do not associate with him, that he may be ashamed.

15 Do not regard him as an enemy, but simply admonish and warn him as [being still] a brother.

16 Now may the Lord of peace Himself grant you His peace [the peace of His kingdom] at all times and in all ways—under all circumstances and conditions, whatever comes. The Lord [be] with you all.

---

f) Alternate translation. (Thayer.)
g) Jamieson, Fausset and Brown.

Living New Testament

17 Comfort your hearts with all comfort, and help you in every good thing you say and do.

Revised Standard

through grace, 17comfort your hearts and
establish them in every good work and word.

CHAPTER 3

Finally, dear brothers, as I come to the end of this letter I ask you to pray for us. Pray first that the Lord's message will spread rapidly and triumph wherever it goes, winning converts everywhere as it did when it came to you.

2 Pray too that we will be saved out of the clutches of evil men, for not everyone loves the Lord.

3 But the Lord is faithful; He will make you strong and guard you from Satanic attacks of every kind.

4 And we trust the Lord that you are putting into practice the things we taught you, and that you always will.

5 May the Lord bring you into an ever deeper understanding of the love of God and of the patience that comes from Christ.

6 Now here is a command, dear brothers, given in the name of our Lord Jesus Christ by His authority: stay away from any Christian who spends his days in laziness and does not follow the ideal of hard work we set up for you.

7 For you well know that you ought to follow our example: you never saw us loafing;

8 We never accepted food from anyone without buying it; we worked hard day and night for the money we needed to live on, in order that we would not be a burden to any of you.

9 It wasn't that we didn't have the right to ask you to feed us, but we wanted to show you, firsthand, how you should work for your living.

10 Even while we were still there with you we gave you this rule: "He who does not work shall not eat."

11 Yet we hear that some of you are living in laziness, refusing to work, and wasting your time in gossiping.

12 In the name of the Lord Jesus Christ we appeal to such people—we command them—to quiet down, get to work, and earn their own living.

13 And to the rest of you I say, dear brothers, never be tired of doing right.

14 If anyone refuses to obey what we say in this letter, notice who he is and stay away from him, that he may be ashamed of himself.

15 Don't think of him as an enemy, but speak to him as you would to a brother who needs to be warned.

16 May the Lord of peace Himself give you His peace no matter what happens. The Lord be with you all.

Appeals for prayer and labor

3 Finally, brethren, pray for us, that the
word of the Lord may speed on and
triumph, as it did among you, 2and that we
may be delivered from wicked and evil men;
for not all have faith. 3But the Lord is faithful; he will strengthen you and guard you
from evil.[d] 4And we have confidence in the
Lord about you, that you are doing and
will do the things which we command. 5May
the Lord direct your hearts to the love of
God and to the steadfastness of Christ.
6 Now we command you, brethren, in the
name of our Lord Jesus Christ, that you
keep away from any brother who is living in
idleness and not in accord with the tradition
that you received from us. 7For you yourselves know how you ought to imitate us; we
were not idle when we were with you, 8we
did not eat any one's bread without paying,
but with toil and labor we worked night and
day, that we might not burden any of you.
9It was not because we have not that right,
but to give you in our conduct an example
to imitate. 10For even when we were with
you, we gave you this command: If any one
will not work, let him not eat. 11For we hear
that some of you are living in idleness, mere
busybodies, not doing any work. 12Now such
persons we command and exhort in the Lord
Jesus Christ to do their work in quietness
and to earn their own living. 13Brethren, do
not be weary in well-doing.
14 If any one refuses to obey what we
say in this letter, note that man, and have
nothing to do with him, that he may be
ashamed. 15Do not look on him as an enemy,
but warn him as a brother.

Benediction

16 Now may the Lord of peace himself
give you peace at all times in all ways. The
Lord be with you all.

[d] Or *the evil one*

King James

17 The salutation of Paul with mine own
hand, which is the token in every epistle: so
I write.
18 The grace of our Lord Jesus Christ *be*
with you all. Amen.

¶ The second *epistle* to the Thessalonians was written from Athens.

Amplified

17 I, Paul, write you this final greeting with my own
hand. This is the mark *and* sign [that it is not a forgery] in
every letter of mine. It is the way I write—my handwriting and signature.
18 The grace (spiritual blessing and favor) of our Lord
Jesus Christ, the Messiah, be with you all. *Amen, so be it.*

Living New Testament

17 Now here is my greeting which I am writing with my own hand, as I do at the end of all my letters, for proof that it really is from me. This is in my own handwriting.

18 May the blessing of our Lord Jesus Christ be upon you all.

Sincerely,
Paul

Revised Standard

17 I, Paul, write this greeting with my
own hand. This is the mark in every letter
of mine; it is the way I write. 18The grace
of our Lord Jesus Christ be with you all.

King James

THE FIRST EPISTLE OF PAUL THE APOSTLE
TO

Timothy

CHAPTER 1

PAUL, an apostle of Jesus Christ by the commandment of God our Saviour, and Lord Jesus Christ, *which is* our hope;

2 Unto Timothy, *my* own son in the faith: Grace, mercy, *and* peace, from God our Father and Jesus Christ our Lord.

3 As I besought thee to abide still at Ephesus, when I went into Macedonia, that thou mightest charge some that they teach no other doctrine,

4 Neither give heed to fables and endless genealogies, which minister questions, rather than godly edifying which is in faith: *so do.*

5 Now the end of the commandment is charity out of a pure heart, and *of* a good conscience, and *of* faith unfeigned:

6 From which some having swerved have turned aside unto vain jangling;

7 Desiring to be teachers of the law; understanding neither what they say, nor whereof they affirm.

8 But we know that the law *is* good, if a man use it lawfully;

9 Knowing this, that the law is not made for a righteous man, but for the lawless and disobedient, for the ungodly and for sinners, for unholy and profane, for murderers of fathers and murderers of mothers, for manslayers,

10 For whoremongers, for them that defile themselves with mankind, for menstealers, for liars, for perjured persons, and if there be any other thing that is contrary to sound doctrine;

11 According to the glorious gospel of the blessed God, which was committed to my trust.

12 And I thank Christ Jesus our Lord, who hath enabled me, for that he counted me faithful, putting me into the ministry;

13 Who was before a blasphemer, and a persecutor, and injurious: but I obtained mercy, because I did *it* ignorantly in unbelief.

14 And the grace of our Lord was exceeding abundant with faith and love which is in Christ Jesus.

15 This *is* a faithful saying, and worthy of all acceptation, that Christ Jesus came into the world to save sinners; of whom I am chief.

Amplified

THE FIRST LETTER OF PAUL
TO

Timothy

CHAPTER 1

PAUL, an apostle (special messenger) of Christ Jesus by appointment *and* command of God our Savior and of Christ Jesus, the Messiah, our Hope,

2 To Timothy, my true son in the faith: Grace (spiritual blessing and favor), mercy and heart peace [be yours] from God the Father and Christ Jesus our Lord.

3 As I urged you when I was on my way to Macedonia, stay on where you are at Ephesus in order that you may warn *and* admonish *and* charge certain individuals not to teach any different doctrine,

4 Nor to give importance to *or* occupy themselves with legends (fables, myths) and endless genealogies which foster *and* promote useless speculations *and* questionings, rather than acceptance in faith of God's administration *and* the divine training that is in faith, [[a]in that leaning of the entire human personality on God in absolute trust and confidence];

5 Whereas the object *and* purpose of our instruction *and* charge is love which springs from a pure heart and a good (clear) conscience and sincere (unfeigned) faith.

6 But certain individuals have missed the mark on this very matter [and] have wandered away into vain arguments *and* discussions *and* purposeless talk.

7 They are ambitious to be doctors of the Law—teachers of the Mosaic ritual—but they have no understanding either of the words *and* terms they use or of the subjects about which they make [such] dogmatic assertions.

8 Now we recognize *and* know that the Law is good, if any one uses it lawfully—for the purpose for which it was designed;

9 Knowing *and* understanding this: that the Law is not enacted for the righteous—the upright and just, who are in right standing with God; but for the lawless and unruly, for the ungodly and sinful, for the irreverent and profane for those who strike *and* beat *and* [even] murder fathers and strike *and* beat *and* [even] murder mothers; for man slayers,

10 [For] impure *and* immoral persons, those who abuse themselves with men, kidnapers, liars, perjurers and whatever else is opposed to wholesome teaching *and* sound doctrine,

11 As laid down by the glorious Gospel of the blessed God, with which I have been entrusted.

12 I give thanks to Him Who has granted me (the needed) strength *and* made me able [for this], Christ Jesus our Lord, because He has judged *and* counted me faithful *and* trustworthy, appointing me to [this stewardship of] the ministry.

13 Though I formerly blasphemed and persecuted and was shamefully *and* outrageously *and* aggressively insulting [to Him], nevertheless I obtained mercy because I had acted out of ignorance in unbelief.

14 And the grace (unmerited favor and blessing) of our Lord [actually] flowed out superabundantly *and* beyond measure for me, accompanied by faith and love that are [to be realized] in Christ Jesus.

15 The saying is sure *and* true and worthy of full *and* universal acceptance, that Christ Jesus, the Messiah, came into the world to save sinners, of whom I am foremost.

---

a) Souter's "Pocket Lexicon to the Greek New Testament."

Living New Testament

I Timothy

CHAPTER 1

From: Paul, a missionary of Jesus Christ, sent out by God our Savior and by Jesus Christ our Lord—our only hope.

2 *To:* Timothy.

Timothy, you are like a son to me in the things of the Lord. May God our Father and Jesus Christ our Lord show you His kindness and mercy and give you great peace of heart and mind.

3, 4 As I said when I left for Macedonia, please stay there in Ephesus and try to stop the men who are teaching such wrong doctrine. Put an end to their myths and fables, and their idea of being saved by finding favor with an endless chain of angels leading up to God—wild ideas that stir up questions and arguments instead of helping people accept God's plan of faith.

5 What I am eager for is that all the Christians there will be filled with love that comes from pure hearts, and that their minds will be clean and their faith strong.

6 But these teachers have missed this whole idea and spend their time arguing and talking foolishness.

7 They want to become famous as teachers of the laws of Moses when they haven't the slightest idea what those laws really show us.

8 Those laws are good when used as God intended.

9 But they were not made for us, whom God has saved; they are for sinners who hate God, have rebellious hearts, curse and swear, attack their fathers and mothers, and murder.

10, 11 Yes, these laws are made to identify as sinners all who are immoral and impure: homosexuals, kidnappers, liars, and all others who do things that contradict the glorious Good News of our blessed God, whose messenger I am.

12 How thankful I am to Christ Jesus our Lord for choosing me as one of His messengers, and giving me the strength to be faithful to Him,

13 Even though I used to scoff at the name of Christ. I hunted down His people, harming them in every way I could. But God had mercy on me because I didn't know what I was doing, for I didn't know Christ at that time.

14 Oh how kind our Lord was, for He showed me how to trust Him and become full of the love of Christ Jesus.

15 How true it is, and how I long that everyone should know it, that Christ Jesus came into the world to save sinners—and I was the greatest of them all.

Revised Standard

THE FIRST LETTER OF PAUL TO

Timothy

Salutation

1 Paul, an apostle of Christ Jesus by com-
mand of God our Savior and of Christ
Jesus our hope,
2 To Timothy, my true child in the faith:
Grace, mercy, and peace from God the
Father and Christ Jesus our Lord.

The problem of unsound doctrine

3 As I urged you when I was going to
Macedonia, remain at Ephesus that you may
charge certain persons not to teach any different doctrine, [4]nor to occupy themselves
with myths and endless genealogies which
promote speculations rather than the divine
training[a] that is in faith; [5]whereas the aim
of our charge is love that issues from a pure
heart and a good conscience and sincere
faith. [6]Certain persons by swerving from
these have wandered away into vain discussion, [7]desiring to be teachers of the law, without understanding either what they are saying or the things about which they make
assertions.
8 Now we know that the law is good, if
any one uses it lawfully, [9]understanding this,
that the law is not laid down for the just
but for the lawless and disobedient, for the
ungodly and sinners, for the unholy and profane, for murderers of fathers and murderers of mothers, for manslayers, [10]immoral
persons, sodomites, kidnapers, liars, perjurers, and whatever else is contrary to sound
doctrine, [11]in accordance with the glorious
gospel of the blessed God with which I have
been entrusted.

The testimony of Paul

12 I thank him who has given me strength
for this, Christ Jesus our Lord, because he
judged me faithful by appointing me to his
service, [13]though I formerly blasphemed and
persecuted and insulted him; but I received
mercy because I had acted ignorantly in unbelief, [14]and the grace of our Lord overflowed for me with the faith and love that
are in Christ Jesus. [15]The saying is sure and
worthy of full acceptance, that Christ Jesus
came into the world to save sinners. And I

[a] Or *stewardship*, or *order*

King James

16 Howbeit for this cause I obtained mercy, that in me first Jesus Christ might shew forth all longsuffering, for a pattern to them which should hereafter believe on him to life everlasting.

17 Now unto the King eternal, immortal, invisible, the only wise God, *be* honour and glory for ever and ever. Amen.

18 This charge I commit unto thee, son Timothy, according to the prophecies which went before on thee, that thou by them mightest war a good warfare;

19 Holding faith, and a good conscience; which some having put away concerning faith have made shipwreck:

20 Of whom is Hymenæus and Alexander; whom I have delivered unto Satan, that they may learn not to blaspheme.

Amplified

16 But I obtained mercy for the reason that in me, as the foremost [of sinners], Jesus Christ might show forth *and* display all His perfect long-suffering *and* patience for an example to [encourage] those who would thereafter believe on Him for [the gaining of] eternal life.

17 Now to the King of eternity, incorruptible *and* immortal, invisible, the only God, be honor and glory forever and ever—to the ages of ages. Amen—so be it.

18 This charge *and* admonition I commit in trust to you, Timothy, my son, [b]in accordance with prophetic intimations which I formerly received concerning you, that inspired *and* aided by them you may wage the good warfare,

19 Keeping fast hold on faith [[c]that leaning of the entire human personality on God in absolute trust and confidence] and a good (clear) conscience. By rejecting *and* thrusting from them [their conscience], some individuals have made shipwreck of their faith.

20 Among them are Hymenaeus and Alexander, whom I have delivered to Satan in order that they may be disciplined [by punishment and learn] not to blaspheme.

CHAPTER 2

I EXHORT therefore, that, first of all, supplications, prayers, intercessions, *and* giving of thanks, be made for all men;

2 For kings, and *for* all that are in authority; that we may lead a quiet and peaceable life in all godliness and honesty.

3 For this *is* good and acceptable in the sight of God our Saviour;

4 Who will have all men to be saved, and to come unto the knowledge of the truth.

5 For *there is* one God, and one mediator between God and men, the man Christ Jesus;

6 Who gave himself a ransom for all, to be testified in due time.

7 Whereunto I am ordained a preacher, and an apostle, (I speak the truth in Christ, *and* lie not;) a teacher of the Gentiles in faith and verity.

8 I will therefore that men pray every where, lifting up holy hands, without wrath and doubting.

9 In like manner also, that women adorn themselves in modest apparel, with shamefacedness and sobriety; not with broided hair, or gold, or pearls, or costly array;

10 But (which becometh women professing godliness) with good works.

11 Let the woman learn in silence with all subjection.

12 But I suffer not a woman to teach, nor to usurp authority over the man, but to be in silence.

13 For Adam was first formed, then Eve.

CHAPTER 2

FIRST of all, then, I admonish *and* urge that petitions, prayers, intercessions and thanksgivings be offered on behalf of all men,

2 For kings and all who are in positions of authority *or* high responsibility, that [outwardly] we may pass a quiet *and* undisturbed life [and inwardly] a peaceable one in all godliness *and* reverence and seriousness in every way.

3 For such [praying] is good *and* right, and [it is] pleasing *and* acceptable to God our Savior,

4 Who wishes all men to be saved and increasingly to perceive *and* recognize *and* discern *and* know precisely *and* correctly the [divine] Truth:

5 That there [is only] one God, and [only] one mediator between God and men, the Man Christ Jesus,

6 Who gave Himself a ransom for all [people, a fac that was] attested to at the right *and* proper time.

7 And of this matter I was appointed a preacher an an apostle (special messenger); I am speaking the truth *i Christ,* I do not falsify [when I say this], a teacher of th Gentiles in [the realm of] faith and truth.

8 I desire therefore that in every place men shoul pray, without anger *or* quarreling *or* resentment or dou [in their minds], lifting up holy hands.

9 Also [I desire] that women should adorn themselve modestly *and* appropriately and sensibly in seemly a parel, not with [elaborate] hair arrangement or gold pearls or expensive clothing,

10 But by doing good deeds—that is, deeds in then selves good, and for the good and advantage of thos contacted by them—as befits women who profess revere tial fear for *and* devotion to God.

11 Let a woman learn in quietness in entire submi siveness.

12 I allow no woman to teach or to have authori over men; she is to remain in quietness *and* keep silen [in religious assemblies].

13 For Adam was first formed, then Eve; [Gen. 2: 21, 22.]

---

b) Vincent's "Word Studies in the New Testament."
c) Souter's "Pocket Lexicon to the Greek New Testament."

Living New Testament

16 But God had mercy on me so that Christ Jesus could use me as an example to show everyone how patient He is with even the worst sinners, so that others will realize that they, too, can have everlasting life.

17 Glory and honor to God for ever and ever. He is the King of the ages, the unseen one who never dies; He alone is God, and full of wisdom. Amen.

18 Now, Timothy, my son, here is my command to you: fight well in the Lord's battles, just as the Lord told us through His prophets that you would.

19 Cling tightly to your faith in Christ and always keep your conscience clear, doing what you know is right. For some people have disobeyed their consciences and have deliberately done what they knew was wrong. It isn't surprising that soon they lost their faith in Christ after defying God like that.

20 Hymenaeus and Alexander are two examples of this. I had to give them over to Satan to punish them until they could learn not to bring shame to the name of Christ.

Revised Standard

am the foremost of sinners; [16]but I received
mercy for this reason, that in me, as the foremost, Jesus Christ might display his perfect
patience for an example to those who were
to believe in him for eternal life. [17]To the
King of ages, immortal, invisible, the only
God, be honor and glory for ever and ever.[b]
Amen.

Timothy urged to pray

18 This charge I commit to you. Timothy,
my son, in accordance with the prophetic utterances which pointed to you, that inspired
by them you may wage the good warfare,
[19]holding faith and a good conscience. By
rejecting conscience, certain persons have
made shipwreck of their faith, [20]among them
Hymenaeus and Alexander, whom I have
delivered to Satan that they may learn not
to blaspheme.

CHAPTER 2

Here are my directions: pray much for others; plead for God's mercy upon them; give thanks for all He is going to do for them.

2 Pray in this way for kings and all others who are in authority over us, or are in places of high responsibility, so that we can live in peace and quietness, spending our time in godly living and thinking much about the Lord.[1]

3 This is good and pleases God our Savior,

4 For He longs for all to be saved and to understand this truth:

5 *That God is on one side and all the people on the other side, and Christ Jesus, Himself man, is between them to bring them together,*

6 *By giving His life for all mankind.* This is the message which at the proper time God gave to the world.

7 And I have been chosen—this is the absolute truth—as God's minister and missionary to teach this truth to the Gentiles, and to show them God's plan of salvation through faith.

8 So I want men everywhere to pray with holy hands lifted up to God, free from sin and anger and resentment.

9, 10 And the women should be the same way, quiet and sensible in manner and clothing. Christian women should be noticed for being kind and good, not for the way they fix their hair or because of their jewels or fancy clothes.

11 Women should listen and learn quietly and humbly.

12 I never let women teach men or lord it over them. Let them be silent in your church meetings.

13 Why? Because God made Adam first, and afterwards He made Eve.

2 First of all, then, I urge that supplications, prayers, intercessions, and thanksgivings be made for all men, [2]for kings and
all who are in high positions, that we may
lead a quiet and peaceable life, godly and
respectful in every way. [3]This is good, and it
is acceptable in the sight of God our Savior,
[4]who desires all men to be saved and to come
to the knowledge of the truth. [5]For there is
one God, and there is one mediator between
God and men, the man Christ Jesus, [6]who
gave himself as a ransom for all, the testimony to which was borne at the proper time.
[7]For this I was appointed a preacher and
apostle (I am telling the truth, I am not
lying), a teacher of the Gentiles in faith and
truth.

The position of women

8 I desire then that in every place the men
should pray, lifting holy hands without anger
or quarreling; [9]also that women should adorn
themselves modestly and sensibly in seemly
apparel, not with braided hair or gold or
pearls or costly attire [10]but by good deeds,
as befits women who profess religion. [11]Let
a woman learn in silence with all submissive-
ness. [12]I permit no woman to teach or to
have authority over men; she is to keep silent.
[13]For Adam was formed first, then Eve;

---

[1]Literally, "in gravity."

[b] Greek *to the ages of ages*

King James

14 And Adam was not deceived, but the woman being deceived was in the transgression.

15 Notwithstanding she shall be saved in childbearing, if they continue in faith and charity and holiness with sobriety.

CHAPTER 3

THIS *is* a true saying, If a man desire the office of a bishop, he desireth a good work.

2 A bishop then must be blameless, the husband of one wife, vigilant, sober, of good behaviour, given to hospitality, apt to teach;

3 Not given to wine, no striker, not greedy of filthy lucre; but patient, not a brawler, not covetous;

4 One that ruleth well his own house, having his children in subjection with all gravity;

5 (For if a man know not how to rule his own house, how shall he take care of the church of God?)

6 Not a novice, lest being lifted up with pride he fall into the condemnation of the devil.

7 Moreover he must have a good report of them which are without; lest he fall into reproach and the snare of the devil.

8 Likewise *must* the deacons *be* grave, not double-tongued, not given to much wine, not greedy of filthy lucre;

9 Holding the mystery of the faith in a pure conscience.

10 And let these also first be proved; then let them use the office of a deacon, being *found* blameless.

11 Even so *must their* wives *be* grave, not slanderers, sober, faithful in all things.

12 Let the deacons be the husbands of one wife, ruling their children and their own houses well.

13 For they that have used the office of a deacon well purchase to themselves a good degree, and great boldness in the faith which is in Christ Jesus.

Amplified

14 And it was not Adam who was deceived, but [the] woman who was deceived *and* deluded and fell into transgression. [Gen. 3:1-6.]

15 Nevertheless (the sentence put upon women [of pain in motherhood] does not hinder their [souls'] salvation), and they will be saved [eternally] if they continue in faith and love and holiness, with self-control; [saved indeed] [d]through the Child-bearing, that is, [e]by the birth of the [divine] Child.

CHAPTER 3

THE saying is true *and* irrefutable: If any man [eagerly] seeks the office of bishop (superintendent, overseer), he desires an excellent task (work).

2 Now a bishop (superintendent, overseer) must give no grounds for accusation *but* must be above reproach, the husband of one wife, circumspect *and* temperate *and* self-controlled; [he must be] sensible *and* well behaved *and* dignified and lead an orderly (disciplined) life; [he must be] hospitable—showing love for and being a friend to the believers, especially strangers or foreigners—[and] be a capable *and* qualified teacher,

3 Not given to wine, not combative but gentle *and* considerate, not quarrelsome *but* forbearing *and* peaceable, not a lover of money—insatiable for wealth and ready to obtain it by questionable means.

4 He must rule his own household well, keeping his children under control, with true dignity, commanding their respect in every way *and* keeping them respectful.

5 For if a man does not know how to rule his own household, how is he to take care of the church of God?

6 He must not be a new convert, or he may [develop a beclouded and stupid state of mind] as the result of pride, [be blinded by] conceit, and fall into the condemnation that the devil [once] did. [Isa. 14:12-14.]

7 Furthermore he must have a good reputation *and* be well thought of by those outside [the church], lest he become involved in slander *and* incur reproach and fall into the devil's trap.

8 In like manner the deacons [must be] worthy of respect, not shifty *and* double talkers *but* sincere in wha they say, not given to much wine, not greedy for base gain—craving wealth and resorting to ignoble and dishon est methods of getting it.

9 They must possess the mystic secret of the fait [Christian truth as hidden from ungodly men,] with a clea conscience.

10 And let them also be tried *and* investigated *an* proved first; then, [if they turn out to be] above reproac let them serve [as deacons].

11 [f][The] women likewise must be worthy of respec *and* serious, not gossipers, but temperate *and* sel controlled, [thoroughly] trustworthy in all things.

12 Let deacons be the husbands of but one wife, ar let them manage [their] children and their own househol well;

13 For those who perform well as deacons acquire good standing for themselves and also gain much con dence *and* freedom *and* boldness in the faith which [founded on and centers] in Christ Jesus.

---

d) Vincent. Doddridge. Macknight. Clark. ASV margin, and othe Cf. Gal. 4:4.
e) Alternate reading.
f) Either their wives or the deaconesses, or both.

Living New Testament

14 And it was not Adam who was fooled by Satan, but Eve, and sin was the result.

15 So God sent pain and suffering to women when their children are born, but He will save their souls if they trust in Him, living quiet, good, and loving lives.

Revised Standard

14 and Adam was not deceived, but the woman was deceived and became a transgressor. 15 Yet woman will be saved through bearing children,[c] if she continues[d] in faith and love and holiness, with modesty.

CHAPTER 3

It is a true saying that if a man wants to be a pastor,[1] he has a good ambition.

2 For a pastor must be a good man whose life cannot be spoken against. He must have only one wife, and he must be hard working and thoughtful, orderly, and full of good deeds. He must enjoy having guests in his home, and must be a good Bible teacher.

3 He must not be a drinker or quarrelsome, but he must be gentle and kind, and not be one who loves money.

4 He must have a well-behaved family, with children who obey quickly and quietly.

5 For if a man can't make his own little family behave, how can he help the whole church?

6 The pastor must not be a new Christian, because he might be proud of being chosen so soon, and pride comes before a fall. (Satan's downfall is an example.)

7 Also, he must be well spoken of by people outside the church—those who aren't Christians—so that Satan can't trap him with many accusations, and leave him without freedom to lead his flock.

8 The deacons must be the same sort of good, steady men as the pastors. They must not be heavy drinkers and must not be greedy for money.

9 They must be earnest, wholehearted followers of Christ who is the hidden Source of their faith.

10 Before they are asked to be deacons they should be given other jobs in the church as a test of their character and ability, and if they do well, then they may be chosen as deacons.

11 Their wives must be thoughtful, not heavy drinkers, not gossipers, but faithful in everything they do.

12 Deacons should have only one wife and they should have happy, obedient families.

13 Those who do well as deacons will be well rewarded both by respect from others and also by developing their own confidence and bold trust in the Lord.

The office of bishop

3 The saying is sure: If any one aspires to the office of bishop, he desires a noble task. 2 Now a bishop must be above reproach, the husband of one wife, temperate, sensible, dignified, hospitable, an apt teacher, 3 no drunkard, not violent but gentle, not quarrelsome, and no lover of money. 4 He must manage his own household well, keeping his children submissive and respectful in every way; 5 for if a man does not know how to manage his own household, how can he care for God's church? 6 He must not be a recent convert, or he may be puffed up with conceit and fall into the condemnation of the devil;[f] 7 moreover he must be well thought of by outsiders, or he may fall into reproach and the snare of the devil.[f]

The office of deacon

8 Deacons likewise must be serious, not double-tongued, not addicted to much wine, not greedy for gain; 9 they must hold the mystery of the faith with a clear conscience. 10 And let them also be tested first; then if they prove themselves blameless let them serve as deacons. 11 The women likewise must be serious, no slanderers, but temperate, faithful in all things. 12 Let deacons be the husband of one wife, and let them manage their children and their households well; 13 for those who serve well as deacons gain a good standing for themselves and also great confidence in the faith which is in Christ Jesus.

---

[1] More literally, "church leader" or "presiding elder."

[c] Or *by the birth of the child*
[d] Greek *they continue*
[f] Or *slanderer*

King James

14 These things write I unto thee, hoping to come unto thee shortly:

15 But if I tarry long, that thou mayest know how thou oughtest to behave thyself in the house of God, which is the church of the living God, the pillar and ground of the truth.

16 And without controversy great is the mystery of godliness: God was manifest in the flesh, justified in the Spirit, seen of angels, preached unto the Gentiles, believed on in the world, received up into glory.

Amplified

14 Although I hope to come to you before long, I am writing these instructions to you so that,

15 If I am detained, you may know how people ought to conduct themselves in the household of God, which is the church of the living God, the pillar and stay—the prop and support—of the Truth.

16 And great *and* important *and* weighty, we confess, is the hidden truth—the mystic secret—of godliness. He [g](God) was made visible in human flesh, justified *and* vindicated in the (Holy) Spirit, was seen by angels, preached among the nations, believed on in the world [and] taken up in glory.

CHAPTER 4

NOW the Spirit speaketh expressly, that in the latter times some shall depart from the faith, giving heed to seducing spirits, and doctrines of devils;

2 Speaking lies in hypocrisy; having their conscience seared with a hot iron;

3 Forbidding to marry, *and commanding* to abstain from meats, which God hath created to be received with thanksgiving of them which believe and know the truth.

4 For every creature of God *is* good, and nothing to be refused, if it be received with thanksgiving:

5 For it is sanctified by the word of God and prayer.

6 If thou put the brethren in remembrance of these things, thou shalt be a good minister of Jesus Christ, nourished up in the words of faith and of good doctrine, whereunto thou hast attained.

7 But refuse profane and old wives' fables, and exercise thyself *rather* unto godliness.

8 For bodily exercise profiteth little: but godliness is profitable unto all things, having promise of the life that now is, and of that which is to come.

9 This *is* a faithful saying and worthy of all acceptation.

10 For therefore we both labour and suffer reproach, because we trust in the living God, who is the Savior of all men, specially of those that believe.

11 These things command and teach.

12 Let no man despise thy youth; but be thou an example of the believers, in word, in conversation, in charity, in spirit, in faith, in purity.

13 Till I come, give attendance to reading, to exhortation, to doctrine.

14 Neglect not the gift that is in thee, which was given thee by prophecy, with the laying on of the hands of the presbytery.

CHAPTER 4

BUT the (Holy) Spirit distinctly *and* expressly declares that in latter times some will turn away from the faith, giving attention to deluding *and* seducing spirits and doctrines that demons teach

2 Through the hypocrisy *and* pretensions of liars whose consciences are seared (cauterized),

3 Who forbid people to marry and [teach them] to abstain from [certain kinds of] foods which God created to be received with thanksgiving by those who believe *and* have (an increasingly clear) knowledge of the truth.

4 For everything God has created is good, and nothing is to be thrown away *or* refused if it is received with thanksgiving.

5 For it is hallowed *and* consecrated by the Word of God and by prayer.

6 If you lay all these instructions before the brethren, you will be a worthy steward *and* a good minister of Christ Jesus, ever nourishing your own self on the truths of the faith and of the good [Christian] instruction which you have closely followed.

7 But refuse *and* avoid irreverent legends—profane and impure and godless fictions, mere grandmothers' tales—and silly myths, *and* express your disapproval of them. Train yourself toward godliness (piety)—keeping yoursel spiritually fit.

8 For physical training is of some value—useful for a little; but godliness [spiritual training] is useful *and* o value in everything *and* in every way, for it holds promis for the present life and also for the life which is to come.

9 This saying is reliable *and* worthy of complete accep ance by everybody.

10 With a view to this we toil *and* strive, [yes] an [h]suffer reproach, because we have [fixed our] hope on th living God, Who is the Savior (Preserver, Maintaine Deliverer) of all men, especially of those who believe- trust in, rely on and adhere to Him.

11 Continue to command these things and to teac them.

12 Let no one despise *or* think less of you because your youth, but be an example (pattern) for the believe in speech, in conduct, in love, in faith and in puri

13 Till I come, devote yourself to [public and priva reading, to exhortation—preaching and personal appeals and to teaching *and* instilling doctrine.

14 Do not neglect the gift which is in you, [that spec inward endowment] which was directly imparted to y [by the Holy Spirit] by prophetic utterance when the eld laid their hands upon you [at your ordination].

---

g) Some authorities read "God."
h) Alternate reading.

Living New Testament

14 I am writing these things to you now, even though I hope to be with you soon,

15 So that if I don't come for awhile you will know what kind of men you should choose as officers for the church of the living God, which contains and holds high the truth of God.

16 It is quite true that the way to live a godly life is not an easy matter. But the answer lies in Christ, who came to earth as a man, was proved spotless and pure in His Spirit, was served by angels, was preached among the nations, was accepted by men everywhere and was received up again to His glory in heaven.

Revised Standard

14 I hope to come to you soon, but I am
writing these instructions to you so that, 15if
I am delayed, you may know how one ought
to behave in the household of God, which is
the church of the living God, the pillar and
bulwark of the truth. 16Great indeed, we confess, is the mystery of our religion:

He[h] was manifested in the flesh,
vindicated[i] in the Spirit,
seen by angels,
preached among the nations,
believed on in the world,
taken up in glory.

CHAPTER 4

But the Holy Spirit tells us clearly that in the last times some in the church will turn away from Christ and become eager followers of teachers with devil-inspired ideas.

2 These teachers will tell lies with straight faces and do it so often that their consciences won't even bother them.

3 They will say it is wrong to be married and wrong to eat meat, even though God gave these things to well-taught Christians to enjoy and be thankful for.

4 For everything God made is good, and we may eat it gladly if we are thankful for it,

5 And if we ask God to bless it, for it is made good by the Word of God and prayer.

6 If you explain this to the others you will be doing your duty as a worthy pastor who is fed by faith and by the true teaching you have followed.

7 Don't waste time arguing over foolish ideas and silly myths and legends. Spend your time and energy in the exercise of keeping spiritually fit.

8 Bodily exercise is all right, but spiritual exercise is much more important and is a tonic for all you do. So exercise yourself spiritually and practice being a better Christian, because that will help you not only now in this life, but in the next life too.

9, 10 This is the truth and everyone should accept it. We work hard and suffer much in order that people will believe it, for our hope is in the living God who died for all, and particularly for those who have accepted His alvation.

11 Teach these things and make sure everyone learns hem well.

12 Don't let anyone think little of you because you are 'oung. Be their ideal; let them follow the way you teach nd live; be a pattern for them in your love, your faith, nd your clean thoughts.

13 Until I get there, read and explain the Scriptures to e church; preach God's Word.

14 Be sure to use the abilities God has given you rough His prophets when the elders of the church laid eir hands upon your head.

Dealing with false doctrine

4 Now the Spirit expressly says that in
later times some will depart from the
faith by giving heed to deceitful spirits and
doctrines of demons, 2through the pretensions
of liars whose consciences are seared, 3who
forbid marriage and enjoin abstinence from
foods which God created to be received with
thanksgiving by those who believe and know
the truth. 4For everything created by God is
good, and nothing is to be rejected if it is
received with thanksgiving; 5for then it is
consecrated by the word of God and prayer.

Instructions for godly living

6 If you put these instructions before the
brethren, you will be a good minister of
Christ Jesus, nourished on the words of the
faith and of the good doctrine which you
have followed. 7Have nothing to do with godless and silly myths. Train yourself in godliness; 8for while bodily training is of some
value, godliness is of value in every way, as
it holds promise for the present life and also
for the life to come. 9The saying is sure and
worthy of full acceptance. 10For to this end
we toil and strive,[j] because we have our hope
set on the living God who is the Savior of
all men, especially of those who believe.

The pastor as an example

11 Command and teach these things.
12Let no one despise your youth, but set the
believers an example in speech and conduct,
in love, in faith, in purity. 13Till I come, attend to the public reading of scripture, to
preaching, to teaching. 14Do not neglect the
gift you have, which was given you by prophetic utterance when the elders laid their

---

[h] Greek *Who;* other ancient authorities read *God;* others, *Which*
[i] Or *justified*
[j] Other ancient authorities read *suffer reproach*

King James

15 Meditate upon these things; give thyself wholly to them; that thy profiting may appear to all.

16 Take heed unto thyself, and unto the doctrine; continue in them: for in doing this thou shalt both save thyself, and them that hear thee.

Amplified

15 Practice *and* cultivate *and* meditate upon these duties, throw yourself wholly into them [your ministry], so that your progress may be evident to everybody.

16 Look well to yourself (to your own personality) and to [your] teaching; persevere in these things—hold to them; for by so doing you will save both yourself and those who hear you.

CHAPTER 5

REBUKE not an elder, but entreat *him* as a father; *and* the younger men as brethren;

2 The elder women as mothers; the younger as sisters, with all purity.

3 Honour widows that are widows indeed.

4 But if any widow have children or nephews, let them learn first to shew piety at home, and to requite their parents: for that is good and acceptable before God.

5 Now she that is a widow indeed, and desolate, trusteth in God, and continueth in supplications and prayers night and day.

6 But she that liveth in pleasure is dead while she liveth.

7 And these things give in charge, that they may be blameless.

8 But if any provide not for his own, and specially for those of his own house, he hath denied the faith, and is worse than an infidel.

9 Let not a widow be taken into the number under threescore years old, having been the wife of one man,

10 Well reported of for good works: if she have brought up children, if she have lodged strangers, if she have washed the saints' feet, if she have relieved the afflicted, if she have diligently followed every good work.

11 But the younger widows refuse: for when they have begun to wax wanton against Christ, they will marry;

12 Having damnation, because they have cast off their first faith.

13 And withal they learn *to be* idle, wandering about from house to house; and not only idle, but tattlers also and busybodies, speaking things which they ought not.

14 I will therefore that the younger women marry, bear children, guide the house, give none occasion to the adversary to speak reproachfully.

15 For some are already turned aside after Satan.

16 If any man or woman that believeth have widows, let them relieve them, and let not the church be charged; that it may relieve them that are widows indeed.

CHAPTER 5

DO not sharply censure *or* rebuke an older man, but entreat *and* plead with him as [you would with] a father; treat younger men like brothers.

2 [Treat] older women like mothers [and] younger women like sisters, in all purity.

3 [Always] treat with great consideration *and* give aid to those who are truly widowed—solitary and without support.

4 But if a widow has children or grandchildren, see to it that these are first made to understand that it is their religious duty (to defray their natural obligation to those) at home, and make return to their parents *or* grandparents [for all their care by contributing to their maintenance], for this is acceptable in the sight of God.

5 Now [a woman] who is a real widow, and is left entirely alone *and* desolate, has fixed her hope on God and perseveres in supplications and prayers night and day;

6 Whereas she who lives in pleasure *and* self-gratification—giving herself up to luxury and self-indulgence—is dead even while she [still] lives.

7 Charge [the people] thus, so that they may be without reproach *and* blameless.

8 If any one fails to provide for his relatives, and especially for those of his own family, he has disowned the faith [by failing to accompany it with fruits], and is worse than an unbeliever [who performs his obligation in these matters].

9 Let no one be put on the roll of widows [who are to receive church support] who is under sixty years of age, or who has been the wife of more than one man;

10 And she must have a reputation for good deeds, as one who has brought up children, who has practiced hospitality to strangers [of the brotherhood], washed the feet of the saints, helped to relieve the distressed, [and devoted herself diligently to doing good in every way.

11 But refuse [to enroll on this list the] younger wid ows, for when they become restive *and* their natura desires grow strong, they withdraw themselves agains Christ [and] wish to marry [again].

12 And so they incur condemnation for having se aside *and* slighted their previous pledge.

13 Moreover, as they go about from house to hous they learn to be idlers, and not only idlers but gossips an busybodies, saying what they should not say *and* talking things they should not mention.

14 So I would have younger [widows] marry, be children, guide the household, [and] not give opponents the faith occasion for slander or reproach.

15 For already some [widows] have turned aside aft Satan.

16 If any believing [i]*man or* woman has [relatives persons in the household who are] widows, let him relie them; let the church not be burdened [with them]; so th it may [be free to] assist those who are truly widows those who are all alone and are dependent.

i) Some ancient authorities so read.

Root causes Root probm

Lack of Love (parents)

1 Surface action	Root
Self criticism	Bitterness
open hostility	wrong Values
over attention on clothes	moral impurity

Surface cause

Dress

Envy

Bordem

Frustration

Guilt

Fear

Eph 4:29 Prov 16:24

Anticipate what the child can become rather than expect him to perform

use of responsibility Phil 2:14

Jam 3:27

acknowledge the childs accomplishments with words of thanks, or praise

enjoy the childs day listen to his actions

Provide time for the ~~[illegible]~~ child to explore

Pslams

Isal 44:24 made by God

Isaiah 45: 9-12 planned by God

Psalm 139-13-18 ordered by God

Mark 10-13-16 Loved by God

Prov 17:6 and given to you

Eph 6: 4

Titus 2:4

Psalm 113-9

God made you I like you
you are special, Thank you God
for making ____ name

Isaih 40:26

1 address the child by his proper name
encorage to call each other by their real names only
animal with names
speak his name with a joy
in the moring, comes to the table, goes to school, comes home from school, goes to bed

Living New Testament

15 Put these abilities to work; throw yourself into your
ısks so that everyone may notice your improvement and
rogress.
16 Keep a close watch on all you do and think. Stay
ue to what is right and God will bless you and use you
help others.

Revised Standard

hands upon you. 15Practice these duties, devote yourself to them, so that all may see
your progress. 16Take heed to yourself and
to your teaching; hold to that, for by so
doing you will save both yourself and your
hearers.

CHAPTER 5

Never speak sharply to an older man, but plead with
him respectfully just as though he were your own
ıther. Talk to the younger men as you would to much-
ved brothers.
2 Treat the older women as mothers, and the girls as
ɔur sisters, thinking only pure thoughts about them.
3 The church should take loving care of women whose
ısbands have died if they don't have anyone else to help
em.
4 But if they have children or grandchildren, these are
e ones who should take the responsibility, for kindness
ould begin at home, supporting needy parents. This is
mething that pleases God very much.
5 The church should care for widows who are poor and
one in the world if they are looking to God for His help,
ıd spending much time in prayer;
6 But not if they are spending their time running
ound gossiping, seeking only pleasure and thus ruining
eir souls.
7 This should be your church rule so that the Christians
ll know and do what is right.
8 But anyone who won't care for his own relatives
ıen they need help, especially those living in his own
mily, has no right to say he is a Christian. Such a person
worse than the heathen.
9 A widow who wants to become one of the special
urch workers[1] should be at least sixty years old and
ve been married only once.
10 She must be well thought of by everyone because of
ɜ good she has done. Has she brought up her children
ɜll? Has she been kind to strangers as well as to other
ıristians? Has she helped those who are sick and hurt? Is
e always ready to show kindness?
11 The younger widows should not become members of
is special group because after awhile they are likely to
sregard their vow to Christ and marry again.
12 And so they will stand condemned because they
ɔke their first promise.
13 Besides, they are likely to be lazy and spend their
ne gossiping around from house to house, getting into
ıer people's business.
14 So I think it is better for these younger widows to
ırry again and have children, and take care of their own
mes; then no one will be able to say anything against
ɜm.
15 For I am afraid that some of them have already
'ned away from the church and been led astray by
tan.
16 Let me remind you again that a widow's relatives
ıst take care of her, and not leave this to the church to
. Then the church can spend its money for the care of
dows who are all alone and have nowhere else to turn.

terally, "enrolled as a widow."

5 Do not rebuke an older man but exhort
him as you would a father; treat younger
men like brothers, 2older women like mothers, younger women like sisters, in all purity.

Pastoral duties to widows

3 Honor widows who are real widows. 4If
a widow has children or grandchildren, let
them first learn their religious duty to their
own family and make some return to their
parents; for this is acceptable in the sight of
God. 5She who is a real widow, and is left
all alone, has set her hope on God and continues in supplications and prayers night and
day; 6whereas she who is self-indulgent is
dead even while she lives. 7Command this,
so that they may be without reproach. 8If
any one does not provide for his relatives,
and especially for his own family, he has
disowned the faith and is worse than an unbeliever.
9 Let a widow be enrolled if she is not
less than sixty years of age, having been the
wife of one husband; 10and she must be well
attested for her good deeds, as one who has
brought up children, shown hospitality,
washed the feet of the saints, relieved the
afflicted, and devoted herself to doing good
in every way. 11But refuse to enrol younger
widows; for when they grow wanton against
Christ they desire to marry, 12and so they
incur condemnation for having violated their
first pledge. 13Besides that, they learn to be
idlers, gadding about from house to house,
and not only idlers but gossips and busybodies, saying what they should not. 14So I
would have younger widows marry, bear
children, rule their households, and give the
enemy no occasion to revile us. 15For some
have already strayed after Satan. 16If any
believing woman[l] has relatives who are widows, let her assist them; let the church not
be burdened, so that it may assist those who
are real widows.

l Other ancient authorities *read man or woman;* others, simply *man*

King James

17 Let the elders that rule well be counted worthy of double honour, especially they who labour in the word and doctrine.

18 For the scripture saith, Thou shalt not muzzle the ox that treadeth out the corn. And, The labourer *is* worthy of his reward.

19 Against an elder receive not an accusation, but before two or three witnesses.

20 Them that sin rebuke before all, that others also may fear.

21 I charge *thee* before God, and the Lord Jesus Christ, and the elect angels, that thou observe these things without preferring one before another, doing nothing by partiality.

22 Lay hands suddenly on no man, neither be partaker of other men's sins: keep thyself pure.

23 Drink no longer water, but use a little wine for thy stomach's sake and thine often infirmities.

24 Some men's sins are open beforehand, going before to judgment; and some *men* they follow after.

25 Likewise also the good works *of some* are manifest beforehand; and they that are otherwise cannot be hid.

Amplified

17 Let the elders who perform the duties of their office well be considered doubly worthy of honor [and of adequate [j]financial support], especially those who labor faithfully in preaching and teaching.

18 For the Scripture says, You shall not muzzle an ox when it is treading out the grain, and again, The laborer is worthy of his hire. [Deut. 25:4.]

19 Listen to no accusation preferred [before a judge] against an elder except it be confirmed by the testimony of two or three witnesses. [Deut. 19:15.]

20 As for those who are guilty *and* persist in sin, rebuke *and* admonish them in the presence of all, so that the rest may be warned *and* stand in wholesome awe *and* fear.

21 I solemnly charge you in the presence of God and of Christ Jesus and of the chosen angels, that you guard *and* keep [these rules] without personal prejudice *or* favor, doing nothing from partiality.

22 Do not be in a hurry in the laying on of hands—giving the sanction of the church too hastily [in reinstating expelled offenders or in ordination in questionable cases]—nor share *or* participate in another man's sins; keep yourself pure.

23 Drink water no longer exclusively, but use a little wine for the sake of your stomach and your frequent illnesses.

24 The sins of some men are conspicuous—openly evident to all eyes—going before them to the judgment [seat] *and* proclaiming their sentence in advance; but the sins of others appear later—following the offender to the bar of judgment and coming into view there.

25 So also good deeds are evident *and* conspicuous, and even when they are not, they cannot remain hidden [indefinitely].

CHAPTER 6

LET as many servants as are under the yoke count their own masters worthy of all honour, that the name of God and *his* doctrine be not blasphemed.

2 And they that have believing masters, let them not despise *them*, because they are brethren; but rather do *them* service, because they are faithful and beloved, partakers of the benefit. These things teach and exhort.

3 If any man teach otherwise, and consent not to wholesome words, *even* the words of our Lord Jesus Christ, and to the doctrine which is according to godliness;

4 He is proud, knowing nothing, but doting about questions and strifes of words, whereof cometh envy, strife, railings, evil surmisings,

5 Perverse disputings of men of corrupt minds, and destitute of the truth, supposing that gain is godliness: from such withdraw thyself.

CHAPTER 6

LET all who are under the yoke as bond servants esteem their own [personal] masters worthy of honor *and* fullest respect, so that the name of God and the teaching may not be brought into disrepute *and* blasphemed.

2 Let those who have believing masters not be disrespectful *or* scornful [to them] on the grounds that they are brothers [in Christ]; rather, they should serve [them all the better] because those who benefit by their kindly service are believers and beloved. Teach and urge these duties.

3 But if any one teaches otherwise and does not [k]assent to the sound *and* wholesome messages of our Lord Jesus Christ, the Messiah, and the teaching which is in agreement with godliness—piety toward God—

4 He is puffed up with pride *and* stupefied with conceit [although he is] woefully ignorant. He has a [l]morbid fondness for controversy and disputes *and* strife about words, which result in (producing) envy *and* jealousy, quarrels *and* dissension, abuse *and* insults *and* slander, an base suspicions,

5 And protracted wrangling *and* wearing discussion an perpetual friction among men who are corrupted in min and bereft of the truth, who imagine that godliness righteousness is a [k]source of profit—a money-makir business, a means of livelihood. *From such withdraw.*

---

j) Vincent.
k) Vincent.
l) Thayer.

Living New Testament

17 Pastors who do their work well should be paid well and should be highly appreciated, especially those who work hard at both preaching and teaching.

18 For the Scriptures say, "Never tie up the mouth of an ox when it is treading out the grain—let him eat as he goes along!" And in another place, "Those who work deserve their pay!"

19 Don't listen to complaints against the pastor unless there are two or three witnesses to accuse him.

20 If he has really sinned, then he should be rebuked in front of the whole church so that no one else will follow his example.

21 I solemnly command you in the presence of God and the Lord Jesus Christ and of the holy angels to do this whether the pastor is a special friend of yours or not. All must be treated exactly the same.

22 Never be in a hurry about choosing a pastor; you may overlook his sins and it will look as if you approve of them. Be sure that you yourself stay away from all sin.

23 (By the way, this doesn't mean you should completely give up drinking wine. You ought to take a little sometimes as medicine for your stomach because you are sick so often.)

24 Remember that some men, even pastors, lead sinful lives and everyone knows it. In such situations you can do something about it. But in other cases only the judgment day will reveal the terrible truth.

25 In the same way, everyone knows how much good some pastors do, but sometimes their good deeds aren't known until long afterward.

Revised Standard

Pastoral duties to elders

17 Let the elders who rule well be considered worthy of double honor, especially
those who labor in preaching and teaching;
[18]for the scripture says, "You shall not muzzle an ox when it is treading out the grain,"
and, "The laborer deserves his wages."
[19]Never admit any charge against an elder
except on the evidence of two or three witnesses. [20]As for those who persist in sin,
rebuke them in the presence of all, so that
the rest may stand in fear. [21]In the presence
of God and of Christ Jesus and of the elect
angels I charge you to keep these rules without favor, doing nothing from partiality.
[22]Do not be hasty in the laying on of hands,
nor participate in another man's sins; keep
yourself pure.

23 No longer drink only water, but use a
little wine for the sake of your stomach and
your frequent ailments.

24 The sins of some men are conspicuous,
pointing to judgment, but the sins of others
appear later. [25]So also good deeds are conspicuous; and even when they are not, they
cannot remain hidden.

CHAPTER 6

Christian slaves should work hard for their owners and respect them; never let it be said that Christ's people re poor workers. Don't let the name of God or His aching be laughed at because of this.

2 If their owner is a Christian, that is no excuse for owing down; rather they should work all the harder ecause a brother in the faith is being helped by their forts. Teach these truths, Timothy, and encourage all to ey them.

3 Some may deny these things, but they are the sound, holesome teachings of the Lord Jesus Christ and are the undation for a godly life.

4 Anyone who says anything different is both proud d stupid. He is quibbling over the meaning of Christ's rds and stirring up arguments ending in jealousy and ger, which only lead to name-calling, and evil suspi- ns.

5 These arguers—their minds warped by sin—don't ow how to tell the truth; to them the Good News is just neans of making money. Keep away from them.

Pastoral duties to slaves

6 Let all who are under the yoke of slavery regard their masters as worthy of all
honor, so that the name of God and the
teaching may not be defamed. [2]Those who
have believing masters must not be disrespectful on the ground that they are brethren;
rather they must serve all the better since
those who benefit by their service are believers and beloved.

Warning against false teachers

Teach and urge these duties. [3]If any one
teaches otherwise and does not agree with
the sound words of our Lord Jesus Christ
and the teaching which accords with godliness, [4]he is puffed up with conceit, he knows
nothing; he has a morbid craving for controversy and for disputes about words, which
produce envy, dissension, slander, base suspicions, [5]and wrangling among men who are
depraved in mind and bereft of the truth,
imagining that godliness is a means of gain.

King James

6 But godliness with contentment is great gain.

7 For we brought nothing into *this* world, *and it is* certain we can carry nothing out.

8 And having food and raiment let us be therewith content.

9 But they that will be rich fall into temptation and a snare, and *into* many foolish and hurtful lusts, which drown men in destruction and perdition.

10 For the love of money is the root of all evil: which while some coveted after, they have erred from the faith, and pierced themselves through with many sorrows.

11 But thou, O man of God, flee these things; and follow after righteousness, godliness, faith, love, patience, meekness.

12 Fight the good fight of faith, lay hold on eternal life, whereunto thou art also called, and hast professed a good profession before many witnesses.

13 I give thee charge in the sight of God, who quickeneth all things, and *before* Christ Jesus, who before Pontius Pilate witnessed a good confession;

14 That thou keep *this* commandment without spot, unrebukeable, until the appearing of our Lord Jesus Christ:

15 Which in his times he shall shew, *who is* the blessed and only Potentate, the King of kings, and Lord of lords;

16 Who only hath immortality, dwelling in the light which no man can approach unto; whom no man hath seen, nor can see: to whom *be* honour and power everlasting. Amen.

17 Charge them that are rich in this world, that they be not highminded, nor trust in uncertain riches, but in the living God, who giveth us richly all things to enjoy;

18 That they do good, that they be rich in good works, ready to distribute, willing to communicate;

19 Laying up in store for themselves a good foundation against the time to come, that they may lay hold on eternal life.

20 O Timothy, keep that which is committed to thy trust, avoiding profane *and* vain babblings, and oppositions of science falsely so called:

21 Which some professing have erred concerning the faith. Grace *be* with thee. Amen.

¶ The first to Timothy was written from Laodicea, which is the chiefest city of Phrygia Pacatiana.

Amplified

6 [And it is, indeed, a source of immense profit, for] godliness accompanied with contentment—that contentment which is a sense of [m]inward sufficiency—is great *and* abundant gain.

7 For we brought nothing into the world, and *obviously* we cannot take anything out of the world;

8 But if we have food and clothing, with these we shall be content (satisfied).

9 But those who crave to be rich fall into temptation and a snare, and into many foolish (useless, godless) and hurtful desires that plunge men into ruin *and* destruction and miserable perishing.

10 For the love of money is a root of all evils; it is through this craving that some have been led astray, *and* have wandered from the faith and pierced themselves through with many [n]acute [mental] pangs.

11 But as for you, O man of God, flee from all these things; aim at *and* pursue righteousness—that is, right standing with God and true goodness; godliness (which is the loving fear of God and Christlikeness), faith, love, steadfastness (patience) and gentle-heartedness.

12 Fight the good fight of the faith; lay hold of the eternal life to which you were summoned, and confessed the good confession [of faith] before many witnesses.

13 In the presence of God Who preserves alive all living things, and Christ Jesus Who in His testimony before Pontius Pilate made the good confession,

14 I [solemnly] charge you to keep all His precepts unsullied *and* flawless, irreproachable until the appearing of our Lord Jesus Christ, the Anointed One.

15 Which will be shown forth in His own proper time by the blessed, only Sovereign, the King of kings and the Lord of lords;

16 Who alone has immortality [in the sense of exemption from every kind of death] and lives in unapproachable light, Whom no man has ever seen or can see. Unto Him be honor and everlasting power *and* dominion. Amen—so be it.

17 As for the rich in this world, charge them not to be proud *and* arrogant *and* contemptuous of others, nor to set their hopes on uncertain riches but on God, Who richly *and* ceaselessly provides us with everything for [our] enjoyment;

18 [Charge them] to do good, to be rich in good works, to be liberal *and* generous-hearted, ready to share [with others],

19 In this way laying up for themselves [the riches tha endure forever] a good foundation for the future, so tha they may grasp that which is life indeed.

20 O Timothy, guard *and* keep the deposit entrusted [t you]! Turn away from the irreverent babble *and* godles chatter, *with* the vain *and* empty *and* worldly phrases, an the subtleties *and* the contradictions in what is falsel called knowledge *and* spiritual illumination.

21 [For] by making such profession some have erred—missed the mark—as regards the faith. Grace (divin favor and blessing) be with you all! *Amen—so be it.*

m) Vincent.
n) Souter.

Living New Testament

6 Do you want to be truly rich? You already are if you are happy and good.

7 After all, we didn't bring any money with us when we came into the world, and we can't carry away a single penny when we die.

8 So we should be well satisfied without money if we have enough food and clothing.

9 But people who long to be rich soon begin to do all kinds of wrong things to get money, things that hurt them and make them evil-minded and finally send them to hell itself.

10 For the love of money is the first step toward all kinds of sin. Some people have even turned away from God because of their love for it, and as a result have pierced themselves with many sorrows.

11 Oh, Timothy, you are God's man. Run from all these evil things and work instead at what is right and good, learning to trust Him and love others, and to be patient and gentle.

12 Fight on for God. Hold tightly to the eternal life which God has given you, and which you have confessed with such a ringing confession before many witnesses.

13 I command you before God who gives life to all, and before Christ Jesus who gave a fearless testimony before Pontius Pilate,

14 That you fulfill all He has told you to do, so that no one can find fault with you from now until our Lord Jesus Christ returns.

15 For in due season Christ will be revealed from heaven by the blessed and only Almighty God, the King of Kings and Lord of Lords,

16 Who alone can never die, who lives in light so terrible that no human being can approach Him. No mere man has ever seen Him, nor ever will. Unto Him be honor and everlasting power and dominion forever and ever. Amen.

17 Tell those who are rich not to be proud and not to trust in their money, which will soon be gone, but their pride and trust should be in the living God who always richly gives us all we need for our enjoyment.

18 Tell them to use their money to do good. They should be rich in good works and should give happily to those in need, always being ready to share with others whatever God has given them.

19 By doing this they will be storing up real treasure for themselves in heaven—it is the only safe investment for eternity! And they will be living a fruitful Christian life down here as well.

20 Oh, Timothy, don't fail to do these things that God entrusted to you. Keep out of foolish arguments with those who boast of their "knowledge" and thus prove their lack of it.

21 Some of these people have missed the most important thing in life—they don't know God. May God's mercy be upon you.

Sincerely,
Paul

Revised Standard

6There is great gain in godliness with contentment; 7for we brought nothing into the world,
and[m] we cannot take anything out of the
world; 8but if we have food and clothing,
with these we shall be content. 9But those
who desire to be rich fall into temptation,
into a snare, into many senseless and hurtful desires that plunge men into ruin and
destruction. 10For the love of money is the
root of all evils; it is through this craving
that some have wandered away from the
faith and pierced their hearts with many
pangs.

The good fight of faith

11 But as for you, man of God, shun all
this; aim at righteousness, godliness, faith,
love, steadfastness, gentleness. 12Fight the
good fight of the faith; take hold of the
eternal life to which you were called when
you made the good confession in the presence
of many witnesses. 13In the presence of God
who gives life to all things, and of Christ
Jesus who in his testimony before Pontius
Pilate made the good confession, 14I charge
you to keep the commandment unstained
and free from reproach until the appearing
of our Lord Jesus Christ; 15and this will be
made manifest at the proper time by the
blessed and only Sovereign, the King of kings
and Lord of lords, 16who alone has immortality and dwells in unapproachable light,
whom no man has ever seen or can see. To
him be honor and eternal dominion. Amen.

The use of wealth

17 As for the rich in this world, charge
them not to be haughty, nor to set their
hopes on uncertain riches but on God who
richly furnishes us with everything to enjoy.
18They are to do good, to be rich in good
deeds, liberal and generous, 19thus laying up
for themselves a good foundation for the
future, so that they may take hold of the
life which is life indeed.

Final charge and benediction

20 O Timothy, guard what has been entrusted to you. Avoid the godless chatter and
contradictions of what is falsely called
knowledge, 21for by professing it some have
missed the mark as regards the faith.
Grace be with you.

[m] Other ancient authorities insert *it is certain that*

King James

THE SECOND EPISTLE OF PAUL THE APOSTLE
TO

Timothy

CHAPTER 1

PAUL, an apostle of Jesus Christ by the will of God, according to the promise of life which is in Christ Jesus,

2 To Timothy, *my* dearly beloved son: Grace, mercy, *and* peace, from God the Father and Christ Jesus our Lord.

3 I thank God, whom I serve from *my* forefathers with pure conscience, that without ceasing I have remembrance of thee in my prayers night and day;

4 Greatly desiring to see thee, being mindful of thy tears, that I may be filled with joy;

5 When I call to remembrance the unfeigned faith that is in thee, which dwelt first in thy grandmother Lois, and thy mother Eunice; and I am persuaded that in thee also.

6 Wherefore I put thee in remembrance that thou stir up the gift of God, which is in thee by the putting on of my hands.

7 For God hath not given us the spirit of fear; but of power, and of love, and of a sound mind.

8 Be not thou therefore ashamed of the testimony of our Lord, nor of me his prisoner: but be thou partaker of the afflictions of the gospel according to the power of God;

9 Who hath saved us, and called *us* with an holy calling, not according to our works, but according to his own purpose and grace, which was given us in Christ Jesus before the world began,

10 But is now made manifest by the appearing of our Saviour Jesus Christ, who hath abolished death, and hath brought life and immortality to light through the gospel:

11 Whereunto I am appointed a preacher, and an apostle, and a teacher of the Gentiles.

12 For the which cause I also suffer these things: nevertheless I am not ashamed: for I know whom I have believed, and am persuaded that he is able to keep that which I have committed unto him against that day.

13 Hold fast the form of sound words, which thou hast heard of me, in faith and love which is in Christ Jesus.

Amplified

THE SECOND LETTER OF PAUL
TO

Timothy

CHAPTER 1

PAUL, an apostle (special messenger) of Christ Jesus by the will of God according to the promise of life that is in Christ Jesus.

2 To Timothy, [my] beloved child: Grace (favor and spiritual blessing), mercy and (heart) peace from God the Father and Christ Jesus our Lord!

3 I thank God Whom I worship with a pure conscience, [[a]in the spirit of] my fathers, when without ceasing I remember you night and day in my prayers,

4 And when as I recall your tears, I yearn to see you, that I may be filled with joy.

5 I am calling up memories of your sincere *and* unqualified faith [the [b]leaning of your entire personality on God in Christ in absolute trust and confidence in His power, wisdom and goodness, a faith] that first lived permanently in (the heart of) your grandmother Lois and your mother Eunice and now, I am [fully] persuaded, (dwells) in you also.

6 That is why I would remind you to stir up—rekindle the embers, fan the flame and keep burning—the [gracious] gift of God, [the inner fire] that is in you by means of the laying on of my hands [[a]with those of the elders at your ordination].

7 For God did not give us a spirit of timidity—of cowardice, of craven and cringing and fawning fear—but [He has given us a spirit] of power and of love and of calm *and* well-balanced mind *and* discipline *and* self-control.

8 Do not blush *or* be ashamed then to testify to *and* for our Lord, nor of me, a prisoner for His sake, but [[c]with me] take your share of the suffering [to which the preaching] of the Gospel [may expose you, and do it] in the power of God.

9 [For it is He] Who delivered *and* saved us and called us with a calling in itself holy *and* leading to holiness—that is, to a life of consecration, a vocation of holiness; [He did it] not because of anything of merit that we have done, but because of *and* to further His own purpose and grace (unmerited favor) which was given us in Christ Jesus before the world began—eternal ages ago.

10 [It is that purpose and grace] which He now has made known *and* has fully disclosed *and* made real [to us] through the appearing of our Savior Christ Jesus Who annulled death *and* made it of no effect, and brought life and immortality—that is, immunity from eternal death—to light through the Gospel.

11 For [the proclaiming of] this [Gospel], I was appointed a herald (preacher) and an apostle (special messenger) and a teacher *of the Gentiles.*

12 And this is why I am suffering as I do. Still I am not ashamed, for I know—I perceive, have knowledge of and am acquainted with Him—Whom I have believed (adhered to and trusted in and relied on), and I am [positively] persuaded that He is able to guard *and* keep that which has been entrusted to me *and* which [d]I have committed [to Him], until that day.

13 Hold fast *and* follow the pattern of wholesome *and* sound teaching which you have heard from me, in [all] the faith and love which are [for us] in Christ Jesus.

---

a) Vincent.
b) Souter.
c) Vincent.
d) Alternate reading.

Living New Testament

II Timothy

CHAPTER 1

From: Paul, Jesus Christ's missionary, sent out by God to tell men and women everywhere about the eternal life He has promised them through faith in Jesus Christ.

2 *To:* Timothy, my dear son. May God the Father and Christ Jesus our Lord shower you with His kindness, mercy and peace.

3 How I thank God for you, Timothy. I pray for you every day, and many times during the long nights I beg my God to bless you richly. He is my fathers' God, and mine, and my only purpose in life is to please Him.

4 How I long to see you again. How happy I would be, for I remember your tears as we left each other.

5 I know how much you trust the Lord, just as your mother Eunice and your grandmother Lois do; and I feel sure you are still trusting Him as much as ever.

6 This being so, I want to remind you to stir into flame the strength and boldness[1] that is in you, that entered into you when I laid my hands upon your head and blessed you.

7 For the Holy Spirit, God's gift, does not want you to be afraid of people, but to be wise and strong, and to love them and enjoy being with them.

8 If you will stir up this inner power, you will never be afraid to tell others about our Lord, or to let them know that I am your friend even though I am here in jail for Christ's sake. You will be ready to suffer with me for the Lord, for He will give you strength in suffering.

9 It is He who saved us and chose us for His holy work, not because we deserved it but because that was His plan long before the world began—to show His love and kindness to us through Christ.

10 And now He has made all of this plain to us by the coming of our Savior Jesus Christ, who broke the power of death and showed us the way of everlasting life through trusting Him.

11 And God has chosen me to be His missionary, to preach to the Gentiles and teach them.

12 That is why I am suffering here in jail and I am certainly not ashamed of it, for I know the one in whom I trust, and I am sure that He is able to safely guard all that I have given Him until the day of His return.

13 Hold tightly to the pattern of truth I taught you, especially concerning the faith and love Christ Jesus offers you.[2]

---

mplied. Literally, "stir up the gift of God."
iterally, "that is in Christ Jesus."

Revised Standard

THE SECOND LETTER OF PAUL TO

Timothy

Salutation

1 Paul, an apostle of Christ Jesus by the
will of God according to the promise of
the life which is in Christ Jesus,
2 To Timothy, my beloved child:
Grace, mercy, and peace from God the Father and Christ Jesus our Lord.

Appeal for faithfulness

3 I thank God whom I serve with a clear
conscience, as did my fathers, when I remember you constantly in my prayers. [4]As
I remember your tears, I long night and day
to see you, that I may be filled with joy. [5]I
am reminded of your sincere faith, a faith
that dwelt first in your grandmother Lois
and your mother Eunice and now, I am sure,
dwells in you. [6]Hence I remind you to rekindle the gift of God that is within you
through the laying on of my hands; [7]for God
did not give us a spirit of timidity but a spirit
of power and love and self-control.
8 Do not be ashamed then of testifying to
our Lord, nor of me his prisoner, but take
your share of suffering for the gospel in the
power of God, [9]who saved us and called us
with a holy calling, not in virtue of our works
but in virtue of his own purpose and the
grace which he gave us in Christ Jesus ages
ago, [10]and now has manifested through the
appearing of our Savior Christ Jesus, who
abolished death and brought life and immortality to light through the gospel. [11]For this
gospel I was appointed a preacher and
apostle and teacher, [12]and therefore I suffer
as I do. But I am not ashamed, for I know
whom I have believed, and I am sure that he
is able to guard until that Day what has been
entrusted to me.[a] [13]Follow the pattern of the
sound words which you have heard from me,
in the faith and love which are in Christ

---

[a] Or *what I have entrusted to him*

King James

14 That good thing which was committed unto thee keep by the Holy Ghost which dwelleth in us.

15 This thou knowest, that all they which are in Asia be turned away from me; of whom are Phygellus and Hermogenes.

16 The Lord give mercy unto the house of Onesiphorus; for he oft refreshed me, and was not ashamed of my chain:

17 But, when he was in Rome he sought me out very diligently, and found *me.*

18 The Lord grant unto him that he may find mercy of the Lord in that day: and in how many things he ministered unto me at Ephesus, thou knowest very well.

Amplified

14 Guard *and* keep [with the greatest care] the precious *and* excellently adapted [Truth] which has been entrusted [to you], by the [help of the] Holy Spirit Who makes His home in us.

15 You already know that all who are in Asia turned away *and* forsook me, Phygelus and Hermogenes among them.

16 May the Lord grant [His] mercy to the family of Onesiphorus, for he often showed me kindness *and* ministered to my needs—comforting and reviving and bracing me like fresh air! He was not ashamed of my chains *and* imprisonment [for Christ's sake].

17 No, rather when he reached Rome he searched diligently *and* eagerly for me and found [me].

18 May the Lord grant to him that he may find mercy from the Lord on that [great] day! And you know how many things he did for me *and* what a help he was at Ephesus better [than I can tell you].

CHAPTER 2

THOU therefore, my son, be strong in the grace that is in Christ Jesus.

2 And the things that thou hast heard of me among many witnesses, the same commit thou to faithful men, who shall be able to teach others also.

3 Thou therefore endure hardness, as a good soldier of Jesus Christ.

4 No man that warreth entangleth himself with the affairs of *this* life; that he may please him who hath chosen him to be a soldier.

5 And if a man also strive for masteries, *yet* is he not crowned, except he strive lawfully.

6 The husbandman that laboureth must be first partaker of the fruits.

7 Consider what I say; and the Lord give thee understanding in all things.

8 Remember that Jesus Christ of the seed of David was raised from the dead according to my gospel:

9 Wherein I suffer trouble, as an evildoer, *even* unto bonds; but the word of God is not bound.

10 Therefore I endure all things for the elect's sakes, that they may also obtain the salvation which is in Christ Jesus with eternal glory.

11 *It is* a faithful saying: For if we be dead with *him,* we shall also live with *him:*

12 If we suffer, we shall also reign with *him:* if we deny *him,* he also will deny us:

13 If we believe not, *yet* he abideth faithful: he cannot deny himself.

14 Of these things put *them* in remembrance, charging *them* before the Lord that they strive not about words to no profit, *but* to the subverting of the hearers.

CHAPTER 2

SO you, my son, be strong—strengthened inwardly—in the grace (spiritual blessing) that is [to be found only] in Christ Jesus.

2 And the [instructions] which you have heard from me, along with many witnesses, transmit *and* entrust (as a deposit) to reliable *and* faithful men who will be competent *and* qualified to teach others also.

3 Take [with me] your share of the hardships *and* suffering [which you are called to endure] as a good (first class) soldier of Christ Jesus.

4 No soldier when in service gets entangled in the enterprises of [civilian] life; his aim is to satisfy *and* please the one who enlisted him.

5 And if any one enters competitive games, he is not crowned unless he competes lawfully—fairly, according to the rules laid down.

6 [It is] the hard-working farmer (who labors to produce) who must be the first partaker of the fruits.

7 Think over these things I am saying—understand them and grasp their application—for the Lord will gran you full insight *and* understanding in everything.

8 Constantly keep in mind Jesus Christ, the Messiah [as] risen from the dead, [as the prophesied King] descended from David, according to the good news (the Gospel that I preach. [Ps. 16:10.]

9 For that [Gospel] I am suffering affliction *and* eve wearing chains, like a criminal. But the Word of God i not chained *or* imprisoned!

10 Therefore I [am ready to] persevere *and* stand m ground with patience *and* endure everything for the sak of the elect [God's chosen], so that they too may obtai [the] salvation which is in Christ Jesus with [the reward o eternal glory.

11 The saying is worthy of confidence *and* sure: If w have died with Him, we shall also live with Him.

12 If we endure, we shall also reign with Him. If w deny *and* disown *and* reject Him, He will also deny *a* disown *and* reject us.

13 If we are faithless (do not believe and are untrue Him), He remains true [faithful to His Word and H righteous character], for He cannot deny Himself.

14 Remind [the people] of these facts, and [solemn charge them in the presence of the Lord to avoid pe controversy over words, which does no good, but ups *and* undermines the faith of the hearers.

Living New Testament

14 Guard well the splendid, God-given ability you received as a gift from the Holy Spirit who lives within you.

15 As you know, all the Christians who came here from Asia have deserted me; even Phygellus and Hermogenes are gone.

16 May the Lord bless Onesiphorus and all his family, because he visited me and encouraged me often. His visits revived me like a breath of fresh air, and he was never ashamed of my being in jail.

17 In fact, when he came to Rome he searched everywhere trying to find me, and finally did.

18 May the Lord give him a special blessing at the day of Christ's return. And you know better than I can tell you how much he helped me at Ephesus.

CHAPTER 2

Oh, Timothy, my son, be strong with the strength Christ Jesus gives you.

2 For you must teach others those things you and many others have heard me speak about. Teach these great truths to trustworthy men who will, in turn, pass them on to others.

3 Take your share of suffering as a good soldier of Jesus Christ, just as I do,

4 And as Christ's soldier do not let yourself become tied up in worldly affairs, for then you cannot satisfy the one who has enlisted you in His army.

5 Follow the Lord's rules for doing His work, just as an athlete either follows the rules or is disqualified and wins no prize.

6 Work hard, like a farmer who gets paid well if he raises a large crop.

7 Think over these three illustrations, and may the Lord help you to understand how they apply to you.

8 Don't ever forget the wonderful fact that Jesus Christ was a Man, born into King David's family; and that He was God, as shown by the fact that He rose again from the dead.

9 It is because I have preached these great truths that I am in trouble here and have been put in jail like a criminal. But the Word of God is not chained, even though I am.

10 I am more than willing to suffer if that will bring salvation and eternal glory in Christ Jesus to those God has chosen.

11 I am comforted by this truth, that when we suffer and die for Christ it only means that we will begin living with Him in heaven.

12 And if we think that our present service for Him is hard, just remember that some day we are going to sit with Him and rule with Him. But if we give up when we suffer, and turn against Christ, then He must turn against us.

13 Even when we are too weak to have any faith left, He remains faithful to us and will help us, for He cannot disown us who are part of Himself, and He will always carry out His promises to us.

14 Remind your people of these great facts, and command them in the name of the Lord not to argue over unimportant things. Such arguments are confusing and useless, and even harmful.

Revised Standard

Jesus; [14]guard the truth that has been entrusted to you by the Holy Spirit who dwells
within us.
15 You are aware that all who are in Asia
turned away from me, and among them
Phygelus and Hermogenes. [16]May the Lord
grant mercy to the household of Onesiphorus,
for he often refreshed me; he was not
ashamed of my chains, [17]but when he arrived
in Rome he searched for me eagerly and
found me—[18]may the Lord grant him to
find mercy from the Lord on that Day—and
you well know all the service he rendered at
Ephesus.

Appeal for endurance

2 You then, my son, be strong in the grace
that is in Christ Jesus, [2]and what you
have heard from me before many witnesses
entrust to faithful men who will be able to
teach others also. [3]Take your share of suffering as a good soldier of Christ Jesus. [4]No
soldier on service gets entangled in civilian
pursuits, since his aim is to satisfy the one
who enlisted him. [5]An athlete is not crowned
unless he competes according to the rules.
[6]It is the hard-working farmer who ought to
have the first share of the crops. [7]Think over
what I say, for the Lord will grant you understanding in everything.
8 Remember Jesus Christ, risen from the
dead, descended from David, as preached in
my gospel, [9]the gospel for which I am suffering and wearing fetters like a criminal.
But the word of God is not fettered. [10]There-
fore I endure everything for the sake of the
elect, that they also may obtain the salvation
which in Christ Jesus goes with eternal glory.
[11]The saying is sure:

If we have died with him, we shall also
live with him;
[12]if we endure, we shall also reign with him;
if we deny him, he will also deny us;
[13]if we are faithless, he remains faithful—
for he cannot deny himself.

A workman approved of God

14 Remind them of this, and charge them
before the Lord[b] to avoid disputing about
words, which does no good, but only ruins

[b] Other ancient authorities read *God*

King James

15 Study to shew thyself approved unto God, a workman that needeth not to be ashamed, rightly dividing the word of truth.

16 But shun profane *and* vain babblings: for they will increase unto more ungodliness.

17 And their word will eat as doth a canker: of whom is Hymenæus and Philetus;

18 Who concerning the truth have erred, saying that the resurrection is past already; and overthrow the faith of some.

19 Nevertheless the foundation of God standeth sure, having this seal, The Lord knoweth them that are his. And, Let every one that nameth the name of Christ depart from iniquity.

20 But in a great house there are not only vessels of gold and of silver, but also of wood and of earth; and some to honour, and some to dishonour.

21 If a man therefore purge himself from these, he shall be a vessel unto honour, sanctified, and meet for the master's use, *and* prepared unto every good work.

22 Flee also youthful lusts: but follow righteousness, faith, charity, peace, with them that call on the Lord out of a pure heart.

23 But foolish and unlearned questions avoid, knowing that they do gender strifes.

24 And the servant of the Lord must not strive; but be gentle unto all *men*, apt to teach, patient,

25 In meekness instructing those that oppose themselves; if God peradventure will give them repentance to the acknowledging of the truth;

26 And *that* they may recover themselves out of the snare of the devil, who are taken captive by him at his will.

Amplified

15 Study *and* be eager *and* do your utmost to present yourself to God approved (tested by trial), a workman who has no cause to be ashamed, correctly analyzing *and* accurately dividing—rightly handling and skillfully teaching—the Word of Truth.

16 But avoid all empty (vain, useless, idle) talk, for it will lead people into more *and* more ungodliness.

17 And their teaching [will devour; it] will eat its way like cancer *or* spread like gangrene. So it is with Hymenaeus and Philetus,

18 Who have missed the mark *and* swerved from the truth by arguing that the resurrection has already taken place. They are undermining the faith of some.

19 But the firm foundation [laid by] God stands, sure *and* unshaken, bearing this seal (inscription): The Lord knows those who are His, and, Let every one who names [himself by] the name of the Lord give up all iniquity *and* stand aloof from it. [Num. 16:5; Isa. 26:13.]

20 But in a great house there are not only vessels of gold and silver but also [utensils] of wood and earthenware, and some for honorable *and* noble [use] and some for menial *and* ignoble [use].

21 So whoever cleanses himself [from what is ignoble *and* unclean]—who separates himself from contact with contaminating and corrupting influences—will [then himself] be a vessel set apart *and* useful for honorable *and* noble purposes, consecrated and profitable to the Master, fit *and* ready for any good work.

22 Shun youthful lusts *and* flee from them, and aim at *and* pursue righteousness—all that is virtuous and good, right living, comformity to the will of God in thought, word and deed. [And aim at and pursue] faith, love, [and] peace—which is harmony and concord with others—in fellowship with all [Christians], who call upon the Lord out of a pure heart.

23 But refuse—shut your mind against, have nothing to do with—trifling (ill-informed, unedifying, stupid) controversies over ignorant questionings, for you know that they foster strife *and* breed quarrels.

24 And the servant of the Lord must not be quarrelsome—fighting and contending. Instead he must be kindly to every one *and* mild-tempered—preserving the bond of peace; he must be a skilled *and* suitable teacher, patient *and* forbearing *and* willing to suffer wrong.

25 He must correct his opponents with courtesy *and* gentleness, in the hope that God may grant that they will repent and come to know the Truth—that is, that they will perceive and recognize and become accurately acquainted with and acknowledge it,

26 And that they may come to their senses [and] escape out of the snare of the devil, having been held captive by him, [henceforth] to do His [God's] will.

CHAPTER 3

THIS know also, that in the last days perilous times shall come.

2 For men shall be lovers of their own selves, covetous, boasters, proud, blasphemers, disobedient to parents, unthankful, unholy,

CHAPTER 3

BUT understand this, that in the last days there will se in perilous times of great stress *and* trouble—hard t deal with and hard to bear.

2 For people will be lovers of self *and* [utterly] sel centered, lovers of money *and* aroused by an inordina (greedy) desire for wealth, proud *and* arrogant *and* co temptuous boasters. They will be abusive (blasphemou scoffers), disobedient to parents, ungrateful, unholy *a* profane.

Living New Testament

15 Work hard so God can say to you, "Well done." Be a good workman, one who does not need to be ashamed when God examines your work. Know what His Word says and means.

16 Steer clear of foolish discussions which lead people into the sin of anger with each other.

17 Things will be said that will burn and hurt for a long time to come. Hymenaeus and Philetus, in their love of argument, are men like that.

18 They have left the path of truth, preaching the lie that the resurrection of the dead has already occurred; and they have weakened the faith of some who believe them.

19 But God's truth stands firm like a great rock, and nothing can shake it. It is a foundation stone with these words written on it: "The Lord knows those who are really His," and "A person who calls himself a Christian should not be doing things that are wrong."

20 In a wealthy home there are dishes made of gold and silver as well as some made from wood and clay. The expensive dishes are used for guests, and the cheap ones are used in the kitchen or to put garbage in.

21 If you stay away from sin you will be like one of these dishes made of purest gold—the very best in the house—so that Christ Himself can use you for His highest purposes.

22 Run from anything that gives you the evil thoughts that young men often have, but stay close to anything that makes you want to do right. Have faith and love, and enjoy the companionship of those who love the Lord and have pure hearts.

23 Again I say, don't get involved in foolish arguments which only upset people and make them angry.

24 God's people must not be quarrelsome; they must be gentle, patient teachers of those who are wrong.

25 Be humble when you are trying to teach those who are mixed up concerning the truth. For if you talk meekly and courteously to them they are more likely, with God's help, to turn away from their wrong ideas and believe what is true.

26 Then they will come to their senses and escape from Satan's trap of slavery to sin which he uses to catch them whenever he likes, and then they can begin doing the will of God.

CHAPTER 3

You may as well know this too, Timothy, that in the last days it is going to be very difficult to be a Christian.

2 For people will love only themselves and their money; they will be proud and boastful, sneering at God, disobedient to their parents, ungrateful to them, and thoroughly bad.

Revised Standard

the hearers. 15Do your best to present yourself to God as one approved, a workman who
has no need to be ashamed, rightly handling
the word of truth. 16Avoid such godless chatter, for it will lead people into more and
more ungodliness, 17and their talk will eat
its way like gangrene. Among them are
Hymenaeus and Philetus, 18who have swerved
from the truth by holding that the resurrection is past already. They are upsetting the
faith of some. 19But God's firm foundation
stands, bearing this seal: "The Lord knows
those who are his," and, "Let every one who
names the name of the Lord depart from
iniquity."
20 In a great house there are not only vessels of gold and silver but also of wood and
earthenware, and some for noble use, some
for ignoble. 21If any one purifies himself
from what is ignoble, then he will be a
vessel for noble use, consecrated and useful
to the master of the house, ready for any
good work. 22So shun youthful passions and
aim at righteousness, faith, love, and peace,
along with those who call upon the Lord
from a pure heart. 23Have nothing to do
with stupid, senseless controversies; you
know that they breed quarrels. 24And the
Lord's servant must not be quarrelsome but
kindly to every one, an apt teacher, forbearing, 25correcting his opponents with gentleness. God may perhaps grant that they will
repent and come to know the truth, 26and
they may escape from the snare of the devil,
after being captured by him to do his will.[c]

The coming apostasy

3 But understand this, that in the last days
there will come times of stress. 2For men
will be lovers of self, lovers of money, proud,
arrogant, abusive, disobedient to their par-

---

[c] Or *by him, to do his* (that is, God's) *will*

King James

3 Without natural affection, trucebreakers, false accusers, incontinent, fierce, despisers of those that are good,

4 Traitors, heady, highminded, lovers of pleasures more than lovers of God;

5 Having a form of godliness, but denying the power thereof: from such turn away.

6 For of this sort are they which creep into houses, and lead captive silly women laden with sins, led away with divers lusts,

7 Ever learning, and never able to come to the knowledge of the truth.

8 Now as Jannes and Jambres withstood Moses, so do these also resist the truth: men of corrupt minds, reprobate concerning the faith.

9 But they shall proceed no further: for their folly shall be manifest unto all *men*, as theirs also was.

10 But thou hast fully known my doctrine, manner of life, purpose, faith, longsuffering, charity, patience,

11 Persecutions, afflictions, which came unto me at Antioch, at Iconium, at Lystra; what persecutions I endured: but out of *them* all the Lord delivered me.

12 Yea, and all that will live godly in Christ Jesus shall suffer persecution.

13 But evil men and seducers shall wax worse and worse, deceiving, and being deceived.

14 But continue thou in the things which thou hast learned and hast been assured of, knowing of whom thou hast learned *them;*

15 And that from a child thou hast known the holy scriptures, which are able to make thee wise unto salvation through faith which is in Christ Jesus.

16 All scripture *is* given by inspiration of God, and *is* profitable for doctrine, for reproof, for correction, for instruction in righteousness:

17 That the man of God may be perfect, throughly furnished unto all good works.

Amplified

3 [They will be] without natural (human) affection (callous and inhuman), relentless—admitting of no truce *or* appeasement. [They will be] slanderers—false accusers, trouble makers; intemperate *and* loose in morals *and* conduct, uncontrolled *and* fierce, haters of good.

4 [They will be] treacherous (betrayers), rash [and] inflated with self-conceit. [They will be] lovers of sensual pleasures *and* vain amusements more than *and* rather than lovers of God.

5 For [although] they hold a form of piety (true religion), they deny *and* reject *and* are strangers to the power of it—their conduct belies the genuineness of their profession. Avoid [all] such people—turn away from them.

6 For among them are those who worm their way into homes and captivate silly *and* weak-natured *and* spiritually dwarfed women, loaded down with [the burden of their] sins, [and easily] swayed *and* led away by various evil desires *and* seductive impulses.

7 [These weak women will listen to anybody who will teach them]; they are forever inquiring *and* getting information, but are never able to arrive at a recognition *and* knowledge of the Truth.

8 Now just as Jannes and Jambres were hostile to *and* resisted Moses, so these men also are hostile to *and* oppose the Truth. They have depraved *and* distorted minds, and are reprobate *and* counterfeit *and* to be rejected as far as the faith is concerned. [Exod. 7:11.]

9 But they will not get very far, for their rash folly will become obvious to everybody, as was that of those [magicians mentioned].

10 Now you have closely observed *and* diligently followed my teaching, conduct, purpose in life, faith, patience, love, steadfastness,

11 Persecutions, sufferings, such as occurred to me at Antioch, at Iconium, and at Lystra, persecutions I endured, but out of them all the Lord delivered me.

12 Indeed all who delight in piety *and* are determined to live a devoted *and* godly life in Christ Jesus will meet with persecution—that is, will be made to suffer because of their religious stand.

13 But wicked men and imposters will go on from bad to worse, deceiving *and* leading astray others and being deceived *and* led astray themselves.

14 But as for you, continue to hold to the things that you have learned and of which you are convinced, knowing from whom you learned [them],

15 And how from your childhood you have had a knowledge of *and* been acquainted with the sacred writings which are able to instruct you *and* give you the understanding for salvation which comes through faith in Christ Jesus [that is, through the [e]leaning of the entire human personality on God in Christ Jesus in absolute trust and confidence in His power, wisdom and goodness].

16 Every Scripture *is* God-breathed—given by His inspiration—and profitable for instruction, for reproof *and* conviction of sin, for correction of error *and* discipline in obedience, *and* for training in righteousness [that is, in holy living, in conformity to God's will in thought, purpose and action],

17 So that the man of God may be complete *and* proficient, well-fitted *and* thoroughly equipped for every good work.

---

e) Souter.

Living New Testament

3 They will be hardhearted and never give in to others; they will be constant liars and troublemakers and will think nothing of immorality. They will be rough and cruel, and sneer at those who try to be good.

4 They will betray their friends; they will be hotheaded, puffed up with pride, and prefer good times to worshiping God.

5 They will go to church,[1] yes, but they won't really believe anything they hear. Don't be taken in by people like that.

6 They are the kind who craftily sneak into other people's homes and make friendships with silly, sin-burdened women and teach them their new doctrines.

7 Women of that kind are forever following new teachers, but they never understand the truth.

8 And these teachers fight truth just as Jannes and Jambres fought against Moses. They have dirty minds, warped and twisted, and have turned against the Christian faith.

9 But they won't get away with all this forever. Some day their deceit will be well-known to everyone, as was the sin of Jannes and Jambres.

10 But you know from watching me that I am not that kind of person. You know what I believe and the way I live and what I want. You know my faith in Christ and how I have suffered. You know my love for you, and my patience.

11 You know how many troubles I have had as a result of my preaching the Good News. You know about all that was done to me while I was visiting in Antioch, Iconium and Lystra, but the Lord delivered me.

12 Yes, and suffering will come to all who decide to live godly lives to please Christ Jesus, from those who hate Him.

13 In fact, evil men and false teachers will become worse and worse, deceiving many, they themselves having been deceived by Satan.

14 But you must keep on believing the things you have been taught. You know they are true for you know that you can trust those of us who have taught you.

15 You know how, when you were a small child, you were taught the holy Scriptures; and it is these that make you wise to accept God's salvation by trusting in Christ Jesus.

16 The whole Bible[2] was given to us by inspiration from God and is useful to teach us what is true and to make us realize what is wrong in our lives; it straightens us out and helps us do what is right.

17 It is God's way of making us well-prepared at every point, fully equipped to do good to everyone.

Literally, "having a form of godliness."
Literally, "every Scripture."

Revised Standard

ents, ungrateful, unholy, 3 inhuman, implacable, slanderers, profligates, fierce, haters of
good, 4 treacherous, reckless, swollen with
conceit, lovers of pleasure rather than lovers
of God, 5 holding the form of religion but
denying the power of it. Avoid such people.
6 For among them are those who make their
way into households and capture weak
women, burdened with sins and swayed by
various impulses, 7 who will listen to anybody and can never arrive at a knowledge of
the truth. 8 As Jannes and Jambres opposed
Moses, so these men also oppose the truth,
men of corrupt mind and counterfeit faith;
9 but they will not get very far, for their
folly will be plain to all, as was that of those
two men.

The defense of the faith

10 Now you have observed my teaching,
my conduct, my aim in life, my faith, my
patience, my love, my steadfastness, 11 my
persecutions, my sufferings, what befell me
at Antioch, at Iconium, and at Lystra, what
persecutions I endured; yet from them all
the Lord rescued me. 12 Indeed all who desire
to live a godly life in Christ Jesus will be
persecuted, 13 while evil men and impostors
will go on from bad to worse, deceivers and
deceived. 14 But as for you, continue in what
you have learned and have firmly believed,
knowing from whom you learned it 15 and
how from childhood you have been acquainted with the sacred writings which are
able to instruct you for salvation through
faith in Christ Jesus. 16 All scripture is inspired by God and[d] profitable for teaching,
for reproof, for correction, and for training
in righteousness, 17 that the man of God may
be complete, equipped for every good work.

[d] Or *Every scripture inspired by God is also*

King James

CHAPTER 4

I CHARGE *thee* therefore before God, and the Lord Jesus Christ, who shall judge the quick and the dead at his appearing and his kingdom;

2 Preach the word; be instant in season, out of season; reprove, rebuke, exhort with all longsuffering and doctrine.

3 For the time will come when they will not endure sound doctrine; but after their own lusts shall they heap to themselves teachers, having itching ears;

4 And they shall turn away *their* ears from the truth, and shall be turned unto fables.

5 But watch thou in all things, endure afflictions, do the work of an evangelist, make full proof of thy ministry.

6 For I am now ready to be offered, and the time of my departure is at hand.

7 I have fought a good fight, I have finished *my* course, I have kept the faith:

8 Henceforth there is laid up for me a crown of righteousness, which the Lord, the righteous judge, shall give me at that day: and not to me only, but unto all them also that love his appearing.

9 Do thy diligence to come shortly unto me:

10 For Demas hath forsaken me, having loved this present world, and is departed unto Thessalonica; Crescens to Galatia, Titus unto Dalmatia.

11 Only Luke is with me. Take Mark, and bring him with thee: for he is profitable to me for the ministry.

12 And Tychicus have I sent to Ephesus.

13 The cloak that I left at Troas with Carpus, when thou comest, bring *with thee,* and the books, *but* especially the parchments.

14 Alexander the coppersmith did me much evil: the Lord reward him according to his works:

15 Of whom be thou ware also; for he hath greatly withstood our words.

16 At my first answer no man stood with me, but all *men* forsook me: *I pray God* that it may not be laid to their charge.

17 Notwithstanding the Lord stood with me, and strengthened me; that by me the preaching might be fully known, and *that* all the Gentiles might hear: and I was delivered out of the mouth of the lion.

18 And the Lord shall deliver me from every evil work, and will preserve *me* unto his heavenly kingdom: to whom *be* glory for ever and ever. Amen.

19 Salute Prisca and Aquila, and the household of Onesiphorus.

20 Erastus abode at Corinth: but Trophimus have I left at Miletum sick.

Amplified

CHAPTER 4

I CHARGE [you] in the presence of God and of Christ Jesus Who is to judge the living and the dead, and by (in the light of) His coming and His kingdom:

2 Herald *and* preach the Word! Keep your sense of urgency (stand by, be at hand and ready, whether the opportunity seems to be favorable or unfavorable, whether it is convenient or inconvenient, whether it be welcome or unwelcome, you as preacher of the Word are to show people in what way their lives are wrong) *and* convince them, rebuking *and* correcting, warning *and* urging *and* encouraging them, being unflagging *and* inexhaustible in patience and teaching.

3 For the time is coming when [people] will not tolerate (endure) sound *and* wholesome instruction, but having ears itching [for something pleasing and gratifying], they will gather to themselves one teacher after another to a considerable number, chosen to satisfy their own liking *and* to foster the errors they hold,

4 And will turn aside from hearing the truth and wander off into myths *and* man-made fictions.

5 As for you, be calm *and* cool *and* steady, accept *and* suffer unflinchingly every hardship, do the work of an evangelist; fully perform all the duties of your ministry.

6 For I am already about to be sacrificed—my life is about to be poured out [as a drink offering]; the time of my [spirit's] release [from the body] is at hand *and* I will soon go free.

7 I have fought the good (worthy, honorable and noble) fight; I have finished the race; I have kept (firmly held) the faith.

8 (As to what remains,) henceforth there is laid up for me the [victor's] crown of righteousness—for being right with God and doing right—which the Lord, the righteous Judge, will award to me *and* recompense me on that [great] day; and not to me only but also to all those who have loved *and* yearned for *and* welcomed His appearing [His return].

9 Make every effort to come to me soon.

10 For Demas has deserted me for love of this present world and has gone to Thessalonica; Crescens [has gone] to Galatia, Titus to Dalmatia.

11 Luke alone is with me. Get Mark and bring him with you, for he is very helpful to me for the ministry.

12 Tychicus I have sent to Ephesus.

13 [When] you come, bring the cloak that I left at Troas with Carpus; also the books, especially the parchments.

14 Alexander the coppersmith did me great wrongs. The Lord will pay him back for his actions.

15 Beware of him yourself, for he opposed *and* resisted our message very strongly *and* exceedingly.

16 At my first trial no one acted in my defense (as my advocate) *or* took my part *or* [even] stood with me, but all forsook me. May it not be charged against them!

17 But the Lord stood by me and strengthened me, so that through me the (Gospel) message might be fully proclaimed and all the Gentiles might hear it. So I was delivered out of the jaws of the lion.

18 [And indeed] the Lord will certainly deliver *and* [f]draw me to Himself from every assault of evil. He will preserve *and* bring [me] safe unto His heavenly kingdom. To Him be the glory forever and ever. Amen—so be it.

19 Give my greetings to Prisca and Aquila, and to the household of Onesiphorus.

20 Erastus stayed on at Corinth, but Trophimus I left ill at Miletus.

---

f) Primary meaning of the Greek: "draw to one's self." Thayer; Abbott-Smith.

Living New Testament

CHAPTER 4

And so I solemnly urge you before God and before Christ Jesus—who will some day judge the living and the dead when He appears to set up His kingdom—

2 To preach the Word of God urgently at all times, whenever you get the chance, in season and out, when it is convenient and when it is not. Correct and rebuke your people when they need it, encourage them to do right, and all the time be feeding them patiently with God's Word.

3 For there is going to come a time when people won't listen to the truth, but will go around looking for teachers who will tell them just what they want to hear.

4 They won't listen to what the Bible says but will blithely follow their own misguided ideas.

5 You must stay awake and watch out for all these dangers. And don't be afraid of suffering for the Lord. Bring others to Christ. Leave nothing undone that you ought to do.

6 I say this because I won't be around to help you very much longer. My time has almost run out. Very soon now I will be on my way to heaven.

7 I have fought long and hard for my Lord, and through it all I have kept true to Him. And now the time has come for me to stop fighting and rest.

8 In heaven a crown is waiting for me which the Lord, the righteous Judge, will give me on that great day of His return. And not just to me, but to all those whose lives show that they are eagerly looking forward to His coming back again.

9 Please come as soon as you can,

10 For Demas has left me. He loved the good things of this life and went to Thessalonica. Crescens has gone to Galatia, Titus to Dalmatia.

11 Only Luke is with me. Bring Mark with you when you come, for I need him.

12 (Tychicus is gone too, as I sent him to Ephesus.)

13 When you come, be sure to bring the coat I left at Troas with Brother Carpus, and also the books, but especially the parchments.

14 Alexander the coppersmith has done me much harm. The Lord will punish him,

15 But be careful of him, for he fought against everything we said.

16 The first time I was brought before the judge no one was here to help me. Everyone had run away. I hope that they will not be blamed for it.

17 But the Lord stood with me and gave me the pportunity to boldly preach a whole sermon for all the vorld to hear. And He saved me from being thrown to he lions.[1]

18 Yes, and the Lord will always deliver me from all vil and will bring me into His heavenly kingdom. To God e the glory for ever and ever. Amen.

19 Please say "hello" for me to Priscilla and Aquila and hose living at the home of Onesiphorus.

20 Erastus stayed at Corinth, and I left Trophimus sick t Miletus.

---

[1] iterally, "I was delivered out of the mouth of the lion."

Revised Standard

Charge to preach sound doctrine

4 I charge you in the presence of God and
of Christ Jesus who is to judge the living
and the dead, and by his appearing and his
kingdom: 2preach the word, be urgent in season and out of season, convince, rebuke, and
exhort, be unfailing in patience and in teaching. 3For the time is coming when people
will not endure sound teaching, but having
itching ears they will accumulate for themselves teachers to suit their own likings, 4and
will turn away from listening to the truth
and wander into myths. 5As for you, always
be steady, endure suffering, do the work of
an evangelist, fulfil your ministry.
6 For I am already on the point of being
sacrificed; the time of my departure has
come. 7I have fought the good fight, I have
finished the race, I have kept the faith.
8Henceforth there is laid up for me the crown
of righteousness, which the Lord, the righteous judge, will award to me on that Day,
and not only to me but also to all who have
loved his appearing.

Greetings and benediction

9 Do your best to come to me soon. 10For
Demas, in love with this present world, has
deserted me and gone to Thessalonica;
Crescens has gone to Galatia,[e] Titus to Dalmatia. 11Luke alone is with me. Get Mark
and bring him with you; for he is very useful
in serving me. 12Tychicus I have sent to
Ephesus. 13When you come, bring the cloak
that I left with Carpus at Troas, also the
books, and above all the parchments. 14Alex-
ander the coppersmith did me great harm;
the Lord will requite him for his deeds. 15Be-
ware of him yourself, for he strongly opposed
our message. 16At my first defense no one
took my part; all deserted me. May it not be
charged against them! 17But the Lord stood
by me and gave me strength to proclaim the
word fully, that all the Gentiles might hear
it. So I was rescued from the lion's mouth.
18The Lord will rescue me from every evil
and save me for his heavenly kingdom. To
him be the glory for ever and ever. Amen.

19 Greet Prisca and Aquila, and the
household of Onesiphorus. 20Erastus remained at Corinth; Trophimus I left ill at

---

[e] Other ancient authorities read *Gaul*

King James

21 Do thy diligence to come before winter. Eubulus greeteth thee, and Pudens, and Linus, and Claudia, and all the brethren.
22 The Lord Jesus Christ *be* with thy spirit. Grace *be* with you. Amen.

¶ The second *epistle* unto Timotheus, ordained the first bishop of the church of the Ephesians, was written from Rome, when Paul was brought before Nero the second time.

Amplified

21 Do hasten *and* try your best to come to me before winter. Eubulus wishes to be remembered to you, as do Pudens and Linus and Claudia and all the brethren.
22 The Lord *Jesus Christ* be with your spirit. Grace (God's favor and blessing) be with you. *Amen.*

Living New Testament

21 Do try to be here before winter. Eubulus sends you greetings, and so do Pudens, Linus, Claudia, and all the others.

22 May the Lord Jesus Christ be with your spirit.

Farewell,
Paul

Revised Standard

Miletus. 21Do your best to come before winter. Eubulus sends greetings to you, as do Pudens and Linus and Claudia and all the brethren.

22 The Lord be with your spirit. Grace be with you.

King James

THE EPISTLE OF PAUL THE APOSTLE TO

Titus

CHAPTER 1

PAUL, a servant of God, and an apostle
of Jesus Christ, according to the faith of
God's elect, and the acknowledging of the
truth which is after godliness;
2 In hope of eternal life, which God, that
cannot lie, promised before the world began;
3 But hath in due times manifested his
word through preaching, which is committed
unto me according to the commandment of
God our Saviour;
4 To Titus, *mine* own son after the common faith: Grace, mercy, *and* peace, from
God the Father and the Lord Jesus Christ
our Saviour.
5 For this cause left I thee in Crete, that
thou shouldest set in order the things that
are wanting, and ordain elders in every city,
as I had appointed thee:
6 If any be blameless, the husband of one
wife, having faithful children not accused of
riot or unruly.
7 For a bishop must be blameless, as the
steward of God; not selfwilled, not soon
angry, not given to wine, no striker, not
given to filthy lucre;
8 But a lover of hospitality, a lover of
good men, sober, just, holy, temperate;
9 Holding fast the faithful word as he
hath been taught, that he may be able by
sound doctrine both to exhort and to convince the gainsayers.
10 For there are many unruly and vain
talkers and deceivers, specially they of the
circumcision:
11 Whose mouths must be stopped, who
subvert whole houses, teaching things which
they ought not, for filthy lucre's sake.
12 One of themselves, *even* a prophet of
their own, said, The Cretians *are* alway
liars, evil beasts, slow bellies.
13 This witness is true. Wherefore rebuke
them sharply, that they may be sound in the
faith;
14 Not giving heed to Jewish fables, and
commandments of men, that turn from the
truth.

Amplified

THE LETTER OF PAUL
TO

Titus

CHAPTER 1

PAUL, a bond servant of God and an apostle (a special
messenger) of Jesus Christ, the Messiah, to stimulate
and promote the faith of God's chosen ones and lead them
on to accurate discernment *and* recognition of *and* acquaintance with the Truth which belongs to *and* harmon-
izes with *and* tends to godliness,
2 (Resting) in the hope of eternal life, [life] which the
ever-truthful God Who cannot deceive, promised before
the world *or* the ages of time began.
3 And [now] in His own appointed time He has made
manifest (made known) His Word *and* revealed it as His
message through the preaching entrusted to me by command of God our Savior;
4 To Titus, my true child according to a common
(general) faith: Grace (favor and spiritual blessing) and
heart-peace from God the Father and *the Lord* Christ
Jesus our Savior.
5 For this reason I left you [behind] in Crete, that you
might set right what was defective *and* finish what was left
undone, and that you might appoint elders *and* set them
over the churches (assemblies) in every city as I directed
you.
6 [These elders should be] men who are of unquestionable integrity *and* are irreproachable, the husband of [but]
one wife, whose children are [well-trained and are] believers, not open to the accusation of being loose in morals
and conduct or unruly *and* disorderly.
7 For the bishop *as* an overseer and God's steward
must be blameless; not self-willed *or* arrogant *or* presumptuous; he must not be quick-tempered *or* given to drink or
pugnacious (brawling, violent); he must not be grasping
and greedy for filthy lucre (financial gain);
8 But he must be hospitable—loving and a friend to
believers, especially to the strangers and foreigners. [He
must be] a lover of goodness—of good people and good
things; sober-minded (sensible, discreet); upright *and* fair-
minded, a devout man *and* religiously right, temperate *and*
keeping himself in hand.
9 He must hold fast to the sure *and* trustworthy Word
of God as he was taught it, so that he may be able both to
give stimulating instruction *and* encouragement in sound
(wholesome) doctrine, and to refute *and* convict those
who contradict *and* oppose it—showing the wayward their
error.
10 For there are many disorderly *and* unruly men who
are idle (vain, empty) *and* misleading talkers and self-
deceivers, *as well as* deceiving others. [This is true] especially of those [who have come over from Judaism] of the
circumcision party.
11 Their mouths must be stopped, for they are mentally distressing *and* subverting whole families by teaching
what they ought not to teach, for the purpose of getting
base advantage *and* disreputable gain.
12 One of their [very] number, a prophet of their own
said, Cretans are always liars, hurtful beasts, idle *and* lazy
gluttons.
13 And this account of them is [really] true. Because i
is [true], rebuke them sharply—deal sternly, [even] severely with them—so that they may be sound in the faith *an*
free from error,
14 [And may show their soundness by] ceasing to giv
attention to Jewish myths *and* fables or to rules [lai
down] by [mere] men who reject *and* turn their backs o
the Truth.

Living New Testament

Titus

CHAPTER 1

From: Paul, the slave of God and the messenger of Jesus Christ. I have been sent to bring faith to those God has chosen and to teach them to know God's truth—the kind of truth that changes lives—so that they can have eternal life, which God promised them before the world began—and He cannot lie.

3 And now in His own good time He has revealed this Good News and permits me to tell it to everyone. By command of God our Savior I have been trusted to do this work for Him.

4 *To:* Titus, who is truly my son in the affairs of the Lord. May God the Father and Christ Jesus our Savior give you His blessings and His peace.

5 I left you there on the island of Crete so that you could do whatever was needed to help strengthen each of its churches, and I asked you to appoint pastors[1] in every city who would follow the instructions I gave you.

6 The men you choose must be well thought of for their good lives; they must have only one wife and their children must love the Lord and not have a reputation for being wild or disobedient to their parents.

7 These pastors[1] must be men of blameless lives because they are God's ministers. They must not be proud or impatient; they must not be drunkards or fighters or greedy for money.

8 They must enjoy having guests in their homes and must love all that is good. They must be sensible men, and fair. They must be clean-minded and level-headed.

9 Their belief in the truth which they have been taught must be strong and steadfast, so that they will be able to teach it to others and show those who disagree with them where they are wrong.

10 For there are many who refuse to obey; this is especially true among those who say that all Christians must obey the Jewish laws. But this is foolish talk; it blinds people to the truth,

11 And it must be stopped. Already whole families have been turned away from the grace of God. Such teachers are only after your money.

12 One of their own men, a prophet from Crete, has said about them, "These men of Crete are all liars; they are like lazy animals, living only to satisfy their stomachs."

13 And this is true. So speak to the Christians there as sternly as necessary to make them strong in the faith,

14 And to stop them from listening to Jewish folk tales and the demands of men who have turned their back on the truth.

---

1 More literally, "elders."

Revised Standard

THE LETTER OF PAUL TO

Titus

Salutation

1 Paul, a servant[a] of God and an apostle
of Jesus Christ, to further the faith of
God's elect and their knowledge of the truth
which accords with godliness, [2]in hope of
eternal life which God, who never lies,
promised ages ago [3]and at the proper time
manifested in his word through the preaching with which I have been entrusted by
command of God our Savior;

4 To Titus, my true child in a common faith:

Grace and peace from God the Father and Christ Jesus our Savior.

Qualifications for elders

5 This is why I left you in Crete, that you
might amend what was defective, and appoint elders in every town as I directed you,
[6]if any man is blameless, the husband of one
wife, and his children are believers and not
open to the charge of being profligate or insubordinate. [7]For a bishop, as God's steward,
must be blameless; he must not be arrogant
or quick-tempered or a drunkard or violent
or greedy for gain, [8]but hospitable, a lover
of goodness, master of himself, upright, holy,
and self-controlled; [9]he must hold firm to the
sure word as taught, so that he may be able
to give instruction in sound doctrine and also
to confute those who contradict it.

Dealing with false teachers

[10]For there are many insubordinate men,
empty talkers and deceivers, especially the
circumcision party; [11]they must be silenced,
since they are upsetting whole families by
teaching for base gain what they have no
right to teach. [12]One of themselves, a prophet
of their own, said, "Cretans are always liars,
evil beasts, lazy gluttons." [13]This testimony
is true. Therefore rebuke them sharply, that
they may be sound in the faith, [14]instead of
giving heed to Jewish myths or to commands

---

a Or *slave*

King James

15 Unto the pure all things *are* pure: but unto them that are defiled and unbelieving *is* nothing pure; but even their mind and conscience is defiled.

16 They profess that they know God; but in works they deny *him*, being abominable, and disobedient, and unto every good work reprobate.

Amplified

15 To the pure [in heart and conscience] all things are pure, but to the defiled *and* corrupt and unbelieving nothing is pure; their very mind and conscience are defiled *and* polluted.

16 They profess to know God—to recognize, perceive and be acquainted with Him—but deny *and* disown *and* renounce Him by what they do; they are detestable *and* loathsome, unbelieving *and* disobedient *and* disloyal *and* rebellious, and [they are] unfit *and* worthless for good work (deed or enterprise) of any kind.

CHAPTER 2

BUT speak thou the things which become sound doctrine:

2 That the aged men be sober, grave, temperate, sound in faith, in charity, in patience.

3 The aged women likewise, that *they be* in behaviour as becometh holiness, not false accusers, not given to much wine, teachers of good things;

4 That they may teach the young women to be sober, to love their husbands, to love their children,

5 *To be* discreet, chaste, keepers at home, good, obedient to their own husbands, that the word of God be not blasphemed.

6 Young men likewise exhort to be sober minded.

7 In all things shewing thyself a pattern of good works: in doctrine *shewing* uncorruptness, gravity, sincerity,

8 Sound speech, that cannot be condemned; that he that is of the contrary part may be ashamed, having no evil thing to say of you.

9 *Exhort* servants to be obedient unto their own masters, *and* to please *them* well in all *things;* not answering again;

10 Not purloining, but shewing all good fidelity; that they may adorn the doctrine of God our Saviour in all things.

11 For the grace of God that bringeth salvation hath appeared to all men,

12 Teaching us that, denying ungodliness and worldly lusts, we should live soberly, righteously, and godly, in this present world;

13 Looking for that blessed hope, and the glorious appearing of the great God and our Saviour Jesus Christ;

CHAPTER 2

BUT [as for] you, teach what is fitting *and* becoming to sound (wholesome) doctrine—the character and right living that identify true Christians.

2 Urge the older men to be temperate, venerable (serious), sensible, self-controlled; sound in the faith, in the love, and in the steadfastness *and* patience [of Christ].

3 Bid the older women similarly to be reverent *and* devout in their deportment, as becomes those engaged in sacred service, not slanderers or slaves to drink. They are to give good counsel *and* be teachers of what is right *and* noble,

4 So that they will wisely train the young women to be [a]sane and sober-minded—temperate, disciplined—and to love their husbands and their children;

5 To be self-controlled, chaste, homemakers, good-natured (kindhearted), adapting *and* subordinating themselves to their husbands, that the word of God may not be exposed to reproach—blasphemed or discredited.

6 In a similar way urge the younger men to be self-restrained *and* to behave prudently—taking life seriously.

7 And show your own self in all respects to be a pattern *and* a model of good deeds *and* works, teaching what is unadulterated, showing gravity—[that is,] having the strictest regard for truth and purity of motive, with dignity and seriousness.

8 And let your instruction be sound *and* fit *and* wise *and* wholesome, vigorous and [b]irrefutable *and* above censure, so that the opponent may be put to shame, finding nothing discrediting *or* evil to say about us.

9 [Tell] bond servants to be submissive to their masters, to be pleasing *and* give satisfaction in every way. [Warn them] not to talk back *or* contradict,

10 Nor to steal by taking things of small value, but to prove themselves truly loyal *and* entirely reliable *and* faithful throughout, so that in everything they may be an ornament *and* do credit to the teaching [which is [c]from and about] God our Savior.

11 For the grace of God—His unmerited favor and blessing—has come forward (appeared) for the deliverance from sin *and* the eternal salvation for all mankind.

12 It has trained us to reject *and* renounce all ungodliness (irreligion) and worldly (passionate) desires, to live discreet (temperate, self-controlled), upright, devout (spiritually-whole) lives in this present world,

13 Awaiting *and* looking for the [fulfillment, the realization of our] blessed hope, even the glorious appearing of our great God and Savior Christ Jesus, the Messiah, the Anointed One,

---

a) The Greek word here for "train" means to make sane, sober minded; to moderate, to discipline. (-Vincent.)
b) Way.
c) Greek, "of."

Living New Testament

15 A person who is pure of heart sees goodness and purity in everything; but a person whose own heart is evil and untrusting finds evil in everything, for his dirty mind and rebellious heart color all he sees and hears.

16 Such persons claim they know God, but from seeing the way they act, one knows they don't. They are rotten and disobedient, worthless so far as doing anything good is concerned.

Revised Standard

of men who reject the truth. [15]To the pure
all things are pure, but to the corrupt and
unbelieving nothing is pure; their very minds
and consciences are corrupted. [16]They profess
to know God, but they deny him by their
deeds; they are detestable, disobedient, unfit
for any good deed.

CHAPTER 2

But as for you, speak up for the right living that goes along with true Christianity.

2 Teach the older men to be serious and unruffled; they must be sensible, knowing and believing the truth and doing everything with love and patience.

3 Teach the older women to be quiet and respectful in everything they do. They must not go around speaking evil of others and must not be heavy drinkers, but they should be teachers of goodness.

4 These older women must train the younger women to live quietly, to love their husbands and their children,

5 And to be sensible and clean minded, spending their time in their own homes, being kind and obedient to their husbands, so that the Christian faith can't be spoken against by those who know them.

6 In the same way, urge the young men to behave carefully, taking life seriously.

7 And here you yourself must be an example to them of good deeds of every kind. Let everything you do reflect your love of the truth and the fact that you are in dead earnest about it.

8 Your conversation should be so sensible and logical that anyone who wants to argue will be ashamed of himself because there won't be anything to criticize in anything you say!

9 Urge slaves to obey their masters and to try their best to satisfy them. They must not talk back,

10 Nor steal, but must show themselves to be entirely trustworthy. In this way they will make people want to believe in our Savior and God.

11 For the free gift of eternal salvation is now being offered to everyone;

12 And along with this gift comes the realization that God wants us to turn from godless living and sinful pleasures and to live good, God-fearing lives day after day,

13 Looking forward to that time when His glory shall be seen—the glory of our great God and Savior Jesus Christ,

Christian doctrine and conduct

2 But as for you, teach what befits sound
doctrine. [2]Bid the older men be temperate, serious, sensible, sound in faith, in love,
and in steadfastness. [3]Bid the older women
likewise to be reverent in behavior, not to be
slanderers or slaves to drink; they are to
teach what is good, [4]and so train the young
women to love their husbands and children,
[5]to be sensible, chaste, domestic, kind, and
submissive to their husbands, that the word
of God may not be discredited. [6]Likewise
urge the younger men to control themselves.
[7]Show yourself in all respects a model of
good deeds, and in your teaching show integrity, gravity, [8]and sound speech that cannot be censured, so that an opponent may be
put to shame, having nothing evil to say of
us. [9]Bid slaves to be submissive to their
masters and to give satisfaction in every
respect; they are not to be refractory, [10]nor
to pilfer, but to show entire and true fidelity,
so that in everything they may adorn the
doctrine of God our Savior.

11 For the grace of God has appeared for
the salvation of all men, [12]training us to renounce irreligion and worldly passions, and
to live sober, upright, and godly lives in this
world, [13]awaiting our blessed hope, the appearing of the glory of our great God and
Savior[c] Jesus Christ, [14]who gave himself for

[c] Or *of the great God and our Savior*

King James

14 Who gave himself for us, that he might redeem us from all iniquity, and purify unto himself a peculiar people, zealous of good works.

15 These things speak, and exhort, and rebuke with all authority. Let no man despise thee.

CHAPTER 3

PUT them in mind to be subject to principalities and powers, to obey magistrates, to be ready to every good work,

2 To speak evil of no man, to be no brawlers, *but* gentle, shewing all meekness unto all men.

3 For we ourselves also were sometimes foolish, disobedient, deceived, serving divers lusts and pleasures, living in malice and envy, hateful, *and* hating one another.

4 But after that the kindness and love of God our Saviour toward man appeared,

5 Not by works of righteousness which we have done, but according to his mercy he saved us, by the washing of regeneration, and renewing of the Holy Ghost;

6 Which he shed on us abundantly through Jesus Christ our Saviour;

7 That being justified by his grace, we should be made heirs according to the hope of eternal life.

8 *This is* a faithful saying, and these things I will that thou affirm constantly, that they which have believed in God might be careful to maintain good works. These things are good and profitable unto men.

9 But avoid foolish questions, and genealogies, and contentions, and strivings about the law; for they are unprofitable and vain.

10 A man that is an heretic after the first and second admonition reject;

11 Knowing that he that is such is subverted, and sinneth, being condemned of himself.

12 When I shall send Artemas unto thee, or Tychicus, be diligent to come unto me to Nicopolis: for I have determined there to winter.

13 Bring Zenas the lawyer and Apollos on their journey diligently, that nothing be wanting unto them.

14 And let ours also learn to maintain good works for necessary uses, that they be not unfruitful.

15 All that are with me salute thee. Greet them that love us in the faith. Grace *be* with you all. Amen.

¶ It was written to Titus, ordained the first bishop of the church of the Cretians, from Nicopolis of Macedonia.

Amplified

14 Who gave Himself on our behalf that He might redeem us (purchase our freedom) from all iniquity and purify for Himself a people—to be peculiarly His own—[people who are] eager *and* enthusiastic about [living a life that is good and filled with] beneficial deeds. [Ps. 130:8; Ezek. 37:23; Deut. 14:2.]

15 Tell [them all] these things. Urge (advise, encourage, warn) and rebuke with full authority. Let no one despise *or* disregard *or* think little of you—conduct yourself and your teaching so as to command respect.

CHAPTER 3

REMIND people to be submissive to [their] magistrates and authorities, to be obedient, to be prepared *and* willing to do any upright *and* honorable work;

2 To slander *or* abuse *or* speak evil of no one, to avoid being contentious, to be forbearing—yielding, gentle and conciliatory—and to show unqualified courtesy toward everybody.

3 For we also were once thoughtless *and* senseless, obstinate *and* disobedient, deluded *and* misled; [we too were once] slaves to all sorts of cravings *and* pleasures, wasting our days in malice and jealousy *and* envy, hateful (hated, detestable) and hating one another.

4 But when the goodness and loving kindness of God our Savior to man [as man] appeared,

5 He saved us, not because of any works of righteousness that we had done, but because of His own pity *and* mercy, by [the] cleansing (bath) of the new birth (regeneration) and renewing of the Holy Spirit,

6 Which He poured out [so] richly upon us through Jesus Christ our Savior.

7 [And He did it in order] that we might be justified by His grace—by His favor, wholly undeserved, that is, that we might be acknowledged and counted as conformed to the Divine will in purpose, thought and action; and that we might become heirs of eternal life according to [our] hope.

8 This message is most trustworthy, and concerning these things I want you to insist steadfastly, so that those who have believed in (trusted, relied on) God may be careful to apply themselves to honorable occupations *and* to doing good, for such things are [not only] excellent *and* right [in themselves], but [they are] good *and* profitable for the people.

9 But avoid stupid *and* foolish controversies and genealogies and dissensions and wrangling about the Law, for they are unprofitable and futile.

10 [As for] a man who is factious—a heretical sectarian and cause of divisions—after admonishing him a first and second time reject (him from your fellowship and have nothing more to do with him),

11 Well aware that such a person has utterly changed—is perverted and corrupted; he goes on sinning [though] he is convicted of guilt *and* self-condemned.

12 When I send Artemas or [perhaps] Tychicus to you, lose no time *but* make every effort to come to me at Nicopolis, for I have decided to spend the winter there.

13 Do your utmost to speed Zenas the lawyer and Apollos on their way; see that they want for nothing.

14 And let our [own people really] learn to apply themselves to good deeds—to honest labor and honorable employment—so that they may be able to meet necessary demands [d]whenever the occasion may require and not be living idle *and* uncultivated *and* unfruitful lives.

15 All who are with me wish to be remembered to you. Greet those who love us in the faith. Grace (God's favor and blessing) be with you all. *Amen, so be it.*

d) Vincent.

Living New Testament

14 Who died under God's judgment against our sins, so that He could rescue us from constant falling into sin and make us His very own people, with cleansed hearts and real enthusiasm for doing kind things for others.

15 You must teach these things and encourage your people to do them, correcting them when necessary as one who has every right to do so. Don't let anyone think that what you say is not important.

CHAPTER 3

Remind your people to obey the government and its officers, and always to be obedient and ready for any honest work.

2 They must not speak evil of anyone, nor quarrel, but be gentle and truly courteous to all.

3 Once we, too, were foolish and disobedient; we were misled by others and became slaves to many evil pleasures and wicked desires. Our lives were full of resentment and envy. We hated others and they hated us.

4 But when the time came for the kindness and love of God our Savior to appear,

5 Then He saved us—not because we were good enough to be saved, but because of His kindness and pity—by washing away our sins and giving us the new joy of the indwelling Holy Spirit

6 Whom He poured out upon us with wonderful fullness—and all because of what Jesus Christ our Savior did

7 So that He could declare us good in God's eyes, all because of His great kindness; and now we can share in the wealth of the eternal life He gives us, and we are eagerly looking forward to receiving it.

8 These things I have told you are all true. Insist on them so that Christians will be careful to do good deeds all the time, for this is not only right, but it brings results.

9 Don't get involved in arguing over unanswerable questions and controversial theological ideas; keep out of arguments and quarrels about obedience to Jewish laws, for this kind of thing isn't worthwhile; it only does harm.

10 If anyone is causing divisions among you, he should be given a first and second warning. After that have nothing more to do with him,

11 For such a person has a wrong sense of values. He is sinning, and he knows it.

12 I am planning to send either Artemas or Tychicus to you. As soon as one of them arrives, please try to meet me at Nicopolis as quickly as you can, for I have decided to stay there for the winter.

13 Do everything you can to help Zenas the lawyer and Apollos with their trip; see that they are given everything they need.

14 For our people must learn to help all who need their assistance, that their lives will be fruitful.

15 Everybody here sends greetings. Please say "hello" to all of the Christian friends there. May God's blessings be with you all.

Sincerely,
Paul

Revised Standard

us to redeem us from all iniquity and to purify for himself a people of his own who are zealous for good deeds.

15 Declare these things; exhort and reprove with all authority. Let no one disregard you.

Faith and works

3 Remind them to be submissive to rulers
and authorities, to be obedient, to be
ready for any honest work, 2to speak evil of
no one, to avoid quarreling, to be gentle, and
to show perfect courtesy toward all men.
3For we ourselves were once foolish, disobedient, led astray, slaves to various passions
and pleasures, passing our days in malice and
envy, hated by men and hating one another;
4but when the goodness and loving kindness
of God our Savior appeared, 5he saved us,
not because of deeds done by us in righteousness, but in virtue of his own mercy, by the
washing of regeneration and renewal in the
Holy Spirit, 6which he poured out upon us
richly through Jesus Christ our Savior, 7so
that we might be justified by his grace and
become heirs in hope of eternal life. 8The
saying is sure.
I desire you to insist on these things, so
that those who have believed in God may be
careful to apply themselves to good deeds;[d]
these are excellent and profitable to men.
9But avoid stupid controversies, genealogies,
dissensions, and quarrels over the law, for
they are unprofitable and futile. 10As for a
man who is factious, after admonishing him
once or twice, have nothing more to do with
him, 11knowing that such a person is perverted and sinful; he is self-condemned.

Closing instruction, benediction

12 When I send Artemas or Tychicus to
you, do your best to come to me at Nicopolis, for I have decided to spend the winter
there. 13Do your best to speed Zenas the
lawyer and Apollos on their way; see that
they lack nothing. 14And let our people learn
to apply themselves to good deeds,[d] so as
to help cases of urgent need, and not to be
unfruitful.
15 All who are with me send greetings to
you. Greet those who love us in the faith.
Grace be with you all.

---

[d] Or *enter honorable occupations*

King James

THE EPISTLE OF PAUL THE APOSTLE TO

Philemon

PAUL, a prisoner of Jesus Christ, and Timothy *our* brother, unto Philemon our dearly beloved, and fellow-labourer,

2 And to *our* beloved Apphia, and Archippus our fellow-soldier, and to the church in thy house:

3 Grace to you, and peace, from God our Father and the Lord Jesus Christ.

4 I thank my God, making mention of thee always in my prayers,

5 Hearing of thy love and faith, which thou hast toward the Lord Jesus, and toward all saints;

6 That the communication of thy faith may become effectual by the acknowledging of every good thing which is in you in Christ Jesus.

7 For we have great joy and consolation in thy love, because the bowels of the saints are refreshed by thee, brother.

8 Wherefore, though I might be much bold in Christ to enjoin thee that which is convenient,

9 Yet for love's sake I rather beseech *thee*, being such an one as Paul the aged, and now also a prisoner of Jesus Christ.

10 I beseech thee for my son Onesimus, whom I have begotten in my bonds:

11 Which in time past was to thee unprofitable, but now profitable to thee and to me:

12 Whom I have sent again: thou therefore receive him, that is, mine own bowels:

13 Whom I would have retained with me, that in thy stead he might have ministered unto me in the bonds of the gospel:

14 But without thy mind would I do nothing; that thy benefit should not be as it were of necessity, but willingly.

15 For perhaps he therefore departed for a season, that thou shouldest receive him for ever;

16 Not now as a servant, but above a servant, a brother beloved, specially to me, but how much more unto thee, both in the flesh, and in the Lord?

17 If thou count me therefore a partner, receive him as myself.

18 If he hath wronged thee, or oweth *thee* aught, put that on mine account;

19 I Paul have written *it* with mine own hand, I will repay *it:* albeit I do not say to thee how thou owest unto me even thine own self besides.

20 Yea, brother, let me have joy of thee in the Lord: refresh my bowels in the Lord.

Amplified

THE LETTER OF PAUL
TO

Philemon

PAUL, a prisoner [for the sake] of Christ Jesus, the Messiah, and our brother Timothy, to Philemon our dearly loved sharer with us in our work,

2 And to Apphia our sister and Archippus our fellow soldier [in the Christian warfare], and to the church (assembly that meets) in your house:

3 Grace (spiritual blessing and favor) be to you all and heart-peace from God our Father and the Lord Jesus Christ, the Messiah.

4 I give thanks to my God for you always when I mention you in my prayers,

5 Because I continue to hear of your love and of your loyal faith which you have toward the Lord Jesus and [which you show] toward all the saints—God's consecrated people.

6 [And I pray] that the participation in *and* sharing of your faith may produce *and* promote full recognition *and* appreciation *and* understanding *and* precise knowledge of every good [thing] that is ours in [our identification with] Christ *Jesus—and* unto [His glory].

7 For I have derived great joy and comfort *and* encouragement from your love, because the hearts of the saints [who are your fellow Christians] have been cheered *and* refreshed through you, [my] brother.

8 Therefore, though I have abundant boldness in Christ to charge you to do what is fitting *and* required *and* your duty to do,

9 Yet for love's sake I prefer to appeal to you just for what I am: I, Paul, an ambassador [of Christ Jesus] *and* an old man and now a prisoner for His sake also.

10 I appeal to you for my [own spiritual] child, Onesimus [meaning profitable], whom I have begotten [in the faith] while a captive in these chains.

11 Once he was unprofitable to you, but now he is indeed profitable to you as well as to me.

12 I am sending him back to you in [a]his own person (and it is like sending) my very heart.

13 I would have chosen to keep him with me, in order that he might minister to my needs in your stead during my imprisonment for the Gospel's sake.

14 But it has been my wish to do nothing about it without first consulting you *and* getting your consent, in order that your benevolence might not seem to be the result of compulsion *or* of pressure but might be voluntary [on your part].

15 Perhaps it was for this reason that he was separated [from you] for a while, that you might have him back as yours forever,

16 Not as a slave any longer but as [something] more than a slave, as a brother [Christian], especially dear to me but how much more to you, both in the flesh [as a servant] and in the Lord [as a fellow believer].

17 If then you consider me a partner *and* a [a]comrade in fellowship, welcome *and* receive him as you would [welcome and receive] me.

18 And if he has done you any wrong in any way, or owes anything [to you], charge that to my account.

19 I, Paul, write it with my own hand, I promise to repay it [in full]—and that is to say nothing [of the fact] that you owe me your very self!

20 Yes, brother, let me have some profit from you in the Lord. Cheer *and* refresh my heart in Christ.

---

a) Vincent.

Living New Testament

Philemon

From: Paul, in jail for preaching the Goods News about Jesus Christ, and from Brother Timothy.

To: Philemon, our much loved fellow worker, and to the church that meets in your home, and to Apphia our sister, and to Archippus who like myself is a soldier of the cross.

3 May God our Father and the Lord Jesus Christ give you His blessings and His peace.

4 I always thank God when I am praying for you, dear Philemon,

5 Because I keep hearing of your love and trust in the Lord Jesus and in His people.

6 And I pray that as you share your faith with others it will grip their lives too, as they see the wealth of good things in you that come from Christ Jesus.

7 I myself have gained much joy and comfort from your love, my brother, because your kindness has so often refreshed the hearts of God's people.

8, 9 Now I want to ask a favor of you. I could demand it of you in the name of Christ because it is the right thing for you to do, but I love you and prefer just to ask you—I, Paul, an old man now, here in jail for the sake of Jesus Christ.

10 My plea is that you show kindness to my child Onesimus, whom I won to the Lord while here in my chains.

11 Onesimus (whose name means "Useful") hasn't been of much use to you in the past, but now he is going to be of real use to both of us.

12 I am sending him back to you, and with him comes my own heart.

13 I really wanted to keep him here with me while I am in these chains for preaching the Good News, and you would have been helping me through him,

14 But I didn't want to do it without your consent. I didn't want you to be kind because you had to but because you wanted to.

15 Perhaps you could think of it this way: that he ran away from you for a little while so that now he can be yours forever,

16 No longer only a slave, but something much better—a beloved brother, especially to me. Now he will mean much more to you too, because he is not only a servant but also your brother in Christ.

17 If I am really your friend, give him the same welcome you would give to me if I were the one who was coming.

18 If he has harmed you in any way or stolen anything from you, charge me for it.

19 I will pay it back (I, Paul, personally guarantee this by writing it here with my own hand) but I won't mention how much you owe me! The fact is, you even owe me your very soul!

20 Yes dear brother, give me joy with this loving act and my weary heart will praise the Lord.

Revised Standard

THE LETTER OF PAUL TO

Philemon

Salutation

1 Paul, a prisoner for Christ Jesus, and
Timothy our brother,
To Philemon our beloved fellow worker
2and Apphia our sister and Archippus our
fellow soldier, and the church in your house:
3 Grace to you and peace from God our
Father and the Lord Jesus Christ.

Words of thanks to Philemon

4 I thank my God always when I remember you in my prayers, 5because I hear of
your love and of the faith which you have
toward the Lord Jesus and all the saints,
6and I pray that the sharing of your faith
may promote the knowledge of all the good
that is ours in Christ. 7For I have derived
much joy and comfort from your love, my
brother, because the hearts of the saints have
been refreshed through you.

Appeal for Onesimus

8 Accordingly, though I am bold enough
in Christ to command you to do what is
required, 9yet for love's sake I prefer to appeal to you—I, Paul, an ambassador[a] and
now a prisoner also for Christ Jesus—10I
appeal to you for my child, Onesimus, whose
father I have become in my imprisonment.
11(Formerly he was useless to you, but now
he is indeed useful[b] to you and to me.) 12I
am sending him back to you, sending my
very heart. 13I would have been glad to keep
him with me, in order that he might serve
me on your behalf during my imprisonment
for the gospel; 14but I preferred to do nothing
without your consent in order that your
goodness might not be by compulsion but of
your own free will.
15 Perhaps this is why he was parted from
you for a while, that you might have him
back for ever, 16no longer as a slave but
more than a slave, as a beloved brother,
especially to me but how much more to you,
both in the flesh and in the Lord. 17So if
you consider me your partner, receive him as
you would receive me. 18If he has wronged
you at all, or owes you anything, charge that
to my account. 19I, Paul, write this with my
own hand, I will repay it—to say nothing of
your owing me even your own self. 20Yes,
brother, I want some benefit from you in the
Lord. Refresh my heart in Christ.

---

[a] Or *an old man*
[b] The name Onesimus means *useful* or (compare verse 20) *beneficial*

King James

21 Having confidence in thy obedience I wrote unto thee, knowing that thou wilt also do more than I say.
22 But withal prepare me also a lodging: for I trust that through your prayers I shall be given unto you.
23 There salute thee Epaphras, my fellow-prisoner in Christ Jesus;
24 Marcus, Aristarchus, Demas, Lucas, my fellow-labourers.
25 The grace of our Lord Jesus Christ *be* with your spirit. Amen.

¶ Written from Rome to Philemon, by Onesimus a servant.

Amplified

21 I write to you [perfectly] confident of your obedient compliance, knowing that you will do even more than I ask.
22 At the same time prepare a guest room [in expectation of extending your hospitality to] me, for I am hoping through your prayers to be granted [the gracious privilege of coming] to you.
23 Greetings to you from Epaphras my fellow prisoner here in [the cause of] Christ Jesus, the Messiah,
24 And [from] Mark, Aristarchus, Demas and Luke, my fellow workers.
25 The grace (blessing and favor) of the Lord Jesus Christ, the Messiah, be with your spirit. *Amen, so be it.*

Living New Testament

21 I've written you this letter because I am positive
that you will do what I ask and even more!
22 Please keep a guest room ready for me, for I am
hoping that God will answer your prayers and let me
come to you soon.
23 Epaphras my fellow prisoner, who is also here for
preaching Christ Jesus, sends you his greetings.
24 So do Mark, Aristarchus, Demas and Luke, my
fellow workers.
25 The blessings of our Lord Jesus Christ be upon your
spirit.

Paul

Revised Standard

21 Confident of your obedience, I write
to you, knowing that you will do even more
than I say. [22]At the same time, prepare a
guest room for me, for I am hoping through
your prayers to be granted to you.

Greetings and benediction

23 Epaphras, my fellow prisoner in Christ
Jesus, sends greetings to you, [24]and so do
Mark, Aristarchus, Demas, and Luke, my
fellow workers.
25 The grace of the Lord Jesus Christ be
with your spirit.

King James

THE EPISTLE OF PAUL THE APOSTLE
TO THE

Hebrews

CHAPTER 1

GOD, who at sundry times and in divers manners spake in time past unto the fathers by the prophets,

2 Hath in these last days spoken unto us by *his* Son, whom he hath appointed heir of all things, by whom also he made the worlds;

3 Who being the brightness of *his* glory, and the express image of his person, and upholding all things by the word of his power, when he had by himself purged our sins, sat down on the right hand of the Majesty on high;

4 Being made so much better than the angels, as he hath by inheritance obtained a more excellent name than they.

5 For unto which of the angels said he at any time, Thou art my Son, this day have I begotten thee? And again, I will be to him a Father, and he shall be to me a Son?

6 And again, when he bringeth in the first begotten into the world, he saith, And let all the angels of God worship him.

7 And of the angels he saith, Who maketh his angels spirits, and his ministers a flame of fire.

8 But unto the Son *he saith*, Thy throne, O God, *is* for ever and ever: a sceptre of righteousness *is* the sceptre of thy kingdom.

9 Thou hast loved righteousness, and hated iniquity; therefore God, *even* thy God, hath anointed thee with the oil of gladness above thy fellows.

10 And, Thou, Lord, in the beginning hast laid the foundation of the earth; and the heavens are the works of thine hands:

11 They shall perish; but thou remainest; and they all shall wax old as doth a garment;

12 And as a vesture shalt thou fold them up, and they shall be changed: but thou art the same, and thy years shall not fail.

13 But to which of the angels said he at any time, Sit on my right hand, until I make thine enemies thy footstool?

14 Are they not all ministering spirits, sent forth to minister for them who shall be heirs of salvation?

Amplified

THE LETTER
TO THE

Hebrews

CHAPTER 1

IN many separate revelations—[a]each of which set forth a portion of the Truth—and in different ways God spoke of old to [our] forefathers in *and* by the prophets.

2 [But] in [c]the last of these days He has spoken to us in [the person of a] Son, Whom He appointed Heir *and* lawful Owner of all things, also by *and* through Whom He created the worlds [b]*and* the reaches of space *and* the ages of time—[that is,] He made, produced, built, operated and arranged them in order.

3 He is the sole expression of the glory of God—the Light-being, the [b]out-raying of the divine—and He is the perfect imprint *and* very image of [God's] nature, upholding *and* maintaining *and* guiding *and* propelling the universe by His mighty word of power. When He had by offering Himself accomplished *our* cleansing of sins *and* riddance of guilt, He sat down at the right hand of the divine Majesty on high,

4 [Taking a place and rank by which] He Himself became as much superior to angels as the glorious Name (title) which He has inherited is different from *and* more excellent than theirs.

5 For to which of the angels did (God) ever say, You are My Son, today I have begotten You [that is, established You in an official Sonship relation, with kingly dignity]? And again, I will be to Him a Father, and He will be to Me a Son? [Ps. 2:7; II Sam. 7:14.]

6 Moreover, when He brings the first-born Son [d]again into the habitable world, He says, Let all the angels of God worship Him.

7 Referring to the angels He says, (God) Who makes His angels [e]winds, and His ministering servants flames of fire; [Ps. 104:4.]

8 But as to the Son, He says to Him, Your throne, O God, is forever and ever (to the ages of the ages), and the scepter of Your kingdom is a scepter of absolute righteousness—of justice and straightforwardness.

9 You have loved righteousness—You have delighted in integrity, virtue and uprightness in purpose, thought and action—and You have hated lawlessness (injustice and iniquity). Therefore God, [even] Your God ([f]Godhead), has anointed You with the oil of exultant joy *and* gladness above *and* beyond Your companions. [Ps. 45:6, 7.]

10 And [further], You, Lord, did lay the foundation of the earth in the beginning, and the heavens are the works of Your hands.

11 They will perish, but You remain *and* continue permanently; they will all grow old *and* wear out like a garment.

12 Like a mantle [thrown about one's self] You will roll them up, and they will be changed *and* replaced by others. But You remain the same and Your years will never end *nor* come to failure. [Ps. 102:25-27.]

13 Besides, to which of the angels has He ever said, Sit at My right hand—associated with Me in My royal dignity—till I make your enemies a stool for your feet? [Ps. 110:1.]

14 Are not the angels all (servants) ministering spirits, sent out in the service [of God for the assistance] of those who are to inherit salvation?

---

a) Vincent.
b) Literal translation.
c) Alford's "Greek Testament."
d) Alford. Expositors. Vincent. Wuest's "Hebrews."
e) Many authorities.
f) Way's "The Letters of Saint Paul and Hebrews."

Living New Testament

Hebrews

CHAPTER 1

Long ago God spoke in many different ways to our fathers through the prophets [in visions, dreams, and even face to face[1]], telling them little by little about His plans.

2 But now in these days He has spoken to us through His Son to whom He has given everything, and through whom He made the world and everything there is.

3 God's Son shines out with God's glory, and all that God's Son is and does marks Him as God. He regulates the universe by the mighty power of His command. He is the one who died to cleanse us and clear our record of all sin, and then sat down in highest honor beside the great God of heaven.

4 Thus He became far greater than the angels, as proved by the fact that His name "Son of God," which was passed on to Him from His Father, is far greater than the names and titles of the angels.

5, 6 For God never said to any angel, "You are My Son, and today I have given You the honor that goes with that name."[2] But God said it about Jesus. Another time He said, "I am His Father and He is My Son." And still another time—when His firstborn Son came to earth—God said, "Let all the angels of God worship Him."

7 God speaks of His angels as messengers swift as the wind and as servants made of flaming fire;

8 But of His Son He says, "Your kingdom, O God, will last forever and ever; its commands are always just and right.

9 You love right and hate wrong; so God, even Your God, has poured out more gladness upon You than on anyone else."

10 God also called Him "Lord" when He said, "Lord, in the beginning You made the earth, and the heavens are the work of Your hands.

11 They will disappear into nothingness, but You will remain forever. They will become worn out like old clothes,

12 And some day You will fold them up and replace them. But You Yourself will never change, and Your years will never end."

13 And did God ever say to an angel, as He does to His Son, "Sit here beside Me in honor until I crush all Your enemies beneath Your feet"?

14 No, for the angels are only spirit-messengers sent out to help and care for those who are to receive His salvation.

[1] Implied.
[2] Literally, "this day I have begotten You."

Revised Standard

THE LETTER TO THE

Hebrews

Christ the revelation of God

1 In many and various ways God spoke of
old to our fathers by the prophets; [2]but
in these last days he has spoken to us by a
Son, whom he appointed the heir of all
things, through whom also he created the
world. [3]He reflects the glory of God and
bears the very stamp of his nature, upholding the universe by his word of power.

Christ the Son of God

When he had made purification for sins, he
sat down at the right hand of the Majesty
on high, [4]having become as much superior
to angels as the name he has obtained is
more excellent than theirs.

[5] For to what angel did God ever say,
"Thou art my Son,
today I have begotten thee"?
Or again,
"I will be to him a father,
and he shall be to me a son"?
[6]And again, when he brings the first-born
into the world, he says,
"Let all God's angels worship him."
[7]Of the angels he says,
"Who makes his angels winds,
and his servants flames of fire."
[8]But of the Son he says,
"Thy throne, O God,[a] is for ever and ever,
the righteous scepter is the scepter of thy[b] kingdom.
[9]Thou hast loved righteousness and hated lawlessness;
therefore God, thy God, has anointed thee
with the oil of gladness beyond thy comrades."
[10]And,
"Thou, Lord, didst found the earth in the beginning,
and the heavens are the work of thy hands;
[11]they will perish, but thou remainest;
they will all grow old like a garment,
[12]like a mantle thou wilt roll them up, and
they will be changed.[c]
But thou art the same,
and thy years will never end."
[13]But to what angel has he ever said,
"Sit at my right hand,
till I make thy enemies
a stool for thy feet"?
[14]Are they not all ministering spirits sent
forth to serve, for the sake of those who are
to obtain salvation?

[a] Or *God is thy throne*
[b] Other ancient authorities read *his*
[c] Other ancient authorities add *like a garment*

King James

CHAPTER 2

THEREFORE we ought to give the more earnest heed to the things which we have heard, lest at any time we should let *them* slip.

2 For if the word spoken by angels was stedfast, and every transgression and disobedience received a just recompence of reward;

3 How shall we escape, if we neglect so great salvation; which at the first began to be spoken by the Lord, and was confirmed unto us by them that heard *him;*

4 God also bearing *them* witness, both with signs and wonders, and with divers miracles, and gifts of the Holy Ghost, according to his own will?

5 For unto the angels hath he not put in subjection the world to come whereof we speak.

6 But one in a certain place testified, saying, What is man, that thou art mindful of him? or the son of man, that thou visitest him?

7 Thou madest him a little lower than the angels; thou crownedst him with glory and honour, and didst set him over the works of thy hands:

8 Thou hast put all things in subjection under his feet. For in that he put all in subjection under him, he left nothing *that is* not put under him. But now we see not yet all things put under him.

9 But we see Jesus, who was made a little lower than the angels for the suffering of death, crowned with glory and honour; that he by the grace of God should taste death for every man.

10 For it became him, for whom *are* all things, and by whom *are* all things, in bringing many sons unto glory, to make the captain of their salvation perfect through sufferings.

11 For both he that sanctifieth and they who are sanctified *are* all of one: for which cause he is not ashamed to call them brethren,

12 Saying, I will declare thy name unto my brethren, in the midst of the church will I sing praise unto thee.

13 And again, I will put my trust in him. And again, Behold I and the children which God hath given me.

14 Forasmuch then as the children are partakers of flesh and blood, he also himself likewise took part of the same; that through death he might destroy him that had the power of death, that is, the devil;

15 And deliver them who through fear of death were all their lifetime subject to bondage.

16 For verily he took not on *him the nature of* angels; but he took on *him* the seed of Abraham.

Amplified

CHAPTER 2

SINCE all this is true, we ought to pay much closer attention than ever to the truths that we have heard, lest in any way we drift past [them] *and* slip away.

2 For if the message given through angels [that is, the Law spoken by them to Moses] was authentic *and* proved sure, and every violation and disobedience received an appropriate (just and adequate) penalty,

3 How shall we escape [appropriate retribution] if we neglect *and* refuse to pay attention to such a great salvation [as is now offered to us, letting it drift past us forever]? For it was declared at first by the Lord [Himself], and it was confirmed to us *and* proved to be real *and* genuine by those who personally heard [Him speak].

4 [Besides these evidences] it was also established *and* plainly endorsed by God, Who showed His approval of it by signs and wonders and various miraculous manifestations of [His] power and by imparting the gifts of the Holy Spirit [to the believers] according to His own will.

5 For it was not to angels that God subjected the habitable world of the future, of which we are speaking.

6 It has been solemnly *and* earnestly said in a certain place, What is man that You are mindful of him, or the son of man that You graciously *and* helpfully care for *and* visit *and* look after him?

7 For some little time You have ranked him lower than *and* inferior to the angels, You have crowned him with glory and honor, *and set him over the works of Your hands,* [Ps. 8:4-6.]

8 For You have put everything in subjection under his feet. Now in putting everything in subjection to man, He left nothing outside [of man's] control. But at present we do not yet see all things subjected to him [man].

9 But we are able to see Jesus, Who was ranked lower than the angels for a little while, crowned with glory and honor because of His having suffered death, in order that by the grace (unmerited favor) of God [to us sinners] He might experience death for every individual person.

10 For it was an act worthy [of God] *and* fitting [to the divine nature] that He, for Whose sake and by Whom all things have their existence, in bringing many sons into glory, should make the Pioneer of their salvation perfect [that is, should bring to maturity the human experience necessary for a perfect equipment for His office as High Priest], through suffering.

11 For both He Who sanctifies—making men holy—and those who are sanctified all have one [Father]. For this reason He is not ashamed to call them brethren,

12 For He says, I will declare Your [the Father's] name to My brethren; in the midst of the (worshipping) congregation I will sing hymns of praise to You. [Ps. 22:22.]

13 And again He says, My trust *and* assured reliance *and* confident hope shall be fixed in Him. And yet again, Here I am, I and the children whom God has given Me. [Isa. 8:17, 18.]

14 Since, therefore, [these His] children share in flesh and blood—that is, in the physical nature of human beings—He [Himself] in a similar manner partook of the same [nature], that by [going through] death He might bring to nought *and* make of no effect him who had the power of death, that is, the devil;

15 And also that He might deliver *and* completely set free all those who through the (haunting) fear of death were held in bondage throughout the whole course of their lives.

16 For, as we all know, He (Christ) did not take hold of angels [[g]the fallen angels]—to give them a helping and delivering hand; but He did take hold of [[g]the fallen] descendants of Abraham—to reach them a helping and delivering hand. [Isa. 41:8, 9.]

---

g) Matthew Henry's Commentary, and others.

Living New Testament

CHAPTER 2

So we must listen very carefully to the truths we have heard, or we may drift away from them.

2 For since the messages from angels have always proved true and people have always been punished for disobeying them,

3 What makes us think that we can escape if we are indifferent to this great salvation announced by the Lord Jesus Himself, and passed on to us by those who heard Him speak?

4 God always has shown us that these messages are true by signs and wonders and various miracles and by giving certain special abilities from the Holy Spirit to those who believe; yes, God has assigned such gifts to each of us.

5 And the future world we are talking about will not be controlled by angels.

6 No, for in the book of Psalms David says to God, "What is mere man that You are so concerned about him? And who is this Son of Man You honor so highly?

7 For though You made Him lower than the angels for a little while, now You have crowned Him with glory and honor.

8 And You have put Him in complete charge of everything there is. Nothing is left out." We have not yet seen all of this take place,

9 But we do see Jesus—who for awhile was a little lower than the angels—crowned now by God with glory and honor because He suffered death for us. Yes, because of God's great kindness, Jesus tasted death for everyone in all the world.

10 And it was right and proper that God, who made everything for His own glory, should allow Jesus to suffer, for in doing this He was bringing vast multitudes of God's people to heaven; for His suffering made Jesus a perfect Leader, one fit to bring them into their salvation.

11 We who have been made holy by Jesus, now have the same Father He has. That is why Jesus is not ashamed to call us His brothers.

12 For He says in the book of Psalms, "I will talk to My brothers about God My Father, and together we will sing His praises."

13 At another time He said, "I will put My trust in God along with My brothers." And at still another time, "See, here am I and the children God gave Me."

14 Since we, God's children, are human beings—made of flesh and blood—He became flesh and blood too by being born in human form; for only as a human being could He die and in dying break the power of the devil who had the power of death.

15 Only in that way could He deliver those who through fear of death have been living all their lives as slaves to constant dread.

16 We all know He did not come as an angel but as a human being—yes, a Jew.

Revised Standard

The role of Christ in salvation

2 Therefore we must pay the closer attention to what we have heard, lest we drift
away from it. 2For if the message declared
by angels was valid and every transgression
or disobedience received a just retribution,
3how shall we escape if we neglect such a
great salvation? It was declared at first by
the Lord, and it was attested to us by those
who heard him, 4while God also bore witness by signs and wonders and various miracles and by gifts of the Holy Spirit
distributed according to his own will.

5 For it was not to angels that God subjected the world to come, of which we are
speaking. 6It has been testified somewhere,

"What is man that thou art mindful of
him,
or the son of man, that thou carest for
him?
7Thou didst make him for a little while
lower than the angels,
thou hast crowned him with glory and
honor,[d]
8Putting everything in subjection under his
feet."

Now in putting everything in subjection to
him, he left nothing outside his control. As
it is, we do not yet see everything in subjection to him. 9But we see Jesus, who for
a little while was made lower than the
angels, crowned with glory and honor because of the suffering of death, so that by
the grace of God he might taste death for
every one.

Christ the high priest

10 For it was fitting that he, for whom
and by whom all things exist, in bringing
many sons to glory, should make the pioneer of their salvation perfect through suffering. 11For he who sanctifies and those
who are sanctified have all one origin. That
is why he is not ashamed to call them
brethren, 12saying,

"I will proclaim thy name to my brethren,
in the midst of the congregation I will
praise thee."

13And again,

"I will put my trust in him."

And again,

"Here am I, and the children God has
given me."

14 Since therefore the children share in
flesh and blood, he himself likewise partook
of the same nature, that through death he
might destroy him who has the power of
death, that is, the devil, 15and deliver all
those who through fear of death were subject to lifelong bondage. 16For surely it is
not with angels that he is concerned but
with the descendants of Abraham. 17There-

[d] Other ancient authorities insert *and didst set him over the works of thy hands*

King James

17 Wherefore in all things it behoved him to be made like unto *his* brethren, that he might be a merciful and faithful high priest in things *pertaining* to God, to make reconciliation for the sins of the people.

18 For in that he himself hath suffered being tempted, he is able to succour them that are tempted.

Amplified

17 So it is evident that it was essential that He be made like His brethren in every respect, in order that He might become a merciful (sympathetic) and faithful High Priest in the things related to God, to make atonement *and* propitiation for the people's sins.

18 For because He Himself [in His humanity] has suffered in being tempted (tested and tried), He is able (immediately) [h]to run to the cry of (assist, relieve) those who are being tempted *and* tested *and* tried [and who therefore are being exposed to suffering].

CHAPTER 3

WHEREFORE, holy brethren, partakers of the heavenly calling, consider the Apostle and High Priest of our profession, Christ Jesus;

2 Who was faithful to him that appointed him, as also Moses *was faithful* in all his house.

3 For this *man* was counted worthy of more glory than Moses, inasmuch as he who hath builded the house hath more honour than the house.

4 For every house is builded by some *man;* but he that built all things *is* God.

5 And Moses verily *was* faithful in all his house, as a servant, for a testimony of those things which were to be spoken after;

6 But Christ as a son over his own house; whose house are we, if we hold fast the confidence and the rejoicing of the hope firm unto the end.

7 Wherefore (as the Holy Ghost saith, To-day if ye will hear his voice,

8 Harden not your hearts, as in the provocation, in the day of temptation in the wilderness:

9 When your fathers tempted me, proved me, and saw my works forty years.

10 Wherefore I was grieved with that generation, and said, They do alway err in *their* heart; and they have not known my ways.

11 So I sware in my wrath, They shall not enter into my rest.)

12 Take heed, brethren, lest there be in any of you an evil heart of unbelief, in departing from the living God.

CHAPTER 3

SO then, brethren, consecrated *and* set apart for God, who share in the heavenly calling, thoughtfully *and* attentively consider Jesus, the Apostle and High Priest Whom we confessed as ours [when we embraced the Christian faith].

2 [See how] faithful He was to Him Who appointed Him [Apostle and High Priest], as Moses was also faithful in the whole household [of God]. [Num. 12:7.]

3 Yet Jesus has been considered worthy of as much greater honor *and* glory than Moses as the builder of a house has more honor than the house [itself].

4 For, [of course,] every house is built *and* furnished by someone, but the Builder of all things *and* the Furnisher [of the entire equipment of all things] is God.

5 And Moses certainly was faithful in the administration of all God's house, [but it was only] as a ministering servant. [In his entire ministry he was but] a testimony to the things which were to be spoken—the revelations to be given afterward [in Christ]. [Num. 12:7.]

6 But Christ, the Messiah, was faithful over His [own Father's] house as a Son [and Master of it]. And it is we who are [now members of] this house, if we hold fast *and firm to the end* our joyful *and* exultant confidence and sense of triumph in our hope [in Christ].

7 Therefore, as the Holy Spirit says, Today, if you will hear His voice,

8 Do not harden your hearts, as [happened] in the rebellion [of Israel] *and* their provocation *and* [i]embitterment [of Me] in the day of testing in the wilderness,

9 Where your fathers tried [My patience] *and* tested [My forbearance] and [j]found I stood their test, and they saw My works for forty years.

10 And so I was provoked (displeased and sorely grieved) with that generation, and said, They always err *and* are led astray in their hearts, and they have not perceived *or* recognized My ways *and* become progressively better *and* more experimentally *and* intimately acquainted with them.

11 Accordingly I swore in My wrath *and* indignation, They shall not enter into My rest. [Ps. 95:7-11.]

12 [Therefore beware,] brethren; take care lest there be in any one of you a wicked, unbelieving heart—which refuses to cleave to, trust in and rely on Him—leading you to turn away *and* desert *or* stand aloof from the living God.

---

h) Wuest's "Hebrews."
i) Souter.
j) Williams.

Living New Testament

17 And it was necessary for Jesus to be like us, His brothers, so that He could be our merciful and faithful High Priest before God, a Priest who would be both merciful to us and faithful to God in dealing with the sins of the people.

18 For since He Himself has now been through suffering and temptation, He knows what it is like when we suffer and are tempted, and He is wonderfully able to help us.

* * * * *

Revised Standard

fore he had to be made like his brethren in
every respect, so that he might become a
merciful and faithful high priest in the service of God, to make expiation for the sins
of the people. 18For because he himself has
suffered and been tempted, he is able to help
those who are tempted.

CHAPTER 3

Therefore, dear brothers whom God has set apart for Himself—you who are chosen for heaven—I want you to think now about this Jesus who is God's Messenger and the High Priest of our faith.

2 For Jesus was faithful to God who appointed Him High Priest, just as Moses also faithfully served in God's house.

3 But Jesus has far more glory than Moses, just as a man who builds a fine house gets more praise than his house does.

4 And many people can build houses, but only God made everything.

5 Well, Moses did a fine job working in God's house, but he was only a servant; and his work was mostly to illustrate and suggest those things that would happen later on.

6 But Christ, God's faithful Son, is in complete charge of God's house. And we Christians are God's house—He lives in us!—if we keep up our courage firm to the end, and our joy and our trust in the Lord.

7, 8 And since Christ is so much superior, the Holy Spirit warns us to listen to Him, to be careful to hear His voice today and not let our hearts become set against Him, as the people of Israel did. They steeled themselves against His love and complained against Him in the desert while He was testing them.

9 But God was patient with them forty years, though they tried His patience sorely; He kept right on doing His mighty miracles for them to see.

10 "But," God says, "I was very angry with them, for their hearts were always looking somewhere else instead of up to Me, and they never found the paths I wanted them to follow."

11 Then God, full of this anger against them, bound Himself with an oath that He would never let them come to His place of rest.

12 Beware then of your own hearts, dear brothers, lest you find that they, too, are evil and unbelieving and are leading you away from the living God.

Christ superior to Moses

3 Therefore, holy brethren, who share in
a heavenly call, consider Jesus, the apostle and high priest of our confession. 2He
was faithful to him who appointed him, just
as Moses also was faithful in[e] God's house.
3Yet Jesus has been counted worthy of as
much more glory than Moses as the builder
of a house has more honor than the house.
4(For every house is built by some one, but
the builder of all things is God.) 5Now
Moses was faithful in all God's house as a
servant, to testify to the things that were to
be spoken later, 6but Christ was faithful
over God's[f] house as a son. And we are his
house if we hold fast our confidence and
pride in our hope.[g]

The disobedient generation

7 Therefore, as the Holy Spirit says,
"Today, when you hear his voice,
8do not harden your hearts as in the rebellion,
on the day of testing in the wilderness,
9 where your fathers put me to the test
and saw my works for forty years.
10 Therefore I was provoked with that
generation,
and said, 'They always go astray in their
hearts;
they have not known my ways.'
11 As I swore in my wrath,
'They shall never enter my rest.' "
12Take care, brethren, lest there be in any
of you an evil, unbelieving heart, leading
you to fall away from the living God. 13But

[e] Other ancient authorities insert *all*
[f] Greek *his*
[g] Other ancient authorities insert *firm to the end*

King James

13 But exhort one another daily, while it is called To-day; lest any of you be hardened through the deceitfulness of sin.

14 For we are made partakers of Christ, if we hold the beginning of our confidence stedfast unto the end;

15 While it is said, To-day if ye will hear his voice, harden not your hearts, as in the provocation.

16 For some, when they had heard, did provoke: howbeit not all that came out of Egypt by Moses.

17 But with whom was he grieved forty years? *was it* not with them that had sinned, whose carcases fell in the wilderness?

18 And to whom sware he that they should not enter into his rest, but to them that believed not?

19 So we see that they could not enter in because of unbelief.

Amplified

13 But instead warn (admonish, urge and encourage) one another every day, as long as it is called Today, that none of you may be hardened [into settled rebellion] by the deceitfulness of sin—[that is,] by the fraudulence, the stratagem, the trickery which the delusive glamor of his sin may play on him.

14 For we [k]have become fellows with Christ, the Messiah, *and* share in all He has for us, if only we hold our first newborn confidence *and* original assured expectation [in virtue of which we are believers] firm *and* unshaken to the end.

15 Then while it is [still] called Today, if you would hear His voice, *and* when you hear it, do not harden your hearts as in the rebellion [in the desert, when the people provoked and irritated and embittered God against them]. [Ps. 95:7, 8.]

16 For who were they that heard *and* yet were rebellious *and* provoked [Him]? Was it not all those who came out of Egypt led by Moses?

17 And with whom was He irritated *and* provoked *and* grieved for forty years? Was it not with those who sinned, whose [l]dismembered bodies were strewn *and* left in the desert?

18 And to whom did He swear that they should not enter His rest, but to those who disobeyed—who had not listened to His word, and who refused to be compliant or be persuaded?

19 So we see that they were not able to enter [into His rest] because of their unwillingness to adhere to *and* trust *and* rely on God—unbelief had shut them out. [Num. 14:1-35.]

CHAPTER 4

LET us therefore fear, lest, a promise being left *us* of entering into his rest, any of you should seem to come short of it.

2 For unto us was the gospel preached, as well as unto them: but the word preached did not profit them, not being mixed with faith in them that heard *it*.

3 For we which have believed do enter into rest, as he said, As I have sworn in my wrath, if they shall enter into my rest: although the works were finished from the foundation of the world.

4 For he spake in a certain place of the seventh *day* on this wise, And God did rest the seventh day from all his works.

CHAPTER 4

THEREFORE, while the promise of entering His rest still holds *and* is offered [today], let us be afraid [[l]to distrust it], lest any of you should [l]think he has come too late *and* has come short of [reaching] it.

2 For indeed we have had the glad tidings [of God] proclaimed to us just as truly as they [the Israelites of old did when the good news of deliverance from bondage came to them]; but the message they heard did not benefit them, because it was not mixed with faith [that is, with [m]the leaning of the entire personality on God in absolute trust and confidence in His power, wisdom and goodness] by those who heard it; *neither* were they [n]united in faith with [Joshua and Caleb] the ones who heard [did believe].

3 For we who have believed—who have adhered to and trusted and relied on God—do enter into that rest, [o]in accordance with His declaration that those [who did not believe] should not enter when He said, As I swore in My wrath, They shall not enter into My rest; and this He said although [His] works had been completed *and* prepared [and waiting for all who would believe] from the foundation of the world. [Ps. 95:11.]

4 For in a certain place He has said this about the seventh day: And God rested on the seventh day from all His works. [Gen. 2:2.]

---

k) Vincent.
l) Vincent.
m) Souter.
n) Many manuscripts so read.
o) Vincent.

Living New Testament

13 Speak to each other about these things every day while there is still time, so that none of you will become hardened against God, being blinded by the glamor[1] of sin.

14 For if we are faithful to the end, trusting God just as we did when we first became Christians, we will share in all that belongs to Christ.

15 But *now* is the time. Never forget the warning, *"Today* if you hear God's voice speaking to you, do not harden your hearts against Him, as the people of Israel did when they rebelled against Him in the desert."

16 And who were these people I speak of, who heard God's voice speaking to them but then rebelled against Him? They were the ones who came out of Egypt with Moses their leader.

17 And who was it who made God angry for all those forty years? These same people who sinned and as a result died in the wilderness.

18 And to whom was God speaking when He swore with an oath that they could never go into the land He had promised His people? He was speaking to all those who disobeyed Him.

19 And why couldn't they go in? Because they didn't trust Him.

Revised Standard

exhort one another every day, as long as it
is called "today," that none of you may be
hardened by the deceitfulness of sin. [14]For
we share in Christ, if only we hold our first
confidence firm to the end, [15]while it is said,
"Today, when you hear his voice,
do not harden your hearts as in the rebellion."
[16]Who were they that heard and yet were
rebellious? Was it not all those who left
Egypt under the leadership of Moses? [17]And
with whom was he provoked forty years?
Was it not with those who sinned, whose
bodies fell in the wilderness? [18]And to
whom did he swear that they should never
enter his rest, but to those who were disobedient? [19]So we see that they were unable
to enter because of unbelief.

CHAPTER 4

Although God's promise still stands—His promise that all may enter His place of rest—we ought to tremble with fear because some of you may be on the verge of failing to get there after all.

2 For this wonderful news—the message that God wants to save us—has been given to us just as it was to those who lived in the time of Moses. But it didn't do them any good because they didn't believe it. They didn't mix it with faith.

3 For only we who believe God can enter into His place of rest. He has said, "I have sworn in My anger that those who don't believe Me will never get in," even though He has been ready and waiting for them since the world began.

4 We know He is ready and waiting because it is written that God rested on the seventh day of creation, having finished all that He had planned to make.

The promise of rest

4 Therefore, while the promise of entering
his rest remains, let us fear lest any of
you be judged to have failed to reach it.
[2]For good news came to us just as to them;
but the message which they heard did not
benefit them, because it did not meet with
faith in the hearers.[h] [3]For we who have believed enter that rest, as he has said,
"As I swore in my wrath,
'They shall never enter my rest,' "
although his works were finished from the
foundation of the world. [4]For he has somewhere spoken of the seventh day in this
way, "And God rested on the seventh day

Literally, "deceitfulness."

[h] Other manuscripts read *they were not united in faith with the hearers*

King James

5 And in this *place* again, If they shall enter into my rest.

6 Seeing therefore it remaineth that some must enter therein, and they to whom it was first preached entered not in because of unbelief:

7 Again, he limiteth a certain day, saying in David, To-day, after so long a time; as it is said, To-day if ye will hear his voice, harden not your hearts.

8 For if Jesus had given them rest, then would he not afterward have spoken of another day.

9 There remaineth therefore a rest to the people of God.

10 For he that is entered into his rest, he also hath ceased from his own works, as God *did* from his.

11 Let us labour therefore to enter into that rest, lest any man fall after the same example of unbelief.

12 For the word of God *is* quick, and powerful, and sharper than any two-edged sword, piercing even to the dividing asunder of soul and spirit, and of the joints and marrow, and *is* a discerner of the thoughts and intents of the heart.

13 Neither is there any creature that is not manifest in his sight: but all things *are* naked and opened unto the eyes of him with whom we have to do.

14 Seeing then that we have a great high priest, that is passed into the heavens, Jesus the Son of God, let us hold fast *our* profession.

15 For we have not an high priest which cannot be touched with the feeling of our infirmities; but was in all points tempted like as *we are, yet* without sin.

16 Let us therefore come boldly unto the throne of grace, that we may obtain mercy, and find grace to help in time of need.

Amplified

5 And [they forfeited their part in it, for] in this [passage] He said, They shall not enter into My rest. [Ps. 95:11.]

6 Seeing then that the promise remains over [from past times] for some to enter that rest, and that those who formerly were given the good news about it *and* the opportunity, failed to appropriate it *and* did not enter because of disobedience,

7 Again He sets a definite day, [a new] Today, [and gives another opportunity of securing that rest,] saying through David after so long a time, in the words already quoted, Today, if you would hear His voice, *and* when you hear it, do not harden your hearts. (Ps. 95:7, 8.]

8 [This mention of a rest was not a reference to their entering into Canaan], for if Joshua had given them rest, He (God) would not speak afterward about another day.

9 So then, there is still awaiting a full *and* complete Sabbath rest reserved for the [true] people of God;

10 For he who has once entered into [God's] rest also has ceased from [the weariness and pain] of human labors, just as God rested from those labors [p]peculiarly His own. [Gen. 2:2.]

11 Let us therefore be zealous *and* exert ourselves *and* strive diligently to enter into that rest [of God]—to know and experience it for ourselves—that no one may fall *or* perish by the same kind of unbelief *and* disobedience [into which those in the wilderness fell].

12 For the Word that God speaks is alive and full of power—making it active, operative, energizing and effective; it is sharper than any two-edged sword, penetrating to the dividing line of the [q]breath of life (soul) and [the immortal] spirit, and of joints and marrow [that is, of the deepest parts of our nature] exposing *and* sifting *and* analyzing *and* judging the very thoughts and purposes of the heart.

13 And not a creature exists that is concealed from His sight, but all things are open *and* exposed, naked *and* defenseless to the eyes of Him with Whom we have to do.

14 Inasmuch then as we have a great High Priest Who has [already] ascended *and* passed through the heavens, Jesus the Son of God, let us hold fast our confession [of faith in Him],

15 For we do not have a High Priest Who is unable to understand *and* sympathize *and* have a fellow feeling with our weaknesses *and* infirmities *and* liability to the assaults of temptation, but One Who has been tempted in every respect as we are, yet without sinning.

16 Let us then fearlessly *and* confidently *and* boldly draw near to the throne of grace—the throne of God's unmerited favor [to us sinners]; that we may receive mercy [for our failures] and find grace to help in good time for every need—appropriate help and well-timed help, coming just when we need it.

CHAPTER 5

FOR every high priest taken from among men is ordained for men in things *pertaining* to God, that he may offer both gifts and sacrifices for sins:

2 Who can have compassion on the ignorant, and on them that are out of the way; for that he himself also is compassed with infirmity.

CHAPTER 5

FOR every high priest chosen from among men is appointed to act in behalf of men in things relating to God, to offer both gifts and sacrifices for sins.

2 He is able to exercise gentleness *and* forbearance toward the ignorant and erring, since he himself also is liable to moral weakness *and* physical infirmity.

---

p) Vincent's "Word Studies in the New Testament."
q) Thayer.

Living New Testament

5 Even so they didn't get in, for God finally said, "They shall never enter my rest."

6 Yet the promise remains and some get in—but not those who had the first chance, for they disobeyed God and failed to enter.

7 But He has set another time for coming in, and that time is now. He announced this through King David long years after man's first failure to enter, saying in the words already quoted, "Today when you hear Him calling, do not harden your hearts against Him."

8 This new place of rest He is talking about does not mean the land of Israel that Joshua led them into. If that were what God meant, He would not have spoken long afterwards about "today" being the time to get in.

9 So there is a full complete rest *still waiting* for the people of God.

10 Christ has already entered there. He is resting from His work, just as God did after the creation.

11 Let us do our best to go into that place of rest, too, being careful not to disobey God as the children of Israel did, thus failing to get in.

12 For whatever God says to us is full of living power: it is sharper than the sharpest dagger, cutting swift and deep into our innermost thoughts and desires with all their parts, exposing us for what we really are.

13 He knows about everyone, everywhere. Everything about us is bare and wide open to the all-seeing eyes of our living God; nothing can be hidden from Him to whom we must explain all that we have done.

14 But Jesus the Son of God is our great High Priest who has gone to heaven itself to help us; therefore let us never stop trusting Him.

15 This High Priest of ours understands our weaknesses, since He had the same temptations we do, though He never once gave way to them and sinned.

16 So let us come boldly to the very throne of God and stay there to receive His mercy and to find grace to help us in our times of need.

Revised Standard

from all his works." 5And again in this place
he said,
"They shall never enter my rest."
6Since therefore it remains for some to enter
it, and those who formerly received the
good news failed to enter because of disobedience, 7again he sets a certain day, "Today," saying through David so long afterward, in the words already quoted,
"Today, when you hear his voice,
do not harden your hearts."
8For if Joshua had given them rest, God[i]
would not speak later of another day. 9So
then, there remains a sabbath rest for the
people of God; 10for whoever enters God's
rest also ceases from his labors as God did
from his.
11 Let us therefore strive to enter that
rest, that no one fall by the same sort of
disobedience. 12For the word of God is
living and active, sharper than any two-
edged sword, piercing to the division of soul
and spirit, of joints and marrow, and discerning the thoughts and intentions of the
heart. 13And before him no creature is hidden, but all are open and laid bare to the
eyes of him with whom we have to do.

Christ the way of approach to God

14 Since then we have a great high priest
who has passed through the heavens, Jesus,
the Son of God, let us hold fast our confession. 15For we have not a high priest who
is unable to sympathize with our weaknesses, but one who in every respect has been
tempted as we are, yet without sinning.
16Let us then with confidence draw near to
the throne of grace, that we may receive
mercy and find grace to help in time of
need.

CHAPTER 5

The Jewish high priest is merely a man like anyone else, but he is chosen to speak for all other men in their dealings with God. He presents their gifts to God and offers to Him the blood of animals that are sacrificed to cover the sins of the people and his own sins too. And

5 For every high priest chosen from
among men is appointed to act on behalf
of men in relation to God, to offer gifts and
sacrifices for sins. 2He can deal gently with
the ignorant and wayward, since he himself

[i] Greek *he*

King James

3 And by reason hereof he ought, as for the people, so also for himself, to offer for sins.

4 And no man taketh this honour unto himself, but he that is called of God, as *was* Aaron.

5 So also Christ glorified not himself to be made an high priest; but he that said unto him, Thou art my Son, to-day have I begotten thee.

6 As he saith also in another *place,* Thou *art* a priest for ever after the order of Melchisedec.

7 Who in the days of his flesh, when he had offered up prayers and supplications with strong crying and tears unto him that was able to save him from death, and was heard in that he feared;

8 Though he were a Son, yet learned he obedience by the things which he suffered;

9 And being made perfect, he became the author of eternal salvation unto all them that obey him;

10 Called of God an high priest after the order of Melchisedec.

11 Of whom we have many things to say, and hard to be uttered, seeing ye are dull of hearing.

12 For when for the time ye ought to be teachers, ye have need that one teach you again which *be* the first principles of the oracles of God; and are become such as have need of milk, and not of strong meat.

13 For every one that useth milk *is* unskilful in the word of righteousness: for he is a babe.

14 But strong meat belongeth to them that are of full age, *even* those who by reason of use have their senses exercised to discern both good and evil.

Amplified

3 And because of this he is obliged to offer sacrifice for his own sins as well as for those of the people.

4 Besides, one does not appropriate for himself the honor [of being high priest], but he is called by God *and* receives it of Him, just as Aaron did.

5 So too Christ, the Messiah, did not exalt Himself to be made a high priest, but was appointed *and* exalted by Him Who said to Him, You are My Son, today I have begotten You; [Ps. 2:7.]

6 As He says also in another place, You are a Priest [appointed] forever after the order (rank) of Melchizedek. [Ps. 110:4.]

7 In the days of His flesh [Jesus] offered up definite, special petitions [for that which He not only wanted [r]but needed], and supplications, with strong crying and tears, to Him Who was [always] able to save Him (out) from death, and He was heard because of His reverence toward God—His godly fear, His piety [[s]that is, in that He shrank from the horrors of separation from the bright presence of the Father].

8 Although He was a Son, He learned [active, special] obedience through what He suffered;

9 And [His completed experience] making Him perfect [in equipment], He became the Author *and* Source of eternal salvation to all those who give heed *and* obey Him, [Isa. 45:17.]

10 Being [t]designated *and* recognized *and* saluted by God as High Priest after the order [with [u]the rank] of Melchizedek. [Ps. 110:4.]

11 Concerning this we have much to say which is hard to explain, since you have become dull in your [spiritual] hearing *and* sluggish, *even* [r]slothful [in achieving spiritual insight].

12 For even though by this time you ought to be teaching others, you actually need some one to teach you over again the very first principles of God's Word. You have come to need milk, not solid food.

13 For every one who continues to feed on milk is obviously inexperienced *and* unskilled in the doctrine of righteousness, [that is, of conformity to the divine will in purpose, thought and action,] for he is a mere infant—not able to talk yet!

14 But solid food is for full-grown men, for those whose senses *and* mental faculties are trained by practice to discriminate *and* distinguish between what is morally good *and* noble and what is evil *and* contrary either to divine or human law.

---

r) Abbott-Smith.
s) Jamieson, Fausset and Brown's "Commentary on the Old an[d] New Testaments."
t) Souter.
u) Thayer.

Living New Testament

because he is a man he can deal gently with other men, though they are foolish and ignorant, for he, too, is surrounded with the same temptations and understands their problems very well.

4 Another thing to remember is that no one can be a high priest just because he wants to be. He has to be called by God for this work in the same way God chose Aaron.

5 That is why Christ did not elect Himself to the honor of being High Priest; no, He was chosen by God. God said to Him, "My Son, today I have honored[1] You."

6 And another time God said to Him, "You have been chosen to be a priest forever, with the same rank as Melchizedek."

7 Yet while Christ was here on earth He pleaded with God, praying with tears and agony of soul to the only one who would save Him from [premature][2] death. And God heard His prayers because of His strong desire to obey God at all times.

8 And even though Jesus was God's Son, He had to learn from experience what it was like to obey, when obeying meant suffering.

9 It was after He had proved Himself perfect in this experience that Jesus became the Giver of eternal salvation to all those who obey Him.

10 For remember that God had chosen Him to be a High Priest with the same rank as Melchizedek.

* * * * *

11 There is much more I would like to say along these lines, but you don't seem to listen, so it's hard to make you understand.

12, 13 You have been Christians a long time now, and you ought to be teaching others, but instead you have dropped back to the place where you need someone to teach you all over again the very first principles in God's Word. You are like babies who can drink only milk, not old enough for solid food. And when a person is still living on milk it shows he isn't very far along in the Christian life, and doesn't know much about the difference between right and wrong. He is still a baby-Christian!

14 You will never be able to eat solid spiritual food and understand the deeper things of God's Word until you become better Christians and learn right from wrong by practicing doing right.

[1] Literally, "begotten You." Probably the reference is to the day of Christ's resurrection.

[2] Implied. Christ's longing was to live until He could die on the cross for all mankind. There is a strong case to be made that Satan's great desire was that Christ should die prematurely, before the mighty work at the cross could be performed. Christ's body, being human, was frail and weak like ours (except that His was sinless). He had said just a few days before, "My soul is exceeding sorrowful *unto death*." And can a human body live long under such pressure of spirit as He underwent in the Garden, that caused sweating of great drops of blood? But God graciously heard and answered His anguished cry in Gethsemane ("Let this cup pass from Me") and preserved Him from seemingly imminent and premature death: for an angel was sent to strengthen Him so that He could live to accomplish God's perfect will at the cross. . . . But some readers may prefer the explanation that Christ's plea was that He be saved *out from* death, at the Resurrection.

Revised Standard

is beset with weakness. [3]Because of this he
is bound to offer sacrifice for his own sins
as well as for those of the people. [4]And one
does not take the honor upon himself, but
he is called by God, just as Aaron was.

5 So also Christ did not exalt himself
to be made a high priest, but was appointed
by him who said to him,

"Thou art my Son,
today I have begotten thee";
[6] as he says also in another place,
"Thou art a priest for ever,
after the order of Melchizedek."

7 In the days of his flesh, Jesus[j] offered
up prayers and supplications, with loud cries
and tears, to him who was able to save him
from death, and he was heard for his godly
fear. [8]Although he was a Son, he learned
obedience through what he suffered; [9]and
being made perfect he became the source of
eternal salvation to all who obey him, [10]be-
ing designated by God a high priest after
the order of Melchizedek.

The immature reproved

11 About this we have much to say which
is hard to explain, since you have become
dull of hearing. [12]For though by this time
you ought to be teachers, you need some
one to teach you again the first principles
of God's word. You need milk, not solid
food; [13]for every one who lives on milk is
unskilled in the word of righteousness, for
he is a child. [14]But solid food is for the
mature, for those who have their faculties
trained by practice to distinguish good from
evil.

[j] Greek *he*

King James

CHAPTER 6

THEREFORE leaving the principles of the doctrine of Christ, let us go on unto perfection; not laying again the foundation of repentance from dead works, and of faith toward God,

2 Of the doctrine of baptisms, and of laying on of hands, and of resurrection of the dead, and of eternal judgment.

3 And this will we do, if God permit.

4 For *it is* impossible for those who were once enlightened, and have tasted of the heavenly gift, and were made partakers of the Holy Ghost,

5 And have tasted the good word of God, and the powers of the world to come,

6 If they shall fall away, to renew them again unto repentance; seeing they crucify to themselves the Son of God afresh, and put *him* to an open shame.

7 For the earth which drinketh in the rain that cometh oft upon it, and bringeth forth herbs meet for them by whom it is dressed, receiveth blessing from God:

8 But that which beareth thorns and briers *is* rejected, and *is* nigh unto cursing; whose end *is* to be burned.

9 But, beloved, we are persuaded better things of you, and things that accompany salvation, though we thus speak.

10 For God *is* not unrighteous to forget your work and labour of love, which ye have shewed toward his name, in that ye have ministered to the saints, and do minister.

11 And we desire that every one of you do shew the same diligence to the full assurance of hope unto the end:

12 That ye be not slothful, but followers of them who through faith and patience inherit the promises.

13 For when God made promise to Abraham, because he could swear by no greater, he sware by himself,

14 Saying, Surely blessing I will bless thee, and multiplying I will multiply thee.

15 And so, after he had patiently endured, he obtained the promise.

16 For men verily swear by the greater: and an oath for confirmation *is* to them an end of all strife.

17 Wherein God, willing more abundantly to shew unto the heirs of promise the immutability of his counsel, confirmed *it* by an oath:

Amplified

CHAPTER 6

THEREFORE let us go on and get past the elementary stage in the teachings *and* doctrine of Christ, the Messiah, advancing steadily toward the completeness *and* perfection that belongs to spiritual maturity. Let us not again be laying the foundation of repentance *and* abandonment of dead works [dead formalism], and of the faith [by which you turned] to God,

2 With teachings about purifying, the laying on of hands, the resurrection from the dead, and eternal judgment *and* punishment. [These are all matters of which you should have been fully aware long, long ago.]

3 If indeed God permits we will [now] proceed [to advanced teaching].

4 For it is impossible [to restore *and* bring again to repentance] those who have been once for all enlightened, who have consciously tasted the heavenly gift, and have become sharers of the Holy Spirit,

5 And have felt how good the Word of God is and the mighty powers of the age *and* world to come,

6 If they then deviate from the faith *and* turn away from their allegiance; [it is impossible] to bring them back to repentance, for (because, [v]while, as long as) they nail up on the cross the Son of God afresh, as far as they are concerned, and are holding [Him] up to contempt *and* shame *and* public disgrace.

7 For the soil which has drunk the rain that repeatedly falls upon it, and produces vegetation useful to those for whose benefit it is cultivated, partakes of a blessing from God.

8 But if [that same soil] persistently bears thorns and thistles, it is considered worthless and near to being cursed, whose end is to be burned. [Gen. 3:17, 18.]

9 Even though we speak this way, yet in your case, beloved, we are now firmly convinced of better things that are near to salvation *and* accompany it.

10 For God is not unrighteous to forget *or* overlook your labor and the love which you have shown for His name's sake in ministering to the needs of the saints—His own consecrated people—as you still do.

11 But we do [[w]strongly and earnestly] desire for each of you to show the same diligence *and* sincerity [all the way through] in realizing *and* enjoying the full assurance *and* development of [your] hope until the end,

12 In order that you may not grow disinterested *and* become [spiritual] sluggards but imitators, behaving as do those who through faith [that is, [x]by their leaning of the entire personality on God in Christ in absolute trust and confidence in His power, wisdom and goodness], and by practice of patient endurance *and* waiting are [now] inheriting the promises.

13 For when God made [His] promise to Abraham, He swore by Himself, since He had no one greater by whom to swear,

14 Saying, Blessing I certainly will bless you and multiplying I will multiply you. [Gen. 22:16, 17.]

15 And so it was that he [Abraham] having waited long *and* endured patiently, realized *and* obtained [in the birth of Isaac as a pledge of what was to come] what God had promised him.

16 Men indeed swear by a greater [than themselves], and with them in all disputes the oath taken for confirmation is final—ending strife.

17 Accordingly God also, in His desire to show more convincingly *and* beyond doubt, to those who were to inherit the promise, the unchangeableness of His purpose *and* plan, intervened (mediated) with an oath.

---

v) Alternate reading.
w) Vincent.
x) Souter.

Living New Testament

CHAPTER 6

Let us stop going over the same old ground again and again, always teaching those first lessons about Christ. Let us go on instead to other things and become mature in our understanding, as strong Christians ought to be. Surely we don't need to speak further about the foolishness of trying to be saved by being good, or about the necessity of faith in God;

2 You don't need further instruction about baptism and spiritual gifts[1] and the resurrection of the dead and eternal judgment.

3 The Lord willing, we will go on now to other things.

4 There is no use trying to bring you back to the Lord again if you have once understood the Good News and tasted for yourself the good things of heaven and shared in the Holy Spirit,

5 And know how good the Word of God is, and felt the mighty powers of the world to come,

6 And then have turned against God. You cannot bring yourself to repent again if you have nailed the Son of God to the cross again by rejecting Him, holding Him up to mocking and to public shame.

7 When a farmer's land has had many showers upon it and good crops come up, that land has experienced God's blessing upon it.

8 But if it keeps on having crops of thistles and thorns, the land is considered no good and is ready for condemnation and burning off.

9 Dear friends, even though I am talking like this I really don't believe that what I am saying applies to you. I am confident you are producing the good fruit that comes along with your salvation.

10 For God is not unfair. How can He forget your hard work for Him, or forget the way you used to show your love for Him—and still do—by helping His children?

11 And we are anxious that you keep right on loving others as long as life lasts, so that you will get your full reward.

12 Then, knowing what lies ahead for you, you won't become bored with being a Christian, nor become spiritually dull and indifferent, but you will be anxious to follow the example of those who receive all that God has promised them because of their strong faith and patience.

* * * *

13 For instance, there was God's promise to Abraham: God took an oath in His own name, since there was no one greater to swear by,

14 That He would bless Abraham again and again, and give him a son and make him the father of a great nation of people.

15 Then Abraham waited patiently until finally God gave him a son, Isaac, just as He had promised.

16 When a man takes an oath, he is calling upon someone greater than himself to force him to do what he has promised, or to punish him if he later refuses to do it; the oath ends all argument about it.

17 God also bound Himself with an oath, so that those He promised to help would be perfectly sure and never need to wonder whether He might change His plans.

[1] Literally, "the laying on of hands."

Revised Standard

Warning against apostasy

6 Therefore let us leave the elementary
doctrines of Christ and go on to maturity, not laying again a foundation of
repentance from dead works and of faith
toward God, 2 with instruction[k] about ablutions, the laying on of hands, the resurrection of the dead, and eternal judgment.
3 And this we will do if God permits.[l] 4 For
it is impossible to restore again to repentance those who have once been enlightened,
who have tasted the heavenly gift, and have
become partakers of the Holy Spirit, 5 and
have tasted the goodness of the word of
God and the powers of the age to come,
6 if they then commit apostasy, since they
crucify the Son of God on their own account and hold him up to contempt. 7 For
land which has drunk the rain that often
falls upon it, and brings forth vegetation
useful to those for whose sake it is cultivated, receives a blessing from God. 8 But
if it bears thorns and thistles, it is worthless and near to being cursed; its end is to
be burned.

True believers encouraged

9 Though we speak thus, yet in your
case, beloved, we feel sure of better things
that belong to salvation. 10 For God is not
so unjust as to overlook your work and the
love which you showed for his sake in serving the saints, as you still do. 11 And we
desire each one of you to show the same
earnestness in realizing the full assurance
of hope until the end, 12 so that you may
not be sluggish, but imitators of those who
through faith and patience inherit the promises.

God's oath unchanging

13 For when God made a promise to
Abraham, since he had no one greater by
whom to swear, he swore by himself, 14 saying, "Surely I will bless you and multiply
you." 15 And thus Abraham,[m] having patiently endured, obtained the promise. 16 Men
indeed swear by a greater than themselves,
and in all their disputes an oath is final for
confirmation. 17 So when God desired to
show more convincingly to the heirs of the
promise the unchangeable character of his
purpose, he interposed with an oath, 18 so

[k] Other ancient manuscripts read *of instruction*
[l] Other ancient manuscripts read *let us do this if God permits*
[m] Greek *he*

King James

18 That by two immutable things, in which *it was* impossible for God to lie, we might have a strong consolation, who have fled for refuge to lay hold upon the hope set before us:

19 Which *hope* we have as an anchor of the soul, both sure and stedfast, and which entereth into that within the veil;

20 Whither the forerunner is for us entered, *even* Jesus, made an high priest for ever after the order of Melchisedec.

Amplified

18 This was so that by two unchangeable things [His promise and His oath], in which it is impossible for God ever to prove false *or* deceive us, we who have fled [to Him] for refuge might have mighty indwelling strength *and* strong encouragement to grasp *and* hold fast the hope appointed for us *and* set before [us].

19 [Now] we have this [hope] as a sure and steadfast anchor of the soul—it cannot slip and it cannot [y]break down under whoever steps out upon it—[a hope] that reaches [y]farther *and* enters into [the very certainty of the Presence] within the veil, [Lev. 16:2.]

20 Where Jesus has entered in for us [in advance], a Forerunner having become a High Priest forever after the order [with [z]the rank] of Melchizedek. [Ps. 110:4.]

CHAPTER 7 (King James)

FOR this Melchisedec, king of Salem, priest of the most high God, who met Abraham returning from the slaughter of the kings, and blessed him;

2 To whom also Abraham gave a tenth part of all; first being by interpretation King of righteousness, and after that also King of Salem, which is, King of peace;

3 Without father, without mother, without descent, having neither beginning of days, nor end of life; but made like unto the Son of God; abideth a priest continually.

4 Now consider how great this man *was*, unto whom even the patriarch Abraham gave the tenth of the spoils.

5 And verily they that are of the sons of Levi, who receive the office of the priesthood, have a commandment to take tithes of the people according to the law, that is, of their brethren, though they come out of the loins of Abraham:

6 But he whose descent is not counted from them received tithes of Abraham, and blessed him that had the promises.

7 And without all contradiction the less is blessed of the better.

8 And here men that die receive tithes; but there he *receiveth them,* of whom it is witnessed that he liveth.

9 And as I may so say, Levi also, who receiveth tithes, payed tithes in Abraham.

10 For he was yet in the loins of his father, when Melchisedec met him.

11 If therefore perfection were by the Levitical priesthood, (for under it the people received the law,) what further need *was there* that another priest should rise after the order of Melchisedec, and not be called after the order of Aaron?

12 For the priesthood being changed, there is made of necessity a change also of the law.

13 For he of whom these things are spoken pertaineth to another tribe, of which no man gave attendance at the altar.

CHAPTER 7 (Amplified)

FOR this Melchizedek, king of Salem [and] priest of the Most High God, met Abraham as he returned from the slaughter of the kings and blessed him;

2 And Abraham gave to him a tenth portion of all [the spoil]. He is primarily, as his name when translated indicates, king of righteousness, and then he is also king of Salem, which means king of peace.

3 Without [record of] father or mother or ancestral line, nor with beginning of days or ending of life, but resembling the Son of God he continues to be a priest without interruption *and* without successor.

4 Now observe *and* consider how great [a personage] this was to whom even Abraham the patriarch gave a tenth—the topmost [the pick] of the heap—of the spoils.

5 And it is true that those descendants of Levi who are charged with the priestly office are commanded in the Law to take tithes from the people, which means from their brethren, though these have descended from Abraham.

6 But this person who has not their Levitical ancestry received tithes from Abraham [himself] and blessed him who possessed the promises [of God].

7 Yet it is beyond all contradiction that it is the lesser person who is blessed by the greater one.

8 Furthermore, here [in the Levitical priesthood] tithes are received by men who are subject to death; while there [in the case of Melchizedek], they are received by one of whom it is testified that he lives [perpetually].

9 A person might even say that through Abraham, Levi [the father of the priestly tribe] himself, who received tithes, paid tithes through Abraham.

10 For he was still in the loins of his forefather [Abraham] when Melchizedek met him [Abraham].

11 Now if perfection [that is, a perfect fellowship between God and the worshipper,] had been attainable by the Levitical priesthood, for under it the people were given the Law, why was it further necessary that there should arise another *and* different kind of Priest, one after the order of Melchizedek, rather than one appointed after the order *and* rank of Aaron?

12 For when there is a change in the priesthood, there is of necessity an alteration of the law [concerning the priesthood] as well.

13 For the One of Whom these things are said belonged [not to the priestly line but] to another tribe, no member of which has officiated at the altar.

---

y) Vincent.
z) Thayer.

Living New Testament

18 He has given us both His promise and His oath, two things we can completely count on, for it is impossible for God to tell a lie. Now all those who flee to Him to save them can take new courage when they hear such assurances from God; now they can know without doubt that He will give them the salvation He has promised them.

19 This certain hope of being saved is a strong and trustworthy anchor for our souls, connecting us with God Himself behind the sacred curtains of heaven.

20 Where Christ has gone ahead to plead for us from His position as[2] our High Priest, with the honor and rank of Melchizedek.

Revised Standard

that through two unchangeable things, in
which it is impossible that God should prove
false, we who have fled for refuge might
have strong encouragement to seize the hope
set before us. [19]We have this as a sure and
steadfast anchor of the soul, a hope that
enters into the inner shrine behind the curtain, [20]where Jesus has gone as a forerunner
on our behalf, having become a high priest
for ever after the order of Melchizedek.

CHAPTER 7

This Melchizedek was king of the city of Salem, and also a priest of the Most High God. When Abraham was returning home after winning a great battle against many kings, Melchizedek met him and blessed him;

2 Then Abraham took a tenth of all he had won in the battle and gave it to Melchizedek. Melchizedek's name means "Justice," so he is the King of Justice; and he is also the King of Peace because of the name of his city, Salem, which means "Peace."

3 Melchizedek had no father or mother[1] and there is no record of any of his ancestors. He was never born and he never died but his life is like that of the Son of God—a priest forever.

4 See then how great this Melchizedek is:

(a) Even Abraham, the first and most honored of all God's chosen people, gave Melchizedek a tenth of the spoils he took from the kings he had been fighting.

5 One could understand why Abraham would do this if Melchizedek had been a Jewish priest, for later on God's people were required by law to give gifts to help their priests because the priests were their relatives.

6 But Melchizedek was not a relative, and yet Abraham paid him.

(b) Melchizedek placed a blessing upon mighty Abraham,

7 And as everyone knows, a person who has the power to bless is always greater than the person he blesses.

8 *(c)* The Jewish priests, though mortal, received tithes; but we are told that Melchizedek lives on.

9 *(d)* One might even say that Levi himself (the ancestor of all Jewish priests, of all who receive tithes), paid tithes to Melchizedek through Abraham.

10 For although Levi wasn't born yet, the seed from which he came was in Abraham when Abraham paid the tithes to Melchizedek.

11 *(e)* If the Jewish priests and their laws had been able to save us, why then did God need to send Christ as a priest with the rank of Melchizedek, instead of sending someone with the rank of Aaron—the same rank all other priests had?

12, 13, 14 And when God sends a new kind of priest, His law must be changed to permit it. As we all know,

---

Literally, "having become."

No one can be sure whether this means that Melchizedek was Christ appearing to Abraham in human form, or simply that there is no *record* of who Melchizedek's father or mother were, no *record* of his birth or death.

Priority of Melchizedek priesthood

7 For this Melchizedek, king of Salem,
priest of the Most High God, met Abraham returning from the slaughter of the
kings and blessed him; [2]and to him Abraham apportioned a tenth part of everything.
He is first, by translation of his name, king
of righteousness, and then he is also king of
Salem, that is, king of peace. [3]He is without father or mother or genealogy, and has
neither beginning of days nor end of life,
but resembling the Son of God he continues
a priest for ever.
4 See how great he is! Abraham the
patriarch gave him a tithe of the spoils.
[5]And those descendants of Levi who receive the priestly office have a commandment in the law to take tithes from the
people, that is, from their brethren, though
these also are descended from Abraham.
[6]But this man who has not their genealogy
received tithes from Abraham and blessed
him who had the promises. [7]It is beyond
dispute that the inferior is blessed by the
superior. [8]Here tithes are received by mortal men; there, by one of whom it is testified
that he lives. [9]One might even say that Levi
himself, who receives tithes, paid tithes
through Abraham, [10]for he was still in the
loins of his ancestor when Melchizedek met
him.
11 Now if perfection had been attainable
through the Levitical priesthood (for under
it the people received the law), what further need would there have been for another priest to arise after the order of
Melchizedek, rather than one named after
the order of Aaron? [12]For when there is
a change in the priesthood, there is necessarily a change in the law as well. [13]For
the one of whom these things are spoken
belonged to another tribe, from which no

King James

14 For *it is* evident that our Lord sprang
out of Juda; of which tribe Moses spake
nothing concerning priesthood.
15 And it is yet far more evident: for
that after the similitude of Melchisedec
there ariseth another priest,
16 Who is made, not after the law of a
carnal commandment, but after the power
of an endless life.
17 For he testifieth, Thou *art* a priest for
ever after the order of Melchisedec.
18 For there is verily a disannulling of
the commandment going before for the
weakness and unprofitableness thereof.
19 For the law made nothing perfect, but
the bringing in of a better hope *did;* by the
which we draw nigh unto God.
20 And inasmuch as not without an oath
he was made priest:
21 (For those priests were made without
an oath; but this with an oath by him that
said unto him, The Lord sware and will not
repent, Thou *art* a priest for ever after the
order of Melchisedec:)
22 By so much was Jesus made a surety
of a better testament.
23 And they truly were many priests, because they were not suffered to continue by
reason of death:
24 But this *man*, because he continueth
ever, hath an unchangeable priesthood.
25 Wherefore he is able also to save
them to the uttermost that come unto God
by him, seeing he ever liveth to make intercession for them.
26 For such an high priest became us,
who is holy, harmless, undefiled, separate
from sinners, and made higher than the
heavens;
27 Who needeth not daily, as those high
priests, to offer up sacrifice, first for his own
sins, and then for the people's: for this he
did once, when he offered up himself.
28 For the law maketh men high priests
which have infirmity; but the word of the
oath, which was since the law, *maketh* the
Son, who is consecrated for evermore.

Amplified

14 For it is obvious that our Lord sprang from the
tribe of Judah, and Moses mentioned nothing about priests
in connection with that tribe.
15 And this becomes more plainly evident when another Priest arises Who bears the likeness of Melchizedek,
[Ps. 110:4.]
16 Who has been constituted a Priest, not on the basis
of a bodily legal requirement—an externally imposed
command concerning His physical ancestry—but on the
basis of the power of an endless *and* indestructible Life.
17 For it is witnessed of Him, You are a Priest forever
after the order [rank] of Melchizedek. [Ps. 110:4.]
18 So, a previous physical regulation *and* command is
cancelled because of its weakness *and* ineffectiveness and
uselessness,
19 For the Law never made anything perfect, but instead a better hope is introduced through which we [now]
come close to God.
20 And it was not without the taking of an oath [that
Christ was made Priest],
21 For those who formerly became priests received
their office without its being confirmed by the taking of an
oath by God, but this One was designated *and* addressed
and saluted with an oath, The Lord has sworn and will
not regret it *or* change His mind, You are a Priest forever
according to the order of Melchizedek. [Ps. 110:4.]
22 In keeping with [the oath's greater strength and
force], Jesus has become the Guarantee of a better
(stronger) agreement—a more excellent and more advantageous covenant.
23 [Again, the former successive line of priests] was
made up of many, because they were each prevented by
death from continuing [perpetually in office];
24 But he holds His priesthood unchangeably because
He lives on forever.
25 Therefore He is able also to save to the uttermost—
completely, perfectly, finally and for all time and eternity—
those who come to God through Him, since He is always
living to make petition to God *and* intercede with Him
and intervene for them.
26 [Here is] the High Priest [perfectly adapted] to our
needs, as was fitting, holy, blameless, unstained by sin,
separated from sinners and exalted higher than the heavens.
27 He has no day by day necessity, as [do each of these
other] high priests, to offer sacrifice first of all for his own
[personal] sins and then for those of the people; because
He [met all the requirements] once for all when He
brought Himself [as a sacrifice] which He offered up.
28 For the Law sets up men in their weakness [frail,
sinful, dying human beings] as high priests, but the word
of [God's] oath, which [was spoken later], after the institution of the Law, [chooses *and* appoints as priest One
Whose appointment is complete and permanent], a Son
Who has been made perfect forever. [Ps. 110:4.]

CHAPTER 8

NOW of the things which we have spoken *this is* the sum: We have such an
high priest, who is set on the right hand of
the throne of the Majesty in the heavens;
2 A minister of the sanctuary, and of the
true tabernacle, which the Lord pitched, and
not man.

CHAPTER 8

NOW the main point of what we have to say is this:
We have such a High Priest, One Who is seated at
the right hand of the majestic [God] in heaven, [Ps.
110:1.]
2 As officiating Priest, a Minister in the holy places *and*
in the true tabernacle which is erected not by man but by
the Lord.

Living New Testament

Christ did not belong to the priest-tribe of Levi, but came from the tribe of Judah, which had not been chosen for priesthood; Moses had never given them that work.

15 So we can plainly see that God's method changed, for Christ, the new High Priest who came with the rank of Melchizedek,

16 Did not become a priest by meeting the old requirement of belonging to the tribe of Levi, but on the basis of power flowing from a life that cannot end.

17 And the Psalmist points this out when he says of Christ, "You are a priest forever with the rank of Melchizedek."

18 Yes, the old system of priesthood based on family lines was canceled because it didn't work. It was weak and useless for saving people.

19 It never made anyone really right with God. But now we have a far better hope, for Christ makes us acceptable to God, and now we may draw near to Him.

20 God took an oath that Christ would always be a Priest,

21 Although He never said that of other priests. Only to Christ He said, "The Lord has sworn and will never change His mind: You are a Priest forever, with the rank of Melchizedek."

22 Because of God's oath, Christ can guarantee forever the success of this new and better arrangement.

23 Under the old arrangement there had to be many priests, so that when the older ones died off, the system could still be carried on by others who took their places.

24 But Jesus lives forever and continues to be a Priest so that no one else is needed.

25 He is able to save completely all who come to God through Him. Since He will live forever, He will always be there to remind God that He has paid for their sins with His blood.

26 He is, therefore, exactly the kind of High Priest we need; for He is holy and blameless, unstained by sin, undefiled by sinners, and to Him has been given the place of honor in heaven.

27 He never needs the daily blood of animal sacrifices, as other priests did, to cover over first their own sins and then the sins of the people; for He finished all sacrifices, once and for all, when He sacrificed Himself on the cross.

28 Under the old system, even the high priests were weak and sinful men who could not keep from doing wrong, but later God appointed by His oath His Son who is perfect forever.

Revised Standard

one has ever served at the altar. [14]For it is
evident that our Lord was descended from
Judah, and in connection with that tribe
Moses said nothing about priests.

Superiority of Christ's priesthood

15 This becomes even more evident when
another priest arises in the likeness of Melchizedek, [16]who has become a priest, not
according to a legal requirement concerning bodily descent but by the power of an
indestructible life. [17]For it is witnessed of
him,

"Thou art a priest for ever,
after the order of Melchizedek."

[18]On the one hand, a former commandment is set aside because of its weakness
and uselessness [19](for the law made nothing
perfect); on the other hand, a better hope
is introduced, through which we draw near
to God.

20 And it was not without an oath.
[21]Those who formerly became priests took
their office without an oath, but this one
was addressed with an oath,

"The Lord has sworn
and will not change his mind,
'Thou art a priest for ever.'"

[22]This makes Jesus the surety of a better
covenant.

23 The former priests were many in number, because they were prevented by death
from continuing in office; [24]but he holds his
priesthood permanently, because he continues
for ever. [25]Consequently he is able for all
time to save those who draw near to God
through him, since he always lives to make
intercession for them.

26 For it was fitting that we should have
such a high priest, holy, blameless, unstained, separated from sinners, exalted
above the heavens. [27]He has no need, like
those high priests, to offer sacrifices daily,
first for his own sins and then for those
of the people; he did this once for all when
he offered up himself. [28]Indeed, the law
appoints men in their weakness as high
priests, but the word of the oath, which
came later than the law, appoints a Son
who has been made perfect for ever.

CHAPTER 8

What we are saying is this: Christ, whose priesthood we have just described, is our High Priest, and is in heaven at the place of greatest honor next to God Himself.

2 He ministers in the temple in heaven, the true place of worship built by the Lord and not by human hands.

Superiority of the new covenant

8 Now the point in what we are saying
is this: we have such a high priest, one
who is seated at the right hand of the throne
of the Majesty in heaven, [2]a minister in the
sanctuary and the true tent[n] which is set up

---

[n] Or *tabernacle*

King James

3 For every high priest is ordained to offer gifts and sacrifices: wherefore *it is* of necessity that this man have somewhat also to offer.
4 For if he were on earth, he should not be a priest, seeing that there are priests that offer gifts according to the law:
5 Who serve unto the example and shadow of heavenly things, as Moses was admonished of God when he was about to make the tabernacle: for, See, saith he, *that* thou make all things according to the pattern shewed to thee in the mount.
6 But now hath he obtained a more excellent ministry, by how much also he is the mediator of a better covenant, which was established upon better promises.
7 For if that first *covenant* had been faultless, then should no place have been sought for the second.
8 For finding fault with them, he saith, Behold, the days come, saith the Lord, when I will make a new covenant with the house of Israel and with the house of Judah:
9 Not according to the covenant that I made with their fathers in the day when I took them by the hand to lead them out of the land of Egypt; because they continued not in my covenant, and I regarded them not, saith the Lord.
10 For this *is* the covenant that I will make with the house of Israel after those days, saith the Lord; I will put my laws into their mind, and write them in their hearts: and I will be to them a God, and they shall be to me a people:
11 And they shall not teach every man his neighbour, and every man his brother, saying, Know the Lord: for all shall know me, from the least to the greatest.
12 For I will be merciful to their unrighteousness, and their sins and their iniquities will I remember no more.
13 In that he saith, A new *covenant*, he hath made the first old. Now that which decayeth and waxeth old *is* ready to vanish away.

Amplified

3 For every high priest is appointed to offer up gifts and sacrifices; so it is essential for this [High Priest] to have some offering to make also.
4 If then He were still living on earth, He would not be a priest at all, for there are [already priests] who offer the gifts in accordance with the Law.
5 [But these offer service merely as] a pattern and as a foreshadowing of [what has its true existence and reality in] the heavenly sanctuary. For when Moses was about to erect the tabernacle, he was warned by God, saying, See to it that you make it all [exactly] according to the copy (the model,) which was shown to you on the mountain. [Exod. 25:40.]
6 But as it now is, He [Christ] has acquired a [priestly] ministry which is as much superior *and* more excellent [than the old] as the covenant—the agreement—of which He is the Mediator (the Arbiter, Agent) is superior *and* more excellent; [because] it is enacted *and* rests upon more important (sublimer, higher and nobler) promises.
7 For if that first covenant had been without defect, there would have been no room for another one *or* an attempt to institute another one.
8 However He finds fault with them, [showing its inadequacy], when He says, Behold, the days will come, says the Lord, when I will make *and* ratify a new covenant *or* agreement with the house of Israel and with the house of Judah.
9 It will not be like the covenant that I made with their forefathers on the day when I grasped them by the hand to help *and* relieve them *and* to lead them out from the land of Egypt, for they did not abide in My agreement with them, and so I withdrew My favor *and* disregarded them, says the Lord.
10 For this is the covenant that I will make with the house of Israel after those days, says the Lord: I will imprint My laws upon their minds, even upon their innermost thoughts *and* understanding, and engrave them upon their hearts, and I will be their God, and they shall be My people.
11 And it will nevermore be necessary for every one to teach his neighbor and his fellow citizen or every one his brother, saying, Know—[that is,] perceive, have knowledge of and get acquainted by experience with—the Lord; for all will know Me, from the smallest to the greatest of them.
12 For I will be merciful *and* gracious toward their sins and I will remember their deeds of unrighteousness no more. [Jer. 31:31-34.]
13 When God speaks of a new [covenant or agreement], He makes the first one obsolete—out of use. And what is obsolete—out of use *and* annulled because of age—is ripe for disappearance *and* to be dispensed with altogether.

CHAPTER 9

THEN verily the first *covenant* had also ordinances of divine service, and a worldly sanctuary.
2 For there was a tabernacle made; the first, wherein *was* the candlestick, and the table, and the shewbread; which is called the sanctuary.

CHAPTER 9

NOW even the first covenant had its own rules *and* regulations for divine worship, and it had a sanctuary, [but one] of this world. [Exod. 25:10-40.]
2 For a tabernacle (tent) was erected, in the outer division *or* compartment of which were the lampstand and the table with [its loaves of] the showbread set forth. [This portion] is called the Holy [Place]. [Lev. 24:5, 6.]

Living New Testament

3 And since every high priest is appointed to offer gifts d sacrifices, Christ must make an offering too.

4 The sacrifice He offers is far better than those offered the earthly priests. (But even so, if He were here on rth He wouldn't even be permitted to be a priest, cause down here the priests still follow the old Jewish stem of sacrifices.)

5 Their work is connected with a mere earthly model the real tabernacle in heaven; for when Moses was tting ready to build the tabernacle, God warned him to low exactly the pattern of the heavenly tabernacle as own to him on Mount Sinai.

6 But Christ, as a Minister in heaven, has been reward- with a far more important work than those who serve der the old laws, because the new agreement which He sses on to us from God contains far more wonderful omises.

7 The old agreement didn't even work. If it had, there ould have been no need for another to replace it.

8 But God Himself found fault with the old one, for said, "The day will come when I will make a new reement with the people of Israel and the people of dah.

9 This new agreement will not be like the old one I ve to their fathers on the day when I took them by the nd to lead them out of the land of Egypt; they did not ep their part in that agreement, so I had to cancel it.

10 But this is the new agreement I will make with the ople of Israel, says the Lord: I will write My laws in eir minds so that they will know what I want them to do thout My even telling them, and these laws will be in eir hearts so that they will want to obey them, and I ll be their God and they shall be My people.

11 And no one then will need to speak to his friend or ighbor or brother, saying, 'You, too, should know the rd,' because everyone, great and small, will know Me eady.

12 And I will be merciful to them in their wrong- ings, and I will remember their sins no more."

13 God speaks of these new promises, of this new reement, as taking the place of the old one; for the old e is out of date now and has been put aside forever.

Revised Standard

not by man but by the Lord. 3For every
high priest is appointed to offer gifts and
sacrifices; hence it is necessary for this
priest also to have something to offer. 4Now
if he were on earth, he would not be a
priest at all, since there are priests who
offer gifts according to the law. 5They serve
a copy and shadow of the heavenly sanctuary; for when Moses was about to erect
the tent,[n] he was instructed by God, saying, "See that you make everything according to the pattern which was shown you on
the mountain." 6But as it is, Christ[o] has
obtained a ministry which is as much more
excellent than the old as the covenant he
mediates is better, since it is enacted on
better promises. 7For if that first covenant
had been faultless, there would have been
no occasion for a second.
8 For he finds fault with them when
he says:

"The days will come, says the Lord, when
I will establish a new covenant with the
house of Israel
and with the house of Judah;
9not like the covenant that I made with
their fathers
on the day when I took them by the hand
to lead them out of the land of Egypt;
for they did not continue in my covenant,
and so I paid no heed to them, says the
Lord.
10This is the covenant that I will make
with the house of Israel
after those days, says the Lord:
I will put my laws into their minds,
and write them on their hearts,
and I will be their God,
and they shall be my people.
11And they shall not teach every one his
fellow
or every one his brother, saying, 'Know
the Lord,'
for all shall know me,
from the least of them to the greatest.
12For I will be merciful toward their iniquities,
and I will remember their sins no more."

13In speaking of a new covenant he treats
the first as obsolete. And what is becoming
obsolete and growing old is ready to vanish
away.

CHAPTER 9

Now in that first agreement between God and His people there were rules for worship and there was a cred tent down here on earth. Inside this place of rship there were two rooms. The first one contained the lden candlestick and a table with special loaves of holy ead upon it; this part was called the Holy Place.

The temporary sacrifices by Levites

9 Now even the first covenant had regulations for worship and an earthly sanctuary. 2For a tent[p] was prepared, the outer
one, in which were the lampstand and the
table and the bread of the Presence;[q] it is
called the Holy Place. 3Behind the second

[n] Or *tabernacle*
[o] Greek *he*
[p] Or *tabernacle*
[q] Greek *the presentation of the loaves*

King James

3 And after the second veil, the tabernacle which is called the Holiest of all;

4 Which had the golden censer, and the ark of the covenant overlaid round about with gold, wherein *was* the golden pot that had manna, and Aaron's rod that budded, and the tables of the covenant;

5 And over it the cherubims of glory shadowing the mercy-seat; of which we cannot now speak particularly.

6 Now when these things were thus ordained, the priests went always into the first tabernacle, accomplishing the service *of God.*

7 But into the second *went* the high priest alone once every year, not without blood, which he offered for himself, and *for* the errors of the people:

8 The Holy Ghost this signifying, that the way into the holiest of all was not yet made manifest, while as the first tabernacle was yet standing:

9 Which *was* a figure for the time then present, in which were offered both gifts and sacrifices, that could not make him that did the service perfect, as pertaining to the conscience;

10 *Which stood* only in meats and drinks, and divers washings, and carnal ordinances, imposed *on them* until the time of reformation.

11 But Christ being come an high priest of good things to come, by a greater and more perfect tabernacle, not made with hands, that is to say, not of this building;

12 Neither by the blood of goats and calves, but by his own blood he entered in once into the holy place, having obtained eternal redemption *for us.*

13 For if the blood of bulls and of goats, and the ashes of an heifer sprinkling the unclean, sanctifieth to the purifying of the flesh:

14 How much more shall the blood of Christ, who through the eternal Spirit offered himself without spot to God, purge your conscience from dead works to serve the living God?

15 And for this cause he is the mediator of the new testament, that by means of death, for the redemption of the transgressions *that were* under the first testament, they which are called might receive the promise of eternal inheritance.

Amplified

3 But [inside], beyond the second curtain *or* veil, [there stood another] tabernacle [division] known as the Holy of Holies. [Exod. 26:31-33.]

4 It had the golden [a]altar of incense and the ark (chest) of the covenant, covered over with wrought gold. This [ark] contained a golden jar which held the manna, and the rod of Aaron that sprouted, and the [two stone] slabs of the covenant, [bearing the Ten Commandments]. [Exod. 30:1-6; 16:32-34; Num. 17:8-10.]

5 Above [the ark] and overshadowing the mercy seat were the representations of the cherubim [winged creatures which were the symbols] of glory. We cannot now go into detail about these things.

6 These arrangements having thus been made, the priests enter habitually into the outer division of the tabernacle, in performance of their ritual acts of worship.

7 But into the second [division of the tabernacle] none but the high priest goes, and he only once a year, and never without taking a sacrifice of blood with him, which he offers for himself and for the errors *and* sins of ignorance *and* thoughtlessness which the people have committed. [Lev. 16:15.]

8 By this the Holy Spirit points out that the way into the [true Holy of] Holies is not yet thrown open as long as the former [the outer portion of the] tabernacle remains a recognized institution *and* is still standing,

9 Seeing that that first [outer portion of the] tabernacle was a parable—a visible symbol or type or picture of the present age. In it gifts and sacrifices are offered, and yet are incapable of perfecting the conscience *or* of cleansing *and* renewing the inner man of the worshipper.

10 For [the ceremonies] deal only with clean and unclean meats and drinks and different washings, [mere] external rules *and* regulations for the body imposed to tide the worshippers over until the time of setting things straight—of reformation, [of the complete new order when Christ, the Messiah, shall establish the reality of what these things foreshadow, a better covenant].

11 But [that appointed time came] when Christ, the Messiah, appeared as a High Priest of the better things that have come *and* [b]are to come. [Then] through the greater and more perfect tabernacle, not made with [human] hands, that is, not a part of this material creation,

12 He went once for all into the [Holy of] Holies [of heaven], not by virtue of the blood of goats and calves [by which to make reconciliation between God and man], but His own blood, having found *and* secured a complete redemption—an everlasting release [for us].

13 For if [the mere] sprinkling of unholy *and* defiled persons with blood of goats and bulls and with the ashes of a burnt heifer is sufficient for the purification of the body, [Lev. 16:6, 16; Num. 19:9, 17, 18.]

14 How much more surely shall the blood of Christ, Who [c]by virtue of [[d]His] eternal Spirit [[d]His own preexistent [e]divine personality] has offered Himself an unblemished sacrifice to God, purify our consciences from dead works *and* lifeless observances to serve the [ever-] living God?

15 [Christ, the Messiah] is therefore the Negotiator *and* Mediator of an [entirely] new agreement (testament covenant), so that those who are called *and* offered it may receive the fulfillment of the promised everlasting inheritance, since a death has taken place which rescues *and* delivers *and* redeems them from the transgressions committed under the [old], first agreement.

---

a) Not kept permanently in the Holy of Holies, but taken in on the Day of Atonement, as the Mischna explains.—Alford. Cited by Wuest in "Hebrews."
b) Alternate reading.
c) Vincent.
d) Many authorities.
e) Alford, cited by Wuest.

Living New Testament

3 Then there was a curtain and behind the curtain was a room called the Holy of Holies.

4 In that room there was a golden incense-altar and the golden chest, called the ark of the covenant, completely covered on all sides with pure gold. Inside the ark were the tablets of stone with the Ten Commandments written on them, and a golden jar with some manna in it, and Aaron's wooden cane that budded.

5 Above the golden chest were statues of angels called the cherubim—the guardians of God's glory—with their wings stretched out over the ark's golden cover, called the mercy seat. But enough of such details.

6 Well, when all was ready the priests went in and out of the first room whenever they wanted to, doing their work.

7 But only the high priest went into the inner room, and then only once a year, all alone, and always with blood which he sprinkled on the mercy seat as an offering to God to cover his own mistakes and sins, and the mistakes and sins of all the people.

8 And the Holy Spirit uses all this to point out to us that under the old system the common people could not go into the Holy of Holies as long as the outer room and the entire system it represents were still in use.

9 This has an important lesson for us today. For under the old system, gifts and sacrifices were offered, but these failed to cleanse the hearts of the people who brought them.

10 For the old system dealt only with certain rituals—what foods to eat and drink, rules for washing themselves, and rules about this and that. The people had to keep these rules to tide them over until Christ came with God's new and better way.

11 He came as High Priest of this better system which we now have. He went into that greater, perfect tabernacle in heaven, not made by men nor part of this world,

12 And once for all took blood into that inner room, the Holy of Holies, and sprinkled it on the mercy seat; but it was not the blood of goats and calves. No, He took His own blood, and with it He, by Himself, made sure of our eternal salvation.

13 And if under the old system the blood of bulls and goats and the ashes of young cows could cleanse men's bodies from sin,

14 Just think how much more surely the blood of Christ will transform our lives and hearts. His sacrifice frees us from the worry of having to obey the old rules, and makes us want to serve the living God. For by the help of the eternal Holy Spirit, Christ willingly gave Himself to God to die for our sins—He being perfect, without a single sin or fault.

15 Christ came with this new agreement so that all who are invited may come and have forever all the wonders God has promised them. For Christ died to rescue them from the penalty of the sins they had committed while still under that old system.

Revised Standard

curtain stood a tent[p] called the Holy of
Holies, 4having the golden altar of incense
and the ark of the covenant covered on all
sides with gold, which contained a golden
urn holding the manna, and Aaron's rod
that budded, and the tables of the covenant;
5above it were the cherubim of glory overshadowing the mercy seat. Of these things
we cannot now speak in detail.
6 These preparations having thus been
made, the priests go continually into the
outer tent,[p] performing their ritual duties;
7but into the second only the high priest
goes, and he but once a year, and not without taking blood which he offers for himself
and for the errors of the people. 8By this
the Holy Spirit indicates that the way into
the sanctuary is not yet opened as long as
the outer tent[p] is still standing 9(which is
symbolic for the present age). According
to this arrangement, gifts and sacrifices are
offered which cannot perfect the conscience
of the worshiper, 10but deal only with food
and drink and various ablutions, regulations
for the body imposed until the time of
reformation.

The eternal sacrifice of Christ

11 But when Christ appeared as a high
priest of the good things that have come,[r]
then through the greater and more perfect
tent[p] (not made with hands, that is, not of
this creation) 12he entered once for all into
the Holy Place, taking[s] not the blood of
goats and calves but his own blood, thus
securing an eternal redemption. 13For if the
sprinkling of defiled persons with the blood
of goats and bulls and with the ashes of
a heifer sanctifies for the purification of the
flesh, 14how much more shall the blood of
Christ, who through the eternal Spirit offered
himself without blemish to God, purify
your[t] conscience from dead works to serve
the living God.

Fulfilment of the new covenant

15 Therefore he is the mediator of a new
covenant, so that those who are called may
receive the promised eternal inheritance,
since a death has occurred which redeems
them from the transgressions under the first

[p] Or *tabernacle*
[r] Other manuscripts read *good things to come*
[s] Greek *through*
[t] Other manuscripts read *our*

King James

16 For where a testament *is,* there must also of necessity be the death of the testator.

17 For a testament *is* of force after men are dead: otherwise it is of no strength at all while the testator liveth.

18 Whereupon neither the first *testament* was dedicated without blood.

19 For when Moses had spoken every precept to all the people according to the law, he took the blood of calves and of goats, with water, and scarlet wool, and hyssop, and sprinkled both the book, and all the people,

20 Saying, This *is* the blood of the testament which God hath enjoined unto you.

21 Moreover he sprinkled with blood both the tabernacle, and all the vessels of the ministry.

22 And almost all things are by the law purged with blood; and without shedding of blood is no remission.

23 *It was* therefore necessary that the patterns of things in the heavens should be purified with these; but the heavenly things themselves with better sacrifices than these.

24 For Christ is not entered into the holy places made with hands, *which are* the figures of the true; but into heaven itself, now to appear in the presence of God for us:

25 Nor yet that he should offer himself often, as the high priest entereth into the holy place every year with blood of others;

26 For then must he often have suffered since the foundation of the world: but now once in the end of the world hath he appeared to put away sin by the sacrifice of himself.

27 And as it is appointed unto men once to die, but after this the judgment:

28 So Christ was once offered to bear the sins of many; and unto them that look for him shall he appear the second time without sin unto salvation.

Amplified

16 For where there is a [last] will *and* testament involved, the death of the one who made it must be established,

17 For a will *and* testament is valid and takes effect only at death, since it has no force *or* legal power as long as the one who made it is alive.

18 So even the (old) first covenant [God's will] was not inaugurated *and* ratified *and* put in force without the shedding of blood.

19 For when every command of the Law had been read out by Moses to all the people, he took the blood of slain calves and goats, together with water and scarlet wool, and with a bunch of hyssop sprinkled both the Book [the roll of the Law and covenant] itself, and all the people,

20 Saying these words: This is the blood that seals *and* ratifies the agreement (the testament, the covenant) which God commanded [me to deliver to] you. [Exod. 24:6-8.]

21 And in the same way he sprinkled with the blood both the tabernacle and all the [sacred] vessels *and* appliances used in [divine] worship.

22 [In fact], under the Law almost everything is purified by means of blood, and without the shedding of blood there is neither release from sin *and* its guilt *nor* the remission of the due *and* merited punishment for sins.

23 By such means therefore it was necessary for the [earthly] copies of the heavenly things to be purified, but the actual heavenly things themselves [required far] better *and* nobler sacrifices than these.

24 For Christ, the Messiah, has not entered into a sanctuary made with [human] hands, only a copy *and* pattern *and* type of the true one, but [He has entered] into heaven itself, now to appear in the [very] presence of God on our behalf.

25 Nor did He [enter into the heavenly sanctuary to] offer Himself regularly again and again, as the high priest enters the [Holy of] Holies every year with blood not his own;

26 For then would He often have had to suffer, [over and over again] since the foundation of the world. But as it now is, He has once for all at the consummation *and* close of the ages appeared to put away *and* abolish sin by His sacrifice [of Himself].

27 And just as it is appointed for [all] men once to die and after that the [certain] judgment,

28 Even so it is that Christ having been offered to take upon Himself *and* bear as a burden the sins of many once *and* [f]once for all, will appear a second time, not carrying any burden of sin *nor* to deal with sin, but to bring to fu salvation those who are (eagerly, constantly and patient ly) waiting for *and* expecting Him.

CHAPTER 10 (King James)

FOR the law having a shadow of good things to come, *and* not the very image of the things, can never with those sacrifices which they offered year by year continually make the comers thereunto perfect.

2 For then would they not have ceased to be offered? because that the worshippers once purged should have had no more conscience of sins.

CHAPTER 10 (Amplified)

FOR since the Law has merely a rude outline (for shadowing) of the good things to come, instead fully expressing those things, it can never by offering th same sacrifices continually year after year make perfe those who approach [its altars].

2 For were it otherwise, would [these sacrifices] n have stopped being offered? Since the worshippers h [g]once for all been cleansed, they would no longer ha any guilt *or* consciousness of sin.

---

f) Abbott-Smith.
g) Abbott-Smith.

Living New Testament

16 Now, if someone dies and leaves a will—a list of things to be given away to certain people when he dies—no one gets anything until it is proved that the person who wrote the will is dead.

17 The will goes into effect only after the death of the person who wrote it. While he is still alive no one can use it to get any of those things he has promised them.

18 That is why blood was sprinkled [as proof of Christ's death[1]] before even the first agreement could go into effect.

19 For after Moses had given the people all of God's laws, he took the blood of calves and goats, along with water, and sprinkled the blood over the book of God's laws and over all the people, using branches of hyssop bushes and scarlet wool to sprinkle with.

20 Then he said, "This is the blood that marks the beginning of the agreement between you and God, the agreement God commanded me to make with you."

21 And in the same way he sprinkled blood on the sacred tent and on whatever instruments were used for worship.

22 In fact we can say that under the old agreement almost everything was cleansed by sprinkling it with blood, and without the shedding of blood there is no forgiveness of sins.

23 That is why the sacred tent down here on earth, and everything in it—all copies from things in heaven—all had to be made pure by Moses in this way, by being sprinkled with the blood of animals. But the real things in heaven, of which these down here are copies, were made pure with far more precious offerings.

24 For Christ has entered into heaven itself, to appear now before God as our Friend. It was not in the earthly place of worship He did this, for that was merely a copy of the real temple in heaven.

25 Nor has He offered Himself again and again, as the high priest down here on earth offered animal blood in the Holy of Holies each year.

26 If that had been necessary, then He would have had to die again and again, ever since the world began. But no! He came once for all, at the end of the age, to put away the power of sin forever by dying for us.

27 And just as it is destined that men die only once, and after that comes judgment,

28 So also Christ died only once as an offering for the sins of many people; and He will come again, but not to deal again with our sins. This time He will come bringing salvation to all those who are eagerly and patiently waiting for Him.

Revised Standard

covenant.[u] 16 For where a will[u] is involved,
the death of the one who made it must be
established. 17 For a will[u] takes effect only
at death, since it is not in force as long as
the one who made it is alive. 18 Hence even
the first covenant was not ratified without
blood. 19 For when every commandment of
the law had been declared by Moses to all
the people, he took the blood of calves and
goats, with water and scarlet wool and
hyssop, and sprinkled both the book itself
and all the people, 20 saying, "This is the
blood of the covenant which God commanded you." 21 And in the same way he
sprinkled with the blood both the tent[p]
and all the vessels used in worship. 22 Indeed, under the law almost everything is
purified with blood, and without the shedding of blood there is no forgiveness of
sins.

Christ the once-for-all sacrifice

23 Thus it was necessary for the copies
of the heavenly things to be purified with
these rites, but the heavenly things themselves with better sacrifices than these. 24 For
Christ has entered, not into a sanctuary
made with hands, a copy of the true one,
but into heaven itself, now to appear in
the presence of God on our behalf. 25 Nor
was it to offer himself repeatedly, as the
high priest enters the Holy Place yearly
with blood not his own; 26 for then he would
have had to suffer repeatedly since the
foundation of the world. But as it is, he has
appeared once for all at the end of the
age to put away sin by the sacrifice of himself. 27 And just as it is appointed for men
to die once, and after that comes judgment, 28 so Christ, having been offered once
to bear the sins of many, will appear a
second time, not to deal with sin but to
save those who are eagerly waiting for him.

CHAPTER 10

The old system of Jewish laws gave only a dim foretaste of the good things Christ would do for us. The sacrifices under the old system were repeated again and again, year after year, but even so they could never save those who lived under their rules.

2 If they could have, one offering would have been enough; the worshipers would have been cleansed once for all, and their feeling of guilt would be gone.

10 For since the law has but a shadow
of the good things to come instead
of the true form of these realities, it can
never, by the same sacrifices which are continually offered year after year, make perfect those who draw near. 2 Otherwise, would
they not have ceased to be offered? If the
worshipers had once been cleansed, they
would no longer have any consciousness

---

[1] Implied.

[u] The Greek word here used means both *covenant* and *will*

[p] Or *tabernacle*

King James

3 But in those *sacrifices there is* a remembrance again *made* of sins every year.

4 For *it is* not possible that the blood of bulls and of goats should take away sins.

5 Wherefore when he cometh into the world, he saith, Sacrifice and offering thou wouldest not, but a body hast thou prepared me:

6 In burnt offerings and *sacrifices* for sin thou hast had no pleasure.

7 Then said I, Lo, I come (in the volume of the book it is written of me,) to do thy will, O God.

8 Above when he said, Sacrifice and offering and burnt offerings and *offering* for sin thou wouldest not, neither hadst pleasure *therein;* which are offered by the law;

9 Then said he, Lo, I come to do thy will, O God. He taketh away the first, that he may establish the second.

10 By the which will we are sanctified through the offering of the body of Jesus Christ once *for all.*

11 And every priest standeth daily ministering and offering oftentimes the same sacrifices, which can never take away sins:

12 But this man, after he had offered one sacrifice for sins for ever, sat down on the right hand of God;

13 From henceforth expecting till his enemies be made his footstool.

14 For by one offering he hath perfected for ever them that are sanctified.

15 *Whereof* the Holy Ghost also is a witness to us: for after that he had said before,

16 This *is* the covenant that I will make with them after those days, saith the Lord, I will put my laws into their hearts, and in their minds will I write them;

17 And their sins and iniquities will I remember no more.

18 Now where remission of these *is, there is* no more offering for sin.

19 Having therefore, brethren, boldness to enter into the holiest by the blood of Jesus,

20 By a new and living way, which he hath consecrated for us, through the veil, that is to say, his flesh;

21 And *having* an high priest over the house of God;

22 Let us draw near with a true heart in full assurance of faith, having our hearts sprinkled from an evil conscience, and our bodies washed with pure water.

Amplified

3 But [as it is], these sacrifices annually bring a fresh remembrance of sins [to be atoned for],

4 Because the blood of bulls and goats is powerless to take sins away.

5 Hence, when He (Christ) entered into the world, He said, Sacrifices and offerings You have not desired, but instead You have made ready a body for Me [to offer];

6 In burnt offerings and sin offerings You have taken no delight.

7 Then I said, Lo, here I am, come to do Your will, O God; [to fulfill] what is written of Me in the volume of the Book. [Ps. 40:6-8.]

8 When He said just before, You have neither desired nor have You taken delight in sacrifices and offerings and burnt offerings and sin offerings, all of which are offered according to the Law,

9 He then went on to say, Lo, [here] I am, come to do Your will. Thus He does away with *and* annuls the first (former) order [as a means of expiating sin] so that He might inaugurate *and* establish the second (latter) order. [Ps. 40:6-8.]

10 And in accordance with this will [of God] we have been made holy (consecrated and sanctified) through the offering made once for all of the body of Jesus Christ, the Anointed One.

11 Furthermore, every [human] priest stands [at his altar of service] ministering daily, offering the same sacrifices over and over again, which never are able to strip (from every side of us) the sins [that envelop us], *and* take them away.

12 Whereas this One (Christ), after He had offered a single Sacrifice for our sins [that shall avail] for all time, sat down at the right hand of God,

13 Then to wait until His enemies should be made a stool beneath His feet. [Ps. 110:1.]

14 For by a single offering He has forever completely cleansed *and* perfected those who are consecrated *and* made holy.

15 And also the Holy Spirit adds His testimony to us [in confirmation of this]. For having said,

16 This is the agreement (testament, covenant) that I will set up *and* conclude with them after those days, says the Lord: I will imprint My laws upon their hearts, and I will inscribe them on their minds—on their inmost thoughts and understanding,

17 He then goes on to say, And their sins and their lawbreakings I will remember no more. [Jer. 31:33, 34.]

18 Now where there is absolute remission—forgiveness and cancellation of the penalty—of these [sins and lawbreakings] there is no longer any offering made to atone for sin.

19 Therefore, brethren, since we have full freedom *and* confidence to enter into the [Holy of] Holies [by the power and virtue] in the blood of Jesus,

20 By this fresh (new) and living way which He initiated *and* dedicated *and* opened for us through the separating curtain [veil of the Holy of Holies], that is, through His flesh;

21 And since we have [such] a great *and* wonderful *and* noble Priest [Who rules] over the house of God,

22 Let us all come forward *and* draw near with true (honest and sincere) hearts in unqualified assurance *and* absolute conviction engendered by faith, [that is, by [h]that leaning of the entire human personality on God in absolute trust and confidence in His power, wisdom and goodness,] having our hearts sprinkled *and* purified from a guilty (evil) conscience and with our bodies cleansed with pure water.

---

h) Souter.

Living New Testament

3 But just the opposite happened: those yearly sacrifices reminded them of their disobedience and guilt instead of relieving their minds.

4 For it is not possible for the blood of bulls and goats to really take away sins.[1]

5 That is why Christ said, as He came into the world, "O God, the blood of bulls and goats cannot satisfy You, so You have made ready this body of Mine for Me to lay as a sacrifice upon Your altar.

6 You were not satisfied with the animal sacrifices, slain and burnt before You as offerings for sin.

7 Then I said, 'See, I have come to do Your will, to lay down My life, just as the Scriptures said that I would.' "

8 After Christ said this, about not being satisfied with the various sacrifices and offerings required under the old system,

9 He then added, "Here I am. I have come to give My life." He cancels the first system in favor of a far better one.

10 Under this new plan we have been forgiven and made clean by Christ's dying for us once and for all.

11 Under the old agreement the priests stood before the altar day after day offering sacrifices that could never take away our sins.

12 But Christ gave Himself to God for our sins as one sacrifice for all time, and then sat down in the place of highest honor at God's right hand,

13 Waiting for His enemies to be laid under His feet.

14 For by that one offering He made forever perfect in the sight of God all those whom He is making holy.

15 And the Holy Spirit testifies that this is so, for He has said,

16 "This is the agreement I will make with the people of Israel, though they broke their first agreement: I will write My laws into their minds so that they will always know My will, and I will put My laws in their hearts so that they will want to obey them."

17 And then He adds, "I will never again remember their sins and lawless deeds."

18 Now, when sins have once been forever forgiven and forgotten, there is no need to offer more sacrifices to get rid of them.

19 And so, dear brothers, now we may walk right into the very Holy of Holies where God is, because of the blood of Jesus.

20 This is the fresh, new, life-giving way which Christ has opened up for us by tearing the curtain—His human body— to let us into the holy presence of God.

21 And since this great High Priest of ours rules over God's household,

22 Let us go right in, to God Himself, with true hearts fully trusting Him to receive us, because we have been sprinkled with Christ's blood to make us clean, and because we have been washed with the pure water.

[1] The blood of bulls and goats merely covered over the sins, taking them out of sight for hundreds of years until Jesus Christ came to die on the cross. There He gave His own blood which forever took those sins away.

Revised Standard

of sin. 3But in these sacrifices there is a
reminder of sin year after year. 4For it is
impossible that the blood of bulls and goats
should take away sins.
5 Consequently, when Christ[v] came into
the world, he said,
"Sacrifices and offerings thou hast not
desired,
but a body hast thou prepared for me;
6in burnt offerings and sin offerings thou
hast taken no pleasure.
7Then I said, 'Lo, I have come to do thy
will, O God,'
as it is written of me in the roll of the
book."
8When he said above, "Thou hast neither
desired nor taken pleasure in sacrifices and
offerings and burnt offerings and sin offerings" (these are offered according to the
law), 9then he added, "Lo, I have come to
do thy will." He abolishes the first in order
to establish the second. 10And by that will
we have been sanctified through the offering of the body of Jesus Christ once for all.
11 And every priest stands daily at his
service, offering repeatedly the same sacrifices, which can never take away sins. 12But
when Christ[w] had offered for all time a
single sacrifice for sins, he sat down at the
right hand of God, 13then to wait until his
enemies should be made a stool for his feet.
14For by a single offering he has perfected
for all time those who are sanctified. 15And
the Holy Spirit also bears witness to us; for
after saying,
16"This is the covenant that I will make
with them
after those days, says the Lord:
I will put my laws on their hearts,
and write them on their minds,"
17then he adds,
"I will remember their sins and their
misdeeds no more."
18Where there is forgiveness of these, there
is no longer any offering for sin.

The appeal to hold firm

19 Therefore, brethren, since we have
confidence to enter the sanctuary by the
blood of Jesus, 20by the new and living
way which he opened for us through the
curtain, that is, through his flesh, 21and
since we have a great priest over the house
of God, 22let us draw near with a true heart
in full assurance of faith, with our hearts
sprinkled clean from an evil conscience
and our bodies washed with pure water.

v Greek *he*
w Greek *this one*

King James

23 Let us hold fast the profession of *our* faith without wavering; (for he *is* faithful that promised;)

24 And let us consider one another to provoke unto love and to good works:

25 Not forsaking the assembling of ourselves together, as the manner of some *is;* but exhorting *one another:* and so much the more, as ye see the day approaching.

26 For if we sin wilfully after that we have received the knowledge of the truth, there remaineth no more sacrifice for sins,

27 But a certain fearful looking for of judgment and fiery indignation, which shall devour the adversaries.

28 He that despised Moses' law died without mercy under two or three witnesses:

29 Of how much sorer punishment, suppose ye, shall he be thought worthy, who hath trodden under foot the Son of God, and hath counted the blood of the covenant, wherewith he was sanctified, an unholy thing, and hath done despite unto the Spirit of grace?

30 For we know him that hath said, Vengeance *belongeth* unto me, I will recompense, saith the Lord. And again, The Lord shall judge his people.

31 *It is* a fearful thing to fall into the hands of the living God.

32 But call to remembrance the former days, in which, after ye were illuminated, ye endured a great fight of afflictions;

33 Partly, whilst ye were made a gazingstock both by reproaches and afflictions; and partly, whilst ye became companions of them that were so used.

34 For ye had compassion of me in my bonds, and took joyfully the spoiling of your goods, knowing in yourselves that ye have in heaven a better and an enduring substance.

35 Cast not away therefore your confidence, which hath great recompence of reward.

36 For ye have need of patience, that, after ye have done the will of God, ye might receive the promise.

37 For yet a little while, and he that shall come will come, and will not tarry.

38 Now the just shall live by faith: but if *any man* draw back, my soul shall have no pleasure in him.

Amplified

23 So let us seize *and* hold fast *and* retain without wavering the [i]hope we cherish *and* confess, *and* our acknowledgment of it, for He Who promised is reliable (sure) *and* faithful to His word.

24 And let us consider *and* give [j]attentive, continuous care to watching over one another, studying how we may stir up (stimulate and incite) to love *and* helpful deeds *and* noble activities;

25 Not forsaking *or* neglecting to assemble together [as believers], as is the habit of some people, but admonishing —warning, urging and encouraging—one another, and all the more faithfully as you see the day approaching.

26 For if we go on deliberately *and* willingly sinning after once acquiring the knowledge of the Truth, there is no longer any sacrifice left to atone for [our] sins—no further offering to which to look forward.

27 [There is nothing left for us then] but a kind of awful *and* fearful prospect *and* expectation of divine judgment and the fury of burning wrath *and* indignation which will consume those who put themselves in opposition [to God]. [Isa. 26:11.]

28 Any person who has violated *and* [thus] rejected *and* set at naught the Law of Moses is put to death without pity *or* mercy on the evidence of two or three witnesses. [Deut. 17:2-6.]

29 How much worse (sterner and heavier) punishment do you suppose he will be judged to deserve who has spurned *and* [thus] trampled under foot the Son of God, and who has considered the covenant blood by which he was consecrated common *and* unhallowed, thus profaning it *and* insulting *and* outraging the (Holy) Spirit [Who imparts] grace—the unmerited favor and blessing of God? [Exod. 24:8.]

30 For we know Him Who said, Vengeance is Mine—retribution and the meting out of full justice rest with Me; I will repay—I will exact the compensation, *says the Lord.* And again, The Lord will judge *and* determine *and* solve *and* settle the cause *and* the cases of His people. [Deut. 32:35, 36.]

31 It is a fearful (formidable and terrible) thing to incur the divine penalties *and* be cast into the hands of the living God!

32 But be ever mindful of the days gone by in which, after you were first spiritually enlightened, you endured a great *and* painful struggle,

33 Sometimes being yourselves a gazingstock, publicly exposed to insults *and* abuse and distress, and sometimes claiming fellowship *and* making common cause with others who were so treated.

34 For you did sympathize *and* suffer along with those who were imprisoned, and you bore cheerfully the plundering of your belongings *and* the confiscation of your property, in the knowledge *and* consciousness that you yourselves had a better and lasting possession.

35 Do not, therefore, fling away your fearless confidence, for it carries a great *and* glorious compensation of reward.

36 For you have need of steadfast patience *and* endurance, so that you may perform *and* fully accomplish the will of God, and thus receive *and* [k]carry away [and enjoy to the full] what is promised.

37 For still a little while—a very little while—and the Coming One will come and He will not delay.

38 But the just shall live by faith [that is, My righteou servant shall live [l]by his conviction respecting man's relationship to God and divine things, and holy fervor born o faith and conjoined with it]; and if he draws back *an*

---

i) Tyndale, Coverdale, and many early Bibles.
j) Vincent.
k) Vincent.
l) Thayer's "Greek-English Lexicon of the New Testament."

Living New Testament

23 Now we can look forward to the salvation God has promised us. There is no longer any room for doubt, and we can tell others that salvation is ours, for there is no question that He will do what He says.

24 In response to all He has done for us, let us outdo each other in being helpful and kind to each other and in doing good.

25 Let us not neglect our church duties and meetings, as some people do, but encourage and warn each other, especially now that the day of His coming back again is drawing near.

26 If anyone sins deliberately by rejecting the Savior after knowing the truth of forgiveness, this sin is not covered by Christ's death; there is no way to get rid of it.

27 There will be nothing to look forward to but the terrible punishment of God's awful anger which will consume all His enemies.

28 A man who refused to obey the laws given by Moses was killed without mercy if there were two or three witnesses to his sin.

29 Think how much more terrible the punishment will be for those who have trampled underfoot the Son of God and treated His cleansing blood as though it were common and unhallowed, and insulted and outraged the Holy Spirit who brings God's mercy to His people.

30 For we know Him who said, "Justice belongs to Me; I will repay them"; who also said "The Lord Himself will handle these cases."

31 It is a fearful thing to fall into the hands of the living God.

* * * * *

32 Don't ever forget those wonderful days when you first learned about Christ. Remember how you kept right on with the Lord even though it meant terrible suffering.

33 Sometimes you were laughed at and beaten, and sometimes you watched and sympathized with others suffering the same things.

34 You suffered with those thrown into jail, and you were actually joyful when all you owned was taken from you, knowing that better things were awaiting you in heaven, things that would be yours forever.

35 Do not let this happy trust in the Lord die away, no matter what happens. Remember your reward!

36 You need to keep on patiently doing God's will if you want Him to do for you all that He has promised.

37 His coming will not be much longer delayed.

38 And those whose faith has made them good in God's sight must live by faith, trusting Him in everything. Otherwise, if they shrink back, God will have no pleasure in them.

Revised Standard

[23]Let us hold fast the confession of our
hope without wavering, for he who promised is faithful; [24]and let us consider how
to stir up one another to love and good
works, [25]not neglecting to meet together,
as is the habit of some, but encouraging
one another, and all the more as you see
the Day drawing near.

26 For if we sin deliberately after receiving the knowledge of the truth, there
no longer remains a sacrifice for sins, [27]but
a fearful prospect of judgment, and a fury
of fire which will consume the adversaries.
[28]A man who has violated the law of Moses
dies without mercy at the testimony of two
or three witnesses. [29]How much worse punishment do you think will be deserved by
the man who has spurned the Son of God,
and profaned the blood of the covenant by
which he was sanctified, and outraged the
Spirit of grace? [30]For we know him who
said, "Vengeance is mine, I will repay."
And again, "The Lord will judge his people." [31]It is a fearful thing to fall into
the hands of the living God.

32 But recall the former days when, after
you were enlightened, you endured a hard
struggle with sufferings, [33]sometimes being
publicly exposed to abuse and affliction, and
sometimes being partners with those so
treated. [34]For you had compassion on the
prisoners, and you joyfully accepted the
plundering of your property, since you knew
that you yourselves had a better possession
and an abiding one. [35]Therefore do not
throw away your confidence, which has a
great reward. [36]For you have need of endurance, so that you may do the will of God and
receive what is promised.

[37]"For yet a little while,
and the coming one shall come and shall
not tarry;
[38]but my righteous one shall live by faith,
and if he shrinks back,
my soul has no pleasure in him."

King James

39 But we are not of them who draw back unto perdition; but of them that believe to the saving of the soul.

CHAPTER 11

NOW faith is the substance of things hoped for, the evidence of things not seen.
2 For by it the elders obtained a good report.
3 Through faith we understand that the worlds were framed by the word of God, so that things which are seen were not made of things which do appear.
4 By faith Abel offered unto God a more excellent sacrifice than Cain, by which he obtained witness that he was righteous, God testifying of his gifts: and by it he being dead yet speaketh.
5 By faith Enoch was translated that he should not see death; and was not found, because God had translated him: for before his translation he had this testimony, that he pleased God.
6 But without faith *it is* impossible to please *him;* for he that cometh to God must believe that he is, and *that* he is a rewarder of them that diligently seek him.
7 By faith Noah, being warned of God of things not seen as yet, moved with fear, prepared an ark to the saving of his house; by the which he condemned the world, and became heir of the righteousness which is by faith.
8 By faith Abraham, when he was called to go out into a place which he should after receive for an inheritance, obeyed; and he went out, not knowing whither he went.
9 By faith he sojourned in the land of promise, as *in* a strange country, dwelling in tabernacles with Isaac and Jacob, the heirs with him of the same promise:
10 For he looked for a city which hath foundations, whose builder and maker *is* God.

Amplified

shrinks in fear, My soul has no delight *or* pleasure in him. [Hab. 2:3, 4.]
39 But our way is not that of those who draw back to eternal misery (perdition) and are utterly destroyed, but we are of those who believe—who cleave to and trust in and rely on God through Jesus Christ, the Messiah—*and* by faith preserve the soul.

CHAPTER 11

NOW faith is the assurance (the confirmation, [m]the title-deed) of the things [we] hope for, being the proof of things [we] do not see *and* the conviction of their reality—faith perceiving as real fact what is not revealed to the senses.
2 For by [faith], *and* [n]trust *and* holy fervor born of faith, the men of old had divine testimony borne to them *and* obtained a good report.
3 By faith we understand that the worlds [during the successive ages] were framed—fashioned, put in order and equipped for their intended purpose—by the word of God, so that what we see was not made out of things which are visible.
4 [Prompted, actuated] by faith Abel brought God a better and more acceptable sacrifice than Cain, because of which it was testified of him that he was righteous—[that is,] that he was upright and in right standing with God—and God bore witness by accepting *and* acknowledging his gifts. And though he died, yet through [the incident] he is still speaking. [Gen. 4:3-10.]
5 Because of faith Enoch was caught up *and* transferred to heaven, so that he did not have a glimpse of death; and he was not found, because God had translated him. For even before he was taken to heaven he received testimony [still on record] that he had pleased *and* been satisfactory to God. [Gen. 5:21-24.]
6 But without faith it is impossible to please *and* be satisfactory to Him. For whoever would come near to God must (necessarily) believe that God exists and that He is the Rewarder of those who earnestly *and* diligently seek Him (out).
7 [Prompted] by faith Noah, being forewarned of God concerning events of which as yet there was no visible sign, took heed *and* diligently *and* reverently constructed *and* prepared an ark for the deliverance of his own family. By this [his faith which relied on God] he passed judgment *and* sentence on the world's unbelief and became an heir *and* possessor of righteousness, [[o]that relation of being right into which God puts the person who has faith]. [Gen. 6:13-22.]
8 [Urged on] by faith Abraham when he was called, obeyed and went forth to a place which he was destined to receive as an inheritance; and he went, although he did not know *or* trouble his mind about where he was to go.
9 [Prompted] by faith he dwelt as a temporary resident in the land which was designated in the promise [of God, though he was as a stranger] in a strange country, living in tents with Isaac and Jacob, fellow heirs with him of the same promise. [Gen. 12:1-8.]
10 For he was waiting expectantly *and* confidently looking forward to the city which has fixed *and* firm foundations, whose Architect *and* Builder is God.

m) Moulton and Milligan.
n) Thayer.
o) Thayer.

Living New Testament

39 But we have never turned our backs on God and sealed our fate. No, our faith in Him assures our souls' salvation.

CHAPTER 11

What is faith? It is the confident assurance that something we want is going to happen. It is the certainty that what we hope for is waiting for us, even though we cannot see it up ahead.

2 Men of God in days of old were famous for their faith.

3 By faith—by believing God—we know that the world and the stars—in fact, all things—were made at God's command; and that they were made from nothing![1]

4 It was by faith that Abel obeyed God and brought an offering that pleased God more than Cain's offering did. God accepted Abel and proved it by accepting his gift; and though Abel is long dead, we can still learn lessons from him about trusting God.

5 Enoch trusted God too, and that is why God took him away to heaven without dying; suddenly he was gone because God took him. Before this happened God had said[1] how pleased He was with Enoch.

6 You can never please God without faith, without depending on Him. Anyone who wants to come to God must believe that there is a God and that He rewards those who sincerely look for Him.

7 Noah was another who trusted God. When he heard God's warning about the future, Noah believed Him even though there was then no sign of a flood, and wasting no time, he built the ark and saved his family. Noah's belief in God was in direct contrast to the sin and disbelief of the rest of the world—which refused to obey—and because of his faith he became one of those whom God has accepted.

8 Abraham trusted God, and when God told him to leave home and go far away to another land which He promised to give him, Abraham obeyed. Away he went, not even knowing where he was going.

9 And even when he reached God's promised land, he lived in tents like a mere visitor, as did Isaac and Jacob, to whom God gave the same promise.

10 Abraham did this because he was confidently waiting for God to bring him to that strong heavenly city whose designer and builder is God.

[1] Implied.

Revised Standard

[39]But we are not of those who shrink back
and are destroyed, but of those who have
faith and keep their souls.

Faith defined

11 Now faith is the assurance of things
hoped for, the conviction of things
not seen. [2]For by it the men of old received divine approval. [3]By faith we understand that the world was created by the
word of God, so that what is seen was
made out of things which do not appear.

Faith of the early patriarchs

4 By faith Abel offered to God a more
acceptable sacrifice than Cain, through which
he received approval as righteous, God bearing witness by accepting his gifts; he died,
but through his faith he is still speaking.
[5]By faith Enoch was taken up so that he
should not see death; and he was not found,
because God had taken him. Now before
he was taken he was attested as having
pleased God. [6]And without faith it is impossible to please him. For whoever would
draw near to God must believe that he exists and that he rewards those who seek
him. [7]By faith Noah, being warned by God
concerning events as yet unseen, took heed
and constructed an ark for the saving of
his household; by this he condemned the
world and became an heir of the righteousness which comes by faith.

Faith of Abraham and his children

8 By faith Abraham obeyed when he
was called to go out to a place which he
was to receive as an inheritance; and he
went out, not knowing where he was to go.
[9]By faith he sojourned in the land of promise, as in a foreign land, living in tents with
Isaac and Jacob, heirs with him of the same
promise. [10]For he looked forward to the
city which has foundations, whose builder

King James

11 Through faith also Sara herself received strength to conceive seed, and was delivered of a child when she was past age, because she judged him faithful who had promised.

12 Therefore sprang there even of one, and him as good as dead, *so many* as the stars of the sky in multitude, and as the sand which is by the sea shore innumerable.

13 These all died in faith, not having received the promises, but having seen them afar off, and were persuaded of *them*, and embraced *them*, and confessed that they were strangers and pilgrims on the earth.

14 For they that say such things declare plainly that they seek a country.

15 And truly, if they had been mindful of that *country* from whence they came out, they might have had opportunity to have returned.

16 But now they desire a better *country*, that is, an heavenly: wherefore God is not ashamed to be called their God: for he hath prepared for them a city.

17 By faith Abraham, when he was tried, offered up Isaac; and he that had received the promises offered up his only begotten *son*,

18 Of whom it was said, That in Isaac shall thy seed be called:

19 Accounting that God *was* able to raise *him* up, even from the dead; from whence also he received him in a figure.

20 By faith Isaac blessed Jacob and Esau concerning things to come.

21 By faith Jacob, when he was a-dying, blessed both the sons of Joseph; and worshipped, *leaning* upon the top of his staff.

22 By faith Joseph, when he died, made mention of the departing of the children of Israel; and gave commandment concerning his bones.

23 By faith Moses, when he was born, was hid three months of his parents, because they saw *he was* a proper child; and they were not afraid of the king's commandment.

24 By faith Moses, when he was come to years, refused to be called the son of Pharaoh's daughter;

25 Choosing rather to suffer affliction with the people of God, than to enjoy the pleasures of sin for a season;

26 Esteeming the reproach of Christ greater riches than the treasures in Egypt: for he had respect unto the recompence of the reward.

Amplified

11 Because of faith also Sarah herself received physical power to conceive a child, even when she was long past the age for it, because she considered [God] Who had given her the promise, reliable *and* trustworthy *and* true to His word. [Gen. 17:19; 18:11-14; 21:2.]

12 So from one man, though he was physically as good as dead, there have sprung descendants whose number is as the stars of heaven, and as countless as the innumerable sands on the seashore. [Gen. 15:5, 6; 22:17; 32:12.]

13 These people all died controlled *and* sustained by their faith, but not having received the tangible fulfillment of [God's] promises, only having seen it *and* greeted it from a great distance by faith, and all the while acknowledging *and* confessing that they were strangers *and* temporary residents *and* exiles upon the earth. [Ps. 39:12; Gen. 23:4.]

14 Now those people who talk as they did show plainly that they are in search of a fatherland—their own country.

15 If they had been thinking with [homesick] remembrance of that country from which they were emigrants, they would have found constant opportunity to return to it;

16 But the truth is that they were yearning for *and* aspiring to a better *and* more desirable country, that is, a heavenly [one]. For that reason God is not ashamed to be called their God—even to be surnamed their God [the God of Abraham, Isaac and Jacob]; for He has prepared a city for them. [Exod. 3:6, 15; 4:5.]

17 By faith Abraham, when he was put to the test—that is, while the testing of his faith was [p]still in progress—[p]had already brought Isaac for an offering; he who had [q]gladly received *and* welcomed [God's] promises was ready to sacrifice his only son, [Gen. 22:1-10.]

18 Of whom it was said, Through Isaac shall your descendants be reckoned. [Gen. 21:12.]

19 For he reasoned that God was able to raise [him] up even from among the dead. Indeed in the sense that Isaac was figuratively dead (potentially sacrificed), he did [actually] receive him back from the dead.

20 [With eyes of] faith Isaac, looking far into the future, invoked blessings upon Jacob and Esau. [Gen. 27:27-29, 39, 40.]

21 [Prompted] by faith Jacob, when he was dying, blessed each of Joseph's sons, and bowed in prayer over the top of his staff. [Gen. 48.]

22 [Actuated] by faith Joseph, when nearing the end of his life, referred to [the promise of God for] the departure of the Israelites out of Egypt, and gave instructions concerning the burial of his own bones. [Gen. 50:24, 25; Exod. 13:19.]

23 [Prompted] by faith Moses after his birth was kept concealed for three months by his parents, because they saw how comely the child was, and they were not overawed *and* terrified by the king's decree. [Exod. 2:2; 1:22.]

24 [Aroused] by faith Moses, when he had grown to maturity *and* [r]become great, refused to be called the son of Pharaoh's daughter, [Exod. 2:10, 15.]

25 Because he preferred rather to share the oppression (suffer the hardships) *and* bear the shame of the people of God than to have the fleeting enjoyment of a sinful life.

26 He considered the contempt *and* abuse *and* shame [borne for] the Christ, the Messiah [Who was to come], to be greater wealth than all the treasures of Egypt, for he looked forward *and* away to the reward (recompense).

---

p) Vincent.
q) American Standard Version.
r) Literal translation.

Living New Testament

11 Sarah, too, had faith, and because of this she was able to become a mother in spite of her old age, for she realized that God, who gave her His promise, would certainly do what He said.

12 And so a whole nation came from Abraham, who was too old to have even one child—a nation with so many millions of people that, like the stars of the sky and the sand on the ocean shores, there is no way to count them.

13 These men of faith I have mentioned died without ever receiving all that God had promised them; but they saw it all awaiting them on ahead and were glad, for they agreed that this earth was not their real home but that they were just strangers visiting down here.

14 And quite obviously when they talked like that, they were looking forward to their real home in heaven.

15 If they had wanted to, they could have gone back to the good things of this world.

16 But they didn't want to. They were living for heaven. And now God is not ashamed to be called their God, for He has made a heavenly city for them.

17 While God was testing him, Abraham still trusted in God and His promises, and so he offered up his son Isaac, and was ready to slay him on the altar of sacrifice;

18 Yes, to slay even Isaac, through whom God had promised to give Abraham a whole nation of descendants!

19 He believed that if Isaac died God would bring him back to life again; and that is just about what happened, for as far as Abraham was concerned, Isaac was doomed to death, but he came back again alive!

20 It was by faith that Isaac knew God would give future blessings to his two sons, Jacob and Esau.

21 By faith Jacob, when he was old and dying, blessed each of Joseph's two sons as he stood and prayed, leaning on the top of his cane.

22 And it was by faith that Joseph, as he neared the end of his life, confidently spoke of God bringing the people of Israel out of Egypt; and he was so sure of it that he made them promise to carry his bones with them when they left!

23 Moses' parents had faith too. When they saw that God had given them an unusual child, they trusted that God would save him from the death the king commanded, and they hid him for three months, and were not afraid.

24, 25 It was by faith that Moses, when he grew up, refused to be treated as the grandson of the king, but chose to share ill-treatment with God's people instead of enjoying the fleeting pleasures of sin.

26 He thought that it was better to suffer for the promised Christ than to own all the treasures of Egypt, for he was looking forward to the great reward that God would give him.

Revised Standard

and maker is God. 11By faith Sarah herself
received power to conceive, even when she
was past the age, since she considered him
faithful who had promised. 12Therefore
from one man, and him as good as dead,
were born descendants as many as the stars
of heaven and as the innumerable grains
of sand by the seashore.

13 These all died in faith, not having
received what was promised, but having
seen it and greeted it from afar, and having acknowledged that they were strangers
and exiles on the earth. 14For people who
speak thus make it clear that they are seeking a homeland. 15If they had been thinking of that land from which they had gone
out, they would have had opportunity to
return. 16But as it is, they desire a better
country, that is, a heavenly one. Therefore
God is not ashamed to be called their God,
for he has prepared for them a city.

17 By faith Abraham, when he was tested, offered up Isaac, and he who had received the promises was ready to offer up
his only son, 18of whom it was said, "Through
Isaac shall your descendants be named."
19He considered that God was able to raise
men even from the dead; hence, figuratively
speaking, he did receive him back. 20By
faith Isaac invoked future blessings on
Jacob and Esau. 21By faith Jacob, when dying, blessed each of the sons of Joseph,
bowing in worship over the head of his
staff. 22By faith Joseph, at the end of his
life, made mention of the exodus of the
Israelites and gave directions concerning his
burial.[x]

Faith of Moses the deliverer

23 By faith Moses, when he was born,
was hid for three months by his parents,
because they saw that the child was beautiful; and they were not afraid of the king's
edict. 24By faith Moses, when he was grown
up, refused to be called the son of Pharaoh's
daughter, 25choosing rather to share ill-treatment with the people of God than to
enjoy the fleeting pleasures of sin. 26He
considered abuse suffered for the Christ
greater wealth than the treasures of Egypt,

---

x Greek ***bones***

King James

27 By faith he forsook Egypt, not fearing the wrath of the king: for he endured, as seeing him who is invisible.

28 Through faith he kept the passover, and the sprinkling of blood, lest he that destroyed the firstborn should touch them.

29 By faith they passed through the Red sea as by dry *land:* which the Egyptians assaying to do were drowned.

30 By faith the walls of Jericho fell down, after they were compassed about seven days.

31 By faith the harlot Rahab perished not with them that believed not, when she had received the spies with peace.

32 And what shall I more say? for the time would fail me to tell of Gedeon, and *of* Barak, and *of* Samson, and *of* Jephthæ; *of* David also, and Samuel, and *of* the prophets:

33 Who through faith subdued kingdoms, wrought righteousness, obtained promises, stopped the mouths of lions,

34 Quenched the violence of fire, escaped the edge of the sword, out of weakness were made strong, waxed valiant in fight, turned to flight the armies of the aliens.

35 Women received their dead raised to life again: and others were tortured, not accepting deliverance; that they might obtain a better resurrection:

36 And others had trial of *cruel* mockings and scourgings, yea, moreover of bonds and imprisonment:

37 They were stoned, they were sawn asunder, were tempted, were slain with the sword: they wandered about in sheepskins and goatskins; being destitute, afflicted, tormented;

38 (Of whom the world was not worthy:) they wandered in deserts, and *in* mountains, and *in* dens and caves of the earth.

39 And these all, having obtained a good report through faith, received not the promise:

40 God having provided some better thing for us, that they without us should not be made perfect.

Amplified

27 [Motivated] by faith he left Egypt behind him, being unawed *and* undismayed by the wrath of the king; for he never flinched *but* held staunchly to his purpose *and* endured steadfastly as one who gazed on Him Who is invisible. [Exod. 2:15.]

28 By faith (simple trust and confidence in God) he instituted *and* carried out the Passover and the sprinkling of the blood [on the doorposts], so that [the angel], the destroyer of the firstborn, might not touch those [of the children of Israel]. [Exod. 12:21-30.]

29 [Urged on] by faith the people crossed the Red Sea as though on dry land, but when the Egyptians tried to do the same thing they were swallowed up [by the sea]. [Exod. 14:21-31.]

30 Because of faith the walls of Jericho fell down after they had been encompassed for seven days [by the Israelites]. [Josh. 6:12-21.]

31 [Prompted] by faith Rahab the prostitute was not destroyed along with those who refused to believe *and* obey, because she had received the spies in peace (without enmity). [Josh. 2:1-21; 6:22-25.]

32 And what shall I say further? For time would fail me to tell of Gideon, Barak, Samson, Jephthah, of David and Samuel and the prophets, [Judg. 6:1-8, 35; 4:1-5, 31; 13:1-16, 31; 11:1-12, 15; I Sam. 1-30; II Sam. 1-24; I Kings 1-2; Acts 3:24.]

33 Who by [the help of] faith subdued kingdoms, administered justice, obtained promised blessings, closed the mouths of lions, [Dan. 6.]

34 Extinguished the power of raging fire, escaped the devourings of the sword, out of frailty *and* weakness won strength *and* became stalwart, even mighty *and* resistless in battle, routing alien hosts. [Dan. 3.]

35 [Some] women received again their dead by a resurrection. Others were tortured [s]to death with clubs, refusing to accept release [offered on the terms of denying their faith], that they might be resurrected to a better life. [I Kings 17:17-24; II Kings 4:25-37.]

36 Others had to suffer the trial of mocking and scourging, and even chains and imprisonment.

37 They were stoned to death; they were lured with tempting offers [to renounce their faith]; they were sawn asunder; they were slaughtered by the sword; [while they were alive] they had to go about wrapped in the skins of sheep and goats, utterly destitute, oppressed, cruelly treated,

38 [Men] of whom the world was not worthy, roaming over the desolate places and the mountains, and [living] in caves *and* caverns and holes of the earth.

39 And all of these, though they won divine approval by [means of] their faith, did not receive the fulfillment of what was promised,

40 Because God had us in mind *and* had something better *and* greater in view for us, so that they [these heroes and heroines of faith] should not come to perfection apart from us, [that is, before we could join them].

CHAPTER 12

WHEREFORE seeing we also are compassed about with so great a cloud of witnesses, let us lay aside every weight, and the sin which doth so easily beset *us*, and let us run with patience the race that is set before us,

CHAPTER 12

THEREFORE then, since we are surrounded by so great a cloud of witnesses [who have borne testimony of the Truth], let us strip off *and* throw aside every encumbrance—unnecessary weight—and that sin which so readily (deftly and cleverly) clings to *and* entangles us, and let us run with patient endurance *and* steady *and* active persistence the appointed course of the race that is set before us,

s) Vincent.

Living New Testament

27 And it was because he trusted God that he left the land of Egypt and wasn't afraid of the king's anger. Moses kept right on going; it seemed as though he could see God right there with him.

28 And it was because he believed God would save His people that he commanded them to kill a lamb as God had told them to and sprinkle the blood on the doorposts of their homes, so that God's terrible Angel of Death could not touch the oldest child in those homes, as he did among the Egyptians.

29 The people of Israel trusted God and went right through the Red Sea as though they were on dry ground. But when the Egyptians chasing them tried it, they all were drowned.

30 It was faith that brought the walls of Jericho tumbling down after the people of Israel had walked around them seven days, as God had commanded them.

31 By faith—because she believed in God and His power—Rahab the harlot did not die with all the others in her city when they refused to obey God, for she gave a friendly welcome to the spies.

32 Well, how much more do I need to say? It would take too long to recount the stories of the faith of Gideon and Barak and Samson and Jephthah and David and Samuel and all the prophets.

33 These people all trusted God and as a result won battles, overthrew kingdoms, ruled their people well, and received what God had promised them; they were kept from harm in a den of lions,

34 And in a fiery furnace. Some, through their faith, escaped death by the sword. Some were made strong again after they had been weak or sick. Others were given great power in battle; they made whole armies turn and run away.

35 And some women, through faith, received their loved ones back again from death.

But others trusted God and were beaten to death, preferring to die rather than turn from God and be free—trusting that they would rise again to a better life afterwards.

36 Some were laughed at and their backs cut open with whips, and others were chained in dungeons.

37, 38 Some died by stoning and some by being sawed in two; others were promised freedom if they would renounce their faith, then were killed with the sword. Some went about in skins of sheep and goats, wandering over deserts and mountains, hiding in dens and caves. They were hungry and sick and ill-treated—too good for this world.

39 And these men of faith, though they trusted God and won His approval, none of them received all that God had promised them;

40 For God wanted them to wait and share the even better rewards that were prepared for us.

Revised Standard

for he looked to the reward. 27 By faith he
left Egypt, not being afraid of the anger
of the king; for he endured as seeing him
who is invisible. 28 By faith he kept the
Passover and sprinkled the blood, so that
the Destroyer of the first-born might not
touch them.

Faith of the Israelites and Rahab

29 By faith the people crossed the Red
Sea as if on dry land; but the Egyptians,
when they attempted to do the same, were
drowned. 30 By faith the walls of Jericho
fell down after they had been encircled for
seven days. 31 By faith Rahab the harlot did
not perish with those who were disobedient,
because she had given friendly welcome to
the spies.

Faith of the judges and prophets

32 And what more shall I say? For time
would fail me to tell of Gideon, Barak,
Samson, Jephthah, of David and Samuel
and the prophets—33 who through faith conquered kingdoms, enforced justice, received
promises, stopped the mouths of lions,
34 quenched raging fire, escaped the edge of
the sword, won strength out of weakness,
became mighty in war, put foreign armies
to flight. 35 Women received their dead by
resurrection. Some were tortured, refusing
to accept release, that they might rise again
to a better life. 36 Others suffered mocking
and scourging, and even chains and imprisonment. 37 They were stoned, they were
sawn in two,[y] they were killed with the
sword; they went about in skins of sheep
and goats, destitute, afflicted, ill-treated—38 of
whom the world was not worthy—wander-
ing over deserts and mountains, and in dens
and caves of the earth.
39 And all these, though well attested
by their faith, did not receive what was
promised, 40 since God had foreseen something better for us, that apart from us they
should not be made perfect.

CHAPTER 12

Since we have such a huge crowd of men of faith watching us from the grandstands, let us strip off anything that slows us down or holds us back, and especially those sins that wrap themselves so tightly around our feet and trip us up; and let us run with patience the particular race that God has set before us.

Christ our example

12 Therefore, since we are surrounded
by so great a cloud of witnesses, let us
also lay aside every weight, and sin which
clings so closely, and let us run with perseverance the race that is set before us, 2 look-

y Other manuscripts add *they were tempted*

King James

2 Looking unto Jesus the author and finisher of *our* faith; who for the joy that was set before him endured the cross, despising the shame, and is set down at the right hand of the throne of God.

3 For consider him that endured such contradiction of sinners against himself, lest ye be wearied and faint in your minds.

4 Ye have not yet resisted unto blood, striving against sin.

5 And ye have forgotten the exhortation which speaketh unto you as unto children, My son, despise not thou the chastening of the Lord, nor faint when thou art rebuked of him:

6 For whom the Lord loveth he chasteneth, and scourgeth every son whom he receiveth.

7 If ye endure chastening, God dealeth with you as with sons; for what son is he whom the father chasteneth not?

8 But if ye be without chastisement, whereof all are partakers, then are ye bastards, and not sons.

9 Furthermore we have had fathers of our flesh which corrected *us*, and we gave *them* reverence: shall we not much rather be in subjection unto the Father of spirits, and live?

10 For they verily for a few days chastened *us* after their own pleasure; but he for *our* profit, that *we* might be partakers of his holiness.

11 Now no chastening for the present seemeth to be joyous, but grievous: nevertheless afterward it yieldeth the peaceable fruit of righteousness unto them which are exercised thereby.

12 Wherefore lift up the hands which hang down, and the feeble knees;

13 And make straight paths for your feet, lest that which is lame be turned out of the way; but let it rather be healed.

14 Follow peace with all *men*, and holiness, without which no man shall see the Lord:

15 Looking diligently lest any man fail of the grace of God; lest any root of bitterness springing up trouble *you*, and thereby many be defiled;

16 Lest there *be* any fornicator, or profane person, as Esau, who for one morsel of meat sold his birthright.

Amplified

2 Looking away [from all that will distract] to Jesus, Who is the Leader *and* the Source of *our* faith [giving the first incentive for our belief] and is also its Finisher, [bringing it to maturity and perfection]. He, for the joy [of obtaining the prize] that was set before Him, endured the cross, despising *and* ignoring the shame, and is now seated at the right hand of the throne of God. [Ps. 110:1.]

3 Just think of Him Who endured from sinners such grievous opposition *and* bitter hostility against Himself—reckon up and consider it all in comparison with your trials—so that you may not grow weary *or* exhausted, losing heart *and* relaxing *and* fainting in your minds.

4 You have not yet struggled *and* fought agonizingly against sin, *nor* have you yet resisted *and* withstood to the point of pouring out your [own] blood.

5 And have you [completely] forgotten the divine word of appeal *and* encouragement in which you are reasoned with *and* addressed as sons? My son, do not think lightly *or* scorn to submit to the correction *and* discipline of the Lord, nor lose courage *and* give up *and* faint when you are reproved *or* corrected by Him;

6 For the Lord corrects *and* disciplines every one whom He loves, and He punishes, even scourges, every son whom He accepts *and* welcomes to His heart *and* cherishes.

7 You must submit to *and* endure [correction] for discipline. God is dealing with you as with sons; for what son is there whom his father does not [thus] train *and* correct *and* discipline?

8 Now if you are exempt from correction *and* left without discipline in which all [of God's children] share, then you are illegitimate offspring *and* not true sons [at all]. [Prov. 3:11, 12.]

9 Moreover, we have had earthly fathers who disciplined us and we yielded [to them] *and* respected [them for training us]. Shall we not much more cheerfully submit to the Father of spirits and so [truly] live?

10 For [our earthly fathers] disciplined us for only a short period of time *and* chastised us as seemed proper *and* good to them, but He disciplines us for our certain good, that we may become sharers in His own holiness.

11 For the time being no discipline brings joy but seems grievous *and* painful, but afterwards it yields peaceable fruit of righteousness to those who have been trained by it—a harvest of fruit which consists in righteousness, [that is, in conformity to God's will in purpose, thought and action, resulting in right living and right standing with God].

12 So then, brace up *and* reinvigorate *and* set right your slackened *and* weakened *and* drooping hands, and strengthen your feeble *and* palsied *and* tottering knees, [Isa. 35:3.]

13 And cut through *and* make firm *and* plain *and* smooth, straight paths for your feet—[yes, make them] safe and upright and happy paths that go in the right direction—so that the lame *and* halting [limbs] may not be put out of joint, but rather may be cured.

14 Strive to live in peace with everybody, and pursue that consecration *and* holiness without which no one will [ever] see the Lord.

15 Exercise foresight *and* be on the watch to look [after one another], to see that no one falls back from *and* fails to secure God's grace (His unmerited favor and spiritual blessing), in order that no root of resentment (rancor, bitterness or hatred) shoot forth and cause trouble *and* bitter torment, and the many become contaminated *and* defiled by it;

16 That no one may become guilty of sexual vice, or become a profane (godless and sacrilegious) person as Esau did, who sold his own birthright for a single meal. [Gen. 25:29-34.]

Living New Testament

2 Keep your eyes on Jesus, our leader and instructor. He was willing to die a shameful death on the cross because of the joy He knew would be His afterwards; and now He sits in the place of honor by the throne of God.

3 If you want to keep from becoming fainthearted and weary, think about His patience as sinful men did such terrible things to Him.

4 After all, you have never yet struggled against sin and temptation until you sweat great drops of blood.

5 And have you quite forgotten the encouraging words God spoke to you, His child? He said, "My son, don't be angry when the Lord punishes you. Don't be discouraged when He has to show you where you are wrong.

6 For when He punishes you, it proves that He loves you. When He whips you it proves you are really His child."

7 Let God train you, for He is doing what any loving father does for his children. Whoever heard of a son who was never corrected?

8 If God doesn't punish you when you need it, as other fathers punish their sons, then it means that you aren't really God's son at all—that you don't really belong in His family.

9 Since we respect our fathers here on earth, though they punish us, should we not all the more cheerfully submit to God's training so that we can begin to really live?

10 Our earthly fathers trained us for a few brief years, doing the best for us that they knew how, but God's correction is always right and for our best good, that we may share His holiness.

11 Being punished isn't enjoyable while it is happening—it hurts! But afterwards we can see the result, a quiet growth in grace and character.

12 So take a new grip with your tired hands, stand firm on your shaky legs,

13 And mark out a straight, smooth path for your feet so that those who follow you, though weak and lame, will not fall and hurt themselves, but become strong.

* * * * *

14 Try to stay out of all quarrels and seek to live a clean and holy life, for one who is not holy will not see the Lord.

15 Look after each other so that not one of you will fail to find God's best blessings. Watch out that no bitterness takes root among you, for as it springs up it causes deep trouble, hurting many in their spiritual lives.

16 Watch out that no one becomes involved in sexual sin or becomes careless about God as Esau did: he traded his rights as the oldest son for a single meal.

Revised Standard

ing to Jesus the pioneer and perfecter of
our faith, who for the joy that was set before him endured the cross, despising the
shame, and is seated at the right hand of the
throne of God.
3 Consider him who endured from sinners such hostility against himself, so that
you may not grow weary or fainthearted.
4In your struggle against sin you have not
yet resisted to the point of shedding your
blood. 5And have you forgotten the exhortation which addresses you as sons?—
"My son, do not regard lightly the discipline of the Lord,
nor lose courage when you are punished by him.
6 For the Lord disciplines him whom he loves,
and chastises every son whom he receives."
7 It is for discipline that you have to endure. God is treating you as sons; for what
son is there whom his father does not discipline? 8If you are left without discipline,
in which all have participated, then you are
illegitimate children and not sons. 9Besides
this, we have had earthly fathers to discipline us and we respected them. Shall
we not much more be subject to the Father
of spirits and live? 10For they disciplined
us for a short time at their pleasure, but he
disciplines us for our good, that we may
share his holiness. 11For the moment all
discipline seems painful rather than pleasant; later it yields the peaceful fruit of
righteousness to those who have been
trained by it.

An appeal for endurance

12 Therefore lift your drooping hands
and strengthen your weak knees, 13and make
straight paths for your feet, so that what
is lame may not be put out of joint but
rather be healed. 14Strive for peace with all
men, and for the holiness without which
no one will see the Lord. 15See to it that
no one fail to obtain the grace of God;
that no "root of bitterness" spring up and
cause trouble, and by it the many become
defiled; 16that no one be immoral or irreli-
gious like Esau, who sold his birthright for

King James

17 For ye know how that afterward, when he would have inherited the blessing, he was rejected: for he found no place of repentance, though he sought it carefully with tears.

18 For ye are not come unto the mount that might be touched, and that burned with fire, nor unto blackness, and darkness, and tempest,

19 And the sound of a trumpet, and the voice of words; which *voice* they that heard entreated that the word should not be spoken to them any more:

20 (For they could not endure that which was commanded, And if so much as a beast touch the mountain, it shall be stoned, or thrust through with a dart:

21 And so terrible was the sight, *that* Moses said, I exceedingly fear and quake:)

22 But ye are come unto mount Sion, and unto the city of the living God, the heavenly Jerusalem, and to an innumerable company of angels,

23 To the general assembly and church of the firstborn, which are written in heaven, and to God the Judge of all, and to the spirits of just men made perfect,

24 And to Jesus the mediator of the new covenant, and to the blood of sprinkling, that speaketh better things than *that of* Abel.

25 See that ye refuse not him that speaketh. For if they escaped not who refused him that spake on earth, much more *shall not* we *escape*, if we turn away from him that *speaketh* from heaven:

26 Whose voice then shook the earth: but now he hath promised, saying, Yet once more I shake not the earth only, but also heaven.

27 And this *word*, Yet once more, signifieth the removing of those things that are shaken, as of things that are made, that those things which cannot be shaken may remain.

28 Wherefore we receiving a kingdom which cannot be moved, let us have grace, whereby we may serve God acceptably with reverence and godly fear:

29 For our God *is* a consuming fire.

Amplified

17 For you understand that later on, when he wanted [to regain title to] his inheritance of the blessing, he was rejected (disqualified and set aside), for he could find no opportunity to repair by repentance [what he had done]—that is, no chance to recall the choice he had made—although he sought for it carefully with [bitter] tears. [Gen. 27:30-40.]

18 For you have not come [as did the Israelites in the wilderness] to a [material] mountain that can be touched, [a mountain] that is ablaze with fire, and to gloom and darkness and a raging storm,

19 And the blast of a trumpet, and a voice whose words make the listeners beg that nothing more be said to them. [Exod. 19:12-22; 2:18-21; Deut. 4:11, 12; 5:22-27.]

20 For they could not bear the command that was given, If even a wild animal touches the mountain, it shall be stoned to death. [Exod. 19:12, 13.]

21 In fact, so awful *and* terrifying was the (phenomenal) sight that Moses said, I am terrified—aghast and trembling with fear. [Deut. 9:19.]

22 But rather, you have approached unto Mount Zion, even to the city of the living God, the heavenly Jerusalem, and to countless multitudes of angels in festal gathering,

23 And to the church (assembly) of the First-born who are registered [as citizens] in heaven, and to the Judge Who is God of all, and to the spirits of the righteous [the redeemed in heaven] who have been made perfect;

24 And to Jesus, the Mediator—Go-between, Agent—of a new covenant, and to the sprinkled blood which speaks [of mercy,] a better *and* nobler *and* more gracious message than the blood of Abel [which cried out for vengeance]. [Gen. 4:10.]

25 So see to it that you do not reject Him *or* refuse to listen to *and* heed Him Who is speaking [to you now]. For if they [the Israelites] did not escape when they refused to listen *and* heed Him Who warned *and* divinely instructed them [here] on earth—revealing with heavenly warnings His will—how much less shall we escape if we reject *and* turn our backs on Him Who cautions *and* admonishes [us] from heaven?

26 Then [at Mount Sinai] His voice shook the earth; but now He has given a promise, Yet once more I will shake *and* make tremble not only the earth but also the (starry) heavens. [Hag. 2:6.]

27 Now this expression, Yet once more, indicates the final removal *and* transformation of all [that can be] shaken, that is, of that which has been created, in order that what cannot be shaken may remain *and* continue. [Ps. 102:26.]

28 Let us therefore, receiving a kingdom that is firm *and* stable *and* cannot be shaken, offer to God pleasing service *and* acceptable worship, with modesty *and* pious care and godly fear *and* awe;

29 For our God [is indeed] a consuming fire. [Deut. 4:24.]

CHAPTER 13

LET brotherly love continue.

2 Be not forgetful to entertain strangers: for thereby some have entertained angels unawares.

CHAPTER 13

LET love for your fellow believers continue *and* be a fixed practice with you—never let it fail.

2 Do not forget *or* neglect *or* refuse to extend hospitality to strangers [in the brotherhood]—being friendly, cordial and gracious, sharing the comforts of your home and doing your part generously—for through it some have entertained angels without knowing it. [Gen. 18:1-8; 19:1-3.]

Living New Testament

17 And afterwards when he wanted those rights back again, it was too late, even though he wept bitter tears of repentance. So remember, and be careful.

* * * * *

18 You have not had to stand face to face with terror, flaming fire, gloom, darkness, and a terrible storm, as the Israelites did at Mount Sinai when God gave them His laws.

19 For there was an awesome trumpet blast, and a voice with a message so terrible that the people begged God to stop speaking.

20 They staggered back under God's command that if even an animal touched the mountain it must die.

21 Moses himself was so frightened at the sight that he shook with terrible fear.

22 But you have come right up into Mount Zion, to the city of the living God, the heavenly Jerusalem, and to the gathering of countless happy angels;

23 And to the church, composed of all those registered in heaven; and to God who is Judge of all; and to the spirits of the redeemed in heaven, already made perfect;

24 And to Jesus Himself, Who has brought us His wonderful new agreement; and to the sprinkled blood which graciously forgives instead of crying out for vengeance as the blood of Abel did.

25 So see to it that you obey Him who is speaking to you. For if the people of Israel did not escape when they refused to listen to Moses, the earthly messenger, how terrible our danger if we refuse to listen to God who speaks to us from heaven!

26 When He spoke from Mount Sinai His voice shook the earth, but, "Next time," He says, "I will not only shake the earth, but the heavens too."

27 By this He means that He will sift out everything without solid foundations, so that only unshakable things will be left.

28 Since we have a kingdom nothing can destroy, let us please God by serving Him with thankful hearts, and with holy fear and awe.

29 For our God is a consuming fire.

Revised Standard

a single meal. 17For you know that afterward, when he desired to inherit the blessing, he was rejected, for he found no
chance to repent, though he sought it with
tears.
18 For you have not come to what may
be touched, a blazing fire, and darkness,
and gloom, and a tempest, 19and the sound
of a trumpet, and a voice whose words made
the hearers entreat that no further messages
be spoken to them. 20For they could not
endure the order that was given, "If even
a beast touches the mountain, it shall be
stoned." 21Indeed, so terrifying was the sight
that Moses said, "I tremble with fear."
22But you have come to Mount Zion and
to the city of the living God, the heavenly
Jerusalem, and to innumerable angels in
festal gathering, 23and to the assembly[z] of
the first-born who are enrolled in heaven,
and to a judge who is God of all, and to
the spirits of just men made perfect, 24and
to Jesus, the mediator of a new covenant,
and to the sprinkled blood that speaks more
graciously than the blood of Abel.
25 See that you do not refuse him who
is speaking. For if they did not escape when
they refused him who warned them on
earth, much less shall we escape if we reject
him who warns from heaven. 26His voice
then shook the earth; but now he has promised, "Yet once more I will shake not only
the earth but also the heaven." 27This phrase,
"Yet once more," indicates the removal of
what is shaken, as of what has been made,
in order that what cannot be shaken may
remain. 28Therefore let us be grateful for
receiving a kingdom that cannot be shaken,
and thus let us offer to God acceptable worship, with reverence and awe; 29for our God
is a consuming fire.

CHAPTER 13

Continue to love each other with true brotherly love.

2 Don't forget to be kind to strangers, for some who have done this have entertained angels without realizing it!

General Christian obligations

13 Let brotherly love continue. 2Do not
neglect to show hospitality to strangers, for thereby some have entertained an-

[z] Or *angels, and to the festal gathering and assembly*

King James

3 Remember them that are in bonds, as bound with them; *and* them which suffer adversity, as being yourselves also in the body.

4 Marriage *is* honourable in all, and the bed undefiled: but whoremongers and adulterers God will judge.

5 *Let your* conversation *be* without covetousness; *and be* content with such things as ye have: for he hath said, I will never leave thee, nor forsake thee.

6 So that we may boldly say, The Lord *is* my helper, and I will not fear what man shall do unto me.

7 Remember them which have the rule over you, who have spoken unto you the word of God: whose faith follow, considering the end of *their* conversation.

8 Jesus Christ the same yesterday, and to-day, and for ever.

9 Be not carried about with divers and strange doctrines. For *it is* a good thing that the heart be established with grace; not with meats, which have not profited them that have been occupied therein.

10 We have an altar, whereof they have no right to eat which serve the tabernacle.

11 For the bodies of those beasts, whose blood is brought into the sanctuary by the high priest for sin, are burned without the camp.

12 Wherefore Jesus also, that he might sanctify the people with his own blood, suffered without the gate.

13 Let us go forth therefore unto him without the camp, bearing his reproach.

14 For here have we no continuing city, but we seek one to come.

15 By him therefore let us offer the sacrifice of praise to God continually, that is, the fruit of *our* lips giving thanks to his name.

16 But to do good and to communicate forget not: for with such sacrifices God is well pleased.

Amplified

3 Remember those who are in prison, as if you were their fellow prisoner; and those who are ill-treated, since you also are liable to bodily sufferings.

4 Let marriage be held in honor—esteemed worthy, precious, [that is,] of great price and especially dear—in all things. And thus let the marriage bed be (kept undishonored,) undefiled; for God will judge *and* punish the unchaste (all guilty of sexual vice) and adulterous.

5 Let your [t]character *or* moral disposition be free from love of money—[including] greed, avarice, lust and craving for earthly possessions—and be satisfied with your present [circumstances and with what you have]; for He (God) [t]Himself has said, I will not in any way fail you *nor* [t]give you up *nor* leave you without support. [I will] not, [u][I will] not, [I will] not in any degree leave you helpless, *nor* forsake *nor* [u]let [you] down, [[t]relax My hold on you].—[v]Assuredly not! [Josh. 1:5.]

6 So we take comfort *and* are encouraged *and* confidently *and* boldly say, The Lord is my Helper, I will not be seized with alarm—I will not fear or dread or be terrified. What can man do to me? [Ps. 118:6; 27:1.]

7 Remember your leaders *and* superiors in authority, [for it was they] who brought to you the Word of God. Observe attentively *and* consider their manner of living—the outcome of their well-spent lives—and imitate their faith [that is, [w]their conviction that God exists and is the Creator and Ruler of all things, the Provider and Bestower of eternal salvation through Christ; and their [v]leaning of the entire human personality on God in absolute trust and confidence in His power, wisdom and goodness].

8 Jesus Christ, the Messiah, [is always] the same, yesterday, today, [yes,] and forever—to the ages.

9 Do not be carried about by different *and* varied and alien teachings; for it is good for the heart to be established *and* ennobled *and* strengthened by means of grace (God's favor and spiritual blessing) and not [to be devoted to] foods (rules of diet and ritualistic meals) which bring no [spiritual] benefit *or* profit to those who observe them.

10 We have an altar from which those who serve *and* [x]worship in the tabernacle have no right to eat.

11 For when the blood of animals is brought into the sanctuary by the high priest as a sacrifice for sin, the victims' bodies are burned outside the limits of the camp. [Lev.16:27.]

12 Therefore Jesus also suffered *and* died outside the [city's] gate in order that He might purify *and* consecrate the people through [the shedding of] His own blood, *and* set them apart as holy—for God.

13 Let us then go forth [from all that would prevent us] to Him outside the camp, [at Calvary,] bearing the contempt *and* abuse *and* shame [with] Him. [Lev. 16:27.]

14 For here we have no permanent city, but we are looking for the one which is to come.

15 Through Him therefore let us constantly *and* at all times offer up to God a sacrifice of praise, which is the fruit of lips that thankfully acknowledge *and* confess *and* glorify His name. [Lev. 7:12; Isa. 57:19; Hos. 14:2.]

16 Do not forget *or* neglect to do kindness *and* good, to be generous *and* distribute *and* contribute to the needy [of the church [y]as embodiment and proof of fellowship], for such sacrifices are well-pleasing to God.

---

t) Vincent.
u) Wuest. Three negatives precede the verb.
v) Souter.
w) Thayer.
x) Vincent.
y) Thayer.

Living New Testament

3 Don't forget about those in jail. Suffer with them as though you were there yourself. Share the sorrow of those being mistreated, for you know what they are going through.

* * * * *

4 Honor your marriage and its vows; and be pure; for God will surely punish all those who are immoral or commit adultery.

* * * * *

5 Stay away from the love of money; be satisfied with what you have. For God has said, "I will never, *never* fail you nor forsake you."

6 That is why we can say without any doubt or fear, "The Lord is my Helper and I am not afraid of anything that mere man can do to me."

7 Remember your leaders who have taught you the Word of God. Think of all the good that has come from their lives, and try to trust the Lord as they do.

* * * * *

8 Jesus Christ is the same yesterday, today and forever.

9 So do not be attracted by strange, new ideas. Your spiritual strength comes as a gift from God, not from ceremonial rules about eating certain foods—a method which, by the way, hasn't helped those who have tried it!

* * * * *

10 We have an altar—the cross where Christ was sacrificed—where those who continue to seek salvation by obeying Jewish laws can never be helped.

11 Under the system of Jewish laws the high priest brought the blood of the slain animals into the sanctuary as a sacrifice for sin, and then the bodies of the animals were burned outside the city.

12 That is why Jesus suffered and died outside the city, where His blood washed our sins away.

13 So let us go out to Him beyond the city walls [that is, outside the interests of this world, being willing to be despised[1]] to suffer with Him there, bearing His shame.

14 For this world is not our home; we are looking forward to our everlasting home in heaven.

* * * * *

15 With Jesus' help we will continually offer our sacrifice of praise to God by telling others of the glory of His name.

16 Don't forget to do good and to share what you have with those in need, for such sacrifices are very pleasing to Him.

* * * * *

[1] Implied.

Revised Standard

gels unawares. [3]Remember those who are in
prison, as though in prison with them; and
those who are ill-treated, since you also are
in the body. [4]Let marriage be held in honor
among all, and let the marriage bed be undefiled; for God will judge the immoral and
adulterous. [5]Keep your life free from love
of money, and be content with what you
have; for he has said, "I will never fail you
nor forsake you." [6]Hence we can confidently say,

"The Lord is my helper,
I will not be afraid;
what can man do to me?"

Warning against apostasy

7 Remember your leaders, those who spoke
to you the word of God; consider the outcome of their life, and imitate their faith.
[8]Jesus Christ is the same yesterday and today
and for ever. [9]Do not be led away by diverse
and strange teachings; for it is well that the
heart be strengthened by grace, not by foods,
which have not benefited their adherents.
[10]We have an altar from which those who
serve the tent[a] have no right to eat. [11]For the
bodies of those animals whose blood is
brought into the sanctuary by the high priest
as a sacrifice for sin are burned outside the
camp. [12]So Jesus also suffered outside the
gate in order to sanctify the people through
his own blood. [13]Therefore let us go forth
to him outside the camp, bearing abuse for
him. [14]For here we have no lasting city, but
we seek the city which is to come. [15]Through
him then let us continually offer up a sacrifice of praise to God, that is, the fruit of lips
that acknowledge his name. [16]Do not neglect
to do good and to share what you have, for
such sacrifices are pleasing to God.

[a] Or *tabernacle*

King James

17 Obey them that have the rule over you, and submit yourselves: for they watch for your souls, as they that must give account, that they may do it with joy, and not with grief: for that *is* unprofitable for you.

18 Pray for us: for we trust we have a good conscience, in all things willing to live honestly.

19 But I beseech *you* the rather to do this, that I may be restored to you the sooner.

20 Now the God of peace, that brought again from the dead our Lord Jesus, that great shepherd of the sheep, through the blood of the everlasting covenant,

21 Make you perfect in every good work to do his will, working in you that which is well-pleasing in his sight, through Jesus Christ; to whom *be* glory for ever and ever. Amen.

22 And I beseech you, brethren, suffer the word of exhortation: for I have written a letter unto you in few words.

23 Know ye that *our* brother Timothy is set at liberty; with whom, if he come shortly, I will see you.

24 Salute all them that have the rule over you, and all the saints. They of Italy salute you.

25 Grace *be* with you all. Amen.

Written to the Hebrews from Italy by Timothy.

Amplified

17 Obey your spiritual leaders and submit to them—continually recognizing their authority over you; for they are constantly keeping watch over your souls *and* guarding your spiritual welfare, as men who will have to render an account [of their trust]. [Do your part to] let them do this with gladness, and not with sighing *and* groaning, for that would not be profitable to you [either].

18 Keep praying for us, for we are convinced that we have a good, (clear) conscience, that we want to walk uprightly *and* to live a noble life, acting honorably *and* in complete honesty in all things.

19 And I beg of you [to pray for us] the more earnestly in order that I may be restored to you the sooner.

20 Now may the God of peace—[Who is] the Author and the Giver of peace—and Who brought again from among the dead our Lord Jesus, that great Shepherd of the sheep, by the blood [that sealed, ratified] the everlasting agreement [covenant, testament], [Isa. 63:11; Zech. 9:11; Isa. 55:3; Ezek. 37:26.]

21 Strengthen (complete, perfect) *and* make you what you ought to be, *and* equip you with everything good that you may carry out His will; [while He Himself] works in you *and* accomplishes that which is pleasing in His sight, through Jesus Christ, the Messiah; to Whom be the glory forever and ever—to the ages of the ages. Amen—so be it.

22 I call on you, brethren, to listen patiently *and* bear with this message of exhortation *and* admonition *and* encouragement, for I have written to you briefly.

23 Notice that our brother Timothy has been released [from prison]. If he comes here soon, I will see you along with him.

24 Give our greetings to all of your spiritual leaders and to all of (God's consecrated believers, your fellow) saints. The Italian Christians send you their greetings [also].

25 Grace (God's favor and spiritual blessing) be with you all. Amen—*so be it.*

Living New Testament

17 Obey your spiritual leaders and be willing to do what they say. For their work is to watch over your souls, and God will judge them on how well they do this. Give them reason to report joyfully about you to the Lord and not with sorrow, for then you will suffer for it too.

18 Pray for us, for our conscience is clear and we want to keep it that way.

19 I especially need your prayers right now so that I can come back to you sooner.

* * * * *

20, 21 And now may the God of peace who brought again from the dead our Lord Jesus, the great Shepherd of the sheep, equip you with all you need for doing His will, through the blood of the everlasting agreement between God and you. And may He produce in you through the power of Christ all that is pleasing to Him, to whom be glory forever and ever. Amen.

* * * * *

22 Brethren, please listen patiently to what I have said in this letter, for it is a short one.

23 I want you to know that Brother Timothy is now out of jail; if he comes here soon, I will come with him to see you.

24, 25 Give my greetings to all your leaders and to the other believers there. The Christians from Italy who are here with me send you their love. God's grace be with you all. Goodbye.

Revised Standard

17 Obey your leaders and submit to them; for they are keeping watch over your souls, as men who will have to give account. Let them do this joyfully, and not sadly, for that would be of no advantage to you.

Request for prayer

18 Pray for us, for we are sure that we
have a clear conscience, desiring to act
honorably in all things. 19I urge you the
more earnestly to do this in order that I
may be restored to you the sooner.

Benediction

20 Now may the God of peace who
brought again from the dead our Lord
Jesus, the great shepherd of the sheep, by
the blood of the eternal covenant, 21equip
you with everything good that you may do
his will, working in you[b] that which is pleasing in his sight, through Jesus Christ; to
whom be glory for ever and ever. Amen.

22 I appeal to you, brethren, bear with
my word of exhortation, for I have written
to you briefly. 23You should understand that
our brother Timothy has been released, with
whom I shall see you if he comes soon.
24Greet all your leaders and all the saints.
Those who come from Italy send you greetings. 25Grace be with all of you. Amen.

[b] Other ancient authorities read ***us***

King James

THE GENERAL EPISTLE OF

James

CHAPTER 1

JAMES, a servant of God and of the Lord Jesus Christ, to the twelve tribes which are scattered abroad, greeting.

2 My brethren, count it all joy when ye fall into divers temptations;

3 Knowing *this*, that the trying of your faith worketh patience.

4 But let patience have *her* perfect work, that ye may be perfect and entire, wanting nothing.

5 If any of you lack wisdom, let him ask of God, that giveth to all *men* liberally, and upbraideth not; and it shall be given him.

6 But let him ask in faith, nothing wavering. For he that wavereth is like a wave of the sea driven with the wind and tossed.

7 For let not that man think that he shall receive any thing of the Lord.

8 A double-minded man *is* unstable in all his ways.

9 Let the brother of low degree rejoice in that he is exalted:

10 But the rich, in that he is made low: because as the flower of the grass he shall pass away.

11 For the sun is no sooner risen with a burning heat, but it withereth the grass, and the flower thereof falleth, and the grace of the fashion of it perisheth: so also shall the rich man fade away in his ways.

12 Blessed *is* the man that endureth temptation: for when he is tried, he shall receive the crown of life, which the Lord hath promised to them that love him.

13 Let no man say when he is tempted, I am tempted of God: for God cannot be tempted with evil, neither tempteth he any man:

14 But every man is tempted, when he is drawn away of his own lust, and enticed.

15 Then when lust hath conceived, it bringeth forth sin: and sin, when it is finished, bringeth forth death.

16 Do not err, my beloved brethren.

17 Every good gift and every perfect gift is from above, and cometh down from the Father of lights, with whom is no variableness, neither shadow of turning.

18 Of his own will begat he us with the word of truth, that we should be a kind of firstfruits of his creatures.

Amplified

THE LETTER
OF

James

CHAPTER 1

JAMES, a servant of God and of the Lord Jesus Christ, to the twelve tribes scattered abroad (among the Gentiles, in the dispersion): Greeting—[a]rejoice!

2 Consider it wholly joyful, my brethren, whenever you are enveloped in *or* encounter trials of any sort, *or* fall into various temptations.

3 Be assured *and* understand that the trial *and* proving of your faith bring out endurance *and* steadfastness *and* patience.

4 But let endurance *and* steadfastness *and* patience have full play *and* do a thorough work, so that you may be [people] perfectly and fully developed (with no defects), lacking in nothing.

5 If any of you is deficient in wisdom, let him ask of [a]the giving God [Who gives] to every one liberally *and* ungrudgingly, without reproaching *or* faultfinding, and it will be given him.

6 Only it must be in faith that he asks, with no wavering—no hesitating, no doubting. For the one who wavers (hesitates, doubts) is like the billowing surge out at sea, that is blown hither *and* thither and tossed by the wind.

7 For truly, let not such a person imagine that he will receive anything [he asks for] from the Lord,

8 [For being as he is] a man of two minds—hesitating, dubious, irresolute—[he is] unstable *and* unreliable *and* uncertain about everything (he thinks, feels, decides).

9 Let the brother in humble circumstances glory in his elevation [as a Christian, called to the true riches and to be an heir of God];

10 And the rich [person ought to glory] in being humbled [by being shown his human frailty], because like the flower of the grass he will pass away.

11 For the sun comes up with a scorching heat and parches the grass; its flower falls off and its beauty fades away. Even so will the rich man wither *and* die in the midst of his pursuits. [Isa. 40:6, 7.]

12 Blessed, happy, [b]to be envied is the man who is patient under trial *and* stands up under temptation, for when he has stood the test *and* been approved he will receive [the victor's] crown of life which God has promised to those who love Him.

13 Let no one say when he is tempted, I am tempted from God; for God is incapable of being tempted by [what is] evil and He Himself tempts no one.

14 But every person is tempted when he is drawn away, enticed *and* baited by his own evil desire (lust, passions).

15 Then the evil desire when it has conceived gives birth to sin, and sin when it is fully matured brings forth death.

16 Do not be misled, my beloved brethren.

17 Every good gift and every perfect ([c]free, large, full) gift is from above; it comes down from the Father of all [that gives] light, in [the shining of] Whom there can be no variation [rising or setting] or shadow cast by His turning [as in an eclipse].

18 And it was of His own [free] will that He gave us birth (as sons) by [His] Word of Truth, so that we should be a kind of first fruits of His creatures—[a sample] of what He created to be consecrated to Himself.

---

a) Literal meaning.
b) Souter.
c) Vincent.

Living New Testament

James

CHAPTER 1

From: James, a servant of God and of the Lord Jesus Christ.

To: Jewish Christians scattered everywhere. Greetings!

2 Dear brothers, is your life full of difficulties and temptations? Then be happy,

3 For when the way is rough, your patience has a chance to grow.

4 So let it grow, and don't try to squirm out of your problems. For when your patience is finally in full bloom, then you will be ready for anything, strong in character, full and complete.

5 If you want to know what God wants you to do, ask Him, and He will gladly tell you, for He is always ready to give a bountiful supply of wisdom to all who ask Him; He will not resent it.

6 But when you ask Him, be sure that you really expect Him to tell you, for a doubtful mind will be as unsettled as a wave of the sea that is driven and tossed by the wind;

7, 8 And every decision you then make will be uncertain, as you turn first this way, and then that. If you don't ask with faith, don't expect the Lord to give you any solid answer.

9 A Christian who doesn't amount to much in this world should be glad, for he is great in the Lord's sight.

10, 11 But a rich man should be glad that his riches mean nothing to the Lord, for he will soon be gone, like a flower that has lost its beauty and fades away, withered—killed by the scorching summer sun. So it is with rich men. They will soon die and leave behind all their busy activities.

12 Happy is the man who doesn't give in and do wrong when he is tempted, for afterwards he will get as his reward the crown of life that God has promised those who love Him.

13 And remember, when someone wants to do wrong it is never God who is tempting him, for God never wants to do wrong and never tempts anyone else to do it.

14 Temptation is the pull of man's own evil thoughts and wishes.

15 These evil thoughts lead to evil actions and afterwards to the death penalty from God.

16 So don't be misled, dear brothers.

17 But whatever is good and perfect comes to us from God, the Creator of all light, and He shines forever without change or shadow.

18 And it was a happy day for Him[1] when He gave us our new lives, through the truth of His Word, and we became, as it were, the first children in His new family.

[1] Literally, "Of His own free will He gave us, etc."

Revised Standard

THE LETTER OF

James

Salutation

1 James, a servant of God and of the
Lord Jesus Christ,
To the twelve tribes in the Dispersion:
Greeting.

True religion patient in temptation

2 Count it all joy, my brethren, when
you meet various trials, 3 for you know that
the testing of your faith produces steadfastness. 4 And let steadfastness have its full
effect, that you may be perfect and complete, lacking in nothing.
5 If any of you lacks wisdom, let him
ask God, who gives to all men generously
and without reproaching, and it will be given
him. 6 But let him ask in faith, with no doubting, for he who doubts is like a wave of the
sea that is driven and tossed by the wind.
7, 8 For that person must not suppose that
a double-minded man, unstable in all his
ways, will receive anything from the Lord.
9 Let the lowly brother boast in his exaltation, 10 and the rich in his humiliation,
because like the flower of the grass he will
pass away. 11 For the sun rises with its scorching heat and withers the grass; its flower
falls, and its beauty perishes. So will the
rich man fade away in the midst of his
pursuits.
12 Blessed is the man who endures trial,
for when he has stood the test he will receive the crown of life which God has
promised to those who love him. 13 Let no
one say when he is tempted, "I am tempted
by God"; for God cannot be tempted with
evil and he himself tempts no one; 14 but
each person is tempted when he is lured
and enticed by his own desire. 15 Then desire
when it has conceived gives birth to sin;
and sin when it is full-grown brings forth
death.
16 Do not be deceived, my beloved
brethren. 17 Every good endowment and
every perfect gift is from above, coming
down from the Father of lights with whom
there is no variation or shadow due to
change.[a] 18 Of his own will he brought us
forth by the word of truth that we should
be a kind of first fruits of his creatures.

[a] Other ancient authorities read *variation due to a shadow of turning*

King James

19 Wherefore, my beloved brethren, let every man be swift to hear, slow to speak, slow to wrath:

20 For the wrath of man worketh not the righteousness of God.

21 Wherefore lay apart all filthiness and superfluity of naughtiness, and receive with meekness the engrafted word, which is able to save your souls.

22 But be ye doers of the word, and not hearers only, deceiving your own selves.

23 For if any be a hearer of the word, and not a doer, he is like unto a man beholding his natural face in a glass:

24 For he beholdeth himself, and goeth his way, and straightway forgetteth what manner of man he was.

25 But whoso looketh into the perfect law of liberty, and continueth *therein,* he being not a forgetful hearer, but a doer of the work, this man shall be blessed in his deed.

26 If any man among you seem to be religious, and bridleth not his tongue, but deceiveth his own heart, this man's religion *is* vain.

27 Pure religion and undefiled before God and the Father is this, To visit the fatherless and widows in their affliction, *and* to keep himself unspotted from the world.

Amplified

19 Understand [this], my beloved brethren. Let every man be quick to hear, (a ready listener,) slow to speak, slow to take offense *and* to get angry.

20 For man's anger does not promote the righteousness God [wishes and requires].

21 So get rid of all uncleanness and the rampant outgrowth of wickedness, and in a humble (gentle, modest) spirit receive *and* welcome the Word which implanted *and* rooted [in your hearts] contains the power to save your souls.

22 But—obey the message; be doers of the Word, and not merely listeners to it, betraying yourselves [into deception by reasoning contrary to the Truth].

23 For if any one only listens to the Word without obeying it *and* being a doer of it, he is like a man who looks carefully at his [own] natural face in a mirror;

24 For he thoughtfully observes himself, then goes off and promptly forgets what he was like.

25 But he who looks carefully into the faultless law, the [law] of liberty, and is faithful to it *and* perseveres in looking into it, being not a heedless listener who forgets, but an active doer [who obeys], he shall be blessed in his doing—in his life of obedience.

26 If any one thinks himself to be religious—piously observant of the external duties of his faith—and does not bridle his tongue, but deludes his own heart, this person's religious service is worthless (futile, barren).

27 External [d]religious worship ([e]religion as it is expressed in outward acts) that is pure and unblemished in the sight of God the Father is this: to visit *and* help *and* care for the orphans and widows in their affliction *and* need, and to keep oneself unspotted *and* uncontaminated from the world.

CHAPTER 2

King James

MY brethren, have not the faith of our Lord Jesus Christ, *the Lord* of glory, with respect of persons.

2 For if there come unto your assembly a man with a gold ring, in goodly apparel, and there come in also a poor man in vile raiment;

3 And ye have respect to him that weareth the gay clothing, and say unto him, Sit thou here in a good place; and say to the poor, Stand thou there, or sit here under my footstool:

4 Are ye not then partial in yourselves, and are become judges of evil thoughts?

5 Hearken, my beloved brethren, Hath not God chosen the poor of this world rich in faith, and heirs of the kingdom which he hath promised to them that love him?

6 But ye have despised the poor. Do not rich men oppress you, and draw you before the judgment seats?

7 Do not they blaspheme that worthy name by the which ye are called?

CHAPTER 2

Amplified

MY brethren, pay no servile regard to people—show no prejudice, no partiality. Do not [attempt to] hold *and* practice the faith of our Lord Jesus Christ [the Lord] of glory together with—snobbery!

2 For if a person comes into your congregation whose hands are adorned with gold rings and who is wearing splendid apparel, and also a poor [man] in shabby clothes comes in,

3 And you pay special attention to the one who wears the splendid clothes and say to him, Sit here in this preferable seat! while you tell the poor [man], Stand there! or, Sit there on the floor at my feet!

4 Are you not discriminating among your own, and becoming critics *and* judges with wrong motives?

5 Listen, my beloved brethren. Has not God chosen those who are poor in the eyes of the world to be rich in faith *and* in their position as believers, and to inherit the kingdom which He has promised to those who love Him?

6 But you [in contrast] have insulted—humiliated, dishonored and shown your contempt for—the poor. Is it not the rich who domineer over you? Is it not they who drag you into the law courts?

7 Is it not they who slander *and* blaspheme that precious name by which you are distinguished *and* called [the name of Christ invoked in baptism]?

---

d) "Religion in its rise interests us about *ourselves;* in its progress, about our *fellow-creatures;* in its highest stage, about the honor of *God.*" (—Jamieson, Fausset and Brown).
e) Abbott-Smith; Moulton and Milligan; Vincent, etc.

Living New Testament

19 Dear brothers, don't ever forget that it is best to listen much, speak little, and not become angry;

20 For anger doesn't make us good, as God demands that we must be.

21 So get rid of all that is wrong in your life, both inside and outside, and humbly be glad for the wonderful message we have received, for it is able to save our souls as it takes hold of our hearts.

22 And remember, it is a message to obey, not just to listen to. So don't fool yourselves.

23 For if a person just listens and doesn't obey, he is like a man looking at his face in a mirror;

24 As soon as he walks away, he can't see himself anymore or remember what he looks like.

25 But if anyone keeps looking steadily into God's law for free men he will not only remember it but he will do what it says, and God will greatly bless him in everything he does.

26 Anyone who says he is a Christian but doesn't control his sharp tongue is just fooling himself, and his religion isn't worth much.

27 The Christian who is pure and without fault, from God the Father's point of view, is the one who takes care of orphans and widows, and whose soul remains true to the Lord—not soiled and dirtied by its contacts with the world.

Revised Standard

True religion evidenced by conduct

19 Know this, my beloved brethren. Let
every man be quick to hear, slow to speak,
slow to anger, [20]for the anger of man does
not work the righteousness of God. [21]There-
fore put away all filthiness and rank growth
of wickedness and receive with meekness
the implanted word, which is able to save
your souls.
22 But be doers of the word, and not
hearers only, deceiving yourselves. [23]For if
any one is a hearer of the word and not a
doer, he is like a man who observes his
natural face in a mirror; [24]for he observes
himself and goes away and at once forgets
what he was like. [25]But he who looks into
the perfect law, the law of liberty, and
perseveres, being no hearer that forgets but
a doer that acts, he shall be blessed in his
doing.
26 If any one thinks he is religious, and
does not bridle his tongue but deceives his
heart, this man's religion is vain. [27]Religion
that is pure and undefiled before God and
the Father is this: to visit orphans and
widows in their affliction, and to keep oneself unstained from the world.

CHAPTER 2

Dear brothers, how can you claim that you belong to the Lord Jesus Christ, the Lord of Glory, if you show favoritism to rich people and look down on poor people?

2 If a man comes into your church dressed in expensive clothes and with valuable gold rings on his fingers, and at the same moment another man comes in who is poor and dressed in threadbare clothes,

3 And you make a lot of fuss over the rich man and give him the best seat in the house and say to the poor man, "You can stand over there if you like, or else sit on the floor"—well,

4 This kind of action casts a question mark across your faith—are you really a Christian at all?—and shows that you are guided by wrong motives.

5 Listen to me, dear brothers: God has chosen poor people to be rich in faith, and the kingdom of heaven is theirs, for that is the gift God has promised to all those who love Him.

6 And yet, of the two strangers, you have despised the poor man. Don't you realize that it is usually the rich men who pick on you and drag you into court?

7 And all too often they are the ones who laugh at Jesus Christ, whose noble name you bear.

True faith impartial

2 My brethren, show no partiality as you
hold the faith of our Lord Jesus Christ,
the Lord of glory. [2]For if a man with gold
rings and in fine clothing comes into your
assembly, and a poor man in shabby clothing also comes in, [3]and you pay attention
to the one who wears the fine clothing and
say, "Have a seat here, please," while you
say to the poor man, "Stand there," or,
"Sit at my feet," [4]have you not made distinctions among yourselves, and become
judges with evil thoughts? [5]Listen, my beloved brethren. Has not God chosen those
who are poor in the world to be rich in
faith and heirs of the kingdom which he
has promised to those who love him? [6]But
you have dishonored the poor man. Is it not
the rich who oppress you, is it not they who
drag you into court? [7]Is it not they who
blaspheme that honorable name by which
you are called?

King James

8 If ye fulfil the royal law according to the scripture, Thou shalt love thy neighbour as thyself, ye do well:
9 But if ye have respect to persons, ye commit sin, and are convinced of the law as transgressors.
10 For whosoever shall keep the whole law, and yet offend in one *point*, he is guilty of all.
11 For he that said, Do not commit adultery, said also, Do not kill. Now if thou commit no adultery, yet if thou kill, thou art become a transgressor of the law.
12 So speak ye, and so do, as they that shall be judged by the law of liberty.
13 For he shall have judgment without mercy, that hath shewed no mercy; and mercy rejoiceth against judgment.
14 What *doth it* profit, my brethren, though a man say he hath faith, and have not works? can faith save him?
15 If a brother or sister be naked, and destitute of daily food,
16 And one of you say unto them, Depart in peace, be *ye* warmed and filled; notwithstanding ye give them not those things which are needful to the body; what *doth it* profit?
17 Even so faith, if it hath not works, is dead, being alone.
18 Yea, a man may say, Thou hast faith, and I have works: shew me thy faith without thy works, and I will shew thee my faith by my works.
19 Thou believest that there is one God; thou doest well: the devils also believe, and tremble.
20 But wilt thou know, O vain man, that faith without works is dead?
21 Was not Abraham our father justified by works, when he had offered Isaac his son upon the altar?
22 Seest thou how faith wrought with his works, and by works was faith made perfect?
23 And the scripture was fulfilled which saith, Abraham believed God, and it was imputed unto him for righteousness: and he was called the Friend of God.
24 Ye see then how that by works a man is justified, and not by faith only.
25 Likewise also was not Rahab the harlot justified by works, when she had received the messengers, and had sent *them* out another way?
26 For as the body without the spirit is dead, so faith without works is dead also.

Amplified

8 If indeed you [really] fulfill the royal Law, in accordance with the Scripture, You shall love your neighbor as [you love] yourself, you do well. [Lev. 19:18.]
9 But if you show servile regard (prejudice, favoritism) for people, you commit sin and are rebuked *and* convicted by the Law as violators *and* offenders.
10 For whosoever keeps the Law [as a] whole, but stumbles *and* offends in one [single instance] has become guilty of [breaking] all of it.
11 For He Who said, You shall not commit adultery, also said, You shall not kill. If you do not commit adultery but do kill, you have become guilty of transgressing the [whole] Law. [Exod. 20:13, 14; Deut. 5:17, 18.]
12 So speak and so act as [people should] who are to be judged under the law of liberty [the moral instruction given by Christ, especially about love].
13 For to him who has shown no mercy the judgment [will be] merciless; but mercy [full of glad confidence] exults victoriously over judgment.
14 What is the use (profit), my brethren, for any one to profess to have faith if he has no [good] works [to show for it]? Can [such] faith save [his soul]?
15 If a brother or sister is poorly clad and lacks food for each day,
16 And one of you says to him, Goodbye! Keep [yourself] warm and well fed, without giving him the necessities for the body, what good does that do?
17 So also faith if it does not have works (deeds and actions of obedience to back it up), by itself is destitute of power—inoperative, dead.
18 But some one will say [to you then], You [say you] have faith and I have [good] works. Now you show me your [alleged] faith apart from any [good] works [if you can], and I by [good] works [of obedience] will show you my faith.
19 You believe that God is one; you do well. So do the demons believe, and shudder [in terror and horror such as [f]make a man's hair stand on end and contract the surface of his skin]!
20 Are you willing to be shown [proof], you foolish, unproductive, spiritually-deficient fellow, that faith apart from [good] works is inactive *and* ineffective *and* worthless?
21 Was not our forefather Abraham [shown to be] justified—made acceptable to God—by [his] works when he brought to the altar as an offering his [own] son Isaac? [Gen. 22:1-14.]
22 You see that [his] faith was cooperating with his works, and [his] faith was completed *and* reached its supreme expression [when he implemented it] by [good] works.
23 And [so] the Scripture was fulfilled that says, Abraham believed—adhered to, trusted in and relied on—God, and this was accounted to him as righteousness [as conformity to God's will in thought and deed], and he was called God's friend. [Gen. 15:6; Isa. 41:8; II Chron. 20:7.]
24 You see that a man is justified (pronounced righteous before God) through what he does and not alone through faith—through works of obedience as well as by what he believes.
25 So also with Rahab the harlot. Was she not shown to be justified (pronounced righteous before God) by [good] deeds when she took in the scouts (spies) and got them away by a different route? [Josh. 2:1-21.]
26 For as the human body apart from the spirit is lifeless, so faith apart from [its] works of obedience is also dead.

---

f) Vincent's "Word Studies in the New Testament."

Living New Testament

8 Yes indeed, it is good when you truly obey our Lord's command, "You must love and help your neighbors just as much as you love and take care of yourself."

9 But you are breaking this law of our Lord's when you favor the rich and fawn over them; it is sin.

10 And the person who keeps every law of God, but makes one little slip is just as guilty as the person who has broken every law there is.

11 For the God who said you must not marry a woman who already has a husband, also said you must not murder, so even though you have not broken the marriage laws by committing adultery, but have murdered someone, you have entirely broken God's laws and stand utterly guilty before Him.

12 You will be judged on whether or not you are doing what Christ wants you to. So watch what you do and what you think;

13 For there will be no mercy to those who have shown no mercy. But if you have been merciful, then God's mercy toward you will win out over His judgment against you.

14 Dear brothers, what's the use of saying that you have faith and are Christians if you aren't proving it by helping others? Will *that* kind of faith save anyone?

15 If you have a friend who is in need of food and clothing,

16 And you say to him, "Well, good-bye and God bless you, stay warm and eat hearty," and then don't give him clothes or food, what good does that do?

17 So you see, it isn't enough just to have faith. You must also do good to prove that you have it. Faith that doesn't show itself by good works is no faith at all—it is dead and useless.

18 But someone may well argue, "You say the way to God is by faith alone, plus nothing; well, I say that good works are important too, for without good works you can't prove whether you have faith or not; but anyone can see that I have faith by the way I act."

19 Are there still some among you who hold that "only believing" is enough? Believing in one God? Well, remember that the devils believe this too—so strongly that they tremble in terror!

20 Dear foolish man! When will you ever learn that "believing" is useless without *doing* what God wants you to? Faith that does not result in good deeds is not real faith.

21 Don't you remember that even our father Abraham was declared good because of what he *did,* when he was willing to obey God, even if it meant offering his son Isaac to die on the altar?

22 You see, he was trusting God so much that he was willing to do whatever God told him to; his faith was made complete by what he did, by his actions, his good deeds.

23 And so it happened just as the Scriptures say, that Abraham trusted God, and the Lord declared him good in God's sight, and he was even called "the friend of God."

24 So you see, a man is saved by what he does, as well as by what he believes.

25 Rahab, the prostitute, is another example of this. She was saved because of what she did when she hid those messengers and sent them safely away by a different road.

26 Just as the body is dead when there is no spirit in it, so faith is dead if it is not the kind that results in good deeds.

Revised Standard

8 If you really fulfil the royal law, according to the scripture, "You shall love your
neighbor as yourself," you do well. [9]But if
you show partiality, you commit sin, and
are convicted by the law as transgressors.
[10]For whoever keeps the whole law but fails
in one point has become guilty of all of it.
[11]For he who said, "Do not commit adultery," said also, "Do not kill." If you do not
commit adultery but do kill, you have become a transgressor of the law. [12]So speak
and so act as those who are to be judged
under the law of liberty. [13]For judgment is
without mercy to one who has shown no
mercy; yet mercy triumphs over judgment.

True faith evidenced by works

14 What does it profit, my brethren, if
a man says he has faith but has not works?
Can his faith save him? [15]If a brother or
sister is ill-clad and in lack of daily food,
[16]and one of you says to them, "Go in
peace, be warmed and filled," without giving them the things needed for the body,
what does it profit? [17]So faith by itself, if
it has no works, is dead.

18 But some one will say, "You have
faith and I have works." Show me your
faith apart from your works, and I by my
works will show you my faith. [19]You believe that God is one; you do well. Even the
demons believe—and shudder. [20]Do you
want to be shown, you foolish fellow, that
faith apart from works is barren? [21]Was not
Abraham our father justified by works, when
he offered his son Isaac upon the altar? [22]You
see that faith was active along with his
works, and faith was completed by works,
[23]and the scripture was fulfilled which says,
"Abraham believed God, and it was reckoned
to him as righteousness"; and he was called
the friend of God. [24]You see that a man is
justified by works and not by faith alone.
[25]And in the same way was not also Rahab
the harlot justified by works when she received the messengers and sent them out
another way? [26]For as the body apart from
the spirit is dead, so faith apart from works
is dead.

King James

CHAPTER 3

MY brethren, be not many masters, knowing that we shall receive the greater condemnation.
2 For in many things we offend all. If any man offend not in word, the same *is* a perfect man, *and* able also to bridle the whole body.
3 Behold, we put bits in the horses' mouths, that they may obey us; and we turn about their whole body.
4 Behold also the ships, which though *they be* so great, and *are* driven of fierce winds, yet are they turned about with a very small helm, whithersoever the governor listeth.
5 Even so the tongue is a little member, and boasteth great things. Behold, how great a matter a little fire kindleth!
6 And the tongue *is* a fire, a world of iniquity: so is the tongue among our members, that it defileth the whole body, and setteth on fire the course of nature; and it is set on fire of hell.
7 For every kind of beasts, and of birds, and of serpents, and of things in the sea, is tamed, and hath been tamed of mankind:
8 But the tongue can no man tame; *it is* an unruly evil, full of deadly poison.
9 Therewith bless we God, even the Father; and therewith curse we men, which are made after the similitude of God.
10 Out of the same mouth proceedeth blessing and cursing. My brethren, these things ought not so to be.
11 Doth a fountain send forth at the same place sweet *water* and bitter?
12 Can the fig tree, my brethren, bear olive berries? either a vine, figs? so *can* no fountain both yield salt water and fresh.
13 Who *is* a wise man and endued with knowledge among you? let him shew out of a good conversation his works with meekness of wisdom.
14 But if ye have bitter envying and strife in your hearts, glory not, and lie not against the truth.
15 This wisdom descendeth not from above, but *is* earthly, sensual, devilish.
16 For where envying and strife *is*, there *is* confusion and every evil work.
17 But the wisdom that is from above is first pure, then peaceable, gentle, *and* easy to be entreated, full of mercy and good fruits, without partiality, and without hypocrisy.
18 And the fruit of righteousness is sown in peace of them that make peace.

Amplified

CHAPTER 3

NOT many [of you] should become teachers [[g]self-constituted censors and reprovers of others], my brethren, for you know that we [teachers] will be judged by a higher standard *and* with greater severity [than other people].—Thus we assume the greater accountability and the more condemnation.
2 For we all often stumble *and* fall *and* offend in many things. And if any one does not offend in speech—never says the wrong things—he is a fully developed character *and* a perfect man, able to control his whole body *and* to curb his entire nature.
3 If we set bits in the horses' mouths to make them obey us, we can turn their whole bodies about.
4 Likewise look at the ships, though they are so great and are driven by rough winds, they are steered by a very small rudder wherever the impulse of the helmsman determines.
5 Even so the tongue is a little member, and it can boast of great things. See how much wood *or* how great a forest a tiny spark can set ablaze!
6 And the tongue [is] a fire. [The tongue is a] world of wickedness set among our members, contaminating *and* depraving the whole body and setting on fire the wheel of birth—the cycle of man's nature—being itself ignited by hell (Gehenna).
7 For every kind of beast and bird, of reptile and sea animal, can be tamed and has been tamed by human genius (nature).
8 But the human tongue can be tamed by no man. It is (an undisciplined, irreconcilable) restless evil, full of death-bringing poison.
9 With it we bless the Lord and Father, and with it we curse men who were made in God's likeness!
10 Out of the same mouth come forth blessing and cursing. These things, my brethren, ought not to be so.
11 Does a fountain send forth [simultaneously] from the same opening fresh water and bitter?
12 Can a fig tree, my brethren, bear olives, or a grapevine figs? Neither can a salt spring furnish fresh water.
13 Who is there among you who is wise and intelligent? Then let him by his noble living show forth his [good] works with the (unobtrusive) humility [which is the proper attribute] of true wisdom.
14 But if you have bitter jealousy (envy) and contention (rivalry, selfish ambition) in your hearts, do not pride yourselves on it and thus be in defiance of *and* false to the Truth.
15 This [superficial] wisdom is not such as comes down from above, but is earthly, unspiritual (animal), even devilish (demoniacal).
16 For wherever there is jealousy (envy) and contention (rivalry and selfish ambition) there will also be confusion (unrest, disharmony, rebellion) and all sorts of evil *and* vile practices.
17 But the wisdom from above is first of all pure (undefiled); then it is peace-loving, courteous (considerate, gentle). [It is willing to] yield to reason, full of compassion and good fruits; it is wholehearted *and* straightforward, impartial *and* unfeigned—free from doubts, wavering and insincerity.
18 And the harvest of righteousness (of conformity to God's will in thought and deed) is [the fruit of the seed] sown in peace by those who work for *and* make peace—in themselves and in others, [that is,] that peace which means concord (agreement, harmony) between individuals, with undisturbedness, in a peaceful mind free from fears and agitating passions and moral conflicts.

---

g) John Calvin, quoted by Jamieson, Fausset and Brown in "A Commentary on the Old and New Testaments."

Living New Testament

CHAPTER 3

Dear brothers, don't be too eager to tell others their faults,[1] for we all make many mistakes; and when we teachers, who should know better, do wrong, our punishment will be greater than it would be for others. If anyone can control his tongue, it proves that he has perfect control over himself in every other way.

3 We can make a large horse turn around and go wherever we want by means of a small bit in his mouth.

4 And a tiny rudder makes a huge ship turn wherever the pilot wants it to go, even though the winds are strong.

5 So also the tongue is a small thing, but what enormous damage it can do. A great forest can be set on fire by one tiny spark.

6 And the tongue is a flame of fire. It is full of wickedness and poisons every part of the body. And the tongue is set on fire by hell itself, and can turn our whole lives into a blazing flame of destruction and disaster.

7 Men have trained, or can train, every kind of animal or bird that lives and every kind of reptile and fish,

8 But no human being can tame the tongue. It is always ready to pour out its deadly poison.

9 Sometimes it praises our heavenly Father, and sometimes it breaks out into curses against men who are made like God.

10 And so blessing and cursing come pouring out of the same mouth. Dear brothers, surely this is not right!

11 Does a spring of water bubble out first with fresh water and then with bitter water?

12 Can you pick olives from a fig tree, or figs from a grape vine? No, and you can't draw fresh water from a salty pool.

13 If you are wise, live a life of steady goodness, so that only good deeds will pour forth. And if you don't brag about them, then you will be truly wise!

14 And by all means don't brag about being wise and good if you are bitter and jealous and selfish; that is the worst sort of lie.

15 For jealousy and selfishness are not God's kind of wisdom. Such things are earthly, unspiritual, inspired by the devil.

16 For wherever there is jealousy or selfish ambition, there will be disorder and every other kind of evil.

17 But the wisdom that comes from heaven is first of all pure and full of quiet gentleness. Then it is peace-loving and courteous. It allows discussion and is willing to yield to others; it is full of mercy and good deeds. It is wholehearted and straightforward and sincere.

18 And those who are peacemakers will plant seeds of peace and reap a harvest of goodness.

Literally, "Not many (of you) should become masters (teachers)."

Revised Standard

True faith evidenced by words

3 Let not many of you become teachers,
my brethren, for you know that we who
teach shall be judged with greater strictness.
2For we all make many mistakes, and if any
one makes no mistakes in what he says he
is a perfect man, able to bridle the whole
body also. 3If we put bits into the mouths
of horses that they may obey us, we guide
their whole bodies. 4Look at the ships also;
though they are so great and are driven by
strong winds, they are guided by a very small
rudder wherever the will of the pilot directs.
5So the tongue is a little member and boasts
of great things. How great a forest is set
ablaze by a small fire!

6 And the tongue is a fire. The tongue is
an unrighteous world among our members,
staining the whole body, setting on fire the
cycle of nature,[b] and set on fire by hell.[c]
7For every kind of beast and bird, of reptile
and sea creature, can be tamed and has been
tamed by humankind, 8but no human being
can tame the tongue—a restless evil, full of
deadly poison. 9With it we bless the Lord
and Father, and with it we curse men, who
are made in the likeness of God. 10From the
same mouth come blessing and cursing. My
brethren, this ought not to be so. 11Does a
spring pour forth from the same opening
fresh water and brackish? 12Can a fig tree,
my brethren, yield olives, or a grapevine figs?
No more can salt water yield fresh.

True and false wisdom

13 Who is wise and understanding among
you? By his good life let him show his works
in the meekness of wisdom. 14But if you have
bitter jealousy and selfish ambition in your
hearts, do not boast and be false to the truth.
15This wisdom is not such as comes down
from above, but is earthly, unspiritual, devilish. 16For where jealousy and selfish ambition exist, there will be disorder and every
vile practice. 17But the wisdom from above
is first pure, then peaceable, gentle, open to
reason, full of mercy and good fruits, without uncertainty or insincerity. 18And the harvest of righteousness is sown in peace by
those who make peace.

[b] Or *wheel of birth*
[c] Greek *Gehenna*

King James

CHAPTER 4

FROM whence *come* wars and fightings among you? *come they* not hence, *even* of your lusts that war in your members?

2 Ye lust, and have not: ye kill, and desire to have, and cannot obtain: ye fight and war, yet ye have not, because ye ask not.

3 Ye ask, and receive not, because ye ask amiss, that ye may consume *it* upon your lusts.

4 Ye adulterers and adulteresses, know ye not that the friendship of the world is enmity with God? whosoever therefore will be a friend of the world is the enemy of God.

5 Do ye think that the scripture saith in vain, The spirit that dwelleth in us lusteth to envy?

6 But he giveth more grace. Wherefore he saith, God resisteth the proud, but giveth grace unto the humble.

7 Submit yourselves therefore to God. Resist the devil, and he will flee from you.

8 Draw nigh to God, and he will draw nigh to you. Cleanse *your* hands, *ye* sinners; and purify *your* hearts, *ye* double-minded.

9 Be afflicted, and mourn, and weep: let your laughter be turned to mourning, and *your* joy to heaviness.

10 Humble yourselves in the sight of the Lord, and he shall lift you up.

11 Speak not evil one of another, brethren. He that speaketh evil of *his* brother, and judgeth his brother, speaketh evil of the law, and judgeth the law: but if thou judge the law, thou art not a doer of the law, but a judge.

12 There is one lawgiver, who is able to save and to destroy: who art thou that judgest another?

13 Go to now, ye that say, To-day or to-morrow we will go into such a city, and continue there a year, and buy and sell, and get gain:

14 Whereas ye know not what *shall be* on the morrow. For what *is* your life? It is even a vapour, that appeareth for a little time, and then vanisheth away.

15 For that ye *ought* to say, If the Lord will, we shall live, and do this, or that.

16 But now ye rejoice in your boastings: all such rejoicing is evil.

17 Therefore to him that knoweth to do good, and doeth *it* not, to him it is sin.

Amplified

CHAPTER 4

WHAT leads to strife (discord and feuds) *and* how do conflicts (quarrels and fightings) originate among you? Do they not arise from your sensual desires that are ever warring in your bodily members?

2 You are jealous *and* covet [what others have] and your desires go unfulfilled; [so] you become murderers. [[h]To hate is to murder as far as your hearts are concerned.] You burn with envy *and* anger and are not able to obtain [the gratification, the contentment and the happiness that you seek], so you fight and war. You do not have because you do not ask.

3 [Or] you do ask [God for them] and yet fail to receive, because you ask with wrong purpose and evil, selfish motives. Your intention is, [when you get what you desire] to spend it in sensual pleasures.

4 You [are like] unfaithful wives [having illicit love affairs with the world] *and* [i]breaking your marriage vow to God! Do you not know that being the world's friend is being God's enemy? So whoever chooses to be a friend of the world takes his stand as an enemy of God.

5 Or do you suppose that the Scripture is speaking to no purpose that says, The Spirit Whom He has caused to dwell in us yearns over us—and [i]He yearns for the Spirit [to be welcome]—with a jealous love? [Jer. 3:14; Hos. 2:19f.]

6 But He gives us more and more grace [[j]power of the Holy Spirit, to meet this evil tendency and all others fully]. That is why He says, God sets Himself against the proud and haughty, but gives grace [continually] to the lowly—those who are humble-minded [enough to receive it]. [Prov. 3:34.]

7 So be subject to God.—Stand firm against the devil; resist him and he will flee from you.

8 Come close to God and He will come close to you. [Recognize that you are] sinners, get your soiled hands clean; [realize that you have been disloyal] wavering individuals with divided interests, and purify your hearts [of your spiritual adultery].

9 [As you draw near to God] be deeply penitent and grieve, even weep [over your disloyalty]. Let your laughter be turned to grief and your mirth to dejection *and* heartfelt shame [for your sins].

10 Humble yourselves—feeling very insignificant—in the presence of the Lord, and He will exalt you.—He will lift you up and make your lives significant.

11 [My] brethren, do not speak evil about or accuse one another. He that maligns a brother or judges his brother is maligning *and* criticizing the Law *and* judging the Law. But if you judge the Law, you are not a practicer of the Law but a censor *and* judge [of it].

12 One only is the Lawgiver *and* Judge—[the One] Who has the absolute power of life and death—Who is able to save and to destroy. [But you], who are you that [you presume to] pass judgment on your neighbor?

13 Come now, you who say, Today or tomorrow we will go into such *and* such a city and spend a year there and carry on our business and make money.

14 Yet you do not know [the least thing] about what may happen tomorrow. What is the nature of your life? You are [really] but a wisp of vapor—a puff of smoke, a mist—that is visible for a little while and then disappears [into thin air].

15 You ought instead to say, If the Lord is willing, we shall live and we shall do this or that [thing].

16 But as it is, you boast [falsely] in your presumption *and* your self-conceit. All such boasting is wrong.

17 So any person who knows what is right to do but does not do it, to him it is sin.

h) I John 3:15.
i) Alternate reading.
j) Adam Clarke.

Living New Testament

CHAPTER 4

What is causing the quarrels and fights among you? Isn't it because there is a whole army of evil desires within you?

2 You want what you don't have so you kill to get it. You long for what others have, and can't afford it, so you start a fight to take it away from them. And yet the reason you don't have what you want is that you don't ask God for it.

3 And even when you do ask you don't get it because your whole aim is wrong—you want only what will give *you* pleasure.

4 You are like an unfaithful wife who loves her husband's enemies. Don't you realize that making friends with God's enemies—the evil pleasures of this world—makes you an enemy of God? I say it again, that if your aim is to enjoy the evil pleasures of the unsaved world, you cannot also be a friend of God.

5 Or what do you think the Scripture means when it says that the Holy Spirit, whom God has placed within us, watches over us with tender jealousy?

6 But He gives us more and more strength to stand against all such evil longings. As the Scripture says, God gives strength to the humble, but sets Himself against the proud and haughty.

7 So give yourselves humbly to God. Resist the devil and he will flee from you.

8 And when you draw close to God, God will draw close to you. Wash your hands, you sinners, and let your hearts be filled with God alone to make them pure and true to Him.

9 Let there be tears for the wrong things you have done. Let there be sorrow and sincere grief. Let there be sadness instead of laughter, and gloom instead of joy.

10 Then when you feel your worthlessness before the Lord, He will lift you up, encourage and help you.

11 Don't criticize and speak evil about each other, dear brothers. If you do, you will be fighting against God's law of loving one another, declaring it is wrong. But your job is not to decide whether this law is right or wrong, but to obey it.

12 Only He who made the law can rightly judge among us. He alone decides to save us or destroy. So what right do you have to judge or criticize others?

13 Look here, you people who say, "Today or tomorrow we are going to such and such a town, stay there a year, and open up a profitable business."

14 How do you know what is going to happen tomorrow? For the length of your lives is as uncertain as the morning fog—now you see it; soon it is gone.

15 What you ought to say is, "If the Lord wants us to, we shall live and do this or that."

16 Otherwise you will be bragging about your own plans, and such self-confidence never pleases God.

17 Remember, too, that knowing what is right to do and then not doing it is sin.

Revised Standard

Friendship and humility

4 What causes wars, and what causes
fightings among you? Is it not your
passions that are at war in your members?
[2]You desire and do not have; so you kill.
And you covet[d] and cannot obtain; so you
fight and wage war. You do not have, because you do not ask. [3]You ask and do not
receive, because you ask wrongly, to spend
it on your passions. [4]Unfaithful creatures!
Do you not know that friendship with the
world is enmity with God? Therefore whoever wishes to be a friend of the world
makes himself an enemy of God. [5]Or do
you suppose it is in vain that the scripture
says, "He yearns jealously over the spirit
which he has made to dwell in us"? [6]But
he gives more grace; therefore it says,
"God opposes the proud, but gives grace to
the humble." [7]Submit yourselves therefore
to God. Resist the devil and he will flee
from you. [8]Draw near to God and he will
draw near to you. Cleanse your hands, you
sinners, and purify your hearts, you men of
double mind. [9]Be wretched and mourn and
weep. Let your laughter be turned to
mourning and your joy to dejection. [10]Hum-
ble yourselves before the Lord and he will
exalt you.

Slander and false confidence

11 Do not speak evil against one another,
brethren. He that speaks evil against a brother or judges his brother, speaks evil against
the law and judges the law. But if you judge
the law, you are not a doer of the law but a
judge. [12]There is one lawgiver and judge, he
who is able to save and to destroy. But who
are you that you judge your neighbor?

13 Come now, you who say, "Today or
tomorrow we will go into such and such a
town and spend a year there and trade and
get gain"; [14]whereas you do not know about
tomorrow. What is your life? For you are a
mist that appears for a little time and then
vanishes. [15]Instead you ought to say, "If the
Lord wills, we shall live and we shall do this
or that." [16]As it is, you boast in your arrogance. All such boasting is evil. [17]Whoever
knows what is right to do and fails to do it,
for him it is sin.

---

[d] Or *you kill and you covet*

King James

CHAPTER 5

GO to now, *ye* rich men, weep and howl for your miseries that shall come upon *you*.

2 Your riches are corrupted, and your garments are motheaten.

3 Your gold and silver is cankered; and the rust of them shall be a witness against you, and shall eat your flesh as it were fire. Ye have heaped treasure together for the last days.

4 Behold, the hire of the labourers who have reaped down your fields, which is of you kept back by fraud, crieth: and the cries of them which have reaped are entered into the ears of the Lord of sabaoth.

5 Ye have lived in pleasure on the earth, and been wanton; ye have nourished your hearts, as in a day of slaughter.

6 Ye have condemned *and* killed the just; *and* he doth not resist you.

7 Be patient therefore, brethren, unto the coming of the Lord. Behold, the husbandman waiteth for the precious fruit of the earth, and hath long patience for it, until he receive the early and latter rain.

8 Be ye also patient; stablish your hearts: for the coming of the Lord draweth nigh.

9 Grudge not one against another, brethren, lest ye be condemned: behold, the judge standeth before the door.

10 Take, my brethren, the prophets, who have spoken in the name of the Lord, for an example of suffering affliction, and of patience.

11 Behold, we count them happy which endure. Ye have heard of the patience of Job, and have seen the end of the Lord; that the Lord is very pitiful, and of tender mercy.

12 But above all things, my brethren, swear not, neither by heaven, neither by the earth, neither by any other oath: but let your yea be yea; and *your* nay, nay; lest ye fall into condemnation.

13 Is any among you afflicted? let him pray. Is any merry? let him sing psalms.

14 Is any sick among you? let him call for the elders of the church; and let them pray over him, anointing him with oil in the name of the Lord:

15 And the prayer of faith shall save the sick, and the Lord shall raise him up; and if he have committed sins, they shall be forgiven him.

16 Confess *your* faults one to another, and pray one for another, that ye may be healed. The effectual fervent prayer of a righteous man availeth much.

17 Elias was a man subject to like passions as we are, and he prayed earnestly that it might not rain: and it rained not on the earth by the space of three years and six months.

18 And he prayed again, and the heaven gave rain, and the earth brought forth her fruit.

Amplified

CHAPTER 5

COME now, you rich [people,] weep aloud and lament over the miseries—the woes—that are surely coming upon you.

2 Your abundant wealth has rotted *and* is ruined and your [many] garments have become moth-eaten.

3 Your gold and silver are completely rusted through, and their rust will be testimony against you and it will devour your flesh as if it were fire. You have heaped together treasure for the last days.

4 [But] look! [Here are] the wages that you have withheld by fraud from the laborers who have reaped your fields, crying out (for vengeance), and the cries of the harvesters have come to the ears of the Lord of hosts.

5 [Here] on earth you have abandoned yourselves to soft (prodigal) living and to [the pleasures of] self-indulgence *and* self-gratification. You have fattened your hearts in a day of slaughter.

6 You have condemned, you have murdered the (innocent) righteous [man, while] he offers no resistance to you.

7 So be patient, brethren, [as you wait] till the coming of the Lord. See how the farmer waits expectantly for the precious harvest from the land. [See how] he keeps up his patient [vigil] over it until it receives the early and late rains.

8 So you also must be patient. Establish your hearts—strengthen and confirm them in the final certainty—for the coming of the Lord is very near.

9 Do not complain, brethren, against one another, so that you [yourselves] may not be judged. Look! The Judge is [already] standing at the very door.

10 [As] an example of suffering and ill-treatment together with patience, brethren, take the prophets who spoke in the name of the Lord—as His messengers.

11 You know how we call those blessed (happy) who were steadfast—who endured. You have heard of the endurance of Job; and you have seen the Lord's [purpose and how He richly blessed him in the] end, in as much as the Lord is full of pity *and* compassion *and* tenderness and mercy. [Job 1:21, 22; 42:10; Ps. 111:4.]

12 But above all [things], my brethren, do not swear either by heaven or by earth or by any other oath; but let your yes be [a simple] yes and your no be [a simple] no, so that you may not sin *and* fall under condemnation.

13 Is any one among you afflicted—ill-treated, suffering evil? He should pray. Is any one glad at heart? He should sing praise [to God].

14 Is any one among you sick? He should call in the church elders—the spiritual guides. And they should pray over him, anointing him with oil in the Lord's name.

15 And the prayer [that is] of faith will save him that is sick, and the Lord will restore him; and if he has committed sins, he will be forgiven.

16 Confess to one another therefore your faults—your slips, your false steps, your offenses, your sins; and pray [also] for one another, that you may be healed *and* restored—to a spiritual tone of mind and heart. The earnest (heart-felt, continued) prayer of a righteous man makes tremendous power available—dynamic in its working.

17 Elijah was a human being with a nature such as we have—with feelings, affections and constitution as ourselves; and he prayed earnestly for it not to rain, and no rain fell on the earth for three years and six months. [I Kings 17:1.]

18 And [then] he prayed again and the heavens supplied rain and the land produced its crops [as usual]. [I Kings 18:42-45.]

Living New Testament

CHAPTER 5

Look here, you rich men, now is the time to cry and groan with anguished grief because of all the terrible troubles ahead of you.

2 Your wealth is even now rotting away, and your fine clothes are becoming mere moth-eaten rags.

3 The value of your gold and silver is dropping fast, yet it will stand as evidence against you, and eat your flesh like fire. That is what you have stored up for yourselves, to receive on that coming day of judgment.

4 For listen! Hear the cries of the field workers whom you have cheated of their pay. Their cries have reached the ears of the Lord of Hosts.

5 You have spent your years here on earth having fun, satisfying your every whim, and now your fat hearts are ready for the slaughter.

6 You have condemned and killed good men who had no power to defend themselves against you.

7 Now as for you, dear brothers who are waiting for the Lord's return, be patient, like a farmer who waits until the autumn for his precious harvest to ripen.

8 Yes, be patient. And take courage, for the coming of the Lord is near.

9 Don't grumble about each other, brothers. Are you yourselves above criticism? For see! the great Judge is coming. He is almost here [let Him do whatever criticizing must be done[1]].

10 For examples of patience in suffering, look at the Lord's prophets.

11 We know how happy they are now because they stayed true to Him then, even though they suffered greatly for it. Job is an example of a man who continued to trust the Lord in sorrow; from his experiences we can see how the Lord's plan finally ended in good, for He is full of tenderness and mercy.

12 But most of all, dear brothers, do not swear either by heaven or earth or anything else; just say a simple yes or no, so that you will not sin and receive God's curse.

13 Is anyone among you suffering? He should keep on praying about it. And those who have reason to be thankful should continually be singing praises to the Lord.

14 Is anyone sick? He should call for the elders of the church and they should pray over him and pour a little oil upon him, calling on the Lord to heal him.

15 And their prayer, if offered in faith, will heal him, for the Lord will make him well; and if his sickness was caused by some sin, the Lord will forgive him.

16 Admit your faults to one another and pray for each other so that you may be healed. The earnest prayer of a righteous man has great power and wonderful results.

17 Elijah was as completely human as we are, and yet when he prayed earnestly that no rain would fall, none fell for the next three and one-half years!

18 Then he prayed again, this time that it *would* rain, and down it poured and the grass turned green and the gardens began to grow again.

[1] Implied.

Revised Standard

The miseries of the rich

5 Come now, you rich, weep and howl for
the miseries that are coming upon you.
2 Your riches have rotted and your garments
are moth-eaten. 3 Your gold and silver have
rusted, and their rust will be evidence against
you and will eat your flesh like fire. You
have laid up treasure[e] for the last days. 4 Behold, the wages of the laborers who mowed
your fields, which you kept back by fraud,
cry out; and the cries of the harvesters have
reached the ears of the Lord of hosts. 5 You
have lived on the earth in luxury and in pleasure; you have fattened your hearts in a day
of slaughter. 6 You have condemned, you
have killed the righteous man; he does not
resist you.

The patience of the saints

7 Be patient, therefore, brethren, until the
coming of the Lord. Behold, the farmer waits
for the precious fruit of the earth, being patient over it until it receives the early and the
late rain. 8 You also be patient. Establish your
hearts, for the coming of the Lord is at hand.
9 Do not grumble, brethren, against one another, that you may not be judged; behold,
the Judge is standing at the doors. 10 As an
example of suffering and patience, brethren,
take the prophets who spoke in the name of
the Lord. 11 Behold, we call those happy who
were steadfast. You have heard of the steadfastness of Job, and you have seen the purpose of the Lord, how the Lord is compassionate and merciful.

12 But above all, my brethren, do not
swear, either by heaven or by earth or with
any other oath, but let your yes be yes and
your no be no, that you may not fall under
condemnation.

Prayer and confession

13 Is any one among you suffering? Let
him pray. Is any cheerful? Let him sing
praise. 14 Is any among you sick? Let him
call for the elders of the church, and let them
pray over him, anointing him with oil in the
name of the Lord; 15 and the prayer of faith
will save the sick man, and the Lord will
raise him up; and if he has committed sins,
he will be forgiven. 16 Therefore confess your
sins to one another, and pray for one another, that you may be healed. The prayer of a
righteous man has great power in its effects.
17 Elijah was a man of like nature with ourselves and he prayed fervently that it might
not rain, and for three years and six months
it did not rain on the earth. 18 Then he prayed
again and the heaven gave rain, and the earth
brought forth its fruit.

[e] Or *will eat your flesh, since you have stored up fire*

King James

19 Brethren, if any of you do err from
the truth, and one convert him;
20 Let him know, that he which con-
verteth the sinner from the error of his way,
shall save a soul from death, and shall hide
a multitude of sins.

Amplified

19 [My] brethren, if any one among you strays from
the Truth *and* falls into error, and another [person] brings
him back [to God],
20 Let the [latter] one be sure that whoever turns a
sinner from his evil course will save [that one's] soul from
death and will cover a multitude of sins [that is, [k]procure
the pardon of the many sins committed by the convert].

---

k) Adam Clarke; Jamieson, Fausset and Brown; Matthew Henry and, many other translators.

Living New Testament

19 Dear brothers, if anyone has slipped away from God and no longer trusts the Lord, and someone helps him understand the Truth again,

20 That person who brings him back to God will have saved a wandering soul from death, bringing about the forgiveness of his many sins.

Sincerely,
James

Revised Standard

19 My brethren, if any one among you wanders from the truth and some one brings
him back, [20]let him know that whoever brings back a sinner from the error of his way will save his soul from death and will cover a multitude of sins.

King James

THE FIRST EPISTLE GENERAL OF

Peter

CHAPTER 1

PETER, an apostle of Jesus Christ, to the strangers scattered throughout Pontus, Galatia, Cappadocia, Asia, and Bithynia,

2 Elect according to the foreknowledge of God the Father, through sanctification of the Spirit, unto obedience and sprinkling of the blood of Jesus Christ: Grace unto you, and peace, be multiplied.

3 Blessed *be* the God and Father of our Lord Jesus Christ, which according to his abundant mercy hath begotten us again unto a lively hope by the resurrection of Jesus Christ from the dead,

4 To an inheritance incorruptible, and undefiled, and that fadeth not away, reserved in heaven for you,

5 Who are kept by the power of God through faith unto salvation ready to be revealed in the last time.

6 Wherein ye greatly rejoice, though now for a season, if need be, ye are in heaviness through manifold temptations:

7 That the trial of your faith, being much more precious than of gold that perisheth, though it be tried with fire, might be found unto praise and honour and glory at the appearing of Jesus Christ:

8 Whom having not seen, ye love; in whom, though now ye see *him* not, yet believing, ye rejoice with joy unspeakable and full of glory:

9 Receiving the end of your faith, *even* the salvation of *your* souls.

10 Of which salvation the prophets have inquired and searched diligently, who prophesied of the grace *that should come* unto you:

11 Searching what, or what manner of time the Spirit of Christ which was in them did signify, when it testified beforehand the sufferings of Christ, and the glory that should follow.

12 Unto whom it was revealed, that not unto themselves, but unto us they did minister the things, which are now reported unto you by them that have preached the gospel unto you with the Holy Ghost sent down from heaven; which things the angels desire to look into.

13 Wherefore gird up the loins of your mind, be sober, and hope to the end for the grace that is to be brought unto you at the revelation of Jesus Christ;

14 As obedient children, not fashioning yourselves according to the former lusts in your ignorance:

15 But as he which hath called you is holy, so be ye holy in all manner of conversation;

Amplified

THE FIRST LETTER OF

Peter

CHAPTER 1

PETER, an apostle (a special messenger) of Jesus Christ, [writing] to the elect exiles of the dispersion scattered (sowed) abroad in Pontus, Galatia, Cappadocia, Asia and Bithynia,

2 Who were chosen *and* foreknown by God the Father and consecrated (sanctified, made holy) by the Spirit to be obedient to Jesus Christ, the Messiah, and to be sprinkled with [His] blood: May grace (spiritual blessing) and peace be given you in increasing abundance—that spiritual peace to be [a]realized in and through Christ, [b]freedom from fears, agitating passions and moral conflicts.

3 Praised (honored, blessed be) the God and Father of our Lord Jesus Christ, the Messiah! By His boundless mercy we have been born again to an ever living hope through the resurrection of Jesus Christ from the dead;

4 [Born anew] into an inheritance which is beyond the reach of change *and* decay (imperishable), unsullied, and unfading, reserved in heaven for you,

5 Who are being guarded (garrisoned) by God's power through [your] faith [till you fully inherit that [c]final] salvation that is ready to be revealed [for you] in the last time.

6 [You should] be exceedingly glad on this account, though now for a little while you may be distressed by trials *and* suffer temptations,

7 So that [the genuineness] of your faith may be tested, [your faith] which is infinitely more precious than the perishable gold which is tested *and* purified by fire. [This proving of your faith is intended] to redound to [your] praise and glory and honor when Jesus Christ, the Messiah, the Anointed One, is revealed.

8 Without having seen Him you love Him; though you do not [even] now see Him you believe in Him, and exult *and* thrill with inexpressible and glorious (triumphant, heavenly) joy.

9 [At the same time] you receive the result (outcome, consummation) of your faith, the salvation of your souls.

10 The prophets who prophesied of the grace [divine blessing] which was intended for you, searched and inquired earnestly about this salvation.

11 They sought [to find out] to whom or when this was to come which the Spirit of Christ working within them indicated when He predicted the sufferings of Christ and the glories that should follow [them].

12 It was then disclosed to them that the services they were rendering were not meant for themselves *and* their period of time, but for you. [It is these very] things which have now already been made known plainly to you by those who preached the good news (the Gospel) to you by the [same] Holy Spirit sent from heaven. Into these things [the very] angels long to look!

13 So brace up your minds; be sober—circumspect [morally alert]; set your hope wholly *and* unchangeably on the grace (divine favor) that is coming to you when Jesus Christ, the Messiah, is revealed.

14 [Live] as children of obedience [to God]; do not conform yourselves to the evil desires [that governed you] in your former ignorance [when you did not know the requirements of the Gospel].

15 But as the One Who called you is holy, you yourselves also be holy in all your conduct *and* manner of living.

---

a) Cremer.
b) Webster, in definition of "peace" in this sense.
c) Williams.

Living New Testament

I Peter

CHAPTER 1

From: Peter, Jesus Christ's missionary.

To: Jewish Christians driven out of Jerusalem and scattered throughout Pontus, Galatia, Cappadocia, Asia, and Bithynia.

2 Dear friends, God the Father chose you long ago and knew you would become His children. And the Holy Spirit has been at work in your hearts, cleansing you with the blood of Jesus Christ and making you to please Him. May God bless you richly and grant you increasing freedom from all anxiety and fear.

3 All honor to God, the God and Father of our Lord Jesus Christ; for it is His boundless mercy that has given us the privilege of being born again, so that we are now members of God's own family. Now we live in the hope of eternal life because Christ rose again from the dead.

4 And God has reserved for His children the priceless gift of eternal life; it is kept in heaven for you, pure and undefiled, beyond the reach of change and decay.

5 And God, in His mighty power, will make sure that you get there safely to receive it, because you are trusting Him. It will be yours in that coming last day for all to see.

6 So be truly glad! There is wonderful joy ahead, even though the going is rough for a while down here.

7 These trials are only to test your faith, to see whether or not it is strong and pure. It is being tested as fire tests gold and purifies it—and your faith is far more precious to God than mere gold; so if your faith remains strong after being tried in the test tube of fiery trials, it will bring you much praise and glory and honor on the day of His return.

8 You love Him even though you have never seen Him; though not seeing Him, you trust Him; and even now you are happy with the inexpressible joy that comes from heaven itself.

9 And your further reward for trusting Him will be the salvation of your souls.

10 This salvation was something the prophets did not fully understand. Though they wrote about it, they had many questions as to what it all could mean.

11 They wondered what the Spirit of Christ within them was talking about, for He told them to write down the events which, since then, have happened to Christ: His suffering, and His great glory afterwards. And they wondered when and to whom all this would happen.

12 They were finally told that these things would not occur during their lifetime, but long years later, during yours. And now at last this Good News has been plainly announced to all of us. It was preached to us in the power of the same heaven-sent Holy Spirit who spoke to them; and it is all so strange and wonderful that even the angels in heaven would give a great deal to know more about it.

13 So now you can look forward soberly and intelligently to more of God's kindness to you when Jesus Christ returns.

14 Obey God because you are His children; don't slip back into your old ways—doing evil because you knew no better.

15 But be holy now in everything you do, just as the Lord is holy, who invited you to be His child.

Revised Standard

THE FIRST LETTER OF

Peter

Salutation

1 Peter, an apostle of Jesus Christ, To the
exiles of the Dispersion in Pontus, Galatia, Cappadocia, Asia, and Bithynia, 2cho-
sen and destined by God the Father and
sanctified by the Spirit for obedience to
Jesus Christ and for sprinkling with his
blood:

May grace and peace be multiplied to you.

The risen Christ

3 Blessed be the God and Father of our
Lord Jesus Christ! By his great mercy we
have been born anew to a living hope through
the resurrection of Jesus Christ from the
dead, 4and to an inheritance which is imperishable, undefiled, and unfading, kept in
heaven for you, 5who by God's power are
guarded through faith for a salvation ready
to be revealed in the last time. 6In this you
rejoice,[a] though now for a little while you
may have to suffer various trials, 7so that the
genuineness of your faith, more precious than
gold which though perishable is tested by
fire, may redound to praise and glory and
honor at the revelation of Jesus Christ.
8Without having seen[b] him you[c] love him;
though you do not now see him you[c] believe
in him and rejoice with unutterable and exalted joy. 9As the outcome of your faith you
obtain the salvation of your souls.

The witness of the prophets

10 The prophets who prophesied of the
grace that was to be yours searched and inquired about this salvation; 11they inquired
what person or time was indicated by the
Spirit of Christ within them when predicting
the sufferings of Christ and the subsequent
glory. 12It was revealed to them that they
were serving not themselves but you, in the
things which have now been announced to
you by those who preached the good news
to you through the Holy Spirit sent from
heaven, things into which angels long to
look.

An appeal for a holy life

13 Therefore gird up your minds, be sober, set your hope fully upon the grace that
is coming to you at the revelation of Jesus
Christ. 14As obedient children, do not be
conformed to the passions of your former
ignorance, 15but as he who called you is
holy, be holy yourselves in all your conduct;

[a] Or *Rejoice in this*
[b] Other ancient authorities read *known*
[c] Or omit *you*

King James

16 Because it is written, Be ye holy; for I am holy.

17 And if ye call on the Father, who without respect of persons judgeth according to every man's work, pass the time of your sojourning *here* in fear:

18 Forasmuch as ye know that ye were not redeemed with corruptible things, *as* silver and gold, from your vain conversation *received* by tradition from your fathers;

19 But with the precious blood of Christ, as of a lamb without blemish and without spot:

20 Who verily was foreordained before the foundation of the world, but was manifest in these last times for you,

21 Who by him do believe in God, that raised him up from the dead, and gave him glory; that your faith and hope might be in God.

22 Seeing ye have purified your souls in obeying the truth through the Spirit unto unfeigned love of the brethren, *see that ye* love one another with a pure heart fervently:

23 Being born again, not of corruptible seed, but of incorruptible, by the word of God, which liveth and abideth for ever.

24 For all flesh *is* as grass, and all the glory of man as the flower of grass. The grass withereth, and the flower thereof falleth away:

25 But the word of the Lord endureth for ever. And this is the word which by the gospel is preached unto you.

Amplified

16 For it is written, You shall be holy, for I am holy. [Lev. 11:44, 45.]

17 And if you call upon Him as [your] Father Who judges each one impartially according to what he does, [then] you should conduct yourselves with true reverence throughout the time of your temporary residence [on the earth, whether long or short].

18 You must know (recognize) that you were redeemed (ransomed) from the useless (fruitless) way of living inherited by tradition from [your] forefathers, not with corruptible things [such as] silver and gold,

19 But [you were purchased] with the precious blood of Christ, the Messiah, like that of a [sacrificial] lamb without blemish or spot.

20 It is true that He was chosen *and* foreordained (destined and foreknown for it) before the foundation of the world, but He was brought out to public view (made manifest) in these last days—at the end of the times—for the sake of you.

21 Through Him you believe—adhere to, rely on—God, Who raised Him up from the dead and gave Him honor *and* glory, so that your faith and hope are [centered and rest] in God.

22 Since by your obedience to the Truth *through the* [*Holy*] *Spirit* you have purified your hearts for the sincere affection of the brethren, [see that you] love one another fervently from a *pure* heart.

23 You have been regenerated—born again—not from a mortal [d]origin ([e]seed, sperm) but from one that is immortal by the *ever* living and lasting Word of God.

24 Because all flesh [mankind] is like grass and all its glory (honor) like [the] flower of grass. The grass withers, and the flower drops off,

25 But the Word of the Lord [[d]divine instruction, the Gospel] endures forever. And this Word is the good news which was preached to you. [Isa. 40:6-9.]

CHAPTER 2

WHEREFORE laying aside all malice, and all guile, and hypocrisies, and envies, and all evil speakings,

2 As newborn babes, desire the sincere milk of the word, that ye may grow thereby:

3 If so be ye have tasted that the Lord *is* gracious.

4 To whom coming, *as unto* a living stone, disallowed indeed of men, but chosen of God, *and* precious,

5 Ye also, as lively stones, are built up a spiritual house, an holy priesthood, to offer up spiritual sacrifices, acceptable to God by Jesus Christ.

6 Wherefore also it is contained in the scripture, Behold, I lay in Sion a chief corner stone, elect, precious: and he that believeth on him shall not be confounded.

CHAPTER 2

SO be done with every trace of wickedness (depravity, malignity) and all deceit and insincerity (pretense, hypocrisy) and grudges (envy, jealousy) and slander *and* evil speaking of every kind.

2 Like newborn babies you should crave—thirst for, earnestly desire—the pure (unadulterated) spiritual milk, that by it you may be nurtured *and* grow unto [completed] salvation;

3 Since you have [already] tasted the goodness *and* kindness of the Lord. [Ps. 34:8.]

4 Come to Him [then, to that] Living Stone which men [f]tried *and* threw away, but which is chosen [and] precious in God's sight. [Ps. 118:22; Isa. 28:16.]

5 [Come] and as living stones be yourselves built [into] a spiritual house, for a holy (dedicated, consecrated) priesthood, to offer up [those] spiritual sacrifices [that are] acceptable *and* well-pleasing to God through Jesus Christ.

6 For thus it stands in Scripture: Behold, I am laying in Zion a chosen, ([g]honored,) precious chief Cornerstone, and he who believes in Him—who adheres to, trusts in and relies on Him—shall never be [h]disappointed *or* put to shame. [Isa. 28:16.]

d) Thayer.
e) Abbott-Smith. cf. Moulton and Milligan.
f) Vincent.
g) Vincent.
h) Thayer.

Living New Testament

16 He Himself has said, "You must be holy, for I am holy."

17 And remember that your heavenly Father to whom you pray has no favorites when He judges. He will judge you with perfect justice for everything you do; so act in reverent fear of Him from now on until you get to heaven.

18 God paid a ransom to save you from the impossible road to heaven which your fathers tried to take, and the ransom He paid was not mere gold or silver, as you very well know.

19 But He paid for you with the precious lifeblood of Christ, the sinless, spotless Lamb of God.

20 God chose Him for this purpose long before the world began, but only recently was He brought into public view, in these last days, as a blessing to you.

21 Because of this your trust can be in God who raised Christ from the dead and gave Him great glory. Now your faith and hope can rest in Him alone.

22 Now you can have real love for everyone because your souls have been cleansed from selfishness and hatred when you trusted Christ to save you; so see to it that you really do love each other warmly, with all your hearts.

23 For you have a new life. It was not passed on to you from your parents, for the life they gave you will fade away. This new one will last forever, for it comes from Christ, God's ever-living Message to men.

24 Yes, our natural lives will fade as grass does when it becomes all brown and dry. All our greatness is like a flower that droops and falls;

25 But the Word of the Lord will last forever. And His message is the Good News that was preached to you.

CHAPTER 2

So get rid of your feelings of hatred. Don't just pretend to be good! Be done with dishonesty and jealousy and talking about others behind their backs.

2, 3 If you have tasted the Lord's goodness and kindness, cry for more, as a baby cries for milk. Eat God's Word—read it, think about it—and grow strong in the Lord and be saved.

4 Come to Christ, who is the living Foundation of Rock upon which God builds; though men have spurned Him, He is very precious to God who has chosen Him above all others.

5 And now you have become living building-stones for God's use in building His house: what's more, you are His holy priests; so come to Him [you are acceptable to Him because of Jesus Christ[1]] and offer to God those things that please Him.

6 As the Scriptures express it, "See, I am sending Christ to be the carefully chosen, precious Cornerstone of My church, and I will never disappoint those who trust in Him."

---

[1] Implied.

Revised Standard

[16]since it is written, "You shall be holy, for
I am holy." [17]And if you invoke as Father
him who judges each one impartially according to his deeds, conduct yourselves
with fear throughout the time of your exile.
[18]You know that you were ransomed from
the futile ways inherited from your fathers,
not with perishable things such as silver or
gold, [19]but with the precious blood of
Christ, like that of a lamb without blemish
or spot. [20]He was destined before the
foundation of the world but was made manifest at the end of the times for your sake.
[21]Through him you have confidence in
God, who raised him from the dead and
gave him glory, so that your faith and hope
are in God.[d]

22 Having purified your souls by your
obedience to the truth for a sincere love of
the brethren, love one another earnestly from
the heart. [23]You have been born anew, not of
perishable seed but of imperishable, through
the living and abiding word of God; [24]for

"All flesh is like grass
and all its glory like the flower of grass.
The grass withers, and the flower falls,
[25]but the word of the Lord abides for ever."

That word is the good news which was
preached to you.

2 So put away all malice and all guile and
insincerity and envy and all slander.
[2]Like newborn babes, long for the pure
spiritual milk, that by it you may grow up
to salvation; [3]for you have tasted the kindness of the Lord.

Christ our cornerstone

4 Come to him, to that living stone, rejected by men but in God's sight chosen and
precious; [5]and like living stones be yourselves
built into a spiritual house, to be a holy
priesthood, to offer spiritual sacrifices acceptable to God through Jesus Christ. [6]For it
stands in scripture:

"Behold, I am laying in Zion a stone,
a cornerstone chosen and precious,
and he who believes in him will not be put
to shame."

---

[d] Or *so that your faith is hope in God*

King James

7 Unto you therefore which believe *he is* precious: but unto them which be disobedient, the stone which the builders disallowed, the same is made the head of the corner,

8 And a stone of stumbling, and a rock of offence, *even to them* which stumble at the word, being disobedient: whereunto also they were appointed.

9 But ye *are* a chosen generation, a royal priesthood, an holy nation, a peculiar people; that ye should shew forth the praises of him who hath called you out of darkness into his marvellous light:

10 Which in time past *were* not a people, but *are* now the people of God: which had not obtained mercy, but now have obtained mercy.

11 Dearly beloved, I beseech *you* as strangers and pilgrims, abstain from fleshly lusts, which war against the soul;

12 Having your conversation honest among the Gentiles: that, whereas they speak against you as evildoers, they may by *your* good works, which they shall behold, glorify God in the day of visitation.

13 Submit yourselves to every ordinance of man for the Lord's sake: whether it be to the king, as supreme;

14 Or unto governors, as unto them that are sent by him for the punishment of evildoers, and for the praise of them that do well.

15 For so is the will of God, that with well-doing ye may put to silence the ignorance of foolish men:

16 As free, and not using *your* liberty for a cloak of maliciousness, but as the servants of God.

17 Honour all *men.* Love the brotherhood. Fear God. Honour the king.

18 Servants, *be* subject to *your* masters with all fear; not only to the good and gentle, but also to the froward.

19 For this *is* thankworthy, if a man for conscience toward God endure grief, suffering wrongfully.

20 For what glory *is it,* if, when ye be buffeted for your faults, ye shall take it patiently? but if, when ye do well, and suffer *for it,* ye take it patiently, this *is* acceptable with God.

21 For even hereunto were ye called: because Christ also suffered for us, leaving us an example, that ye should follow his steps:

22 Who did no sin, neither was guile found in his mouth:

23 Who, when he was reviled, reviled not again; when he suffered, he threatened not; but committed *himself* to him that judgeth righteously:

Amplified

7 To you then who believe—who adhere to, trust in and rely on Him— is the preciousness; but for those who disbelieve [it is true], The [very] Stone which the builders rejected has become the main Cornerstone, [Ps. 118:22.]

8 And a Stone that will cause stumbling and a Rock that will give [men] offense; they stumble because they disobey *and* disbelieve [God's] Word, as those [who reject Him] were destined (appointed) to do.

9 But you are a chosen race, a royal priesthood, a dedicated nation, [[i]God's] own [j]purchased, special people, that you may set forth the wonderful deeds *and* display the virtues *and* perfections of Him Who called you out of darkness into His marvelous light. [Exod. 23:22.]

10 Once you were not a people [at all], but now you are God's people; once you were unpitied, but now you are pitied *and* have received mercy. [Hos. 2:23.]

11 Beloved, I implore you as sojourners, strangers *and* exiles [in this world] to abstain from the sensual urges—the evil desires, the passions of the flesh [your lower nature]—that wage war against the soul.

12 Conduct yourselves properly (honorably, righteously) among the Gentiles, so that although they may slander you as evildoers, [yet] they may by witnessing your good deeds [come to] glorify God in the day of inspection [[k]when God shall look upon (you) wanderers, as a pastor (shepherd) over his flock].

13 Be submissive to every human institution *and* authority for the sake of the Lord, whether it be to the emperor as supreme,

14 Or to governors as sent by him to bring vengeance (punishment, justice) to those who do wrong, and to encourage those who do good service.

15 For it is God's will *and* intention that by doing right [your] good *and* honest lives should silence (muzzle, gag) the ignorant charges *and* ill-informed criticisms of foolish persons.

16 [Live] as free people, [yet] without employing your freedom as a pretext for wickedness; but [live at all times] as servants of God.

17 Show respect for all men—treat them honorably. Love the brotherhood [the Christian fraternity of which Christ is the Head]. Reverence God. Honor the emperor.

18 [You who are] household servants, be submissive to your masters with all (proper) respect, not only to those who are kind, considerate *and* reasonable but also to those who are surly—overbearing, unjust and crooked.

19 For one is regarded favorably (is approved, acceptable and thankworthy) if, as in the sight of God, he endures the pain of unjust suffering.

20 [After all] what [l]kind of glory [is there in it] if when you do wrong and are punished for it you take it patiently? But if you bear patiently with suffering [which results] when you do right *and* that is undeserved, it is acceptable *and* well-pleasing to God.

21 For even to this were you called—it is inseparable from your vocation. For Christ also suffered for you, leaving you [His personal] example, so that you should follow on in His footsteps.

22 He was guilty of no sin; neither was deceit (guile) ever found on His lips. [Isa. 53:9.]

23 When He was reviled *and* insulted, He did not revile *or* offer insult in return; [when] He was abused *and* suffered He made no threats [of vengeance]; but He trusted [Himself and everything] to Him Who judges fairly.

---

i) ASV.
j) Wycliffe.
k) J. Rawson Lumby in "Speaker's Commentary."
l) Literal meaning.

Living New Testament

7 Yes, He is very precious to you who believe; and to those who reject Him, well—"The same Stone that was rejected by the builders has become the Cornerstone, the most honored and important part of the building."

8 And the Scriptures also say, "He is the Stone that some will stumble over, and the Rock that will make them fall." They will stumble because they will not listen to God's Word, nor obey it, and so this punishment must follow—that they will fall.

9 But you are not like that, for you have been chosen by God Himself—you are priests of the King, you are holy and pure, you are God's very own—all this so that you may show to others how God called you out of the darkness into His wonderful light.

10 Once you were less than nothing; now you are God's own. Once you knew very little of God's kindness; now your very lives have been changed by it.

11 Dear brothers, you are only visitors here. Since your real home is in heaven I beg you to keep away from the evil pleasures of this world; they are not for you, for they fight against your very souls.

12 Be careful how you behave among your unsaved neighbors; for then, even if they are suspicious of you and talk against you, they will end up praising God for your good works when Christ returns.

13 For the Lord's sake, obey every law of your government: those of the king as head of the state,

14 And those of the king's officers, for he has sent them to punish all who do wrong, and to honor those who do right.

15 It is God's will that your good lives should silence those who foolishly condemn the Gospel without knowing what it can do for them, having never experienced its power.

16 You are free from the law, but that doesn't mean you are free to do wrong. Live as those who are free to do only God's will at all times.

17 Show respect for everyone. Love Christians everywhere. Fear God and honor the government.

18 Servants, you must respect your masters and do whatever they tell you—not only if they are kind and reasonable, but even if they are tough and cruel.

19 Praise the Lord if you are punished for doing right!

20 Of course, you get no credit for being patient if you are beaten for doing wrong; but if you do right and suffer for it, and are patient beneath the blows, God is well pleased.

21 This suffering is all part of the work God has given you. Christ, who suffered for you, is your example. Follow in His steps:

22 He never sinned, never told a lie,

23 Never answered back when insulted; when He suffered He did not threaten to get even; He left His case in the hands of God who always judges fairly.

Revised Standard

7 To you therefore who believe, he is precious,
but for those who do not believe,
"The very stone which the builders rejected
has become the head of the corner,"
8 and
"A stone that will make men stumble,
a rock that will make them fall";
for they stumble because they disobey the
word, as they were destined to do.
9 But you are a chosen race, a royal priesthood, a holy nation, God's own people,[e] that
you may declare the wonderful deeds of him
who called you out of darkness into his marvelous light. 10 Once you were no people but
now you are God's people; once you had not
received mercy but now you have received
mercy.

The Christian and unbelievers

11 Beloved, I beseech you as aliens and
exiles to abstain from the passions of the
flesh that wage war against your soul. 12 Maintain good conduct among the Gentiles, so that
in case they speak against you as wrongdoers,
they may see your good deeds and glorify
God on the day of visitation.

The Christian and the state

13 Be subject for the Lord's sake to every
human institution,[f] whether it be to the emperor as supreme, 14 or to governors as sent
by him to punish those who do wrong and to
praise those who do right. 15 For it is God's
will that by doing right you should put to
silence the ignorance of foolish men. 16 Live
as free men, yet without using your freedom
as a pretext for evil; but live as servants of
God. 17 Honor all men. Love the brotherhood.
Fear God. Honor the emperor.

The servant and his master

18 Servants, be submissive to your masters with all respect, not only to the kind and
gentle but also to the overbearing. 19 For one
is approved if, mindful of God, he endures
pain while suffering unjustly. 20 For what
credit is it, if when you do wrong and are
beaten for it you take it patiently? But if
when you do right and suffer for it you take
it patiently, you have God's approval.

Christ our great example

21 For to this you have been called, because
Christ also suffered for you, leaving you an
example, that you should follow in his steps.
22 He committed no sin; no guile was found
on his lips. 23 When he was reviled, he did
not revile in return: when he suffered, he did
not threaten; but he trusted to him who

---

[e] Greek *a people for his possession*
[f] Or *every institution ordained for men*

King James

24 Who his own self bare our sins in his own body on the tree, that we, being dead to sins, should live unto righteousness: by whose stripes ye were healed.

25 For ye were as sheep going astray; but are now returned unto the Shepherd and Bishop of your souls.

Amplified

24 He personally bore our sins in His [own] body to the tree [m][as to an altar and offered Himself on it], that we might die (cease to exist) to sin and live to righteousness. By His wounds you have been healed.

25 For you were going astray like [so many] sheep, but now you have come back to the Shepherd and Guardian (the Bishop) of your souls. [Isa. 53:5, 6.]

CHAPTER 3

LIKEWISE, ye wives, *be* in subjection to your own husbands; that, if any obey not the word, they also may without the word be won by the conversation of the wives;

2 While they behold your chaste conversation *coupled* with fear.

3 Whose adorning let it not be that outward *adorning* of plaiting the hair, and of wearing of gold, or of putting on of apparel;

4 But *let it be* the hidden man of the heart, in that which is not corruptible, *even the ornament* of a meek and quiet spirit, which is in the sight of God of great price.

5 For after this manner in the old time the holy women also, who trusted in God, adorned themselves, being in subjection unto their own husbands:

6 Even as Sara obeyed Abraham, calling him lord: whose daughters ye are, as long as ye do well, and are not afraid with any amazement.

7 Likewise, ye husbands, dwell with *them* according to knowledge, giving honour unto the wife, as unto the weaker vessel, and as being heirs together of the grace of life; that your prayers be not hindered.

8 Finally, *be ye* all of one mind, having compassion one of another, love as brethren, *be* pitiful, *be* courteous:

9 Not rendering evil for evil, or railing for railing: but contrariwise blessing; knowing that ye are thereunto called, that ye should inherit a blessing.

CHAPTER 3

IN like manner you married women, be submissive to your own husbands—subordinate yourselves as being secondary to and dependent on them, and adapt yourselves to them. So that even if any do not obey the Word [of God], they may be won over not by discussion but by the [godly] lives of their wives,

2 When they observe the pure *and* modest way in which you conduct yourselves, together with your [n]reverence [for your husband. That is, you are to feel for him all that reverence includes]—[o]to respect, defer to, revere him; [revere means] [o]to honor, esteem (appreciate, prize), and [in the human sense] adore him; [and adore means] [o]to admire, praise, be devoted to, deeply love and [o]enjoy [your husband].

3 Let not yours be the [merely] external adorning with [elaborate] [n]interweaving *and* knotting of the hair, the wearing of jewelry, or changes of clothes;

4 But let it be the inward adorning *and* beauty of the hidden person of the heart, with the incorruptible *and* unfading charm of a gentle and peaceful spirit, which (is not anxious or wrought up, but) is very precious in the sight of God.

5 For it was thus that the pious women of old who hoped in God were (accustomed) to beautify themselves, and were submissive to their husbands—adapting themselves to them as themselves secondary and dependent upon them.

6 It was thus that Sarah obeyed Abraham (following his guidance and acknowledging his headship over her by) calling him lord—master, leader, authority. And you are now her true daughters if you do right and let nothing terrify you—not giving way to hysterical fears or letting anxieties unnerve you.

7 In the same way you married men should live considerately with [your wives], with an [p]intelligent recognition [of the marriage relation], honoring the woman as [physically] the weaker, but [realizing that you] are joint heirs of the grace (God's unmerited favor) of life, in order that your prayers may not be hindered *and* cut off.—Otherwise you cannot pray effectively.

8 Finally, all [of you] should be of one *and* the same mind (united in spirit), sympathizing [with one another], loving [each the others] as brethren (of one household), compassionate *and* courteous—tenderhearted and humble-minded.

9 Never return evil for evil or insult for insult—scolding, tongue-lashing, berating; but on the contrary blessing—praying for their welfare, happiness and protection, and truly pitying and loving them. For *know that* to this you have been called, that you may yourselves inherit a blessing [from God]—obtain a blessing as heirs, bringing welfare and happiness and protection.

---

m) Vincent.
n) Thayer.
o) English synonyms of the preceding to-be-defined word.
p) Vincent.

Living New Testament

24 He personally carried the load of our sins in His own body when He died on the cross, so that we can be finished with sin, and live a good life from now on. For His wounds have healed ours!

25 Like sheep you wandered away from God, but now you have returned to your Shepherd, the Guardian of your souls who keeps you safe from all attacks.

CHAPTER 3

Wives, fit in with your husband's plans; for then if they refuse to listen when you talk to them about the Lord, they will be won by your respectful, pure behavior. Your godly lives will speak to them better than any words.

3 Don't be concerned about the outward beauty that depends on jewelry, or beautiful clothes, or hair arrangement.

4 Be beautiful inside, in your hearts, with the lasting charm of a gentle and quiet spirit which is so precious to God.

5 That kind of deep beauty was seen in the saintly women of old, who trusted God and fitted in with their husbands' plans.

6 Sarah, for instance, obeyed her husband Abraham, honoring him as head of the house. And if you do the same, you will be following in her steps like good daughters and doing what is right; then you will not need to fear [offending your husbands[1]].

7 You husbands must be careful of your wives, being thoughtful of their needs and honoring them as the weaker sex. Remember that you and your wife are partners in receiving God's blessings, and if you don't treat her as you should, your prayers will not get ready answers.

8 And now this word to all of you: You should be like one big happy family, full of sympathy toward each other, loving one another with tender hearts and humble minds.

9 Don't repay evil for evil. Don't snap back at those who say unkind things about you. Instead, pray for God's help for them, for we are to be kind to others, and God will bless us for it.

[1]Implied.

Revised Standard

judges justly. 24He himself bore our sins in
his body on the tree,[g] that we might die to
sin and live to righteousness. By his wounds
you have been healed. 25For you were straying like sheep, but have now returned to the
Shepherd and Guardian of your souls.

The husband and the wife

3 Likewise you wives, be submissive to
your husbands, so that some, though
they do not obey the word, may be won
without a word by the behavior of their
wives, 2when they see your reverent and
chaste behavior. 3Let not yours be the outward adorning with braiding of hair, deco-
ration of gold, and wearing of robes, 4but let
it be the hidden person of the heart with the
imperishable jewel of a gentle and quiet spirit, which in God's sight is very precious. 5So
once the holy women who hoped in God used
to adorn themselves and were submissive to
their husbands, 6as Sarah obeyed Abraham,
calling him lord. And you are now her children if you do right and let nothing terrify
you.
7 Likewise you husbands, live considerately with your wives, bestowing honor on
the woman as the weaker sex, since you are
joint heirs of the grace of life, in order that
your prayers may not be hindered.

Christian conduct in review

8 Finally, all of you, have unity of spirit,
sympathy, love of the brethren, a tender
heart and a humble mind. 9Do not return
evil for evil or reviling for reviling; but on
the contrary bless, for to this you have been
called, that you may obtain a blessing. 10For

[g] Or *carried up . . . to the tree*

King James

10 For he that will love life, and see good days, let him refrain his tongue from evil, and his lips that they speak no guile:

11 Let him eschew evil, and do good; let him seek peace, and ensue it.

12 For the eyes of the Lord *are* over the righteous, and his ears *are open* unto their prayers: but the face of the Lord *is* against them that do evil.

13 And who *is* he that will harm you, if ye be followers of that which is good?

14 But and if ye suffer for righteousness' sake, happy *are ye:* and be not afraid of their terror, neither be troubled;

15 But sanctify the Lord God in your hearts: and *be* ready always to *give* an answer to every man that asketh you a reason of the hope that is in you with meekness and fear:

16 Having a good conscience; that, whereas they speak evil of you, as of evildoers, they may be ashamed that falsely accuse your good conversation in Christ.

17 For *it is* better, if the will of God be so, that ye suffer for well-doing, than for evil-doing.

18 For Christ also hath once suffered for sins, the just for the unjust, that he might bring us to God, being put to death in the flesh, but quickened by the Spirit:

19 By which also he went and preached unto the spirits in prison;

20 Which sometime were disobedient, when once the long-suffering of God waited in the days of Noah, while the ark was a-preparing, wherein few, that is, eight souls were saved by water.

21 The like figure whereunto *even* baptism doth also now save us (not the putting away of the filth of the flesh, but the answer of a good conscience toward God,) by the resurrection of Jesus Christ:

22 Who is gone into heaven, and is on the right hand of God; angels and authorities and powers being made subject unto him.

CHAPTER 4

FORASMUCH then as Christ hath suffered for us in the flesh, arm yourselves likewise with the same mind: for he that hath suffered in the flesh hath ceased from sin;

Amplified

10 For let him who wants to enjoy life and see good days (good whether apparent or not), keep his tongue free from evil, and his lips from guile (treachery, deceit).

11 Let him turn away from wickedness *and* shun it; and let him do right. Let him search for peace—harmony, undisturbedness from fears, agitating passions and moral conflicts—and seek it eagerly.—Do not merely desire peaceful relations [with God, with your fellowmen, and with yourself], but pursue, go after them!

12 For the eyes of the Lord are upon the righteous—those who are upright and in right standing with God—and His ears are attentive to their prayer. But the face of the Lord is against those who practice evil—to oppose them, to frustrate and defeat them. [Ps. 34:12-16.]

13 Now who is there to hurt you if you are [q]zealous followers of that which is good?

14 But even in case you should suffer for the sake of righteousness, [you are] blessed—happy, to be envied. Do not dread *or* be afraid of their threats, nor be disturbed [by their opposition].

15 But in your hearts set Christ apart as holy [and acknowledge Him] as Lord. Always be ready to give a logical defense to any one who asks you to account for the hope that is in you, but do it courteously and respectfully. [Isa. 8:12, 13.]

16 [And see to it that] your conscience is [r]entirely clear, so that, when you are falsely accused as evildoers, those who threaten you abusively *and* revile your right behavior in Christ may come to be ashamed [of slandering your good lives].

17 For [it is] better to suffer [unjustly] for doing right, if that should be God's will, than to suffer [justly] for doing wrong.

18 For Christ, the Messiah, [Himself] died for sins once [s]for all, the Righteous for the unrighteous—the Just for the unjust, the Innocent for the guilty—that He might bring us to God. In His human body He was put to death but He was made alive in the spirit,

19 In which He went and preached to the spirits in prison,

20 [The souls of those] who long before in the days of Noah had been disobedient, when God's patience waited during the building of the ark in which a few [people], actually eight in number, were saved through water. [Gen. 6-8.]

21 And baptism, which is a figure [of their deliverance], does now also save you [from inward questionings and fears], not by the removing of outward body filth (bathing), but by [providing you with] the answer of a good and clear conscience [inward cleanness and peace] before God, [because you are demonstrating what you believe to be yours] through the resurrection of Jesus Christ.

22 [And He] has now entered into heaven and is at the right hand of God, with [all] angels and authorities and powers made subservient to Him.

CHAPTER 4

SO, since Christ suffered in the flesh [[t]for us, for you] arm yourselves with the same thought *and* [u]purpo[se] [patiently to suffer rather than fail to please God]. F[or] whoever has suffered in the flesh [having [v]the mind o[f] Christ] has done with [intentional] sin—has stopped plea[s]ing himself and the world, and pleases God.

q) Best authorities read "zealous."
r) Vincent: "unimpaired."
s) Thayer.
t) Some ancient authorities read "for us," some "for you."
u) Abbott-Smith.
v) Cambridge Bible (—Gray and Adams).

Living New Testament

10 If you want a happy, good life, keep control of your tongue, and guard your lips from telling lies.

11 Turn away from evil and do good. Try to live in peace even if you must run after it to catch and hold it!

12 For the Lord is watching His children, listening to their prayers; but the Lord's face is hard against those who do evil.

13 Usually no one will hurt you for wanting to do good.

14 But even if they should, you are to be envied, for God will reward you for it.

15 Quietly trust yourself to Christ your Lord and if anybody asks why you believe as you do, be ready to tell him, and do it in a gentle and respectful way.

16 Do what is right; then, if men speak against you, calling you evil names, they will become ashamed of themselves for falsely accusing you when you have only done what is good.

17 Remember, if God wants you to suffer, it is better to suffer for doing good than for doing wrong!

18 Christ also suffered. He died once for the sins of all us guilty sinners, although He Himself was innocent of any sin at any time, that He might bring us safely home to God. But though His body died, His spirit lived on,

19 And it was in the spirit that He visited the spirits in prison, and preached to them—

20 Spirits of those who, long before in the days of Noah, had refused to listen to God, though He waited patiently for them while Noah was building the ark. Yet only eight persons were saved from drowning in that terrible flood.

21 (That, by the way, is what baptism pictures for us: in baptism we show that we have been saved from death and doom by the resurrection of Christ;[2] not because our bodies are washed clean by the water, but because in being baptized we are turning to God and asking Him to cleanse our *hearts* from sin.)

22 And now Christ is in heaven, sitting in the place of honor next to God the Father, with all the angels and powers of heaven bowing before Him and obeying Him.

CHAPTER 4

Since Christ suffered and underwent pain, you must have the same attitude He did; you must be ready to suffer, so. For remember, when your body suffers, sin loses its power,

Or, "Baptism, which corresponds to this, now saves you through the Resurrection."

Revised Standard

"He that would love life
and see good days,
let him keep his tongue from evil
and his lips from speaking guile;
11 let him turn away from evil and do right;
let him seek peace and pursue it.
12 For the eyes of the Lord are upon the righteous,
and his ears are open to their prayer.
But the face of the Lord is against those that do evil."

The Christian and persecution

13 Now who is there to harm you if you
are zealous for what is right? 14 But even if
you do suffer for righteousness' sake, you will
be blessed. Have no fear of them, nor be
troubled, 15 but in your hearts reverence
Christ as Lord. Always be prepared to make
a defense to any one who calls you to account for the hope that is in you, yet do it
with gentleness and reverence; 16 and keep
your conscience clear, so that, when you are
abused, those who revile your good behavior
in Christ may be put to shame. 17 For it is
better to suffer for doing right, if that should
be God's will, than for doing wrong. 18 For
Christ also died[h] for sins once for all, the
righteous for the unrighteous, that he might
bring us to God, being put to death in the
flesh but made alive in the spirit; 19 in which
he went and preached to the spirits in prison,
20 who formerly did not obey, when God's
patience waited in the days of Noah, during
the building of the ark, in which a few, that
is, eight persons, were saved through water.
21 Baptism, which corresponds to this, now
saves you, not as a removal of dirt from the
body but as an appeal to God for a clear
conscience, through the resurrection of Jesus
Christ, 22 who has gone into heaven and is
at the right hand of God, with angels, authorities, and powers subject to him.

The Christian in the end times

4 Since therefore Christ suffered in the flesh,[i] arm yourselves with the same thought, for whoever has suffered in the flesh

[h] Other ancient authorities read *suffered*
[i] Other ancient authorities add *for us;* some *for you*

King James

2 That he no longer should live the rest of *his* time in the flesh to the lusts of men, but to the will of God.

3 For the time past of *our* life may suffice us to have wrought the will of the Gentiles, when we walked in lasciviousness, lusts, excess of wine, revellings, banquetings, and abominable idolatries:

4 Wherein they think it strange that ye run not with *them* to the same excess of riot, speaking evil of *you:*

5 Who shall give account to him that is ready to judge the quick and the dead.

6 For for this cause was the gospel preached also to them that are dead, that they might be judged according to men in the flesh, but live according to God in the spirit.

7 But the end of all things is at hand: be ye therefore sober, and watch unto prayer.

8 And above all things have fervent charity among yourselves: for charity shall cover the multitude of sins.

9 Use hospitality one to another without grudging.

10 As every man hath received the gift, *even so* minister the same one to another, as good stewards of the manifold grace of God.

11 If any man speak, *let him speak* as the oracles of God; if any man minister, *let him do it* as of the ability which God giveth: that God in all things may be glorified through Jesus Christ, to whom be praise and dominion for ever and ever. Amen.

12 Beloved, think it not strange concerning the fiery trial which is to try you, as though some strange thing happened unto you:

13 But rejoice, inasmuch as ye are partakers of Christ's sufferings; that, when his glory shall be revealed, ye may be glad also with exceeding joy.

14 If ye be reproached for the name of Christ, happy *are ye;* for the spirit of glory and of God resteth upon you: on their part he is evil spoken of, but on your part he is glorified.

15 But let none of you suffer as a murderer, or *as* a thief, or *as* an evildoer, or as a busybody in other men's matters.

16 Yet if *any man suffer* as a Christian, let him not be ashamed; but let him glorify God on this behalf.

Amplified

2 So that he can no longer spend the rest of his natural life living by [his] human appetites *and* desires, but [he lives] for what God wills.

3 For the time that is past already suffices for doing what the Gentiles like to do, living (as you have done) in shameless, insolent wantonness, in lustful desires, drunkenness, reveling, drinking bouts *and* abominable, lawless idolatries.

4 They are astonished *and* think it very queer that you do not now run hand in hand with them in the same excesses of dissipation, and they abuse [you].

5 But they will have to give an account to Him Who is ready to judge *and* pass sentence on the living and the dead.

6 For this is why the good news (the Gospel) was preached [[w]in their lifetime] even to the dead, that though judged in fleshly bodies as men are, they might live in the spirit as God does.

7 But the end *and* culmination of all things has now come near; keep sound-minded *and* self-restrained and alert therefore for [the practice of] prayer.

8 Above all things have intense *and* unfailing love for one another, for love covers a multitude of sins—forgives and [x]disregards the offenses of others. [Prov. 10:12.]

9 Practice hospitality to one another—that is, those of the household of faith. (Be hospitable, that is, be a lover of strangers, with brotherly affection for the unknown guests, the foreigners, the poor and all others who come your way who are of Christ's body.) And [in each instance] do it ungrudgingly—cordially and graciously without complaining [but as representing Him].

10 As each of you has received a gift (a particular spiritual talent, a gracious divine endowment), employ it for one another as [befits] good trustees of God's many-sided grace—faithful stewards of the [x]extremely diverse [powers and gifts granted to Christians by] unmerited favor.

11 Whoever speaks, [let him do it as one who utters] oracles of God; whoever renders service, [let him do it] as with the strength which God furnishes [x]abundantly; so that in all things God may be glorified through Jesus Christ, the Messiah. To Him be the glory and dominion for ever and ever—through endless ages. Amen—so be it.

12 Beloved, do not be amazed *and* bewildered at th fiery ordeal which is taking place to test your quality, a though something strange—unusual and alien to you an your position—were befalling you.

13 But in so far as you are sharing Christ's sufferings rejoice, so that when His glory (full of radiance an splendor) is revealed you may also rejoice with triumph—exultantly.

14 If you are censured *and* suffer abuse [because yo bear] the name of Christ, blessed [are you]—happy, fortu nate, [y]to be envied, [z]with life-joy and satisfaction in God favor and salvation, regardless of your outward condition—because the Spirit of glory, the Spirit of God, is restir upon you. *On their part He is blasphemed, but on yo part He is glorified.* [Isa. 11:2.]

15 But let none of you suffer as a murderer, or a thie or any sort of criminal; or as a mischief-maker (a me dler) in the affairs of others—infringing on their rights.

16 But if [one is ill-treated and suffers] as a Christi [which he is contemptuously called], let him not ashamed, but give glory to God that he is [deem worthy] to suffer in this name.

---

w) Many commentators.
x) Thayer.
y) Souter.
z) Cremer.

Living New Testament

2 And you won't be spending the rest of your life chasing after evil desires, but will be anxious to do the will of God.

3 You have had enough in the past of the evil things the godless enjoy—sex sin, lust, getting drunk, wild parties, drinking bouts, and the worship of idols—and other terrible sins.[1]

4 Of course, your former friends will be very surprised when you don't eagerly join them any more in the wicked things they do, and they will laugh at you in contempt and scorn.

5 But just remember that they must face the Judge of all, living and dead; they will be punished for the way they have lived.

6 That is why the Good News was preached even to those who were dead[2]—killed by the flood[3]—so that although their bodies were punished with death, they could still live in their spirits as God lives.

7 The end of the world is coming soon. Therefore be earnest, thoughtful men of prayer.

8 Most important of all, continue to show deep love for each other, for love makes up for many of your faults.[4]

9 Cheerfully share your home with those who need a meal or a place to stay for the night.

10 God has given each of you some special abilities; be sure to use them to help each other, passing on to others God's many kinds of blessings.

11 Are you called to preach? Then preach as though God Himself were speaking through you. Are you called to help others? Do it with all the strength and energy that God supplies, so that God will be glorified through Jesus Christ—to Him be glory and power forever and ever. Amen.

12 Dear friends, don't be bewildered or surprised when you go through the fiery trials ahead, for this is no strange, unusual thing that is going to happen to you.

13 Instead, be really glad—because these trials will make you partners with Christ in His suffering, and afterwards you will have the wonderful joy of sharing His glory in that coming day when it will be displayed.

14 Be happy if you are cursed and insulted for being a Christian, for when that happens the Spirit of God will come upon you with great glory.[5]

15 Don't let me hear of your suffering for murdering or stealing or making trouble or being a busybody and prying into other people's affairs.

16 But it is no shame to suffer for being a Christian. Praise God for the privilege of being in Christ's family and being called by His wonderful name!

Literally, "lawless idolatries."
Peter's meaning is unclear to all commentators. God's program 'or the unsaved today is "the wages of sin is death and after that :he judgment." The Bible does not teach that those who are alive oday will have a second chance to hear and accept the Gospel. 'or this reason some believe that verse 6 would be more accurately nterpreted: "And that is why the Good News of salvation was preached (in their lifetime) to those who were going to die. For hough their bodies would be given the death penalty, like anyone lse, they could still be alive in the spirit, as God is."
mplied. See I Peter 3:19, 20.
)r, "love overlooks each other's many faults."
)r, "the glory of the Spirit of God is being seen in you."

Revised Standard

has ceased from sin, [2]so as to live for the rest
of the time in the flesh no longer by human
passions but by the will of God. [3]Let the
time that is past suffice for doing what the
Gentiles like to do, living in licentiousness,
passions, drunkenness, revels, carousing, and
lawless idolatry. [4]They are surprised that
you do not now join them in the same wild
profligacy, and they abuse you; [5]but they
will give account to him who is ready to
judge the living and the dead. [6]For this is
why the gospel was preached even to the
dead, that though judged in the flesh like
men, they might live in the spirit like God.
7 The end of all things is at hand; therefore keep sane and sober for your prayers.
[8]Above all hold unfailing your love for one
another, since love covers a multitude of
sins. [9]Practice hospitality ungrudgingly to
one another. [10]As each has received a gift,
employ it for one another, as good stewards
of God's varied grace: [11]whoever speaks, as
one who utters oracles of God; whoever
renders service, as one who renders it by
the strength which God supplies; in order
that in everything God may be glorified
through Jesus Christ. To him belong glory
and dominion for ever and ever. Amen.

The Christian and suffering

12 Beloved, do not be surprised at the
fiery ordeal which comes upon you to prove
you, as though something strange were happening to you. [13]But rejoice in so far as you
share Christ's sufferings, that you may also
rejoice and be glad when his glory is revealed. [14]If you are reproached for the name
of Christ, you are blessed, because the spirit
of glory[j] and of God rests upon you. [15]But
let none of you suffer as a murderer, or a
thief, or a wrongdoer, or a mischief-maker;
[16]yet if one suffers as a Christian, let him
not be ashamed, but under that name let

---

j Other ancient authorities insert *and of power*

King James

17 For the time *is come* that judgment must begin at the house of God: and if *it* first *begin* at us, what shall the end *be* of them that obey not the gospel of God?

18 And if the righteous scarcely be saved, where shall the ungodly and the sinner appear?

19 Wherefore let them that suffer according to the will of God commit the keeping of their souls to *him* in well doing, as unto a faithful Creator.

Amplified

17 For the time [has arrived] for judgment to begin with the household of God; and if it begins with us, what will [be] the end of those who do not respect *or* believe *or* obey the good news (the Gospel) of God?

18 And if the righteous are barely saved, what will become of the godless and wicked? [Prov. 11:31.]

19 Therefore, those who are ill-treated *and* suffer in accordance with God's will must do right, and commit their souls (in charge as a deposit) to the One Who created them *and* will never fail [them].

CHAPTER 5

THE elders which are among you I exhort, who am also an elder, and a witness of the sufferings of Christ, and also a partaker of the glory that shall be revealed:

2 Feed the flock of God which is among you, taking the oversight *thereof*, not by constraint, but willingly; not for filthy lucre, but of a ready mind;

3 Neither as being lords over *God's* heritage, but being ensamples of the flock.

4 And when the chief Shepherd shall appear, ye shall receive a crown of glory that fadeth not away.

5 Likewise, ye younger, submit yourselves unto the elder. Yea, all *of you* be subject one to another, and be clothed with humility: for God resisteth the proud, and giveth grace to the humble.

6 Humble yourselves therefore under the mighty hand of God, that he may exalt you in due time:

7 Casting all your care upon him; for he careth for you.

8 Be sober, be vigilant; because your adversary the devil, as a roaring lion, walketh about, seeking whom he may devour:

9 Whom resist stedfast in the faith, knowing that the same afflictions are accomplished in your brethren that are in the world.

10 But the God of all grace, who hath called us unto his eternal glory by Christ Jesus, after that ye have suffered a while, make you perfect, stablish, strengthen, settle *you*.

CHAPTER 5

I WARN *and* counsel the elders among you—the pastors and spiritual guides of the church—as a fellow elder and as an eyewitness [called to testify] of the sufferings of Christ, as well as a sharer in the glory (the honor and splendor) that is to be revealed (disclosed, unfolded):

2 Tend—nurture, guard, guide and fold—the flock of God that is [your responsibility], not by coercion *or* constraint but willingly; not dishonorably motivated by the advantages *and* profits [belonging to the office] but eagerly *and* cheerfully.

3 Not (as arrogant, dictatorial and overbearing persons) domineering over those in your charge, but being examples—patterns and models of Christian living—to the flock (the congregation).

4 And [then] when the Chief Shepherd is revealed you will win the [a]conqueror's crown of glory.

5 Likewise you that are younger *and* of lesser rank be subject to the elders—the ministers and spiritual guides of the church, giving them due respect and yielding to their counsel. Clothe (apron) yourselves, all of you, with humility—as the garb of a servant, [b]so that its covering cannot possibly be stripped from you, with freedom from pride and arrogance—toward one another. For God sets Himself against the proud—the insolent, the overbearing, the disdainful, the presumptuous, the boastful, and opposes, frustrates and defeats them—but gives grace (favor, blessing) to the humble. [Prov. 3:34.]

6 Therefore humble yourselves (demote, lower yourselves in your own estimation) under the mighty hand of God, that in due time He may exalt you.

7 Casting the [c]whole of your care—all your anxieties, all your worries, all your concerns, [c]once and for all—on Him; for He cares for you affectionately, *and* cares about you [c]watchfully. [Ps. 55:22.]

8 Be well-balanced—temperate, sober-minded; be vigilant *and* cautious at all times, for that enemy of yours, the devil, roams around like a lion roaring [[c]in fierce hunger], seeking someone to seize upon *and* devour.

9 Withstand him; be firm in faith [against his onset],—rooted, established, strong, immovable and determined—knowing that the same ([c]identical) sufferings are appointed to your brotherhood (the whole body of Christians) throughout the world.

10 And after you have suffered a little while, the God of all grace—Who imparts all blessing and favor—Who has called you to His [own] eternal glory in Christ *Jesus*, will Himself complete *and* make you what you ought to be, establish *and* ground you securely, *and* strengthen (and [d]settle) you.

a) Vincent: "In Paul . . . always the *conqueror's* crown."
b) Bengel.
c) Vincent.
d) Many ancient authorities so read.

Living New Testament

17 For the time has come for judgment, and it must begin first among God's own children. And if even we who are Christians must be judged, what terrible fate awaits those who have never believed in the Lord?

18 If the righteous are barely saved, what chance will the godless have?

19 So if you are suffering according to God's will, keep on doing what is right and trust yourself to the God who made you, for He will never fail you.

Revised Standard

him glorify God. 17For the time has come
for judgment to begin with the household of
God; and if it begins with us, what will be
the end of those who do not obey the gospel
of God? 18And

"If the righteous man is scarcely saved,
where will the impious and sinner appear?"

19Therefore let those who suffer according
to God's will do right and entrust their souls
to a faithful Creator.

CHAPTER 5

And now, a word to you elders of the church. I, too, am an elder; with my own eyes I saw Christ dying on the cross; and I, too, will share His glory and His honor when He returns. Fellow elders, this is my plea to you:

2 Feed the flock of God; care for it willingly, not grudgingly; not for what you will get out of it, but because you are eager to serve the Lord.

3 Don't be tyrants, but lead them by your good example,

4 And when the Head Shepherd comes, your reward will be a never-ending share in His glory and honor.

5 You younger men, follow the leadership of those who are older. And all of you serve each other with humble spirits, for God gives special blessings to those who are humble, but sets Himself against those who are proud.

6 If you will humble yourselves under the mighty hand of God, in His good time He will lift you up.

7 Let Him have all your worries and cares, for He is always thinking about you and watching everything that concerns you.

8 Be careful—watch out for attacks from Satan, your great enemy. He prowls around like a hungry, roaring lion, looking for some victim to tear apart.

9 Stand firm when he attacks. Trust the Lord; and remember that other Christians all around the world are going through these sufferings too.

10 After you have suffered a little while, our God, who is full of kindness through Christ, will give you His eternal glory. He personally will come and pick you up, and set you firmly in place, and make you stronger than ever.

Christian life in God's care

5 So I exhort the elders among you, as a
fellow elder and a witness of the sufferings of Christ as well as a partaker in the
glory that is to be revealed. 2Tend the flock
of God that is your charge,[k] not by constraint but willingly,[l] not for shameful
gain but eagerly, 3not as domineering over
those in your charge but being examples
to the flock. 4And when the chief Shepherd
is manifested you will obtain the unfading
crown of glory. 5Likewise you that are
younger be subject to the elders. Clothe
yourselves, all of you, with humility toward
one another, for "God opposes the proud,
but gives grace to the humble."

6 Humble yourselves therefore under the
mighty hand of God, that in due time he may
exalt you. 7Cast all your anxieties on him,
for he cares about you. 8Be sober, be watchful. Your adversary the devil prowls around
like a roaring lion, seeking some one to devour. 9Resist him, firm in your faith, knowing that the same experience of suffering is
required of your brotherhood throughout the
world. 10And after you have suffered a little
while, the God of all grace, who has called
you to his eternal glory in Christ, will himself restore, establish, and strengthen[m] you.

---

[k] Other ancient authorities add *exercising the oversight*

[l] Other ancient authorities add *as God would have you*

[m] Other ancient authorities read *restore, establish, strengthen and settle*

King James

11 To him *be* glory and dominion for ever and ever. Amen.

12 By Silvanus, a faithful brother unto you, as I suppose, I have written briefly, exhorting, and testifying that this is the true grace of God wherein ye stand.

13 The *church that is* at Babylon, elected together with *you,* saluteth you; and *so doth* Marcus my son.

14 Greet ye one another with a kiss of charity. Peace *be* with you all that are in Christ Jesus. Amen.

Amplified

11 To Him be the dominion—power, authority, rule—forever and ever. Amen—so be it.

12 By Silvanus, a true (loyal, consistent, incorruptible) brother, as I consider him, I have written briefly to you, to counsel *and* urge *and* stimulate [you] and to declare [to you] that this is the true [account of the] grace (the undeserved favor) of God. Be steadfast *and* persevere in it.

13 She [your sister-church(?) here] in Babylon, [who is] elect (chosen) with [yourselves], sends you greetings, and [so does] my son (disciple) Mark.

14 Salute one another with a kiss of love—the symbol of mutual affection. To all of you that are in Christ *Jesus,* the Messiah, may there be peace—[e]every kind of peace (blessing), especially peace with God, and [f]freedom from fears, agitating passions and moral conflicts. *Amen—so be it.*

---

e) Thayer.
f) Webster, in definition of "peace" in this sense.

Living New Testament

11 To Him be all power over all things, forever and ever. Amen.

12 I am sending this note to you through the courtesy of Silvanus who is, in my opinion, a very faithful brother. I hope I have encouraged you by this letter for I have given you a true statement of the way God blesses. What I have told you here should help you to stand firmly in His love.

13 My wife[1] here in Rome—she is your sister in the Lord—sends you her greetings; so does my son Mark.

14 Give each other the handshake of Christian love. Peace be to all of you who are in Christ.

Peter

Revised Standard

11To him be the dominion for ever and ever. Amen.

Conclusion and benediction

12 By Silvanus, a faithful brother as I regard him, I have written briefly to you, exhorting and declaring that this is the true
grace of God; stand fast in it. 13She who is
at Babylon, who is likewise chosen, sends you
greetings; and so does my son Mark. 14Greet
one another with the kiss of love.
Peace to all of you that are in Christ.

---

terally, "She who is at Babylon, is likewise chosen"; but bylon was the Christian nickname for Rome, and the "she" thought by many to be Peter's wife to whom reference is de in Matthew 8:14, I Corinthians 9:5, etc. Others believe s should read "Your sister church here in Babylon salutes you, d so does my son Mark."

King James

THE SECOND EPISTLE GENERAL OF

Peter

CHAPTER 1

SIMON Peter, a servant and an apostle of Jesus Christ, to them that have obtained like precious faith with us through the righteousness of God and our Saviour Jesus Christ:

2 Grace and peace be multiplied unto you through the knowledge of God, and of Jesus our Lord,

3 According as his divine power hath given unto us all things that *pertain* unto life and godliness, through the knowledge of him that hath called us to glory and virtue:

4 Whereby are given unto us exceeding great and precious promises: that by these ye might be partakers of the divine nature, having escaped the corruption that is in the world through lust.

5 And beside this, giving all diligence, add to your faith virtue; and to virtue knowledge;

6 And to knowledge temperance; and to temperance patience; and to patience godliness;

7 And to godliness brotherly kindness; and to brotherly kindness charity.

8 For if these things be in you, and abound, they make *you that ye shall* neither *be* barren nor unfruitful in the knowledge of our Lord Jesus Christ.

9 But he that lacketh these things is blind, and cannot see afar off, and hath forgotten that he was purged from his old sins.

10 Wherefore the rather, brethren, give diligence to make your calling and election sure: for if ye do these things, ye shall never fall:

11 For so an entrance shall be ministered unto you abundantly into the everlasting kingdom of our Lord and Saviour Jesus Christ.

12 Wherefore I will not be negligent to put you always in remembrance of these things, though ye know *them*, and be established in the present truth,

13 Yea, I think it meet, as long as I am in this tabernacle, to stir you up by putting *you* in remembrance;

14 Knowing that shortly I must put off *this* my tabernacle, even as our Lord Jesus Christ hath shewed me.

Amplified

THE SECOND LETTER
OF

Peter

CHAPTER 1

SIMON Peter, a servant and apostle (special messenger) of Jesus Christ, to those who have received (obtained an equal privilege of) like precious faith with ourselves in *and* through the righteousness of our God and Savior Jesus Christ:

2 May grace (God's favor) and peace, (which is [a]perfect well-being, all necessary good, all spiritual prosperity and [b]freedom from fears and agitating passions and moral conflicts) be multiplied to you in (the full, personal, [d]precise and correct) knowledge of God and of Jesus our Lord.

3 For His divine power has bestowed upon us all things that [are requisite and suited] to life and godliness, through the ([c]full, personal) knowledge of Him Who called us by *and* to His own glory and excellence (virtue).

4 By means of these He has bestowed on us His precious and exceedingly great promises, so that through them you may escape (by flight) from the moral decay (rottenness and corruption) that is in the world because of covetousness (lust and greed), and become sharers (partakers) of the divine nature.

5 For this very reason, [c]adding your diligence [to the divine promises], employ every effort in [c]exercising your faith to develop virtue (excellence, resolution, Christian energy); and in [exercising] virtue [develop] knowledge (intelligence),

6 And in [exercising] knowledge [develop] self-control and in [exercising] self-control [develop] steadfastness (patience, endurance), and in [exercising] steadfastness [develop] godliness (piety),

7 And in [exercising] godliness [develop] brotherly affection, and in [exercising] brotherly affection [develop] Christian love.

8 For as these qualities are yours and increasingl abound in you, they will keep [you] from being idle o unfruitful unto the ([e]full personal) knowledge of ou Lord Jesus Christ, the Messiah, the Anointed One.

9 For whoever lacks these qualities is blind, [[e]spiritua ly] shortsighted, [f]seeing only what is near to him; and ha become oblivious [of the fact] that he was cleansed fro his old sins.

10 Because of this, brethren, be all the more solicito *and* eager to make sure (to ratify, to strengthen, to mak steadfast) your calling and election; for if you do this yc will never stumble *or* fall.

11 Thus there will be richly *and* abundantly provide for you entry into the eternal kingdom of our Lord a Savior Jesus Christ.

12 So I intend always to remind you about the things, although indeed you know them and are firm in t truth that [you] now [hold].

13 I think it right, as long as I am in this tabernac (tent, body), to stir you up by way of remembrance;

14 Since I know that the laying aside of this body mine will come speedily, as our Lord Jesus Christ ma clear to me.

---

a) Matthew Henry.
b) Webster, defining "peace" in this sense.
c) Vincent.
d) Thayer.
e) Vincent.
f) Rotherham's "Emphasized Bible."

Living New Testament

II Peter

CHAPTER 1

From: Simon Peter, a servant and missionary of Jesus
Christ.
To: All of you who have our kind of faith. The faith I
speak of is the kind that Jesus Christ our God and Savior
gives to us. How precious it is, and how just and good He
is to give this same faith to each of us.
2 Do you want more and more of God's kindness and
peace? Then learn to know Him better and better.
3 For as you know Him better, He will give you,
through His great power, everything you need for living a
truly good life: He even shares His own glory and His
own goodness with us!
4 And by that same mighty power He has given us all
the other rich and wonderful blessings He promised; for
instance, the promise to save us from the lust and rottenness all around us, and to give us His own character.
5 But to obtain these gifts, you need more than faith;
you must also work hard to be good, and even that is not
enough. For then you must learn to know God better and
discover what He wants you to do.
6 Next, learn to put aside your own desires so that you
will become patient and godly, gladly letting God have His
way with you.
7 This will make possible the next step, which is for
you to enjoy other people and to like them, and finally
you will grow to love them deeply.
8 The more you go on in this way, the more you will
grow strong spiritually and become fruitful and useful to
our Lord Jesus Christ.
9 But anyone who fails to go after these additions to
aith is blind indeed, or at least very shortsighted, and has
orgotten that God delivered him from the old life of sin
o that now he can live a strong, good life for the Lord.
10 So, dear brothers, work hard to prove that you
eally are among those God has called and chosen, and
hen you will never stumble or fall away.
11 And God will open wide the gates of heaven for you
o enter into the eternal kingdom of our Lord and Savior
esus Christ.
12 I plan to keep on reminding you of these things
ven though you already know them and are really getting
long quite well!
13, 14 But the Lord Jesus Christ has showed me that
y days here on earth are numbered, and I am soon to
e. As long as I am still here I intend to keep sending
ese reminders to you,

Revised Standard

THE SECOND LETTER OF

Peter

Salutation

1 Simon Peter, a servant and apostle of
Jesus Christ,
To those who have obtained a faith of
equal standing with ours in the righteousness of our God and Savior Jesus Christ:[a]
2 May grace and peace be multiplied to
you in the knowledge of God and of Jesus
our Lord.

The growth of true knowledge

3 His divine power has granted to us all
things that pertain to life and godliness,
through the knowledge of him who called
us to[b] his own glory and excellence, [4]by
which he has granted to us his precious and
very great promises, that through these you
may escape from the corruption that is in the
world because of passion, and become partakers of the divine nature. [5]For this very
reason make every effort to supplement your
faith with virtue, and virtue with knowledge,
[6]and knowledge with self-control, and self-
control with steadfastness, and steadfastness
with godliness, [7]and godliness with brotherly
affection, and brotherly affection with love.
[8]For if these things are yours and abound,
they keep you from being ineffective or unfruitful in the knowledge of our Lord Jesus
Christ. [9]For whoever lacks these things is
blind and shortsighted and has forgotten that
he was cleansed from his old sins. [10]There-
fore, brethren, be the more zealous to confirm your call and election, for if you do
this you will never fall; [11]so there will be
richly provided for you an entrance into the
eternal kingdom of our Lord and Savior
Jesus Christ.

The basis of true knowledge

12 Therefore I intend always to remind
you of these things, though you know them
and are established in the truth that you have.
[13]I think it right, as long as I am in this
body,[c] to arouse you by way of reminder,
[14]since I know that the putting off of my
body[c] will be soon, as our Lord Jesus Christ

[a] Or *of our God and the Savior Jesus Christ*
[b] Or *by*
[c] Greek *tent*

King James

15 Moreover I will endeavour that ye may be able after my decease to have these things always in remembrance.

16 For we have not followed cunningly devised fables, when we made known unto you the power and coming of our Lord Jesus Christ, but were eyewitnesses of his majesty.

17 For he received from God the Father honour and glory, when there came such a voice to him from the excellent glory, This is my beloved Son, in whom I am well pleased.

18 And this voice which came from heaven we heard, when we were with him in the holy mount.

19 We have also a more sure word of prophecy; whereunto ye do well that ye take heed, as unto a light that shineth in a dark place, until the day dawn, and the day star arise in your hearts:

20 Knowing this first, that no prophecy of the scripture is of any private interpretation.

21 For the prophecy came not in old time by the will of man: but holy men of God spake *as they were* moved by the Holy Ghost.

Amplified

15 Moreover, I will diligently endeavor [to see to it] that [even] after my departure (decease) you may be able at all times to call these things to mind.

16 For we were not following out cleverly devised stories when we made known to you the power and coming of our Lord Jesus Christ, the Messiah, but we were eyewitnesses of His majesty—grandeur, authority of sovereign power.

17 For when He was invested with honor and glory from God the Father and a voice was borne to Him by the (splendid) Majestic Glory [in the bright cloud that overshadowed Him, saying], This is My beloved Son in Whom I am well pleased *and* delight,

18 We [actually] heard this voice borne out of heaven, for we were together with Him on the holy mountain.

19 And we have the prophetic word [made] firmer still. You will do well to pay close attention to it as to a lamp shining in a dismal (squalid and dark) place, until the day breaks through [the gloom] and the Morning Star rises ([g]comes into being) in your hearts.

20 [Yet] first [you must] understand this, that no prophecy of Scripture is [a matter] of any personal *or* private *or* special interpretation (loosening, solving).

21 For no prophecy ever originated because some man willed it [to do so]—it never came by human impulse—but as men spoke from God who were borne along (moved and impelled) by the Holy Spirit.

CHAPTER 2

BUT there were false prophets also among the people, even as there shall be false teachers among you, who privily shall bring in damnable heresies, even denying the Lord that bought them, and bring upon themselves swift destruction.

2 And many shall follow their pernicious ways; by reason of whom the way of truth shall be evil spoken of.

3 And through covetousness shall they with feigned words make merchandise of you: whose judgment now of a long time lingereth not, and their damnation slumbereth not.

4 For if God spared not the angels that sinned, but cast *them* down to hell, and delivered *them* into chains of darkness, to be reserved unto judgment;

5 And spared not the old world, but saved Noah the eighth *person*, a preacher of righteousness, bringing in the flood upon the world of the ungodly;

6 And turning the cities of Sodom and Gomorrha into ashes condemned *them* with an overthrow, making *them* an ensample unto those that after should live ungodly;

7 And delivered just Lot, vexed with the filthy conversation of the wicked:

8 (For that righteous man dwelling among them, in seeing and hearing, vexed *his* righteous soul from day to day with *their* unlawful deeds;)

CHAPTER 2

BUT also [in those days] there arose false prophets among the people, just as there will be false teachers among yourselves, who will subtly *and* stealthily introduce heretical doctrines—destructive heresies—even denying *and* disowning the Master Who bought them, bringing upon themselves swift destruction.

2 And many will follow their immoral ways *and* lascivi-ous doings; because of them the true Way will b maligned *and* defamed.

3 And in their covetousness (lust, greed) they wi exploit you with (cunning) false arguments. From of ol the sentence [of condemnation] for them has not bee idle; their destruction (eternal misery) has not bee asleep.

4 For God [even] spared not angels that sinned, b cast them into hell, delivering them to be kept there in pi of gloom till the judgment *and* their doom.

5 And He spared not the ancient world, but preserve Noah, a preacher of righteousness, with seven other pe sons, when He brought a flood upon the world of ungod [people]. [Gen. 8:18; 6-8.]

6 And He condemned to ruin *and* extinction the citi of Sodom and Gomorrah, reducing them to ashes [a thus] set them forth as an example to those who would ungodly. [Gen. 19:24.]

7 And He rescued righteous Lot, greatly worn out *a* distressed by the wanton ways of the ungodly *and* lawle [Gen. 19:16, 29.]

8 For that just man, living [there] among them, t tured his righteous soul every day with what he saw a heard of [their] unlawful and wicked deeds.

---

g) Abbott-Smith.

Living New Testament

15 Hoping to impress them so clearly upon you that you will remember them long after I have gone.

16 For we have not been telling you fairy tales when we explained to you the power of our Lord Jesus Christ and His coming again. My own eyes have seen His splendor and His glory:

17, 18 I was there on the holy mountain when He shone out with honor given Him by God His Father; I heard that glorious, majestic voice calling down from heaven, saying, "This is My much-loved Son; I am well pleased with Him."

19 So we have seen and proved that what the prophets said came true. You will do well to pay close attention to everything they have written, for, like lights shining into dark corners, their words help us to understand many things that otherwise would be dark and difficult. But when you consider the wonderful truth of the prophets' words, then the light will dawn in your souls and Christ the Morning Star will shine in your hearts.

20, 21 For no prophecy recorded in Scripture was ever thought up by the prophet himself. It was the Holy Spirit within these godly men who gave them true messages from God.

Revised Standard

showed me. 15And I will see to it that after
my departure you may be able at any time
to recall these things.
16 For we did not follow cleverly devised
myths when we made known to you the power and coming of our Lord Jesus Christ, but
we were eye-witnesses of his majesty. 17For
when he received honor and glory from God
the Father and the voice was borne to him
by the Majestic Glory, "This is my beloved
Son,[d] with whom I am well pleased," 18we
heard this voice borne from heaven, for we
were with him on the holy mountain. 19And
we have the prophetic word made more sure.
You will do well to pay attention to this as
to a lamp shining in a dark place, until the
day dawns and the morning star rises in your
hearts. 20First of all you must understand
this, that no prophecy of scripture is a matter
of one's own interpretation, 21because no
prophecy ever came by the impulse of man,
but men moved by the Holy Spirit spoke
from God.[e]

CHAPTER 2

But there were false prophets, too, in those days, just as there will be false teachers among you. They will leverly tell their lies about God, turning against even heir Master who bought them; but theirs will be a swift .nd terrible end.

2 Many will follow their evil teaching that there is othing wrong with sexual sin. And because of them ;hrist and His way will be scoffed at.

3 These teachers in their greed will tell you anything to et hold of your money. But God condemned them long go and their destruction is on the way.

4 For God did not spare even the angels who sinned, ıt threw them into hell, chained in gloomy caves and arkness until the judgment day.

5 And He did not spare any of the people who lived in ıcient times before the flood except Noah, the one man ho spoke up for God, and his family of seven. At that ne God completely destroyed the whole world of ungodmen with the vast flood.

6 Later, He turned the cities of Sodom and Gomorrah to heaps of ashes and blotted them off the face of the ırth, making them an example for all the ungodly in the ture to look back upon and fear.

7, 8 But at the same time the Lord rescued Lot out of dom because he was a good man, sick of the terrible ckedness he saw everywhere around him day after day.

False prophets and false teachers

2 But false prophets also arose among the
people, just as there will be false teachers among you, who will secretly bring in
destructive heresies, even denying the Master
who bought them, bringing upon themselves
swift destruction. 2And many will follow their
licentiousness, and because of them the way
of truth will be reviled. 3And in their greed
they will exploit you with false words; from
of old their condemnation has not been idle,
and their destruction has not been asleep.
4 For if God did not spare the angels
when they sinned, but cast them into hell[f]
and committed them to pits of nether gloom
to be kept until the judgment; 5if he did not
spare the ancient world, but preserved Noah,
a herald of righteousness, with seven other
persons, when he brought a flood upon the
world of the ungodly; 6if by turning the cities
of Sodom and Gomorrah to ashes he condemned them to extinction and made them
an example to those who were to be ungodly;
7and if he rescued righteous Lot, greatly distressed by the licentiousness of the wicked
8(for by what that righteous man saw and
heard as he lived among them, he was vexed
in his righteous soul day after day with their

[d] Or *my Son, my* (or *the*) *Beloved*
[e] Other authorities read *moved by the Holy Spirit holy men of God spoke*
[f] Greek *Tartarus*

King James

9 The Lord knoweth how to deliver the godly out of temptations, and to reserve the unjust unto the day of judgment to be punished:

10 But chiefly them that walk after the flesh in the lust of uncleanness, and despise government. Presumptuous *are they*, selfwilled, they are not afraid to speak evil of dignities.

11 Whereas angels, which are greater in power and might, bring not railing accusation against them before the Lord.

12 But these, as natural brute beasts, made to be taken and destroyed, speak evil of the things that they understand not; and shall utterly perish in their own corruption;

13 And shall receive the reward of unrighteousness, *as* they that count it pleasure to riot in the day time. Spots *they are* and blemishes, sporting themselves with their own deceivings while they feast with you;

14 Having eyes full of adultery, and that cannot cease from sin; beguiling unstable souls: an heart they have exercised with covetous practices; cursed children:

15 Which have forsaken the right way, and are gone astray, following the way of Balaam *the son* of Bosor, who loved the wages of unrighteousness;

16 But was rebuked for his iniquity: the dumb ass speaking with man's voice forbad the madness of the prophet.

17 These are wells without water, clouds that are carried with a tempest; to whom the mist of darkness is reserved for ever.

18 For when they speak great swelling *words* of vanity, they allure through the lusts of the flesh, *through much* wantonness, those that were clean escaped from them who live in error.

19 While they promise them liberty, they themselves are the servants of corruption: for of whom a man is overcome, of the same is he brought in bondage.

20 For if after they have escaped the pollutions of the world through the knowledge of the Lord and Saviour Jesus Christ, they are again entangled therein, and overcome, the latter end is worse with them than the beginning.

21 For it had been better for them not to have known the way of righteousness, than, after they have known *it*, to turn from the holy commandment delivered unto them.

22 But it is happened unto them according to the true proverb, The dog *is* turned to his own vomit again; and the sow that was washed to her wallowing in the mire.

Amplified

9 Now if [all these things be true, then be sure] the Lord knows how to rescue the godly out of temptations *and* trials, and how to keep the ungodly under chastisement until the day of judgment *and* doom;

10 And particularly those who walk after the flesh and indulge in the lust of polluting passion, and scorn *and* despise authority. Presumptuous *and* daring—self-willed *and* self-loving [creatures]! They scoff at *and* revile dignitaries (glorious ones) without trembling,

11 Whereas [even] angels, though superior in might and power, do not bring a defaming charge against them before the Lord.

12 But these [people]! Like unreasoning beasts, mere creatures of instinct, born [only] to be captured and destroyed, railing at things of which they are ignorant, they shall utterly perish in their [own] corruption—in their destroying they shall surely be destroyed,

13 Being destined to receive [punishment as] the reward of [their] unrighteousness—suffering wrong as the hire for [their] wrongdoing. They count it a delight to revel in the daytime—living luxuriously and delicately. They are blots and blemishes, revelling in their [h]deceptions (at love feasts) *and* carousing together [even] as they feast with you.

14 They have eyes full of harlotry, insatiable for sin. They beguile *and* bait *and* lure away unstable souls. Their hearts are trained in covetousness—lust, greed. [They are [i]exposed to cursing,] children of a curse!

15 Forsaking the straight road they have gone astray; they have followed the way of Balaam, [the son] of Beor, who loved the reward of wickedness. [Num. 22:5, 7.]

16 But he was rebuked for his own transgression when a dumb beast of burden spoke with human voice and checked the prophet's madness. [Num. 22:21-31.]

17 These are springs without water and mists driven along before a tempest, for whom is reserved *forever* the gloom of darkness.

18 For uttering loud boasts of folly, they beguile *and* lure with lustful desires of the flesh those who are barely escaping from them who are wrongdoers.

19 They promise them liberty, when they themselves are the slaves of depravity *and* defilement, for by whatever any one is made inferior *or* overcome *or* worsted, to that [person or thing] he is enslaved.

20 For if, after they have escaped the pollutions of the world through (the full, personal) knowledge of our Lord and Savior Jesus Christ, they again become entangled in them and are overcome, their last condition is worse [for them] than the first.

21 For never to have obtained a (full, personal) knowledge of the Way of righteousness would have been better for them than, having obtained [such knowledge], to turn back from the holy commandment which was (verbally) delivered to them.

22 There has befallen them the thing spoken of in the true proverb, The dog turns back to his own vomit, and the sow is washed only to wallow again in the mire. [Prov. 26:11.]

h) Some ancient authorities read "love feasts."
i) Thayer.

Living New Testament

9 So also the Lord can rescue you and me from the temptations that surround us, and continue to punish the ungodly until the day of final judgment comes.

10 He is especially hard on those who follow their own evil, lustful thoughts, and those who are proud and willful, daring even to scoff at the Glorious Ones[1] without so much as trembling,

11 Although the angels in heaven who stand in the very presence of the Lord, and are far greater in power and strength than these false teachers, never speak out disrespectfully against these evil Mighty Ones.

12 But false teachers are fools—no better than animals. They do whatever they feel like; born only to be caught and killed, they laugh at the terrifying powers of the underworld[2] which they know so little about; and they will be destroyed along with all the demons and powers of hell.[3]

13 That is the pay these teachers will have for their sin. For they live in evil pleasures day after day. They are a disgrace and a stain among you, deceiving you by living in foul sin on the side while they join your love feasts as though they were honest men.

14 No woman can escape their sinful stare, and of adultery they never have enough. They make a game of luring unstable women. They train themselves to be greedy; and are doomed and cursed.

15 They have gone off the road and become lost like Balaam, the son of Beor, who fell in love with the money he could make by doing wrong;

16 But Balaam was stopped from his mad course when his donkey spoke to him with a human voice, scolding and rebuking him.

17 These men are as useless as dried-up springs of water, promising much and delivering nothing; they are as unstable as clouds driven by the storm winds. They are doomed to the eternal pits of darkness.

18 They proudly boast about their sins and conquests, and, using lust as their bait, they lure back into sin those who have just escaped from such wicked living.

19 "You aren't saved by being good," they say, "so you might as well be bad. Do what you like, be free." But these very teachers who offer this "freedom" from law are themselves slaves to sin and destruction. For a man is a slave to whatever controls him.

20 And when a person has escaped from the wicked ways of the world by learning about our Lord and Savior Jesus Christ, and then gets tangled up with sin and becomes its slave again, he is worse off than he was before.

21 It would be better if he had never known about Christ at all than to learn of Him and then afterwards turn his back on the holy commandments that were given to him.

22 There is an old saying that "A dog comes back to what he has vomited, and a pig is washed only to come back and wallow in the mud again." That is the way it is with those who turn again to their sin.

Or, "the glories of the unseen world."
Literally, "the things they do not understand."
Implied. Literally, "will be destroyed in the same destruction with them."

Revised Standard

lawless deeds), [9]then the Lord knows how
to rescue the godly from trial, and to keep
the unrighteous under punishment until the
day of judgment, [10]and especially those who
indulge in the lust of defiling passion and
despise authority.

Character and conduct of deceivers

Bold and wilful, they are not afraid to
revile the glorious ones, [11]whereas angels,
though greater in might and power, do not
pronounce a reviling judgment upon them
before the Lord. [12]But these, like irrational
animals, creatures of instinct, born to be
caught and killed, reviling in matters of which
they are ignorant, will be destroyed in the
same destruction with them, [13]suffering
wrong for their wrongdoing. They count it
pleasure to revel in the daytime. They are
blots and blemishes, reveling in their dissipation,[g] carousing with you. [14]They have
eyes full of adultery, insatiable for sin. They
entice unsteady souls. They have hearts
trained in greed. Accursed children! [15]For-
saking the right way they have gone astray;
they have followed the way of Balaam, the
son of Beor, who loved gain from wrongdoing, [16]but was rebuked for his own transgression; a dumb ass spoke with human voice
and restrained the prophet's madness.

The consequences of deception

17 These are waterless springs and mists
driven by a storm; for them the nether gloom
of darkness has been reserved. [18]For, uttering loud boasts of folly, they entice with licentious passions of the flesh men who have
barely escaped from those who live in error.
[19]They promise them freedom, but they
themselves are slaves of corruption; for whatever overcomes a man, to that he is enslaved.
[20]For if, after they have escaped the defile-
ments of the world through the knowledge of
our Lord and Savior Jesus Christ, they are
again entangled in them and overpowered,
the last state has become worse for them
than the first. [21]For it would have been better
for them never to have known the way of
righteousness than after knowing it to turn
back from the holy commandment delivered
to them. [22]It has happened to them according
to the true proverb, The dog turns back to
his own vomit, and the sow is washed only to
wallow in the mire.

---

g Other ancient authorities read *love feasts*

King James

CHAPTER 3

THIS second epistle, beloved, I now write unto you; in *both* which I stir up your pure minds by way of remembrance:

2 That ye may be mindful of the words which were spoken before by the holy prophets, and of the commandment of us the apostles of the Lord and Saviour:

3 Knowing this first, that there shall come in the last days scoffers, walking after their own lusts,

4 And saying, Where is the promise of his coming? for since the fathers fell asleep, all things continue as *they were* from the beginning of the creation.

5 For this they willingly are ignorant of, that by the word of God the heavens were of old, and the earth standing out of the water and in the water:

6 Whereby the world that then was, being overflowed with water, perished:

7 But the heavens and the earth, which are now, by the same word are kept in store, reserved unto fire against the day of judgment and perdition of ungodly men.

8 But, beloved, be not ignorant of this one thing, that one day *is* with the Lord as a thousand years, and a thousand years as one day.

9 The Lord is not slack concerning his promise, as some men count slackness; but is longsuffering to us-ward, not willing that any should perish, but that all should come to repentance.

10 But the day of the Lord will come as a thief in the night; in the which the heavens shall pass away with a great noise, and the elements shall melt with fervent heat, the earth also and the works that are therein shall be burned up.

11 *Seeing* then *that* all these things shall be dissolved, what manner *of persons* ought ye to be in *all* holy conversation and godliness,

12 Looking for and hasting unto the coming of the day of God, wherein the heavens being on fire shall be dissolved, and the elements shall melt with fervent heat?

13 Nevertheless we, according to his promise, look for new heavens and a new earth, wherein dwelleth righteousness.

14 Wherefore, beloved, seeing that ye look for such things, be diligent that ye may be found of him in peace, without spot, and blameless.

15 And account *that* the long suffering of our Lord *is* salvation; even as our beloved brother Paul also according to the wisdom given unto him hath written unto you;

16 As also in all *his* epistles, speaking in them of these things; in which are some things hard to be understood, which they that are unlearned and unstable wrest, as *they do* also the other scriptures, unto their own destruction.

Amplified

CHAPTER 3

BELOVED, I am now writing you this second letter. In [both of] them I have stirred up your unsullied (sincere) mind by way of remembrance;

2 That you should recall the predictions of the holy (consecrated, dedicated) prophets and the commandment of the Lord and Savior [given] through your apostles, [His] special messengers.

3 To begin with, you must know *and* understand this, that scoffers (mockers) will come in the last days with scoffing; [people who] walk after their own fleshly desires

4 And saying, Where is the promise of His coming? For since the forefathers fell asleep, all things have continued exactly as they did from beginning of creation.

5 For they wilfully overlook *and* forget this [fact], that heavens [came into] existence long ago by the word of God, and an earth also which was formed out of water and by means of water,

6 Through which the world that then [existed] was deluged with water and perished. [Gen. 1:6-8; 7:11.]

7 But by the same word the present heavens and earth have been stored up (reserved) for fire, being kept until the day of judgment and destruction of the ungodly people.

8 Nevertheless do not let this one fact escape you, beloved, that with the Lord one day is as a thousand years, and a thousand years as one day. [Ps. 90:4.]

9 The Lord does not delay *and* be tardy *or* slow about what He promises, according to some people's conception of slowness, but He is long-suffering (extraordinarily patient) toward you, not desiring that any should perish, but that all should turn to repentance.

10 But the day of the Lord will come as a thief, and then the heavens will vanish (pass away) with a thunderous crash, and the [[j]material] elements [of the universe] will be dissolved with fire, and the earth and the works that are upon it will be burned up.

11 Since all these things are thus [k]in the process of being dissolved, what kind of person ought [each of] you to be [in the meanwhile] in consecrated *and* holy behavior and devout *and* godly qualities?

12 While you wait and earnestly long for—expecting and [l]hastening—the coming of the day of God by reason of which the flaming heavens will be dissolved, and the [[j]material] elements [of the universe] will flare *and* melt with fire. [Isa. 34:4.]

13 But we look for new heavens and a new earth according to His promise, in which righteousness (uprightness, freedom from sin, and right standing with God) is to abide. [Isa. 65:17; 66:22.]

14 So, beloved, since you are expecting these things, be eager to be found by Him [at His coming] without spot or blemish, and at peace—in serene confidence, free from fears and agitating passions and moral conflicts.

15 And consider that the long-suffering of our Lord [[m]His slowness in avenging wrongs and judging the world] is salvation, [[m]that which conduces to the soul's safety] even as our beloved brother Paul also wrote to you according to the spiritual insight given him,

16 Speaking of this as he does in all of his letters. There are some things in those [epistles of Paul] that are difficult to understand, which the ignorant and unstable twist *and* misconstrue to their own [n]utter destruction, just as [they distort and misinterpret] the rest of the Scriptures.

---

j) Abbott-Smith.
k) Vincent.
l) Alternate reading.
m) Thayer.
n) Thayer.

Living New Testament

CHAPTER 3

This is my second letter to you, dear brothers, and in both of them I have tried to remind you—if you will let me—about facts you already know: facts you learned from the holy prophets and from us apostles who brought you the words of our Lord and Savior.

3 First, I want to remind you that in the last days there will come scoffers who will do every wrong they can think of, and laugh at the truth.

4 This will be their line of argument: "So Jesus promised to come back, did He? Then where is He? He'll never come! Why, as far back as anyone can remember everything has remained exactly as it was since the first day of creation."

5, 6 They deliberately forget this fact: that God did destroy the world with a mighty flood, long after He had made the heavens by the word of His command, and had used the waters to form the earth and surround it.

7 And God has commanded that the earth and the heavens be stored away for a great bonfire at the judgment day, when all ungodly men will perish.

8 But don't forget this, dear friends, that a day or a thousand years from now is like tomorrow to the Lord.

9 He isn't really being slow about His promised return, even though it sometimes seems that way. But He is waiting, for the good reason that He is not willing that any should perish, and He is giving more time for sinners to repent.

10 The day of the Lord is surely coming, as unexpectedly as a thief, and then the heavens will pass away with a terrible noise and the heavenly bodies will disappear in fire, and the earth and everything on it will be burned up.

11 And so since everything around us is going to melt away, what holy, godly lives we should be living!

12 You should look forward to that day and hurry it along—the day when God will set the heavens on fire, and the heavenly bodies will melt and disappear in flames.

13 But we are looking forward to God's promise of new heavens and a new earth afterwards, when there will be only goodness.[1]

14 Dear friends, while you are waiting for these things to happen and for Him to come, try hard to live without sinning; and be at peace with everyone so that He will be pleased with you when He returns.

15, 16 And remember why He is waiting. He is giving us time to get His message of salvation out to others. Our wise and beloved brother Paul has talked about these same things in many of his letters. Some of his comments are not easy to understand, and there are people who are deliberately stupid, and always demand some unusual interpretation—they have twisted his letters around to mean something quite different from what he meant, just as they do the other parts of the Scriptures—and the result is disaster for them.

---

[1] Literally, "wherein righteousness dwells."

Revised Standard

The promise of Christ's coming

3 This is now the second letter that I have written to you, beloved, and in both of them I have aroused your sincere mind by way of reminder; 2that you should remember the predictions of the holy prophets and the commandment of the Lord and Savior through your apostles. 3First of all you must understand this, that scoffers will come in the last days with scoffing, following their own passions 4and saying, "Where is the promise of his coming? For ever since the fathers fell asleep, all things have continued as they were from the beginning of creation." 5They deliberately ignore this fact, that by the word of God heavens existed long ago, and an earth formed out of water and by means of water, 6through which the world that then existed was deluged with water and perished. 7But by the same word the heavens and earth that now exist have been stored up for fire, being kept until the day of judgment and destruction of ungodly men.

Time and circumstances of the coming

8 But do not ignore this one fact, beloved, that with the Lord one day is as a thousand years, and a thousand years as one day. 9The Lord is not slow about his promise as some count slowness, but is forbearing toward you,[h] not wishing that any should perish, but that all should reach repentance. 10But the day of the Lord will come like a thief, and then the heavens will pass away with a loud noise, and the elements will be dissolved with fire, and the earth and the works that are upon it will be burned up.

11 Since all these things are thus to be dissolved, what sort of persons ought you to be in lives of holiness and godliness, 12waiting for and hastening[i] the coming of the day of God, because of which the heavens will be kindled and dissolved, and the elements will melt with fire! 13But according to his promise we wait for new heavens and a new earth in which righteousness dwells.

The concluding appeal

14 Therefore, beloved, since you wait for these, be zealous to be found by him without spot or blemish, and at peace. 15And count the forbearance of our Lord as salvation. So also our beloved brother Paul wrote to you according to the wisdom given him, 16speaking of this as he does in all his letters. There are some things in them hard to understand, which the ignorant and unstable twist to their own destruction, as they do the other

---

[h] Other ancient authorities read *on your account*

[i] Or *earnestly desiring*

King James

17 Ye therefore, beloved, seeing ye know *these things* before, beware lest ye also, being led away with the error of the wicked, fall from your own stedfastness.
18 But grow in grace, and *in* the knowledge of our Lord and Saviour Jesus Christ. To him *be* glory both now and for ever. Amen.

Amplified

17 Let me warn you therefore, beloved, that knowing these things beforehand, you should be on your guard lest you be carried away by the error of lawless *and* wicked [persons and] fall from your own [present] firm condition—your own steadfastness [of mind].
18 But grow in grace (undeserved favor, spiritual strength) and [o]recognition *and* knowledge *and* understanding of our Lord and Savior Jesus Christ, the Messiah. To Him [be] glory (honor, majesty and splendor) both now and to the day of eternity. Amen—so be it!

o) Cremer.

Living New Testament

17 I am warning you ahead of time, dear brothers, so that you can watch out and not be carried away by the mistakes of these wicked men, lest you yourselves become mixed up too.

18 But grow in spiritual strength and become better acquainted with our Lord and Savior Jesus Christ. To Him be all glory and splendid honor, both now and forevermore. Good-bye.

Peter

Revised Standard

scriptures. 17 You therefore, beloved, knowing this beforehand, beware lest you be carried away with the error of lawless men and
lose your own stability. 18 But grow in the
grace and knowledge of our Lord and Savior
Jesus Christ. To him be the glory both now
and to the day of eternity. Amen.

King James

THE FIRST EPISTLE GENERAL OF

John

CHAPTER 1

THAT which was from the beginning,
which we have heard, which we have
seen with our eyes, which we have looked
upon, and our hands have handled, of the
Word of life;
2 (For the life was manifested, and we
have seen *it*, and bear witness, and shew
unto you that eternal life, which was with
the Father, and was manifested unto us;)
3 That which we have seen and heard
declare we unto you, that ye also may have
fellowship with us: and truly our fellowship
is with the Father, and with his Son Jesus
Christ.
4 And these things write we unto you,
that your joy may be full.
5 This then is the message which we have
heard of him, and declare unto you, that
God is light, and in him is no darkness at
all.
6 If we say that we have fellowship with
him, and walk in darkness, we lie, and do
not the truth:
7 But if we walk in the light, as he is in
the light, we have fellowship one with another, and the blood of Jesus Christ his Son
cleanseth us from all sin.
8 If we say that we have no sin, we deceive ourselves, and the truth is not in us.
9 If we confess our sins, he is faithful and
just to forgive us *our* sins, and to cleanse us
from all unrighteousness.
10 If we say that we have not sinned, we
make him a liar, and his word is not in us.

Amplified

THE FIRST LETTER
OF

John

CHAPTER 1

[WE are writing] about the Word of Life [[a]in] Him
Who existed from the beginning, Whom we have
heard, Whom we have seen with our [own] eyes, Whom
we have gazed upon [for ourselves] and have touched with
our [own] hands.
2 And the Life [[a]an aspect of His being] was revealed
(made manifest, demonstrated), and we saw (as eyewitnesses) and are testifying to and declare to you the Life,
the eternal Life [[a]in Him] Who already existed with the
Father and Who [actually] was made visible—was revealed—to us [His followers].
3 What we have seen and [ourselves] heard we are also
telling you, so that you too may [a]realize *and* enjoy fellowship as partners *and* partakers with us. And [this] fellowship that we have (which is a [a]distinguishing mark of
Christians) is with the Father and with His Son Jesus
Christ, the Messiah.
4 And we are now writing these things to you so that
our joy [in seeing you included] may be full—and [b]your
joy may be complete.
5 And this is the message—the message of [a]promise—
which we have heard from Him and now are reporting to
you: God is Light and there is no darkness in Him at
all—[c]no, not in any way.
6 [So] if we say we are partakers together *and* enjoy
fellowship with Him when we live *and* move *and* are
walking about in darkness, we are [both] speaking falsely
and do not live *and* practice the Truth [of the Gospel].
7 But if we [really] are living *and* walking in the Light
as He [Himself] is in the Light, we have [true, unbroken]
fellowship with one another, and the blood of Jesus *Christ*
His Son cleanses (removes) us from all sin *and* guilt—
keeps us cleansed from sin in all its forms *and* manifestations.
8 If we say we have no sin—refusing to admit that we
are sinners—we delude *and* lead ourselves astray, and the
Truth [which the Gospel presents] is not in us—does not
dwell in our hearts.
9 If we [freely] admit that we have sinned *and* confess
our sins, He is faithful and just [true to His own nature
and promises] and will forgive our sins (dismiss our
lawlessness) and continuously cleanse us from all unrighteousness—everything not in conformity to His will in
purpose, thought and action.
10 If we say (claim) we have not sinned, we contradict
His Word *and* make Him out to be false *and* a liar, and
His Word is not in us—the divine message of the Gospel is
not in our hearts.

King James

CHAPTER 2

MY little children, these things write I
unto you, that ye sin not. And if any
man sin, we have an advocate with the Father, Jesus Christ the righteous:

Amplified

CHAPTER 2

MY little children, I write you these things so that you
may not violate God's law *and* sin; but if any one
should sin, we have an Advocate (One Who will intercede
for us) with the Father; [it is] Jesus Christ [the all
righteous—upright, just, Who conforms to the Father's
will in every purpose, thought and action.

a) Vincent.
b) Many ancient texts read "your joy."
c) Literal meaning.

Living New Testament

I John

CHAPTER 1

Christ was alive when the world began, yet I myself have seen Him with my own eyes and listened to Him speak. I have touched Him with my own hands. He is God's message of Life.

2 This one who is Life from God has been shown to us and we guarantee that we have seen Him; I am speaking of Christ, who is eternal Life. He was with the Father and then was shown to us.

3 Again I say, we are telling you about what we ourselves have actually seen and heard, so that you may share the fellowship and the joys we have with the Father and with Jesus Christ His Son.

4 And if you do as I say in this letter, then you, too, will be full of joy, and so will we.

5 This is the message God has given us to pass on to you; That God is Light and in Him is no darkness at all.

6 So if we say we are His friends, but go on living in spiritual darkness and sin, we are lying.

7 But if we are living in the light of God's presence, just as Christ does, then we have wonderful fellowship and joy with each other, and the blood of Jesus His Son cleanses us from every sin.

8 If we say that we have no sin, we are only fooling ourselves, and refusing to accept the truth.

9 But if we confess our sins to Him,[1] He can be depended on to forgive us and to cleanse us from every wrong. [And it is perfectly proper for God to do this for us because Christ died to wash away our sins.[2]]

10 If we claim we have not sinned, we are lying and calling God a liar, *for He says we have sinned.*

Revised Standard

THE FIRST LETTER OF

John

Introduction

1 That which was from the beginning,
which we have heard, which we have
seen with our eyes, which we have looked
upon and touched with our hands, concerning the word of life—2the life was made
manifest, and we saw it, and testify to it,
and proclaim to you the eternal life which
was with the Father and was made manifest to us—3that which we have seen and
heard we proclaim also to you, so that you
may have fellowship with us; and our fellowship is with the Father and with his Son
Jesus Christ. 4And we are writing this that
our[a] joy may be complete.

The test of righteousness

5 This is the message we have heard from
him and proclaim to you, that God is light
and in him is no darkness at all. 6If we say
we have fellowship with him while we walk
in darkness, we lie and do not live according
to the truth; 7but if we walk in the light, as
he is in the light, we have fellowship with
one another, and the blood of Jesus his Son
cleanses us from all sin. 8If we say we have
no sin, we deceive ourselves, and the truth is
not in us. 9If we confess our sins, he is faithful and just, and will forgive our sins and
cleanse us from all unrighteousness. 10If we
say we have not sinned, we make him a liar,
and his word is not in us.

CHAPTER 2

My little children, I am telling you this so that you will stay away from sin. But if you sin, there is omeone to plead for you before the Father. His name is esus Christ, the one who is all that is good and who leases God completely.

2 My little children, I am writing this to
you so that you may not sin; but if any
one does sin, we have an advocate with the

Implied. Literally, "if we confess our sins."
Literally, "He is . . . just."

[a] Other ancient authorities read *your*

King James

2 And he is the propitiation for our sins: and not for ours only, but also for *the sins of* the whole world.

3 And hereby we do know that we know him, if we keep his commandments.

4 He that saith, I know him, and keepeth not his commandments, is a liar, and the truth is not in him.

5 But whoso keepeth his word, in him verily is the love of God perfected: hereby know we that we are in him.

6 He that saith he abideth in him ought himself also so to walk, even as he walked.

7 Brethren, I write no new commandment unto you, but an old commandment which ye had from the beginning. The old commandment is the word which ye have heard from the beginning.

8 Again, a new commandment I write unto you, which thing is true in him and in you: because the darkness is past, and the true light now shineth.

9 He that saith he is in the light, and hateth his brother, is in darkness even until now.

10 He that loveth his brother abideth in the light, and there is none occasion of stumbling in him.

11 But he that hateth his brother is in darkness, and walketh in darkness, and knoweth not whither he goeth, because that darkness hath blinded his eyes.

12 I write unto you, little children, because your sins are forgiven you for his name's sake.

13 I write unto you, fathers, because ye have known him *that is* from the beginning. I write unto you, young men, because ye have overcome the wicked one. I write unto you, little children, because ye have known the Father.

14 I have written unto you, fathers, because ye have known him *that is* from the beginning. I have written unto you, young men, because ye are strong, and the word of God abideth in you, and ye have overcome the wicked one.

15 Love not the world, neither the things *that are* in the world. If any man love the world, the love of the Father is not in him.

16 For all that *is* in the world, the lust of the flesh, and the lust of the eyes, and the pride of life, is not of the Father, but is of the world.

Amplified

2 And He—[d]that same Jesus Himself—is the propitiation (the atoning sacrifice) for our sins, and not for ours alone but also for [the sins of] the whole world.

3 And this is how we may discern [[d]daily by experience] that we are coming to know Him—to perceive, recognize, understand and become better acquainted with Him: if we keep (bear in mind, observe, practice) His teachings (precepts, commandments).

4 Whoever says, I know Him—I perceive, recognize, understand and am acquainted with Him—but fails to keep *and* obey His commandments (teachings) is a liar, and the Truth [[e]of the Gospel] is not in him.

5 But he who keeps [treasures] His Word—who bears in mind His precepts, who observes His message in its entirety—truly in him has the love of *and* for God been perfected (completed, reached maturity). By this we may perceive *and* know *and* recognize *and* be sure that we are in Him:

6 Whoever says he abides in Him ought—as [d]a personal debt—to walk *and* conduct himself in the same way in which He walked *and* conducted Himself.

7 Beloved, I am writing you no new commandment, but an old commandment which you have had *from the beginning;* the old commandment is the message which you have heard—the [e]doctrine [of salvation through Christ].

8 Yet I am writing you a new commandment, which is true—is realized—in Him and in you, because the darkness ([f]moral blindness) is clearing away and the true Light [[f]the revelation of God in Christ] is already shining.

9 Whoever says he is in the Light and [yet] hates his brother [Christian, [g]born-again child of God his own Father] is in darkness even until now.

10 Whoever loves his brother [believer] abides (lives) in the Light, and in It *or* in [h]him there is no occasion for stumbling *or* cause for error *or* sin.

11 But he who hates (detests, despises) his brother [[g]in Christ] is in darkness and walking (living) in the dark; he is straying *and* does not perceive *or* know where he is going, because the darkness has blinded his eyes.

12 I am writing to you, little children, because for His name's sake your sins are forgiven—pardoned through His name and on account of confessing His name.

13 I am writing to you, fathers, because you have come to know (recognize, be aware of and understand) Him Who [has existed] from the beginning. I am writing to you, young men, because you have been victorious over the wicked [one]. I write to you, [i]boys (lads), because you have come to know *and* recognize *and* be aware of the Father.

14 I write to you, fathers, because you have come to know (recognize, be conscious of and understand) Him Who [has existed] from the beginning. I write to you young men, because you are strong *and* vigorous, and the Word of God is (always in your hearts) abiding in you and you have been victorious over the wicked one.

15 Do not love *or* cherish the world or the things that are in the world. If any one loves the world, love for the Father is not in him.

16 For all that is in the world, the lust of the flesh [craving for sensual gratification], and the lust of the eyes [greedy longings of the mind] and the pride of life [assurance in one's own resources *or* in the stability of earthly things]—these do not come from the Father but are from the world [itself].

d) Vincent.
e) Thayer.
f) Vincent.
g) Thayer.
h) Alternate reading, "it" or "him."
i) Abbott-Smith.

Living New Testament

2 He is the one who took God's wrath against our sins upon Himself, and brought us into fellowship with God; and He is the forgiveness[1] for our sins, and not only ours but all the world's.

3 And how can we be sure that we belong to Him? By looking within ourselves: are we really trying to do what He wants us to?

4 Someone may say, "I am a Christian; I am on my way to heaven; I belong to Christ." But if he doesn't do what Christ tells him to, he is a liar.

5 But those who do what Christ tells them to will learn to love God more and more. That is the way to know whether or not you are a Christian.

6 Anyone who says he is a Christian should live as Christ did.

7 Dear brothers, I am not writing out a new rule for you to obey, for it is an old one you have always had, right from the start. You have heard it all before.

8 Yet it is always new, and works for you just as it did for Christ; and as we obey this commandment, *to love one another,* the darkness in our lives disappears and the new light of life in Christ shines in.

9 Anyone who says he is walking in the light of Christ but hates his brother Christian is still in darkness.

10 But whoever loves his brother Christian is "walking in the light" and can see his way without stumbling around in darkness and sin.

11 For he who hates his Christian brother is wandering around in spiritual darkness and doesn't know where he is going, for the darkness has made him blind so that he cannot see the way.

12 I am writing these things to all of you, my little children, because your sins have been forgiven in the name of Jesus our Savior.

13 I am saying these things to you older men because you really know Christ, the one who has been alive from the beginning. And you young men, I am talking to you because you have won your battle with Satan. And I am writing to you younger boys and girls because you, too, have learned to know God our Father.

14 And so I say to you fathers who know the eternal God, and to you young men who are strong, with God's Word in your hearts, and have won your struggle against Satan:

15 Stop loving this evil world and all that it offers you, for when you love these things you show that you do not really love God;

16 For all these worldly things, these evil desires—the craze for sex, the ambition to buy everything that appeals to you, and the pride that comes from wealth and importance—these are not from God. They are from this evil world itself.

[1] Or, "atoning sacrifice."

Revised Standard

Father, Jesus Christ the righteous; 2and he is
the expiation for our sins, and not for ours
only but also for the sins of the whole
world. 3And by this we may be sure that we
know him, if we keep his commandments.
4He who says "I know him" but disobeys his
commandments is a liar, and the truth is not
in him; 5but whoever keeps his word, in him
truly love for God is perfected. By this we
may be sure that we are in him: 6he who
says he abides in him ought to walk in the
same way in which he walked.

The test of love

7 Beloved, I am writing you no new
commandment, but an old commandment
which you had from the beginning; the old
commandment is the word which you have
heard. 8Yet I am writing you a new commandment, which is true in him and in you,
because[b] the darkness is passing away and
the true light is already shining. 9He who
says he is in the light and hates his brother
is in darkness still. 10He who loves his brother
abides in the light, and in it[c] there is no
cause for stumbling. 11But he who hates
his brother is in the darkness and walks in
the darkness, and does not know where he is
going, because the darkness has blinded his
eyes.
12 I am writing to you, little children,
because your sins are forgiven for his sake.
13I am writing to you, fathers, because you
know him who is from the beginning. I am
writing to you, young men, because you have
overcome the evil one. I write to you, children, because you know the Father. 14I write
to you, fathers, because you know him who
is from the beginning. I write to you, young
men, because you are strong, and the word
of God abides in you, and you have overcome the evil one.
15 Do not love the world or the things in
the world. If any one loves the world, love
for the Father is not in him. 16For all that is
in the world, the lust of the flesh and the
lust of the eyes and the pride of life, is not

[b] Or *that*
[c] Or *him*

King James

17 And the world passeth away, and the lust thereof: but he that doeth the will of God abideth for ever.

18 Little children, it is the last time: and as ye have heard that antichrist shall come, even now are there many antichrists; whereby we know that it is the last time.

19 They went out from us, but they were not of us; for if they had been of us, they would *no doubt* have continued with us: but *they went out*, that they might be made manifest that they were not all of us.

20 But ye have an unction from the Holy One, and ye know all things.

21 I have not written unto you because ye know not the truth, but because ye know it, and that no lie is of the truth.

22 Who is a liar but he that denieth that Jesus is the Christ? He is antichrist, that denieth the Father and the Son.

23 Whosoever denieth the Son, the same hath not the Father: [*but*] *he that acknowledgeth the Son hath the Father also.*

24 Let that therefore abide in you, which ye have heard from the beginning. If that which ye have heard from the beginning shall remain in you, ye also shall continue in the Son, and in the Father.

25 And this is the promise that he hath promised us, *even* eternal life.

26 These *things* have I written unto you concerning them that seduce you.

27 But the anointing which ye have received of him abideth in you, and ye need not that any man teach you: but as the same anointing teacheth you of all things, and is truth, and is no lie, and even as it hath taught you, ye shall abide in him.

28 And now, little children, abide in him; that, when he shall appear, we may have confidence, and not be ashamed before him at his coming.

29 If ye know that he is righteous, ye know that every one that doeth righteousness is born of him.

Amplified

17 And the world passes away *and* disappears, and with it the forbidden cravings (the passionate desires, the lust) of it; but he who does the will of God and carries out His purposes in his life, abides (remains) forever.

18 [j]Boys (lads), it is the last time—hour [the end of this age]. And as you have heard that Antichrist [he who will oppose Christ in the guise of Christ] is coming, even now many antichrists have arisen, which confirms our belief that it is the final (the end) time.

19 They went out from our number, but they did not [really] belong to us; for if they had been of us, they would have remained with us. But [they withdrew] that it might be plain that they all are not of us.

20 But—you hold a sacred appointment, you have been given an unction—you have been anointed by the Holy One, and you all know [the Truth].

21 I write to you, not because you are ignorant *and* do not perceive *and* know the Truth, but because you do perceive *and* know it, and [know positively] that nothing false—no deception, no lie—is of the Truth.

22 Who is [such a] liar as he who denies that Jesus is the Christ, the Messiah? He is antichrist, (the antagonist of Christ), who [k]habitually denies *and* refuses to acknowledge the Father and the Son.

23 No one who [k]habitually denies (disowns) the Son [k]even has the Father. *Whoever confesses (acknowledges and has) the Son has the Father also.*

24 As for you, keep in your hearts what you have heard from the beginning. If what you heard from the first dwells *and* remains in you, then you will dwell in the Son and in the Father (always).

25 And this is what He Himself has promised us, the life, the eternal [life].

26 I write this to you with reference to those who would deceive you—seduce and lead you astray;

27 But as for you, (the sacred appointment, the unction) the anointing which you received from Him, abides ([l]permanently) in you; [so] then you have no need that any one should instruct you. But just as His anointing teaches you concerning everything, and is true, and is no falsehood, so you must abide—live, never to depart [[l]rooted in Him, knit to Him] just as [His anointing] has taught you [to do].

28 And now, little children, abide (live, remain [l]permanently) in Him, so that when He is made visible, we may have *and* enjoy perfect confidence (boldness, assurance) and not be ashamed *and* shrink from Him at His coming.

29 If you know (perceive and are sure) that He [Christ] is absolutely righteous (conforming to the Father's will in purpose, thought and action), you may also know (be sure) that every one who does righteously [and is therefore in like manner conformed to the divine will] is born (begotten) of Him [[m]God].

CHAPTER 3

BEHOLD, what manner of love the Father hath bestowed upon us, that we should be called the sons of God: therefore the world knoweth us not, because it knew him not.

CHAPTER 3

SEE what [[n]an incredible] quality of love the Fathe has given (shown, bestowed on) us, that we should [b permitted to] be named *and* called *and* counted the chi dren of God! And so we are! The reason that the worl does not know (recognize, acknowledge) us, is that it do not know (recognize, acknowledge) Him.

j) Abbott-Smith.
k) Vincent.
l) Thayer.
m) Westcott: When John thinks of God in relation to men he nev thinks of Him apart from Christ.
n) Vincent.

Living New Testament

17 And this world is fading away, and these evil, forbidden things will go with it, but whoever keeps doing the will of God will live forever.

18 Dear children, this world's last hour has come. You have heard about the Antichrist who is coming—the one who is against Christ—and already many such persons have appeared. This makes us all the more certain that the end of the world is near.

19 These "against-Christ" people used to be members of our churches, but they never really belonged with us or else they would have stayed. When they left us it proved that they were not of us at all.

20 But you are not like that, for the Holy Spirit has come upon you, and you know the truth.

21 So I am not writing to you as to those who need to know the truth, but I warn you as those who can discern the difference between true and false.

22 And who is the greatest liar? The one who says that Jesus is not Christ. Such a person is antichrist, for he does not believe in God the Father and in His Son.

23 For a person who doesn't believe in Christ, God's Son, can't have God the Father either. But he who has Christ, God's Son, has God the Father also.

24 So keep on believing what you have been taught from the beginning. If you do, you will always be in close fellowship with both God the Father and His Son.

25 And He Himself has promised us this: *eternal life.*

26 These remarks of mine about the Antichrist are pointed at those who would dearly love to blindfold you and lead you astray.

27 But you have received the Holy Spirit and He lives within you, in your hearts, so that you don't need anyone to teach you what is right. For He teaches you all things, and He is the Truth, and no liar; and so, just as He has said, you must live in Christ, never to depart from Him.

28 And now, my little children, stay in happy fellowship with the Lord so that when He comes you will be sure that all is well, and will not have to be ashamed and shrink back from meeting Him.

29 Since we know that God is always good and does only right, we may rightly assume that all those who do right are His children.

Revised Standard

of the Father but is of the world. 17 And
the world passes away, and the lust of it;
but he who does the will of God abides for
ever.

The test of belief

18 Children, it is the last hour; and as
you have heard that antichrist is coming, so
now many antichrists have come; therefore
we know that it is the last hour. 19 They went
out from us, but they were not of us; for if
they had been of us, they would have continued with us; but they went out, that it
might be plain that they all are not of us.
20 But you have been anointed by the Holy
One, and you all know.[d] 21 I write to you,
not because you do not know the truth, but
because you know it, and know that no lie
is of the truth. 22 Who is the liar but he who
denies that Jesus is the Christ? This is the
antichrist, he who denies the Father and
the Son. 23 No one who denies the Son has
the Father. He who confesses the Son has the
Father also. 24 Let what you heard from the
beginning abide in you. If what you heard
from the beginning abides in you, then you
will abide in the Son and in the Father.
25 And this is what he has promised us,[e]
eternal life.
26 I write this to you about those who
would deceive you; 27 but the anointing which
you received from him abides in you, and you
have no need that any one should teach you;
as his anointing teaches you about everything, and is true, and is no lie, just as it
has taught you, abide in him.
28 And now, little children, abide in him,
so that when he appears we may have confidence and not shrink from him in shame at
his coming. 29 If you know that he is righteous, you may be sure that every one who
does right is born of him.

CHAPTER 3

See how very much our heavenly Father loves us, for He allows us to be called His children—think of it—and we really *are!* But since most people don't know God, naturally they don't understand that we are His children.

Obedience in action

3 See what love the Father has given us,
that we should be called children of
God; and so we are. The reason why the
world does not know us is that it did not

[d] Other ancient authorities read *you know everything*
[e] Other ancient authorities read *you*

King James

2 Beloved, now are we the sons of God, and it doth not yet appear what we shall be: but we know that, when he shall appear, we shall be like him; for we shall see him as he is.

3 And every man that hath this hope in him purifieth himself, even as he is pure.

4 Whosoever committeth sin transgresseth also the law: for sin is the transgression of the law.

5 And ye know that he was manifested to take away our sins; and in him is no sin.

6 Whosoever abideth in him sinneth not: whosoever sinneth hath not seen him, neither known him.

7 Little children, let no man deceive you: he that doeth righteousness is righteous, even as he is righteous.

8 He that committeth sin is of the devil; for the devil sinneth from the beginning. For this purpose the Son of God was manifested, that he might destroy the works of the devil.

9 Whosoever is born of God doth not commit sin; for his seed remaineth in him: and he cannot sin, because he is born of God.

10 In this the children of God are manifest, and the children of the devil: whosoever doeth not righteousness is not of God, neither he that loveth not his brother.

11 For this is the message that ye heard from the beginning, that we should love one another.

12 Not as Cain, *who* was of that wicked one, and slew his brother. And wherefore slew he him? Because his own works were evil, and his brother's righteous.

13 Marvel not, my brethren, if the world hate you.

14 We know that we have passed from death unto life, because we love the brethren. He that loveth not *his* brother abideth in death.

15 Whosoever hateth his brother is a murderer: and ye know that no murderer hath eternal life abiding in him.

16 Hereby perceive we the love *of God*, because he laid down his life for us: and we ought to lay down *our* lives for the brethren.

Amplified

2 Beloved, we are [even here and] now God's children; it is not yet disclosed (made clear) what we shall be [hereafter], but we know that when He comes *and* is manifested we shall [[o]as God's children] resemble *and* be like Him, for we shall see Him [n]just as He [really] is.

3 And every one who has this hope [resting] on Him cleanses (purifies) himself just as He is pure—chaste, undefiled, guiltless.

4 Every one who commits (practices) sin is guilty of lawlessness; for [that is what] sin is, lawlessness [the breaking, violating of God's law by transgression or neglect; being unrestrained and unregulated by His commands and His will].

5 You know that He appeared in visible form *and* became Man to take away [upon Himself] sins, and in Him there is no sin—[n]essentially and forever.

6 No one who abides in Him—who lives and remains [p]in communion with and in obedience to Him, [deliberately and knowingly] [p]habitually commits (practices) sin. No one who habitually sins has either seen *or* known Him—recognized, perceived or understood Him, or has had an experimental acquaintance with Him.

7 [q]Boys (lads), let no one deceive *and* lead you astray. He who practices righteousness—who is upright, conforming to the divine will in purpose, thought and action, living a consistently conscientious life—is righteous, even as He is righteous.

8 [But] he who commits sin (who practices evil doing) is of the devil—takes his character from the evil one; for the devil has sinned (has violated the divine law) from the beginning. The reason the Son of God was made manifest (visible) was to undo (destroy, loosen and dissolve) the works the devil [has done].

9 No one born (begotten) of God [deliberately and knowingly] [p]habitually practices sin, for God's nature abides in him—His principle of life, the divine sperm, remains permanently within him—and he cannot practice sinning because he is born (begotten) of God.

10 By this it is made clear who take their nature from God *and* are His children, and who take their nature from the devil *and* are his children: no one who does not practice righteousness—who does not conform to God's will in purpose, thought and action—is of God; neither is any one who does not love his brother [his fellow [r]believer in Christ].

11 Because this is the message—the announcement—which you have heard from the first, that we should love one another,

12 [And] not be like Cain who [took his nature and got his motivation] from the evil one and slew his brother. And why did he slay him? Because his deeds (activities, works) were wicked *and* malicious and his brother's were righteous—virtuous.

13 Do not be surprised *and* wonder, brethren, that the world detests *and* pursues you with hatred.

14 We know that we have passed over out of the death into the Life by the fact that we love the brethren, [our fellow Christians]. He who does not love abides—remains is [s]held and kept continually—in [spiritual] death.

15 Any one who (abominates, detests) hates his brother [in Christ] is [at heart] a murderer, and you know that no murderer has eternal life abiding ([s]persevering) within him.

16 By this we come to know—progressively to recognize, to perceive, to understand the [essential] love: that He laid down His [own] life for us; and we ought to lay [our] lives down for [those who are our] brothers [[s]in Him

n) Vincent.
o) Jamieson, Fausset and Brown.
p) Vincent.
q) Abbott-Smith.
r) Thayer.
s) Thayer.

Living New Testament

2 Yes, dear friends, we are already God's children, right now, and we can't even imagine what it is going to be like later on. But we do know this, that when He comes we will be like Him, as a result of seeing Him as He really is.

3 And everyone who really believes this will try to stay pure because Christ is pure.

4 But those who keep on sinning are against God, for every sin is done against the will of God.

5 And you know that He became a man so that He could take away our sins, and that there is no sin in Him, no missing of God's will at any time in any way.

6 So if we stay close to Him, obedient to Him, we won't be sinning either; but as for those who keep on sinning, they should realize this: they sin because they have never really known Him or become His.

7 Oh, dear children, don't let anyone deceive you about this: if you are constantly doing what is good, it is because you *are* good, even as He is.

8 But if you keep on sinning, it shows that you belong to Satan, who since he first began to sin has kept steadily at it. But the Son of God came to destroy these works of the devil.

9 The person who has been born into God's family does not make a practice of sinning, because now God's life is in him; so he can't keep on sinning, for this new life has been born into him and controls him—he has been *born again.*

10 So now we can tell who is a child of God and who belongs to Satan. Whoever is living a life of sin and doesn't love his brother shows that he is not in God's family;

11 For the message to us from the beginning has been that we should love one another.

12 We are not to be like Cain, who belonged to Satan and killed his brother. Why did he kill him? Because Cain had been doing wrong and he knew very well that his brother's life was better than his.

13 So don't be surprised, dear friends, if the world hates you.

14 If we love other Christians it proves that we have been delivered from hell and given eternal life. But a person who doesn't have love for others is headed for eternal death.

15 Anyone who hates his Christian brother is really a murderer at heart; and you know that no one wanting to murder has eternal life within.

16 We know what real love is from Christ's example in dying for us. And so we also ought to lay down our lives for our Christian brothers.

Revised Standard

know him. [2]Beloved, we are God's children
now; it does not yet appear what we shall
be, but we know that when he appears we
shall be like him, for we shall see him as
he is. [3]And every one who thus hopes in
him purifies himself as he is pure.
4 Every one who commits sin is guilty of
lawlessness; sin is lawlessness. [5]You know
that he appeared to take away sins, and in
him there is no sin. [6]No one who abides in
him sins; no one who sins has either seen
him or known him. [7]Little children, let no
one deceive you. He who does right is righteous, as he is righteous. [8]He who commits
sin is of the devil; for the devil has sinned
from the beginning. The reason the Son of
God appeared was to destroy the works of
the devil. [9]No one born of God commits sin;
for God's[f] nature abides in him, and he cannot sin because he is[g] born of God. [10]By
this it may be seen who are the children of
God, and who are the children of the devil:
whoever does not do right is not of God, nor
he who does not love his brother.

Love in action

11 For this is the message which you have
heard from the beginning, that ye should
love one another, [12]and not be like Cain who
was of the evil one and murdered his brother.
And why did he murder him? Because his
own deeds were evil and his brother's righteous. [13]Do not wonder, brethren, that the
world hates you. [14]We know that we have
passed out of death into life, because we
love the brethren. He who does not love remains in death. [15]Any one who hates his
brother is a murderer, and you know that no
murderer has eternal life abiding in him. [16]By
this we know love, that he laid down his life
for us; and we ought to lay down our lives

[f] Greek *his*

[g] Or *for the offspring of God abide in him, and they cannot sin because they are*

King James

17 But whoso hath this world's good, and seeth his brother have need, and shutteth up his bowels *of compassion* from him, how dwelleth the love of God in him?

18 My little children, let us not love in word, neither in tongue; but in deed and in truth.

19 And hereby we know that we are of the truth, and shall assure our hearts before him.

20 For if our heart condemn us, God is greater than our heart, and knoweth all things.

21 Beloved, if our heart condemn us not, *then* have we confidence toward God.

22 And whatsoever we ask, we receive of him, because we keep his commandments, and do those things that are pleasing in his sight.

23 And this is his commandment, That we should believe on the name of his Son Jesus Christ, and love one another, as he gave us commandment.

24 And he that keepeth his commandments dwelleth in him, and he in him. And hereby we know that he abideth in us, by the Spirit which he hath given us.

Amplified

17 But if any one has this world's goods—resources for sustaining life—and sees his brother *and* [s]fellow believer in need, yet closes his heart of compassion against him, how can the love of God live *and* remain in him?

18 Little children, let us not love [merely] in theory *or* in speech but in deed and in truth—in practice and in sincerity.

19 By this we shall come to know—perceive and recognize and understand—that we are of the Truth, and can reassure (quiet, conciliate and pacify) our hearts in His presence

20 In whatever our hearts in [[t]tormenting] self-accusation make us feel guilty *and* condemn us. For [[t]we are in God's hands]; He is above *and* greater than our consciences (our hearts), and He knows (perceives and understands) everything—nothing is hidden from Him.

21 And, beloved, if our consciences (our hearts) do not accuse us—if they do not make us feel guilty and condemn us—we have confidence (complete assurance and boldness) before God;

22 And we receive from Him whatever we ask for, because we ([t]watchfully) obey His orders—observe His suggestions and injunctions, follow His plan for us—*and* ([t]habitually) practice what is pleasing to Him.

23 And this is His order (His command, His injunction), that we should believe—put our faith and trust in and adhere to and rely—on the name of His Son Jesus Christ, the Messiah, and that we should love one another, just as He has commanded us.

24 All who keep His commandments (who obey His orders and follow His plan, live and continue to live, to stay and) abide in Him, and He in them.—[u]They let Christ be a home to them and they are the home of Christ. And by this we know *and* understand *and* have the proof that He [really] lives *and* makes His home in us, by the (Holy) Spirit Whom He has given us.

CHAPTER 4

BELOVED, believe not every spirit, but try the spirits whether they are of God: because many false prophets are gone out into the world.

2 Hereby know ye the Spirit of God: Every spirit that confesseth that Jesus Christ is come in the flesh is of God:

3 And every spirit that confesseth not that Jesus Christ is come in the flesh is not of God: and this is that *spirit* of antichrist, whereof ye have heard that it should come; and even now already is it in the world.

4 Ye are of God, little children, and have overcome them: because greater is he that is in you, than he that is in the world.

CHAPTER 4

BELOVED, do not put faith in every spirit, but prove (test) the spirits to discover whether they proceed from God; for many false prophets have gone forth into the world.

2 By this you may know (perceive and recognize) the Spirit of God: every spirit which acknowledges *and* confesses [the fact] that Jesus Christ, the Messiah, [actually] has become man *and* has come in the flesh is of God—has God for its source.

3 And every spirit which does not acknowledge *and* confess *that* Jesus *Christ has come in the flesh* [but would [v]annul, destroy, [w]sever, disunite Him] is not of God—does not proceed from Him. This [[x]non-confession] is the [spirit] of antichrist, [of] which you heard that it was coming, and now it is already in the world.

4 Little children, you are of God—you belong to Him—and have [already] defeated *and* overcome them [the agents of antichrist], because He Who lives in you is greater (mightier) than he who is in the world.

---

s) Thayer.
t) Vincent.
u) After Bede.
v) An ancient reading.
w) The Vulgate translation.
x) Vincent.

Living New Testament

17 But if someone who is supposed to be a Christian has money enough to live well, and sees a brother in need, and won't help him—how can God's love be within *him?*

18 Little children, let us stop just *saying* we love people; let us *really* love them, and *show it* by our *actions.*

19 Then we will know for sure, by our actions, that we are on God's side and our consciences will be clear, even when we stand before the Lord.

20 But if we have bad consciences and feel that we have done wrong, the Lord will surely feel that way about us even more,[1] for He knows everything we do.

21 But, dearly loved friends, if our consciences are clear, we can come to the Lord with perfect assurance and trust,

22 And get whatever we ask for because we are obeying Him and doing the things that please Him.

23 And this is what God says we must do: believe on the name of His Son Jesus Christ, and love one another.

24 Those who do what God says—they are living with God and He with them. We know this is true because the Holy Spirit He has given us tells us so.

Revised Standard

for the brethren. [17]But if any one has the
world's goods and sees his brother in need,
yet closes his heart against him, how does
God's love abide in him? [18]Little children,
let us not love in word or speech but in deed
and in truth.
19 By this we shall know that we are of
the truth, and reassure our hearts before him
[20]whenever our hearts condemn us; for God
is greater than our hearts, and he knows everything. [21]Beloved, if our hearts do not condemn us, we have confidence before God;
[22]and we receive from him whatever we ask,
because we keep his commandments and do
what pleases him. [23]And this is his commandment, that we should believe in the name of
his Son Jesus Christ and love one another,
just as he has commanded us. [24]All who keep
his commandments abide in him, and he in
them. And by this we know that he abides in
us, by the Spirit which he has given us.

CHAPTER 4

Dearly loved friends, don't always believe everything you hear just because someone says it is a message from God: test it first to see if it really is. For there are many false teachers around,

2 And the way to find out if their message is from the Holy Spirit is to ask: Does it really agree that Jesus Christ, God's Son, actually became man with a human body? If so, then the message is from God.

3 If not, the message is not from God but from one who is against Christ, like the "Antichrist" you have heard about who is going to come, and his attitude of enmity against Christ is already abroad in the world.

4 Dear young friends, you belong to God and have already won your fight with those who are against Christ, because there is Someone in your hearts who is stronger than any evil teacher in this wicked world.

Faith in action

4 Beloved, do not believe every spirit, but
test the spirits to see whether they are of
God; for many false prophets have gone out
into the world. [2]By this you know the Spirit
of God: every spirit which confesses that
Jesus Christ has come in the flesh is of God,
[3]and every spirit which does not confess Jesus
is not of God. This is the spirit of antichrist,
of which you heard that it was coming, and
now it is in the world already. [4]Little children, you are of God, and have overcome
them; for he who is in you is greater than
he who is in the world. [5]They are of the

[1] Or, perhaps, "the Lord will be merciful anyway." Literally, "If our heart condemns us, God is greater than our heart."

King James

5 They are of the world: therefore speak they of the world, and the world heareth them.

6 We are of God: he that knoweth God heareth us; he that is not of God heareth not us. Hereby know we the spirit of truth, and the spirit of error.

7 Beloved, let us love one another: for love is of God; and every one that loveth is born of God, and knoweth God.

8 He that loveth not knoweth not God; for God is love.

9 In this was manifested the love of God toward us, because that God sent his only begotten Son into the world, that we might live through him.

10 Herein is love, not that we loved God, but that he loved us, and sent his Son *to be* the propitiation for our sins.

11 Beloved, if God so loved us, we ought also to love one another.

12 No man hath seen God at any time. If we love one another, God dwelleth in us, and his love is perfected in us.

13 Hereby know we that we dwell in him, and he in us, because he hath given us of his Spirit.

14 And we have seen and do testify that the Father sent the Son *to be* the Saviour of the world.

15 Whosoever shall confess that Jesus is the Son of God, God dwelleth in him, and he in God.

16 And we have known and believed the love that God hath to us. God is love; and he that dwelleth in love dwelleth in God, and God in him.

17 Herein is our love made perfect, that we may have boldness in the day of judgment: because as he is, so are we in this world.

18 There is no fear in love; but perfect love casteth out fear: because fear hath torment. He that feareth is not made perfect in love.

19 We love him, because he first loved us.

20 If a man say, I love God, and hateth his brother, he is a liar: for he that loveth not his brother whom he hath seen, how can he love God whom he hath not seen?

Amplified

5 They proceed from the world *and* are of the world, therefore it is out of the world [its [x]whole economy morally considered] that they speak, and the world listens (pays attention) to them.

6 We are [children] of God. Whoever is learning to know God—progressively to perceive, recognize and understand God [by observation and experience] and to [x]get an ever clearer knowledge of Him—listens to us; and he who is not of God does not listen *or* pay attention to us. By this we know (recognize) the Spirit of Truth and the spirit of error.

7 Beloved, let us love one another; for love [springs] from God, and he who loves [his fellow men] is begotten (born) of God and is coming (progressively) to know *and* understand God—to perceive and recognize and get a better and clearer knowledge of Him.

8 He who does not love has not become acquainted with God—does not *and* never did know Him; for God is love.

9 In this the love of God was made manifest (displayed), where we are concerned, in that God sent His Son, the only begotten *or* [y]unique [Son], into the world so that we might live through Him.

10 In this is love, not that we loved God, but that He loved us and sent His Son to be the propitiation (the atoning sacrifice) for our sins.

11 Beloved, if God loved us so [very much], we also ought to love one another.

12 No man has at any time [yet] seen God. But if we love one another, God abides (lives and remains) in us and His love [that love which is essentially His] is brought to completion—to its full maturity, runs its full course, is perfected—in us!

13 By this we come to know (perceive, recognize and understand) that we abide (live and remain) in Him and He in us: because He has given (imparted) to us of His (Holy) Spirit.

14 And [besides] we ourselves have seen [have deliberately and steadfastly contemplated], and bear witness that the Father has sent the Son [as the] Savior of the world.

15 Any one who confesses (acknowledges, owns) that Jesus is the Son of God, God abides (lives, makes His home) in him, and he (abides, lives, makes his home) in God.

16 And we know (understand, recognize, are conscious of, by observation and by experience), and believe (adhere to and put faith in and rely on) the love God cherishes for us. God is love, and he who dwells *and* continues in love dwells *and* continues in God, and God dwells *and* continues in him.

17 In this [union and communion with Him] love is brought to completion *and* attains perfection with us, that we may have confidence for the day of judgment—with assurance and boldness to face Him—because as He is, so are we in this world.

18 There is no fear in love—dread does not exist; but full-grown (complete, perfect) love [z]turns fear out of doors *and* expels every trace of terror! For fear [a]brings with it the thought of punishment, and [so] he who is afraid has not reached the full maturity of love—is not yet grown into love's complete perfection.

19 We love *Him,* because He first loved us.

20 If any one says, I love God, and (detests, abominates) hates his brother [[a]in Christ], he is a liar; for he who does not love his brother whom he has seen, cannot love God Whom he has not seen.

---

x) Vincent.
y) Moulton and Milligan.
z) Vincent.
a) Thayer.

Living New Testament

5 These men belong to this world, so, quite naturally, they are concerned about worldly affairs and the world pays attention to them.

6 But we are children of God; that is why only those who have walked and talked with God will listen to us. Others won't. That is another way to know whether a message is really from God; for if it is, the world won't listen to it.

7 Dear friends, let us practice loving each other, for love comes from God and those who are loving and kind show that they are the children of God, and that they are getting to know Him better.

8 But if a person isn't loving and kind, it shows that he doesn't know God—for God is love.

9 God showed how much He loved us by sending His only Son into this wicked world to bring to us eternal life through His death.

10 In this act we see what real love is: it is not our love for God, but His love for us when He sent His Son to satisfy God's anger against our sins.

11 Dear friends, since God loved us as much as that, we surely ought to love each other too.

12 For though we have never yet seen God, when we love each other God lives in us and His love within us grows ever stronger.

13 And He has put His own Holy Spirit into our hearts as a proof to us that we are living with Him and He with us.

14 And furthermore, we have seen with our own eyes and now tell all the world that God sent His Son to be their Savior.

15 Anyone who believes and says that Jesus is the Son of God has God living in him, and he is living with God.

16 We know how much God loves us because we have felt His love and because we believe Him when He tells us that He loves us dearly. God is love, and anyone who lives in love is living with God and God is living in Him.

17 And as we live with Christ, our love grows more perfect and complete; so we will not be ashamed and embarrassed at the day of judgment, but can face Him with confidence and joy, because He loves us and we love Him too.

18 We need have no fear of someone who loves us perfectly; His perfect love for us eliminates all dread of what He might do to us. If we are afraid, it is for fear of what He might do to us, and shows that we are not fully convinced that He really loves us.

19 So you see, our love for Him comes as a result of His loving us first.

20 If anyone says,"I love God," but keeps on hating his brother, he is a liar; for if he doesn't love his brother who is right there in front of him how can he love God whom he has never seen?

Revised Standard

world, therefore what they say is of the
world, and the world listens to them. [6]We are
of God. Whoever knows God listens to us,
and he who is not of God does not listen
to us. By this we know the spirit of truth and
the spirit of error.

The source of love

7 Beloved, let us love one another; for
love is of God, and he who loves is born of
God and knows God. [8]He who does not love
does not know God; for God is love. [9]In
this the love of God was made manifest
among us, that God sent his only Son into
the world, so that we might live through him.
[10]In this is love, not that we loved God but
that he loved us and sent his Son to be the
expiation for our sins. [11]Beloved, if God so
loved us, we also ought to love one another.
[12]No man has ever seen God; if we love one
another, God abides in us and his love is
perfected in us.

13 By this we know that we abide in him
and he in us, because he has given us of his
own Spirit. [14]And we have seen and testify
that the Father has sent his Son as the Savior of the world. [15]Whoever confesses that
Jesus is the Son of God, God abides in him,
and he in God. [16]So we know and believe
the love God has for us. God is love, and
he who abides in love abides in God, and
God abides in him. [17]In this is love perfected
with us, that we may have confidence for the
day of judgment, because as he is so are we
in this world. [18]There is no fear in love, but
perfect love casts out fear. For fear has to do
with punishment, and he who fears is not
perfected in love. [19]We love, because he
first loved us. [20]If any one says, "I love
God," and hates his brother, he is a liar;
for he who does not love his brother whom
he has seen, cannot[h] love God whom he has

---

h Other ancient authorities read *how can he*

King James

21 And this commandment have we from him, That he who loveth God love his brother also.

CHAPTER 5

WHOSOEVER believeth that Jesus is the Christ is born of God: and every one that loveth him that begat loveth him also that is begotten of him.

2 By this we know that we love the children of God, when we love God, and keep his commandments.

3 For this is the love of God, that we keep his commandments: and his commandments are not grievous.

4 For whatsoever is born of God overcometh the world: and this is the victory that overcometh the world, *even* our faith.

5 Who is he that overcometh the world, but he that believeth that Jesus is the Son of God?

6 This is he that came by water and blood, *even* Jesus Christ; not by water only, but by water and blood. And it is the Spirit that beareth witness, because the Spirit is truth.

7 For there are three that bear record in heaven, the Father, the Word, and the Holy Ghost: and these three are one.

8 And there are three that bear witness in earth, the Spirit, and the water, and the blood: and these three agree in one.

9 If we receive the witness of men, the witness of God is greater: for this is the witness of God which he hath testified of his Son.

10 He that believeth on the Son of God hath the witness in himself: he that believeth not God hath made him a liar; because he believeth not the record that God gave of his Son.

11 And this is the record, that God hath given to us eternal life, and this life is in his Son.

12 He that hath the Son hath life; *and* he that hath not the Son of God hath not life.

13 These things have I written unto you that believe on the name of the Son of God; that ye may know that ye have eternal life, and that ye may believe on the name of the Son of God.

Amplified

21 And this command (charge, order, injunction) we have from Him, that he who loves God shall love his brother [[a]believer] also.

CHAPTER 5

EVERY one who believes—adheres to, trusts in and relies [on the fact]—that Jesus is the Christ, the Messiah, is a born-again child of God; and every one who loves the Father also loves the one born of Him—His offspring.

2 By this we come to know (recognize and understand) that we love the children of God: when we love God and obey His commands—orders, charges; when we keep His ordinances and are mindful of His precepts and His teaching.

3 For the [true] love of God is this, that we do His commands—keep His ordinances and are mindful of His precepts and teaching. And these orders of His are not irksome—burdensome, oppressive or grievous.

4 For whatever is born of God is victorious over the world; and this is the victory that conquers the world, even our faith.

5 Who is it that is victorious over (that conquers) the world but he who believes that Jesus is the Son of God—who adheres to, trusts in and relies [on that fact]?

6 This is He Who came by (with) water and blood [[b]His baptism and His death], Jesus Christ, the Messiah; not by (in) the water only but by (in) the water and the blood.

7 And it is the (Holy) Spirit Who bears witness, because the (Holy) Spirit is the Truth.

8 So there are three witnesses *in heaven, the Father, the Word and the Holy Spirit, and these three are One; and there are three witnesses on the earth,* the Spirit, the water and the blood; and these three agree—are in unison, their testimony coincides.

9 If we accept [as we do] the testimony of men (if we are willing to take human authority), the testimony of God is greater (stronger authority), for this is the testimony of God; even the witness which He has borne regarding His Son.

10 He who believes in the Son of God—who adheres to and trusts in and relies on Him, possesses this divine attestation—has the testimony within himself. He who does not believe God (in this way) has made Him out to be *and* represented Him as a liar, because he has not believed—put his faith in and adhered to and relied on the testimony—the evidence that God has borne regarding His Son.

11 And this is that testimony—that evidence: God gave us eternal life, and this life is in His Son.

12 He who possesses the Son has that life; he who does not possess the Son of God does not have that life.

13 I write this to you who believe in (adhere to, trust in and rely on) the name of the Son of God—that is, in [c]the peculiar services and blessings conferred by Him on men—so that you may know (with settled and absolute knowledge) that you [already] have life, [d]yes, eternal life.

a) Thayer.
b) Vincent.
c) Thayer.
d) Westcott in Speaker's Commentary.

Living New Testament

21 And God Himself has said that one must not only love God, but his brother too.

CHAPTER 5

If you believe that Jesus is the Christ—that He is God's Son and your Savior—then you are a child of God. And all who love the Father love His children too.

2 So you can find out how much you love God's children—your brothers and sisters in the Lord—by how much you love and obey God.

3 Loving God means doing what He tells us to do, and really, that isn't hard at all;

4 For every child of God can obey Him, defeating sin and evil pleasure by trusting Christ to help him.

5 But who could possibly fight and win this battle except by believing that Jesus is truly the Son of God?

6, 7, 8 And we know He is, because God said so with a voice from heaven when Jesus was baptized, and again as He was facing death[1]—yes, not only at His baptism but also as He faced death.[2] And the Holy Spirit, forever truthful, says it too. So we have these three witnesses: the voice of the Holy Spirit in our hearts, the voice from heaven at Christ's baptism, and the voice before He died.[3] And they all say the same thing: that Jesus Christ is the Son of God.[4]

9 We believe men who witness in our courts, and so surely we can believe whatever God declares. And God declares that Jesus is His Son.

10 All who believe this know in their hearts that it is true. If anyone doesn't believe this, he is actually calling God a liar, because he doesn't believe what God has said about His Son.

11 And what is it that God has said? That He has given us eternal life, and that this life is in His Son.

12 So whoever has God's Son has life; whoever does not have His Son, does not have life.

13 I have written this to you who believe in the Son of God so that you may know you have eternal life.

Revised Standard

not seen. [21]And this commandment we have
from him, that he who loves God should love
his brother also.

Victory through faith

5 Every one who believes that Jesus is the
Christ is a child of God, and every one
who loves the parent loves the child. [2]By
this we know that we love the children of
God, when we love God and obey his commandments. [3]For this is the love of God,
that we keep his commandments. And his
commandments are not burdensome. [4]For
whatever is born of God overcomes the
world; and this is the victory that overcomes the world, our faith. [5]Who is it that
overcomes the world but he who believes
that Jesus is the Son of God?

Faith through the Son

6 This is he who came by water and blood,
Jesus Christ, not with the water only but
with the water and the blood. [7]And the
Spirit is the witness, because the Spirit is the
truth. [8]There are three witnesses, the Spirit,
the water, and the blood; and these three
agree. [9]If we receive the testimony of men,
the testimony of God is greater; for this is
the testimony of God that he has borne witness to his Son. [10]He who believes in the
Son of God has the testimony in himself.
He who does not believe God has made him
a liar, because he has not believed in the
testimony that God has borne to his Son.
[11]And this is the testimony, that God gave us
eternal life, and this life is in his Son. [12]He
who has the Son has life; he who has not
the Son of God has not life.

The certainties of faith

13 I write this to you who believe in the
name of the Son of God, that you may know

---

[1] Literally, "This is He who came by water and blood." See Matthew 3:16, 17; Luke 9:31, 35; John 12:27, 28, 32, 33. Other interpretations of this verse are equally possible.
[2] Literally, "not by water only, but by water and blood."
[3] Literally, "the Spirit, and the water, and the blood."
[4] Implied.

King James

14 And this is the confidence that we have in him, that, if we ask any thing according to his will, he heareth us:

15 And if we know that he hear us, whatsoever we ask, we know that we have the petitions that we desired of him.

16 If any man see his brother sin a sin *which* is not unto death, he shall ask, and he shall give him life for them that sin not unto death. There is a sin unto death: I do not say that he shall pray for it.

17 All unrighteousness is sin: and there is a sin not unto death.

18 We know that whosoever is born of God sinneth not; but he that is begotten of God keepeth himself, and that wicked one toucheth him not.

19 *And* we know that we are of God, and the whole world lieth in wickedness.

20 And we know that the Son of God is come, and hath given us an understanding, that we may know him that is true, and we are in him that is true, *even* in his Son Jesus Christ. This is the true God, and eternal life.

21 Little children, keep yourselves from idols. Amen.

Amplified

14 And this is the confidence—the assurance, the [privilege of] boldness—which we have in Him: [we are sure] that if we ask anything (make any request) according to His will (in agreement with His own plan) He listens to *and* hears us.

15 And if (since) we [positively] know that He listens to us in whatever we ask, we also know [with settled and absolute knowledge] that we have [granted us as our present possessions] the requests made of Him.

16 If any one sees his brother [believer] committing a sin that does not [lead to] death [the extinguishing of life], he will pray and (God) will give him life—yes, He will grant life to all those whose sin is not [one leading] to death. There is a sin [that leads] to death; I do not say that one should pray for that.

17 All wrongdoing is sin, and there is sin which does not [involve] death—that may be repented of and forgiven.

18 We know [absolutely] that any one born of God does not [deliberately and knowingly] practice committing sin, but the One Who was begotten of God carefully watches over *and* protects him—Christ's divine presence within him preserves him against the evil—and the wicked one does not lay hold (get a grip) on him *or* touch [him].

19 We know [positively] that we are of God, and the whole world [around us] is under the power of the evil one.

20 And we [have seen and] know [positively] that the Son of God has [actually] come to this world and has given us understanding *and* insight progressively to perceive (recognize) *and* come to know better *and* more clearly Him Who is true; and we are in Him Who is true, in His Son Jesus Christ, the Messiah. This is the true God and Life eternal.

21 Little children, keep yourselves from idols—false gods, [from anything and everything that would occupy the place in your heart due to God, from any sort of substitute for Him that would take first place in your life]. *Amen. So let it be.*

Living New Testament

14 And we are sure of this, that He will listen to us whenever we ask Him for anything in line with His will.

15 And if we really know He is listening when we talk to Him and make our requests, then we can be sure that He will answer us.

16 If you see a Christian sinning in a way that does not end in death, you should ask God to forgive him and God will give him life, unless he has sinned that one fatal sin. But there is that one sin which ends in death and if he has done that, there is no use praying for him.

17 Every wrong is a sin, of course. I'm not talking about these ordinary sins; I am speaking of that one that ends in death.[5]

18 No one who has become part of God's family makes a practice of sinning, for Christ, God's Son, holds him securely and the devil cannot get his hands on him.

19 We know that we are children of God and that all the rest of the world around us is under Satan's power and control.

20 And we know that Christ, God's Son, has come to help us understand and find the true God. And now we are in God because we are in Jesus Christ His Son, who is the only true God; and He is eternal Life.

21 Dear children, keep away from anything that might take God's place in your hearts. Amen.

Sincerely,
John

[5] Commentators differ widely in their thoughts about what sin this is, and whether it causes physical death or spiritual death. Blasphemy against the Holy Spirit results in spiritual death (Mark 3:29) but can a Christian ever sin in such a way? Impenitence at the Communion Table sometimes ends in physical death (I Cor. 11:30). And Hebrews 6:4-8 speaks of the terrible end of those who fall away.

Revised Standard

that you have eternal life. [14]And this is the
confidence which we have in him, that if we
ask anything according to his will he hears
us. [15]And if we know that he hears us in
whatever we ask, we know that we have obtained the requests made of him. [16]If any
one sees his brother committing what is not
a mortal sin, he will ask, and God[i] will give
him life for those whose sin is not mortal.
There is sin which is mortal; I do not say
that one is to pray for that. [17]All wrongdoing is sin, but there is sin which is not mortal.

18 We know that any one born of God does not sin, but He who was born of God keeps him, and the evil one does not touch him.

19 We know that we are of God, and the whole world is in the power of the evil one.

20 And we know that the Son of God
has come and has given us understanding, to
know him who is true; and we are in him
who is true, in his Son Jesus Christ. This is
the true God and eternal life. [21]Little children, keep yourselves from idols.

[i] Greek *he*

King James

THE SECOND EPISTLE OF

John

THE elder unto the elect lady and her children, whom I love in the truth; and not I only, but also all they that have known the truth;

2 For the truth's sake, which dwelleth in us, and shall be with us for ever.

3 Grace be with you, mercy, *and* peace, from God the Father, and from the Lord Jesus Christ, the Son of the Father, in truth and love.

4 I rejoiced greatly that I found of thy children walking in truth, as we have received a commandment from the Father.

5 And now I beseech thee, lady, not as though I wrote a new commandment unto thee, but that which we had from the beginning, that we love one another.

6 And this is love, that we walk after his commandments. This is the commandment, That, as ye have heard from the beginning, ye should walk in it.

7 For many deceivers are entered into the world, who confess not that Jesus Christ is come in the flesh. This is a deceiver and an antichrist.

8 Look to yourselves, that we lose not those things which we have wrought, but that we receive a full reward.

9 Whosoever transgresseth, and abideth not in the doctrine of Christ, hath not God. He that abideth in the doctrine of Christ, he hath both the Father and the Son.

10 If there come any unto you, and bring not this doctrine, receive him not into *your* house, neither bid him God speed:

11 For he that biddeth him God speed is partaker of his evil deeds.

12 Having many things to write unto you, I would not *write* with paper and ink: but I trust to come unto you, and speak face to face, that our joy may be full.

13 The children of thy elect sister greet thee. Amen.

Amplified

THE SECOND LETTER
OF

John

THE elderly elder [of the church addresses this letter] to the elect (chosen) lady (Cyria) and her children, whom I truly love, and not only I but also all who are progressively learning to recognize *and* know *and* understand the Truth,

2 Because of the Truth which lives *and* stays on in our hearts and will be with us forever:

3 Grace (spiritual blessing), mercy and soul-peace will be with us, from God the Father and from Jesus Christ, the Messiah, the Father's Son, in all sincerity (truth) and love.

4 I was greatly delighted to find some of your children walking (living) in [the] Truth, just as we have been commanded by the Father [Himself].

5 And now I beg you, lady (Cyria), not as if I were issuing a new charge (injunction or command), but [simply recalling to your mind] the one we have had from the beginning, that we love one another.

6 And what this love consists in is this, that we live *and* walk in accordance with *and* guided by His commandments—His orders, ordinances, precepts, teaching. This is the commandment, as you have heard from the beginning, that you continue to walk in love—guided by it and following it.

7 For many imposters—seducers, deceivers and false leaders—have gone out into the world, men who will not acknowledge (confess, admit) the coming of Jesus Christ, the Messiah, in bodily form; such a one is the imposter—the seducer, the deceiver, the false leader, the antagonist of Christ—and the Antichrist.

8 —Take care; look to yourselves that you may not lose (throw away or destroy) all that we *and* you have labored for, but that you may [persevere until you] win *and* receive back a perfect reward—in full.

9 Any one who runs on ahead [of God] and does not abide in the doctrine of Christ—who is not content with what He taught—does not have God; but he who continues to live in the doctrine (teaching) of Christ—does have God; he has both the Father and the Son.

10 If any one comes to you and does not bring this doctrine (is disloyal to what Jesus Christ taught), do not receive him—do not accept him, do not welcome *or* admit him—into [your] house or bid him Godspeed *or* give him any encouragement.

11 For he who wishes him success—who encourages him, wishing him Godspeed—is a partaker in his evil doings.

12 Although I have many things to write to you, I prefer not to do so with paper and ink, but I hope to come to see you and talk with you by word of mouth, so that our joy may be complete.

13 The children of your elect (chosen) sister wish to be remembered to you. *Amen. So be it.*

Living New Testament

II John

From: John, the old Elder of the church.

To: That dear woman Cyria, one of God's very own, and to her children whom I love so much, as does everyone else in the church.

2 Since the Truth is in our hearts forever,

3 God the Father and Jesus Christ His Son will bless us with great mercy and much peace, and with truth and love.

4 How happy I am to find some of your children here, and to see that they are living as they should, following the Truth, obeying God's command.

5 And now I want to urgently remind you, dear friends, of the old rule God gave us right from the beginning, that Christians should love one another.

6 If we love God, we will do whatever He tells us to. And He has told us from the very first to love each other.

7 Watch out for the false leaders—and there are many of them around—who don't believe that Jesus Christ came to earth as a human being with a body like ours. Such people are against the truth and against Christ.

8 Beware of being like them, and losing the prize that you and I have been working so hard to get. See to it that you win your full reward from the Lord.

9 For if you wander beyond the teaching of Christ, you will leave God behind; while if you are loyal to Christ's teachings, you will have God too. Then you will have both the Father and the Son.

10 If anyone comes to teach you, and he doesn't believe what Christ taught, don't even invite him into your home. Don't encourage him in any way.

11 If you do you will be a partner with him in his wickedness.

12 Well, I would like to say much more, but I don't want to say it in this letter, for I hope to come to see you soon and then we can talk over these things together and have a joyous time.

13 Greetings from the children of your sister—another choice child of God.

Sincerely,
John

Revised Standard

THE SECOND LETTER OF

John

Salutation

1 The elder to the elect lady and her children, whom I love in the truth, and not only
I but also all who know the truth, [2]because
of the truth which abides in us and will be
with us for ever:
3 Grace, mercy, and peace will be with
us, from God the Father and from Jesus
Christ the Father's Son, in truth and love.

Counsel and warnings

4 I rejoiced greatly to find some of your
children following the truth, just as we have
been commanded by the Father. [5]And now I
beg you, lady, not as though I were writing
you a new commandment, but the one we
have had from the beginning, that we love
one another. [6]And this is love, that we follow
his commandments; this is the commandment, as you have heard from the beginning,
that you follow love. [7]For many deceivers
have gone out into the world, men who will
not acknowledge the coming of Jesus Christ
in the flesh; such a one is the deceiver and
the antichrist. [8]Look to yourselves, that you
may not lose what you[a] have worked for, but
may win a full reward. [9]Any one who goes
ahead and does not abide in the doctrine of
Christ does not have God; he who abides in
the doctrine has both the Father and the Son.
[10]If any one comes to you and does not
bring this doctrine, do not receive him into
the house or give him any greeting; [11]for he
who greets him shares his wicked work.

Conclusion

12 Though I have much to write to you,
I would rather not use paper and ink, but
I hope to come to see you and talk with you
face to face, so that our joy may be complete.
13 The children of your elect sister greet
you.

[a] Other ancient authorities read *we*

King James

THE THIRD EPISTLE OF

John

THE elder unto the well-beloved Gaius,
whom I love in the truth.
2 Beloved, I wish above all things that
thou mayest prosper and be in health, even
as thy soul prospereth.
3 For I rejoiced greatly, when the brethren came and testified of the truth that is
in thee, even as thou walkest in the truth.
4 I have no greater joy than to hear that
my children walk in truth.
5 Beloved, thou doest faithfully whatsoever thou doest to the brethren, and to
strangers;
6 Which have borne witness of thy charity before the church: whom if thou bring
forward on their journey after a godly sort,
thou shalt do well:
7 Because that for his name's sake they
went forth, taking nothing of the Gentiles.
8 We therefore ought to receive such,
that we might be fellow-helpers to the truth.
9 I wrote unto the church: but Diotrephes, who loveth to have the preeminence
among them, receiveth us not.
10 Wherefore, if I come, I will remember
his deeds which he doeth, prating against us
with malicious words: and not content
therewith, neither doth he himself receive
the brethren, and forbiddeth them that
would, and casteth *them* out of the church.
11 Beloved, follow not that which is evil,
but that which is good. He that doeth good
is of God: but he that doeth evil hath not
seen God.
12 Demetrius hath good report of all
men, and of the truth itself: yea, and we
also bear record; and ye know that our
record is true.
13 I had many things to write, but I will
not with ink and pen write unto thee:
14 But I trust I shall shortly see thee, and
we shall speak face to face. Peace *be* to
thee. *Our* friends salute thee. Greet the
friends by name.

Amplified

THE THIRD LETTER
OF

John

THE elderly elder [of the church addresses this letter]
to the (esteemed) beloved Gaius, whom I truly love.
2 Beloved, I pray that you may prosper in every way
and [that your body] may keep well, even as [I know] your
soul keeps well *and* prospers.
3 In fact, I greatly rejoiced [when some of] the brethren from time to time arrived and spoke [so highly] of
the sincerity *and* fidelity of your life, as indeed you do live
in the Truth [the whole Gospel presents].
4 I have no greater joy than this, to hear that my
[spiritual] children are living their lives in the Truth.
5 Beloved, it is a fine *and* faithful work that you are
doing when you give any service to the [Christian] brethren, and [especially when they are] strangers.
6 They have testified before the church of your love
and friendship. You will do well to forward them on their
journey, [and you will please do so] in a way worthy of
God's [service].
7 For these [traveling missionaries] have gone out for
the Name's sake—for His sake—and are accepting nothing from the heathen (the Gentiles, the non-Israelites).
8 So we ourselves ought to support such people—to
welcome and provide for them—in order that we may be
fellow workers in the Truth (the whole Gospel) *and*
co-operate with its teachers.
9 I have written briefly to the church; but Diotrephes,
who likes to take the lead among them *and* put himself
first, does not acknowledge my authority *and* refuses to
accept my suggestions *or* to listen to me.
10 So when I arrive, I will call attention to what he is
doing, his boiling over *and* casting malicious reflections
upon us with insinuating language. And not satisfied with
that, he refuses to receive *and* welcome the [missionary]
brethren himself, and also interferes with *and* forbids
those who would welcome them, and tries to expel (excommunicate) them from the church.
11 Beloved, do not imitate evil, but imitate good. He
who does good is of God; he who does evil has not seen
(discerned or experienced) God—has enjoyed no vision of
Him and does not know Him at all.
12 Demetrius has warm commendation from everyone,
and from the Truth itself; we add our testimony also, and
you know that our testimony is true.
13 I had much [to say to you when I began] to write,
but I prefer not to put it down with pen (a reed) and
ink;
14 I hope to see you soon, and we will talk together by
word of mouth.
15 [Goodbye!] Peace be to you! The friends here send
you greetings. Remember me to the friends there, (to
every one of them personally) by name.

Living New Testament

III John

From: John, the Elder.
To: Dear Gaius, whom I truly love.

2 Dear friend, I am praying that all is well with you and that your body is as healthy as I know your soul is.

3 Some of the brothers traveling by have made me very happy by telling me that your life stays clean and true, and that you are living by the standards of the Gospel.

4 I could have no greater joy than to hear such things about my children.

5 Dear friend, you are doing a good work for God in taking care of the traveling teachers and missionaries who are passing through.

6 They have told the church here of your friendship and your loving deeds. I am glad when you send them on their way with a generous gift.

7 For they are traveling for the Lord, and take neither food, clothing, shelter, nor money from those who are not Christians, even though they have preached to them.

8 So we ourselves should take care of them in order that we may become partners with them in the Lord's work.

9 I sent a brief letter to the church about this, but proud Diotrephes, who loves to push himself forward as the leader of the Christians there, does not admit my authority over him and refuses to listen to me.

10 When I come I will tell you some of the things he is doing and what wicked things he is saying about me and what insulting language he is using. He not only refuses to welcome the missionary travelers himself, but tells others not to, and when they do he tries to put them out of the church.

11 Dear friend, don't let this bad example influence you. Only follow what is good. Remember that those who do what is right prove that they are God's children; and those who continue in evil prove that they are far from God.

12 But everyone, including Truth itself, speaks highly of Demetrius. I myself can say the same for him, and you know I speak the truth.

13 I have much to say but I don't want to write it,

14 For I hope to see you soon and then we will have much to talk about together.

15 So good-bye for now. Friends here send their love, and please give each of the folks there a special greeting from me.

Sincerely,
John

Revised Standard

THE THIRD LETTER OF

John

Salutation

1 The elder to the beloved Gaius, whom
I love in the truth.
2 Beloved, I pray that all may go well
with you and that you may be in health; I
know that it is well with your soul. [3]For I
greatly rejoiced when some of the brethren
arrived and testified to the truth of your life,
as indeed you do follow the truth. [4]No greater joy can I have than this, to hear that my
children follow the truth.

Encouragement for Gaius

5 Beloved, it is a loyal thing you do when
you render any service to the brethren, especially to strangers, [6]who have testified to
your love before the church. You will do
well to send them on their journey as befits
God's service. [7]For they have set out for his
sake and have accepted nothing from the
heathen. [8]So we ought to support such men,
that we may be fellow workers in the truth.

Reproof for Diotrephes

9 I have written something to the church;
but Diotrephes, who likes to put himself first,
does not acknowledge my authority. [10]So if
I come, I will bring up what he is doing, prating against me with evil words. And not content with that, he refuses himself to welcome
the brethren, and also stops those who want
to welcome them and puts them out of the
church.

Commendation for Demetrius

11 Beloved, do not imitate evil but imitate good. He who does good is of God; he
who does evil has not seen God. [12]Demetri-
us has testimony from every one, and from
the truth itself; I testify to him too, and you
know my testimony is true.

Conclusion

13 I had much to write to you, but I
would rather not write with pen and ink;
[14]I hope to see you soon, and we will talk
together face to face.
15 Peace be to you. The friends greet you.
Greet the friends, every one of them.

King James

THE GENERAL EPISTLE OF

Jude

JUDE, the servant of Jesus Christ, and brother of James, to them that are sanctified by God the Father, and preserved in Jesus Christ, *and* called:

2 Mercy unto you, and peace and love, be multiplied.

3 Beloved, when I gave all diligence to write unto you of the common salvation, it was needful for me to write unto you, and exhort *you* that ye should earnestly contend for the faith which was once delivered unto the saints.

4 For there are certain men crept in unawares, who were before of old ordained to this condemnation, ungodly men, turning the grace of our God into lasciviousness, and denying the only Lord God, and our Lord Jesus Christ.

5 I will therefore put you in remembrance, though ye once knew this, how that the Lord, having saved the people out of the land of Egypt, afterward destroyed them that believed not.

6 And the angels which kept not their first estate, but left their own habitation, he hath reserved in everlasting chains under darkness unto the judgment of the great day.

7 Even as Sodom and Gomorrha, and the cities about them in like manner, giving themselves over to fornication, and going after strange flesh, are set forth for an example, suffering the vengeance of eternal fire.

8 Likewise also these *filthy* dreamers defile the flesh, despise dominion, and speak evil of dignities.

9 Yet Michael the archangel, when contending with the devil he disputed about the body of Moses, durst not bring against him a railing accusation, but said, The Lord rebuke thee.

10 But these speak evil of those things which they know not: but what they know naturally, as brute beasts, in those things they corrupt themselves.

11 Woe unto them! for they have gone in the way of Cain, and ran greedily after the error of Balaam for reward, and perished in the gainsaying of Core.

Amplified

THE LETTER
OF

Jude

JUDE, a servant of Jesus Christ, the Messiah, and brother of James, [writes this letter] to those who are called (chosen), dearly loved by God the Father ([a]and separated, set apart), and kept for Jesus Christ:

2 May mercy, soul-peace and love be multiplied to you.

3 Beloved, my whole concern was to write to you in regard to our common salvation. [But] I found it necessary *and* was impelled to write you and urgently appeal to *and* exhort [you] to contend for the faith which was once for all [b]handed down to the saints—the faith [which is that sum of Christian belief] which was delivered [b]verbally to the holy people of God.

4 For certain men have crept in stealthily—[c]gaining entrance secretly by a side [door]. Their doom was predicted long ago, (impious, profane) ungodly persons who pervert the grace (the spiritual blessing and favor) of our God into lawlessness *and* wantonness *and* immorality, and disown *and* deny our sole Master and Lord, Jesus Christ, the Messiah, the Anointed One.

5 Now I want to remind you, though you were fully informed once for all, that though the Lord [at one time] delivered a people out of the land of Egypt, He subsequently destroyed those [of them] who did not believe—who [refused] to adhere to, trust in and rely upon Him.

6 And angels that did not keep (care for, guard and hold to) their own first place of power but abandoned their proper dwelling place, He has reserved in custody in eternal chains (bonds) under the thick gloom of utter darkness until the judgment *and* doom of the great day.

7 Just as Sodom and Gomorrah and the adjacent towns, which likewise gave themselves over to impurity and indulged in unnatural vice *and* sensual perversity, are laid out [in plain sight] as an exhibit of perpetual punishment [to warn] of everlasting fire [the wicked are sentenced to suffer]. [Gen. 19.]

8 Nevertheless in like manner these dreamers also corrupt the body, scorn *and* reject authority *and* government, and revile *and* libel *and* scoff at [heavenly] glories (the glorious ones).

9 But when [even] the archangel Michael, contending with the devil, judicially argued (disputed) about the body of Moses, he dared not (presume to) bring an abusive condemnation against him, but [simply] said, The Lord rebuke you! [Zech. 3:2.]

10 But these men revile (scoff and sneer at) anything they do not happen to be acquainted with *and* do not understand; and whatever they do understand physically, [that which they know by mere instinct] like irrational beasts, by these they corrupt themselves *and* are destroyed (perish).

11 Woe to them! For they have run riotously in the way of Cain, and have abandoned themselves for the sake of gain [it offers them] to the error of Balaam, and have perished in rebellion [like that] of Korah! [Gen. 4:3-8; Num. 22-24; 16.]

---

a) Some texts so read.
b) Abbott-Smith.
c) Meaning of the verb.

Living New Testament

Jude

From: Jude, a servant of Jesus Christ, and a brother of James.

To: Christians everywhere, for God the Father has chosen you and Jesus Christ has kept you safe.

2 May you be given more and more of God's kindness, peace, and love.

3 Dearly loved friends, I had been planning to write you some thoughts about the salvation God has given us, but now I find I must write of something else instead, urging you to stoutly defend the truth which God gave, once for all, to His people to keep without change through the years.

4 I say this because some godless teachers have wormed their way in among you, saying that after we become Christians we can do just as we like without fear of God's punishment. The fate of such people was written long ago, for they have turned against our only Master and Lord, Jesus Christ.

5 My answer to them is: remember this fact—which you know already—that the Lord saved a whole nation of people out of the land of Egypt, and then killed every one of them who did not trust and obey Him.

6 And I remind you of those angels who were once pure and holy, but willingly turned to a life of sin. Now God has them chained up in prisons of darkness, waiting for the judgment day.

7 And don't forget the cities of Sodom and Gomorrah and their neighboring towns, all full of lust of every kind including lust of men for other men. Those cities were destroyed by fire and continue to be a warning to us that there is a hell in which sinners are punished.

8 Yet these false teachers go on living their evil, immoral lives, degrading their bodies and laughing at those in authority over them, even scoffing at the Glorious Ones [those mighty powers of awful evil who left their first estate[1]].

9 Yet Michael, one of the mightiest of the angels, when he was arguing with Satan about Moses' body, did not dare to accuse Satan, or jeer at him, but simply said, "The Lord rebuke you."

10 But these men mock and curse at anything they do not understand, and, like animals, they do whatever they feel like, thereby ruining their souls.

11 Woe upon them! For they follow the example of Cain who killed his brother; and, like Balaam, they will do anything for money; and like Korah, they have disobeyed God in the hope of gain and will die under His curse.

[1] Implied.

Revised Standard

THE LETTER OF

Jude

Introduction

1 Jude, a servant of Jesus Christ and
brother of James,
To those who are called, beloved in God
the Father and kept for Jesus Christ:
2 May mercy, peace, and love be multiplied to you.
3 Beloved, being very eager to write to
you of our common salvation, I found it necessary to write appealing to you to contend
for the faith which was once for all delivered
to the saints. [4]For admission has been secretly gained by some who long ago were designated for this condemnation, ungodly persons
who pervert the grace of our God into licentiousness and deny our only Master and
Lord, Jesus Christ.[a]

Character and doom of false teachers

5 Now I desire to remind you, though
you were once for all fully informed, that
he[b] who saved a people out of the land of
Egypt, afterward destroyed those who did not
believe. [6]And the angels that did not keep
their own position but left their proper
dwelling have been kept by him in eternal
chains in the nether gloom until the judgment of the great day; [7]just as Sodom and
Gomorrah and the surrounding cities, which
likewise acted immorally and indulged in
unnatural lust, serve as an example by un-
dergoing a punishment of eternal fire.
8 Yet in like manner these men in their
dreamings defile the flesh, reject authority,
and revile the glorious ones.[c] [9]But when the
archangel Michael, contending with the devil,
disputed about the body of Moses, he did
not presume to pronounce a reviling judgment upon him, but said, "The Lord rebuke
you." [10]But these men revile whatever they
do not understand, and by those things that
they know by instinct as irrational animals
do, they are destroyed. [11]Woe to them! For
they walk in the way of Cain, and abandon
themselves for the sake of gain to Balaam's

[a] Or *the only Master and our Lord Jesus Christ*
[b] Ancient authorities read *Jesus* or *the Lord* or *God*
[c] Greek *glories*

King James

12 These are spots in your feasts of charity, when they feast with you, feeding themselves without fear: clouds *they are* without water, carried about of winds; trees whose fruit withereth, without fruit, twice dead, plucked up by the roots;

13 Raging waves of the sea, foaming out their own shame; wandering stars, to whom is reserved the blackness of darkness for ever.

14 And Enoch also, the seventh from Adam, prophesied of these, saying, Behold, the Lord cometh with ten thousands of his saints,

15 To execute judgment upon all, and to convince all that are ungodly among them of all their ungodly deeds which they have ungodly committed, and of all their hard *speeches* which ungodly sinners have spoken against him.

16 These are murmurers, complainers, walking after their own lusts; and their mouth speaketh great swelling *words*, having men's persons in admiration because of advantage.

17 But, beloved, remember ye the words which were spoken before of the apostles of our Lord Jesus Christ;

18 How that they told you there should be mockers in the last time, who should walk after their own ungodly lusts.

19 These be they who separate themselves, sensual, having not the Spirit.

20 But ye, beloved, building up yourselves on your most holy faith, praying in the Holy Ghost,

21 Keep yourselves in the love of God, looking for the mercy of our Lord Jesus Christ unto eternal life.

22 And of some have compassion, making a difference:

23 And others save with fear, pulling *them* out of the fire; hating even the garment spotted by the flesh.

24 Now unto him that is able to keep you from falling, and to present *you* faultless before the presence of his glory with exceeding joy,

25 To the only wise God our Saviour, *be* glory and majesty, dominion and power, both now and ever. Amen.

Amplified

12 These are (elements of danger,) hidden reefs in your love feasts, where they boldly feast sumptuously—carousing together [in your midst]—without scruple providing for themselves [alone]. They are clouds without water, swept along by the winds, trees without fruit at the late autumn gathering time, twice (doubly) dead, [lifeless and] plucked up by the roots;

13 Wild waves of the sea, flinging up the foam of their own shame *and* disgrace; wandering stars for whom the gloom of eternal darkness has been reserved forever.

14 It was of these people moreover that Enoch in the seventh [generation] from Adam prophesied when he said, Behold, the Lord comes with His myriads of holy ones—ten thousands of His saints;

15 To execute judgment upon all, and to convict all the impious (unholy ones) of all their ungodly deeds which they have committed [in such an] ungodly [way], and of all the severe—abusive, soul-jarring—things which ungodly sinners have spoken against Him.

16 These are inveterate murmurers (grumblers), that complain [of their lot in life], going after their own desires—controlled by their passions; their talk is boastful *and* arrogant, [and they claim to] admire men's persons *and* pay people flattering compliments to gain advantage.

17 But you must remember, beloved, the predictions which were made by the apostles (the special messengers) of our Lord Jesus Christ, the Messiah, the Anointed One.

18 They told you beforehand, In the last days (in the end time) there will be scoffers—who seek to gratify their own unholy desires—following after their own ungodly passions.

19 It is these who are (agitators) setting up distinctions *and* causing divisions; merely sensual [creatures]—carnal, worldly-minded people—devoid of the (Holy) Spirit *and* destitute of any higher spiritual life.

20 But you, beloved, build yourselves up [founded] on your most holy faith—[d]make progress, rise like an edifice higher and higher—praying in the Holy Spirit;

21 Guard *and* keep yourselves in the love of God; expect *and* patiently wait for the mercy of our Lord Jesus Christ, the Messiah, [which will bring you] unto life eternal.

22 And ([e]refute [so as to] convict some who dispute with you, *and*) on some have mercy who waver *and* doubt.

23 [Strive to] save others, snatching [them] out of [the] fire; on others take pity [but] with fear, loathing even the garment spotted by the flesh *and* polluted by their sensuality. [Zech. 3:2-4.]

24 Now to Him Who is able to keep you without stumbling, *or* slipping, *or* falling and to present [you] unblemished (blameless and faultless) before the presence of His glory—with unspeakable, ecstatic delight—in triumphant joy *and* exultation,

25 To the one only God, our Savior through Jesus Christ our Lord, be glory (splendor), majesty, might *and* dominion, and power *and* authority, before all time and now and forever—unto all the ages of eternity. Amen—so be it.

---

d) Quoted by Thayer.
e) Some ancient authorities so read.

Living New Testament

12 When these men join you at the love feasts of the church, they are evil smears among you, laughing and carrying on, gorging and stuffing themselves without a thought for others. They are like clouds blowing over dry land without giving rain, promising much, but producing nothing. They are like fruit trees without any fruit at picking time. They are not only dead, but doubly dead, for they have been pulled out, roots and all, to be burned.

13 All they leave behind them is shame and disgrace like the dirty foam along the beach left by the wild waves. They wander around looking as bright as stars, but ahead of them is the everlasting gloom and darkness that God has prepared for them.

14 Enoch, who lived long ago, soon after Adam, knew about these men and said this about them: "See, the Lord is coming with millions of His holy ones.

15 He will bring the people of the world before Him in judgment, to receive just punishment, and to prove the terrible things they have done in rebellion against God, revealing all they have said against Him."

16 These men are constant gripers, never satisfied, doing whatever evil they feel like; they are loud-mouthed "show-offs," and when they show respect for others, it is only to get something from them in return.

17 Dear friends, remember what the apostles of our Lord Jesus Christ told you,

18 That in the last times there would come these scoffers whose whole purpose in life is to enjoy themselves in every evil way imaginable.

19 They stir up arguments; they love the evil things of the world; they do not have the Holy Spirit living in them.

20 But you, dear friends, must build up your lives ever more strongly upon the foundation of our holy faith, learning to pray in the power and strength of the Holy Spirit.

21 Stay always within the boundaries where God's love can reach and bless you. Wait patiently for the eternal life that our Lord Jesus Christ in His mercy is going to give you.

22 Try to help those who argue against you. Be merciful to those who doubt.

23 Save some by snatching them as from the very flames of hell itself. And as for others, help them to find the Lord by being kind to them, but be careful that you yourselves aren't pulled along into their sins. Hate every trace of their sin while being merciful to them as sinners.

24, 25 And now—all glory to Him who alone is God, who saves us through Jesus Christ our Lord; yes, splendor and majesty, all power and authority are His from the beginning; His they are and His they evermore shall be. And He is able to keep you from slipping and falling away, and to bring you, sinless and perfect, into His glorious presence with mighty shouts of everlasting joy. AMEN.

Jude

Revised Standard

error, and perish in Korah's rebellion.[12]These
are blemishes[d] on your love feasts, as they
boldly carouse together, looking after themselves; waterless clouds, carried along by
winds; fruitless trees in late autumn, twice
dead, uprooted; [13]wild waves of the sea, casting up the foam of their own shame; wandering stars for whom the nether gloom of
darkness has been reserved for ever.

14 It was of these also that Enoch in the
seventh generation from Adam prophesied,
saying, "Behold, the Lord came with his
holy myriads, [15]to execute judgment on all,
and to convict all the ungodly of all their
deeds of ungodliness which they have committed in such an ungodly way, and of all
the harsh things which ungodly sinners have
spoken against him." [16]These are grumblers,
malcontents, following their own passions,
loud-mouthed boasters, flattering people to
gain advantage.

Admonition to hold the true faith

17 But you must remember, beloved, the
predictions of the apostles of our Lord Jesus
Christ; [18]they said to you, "In the last time
there will be scoffers, following their own
ungodly passions." [19]It is these who set up
divisions, worldly people, devoid of the Spirit. [20]But you, beloved, build yourselves up
on your most holy faith; pray in the Holy
Spirit; [21]keep yourselves in the love of God;
wait for the mercy of our Lord Jesus Christ
unto eternal life. [22]And convince some, who
doubt; [23]save some, by snatching them out
of the fire; on some have mercy with fear,
hating even the garment spotted by the flesh.[e]

Benediction

24 Now to him who is able to keep you
from falling and to present you without blemish before the presence of his glory with rejoicing, [25]to the only God, our Savior through
Jesus Christ our Lord, be glory, majesty, dominion and authority, before all time and
now and for ever. Amen.

[d] Or *reefs*
[e] The Greek text in this sentence is uncertain at several points

King James

THE

Revelation

OF ST. JOHN THE DIVINE

CHAPTER 1

THE Revelation of Jesus Christ, which
God gave unto him, to shew unto his
servants things which must shortly come to
pass; and he sent and signified *it* by his
angel unto his servant John:
2 Who bare record of the word of God,
and of the testimony of Jesus Christ, and of
all things that he saw.
3 Blessed *is* he that readeth, and they
that hear the words of this prophecy, and
keep those things which are written therein:
for the time *is* at hand.
4 John to the seven churches which are
in Asia: Grace *be* unto you, and peace, from
him which is, and which was, and which is
to come; and from the seven Spirits which
are before his throne;
5 And from Jesus Christ, *who is* the
faithful witness, *and* the first begotten of the
dead, and the prince of the kings of the
earth. Unto him that loved us, and washed
us from our sins in his own blood,
6 And hath made us kings and priests
unto God and his Father; to him *be* glory
and dominion for ever and ever. Amen.
7 Behold, he cometh with clouds; and
every eye shall see him, and they *also* which
pierced him: and all kindreds of the earth
shall wail because of him. Even so, Amen.
8 I am Alpha and Omega, the beginning
and the ending, saith the Lord, which is, and
which was, and which is to come, the Almighty.
9 I John, who also am your brother, and
companion in tribulation, and in the kingdom and patience of Jesus Christ, was in the
isle that is called Patmos, for the word of
God, and for the testimony of Jesus Christ.
10 I was in the Spirit on the Lord's day,
and heard behind me a great voice, as of a
trumpet,
11 Saying, I am Alpha and Omega, the
first and the last: and, What thou seest,
write in a book, and send *it* unto the seven
churches which are in Asia; unto Ephesus,
and unto Smyrna, and unto Pergamos, and
unto Thyatira, and unto Sardis, and unto
Philadelphia, and unto Laodicea.

Amplified

THE REVELATION
TO

John

CHAPTER 1

[THIS is] the revelation of Jesus Christ—His unveiling
of the divine mysteries. God gave it to Him to
disclose *and* make known to His bond servants certain
things which must shortly *and* speedily come to pass [a]in
their entirety. And He sent and communicated it through
His angel (messenger) to His bond servant John,
2 Who has testified to *and* vouched for all that he saw
[[a]in his visions], the Word of God and the testimony of
Jesus Christ.
3 Blessed (happy, [b]to be envied) is the man who reads
aloud [in the assemblies] the word of this prophecy; and
blessed (happy, [b]to be envied) are those who hear [it
read] and who keep themselves true to the things which
are written in it—heeding them and laying them to heart—
for the time [for them to be fulfilled] is near.
4 John to the seven assemblies (churches) that are in
Asia: May grace (God's unmerited favor) be granted to
you and spiritual peace [[c]the peace of Christ's kingdom]
from Him Who is and Who was and Who is to come. And
from the seven Spirits—that is, [d]the sevenfold Holy Spirit—
before His throne. [Isa. 11:2.]
5 And from Jesus Christ the faithful *and* trustworthy
Witness, the First-born of the dead [that is, first to be
brought back to life] and the Prince (Ruler) of the kings
of the earth. To Him Who [e]ever loves us and has [e]once
[for all] loosed *and* freed us from our sins by His own
blood, [Ps. 89:27.]
6 And formed us into a kingdom [a royal race], priests
to His God and Father, to Him be the glory and the
power *and* the majesty and the dominion throughout the
ages *and* forever and ever. Amen, so be it. [Exod. 19:6;
Isa. 61:6.]
7 Lo, He is coming with the clouds, and every eye will
see Him, even those who pierced Him; and all the tribes
of the earth shall gaze upon Him *and* beat their breasts
and mourn *and* lament over Him. Even so [must it be].
Amen—so be it. [Dan. 7:13; Zech. 12:10.]
8 I am the Alpha and the Omega *the Beginning and the
End,* says the Lord God, He Who is and Who was and
Who is to come, the Almighty—the Ruler of all. [Isa.
9:6.]
9 I, John, your brother *and* companion—sharer and
participator—with you in the tribulation and kingdom and
patient endurance [which are] in Jesus *Christ*, was on the
isle called Patmos, [banished] on account of [my witnessing to] the Word of God and the testimony—the proof,
the evidence—for Jesus *Christ.*
10 I was in the Spirit—rapt in His power—on the
Lord's day, and I heard behind me a great voice like the
calling of a [f]war trumpet,
11 Saying, *I am the Alpha and the Omega, the First
and the Last.* Write promptly what you see (your vision)
in a book and send it to the seven churches *which are in
Asia*—to Ephesus and to Smyrna and to Pergamum and
to Thyatira and to Sardis and to Philadelphia and to
Laodicea.

---

a) Vincent.
b) Souter.
c) Abbott-Smith, "Manual Greek Lexicon of the New Testament."
d) Trench and many others.
e) Williams: "ever" and "once" found in the tenses.
f) Vincent.

Living New Testament

The Revelation

CHAPTER 1

This book unveils some of the future activities soon to occur in the life of Jesus Christ.[1] God permitted Him to reveal these things to His servant John in a vision; and then an angel was sent from heaven to explain the vision's meaning.

2 John wrote it all down—the words of God and Jesus Christ and everything he heard and saw.

3 If you read this prophecy aloud to the church, you will receive a special blessing from the Lord. Those who listen to it being read and do what it says will also be blessed. For the time is near when these things will all come true.

* * * *

4 *From*: John
To: The seven churches in Turkey.[2]

Dear Friends:

May you have grace and peace from God who is, and was, and is to come! and from the seven-fold Spirit[3] before His throne;

5 And from Jesus Christ who faithfully reveals all truth to us. He was the first to rise again from death, to die no more.[4] He is far greater than any king in all the earth. All praise to Him who always loves us and who set us free from our sins by pouring out His life blood for us.

6 He has gathered us into His kingdom and made us priests of God His Father. Give to Him everlasting glory! He rules forever! Amen!

7 See! He is arriving, surrounded by clouds; and every eye shall see Him—yes, and those who pierced Him.[5] And the nations will weep in sorrow and in terror when He comes. Yes! Amen! Let it be so!

8 "I am the A and Z,[6] the Beginning and the Ending of all things," says God, who is the Lord, the All Powerful One who is, and was, and is coming again![7]

9 It is I, your brother John, a fellow sufferer for the Lord's sake, who is writing this letter to you. I, too, have shared the patience Jesus gives, and we will share His kingdom!

I was on the island of Patmos, exiled there for preaching the Word of God, and for telling what I knew about Jesus Christ.

10 It was the Lord's Day and I was worshiping, when suddenly I heard a loud voice behind me, a voice that sounded like a trumpet blast,

11 Saying, "I am A and Z, the First and Last!" And then I heard Him say, "Write down everything you see, and send your letter to the seven churches in Turkey:[8] to the church in Ephesus, the one in Smyrna, and

---

[1] Literally, "the revelation *of* (*concerning*, or, *from*) Jesus Christ."
[2] Literally, "in Asia."
[3] Literally, "the seven spirits." But see Isaiah 11:2, where various aspects of the Holy Spirit are described, and Zech. 4:2-6, giving probability to the paraphrase; also see Revelation 2:7.
[4] Literally, "the First-born from the dead." Others (Lazarus, etc.) rose to die again. As used here the expression therefore implies "to die no more."
[5] John saw this happen with his own eyes—the piercing of Jesus—and never forgot the horror of it.
[6] Literally, "I am Alpha and Omega"; these are the first and last letters of the Greek alphabet.
[7] Literally, "who comes" or "who is to come."
[8] "The seven churches in Asia."

Revised Standard

THE

Revelation

TO JOHN

The source of the revelation

1 The revelation of Jesus Christ, which God
gave him to show to his servants what
must soon take place; and he made it known
by sending his angel to his servant John,
[2]who bore witness to the word of God and
to the testimony of Jesus Christ, even to all
that he saw. [3]Blessed is he who reads aloud
the words of the prophecy, and blessed are
those who hear, and who keep what is written therein; for the time is near.

The salutation

4 John to the seven churches that are in
Asia:
Grace to you and peace from him who is
and who was and who is to come, and from
the seven spirits who are before his throne,
[5]and from Jesus Christ the faithful witness,
the firstborn of the dead, and the ruler of
kings on earth.
To him who loves us and has freed us
from our sins by his blood [6]and made us a
kingdom, priests to his God and Father, to
him be glory and dominion for ever and ever.
Amen. [7]Behold, he is coming with the clouds,
and every eye will see him, every one who
pierced him; and all tribes of the earth will
wail on account of him. Even so. Amen.
8 "I am the Alpha and the Omega," says
the Lord God, who is and who was and who
is to come, the Almighty.

The voice and the vision

9 I John, your brother, who share with
you in Jesus the tribulation and the kingdom and the patient endurance, was on the
island called Patmos on account of the word
of God and the testimony of Jesus. [10]I was
in the Spirit on the Lord's day, and I heard
behind me a loud voice like a trumpet [11]say-
ing, "Write what you see in a book and send
it to the seven churches, to Ephesus and to
Smyrna and to Pergamum and to Thyatira
and to Sardis and to Philadelphia and to
Laodicea."

King James

12 And I turned to see the voice that spake with me. And being turned, I saw seven golden candlesticks;

13 And in the midst of the seven candlesticks *one* like unto the Son of man, clothed with a garment down to the foot, and girt about the paps with a golden girdle.

14 His head and *his* hairs *were* white like wool, as white as snow; and his eyes *were* as a flame of fire;

15 And his feet like unto fine brass, as if they burned in a furnace; and his voice as the sound of many waters.

16 And he had in his right hand seven stars: and out of his mouth went a sharp two-edged sword: and his countenance *was* as the sun shineth in his strength.

17 And when I saw him, I fell at his feet as dead. And he laid his right hand upon me, saying unto me, Fear not; I am the first and the last:

18 I *am* he that liveth, and was dead; and, behold, I am alive for evermore, Amen; and have the keys of hell and of death.

19 Write the things which thou hast seen, and the things which are, and the things which shall be hereafter;

20 The mystery of the seven stars which thou sawest in my right hand, and the seven golden candlesticks. The seven stars are the angels of the seven churches: and the seven candlesticks which thou sawest are the seven churches.

Amplified

12 Then I turned to see [whose was] the voice that was speaking to me, and on turning I saw seven golden lampstands,

13 And in the midst of the lampstands [One] like a Son of man, clothed with a robe which reached to His feet and with a girdle of gold about His breast. [Dan. 7:13; 10:5.]

14 His head and His hair were white like white wool, [as white] as snow, and His eyes [flashed] like a flame of fire. [Dan. 7:9.]

15 His feet glowed like (bright,) burnished bronze as it is refined in a furnace, and His voice was like the sound of many waters. [Dan. 10:6.]

16 In His right hand He held seven stars, and from His mouth there came forth a sharp two-edged sword, and His face was like the sun shining in full power at midday. [Exod. 34:29.]

17 When I saw Him I fell at His feet as if dead. But He laid His right hand on me and said, Do not be afraid! I am the First and the Last, [Isa. 44:6.]

18 And the Ever-living One—I am living in the eternity of the eternities. I died, but see, I am alive for evermore; and I possess the keys of Death and Hades [the realm of the dead].

19 Write therefore the things you see, what they are [and signify], and what is to take place hereafter.

20 As to the hidden meaning (the mystery) of the seven stars which you saw on My right hand and the seven lampstands of gold, the seven stars are the seven angels (messengers) of the seven churches (assemblies) and the seven lampstands are the seven churches.

CHAPTER 2

UNTO the angel of the church of Ephesus write; These things saith he that holdeth the seven stars in his right hand, who walketh in the midst of the seven golden candlesticks;

2 I know thy works, and thy labour, and thy patience, and how thou canst not bear them which are evil: and thou hast tried them which say they are apostles, and are not, and hast found them liars:

3 And hast borne, and hast patience, and for my name's sake hast laboured, and hast not fainted.

4 Nevertheless I have *somewhat* against thee, because thou hast left thy first love.

5 Remember therefore from whence thou art fallen, and repent, and do the first works; or else I will come unto thee quickly, and will remove thy candlestick out of his place, except thou repent.

6 But this thou hast, that thou hatest the deeds of the Nicolaitans, which I also hate.

CHAPTER 2

TO the angel (messenger) of the assembly (church) in Ephesus write: These are the words of Him Who holds the seven stars [which are the messengers of the seven churches] in His right hand, Who goes about among the seven golden lampstands [which are the seven churches].

2 I know your industry *and* activities, laborious toil *and* trouble, and your patient endurance, and how you cannot tolerate wicked [men] and have tested *and* critically appraised those who call [themselves] apostles (special messengers [of Christ]) and yet are not, and have found them to be imposters *and* liars.

3 I know you are enduring patiently and are bearing up for My name's sake, and you have not fainted *or* become exhausted *or* grown weary.

4 But I have this [one charge to make] against you, that you have left (abandoned) the love that you had at first—you have deserted [Me], your first love.

5 Remember then from what heights you have fallen. Repent—change the inner man to meet God's will—and do the works you did previously [when first you knew the Lord]. Or else I will visit you and remove your lampstand from its place, unless you change your mind *and* repent.

6 Yet you have this—in your favor and to your credit—you detest the works of the Nicolaitans [what they are doing as corrupters of the people], which I Myself also detest.

Living New Testament

those in Pergamos, Thyatira, Sardis, Philadelphia, and Laodicea."

12 When I turned to see who was speaking, there behind me were seven candlesticks of gold.

13 And standing among them was one who looked like Jesus who called himself the Son of Man,[9] wearing a long robe circled with a golden band across His chest.

14 His hair[10] was white as wool or snow, and His eyes penetrated like flames of fire.

15 His feet gleamed like burnished bronze, and His voice thundered like the waves against the shore.

16 He held seven stars in His right hand and a sharp, double-bladed sword in His mouth,[11] and His face shone like the power of the sun in unclouded brilliance.

17, 18 When I saw Him, I fell at His feet as dead; but He laid His right hand on me and said, "Don't be afraid! Though I am the First and Last, the Living One who died, who is now alive forevermore, who has the keys of hell and death—don't be afraid!

19 Write down what you have just seen, and what will soon be shown to you.

20 This is the meaning of the seven stars you saw in My right hand, and the seven golden candlesticks: The seven stars are the leaders[12] of the seven churches, and the seven candlesticks are the churches themselves.

Revised Standard

12 Then I turned to see the voice that
was speaking to me, and on turning I saw
seven golden lampstands, [13]and in the midst
of the lampstands one like a son of man,
clothed with a long robe and with a golden
girdle round his breast; [14]his head and his
hair were white as white wool, white as
snow; his eyes were like a flame of fire, [15]his
feet were like burnished bronze, refined as
in a furnace, and his voice was like the
sound of many waters; [16]in his right hand he
held seven stars, from his mouth issued a
sharp two-edged sword, and his face was
like the sun shining in full strength.
17 When I saw him, I fell at his feet as
though dead. But he laid his right hand upon
me, saying, "Fear not, I am the first and the
last, [18]and the living one; I died, and behold
I am alive for evermore, and I have the keys
of Death and Hades. [19]Now write what you
see, what is and what is to take place hereafter. [20]As for the mystery of the seven stars
which you saw in my right hand, and the
seven golden lampstands, the seven stars are
the angels of the seven churches and the sev-
en lampstands are the seven churches.

CHAPTER 2

Write a letter to the leader[1] of the church at Ephesus and tell him this:

I write to inform you of a message from Him who walks among the churches[2] and holds their leaders in His right hand. He says to you:

2 I know how many good things you are doing. I have watched your hard work and your patience; I know you don't tolerate sin among your members, and you have carefully examined the claims of those who say they are apostles but aren't. You have found out how they lie.

3 You have patiently suffered for Me without quitting.

4 Yet there is one thing wrong: you don't love Me as at first!

5 Think about those times of your first love (how different now!) and turn back to Me again and work as you did before; or else I will come and remove your candlestick from its place among the churches.

6 But there is this about you that is good: you hate the deeds of the licentious Nicolaitans,[3] just as I do.

The message to Ephesus

2 "To the angel of the church in Ephesus
write: 'The words of him who holds the
seven stars in his right hand, who walks
among the seven golden lampstands.
2 " 'I know your works, your toil and
your patient endurance, and how you cannot
bear evil men but have tested those who call
themselves apostles but are not, and found
them to be false; [3]I know you are enduring
patiently and bearing up for my name's
sake, and you have not grown weary. [4]But
I have this against you, that you have abandoned the love you had at first. [5]Remember
then from what you have fallen, repent and
do the works you did at first. If not, I will
come to you and remove your lampstand
from its place, unless you repent. [6]Yet this
you have, you hate the works of the Nico-

---

[9] Literally, "like unto a Son of Man"; John recognizes Him from having lived with Him for three years, and from seeing Him in glory at the Transfiguration.

[10] Literally, "His head—the hair—was white like wool."

[11] Literally, "coming out from His mouth."

[12] Literally, "angels." Some expositors (Origen, Jerome, etc.) believe from this that an angelic being is appointed by God to oversee each local church.

Literally, "angel," as in 1:20.

Literally, "from Him who holds the seven stars in His right hand and walks among the seven golden candlesticks."

Nicolaitans, when translated from Greek to Hebrew, becomes Balaamites; followers of the man who induced the Israelites to fall by lust, (See Rev. 2:14 and Num. 31:15, 16.)

King James

7 He that hath an ear, let him hear what the Spirit saith unto the churches; To him that overcometh will I give to eat of the tree of life, which is in the midst of the paradise of God.

8 And unto the angel of the church in Smyrna write; These things saith the first and the last, which was dead, and is alive;

9 I know thy works, and tribulation, and poverty, (but thou art rich) and *I know* the blasphemy of them which say they are Jews, and are not, but *are* the synagogue of Satan.

10 Fear none of those things which thou shalt suffer: behold, the devil shall cast *some* of you into prison, that ye may be tried; and ye shall have tribulation ten days: be thou faithful unto death, and I will give thee a crown of life.

11 He that hath an ear, let him hear what the Spirit saith unto the churches; He that overcometh shall not be hurt of the second death.

12 And to the angel of the church in Pergamos write; These things saith he which hath the sharp sword with two edges;

13 I know thy works and where thou dwellest, *even* where Satan's seat *is:* and thou holdest fast my name, and hast not denied my faith, even in those days wherein Antipas *was* my faithful martyr, who was slain among you, where Satan dwelleth.

14 But I have a few things against thee, because thou hast there them that hold the doctrine of Balaam, who taught Balac to cast a stumblingblock before the children of Israel, to eat things sacrificed unto idols, and to commit fornication.

15 So hast thou also them that hold the doctrine of the Nicolaitans, which thing I hate.

16 Repent; or else I will come unto thee quickly, and will fight against them with the sword of my mouth.

17 He that hath an ear, let him hear what the Spirit saith unto the churches; To him that overcometh will I give to eat of the hidden manna, and will give him a white stone, and in the stone a new name written, which no man knoweth saving he that receiveth *it.*

18 And unto the angel of the church in Thyatira write; These things saith the Son of God, who hath his eyes like unto a flame of fire, and his feet *are* like fine brass;

19 I know thy works, and charity, and service, and faith, and thy patience, and thy works; and the last *to be* more than the first.

20 Notwithstanding I have a few things against thee, because thou sufferest that woman Jezebel, which calleth herself a prophetess, to teach and to seduce my servants to commit fornication, and to eat things sacrificed unto idols.

21 And I gave her space to repent of her fornication; and she repented not.

Amplified

7 He who is able to hear, let him listen to *and* give heed to what the Spirit says to the assemblies (the churches). To him who overcomes (is victorious) I will grant to eat [of the fruit] of the tree of life, which is in the paradise of God. [Gen. 2:9; 3:24.]

8 And to the angel (messenger) of the assembly (church) in Smyrna write, These are the words of the First and the Last, Who died and came to life again: [Isa. 44:6.]

9 I know your affliction *and* distress *and* pressing trouble, and your poverty; but you are rich! and how you are abused *and* reviled *and* slandered by those who say they are Jews and are not, but are a synagogue of Satan.

10 Fear nothing that you are about to suffer.—Dismiss your dread and your fears! Behold, the devil is indeed about to throw some of you into prison, that you may be tested *and* proved *and* critically appraised; and for ten days you will have affliction. Be loyally faithful unto death—[that is,] even if you must die for it—and I will give you the crown of life. [Rev. 3:10, 11.]

11 He who is able to hear, let him listen to *and* heed what the Spirit says to the assemblies (the churches). He who overcomes (is victorious) shall in no way be injured by the second death.

12 Then to the angel (messenger) of the assembly (church) in Pergamum write: These are the words of Him Who has *and* wields the sharp two-edged sword.

13 I know where you live, a place where Satan sits enthroned. [Yet] you are clinging to *and* holding fast My name and you did not deny My faith even in the days of Antipas, My witness, My faithful one, who was killed [martyred] in your midst where Satan dwells.

14 Nevertheless I have a few things against you: you have some people there who are clinging to the teaching of Balaam, who taught Balak to set a trap *and* a stumbling block before the sons of Israel, [to entice them] to eat food that had been sacrificed to idols and to practice lewdness—giving themselves up to sexual vice. [Num. 31:16; 25:1, 2.]

15 You also have some who in a similar way are clinging to the teaching of the Nicolaitans [those corrupters of the people], which thing I hate.

16 Repent [then]! Or else I will come to you quickly and fight against them with the sword of My mouth.

17 He who is able to hear, let him listen to *and* heed what the Spirit says to the assemblies (the churches). To him who overcomes (who conquers) I will give to eat of the manna that is hidden, and I will give him a white stone, with a new name engraved on the stone which no one knows *or* understands except he who receives it. [Ps. 78:24; Isa. 62:2.]

18 And to the angel (the messenger) of the assembly (church) in Thyatira write: These are the words of the Son of God, Who has eyes that flash like a flame of fire, and Whose feet glow like bright *and* burnished *and* white-hot bronze. [Dan. 10:6.]

19 I know your record *and* what you are doing, your love and faith and service and patient endurance, and that your recent works are more numerous *and* greater than your first ones.

20 But I have this against you, that you tolerate the woman Jezebel, who calls herself a prophetess (claiming to be inspired), and who is teaching and leading astray my servants *and* beguiling them into practicing sexual vice and eating food sacrificed to idols. [I Kings 16:31; II Kings 9:22, 30.]

21 I gave her time to repent, but she has no desire to repent ([g]out) of her immorality [symbolic of idolatry] *and* refuses to do so.

---

g) Literal meaning.

Living New Testament

7 Let this message sink into the ears of anyone who listens to what the Spirit is saying to the churches: To everyone who is victorious, I will give fruit from the Tree of Life in the Paradise of God.

* * * *

8 *To the leader*[4] *of the church in Smyrna write this letter:*

This message is from Him who is the First and Last, who was dead and then came back to life.

9 I know how much you suffer for the Lord, and I know all about your poverty (but you have heavenly riches!). I know the slander of those opposing you, who say that they are Jews—the children of God—but they aren't, for they support the cause of Satan.

10 Stop being afraid of what you are about to suffer—for the Devil will soon throw some of you into prison to test you. You will be persecuted for 'ten days.' Remain faithful even when facing death and I will give you the crown of life—an unending, glorious future.[5]

11 Let everyone who can hear, listen to what the Spirit is saying to the churches: He who is victorious shall not be hurt by the Second Death.

* * * *

12 *Write this letter to the leader*[4] *of the church in Pergamos:*

This message is from Him who wields the sharp and double-bladed sword.

13 I am fully aware that you live in the city where Satan's throne is, at the center of Satanic worship; and yet you have remained loyal to Me, and refused to deny Me, even when Antipas, My faithful witness, was martyred among you by Satan's devotees.

14 And yet I have a few things against you. You tolerate some among you who do as Balaam did when he taught Balak how to ruin the people of Israel by involving them in sexual sin, and encouraging them to go to idol feasts.

15 Yes, you have some of these very same followers of Balaam[6] among you!

16 Change your mind and attitude, or else I will come to you suddenly and fight against them with the sword of My mouth.

17 Let everyone who can hear, listen to what the Spirit is saying to the churches: Every one who is victorious shall eat of the hidden manna, the secret nourishment from heaven; and I will give to each a white stone, and on the stone will be engraved a new name that no one else knows except the one receiving it.

* * * *

18 *Write this letter to the leader*[7] *of the church in Thyatira:*

This is a message from the Son of God, whose eyes penetrate like flames of fire, whose feet are like glowing brass.

19 I am aware of all your good deeds—your kindness to the poor, your gifts and service to them; also I know your love and faith and patience, and I can see your constant improvement in all these things.

20 Yet I have this against you: You are permitting that woman Jezebel, who calls herself a prophetess, to teach My servants that sex sin is not a serious matter; she urges them to practice immorality and to eat meat that has been sacrificed to idols.

21 I gave her time to change her mind and attitude, but she refused.

---

[4] Literally, "angel." See note on 1:20.
[5] Implied.
[6] Literally, "Nicolaitans," Greek form of "Balaamites."
[7] Literally, "angel." See note on 1:20.

Revised Standard

laitans, which I also hate. 7 He who has an
ear, let him hear what the Spirit says to the
churches. To him who conquers I will grant
to eat of the tree of life, which is in the paradise of God.'

The message to Smyrna

8 "And to the angel of the church in
Smyrna write: 'The words of the first and
the last, who died and came to life.
9 " 'I know your tribulation and your
poverty (but you are rich) and the slander
of those who say that they are Jews and are
not, but are a synagogue of Satan. 10 Do not
fear what you are about to suffer. Behold,
the devil is about to throw some of you into
prison, that you may be tested, and for ten
days you will have tribulation. Be faithful
unto death, and I will give you the crown
of life. 11 He who has an ear, let him hear
what the Spirit says to the churches. He who
conquers shall not be hurt by the second
death.'

The message to Pergamum

12 "And to the angel of the church in
Pergamum write: 'The words of him who has
the sharp two-edged sword.
13 " 'I know where you dwell, where Satan's throne is; you hold fast my name and
you did not deny my faith even in the days
of Antipas my witness, my faithful one, who
was killed among you, where Satan dwells.
14 But I have a few things against you: you
have some there who hold the teaching of
Balaam, who taught Balak to put a stumbling
block before the sons of Israel, that they
might eat food sacrificed to idols and practice
immorality. 15 So you also have some who
hold the teaching of the Nicolaitans. 16 Repent then. If not, I will come to you soon
and war against them with the sword of my
mouth. 17 He who has an ear, let him hear
what the Spirit says to the churches. To
him who conquers I will give some of the
hidden manna, and I will give him a white
stone, with a new name written on the stone
which no one knows except him who receives
it.'

The message to Thyatira

18 "And to the angel of the church in
Thyatira write: 'The words of the Son of
God, who has eyes like a flame of fire, and
whose feet are like burnished bronze.
19 " 'I know your works, your love and
faith and service and patient endurance, and
that your latter works exceed the first. 20 But
I have this against you, that you tolerate the
woman Jezebel, who calls herself a prophetess and is teaching and beguiling my servants
to practice immorality and to eat food sacrificed to idols. 21 I gave her time to repent,
but she refuses to repent of her immorality.

King James

22 Behold, I will cast her into a bed, and them that commit adultery with her into great tribulation, except they repent of their deeds.

23 And I will kill her children with death; and all the churches shall know that I am he which searcheth the reins and hearts: and I will give unto every one of you according to your works.

24 But unto you I say, and unto the rest in Thyatira, as many as have not this doctrine, and which have not known the depths of Satan, as they speak; I will put upon you none other burden.

25 But that which ye have *already* hold fast till I come.

26 And he that overcometh, and keepeth my works unto the end, to him will I give power over the nations:

27 And he shall rule them with a rod of iron; as the vessels of a potter shall they be broken to shivers: even as I received of my Father.

28 And I will give him the morning star.

29 He that hath an ear, let him hear what the Spirit saith unto the churches.

Amplified

22 Take note: I will throw her on a bed [[h]of anguish], and those [her paramours] who commit adultery with her I will bring down to [g]pressing distress *and* severe affliction, unless they turn away their minds from conduct [such as] hers *and* repent of ([i]their) doings.

23 And I will strike her children [her proper followers] dead—thoroughly exterminating them. And all the assemblies (the churches) shall recognize *and* understand that I am He Who searches minds—the thoughts, feelings and purposes—and the [inmost] hearts, and I will give to each of you [the reward for what you have done] as your work deserves. [Jer. 17:10; Ps. 62:12.]

24 But to the rest of you in Thyatira, who do not hold this teaching, who have not explored *and* known the depths of Satan, as they say, I tell you that I do not lay upon you any other (fresh) burden;

25 Only hold fast to what you have until I come.

26 And He who overcomes, (is victorious) and who obeys My commands to the [very] end—doing the works [that please Me]—I will give him authority *and* power over the nations;

27 And he shall rule them with a sceptre (rod) of iron, as when earthen pots are broken in pieces, and [his power over them shall be] like that which I Myself have received from My Father; [Ps. 2:8, 9.]

28 And I will give him the Morning Star.

29 He who is able to hear, let him listen to *and* heed what the (Holy) Spirit says to the assemblies (the churches).

CHAPTER 3

AND unto the angel of the church in Sardis write; These things saith he that hath the seven Spirits of God, and the seven stars; I know thy works, that thou hast a name that thou livest, and art dead.

2 Be watchful, and strengthen the things which remain, that are ready to die: for I have not found thy works perfect before God.

3 Remember therefore how thou hast received and heard, and hold fast, and repent. If therefore thou shalt not watch, I will come on thee as a thief, and thou shalt not know what hour I will come upon thee.

4 Thou hast a few names even in Sardis which have not defiled their garments; and they shall walk with me in white: for they are worthy.

5 He that overcometh, the same shall be clothed in white raiment; and I will not blot out his name out of the book of life, but I will confess his name before my Father, and before his angels.

6 He that hath an ear, let him hear what the Spirit saith unto the churches.

CHAPTER 3

AND to the angel (the messenger) of the assembly (the church) in Sardis write: These are the words of Him Who has the seven Spirits of God [that is, [j]the sevenfold Holy Spirit] and the seven stars: I know your record *and* what you are doing; you are supposed to be alive, but [in reality] you are dead.

2 Rouse yourselves *and* keep awake, and strengthen *and* invigorate what remains and is on the point of dying; for I have not found a thing that you have done—any work of yours—meeting the requirements of My God *or* perfect in His sight.

3 So call to mind the lessons you received and heard; continually lay them to heart *and* obey them, and repent. In case you will not rouse yourselves *and* keep awake *and watch* I will come upon you like a thief, and you will not know *or* suspect at what hour I will come.

4 Yet you still have a few [persons'] names in Sardis who have not soiled their clothes, and they shall walk with Me in white, because they are worthy *and* deserving.

5 Thus shall he who conquers (is victorious) be clad in white garments, and I will not erase *or* blot out his name from the Book of Life; I will acknowledge him [as Mine], *and* I will confess his name openly before My Father and before His angels. [Ps. 69:28; Dan. 12:1.]

6 He who is able to hear, let him listen to *and* heed what the (Holy) Spirit says to the assemblies (the churches).

---

g) Literal meaning.
h) Vincent.
i) Many ancient authorities so read.
j) Trench.

Living New Testament

22 Pay attention now to what I am saying: I will lay
her upon a sickbed of intense affliction, along with all her
immoral followers,[8] unless they turn again to Me, repenting of their sin with her;
23 And I will strike her children dead. And all the
churches shall know that I am He who searches deep
within men's hearts and minds; I will give to each of you
whatever you deserve.
24, 25 As for the rest of you in Thyatira who have not
followed this false teaching ("deeper truths," as they call
them—depths of Satan, really), I will ask nothing further
of you; only hold tightly to what you have until I come.
26 To every one who overcomes—who to the very end
keeps on doing the things that please Me—I will give
power over the nations.
27 You will rule them with a rod of iron just as My
Father gave Me the authority to rule them; they will be
shattered like a pot of clay that is broken into tiny pieces.
28 And I will give you the Morning Star!
29 Let all who can hear, listen to what the Spirit says
to the churches.

Revised Standard

22 Behold, I will throw her on a sickbed, and
those who commit adultery with her I will
throw into great tribulation, unless they repent of her doings; 23 and I will strike her
children dead. And all the churches shall
know that I am he who searches mind and
heart, and I will give to each of you as your
works deserve. 24 But to the rest of you in
Thyatira, who do not hold this teaching,
who have not learned what some call the
deep things of Satan, to you I say, I do not
lay upon you any other burden; 25 only hold
fast what you have, until I come. 26 He who
conquers and who keeps my works until the
end, I will give him power over the nations,
27 and he shall rule them with a rod of iron,
as when earthen pots are broken in pieces,
even as I myself have received power from
my Father; 28 and I will give him the morning star. 29 He who has an ear, let him hear
what the Spirit says to the churches.'

CHAPTER 3

To the leader[1] *of the church in Sardis write this letter:*
This message is sent to you by the one who has the
seven-fold Spirit[2] of God and the seven stars.
I know your reputation as a live and active church, but
you are dead.
2 Now wake up! Strengthen what little remains—for
even what is left is at the point of death. Your deeds are
far from right in the sight of God.
3 Go back to what you heard and believed at first; hold
to it firmly and turn to Me again. Unless you do, I will
come suddenly upon you, unexpected as a thief, and
punish you.
4 Yet even there in Sardis some haven't soiled their
garments with the world's filth; they shall walk with Me in
white, for they are worthy.
5 Everyone who conquers will be clothed in white, and
I will not erase his name from the Book of Life, but I will
announce before My Father and His angels that he is
Mine.
6 Let all who can hear, listen to what the Spirit is
saying to the churches.

The message to Sardis

3 "And to the angel of the church in Sardis
write: 'The words of him who has the
seven spirits of God and the seven stars.
" 'I know your works; you have the name
of being alive, and you are dead. 2 Awake,
and strengthen what remains and is on the
point of death, for I have not found your
works perfect in the sight of my God. 3 Remember then what you received and heard;
keep that, and repent. If you will not awake,
I will come like a thief, and you will not
know at what hour I will come upon you.
4 Yet you have still a few names in Sardis,
people who have not soiled their garments;
and they shall walk with me in white, for
they are worthy. 5 He who conquers shall be
clad thus in white garments, and I will not
blot his name out of the book of life; I will
confess his name before my Father and before his angels. 6 He who has an ear, let him
hear what the Spirit says to the churches.'

---

8 Literally, "together with all those who commit adultery with her."
1 Literally, "angel." See note on 1:20.
2 Literally, "the seven spirits of God." See note on 1:4.

King James

7 And to the angel of the church in Philadelphia write; These things saith he that is holy, he that is true, he that hath the key of David, he that openeth, and no man shutteth; and shutteth and no man openeth;

8 I know thy works: behold, I have set before thee an open door, and no man can shut it: for thou hast a little strength, and hast kept my word, and hast not denied my name.

9 Behold, I will make them of the synagogue of Satan, which say they are Jews, and are not, but do lie; behold, I will make them to come and worship before thy feet, and to know that I have loved thee.

10 Because thou hast kept the word of my patience, I also will keep thee from the hour of temptation, which shall come upon all the world, to try them that dwell upon the earth.

11 Behold, I come quickly: hold that fast which thou hast, that no man take thy crown.

12 Him that overcometh will I make a pillar in the temple of my God, and he shall go no more out: and I will write upon him the name of my God, and the name of the city of my God, *which is* new Jerusalem, which cometh down out of heaven from my God: and *I will write unto him* my new name.

13 He that hath an ear, let him hear what the Spirit saith unto the churches.

14 And unto the angel of the church of the Laodiceans write; These things saith the Amen, the faithful and true witness, the beginning of the creation of God;

15 I know thy works, that thou art neither cold nor hot: I would thou wert cold or hot.

16 So then because thou art lukewarm, and neither cold nor hot, I will spue thee out of my mouth.

17 Because thou sayest, I am rich, and increased with goods, and have need of nothing; and knowest not that thou art wretched, and miserable, and poor, and blind, and naked:

18 I counsel thee to buy of me gold tried in the fire, that thou mayest be rich; and white raiment, that thou mayest be clothed, and *that* the shame of thy nakedness do not appear; and anoint thine eyes with eyesalve, that thou mayest see.

19 As many as I love, I rebuke and chasten: be zealous therefore, and repent.

20 Behold, I stand at the door, and knock: if any man hear my voice, and open the door, I will come in to him, and will sup with him, and he with me.

21 To him that overcometh will I grant to sit with me in my throne, even as I also overcame, and am set down with my Father in his throne.

22 He that hath an ear let him hear what the Spirit saith unto the churches.

Amplified

7 And to the angel (the messenger) of the assembly (the church) in Philadelphia write: These are the words of the Holy One, the True One, He Who has the key of David, Who opens and no one shall shut, Who shuts and no one shall open. [Isa. 22:22.]

8 I know your [record of] works *and* what you are doing. See! I have set before you a door wide open, which no one is able to shut; I know that you have but little power, and yet you have kept My Word *and* guarded My message, and have not renounced *or* denied My name.

9 Take note! I will make those of the synagogue of Satan who say they are Jews and are not, but lie, behold, I will make them come and bow down before your feet, and learn *and* acknowledge that I have loved you. [Isa. 60:14; 49:23; 43:4.]

10 Because you have guarded *and* kept My word of patient endurance—have held fast the [k]lesson of My patience with the [k]expectant endurance that I give you—I also will keep you (safe) from the hour of trial (testing) which is coming on the whole world, to try those who dwell upon the earth.

11 I am coming quickly; hold fast what you have, so that no one may rob you *and* deprive you of your crown.

12 He who overcomes (is victorious), I will make him a pillar in the sanctuary of My God; he shall never be put out of it *or* go out of it, and I will write on him the name of My God, and the name of the city of My God, the new Jerusalem which descends from My God out of heaven, and My own new name. [Isa. 62:2; Ezek. 48:35.]

13 He who can hear, let him listen to *and* heed what the Spirit says to the assemblies (the churches).

14 And to the angel (messenger) of the assembly (the church) in Laodicea write: These are the words of the Amen, the trusty *and* faithful and true Witness, the Origin *and* Beginning *and* Author of God's creation. [Isa. 55:4; Prov. 8:22.]

15 I know your [record of] works *and* what you are doing; you are neither cold nor hot. Would that you were cold or hot!

16 So, because you are lukewarm, and neither cold nor hot, I will spue you out of My mouth!

17 For you say, I am rich, I have prospered *and* grown wealthy, and I am in need of nothing; and do not realize *and* understand that you are wretched, pitiable, poor, blind and naked. [Hos. 12:8.]

18 Therefore I counsel you to purchase from Me gold refined *and* tested by fire, that you may be [truly] wealthy, and white clothes to clothe you and to keep the shame of your nudity from being seen, and salve to put on your eyes that you may see.

19 Those whom I [dearly and tenderly] love, I tell their faults and convict *and* convince *and* reprove and chasten—[that is,] I discipline and instruct them. So be enthusiastic *and* in earnest *and* burning with zeal, and repent—changing your mind and attitude. [Prov. 3:12.]

20 Behold, I stand at the door and knock; if any one hears *and* listens to *and* heeds My voice and opens the door, I will come in to him and will eat with him, and he [shall eat] with Me.

21 He who overcomes (is victorious), I will grant him to sit beside Me on My throne, as I Myself overcame (was victorious) and sat down beside My Father on His throne.

22 He who is able to hear, let him listen to *and* heed what the (Holy) Spirit says to the assemblies (the churches).

---

k) Greek, "of my endurance"; "a patient, steadfast waiting for" (Thayer).

Living New Testament

* * * *

7 *Write this letter to the leader*[3] *of the church in Philadelphia:*

This message is sent to you by the one who is holy and true, and has the key of David to open what no one can shut and to shut what no one can open.

8 I know you well: you aren't strong, but you have tried to obey[4] and have not denied My Name. Therefore I have opened a door to you that no one can shut.

9 Note this: I will force those supporting the causes of Satan while claiming to be Mine[5] (but they aren't—they are lying) to fall at your feet and acknowledge that you are the ones I love.

10 Because you have patiently obeyed Me despite the persecution, therefore I will protect you from[6] the time of Great Tribulation and temptation, which will come upon the world to test everyone alive.

11 Look, I am coming soon![7] Hold tightly to the little strength you have—so that no one will take away your crown.

12 As for the one who conquers, I will make him a pillar in the temple of My God; he will be secure, and will go out no more; and I will write My God's Name on him, and he will be a citizen in the city of My God—the New Jerusalem, coming down from heaven from My God; and he will have My new Name inscribed upon him.

13 Let all who can hear, listen to what the Spirit is saying to the churches.

* * * *

14 *Write this letter to the leader*[8] *of the church in Laodicea:*

This message is from the one who stands firm,[9] the faithful and true Witness [of all that is or was or evermore shall be[10]], the primeval source of God's creation:

15 I know you well—you are neither hot nor cold; I wish you were one or the other!

16 But since you are merely lukewarm, I will spit you out of My mouth!

17 You say, 'I am rich, with everything I want; I don't need a thing!' And you don't realize that spiritually you are wretched and miserable and poor and blind and naked.

18 My advice to you is to buy pure gold from Me, gold purified by fire—only then will you truly be rich. And to purchase from Me white garments, clean and pure, so you won't be naked and ashamed; and to get medicine from Me to heal your eyes and give you back your sight.

19 I continually discipline and punish everyone I love; so I must punish you, unless you turn from your indifference and become enthusiastic about the things of God.

20 Look! I have been standing at the door and I am constantly knocking. If anyone hears Me calling him and opens the door, I will come in and fellowship with him and he with Me.

21 I will let every one who conquers sit beside Me on My throne, just as I took My place with My Father on His throne when I had conquered.

22 Let those who can hear, listen to what the Spirit is saying to the churches."

[3] Literally, "angel." See note on 1:20.
[4] Literally, "you have kept My word."
[5] Literally, "say they are Jews but are not."
[6] Or, "I will keep you from falling in the hour of testing . . ." The inference is not clear in the Greek as to whether this means "kept from" or "kept through" the coming horror.
[7] Or, "suddenly," "unexpectedly."
[8] Literally, "angel." See note on 1:20.
[9] Literally, "from the Amen."
[10] Implied.

Revised Standard

The message to Philadelphia

7 "And to the angel of the church in Philadelphia write: 'The words of the holy one, the true one, who has the key of David, who opens and no one shall shut, who shuts and no one opens.

8 " 'I know your works. Behold, I have set before you an open door, which no one is able to shut; I know that you have but little power, and yet you have kept my word and
have not denied my name. 9Behold, I will make those of the synagogue of Satan who say that they are Jews and are not, but lie—behold, I will make them come and bow down before your feet, and learn that I have
loved you. 10Because you have kept my word of patient endurance, I will keep you from the hour of trial which is coming on the whole world, to try those who dwell upon
the earth. 11I am coming soon; hold fast what you have, so that no one may seize your
crown. 12He who conquers, I will make him a pillar in the temple of my God; never shall he go out of it, and I will write on him the name of my God, and the name of the city of my God, the new Jerusalem which comes down from my God out of heaven, and my
own new name. 13He who has an ear, let him hear what the Spirit says to the churches.'

The message to Laodicea

14 "And to the angel of the church in Laodicea write: 'The words of the Amen, the faithful and true witness, the beginning of God's creation.

15 " 'I know your works: you are neither cold nor hot. Would that you were cold or
hot! 16So, because you are lukewarm, and neither cold nor hot, I will spew you out of
my mouth. 17For you say, I am rich, I have prospered, and I need nothing; not knowing that you are wretched, pitiable, poor, blind,
and naked. 18Therefore I counsel you to buy from me gold refined by fire, that you may be rich, and white garments to clothe you and to keep the shame of your nakedness from being seen, and salve to anoint your eyes,
that you may see. 19Those whom I love, I reprove and chasten; so be zealous and re-
pent. 20Behold, I stand at the door and knock; if any one hears my voice and opens the door, I will come in to him and eat with
him, and he with me. 21He who conquers, I will grant him to sit with me on my throne, as I myself conquered and sat down with my
Father on his throne. 22He who has an ear, let him hear what the Spirit says to the churches.' "

King James

CHAPTER 4

AFTER this I looked, and, behold, a door *was* opened in heaven: and the first voice which I heard *was* as it were of a trumpet talking with me; which said, Come up hither, and I will shew thee things which must be hereafter.

2 And immediately I was in the spirit; and, behold, a throne was set in heaven, and *one* sat on the throne.

3 And he that sat was to look upon like a jasper and a sardine stone: and *there was* a rainbow round about the throne, in sight like unto an emerald.

4 And round about the throne *were* four and twenty seats: and upon the seats I saw four and twenty elders sitting, clothed in white raiment; and they had on their heads crowns of gold.

5 And out of the throne proceeded lightnings and thunderings and voices: and *there were* seven lamps of fire burning before the throne, which are the seven Spirits of God.

6 And before the throne *there was* a sea of glass like unto crystal: and in the midst of the throne, and round about the throne, *were* four beasts full of eyes before and behind.

7 And the first beast *was* like a lion, and the second beast like a calf, and the third beast had a face as a man, and the fourth beast *was* like a flying eagle.

8 And the four beasts had each of them six wings about *him;* and *they were* full of eyes within: and they rest not day and night, saying, Holy, holy, holy, Lord God Almighty, which was, and is, and is to come.

9 And when those beasts give glory and honour and thanks to him that sat on the throne, who liveth for ever and ever,

10 The four and twenty elders fall down before him that sat on the throne, and worship him that liveth for ever and ever, and cast their crowns before the throne, saying,

11 Thou art worthy, O Lord, to receive glory and honour and power: for thou hast created all things, and for thy pleasure they are and were created.

CHAPTER 5

AND I saw in the right hand of him that sat on the throne a book written within and on the backside, sealed with seven seals.

2 And I saw a strong angel proclaiming with a loud voice, Who is worthy to open the book, and to loose the seals thereof?

Amplified

CHAPTER 4

AFTER this I looked, and lo, a door standing open in heaven! And the first voice, which I had heard addressed to me like [the calling of] a [l]war trumpet, said, Come up here, and I will show you what must take place in the future.

2 At once I came under the (Holy) Spirit's power, and lo, a throne stood in heaven, with One seated on the throne! [Ezek. 1:26.]

3 And He Who sat there appeared like [the crystalline brightness of] jasper and [the fiery] sardius, and encircling the throne there was a halo that looked like [a rainbow of] emerald. [Ezek. 1:28.]

4 Twenty-four other thrones surrounded the throne and seated on these thrones were twenty-four elders, [[m]the members of the heavenly Sanhedrin], arrayed in white clothing, with crowns of gold upon their heads.

5 Out from the throne came flashes of lightning and rumblings and peals of thunder, and in front of the throne seven blazing torches burned, which are the seven Spirits of God [[n]the sevenfold (Holy) Spirit];

6 And in front of the throne there is also what looks like a transparent glassy sea, as if of crystal. And around the throne, in the center at each side of the throne, are four living creatures (ones, or beings) that are full of eyes in front and behind [with intelligence as to what is before and at the rear of them]. [Ezek. 1:5, 18.]

7 The first living creature (one, or being) was like a lion, the second living creature like an ox, the third living creature had the face of a man, and the fourth living creature [was] like a flying eagle. [Ezek. 1:10.]

8 And the four living creatures, individually having six wings, are full of eyes all over and within [underneath their wings]; and day and night they never stop saying, Holy, holy, holy is the Lord God Almighty (Omnipotent), Who was and Who is and Who is to come. [Isa. 6:1-3.]

9 And whenever the living creatures offer glory and honor and thanksgiving to Him Who sits on the throne, Who lives forever and ever—through the eternities of the eternities—[Ps. 47:8.]

10 The twenty-four elders [[o]the members of the heavenly Sanhedrin] fall prostrate before Him Who is sitting on the throne and they worship Him Who lives forever and ever; and they throw down their crowns before the throne, crying out,

11 Worthy are You, our Lord and God, to receive the glory and the honor and dominion, for You created all things; by Your will they were [brought into being] and were created. [Ps. 19:1.]

CHAPTER 5

AND I saw lying on the [p]open hand of Him Who was seated on the throne a (book) scroll written within and on the back, closed *and* sealed with seven seals; [Ezek. 2:9, 10; Isa. 29:11; Dan. 12:4.]

2 And I saw a strong angel announcing in a loud voice, Who is worthy to open the scroll? And—who is entitled and deserves and is morally fit—to break its seals?

---

l) Vincent.
m) Berry's "Greek-English Lexicon to the New Testament," and others.
n) Richard of St. Victor, cited by Trench.
o) Berry.
p) Vincent.

Living New Testament

CHAPTER 4

Then as I looked, I saw a door standing open in heaven, and the same voice I had heard before, that sounded like a mighty trumpet blast, spoke to me and said,

"Come up here and I will show you what must happen in the future!"

2 And instantly I was, in spirit, there in heaven and saw—oh, the glory of it!—a throne and Someone sitting on it!

3 Great bursts of light flashed forth from Him as from a glittering diamond, or from a shining ruby, and a rainbow glowing like an emerald encircled His throne.

4 Twenty-four smaller thrones surrounded His, with twenty-four elders sitting on them; all were clothed in white, with golden crowns upon their heads.

5 Lightning and thunder issued from the throne, and there were voices in the thunder. Directly in front of His throne were seven lighted lamps representing the sevenfold Spirit[1] of God.

6 Spread out before it was a shiny crystal sea. Four Living Beings, dotted front and back with eyes, stood at the throne's four sides.

7 The first of these Living Beings was in the form of a lion; the second looked like an ox; the third had the face of a man; and the fourth, the form of an eagle, with wings spread out as though in flight.

8 Each of these Living Beings had six wings, and the central sections of their wings were covered with eyes. Day after day and night after night they kept on saying, "Holy, holy, holy, Lord God Almighty—the one who was, and is, and is to come."

9 And when the Living Beings give glory and honor and thanks to the one sitting on the throne, who lives forever and ever,

10 The twenty-four Elders fell down before Him and worshiped Him, the Eternal Living One, and cast their crowns before the throne, singing,

11 "O Lord, You are worthy to receive the glory and the honor and the power, for You have created all things. They were created and called into being by Your act of will."

Revised Standard

The heavenly worship

4 After this I looked, and lo, in heaven an
open door! And the first voice, which I
had heard speaking to me like a trumpet, said,
"Come up hither, and I will show you what
must take place after this." [2]At once I was
in the Spirit, and lo, a throne stood in heav-
en, with one seated on the throne! [3]And he
who sat there appeared like jasper and carnelian, and round the throne was a rainbow
that looked like an emerald. [4]Round the
throne were twenty-four thrones, and seated
on the thrones were twenty-four elders, clad
in white garments, with golden crowns upon
their heads. [5]From the throne issue flashes
of lightning, and voices and peals of thunder,
and before the throne burn seven torches of
fire, which are the seven spirits of God; [6]and
before the throne there is as it were a sea
of glass, like crystal.
And round the throne, on each side of the
throne, are four living creatures, full of eyes
in front and behind: [7]the first living creature
like a lion, the second living creature like an
ox, the third living creature with the face of
a man, and the fourth living creature like a
flying eagle. [8]And the four living creatures,
each of them with six wings, are full of eyes
all round and within, and day and night they
never cease to sing,

"Holy, holy, holy, is the Lord God Almighty,
who was and is and is to come!"

[9]And whenever the living creatures give glory
and honor and thanks to him who is seated
on the throne, who lives for ever and ever,
[10]the twenty-four elders fall down before
him who is seated on the throne and worship
him who lives for ever and ever; they cast
their crowns before the throne, singing,
[11]"Worthy art thou, our Lord and God,
to receive glory and honor and power,
for thou didst create all things,
and by thy will they existed and were created."

Living New Testament

CHAPTER 5

And I saw a scroll in the right hand of the one who was sitting on the throne, a scroll with writing on the inside and on the back, and sealed with seven seals.

2 A mighty angel with a loud voice was shouting out this question: "Who is worthy to break the seals on this scroll, and to unroll it?"

Revised Standard

Prelude to the seven seals

5 And I saw in the right hand of him who
was seated on the throne a scroll written
within and on the back, sealed with seven
seals; [2]and I saw a strong angel proclaiming
with a loud voice, "Who is worthy to open

Literally, "the seven spirits of God." But see Zech. 4:2-6, where the lamps are equated with the one Spirit.

King James

3 And no man in heaven, nor in earth, neither under the earth, was able to open the book, neither to look thereon.

4 And I wept much, because no man was found worthy to open and to read the book, neither to look thereon.

5 And one of the elders saith unto me, Weep not: behold, the Lion of the tribe of Juda, the Root of David, hath prevailed to open the book, and to loose the seven seals thereof.

6 And I beheld, and, lo, in the midst of the throne and of the four beasts, and in the midst of the elders, stood a Lamb as it had been slain, having seven horns and seven eyes, which are the seven Spirits of God sent forth into all the earth.

7 And he came and took the book out of the right hand of him that sat upon the throne.

8 And when he had taken the book, the four beasts and four *and* twenty elders fell down before the Lamb, having every one of them harps, and golden vials full of odours, which are the prayers of saints.

9 And they sung a new song, saying, Thou art worthy to take the book, and to open the seals thereof: for thou wast slain, and hast redeemed us to God by thy blood out of every kindred, and tongue, and people, and nation;

10 And hast made us unto our God kings and priests: and we shall reign on the earth.

11 And I beheld, and I heard the voice of many angels round about the throne and the beasts and the elders: and the number of them was ten thousand times ten thousand, and thousands of thousands;

12 Saying with a loud voice, Worthy is the Lamb that was slain to receive power, and riches, and wisdom, and strength, and honour, and glory, and blessing.

13 And every creature which is in heaven, and on the earth, and under the earth, and such as are in the sea, and all that are in them, heard I saying, Blessing, and honour, and glory, and power, *be* unto him that sitteth upon the throne, and unto the Lamb for ever and ever.

14 And the four beasts said, Amen. And the four *and* twenty elders fell down and worshipped him that liveth for ever and ever.

Amplified

3 And no one in heaven or on earth or under the earth [in the realm of the dead, Hades] was able to open the scroll or to take a [single] look at its contents.

4 And I wept audibly *and* bitterly because no one was found fit to open the scroll or to inspect it.

5 Then one of the elders [[q]of the heavenly Sanhedrin] said to me, Stop weeping! See, the Lion of the tribe of Judah, the [r]Root (Source) of David, has won—has overcome *and* conquered! He can open the scroll and break its seven seals! [Gen. 49:9, 10; Isa. 11:1, 10.]

6 And there between the throne and the four living creatures (ones, or beings) and among the elders [[q]of the heavenly Sanhedrin], I saw a Lamb standing, as though it had been slain, with seven horns and with seven eyes, which are the seven Spirits of God [that is, [s]the sevenfold Holy Spirit] Who have been sent [on duty far and wide] into all the earth. [Isa. 53:7; Zech. 4:10; 3:8, 9.]

7 He then went and took the scroll from the right hand of Him Who sat on the throne.

8 And when He had taken the scroll (book), the four living creatures and the twenty-four elders [[q]of the heavenly Sanhedrin] prostrated themselves before the Lamb. Each was holding a harp [lute or guitar], and they had golden bowls full of incense [fragrant spices and gums for burning], which are the prayers of God's people—the saints.

9 And [now] they sing a new song, saying, You are worthy to take the scroll and to break the seals that are on it, for You were slain (sacrificed) and with Your blood You purchased men unto God from every tribe and language and people and nation. [Ps. 33:3.]

10 And You have made them a kingdom [royal race] and priests to our God, and they shall reign [as kings] over the earth! [Exod. 19:6; Isa. 61:6.]

11 Then I looked, and I heard the voices of many angels on every side of the throne, and of the living creatures and the elders [[q]of the heavenly Sanhedrin], and they numbered ten thousand times ten thousand and thousands of thousands, [Dan. 7:10.]

12 Saying in a loud voice, Deserving is the Lamb that was sacrificed, to receive all the power and riches and wisdom and might and honor and majesty (glory, splendor) and blessing!

13 And I heard every created thing in heaven and on earth and under the earth [in Hades, the place of departed spirits] and on the sea and all that is in it, crying out together, To Him Who is seated on the throne and to the Lamb be ascribed the blessing and the honor and the majesty (glory, splendor) and the power (might and dominion) forever and ever—through the eternities of the eternities! [Dan. 7:13, 14.]

14 Then the four living creatures (ones, or beings) said, Amen—so be it! and the elders [[t]of the heavenly Sanhedrin] prostrated themselves and worshipped *Him Who lives forever and ever.*

CHAPTER 6

AND I saw when the Lamb opened one of the seals, and I heard, as it were the noise of thunder, one of the four beasts saying, Come and see.

CHAPTER 6

THEN I saw as the Lamb broke open one of the seven seals, and as if in a voice of thunder I heard one of the four living creatures call out, Come!

---

q) Berry's "Greek-English Lexicon to the New Testament," and others.
r) Rev. 22:16.
s) Vincent.
t) Berry's "Greek-English Lexicon to the New Testament," and others.

Living New Testament

3 But no one in all heaven or earth or from among the dead was permitted to open and read it.

4 Then I wept with disappointment[1] because no one anywhere was worthy; no one could tell us what it said.

5 But one of the twenty-four Elders said to me, "Cease weeping, for look! The Lion of the tribe of Judah, the Root of David, has conquered, and proved Himself worthy to open the scroll and to break its seven seals."

6 I looked and saw a Lamb standing there before the twenty-four Elders, in front of the throne and the Living Beings, and on the Lamb were wounds that once had caused His death. He had seven horns and seven eyes, which represent the seven-fold Spirit[2] of God, sent out into every part of the world.

7 He stepped forward and took the scroll from the right hand of the one sitting upon the throne.

8 And as He took the scroll, the twenty-four Elders fell down before the Lamb, each with a harp and golden vials filled with incense—the prayers of God's people!

9 They were singing[3] Him a new song with these words: "You are worthy to take the scroll and break its seals and open it; for You were slain, and Your blood has bought people from every nation as gifts for God.

10 And You have gathered them into a kingdom and made them priests of our God; they shall reign upon the earth."

11 Then in my vision I heard the singing[3] of millions of angels surrounding the throne and the Living Beings and the Elders:

12 "The Lamb is worthy" (loudly they sang[3] it!) "—the Lamb who was slain. He is worthy to receive the power, and the riches, and the wisdom, and the strength, and the honor, and the glory, and the blessing."

13 And then I heard everyone in heaven and earth, and from the dead beneath the earth and in the sea, exclaiming, "The blessing and the honor and the glory and the power belong to the one sitting on the throne, and to the Lamb forever and ever."

14 And the four Living Beings kept saying, "Amen!" And the twenty-four Elders fell down and worshiped Him.

Revised Standard

the scroll and break its seals?" [3]And no one
in heaven or on earth or under the earth was
able to open the scroll or to look into it, [4]and
I wept much that no one was found worthy
to open the scroll or to look into it. [5]Then
one of the elders said to me, "Weep not; lo,
the Lion of the tribe of Judah, the Root of
David, has conquered, so that he can open
the scroll and its seven seals."

The scroll and the Lamb

6 And between the throne and the four
living creatures and among the elders, I saw
a Lamb standing, as though it had been slain,
with seven horns and with seven eyes, which
are the seven spirits of God sent out into
all the earth; [7]and he went and took the
scroll from the right hand of him who was
seated on the throne. [8]And when he had
taken the scroll, the four living creatures and
the twenty-four elders fell down before the
Lamb, each holding a harp, and with golden
bowls full of incense, which are the prayers
of the saints; [9]and they sang a new song,
saying,

"Worthy art thou to take the scroll and to
 open its seals,
for thou wast slain and by thy blood didst
 ransom men for God
from every tribe and tongue and people
 and nation,
[10]and hast made them a kingdom and priests
 to our God,
and they shall reign on earth."

[11]Then I looked, and I heard around the
throne and the living creatures and the elders the voice of many angels, numbering
myriads of myriads and thousands of thousands, [12]saying with a loud voice, "Worthy
is the Lamb who was slain, to receive power
and wealth and wisdom and might and honor
and glory and blessing!" [13]And I heard every
creature in heaven and on earth and under
the earth and in the sea, and all therein,
saying, "To him who sits upon the throne
and to the Lamb be blessing and honor and
glory and might for ever and ever!" [14]And
the four living creatures said, "Amen!" and
the elders fell down and worshiped.

CHAPTER 6

As I watched, the Lamb broke the first seal and began to unroll the scroll. Then one of the four Living Beings, with a voice that sounded like thunder, said, "Come!"

Six of the seals opened

6 Now I saw when the Lamb opened one
of the seven seals, and I heard one of the
four living creatures say, as with a voice of

---

[1] Implied.

[2] Literally, "the seven spirits of God"; but see Zechariah 4:2-6, 10, where the seven eyes are equated with the seven lamps and the one Spirit.

[3] Literally, "saying" or "said."

King James

2 And I saw, and behold a white horse: and he that sat on him had a bow; and a crown was given unto him: and he went forth conquering, and to conquer.

3 And when he had opened the second seal, I heard the second beast say, Come and see.

4 And there went out another horse *that was* red: and *power* was given to him that sat thereon to take peace from the earth, and that they should kill one another: and there was given unto him a great sword.

5 And when he had opened the third seal, I heard the third beast say, Come and see. And I beheld, and lo a black horse; and he that sat on him had a pair of balances in his hand.

6 And I heard a voice in the midst of the four beasts say, A measure of wheat for a penny, and three measures of barley for a penny; and *see* thou hurt not the oil and the wine.

7 And when he had opened the fourth seal, I heard the voice of the fourth beast say, Come and see.

8 And I looked, and behold a pale horse: and his name that sat on him was Death, and Hell followed with him. And power was given unto them over the fourth part of the earth, to kill with sword, and with hunger, and with death, and with the beasts of the earth.

9 And when he had opened the fifth seal, I saw under the altar the souls of them that were slain for the word of God, and for the testimony which they held:

10 And they cried with a loud voice, saying, How long, O Lord, holy and true, dost thou not judge and avenge our blood on them that dwell on the earth?

11 And white robes were given unto every one of them; and it was said unto them, that they should rest yet for a little season, until their fellow-servants also and their brethren, that should be killed as they *were,* should be fulfilled.

12 And I beheld when he had opened the sixth seal, and, lo, there was a great earthquake; and the sun became black as sackcloth of hair, and the moon became as blood;

13 And the stars of heaven fell unto the earth, even as a fig tree casteth her untimely figs, when she is shaken of a mighty wind.

14 And the heaven departed as a scroll when it is rolled together; and every mountain and island were moved out of their places.

15 And the kings of the earth, and the great men, and the rich men, and the chief captains, and the mighty men, and every bondman, and every free man, hid themselves in the dens and in the rocks of the mountains;

16 And said to the mountains and rocks, Fall on us, and hide us from the face of him that sitteth on the throne, and from the wrath of the Lamb:

17 For the great day of his wrath is come; and who shall be able to stand?

Amplified

2 And I looked, and saw there a white horse whose rider carried a bow. And a crown was given him, and he rode forth conquering and to conquer. [Zech. 1:8; 6:1-3; Ps. 45:4, 5.]

3 And when He broke the second seal, I heard the second living creature call out, Come!

4 And another horse came out, flaming red. And its rider was empowered to take the peace from the earth, so that men slaughtered one another; and he was given a huge sword.

5 When He broke open the third seal, I heard the third living creature call out, Come *and look!* And I saw, and behold, a black horse, and in his hand the rider had a pair of scales (a balance).

6 And I heard what seemed to be a voice from the midst of the four living creatures saying, A quart of wheat for a denarius [a whole day's wages], and three quarts of barley for a denarius; but do not harm the oil and the wine! [II Kings 6:25.]

7 When the Lamb broke open the fourth seal, I heard the fourth living creature call out, Come!

8 So I looked, and behold, an ashy pale horse [[u]black and blue as if made so by bruising], and its rider's name was Death, and Hades [the realm of the dead] followed him closely; and they were given authority *and* power over a fourth part of the earth, to kill with the sword and with famine and with plague (pestilence, disease) and with wild beasts of the earth. [Hos. 13:14; Ezek. 5:12.]

9 When the Lamb broke open the fifth seal, I saw at the foot of the altar the souls of those whose lives had been sacrificed for [adhering to] the Word of God and for the testimony they had borne.

10 They cried in a loud voice, O (Sovereign) Lord, holy and true, how long now before You will sit in judgment and avenge our blood upon those who dwell on the earth? [Zech. 1:12; Ps. 79:5; Gen. 4:10.]

11 Then they were each given a [v]long *and* flowing *and* festive white robe and told to rest *and* wait patiently a little while longer, until the number should be complete of their fellow servants and their brethren, who were to be killed as they themselves had been.

12 When He [the Lamb] broke open the sixth seal, I looked, and there was a great earthquake; and the sun grew black as sackcloth of hair, (the full disc of) the moon became like blood. [Joel 2:10, 31.]

13 And the stars of the sky dropped to the earth like a fig tree shedding its unripe fruit out of season when shaken by a strong wind. [Isa. 34:4.]

14 And the [w]sky rolled up like a scroll *and* vanished, and every mountain and island was dislodged from its place.

15 Then the kings of the earth and their noblemen and their magnates and their military chiefs and the wealthy and the strong and [everyone, whether] slave or free, hid themselves in the caves and among the rocks of the mountains, [Isa. 2:10.]

16 And they called to the mountains and the rocks, Fall on (before) us and hide us from the face of Him Who sits on the throne, and from the [x]deep-seated indignation *and* wrath of the Lamb. [Hos. 10:8; Isa. 2:19-21.]

17 For the great day of His wrath (vengeance, retribution, indignation) has come, and who is able to stand before it? [Joel 2:11; Mal. 3:2.]

---

u) Definition of "livid," symbolizing death and pestilence.
v) Vincent.
w) Moulton and Milligan.
x) Vincent.

Living New Testament

2 I looked, and there in front of me was a white horse. Its rider carried a bow, and a crown was placed upon his head; he rode out to conquer in many battles and win the war.

3 Then He unrolled the scroll to the second seal, and broke it open, too. And I heard the second Living Being say, "Come!"

4 This time a red horse rode out. Its rider was given a long sword and the authority to banish peace and bring anarchy to the earth; war and killing broke out everywhere.

5 When He had broken the third seal, I heard the third Living Being say, "Come!" And I saw a black horse, with its rider holding a pair of balances in his hand.

6 And a voice from among the four Living Beings said, "A loaf of bread for a dollar, or three pounds of barley flour,[1] but there is no olive oil or wine."[2]

7 And when the fourth seal was broken, I heard the fourth Living Being say, "Come!"

8 And now I saw a pale horse, and its rider's name was Death. And there followed after him another horse whose rider's name was Hell. They were given control of one-fourth of the earth, to kill with war and famine and disease and wild animals.

9 And when He broke open the fifth seal, I saw an altar, and underneath it all the souls of those who had been martyred for preaching the Word of God and for being faithful in their witnessing.

10 They called loudly to the Lord and said, "O Sovereign Lord, holy and true, how long will it be before You judge the people of the earth for what they've done to us? When will You avenge our blood against those living on the earth?"

11 White robes were given to each of them, and they were told to rest a little longer until their other brothers, fellow servants of Jesus, had been martyred on the earth and joined them.

12 I watched as He broke the sixth seal, and there was a vast earthquake; and the sun became dark like black cloth, and the moon was blood-red.

13 Then the stars of heaven appeared to be falling to earth[3]—like green fruit from fig trees buffeted by mighty winds.

14 And the starry heavens disappeared[4] as though rolled up like a scroll and taken away; and every mountain and island shook and shifted.

15 The kings of the earth, and world leaders and rich men, and high-ranking military officers, and all men great and small, slave and free, hid themselves in the caves and rocks of the mountains,

16 And cried to the mountains to crush them. "Fall on us," they pleaded, "and hide us from the face of the one sitting on the throne, and from the anger of the Lamb,

17 Because the great day of Their anger has come, and who can survive it?"

---

[1] Literally, "A choenix of wheat for a denarius, and three choenix of barley for a denarius. . . ."
[2] Literally, "do not damage the oil and wine."
[3] Literally, "the stars of heaven fell to the earth."
[4] Literally, "the sky departed."

Revised Standard

thunder, "Come!" 2 And I saw, and behold,
a white horse, and its rider had a bow; and
a crown was given to him, and he went out
conquering and to conquer.
3 When he opened the second seal, I
heard the second living creature say, "Come!"
4 And out came another horse, bright red;
its rider was permitted to take peace from
the earth, so that men should slay one another; and he was given a great sword.
5 When he opened the third seal, I heard
the third living creature say, "Come!" And
I saw, and behold, a black horse, and its
rider had a balance in his hand; 6 and I heard
what seemed to be a voice in the midst of
the four living creatures saying, "A quart of
wheat for a denarius,[a] and three quarts of
barley for a denarius;[a] but do not harm oil
and wine!"
7 When he opened the fourth seal, I heard
the voice of the fourth living creature say,
"Come!" 8 And I saw, and behold, a pale
horse, and its rider's name was Death, and
Hades followed him; and they were given
power over a fourth of the earth, to kill
with sword and with famine and with pestilence and by wild beasts of the earth.
9 When he opened the fifth seal, I saw
under the altar the souls of those who had
been slain for the word of God and for the
witness they had borne; 10 they cried out
with a loud voice, "O Sovereign Lord, holy
and true, how long before thou wilt judge
and avenge our blood on those who dwell
upon the earth?" 11 Then they were each
given a white robe and told to rest a little
longer, until the number of their fellow
servants and their brethren should be complete, who were to be killed as they themselves had been.
12 When he opened the sixth seal, I
looked, and behold, there was a great earthquake; and the sun became black as sackcloth, the full moon became like blood,
13 and the stars of the sky fell to the earth
as the fig tree sheds its winter fruit when
shaken by a gale; 14 the sky vanished like
a scroll that is rolled up, and every mountain and island was removed from its place.
15 Then the kings of the earth and the great
men and the generals and the rich and the
strong, and every one, slave and free, hid
in the caves and among the rocks of the
mountains, 16 calling to the mountains and
rocks, "Fall on us and hide us from the face
of him who is seated on the throne, and
from the wrath of the Lamb; 17 for the great
day of their wrath has come, and who can
stand before it?"

---

[a] The denarius was worth about twenty cents

King James

CHAPTER 7

AND after these things I saw four angels standing on the four corners of the earth, holding the four winds of the earth, that the wind should not blow on the earth, nor on the sea, nor on any tree.

2 And I saw another angel ascending from the east, having the seal of the living God: and he cried with a loud voice to the four angels, to whom it was given to hurt the earth and the sea,

3 Saying, Hurt not the earth, neither the sea, nor the trees, till we have sealed the servants of our God in their foreheads.

4 And I heard the number of them which were sealed: *and there were* sealed an hundred *and* forty *and* four thousand of all the tribes of the children of Israel.

5 Of the tribe of Juda *were* sealed twelve thousand. Of the tribe of Reuben *were* sealed twelve thousand. Of the tribe of Gad *were* sealed twelve thousand.

6 Of the tribe of Aser *were* sealed twelve thousand. Of the tribe of Nepthalim *were* sealed twelve thousand. Of the tribe of Manasses *were* sealed twelve thousand.

7 Of the tribe of Simeon *were* sealed twelve thousand. Of the tribe of Levi *were* sealed twelve thousand. Of the tribe of Issachar *were* sealed twelve thousand.

8 Of the tribe of Zabulon *were* sealed twelve thousand. Of the tribe of Joseph *were* sealed twelve thousand. Of the tribe of Benjamin *were* sealed twelve thousand.

9 After this I beheld, and, lo, a great multitude, which no man could number, of all nations, and kindreds, and people, and tongues, stood before the throne, and before the Lamb, clothed with white robes, and palms in their hands;

10 And cried with a loud voice, saying, Salvation to our God which sitteth upon the throne, and unto the Lamb.

11 And all the angels stood round about the throne, and *about* the elders and the four beasts, and fell before the throne on their faces, and worshipped God,

12 Saying, Amen: Blessing, and glory, and wisdom, and thanksgiving, and honour, and power, and might, *be* unto our God for ever and ever. Amen.

13 And one of the elders answered, saying unto me, What are these which are arrayed in white robes? and whence came they?

14 And I said unto him, Sir, thou knowest. And he said to me, These are they which came out of great tribulation, and have washed their robes, and made them white in the blood of the Lamb.

15 Therefore are they before the throne of God, and serve him day and night in his temple: and he that sitteth on the throne shall dwell among them.

16 They shall hunger no more, neither thirst any more; neither shall the sun light on them, nor any heat.

17 For the Lamb which is in the midst of the throne shall feed them, and shall lead them unto living fountains of waters: and God shall wipe away all tears from their eyes.

Amplified

CHAPTER 7

AFTER this I saw four angels stationed at the four corners of the earth, [x]firmly holding back the four winds of the earth, so that no wind should blow on the earth or sea or upon any tree. [Zech. 6:5.]

2 Then I saw a second angel coming up from the east (the rising of the sun), and carrying the seal of the living God. And with a loud voice he called out to the four angels who had been given authority *and* power to injure earth and sea,

3 Saying, Harm neither the earth nor the sea nor the trees, until we have sealed the bond servants of our God upon their foreheads. [Ezek. 9:4.]

4 And [then] I heard how many were sealed (marked) out of every tribe of the sons of Israel; there were a hundred and forty-four thousand sealed.

5 Twelve thousand were sealed (marked) out of the tribe of Judah, twelve thousand of the tribe of Reuben, twelve thousand of the tribe of Gad,

6 Twelve thousand of the tribe of Asher, twelve thousand of the tribe of Naphtali, twelve thousand of the tribe of Manasseh,

7 Twelve thousand of the tribe of Simeon, twelve thousand of the tribe of Levi, twelve thousand of the tribe of Issachar,

8 Twelve thousand of the tribe of Zebulun, twelve thousand of the tribe of Joseph, twelve thousand of the tribe of Benjamin.

9 After this I looked and a vast host appeared which no one could count, [gathered out] of every nation, from all tribes and peoples and languages. These stood before the throne and before the Lamb; they were attired in white robes, with palm branches in their hands.

10 In loud voice they cried, saying, [Our] salvation is due to our God Who is seated on the throne, and to the Lamb—to Them [we owe our] deliverance!

11 And all the angels were standing round the throne and round the elders [[y]of the heavenly Sanhedrin] and the four living creatures, and they fell prostrate before the throne and worshipped God.

12 Amen! (So be it!) they cried. Blessing and glory *and* majesty *and* splendor and wisdom and thanks and honor and power and might [be ascribed] to our God to the ages and ages—forever and ever, throughout the eternities of the eternities! Amen! (So be it!)

13 Then, addressing me, one of the elders [[y]of the heavenly Sanhedrin] said, Who are these [people] clothed in the long white robes? And from where have they come?

14 I replied, Sir, you know. And he said to me, These are they who have come out of the great tribulation (persecution), and have washed their robes and made them white in the blood of the Lamb. [Dan. 12:1; Gen. 49:11.]

15 For this reason they are [now] before the [very] throne of God, and serve Him day and night in His (temple) sanctuary; and He Who is sitting upon the throne will protect *and* spread His tabernacle over *and* shelter them with His presence.

16 They shall hunger no more, neither thirst any more, neither shall the sun smite them, nor any [z]scorching heat. [Isa. 49:10; Ps. 121:6.]

17 For the Lamb Who is in the midst of the throne will be their Shepherd, and He will guide them to the springs of the waters of Life; and God will wipe every tear away from their eyes. [Ezek. 34:23; Ps. 23:2; Isa. 25:8.]

---

x) Vincent.
y) Souter: "A Pocket Lexicon to the Greek New Testament," and others.
z) Berry: "Greek-English Lexicon to the New Testament," and others.

Living New Testament

CHAPTER 7

Then I saw four angels standing at the four corners of the earth, holding back the four winds from blowing, so that not a leaf rustled in the trees, and the ocean became as smooth as glass.

2 And I saw another angel coming from the east, carrying the Great Seal of the Living God. And he shouted out to those four angels who had been given power to injure earth and sea,

3 "Wait! Don't do anything yet—hurt neither earth nor sea nor trees—until we have placed the Seal of God upon the foreheads of His servants."

4, 5, 6, 7, 8 How many were given this mark? I heard the number—it was 144,000, out of all twelve tribes of Israel, as listed here:

Judah	12,000
Reuben	12,000
Gad	12,000
Asher	12,000
Naphtali	12,000
Manasseh	12,000
Simeon	12,000
Levi	12,000
Issachar	12,000
Zebulun	12,000
Joseph	12,000
Benjamin	12,000

9 After this I saw a vast crowd, too great to count, from all the nations and provinces and languages, standing in front of the throne and before the Lamb, clothed in white, with palm branches in their hands.

10 And they were shouting with a mighty shout, "Salvation comes from our God upon the throne, and from the Lamb."

11 And now all the angels were crowding around the throne and around the Elders and the four Living Beings, and falling face down before the throne and worshiping God.

12 "Amen!" they said. "Blessing, and glory, and wisdom, and thanksgiving, and honor, and power, and might be to our God forever and forever. Amen!"

13 Then one of the twenty-four Elders asked me, "Do you know who these are, who are clothed in white, and where they come from?"

14 "No, sir," I replied. "Please tell me."

"These are the ones coming out of the Great Tribulation," he said; "they washed their robes and whitened them by the blood of the Lamb.

15 That is why they are here before the throne of God, serving Him day and night in His temple. The one sitting on the throne will shelter them;

16 They will never be hungry again, nor thirsty, and they will be fully protected from the scorching noontime heat.

17 For the Lamb standing in front of[1] the throne will feed them and be their Shepherd and lead them to the springs of the Water of Life. And God will wipe their tears away."

[1] Literally, "in the center of the throne"; i.e., directly in front, not to one side. An alternate rendering might be, "at the heart of the throne."

Revised Standard

The sealing of God's servants

7 After this I saw four angels standing
at the four corners of the earth, holding
back the four winds of the earth, that no
wind might blow on earth or sea or against
any tree. [2]Then I saw another angel ascend
from the rising of the sun, with the seal of
the living God, and he called with a loud
voice to the four angels who had been given
power to harm earth and sea, [3]saying, "Do
not harm the earth or the sea or the trees,
till we have sealed the servants of our God
upon their foreheads." [4]And I heard the
number of the sealed, a hundred and forty-
four thousand sealed, out of every tribe of
the sons of Israel, [5]twelve thousand sealed
out of the tribe of Judah, twelve thousand
of the tribe of Reuben, twelve thousand of
the tribe of Gad, [6]twelve thousand of the
tribe of Asher, twelve thousand of the tribe
of Naphtali, twelve thousand of the tribe
of Manasseh, [7]twelve thousand of the tribe
of Simeon, twelve thousand of the tribe of
Levi, twelve thousand of the tribe of Issachar,
[8]twelve thousand of the tribe of Zebulun,
twelve thousand of the tribe of Joseph, twelve
thousand sealed out of the tribe of Benjamin.

The saints in white robes

9 After this I looked, and behold, a great
multitude which no man could number, from
every nation, from all tribes and peoples and
tongues, standing before the throne and before the Lamb, clothed in white robes, with
palm branches in their hands, [10]and crying
out with a loud voice, "Salvation belongs to
our God who sits upon the throne, and to
the Lamb!" [11]And all the angels stood round
the throne and round the elders and the four
living creatures, and they fell on their faces
before the throne and worshiped God, [12]say-
ing, "Amen! Blessing and glory and wisdom
and thanksgiving and honor and power and
might be to our God for ever and ever!
Amen."
13 Then one of the elders addressed me,
saying, "Who are these, clothed in white
robes, and whence have they come?" [14]I said
to him, "Sir, you know." And he said to me,
"These are they who have come out of the
great tribulation; they have washed their
robes and made them white in the blood
of the Lamb.

[15]Therefore are they before the throne of God,
and serve him day and night within his temple;
and he who sits upon the throne will shelter them with his presence.
[16]They shall hunger no more, neither thirst any more;
the sun shall not strike them, nor any scorching heat.
[17]For the Lamb in the midst of the throne will be their shepherd,
and he will guide them to springs of living water;
and God will wipe away every tear from their eyes."

King James

CHAPTER 8

AND when he had opened the seventh seal, there was silence in heaven about the space of half an hour.

2 And I saw the seven angels which stood before God; and to them were given seven trumpets.

3 And another angel came and stood at the altar, having a golden censer; and there was given unto him much incense, that he should offer *it* with the prayers of all saints upon the golden altar which was before the throne.

4 And the smoke of the incense, *which came* with the prayers of the saints, ascended up before God out of the angel's hand.

5 And the angel took the censer, and filled it with fire of the altar, and cast *it* into the earth: and there were voices, and thunderings, and lightnings, and an earthquake.

6 And the seven angels which had the seven trumpets prepared themselves to sound.

7 The first angel sounded, and there followed hail and fire mingled with blood, and they were cast upon the earth: and the third part of trees was burnt up, and all green grass was burnt up.

8 And the second angel sounded, and as it were a great mountain burning with fire was cast into the sea: and the third part of the sea became blood;

9 And the third part of the creatures which were in the sea, and had life, died; and the third part of the ships were destroyed.

10 And the third angel sounded, and there fell a great star from heaven, burning as it were a lamp, and it fell upon the third part of the rivers, and upon the fountains of waters;

11 And the name of the star is called Wormwood: and the third part of the waters became wormwood; and many men died of the waters, because they were made bitter.

12 And the fourth angel sounded, and the third part of the sun was smitten, and the third part of the moon, and the third part of the stars; so as the third part of them was darkened, and the day shone not for a third part of it, and the night likewise.

13 And I beheld, and heard an angel flying through the midst of heaven, saying with a loud voice, Woe, woe, woe, to the inhabiters of the earth by reason of the other voices of the trumpet of the three angels, which are yet to sound!

Amplified

CHAPTER 8

WHEN He [the Lamb] broke open the seventh seal, there was silence for about half an hour in heaven.

2 Then I saw the seven angels who stand before God, and to them were given seven trumpets.

3 And another angel came and stood over the altar. He had a golden censer, and he was given very much incense [fragrant spices and gums which exhale perfume when burned], that he might mingle it with the prayers of all the people of God (the saints) upon the altar of gold before the throne. [Ps. 141:2.]

4 And the smoke of the incense (the perfume) arose in the presence of God with the prayers of the people of God (the saints) from the hand of the angel.

5 So the angel took the censer and filled it with fire from the altar and cast it upon the earth. Then there followed thunder peals *and* loud rumblings *and* blasts *and* noises, and lightning flashes, and an earthquake. [Lev. 16:12; Ezek. 10:2.]

6 Then the seven angels who had the seven trumpets prepared to sound them.

7 The first angel blew [his] trumpet, and there was a storm of hail and fire mingled with blood, cast upon the earth. And a third part of the earth was burned up, and a third of the trees was burned up and all the green grass was burned up. [Exod. 9:23-25.]

8 The second angel blew his trumpet, and something resembling a great mountain, blazing with fire, was hurled into the sea. [Jer. 51:25.]

9 And a third of the sea was turned to blood, a third of the living creatures in the sea perished, and a third of the ships were destroyed.

10 The third angel blew [his] trumpet, and a huge star fell from heaven, burning like a torch, and it dropped on a third of the rivers and on the springs of water.

11 And the name of the star is Wormwood. A third part of the waters was changed into wormwood, and many people died from using the water, because it had become bitter.

12 Then the fourth angel blew [his] trumpet, and a third of the sun was smitten, and a third of the moon, and a third of the stars, so that [the light of] a third of them was darkened, and a third of the daylight [itself] was withdrawn and likewise a third [of the light] of the night was kept from shining.

13 Then I [looked and I] saw a solitary eagle flying in midheaven, and as it flew I heard it crying with a loud voice, Woe, woe, woe to those who dwell on the earth, because of the rest of the trumpet blasts which the three angels are about to sound!

Living New Testament

CHAPTER 8

When the Lamb had broken the seventh seal, there was silence throughout all heaven for what seemed like half an hour.

2 And I saw the seven angels that stand before God, and they were given seven trumpets.

3 Then another angel with a golden censer came and stood at the altar; and a great quantity of incense was given to him to mix with the prayers of God's people, to offer upon the golden altar before the throne.

4 And the perfume of the incense mixed with prayers ascended up to God from the altar where the angel had poured them out.

5 Then the angel filled the censer with fire from the altar and threw it down upon the earth; and thunder crashed and rumbled, lightning flashed, and there was a terrible earthquake.

6 Then the seven angels with the seven trumpets prepared to blow their mighty blasts.

7 The first angel blew his trumpet, and hail and fire mixed with blood were thrown down upon the earth. One-third of the earth was set on fire so that one-third of the trees were burned, and all the green grass.

8, 9 Then the second angel blew his trumpet, and what appeared to be a huge burning mountain was thrown into the sea, destroying a third of all the ships; and a third of the sea turned red as[1] blood; and a third of the fish were killed.

10 The third angel blew, and a great flaming star fell from heaven upon a third of the rivers and springs.

11 The star was called "Bitterness"[2] because it poisoned a third of all the water on the earth and many people died.

12 The fourth angel blew his trumpet and immediately a third of the sun was blighted and darkened, and a third of the moon and the stars, so that the daylight was dimmed by a third, and the nighttime darkness deepened.

13 As I watched, I saw a solitary eagle flying through the heavens crying loudly, "Woe, woe, woe to the people of the earth because of the terrible things that will soon happen when the three remaining angels blow their trumpets."

[1] Literally, "became blood."
[2] Literally, "Wormwood."

Revised Standard

The seventh seal

8 When the Lamb opened the seventh
seal, there was silence in heaven for
about half an hour. 2Then I saw the seven
angels who stand before God, and seven
trumpets were given to them. 3And another
angel came and stood at the altar with a
golden censer; and he was given much
incense to mingle with the prayers of all
the saints upon the golden altar before the
throne; 4and the smoke of the incense rose
with the prayers of the saints from the hand
of the angel before God. 5Then the angel
took the censer and filled it with fire from
the altar and threw it on the earth; and
there were peals of thunder, loud noises,
flashes of lightning, and an earthquake.
6 Now the seven angels who had the
seven trumpets made ready to blow them.
7 The first angel blew his trumpet, and
there followed hail and fire, mixed with
blood, which fell on the earth; and a third
of the earth was burnt up, and a third of
the trees were burnt up, and all green grass
was burnt up.
8 The second angel blew his trumpet,
and something like a great mountain, burning with fire, was thrown into the sea; 9and
a third of the sea became blood, a third of
the living creatures in the sea died, and a
third of the ships were destroyed.
10 The third angel blew his trumpet, and
a great star fell from heaven, blazing like
a torch, and it fell on a third of the rivers
and on the fountains of water: 11The name
of the star is Wormwood. A third of the
waters became wormwood, and many men
died of the water, because it was made bitter.
12 The fourth angel blew his trumpet,
and a third of the sun was struck, and a
third of the moon, and a third of the stars,
so that a third of their light was darkened;
a third of the day was kept from shining,
and likewise a third of the night.
13 Then I looked, and I heard an eagle
crying with a loud voice, as it flew in midheaven, "Woe, woe, woe to those who dwell
on the earth, at the blasts of the other
trumpets which the three angels are about
to blow!"

King James

CHAPTER 9

AND the fifth angel sounded, and I saw a star fall from heaven unto the earth: and to him was given the key of the bottomless pit.

2 And he opened the bottomless pit; and there arose a smoke out of the pit, as the smoke of a great furnace; and the sun and the air were darkened by reason of the smoke of the pit.

3 And there came out of the smoke locusts upon the earth: and unto them was given power, as the scorpions of the earth have power.

4 And it was commanded them that they should not hurt the grass of the earth, neither any green thing, neither any tree; but only those men which have not the seal of God in their foreheads.

5 And to them it was given that they should not kill them, but that they should be tormented five months: and their torment *was* as the torment of a scorpion, when he striketh a man.

6 And in those days shall men seek death, and shall not find it; and shall desire to die, and death shall flee from them.

7 And the shapes of the locusts *were* like unto horses prepared unto battle; and on their heads *were* as it were crowns like gold, and their faces *were* as the faces of men.

8 And they had hair as the hair of women, and their teeth were as *the teeth* of lions.

9 And they had breastplates, as it were breastplates of iron; and the sound of their wings *was* as the sound of chariots of many horses running to battle.

10 And they had tails like unto scorpions, and there were stings in their tails: and their power *was* to hurt men five months.

11 And they had a king over them, *which is* the angel of the bottomless pit, whose name in the Hebrew tongue *is* Abaddon, but in the Greek tongue hath *his* name Apollyon.

12 One woe is past; *and*, behold, there come two woes more hereafter.

13 And the sixth angel sounded, and I heard a voice from the four horns of the golden altar which is before God,

14 Saying to the sixth angel which had the trumpet, Loose the four angels which are bound in the great river Euphrates.

15 And the four angels were loosed, which were prepared for an hour, and a day, and a month, and a year, for to slay the third part of men.

16 And the number of the army of the horsemen *were* two hundred thousand thousand: and I heard the number of them.

17 And thus I saw the horses in the vision, and them that sat on them, having breastplates of fire, and of jacinth, and brimstone: and the heads of the horses *were* as the heads of lions; and out of their mouths issued fire and smoke and brimstone.

18 By these three was the third part of men killed, by the fire, and by the smoke, and by the brimstone, which issued out of their mouths.

Amplified

CHAPTER 9

THEN the fifth angel blew [his] trumpet, and I saw a star that had fallen from the sky to the earth, and to the angel was given the key [a]of the shaft of the abyss—the bottomless pit.

2 He opened the [a]long shaft of the abyss—the bottomless pit—and smoke like the smoke of a huge furnace puffed out of the [a]long shaft, so that the sun and the atmosphere were darkened by the smoke from the long shaft. [Gen. 19:28; Exod. 19:18; Joel 2:10.]

3 Then out of the smoke locusts came forth on the earth, and such power was granted them as the power the earth's scorpions have. [Exod. 10:12-15.]

4 They were told not to injure the herbage of the earth nor any green thing nor any tree, but only [to attack] such human beings as do not have the seal (mark) of God on their foreheads. [Ezek. 9:4.]

5 They were not permitted to kill them, but to torment (distress, vex) them for five months, and the pain caused them was like the torture of a scorpion when it stings a person.

6 And in those days people will seek death and will not find it, and they will yearn to die, but death evades *and* flees from them. [Job 3:21.]

7 The locusts resembled horses equipped for battle. On their heads was something like golden crowns. Their faces resembled the faces of people. [Joel 2:4.]

8 They had hair like the hair of women, and their teeth were like lions' teeth. [Joel 1:6.]

9 Their breastplates [scales] resembled breastplates made of iron, and the [whirring] noise made by their wings was like the roar of a vast number of horse-drawn chariots going at full speed into battle. [Joel 2:5.]

10 They have tails like scorpions, and they have stings, and in their tails lies their ability to hurt men for (the) five months.

11 Over them as king they have the angel of the abyss—of the bottomless pit. In Hebrew his name is Abaddon [destruction], but in Greek he is called Apollyon [destroyer].

12 The first woe (calamity) has passed; lo, two others are yet to follow.

13 Then the sixth angel blew [his] trumpet, and from the four horns of the altar of gold which stands before God I heard a solitary voice,

14 Saying to the sixth angel who had the trumpet, Liberate the four angels who are bound at the great river Euphrates.

15 So the four angels, who had been in readiness for that hour in the appointed day, month and year, were liberated to destroy a third of mankind.

16 The number of their troops of cavalry was twice ten thousand times ten thousand (200,000,000); I heard what their number was.

17 And in [my] vision the horses and their riders appeared to me like this: the riders wore breastplates the color of fiery red and sapphire blue and sulphur (brimstone) yellow. The heads of the horses looked like lions' heads, and from their mouths there poured fire and smoke and sulphur (brimstone).

18 A third of mankind was killed by these three plagues, by the fire and the smoke and the sulphur (brimstone) that poured from the mouths of the horses.

---

a) Vincent.

Living New Testament

CHAPTER 9

Then the fifth angel blew his trumpet and I saw one[1] who was fallen to earth from heaven, and to him was given the key to the bottomless pit.

2 When he opened it, smoke poured out as though from some huge furnace, and the sun and air were darkened by smoke.

3 Then locusts came from the smoke and descended onto the earth and were given power to sting like scorpions.

4 They were told not to hurt the grass or plants or trees, but to attack those people who did not have the mark of God on their foreheads.

5 They were not to kill them, but to torture them for five months with agony like the pain of scorpion stings.

6 In those days men will try to kill themselves but won't be able to—death will not come. They will long to die—but death will flee away!

7 The locusts looked like horses armored for battle. They had what looked like golden crowns on their heads, and their faces looked like men's.

8 Their hair was long like women's, and their teeth were those of lions.

9 They wore breastplates that seemed to be of iron, and their wings roared like an army of chariots rushing into battle.

10 They had stinging tails like scorpions, and their power to hurt, given to them for five months, was in their tails.

11 Their king is the Prince of the bottomless pit whose name in Hebrew is Abaddon, and in Greek, Apollyon [and in English, the Destroyer[2]].

12 One terror now ends, but there are two more coming!

13 The sixth angel blew his trumpet and I heard a voice speaking from the four horns of the golden altar that stands before the throne of God,

14 Saying to the sixth angel, "Release the four mighty demons[3] held bound at the great River Euphrates."

15 They had been kept in readiness for that year and month and day and hour, and now they were turned loose to kill a third of all mankind.

16 They led an army of 200,000,000[4] warriors[5]—I heard an announcement of how many there were.

17, 18 I saw their horses spread out before me in my vision; their riders wore fiery-red breastplates, though some were sky-blue and others yellow. The horses' heads looked much like lions', and smoke and fire and flaming sulphur billowed from their mouths, killing one-third of all mankind.

[1] Literally, "a star fallen from heaven"; it is unclear whether this person is of Satanic origin, as most commentators believe, or whether the reference is to Christ.
[2] Implied.
[3] Literally, "(fallen) angels."
[4] If this is a literal figure, it is no longer incredible, in view of a world population of 6,000,000,000 in the near future. In China alone, in 1961, there were an "estimated 200,000,000 armed and organized militiamen" (Associated Press Release, April 24, 1964).
[5] Literally, "horsemen."

Revised Standard

The plague of locusts

9 And the fifth angel blew his trumpet,
and I saw a star fallen from heaven
to earth, and he was given the key of the
shaft of the bottomless pit; [2]he opened the
shaft of the bottomless pit, and from the
shaft rose smoke like the smoke of a great
furnace, and the sun and the air were
darkened with the smoke from the shaft.
[3]Then from the smoke came locusts on the
earth, and they were given power like the
power of scorpions of the earth; [4]they were
told not to harm the grass of the earth or
any green growth or any tree, but only
those of mankind who have not the seal of
God upon their foreheads; [5]they were allowed
to torture them for five months, but
not to kill them, and their torture was like
the torture of a scorpion, when it stings a
man. [6]And in those days men will seek
death and will not find it; they will long
to die, and death will fly from them.
7 In appearance the locusts were like
horses arrayed for battle; on their heads
were what looked like crowns of gold; their
faces were like human faces, [8]their hair like
women's hair, and their teeth like lions' teeth;
[9]they had scales like iron breastplates, and
the noise of their wings was like the noise
of many chariots with horses rushing into
battle. [10]They have tails like scorpions, and
stings, and their power of hurting men for
five months lies in their tails. [11]They have
as king over them the angel of the bottomless
pit; his name in Hebrew is Abaddon,
and in Greek he is called Apollyon.[b]
12 The first woe has passed; behold, two
woes are still to come.

The cavalry from the Eu-phrates

13 Then the sixth angel blew his trumpet,
and I heard a voice from the four horns of
the golden altar before God, [14]saying to the
sixth angel who had the trumpet, "Release
the four angels who are bound at the great
river Eu-phrates." [15]So the four angels were
released, who had been held ready for the
hour, the day, the month, and the year, to
kill a third of mankind. [16]The number of the
troops of cavalry was twice ten thousand
times ten thousand; I heard their number.
[17]And this was how I saw the horses in my
vision: the riders wore breastplates the color
of fire and of sapphire[c] and of sulphur, and
the heads of the horses were like lions' heads,
and fire and smoke and sulphur issued from
their mouths. [18]By these three plagues a third
of mankind was killed, by the fire and smoke
and sulphur issuing from their mouths. [19]For

[b] Or *Destroyer*
[c] Greek ***hyacinth***

King James

19 For their power is in their mouth, and in their tails: for their tails *were* like unto serpents, and had heads, and with them they do hurt.

20 And the rest of the men which were not killed by these plagues yet repented not of the works of their hands, that they should not worship devils, and idols of gold, and silver, and brass, and stone, and of wood: which neither can see, nor hear, nor walk:

21 Neither repented they of their murders, nor of their sorceries, nor of their fornication, nor of their thefts.

Amplified

19 For the power of the horses to do harm is in their mouths and also in their tails. Their tails are like serpents, for they have heads, and it is by means of them that they wound people.

20 And the rest of humanity, who were not killed by these plagues, even then did not repent (out) of [the worship of] the works of their [own] hands, so as to cease paying homage to the demons and idols of gold and silver and bronze and stone and wood, which can neither see nor hear nor move. [Isa. 17:8; Ps. 115:4-7; 135:15-17.]

21 And they did not repent (out) of their murders or their practice of magic (sorceries) or their sexual vice or their thefts.

CHAPTER 10

AND I saw another mighty angel come down from heaven, clothed with a cloud: and a rainbow *was* upon his head, and his face *was* as it were the sun, and his feet as pillars of fire:

2 And he had in his hand a little book open: and he set his right foot upon the sea, and *his* left *foot* on the earth,

3 And cried with a loud voice, as *when* a lion roareth: and when he had cried, seven thunders uttered their voices.

4 And when the seven thunders had uttered their voices, I was about to write: and I heard a voice from heaven saying unto me, Seal up those things which the seven thunders uttered, and write them not.

5 And the angel which I saw stand upon the sea and upon the earth lifted up his hand to heaven,

6 And sware by him that liveth for ever and ever, who created heaven, and the things that therein are, and the earth, and the things that therein are, and the sea, and the things which are therein, that there should be time no longer:

7 But in the days of the voice of the seventh angel, when he shall begin to sound, the mystery of God should be finished, as he hath declared to his servants the prophets.

8 And the voice which I heard from heaven spake unto me again, and said, Go *and* take the little book which is open in the hand of the angel which standeth upon the sea and upon the earth.

9 And I went unto the angel, and said unto him, Give me the little book. And he said unto me, Take *it*, and eat it up; and it shall make thy belly bitter, but it shall be in thy mouth sweet as honey.

10 And I took the little book out of the angel's hand, and ate it up; and it was in my mouth sweet as honey: and as soon as I had eaten it, my belly was bitter.

11 And he said unto me, Thou must prophesy again before many peoples, and nations, and tongues, and kings.

CHAPTER 10

THEN I saw another mighty angel coming down from heaven, robed in a cloud, with a [halo like a] rainbow over his head; his face was like the sun, and his feet [legs] were like columns of fire.

2 He had a little book (scroll) open in his hand. He set his right foot on the sea and his left foot on the land,

3 And he shouted with a loud voice like the roaring of a lion; and when he had shouted, the seven thunders gave voice *and* uttered their message in distinct words.

4 And when the seven thunders had spoken (sounded), I was going to write [it down], but I heard a voice from heaven saying, Seal up what the seven thunders have said! Do not write it down!

5 Then the [mighty] angel whom I had seen stationed on sea and land raised his right hand to heaven (the [b]sky), [Deut. 32:40; Dan. 12:6, 7.]

6 And swore in the name of (by) Him Who lives forever and ever, Who created the heavens ([b]sky) and all they contain, and the earth and all that it contains, and the sea and all that it contains. [He swore] that no more time should intervene *and* there should be no more waiting *or* delay,

7 But that when the days come that the trumpet call of the seventh angel is about to be sounded, then God's mystery—His secret design, His hidden purpose—as He had announced the glad tidings to His servants the prophets, should be fulfilled (accomplished, completed). [Dan. 12:6, 7.]

8 Then the voice that I heard from heaven spoke again to me, saying, Go and take the little book (scroll) which is open on the hand of the angel who is standing on the sea and on the land.

9 So I went up to the angel and asked him to give me the little book. And he said to me, Take it and eat it. It will embitter your stomach, though in your mouth it will be sweet as honey. [Ezek. 2:8, 9; 3:1-3.]

10 So I took the little book from the angel's hand and ate *and* swallowed it; it was sweet as honey in my mouth, but once I had swallowed it my stomach was embittered.

11 Then they said to me, You are to make a fresh prophecy concerning many peoples *and* races and nations and languages and kings. [Jer. 1:10.]

---

b) Abbott-Smith.

Living New Testament

19 Their power of death was not only in their mouths, but in their tails as well, for their tails were similar to serpents' heads that struck and bit with fatal wounds.

20 But the men left alive after these plagues *still refused to worship God!* They would not renounce their demon-worship, nor their idols made of gold and silver, brass, stone, and wood—which neither see nor hear nor walk!

21 Neither did they change their mind and attitude about all their murders and witchcraft, their immorality and theft.

Revised Standard

the power of the horses is in their mouths and in their tails; their tails are like serpents, with heads, and by means of them they wound.

20 The rest of mankind, who were not killed by these plagues, did not repent of the works of their hands nor give up worshiping demons and idols of gold and silver and bronze and stone and wood, which cannot either see or hear or walk; 21nor did they repent of their murders or their sorceries or their immorality or their thefts.

CHAPTER 10

Then I saw another mighty angel coming down from heaven, surrounded by a cloud, with a rainbow over his head; his face shone like the sun and his feet flashed with fire.

2 And he held open in his hand a small scroll. He set his right foot on the sea and his left foot on the earth,

3 And gave a great shout—it was like the roar of a lion—and the seven thunders crashed their reply.

4 I was about to write what the thunders said when a voice from heaven called to me, "Don't do it. Their words are not to be revealed."

5 Then the mighty angel standing on the sea and land lifted his right hand to heaven,

6 And swore by Him who lives forever and ever, who created heaven and everything in it and the earth and all that it contains and the sea and its inhabitants, that there should be no more delay,

7 But that when the seventh angel blows his trumpet, then God's veiled plan—mysterious through the ages ever since it was announced by His servants the prophets—will be fulfilled.

8 Then the voice from heaven spoke to me again, "Go and get the unrolled scroll from the mighty angel standing there upon the sea and land."

9 So I approached him and asked him to give me the scroll. "Yes, take it and eat it," he said. "At first it will taste like honey, but when you swallow it, it will make your stomach sour!"

10 So I took it from his hand, and ate it! and just as he had said, it was sweet in my mouth but it gave me a stomach ache when I swallowed it.

11 Then he told me, "You must prophesy further about many peoples, nations, tribes and kings."

John eats the scroll

10 Then I saw another mighty angel coming down from heaven, wrapped in a cloud, with a rainbow over his head, and his face was like the sun, and his legs like pillars of fire. 2He had a little scroll open in his hand. And he set his right foot on the sea, and his left foot on the land, 3and called out with a loud voice, like a lion roaring; when he called out, the seven thunders sounded. 4And when the seven thunders had sounded, I was about to write, but I heard a voice from heaven saying, "Seal up what the seven thunders have said, and do not write it down." 5And the angel whom I saw standing on sea and land lifted up his right hand to heaven 6and swore by him who lives for ever and ever, who created heaven and what is in it, the earth and what is in it, and the sea and what is in it, that there should be no more delay, 7but that in the days of the trumpet call to be sounded by the seventh angel, the mystery of God, as he announced to his servants the prophets, should be fulfilled.

8 Then the voice which I had heard from heaven spoke to me again, saying, "Go, take the scroll which is open in the hand of the angel who is standing on the sea and on the land." 9So I went to the angel and told him to give me the little scroll; and he said to me, "Take it and eat; it will be bitter to your stomach, but sweet as honey in your mouth." 10And I took the little scroll from the hand of the angel and ate it; it was sweet as honey in my mouth, but when I had eaten it my stomach was made bitter. 11And I was told, "You must again prophesy about many peoples and nations and tongues and kings."

King James

CHAPTER 11

AND there was given me a reed like unto a rod: and the angel stood, saying, Rise, and measure the temple of God, and the altar, and them that worship therein.

2 But the court which is without the temple leave out, and measure it not; for it is given unto the Gentiles: and the holy city shall they tread under foot forty *and* two months.

3 And I will give *power* unto my two witnesses, and they shall prophesy a thousand two hundred *and* threescore days, clothed in sackcloth.

4 These are the two olive trees, and the two candlesticks standing before the God of the earth.

5 And if any man will hurt them, fire proceedeth out of their mouth, and devoureth their enemies: and if any man will hurt them, he must in this manner be killed.

6 These have power to shut heaven, that it rain not in the days of their prophecy: and have power over waters to turn them to blood, and to smite the earth with all plagues, as often as they will.

7 And when they shall have finished their testimony, the beast that ascendeth out of the bottomless pit shall make war against them, and shall overcome them, and kill them.

8 And their dead bodies *shall lie* in the street of the great city, which spiritually is called Sodom and Egypt, where also our Lord was crucified.

9 And they of the people and kindreds and tongues and nations shall see their dead bodies three days and an half, and shall not suffer their dead bodies to be put in graves.

10 And they that dwell upon the earth shall rejoice over them, and make merry, and shall send gifts one to another; because these two prophets tormented them that dwelt on the earth.

11 And after three days and an half the Spirit of life from God entered into them, and they stood upon their feet; and great fear fell upon them which saw them.

12 And they heard a great voice from heaven saying unto them, Come up hither. And they ascended up to heaven in a cloud; and their enemies beheld them.

13 And the same hour was there a great earthquake, and the tenth part of the city fell, and in the earthquake were slain of men seven thousand: and the remnant were affrighted, and gave glory to the God of heaven.

14 The second woe is past; *and*, behold, the third woe cometh quickly.

15 And the seventh angel sounded; and there were great voices in heaven, saying, The kingdoms of this world are become *the kingdoms* of our Lord, and of his Christ; and he shall reign for ever and ever.

Amplified

CHAPTER 11

A REED [as a measuring rod] was then given to me, [shaped] like a staff, and I was told: Rise up and measure the sanctuary of God and the altar [of incense], and [number] those who worship there; [Ezek. 40:3.]

2 But leave out of your measuring the court outside the sanctuary of God; omit that, for it is given over to the Gentiles (the nations), and they will trample the holy city under foot for forty-two months [three and one-half years]. [Zech. 12:3; Isa. 63:18.]

3 And I will grant the power of prophecy to My two witnesses for twelve hundred and sixty days [forty-two months; three and one-half years], dressed in sackcloth.

4 These [witnesses] are the two olive trees and the two lampstands which stand before the Lord of the earth. [Zech. 4:3, 11-14.]

5 And if any one attempts to injure them, fire pours from their mouth and consumes their enemies; if any one should attempt to harm them, thus he is doomed to be slain. [II Kings 1:10; Jer. 5:14.]

6 These [two witnesses] have power to shut up the sky, so that no rain may fall during the days of their prophesying [their [c]prediction of events relating to Christ's kingdom and its speedy triumph] and they also have power to turn the waters into blood, and to smite *and* scourge the earth with all manner of plagues, as often as they choose. [I Kings 17:1; Exod. 7:17, 19.]

7 But when they have finished their testimony *and* their evidence is all in, the beast (monster) that comes up out of the abyss (bottomless pit) will wage war on them and conquer them and kill them. [Dan. 7:3, 7, 21.]

8 And their dead bodies [will lie exposed] in the open street ([d]a public square) of the great city which is in a spiritual sense called by the mystical *and* allegorical names of Sodom and Egypt, where also their Lord was crucified. [Isa. 1:9.]

9 For three and a half days men from the races and tribes and languages and nations will gaze at their dead bodies and will not allow them to be put in a tomb.

10 And those who dwell on the earth will gloat *and* exult over them *and* rejoice exceedingly, taking their ease and sending presents (in congratulation) to one another, because these two prophets had been such a vexation *and* trouble *and* torment to all the dwellers on the earth.

11 But after three and a half days, by God's gift the breath of life again entered into them, and they rose up on their feet and great dread and terror fell on those who watched them. [Ezek. 37:5, 10.]

12 Then [the two witnesses] heard a strong voice from heaven calling to them, Come up here! And before the very eyes of their enemies they ascended into heaven in a cloud. [II Kings 2:11.]

13 And at that [very] hour there was a tremendous earthquake and one tenth of the city was destroyed (fell); seven thousand people perished in the earthquake, and those who remained were filled with dread *and* terror *and* were awe-struck, and they glorified the God of heaven.

14 The second woe (calamity) has passed; now the third woe is speedily to come.

15 The seventh angel then blew his trumpet and there were mighty voices in heaven, shouting, The dominion (kingdom, sovereignty, rule) of the world has now come into the possession and become the kingdom of our Lord and of His Christ, the Messiah, and He shall reign forever and ever—for the eternities of the eternities! [Ps. 22:28; Dan. 7:13, 14, 27.]

---

c) Thayer.
d) Souter.

Living New Testament

CHAPTER 11

Now I was given a measuring stick and told to go and measure the temple of God, including the inner court where the altar stands, and to count the number of worshipers.[1]

2 "But do not measure the outer court," I was told, "for it has been turned over to the nations. They will trample over the Holy City for forty-two months.[2]

3 And I will give power to My two witnesses to prophesy 1260 days[2] clothed in sackcloth."

4 These two prophets are the two olive trees,[3] and two candlesticks standing before the God of all the earth.

5 Anyone trying to harm them will be killed by bursts of fire shooting from their mouths.

6 They have power to shut the skies so that no rain will fall during the three and a half years they prophesy, and to turn rivers and oceans to blood, and to send every kind of plague upon the earth as often as they wish.

7 When they complete the three and a half years of their solemn testimony, the tyrant who comes out of the bottomless pit[4] will declare war against them and conquer and kill them;

8, 9 And for three and a half days their bodies will be exposed in the streets of Jerusalem (the city fittingly described as "Sodom" or "Egypt")—the very place where their Lord was crucified. No one will be allowed to bury them, and people from many nations will crowd around to gaze at them.

10 And there will be a worldwide holiday—people everywhere will rejoice and give presents to each other and throw parties to celebrate the death of the two prophets who had tormented them so much!

11 But after three and a half days, the spirit of life from God will enter them and they will stand up! And great fear will fall on everyone.

12 Then a loud voice will shout from heaven, "Come up!" And they will rise to heaven in a cloud as their enemies watch.

13 The same hour there will be a terrible earthquake that levels a tenth of the city leaving 7000 dead. Then everyone left will, in their terror, give glory to the God of heaven.

14 The second woe is past, but the third quickly follows:

15 For just then the seventh angel blew his trumpet, and there were loud voices shouting down from heaven, "The kingdom of this world now belongs to our Lord, and to His Christ; and He shall reign forever and ever."[5]

[1] Literally, "Rise and measure the temple of God, and the altar, and them that worship therein."
[2] Three and one-half years, as in Daniel 12:7.
[3] Zechariah 4:3, 4, 11.
[4] Revelation 9:11.
[5] Or, "The Lord and His Anointed shall now rule the world from this day to eternity."

Revised Standard

The two witnesses

11 Then I was given a measuring rod like a staff, and I was told: "Rise and measure the temple of God and the altar and those who worship there, 2but do not measure the court outside the temple; leave that out, for it is given over to the nations, and they will trample over the holy city for forty-two months. 3And I will grant my two witnesses power to prophesy for one thousand two hundred and sixty days, clothed in sackcloth."

4 These are the two olive trees and the two lampstands which stand before the Lord of the earth. 5And if any one would harm them, fire pours from their mouth and consumes their foes; if any one would harm them, thus he is doomed to be killed. 6They have power to shut the sky, that no rain may fall during the days of their prophesying, and they have power over the waters to turn them into blood, and to smite the earth with every plague, as often as they desire. 7And when they have finished their testimony, the beast that ascends from the bottomless pit will make war upon them and conquer them and kill them, 8and their dead bodies will lie in the street of the great city which is allegorically[d] called Sodom and Egypt, where their Lord was crucified. 9For three days and a half men from the peoples and tribes and tongues and nations gaze at their dead bodies and refuse to let them be placed in a tomb, 10and those who dwell on the earth will rejoice over them and make merry and exchange presents, because these two prophets had been a torment to those who dwell on the earth. 11But after the three and a half days a breath of life from God entered them, and they stood up on their feet, and great fear fell on those who saw them. 12Then they heard a loud voice from heaven saying to them, "Come up hither!" And in the sight of their foes they went up to heaven in a cloud. 13And at that hour there was a great earthquake, and a tenth of the city fell; seven thousand people were killed in the earthquake, and the rest were terrified and gave glory to the God of heaven.

14 The second woe has passed; behold, the third woe is soon to come.

Seventh trumpet: the reign of Christ

15 Then the seventh angel blew his trumpet, and there were loud voices in heaven, saying, "The kingdom of the world has become the kingdom of our Lord and of his Christ, and he shall reign for ever and

[d] Greek *spiritually*

King James

16 And the four and twenty elders, which sat before God on their seats, fell upon their faces, and worshipped God,

17 Saying, We give thee thanks, O Lord God Almighty, which art, and wast, and art to come; because thou hast taken to thee thy great power, and hast reigned.

18 And the nations were angry, and thy wrath is come, and the time of the dead, that they should be judged, and that thou shouldest give reward unto thy servants the prophets, and to the saints, and them that fear thy name, small and great; and shouldest destroy them which destroy the earth.

19 And the temple of God was opened in heaven, and there was seen in his temple the ark of his testament: and there were lightnings, and voices, and thunderings, and an earthquake, and great hail.

Amplified

16 Then the twenty-four elders [of [e]the heavenly Sanhedrin] who sit on their thrones before God prostrated themselves before Him and worshiped,

17 Exclaiming, To You we give thanks, Lord God Omnipotent, Who are and [ever] were, for assuming the high sovereignty *and* the great power that are Yours and beginning to reign.

18 And the heathen (the nations) raged, but Your wrath (retribution, indignation) came, the time when the dead will be judged and to reward Your servants, the prophets and saints, and those who revere (fear) Your name, both low and high *and* small and great; and [the time] for destroying the corrupters of the earth. [Ps. 2:1.]

19 Then the sanctuary of God in heaven was thrown open, and the ark of His covenant was seen standing inside in His sanctuary; and there were lightning flashes, loud rumblings (blasts, mutterings), peals of thunder, an earthquake, and a terrific hailstorm. [I Kings 8:1-6.]

CHAPTER 12

AND there appeared a great wonder in heaven; a woman clothed with the sun, and the moon under her feet, and upon her head a crown of twelve stars:

2 And she being with child cried, travailing in birth, and pained to be delivered.

3 And there appeared another wonder in heaven; and behold a great red dragon, having seven heads and ten horns, and seven crowns upon his heads.

4 And his tail drew the third part of the stars of heaven, and did cast them to the earth: and the dragon stood before the woman which was ready to be delivered, for to devour her child as soon as it was born.

5 And she brought forth a man child, who was to rule all nations with a rod of iron: and her child was caught up unto God, and *to* his throne.

6 And the woman fled into the wilderness, where she hath a place prepared of God, that they should feed her there a thousand two hundred *and* threescore days.

7 And there was war in heaven: Michael and his angels fought against the dragon; and the dragon fought and his angels,

8 And prevailed not; neither was their place found any more in heaven.

9 And the great dragon was cast out, that old serpent, called the Devil, and Satan, which deceiveth the whole world: he was cast out into the earth, and his angels were cast out with him.

10 And I heard a loud voice saying in heaven, Now is come salvation, and strength, the kingdom of our God, and the power of his Christ: for the accuser of our brethren is cast down, which accused them before our God day and night.

CHAPTER 12

AND a great sign [wonder warning of future events of ominous significance] appeared in heaven, a woman clothed with the sun, with the moon under her feet, and with a crownlike garland (tiara) of twelve stars on her head.

2 She was pregnant and she cried out in her birth pangs, in the anguish of her delivery.

3 Then another ominous sign (wonder) was seen in heaven. Behold, a huge, fiery-red dragon, with seven heads and ten horns, and seven kingly crowns (diadems) upon his heads. [Dan. 7:7.]

4 His tail swept [across the sky] *and* dragged down a third of the stars, and flung them to the earth. And the dragon stationed himself in front of the woman who was about to be delivered, so that he might devour her child as soon as she brought it forth. [Dan. 8:10.]

5 And she brought forth a male Child, One Who is destined to shepherd (rule) all the nations with an iron staff (scepter), and her Child was caught up to God and to His throne. [Ps. 2:8, 9; 110:1, 2.]

6 And the woman [herself] fled into the desert (wilderness), where she has a retreat prepared [for her] by God, in which she is to be fed *and* kept safe for one thousand two hundred and sixty days [forty-two months; three and one-half years].

7 Then war broke out in heaven, Michael and his angels going forth to battle with the dragon; and the dragon and his angels fought,

8 But they were defeated and there was no room found for them in heaven any longer.

9 And the huge dragon was cast down *and* out, that ages-old serpent, who is called the Devil and Satan, he who is the seducer (deceiver) of all humanity the world over; he was forced out *and* down to the earth, and his angels were flung out along with him. [Gen. 3:1, 14, 15; Zech. 3:1.]

10 Then I heard a strong voice in heaven, saying, Now it has come, the salvation and the power and the kingdom (the dominion, the reign) of our God and the power (the sovereignty, the authority) of His Christ, the Messiah; for the accuser of our brethren, he who keeps bringing before our God charges against them day and night, has been cast out! [Job 1:9-11.]

---

e) Souter, and others.

Living New Testament

16 And the twenty-four Elders sitting on their thrones before God threw themselves down in worship, saying,

17 "We give thanks, Lord God Almighty, who is and was, for now You have assumed Your great power and have begun to reign.

18 The nations were angry with You, but now it is Your turn to be angry with them. It is time to judge the dead, and reward Your servants—prophets and people alike, all who fear Your Name, both great and small—and to destroy those who have caused destruction upon the earth."

19 Then, in heaven, the temple of God was opened and the ark of His covenant could be seen inside. Lightning flashed and thunder crashed and roared, and there was a great hailstorm and the world was shaken by a mighty earthquake.

Revised Standard

ever." [16]And the twenty-four elders who sit on their thrones before God fell on their faces and worshiped God, [17]saying,

"We give thanks to thee, Lord God Almighty, who art and who wast,
that thou hast taken thy great power and begun to reign.
[18]The nations raged, but thy wrath came,
and the time for the dead to be judged,
for rewarding thy servants, the prophets and saints,
and those who fear thy name, both small and great,
and for destroying the destroyers of the earth."

19 Then God's temple in heaven was opened, and the ark of his covenant was seen within his temple; and there were flashes of lightning, loud noises, peals of thunder, an earthquake, and heavy hail.

CHAPTER 12

Then a great pageant appeared in heaven, portraying things to come. I saw a woman clothed with the sun, with the moon beneath her feet, and a crown of twelve stars on her head.

2 She was pregnant and screamed in the pain of her labor, awaiting her delivery.

3 Suddenly a red Dragon appeared, with seven heads and ten horns, and seven crowns on his heads.

4 His tail drew along behind him a third of the stars, which he plunged to the earth. He stood before the woman as she was about to give birth to her child, ready to eat the baby as soon as it was born.

5 She gave birth to a boy who was to rule all nations with a heavy hand, and He was caught up to God and to His throne.

6 The woman fled into the wilderness, where God had prepared a place for her, to take care of her for 1,260 days.

7 Then there was war in heaven; Michael and the angels under his command fought the Dragon and his hosts of fallen angels.

8 And the Dragon lost the battle and was forced from heaven.

9 This great Dragon—the ancient serpent called the Devil, or Satan, the one deceiving the whole world—was thrown down onto the earth with all his army.

10 Then I heard a loud voice shouting across the heavens, "It has happened at last! God's salvation and the power and the rule, and the authority of His Christ are finally here; for the Accuser of our brothers has been thrown down from heaven onto earth—he accused them day and night before our God.

The dragon; the mother with child

12 And a great portent appeared in heaven, a woman clothed with the sun, with the moon under her feet, and on her head a crown of twelve stars; [2]she was with child and she cried out in her pangs of birth, in anguish for delivery. [3]And another portent appeared in heaven; behold, a great red dragon, with seven heads and ten horns, and seven diadems upon his heads. [4]His tail swept down a third of the stars of heaven, and cast them to the earth. And the dragon stood before the woman who was about to bear a child, that he might devour her child when she brought it forth; [5]she brought forth a male child, one who is to rule all the nations with a rod of iron, but her child was caught up to God and to his throne, [6]and the woman fled into the wilderness, where she has a place prepared by God, in which to be nourished for one thousand two hundred and sixty days.

The angel Michael

7 Now war arose in heaven, Michael and his angels fighting against the dragon; and the dragon and his angels fought, [8]but they were defeated and there was no longer any place for them in heaven. [9]And the great dragon was thrown down, that ancient serpent, who is called the Devil and Satan, the deceiver of the whole world—he was thrown down to the earth, and his angels were thrown down with him. [10]And I heard a loud voice in heaven, saying, "Now the salvation and the power and the kingdom of our God and the authority of his Christ have come, for the accuser of our brethren has been thrown down, who accuses them day and

King James

11 And they overcame him by the blood of the Lamb, and by the word of their testimony; and they loved not their lives unto the death.

12 Therefore rejoice, *ye* heavens, and ye that dwell in them. Woe to the inhabiters of the earth and of the sea! for the devil is come down unto you, having great wrath, because he knoweth that he hath but a short time.

13 And when the dragon saw that he was cast unto the earth, he persecuted the woman which brought forth the man *child*.

14 And to the woman were given two wings of a great eagle, that she might fly into the wilderness, into her place, where she is nourished for a time, and times, and half a time, from the face of the serpent.

15 And the serpent cast out of his mouth water as a flood after the woman, that he might cause her to be carried away of the flood.

16 And the earth helped the woman, and the earth opened her mouth, and swallowed up the flood which the dragon cast out of his mouth.

17 And the dragon was wroth with the woman, and went to make war with the remnant of her seed, which keep the commandments of God, and have the testimony of Jesus Christ.

Amplified

11 And they have overcome (conquered) him by means of the blood of the Lamb and by the utterance of their testimony, for they did not love *and* cling to life even when faced with death—holding their lives cheap till they had to die [for their witnessing].

12 Therefore be glad (exult), O heavens and you that dwell in them! But woe to you, O earth and sea, for the devil has come down to you in fierce anger (fury), because he knows that he has [only] a short time [left]! [Isa. 44:23; 49:13.]

13 And when the dragon saw that he was cast down to the earth, he went in pursuit of the woman who had given birth to the male Child.

14 But the woman was supplied with the two wings of a giant eagle, so that she might fly from the presence of the serpent into the desert (wilderness, to the retreat) where she is to be kept safe *and* fed for a time, and times, and half a time [three and one-half years, or twelve hundred sixty days]. [Dan. 7:25; 12:7.]

15 Then out of his mouth the serpent spouted forth water like a flood after the woman, that she might be carried off with the torrent.

16 But the earth came to the rescue of the woman, and the ground opened its mouth and swallowed up the stream of water which the dragon had spouted from his mouth.

17 So then the dragon was furious (enraged) at the woman, and he went away to wage war on the remainder of her descendants, [on those] who obey God's commandments and who have the testimony of Jesus *Christ*—and adhere to it and [f]bear witness to Him.

CHAPTER 13

AND I stood upon the sand of the sea, and saw a beast rise up out of the sea, having seven heads and ten horns, and upon his horns ten crowns, and upon his heads the name of blasphemy.

2 And the beast which I saw was like unto a leopard, and his feet were as *the feet* of a bear, and his mouth as the mouth of a lion: and the dragon gave him his power, and his seat, and great authority.

3 And I saw one of his heads as it were wounded to death; and his deadly wound was healed: and all the world wondered after the beast.

4 And they worshipped the dragon which gave power unto the beast: and they worshipped the beast, saying, Who *is* like unto the beast? who is able to make war with him?

5 And there was given unto him a mouth speaking great things and blasphemies; and power was given unto him to continue forty *and* two months.

6 And he opened his mouth in blasphemy against God, to blaspheme his name, and his tabernacle, and them that dwell in heaven.

7 And it was given unto him to make war with the saints, and to overcome them: and power was given him over all kindreds, and tongues, and nations.

CHAPTER 13

[AS] [g]I stood on the sandy beach, I saw a beast coming up out of the sea with ten horns and seven heads. On his horns he had ten royal crowns (diadems) and blasphemous titles (names) on his heads.

2 And the beast that I saw resembled a leopard, his feet were like those of a bear, and his mouth was like that of a lion. And to him the dragon gave his [own] might *and* power, and his [own] throne and great dominion.

3 And one of his heads seemed to have a deadly wound. But his death stroke was healed, and the whole earth went after the beast in amazement *and* admiration.

4 They fell down *and* did homage to the dragon, because he had bestowed on the beast all his dominion *and* authority; they also praised *and* worshipped the beast, exclaiming, Who is a match for the beast, and who can make war against him?

5 And the beast was given the power of speech, uttering boastful and blasphemous words, and he was given freedom to exert his authority *and* to exercise his will during forty-two months [three and a half years]. [Dan. 7:8.]

6 And he opened his mouth to speak slanders against God, blaspheming His name and His abode, [even vilifying] those who live in heaven.

7 He was further permitted to wage war on God's holy people (the saints) and to overcome them. And power was given him to extend his authority over every tribe and people and tongue and nation, [Dan. 7:21, 25.]

---

f) Williams.
g) Many ancient authorities read "he."

Living New Testament

11 They defeated him by the blood of the Lamb, and by their testimony; for they did not love their lives but laid them down for Him.

12 Rejoice, O heavens! you citizens of heaven, rejoice! be glad! But woe to you people of the world, for the Devil has come down to you in great anger, knowing that he has little time."

13 And when the Dragon found himself cast down to earth, he persecuted the woman who had given birth to the child.

14 But she was given two wings like those of a great eagle, to fly into the wilderness to the place prepared for her, where she was cared for and protected from the Serpent, the Dragon, for three and a half years.[1]

15 And from the Serpent's mouth a vast flood of water gushed out and swept toward the woman in an effort to get rid of her;

16 But the earth helped her by opening its mouth and swallowing the flood!

17 Then the furious Dragon set out to attack the rest of her children—all who were keeping God's commandments and confessing that they belong to Jesus. He stood waiting on an ocean beach.

Revised Standard

night before our God. 11And they have conquered him by the blood of the Lamb and
by the word of their testimony, for they
loved not their lives even unto death. 12Re-
joice then, O heaven and you that dwell
therein! But woe to you, O earth and sea,
for the devil has come down to you in
great wrath, because he knows that his time
is short!"

13 And when the dragon saw that he had
been thrown down to the earth, he pursued
the woman who had borne the male child.
14But the woman was given the two wings
of the great eagle that she might fly from
the serpent into the wilderness, to the place
where she is to be nourished for a time,
and times, and half a time. 15The serpent
poured water like a river out of his mouth
after the woman, to sweep her away with
the flood. 16But the earth came to the help
of the woman, and the earth opened its
mouth and swallowed the river which the
dragon had poured from his mouth. 17Then
the dragon was angry with the woman, and
went off to make war on the rest of her
offspring, on those who keep the commandments of God and bear testimony to Jesus.
And he stood[e] on the sand of the sea.

CHAPTER 13

And now, in my vision, I saw a strange Creature rising up out of the sea. It had seven heads and ten horns, and ten crowns upon its horns. And written on each head were blasphemous names, each one defying and insulting God.

2 This Creature looked like a leopard but had bear's feet and a lion's mouth! And the Dragon gave him his own power and throne and great authority.

3 I saw that one of his heads seemed wounded beyond recovery—but the fatal wound was healed! All the world marveled at this miracle and followed the Creature in awe.

4 They worshiped the Dragon for giving him such power, and they worshiped the strange Creature. "Where is there anyone as great as he?" they exclaimed. "Who is able to fight against him?"

5 Then the Dragon encouraged the Creature to speak great blasphemies against the Lord; and gave him authority to control the earth for forty-two months.

6 All that time he blasphemed God's name and His temple and all those living in heaven.

7 The Dragon gave him power to fight against God's people[1] and to overcome them, and to rule over all nations and language groups throughout the world.

The beast from the sea

13 And I saw a beast rising out of
the sea, with ten horns and seven
heads, with ten diadems upon its horns
and a blasphemous name upon its heads.
2And the beast that I saw was like a leopard,
its feet were like a bear's, and its mouth was
like a lion's mouth. And to it the dragon
gave his power and his throne and great
authority. 3One of its heads seemed to have
a mortal wound, but its mortal wound was
healed, and the whole earth followed the
beast with wonder. 4Men worshiped the
dragon, for he had given his authority to
the beast, and they worshiped the beast,
saying, "Who is like the beast, and who
can fight against it?"

5 And the beast was given a mouth uttering haughty and blasphemous words, and it
was allowed to exercise authority for forty-
two months; 6it opened its mouth to utter
blasphemies against God, blaspheming his
name and his dwelling, that is, those who
dwell in heaven. 7Also it was allowed to
make war on the saints and to conquer
them.[f] And authority was given it over
every tribe and people and tongue and na-

[1] Literally, "a time and times and half a time."
[1] Literally, "It was permitted to fight against God's people."

[e] Other ancient authorities read *And I stood*, connecting the sentence with 13.1
[f] Other ancient authorities omit this sentence

King James

8 And all that dwell upon the earth shall worship him, whose names are not written in the book of life of the Lamb slain from the foundation of the world.
9 If any man have an ear, let him hear.
10 He that leadeth into captivity shall go into captivity: he that killeth with the sword must be killed with the sword. Here is the patience and the faith of the saints.
11 And I beheld another beast coming up out of the earth; and he had two horns like a lamb, and he spake as a dragon.
12 And he exerciseth all the power of the first beast before him, and causeth the earth and them which dwell therein to worship the first beast, whose deadly wound was healed.
13 And he doeth great wonders, so that he maketh fire come down from heaven on the earth in the sight of men,
14 And deceiveth them that dwell on the earth by *the means of* those miracles which he had power to do in the sight of the beast; saying to them that dwell on the earth, that they should make an image to the beast, which had the wound by a sword, and did live.
15 And he had power to give life unto the image of the beast, that the image of the beast should both speak, and cause that as many as would not worship the image of the beast should be killed.
16 And he causeth all, both small and great, rich and poor, free and bond, to receive a mark in their right hand, or in their foreheads:
17 And that no man might buy or sell, save he that had the mark, or the name of the beast, or the number of his name.
18 Here is wisdom. Let him that hath understanding count the number of the beast: for it is the number of man; and his number *is* Six hundred threescore *and* six.

Amplified

8 And all the inhabitants of the earth will fall down in adoration *and* pay him homage, every one whose name has not been recorded from the foundation of the world in the Book of Life of the Lamb that was slain [in sacrifice] [h]from the foundation of the world.
9 If any one is able to hear, let him listen:
10 Whoever leads into captivity will himself go into captivity; if any one slays with the sword, with the sword must he be slain. Herein is [the call for] the patience and the faith *and* fidelity of the saints (God's people). [Jer. 15:2.]
11 Then I saw another beast rising up out of the land [itself]; he had two horns like a lamb and he spoke (roared) like a dragon.
12 He exerts all the power *and* right of control of the former beast in his presence, and causes the earth and those who dwell upon it to exalt *and* deify the first beast, whose deadly wound was healed, *and* worship him.
13 He performs great signs—startling miracles—even making fire fall from the sky to the earth in men's sight.
14 And because of the signs (miracles) which he is allowed to perform in the presence of the [first] beast, he deceives those who inhabit the earth, commanding them to erect a statue (an image) in the likeness of the beast which was wounded by the (small) sword and still lived. [Deut. 13:1-5.]
15 And he was permitted [also] to impart the breath of life into the beast's image so that the statue of the beast could actually talk, and to cause to be put to death those who would not bow down *and* worship the image of the beast. [Dan. 3:5.]
16 Also he compels all [alike], both small and great, both the rich and the poor, both free and slave to be marked with an inscription ([i]stamped) on their right hands or on their foreheads.
17 So that no one will have power to buy or sell unless he bears the stamp (mark, inscription), [that is,] the name of the beast or the number of his name.
18 Here is [room for] discernment—a call for the wisdom [[i]of interpretation]; let any one who has intelligence (penetration and insight enough) calculate the number of the beast, for it is a human number—the number of a certain man; his number is six hundred and sixty-six.

CHAPTER 14

AND I looked, and, lo, a Lamb stood on the mount Sion, and with him an hundred forty *and* four thousand, having his Father's name written in their foreheads.
2 And I heard a voice from heaven, as the voice of many waters, and as the voice of a great thunder: and I heard the voice of harpers harping with their harps:
3 And they sung as it were a new song before the throne, and before the four beasts, and the elders: and no man could learn that song but the hundred *and* forty *and* four thousand, which were redeemed from the earth.

CHAPTER 14

THEN I looked and lo, the Lamb stood on Mount Zion, and with Him a hundred and forty-four thousand [men] who had His name and His Father's name inscribed on their foreheads.
2 And I heard a voice from heaven like the sound of great waters and like the rumbling of mighty thunder; the voice I heard [seemed like the music] of harpists [j]accompanying themselves on their harps.
3 And they sing a new song before the throne [of God] and before the four living creatures and before the elders [of [k]the heavenly Sanhedrin]. No one could learn [to sing] that song except the hundred and forty-four thousand who had been ransomed (purchased, redeemed) from the earth.

---

h) Alternate reading: construing these words with *slain* or with *recorded*.
i) Thayer.
j) Vincent.
k) Souter, and others.

Living New Testament

8 And all mankind—whose names were not written down before the founding of the world in the slain[2] Lamb's Book of Life—worshiped the evil Creature.

9 Anyone who can hear, listen carefully:

10 The people of God who are destined for prison will be arrested and taken away; those destined for death will be killed.[3] But do not be dismayed, for here is your opportunity for endurance and confidence.

11 Then I saw another strange animal, this one coming up out of the earth, with two little horns like those of a lamb but a fearsome voice like the Dragon's.

12 He exercised all the authority of the Creature whose death-wound had been healed, whom he required all the world to worship.

13 He did unbelievable miracles such as making fire flame down to earth from the skies while everyone was watching.

14 By doing these miracles, he was deceiving people everywhere. He could do these marvelous things whenever the first Creature was there to watch him. And he ordered the people of the world to make a great statue of the first Creature, who was fatally wounded and then came back to life.

15 He was permitted to give breath to this statue and even make it speak! Then the statue ordered that anyone refusing to worship it must die!

16 He required everyone—great and small, rich and poor, slave and free—to be tattooed with a certain mark on the right hand or on the forehead.

17 And no one could get a job or even buy in any store without the permit of that mark, which was either the name of the Creature or the code number of his name.

18 Here is a puzzle that calls for careful thought to solve it. Let those who are able, interpret this code: the numerical values of the letters in his name add to 666![4]

Revised Standard

tion, 8and all who dwell on earth will worship it, every one whose name has not
been written before the foundation of the
world in the book of life of the Lamb
that was slain. 9If any one has an ear, let
him hear:

10If any one is to be taken captive, to captivity he goes;
if any one slays with the sword,
with the sword must he be slain.
Here is a call for the endurance and faith
of the saints.

The beast from the earth

11 Then I saw another beast which rose
out of the earth; it had two horns like a
lamb and it spoke like a dragon. 12It exercises all the authority of the first beast in
its presence, and makes the earth and its
inhabitants worship the first beast, whose
mortal wound was healed. 13It works great
signs, even making fire come down from
heaven to earth in the sight of men; 14and
by the signs which it is allowed to work in
the presence of the beast, it deceives those
who dwell on earth, bidding them make an
image for the beast which was wounded by
the sword and yet lived; 15and it was allowed
to give breath to the image of the beast so
that the image of the beast should even speak,
and to cause those who would not worship
the image of the beast to be slain. 16Also it
causes all, both small and great, both rich
and poor, both free and slave, to be marked
on the right hand or the forehead, 17so that
no one can buy or sell unless he has the
mark, that is, the name of the beast or the
number of its name. 18This calls for wisdom: let him who has understanding reckon
the number of the beast, for it is a human
number, its number is six hundred and
sixty-six.[g]

CHAPTER 14

Then I saw a Lamb standing on Mount Zion in Jerusalem, and with Him were 144,000 who had His Name and His Father's Name written on their foreheads.

2 And I heard a sound from heaven like the roaring of a great waterfall or the rolling of mighty thunder. It was the singing of a choir accompanied by harps.

3 This tremendous choir—144,000 strong—sang a wonderful new song in front of the throne of God, and before the four Living Beings and the twenty-four Elders; and no one could sing this song except these 144,000 who had been redeemed from the earth.

The Lamb on Mount Zion

14 Then I looked, and lo, on Mount
Zion stood the Lamb, and with him a
hundred and forty-four thousand who had his
name and his Father's name written on their
foreheads. 2And I heard a voice from heaven
like the sound of many waters and like the
sound of loud thunder; the voice I heard was
like the sound of harpers playing on their
harps, 3and they sing a new song before the
throne and before the four living creatures
and before the elders. No one could learn
that song except the hundred and forty-four
thousand who had been redeemed from the

---

[2] Or, "those whose names were not written in the Book of Life of the Lamb slain before the founding of the world." That is, regarded as slain in the eternal plan and knowledge of God.

[3] Or, "If anyone imprisons you, he will be imprisoned! If anyone kills you, he will be killed!"

[4] Some manuscripts read "616."

[g] Other ancient authorities read *six hundred and sixteen*

King James

4 These are they which were not defiled with women; for they are virgins. These are they which follow the Lamb whithersoever he goeth. These were redeemed from among men, *being* the first fruits unto God and to the Lamb.

5 And in their mouth was found no guile: for they are without fault before the throne of God.

6 And I saw another angel fly in the midst of heaven, having the everlasting gospel to preach unto them that dwell on the earth, and to every nation, and kindred, and tongue, and people,

7 Saying with a loud voice, Fear God, and give glory to him; for the hour of his judgment is come: and worship him that made heaven, and earth, and the sea, and the fountains of waters.

8 And there followed another angel, saying, Babylon is fallen, is fallen, that great city, because she made all nations drink of the wine of the wrath of her fornication.

9 And the third angel followed them, saying with a loud voice, If any man worship the beast and his image, and receive *his* mark in his forehead, or in his hand,

10 The same shall drink of the wine of the wrath of God, which is poured out without mixture into the cup of his indignation; and he shall be tormented with fire and brimstone in the presence of the holy angels, and in the presence of the Lamb:

11 And the smoke of their torment ascendeth up for ever and ever: and they have no rest day nor night, who worship the beast and his image, and whosoever receiveth the mark of his name.

12 Here is the patience of the saints: here *are* they that keep the commandments of God, and the faith of Jesus.

13 And I heard a voice from heaven saying unto me, Write, Blessed *are* the dead which die in the Lord from henceforth: Yea, saith the Spirit, that they may rest from their labours; and their works do follow them.

14 And I looked, and behold a white cloud, and upon the cloud *one* sat like unto the Son of man, having on his head a golden crown, and in his hand a sharp sickle.

15 And another angel came out of the temple, crying with a loud voice to him that sat on the cloud, Thrust in thy sickle, and reap: for the time is come for thee to reap; for the harvest of the earth is ripe.

16 And he that sat on the cloud thrust in his sickle on the earth; and the earth was reaped.

17 And another angel came out of the temple which is in heaven, he also having a sharp sickle.

18 And another angel came out from the altar, which had power over fire; and cried with a loud cry to him that had the sharp sickle, saying, Thrust in thy sharp sickle, and gather the clusters of the vine of the earth; for her grapes are fully ripe.

Amplified

4 These are they who have not defiled themselves by relations with women, for they are [[l]pure as] virgins. These are they who follow the Lamb wherever He goes. These are they who have been ransomed (purchased, redeemed) from among men as the first fruits for God and the Lamb.

5 No lie was found to be upon their lips, for they are blameless—spotless, untainted, without blemish—*before the throne of God.*

6 Then I saw another angel flying in mid-air, with an eternal Gospel (good news) to tell to the inhabitants of the earth, to every race and tribe and language and people.

7 And he cried with a mighty voice, Revere God and give Him glory (honor and praise in worship), for the hour of His judgment has arrived. Fall down before Him; pay Him homage *and* adoration *and* worship Him Who created heaven and earth, the sea and the springs (fountains) of water.

8 Then another angel, a second, followed, declaring, Fallen, fallen is Babylon the great! She who made all nations drink of the [maddening] wine of her passionate unchastity [[m]idolatry]. [Isa. 21:9.]

9 Then another angel, a third, followed them, saying with a mighty voice, Whoever pays homage to the beast and his statue and permits the [beast's] stamp (mark, inscription) to be put on his forehead or on his hand,

10 He too shall [have to] drink of the wine of God's indignation *and* wrath, poured undiluted into the cup of His anger, and he shall be tormented with fire and brimstone in the presence of the holy angels and in the presence of the Lamb. [Gen. 19:24.]

11 And the smoke of their torment ascends forever and ever, and they have no respite—no pause, no intermission, no rest, no peace—day or night, these who pay homage to the beast and to his image, and whoever receives the stamp of his name upon him. [Isa. 34:10.]

12 Here [comes in a call for] the steadfastness of the saints—the patience, the endurance of the people of God—those who (habitually) keep God's commandments and [their] faith in Jesus.

13 Then I heard further, [[m]perceiving the distinct words of] a voice from heaven saying, Write this: Blessed—happy, [n]to be envied—are the dead from now on who die in the Lord! Yes, blessed—happy, [n]to be envied indeed—says the Spirit, [in] that they may rest from their labors, for their works (deeds) do follow (attend, accompany) them!

14 Again I looked, and lo, [I saw] a white cloud, and sitting on the cloud [o]*O*ne resembling a [o]*S*on of man, with a crown of gold on *H*is head, and a sharp scythe (sickle) in *H*is hand. [Dan. 7:13.]

15 And another angel came out of the temple sanctuary, calling with a mighty voice to [o]*H*im *W*ho was sitting upon the cloud, Put in *Y*our scythe and reap, for the hour has arrived to gather the harvest, for the earth's crop is fully ripened. [Joel 3:13.]

16 So [o]*H*e *W*ho was sitting upon the cloud swung *H*is scythe (sickle) on the earth and the earth's crop was harvested.

17 Then another angel came out of the temple sanctuary in heaven, and he also carried a sharp scythe (sickle).

18 And another angel came forth from the altar, [the angel] who has authority *and* power over fire, and he called with a loud cry to him who had the sharp scythe (sickle), Put forth your scythe and reap the fruitage of the vine of the earth, for its grapes are entirely ripe.

l) Williams.
m) Thayer.
n) Souter.
o) Capitals suppositional. Many question whether this refers to Christ.

Living New Testament

4 For they are spiritually undefiled, pure as virgins,[1] following the Lamb wherever He goes. They have been purchased from among the men on the earth as a consecrated offering to God and the Lamb.

5 No falsehood can be charged against them; they are blameless.

6 And I saw another angel flying through the heavens, carrying the everlasting Good News to preach to those on earth—to every nation, tribe, language and people.

7 "Fear God," he shouted, "and extol His greatness. For the time has come when He will sit as Judge. Worship Him who made the heaven and the earth, the sea and all its sources."

8 Then another angel followed him through the skies, saying, "Babylon is fallen, is fallen—that great city—because she seduced the nations of the world and made them share the wine of her intense impurity and sin."

9 Then a third angel followed them shouting, "Anyone worshiping the Creature from the sea[2] and his statue and accepting his mark on the forehead or the hand,

10 Must drink the wine of the anger of God; it is poured out undiluted into God's cup of wrath. And they will be tormented with fire and burning sulphur in the presence of the holy angels and the Lamb.

11 The smoke of their torture rises forever and ever, and they will have no relief day or night, for they have worshiped the Creature and his statue, and have been tattooed with the code of his name.

12 Let this encourage God's people to endure patiently every trial and persecution, for they are His saints who remain firm to the end in obedience to His commands and trust in Jesus."

13 And I heard a voice in the heavens above me saying, "Write this down: At last the time has come for His martyrs[3] to enter into their full reward. Yes, says the Spirit, they are blest indeed, for now they shall rest from all their toils and trials; for their good deeds follow them to heaven!"

14 Then the scene changed and I saw a white cloud, and Someone sitting on it who looked like Jesus, who was called "The Son of Man,"[4] with a crown of solid gold upon His head and a sharp sickle in His hand.

15 Then an angel came from the temple and called out to Him, "Begin to use the sickle, for the time has come for You to reap; the harvest is ripe on the earth."

16 So the One sitting on the cloud swung His sickle over the earth, and the harvest was gathered in.

17 After that another angel came from the temple in heaven, and he also had a sharp sickle.

18 Just then the angel who has power to destroy the world with fire,[5] shouted to the angel with the sickle, "Use your sickle now to cut off the clusters of grapes from the vines of the earth, for they are fully ripe for judgment."

---

[1] Literally, "They have not defiled themselves with women, for they are virgins."

[2] Implied.

[3] Literally, "those who die in the faith of Jesus." Verse 12 implies death from persecution for Christ's sake.

[4] Literally, "one like a Son of Man."

[5] Literally, "who has power over fire."

Revised Standard

earth. 4It is these who have not defiled themselves with women, for they are chaste;[h] it is
these who follow the Lamb wherever he
goes; these have been redeemed from mankind as first fruits for God and the Lamb,
5and in their mouth no lie was found, for
they are spotless.

The angelic messages

6 Then I saw another angel flying in midheaven, with an eternal gospel to proclaim
to those who dwell on earth, to every nation and tribe and tongue and people; 7and
he said with a loud voice, "Fear God and
give him glory, for the hour of his judgment
has come; and worship him who made heaven
and earth, the sea and the fountains of
water."

8 Another angel, a second, followed,
saying, "Fallen, fallen is Babylon the great,
she who made all nations drink the wine of
her impure passion."

9 And another angel, a third, followed
them, saying with a loud voice, "If any one
worships the beast and its image, and receives a mark on his forehead or on his
hand, 10he also shall drink the wine of
God's wrath, poured unmixed into the cup
of his anger, and he shall be tormented with
fire and brimstone in the presence of the
holy angels and in the presence of the
Lamb. 11And the smoke of their torment
goes up for ever and ever; and they have
no rest, day or night, these worshipers of
the beast and its image, and whoever receives the mark of its name."

12 Here is a call for the endurance of
the saints, those who keep the commandments of God and the faith of Jesus.

13 And I heard a voice from heaven
saying, "Write this: Blessed are the dead
who die in the Lord henceforth." "Blessed
indeed," says the Spirit, "that they may rest
from their labors, for their deeds follow
them!"

14 Then I looked, and lo, a white cloud,
and seated on the cloud one like a son of
man, with a golden crown on his head, and
a sharp sickle in his hand. 15And another
angel came out of the temple, calling with
a loud voice to him who sat upon the cloud,
"Put in your sickle, and reap, for the hour
to reap has come, for the harvest of the
earth is fully ripe." 16So he who sat upon
the cloud swung his sickle on the earth,
and the earth was reaped.

17 And another angel came out of the
temple in heaven, and he too had a sharp
sickle. 18Then another angel came out from
the altar, the angel who has power over
fire, and he called with a loud voice to him
who had the sharp sickle, "Put in your
sickle, and gather the clusters of the vine

---

[h] Greek *virgins*

King James

19 And the angel thrust in his sickle into the earth, and gathered the vine of the earth, and cast *it* into the great winepress of the wrath of God.

20 And the winepress was trodden without the city, and blood came out of the winepress, even unto the horse bridles, by the space of a thousand *and* six hundred furlongs.

Amplified

19 So the angel swung his scythe on the earth and stripped the grapes *and* gathered the vintage from the vines of the earth, and cast it into the huge wine press of God's indignation *and* wrath.

20 And [the grapes in] the wine press were trodden outside the city, and blood poured from the wine press, [reaching] as high as horses' bridles, for a distance of one thousand and six hundred stadia [about two hundred miles]. [Joel 3:13.]

CHAPTER 15 (King James)

AND I saw another sign in heaven, great and marvellous, seven angels having the seven last plagues; for in them is filled up the wrath of God.

2 And I saw as it were a sea of glass mingled with fire: and them that had gotten the victory over the beast, and over his image, and over his mark, *and* over the number of his name, stand on the sea of glass, having the harps of God.

3 And they sing the song of Moses the servant of God, and the song of the Lamb, saying, Great and marvellous *are* thy works, Lord God Almighty; just and true *are* thy ways, thou King of saints.

4 Who shall not fear thee, O Lord, and glorify thy name? for *thou* only *art* holy: for all nations shall come and worship before thee; for thy judgments are made manifest.

5 And after that I looked, and, behold, the temple of the tabernacle of the testimony in heaven was opened:

6 And the seven angels came out of the temple, having the seven plagues, clothed in pure and white linen, and having their breasts girded with golden girdles.

7 And one of the four beasts gave unto the seven angels seven golden vials full of the wrath of God, who liveth for ever and ever.

8 And the temple was filled with smoke from the glory of God, and from his power; and no man was able to enter into the temple, till the seven plagues of the seven angels were fulfilled.

CHAPTER 15 (Amplified)

THEN I saw another wonder (sign, token, symbol) in heaven, great and marvelous [warning of events of ominous significance]. There were seven angels bringing seven plagues (afflictions, calamities), which are the last, for with them God's wrath (indignation) is completely expressed—reaches its climax and is ended. [Lev. 26:21.]

2 Then I saw what seemed to be a glassy sea blended with fire, and those who had come off victorious from the beast, and from his statue and from the number corresponding to his name, were standing beside the glassy sea with harps of God in their hands.

3 And they sing the song of Moses, the servant of God, and the song of the Lamb, saying, Mighty and marvelous are Your works, O Lord God the Omnipotent! Righteous (just) and true are Your ways, O Sovereign of the ages—King of the [p]nations! [Exod. 15:1; Ps. 145:17.]

4 Who shall not reverence and glorify Your name, O Lord—giving You honor and praise in worship? For You only are holy. All the nations shall come and pay homage *and* adoration to You, for Your just judgments—Your righteous sentences and deeds—have been made known *and* displayed. [Jer. 10:7; Ps. 86:9, 10.]

5 After this I looked and the sanctuary of the tent of the testimony in heaven was thrown open

6 And there came out of the temple sanctuary the seven angels bringing the seven plagues (afflictions, calamities). They were arrayed in pure gleaming linen, and around their breasts they wore girdles of gold.

7 And one of the four living creatures [then] gave the seven angels seven bowls of gold full of the wrath *and* indignation of God Who lives forever and ever—in the eternities of the eternities.

8 And the sanctuary was filled with smoke from the glory (the radiance, the splendor) of God and from His might *and* power, and no one was able to go into the sanctuary until the seven plagues (afflictions, calamities) of the seven angels were ended. [I Kings 8:10; Isa. 6:4; Ezek. 44:4.]

CHAPTER 16 (King James)

AND I heard a great voice out of the temple saying to the seven angels, Go your ways, and pour out the vials of the wrath of God upon the earth.

CHAPTER 16 (Amplified)

THEN I heard a mighty voice from the temple sanctuary saying to the seven angels, Go and empty out on the earth the seven bowls of God's wrath *and* indignation. [Isa. 66:6; Ps. 69:24.]

p) Many authorities read "nations."

Living New Testament

19 So the angel swung his sickle on the earth and loaded the grapes into the great winepress of God's wrath.

20 And the grapes were trodden in the winepress outside the city, and blood flowed out in a stream 200 miles long and as high as a horse's bridle.

Revised Standard

of the earth, for its grapes are ripe." [19]So the angel swung his sickle on the earth and gathered the vintage of the earth, and threw it into the great wine press of the wrath of God; [20]and the wine press was trodden outside the city, and blood flowed from the wine press, as high as a horse's bridle, for one thousand six hundred stadia.[i]

CHAPTER 15

And I saw in heaven another mighty pageant showing things to come: seven angels were assigned to carry down to earth the seven last plagues—and then at last God's anger will be finished.

2 Spread out before me was what seemed to be an ocean of fire and glass, and on it stood all those who had been victorious over the Evil Creature and his statue and his mark and number. All were holding harps of God,

3 And they were singing the song of Moses, the servant of God, and the song of the Lamb:

"Great and marvelous
Are Your doings,
Lord God Almighty.
Just and true
Are Your ways,
O King of Ages.[1]
4 Who shall not fear,
O Lord,
And glorify Your Name?
For You alone are holy.
All nations will come
And worship before You,
For Your righteous deeds
Have been disclosed."

5 Then I looked and saw that the Holy of Holies of the temple in heaven was thrown wide open!

6 The seven angels who were assigned to pour out the seven plagues then came from the temple, clothed in spotlessly white linen, with golden belts across their chests.

7 And one of the four Living Beings handed each of them a golden flask filled with the terrible wrath of the Living God who lives forever and forever.

8 The temple was filled with smoke from His glory and power; and no one could enter until the seven angels had completed pouring out the seven plagues.

The seven bowls of wrath

15 Then I saw another portent in heaven, great and wonderful, seven angels with seven plagues, which are the last, for with them the wrath of God is ended.

2 And I saw what appeared to be a sea of glass mingled with fire, and those who had conquered the beast and its image and the number of its name, standing beside the sea of glass with harps of God in their hands. [3]And they sing the song of Moses, the servant of God, and the song of the Lamb, saying,

"Great and wonderful are thy deeds,
O Lord God the Almighty!
Just and true are thy ways,
O King of the ages![j]
[4]Who shall not fear and glorify thy name,
O Lord?
For thou alone art holy.
All nations shall come and worship thee,
for thy judgments have been revealed."

5 After this I looked, and the temple of the tent of witness in heaven was opened, [6]and out of the temple came the seven angels with the seven plagues, robed in pure bright linen, and their breasts girded with golden girdles. [7]And one of the four living creatures gave the seven angels seven golden bowls full of the wrath of God who lives for ever and ever; [8]and the temple was filled with smoke from the glory of God and from his power, and no one could enter the temple until the seven plagues of the seven angels were ended.

CHAPTER 16

And I heard a mighty voice shouting from the temple to the seven angels, "Now go your ways and empty out the seven flasks of the wrath of God upon the earth."

The plagues upon men

16 Then I heard a loud voice from the temple telling the seven angels, "Go and pour out on the earth the seven bowls of the wrath of God."

[1] Some manuscripts read, "King of the Nations."

[i] About two hundred miles
[j] Other ancient authorities read *the nations*

King James

2 And the first went, and poured out his vial upon the earth; and there fell a noisome and grievous sore upon the men which had the mark of the beast, and *upon* them which worshipped his image.

3 And the second angel poured out his vial upon the sea; and it became as the blood of a dead *man;* and every living soul died in the sea.

4 And the third angel poured out his vial upon the rivers and fountains of waters; and they became blood.

5 And I heard the angel of the waters say, Thou art righteous, O Lord, which art, and wast, and shalt be, because thou hast judged thus.

6 For they have shed the blood of saints and prophets, and thou hast given them blood to drink; for they are worthy.

7 And I heard another out of the altar say, Even so, Lord God Almighty, true and righteous *are* thy judgments.

8 And the fourth angel poured out his vial upon the sun; and power was given unto him to scorch men with fire.

9 And men were scorched with great heat, and blasphemed the name of God, which hath power over these plagues: and they repented not to give him glory.

10 And the fifth angel poured out his vial upon the seat of the beast; and his kingdom was full of darkness; and they gnawed their tongues for pain,

11 And blasphemed the God of heaven because of their pains and their sores, and repented not of their deeds.

12 And the sixth angel poured out his vial upon the great river Euphrates; and the water thereof was dried up, that the way of the kings of the east might be prepared.

13 And I saw three unclean spirits like frogs *come* out of the mouth of the dragon, and out of the mouth of the beast, and out of the mouth of the false prophet.

14 For they are the spirits of devils, working miracles, *which* go forth unto the kings of the earth and of the whole world, to gather them to the battle of that great day of God Almighty.

15 Behold, I come as a thief. Blessed *is* he that watcheth, and keepeth his garments, lest he walk naked, and they see his shame.

16 And he gathered them together into a place called in the Hebrew tongue Armageddon.

17 And the seventh angel poured out his vial into the air; and there came a great voice out of the temple of heaven, from the throne, saying, It is done.

18 And there were voices, and thunders, and lightnings; and there was a great earthquake, such as was not since men were upon the earth, so mighty an earthquake, *and* so great.

19 And the great city was divided into three parts, and the cities of the nations fell: and great Babylon came in remembrance before God, to give unto her the cup of the wine of the fierceness of his wrath.

Amplified

2 So the first [angel] went and emptied his bowl on the earth, and foul and painful ulcers (sores) came on the people who were marked with the stamp of the beast and who did homage to his image. [Exod. 9:10, 11; Deut. 28:35.]

3 The second *angel* emptied his bowl into the sea, and it turned into blood like that of a corpse [thick, corrupt, ill-smelling and disgusting], and every living thing that was in the sea perished.

4 Then the third *angel* emptied out his bowl into the rivers and the springs of water, and they turned into (became) blood. [Exod. 7:17-21.]

5 And I also heard the angel of the waters say, Righteous (just) are You in these Your decisions *and* judgments, You who are and were, O Holy One!

6 Because they have poured out the blood of (the saints) Your people and the prophets, and You have given them blood to drink. Such is their due—they deserve it! [Ps. 79:3.]

7 And [from] the altar I heard [the] cry, Yes, Lord God the Omnipotent, Your judgments (sentences, decisions) are true and just *and* righteous! [Ps. 119:137.]

8 Then the fourth *angel* emptied out his bowl upon the sun, and it was permitted to burn (scorch) humanity with [fierce, glowing] heat (fire).

9 People were severely burned (scorched) by the fiery heat, and they reviled *and* blasphemed the name of God Who has control of these plagues, and they did not repent of their sins—felt no regret, contrition and compunction for their waywardness, refusing to amend their ways—to give Him glory.

10 Then the fifth *angel* emptied his bowl on the throne of the beast, and his kingdom was [plunged] in darkness, and people gnawed their tongues for the torment—of their excruciating distress and severe pain—[Exod. 10:21.]

11 And blasphemed the God of heaven because of their anguish and their ulcers (sores), and they did not deplore their wicked deeds *or* repent—for what they had done.

12 Then the sixth *angel* emptied his bowl on the mighty river Euphrates, and its water was dried up to make ready a road for [the coming of] the kings of the east (from the rising sun). [Isa. 11:15, 16.]

13 And I saw three loathsome spirits like frogs, [leaping] from the mouth of the dragon and from the mouth of the beast and from the mouth of the false prophet. [I Kings 22:21-23; Exod. 8:3.]

14 For really they are the spirits of demons that perform signs (wonders, miracles). And they go forth to the rulers *and* leaders all over the world, to gather them together for war on the great day of God the Almighty.

15 Lo, I am going to come like a thief! Blessed—happy, [q]to be envied—is he who stays awake (alert) and who guards his clothes so that he may not be naked and [have the shame of being] seen exposed!

16 And they gathered them together at the place which in Hebrew is called Armageddon. [II Kings 9:27.]

17 Then the seventh *angel* emptied out his bowl into the air, and a mighty voice came out of the sanctuary *of heaven* from the throne [of God], saying, It is done! (It is all over, it is all accomplished, it has come!) [Isa. 66:6.]

18 And there followed lightning flashes, loud rumblings, peals of thunder, and a tremendous earthquake; nothing like it has ever occurred since men dwelt on the earth, so severe *and* far reaching was that earthquake. [Exod. 19:16; Dan. 12:1.]

19 The mighty city was broken into three parts, and the cities of the nations fell. And God kept in mind mighty Babylon, to make her drain the cup of His furious wrath *and* indignation.

---

q) Souter.

Living New Testament

2 So the first angel left the temple and poured out his flask over the earth, and horrible, malignant sores broke out on everyone who had the mark of the Creature and was worshiping his statue.

3 The second angel poured out his flask upon the oceans, and they became like the watery blood of a dead man; and everything in all the oceans died.

4 The third angel poured out his flask upon the rivers and springs and they became blood.

5 And I heard this angel of the waters declaring, "You are just in sending this judgment, O Holy One, who is and was,

6 For Your saints and prophets have been martyred and their blood poured out upon the earth; and now, in turn, You have poured out the blood of those who murdered them; it is their just reward."

7 And I heard the angel of the altar[1] say, "Yes, Lord God Almighty, Your punishments are just and true."

8 Then the fourth angel poured out his flask upon the sun, causing it to scorch all men with its fire.

9 Everyone was burned by this blast of heat, and they cursed the name of God who sent the plagues—they did not change their mind and attitude to give Him glory.

10 Then the fifth angel poured out his flask upon the throne of the Creature from the sea,[2] and his kingdom was plunged into darkness. And his subjects gnawed their tongues in anguish,

11 And cursed the God of heaven for their pains and sores, but they refused to repent of all their evil deeds.

12 The sixth angel poured out his flask upon the great River Euphrates and it dried up so that the kings from the east could march their armies westward without hindrance.

13 And I saw three evil spirits disguised as frogs leap from the mouth of the Dragon, the Creature, and his False Prophet.[3]

14 These miracle-working demons conferred with all the rulers of the world to gather them for battle against the Lord on that great coming Judgment Day of God Almighty.

15 "Take note: I will come as unexpectedly as a thief! Blessed are all who are awaiting Me, who keep their robes in readiness and will not need to walk naked and ashamed."

16 And they gathered all the armies of the world near a place called, in Hebrew, Armageddon—the Mountain of Megiddo.

17 Then the seventh angel poured out his flask into the air; and a mighty shout came from the throne of the temple in heaven, saying, "It is finished!"[4]

18 Then the thunder crashed and rolled, and lightning flashed; and there was a great earthquake of a magnitude unprecedented in human history.

19 The great city of "Babylon" split into three sections, and cities around the world fell in heaps of rubble; and so all of "Babylon's" sins were remembered in God's thoughts, and she was punished to the last drop of anger in the cup of the wine of the fierceness of His wrath.

[1] Literally, "I heard the altar cry. . . ."
[2] Implied.
[3] Described in Chap. 13:11-15 and 19:20.
[4] Literally, "it has happened." An epoch of human history has come to an end.

Revised Standard

2 So the first angel went and poured his bowl on the earth, and foul and evil sores came upon the men who bore the mark of the beast and worshiped its image.

3 The second angel poured his bowl into the sea, and it became like the blood of a dead man, and every living thing died that was in the sea.

4 The third angel poured his bowl into the rivers and the fountains of water, and they became blood. 5And I heard the angel of water say,

"Just art thou in these thy judgments,
thou who art and wast, O Holy One.
6For men have shed the blood of saints
and prophets,
and thou hast given them blood to drink.
It is their due!"
7And I heard the altar cry,
"Yea, Lord God the Almighty,
true and just are thy judgments!"

8 The fourth angel poured his bowl on the sun, and it was allowed to scorch men with fire; 9men were scorched by the fierce heat, and they cursed the name of God who had power over these plagues, and they did not repent and give him glory.

10 The fifth angel poured his bowl on the throne of the beast, and its kingdom was in darkness; men gnawed their tongues in anguish 11and cursed the God of heaven for their pain and sores, and did not repent of their deeds.

The kings assembled at Armageddon

12 The sixth angel poured his bowl on the great river Eu-phrates, and its water was dried up, to prepare the way for the kings from the east. 13And I saw, issuing from the mouth of the dragon and from the mouth of the beast and from the mouth of the false prophet, three foul spirits like frogs; 14for they are demonic spirits, performing signs, who go abroad to the kings of the whole world, to assemble them for battle on the great day of God the Almighty. 15("Lo, I am coming like a thief! Blessed is he who is awake, keeping his garments that he may not go naked and be seen exposed!") 16And they assembled them at the place which is called in Hebrew Armageddon.

The earthquake

17 The seventh angel poured his bowl into the air, and a great voice came out of the temple, from the throne, saying, "It is done!" 18And there were flashes of lightning, loud noises, peals of thunder, and a great earthquake such as had never been since men were on the earth, so great was that earthquake. 19The great city was split into three parts, and the cities of the nations fell, and God remembered great Babylon, to make her

King James

20 And every island fled away, and the mountains were not found.

21 And there fell upon men a great hail out of heaven, *every stone* about the weight of a talent: and men blasphemed God because of the plague of the hail; for the plague thereof was exceeding great.

Amplified

20 And every island fled and no mountains could be found.

21 And great—excessively oppressive—hailstones, as heavy as a talent [between fifty and sixty pounds], of immense size, fell from the sky on the people, and men blasphemed God for the plague of the hail, so very great was [the torture] of that plague. [Exod. 9:23.]

CHAPTER 17

AND there came one of the seven angels which had the seven vials, and talked with me, saying unto me, Come hither; I will shew unto thee the judgment of the great whore that sitteth upon many waters:

2 With whom the kings of the earth have committed fornication, and the inhabitants of the earth have been made drunk with the wine of her fornication.

3 So he carried me away in the spirit into the wilderness: and I saw a woman sit upon a scarlet coloured beast, full of names of blasphemy, and having seven heads and ten horns.

4 And the woman was arrayed in purple and scarlet colour, and decked with gold and precious stones and pearls, having a golden cup in her hand full of abominations and filthiness of her fornication:

5 And upon her forehead *was* a name written, MYSTERY, BABYLON THE GREAT, THE MOTHER OF HARLOTS AND ABOMINATIONS OF THE EARTH.

6 And I saw the woman drunken with the blood of the saints, and with the blood of the martyrs of Jesus: and when I saw her, I wondered with great admiration.

7 And the angel said unto me, Wherefore didst thou marvel? I will tell thee the mystery of the woman, and of the beast that carrieth her, which hath the seven heads and ten horns.

8 The beast that thou sawest was, and is not; and shall ascend out of the bottomless pit, and go into perdition: and they that dwell on the earth shall wonder, whose names were not written in the book of life from the foundation of the world, when they behold the beast that was, and is not, and yet is.

9 And here *is* the mind which hath wisdom. The seven heads are seven mountains, on which the woman sitteth.

10 And there are seven kings: five are fallen, and one is, *and* the other is not yet come; and when he cometh, he must continue a short space.

11 And the beast that was, and is not, even he is the eighth, and is of the seven, and goeth into perdition.

12 And the ten horns which thou sawest are ten kings, which have received no kingdom as yet; but receive power as kings one hour with the beast.

CHAPTER 17

ONE of the seven angels who had the seven bowls then came and spoke to me, saying, Come with me! I will show you the doom (sentence, judgment) of the great harlot [idolatress] who is seated on many waters, [Jer. 51:13.]

2 [She] with whom the rulers of the earth have joined in prostitution [idolatry], and with the wine of whose immorality [idolatry] the inhabitants of the earth have become intoxicated. [Jer. 25:15, 16.]

3 And [the angel] bore me away [rapt] in the Spirit into a desert (wilderness), and I saw a woman seated on a scarlet beast that was all covered with blasphemous titles (names), and he had seven heads and ten horns.

4 The woman was robed in purple and scarlet, and bedecked with gold, precious stones and pearls, [and she was] holding in her hand a cup of gold full of the accursed offenses and the filth of her lewdness *and* vice. [Jer. 51:7.]

5 And on her forehead there was inscribed a name of mystery—with a secret symbolic meaning: Babylon the great, the mother of prostitutes [idolatresses] and of the filth *and* atrocities *and* abominations of the earth.

6 I also saw that the woman was drunk, [drunk] with the blood of the saints (God's people), and the blood of the martyrs [who witnessed] for Jesus. And when I saw her I was utterly amazed *and* wondered greatly.

7 But the angel said to me, Why do you wonder? I will explain to you the [secret symbolic meaning of the] mystery of the woman, as well as of the beast having the seven heads and ten horns that carries her.

8 The beast that you saw [once] was, but [now] is no more, and he is going to come up out of the abyss (the bottomless pit) and proceed to go to perdition; and the inhabitants of the earth whose names have not been recorded in the Book of Life from the foundation of the world, will be astonished when they look at the beast, because he [once] was, but [now] is no more, and he is [yet] to come. [Dan. 7:3.]

9 This calls for a mind [to consider that is packed] with wisdom *and* intelligence—it is something for a particular mode of thinking and judging of thoughts, feelings and purposes. The seven heads are seven hills upon which the woman is sitting;

10 And they are also seven kings, five of whom have fallen, one still exists—and is reigning; the other [the seventh] has not yet appeared, and when he does arrive he must stay [but] a brief time.

11 And as for the beast that [once] was, but now is no more, he [himself] is an eighth ruler (king, head), but he is of the seven *and* belongs to them, and he goes to perdition.

12 Also the ten horns that you observed are ten rulers (kings) who have as yet received no royal dominion, but together they are to receive power *and* authority as rulers for a single hour, along with the beast. [Dan. 7:20-24.]

Living New Testament

20 And islands vanished, and mountains flattened out,

21 And there was an incredible hailstorm from heaven; hailstones weighing a hundred pounds fell from the sky onto the people below, and they cursed God because of the terrible hail.

CHAPTER 17

One of the seven angels who had poured out the plagues came over and talked with me, "Come with me," he said, "and I will show you what is going to happen to the Notorious Prostitute, who sits upon the many waters of the world.

2 The kings of the world have had immoral relations with her, and the people of the earth have been made drunk by the wine of her immorality."

3 So the angel took me in spirit into the wilderness. There I saw a woman sitting on a scarlet animal that had seven heads and ten horns,[1] written all over with blasphemies against God.

4 The woman wore purple and scarlet clothing and beautiful jewelry made of gold and precious gems and pearls, and held in her hand a golden goblet full of obscenities.

5 A mysterious caption was written on her forehead: "Babylon the Great, Mother of Prostitutes and of Idol Worship Everywhere around the World."

6 I could see that she was drunk—drunk with the blood of the martyrs of Jesus she had killed. I stared at her in horror.

7 "Why are you so surprised?" the angel asked. "I'll tell you who she is and what the animal she is riding represents.

8 He was alive but isn't now. And yet, soon, he will come up out of the bottomless pit and go to eternal destruction;[2] and the people of earth, whose names have not been written in the Book of Life before the world began, will be dumbfounded at his reappearance after being dead.[3]

9 And now think hard: His seven heads represent a certain city[4] built on seven hills where this woman has her residence.

10 They also represent seven kings. Five have already fallen, the sixth now reigns, and the seventh is yet to come, but his reign will be brief.

11 The scarlet animal that died is the eighth king, having reigned before as one of the seven; after his second reign, he too will go to his doom.[2]

12 His ten horns are ten kings who have not yet risen to power; they will be appointed to their kingdoms for one brief moment, to reign with him.

---

[1] As the Dragon—Satan—and the Creature from the sea are also described in 12:3, 9 and 13:1.
[2] Literally, "go to perdition."
[3] Literally, "dumbfounded at the ruler who was, and is not, and will be present."
[4] Implied in verse 18.

Revised Standard

drain the cup of the fury of his wrath. [20]And every island fled away, and no mountains were to be found; [21]and great hailstones, heavy as a hundred-weight, dropped on men from heaven, till men cursed God for the plague of the hail, so fearful was that plague.

Judgment of Babylon, the harlot

17 Then one of the seven angels who had the seven bowls came and said to me, "Come, I will show you the judgment of the great harlot who is seated upon many waters, [2]with whom the kings of the earth have committed fornication, and with the wine of whose fornication the dwellers on earth have become drunk." [3]And he carried me away in the Spirit into a wilderness, and I saw a woman sitting on a scarlet beast which was full of blasphemous names, and it had seven heads and ten horns. [4]The woman was arrayed in purple and scarlet, and bedecked with gold and jewels and pearls, holding in her hand a golden cup full of abominations and the impurities of her fornication; [5]and on her forehead was written a name of mystery: "Babylon the great, mother of harlots and of earth's abominations." [6]And I saw the woman, drunk with the blood of the saints and the blood of the martyrs of Jesus.

Explanation of the harlot and beast

When I saw her I marveled greatly. [7]But the angel said to me, "Why marvel? I will tell you the mystery of the woman, and of the beast with seven heads and ten horns that carries her. [8]The beast that you saw was, and is not, and is to ascend from the bottomless pit and go to perdition; and the dwellers on earth whose names have not been written in the book of life from the foundation of the world, will marvel to behold the beast, because it was and is not and is to come. [9]This calls for a mind with wisdom: the seven heads are seven hills on which the woman is seated; [10]they are also seven kings, five of whom have fallen, one is, the other has not yet come, and when he comes he must remain only a little while. [11]As for the beast that was and is not, it is an eighth but it belongs to the seven, and it goes to perdition. [12]And the ten horns that you saw are ten kings who have not yet received royal power, but they are to receive authority as kings for one hour, together with the beast.

King James

13 These have one mind, and shall give their power and strength unto the beast.

14 These shall make war with the Lamb, and the Lamb shall overcome them: for he is Lord of lords, and King of kings: and they that are with him *are* called, and chosen, and faithful.

15 And he saith unto me, The waters which thou sawest, where the whore sitteth, are peoples, and multitudes, and nations, and tongues.

16 And the ten horns which thou sawest upon the beast, these shall hate the whore, and shall make her desolate and naked, and shall eat her flesh, and burn her with fire.

17 For God hath put in their hearts to fulfil his will, and to agree, and give their kingdom unto the beast, until the words of God shall be fulfilled.

18 And the woman which thou sawest is that great city, which reigneth over the kings of the earth.

Amplified

13 These have one common policy (opinion, purpose), and they deliver their power and authority to the beast.

14 They will wage war against the Lamb, and the Lamb will triumph over them; for He is Lord of lords and King of kings, and those with Him *and* on His side are chosen and called [elected] and loyal *and* faithful followers. [Dan. 2:47.]

15 And [the angel further] said to me, The waters that you observed, where the harlot is seated, are races and multitudes and nations and dialects (languages).

16 And the ten horns that you saw, they and the beast will [be the very ones to] hate the harlot [the idolatrous woman]; they will make her cheerless (bereaved, desolate) and they will strip her, and eat up her flesh and utterly consume her with fire.

17 For God has put it into their hearts to carry out His own purpose by acting in harmony in surrendering their royal power *and* authority to the beast, until the prophetic words—intentions and promises—of God shall be fulfilled.

18 And the woman that you saw is herself the great city which dominates *and* controls the rulers *and* the leaders of the earth.

CHAPTER 18

AND after these things I saw another angel come down from heaven, having great power; and the earth was lightened with his glory.

2 And he cried mightily with a strong voice, saying, Babylon the great is fallen, is fallen, and is become the habitation of devils, and the hold of every foul spirit, and a cage of every unclean and hateful bird.

3 For all nations have drunk of the wine of the wrath of her fornication, and the kings of the earth have committed fornication with her, and the merchants of the earth are waxed rich through the abundance of her delicacies.

4 And I heard another voice from heaven, saying, Come out of her, my people, that ye be not partakers of her sins, and that ye receive not of her plagues.

5 For her sins have reached unto heaven, and God hath remembered her iniquities.

6 Reward her even as she rewarded you, and double unto her double according to her works: in the cup which she hath filled fill to her double.

7 How much she hath glorified herself, and lived deliciously, so much torment and sorrow give her: for she saith in her heart, I sit a queen, and am no widow, and shall see no sorrow.

8 Therefore shall her plagues come in one day, death, and mourning, and famine; and she shall be utterly burned with fire: for strong *is* the Lord God who judgeth her.

CHAPTER 18

THEN I saw another angel descending from heaven, possessing great authority, and the earth was illuminated with his radiance *and* splendor.

2 And he shouted with a mighty voice, She is fallen! Mighty Babylon is fallen! She has become a resort *and* dwelling place for demons, a dungeon haunted by every loathsome spirit, an abode for every filthy and detestable bird;

3 Because all nations have drunk the wine of her passionate unchastity, and the rulers *and* leaders of the earth have joined with her in committing fornication [idolatry], and the businessmen of the earth have become rich with the wealth of her excessive luxury *and* wantonness. [Jer. 25:15, 27.]

4 I then heard another voice from heaven saying, Come out from her, my people, so that you may not share in her sins, neither participate in her plagues. [Isa. 48:20; Jer. 50:8.]

5 For her iniquities—her crimes and transgressions—are piled up as high as heaven, and God has remembered her wickedness *and* [her] crimes—and calls them up for settlement. [Jer. 51:9.]

6 Repay to her what she herself has paid [to others] and double [her doom] in accordance with what she has done. Mix a double portion for her in the cup she mixed [for others]. [Ps. 137:8.]

7 To the degree that she glorified herself and reveled in her wantonness—living deliciously and luxuriously—to that measure impose on her torment *and* anguish and tears *and* mourning. Since in her heart she boasts, I am not a widow; as a queen [on a throne] I sit, and I shall never see suffering *or* experience sorrow, [Isa. 47:8, 9.]

8 So shall her plagues (afflictions, calamities) come thick upon her in a single day, pestilence and anguish *and* sorrow and famine, and she shall be utterly consumed—burned up with fire; for mighty is the Lord God Who judges her.

Living New Testament

13 They will all sign a treaty giving their power and strength to him.

14 Together they will wage war against the Lamb, and the Lamb will conquer them; for He is Lord over all lords, and King of kings, and His people are the called and chosen and faithful ones.

15 The oceans, lakes and rivers that the woman is sitting on represent masses of people of every race and nation.

16 The scarlet animal and his ten horns—which represent ten kings who will reign with him—all hate the woman, and will attack her and leave her naked and ravaged by fire.

17 For God will put a plan into their minds, a plan that will carry out His purposes: they will mutually agree to give their authority to the scarlet animal, so that the words of God will be fulfilled.

18 And this woman you saw in your vision represents the great city that rules over the kings of the earth."

Revised Standard

[13]These are of one mind and give over
their power and authority to the beast;
[14]they will make war on the Lamb, and the
Lamb will conquer them, for he is Lord of
lords and King of kings, and those with him
are called and chosen and faithful."
15 And he said to me, "The waters that
you saw, where the harlot is seated, are
peoples and multitudes and nations and
tongues. [16]And the ten horns that you saw,
they and the beast will hate the harlot;
they will make her desolate and naked, and
devour her flesh and burn her up with fire,
[17]for God has put it into their hearts to
carry out his purpose by being of one mind
and giving over their royal power to the
beast, until the words of God shall be fulfilled. [18]And the woman that you saw is
the great city which has dominion over
the kings of the earth."

CHAPTER 18

After all this I saw another angel come down from heaven with great authority, and the earth grew bright with his splendor.

2 He gave a mighty shout, "Babylon the Great is fallen, is fallen; she has become a den of demons, a haunt of devils and every kind of evil spirit.[1]

3 For all the nations have drunk the fatal wine of her intense immorality. The rulers of the earth have enjoyed themselves[2] with her, and businessmen throughout the world have grown rich from all her luxurious living."

4 Then I heard another voice calling from heaven, "Come away from her, My people; do not take part in her sins, or you will be punished with her.

5 For her sins are piled as high as heaven and God is ready to judge her for her crimes.

6 Do to her as she has done to you, and more—give double penalty for all her evil deeds. She brewed many a cup of woe for others—give twice as much to her.

7 She has lived in luxury and pleasure—match it now with torments and with sorrows. She boasts, 'I am queen upon my throne. I am no helpless widow. I will not experience sorrow.'

8 Therefore the sorrows of death and mourning and famine shall overtake her in a single day, and she shall be utterly consumed by fire; for mighty is the Lord who judges her."

[1] Literally, "of every foul and hateful bird."
[2] Literally, "have committed fornication with her."

The doom of Babylon announced

18 After this I saw another angel coming down from heaven, having great
authority; and the earth was made bright
with his splendor. [2]And he called out with
a mighty voice,
"Fallen, fallen is Babylon the great!
It has become a dwelling place of demons,
a haunt of every foul spirit,
a haunt of every foul and hateful bird;
[3]for all nations have drunk[k] the wine of her impure passion,
and the kings of the earth have committed fornication with her,
and the merchants of the earth have grown rich with the wealth of her wantonness."
[4]Then I heard another voice from heaven
saying,
"Come out of her, my people,
lest you take part in her sins,
lest you share in her plagues;
[5]for her sins are heaped high as heaven,
and God has remembered her iniquities.
[6]Render to her as she herself has rendered,
and repay her double for her deeds;
mix a double draught for her in the cup she mixed.
[7]As she glorified herself and played the wanton,
so give her a like measure of torment and mourning.
Since in her heart she says, 'A queen I sit,
I am no widow, mourning I shall never see,'
[8]so shall her plagues come in a single day,
pestilence and mourning and famine,
and she shall be burned with fire;
for mighty is the Lord God who judges her."

k Other ancient authorities read *fallen by*

King James

9 And the kings of the earth, who have committed fornication and lived deliciously with her, shall bewail her, and lament for her, when they shall see the smoke of her burning,

10 Standing afar off for the fear of her torment, saying, Alas, alas that great city Babylon, that mighty city! for in one hour is thy judgment come.

11 And the merchants of the earth shall weep and mourn over her; for no man buyeth their merchandise any more:

12 The merchandise of gold, and silver, and precious stones, and of pearls, and fine linen, and purple, and silk, and scarlet, and all thyine wood, and all manner vessels of ivory, and all manner vessels of most precious wood, and of brass, and iron, and marble,

13 And cinnamon, and odours, and ointments, and frankincense, and wine, and oil, and fine flour, and wheat, and beasts, and sheep, and horses, and chariots, and slaves, and souls of men.

14 And the fruits that thy soul lusted after are departed from thee, and all things which were dainty and goodly are departed from thee, and thou shalt find them no more at all.

15 The merchants of these things, which were made rich by her, shall stand afar off for the fear of her torment, weeping and wailing,

16 And saying, Alas, alas, that great city, that was clothed in fine linen, and purple, and scarlet, and decked with gold, and precious stones, and pearls!

17 For in one hour so great riches is come to nought. And every shipmaster, and all the company in ships, and sailors, and as many as trade by sea, stood afar off,

18 And cried when they saw the smoke of her burning, saying, What *city is* like unto this great city!

19 And they cast dust on their heads, and cried, weeping and wailing, saying, Alas, alas, that great city, wherein were made rich all that had ships in the sea by reason of her costliness! for in one hour is she made desolate.

20 Rejoice over her, *thou* heaven, and *ye* holy apostles and prophets; for God hath avenged you on her.

21 And a mighty angel took up a stone like a great millstone, and cast *it* into the sea, saying, Thus with violence shall that great city Babylon be thrown down, and shall be found no more at all.

22 And the voice of harpers, and musicians, and of pipers, and trumpeters, shall be heard no more at all in thee; and no craftsman, of whatsoever craft *he be*, shall be found any more in thee; and the sound of a millstone shall be heard no more at all in thee;

Amplified

9 And the rulers *and* leaders of the earth, who joined her in her immorality [idolatry] and luxuriated with her, will weep *and* beat their breasts and lament over her when they see the smoke of her conflagration. [Ezek. 26:16, 17.]

10 They will stand a long way off, in terror of her torment, and they will cry, Woe *and* alas! the great city! the mighty city, Babylon! In one single hour how your doom (judgment) has overtaken you!

11 And earth's businessmen weep and grieve over her, because no one buys their freight (cargo) any more. [Ezek. 27:36.]

12 Their merchandise is of gold, silver, precious stones and pearls; of fine linen, purple, silk and scarlet [stuffs]; all kinds of scented wood, all sorts of articles of ivory, all varieties of objects of costly woods, bronze, iron and marble; [Ezek. 27:12, 13, 22.]

13 Of cinnamon, spices, incense, ointment *and* perfume, and frankincense; of wine and olive oil, fine flour and wheat; of cattle and sheep, horses and conveyances; and of slaves, [that is,] the bodies, and souls of men!

14 The ripe fruits *and* delicacies for which your soul longed have gone from you, and all your luxuries *and* dainties, your elegance *and* splendor are lost to you, never again to be recovered *or* experienced!

15 The dealers who handled these articles, who grew wealthy through their business with her, will stand a long way off, in terror of her doom *and* torment, weeping and grieving aloud, and saying,

16 Alas, alas for the great city that was robed in fine linen, in purple and scarlet, bedecked *and* glittering with gold, with precious stones, and with pearls! [Ezek. 27:36, 31.]

17 Because in one [single] hour all the vast wealth has been destroyed—wiped out. And all ship captains *and* pilots, navigators and all who live by seafaring, the crews and all who ply their trade on the sea, stood a long way off, [Isa. 23:14; Ezek. 27:26-30.]

18 And exclaimed as they watched the smoke of her burning, What city could be compared to the great city!

19 And they threw dust on their heads, as they wept and grieved, exclaiming, Woe *and* alas, for the great city where all who had ships on the sea grew rich [through her extravagance] from her great wealth! In one single hour she has been destroyed *and* has become a desert! [Ezek. 27:30-34.]

20 Rejoice (celebrate) over her, O heaven! O saints (people of God) and apostles and prophets, because God has executed vengeance for you upon her! [Isa. 44:23; Jer. 51:48.]

21 Then a single powerful angel took up a boulder like a great millstone and flung it into the sea, crying, With such violence shall Babylon the great city be hurled down to destruction and shall never again be found. [Jer. 51:63, 64; Ezek. 26:21.]

22 And the sound of harpists and minstrels and flute players and trumpeters shall never again be heard in you, and no skilled artisan of any craft shall ever again be found in you, and the sound of the millstone shall never again be heard in you. [Isa. 24:8; Ezek. 26:13.]

Living New Testament

9 And the world leaders, who took part in her immoral acts and enjoyed her favors, will mourn for her as they see the smoke rising from her charred remains.

10 They will stand far off, trembling with fear and crying out, "Alas, Babylon, that mighty city! In one moment her judgment fell."

11 The merchants of the earth will weep and mourn for her, for there is no one left to buy their goods.

12 She was their biggest customer for gold and silver, precious stones, pearls, finest linens, purple silks, and scarlet; and every kind of perfumed wood, and ivory goods and most expensive wooden carvings, and brass and iron and marble;

13 And spices and perfumes and incense, ointment and frankincense, wine, olive oil, and fine flour; wheat, cattle, sheep, horses, chariots, and slaves—and even the souls of men.

14 "All the fancy things you loved so much are gone," they cry. "The dainty luxuries and splendor that you prized so much will never be yours again. They are gone forever."

15 And so the merchants who have become wealthy by selling her these things shall stand at a distance, fearing danger to themselves, weeping and crying,

16 "Alas, that great city, so beautiful—like a woman clothed in finest purple and scarlet linens, decked out with gold and precious stones and pearls!

17 In one moment, all the wealth of the city is gone!" And all the shipowners and captains of the merchant ships and crews will stand a long way off,

18 Crying as they watch the smoke ascend and saying, "Where in all the world is there another city such as this?"

19 And they will throw dust on their heads in their sorrow and say, "Alas, alas, for that great city! She made us all rich from her great wealth. And now in a single hour all is gone. . . . "

20 But you, O heaven, rejoice over her fate; and you, O children of God and the prophets and the apostles! For at last God has given judgment against her for you.

21 Then a mighty angel picked up a boulder shaped like a millstone and threw it into the ocean and shouted, "Babylon, that great city, shall be thrown away as I have thrown away this stone, and she shall disappear forever.

22 Never again will the sound of music be there—no more pianos, saxophones, and trumpets.[3] No industry of any kind will ever again exist there, and there will be no more milling of the grain.

Literally, "harpers . . . pipers . . . and trumpeters."

Revised Standard

The lament over Babylon

9 And the kings of the earth, who committed fornication and were wanton with
her, will weep and wail over her when they
see the smoke of her burning; [10]they will
stand far off, in fear of her torment, and
say,

"Alas! alas! thou great city,
thou mighty city, Babylon!
In one hour has thy judgment come."

11 And the merchants of the earth weep
and mourn for her, since no one buys their
cargo any more, [12]cargo of gold, silver,
jewels and pearls, fine linen, purple, silk
and scarlet, all kinds of scented wood, all
articles of ivory, all articles of costly wood,
bronze, iron and marble, [13]cinnamon, spice,
incense, myrrh, frankincense, wine, oil, fine
flour and wheat, cattle and sheep, horses
and chariots, and slaves, that is, human
souls.

[14]"The fruit for which thy soul longed
has gone from thee,
and all thy dainties and thy splendor
are lost to thee, never to be found
again!"

[15]The merchants of these wares, who gained
wealth from her, will stand far off, in fear
of her torment, weeping and mourning
aloud,

[16]"Alas, alas, for the great city
that was clothed in fine linen, in purple
and scarlet,
bedecked with gold, with jewels, and with
pearls!

[17]In one hour all this wealth has been laid
waste."

And all shipmasters and seafaring men,
sailors and all whose trade is on the sea,
stood far off [18]and cried out as they saw
the smoke of her burning,

"What city was like the great city?"

[19]And they threw dust on their heads, as
they wept and mourned, crying out,

"Alas, alas, for the great city
where all who had ships at sea grew rich
by her wealth!
In one hour she has been laid waste.

[20]Rejoice over her, O heaven,
O saints and apostles and prophets,
for God has given judgment for you
against her!"

The desolation of Babylon

21 Then a mighty angel took up a stone
like a great millstone and threw it into the
sea, saying,

"So shall Babylon the great city be
thrown down with violence,
and shall be found no more;

[22]and the sound of harpers and minstrels,
of flute players and trumpeters,
shall be heard in thee no more;
and a craftsman of any craft
shall be heard in thee no more;
and the sound of the millstone
shall be found in thee no more;

King James

23 And the light of a candle shall shine no more at all in thee; and the voice of the bridegroom and of the bride shall be heard no more at all in thee: for thy merchants were the great men of the earth; for by thy sorceries were all nations deceived.

24 And in her was found the blood of prophets, and of saints, and of all that were slain upon the earth.

Amplified

23 And never again shall the light of a lamp shine in you, and the voice of bridegroom and bride shall never be heard in you again; for your businessmen were the great *and* prominent men of the earth, and by your magic spells *and* poisonous charm all nations were led astray—seduced and deluded.

24 And in her was found the blood of prophets and of saints, and of all those who have been slain (slaughtered) on earth. [Jer. 51:49.]

CHAPTER 19

AND after these things I heard a great voice of much people in heaven saying, Alleluia; Salvation, and glory, and honour, and power, unto the Lord our God:

2 For true and righteous *are* his judgments: for he hath judged the great whore, which did corrupt the earth with her fornication, and hath avenged the blood of his servants at her hand.

3 And again they said, Alleluia. And her smoke rose up for ever and ever.

4 And the four and twenty elders and the four beasts fell down and worshipped God that sat on the throne, saying, Amen; Alleluia.

5 And a voice came out of the throne, saying, Praise our God, all ye his servants, and ye that fear him, both small and great.

6 And I heard as it were the voice of a great multitude, and as the voice of many waters, and as the voice of mighty thunderings, saying, Alleluia: for the Lord God omnipotent reigneth.

7 Let us be glad and rejoice, and give honour to him: for the marriage of the Lamb is come, and his wife hath made herself ready.

8 And to her was granted that she should be arrayed in fine linen, clean and white: for the fine linen is the righteousness of saints.

9 And he saith unto me, Write, Blessed *are* they which are called unto the marriage supper of the Lamb. And he saith unto me, These are the true sayings of God.

10 And I fell at his feet to worship him. And he said unto me, See *thou do it* not: I am thy fellow-servant, and of thy brethren that have the testimony of Jesus: worship God: for the testimony of Jesus is the spirit of prophecy.

CHAPTER 19

AFTER this I heard what sounded like a mighty shout of a great crowd in heaven, exclaiming, Hallelujah—praise the Lord! Salvation and glory (splendor and majesty) and power (dominion and authority [belong]) to our God!

2 Because His judgments—His condemnation and punishment, His sentences of doom—are true *and* sound just *and* upright. He has judged—convicted, pronounced sentence and doomed the great *and* notorious harlot [idolatress] who corrupted *and* demoralized *and* poisoned the earth with her lewdness *and* adultery [idolatry]. And He has avenged—visited on her the penalty for—the blood of His servants. [Deut. 32:43.]

3 And again they shouted, Hallelujah—praise the Lord! The smoke of her [burning] shall continue to ascend forever and ever—through the eternities of the eternities. [Isa. 34:10.]

4 Then the twenty-four elders [of [r]the heavenly Sanhedrin] and the four living creatures fell prostrate and worshipped (paying divine honors to) God Who sits on the throne, saying, Amen! Hallelujah—praise the Lord!

5 Then from the throne there came a voice saying, Praise our God, all you servants of His, you who reverence Him, both small and great! [Ps. 115:13.]

6 After that I heard what sounded like the shout of a vast throng, like the boom of many pounding waves and like the roar of terrific *and* mighty thunderpeals, exclaiming, Hallelujah—praise the Lord! For now the Lord our God the Omnipotent—the All-Ruler—reigns!

7 Let us rejoice—and shout for joy—exulting *and* triumphant! Let us celebrate *and* ascribe to Him glory *and* honor, for the marriage of the Lamb [at last] has come and His bride has prepared herself. [Ps. 118:24.]

8 She has been permitted to dress in fine (radiant) linen—dazzling and white, for the fine linen is (signifies, represents) the righteousness—the upright, just and godly living [deeds, conduct] and right standing with God—of the saints (God's holy people).

9 Then [the angel] said to me, Write this down: Blessed—happy, [s]to be envied—are those who are summoned (invited, called) to the marriage supper of the Lamb. And he said to me [further], These are the true words—the genuine *and* exact declarations—of God.

10 Then I fell prostrate at his feet to worship—to pay divine honors—to him, but he [restrained me] and said, Refrain!—You must not do that! I am [only] another servant with you and your brethren who have [accepted

---

r) Berry, and others.
s) Souter.

Living New Testament

23 Dark, dark will be her nights; not even a lamp in a window will ever be seen again. No more joyous wedding bells and happy voices of the bridegrooms and the brides. Her businessmen were known around the world and she deceived all nations with her sorceries.

24 And she was responsible for the blood of all the martyred prophets and the saints."

CHAPTER 19

After this I heard the shouting of a vast crowd in heaven, "Hallelujah! Praise the Lord! Salvation is from our God. Honor and authority belong to Him alone;

2 For His judgments are just and true. He has punished the Great Prostitute who corrupted the earth with her sin;[1] and He has avenged the murder of His servants."

3 Again and again their voices rang, "Praise the Lord! The smoke from her burning ascends forever and forever!"

4 Then the twenty-four elders and four Living Beings fell down and worshiped God, who was sitting upon the throne, and said, "Amen! Hallelujah! Praise the Lord!"

5 And out of the throne came a voice that said, "Praise our God, all you His servants, small and great, who fear Him."

6 Then I heard again what sounded like the shouting of a huge crowd, or like the waves of a hundred oceans crashing on the shore, or like the mighty rolling of great thunder, "Praise the Lord. For the Lord our God, the Almighty, reigns.

7 Let us be glad and rejoice and honor Him; for the time has come for the wedding banquet of the Lamb, and His bride has prepared herself.

8 She is permitted to wear the cleanest and whitest and finest of linens." (Fine linen represents the good deeds done by the people of God.)

9 And the angel[2] dictated this sentence to me: "Blessed are those who are invited to the wedding feast of the Lamb." And he added, "God Himself has stated this."[3]

10 Then I fell down at his feet to worship him, but he said, "No! Don't! For I am a servant of God just as you are, and as your brother Christians are, who testify of their faith in Jesus. The purpose of all prophecy and of all I have shown you is to tell about Jesus."[4]

[1] Literally, "fornication," the word used symbolically through the prophets for the worship of false gods.
[2] Literally, "he"; the exact antecedent is unclear.
[3] Literally, "These are the true words of God."
[4] Literally, "The testimony of Jesus is the spirit of prophecy."

Revised Standard

23 and the light of a lamp
shall shine in thee no more;
and the voice of bridegroom and bride
shall be heard in thee no more;
for thy merchants were the great men of the earth,
and all nations were deceived by thy sorcery.
24 And in her was found the blood of prophets and of saints,
and of all who have been slain on earth."

The marriage supper of the Lamb

19 After this I heard what seemed to be
the mighty voice of a great multitude
in heaven, crying,
"Hallelujah! Salvation and glory and power belong to our God,
2 for his judgments are true and just;
he has judged the great harlot who corrupted the earth with her fornication,
and he has avenged on her the blood of his servants."
3 Once more they cried,
"Hallelujah! The smoke from her goes up for ever and ever."
4 And the twenty-four elders and the four
living creatures fell down and worshiped
God who is seated on the throne, saying,
"Amen. Hallelujah!" 5 And from the throne
came a voice crying,
"Praise our God, all you his servants,
you who fear him, small and great."
6 Then I heard what seemed to be the voice
of a great multitude, like the sound of
many waters and like the sound of mighty
thunderpeals, crying,
"Hallelujah! For the Lord our God the Almighty reigns.
7 Let us rejoice and exult and give him the glory,
For the marriage of the Lamb has come,
and his Bride has made herself ready;
8 it was granted her to be clothed with fine linen, bright and pure"—
for the fine linen is the righteous deeds
of the saints.
9 And the angel said[l] to me, "Write
this: Blessed are those who are invited to
the marriage supper of the Lamb." And
he said to me, "These are true words of
God." 10 Then I fell down at his feet to
worship him, but he said to me, "You must
not do that! I am a fellow servant with you

[l] Greek *he said*

King James

11 And I saw heaven opened, and behold a white horse; and he that sat upon him *was* called Faithful and True, and in righteousness he doth judge and make war.

12 His eyes *were* as a flame of fire, and on his head *were* many crowns; and he had a name written, that no man knew, but he himself.

13 And he *was* clothed with a vesture dipped in blood: and his name is called The Word of God.

14 And the armies *which were* in heaven followed him upon white horses, clothed in fine linen, white and clean.

15 And out of his mouth goeth a sharp sword, that with it he should smite the nations: and he shall rule them with a rod of iron: and he treadeth the winepress of the fierceness and wrath of Almighty God.

16 And he hath on *his* vesture and on his thigh a name written, KING OF KINGS, AND LORD OF LORDS.

17 And I saw an angel standing in the sun; and he cried with a loud voice, saying to all the fowls that fly in the midst of heaven, Come and gather yourselves together unto the supper of the great God;

18 That ye may eat the flesh of kings, and the flesh of captains, and the flesh of mighty men, and the flesh of horses, and of them that sit on them, and the flesh of all *men, both* free and bond, both small and great.

19 And I saw the beast, and the kings of the earth, and their armies, gathered together to make war against him that sat on the horse, and against his army.

20 And the beast was taken, and with him the false prophet that wrought miracles before him, with which he deceived them that had received the mark of the beast, and them that worshipped his image. These both were cast alive into a lake of fire burning with brimstone.

21 And the remnant were slain with the sword of him that sat upon the horse, which *sword* proceeded out of his mouth: and all the fowls were filled with their flesh.

Amplified

and hold] the testimony borne by Jesus. Worship God! For the substance (essence) of the truth revealed by Jesus is the spirit of all prophecy—the vital breath, the inspiration of all inspired preaching and interpretation of the divine will and purpose [including both mine and yours].

11 After that I saw heaven opened, and behold, a white horse [appeared]! The One Who was riding it is called Faithful (trustworthy, loyal, incorruptible, steady) and True, and He passes judgment and wages war in righteousness—holiness, justice and uprightness. [Ezek. 1:1.]

12 His eyes [blaze] like a flame of fire, and on His head are many kingly crowns (diadems); and He has a title (name) inscribed which He alone knows *or* can understand. [Dan. 10:6.]

13 He is dressed in a robe dyed by [t]dipping in blood, and the title by which He is called is The Word of God.

14 And the troops of heaven, clothed in fine linen, dazzling and clean, followed Him on white horses.

15 From His mouth goes forth a sharp sword with which He can smite (afflict, strike) the nations, and He will shepherd *and* control them with a staff (scepter, rod) of iron. He will tread the wine press of the fierceness of the wrath *and* indignation of God the All-Ruler—the Almighty, the Omnipotent. [Ps. 2:9.]

16 And on His garment (robe) and on His thigh He has a name (title) inscribed, KING OF KINGS AND LORD OF LORDS. [Deut. 10:17; Dan. 2:47.]

17 Then I saw a single angel stationed in the sun's [u]light, and with a mighty voice he shouted to all the birds that fly across the sky, Come, gather yourselves together for the great supper of God, [Ezek. 39:4, 17-20.]

18 That you may feast on the flesh of rulers, the flesh of generals *and* captains, the flesh of powerful *and* mighty men, the flesh of horses and their riders, and the flesh of all humanity, both free and slave, both small and great!

19 Then I saw the beast and the rulers *and* leaders of the earth with their troops mustered to go into battle *and* make war against Him Who is mounted on the horse and against His troops.

20 And the beast was seized *and* overpowered, and with him the false prophet who in his presence had worked wonders *and* performed miracles by which he led astray those who had accepted *or* permitted to be placed upon them the stamp (mark) of the beast, and those who paid homage *and* gave divine honors to his statue. Both of the two were hurled alive into the fiery lake that burns *and* blazes with brimstone.

21 And the rest were killed with the sword that issues from the mouth of Him Who is mounted on the horse, and all the birds fed ravenously *and* glutted themselves with their flesh.

CHAPTER 20 (King James)

AND I saw an angel come down from heaven, having the key of the bottomless pit and a great chain in his hand.

2 And he laid hold on the dragon, that old serpent, which is the Devil, and Satan, and bound him a thousand years,

3 And cast him into the bottomless pit, and shut him up, and set a seal upon him, that he should deceive the nations no more, till the thousand years should be fulfilled: and after that he must be loosed a little season.

CHAPTER 20 (Amplified)

THEN I saw an angel descending from heaven; he was holding the key of the abyss—the bottomless pit—and a great chain was in his hand.

2 And he gripped *and* overpowered the dragon, that old serpent of primeval times, who is the devil and Satan, and [securely] bound him for a thousand years.

3 Then he hurled him into the abyss—the bottomless pit—and closed it and sealed it above him, so that he should no longer lead astray *and* deceive *and* seduce the nations until the thousand years were at an end. After that he must be liberated for a short time.

---

t) Some ancient authorities read "sprinkled with blood."
u) Thayer, Berry, etc.

Living New Testament

11 Then I saw heaven opened and a white horse standing there; and the one sitting on the horse was named "Faithful and True"—the one who justly punishes and makes war.

12 His eyes were like flames, and on His head were many crowns. A name was written on His forehead,[5] and only He knew its meaning.

13 He was clothed with garments dipped in blood, and His title was "The Word of God."[6]

14 The armies of heaven, dressed in finest linen, white and clean, followed Him on white horses.

15 In His mouth He held a sharp sword to strike down the nations; He ruled them with an iron grip; and He trod the winepress of the fierceness of the wrath of Almighty God.

16 On His robe and thigh were written this title: "KING OF KINGS AND LORD OF LORDS."

17 Then I saw an angel standing in the sunshine, shouting loudly to the birds, "Come! Gather together for the supper of the Great God!

18 Come and eat the flesh of kings, and captains, and great generals; of horses and riders; and of all humanity, both great and small, slave and free."

19 Then I saw the Evil Creature gathering the governments of the earth and their armies to fight against the one sitting on the horse and His army.

20 And the Evil Creature was captured, and with him the False Prophet,[7] who could do mighty miracles when the Evil Creature was present—miracles that deceived all who had accepted the Evil Creature's mark, and who worshiped his statue. Both of them—the Evil Creature and his False Prophet—were thrown alive into the Lake of Fire that burns with sulphur.

21 And their entire army was killed with the sharp sword in the mouth of the one riding the white horse, and all the birds of heaven were gorged with their flesh.

Revised Standard

and your brethren who hold the testimony
of Jesus. Worship God." For the testimony
of Jesus is the spirit of prophecy.

Defeat of the beast and false prophet

11 Then I saw heaven opened, and behold, a white horse! He who sat upon it is
called Faithful and True, and in righteousness he judges and makes war. 12His eyes
are like a flame of fire, and on his head
are many diadems; and he has a name inscribed which no one knows but himself.
13He is clad in a robe dipped in[m] blood,
and the name by which he is called is The
Word of God. 14And the armies of heaven,
arrayed in fine linen, white and pure, followed him on white horses. 15From his
mouth issues a sharp sword with which to
smite the nations, and he will rule them
with a rod of iron; he will tread the wine
press of the fury of the wrath of God the
Almighty. 16On his robe and on his thigh
he has a name inscribed, King of kings and
Lord of lords.
17 Then I saw an angel standing in the
sun, and with a loud voice he called to all
the birds that fly in midheaven, "Come,
gather for the great supper of God, 18to eat
the flesh of kings, the flesh of captains, the
flesh of mighty men, the flesh of horses and
their riders, and the flesh of all men, both
free and slave, both small and great." 19And
I saw the beast and the kings of the earth
with their armies gathered to make war
against him who sits upon the horse and
against his army. 20And the beast was captured, and with it the false prophet who in
its presence had worked the signs by which
he deceived those who had received the
mark of the beast and those who worshiped
its image. These two were thrown alive into
the lake of fire that burns with brimstone.
21And the rest were slain by the sword of
him who sits upon the horse, the sword that
issues from his mouth; and all the birds
were gorged with their flesh.

CHAPTER 20

Then I saw an angel come down from heaven with the key to the bottomless pit and a heavy chain in his hand.

2 He seized the Dragon—that old Serpent, the Devil, Satan—and bound him in chains for 1000 years,

3 And threw him into the bottomless pit, which he then shut and locked, so that he could not fool the nations any more until the thousand years were finished. Afterwards he would be released again for a little while.

[5] Implied.
[6] Literally, "The Logos," as in John 1:1—the ultimate method of God's revealing Himself to man.
[7] See chapter 13, verses 11-16.

The binding of Satan

20 Then I saw an angel coming down
from heaven, holding in his hand the
key of the bottomless pit and a great chain.
2And he seized the dragon, that ancient serpent, who is the Devil and Satan, and bound
him for a thousand years, 3and threw him
into the pit, and shut it and sealed it over
him, that he should deceive the nations no
more, till the thousand years were ended.

[m] Other ancient authorities read *sprinkled with*

King James

4 And I saw thrones, and they sat upon them, and judgment was given unto them: and *I saw* the souls of them that were beheaded for the witness of Jesus, and for the word of God, and which had not worshipped the beast, neither his image, neither had received *his* mark upon their foreheads, or in their hands; and they lived and reigned with Christ a thousand years.

5 But the rest of the dead lived not again until the thousand years were finished. This *is* the first resurrection.

6 Blessed and holy *is* he that hath part in the first resurrection: on such the second death hath no power, but they shall be priests of God and of Christ, and shall reign with him a thousand years.

7 And when the thousand years are expired, Satan shall be loosed out of his prison,

8 And shall go out to deceive the nations which are in the four quarters of the earth, Gog and Magog, to gather them together to battle: the number of whom *is* as the sand of the sea.

9 And they went up on the breadth of the earth, and compassed the camp of the saints about, and the beloved city: and fire came down from God out of heaven, and devoured them.

10 And the devil that deceived them was cast into the lake of fire and brimstone, where the beast and the false prophet *are*, and shall be tormented day and night for ever and ever.

11 And I saw a great white throne, and him that sat on it, from whose face the earth and the heaven fled away; and there was found no place for them.

12 And I saw the dead, small and great, stand before God; and the books were opened: and another book was opened, which is *the book* of life: and the dead were judged out of those things which were written in the books, according to their works.

13 And the sea gave up the dead which were in it; and death and hell delivered up the dead which were in them: and they were judged every man according to their works.

14 And death and hell were cast into the lake of fire. This is the second death.

15 And whosoever was not found written in the book of life was cast into the lake of fire.

Amplified

4 Then I saw thrones, and sitting on them were those to whom authority to act as judges *and* pass sentence was entrusted. Also I saw the souls of those who had been slain with axes (beheaded) for their witnessing to Jesus and [for preaching and testifying] for the Word of God, and who had refused to pay homage to the beast or his statue and had not accepted his mark *or* permitted it to be stamped on their foreheads or on their hands. And they lived again, and ruled with Christ, the Messiah, a thousand years. [Dan. 7:9, 22, 27.]

5 The remainder of the dead were not restored to life again until the thousand years were completed. This is the first resurrection.

6 Blessed (happy, [v]to be envied) and holy—spiritually whole, of unimpaired innocence and proved virtue—is the person who takes part (shares) in the first resurrection! Over them the second death exerts no power *or* authority, but they shall be ministers of God and of Christ, the Messiah, and they shall rule along with Him a thousand years.

7 And when the thousand years are completed, Satan will be released from his place of confinement,

8 And he will go forth to deceive *and* seduce *and* lead astray the nations which are in the four quarters of the earth, that is, Gog and Magog, to muster them for war; their number is as the sand of the sea. [Ezek. 38:2, 9, 15, 22.]

9 And they swarmed up over the broad plain of the earth and encircled the fortress (camp) of God's people (the saints) and the beloved city; but fire descended from heaven and consumed them. [II Kings 1:10-12; Ezek. 38:2, 22.]

10 Then the devil who had led them astray—deceiving and seducing them—was hurled into the fiery lake of burning brimstone where the beast and false prophet were; and they will be tormented day and night forever and ever—through the ages of the ages.

11 Then I saw a great white throne and the One Who was seated upon it, from Whose presence *and* from the sight of Whose face earth and sky fled away and no place was found for them.

12 I [also] saw the dead, great and small; they stood before the throne, and books were opened. Then another book was opened, which is [the Book] of Life. And the dead were judged (sentenced) by what they had done [[w]their whole way of feeling and acting, their aims and endeavors] in accordance with what was recorded in the books.

13 And the sea delivered up the dead who were in it, Death and Hades [[x]the state of death or disembodied existence] surrendered the dead in them; and all were tried *and* their cases determined by what they had done—according to their motives, aims and works.

14 Then death and Hades [[x]the state of death or disembodied existence] were thrown into the lake of fire. This is the second death, the lake of fire.

15 And if any one's [name] was not found recorded in the Book of Life, he was hurled into the lake of fire.

---

v) Souter.
w) Thayer.
x) "The International Bible Encyclopedia."

Living New Testament

4 Then I saw thrones, and sitting on them were those who had been given the right to judge. And I saw the souls of those who had been beheaded for their testimony about Jesus, for proclaiming the Word of God, and who had not worshiped the Creature or his statue, nor accepted his mark on their foreheads or their hands. They had come to life again and now they reigned with Christ for a thousand years.

5 This is the First Resurrection. (The rest of the dead did not come back to life until the thousand years had ended.)

6 Blessed and holy are those who share in the First Resurrection. For them the Second Death holds no terrors, for they will be priests of God and of Christ, and shall reign with Him a thousand years.

7 When the thousand years end, Satan will be let out of his prison.

8 He will go out to deceive the nations of the world and gather them together, with Gog and Magog, for battle—a mighty host, numberless as sand along the shore.

9 They will go up across the broad plain of the earth and surround God's people and the beloved city of Jerusalem[1] on every side. But fire from God in heaven will flash down on the attacking armies and consume them.

10 Then the Devil who had betrayed them will again[2] be thrown into the Lake of Fire burning with sulphur where the Creature and False Prophet are, and they will be tormented day and night forever and ever.

11 And I saw a great white throne and the one who sat upon it, from whose face the earth and sky fled away, but they found no place to hide.[3]

12 I saw the dead, great and small, standing before God; and The Books were opened, including the Book of Life. And the dead were judged according to the things written in The Books, each according to the deeds he had done.

13 The oceans surrendered the bodies buried in them; and the earth and the underworld gave up the dead in them. Each was judged according to his deeds.

14 And Death and Hell were thrown into the Lake of Fire. This is the Second Death—the Lake of Fire.

15 And if anyone's name was not found recorded in the Book of Life, he was thrown into the Lake of Fire.

Implied.
Implied; Revelation 20:3.
Literally, "There was no longer any place for them."

Revised Standard

After that he must be loosed for a little while.

The millennial reign

4 Then I saw thrones, and seated on
them were those to whom judgment was
committed. Also I saw the souls of those
who had been beheaded for their testimony
to Jesus and for the word of God, and who
had not worshiped the beast or its image
and had not received its mark on their foreheads or their hands. They came to life, and
reigned with Christ a thousand years. [5]The
rest of the dead did not come to life until
the thousand years were ended. This is the
first resurrection. [6]Blessed and holy is he
who shares in the first resurrection! Over
such the second death has no power, but
they shall be priests of God and of Christ,
and they shall reign with him a thousand
years.

The loosing of Satan

7 And when the thousand years are ended, Satan will be loosed from his prison
[8]and will come out to deceive the nations
which are at the four corners of the earth,
that is, Gog and Magog, to gather them
for battle; their number is like the sand of
the sea. [9]And they marched up over the
broad earth and surrounded the camp of
the saints and the beloved city; but fire
came down from heaven[n] and consumed
them, [10]and the devil who had deceived
them was thrown into the lake of fire and
brimstone where the beast and the false
prophet were, and they will be tormented
day and night for ever and ever.

The great white throne judgment

11 Then I saw a great white throne and
him who sat upon it; from his presence
earth and sky fled away, and no place was
found for them. [12]And I saw the dead, great
and small, standing before the throne, and
books were opened. Also another book was
opened, which is the book of life. And the
dead were judged by what was written in
the books, by what they had done. [13]And
the sea gave up the dead in it, Death and
Hades gave up the dead in them, and all
were judged by what they had done. [14]Then
Death and Hades were thrown into the
lake of fire. This is the second death, the
lake of fire; [15]and if any one's name was
not found written in the book of life, he
was thrown into the lake of fire.

[n] Other ancient authorities read *from God, out of heaven,* or *out of heaven from God*

King James

CHAPTER 21

AND I saw a new heaven and a new earth: for the first heaven and the first earth were passed away; and there was no more sea.

2 And I John saw the holy city, new Jerusalem, coming down from God out of heaven, prepared as a bride adorned for her husband.

3 And I heard a great voice out of heaven saying, Behold, the tabernacle of God *is* with men, and he will dwell with them, and they shall be his people, and God himself shall be with them, *and be* their God.

4 And God shall wipe away all tears from their eyes; and there shall be no more death, neither sorrow, nor crying, neither shall there be any more pain: for the former things are passed away.

5 And he that sat upon the throne said, Behold, I make all things new. And he said unto me, Write: for these words are true and faithful.

6 And he said unto me, It is done. I am Alpha and Omega, the beginning and the end. I will give unto him that is athirst of the fountain of the water of life freely.

7 He that overcometh shall inherit all things; and I will be his God, and he shall be my son.

8 But the fearful, and unbelieving, and the abominable, and murderers, and whoremongers, and sorcerers, and idolaters, and all liars, shall have their part in the lake which burneth with fire and brimstone: which is the second death.

9 And there came unto me one of the seven angels which had the seven vials full of the seven last plagues, and talked with me, saying, Come hither, I will shew thee the bride, the Lamb's wife.

10 And he carried me away in the spirit to a great and high mountain, and shewed me that great city, the holy Jerusalem, descending out of heaven from God,

11 Having the glory of God: and her light *was* like unto a stone most precious, even like a jasper stone, clear as crystal;

12 And had a wall great and high, *and* had twelve gates, and at the gates twelve angels, and names written thereon, which are *the names* of the twelve tribes of the children of Israel:

13 On the east three gates; on the north three gates; on the south three gates; and on the west three gates.

14 And the wall of the city had twelve foundations, and in them the names of the twelve apostles of the Lamb.

15 And he that talked with me had a golden reed to measure the city, and the gates thereof, and the wall thereof.

16 And the city lieth foursquare, and the length is as large as the breadth: and he measured the city with the reed, twelve thousand furlongs. The length and the breadth and the height of it are equal.

Amplified

CHAPTER 21

THEN I saw a new [y]sky (heaven) and a new earth; for the former [y]sky and the former earth had passed away (vanished), and there no longer existed any sea. [Isa. 65:17; 66:22.]

2 And I saw the holy city, the new Jerusalem, descending out of heaven from God, all arrayed like a bride beautified *and* adorned for her husband;

3 Then I heard a mighty voice from the throne *and* I perceived its distinct words, saying, See! The abode of God is with men, and He will live (encamp, tent) among them, and they shall be His people and God shall personally be with them and be their God. [Ezek. 37:27.]

4 God will wipe away every tear from their eyes, and death shall be no more, neither shall there be anguish—sorrow and mourning—nor grief nor pain any more; for the old conditions *and* the former order of things have passed away. [Isa. 25:8; 35:10.]

5 And He Who is seated on the throne said, See! I make all things new. Also He said, Record this, for these sayings are faithful—accurate, incorruptible and trustworthy—and true (genuine). [Isa. 43:19.]

6 And He [further] said to me, It is done! I am the Alpha and the Omega, the Beginning and the End. To the thirsty I [Myself] will give water without price from the fountain (springs) of the water of Life. [Isa. 55:1.]

7 He who is victorious shall inherit all these things, and I will be God to him and he shall be My son.

8 But as for the cowards *and* the ignoble *and* the contemptible *and* the cravenly lacking in courage *and* the cowardly submissive; and as for the unbelieving and faithless; and as for the depraved and defiled with abominations; and as for murderers and the lewd and adulterous and the practicers of magic arts and the idolaters [those who give supreme devotion to any one or anything other than God] and all liars [those who knowingly convey untruth by word or deed, all of these shall have] their part in the lake that blazes with fire and brimstone. This is the second death. [Isa. 30:33.]

9 Then one of the seven angels who had the seven bowls filled with the seven final plagues (afflictions, calamities) came and spoke to me. He said, Come with me! I will show you the bride, the Lamb's wife.

10 Then in the Spirit He conveyed me away to a vast and lofty mountain, and exhibited to me the holy (hallowed, consecrated) city of Jerusalem descending out of heaven from God, [Ezek. 40:2.]

11 Clothed in God's glory—in all its splendor and radiance. The luster of it resembled a rare *and* most precious jewel, like jasper, shining clear as crystal.

12 It had a massive and high wall with twelve [large] gates, and at the gates [there were stationed] twelve angels, and [on the gates] the names of the twelve tribes of the sons of Israel were written; [Ezek. 48:30-35; Exod. 28:21.]

13 On the east side three gates, on the north side three gates, on the south side three gates, and on the west side three gates.

14 And the wall of the city had twelve foundatio[illegible] [stones], and on them the twelve names of the twelv[illegible] apostles of the Lamb.

15 And he who spoke to me had a golden measurin[illegible] reed (rod) to measure the city and its gates and its wall [Ezek. 40:5.]

16 The city lies in a square, its length being the same a[illegible] its width. And he measured the city with his reed, twelv[illegible] thousand stadia [about fifteen hundred miles]; its lengt[illegible] and width and height are the same.

---

y) Thayer.

Living New Testament

CHAPTER 21

Then I saw a new earth (with no oceans!) and a new sky, for the present earth and sky had disappeared.

2 And I, John, saw the Holy City, the new Jerusalem, coming down from God out of heaven. It was a glorious sight, beautiful as a bride at her wedding.

3 I heard a loud shout from the throne saying, "Look, the home of God is now among men, and He will live with them and they will be His people; yes, God Himself will be among them.[1]

4 He will wipe away all tears from their eyes, and there shall be no more death, or sorrow, or crying, or pain. All of that has gone forever."

5 And the one sitting on the throne said, "See, I am making all things new!" And then He said to me, "Write this down, for what I tell you is trustworthy and true:

6 It is finished! I am the A and Z—the Beginning and the End. I will give to the thirsty the springs of the Water of Life—as a gift!

7 Everyone who conquers will inherit all these blessings, and I will be his God and he will be My son.

8 But cowards who turn back from following Me, and those who are unfaithful to Me, and the corrupt, and murderers, and the immoral, and those conversing with demons, and idol worshipers and all liars—their doom is in the Lake that burns with fire and sulphur. This is the Second Death."

9 Then one of the seven angels, who had emptied the flasks containing the seven last plagues came and said to me, "Come with me and I will show you the bride, the Lamb's wife."

10 In a vision he took me to a towering mountain peak and from there I watched that wondrous city, the holy Jerusalem, descending out of the skies from God.

11 It was filled with the glory of God, and flashed and glowed like a precious gem, crystal clear like jasper.

12 Its walls were broad and high, with twelve gates guarded by twelve angels. And the names of the twelve tribes of Israel were written on the gates.

13 There were three gates on each side—north, south, east, and west.

14 The walls had twelve foundation stones, and on them were written the names of the twelve apostles of the Lamb.

15 The angel held in his hand a golden measuring stick to measure the city and its gates and walls.

16 When he measured it, he found it was a square as wide as it was long; in fact, it was in the form of a cube, for its height was exactly the same as its other dimensions—1,500 miles each way.

---

[1] Some manuscripts add, "and be their God."

Revised Standard

The new heaven and the new earth

21 Then I saw a new heaven and a new
earth; for the first heaven and the
first earth had passed away, and the sea
was no more. 2And I saw the holy city, new
Jerusalem, coming down out of heaven
from God, prepared as a bride adorned for
her husband; 3and I heard a great voice
from the throne saying, "Behold, the dwelling of God is with men. He will dwell with
them, and they shall be his people,[o] and
God himself will be with them;[p] 4he will
wipe away every tear from their eyes, and
death shall be no more, neither shall there
be mourning nor crying nor pain any more,
for the former things have passed away."
5 And he who sat upon the throne said,
"Behold, I make all things new." Also he
said, "Write this, for these words are trustworthy and true." 6And he said to me, "It
is done! I am the Alpha and the Omega,
the beginning and the end. To the thirsty I
will give water without price from the
fountain of the water of life. 7He who conquers shall have this heritage, and I will be
his God and he shall be my son. 8But as
for the cowardly, the faithless, the polluted,
as for murderers, fornicators, sorcerers,
idolaters, and all liars, their lot shall be in
the lake that burns with fire and brimstone,
which is the second death."

The new Jerusalem

9 Then came one of the seven angels
who had the seven bowls full of the seven
last plagues, and spoke to me, saying,
"Come, I will show you the Bride, the wife
of the Lamb." 10And in the Spirit he carried me away to a great, high mountain,
and showed me the holy city Jerusalem
coming down out of heaven from God,
11having the glory of God, its radiance like
a most rare jewel, like a jasper, clear as
crystal. 12It had a great, high wall, with
twelve gates, and at the gates twelve angels,
and on the gates the names of the twelve
tribes of the sons of Israel were inscribed;
13on the east three gates, on the north three
gates, on the south three gates, and on the
west three gates. 14And the wall of the city
had twelve foundations, and on them the
twelve names of the twelve apostles of the
Lamb.
15 And he who talked to me had a measuring rod of gold to measure the city and
its gates and walls. 16The city lies foursquare, its length the same as its breadth;
and he measured the city with his rod,
twelve thousand stadia;[q] its length and

---

[o] Other ancient authorities read *peoples*
[p] Other ancient authorities add *and be their God*
[q] About fifteen hundred miles

King James

17 And he measured the wall thereof, an hundred *and* forty *and* four cubits, *according to* the measure of a man, that is, of the angel.

18 And the building of the wall of it was *of* jasper: and the city *was* pure gold, like unto clear glass.

19 And the foundations of the wall of the city *were* garnished with all manner of precious stones. The first foundation *was* jasper; the second, sapphire; the third, a chalcedony; the fourth, an emerald;

20 The fifth, sardonyx; the sixth, sardius; the seventh, chrysolyte; the eighth, beryl; the ninth, a topaz; the tenth, a chrysoprasus; the eleventh, a jacinth; the twelfth, an amethyst.

21 And the twelve gates *were* twelve pearls: every several gate was of one pearl: and the street of the city *was* pure gold, as it were transparent glass.

22 And I saw no temple therein: for the Lord God Almighty and the Lamb are the temple of it.

23 And the city had no need of the sun, neither of the moon, to shine in it: for the glory of God did lighten it, and the Lamb *is* the light thereof.

24 And the nations of them which are saved shall walk in the light of it: and the kings of the earth do bring their glory and honour into it.

25 And the gates of it shall not be shut at all by day: for there shall be no night there.

26 And they shall bring the glory and honour of the nations into it.

27 And there shall in no wise enter into it any thing that defileth, neither *whatsoever* worketh abomination, or *maketh* a lie: but they which are written in the Lamb's book of life.

Amplified

17 He measured its wall also, one hundred and forty-four cubits (about seventy-two yards) by a man's measure [[z]of a cubit from his elbow to his third finger tip] which is [the measure] of the angel.

18 The wall was built of jasper, while the city [itself was of] pure gold, clear and transparent like glass.

19 The foundation [stones] of the wall of the city were ornamented with all of the precious stones. The first foundation [stone] was jasper, the second sapphire, the third chalcedony (or white agate), the fourth emerald, [Isa. 54:11, 12.]

20 The fifth onyx, the sixth sardius, the seventh chrysolite, the eighth beryl, the ninth topaz, the tenth chrysoprase, the eleventh jacinth, the twelfth amethyst.

21 And the twelve gates were twelve pearls, each separate gate being built of one solid pearl. And the main street (the broadway) of the city was of gold as pure *and* translucent as glass.

22 I saw no temple in the city, for the Lord God Omnipotent [Himself] and the Lamb [Himself] are its temple.

23 And the city has no need of the sun nor of the moon to give light to it, for the splendor *and* radiance (glory) of God illuminate it, and the Lamb is its lamp. [Isa. 24:23; 60:1, 19.]

24 The nations shall walk by its light and the rulers *and* leaders of the earth shall bring into it their glory.

25 And its gates shall never be closed by day, and there shall be no night there. [Isa. 60:11.]

26 They shall bring the glory—the splendor and majesty—and the honor of the nations into it.

27 But nothing that defiles *or* profanes *or* is [a]unwashed shall ever enter it, nor any one who commits abominations—that is, unclean, detestable, morally repugnant things—or practices falsehood, but only those whose names are recorded in the Lamb's Book of Life.

CHAPTER 22

AND he shewed me a pure river of water of life, clear as crystal, proceeding out of the throne of God and of the Lamb.

2 In the midst of the street of it, and on either side of the river, *was there* the tree of life, which bare twelve *manner of* fruits, *and* yielded her fruit every month: and the leaves of the tree *were* for the healing of the nations.

3 And there shall be no more curse: but the throne of God and of the Lamb shall be in it; and his servants shall serve him:

4 And they shall see his face; and his name *shall be* in their foreheads.

5 And there shall be no night there; and they need no candle, neither light of the sun; for the Lord God giveth them light: and they shall reign for ever and ever.

CHAPTER 22

THEN he showed me the river whose waters give life, sparkling like crystal, flowing out from the throne of God and of the Lamb

2 Through the middle of the broad way of the city; also, on either side of the river, the tree of life with its twelve varieties of fruit, yielding each month its fresh crop; and the leaves of the tree were for the healing *and* the restoration of the nations. [Gen. 2:9.]

3 There shall no longer exist there anything that is accursed—detestable, foul, offensive, impure, hateful or horrible. But the throne of God and of the Lamb shall be in it, and His servants shall worship Him—pay divine honors to Him and do Him holy service. [Zech. 14:21.]

4 They shall see His face, and His name shall be on their foreheads. [Ps. 17:15.]

5 And there shall be no more night; they have no need for lamplight or sunlight, for the Lord God will illuminate them *and* be their light, and they shall reign (as kings) forever and ever—through the eternities of the eternities.

z) Clarke's Commentary.
a) Souter.

Living New Testament

17 Then he measured the thickness of the walls and found them to be 216 feet across (the angel called out these measurements to me, using standard units.)[2]

18, 19 The city itself was pure, transparent gold, like glass! The wall was made of jasper, and was built on twelve layers of foundation stones inlaid with gems.

The first layer[3] with jasper;
The second with sapphire;
The third with chalcedony;
The fourth with emerald;
The fifth with sardonyx;
20 The sixth layer with sardius;
The seventh with chrysolite;
The eighth with beryl;
The ninth with topaz;
The tenth with chrysoprase;
The eleventh with jacinth;
The twelfth with amethyst.

21 The twelve gates were made of pearls—each gate from a single pearl! And the main street was pure transparent gold, like glass.

22 No temple could be seen in the city, for the Lord God Almighty and the Lamb are worshiped in it everywhere.[4]

23 And the city has no need of sun or moon to light it, for the glory of God and of the Lamb illuminate it.

24 Its light will light the nations of the earth, and the rulers of the world will come and bring their glory to it.

25 Its gates never close: they stay open all day long—and there is no night!

26 And the glory and honor of all the nations shall be brought into it.

27 Nothing evil will be permitted in it—no one immoral or dishonest—but only those whose names are written in the Lamb's Book of Life.

Revised Standard

breadth and height are equal. 17He also measured its wall, a hundred and forty-four cubits by a man's measure, that is, an angel's. 18The wall was built of jasper, while the city was pure gold, clear as glass. 19The foundations of the wall of the city were adorned with every jewel; the first was jasper, the second sapphire, the third agate, the fourth emerald, 20the fifth onyx, the sixth carnelian, the seventh chrysolite, the eighth beryl, the ninth topaz, the tenth chrysoprase, the eleventh jacinth, the twelfth amethyst. 21And the twelve gates were twelve pearls, each of the gates made of a single pearl, and the street of the city was pure gold, transparent as glass.

22 And I saw no temple in the city, for its temple is the Lord God the Almighty and the Lamb. 23And the city has no need of sun or moon to shine upon it, for the glory of God is its light, and its lamp is the Lamb. 24By its light shall the nations walk; and the kings of the earth shall bring their glory into it, 25and its gates shall never be shut by day—and there shall be no night there; 26they shall bring into it the glory and the honor of the nations. 27But nothing unclean shall enter it, nor any one who practices abomination or falsehood, but only those who are written in the Lamb's book of life.

CHAPTER 22

And he pointed out to me a river of pure Water of Life, clear as crystal, flowing from the throne of God and the Lamb,

2 Coursing down the center of the main street. On each side of the river grew Trees[1] of Life, bearing twelve crops of fruit, with a fresh crop each month; the leaves were used for medicine to heal the nations.

3 There shall be nothing in the city which is evil; for the throne of God and of the Lamb will be there, and His servants will worship Him.

4 And they shall see His face; and His name shall be written on their foreheads.

5 And there will be no night there—no need for lamps or sun—for the Lord God will be their light; and they shall reign forever and ever.

The water and tree of life

22 Then he showed me the river of the water of life, bright as crystal, flowing from the throne of God and of the Lamb 2through the middle of the street of the city; also, on either side of the river, the tree of life[r] with its twelve kinds of fruit, yielding its fruit each month; and the leaves of the tree were for the healing of the nations. 3There shall no more be anything accursed, but the throne of God and of the Lamb shall be in it, and his servants shall worship him; 4they shall see his face, and his name shall be on their foreheads. 5And night shall be no more; they need no light of lamp or sun, for the Lord God will be their light, and they shall reign for ever and ever.

---

2 Literally, "144 cubits by human measurements." A cubit was the average length of a man's arm—not an angel's! The angel used normal units of measurement that John could understand.
3 Implied.
4 Literally, "are its temple."
1 Literally, "the tree of life"—used here as a collective noun, implying plurality.

r Or *the Lamb. In the midst of the street of the city, and on either side of the river, was the tree of life,* etc.

King James

6 And he said unto me, These sayings *are* faithful and true: and the Lord God of the holy prophets sent his angel to shew unto his servants the things which must shortly be done.

7 Behold, I come quickly: blessed *is* he that keepeth the sayings of the prophecy of this book.

8 And I John saw these things, and heard *them*. And when I had heard and seen, I fell down to worship before the feet of the angel which shewed me these things.

9 Then saith he unto me, See *thou do it* not: for I am thy fellow-servant, and of thy brethren the prophets, and of them which keep the sayings of this book: worship God.

10 And he saith unto me, Seal not the sayings of the prophecy of this book: for the time is at hand.

11 He that is unjust, let him be unjust still: and he which is filthy, let him be filthy still: and he that is righteous, let him be righteous still: and he that is holy, let him be holy still.

12 And, behold, I come quickly; and my reward *is* with me, to give every man according as his work shall be.

13 I am Alpha and Omega, the beginning and the end, the first and the last.

14 Blessed *are* they that do his commandments, that they may have right to the tree of life, and may enter in through the gates into the city.

15 For without *are* dogs, and sorcerers, and whoremongers, and murderers, and idolaters, and whosoever loveth and maketh a lie.

16 I Jesus have sent mine angel to testify unto you these things in the churches. I am the root and the offspring of David, *and* the bright and morning star.

17 And the Spirit and the bride say, Come. And let him that heareth say, Come. And let him that is athirst come. And whosoever will, let him take the water of life freely.

18 For I testify unto every man that heareth the words of the prophecy of this book, If any man shall add unto these things, God shall add unto him the plagues that are written in this book:

Amplified

6 And he [of the seven angels further] said to me, These statements are reliable—worthy of confidence—and genuine (true). And the Lord, the God of the spirits of the prophets, has sent His messenger (angel) to make known *and* exhibit to His servants what must soon come to pass.

7 And behold, I am coming speedily. Blessed (happy and [b]to be envied) is he who observes *and* lays to heart *and* keeps the truths of the prophecy—the predictions, consolations and warnings—contained in this little book.

8 And I John am he who heard and witnessed these things. And when I heard and saw them, I fell prostrate before the feet of the messenger (angel) who showed them to me, to worship him.

9 But he said to me, Refrain!—You must not do that! I am [only] a fellow servant along with yourself and of your brethren the prophets, and of those who are mindful *and* practice [the truths contained in] the messages of this book. Worship God!

10 And he [further] told me, Do not seal up the words of the prophecy of this book *and* make no secret of them; for the time [c]when things are brought to a crisis *and* the period of their fulfillment is near.

11 He who is unrighteous (unjust, wicked) let him be unrighteous still, and he that is filthy (vile, impure) let him be filthy still, and he that is righteous (just, upright, in right standing with God) let him do right still, and he who is holy let him be holy still. [Dan. 12:10.]

12 Behold, I am coming soon, and I shall bring My wages *and* rewards with Me, to repay *and* render to each one just what his own actions *and* his own work merit. [Isa. 40:10; Jer. 17:10.]

13 I am the Alpha and the Omega, the First and the Last (the Before all and at the End of all). [Isa. 44:6; 48:12.]

14 Blessed (happy and [d]to be envied) are those who cleanse their garments that they may have the authority *and* right to [approach] the tree of life and to enter in through the gates to the city. [Gen. 2:9; 3:22, 24.]

15 [But] without are the dogs and those who practice sorceries (magic arts) and impurity (the lewd, adulterers) and the murderers and idolaters and every one who loves and deals in falsehood—untruth, error, deception, cheating.

16 I, Jesus, have sent My messenger (angel) to you to witness *and* to give you assurance of these things for the churches (assemblies). I am [both] the Root (the Source) and the Offspring of David, the radiant *and* brilliant Morning Star. [Isa. 11:1, 10.]

17 The (Holy) Spirit and the bride [the church, the true Christians] say, Come! And let him who is listening say, Come! And let every one come who is thirsty [who is painfully conscious of his need [e]of those things by which the soul is refreshed, supported and strengthened]; and whoever [earnestly] desires to do it, let him come and take *and* appropriate (drink) the Water of Life without cost. [Isa. 55:1.]

18 I [personally solemnly] warn every one who listens to the statements of the prophecy [the [e]predictions and the consolations and admonitions pertaining to them] in this book: if any one shall add anything to them, God will add *and* lay upon him the plagues—the afflictions and the calamities—that are recorded *and* described in this book.

---

b) Souter.
c) Thayer.
d) Souter.
e) Thayer.

Living New Testament

* * * *

6, 7 Then the angel said to me, "These words are trustworthy and true: 'I am coming soon!'[2] God, who tells His prophets what the future holds, has sent His angel to tell you this will happen soon. Blessed are those who believe it and all else written in the scroll."

8 I, John, saw and heard all these things, and fell down to worship the angel who showed them to me;

9 But again he said, "No, don't do anything like that. I, too, am a servant of Jesus as you are, and as your brothers the prophets are, as well as all those who heed the truth stated in this Book. Worship God alone."

10 Then he instructed me, "Do not seal up what you have written, for the time of fulfillment is near.

11 And when that time comes, all doing wrong will do it more and more; the vile will become more vile; good men will be better; those who are holy will continue on in greater holiness."

* * * *

12 "See, I am coming soon,[2] and My reward is with Me, to repay everyone according to the deeds he has done.

13 I am the A and Z, the Beginning and the End, the First and Last.

14 Blessed forever are all who are washing their robes, to have the right to enter in through the gates of the city, and to eat the fruit from the Tree of Life.

15 Outside the city are those who have strayed away from God, and the sorcerers and the immoral and murderers and idolaters, and all who love to lie, and do so.

16 I, Jesus, have sent My angel to you to tell the churches all these things. I am both David's Root and his Descendant. I am the bright Morning Star.

17 The Spirit and the bride say, 'Come.' Let each one who hears them say the same, 'Come.' Let the thirsty one come—anyone who wants to; let him come and drink the Water of Life without charge.

18 And I solemnly declare to everyone who reads this book: if anyone adds anything to what is written here, God shall add to him the plagues described in this book.

Or, "suddenly," "unexpectedly."

Revised Standard

Epilogue

6 And he said to me, "These words are trustworthy and true. And the Lord, the God of the spirits of the prophets, has sent his angel to show his servants what must soon take place.

7 And behold, I am coming soon."

Blessed is he who keeps the words of the prophecy of this book.

8 I John am he who heard and saw these things. And when I heard and saw them, I fell down to worship at the feet of the angel who showed them to me;
9but he said to me, "You must not do that! I am a fellow servant with you and your brethren the prophets, and with those who keep the words of this book. Worship God."

10 And he said to me, "Do not seal up the words of the prophecy of this book, for the time is near.
11Let the evildoer still do evil, and the filthy still be filthy, and the righteous still do right, and the holy still be holy."

12 "Behold, I am coming soon, bringing my recompense, to repay every one for what he has done.
13I am the Alpha and the Omega, the first and the last, the beginning and the end."

14 Blessed are those who wash their robes,[s] that they may have the right to the tree of life and that they may enter the city by the gates.
15Outside are the dogs and sorcerers and fornicators and murderers and idolaters, and every one who loves and practices falsehood.

16 "I Jesus have sent my angel to you with this testimony for the churches. I am the root and the offspring of David, the bright morning star."

17 The Spirit and the Bride say, "Come." And let him who hears say, "Come." And let him who is thirsty come, let him who desires take the water of life without price.

18 I warn every one who hears the words of the prophecy of this book: if any one adds to them, God will add to him the plagues described in this book,
19and if

[s] Other ancient authorities read *do his commandments*

King James

19 And if any man shall take away from the words of the book of this prophecy, God shall take away his part out of the book of life, and out of the holy city, and *from* the things which are written in this book.
20 He which testifieth these things saith, Surely I come quickly. Amen. Even so, come, Lord Jesus.
21 The grace of our Lord Jesus Christ *be* with you all. Amen.

Amplified

19 And if any one cancels *or* takes away from the statements of the book of this prophecy—these [e]predictions relating to Christ's kingdom and its speedy triumph, together with the consolations and admonitions (warnings) pertaining to them—God will cancel *and* take away from him his share in the tree of life and in the city of holiness (pure and hallowed) which are described *and* promised in this book.
20 He Who gives this warning *and* affirms *and* testifies to these things, says, Yes—it is true. [Surely] I am coming quickly—swiftly, speedily. Amen—so let it be! Yes, come, Lord Jesus!
21 The grace (blessing and favor) of the Lord Jesus *Christ, the Messiah* be [f]with all the saints—God's holy people) [[e]those set apart for God, to be, as it were, exclusively His]. Amen—so let it be!

---

e) Thayer.

Living New Testament

19 And if anyone subtracts any part of these prophecies, God shall take away his share in the Tree of Life,
and in the Holy City just described.
20 He who has said all these things declares: Yes, I am
coming soon!"[3]
Amen! Come, Lord Jesus!
21 The grace of our Lord Jesus Christ be with you all.
Amen!

[3] Or, "suddenly," "unexpectedly."

Revised Standard

any one takes away from the words of the
book of this prophecy, God will take away
his share in the tree of life and in the holy
city, which are described in this book.
20 He who testifies to these things says,
"Surely I am coming soon." Amen. Come,
Lord Jesus!
21 The grace of the Lord Jesus be with
all the saints.[t] Amen.

[t] Other ancient authorities omit *all;* others omit *the saints*

Jesus did not need to experience every temptation men have experienced. but every Kind of temptation

In John 2:14 it states that men are tempted along 3 avenues. the lust of the flesh, the lust of the eye and the pride of Life.

These were the avenues along Eve was tempted in the garden

. and also that Satan brought to Jesus in the Wilderness Matt 4-1-10